The Hornbook

Dr. Johnson described the hornbook as "the first book of children, covered with horn to keep it unsoiled." Pardon's *New General English Dictionary* (1758) defined it as "A leaf of written or printed paper pasted on a board, and covered with horn, for children to learn their letters by, and to prevent their being torn and daubed."

It was used throughout Europe and America between the late 1400s and the middle 1700s.

Shaped like an old-fashioned butter paddle, the first hornbooks were made of wood. The paper lesson the child was to learn was fastened to the wooden paddle and covered with a piece of horn. The transparent strip of horn was made by soaking a cow's horn

in hot water and peeling it away at the thickness of a piece of celluloid. The horn was necessary to protect the lesson from the damp and perhaps grubby hands of the child. Hornbooks commonly contained the alphabet, the vowels, and the Lord's Prayer. Later hornbooks were made of various materials: brass, copper, silver, ivory, bronze, leather, and stone.

As the art of printing advanced, the hornbook was supplanted by the primer in the book form we know today. Subsequently, West Publishing Company developed its "Hornbook Series", a series of scholarly and well-respected one volume treatises on particular areas of law. Today they are widely used by law students, lawyers and judges.

*

LAW OF REMEDIES

DAMAGES–EQUITY–RESTITUTION

Second Edition

By

Dan B. Dobbs

Professor of Law
University of Arizona

This book is an abridgement of Dobbs' "Law of Remedies, Second Edition, Volumes 1–3," Practitioner Treatise Series.

HORNBOOK SERIES®

WEST PUBLISHING CO.
ST. PAUL, MINN., 1993

This is an abridgement of Dobbs' "Law of Remedies, Second Edition, Volumes 1–3", Practitioner Treatise Series, West Publishing Co., 1993.

Hornbook Series, Westlaw, the West Publishing Co. Logo and the key symbol appearing on the front cover are registered trademarks of West Publishing Co. Registered in U.S. Patent and Trademark Office.

Library of Congress Cataloging-in-Publication Data
Dobbs, Dan B.
  Law of remedies : damages, equity, restitution / by Dan B. Dobbs. —
2nd ed.
   p. cm. — (Hornbook series)
  Rev. ed. of : Handbook on the law of remedies. 1973. Includes index.
  ISBN 0–314–01123–4
  1. Remedies (Law)—United States. I. Dobbs, Dan B. Handbook on
the law of remedies. II. Title. III. Series.
  KF9010.D6 1993b
  347.73'77—dc20
  [347.30777]   93–10776
                 CIP

ISBN 0–314–01123–4

Dobbs, Remedies, 2nd Ed. HB
1st Reprint—1995

Preface

This abridgement is meant to provide a text for law students, teachers, and lawyers. To provide a portable and reasonably priced volume, substantial cuts were made in both text and footnotes. Cuts require the user to read with a degree of tolerance and creativity.

What remains is still a very large volume. Although it covers the field of remedies, it covers some topics in more detail than others. This volume usually places more reliance upon the general rules found in Chapters 1–4 (and for contracts in the first part of Chapter 12). Correspondingly, it provides less detail about remedies in particular settings.

It is my hope and expectation that students, teachers, and lawyers will find this one-volume edition useful on an everyday basis. It should be a good desk book or office volume for lawyers and teachers and a good source of general information about remedies for the student.

Cuts were made in virtually every section of the three-volume edition. To show where all these cuts were made would create an aggravating clutter. Some of the longer cuts are identified by subject matter, but not all of them. (See USING THIS ABRIDGEMENT.) The first edition of this book was well-received by practicing lawyers. This edition should be even more useful standing alone. I hope it gains added value because lawyers can turn to the three-volume work when critical professional detail becomes important.

DAN B. DOBBS

Tucson, Arizona
May, 1993

*

Using This Abridgement

This book is an abridgement. The full text is found in the three-volume Practitioner Treatise edition. Sections and parts of sections that appear in the three-volume work have been omitted here. Footnotes and parts of footnotes have likewise been omitted.

In some instances the reader can determine whether additional material can be found in the unabridged edition. However, to avoid clutter, many shorter omissions are not marked.

To find out more detailed information about omissions and how to interpret what you see in this book, read the material below.

Text Omissions

1. When entire sections are omitted from this edition, their titles are retained in this volume without accompanying text. The title without text will indicate the general subject matter. The text will be found in the three-volume edition. Many omitted subsections are shown in the same way.

2. When substantial discussions on a discrete topic are omitted (but not an entire subsection or section) a bracketed note will usually indicate the general topics covered by the omitted material and refer the reader to the three-volume edition. Some such notes will also suggest related summaries in the present volume.

3. When the omission of text material is shorter, or includes mainly examples, additional explanations, or footnotes, no direct indication of the omission is given. This occasional inconvenience is preferable to a repeated intrusive indication that something has been cut.

4. When the removed texts contained footnote references, the text note numbers will not be consecutive. The user will be able to determine that text containing those note numbers has been removed. For example, suppose the first paragraph contains references to footnotes 1 and 2, the second paragraph to footnotes 3–5, and the third paragraph to footnotes 6–10. If the second paragraph has been cut, only two paragraphs will appear. Their footnote numbers remain the same as those in the three-volume edition, however, so the reader will perceive that the text references skip from notes 1 and 2 in the first paragraph to notes 6 through 10 in the next. This skip will serve as a notice that some material has been omitted.

Footnotes

1. All original footnote numbers remain unchanged. All superior numbers in the text remain there, whether or not there are accompanying footnotes in this edition. If you find a superior number "14" in the text but no footnote 14 at the bottom of the page, that means that footnote 14 appears only in the three-volume work. In this way you can see at all times whether

additional note material is available to you in the larger work. I have tried to keep most footnotes. Many that have been stricken are notes of convenience (for cross-reference) or added detail or qualification.

2. Some cross-references refer to materials that do not appear in this one-volume edition. The reader may find this aggravating at times. There is a point to this arrangement, however. Such references will identify both the subject matter and the location of the referenced material in the three-volume work.

3. Omissions within footnotes are NOT indicated. Some footnotes have not been cut at all; others have been cut substantially.

WESTLAW® Overview

Dobbs' *Law of Remedies* offers a detailed and comprehensive treatment of principles and issues in remedies law. To supplement the information in this book, you can access WESTLAW, a computer-assisted legal research service of West Publishing Company. WESTLAW contains a broad library of resources, including case law, statutes, administrative materials, commentary, and current legal and news developments.

Learning how to use these materials effectively will enhance your legal research. So that you can coordinate your book and WESTLAW research, this volume contains an appendix listing WESTLAW databases, search techniques and sample problems.

THE PUBLISHER

*

Summary of Contents

Chapter   **Page**

1. Introduction to Remedies — 1
2. Equity and Nonmonetary Remedies — 47
   - A. History, Development and Meanings of Equity — 48
   - B. Discretion in Equity — 66
   - C. Procedures, Jurisdiction, and Enforcement — 101
   - D. Injunctions — 162
3. Principles of Damages — 207
4. Restitution — 364
   - A. The Nature of Restitution — 365
   - B. Defenses and Limitations — 448
5. Harms to Interests in Tangible Property — 492
   - A. Land — 494
     - (1) In General — 494
     - (2) Interests in Physical Integrity of Land and Structures — 497
     - (3) Interests in Use and Enjoyment — 513
     - (4) Harms to Interests in Exclusive Possession — 528
     - (5) Procedural and Remedial Impacts of Permanent Invasions — 542
     - (6) Consequential and Punitive Measures in Land Cases — 544
   - B. Personal Property — 545
6. Interference With Economic Rights — 596
7. Invasion of Civil Rights and Dignitary Interests — 622
8. Personal Injury and Death — 646
9. Fraud and Misrepresentation — 694
10. Duress, Undue Influence, and Other Unconscionable Conduct — 718
11. Mistake in Contracting and Gift Transactions — 736
12. Remedies for Breach of Contract — 747
    - A. General Remedial Rules — 749
      - (1) Money Remedies — 762
      - (2) Specie and Non-monetary Remedies — 805
    - B. Particular Contracts — 819
      - (1) Land Contracts — 819
      - (2) Chattel Sales Contracts — 838
      - (3) Building Contracts — 844
      - (4) Other Contracts — 853
13. Unenforceable Contracts — 856

APPENDIX: REMEDIES LAW RESEARCH ON WESTLAW — 881
TABLE OF CASES — 893
INDEX — 921

*

Table of Contents

CHAPTER 1. INTRODUCTION TO REMEDIES

§ 1.1 THE BASIC REMEDIES

Page

The Province of Remedies Law 1
    The remedial issues 1
    Remedial law vs. substantive law 1
    Remedial law vs. procedural law 2
    The main kinds of remedies 2
    Availability 2
Damages 3
    Damages as compensation 3
    Forms of the damages remedy 3
    Noncompensatory money awards 3
    Conventional damages 4
Restitution 4
    Restitution as restoration to prevent unjust enrichment 4
    Example 4
    The special sense of "restoration" to mean disgorgement of gains 4
    Restitution in specie 5
    Special forms of restitution 5
Coercive Remedies 5
    Injunctive remedies and the contempt power 5
    Named forms of coercive remedies 6
    Other forms of injunction 6
    Expanding injunctive relief 6
    Provisional injunctions 7
Declaratory Remedies 7
Non-judicial Remedies: Alternative Dispute Resolution and Self–Help .. 8
    Self-help 8
    Administrative relief 8
    Alternative dispute resolution 8
Essential Issues 9

§ 1.2 REMEDIES "AT LAW" AND REMEDIES "IN EQUITY"

Classification of Remedies as Legal or Equitable *
Effect on Jury Trial *
Discretion to Deny or Limit Remedy *

* For the full text of this section, see Dobbs, Law of Remedies, Second Edition, Practitioner Treatise Series, Vol. 1 (§§ 1.1–5.18).

§ 1.3 PROVISIONAL AND PERMANENT REMEDIES

Characteristics of Provisional Remedies *
Types of Provisional Remedies *
Attachment and Garnishment *
Preliminary Injunctions *
Temporary Restraining Order *
Special Constraints on Provisional Remedies *

§ 1.4 REMEDIES AND ENFORCEMENT DEVICES

	Page
Execution of Money Judgments "at Law"	12
Adjudication of liability, not a command to pay	12
Traditional execution writs	12
Statutory base in modern law	12
Contempt Sentences to Enforce Coercive Remedies	13
Decree issuing a command in personam	13
Law and equity and coercive orders	13
Examples of contempt powers	13
Non-contempt enforcement of in personam orders	14
Garnishment	14
Supplementary Proceedings or Creditors Bills in Equity	14
Equitable Liens and Constructive Trusts	15
Judgments for Possession of Property at Law	15
Receivers and Masters	16
Receivers	16
Masters	16
Receiver-masters under civil rights or restructuring injunctions	16

§ 1.5 PUBLIC LAW AND PRIVATE LAW REMEDIES

Public Law Remedies Generally	17
Public issue litigation	17
Public law remedies generally	17
Factual variation and the variability of injunctive relief	18
Institutional Restructuring Litigation	18
Discrete and Particular Differences in Public and Private Remedies	19
Statutory injunctions	19
Attorney fees	20

§ 1.6 THE SCOPE OF REMEDIAL ISSUES

The Importance of Remedial Scope	20
The Scope of Remedial Issues	21
Remedial issues arise when the plaintiff has a cause of action	21
Remedial issues	21
Applying the Limitations	21
Substantive law	21
Process or procedural law	21
Theories are not remedies	22

* For the full text of this section, see Dobbs, Law of Remedies, Second Edition, Practitioner Treatise Series, Vol. 1 (§§ 1.1–5.18).

§ 1.7 REMEDIAL ANALYSIS: MATCHING RIGHT
AND REMEDY

	Page
Rights and Remedies	22
Principle: remedies congruent with rights	22
Examples	22
Corollary	23
Knowing the right by knowing the remedy	23
Denying rights in the belief that remedies are not measurable or practical	23
The puzzle of discorrelate rights and remedies	24
Practical Constraints and Conventional Remedies	24
Judicial resources	24
Judicial roles	25
The limits of proof: conventional remedies	25
Forms of conventional remedies	25
Examples of conventional remedies	25
Reasons for conventional remedies	26
Importance of conventional measures	26
Remedies exceeding rights	26
Choosing Among Several Potentially Acceptable Remedies	27

§ 1.8 REMEDIAL ANALYSIS: COMPARING REMEDIES

Arguments From Remedial Equivalence *
Equivalence Must Be Established *
Granting a Remedy Because Equivalent Remedy Would Be Granted *
Denying a Remedy Because Equivalent Remedy Would Be Denied *

§ 1.9 REMEDIAL ANALYSIS: COUNTING COSTS
AND BENEFITS

Choosing Remedies in the Light of Costs and Benefits	29
Efficiency	30
Efficiency as maximizing human satisfactions	30
The Pareto superior idea of efficiency	30
The Kaldor–Hicks test of efficiency	30
Efficiency vs. right	31
Efficiency in selecting a remedy: the painting sale example	31
Efficient breach	33
The music group example	33
Applying efficient breach ideas to the music group case	33
Arguments against efficient breach	34
Waste	35
Remedy Costs Exceeding Relevant Legal Benefits	36
Remedy Costs Exceeding Legal Loss or Harm	36
Measuring Remedy Benefits: The Subjective Benefit Case	37
Counting on conventions	37

* For the full text of this section, see Dobbs, Law of Remedies, Second Edition, Practitioner Treatise Series, Vol. 1 (§§ 1.1–5.18).

Page

The logger and the plaintiff's tree 37
Proven subjective value to the plaintiff 37
Waste, entitlement and efficiency in the tree replacement 38
Measuring Remedy Benefits: The Case of Benefits to Third Persons or
the Public 38
Considering public benefit from tree replacement 38
Is it correct to consider benefits to those who have no rights? 39
Considering public rights in natural resources 39
Measuring Remedy Costs and Deterrence 39
Net cost to the defendant after considering his gains 39
Externalized costs 40
Effective deterrence 40
Transaction Costs 41
Rights and Efficiencies 41

§ 1.10 REMEDIES AND TRIAL STRATEGY

Remedy Chosen to Maximize Threat to the Defendant 42
The costly injunction example 42
The constructive trust—lis pendens example 43
Remedy Chosen to Enhance Procedural Advantage or Avoid Disadvan-
tage 43
The equity non-jury trial example 43
The discovery and proof example 44
The injunction bond example 44
Remedy Chosen to Avoid Defenses 45
Discretionary defenses to equitable remedies 45
Remedial immunities 45
Remedy Chosen to Enhance Enforcement of Decrees or Collection of
Judgments 45
The claim of equitable ownership or security interest example 45
The coercive order example 45

CHAPTER 2. EQUITY AND NONMONETARY REMEDIES

A. HISTORY, DEVELOPMENT AND MEANINGS OF EQUITY

§ 2.1 INTRODUCTION TO EQUITY AND EQUITABLE REMEDIES

§ 2.1(1) An Introductory Overview 48
Historical Law and Equity Court Systems 48
Coercive Remedies in Equity 49
Contempt in Equity 49
Substantive Law in Equity 49
Procedure in Equity 49
Discretion in Equity 50
—Equitable Defenses 50
—Measure of Relief 50
Adequacy of Legal Remedy or Irreparable Harm Test 50

Page

Merger of Law and Equity -- 51
Terminology: "Equity" -- 51

§ 2.1(2) Equitable Remedies ------------------------------------- 51
Coercive Remedies -- 51
    Injunctive relief -- 51
    Example of injunctive relief ------------------------------------ 52
    Injunctions under other names ---------------------------------- 52
    Specific performance --- 53
Declaratory Remedies -- 53
Restitutionary Remedies -- 53

§ 2.1(3) Meanings of Equity -------------------------------------- 55
Meanings of Equity and "Equitable" ------------------------------- 55
    Fairness, morality, and flexibility ------------------------------ 55
    The body of equity precedent, doctrine, and attitude ------------ 56
    Distinctive remedies --- 56
Effect of Determination that a Claim or Defense is Equitable ------------ 57
    What makes a claim "equitable" today? -------------------------- 57
    Equitable in the sense of fair, moral, or just ------------------- 57
    Equitable in the sense that an equitable remedy is sought ---------- 57
    Strategic possibilities -- 58

§ 2.2 THE DEVELOPMENT OF THE EQUITY COURT
The Chancellor as Writ Maker ------------------------------------- 58
Limits on the Effectiveness of Common Law Courts --------------------- 59
The Chancellor as a Political Power ------------------------------ 59
The Chancellor as a Judge -- 60
    The chancellor's court -- 60
    The chancellor's procedure -------------------------------------- 60
    The chancellor's rules -- 61
    The chancellor's jurisdiction ----------------------------------- 61
    The chancellor's theory of power: The dual system and the in personam order --- 62

§ 2.3 SUBSTANTIVE RULES DEVELOPED FROM ETHICAL PRINCIPLES OF EQUITY

§ 2.3(1) The Remedial and the Substantive ------------------------ 63
Remedial Equity -- 63
Substantive Equity -- 64

§ 2.3(2) Equity's Place in the Law of Uses and Trusts ------------- 64
Medieval Limits on Disposition of Land at Death *
Circumventing the Rule by "Uses" *
The Statute of Uses *
The Active Use Develops Into the Trust *

* For the full text of this section, see Dobbs, Law of Remedies, Second Edition, Practitioner Treatise Series, Vol. 1 (§§ 1.1–5.18).

The Bargain and Sale Development *
How Equity Characteristics Made the Trust Work *

                                                                          Page
§ 2.3(3) Equity's Place in the Law of Mortgages 64
The Common Law Mortgage as Absolute Deed *
The Equitable View of the Borrower's Rights *
The Borrower's "Equity" in the Mortgaged Land *
The Defaulting Borrower's Rights *
The Borrower's Equity of Redemption *
Foreclosing the Equity of Redemption *

§ 2.3(4) Equitable Conversion and Other Substantive Equity 64
The Equitable Conversion Doctrine *
Other Substantive Rules of Equity *

§ 2.3(5) Substantive Equitable Defenses: Equitable Estoppel
              and Similar Conceptions ------------------------------- 64
Meaning of Estoppel *
Kinds of Estoppel *
Example of Equitable Estoppel *
Elements *
Estoppel Applied in "Law" *
Public Entities and Public Policies *
Estoppel and Fraud *
Estoppel and Promise; Promissory Estoppel *
Estoppel and Restitution *
Estoppel and Waiver *
Estoppel and Laches *
Estoppel and Ratification *
Estoppel and Other Related Doctrines *
Estoppel and Analysis *

B. DISCRETION IN EQUITY

§ 2.4 THE ROLE OF DISCRETION: LIMITING AND TAILORING EQUITABLE RELIEF ON ETHICAL GROUNDS

§ 2.4(1) In Summary --- 66
Discretion to Deny or Limit Relief in Equity -------------------------- 66
Equitable Defenses -- 66
Balancing --- 67
Measuring or Shaping the Remedy ------------------------------------ 67
The Appropriate Role of Discretion ---------------------------------- 67

§ 2.4(2) Unclean Hands --- 68
General Rule and Its Effect -- 68
      General rule --- 68
      As a purely equitable defense --------------------------------- 68

* For the full text of this section, see Dobbs, Law of Remedies, Second Edition, Practitioner Treatise Series, Vol. 1 (§§ 1.1–5.18).

Page

Spurious unclean hands cases: substantive meanings and pari delicto   68
Extending judicial discretion to bar rights 69
Relatedness of Improper Conduct to Claim 69
   Related misconduct required to invoke the defense 69
   A narrow formula 70
   A discretionary formula 70
   Improper conduct not causing injury to defendant 70
Commentary: A Suggested Analysis 71
   Excluding rule-of-law and substantive defenses 71
   Excluding equitable defenses that would bar a legal claim 71
   If a pure equitable defense is invoked, is the misconduct serious?   71
   Determining relatedness 71
   Values at stake and alternative sanctions 72

§ 2.4(3) Contract Defenses in Equity 72
Unconscionability 73
Mutuality of Remedy 74

§ 2.4(4) Laches 75
Generally 75
   Laches a bar to equitable claims 75
   Laches defined 75
   Limitations on the defense 75
   Bases 76
   Law and equity 76
   Laches as a partial defense only 76
   Public interests 77
Effect of Statutes of Limitations 77
   Application of statutes of limitations to equitable claims 77
   The "analogous" statutes of limitations 77

§ 2.4(5) Balancing Equities, Hardships and Public Interests 78
In General 78
   Equitable defenses without balancing 78
   Balancing equities and hardships 78
Balancing Equities 79
   Equities 79
   Examples 79
   Good faith, fault, motive 79
Balancing Hardships 79
   Hardship rules 79
   Hardship to the defendant 80
   Hardships to the plaintiff 80
Balancing Interests of the Public and Third Persons 80
   Balancing to deny injunctive relief *
   Balancing to favor injunctive relief *
   Statutory balance *
   Public interest balancing as cost-benefit analysis 81

* For the full text of this section, see Dobbs, Law of Remedies, Second Edition, Practitioner Treatise Series, Vol. 1 (§§ 1.1–5.18).

Page

§ 2.4(6) Measuring, Shaping, or Tailoring the Remedy 81
The Measuring, Shaping, or Tailoring Stage *
Measuring up to the Right *
Narrowing Down to Hardships or Equities *
Examples of Measuring or Shaping the Remedy *
Remedies Exceeding Rights *

§ 2.4(7) The Role of Equitable Discretion in Equity 84
The Dilemma of Discretion *
    Limits on discretion *
    Limits on the limits of discretion *
    Uncertainties in the balancing process *
    Disadvantages of discretion *
Discretion and the Rightful Position: Discretion Limiting Rights *
    Aiming at protecting the plaintiff's entitlement or rightful position *
    Practical constraints and lesser goals *
    Traditional view that equitable discretion does not deny the plaintiff
      her rightful position *
    Redefining the plaintiff's rightful position to include equitable pro-
      tection *
    Circularity in rightful position arguments *
    The modest proposition *
    Rejecting discretion to deny all rights *
    Statutory rights and equitable discretion *
Discretion to Expand Rights? *
    Rightful position goals and the expansion of remedies in equity *
    Assuring full rights by giving relief beyond the entitlement *
    Affecting third persons *
    Incidental burdens *
    Substantial burdens *

**§ 2.5   REMEDIAL LIMITS BASED ON POWER AND POLICY:
ADEQUACY AND PRACTICABILITY**

**§ 2.5(1) Adequacy of Legal Remedy or the Irreparable Harm
      Rule** 86
Adequacy Test 86
Historical Basis 86
The Irreparable Harm Formulation 87
Relative Adequacy 88
Adequacy as a Non-discretionary Rule; "Equity Jurisdiction" 88
Distinguishing Other Rules 88
Examples 89
Rule Inapplicable to Substantive Equitable Rights 89
Attacks and Doubts *

* For the full text of this section, see Dobbs, Law of Remedies, Second Edition, Practitioner Treatise Series, Vol. 1 (§§ 1.1–5.18).

Page

§ 2.5(2) **Establishing Irreparable Harm** ----------------------------------- 90

Patterns of Irreparable Harm/Inadequate Legal Remedy ------------------- 90

    Patterns and factors in determining inadequacy ------------------------ 90

    (1) "Unique" or special entitlements ---------------------------------- 90

    (2) Repeated acts, multiplicity of suits -------------------------------- 91

    (3) Legal remedy available but not collectible --------------------------- 91

    (4) Damages cannot be measured with reasonable certainty --------- 91

Applications in Specific Performance Cases *

    The uniqueness pattern *

    The measurement difficulty pattern *

    Specific performance for sellers *

Applications in Tort Cases *

    The uniqueness pattern *

    The repeated harm, multiplicity of suit pattern *

    The measurement difficulty pattern *

§ 2.5(3) **The Adequacy Test Today: Reality and Debate** ------------ 92

Adequacy Today --- 92

    The rule declines -- 92

    Emerging issues --- 92

Coercive Remedies: The Advocates --- 93

    Owen Fiss -- 93

    Douglas Laycock -- 93

Coercive Remedies: Doubters and Disbelievers ----------------------------- 94

    Doug Rendleman -- 94

    Edward Yorio --- 95

Specific Performance --- 95

    Disfavoring specific performance ------------------------------------- 95

    Favoring specific performance --------------------------------------- 96

    Moral theories of performance --------------------------------------- 96

    Party autonomy --- 97

Some Assessments --- 97

§ 2.5(4) **Practicality and Public Policy as Limits On or Guides
      to Equitable Remedies** --- 98

Substantive Policy --- 98

    Compelling personal service --- 98

    Forbidding speech -- 98

    Weighing public needs -- 98

Practicality, Convenience, Judicial Resources ------------------------------ 99

    Supervision --- 99

    Certainty in specific performance ------------------------------------- 99

Deference and Practical Caution -- 100

    State court injunctions against other state courts -------------------- 100

    Federal courts enjoining state court proceedings -------------------- 100

    Administrative proceedings *

    Enjoining the executive *

---

* For the full text of this section, see Dobbs, Law of Remedies, Second Edition, Practitioner Treatise Series, Vol. 1 (§§ 1.1–5.18).

Enjoining acts in other states *
Adequacy and policy *
Relevance to remedies *

C. PROCEDURES, JURISDICTION, AND ENFORCEMENT

§ 2.6 LAW AND EQUITY TODAY—THE MERGER OF LAW AND EQUITY AND THE RIGHT OF JURY TRIAL

Page

§ 2.6(1) The Merger of Law and Equity 101
Generally 101
    Merger 101
    Scope 102
Substantive and Procedural Merger 102
    Procedural merger and the jury 102
    Merger and substantive law 103
Remedial Merger 103
    Merger and remedial law 103
    Adequacy or irreparable harm rules *
    Equitable discretion *
    Unclean hands *
    Laches *
    Coercive orders and enforcement of money awards *

§ 2.6(2) Merger and Jury Trial—Equity Jury Rules 104
Constitutional Rights to Jury Trial "at Common Law" 104
States Granting Equity Jury Trial 105
Advisory Juries in Equity 105

§ 2.6(3) Characterizing a Case: Equitable or Legal? 105
In Summary 105
    Distinguishing characteristics 105
    Substantive and remedial tests of equitable status 105
    Judicial approaches generally 106
Remedies Sought as Test of Equitable or Legal Character 106
    The remedial test 106
    Money claims for restitution 106
    Money claims for restitution with equitable enforcement: constructive trusts 107
    Money claims for restitution with equitable enforcement: accounting for profits 107
    The Dairy Queen case 108
    The stockholder's derivative suit 108
    The preference/fraudulent conveyance litigation; bankruptcy 110
Substantive Tests of Legal or Equitable Character: Equity without Coercion 111
    The substantive test 111

---

* For the full text of this section, see Dobbs, Law of Remedies, Second Edition, Practitioner Treatise Series, Vol. 1 (§§ 1.1–5.18).

Page

Mortgages 111
Trusts 112
Rescission and other declaratory decrees 112
Estoppel and other equitable doctrines 113
Statutory Claims 114
Generally 114
Power of the legislature to prescribe non-jury trials 114
Indiscriminate equity: the case of Title VII 115
Evaluating Approaches 116

§ 2.6(4) Jury Trial in Mixed Law and Equity Cases 117
Clean-up or Incidental Jurisdiction 117
Whole case tried in equity 117
Examples 117
Efficiency and waiver theories 117
Severance or Separate Trials 118
Trial of equity issues first, controlling legal issues by res judicata . 118
Trial of the law claim first 118
The Dairy Queen Rule 118
Abolishing incidental jurisdiction? 119
Mode of trial after incidental jurisdiction is abolished 119
Example 119
Effects and strategies 119
Current status 120
In the states 120
Equitable Claim with Legal Counterclaim: Beacon Theatres 121
The Federal rule 121
In the states 122
Affecting Jury Trial by Res Judicata: The Order of Trial 122

§ 2.6(5) Effect of Jury Trial on Tailoring or Modifying the Decree 124
Discretion and Other Equity Power 124
Preliminary Relief Unaffected by Dairy Queen 124
Judge's Power to Limit Remedy Independent of Jury Findings *
Practice in States Allowing Jury Trial *
Jury's Role in Finding Facts Upon Which Judge's Discretion is Based *
Jury's Role in Measuring Damages Given in Substitution for Equitable Relief *
Modification *

§ 2.7 "JURISDICTIONAL" ISSUES IN EQUITY COURTS

Jurisdiction and Power 124
Spurious Jurisdiction 124
"Equity jurisdiction" 124
"Clean-up jurisdiction" *

* For the full text of this section, see Dobbs, Law of Remedies, Second Edition, Practitioner Treatise Series, Vol. 1 (§§ 1.1–5.18).

                                                                     Page
Jurisdiction to Preserve the Court's Power to Act 125
    Error distinguished 125
    True jurisdictional limitations 125
    The bootstrap corollary 125
    The Mineworkers case 126
Interstate Equity 127
    Jurisdiction over person or property required 127
    Remedial limits of jurisdiction quasi-in rem 127
    Contract to sell land example 127
    Expanded personal jurisdiction permitting in personam remedies .. 127
    Affecting foreign land titles 128
    Example 128
    In personam orders affecting foreign land 129
    Compelling acts in foreign states 129

§ 2.8 ENFORCEMENT OF EQUITY DECREES

§ 2.8(1) Methods of Enforcement 130
Contempt Sanctions 130
Non-parties Subject to Liability for Contempt 130
Raising Defenses to the Contempt Charge 131
Decretal Transfer of Title, Liens and Trusts 131
Enforcing Possession Through the Sheriff's In Rem Seizure 132
Receivers 132
Masters 133
Enforcing Money Decrees 133
Supplemental Proceedings 134

§ 2.8(2) Sanctions for Contempt 135
General Categories 135
Imprisonment 135
Imprisonment for Debt 135
Coercive Fines 136
Compensatory or Remedial Sanctions 136
Defendant's Profits as a Remedial Sanction 137
Denying the Right to Litigate 137
Other Sanctions 138

§ 2.8(3) Enforcement of Equity Decrees by Contempt Powers—
         Civil vs. Criminal 138
Determinate, Coercive and Remedial Sanctions 138
    Criminal sanctions require criminal trial procedures 138
    Sanction imposed determines civil or criminal nature 138
    Tests applied 139
    Examples of criminal and civil sanctions 139
    When a determinate sanction is coercive 139
    The special rule for remedial or compensatory sanctions 140
Where Coercive Effects Are Impossible, Diminished, Unnecessary or Ex-
    hausted 140
    The core cases: when the court's decree has no further force 140

Page

—Decree reversed on appeal 141
—Prohibitory and mandatory decrees 141
—Orders to testify 141
Beyond the core: when the injunction prohibits but does not man-
   date acts 142
—The Michigan rule 142
—The Pennsylvania rule 142
—Decisions approving coercive contempt in prohibitory injunction
   cases 143
—Evaluations 144
Exhausted or diminished coercive effect 144
The Supreme Court's test 145

§ 2.8(4) Consequences of the Criminal Contempt Classification 145
General Rule: Criminal Protections Apply 145
Examples 146
Jury Trial 146
Limited Punishment 147

§ 2.8(5) Persons Subject to Contempt 148
General Rule 148
Parties, Persons in Concert or Abetting Them 148
Independent Interest or Activity of the Contemnor Negating Concert .. 149
Agents 150
Successors and Privies 150
Injunctions In Rem and Other Expansive Injunctions 151
Resurrecting In Rem Injunctions? 152
Contempt Liability of Named Defendant for Acts of Third Persons 153

§ 2.8(6) Review: The Collateral Bar Rule 153
Liability for Disobedience of Unreversed Erroneous Order 153
Nonliability for Disobedience of Void Order 153
The Example of Walker v. City of Birmingham 154
Exception: Opportunity for Meaningful Hearing on the Merits 154
Exception: Lack of Jurisdiction 155
The Mine Workers Bootstrap Rule 155
State Cases 156
Media Restraints 156
Non-media Defendants 157
Comment 157

§ 2.8(7) Inability to Comply and Related Defenses 158
Burden of Proving Ability or Inability to Comply 158
Compensatory Fines 159
Nebulous Injunctions: The Order That Cannot Be Understood 159

§ 2.8(8) Modification of Decrees 160
Modification Permitted Generally 160
Role of Modification in Enforcement 160
Consent Decrees: Modification Permitted 161

	Page
The Swift Case	161
Modifying the Rigid Rule	161
Discretion	162

D. INJUNCTIONS

§ 2.9 PERMANENT INJUNCTIONS

§ 2.9(1) Injunctions Generally	162
Injunction as a Coercive Order	162
Mandatory vs. Prohibitory Injunctions	163
Classification	163
Formal but not substantive differences	163
Reluctance to use mandatory injunctions	163
Preventive, Reparative and Structural Injunctions	164
Reparative and preventive injunctions	164
Structural injunctions	164
Other Compulsions	164
Injunctions with specific names	164
Prerogative writs	165
Prohibition and mandamus	165

§ 2.9(2) Bases for Grant or Denial of Injunctive Relief	165
Grounds and Cases for Injunctive Relief	165
The Adequate Legal Remedy and Balance of Equities and Costs	166
Traditional adequacy or irreparable harm rule	166
Balance of benefits and costs or disadvantages	166
Non-monetary costs	166
Economic costs	166
Alternative remedies as a benchmark for measuring benefit of the injunction	167
Injunctions undercutting rule for minimizing damages	167
Risk of error	167

§ 2.9(3) Subject Matter: Injunctions Protecting or Limiting Property and Economic Rights	168
Property Rights	168
Economic Rights	168
Crimes	169

§ 2.9(4) Subject Matter: Injunctions Facilitating Procedure, Tactics, or Review	170
Tactical, Procedural and Review Injunctions	170
Enjoining Civil Litigation	171
Enjoining abusive litigation	171
Enjoining litigation temporarily to prevent irreparable loss of rights	171
Enjoining litigation to control choice of forum	171
Federal courts enjoining state litigation	172
Bills of peace	172
Interpleader	173
Traditional interpleader	173

Page

Examples 173
Traditional limiting rules 173
Federal statutory interpleader 174
Federal rule interpleader; comparisons 175
Interpleader to compel equitable distribution of limited funds 175
Potentials for expanding interpleader 175
Enjoining Criminal Prosecutions 176

§ 2.9(5) Subject Matter: Injunctions Protecting Personal Rights 177
Property Right/Personal Right Distinction 177
Political and Civil Rights 177
Religious Matters 179
Defamation 179
Other Cases 179

§ 2.10 STATUTORY INJUNCTIONS

Adequacy or Irreparable Injury Requirement in Statutory Injunction
  Cases 180
Statutory construction in mandatory and permissible statutes 180
Authorization read to eliminate irreparable injury requirement 180
In preliminary relief cases 181
Discretion to Deny the Statutory Injunction 181
Statutory construction issues 181
The Schoenbrod principle 181
Refusing and tailoring the statutory injunction 182
Insisting on the statutory injunction 182
Discretion to deny remedies, not discretion to deny rights 182
Adding Relief Not Specified in Statutes 183

§ 2.11 PROVISIONAL INJUNCTIONS AND OTHER INJUNCTIVE PROCEDURES

§ 2.11(1) Preliminary Injunctions and Temporary Restraining Orders Generally 184
Types of Provisional Relief 184
Permanent injunctions 184
Preliminary injunctions 184
Temporary restraining orders 184
Other forms of provisional relief 185
Types of Cases 185
Tangible and intangible property 185
Economic and contract rights 186
Constitutional, personal, and public rights 186
Error potential 187

§ 2.11(2) Standards for Issuance of Provisional Injunctive Orders 187
Standards 187
Main factors 187
The special irreparable harm requirement 187

	Page
Unstructured factors	187
Structured factors	188
Imperfections	188
The Leubsdorf rationale and reformulation	189
Example under the Leubsdorf formulation	189
Preliminary injunction when the plaintiff is unlikely to win	190
Role of quantification	190
Judicial acceptance of the Leubsdorf standard	191
Critics and Evaluations	192
Critics	192
Tune-up changes wrought by the Leubsdorf formula	193
Significant change wrought by the Leubsdorf formula	193
What Counts as Irreparable Harm	193
Harm not preventable by permanent injunction and not compensable in damages	193
Timber cutting example	194
Timing of the final hearing as a factor	194
The museum example	194
Tailoring to avoid or limit irreparable harm	195
Irreparable harm to public or third-party interests	195
Remote irreparable harm	195
§ 2.11(3) The Security Requirement	196
General Rule	196
Bond required	196
Purposes	197
Bond as Limit of Liability	197
Majority view: liability limited to amount of the bond	197
Minority view: plaintiff is personally liable	198
Expanding liability by a special undertaking	198
Alternative damages claims by the wronged defendant	199
Restitution claims by the wronged defendant	199
Discretion to Dispense with Bond or Refuse Claims against It	199
Mandatory bond	199
Discretionary bond under state statutes	200
Four stages or points for the exercise of discretion	200
Open-ended discretion	201
Limited discretion	202
Triggering the Bond Liability	202
Damages Recoverable	203
Comments on the Bond Requirement	205
§ 2.11(4) Judicial Review of Injunctions	206
Appeals of Injunctive Orders	206
Stays of Injunctive Orders *	
Mandatory Injunctions *	

* For the full text of this section, see Dobbs, Law of Remedies, Second Edition, Practitioner Treatise Series, Vol. 1 (§§ 1.1–5.18).

CHAPTER 3. PRINCIPLES OF DAMAGES

§ 3.1 INTRODUCING DAMAGES LAW: TERMS, GOALS AND METHODS

Page

Terminology and Concepts -------------------------------------- 208
 Money award and in rem enforcement ---------------------- 208
 Harm or loss distinguished ----------------------------------- 209
 Specie remedies distinguished ------------------------------- 209
 Restitution distinguished ------------------------------------ 210
Compensatory and Non-compensatory Goals --------------------- 210
 Non-pecuniary injury --- 211
 Non-compensatory characteristics of non-pecuniary injury damages 211
 Three reasons for awarding non-compensatory damages ------ 211
 Punitive damages --- 212
Proof, Convention and Substantive Policy in Damages Measurement --- 212
 Substantive goals guiding damages measurement ------------ 212
 —Legal theory of the complaint ------------------------------ 212
 —Incentive damages; a nuisance example ------------------- 213
 —Incentive damages; a contract example -------------------- 213
 —Economic waste --- 213
 Conventions in damages measurement ----------------------- 213
Major Issues in Damages Law ----------------------------------- 214
 The role of damages in the remedial scheme ---------------- 214
 The role of compensation in damages remedies ------------- 215
 Caps on damages and multipliers of damages --------------- 215
 The attorney fees issue -------------------------------------- 215
 Damages administration: periodic payments ----------------- 215

§ 3.2 SUMMARIZING DAMAGES RULES

Measures of Damages -- 216
 General or market damages ---------------------------------- 216
 Special or consequential damages --------------------------- 217
 Substitution cost damages ------------------------------------ 217
 Standardized and pattern damages -------------------------- 217
 Punitive damages --- 218
 Litigation costs -- 218
Adjustments for Time Differentials: Delay and Prepayment ------- 218
 Interest -- 218
 Reduction to present value ----------------------------------- 219
Adjustments for Benefits Reaped or Harms Avoided by the Plaintiff ---- 219
 Collateral source benefits ----------------------------------- 219
 Direct benefits --- 219
 Avoided and avoidable consequences ------------------------ 219

§ 3.3 BASIC DAMAGES MEASURES OR APPROACHES

§ 3.3(1) Measures and Elements of Damages ------------------ 220
The Specific Element Approach: Personal Injury and Related Cases ----- 220

Page

The Yardstick or Measured Approach: Property and Contract Cases 220
    Three types of damages measurement ------------------------------------ 220
    Standardization and individuation *
    Duplication and overcompensation *

§ 3.3(2) Nominal Damages and Standardized Surrogate Damages -- 221
Nominal Damages -- 221
    Meaning -- 221
    Where the plaintiff has no cause of action ----------------------------- 221
    When substantial damages are recoverable ---------------------------- 221
    When nominal damages are recoverable ------------------------------ 221
    Why nominal damages --- 221
Standardized Surrogate Damages -- 222

§ 3.3(3) General Damages or Market Measures ------------------------ 223
General Damages—The Pleading Rule *
General Damages as a Market Damages Measure *
The Tort Example *
The Contract Example *
Loss of Market "Gains," Not Loss of Profits *
Characteristics of Market Damages: Unrealized Losses *
Characteristics of Market Damages: A Closing Date for Party Accounting *
Characteristics of Market Damages: Transaction Costs Ignored *
Why Market Measures? *

§ 3.3(4) Consequential Damages ------------------------------------- 226
Meaning of Special or Consequential Damages *
Income or Profit Lost *
Expense Incurred *
Characteristics of Consequential Damages *
Market Gains Distinguished *
Problems With Consequential Damages *

§ 3.3(5) Substitution Costs -- 229
What is Measured by Substitution Costs *
Two Uses of Substitution Cost Measures *
Relation to Market Measure *
Characteristics *
Problems With Substitution Cost Measures *

§ 3.3(6) Individuating Damages: Protecting the Plaintiff's Personal Values -- 231
Objectified Measures of Damages *
Idiosyncratic Values vs. Objective Measures: Substitution Cost vs. Market Measures *
Profits vs. Gains: Consequential vs. Market Measures *

* For the full text of this section, see Dobbs, Law of Remedies, Second Edition, Practitioner Treatise Series, Vol. 1 (§§ 1.1–5.18).

Page

§ 3.3(7) Duplication of Damages --- 231

Adding Two Measures for One Loss or Wrong ----------------------------- 231

    General damages plus substitution cost damages ---------------------- 231

    General damages and profits --- 232

    The nuisance example *

    Limits to the duplication argument *

    Other forms of overcompensation *

Awarding Damages under Several Substantive Theories *

Awarding Damages and other Remedies *

§ 3.3(8) The Relative Accuracy of Damages Measures: A Comment --- 232

§ 3.4 PROVING CONSEQUENTIAL DAMAGES: SPECIAL REQUIREMENTS, LIMITED ALTERNATIVES

Rules Inhibiting Consequential Damages Claims -------------------------- 234

    Pleading --- 234

    Certainty: pecuniary loss must be realized ------------------------------ 234

    Certainty: proof as to amount --- 234

    Proximate cause and Hadley limits -- 235

    Avoidable consequences --- 236

Alternative Claims to Escape the Limitations ------------------------------ 236

    Objective substitutes for profit loss -------------------------------------- 236

    Value of the chance; preponderance of the evidence ------------------ 236

    Value of chances that are bought and sold ----------------------------- 236

    Value of chances for which there is no market ------------------------- 237

    Percentage chance without a market: the pig that missed the fair - 237

    Authority for and against value of the chance ------------------------- 237

    Would value-of-the chance always limit the recovery to less than compensation? --- 238

§ 3.5 CONSTRUCTING MARKET VALUE: DEFINITIONS AND EVIDENCE

Constructing a Hypothetical Market -- 238

    No market --- 238

    Willing buyer and seller: looking for information to construct a "market" -- 239

    Scope and related material --- 239

Opinion Evidence of Value --- 239

    Expert opinion -- 239

    Owner opinion -- 240

    Other opinion testimony -- 240

Data for Constructing a Value -- 240

    Market reports -- 240

    Comparable sales --- 240

    Offers and prior sales --- 241

    "Capitalization of income" or discounted cash flow -------------------- 241

* For the full text of this section, see Dobbs, Law of Remedies, Second Edition, Practitioner Treatise Series, Vol. 1 (§§ 1.1–5.18).

                                                                 Page

Capitalization: passive income requirement 242
Capitalization: figuring the discount rate 242
Other methods 244

§ 3.6 INTEREST ADJUSTMENTS

§ 3.6(1) Interest and Prejudgment Interest 244
Background and Summary 244
    Interest as compensation, restitution and incentive 244
    Historic attitudes towards interest 245
    Residual reluctance to award interest for pre-judgment losses 245
    Computation 245
Categories of Interest 245
General Rules 246
    Rule against interest on unliquidated sums 246
    Interest permitted on liquidated or "ascertainable" damages 247
    Example of ascertainable damages 247
    Effect of disputes, defenses and counterclaims 248
    Other limitations on interest 248

§ 3.6(2) Sidestepping the Traditional Limitations 248
Extending the Realm of the Ascertainable 248
    Generally 249
    Examples of extension 249
    The future of the "ascertainable" standard 250
Claiming Interest or Costs as Special Damages 250
Claiming Interest in Lieu of Rental Value or Lost Profits 250
Claiming Interest as Restitution 251
Contract, Express or Implied 252
Statutes 252

§ 3.6(3) Attacking the Traditional Limitations 254
    Compensation, restitution, and incentives 254
    Plaintiff's real losses 254
    The defendant's real gains 255
    Incentives to delay 255
    Reduction to present value argument 255
    Fairness to defendant arguments 255

§ 3.6(4) Computation of Interest 256
Financing Costs as Special Damages *
Prejudgment Interest When Special Damages Have Not Been Proven *
Legal or Statutory Rate *
Market Rates *
Simple Interest *
Types of Compounding Permitted *
Accrual 257
Elements of Damages Included 258

* For the full text of this section, see Dobbs, Law of Remedies, Second Edition, Practitioner Treatise Series, Vol. 1 (§§ 1.1–5.18).

Page

§ 3.6(5) Other Limitations on Prejudgment Interest 258
Underlying Claim Not Matured or Accrued *
Duplication *
Discretion *

§ 3.6(6) Judgment Interest 259
Rate and Compounding *
Verdict or Judgment? *
Which Judgment? *
Affirmance of Judgment After Plaintiff Appeals *
Modification as to Amount or New Judgment Favorable to Plaintiff *

§ 3.7 DAMAGES AND VARIATIONS IN DOLLAR VALUE

Topic and Scope 259
Reduction to Present Value 260
    Reduction to present value required 260
    Reasons for rule 260
    Methods for computing 260
Inflation 260
    Effect of future inflation on future losses considered 260
    General methods for considering inflation 261
    Adjusting for inflation by finding the "real" interest rate ... 261
    Treating future inflation and present value reductions as a wash .. 261
    Periodic payments 261
    Distinguishing other adjustments from inflation adjustments 261
Foreign Currency Fluctuations against the Dollar 262
    Dollar judgments; conversion from foreign currency 262
    Example of conversion date options 262
    Breach date rule 263
    Judgment date rule 263
    Payment date rule 263
    Criticizing the breach date rule 263
    Supporting the payment date rule 264
    Making payment date work 264
    Judgments in foreign currency 264
    Which currency is the rightful currency 265
    Making the plaintiff whole 265
    Restitution 265

§ 3.8 BENEFITS TO THE PLAINTIFF FROM THE DEFENDANT'S ACTS

§ 3.8(1) Collateral Source Benefits 266
General Rule 266
    No credit to the defendant for collateral benefits to the plaintiff ... 266
    Insurance and similar benefits 267

* For the full text of this section, see Dobbs, Law of Remedies, Second Edition, Practitioner Treatise Series, Vol. 1 (§§ 1.1–5.18).

                                                                                Page
Gifts and public benefits -- 267
Replacement of support and tax savings ---------------------------- 267
Rationales -- 267
Donor's intent -- 267
Subrogation --- 268
Plaintiff paid --- 268
Windfall --- 268
Measurement and prejudice --------------------------------------- 268
Unspoken rationales -- 269
Statutory Changes --- 269
Statutes fostering a credit --- 269
Allocating and computing the credit --------------------------- 269

§ 3.8(2) Direct Benefits -- 269
General Rule --- 269
Exceptions or Limitations --- 270
Benefits common to the community *
Benefits to "different interests" *
Unwanted benefits *
Causation *
Time for valuing the plaintiff's loss *

§ 3.9   MINIMIZING DAMAGES: AVOIDABLE CONSEQUENCES RULES

General Rule -- 270
General scope of avoidable consequences rules ------------------ 270
The four rules of avoidable consequences ---------------------- 271
Example --- 271
Burden of proof -- 272
Applications and Amplifications --------------------------------------- 272
First rule -- 272
Second rule: reasonableness assessments ------------------------ 272
Third rule --- 273
When minimizing adds assets -- 273
Special rule for leases --- 274
Rationales and Limitations -- 274
Efficiency and fairness -- 274
Relative fault or ability to minimize ------------------------------ 274
Substantial rights -- 274
Strategically placed defendants ------------------------------------- 275
Comparative Fault vs. Avoidable Consequences --------------------- 275

§ 3.10   RECOVERY OF ATTORNEY FEES AND COSTS IN LITIGATION

§ 3.10(1) General Rule and Summary ---------------------------- 276
The General Rule -- 276
The general rule -- 276

* For the full text of this section, see Dobbs, Law of Remedies, Second Edition, Practitioner
Treatise Series, Vol. 1 (§§ 1.1–5.18).

Page
Development of the American Rule --------------------------------- 277
Rationales --- 277
The Attacking Arguments --- 277
Other legal systems -- 277
The main arguments --- 278
(1) Indemnity: two way fee shifting ------------------------------ 278
(2) Fees as damages: one way fee shifting ---------------------- 278
(3) Fees as incentives -- 278
Scope and Exceptions *
Functional exceptions *
Scope: recovery from litigation allies *
Traditional exceptions *
Exceptions: statutes and private attorney generals *
Entitlement *
Measurement of fees *

§ 3.10(2) The Common Fund, Substantial Benefit and Private
         Attorney General -- 279
Fee Sharing under the Common Fund Rule ------------------------ 279
The common fund rule --- 279
Examples -- 280
Restitutionary basis for fee sharing ----------------------------- 280
Restitution and the "volunteers" rule --------------------------- 281
Common fund and conflict of interest --------------------------- 281
Fee Shifting under the "Substantial Benefit" Extension -------- 281
Extending common fund ideas ----------------------------------- 281
Hall v. Cole -- 282
Potential coverage --- 282
Criticizing the restitutionary argument in substantial benefit cases 282
Unspoken reasons *
The Private Attorney General ------------------------------------- 283
Serrano v. Priest -- 283
Status of the private attorney general doctrine ----------------- 283
The benefit element --- 284
Comparisons to substantial benefit rule ------------------------- 284
Coincidence of burden and benefit ------------------------------- 285
The public policy elements --------------------------------------- 285

§ 3.10(3) Attorney Fees as Damages and Sanctions ------------- 285
Fee Recovery as Damages: The Principle ------------------------- 285
Contractual Obligations to Protect against Litigation Costs ---- 286
Explicit contracts --- 286
Indemnity and hold harmless agreements generally *
Injunction bonds -- 286
Title warranty --- 287
Liability insurer's promise to defend *
First party insurer's bad faith failure to pay policy benefits *

* For the full text of this section, see Dobbs, Law of Remedies, Second Edition, Practitioner Treatise Series, Vol. 1 (§§ 1.1–5.18).

                                                                 Page

Promises to arbitrate, not litigate *
Other implicit agreements 287
Tort, Indemnity, and Sanction: Obligations Imposed by Law 288
Indemnity without express contract 288
Third person litigation 289
Beyond the third party limitation 289
Malicious prosecution and similar damages cases 290
Litigation misconduct 290
Contempt of court 291

§ 3.10(4) Development of the Civil Rights Fee Statutes 291
Fee Award Statutes Generally 291
Development of the Civil Rights Fee Award 292
Narrow fee statutes 292
The private attorney general rationale in Piggie Park 292
Attempts to extend the rationale 293
Alyeska: the Supreme Court rejects the extension 293
Section 1988 293

§ 3.10(5) Eligibility and Entitlement Generally 293
Entitlement Issues *
Scope: Civil Rights Statutes *
Entitlement in Summary *
(1) Routinely awarded to prevailing plaintiffs 294
(2) Routinely denied to prevailing defendants 294
(3) Awarded as costs, not "damages" 294
(4) Fee awards can be claimed by clients' lawyers 294
(5) Only prevailing plaintiffs recover 295

§ 3.10(6) Eligibility and Entitlement: Prevailing Party Rules 295
General Rules 295
Standard 295
Prevailing without relief 295
Relief without prevailing: interim success 295
Preliminary injunction shown to have been erroneous 296
Preliminary injunction mooted 297
Preliminary injunction with immediate fees 297
Criticisms and limits on immediate fees 297
Prevailing by settlement 298
Prevailing by defendant's unilateral reform; moot cases 299
Collateral Disputes within the Litigation *
Pre-litigation administrative proceedings *
Prevailing on a non-fee claim *
Liability limited to losing parties; intervenors *
Joint and several liability *
Apportionment of fee liability *

* For the full text of this section, see Dobbs, Law of Remedies, Second Edition, Practitioner Treatise Series, Vol. 1 (§§ 1.1–5.18).

Page

§ 3.10(7) Fee Measurement: In Summary ------------------------------ 300
Hourly Rate Measure *
Factors and Percentages *
Effect of Small Recovery *
Reduction for Limited Success *
Addition for Risks *
Effect of Fee Contract With Client *
Other Litigation Costs *

§ 3.10(8) Fee Measurement: Basic Methods ---------------------------- 301
In General *
The Johnson Factors Method *
    Factors used by lawyers *
    Factors adopted for court awarded fees *
    Subjective and non-quantitative characteristics *
Hourly Rate Method *
    Hourly rates: the lodestar method *
    Objectified characteristics *
    Disadvantages of hourly rate method *
The Rate Element in the Hourly Method *
    Standards under Blum v. Stenson *
    Ambiguities *
    Rate in different communities *
    Rates for lawyers whose usual charges are less than market *
    Historic rates vs. market rates: lawyers who charge more *
The Time Element in the Hourly Method *
    Time proof required *
    Fees for work in claiming fees *
    Reasonableness of hours claimed *
    Three types of appraisals of time claimed *
Evaluating Time Invested by Cost–Benefit Analysis: The Private Case
    Comparison -- 301
        Disproportionate fees -- 301
        Riverside -- 301
        Riverside dissenters -- 302
        Riverside plurality; weighing social benefits against fee costs ----- 302
        Reciprocity in litigation costs --------------------------------- 303
        Alternative grounds for attacking time invested --------------- 303
Percentage Fees -- 303
Standardized Fees -- 304

§ 3.10(9) Fee Measurement: Reduction for Partial Success -------- 305
General Rule --- 305
Difficulty in Applying the Limited Success Rule --------------------- 305
    Judging success --- 305
    (1) The complaint-judgment test --------------------------------- 305
    (2) The reasonable expectation test ------------------------------ 305

* For the full text of this section, see Dobbs, Law of Remedies, Second Edition, Practitioner Treatise Series, Vol. 1 (§§ 1.1–5.18).

                                                                    Page

(3) Proportionality test -- 305

Reductions --- 306

Why are reductions required? *

§ 3.10(10) Fee Measurement: Enhancement and Multipliers ------ 306

Enhancements for Quality, Difficulty, Results or Like Factors ------ 306

   Enhancements under Johnson factors approach ------------------ 306

   Enhancements/multipliers denied under hourly rate or lodestar approach --- 306

   Permissible enhancements under the hourly rate method ----------- 307

Contingency or Risk Enhancements ---------------------------------- 308

   The risk problem -- 308

   The Leubsdorf proposal -- 308

   Pre–Blum decisions -- 309

   Delaware Valley II -- 309

   Justice O'Connor's opinion in Delaware Valley II *

   Granting enhancements under Justice O'Connor's opinion *

   Denying enhancements in spite of Justice O'Connor's opinion *

Delay Enhancement --- 309

§ 3.10(11) Fee Measurement: Effect of Client's Fee Contract ---- 310

Effect on Contingency Enhancement *

Effect on Defendant's Base Liability *

Effect of Defendant's Statutory Liability on Client's Contract Liability *

§ 3.11 PUNITIVE DAMAGES

The General Rules

§ 3.11(1) Punitive Damages Allowable -------------------------- 310

Introduction and Summary -- 310

Punitive Damages Generally -- 312

   Definition, basis, and terms ------------------------------------ 312

   In-court misconduct --- 313

   Origin and discretion as to amount ------------------------------ 313

   State of authority for punitive damages -------------------------- 313

   Traditional jury role and amounts ------------------------------- 314

   New limitations on or review of jury's role ---------------------- 315

Settings for Exclusion of Punitive Damages ------------------------ 315

   Equity -- 315

   Contract claims --- 315

   Arbitration --- 315

   Free speech areas --- 315

   Statutory claims -- 316

Settings for Grant of Punitive Damages ---------------------------- 316

Persons Liable -- 317

   Mental capacity --- 317

   Minors -- 318

* For the full text of this section, see Dobbs, Law of Remedies, Second Edition, Practitioner Treatise Series, Vol. 1 (§§ 1.1–5.18).

Page

Employers, public entities, public utilities ----------------------------- 318
Persons Who May Sue --- 318

§ 3.11(2) Bases of the Traditional Punitive Damages Award ----- 318
Punishment and Retribution: Just Deserts -------------------------------- 318
The Mental State Required -- 319
    Conduct --- 319
    Tests for state of mind --- 319
    State of mind: intentional risk-taking vs. intentional harm ---------- 319
    Limited value of tests -- 320
    Illustrative cases -- 320
Gross Negligence and Mental States -------------------------------------- 320
Torts Based on Bad Faith, Malice or Serious Wrongs ---------------------- 321
Deviant Applications of the Rules --------------------------------------- 321
Abuse of Power --- 321

§ 3.11(3) Deterrence and Other Purposes of Punitive Damages --- 322
Deterrence -- 322
    Deterrence as a goal and measure ------------------------------------- 322
    Deterrence by removing profit from profitable torts ------------------ 323
    How tortious activity may continue to be profitable after paying
      compensatory damages -- 323
    "General" deterrence by imposing costs of all harms done to
      everyone --- 324
    Injunctive deterrence with punitive awards --------------------------- 325
    Deterrence by example to others -------------------------------------- 326
    Deterrence and just deserts -- 326
Litigation Finance and Added Compensation ------------------------------- 327
    Litigation finance; compensation for attorney fees ------------------- 327
    Litigation finance; incentives to sue -------------------------------- 327
    Forcing a choice between attorney fee and punitive damages --------- 328
    Litigation finance vs. punishment *
    Added compensation *

Punitive Damage Litigation: The Main Problem

§ 3.11(4) Proof Standards -------------------------------- ------------------- 328

§ 3.11(5) Financial Condition of Defendant ---------------------------- 328
Permitting Evidence of the Defendant's Finances ------------------------- 328
    General rule admitting proof of financial condition ------------------ 328
    Theory of the rule --- 329
    Is proof required? --- 329
    California requirement of proof -------------------------------------- 329
Countering Prejudice Resulting from Wealth Evidence -------------------- 330
    Defendant's introduction of financial evidence ----------------------- 330
    Limits on wealth discovery --- 330
    Prejudice at trial; bifurcation -------------------------------------- 330

* For the full text of this section, see Dobbs, Law of Remedies, Second Edition, Practitioner Treatise Series, Vol. 1 (§§ 1.1–5.18).

	Page
Types of Financial Information Admissible	331
Types of wealth—net worth, income	331
Other uses of profits evidence	332
Surrogates for profits proof	333
Proof of insurance against punitive damages	333
Whose Wealth? Third Parties and Vicarious Liability *	
Whose wealth? *	
Proof of wealth and vicarious liability *	

§ 3.11(6) Vicarious Liability for Punitive Damages 334
Scope *
The Restatement Complicity Rule 334
The Liberal Rule 334
Alternatives 334
Differential in Punitive Awards Between Principal and Agent 335
Differential in Punitive Awards in Other Cases of Joint and Several Liability *

§ 3.11(7) Punitive Liabilities of Insurers for Wrongs of Insureds 335

§ 3.11(8) Multiple Punitive Liability 337
Multiple Liability Problems *
Authority Generally *
Defendants' Arguments *
Judicial Response *
The Plaintiffs' Concern: Exhausting Funds to the Prejudice of Later Claimant *
Judicial Solutions *
Multiple Punishments for Multiple Acts *
Where There is Only One Wrongful Act *
Non-punitive "Punitive" Damages *
State Legislation and Proposals *
Federal Solutions Proposed *

§ 3.11(9) Scope of Punitive Liability: Causation and Persons and Injuries Outside the Risk 341
Derivative Liability *
    Excluding recovery by persons not directly injured *
    Allowing recovery by persons not directly injured *
    Scope of the exclusion *
Injuries and Persons within the Risk *
    Negligence law rule of proximate cause *
    Example as applied to punitive damages *
    Cover-ups and other post-injury behavior *
    Torts to different persons *
    Torts by two different agents *

* For the full text of this section, see Dobbs, Law of Remedies, Second Edition, Practitioner Treatise Series, Vol. 1 (§§ 1.1–5.18).

Page

§ 3.11(10) The Actual Damages Requirement 341
The Rule 341
Interpretations of the Rule 341
Criticisms of the Rule 342
Reinterpreting the Rule 342
Case Development 343

§ 3.11(11) The Ratio Rule 343
Relationship of Punitive to Compensatory Damages 343
Relationship of Punitive Damages to Potential Harm From Defendant's
  Conduct 344
Criticisms 344
The Ratio Rule and Judicial Review 345
The Ratio Rule and Jury Instructions 345

**§ 3.11(12) Constitutional and Statutory Challenges to Punitive
       Damages** 345
Constitutional Attacks on Punitive Damages 345
  Double jeopardy 345
  Excessive fines under the Eighth Amendment 347
  Due process 347
  Due process and jury guidance 347
  Due process and post-trial review 347
  First Amendment 348
Legislative Limitations on Punitive Damages 349
  Multiple damages statutes as caps 349
  "Tort reform" legislative caps and limitations 349
  Constitutionality of caps 350
  Construction of capping statutes 350
  Redirecting the award from plaintiff to the state 351
  Statutory confrontation of fairness issues 351
  Statutory enhancement of judicial control 351

§ 3.11(13) Adjustments and Computations 352
Reduction in Punitive Award When Compensatory Award is Reduced *
Comparative Fault Reductions *
Other Reductions and Adjustments *

§ 3.11(14) Factors in Fixing the Amount of Punitive Damages 352
"Factors" 352
  Culpability factors 353
  Deterrence factors 353
  Litigation support factors 354
Criticisms 354
  Disharmony among the factors 354
  Absence of evidence 354

* For the full text of this section, see Dobbs, Law of Remedies, Second Edition, Practitioner Treatise Series, Vol. 1 (§§ 1.1–5.18).

Page

§ 3.11(15) The Debate Over Punitive Damages 355

Criticizing, Defending and Reforming Punitive Damages

Fairness Criticisms 355
Economic Criticisms 356
Evaluating the Criticisms 356

§ 3.12 MULTIPLIED DAMAGES

Nature of Multiple Damages Statutes 358
    Typical statutes 358
    Differences between multiplied and punitive damages 359
    Non-punitive purposes under some statutes 359
Issues Affected by Punitive or Nonpunitive Nature 360
    Punitive multiplication precluding common law punitive damages . 360
    Nonpunitive multiplication—effect on common law punitive damages 360
    Nature of statutory damages as affecting compensatory award 361
    Nature of statutory damages as affecting other issues 361
Computation under Multiple Damages Statutes 361
    Which measure of damages is multiplied? 361
    Order of credits and multiplication 362

CHAPTER 4. RESTITUTION

A. THE NATURE OF RESTITUTION

§ 4.1 RESTITUTION AND UNJUST ENRICHMENT

§ 4.1(1) Core Ideas of Restitution 365
Definitions and Goals 365
    Defendant's gains, not plaintiff's losses 365
    Money restitution in excess of damages 366
    Unjust enrichment basis of restitution claims 366
    Substantive and remedial sides of unjust enrichment 366
Applications 366
    Contract breach; unenforceable contracts 366
    Mistake 367
    Torts and subtortious wrongs 367
    Other cases 368
Measuring Benefits for Restitution 368
    Different measures 368
    Identifying benefits with the gains they produce 368
Relation of Restitution to Damages 369
    Remedial differences 369
    Remedial similarities 369
    Characterizing the award as restitution or damages 369
Relation of Restitution to Equity 370
Terminology 370

Page

§ 4.1(2) The Substantive Side of Restitution: Unjust Enrichment 371
Introducing the Meanings of Unjust Enrichment 371
  Unjust enrichment as the basis of liability 371
  Group 1 Cases: Benefits to defendant where title remains in the plaintiff 372
  Group 2 Cases: Benefits to defendant where title passes through misconduct 372
  Group 3 Cases: Benefits to defendant resulting from breach of contract 373
  Group 4 Cases: Benefits to defendant from money or services without misconduct—Mistakes and other disruptions in contracting .. 373
  Benefits conferred without mistake or contract 374
  Where restitution is the only basis of liability: substantive unjust enrichment issues 374
Restitution/Unjust Enrichment Claims to Establish New Rights 375
  Restitution as a means for recognizing rights in intangibles 375
  Is "unjust enrichment" too vague? 376
Qualifying and Limiting Unjust Enrichment Claims: Protecting Innocence and Autonomy 376
  Protecting autonomy under the volunteers rules 376
  Protecting innocent purchasers 376
  Protecting defendants who have changed position 377
  Protecting public policy 377

§ 4.1(3) Introducing the Procedural and Terminological Side of Restitution 377
Diversity and Unity 377
Equity 378
Law 378
In Personam and In Rem Procedures 378

§ 4.1(4) The Measurement of Restitution—The Remedial Side of Restitution 379
Remedial Problems: Choosing Restitution and Its Measure 379
  The remedial issues in restitution 379
  Measurement of defendant's benefits 379
  Major measures 379
  Choosing among the measures 380
  Unjust enrichment and punitive damages 380
  Remedy choice 380
Relation of Substance and Remedy 381
  Substantive–remedial entanglement 381
  Example of services under an unenforceable contract 381
  Which decision comes first, substantive or remedial? 382
  Substantive decisions influenced by existence of a mild remedy 382
  Substantive decisions influenced by radical remedy 382

§ 4.2 RESTITUTION AT LAW—TERMINOLOGY AND DEVELOPMENT

Page

§ 4.2(1) In Summary 383
Plaintiff Has Legal Title: Ejectment and Replevin 383
Plaintiff Has no Legal Title But Claims in Assumpsit on Analogy to
    Contract 383
Implying a Contract to Do Justice 383
An Example 384
The Terminology 384

§ 4.2(2) Development of Restitution When Plaintiff Had Title:
            Ejectment and Replevin 384
Ejectment *
    Earliest actions *
    Ejectment action *
    Sheriff's role *
    When ejectment was not adequate *
    Peculiar characteristics in earlier law *
Replevin and Detinue *
    Detinue *
    Replevin and the self-help remedy of distress *
    Restitution based in property right *
Special Procedures Developed in Replevin Cases *

§ 4.2(3) Development of Restitution When Plaintiff Had No Title 384
When the Plaintiff Did Not Have Title: Assumpsit *
    The limits of early contract enforcement—covenant and debt ac-
        tions *
    The development of assumpsit out of trespass and case *
    Trespass on the case *
    The defendant's undertaking becomes contract *
    Debt and assumpsit *
    Implied in fact contracts 384
    Implied in law contracts—quasi-contract and restitution in assump-
        sit 385
    Examples 385
    Quasi-contract: meaning, function and confusion 385
    Unjust enrichment basis first recognized 386
    The common counts 386
    —Money paid to the defendant's use 386
    —Money had and received 387
    —Use and occupation of land 387
    —Goods sold and delivered 387
    —Quantum meruit 388
    —Quantum valebant 388

* For the full text of this section, see Dobbs, Law of Remedies, Second Edition, Practitioner Treatise Series, Vol. 1 (§§ 1.1–5.18).

Page

Waiver of Tort and Suit in Assumpsit --------------------------------- 388
    Lamine v. Dorrell --- 388
    The agency theory -- 389
    Limitations on waiver of tort --------------------------------------- 389
The Future of Restitution Law -- 390

§ 4.3 RESTITUTION IN EQUITY—TERMINOLOGY AND PROCEDURE

§ 4.3(1) Equitable Restitutionary Devices Generally ------------------ 391
Law Courts' Limits: Protection of Legal Title ------------------------- 391
Equity Courts' Ability to Ignore Legal Title -------------------------- 391
Major Restitutionary Remedies in Equity ------------------------------ 391
Constructive Trust *
The Equitable Lien *
Subrogation *
Accounting for Profits *
Four Potential Effects of Tracing Remedies --------------------------- 392

§ 4.3(2) The Constructive Trust ------------------------------------- 392
In Summary -- 392
The Mechanism of the Constructive Trust ------------------------------ 392
    The constructive trust and quasi-contract --------------------------- 392
    Mechanisms and procedures of the constructive trust ---------------- 393
    Requirement of res or property ------------------------------------- 393
    Other liabilities not excluded --------------------------------------- 394
Operation and Effects of the Constructive Trust ---------------------- 394
    (1) Capturing the defendant's gains --------------------------------- 394
      —Example --- 395
      —Tracing --- 395
    (2) Preferences and priorities --------------------------------------- 395
      —Example --- 395
      —Combining profits and priorities ------------------------------- 396
      —Priorities and tracing --- 396
    (3) Recovery of specific property ------------------------------------ 397
    (4) Equity trials—Nonjury trial ------------------------------------ 397
      —Adequate remedy at law --------------------------------------- 397
    Constructive trust effects without constructive trust terminology -- 398
Grounds for the Constructive Trust ----------------------------------- 398
    Basis in unjust enrichment --- 398
    Earlier limitations --- 399
    Application of constructive trusts today ----------------------------- 399
    When constructive trust is limited to cases of wrongdoing ---------- 400
    Donees and purchasers --- 400
Constructive Trust in Relation to Other Trusts ---------------------- 401
    The express trust *
    The resulting trust *

* For the full text of this section, see Dobbs, Law of Remedies, Second Edition, Practitioner Treatise Series, Vol. 1 (§§ 1.1–5.18).

Page

§ 4.3(3) The Equitable Lien 401
Liens Generally 401
Agreements and Other Lien Sources 401
Equitable Liens by Agreement 401
Equitable Liens Judicially Implied to Prevent Unjust Enrichment 402
Where Constructive Trust is Excessive 402
Where the Constructive Trust Assets are Deficient 403
Lien and Trust Comparisons 403
Lien and Trust Differences 404

§ 4.3(4) Subrogation 404
Subrogation as Substitution 404
Subrogation Based on Unjust Enrichment; Terminology 405
The Surety and Insurer Examples 405
The Mortgage Example 406
Priorities 406
Tracing 407
Garnishment and Subrogation 407
Contribution and Indemnity and Subrogation 408

§ 4.3(5) Accounting and Accounting for Profits 408
Development of Common Law and Equitable Accounting 408
   Common law action of account 408
   Equity accounting 409
Accounting for Profits Today 409
   Accounting to deal with complex accounts 409
   Accounting as discovery 410
   Accounting to capture profits and force proof from the defendant 410
   Grounds for the accounting for profits; is accounting limited to fidu-
     ciaries? 410
   Profit recovery against non-fiduciaries 411
   Burden of proof against non-fiduciaries 411
   Burden to prove business expense deductions 412
   Burden to prove basis for apportionment of profit between innocent
     and wrongful acts 412
   Accounting for profits in law and equity 413

§ 4.3(6) Rescission 414
Meaning of Rescission 414
   Rescission 414
   Avoidance 414
   Termination 414
   Distinct from restitution 415
Methods of Rescission 415
   Mutual agreement 415
   Unilateral rescission; rescission at law 415
   Judicial rescission; rescission in equity 415
   Grounds for rescission and restitution 416

Page

§ 4.3(7) Reformation ---- 416
Reforming Documents to the Parties' Intent ---- 416
Constructive Trust Compared ---- 417
Rescission Compared ---- 417
Law and Equity; Reformation With or Without Physical Alteration ---- 417
Some Nontraditional Reformation ---- 418

§ 4.3(8) Equitable Conversion ---- 419
Raw Doctrine ---- 419
    The seller as trustee under a specifically performable contract ---- 419
    The tracing element ---- 419
Consequences of Equitable Conversion ---- 420
    Profit from the vendor's breach ---- 420
    Risk of loss ---- 421
    Affecting nature of the property as personalty or realty ---- 421
A Comment ---- 422

§ 4.4 SPECIFIC AND SUBSTITUTIONARY RESTITUTION

Specific Restitution *
Combining Specific and Substitutionary Restitution *
    Mixed restitution *
    Restitution owed by the plaintiff *
    More flexible adjustments *
Substitutionary Restitution *

§ 4.5 MEASUREMENT OF RESTITUTION

§ 4.5(1) General Principles and Substantive Policy ---- 423
Scope and Direction ---- 423
Unjust Enrichment ---- 423
Types of Benefit and Measures ---- 423
Substantive Policy and Measurement ---- 424

§ 4.5(2) Market Measures of Restitution ---- 425
Direct Money Payments ---- 425
Increase in Market Value of Defendant's Assets ---- 426
    General rule ---- 426
    Example: mistaken improvements to property add to its value ---- 426
    Defendant's subjective purpose affecting value ---- 426
    Measuring personal use value ---- 426
    Date for measurement ---- 427
    Unrealized gains ---- 427
Value of Services in the Labor Market ---- 428
    Market value of services, regardless of assets they produce ---- 428
    When increased asset value is a limitation ---- 429
    Market rate for services includes normal "profits" ---- 429
Market Use Value ---- 429

* For the full text of this section, see Dobbs, Law of Remedies, Second Edition, Practitioner Treatise Series, Vol. 1 (§§ 1.1–5.18).

Page

§ 4.5(3) Consequential Benefits Measures of Restitution 431
Consequential Damages and Consequential Benefits 431
    Consequential benefits compared to consequential damages 431
    Distinctions between consequential and market measures 431
    Levels of consequential benefits 432
Consequential Benefits from Transfer of Entitlements 432
    Gains from transfer in a rising market 432
    Gains from a transfer above market rate 432
Consequential Benefits from Use 433
    Receipt of rental or interest income 433
    Savings from defendant's own use of the plaintiff's entitlement 433
    Collateral profit 434
Adjustments and Problems in Collateral Profit Cases 434
    Expense deductions 434
    The apportionment problem 435
    The trademark-copyright examples 435
    Apportionment required 435
    Burden of proving apportionment 436
    Counterpart problems in damages law 436
    Profits recovery and the separation of risk from opportunity 437
The Breacher's Profits in Contract Cases 438
    General rule 438
    The trust or equitable conversion exception 438
    Fiduciary breach: the Snepp case 438
When Is Restitution Properly Measured by Consequential Benefits? 439
    Factors 439
    A generalization 439
    Measure to limit vs. measure to expand liability 439
    Consequential benefits from property title to which remains in the
      plaintiff 439
    Consequential benefits from property or money, to which the plain-
      tiff has no legal title 441

§ 4.5(4) Guides to and Limitations on Measures of Restitution 441
Contract Price As a Guide or Ceiling 441
    Contract transactions permitting restitution 441
    Contract price as evidence of amount of benefit 442
    Contract price or expectancy not a ceiling on buyer's restitution ... 442
    Contract price or expectancy not a ceiling on seller's restitution ... 442
    The full performance liquidated sum rule 443
Costs and Reliance Expenses 443
Benefits Passed on, Consumed, Destroyed or Offset by Losses 444
    Benefits passed on 444
    Benefits consumed or destroyed 444
    Benefits offset by loss 445

§ 4.5(5) Combining Restitution With Other Remedies 446
Compensatory Damages and Restitution 446
Punitive Damages and Restitution 447

B. DEFENSES AND LIMITATIONS

§ 4.6 DEFENDANT'S CHANGE OF POSITION

		Page
Changed Position May Defeat Restitution		448
Related Rules		448
Types of Cases		449
Benefits Passed on		449
Benefits Expended or Consumed		449
Loss, Harm, or Destruction		450

§ 4.7 BONA FIDE PURCHASERS FOR VALUE AND DISCHARGE FOR VALUE

§ 4.7(1) Bona Fide Purchasers 450
Rule Summary 450
General Rule—Legal versus Equitable Title 451
    Where legal title remains in O 451
    Where legal title passes to purchaser 451
    Trust example 451
    Fraudulent purchase example 452
    Equitable remedies against bona fide purchasers who take legal title 452
    Restating the rule 452
    Purchase and value 453
General Rule—Equitable Title versus Equitable Title 453
    Conflicting equitable interests illustrated 453
    First in time, first in right 453
    Qualifying and limiting the first in time rule 453
Modifications and Exceptions: Commercial Sales, Land Titles and Security Transactions 454
    Traditional rules undesirable in commercial sales 454
    Voidable title technique 455
    Entrusting statutes 455
    Land title recording 455
    Motor vehicle purchases 456
Modifications and Exceptions: Money, Choses in Action and Negotiable Instruments 456
    A chose in action *
    Cash money *
    Negotiable instruments *

§ 4.7(2) Discharge for Value 456
Mistaken Payment Used to Satisfy a Valid Claim Against a Third Person 456
    General rule 456
    The example of Weiner v. Roof 456
    The example of Banque Worms 457
    The example of Gaffner v. American Finance Co. 457
Mistaken Payment Used to Satisfy a Void Claim 458

---

* For the full text of this section, see Dobbs, Law of Remedies, Second Edition, Practitioner Treatise Series, Vol. 1 (§§ 1.1–5.18).

	Page
Rationales and Policies	459
Discharge for value as a changed position rule	459
Discharge for value as a bona fide purchaser rule	460
Policies	460

§ 4.8 THE REQUIREMENT OF RESTORATION OR TENDER BY THE PLAINTIFF

"At Law"	461
Pre-suit restoration or tender required for rescission "at law"	461
What is rescission "at law"	461
What counts as a tender	462
"In Equity"	463
Pre-suit tender or restoration not required for rescission "in equity"	463
Restoration ultimately determined at trial in equity rescission	463
Qualifications to the Requirement of Tender at Law	464
Items the plaintiff is entitled to keep	464
Where tender would be useless	464
Amounts to be tendered indeterminate	464
Where the adjustment remedy is not rescission	464
Reform of the Tender Rules	465
Measure of Restoration Required of the Plaintiff	466

§ 4.9 UNSOLICITED BENEFITS—VOLUNTEERS AND INTERMEDDLERS

§ 4.9(1) Rule, Background and Summary	467
Factual Context	467
Denial of Restitution to "Volunteers and Intermeddlers"	467
Arguing and Resolving Cases	468
Unifying Principles	468
Categorizing Cases	469
§ 4.9(2) Underlying Principles in Unsolicited Benefit Cases	469
Incidental Reasons for Denying Relief	469
Economic and Moral Reasons	470
Personal Autonomy: the Defendant's Right of Free Choice	470
Free Choice in Non-consensual Transactions	470
Choice in Contracts and Consensual Transactions	471
Limits of Choice	472
Limits of Principle	472
§ 4.9(3) Benefits in Cash or Specific Chattels	472
Restitution Generally Allowed	473
Mistaken cash payments	473
Specific chattels	473
Contribution for cotenant improvements later realized in cash	473
Restitution Sometimes Denied	474
Payment of another's debt	474
Overpayment of taxes	476

Page

§ 4.9(4) Intentionally Conferring Non-cash Benefits Where Parties Could or Did Contract ------------------------------------ 476
Situations and Principles -- 476
Tacit, Vague or Ambiguous Understandings ------------------------- 477
    Implications derived from parties' dealings ------------------ 477
    Family and neighborly services ------------------------------- 477
    Submission of ideas --- 478
    Business or professional services ----------------------------- 478
No Contract Between Parties Who Are in Position to Bargain ----------- 479
    Non-liability --- 479
    Freeriders problems --- 480
Contract Between Parties on General Subject Matter ------------------- 480
    Existence of an express contract ------------------------------ 480
    Example of the failed land purchase --------------------------- 480
    Example of the insured's expense saving the insurer liability ------- 481
    Variations on the insurer example ----------------------------- 482
Three–Party Dealings; Improvement by Subcontractors ---------------- 482
    Implications of non-contracting -------------------------------- 482
    Examples --- 482
    Subcontractors enriching a landowner ------------------------- 483
Non-cash Benefits Realized in Cash Later --------------------------- 484

§ 4.9(5) Intentionally or Innocently Conferring Non–cash Benefits Where Bargaining Is Not Possible ---------------- 484
Emergency, Preservation of Property or Life, Necessaries ---------------- 485
Improvers of Chattels, Extenders of Credit ------------------------- 486
Mistaken Improvers of Land --------------------------------------- 488

§ 4.9(6) Acceptance or Opportunity to Reject: Lawyers and the Common Fund -- 489
Acceptance of a Benefit --- 489
Realization of a Benefit in Cash ---------------------------------- 489
Ambiguities in Acceptance and Realization ------------------------- 489
Ability to Reject the Benefit and the Common Fund Attorney Fee Rule 490

CHAPTER 5.   HARMS TO INTERESTS IN TANGIBLE PROPERTY

A.   LAND

(1) IN GENERAL

§ 5.1   HARMS TO INTERESTS IN LAND GENERALLY

Elements in Selecting and Measuring Remedies ---------------------- 494
    Types of remedies -- 494
    Interests in land --- 494
    Physical security, use and enjoyment and pure possession interests 494
    Role of legal theory -- 494
    Means of harm -- 495
    Defendant's state of mind ------------------------------------- 495

Page

Damages Generally --- 495
    Physical harms to the land ------------------------------- 495
    Interference with possession ----------------------------- 496
    Interference with use and enjoyment --------------------- 496
    Adjustments --- 496
Restitution Generally --- 496
Injunction and Possessory Relief ---------------------------------- 496
    Threat of future harm, inadequate remedy at law --------- 496
    Injunction to affect title and possession ---------------- 497
    Encroachment cases ------------------------------------ 497
    Costs and benefits of injunctive relief ------------------ 497

(2) INTERESTS IN PHYSICAL INTEGRITY OF LAND AND STRUCTURES

§ 5.2 HARMS TO INTERESTS IN PHYSICAL INTEGRITY OF LAND AND STRUCTURES: DAMAGES

§ 5.2(1) Basic Measures of Damages for Physical Harm to Property: Diminished Value vs. Repair Costs ------------------- 497
Alternative Measures -- 497
Windfall and Waste --- 498
Idiosyncratic and Personal Uses ---------------------------------- 499

§ 5.2(2) Choosing Between Diminished Value and Repair Costs: The Permanency Test and Restatement Test ------------ 500
The Permanency Test *
Permanency Test as Shorthand for Policy Decision *
Limits of the Permanency Test *
The Restatement Test *
Limits of the Restatement Rule *
Pragmatic Eclecticism *
Where There Is No Conflict *

§ 5.2(3) Ceilings on Repair Costs Recoveries -------------------- 500
Diminution in Value as Ceiling *
Pre-injury Value as a Ceiling *
Rationales *
Other Solutions *

§ 5.2(4) Repair Costs as a Ceiling on Diminished Value Claim 501

§ 5.2(5) Allowance of Repair Costs in Environmental Damage Cases --- 502
Repair or Restoration Costs to Prevent or Minimize External Harm ---- 502
Analogies under Environmental Statutes --------------------------- 502
    The Superfund Act ------------------------------------ 503
    Persons liable -- 503
    Elements of recovery ---------------------------------- 503

* For the full text of this section, see Dobbs, Law of Remedies, Second Edition, Practitioner Treatise Series, Vol. 1 (§§ 1.1–5.18).

                                                          Page

Response costs -- 504

Natural resource damage ------------------------------------- 504

Restoration costs in excess of resource value? The efficiency argument -- 505

Restitution or damages -------------------------------------- 505

§ 5.2(6) Limits on Replacement Costs in Analogous Eminent Domain Cases -- 506

General Market Measured Compensation in Federal Eminent Domain Cases *

The Role of Replacement Costs in Figuring Market Value *

Distinguishing Replacement Cost From Substitute Facilities *

General Federal Rule Excluding Substitute Facilities Costs *

The Duncanville, Texas Case *

The Lutheran Synod Case *

Substitute Costs With Adjustment for Appreciated Assets *

Criticizing Duncanville *

State Cases *

§ 5.2(7) Adjustments Required When Repair Costs Are Allowed 509

Deduction for Appreciated Value ---------------------------- 509

Figuring the Adjustments *

Denial of Deduction *

Allowance of Deduction for Appreciation With Adjustment for Plaintiff's Costs of Early Replacement *

Overhead Adjustments *

§ 5.2(8) Waste -- 510

Damages *

　　Detriment to a future estate *

　　Damages measures *

　　Waste by increasing the value of the land *

Injunctions *

　　Injunctions against voluntary waste *

　　Injunctions against permissive waste *

§ 5.3   HARMS TO INTERESTS IN PHYSICAL INTEGRITY OF LAND AND STRUCTURES: DAMAGES FOR SEVERANCE

§ 5.3(1) Severance Cases Generally --------------------------- 510

§ 5.3(2) Good Faith Trespassers -------------------------------- 511

Minerals and Timber *

　　Royalty and stumpage *

　　Price less production costs *

　　Multiple damages *

　　Ornamental trees and shrubs *

---

* For the full text of this section, see Dobbs, Law of Remedies, Second Edition, Practitioner Treatise Series, Vol. 1 (§§ 1.1–5.18).

Crops *
    Mature value less cost of cultivation and harvest *
    Alternative damages claims *
Sand, Gravel and Dirt *

                                                           Page

§ 5.3(3) Bad Faith Trespassers: Three Punitive Approaches 511
Harsh Measure of Damages 511
Double and Treble Damages Under Statutes *
Punitive Damages *
Punitive Approaches Compared Generally 511
Approaches Compared—Burden of Proof *
Recovery of Several Punitive Elements *

§ 5.3(4) Traders Who Purchase Severed Articles 511

**§ 5.4   HARMS TO INTERESTS IN PHYSICAL INTEGRITY OF
LAND AND STRUCTURES: RESTITUTION FOR SEVERANCE**

Trespasses That Do Not Justify Restitution 511
Restitution for Taking 512
Restitution as a Fictional Contract *
Restitution to Capture the Defendant's Gains 512
Gain in Market or Exchange Transaction *
Gain in Profit–Making Activity or Use *

**§ 5.5   HARMS TO INTERESTS IN PHYSICAL INTEGRITY OF
LAND AND STRUCTURES: INJUNCTIVE RELIEF**

Scope *
Inadequacy of Legal Remedy *
Injunctions Against Physical Harm *
Mandatory Injunctions to Restore Physical Integrity *
Repeated or Continuous Trespasses *
Encroachments and Injuries to Non-unique Interests *
Self–Help and Reverse Injunctions *
Boundary Disputes and Preliminary Injunction Risks *

(3) INTERESTS IN USE AND ENJOYMENT

**§ 5.6   HARMS TO INTERESTS IN USE AND ENJOYMENT:
DAMAGES FOR NUISANCE**

§ 5.6(1) Substantive Background: Nuisance and Trespass 513

§ 5.6(2) Nuisance Damages Generally 514
Objective or Market Measures 514
    Diminished market value 514
    Diminished rental value 515
    Costs of repair or abatement 515
    Ceilings on recovery of repair or abatement costs 515

* For the full text of this section, see Dobbs, Law of Remedies, Second Edition, Practitioner Treatise Series, Vol. 1 (§§ 1.1–5.18).

Page

Added value to land affecting ceiling on repair costs recovery *
Damages Not Based on Property Value or Repair ---------------------------- 515
Personal discomfort, illness and anguish ------------------------------------ 515
Combining claims for discomfort and claims for diminished
value -- 516
Nuisance claims of non-owners *
Public claims for nuisance damages *

§ 5.6(3) Damages Incentives to Abate ---------------------------------- 517

§ 5.6(4) Regulatory Takings -- 517

§ 5.7 HARMS TO INTERESTS IN USE AND ENJOYMENT:
INJUNCTIVE RELIEF

§ 5.7(1) Substantive Background and Summary ------------------------ 517

§ 5.7(2) Doctrine Limiting Nuisance Injunctions -------------------- 518
Adequacy of Legal Remedy, Irreparable Harm ---------------------------------- 518
Adequacy test -- 518
Injunctions issued *
Balancing Hardships and Equities -- 518
Threshold, rights, and remedies types of balancing -------------------- 518
Rights-balancing -- 518
Remedies balancing generally -- 519
Equities and misconduct -- 519
Hardships and economic waste -- 520
Public interests and social utility -- 521
Public interests against the injunction -- 521
Public interests favoring the injunction ------------------------------------ 521

§ 5.7(3) The Remedial Options in Nuisance Cases ------------------ 522
Four Basic Remedial Choices -- 522
Traditional choices -- 522
The fourth option: a compensated injunction ------------------------------ 523
Spur Industries -- 523
Acceptance of Spur Industries -- 523
Form and Terms of the Remedy: Fine–Tuning Injunctions ------------ 523
Nebulous injunctions -- 523
Scope and limits of injunction -- 524
Incentive injunctions and incentive damages ---------------------------- 525

§ 5.7(4) Economic and Other Perspectives -------------------------------- 525
Complexities in Forecasting Relative Costs *
Post-judgment Bargaining; Injunction as the Preferred Remedy *
Economic Efficiency Claims; Damages as the Preferred Remedy *
Limits on Efficiency of Party–Bargaining; View That Efficiency of Rem-
edy Depends on Facts of the Case *
Is There a Special Role for the Compensated Injunction? *

* For the full text of this section, see Dobbs, Law of Remedies, Second Edition, Practitioner
Treatise Series, Vol. 1 (§§ 1.1–5.18).

Page

§ 5.7(5) Effects of Statutes on Nuisance Injunctions 528
Adequacy and Hardships under Statutes *
   Adequacy or irreparable harm tests under statutes *
   Relative hardships or balancing under statutes; the mandatory rule *
   Qualifications to the mandatory rule *
   Construing statutes *
Preemption and Exhaustion of Remedies *
   Does a statute exclude ADDED judicial relief? *
   Preemption and remedial preemption *
   Judicial remedies as a supplement to statutory remedies *

§ 5.7(6) Easements -- 528
Non-possessory Rights *
Adequacy of Legal Remedy *
Relief Granted *
Easement in Dispute *

(4) HARMS TO INTERESTS IN EXCLUSIVE POSSESSION

§ 5.8 HARMS TO INTERESTS IN EXCLUSIVE POSSESSION: DAMAGES FOR NON–HARMFUL TRESPASSES, USE, OR OCCUPATION OF LAND

§ 5.8(1) In General -- 528

§ 5.8(2) Damages and Mesne Profits ------------------------------- 529
Nominal Damages -- 529
Rental Value or Mesne Profits ------------------------------------ 529
   Generally -- 529
   Objective or market measure; irrelevance of defendant's losses ----- 530
   Objective measure; irrelevance of plaintiff's lack of loss -------------- 530
   Trespasser's profits; damages and restitution distinguished ---------- 531
   Subjective tests --- 531
Occupation of Part of a Tract *
Periodic and Sub-optimal Uses ------------------------------------ 532

§ 5.8(3) Improvements Added by Trespasser -------------------------- 532
Traditional Rules *
   Affirmative relief denied the mistaken improver *
   Owner invoking equity; offset rules *
   Practical limits offset rules *
   Recognizing affirmative claims by the trespasser *
Statutory Solutions *
   Betterments statutes *
   Expanded liability for improvements *
Remedy Choice *
   Removal of the improvement *
   Postponed lien *
   Installment payments *

* For the full text of this section, see Dobbs, Law of Remedies, Second Edition, Practitioner Treatise Series, Vol. 1 (§§ 1.1–5.18).

Forced sale *
Ceilings on recovery *
Related Rules and Policy Issues *

§ 5.9 DISPOSSESSION—RESTITUTION FOR USE
AND OCCUPATION

Appropriation of Tangible Property *
Rule Against "Assumpsit" for Use and Occupation *
Effects on Damages and Procedural Incidents of the Claim *
Under Modern Procedure *
Precluding Profit Recovery *
Allowing Profits Recovery *
Allowing "Negative Unjust Enrichment" *

§ 5.10 HARMS TO INTERESTS IN EXCLUSIVE POSSESSION—
INJUNCTION, EJECTMENT AND SUMMARY RELIEF

Page

§ 5.10(1) Ejectment 534

§ 5.10(2) Forcible Entry and Detainer, Summary Ejectment 535
Force Against One in Peaceable Possession *
Unlawful Detainer or Summary Process *
Res Judicata *

§ 5.10(3) Injunctive Protection of Possession Generally 535
Adequacy and Irreparability Rules 536
    General rules 536
    Repeated or continuing trespasses 536
    Effects *
Injunctions Where Title to Land Is in Issue 536
    General rule 536
    Provisional relief 537
    Enjoining economic activity while title is in issue 537
    Exceptions to the title rules 538
Injunctions Transferring Possession of Land 538
    No transfer of possession by preliminary injunction 538
    Broader rule statements 538
Easements 539

§ 5.10(4) Injunctive Protection Against Encroaching Structures 539
Adequacy, Title and Possession in Encroachment Cases 539
    Adequacy 539
    Title and possession 540
Hardships and Equities 540
    Balancing hardships 540
    Guiding policies 540
    Equities 540

* For the full text of this section, see Dobbs, Law of Remedies, Second Edition, Practitioner Treatise Series, Vol. 1 (§§ 1.1–5.18).

Page

Hardships or economic costs 541
Refusing to balance hardships and equities 541

(5) PROCEDURAL AND REMEDIAL IMPACTS OF PERMANENT INVASIONS

§ 5.11 STATUTES OF LIMITATIONS, RES JUDICATA AND THE PERMANENT HARM DOCTRINES

§ 5.11(1) General Rules for Permanent Invasions 542
Terminology *
Permanent Damages for Permanent Invasions *
Res Judicata Rules for Permanent Harms *
Statute of Limitations Rules for Permanent Harms *
Res Judicata and Statute of Limitations Rules for Temporary Nuisances *

§ 5.11(2) What Invasions Are "Permanent"? 543
Narrow and Liberal Tests of Permanence *
Invasions Subject to Abatement *
Invasions Not Subject to Abatement *
Physical Permanence *
A Double Standard *

§ 5.11(3) Incentives in the Permanent Nuisance Issue 543
The Place of Incentives in the Permanency Issue *
Disincentives for Correction: Permanent Nuisance *
Incentives for Correction: Temporary Nuisance *
Counter–Concerns *

§ 5.11(4) The Plaintiff's Dilemma 544
The Plaintiff's Dilemma and Right of Election *
Public Concerns Affecting Plaintiff's Election *

(6) CONSEQUENTIAL AND PUNITIVE MEASURES IN LAND CASES

§ 5.12 CONSEQUENTIAL, MULTIPLE AND PUNITIVE DAMAGES

§ 5.12(1) General Rules *

§ 5.12(2) Duplicative Recoveries: Recovering Both Consequential and General Damages 544
Improper Duplication *
General Damages *
Special Damages *
Where Plaintiff Can Recover Both General and Special Damages *
Testimonial Ambiguity and Duplicated Damages *
Other Cases of Duplication When Both Special and General Damages Can Be Recovered *

* For the full text of this section, see Dobbs, Law of Remedies, Second Edition, Practitioner Treatise Series, Vol. 1 (§§ 1.1–5.18).

Diminished Rental Value Plus Mental Distress in Nuisance Cases *
The Loss of Profits Claim *
Where the Plaintiff Is Limited to Special Damages Recoveries *

Page

§ 5.12(3) **Punitive Damages** -------------------------------------- 545
Statutory Multiple Damages *
Common Law Punitive Damages *

B. PERSONAL PROPERTY

§ 5.13 GENERAL DAMAGES: DIMINISHED MARKET VALUE

§ 5.13(1) **General Rules** --- 545
General Damages Rules -- 545
    Taking and destruction -------------------------------------- 545
    Taking: supplementary measures ----------------------------- 545
    Harm to chattels -- 546
    Applications --- 546
Alternatives and Special Damages ---------------------------------- 546
    Repair or replacement costs --------------------------------- 546
    Adjustments when repair or replacement costs are awarded --------- 546
    Unique goods, goods without market value ------------------- 547
    Special and punitive damages -------------------------------- 547

§ 5.13(2) **Time for Assessment of Market Value** ----------------- 547
Steady Markets -- 547
Delayed Replacement and Fluctuating Markets ----------------------- 548
    The problem --- 548
    The stand-pat rule -- 548
    Highest value to trial rule --------------------------------- 549
    New York rule: highest value in reasonable time ------------ 549

§ 5.13(3) **Place or Market for Assessment of Market Value** ------- 550
Geographical Markets -- 550
    "No market" --- 550
    Adjustments for transportation costs ------------------------ 550
Economic Markets—Wholesale versus Retail Markets ------------------ 551
    Retailer and consumer -------------------------------------- 551
    Manufacturer, maker or shipper ----------------------------- 551
    Manipulation of the market test versus special damages allowances *

§ 5.13(4) **Evidence of Value** ----------------------------------- 552
Generally *
Opinion Testimony *
    Experts *
    Admissible owner-opinion and extensions *
    Non-market damages *
    Limits on owner-opinion *

* For the full text of this section, see Dobbs, Law of Remedies, Second Edition, Practitioner Treatise Series, Vol. 1 (§§ 1.1–5.18).

§ 5.14 REPLACEMENT AND REPAIR COSTS

Page

§ 5.14(1) Replacement and Repair Costs as Alternative Measures of Damages or as Limits on Recovery 552
Alternate Measures of Damages and the Ceiling Problem *
The No–Problem Case: Repair Costs as Evidence of Diminished Value *
Diminished Value as a Ceiling *
Diminished Value Not a Ceiling *
Cost of Repair a Ceiling? *
    Minimizing damages rule has no application to general damages *
    Practical reasons for full diminished value recovery *
Ceilings Not a Limit on Loss of Use *

§ 5.14(2) Accounting for Overhead in Repairs Cases 552
Direct Costs of Repairs -- 552
Overhead Costs Attributable to Repairs ------------------------------- 553
    The overhead claim -- 553
    Rejection of overhead claims --------------------------------- 553
    Acceptance of overhead claims -------------------------------- 554
    Overhead and profits recovery -------------------------------- 554
    The simple calculation --------------------------------------- 554
    The cumbersome calculation ----------------------------------- 554
    Why the gross profit recovery is right ----------------------- 555
    Proof; spurious overhead ------------------------------------- 555

§ 5.14(3) Credits for Appreciation in Value Resulting From Repair or Replacement ------------------------------- 555
General Rule: Deduction for Increased Value ------------------------- 556
    Deduction allowable -- 556
    Types of increased value ------------------------------------- 556
    Qualifications to the rule ----------------------------------- 556
Unwanted Benefits; Consumer Goods *
    Conflicting principles *
    The Restatement compromise *
    Consumer goods *
    Public property *
Benefits Not Captured or Realized *
Proof of Enhanced Value: Accounting Depreciation vs. Market Value --- 557
    Accounting for enhancement by use of diminished market value test 557
    Accounting for enhancement by use of depreciation formulas ------- 557
    Depreciation formulas -- 557
    Intuitive and other adjustments for depreciation ------------- 558
    Cases demanding extraordinary proof or extreme degrees of depreciation --- 558
Calculating Depreciation Adjustments ------------------------------- 559
    Depreciation --- 559
    "Appreciation" --- 559

* For the full text of this section, see Dobbs, Law of Remedies, Second Edition, Practitioner Treatise Series, Vol. 1 (§§ 1.1–5.18).

Page

Additional adjustment when plaintiff will not realize enhanced value
   immediately --- 559
Integral parts of a larger whole ---------------------------------- 560

§ 5.14(4) Credits for Return of Converted Chattel or Its Use   in
   Plaintiff's Interest --------------------------------------- 561
Mitigation by Return of Converted Chattel *
Mitigation by Use of Chattel to Benefit of Plaintiff *

**§ 5.15 SPECIAL OR CONSEQUENTIAL DAMAGES FOR HARM
TO, TAKING OR DESTRUCTION OF
PERSONAL PROPERTY**

§ 5.15(1) Special or Consequential Damages Generally ------------ 561
Consequential or Special Damages *
   Special damages allowable *
   In lieu of or in addition to general damages? *
   Types of special damages *
Loss of Use Damages, Including Lost Profit *
   Lost use recoverable *
   Measures of lost use generally *
   Actual vs. bookkeeping losses *
Intangible and Sentimental Losses; Emotional Harm *
Expenses Incurred *

§ 5.15(2) Loss of Profits and Other Loss of Use Claims ------------ 561
Measures: Loss of Profits, Increase of Expense ------------------------- 561
   Profits and increased expenses recoverable --------------------------- 561
   Proof required --- 561
   The avoidable consequences rules ------------------------------------ 562
   Duplication -- 562
Measures: Cost of Hiring a Substitute Chattel—"Lease-in" Costs -------- 562
   Rental value distinguished; rule ------------------------------------ 562
   Recovery when no substitute is actually hired ---------------------- 562
   Limited recovery for overworked substitutes ------------------------ 563
   The spare boat doctrine -- 563
Measures: Rental Value—The "Lease–Out" Value ------------------------- 563
   Rental value vs. substitute chattel cost ---------------------------- 563
   Rental value as general damages ------------------------------------ 564
Measures: Interest -- 564
   Mandatory or optional measure ------------------------------------- 564
   Prejudgment interest rules --- 565
Probable Use—Market Value of the Use or Actual Loss? ----------------- 566
   Three types of limited loss -- 566
   Brooklyn Terminal --- 566
   Private automobile cases -- 567
   Other commercial chattels --- 567

* For the full text of this section, see Dobbs, Law of Remedies, Second Edition, Practitioner Treatise Series, Vol. 1 (§§ 1.1–5.18).

Page

General damages/special damages dichotomy and the actual loss prob-
lem -- 568
The anomaly in lost use cases --- 568
Choosing a measure of damages --- 569
The interest compromise --- 569
Characterization and the Question of Deductions --------------------------- 570
Erroneous characterizations as rental value claims ----------------------- 570
AT & T v. Connecticut Light --- 570
The deduction problem --- 570
Conversion and Destruction Cases --- 571
Traditional conversion rule --- 571
Destruction rules --- 571
Contemporary rules --- 571
Time Period --- 572

§ 5.15(3) Intangible and Sentimental Losses; Emotional Harms
and Punitive Damages --- 572
General Rules *
Intentional Infliction of Distress *
Negligent Damage to Property: General Rule Against Mental Anguish
Awards *
When Damaging Events Implicate the Person as Well as Property: Negli-
gent Infliction Of Emotional Distress *
Special Property: Pets and Other Animals ----------------------------------- 574
Other Personal Property -- 575

§ 5.16 UNIQUE GOODS AND THOSE
WITHOUT MARKET VALUE

§ 5.16(1) In General --- 575
No–Market: Personal and Artistic Items *
No–Market: Income Producing Goods *
Special and Nominal Damages *
Constructive Market Value *

§ 5.16(2) Property Used in Production of Income ----------------------- 576
Major Factors in Valuing No–Market Income Property -------------------- 576
Depreciation --- 577
"New for old" --- 577
Depreciation and the Standard Oil Case --------------------------------- 577
"Capitalization" of Income or Earnings *
Earnings reflect capital value *
Earnings not attributable to property *
Unknown rate of capitalization or discount *

§ 5.16(3) Property Held for Personal Use ----------------------------------- 577
Clothing, Household Goods *
Goods With Associational or Affect Value *

* For the full text of this section, see Dobbs, Law of Remedies, Second Edition, Practitioner
Treatise Series, Vol. 1 (§§ 1.1–5.18).

Page

§ 5.16(4) Property With Artistic or Historic Value ------------------ 579
Use of Market Value --- 579
    Markets for unique historical and artistic items ---------------------- 579
    Where there is no market --- 579
Artist's Remedies for Alteration of Art after Sale: "Moral Rights" Legis-
    lation --- 580
    Common law and civil law -- 580
    Statutory changes --- 581
    The federal Visual Artists Act --- 581
    Remedies under the federal statute --------------------------------------- 582
Salvage Value of Art and "Moral Rights of Artists" --------------------- 582
    Diminished value rule --- 582
    Dilution of artist's standards or goodwill by sales of damaged work 582
    Moral right and economic waste --- 582
Wholesale or Retail Value of Art --- 583

Appended Note to § 5.16(4) -- 583
Note on Remedies Under State Moral Rights Statutes Possibly Preempted
    Under Federal Law --- 583
    Federal preemption *
    Actual damages under state statutes *
    Reputational harms *
    Affront to personality *
    Public rights or interests *
    Surrogate damages *
    Rescission or forfeiture of despoiler's interests *

§ 5.17 SPECIFIC RECOVERY OF CHATTELS

§ 5.17(1) Generally --- 583
Specific Recovery; Self–Help *
Judicial Relief Generally *

§ 5.17(2) Replevin: Recovery at Law and Due Process --- -------- 583
Traditional Procedure --- 583
Provisional Relief With No Hearing *
Constitutional Limitations --- 584
Scope *
Statutory Change: the Mitchell Statutes *
Statutory Change: the Fuentes Statutes *

§ 5.17(3) Injunction: Equitable Recovery of Chattels ---------------- 586
Inadequate Legal Remedy -- 586
Provisional Equitable Relief and Constitutional Requirements ----------- 587

* For the full text of this section, see Dobbs, Law of Remedies, Second Edition, Practitioner
Treatise Series, Vol. 1 (§§ 1.1–5.18).

§ 5.18 RESTITUTION IN MONEY

Page
§ 5.18(1) Waiver of Tort and Suit in Assumpsit for Conversion 588
Rule and Its Setting *
Plaintiff's Option *
Assumpsit—Waiver of Tort Theory *
Effects of Assumpsit Theory: Tort Becomes Contract; the Statute of Limitations *
Effects of Assumpsit Theory Under Modern Cases *
Necessity of Sale by Tortfeasor *
Enrichment Required *
Formal Requirements *

§ 5.18(2) Measure of Recovery in Assumpsit for Converted Chattels 589
Sale Price and Market Value 589
  General rules 589
  Variations: market value of goods sold 590
  Variations: subjective value to converter 590
Savings to the Defendant 590
  The Olwell case 590
  Observations on Olwell 591
  The Ablah case 591
Profits of the Defendant From Use of Goods 591
  Profits generally 591
  Measuring the benefit 592
  Attributing benefit to plaintiff's goods rather than to defendant's labor 592

§ 5.18(3) Constructive Trusts and Equitable Liens 592
Equitable Relief and Its Advantages 592
Relief Against Fiduciaries 593
Non-fiduciary Cases 593
Reasons for Limiting Equitable Relief 594
Adequacy of Legal Remedy 594
Adequacy Test in Fiduciary Cases 594
Is the Legal Remedy Adequate in Non-fiduciary Cases? 594
Judicial Response to Adequacy Test in Non-fiduciary Cases ... 595

CHAPTER 6. INTERFERENCE WITH ECONOMIC RIGHTS

§ 6.1 MISAPPROPRIATION OF MONEY—TRACING

§ 6.1(1) Conversion and "Assumpsit" 597
Conversion of Money Impossible at Common Law **
Conversion and Assumpsit Claims for Misappropriated Money Today **
Assumpsit Fictions **

* For the full text of this section, see Dobbs, Law of Remedies, Second Edition, Practitioner Treatise Series, Vol. 1 (§§ 1.1–5.18).

** For the full text of this section, see Dobbs, Law of Remedies, Second Edition, Practitioner Treatise Series, Vol. 2 (§§ 6.1–11.10).

No Liability Cases *
Replevin of Money *

Page

§ 6.1(2) Constructive Trusts, Equitable Liens and Subrogation in
General 598
Remedies Available in General *
Restitutionary Results *
Grounds for Trusts and Liens *
Significance of Trust or Lien *
  (1) Non-jury trials *
  (2) Capturing the wrongdoer's gains *
  (3) Capturing specific property *
  (4) Gaining priorities over other creditors and avoiding exemptions *
Limiting Relief to an Equitable Lien Where Other Creditors Would Be
  Prejudiced by a Constructive Trust *
Equitable Lien or Constructive Trust on Proportionate Share? *
Investment of the Plaintiff's Funds in Life Insurance *

§ 6.1(3) The Necessity of Tracing 599
Tracing or Identification Required 599
Tracing Monies; Debt vs. Constructive Trust 599
Swollen Assets 600
Circumstantial Evidence in Tracing 601

§ 6.1(4) Mingled Funds 601
Tracing to a Commingled Fund 601
  Proportionate share in the fund 601
  Property purchased by use of the entire fund 602
Rules for Tracing After Withdrawals 602
  (1) First in, first out rule 602
  (2) Hallett Rule: wrongdoer's funds withdrawn first 602
  (3) "Evidence" tracing to withdrawals 603
  (4) Option rule 603
  (5) The Restatement Proportionate Shares Rule 604
Limits on Tracing to a Fund Partially Depleted and Restored—The Low-
  est Balance Rule 605
  Trust or lien on fund's lowest balance 605
  Denial of recovery where low balance not provable 605
  Computing low balance 605
  Wrongdoer's purpose to restore trust funds 606
Mingling Funds of Several Victims 606
Assessing the Tracing Problem 607

§ 6.1(5) Injunctive Recovery of Money—Freezing Assets 607
Freezing Funds by Attachment Before Trial *
Denial of Injunctive Orders to Freeze Funds *
Grant of Injunctive Orders to Freeze Funds in Debt Claims *

* For the full text of this section, see Dobbs, Law of Remedies, Second Edition, Practitioner
Treatise Series, Vol. 2 (§§ 6.1–11.10).

Grant of Injunctive Orders to Freeze Funds in Equitable Ownership
    Claims *
Terms or Scope of the Injunction *
Lis Pendens Against Real Property *
Specific Property Must Be Identified for Lis Pendens *

§ 6.2   PATENT INFRINGEMENT

§ 6.2(1) Substantive Background *
Federal Role *
Monopoly for a Limited Period *
Patent Process *
Patentable Items *
Infringement *

§ 6.2(2) Summary of Remedies *
Damages *
Restitution: Profits of the Infringer *
Attorney Fees *
Injunctions *
Equitable Defenses *

§ 6.2(3) Compensatory Damages *
Royalty and Lost Profits *
Reasonable Royalty *
    As a market measure *
    Hypothetical royalty in absence of a market *
    Relevant economic facts in determining hypothetical reasonable roy-
        alty *
    Royalty base *
Lost Profits and other Special Damages *
    General rule *
    "Direct" proof of lost profits *
    Indirect proof of lost profits—defendant's sales as proof of plaintiff's
        losses *
    Overhead and the incremental income method *
Prejudgment Interest *
    General rule: prejudgment interest routinely awarded *
    No prejudgment interest on punitive or "increased" damages *
    Interest rates *

§ 6.2(4) Restitution, Including Infringer's Profits *
Denial of Restitution in Patent Cases *
    Tortfeasor's profits generally *
    Infringer's profits in patent cases *
    Patentee's loss recoverable, though equivalent to infringer's gain *
    Infringer's profits as bearing on reasonable royalty *
    Deterrence *

* For the full text of this section, see Dobbs, Law of Remedies, Second Edition, Practitioner
Treatise Series, Vol. 2 (§§ 6.1–11.10).

Profits as Contempt Sanctions Against Infringer Who Violates an Injunction *
    Earlier awards of profits in patent infringement contempt cases *
    Current doubts *

§ 6.2(5) Injunctive Relief and Destruction of Infringing Articles *
Permanent Injunctions *
    Adequacy and irreparability tests *
    Injunctions denied on other grounds *
Preliminary Injunctions *
    General availability in contemporary patent cases *
    Factors in determining grant of preliminary injunction *
    Application *
Scope of Injunction—Impoundment and Destruction *
    Specificity vs. nebulosity *
    Chilling inventive modification *
    The limited contempt rule *
    Impoundment or destruction *
Licensee vs. Patentee *
    Declaratory judgment on validity of patent *
    Royalty obligations during litigation over validity? *
    Freezing the royalty payments in escrow? *

§ 6.2(6) Equitable Defenses *
Estoppel *
    Applied to both legal and equitable claims *
    Abandonment and delay *
Laches *
    Prejudicial delay *
    Effect in legal and equitable claims *
    No bar to future patent infringement claims *
Unclean Hands *
    Rule *
    Public interest *

§ 6.2(7) Attorney Fees *
General Rule *
Exceptional Case Standard; Discretion *
Prevailing Party Test *
Fee Computation *

§ 6.2(8) Punitive and Multiple Damages *
Statutory "Increased" Damages *
Willful Infringement Requirement *
Punitive Character of Increased Damages *
Effect of Comprehensive Statutory Scheme *

* For the full text of this section, see Dobbs, Law of Remedies, Second Edition, Practitioner Treatise Series, Vol. 2 (§§ 6.1–11.10).

§ 6.3 COPYRIGHT INFRINGEMENT

§ 6.3(1) Substantive Background *
The Federal Role in Copyright *
Protection of Specific Expression Only *
Subject-matter *
Free Speech and Copyright *

§ 6.3(2) Summary of Remedies *
Damages *
Restitution of the Infringer's Profits *
Injunction *
Impoundment and Destruction of Infringing Articles *
Equitable Defenses *
Attorney Fees *

§ 6.3(3) Compensatory Damages *
Actual Damages *
Statutory Damages *
Moral Rights Cases *
Additional Damages in Cases of Willful Infringements *
Interest *

§ 6.3(4) Restitution, Including the Infringer's Profits *
Damages and Profits *
    Infringer's profits recoverable *
    Profits contrasted with damages *
    The non-duplication rule *
The Meaning of Profit, Gross and Net *
    Profit and gain *
    Statutory entitlement and burden of proof *
    Role of fault? *
    Deduction of direct costs and overhead *
    Deduction limited to expense of producing infringement profits *
Apportionment, Denial and Grant of Profits *
    The problem of attributing or allocating profit to the infringement *
    Statutory entitlement and burden of proof in attribution cases *
    Meliorating the statutory burden *
    Denial in absence of apportionment *

§ 6.3(5) Injunctive Relief and Destruction *
Injunctions Generally *
    Adequacy and irreparable harm *
    Preliminary injunctions and restraining orders *
    Scope *
Impoundment of Infringing Articles *
    Impoundment authorized *
    Procedure and constitutionality *
    Theories for providing a hearing *

* For the full text of this section, see Dobbs, Law of Remedies, Second Edition, Practitioner Treatise Series, Vol. 2 (§§ 6.1–11.10).

Destruction of Infringing Articles *
Economic Waste and Bargaining *

§ 6.3(6) Equitable Defenses *
Estoppel *
Unclean Hands *

§ 6.3(7) Attorney Fees *
Entitlement *
 Conditions for granting the award generally *
 Requirement of copyright registration *
 Denial of the fee award *
 Prevailing party *
Calculating the Award *
 Changing the view of the reasonable fee award *
 Market rates for fee awards *
 Partial success *
 Argument for apportionment between fee-bearing and non-fee-bearing claims *
 Possible solutions to the apportionment argument *

§ 6.3(8) Punitive and Multiple Damages *
Increased Damages Provision as Excluding Punitive Damages *
Rationales *
The Anomaly Argument for Additional Punitive Damages *
Complete Statutory Scheme of Remedies *

§ 6.4 TRADEMARK INFRINGEMENT

§ 6.4(1) Substantive Background *
Common Law Protection for Trademarks *
Extensions and Limits *
Product Design and Packaging *
Federal Approaches: Registration and Federal Remedies for State–Created Trademarks *
Federal Approaches: a New Cause of Action *

§ 6.4(2) Summary of Remedies *
Damages *
Restitution; the Infringer's Profits *
Injunctive Relief; Destruction of Infringing Goods *
Additional Relief *
Equitable Defenses *
Situational Differences *

§ 6.4(3) Compensatory Damages *
Registered and Unregistered Marks *
Damages for Infringement *
Liberality and Discretion in Fixing or Denying Damages *

---

* For the full text of this section, see Dobbs, Law of Remedies, Second Edition, Practitioner Treatise Series, Vol. 2 (§§ 6.1–11.10).

Royalties or License Fees for Use of Registered Trademark *
Lost Sales: Profits Resulting From Infringement of Registered Mark *
Profits as Damages v. Profits as Restitution *
Lost Profits Claims Against Noncompeting Infringers *
Other Forms of Lost Profit Proof *
Reputation and Goodwill *
Expenses *
Interest *

§ 6.4(4) Restitution, Including the Infringer's Profits *
Triggering a Recovery of the Infringer's Profits *
    Recovery of infringer's profits authorized *
    Statutory limitations *
    Is fault required? *
Measuring the Infringer's Profits *
    Gross profit proof *
    Profits as evidence of damages distinguished *
    Deductions generally *
    Deduction for overhead expense *
    Deduction for income taxes *
    Deduction for losses in some years or some segments of infringing
      business *
    Other deductions *
Apportioning Profits to the Infringement *
    The apportionment problem *
    The defendant's burden in apportionment issues *
Profits of Noncompeting Infringers *

§ 6.4(5) Injunctive Relief and Destruction of Infringing Goods *
Injunctive Relief Generally *
    Authority to issue injunctions *
    Basis for injunction *
    Adequacy of legal remedy *
Scope of the Injunction *
    "Cease sales" and other intrusive injunctions *
    Injunctions to alter labels or to couple mark with disclaimers *
    Avoiding economic waste *
Destruction of Infringing Articles *
    Destruction of labels, printing plates and the like *
    Destruction of goods themselves *
Preliminary Injunctions *
    General rules *
    Irreparable harm in trademark cases *
Temporary Restraining Orders and Ex Parte Seizures *
    TRO generally *
    Statutory ex parte seizure orders generally *
    Equitable and similar prerequisites to statutory order *

* For the full text of this section, see Dobbs, Law of Remedies, Second Edition, Practitioner
Treatise Series, Vol. 2 (§§ 6.1–11.10).

Other prerequisites to the statutory order *
Execution of seizure *
Erroneous Seizure or Provisional Injunction *
Recovery against the bond *
Recovery beyond the bond; damages of third persons *

§ 6.4(6) Equitable Defenses *
Estoppel and Acquiescence *
Laches *
Generally *
Effect *
Prejudice; statute of limitations *
Discretion *
Unclean Hands *
Generally *
In trademark cases *
What counts as unclean hands *
Misconduct must be related *

§ 6.4(7) Attorney Fees *
Generally *
Basic rules *
Entitlement *
Prevailing party *
The exceptional case standard *
"Discretion" under exceptional case standard *
The counterfeit mark standard *
Calculating the Award *
General guides from other fee-award litigation *
Statutory Differences *

§ 6.4(8) Punitive and Multiple Damages *
Multiple Damages Authorized *
Punitive Damages Under the Lanham Act *
Punitive Damages Under State Law *

§ 6.5   MISAPPROPRIATION OF INTANGIBLE WORK PRODUCT NOT PROTECTED BY COPYRIGHT OR PATENT

§ 6.5(1) Misappropriation: Scope and Substantive Background *

Page

§ 6.5(2) Privately Communicated Ideas: Submission of Ideas in Expectation of Payment 612
Elements of a Claim 612
Submission of ideas 612
Elements of the claim 612
Property versus Contract Theories *
Damages *

* For the full text of this section, see Dobbs, Law of Remedies, Second Edition, Practitioner Treatise Series, Vol. 2 (§§ 6.1–11.10).

Value of the idea *
Royalty and the like *
"Owner" testimony as to value *
Value and continued protection of the idea *
Value of work or services in producing idea or investment in it *
Value reflected in defendant's savings or profits *
Punitive damages *
Restitution *
Injunction *

                                                                   Page
§ 6.5(3) Publicly Communicated Ideas or Work Products: Misap-
      propriation -- 613
Substance and Remedy -- 613
    Substantive and remedial interaction ------------------------------- 613
    General rule --- 613
INS v. AP: The Tangible Work Product and Unjust Enrichment *
    The trademark/unfair competition qualification *
    Unjust enrichment: International News Service *
    Did Sears overrule International News Service? *
    Zacchini *
    Distinguishing Sears from Zacchini; the Bonito difficulty *
The Right of Publicity: Celebrity Characteristics, Performances and other
    Intangibles *
    Names, likenesses, celebrity characteristics *
    Potential limits *
Remedies *
    Injunction *
    Preliminary injunction *
    Restitution *
    Damages *

§ 6.6 INTERFERENCE WITH CONTRACTS AND OPPORTUNITIES GENERALLY

§ 6.6(1) Scope and Substantive Background *
Economic Interests and Interference Torts *
    The meaning of economic harm *
    Interference with contract *
    Interference with opportunity *
Related Torts and Scope of Section *
Remedies Generally *

§ 6.6(2) Damages -- 613
In Summary *
General Damages *
Consequential Damages *
    The contract measure *
    The tort measure *

---

* For the full text of this section, see Dobbs, Law of Remedies, Second Edition, Practitioner Treatise Series, Vol. 2 (§§ 6.1–11.10).

Proximate cause limits *
Avoidable consequences *
Reasonable Certainty in Consequential Damages *
    Requirement of reasonable certainty; nominal damages *
    Inducing breach *
    Interference with mere opportunity *
    Case examples *
    Examples of evidence *
    Elaboration of evidence *
    Excluding cause of action for uncertainty *
Punitive Damages *
Mental or Emotional Distress *
    Recoverability *
    Tests or conditions for recovery *
The Role of Extracontractual Damages *
Damages Against Both the Tortfeasor and Contracting Party *
The Rule Against Recovery for Negligently Inflicted Economic Loss *
    Traditional rule against recovery of negligently inflicted economic
        loss without physical harm *
    The Baker example *
    Contract and third party beneficiary cases *
    Physical harm with economic loss cases *
    Subrogation pattern cases *
    Type of economic damages claimed affecting the subrogation pat-
        tern *
    Interference with a specifically performable contract *

                                                                 Page
§ 6.6(3) Restitution --- 614
Older View *
Wrongdoer's Gains Recoverable ------------------------------------ 614
Example of Restitutionary Recovery *
Trust and Lien *
Tracing and Measuring *
The Harper Case *

§ 6.6(4) Injunction and Specific Performance ----------------- 614
Against the Contracting Party ---------------- --------------------- 614
Against the Interfering Tortfeasor *
    The adequacy test *
    Granting injunction: trade libel, trade secrets, soliciting employees *
    Denying injunctions *

§ 6.6(5) Efficient Breach and Remedies for Interference With Con-
        tract or Opportunities ------------------------------------ 615
Damages in an Efficient Breach Regime *
    The right to breach and pay the costs *
    Extracontractual remedies in an efficient breach regime *
    Rejection of efficient breach supports extracontractual damages *

* For the full text of this section, see Dobbs, Law of Remedies, Second Edition, Practitioner Treatise Series, Vol. 2 (§§ 6.1–11.10).

Injunction in an Efficient Breach Regime *
Cases Outside an Efficient Breach Regime *
    Interference with property rather than contract *
    Interference by independent tort *
    Interference to accomplish illegal purposes *
    Interference with specifically performable contracts *
    Unique or personal goods or services *

§ 6.7 INTERFERENCE BY WRONGFUL ACQUISITION OF PROPERTY AT DEATH OF ANOTHER

	Page
Types of Claims	615
Forms of interference: murder, fraud, and other wrongs	615
Relevance of factual differences	615

    Potential remedies *
Probate Proceedings *
    Where adequate *
    Example of probate adequacy *
    Example of probate inadequacy *
Damages or Constructive Trust *
    Tort damages and constructive trust *
    Similarities *
    Advantages of the tort-damages claim *
    Advantages of the constructive trust claim *
Damages Measurement Generally *
Remedies and Measurement in Accelerated Expectancy Cases *
    Gaining an earlier inheritance *
    Interest as measure of anticipatory gains *
    Complete disgorgement of gains *
Measurement in Cotenant Survivorship Cases *
    The problem and its solutions *
    (1) Complete disgorgement *
    (2) Murderer retains interest for life *
    (3) The partition analogy; murderer takes one-half interest *
    (4) Respecting equities of ownership *
    (5) Murderer becomes joint tenant with victim's heirs *

§ 6.8 INTERFERENCE BY COMMERCIAL DISPARAGEMENT OR INJURIOUS FALSEHOOD

§ 6.8(1) Substantive Background *
Generally *
Product Disparagement Version *
Slander of Title Version *
Relation to Other Torts *
Constitutional Limits? *

* For the full text of this section, see Dobbs, Law of Remedies, Second Edition, Practitioner Treatise Series, Vol. 2 (§§ 6.1–11.10).

Libel and Injurious Falsehood *
Anomalies and Remedial Strategies *

§ 6.8(2) Damages *
Pecuniary Damages Required *
Meaning of Special Damages Requirement: Realized Pecuniary Losses *
Proof *
Punitive Damages *
Attorney Fees *

§ 6.8(3) Injunctions *
General Rules *
    Traditional equity view *
    Holding the injunction permissible *
    Holding the injunction impermissible *
    Fact-specific and policy-specific solutions *
Case Patterns *
    Slander of title cases *
    Statutory claims; disparagement without issues of social concern *
    Disparagement combined with social or political comment or criticism *
Remedial versus Substantive Solutions *
    Public versus commercial issues *
    Substantive law limitations *
    Added remedial limitations *

§ 6.9 INTERFERENCE BY UNCONSTITUTIONAL
REGULATION OF LAND USE: "REGULATORY TAKINGS"

§ 6.9(1) Substantive Background *

                                                                    Page
§ 6.9(2) Taking by Regulation ---------------------------------- 616
Diminished Rental Value or Equivalent -------------------------- 616
Undeveloped Land; Option Value *
Discounting for Uncertainty of the Restriction's Effects *
Causal Doubts in General Damages Cases *
Role of Special Damages *
Duplication of Special and General Damages *

§ 6.9(3) Civil Rights Theories—Due Process or Equal Protection *
Attorney Fee Awards *
Punitive Damages *
Special Damages Versus General Damages *

§ 6.9(4) Limiting Recoveries to Special Damages *

* For the full text of this section, see Dobbs, Law of Remedies, Second Edition, Practitioner Treatise Series, Vol. 2 (§§ 6.1–11.10).

§ 6.10 WRONGFUL DISCHARGE AND JOB DISCRIMINATION

                                                              Page
§ 6.10(1) Scope, Background and Summary ----------------------- 617
Traditional At–Will Employees and Common Law Wrongful Discharge . 617
Advent of Statutory Law -- 618
Strategy Issues -- 618
Law and Equity --- 619
Summary -- 619

§ 6.10(2) Common Law Wrongful Discharge *
Theories of Relief *
Wrongful Discharge—The Public Policy Theory *
    Tort or contract *
    Tort damages *
    Contract damages *
    Economic harm: back pay *
    Economic harm: front pay *
    Economic harm: special damages *
    Minimizing damages *
    Reinstatement *
Wrongful Discharge—The Bad Faith Theory *
    Tort vs. contract theories *

§ 6.10(3) Statutory Wrongful Discharge: The Legislative Back-
            ground *
Statutory Characteristics *
    Scope *
    Statutory groupings *
    (1) Whistleblower and anti-retaliation statutes *
    (2) Employment discrimination, retirement security, and civil serv-
        ice systems *
    (3) Civil rights statutes and common law mental distress claims *
    Remedial strategy choices required *
Employment Discrimination Statutes *
    Title VII *
    Equal Pay Act, Age Discrimination Act and others *
    General remedial approach *
Civil Rights Statutes and Related Claims *
    Sections 1983 and 1981 *
    State tort rules *
    General remedial approach *

§ 6.10(4) Statutory Wrongful Discharge—The Remedies *
Summary of Remedies *
    Back pay, reinstatement and front pay *
    Emotional distress, punitive and consequential damages *
    Prejudgment interest *

* For the full text of this section, see Dobbs, Law of Remedies, Second Edition, Practitioner
Treatise Series, Vol. 2 (§§ 6.1–11.10).

Attorney fees *
Avoidable consequences and collateral source *
Back Pay *
    Back pay generally available *
    Back pay measures and elements *
Reinstatement, Retention, Hiring *
    Specific relief—hiring or reinstatement *
    Effect on estimating other losses *
    Postponed reinstatement *
    Seniority *
Preliminary Relief *
    Reinstatement by preliminary injunction *
    Deference to administrative process and similar elements *
    Proving irreparable harm *
    Presuming irreparable harm *
    Variables in determining whether the plaintiff must show irreparable
        harm *
    Irreparable harm requirement and deference to administrative proc-
        esses *
    Other requirements for preliminary injunction *
    Civil rights claims under § 1981 and § 1983 *
Front Pay *
Consequential, Intangible and Punitive Damages *
    Traditional limits under job discrimination statutes *
    The 1991 Civil Rights Act *
    Caps under the 1991 Civil Rights Act *
    Claims under older civil rights statutes and the like *
Interest *
    Common law rules *
    Title VII, ERISA, §§ 1981, 1983 *
    Equal Pay and Age Discrimination Acts *
Attorney Fees *
Avoidable Consequences—Mitigation of Damages *
    General rule *
    Substitute employment *
    Burden of proof *
    Collateral source payments; unemployment compensation, social se-
        curity *

§ 6.10(5) Statutory Job Discrimination and Equity: Jury Trial *
Law, Equity, Jury and Discretion *
    Consequences of characterization *
    Purpose of characterization *
Jury Trial *
    The constitutional rule *
    Applying the rule to back pay and reinstatement claims? *
    Title VII rules *

* For the full text of this section, see Dobbs, Law of Remedies, Second Edition, Practitioner
Treatise Series, Vol. 2 (§§ 6.1–11.10).

Theories for denying Title VII jury trial *
ERISA claims; the trust theory as a basis for denying jury trial *
Statutes keyed to the FLSA remedial provisions: Age Discrimination in Employment Act *
Title VII jury trial after the 1991 Civil Rights Act *
Jury right for compensatory damages and punitive claims under Sections 1981 and 1983 *
Jury right for back pay claims under Sections 1981 and 1983 *

§ 6.10(6) Statutory Job Discrimination and Equity: Discretion *
Cases Equitable for One Purpose but Legal for Another *
Traditional Equity Discretion *
Forms of Discretion *
Discretion Asserted in Title VII *
The Doubtful Scope of Discretion *
Discretion as a Shorthand Expression *
Discretion in Formulating Scope and Details of Remedy *

§ 6.10(7) Statutory Job Discrimination and Equity: Equitable Defenses *
Equitable Defenses Available "at Law" *
Laches *
Time Limits Under Title VII *
Delay Possible Under Title VII *
Application of Laches *

§ 6.11 LAWYER MALPRACTICE

	Page
Context and Scope	620
Primarily an economic tort	620
Non-representational lawyer torts	620
Representational settings	620
Litigation malpractice	620
Damages Summary	620

Basic Damages for the Case Within the Case Recovery *
Measure of damages: substituted liability *
Recoverable elements *
Credits *
Client's losses reduced by collateral payments *
Fees the client otherwise would have paid *
Proof *
As special damages *
Damages must be caused in fact *
Reasonable basis for estimating amount must be shown *
Consequential Damages *
The second layer damages *

* For the full text of this section, see Dobbs, Law of Remedies, Second Edition, Practitioner Treatise Series, Vol. 2 (§§ 6.1–11.10).

Emotional distress *
Attorney fees *
Damages Arising from the Malpractice Trial Itself *
Attorney fees generally denied *
Extending the basic measure recovery to include malpractice suit
fees *
Third party litigation exception *
Extending the third party rule *
Indirect fee compensation *
Interest *
Punitive Damages *

§ 6.12 BAD FAITH BREACH OF CONTRACT

Substantive Background and Remedial Interaction *
Tort vs. contract damages *
Good faith rule in contract *
Good faith rule in tort *
(1) Third-party or excess judgment cases *
(2) First-party or insurance benefits cases *
(3) Beyond insurance *
(4) Moving back? *
Damages *
Economic harm *
Consequential economic harms *
Emotional distress damages *
Punitive damages *
Efficient breach *

CHAPTER 7. INVASION OF CIVIL RIGHTS AND DIGNITARY INTERESTS

§ 7.1 DIGNITARY INVASIONS GENERALLY

Page

§ 7.1(1) Background and Scope -- 623
Contrasted With Economic Injuries *
Examples of Dignitary Torts *
Economic and Presumed Damages *
Free Speech Interests *
Interaction of Substance and Remedy *
Scope and Chapter Approach *

§ 7.1(2) Presumed and General Damages -------------------------------- 624
Substantial Unproven Damages Awards *
Terminology and Purposes *
"Presumption" as a Fair Inference of Damages in Fact *
Damages to Reflect Inherent Value of Rights *
Damages to Provide Incentive to Sue *

* For the full text of this section, see Dobbs, Law of Remedies, Second Edition, Practitioner Treatise Series, Vol. 2 (§§ 6.1–11.10).

The Critical Problem of Damages Measurement or Limit *
Statutory Minimum Damages *
Common Law Minimum Damages and Limits? *

§ 7.2 REMEDIES FOR DEFAMATION

                                                                    Page
§ 7.2(1) Substantive Background ---------------------------------- 626
Defamation and Other Torts *
Libel and Slander *
Common Law "Strict Liability" *
Constitutional Abrogation of Strict Liability *

§ 7.2(2) Summary of Remedies ------------------------------------ 627
Restitution and Injunction *
Damages Generally *
Economic and Nominal Damages *
Presumed Damages and Emotional Distress *
Reputational Loss *
Punitive Damages *

**§ 7.2(3) Presumed or General Damages Under Common Law
            Rules** --- 628
Libel *
Slander and Slander per se *
Libel per quod *
State Statutes *
Presumed Damages: Common Law Summary *

**§ 7.2(4) Constitutional Limits on Presumed and Punitive Dam-
            ages** --- 629
Public Official, Public Figure Suits *
Private Person Suits Where Defamation Deals With Issue of Public Con-
  cern *
Private Person Suits Where Defamation Deals With Issue of Purely Pri-
  vate Concern *
Summary *

**§ 7.2(5) Presumed or General Damages: Relationship to Emo-
            tional, Reputational, and Nominal Damages** ------------- 630
Vindicating Dignitary Rights *
    Nominal and presumed damages *
    No measure of presumed damages *
    Analysis required *
Presumption of Harm vs. Presumption of Amount of Harm *
    The ambiguity of presumed damages *
    Against presumed harm *
    The sting of the second meaning *
Types of Reputational Harm *
Is Reputational Harm Really Emotional Distress? *

* For the full text of this section, see Dobbs, Law of Remedies, Second Edition, Practitioner
Treatise Series, Vol. 2 (§§ 6.1–11.10).

Page

§ 7.2(6) The Free Standing Claim for Emotional Distress Damages 630
Emotional Distress Without Defamation: Constitutional Concerns 630
  Constitutionally permissible 630
  Criticisms; state law *
  As a means of ignoring plaintiff's bad reputation *
Limits and Forms of Mental Distress Damages *
  Generally *
  A chain of emotional consequences and the thin skull rules *
  Consortium *

§ 7.2(7) Reputational Harm Generally 631
Reputational Harm—Elements of Damage Causation *
Factors in Assessing Reputational Harm *

§ 7.2(8) Reputational Harm—Understanding and Belief of Accusations 631
Understanding vs. Belief *
Understanding the Meaning of an Accusation *
Audience Belief in the Truth of an Accusation *
Where Presumed Damages Are Forbidden *
Proof by the Defendant That Audience Disbelieved the Words *
Refusal to Admit Testimony *
Indirect Evidence of Belief or Disbelief *

§ 7.2(9) Reputational Harm—Prior Reputation, Prior Publications, and the Libel Proof Plaintiff 631
The Third Causal Element and Judicial Responses *
  Diminished reputation *
  Three consequences of the plaintiff's prior bad reputation *
Plaintiff's Prior Reputation Generally *
  Plaintiff's good reputation *
  Plaintiff's bad reputation *
Prior Publications Causing Plaintiff's Bad Reputation *
Libel-Proof Plaintiffs: Denying the Claim or Limiting the Damages? *
  Dismissal of the claim under libel-proof plaintiff doctrine *
Five Case–Categories *
  Type I—Reputation already destroyed on same issue; the issue-specific case *
  Type II—False and defamatory evidence pointing to derogatory truth; the subsidiary fact case *
  Type III—Reputation already destroyed on a different issue; the case of the shoplifting traitor *
  Type IV—Undeserved prior bad reputation *
  Type V—Plaintiff's bad reputation from prior publications *

* For the full text of this section, see Dobbs, Law of Remedies, Second Edition, Practitioner Treatise Series, Vol. 2 (§§ 6.1–11.10).

Page

§ 7.2(10) Reputational Harm—Retraction 631
Rehabilitated Reputation *
Effect of Retraction *
Refusal to Retract *
Retraction Statutes *
Importance of Statutes *
Constitutionality *

§ 7.2(11) Economic Damages 631
Lost Wages, Commissions and Business Opportunities *
Expenses Incurred to Counter Defamation *
Medical Expenses *
Avoidable Consequences *

§ 7.2(12) Punitive Damages 632
Constitutional Constraints on Punitive Damages *
Where Constraints Do Not Apply *
State–Law Rules *

§ 7.2(13) Restitution 632
Restitution Denied *
Apportionment and Free Speech Reasons *
Publisher's Profits in Non-defamation Cases 632
Where Publication Counts as Some Other Tort *
Commentators *

§ 7.2(14) Non–monetary Relief: Injunction, Reply, and Declaratory Judgment and Reform Proposals 632
Injunctions *
    Injunctions denied 632
    Free speech 633
    Injunction against commercial disparagement *
    Incidental effect of injunctions against other torts *
    Expungement orders 633
Retraction and Right of Reply 634
The Declaratory Judgment or Lie Bill *
The Annenberg Proposals 634

§ 7.3 REMEDIES FOR OTHER DIGNITARY CLAIMS

§ 7.3(1) Dignitary Torts Generally 635
Scope *
    Dignitary torts *
    Examples *
    Civil rights torts *
The Constitutional Connection *
    The defamation template *
    Communicative and non-communicative torts *
Remedies Generally *

* For the full text of this section, see Dobbs, Law of Remedies, Second Edition, Practitioner Treatise Series, Vol. 2 (§§ 6.1–11.10).

Page

§ 7.3(2) Dignitary Torts: Damages ---------------------------------- 635
Presumed General Damages --- 635
    Presumed damages rules --- 635
    Application to particular torts --------------------------------- 636
Bases of Presumed Damages *
    Inferences of fact *
    Litigation finance *
    Definitional harm *
Emotional Distress Damages *
    Presumed emotional distress damages *
    Risk of duplication when plaintiff has multiple theories of recovery *
Other Damages *
    Punitive damages—dual relevance of defendant's serious misbehavior *
    Punitive damages—risk of duplication *
    Pecuniary or special damages *
    Attorney fees or litigation costs *
Limitations on Damages *
    Limits where publication is basis *
    Minimizing damages: the avoidable consequences rule *
    Mitigation of damages *
Critiques *

§ 7.3(3) Constitutional Limits Generally -------------------------- 637
Constitutional Free Speech Limitations? *
Knowing or Reckless Falsehood Requirement *
The "Some Fault" Requirement *
Effect on Presumed Damages Recoveries *
Other Communicative Torts *
Non-communicative Dignitary Torts *

§ 7.3(4) The Special Case of Privacy Invasion --------------------- 638
Initial Distinctions *
Types of Privacy Right *
Intrusion Upon Seclusion *
Intrusion: Economic and Emotional Distress Damages *
Statutory Presumed Damages *
Commercial Appropriation *
Non-dignitary Versions of Appropriation; the Right of Publicity *
False Light *
Constitutional Limitations *
State–Law Remedial Limitations *
Private Facts *
Improper Means *
Truth Published Without Improper Means; Potential Limitations *
Do the Defamation Rules Apply? *

* For the full text of this section, see Dobbs, Law of Remedies, Second Edition, Practitioner Treatise Series, Vol. 2 (§§ 6.1–11.10).

Page

§ 7.3(5) Injunctive Relief 638
General Rules 638
  Traditional view: no equitable protection *
  Contemporary view 638
  Adequacy of legal remedy 638
  Personal rights protectible *
  Grounds for denial of injunction 638
Injunctions against Criminal Prosecution *
  Prosecutions harassing the plaintiff *
  Testing constitutionality of statute *
  Federal-state relationships *
Injunctions against Civil Litigation *
  Strategic and economic claims for injunction *
  Dignitary claims for injunction *
Injunctions Against Privacy Invasion and Other Harassments *
  Assault and battery *
  Intrusive privacy invasion *
  Privacy invasion by publications *
Injunctions to Protect Family and Family Relationships *
  Injunctions to protect influence and control over children *
  Injunction to protect affections of a spouse *
  Injunction to require medical attention *
Injunctions to Protect Political Relations *
  Political participation *
  Public information *
Injunctions to Protect Social Relations *
  Public accommodations *
  Social associations *
Injunctions to Protect Religious Interests *
  Older practice *
  Constitutional limits on judicial decisions grounded in church doctrine *
  Church procedures *
  Neutral principles of property *

§ 7.4 CONSTITUTIONAL CIVIL RIGHTS TORTS

§ 7.4(1) Scope and Substantive Background *
Civil Rights Torts as Dignitary Torts *
Constitutional Violations Under "Color of Law" *
"1983" and "Bivens" Actions *
State–Law Civil Rights *
Non-dignitary, Economic Aspects *
Forms of Civil Rights Violations *

§ 7.4(2) Presumed General Damages 638
The Federal Rule against Presumed Damages 638
  The rule in Carey v. Piphus 638
  Resolving the ambiguity: Stachura 639

* For the full text of this section, see Dobbs, Law of Remedies, Second Edition, Practitioner Treatise Series, Vol. 2 (§§ 6.1–11.10).

Page

What Counts as Actual Injury? -- 640
    No injury in rights violation -------------------------------------- 640
    Emotional and other consequences of a rights violation -------------- 640
Permitted Presumptions of Damages *
    Presumption in the sense of inference *
    Common law analogies *
Comment *

§ 7.4(3) Compensatory and Punitive Damages ----------------------- 640
Low and Variable Awards *
Traditional Rules of Damage Causation *
    Cause in fact *
    Apportionment *
    All damages naturally resulting *
Pain and Emotional Distress *
    Deterrence through emotional distress damages *
    Physical harm, emotional distress *
    Illustrative cases *
    A lower scale of evaluation? *
    Review of awards *
    Effectiveness of Carey–Stachura limits *
    Replacing presumed damages with emotional harm claims? *
Pecuniary Losses *
    Pecuniary losses recoverable *
    Wrongful death *
    Survival claim *
Punitive Damages *

§ 7.4(4) Injunctive Relief --- 640
"Private" or Individual Injunctions -------------------------------- 640
Structural or Institutional Injunctions --------------------------- 641
    Re-structuring institutions -------------------------------------- 641
    Bi-polar vs. representative or "legislative" litigation ------------- 641
    Terminal remedies vs. ongoing administration -------------------- 642
    Judicial supervision of institutional reform; masters and receivers - 642
    Right-remedy: correlation vs. dis-correlation --------------------- 643
    Remedies for rights vs. remedies against social attitudes ----------- 644
Comment on Structural Injunctions -------------------------------- 644

§ 7.4(5) Attorney Fees and Remedial Strategy Issues -------------- 645
Recoverable Attorney Fees *
    The American Rule *
    Fee recovery in civil rights cases *
    Fee measurement rules *
Remedial Strategy *

* For the full text of this section, see Dobbs, Law of Remedies, Second Edition, Practitioner Treatise Series, Vol. 2 (§§ 6.1–11.10).

CHAPTER 8. PERSONAL INJURY AND DEATH

§ 8.1 DAMAGES FOR PERSONAL INJURY

Page

§ 8.1(1) Damages for Personal Injury 647
Compensation Elements Generally 647
    Compensatory, lump-sum awards 647
    Elements 647
    Permanent or future harm 647
    Elements apply in injury claims generally 648
    Compensation systems awards *
Limits and Adjustments 648
    Limits; attorney fees 648
    Adjustments for delayed payment 648
    Adjustments for inflation and present value 648
    Comparative fault reductions 649
    Tax savings adjustments 649
    Avoidable consequences and collateral sources 649
Criticisms and Changes *

§ 8.1(2) Earning Capacity and Lost Income 649
Earning Capacity—Wage Distinction 649
    Recovery for wage and other income loss 649
    Recovery for impaired earning capacity 649
    Evidentiary differences and limits *
Lost Capacity Without Lost Income *
    Lost capacity without wage loss *
    Rules applied 650
    Homemakers 650
    Investment or business income after injury *
    Rationales *
    Limits *
    Avoidable consequences *
Proving Specific Losses or Diminished Capacity *
    Wages or salary relevant *
    Injury and diminished capacity *
    Non-wage opportunity losses *
    Speculative claims *
    Lost profit opportunities *
Future Losses *
    Generally *
    Reduced life expectancy *
Alternative Systems *
    Scheduled injuries *
    Percentage disability *

§ 8.1(3) Medical and Other Expenses 650
Expenses Generally 650

* For the full text of this section, see Dobbs, Law of Remedies, Second Edition, Practitioner Treatise Series, Vol. 2 (§§ 6.1–11.10).

Page

General rule --- 650
    Proximate cause, certainty and policy limits; wrongful pregnancy and
        wrongful birth *
Proof and Apportionment *
    Reasonable value not actual cost of services or supplies *
    Proof of reasonableness required *
    Proof of reasonableness inferred *
    Apportionment of medical costs between injury and other causes *
Diagnostic, Medical Monitoring or Medical Surveillance Expenses ------- 651
    Recovery for diagnosis in absence of symptoms ----------------------- 651
    Medical surveillance --- 651

§ 8.1(4) Mental and Physical Pain and Suffering -------------------- 652
Recoverability -- 652
    All forms of suffering recoverable generally *
    Proof of pain *
    Pain award required --- 652
Standards of Measurement *
    Noneconomic and noncompensatory damages *
    Standards for measurement; the "Golden Rule" argument *
Scope of Pain, Suffering and Distress *
    Physical pain and loss *
    Emotional states produced by injury ------------------------------- 652
    Loss of enjoyment of life --- 653
    Is loss of enjoyment independent of pain and suffering? ------------ 653
    Is consciousness of pain or loss required? ----------------------- 654
Lost Years *
    Recovery for distress at reduced life expectancy ------------------- 655
    Traditional view: no additional independent recovery for reduced ex-
        pectancy --- 655
    Cases allowing recovery for reduced expectancy independent of emo-
        tional or pecuniary harm ------------------------------------- 656
Fear of Future Harm -- 656
    Types of recovery for future harm ---------------------------------- 656
    Fear recovery permissible -- 656
    Where there is no present injury or tort --------------------------- 657
The Per Diem Argument *
    Per diem or mathematical formula *
    Per diem argument permissible *
    Minority view *
Abolishing or Limiting Pain and Suffering Awards ----------------------- 657
    Proposals and statutes -- 657
    Criticisms: overdeterrence without compensatory function ---------- 658
    Criticisms: no measurement, unfairly inconsistent awards ---------- 659
    Limited symbolic value of pain award ------------------------------ 659
    Compelled purchase of insurance ----------------------------------- 659
    Financing litigation costs with pain awards ----------------------- 659

* For the full text of this section, see Dobbs, Law of Remedies, Second Edition, Practitioner Treatise Series, Vol. 2 (§§ 6.1–11.10).

Page

§ 8.1(5) Consortium -- 660
Common Law *
Scope of Consortium Rights Today *
Economic Services and Duplicated Damages *
Noneconomic Aspects of Consortium *
Consortium and Mental Distress Claims *

§ 8.1(6) Punitive Damages --- 661
General Rules *
    Recoverability *
    Serious misconduct and state of mind *
    Illustrative cases *
    Jury discretion *
    Liability insurance for punitive damages *
    Vicarious liability *
    Multiple punitive liability *
Measurement and Caps *
    Factors *
    Direct and indirect caps *
    Adjustments: comparative fault, present value and interest *

§ 8.1(7) Future Damages --- 661
Proof Standards Generally *
    Single claim for all future damages *
    Preponderance or 50%–plus rule *
Alternatives to Preponderantly Proved Future Harm *
    Insuring against future harms *
    Fear of future harm, medical surveillance *
    "Splitting" the cause of action *
    Value of the chance or enhanced risk theories *
Value of the Chance/Enhanced Risk Arguments in Court *
    Medical malpractice *
    Market-share liability in products liability cases *
    Toxic tort cases *
    Comment *

§ 8.2 THE SPECIAL CASES OF WRONGFUL PREGNANCY, WRONGFUL BIRTH, AND WRONGFUL LIFE CLAIMS

Substantive Background --- 661
    Wrongful conception or pregnancy ------------------------- 661
    Wrongful birth --- 661
    Wrongful life --- 662
Wrongful Birth, Wrongful Life and Misadoption ------------------- 662
    Child-rearing expense --------------------------------------- 662
    Pain and emotional distress -------------------------------- 663

* For the full text of this section, see Dobbs, Law of Remedies, Second Edition, Practitioner Treatise Series, Vol. 2 (§§ 6.1–11.10).

Page

Wrongful Conception or Pregnancy -- 664
    Generally: expense, wage loss, pain and distress ------------------------ 664
    Child-rearing expense—the majority ------------------------------------ 664
    Child-rearing expense—the minority ------------------------------------ 665
    Genetic defects in wrongful pregnancy cases --------------------------- 666
Offsets --- 666
    Offsets; the "benefits" rule -- 666
    Wrongful pregnancy and presumed benefit ------------------------------ 666
    Wrongful pregnancy and "actual" benefit ------------------------------- 667
    Wrongful pregnancy: emotional benefits offsetting economic loss? -- 667
    Wrongful pregnancy: undiminished recovery of child-rearing expenses 667
    Wrongful birth -- 668
    Comment -- 668
Avoidable Consequences—"Mitigation" of Damages ---------------------- 669

§ 8.3 WRONGFUL DEATH AND SURVIVAL ACTIONS

§ 8.3(1) Substantive Background and Remedial Summary -------- 670
Substantive Common Law Rules --- 670
    Three rules --- 670
    Effect --- 671
American Survival and Death Statutes ----------------------------------- 671
    Judge-made claims --- 671
    Development of statutory claims *
    Wrongful death statutes -- 671
    Survival statutes -- 672
    Hybrid statutes -- 672
Changing Purposes and Enduring Problems ------------------------------- 672
    Social welfare purposes --- 672
    Property protection purposes -- 672
    Maldistribution of dependents' recoveries -------------------------- 672
    Pecuniary vs. non-pecuniary claims --------------------------------- 673

§ 8.3(2) Survival Statute Damages ------------------------------- 673
General Rules *
    Two forms of survival actions -------------------------------------- 673
    General rule --- 673
    Exclusion of particular elements ------------------------------------ 673
    Recovery of particular elements ------------------------------------- 673
Lost Earnings *
    Earnings lost from injury to death *
    "Future" lost earnings *
    Duplication risks *
Punitive Damages -- 674
    Recoverable in first type of survival action *
    Not recoverable in second type of survival action *
Allocating Damages between Survival and Death Actions *

* For the full text of this section, see Dobbs, Law of Remedies, Second Edition, Practitioner Treatise Series, Vol. 2 (§§ 6.1–11.10).

Page

§ 8.3(3) Wrongful Death Statute Damages—Summary 674
Two Measures of Economic Harm *
Non-economic Harm *
Punitive Damages *
Future Loss *

§ 8.3(4) Wrongful Death Statute Damages—Economic Damages 674
Economic Measures Generally *
Loss to Dependents Measure *
    General adoption *
    Measure: contributions *
    Form of contributions *
    Effect of death benefits or inheritance from decedent *
    Entitlement or welfare? *
    Proof *
    Time period for support *
    Relevance of past earnings, personal qualities *
    The non-working or non-contributing deceased *
Loss to Estate Measure *
    Measure generally *
    Limits *
    Basis *
    Advantages *
    Retired persons, homemakers *
Lost Inheritance Claims *
    Adding loss of inheritance to the loss to dependents approach *
    The added costs/uncertainty argument *
    The duplication argument *
Caps on Damages *
    Generally *
    Tort reform statutes *
    The Warsaw Convention *

§ 8.3(5) Non–Economic Damages -- 675
Traditional Rule and Its Problems *
    Traditional rule against non-economic damages *
    Problem cases *
Recovery for Services, Society or Mental Anguish *
    The services solution *
    The companionship, society, love, advice, and guidance solution *
    The mental anguish solution *
Ante-mortem Losses to Survivors *
    Ante-mortem consortium loss *
    Ante-mortem mental anguish *
"Hedonic Damages" *
    Lost enjoyment in personal injury claims *
    Deceased's loss of life's pleasures in wrongful death claim *

* For the full text of this section, see Dobbs, Law of Remedies, Second Edition, Practitioner Treatise Series, Vol. 2 (§§ 6.1–11.10).

Intractable Problems and Unpleasant Solutions *
   Absence of measurement standards *
   Proposals and enactments *

Page

§ 8.3(6) **Nominal Damages, Punitive Damages, Interest** 675
Nominal Damages *
Interest *
Punitive Damages *
   Wrongful death *
   Survival actions *

§ 8.3(7) **Death Damages—Damages Affected by Events Subsequent to Death** --- 675
Post-death Changes in Damages Generally ------------------------------- 675
   Are damages fixed at the time of death? ---------------------------- 675
   Events bearing on damages to survivors ---------------------------- 675
   Remarriage of a spouse, death of a survivor and altered needs of
      dependents --- 675
Remarriage of Decedent's Spouse, Adoption of Children *
   Relevance of remarriage to damages *
   General rule as excluding remarriage evidence *
   General rule as permitting affirmative claims by the plaintiff *
   Rationale *
   Criticisms of rationales *
   Admitting remarriage evidence *
   Raising remarriage on voir dire *
Survival of the Wrongful Death Action after Survivor's Death *
   The problem *
   Judicial solutions *
   (1) Abatement of the wrongful death action *
   (2) Survival of the wrongful death action to the beneficiary's estate *
   (3) Transfer of the wrongful death action to other or secondary beneficiaries *
   Thrust of the cases *
   Damages not fixed at time of death *
Post-Death Events Affecting Beneficiaries' Need for Support *
   Increased need for support *
   Decreased need for support *
   Benefits resulting from death *

§ 8.4 ADJUSTMENTS: DELAYED PAYMENT OF PAST DAMAGES—INTEREST

Judgment Interest *
Prejudgment Interest—When Allowed *
   Prejudgment interest generally *
   Interest on damages for future losses *
   Nonpecuniary damages *
   Statutes *

---

* For the full text of this section, see Dobbs, Law of Remedies, Second Edition, Practitioner Treatise Series, Vol. 2 (§§ 6.1–11.10).

Prejudgment Interest—Computational Issues *
    Triggering interest accrual *
    Rate *
    Compounding *
    Discretion *
    Statutory enigmas *

§ 8.5 ADJUSTMENTS: FUTURE DAMAGES: REDUCTION TO PRESENT VALUE AND INFLATION ADJUSTMENT

                                                                    Page
§ 8.5(1) Summary 676
Loss Period *
Reduction to Present Value *
Inflation *
Periodic Payments, Structured Settlements *

§ 8.5(2) Adjustments for Future Damages Generally: Establishing the Loss Period 676
Loss Periods Generally 676
    Relevance of loss period 676
    Loss periods in permanent injury cases 676
The Life Expectancy Loss Period 676
    Mortality tables admissible 676
    Nature of mortality tables 676
    Limits of mortality tables 677
    Individualized health information 677
    Prejudicial health information 677
Policy Issues on Mortality Tables 677
    Ethnic and gender distinctions 677
    Implications of a compensatory purpose 678
    Gender discrimination rulings on mortality tables 678
The Work Life Expectancy Loss Period *
    Casual estimates *
    Work life tables *
    Gender and race in work-life tables *
    Limits of work-life tables *
    Legal effect of tables *
    The earning capacity problem *

§ 8.5(3) Reduction to Present Value *
Traditional Reduction Requirement *
    General rule *
    Goal and basis for reduction *
Computation *
    Variables in computation *
    Two types of present value computation *
    Practical methods available *

* For the full text of this section, see Dobbs, Law of Remedies, Second Edition, Practitioner Treatise Series, Vol. 2 (§§ 6.1–11.10).

Choosing a Discount Rate *
    Effect of choice *
    Legal interest vs. judicial choice *
    Policy choice to control for inflation *
    Jury choice of rate *
Proof of Present Value *
    Instructions in lieu of proof *
    Burden of proof *

§ 8.5(4) Inflation and Loss of Increased Future Income *
General Rules *
    Traditional rule against taking inflation into account *
    Inequity of the traditional rule *
    The current practice *
Methods for Inflation Adjustment *
    (1) Proof of expected wage growth *
    (2) Proof of expected inflation rates for loss period *
    (3) Adjusting the discount rate to reflect inflation *
    (4) Adjusting the discount rate on the basis of past correlation between interest and inflation *
    (5) Standardizing a reduced discount rate *
    (6) A presumed rate *
    Weighing the practical problems *

§ 8.5(5) Periodic Payments, Structured Settlements and Court Ordered Funds *
Adjustable Awards and Settlements *
    Lump-sum finality vs. flexible awards *
    A thoroughgoing adjustable award system *
    Adjustments for the plaintiff's changed condition *
    Adjustments for economic changes *
    Partial adjustment systems *
The Claimed Advantages of Adjustable Award Systems *
    Advantages to the public *
    Advantages to the victim *
    Advantages to the defendant/insurer *
    Main forms of adjustable damages *
Structured Settlements *
    Nature of structured settlements *
    Qualified assignments *
    Structuring for future needs *
    Lawyers' financial assessments *
    Tax liability of the plaintiff's lawyer on delayed fees *
Periodic Payment Statutes *
    Adoption *
    Limitations *

* For the full text of this section, see Dobbs, Law of Remedies, Second Edition, Practitioner Treatise Series, Vol. 2 (§§ 6.1–11.10).

Issues *
The insured future cost alternative *
Court Ordered Funds *

§ 8.6 ADJUSTMENTS: BENEFITS TO THE PLAINTIFF

§ 8.6(1) Summary *

§ 8.6(2) Direct Benefits to the Plaintiff *
Direct Benefits Rule *
Types of Benefit *
Credit Limited to Types of Interest Matching Types of Benefit *
Tracing the Benefit Back to the Plaintiff *
Public Benefits, Public Defendant *
Public Benefits, Private Defendant *
Savings *
Comment *

§ 8.6(3) Collateral Source or Collateral Benefit Rule *
Common Law Rule *
    General rule *
    Scope and application *
Rationale and Debates *
    Litigation finance motivation *
    Donor intends to benefit the plaintiff, not defendant *
    The plaintiff paid *
    Subrogation *
    The wrongdoer should not get a windfall *
Statutory Changes *
    Coordination of benefits *
    "Tort reform" statutes *
    Limiting offset or credit to corresponding types of damages *
    Order of offset or credit *
Evaluating Collateral Source Solutions *

                                                                          Page
§ 8.6(4) Plaintiff's Income Tax Benefits ---------------------------------- 679
Plaintiff's Tax Savings *
    Injury awards not taxed *
    Scope of tax rule *
Effect on Damages Measurement *
    Traditional state-court rules *
    Rationales for refusal to adjust the award *
    The rule in wrongful death actions *
    Alternative approaches *
    The "federal" rule *
    Scope of the Liepelt rule *
    The federal impact *
Jury Instructions *
    The problem *

* For the full text of this section, see Dobbs, Law of Remedies, Second Edition, Practitioner Treatise Series, Vol. 2 (§§ 6.1–11.10).

Traditional rule *
The minority group *
Rationales *

§ 8.7 ADJUSTMENTS: AVOIDABLE CONSEQUENCES AND COMPARATIVE NEGLIGENCE

Page

§ 8.7(1) Apportionment Systems: Causal Apportionment, Avoidable Consequences and Comparative Fault -------------- 679
Assignment of Responsibility vs. Measurement *
Systems for Allocating Responsibility *
    Causal apportionment *
    Comparative fault *

§ 8.7(2) Avoidable Consequences Rules: Minimizing Damages --- 680
General Rules *
Factual Settings *
Reasonableness Test; Factors *
Personal Autonomy: Wide Latitude for Plaintiff's Choice *
Personal Autonomy in Wrongful Birth and Wrongful Pregnancy Cases *
Burden of Proof *

§ 8.7(3) Comparative Negligence ------------------------------- 680
Principles of Damage Allocation *
Assigning Fault *
Damage Reduction in Percentages *
Punitive Damages *
Pure and Modified Forms of Comparative Fault *
Choosing Comparative Fault vs. Avoidable Consequences Apportionment *

§ 8.7(4) "Seat Belt" Defenses ------------------------------- 682
Comparative Negligence or Avoidable Consequences? *
    Scope of the "seat belt" issue *
    Comparisons to contributory negligence and avoidable consequences *
    Accidental elements in the problem *
Judicial Choices *
    Rejecting the seat belt defenses altogether *
    Choosing between causal and fault-based apportionment *
    Sidestepping the difficulties *
Effects of Different Apportionment Methods *
    (1) The avoidable consequences solution *
    (2) A comparative negligence solution *
    (3) A dual or combined approach *
    Comment *
Arbitrary Limits *

* For the full text of this section, see Dobbs, Law of Remedies, Second Edition, Practitioner Treatise Series, Vol. 2 (§§ 6.1–11.10).

§ 8.8 STATUTORY CAPS ON DAMAGES— "TORT REFORM" LIMITS

Page

Summary ----- 683
  The tort reform movement ----- 683
  Tort reform changes ----- 683
  Types of statutes ----- 684
Types of Damages Capped ----- 684
  (1) Noneconomic limits only ----- 684
  (2) Limit on recovery of actual damages ----- 684
  (3) Dual caps ----- 684
Types of Cases or Defendants to Which Cap Applies ----- 684
  (1) Application to cases generally ----- 684
  (2) Application of specified claims or defendants ----- 685
Indirect Caps and Substitute Compensation Systems ----- 685
Constitutionality ----- 686
  Statutes unconstitutional ----- 686
  Statutes constitutional ----- 686
Construction ----- 687
Effects ----- 688
Alternatives ----- 689

§ 8.9 RESTITUTION IN PERSONAL INJURY CASES

Nature of the Victim's Claim for Wrongdoer Profits *
  Restitution as wrongdoer's gains *
  Murder-and-inherit cases ----- 689
  Murder-and-publish cases ----- 690
  Possible expansions *
  Absence of a non-statutory claim *
Statutory Claims *
  Adoption of "Son of Sam" statutes ----- 690
  Effect on wrongdoer's profits ----- 690
  Effect on victim's recovery ----- 690
  Constitutional challenges to the statutes ----- 690

§ 8.10 EQUITABLE RELIEF IN PERSONAL INJURY CLAIMS

Summary ----- 692
Traditional Practice and Changing Attitudes *
  Traditional practice *
  Changed recognition of institutional responsibility *
  Changed attitudes toward injunction and public litigation *
  Increased regulation of safety *
  Victim's loss of self-protecting capacity *
  The litigation finance problem *
  The "standing" problem *
  Injunction and punitive damages deterrence *

* For the full text of this section, see Dobbs, Law of Remedies, Second Edition, Practitioner Treatise Series, Vol. 2 (§§ 6.1–11.10).

Page

Injunctive Enforcement of Liability—Enjoining Payment 692
    Securing payment before judgment 692
    Injunctive creation of medical monitoring funds 692

CHAPTER 9. FRAUD AND MISREPRESENTATION

§ 9.1 SUBSTANTIVE BACKGROUND AND REMEDIAL SUMMARY

Scope *
    Generally *
    Intended and negligent deception *
    Statutes; securities; RICO *
Interests Protected *
    Misrepresentation as a tort to economic interests *
    Misrepresentation as element of other torts allowing non-pecuniary
        damages *
Fraud, Deceit and Misrepresentation *
    Fraud as misrepresentation *
    "Deceit" vs. negligent misrepresentation *
    Fraud in inducement, factum and integration *
Fraud and Contract *
    Misrepresentation and promise *
    Illustrative differences *
    Damages: contract or tort? *
Fraud and other Misconduct *
Remedies for Misrepresentation *
    Damages *
    Rescission and defenses *
    Restitution: constructive trusts and equitable lien *
    Reformation *
    Restoration by the plaintiff *

§ 9.2 DAMAGES FOR DECEPTION

§ 9.2(1) Damages Measure in Intentional Fraud Cases 694
In General 694
    Complexity and convention *
    Financial damage required *
The "Out-of-Pocket" Measure 695
    General damages: out-of-pocket measure 695
    Special meaning of "out-of-pocket" 695
    Date for valuation: buyer-plaintiffs *
    Date for valuation: seller-plaintiffs *
    Example of out-of-pocket measure 695
The "Loss of Bargain" Measure 695
    General damages: the benefit of the bargain or loss of bargain meas-
        ure 695
    The "value" form of the loss of bargain measure 696

* For the full text of this section, see Dobbs, Law of Remedies, Second Edition, Practitioner Treatise Series, Vol. 2 (§§ 6.1–11.10).

Page

Example of the value form ------ 696
The "cost" form of the loss of bargain measure ------ 696
Example of the cost form ------ 696
Flexible Measures ------ 697
Measure optional with the plaintiff or flexibly applied by the court 697
Consequential Damages ------ 697
Special or consequential damages ------ 697
Example of special damages *

§ 9.2(2) Measures of Damages for Negligent or Innocent Representations ------ 697
Negligent Misrepresentation Cases *
Innocent Misrepresentation Cases *
Liabilities for innocent misrepresentation ------ 697
Rescission for innocent misrepresentations ------ 697
Out-of-pocket as financial equivalent of rescission *
Recovery of out-of-pocket damages for innocent representations ---- 698

§ 9.2(3) Consequential or Special Damages ------ 698
Specials Recoverable in Addition to General Damages ------ 698
In general *
Limiting rules *
Exclusion of emotional distress damages *
Expenses incurred as a result of misrepresentation *
Profits lost as a result of misrepresentation *
Where Specials Duplicate General Damages *
The principle *
How duplication occurs *
Denial of duplicated awards *
Non-duplicative awards *

§ 9.2(4) Emotional Distress Damages in Misrepresentation Cases 698
Interests Protected—General Rule ------ 698
Emotional distress recovery denied ------ 698
Emotional distress recovery allowed ------ 699
Scope of the rule against emotional distress recovery ------ 699
Recovery of Non-economic Damages on Other Theories *
Misrepresentation as element in other torts *
Where the other tort warrants emotional distress damages *
Recovery of Non–economic Damages on a Fraud Theory? *
A commentator's proposals *
Casual decisions *
Emotional distress claims clothed as fraud cases *
Other highly personal harms resulting from fraud *
Comment *

* For the full text of this section, see Dobbs, Law of Remedies, Second Edition, Practitioner Treatise Series, Vol. 2 (§§ 6.1–11.10).

Page

§ 9.2(5) **Punitive Damages in Misrepresentation Cases** 699
Punitive Damages Recoverable for Fraud *
    General rules of punitive damages apply *
    Intentional deception as a sufficient basis for punitive damages *
    Intentional deception insufficient? *
    Favoring the rule that fraud alone is sufficient *
    Attenuated fraud as ground for denial of punitive damages *
    Negligent misrepresentation *
Statutory and Multiple Damages *
Punitive Damages and Emotional Distress Damages *

§ 9.2(6) **Limitations of Damages under Causation and Proximate**
      Causation Doctrines --- 699
Scope of Risk and Loss Problems ----------------------------------- 699
Cause in Fact -- 700
    The but-for rule --- 700
    Transaction causation where same loss would have occurred anyway 700
    Transaction causation where loss causation can also be fairly as-
      sumed -- 700
    When defendant could have fulfilled his duty by either a causal or
      non-causal act --- 701
Proximate Cause: Losses Outside the Risks Associated with the Rep-
    resentation --- 702
    Cause-in-fact with unrelated losses ------------------------------- 702
    The factory explosion example ----------------------------------- 702
    Transaction causation, price causation --------------------------- 702
Four Approaches to the "Proximate Cause" Problem ---------------- 702
    (1) Allowing full recovery -------------------------------------- 702
    (2) Denying all recovery -- 703
    (3) Full recovery in limited cases: misrepresentation interpreted
      broadly to cover all risks ----------------------------------- 704
    (4) Proximate cause approach: allowance of true general damages - 704
Segregating Misrepresentation Damages from Extraneous–Force Damages 705
    Market value at purchase date as basis --------------------------- 705
    General (unrealized) damages ------------------------------------ 706
    Out-of-pocket measure example ---------------------------------- 706
    Loss of bargain measure example -------------------------------- 707
Comment --- 707

§ 9.3 RESTITUTIONARY REMEDIES FOR DECEPTION: RESCISSION, CONSTRUCTIVE TRUSTS AND OTHER REMEDIES

§ 9.3(1) **Rescission and Restitution** ------------------------------- 708
In Fraud Cases *
Innocent Misrepresentation Cases *
Out-of-Pocket Damages Equivalence *
Specie or Money Restitution *

* For the full text of this section, see Dobbs, Law of Remedies, Second Edition, Practitioner Treatise Series, Vol. 2 (§§ 6.1–11.10).

                                                                     Page
§ 9.3(2) Is Damages Causation Required to Support Rescission? 708
Existence of Damage as a Prerequisite to Restitution ----------------------- 708
    General rule -- 708
    View requiring pecuniary loss *
    Appropriate use of the no-damage finding *
Causal Requirements in Rescission/Restitution Claims *
    "Proximate cause" limits -- 708
    Avoiding proximate cause limits by claiming rescission? -------------- 708
    The damages solution -- 709

§ 9.3(3) Restoration Required of the Plaintiff ------------------------ 709
A Generalization *
General Rules *
    Plaintiff required to make restoration *
    Ultimate restoration vs. pre-suit restoration *
Rescission at Law or in Equity *
    Equity suit *
    Rescission "at law"—traditional requirement of pre-suit return *
    Rescission after merger of law and equity *
Ultimate Restoration in Specie Required of the Plaintiff *
Excuses Permitting Substitutionary Restitution *
    (a) Money, fungible property *
    (b) Services, intangibles and use value *
    (c) Property worthless when received *
    (d) Disposal without knowledge of the fraud *
Restoration of Damaged or Depreciated Property *
    Property devalued because of plaintiff's fault *
    Property devalued by forces fraudulently misrepresented by defendant *
    Property devalued by neutral forces, extraneous to the defendant's
        misrepresentation *
    Innocent and negligent misrepresentation *
    Restoration of altered property *
Restoration in Release Cases *
Restoration of other Benefits Resulting From Transaction *

§ 9.3(4) Restitution Required of the Defendant ---------------------- 709
Restitution Allowable -- 709
    Benefits to be restored to the plaintiff generally ----------------------- 709
    Third person liability for restitution ---------------------------------- 710
Specific Restitution; Drawing on the Court's Equity Powers *
    Specie restitution "at law" *
    Constructive trust to obtain specific restitution in equity *
    Constructive trust and tracing *
    Adequacy of legal remedy test where plaintiff seeks recovery of spe-
        cific property *
    Adequacy test where plaintiff seeks recovery of money *
    Constructive trust, equitable lien, subrogation *

* For the full text of this section, see Dobbs, Law of Remedies, Second Edition, Practitioner
Treatise Series, Vol. 2 (§§ 6.1–11.10).

Page

Substitutionary Restitution for Values Retained by Defendant *
Recovery of Gains or Appreciation Derived From Transferred Property *
   Recovering defendant's gains from a sale ------------------------------- 710
   Gains the plaintiff would not have made ------------------------------- 711
   Gains the defendant would have made anyway ------------------------- 711
   Recovering appreciation in value in excess of defendant's gains—
      possible options --- 711
   —The Rothko case --- 712
   —Non-fiduciaries; damages vs. restitution *
Recovery of Use Values *
   Rental value *
   Interest *
   Profits from operating the transferred property *
Security for a Money Recovery *
   Constructive trust to exclude other creditors *
   Equitable lien to exclude other creditors *
   Security plus a personal (deficiency) judgment *

§ 9.4   RESTITUTION PLUS DAMAGES: ELECTION OF REMEDIES

Traditional Rules Generally -- 712
   General rule --- 712
   Examples -- 712
   Election rules inapplicable to inconsistent theories --------------------- 713
Rationales for Election Doctrine -- 713
   The duplication theory of election doctrine ----------------------------- 713
   Estoppel theory of election doctrine *
Two Types of "Election" *
   Affirmance vs. disaffirmance remedies *
   The first rule: the either/or rule --- 713
   The second rule: pre-trial election forced -------------------------------- 713
Operation and Status of the Pre-trial Forced Election Rule *
   Operation of the second rule *
   Criticisms of the second rule *
Operation of Rule against Both Affirmance and Disaffirmance Relief *
   Apparent support for the either/or rule *
   Criticisms: injustice *
   Criticisms: illogic *
Nontraditional Recoveries --- 714
   Allowing both restitution and compensatory consequential damages 714
   Restitution plus loss-of-bargain damages ------------------------------- 714
   Restitution, election and punitive damages ----------------------------- 715

§ 9.5   REFORMATION AS A REMEDY FOR DECEPTION

Reformation Generally --- 715
   Reformation to reflect the true agreement ------------------------------ 715

* For the full text of this section, see Dobbs, Law of Remedies, Second Edition, Practitioner Treatise Series, Vol. 2 (§§ 6.1–11.10).

                                                                    Page
Reformation to reflect legal standard ----------------------------- 716
Reformation vs. rescission --------------------------------------- 716
Substantive bases *
Reformation in Law and Equity ----------------------------------- 716
Physical reformation as equitable remedy ----------------------- 716
"Reformation" without physical re-writing ----------------------- 716
Rescission or Reformation—Fraud in Forming or Fraud in Expressing
    the Contract? --- 716
The formation-integration distinction --------------------------- 716
Classifying as formation or expression *
The formula or principle vs. the application as embodying the agree-
    ment --- 716
Standard legal terms *
Objective manifestation of intent *
Requirement of Writing and Parol Evidence: Effect of Statute, Rule or
    Contract *
Effect of statute of frauds *
Overconveyance *
Underconveyance *
Executory contracts *
Effect of parol evidence rule *
Disclaimers and merger clauses *

§ 9.6 EQUITABLE DEFENSES IN MISREPRESENTATION CASES

Equitable Defenses and Equitable Discretion Generally -------------------- 717
Substantive defenses *
Remedial defenses *
Discretion to Deny Rescission *
Minor deficiencies and adequate compensation *
Plaintiff's delay *
Estoppel *
Unclean hands *
Generally limited to "equity" suits *
Effect in "Law" Actions for "rescissory" damages *
Bona Fide Purchaser Rules *
The "no title" rule *
The voidable title rule *
Donees and others who do not qualify as bona fide purchasers *
Forgery: "void" transactions *
Fraud in the factum or execution *
Related Doctrines *
Holder in due course *
Discharge for value *

* For the full text of this section, see Dobbs, Law of Remedies, Second Edition, Practitioner Treatise Series, Vol. 2 (§§ 6.1–11.10).

CHAPTER 10. DURESS, UNDUE INFLUENCE, AND OTHER UNCONSCIONABLE CONDUCT

§ 10.1 SUBSTANCE AND REMEDY IN MISCONDUCT CASES

        Page

Scope the Substantive Wrongs --- 718
Public Policy or Private Morality? *
    Wrong and remedy *

§ 10.2 DURESS AND ECONOMIC COMPULSION

§ 10.2(1) **Avoidance For Duress Generally** ----------------------------- 719
General Rule --- 719
Physical Compulsion *
Threats of Physical Harm *
Economic Compulsion *
Remedies *
Primary Issues: Wrongfulness of Threats *
Primary Issues: Coercion *
Duress Distinguished From Tort and Other Claims *
Torts Related to Duress *

§ 10.2(2) **What Threats Are Wrongful Generally** ---------------------- 719
Wrongful Threat Required -- 719
Threats That Are Not Wrongful *
Threats That Are Wrongful *
The Dalzell Community Standard *
The Restatement Abuse of Contracting Process Standard: Loss Without
    Gain *

§ 10.2(3) **Threats in Particular Settings** -------------------------------- 719
Duress of Person or Goods *
    Duress of person *
    Duress of goods *
Railroads, Utilities and Taxing Authorities *
    Refusal to deal by railroads and utilities *
    Taxes, fees and assessments *
Threats of Prosecution *
    The "right" to prosecute *
    Limiting the "right" to prosecute for private advantage *
    Threat of public exposure *
Threats of Civil Litigation *
    Threats of civil litigation not generally wrongful *
    Threats of civil litigation not generally sufficiently coercive *
    When civil process limits use of property *
    Example *
    Forms of process limiting use of property *

* For the full text of this section, see Dobbs, Law of Remedies, Second Edition, Practitioner Treatise Series, Vol. 2 (§§ 6.1–11.10).

Threat to Breach Contract *
     Efficient breaches and self-protecting breaches *
     Rule that threat of breach is not wrongful *
     When threat of breach is wrongful *
     Example: Loral *
     Example: Hochman *
     Matching the examples to the Restatement's formulation *
     Good faith and fair dealing *
     Specifically performable contracts *
     Refusal to modify contract *
     Threats to interfere with contractor's economic relations with others *
     Threats to refuse to contract *
     Other threats *

§ 10.3   UNDUE INFLUENCE

                                                      Page
General Rules 719
     Influence by dominant party 719
     What influence is undue *
     Examples *
     Undue influence, fraud and duress *
     Undue influence and mental incapacity *
     Remedies for undue influence *
Evidence and Presumptions *
     Formulaic guides *
     Evidence *
     Presumption from gift to dominant party in confidential relationship *
     The presumption in testamentary transactions *

§ 10.4   BREACH OF FIDUCIARY OBLIGATION OR ABUSE OF CONFIDENTIAL RELATIONSHIP

Equitable Duties of Those in Special Relationships *
     In general *
     Fiduciary obligations 720
     Confidential relationship 721
     Special relationships, undue influence, and the burden of proof *
     Special relationships and fraud *
     Special relationships and inside information *
     Special relationships and unjust gains *
     Special relationships and unclean hands or pari delicto 722
Remedies for Breach of Fiduciary Obligation or Abuse of Confidential Relationship 722

* For the full text of this section, see Dobbs, Law of Remedies, Second Edition, Practitioner Treatise Series, Vol. 2 (§§ 6.1–11.10).

§ 10.5 MISUSE OF CONFIDENTIAL ECONOMIC INFORMATION

Page

§ 10.5(1) Duties of Loyalty and Confidentiality and the Real Estate Broker's Secret Profits ---------------------------------- 724
Special Duties of Loyalty and Confidentiality ------------------------------- 724
The Broker's Profit Cases --- 725
    Agent's duty to principal -- 725
    Agent's duty to buyers or third persons ------------------------------- 725
    The Harper case -- 725
    The Ward case -- 726
    The meanings of Harper and Ward -------------------------------------- 726
    Agent's misrepresentation of the vendor's price ----------------------- 727
Remedies --- 727
    Restitution --- 727
    Effect of vendor's rights to restitution in same property ------------ 728
    When the agent's or insider's gain is in the form of money -------- 728
    Damages -- 729
    Punitive damages --- 729

§ 10.5(2) Insider Transactions in Securities ---------------------------- 729
Traditional Fiduciary Law *
    Corporate opportunity *
    Disgorgement of gains made from fiduciary's use of inside information *
    Damages to traders *
    Scope *
Federal Statutory Liabilities for Insider's Short Swing Profits *
    Section 16(b) *
Federal Statutory Duties under Rule 10b–5 and other Statutes *
    Disclosure required under Rule 10b–5 *
    Insider's misuse of inside information under Rule 10b–5 *
    Insider's liability for tippee's profits *
    Liability of outsiders or tippees when information is about a different company *
    Participating outsiders; misappropriation *
    Statutory liability to contemporaneous traders *
Remedies under Federal Statutes *
    Public remedies *
    Damages and the restitution ceiling *
    Restitution *
    Attorney fees and prejudgment interest *
Measuring Disgorgement *
    Single transactions: matched purchase and sale *
    Multiple transactions: unmatched purchases and sales *
    Deductions: the insider's losses on some improper transactions *

* For the full text of this section, see Dobbs, Law of Remedies, Second Edition, Practitioner Treatise Series, Vol. 2 (§§ 6.1–11.10).

Page

§ 10.5(3) Trade Secrets and Confidential Information -------------- 729
Protecting Trade Secrets by Law and Covenant *
    Fiduciary principles *
    Trade secrets and covenants not to compete *
    Trade secrets protected *
    Public domain and rightfully acquired information *
    Wrongful acquisition or appropriation *
    Non-competition and other restrictive covenants *
Remedies: Restitution -- 729
    The wrongdoer's profits -------------------------------------- 729
    The wrongdoer's savings ------------------------------------- 729
    Adjustments in profit recoveries: apportionment and deductions ---- 730
Remedies: Damages *
    "General" or market value damages *
    Constructed market value *
    Consequential damages *
    Royalty measured damages *
    Damages in addition to restitution *
    Punitive damages *
Remedies: Injunctions --- 730
    Be-good injunctions -- 730
    No-competition injunctions against former employee ----------- 730
    Injunctions against competitor ------------------------------- 731
    Scope and duration of injunctions --------------------------- 731

§ 10.6 LIABILITIES FOR COMMERCIAL AND POLITICAL BRIBERY AND RELATED WRONGS

Bribing Seller's Liability to Buyer—Common Law Damages and Restitution -- 733
    Illustrative cases; the fiduciary's liability -------------------- 733
    Basis in fiduciary rules ------------------------------------- 733
    Briber's liability -- 734
    Damages *
    Restitution *
    Political bribery *
    Recovery from both briber and bribee *
    Recovery from those who profit *
Bribing Seller's Liability to Competitors *

§ 10.7 UNCONSCIONABLE CONDUCT AND THE UCC

Equity Unconscionability *
UCC or Code–Type Unconscionability *
    Code unconscionability *
    Distinguishing Code and equity unconscionability *
    The Walker–Thomas example *
    Procedural vs. substantive unconscionability *

* For the full text of this section, see Dobbs, Law of Remedies, Second Edition, Practitioner Treatise Series, Vol. 2 (§§ 6.1–11.10).

Unfair price *
Limited remedy *
Evaluating Unconscionability *
Equity unconscionability *
Process unconscionability *
Substantive Code-type unconscionability *

CHAPTER 11. MISTAKE IN CONTRACTING AND GIFT
TRANSACTIONS

§ 11.1 VARIETIES OF MISTAKE AND REMEDIES
FOR MISTAKE

Scope *
Substantive Law *
Mistake vs. Impossibility, Impracticability or Frustration of Purpose *
Mutual Mistake of Fact *
Mistakes in Formation *
Mistakes in Performance *
Mistakes in Integration or Writing of the Contract *
Mistakes as a Cause or Condition of Tort Liability *
Mistakes as a Cause or Condition of Contract Liability *

§ 11.2 THE MEANING OF MISTAKE—ERRONEOUS BELIEF,
MISUNDERSTANDING AND CONSCIOUS IGNORANCE

Page
Mistake of Fact or Law 738
  Mistake as state of mind 738
  Conduct distinguished *
  Mistake of fact as including mistake of law *
  Facts vs. expectations *
  Legal policy: respecting parties' risk allocations 739
  When fact and future are not readily distinguishable *
Conscious Ignorance, Assumed Risk and Doubt 739
  Formation of the contract 739
  Performance of a contract 740
  Expression or integration of a contract 740
  Assumed risks formulation of the principle 740
  Degrees of ignorance and risk allocation *
  Relation of conscious ignorance and negligence *
Misunderstanding 740

§ 11.3 MISTAKE IN THE ATTEMPTED FORMATION OF A
CONTRACT—MUTUAL MISTAKE

General Rule *
  The contract enforcing principle 741
  Basic mistake analysis *

* For the full text of this section, see Dobbs, Law of Remedies, Second Edition, Practitioner Treatise Series, Vol. 2 (§§ 6.1–11.10).

                                                                    Page
Restitution *
Example --- 741
Defining mistake to exclude relief for erroneous predictions *
Contract allocating risk *
Implicit risk allocation based on parties' knowledge of risk *
When the risk is not allocated or is allocated to the defendant *
Mistakes as to Existence or Identity of Subject Matter *
Requiring mistake as to identity or existence of subject matter ----- 741
Mistake as to existence example -------------------------------------- 742
Identity of the physical thing *
Identity of intangible "things" *
Mistake as to thing's function *
Comment --- 742
Court Allocation of Risks *
Defenses and Limitations *

§ 11.4 MISTAKE IN ATTEMPTED FORMATION OF A
CONTRACT—UNILATERAL MISTAKE

General Rules --- 743
Unilateral mistake alone insufficient ------------------------------- 743
Public policy *
Other party knows of the mistake *
The additional Restatement rule: unconscionable hardship plus a fa-
vorable allocation of risk of mistake ------------------------------ 743
Bidding Cases *
Known or suspected error *
Error not known or suspected *
Public bidding process *
Effectuating avoidance *
The Restatement rule on bidders *
Characteristics of bidding cases *
Extending the bidding rules to other cases *
Commenting on the Restatement Rule *
Restating the Restatement *
Is unconscionability or hardship relevant? *
Allocating risks of mistake to non-mistaken party? *

§ 11.5 RESTITUTION AS A REMEDY FOR MISTAKE IN
FORMATION OF A CONTRACT—MEASUREMENT
OF RESTITUTION

Avoidance and Restitution Generally *
Restitution in Money *
Restitution after avoidance *
Multiple measures of restitution *
Reliance expenses generally unrecoverable ------------------------- 744
Reliance expenses in unilateral mistake cases *

* For the full text of this section, see Dobbs, Law of Remedies, Second Edition, Practitioner
Treatise Series, Vol. 2 (§§ 6.1–11.10).

Page

Benefits conferred but not as part of bargained for performance --- 744
Benefits conferred as part of the performance under the contract - 744
Contract price as measure or evidence *
Contract price as floor or ceiling on restitution *
Restitution in Specie and Adjustments on Both Sides *
Unwinding Contracts: Is Restitution the Limit? *
Leaving loss where it falls *
Dividing losses *
Loss sharing and relational contracts *
Gain sharing *

§ 11.6 REFORMATION FOR MISTAKE IN EXPRESSION

§ 11.6(1) Grounds and Cases for Reformation ------------------------- 745
General Rules *
Reformation to correct discrepancy between writing and agreement *
Evidence and burden of proof *
How discrepancy can arise *
Examples *
Effect of the statute of frauds *
Effect of the parol evidence rule *
Mutual Mistakes *
Reformulating the mutual mistake language *
Scrivener's mistakes *
Unilateral mistake known to other party *
Relief to third persons *

§ 11.6(2) Reformation and the Alternatives --------------------------- 745
Choosing Rescission, Specific Performance or Reformation *
Examples: Reformation Inappropriate *
When the Choice Is Between Rescission and an Action for Breach *
Rescission vs. Reformation: Two Mistakes *
Rescission or No Relief vs. Reformation: When General Provisions Differ
  From Specific Provisions *

**§ 11.6(3) Effectuating, Extending and Defending Reformation
        Claims** -- 745
Effectuating Reformation *
Physical reformation, revised instruments *
Interpretation in lieu of reformation *
Defensive reformation *
Implicit reformation followed by enforcement *
Equitable Discretion and the Extension of Reformation *
Reformation and equitable discretion *
Downwriting agreements to comply with legal restrictions *
Judicial price and other adjustments *
Equities and hardships *

* For the full text of this section, see Dobbs, Law of Remedies, Second Edition, Practitioner
Treatise Series, Vol. 2 (§§ 6.1–11.10).

Defenses *
  Bona fide purchasers *
  Changed position *

§ 11.7 MISTAKE IN THE PERFORMANCE OF AN OBLIGATION—RESTITUTION REMEDIES

General Rules: Restitution for Mistakenly Conferred Benefits *
  Restitution for mistaken overperformance *
  Examples *
  Unilateral mistake *
  Plaintiff's negligence *
Remedies *
Affirmative Defenses *
Is the Mistake One in Performance of the Old Contract or Formation of
  a New One? *

§ 11.8 CHANGE OF POSITION

General Principles *
  The changed position principle *
  Limitations and qualifications *
  Burden of proof *
  Types of cases *
Payments to a Known Intermediary Have Been Passed on *
  General rule *
  Examples *
  Credits to an undisclosed principal *
  Where passed-on benefit could be recovered *
  Suits against the recipient of the passed-on benefit *
Was the Benefit Passed on? Tracing the Connection between Pay-In and
  Pay-Out *
  Connection between benefit received and credit or payment out *
  Is a benefit passed on by a bookkeeping entry? *
  Tracing benefits back to the plaintiff *
Changed Position—Expenditure or Consumption *
  General rule *
  Underlying concept of benefit *
  Hardships and equities on consumption-expenditure cases *
  Hardship and autonomy *
  Partial restitution *
Destruction, Damages, Loss of Benefit *
  General rule *
  Where depreciation or loss results from defendant's consumption-
    expenditure decisions *
  Loss of or damage to benefits conferred in contracting *

* For the full text of this section, see Dobbs, Law of Remedies, Second Edition, Practitioner Treatise Series, Vol. 2 (§§ 6.1–11.10).

§ 11.9   SETTLEMENT OF CLAIMS AND PERSONAL INJURY RELEASES

General Rules *
    Grounds for avoidance *
    Scope *
    Setting *
    Principle and general rule *
    Mistake about existence or nature of injury *
    Examples *
    Mistake about extent of injury or its consequences *
    Example *
    Effect of language releasing claims for unknown injuries *
    Manipulating the distinction between unknown injury and consequences *
Restoration or Tender by the Plaintiff *
Comment *

§ 11.10   MISTAKE IN GIFT TRANSACTION

Gifts Induced by Mistake—Donor versus Donee *
    Reformation or restitution for basic mistake *
    Unilateral mistake in donation *
    Mistaken gift examples *
    Mistake not causing donation *
    Form of benefit conferred by mistake *
    Forms of restitution *
Gifts Limited by Mistake—Donee versus Donor or Donor's Transferees *
    Intention to give not enforced *
    Attempted but ineffective gift followed by donor's death *
    Case authority *
    Evidence rather than rule *
    "Meritorious consideration" *

CHAPTER 12.   REMEDIES FOR BREACH OF CONTRACT

A.   GENERAL REMEDIAL RULES

§ 12.1   CONTRACT REMEDIES GENERALLY

	Page
§ 12.1(1) Damages, Restitution and Specific Performance	749
Contract Remedies Generally	749
Traditional remedies	750
Flexible remedies	750
Combining and "electing" remedies	751
Damages—Compensation and Convention	751
Compensation goals	751
Practical constraints and conventional limits	751
Policy constraints: defining compensation	751
Expectancy damages	752

* For the full text of this section, see Dobbs, Law of Remedies, Second Edition, Practitioner Treatise Series, Vol. 2 (§§ 6.1–11.10).

	Page
General and consequential measures of expectancy	752
Certainty and foreseeability limitations on consequential damages	752
Attorney fees	752
Reliance damages	752
Liquidated damages	752
Punitive damages and mental anguish damages	753
Avoidable consequences and collateral sources	753
Other adjustments	753
Restitution	753
Defendant's gain	753
Specific restitution	753
Money restitution	754
Defendant's collateral gains or profits	754
Specific Performance	754
Generally; adequacy test	754
Equitable discretion and equitable defenses	754
Equitable conversion based on specific performability	755
Security for Performance: Liens	755
Security as remedy	755
Mechanic's and materialman's lien	755
Liens for the vendor and purchaser of land	756
Dealing in the property for the breacher's account	756
Options and issues	756
§ 12.1(2) Policy and Practicality in Selecting and Measuring Contract Remedies	757
Contract Policy and Remedial Outlook	757
Contract policy *	
The values of enforcement	757
Contract policy affecting remedial attitudes	758
Relational contracts	758
Rigorous enforcement attitudes	759
Economic considerations	759
Remedial Purposes and Limits	760
Practical constraints	760
Contracting purposes	761
Subjective vs. objective measurement	761
Type of branch	761
Economic setting	762
Remedial implications	762

(1) MONEY REMEDIES

§ 12.2 DAMAGES TO COMPENSATE FOR EXPECTANCY

§ 12.2(1) Expectancy and Compensation Generally	762
General Rules of Expectation Damages	762
A rough rule	762

---

* For the full text of this section, see Dobbs, Law of Remedies, Second Edition, Practitioner Treatise Series, Vol. 3 (§§ 12.1–End).

Page

A buy-sell contract -- 763
A services contract -- 763
Compensation as a Goal -- 763
The goal of "compensation" -------------------------------------- 763
Putting plaintiff in the performance position ------------------- 763
Defining "compensation" --- 763
Practical limits on the compensation goal ----------------------- 764
Expectancy *
Expectancy *
Objective and economic meaning of expectancy *
Grounds for Protecting the Expectancy *
Economic activity encouraged *
Expectancy as a default remedy *
Efficient breach *
Remedial structure *

§ 12.2(2) Market Value vs. Cost Expectancy Measures -------------- 764
Expectancy Goals and Measurement Choices *
Market and Cost Measures of Expectancy -------------------------- 764
Market measures --- 764
Conventions in market measures ---------------------------------- 765
Cost measures --- 765
How Market and Cost Measures May Yield Different Awards ---------- 765
(1) Measurement date: rising cost of substitute performance ----- 765
(2) Acceptable similar but different substitute performance under
    UCC --- 766
(3) Substitute performance at less than market price ------------ 766
(4) Repair-replacement with destruction of existing work as a substi-
    tute performance -- 766
(5) Idiosyncratic values -- 767
Market Value Measurements as Minimum or Standardized Damages *
Choosing between Market and Cost Measures ----------------------- 767
Cost measures not invariably available at the plaintiff's option ----- 767
"Economic waste" and associated dilemmas ------------------------ 767
Windfall or compensation? --------------------------------------- 767
Added benefits or useful life from substitute performance ------- 768
Determining what counts as a substitute performance ------------- 768
Advantageous use of the cost measure ---------------------------- 769

§ 12.2(3) General vs. Special Measures of Expectancy ------------- 769
Expectancy Via General or Special Damages ----------------------- 769
Recovery of both general and special damages -------------------- 769
Limitations on consequential or special damages ----------------- 770
The General–Special Distinction *
General damages: present value of the thing promised *
General damages: date for computing unrealized loss *
General damages: formal definitions *

Page

General damages illustrated *

Special or consequential damages: benefits that would have resulted
  from performance --- 770

Consequential damages illustrated --------------------------------------- 770

"Profits" and consequential damages ------------------------------------- 770

Structuring proof to claim either general or special damages *

Locating the Cost Measures in the General–Special Scheme *

General Damages Exceeding or Falling Short of Perfect Compensation *

Accurate compensation measured by the plaintiff's net worth on the
  relevant date *

Imperfect compensation as measured by consequential losses *

Example of general damages exceeding compensation *

Movements to limit use of general damages *

Some Functions and Limits of General Damages *

Are market damages an attempt to accurately measure the cost of
  substitute performance? *

The function of general damages as reflecting the scope of the parties' guarantees *

The function of general damages as reflecting a minimum standardized recovery or "default" measure in the absence of party
  agreement *

The function of general damages in reflecting subjective compensation at low cost *

The ultimate impossibility of awarding perfect compensation *

RULES VS. INDETERMINATE RECOVERIES *

§ 12.3 DAMAGES TO COMPENSATE FOR RELIANCE LOSS AND OPPORTUNITY COSTS

§ 12.3(1) Reliance Loss as Measure of Damages ---------------------- 771

Recoverability of Reliance Damages ------------------------------------- 771

Reliance loss damages generally -------------------------------------- 771

Illustration -- 772

Motivation to claim -- 772

Reliance and Expectancy --- 772

Secondary role of reliance damages *

Reliance expense incurred regardless of performance *

Recoupment through performance: pre-contract expenses and fixed
  overhead --- 772

Opportunity cost --- 773

Reliance expense exceeding expectancy *

Reliance and Restitution -- 773

The Other Relevance of Reliance—Transactions Unenforceable as Contracts -- 774

* For the full text of this section, see Dobbs, Law of Remedies, Second Edition, Practitioner
Treatise Series, Vol. 3 (§§ 12.1–End).

Page

§ 12.3(2) Expectancy as a Cap on Reliance Damages 774
General Rules: Expectancy Caps Reliance ----------------------------------- 774
    Zero expectancy cases --- 774
    Recovery of reliance expenses when they exceed expectancy 774
    Burden of proof rule --- 775
Reliance as Special Damages: Essential and Incidental Reliance 775
    Essential reliance expenses as specials ------------------------------- 775
    Essential reliance and the expectancy cap ---------------------------- 775
    Incidental reliance expense as consequential damage ----------------- 775
    Incidental reliance and the expectancy cap --------------------------- 775
Measurement of Reliance Expenditures against Caps *
    Formulation of the cap rules *
    Conforming the rules to the principle *
    Application of the cap: market measured expectancy *
    Application of the cap: consequential damages measure of expectancy *
Defending on the Expectancy Cap *
    What must defendant prove? *
    Defendant's difficulty increases with improbability of the plaintiff's claim *
    Reliance damages as flexible damage award; reduced proof required to limit reliance damages? *

§ 12.4 THE SPECIAL PROBLEMS OF CONSEQUENTIAL DAMAGES

§ 12.4(1) Special or Consequential Damages: Limiting Rules 776

§ 12.4(2) Causation Requirements ------------------------------- 777
Rules Generally *
"Proximate Cause" and Cause in Fact *
Application of Cause in Fact Requirement *
Multiple Causes *
Causal Rules Expressed in Other Doctrines *

§ 12.4(3) Proof Requirements ----------------------------------- 779
General Rule -- 779
    Certainty rule --- 779
    Hard and soft approaches -- 779
    Consequential damages in issue *
Lost Profits *
    Lost market gains distinguished *
    Profits derived from business or ongoing operations *
    Past profit history and the new business rule *
    Plaintiff's own comparable past experience *
    Competitor's and others' comparable experience; yardstick evidence *
    Parties' assessments in contracting *
    Other items of profits evidence *
    Nature of the enterprise *

* For the full text of this section, see Dobbs, Law of Remedies, Second Edition, Practitioner Treatise Series, Vol. 3 (§§ 12.1–End).

Good will *
"Secondary" good will *
Capital and Income Versions of "Profits"—Profits as Evidence of Market
    Value *
    Case 1: Profits as consequential damages *
    Case 2: Profits as evidence of market value *
    Duplicated damages *
    Proof required when profits prove market value *
Adjustments to Prevent Excessive Recovery *
    Duplication of special damages *
    Where plaintiff saves capital for other investments *

§ 12.4(4) The Contemplation of the Parties Rule *
Liability Limited *
Examples *
Acceptance of the Rule *
Scope and Rationale Generally *
Formulations of the Rules *
Hadley Inapplicable to General Damages Claims *
Applications *

                                                                      Page
§ 12.4(5) The Contemplation of the Parties Rule: Rationales 780
The Moral Basis for a Contemplation of the Parties' Limitation 781
    Scope of liability determined by scope of promise 781
    Necessary conditions: party autonomy 781
    Necessary conditions: parties' implicit understandings can be deter-
        mined 782
    A qualification: contract as risk assignment 782
The Economic Basis for a Contemplation of the Parties' Limitation 783
    Increased costs, cross-subsidies, efficient use of resources 783
    The business trip example 783
    Increased costs 784
    Cross-subsidies 785
The Pragmatic Limitation 785

§ 12.4(6) The Contemplation of the Parties Rule: Formulations . 785
Tests Based on the Moral Rationale of Hadley 785
    Contemplation of the parties formulation 785
    Tacit agreement formulation and its liberalization 786
Foreseeability Tests 786
    Foreseeability formulation 786
    Foreseeability as a misinterpretation? 787
    Foreseeability as shorthand for contemplation of the parties? *
    Negative and positive foreseeability tests conflated? *
    Non-literal applications of foreseeability 787
The Restatement Second of Contracts Formulations 788
    Discretionary limits on damages 788

* For the full text of this section, see Dobbs, Law of Remedies, Second Edition, Practitioner
Treatise Series, Vol. 3 (§§ 12.1–End).

Page

Unassumed risks and disproportionate pricing ------------------------- 788

Unallocated risks, judicial discretion -------------------------------- 789

§ 12.4(7) Contemplation of the Parties: Applications and Subsidiary Principles -- 789

Meaning and Scope of Contemplation and Foreseeability *

    Time of contracting governs *

    Contemplation/foreseeability of general type of harm suffices *

    Objective test *

    Probability *

General Damages *

    Limits inapplicable to general damages *

    Buy-sell contracts *

    Specified sums of money as general damages *

    When interest can be general damages *

Applying the Rule in Consequential Damages Claims: What Risks Were Guaranteed? *

    Standardized goods or services at standardized prices *

    Illustrations: telegraphic transmissions *

    Buy-sell contracts *

    Substitute performance and minimizing damages *

    Loan contracts *

Reliance Damages *

Hybrid Damages, Bad Faith, and Tort Claims *

§ 12.5 EXTRACONTRACTUAL DAMAGES: EMOTIONAL DISTRESS AND PUNITIVE DAMAGES

§ 12.5(1) Emotional Distress Damages ------------------------------- 789

Rule and Exceptions Generally -- 789

    General Rule --- 789

    Rationale *

    Escaping the rule under contract theory ---------------------- 789

    Escaping the rule under tort theory -------------------------- 790

Traditional Exceptions—Combining Tort and Contract Theories *

The Tort Exception Today *

    Independent misconduct *

    Contract creating tort duty *

    The "bad faith" tort *

The Contract Exception Today *

    "Personal" element contracts generally *

    The vacation cases *

    Contracts for personal well-being *

    Warranty cases *

    Commercial contracts *

Critiquing the Rules *

    Should liability be expanded? *

* For the full text of this section, see Dobbs, Law of Remedies, Second Edition, Practitioner Treatise Series, Vol. 3 (§§ 12.1–End).

The serenity surcharge *
Is liability expanding in fact? *

    Page

§ 12.5(2) **Punitive Damages for Breach of Contract** 790
General Rules 790
    Rule against punitive awards 790
    The "exceptions" to the rule 790
    Rationales 791
To Expand Liability or Not *
    Discarding the restrictions? *
    Finding a tort *
    The bad faith tort *
    The "bad faith" tort in insurance cases *
    Limiting the bad faith tort in employment cases *
    Seeking the appropriate scope for the bad faith tort *

§ 12.6   ADJUSTMENTS IN DAMAGES

§ 12.6(1) **Summary of Adjustments** 791
(1) Credits for Prepayments and Benefits Bestowed 791
(2) Savings Effected 791
(3) Interest 791
(4) Reduction to Present Value 792
(5) Attorney Fees 792
(6) Avoidable Consequences, Minimizing Damages 792
(7) Collateral Source Payments 792

§ 12.6(2) **The Avoidable Consequences Rules** 793
General Rules *
First Rule Reductions *
    Credit for actual gains received by the plaintiff in substitute transactions *
    Credit for actual gains in substitute but unsuitable transactions *
    Rule limited to "substitute" transactions *
    Different time periods *
    Cover and resale transactions *
Second Rule Reductions *
    Rule formulation; causation requirement *
    The reasonableness issue *
    Minimizing by stopping harms or ceasing costly production *
    Minimizing by substitute transactions *
    Substitute transactions after anticipatory repudiation *
    Minimizing by renegotiating a substitute transaction with the breacher *
    Minimizing by seeking specific performance *
    Do minimizing rules apply to specifically performable contracts? *
Third Rule Additions *
    Recoverable expenses *

* For the full text of this section, see Dobbs, Law of Remedies, Second Edition, Practitioner Treatise Series, Vol. 3 (§§ 12.1–End).

Effect of contemplation-of-the-parties rules *
Expenses incurred recaptured by increase in assets or income *
Expenses adding value that cannot be captured or is unwanted *
Is There a Fourth Rule? *
    Rule pattern *
    Offset for hypothetical expenditure that would have reduced damages *
    Choice among several reasonable but hypothetical expenditures *
    Hypothetical expenditure that would not have reduced damages *
    Defendant's expenditure in unsuccessful attempt to reduce damages *
The Special Problem of Leases and Contracts to Lease *
    Contracts to lease *
    Leases: traditional rule that minimizing is not required *
    Rationale of the rule *
    Criticisms and changes; the tendency to require minimizing *
    Comments *
Limitations on Application of Minimizing Damages Rule *

                                                                    Page
§ 12.6(3) Must General Damages Be Minimized? ---------------------- 793
Two Views *
Three Cases *
    (1) The case of defective plumbing work for the homeowner *
    (2) The seller of a residence reneges *
    (3) The buyer reneges on the purchase of a market commodity *
§ 12.6(4) The Collateral Source Rule ------------------------------ 793
Collateral Source Rule and Offsetting Benefits *
Collateral Source Rule vs. Minimizing Damages Rules *
General Scope of Collateral Source Rule *
Application to Contract Cases Generally *
Cases With Tort Elements *
Public Benefits Resulting to the Plaintiff From Defendant's Breach *
Other Cases *
Collateral Source Rule and Subrogation *
Collateral Source Rule and "Efficient Breach" *
Collateral Source and Market–Measured Damages *

§ 12.7 MONEY AWARDS AS RESTITUTION FOR
            BREACH OF CONTRACT

§ 12.7(1) General Rules Permitting Restitution --------------------- 793
Roles of Restitution in Contracting ------------------------------- 793
    Restitution --- 793
    Avoidable or unenforceable contracts -------------------------- 793
    Restitution to the party in default --------------------------- 793
    Restitution for breach of enforceable contract ---------------- 794
General Rules Permitting Restitution for Contract Breach ---------- 794
    Restitution vs. damages --------------------------------------- 794
    General rules --- 794
    Restitution illustrated --------------------------------------- 794

* For the full text of this section, see Dobbs, Law of Remedies, Second Edition, Practitioner Treatise Series, Vol. 3 (§§ 12.1–End).

                                                                    Page
Restitution and expectancy -- 794
Restitution and reliance -- 795
Limits on restitution for breach *

§ 12.7(2) Form of Restitution—Specific vs. Monetary --------------- 795
Specific Restitution: Unique Goods and Security Interests *
Palmer–Restatement Approach: Specific Restitution Generally Available *
UCC Limiting Specific Restitution *
Discretion Limiting Specific Restitution Under the Restatement *
Executed Contracts to Convey Real Property *

§ 12.7(3) Mode of Measurement for Money Restitution ------------- 797
Generally --- 797
    Different measures available *
    Factors in choosing the more or less generous measure *
Benefits Conferred in Performance of the Contract ----------------- 797
    Restitution of price -------------------------------------- 797
    Restitution of the defendant's profits -------------------- 797
    Value of performance bargained for ------------------------ 797
    Additions to the defendant's wealth from plaintiff's performance -- 798
    Limiting the choice? *
Benefits Conferred in Reliance but not in Performance ------------- 798

**§ 12.7(4) Restitution Based on Defendant's Profits in Connection
       with Breach** -- 799
General Rule -- 799
    Wrongdoer's profits recoverable in tort cases ------------- 799
    Breacher's profits generally denied in contract cases ----- 799
    Illustration of the contract rule ------------------------- 799
Bases for the No–Restitution Rule *
    Compared to restitution permitted in contract cases *
    Compared to restitution permitted in tort cases *
    The Farnsworth arguments *
Scope of or Exceptions to the Rule -------------------------------- 799
    (1) Contract combined with tort or fiduciary breach ------- 799
    (2) Plaintiff acquires a property right in the defendant's promised
        performance: equitable conversion --------------------- 800
    (3) Plaintiff's own performance used to generate profits for breach-
        ing defendant --- 801
    (4) "Abuse of contract" ----------------------------------- 801

§ 12.7(5) Expectancy or Price as a Limit on Restitution ---------- 802
Summary and Background *
    Rule summary --- 802
    Expectancy vs. restitution goals *
    The defendant's profits case *
    The losing contract case *

* For the full text of this section, see Dobbs, Law of Remedies, Second Edition, Practitioner
Treatise Series, Vol. 3 (§§ 12.1–End).

When Expectancy Operates as a Ceiling on Recovery *
    Plaintiff's expectancy a ceiling: restitution would be measured by
      defendant's collateral gains *
    Plaintiff's expectancy a ceiling: full performance except for defen-
      dant's payment of liquidated sum *
When Expectancy Does Not Operate as a Ceiling on Restitution *
    Restitution of price payment *

                                                                          Page
    Restitution for value of non-money partial performance 803
Comments on Recovery of Restitution in Excess of Expectancy *
    Anomalies *
    Discarding rhetoric *
    Equities *
    Breach effecting savings to the non-breaching party *
    Causation *
    Measurement *
    Plaintiff's costs; not good evidence of value in a loss contract *
    Judicial reallocation of risks allocated by contract *
    Unallocated risks and the expectancy ceiling *
    Minimum proof suggested *

**§ 12.7(6) Recovery of Both Restitution and Damages: Election of
          Remedies** 803
Generally *
    General requirement of "election" *
    Affirmance vs. disaffirmance remedies *
    "Inconsistent" remedies *
The Four Settings for the Election Doctrine *
    (1) Serial assertion of "inconsistent" remedies *
    (2) Simultaneous assertion of "inconsistent" remedies *
    (3) Procedural choice *
    (4) Pre-suit delay *

§ 12.7(7) Restitution Claims Against Non-parties 803

(2) SPECIE AND NON–MONETARY REMEDIES

§ 12.8 NON–MONETARY REMEDIES—SPECIFIC PERFORMANCE AND DECLARATORY JUDGMENT

§ 12.8(1) Specific Performance Generally 805
Specific Performance Generally 805
    Elements in grant or denial of relief 805
    Specific performance as injunction *
    Traditional characteristics as equitable remedy; procedure *
    Traditional characteristics as equitable remedy; adequacy *
    Traditional characteristics as equitable remedy; discretion, practicality *
    Partial specific performance *
    Combined with other remedies *

* For the full text of this section, see Dobbs, Law of Remedies, Second Edition, Practitioner Treatise Series, Vol. 3 (§§ 12.1–End).

	Page
The Role of Specific Performance	805
Remedial role for the plaintiff	805
Strategic role in litigation	805
Strategic role in price speculation	806
Role in the judicial system *	
Implications of Specific Performance—Equitable Conversion	806
Implication for damages measurements	807
Implications of equitable "ownership" affecting risks and opportunities	807
Two effects of "equitable ownership" theory	807

§ 12.8(2) The Adequacy Test 808
The Traditional Adequacy Test *
   Old and new *
   Iterations of the adequacy test *
   What remedies are inadequate *
   Applications *
Rethinking the Adequacy Test *
   Merger of law and equity eliminates one basis *
   The Laycock position *
   The Yorio position *
   Economic arguments *
   The freedom of contract solution *
Comment: Procedural Reforms in Applying the Adequacy Test *
   Procedural components of the adequacy test *
   Dropping adequacy from the prima facie cases *
   Adequacy rules of law for homogenous classes of cases *
   A conceptual overhaul, utilitarian tune-up *
Comment: The Inadequate Adequacy Test *
   Misformulation and residual policy concerns *
   Jury trial, contempt power, and discretion *
   Strategic use of specific performance *

§ 12.8(3) Practicability and Policy Limitations 808
Generally 808
Enforcement and Supervision Problems 809
   Traditional refusal to enforce 809
   Meliorating rules 809
   Weighing relative costs and advantages; arbitrators *
   Reasons for caution *
   Reasons to afford relief *
   Is supervision likely to be necessary? *
Uncertainty of Contract Terms *
   The certainty requirement *
   Proving too much *
   Balance of advantages *

* For the full text of this section, see Dobbs, Law of Remedies, Second Edition, Practitioner Treatise Series, Vol. 3 (§§ 12.1–End).

                                                          Page
Personal Service Contracts 810
    Traditional rule against compulsion 810
    Legislative and judicial change 810

§ 12.8(4) Fairness and Hardship Limitations 810
In General 810
Unconscionable Contracts—Fairness Defenses *
    Substantive defenses *
    Unfairness as a remedial or "equitable" defense *
    Unfairness types—process vs. substantive unfairness *
    Substantive unfairness *
    Price fairness *
    Typical cases *
    Punitive denial of relief *
Estoppel, Laches and Unclean Hands *
    Estoppel *
    Laches *
    Unclean hands *
Hardship and Economic Considerations *
    Hardship reasoning *
    Changed circumstances as basis *
    Disparity in cost and legitimate value to the plaintiff *
    Price hardship due to inflation *
    Hardship on third parties *
Critiquing Hardship Reasoning *
    Re-writing the contract? *
    Restating the frustration doctrine? *
    Appropriate roles for hardship reasoning *
    An application *
Mutuality of Remedy—Inability to Secure Performance on Both Sides *
    Generally *
    Examples *
    Affirmative mutuality *
    Acceptance, revision and decline of the doctrine *
    The Restatement version *
    Example of specific performance conditioned upon security *
    Unfairness or hardship versions *

§ 12.8(5) Discretion and the Effect of Equitable Defenses on Le-
        gal Relief 811
Discretion: Substantive and Remedy, Law and Equity *
    No discretion on substantive rights *
    Legal and equitable discretion as to remedies *
    Is equitable discretion different from legal discretion on remedies? *
Effect of Denying Equitable Relief *
    When denial of specific performance is res judicata; claim preclusion *
    Issue preclusion *

* For the full text of this section, see Dobbs, Law of Remedies, Second Edition, Practitioner Treatise Series, Vol. 3 (§§ 12.1–End).

Equitable defenses not barring legal claims *
Predictable loss of legal claim after loss of equitable remedy *
Dilemma: is equitable discretion barring substantive rights? *
Dilemma: is the system pursuing a moral double standard? *
Answer 1: equitable defenses as legal defenses in disguise *
Answer 2: cases which warrant one remedy but not another *
Where damages would cost less than specific performance *
Where specific performance but not damages would give plaintiff a free ride *
Minimizing discretion, maximizing analysis *

Page

§ 12.8(6) Specific Performance and Contemplation of the Parties 811
Hadley v. Baxendale *
When Hadley is Irrelevant to Specific Performance Claims *
Limitation of Liability Clauses and the Sale of Carrots Example *
Specific Performance Inconsistent With a Limited Liability/Exclusive Remedy Clause *
The Hadley Rule as an Implied Limitation on Liability *
Uncontemplated Remedies *
Denial of Lost Profits Under Hadley and Certainty Rules *
The Example of the Resort Hotel's Water Supply *
Specific Performance When Lost Profits Are Not Provable Under Certainty Rules *

§ 12.8(7) Declaratory Judgment 811
Statutory Authorizations *
Case or Controversy Requirement *
Discretion and Other Grounds for Denial of Relief *
Jury Trial *
Declaratory Judgment Examples *

§ 12.9   AGREED REMEDIES

§ 12.9(1) Summary 812
Liquidated Damages Agreements Enforceable *
Penalty Agreements Unenforceable *
Approximating Damages at Time of Contract or Breach *
Unconscionability Rationales *
Compulsion and Efficient Breach Rationales *
Options and Alternative Performances Permitted *
Drafting and Interpretation *
Agreements for Arbitration and Specific Performance *

§ 12.9(2) Liquidated Damages and Penalties: General Rules 813
Agreed Remedies; Penalties Unenforceable *
Limitations and Penalties *
Alternative Tests: Approximation of Anticipated or Actual Damages *

* For the full text of this section, see Dobbs, Law of Remedies, Second Edition, Practitioner Treatise Series, Vol. 3 (§§ 12.1–End).

When the First Alternative Is Not Sufficient *
Must Loss Be Difficult to Prove? *
Subjective Intent *
Single Liquidation Covering Two or More Covenants *
Burden of Proof *
Applications and Examples *

Page

§ 12.9(3) Liquidated Damages: Rationales and Critiques 815
Four Arguments in Support of the Traditional Rules *
Advantages of Liquidated Damages Provisions *
Answering the Unconscionability Argument *
Answering Efficient Breach Arguments *
Answering Incentive to Induce Breach Arguments *

§ 12.9(4) Liquidated Damages: Alternative Analysis, Alternative Clauses 815
Alternative Perceptions of "Penalty" Clauses *
Defendant Is Taking Back Something He Has Sold *
Defendant is Buying Something *
Where the Sum Is the Contract Obligation, Not Damages for Breach *
Alternative Contracts *
Deposits and Forfeitures *
Affirmative Incentive Provisions *

§ 12.9(5) Liquidated Damages: Drafting and Interpretation 817
Exclusive Versus Nonexclusive Remedy *
Validity of Nonexclusive Clauses *
Recovery of Both Actual and Liquidated Damages *
Specific Performance *
What Breaches are Covered; Delay 818

§ 12.9(6) Agreements for or against Specific Performance and Other Remedies 818
General Rule 818
Melioration of the General Rule 819
Agreements for Specific Performance *
    Equity rules for specific performance *
    General rule *
    Melioration of the general rule *
    The jurisdictional rationales *
    The equitable discretion rationale *
    Comments on discretion *
    Weight to be given to contract provision *
Agreements for Arbitration and other Restrictions on Relief *
    Arbitration ousting specific performance remedy *
    Liquidated damages and other clauses ousting specific performance *

* For the full text of this section, see Dobbs, Law of Remedies, Second Edition, Practitioner Treatise Series, Vol. 3 (§§ 12.1–End).

B. PARTICULAR CONTRACTS

(1) LAND CONTRACTS

§ 12.10 VENDOR AND PURCHASER OF LAND: REMEDIES AND RISK OF LOSS IN SUMMARY

                                                              Page
Land Contract Types --- 819
    Earnest money contracts ----------------------------- 819
    Installment contracts ------------------------------- 819
    Scope --- 820
Purchaser's Remedies -- 820
    Damages --- 820
    Restitution --- 820
    Specific performance -------------------------------- 820
    Deed covenants -------------------------------------- 820
Vendor's Remedies --- 821
    Damages --- 821
    Specific performance -------------------------------- 821
    Restitution --- 821
    Vendor's lien --------------------------------------- 821
Risk of Loss -- 821

§ 12.11 PURCHASER'S REMEDIES FOR VENDOR'S BREACH

§ 12.11(1) Purchaser's Damages ---------------------------- 822
Intended Breach *
Breach Because of Innocent Title Defect ----------------------- 822
    The English rule: Flureau v. Thornhill -------------- 822
    The American rule *
    Limitations on the Flureau rule --------------------- 822
    Basis for rules *
Partial Breach -- 822
    Deficiencies -- 822
    Acreage deficiencies -------------------------------- 823
    Under an English–rule approach—reduction proportioned to price - 823
    —Reduction only as needed to equalize value on contract as a whole 823
    Under an American-rule approach --------------------- 824
    Improvements and variably valued acres -------------- 824
    Qualitative defects—market valuation *
    —Proportionate price reduction *
    —Spousal interests *
    Delay damages *
Special Damages *
    Generally *
    Lost profits and contemplation of the parties *
    Lost profits and reasonable certainty *
    Cost of cover or substitute property *

* For the full text of this section, see Dobbs, Law of Remedies, Second Edition, Practitioner Treatise Series, Vol. 3 (§§ 12.1–End).

"Essential" and customary reliance expense *
"Incidental" reliance expense *   **Page**
Vendor's Breach of Deed Covenants ------------------------------------- 824
    Merger in deed; covenants -------------------------------------- 824
    Damages limited to contract price ----------------------------- 825
    Measures of damages --- 825

§ 12.11(2) Rescission and Restitution for the Purchaser ---------- 825
Executory Contracts --- 825
    Rescission and restitution permitted *
    Rescission denied for minor or collateral breaches *
Restitution of the Vendor's "Profits"? *
    Gains from resale to third person *
    Cases allowing recovery of vendor's gain; equitable conversion *
    Vendor's gain as evidence of market value *
    Recovering vendor's gains to avoid the English-rule limitation *
    Punitive restitution *
Restoration Required on Both Sides *
    General rule *
    Obligation to restore value of land use *
    Right to recover for value of improvements made on land to be
        returned *
Executed Contracts: Deed Covenants ---------------------------------- 825

§ 12.11(3) Specific Performance in Favor of the Purchaser ------- 826
General Rule Favoring Specific Performance *
    Legal remedy presumptively inadequate *
    Putative exceptions *
    Interstate specific performance *
Equitable Defenses *
    Discretionary balancing generally *
    The speculating land buyer *
Partial Specific Performance *
    Deficiencies *
    Change of property or its status *

§ 12.11(4) The Purchaser's Lien ---------------------------------- 826
Right to a Lien *
Examples of Lien and Rights Secured *
Property Covered *
Third Persons Subject to Lien *
Enforcement and Lis Pendens Notice *

§ 12.12   VENDOR'S REMEDIES FOR PURCHASER'S BREACH

§ 12.12(1) Vendor's Damages Remedy ------------------------------ 826
General Damages --- 826
    In summary -- 826

---

* For the full text of this section, see Dobbs, Law of Remedies, Second Edition, Practitioner Treatise Series, Vol. 3 (§§ 12.1–End).

General damages: market-contract differential *
Measurement date; subsequent sale or market price *
Purchase price *
Special Damages *
   Recoverable consequential damages *
   Avoidable consequences *
   Duplicative damages *   **Page**
   Rental value recoveries --- 826
Liquidated Damages and Money Forfeitures *
   Earnest money forfeitures *
   Vendor's option to claim actual damages or forfeiture *
   "Election of remedies" preventing full damages *
   Contract limiting remedy to forfeiture *
Care of Grantor Contracts *
   Damages measure *
   Minimizing rules vs. collateral source rules *

§ 12.12(2) Restitution to the Vendor -------------------------------- 827
Executory Contracts *
   Absence of restitution *
   Clearing title *
Purchaser's Pre-closing Occupancy ----------------------------------- 827
   Traditional denial of restitution for rental value *
   Does breach of the purchase agreement affect the rental value claim? 828
   No assumpsit for use rule and implicit contractual exclusion ------- 828
   Bases for liability for the pre-closing rental ----------------------- 828
Executed Contracts -- 829
   Denial of rescission for purchaser's breach of money obligation ----- 829
   Denial of rescission for purchaser's breach of non-money covenants *
   Reasons for denial *
   Conditions and covenants *
   Money restitution for breach of non-money covenant *
Support of Grantor Contracts *
   Rescission and cancellation granted *
   Adjustments required *
   Equitable grounds for denying cancellation *
   Money restitution *

§ 12.12(3) Specific Performance in Favor of the Vendor ----------- 829
General Rules *
   The adequacy test *
   Adequacy test no bar to specific performance for the vendor *
   Argument that vendor's damages are inadequate *
   Argument based on mutuality of remedy *
   Comment: Case by case analysis or rule of law? *
   Discretion and defenses *

* For the full text of this section, see Dobbs, Law of Remedies, Second Edition, Practitioner Treatise Series, Vol. 3 (§§ 12.1–End).

Damages in Specific Performance Suits *
    Claiming damages in the specific performance suit *
    "Equivalent" action at law for the purchase price *
Deficiency and Excess of Acreage *
    Deficient acreage *
    Excess acreage *

                                                          Page

§ 12.12(4) The Vendor's Lien -- 830

§ 12.13 SOME PROBLEMS OF INSTALLMENT CONTRACTS REMEDIES

Installment Land Sales Contracts *
    Installment contract and mortgages *
    Remedial provisions of the installment contract *
Vendor's Remedies under Installment Contracts *
    Vendor's remedies *
    Forfeiture of payments made, not substantially exceeding the vendor's recoverable damages *
    Forfeiture as preventing deficiency judgment or other damages *
    Election of remedies reasoning to bar expectancy damages *
    Criticizing election reasoning: termination vs. rescission *
    Criticizing election reasoning: flaws in the election doctrine *
    Problems with price actions *
    Foreclosure of the purchaser's rights *
    Integrating forfeiture into the damages remedies *
Restitution to the Purchaser in Default—Traditional and Modern Rules and their Bases *
    Buyer protection and the restitutionary issue *
    No restitution of sums forfeited as earnest money *
    Installment payments: traditional and modern rules *
    Traditionalist arguments and their counters *
    Restitutionary support in the mortgage analogy *
Protecting the Vendor's Remedies in a Restitutionary Regime *
    Protecting the vendor's damages remedy; burden of proof *
    Protecting the vendor's specific performance remedy *
    Terminating the vendor's claim to specific performance *
Measuring the Purchaser's Restitution *
    Termination vs. rescission theories *
    Restitution under a rescission theory *
    Restitution under a termination theory *
    Comparing results *
    Mixing the theories *

§ 12.14 LOSS OR DAMAGE TO PROPERTY BEFORE CONVEYANCE

Contract, Tort and Statutory Solutions *
The Equitable Conversion Solution *

---

* For the full text of this section, see Dobbs, Law of Remedies, Second Edition, Practitioner Treatise Series, Vol. 3 (§§ 12.1–End).

The Possession or Title Solution *
Avoidance or Excused Performance *
Insurance Proceeds *
Price Abatement *

§ 12.15 LEASES AND LEASE CONTRACTS

Page

§ 12.15(1) Background and Scope ---------------------------------- 832
Scope *
Conveyance vs. Contract; Rent vs. Damages *
Independent Obligations *
Changing Traditional Views *
Legislation *
Scope of Coverage *

§ 12.15(2) Lessee's Remedies for Lessor's Breach Affecting Use
              Premises -- 832
Damages *
    General Damages -- 832
    Consequential damages generally ----------------------------- 833
    Entrepreneurial losses as consequential damages *
Rent Withholding and Rent Abatement *
    Rent withholding and abatement ------------------------------ 833
    Measure of abatement based on general damages or expectancy ---- 834
    Measure of abatement based on cost of substitute performance ----- 834
Rescission, Termination and Restitution *
    Traditional common law views *
    Contemporary view permitting rescission --------------------- 834
    Restitution of payments, improvement values *
Specific Performance and Injunction *
    Specific performance *
    Injunctive specific performance *

§ 12.15(3) Lessor's Remedies Against Lessee Who Defaults or
              Abandons the Premises ------------------------------- 835
Remedies Generally *
    Recovery of accrued rental and repair costs ----------------- 835
    Remedies when tenant abandons the lease --------------------- 835
Termination vs. the Tenant's Account Remedy *
    Termination vs. re-letting for the tenant's account *
    Notice to the tenant *
Rents Accrued and Accelerated *
    Collecting rents as due; acceleration clauses *
    Acceleration clauses unenforceable *
    Making acceleration reasonable: discount to present value *
Termination Plus a Deficiency Judgment *
    Termination plus damages for the deficiency? *
    Basis in statutes, covenants, and contract theory *

* For the full text of this section, see Dobbs, Law of Remedies, Second Edition, Practitioner Treatise Series, Vol. 3 (§§ 12.1–End).

Measurement of Future Loss *
    Measurement as general (market) damages *
    Application of market measure *
    Measurement as special damages with an avoidable consequences
      reduction *   **Page**
Minimizing or "Mitigating" Damages ----------------------------------- 836
    Traditional view *
    Modern view --- 836
    Rationales: lease as conveyance ------------------------------------- 836
    Rationales: lease as contract with specific performance --------------- 836
    Comment: residential leases *
    Comment: commercial transactions *
Computing Credits to the Tenant ------------------------------------- 837
    The problem of excess substitute rents ------------------------------- 837
    Choice of termination vs. tenant's account remedy determining credit 837
    Assessing the rule against credit *

(2) CHATTEL SALES CONTRACTS

§ 12.16 BUYER'S REMEDIES FOR BREACH OF CHATTEL SALES CONTRACT

§ 12.16(1) Buyer's Remedies: Background and Summary ---------- 838
Damages *
    Common law contract-market differential *
    Common law adjustments *
    Code similarities *
    Code differences --- 838
    Liquidated damages -- 838
Restitution *
Specific Performance *

§ 12.16(2) Buyer's Market Measured Damages ----------------------- 839
General Rule for Breach *
Example *
Time for Market Measurement *
Place for Market Measurement *
Type of Market Used for Measurement *
Relationship to Other Damages Claims *

§ 12.16(3) Buyer's Cover Damages Under the Code ----------------- 839
Cover under the Code Generally ------------------------------------- 839
    Damages measured by added cost of getting substitute performance 839
    What counts as cover? --- 839
    Two remedial meanings of cover ------------------------------------ 840
Cover as a Measure of Damages *
    Cover and market *
    Cover as shifting a market date *

* For the full text of this section, see Dobbs, Law of Remedies, Second Edition, Practitioner Treatise Series, Vol. 3 (§§ 12.1–End).

Cover when market is undeveloped *
More radical changes effected by cover rules *
Substitute goods worth more than contract goods *
Four types of "worth more" substitutes *
(1) Higher value goods do not count as a cover *
(2) Higher value goods count as a cover *
(3) Higher value goods count as cover, subject to offset for increased
    profitability *
(4) Higher value goods increase assets but not income *
Where buyer will realize "added profits" *
Where buyer will realize gain in other forms *
Non-transient added asset value *
Attributing new purchases to the breach; measuring cover when the
    buyer makes multiple purchases *
Cover as Minimizing: Must Market Damages Be Minimized? *
Cover to minimize damages *
When damages are limited by the cover measure *
Example of market damages not limited by cover *
Example of cover limiting market damages *
The White and Summers arguments *
When market damages may be recovered after purchase of substitute
    goods *

                                                                     Page
§ 12.16(4) Buyer's Incidental and Consequential Damages **840**
Incidental and Consequential Damages Generally *
Consequential damages *
Incidental damages *
Consequential or "Actual" Damages as a Limit on Market Damages *
The problem *
Authority limiting market damages under the UCC *
Seller's burden of proof *
Limiting the limit on market damages *

**§ 12.16(5) Buyer's Damages after Seller's Anticipatory Repudia-
        tion** --- **840**
Market Damages: Possible Dates *
Learned of Repudiation Date *
Time of Performance or Repudiation Plus Reasonable Time *
Cover After Anticipatory Repudiation *

§ 12.16(6) Buyer's Restitutionary Claims ---------------------------------- **841**
Restitution of Price Generally *
Restitution Plus Damages *
Loss Contract: Restitution of Prepayments in Excess of Expectancy Dam-
    ages *
Restitution of the Seller's Profit *
Restitution in Favor of the Breaching Buyer *

* For the full text of this section, see Dobbs, Law of Remedies, Second Edition, Practitioner
Treatise Series, Vol. 3 (§§ 12.1–End).

Page

§ 12.16(7) Buyer's Specific Performance Remedy 841
Where Buyer Has Contract but no Property Interest *
    Traditional adequacy rule *
    Physically unique goods *
    Associationally unique goods *
    Functionally unique goods *
    The Uniform Commercial Code *
    Factors *
    Judicial attitude *
Where the Buyer Has Acquired a "Property" in the Goods *
    Replevin where title but not possession has passed *
    Adequacy issue and equitable discretion eliminated *
    In rem vs. in personam enforcement *
    The possibility of equitable relief *
    UCC: Right to goods identified to the contract; replevin and specific
      performance *
    Narrow limits of the Code rule *
    Does the UCC permit specific performance and/or discretion? *

**§ 12.17 SELLER'S REMEDIES FOR BREACH OF
CHATTEL SALES CONTRACT**

§ 12.17(1) Seller's Remedies—Background and Summary 842
Common Law Damages *
Uniform Commercial Code Remedies *
    Basic measures under the Code: market and resale measures 842
    Special-case measures: lost profits and price recovery 842
    Incidental damages -- 842
    Consequential damages --- 842
    Liquidated damages, limited remedies ------------------------------- 843
    Restitution --- 843
    Specific performance --- 843
    Problem areas *

§ 12.17(2) Seller's Market Measured Damages --------------------- 843
General Rule for Breach or Repudiation *
Example *
Time and Place for Market Measurement *
Relationship to Other Damages Claims *

§ 12.17(3) Seller's Resale Measured Damages --------------------- 843
Resale under the Code *
    Resale price/contract price differential *
    Example *
    What counts as resale *
    Conceptions and functions of resale *
Resale Losses as a Ceiling on Market Damages *
    Resale as optional remedy *

* For the full text of this section, see Dobbs, Law of Remedies, Second Edition, Practitioner Treatise Series, Vol. 3 (§§ 12.1–End).

Are resale damages a ceiling on recovery? *
Avoidable consequences/"mitigating damages" rules distinguished *
The position of performance argument *
Is tracing goods a workable conceptual tool for imposing a ceiling? *
Anomalies *
Resale and lost volume *

Page

§ 12.17(4) Seller's Incidental and Consequential Damages 843
Consequential Damages: Incidental Damages and Lost Profits *
    Common law structure *
    Code structure: lost profits recoverable *
    Code structure: incidental damages recoverable *
    Code structure: (other) consequential damages *
Damages Allowable as Incidental Damages *
    Meanings of incidental damages *
    Incidental as adjunctive damages *
    Incidental damages as expenses of reliance and minimizing *
    As expenses of dealing directly with the rejected goods *
    Incidental damages: a tentative conclusion *

§ 12.17(5) Seller's "Lost Profit" Damages ----------------------------------- 844
Invoking the Lost Profits Recovery: Three Types of Lost Profit Cases *
    General rule under the Code *
    Lost volume sellers *
    Manufacturers stopped in midstream; the "components seller" *
    "Jobbers" *
Limitations *
    Is lost volume real? *
    Statistical planning: overbooking *
Calculating Profits and Overhead *
    Measurement generally *
    Overhead *
    Example *
    Other overhead methods *
    Computing lost profits to include (other) consequential damages *
    Recovering lost profits to recover reliance expenses *
Relationship to Other Damages Measures *

§ 12.17(6) Seller's Restitutionary Remedies ----------------------------- 844
Full Performance *
Part Performance *
The Wellston Case *
Does the Part Performance Rule Apply After Adoption of the Code? *
Cash Sales and Reclamation *

§ 12.17(7) Seller's Specific Performance Remedy: The Price Action --- 844
Specific Performance and Money Recoveries of the Price *

* For the full text of this section, see Dobbs, Law of Remedies, Second Edition, Practitioner Treatise Series, Vol. 3 (§§ 12.1–End).

When the Price Action Is Permitted *
Buyer's Rights *

§ 12.18 REMEDIES FOR BREACH OF LEASE OF GOODS

Background and Examples *
    Inauguration *
    Leases vs. other transactions *
    Related remedial issues *
Liquidated Damages *
    Policy in favor of liquidated damages *
    Approved formulas *
    Terms of judging reasonableness *
    Code liquidation of damages *
Lessee's Remedies *
    Market measured damages *
    Cover measured damages *
    Incidental and consequential damages *
    Using the goods as security *
    Specific performance or replevin *
    Problems *
Lessor's Remedies *
    Market measured damages *
    Re-leasing measure of damages *
    Incidental, consequential and lost profits measures *
    "Lost profit" measure of damages *
    Specific performance, rent action *
    Recovery of possession *

(3) BUILDING CONTRACTS

§ 12.19 OWNER'S REMEDIES FOR BREACH OF BUILDING OR REPAIR CONTRACT

     Page
§ 12.19(1) Owner's Damages Remedy 844
General Rules—Nonperformance or Defective Performance 844
    Basic alternative rules 844
    Factors in choosing 844
    Related situations and claims 844
The Cost Rule: Conditions and Qualifications 845
    Completion or repair must be a substitute for contract performance 845
    Reasonableness of substitute performance *
    Substitute performance more beneficial to owner *
    Events subsequent to breach as affecting measure of compensation *
Choosing Between Cost and Value Rules in Waste or Windfall Cases *
    Waste, windfall and expectancy 845
    Disproportion: costs to lost value 845

* For the full text of this section, see Dobbs, Law of Remedies, Second Edition, Practitioner Treatise Series, Vol. 3 (§§ 12.1–End).

Disproportion in purely pecuniary contracts *
Disproportion in non-pecuniary, personal taste contracts *
Risks of overvaluing subjective preferences of owner *

Page

Role of wilfulness in the breaching --------------------------------------- 846
Criticizing wilfulness analysis --- 846
Unjust enrichment of the contractor ------------------------------------- 847
Four solutions --- 847
Consequential Damages *
Delay in performance: rental value *
Delay: interest and finance charges *
Lost profits *
Delay: liquidated damages *

§ 12.19(2) Owner's Restitutionary Remedies --------------------------- 848

§ 12.19(3) Owner's Specific Performance Remedy -------------------- 848
General Rules *
Adequacy of Legal Remedy *
When cost of completion measure is adequate *
When cost measure is not adequate; buildings on the defendant's land *
When cost measure is not adequate; complex contracts *
Where damages would be measured by loss in value; costs greater
than benefits *
Practicality: Supervision *
Traditional rule *
Practical inducements to perform as minimizing supervision *
Balance of need for relief; public interest *

§ 12.20 CONTRACTOR'S REMEDIES FOR OWNER'S
BREACH OF CONSTRUCTION OR
REPAIR CONTRACT

§ 12.20(1) Contractor's Damages Remedies ---------------------------- 848
Scope and Background *
Contractor's Expectancy Damages *
Full performance and no performance cases ---------------------------- 848
Price less saved expenses -- 848
Alternate calculations: profits plus costs incurred and proportionate
payment for proportionate work --------------------------------------- 848
When the rules are equivalent --- 849
Illustrations *
Losing contracts --- 849
Contractor's Reliance and Consequential Damages *
Consequential damages generally *
Reliance expenses *
Reliance expense recovery built into general damages measures *
Delay costs generally *
Delay: total cost method *
Provisions for no damages or liquidated damages *

* For the full text of this section, see Dobbs, Law of Remedies, Second Edition, Practitioner
Treatise Series, Vol. 3 (§§ 12.1–End).

Page

§ 12.20(2) Contractor's Restitutionary Remedies 849

General Rules --- 849

    Restitution allowable for benefits conferred on owner or general contractor -- 849

    Measures of restitution --- 850

    Subcontractors and others not in privity with owner *

    When restitution is the preferred remedy *

    Restitution to Put Contractor in Better Position by Reason of Breach 850

    General rule *

Limitations on Excess Restitution *

Application *

    Policy against unjust enrichment *

    Measurement of the landowner's enrichment in accordance with contractual risk allocation *

    Distinguishing losses from unallocated risks from contractor's management losses *

    Relevance of landowner's breach *

    Realistic estimates of benefits *

Restitution to the Defaulting Contractor *

    Suit for contract damages *

    Suit for restitution *

    Measurement of restitution *

Restitution for Additional or Extra Work *

    Extra work situations *

    Restitution or judicial readjustment of the contractual relation? *

    Implied in fact contract *

    Work not requested *

    Unexpected difficulties adding to costs *

    Measurement *

§ 12.20(3) Third Party Restitution Claims of Subcontractors and Others: Mechanics' Liens and Other Devices 850

Subcontractors', Laborers' and Suppliers' Claims Generally --------------- 850

    The third party situations --- 850

    Three general rules --- 851

Subrogation and Restitution Claims *

    The subcontractor's subrogation claim against retained funds ------- 851

    Landowner's limited liability when there are competing claims against the fund *

    General rule against restitution ----------------------------------- 851

    Reasons for the general rule *

    Landlord's benefit from tenant's improvements at the expense of contractors or materialmen ----------------------------------- 852

Mechanics' and Materialmen's Liens and Other Solutions *

    Statutory liens against the owner ------------------------------------- 852

    Statutory and bond coverage *

    Foreclosure *

* For the full text of this section, see Dobbs, Law of Remedies, Second Edition, Practitioner Treatise Series, Vol. 3 (§§ 12.1–End).

Stop notices *
Avoiding the lien; payment bonds *
The Miller Act and State Counterparts *

(4) OTHER CONTRACTS

§ 12.21 EMPLOYEE'S REMEDIES FOR EMPLOYER'S BREACH OF EMPLOYMENT CONTRACT

                                      Page

§ 12.21(1) Scope and Related Materials 853

§ 12.21(2) Employee's Damages Remedy 853
Basic Rules *
    General rule: contract price with deduction for replacement income *
    Compared to the market-contract differential *
Avoidable Consequences: Minimizing Damages *
    The first and second rules of avoidable consequences *
    "Reasonable diligence" *
    Income earnable while continuing employment *
    Suitable, comparable, or substitute employment *
    Going into business *
    Deductions for replacement income: burden of proof *
Collateral Source Benefits *
Consequential and Punitive Damages *
    Limiting rules; Hadley v. Baxendale *
    Perquisites and collateral advantages of the job *
    Reasonable certainty rule and collateral employment advantage *
    Reputation and emotional harm *
    Punitive damages *
Liquidated Damages *

§ 12.21(3) Employee's Restitutionary Remedies 853
General Rule *
Recovery in Excess of the Contract Price *
Respecting Contractual Risk and Cost Allocation *
Employee in Default *

§ 12.21(4) Specific Performance and Injunction in Favor of Employee 853
Traditional Rule Against Specific Performance *
Four Reasons Against Relief *
Mutuality *
Adequate Legal Remedy *
Difficulty of Judicial Supervision *
The Difficulty of Estimating Difficulty *
Forcing an Unwanted Relationship *
Parties' Contemplation as a Limit on Relief *
Reputational Loss *

* For the full text of this section, see Dobbs, Law of Remedies, Second Edition, Practitioner Treatise Series, Vol. 3 (§§ 12.1–End).

§ 12.22 EMPLOYER'S REMEDIES FOR EMPLOYEE'S BREACH OF EMPLOYMENT CONTRACT

Page

§ 12.22(1) The Employer's Money Remedies ------------------------------- 853
Scope *
General Rule *
Consequential Damages *
Lost Profits *
Restitution *

§ 12.22(2) The Employer's Equitable Remedies ----------------------- 853
Specific Performance Generally *
    General rule *
    Moral basis *
    Practical basis *
    Scope *
Enforcement of Negative Covenants *
    Negative promises: covenants not to compete ---------------------------- 853
    The Lumley v. Wagner case --- 853
    Enforcement of the negative against skilled employees --------------- 854
    Negative injunctions against sellers of good will ----------------------- 854
    Limiting considerations -- 854
    Hard line limits *
    The negative injunction in trade secret thefts *
    Reformation of illegal clauses *

§ 12.23 REMEDIES UNDER ARBITRATION CONTRACTS

The Nature of Arbitration *
    Contracting for arbitration *
    Arbitration and alternative dispute resolution *
    Advantages of arbitration *
    Arbitration as a remedy and as engendering remedies by the arbitrator *
Common Law and Equity: Limited Enforcement *
    Common law rule of revocability *
    Equity follows the law *
    Enforcement of the final award *
Statutory Enforcement of Arbitration Agreements *
    Governing statutes *
    Specific performance and other enforcement *
Judge and Arbitrator *
    Forms and limits of judicial review *
    The arbitrator's powers *
    Bootstrap: does the arbitrator have the power to determine arbitrability? *
    Determining whether the contract was procured by fraud or otherwise subject to avoidance *
    Determining "jurisdictional" facts *

* For the full text of this section, see Dobbs, Law of Remedies, Second Edition, Practitioner Treatise Series, Vol. 3 (§§ 12.1–End).

The Arbitrator's Remedies *
    Compensatory damages *
    Equitable or non-monetary relief *
    Relief courts would refuse *
    Relief courts are prohibited from giving *
    Punitive damages *

CHAPTER 13.   UNENFORCEABLE CONTRACTS

§ 13.1   RESTITUTION IN UNENFORCEABLE CONTRACTS: SCOPE AND SUMMARY

The Problem Situations *
Restitution for Part Performance *
Reliance Expenses Apart From Restitution *
Measuring Restitution *
Differential Policy *
Restitution Versus Readjustment *

§ 13.2 RESTITUTION FOR BENEFITS CONFERRED UNDER CONTRACTS UNENFORCEABLE FOR LACK OF A WRITING

	Page
§ 13.2(1) Restitution Permitted under Statute of Frauds Policy	857
General Rules	857
Restitution and the Statute of Frauds Policy	857
Statutory policy does not prevent a recovery of the defendant's unjust enrichment	857
Example	858
Relevance of the contract	858
§ 13.2(2) Restitution and Its Measure	858
Measures of Restitution	858
General rule permitting restitution	858
Exception where plaintiff is in default	858
Measurement options	859
Benefits Conferred in Performance of the Contract Obligation	859
Payments made, market value of performance, or increase in defendant's wealth	859
Rationale	860
Improvements on land by vendor or lessor	860
Improvements on land by purchaser or lessee	861
Services rendered under employment and care contracts	861
Expenses Incurred in Reliance on But Not in Performance of the Contract *	
Limiting recovery to defendant's increased wealth *	
Distinguishing requested from unrequested benefits *	

* For the full text of this section, see Dobbs, Law of Remedies, Second Edition, Practitioner Treatise Series, Vol. 3 (§§ 12.1–End).

Page

Contract Price as Evidence of Benefit --------------------------------- 861
    Contract price and restitution measures ---------------------------- 861
    Contract price as a ceiling on recovery --------------------------- 862

§ 13.2(3) Restitution in Specie --------------------------------------- 862
Specific Restitution Generally Denied *
Personal Care Contracts in Exchange for Land *
Conveyance to Be Held in Trust for Grantor *
Conveyance to Be Held in Trust for Third Person *

§ 13.2(4) Reliance Expenses vs. Restitution ---------------------- 863
Distinguishing Reliance Expense From Restitution --------------- 863
    Contracting for process vs. contracting for end-result --------- 863
    Contracting for manufactured product not for steps in manufacture 863
    Contracting to employ, not employee's preparation to work --------- 864
    Doubting the distinction --------------------------------------- 864
    Three levels of reliance --------------------------------------- 864
    Recognizing essential steps as requested performance ---------- 865
Direct or Indirect Allowance of Reliance Damages ---------------- 865

§ 13.2(5) Estoppel and Part Performance ------------------------- 865
Part Performance -- 865
    Incorporated in UCC -- 865
    Judicial doctrine of part performance -------------------------- 866
    Limitations --- 866
Estoppel, Equitable and Promissory ---------------------------------- 866
    Equitable estoppel --- 866
    Promissory estoppel -- 867
    Promissory estoppel examples ----------------------------------- 868
Limitations on the Doctrine and the Remedy ---------------------- 868
    Limiting remedy to restitution or to reliance damages --------- 868
    Requirement of unjust enrichment to defendant or unconscionable
      harm to the plaintiff *
    Nature of reliance required *
    Other limitations *

§ 13.3 REMEDIES WHEN PERFORMANCE IS EXCUSED
UNDER DOCTRINES OF FRUSTRATION
OR IMPRACTICALITY

§ 13.3(1) Substantive Framework ----------------------------------- 869
Strict Liability and Its Scope *
Discharging Liability for Risks Outside the Scope of the Contract ------- 869
Supervening Impossibility *
Supervening Impracticality *
Supervening Frustration of Purpose: a Room Without a View *
Existing Impossibility, Impracticality or Frustration *

* For the full text of this section, see Dobbs, Law of Remedies, Second Edition, Practitioner Treatise Series, Vol. 3 (§§ 12.1–End).

Page

§ 13.3(2) **Remedial Alternatives and Problems** ---------------------- 869
Restitution Generally --- 869
   "Rescission ab initio" vs. excuse of future performance -------------- 869
   The future excuse rule of Chandler v. Webster ------------------------ 869
   The full restitution rule of Fibrosa ------------------------------- 870
   American rule generally --- 871
Restitutionary Measures --- 871
   Money payments and the value of services generally ----------------- 871
   Contract rate; divisible contracts --------------------------------- 871
   Benefit received but its value lost -------------------------------- 871
   Unrealized benefit --- 872
Reliance Damages and Net Value Restitution ---------------------------- 873
   Reliance expense award inappropriate ------------------------------ 873
   Reliance expense award appropriate -------------------------------- 873
Other Remedial Solutions -- 874
   Economic efficiency vs. division of losses -------------------------- 874
   Court-made adjustments -- 874
   Comment *

§ 13.4 **REMEDIES FOR BENEFITS CONFERRED UNDER CONTRACTS AVOIDED FOR DEFECTIVE CAPACITY**

§ 13.4(1) **Power of Avoidance** ------------------------------------- 875
Avoidance for Incapacity *
Public Policy Avoidances: the Lawyer Cases *
Section Coverage *

§ 13.4(2) **Infancy** -- 875
Substantive Right to Avoid Contract *
   Substantive rules: contracts voidable ----------------------------- 875
   Exceptions -- 875
Restitution to the Minor --- 875
Restitution From the Minor --- 876
   The harsh rule for damaged or depreciated property ---------------- 876
   Services or intangibles received and used *
   Moderate rules requiring restitution ------------------------------ 876
   Tracing the minor's benefits *
   Policy issues *

§ 13.4(3) **Mental Incompetency** ---------------------------------- 876
Incompetency and Related Grounds for Avoidance *
Void or Voidable; Bona Fide Purchasers *
Restitution *
Fair Contracts *

* For the full text of this section, see Dobbs, Law of Remedies, Second Edition, Practitioner Treatise Series, Vol. 3 (§§ 12.1–End).

§ 13.5 ATTORNEY'S REMEDY WHEN CLIENT AVOIDS CONTRACT

Restitution and the Alternatives *
  Limiting the attorney's recovery to quantum meruit *
  Permitting the attorney a recovery on the contract *
  Apportioning a single fee *
  Accrual of restitutionary claim *
Measure of the Attorney's Restitution *
  Major options for measurement *
  Factors and unquantified estimates *
  Contract price as ceiling *
Comments on Measurement and Limitation Options *
  Relevance of the percentage fee *
  Difficulty of percentage fee measurements *
  Percentage measurement and the client's right to discharge *
  Other measures and the client's right to discharge *

§ 13.6 RESTITUTION IN CONNECTION WITH ILLEGAL CONTRACTS AND ACTIVITIES

Summary of Rules *
  Illegal contracts not enforceable *

                                                                    Page
  General rule against restitution ------------------------------- 877
  Rationale and extensions --------------------------------------- 877
Examples *
  Gambling *
  Licensing *
  Public entity contracts *
  Property transfers to defeat creditors or ownership restrictions *
Exceptions Permitting Restitution *
  Restitution when the contract is enforceable *
  Exceptions generally --- 875
  (1) The plaintiff is ignorant of the illegality ---------------- 875
  (2) The plaintiff is the victim of fraud, duress, or similar misconduct 875
  (3) Recovery will prevent unjust enrichment of a fiduciary ----- 875
  (4) The plaintiff is within a class of persons for whose protection the transaction was made illegal ---------------------------- 875
  (5) The illegality is not closely related to the plaintiff's claim or is a segment in a "divisible" contract ------------------ 879
  (6) Restitution is consistent with preventing accomplishment of the illegality --- 879
  (7) Public policy will be served by granting restitution or enforcement -- 879
  Generalizing and reformulating exceptions --------------------- 879

* For the full text of this section, see Dobbs, Law of Remedies, Second Edition, Practitioner Treatise Series, Vol. 3 (§§ 12.1–End).

Scope of Tolerance Under Pari Delicto *
    Pari delicto and statutory or public policy *

Page

    Pari delicto and unclean hands -- 879
Policy Considerations and New Solutions *
    The dilemma: leaving benefits in the hands of one wrongdoer *
    Effective deterrence *
    The John Wade solution *
Illegal Transactions Outside Contract *

APPENDIX: REMEDIES LAW RESEARCH ON WESTLAW ------------------------------ 881
TABLE OF CASES --- 893
INDEX -- 921

* For the full text of this section, see Dobbs, Law of Remedies, Second Edition, Practitioner Treatise Series, Vol. 3 (§§ 12.1–End).

LAW OF REMEDIES

DAMAGES–EQUITY–RESTITUTION

Second Edition

*

Chapter 1

INTRODUCTION TO REMEDIES

Analysis

Sec.
1.1   The Basic Remedies.
1.2   Remedies "At Law" and Remedies "In Equity".
1.3   Provisional and Permanent Remedies.
1.4   Remedies and Enforcement Devices.
1.5   Public Law and Private Law Remedies.
1.6   The Scope of Remedial Issues.
1.7   Remedial Analysis: Matching Right and Remedy.
1.8   Remedial Analysis: Comparing Remedies.
1.9   Remedial Analysis: Counting Costs and Benefits.
1.10 Remedies and Trial Strategy.

§ 1.1   The Basic Remedies

The Province of Remedies Law

The remedial issues. The law of judicial remedies determines the nature and scope of the relief to be given to a plaintiff once that plaintiff has established a substantive right by appropriate in-court procedures. The two major remedial questions are (1) what remedy or combination of remedies can or should be awarded? and (2) what is the measure, or the scope, of the remedy chosen?

Remedial rules that answer these questions point lawyers to proof required in the same way that substantive rules do. For instance, a rule that measures damages for breach of a contract to sell a house by the difference between the contract price and the market price of the house tells the lawyer that she must prove *both* the contract price *and* the market price.[1] There are, however, important differences between remedial and substantive law.

Remedial law vs. substantive law. The question whether a given set of facts shows a right in the plaintiff is a substantive question. For example, the question whether the plaintiff can recover for trespass or breach of contract is substantive, and so is the question whether a given set of facts amounts to a trespass or breach of contract. Those questions are answered by turning to the law of torts or contract. When the plaintiff's substantive rights are known, the remedies questions can be asked. What relief is to be given for violation of the substantive right? More specific remedial ques-

1

tions might be "Can the plaintiff recover damages for trespass, and if so by what measure?" [2]

Remedial law vs. procedural law. The law of remedies is thus sharply distinguished from the substantive law of rights. It is also distinguished from the law of procedure. Procedural law deals with process of getting from right to remedy. Getting there is the important thing for the law of procedure. The methods for presenting both substantive and remedial issues are its concern. Some remedies questions are closely connected with the substantive law or with procedural problems and more is to be said about that later. For most purposes, however, remedies questions and remedies law are quite distinct from both substance and procedure.

The main kinds of remedies. Judicial remedies usually fall in one of four major categories: (1) Damages remedies, (2) Restitutionary remedies, (3) Coercive remedies such as injunctions, or (4) Declaratory remedies. In public law or institutional reform cases such as those involving school integration, coercive remedies can take many special forms.[3] This four-part classification of remedies is not the only relevant classification to be made,[4] but it is the most important one for an initial survey of the field.

These major remedial categories were treated as separate fields of legal study until about the middle of the twentieth century when Charles Alan Wright's casebook on remedies brought them together.[5] In practice, litigated cases often present a choice among remedies, so the lawyer must consider all the options. For this reason and others similar to it, the unified treatment of all remedies has become generally accepted, and the field has now generated a major body of literature,[6] although important works on particular remedial categories remain useful.[7]

Availability. Availability of particular remedies depends much on the facts of the case. The plaintiff who suffers personal injury will have little use for an injunction. In many instances, however, the plaintiff will be given a choice among remedies, for instance, a choice between rescission and damages.[8] At other times courts may limit the plaintiff's remedy to dam-

---

§ 1.1

5. Charles Alan Wright, Cases on Remedies (1955).

6. As reflected in increasingly sophisticated casebooks: Douglas Laycock, Modern American Remedies, Cases and Materials (1985); Robert Leavell, Jean Love & Grant Neslon, Cases and Materials on Equitable Remedies, Restitution and Damages (4th ed. 1986); Edward D. Re and Stanton D. Krauss, Cases and Materials on Remedies (1992); David Schoenbrod, Angus Macbeth, David Levine & David Jung, Remedies: Public and Private (1990); Elaine W. Shoben and Wm. Murray Tabb, Cases and Problems on Remedies (1989); Robert S. Thompson and John A. Sebert, Jr., Remedies: Damages, Equity and Restitution (2d ed. 1989); Kenneth York, John Bauman & Doug Rendleman, Cases and Materials on Remedies (5th ed. 1992). The Restatements of Torts and Contracts both contain substantial segments stating an integrated set of remedial rules. Owen Fiss, The Civil Rights Injunction (1978) and Douglas Laycock, The Death of the Irreparable Harm Rule (1991) discuss mainly injunctions but both argue for a more integrated approach. Edward Yorio, Contract Enforcement: Specific Performance and Injunctions (1989) emphasizes specific performance but constantly compares or contrasts damages remedies.

7. The most notable work is that of Professor Palmer in his four-volume work on restitution. See George Palmer, Law of Restitution (1978 & Supps.). There is a special reason why restitution deserves separate treatment as well as treatment in the unified area of remedies. That reason is that restitution has a substantive as well as a remedial aspect. Other separate remedies are covered in see Charles T. McCormick, Damages (1935); E. Borchard, Declaratory Judgments (2d ed. 1941).

ages even if the plaintiff would benefit by and would prefer a coercive remedy such as specific performance.[9] This reflects a general preference in the courts for the damages remedy, but in spite of that preference, coercive remedies are widely available. In some instances the plaintiff can have more than one remedy so long as the total does not provide more than one complete compensation or one complete restitution. In the same way the plaintiff can have more than one measure of damages so long as the elements do not duplicate one another.[10]

Damages

Damages as compensation. The damages remedy is a money remedy aimed at making good the plaintiff's losses.[11] For any given breach of the plaintiff's rights, damages are traditionally awarded in American dollars,[12] in a single lump sum to compensate both for past harms and those anticipated in the future.[13] There are other money remedies with other purposes, and it is therefore necessary to emphasize that the term *damages* usually refers to compensation.[14] For instance, if the defendant sets fire to the plaintiff's house, the damages remedy gives compensation. A remedial issue might be whether to measure compensation by the cost of repair of the house or the diminished value of the house due to the fire. Compensation can include payment to make good a loss and also payment for failure to harvest a gain to which the plaintiff was entitled.

Forms of the damages remedy. Courts recognize many particular kinds or measures of damages. Damages can often be conveniently measured by assessing the market value of what the plaintiff lost at the time the loss occurred. For instance, if the plaintiff's car is harmed by defendant's fault, it may be worth less by $1,000 and the plaintiff can ordinarily recover such a sum. A market measure like this is often called general damages. At other times damages are measured by trying to estimate the costs the plaintiff may incur after the primary harm has been done and in consequence of that primary loss. For instance, if the plaintiff cannot work one day while the car is being repaired, consequential damages might include loss of wages. These distinctions carry with them some particular rules and problems. In addition, many particular elements of harm are the subject of special rules. For instance, the American Rule does not allow a prevailing party to recover anything for attorney fee expense. A substantial part of remedies is devoted to rules and problems about different forms or particular elements of damages.

Noncompensatory money awards. A few money awards that are not compensatory in nature are nevertheless traditionally called damages. The award of punitive or exemplary damages, intended partly to punish or deter the defendant, is in this category. The award is not truly a damages award based on measuring compensation; it is merely called damages for convenience. There may be a few other similar instances in which money awards are called damages even though they are seemingly not compensatory.[15]

14. Damages may also refer to the harm done to the plaintiff, for instance, a crushed fender or a broken arm. So common usage gives damages two meanings, one in reference to the fact of harm and one in reference to the legal recovery. This treatise attempts, possibly not always successfully, to use the term only in its legal sense as compensation for harm. The term harm is used to refer to the objective fact of injury.

Conventional damages. A more important qualification to the idea that damages are compensatory is that in many, many instances, damages are assessed by resort to conventional measurements. For instance, you might be permitted to recover interest from a defendant who has delayed paying a debt to you. If interest is awarded, the court may not ask whether or not you would have earned interest if the defendant had paid you earlier. The court may also fail to ask whether or not you actually incurred an interest expense, say, because you had to borrow money when the defendant was late in paying. Rather than pursue such questions, the court may simply award a fixed interest rate.[16] In much the same way, statutes may fix a standard amount for recovery, or a standardized minimum recovery,[17] or a standardized multiple recovery.[18] Judicially developed formulas may have a similar effect.[19]

The role of convention in damage measure deserves more comment later.[20] The important point here is that, conventions aside, the aim of damages is compensation for the plaintiff's loss, or at least some substitute for compensation. In particular, damages is not measured by the defendant's gain, which is the province of the restitutionary remedies.

Restitution

Restitution as restoration to prevent unjust enrichment. Restitution is literally restoration of something. Although an award of restitution may in fact provide compensation for the plaintiff in some cases, the restitutionary goal is different. The restitutionary goal is to prevent unjust enrichment of the defendant by making him give up what he wrongfully obtained from the plaintiff. So restitution is measured by the defendant's gains, not by the plaintiff's losses. If the plaintiff's losses and the defendant's gains were always in the same amount, the distinction between compensatory damages and restitution would not be very important today.[21] However, the defendant's gains in a transaction exceed the plaintiff's losses in some cases, and if so, restitution would be a better remedy.

Example. For example, suppose the defendant misappropriates $1,000 which the plaintiff had hidden away in a mattress. The defendant invests the $1,000 in shares of corporate stock, something the plaintiff himself would never do. As it happens, the stock rises in value and the shares are now worth $2,000. The plaintiff's loss is only $1,000, but the defendant's gain is $2,000. A restitution recovery is $2,000, while a compensatory damages recovery would be only $1,000.

The special sense of "restoration" to mean disgorgement of gains. Restitution might sound like the wrong word to use for a recovery of the defendant's gain in the example just given, since the plaintiff never had $2,000 or shares of stock, but it is the word used in such cases because courts see the shares purchased by the defendant as substitutes for the plaintiff's money. Although the defendant is not "restoring" the money, he is "restoring" or making restitution of the shares that were substituted for it, or their money value.[22] The important point is that the restitutionary remedy gives the plaintiff the defendant's unjust gains rather than the plaintiff's losses. Frequently the plaintiff will have a choice between damages or restitution.

In the example just given, the plaintiff would choose restitution because it yields a higher award.

Restitution in specie. The example just given is not exhaustive. In many instances, restitution will be *in specie* or in kind rather than in money.[23] In the example given above, the plaintiff might well recover the shares of stock in which his money was invested.[24] Restitution *in specie* might be important to a plaintiff who is more interested in recovering the specific thing than in its money value. For instance, if the defendant fraudulently got title to the plaintiff's homestead, the plaintiff might want restitution *in specie* because the homestead was more important than its money value. In some instances restitution takes on more subtle forms, as where the parties are restored to a previous position by rescission or cancellation of an instrument,[25] or where a contract is reformed to reflect an earlier and more accurate statement of the parties' agreement.[26]

Special forms of restitution. The law of restitution can be difficult and confusing because restitution may be identified by terms that refer to some particular form of restitution or some particular piece of remedial history. For example, some particular restitution claims may be identified as quasi-contract claims, or as claims in *assumpsit* or *quantum meruit.*[27] Claims for a constructive trust,[28] for an equitable lien,[29] or for subrogation are all restitutionary claims.[30] The list goes on.[31] So restitution today is a general term for diverse kinds of recoveries aimed at preventing unjust enrichment of the defendant and measured by the defendant's gains, but it has many specific forms, each of which must be addressed separately.

One other caution must be given about restitution. Although there is a clear distinction between damages based on the plaintiff's loss and restitution of benefits based on the defendant's unjust gains, many judges have used the term "damages" to refer to *any* monetary award. So judges frequently speak of "damages" when they mean restitution. The reader of restitutionary material is always challenged by its archaic terminology and by loose usage to analyze cases by their content rather than their terms.

Coercive Remedies

Injunctive remedies and the contempt power. Coercive remedies are typified by the injunction.[32] The injunction is a personal command to the defendant to act or to avoid acting in a certain way. The defendant who wilfully disobeys may be jailed or fined or otherwise sanctioned for "contempt."[33] Courts ordinarily have no comparable contempt power for the enforcement of damages awards.[34] The potential for contempt enforcement of injunctive orders is an important distinguishing characteristic of injunctive awards and one that makes them especially threatening.

23. See generally §§ 4.2(2) and 4.3 below.

24. See § 4.3(2), below (constructive trusts).

25. See generally § 4.3(6) below.

26. See generally § 4.3(7) below.

27. See § 4.2(3) below.

28. See § 4.3(2) below.

29. See § 4.3(3) below.

30. See § 4.3(4) below.

31. Other forms of restitution, identified by procedural labels, include rescission, accounting for profits, replevin and ejectment.

The coercive order is sometimes also called an *in personam* order, meaning mainly that it is a personal directive enforceable "against the person" by use of the contempt power, in contrast to a remedy like an ordinary damages judgment that is enforceable only against the defendant's property.[35]

Named forms of coercive remedies. Some forms of coercive remedies have become common enough or standardized enough that they have names of their own, just as some forms of restitution do. For example, specific performance is an injunctive or coercive remedy in which the defendant is ordered to perform contract obligations. Injunctive orders may lie as the basis of named actions like interpleader.[36]

Other forms of injunction. More commonly, the injunction has no special name. The forms and directions of such injunctions are almost limitless. The injunction may be prohibitory in form or it may be mandatory, compelling some affirmative action. It may attempt to prevent harm or to compel some form of reparation for harm already done.[37] In fact some restitution is compelled by resort to a form of injunction which requires the defendant to restore some specific thing to the plaintiff.[38]

The last half of the twentieth century saw the development of "structural" injunctions, used to restructure major public institutions such as schools and prisons, to force compliance with constitutional demands.[39] The injunction has become a major force in many public law decisions, not only in restructuring cases but also under many regulatory statutes which authorize or require injunctive relief.[40]

Expanding injunctive relief. Injunctive relief has probably expanded in private as well as in public law cases. An old tradition said that the injunction would not be issued if other remedies were "adequate."[41] That tradition meant that the plaintiff who preferred injunctive relief might be left to a damages remedy instead. A number of contemporary thinkers have argued that the traditional rule is wrong and that injunctive relief should be awarded when it is appropriate.[42] Douglas Laycock has argued that in fact courts seldom deny injunctions on the basis of the adequacy or irreparable harm rule.[43] Other writers believe that the adequacy test should continue to guard access to injunctive relief,[44] and courts do in fact sometimes deny injunctions when they believe damages to provide a sufficient remedy. It

36. Interpleader: the nominal plaintiff deposits in court a fund or thing claimed by two or more other people, obtaining an injunction which compels them to present their claims where the fund is deposited, thus avoiding multiple suits. See § 2.9(4) below.

37. See § 2.9(1) below.

38. See § 4.3(2) below (constructive trust).

39. See §§ 2.9(1) & 7.4(4) below.

40. See § 2.10 below.

41. See § 2.5 below. An alternative form of the statement is that the injunction will not issue unless, without it, the plaintiff will suffer irreparable harm.

42. Traditional discretion exercised by equity courts would allow the court to withhold an injunction if it deemed such relief inappropriate, even if there is no adequacy or irreparable harm test.

43. Douglas Laycock, The Death of the Irreparable Injury Rule (1991) (book); Laycock, The Death of the Irreparable Injury Rule, 103 Harv.L.Rev. 687 (1990).

44. The notable arguments have been made with reference to specific performance. See Edward Yorio, Contract Enforcement: Specific Performance and Injunctions (1989). See § 2.5(3) for more on this topic.

does seem clear, however, that injunctions generally go today more readily than they once did.

Provisional injunctions. One special form of injunction requires separate attention. Provisional injunctions can be issued as temporary measures before a trial is held, usually because of some pressing emergency. One provisional injunction is usually called the temporary restraining order, and it is issued in limited circumstances without giving the defendant an opportunity to be heard. The other form is usually called the preliminary injunction. As to this the defendant has notice and an opportunity to be heard, but the hearing is held before the defendant has extensive time to prepare and the hearing is quite limited, sometimes merely a presentation of affidavits. These provisional injunctions are especially dangerous and some special rules have developed to limit the occasions for their use and to protect the defendant from loss when they are in fact used improperly.[45]

Declaratory Remedies

Declaratory remedies furnish an authoritative and reliable statement of the parties' rights.[46] Other remedies may be added if necessary, but the declaratory remedy itself makes no award of damages, restitution, or injunction.

The chief problem in obtaining declaratory relief lies in the rules of justiciability, rules that courts will not issue advisory opinions, decide moot cases or those that are not ripe, or deal in any dispute that does not count as a case or controversy. Although people might settle legal arguments between themselves by going to the law library or calling the librarian, they cannot call on the courts in the same way. These concerns grow out of procedural and process values; they have to do with what we think about the nature of courts and judicial work.

Before declaratory judgment statutes were enacted, plaintiffs obtained relief that was sometimes essentially declaratory by suing for injunctive relief, or to quiet title to land, or to rescind a contract.[47] When the declaratory judgment performs an analogous function, the case is justiciable and such relief is appropriate. Yet it is not possible to describe adequately all the instances in which these concerns will prevent declaratory relief.

Declaratory relief is often useful in contract disputes. A good example is the dispute over liability insurance coverage. The insured tortfeasor, the insurer and the injured victim all need to know whether insurance covers the claim. When the insurer insists that it does not cover the claim and the others insist that it does, declaratory judgment is a good resolution.[48]

Another case for declaratory relief may arise when a citizen is confronted with a regulatory demand that may be unconstitutional. For example, suppose a law prohibits selling groceries on Sunday. A grocer who wishes to sell groceries on Sunday can test the law by violating it and then objecting to its constitutionality in a criminal prosecution, but to do so the citizen risks suffering criminal penalties. If the grocer is really ready to open the doors of the store on Sunday and the prosecutor is really threatening to prosecute,

---

45. See § 2.11 below.

46. See generally, E. Borchard, Declaratory Judgments (2d ed. 1941).

the case is indeed a real case and controversy, and declaratory judgment is most appropriate, although sometimes the same thing can be accomplished by enjoining enforcement of the statute.[49]

Non-judicial Remedies: Alternative Dispute Resolution and Self–Help

Although non-judicial remedies are outside the scope of this treatise, they help define the scope of judicial remedies by exclusion. Three kinds of non-judicial remedies are important: (1) self-help remedies, (2) administrative remedies, and (3) alternative dispute resolution remedies.

Self-help. Self-help remedies are sometimes actually recognized by law. A landowner, for example, might have a privilege to remove a trespassing object from the land or even to abate a nuisance. Much less formal self-help remedies for some invasions might include such simple acts as calling the police if neighbors are too noisy, or actually negotiating with the neighbors. Good reasons exclude discussion of such self-help remedies from this treatise, but lawyers should not overlook them in appropriate cases.

Administrative relief. The law of administrative agencies is itself a very large and specialized subject and it includes administrative remedies, some of which may be quite complex.[50] Some administrative remedies, such as orders to cease and desist a particular course of conduct, must be enforced by courts if the parties resist. Others may be more or less self-executing, as where an agency denies a license.

Administrative remedies may impact judicial remedies indirectly. If an administrative agency has jurisdiction of a given subject matter, judicial remedies may be inappropriate, at least until the agency has acted. So, for example, a discharged government worker might have civil service rights enforceable by an administrative agency. If so, a court might refuse to issue a preliminary injunction to restore the worker to her job, leaving the matter to the agency, at least temporarily.[51] The only remedial point that can be made here is that, within the scope of an administrative agency's jurisdiction, judicial remedies may be displaced and the lawyer may be wise to consider the administrative relief available.

Alternative dispute resolution. Alternative dispute resolution is usually not a remedy but a means of procedure for determining appropriate remedies. Alternative dispute resolution (ADR) is a general term applied to non-judicial and non-official systems for resolving disputes. Mechanisms for dispute resolution might include arbitration or mediation.[52] In such systems, the dispute is resolved outside the courts and outside the administrative agencies because the parties have agreed on ADR in advance. The remedy awarded in some disputes might resemble one of the basic remedies discussed above. For example, an arbitrator might award damages or might

---

50. Remedies may include money awards, as in the case of workers' compensation, cease and desist orders as in the case of some regulatory agencies, arrangements for elections in labor management cases and many others. For a very brief description see Bernard Schwartz, Administrative Law § 2.23 (2d ed. 1984).

51. E.g., Sampson v. Murray, 415 U.S. 61, 94 S.Ct. 937, 39 L.Ed.2d 166 (1974).

52. See Corinne Cooper & Bruce Meyerson, A Drafter's Guide to Alternative Dispute Resolution (1991) (introductory review of mechanisms and their use, with bibliography and resources such as helpful organizations).

award what amounts to an injunction, although if the defendant resists, the plaintiff might be required to look to the courts for enforcement of the award.[53]

Essential Issues

The classification of remedies is useful because it provides an overview and because it provides the terms necessary for discourse on remedial topics. Otherwise, however, the classification is of limited significance. The essential remedial questions are much more involved than a classification suggests.

The plaintiff must, in the first place, select the remedy that will best serve the interests involved. For example, the plaintiff may be required to choose damages or specific performance. The remedy must match the plaintiff's substantive right, and it must be selected to avoid serious defenses if possible. It must also be selected with a view to whatever procedural or tactical advantage may be carried with a given remedy. All this done, the plaintiff must be prepared to estimate and offer evidence to show the appropriate measure or scope of the remedy. Classifying and identifying remedial alternatives is thus only the first step.

§ 1.2 Remedies "At Law" and Remedies "In Equity"

The damages remedy was historically a legal remedy. The injunction and most other coercive remedies were equitable. Restitution, on the other hand, was a remedy available in certain cases at law, and in certain others in equity. With restitution, the classification depended upon the specific kind of restitution the plaintiff sought.[2] Relief under declaratory judgment statutes has been widely regarded as a hybrid, sometimes analogous to a legal remedy,[3] sometimes to an equitable one,[4] often depending on how the issue comes up.

Although the distinction between law and equity has been abolished in most judicial systems and in most ways, the classification of a remedy as legal or equitable remains important for at least two reasons of general significance, besides the fact that equitable remedies are generally enforceable by contempt while legal remedies are not.[5] First, jury trial is still, in many courts, granted or refused according to whether the remedy sought is legal or equitable. Jury trial is traditionally granted as of right in law cases, which usually means when the remedy sought is purely legal. Jury trial is not granted in equity cases, which usually means when the remedy sought is equitable.[6]

---

53. On arbitration generally, see § 12.23.

§ 1.2

2. Ejectment, replevin, and assumpsit (including the common counts under assumpsit like quantum meruit) were all legal claims for restitution. See § 4.2 below. Constructive trust, equitable lien and subrogation were all equitable remedies yielding restitution. See § 4.3 below.

3. Beacon Theatres, Inc. v. Westover, 359 U.S. 500, 79 S.Ct. 948, 3 L.Ed.2d 988 (1959) (treating it as legal).

4. See § 2.6(3) below.

5. See § 1.3 below.

6. Sometimes the old separate equity courts granted remedies that today would be considered legal. Classification of a case as equitable or legal is difficult when equitable history conflicts with the nature of the remedy. See generally § 2.6 below.

A second reason for the classification of remedy as legal or equitable lies in the tradition that equitable relief is discretionary. The old separate courts of equity could refuse the remedy or condition it in some way, even if the plaintiff proved a good case and the defendant proved no defense that would defeat the plaintiff's legal rights. In contrast, the old separate law courts emphasized rights, not discretion of the judge, and naturally assumed that the legal remedy went as a matter of course when the right was established. Although the courts of law and equity are merged almost everywhere, this dichotomy remains in the remedial language today; perhaps it actually determines results in some cases.[7]

§ 1.3 Provisional and Permanent Remedies

A third kind of classification of remedies distinguishes between permanent remedies and provisional remedies. Permanent remedies are those awarded after a trial has established rights and appropriate remedial measures. All of the remedies discussed so far—damages, restitution, injunction, and declaratory judgment—are usually permanent remedies.

Provisional remedies on the other hand give relief before a full trial can be held, although the plaintiff may be required to make at least a brief appearance before a judge before relief is granted. The occasions for provisional remedies are limited by court rules, statutes, and constitutional considerations. Provisional remedies are nearly always denied unless the judge believes or at least assumes that the remedy can be given back if a trial shows it was not warranted. As courts frequently say, provisional remedies aim only at preserving the status quo.[1] Provisional remedies are also denied unless there is a pressing reason to grant them.

The most familiar provisional remedies are attachment of money or property before trial, replevin,[2] garnishment, the preliminary injunction and the temporary restraining order. Appointment of a receiver for the defendant's property before trial may have the same effect. Unilateral recording of liens or other claims may also have the effect of tying up the defendant's property before trial.[3] Some of these remedies are discussed in more detail later; only a brief explanation is useful here.

Statutes provide for attachment of the defendant's funds or property before trial, but only in exigent circumstances, as where the defendant is about to flee the jurisdiction or fraudulently dispose of the money or property.[4] The attachment does not give the money to the plaintiff; it only holds it so that it is available if the trial shows the plaintiff is entitled to reach it to satisfy his claim. Garnishment is similar to attachment, but with garnishment the plaintiff does not reach property or money held by the defendant; instead the plaintiff reaches a claim the defendant has against someone else. A writ of garnishment against a bank, for example, might

7. See § 2.4 below.

§ 1.3

1. E.g., Cameron v. Bartels, 214 Ill.App.3d 69, 573 N.E.2d 273 (1991) (preliminary injunction).

2. Replevin allows the plaintiff to post a bond and to recover, before trial, a chattel to which he claims the right to possession. See § 5.17 below. In this respect replevin differs from the usual provisional remedy which normally attempts merely to preserve the status quo.

3. See § 6.1(5) below.

have the effect of freezing the defendant's bank account until trial could be held.[5]

Attachment and garnishment may be used as devices to enforce a judgment in favor of the plaintiff by seizing the defendant's property, funds, or claim against others and using it under procedures prescribed by law to satisfy the plaintiff's judgment.[6] As provisional remedies, however, attachment and garnishment are invoked before trial and only serve to impound the property, funds, or claims of the defendant as security for payment of a judgment that might or might not be entered in the plaintiff's favor.

Preliminary injunctions, issued on short notice to the defendant and after a very attenuated hearing, are intended, like attachment before trial, to prevent irreparable harm. For example, suppose the plaintiff claims that the defendant has defrauded the plaintiff and has $100,000 of the plaintiff's money in the defendant's bank account. Sometimes a preliminary injunction is issued to freeze the funds until a trial can be held, much in the same way an attachment or garnishment might do.[7]

Preliminary injunctions, however, are not limited to money or property cases and have a wide potential both for averting and for causing harm. Suppose that a city enacts an ordinance that, if enforced, would put the plaintiff out of business, or would prevent the plaintiff from exercising some important right, such as the right of free speech. If the city is about to enforce the ordinance immediately, the plaintiff may be ruined or irreparably lose important rights unless an injunction is issued immediately. Yet a full trial cannot be scheduled for months at best. In such cases the plaintiff may seek a preliminary injunction that forbids enforcement of the ordinance until a trial can be held and a final decision made.[8]

An even more stringent form of pre-trial injunctive relief is the temporary restraining order. Unlike the preliminary injunction, the temporary restraining order (TRO) is issued without any notice at all to the defendant, who has no opportunity to appear and offer a defense. The defendant is not bound by a TRO, however, until he has been notified of its terms. It terminates, in federal practice, in a matter of days, and the defendant may ask the court to dissolve the order sooner.[9]

All provisional remedies risk unjust harm to the defendant, because they impinge upon the defendant's rights and freedoms before a due process trial can be held. For these reasons, provisional remedies are usually carefully limited by statute, or by judicial decisions. The United States Constitution as well as state constitutions may condemn the use of provisional remedies unless the plaintiff shows (1) a pressing need for immediate relief, and (2) that the relief given is more or less reversible, so that if a trial shows the provisional remedy was wrongly invoked, the harm to the defendant can be undone. In addition some kind of attenuated judicial hearing may be required. The plaintiff is commonly required to post a bond or other

5. E.g., Barbouti v. Lysandrou, 559 So.2d 648 (Fla.App.1990).

6. E.g., Strande v. Mershon, 814 S.W.2d 704 (Mo.App.1991).

7. See § 6.1(5) below.

8. E.g., Planned Parenthood Ass'n of Cincinnati, Inc. v. City of Cincinnati, 822 F.2d 1390 (6th Cir.1987). Other illustrative instances can be found in § 2.11(1) below.

9. See generally § 2.11(1).

security, and conceivably this is a constitutional requirement in some cases. Some of these constraints are discussed in connection with discussions of preliminary injunctions and TROs generally,[10] in connection with replevin and related remedies,[11] and in connection with the use of preliminary injunctions to freeze bank accounts or other funds.[12]

§ 1.4 Remedies and Enforcement Devices

The law of remedies is only indirectly concerned with devices for enforcement of judgments and decrees against defendants who do not voluntarily comply with the court's decisions. That indirect concern is sometimes important, however, because the plaintiff's choice of a remedy may govern the procedures for enforcement of the final judgment. So remedial strategy must always take enforcement into account and for this reason the major enforcement devices are outlined in this section.

Execution of Money Judgments "at Law"

Adjudication of liability, not a command to pay. Ordinary money judgments reflect an adjudication of liability but they do not enter any command to the defendant. Money judgments rendered by the old separate law courts and most money judgments today are in a form which says that the plaintiff shall have and recover of the defendant the sum of $10. Since this was not a personal order, the defendant who does not pay is not jailed for contempt. Instead, enforcement is achieved indirectly by seizing the defendant's property. Enforcement is *in rem,* that is against things or property, not against persons. The process is referred to as execution.

Traditional execution writs. Execution was, in England, carried out by the use of several distinct execution writs with peculiar names like *fieri facias* and even more peculiar abbreviations like *fi. fa.* Such names can be found often in older American usage as well and are still used in some states. All the execution writs entailed seizure of property, either actually or symbolically. The writs commanded the sheriff to sell goods, or (at a later period of history) to sell land of the judgment debtor in order to provide money for the payment of the judgment.[1]

Statutory base in modern law. Execution to enforce judgments at law today is carried out largely under statutory provisions, but the main outlines remain the same. After the judgment is rendered for a certain sum of money,[2] an execution or execution writ is issued out of the clerk's office and

---

10. See §§ 2.11(2) & 2.11(3).

11. See § 5.17(2) below.

12. See § 6.5(1).

§ 1.4

1. The principle writs, each providing for execution on a different sort of interest of the debtor, were (1) fieri facias, calling upon the sheriff to sell the goods and chattels of the debtor; (2) levari facias, calling upon the sheriff to seize lands and goods for the purpose of getting rents and profits; (3) elegit, permitting seizure of goods for delivery to the creditor at appraised value, and then, if necessary, permitting installation of the creditor on one-half

of the debtor's land. See R. Millar, Civil Procedure of the Trial Court in Historical Perspective 422 ff. (1952). Provisions for personal arrest of the defendant in certain cases are largely obsolete.

2. The money judgment issued by the old separate law courts was for a sum certain, not installments. Execution issues only to enforce a judgment for a sum certain. See Roach v. Roach, 164 Ohio St. 587, 132 N.E.2d 742, 59 A.L.R.2d 685 (1956) (child support installments due but not reduced to lump sum judgment are not subject to execution). Courts today can draw on the powers of the old separate courts of equity to enforce install-

given to the sheriff, who is commanded by the writ to levy on the property of the debtor.[3] The sheriff usually does this by actually taking possession of the property or, at times, symbolically doing so.[4] He then publishes notice of the intended sale [5] of the property and a sale is held. This is usually regulated in some detail by statute. The money obtained from the sale is used to pay the court costs, sheriff's fees, and, so far as possible, the plaintiff's judgment.[6] If any of the proceeds remain, those proceeds may be applied to claims of other judgment creditors. If all such creditors are paid and money still remains, the excess is paid to the defendant.

In rem enforcement of money judgments is usually cumbersome and slow. Fairness requires notice to the debtor. Both fairness and efficiency require notice to potential buyers and the conduct of the sale at a time that is most likely to obtain a good price for the goods or land. Buyers, especially buyers of real property, will not pay full prices unless they are assured that the execution and sale were procedurally sound so that they can get good title. When there are several judgment creditors, issues of priority complicate the distribution of proceeds. These and other issues raised by *in rem* enforcement are left for more specialized treatment elsewhere.

Contempt Sentences to Enforce Coercive Remedies

Decree issuing a command in personam. In the old separate court system, law courts adjudicated rights and liabilities but they issued no commands. Instead they preferred to enforce judgments *in rem*. The old separate equity courts worked the other way around. Their decrees ended in a personal command telling the defendant to do something or to cease doing something. You could not disobey the judgment of a law court because it ordered nothing. But you could disobey the decree in equity because it commanded you to act in a specified way. This difference wrought a difference in enforcement. The old separate equity court often enforced its decree by using contempt powers, fining or imprisoning the defendant until he complied with the degree. This is sometimes called *in personam* enforcement, in contrast to the *in rem* enforcement at law.

Law and equity and coercive orders. Most judicial systems have long since combined law and equity courts in a single court having the powers of both the old law and the old equity courts. So it is technically no longer right in most states to say that equity enforces decrees *in personam* while law enforces them *in rem*. However, the kind of decree equity once issued, a coercive, *in personam* order directing the defendant to act in a specified way, is enforceable by contempt just as it was when there were separate equity courts. It is still common, by way of shorthand, to associate contempt powers with "equity," although it is more accurate to associate them with a valid coercive order.

Examples of contempt powers. A coercive order might command the defendant to disclose the presence of her daughter so that her former husband can exercise his visitation rights. If the defendant refuses to make disclosure as ordered, the contempt power allows the judge to impose either

---

ments in a different way, by contempt power if necessary. There are a few changes in attitudes about installment judgments. See the discussion of periodic payment statutes and structured settlements in personal injury litigation, § 8.5(5) below. See also § 8.10 on injunctive enforcement of payment in personal injury cases.

criminal or civil sanctions. A criminal sanction might be, for example, a $1,000 fine or 10 days in jail. A civil sanction is one designed to coerce the defendant to comply with the order, so it would not be a fixed fine or jail sentence. Instead, a civil contempt sanction would be a daily fine, say $100 per day until the defendant complies with the decree, or an indefinite jail sentence until the defendant complies.

The contempt power is dangerous but often effective and efficient. The implicit threat of that power lies behind most injunctive orders, and that threat may play a part in the plaintiff's strategic choice of the injunctive remedy in some cases. The contempt power also raises complex technical and policy issues that require a more complete discussion in connection with equitable remedies generally.[7]

Non-contempt enforcement of in personam orders. Although contempt is the enforcement device most commonly associated with coercive remedies, courts are not necessarily required to resort to that power. If, for example, a court were to order the defendant to make periodic payments of money, the decree would be coercive and would not qualify for ordinary *in rem* enforcement because of the rule that execution issues only on a judgment for a specified sum of money.[8] But a court could avoid invoking the drastic power of contempt by reducing the past due payments to a separate judgment and authorizing execution on that judgment. Or if a court ordered specific performance of a contract to sell Blackacre, it could jail the defendant for refusing to comply, but it could avoid such extremes by making the conveyance itself.[9]

Garnishment

Execution clearly doesn't work where the debtor has no tangible assets. However, the debtor may have intangible rights that can be reached by the judgment creditor. Garnishment has been mentioned as a provisional remedy;[10] it is also an enforcement device. Suppose T owes money to the judgment debtor. The judgment creditor may be permitted to bring T into court and require T to pay what he owes the debtor. If T admits the debt and pays it into court, the money is used toward the satisfaction of the creditor's judgment. If T does not answer the process served upon him, a default judgment may be taken against him. The details of this process are controlled by statute and vary with local practice.[11] Particular states may call this kind of garnishment by other names. Such a garnishment to enforce a final judgment should be distinguished from the provisional remedy of garnishment before trial, which is aimed at preserving assets of the debtor until a final decision can be had on the merits.

Supplementary Proceedings or Creditors Bills in Equity

Sometimes neither execution nor garnishment is effective to reach intangible or equitable assets of the debtor, even when those assets are not subject to exemption. In cases of this sort, the judgment creditor may be compelled to resort to a device that used to be called a creditor's bill or supplementary proceeding in equity. With the merger of law and equity, a separate suit is no longer required, but such proceedings remain equitable in

7. See § 2.8 below.

the sense that enforcement is achieved, not through seizure of the property, but through the coercive power of the old separate equity court.

For example, if the plaintiff recovers a money judgment at law against the defendant, and finds no assets except the defendant's share in a patent right, the plaintiff may ask the court to order the defendant to sell his share of the patent, or to execute an assignment of it toward satisfaction of the money judgment. The court may do this, and enforce its order by contempt if necessary, or it may appoint a trustee or other officer of the court to execute the assignment of the patent in the name of the debtor.[12] Other intangible interests can be reached in the same way.

Equitable Liens and Constructive Trusts

The old separate equity courts gave remedies that were not obviously coercive and that were not called injunctions. The plaintiff could seek certain restitutionary remedies in the old equity courts, notably equitable liens, constructive trusts, and an accounting for profits. Those remedies must be discussed in detail later.[13] An illustration is enough to suggest their distinctive quality. Suppose the defendant embezzles the plaintiff's money and uses it to purchase Blackacre. When the plaintiff discovers these facts, she might sue for damages or money restitution equal to the amount taken. But if Blackacre has risen in value, the plaintiff might instead seek a constructive trust. The constructive trust remedy says that the defendant, holding legal title to Blackacre, will be treated as if he were holding it in trust for the plaintiff. The court will then order the defendant to execute his trust by conveying to the plaintiff. One effect is to give the plaintiff the increase in value of Blackacre itself. Another is to give her priority over other creditors who might otherwise seek to levy upon Blackacre for payment of their judgments.

The equitable lien is similar, but as its name suggests, it gives the plaintiff a lien or security interest in Blackacre rather than ultimate ownership. The equitable lien might be more appropriate if the defendant purchased Blackacre with both his own and the plaintiff's money. The equitable lien would hold Blackacre hostage for repayment of the plaintiff's money but would not give her title. The lien could be foreclosed much as a mortgage is foreclosed if necessary.[14]

The constructive trust and the equitable lien are perhaps most conventionally thought of as remedies rather than as enforcement devices. However, lurking behind the constructive trust is the *in personam* power of the old equity courts. Implicitly, if not actually, the defendant who is subjected to a constructive trust will be subjected to a coercive order to make the required transfer of property or funds. The equitable lien would normally be enforced by foreclosure, which bears some resemblance to an execution sale, although foreclosure is traditionally considered to be "equitable."

Judgments for Possession of Property at Law

Where the plaintiff sued, not for money, but to regain possession of property to which he claimed a right, law courts again approached enforce-

13. See § 4.3 below.   14. See § 4.3(3) below.

ment by an *in rem* procedure using the sheriff. In ejectment cases, the sheriff was told to put the plaintiff in possession of real property (by ousting the defendant if necessary).[15] In replevin cases, the sheriff was told to bring personal property either to the plaintiff or to the court when the plaintiff put up a bond.[16] In both cases, the method was cumbersome, and there were things the sheriff might not wish to do, such as put the plaintiff in possession of Blackacre by removing an encroaching 10–story building. In replevin cases the sheriff might not be able to find the personal property claimed in the writ. Thus ultimate enforcement of legal rights of possession might require the attention of the equity court, which could make a coercive order to compel the defendant to remove the encroachment [17] or give up the personal property.[18]

Receivers and Masters

Receivers. Two other enforcement devices can be especially important in some cases. Courts may appoint receivers to manage property.[19] A receiver might be appointed before trial to preserve the property or manage it pending decisions on the merits. Receivers may be especially useful to manage an ongoing operation such as a business. Receivers may also be appointed to execute a judgment, for example by selling off property gradually to obtain the best prices over a period of time, or simply to locate and return property.[20]

Masters.[21] Sometimes courts appoint masters, who act as officers of the court, usually to assist in managing complex trials by taking testimony and making a report or recommendation, or by managing a large, complex discovery process.[22] A master used in this way is a procedural, not an enforcement device. On the other hand, a master might be appointed to monitor the execution of and compliance with a complex decree and report to the court if the defendant fails to comply.[23] In that role, the master is a means of assisting enforcement.

Receiver-masters under civil rights or restructuring injunctions. Courts have made dramatic use of receivers and masters or some combination in some major civil rights injunctions. When courts undertake to restructure a social institution such as a school system or a prison, to make it conform to constitutional standards,[24] legal rules may be pitted against strongly ingrained cultures that are not amenable to change merely because the court orders it. So in some cases courts have displaced elected or other local authority by appointing a receiver to manage a school system to bring it into compliance with court orders.[25] Such remedies are obviously extreme and reserved for extreme cases or last resorts.

---

15. See §§ 4.2(2) & 5.10(1) below.

16. See § 5.17 below.

17. See § 5.10(4) below.

18. See § 5.17(3) below.

19. See Fed.R.Civ.Proc. Rule 66.

22. Fed.R.Civ.Proc.R. 53 authorizes appointment of masters. Federal magistrates may now perform masters' functions, but traditionally a master was a lawyer appointed for the specific task assigned.

23. See Ruiz v. Estelle, 679 F.2d 1115, 1159–1163 (5th Cir.1982), cert. denied, 460 U.S. 1042, 103 S.Ct. 1438, 75 L.Ed.2d 795 (1983).

24. See § 7.4(4) below.

25. Morgan v. McDonough, 540 F.2d 527 (1st Cir.1976), cert. denied, 429 U.S. 1042, 97 S.Ct. 743, 50 L.Ed.2d 755 (1977).

§ 1.5   Public Law and Private Law Remedies

Public Law Remedies Generally

Public issue litigation. Public law litigation on the civil side includes litigation pursued by public officials like the attorney general of a state and by public agencies like the Securities and Exchange Commission. With the 1954 decision in *Brown v. Board of Education* [1] that school segregation was unconstitutional, and with renewed legislative attempts to enforce civil rights in the 1960s and after, lawyers and judges have understood public law litigation more broadly. Public law litigation is now understood to include litigation that raises important public issues, even if that litigation is instituted by private individuals.

There is actually nothing new in the idea that all litigation raises issues that have at least some importance to the public. Otherwise the use of public facilities to resolve those issues would not be justified. So what is a public law issue is a matter of degree, but it certainly includes private litigation brought to enforce civil rights or to litigate environmental issues, or issues about the disposal or management of public resources.[2] On such matters the private plaintiff is regarded as one who performs the public's work; the private plaintiff in such cases is a "private attorney general." [3]

Public law remedies generally. Courts impose no across-the-board distinctions between public and private law remedies. Remedial principles remain the same, and public law remedies are, in the broad sense, the same as those used in private law. For instance, public agencies recover statutory damages,[4] injunctions,[5] and even restitution of improper gains made by the defendant at public expense.[6] Private individuals, pursuing litigation of public importance, recover the same general remedies. Private plaintiffs recover both damages [7] and injunctions [8] in civil rights cases, and private individuals may similarly serve the public interest when they force a law violator to disgorge or make restitution of his wrongful gains.[9]

§ 1.5

1. 347 U.S. 483, 74 S.Ct. 686, 98 L.Ed. 873, 38 A.L.R.2d 1180 (1954); Brown v. Board of Educ., 349 U.S. 294, 75 S.Ct. 753, 99 L.Ed.2d 1083 (1955) (injunctive remedy ordered).

2. Conceptions of "public law" in this context differ. Many writers on the topic of public law remedies often have in mind the institutional restructuring cases, in which public institutions like schools or prisons are restructured by injunction. But suits for damages to natural resources by oil spills or hazardous substances, see § 5.2(5) below, are assuredly as public as institutional restructuring cases. See, discussing some definitions or inclusions, Sturm, A Normative Theory of Public Law Remedies, 79 Geo.L.Rev. 1355, 1357, n. 1 (1991).

3. Newman v. Piggie Park Enterprises, Inc., 390 U.S. 400, 88 S.Ct. 964, 19 L.Ed.2d 1263 (1968) (a phrase used to justify the automatic award of attorney fees to the prevailing plaintiff in discrimination litigation where Congress had authorized such an award but had not mandated it).

4. E.g., United States v. Bornstein, 423 U.S. 303, 96 S.Ct. 523, 46 L.Ed.2d 514 (1976).

5. As where an agency seeks injunctive enforcement of a regulatory statute. See § 2.10 below on statutory injunctions.

6. As in political bribery cases, where both the outside briber and the governmental bribee are held liable. See § 10.6 below.

7. E.g., Brooks v. Andolina, 826 F.2d 1266, 1270 (3d Cir.1987).

8. It should be remembered that the plaintiffs in Brown v. Board of Educ. secured injunctive relief that ordered a reversal of the whole pattern of segregation in schools. See Brown v. Board of Educ., 349 U.S. 294, 75 S.Ct. 753, 99 L.Ed.2d 1083 (1955) (injunctive remedy ordered).

9. As where a corporation recovers profits of its officers or directors who use inside cor-

When enormous differences are perceived between public and private remedies, the differences perceived are often closely related to substantive or process issues rather than to the choice or measure of remedies as such.[10] The remainder of this section is mainly devoted to explanation and qualification of these statements.

Factual variation and the variability of injunctive relief. Public law remedies are very often injunctive remedies. Injunctions can be varied infinitely. An injunction that tells a school board only to stop discriminating looks very much like an injunction that tells a landowner only to stop committing a nuisance; but if either injunction adds specific standards or definitions, or specifies the means for accomplishing the goal, the two injunctions will look very different indeed. One injunction might describe required smokestack filters while the other might describe a required process or standard for drawing school district boundaries. But those differences reflect the infinite variability of injunctive relief to suit the infinitely varied facts of cases and the infinitely varied sensibilities of the chancellors. Two different private nuisance injunctions might differ as much as a private nuisance injunction differs from a public desegregation injunction. The factual content of public law litigation does not in itself make the remedies or the remedial issues different.

Institutional Restructuring Litigation

One kind of public litigation seems to be different in important ways from private litigation and also from most kinds of public litigation. Institutional restructuring litigation attempts to force a public institution such as a prison or school into conformity with constitutional standards.[11] Structural litigation is likely to be large and to implicate many people and many interests. School integration, for example, may take on political overtones because many different solutions might be acceptable and because interest groups compete for the court's attention and seek to impose solutions. Because many solutions might be acceptable and there are no particular rules to force the choice of one of them, political interests and biases are in the foreground. Beyond this, the remedies chosen will not work easily because almost by definition, the institutionalized culture will be at odds with the court's decree.

These cases are different, something new under the legal sun. They differ from much private litigation (and also from much public litigation) in their size and scope and in their peculiar facts. But how different are they when it comes to remedies? Differences in facts of these cases implicate remedial issues only in the way that different facts of different cases always implicate remedial issues; the remedy must respond to the facts and the law.

It is true that old remedies may be used in more or less new ways in restructuring litigation. For example, the school may be enjoined to integrate along specified guidelines and if it refuses, the court might appoint a receiver to manage the school and bring it into conformity.[12] The use of a

porate information to profit from purchase or sale of investments. See § 10.5(2) below.

10. See § 1.6 below.

11. See § 7.4(4) below.

12. See § 1.4 above.

receiver, however, is not in itself new and does not differ in general outlines from the use of a receiver as a private law remedy.

It is also true that these institutional restructuring cases raise difficult process issues. Should judges undertake to reform all or substantial parts of society in their own image? How political should they be? Should they invite the public at large to "testify" or submit arguments? How much can judges remain adjudicators if they administer prisons or schools? If answered fairly, the questions are not answered easily. The point here is not to answer them but to say they are not primarily remedial questions at all. They are questions about the nature of the judicial process and the role of judges in society. They are not unimportant or even irrelevant to remedies, but they are not essentially remedial questions.

The remedially connected differences of restructuring litigation have to do mainly with process and policy. Interference with state institutions, and especially with elected officials, must not be taken lightly, no matter how the remedy is shaped. Once a remedy like receivership for a school is proposed, courts do indeed face policy conflicts that differ from those normally encountered in private litigation, and those conflicts implicate remedial decisions.[13] In addition, to make a remedy effective, the court may be forced to order the defendant to do things that go far beyond the plaintiff's rights.[14] So restructuring litigation, at least, does seem to involve some special if not unique remedial issues, even if the ultimate remedy granted is formally the same as remedies granted in private cases.

Discrete and Particular Differences in Public and Private Remedies

With the possible exception of restructuring litigation, remedial issues, remedial principles, and actual remedies awarded are much the same in public law and private cases. Nevertheless, there are some discrete rules that may point to occasional very specific differences. The following paragraphs point to some of these.

Statutory injunctions. Where a statute authorizes an injunction at the behest of a public agency, courts sometimes issue injunctions without requiring the agency to show any threat that irreparable harm will follow if the injunction is denied.[15] Yet in theory, private litigants must always show such a threat in order to obtain an injunction. The distinction is not a large one. The irreparable injury requirement imposed upon private litigants seems to have less and less significance in actual operation.[16] In any event, a plaintiff who pursues a statutory right takes the statutory remedy as the statute gives it. If a statute authorizes injunctive relief without regard to the traditional irreparable injury requirement, then a private as well as a

13. I do not wish to overstate this point. Official interference with people's activities is always undesirable if it can be avoided. Judges are often called upon to decide when interference is and when it is not justified. A judge considering a polluting factory has a wide range of injunctive choices and the same questions about interference with the factory that the judge has when considering a segregated school system. The different facts and the different intensities of policy and feeling may distinguish the two situations; but at the core, the policy decisions involve similar choices.

14. See §§ 1.7 & 2.4(7) below.

15. See § 2.10 below.

16. See § 2.5 below.

public plaintiff can have such relief.[17] The differential treatment of public litigants on this point seems minimal at best.

Attorney fees. Perhaps the largest single difference in public and private remedial rules arises from the general American Rule that neither litigant can recover attorney fee expenses from the other.[18] This rule is subject only to some discrete exceptions in private litigation. When the private litigant takes up the public sword and prevails in public issue litigation, however, that litigant is often allowed to recover attorney fee expense. In the most notable instances, the recovery is authorized by civil rights, environmental, or other statutes.[19] In a few states, the private litigant who acts as a "private attorney general" is allowed to recover attorney fees from the losing defendant under a court-made rule.[20]

Other particular differences between public and private remedial rules may exist,[21] but except as noted below they do not represent the use of radically different remedies or the use of different remedial principles.

§ 1.6 The Scope of Remedial Issues

The Importance of Remedial Scope

Lawyers use the word remedies in a host of different ways. Sometimes they characterize a problem or issue as a remedial problem because such a characterization fits their theory of a case or an article. Some authors have preferred to characterize certain problems as remedial in nature because they associated remedies with flexible balancing of many factors.[1] Sometimes lawyers use the word less artfully, but still in ways that make it difficult to know how a remedies question differs from a procedural or some other kind of question.

Effective use of this book by the reader requires some idea about its scope. Its scope is also important because the field of remedies needs suitable boundaries. In a broad sense, almost any solution to any kind of problem can be regarded as a remedy. One could say "education is a remedy for discrimination." One could even say "getting out the vote" is a remedy for some problems. It is important to exclude such solutions from the field of legal remedies. That is not because they are undesirable or insignificant but because any field of study must be sufficiently coherent to permit practical and meaningful discussion about it. It must also be sufficiently coherent to permit those who study the field to master it in its entirety. By any definition, the field of remedies is so large that its mastery is very

---

18. On the American Rule and its common law and statutory exceptions, see § 3.10 below.

21. One possible difference is the rule that one cannot recover substantial damages for violation of a constitutional right without proving some harm other than the loss of the right itself. See Carey v. Piphus, 435 U.S. 247, 98 S.Ct. 1042, 55 L.Ed.2d 252 (1978) and the discussion in § 7.4(2) below. If one interprets common law decisions in such cases as assault to permit substantial damages, then this rule is a departure. The Supreme Court,

however, thinks it is no departure at all. A second possible difference is that in mass product liability cases, courts may be awarding punitive damages as a means of financing litigation that in effect helps regulate an industrial defendant who is willing to risk substantial public harm. See § 3.11(3) below.

§ 1.6

1. Fallon & Meltzer, New Law, Non–Retroactivity, and Constitutional Remedies, 104 Harv.L.Rev. 1733, 1765 (1991).

difficult at best. Common communication within the field is defeated by the Balkanization that results when the whole field cannot be mastered.

This section attempts to state a view of what counts as a remedial issue, to provide an indication of coverage if nothing else. The next section takes up a related question, the reciprocal relationship between rights and remedies.

The Scope of Remedial Issues

Remedial issues arise when the plaintiff has a cause of action. For this book, remedies law is not substantive law and not procedural law. The remedial issues arise only when substantive law tells us that the plaintiff's right has been infringed in a way that gives the plaintiff a legal claim or cause of action.

Remedial issues. A remedy is some form of damages, injunction, restitution, or declaratory judgment, or some combination of the four. The main remedial issues are (1) What remedies are available and which of those is most suitable? and (2) What is the measure or scope of the preferred remedy? Subsidiary questions abound. For instance, in determining which remedy is most suited or preferred, a lawyer might consider the strategy effects of the remedy choices, the most obvious of which is that if the claim is for a purely equitable remedy, the plaintiff might get no jury trial.

Applying the Limitations

Substantive law. The question, "Do I have *any* remedy?" is a substantive law question, not a remedial question. Whether or not a wrong was committed or a right violated is a substantive question, although it is one sometimes easy to confuse with remedial issue. If no legal wrong at all has been done to the plaintiff, there is no case and no remedial issue.

Suppose you lean against the plaintiff's new car, but do not cause any harm to it and do not interfere with the plaintiff's possession. You might attempt to escape liability to the proud new owner on the ground that no harm was done and so no damages could be recovered. Phrased in that way the issue sounds remedial. But the logically anterior question is whether the plaintiff had any right against you at all. The law of trespass to chattels says he does not. The substantive rule is that one cannot recover for non-harmful touching of chattels that does not involve dispossession. Although the substantive rule turns on the presence or absence of harm and the presence of harm is also often important on remedial issues, the issue is not a remedial issue here. We can be sure of that because it eliminates the cause of action and does not merely affect the amount of recovery or the choice among remedial alternatives.

Process or procedural law. Sometimes the plaintiff suffers a wrong in some important sense but not one for which a cause of action is recognized. For example, if a trial judge admits evidence over the plaintiff's objection and the plaintiff ultimately loses the case at the trial level, the plaintiff has a procedural right to appeal. But the plaintiff does not have a cause of action based on the judge's error. Speaking loosely, one could say the plaintiff's remedy is to appeal. But the right to use some particular procedure like appeal is not a remedy as that term is used in this book. It is not a remedy because the plaintiff has no cause of action at all; no remedial issues arise, only a procedural issue.

Substance, procedure, and process are of course important to lawyering a case. They are even important in connection with remedies. For example, one might argue that in a large restructuring litigation such as a school integration suit, the judge should invite community representatives as well as parties to deliberate over remedial alternatives.[2] Extreme and diverse groups sometimes come to a consensus on solutions,[3] and such a process might produce a better remedy than the judge could think of on the basis of adversarial arguments. In addition, the participation of diverse elements of the community in a deliberative setting may have values of its own and even if it did not, and their participation would be more likely to induce their compliance and satisfaction with the ultimate decree. There are also arguments against such a process for selecting a remedy, but whatever their merits, the question of *who decides* the remedy is not a remedies question. It is a question instead about the process by which the remedies question is decided.

Theories are not remedies. The theory invoked to justify relief is not a remedy. Nor is a named cause of action. For instance, "assumpsit," was a form of action at common law which connoted both a certain theoretical justification for relief and a remedy. The term assumpsit might be used loosely to refer to the remedy available, but the cause of action itself is not a remedy, nor is the form used to prosecute it.

§ 1.7 Remedial Analysis: Matching Right and Remedy

Rights and Remedies

Principle: remedies congruent with rights. Although earlier discussions have emphasized that questions about substantive rights are quite different from questions about remedies, it is nevertheless true that remedies are means of carrying into effect the substantive right. Subject to certain qualifications, the remedy should reflect the right or the policy behind that right as precisely as possible.

Examples. For example, if the right is a right against *A*, then the remedy must not run against *B*.[1] *B* may be unavoidably affected by what happens to *A*, but no remedy should run against *B* when *B* has violated no rights.[2] If the right is purely an economic right, such as a right to be paid $100 on a promissory note, then the remedy should not include damages for emotional distress that occurs when the payment is late.[3] Although these points seem obvious when stated, they are in fact sometimes overlooked.

---

2. See Sturm, A Normative Theory of Public Law Remedies, 79 Geo.L.Rev. 1355 (1991).

3. See Smolla, The Annenberg Libel Reform Proposal: The Case for Enactment, 31 Wm. & Mary L.Rev. 25 (1989).

§ 1.7

1. General Building Contractors Ass'n, Inc. v. Pennsylvania, 458 U.S. 375, 102 S.Ct. 3141, 73 L.Ed.2d 835 (1982) (contractors who violated no rights could not be forced to help reme-

dy discrimination caused by union). Accord: Rizzo v. Goode, 423 U.S. 362, 96 S.Ct. 598, 46 L.Ed.2d 561 (1976) (no injunction requiring procedure for citizen complaints about police, since city officials, who were defendants, had not themselves violated the constitution). Cf. Laycock, Consent Decrees without Consent: The Rights of Nonconsenting Third Parties, 1987 U.Chi.Legal F. 103 (1987).

The principle applies both to the selection of a remedy and to its measurement. Courts would not select punitive damages as a remedy for most ordinary contract breaches. Punishment would go far beyond the plaintiff's bargained for right in most instances.[4] If the plaintiff recovers restitution for work done under a contract that is unenforceable under the statute of frauds, the measure of that remedy must reflect its purpose: it must prevent the defendant's unjust enrichment, but it must not go further and give the plaintiff the profit she would have made on the deal.[5]

Corollary. If remedies should reflect the substantive right, then anyone who wishes to formulate an appropriate remedy must know the nature and scope of the underlying right. Serious study of remedies thus has the effect of bringing into question matters of substantive policy and renewing analysis of that policy. This point means that the study of remedies is hampered at the outset by practical limitations. One must know the substantive law and policy to select and measure remedies, but no one could know all law and all substantive policy and no book could adequately state it. So as a practical matter a book on remedies is necessarily selective both as to the topics covered and as to the amount of substantive law mentioned. In this book substantive law is stated only in a limited fashion and only when it might not be generally familiar.

Knowing the right by knowing the remedy. The scheme of analysis just presented works when we have a clear conception of the plaintiff's right and want to know what the remedy is. Sometimes, however, the process is reversed and we know what the right is only because we see it exemplified in the remedy. An example of this reversed process occurs under the traditionally accepted rule that courts do not order specific performance of ordinary contracts to buy and sell goods.[6] Because we know that specific performance would be routinely denied in such cases, we could reasonably say that, as far as the law was concerned, the plaintiff has no right to prevent a breach of the contract. That in turn made it clear that the defendant had the legal right to breach a contract, although he would be obliged to pay damages if he did so.

This particular kind of insight later became the simple basis of complex economic analysis of contract rights. It was an insight about *rights* derived from knowledge about *remedies.* It did not work the way the right-remedy logic suggests, but just the other way around: knowing the remedy or its limits helped us see that in reality the right was limited.

Denying rights in the belief that remedies are not measurable or practical. The purest kind of remedies question addresses the remedy for a known right and attempts to correlate the two. But sometimes the remedial tail wags the substantive dog.

The wrongful life claim is one asserted by a child who is born with a genetic constitution which will cause pain and a severely limited life.[7] He

---

5. See § 13.2(2).

6. See § 12.8 generally for this rule and contemporary doubters.

7. See § 8.2 below. *Wrongful life* refers to the child's claim that he should not have been

born and suffers harm because he was. A related but distinct claim is *wrongful birth,* a claim by *parents* who must bear the cost and emotional harm because the defendant physician did not advise them of genetic difficulties in time to terminate the pregnancy. A third asserts that the defendant physician negligently failed to provide genetic counseling that would have allowed the mother to terminate her pregnancy and thus avoid the pain he is suffering. There is no doubt that the child suffers and that it could have been avoided only if he had not been allowed to live. If the physician was in fact negligent in failing to diagnose the condition (and if the mother would have properly terminated the pregnancy), it looks very much as if some kind of wrong has been done to the child.

Nevertheless, courts have not generally recognized a right in the child.[8] A number of reasons and feelings swirl through these cases. One of those reasons is that it is difficult to imagine a suitable remedy. If, as some writers have suggested,[9] a meaningful measure of money damages could be worked out, courts might be willing to say that the child was wronged. In such a case, the question of rights turns in part on whether courts can see a practical remedy. Although remedy normally follows the right, rights will not be established unless a remedy can be administered.

The puzzle of discorrelate rights and remedies. When the law seems to provide a remedy that does not correlate with the right, the first line of analysis suggested above would indicate that the remedy is wrong in some way. It should either be augmented or diminished to reflect the right. But because some rights are best understood by knowing their remedies, we must now recognize that a right-remedy discorrelation could mean that we have misstated the right rather than the remedy. In that case, we might want to revise our picture of the right in issue and not revise the remedy at all. When the right and remedy do not correlate, it looks as if something needs to be changed, but one cannot determine in the abstract whether the remedy should be changed to match the right or vice versa.

But there is still another possibility in this analysis. The general principle states that remedies should reflect rights and should not give the plaintiff either more or less than her right or entitlement. But there are some important qualifications to that principle to be stated below. If those qualifications can be invoked, then a discorrelation between right and remedy may be appropriate.

Practical Constraints and Conventional Remedies

Remedies may be limited by practical considerations. Courts may consciously provide a remedy that fails to fulfill or vindicate the plaintiff's right because the costs of granting the remedy are deemed to be too high. When this happens, discorrelation between right and remedy is accepted as the lesser of evils.

Judicial resources. One constraint on remedies is the court's own time and expertise. Courts traditionally refused to give the specific performance remedy if they feared they might be required to deal with the case repeatedly. They liked to give such a remedy to enforce a simple land contract where a deed could be ordered the case would be over, but they did not like

claim is *wrongful pregnancy* or *wrongful conception,* in which the physician negligently performed a procedure to prevent conception and a child is conceived. This paragraph deals only with the wrongful birth claim.

9. Kelly, The Rightful Position in "Wrongful Life" Actions, 42 Hast.L.J. 505 (1991).

to give it to enforce a building contract, which might require repeated judicial action.[10]

Judicial roles. Another constraint is the courts view of their own role in society. Earlier discussions reflected the possibility that a court would enforce integration of a school by appointing a receiver to manage it and displacing the school board and administrators.[11] Given the importance of the rights involved, a court might well be willing to use its limited time to enforce an integration order. Yet to a degree, a judge who undertakes to administer a school or prison must step out of the traditional judicial role. So some judges might hesitate to become deeply involved in details of school administration in such cases, even if that meant that their injunction remedy was less effective.

The limits of proof: conventional remedies. A third reason for remedies that do not match rights is found in the limits of proof and particularly in the limits of causal proof, combined with the convenience of standardized or conventional remedies. Conventional remedies do not correlate with rights except by happenstance. They may give the plaintiff either more or less than her entitlement. In the case of conventionalized restitution, they may force the defendant to disgorge more, or less, than his unjust gain.[12] Even the injunctive remedy can be conventionalized.[13]

Forms of conventional remedies. Conventional remedies may be given in the form of conventional measurements or standardized sums of money. A *measure,* such as a damages measure, is a formula or yardstick by which the remedy is measured. If a measure is selected for convenience or efficiency rather than for accuracy, it is conventional. It is not necessarily accurate to use standardized methods for figuring depreciation when that is relevant to the award of damages; but it is wonderfully efficient and close enough to make efficiency more important than precise accuracy. A standardized *sum* is also a conventional remedy. For example, a statute might provide that the victim of telephone eavesdropping is entitled to $1,000 for every offense.

Examples of conventional remedies. The example of a conventional remedy given at the beginning of this chapter was the award of interest as damages to represent compensation for delay in paying the plaintiff money due. Suppose *A* owes *B* $100, payment due one year ago. But *A* lost his job, had no money and could borrow none, so he was a year late in making payment. Even if the contract did not call for interest, the courts will award interest as "damages" in such cases. What were *B's* damages in reality? *B's* damages depend on proof that he incurred expense or failed to reap a gain *because* he did not have the $100. Causal proof of that kind always asks hypothetically what would have happened differently if the money had been paid. There are many possibilities. *B* might testify that had she been

12. The examples in this section are damages examples for reasons of convenience and simplicity. One set of conventions in measuring restitution can readily be seen in the tracing rules discussed in § 6.1(3).

13. Injunctions are least likely to be conventional because they are almost always tailored in some degree. But even injunctions may use convenient surrogates for the plaintiff's entitlement. The plaintiff whose entitle-

ment is not to be harassed may be protected by an injunction that tells the harassing defendant to stay at least 25 feet from the plaintiff. The plaintiff has no right to hold the defendant at a 25–foot distance, only to prevent harassment, but the 25–foot injunction may be the only one that can be practically enforced. See Galella v. Onassis, 487 F.2d 986, 28 A.L.R.Fed. 879 (2d Cir.1973).

paid on time she would have invested the $100 in stock that has since risen greatly in value. If we believed that testimony, then ordinary interest would not be a good representation of *B's* actual damages. Or *B* might admit that she would have kept the $100 buried beneath a floor board. The truth is that except in rare cases no one is likely to know how things would have turned out. *B might* have invested in good stock but she might have lost the money to a mugger or invested in bad stock.

Courts do not require *B* to convince the trier what she would have done and they might not permit her to do so. Instead they award interest, whether or not she would have earned interest upon timely payment of the money and whether or not she incurred interest expense because she did not have it. Other examples of conventional remedies include especially the convention of market-measured or general damages.[14]

Reasons for conventional remedies. A number of reasons that support the use of conventional measures of remedy for some cases can best be understood in context.[15] A brief statement is that the conventional measure relieves the plaintiff of the burden of proving precise losses when such proof is difficult, impossible and costly and when in any event it is unlikely to produce figures in which one can be confident.

Importance of conventional measures. Conventions in damages and money restitution measurement are far more important and more pervasive than has been generally recognized. When writers criticize particular damages measures on the ground that they imperfectly measure the precise loss suffered, they sometimes fail to consider the conventional nature of market measured damages. Precise damages measures are frequently impossible and almost always extremely difficult and costly to establish. The appropriate question is not merely whether the remedy precisely measures the right but whether a conventional measure is acceptable.

Remedies exceeding rights. The most commonly recognized disparity between right and remedy occurs when the remedy fall short and the plaintiff obtains something less than her entitlement. That might happen, for instance, if a court were to deny an injunction or specific performance on discretionary grounds but granted the plaintiff's relatively inadequate damages remedy. It would also happen if the plaintiff has a loss but cannot prove the amount with sufficient certainty. However, remedies may also exceed rights by giving the plaintiff something to which she is not entitled. When that is merely a conventional substitute for relief that is impossible to mete out with precision, a remedy in excess of rights seems easily justified.

Suppose, however, that the plaintiff has a right not to suffer job discrimination and that the defendant employer has a right to discharge employees for good, non-discriminatory reasons. If the defendant wrongfully discharges the plaintiff, she has a right to reinstatement; and an injunction against further discrimination in employment might be appropriate. Those remedies would reflect the rights of the plaintiff and other employees. Suppose the injunction goes further, however, and requires the employer to post notices to employees of their right to sue in the event of a discharge,

14. See §§ 3.1; 3.3(2); 3.3(3); 12.2(2) & 12.- 2(3) below.   15. See e.g., §§ 3.3(2) & 3.3(3) below.

and even further requires the employer to make available to all employees a list of lawyers who specialize in wrongful discharge cases. These latter provisions go beyond the plaintiff's rights and also tend to invade rights of the defendant. An injunction framed precisely to the plaintiff's right would be feasible. It will be difficult to justify extending the injunction so far beyond the plaintiff's right unless it is reasonably necessary to effectuate the plaintiff's rights or those of other employees whom she represents.[16]

Choosing Among Several Potentially Acceptable Remedies

The plaintiff's choice of remedy is of course governed by her own interests in maximum recovery or in strategy for trial and settlement. The public interest, however, is not necessarily to maximize the plaintiff's recovery or her strategic position. How should a judge choose between two or more potential remedies, each of which provides an acceptable match for the plaintiff's right?

Where all the available remedies are approximately equivalent in effect upon both to the plaintiff and to the defendant,[17] and none imposes special costs upon the court or the public, the plaintiff's choice of remedy should be respected. This is not to say that all remedies should be equally available. Policy or tradition may dictate a rule against specific performance of many contracts, and when it does, the plaintiff is left to her damages remedy only. When specific performance is an available option, however, the plaintiff's preference for or against that remedy should be and usually is respected if it imposes no special costs upon the court, the public, or the defendant.

Very difficult remedial decisions must be made when two or more remedies will each provide appropriate redress of the plaintiff's entitlement but one of them will entail onerous costs to the defendant or economic waste. In general we wish to fully redress the plaintiff's rights, but at the same time we wish to count the costs. Remedies that cost more than the benefits they produce are suspect. No remedial analysis is complete until the costs and benefits have been counted. But as will be indicated, counting costs and benefits of remedial action is not so easy.[18]

§ 1.8 Remedial Analysis: Comparing Remedies

Lawyers compare remedies chiefly to find the remedy likely to produce the most satisfactory relief or to produce the best strategic position. But comparison of remedies is sometimes a useful tool in analysis of the remedial aspects of a case. Sometimes comparison simply yields insight about the nature of a remedy at issue in a case, or reveals that the remedy is not so exotic as it seems. Some of the mystery of equitable subrogation may disappear, for example, if it is compared to a kind of equitable assignment or to ordinary garnishment.[1]

More pointedly, however, the approximate equivalence of one remedy to another may support arguments that if one remedy is available, then its equivalent should also be available, or the reverse argument that if one

---

16. See §§ 2.4(6) & 7.4(4) below.

17. See § 1.8 on remedial equivalence arguments.

18. See § 1.9 below.

§ 1.8

1. Subrogation is explained in § 4.3(4) below.

remedy is not permissible, than its equivalent should also be denied. The disequivalence of two remedies is relevant in the opposite direction.

Arguments from remedial equivalence only work when approximate equivalence can be established. Sometimes two remedies are financially equivalent but so different conceptually that courts do not treat them as equivalent at all. Federal courts applying the Eleventh Amendment immunity of states hold that injunctions are at times permissible against state officers, even though the effect will be to compel the state to spend money to comply with the injunction. Yet money damages in the same amount are not permissible.[2]

An example of approximate remedial equivalence as a ground for granting a new remedy can be found in the case of innocent misrepresentation. Traditional tort law held that the plaintiff could recover damages for the defendant's misrepresentation only if the plaintiff established scienter, an intent to deceive. Innocent misrepresentations were not actionable for damages, but many innocent misrepresentations would represent mutual mistakes that would justify rescission. So the rule was that the rescission remedy might be available but not the damages remedy. But it is now perceived that some measures of damages closely approximate rescission by giving the parties the same asset value they would have if rescission took place.

Suppose the defendant innocently misrepresents facts about Blackacre. On the strength of those representations, the plaintiff purchases Blackacre for $100,000. Blackacre is in fact worth only $90,000. The plaintiff can get out of the financial hole by rescission; she gives back Blackacre and gets back her $100,000. Her assets relevant to the transaction then remain where they started, at $100,000. The defendant's also remain where they started; he has a house worth only $90,000. If for any reason rescission was inappropriate, the plaintiff should usually be permitted to claim the financial equivalent, or $10,000 in cash. The Second Restatement of Torts has so provided.[3]

Remedial equivalence may be grounds for denying one remedy if its equivalent would be denied. In *Ohio v. Kovacs*[4] the Supreme Court held that a costly obligation under an injunction to clean up a hazardous waste cite was dischargeable in bankruptcy just as a money obligation would be. The case turned in part on statutory language, but in part on the recognition that an injunctive obligation costing money was largely equivalent to a money obligation that would be discharged. On essentially similar principles it can be said that since one who commits no wrongs cannot be held liable in money, he cannot be held liable to costly injunctive relief either.[5]

The field of remedies is not as coherent as lawyers might expect. Sometimes similar or almost equivalent remedies are subjected to inconsis-

2. See Edelman v. Jordan, 415 U.S. 651, 94 S.Ct. 1347, 39 L.Ed.2d 662 (1974); cf. Hutto v. Finney, 437 U.S. 678, 98 S.Ct. 2565, 57 L.Ed.2d 522 (1978).

3. This topic of rescission-equivalent damages is discussed in § 9.2(2) below.

4. 469 U.S. 274, 105 S.Ct. 705, 83 L.Ed.2d 649 (1985).

5. General Building Contractors Ass'n, Inc. v. Pennsylvania, 458 U.S. 375, 102 S.Ct. 3141, 73 L.Ed.2d 835 (1982). Accord: Rizzo v. Goode, 423 U.S. 362, 96 S.Ct. 598, 46 L.Ed.2d 561 (1976) (no injunction requiring procedure for citizen complaints about police, since city officials, who were defendants, had not themselves violated the constitution).

tent rules. A lawyer furthers analysis and tends to foster more consistent approaches by comparing remedies, not only for their conceptual similarities or differences, but also for their impact on human wants. Even without such lofty goals, however, close comparison of remedies and remedial rules may increase the analytic support for lawyers' arguments.

§ 1.9 Remedial Analysis: Counting Costs and Benefits

Choosing Remedies in the Light of Costs and Benefits

To impose a remedy is to impose costs and to create benefits. Any remedy, including injunctive and other non-money remedies, will impose costs upon the defendant. Any effective remedy will also create benefits for the plaintiff. Remedies may also impose costs upon or provide benefits for third persons or the public.

In choosing between two remedies (or two measures of a single remedy), courts usually attempt to choose a remedy that will approximately vindicate the plaintiff's right.[1] But costs and benefits of a remedy must also be considered. A remedy that costs more than the benefit it provides may be an inefficient means of vindicating the plaintiff's right. Because rights are more important than efficiencies in some cases, a costly, inefficient remedy is not necessarily "wrong." But judges will want to consider the alternatives before inflicting a remedy that costs more to the defendant than it is worth to the plaintiff. So counting costs and benefits of remedies is worthwhile. This section introduces some of the problems to be considered when remedies are selected with costs and benefits in mind.

Economic analysis is important in legal thought.[2] Perhaps that analysis is most effective in helping to determine how rights are assigned in the first place, but it cannot be disregarded in choosing remedies and a certain amount of economic discussion will appear in connection with particular remedial topics in this book, ranging from the rules for minimizing damages[3] to the appropriate remedial choices in nuisance cases[4] and on to the economics of liquidated damages clauses in contracts.[5] This section does not attempt to introduce, much less to survey, economic analysis of law as it might affect remedies. The modest goal of this section is to illustrate some ways in which lawyers and judges may compare remedial options by counting the costs and benefits of each proposed remedy. It also suggests some situations in which counting costs and benefits may itself be too expensive or even irrelevant.

§ 1.9

1. See § 1.7 above.

2. Economic analysis of law, or law and economics, has developed primarily since the early 1970s and has produced legions of writers, as well as work ranging from homey example to high theory. For a general introduction see Richard Posner, Economic Analysis of Law (3d ed. 1986) (a non-technical, understandable book by the best-known proponent of economic analysis); A. Mitchell Polinsky, An Introduction to Law and Economics (1983) (short and readable).

3. The general rule requires the plaintiff to take reasonable steps to hold her damages at a minimum and refuses compensation for harms the plaintiff could reasonably have avoided. See § 3.9 generally and § 12.6(2) as to minimizing in contracts cases.

4. See §§ 5.6 & 5.7 below.

5. See § 12.9 on agreed remedies generally, including liquidated damages.

Efficiency

Efficiency as maximizing human satisfactions. Economist-lawyers sometimes say that economic efficiency only means a respect for human wants. Goods have value because human beings want them. Economic value is thus viewed as a reflection of human desires, and efficiency is merely a word used to talk about maximizing human satisfaction. For instance, suppose that you build your house on the wrong lot by mistake and the owner proposes to remedy the matter by forcing its removal, which will substantially destroy the house. Even though the house is built in violation of the plaintiff's property rights, it has value to human beings. Destruction of the house is "inefficient" enough to make us consider whether other remedies will suffice.

The Pareto superior idea of efficiency. What counts as maximizing human satisfactions? You could measure human satisfaction or utility solely in terms of wealth. Some economic thinkers do indeed emphasize wealth maximization as a measure of efficiency because wealth can be measured more readily than increased subjective satisfactions. A more general definition of efficiency is called Pareto superior efficiency. This type of efficiency is said to occur if, as a result of the transaction (or judicial decision) no one is worse off and at least one person is better off. Worse off and better off require comparisons to something. Usually people mean worse off or better off in comparison to no transaction at all.

It may not be possible to show that any transaction is in fact Pareto superior or otherwise efficient.[6] Nor is it entirely clear that Pareto superior ideas of efficiency can be readily translated to decisions of courts about remedies, as distinct from decisions about rights. Most economic analysis is really about the efficiency of assigning underlying rights to one person or another rather than about the relative efficiency of remedies in a practical litigation context. However, a rough application of the idea to remedies might be intelligible. If two remedies both vindicate the plaintiff's right, but one costs more than the other, the more costly remedy is less efficient. The defendant is worse off in comparison to the more efficient remedy.

The Kaldor–Hicks test of efficiency. Efficiency is not a simple idea. Economists also recognize other types of efficiency that are important in economic analysis and in philosophical arguments about the merits of efficiency goals.[7] Instead of measuring efficiency by the Pareto superior

---

6. See Hovenkamp, Positivism in Law and Economics, 78 Calif.L.Rev. 815 (1990) (Pareto analysis has "almost no application to real world policymaking because its conditions are never satisfied"); Calabresi, The Pointlessness of Pareto: Carrying Coase Further, 100 Yale L.J. 1211 (1991) (arguing that when all relevant costs are considered, including the cost of change, Pareto superior conditions cannot be met).

In the limited world of litigation, Pareto comparisons may be possible because we accept a platform of assumptions or positive conventions from which to launch them. But even this platform may not provide a sufficient foundation when the plaintiff claims to have subjective valuations of entitlements in issue, as where the owner of an ordinary alley cat claims, "My cat is worth a million dollars to me."

7. Jules Coleman neatly outlines these definitions in Coleman, Efficiency, Utility, and Wealth Maximization, 8 Hofstra L.Rev. 509 (1980). They are: (1) Pareto superior: compared to the alternative, no one is worse off by the allocation of resources in question and at least one person is better off. (2) Pareto optimal: no further reallocation of resources can make one person better off without making another worse off; (3) Kaldor–Hicks efficiency: compared to the alternative, the allocation of

definition, you could use the Kaldor–Hicks test: whether the proposed allocation of resources (or remedy), as compared to the alternative, will make at least one person better off in such a degree that the gain will be sufficient to compensate all persons who are made worse-off.

The Kaldor–Hicks test for efficiency, as it might be applied in litigation or remedial analysis, seems to emphasize satisfactions measurable in money or wealth. The Pareto superior test allows one person to veto the proposed change with the claim "I will be worse off." Kaldor–Hicks does not; it adds up total gains and subtracts total losses. Kaldor–Hicks applied in a remedies context would require us to evaluate all interests in dollars. Such a test of efficiency is hard to use effectively when the plaintiff claims an injunction on the ground that dollars will not adequately vindicate her rights.

Suppose the defendant, to save the cost of using a longer and less risky route, is trucking toxic wastes through a neighborhood full of children where there is also an increased risk of overturned trucks which might allow the toxic material to escape. The risk is small and the savings great enough to pay the potential damages as discounted by the probability of their occurrence. The Kaldor–Hicks idea of efficiency might tell the judge to refuse an injunction against the trucking of toxic materials through a residential neighborhood. The judge would be required to estimate the neighborhood plaintiffs' prospective damages in dollars, and also to convert the plaintiffs' present fears into dollars. Yet the plaintiffs in the neighborhood might prefer to do without the dollars and recover their sense of peace and safety.[8]

Efficiency vs. right. Lawyers are quick to point out that a decision that is efficient in some economic sense may also be unfair or require a redistribution of resources that offends our sense of rightness. Some such apparently efficient decisions might even turn out to be inefficient if human satisfaction or "welfare" is not measured solely in dollars. Some economists have been thinking along similar lines.[9] If these criticisms are sound, it means that at times it may be important to discard the "efficient" solution. Yet, within the practical limitations imposed in litigation and in some particular cases, it is still desirable to do the best we can to estimate costs and benefits in trying to solve remedies problems.

Efficiency in selecting a remedy: the painting sale example. How does this efficiency idea work in choosing among remedies or measures of a single remedy?

Suppose the plaintiff, Paloma, operates an art gallery and has contracted to purchase a painting from Dufy for $10,000. She is certain she can resell it to Mrs. Momar for $15,000, although she has no contract to do so. Dufy, however, decides to keep the painting for himself and refuses to go through with the sale to Paloma. The plaintiff may sue for damages for breach of the contract, but she might also consider suing for specific

---

resources under consideration will make at least one person better off in such a degree that the gain will be sufficient to compensate all persons who are made worse-off. With Kaldor–Hicks compare the discussion in the paragraph "Efficient breach" below.

8. A broader form of the criticism of Kaldor–Hicks is that it embodies a double assumption that each dollar awarded is worth the same as each other dollar and that a dollar awarded to P is worth the same to her as the dollar taken from D. See Hovenkamp, Positivism in Law and Economics, 78 Calif.L.Rev. 815 (1990).

9. See Cirace, A Synthesis of Law and Economics, 44 Sw.L.J. 1139 (1990).

performance. If the plaintiff wanted the painting for her own aesthetic satisfaction, her claim for specific performance would be especially appealing because a recovery of damages would not give her the same satisfaction. Because she wanted the painting only to re-sell, however, her wants can be satisfied by paying her the resale price less the contract price for the painting. If the defendant values the painting more than he values the $5,000, he would prefer to pay the damages. The plaintiff's wants, on the other hand, would be equally satisfied either by receiving the painting for resale or receiving the $5,000.

In this example, the court can seek efficiency or maximum human satisfaction in its choice between the damages remedy and the specific performance remedy. At least on the surface, it looks as if the damages remedy tends to produce the more total satisfaction of the parties than the specific performance remedy. The plaintiff will be just as well off with damages because it will give her the same "profit" she would have made upon resale. The defendant will be better off because, although he must pay $5,000 for breach of contract, he retains something he now values more than he values that amount of money, namely, the painting. Only if one felt vindictive about mind-changing promisors would it be desirable to minimize the defendant's satisfaction.[10]

Counting costs and benefits, however, is at best difficult. Conventions or practicalities may limit the costs and benefits that can be counted. In the painting example, remember that the plaintiff buyer was intending to re-sell the painting to Mrs. Momar. We have no obvious way of comparing Mrs. Momar's loss of satisfaction with the reneging seller's gain in satisfaction when the sale is stopped. Nor is it clear that we should do so. The impracticality of measuring costs and benefits to all people and throughout all time may induce us to accept as a convention what some thinkers accept as an article of faith: that if Mrs. Momar's disappointment is great enough, she will offer enough money to buy the painting from the reneging seller. In that case, the total satisfaction would again be maximized.[11]

Economic thinkers differ among themselves about particular solutions. Some might disagree that the award of damages in the painting example would be more efficient;[12] some might even seek to shift the focus away from traditional notions of efficiency in order to consider more explicitly

---

10. Some cases for comparison or contrast are Groves v. John Wunder Co., 205 Minn. 163, 286 N.W. 235, 123 A.L.R. 502 (1939) and Peevyhouse v. Garland Coal & Min. Co., 382 P.2d 109 (Okl.1962), aff'd on rehearing, 382 P.2d 116 (Okl.1963), cert. denied, 375 U.S. 906, 84 S.Ct. 196, 11 L.Ed.2d 145 (1963), both discussed in § 12.19(1) below.

11. In this scenario, suppose that Mrs. Momar believes she will have more than $20,000 satisfaction from owning the painting. The reneging seller, remember, has kept the painting by paying the gallery owner's expected profit of $5,000. Momar can offer $20,000 to the reneging seller. If he accepts the offer, Momar improves her satisfaction level because the painting is worth more to her. The reneging seller improves his satisfaction, too.

We know that because he would not sell unless he regarded the $20,000 cash as worth more to him than the painting. If the reneging seller refuses to sell for what Momar will pay, then we know that he gets more than $20,000 satisfaction from the painting, so the painting stays home where it produces the most total satisfaction. Dr. Pangloss would love it, and so, for a while, would Candide. It is the best of all possible worlds.

12. Cf. Schwartz, The Case for Specific Performance, 89 Yale L.J. 271 (1979). Schwartz argued in favor of specific performance as a routinely available remedy on the ground that if it was the plaintiff's preferred remedy it would provide better compensation for breach and would generate efficiencies for that reason. See also § 12.8(2) below.

proper distribution of goods,[13] fairness, or even right for right's sake. The point of the present discussion, however, is not to reach an ultimate conclusion about the relative efficiency of the damages and the specific performance remedy. It is rather to point out that from a remedies point of view, the desire to maximize human satisfaction arises when the lawyer or judge must choose between remedies or between measures or adjustments of them. It also serves to show that the satisfactions protected by considering costs and benefits are not necessarily limited to pecuniary satisfactions. In the painting example the reneging seller's aesthetic interests and the disappointed gallery owner's pecuniary interests are both protected.[14]

Efficient breach. An idea of efficient breach of contract is tucked away below the surface in the painting example. The idea of efficient breach excites controversy. The notion is that sometimes a contract *should* be breached to achieve efficiency in the sense of maximum satisfactions as shown by measurable economic gains. The efficient breach idea does not relieve the defendant from liability for his breach. On the contrary, it regards the breach as efficient only if the breaching party can earn or save enough by breaching to pay all of the damages caused by that breach and then pays those damages.

The music group example. Suppose that three young people in a small city form a music group. After a few successful appearances in local establishments, they sign a three-year record contract with a local recording studio. The group cuts a record and the studio distributes it according to contract, but the studio's resources are limited; it cannot provide national distribution or publicity. Given its limited resources, the studio can expect to make no more than $10,000 per year and the music group can expect even less. Nevertheless, the record falls into the hands of a national record company, which is impressed with the group's talent and offers the group hundreds of thousands of dollars for a contract. The national contract would provide the group with an opportunity for national recognition and distribution. But the local recording studio objects, claiming that the group is already bound by a contract with the local studio. Should it be permitted to enjoin the music group from accepting the offer from the national company? Or alternatively, to reap some or all of the national profits? Or should the local recording studio be limited to a recovery of its actual damages under the contract, not more than $10,000 a year?

Applying efficient breach ideas to the music group case. The efficient breach idea says that the music group should breach the contract with the local studio, using the gains from the new contract to pay the damages. Such a result would comport with the Kaldor–Hicks notion of efficiency.[15] The group will enjoy increased opportunities and a chance to exploit its

---

13. Calabresi, The Pointlessness of Pareto: Carrying Coase Further, 100 Yale L.J. 1211 (1991); Cirace, A Synthesis of Law and Economics, 44 Sw.L.J. 1139 (1990) (efficiency by any standard does not correlate "to wealth maximization because the total amount of wealth a society generates depends upon both the efficiency and the distribution of income").

14. The efficiency of the solution does not turn on whether the owner wants the painting for his own aesthetic satisfaction or because

he has a better sales opportunity elsewhere. The point is only that subjective and personal satisfactions are equally protected by the efficiency analysis.

15. Kaldor–Hicks efficiency is achieved whether or not the group's gains are used to pay damages. Even so, arguments for efficient breach do not propose to relieve the music group from liability for damages.

talent, the national company will reap business profits, and audiences will reap greater enjoyment through wider exposure of the group. The local studio is not worse off, because its lost profits have been compensated for by the damages payment. If the local studio were allowed to enjoin the music group from performing nationally, or to effectively inhibit that performance by imposing punitive damages on the group or on the national company, the group, the national company, and the potential audience would all be worse off, but the local studio would be no better off. The world's wealth, as measured by the development of the musical talent and the price people pay for it, would be less.

Arguments against efficient breach. One argument often raised against efficient breach notions is that the local studio (in this example) ought to be entitled to a share of the surplus that breach makes possible. If a court were to issue an injunction against the national contract, the national company would have to buy out the local studio. The local studio would charge enough to give it some share in the new-found value. But unless a contract right is equivalent to a property right, it is not so clear that the victim of breach should be entitled to share in the surplus created by the breach. In this example, it is not the studio's talent, not its investment, not its labor, and not its publicity or distribution that will produce the gains of the new deal. A second point, and one much discussed, is that the costs of bargaining and buying out the old contract—renegotiation costs—may be so high that the national company will drop the deal altogether. So if you want to preserve the benefits of efficient breach, you may want to avoid taxing the opportunity that leads to the breach by compelling a costly buyout.[16]

Most people can think of several reasons to question the efficient breach idea. Some say it is immoral because the group has made a promise and should be required to keep it, or at least not to profit by its breach.[17] Some might say that at least when the parties contract about property rather than services, the buyer acquires a kind of equitable property interest as soon as the contract is signed and so should enjoy any profits the seller makes from re-selling at a higher price. In the painting example, if Dufy simply sold the painting to a new buyer instead of to Paloma, you could view the case as almost like a conversion of a painting that equitably belongs to Paloma.[18]

Other critics might argue that the breach victim never recovers full damages, so that fair conditions for essential breach never occur.[19] Still

16. See § 12.1(2) below.

17. Some promises are as this argument assumes, but commercial promises that are not specifically performable are usually construed to mean something like "I will perform as stated in this contract, else pay legal damages." If the defendant has promised only to perform or pay, there is no immorality if he chooses the second option rather than the first.

18. This is a kind of equitable conversion reasoning. It is occasionally applied to real property to permit the would-be purchaser to take the gains made by the reneging seller,

see § 12.7(4) below. It is a formal conception that may express results, not a reason for regarding the contract right as property.

19. One form of this argument is that some elements of damages are almost never recoverable in civil suits. The plaintiff usually must pay her own attorney fees, for example. So far as the argument against efficient breach relies on this proposition, it seems better addressed to the rule against attorney fee recovery. Another form of the argument is that some losses cannot be compensated in money because they are subjective or too difficult to prove. But the plaintiff is fully compensated according to the terms of the con-

others argue that although efficiency might result if you measure it in money, you might get a different answer if you measured it in total utility. In the music group case maybe more people achieve more satisfaction if the contract is breached, but maybe not in some other examples. Suppose in the painting hypothetical that Dufy reneges on his contract to sell to Paloma because a Mr. Getty gives him $20,000 for it. Although Mr. Getty paid more than Paloma or Mrs. Momar could afford, the breach and sale to Getty may not have increased satisfactions at all unless you are willing to say that satisfactions are measured only in the money payment. (Mr. Getty might let only his rich friends see the painting while anyone would be allowed to see it in Mrs. Momar's house.)

Economic thinkers do not fully agree about the role for efficient breach, if any.[20] Perhaps much depends on the underlying assumptions of the parties; perhaps something depends on the facts of individual cases. But if efficient breach ideas apply in any cases, it pays lawyers and judges to consider the costs in all cases.

Waste

Efficiency considerations count heavily when a remedy will actually require waste. Courts almost always try to avoid imposing remedies that entail unnecessary waste. When persons who suffer legally relevant harm can be made substantially whole without waste it is preferable to use a remedy that avoids it. Waste usually refers to destruction of economic value (and hence destruction of something some people want).

For example, suppose that under a contract, the defendant builds a house for the plaintiff. Upon its completion, the parties discover that the wall studs were not offset to minimize transmission of sound between rooms. To comply with contract specifications now would require destruction of the house or substantial parts of it. A sound-absorbing material can be pumped into the wall space to achieve almost as good a result as offset studs. A remedy that requires the insulation plus damages for any remaining detriment is probably preferable to a remedy that requires destruction of substantial portions of the house.[21]

Even if avoidance of waste were an absolute rule, some remedies that entail waste would be permitted, because the alternative remedy may entail even greater waste. Comparison of the remedial alternatives is always required. Suppose the defendant innocently develops a trademark which, as it happens, is closely similar to the plaintiff's trademark. Both marks have value, but neither will be so valuable if both are used. If the defendant's mark is an infringing mark, the court may enjoin its further use.[22] This is analogous to destruction of the house because it effectively destroys the economic value of the defendant's mark.

tract if she recovers either the performance promised or the legal damages; she may have other losses, but they are not losses the defendant agreed to cover.

20. See Harrison, Egoism, Altruism, and Market Illusions: The Limits of Law and Economics, 33 U.C.L.A. L.Rev. 1309 (1986) (doubting values and assumptions of some economic analysis); A. Polinsky, An Introduction to Law and Economics, 32–36 (1983) (right amount of efficient breach might lead to the wrong amount of efficient investment in reliance on the contract).

21. See § 12.19(1) for the specific rules and cases.

22. See § 6.4(5) below.

But the injunction that requires waste of the defendant's mark would still be the best solution because it is less wasteful than the alternative, which would reduce the value of the plaintiff's mark by allowing the defendant to confuse customers with his similar mark. It may also be the better solution for a very different reason: destruction of the values in the defendant's mark may be necessary to provide a remedy that respects the plaintiff's rights. Sometimes waste is necessary if rights are respected.

So there is no flat principle that remedies cannot be wasteful. The waste principle, like most economic ideas, asks us to consider the consequences of the remedial alternatives and to count the consequences as important, but not necessarily determinative.

Remedy Costs Exceeding Relevant Legal Benefits

Even when waste is not in issue, courts are properly reluctant to impose a more costly remedy upon the defendant when a less costly remedy will make whole all relevant legal harm. The cost of a remedy should not exceed the benefit it produces if equal benefits can be achieved more cheaply. A remedy is more desirable or efficient if, as compared to the alternative remedy, it leaves the defendant better off without leaving the plaintiff worse off.

For example, suppose that the defendant, who operates an automobile repair garage, negligently demolishes the plaintiff's old car. Immediately before its destruction the car had a market value of $1,000. A replacement car of equal value and equal performance is available at that cost. Alternatively, the defendant could repair the car in his garage at a cost of $2,000. Courts will probably not order the defendant to repair the car. Although there may be several good reasons for refusing such a remedy,[23] one economic reason is that an expensive repair would give the plaintiff no greater benefit than a cheaper replacement.

Remedy Costs Exceeding Legal Loss or Harm

The compensation principle more than an efficiency principle dictates a similar result in a similar factual setting. Courts should not impose a remedy that exceeds full compensation for legally recognized loss or harm, even if the defendant's cost and the plaintiff's benefit would be equal and even if no waste is required.

Suppose the same facts as the previous example, except that the plaintiff does not seek a remedy requiring the defendant personally to repair the car. Instead, the plaintiff demands $2,000 in cash as the cost of repair (rather than $1,000 as the cost of procuring a substitute car). In the absence of special reasons to hold otherwise, the court will often limit the recovery to the less costly remedy, in this case, the cost of replacement. Notice that a recovery of $2,000 would not cost more to the defendant than it was worth to the plaintiff, because $2,000 is worth the same to both the defendant and the plaintiff. Nor would the recovery entail economic waste. However, unless the destroyed car is in some way unique and the unique qualities can be

---

23. Traditional dislike for direct compulsion is a reason for refusing to order the defendant to repair the car that is grounded in social and political ideals about human beings and their relationships rather than in efficiency as such.

restored by repair, $2,000 exceeds the plaintiff's loss or harm. So the remedy should still be limited to $1,000.

Measuring Remedy Benefits: The Subjective Benefit Case

Counting on conventions. Counting costs and benefits of a remedy requires us to measure the benefits a remedy would provide the plaintiff and the costs that would be imposed upon the defendant. Neither measurement is always simple. A very large number of remedies problems arise because we are not sure whether the proposed remedy will provide a benefit that is equal to either its total costs or to the value of the plaintiff's underlying right. In fact, it would be realistic to say that completely accurate counting is not really possible. Counting or measurement, in remedial law at least, is almost always possible only from a platform of positive conventions. For instance, if the defendant damages an old machine that must be replaced, we might resort to useful accounting conventions for figuring depreciation of that property.[24] We come to common agreement about damages in part by relying on such conventions.

In counting costs and benefits of a given remedy, we are likely also to build on the basis of conventions about which costs and benefits are to be considered. In particular, practical proof limits may induce us to ignore some (but not all) subjective benefits or costs and some (but not all) benefits or costs to the public or to third persons.

The logger and the plaintiff's tree. Suppose the defendant is a logger who negligently locates a boundary line and cuts a large tree on the plaintiff's land in addition to the trees on adjoining property where he is entitled to cut. Fortunately, its loss does not much affect the market value of the land, so the plaintiff's property is worth only $500 less than it was worth when the tree was standing. But what if the plaintiff wants the tree replaced and replacement cost will be $5,000? At first glance this might seem a great deal like the case in which the defendant destroyed the plaintiff's old car. In that case we opted for the less costly remedy because either remedy would substantially make the plaintiff whole. But that may not be so in the tree case.

Proven subjective value to the plaintiff. In the tree case suppose we knew two things: (1) the plaintiff really subjectively valued the tree as being worth at least $5,000, so she would replace the tree from her own funds if the defendant were not liable for replacement costs;[25] and (2) the plaintiff had a legal right to protection of her subjective values in the tree and not merely to protection of her transferable economic values.[26] At least in all

---

24. On depreciation in figuring damages, see § 5.2(7) below. On conventions in damages measurements generally, see §§ 3.1 & 3.5 below.

25. We might not want to accept the plaintiff's testimony about this standing alone, but sometimes objective evidence points to subjective valuation. The plaintiff might have expended $5,000 of her own funds to replace the tree at a time when she believed that the tree cutter could not be identified. In some other situations, the plaintiff's pre-injury purchase

of expensive insurance might provide evidence about how she values property. See Levmore, Self–Assessed Valuation Systems for Tort and Other Law, 68 Va.L.Rev. 771 (1982).

26. Some legal rights are established to protect transferable economic interests only. The landowner's right to just compensation when government takes her land is usually only a right to compensation for interests of pecuniary value that could be transferred to others. See § 5.2(6) below. Somewhat similarly, not all but most contract rights are

cases where both these things are shown, the high cost of replacement, $5,000, may be economically appropriate, even though it far exceeds the plaintiff's losses as measured by the real estate market.

Waste, entitlement and efficiency in the tree replacement. Notice first that replacement of the tree does not entail waste. Nothing is destroyed in replacing the tree. Then notice that the plaintiff does not get more than she is entitled to. We know that because we accepted proposition (2) above, at least for purposes of this discussion. (The answer would be different if we thought that her right was limited to transferable economic values. This is a point on which some economic analysis might focus.) Finally, notice that a remedy that provides replacement or the cost of replacement does not violate efficiency ideals. We know that because we accepted proposition (1) above; the plaintiff really does value the tree as worth at least $5,000, so the defendant's cost in replacing the tree (or paying for its replacement) does not exceed the benefit provided the plaintiff or the one she is entitled to have.

This example reminds us that efficiency ideals do not preclude protection of subjective, non-market values because the plaintiff's satisfactions need not be measured by market value of the plaintiff's entitlements. Efficiency ideals, in fact, seem to have little to say about this particular situation. If we knew the plaintiff cared nothing for the tree, the ideal of efficiency and the ideal of compensation would jointly call for a recovery limited to $500, the diminished land value. If, however, we know that the plaintiff's valuation of the tree exceeds replacement costs and that she is entitled to protection of her subjective feelings, then those ideals do not counsel against the recovery of the high replacement costs. A recovery of replacement costs would be right in that case as the cheapest means to vindicate the plaintiff's right.[27]

Whether a jury should be permitted to believe the plaintiff's claim that she values the tree at such a high figure is another matter; it does not turn directly on economic analysis but on a sense of the practical limitations of litigation, including the limitations of proof.

Measuring Remedy Benefits: The Case of Benefits to Third Persons or the Public

Considering public benefit from tree replacement. Benefits of a proposed remedy may be difficult to measure for a second reason. If a proposed remedy, such as replacement of the destroyed tree, will benefit the plaintiff only by $500 but will benefit the public by $5,500, then the $5,000 cost of replacement is not inefficient. The defendant will incur a cost of $5,000 but will thereby secure benefits for a total of $5,500. It is difficult to value the

pecuniary rights; the plaintiff does not usually recover for emotional harm when the defendant breaches a contract. See § 12.5(1). But in a society that respects the autonomy of individuals, the plaintiff's subjective valuations should be respected in the remedy if that can be done without unfairness to the defendant and if practical proof shows such a valuation.

27. If the plaintiff valued the tree at $1 million, replacement costs would be the more appropriate method for getting the $1 million in satisfaction to which the plaintiff is entitled, so she would not recover $1 million. If all the conditions are met for recovery based on her subjective valuation, however, she would be logically entitled to recover replacement costs plus some amount of money for the time period in which she had neither the original tree nor its replacement.

public benefits in this example, but in fact such valuation is possible.[28] If tree replacement really does create a total additional wealth of $500, as it does in this example, then the replacement is not inefficient. In fact, it may add to efficiency in providing appropriate deterrence.

Is it correct to consider benefits to those who have no rights? But even if the public does benefit to the extent of $5,000 from the tree's replacement there are reasons to be cautious about imposing a cost-of-replacement remedy upon the defendant where the owner of the tree values it at only $500. One reason is that the cost of proving the benefits will itself be high and we are not likely to feel very confident about the results. Another is that while the cost of replacement remedy is not inefficient, it is misdirected. It makes the defendant pay not only for violation of the plaintiff's right (worth $500) but also for losses suffered by people who have no rights in the tree at all. We all benefit from trees, even when trees are grown on the land of others, but we have no rights to those trees, a point that is demonstrated by the fact that if the plaintiff herself removed her own tree, we could not recover damages from her. So the defendant's liability should not be measured by the public's loss, only by the rights that were invaded.[29]

Considering public rights in natural resources. The answer is different when it comes to public resources. By statute, government trustees may recover for the harm suffered by the public when natural resources are damaged by oil spills or hazardous substances.[30] The statute supplies the element that is missing in the case of the private landowner's trees; it creates a right in the public. Valuation of the damaged resource is still difficult, but it is no longer anomalous: the defendant is made to expend large sums of money to protect public rights in the resources, but not made to protect individuals who have no rights. In addition, liability for the cost of restoring the resource (or some similar liability) may have important deterrence effects.

Measuring Remedy Costs and Deterrence

Although efficiency ideals ask us to measure and compare costs and benefits of any proposed remedy, we have seen that measuring benefits is not always easy. Neither is measuring costs.

Net cost to the defendant after considering his gains. Take the logger's case with the same figures; the plaintiff's land is still worth $500 less than before the tree was destroyed and the cost of replacement is still $5,000. Suppose that the tree was destroyed in the first place because the defendant does not run surveys or mark boundaries and that his failure to do so violates the standard of care owed to the plaintiff. The refusal to do the required surveys saves the defendant the cost of making the survey and also results in his getting a few added trees that do not belong to him in the same

---

28. See § 5.2(5) below (natural resource damages under federal statutes).

29. But cf. Galligan, Augmented Awards: The Efficient Evolution of Punitive Damages, 51 La.L.Rev. 3 (1990) (proposing to augment the plaintiff's damages recoveries to account for all damages resulting from a negligent activity such as a toxic spill, including damages that accrue to third persons who, like the

non-tree owners, have no legally recognized rights).

30. See The Comprehensive Environmental Response, Compensation, and Liability Act, 42 U.S.C.A. § 9601 et seq. (also known as the Superfund Act or CERCLA), discussed in § 5.2(5) below.

way he obtained the plaintiff's tree. The saved costs and the value of the added trees for which no one sues could add up to an average of $5,000 for each area he logs.

On these facts it is plausible to view the logger's net cost of replacing the tree as zero, not $5,000. He destroys the tree by conduct that gives him a $5,000 gain. To charge him $5,000 for the cost of replacement is only to eliminate his gain. In fact, not to charge him the full cost of replacement on these facts is to give him incentive to continue his negligent or trespassory conduct.

Externalized costs. One way to see this kind of case is to think of the logger as making other people bear costs of running his business. He saves the survey costs by forcing the landowners adjoining his cutting areas to pay the price in lost trees. The logger is like the fathers in Jeremiah's adage: "The fathers have eaten a sour grape, and the children's teeth are set on edge." [31] Economic writers might speak of externalization of costs. Externalization might be regarded as one kind of inefficiency, partly because it does not lead people like the logger to take the efficient amount of precautions. If all landowners, including those who never sue, suffer tree losses of $100,000, and the logger obtains gains of $50,000, his refusal to survey is inefficient because it leads to more losses than gains.

Effective deterrence. This example suggests that measurement of costs and benefits is important to provide the right deterrence. If the contractor has saved monies by his misconduct, damages must be measured at a level sufficient to make sure he will not think of saving monies that way in the future. It also shows that net costs to a defendant require us to consider his savings as well. And finally, considering his savings may require us to consider savings in all his logging transactions as a unit in order to see the total correctly.

This line of reasoning would not work if we were trying to decide whether the logger should exercise care in the first place. If that were the issue, maybe we would decide that landowners should have to fence out trespassers and protect themselves because it would be cheaper to do that than to require loggers to make surveys.[32] Fortunately, however, the landowner's right to her trees is already decided by law. Once that is given, it is useful to view the logger's gains from violating that right as a reduction in

---

31. Jeremiah 30:29. Jeremiah promises a better day, one in which a person is punished for his own iniquity, not another's.

32. Although the idea sounds highly implausible on the facts, there are endless variations on it in the literature, mostly derived from the famous exposition of the Coase Theorem in Ronald Coase, The Problem of Social Cost, 3 J.L. & Econ. 1 (1960). In these workouts, adjoining landowners have incompatible uses, in that the activities of one imposes costs on the other, as where the railroad's operation repeatedly causes fires that burn the farmer's crops. But it takes both uses to create a problem, so it is difficult in the abstract to say whether the railroad should pay the farmer or

the farmer should provide protection for his crops. Coase thought it would not matter (on efficiency issues) which solution the law adopted if the parties could bargain for their own solution without costs. There are many discussions. See e.g., Richard Posner, Economic Analysis of Law (3d ed. 1986). Some other qualifications of the theorem are explicated in Hovenkamp, Marginal Utility and the Coase Theorem, 75 Cornell L.Rev. 783 (1990). Since there are always transaction costs such as the cost of bargaining, the amount of those costs and best way to minimize them is a primary feature in many economic discussions.

his costs of providing a remedy and to calculate the deterrent effect of a replacement remedy accordingly.

Transaction Costs

Economist-lawyers frequently discuss transaction costs. Transaction costs are costs that will be incurred to enter into an exchange (or by analogy, to impose a remedy). If you want to buy or sell, repair, or replace, you will have transaction costs. For instance, if you want to buy a house, you will have information costs in locating the house and locating the seller. Other transaction costs will include attorney fees, title insurance, the time it takes to bargain for the price, to arrange for the shift of your present homeowner's insurance, and the money you spend to get to the closing. Some transactions entail substantial information costs. Finding the cheapest and most reliable person to repair your car or replace your tree will require time and probably cash as well.

Economic thinkers often discuss transaction costs in considering how rights should be assigned between parties. For instance, in deciding whether parties should be permitted to contract freely for any kind of penalty or liquidated damages clause, you might want to consider whether such a right would add to the costs of contracting because of the added time that would be required if parties had an infinite range of options about liquidated damages. Or you might want to consider whether free bargaining about liquidated damages would have the effect of revealing important information to each bargainer about the intentions of the other, perhaps with the effect of saving some investigation costs.

Remedies impose transaction costs in several ways. Some remedies may in effect encourage the parties to bargain to a final solution from a platform the court sets. For example, if the court enjoins the defendant to destroy a house erroneously built on the plaintiff's lot, the defendant will probably bargain to buy the lot at a high price or sell the house to the plaintiff at a low price as a cheaper solution than total destruction.[33]

Public and private costs of figuring remedies are themselves transaction costs of a kind. When judges and lawyers attempt to estimate costs and benefits of a given remedy, they are engaging in an activity that itself is costly. In fact cost estimates are infinitely regressive: you could attempt to figure the cost of figuring costs, and the costs of figuring the cost of figuring costs and so on. At some point the court must conclude that the benefits of more remedial analysis and more accurate estimates is too costly. So at some point courts may opt for conventional remedial formulas or standardized remedies or for conventions that consider only a limited number of costs and benefits (as where the court disregards costs of benefits to third persons).

Rights and Efficiencies

This section has suggested that in the law of remedies it is usually worthwhile to count the costs and benefits of a remedy. But this section does not suggest that efficiency trumps rights. In litigated cases, efficiency is most important in determining the scope of one's rights in a doubtful case. Once the right is clearly established and its scope is firm, remedies must

---

33. On post-remedy bargaining, see § 5.7(4) below.

match that right and vindicate it, subject only to practical constraints of knowledge and litigation procedure.

So, as always, a person's conception of the underlying right will determine much about remedies in general and about the role of efficiency arguments in particular. I send a parcel by a high-priced next-day-delivery service, paying $100 for the guaranteed delivery. But the parcel is not delivered the next day; it is delivered two days late. As a result I lose a sale that would have made me a profit of $2,000. The carrier has breached its contract with me. Does it owe $100 or $2,000? Does the answer turn on any kind of efficiency assessment? Or solely on the scope of my contractual right?

The view expressed in this book [34] is that in the absence of reason to think otherwise, the agreement in the example is best understood to mean this: the carrier will either make delivery as promised or else will pay the plaintiff the value of the one-day-delivery service for such a parcel (presumably the $100 price). If the contract means that, the recovery cannot include my loss of profits. Other people may read the meaning of such a contract differently, but if that is the meaning and what the parties intended, then no question of efficiency arises. We have identified the plaintiff's right fully. The only task for the law of remedies is then to enforce that right by awarding $100. Counting costs and benefits is always enlightening, but it does not always determine the remedy.

§ 1.10 Remedies and Trial Strategy

In some cases the plaintiff's lawyer will have no choice of remedy; the only remedial issue will be the measure or scope of the remedy. When a choice among remedies is available, the selection of remedy is most obviously important to maximize the client's desired recovery. However, the plaintiff's lawyer may also claim a remedy for strategic reasons, to improve chances of success at trial or to improve the plaintiff's position in settlement. The choice of remedy frequently must be made at the outset, in the initial complaint if not sooner.[1] For strategy purposes, the remedy can be chosen only after planning and forecasting all the possible future procedures, defenses, and negotiations in the case.

The plaintiff's claim of a remedy may have at least three distinct kinds of strategic effects. First, one remedy claim may threaten the defendant more than another. A more threatening claim, if credible, may tend to induce a quicker or better settlement. Second, one remedy claim may provide the plaintiff with a procedural advantage not available with another remedy. Third, one remedy may avoid defenses that would be interposed if another remedy were chosen.

Remedy Chosen to Maximize Threat to the Defendant

The costly injunction example. Suppose the plaintiff can get her remedial entitlement by a recovery of $5,000 in damages or by getting an injunction

---

34. See §§ 12.4(4)–12.4(7) below.

§ 1.10

1. Amendments of pleadings are of course possible under modern procedures, but the unfortunate doctrine of election of remedies in some of its forms may foreclose some remedies because of pre-complaint conduct of the plaintiff. See §§ 9.4, 12.7(6), 12.12(1) & 12.13 below.

requiring the defendant to remove his building which encroaches three inches on the plaintiff's property. Either way the plaintiff will be satisfied, but if the defendant must remove the building, it will cost him $200,000. The plaintiff may claim an injunctive remedy even if damages would fully compensate, because the threat of a $200,000 loss to the defendant is likely to induce a quick settlement and a payment of much more than the $5,000 in actual damages.[2] Strategy decisions are matters of art.

The constructive trust—lis pendens example. The injunctive claim is by no means the only claim likely to increase pressure on a defendant. Suppose the defendant obtains money from the plaintiff by fraud, then uses the money to purchase Blackacre. The plaintiff could claim money damages, but for more than one good reason the plaintiff may prefer to claim a constructive trust on Blackacre, that is, that she should be regarded as the equitable owner of the land. Such a claim made in good faith would probably allow her to file a *lis pendens* or public notice of her claim to title. Prospective purchasers of Blackacre would be on notice of the claim and probably would not buy it, and certainly would not do so at its full value. Prospective lenders would not lend money on the strength of Blackacre as security. The effect of the *lis pendens,* then, would probably be to tie up the property and the defendant may again be pressured to settle more quickly or on better terms. This is a pressure that could not be generated by an ordinary money claim because *lis pendens* can usually be invoked only when the plaintiff claims an interest in the property itself. It is interesting to notice that this strategy can be invoked only by the lawyer who knows both of the constructive trust remedy and the *lis pendens* rules.

These two examples suggest but do not exhaust possibilities. The possibility of pressure, however, should not always be acted upon. Strategy is an art and sometimes it is bad strategy to increase the stakes of the game. Some adversaries merely increase their resistance when the stakes go up or when they believe they are being manipulated. So the point is not that the toughest remedy should always be asserted. It is rather that the choice of a remedy claim is one that may have strategy implications to be considered at the outset of the case.

Remedy Chosen to Enhance Procedural Advantage or Avoid Disadvantage

The equity non-jury trial example. Some remedy claims may affect procedures and procedures sometimes offer an advantage to one party or the other. In most states the claim of an equitable remedy like an injunction or constructive trust is tried without a jury.[3] The claim of damages, on the other hand, may carry with it a constitutional jury trial right. The choice between a jury and non-jury trial is not always significant, but sometimes it can be critical to a winning strategy. The obvious reason is that the jury may be inclined to favor a sympathetic or popular party and disfavor an unpopular one. Sometimes, the jury trial strategy has less obvious elements. It may take much longer to get to a trial by jury than to get to a trial before a judge. When timing matters in the strategy of either party, then the

---

2. For discussions of the remedial merits in such cases, see §§ 5.7(2), 5.7(4) & 5.10(4) below.

3. The jury trial rules are covered in § 2.6 below.

choice between jury and non-jury trial may matter, too. One means of guaranteeing a right to a jury trial is to claim a purely "legal" remedy; one means of getting a non-jury trial is to claim a purely equitable remedy.

The discovery and proof example. The kind of evidence that is relevant at trial (and the kind of discovery permitted) depends in part on the remedy claimed. Plaintiffs would always show that the defendant is rich if they were permitted to do so, because they would hope that the defendant's wealth would influence the trier both as to liability and as to the extent of the remedy. Such proof is ordinarily excluded as prejudicial and irrelevant to any legitimate issue in the case. But if the plaintiff can claim the punitive damages remedy in good faith, she will ordinarily be permitted to discover the defendant's financial information and to prove it at trial.[4]

For different reasons, the defendant's financial condition becomes relevant if the plaintiff can legitimately claim restitution based on the defendant's profits. For example if the defendant profits in its business by using the plaintiff's property, the plaintiff is allowed in some cases to recover those profits. Both discovery of the profit information and detailed proof of it are thus proper.

Both the punitive damages claim and the restitution of profits claim are valuable to the plaintiff in themselves, not merely for strategic reasons, so it is not very likely that a plaintiff would claim such remedies solely for the purpose of making the defendant's wealth an issue in the case. However, plaintiffs do use the strategic advantage of showing the defendant's financial condition when those remedies are claimed for other reasons.

The injunction bond example. The plaintiff may choose a remedy not only to gain an estimated procedural advantage but to avoid a procedural disadvantage or a strategically vulnerable position. The plaintiff might in the first instance consider seeking a preliminary injunction against the defendant, say to enjoin the defendant's alleged infringement of the plaintiffs' trademark. Such a remedy could exert much pressure on a defendant because the injunction might prevent the defendant from marketing its products without changing the infringing mark.

Unless the infringement is abundantly clear, however, the plaintiff must also consider that she might lose at trial. If the plaintiff seeks a preliminary injunction, she will be required to post a bond to guarantee that she will pay the defendant's damages if it turns out that the preliminary injunction was erroneously issued. The plaintiff's liability on the bond subjects the plaintiff to a threat of loss. It puts the plaintiff in a strategically vulnerable position if the defendant can mount a credible defense. In that event the plaintiff facing potential liability on the injunction bond may be under pressure to settle on unfavorable terms. In thinking through these possible steps in the case, the plaintiff's lawyer may sometimes prefer to avoid a claim for preliminary relief to avoid the potential for liability. The ultimate decision on that point of course turns in part on how badly the plaintiff needs the preliminary injunction.

---

4. Sometimes the plaintiff must establish a prima facie case for punitive damages before discovery or proof at trial is allowed. § 3.11(5) below.

Remedy Chosen to Avoid Defenses

Discretionary defenses to equitable remedies. Defenses sometimes operate differentially among remedies, so plaintiffs may at times choose a remedy to avoid a potential defense. Judges claim the power to refuse equitable remedies as a matter of discretion and defendants may invoke a number of equitable defenses that have little or no application to bar claims to legal remedies.[5] In many such cases the plaintiff's main claim is an equitable claim, so that she will have little choice in the matter. Where a choice is possible, however, the plaintiff may prefer to assert a legal remedy rather than to invite an exploration of her unclean hands or other moral characteristics that judges feel free to consider when an equitable remedy is asserted.

Remedial immunities. More dramatically, the plaintiff may be compelled to forego a damages remedy altogether when the defendant can assert an immunity against damages but not against an injunction. The Eleventh Amendment bars suits against states, but permits injunctions against state officers to compel future action, even when the indirect effect is to compel the state to spend money to comply with the injunction.[6]

Remedy Chosen to Enhance Enforcement of Decrees or Collection of Judgments

When the plaintiff's rights are clear she may not need to make strategic decisions to enhance procedural advantage or pressure the defendant. She may, however, need to choose a remedy claim to improve chances of collection or enforcement of her right if the defendant flees or is short of funds.

The claim of equitable ownership or security interest example. Good faith remedy claims that assert either an equitable ownership interest or a security interest in the defendant's property can give the plaintiff great advantage at the enforcement stage. If the plaintiff recovers only a money judgment, other creditors of the defendant may enforce their claims first and may exhaust all the defendant's property in the process. If the plaintiff is able to claim a constructive trust on the defendant's property, however, the court will compel the defendant to convey that property to the plaintiff, in effect giving the plaintiff priority over other creditors of the defendant, as well as some other advantages. Similarly, if the plaintiff can claim an equitable or other lien against the defendant's property, the plaintiff may be allowed to satisfy her money claim out of that property ahead of other creditors.

The coercive order example. Another way to improve chances of collecting a money claim is to seek a court order to pay it rather than an ordinary judgment that would be enforced by levy on the defendant's property. The threat of an ordinary money judgment is meaningless to a defendant who has no property, but the threat of the contempt power, with its potential jail sentence, may be quite effective indeed. This treatise does not advocate the use of contempt powers to collect money judgments, but there are a few

---

5. See § 2.4 below.

6. Edelman v. Jordan, 415 U.S. 651, 94 S.Ct. 1347, 39 L.Ed.2d 662 (1974); cf. Hutto v.

Finney, 437 U.S. 678, 98 S.Ct. 2565, 57 L.Ed.2d 522 (1978).

kinds of cases in which such powers may be used and may be the only hope for enforcement of the plaintiff's claim.   Child support cases are the best example.[7]

7. On the topic of orders to pay money with potential for contempt enforcement, see § 2.8(2) below.

Chapter 2

EQUITY AND NONMONETARY REMEDIES

Analysis

A. HISTORY, DEVELOPMENT AND MEANINGS OF EQUITY

Sec.
2.1   Introduction to Equity and Equitable Remedies.
    2.1(1) An Introductory Overview.
    2.1(2) Equitable Remedies.
    2.1(3) Meanings of Equity.
2.2   The Development of the Equity Court.
2.3   Substantive Rules Developed From Ethical Principles of Equity.
    2.3(1) The Remedial and the Substantive.
    2.3(2) Equity's Place in the Law of Uses and Trusts.
    2.3(3) Equity's Place in the Law of Mortgages.
    2.3(4) Equitable Conversion and Other Substantive Equity.
    2.3(5) Substantive Equitable Defenses: Equitable Estoppel and Similar Conceptions.

B. DISCRETION IN EQUITY

2.4   The Role of Discretion: Limiting and Tailoring Equitable Relief on Ethical Grounds.
    2.4(1) In Summary.
    2.4(2) Unclean Hands.
    2.4(3) Contract Defenses in Equity.
    2.4(4) Laches.
    2.4(5) Balancing Equities, Hardships and Public Interests.
    2.4(6) Measuring, Shaping, or Tailoring the Remedy.
    2.4(7) The Role of Equitable Discretion in Equity.
2.5   Remedial Limits Based on Power and Policy: Adequacy and Practicability.
    2.5(1) Adequacy of Legal Remedy or the Irreparable Harm Rule.
    2.5(2) Establishing Irreparable Harm.
    2.5(3) The Adequacy Test Today: Reality and Debate.
    2.5(4) Practicality and Public Policy as Limits on or Guides to Equitable Remedies.

C. PROCEDURES, JURISDICTION, AND ENFORCEMENT

2.6   Law and Equity Today—The Merger of Law and Equity and the Right of Jury Trial.
    2.6(1) The Merger of Law and Equity.
    2.6(2) Merger and Jury Trial—Equity Jury Rules.
    2.6(3) Characterizing a Case: Equitable or Legal?
    2.6(4) Jury Trial in Mixed Law and Equity Cases.
    2.6(5) Effect of Jury Trial on Tailoring or Modifying the Decree.

Sec.
2.7 "Jurisdictional" Issues in Equity Courts.
2.8 Enforcement of Equity Decrees.
  2.8(1) Methods of Enforcement.
  2.8(2) Sanctions for Contempt.
  2.8(3) Enforcement of Equity Decrees by Contempt Powers—Civil vs. Criminal.
  2.8(4) Consequences of the Criminal Contempt Classification.
  2.8(5) Persons Subject to Contempt.
  2.8(6) Review: The Collateral Bar Rule.
  2.8(7) Inability to Comply and Related Defenses.
  2.8(8) Modification of Decrees.

D. INJUNCTIONS

2.9 Permanent Injunctions.
  2.9(1) Injunctions Generally.
  2.9(2) Bases for Grant or Denial of Injunctive Relief.
  2.9(3) Subject Matter: Injunctions Protecting or Limiting Property and Economic Rights.
  2.9(4) Subject Matter: Injunctions Facilitating Procedure, Tactics, or Review.
  2.9(5) Subject Matter: Injunctions Protecting Personal Rights.
2.10 Statutory Injunctions.
2.11 Provisional Injunctions and Other Injunctive Procedures.
  2.11(1) Preliminary Injunctions and Temporary Restraining Orders Generally.
  2.11(2) Standards for Issuance of Provisional Injunctive Orders.
  2.11(3) The Security Requirement.
  2.11(4) Judicial Review of Injunctions.

———————

A. HISTORY, DEVELOPMENT AND MEANINGS OF EQUITY

§ 2.1 Introduction to Equity and Equitable Remedies

§ 2.1(1) An Introductory Overview

Historical Law and Equity Court Systems

Two systems of courts once existed in Anglo–American law. One court system was that of the law courts, presided over by judges. The other was that of the equity court, presided over by the Chancellor.[1] The Chancellor invented a body of substantive rules which in effect (but not in theory) could trump the rules of the law courts. More importantly for remedies, the Chancellors also invented remedies. Even today, when the two systems of courts are substantially merged, lawyers speak of "legal" remedies, meaning those traditionally recognized by the old separate law courts, and "equitable" remedies, meaning those distinctive remedies utilized by the Chancellors.

§ 2.1(1)

1. Some other minor courts in England exercised "equity" powers, but for most purposes it is correct to speak of "the" equity court, meaning the Court of Chancery.

Coercive Remedies in Equity

Equity courts traditionally awarded and continue to award a variety of remedies. Some equitable remedies are restitutionary, in money or otherwise.[2] Some are declaratory remedies. Most often, however, equitable remedies are coercive. The coercive remedies in equity are variants of the injunction.[3] The injunction is a personal order to the defendant. It is not merely a judgment such as the law courts might issue. It did not merely declare the defendant's debt or obligation, but instead commanded the defendant to do or refrain from a specified act. For example, the defendant might be enjoined to cease acts that constitute a nuisance,[4] or enjoined to remove boulders wrongly deposited on the plaintiff's land.[5] Variations on the injunctive remedy will quickly appear. The essence of the remedy in most instances, however, is the *in personam* order, enforced by the distinctive power of contempt.

Contempt in Equity

These coercive remedies were distinctive. They were enforced by the power of contempt if necessary. That is, the defendant might be fined or imprisoned for failure to comply with the order and might be held in prison until he complied or indicated a willingness to do so.[6] The old separate law courts did not issue injunctive orders; they rendered judgments instead. The law courts did not seek to enforce their orders by contempt powers, but by seizure of property.

Substantive Law in Equity

The separate equity court also developed a body of substantive law, including much of the law of mortgages and trusts.[7] Some of the substantive law rules developed by equity courts are important to an understanding of remedies. For the moment, however, the important point is more limited. It is that the body of rules and doctrines that make up "equity," has both a substantive and a remedial side, a distinction that turns out to be important.

Procedure in Equity

Separate equity courts also had a procedural side and some of it survives in today's merged court system. Equity procedure was a substantial advance over trial by wager of law, because the Chancellor in equity actually concerned himself with the evidence of witnesses. The Chancellor (or his deputy) sat as a single judge who was both trier of facts and law.[8] The parties got no jury trial in Chancery. The non-jury trial remains today one of the three or four most outstanding characteristics of an "equity" trial today.[9]

2. For restitutionary remedies, see Chapter 4 generally.

3. See generally § 2.9 below.

4. See § 5.7 below.

5. Wheelock v. Noonan, 108 N.Y. 179, 15 N.E. 67 (1888); § 5.5 below.

6. See § 2.8 below.

7. See § 2.3 below.

8. On traditional equity procedure and its difference from the procedure of the law courts, see F.W. Maitland, Equity (1932).

9. See § 2.6 below.

Discretion in Equity

One other striking characteristic of equity and equitable remedies is a high degree of discretion.[10] The legal system, the system of the law courts, emphasizes rights. The equity system treats access to its remedies as at least in part a privilege. Even if a plaintiff makes out a case for relief according to all the preexisting rules, the court of equity may in its discretion refuse its aid. Equity courts saw their discretion as a reflection of their flexibility and as a means to justice apart from law. Law courts at times saw it as a kind of lawlessness. Both were partly right. Today the two "systems" are quite a bit alike, but the difference between right and privilege remains not only in the language of the courts but also in many actual decisions that turn on equitable discretion.

—Equitable Defenses

In particular, equitable relief is likely to be denied if the plaintiff is subject to "equitable defenses," as where he "comes into court with unclean hands," [11] or is guilty of laches by delay in enforcing his rights.[12] Some equitable defenses, such as estoppel, have been adopted in purely legal actions.[13] Others, such as defenses or partial defenses based on hardship to the defendant, remain primarily equitable, to be invoked only to defeat an equitable remedy.[14]

—Measure of Relief

Discretion as to equitable remedies goes beyond the power to deny relief; it extends as well to the power of shaping relief, determining its extent, scope, and particular incidents. For example, an injunction might be shaped to compel the defendant to cease operating a polluting factory, or it might instead only compel the defendant to reduce the amount of pollutants.[15]

Adequacy of Legal Remedy or Irreparable Harm Test

One of the chief remedial doctrines of equity is called the adequacy test or the irreparable harm rule.[16] If equity created a substantive right not recognized at law, then equity would create whatever remedy it thought appropriate. The adequacy of legal remedies as enforced by law courts was of no concern. But if the plaintiff's substantive right was one created by the law courts in the first place, then what was equity's role? The plaintiff who sought to enjoin a trespass was not asking equity to recognize some new substantive right; the plaintiff's property right was already recognized by law courts. In such a case the plaintiff was only asking for an *equitable* remedy to enforce a *legal* right. In those cases the equity courts traditionally said that the equitable remedy would be granted only if the legal remedy was inadequate. Put in more forceful language, equity would not grant a remedy for a legal right unless, without the equitable remedy, the plaintiff would suffer irreparable harm.

---

10. See § 2.4 below.

11. See § 2.4(2) below.

12. See § 2.4(4) below.

13. See § 2.3(5) below.

14. See § 2.4(5) below.

15. See §§ 2.4(6) & 5.7(3) below.

16. See generally § 2.5 below. For the adequacy test in contract (specific performance) cases, see § 12.8 below.

So a whole body of decision concerns the problem of what counts as irreparable harm or inadequate legal remedy. Since the 1970s, a new issue has arisen. Writers now question the adequacy rule.[17] Some say it should not exist at all, others say that in reality it does not exist, or not in any substantial way.[18] A substantial portion of "equity" law deals with one or more of these adequacy-irreparability questions.

Merger of Law and Equity

In the federal court system and in most state court systems today, the separate courts of law and equity have long since been merged into a single court of general jurisdiction.[19] That court exercises the powers and grants the remedies of both the old kinds of courts. The plaintiff might sue to enjoin the defendant's repeated trespasses and in the same case ask for damages for harm already done by past trespasses and the judge might grant both kinds of relief.

In the light of this merger, why bother to label a claim as "equitable" or "legal"? What difference does it make? First, if the plaintiff claims a purely coercive equitable remedy and nothing more, the trial will be a non-jury trial, just as it was when the plaintiff sought such a remedy in a separate equity court. (If the plaintiff claims both an equitable and a legal remedy, such as an injunction and damages, the jury trial issue becomes more complicated, but that point can wait.)[20] Second, to the extent that the plaintiff claims an equitable remedy, the trial judge will enjoy great discretion to refuse the remedy or to limit it. Whether this should be so is another matter.

Terminology: "Equity"

The merger of law and equity powers makes it anomalous to refer to "equitable" remedies and some writers try to avoid such terms. Because equitable remedies are usually coercive, the term coercive remedy can be substituted for the term equitable remedy, as it sometimes is in this treatise. Professional usage changes slowly, however, so sometimes the term equitable remedy or some similar term will be used here to refer to remedies that, historically, were separately administered and may still have distinctive qualities associated with coercion and discretion.

§ 2.1(2) Equitable Remedies

Coercive Remedies

Injunctive relief. The most common equitable remedies are coercive. They are intended to force the defendant to act or to cease from acting in specified ways. The most general term for a coercive remedy is "injunction."[1] The defendant is enjoined by a prohibitory injunction to refrain from doing specified acts; or he is commanded by a mandatory injunction to carry out specified acts. Sometimes provisional injunctive orders are grant-

---

17. See §§ 2.5(3) & 12.8 below.

18. Laycock, The Death of the Irreparable Injury Rule (1991); Laycock, The Death of the Irreparable Injury Rule, 103 Harv.L.Rev. 687 (1990).

19. See § 2.6 below.

20. See §§ 2.6(3) & 2.6(4) below.

§ 2.1(2)

1. On injunctions generally, see § 2.9 below.

ed to protect the plaintiff before a full scale trial, in which case the injunction may be referred to as a preliminary injunction or a temporary restraining order.[2] In all these cases, the injunctive order carries an implicit threat: failure to comply can lead to a sanction for contempt of court.[3]

Example of injunctive relief. The injunction can be seen at work when the judge orders the defendant to cease a repeated trespass,[4] or to cease acts that constitute a nuisance.[5] The injunction is often especially important when the defendant in some way interferes with the plaintiff's economic opportunities. So the injunction is often used to stop trademark infringement,[6] or misappropriation of the plaintiff's intangible work product,[7] and simple interference with contract.[8] Any systematic violation of the plaintiff's civil rights is likely to call for injunctive relief, too, and restructuring of major institutions of society initiated by injunction which compels integration of schools, or minimum standards of humane treatment for persons held in the state's custody.[9]

Injunctions under other names. Sometimes *in personam,* injunctive orders are given names that refer to their factual context. Their injunctive character, however, remains affected by the label. The plaintiff who is discharged from employment as a result of job discrimination may be entitled to a remedy often called "reinstatement." [10] Reinstatement is specific relief and it is backed by the power of compulsion through contempt sanctions. When the order is written to reinstate the plaintiff in the job, its injunctive character becomes apparent.

Another example is the interpleader case. When two or more persons assert conflicting claims against the plaintiff, the plaintiff is in danger of a double liability as well as the cost of defending many suits. For example, if two people claim to be the named beneficiary of a life insurance policy, the insurer should only pay one of them, but if they sue in different courts, different juries and judges might hold the insurer liable to each. In this situation the insurer might seek an injunction to compel all claims to be brought in a single suit. This is definitely an injunction, but it travels under the descriptive name of interpleader.[11]

A third example is the cancellation of instruments. Equity might order a defendant to surrender up a document for cancellation, and the entire case is likely to be characterized and digested as a case of cancellation. But cancellation, too, may entail the use of the injunction and coercive penalties if necessary to force actual surrender of the document or to direct an official to make changes in an official record.[12]

2. See § 2.11 below.

3. Contempt: § 2.8 below.

4. See for example, § 5.5 below.

5. See § 5.7 generally.

6. See § 6.4(5).

7. See § 6.5(3) below.

8. See § 6.6(4) below.

9. See § 7.4(4) below.

10. See § 6.10(4).

11. See § 2.9(4) below.

12. E.g., First Family Mortgage Corp. of Florida v. White, 549 So.2d 1049 (Fla.App. 1989) (mortgage satisfaction canceled, mortgage reinstated after mortgagee mistakenly satisfied the mortgage); Armstrong v. Dantoni, 19 So.2d 293 (La.App.1944) (mortgage canceled when it appeared that vendor did not have title to the land sold and subject to mortgage).

Specific performance. One form of the injunction is usually called by the name of specific performance. Specific performance is an injunctive order compelling the defendant to perform his contract (not merely to pay damages for breach).[13] The most common example is the order to convey land as promised by a valid contract,[14] but some other contracts are specifically enforced, too.[15]

Declaratory Remedies

Some equitable remedies were injunctive in form but declaratory in effect. A declaratory judgment provides an authoritative declaration of the parties' disputed rights. For example, the parties might have different interpretations of a contract. If neither wants to breach, it will be helpful if they can obtain a judicial decision about what the contract requires.[16] The declaratory judgment is now an established remedy by federal [17] and state statutes.[18] Before the statutes were passed, however, equity sometimes achieved a declaratory judgment effect by issuing some form of injunctive order.

Many claims in equity for rescission of a transaction or cancellation of an instrument,[19] claims for reformation,[20] and interpleader,[21] had as their major purpose a declaration of rights, so that the plaintiff might proceed with an intelligent understanding of what he could and could not legally do.[22] Such claims still exist in equity, as where the plaintiff seeks to enjoin the enforcement of a statute alleged to be unconstitutional.[23] In many instances, though he does indeed wish an injunction, his main purpose is to test the constitutionality. He knows that if he establishes the invalidity of the law, the injunction is usually not needed, so a major function of the claim is to obtain an authoritative pronouncement about the law's validity. In this and other cases, the availability today of a declaratory judgment under the declaratory judgment statutes has slowly eroded the need for coercive relief, though such relief may still be granted where needed.

Restitutionary Remedies

Restitution is a large topic in itself.[24] It includes all cases in which the plaintiff can recover things or money to prevent the defendant's unjust

---

13. See § 12.8 below.

14. See § 12.11(3) below.

15. See §§ 12.12(3) (in favor of land seller); 12.16(7) (chattel buyer); 12.17(7) (chattel seller, price action); 12.18 (lease of goods); 12.-19(3) (building, construction contracts); 12.-22(2) (employer's partial specific enforcement of employee's covenants not to work for others); 12.23 (arbitration contract).

16. Further on declaratory judgments, see § 12.8(7) below.

17. 28 U.S.C.A. § 2201(a).

18. Most states have adopted the declaratory act, and those that have not sometimes have declaratory judgment acts of their own. See 9A Uniform L.Ann. (1965) for a list of those states having the Uniform Act.

19. For examples of rescission, see § 9.3 below (fraud). When the rescinded transac-

tion was represented in a document that might be transferred to a bona fide purchaser or that was placed on public records, rescission alone would not suffice; it would be necessary to order actual cancellation of the document. The latter is the injunctive portion of the rescission; the decision to rescind itself is merely declaratory.

20. See §§ 9.5 & 11.6(1)–11.6(3) below.

21. See § 2.9(4) below.

22. This point is made in several places in E. Borchard, Declaratory Judgments (2d ed. 1941).

23. Not always with success, see § 2.9(4) below.

24. On restitution generally, see Chapter 4 below. Restitution is frequently an issue in contract cases when the contract is breached.

enrichment. The fundamental idea of restitution is that the defendant must restore, (make restitution of) something which, in good conscience, belongs to the plaintiff.[25] A familiar example occurs when a contract is rescinded. In such a case, each party must make restitution of what she received under the contract. A less obvious example is reformation, in which equity powers might be used to reform or re-write a contract or deed to make it conform to the parties' true agreement. Such a reformation is restitutionary in that it takes from the defendant a spurious contract to which he was never entitled. Restitution is awarded in many other and quite different kinds of cases and measured in different ways as well.

Detailed discussion of restitutionary remedies can wait for discussion in Chapter 4. Here it is enough to recognize that both law courts and equity courts made restitutionary awards or orders, but that the traditional equity versions of restitution were usually distinct from the law versions.[26] The moral basis of restitution was the same both for law and for equity courts: the defendant had something which in equity in good conscience belonged to the plaintiff, and the defendant must be made to disgorge it. But in the equity versions of restitution, restoration might be enforced, implicitly or explicitly, by equity's coercive powers. That is, the injunctive order or the threat of it lay behind the operation of restitution in equity. One case will suffice as an illustration, and other equitable aspects of restitution can be left for consideration later.

Suppose that the defendant is an employee and that the plaintiff is the employer. The defendant secretly uses $100,000 of the plaintiff's business funds to purchase Blackacre in his own name. When the plaintiff discovers this embezzlement, she wants restitution. Money restitution of the $100,000 might be preferable in some cases, and if so, the plaintiff can easily enforce the money claim "at law," that is, without resort to any special equity powers.

But equity courts recognized that if the plaintiff's money purchased Blackacre, then in an "equitable" sense, the plaintiff was the "owner" of Blackacre itself. In this situation equity could treat the defendant as a trustee of Blackacre, that is, as if he were holding Blackacre on behalf of the plaintiff. The point is not limited to embezzlement cases. For example, one who gains Blackacre by fraud[27] or duress[28] or undue influence[29] may be subjected to the same constructive trust. Having declared the defendant to be a constructive trustee, equity courts would then order him to convey Blackacre to the plaintiff. If Blackacre were by that time worth more than $100,000, the plaintiff might much prefer this constructive trust remedy.

The important thing here is that even in these restitutionary remedies, equity characteristically operated through an element of compulsion or coercion. Whether the equitable remedy is called restitution, interpleader, or specific performance, then, at root it is commonly an injunction in some form.

See generally § 12.7 below; and also when it proves to be unenforceable. See Chapter 13 generally. Mistake, Chapter 11, and fraud, Chapter 9, are frequently grounds for restitution as well.

25. See § 4.1(1) below.

26. See § 4.2 (law) and § 4.3 (equity).

27. See § 9.3(4) below.

28. See § 10.2 below.

29. See § 10.3 below.

§ 2.1(3) Meanings of Equity

The preceding subsection showed that equitable remedies usually contain a coercive or injunctive element. So if the plaintiff seeks an injunction, it is easy to say that she is seeking equitable relief. However, the terms *equity* and *equitable* are not always used to refer to remedial characteristics of a case. Instead, the terms are sometimes given a quite different meaning. Two important questions are bound up in the definitions or connotations of these terms. One question asks what different meanings such terms have. The second question asks why it matters, given that law courts and equity courts have merged and that in most states one court administers a unitary system of justice. The answer to the second question turns in part on the different meanings of *equitable,* which sometimes refers to fairness, sometimes to the juridical mass of equity precedent, sometimes to remedies. First consider the different meanings of equity and equitable, and then consider when and why it matters that a case, claim, or defense is equitable.

Meanings of Equity and "Equitable"

Fairness, morality, and flexibility. One group of ideas associated with the term equity suggests fairness and moral quality. The law of fiduciary and confidential relationships developed by equity courts and carried on today in many forms, derived from equity's early emphasis on moral rectitude. When an elderly client gives her estate to her lawyer in whom she reposes the utmost confidence and trust, equity became suspicious and might force the lawyer to disgorge the estate even though he had good legal title.[1]

This idea that equity means moral rectitude is frequently coupled with the idea of flexibility. Equity is said to be flexible rather than rigid, its interest justice rather than law. Suppose a tenant is one day late in paying her rent, as the result, say, of a mistake or an accident that put her in the hospital. The landlord seeks to oust her in accord with the terms of the lease. A court may say that equity relieves from a forfeiture, allow the tenant to pay the landlord and keep the tenancy.[2] Something very much like this is in fact the source of the law of mortgages, which equity courts invented to prevent forfeitures of land when a debtor was late in paying the debt.[3] Illustrations like these suggest both fairness and flexibility, and also attention to the inequality of the parties.

When a decision is explained on the ground that it is equitable in the sense that it is fair, compassionate, or flexible, as in the forfeiture example, several things stand out. First, equity courts originated such approaches to judicial decision making. Second, the judge may give "equity" as a *reason for the decision* regardless whether the case itself is equitable or not. Third, to say that equity should relieve the tenant from a forfeiture is not to say anything about equity courts or equity procedure, perhaps not even about remedies; it is to say that commonly accepted feelings of fairness demand more flexibility than pure, straight-faced "law" would allow. In other

---

§ 2.1(3)

1. See §§ 10.3 & 10.4 below on undue influence and confidential relationships generally.

2. E.g., Thomas v. Given, 75 Ariz. 68, 251 P.2d 887 (1952). Compare the equity maxims, § 2.3(4) below.

3. See § 2.3(3) below.

words, *equity* and *equitable* in this sense appeal to substantive grounds for action.

To keep a balanced perception of equity's flexibility and justice, however, it is important to notice that "law" courts might get the same result in some cases without the moralistic language or the claim to a wide-ranging discretion: a law court might simply say that time is not of the essence so a late payment is not a substantial breach. In addition, legal remedies like damages might be *more* rather than less flexible than equitable remedies like specific performance in some cases.[4] For example, the damages remedy might be adjusted downward to reflect the fact that some of the harm could have been avoided by the plaintiff.[5]

The body of equity precedent, doctrine, and attitude. In another sense, the term equitable refers simply to the body of precedent or practice or attitude of equity courts. Since that body of work often turned on fairness notions, the two ways of speaking about equity may be equivalent in some cases. But equity courts developed distinctive procedures, which were of course "equitable" in the sense that they were connected to the equity court, but not necessarily any more moral than some alternatives.[6] In addition, equity courts developed some more or less specific rules that are not obviously related to equity in the sense of fairness and flexibility. So you can read such strange locutions as "equitable conversion"[7] and "equitable fraud."[8] Equitable fraud is of course not a reference to a kind of fraud that is fair, moral or flexible. It refers to conduct a Chancellor historically would recognize as "fraud" even though law courts would not.

When lawyers and judges use equity and equitable to refer to the whole body of equitable precedent or to some particular portion of it, only someone who knows the equity precedent can understand the exact meaning of the term. We can say, however, that when the terms equity and equitable refer to a body of precedent or attitudes of the Chancellors, that does not necessarily make the case "equitable" in any other sense at all. For instance, equitable estoppel originated in equity, but judges deciding purely "law" issues apply the equitable estoppel doctrine quite readily.[9] So in a case that is tried to a jury as a "law" case, the judge might still make important decisions turn on equitable estoppel or other equity doctrines.

Distinctive remedies. As already indicated, the Chancellor's remedies were quite different from those "at law." The term equitable, when applied to a remedy, usually has a precise meaning. It means a remedy based on a personal order, commanding specified conduct of the defendant, such an

---

4. See Yorio, A Defense of Equitable Defenses, 51 Ohio St.L.J. 1201 (1991).

5. The avoidable consequences rules require the plaintiff to minimize damages where that is reasonable. See § 3.9 below. Specific performance, on the other hand, might be an all-or-nothing proposition.

6. As to the characteristics of the equity hearing, see F. Maitland, Equity 5 (Rev. ed. 1936, 1969 reprint); W. Clephane, Equity Pleading and Practice 287–292 (1926). So far as equity disdained primitive modes of trial by battle, the equity procedure might be said to

be more fair or moral. But a trial without a jury, and by a judge who invariably insists on written, not oral testimony, is not a procedure that has any particular moral quality.

7. See § 2.3(4) below.

8. E.g., Stearns v. Emery–Waterhouse Co., 596 A.2d 72 (Me.1991) ("a promisor's acceptance of partial performance may estop a defense under the statute on the ground of equitable fraud").

9. See § 2.3(5) below.

injunction, an order for specific performance, or a constructive trust or similar remedy coupled with an in personam order.[10]

When the plaintiff's complaint asks for an equitable remedy and no other, the case is indisputably an equitable one. It will invoke "equity" in the first sense of fairness and morality, and equity procedures and attitudes and precedent, such as nonjury trials and discretionary dismissals.

Effect of Determination that a Claim or Defense is Equitable

What makes a claim "equitable" today? The powers of law courts and those of equity courts were combined long ago, in reforms that began about 1850. The trial courts of general jurisdiction in almost all states now exercise both kinds of powers, as do the Federal District Courts. So to say that a case or a claim within a case is "equitable" does not mean that the plaintiff sues in a separate court. What, then, is the effect of saying that a claim or defense is equitable? The answer is that the effect depends on the sense in which "equitable" is used.

Equitable in the sense of fair, moral, or just. When the term "equitable" is used only to describe the moral basis of a claim or defense, the conclusion that the claim is equitable has no necessary legal effect on the remedy or on the procedure. Take this sentence: "The defendant stole the plaintiff's watch, worth only $10, but the defendant sold it for $100; it is only just and equitable that the defendant pay the plaintiff the $100. Good conscience demands it." In these sentences, the writer is stating a substantive ground for relief. He is not addressing the remedy. In fact, in such cases as those described in this sentence, the plaintiff can simply sue for the money ($100) and recover it "at law," with a jury trial if he wishes. It is not wrong to say that such a claim is "equitable," but it is equitable only in a very limited way: it appeals to "the equities," the sense of justice. It does not necessarily involve equity remedies, equitable defenses, or equitable procedures like the non-jury trial.[11]

Equitable in the sense that an equitable remedy is sought. In contrast to the substantive uses of the term "equitable," courts and lawyers often use the term much more precisely to mean that the plaintiff has sought an equitable remedy, usually one involving coercive elements. When that is the case, there are two major legal effects of concluding that the case, claim or remedy is equitable.

First, when the plaintiff asserts an equitable remedy, equitable defenses can be invoked even if they could not be invoked against a "legal" claim. More broadly, the judge will feel free to exercise discretion in denying the remedy and, if she grants it, in shaping the remedy.

Second, subject to an important exception, if the plaintiff claims an equitable remedy, then neither party has a right to a jury trial. If the plaintiff seeks only damages for the defendant's trespass, the case goes to a jury on demand; if the plaintiff seeks only an injunction to prevent future

---

10. See § 2.1(2) above.

11. In some state courts, the appeal to equitable principles or at least to substantive equitable rules is enough to make the case equitable for jury trial purposes, so that, for example, mortgage foreclosure, a substantive law developed in historic equity courts, may call for a non-jury trial.

trespasses, the case is tried to the judge sitting as Chancellor and without a jury. The exception to the non-jury trial rule occurs if both remedies are sought together, damages for the past trespass and injunction to prevent the future trespass. In the federal system, all facts relevant to both remedies are tried to a jury.[12]

Strategic possibilities. For a plaintiff with feasible options about the type of relief that is acceptable, the existence of two systems of remedies offers strategic possibilities. The most obvious of these is the possibility that the plaintiff can elect either to have or to avoid a jury, simply by choosing an equitable or a legal remedy.

§ 2.2   The Development of the Equity Court[1]

The Chancellor as Writ Maker

Long before the Chancellor of England was a judge of an equity court,[2] he was an administrator. An understanding of modern equity still depends on an understanding of some of the roles he played.[3]

First of all, the medieval chancellor was a high minister of the king, more closely analogous to a prime minister than to anything else we are familiar with. He was often a Bishop of the Church. As a kind of prime minister, the Chancellor did the sort of administrative work ministers do—he was an advisor, negotiator, ambassador, propagandist and stand-in for the king.

The other task of the medieval chancellor was more routine. Medieval England was not a highly literate society. Many of the clergy, however, could write, and the chancellor as a literate man served not only as a "prime minister", but also as head of the royal writing department, supervising literate clerks. Writings from the king to subjects or officers were drawn up in the chancery. One important kind of writing drawn up in Chancery was the original writ—the document that was used to begin a common law action. Some forms of action were quite common and many of the writs for such actions were drawn by low level clerks and given as a matter of course, each based on some more or less standard form. Others were a bit more novel and hence controversial—controversial because any new writ was an assertion of power in the king's courts, and any assertion of power in the king's courts took away power from the lords or other local influences.

12. See § 2.6 below.

§ 2.2

1. See W. Holdsworth, History of English Law 395–477 (1922) (the Court of Chancery, including its bankruptcy jurisdiction); S.F.C. Milsom, Historical Foundations of the Common Law, Chapter 4, pp. 82–96 (2d ed. 1980) (succinct, clear treatment); F.W. Maitland, Equity 1–11 (Rev. by John Brunyate 1969); E. Morgan, Introduction to the Study of Law 9–13 (1926); 1 G. Spence, Equitable Jurisdiction of the Court of Chancery, 321–354 (1846, reprinted 1981) (also reprinted in 2 Select Essays in Anglo–American Legal History 219

(1908)); W. Baildon, Introduction to Select Cases in Chancery, 1364–1471 (Selden Society v. 10, 1896).

2. Various other courts besides chancery had some degree of equitable power at one time or another, usually minor. These courts are not significant in the history of equity and are not considered here. See G. Spence, supra n. 1 at 349–354.

3. Not surprisingly, the Chancellor was historically a male. The invariant use of the pronoun "he" is historically correct in this section.

When the plaintiff came to the chancery for help with an unusual set of facts to which the old writs did not fit, the chancellor sometimes issued a new kind of writ.

Limits on the Effectiveness of Common Law Courts

The common law was not radical, innovative or even moderately responsive as was indicated by the fact that it could not invent the simple contract in less than two or three hundred years.[4] The sluggishness of the common law might not have resulted from the Provisions of Oxford, but that enactment illustrated some of the pressure upon the courts and the central administration to respect local rights and local administration of justice. The Statute of Westminster might not have been responsible for the writ of Trespass on the Case, but it did illustrate the counter-thrust—slow analogical development of national power in the common law courts.

Thus the situation as it existed in, say, the year 1300, was a system of common law courts with limited powers: they could grow and develop, but only over long generations. For the special case that did not fit the existing writs and was not similar enough to the old ones, some special aid was required if national justice was to be obtained. As in many cases since that time, national justice might furnish the only justice available, if the plaintiff's complaint was against the local lord, or if it was against the king's own agents or officers. This was where the chancellor's second role, as an official of high power in the central administration, became important.

The Chancellor as a Political Power

The chancellor of the medieval period was a powerful man. He was, first of all, a member of the Council and sat there with other lords of the realm. In addition, the chancellor was often a prelate with the weight of the church behind him. But beyond all this, he was the king's right hand man and acted in the king's name on many occasions.

The king as the fountain of justice would be petitioned by subjects for political favors, that is, for help where law did not reach.

The chancellor was naturally a little cautious about interfering with powerful persons. Somewhere along the line he developed two habits of considerable importance. One habit was to try to get the facts before he acted. Since he was acting administratively or politically, it did not occur to him to use juries or to go through some elaborate feudal wager of law; he wanted the facts, so he got witnesses before him and asked them questions about the petition of the plaintiff, going through each assertion of the petition.

The other habit developed by the chancellor along the way was the habit of giving very pious reasons for his actions. Since he did not act under "law", but apart from it, he needed both power and propaganda to back him up, and he in fact had them both. The propaganda—an appeal to justice, conscience, and religion—was essentially religious. The power was essentially royal. The chancellor, so to speak, carried a Bible in a mailed fist.

---

4. See § 4.2(3) below.

The Chancellor as a Judge

The chancellor's court. Over a long period of time, the chancellor's role evolved. He gradually became not merely an administrative official dispensing political favors, but a judge deciding facts and applying more or less definite principles to those facts. Petitioners, aware that the king would refer their petitions to the chancellor, began to go directly to him. His procedures became standardized, his substantive principles developed into a vague but more or less coherent body, and he developed devices for enforcing his orders, as well as theories to support his rules.

The distinction between political action and judicial action was not very clear in medieval England and even the common law courts sometimes entertained bills for special relief, so that on occasion they, too, looked a little like "equity courts".[5] However, by the 15th century the chancellor was clearly a judge, recognized as such and acting as such: he was acting regularly in a class of cases where the common law courts or the common law itself seemed inadequate to him, and acting without specific authority from the king to hear the particular case.

The chancellor's procedure. The chancellor's judicial work was rather different from that of the common law judges in several important respects. First, the suit in equity—that was in chancery court—was originated by petition or bill, rather than by a writ. Where the writ used in law courts was full of forms, the petition was full of allegations of fact and a certain amount of argumentation. The writ of Trespass varied little from one case to another. The petition to the chancellor for equity was formal in the sense that it contained repeated elements—humble, pious and piteous cries of the downtrodden [6]—but it was nevertheless factual in the sense that it made particular charges or allegations that might vary from case to case.

Another difference was in the trial itself. The trial at law might have proceeded without any actual testimony at all, by elaborate pleading and counterpleading done orally, with a high chance of decision based upon one lawyer's technical slip. An equity trial commenced with a subpoena, that was, with an order to the defendant to appear "under penalty" of some punishment and to testify. Equity developed its own elaborate forms of pleading in due time, but in this simple essence at least, it introduced a strong emphasis on fact-gathering and fact-decision that permeated modern trials in both law and equity.

There was, of course, no jury. The chancellor had begun this business thinking of himself not as a judge, but as a politician or administrator, and naturally he had not called a jury in to help him administer his office. Later, however, it was apparent that the absence of a jury was a positive advantage in some cases, as where the petitioner's chief complaint about the law courts was that the defendant was rich and would bribe the juries.

---

5. Sayles, The Court of King's Bench in Law and History (Selden Society Lecture, 1959).

6. However, at a fairly early date, a businesslike tone appears in many petitions. For instance, the allegation that the defendant has got money belonging (in some sense) to the plaintiff, appeals to the chancellor because the common law remedies were aimed initially at the protection of land in a feudal economy and were not yet adapted to the protection of money in a society that was beginning to change its economic operations. See W. Baildon, Select Cases in Chancery, 1364–1471 (10 Selden Society 1896).

Later still, the absence of a jury suggested that more complex issues might be taken up than could readily be understood by randomly selected jurors.

Finally, the enforcement of equity decrees differed from the enforcements of judgments at law in a great many cases. Although equity could act against property where need be—by getting possession of it and selling it and disposing of the proceeds in a proper way—this method of enforcing judgments was more common to law courts. Equity tended to use the contempt power instead. This was consistent with equity's theory that it was acting *in personam,* as a pressure on the conscience of the defendant, not *in rem* as a declarer of law. Thus if the defendant's conscience was not moved enough for him to obey an equity decree, equity would likely imprison him until his conscience was so moved.[7]

The chancellor's rules. The chancellors eventually developed some specific rules for specific situations, but for many years equity was criticized as a lawless thing, where only the chancellor's discretion governed and there was no law by which to measure a person's rights. A general rule to do the right thing and follow good conscience didn't give much guidance. There was a lot to this criticism. The chancellors were mostly churchmen until after Henry VIII put Thomas More's head on a pike. As churchmen they tended to rely on unctuous sentiments about conscience, and as Selden pointed out, in the most famous of all comments about equity, the conscience of chancellors was as apt to vary as the length of their feet. Equity, he said, was a "roguish thing," for just that reason.[8]

On the other hand equity favored the things that society has always said it favored—some sort of fair dealing amongst all people, and relief from mistake, oppression, and fraud. Eventually some of these notions of fair play and good conscience resulted in several major institutions of the law. On purely moral grounds equity enforced simple contracts (after all, one should keep one's promises), created the law of uses and trusts (people should perform duties entrusted to them), and developed the law of mortgage security with the mortgagor's right of redemption (forfeiture of the borrower's land was a harsh thing). These aspects of equity are a reminder that major legal devices of a substantive nature could grow out of equity's efforts to enforce good conscience.

The chancellor's jurisdiction. Chief Justice Fuller is quoted as saying, perhaps with some implied criticism of a colleague: "Brother B. would codify all laws in an act of two sections: 1st, All people must be good; 2d, Courts of equity are hereby given full power and authority to enforce the provisions of

---

7. On contempt, see § 2.8, below.

8. J. Selden, Table Talk (Pollock Ed.1927). Selden's comment, made in the early 17th century, is given here in modernized spelling and punctuation:

Equity in law is to say that the spirit is in Religion, what ever one please to make it. Sometimes [equity] goes according to conscience, sometimes according to law, sometimes according to the rule of the Court.

Equity is a roguish thing. For law we have a measure, know what to trust to. Equity is according to the conscience of him that is Chancellor, and as that is larger or narrower, so is equity. Tis all one, as if they should make the standard for measure we call a foot to be the Chancellor's foot. What an uncertain measure this would be; one chancellor has a long foot, another a short foot, a third an indifferent foot; tis the same thing in the Chancellor's conscience.

this act." [9]   Such a statute would, of course, be an intolerable one in a free society. If equity had acted on any such roving commission to do good, it probably would not have survived, since practically everyone would have been frightened of a powerful court heaven-bent on goodliness—which might, as Selden had said, mean almost anything.

Equity never fell into this trap. In the first place, its major substantive efforts—enforcement of simple contracts on the ground of conscience, for example—seemed to serve other, more commercial or practical purposes as well as the stated purpose of good conscience. In the second place, equity purported to limit its activities to cases in which the law had proved in some manner inadequate. Sometimes equity's refusal to act is expressed in the phrase that says there was no equity jurisdiction. The term was unfortunate and misleading, as will be shown later.[10] However, it was a term that marked the fact that there were some limits on what equity would do and what it wouldn't do.

The chancellor's theory of power: The dual system and the in personam order. The English law from the 15th century onward, then, was a dual system of common law on one side and equity on the other. This is a simplification, since there were also courts of admiralty, and some remnants of the ecclesiastical courts, local courts and occasional special courts, such as the Star Chamber. Each of these applied its own legal rules, different from the legal rules of the law that applied in common to all Englishmen. Nevertheless, these other courts had some excuse and tradition: admiralty was an international law and a commercial one, and no state could afford to use its own traditions, especially if they were as arcane as some of those of the common law, in such a field. Equity, however, was for home consumption by English subjects, and it was a little difficult to know exactly why it was that the king's judges in the Common Pleas Court dictated one law, while the king's judge in Chancery dictated another.

The answer of the chancellors was that they were not speaking law at all; far be it from them to change the law of England. No; the chancellors were keeping the law intact and making personal orders to the defendant. The importance of this was enormous in the later development of equity, both substantively and remedially.

This notion converted equity's weakness—the lack of any hard rules—into its strength. The idea was that equity's pronouncements in an individual case did not make law; hence, the common law rule retained its generality and authority as "law". Equity's decree simply commanded an individual to act in some certain way. When he acted in that way, of course, he might have changed his legal status or his legal rights, but that would be by operation of "law". Equity did not therefore, change law, it changed the acts of persons. The law could ascribe whatever significance it liked to these acts.

What it meant was expressed in the phrase, by "equity acts *in personam*." The phrase was not entirely accurate because in some sense equity could act *in rem* by sequestering property and selling it if necessary. But

9. Gregory, Government by Injunction, 11 Harv.L.Rev. 487, 510 (1898).

10. On the meanings of jurisdiction see § 2.7 below.

equity did not act *in rem* by making or creating legal rules as the law of the land. It could not affect title to property (so it said); only law could do that. What equity could do was simple: it could tell a defendant, under pain of personal imprisonment, to use the law or legal rule in a particular *manner*. It could not say what counted as legal title, but it could say that if the defendant had such a title, he must convey it to the plaintiff.

The idea that equity acted *in personam* was an important one for describing the way an equity decree worked and the way it contrasted with a judgment at law. The equity decree would tell a defendant to do something, or not to do something, for example, to convey land. The judgment at law was a complete contrast. It told the defendant neither to act nor to avoid acting. It declared the law, as applied to his case. It said: the plaintiff owned Blackacre, and title was in him. Or the defendant owed the plaintiff thirty pounds. This was law-saying, not a personal order. Consequently, the court was not offended if the defendant did not pay the 30 pounds or turn over Blackacre. The court would enforce its judgment as the law, by taking some action with respect to property. The sheriff would put the defendant out of Blackacre and put the plaintiff in, or the defendant's goods would be sold to make money to pay the 30 pounds. But the defendant who ignored a judgment at law was not contumacious. He had ignored law, but he had not disobeyed a personal directive.

The defendant who failed to act as equity decreed, however, was in a different position. Equity commanded he convey Blackacre; it did not merely decide the ownership. The command was personal and there were echoes in it of the king's political power of an earlier era. When he disobeyed, there was something like lese majesty, and he was clamped in irons as punishment for his disobedience.

The difference between the judgment at law, which declared rights in things—*in rem*—and the decree in equity which commanded the defendant's conscience to act—*in personam*—was thus a very considerable one. The chancellors used it constantly to explain why there could be apparently contradictory systems at work on English soil, yielding different results: one was law, the other was merely a personal matter.

This *in personam* character showed up not only in the remedy—the injunction was a personal order to act or refrain from acting, while the money judgment at law was not—but also in the substantive development of equity. This latter requires a brief discussion, even in a book on remedies.

§ 2.3 Substantive Rules Developed From Ethical Principles of Equity

§ 2.3(1) The Remedial and the Substantive

Remedial Equity

Remedial rules historically derived from equity courts either created or barred a remedy, but did not affect the underlying right. For example, a plaintiff might assert his purely legal right to possession of land by asking equity to enjoin the defendant's trespass. The injunctive remedy was equitable, added as an alternative to the legal remedy of damages. No new right was created by equity courts in granting such an injunction. Instead, the right recognized at law was given an added remedy. Equitable defenses worked to deny rather than create a new remedy, but again, they left the underlying right intact and left the plaintiff to any legal remedies he might have.

Substantive Equity

Substantive equity is different in important ways. Substantive equity could create an entirely new right, not recognized in the old law courts. Similarly, substantive equity could deny *all* remedies, with the effect that it eliminated the underlying legal right as well as any equitable remedy. That would mean the plaintiff could not recover any remedy, either legal or equitable.

Although this treatise is addressed to remedies, not substantive law, equitable remedies may be understood partly in comparison to substantive equity. Perhaps more importantly, the meaning of the merger of law and equity becomes clear partly by distinguishing substantive and remedial equity. Some, but not all, substantive equity is sketched in this section.

Much of substantive equity derives from the duel role of the early Chancellors as both judge and bishop. Moral behavior and good conscience were the constantly stated guides for the chancellors in developing substantive rules. Two important fields of law, that of mortgages and that of trusts, grew out of these ideals of conscience, and from those fields sprung many modern equitable ideas. Relief from a forfeiture today [1] is a direct product of equity's role in developing the law of mortgages, and indeed, much of modern land finance is a result of that development. Likewise the modern law of fiduciary and confidential relationships,[2] of supreme importance in a wide range of contemporary decisions, is a product of equity's role in the law of trusts.

Equity's historic role in mortgages and trusts is summarized in the following two subsections.

§ 2.3(2) Equity's Place in the Law of Uses and Trusts [1]

[For the text of this section, see the unabridged Practitioner Treatise edition.]

§ 2.3(3) Equity's Place in the Law of Mortgages [1]

[For the text of this section, see the unabridged Practitioner Treatise edition.]

§ 2.3(4) Equitable Conversion and Other Substantive Equity

[Consult § 4.3(8) below and this section in the Practitioner Treatise edition.]

§ 2.3(5) Substantive Equitable Defenses: Equitable Estoppel and Similar Conceptions

A final illustration of a purely substantive equity is the estoppel concept and several close relations. This marks a considerable departure from the materials just discussed, because estoppel does not necessarily involve any form of equitable ownership. The word means simply that someone is "stopped" from claiming or saying something; usually he is stopped from saying the truth or claiming a lawful claim, and usually this is because of some prior inconsistent statement or activity.

X begins building a garage while N, a neighbor, stands by watching. N makes no objection, but when X completes the job, N says politely, "I think you have built the garage on my land." He then orders a survey and finds that it is indeed so. N then sues in equity to force removal of the offending structure. Almost certainly relief will be denied for one reason or another.[1] A court might say he is estopped from asserting the true location of the lot line, because his conduct (including silence here) misled X, and that if N is allowed to assert the truth now, this will combine with his earlier inconsistent conduct to cause harm to X. More moderately, N might merely be estopped to deny his own liability for the value of the improvements.[2]

First, the actor, who usually must have knowledge, notice or suspicion of the true facts,[4] communicates something to another in a misleading way, either by words, conduct or silence.[5] Second, the other in fact relies, and relies reasonably or justifiably, upon that communication.[6] And third, the other would be harmed materially if the actor is later permitted to assert any claim inconsistent with his earlier conduct.[7] A fourth element is that the actor knows, expects or foresees that the other would act upon the information given, or that a reasonable person in the actor's position would expect or foresee such action.[8]

Some other equitable defenses do not require reliance or prejudicial impact as a result of that reliance. The plaintiff might be barred by a knowing waiver of rights[9] or by "unclean hands,"[10] for example. Sometimes courts say they are barring a plaintiff because of estoppel even when the defendant has not relied or suffered prejudice in reliance on the appearances created by the plaintiff.[11] Such cases often appear to be waiver or

§ 2.3(5)

1. See § 5.10(4) below (balancing hardships and equities).

2. See § 5.8(3) below. Cf. Benedict v. Little, 288 Ala. 638, 264 So.2d 491, 495 (1972) (landowner who stood by while improver mistakenly added improvements to landowner's land estopped from denying liability for their value).

4. E.g., County of Sonoma v. Rex, 231 Cal. App.3d 1289, 282 Cal.Rptr. 796, 800 (1991); Post v. Commissioner of Dept. of Environmental Quality Engineering, 403 Mass. 29, 525 N.E.2d 666, 669 (1988). Knowledge of the facts does not imply that the party to be estopped is guilty of an intent to deceive. See the paragraph "Estoppel and Fraud," below.

5. See In re Marriage of Umphrey, 218 Cal.App.3d 647, 267 Cal.Rptr. 218, 222 (1990) (a "representation or promise"); First Fed. Sav. & Loan Ass'n v. Perry's Landing, Inc., 11 Ohio App.3d 135, 463 N.E.2d 636, 648 (1983) ("there must be something in the nature of a representation by words, acts, or silence"). The distinction between representations of law and fact was invoked in Chemical Bank v. Washington Public Power Supply System, 102 Wash.2d 874, 691 P.2d 524, 542 (1984), cert.

denied, 471 U.S. 1065, 105 S.Ct. 2140, 85 L.Ed.2d 497 (1985), where the court held that representations of law could not form the basis for an estoppel, at least on the facts of that case.

6. See Simineo v. Kelling, 199 Colo. 225, 607 P.2d 1289 (1980). Sometimes it is said that the party asserting estoppel must "lack knowledge of the true facts," E.g., Broadworth Realty Associates v. Chock 336 B'way Operating, Inc., 168 A.D.2d 299, 562 N.Y.S.2d 630 (1990). Ordinarily, however, this requirement would be covered by the requirement of reliance or the requirement of reasonable reliance.

11. Thus in Hershey v. Hershey, 467 N.W.2d 484 (S.D.1991) a father owed child support, but the mother concealed the child and herself for many years. Later she claimed child support. The father argued that she was estopped to claim support because of the concealment. The court approved the idea that the mother might be estopped, shifting to an implied waiver theory. Note that no misleading appearance was created and there was nothing upon which the father could rely. He lost an important right,

unclean hands cases in disguise. Put differently, the term estoppel is often used more loosely than might be expected.

Equitable estoppel originated in decisions of equity courts, as its name implies; but it has long since "worked over" into law. This means that estoppel, when established, affects not only equitable remedies, but also legal remedies. It is, in other words, a substantive doctrine which may bar the underlying right altogether, not merely the equitable enforcement of it.

Because estoppel is a substantive rule and can bar (or sometimes establish) a right, it is no surprise that courts have been reluctant to apply estoppel against governmental entities. Such a rule is especially appropriate when estoppel would interfere with acts of government or would effectively exempt the litigant from a government rule that ought to apply uniformly and even-handedly to all citizens.[12] Although the rule is formulated in various ways, the essence is that estoppel is not applied against governmental entities when to do so would frustrate or impede public policy.[13]

[*For discussion of estoppel compared to fraud, promissory estoppel, ratification and other doctrines, see this section in the Practitioner Treatise edition, vol. 1, pp. 84–90.*]

B. DISCRETION IN EQUITY

§ 2.4   The Role of Discretion: Limiting and Tailoring Equitable Relief on Ethical Grounds

§ 2.4(1) In Summary

Discretion to Deny or Limit Relief in Equity

When equitable relief is sought, courts claim the power to deny that relief as a matter of discretion. In some instances, discretion has been limited by appellate decisions, so that, for instance, specific performance is almost routinely granted in land sales contracts if the plaintiff prefers that remedy.[1] Discretion to deny or to limit equitable relief is normally invoked by considering an equitable defense which permits wide latitude in decision-making, or by "balancing" equities, hardships, and the interests of the public and of third persons. Discretion allows the court to grant full relief, deny all equitable relief and leave the plaintiff to her legal remedies, or to limit relief.

Equitable Defenses

Equitable defenses may be substantive or remedial. That is, they may bar the cause of action entirely, or bar only the equitable remedy. Most equitable defenses only bar the equitable remedy. As already shown, however, estoppel is an equitable defense that works in "legal" as well as "equitable" cases.[2]

The chief remedial defenses to equitable claims are the unclean hands[3] defenses and laches.[4] The plaintiff who comes into equity with "unclean

but he was not misled to his prejudice, so the case looks more like one of "unclean hands."

hands," may be denied equitable relief and so may the plaintiff who is "guilty" of unreasonable delay in protecting her right. Similarly, the plaintiff who has made an unconscionable deal may be denied equitable relief, but in theory still has full legal remedies.[5]

Balancing

Aside from these remedial defenses, equity has often followed a principle of balancing various ethical and hardship considerations.[6] Sometimes this balancing idea is a way in which economic considerations are taken into account.

The balancing idea is entirely different from the defense idea. It is quite possible, for example, that the plaintiff has delayed bringing suit, but not enough to warrant barring her completely by the laches defense. However, the court may wish to consider her delay along with other equitable factors, such as the fault, if any, of the plaintiff. It may also wish to balance the respective hardships to the parties. Even when an equitable defense does not bar the claim, the total balance of equities and hardships might do so. And vice versa: where equities strongly favor the plaintiff, a relatively minor inequity may not constitute a defense that bars the claim entirely, even though the same inequity might do so if the equities more strongly favored the defendant.

By balancing public interests and those of third persons, the courts are able to consider all the costs and all the benefits of the defendant's conduct and likewise all the costs and benefits of issuing an injunction. If the injunction benefits others besides the plaintiff, those benefits may be weighed in the balance in favor of the injunction.[7]

Measuring or Shaping the Remedy

Balancing of equities and hardships may lead the court to grant some equitable relief but not as much as the plaintiff might want. Put differently, the court has the power to measure, shape or tailor relief to fit its view of the balance of equities and hardships. For example, instead of granting an injunction to compel the defendant to stop a pollution nuisance, the court may grant the injunction only to take effect at a certain time in the future.[8]

The Appropriate Role of Discretion

Discretion of equity courts is long established. It makes possible decisions that are flexible, intuitive, and tailored to the particular case. It also makes possible decisions that are unanalyzed, unexplained, and un-thoughtful. The precise role for discretion of judges has not been worked out. Discretion of the chancellor originated in a society where authority counted for more than democracy, and the wishes of the powerful for more than their explanations. Two particular arguments about discretion have suggested that it should not be permitted to limit a remedy provided by statute,[9] and that it should not be used to grant the plaintiff more than her original entitlement.[10]

§ 2.4(2) Unclean Hands

General Rule and Its Effect

General rule. "One who comes into equity must come with clean hands." This maxim of equity courts states a general principle under which the plaintiff seeking equitable relief such as an injunction may be denied the equitable remedy on the basis of his "unclean hands"—that is, his misconduct—provided that misconduct is sufficiently related to his claim.

The unclean hands defense is closely related to other equitable defenses such as unconscionability or unfairness in contracts,[1] and even to equitable concerns over hardship. Almost any kind of conduct the chancellor may consider to be unethical or improper might suffice to bar the plaintiff's claim, even if the conduct is not actually illegal. The point, the courts often say, is not that the plaintiff's unclean hands furnish a "defense" to the defendant, but rather that the court itself wishes to avoid participating in iniquity.[2] For this reason, the issue may be raised by the court sua sponte even if counsel does not raise it.[3]

As a purely equitable defense. The most orthodox view of the unclean hands doctrine makes it an equitable defense, that is, one that can be raised to defeat an equitable remedy, but not one that defeats other remedies. Courts repeatedly refer to the defense in that light.[4] Some scholars think there is no justification for any separate doctrine of "unclean hands." If there is any justification for such a doctrine, however, it is that it may express the chancellor's discretion to deny a purely equitable remedy, while leaving the plaintiff full access to her legal remedies. Courts do not seem to limit themselves invariably to such a usage.

Spurious unclean hands cases: substantive meanings and pari delicto. The unclean hands phrase is too pithy and convenient; sometimes it is tossed on the conference table like a wild card in a poker game, used to mean whatever one needs it to mean. Sometimes it seems to mean only that some legal rule or policy opposes the plaintiff's claim and that both legal and equitable relief should be denied.[5] Used in this way, "unclean hands" is only one way of expressing a result that would be reached whether or not such a phrase or doctrine ever existed.

For example, the unclean hands doctrine may be invoked when the plaintiff has engaged in illegal activity and seeks to reap the fruits of his illegal conduct, but that situation is already covered by the pari delicto rules concerning illegality.[6] Or again, unclean hands doctrine is often raised in

---

§ 2.4(2)

1. See § 2.4(3) below and the primary discussion in §§ 12.8(4) & 12.8(5) below. The separate mutuality defense in contract cases is also considered in § 12.8(4).

2. E.g., Northeast Women's Center, Inc. v. McMonagle, 868 F.2d 1342, 1354 (3d Cir.1989), cert. denied, 493 U.S. 901, 110 S.Ct. 261, 107 L.Ed.2d 210 (1989).

5. See Chafee, Equity and Unclean Hands, 47 Mich.L.Rev. 877 (Pt. I) & 1065 (Pt. II) (1949).

6. The unclean hands defense used in this way may be just another phrase for the illegality rule under the pari delicto doctrine, and courts frequently seem to use the phrases interchangeably. E.g., Dillon v. Dean, 158 A.D.2d 579, 551 N.Y.S.2d 547 (1990). On pari delicto generally, see § 13.6 below. See also, comparing contributory negligence (under either the complete-bar or the comparative fault systems), assumed risk, and the justifiable reliance rules in fraud cases, Gabaldon, Unclean Hands and Self–Inflicted Wounds: The Significance of Plaintiff Conduct in Actions for Misrepresentation under Rule 10b–5, 71 Minn. L.Rev. 317 (1986).

marital disputes, custody and adoption battles; but used in such cases it may only be a fuzzy version of some other standard, such as the "best interest of the child" standard.[7] In all of these cases the doctrine is spurious in the sense that it adds nothing to the more precise rules that would deny the plaintiff the relief sought.[8]

Extending judicial discretion to bar rights. There is room for concern that the phrase is occasionally used in a very different and disturbing manner, as authority for discretion to reject the plaintiff's legal rights. If judges had the power to deny damages and other legal remedies because a plaintiff came into court with unclean hands, citizens would not have rights, only privileges. Discretion to deny legal relief would mean that the judge might refuse to permit recovery of personal injury damages to a pedestrian struck down in a crosswalk on the ground that she was on her way to an illicit rendezvous and would not have been injured had she stayed home with her family. The merger of law and equity suggests that substantive defenses, based on identifiable legal rules or policy, should apply in both law and equity, as in fact is the case with estoppel. But the merger does not suggest that a judge has discretion to bar rights as well as to limit remedies.[9]

Although discretion in an official, including that reposed in a judge, is always a matter of some concern in a society based on rights of citizens, discretion to deny one remedy but to leave another standing is much more modest than discretion to deny all of the plaintiff's remedies and therefore all of her rights. The courts have not advocated the power to deny all rights as a matter of discretion, but some of the cases may have that effect.[10]

Relatedness of Improper Conduct to Claim

Related misconduct required to invoke the defense. Although many cases in which the unclean hands doctrine is invoked are actually cases of outright illegality, the implication of the cases is that any improper or unethical conduct will suffice to permit the chancellor to close the doors of the court to the plaintiff. However, courts are agreed that the plaintiff's improper conduct, whatever it is, must be related in some substantial and significant way to the claim he now asserts.[12] "Equity does not demand that

---

7. See Matter of Adoption of W.A.T., etc., 808 P.2d 1083 (Utah 1991) (polygamous adoptive parents; court rejects a clean hands approach in favor of a best interest of the child approach in adoption cases).

8. This point is explored further in § 12.-8(5) in connection with the chancellor's discretion in the enforcement of contracts.

9. In Byron v. Clay, 867 F.2d 1049 (7th Cir.1989) Judge Posner suggested that merger warranted the application of equitable defenses to purely "legal" claims, but as to unclean hands he evidently had in mind violation of explicit legal policy, not merely discretion, because he compared that doctrine to the pari delicto doctrine.

10. Legal relief as well as equitable relief has been barred in some cases, possibly on discretionary grounds rather than on the basis of a determinable legal policy. See Tempo

Music, Inc. v. Myers, 407 F.2d 503 (4th Cir. 1969); North Pacific Lumber Co. v. Oliver, 286 Or. 639, 596 P.2d 931 (1979).

12. Knaebel v. Heiner, 663 P.2d 551 (Alaska 1983) (the plaintiff's "wrongful act" must be "related to the action being litigated;" he must have "acted fairly and without fraud or deceit as to the controversy in issue"); Calcote v. Calcote, 583 So.2d 197, 200 (Miss.1991) ("when his conduct with respect to the transaction in question has been characterized by wilful inequity, or illegality * * *. It may be described as such wilful misconduct, inequity or fraud with respect to the immediate transaction as would be condemned and pronounced wrongful by honest and fair-minded men," quoting Griffith, Mississippi Chancery Practice).

its suitors shall have led blameless lives" and even outright illegality is no defense when it is collateral or has been terminated.[13]

A narrow formula. Under one formula, the plaintiff's improper conduct does not preclude equitable relief unless the rights he now asserts were acquired, at least in part, by that improper conduct. "What is material is not that the plaintiff's hands are dirty, but that he dirties them in acquiring the right he now asserts * * *."[14] A variation on this formula limits the clean hands defense to cases in which the plaintiff is seeking to secure a benefit "from the very conduct" which is inequitable.[15]

A discretionary formula. Other courts, though insisting on a relationship between the improper conduct and the claim, have ignored the narrow formula or have been content to treat the question as a part of equity's traditional discretion. The Oregon Court thought it enough to say that the improper conduct "sufficiently affected the equitable relations between the parties" to justify the denial of relief.[16] Discretion may work the other way around as well. In a Pennsylvania case, a trustee was guilty of self-dealing and mismanagement and the beneficiary sought to have him removed. However, the beneficiary had failed to apply the trust funds for scholarships as directed by the trust. The trustee tried to defend on the basis of unclean hands. The court refused to bar the beneficiary's claim. Among other things the court said, that the doctrine need not be applied "where its application will produce inequitable results, especially where the rights of innocent parties are involved," and that the chancellor had discretion to ignore the doctrine.[17]

Improper conduct not causing injury to defendant. In some cases, the plaintiff's improper conduct might be unrelated in that it was directed at and injured only third persons. Chafee long ago pointed out that the original line of clean hands cases invoked the doctrine only when the plaintiff had dirtied his hands by wronging the defendant himself, not by harming third persons or by being a "bad" person.[18] Since that time, cases have often offered "unclean hands" as ground for denying relief even though the defendant has not been harmed by the plaintiff's improper conduct. Many of these are no doubt cases in which the unclean hands terminology was misused in the first place, that is, cases in which there were nondiscretionary legal rules or public policies that provided substantive defenses to the plaintiff's claim.

If there are any cases at all in which there is room for "unclean hands" as a purely equitable defense based on discretion to deny equitable remedies, the plaintiff's remedy against the defendant should not be denied unless his misconduct has actually harmed the defendant, or has at least put the defendant in substantial risk of harm from that misconduct. Thus, for example, the owner of a valid copyright in an obscene movie should be

---

13. Loughran v. Loughran, 292 U.S. 216, 54 S.Ct. 684, 78 L.Ed. 1219 (1934). See also § 13.6 below.

14. Republic Molding Corp. v. B.W. Photo Utilities, 319 F.2d 347 (9th Cir.1963); see also Tami v. Pikowitz, 138 N.J.Eq. 410, 48 A.2d 221 (1946).

16. North Pacific Lumber Co. v. Oliver, 286 Or. 639, 596 P.2d 931 (1979).

17. In re Francis Edward McGillick Foundation, 406 Pa.Super. 249, 594 A.2d 322, 329 (1991).

18. Chafee, Equity and Unclean Hands, 47 Mich.L.Rev. 877, 881 (1949).

allowed an injunction against an infringer to prevent the infringer's showing of the movie; [19] one who has a valid contract to buy land should be given specific performance even though he was convicted of an unrelated crime against unrelated persons a decade ago.[20] The moral misconduct of the plaintiff has not harmed the infringer and the courts are not authorized to confiscate a person's property—the copyright—merely because he is not a nice person.

Commentary: A Suggested Analysis

Excluding rule-of-law and substantive defenses. The first step in analysis of a putative unclean hands defense is to determine whether the defense really appeals to (or seeks to generate) a rule of law grounded in legal policy and applicable to a describable class of cases. For example, the defense might really be the defense that the plaintiff is attempting to enforce an illegal contract. If this is the case, the term "unclean hands" should be dropped altogether and the analysis should proceed on the basis of the rule of law in issue.

Excluding equitable defenses that would bar a legal claim. If the defense is really an appeal to equitable discretion, then it should apply only to bar equitable remedies. It should be dropped entirely if it is asserted as a defense against a legal remedy. This means that the genuine defense of illegality or a describable public policy would still bar both legal and equitable relief, but the judge would not enjoy "discretion" to bar the plaintiff entirely.

If a pure equitable defense is invoked, is the misconduct serious? The third step in analysis must be taken if, after all, the defense is a purely equitable defense, asking the chancellor to exercise discretion or judgment to deny equitable relief. If this is the case, then three subsidiary questions arise. The first of these is whether the plaintiff's misconduct is serious enough to warrant courts in withholding relief that otherwise would be forthcoming. This appears to appeal directly to the chancellor's discretion or judgment.

Determining relatedness. The second question is whether the misconduct of the plaintiff is closely related to the claim she asserts. Relatedness can be described in legal terms. Much law in various fields is devoted to issues of relatedness, often under the rubric of proximate cause. Unclean hands rules can be congruent with the rules of relatedness in other legal settings by adopting the general principle that the plaintiff's misconduct does not count against him unless it harmed or at least threatened the defendant or a small class of persons with which the defendant is importantly identified; and it does not count against him unless the harm that came to the defendant was the same kind of harm the plaintiff intended or unreasonably risked.[21]

19. Mitchell Bros. Film Group v. Cinema Adult Theater, 604 F.2d 852, 50 A.L.R.Fed. 786 (5th Cir.1979), cert. denied, Bora v. Mitchell Bros. Film Group, 445 U.S. 917, 100 S.Ct. 1277, 63 L.Ed.2d 601 (1980). The usual view is that obscenity does not prevent a valid copyright. See § 6.3(6) below.

20. Morey v. Sings, 174 A.D.2d 870, 570 N.Y.S.2d 864 (1991).

21. This is a non-technical statement of the risk rules applied in legal or proximate cause cases. Although some courts rest their proximate cause rules on elaborate analysis of intervening causes, to a very large extent this

Values at stake and alternative sanctions. The third subsidiary issue is whether invocation of the unclean hands defense will interfere with other legal values or goals. Some plaintiffs, such as civil rights plaintiffs, sue for themselves but in so doing also vindicate public policy. Less vaunted actions by other plaintiffs can have public benefit which should not be put aside on unclean hands grounds.[23] To dismiss such a plaintiff's claim may be to interfere with the rights of third persons or the public, so at the very least added caution is required.[24]

Another value at stake is the plaintiff's own rights. A plaintiff does not become an outlaw or a non-citizen because he is guilty of wrongdoing. If application of the clean hands defense would deny the plaintiff her rights, it goes too far for a free society.

In judging the other values at stake, alternative sanctions should be considered. One possibility is that the defendant will have a tort claim against the plaintiff who has wronged him.[27] Such a claim may adequately sanction the plaintiff's misconduct and the unclean hands defense will not be needed for that purpose.[28]

§ 2.4(3) Contract Defenses in Equity

As a limitation on remedies, the unclean hands doctrine closely resembles equity unconscionability rules under which equity courts may refuse to give specific enforcement to a contract which the courts deem unfair, unconscionable or too one-sided. (A similar rule embodied in the Uniform Commercial Code permits courts to strike unconscionable provisions in sales contracts.)[1] The equitable defenses to specific performance of contracts are discussed primarily in Chapter 12, but they are discussed here illustratively to show the relationship to the general pattern of equitable approaches. As with the orthodox view of the unclean hands defense, unconscionability and mutuality defenses purport to be equitable defenses, that is, defenses that bar the remedy but leave the plaintiff free to claim damages or other legal relief.[2]

---

is a matter of style, and the great majority of proximate cause cases are consistent with the risk rule.

Compare the formulation in Northeast Women's Center, Inc. v. McMonagle, 868 F.2d 1342, 1354 (3d Cir.1989), cert. denied, 493 U.S. 901, 110 S.Ct. 261, 107 L.Ed.2d 210 (1989) where a clinic sought to enjoin pro-life or anti-abortion protestors from trespass and violence at the clinic. The defendants claimed the clinic had unclean hands that prevented the injunction because some of the aborted fetuses had been inspected for completeness by a doctor who was not board certified. A statute required a board-certified or eligible doctor to inspect. The court held that the plaintiff's fault, if any, was "collateral to the matter involved in this lawsuit," and that it had "no connection at all to the Defendants' actions which the jury found violated both federal and state law." This is not an explicit risk-rule analysis, but it is consistent with it and uses

the language of the alternate "direct cause" test of proximate cause.

23. See Chicago & W.I.R. Co. v. Brotherhood of Ry. Clerks, 221 F.Supp. 561 (N.D.Ill. 1963) (labor dispute, injunction against work stoppage might issue in spite of unclean hands because of public concern).

24. "The doctrine of unclean hands, functionally rather than moralistically conceived, gives recognition to the fact that equitable decrees may have effects on third parties—persons who are not parties to a lawsuit, including taxpayers and members of the law-abiding public—and so should not be entered without consideration of those effects." Byron v. Clay, 867 F.2d 1049 (7th Cir.1989) (Judge Posner).

§ 2.4(3)

1. UCC § 2–302. See § 10.7 below.

2. See the discussion in § 12.8(5) below.

Unconscionability

A famous case involving this problem is *Campbell Soup Co. v. Wentz.*[3] In this case Campbell developed a special kind of carrot, which it deemed more suitable for its canned soups. It provided seeds of this carrot to people named Wentz, who agreed to raise carrots on their land and to sell them all to Campbell at a specified price. Campbell's contract was rather favorable to Campbell in several respects. Campbell was allowed to refuse carrots that were too large, and it was also allowed to refuse carrots it was unable to inspect, grade, or receive because of circumstances beyond its control, or because of a labor dispute. And, even if Campbell refused deliveries of carrots under this clause, the Wentzes were forbidden to sell elsewhere without Campbell's permission.

This was a fairly hard contract. Knowledgeable business persons with a reasonable amount of bargaining power probably would not wish to accept the risk that a season's work and investment would be entirely lost if Campbell had a strike. Yet the contract called upon the Wentzes to accept this risk. Judge Goodrich thought that, taken as a whole, the contract was too harsh, and for that reason he refused to order specific performance in favor of Campbell and against the Wentzes.

Yet the Wentzes were in breach, and for a fairly clear reason. The price of the carrots on the market had gone up spectacularly and the Wentzes could obtain a better price in the market by violating their contract. Quite possibly Campbell would be limited, in a recovery at law, to liquidated damages in a relatively small sum.[4] Thus by breaching a contract of the sort that would ordinarily be specifically enforced in equity, the grower could obtain a better price and might limit their liability at law so that breach gave them a profit even after payment of damages.

Put another way, none of the elements that made the contract a potentially harsh one ever came about. If anyone was guilty of misbehavior on the actual facts of the case, it was the grower, not Campbell. Yet it was Campbell who was denied equitable relief.

Since Campbell's contract clauses caused no harm to the growers, it is possible to interpret this decision as one that punishes Campbell for its bad state of mind, even though that state of mind caused no harm to the other parties, and even though the rights asserted were not in any sense acquired through that bad state of mind. This suggests that the decision is more like that of an ecclesiastical court commanding a penance for sinful thoughts than anything else. To speak of the case in terms of unclean hands, one could say that Campbell's misconduct was not related to the claim it sought to enforce.

However, the court probably felt that the clauses in question were against public policy and probably felt that it was important to strike them down for that reason. If the court had enforced the contract, with nothing more than a dictum that such clauses were improper, there was the possibility that Campbell would continue to use such contracts in their dealings with farmers and reap the benefits of them until some aggressive, knowledgeable

---

3. 172 F.2d 80 (3d Cir.1948).

4. See § 12.8(6) below discussing this aspect of *Campbell Soup.*

farmer took the matter to court on the specific issue. In other words, unless relief were denied, Campbell would have no incentive to use fairer contracts in dealings with others. Caught between two such unpalatable choices, the court decided to give Campbell some incentive to draft fair agreements with its growers.

There are two important characteristics to notice about this kind of case, besides the ones just discussed. One is that the choice is all or nothing. Equity will enforce the contract specifically, or it will not. There is little room in equity's doctrine for rewriting the contract or striking some clauses of it and then enforcing it as rewritten.

The second thing to notice here is that the only remedy withheld is the equity remedy. The legal remedy for damages remains at least theoretically available to the plaintiff, just as in the case of unclean hands generally. There is no reason to think that the merger of law and equity should affect this, except to make it clear that the plaintiff had better claim damages in the same suit or be barred by res judicata.[5]

The *Campbell Soup* case and other issues of unfairness and hardship are discussed further in connection with contract remedies. The distinction between remedial and substantive defenses is also considered further in the same place.[6]

Mutuality of Remedy [7]

The mutuality of remedy doctrine as it was originally applied held that the equitable remedy of specific performance should be equally available to both parties, or equally unavailable to them.[8] In the abstract this sounded entirely equitable in the sense that it seemed just or fair. According to one judge, the mutuality of remedies doctrine "stands upon the foundation of all equitable jurisprudence, which distributes justice with an impartial hand, and withholds its extraordinary remedies from those who have not submitted themselves freely to its jurisdiction."[9]

In theory the doctrine was fair and operated only as a remedial defense, to bar the equitable but not the legal remedy. In practice, the doctrine could work unfairly and unpredictably. The doctrine arose in cases where parties made a valid contract. The defendant validly promised some performance that ordinarily could be compelled in a suit for specific performance—for instance, he promised to convey land to the plaintiff. If the plaintiff had promised money in return, he had no difficulty in getting specific performance from the defendant, since land is unique and money damages are not adequate to compensate for a specific parcel of land. But if the plaintiff had promised to render services in exchange for the land, there was trouble. If the plaintiff failed to perform his services, he would be liable in damages, but equity would not specifically compel him to perform, since this would result in something like involuntary servitude and would be against public policy if not actually in violation of the constitution.[10] Since equity would

5. See § 12.8(5) below.

6. See §§ 12.8(4) & 12.8(5) below.

7. The primary treatment for this topic is found in § 12.8(4) below.

8. See E. Fry, Specific Performance of Contracts § 460 (6th ed. 1921).

9. McCall v. Atchley, 256 Mo. 39, 54–55, 164 S.W. 593, 598 (1914).

10. See § 12.22(2) below.

not force the plaintiff to perform the services promised, it took the position that it would not force the defendant to convey the land promised.

The negative mutuality rule has been largely abandoned, but it is still often mentioned, along with particular exceptions. The Restatement waters it down to a factor in the court's discretion.[12] The absence of mutuality is rightly considered if the contract otherwise appears to be the result of a tainted bargaining process. In such a case it may be a sign that the defendant did not understand the deal, or lacked mental capacity, or was victimized by misrepresentations.

§ 2.4(4) Laches

Generally

Laches a bar to equitable claims. A plaintiff guilty of laches may be barred from recovery of any kind of equitable remedy, including injunctions,[1] specific performance,[2] and equitable accounting.[3] Laches can also be applied to bar a mortgage foreclosure,[4] a quiet title suit,[5] and even reinstatement in a job under discrimination statutes[6] or an administrative claim.[7]

Laches defined. In its most orthodox form, laches is unreasonable delay by the plaintiff in prosecuting a claim or protecting a right of which the plaintiff knew or should have known, and under circumstances causing prejudice to the defendant.[8] The plaintiff may be barred not only by delay occurring before suit is filed, but also delay in prosecuting the claim afterward.[9] Delay by the plaintiff might also suggest the possibilities of ordinary estoppel, waiver, acquiescence,[10] and even ratification. It is common to see several of these terms used in a single opinion. Because all equitable terms tend to be softly defined and loosely used, a certain amount of confusion results.

Limitations on the defense. The laches defense is said to be an affirmative one, with the burden of proving it upon the defendant.[11] It may not be

12. Restatement Second of Contracts § 363 (1981).

§ 2.4(4)

8. E.g., Equal Employment Opportunity Com'n v. Radiator Specialty Co., 610 F.2d 178, 183 (4th Cir.1979) (rejecting defense because prejudice was not shown); Landis v. Hodgson, 109 Idaho 252, 706 P.2d 1363 (1985) (laches is delay by plaintiff with injury resulting to defendant if relief is granted); State ex rel. Casale v. McLean, 58 Ohio St.3d 163, 569 N.E.2d 475 (1991) (prejudice cannot be inferred from mere lapse of time); Weinberg v. Commonwealth, State Bd. of Examiners of Public Accountants, 509 Pa. 143, 501 A.2d 239 (1985) (both unjustified delay and prejudice to the defendant). As formulated by many courts, the defendant must show his own "lack of knowledge" that the plaintiff would assert the right as well as prejudice. This seems, however, to be another way of stating that the defendant must rely in fact and must rely reasonably upon the delay; if the defendant knew the delay meant nothing, he would

not rely, or would not reasonably rely to his prejudice.

9. Beech v. Ragnar Benson, Inc., 402 Pa.Super. 449, 587 A.2d 335 (1991). In Title VII job discrimination claims the plaintiff's right to sue matures only when she receives a right to sue letter from the EEOC. This may take many years and the plaintiff is entitled to prompt the EEOC and obtain such a letter after a specified waiting period. One court has held that even though the suit was brought soon after the letter was received, the plaintiff's failure to prompt the EEOC could constitute laches. Cleveland Newspaper Guild v. Plain Dealer Pub. Co., 839 F.2d 1147 (6th Cir.1988), cert. denied, 488 U.S. 899, 109 S.Ct. 245, 102 L.Ed.2d 234 (1988). For a discussion of this problem and contrary authorities see § 6.10(7) below.

10. As to these three terms, see § 2.3(5) above.

11. E.g., Weinberg v. Commonwealth, State Bd. of Examiners of Public Accountants, 509 Pa. 143, 501 A.2d 239, 242 (1985).

invoked at all to defeat the public interest,[12] and it may not be invoked by a trustee to defeat the claim of a beneficiary, unless the trustee has first repudiated the trust relationship and communicated that repudiation to the beneficiary.[13] When laches does not amount to estoppel or waiver, it does not ordinarily bar legal claims, only equitable remedies.[14]

Bases. Decisions and commentaries seem to imply several different reasons for the laches rule, but those reasons are not usually explored in the discussions. First, the laches rule may have originated in equity because no statute of limitations applied,[15] and clearly enough it functions in part as a kind of "flexible"[16] statute of limitations, barring long-delayed claims where no statute of limitations was available for that purpose. This traditional function suggests that laches should be limited to cases in which no statute of limitations applies.

Second, the laches rule is associated with an equitable maxim, that equity aids the vigilant, not those who sleep on their rights. Sometimes the focus of this and similar statements seems to be on the plaintiff's fault, so that he is barred partly because he is guilty of something like contributory fault.[17] The plaintiff's fault, if any, is indeed relevant, but not perhaps because equity should punish him. Rather it is that if delay has prejudiced the defendant, the plaintiff may fairly be asked to bear the responsibility for that prejudice, but not otherwise.

Third, the laches rule sometimes seems based on actual prejudice to the defendant, irrespective of any applicable statute of limitations. The formula for the laches rule might be read as combining some fault on the plaintiff's part with prejudice to the defendant. However, the formula does not directly take into account the existence or non-existence of a statute of limitations, and as will appear, courts do not always require a demonstration of prejudice to the defendant in order to bar the plaintiff.

Law and equity. Courts have routinely referred to laches as an equitable defense, that is, a defense to equitable remedies but not a defense available to bar a claim of legal relief.[18] However, delay in pursuing a right might well qualify as an estoppel[19] or even a waiver or abandonment of a right,[20] as courts sometimes recognize. If the plaintiff "unreasonably" delays under circumstances suggesting that he intends not to pursue a claim and the defendant relies on this appearance to his detriment, all the elements of ordinary estoppel are present, and perhaps even the elements of waiver or abandonment. Because estoppel and waiver are substantive defenses that reach all remedies, both legal and equitable, they are applicable "at law." Presumably when delay misleads the defendant to his prejudice, estoppel or waiver may defeat the plaintiff's claim even when the plaintiff seeks purely legal relief.[21] When the plaintiff's delay causes prejudice to the defendant but not because it misleads him or misrepresents any fact, it is not clear that the delay should bar even equitable remedies. However, if it does, the bar should not be extended to legal relief which comes as of right.

Laches as a partial defense only. Because laches is based on prejudice to the defendant, the bar it raises should be no broader than the prejudice shown. So it is not surprising that some trademark cases have said that laches bars relief for past infringements but not for future claims.[22]

Somewhat differently, the bar of laches might be limited monetarily where the plaintiff's delay induces the defendant to make expenditures that he would not otherwise have made. In such case the plaintiff might be allowed a recovery, with an offsetting liability for the costs attributable to the delay period. Justice White once suggested something like this when the plaintiff in a job discrimination case had delayed in enforcing job rights. He suggested that the plaintiff might be allowed to proceed with the claim, but that backpay that was otherwise due under the statute could be eliminated for the period of unreasonable delay.[24]

Public interests. Laches is a defense that may on occasion be raised by public entities, either as a defense [25] or as a factor to be considered in exercising discretion whether to issue an injunction or to limit its terms.[26] But laches, whether raised by or against a public entity, is not to be used to defeat an overriding public interest, so an entity's delay in suing to enjoin a public nuisance may not always defeat the injunction.[27] Similarly, a citizen suit attacking constitutionality of legislation is not necessarily defeated because government agencies have invested time and funds in implementing it.[28]

Effect of Statutes of Limitations

Application of statutes of limitations to equitable claims. If a statute of limitations addresses the kind of claim brought by the plaintiff, and bars the claims, neither laches nor its absence is relevant; the claim is barred by the statute.[29] However, a long tradition holds that at least some statutes of limitation do not apply to equitable claims.[30] This view may be justified or required where the statute addresses only claims for "damages" [31] or where, as in the case of many federal statutes, a cause of action is created that does not fit within the coverage of any existing statute of limitations.[32]

The "analogous" statutes of limitations. Where no statute of limitations applies to the equitable claim, laches doctrine provides a kind of flexible substitute. In such cases, however, courts may look to an "analogous" statute of limitations. An analogous statute is one that applies to a similar cause of action or one that applies to the same cause of action when a different remedy is sought.

---

24. See Kamberos v. GTE Automatic Elec., Inc., 454 U.S. 1060, 102 S.Ct. 612, 70 L.Ed.2d 599 (1981) (Justice White dissenting from denial of certiorari).

25. See Weinberg v. Commonwealth, State Bd. of Examiners of Public Accountants, 509 Pa. 143, 501 A.2d 239 (1985).

26. See Matter of Chicago, Rock Island and Pac. R. Co. v. Iowa Dept. of Transp., 756 F.2d 517 (7th Cir.1985) (fact that public entity had slept on its rights played an indirect part in deciding not to issue an injunction against prospective nuisance).

27. See e.g., Liller v. State Highway Admin., 25 Md.App. 276, 333 A.2d 644 (1975) and § 5.7(2) below.

28. Chemical Specialties Mfrs. Ass'n, Inc. v. Deukmejian, 227 Cal.App.3d 663, 673, 278 Cal.Rptr. 128, 134 (1991) ("The overriding public interest in compliance with this mandate outweighs any minimal prejudice suffered by respondents. Under the circumstances presented in this case, the public's interest in adherence to the single-subject requirement should not be subordinated to its interest in economical government").

30. See Allcard v. Skinner, [1887] 36 Ch. Div. 145; 2 Pomeroy Equity Jurisprudence § 419a (5h ed. Symons 1941). This is sometimes stated as if governed by a judge-made rule to which the statutory terms were irrelevant. See, e.g., Meyers v. Kissner, 217 Ill. App.3d 136, 160 Ill.Dec. 140, 576 N.E.2d 1094 (1991) ("As a general rule, suits in equity are not subject to statutory limitations periods").

When courts look to an analogous statute of limitations for guidance, and that statute has run, they may (1) presume unreasonable delay and prejudice, but permit the plaintiff to rebut the presumption; [35] (2) treat the statute as one element "in the congeries of factors to be considered." [36] Some authority has gone beyond either of these rules by holding that equity will follow the law and (3) give the statute conclusive effect.[37] The effect of the last view is to say that, after all, statutes of limitations do apply to equitable claims.

When courts look to an analogous statute of limitations for guidance and that statute has *not* run, the orthodox view is that the defendant may still defeat the claim by showing "inexcusable delay and resulting prejudice." [38] This seems right if it refers either to a genuine estoppel or to a genuine waiver. But however long the plaintiff's delay may be, if she sues within the time permitted by statute and does not mislead the defendant to his prejudice, denial of relief seems unwarranted. Sometimes, however, courts have barred a plaintiff who sues within the permitted period and whose delay has not misled the defendant.[39] In some such cases the defendant may suffer because of the delay, but not because he relied upon misleading appearances created by the plaintiff. Yet if the plaintiff has done only what she is permitted to do by statute, and has not misled the defendant, the basis for barring the plaintiff seems to have disappeared.

§ 2.4(5) Balancing Equities, Hardships and Public Interests

In General

Equitable defenses without balancing. Equity courts are traditionally free to balance equities and hardships in determining whether or not to grant an equitable remedy. Balancing of hardships and equities differs from the recognition of defenses such as the unclean hands defense. Equitable *defenses* invite the court to consider only the plaintiff's ethical standing and to deny all remedies if the plaintiff does not meet equity's standards. The *Campbell Soup* case discussed earlier [1] is a good example of an equitable defense that definitely does not involve balancing. In that case the court looked only at the unconscionable provisions of the plaintiff's contract and did not attempt to compare the plaintiff's behavior in drafting his contract with the defendant's behavior in breaching.

Balancing equities and hardships. In contrast, the balancing of equities and hardships looks at the conduct of both parties and the potential hardships that might result from a judicial decision either way. For example, the plaintiff's delay might, when viewed as a defense, simply bar the

---

35. "A defendant has the burden to show laches before the statutory period; a plaintiff has the burden to disprove laches after the statutory period." Oregon State Bar v. Wright, 309 Or. 37, 785 P.2d 340, 342 (1990).

36. Goodman v. McDonnell Douglas Corp., 606 F.2d 800 (8th Cir.1979), cert. denied, 446 U.S. 913, 100 S.Ct. 1844, 64 L.Ed.2d 267 (1980).

37. Meyers v. Kissner, 217 Ill.App.3d 136, 160 Ill.Dec. 140, 576 N.E.2d 1094 (1991) ("where a claim for equitable relief is not brought until after the limitations period for the corresponding legal action has expired, it too will be time-barred, even if the delay in filing suit has caused no prejudice to the defendant").

38. See Barrois v. Nelda Faye, Inc., 597 F.2d 881 (5th Cir.1979).

39. See Cleveland Newspaper Guild v. Plain Dealer Pub. Co., 839 F.2d 1147 (6th Cir.1988), cert. denied, 488 U.S. 899, 109 S.Ct. 245, 102 L.Ed.2d 234 (1988) and the discussion in § 6.10(7) below.

plaintiff's claim altogether. If the delay is not sufficient to bar the plaintiff, that delay may nevertheless be considered in the total balance of all factors affecting the equities. The equities in favor of, as well as those against the plaintiff would be considered in balancing, and the equities in favor of and against the defendant are likewise considered. So the plaintiff's delay, coupled with minimal prejudice to the defendant might lead the court to strike the balance of equities in the plaintiff's favor and permit the claim to proceed.[2]

Balancing Equities

Equities. The equities of a case are usually taken to refer to matters of fault, ethical position, and delay. Thus if one party has been guilty of some misleading conduct, this may be considered, even if it does not in itself amount to an estoppel or unclean hands. Hardships, changed position and various forms of prejudice or harm to the parties are also considered in this balancing.

Examples. All or almost all equitable remedies are discretionary in some degree. Balancing of equities and hardships is the process through which discretion is informed and expressed. Examples of cases in which balancing occurs are cases in which injunctions are sought to compel removal of encroaching structures,[3] to force removal of structures erected in violation of building restrictions,[4] or to force removal of nuisances.[5] In such cases and many others, the courts may recognize the plaintiff's right, and yet refuse to enforce it, or enforce it in limited ways. For instance, the defendant may be committing a nuisance, but the court may refuse to enjoin it because of the total set of concerns about (1) the relative ethical standing of the parties and (2) the hardship to the defendant and to the public that might be imposed if an injunction issued.

Good faith, fault, motive. One equity obviously important here is the good faith of the defendant; if he acted negligently or intentionally in erecting his garage on the plaintiff's land, the equities are weighed pretty heavily against him.[6] If he is in good faith, however, other equities and hardships may be considered: Did the complaining plaintiff engage in delay or misleading conduct? Would the grant of an injunction encourage the plaintiff to exact extortion, that is, is he merely seeking to force the defendant to "buy him out?" Even if he is trying to use the pressure generated by an injunction to force a buy-out by the defendant, might the buy-out price be a good reflection of the plaintiff's damages?[7] Is the plaintiff seriously damaged and does he assert his claim in good faith? Even if the answers to such questions are unfavorable to the plaintiff, it yet remains to compare his conduct in these respects with that of the defendant and to balance the two.[8]

Balancing Hardships

Hardship rules. In addition to these equities, courts consider the hardships likely to result to the plaintiff if the relief is denied compared to the hardship likely to result to the defendant if relief is granted. Sometimes

§ 2.4(5)

7. See § 5.7(4) below.

Dobbs, Remedies, 2nd Ed. HB—6

8. See Keeton and Morris, Notes on "Balancing the Equities," 18 Tex.L.Rev. 412 (1940) (discussing most of these equities).

hardship is not balanced as one factor but instead is represented in more or less specific defensive rules. In some cases the defendant's detrimental change of position will be a defense.[9] The bona fide purchaser defense is also sometimes a specific form of hardship defense.[10]

Hardship to the defendant. Such specific defenses aside, hardship that will result to the defendant if the court awards equitable relief is merely one factor to be considered. Hardship to the defendant may be grounds for denying an equitable remedy unless the remedy will help the plaintiff more than it harms the defendant. For example, the New York Court of Appeals once refused to enforce a building restriction which had become largely obsolete, saying that if the restriction had great value to the plaintiff, the court might enforce it in spite of harm that enforcement would cause to the defendant.[11] But because enforcement of the restriction would not have been useful to the plaintiff on the facts of that case, the court refused to extend the "long arm" of equity "to harm one party without helping the other, for that would be unjust." The court then added: "An injunction that bears heavily on the defendant without benefiting the plaintiff will always be withheld as oppressive." The language of hardship is the language of equity courts, but the quoted sentence reveals a kind of cost-benefit meaning of "hardship," and a lurking economic concern that courts should not impose costs on one party without securing benefits for the other.[12]

It is difficult to apply the hardship factor in a proper way, apart from specific rules such as those of the bona fide purchaser defense. Some hardships to the defendant are inseparable incidents of the plaintiff's right. The defendant will always suffer a hardship if he must comply with his contract when it has become expensive or if he must cease operating a factory that earns profits but also pollutes. The plaintiff's contract should not be rewritten to avoid hardship to the defendant;[13] the public's right to clean air should not be degraded to support polluting factories.[14] Hardship to the defendant is perhaps best considered in the balance when the hardship to the defendant is not an inseparable part of the plaintiff's right, or when the cost or hardship to the defendant far exceeds the benefit to which the plaintiff is entitled, or when hardship to the defendant suggests that the plaintiff's right was unfairly acquired in the first place.[15]

Hardships to the plaintiff. Hardships to the plaintiff come in for consideration, too. Usually, however, "hardship" is not an independent ground for relief. Instead, hardship to the plaintiff is part of the reasons for the doctrine that equity will relieve from forfeitures[16] and refuse its enforcement to harsh contracts.[17] Hardship to one of the parties is part of the basis for relieving from mistake,[18] and from impossibility and frustration of contracts.[19]

Balancing Interests of the Public and Third Persons

Courts have traditionally said they would balance the public interest and even the interests of third persons in determining whether or not to

10. § 4.7(1) below; cf. § 4.7(2) (discharge for value).

11. McClure v. Leaycraft, 183 N.Y. 36, 75 N.E. 961 (1905).

12. See § 5.7 generally and 5.7(4) in particular.

issue equitable relief.[20]   Sometimes a public interest is opposed to the injunction, but not sufficient to outweigh the plaintiff's right or some other public interest.[21]   At other times the public interest is perceived to correlate with the defendant's interest and to warrant denial of the injunction.   When the defendant is a public utility, carrier, or public agency, courts might be especially ready to take public interest into account and to deny or limit equitable relief that might interfere with that interest.[22]   If a factory constitutes a polluting nuisance, courts may concentrate on the fact that the public benefits from jobs created by the factory and the fact that third persons (the employees) benefit from holding those jobs.   With these interests in mind the court may deny the injunction,[23] just as it might do by focusing on the hardship to the defendant.   An Oregon decision refused to let an injunction go on behalf of a shopping center owner to prevent trespass by defendants, because the defendants were seeking signatures to initiate legislation and because the public interest outweighed the landowner's interests in injunctive relief.[24]

Public interest balancing as cost-benefit analysis.   Perceptions of public interest shift over time.   The balancing of public interests and third person rights is the method by which courts may consider all the costs and benefits of the defendant's activity in deciding whether to enjoin it.   It is, in other words, the traditional door which admits a modicum of economic analysis into the equity case.[27]

For instance, trademark infringement tends to cause customer confusion and may lead consumers to buy a product they did not intend to buy; the public interest represented by customer confusion weighs in favor of an injunction because it represents a cost being imposed by the defendant's conduct, although not one imposed directly upon the plaintiff.   Similarly, civil rights violations, unabated by injunctions, threaten many third persons who could never bring suit, so that the injunction creates a benefit far beyond the benefit to the individual plaintiff.   If these interests were not considered, courts would deny the injunction in some cases either because they would not be counting all the costs of the defendant's activity or all the benefits of the injunction.

§ 2.4(6) Measuring, Shaping, or Tailoring the Remedy

After balancing the equities and hardships a court might deny all relief to the plaintiff.   Alternatively, however, the court might simply limit relief in accord with its view of the equities or hardships.   The measurement or shaping of the remedy is partly a product of the court's ideas about the

20. E.g., City of Harrisonville, Mo. v. W.S. Dickey Clay Mfg. Co., 289 U.S. 334, 53 S.Ct. 602, 77 L.Ed. 1208 (1933).

21. Cf. In re T.R., 52 Ohio St.3d 6, 556 N.E.2d 439 (1990) (supporting a gag order and a closed hearing on the custody battle concerning a child born of a surrogate mother; the efforts of some parties to try the case in supermarket tabloids and on television talk shows was detrimental to the child's best interests; public interest was an insufficient counterweight).

22. See Loma Portal Civic Club v. American Airlines, Inc., 61 Cal.2d 582, 39 Cal.Rptr. 708, 394 P.2d 548 (1964) (damages but not injunction against public service corporation which has taken private property in the public interest).

23. E.g., Riter v. Keokuk Electro–Metals Co., 248 Iowa 710, 82 N.W.2d 151 (1957).

24. Lloyd Corp., Ltd. v. Whiffen, 307 Or. 674, 773 P.2d 1294 (1989) (also citing shopping mall cases decided on constitutional grounds and reflecting a majority favoring the landowner).

nature and scope of the underlying right and partly a product of balancing. The term tailoring is sometimes used to refer only to the latter, but it is used here to include any effort to determine the details of the injunctive remedy.

When the court believes the underlying right to be highly significant, it may write injunctive relief as broad as the right itself, even when the injunctive relief is highly intrusive and risks serious harms to the defendant's interests. For example, injunctions enforcing anti-discrimination statutes have been used to force a university to grant tenure to a candidate it said it considered to be unqualified,[1] and to force a partnership to accept an associate as a full partner,[2] although similar enforcement is traditionally denied to employees who merely assert a contract right.[3]

On the other hand, courts may narrow the remedy to reflect something less than the right the plaintiff began with. A court may read the hardships or economic concerns to suggest that an injunction should not issue to close down a polluting factory even though it is doing serious harm. In that case the court will begin to think of alternatives, such as an injunction that will close the factory down at some time in the future, or one that would require experimenting with devices to control pollution. The decisions are polycentric so that a decision to grant limited relief of a particular kind may require further balancing.[4]

In some situations the chancellor has a large range of possibilities for measuring out relief. For example, a factory's operation may cause a nuisance. The chancellor might consider an injunction forbidding: (1) Creating or continuing a nuisance;[5] (2) operating certain specified engines;[6] (3) operating any engines producing a noise level at the property line in excess of so many decibels;[7] (4) operating after 5:00 p.m.;[8] (5) any operation. The list can be extended to reflect all of the potential options.

The first kind of injunction in the list is so nebulous that it might be objectionable on due process grounds.[9] The rest are all within the realm of reason, depending on the facts. And, indeed, there are still other possibili-

§ 2.4(6)

1. Brown v. Trustees of Boston University, 891 F.2d 337 (1st Cir.1989) ("We agree that courts should be 'extremely wary of intruding into the world of university tenure decisions,' * * *. However, once a university has been found to have impermissibly discriminated in making a tenure decision, as here, the University's prerogative to make tenure decisions must be subordinated to the goals embodied in Title VII").

2. Hopkins v. Price Waterhouse, 920 F.2d 967, 969 (D.C.Cir.1990) (Title VII job discrimination; "We find it inconceivable * * * that the Supreme Court intended to open up a partnership's admission decisions to judicial scrutiny while placing them beyond effective judicial remedy").

3. See § 12.21(4) below.

4. Cf. Schoenbrod, The Measure of an Injunction: A Principle to Replace Balancing the Equities and Tailoring the Remedy, 72 Minn.L.Rev. 627, 636, n. 38 (1988).

5. E.g., Bishop Processing Co. v. Davis, 213 Md. 465, 132 A.2d 445 (1957) (injunction to avoid escape of noxious gases that interfere with plaintiff's use and enjoyment of property).

6. Cf. Milling v. Berg, 104 So.2d 658 (Fla. App.1958) (temporary order against boatyard's work, on any steel boat, which made more noise than others).

7. Cf. MacArtor v. Graylyn Crest III Swim Club, Inc., 41 Del.Ch. 26, 187 A.2d 417 (1963) (stop to be placed on volume control of loudspeaker at swimming pool).

8. Cf. Smith v. Stasco Milling Co., 18 F.2d 736 (2d Cir.1927) (blasting at night forbidden).

9. See International Longshoremen's Ass'n, Local 1291 v. Philadelphia Marine Trade Ass'n, 389 U.S. 64, 88 S.Ct. 201, 19 L.Ed.2d 236 (1967). For additional cases and for the nebulosity defense to contempt, see § 2.8(7) below.

ties. The chancellor might, for example, decide to order experiments for controlling the nuisance, or to give the defendant time to do so.[10] The chancellor might even conceivably order the defendant to move the polluting factory to a location that causes less interference, but order the plaintiff to pay the cost of the move.[11]

If remedies should enforce rights, then the tailoring stage should shape the remedy to reflect the rights in question, subject only to practical constraints. Because injunctions can provide many different means and terms, they may at times be tailored to forbid acts that are not themselves wrongs, or to command acts that are not in themselves part of the plaintiff's entitlement.

For example, it is not wrong for a photographer to be within 25 feet of a celebrity on a public sidewalk, but if the photographer has been harassing the celebrity for a long period the court might be faced with a difficult choice in framing the injunction. A "no harassment" injunction is nebulous or vague and it will be difficult to enforce by contempt. So the court might consider an injunction which clearly forbids the photographer from exercising his own rights by forbidding him from approaching within 25 feet of the celebrity. Such an injunction exceeds the celebrity's rights, because she has no right to preclude use of a sidewalk by others. Yet the decree might be justified as a means of providing reparation for rights she has already lost, or as a means of protecting those rights that she indisputably does have.[12]

Many kinds of cases can raise similar issues about the breadth of the injunction as compared to the scope of the right.[13] Sometimes the injunction seems to go far beyond the right. In one case the court found that the state had failed properly to pay hospitals under a medical assistance program. It then approved an order compelling the state to pay $2 million, but not for past due payments; the state was ordered to pay the hospital as advances on future obligations that had not accrued and for which no payment was due.[14] In a Supreme Court decision,[15] a statute proscribed structures in rivers; the Court approved an injunction that would prohibit discharge of pollution into the river. Such cases may be subject to serious criticism unless they can be justified on the ground that the decree, if going beyond the right, at least compels acts that will have the primary effect of enforcing the right. That might be the case with the celebrity photographer, but it is not so obviously so in other instances. Cases raising this problem reflect the extraordinary

10. See Restatement (Second) of Torts § 941 Comment *e* (1979).

11. This is the "compensated injunction" or fourth option. See Spur Indus. Inc. v. Del E. Webb Dev. Co., 108 Ariz. 178, 494 P.2d 700, 53 A.L.R.3d 861 (1972); § 5.7(3) below; cf. Emery Industries, Inc. v. Cottier, 202 U.S.P.Q. 829 (D.Ohio 1978) (former employee enjoined from working for plaintiff's competitor because trade secret revelation would be inevitable, but as condition of the injunction the plaintiff had to compensate former employee at a stated rate); see § 10.5(3).

12. Galella v. Onassis, 487 F.2d 986, 28 A.L.R.Fed. 879 (2d Cir.1973) (TRO against ha-

rassing photographer initially forbidding harassment; when this general prohibition proved ineffective the Court of Appeals ultimately approved a specific injunction requiring the photographer to stay 25-feet from the plaintiff).

13. As to some of the argument in civil rights cases, see § 7.4(4) below.

14. Temple University v. White, 941 F.2d 201, 216–221 (3d Cir.1991), cert. denied, ___ U.S. ___, 112 S.Ct. 873, 116 L.Ed.2d 778 (1992).

15. United States v. Republic Steel Corp., 362 U.S. 482, 80 S.Ct. 884, 4 L.Ed.2d 903 (1960).

power of injunctions and provide a warning that they can be overdrawn as well as underdrawn.

§ 2.4(7) The Role of Equitable Discretion in Equity

The chancellor's discretion to deny relief is a peculiar tradition to encounter in a democratic society where citizens possess rights under the law, not merely the hope of indulgence. The chancellor-bishop's discretion to refuse enforcement of established rights may have seemed normal in 16th century England. He was authoritative bishop who gave relief as a matter of grace and discretion to individuals who were subjects of the Crown, not citizens of a democracy.

Few American citizens, however, would think of themselves in court as humble petitioners, on their knees before the judge who may deny relief on grounds that cannot be stated as principles or applied even-handedly to all suitors. Nor would they see themselves like Kafka's agonists, controlled by unknown and unknowable laws.[1] So a full-blown discretion in the chancellor to deny relief may be hard to reconcile with the ideal of rights under the law. What is the appropriate role for discretion in either limiting or expanding equitable remedies? This subsection points to some of the particular issues raised by such large questions.

[*For discussion of the problems of discretion and the power of judges to limit rights by discretionary decisions, see this section in the Practitioner Treatise edition, vol. 1, pp. 115–123.*]

If, on the facts of the case, the only meaningful relief is equitable relief, or if denial of equitable relief would in fact operate to deny legal relief as well, then a discretionary denial of the remedy is also a denial of the right. That is so because denial of *all* available remedies is exactly equivalent to saying the plaintiff has no right at all.

Equity courts never claimed the power to deny a plaintiff's legal rights except by substantive defenses like estoppel. If the modest proposition is correct, then equity should not exercise discretion to deny even purely equitable remedies where equitable remedies represent the only practical remedy or the only one that protects the core rights. Although denial of the right might be appropriate if based on estoppel, or the plaintiff's closely related illegal conduct, it would not be appropriate if based merely on a vague and general balancing of equities and hardships. Some authority can be understood as representing such a view.

In *Tennessee Valley Authority v. Hill*, (the *Snail Darter Case*)[9] a federal statute aimed at protecting endangered species authorized an injunction. The statute was invoked as grounds for enjoining completion of a dam in the TVA system because the dam, if completed, would destroy the habitat of the snail darter, a unique species of perch. The injunction would have the effect

1. Compare: "The first principle of due process embraces a rule of law which contains standards that can be known in advance, conformed to, and applied rationally. The doctrine of the supremacy of law is 'a doctrine that the sovereign and all its agencies are bound to act upon principles, not according to arbitrary will; are obliged to follow reason instead of being free to follow caprice.' " Mattison v. Dallas Carrier Corp., 947 F.2d 95 (4th Cir.1991) (quoting Roscoe Pound, The Spirit of the Common Law 183 (1963).

9. 437 U.S. 153, 98 S.Ct. 2279, 57 L.Ed.2d 117 (1978).

of discarding considerable work already done and destroying the benefits, whatever they might be, of having the dam completed. Balancing of hardships might suggest that considering the enormous cost already invested, as well as the human benefits the dam might bring, the injunction should be denied.

But the Supreme Court of the United States refused to balance hardships or equities and held that the injunction should run to forbid completion of the dam. Alternative remedies were not available. In practical effect it would not be merely denial of an equitable remedy, but denial of a substantive right created by Congress. Although the Court did not express itself in precisely these terms, the decision against discretion is completely in accord with the view that equity must not use discretion and balancing to deny substantive rights.

Statutory rights and equitable discretion. The *Snail Darter* case can be seen in a different perspective as a case of statutory rights. Some thinkers assert that courts have no power to dispense with statutory remedies in their discretion unless the statute itself so provides or implies.[10] But this seems right only when denial of the statutory remedy is a denial of all remedies. After the *Snail Darter's* case, the Supreme Court held that equitable discretion could be invoked to deny equitable relief against the Navy, which was polluting waters by dropping bombs without the requisite administrative approval. Administrative approval was not exactly a "remedy" for the plaintiffs who sought to enjoin the Navy, but it did represent alternative solutions to the case. Under those circumstances, the Court thought that an injunction could be denied to permit the Navy to seek such approval.[11]

So it would seem that the equity court must grant the equitable relief without room for discretion (a) when the statutory command is absolute and does not brook equitable discretion, and (b) when the statutory scheme permits *only* equitable relief and denial of that relief would be a denial of the right granted by the statute. Conversely, equitable relief such as an injunction could be denied according to the usual balancing and discretion of equity courts if, in spite of past violations of the statute, the defendant presented no threat of future violation,[12] or if the statute itself explicitly or implicitly authorized balancing or discretion to reject remedies.

[For discussion of equitable discretion to expand rights, and to affect third persons, see this section in the Practitioner Treatise edition, vol. 1, pp. 121–123.]

10. See Plater, Statutory Violations and Equitable Discretion, 70 Calif.L.Rev. 524 (1982); § 5.7(5) below.

11. Weinberger v. Romero–Barcelo, 456 U.S. 305, 102 S.Ct. 1798, 72 L.Ed.2d 91 (1982). A debate ensued. See Farber, Equitable Discretion, Legal Duties, and Environmental Injunctions, 45 U.Pitt.L.Rev. 513 (1984) (compliance was required by the statute, but immediate compliance was not); Plater, Statutory Violations and Equitable Discretion, 70 Calif.L.Rev. 524 (1982) (opposing *Weinberger* as plainly rejecting a statutory command); Schoenbrod, The Measure of an Injunction: A

Principle to Replace Balancing the Equities and Tailoring the Remedy, 72 Minn.L.Rev. 627, 647 (1988) (a court which allows departure from the statute by refusing the injunction must do so only if it finds a factor present in the case that "was not reflected in [the statute's] formulation").

12. Hecht Co. v. Bowles, 321 U.S. 321, 64 S.Ct. 587, 88 L.Ed. 754 (1944) was such a case and the Court thought an injunction was not required. See the discussion in Plater, Statutory Violations and Equitable Discretion, 70 Calif.L.Rev. 524, 562–67 (1982); § 5.7(5) below.

§ 2.5 Remedial Limits Based on Power and Policy: Adequacy and Practicability

Equitable relief is traditionally denied on two grounds that are not even nominally associated with the traditional ethical rules. First, when the plaintiff claims equitable relief for a right created or recognized "at law," it is said that equitable relief must be denied unless the legal remedy is inadequate and denial will not cause irreparable harm to the plaintiff. In theory, this is not a rule of discretion but a rule of policy or even a limitation on judicial power. This rule has come upon heavy attack today and its existence has been called into doubt.[1] Second, equitable relief may be denied, in the court's discretion, for reasons of convenience or policy, as where enforcement of an injunction might require excessive investment of judicial resources or might interfere with resolution of the case by other courts, agencies or departments.[2]

§ 2.5(1) Adequacy of Legal Remedy or the Irreparable Harm Rule

Adequacy Test

When the plaintiff sought an equitable remedy for a right that had already been created or recognized by law courts, the equity courts historically held that equitable relief would be denied unless the plaintiff could show that the legal remedy was in some way inadequate. For example, if the defendant was in possession of the plaintiff's land, the plaintiff might seek to remove him by a mandatory injunction requiring him to leave. However, the legal action of ejectment would accomplish the same thing and a court might refuse the injunction on that ground.[1]

Historical Basis

After separate equity courts had developed in England, equity sometimes acted to create new substantive rights, even in opposition to legal rules, as where it prevented enforcement of mortgages against debtors.[2] It might even enjoin enforcement of solemn legal judgments.[3] Equity's expansive power ignited opposition from law court judges, not only because their turf was threatened, but also because their ideologies and methodologies differed from the chancellor.[4] When the equity courts did *not* create a new right, but instead merely added a remedy to rights already recognized by the law courts, they prudently stated the adequacy rule.

In this setting, the adequacy rule represented some kind of accommodation between the two kinds of courts. It also represented a kind of self-serving propaganda by equity courts, the effect of which was to say they were not trespassing on the jurisdiction of the law courts.[5] With the merger of law and equity courts into a unitary system of justice,[6] this history offers no basis for continued use of the rule, and it remains today primarily as a

§ 2.5(1)

3. This was settled in the famous Coke–Ellesmere dispute. Coke, Chief Justice of the King's Bench who liked to style himself Chief Justice of England attempted to prohibit the Chancellor, Ellesmere, from enjoining enforcement of judgments rendered by the law courts. King James I, an autocratically-minded man, naturally favored his Chancellor over Coke, a supporter of Parliament and a believer that the king himself was subject to the common law. There are many surveys of the dispute, which, of course, Chancery won. See F. Maitland, Equity 9 (2d ed. 1947); Dawson, Coke and Ellesmere Disinterred: The Attack on the Chancery in 1616, 36 Ill.L.Rev. 127 (1941).

convenient (but perhaps misleading and overstated) expression for entirely different policies.

The Irreparable Harm Formulation

In many instances courts formulate the adequate legal remedy rule by saying that equitable relief is denied unless the plaintiff could show that, without such relief, he would suffer an irreparable harm.[7] The two formulas represent the same core ground for refusing equitable relief when noncoercive relief "at law" is available.[8]

However, the irreparable harm formulation is sometimes used, not to compare the legal remedy, but for other purposes, for which it is given a different meaning. First, "irreparable harm" may be a short (and misleading) way of saying that, if the plaintiff seeks a preventive injunction to forestall harm, the threat of harm must be real.[9]

Second, "irreparable harm" may be used by the plaintiff to assert an argument for the creation of a new *substantive* right rather than as a ground for a coercive remedy for an existing right. Suppose you say to the court, "my former spouse has custody of our children, has remarried, and is about to change their names to that of her new spouse. I ask an injunction because if you do not grant it, my relationship with my children might be irreparably harmed." Your former spouse would not be committing a tort in changing the children's name. You are not asking for injunction because damages are inadequate. You are asking for injunction because you have *no right at all* unless a court will recognize one in this proceeding. Your assertion of "irreparable injury" in this case is an appeal to equity to create a new, equitable right, one that would *not* be enforced by a damages judgment. It is equivalent to saying "justice demands judicial intervention," not equivalent to saying "I can get damages but that is a poor remedy."

Many cases have listed both inadequate remedy at law *and* irreparable harm as separate prerequisites to coercive relief. This seems to be an erroneous conflation of the two different kinds of cases, remedial and substantive. Where the issue is remedial, the adequacy and irreparability rules mean the same thing. Where the issue is substantive, whether the court should create a new right, irreparable harm has a meaning that is different, but one that is not involved at all in the question whether to leave the plaintiff to a noncoercive remedy.

This section addresses the question whether coercive relief is to be denied because some noncoercive relief is available. On that point, the courts have stated the adequacy/irreparability rule over and over, as a routine introduction to the issue.[12]

---

8. See D. Laycock, The Death of the Irreparable Injury Rule 8 (1991). One commentator believes the two formulations, inadequate legal remedy and irreparable injury, represent two different ideas. See Shreve, Federal Injunctions and the Public Interest, 51 Geo. Wash.L.Rev. 382 (1983). Cases sometimes say that the plaintiff must show inadequate remedy at law and also irreparable harm, as if the two tests were separate requirements. See,

e.g., Kugler v. Ryan, 682 S.W.2d 47 (Mo.App. 1984).

12. E.g., Knaebel v. Heiner, 663 P.2d 551 (Alaska 1983); Brownfield v. Daniel Freeman Marina Hosp., 208 Cal.App.3d 405, 256 Cal. Rptr. 240 (1989); B.G.H. Ins. Syndicate, Inc. v. Presidential Fire & Casualty Co., 549 So.2d 197 (Fla.App.1989); In re Marriage of Strauss, 183 Ill.App.3d 424, 132 Ill.Dec. 245, 539 N.E.2d 808 (1989); Borom v. City of St. Paul,

Relative Adequacy

Authoritative federal decisions hold that the adequacy rule is relative. Before equitable relief is foreclosed, the legal remedy must be as complete, practical and efficient as the equitable remedy available.[13] That is, the content of the legal remedy is judged relative to the content of the equitable remedy. This comparison of remedies seems to cover their content, not their enforcement procedures.[14]

Although the adequacy rule is relative, it is also negative. Equitable relief is foreclosed when the legal remedy is deemed adequate, but equitable relief is not correspondingly available when the legal remedy is not.

Adequacy as a Non-discretionary Rule; "Equity Jurisdiction"

A traditional locution of equity courts referred to the body of equity precedent and practice as "equity jurisdiction." Sometimes a bill in equity would be dismissed because there was no "equity jurisdiction," and sometimes this phrase was used in dismissing an equitable claim under the adequacy rule. But equity jurisdiction is not jurisdictional in the modern procedural sense. If a court were to grant an injunction when the plaintiff had an adequate remedy at law, the injunction assuredly would not be void; the defendant would disobey it at risk of contempt sanctions. So the adequacy rule is not a jurisdictional rule, as courts and writers have recognized.[15]

Distinguishing Other Rules

The adequacy rule is often confused with or collapsed into some other rules which are quite distinct. When the plaintiff sues for a preventive

289 Minn. 371, 184 N.W.2d 595 (1971) (injunction sought against city to restrain contracting with employer who racially discriminated, held, denied because plaintiff had adequate remedy at law); Presto–X–Co. v. Ewing, 442 N.W.2d 85 (Iowa 1989); Nebraska Public Power Dist. v. Lockard, 237 Neb. 589, 467 N.W.2d 53 (1991); Smith v. Smith, 4 Wash.App. 608, 484 P.2d 409 (1971) (contract by H to pay child support to W not specifically enforceable since money judgment at law would be adequate).

As will be suggested later, some of the cases relying upon the adequacy rule will be better understood on other grounds. See § 2.5(3) below.

13. See Terrace v. Thompson, 263 U.S. 197, 214, 44 S.Ct. 15, 17, 68 L.Ed. 255, 274 (1923) ("a suit in equity does not lie where there is a plain, adequate and complete remedy at law * * *. But the legal remedy must be as complete, practical and efficient as that which equity could afford"); Fischer v. Brombolich, 207 Ill.App.3d 1053, 152 Ill.Dec. 908, 566 N.E.2d 785, 793 (1991) ("For there to be an adequate remedy at law, the remedy must be clear, complete, and as practical and efficient to the ends of justice and its prompt administration as an equitable remedy"). Some similar formulations emphasize the importance of a complete remedy at law without capturing the idea that the legal remedy must be compared to the equitable relief. E.g., Wilcox v. Timberon Protective Ass'n, 111 N.M. 478, 806 P.2d 1068, 1076 (App.1990) ("adequate and complete remedy at law", under a heading in the opinion styled "Relative Adequacy of Injunction"); Isuani v. Manske–Sheffield Radiology Group, 805 S.W.2d 602 (Tex.App.1991).

The federal formula, from which some of the other formulas seem to have been taken, appears to be an affirmative and slightly more liberal version of the limits imposed in the Judiciary Act of 1789, § 16: "That suits in equity shall not be sustained in either of the courts of the United States, in any case where plain, adequate and complete remedy may be had at law."

14. Thus the legal remedy does not become inadequate merely because enforcement of money judgments by the impersonal processes of the law is more cumbersome than simply ordering the defendant to act and jailing him if he does not.

15. Moore v. McAllister, 216 Md. 497, 141 A.2d 176 (1958); Duvall v. Duvall, 224 Miss. 546, 80 So.2d 752 (1955); Chafee, Some Problems of Equity, 296–380 (1950) (detailed discussion).

injunction, the plaintiff must show a threat of future harm, else the injunction will be denied. The requirement of a threatened harm in such cases is sometimes expressed in terms of the adequacy or irreparable harm rules. But the problem in such cases is not whether there is an adequate legal remedy but whether there is anything to redress at all.

Examples

The most common instances of an adequate legal remedy occur when the plaintiff seeks to enforce a right the primary value of which is economic and which can be compensated in money. Two examples can illustrate a benign application of the rule in contract and in tort.

Suppose the defendant contracts to sell the plaintiff shares of stock that are sold on the New York Stock Exchange, or futures in grain sold on a commodity exchange. When the defendant later reneges, the plaintiff might sue for specific performance, an equitable remedy that would force the defendant to supply the promised performance. But in such a case the legal remedy is adequate; the plaintiff simply picks up the telephone and orders a replacement supply from the broker. If the market price has risen so that he must pay more than the contract price, then he can recover the additional costs from the defendant. Specific performance is traditionally denied in such cases (and in some more arguable than this), because the remedy at law is adequate.[21]

For a tort example, suppose that the defendant steals the plaintiff's law library. If the plaintiff can identify the books, he can recover them by the old legal action of replevin, in which the sheriff will be told to seize the books and deliver them to the plaintiff.[22] Except in most unusual cases, this action "at law" is quite adequate; the plaintiff does not need an injunction and the adequacy rule says he cannot have it.[23]

Rule Inapplicable to Substantive Equitable Rights

As already explained, a court considering whether to recognize or create a new kind of right may wish to know whether the injury to the plaintiff is a serious one and for this purpose may ask whether it is "irreparable." This substantive usage of the term "irreparable" is not related to the remedial question, whether to deny coercive remedies but allow noncoercive ones. Once the court creates a substantive equitable right, the question of irreparable harm or adequate legal remedy passes from the picture, and the new right is enforced by the coercive remedy without concern over adequate legal remedies.

The point is easier to see in connection with rules established when equity courts had a separate existence. Sometimes the separate equity courts, instead of adding a remedy to a right created by law courts, created a wholly new right which was flatly contradictory to the rights created in the

---

21. See Klein v. PepsiCo, Inc., 845 F.2d 76 (4th Cir.1988) (aircraft sale, money remedy "at law" adequate); Restatement Second of Contracts § 359(1) (1981). As to the adequacy test in specific performance cases generally, see § 12.8(2) below; as to the test in UCC suits by the buyer of goods, see § 12.16(7) below.

22. See § 5.17(2) below.

23. E.g., Charles Simkin & Sons, Inc. v. Massiah, 289 F.2d 26 (3d Cir.1961); see § 5.17(3) below.

law courts. For example, equity created the right of redemption in mortgage cases.[24] Equity created rights of beneficiaries of express trusts,[25] later expanding these rights to include constructive trusts.[26] In both mortgage and trust cases, equity courts imposed results that ignored and effectively abolished "legal" rights. In these cases of substantive equity, the adequacy of legal remedy was largely irrelevant.

These were cases in which equity courts did not seek accommodation with the law courts as they did when they only enforced legal rights with a better remedy. Instead, equity courts in these cases sought to completely undermine the "legal" title to property. So the adequate legal remedy rule has no application where equitable intervention is substantive rather than remedial,[27] as in the case of a constructive trust suit [28] or a suit against a fiduciary.[29]

§ 2.5(2) Establishing Irreparable Harm

Patterns of Irreparable Harm/Inadequate Legal Remedy

Patterns and factors in determining inadequacy. There is no general formula for determining when a legal remedy is inadequate. In a few situations, injunctions are so routinely given that they are sometimes regarded as the normal remedy, to be given irrespective of the adequacy test.[1] In addition, there are some common patterns of evidence which shows an inadequate legal remedy. The legal remedy is usually inadequate, and the equitable remedy usually granted, in cases like these:

(1) "Unique" or special entitlements. The plaintiff is deprived of some thing to which he is entitled, because the defendant has committed a tort or a breach of contract. The plaintiff needs the thing and cannot get it in the market. The legal remedy of damages will not do because he needs the thing itself. He will probably get equitable relief by way of injunction or specific performance. Some constitutional rights, such as free speech rights, are in this category;[2] so are rights of children in the state's custody to receive physical or emotional protection.[3] Parcels of land are unique, and

---

28. See Heckmann v. Ahmanson, 168 Cal. App.3d 119, 214 Cal.Rptr. 177 (1985).

29. I George Palmer, Law of Restitution § 1.6 (1978 & Supps.). Palmer, the leading authority on restitution, believes that results are less predictable when the "trust" claim is not against a fiduciary.

§ 2.5(2)

1. KSM Fastening Systems, Inc. v. H.A. Jones Co., 776 F.2d 1522 (Fed.Cir.1985) (injunction against infringement is the norm); United States Jaycees v. Cedar Rapids Jaycees, 794 F.2d 379, 382 (8th Cir.1986) (trademark infringement, injunction "denied only in the most unusual of cases"); Hibbett Sporting Goods, Inc. v. Biernbaum, 375 So.2d 431 (Ala. 1979) (covenant that lessor would not lease to lessee's competitors to be enforced by injunction; the only issue is whether the proposed leases would violate the covenant); Capraro v. Lanier Business Products Inc., 466 So.2d 212 (Fla.1985) (Irreparable harm need not be

shown to justify preliminary injunction for violation of covenant not to compete). Specific performance of land contracts is given routinely when the only issue is adequacy. See paragraph, "The uniqueness pattern" below.

2. See, e.g., Paulsen v. County of Nassau, 925 F.2d 65 (2d Cir.1991) (even minimal loss of First Amendment rights would be irreparable harm, preliminary injunction against interference with distribution of leaflets upheld).

3. Artist M. v. Johnson, 917 F.2d 980 (7th Cir.1990) (preliminary injunction requiring prompt attention to child required after state intervenes for child's protection to prevent "increased likelihood that families would be broken up or remain apart, that plaintiffs would be deprived of protective services, and that, in the absence of timely case plans and case reviews, children would be left in "unnecessarily restrictive or dangerous placements"), rev'd on other grounds, ___ U.S. ___, 112 S.Ct. 1360, 114 L.Ed.2d 97 (1992).

the adequacy rule seldom prevents protecting this unique interest by injunction.[4] Although "unique" is the term used in this kind of case, the term may include entitlements that are not literally one-of-a-kind. Entitlements are legally unique if they cannot be assuredly replaced with equivalents. One example is a share of stock in a closely held corporation,[5] or an heirloom or a painting that holds a unique place in the plaintiff's affections.

(2) Repeated acts, multiplicity of suits. The defendant acts in such a way that the plaintiff may be required to bring (or defend) more than one suit to effectuate his legal remedy (or to protect his legal right). This is a hardship, and equity may avoid it by awarding more adequate relief. For instance, if the defendant repeatedly trespasses on the plaintiff's land, equity may enjoin the trespass rather than force repeated actions at law to redress the injury.[6] Similarly, if the defendant has subjected the plaintiff to repeated malicious suits over the same subject matter, he may be enjoined from bringing further actions.[7]

(3) Legal remedy available but not collectible. The plaintiff is entitled either to money or certain performance by the defendant. Money, recoverable at law, would be an entirely adequate remedy, but the defendant is insolvent and it is not collectible. However, the defendant is still capable of rendering the performance to which the plaintiff is entitled, even though he could not pay money damages. Equity may be willing to order the performance in such a case,[8] although if the defendant's debt is discharged in bankruptcy his obligation under an injunction may be discharged as well, at least where compliance with the equity order will require a financial outlay.[9]

(4) Damages cannot be measured with reasonable certainty. The plaintiff is entitled to damages at law and this would be adequate if damages could be measured with any reasonable degree of accuracy, but under the facts damages are so speculative that any award is likely to be inadequate. This may be sufficient reason for equity to give its relief. For example, the defendant's infringement of the plaintiff's trademark is likely to confuse customers and cause losses to the plaintiff that cannot be measured, so

4. E.g., Dixon v. Thatcher, 103 Nev. 414, 742 P.2d 1029 (1987) (enjoining sale of plaintiff's log house under deed of trust).

5. E.g., Aldrich v. Geahry, 367 Pa. 252, 80 A.2d 59 (1951).

8. See Rose v. Rose, 66 N.C.App. 161, 310 S.E.2d 626 (1984) (separation agreement). Insolvency tends to be a make-weight or minor factor. See R.H. Sanders Corp. v. Haves, 541 S.W.2d 262 (Tex.App.1976) (apparently an alternative ground in the trial court, injunction held proper on the ground that damages were difficult to calculate). In Willing v. Mazzocone, 482 Pa. 377, 393 A.2d 1155 (1978) the court refused to enjoin a continuing demonstration/libel in spite of the defendant's insolvency.

The best discussion of the insolvency decisions is two and one-half pages long. D. Laycock, The Death of the Irreparable Injury Rule 75–77 (1991). The problem only arises with claims for preventive relief; as to past harms and reparative injunctions, the plaintiff is a creditor of the insolvent and must share with other creditors in the absence of property or restitutionary claims. Distinguish freeze orders issued before a trial on the merits, as to which see § 6.1(5) below.

9. Ohio v. Kovacs, 469 U.S. 274, 105 S.Ct. 705, 83 L.Ed.2d 649 (1985). *Kovacs* involved a reparative rather than a preventive injunction; it required the defendant to clean up a hazardous waste site and would have entailed actual expenditure of funds. A preventive injunction that prevents the defendant from competing in business or infringing a trademark is presumably a different matter. Such an injunction affects income, not outlay, and prevents earnings by the bankrupt but does not interfere with the clean-slate that discharge otherwise provides.

injunction may be routinely issued in such cases and others causing business losses that cannot be identified.[10]

[For applications in contract and tort cases, see this section in the Practitioner Treatise edition, vol. 1, pp. 132–135.]

§ 2.5(3)   The Adequacy Test Today: Reality and Debate

Adequacy Today

The rule declines. The adequacy test is repeatedly invoked today when the plaintiff seeks equitable relief. Nevertheless its importance has declined. Many cases do not mention the test at all. Some cases mention the test but find plenty of grounds for saying that the legal remedy is not adequate. Adequacy of the legal remedy is often judged quite liberally in favor of the equitable remedy. When equitable relief is denied, it is quite often on grounds entirely distinct from the adequacy grounds. For instance, as shown in the next subsection, the adequacy rule may be invoked even when equitable relief is denied on grounds of practicality or policy.[1] So although the rule is often invoked, it is also often ignored, sidestepped, or invoked in a way that means something else altogether. It is probably fair to say that the adequacy test has been evolving from a rule to a factor in the court's balance of costs and benefits.[2] The giant that guarded equity's gate is dying.

Emerging issues. In this setting a major debate has erupted. Most of the debate has purported to center on the adequacy/irreparability rule. The first issue is whether the adequacy test should or does continue to bar access to coercive remedies such as the injunction. Many contemporary thinkers have argued against the adequacy test. The second issue, often submerged in the debate over the adequacy test, is whether coercive remedies should be granted on demand (or presumptively or routinely). No thinker seems to favor an *invariable* award of coercive remedies, but some argue that when the plaintiff demands such a remedy, it should ordinarily be granted.

The two issues are similar; and because the adequacy rule was the traditional gatekeeper that forestalled coercive remedies on demand, it is easy to confuse the adequacy and "on demand" issues. But one could reject the adequacy test completely without deciding that plaintiffs should be presumptively entitled to coercive remedies whenever they asked for them.

The adequacy rule is already much reduced in practical operation, so the second issue may be the much more important one. It can be reduced to a simple question. If the plaintiff can have coercive remedies, even when her

---

10. See United States Jaycees v. Cedar Rapids Jaycees, 794 F.2d 379, 382 (8th Cir. 1986) (trademark infringement injunction denied only in unusual cases); § 6.4(5) below.

§ 2.5(3)

1. See § 2.5(4) below. In the same vein, the adequacy test can be seen as a kind of inept corollary to the rule requiring the plaintiff to minimize damages. It is sound enough to require a defendant to remove boulders he

has deposited upon the plaintiff's land, but it would not be equally sound to issue an injunction to require him to remove a cardboard box; the plaintiff can minimize the problem by removing it himself.

2. That approach is discussed in § 2.9(2) below. See Edward Yorio, Contract Enforcement: Specific Performance and Injunctions § 2.5 (1989); Douglas Laycock, The Death of the Irreparable Injury Rule 10 (1991).

damages remedy is adequate, what limiting rules, if any, bar or limit coercive orders?

This section points to some of the main contentions in the debate over increased access to coercive remedies, first as to injunctions generally, then as to specific performance of contracts in particular.

Coercive Remedies: The Advocates

Owen Fiss. In 1978 Professor Owen Fiss attacked the traditional "hierarchy" of remedies embodied in the traditional preference for damages over injunctions and specific performance.[3] Fiss attacked the adequacy/irreparable harm rule, arguing that, although "reactionary forces" wanted to subordinate the injunction, there was really "no reason why the injunction should be disfavored".[4] For him, injunctions were at least as desirable a remedy as damages. He saw in injunctions no threat to liberty when they compelled conduct, no danger to free speech when they shut off publication, and no impediment to any desirable economic efficiency when they compelled performance of contracts. He was also willing to invoke coercive orders independent of the substantive rights they were meant to enforce.[5] In part at least, Fiss seemed to favor coercive remedies because he saw the task of courts as effectuating social reform, not because their task is individual justice or economic efficiency.[6]

Fiss opposed the adequacy rule and his overall exposition might sound as if he also favored coercive remedies on demand. But Fiss explicitly said otherwise. He opposed any "hierarchy" of remedies; the remedy choice was to be made on the basis of the advantages and disadvantages in each case. The superiority of an injunction would not be presumed.[7]

Douglas Laycock. In 1991, following publication of an article in the Harvard Law Review,[8] Douglas Laycock published an important and scholarly book called The Death of the Irreparable Injury Rule.[9] Discussing the adequacy/irreparable harm test, Laycock analyzed virtually every category of injunction and specific performance case in modern law. He had reviewed Fiss's proposals and had approved what he considered to be their thrust, but not all the details.[10] Then after studying a large sample of actual cases, Laycock came to a startling conclusion. He decided that no plaintiff

3. O. Fiss, The Civil Rights Injunction (1978), hereafter in this Section, cited as Fiss. Judge Wisdom and several eminent remedies scholars reviewed the Fiss book in essays that are themselves illuminating. See Laycock, Book Review, Injunctions and the Irreparable Injury Rule, 57 Tex.L.Rev. 1065, 1068 (1979); Rendleman, Book Review, 47 U.Chi.L.Rev. 199 (1979); Veitch, Book Review, 58 Can.B.Rev. 235 (1980); Wisdom, Book Review, 89 Yale L.J. 825 (1980).

4. Fiss, 5–6.

5. See § 7.4(4) below.

6. See Fiss, The Supreme Court 1978 Term, Foreword: The Forms of Justice, 93 Harv.L.Rev. 1, 29 (1979) ("courts exist to give meaning to our public values, not to resolve disputes"); cf. Laycock, Book Review, Injunctions and the Irreparable Injury Rule, 57 Tex.

L.Rev. 1065, 1068 (1979) ("he seems to impute to the world his view that injunctions were redeemed by the civil rights experience").

7. Fiss at 6.

8. Laycock, The Death of the Irreparable Injury Rule, 103 Harv.L.Rev. 687 (1990).

9. D. Laycock, The Death of the Irreparable Injury Rule (1991), hereafter cited in this section as Laycock. The book is cited in the remainder of this section, but the article is almost identical. The book has the convenience of a detailed index. The article is available on Westlaw, so word searches in the article are possible.

10. Laycock, Injunctions and the Irreparable Injury Rule, 57 Tex.L.Rev. 1065 (1979).

with a plausible need for specific equitable relief would be barred by the adequacy rule.[11] Although the rule is often invoked by the courts, Laycock concluded that it is always irrelevant. When equitable relief is properly denied, it is almost always for other reasons, even though the adequacy rule might be used as a stand-in or for those other reasons or as a convenient way of disposing of the case. In any event, the courts were not either motivated or logically compelled by the adequacy/irreparability rule.

Laycock pointed to and analyzed a wide spectrum of contemporary cases. For example, courts might refuse to give equitable relief because the plaintiff has no substantive right at all,[12] because the plaintiff sought preliminary relief before trial without a sufficiently strong ground to deny the defendant the protections of a full due process hearing,[13] or because other courts or forums should resolve the case.[14] Yet in each instance the court may give the convenient reason that the plaintiff has an adequate non-coercive remedy.

Similarly, courts may refuse an injunction as a balancing of hardships and equities, after considering in the balance the fact that the plaintiff has other remedies,[15] or because injunctions run too many risks or compel conduct we are socially unwilling to compel, as where they would shut off speech or would enlist the defendant in the plaintiff's personal service.[16] Again, the rule selected to explain these results may be the adequacy rule. But the rule seems to be selected for its convenience in statement, not for its fit to the facts.

The affirmative side of Laycock's perceptions may be more important. He believed that the law of remedies can be accurately stated without reference to the adequacy/irreparable injury rule, and that the resulting shift exposes the important policy issues that were cloaked by that rule.[17]

On the second issue, whether coercive remedies should be available on demand, Laycock was more precise than Fiss. He proposed a carefully drafted set of rules.[18] The adequacy rule would be abolished, but coercive remedies would not become automatic, because the courts would still be required or permitted to deny such remedies either as a result of balancing equities, hardships, and practicalities, or under some specific rule. Nevertheless, Laycock went beyond Fiss because he proposed to make coercive remedies "presumptively" available.[19]

Coercive Remedies: Doubters and Disbelievers

Doug Rendleman. Support for the adequacy rule is almost always less universal in scope than the attacks on it. Some support for the adequacy rule comes from equity skeptics who worry more about intrusive, coercive remedies than about the adequacy rule as such. That is, some thinkers seem to worry more about the question whether coercive remedies should be given on demand than about the adequacy test as a criterion. Coercive equitable remedies can sometimes create more problems than they solve. They may interfere with jury trial rights, they raise the potential for enforcement by jail sentences that might never end, and they may impose costs that exceed the harvest of benefits.

Doug Rendleman, long an important remedies scholar, cautions that specific performance and other forms of coercion may be important and may be the only satisfactory remedy in some cases, but that the remedy must be considered against its intrusive and potentially costly effects. In particular, Rendleman has mentioned the potential abuses of the contempt power and the lost right of jury trial that may follow when coercive remedies are used. In some cases coercive enforcement can be "psychologically taxing, protracted, and costly." [20]

Rendleman may not directly support the adequacy test as such, but he appears to oppose the view that all remedies are equally available to the plaintiff.[21] His is a voice of caution and doubt.

Edward Yorio. Professor Edward Yorio addresses only the specific performance remedy, but he should be mentioned here because of the strong positions he has taken against the use of that particular coercion. As to the adequacy rule, Yorio seems to justify it only as a kind of balancing test used to figure total costs and benefits of equitable relief as compared to other available remedies, rather than as an automatic bar.[22] In that respect, he seems to be on the same side of the table as Douglas Laycock.

Yorio, however, does not share the view that coercive remedies should be granted routinely. Still addressing specific performance in particular, he argues that both the defendant-promisor and the court have interests in the nature and scope of the remedy.[23] The parties' failure to specify a remedy should be read as leaving the remedy to the court's judgment, not as leaving the remedy to the promisee's choice.[24] Yorio also sided with the economic arguments that favor the present regime, believing that specific performance is efficient when the subject matter of the contract is more or less unique, otherwise not.[25]

Specific Performance

The specific performance remedy is a form of injunction and thus encompassed in the comments of thinkers like Laycock. However, specific performance arises in a contractual setting. Because within limits the parties can bargain about remedies, some approaches to specific performance might be different.

Disfavoring specific performance. Kronman, doing an economic analysis, argued that the adequacy rule produces about the same results the parties would bargain for if they were to bargain about remedies.[26] When performance is unique, the parties would probably prescribe specific performance and in addition the courts would find specific performance administratively convenient because damages would be hard to assess in such a case. So the traditional approach favoring specific performance in such cases is doubly right. When the performance contracted for is *not* unique, however, the parties probably would not want to bargain for specific performance. If the court refuses specific performance in such non-unique cases, it saves the costs of negotiation about the remedy.[27]

20. Rendleman, The Inadequate Remedy at Law Prerequisite for an Injunction, 33 U.Fla.L.Rev. 346, 356 (1981).

21. See Rendleman, supra n. 20 at 358.

22. See, among many references, Yorio, § 2.5 (1989).

26. Kronman, Specific Performance, 45 U.Chi.L.Rev. 351 (1978).

27. In actuality the parties seem to have little freedom to prescribe their own remedies, see § 12.9(6) below. However, courts often assume that a liquidated damages clause,

Goetz and Scott also doubted that specific performance should be granted on demand. They argued that specific performance fails to set the right amount of minimizing behavior in "specialized" (non-market) contracts, and that it makes no difference, economically, where there was a well-developed market for the goods in question.[28]

Favoring specific performance. A number of other writers have taken a view about specific performance more closely aligned with the Fiss view about coercive remedies generally, except that they justify the coercive remedy by economic analysis or moral assertions.[29] Schwartz argued that specific performance was a more efficient remedy, partly because damages are likely to be undercompensatory.[30] Sometimes writers have explicitly sought to protect the promisee's subjective valuation of the performance due by making specific performance readily available.[31]

Other economic arguments pro and con turn in part on whether breach should be encouraged when it will allow full payment of damages to the promisee and still permit a gain to the promisor. If so, specific performance on its face seems to undercut the policy of this efficient breach. On the other hand, some economists argue that when the promisor is given a chance to sell his performance at a higher price elsewhere, he can "buy out" of the contract with the original promisee. This in turn leads to a debate over whether the post-breach negotiations would themselves be costly and inefficient.[32]

Moral theories of performance. The leading theories favoring routine specific performance are expressly economic in nature and depend on economic analysis, but they find support as well in theories of contract that are expressly moral in nature. The moral theory of a contract promise assumes that the promise cannot be understood as a promise that "I will perform as

where valid, is also exclusive. Operating in an arena governed by this assumption, parties can provide for liquidated damages as a means of excluding specific performance, even though they cannot provide a clause in favor of specific performance. Even if this is not thought to represent sufficient party control over the remedy to show an actual savings of dollar costs in negotiation, it is important that the remedies prescribed by the courts reflect the parties' preferences.

28. Goetz & Scott, The Mitigation Principle: Toward a General Theory of Contractual Obligation, 69 Va.L.Rev. 967 (1983).

29. See Schwartz, The Case for Specific Performance, 89 Yale L.J. 271 (1979); Ulen, The Efficiency of Specific Performance: Towards a Unified Theory of Contract Remedies, 83 Mich.L.Rev. 341 (1984).

30. Schwartz, The Case for Specific Performance, 89 Yale L.J. 271 (1979). This treatise takes the view that "compensation" in contract cases is properly fixed at the level of the plaintiff's contract entitlement but that this is not the same as all losses resulting from breach, because the contract is usually meant to guarantee only against certain losses. Under this view, the damages remedy is not necessarily undercompensatory merely because it leaves the promisee with losses. Whether the damage award is compensatory does not depend on the loss so much as on the entitlement the plaintiff "bought" in the contract. See § 12.2(1). The point is also related to Hadley v. Baxendale rules, as to which see §§ 12.4(4)–12.4(7).

31. As implied in the preceding note, subjective preference or valuations of the performance should not be compensated unless they were part of the entitlement the plaintiff bought and paid for. If I contract to buy a lamb for $20 and the seller breaches, he would be very surprised to hear that I subjectively valued that lamb at $100,000. If he thought he was dealing in lambs and not in a golden fleece, he should not be held liable for my idiosyncratic values. My idiosyncratic values can be fairly communicated to him if I demand a $100,000 liquidated damages clause, in which case one suspects the price of the lamb will rise dramatically. Protecting idiosyncratic values is a tricky business and not invariably a good ground for specific performance.

32. See § 12.8(2) below.

stated, else pay damages." Instead, the moral view is that the promise is "I will perform as stated, no ifs, ands, buts or substitutes." Given the promise so interpreted, specific performance is said to be "simply right." [33] Enforced morality is an ancient idea of the chancellors, so if the contract is a plain vanilla promise and if morality should be enforced by compelled performance, then specific performance, if not injunctions in general, should become routine. The double premise required for this conclusion is of course subject to dispute.

Party autonomy. Part of the objection to routine specific performance is the lurking suspicion that such a remedy is definitely *not* what the parties expected and not the basis for pricing their respective performances. Courts do not allow the parties complete freedom to bargain about remedies.[34] Allowing the parties complete freedom of contract about remedies would not solve all the problems, but it would reduce the significance of the issue and it would facilitate pricing of performance in the light of the remedies bargained for. Opening up any area for bargaining adds to the potential costs of contracting, but also to the freedom and the information necessary to make desirable contracts. In specific performance cases the adequacy/coercive remedy problem can be much minimized by allowing genuine freedom of contract on remedial issues.

Some Assessments

The adequacy rule, as a rule that simply bars the gate, is virtually dead and probably should be. Laycock's immense scholarship and biting analysis will make it difficult to return to that simple shibboleth as a means for exercising discretion, even if we would like to do so. Unqualified support for a general adequacy rule is hard to find. The rule today seems to be one of those rules judges grab off the rack without really trying it on; it doesn't fit, but it is easy to state with citations.

Realistically speaking, the much more important matter is the second issue. Should the coercive remedy be available to the plaintiff routinely or presumptively, unless there is some particular reason to deny it? Or should courts be reluctant to use coercion even after the adequacy rule is abolished?

On this second issue, attitude and personality may control preferences. Optimists do not worry about judges who like to exercise coercive remedies. They are confident that jury trial rights are either not so important or can be protected. They believe that imprisonment for debt can be avoided by using contempt fines instead of contempt imprisonment. Pessimists doubt the benignant use of power and may mistrust those who favor coercion when other solutions are available. Balancing of equities, hardships, and practicalities, supplemented by a few more particular rules,[35] might suffice. But the critical weight in the balance may turn out to be the weight of one's attitude about coercion and its intrusive effects. The adequacy test can be discarded, but a pessimistic presumption that disfavors coercion may prove to be a more difficult matter.

33. See Linzer, On the Amorality of Contract Remedies—Efficiency, Equity, and the Second Restatement, 1981 Colum.L.Rev. 111, 138 (1981).

34. See § 12.9 generally, § 12.9(6) as to agreements for specific performance.

§ 2.5(4) Practicality and Public Policy as Limits on or Guides to Equitable Remedies

Previous sections have shown how coercive remedies in particular may be limited by ethical or justice considerations, and by the adequacy rule. Such remedies may also be limited by considerations of policy and practicality. This section lists several important examples and in some instances refers the reader to more developed discussions elsewhere.

Substantive Policy

Compelling personal service. Substantive policy opposes orders that compel personal servitude. The defendant who promises to do personal service for another may be held in damages, but may not be compelled to do personal work for another.[1] This is a substantive policy with a precise remedial effect: it limits the injunctive or specific performance remedy but not the damages remedy. It does not turn on adequacy or even ethics, but on a strong policy about the limits of judicial power and the strength of personal autonomy.

Forbidding speech. Speech is important in our society not only as a source of public values but also as a central part of one's personality. The right to speak is an intimate value closely related with the right to refuse personal service; an injunction against either invades personhood in serious ways. Because of both the social and the personal values in speech, damages for some kinds of speech like libel may be circumscribed.[2] Injunctions, more intrusive and more serious in their limitations, are usually even more circumscribed. Tradition has it that libel is not enjoined.[3]

Some writers would narrow that tradition by saying that injunctions are permissible so long as they are not a prior restraint. Restraints on additional speech are always prior to that additional speech and always run the risk that ideas and deeply personal values will be shut off by a judge who believes he knows the truth. Whatever the exact line, however, it is clear the coercive remedy is more intrusive in matters of speech and also that in some degree coercive remedies like injunctions are limited in ways that damages remedies are not.

Weighing public needs. Equity courts have long recognized that public interests are to be weighed whenever equity's power is called upon. This may outweigh all other considerations. A court may be unwilling to issue an order that will require long supervision,[4] but willing to issue the same order if a public interest calls for it.[5] Similarly, the plaintiff's unclean hands may not furnish a defense if the public interest decrees otherwise.[6] The operation of railroads, buses, public utilities and the like is frequently identified with public interest in this sense, and the utility may be permitted to obtain relief that would not necessarily be available to others,[7] or to avoid

---

§ 2.5(4)

1. The topic is discussed in § 12.22(2).

2. See § 7.2(4) below.

3. See § 7.2(14).

4. See the paragraph, "Supervision" below.

5. See Virginian Ry. Co. v. System Federation, 300 U.S. 515, 57 S.Ct. 592, 81 L.Ed. 789 (1937); § 12.8(3) below.

6. E.g., Radich v. Kruly, 226 Cal.App.2d 683, 38 Cal.Rptr. 340 (1964).

7. Edison Illuminating Co. v. Eastern Pa. Power Co., 253 Pa. 457, 98 A. 652 (1916) (spe-

orders that others would not be permitted to avoid, because of the public interest involved.[8]

Practicality, Convenience, Judicial Resources

Supervision. Injunctive decrees might order a single act by the defendant. For example, the court might order the defendant to convey Blackacre to the plaintiff as he contracted to do. Other injunctive decrees might order complex operations that would take place over a long period of time. An order requiring a contractor to build a building, or a railroad to install a station and provide service as contracted would be like this. Courts traditionally worried about the second kind of order. They anticipated that new disputes would arise constantly and sap judicial resources. Perhaps they also feared that constant supervision would precipitate a metamorphosis by which they would become administrators rather than judges. At any rate, important cases have refused to order specific performance where the performance would require complex or continuing acts.[9]

The fear of long supervisory problems is probably overdone, and some decisions refusing relief seem wrong.[10] But in any event it does not raise a rule of law, only a guide to the chancellor's discretion. The stronger the need for coercive relief, the more willing the chancellor to grant the relief in spite of fearful anticipations. So some cases grant specific performance of contracts that call for continuing work and relationships in the future.[11]

The same is true with injunctions. Some of the most important civil rights injunctions—the structural injunctions as Fiss called them—undertake almost incredibly complex restructuring of public institutions to bring them into conformity with constitutional demands.[12] If the defendants are recalcitrant and the alternatives ineffective, then the demand on judicial resources in such cases is worth the cost of judicial time. So the long-continued supervision problem represents a factor in the balance of decision-making, not a rule.

Certainty in specific performance. The cases are replete with the assertion that a contract, to warrant specific performance, must be certain and complete. Sometimes the meaning of this requirement is obscure, since a contract is not a contract at all unless it expresses some kind of promise that can be understood by intelligent beings. The theoretical explanation is that this is a practicality rule. It avoids a specific performance decree (it is said) because the chancellor will not know what terms to insert. The suggestion is that the same uncertain contract could support a claim for damages, even

cific performance of contract in favor of power company, even though longer supervision might be required; power company was public service corporation and there was a public interest).

8. Sexton v. Public Serv. Coordinated Transport, 5 N.J.Super. 555, 68 A.2d 648 (1949) (no preliminary injunction against bus company; public interest was involved).

9. See generally § 12.8(3) below.

10. E.g., Besinger v. National Tea Co., 75 Ill.App.2d 395, 221 N.E.2d 156 (1966), discussed in § 12.8(3) below. Professor Yorio

thinks the decision got the right result because he believes the legal remedy was adequate enough. See E. Yorio, Contract Enforcement: Specific Performance and Injunctions § 13.4.3 (1989).

11. City Stores Co. v. Ammerman, 266 F.Supp. 766, 776 (D.D.C.1967), aff'd, 394 F.2d 950, 38 A.L.R.3d 1042 (D.C.Cir.1968); § 12.8(3) below.

12. See Fiss, The Civil Rights Injunction 36–37 (1978) (describing some aspects of the restructuring injunctions).

though it is too uncertain to permit a good decree. The likelihood is to the contrary; if the contract is not certain enough to order performance, it probably is not certain enough to permit a good calculation of damages either. So the certainty rule, allegedly a remedial rule directed at injunctions, may be equally applicable to damages claims and hence a substantive rather than a remedial rule.[13]

Deference and Practical Caution

Professor Laycock identifies a category of policy he calls deference to other authority.[14] Sometimes a plaintiff who is subject to another court, or to some adverse action by the executive branch of government, will seek injunctive relief. The plaintiff may seek to enjoin the defendant from litigating a claim or from prosecuting a criminal charge in another court, for example. Or the plaintiff may seek to enjoin an administrative proceeding or some other executive action.

State court injunctions against other state courts. In such cases it is often better policy not to issue the injunction. Sometimes practical limits on the court's power suggest that the injunction should not issue. If the Illinois court enjoins X from litigating against Y in Michigan, the Michigan Court may respond by enjoining Y not to enforce the injunction.[15] Because injunctive orders are not ordinarily res judicata or subject to full faith and credit in other court systems, the court war may continue until the parties' funds are exhausted. So, as Justice Wallace Schaefer once said, the best place to stop will be before the first injunction is issued.[16]

In such cases an injunction in one court to halt proceedings in another is one way to allocate power between the courts. Allocation of this power is always significant to the parties, who have their own preferred forums for trial. Allocation of power among governments and among branches of government is also socially and politically important. Policy conflicts are often serious.

Federal courts enjoining state court proceedings. One pattern that has engaged many lawyers is the suit in federal court to enjoin a state proceeding (or some other state action) on the ground that the state proceeding is based on an unconstitutional law or some unconstitutional acts. Because federal constitutional issues can be raised in state courts, and a federal injunction against state litigation may create an unnecessary friction between the two systems, the injunction against criminal prosecution in state courts may be denied.[17] In a few cases it is granted.[18] Similar concerns limit federal injunctions against state civil and administrative proceedings.[19]

---

13. See § 12.8(3) below.

14. D. Laycock, The Death of the Irreparable Injury Rule, Chapter 6 (1991).

15. See James v. Grand Trunk W.R.Co., 14 Ill.2d 356, 152 N.E.2d 858, 74 A.L.R.2d 814 (1958), cert. denied, 358 U.S. 915, 79 S.Ct. 288, 3 L.Ed.2d 239 (1958).

16. Id. (Schaeffer, J. dissenting).

17. Younger v. Harris, 401 U.S. 37, 91 S.Ct. 746, 27 L.Ed.2d 669 (1971); § 7.3(5) below.

18. Dombrowski v. Pfister, 380 U.S. 479, 85 S.Ct. 1116, 14 L.Ed.2d 22 (1965); § 7.3(5) below.

19. See § 7.3(5) below. Cf. Pennzoil Co. v. Texaco, Inc., 481 U.S. 1, 107 S.Ct. 1519, 95 L.Ed.2d 1 (1987) (no injunction against enforcement of state's judgment, though denial of injunction would mean de facto denial of any review).

These concerns find expression in some federal statutes limiting injunctive interference with state proceedings as well.[20]

The policy conflicts are jurisdictional and substantive, so the court must decide the appropriate sphere of judicial action for each court system and must also consider the importance of the substantive constitutional rights in issue. Both those issues are outside the scope of remedies law, but they come to head as almost all issues do in connection with a particular remedy. When those issues come to a head in an injunction suit the courts sometimes speak the language of irreparable harm or adequate legal remedy, meaning that the party seeking a federal injunction may raise his constitutional issue in the state court suit or prosecution. The point is not irrelevant, but the central decision is really less about adequacy or irreparable harm than it is about the appropriate allocation of power on issues of federal constitutional rights.

[For discussion of these issues in connection with injunctions against administrative agencies, executive acts, and conduct in other states, see this section in the Practitioner Treatise edition, vol. 1, pp. 146–148.]

C. PROCEDURES, JURISDICTION, AND ENFORCEMENT

§ 2.6 Law and Equity Today—the Merger of Law and Equity and the Right of Jury Trial

§ 2.6(1) The Merger of Law and Equity

Generally

Merger. In the 19th century both England and the American states adopted major procedural reforms. In America the reform began with constitutional amendments and the adoption of Code procedure in the Field Code in New York in 1848 and its spread to other states. For students of remedies, the central reform is that the constitutions and codes abolished separate equity or chancery courts and created one form of action, the civil action.[1] This reform is commonly referred to as the merger of law and equity. Similar provisions for merger can be found in the Federal Rules of Civil Procedure.[2]

20. 28 U.S.C.A. § 2283 provides: "A court of the United States may not grant an injunction to stay proceedings in a State court except as expressly authorized by Act of Congress, or where necessary in aid of its jurisdiction, or to protect or effectuate its judgments." See County of Imperial v. Munoz, 449 U.S. 54, 101 S.Ct. 289, 66 L.Ed.2d 258 (1980). Cf. 28 U.S.C.A. § 1341 & 28 U.S.C.A. § 1342 (federal courts not to enjoin state tax collections or state utility rate making where state remedies are available).

§ 2.6(1)

1. See Fleming James, Jr. and Geoffrey Hazard, Jr., Civil Procedure § 1.6 (3d ed. 1985).

2. The federal courts always had equity powers as well as law power, but they operated, until the Federal Rules of Civil Procedure, by distinctly separating equity cases and even had separate equity rules. On the debates over equity jurisdiction in federal courts see Warren, New Light on the History of the Federal Judiciary Act of 1798, 37 Harv.L.Rev. 49, 96 ff (1923). The power to combine the courts is considered in McCormick, The Fusion of Law and Equity in United States Courts, 6 N.C.L.Rev. 283 (1928).

Merger has not been uniform throughout the United States. A few states maintain separate equity courts, or separate divisions of a single court, usually with provisions for free transfer of cases between the courts or divisions. Where this is so, special rules or practices may be required, sometimes necessitating two trials.[3] But the judge of a court of general jurisdiction in most states and the judges of the United States District Courts enjoy both the powers of the old chancellors and the powers of the old law judges. Many other states maintain a tier of minor courts of limited jurisdiction, such as justice courts or magistrates who are typically not given equity powers.[4] But these limited exceptions come down to saying that, overwhelmingly, the courts of general jurisdiction in America enjoy both law and equity powers.

Scope. This section outlines some of the meanings and effects of merger. Because equity courts granted no jury trials, the most significant issue considered here is the effect of merger on jury trial rights and the strategy issues that accompany jury trial issues. The general question asked in this section is whether merger of law and equity makes the old distinction between the two kinds of cases or remedies obsolete.

Substantive and Procedural Merger

Procedural merger and the jury. In most states and in the federal system, there are no longer separate equity rules of procedure.[5] With one exception, the same procedures are available to the parties whether the plaintiff seeks an injunction or money damages. Only a few states have retained separate equity courts, or, short of that, docket cases separately and use slightly different rules. Overwhelmingly, however, the judicial systems are procedurally unitary. The exception to procedural unification is the jury trial.

Equity courts did not grant jury trials; law courts did.[6] Merger has not obliterated the difference between the two court systems as to jury trials. Pure "equity" cases are still tried without a jury. Pure common law cases, in contrast, carry constitutional jury trial rights. In such pure cases, merger has had little or no formal effect. However, merger may have contributed to a contracting conception of what is uniquely equitable. The result is that jury trial is now available in some cases because the claim is considered to be a common law claim, even though at one time it was thought of as equitable.[7]

In addition, procedural reform and merger make it possible to join claims that are both legal and equitable in a way that was not usually possible before. When a case involves both legal and equitable issues, rules, or remedies, however, some kind of accommodation is required. In these mixed cases merger has sometimes pushed courts to expand jury trial so that

3. See Stanardsville Volunteer Fire Co., Inc. v. Berry, 229 Va. 578, 584–585, 331 S.E.2d 466, 470 (1985) (proper procedure to try the plaintiff's easement by estoppel claim would be to sue for preliminary injunctive relief on equity side, then to have a jury trial on the law side if the plaintiff lost the equity claim, or to have the injunction made permanent if the plaintiff won it).

4. See Lash Furniture Co. v. Norton, 124 Vt. 58, 196 A.2d 506 (1963).

5. As to "jurisdiction" in equity, see § 2.7 below.

6. See § 2.6(2) below.

7. See § 2.6(3) below.

some equitable issues may be governed by a jury verdict, as explained in the next subsection.[8]

Merger and substantive law. Merger reinforced the tendency of the old law courts to adopt equity's more modern ways. As to substantive rules, merger is now virtually complete. A court today will ordinarily apply the substantive rules appropriate to the facts, regardless whether those rules originated in equity courts or in law courts. A single case may thus involve some issues and rules that originated in equity and some that originated at law. Actually, the merger of substantive rules had been constantly taking place even before formal merger. Law courts were routinely assimilating equity's substantive ideas. For example, it has been a long time since "equitable estoppel" was purely equitable.

So today the judge deciding an undue influence case may apply rules that originated in equity because those are the rules that govern the facts; it will not be necessary to ask whether the court sits as an equity court or a law court because it always sits as both. If an equity court would have given the plaintiff standing to sue, then the merged court can do so, even if the plaintiff does not seek a coercive or "equitable" remedy.[9] This almost complete merger of the two court systems on issues of substance turns out to be important in understanding the appropriate scope of jury trial rights.[10]

Remedial Merger

Merger and remedial law. After merger, a court having both law and equity powers may give the plaintiff any remedy justified by pleading and proof. For example, the court might grant specific performance, which is a coercive remedy of equitable origin; or it might grant damages, which is a remedy of legal origin; or it might grant some combination. To this extent, remedial merger is complete.

Three qualifications impinge on this apparently complete merger: (1) The adequacy/irreparable harm rules may still operate to limit coercive but not other remedies; (2) Most equitable discretion to deny relief has traditionally been applied remedially, to bar specific performance or injunction but not to bar damages, and these rules can appropriately be applied in the merged court system; (3) Something similar can be said about the equitable defenses of unclean hands and laches.

[*For the effect of merger on the adequacy rule, discretion and equitable defenses, see this section in the Practitioner Treatise edition, vol. 1, pp. 150–153.*]

Coercive orders and enforcement of money awards. Two other differences between traditional law and traditional equity remain after merger. A complete merger means that the court would have the power to issue an injunction to compel a tort defendant to pay money to the injured tort plaintiff, just as it has the power to compel specific performance of a contract. The practice, however, has not been to compel money payments by injunctive orders except in very special cases. Instead, a *judgment* is

---

8. See § 2.6(4) below.

9. See Ross v. Bernhard, 396 U.S. 531, 90 S.Ct. 733, 24 L.Ed.2d 729 (1970).

10. See § 2.6(2) below.

rendered for most ordinary money obligations. The differences between the injunctive order and the judgment is in the enforcement. The injunctive decree can be enforced by contempt; the judgment is enforced by seizing assets. The law-equity distinction does not prevent injunctions to require money payments, but good sense or caution will often do so. Put differently, the occasions for invoking coercive power are not necessarily changed by merger.

Even so, there are cases in which injunctive orders compel the payment of money. Courts may compel the payment of money due as part of a status obligation, such as the obligation of child or spousal support.[18] In such cases no fixed sum is due for a fixed period, so a judgment for a sum certain is often impractical. Courts might also order money payments as part of an accounting.[19] A constructive trust or similar remedy applied against a fund of money such as a bank account may in fact be enforced ultimately by a compelled transfer of the fund.[20] Sometimes courts also freeze bank accounts or other funds before a full trial where the plaintiff makes a strong showing of ownership.[21] One court ordered a public agency to make advance payments to a hospital toward the agency's future liabilities under a medical assistance program.[22] In very recent years some courts have ordered tortfeasors to make partial payments to permit medical monitoring of victims, once the defendants' tort liability established.[23] The last instance is decidedly a case that would have been brought "at law" under the pre-merger system, and it reflects the new flexibility available with merger.

§ 2.6(2) Merger and Jury Trial—Equity Jury Rules

Constitutional Rights to Jury Trial "at Common Law"

The old separate courts of equity did not afford jury trial as of right. The chancellor acted as trier of fact as well as decision-maker on issues of conscience or rules. Merger did not affect this practice in most courts. The United States Constitution guarantees a right to jury trial as it is existed when the Seventh Amendment was adopted in 1791,[1] but the jury trial right so preserved applies only to "common law" actions, not to equity suits.[2]

---

18. See Brown v. Brown, 287 Md. 273, 412 A.2d 396 (1980) (orders compelling payment for support of own child are permissible and can be enforced by imprisonment for contempt, but not orders for support of a stepchild); In re the Marriage of Griffin, 141 Wis.2d 699, 416 N.W.2d 612 (1987) (past due child support enforceable by contempt). Such cases may lead to enforcement by the contempt power, as in Hicks on Behalf of Feiock v. Feiock, 485 U.S. 624, 108 S.Ct. 1423, 99 L.Ed.2d 721 (1988), discussed in § 2.8(3) below.

19. As to accounting, see § 4.3(5) below.

20. As to constructive trusts and similar remedies, see § 4.3(2) below.

21. See § 6.1(5) below.

22. See Temple University v. White, 941 F.2d 201, 216–221 (3d Cir.1991).

23. See § 8.10 below.

§ 2.6(2)

1. The text states the usual view. But Professor Charles Wolfram has given a scholarly and vigorous argument that "common law" in the Seventh Amendment should be read to mean the common law process of adjudication and that the jury trial right was thus not fixed by historical precedents that existed in 1791. He calls this the "dynamic reading" of the Seventh Amendment. Wolfram, The Constitutional History of the Seventh Amendment, 57 Minn.L.Rev. 730 (1973).

2. U.S. Const.Amend. VII: "In suits at common law, where the value in controversy shall exceed twenty dollars, the right of trial by jury shall be preserved, and no fact tried by a jury shall be otherwise re-examined in any court of the United States than according to the rules of the common law." Only a few states have no similar guarantee. See James,

State constitutions usually preserve the right from the various times of their adoption.

States Granting Equity Jury Trial

Statutes as well as state constitutional provisions may augment the constitutional and historical right to jury trial. Several American states created a novel system in which jury trial is afforded even in core equity cases. Van Hecke concluded that at one time 13 states permitted a binding jury verdict in equity trials. At the time he wrote, only four states continued to use this practice.[3] The actual use of binding jury verdicts in equity, however, appears to be somewhat more attenuated than this picture suggests. In Georgia, there is no general right to equity jury, and the parties can have a jury only by virtue of a statutory provision for juries in damages claims in equity.[4] Texas has a strong constitutional provision for jury trial in "all causes," and strong judicial recognition of that right,[5] but not every proceeding counts as a "cause" for which such a trial is required.[6]

Advisory Juries in Equity

Equity courts have the power to call an advisory jury and to accept its verdict or reject it as mere advice and to substitute the judge's own findings of fact.[7]

§ 2.6(3)   Characterizing a Case: Equitable or Legal?

In Summary

Distinguishing characteristics. When equity courts were separate courts, they could be distinguished from law courts in three important ways. Their substantive rules were different when they created an equitable right contrary to rights that would exist at law; their procedure was different; and their remedies were different whenever they gave coercive relief. In addition, they claimed the power to deny relief as a matter of discretion.

Substantive and remedial tests of equitable status. These characteristics suggest at least two [1] distinct tests for determining equitable status today. *First,* a claim could be deemed equitable if it sought a coercive remedy like injunction, otherwise not. *Second,* a claim could be deemed equitable if the plaintiff sought to enforce a right that was originally created in the equity courts, or a right that was traditionally decided according to equitable principles.

For instance, trademark rights might be decided by stressing fairness or similar principles of equity substance.[2] Rights arising from mortgages[3] or trusts,[4] were created in equity courts to begin with, so it is plausible to say

Right to a Jury Trial in Civil Actions, 72 Yale L.J. 655 (1963).

3. Van Hecke, Trial by Jury in Equity Cases, 31 N.C.L.Rev. 157 (1953). The four states Professor Van Hecke listed were Georgia, North Carolina, Tennessee and Texas.

4. See Clayton v. Deverell, 257 Ga. 653, 362 S.E.2d 364, 367 (1987).

5. E.g., Citizens State Bank of Sealy, Texas v. Caney Investments, 746 S.W.2d 477 (Tex.

1988) (recognizing jury trial right in suit for permanent injunction).

6. See State v. Credit Bureau of Laredo, Inc., 530 S.W.2d 288 (Tex.1975).

7. E.g., Sheila's Shine Prods., Inc. v. Sheila Shine, Inc., 486 F.2d 114, 121–122 (5th Cir. 1973); Posey v. Leavitt, 229 Cal.App.3d 1236, 280 Cal.Rptr. 568 (1991); Stanardsville Volunteer Fire Co., Inc. v. Berry, 229 Va. 578, 331 S.E.2d 466 (1985).

that cases involving those topics are "equitable" in some substantive sense, provided that right was still being treated as a purely "equitable" right when the constitution was adopted. If this substantive test of equitable status were used, a case might be considered as "equitable" even though no coercive remedy was invoked or needed. One difficulty with this kind of "historical" or substantive test was that law and equity were not fixed categories of logical thought but shifting sands of history: a case might be equitable or legal, depending on the moment at which the question was asked.[5]

Judicial approaches generally. The courts have not settled fully on any firm approach. In general, a case will be treated as equitable if an equitable, coercive remedy is invoked. However, even when no such remedy is at issue, some cases, such as mortgage foreclosures, are treated as equitable. The Supreme Court of the United States, in decisions governing federal trials, has said it would consider *both* historic analogies *and* remedies to determine the equitable or legal status of a claim. If equity courts traditionally tried an analogous claim at the time the Seventh Amendment was adopted, then the substantive analogy suggests that the claim is equitable and that no jury trial is required. However, if the remedy sought is merely an ordinary damages award, the remedial test suggests that the claim is a "common law" claim triable to a jury. The Supreme Court has not suggested how to weigh these two tests when they conflict, but it has said that the remedy sought is the more weighty consideration.[6]

Remedies Sought as Test of Equitable or Legal Character

The remedial test. Courts agree that the plaintiff's label on the claim does not control the status as an equitable or legal claim.[7] They also agree that a case does not become equitable merely because the defendant raises an equitable defense such as estoppel.[8] And, overwhelmingly, courts characterize claims according to the remedies sought rather than according to subject matter or substantive rules involved.

If the remedy sought is a coercive order, the claim is equitable; if the remedy sought is a judgment to be enforced in rem by seizure of property, the claim is legal. An action for an ordinary[9] money judgment,[10] for replevin,[11] or for ejectment[12] is an action at law. In contrast, a suit for injunction[13] or one for specific performance is equitable.[14]

Money claims for restitution. Some money claims are not "damages" representing the plaintiff's loss but "restitution" representing the defendant's unjust gains in a transaction. As indicated below, some restitution claims were equitable. However, many were not. Many restitution claims were brought under the common law writ of assumpsit, using its common counts such as the count for money had and received. These claims are claims at law in every sense, first because they seek simply money relief, and second because they were historically brought in the separate law courts.[15]

§ 2.6(3)

5. The "borrowing" of law from equity and vice versa is classically described in Fleming James, Jr. & Geoffrey Hazard, Jr., Civil Procedure § 8.2 (3d ed. 1985).

6. Tull v. United States, 481 U.S. 412, 421, 107 S.Ct. 1831, 1837, 95 L.Ed.2d 365 (1987); Granfinanciera, S.A. v. Nordberg, 492 U.S. 33, 109 S.Ct. 2782, 106 L.Ed.2d 26 (1989).

Money claims for restitution with equitable enforcement: constructive trusts. Just the opposite is true for some other kinds of restitution claims. The constructive trust is the most familiar case. If the defendant obtains a fund of money from the plaintiff (by fraud or embezzlement, for example) and deposits it in a bank account, the plaintiff might recover a constructive trust on the bank account. This is not merely a remedy created in equity; it is also a substantive rule created by equity. The upshot of the constructive trust is an order compelling the defendant (or the bank) to place the fund in the plaintiff's name. It differs from an ordinary judgment at law, which would adjudicate the plaintiff's right to recover *an* amount of money from the defendant, but would not identify the particular source.[16] The constructive trust has great advantages, one of which is to permit the plaintiff to recover the fund without sharing it with any other creditors, because in the eyes of equity it is his.

Because the constructive trust is ultimately enforceable by a personal order (convey Blackacre or transfer the specific fund of money), it has at least a latent injunctive or coercive quality. And because it was historically and substantively equitable as well, the constructive trust suit is almost always regarded as equitable in nature, even though it might ultimately reach a fund of money.[17]

If no particular property is identified as belonging to the plaintiff in equity and good conscience, the plaintiff's claim for money restitution looks like an ordinary claim for a money judgment. In that case, the claim seems to be legal by ordinary standards.[18] Sometimes courts have used the term constructive trust in adjudicating cases where there is no res to which a trust can attach. The term cannot refer in such cases to a trust duty about specific property or an identified fund, so it looks like a way of referring to an ordinary obligation to make restitution of money which would be enforceable at law. Nevertheless a court may characterize such cases as equitable so as to deny a right to jury trial.[19]

Money claims for restitution with equitable enforcement: accounting for profits. Several remedies parallel the constructive trust.[20] The remedy known as accounting or accounting for profits is usually regarded as equitable, but it can ultimately resemble a money judgment. The accounting claim is that the defendant (often a fiduciary) has profited by using something which in good conscience belongs to the plaintiff and that the defendant ought to disgorge his profits in much the same way that a constructive trustee would be required to do. The old equity courts ordered an accounting in two kinds of cases. In one, the accounts were too complicated for a jury, so in a sense the legal remedy was inadequate because the procedure by way of jury trial was inadequate. In the other, equity appeared to take jurisdiction because equity courts were interested in the *substantive* rules involved; they wanted to enforce an equitable duty to account. Equity recognized and enforced fiduciary duties, so it naturally gave an accounting

---

18. See Blue Cross Health Servs., Inc. v. Sauer, 800 S.W.2d 72 (Mo.App.1990); 4.3(2) below.

19. People ex rel. Daley v. Warren Motors, Inc., 114 Ill.2d 305, 102 Ill.Dec. 400, 500 N.E.2d 22 (1986).

20. Notably, equitable liens, subrogation, accounting for profits, rescission, reformation. See §§ 4.3(3)–4.3(7), below.

remedy against fiduciaries.[21] The accounting claim is usually regarded as equitable and jury trial in accounting claims is often denied.[22]

Nevertheless, the accounting also bears a considerable resemblance to an ordinary money judgment. It ends with a determination that the defendant owes a fixed sum of money. Although it might be possible to compel payment of that money by an in personam order enforceable by contempt, such a procedure may be unwise if it is not needed. If no personal order is used to enforce the award of a fixed sum at the end of the accounting, the ultimate judgment would look like an ordinary money judgment "at law." There is nothing especially equitable about the fact that the plaintiff recovers the defendant's profits or gains; quasi-contract claims permit recovery of such gains, and quasi-contract claims are indisputably claims "at law."[23] So if the ultimate award in the accounting is merely a non-coercive money judgment, the accounting claim might be thought to require a jury trial.[24] This is the setting that led to a major decision of the United States Supreme Court in the *Dairy Queen* case.

The Dairy Queen case. In *Dairy Queen, Inc. v. Wood*,[25] the Supreme Court focused on the remedy to determine whether the case was equitable or not. The plaintiff claimed an accounting for profits, alleging that the defendants owed the plaintiffs a percentage of profits in connection with a Dairy Queen franchise. The plaintiffs resisted jury trial on the ground that an accounting is equitable. To determine whether the claim was equitable or not, the Court focused on the remedy. The remedy was not coercive, but only a claim for money. Judging by this remedy, the case appeared to be an ordinary claim at law.

Because the claim was one for money, the case would be equitable only if the equity court could somehow provide a more adequate remedy by its form of trial. The legal remedy with a jury trial might be inadequate if the accounting would be too complex for a jury; in that case, the more adequate equity remedy would be a non-jury trial. But the Court thought that adequacy of the legal remedy should be judged in the light of modern procedures, including merger, not by purely historical standards. The jury would very likely be adequate to the task of figuring net profits if the court appointed a master to "unravel" the accounts and present findings or recommendations to the jury. So the equity mode of trial (without a jury) was not itself a part of the remedy needed. That left a claim for a money recovery, and as judged by that remedy, the case was purely legal. Consequently a jury trial was required.

The stockholder's derivative suit. *Dairy Queen* seemed to focus on the remedy as a major basis for characterizing a claim as legal. In addition, it

21. See Eichengrun, Remedying the Remedy of Accounting, 60 Ind.L.J. 463 (1985); § 4.3(5) below.

22. See Phillips v. Kaplus, 764 F.2d 807 (11th Cir.1985) (plaintiff sought to be restored to partnership interests, which defendant allegedly obtained from plaintiffs by fraud, with dissolution of partnership as the second stage of relief, and with distribution of assets by way of accounting as the third; held, the claim is equitable); Van de Kamp v. Bank of

America Nat. Trust & Savings Ass'n, 204 Cal. App.3d 819, 251 Cal.Rptr. 530 (1988); Dick v. Dick, 167 Conn. 210, 355 A.2d 110 (1974); § 4.3(5) below.

23. See §§ 4.2(3), 4.5 below.

24. See John A. McCarthy & Co., Inc. v. Hill, 295 N.Y. 320, 67 N.E.2d 375 (1946).

25. 369 U.S. 469, 82 S.Ct. 894, 8 L.Ed.2d 44 (1962).

seemed to emphasize the enhanced powers and procedures of the merged court in determining whether trial at law with a jury would provide adequate redress. The Supreme Court applied these concepts in *Ross v. Bernhard,*[26] a stockholder's derivative suit.

Equity's connection with stockholder derivative suits comes about this way. If directors of a corporation misuse company assets or opportunities, the corporation has a legal right to sue. But the corporation would not do so, because it was under the control of the directors. Because the corporation is the legal entity with the right to sue, shareholders were not permitted to do so. So shareholders went to equity, where they could sometimes show the chancellor sufficient preliminary facts to obtain permission to sue on behalf of the besieged corporation. In effect, the equity court gave the shareholder standing as a kind of temporary and limited trustee for the company.

Traditionally, the equity court, having taken the case to create standing for the plaintiff would proceed to adjudicate the merits, even if the merits only involved an ordinary money claim. The Supreme Court in *Ross v. Barnard* changed this; it held that once the judge-as-chancellor established the stockholder's right to sue for the corporation, the case would proceed exactly as it would have proceeded in a suit by the corporation itself. The merger of law and equity meant that "it is no longer tenable for a distinct court, administering both law and equity in the same action, to deny legal remedies to a corporation, merely because the corporation's spokesmen are its shareholders rather than its directors."[27] If the claim was a money judgment claim, or otherwise presented a "legal issue," a jury trial would be available on demand.[28]

As in *Dairy Queen,* the Court discarded historical practice. It focused first on the flexibility that comes with merger; the judge of the merged court can try the "equity" issue by itself, deciding initially whether the stockholder should have standing to sue, and if so, then set the remainder of the case down for a jury trial if the remaining matters in dispute are "legal." And second, the Court focused on the remedy sought; money damages is not equitable, so in the second stage, a jury trial is appropriate.

This kind of decision would seem to be a good model for some others. For example, in interpleader cases, equity uses its coercive power to force all claimants to a fund or property to present their claims in a single court, so that the stakeholder will not be forced to litigate separately with all of them. Once that equitable power has been exercised, the underlying litigation proceeds. If that litigation is over purely "legal" claims to the fund, the principle in *Ross* suggests that the trial should be to a jury if one is demanded.[29]

26. 396 U.S. 531, 90 S.Ct. 733, 24 L.Ed.2d 729 (1970).

27. Id. at 540, 90 S.Ct. at 739, 24 L.Ed.2d at 737.

28. " * * * we have no doubt that the corporation's claim is, at least in part, a legal one. The relief sought is money damages * * *." Id. at 512, 90 S.Ct. at 740, 24 L.Ed.2d at 738.

29. Poss v. Franklin Federal Sav. & Loan Ass'n of Russellville, Ala., 455 So.2d 9 (Ala. 1984); Geddes v. Rosen, 22 A.D.2d 394, 255 N.Y.S.2d 585 (1965). See Wright & Miller, Federal Practice and Procedure § 74 (1986 & Supp.). Some state decisions are to the contrary. In Waggoner v. Johnston, 408 P.2d 761 (Okl.1965) both claimants brought in had "legal," not equitable claims to the fund. Never-

The preference/fraudulent conveyance litigation; bankruptcy. A good illustration of how a suit is characterized as legal or equitable according to the remedy sought was suggested in a Supreme Court decision, *Granfinanciera, S.A. v. Nordberg.*[30] It considered cases of preferences or fraudulent transfers[31] by debtors who attempt to siphon off their assets before creditors could reach them. Under some circumstances such transfers to defeat claims of creditors are improper. For instance, *B,* about to become bankrupt, transfers all his money to a friend or favored creditor, *T.* When the bankruptcy court takes over *B*'s assets to share them out among creditors, there will be no funds because *B* has already transferred them to *T.* So legal rules permit creditors, or the trustee in bankruptcy who represents all the creditors as a group, to recover the transferred assets from *T.* Such a recovery permits the assets to be applied to payments of creditors' claims and defeats the effort to secrete them or to favor one creditor over others.

Is the suit by the trustee to recover the preferential transfer a suit "in equity" or "at law"? Under the remedial test, the answer depends on the remedy sought. If the asset transferred was money or personal property, a money recovery or a specific recovery of the chattel by way of replevin would be available "at law," and in that case a jury trial would be constitutionally available upon demand. On the other hand, if the asset transferred was real property, the plaintiff might need an in personam order compelling the defendant to deed back the property or some other equitable relief. If the plaintiff sought equitable relief, a non-jury trial would then be the traditional response. The *Granfinanciera* Court did not rely exclusively on a remedial test. It also found some disputed history showing that some 18th century suits to recover transfers were often brought at law. Nevertheless, the Court emphasized that the remedy sought is a more important factor than historical practice.[32] So a suit to recover a preferential transfer of money requires a jury trial.

The point is that the substantive law of preference and fraudulent conveyances is the same whether the plaintiff seeks to recover money or real property, but that the remedy is different and that the remedial difference is the chief factor in deciding whether the case is legal or equitable. In the *Granfinanciera* case itself, the suit to recover the debtor's pre-bankruptcy transfer of assets was in the bankruptcy court itself, not in some court of general jurisdiction. Bankruptcy is traditionally regarded as an equitable proceeding. If a creditor of the bankrupt submits a claim and the trustee

---

theless, in accord with what it described as the vast weight of authority, the court denied jury trial on the ground that "interpleader, from beginning to end, is an equitable action," because of the initial use of equity power. Cf. Williams v. Overstreet, 230 Ga. 112, 195 S.E.2d 906 (1973) (begun as suit to enforce equitable lien on funds, concluded as interpleader after funds paid into court, case is in equity, no jury). As to interpleader see § 2.9(4) below.

30. 492 U.S. 33, 109 S.Ct. 2782, 106 L.Ed.2d 26 (1989).

31. Preferences are payments of an antecedent debt by an insolvent; fraudulent con-

veyances or transfers are transfers made in an effort to hide assets from creditors. Both are recoverable on slightly different theories. Professor McCoid thinks that the action at law was commonly accepted for the recovery of preferences but that suits in equity came to be used for the recovery of fraudulent conveyances. See McCoid, Right to Jury Trial in Bankruptcy: Granfinanciera, S.A. v. Nordberg, 65 Am. Bankruptcy L.J. 15, 23–28 (1991).

32. See Granfinanciera, S.A. v. Nordberg, 492 U.S. 33, 42, 109 S.Ct. 2782, 2790, 106 L.Ed.2d 26 (1989).

disputes it, the court decides the issue without a jury. Nevertheless, the Court in *Granfinanciera* held that if the trustee claims against *T* for a money recovery in the bankruptcy proceeding where *T* has submitted no claim,[33] the Constitution requires a jury trial if it is demanded.[34]

Substantive Tests of Legal or Equitable Character: Equity without Coercion

The substantive test. An alternative to the *Dairy Queen* remedial approach ignores the remedy sought. The alternative asks whether the claim is substantively equitable, not whether it is remedially so. Under this approach, the claim is equitable if equity historically entertained similar claims or if substantive equitable doctrines or rules would govern the case, or if the case was simply regarded as equitable in some important sense before the constitutions were adopted. Several important kinds of cases fell in this substantive or historical category—mortgage foreclosures,[35] trust litigation,[36] bankruptcy,[37] even divorce.[38]

History does not always speak clearly about many other cases, however.[39] When history is deficient, as it always is when the claim in issue is one unknown to the 18th century, the courts resort to analogies. Had the alternative approach been adopted in *Dairy Queen,* the Court would have treated the case as "equitable" because accounting was historically the province of the separate equitable courts and invoked the equity court's ideas of substantive law. It would not matter under this test that no coercive remedy would be granted.

Mortgages. As already shown, the old separate equity courts developed the substantive law of trusts and mortgages.[40] The equitable doctrines of mortgages in effect forgave debtors their letter-of-the law obligations, and then, by foreclosure, put a limit on how long debtors could take to pay their debts. Sometimes equity's coercive powers were involved in these cases, but not always. The mortgage foreclosure declared the parties' status and removed the impediment which equity itself had placed in the way of the creditor. Foreclosure and the associated claims eventually produce a money judgment or its equivalent; and it in effect schedules a sale of the mortgaged land to pay the debt. So, like accounting, foreclosure is historically and substantively equitable, but it can be accomplished without coercive remedies. Most courts impliedly accept the substantive or "historical" test in

33. Where the transferee, *T,* himself submits a claim in bankruptcy, and the trustee counterclaims to recover a preferential transfer, both the claim and the counterclaim are tried as "equity," non-jury proceedings. Katchen v. Landy, 382 U.S. 323, 86 S.Ct. 467, 15 L.Ed.2d 391 (1966).

34. Strangely enough, the issue whether bankruptcy courts themselves can provide the Seventh Amendment jury trial was not decided; even the constitutionality of some of the bankruptcy court's powers remain in doubt. On these and related points see Gibson, Jury Trials and Core Proceedings: The Bankruptcy Judge's Uncertain Authority, 65 Am. Bankruptcy L.J. 143 (1991).

35. See the paragraph, "Mortgages," immediately below.

36. See the paragraph "Trusts," below.

37. See the paragraph, "The preference/fraudulent conveyance litigation; bankruptcy," above.

38. See the paragraph "Rescission and other declaratory decrees," below.

39. See Professor John McCoid's discussion of the Granfinanciera case and some alternative historical interpretations, supra n. 31.

40. See § 2.3 above generally.

foreclosure cases, holding that actions to foreclose mortgages [41] or mechanics' or other liens [42] are equitable even though no particular coercive remedy is sought.[43]

Trusts. The equitable doctrines recognized trusts and substantive fiduciary duties not originally recognized by the separate law courts. So equity naturally enforced the duties it created. Sometimes the coercive power was implicated, as where a trustee was compelled to reconvey property he had wrongfully taken. Equity might also require him to account for profits made with trust property, which, as already seen, might or might not entail a coercive remedy. In other cases, the trustee might be subjected merely to a money judgment. So trust and fiduciary cases are historically and substantively equitable, but remedially speaking they might be legal. In these cases, authorities sometimes seem to apply a substantive or historical test and sometimes a remedial test. The trust beneficiary's remedies against the trustee are said to be equitable, but at the same time courts recognize that if the plaintiff seeks merely to recover a fixed sum of money or the replevin of a chattel, the remedy is "at law" with a jury trial.[44]

Rescission and other declaratory decrees. Another example of equitable intervention without the use of coercive orders includes some kinds of rescission. Equity might rescind contracts by actually canceling instruments, a remedy that might require use of equity's coercive power (an order to surrender the instrument for cancellation). But at other times, equity's rescission operated, like equity's decree quieting title, merely to declare a status in a way that would be binding. Although an injunction or other coercive order might be useful in particular cases, it was by no means necessary to effect rescission. Something similar can be said of reformation: sometimes it required coercive power, or at least direct judicial intervention, but at other times it was merely a kind of declaratory judgment.

Because a declaratory judgment is not a coercive remedy, it can be regarded as a purely legal remedy, and the Supreme Court has so regarded it.[45] However, the declaratory effects of equitable remedies like rescission

---

41. Jamaica Savings Bank v. M.S. Investing Co., 274 N.Y. 215, 8 N.E.2d 493, 112 A.L.R. 1485 (1937) (excellent discussion of different possibilities, foreclosure, deficiency, separate suit on the bond or debt at law); State Bank of Lehi v. Woolsey, 565 P.2d 413 (Utah 1977) (nonjury trial in foreclosure action even as to underlying money claims).

42. First Nat. Bank of Meeker v. Theos, 794 P.2d 1055 (Colo.App.1990); Weisman v. Hopf–Himsel, Inc., 535 N.E.2d 1222 (Ind.App. 1989); Kahle v. John McDonough Builders, Inc., 85 Md.App. 141, 582 A.2d 557 (1990). In *Theos, supra,* the court summarized a common attitude as follows:

Actions seeking judicial foreclosure of liens have traditionally been considered equitable proceedings. Although such actions typically involve determinations of the existence and amount of indebtedness, and although any ensuing foreclosure decree typically includes a personal monetary award against

the debtor founded in contract, the basic thrust of foreclosure proceedings has nevertheless been held to be equitable.

Although granting that foreclosure of a mechanic's lien is equitable, the court may simply state, without advancing reasons, that the claim in the particular case is "essentially" a claim on a contract and hence one at law. Stokes v. Johnston, 138 A.D.2d 481, 526 N.Y.S.2d 27 (1988).

43. Indeed, at some times and places foreclosure of a mechanics lien was once treated as a purely legal action. See the good discussion in Suburbia Pools, Inc. v. Fischer, 661 S.W.2d 823 (Mo.App.1983).

44. See Kahle v. John McDonough Builders, Inc., 85 Md.App. 141, 582 A.2d 557 (1990) (relying on the Restatement Second of Trusts §§ 197, 198).

45. Beacon Theatres, Inc. v. Westover, 359 U.S. 500, 79 S.Ct. 948, 3 L.Ed.2d 988 (1959).

suggest a historical equitable connection, and where the declaratory judgment resembles a traditional equitable remedy that had declaratory effects, some courts treat the declaratory judgment as equitable,[46] along with rescission itself.[47] More commonly the declaratory action is regarded as equitable when the underlying dispute is equitable, otherwise it is legal.[48]

Determinations of status are often vaguely connected with equity. Divorce has long been associated with equity and non-jury divorce trials are common, although a number of states have permitted jury trials in divorce actions, or as to some particular issues in those actions.[49] Quiet title suits operate most fundamentally to declare landowning status, are traditionally regarded as purely equitable.[50] Some other status determinations, such as those made in juvenile court, are usually made without juries and sometimes on the explicit ground that they have equitable characteristics.[51]

Estoppel and other equitable doctrines. Many substantive equitable doctrines or attitudes may become involved in any given case. An extreme application of the substantive test suggests that if some equitable doctrine like estoppel or unclean hands is considered or applied in a case, the case becomes equitable. Probably most courts would not consider going so far, but at least one court converted an ordinary contract claim to a suit in equity and denied the jury trial right on the ground that the plaintiff claimed a promissory estoppel.

The case is *C & K Engineering Contractors.*[52] A general contractor sued a subcontractor who had reneged on its promise to do certain work on a large project. When the sub reneged, the general contractor was required to do the sub's work at a higher cost than the price bid by the sub. The general contractor sued for the excess cost. The general contractor's theory was that the subcontractor had promised to adhere to its bid and that the general contractor had relied on the promise. Such reliance is an accepted substitute for consideration in many cases.[53] The doctrine that permits foreseeable reliance to substitute for consideration is often called promissory estoppel, and regarded as a modern outgrowth of equitable estoppel.[54] Equi-

---

46. See Fowler v. Ross, 142 Cal.App.3d 472, 191 Cal.Rptr. 183 (1983); First–Citizens Bank and Trust Co. of S.C. v. Hucks, 305 S.C. 296, 408 S.E.2d 222 (1991).

47. Motor Vehicle Mfrs. Ass'n of the U.S., Inc. v. State, 75 N.Y.2d 175, 551 N.Y.S.2d 470, 550 N.E.2d 919 (1990); Johnson v. South Carolina Nat. Bank, 292 S.C. 51, 354 S.E.2d 895 (1987). Even when the plaintiff seeking rescission had already rescinded by its unilateral notification (see § 4.8 below), the later suit for rescission in equity was said to permit no jury trial. Phoenix Mut. Life Ins. Co. v. Conway, 11 N.Y.2d 367, 229 N.Y.S.2d 740, 183 N.E.2d 754 (1962).

48. If the declaratory judgment is not analogous to a traditional equitable remedy but merely an "inverted lawsuit," jury trial is granted. See Fleming James & Geoffrey Hazard, Civil Procedure § 8.10 (3d ed. 1985). See Annotation, Right to jury trial in action for declaratory relief in state court, 33 A.L.R. 4th 146.

49. See Annotation, Right to jury trial in state court divorce proceedings, 56 A.L.R. 4th 955.

50. E.g., Estate of Phelps v. Odekerken, 223 Cal.App.3d 332, 273 Cal.Rptr. 2 (1990).

51. In re R.Y., 189 N.W.2d 644 (N.D.1971).

52. C & K Engineering Contractors v. Amber Steel Co., Inc., 23 Cal.3d 1, 151 Cal.Rptr. 323, 587 P.2d 1136 (1978).

53. See Restatement Second of Contracts § 90 (1981).

54. The promissory estoppel doctrine started as a peaceful plowshare that allowed the plaintiff to show reliance as a consideration substitute. Later, courts beat it into a substantial sword for hacking away the statute of frauds. See § 13.2(5) below. Only the simple plowshare version was involved in *C & K Engineering Contractors.*

table estoppel was a doctrine with roots in law that was expanded in the equity courts. So the court characterized the suit as "equitable" and denied a jury trial, even though the remedy sought was a simple money judgment and even though estoppel is regularly applied today in cases that are purely legal in nature.

The dissenting judge in *C & K Engineering Contractors* argued that jury trial rights should be determined by asking whether equity *remedies* were in issue, not by asking whether equitable *rights* or equitable doctrines were invoked. The doctrine of promissory estoppel was not a doctrine that created a remedy; it was one that created a right. So in the dissenter's view, the case was not an equity case at all, but a simple case at law, for which a jury should be granted on demand.

Statutory Claims

Generally. The preceding discussion shows that courts have sometimes considered a case to be equitable because the remedy is equitable and sometimes because the substantive rules to be applied are historically equitable. But suppose the claim is a new one, newly recognized by courts or newly created by a statute. Is such a claim to be regarded as one "at law" with a jury trial or as one "in equity," without a jury trial?

In general, the answer is found by analogy, where, once again, the remedy prescribed tends to dictate the characterization. So it is no surprise that a statutory claim for *damages* is regarded as a common law claim that requires a jury trial,[55] at least where the claim is analogous to the general kinds of claims permitted at common law.[56] On the other hand, if the statutory remedy is injunctive relief, courts can be expected to treat the claim as equitable.[57]

Power of the legislature to prescribe non-jury trials. Suppose that the statute itself addresses the jury trial question, either by providing for a jury trial, providing against a jury trial, or assigning the claim to an administrative agency or some other tribunal in which jury trial would not be possible. Has the legislative branch the power to affect jury trial if the statutory claim is analogous to a common law claim? The Supreme Court has said that Congress could create a claim and assign it to a tribunal with no jury if, but only if, the claim litigates "public rights." In such cases Congress may assign the litigation to a non-Article III court and by the same token, Congress may prescribe a non-jury trial. But if the claim is otherwise a

---

55. Curtis v. Loether, 415 U.S. 189, 94 S.Ct. 1005, 39 L.Ed.2d 260 (1974) (civil rights claims for housing discrimination, jury trial); cf. Department of Revenue v. Jarvenpaa, 404 Mass. 177, 534 N.E.2d 286, 293 (1989) (suit for money for support of defendant's child, jury trial).

56. See Tull v. United States, 481 U.S. 412, 107 S.Ct. 1831, 95 L.Ed.2d 365 (1987) (considering whether a statutory "civil penalty" in a pollution type claim under the federal Clean Water Act was analogous to a common law action for debt, for abatement of a nuisance, for disgorgement of profits); Ford v. Blue Cross and Blue Shield Conn., Inc., 216 Conn. 40, 578 A.2d 1054, 1059 (1990) (statutory

wrongful discharge action, right to jury trial for common law cases and all those "substantially similar thereto"). The Massachusetts Court said that "If a wholly new cause of action is created, a jury trial right does not attach to that claim," but it also held that a statutory claim against a putative father for support of an illegitimate child is not a wholly new type of claim. Hence a jury trial was required. Department of Revenue v. Jarvenpaa, 404 Mass. 177, 534 N.E.2d 286, 293 (1989).

57. Commonwealth v. Guilfoyle, 402 Mass. 130, 521 N.E.2d 984 (1988) (suit to enjoin a juvenile's violation of civil rights of other juveniles properly tried without a jury).

"legal cause of action," Congress cannot deprive the parties of a jury trial when they litigate that right unless "public rights" are involved, as in public regulatory schemes.[58]

Indiscriminate equity: the case of Title VII. Courts have generally accepted no one clear guide to determine the equitable-legal status of a claim. Uncertainty permits courts to characterize claims as equitable (or not) almost on the basis of a feeling or a personal preference, without considering either the coercive nature of the remedy or the substantive, historical practice.

The 1964 Civil Rights Act, in Title VII, created a cause of action against employers for certain acts of job discrimination. Remedies included reinstatement in any job lost because of discrimination and back pay.[59] Reinstatement clearly invoked an equitable remedy; it is a form of injunction. Back pay, on the other hand, is a money remedy, and looks on its face like a "law" claim, for which a jury would be routinely granted.[60]

The federal courts of appeals, however, insisted that the back pay remedy in Title VII was "equitable."[61] One reason advanced for this conclusion was that back pay was somehow "restitutionary" and that it was therefore equitable. Even if back pay was restitutionary, which does not appear to be the case,[62] restitution claims were routinely claims brought "at law," in the absence of some added claim for an equitable remedy. Some courts seemed to reason that they should have discretion to deny relief, and that therefore the claim must be equitable.[63] Finally, courts sometimes suggested that the legislative branch could do an end run around the Seventh Amendment by declaring a legal claim to be equitable, and that it had done so in Title VII.[64]

Whatever the merits of jury trial, the right to have it should not depend upon ad hoc judicial fiat. None of the reasons given for its denial comports with either the substantive or remedial tests for determining equitable status of a claim. The 1991 Civil Rights Act resolved the issue where it

58. Granfinanciera, S.A. v. Nordberg, 492 U.S. 33, 53, 109 S.Ct. 2782, 2796, 106 L.Ed.2d 26 (1989).

59. The topic, including the right to jury trial, is given primary attention in § 6.10(5) below.

60. For the method of dealing with claims for two remedies, one legal and one equitable, see § 2.6(4) below.

61. E.g., Walton v. Eaton Corp., 563 F.2d 66 (3d Cir.1977); Pons v. Lorillard, 549 F.2d 950, 953 (4th Cir.1977), aff'd on other issues, 434 U.S. 575, 98 S.Ct. 866, 55 L.Ed.2d 40 (1978) (Title VII backpay remedy was equitable because it was tied to equitable relief and because it was discretionary, but Age Act back pay was "legal"); Harkless v. Sweeny Independent School Dist., 427 F.2d 319, 324 (5th Cir.1970), cert. denied, 400 U.S. 991, 91 S.Ct. 541, 27 L.Ed.2d 439 (1971). One district court has held to the contrary. Beesley v. Hartford Fire Ins. Co., 717 F.Supp. 781 (N.D.Ala.1989), on reconsideration, 723 F.Supp. 635 (1989). Note, Judge Acker's Last Stand: The North-

ern District of Alabama's Lonesome Battle for the Right to Trial by Jury under Title VII, 39 Wash.U.J.Urb. & Contemp.L. 135 (1991).

62. The term "restitution" can be used merely to mean something like damages, as where a judge grants probation to one convicted of crime on condition that he make "restitution" to his victim. In the law of remedies the terms usually refers to restoration of gains received by the defendant. Employers who refuse to promote an employee for discriminatory reasons might in some sense gain the salary differential. However, employers who hire others for the job instead of the plaintiff seem to make no gain at all.

63. Described as a "novel and aberrant view" in Rendleman, Chapters of the Civil Jury, 65 Ky.L.J. 769, 777–780 (1977).

64. These reasons are discussed further, with citations to authorities, in § 6.10(5) below.

counted most; that act provided for a jury trial in cases of intentional discrimination.[65] The decisions against jury trial, however, will remain as a caution, even if the issue does not arise again under that particular statute.[66]

Evaluating Approaches

The historical or substantive approach breaks down quickly when history furnishes no precise guide, when history cannot be discovered in detail, and when we think we know more history than we do in fact. Resort to analogy has seemed the next best thing to courts trying to estimate substantive equity as a test, but analogy is no guide whatever to what equity courts actually *did*. At best analogy decides what equity would have done had things been different. When analogy becomes strained or difficult it merely adds to an armory of manipulative devices by which jury trial may or may not be granted.

In *Tull v. United States*,[67] the government sought civil penalties in a pollution claim under the Clean Water Act. In determining whether the claim was legal or equitable the Court considered whether the claim might be analogous to the 18th century action of debt or alternatively to a suit to abate a nuisance or even a restitution claim.[68] This kind of approach is less than speculation about historical facts; it is the imaginative construction of legal culture that never existed. Justice Brennan was led to conclude that the courts should abandon all analysis of analogies to substantive equity. Instead he would consider whether the remedy was legal or equitable. "If the relief is legal in nature, i.e., if it is the kind of relief that historically was available from courts of law, I would hold that the parties have a constitutional right to trial by jury * * *."[69]

The substantive or historical approach can easily slip into an almost mystic and completely anti-historical approach when courts identify "equity" with justice and fairness. Equity courts were indeed identified with justice and fairness, but it is not true that a case fell within separate equity jurisdiction if a judge decided to be fair. Law courts could and can be fair and just as well as equity courts; they did not become equity courts by adverting to concerns of justice. The suggestion that a case becomes equitable if the point is to do justice may deny a jury trial right for a completely ahistorical reason. Mystic declarations that a case is "inherently" equitable are similar. They may reflect merely a desire of a particular court on a particular occasion to eliminate a jury trial and at the same time to be forgiven the job of analyzing the problem.

---

65. To be codified as 42 U.S.C.A. § 1981a. See § 6.10(5) below.

66. Perhaps the issue could still arise as to disparate impact (unintended discrimination) cases, but that does not seem likely. If it should arise, a non jury trial might be justified on the ground that Congress can declare a remedy to be equitable in Title VII cases because "public rights" are involved; but that was not the analysis of the Courts of Appeals in declaring that the original Title VII claims were "equitable."

67. 481 U.S. 412, 421, 107 S.Ct. 1831, 1837, 95 L.Ed.2d 365 (1987).

68. Tull v. United States, 481 U.S. 412, 421, n. 6, 107 S.Ct. 1831, 1837, n. 6, 95 L.Ed.2d 365 (1987) (rejecting the government's argument that the remedy was for "disgorgement").

69. Chauffeurs, Teamsters and Helpers, Local No. 391 v. Terry, 494 U.S. 558, 572, 110 S.Ct. 1339, 1349, 108 L.Ed.2d 519 (1990) (Brennan, J. concurring in part and concurring in the judgment).

The remedy test may be much better, but it, too, has been subject to manipulation. The suggestion in some cases that all restitution remedies fall within the jurisdiction of the chancellors is simply not historically true,[70] but even well-understood history has not prevented some courts from advancing the argument that a jury trial must be denied in restitution cases. Nevertheless, the remedy test is far clearer. It, too, is a historical test of equity, but it asks whether law courts would have given the remedy sought, not whether they would have entertained the particular substantive claim.

§ 2.6(4)　Jury Trial in Mixed Law and Equity Cases

Mixed law and equity issues may arise because the plaintiff seeks both legal and equitable relief for a single claim, or because the plaintiff seeks equitable relief and the defendant asserts a legal counterclaim.

Clean-up or Incidental Jurisdiction

Whole case tried in equity. At least in some stages of history, equity courts asserted incidental or "clean-up" jurisdiction to decide all issues in a case, including legal issues, once they had taken jurisdiction to decide the equitable issues.[1] If the case is "essentially equitable," a court might say, then the whole case, including legal issues, could be tried to the judge without a jury.[2] The same effect is often achieved without reference to incidental or clean up jurisdiction. Courts often simply characterize the case as a single unit; if they find the gist, the essence, or the primary point to be "equitable," then the whole case including the legal issue is tried without a jury.[3]

Examples. For example, if the plaintiff sued for specific performance and damages, the judge might grant both the equitable and legal remedies, or deny one of them, without a jury trial on either.[4] Or if the plaintiff sued to reform a contract and also for damages from breach of the contract as reform, the chancellor could grant the reformation and also the damages. A similar idea could be applied when the defendant asserted a legal counterclaim: equity might try the entire package as a non-jury matter.[5]

Efficiency and waiver theories. One argument for the incidental jurisdiction idea is that it is efficient; it will avoid a multiplicity of suits.[6] Another theory for trying the whole action together as an equity case is that a plaintiff who joins legal and equitable claims,[7] or a defendant who files a legal counterclaim in an equity suit "waives" jury trial rights.[8] The same

---

70. See § 4.2 below.

§ 2.6(4)

1. See Levin, Equitable Clean–Up and the Jury, 100 U.Pa.L.Rev. 320, 326–331 (1951); § 2.7 below. But the court might insist that "equity" jurisdiction attaches only if equitable issues appear when the suit is commenced. See Suburbia Pools, Inc. v. Fischer, 661 S.W.2d 823 (Mo.App.1983).

2. See Motor Vehicle Mfrs. Ass'n of the U.S., Inc. v. O'Neill, 203 Conn. 63, 523 A.2d 486, 493 (1987); Weisman v. Hopf–Himsel, Inc., 535 N.E.2d 1222 (Ind.App.1989).

3. E.g., Dick v. Dick, 167 Conn. 210, 355 A.2d 110 (1974).

6. E.g., Eckerd Drugs of N.J., Inc. v. S.R. 215, Rite–Aid Corp., 170 N.J.Super. 37, 40, 405 A.2d 474, 476 (1979) ("once equity jurisdiction attaches it will be retained in order to avoid a multiplicity of suits"; suit to compel sale of business and for tortious interference with contract was mainly equitable, no jury trial).

7. E.g. John W. Cowper Co., Inc. v. Buffalo Hotel Dev. Venture, 99 A.D.2d 19, 471 N.Y.S.2d 913, 915 (1984) ("joinder in a complaint of both legal and equitable causes of action arising from the same transaction constitutes a waiver by plaintiff of his right to a trial by jury").

idea may be advanced by saying that the plaintiff who voluntarily submits a claim in equity, takes an equity trial, even as to a legal counterclaim.[9]

Severance or Separate Trials

Trial of equity issues first, controlling legal issues by res judicata. The same effect is achieved if the judge in a modern court decides to sever the claims and try them separately, but decides to try the equity claim first.[10] The equity decision will then be res judicata or collateral estoppel as to all facts decided. When the clean-up rule is used, or when the claims are severed and the equity trial comes first, the effect is to eliminate jury trial on any facts the legal and equity claims have in common.[11] Even if there are no factual issues in common, a non-jury trial of an equitable defense might have the effect of barring the claim entirely, regardless of what a jury would have found on the legal issues. For instance, in one case, the judge found that the plaintiff's conduct was inequitable, and hence barred relief without ever submitting an issue to the jury on the merits.[12]

Trial of the law claim first. The clean-up rule did not apply in every case. Sometimes equitable relief was considered to depend entirely on whether a legal right was first established.[13] In that case, equity would not proceed until the right was established in the law courts, and then would act in accord with the legal ruling. The effect of this procedure was to accord a jury trial on all factual disputes the two claims had in common, because the equity courts followed the ruling of the earlier trial at law.[14] With merger of law and equity, the same thing can be accomplished in the single court by severing the claims and trying the legal claim first, or by trying them together and accepting the jury's verdict as binding on both the legal and equitable issues.

The Dairy Queen Rule

The preceding materials indicate that in the days of separate equity courts the plaintiff might or might not have a jury trial right when he asserts both a legal and equitable claim, depending on whether the court would try all issues in equity as part of its incidental jurisdiction or whether it would await a decision on some issues at law.

---

9. Gulesian v. Newton Trust Co., 302 Mass. 369, 19 N.E.2d 312 (1939).

12. Garco Mfg., Inc. v. Herst Lighting Co., 820 F.2d 1209 (Fed.Cir.1987).

13. A leading case was Scott v. Neely, 140 U.S. 106, 11 S.Ct. 712, 35 L.Ed. 358 (1891), holding that the plaintiff who wanted equity's aid in collecting a debt would be required to establish the debt first at law.

14. E.g., Dick v. Dick, 167 Conn. 210, 355 A.2d 110 (1974) (jury trial as to authenticity of defendant's signature on an agreement, equity trial on the accounting and constructive trust issues that arose when authenticity was established); Torphy v. Reder, 357 Mass. 153, 257 N.E.2d 435 (1970) (enforcement of certain lien claims have both legal and equitable aspects;

one is entitled to a jury trial as to the existence of the debt, and a non-jury equity trial as to the lien or remedial aspect).

The best discussion is Fleming James and Geoffrey Hazard, Civil Procedure § 8.7 (3d ed. 1985). These authorities also discuss a third situation, one in which the plaintiff can control the jury trial issue by controlling the order of trial. That is, the plaintiff could sue on an equitable claim first or then a legal claim, or vice versa. Factual determinations made in the first trial would bind the second, so the plaintiff's choice of law would mean that a jury's decision governed equitable relief, too, while the plaintiff's choice of equity would work the other way around. Such cases seem to have been rare.

Abolishing incidental jurisdiction? In *Dairy Queen, Inc. v. Wood,*[15] the Supreme Court of the United States instituted a new and different system for determining jury trial rights in federal courts. First, as indicated in the previous section, the Court limited the kinds of claims that could be considered equitable, non-jury claims. Second, the Court seemed to outlaw the clean-up or incidental jurisdiction doctrine as a basis for avoiding jury trial. Justice Black said:

> At the outset, we may dispose of one of the grounds upon which the trial court acted in striking the demand for trial by jury—that based upon the view that the right to trial by jury may be lost as to legal issues where those issues are characterized as 'incidental' to equitable issues— for our previous decisions make it plain that no such rule may be applied in the federal courts.

Mode of trial after incidental jurisdiction is abolished. If incidental jurisdiction is no longer acceptable, how is the case to be tried in the modern court with both legal and equitable powers? Justice Black's idea was simple. The whole case is normally tried at once, with the judge submitting to the jury all factual disputes that arise on the "legal" claim. The jury's determination of facts is then binding on the "equitable" claim, and the judge must determine equitable issues in accordance with the facts found by the jury. (If the equitable claim raises factual issues not relevant to the legal claim and not decided by the jury, the judge would be free to decide those independently.)

Example. Suppose the plaintiff asserts a contract to purchase Blackacre from the defendant and demands specific performance plus damages for the delay in conveyance. Perhaps the only real dispute is whether the defendant promised to convey Blackacre. Apparently what Justice Black had in mind was something like this: the case would be tried as a unit, with only the damages issue submitted to the jury. The jury would be required to determine whether or not a contract existed. If it found a contract and awarded damages, the judge would not be permitted to deny equitable relief on the ground that no contract existed;[16] instead, the judge would be bound by the jury's verdict.

Effects and strategies. The effect is to afford jury trial rights to either party in any case in which the plaintiff sues for both legal and equitable relief and in which the common issues of fact are relevant to both kinds of relief. The plaintiff who wishes to avoid a potentially hostile jury may confront a strategic decision. She might simply claim the specific performance without damages. Such a claim is equitable by any standard, so no jury trial would be available to the defendant. If the money claim is minor and the jury risk is great, this might be the plaintiff's choice. On the other hand, if the plaintiff wants a jury trial in an equitable claim, it behooves her to find a plausible damages claim that will raise the same issues of fact.

15. 369 U.S. 469, 82 S.Ct. 894, 8 L.Ed.2d 44 (1962).

16. Whether the trial judge could deny relief as a matter of discretion, or fashion relief by ordering a partial specific performance, is considered in § 2.6(5) below.

Current status. The Supreme Court has reiterated its position that incidental jurisdiction theories cannot diminish a jury trial right.[17] However, some federal courts, notably in Title VII job discrimination cases before the 1991 Civil Rights Act, continued to use incidental jurisdiction theories as a justification for committing job discrimination cases to a non-jury trial.[18]

In the states. The states have not overwhelmingly embraced *Dairy Queen* and they are not required to do so, since *Dairy Queen* governs only trials in federal courts.[19] Some states have accepted the *Dairy Queen* idea for at least some mixed equity-law claims,[20] or at least have cited cases in the

---

17. Tull v. United States, 481 U.S. 412, 107 S.Ct. 1831, 95 L.Ed.2d 365 (1987); Curtis v. Loether, 415 U.S. 189, 196, 94 S.Ct. 1005, 1009, 39 L.Ed.2d 260, 267 (1974) ("The right cannot be abridged by characterizing the legal claim as 'incidental' to the equitable relief sought"); Ross v. Bernhard, 396 U.S. 531, 537, 90 S.Ct. 733, 738, 24 L.Ed.2d 729, 736 (1970) ("where equitable and legal claims are joined in the same action, there is a right to jury trial on the legal claims which must not be infringed either by trying the legal issues as incidental to the equitable ones or by a court trial of a common issue existing between the claims").

There is a curious statement in Chauffeurs, Teamsters and Helpers, Local No. 391 v. Terry, 494 U.S. 558, 110 S.Ct. 1339, 1348, 108 L.Ed.2d 519 (1990) that "a monetary award 'incidental to or intertwined with injunctive relief' may be equitable." Justice Marshall, who made this statement, also said that jury trial rights could not be abridged by the incidental jurisdiction theory. *Curtis v. Loether,* supra. In the *Terry* case he seems to be addressing another point, namely, whether some monetary awards can be equitable. (Money awarded under a constructive trust would be a good candidate). So the statement does not appear to cast any doubt on *Dairy Queen's* rule on incidental jurisdiction.

18. Williams v. Owens–Illinois, Inc., 665 F.2d 918, 929 (9th Cir.1982), cert. denied, 459 U.S. 971, 103 S.Ct. 302, 74 L.Ed.2d 283 (1982) (back pay claim "was properly viewed as either equitable or as a legal remedy incidental to an equitable cause of action and accordingly not sufficient to create a right to jury trial"). See §§ 2.6(3) above & 6.10(5) below.

19. *Dairy Queen* governs all federal trials, including diversity trials. Simler v. Conner, 372 U.S. 221, 83 S.Ct. 609, 9 L.Ed.2d 691 (1963).

20. All of the following cases, in varying degrees, and in dicta or otherwise, accept one or more of the ideas in the *Dairy Queen* line, as a matter of local procedural or local constitutional rules, but some of the cases may have failed to accept the full import of those ideas as Justice Black advanced them. See Habib v. Thurston, 517 A.2d 1 (D.C.App.1985) (adverse claims to rents paid into court by tenant during dispute with landlord; although the fund

in court originates in an "equitable" protective order, claims to the money are legal and parties have jury trial right); Evans v. Evans, 547 So.2d 459 (Ala.1989) ("Under the Alabama Rules of Civil Procedure, * * * [t]he trial must be arranged so that the decision of the equitable issues by the judge does not operate to deny a trial by jury of the legal issues," citing *Dairy Queen*); Selby Constructors v. McCarthy, 91 Cal.App.3d 517, 154 Cal.Rptr. 164 (1979) (mechanic's lien foreclosure is equitable, but when claim for personal liability is included, all issues except procedural issues about perfection of the lien become legal and a jury trial is required); Cerrito v. Kovitch, 457 So.2d 1021 (Fla.1984); David Steed and Associates, Inc. v. Young, 115 Idaho 247, 766 P.2d 717, 720 (1988) (irrelevant that legal issues are "incidental" to equitable claims, legal counterclaims in mortgage foreclosure suit to be tried to a jury); Life for God's Stray Animals, Inc. v. New North Rockdale County Homeowners Ass'n, 253 Ga. 551, 322 S.E.2d 239, 241 (1984) (jury trial on damages should precede non-jury equity trial, citing *Dairy Queen* and *Beacon*); Hashem v. Taheri, 82 Md.App. 269, 571 A.2d 837 (1990) (stockholder's derivative action, federal rules used); Bendick v. Cambio, 558 A.2d 941, 944 (R.I. 1989) ("we have followed a course substantially parallel to that of the United States Supreme Court in *Dairy Queen* "); Perilli v. Board of Educ., Monongalia County, 182 W.Va. 261, 387 S.E.2d 315 (1989) (teacher's sex discrimination claim under state law entitled her to jury on factual claims that would result in money recovery, *Dairy Queen* and other federal cases are "persuasive authority"); Hyatt Bros., Inc. v. Hyatt, 769 P.2d 329, 334 (Wyo.1989) ("If both legal relief * * * and equitable relief * * * are involved, the jury decides the facts involved in the legal matter, and the judge then may add such equitable relief as may be consistent with the jury's determination"). Vermont appears to have reached a *Dairy Queen* result through the combined effects of rule and decisions. See also, Vt.R.C.Proc. 39 and Reporters Notes thereto.

Dairy Queen line with a degree of tacit or explicit approval.[21]   Others historically used incidental jurisdiction theories to try the entire case as an "equity" case and continue to state the incidental or clean-up jurisdiction approach [22] or to decide ad hoc on the order of trial of the two claims.[23]   For instance, without adopting *Beacon* or *Dairy Queen* as a principle, a New York court decided that the trial judge should have discretion to characterize a case as either legal or equitable when the equitable issues were a relatively small part of the case.[24]

Although the states have been friendly to *Dairy Queen,* it does not seem right to say that they have accepted all the implications of that case.   But for that matter, it is not always clear that the federal courts have fully accepted *Dairy Queen* either.

Equitable Claim with Legal Counterclaim: Beacon Theatres

The Federal rule.   In *Beacon Theatres, Inc. v. Westover,*[25] Beacon and Fox were competitors in the movie theatre business.   Beacon threatened to sue Fox for antitrust violations.   Fox was concerned that this threat or the attendant publicity would cause him difficulty in obtaining first-run movie contracts, so he wanted the matter determined.   To get a determination, he sued Beacon (1) to enjoin Beacon from pursuing an antitrust action and (2) for declaratory judgment.   Beacon counterclaimed, asserting the very antitrust suit that Fox wanted to enjoin.

Both the plaintiff's claim and the defendant's counterclaim raised the same underlying issues about the validity of Fox's business arrangements. In the plaintiff's complaint the issues arise in an equitable context because the plaintiff sought an injunction.   In the defendant's counterclaim the issues arise in a "law" context because the defendant sought damages.   In pre-merger days this kind of case might have called for the chancellor's

---

21.   See Thompson v. First Mississippi Nat. Bank & Mut. Savings Life Ins. Co., 427 So.2d 973, 976 (Miss.1983) (party cannot avoid jury trial by "camouflage" of money claim as an accounting, citing *Dairy Queen,* seemingly a less than complete acceptance of the principle but friendly to it); Gray v. Billings, 213 Mont. 6, 689 P.2d 268, 271 (1984); Kenney v. Scientific, Inc., 212 N.J.Super. 6, 512 A.2d 1142, 1147 (1986) (friendly citations to *Dairy Queen* and other cases, but concluding that the case was too complex for a jury trial); Scott v. Woods, 105 N.M. 177, 730 P.2d 480 (App.1986) (adopting the line of federal cases to govern jury trial in stockholders' derivative suit); John W. Cowper Co., Inc. v. Buffalo Hotel Dev. Venture, 99 A.D.2d 19, 471 N.Y.S.2d 913 (1984); Rexnord, Inc. v. Ferris, 294 Or. 392, 657 P.2d 673, 679, n. 4 (1983) (suggesting that in "some cases" trying the legal issue first is preferable).

22.   E.g., Motor Vehicle Mfrs. Ass'n of the U.S., Inc. v. O'Neill, 203 Conn. 63, 523 A.2d 486 (1987); Linville v. Wilson, 628 S.W.2d 422 (Mo.App.1982); Motor Vehicle Mfrs. Ass'n of the U.S., Inc. v. State, 75 N.Y.2d 175, 183, 551 N.Y.S.2d 470, 474, 550 N.E.2d 919, 923 (1990) (incidental fees and charges recoverable under Lemon Law; no jury required because incidental award does not affect "equitable nature of the action"); State Bank of Lehi v. Woolsey, 565 P.2d 413 (Utah 1977) (mortgage foreclosure, money debt issues triable to judge, not jury, as part of incidental jurisdiction).

23.   Cf. New Jersey Highway Authority v. Renner, 18 N.J. 485, 114 A.2d 555 (1955) (legal counterclaim situation, on the facts a jury trial should be granted).

24.   John W. Cowper Co., Inc. v. Buffalo Hotel Dev. Venture, 99 A.D.2d 19, 23, 471 N.Y.S.2d 913, 917 (1984) (eight claims for money damages, nine counterclaims for money damages, and one equitable claim (for foreclosure), trial judge "can direct the method by which the issues are tried and may minimize the danger of conflicting verdicts by permitting the jury to hear testimony on both the legal issues and the Lien Law claims, treating the jury's determination on the latter as advisory").

25.   359 U.S. 500, 79 S.Ct. 948, 3 L.Ed.2d 988 (1959).

discretion about jury trial, or the court might use some form of clean-up or incidental jurisdiction theories to decide the whole case as an equity case. The Supreme Court in *Beacon,* however, held that the federal judge has no discretion to deny jury trial, by trying the equitable issues first or otherwise. The result is in accord with *Dairy Queen's* vision of the trial: the "legal" issues are tried (first, or along with) the equitable issues; the jury's determination of facts on those issues is also the determination that governs the judge on issues of equitable relief.

In the states. Beacon does not control state courts. The states traditionally took a quite different view about legal counterclaims, holding that the defendant has no right to a jury trial when he files a counterclaim in an equity suit.[26] So in a state following traditional law, the counterclaimant will get a jury trial if the plaintiff has filed in federal court but not if the plaintiff has filed in state court.[27]

Where the counterclaim was not compulsory, it was plausible to suggest that the counterclaiming defendant waived his jury claim by choosing to counterclaim rather than to sue in a separate suit. After merger, however, counterclaims arising from the same set of facts would ordinarily be compulsory, so that the defendant would have no real choice about presenting all his claims or losing them. At least in the case of compulsory counterclaims, the traditional rule compels the defendant to give up his claim or give up his jury trial right. So in those cases, if not in all counterclaim cases, state courts have sometimes followed *Beacon* at least to the extent of requiring a jury trial on the counterclaim issues.[28] In addition, as in the *Dairy Queen* situation, some courts will make ad hoc decisions in favor of jury trials without adopting a general principle like that in *Beacon.*[29]

Affecting Jury Trial by Res Judicata: The Order of Trial

The Supreme court in *Beacon* and *Dairy Queen* insisted that when mixed issues of law and equity were involved, the equity issues should not be tried first, because to do that would be to control the results on the law side by a non-jury trial, either through res judicata or some analogous doctrine. There are two points embedded in this idea. *One, if* for any reason the equity issue is properly determined first, *then* the facts decided on that issue

26. E.g., Adolph Rub Trust, First Trust Co. of N.D. v. Rub, 474 N.W.2d 73 (N.D.1991); Comstock v. Little, 359 P.2d 704 (Okl.1961) (claim to establish a boundary line by acquiescence is equitable; counterclaim for ejectment, which raised same issues, is legal; no jury trial right, the case remains equitable); Westwood Corp. v. Bowen, 108 Or.App. 310, 815 P.2d 1282 (1991). See Annotation, Right in Equity Suit to Jury Trial of Counterclaim Involving Legal Issue, 17 A.L.R.3d 1321 (1968).

27. Compare Eldredge v. Gourley, 505 F.2d 769 (3d Cir.1974) (arising in Pennsylvania, a dispute involving Pennsylvania land, jury trial on counterclaim) with Rosenberg v. Rosenberg, 276 Pa.Super. 203, 419 A.2d 167 (1980) (no jury trial on counterclaim, on the assertion that it would create collateral estoppel problems and would be cumbersome).

28. See First Western Bank, Sturgis v. Livestock Yards Co., 466 N.W.2d 853 (S.D. 1991); First–Citizens Bank & Trust Co. of South Carolina v. Hucks, 305 S.C. 296, 408 S.E.2d 222 (1991) ("A party does not waive its rights to a jury trial on a counterclaim asserted in an equity action if the counterclaim is legal and compulsory in nature").

29. See New Jersey Highway Auth. v. Renner, 18 N.J. 485, 114 A.2d 555 (1955) (trial judge has discretion as to whether legal or equitable claims are tried first, and decision on facts first tried becomes binding, but parties here treated legal counterclaim as an independent suit and counterclaimant should have a jury trial).

will control in any subsequent legal proceeding. And *two, because* such control poses a potential threat to effective jury trial rights, the Court will limit the occasions in which equity issues can be first tried, as the Court held in *Beacon* and *Dairy Queen.*

The first point is illustrated in the Supreme Court's decision in *Parklane Hosiery Co. v. Shore.*[30] In the SEC sought to enforce federal security laws by obtaining an injunction against Parklane's use of misleading statements made in the course of a merger transaction. The trial judge found the statements to be misleading and granted the injunction. Shore, an individual, had earlier brought an action for damages based on the same statements, but the separate SEC injunction suit was tried first. After the injunction issued in that suit, Shore wanted to take advantage of the decision there by claiming that the findings in the injunction suit established the misleading character of the statements in issue. Parklane resisted on the ground that to so hold would be to deprive Parklane of a jury trial on that issue. The Court held, however, it was proper for the SEC injunction suit to proceed "in equity" and that once it had properly come to a final judgment, the contemporary doctrines of res judicata and collateral estoppel would apply as in any other case. So the facts in the damages action were controlled, not by a jury determination, but by the decision of a judge in an injunction suit.

The second point is illustrated in *Lytle v. Household Manufacturing, Inc.*[31] The plaintiff there was an African–American who was discharged by the defendant employer and allegedly mistreated in some other ways as well. The plaintiff brought a suit under Title VII, based on employment discrimination, which was assumed to be equitable.[32] The plaintiff also asserted a claim under § 1981,[33] which prohibits interference with rights to contract. Section 1981 claims are usually assumed to be purely "legal" claims.[34]

The trial judge erroneously concluded that Title VII was the exclusive remedy, so he dismissed the § 1981 claim. He then tried the Title VII claim without a jury on the assumption that it was equitable in character. He found for the defendant. The Court of Appeals recognized that the trial judge was in error in dismissing the § 1981 claim, but thought that it did not matter because the judge's findings on Title VII would be res judicata on that claim and would foreclose any liability even if it were to send the case back for trial on the § 1981 claim.

The Supreme Court held it improper to eliminate jury trial rights by erroneously trying the supposedly equity claim first. *Dairy Queen's* approach would have required the trial court to treat the legal issue (§ 1981) as having been tried first, so as to preserve the jury trial rights. It was not in fact tried first in *Lytle,* just as it was not in *Parklane.* But there is a big difference. In *Parklane* it was proper to try the injunction issue first and because it was proper under existing procedures, the decision would be res judicata in the same way other decisions are. In *Lytle* it was decidedly *not*

---

30. 439 U.S. 322, 99 S.Ct. 645, 58 L.Ed.2d 552 (1979).

31. 494 U.S. 545, 110 S.Ct. 1331, 108 L.Ed.2d 504 (1990).

32. As to the dubious view that Title VII claims are "equitable" see §§ 2.6(3) above & 6.10(5) below.

33. 42 U.S.C.A. § 1981.

34. See § 6.10(5) below.

proper to try the equitable issue first; that trial was possible only because of an erroneous dismissal of the "law" claim under § 1981.

All of this is important only when the legal and the equitable claim share common issues of fact. If the two claims are factually independent, then the order of trial doesn't matter, because the decision on one claim will not affect the other.[35]

§ 2.6(5) Effect of Jury Trial on Tailoring or Modifying the Decree

Discretion and Other Equity Power

Equity courts traditionally exercised powers that might not fit well with the jury trial required by the *Beacon* and *Dairy Queen* cases where mixed issues of law and equity are involved. Equity also enforced its orders by contempt of court sanctions. Where those sanctions are "civil," a jury is not usually required, as explained more fully elsewhere.[1]

In addition, equity courts have traditionally exercised four kinds of power that seem largely unsuited for any jury determination: (1) They granted provisional relief in the form of temporary restraining orders and preliminary injunctions, sometimes literally on a moment's notice. (2) They exercised discretion to deny relief in some cases even when the facts were determined in the plaintiff's favor. (3) Relatedly, they tailored, measured or limited the remedy to something less than the factual findings might warrant, again as a matter of discretion. (4) They retained the power to modify "permanent" injunctions long after they were issued.

[*For discussion of jury roles in each of these categories, see this section in the Practitioner Treatise edition.*]

§ 2.7 "Jurisdictional" Issues in Equity Courts

Jurisdiction and Power

Jurisdiction is the power to render a legally binding judgment or decree. Constitutions limit judicial power and may permit legislatures to do so as well.[1] The limitation is sometimes phrased in terms of the subject matter. A justice of the peace court is usually denied power to grant divorces or specific performance, for example. State courts may be denied the power to administer bankruptcy.

The decree or judgment of a court acting without jurisdiction is not merely erroneous; it is void. A judgment that is merely erroneous must be attacked directly if at all (usually by appeal or by motion in the case to set the judgment aside). A void order, on the other hand, may be attacked collaterally by resisting its enforcement in subsequent judicial proceedings.[2] Distinguishing between the court's error and its want of power is sometimes difficult,[3] but once the distinction is drawn, the legal consequences are clear.

Rules about the jurisdiction or power of courts are important regardless whether a case is "legal" or "equitable." Jurisdictional limitations are especially important in connection with contempt punishments. The rule is

---

35. See Dollar Systems, Inc. v. Avcar Leasing Systems, Inc., 890 F.2d 165, 170–171 (9th Cir.1989).

§ 2.7

3. See Dobbs, Trial Court Error as an Excess of Jurisdiction, 43 Tex.L.Rev. 854 (1965).

that one must obey a coercive order such as an injunction until it is reversed, and one who disobeys is subject to sanctions for contempt of court. In most instances the disobedient defendant can defend against the sanctions only by showing that the underlying injunction was void, not merely erroneous. Some of these jurisdictional issues are thus especially important in contempt cases and they are discussed later in that connection. But enough has been said to show that jurisdictional rules in general and the distinction between a decree that is void and one that is merely erroneous is significant.

Although the distinction between error and want of power is important, courts and writers sometimes use the term jurisdiction loosely and in divergent ways. This section attempts to collect in one place several of these usages. Because the term jurisdiction is used or misused in such a variety of ways, some of the materials sketched here have little in common with some of the other materials except the terminology. Nevertheless it is useful to consider these diverse materials together.

Spurious Jurisdiction

"Equity jurisdiction". The term "equity jurisdiction" was traditionally used to refer to the body of equitable precedents, practices, and attitudes. The term did not usually mean jurisdiction in the sense of fundamental power. Sometimes courts would say that if the plaintiff had an adequate remedy at law, they would dismiss the claim "for want of equity jurisdiction." If this locution truly referred to jurisdiction, then it would mean that if an equity judge granted an injunction when the plaintiff really had an adequate remedy at law, the decree would be void. But the phrase means no such thing, as Chafee long ago showed [4] and as the cases recognize when the issue actually arises.[5] For clarity, the term equity jurisdiction might well be avoided.

[For discussion of clean-up jurisdiction, see this section in the Practitioner's Treatise edition.]

Jurisdiction to Preserve the Court's Power to Act

Error distinguished. Courts are bound to follow a constitutional statute which instructs them to grant relief in stated circumstances or to deny it in others. When a court does not comply with a statutory (or constitutional) rule, however, the means of correction is by appeal or other review. The court's judgment is erroneous but not void.

True jurisdictional limitations. Occasionally, however, a statutory rule is not merely a rule of substantive law but is instead a jurisdictional limitation. That is, a statute might limit the very *power* of the court to act. A court without jurisdiction of the subject matter cannot enter a valid judgment. On the contrary, its judgment is utterly void, is not res judicata, and may be freely disobeyed.[11]

The bootstrap corollary. A corollary rule, however, is that only judges can decide whether or not they have jurisdiction or judicial power. The legislature that restricts jurisdiction must expect judges to decide the question because there is no one else to do so. So judges ordinarily have

---

11. See Dobbs, The Decline of Jurisdiction by Consent, 40 N.C.L.Rev. 49 (1961); Dobbs, Trial Court Error as an Excess of Jurisdiction, 43 Tex.L.Rev. 854 (1965).

jurisdiction or power to decide their own jurisdiction. The judge's decision that she has jurisdiction or power to act in a case may be erroneous, but nevertheless may itself be valid until reversed. If it is not reversed, then the judge's decision about jurisdiction itself becomes valid by operation of res judicata rules. This corollary rule is sometimes called the bootstrap rule, with the implication that judges could pull themselves up by their own bootstraps.[12]

The Mineworkers case. None of this is a matter peculiar to equity, but it leads to a special problem that arose in the exercise of equity's strong arm. In *United States v. United Mine Workers,*[13] the government had been operating coal mines during difficulties associated with World War II. It had a contract with the Mine Workers union, headed by Mr. John L. Lewis. Mr. Lewis took the position that the union could terminate the contract, and that if a new contract of his liking was not signed, he would call a strike under the principle of "no contract, no work." The government, as operator of the mines, went to court. It sought a declaratory judgment to the effect that the union could not terminate the existing contract.

It also sought and obtained a temporary restraining order[14] to prevent Mr. Lewis from calling or supporting a strike. Mr. Lewis and his union violated this order and were later charged with contempt of court for doing so. The defendants defended the contempt charge on the ground that the court lacked any jurisdiction to issue any injunction in the case, that its order was void and therefore obedience was not required and disobedience could not be punished. The defendants pointed to the Norris–LaGuardia Act, which virtually eliminated federal court "Jurisdiction to issue any restraining order in any case * * * involving or growing out of any labor dispute * * *."[15]

The position asserted by the defendants was traditionally the sound one: an order issued without jurisdiction was void and no one could be charged with contempt for disobeying it. Nevertheless fines against the defendants were upheld by the Supreme Court. The Court gave alternative grounds, one of them of no interest here. The other was a corollary to the bootstrap principle. It was that

> "the District Court unquestionably had the power to issue a restraining order for the purpose of preserving existing conditions pending upon its own jurisdiction."

In other words, since the court had the power to decide its own jurisdiction (including a power to decide erroneously until reversed), it also had the power to make its decision effective, or at least to keep the way open for a meaningful decision.

Thus a court having equity powers may be given jurisdiction to decide its own jurisdiction, just as any other court may be given such power. However, if a court has equity powers, it may have the additional authority

---

12. See Dobbs, The Validation of Void Judgments: The Bootstrap Principles, 53 Va. L.Rev. 1003, 1241 (Pts. and II) (1967).

13. 330 U.S. 258, 67 S.Ct. 677, 91 L.Ed. 884 (1947).

14. A form of provisional injunctive relief issued without an adversary hearing. See § 2.11(1) below.

15. 29 U.S.C.A. § 104.

to preserve the status quo by way of an injunction, so that its jurisdiction to decide its own jurisdiction is preserved.

Interstate Equity

Jurisdiction over person or property required. In addition to having jurisdiction over the class of case involved, the court must obtain jurisdiction over the person of the defendant or over the defendant's property if it is to render a valid decree. Any decree rendered without jurisdiction may be void as violating due process, and it is certainly not enforceable in any other state under the Full Faith and Credit Clause of the constitution. The jurisdiction over the person rules applied both in law and equity and they continue to apply after merger.

Remedial limits of jurisdiction quasi-in rem. Under older law, a court gained jurisdiction over a person when that person was served with process within the state. If the defendant was a non-resident and not physically present in the state, the court could also obtain jurisdiction of very limited scope by obtaining jurisdiction over the defendant's property within the state. The first kind was called personal jurisdiction and the second quasi in rem jurisdiction. There were important remedial differences. Jurisdiction quasi in rem allowed the plaintiff to recover the property (or the money it produced on sale), but did not allow the plaintiff to recover any judgment that could be collected against the defendant personally from the defendant's other assets. Similarly, quasi in rem jurisdiction would not support an in personam decree in equity.

Contract to sell land example. For example, suppose the defendant, residing in California, contracts to sell Blackacre, located in North Carolina. If the plaintiff sues in North Carolina and the defendant did not leave California, personal jurisdiction probably could not be obtained under traditional law. However, the North Carolina court could have seized the defendant's property and rendered a decree about the property, perhaps even conveying title to the plaintiff.[16] However, the court's direct transfer of property to the plaintiff would not give the plaintiff an important element of the bargain. Contracts to convey real property are usually contracts to convey property by a warranty deed, with certain personal covenants guaranteeing title, right to possession and other matters.[17] If the court's jurisdiction was quasi in rem, only over the property, it could not order specific performance and therefore could not secure the plaintiff the benefit of the covenants the defendant had been promised.[18]

Expanded personal jurisdiction permitting in personam remedies. There may still be some room for quasi in rem jurisdiction.[19] But it is largely if not completely obsolete, because the Supreme Court's decisions have permitted the much broader personal jurisdiction whenever the defendant has some

---

16. Traditional views held that "equity acts in personam," but this has never prevented equity from acting in rem (against property directly) where that was appropriate. See Cook, The Powers of Courts of Equity, 15 Colum.L.Rev. 106, 228 (Pts. 1–3) (1915). Statutes or court rules permit the direct transfer of title by court decree or similar device. E.g., N.C.Gen.Stat. § 1–228.

17. See § 12.11(1) below.

18. Otis Oil & Gas Corp. v. Maier, 74 Wyo. 137, 284 P.2d 653 (1955).

19. See Jack Friedenthal, Mary Kay Kane, Arthur Miller, Civil Procedure 155 (1985).

minimum contacts with the state.[20] The fact that the defendant's land, the very land promised to the plaintiff, is in the state, is itself an important contact, so in many if not all cases like the one supposed, the plaintiff can probably obtain personal jurisdiction. That in turn means that the plaintiff would be permitted to have the specific performance (or other appropriate in personam remedy).

Getting the decree is only the first step. It is not the same as enforcing it. If the defendant is not in the state and does not ever need to be there, the North Carolina court would find it difficult or impossible to effectuate its specific performance decree by contempt power. Because the in personam, non-money decree is usually not entitled to recognition in other states, enforcement where the defendant lives will also be difficult or impossible. So personal jurisdiction over the defendant may not always make a fully satisfactory remedy readily available.

Affecting foreign land titles. In the situation just presented, suit was brought in the state where the land lay, and the court could reach the land, but maybe not the person of the defendant. A different problem arises where the situation is reversed and suit is brought where the defendant can be personally served, but the land lies elsewhere. In that case, the court can reach the person of the defendant and can validly issue an *in personam* order; but it cannot directly reach the land of another state.

Example. For instance, A, in California, promises to sell Blackacre, which lies in North Carolina. When he reneges, B goes to California and brings a suit for specific performance. Assuming local procedures permit it, the California court may order A to convey the North Carolina land. If he obeys this decree, and makes out a deed to B, B must still take some steps to protect himself. For example, he must record the deed in the appropriate county in North Carolina so as to protect against the possibility that A will make a deed to someone else. However, having done this, B will be the record title owner in North Carolina. This will be so because North Carolina controls title to her land, and she says that duly recorded deeds operate to have that effect.

If A refuses to obey the California court decree, B will have no deed from him to record in North Carolina. California, not having jurisdiction of the land in North Carolina and not having sovereignty of it, cannot properly affect its title in any direct way. The California court, for example, could not simply issue a decree saying that land title in North Carolina "is hereby transferred." Nor can the California court do what amounts to the same thing, by making out a deed itself. If it attempts such devices as these, North Carolina will be free to disregard them.[21]

This rule is not concerned with fundamental fairness to the defendant. There would be nothing unfair to the defendant if the California court transferred North Carolina land. Indeed, the California defendant is much better off to have had the hearing in California than in North Carolina. The

20. See Shaffer v. Heitner, 433 U.S. 186, 97 S.Ct. 2569, 53 L.Ed.2d 683 (1977); Jack Friedenthal, Mary Kay Kane, Arthur Miller, Civil Procedure §§ 3.14–3.15 (1985).

21. See Fall v. Eastin, 215 U.S. 1, 30 S.Ct. 3, 54 L.Ed. 65 (1909); Fenner v. Fenner, 106 N.M. 36, 738 P.2d 908 (1987); Reese, Full Faith & Credit to Foreign Equity Decrees, 42 Iowa L.Rev. 183 (1956).

reason for this rule is that the sovereignty of North Carolina over its own land is an important thing, and it should not be subjected to the direct decrees of the California court, especially where there is no provision for recording those decrees as documents of title so as to keep North Carolina land titles reasonably clear. Perhaps this reason puts too much weight on the symbolic side of sovereignty, when the practical concern ought to be only the protection of clear land titles and recording in other states.

The only objection that can be made to a direct transfer of North Carolina land by a California Court is the one that can be made by North Carolina. But to say that California has "no jurisdiction" to make the direct transfer suggests that North Carolina would not be permitted to enforce the California order even if it wanted to; how could it enforce a void order? California should not be permitted to force a change in North Carolina's land titles against North Carolina's will, but if North Carolina wants to enforce the California decree it should be permitted to do so. If North Carolina *can* enforce the California decree, as seems to be the case,[22] then the limit to California's power is not really "jurisdictional" at all. The limitation is a privilege vested in North Carolina to disregard the California judgment.

In personam orders affecting foreign land. Nevertheless, interstate coercive remedies leave a lot of uncertainty. Where land title is involved, uncertainty is anathema. So in interstate cases, the plaintiff prefers personal jurisdiction over a defendant who is present in the state and who can be coerced. If the defendant refuses to execute the deed as required by an *in personam* order of a court having jurisdiction of his person, the plaintiff may apply for civil contempt sanctions. Under these sanctions, the defendant might be jailed until he signs the deed. Once it signs it, the plaintiff will have the deed, record it in North Carolina and acquire a full North Carolina title.

Compelling acts in foreign states. As already noted, courts have traditionally been reluctant to compel the defendant to do acts in a foreign state. This reluctance has sometimes been expressed in jurisdictional terms, but the problem is not jurisdictional. It is rather a question of practicality and reasonable deference to the interests of other states. So injunction are issued to compel acts elsewhere when the circumstances are appropriate and where contempt enforcement at home appears to be reasonably possible.[23]

---

22. (1) North Carolina might treat California's factual findings as a collateral estoppel and simply re-issue the California decree with North Carolina's imprimatur. Rozan v. Rozan, 49 Cal.2d 322, 317 P.2d 11 (1957); Phelps v. Williams, 192 A.2d 805 (D.C.App.1963); Andre v. Morrow, 106 Idaho 455, 680 P.2d 1355 (1984); Fenner v. Fenner, 106 N.M. 36, 738 P.2d 908 (1987); Bailey v. Tully, 242 Wis. 226, 7 N.W.2d 837, 145 A.L.R. 578 (1943). (2) A California in personam decree might be enforced in North Carolina as a matter of comity. McElreath v. McElreath, 162 Tex. 190,

345 S.W.2d 722 (1961). (3) North Carolina might overlook the symbolic invasion of its sovereignty committed by a California in rem/direct transfer decree and proceed to enforce it. Allis v. Allis, 378 F.2d 721 (5th Cir.1967).

There is a possibility that facts found in the California suit would be given collateral estoppel effect via the full faith and credit clause.

23. See § 2.5(4) above.

§ 2.8 Enforcement of Equity Decrees

§ 2.8(1) Methods of Enforcement

As already indicated,[1] equitable decrees are traditionally *in personam,* that is, personal orders to the defendant to act in a particular way, and they differ from traditional judgments at law in this respect. Because they are personal orders, they are often enforced coercively, through the contempt power. They may also be enforced in other, less drastic ways, however. This section sketches the means of enforcing equitable orders and the rules for enforcement through contempt.

Contempt Sanctions

Equitable decrees may take several different forms. The method of enforcement may be varied with the form of the decree and with practical considerations. The ordinary judgment cannot be enforced by the contempt power. However, courts claim inherent power, independent of statute,[2] to enforce coercive orders like injunctions by contempt.[3] Under the contempt power, the disobedient defendant may be subjected to imprisonment or fine (among other sanctions).[4]

Except in the case of certain acts of contempt committed in the presence of the judge,[5] the court must hold a hearing to determine whether the court's order has been disobeyed and whether the putative contemnor has any defenses.[6] If the contempt is established, the sanctions are usually in the form of fines or imprisonment, or less commonly a remedial fine, payable to the aggrieved party.[7]

The sanction may be "determinate," that is, a fine in a fixed sum or imprisonment for a fixed period. Alternatively the sanction may be indeterminate and continuing, that is, a fine of $100 per day or imprisonment until the court's order is complied with. The determinate sanction is regarded as a criminal sanction, imposed to punish and to vindicate the court's authority.[8] When that is the case, the incidents of trial must comport with all the relevant rules of criminal procedure, including the constitutional protections afforded to those charged with crime. This rule may require a jury trial and proof beyond a reasonable doubt.[9]

When the sanction is indeterminate and continuing, it is usually intended to coerce compliance with the court's decree; the sanction can be lifted when compliance occurs. In that case, the contemnor can stop the accrual of the fine and obtain release from prison simply by obeying the court's order. When this is the kind of sanction for contempt, the contempt trial is considered civil and the criminal rules do not apply.[10]

Non-parties Subject to Liability for Contempt

A court's injunctive decree may indirectly or factually affect conduct of many people. For example, if a court orders a wholesaler to supply goods to

---

§ 2.8(1)

5. Acts in the presence of the judge are usually called direct contempts, and as to these no separate trial or evidence is required. Otherwise, at least some kind of evidentiary hearing is required. See State v. Ryan, 59 Hawaii 425, 583 P.2d 329 (1978) (nonappearance of attorney was not to be classified as direct contempt). Direct contempts raise a number of issues, such as the ability of the judge to provide a fair determination of issues. See generally Dobbs, Contempt of Court: A Survey, 56 Cornell L.Rev. 183, 224 (1971). Direct contempts are outside the scope of the present coverage.

one retailer, the effect may be that the wholesaler cannot supply goods to some other retailer.[11]   But some injunctions may legally as well as factually affect persons who are not parties.   In general, under Rule 65 of the Federal Rules and similar state practice, the injunction may bind parties and also those who are in active concert with parties in violating the injunction.[12]

Raising Defenses to the Contempt Charge

The traditional rule is that one charged with civil contempt may defend by showing that he did not know of the order, or violate it, or that he lacked ability to comply with the order.[13]   One charged with criminal contempt has the benefit of the rule which puts the burden on the prosecution to show a wilful violation, that is, that the defendant knew of the order, had the ability to comply, and refused to do so.   Both criminal and civil contempt charges could be defended as well on the ground that the court issuing the injunction lacked jurisdiction of the person or subject matter.   In neither the civil or criminal case, however, was the contemnor allowed to defend by showing that the injunction was erroneous.   A few cases today take a more generous view, allowing the contemnor to defend the contempt charge when no other practical way existed to challenge its merits.   In addition, some courts have described some erroneous orders as going beyond the court's jurisdiction and hence void, with the effect of allowing the contemnor to defend the contempt charge.[14]

Decretal Transfer of Title, Liens and Trusts

In personam orders can often be enforced by some means short of, and sometimes by means more efficient than, contempt proceedings.   When a court orders specific performance of a contract to convey Blackacre, or determines that the defendant holds Blackacre as a constructive trustee for the plaintiff, the court may order the defendant to convey that property and enforce the order by contempt sanctions if necessary.   But it is also possible for the court to transfer title directly by its decree [15] or by ordering an officer of the court to make a deed.[16]   This is subject to the qualification that decretal transfers, and those made by an officer of the court are effective only as to land within the state,[17] and to the practical necessity that such decrees be recorded amongst appropriate deed records so as to appear in the chain of title.   With these qualifications, however, it is apparent that decretal transfer is a very efficient method of enforcing the court's specific performance or constructive trust decree.

Another device which may avoid contempt proceedings is the equitable lien.   If the defendant attempts to defeat a court order by transferring his property to another who is not a bona fide purchaser, the court may impose

---

11. E.g., Leonard E. Warner, Inc. v. Nissan Motor Corp. in U.S.A., 66 N.C.App. 73, 311 S.E.2d 1 (1984).

15. E.g., Associated Truck Lines, Inc. v. Baer, 346 Mich. 106, 77 N.W.2d 384 (1956) (specific performance, decretal transfer); Alpern v. Coe, 352 Pa. 208, 42 A.2d 542, 161 A.L.R. 1046 (1945) (constructive trust, court can transfer by decree).

16. E.g., Cooley v. Scarlett, 38 Ill. 317 (1865).   Federal Rule 70 provides in part: "If

a judgment directs a party to execute a conveyance of land or to deliver deeds or other documents or to perform any other specific act and the party fails to comply within the time specified, the court may direct the act to be done at the cost of the disobedient party by some other person appointed by the court and the act when so done has like effect as if done by the party."

a lien or trust upon the property in the hands of that other person.[18] The property may thus be recaptured for the plaintiff's benefit without contempt sanctions.

Enforcing Possession Through the Sheriff's In Rem Seizure

When possession rather than title was in issue, the action was often a legal rather than equitable one, and when the law court determined that the plaintiff was entitled to possession, the court issued a writ requiring the sheriff to put the plaintiff in possession.[19] The old separate law court would not, of course, issue an *in personam* order to the defendant to give up possession, but would use the sheriff as the officer of the court to effect the decree indirectly. When possession became an issue in equity cases, equity would issue an *in personam* order, enjoining the defendant to give up possession to the plaintiff. Since equity obviously has sufficient power to enforce this kind of order through contempt proceedings, the order was no doubt often effective without any further compulsion. If more was needed, however, equity courts could utilize the sheriff's services in the same way as law courts, and to this end would issue a writ of assistance, directing the sheriff to put the plaintiff in possession.[20] Here again, equity relief is "*in rem*" rather than "*in personam*" and it is now sometimes specifically authorized by rules or statutes.[21]

Receivers

Other *in personam* orders may also be enforceable without use of the contempt power. Receivers are appointed by the court to take charge of or manage property until some final disposition is made.[22] For example, receivers might be appointed to take charge of partnership assets as a part of winding up the partnership, or to manage the business of an incompetent.[23] In one well known case, a New York court ordered a defendant to bring a

---

18. E.g., Martian v. Martian, 399 N.W.2d 849 (N.D.1987).

19. Sometimes called a writ of possession, or writ habere facias possessionem. As to ejectment and similar actions at law to regain possession, see § 5.10 below.

20. R. Millar, Civil Procedure of the Trial Court in Historical Perspective 475–76 (1952). The older procedure had it that equity courts proceeded first by way of other enforcement devices, such as contempt, and the writ of assistance as a last resort. This is now obsolete, and the writ of assistance, at least in systems where law and equity are merged, may issue as the preferred form of relief. Federal Rule 70 provides for the issuance as a matter of course by the clerk: "When any order or judgment is for delivery of possession, the party in whose favor it is entered is entitled to a writ of execution or assistance upon application to the clerk."

21. Fed.R.Civ.Proc.R. 70 provides in part:

On application of the party entitled to performance, the clerk shall issue a writ of attachment or sequestration against the property of the disobedient party to compel obedience to the judgment. The court may also in proper cases adjudge the party in contempt. If real or personal property is within the district, the court in lieu of directing a conveyance thereof may enter a judgment divesting the title of any party and vesting it in others and such judgment has the effect of a conveyance executed in due form of law. When any order or judgment is for the delivery of possession, the party in whose favor it is entered is entitled to a writ of execution or assistance upon application to the clerk.

22. In the federal system receivers are authorized by Fed.R.Civ.Proc. Rule 66. State statutes may authorize or regulate the appointment and powers of receivers. E.g., West's Ann.Cal.Code Civ.Proc. § 699.070 (court may vest receiver with power to sell the property if it is perishable or will deteriorate, similar powers vested in levying officer, fees fixed by the court and may be charged against judgment creditor).

23. See 4 J. Pomeroy, Equity Jurisprudence §§ 1332–1336 (5th ed. Symons 1941).

race horse from California to another state. When the defendant refused, the court appointed a receiver to go to California and take possession of the horse, and return the animal at the defendant's expense.[24] The receiver's fees and costs were also chargeable to the defendant.[25]

Masters

Masters were traditional officers of equity courts, appointed to carry out some specific judicial task, usually associated with taking evidence.[26] United States Magistrates are authorized to serve if the judge orders a reference to a master. The scope of the master's duty is governed by the judge's order of reference. Masters traditionally served an important role in sifting through voluminous evidence in complex cases, such as accountings. Masters might also function as a third person who can be appointed by the judge to convey property when the defendant refuses to do so.[27] Most commonly the masters took evidence and made a report to the judge, who might adopt the findings or not, so they were not primarily enforcers. In recent years some courts have appointed masters or other similar officers of the court to carry out some enforcement functions. When injunctions are used in civil rights cases to restructure institutions such as prisons, a master appointed by the court may be installed to supervise the changes and even to virtually administer the system when the defendant authorities are recalcitrant.[28]

Enforcing Money Decrees

Sometimes equity courts have occasion to issue money decrees. These may be made in the form of *in personam* orders, as is commonly the case where a defendant is ordered to pay alimony or child support in certain regular amounts. A money decree in equity in modern times could also be couched in the form of an adjudication of liability, though in practice the *in personam* order to pay is more common. The difference is that the adjudication of liability is not a personal order and it would not be enforceable by contempt proceedings. In such a case the money decree of equity could be enforced under statutes in the same way that money judgments at law are enforced—by execution on property of the defendant, with a sale and application of the proceeds to the debt.

The same process for enforcement of a money decree may be used where the decree is phrased in terms of an *in personam* order to pay money. In other words, the fact that the decree is an *in personam* order does not prevent enforcement "*in rem.*" The older practice was otherwise, under the maxim that "equity acts *in personam*", and under that practice execution in equity was a limited procedure. Today, however, equity money decrees are

---

24. Madden v. Rosseter, 114 Misc. 416, 187 N.Y.S. 462 (Sup.Ct.1921), aff'd without opinion, 196 A.D. 891, 187 N.Y.S. 943 (1921).

25. Madden v. Rosseter, 117 Misc. 244, 192 N.Y.S. 113 (1921) ($5,000 for receiver's fee, $500 for his counsel, fees taxed as costs against defendant).

26. Fed.R.Civ.Proc.R. 53 governs the appointment of masters in federal courts. Except when the magistrate serves as a master,

the master is paid compensation fixed by the court and charged against one or more parties or against any fund in the court's custody in connection with the case. As to calculating the fee, see Levine, Calculating Fees of Special Masters, 37 Hast.L.J. 141 (1985).

27. See n. 16, supra.

28. See § 7.4(4) below.

treated as virtually identical with money judgments at law for purposes of enforcement, at least where the plaintiff so desires.

Under these rules, money decrees in equity for specific sums may be entitled to full faith and credit in other states,[29] though some *in personam* decrees are not. Similarly, the equity money decree may be enforced by execution.[30] Indeed, state constitutional provisions against imprisonment for debt may prohibit enforcement by contempt power using jail sentences as sanctions.[31] In line with this, statutes may require use of execution rather than contempt where execution is possible,[32] and in any event, execution is probably the preferred mode of enforcing a purely money decree.[33]

Supplemental Proceedings

When the defendant was subjected to a money judgment, either at law or in equity, the equity courts traditionally aided enforcement by supplemental proceedings in some cases. Such proceedings were used partly as a kind of post-trial discovery to compel the defendant to reveal assets upon which the judgment could be executed, or to order transfer of intangible assets such as rights in trademarks or copyrights that could not be reached at all by execution.[34] This kind of aid to enforcement is still authorized[35] and still used, once it appears that ordinary execution is ineffective because assets are intangible and cannot be seized for levy of execution, or because they are held in the hands of third persons.[36]

29. See Reese, Full Faith & Credit to Foreign Equity Decrees, 42 Iowa L.Rev. 183 (1957). Decrees ordering future payments of alimony or child support may be subject to modification in the court that rendered the decree, and where this is so, a number of difficulties have arisen in obtaining full faith and credit and in modifying the decree. See Robert Leflar, Luther McDougal III, & Robert Felix, American Conflicts Law §§ 227–228 (4th ed. 1986).

30. See Messenger v. Messenger, 46 Cal.2d 619, 297 P.2d 988 (1956) (alimony decree, trial court may enforce in its discretion by either contempt or execution); White v. White, 233 Mass. 39, 123 N.E. 389 (1919) (contempt or execution in alimony decree). See also, Dolan v. Hudson, 83 S.D. 144, 156 N.W.2d 78 (1968). Statutes and court rules may compel or permit execution rather than contempt enforcement. Fed.R.Civ.Proc.R. 69 provides in part:

(a) In General. Process to enforce a judgment for the payment of money shall be a writ of execution, unless the court directs otherwise. The procedure on execution, in proceedings supplementary to and in aid of a judgment, and in proceedings on and in aid of execution shall be in accordance with the practice and procedure of the state in which the district court is held, existing at the time the remedy is sought, except that any statute of the United States governs to the extent that it is applicable. In aid of the judgment or execution, the judgment creditor or a successor in interest when that interest appears of record, may obtain dis-

covery from any person, including the judgment debtor, in the manner provided in these rules or in the manner provided by the practice of the state in which the district court is held.

31. See § 2.8(2) below.

32. E.g., N.C.Gen.Stat. § 5–8(2). See Warehouse Carpet Sales & Serv., Inc. v. S.C.J. Assocs., Inc., 170 Ga.App. 352, 317 S.E.2d 328, 329–330 (1984) ("A money judgment may normally be enforced only by execution thereon, not by contempt proceedings" but contempt can be used where "the order to pay is interlocutory in nature [and] contempt is the only method of enforcement available").

33. Cf. Fed.R.Civ.Proc. Rule 69: "Process to enforce a judgment for the payment of money shall be a writ of execution, unless the court directs otherwise."

34. See generally J. Pomeroy, Equity Jurisprudence § 1415 (5th ed. 1941).

35. By Rule 69, Fed.R.Civ.Proc. in the federal courts, and often by statute in the states.

36. The supplemental proceedings may thus be used to reach fraudulent conveyances. See e.g., Allied Industries Intern., Inc. v. AGFA–Gevaert, Inc., 688 F.Supp. 1516 (S.D.Fla.1988), aff'd, 900 F.2d 264 (11th Cir. 1990). Some states may permit supplemental proceedings to bring in third persons yet require a separate but similar action if the third person claims to own the property. See Federal Deposit Ins. Corp. v. British–American Corp., 726 F.Supp. 622 (E.D.N.C.1989).

§ 2.8(2) Sanctions for Contempt

Sanctions for violation of a coercive personal order such as an injunction or specific performance decree may be considered to be either criminal or civil. The rules for distinguishing between criminal and civil sanctions and the special rules which limit criminal sanctions and criminal contempt hearings are discussed in the subsections that follow.[1]

General Categories

Sanctions for contempt fall in three categories. (1) Determinate sanctions, such as a jail sentence of 30 days. These are criminal sanctions. (2) Coercive sanctions, such as imprisonment until the contemnor complies with the court's order, or a fine to be applied unless or until the contemnor complies. This is a civil sanction even though it entails imprisonment. (3) Remedial or compensatory sanctions, such as a civil fine payable to the plaintiff in compensation for losses suffered as a result of the defendant's non-compliance with the court's order.

Imprisonment

Coercive sanctions may take almost any form. Imprisonment until the contemnor complies with the court's order is a permissible form of civil sanction for contempt, because it provides the defendant or contemnor with continuing incentive to comply. As the saying goes, he carries the keys to the jail in his own pocket.[2] The characteristic of this coercive imprisonment is that it has no definite term in the way a criminal sentence would. It may last indefinitely, at least as long as it carries coercive potential.[3] Another form of coercive and civil imprisonment is the *in terrorem* sentence. The court may sentence the defendant to a definite jail term but suspend the sentence or put the defendant on probation so long as he obeys the court's order in the future.[4]

Imprisonment for Debt

Most states constitutionally proscribe imprisonment for debt.[5] Under these provisions, coercive imprisonment may not be used to enforce orders to pay debts.[6] Few such orders are entered, however. The ordinary debt claim can be enforced by execution rather than contempt, even if the court enters a personal, coercive order to pay it.[7]

The typical *in personam* order to pay money is not an order to pay a "debt" but an order to pay money arising from a status obligation. Obligations imposed by law to support a spouse or minor child are in this category, so orders to make support payments may be enforced by imprison-

---

§ 2.8(2)

1. See §§ 2.8(3) & 2.8(4) below.

2. In re Nevitt, 117 Fed. 448, 461, 54 C.C.A. 622 (1902).

3. See § 2.8(3) below as to the possibility that coercive effect will be exhausted.

4. See Hicks on Behalf of Feiock v. Feiock, 485 U.S. 624, 108 S.Ct. 1423, 99 L.Ed.2d 721 (1988), discussed further in § 2.8(3) below.

5. E.g., Ariz. R.S. Const. Art. 2, § 18; West's Ann.Cal. Const. art. 1, § 10; Vernon's Ann.Tex. Const. Art. 1, § 18.

6. E.g., Brown v. Brown, 287 Md. 273, 412 A.2d 396 (1980). Distinguish restitution ordered as a condition of probation, which has been upheld. See People v. Baumann, 176 Cal.App.3d 67, 222 Cal.Rptr. 32 (1985).

7. See § 2.8(1) above.

ment for contempt if necessary,[8] although obligations arising only from agreement of the parties are not.[9]

Sometimes fiduciary obligations are treated as obligations of status rather than debt, so that, again, payment may be ordered and disobedience sanctioned by imprisonment.[10] Other obligations, such as obligations arising from fraud, may be textually exempted from the constitutional stricture. New York once held that a court could order payment of an ordinary contract debt and enforce the order by contempt and imprisonment, provided only that the defendant was able to pay.[11]

When a decree ordering payment of money is entered because of the consent or agreement of the parties, some decisions have held that the obligation thus created is assimilated to a contract or debt, and cannot be enforced by contempt.[12] Other courts have viewed the decree as "independent" of the agreement on which it is based and have permitted contempt enforcement and imprisonment if the decree otherwise warrants such a sanction.[13]

Coercive Fines

Instead of imprisonment, the court may impose a fine upon the defendant. A simple fine in a specified amount is a criminal contempt sanction. But if the fine is coercive in nature, it is a civil sanction. One form of coercive or civil fine compels the defendant to pay a daily fine until compliance is shown or the contempt purged.[14] Variations include the conditional fine that is stated in a determined amount, but not to be imposed unless the defendant again violates the court's decree.

Compensatory or Remedial Sanctions [15]

The Supreme Court has long recognized that one appropriate kind of sanction for civil contempt is remedial rather than coercive.[16] That is, the sanction provides the plaintiff with a substitute for the defendant's obedience without compelling that obedience itself. The most straightforward version of the remedial sanction is the compensatory fine, paid to the plaintiff as compensation.[17] If the fine is to be justified because it is

8. E.g., Smith v. Smith, 427 A.2d 928 (D.C.App.1981); Johnson v. Johnson, 241 Md. 416, 216 A.2d 914 (1966); See Ex parte Preston, 162 Tex. 379, 347 S.W.2d 938 (1961); Annotation, 30 A.L.R. 130 (1924).

9. Ordinary contract obligations, even though they may run to family members, are debts, so that contempt imprisonment for these is impermissible. E.g., Ruhsam v. Ruhsam, 110 Ariz. 326, 518 P.2d 576 (1974).

10. E.g., People v. La Mothe, 331 Ill. 351, 163 N.E. 6 (1928) (trustee).

11. Reeves v. Crownshield, 274 N.Y. 74, 8 N.E.2d 283 (1937).

12. Holden v. Holden, 245 N.C. 1, 95 S.E.2d 118 (1956).

13. Goodman v. Goodman, 695 S.W.2d 865, 867 (Ky.1985); Scheldrup v. Gaffney, 243 Iowa 1297, 55 N.W.2d 272 (1952); Ex parte Gorena, 595 S.W.2d 841, 844 (Tex.1979) ("Despite the fact that a judgment has its genesis in an agreement between the parties, the judgment itself has an independent status").

14. Sunbeam Corp. v. Golden Rule Appliance Co., 252 F.2d 467 (2d Cir.1958).

15. The complete study of compensatory contempt sanctions is Rendleman, Compensatory Contempt: Plaintiff's Remedy When A Defendant Violates An Injunction, 1980 Ill.L.Forum 971.

16. Gompers v. Buck's Stove & Range Co., 221 U.S. 418, 31 S.Ct. 492, 55 L.Ed. 797 (1911).

17. United States v. United Mine Workers of America, 330 U.S. 258, 303–304, 67 S.Ct. 677, 701, 91 L.Ed. 884 (1947). The *Mine Workers* Court said, citation omitted:

Judicial sanctions in civil contempt proceedings may, in a proper case, be employed for either or both of two purposes; to coerce the

remedial, courts have said that it must be based on evidence, either of the plaintiff's loss [18] or the defendant's gains.[19] Related, a court may impose money sanctions under Rule 11 or under the court's inherent power for obstructive or harassing acts, and in such cases the sanction may be measured by some or all of the plaintiff's attorney fee costs.[20] Some courts have questioned the remedial or compensatory fine, on the ground that it really awards damages without preserving right to jury trial, or on somewhat less certain grounds.[21]

Defendant's Profits as a Remedial Sanction

Quite apart from contempt sanctions, a defendant who gains benefits as a result of a wrong done to the plaintiff may be made to disgorge those benefits under the law of restitution and on the ground that such disgorgement is required to prevent the defendant's unjust enrichment.[22] Could a court award restitution of the defendant's unjust gains as a remedial sanction for contempt? Although a few courts have been negative, a number have permitted a civil contempt sanction in this form.[23]

Denying the Right to Litigate

Imprisonment, fines and disgorgements do not exhaust the courts' repertoire of sanctions. Sometimes courts have held that a contumacious party can be refused even the right to litigate. In *Hovey v. Elliott*,[24] the defendant was ordered, in an early stage of the case, to deposit a disputed sum in court. He refused to do so. The judge then struck his answer and entered a default against him. The United States Supreme Court overturned this action as a denial of due process.

A few years later the Court cast doubt on *Hovey* by deciding a very similar case in a different way. In *Hammond Packing Co. v. Arkansas*,[25] the state sued Hammond, a foreign corporation. After Hammond answered, the state sought to examine its records in Chicago. Hammond refused to comply with a court order that required it to make its books available, asserting

---

defendant into compliance with the court's order, and to compensate the complainant for losses sustained.

18. *United States v. United Mine Workers of Am.,* supra n. 17 ("Where compensation is intended, a fine is imposed, payable to the complainant. Such fine must of course be based upon evidence of complainant's actual loss, and his right, as a civil litigant, to the compensatory fine is dependent upon the outcome of the basic controversy"); New York State Nat. Organization for Women v. Terry, 886 F.2d 1339 (2d Cir.1989) (fact that fine was payable to plaintiff might enhance its coercive effect, but it was not justified unless it represented at least a general estimate of the loss or proof showed that its coercive effect would be enhanced because it was payable to the plaintiff).

19. See paragraph "Defendant's profits as a remedial sanction," below.

20. Chambers v. NASCO, Inc., ___ U.S. ___, 111 S.Ct. 2123, 115 L.Ed.2d 27 (1991) (series of obstructive, delaying, harassing acts, some of which would apparently amount to contempt, plaintiff's entire litigation costs, just short of $1 million, awarded as sanction).

21. See H.J. Heinz Co. v. Superior Court, 42 Cal.2d 164, 266 P.2d 5 (1954); Eberle v. Greene, 71 Ill.App.2d 85, 217 N.E.2d 6 (1966); Morris v. Whitehead, 65 N.C. 637 (1871).

22. See Chapter 4 generally.

23. *Civil contempt:* Leman v. Krentler–Arnold Hinge Last Co., 284 U.S. 448, 52 S.Ct. 238, 76 L.Ed. 389 (1932); Connolly v. J.T. Ventures, 851 F.2d 930 (7th Cir.1988). *Criminal contempt:* Chicago v. Hart Bldg. Corp., 116 Ill.App.2d 39, 253 N.E.2d 496 (1969), cert. denied, 398 U.S. 950, 90 S.Ct. 1870, 26 L.Ed.2d 290 (1970).

24. 167 U.S. 409, 17 S.Ct. 841, 42 L.Ed. 215 (1897).

25. 212 U.S. 322, 29 S.Ct. 370, 53 L.Ed. 530 (1909).

constitutional rights. When Hammond refused to comply with the order, the court struck Hammond's answer and entered judgment against it. The Supreme Court upheld this procedure. There was statutory authorization for the procedure thus adopted, but the Court refused to distinguish *Hovey* on that basis. Instead, the Court held that the statute created a valid presumption of fact.

However these two cases are to be explained, there seems to be no constitutional inhibition against a contempt sanction that deprives the litigant of his right to attack or seek affirmative relief.[26]

Other Sanctions

In *Lance v. Plummer*,[27] a honorary deputy was enjoined from harassing the plaintiffs. When he was found in contempt, the court deprived him of his badge, subject to restoration if he purged himself of contempt. The effect was a partial remedy; it might not prevent harassment of the plaintiffs, but it might have prevented harassment under color of law and with whatever authority the badge conferred. There seems to be no general rule limiting the form of the sanction, although some sanctions that are imaginable would run into due process objections.

§ 2.8(3) Enforcement of Equity Decrees by Contempt Powers—Civil vs. Criminal

Determinate, Coercive and Remedial Sanctions

Criminal sanctions require criminal trial procedures. It is almost always necessary to distinguish between "civil" and "criminal" contempt hearings and sanctions.[1] The kind of trial procedure used in a contempt hearing must correlate with the sanction: if the sanction is "criminal," then the constitutional and procedural rules applied to criminal trials must be observed. A discorrelation between the procedure and the sanction annuls the conviction. In addition, if the contempt is criminal, the maximum punishment will be set by statute or by constitutional rules. Two points become important in consequence of this rule. First, criminal sanctions must be distinguished from civil sanctions. Second, the procedural requirements of a criminal-type contempt trial must be identified and provided when a criminal sanction is contemplated.[2]

Sanction imposed determines civil or criminal nature. The term criminal contempt does not refer to the nature of the act of contempt.[3] Although some acts committed in disobeying a court order may violate criminal statutes, almost any knowing act of disobedience of a court order is sufficiently criminal to permit the court to impose criminal sanctions. The question whether the contempt hearing must respect the criminal procedures or not depends, not on the contemnor's act, but on the sanction to be imposed.

26. See National Union of Marine Cooks & Stewards v. Arnold, 348 U.S. 37, 75 S.Ct. 92, 99 L.Ed. 46 (1954) (denial of right to appeal as coercive or remedial, but not as punitive measure); Garrett v. Garrett, 341 Ill. 232, 173 N.E. 107 (1930). See Annotation, 49 A.L.R.2d 1425 (1956) (dismissal of appeal); Annotation, 14 A.L.R.2d 580 (1950) (striking pleading).

27. 353 F.2d 585 (5th Cir.1965), cert. denied, 384 U.S. 929, 86 S.Ct. 1380, 16 L.Ed.2d 532 (1966).

Tests applied. It is traditionally said that the sanction is criminal when it punishes or vindicates the court's authority. In contrast, the sanction is civil when it operates coercively to induce compliance with the court's decree or remedially to obtain for the plaintiff a substitute for the defendant's compliance.[4] Many contempt sanctions probably have both punishment and compliance effects. But neither the personal effect on the individual defendant nor the judge's subjective purpose in imposing the sanction govern the classification as civil or criminal.[5] Instead, the sanction is usually regarded as criminal whenever it is a determinate fine or jail sentence, and when it has no possible or permissible coercive effect.[6]

Examples of criminal and civil sanctions. For example, a fine of $10,000, imposed without condition, is a criminal sanction. An unconditional jail sentence of ten days is a criminal sanction. On the other hand, a fine of $1,000 per day until the contemnor complies with the court's order is a civil sanction. So is a jail sentence to last indefinitely but to terminate when the contemnor complies or shows a disposition to do so. The reason for these rules is not hard to see in connection with these examples. An unconditional fine or jail sentence does not provide incentive for compliance with the decree; the sanction will proceed whether or not the defendant decides to yield to the court's authority. So it must be punishment. A conditional or indeterminate fine or sentence, however, leaves the keys to the jail in the contemnor's own pocket; he has incentive to comply to secure release and to minimize the fine. So the indeterminate sanction is almost always coercive and civil, at least where something is left in fact to coerce.

When a determinate sanction is coercive. Although a simple determinate sanction is always punitive and criminal in nature, a determinate sanction might be made conditional. Any form of conditional fine or imprisonment is also coercive and therefore civil. For instance, the court might impose a suspended sentence of imprisonment, with incarceration to take place only if the defendant again violates the court's order. Or the court might impose a jail term but put the plaintiff on probation so long as he continues to obey the decree.

§ 2.8(3)

4. E.g., Labor Relations Com'n v. Fall River Educators' Ass'n, 382 Mass. 465, 416 N.E.2d 1340 (1981); Mason Furniture Corp. v. George, 116 N.H. 451, 362 A.2d 188, 189 (1976) ("A civil contempt * * * is an order committing the judgment debtor to custody until he makes a prescribed payment" and "to secure a payment, not to punish"); Jolly v. Wright, 300 N.C. 83, 265 S.E.2d 135, 142 (1980) ("its purpose is to use the court's power to impose fines or imprisonment as a method of coercing the defendant to comply with an order"); State, Fall River County v. Dryden, 409 N.W.2d 648 (S.D.1987); In re Yoho, 171 W.Va. 625, 301 S.E.2d 581, 585 (1983); see Matter of Hanks, 290 Or. 451, 623 P.2d 623, 626 (1981) ("Civil contempt is contempt in which the court's sanction is intended to compel compliance with the court's order * * *.").

5. Hicks on Behalf of Feiock v. Feiock, 485 U.S. 624, 635, 108 S.Ct. 1423, 1431, 99 L.Ed.2d 721, 734 (1988) ("Although the purposes that lie behind particular kinds of relief are germane to understanding their character, this Court has never undertaken to psychoanalyze the subjective intent of a State's laws and its courts * * * *"). The rule has often been expressed as turning on the purpose of the punishment, e.g., Commonwealth v. Charlett, 481 Pa. 22, 391 A.2d 1296 (1978), but that expression usually was not intended to suggest that the judge's subjective purpose controlled.

6. Anderson v. St. Mary's Hospital, 101 Ill.App.3d 596, 56 Ill.Dec. 936, 428 N.E.2d 528 (1981); State ex rel. Kandt v. North Platte Baptist Church, 219 Neb. 694, 365 N.W.2d 813 (1985); Wides v. Wides, 96 A.D.2d 592, 465 N.Y.S.2d 285 (1983); Bishop v. Bishop, 90 N.C.App. 499, 369 S.E.2d 106 (1988). As to the possible or permissible coercive effect, see segment, *Where Coercive Effects Are Impossible, Diminished, Unnecessary or Exhausted,* below.

Hicks v. Feiock,[7] is an example. The defendant was under a court order to make child-support payments to his former wife. After he made only sporadic payments for six years, the court again ordered payment. The next year his former wife sought contempt enforcement, showing that he had made only two of the payments required and that undetermined amount of arrearage existed. The court found that the defendant was unable to pay during some months, and consequently not in contempt for those. It then imposed jail sentence for the other months of nonpayment, but suspended the sentence and put the defendant on probation. One condition of the probation was payment of support and arrearages at a specified rate. The Supreme Court held that for constitutional purposes, the sanction would be coercive if full payment would have the effect of relieving the defendant of liability for contempt. Although the sanction was determinate, if the sanction was truly conditional, it was also coercive and civil.

The special rule for remedial or compensatory sanctions. The tests just discussed do not fit quite so neatly when the sanction is remedial but not coercive. Suppose the judge concludes that the defendant will not comply with the court's decree or that he has made full compliance impossible. For instance, suppose the judge issues a specific performance decree, ordering the defendant to convey Blackacre to the plaintiff. The defendant instead conveys to an innocent purchaser. In this situation coercive contempt sanctions against the defendant may not be possible. The judge might therefore impose a criminal contempt sanction by jailing the defendant for a stated time period or fining him for a stated amount.

However, the judge might conclude instead that the plaintiff, whose right to the land has been frustrated by the defendant's disobedience, should at least obtain a substitute by way of money. For this purpose the judge might impose a remedial fine, in an amount approximating the plaintiff's damages.[8] A compensatory fine is a determinate amount and as such bears one of the marks of a criminal sanction. On the other hand, if it is proportioned to the loss suffered and payable to the party aggrieved, its remedial function seems predominant, and the Supreme Court has recognized the remedial fine as a civil sanction when it is payable to the injured party.[9]

Where Coercive Effects Are Impossible, Diminished, Unnecessary or Exhausted

The core cases: when the court's decree has no further force. An important implication of the rules for distinguishing civil from criminal contempt is that if the degree by its terms does not compel future or post-

7. 485 U.S. 624, 108 S.Ct. 1423, 99 L.Ed.2d 721 (1988).

8. United States v. United Mine Workers of America, 330 U.S. 258, 304, 67 S.Ct. 677, 701, 91 L.Ed. 884, 918 (1947) ("Such fine must of course be based upon evidence of complainant's actual loss, and his right, as a civil litigant, to the compensatory fine is dependent upon the outcome of the basic controversy"). See N.Y.Jud.L. § 774 ("a fine, sufficient to indemnify the aggrieved party").

9. "If the relief provided is a fine, it is remedial when it is paid to the complainant, and punitive when it is paid to the court, though a fine that would be payable to the court is also remedial when the defendant can avoid paying the fine simply by performing the affirmative act required by the court's order." Hicks on Behalf of Feiock v. Feiock, 485 U.S. 624, 632, 108 S.Ct. 1423, 1429–30, 99 L.Ed.2d 721, 731 (1988).

violation conduct, there is nothing to coerce and any sanction for its past violation must necessarily be criminal.[10] This idea has proved to be complex. The Supreme Court may have cast doubt upon the broadest version of this idea, but probably not upon its core principle.[11]

—*Decree reversed on appeal.* One major example is the case of a decree that is reversed on appeal. The defendant is not free to violate a court's injunction merely because he appeals it.[12] If the defendant does violate the order while appeal is pending, and later obtains reversal of the order on the merits, the court may still sanction his violation as a contempt. However, because the order has been reversed, it has no future force. The power of the injunctive order itself is exhausted and for this reason there is nothing left to coerce. Consequently, the contempt sanction, unless compensatory, must be criminal in nature.[13]

—*Prohibitory and mandatory decrees.* Other examples show that the core principle applies whether the court's order forbids an act or compels one. Suppose the order prohibits the defendant from conducting a May Day demonstration and that the defendant violates the order. After May Day has come and gone, the case is like the case of the order that is reversed on appeal: the court's order has no remaining future effect. In this instance, it is exhausted by its own terms. There is quite literally nothing to coerce. The past violation may be remedied by a compensatory fine or a criminal contempt sanction,[14] but no coercive civil contempt is possible or permissible.[15]

—*Orders to testify.* The same principle applies if the court order affirmatively orders the defendant to testify before a grand jury. Once the grand jury is dissolved, the order by its terms requires no further conduct of the contemnor, and nothing to coerce. He may be held in civil contempt until the grand jury is dissolved, but after its dissolution he may be held only for criminal contempt.[16]

10. This setting is similar to the setting in which the defendant finds future compliance impossible but was had the ability to comply in the past. The two settings may be conflated. The California statute provides, subject to an exception, "when the contempt consists of the omission to perform an act which is yet in the power of the person to perform, he or she may be imprisoned until he or she has performed it * * *." West's Ann.Cal.Code Civ. Proc. § 1219. The "power to perform" language may have been addressed to personal ability to perform, but could also address the case in which no future act is required. These two situations can be treated together as to future compliance; when they are lumped together in discussions about liability for *past* compliance, confusing difficulties result. See the paragraph "Beyond the core: when the injunction prohibits but does not mandate acts," below.

11. See paragraph, "The Supreme Court's test" below.

12. If the order is stayed during appeal, the defendant's acts will not be a violation of the order. As to stays of an injunctive order, see § 2.11(4) below.

13. See nn. 14 & 15 below. As to criminal contempt liability for violation of an order that is later reversed, consult § 2.8(6) below.

14. See Worden v. Searls, 121 U.S. 14, 7 S.Ct. 814, 30 L.Ed. 853 (1887); United States v. United Mine Workers of America, 330 U.S. 258, 67 S.Ct. 677, 91 L.Ed. 884 (1947) ("Violations of an order are punishable as criminal contempt even though the order is set aside on appeal"). The liability to criminal punishment has been criticized, see below § 2.8(6). But there is no claim that civil, coercive punishment is permissible.

15. In re Novak, 932 F.2d 1397, 1401 & n. 6 (11th Cir.1991); see Worden v. Searls, 121 U.S. 14, 7 S.Ct. 814, 30 L.Ed. 853 (1887).

16. Shillitani v. United States, 384 U.S. 364, 86 S.Ct. 1531, 16 L.Ed.2d 622 (1966).

Beyond the core: when the injunction prohibits but does not mandate acts. The core principles just discussed turn on the order itself and whether it requires further action that can be coerced. Some courts have extended those core ideas by distinguishing between injunctions that require the defendant to carry out affirmative acts and those that prohibit acts. For these courts, the injunction that requires affirmative conduct can be enforced coercively by civil contempt sanctions, but the injunction that prohibits conduct seemingly cannot.

—The Michigan rule. In a Michigan case, *Dougherty,*[17] protestors broke into the plaintiff's premises to protest the plaintiff's production of missile parts. They damaged some property and defaced buildings. The court then prohibited further trespass and also any blocking of ingress and egress. The contemnors knowingly violated the injunction and the trial court found them in contempt. It imposed a civil sanction, namely imprisonment until they assured the court that they would not further violate the order. The Michigan Supreme Court, in a divided decision, held that no coercive contempt sanction would be permissible. It distinguished between orders that compel acts and those that prohibit them. When acts are prohibited, a violation of the injunction warranted criminal sanctions or perhaps remedial compensatory fines, but not coercive sanctions. This was so, the majority thought, because although the defendant has violated the order by his past acts, he was not in present violation because he was not trespassing at the moment the contempt trial was held. The majority thought that this meant "there is no need to coerce compliance, since, of course, there is already compliance."[18]

The *Dougherty* decision finds an uncertain degree of support in some of the language of a Supreme Court decision, *Gompers v. Buck's Stove and Range Co.*[19] But the *Gompers'* Court did not address the case of a defendant who has violated the court's order and who threatens to continue violation. An injunction which prohibits a May Day demonstration has no further force after May Day has come and gone, but an injunction which prohibits any future trespass has continuing force. It would be wrong to use coercive sanctions in the May Day case because the decree itself leaves nothing to enforce. It would also be wrong to use a coercive sanction if no future violation is threatened. The *Dougherty* decision appears to go further, however. It appears to hold that even when the defendant has violated the injunction, is still subject to its continuing terms, and proposes to violate it in the future, a coercive sanction is not available.

—The Pennsylvania rule. A Pennsylvania case[20] reached a similar result where the trial judge attempted to impose a conditional fine rather than indeterminate imprisonment. In that case, an abortion protester,

17. In re Contempt of Dougherty, 429 Mich. 81, 413 N.W.2d 392, 81 A.L.R.4th 971 (1987).

18. Id. at 399.

19. 221 U.S. 418, 442, 31 S.Ct. 492, 498, 55 L.Ed. 797, 806 (1911) ("But imprisonment for civil contempt is ordered where the defendant has refused to do an affirmative act required by the provisions of an order which, either in form or substance, was mandatory in its char- acter * * *. On the other hand, if the defendant does that which he has been commanded not to do, the disobedience is a thing accomplished. Imprisonment cannot undo or remedy what has been done, nor afford any compensation for the pecuniary injury caused by the disobedience.").

20. Crozer–Chester Medical Center v. Moran, 522 Pa. 124, 560 A.2d 133 (1989).

harassing patients and a clinic, was repeatedly enjoined and repeatedly subjected to contempt hearings. The trial court found the defendant in contempt, but acted with restraint by imposing a "conditional fine" of $1,000 that would not be payable unless the defendant violated the injunction again. This is a coercive fine because it can be avoided by compliance with the court's order. The defendant did not comply, however, but continued to carry out the prohibited activities. After three rounds, the court ordered the defendant to pay the accrued fine. Although the fine began as a coercive fine, it could not be coercive after the defendant had refused to obey the court's order. Instead of evaluating the fine as of the time it was originally imposed in conditional and coercive form, the Pennsylvania Court evaluated it at the time the court ordered its collection. At that time, because the defendant could not purge himself of past contempts to avoid the fine, the court held that the fine had become criminal. So the whole contempt proceeding would have to meet the criminal procedure rules and the fine would be limited by whatever statutory limits might apply to criminal contempt fines.

—Decisions approving coercive contempt in prohibitory injunction cases. Several cases, recent at this writing, are essentially contrary to the Michigan and Pennsylvania rules. In *Aradia Women's Health Center v. Operation Rescue,*[21] an injunction issued against an association, prohibiting interference with women's access to a clinic for legal abortions. The injunction applied to non-parties who had notice of the injunction and who acted in concert with the organization.[22] Individuals appeared at the clinic to block access. The plaintiff's attorney then read them the injunctive order which also provided prospectively that a fine of $500 per day would be imposed for each violation.

The demonstrators refused to leave and were held in contempt under the original terms of the order. They argued as the demonstrators in Michigan and Pennsylvania did, but without success. The Ninth Circuit observed that the penalties were fixed prospectively, in the original decree, and that a prospective penalty was a hallmark of civil or coercive contempt. Although the *hearing* to determine whether a violation occurred was necessarily held *after* the conduct and not before, that fact "does not turn an otherwise civil contempt sanction into a criminal one."[23]

A similar result on similar facts was reached earlier in decisions of the Second and Third Circuits,[24] and in some state courts.[25] Even if some of these decisions may be technically distinguished from the Michigan and

---

21. 929 F.2d 530 (9th Cir.1991).

22. As to the liability of non-parties to contempt, see § 2.8(5) below.

23. The court continued: "As with many civil contempt fines, '[t]he factual determination of noncompliance—the assessment of whether the standards showing contempt were satisfied—and the resulting imposition of fines necessarily occurred after defendants' ample opportunity to comply had come and gone.'"

24. New York State Nat. Organization for Women v. Terry, 886 F.2d 1339 (2d Cir.1989); Roe v. Operation Rescue, 919 F.2d 857, 869 (3d Cir.1990) (refusing to follow Pennsylvania's decision in *Crozer–Chester Medical Center* on the ground that federal, not state law controlled federal court contempt practice); see also Northeast Women's Center, Inc. v. McMonagle, 939 F.2d 57 (3d Cir.1991).

25. Lovejoy Specialty Hosp., Inc. v. Advocates For Life, Inc., 104 Or.App. 596, 802 P.2d 684 (1990).

Pennsylvania counterparts, their thrust and outlook seems to be essentially contrary.

—*Evaluations.* Both the Michigan and Pennsylvania cases reflect appropriate concern about contempt sanctions, but they withdraw the power of coercive sanctions from a broad range of cases. Both decisions disregard threat of future violation as an element in determining whether a coercive sanction is appropriate for a past violation, and both decisions appear to make it impossible to use coercive remedies to obtain compliance of prohibitory orders. An alternative approach might be to refuse coercive sanctions in all the core cases (where the decree itself has no future functions) and all the cases in which a threat of future violation is insufficiently demonstrated, but otherwise to follow the federal decisions.

Exhausted or diminished coercive effect. A narrower proposal to limit coercive sanctions has been advanced in some cases. Their proposition is that a coercive sanction may gradually lose its potential incentive effect and that when it becomes demonstrable that the sanction has lost its coercive effect, the sanction must be dissolved.

For instance, suppose that a witness refuses to testify before the grand jury after being ordered to do so. He says he fears for the life of his family. The judge holds him in contempt and sanctions the contempt by a coercive jail sentence. He must remain until he testifies or the grand jury's term is over or until eighteen months have elapsed under a statutory limit. He remains adamant after imprisonment. After, say 17 months of imprisonment, only one month remains during which he could be coerced to testify. What is the likelihood that the contemnor will suddenly change his mind with only one more month left? The argument is that the contempt sanction has become non-coercive and hence criminal, and that to continue imprisonment when coercion is no longer reasonably likely violates due process of law. Several courts have accepted the argument and ruled that a contemnor must be released when the coercive sanction appears to fail of its purpose.[26]

One of these cases became notorious and something of a cause in the 1980s. Dr. Elizabeth Morgan was ordered to make her child available for visitation by the child's father. Believing this to represent a serious threat to the child, she refused and hid the child. She was jailed for contempt and remained in jail for almost two years before obtaining release on the ground that her continued confinement violated due process.[27]

26. Lambert v. Montana, 545 F.2d 87 (9th Cir.1976) (contemnor, refusing to testify, had served 16 months; given that length of time, the substantial likelihood is that continued confinement has lost its coercive force and is now criminal in nature); In re Farr, 36 Cal. App.3d 577, 584, 111 Cal.Rptr. 649, 653 (1974) ("it is necessary to determine the point at which the commitment ceases to serve its coercive purpose and become punitive in character. When that point is reached so that the incarceration of the contemnor becomes penal, its duration is limited by the five day maximum sentence provided in Code of Civil Procedure section 1218"); Catena v. Seidl, 65 N.J. 257, 262, 321 A.2d 225, 228 (1974) ("It is abhorrent to our concept of personal freedom that the process of civil contempt can be used to jail a person indefinitely, possibly for life, even though he or she refuses to comply with the court's order * * * in civil contempt proceedings involving an adamant contemnor, continued imprisonment may reach a point where it becomes more punitive than coercive and thereby defeats the purpose of the commitment").

27. See Morgan v. Foretich, 564 A.2d 1 (D.C.App.1989).

Other courts have not accepted the exhausted coercion idea.[28] Even when a court accepts the idea in principle, its application is a problem. How does the court know that the jail sentence will never have coercive effect? In *Catena v. Seidl,*[29] the court endorsed the exhausted coercion principle in ringing terms, but refused to release the contemnor. The fact that the contemnor had suffered prison for four years, persistently refusing to testify, the fact that he was over 70 years of age, and the fact that he was in poor health were not, taken together, enough to warrant the conclusion that coercive effect was no longer possible. The court placed the burden on the contemnor to show "that there is no reasonable likelihood that continued incarceration will cause him to break his silence." This and some other decisions look like efforts to find a middle ground between lifetime imprisonment and automatic release for any truly determined contemnor.[30] Professor Doug Rendleman has suggested that a legislative cap on coercive imprisonment terms would be fairer. He thought six or twelve months would suffice, or that a six month cap coupled with a possibility of renewal on the recommendations of a panel of judges would be a better solution.[31]

The Supreme Court's test. In *Hicks v. Feiock*[32] the Supreme Court made a point of saying that the civil-criminal classification did not depend upon the subjective purposes of the judge in imposing the sanction. The classification is made rather by "an examination of the character of the relief itself."[33] This approach might be read to mean that the Court would also disregard subjective or individualized *effects* of the contempt sanction, so that it would never inquire into the question of exhausted coercive effect. Some courts have suggested that this is a possible reading.[34] If this view is adopted, the "character of the relief" would be judged at the time the sanction is imposed and subsequent effects would not be relevant except to modify the underlying order itself.

§ 2.8(4) Consequences of the Criminal Contempt Classification

General Rule: Criminal Protections Apply

To classify a contempt sanction as criminal is to trigger two distinct effects. First, if the contempt sanction is criminal in nature, the contempt trial or show-cause hearing must satisfy most of the rules for criminal trials and proof.[1] Second, and, perhaps more importantly in some cases, if the

---

28. E.g., In re Grand Jury Investigation (Braun), 600 F.2d 420 (3d Cir.1979).

29. Catena v. Seidl, 65 N.J. 257, 321 A.2d 225 (1974).

30. One middle ground was suggested by Judge Posner. He thought that when the witness refuses to testify for fear of harm to his family, the government might be required to show that it could provide reasonable protection before contempt could be found, and even then contempt would be improper if the government could obtain evidence elsewhere. In re Grand Jury Proceedings (Freligh), 894 F.2d 881 (7th Cir.1989).

31. Rendleman, Disobedience and Coercive Contempt Confinement: The Terminally Stub-

born Contemnor, 48 Wash. & Lee L.Rev. 185 (1991).

32. 485 U.S. 624, 108 S.Ct. 1423, 99 L.Ed.2d 721 (1988).

33. Id. at 636, 108 U.S. at 1432, 99 L.Ed.2d at 734.

34. See United States v. Jones, 880 F.2d 987 (7th Cir.1989).

§ 2.8(4)

1. Cliett v. Hammonds, 305 F.2d 565, 569–570 (5th Cir.1962) ("In a proceeding as for criminal contempt, the defendant-respondent must be accorded all of the protections due one standing a traditional trial of a criminal offense charged by indictment").

sanction can only be criminal in nature, then the sentence must be limited to the criminal sentences provided by law.[2] "Criminal contempt," the Supreme Court has said, "is a crime in the ordinary sense * * *."[3]

Examples

In criminal as distinct from civil cases, the burden of proof is upon the prosecution to show beyond a reasonable doubt that the defendant was guilty.[4] Guilt requires an intent to violate the order and an ability to comply, so the prosecution must also show that the defendant had the ability to comply and that he wilfully violated the decree.[5] In a civil contempt case, in contrast, the burden may be placed upon the defendant who has violated a decree to show that he lacked the ability to comply.[6] As in any case, the defendant may not be compelled to testify against himself or give up constitutional rights.[7] A host of other substantive and procedural rights may be accorded the criminal contempt defendant. Substantively, the protections against double jeopardy apply, for example.[8] Conceivably even *Miranda* rights apply in contempt.[9] In more serious criminal contempt cases, the defendant will have a jury trial right not available in civil contempt hearings.[10]

In addition, if the contempt hearing is criminal in nature, the courts may show special concern in some sensitive areas, such as the judge's impartiality.[11] The plaintiff may be entitled to notice not only that she is charged with contempt, but that the claim is criminal in nature.[12] The Supreme Court has now held that the lawyer for the aggrieved party should not prosecute criminal contempt charges; instead, the public prosecutor should present the case for criminal contempt. In any event, if a private prosecutor is used in criminal contempt cases, that attorney must not be the plaintiff's own counsel.[13]

Jury Trial

Equity courts did not empanel juries for the trial on the merits and they

---

2. In re Contempt of Dougherty, 429 Mich. 81, 413 N.W.2d 392, 81 A.L.R.4th 971 (1987).

3. Bloom v. Illinois, 391 U.S. 194, 88 S.Ct. 1477, 20 L.Ed.2d 522 (1968).

4. Gompers v. Buck's Stove & Range Co., 221 U.S. 418, 444, 31 S.Ct. 492, 499, 55 L.Ed. 797, 807 (1911) ("it is certain that in proceedings for criminal contempt the defendant is presumed to be innocent, he must be proved to be guilty beyond a reasonable doubt"); Phillips v. Iowa Dist. Court of Johnson County, 380 N.W.2d 706, 708 (Iowa 1986); Mabry v. Howington, 569 So.2d 1165 (Miss.1990).

5. See Midland Steel Products Co. v. International Union, United Auto. Aerospace and Agricultural Implement Workers of America, Local 486, 61 Ohio St.3d 121, 127, 128, 573 N.E.2d 98, 103, 104 (1991) (intent to defy the court must be shown; but state of mind can be shown by circumstantial evidence); Dobbs, Contempt of Court: A Survey, 56 Cornell L.Rev. 183, 261–267 (1971).

6. See Hicks v. Feiock, 485 U.S. 624, 108 S.Ct. 1423, 99 L.Ed.2d 721 (1988).

7. Gompers v. Buck's Stove & Range Co., 221 U.S. 418, 31 S.Ct. 492, 55 L.Ed. 797 (1911); see Maness v. Meyers, 419 U.S. 449, 95 S.Ct. 584, 42 L.Ed.2d 574 (1975).

8. For this and other examples, see Dobbs, Contempt of Court: A Survey, 56 Cornell L.Rev. 183, 242 (1971).

9. See Furtado v. Furtado, 380 Mass. 137, 402 N.E.2d 1024 (1980) discussing some of these possibilities.

10. See the paragraph "Jury trial," below.

11. See Mayberry v. Pennsylvania, 400 U.S. 455, 91 S.Ct. 499, 27 L.Ed.2d 532 (1971).

12. See Premeaux v. Smith, 569 So.2d 681, 684 (Miss.1990).

13. Young v. United States ex rel. Vuitton et Fils S.A., 481 U.S. 787, 107 S.Ct. 2124, 95 L.Ed.2d 740 (1987).

did not do so in contempt cases, either.[14]   However, the United States Supreme Court in a series of cases first recognized a right to jury trial in criminal contempt cases in federal courts,[15] then recognized the right for trials in state courts as well.[16]   There is no corresponding jury trial right in civil contempt cases.[17]

The Constitutional jury trial in criminal contempt cases applies only when the charge is considered to be a serious one.   The seriousness is measured roughly.   The rule of thumb was that if the penalty prescribed is imprisonment of less than six months, or a fine of $500 or less, then the contempt is a "petty offense" for which no jury is required.[18]   Some contempt sanctions do not fit this rule of thumb test well.   In one case the sanction was a three year sentence with probation; the Court held no jury was required.[19]   In another a $10,000 criminal fine imposed upon a union with 13,000 dues-paying members was regarded as sufficiently petty to permit a non-jury trial.[20]   But sometimes much smaller fines are regarded as serious enough to require a jury trial.[21]

Because the federal judge presumably does not know in advance of trial the fine or imprisonment that will be imposed, the judge must either empanel a jury when a serious sanction is a possibility, or else impose a sanction that is petty.   State courts are not so likely to have this problem because state statutes frequently provide the criminal contempt punishment.

Limited Punishment

In some cases the real importance of saying that the contempt is criminal rather than civil lies in the fact that the imprisonment permitted by state statutes, may be quite small indeed, while the civil or coercive sanction might last indefinitely.   To the determined defendant who means to repeat his violation of the court order over and over (as in the case of some protesters), the criminal punishment is far preferable.   It may serve to provide publicity for the protest without coercing compliance when criminal sentences are limited by short statutory terms.[22]

14. 4 W. Blackstone, Commentaries 286–287; 3 W. Holdsworth, History of English Law 391–394 (5th ed. 1942).   But there is a difference of opinion whether jury trial was ever afforded for contempt outside the court's presence.   See Green v. United States, 356 U.S. 165, 203, 78 S.Ct. 632, 648, 2 L.Ed.2d 672, 693 (1958) (Justice Black dissenting).

15. Cheff v. Schnackenberg, 384 U.S. 373, 86 S.Ct. 1523, 16 L.Ed.2d 629 (1966) (jury trial if more than six months sentence, held as a matter of the Court's supervisory power over lower federal courts).

16. Duncan v. Louisiana, 391 U.S. 145, 88 S.Ct. 1444, 20 L.Ed.2d 491 (1968) (Sixth Amendment right to jury trial for serious offenses applies to the States through the Fourteenth Amendment); Bloom v. Illinois, 391 U.S. 194, 88 S.Ct. 1477, 20 L.Ed.2d 522 (1968) (jury trial is required in contempt cases after all, and under *Duncan* this applies to the states, too).

17. Shillitani v. United States, 384 U.S. 364, 86 S.Ct. 1531, 16 L.Ed.2d 622 (1966).

18. See Cheff v. Schnackenberg, supra n. 15.

19. Frank v. United States, 395 U.S. 147, 89 S.Ct. 1503, 23 L.Ed.2d 162 (1969), reh. denied, 396 U.S. 869, 90 S.Ct. 34, 24 L.Ed.2d 123 (1969) (three year sentence with probation does not require jury trial under 6–month test).

20. Muniz v. Hoffman, 422 U.S. 454, 95 S.Ct. 2178, 45 L.Ed.2d 319 (1975).

21. Douglass v. First Nat. Realty Corp., 543 F.2d 894 (D.C.Cir.1976) ($5,000, imposed upon individuals).

22. See In re Contempt of Dougherty, 429 Mich. 81, 413 N.W.2d 392, 81 A.L.R.4th 971 (1987) discussed in § 2.8(3) above.   But cf. Markley v. State, 507 So.2d 1043 (Ala.Crim. App.1987) (conditions of probation operated like injunction against burglar-priest's further participation in anti-abortion violence, full criminal sentence invoked when priest violated condition by further participation).

§ 2.8(5) Persons Subject to Contempt [1]

General Rule

All persons who are bound to obey an injunctive order and who have the ability to comply are subject to sanction for contempt if they knowingly disobey the order. Conversely, persons who are not bound by the injunction are not subject to the court's contempt power for disobedience.[2]

Parties, Persons in Concert or Abetting Them

Parties to the litigation in which the injunctive order is issued are bound by the injunction. So are "their officers, agents, servants, employees, and attorneys." In addition, by Rule 65(d) of the Federal Rules and by similar state-law rules, the injunction binds persons who have notice [3] of the order and who act in "active concert or participation" with parties.[4] Sometimes courts express this or a similar idea by saying that those who aid and abet the defendant are also covered by the injunction.[5]

A West Virginia case provides a good illustration of the rule binding those in concert or participation with parties. A court order gave custody of a child to W, ordering H to turn the child over. H did not do so and H's parents absconded with the child. The parents knew of the court order. They were arrested and charged with contempt. H's father was not a party, but was a witness in the proceeding and he had actual notice of the custody award. He was "acting in concert [with H] to frustrate the court's order." For this reason he was subject to contempt charges.[6] Such a person may

§ 2.8(5)

1. The leading discussion is Rendleman, Beyond Contempt: Obligors to Injunctions, 53 Tex.L.Rev. 873 (1975); see also Dobbs, Contempt of Court: A Survey, 56 Cornell L.Rev. 183, 249–258 (1971).

2. See Rendleman, supra n. 1.

3. Notice that an injunction has issued, or even of its general import, may not suffice. In Midland Steel Products Co. v. International Union, United Auto. Aerospace and Agricultural Implement Workers of America, Local 486, 61 Ohio St.3d 121, 573 N.E.2d 98, 102–103 (1991) the court insisted that non-parties are not to be bound until they have notice of the order's specific terms. "A court's order is an "order" only to the extent of its terms. To know an order, one must know its terms."

4. Rule 65 provides:

(d) *Form and Scope of Injunction or Restraining Order.* Every order granting an injunction and every restraining order shall set forth the reasons for its issuance; shall be specific in terms; shall describe in reasonable detail, and not by reference to the complaint or other document, the act or acts sought to be restrained; and is binding only upon the parties to the action, their officers, agents, servants, employees, and attorneys, and upon those persons in active concert or participation with them who receive actual notice of the order by personal service or otherwise.

See, e.g., Northeast Women's Center, Inc. v. McMonagle, 868 F.2d 1342 (3d Cir.1989), cert. denied, 493 U.S. 901, 110 S.Ct. 261, 107 L.Ed.2d 210 (1989); Fed.R.Civ.Proc. Rule 65(d) and its counterparts. See Annotation, Who, under rule 65(d) * * * are persons "in active concert or participation" with parties to action so as to be bound by order granting injunction," 61 A.L.R.Fed. 482 (1983).

5. See Regal Knitwear Co. v. National Labor Relations Bd., 324 U.S. 9, 14, 65 S.Ct. 478, 481, 89 L.Ed. 661 (1945) (Rule 65 is derived from "doctrine that a decree of injunction not only binds the parties defendant but also those identified with them in interest, in 'privity' with them, represented by them or subject to their control. In essence it is that defendants may not nullify a decree by carrying out prohibited acts through aiders and abettors, although they were not parties to the original proceeding"). Roe v. Operation Rescue, 919 F.2d 857, 871 (3d Cir.1990) ("those who have knowledge of a valid court order and abet others in violating it are subject to the court's contempt powers").

6. Hendershot v. Handlan, 162 W.Va. 175, 248 S.E.2d 273, 7 A.L.R.4th 874 (1978).

have a defense, but it will not be a defense based on the fact that he was a non-party.

Similarly, If Mr. Weiss is enjoined from using premises for illegal liquor or prostitution, he is liable to contempt if he continues, and so is Fifi Belondon if she engages in the forbidden sale or service on his behalf.[7] Similarly, if the order requires the defendant to sell Blackacre to the plaintiff, or not to sell it to anyone else, the defendant is bound, and so is the purchaser who knowingly aids his violation of the order by buying the property.[8]

Independent Interest or Activity of the Contemnor Negating Concert

When an injunction prohibits an act by *A*, the same act by *B*, who was not a party to the injunction suit, is not necessarily a violation of the injunction at all, even if *B* knows of the injunction. Furthermore, if the non-party has an independent interest of his own, to bind him by the injunction when that interest has not been represented might run on the foul side of due process.[9]

Suppose two men claim to be the father of a child. The court enjoins one of them, *A* to give the baby up to its mother. But the other putative father is not a party and his interests were never represented by anyone who was. *B* obtains the baby from the mother and refuses to give the child up. In cases of this kind, it is easy to perceive that *B* is not aiding and abetting *A*, but is instead acting on his own interest; he is not in violation of the injunction because it was not directed to him and he has done no act that counts as aiding *A*. In such cases *B's* rights and claims are independent of *A's* and that fact may help us to see that he is not violating the injunction at all.

In *Rigas v. Livingston,*[10] the plaintiff occupied a fruit stand on the sidewalk in front of a store occupied by one Levy as a tenant. Levy tried to have the stand moved by city authorities, and the plaintiff obtained an injunctive order forbidding Levy's interference with the stand. The order by its terms bound all persons having knowledge of the order. After that, Levy's landlord had the stand removed. The plaintiff then sought to hold the landlord in contempt. Although there was some reason to believe that the landlord acted at least in part to aid Levy in violating the order and might be guilty of a tort to the plaintiff, the court held that no contempt sanction was justified. Quoting a text, the New York Court concluded that "One who was not a party to the proceeding, and who has acquired no rights from any of the parties defendant pendente lite, is not guilty of a breach of

7. Weiss v. State ex rel. Cardine, 455 P.2d 904 (Wyo.1969), cert. denied, 398 U.S. 927, 90 S.Ct. 1815, 26 L.Ed.2d 89 (1970).

8. Reich v. United States, 239 F.2d 134 (1st Cir.1956), cert. denied, 352 U.S. 1004, 77 S.Ct. 563, 1 L.Ed.2d 549 (1957) (buyer of energy accumulator which Dr. Reich had been forbidden to sell); cf. Catalano v. Catalano, 158 A.D.2d 570, 551 N.Y.S.2d 539 (1990) (restraining order in divorce proceedings enjoining transfer of property by either party, purchaser who knew of injunction was bound, was not a bona fide purchaser, and took a title that was "null and void").

9. See Rendleman, supra n. 1 at 880–881, 892–895.

10. 178 N.Y. 20, 70 N.E. 107 (1904).

injunction by exercising a right which belonged to him before suit." [11]

Agents

The rule is almost universally stated to be that agents and officers of the enjoined defendant are bound by the order if they have notice of it and are in contempt if they violate it. So far as coercive contempt is concerned, it may be good policy in some cases to use the contempt power against the principal before seeking to coerce the agent.[12] In any event, the agent is properly held in contempt only if the agent was acting *as* an agent within the scope of employment at the time he allegedly violates the court's order. Even an agent is free to act for himself rather than for his principal. Under the independent interest rule, the agent who acting for his own interest and not that of his principal would not be in violation of the injunction or liable for contempt. In *Alemite Mfg. Corp. v. Staff*[13] an order ran against a principal and bound the agent. But the agent later left employment and acted on his own. He could not be held in contempt for his acts, even though, had those acts been committed in employment, he would have been liable.

When the agent remains in employment, the same rule applies, but it may be difficult in that case to determine whether any given act by the agent is his own or his principal's. The independent interest rule tells us in that case what conclusions to look for, but not how to find them. The right strategy in some cases will be to name the agent as a party defendant. In others, plaintiffs and judges may be required to recognize that contempt sanctions may not provide an immediate solution. In some cases the solution will be to require the plaintiff to enjoin new parties after they have had their day in court.[14] In others, the solution may be to hold the contemnor in tort rather than in contempt.[15]

Successors and Privies

It is traditionally said that an injunction against public officers in their official capacity ordinarily binds their successors in office and perhaps others in privity with the defendants as well.[16] Other successors, such as those who

---

11. Id. at 108, quoting James Lambert High on Injunctions.

12. In Spallone v. United States, 493 U.S. 265, 110 S.Ct. 625, 107 L.Ed.2d 644 (1990) a city was bound by a consent judgment to disperse public housing into various areas, but the council members refused to vote for the required ordinance. They, and the city as an entity, were held in contempt. The Supreme Court, however, thought that the individual council members should not be punished to compel their vote, at least until coercive efforts against the city as an entity were exhausted. Otherwise, the Court thought, individual legislators would vote their financial interests to avoid punishment, not interest of their constituents and that this would pervert the normal legislative process. It might be argued that this case cannot be generalized beyond its facts.

13. 42 F.2d 832 (2d Cir.1930).

14. See Rendleman, supra n. 1.

15. In Rigas v. Livingston, supra n. 10, the landlord may have been helping his tenant circumvent the injunction protecting the plaintiff's fruit stand. Doubts on that point properly lead a court to deny contempt punishment, but do not affect the landlord's liability in tort for abuse of process, trespass, conversion of chattels or any other tort that might be involved.

16. See e.g., Channell v. Applied Research, Inc., 472 So.2d 1260, 1262 (Fla.App.1985) ("A decree of injunction not only binds the parties defendant, but also those identified with them in interest, those in privity with them, and those represented by them or subject to their control"); Kelly v. City of Cape Girardeau, 230 Mo.App. 137, 89 S.W.2d 693, 695 (1936) ("privies are equally bound in respect to the subject-matter of the litigation with the particular parties * * * and, therefore, since suc-

purchase property connected with the injunction, may also be bound.[17] All such persons, being bound by the injunction, are subject to contempt sanctions if they violate its terms or assist others in doing so.

Injunctions in Rem and Other Expansive Injunctions

As Professor Rendleman has said, a majority's social policy is difficult to enforce against an "implacable minority" which is united by "unrelenting zeal." [18] An individual who harasses school children trying to attend an integrated school or women attempting to reach a legal abortion clinic may be enjoined and held in contempt, but one can be sure that another will take his place. At one time courts sought to deal with this problem by proclaiming that their injunctive orders operated like statutes, to compel appropriate conduct by all persons who had notice, not merely of parties and those in concert with them.[19]

The in rem injunction purported to bind the world, enjoining all persons from using premises for illegal purposes (usually in connection with illegal alcohol consumption). In Paris, Arkansas, one Flannery was enjoined from operating a snooker parlor. Flannery sold his equipment to Rogers for almost $3,000 and Rogers opened a snooker parlor with the equipment in a different building. The lower court held Rogers in contempt. This was reversed on appeal,[20] no doubt to the unending happiness of the Parisian snooker lovers.

But other cases, ignoring the distinction between adjudication of title and regulation of conduct, held that injunctions regulating conduct on property could bind the world, including those who were not parties to the litigation, who were not acting in concert with parties, and who even lacked

cessors in public office are in privity with their predecessors as to official matters, it must follow that the subsequent changes occurring in the identify of the officers of the defendant city did not in any way destroy the conclusive effect"). See Annotation, Violation of state court order by one other than party as contempt, 7 A.L.R.4th 893 (1981). Rendleman criticizes "privity" as meaningless and likely to be misused. See Rendleman, supra n. 1 at 879–880. In the narrow kind of case in which an injunction requires a landowner to recognize the plaintiff's easement, however, a successive landowner is a privy in a meaningful sense.

17. See Golden State Bottling Co., Inc. v. N.L.R.B., 414 U.S. 168, 94 S.Ct. 414, 422–423, 38 L.Ed.2d 388 (1973) (bona fide purchaser of business bound by order affording remedies for unfair labor practices of its predecessor, when purchaser knew that the violation had not been remedied). See also Regal Knitwear Co. v. National Labor Relations Bd., 324 U.S. 9, 14, 65 S.Ct. 478, 481, 89 L.Ed. 661 (1945).

The Court in Regal Knitwear said that "The term 'successors and assigns' in an enforcement order of course may not enlarge its scope beyond that defined by the Federal Rules of

Civil Procedure." But it recognized two bases on which successors or transferees of the defendant might be held. First, "Successors and assigns may * * * be instrumentalities through which defendant seeks to evade an order or may come within the description of persons in active concert or participation with them in the violation of an injunction. If they are, by that fact they are brought within scope of contempt proceedings by the rules of civil procedure." Second, an injunction " 'may also, in appropriate circumstances, be enforced against those to whom the business may have been transferred, whether as a means of evading the judgment or for other reasons.' "

18. Rendleman, supra n. 1 at 898, 902.

19. Professor Rendleman treats this topic historically, reviewing the cases that claimed the power of controlling non-parties to prevent obstruction of justice and those which operated more or less in rem. See Rendleman, supra n. 1 at 899–924. See also Dobbs, supra n. 1 at 254–258.

20. Rogers v. State ex rel. Robinson, 194 Ark. 633, 109 S.W.2d 120 (1937).

notice of the injunction.[21]   In rem injunctions are doctrinally obsolete.   Even if they were limited to those who received due process notice of the injunctive order, they would fail the "active concert" test that currently controls contempt liability for non-parties.[22]   But it may rise again as dead doctrine does so often.

Resurrecting in Rem Injunctions?

A cautionary case is United States v. Hall,[23] where the court issued a blanket injunction prohibiting the world at large from entering the grounds of a school during a time of unrest over desegregation orders.   The order exempted only students, employees, parents and the like.   The order was issued in the desegregation litigation, not in a separate suit.   The activities of Hall formed one ground for the order, but Hall was not a party to this litigation.   He never had an opportunity to contest the injunction, its scope, or its application to him, and under the collateral bar rule ordinarily could not do so on a later contempt hearing.[24]   Hall entered the school ground to express his feelings about the way things were going after he had notice of the injunction.   The court upheld the ensuing contempt conviction in spite of the fact that Hall had not been made a party and was not acting in concert with anyone who was.

The *Hall* decision does not represent a full return to the in rem injunction because Hall in fact had notice of the injunction; the defect for Hall was not notice but fundamental fairness and a due process opportunity to be represented in the determination to issue the order.   Even though the case is not a full return to the in rem injunction, the court justified the blanket order against non-parties partly on analogy to the in rem injunction. Like the in rem injunction, such orders operate more like legislation than adjudication.[25]   This fact led Professor Rendleman to conclude that the in rem injunction was in reality a "judicial abrogation of legislative power," [26] in addition to whatever fundamental unfairness is to be found in binding a person who has never had a day in court.

Federal courts have also favored expansive use of injunctions to control non-parties in some cases to preserve their jurisdiction and effectuate their judgments, sometimes claiming to act in rem.[27]

21.   Silvers v. Traverse, 82 Iowa 52, 47 N.W. 888 (1891).

22.   See Rendleman, supra n. 1 at 914; Dobbs, supra n. 1 at 257–261.

23.   472 F.2d 261 (5th Cir.1972).

24.   See § 2.8(6) below as to the collateral bar rule.

25.   See State of New Hampshire v. Gross, 117 N.H. 853, 379 A.2d 804 (1977), citing Dobbs, supra n. 1 at 250.

26.   Rendleman, supra n. 1 at 929.

27.   See In re Baldwin–United Corp., Single Premium Deferred Annuities Ins. Litigation, 770 F.2d 328 (2d Cir.1985); but cf. County of Imperial v. Munoz, 449 U.S. 54, 101 S.Ct. 289, 66 L.Ed.2d 258 (1980) (order not to sell water did not necessarily foreclose attack on that order by non-party buyer of the water).

The court in *Baldwin–United*, supra, observed: "Federal courts have authority under the All–Writs Act, 28 U.S.C.A. § 1651 (1982), to 'issue all writs necessary or appropriate in aid of their respective jurisdictions and agreeable to the usages and principles of law.'" Although "the mere existence of a parallel lawsuit in state court that seeks to adjudicate the same in personam cause of action does not in itself provide sufficient grounds for an injunction against a state action in favor of a pending federal action," "when federal courts have jurisdiction over a res in an in rem action; in such a case, because the "exercise by the state court of jurisdiction over the same res necessarily impairs, and may defeat, the jurisdiction of the federal court already attached," the federal court is empowered to enjoin any state court proceeding affecting that res." Notice that the effect of this rea-

Contempt Liability of Named Defendant for Acts of Third Persons

In the usual case, the question is whether a third person, not a named defendant, can be held liable in contempt for violating the injunction. A third person's violation can also raise the question of contempt liability for the named defendant. Presumably the named defendant is liable to contempt if he directs the third person to assist him in violating the decree, or participates with the third person. But it does not follow that the named defendant is liable for contempt merely because his agent violates the injunction without the tacit or explicit approval of the defendant.

In *NBA Properties, Inc. v. Gold,*[28] a franchisor was infringing the plaintiff's trademarks, partly through its franchisees. The trademark owner sued the franchisor and obtained an injunction forbidding infringement. Some of its franchisees, however, continued infringement in spite of the fact that the franchisor had given them notice of the injunction. The court held that the franchisor was not in contempt. It had taken no steps to abet the franchisees' infringements and it was not legally identified with the franchisees, who were legally separate entities.

§ 2.8(6) Review: The Collateral Bar Rule[1]

Liability for Disobedience of Unreversed Erroneous Order

One who disobeys an injunctive order that is later reversed on appeal for error may be held in criminal contempt for the disobedience in spite of the reversal. Stated differently, the fact that an injunction is erroneously issued constitutes no defense to a criminal contempt charge; the court's order must be obeyed until reversed.[2]

Nonliability for Disobedience of Void Order

A radical distinction is drawn between an erroneous order and one made without jurisdiction. An injunction issued by a court which lacks jurisdiction of the subject matter or the person is void. Such an order has no legal effect and if the defendant disobeys that order he is not in contempt. Stated differently, the fact that the order is void constitutes a defense to a subsequent charge of contempt.[3]

soning is like the in rem reasoning use in the liquor control cases: possession of the res gives the court power not only to adjudicate the res but also to control conduct of non-parties.

28. 895 F.2d 30 (1st Cir.1990).

§ 2.8(6)

1. The leading contemporary discussion is Rendleman, More on Void Orders, 7 Ga.L.Rev. 246 (1973). See also Z. Chafee, Some Problems of Equity 349 ff. (1950).

2. Cologne v. Westfarms Associates, 197 Conn. 141, 496 A.2d 476, 481 (1985); Balter v. Regan, 63 N.Y.2d 630, 631, 479 N.Y.S.2d 506, 507, 468 N.E.2d 688 (1984), cert. denied, 469 U.S. 934, 105 S.Ct. 333, 83 L.Ed.2d 269 (1984) ("However misguided and erroneous the court's order may have been, petitioner was not free to disregard it"); Menard v. Woon-

socket Teachers' Guild–AFT, 117 R.I. 121, 363 A.2d 1349 (1976).

3. See, e.g., Phoenix Newspapers, Inc. v. Superior Court, 101 Ariz. 257, 418 P.2d 594 (1966); In the Matter of Wharton, 305 N.C. 565, 290 S.E.2d 688 (1982); Boyls v. Boyls, 463 A.2d 1307 (R.I.1983) (Illinois divorce, if entitled to full faith and credit, divested Rhode Island family court of jurisdiction, and if it lacked jurisdiction its contempt orders could be attacked collaterally); Ex parte Olivares, 662 S.W.2d 594 (Tex.1983) (trial court had no jurisdiction to issue order after case was dismissed, contempt reviewable by habeas corpus); cf. Karras v. Gannon, 345 N.W.2d 854, 857 (S.D.1984) ("we do not view the verbal [oral] order as constituting an injunction as such," contempt reversed); In re Contempt of Reeves, 112 Idaho 574, 580, 733 P.2d 795, 801 (App.1987) (term "jurisdiction" is unsatisfacto-

The Example of Walker v. City of Birmingham

Although the rules have been recognized for many years, the best known example is a Supreme Court decision in 1967, *Walker v. City of Birmingham.*[4] That case arose from a planned demonstration by Dr. Martin Luther King and others, to take place on Good Friday and Easter Sunday. On Wednesday a state court issued an ex parte order forbidding the marches or demonstrations. Leaders of the proposed march had notice of the order, but they led a march anyway, and were held in contempt. At the contempt hearing these leaders attempted to justify their apparent violation of the order on the ground that the statute on which it was based was unconstitutional and that it had been applied in a discriminatory fashion. The Alabama courts refused to entertain these matters in defense. The Supreme Court affirmed, holding that such an application of the collateral bar rule was constitutional.

The decision reinforces the collateral bar rule in a case where the rule has little appeal, partly because it is applied to an ex parte restraining order of which the defendants had no advance notice and no opportunity to contest. In effect, the Court held that the merits of the case could be tried only on a motion to dissolve or modify the temporary restraining order or on appeal from the order, not in the contempt hearing. Unconstitutionality of the injunction, or the statute did not deprive the court of jurisdiction to issue the order, no matter how erroneous it was.

Exception: Opportunity for Meaningful Hearing on the Merits

The *Walker* Court seemed to recognize two possible exceptions to the general collateral bar rule, or more accurately, two kinds of cases in which due process might require courts to hear objections to the merits of the injunctive order in the contempt trial itself. The Court seems to have implied that the contemnors should be allowed to defend by showing that they had sought modification of the unconstitutional order and had been denied relief, or possibly by showing that they had not sought a modification but would have been denied relief had they done so.[5] As the Eleventh Circuit said, "the collateral bar rule presupposes that adequate and effective remedies exist for orderly review of the challenged ruling; in the absence of such an opportunity for review, the accused contemnor may challenge the validity of the disobeyed order on appeal from his criminal contempt conviction and escape punishment if that order is deemed invalid".[6] Similarly, if orders to testify or make discovery can be meaningfully reviewed only by noncompliance, then the collateral bar rule does not prevent the contemnor

---

ry and "[i]n light of the historical implications of this term, we decline to use it. Nevertheless, one example of a 'transparently invalid' order would be an order obviously outside the subject matter or personal jurisdiction of the court").

4. 388 U.S. 307, 87 S.Ct. 1824, 18 L.Ed.2d 1210 (1967).

5. "This case would arise in quite a different constitutional posture if the petitioners,

before disobeying the injunction, had challenged it in the Alabama courts, and had been met with delay or frustration of their constitutional claims. But there is no showing that such would have been the fate of a timely motion to modify or dissolve the injunction." Id. at 318, 87 S.Ct. at 1831, 18 L.Ed.2d at 1218.

6. In re Novak, 932 F.2d 1397, 1401–1402 (11th Cir.1991).

from defending the contempt charge because the disclosure order was invalid.[7]

Exception: Lack of Jurisdiction

The *Walker* Court also recognized that the contemnors could defend by showing that the court not only lacked jurisdiction, but lacked even the semblance of it.[8] That would seldom be the case and was not the case in *Walker* itself. The lack of jurisdiction exception would seem to have little scope. Courts of general jurisdiction—the general trial courts of a state, or the United States District Court—enjoy wide powers. Unless a statute or constitutional rule excludes their power from a particular kind of case, these courts have jurisdiction over that class of cases. Courts do not merely have jurisdiction or power to make correct decisions; they also have jurisdiction to make erroneous decisions. A bad decision, in other words, is not void; it is merely reversible on appeal.[9]

The Mine Workers Bootstrap Rule

Even when the court's jurisdiction on the merits is doubtful, the issue of jurisdiction itself must be resolved by the court, not by one of the parties. So it is said that courts have jurisdiction to determine their own jurisdiction. The famous *United Mine Workers* case [10] illustrates one of the consequences of this rule. A statute provided that federal courts had no "jurisdiction to issue any restraining order" in labor disputes. The mine workers struck coal mines at a time when, as a result of World War II arrangements the government was operating the mines. The government sought to enjoin the strike in spite of the statutory proscription. Perhaps the statute could be construed not to cover cases in which the operator was the government, but that issue would require careful consideration by the court. The trial court issued a temporary restraining order to preserve the status quo until it could consider the question. However, the union violated the order. Its position was, naturally enough, that the court had no jurisdiction under the plain provisions of the statute. Nevertheless, the court imposed contempt sanctions.

The Supreme Court upheld the sanctions. Although the court may have lacked plenary or ultimate jurisdiction over the merits, it did have a kind of

---

7. See Maness v. Meyers, 419 U.S. 449, 95 S.Ct. 584, 42 L.Ed.2d 574 (1975); State v. Crenshaw, 307 Or. 160, 764 P.2d 1372 (1988) (emphasizing the availability or not of meaningful review as the test); cf. United States Catholic Conference v. Abortion Rights Mobilization, Inc., 487 U.S. 72, 108 S.Ct. 2268, 101 L.Ed.2d 69 (1988) (non-party witness may attack court's jurisdiction even if jurisdiction is colorable); People v. Shukovsky, 128 Ill.2d 210, 131 Ill.Dec. 69, 538 N.E.2d 444 (1988).

8. Walker v. City of Birmingham, 388 U.S. 307, 315, 87 S.Ct. 1824, 1829, 18 L.Ed.2d 1210, 1217 (1967) (suggesting that attack would be permissible if the "injunction was transparently invalid or had only a frivolous pretense to validity"); but cf. United States Catholic Conference v. Abortion Rights Mobilization, Inc., 487 U.S. 72, 108 S.Ct. 2268, 101 L.Ed.2d

69 (1988) (non-party witness may attack court's jurisdiction even if jurisdiction is colorable).

9. See Dobbs, Trial Court Error as an Excess of Jurisdiction, 43 Tex.L.Rev. 854 (1965). California, however, has treated some important errors as an excess of jurisdiction, thus permitting collateral attack in the contempt hearing. See In re Berry, 68 Cal.2d 137, 65 Cal.Rptr. 273, 436 P.2d 273 (1968). In In re Misener, 38 Cal.3d 543, 213 Cal.Rptr. 569, 698 P.2d 637 (1985) the court made a bald statement that "An order of contempt cannot stand if the underlying order is invalid." See also the paragraph, "Media restraints" below.

10. United States v. United Mine Workers, 330 U.S. 258, 67 S.Ct. 677, 91 L.Ed. 884 (1947).

preliminary jurisdiction—enough to consider any arguable claim that it had jurisdiction on the merits. As long as the claim that the court had power was not frivolous or transparently invalid, the court had "incipient" jurisdiction to consider *that* claim. Having *that* much power, it could also issue an injunctive order to protect that power by preserving the status quo until a decision could be made. The injunctive order performing that limited function was thus valid and obedience was required until the order was stayed, modified or reversed.[11]

Although the decision has been rejected in some states[12] and strongly criticized by important scholars,[13] its principles have not been overturned. It is usually difficult to claim that an error, even a very large error, represents a defect in the court's jurisdiction. The *Mine Workers* case shows that even when an error is to be treated as jurisdictional, incipient or "bootstrap" jurisdiction may nevertheless require obedience until the order is reversed.

State Cases

With the exceptions noted, the Court's decision in *Walker* permits but does not require states to impose contempt sanctions for violation of an unconstitutional order. State courts usually follow the collateral bar rule and exercise their contempt powers even when the underlying injunction is unconstitutional and even when it has already been held so at the time of the contempt hearing.[14] But states are free to reject the permission given in *Walker* and to write into their laws a more liberal procedure for raising constitutional issues in contempt cases.[15] In addition, courts wishing to permit the attack on a contempt conviction may at times simply consider substantive error as if it were a lack of jurisdiction.

Media Restraints

Many of the cases involve provisional injunctive orders that appear to restrain the exercise of First Amendment rights, such as the right to picket peacefully, to sell books, or to publish news. When an order runs against a newspaper or other public medium, and turns out to be an erroneous invasion of constitutional rights, a number of courts have been ready to say that the order was not merely error and that instead it exceeded the court's jurisdiction. The result of these decisions is that the publisher may raise the constitutional issue at the contempt hearing and may escape all liability for contempt if the underlying order was constitutionally erroneous. Constitu-

11. See Dobbs, Beyond Bootstrap: Foreclosing the Issue of Subject–Matter Jurisdiction Before Final Judgment, 51 Minn.L.Rev. 491, 496–98 (1967). See also Dobbs, The Validation of Void Judgments: The Bootstrap Principles, 53 Va.L.Rev. 1003, 1241 (Pts. I and II) (1967).

12. In re Berry, 68 Cal.2d 137, 65 Cal.Rptr. 273, 280, 436 P.2d 273, 280 (1968).

13. See Rendleman, More on Void Orders, 7 Ga.L.Rev. 246, 251–255 (1973).

14. People v. Sequoia Books, Inc., 172 Ill. App.3d 627, 122 Ill.Dec. 678, 527 N.E.2d 50 (1988), modified and aff'd, 127 Ill.2d 271, 130 Ill.Dec. 235, 537 N.E.2d 302 (1989) (anti-obscenity injunction); see Cologne v. Westfarms Associates, 197 Conn. 141, 496 A.2d 476, 481 (1985).

15. See In re Berry, 68 Cal.2d 137, 65 Cal. Rptr. 273, 436 P.2d 273 (1968) (rejecting *Mine Workers* bootstrap type of jurisdiction and finding a jurisdiction defect in a constitutional error).

tional error in these cases is treated as a jurisdictional defect, not as merely error.[16]

Non-media Defendants

Non-media defendants whose First Amendment rights are invaded by an injunctive order do not generally fare so well. The *Walker* defendants were not allowed to raise their constitutional rights in the contempt hearing. In Arizona, farmworkers whose strike was enjoined by an order that enjoined speech as well as violence, were similarly held in contempt in spite of the order's constitutional error.[17] In Illinois a bookseller who was enjoined from distributing "obscenity" under an unconstitutional statute was nevertheless held in contempt for violating the order before the statute was excised.[18] An attorney who advises his client to ignore a court's order may be held in contempt even if the order is erroneous and the attorney's advice to the client is necessarily a form of speech.[19] In these cases courts thought the constitutional transgressions of the order were merely errors and they did not render the decrees void for want of jurisdiction.

Sometimes the distinction between the treatment of media and non-media defendants may be explained on the ground that the injunctions in media cases are often efforts to impose prior restraint on speech. But all restraint of speech is prior to the speech rights the defendant wishes to exercise. Some of it is prior restraint even in a narrower sense.

Comment

Professor Rendleman has been the most outspoken critic of the collateral bar rule. Cases like *Walker* combine several extreme elements. The injunction there ran ex parte, without a hearing for those enjoined, much less for those who might not have been named at all. In addition, one might doubt that the defendants had a very real opportunity to contest the order before time for the Good Friday march, and certainly they had no practical opportunity for review. Professor Rendleman proposed a change in the collateral bar rule to require that if a temporary restraining order would have "practical finality," then the defendant must be served with notice in advance of adjudication. In the absence of such a notice, he proposed to make the injunction void.[20]

16. Phoenix Newspapers, Inc. v. Superior Court, 101 Ariz. 257, 418 P.2d 594 (1966) (prohibition to prevent trial of contempt on the ground that it was beyond the court's jurisdiction); State v. Coe, 101 Wash.2d 364, 679 P.2d 353, 357 (1984) (radio station published trial information in violation of court order; the "jurisdiction test measures whether a court, in issuing an order or holding in contempt those who defy it, was performing the sort of function for which judicial power was vested in it * * * 'Only when a court is so obviously traveling outside its orbit as to be merely usurping judicial forms and facilities, may [its order] be disobeyed * * * ' "; as a prior restraint on speech, the order against publication was void).

17. State v. Chavez, 123 Ariz. 538, 601 P.2d 301 (App.1979).

18. People v. Sequoia Books, Inc., 172 Ill. App.3d 627, 122 Ill.Dec. 678, 527 N.E.2d 50 (1988), modified and aff'd, 127 Ill.2d 271, 130 Ill.Dec. 235, 537 N.E.2d 302 (1989).

19. See In re Contempt of Reeves, 112 Idaho 574, 733 P.2d 795 (App.1987) (attorney who advised client to ignore a restraining order affecting child custody held in criminal contempt, principles in *Walker* and like cases applied).

20. Rendleman, supra n. 1 at 291.

Since Professor Rendleman's criticism was published in 1973, courts seem to have been working toward a similar idea. Without holding the order void, they have nevertheless begun to insist that the defendant must have some realistic opportunity to contest its merits, permitting him to do so in the contempt hearing if earlier opportunities were not available as practical possibilities.[21]   Full recognition of such a rule would probably minimize the spurious claim that the trial court had no jurisdiction to make errors, while satisfying the American commitment to fair trials.   At the same time, in most cases of permanent and even preliminary injunctions, it would leave the collateral bar rule intact, requiring the defendant to raise his constitutional objections at the initial stages of the underlying litigation.

§ 2.8(7) Inability to Comply and Related Defenses

Those charged with contempt may of course defend on many grounds— that they did not disobey the injunctive order, or that it was void.[1]   It has even been held that laches could bar the prosecution of contempt.[2]   This subsection discusses the defense that the defendant lacked the ability to comply with the court's order, either because he lacked the physical or financial means to do so or because the order was so nebulous that the defendant could not determine what conduct was required.

Burden of Proving Ability or Inability to Comply

In a criminal contempt, the prosecution must prove in the first instance that the violation of the injunctive order was wilful.   This seems to require proof that the contemnor had the ability to comply with the order.[3]   When the contempt is civil, on the other hand, the burden is commonly placed upon the contemnor to prove his inability to comply with the injunction.[4]

The placement of the burden of proof becomes significant when the defendant is ordered to act affirmatively in some manner.   Defendants commonly raise inability to comply arguments when they have failed to make payments ordered for child or spousal support.[5]   Some of the excuses offered merit high marks for inventiveness but low marks for credibility. One defendant, ordered to divide community assets of $21,000 with his former wife claimed he had flushed the money down the toilet and into the sewers of Fort Worth.[6]   Another defendant, ordered to turn over $18,000 to a receiver, said he had that sum in cash while bird hunting and lost it somewhere in the woods.[7]   Another offered a more elevated excuse: he had transferred all his property to a religious organization because he had "decided to follow the lifestyle of St. Francis of Assisi: chastity, obedience,

---

21. See cases cited supra n. 7, for instance.

§ 2.8(7)

1. See §§ 2.7 & 1.8(6) above.

2. Oregon State Bar v. Wright, 309 Or. 37, 785 P.2d 340, 342 (1990).

3. See Hicks on Behalf of Feiock v. Feiock, 485 U.S. 624, 108 S.Ct. 1423, 99 L.Ed.2d 721 (1988); see Dobbs, Contempt of Court: A Survey, 56 Cornell L.Rev. 183, 261 (1971).

4. E.g., Diver v. Diver, 402 Mass. 599, 524 N.E.2d 378 (1988).

5. See, e.g., Hicks on Behalf of Feiock v. Feiock, 485 U.S. 624, 108 S.Ct. 1423, 99 L.Ed.2d 721 (1988); Ickowitz v. Iowa District Court for Polk County, 452 N.W.2d 446 (1990).

6. Ex parte Preston, 162 Tex. 379, 347 S.W.2d 938 (1961).

7. Drake v. National Bank of Commerce of Norfolk, 168 Va. 230, 190 S.E. 302, 109 A.L.R. 1517 (1937).

and poverty." [8] By placing the burden of proof on the defendant to show inability to comply, courts make it easy to resolve such civil contempt cases against the defendant.

Compensatory Fines

When the civil contempt sanction is a compensatory fine, intended to reimburse the plaintiff for losses suffered by reason of the defendant's violation of a court's order, inability to comply with the initial order is arguably irrelevant. To impose a remedial fine to compensate the plaintiff for the defendant's breach may be no more than to impose damages, as to which the defendant's intent and ability to comply are wholly insignificant. A remedial contempt fine to be collected by execution rather than by further contempts, then, may be justified even if the defendant lacked ability to comply with the original order.[9]

Nebulous Injunctions: the Order That Cannot Be Understood

As a matter of substantive and procedural justice, injunctions must be understandable to reasonable people when they are issued [10] and also later when the defendant is attempting to comply. They should not depend for interpretation upon outside materials [11] and they must not be too vague for intelligent understanding. If they defeat fair efforts to comprehend, they must not be enforced by contempt. Ordinary legal rules require this much,[12] and so, seemingly, does the due process clause of the Constitution.[13] The result is that contempt will be impermissible when the injunction is nebulous.

In addition, when an injunction is ambiguous rather than vague or nebulous, the ambiguity should be interpreted in favor of the defendant, so that contempt is not proper if the defendant complied with either reading of the order.[14]

When an order affects a broad course of future conduct, it may necessarily leave some uncertainties. It is not too much to expect the parties to read the injunction intelligently and in context in such cases.[15] Parties are

8. Martian v. Martian, 399 N.W.2d 849 (N.D.1987).

9. Cf. United Factory Outlet, Inc. v. Jay's Stores, Inc., 361 Mass. 35, 278 N.E.2d 716 (1972) (remedial fine for inadvertent contempt by a corporation).

10. Fed.R.Civ.Proc.R. 65(d) requires that injunctions "shall be specific in terms; shall describe in reasonable detail, and not by reference to the complaint or other document, the act or acts sought to be restrained * * *."

11. Labbadia v. Bailey, 147 Conn. 82, 157 A.2d 237 (1959). See also Fed.R.Civ.Proc.R. 65(d).

12. Baldwin v. Miles, 58 Conn. 496, 502, 20 A. 618, 620 (1890) (" 'Injunctions ought to be made plain and distinct. No respondent is to be entrapped into a contempt by vague or general orders' ").

13. Cf. International Longshoremen's Ass'n, Local 1291 v. Philadelphia Marine Trade Ass'n, 389 U.S. 64, 76, 88 S.Ct. 201, 208, 19 L.Ed.2d 236, 245 (1967) ("The most fundamental postulates of our legal order forbid the imposition of a penalty for disobeying a command that defies comprehension"); Schmidt v. Lessard, 414 U.S. 473, 476, 94 S.Ct. 713, 715, 38 L.Ed.2d 661, 665 (1974) ("basic fairness requires that those enjoined receive explicit notice of precisely what conduct is outlawed").

14. NBA Properties, Inc. v. Gold, 895 F.2d 30, 32 (1st Cir.1990) (similar to above, "Also, we must read any 'ambiguities' or 'omissions' in such a court order as 'redound[ing] to the benefit of the person charged with contempt.' "); Eavenson, Auchmuty & Greenwald v. Holtzman, 775 F.2d 535 (3d Cir.1985) (similar in Rule 11 cases, express analogy to contempt).

15. See Planned Parenthood League of Mass., Inc. v. Operation Rescue, 406 Mass. 701, 550 N.E.2d 1361 (1990) ("obstruction" is a

protected by their ability to resort to the court for further interpretations of the order as required [16] and by the rule that forbids contempt sanctions when the order is uncertain.

§ 2.8(8) Modification of Decrees

Modification Permitted Generally

Courts traditionally retain the power to modify final coercive decrees prospectively.[1] The extreme form of such modification is dissolution of the decree as to the future. The modification or dissolution discussed here is not based on new evidence but upon changed circumstances.[2] It does not relitigate facts already decided but considers changes in the conditions that occur subsequent to the decree. Sometimes the change is factual, as where a father's obligation to pay child support is reduced because, after the decree, he lost his job.[3] Sometimes the relevant change is change in a legal rule on which the decree is based.[4]

A less traditional reason for modifying an injunction is simply that experience in operating under it demonstrates that it is flawed, ineffective, or excessive. For instance, civil rights injunctions aimed at restructuring institutions such as schools are often modified many times as experience shows flaws or inadequacies.[5]

Role of Modification in Enforcement

Modification is important in enforcement of injunctions and other decrees, first because modification may be needed to secure the plaintiff complete relief to which she is entitled and second because modification may be necessary to protect the defendant against a decree which is proving to be excessively demanding. In the second case, defendants who do not seek appropriate modification when circumstances change may find themselves in contempt of court that could have been avoided by a motion to modify the decree.

A third significance of modification has less to do with enforcement of decrees and more with their initial formulation. The power to modify later is a proleptic consideration: the judge writes the initial decree with knowl-

---

word ordinarily understandable and construed in the factual situation of abortion clinic protests is a sufficiently meaningful description of the forbidden conduct).

16. See Infusaid Corp. v. Intermedics Infusaid, Inc., 756 F.2d 1 (1st Cir.1985).

§ 2.8(8)

1. See Fed.R.Civ.Proc.R. 60(b) ("On motion and upon such terms as are just, the court may relieve a party or a party's legal representative from a final judgment, order, or proceeding for the following reasons: * * *. (5) * * * it is no longer equitable that the judgment should have prospective application; or (6) any other reason justifying relief from the operation of the judgment").

2. System Federation No. 91, Ry. Employees' Dept. v. Wright, 364 U.S. 642, 81 S.Ct. 368, 5 L.Ed.2d 349 (1961) ("sound judicial discretion may call for the modification of the terms of an injunctive decree if the circumstances, whether of law or fact, * * * have changed, or new ones have since arisen").

3. See, e.g., Sweeney v. Hoff, 478 N.W.2d 9 (N.D.1991) ("It is well-settled that courts which issue divorces and award child support retain the authority to modify the amount to be paid, or the method of payment, when there has been a showing that the circumstances of the parties have materially changed").

4. See Turner v. Turner, 219 Conn. 703, 595 A.2d 297 (1991) (new statutory child support guidelines applied retrospectively to permit modification of child support decree already existing when guidelines were passed; construing statutory purpose and using analogy to changed circumstances).

5. See § 7.4(4) below.

edge that if it is too broadly formulated, it can be modified if it proves to be too demanding.[6]

Consent Decrees: Modification Permitted

Consent decrees may also be modified. The consent decree has contractual aspects; it is based upon the parties' agreement. But it has public aspects as well; it is enforceable as a judgment. Besides that, injunctive decrees always have strong impacts on third persons and on public interests. The public interest might require modification of a child support decree for example, even though the initial decree was based wholly upon the contract of the divorcing parents.[7]

The Swift Case

In *United States v. Swift & Co.*,[8] a number of meatpackers consented to an antitrust decree which broke up their combinations in restraint of trade. Later, some defendants and others affected by the decree sought modification of it. The trial court granted a limited modification but the Supreme Court held the modification to be improper. In so holding, the Court, through Justice Cardozo, seemed to impose heavy limitations on the power to modify consent decrees:

> "The injunction, whether right or wrong, is not subject to impeachment in its application to the conditions that existed at its making * * *. Nothing less than a clear showing of grievous wrong evoked by new and unforeseen conditions should lead us to change what was decreed after years of litigation with the consent of all concerned." [9]

Although there are special reasons for caution when it comes to modification of consent decrees, the formulation in *Swift* and some decisions based upon it, appears to go beyond caution.

Modifying the Rigid Rule

The rigid rule in *Swift* has been doubted or manipulated in some later cases, especially those involving institutional reform. A consent decree enjoins double-bunking or other crowded conditions in a county jail. Ten years later, the sheriff-defendant, unable to comply without releasing prisoners or detainees, seeks a modification. In situations similar to this, some courts have held that modification is permissible without complying with the onerous standard in *Swift*. Under this more relaxed view, a court could modify a decree if modification would be in line with basic principles of contract law, which themselves have become more amenable to modifica-

---

6. Ozark Bi–Products v. Bohannon, 224 Ark. 17, 271 S.W.2d 354, 357 (1954).

7. Alexander v. Alexander, 12 Va.App. 691, 406 S.E.2d 666 (1991).

8. 286 U.S. 106, 52 S.Ct. 460, 76 L.Ed. 999 (1932).

9. 286 U.S. at 119, 52 S.Ct. at 464. This rigid position seems to result from a swirl of mixed feelings. The defendants consented "with their eyes open," a point that seems to treat the decree as a contract. "We are not at liberty to reverse under the guise of readjusting," a point that seems to view modification as belated appeal or as a collateral attack, although it is neither. Cardozo, notable for his flexibility in interpreting the common law, as where he abolished the privity requirement in products negligence cases, could be quite inflexible when it came to enforcing statutes, as in Martin v. Herzog, 228 N.Y. 164, 126 N.E. 814 (1920), and decrees, as in *Swift*.

tion.[10]   A court could also modify a decree if experience indicates the decree was not adapted to its purpose.[11]

Rule 60(b) of the Federal Rules of Civil Procedure permits modification of decrees "upon such terms as are just." The rule seems to provide a more flexible standard for modification than the "grievous wrong" standard in *Swift*. The Supreme Court has now said that Rule 60(b) governs the modification of consent decrees as well as others and that modification will be permissible when one who seeks a modification establishes a significant change in factual or legal circumstances which makes it inequitable to give the original decree prospective application.[12] Modification is not necessarily to be denied merely because changes were foreseeable, but it should ordinarily be denied when the change was actually foreseen or was assumed as a basis for entering the decree.[13] Modification may be affirmatively required if the decree imposes obligations that have become legally impermissible.[14]

Discretion

The motion to modify a decree traditionally appeals largely to the court's discretion. Careful commentary suggests that the discretion should be exercised cautiously,[15] a rule that seems sound regardless whether the decree is or is not entered by consent. So unless modification is clearly demanded by "equity," policy, or justice, the chancellor in the first instance is usually free to deny it. That freedom puts a great deal of responsibility upon the chancellor, however, fully to consider the grounds for relief. An automatic rejection of relief by way of modification is no more justified than automatic acceptance. The modification itself, of course, must be tailored to reflect the parties' rights under the changed conditions and to reflect the equities the court now perceives.

D. INJUNCTIONS

§ 2.9 Permanent Injunctions

§ 2.9(1) Injunctions Generally

Injunction as a Coercive Order

An injunction is a remedy in the form of an *in personam* order, usually issued by a trial court of general jurisdiction. It directs the defendant to act, or to refrain from acting in a specified way, and it is enforceable by the contempt power.[1] The injunction must be obeyed until it is stayed, dissolved, or reversed, even if it is erroneously issued.[2]

Any *in personam* order that is enforceable by contempt power is an injunctive order, although more specific names are sometimes used to

---

10. As to the increased possibility of modifying contracts, see, e.g., Oglebay Norton Co. v. Armco, Inc., 52 Ohio St.3d 232, 556 N.E.2d 515 (1990), discussed in § 12.1(2). As to increasingly flexible doctrines of frustration and impracticability, see § 13.3 below. See also Jost, From Swift to Stotts and Beyond: Modification of Injunctions in the Federal Courts, 64 Tex.L.Rev. 1101 (1986).

11. E.g., Heath v. De Courcy, 888 F.2d 1105 (6th Cir.1989), reviewing a number of cases.

12. Rufo v. Inmates of the Suffolk County Jail, ___ U.S. ___, 112 S.Ct. 748, 116 L.Ed.2d 867 (1992).

15. Jost, From Swift to Stotts and Beyond: Modification of Injunctions in the Federal Courts, 64 Tex.L.Rev. 1101 (1986).

indicate the factual context to which the injunction belongs. For instance, specific performance is a remedy by which the defendant is ordered to perform a contract and the specific performance order is thus a form of injunction.[3] Reinstatement in a job is a remedy for job discrimination in some cases and the reinstatement order is a form of injunction.[4] Preliminary injunctions and temporary restraining orders are likewise injunctive forms.[5] Even the automatic stay in bankruptcy[6] operates like an injunction.[7]

An injunction may form the only remedy in a case, or it may be one part of more complex remedies. As the only remedy, the injunction might simply enjoin the defendant's repeated trespass on the plaintiff's land or prohibit infringement of a trademark. As one part of complex remedies, the injunction might be used ancillary to some other remedy, as it is in interpleader cases, where it operates to bring all potential claimants to a fund into court, after which the case proceeds to entirely different remedial conclusions.[8] Or it might be used ultimately to enforce the court's declaration of a constructive trust,[9] or to enforce a court's decision that some legal instrument should be canceled. Injunctions that forbid future misconduct are also frequently coupled with an award of damages for harms already done.

Mandatory vs. Prohibitory Injunctions

Classification. Injunctions are sometimes classified as being either mandatory or prohibitory. The prohibitory injunction forbids an act. "The defendant is hereby enjoined from trespassing upon Blackacre," is a prohibitory injunction. The mandatory injunction orders an affirmative act or course of conduct. "The defendant is hereby ordered to remove all boulders he has previously deposited upon Blackacre," is a mandatory injunction.

Formal but not substantive differences. In both of the examples given above, the defendant's trespass on Blackacre might have been the result of identical acts—deposit of boulders on the plaintiff's land. One of the injunctions, however, addresses the trespass as a continuing trespass or frames the order prohibitively; the other frames the order as a mandatory injunction. In many situations the two kinds of injunctions are different in form, but not in purpose or effect. Courts say that they will ignore the prohibitory locutions and classify the injunction as mandatory if it is "really" mandatory. This practice calls on standards even less certain than the formal language of the injunction, however. For instance, one court held that an injunction against working for the plaintiff's competitors was mandatory.[10]

Reluctance to use mandatory injunctions. Although the difference between mandatory and prohibitory injunctions is often formal, simply a way of phrasing the order, courts sometimes attach significance to that difference. Sometimes the distinction has a procedural effect discussed later.[11] At other times, courts may be reluctant to award a mandatory injunction because it may be especially intrusive, or more difficult to supervise and

§ 2.9(1)

10. Paramount Pictures Corp. v. Davis, 228 Cal.App.2d 827, 39 Cal.Rptr. 791 (1964), dis-   cussed in § 2.11(4) below.

enforce. Such intrusions or difficulties, however, usually result, if at all, only because of the injunction's content rather than its mandatory form.[12] Courts are right to weigh intrusion carefully in injunction cases, but the mandatory form of the injunction is not often a good measure of that intrusion and in any event the intrusion effected must be weighed against the intrusion required to provide a suitable remedy.

Preventive, Reparative and Structural Injunctions

Reparative and preventive injunctions. A second set of classifications for injunctions may be more meaningful. The second set describes injunctions as reparative, preventive, or structural.[13] The reparative injunction requires the defendant to restore the plaintiff to a preexisting entitlement. The mandatory injunction requiring a trespasser to remove the boulders he deposited is in this category. A preventive injunction attempts to prevent the loss of an entitlement in the future. It might be prohibitory, as where the defendant is enjoined not to obstruct ingress into the plaintiff's premises. Of course some injunctive orders both repair and prevent harm.

The difference between reparative and preventive injunctions is important in presenting evidence and formulating decrees. The reparative injunction goes when the evidence shows that an existing right has been violated but can be repaired or restored effectively. The preventive injunction, on the other hand, is not proper unless the defendant is threatening to commit a wrong in the future. The defendant's past trespass upon the plaintiff's land by dumping boulders on it is not by that act alone threatening to wrong the plaintiff in the future. So a reparative injunction might go to require removal of the boulders, but not a preventive injunction to forbid future trespasses. On the other hand, when demonstrators show intransigent determination to continue trespassing indefinitely, an preventive injunction may be appropriate.

Structural injunctions. Professor Owen Fiss has argued that there is a third type of injunction that belongs in this set.[14] The structural or restructuring injunction attempts to remodel an existing social or political institution to bring it into conformity with constitutional demands. Examples are the injunction that restructures a school system to facilitate equality of educational opportunity, or restructures a prison to eliminate cruel and inhuman punishments. Such injunctions would be simple reparative or preventive injunctions if they merely ordered authorities to carry out or to cease some specific act. However, restructuring injunctions are typically complex and invasive. They are likely to involve the judge in tasks traditionally considered to be non-judicial, that is, less about rights and duties and more about management. For this reason, structural injunctions are likely to be used, as they are now, only as public law remedies for serious and pervasive rights violations.[15]

Other Compulsions

Injunctions with specific names. As already noted, many orders that are injunctive in nature, may be called by some more descriptive name. One

13. See Owen Fiss, The Civil Rights Injunction (1978).

15. See § 7.4(4) below.

obscure prerogative writ issued out of Chancery under the quaint name of *ne exeat regno.* This writ forbade one from leaving the realm. It was eventually used to prevent one from leaving the jurisdiction to escape liabilities.[16] Many common compulsory orders today get their own names. Specific performance, interpleader, reinstatement in a job, divestiture of holdings to comply with antitrust laws, destruction of property by court order—these are all injunctive orders. The list will grow as long as judges and lawyers use special words to describe the factual situation in which the injunction goes.

Prerogative writs. One special group of compulsory orders was known collectively as prerogative writs [17] or extraordinary remedies. These writs could be used by law courts, in spite of the fact that they were coercive orders. The main writs in this group were *habeas corpus, prohibition,* and *mandamus.*[18] The *habeas* writ is most familiar; it orders the named defendant to produce the body of a named person, that is, to release the person from imprisonment. Like the other prerogative writs, it was issued by law courts in spite of its form as a direct compulsory order.

Prohibition and mandamus. The writ of *prohibition* was likewise a coercive order, but issued by a superior to an inferior judge, ordering the inferior to cease trial of a case or to cease certain actions in the case.[19] The writ of *mandamus* was similar except that the inferior judge was compelled by the writ to take some affirmative action in the case,[20] or the writ was used to compel a public officer to carry out a ministerial duty about which the office had no discretion. Remnants of these writs remain today, mainly to provide review by appellate courts in extraordinary cases in which appeal is not possible. In some states, the prerogative writs are abolished and special actions substituted.

§ 2.9(2) Bases for Grant or Denial of Injunctive Relief

Grounds and Cases for Injunctive Relief

Injunctions may be granted to prevent violation of rights or to restore the plaintiff to rights that have already been violated. The ground for relief and the scope of that relief are both found in the right itself. If the right is to be a partner or a tenured professor, then the injunctions may so require in spite of the risk of judicial error and the intrusiveness of injunctive relief.[1] Sometimes they are also granted to establish rights that did not theretofore exist,[2] or to effectuate rights by compelling some change in normal legal

16. See 1 W. Holdsworth, History of English Law 226 ff. (7th ed. 1956).

17. Distinguish *original writ* by which, at common law, the suit was begun. The original writ was the writ in assumpsit or trespass or the like. Distinguish also execution writs, such as *fieri facias* and *elegit.* These were the writs or court orders by which judgments were enforced through seizure of property. See R. Millar, Civil Procedure of the Trial Court in Historical Perspective 426 ff (1952). At one time appellate review was fostered through the use of some writs, one of which, *certiorari,* still runs.

18. Other prerogative writs included certiorari, to review lower court decisions, and quo warranto, to try the question of official authority to act or right to office. There are several more obscure examples. See 1 W. Holdsworth, History of English Law 226 ff. (7th ed. 1956).

19. F. Ferris & F. Ferris, Jr., The Law of Extraordinary Legal Remedies, §§ 303–306 (1926).

20. H. Potter, Historical Introduction to English Law 130 (1948).

procedure.[3] No general principle limits injunctive relief to any particular kind of case or constellation of facts.

Injunctions are denied in particular cases when the plaintiff fails to establish any underlying right. They are also denied in individual cases when the judge concludes that some other remedy ought to be used instead. Otherwise, the injunction is a potential remedy in any case in which it may provide significant benefits that are greater than its costs or disadvantages. Limitations on the injunction come when the judge weighs benefits or disadvantages in particular cases, not by dint of any general subject matter limitation.

The Adequate Legal Remedy and Balance of Equities and Costs

Traditional adequacy or irreparable harm rule. The traditional rule denied injunctions, including specific performance orders, if the remedy at law was regarded as adequate. Stated otherwise, the traditional rule denied injunctive relief unless, without it, the plaintiff would suffer irreparable harm.[6] That rule, as a free-standing rule, probably has little direct effect today.[7]

Balance of benefits and costs or disadvantages. Adequacy of legal remedy today is, however, relevant in balancing the costs and benefits of a potential injunction. Injunctions are denied if the total estimated balance of benefits from the injunction outweighs its estimated total costs or disadvantages.[8] The costs and benefits are not necessarily quantifiable or expressed in money terms. For example, the injunction is a benefit if it provides the plaintiff the very thing to which he is entitled, whether or not that entitlement is worth any particular amount of money. If an injunction forces the defendant to return the plaintiff's portrait of his Great Aunt Gilda, that is a benefit even if the portrait has no market value.

Non-monetary costs. The costs of an injunction may also be impossible to state in money terms. Costs include risks that an injunction may impose. Risks of an injunction include the possibility of undue intrusion and coercion, the possibility that the contempt power might be invoked, hardships or costs to the defendant that would not be entailed by damages remedies,[9] and even the disruption of orderly alternative processes for resolution of the dispute.[10] In addition, injunctive relief might have inappropriate collateral effects; it may shift the normal burden of proof,[11] or provide the plaintiff with undeserved or impolitic priorities or preferences over other creditors; [12] it might shift the trial forum and change the mode of trial from jury to non-jury trial.

Economic costs. Some injunctions have definite economic costs and risks as well. An injunction that requires destruction of a building or closure of a productive factory must be considered a high-cost remedy even in purely economic terms, although there may be ways of minimizing that cost, and if so that, too, must be counted.

§ 2.9(2)

3. As in interpleader cases. See § 2.9(3) below. And in cases when the court freezes the defendant's bank account to preserve the fund claimed by the plaintiff. See § 6.1(5) below. Or orders payment of part of the defendant's obligation before the amount of the obligation has been finally determined. See § 8.10 below.

For instance, a court has good reason to enjoin operation of a polluting factory when the pollution cannot be halted in any other way. But the high economic costs of the closing—lost production, lost jobs, lost property value— would encourage the court to evaluate other solutions carefully. If the pollution does no permanent environmental harm and only the plaintiff suffers from it, courts might consider refusing the injunction because of its high cost.[13] But alternatively, they might consider issuing the injunction with the expectation that the factory could buy out of it by purchasing the plaintiff's property or at least an easement that would permit it to contin- ue.[14] As this illustration suggests, weighing economic costs and benefits of an injunction is not necessarily easier than weighing intangible benefits.

Alternative remedies as a benchmark for measuring benefit of the injunc- tion. In determining the benefits of an injunction the court must necessari- ly measure the benefit from a benchmark of alternative remedies. If the plaintiff does not care about the portrait of his great aunt Gilda for sentimental reasons but only wants the canvas for its economic value, then the damages remedy might be just as good and the benefits of the injunction are thus not very great. In such a case the costs of an injunction might outweigh the benefits because the benefits are so attenuated. The legal remedy may not be as adequate as an injunction, but it may be adequate enough, considering risks or costs that an injunction can create.

Injunctions undercutting rule for minimizing damages. Likewise, an injunction might circumvent the policy of minimizing damages: it is a good idea to force the defendant to remove boulders he has deposited on the plaintiff's land, but not a good idea to enjoin him to remove a cardboard box he dropped there; as to the box, the plaintiff may be best situated to effect an efficient removal. Besides these specific instances, the general prefer- ence, especially in private-law remedies, runs against coercive remedies.

Risk of error. Any legal decision might be erroneous, even after a full trial in which the judicial system has done its best to find truth and achieve justice. Because injunctions might sometimes be more intrusive than an alternative remedy, an erroneous injunction might be more harmful to the defendant and less respectful of the defendant's rights. There is no way to be sure that any given legal decision is "right," but it may be possible to minimize the harm than could result from an erroneous decision by refusing injunctive relief when that form of relief would be especially destructive to the defendant's rights if it is erroneous, provided that the plaintiff's rights can be substantially protected by other remedies.

Suppose a defendant violates a building restriction by constructing a home with a roofline too high and the court thinks the defendant may have done so purposely. The defendant's wilful violation suggests that an injunc- tion might be justified to force reconstruction of the house. On the other hand, such an injunction would be costly and the conclusion that the defendant acted wilfully might be erroneous. If the neighboring plaintiffs have not suffered harm, an award of damages might be less intrusive than

---

13. As in Boomer v. Atlantic Cement Co., 26 N.Y.2d 219, 309 N.Y.S.2d 312, 257 N.E.2d 870, 40 A.L.R.3d 590 (1970). See § 5.7(2) be- low.

14. See §§ 5.7(3) & 5.7(4) below.

an injunctive reconstruction; given the risk of error, *and* the loss in value that results when a building must be partially destroyed, the injunction may seem too costly compared to the benefits it produces. If so, the court would limit the plaintiffs' relief to damages.

§ 2.9(3) Subject Matter: Injunctions Protecting or Limiting Property and Economic Rights

The broad potential for injunctive remedies is shown by the cases in which it is invoked. Many of those cases are considered in more detail elsewhere. This subsection and those that follow point to some illustrative situations for injunctions.

Property Rights

Injunctions are commonly sought and appropriately issued to prevent many kinds of threatened torts to property interests, as well as to restore property already tortiously harmed. For example, injunctions go in cases of torts to tangible property such as trespass,[1] waste,[2] and nuisance,[3] where the defendant threatens to continue or repeat such torts. Injunctions may compel defendants to remove encroaching structures,[4] or to bring their homes into accord with zoning requirements or building restrictions,[5] and to return stolen chattels.[6]

Economic Rights

Injunctions are quite commonly used to redress commercial torts, rights in intangible property, and other economic interests. Injunctions run to prevent infringement of patents,[7] trademarks[8] and copyrights,[9] as well as misappropriation of commercial values,[10] and interference with contract.[11] Sometimes, too, the injunction is used to prohibit injurious falsehoods such as commercial disparagement.[12] It is now used to restore discrimination victims to their job rights under Title VII.[13] In the form of specific performance, the injunction is used quite routinely in land sale contracts,[14] and less often to enforce some others.[15]

One form of the injunction used to protect economic (and other) interests is the injunction against enforcement of a regulatory statute on the ground that it is unconstitutional[16] or that it conflicts with some other regulatory

§ 2.9(3)

1. See § 5.10(3) below.
2. See § 5.2(8) below.
3. See § 5.7 below.
4. See §§ 5.10(4) & 5.5 below.
5. See § 5.7(2) below.
6. See § 5.17(3) below.
7. See § 6.2(5).
8. See § 6.4(5).
9. See § 6.3(5), below.
10. See § 6.5 below.
11. See § 6.6(4) below.
12. See § 6.8(3) below.
13. See § 6.10(4) below; cf. § 12.21(4) (specific performance for breach of job contract).

14. See § 12.8 generally, and §§ 12.11(3) & 12.12(3) as to land sale contracts in particular.

15. See, e.g., §§ 12.16(7) & 12.17(7) (goods buyer's and goods seller's specific performance rights respectively); § 12.23 (arbitration contracts).

16. E.g., Planned Parenthood Ass'n of Cincinnati, Inc. v. City of Cincinnati, 822 F.2d 1390 (6th Cir.1987) (enjoining enforcement of city ordinance regulating disposal of "fetal remains" resulting from abortions). Imperial County v. Munoz, 449 U.S. 54, 101 S.Ct. 289, 66 L.Ed.2d 258 (1980) (if statute violated federal constitution, then court could also enjoin enforcement of state-court decree enforcing that statute).

scheme.[17] Sometimes such injunctions are refused when the constitutionality of the statute will be resolved in other forums without undue delay or threat.[18] Injunctions against collection of taxes seriously threaten government operations and are likely to be denied.[19] But the rules are not categorically negative; they involve an evaluation of the facts in each case.

The injunction may be used to protect economic interests by requiring the defendant to obey a statutory command. In *Temple University v. White*,[20] a court went so far as to compel a state agency to make payments of monies to a hospital on the ground that the state had not properly calculated payments due in the past and that the payments would serve as advances on the state's future obligations to the hospital.

Injunctions to protect economic rights are not necessarily limited to prohibitory injunctions or to cases in which the plaintiff has a formal cause of action for damages. In a Texas case, a newspaper publisher obtained an injunction against a district attorney requiring him to give the newspaper access to the district attorney's office equal to the access given to other news media.[21] Although in one sense the injunction protects civil rights by securing equal treatment, in fact it seems to be an injunction that secures the access necessary for the newspaper's economic success.

Crimes

The rule often repeated is that courts will not enjoin a crime in order to protect personal rights.[22] On the other hand, they would enjoin a crime to protect property rights, as in the case of nuisances. In modern practice many crimes are enjoined under regulatory statutes,[23] civil rights statutes,[24] under a broadened definition of nuisance or property right, and when the crime is "incidental."[25] Regulatory injunctions, issued at the behest of administrative agencies today often run to prohibit regulated activity which is also criminal.

17. See Rice v. Norman Williams Company, 458 U.S. 654, 102 S.Ct. 3294, 73 L.Ed.2d 1042 (1982) (injunction can go to prevent enforcement of state statute that is preempted by federal antitrust laws); Cohen v. County of San Francisco Bd. of Supervisors, 40 Cal.2d 277, 219 Cal.Rptr. 467, 707 P.2d 840 (1985) (upholding ordinance in most respects but remanding for determining whether preliminary injunction would be proper to the extent that ordinance was preempted by state statute).

18. See § 2.9(4) below (enjoining criminal prosecutions).

19. W.T. Grant Co. v. Srogi, 52 N.Y.2d 496, 438 N.Y.S.2d 761, 420 N.E.2d 953 (1981) (cases approving injunction "have usually involved situations in which there has been a clear showing of intentional overassessment of property tantamount to fraud on the part of the tax authority and the taxpayer was without relief from the imminent deprivation of his property while he attempted to challenge the unauthorized tax;" but "an injunction is not available to avoid an excessive assessment which is the product of inadvertence or mistake and the taxpayer in such instances is left solely to his administrative remedies"). Federal courts are told by statute not to enjoin state tax collections or utility rate making decisions as long as state remedies are available. 28 U.S.C.A. §§ 1341 & 1342.

20. 941 F.2d 201, 216–221 (3d Cir.1991).

21. Southwestern Newspapers Corp. v. Curtis, 584 S.W.2d 362 (Tex.Civ.App.1979).

22. See Developments in the Law—Injunctions, 78 Harv.L.Rev. 994, 1013 (1965).

23. E.g., Ginsburg v. Kovrak, 392 Pa. 143, 139 A.2d 889 (1958) (injunction against practice of law by attorney not licensed in Pennsylvania).

24. Everett v. Harron, 380 Pa. 123, 110 A.2d 383 (1955).

25. E.g., Harvey v. Prall, 250 Iowa 1111, 97 N.W.2d 306 (1959) (hauling garbage without a permit is a nuisance and enjoinable).

When injunctions are a part of the criminal enforcement scheme, they may be the most appropriate remedy as in many cases of shabby business practices outlawed by consumer protection statutes. In other cases, however, injunctions against crime may operate to deprive the defendant of a jury trial, or to take him into a hostile venue or forum, or to add a penalty to his "crime" that the legislature never intended and certainly did not provide for. The injunction may also risk a contempt punishment or coercive contempt sanction that far exceeds the criminal punishment provided by the statute. Courts have recognized many of these reasons against "criminal equity." [26]

Whether a crime should be enjoined depends on the risks and costs as compared to the benefits it will produce. The costs just listed are substantial, including possible loss of a jury trial right and the addition of unwarranted penalties. On the other hand, the fact that the defendant's conduct is somehow criminal in addition to the fact that it violates the plaintiff's rights should not operate to protect the defendant. For instance, protective orders are routinely issued in domestic cases to prevent intimidation, harassment or injury by the defendant spouse. [27] Once again, the supposed rule appears to be a matter of analyzing the case to obtain the best net remedy. The overwhelming danger that some spouses face justifies the injunction in spite of the fact that it is also enjoining a crime.

§ 2.9(4) Subject Matter: Injunctions Facilitating Procedure, Tactics, or Review

Tactical, Procedural and Review Injunctions

Sometimes injunctions do not protect primary private rights at all, but instead change normal procedures to help secure the plaintiff's right or to provide a procedural or tactical advantage in pursuing it. Similarly, a plaintiff may seek to enjoin enforcement of an administrative decision as a means of obtaining judicial review.

In a sense all such injunctions may give the plaintiff something that, literally, is not his substantive right, or something that exceeds his right. For example, if the defendant has a history of wrongfully discharging employees in violation of their rights, an injunction might not only forbid such discharges but might also require the defendant to post workplace notices explaining to employees what their rights are. [1] The injunction forbidding wrongful discharge is aimed at the plaintiff's rights; the injunction requiring notice is aimed at facilitating those rights through procedures to which the plaintiff has no legal claim at all.

Other injunctions serve to protect or secure primary rights but also provide procedural or significant tactical advantage. An injunction freezing the defendant's assets pending a determination of the plaintiff's rights secures any primary right the plaintiff turns out to have, but it also has an enormous tactical impact. [2] A preliminary injunction or temporary restrain-

---

26. See Commonwealth v. Stratton Finance Co., 310 Mass. 469, 38 N.E.2d 640 (1941).

27. Frequently these injunctions are authorized by statute, as in West's Ann.Cal.Civ. Code § 4359; N.Y.–McKinney's Jud.L. § 828; N.Y.–McKinney's Dom.Rel.L. § 251.

§ 2.9(4)

1. See § 7.4(4) below.

2. See § 6.1(5) below.

ing order[3] may protect the plaintiff's primary right (if any), but it will also put the defendant at a disadvantage that may induce a more compliant attitude in settlement.

The ways in which injunctions can enhance a plaintiff's tactical position are without any theoretical limit. Some of the major instances of "procedural" injunctions are those used to enjoin criminal prosecution, to enjoin civil litigation in other courts, and those used to compel potential claims to assert claims in a single court.

Enjoining Civil Litigation

Enjoining abusive litigation. Access to courts is an important part of the American system of law. Sometimes the right to resort to court is abused, as the law of malicious prosecution and abuse of process shows. Sometimes courts respond to that abuse by enjoining the abuser from going to court, but only rarely and usually only to prevent relitigation of issues already determined,[4] or to enforce agreements to arbitrate which exclude resort to courts.[5] The costs of damages actions against abusers of the judicial system are high enough because they risk chilling the citizen's use of courts to resolve disputes. The costs of injunctive relief may be higher because that relief will prevent courts from hearing the citizen's complaint altogether and will make a judgment about its merits impossible.

Enjoining litigation temporarily to prevent irreparable loss of rights. A second kind of injunction is very limited. It might enjoin a mortgage foreclosure or summary eviction of a tenant if those actions gave the mortgagee or tenant no opportunity to raise appropriate defenses.[6] If the injunction plaintiff can present her side of the case in the foreclosure or eviction suit, however, an injunction in such cases merely becomes an instrument for controlling the choice of forum. In that case, as indicated below, the injunction is usually hard to justify.[7]

Enjoining litigation to control choice of forum. A different kind of injunction against litigation is presented when two disputing parties attempt to prevent the other's resort to a favorable forum. One obtains a Michigan injunction forbidding the other from pursuing a suit in Illinois. If obeyed, such an injunction intrudes on the appropriate power of Illinois courts. But the injunction-defendant might not obey it. Because most injunctive orders are not entitled to full faith and credit under the constitution,[8] Illinois is free to issue its own injunction, forbidding the plaintiff in the first injunction

---

3. See § 2.11 below.

4. See Steinberg v. McKay, 295 Mass. 139, 3 N.E.2d 23, 25 (1936) ("litigation instituted by the present defendant is not only without merit, but is part of a systematic harassment of the plaintiff by groundless suits," injunction proper). For other cases, see § 7.3(5) below.

5. See § 12.23 below.

6. Triple J Cattle, Inc. v. Chambers, 551 So.2d 280 (Ala.1989) (mortgagor who stood ready to pay off note was entitled to injunctive relief against foreclosure until amount due could be determined); cf. Long v. Zirkle, 811 S.W.2d 840 (Mo.App.1991) (church mem-

bers' derivative suit for injunction against foreclosure, injunction issued).

7. See Kanter & Eisenberg v. Madison Associates, 116 Ill.2d 506, 108 Ill.Dec. 476, 508 N.E.2d 1053 (1987) (no injunction for tenant against eviction because he may pay rent under protest and sue to recover if it is excessive).

8. See Laker Airways Limited v. Sabena, Belgian World Airlines, 731 F.2d 909, 78 A.L.R.Fed. 751 (D.C.Cir.1984); Reese, Full Faith & Credit to Foreign Equity Decrees, 42 Iowa L.Rev. 183 (1957).

from enforcing the Michigan decree.[9] This "unseemly kind of judicial disorder" Justice Schaefer said, ought to stop where it begins.[10]

By and large courts silently observe Justice Schaefer's admonition. The injunction would be helpful to the plaintiff; if the one forum is unfair or hostile to one of the parties, injunction may be the *only* remedy. But unless unfairness can be established by neutral standards, one court's intervention in another's work costs more to the system than the benefits it can attain. Nevertheless, one court occasionally "protects its jurisdiction" by issuing an injunction that forbids parties to litigate elsewhere,[11] or forbids their enforcement of another court's decree.[12] Sometimes, however, courts resolve the problem by staying their proceedings and permitting the litigation to continue its course in another forum.[13]

Federal courts enjoining state litigation. Federal courts are told expressly by statute that they "may not grant an injunction to stay proceedings in a State court except as expressly authorized by Act of Congress, or where necessary in aid of [their] jurisdiction, or to protect or effectuate [their] judgments."[14] Even so, federal courts may enjoin enforcement of state court judgments or decrees where necessary to effectuate the federal court's decision that a statute is unconstitutional.[15]

Bills of peace. Before the development of modern class actions and other procedures, equity courts sometimes issued injunctions to compel numbers of suitors, each of whom had independent claims against one defendant, to bring their claims into one forum. For instance, one polluter faced with 25 claims by 25 people in 25 different courts might bring a "bill of peace" suit to injunctively bring all 25 claimants into a single court where their claims could be presented in one suit.[16] If the separate equity court had independent grounds for taking jurisdiction, such an injunction might be issued.[17] Even if all claims were claims "at law" with no equitable aspects, some courts issued the injunction and compelled all claimants to submit to a single equity forum.[18]

This procedure could have been adapted to permit a jury trial once the injunction had served its purpose.[19] However, modern procedure after

---

9. James v. Grand Trunk Western R. Co., 14 Ill.2d 356, 152 N.E.2d 858, 74 A.L.R.2d 814 (1958), cert. denied, 358 U.S. 915, 79 S.Ct. 288, 3 L.Ed.2d 239 (1958) (issuing a counter injunction like that described in the text).

10. Id. (Schaefer, J., dissenting).

11. See Laker Airways Limited v. Sabena, Belgian World Airlines, 731 F.2d 909, 78 A.L.R.Fed. 751 (D.C.Cir.1984) (federal court enjoining some parties in antitrust litigation from pursuing an English-court injunction against the American litigation).

12. See Imperial County v. Munoz, 449 U.S. 54, 101 S.Ct. 289, 66 L.Ed.2d 258 (1980).

13. LaDuke v. Burlington Northern R. Co., 879 F.2d 1556 (7th Cir.1989) (federal court could properly stay suit to permit a state court proceeding to resolve the dispute if it could); Microsoftware Computer Systems, Inc. v. Ontel Corp., 686 F.2d 531 (7th Cir.1982).

14. 28 U.S.C.A. § 2283.

15. See Imperial County v. Munoz, 449 U.S. 54, 101 S.Ct. 289, 66 L.Ed.2d 258 (1980).

16. See Chafee, Bills of Peace with Multiple Parties, 45 Harv.L.Rev. 1297 (1932), reprinted substantially in Chafee, Some Problems of Equity 149–198 (1950); 2 Pomeroy, Equity Jurisprudence §§ 243–275 (5th ed. 1941). Some of this is pretty tedious going.

17. Sovereign Camp W.O.W. v. O'Neill, 266 U.S. 292, 45 S.Ct. 49, 69 L.Ed. 293 (1924); see Georgia Power Co. v. Hudson, 49 F.2d 66, 75 A.L.R. 1439 (4th Cir.1931) (dictum).

18. Tribbette v. Illinois Cent. R. Co., 70 Miss. 182, 12 So. 32, 19 A.L.R. 660 (1892).

19. See § 2.6(3) (jury trial in interpleader cases).

merger of law and equity has largely supplanted the bill of peace; consolidation of claims, transfers of actions to other venues, class actions and other procedural devices, not independent injunctions, are more commonly used to compel joinder or to facilitate a single trial.[20] The injunction is used to compel joinder in one remaining situation, however. That is the interpleader situation.

Interpleader

Traditional interpleader. One kind of injunction against litigation in other courts is the interpleader injunction. Interpleader was once brought as a suit in the separate equity court.[21] The interpleader plaintiff deposited a fund or property, to which he asserted no claim. The interpleader plaintiff is often designated as a Stakeholder. He brought in A and B (and perhaps others) as defendants. The interpleader plaintiff asked the court (a) to require A and B to assert any claims they might have to the fund or property in the interpleader case and (b) to enjoin them from proceeding to assert claims elsewhere. This injunction was an essential step in the process. Without it, the Stakeholder could get none of the protection sought, because without the injunction both A and B could also assert separate claims in other courts and the Stakeholder would be forced to defend both or risk double liability. Once the injunction was issued, however, A and B asserted their claims against the fund or property in the court chosen by the Stakeholder. At that point, the Stakeholder could leave the case free of further responsibility and free as well of the costs of defending multiple claims over one liability.

Examples. Interpleader made sense when the Stakeholder was liable only to one party but two or more claims might be asserted. For instance, a bailee might be obliged to return the bailed fur coat, but two people might claim it. Or an insurer is obliged to pay a sum of money to the surviving spouse of the deceased, but two different people claim to be that spouse. The bailee and the insurer have only one obligation, so interpleader is a good solution. Interpleader is not appropriate when the interpleader plaintiff could be liable to each of several persons.[22] If a charity runs a lottery and by its terms owes $10,000 to the holder of winning numbers, then it is liable for that sum to all holders of the right numbers, not just to one. Such a case is no case for interpleader at all.

Traditional limiting rules. The sense of what cases were "right" for interpleader eventually crystallized in several supposed rules [23] which came to be interpreted technically and constrictively in ways indicated in footnotes.[24]

---

20. The common problems in all these representative devices—why one person can represent and bind another—is considered in Stephen Yeazell, From Medieval Group Litigation to the Modern Class Action (1987), which gives some attention to bills of peace and other early group litigations.

21. An earlier common law interpleader was quite narrow and has long been obsolete. See Hazard and Moskovitz, An Historical and Critical Analysis of Interpleader, 52 Calif.L.Rev. 706, 709 (1964).

22. See the paragraph "Bills of peace" below.

23. The rules are traceable to Pomeroy. See, Pomeroy, Equitable Jurisprudence § 1322 (5th ed. 1941) (the rule statements trace back to the 1883 edition).

24. See Hazard and Moskovitz, An Historical and Critical Analysis of Interpleader, 52 Calif.L.Rev. 706 (1964). These authors conclude that the rules, far from classic, were generalized improperly by Pomeroy. See also

(1) The adverse claimants must claim the same thing, debt or duty. This is referred to as the identity rule.[25]

(2) The claimants must derive their claims to title from a common source or origin. This is sometimes referred to as the privity rule.[26]

(3) The Stakeholder must not assert any claim or have any interest in the subject matter. This meant that the Stakeholder could not get the benefit of interpleader if he himself had any claim, however legitimate it might be.[27]

(4) The Stakeholder must have incurred no independent liability to either of the claimants.[28]

Federal statutory interpleader. Professor Chafee set out to modernize interpleader and wrote major articles on the subject from 1921 to 1943.[29] The congress enacted several federal interpleader statutes, culminating in the 1936 statute, with some amendments since that time.[30] In general the impact has been to liberalize interpleader and to free it at least in part from the artificial constraints. The federal statute specifically permits actions "in the nature of interpleader," which allows the stakeholder-plaintiff to assert a claim to the fund or property even though he brings in adverse claimants. It also provides that the "action may be entertained although the titles or claims of the conflicting claimants do not have a common origin, or are not identical, but are adverse to and independent of one another." These

Chafee, Modernizing Interpleader, n. 29 below.

25. If the identity rule meant only that the claims must be, in part, mutually exclusive, it might be an appropriate rule; but in fact this identity rule was interpreted to mean that if the adverse claimants claimed in different amounts, the identity requirement was not met and there could be no interpleader.

26. This requirement was given a highly technical interpretation. If each claimant claimed to derive his rights to the property directly from X, there was privity and the interpleader could be maintained. However, in many cases claimant A derived his rights from X, while claimant B derived his rights from Y, and claimed they were superior. In such a case there was no privity and interpleader would be denied. This situation also often raised other, more or less overlapping reasons for denial of interpleader but no real reason of policy seemed involved to prevent this relief.

27. This requirement was relaxed where there was an independent ground for equity jurisdiction, in which case the Stakeholder's suit was referred to as a bill in the *nature* of interpleader.

28. This rule sounds good. In fact it sounds like a special form of the requirement that claims must be mutually exclusive to justify interpleader. However, the Stakeholder's problem is partly his uncertainty about the whole thing. It is possible that the holder of the fur coat is liable to B, as the owner, and also liable to A on the basis of contract liability incurred when A bailed the fur. For instance, the Stakeholder may have given A a receipt that creates an independent basis for A's claim, regardless of whether B is the true owner or not. This has been enough to bar interpleader in some cases. But the fact is that the Stakeholder's uncertainty in this case creates the need for interpleader here as much as in any other case. It is true that if he owes both A and B, interpleader is unnecessary. On the other hand, if it turns out that the Stakeholder is "really" only liable to one of the two claimants, but is denied interpleader because of a merely possible independent liability to both, he may be vested with two suits and subjected to two liabilities on a single obligation. Thus interpleader is needed in such a situation as well as in situations where lack of independent liability is clear.

29. Chafee, Modernizing Interpleader, 30 Yale L.J. 814 (1921); Chafee, Interstate Interpleader, 33 Yale L.J. 685 (1924); Chafee, Interpleader in the United States Courts, 41 Yale L.J. 1134 (1932), 42 Yale L.J. 41 (1932) (Pts. I & II); Chafee, The Federal Interpleader Act of 1936, 45 Yale L.J. 963, 1161 (1936) (Pts. I & II); Chafee, Federal Interpleader Since the Act of 1936, 49 Yale L.J. 377 (1940); Chafee, Broadening the Second Stage of Interpleader, 56 Harv.L.Rev. 541 (1943).

30. 28 U.S.C.A. §§ 1335, 1397, 2361. See Charles Alan Wright, Arthur R. Miller and Mary Kay Kane, Federal Practice and Procedure § 1701 (1986 & Supp.).

substantive reforms make interpleader widely available when the federal statute applies.

Federal rule interpleader; comparisons. In addition to the federal statute, the Federal Rules of Civil Procedure provide for a non-statutory interpleader, based on the equity powers of the federal courts under "federal question" jurisdiction and in diversity of citizenship cases. Under Rule 22, the controversy must concern more than $10,000 and the plaintiff-stakeholder must be diverse in citizenship from the claimants. In contrast, the federal statute permits federal jurisdiction if the claimants are diverse in citizenship among themselves and if the fund or property in question is valued at $500 or more.[31] Statutory interpleader also has the advantage of a nationwide service of process.[32]

Interpleader to compel equitable distribution of limited funds. Interpleader offers opportunities for equitable development to resolve some difficult problems. Suppose a liability insurer issues a policy to pay the legal liability of its insured up to a policy limit of $100,000. The insured causes serious injuries to 25 people in a bus collision, and each claims injuries exceeding $100,000. Any one claimant might exhaust the entire insurance fund if her claim proves good. Under usual rules, if claimant A recovers a judgment of $100,000 or more before others recover, she will be able to enforce that judgment against the insurer, thus absorbing the entire fund. Could the insurer use interpleader to deposit the $100,000 in court and bring in all 25 claimants? If so, the judge might be able to parcel out the limited fund in an equitable manner, much as a bankruptcy judge converts each claim against the bankruptcy to an equitable share of the limited assets.

One problem is that the insurer does not stand to lose $100,000 to each claimant. Its obligation will be satisfied when it pays to any claimant the entire policy amount. Nevertheless, the Supreme Court has permitted interpleader in this situation.[33]

Potentials for expanding interpleader. A more developed interpleader practice could deal with some other problems of multiple claims. For instance, one problem of punitive damages is that a single defendant may be struck with many punitive damages verdicts by many different plaintiffs in many different suits.[34] To the extent that multiple punitive awards can be unfair or inefficient, a developed and flexible interpleader practice could help deal with the problem. For example, if authorized to do so, the court permit all claimants to pursue their claims to judgment in the court of their choice, but order them not to enforce their punitive damages judgment. Instead, the punitive damages portion of the judgment would be injunctively brought into the single "interpleader" court, where a judge or jury could decide an appropriate total punitive liability and share that total among all claimants ratably according to their existing judgments.[35] This solution does

31. For these and other differences, consult Charles Alan Wright, Arthur R. Miller and Mary Kay Kane, Federal Practice and Procedure § 1703 (1986 & Supp.).

32. 28 U.S.C.A. § 2361.

33. State Farm Fire & Cas. Co. v. Tashire, 386 U.S. 523, 87 S.Ct. 1199, 18 L.Ed.2d 270

(1967). See Charles Alan Wright, Arthur R. Miller and Mary Kay Kane, Federal Practice and Procedure § 1705 (1986 & Supp.).

34. See § 3.11(8) below.

35. Cf. In re Asbestos School Litigation, 620 F.Supp. 873 (E.D.Pa.1985) (class action, judge permitted individuals to opt-out of the

not appear to be on the horizon, but even to sketch it is to suggest continuing possibility of developing interpleader to resolve procedural problems.

Enjoining Criminal Prosecutions [36]

Courts usually refuse to enjoin criminal prosecutions, once they have been instituted. If the injunction-seeker has a good defense, he can usually present it in the criminal prosecution itself, perhaps even obtain dismissal in an early probable cause hearing. While an injunction might be a preferable remedy for any number of reasons, the normal rules of criminal procedure are quite protective and the interest in orderly procedure may be thought to require that courts keep hands off the criminal process. If the court hears all the evidence in the injunction suit and decides that the prosecution can proceed, then all the evidence will be produced again, before another judge in the criminal suit. If the evidence is not heard in the injunction suit, the question may tend to be abstract and not suited for a final determination. Either way, it seems better to use the criminal process unless its use can be shown to be a wrong and also one that threatens important rights of the plaintiff. When a federal court is asked to enjoin a state court's criminal prosecution, additional reasons against injunctive relief appear; the federal government should not precipitate a conflict with state governments without a strong reason. So in general, courts do not enjoin pending criminal prosecutions.[37]

If equity refused to protect personal rights, as a judge once said,[38] courts would refuse to enjoin *any* criminal prosecution. But the reasons for refusing the injunction are not so broad. Because the reasons are narrow, courts do in fact enjoin criminal prosecutions in at least two kinds of cases. *First,* they enjoin criminal prosecutions that amount to an abuse of process because the prosecution is not only without justification but is repeated as a form of official harassment.[39] *Second,* they enjoin criminal prosecutions or other enforcement under unconstitutional statutes when no prosecution is pending and the plaintiff attacks the constitutionality of the criminal statute. If the plaintiff does not engage in the activity prohibited by the statute, he may be forfeiting constitutional rights because he cannot afford to risk fines or penalties. If he engages in the activity in order to test the statute's validity, it may turn out to be a valid statute after all and he may be fined or jailed. The Supreme Court has repeatedly approved anti-prosecution injunctions in this situation,[40] and so have state courts.[41]

class litigation but with the proviso that if they opted out they could not claim punitive damages in individual litigation; injunction against opt-out litigants in another jurisdiction to prohibit punitive claims).

36. See also § 7.3(5) below.

37. See Younger v. Harris, 401 U.S. 37, 91 S.Ct. 746, 27 L.Ed.2d 669 (1971).

38. See § 2.9(5) below.

39. E.g., United States v. Wood, 295 F.2d 772 (5th Cir.1961), cert. denied, 369 U.S. 850, 82 S.Ct. 933, 8 L.Ed.2d 9 (1962) (suit to enjoin prosecution of an African–American, alleging prosecution was used to intimidate blacks and discourage their registration as voters; TRO should issue); Kenyon v. City of Chicopee, 320 Mass. 528, 70 N.E.2d 241, 175 A.L.R. 430 (1946).

40. See Steffel v. Thompson, 415 U.S. 452, 94 S.Ct. 1209, 39 L.Ed.2d 505 (1974) (declaratory relief appropriate after request for injunction abandoned; court's reasoning appears to apply as well to injunctions); Douglas Laycock, The Death of the Irreparable Injury Rule, 78–80 (1991). See also § 7.3(5) below.

41. Majmundar v. Veline, 256 Ga. 8, 342 S.E.2d 682 (1986). See also § 7.3(5) below.

§ 2.9(5) Subject Matter: Injunctions Protecting Personal Rights

Courts today issue injunctions to protect many kinds of personal rights that are not associated with property or economic interests, of which civil rights in various forms is a very large category. In most instances, injunctions are denied only because the costs, including intangible costs, are thought to outweigh the benefits, and a case by case determination is required to make such a judgment. In several important classes, of cases, however, the cost-benefit assessment regularly tends to be negative as already seen in the case of suits to enjoin litigation in other courts.[1] A few similar negative tendencies can be found in personal right cases. In such cases the injunction may serve great ideals, but it may also intrude seriously upon rights of the defendant or convert the judge into an administrator engaged in non-judicial tasks.

Property Right/Personal Right Distinction

In 1818 a Chancellor, in an oral discussion, tossed off a dictum to the effect that equity would not protect personal rights, only property rights.[2] The notion that equity would not protect personal rights, if ever true, is no longer the law in most courts; it is explicitly repudiated or simply ignored in most cases.[3] The subsidiary notion that equity will not enjoin certain acts that do not invade property rights sometimes gets to the right conclusion, but the reasons have nothing to do with the property-personal right distinction. Instead, courts may refuse certain acts for the reasons already mentioned—because the total risks or costs of injunctive relief are too great considering that the plaintiff who seeks the injunction has a some other means of vindicating his rights and that the alternative is almost as satisfactory as the injunction but without its costs. A few examples follow.

Political and Civil Rights

The traditional personal-property right dichotomy also led to the routine statement that injunctions would not go to protect political and civil rights, because such rights were not grounded in "property." Since the middle of the 20th century, this notion has been obsolete, at least in the federal courts. *Brown v. Board of Education,*[4] approved the injunction to attack segregated schooling in 1955. Since that time the injunction has been a major tool in a variety of civil rights cases. It has been used to establish and protect political rights by outlawing gerrymandering and compelling fair apportion-

---

§ 2.9(5)

1. See § 2.9(4) above.

2. Gee v. Pritchard, 2 Swanst. 402, 36 Eng. Rep. 670 (Ch. 1818). Courts attempted to preserve the formal truth of the dictum by giving wild definitions to property rights. In Stark v. Hamilton, 149 Ga. 227, 99 S.E. 861 (1919) it was said that a young woman's father has a property right that would warrant an injunction against her debaucher. Economic rights not represented in any tangible property or any document also counted. See Doyle v. Clark, 220 Ind. 271, 41 N.E.2d 949 (1942) (statute against sale of cold beer by grocery store invades property right). Other courts sometimes carried out the letter of the dictum. E.g., Law v. Texas Delivery Service, Inc., 335 S.W.2d 653 (Tex.Civ.App.1960) (statute regulating motor carriers not an invasion of vested property right).

3. See Knighton v. Knighton, 252 Ala. 520, 41 So.2d 172 (1949) (dictum); Kenyon v. City of Chicopee, 320 Mass. 528, 70 N.E.2d 241, 175 A.L.R. 430 (1946); Smith v. State, 242 So.2d 692 (Miss.1970); Streeter v. Brogan, 113 N.J.Super. 486, 274 A.2d 312 (1971).

4. 349 U.S. 294, 75 S.Ct. 753, 99 L.Ed. 1083 (1955).

ment of congressional and other districts.[5] It has even been used to compel distribution of public housing geographically throughout the city.[6] Some civil rights have been regarded as so significant that courts have sometimes undertaken, not merely to order their protection in general terms, but to engage in a substantial restructuring of institutions whose ingrained practices violate civil rights.[7]

Political and civil rights are not the sole province of the federal government or the federal courts. States also recognize and enforce such rights. Sometimes a state statute provides expressly for injunctive relief in political or civil rights cases. For instance, open meeting laws, which guarantee public access to important governmental activities, usually authorize injunctive enforcement.[8] But even without statutory authorization, courts sometimes enjoin officials to guarantee equal treatment.[9]

In these cases as elsewhere, injunctions generate costs. It is at best impolitic for judges to take over part of the executive branch or to interfere with legislative processes by injunction. For instance, although courts can and do use injunctions to assure constitutional apportionment in some cases, they are reluctant to enjoin elections and try to avoid doing so.[10]

More importantly, judicial control of legislative or executive branch decisions interferes substantially with the separation of powers system of government. If the judicial interference is substantial, judges themselves may lose their distinctive judicial character if they become managers of executive departments by way of injunction. Such costs are very significant ones in the American system of government, but so are the costs of letting executive departments systematically violate civil rights. The costs or risks or disadvantages of issuing injunctions in these cases are weighed against benefits, and not surprisingly there are cases in which courts have found reasons to avoid injunctions that intrude on the executive branch if the intrusion would be extensive,[11] even though in other cases courts have been

---

5. Beginning with Baker v. Carr, 369 U.S. 186, 82 S.Ct. 691, 7 L.Ed.2d 663 (1962) and followed in a number of other cases.

6. See Spallone v. United States, 493 U.S. 265, 110 S.Ct. 625, 107 L.Ed.2d 644 (1990) (reflecting the order and approving contempt sanctions against city).

7. See § 7.4(4) below.

8. E.g., Common Council of City of Peru v. Peru Daily Tribune, Inc., 440 N.E.2d 726 (Ind. App.1982).

9. E.g., Southwestern Newspapers Corp. v. Curtis, 584 S.W.2d 362 (Tex.Civ.App.1979).

10. See Bardwell v. Parish Council of Parish of East Baton Rouge, 216 La. 537, 44 So.2d 107, 19 A.L.R.2d 514 (1949) (election that would produce unconstitutional initiated act not enjoined); Adams County Election Com'n v. Sanders, 586 So.2d 829 (Miss.1991) (although districts were malapportioned, no injunction should go against present election, because authorities would call special elections later when Justice Department approved plan, and special election in reapportioned

districts would ultimately protect the constitutional rights). Post-election determinations as to validity of the election call for a different balance. Thus in Kaiser Hawaii Kai Development Co. v. City and County of Honolulu, 70 Hawaii 480, 777 P.2d 244 (1989) the court first insisted that an initiative election to rezone property could go forward, then after the initiative passed, held its product to be invalid on the ground that the statutes did not permit zoning by initiative. In Tully v. State, 143 Ill.2d 425, 158 Ill.Dec. 546, 574 N.E.2d 659 (1991) the court barred a judge from office when, after reaching the mandatory retirement age, he did not make other candidates for office aware of his claim that the mandatory retirement provision was unconstitutional and that he intended to run.

11. City of Los Angeles v. Lyons, 461 U.S. 95, 103 S.Ct. 1660, 75 L.Ed.2d 675 (1983) (Court refused to approve injunctions against police chokeholds, victim who might never suffer chokehold again had no standing); Rizzo v. Goode, 423 U.S. 362, 96 S.Ct. 598, 46 L.Ed.2d 561 (1976) (lower level police miscon-

willing to engage in extensive restructuring of schools or prisons to guarantee effective protection of civil rights.[12]

Religious Matters [13]

Any judicial interference in religious matters runs serious constitutional risks of violating religious freedom guarantees. The injunction is likely to be an especially intrusive remedy and hence likely to interfere more seriously. So courts try to stay out of religious disputes. They do not decide, for example, matters of religious doctrine, or which of two contending groups in a church has departed from the true faith.[14] Courts may decide property ownership in churches or among contending church groups, but only on neutral issues of property law, not on issues of religious faith.[15] The line is hard to draw sometimes, but the religious freedom right is singular in the American system and by its terms it requires the government to keep hands off. The result is a unique balance of the costs and benefits of the injunction, and one which leaves injunctions almost wholly out of the picture.

Defamation [16]

Another First Amendment right, free speech, suggests that injunctions should not go to prohibit speech any more than they should go to determine religious questions. The traditional equity view forbad injunctions against defamation, preferring to leave the plaintiff to the damages remedy. Today the refusal to enjoin speech finds renewed support in free speech values, whether or not the constitution precludes the injunction.[17]

Other Cases

Injunctions are potentially issued in almost any kind of case, including no doubt many that have yet to be conceived. Injunctions sometimes issue to require medical treatment, or to forbid it; to forbid or permit the change of a child's name; to prevent privacy invasion or harassment, or physical attack; and even protection of membership in a group.[18] As long as official control seems better than private destructiveness, the list is likely to grow.

§ 2.10 Statutory Injunctions

When a statute either authorizes or requires an injunctive remedy, the courts tend to regard the statutory authorization as a substitute for the irreparable injury rule, so that, at least prima facie, a statutory injunction can go even if the plaintiff would otherwise be denied relief because he has an adequate remedy at law. On the other hand, courts tend to claim the

duct did not entitle anyone to injunction against officials who did not sponsor that misconduct).

12. Hutto v. Finney, 437 U.S. 678, 683, 98 S.Ct. 2565, 57 L.Ed.2d 522 (1978).

13. See § 7.3(5) below.

14. See Presbyterian Church in the United States v. Mary Elizabeth Blue Hull Memorial Presbyterian Church, 393 U.S. 440, 89 S.Ct. 601, 21 L.Ed.2d 658 (1969).

15. See Jones v. Wolf, 443 U.S. 595, 99 S.Ct. 3020, 61 L.Ed.2d 775 (1979).

16. See generally § 7.2(14) below.

17. E.g., Kramer v. Thompson, 947 F.2d 666 (3d Cir.1991); High Country Fashions, Inc. v. Marlenna Fashions, Inc., 257 Ga. 267, 357 S.E.2d 576, 577 (1987). Other authorities are cited in § 7.2(14) below.

18. All these instances are discussed in § 7.4(5) below.

power to deny the statutory injunction on the usual equitable grounds, at least where denial does not defeat the statutory policy or substance.

Adequacy or Irreparable Injury Requirement in Statutory Injunction Cases

Statutory construction in mandatory and permissible statutes. Should a statutory injunction go without proof of irreparable harm? The answer is a matter of statutory construction. The statute might mean to authorize the injunction without the usual showing that the legal remedy is inadequate or that the plaintiff will be irreparably harmed. Or it might mean merely to invoke the usual rules of equity, including the usual irreparable harm rules.[1] The question is one of statutory construction, not common law principle.[2] So long as the statute is constitutionally valid,[3] its construction governs.

Authorization read to eliminate irreparable injury requirement. Because construction may vary greatly from statute to statute, it seems unsound to state any general rule. It is a fact, however, that a number of cases have dispensed with the usual adequacy or irreparable harm rule when the statute has authorized injunctive relief.[4] Some of the cases involve public injunctions,[5] but others have involved private civil suits only.[6]

The court's reasons for permitting a public entity to sue without showing irreparable harm may at times seem equally applicable to private suits.

Sometimes courts claim to be acting on statutory authority in dispensing with the irreparable harm rule, but sometimes they seem to claim the power to do so without regard to the statute's authority.[10] If the courts have in fact shed themselves of the irreparable injury rule anyway,[11] the statutory authorization would seem important only to signify that the statute did not exclude injunctive relief.

§ 2.10

1. Cf. Hecht Co. v. Bowles, 321 U.S. 321, 64 S.Ct. 587, 88 L.Ed. 754 (1944) (statute's direction that court "shall" grant injunction read to permit equitable balancing). Later decisions have read *Hecht* to insist on the irreparable injury requirement as a condition to relief. See Rondeau v. Mosinee Paper Corp., 422 U.S. 49, 95 S.Ct. 2069, 45 L.Ed.2d 12 (1975). *Hecht* and a number of other cases are given intense scrutiny in Plater, Statutory Violations and Equitable Discretion, 70 Calif.L.Rev. 524 (1982).

4. See, e.g., IT Corp. v. County of Imperial, 35 Cal.3d 63, 196 Cal.Rptr. 715, 672 P.2d 121 (1983); Times Publishing Co. v. Williams, 222 So.2d 470 (Fla.App.1969), overruled on different issues, Neu v. Miami Herald Publishing Co., 462 So.2d 821 (Fla.1985) (open meeting law, "if the provision granting jurisdiction * * * to issue injunctions to enforce this act is to be given any legal effect, it must be said that it is the equivalent of a legislative declaration that a violation of the statutory mandate constitutes an irreparable public injury"); Common Council of City of Peru v. Peru Daily Tribune, Inc., 440 N.E.2d 726 (Ind.App.1982) (same); Douglas Laycock, The Death of the Irreparable Injury Rule 82–84 & 96–98 nn. 92–95 (1991) (citing and summarizing cases). Cf. Little Joseph Realty, Inc. v. Town of Babylon, 41 N.Y.2d 738, 395 N.Y.S.2d 428, 363 N.E.2d 1163 (1977) (zoning ordinance violation establishes legislative balance).

6. Stark v. Borner, 226 Mont. 356, 735 P.2d 314 (1987) (land purchase litigation between private parties; injunction can be granted on any ground authorized in statute, irreparable harm need not be demonstrated); Matawan Regional Teachers Ass'n v. Matawan–Aberdeen Regional Board of Education, 212 N.J.Super. 328, 514 A.2d 1361 (1986) (open meeting law claim by teacher's association, "where injunctions are creatures of statute, all that need be proven is a statutory violation"); Common Council of Peru, Ind. v. Peru Daily Tribune, Inc., supra n. 4; Times Publishing Co. v. Williams, 222 So.2d 470 (Fla.App.1969).

10. See Douglas Laycock, The Death of the Irreparable Injury Rule 82–84 (1991).

11. See § 2.5 above generally.

In preliminary relief cases. Professor Leubsdorf pointed out [12] that the practice of dispensing with the irreparable injury rule had sometimes "spread without much thought" to provisional injunction cases. [13] It is quite doubtful that a statute authorizing injunctions without irreparable harm is also intended to authorize a lunch-time restraining order without a showing of irreparable harm. The adequacy or irreparable harm rule serves a very different purpose in preliminary injunction and TRO cases. In those cases it guards against serious loss due to an inadequate hearing. [14] Even if the statute can constitutionally dispense with the irreparable injury rule in provisional relief cases, statutes should not be readily construed either to permit or to require such a drastic removal of a protection that is all too limited in any event.

Discretion to Deny the Statutory Injunction

Statutory construction issues. Equity courts traditionally maintained a power of discretion to deny relief on a wide variety of grounds, including the chancellor's belief that unfairness lurked in the background, or that the plaintiff had unclean hands, or was guilty of laches. [15] Quite commonly today relief is denied on the basis of a "balancing" hardships and equities, often without much real explanation how such factors are weighted or why. A major issue is whether some forms or possibly all forms of equitable discretion can be invoked to refuse an injunction that is authorized or required by a statute.

At least in the first instance, the issue is once again an issue of statutory construction. If the statute authorizes the injunction, but is construed not to require an injunction, the answer seems straightforward: if the injunction is not required, then it is not required; the court may refuse it. If the statute on its face seems to require the injunction, the answer is complex. The statute might require an injunction, but on the assumption that the usual rules about injunctions apply. Read that way, the statute might be understood to say to the judge, "Issue the injunction when this statute is violated, unless you find some traditional equitable reason to deny it and the reason you find is consistent with this statute's goals." In addition, of course, the statutory "shall" might in some cases be understood as something less than a command.

The Schoenbrod principle. Professor Schoenbrod proposes a similar idea, which he states as a principle but which seems also to be a good guide to construction of the statutes: the judge may withhold injunctive relief apparently mandated by the statute only when to do so is consistent with the

---

12. See Leubsdorf, The Standards for Preliminary Injunctions, 91 Harv.L.Rev. 525, 562 (1978).

13. E.g., People v. Mika Timber Co., Inc., 221 Ill.App.3d 192, 163 Ill.Dec. 741, 581 N.E.2d 895 (1991) ("the legislature has already determined, in passing the applicable statute, that violations of the statute cause irreparable injury for which no adequate remedy exists * * * once a violation has been shown, the trial court has no discretion to refuse to issue an injunction to enforce the terms of the Act"; preliminary injunction approved). Permitting

preliminary injunctions without a showing of irreparable harm seems so unjustified that the defendant will argue for other limitations to be substituted. Cf. Securities and Exchange Com'n v. Unifund SAL, 910 F.2d 1028 (2d Cir.1990) (probable success on merits required, and the ordinary alternative in the Second Circuit, irreparable harm plus serious questions on the merits, is not available).

14. See below § 2.11.

15. See §§ 2.3(5) & 2.4 above.

statute's goal, and even then only if the court's departure from the apparent command of the statute is based on some factor in the case not reflected in the statute's formulation.[16]

Refusing and tailoring the statutory injunction. A leading case is *Hecht Co. v. Bowles.*[17] The statute said the court "shall" grant an injunction. But as Professor Plater has argued,[18] the *Hecht* case was one in which no future violation was threatened. The court did not deny an injunction because it balanced equities and hardships, but only because there was no threat of future misconduct to enjoin. That makes *Hecht* a rather limited authority.

Nevertheless, the Supreme Court has subsequently seemed to take the view that statutorily mandated injunctions could be withheld, or at least postponed, as a matter of equitable discretion, even when future statutory violations were threatened,[19] so long as the statutory policy can be respected even as the injunction is denied.[20] Similarly, the terms of the injunction might be tailored to provide less literal relief than called for if the relief actually given fully supports the statutory aims.[21]

Insisting on the statutory injunction. Statutes are often silent, incoherent, or opaque, but a construction that respects legislative purpose may still be possible. The Snail Darters case is an example. The statute protected endangered species and authorized an injunction to carry out its terms. A unique species of perch was found near the site of a dam about to be completed as part of the TVA system. The species would be destroyed if the dam went into operation. The usual balancing of hardships and equities, costs and benefits, might suggest that the perch had to take second place to economic development of the Tennessee Valley, especially given the large investment already poured into the dam's construction. The Supreme Court held otherwise, saying that the injunction had to be issued under the statute.[22]

Discretion to deny remedies, not discretion to deny rights. Some commentators read this decision as an inflexible insistence that the mandated injunction must always issue, a view that makes later decisions puzzling.[23]

16. Schoenbrod, The Measure of an Injunction: A Principle to Replace Balancing the Equities and Tailoring the Remedy, 72 Minn. L.Rev. 627, 647 (1988).

17. 321 U.S. 321, 64 S.Ct. 587, 88 L.Ed. 754 (1944).

18. See Plater, Statutory Violations and Equitable Discretion, 70 Cal.L.Rev. 524 (1982).

19. See Weinberger v. Romero–Barcelo, 456 U.S. 305, 102 S.Ct. 1798, 72 L.Ed.2d 91 (1982) (withholding injunction while defendant attempted to comply with environmental statute). The significance of this decision is much debated. See Plater, supra n. 18; Farber, Equitable Discretion, Legal Duties, and Environmental Injunctions, 45 U.Pitt.L.Rev. 513 (1984) (suggesting that compliance with the statute was required even if immediate compliance was not). See also Rondeau v. Mosinee Paper Corp., 422 U.S. 49, 95 S.Ct. 2069, 45 L.Ed.2d 12 (1975) read *Hecht* to mean

that the court could deny the injunction on the ground that the plaintiff had failed to show irreparable injury, but the point seems to have been unnecessary as the statute there did not in terms create any private right of action at all.

20. See Amoco Production Co. v. Village of Gambell, Alaska, 480 U.S. 531, 107 S.Ct. 1396, 94 L.Ed.2d 542 (1987) (statutory policy, not statutory procedure is central).

21. See State of Oregon ex rel. Cox v. Davidson Industries, Inc., 291 Or. 839, 635 P.2d 630 (1981) (defendant not required to remove illegal fill from waters, but would be required to do certain construction to achieve environmental purposes of the statute).

22. Tennessee Valley Authority v. Hill, 437 U.S. 153, 98 S.Ct. 2279, 57 L.Ed.2d 117 (1978).

23. See Weinberger v. Romero–Barcelo, supra n. 19.

But the Snail Darters case is probably simpler. The *only* remedy in that case was an injunction. No one could have sued for damages for the destruction of the Snail Darters. So the case was not one in which the court could deny equitable relief in its discretion and leave the plaintiff with some legal relief. It was injunction or nothing. To deny *all* remedy is to deny the right itself. Judges can deny any enforcement of the plaintiff's *right* where the plaintiff has forfeited the right by his conduct, as in estoppel cases. Judges can also deny *remedies* on the basis of cost-benefit balances. But not so easy to think that the Congress means statutory *rights* to come and go in the discretion of a federal judge. Indeed, the concept of a right is at odds with the concept of discretion to deny the right. So when the statute provided for an injunctive remedy and *only* an injunctive remedy, it provided strong reasons to think the court had no discretion to deny the only remedy there was. By the same token, the Snail Darters case says nothing about the power of a court to refuse a statutory injunction when the statute authorizes several different remedies.

Courts probably should not be quick to minimize any rights by exercising discretion, and certainly should not undermine statutory rights by doing so. The statute remains the best beginning place for identifying the rights and the permissible range of discretion in administering remedies.

Adding Relief Not Specified in Statutes [24]

Although there is no general rule that prevents courts from adding remedies to those specified in statutes, several doctrines may persuade them not to do so in particular cases. First, a statutory cause of action may implicitly exclude other causes of action or preempt the field.[25] In that case no other cause of action can furnish a ground for a remedy. Second, a statutory authorization of one remedy may implicitly exclude all others not named in the statute. This is the most likely to be a fair construction when the statutory remedies are extensively provided and qualified.[26] Third, even when the statute does not present a full remedial scheme, the statutory policy may be deemed to exclude some remedies.[27] Fourth, judicial remedies may also be limited when administrative agencies are given regulatory authority over the issues in question. Doctrine may require the plaintiff to exhaust administrative remedies before resorting to court, or to acknowledge the "primary jurisdiction" of an administrative agency.[28]

---

24. See also § 5.7(5) below.

25. E.g., Middlesex County Sewerage Auth. v. National Sea Clammers Ass'n, 453 U.S. 1, 101 S.Ct. 2615, 69 L.Ed.2d 435 (1981).

26. For example, Title VII, prohibiting job discrimination, sets up a remedial scheme based on back pay, reinstatement, and equitable relief. The statute can be fairly construed to exclude punitive damages by its omission from a coherent scheme. Courts in fact do exclude punitive damages, although sometimes for slightly different reasons. See § 6.10(4) below.

27. See Loma Portal Civic Club v. American Airlines, Inc., 61 Cal.2d 582, 39 Cal.Rptr. 708, 394 P.2d 548 (1964), discussed in § 5.7(5) below.

28. See Douglas Laycock, The Death of the Irreparable Injury Rule 136–140 (1991).

§ 2.11 Provisional Injunctions and Other Injunctive Procedures

§ 2.11(1) Preliminary Injunctions and Temporary Restraining Orders Generally

Types of Provisional Relief

Permanent injunctions. Injunctions issued after an appropriate trial on the merits are sometimes called permanent injunctions. Permanent injunctions are not necessarily permanent in fact, because they may be modified on motion by either party if circumstances warrant.[1] Some kinds of permanent injunctions are more or less consciously experimental, issued in the expectation that changes will be made, especially where major institutions are restructured to correspond to constitutional architecture.[2] So the permanent injunction is merely one issued after a full trial, and the term merely distinguishes them from temporary injunctive orders issued before a full trial.

Preliminary injunctions. Two kinds of provisional or pre-trial injunctive orders may be issued. The most common is the preliminary injunction. Under the federal scheme and terminology with counterparts in many states, the preliminary injunction is issued only after notice is given to the defendant that the plaintiff will move for such relief, so that the defendant has an opportunity to be heard before the preliminary injunction is issued.[3] The hearing, however, is usually attenuated and much less than due process would require for a full trial. Evidence may be taken by affidavit, for example. The preliminary injunction remains in effect until dissolved or until the permanent injunction is in place or the case dismissed. In general, preliminary relief is denied except to prevent irreparable harm. Standards for granting such relief are explained in the following subsection.

Temporary restraining orders. The temporary restraining order, often called a TRO, can put an even greater strain on due process. The TRO is not to be issued unless the plaintiff shows irreparable injury will otherwise result and also "certifies to the court in writing the efforts, if any, which have been made to give the notice and the reasons supporting his claim that notice should not be required."[4] In some cases, this rule requires the plaintiff to give notice that he will apply for a TRO, so that the defendant may appear and oppose the order. But it also permits the court to dispense with notice in some cases,[5] so the TRO may be issued *ex parte.* Under this

§ 2.11(1)

1. See United States v. United Shoe Machinery Corp., 391 U.S. 244, 88 S.Ct. 1496, 20 L.Ed.2d 562 (1968).

2. See O. Fiss, The Civil Rights Injunction, 36 (1978); § 7.4(4) below.

3. Fed.R.Civ.Proc.Rule 65(a).

4. Rule 65(b) provides in part: "A temporary restraining order may be granted without written or oral notice to the adverse party or his attorney only if (1) it clearly appears from specific facts shown by affidavit or by the verified complaint that immediate and irreparable injury, loss, or damage will result to the applicant before the adverse party or his attorney can be heard in opposition, and (2) the applicant's attorney certifies to the court in writing the efforts, if any, which have been made to give the notice and the reasons supporting his claim that notice should not be

required." The order itself must "define the injury and state why it is irreparable and why the order was granted without notice".

5. The plaintiff normally wishes to avoid notice when notice would give the defendant an opportunity to take evasive action before the TRO is issued, for example, by hiding or conveying property. A good example is Chambers v. NASCO, Inc., ___ U.S. ___, 111 S.Ct. 2123, 115 L.Ed.2d 27 (1991). The plaintiff there was seeking specific performance of a contract to transfer a television station; it gave notice that it would seek a TRO to prevent the defendant's transfer of the property. Before the TRO could be issued, the defendant transferred the property. The plaintiff ultimately got the property, but only after extensive and costly litigation.

procedure, the defendant is not bound until he receives notice that the order has been issued, but he is put under its constraints without an initial opportunity to present facts or argue his side of the question.

Unless extended, the TRO must terminate within ten days. It must terminate sooner if the court dissolves it on the defendant's motion. It also terminates when the preliminary injunction hearing is held, at which time the judge may decide to withhold further provisional relief altogether or may substitute the preliminary injunction. The preliminary injunction hearing must be expedited.[6]

Other forms of provisional relief. Provisional relief is not uniquely injunctive or equitable. Courts give provisional relief before trial "at law" by way of attachment, garnishment, or replevin.[7] Some important security for a plaintiff can be obtained *ex parte* without any judicial process at all, as where the plaintiff files a *lis pendens* notice [8] or a notice of a mechanics' lien.[9]

Types of Cases

Provisional relief by way of preliminary injunctions or temporary restraining orders always turns on the facts of the individual case because the judge must estimate the irreparable harm at stake for both parties as well as their chance of success.[10] When the facts otherwise warrant, and the plaintiff establishes a substantive right, provisional relief can be appropriate in a wide variety of cases. The following paragraphs sketch some of the possible uses for such relief.

Tangible and intangible property. Preliminary injunctions or TROs issue to protect a variety of property interests. For example, such provisional relief may prevent defendants from cutting the plaintiff's timber,[11] or from carrying on political activities in the plaintiff's shopping center.[12] Even mandatory preliminary injunctions are sometimes issued to vindicate property rights.[13] Likewise, preliminary injunctions go in intellectual prop-

---

6. Rule 65(b) provides in part: "Every temporary restraining order granted without notice shall be endorsed with the date and hour of issuance; shall be filed forthwith in the clerk's office and entered of record * * * and shall expire by its terms within such time after entry, not to exceed 10 days, as the court fixes, unless within the time so fixed the order, for good cause shown, is extended for a like period or unless the party against whom the order is directed consents that it may be extended for a longer period. The reasons for the extension shall be entered of record. In case a temporary restraining order is granted without notice, the motion for a preliminary injunction shall be set down for hearing at the earliest possible time and takes precedence of all matters except older matters of the same character; and when the motion comes on for hearing the party who obtained the temporary restraining order shall proceed with the application for a preliminary injunction and, if he does not do so, the court shall dissolve the temporary restraining order. On 2 days' notice to the party who obtained the temporary restraining order without notice or on such

shorter notice to that party as the court may prescribe, the adverse party may appear and move its dissolution or modification and in that event the court shall proceed to hear and determine such motion as expeditiously as the ends of justice require."

7. See § 5.17 below.

8. See § 6.1(5).

9. See § 12.20(3).

10. These standards, and their various formulations, are considered in § 2.11(2) below.

11. Cameron v. Bartels, 214 Ill.App.3d 69, 157 Ill.Dec. 855, 573 N.E.2d 273 (1991). See § 5.5 below.

12. Fiesta Mall Venture v. Mecham Recall Committee, 159 Ariz. 371, 767 P.2d 719 (App. 1988). If the defendants have a protected right to be in the shopping center, then of course the injunction does not issue.

13. Doré v. Jefferson Guaranty Bank, 543 So.2d 560 (La.App.1989) (compelling defendant to remove trash deposited on the plaintiff's land).

erty cases, to protect against copyright,[14] patent [15] or trademark [16] infringement, or to prevent other misappropriation of creative materials,[17] or of trade secrets.[18] When the plaintiff claims an equitable interest in property or a fund of money, the court may also use the preliminary injunction to seize the property [19] or freeze the funds [20] until the trial can resolve the dispute.

Economic and contract rights. Preliminary relief is also granted to protect economic rights not based on property interests. Preliminary injunctions may issue to enforce contracts, for example, in effect providing preliminary specific performance,[21] or to protect a contractor's bidding rights in a contract with the city.[22] When non-competition covenants are valid, enforcement of such covenants by preliminary injunction is sometimes appropriate.[23] Preliminary injunction to protect job rights is unusual, but even that relief is occasionally granted.[24]

Constitutional, personal, and public rights. Provisional relief to protect constitutional and personal rights is often especially appropriate because such rights are often truly irreplaceable. So a preliminary injunction might issue, for example, to prohibit interference with the plaintiff's free speech rights in a public forum.[25] For similar reasons, a preliminary injunction may issue to require government agencies to meet statutory standards for the protection of children under their care.[26] Likewise, protestors who are

14. Salinger v. Random House, Inc., 811 F.2d 90 (2d Cir.1987), cert. denied, 484 U.S. 890, 108 S.Ct. 213, 98 L.Ed.2d 177 (1987). As to injunctions in copyright cases generally see § 6.3(5) below.

15. See Smith International, Inc. v. Hughes Tool Co., 718 F.2d 1573 (Fed.Cir.1983), cert. denied, 464 U.S. 996, 104 S.Ct. 493, 78 L.Ed.2d 687 (1983); see § 6.2(5) below as to injunctions in patent cases.

16. Processed Plastic Co. v. Warner Communications, Inc., 675 F.2d 852, 858 (7th Cir. 1982) (trademark infringement harm is irreparable by nature); as to injunctive remedies in trademark cases generally see § 6.4(5) below.

17. Cf. Estate of Presley v. Russen, 513 F.Supp. 1339 (D.N.J.1981) (Presley imitator enjoined preliminarily on unfair competition theory). As to remedies for misappropriation generally, see § 6.5(3) below.

18. E.g., Courtesy Temporary Service, Inc. v. Camacho, 222 Cal.App.3d 1278, 272 Cal. Rptr. 352 (1990). As to trade secret remedies generally see § 10.5(3) below.

19. Ferry–Morse Seed Co. v. Food Corn, Inc., 729 F.2d 589 (8th Cir.1984) (preliminary mandatory injunction requiring defendant to turn over 6000 bags of unique seed corn pursuant to a contract). See, as to this equitable replevin, § 5.17(3) below.

20. Silverman v. Blaustein, 369 So.2d 86 (Fla.App.1979). As to freezing bank accounts and other funds by preliminary injunction, see § 6.1(5) below.

21. E.g., Gold v. Ziff Communications Co., 196 Ill.App.3d 425, 142 Ill.Dec. 890, 553 N.E.2d 404 (1989) (mandatory preliminary injunction requiring defendant publisher to continue plaintiff's advertising). See § 12.8(1) below.

22. Cf. Glenwood Bridge, Inc. v. City of Minneapolis, 940 F.2d 367 (8th Cir.1991) (after contractor was low bidder, city rejected all bids out of concern about labor strikes and prepared for rebidding with a labor clause in the contract that probably was preempted by federal law; preliminary relief appropriate).

23. See Hamer Holding Group, Inc. v. Elmore, 202 Ill.App.3d 994, 148 Ill.Dec. 310, 560 N.E.2d 907 (1990) (reversing denial of preliminary injunction for determination of reasonableness issues). See § 12.22(2) as to remedies generally.

24. See generally § 6.10(4) below.

25. Paulsen v. County of Nassau, 925 F.2d 65 (2d Cir.1991) (Christian Joy Fellowship members attempting to give guidance to rock concert fans; only content neutral limitations can be imposed on public forum speech, and even minimal loss of First Amendment freedoms is irreparable injury).

26. Artist M. v. Johnson, 917 F.2d 980 (7th Cir.1990) (Illinois family service department required to act promptly to assign caseworkers to child after department intervenes for child's protection, irreparable harm threatened by "increased likelihood that families would be broken up or remain apart, that plaintiffs would be deprived of protective ser-

picketing at the plaintiff's residence might be enjoined to protect against the intrusion on privacy if the protestor's free speech rights can be fully respected by requiring them to protest at another location.[27] Sometimes the plaintiff obtains preliminary relief that protects public rights, as when the court protects environment rights by enjoining pollution.[28]

Error potential. The potential for abuse and error in injunctive orders is usually very large. To minimize this potential, courts and rules impose two special requirements before provisional injunctions go. First, the plaintiff must show a comparatively high level of net irreparable harm. Second, the plaintiff must post a bond or other security to guarantee payment to the defendant for harms he suffers if the injunction is erroneously issued. These two requirements are considered in the next two subsections.

§ 2.11(2) Standards for Issuance of Provisional Injunctive Orders
Standards

Main factors. To obtain a preliminary injunction the plaintiff must show special justifications. Bearing in mind the possibility that preliminary relief will prove to be erroneous when a full trial on the merits is held, courts have mainly been concerned with three factors: (1) irreparable harm the plaintiff may suffer if relief is denied; (2) irreparable harm the defendant or third parties will suffer if relief is granted; (3) the probability that the plaintiff will prevail on the merits.

The special irreparable harm requirement. The irreparable harm required in preliminary injunction cases differs from that required in permanent injunction cases.[1] In preliminary relief cases the irreparable harm requirement serves a special purpose; it provides a barrier against the easy use of public power without a trial. Even if irreparable harm (or the adequate-legal-remedy rule) is no longer so important in permanent injunction cases, it remains most significant in preliminary injunction cases. Consequently, facts that would show sufficient "irreparable harm" in a permanent injunction case may not suffice at the preliminary stage.[2]

Unstructured factors. Courts often provide an unstructured list of several factors bearing on the decision to grant or deny preliminary injunctions.[3] The lists often resemble that already given.[4] However, courts

vices", and that, in the absence of timely case plans and case reviews, children would be left in "unnecessarily restrictive placement"), rev'd on other grounds, __ U.S. __, 112 S.Ct. 1360, 118 L.Ed.2d 1 (1991).

27. Boffard v. Barnes, 248 N.J.Super. 501, 591 A.2d 699 (1991) (anti-abortion protestors, residential picketing enjoined, though not other picketing). In this and many other cases, the most significant question is the substantive question whether the defendants enjoy free speech rights.

28. People v. Mika Timber Co., Inc., 221 Ill.App.3d 192, 163 Ill.Dec. 741, 581 N.E.2d 895 (1991).

§ 2.11(2)

1. As to the irreparable harm or adequate-remedy-at-law rule for permanent injunction cases, see § 2.5 above.

2. See Laycock, The Death of the Irreparable Injury Rule 113 (1991) (also pointing out that the irreparable injury in issue at the provisional stage is only that which cannot be prevented by a later injunction after a more complete hearing, rather than one that which cannot be prevented by a remedy at law).

3. E.g., W.T. Grant Co. v. Srogi, 52 N.Y.2d 496, 438 N.Y.S.2d 761, 420 N.E.2d 953 (1981) ("(1) the likelihood of success on the merits; (2) irreparable injury absent granting the preliminary injunction; and (3) a balancing of the equities"); Solow v. Liebman, 175 A.D.2d 120, 572 N.Y.S.2d 19 (1991).

4. See footnote 4 on page 188.

commonly give no explanation how the several factors are to be weighed or how they work together. For example, suppose the plaintiff has only a so-so chance of success on the merits but is threatened with enormous irreparable harm and that the defendant will suffer very little such harm if the preliminary injunction is issued. The unstructured list invites the judge to exercise her conscience but it does not suggest any particular analysis or reasoning. In particular, the unstructured list does not suggest anything about the relative importance of the irreparable harm as compared to the plaintiff's chance of winning on the merits.

Structured factors. Other courts have tried to provide more structure and to recognize that even the plaintiff who is not very likely to prevail on the merits, may be faced with such irreparable loss that the preliminary injunction should go. The Second Circuit has repeatedly said that the plaintiff must show (1) irreparable harm and (2) *either* (a) "probable success on the merits," *or* (b) a balance of hardships "tipping decidedly" in the plaintiff's favor plus serious questions on the merits.[5] The "balance of hardships" seems to be about the equivalent of irreparable loss.

Imperfections. Although neither the list of factors nor the Second Circuit's structured formula seems to be perfectly complete, they can be read

4. One typical list, for example, tells the judge to consider

"1. Whether the movant has shown a strong or substantial likelihood or probability of success on the merits. 2. Whether the movant has shown irreparable injury. 3. Whether the preliminary injunction could harm third parties. 4. Whether the public interest would be served by issuing the preliminary injunction."

See Planned Parenthood Ass'n of Cincinnati, Inc. v. City of Cincinnati, 822 F.2d 1390 (6th Cir.1987); Friendship Materials, Inc. v. Michigan Brick, Inc., 679 F.2d 100 (6th Cir.1982) (similar); First–Citizens Bank & Trust Co. v. Camp, 432 F.2d 481 (4th Cir.1970) (similar); Adams County Election Com'n By and Through McMillian v. Sanders, 586 So.2d 829 (Miss.1991) (similar).

The list given in the first paragraph of this section is a version of the list just quoted. In the quoted list, the third and fourth factors could be grouped together because both are concerned with harm to third persons. They can also be expressed in terms parallel to those in the second factor, so that "harm" becomes irreparable harm, which is presumably what the courts mean. When put in uniform terminology, this list seems to say that irreparable harm to third persons is considered, but it omits to say that irreparable harm to the defendant himself is considered. Courts probably do not mean to say that, hence the list formulated in the text adds irreparable harm to the defendant.

5. See Triebwasser & Katz v. American Tel. & Tel. Co., 535 F.2d 1356 (2d Cir.1976); Consolidated Gold Fields PLC v. Minorco, 871

F.2d 252 (2d Cir.1989), modified by, 890 F.2d 569 (1989); Securities and Exchange Com'n v. Unifund SAL, 910 F.2d 1028 (2d Cir.1990).

The formula is murky, but fairly translated into common terminology it seems to mean that if the probability of the plaintiff's success on the merits is more-likely-than-not, that fact plus proof of irreparable harm will justify the injunction. If the plaintiff cannot show such a good probability of success but only shows "serious questions on the merits," then the plaintiff will have to show that her irreparable loss of rights will be greater than the defendant's. This formula does not seem as clear or as complete as Leubsdorf's; the defendant's irreparable loss of rights are important even when the plaintiff has a probability of success more likely than not, and the Second Circuit's formula seems not to consider that. But the formula surely aims at minimizing irretrievable loss from hasty decisions on preliminary injunction, even if it is less precise than Leubsdorf's.

Approving a preliminary injunction to prevent a merger, the court in *Consolidated Gold Fields,* supra, emphasized that the irreparable harm was so overwhelming that doubts were to be resolved *in favor* of the preliminary relief. "Were the merger to be consummated, the Minorco group will likely dominate the strategically important world gold market. Gold Fields and its associated entities would cease to be viable competitors in the market. Such a possibility alone suggests that 'doubts as to whether a [preliminary] injunction * * * is necessary to safeguard [the target group] * * * should be resolved in favor of granting the injunction.'"

as imperfect statements about similar goals. The statements are imperfect if they are read like statutes or Restatement black letter text. Read that way, the list of factors cannot be right because it tells the judge to consider the hardships or irreparable loss of rights that third persons would suffer if the preliminary injunction is issued erroneously; but it makes no similar provision for the person most likely to be affected, the defendant himself. A similar observation could be made about the first prong of the Second Circuit's formula.

It is most unlikely that courts intend to ignore the potential harm an erroneous injunction could cause to the defendant. In fact, courts have long considered the possibility that error at the preliminary stage could cause irreparable harm to *either* party and have long tried to take that risk of error into account in deciding whether an injunction should go before trial.[6]

So the gist of the standards is probably easy to understand in common sense terms even if the expression is imperfect: the judge should grant or deny preliminary relief with the possibility in mind that an error might cause irreparable loss to either party. Consequently the judge should attempt to estimate the magnitude of that loss on each side and also the risk of error.

The Leubsdorf rationale and reformulation. Professor John Leubsdorf, recognized that the standards stated by courts were diverse but they probably had similar goals. He suggested that the standard should operate to "minimize the probable irreparable loss of rights caused by errors incident to hasty decision."[7] He went on to show how that process would work, using the major traditional factors. The judge would estimate the irreparable loss that would result to each party if the preliminary injunction is either erroneously granted or erroneously denied. She would then estimate each party's chance of winning at the permanent injunction stage. The first estimate of irreparable loss would then be discounted to reflect each party's probability of success on the merits. If the plaintiff's discounted irreparable loss is greater than the defendant's, the preliminary injunction would go; otherwise not.

Example under the Leubsdorf formulation. Judges probably will be unable to put figures to many estimates, but figures can be used to illustrate the Leubsdorf formula. Suppose the plaintiff demonstrates that, without the injunction, she will suffer irreparable harm and that, although it is not the equivalent of damages, the irreparable harm can be roughly valued at $100,000.[8] The judge then estimates the plaintiff's chance of winning and

6. "In a doubtful case, where the granting of the injunction would, on the assumption that the defendant ultimately will prevail, cause greater detriment to him than would, on the contrary assumption, be suffered by the complainant through its refusal, the injunction usually should be denied." Harriman v. Northern Securities Co., 132 Fed. 464 (D.N.J. 1904), aff'd, 197 U.S. 244, 25 S.Ct. 493, 49 L.Ed. 739 (1905).

7. Leubsdorf, The Standard for Preliminary Injunctions, 91 Harv.L.Rev. 525 (1978).

8. By definition, irreparable harm cannot be measured in damages, but not all irreparable harm is equal. Some irreparable harm is very substantial and some not so substantial. It is useful to represent that harm in dollar figures, just as it is useful to represent pain and suffering in dollar figures. More to the point here, the numbers merely stand for *relative* amounts of irreparable harm suffered by plaintiff and defendant. If each party will suffer approximately the same amount of irreparable harm through an erroneous decision to issue or deny the injunction, that harm can

concludes that it is a fair chance but not overwhelming, say 60%. On those estimates, the judge would discount the plaintiff's irreparable harm to reflect the possibility that the plaintiff would lose on the merits at the permanent injunction stage. The plaintiff has a 60% chance of winning, so the irreparable harm would be worth about $60,000, not $100,000.

The judge would then consider irreparable harm that would be suffered by the defendant if a preliminary injunction were erroneously issued. Suppose she estimates the potential irreparable harm to the defendant to be $120,000. That estimate means the defendant's raw potential irreparable harm is greater than the plaintiff's. Yet the defendant's chance of success is only 40%. Discounting the defendant's irreparable harm to reflect his probable success, the judge multiplies $120,000 by the 40% figure. That calculation shows that the defendant's discounted irreparable harm is only $48,000.

The judge is now in position to compare the irreparable harm that would be suffered by each party if the judge's decision about preliminary relief proves to be erroneous when a full hearing is held at the permanent stage. The plaintiff's gross risk is smaller than the defendant's ($100,000 compared to $120,000); but when the irreparable losses are weighted to consider that the plaintiff will probably win, the plaintiff's risk is noticeably higher—$60,000 against $48,000. So on these estimates, the judge would grant the preliminary injunction.

Preliminary injunction when the plaintiff is unlikely to win. Under this system, the plaintiff might be given a preliminary injunction even if the judge thought the plaintiff had less than a 50% chance of winning on the merits. That is so because she might have enormous irreparable loss at stake while the defendant had almost none. In that case, the discounted irreparable harm for the plaintiff might still far exceed the discounted irreparable harm for the defendant. In fact, if all the losses for the defendant can be made up in damages, the defendant might be threatened with no irreparable loss at all, only money damages that would be fully recoverable in the event of error. In that case, the preliminary injunction should surely go if the plaintiff shows any significant degree of irreparable harm.

Many rules or standards work poorly at the fringe of their domain, and the Leubsdorf standard might be one of them. A judge might not want to accept the Leubsdorf standard for the plaintiff with a 1% chance of success [9] but could consistently apply it to plaintiffs with only a 30% or 40% chance.

Role of quantification. Leubsdorf's formula is easy to understand when examples are given and the estimates of probable success and risk of irreparable harm are reduced to numbers. Quantifying intangible values is

be represented by any number. $1 will do as well as $100,000 for the ultimate comparison. If the plaintiff will suffer twice as much harm as the defendant, the numbers could be $2 and $1, or equally $200,000 and $100,000. Because the purpose of assigning numbers is merely to illustrate that the net irreparable harm of one party is greater than that of the other, relative size is all we need to know.

9. An improbable calculation. The judge is not likely to believe that she can figure probabilities as closely as 1%, so the judge who thinks that the plaintiff's chances are that poor is more likely to come up with the estimate of zero.

not a scientific exercise, but lawyers routinely make settlements on the basis of their estimates about probable success; and juries quantify such unlikely intangibles as comparative negligence of plaintiffs and defendants. So the quantification suggested by the illustration is not in itself an unusual operation, provided it is understood to be an estimate and a mode of expression rather than a hard datum.

In any event, the formula does not depend on using actual numbers. It is a map for making mental judgments, many of which will necessarily be qualitative and rough rather than quantitative and precise. For instance, loss of a constitutional right is irreparable injury[10] but certainly one that cannot be readily reduced to a dollar amount.[11] The judge may be able to make no clearer estimate of the plaintiff's irreparable loss than to say it is likely to be "very substantial." Nevertheless, the Leubsdorf formula reveals the ultimate *kind* of estimate to be made. Sometimes judges may find it helpful to replace gross verbal estimates of irreparable harm with more precise figures; when they cannot do so, they may believe that the plaintiff has failed to satisfy the burden of proof. Even so, nothing in the formula's directives requires quantification. The object, after all, is to minimize irreparable harm, whether it is harm to defendants or harm to plaintiffs.

Judicial acceptance of the Leubsdorf standard. A number of cases now adopt the Leubsdorf formula, or one that seems practically indistinguishable,[12] in preference to the undifferentiated list of factors. For instance, the

---

10. E.g., Planned Parenthood Ass'n of Cincinnati, Inc. v. City of Cincinnati, 822 F.2d 1390 (6th Cir.1987).

11. Cf. Carey v. Piphus, 435 U.S. 247, 98 S.Ct. 1042, 55 L.Ed.2d 252 (1978) (nominal damages only for loss of due process right), discussed in § 7.4(2) below.

12. American Hospital Supply Corp. v. Hospital Products Ltd., 780 F.2d 589 (7th Cir. 1986); Friendship Materials, Inc. v. Michigan Brick, Inc., 679 F.2d 100 (6th Cir.1982); IT Corp. v. County of Imperial, 35 Cal.3d 63, 196 Cal.Rptr. 715, 672 P.2d 121 (1983) ("if it appears fairly clear that the plaintiff will prevail on the merits, a trial court might legitimately decide that an injunction should issue even though the plaintiff is unable to prevail in a balancing of the probable harms. On the other hand, the harm which the defendant might suffer if an injunction were issued may so outweigh that which the plaintiff might suffer in the absence of an injunction that the injunction should be denied even though the plaintiff appears likely to prevail on the merits"; the goal is "to minimize the harm which an erroneous interim decision may cause," citing Leubsdorf); American Academy of Pediatrics v. Van de Kamp, 214 Cal.App.3d 831, 263 Cal.Rptr. 46 (1989) ("In deciding whether to issue a preliminary injunction, a trial court must review two interrelated factors: ' "The first is the likelihood that the plaintiff will prevail on the merits at trial. The second is the interim harm that the plaintiff is likely to sustain if the injunction were denied as compared to the harm that the defendant is likely to suffer if the preliminary injunction were issued" ' "); Kanter & Eisenberg v. Madison Associates, 116 Ill.2d 506, 108 Ill.Dec. 476, 508 N.E.2d 1053 (1987) ("Certain threads, however, run through virtually all statements of the test: the possibility of irreparable harm to the plaintiff's legal rights pending the outcome of trial if the preliminary injunction does not issue, the potential irreparable harm to defendant's rights if it does, and the plaintiff's likelihood of success on the merits," the aim is to minimize risk of "choosing wrongly," citing Leubsdorf; Packaging Industries Group, Inc. v. Cheney, 380 Mass. 609, 405 N.E.2d 106 (1980) (judge is to evaluate "in combination the moving party's claim of injury and chance of success on the merits. If the judge is convinced that failure to issue the injunction would subject the moving party to a substantial risk of irreparable harm, the judge must then balance this risk against any similar risk of irreparable harm which granting the injunction would create for the opposing party. What matters as to each party is not the raw amount of irreparable harm the party might conceivably suffer, but rather the risk of such harm in light of the party's chance of success on the merits," citing Leubsdorf); cf. Williams v. Greene, 36 N.C.App. 80, 243 S.E.2d 156 (1978) ("The judge in exercising his discretion should engage in a balancing process, weighing potential harm to the plaintiff if the injunction is not issued against the potential harm to the defendant if injunctive relief is granted," citing Leubsdorf).

Sixth Circuit accepted at least a part of the Leubsdorf formula when it said that "the likelihood of success that need be shown * * * will vary inversely with the degree of injury the plaintiff will suffer absent an injunction." [13] The leading case is *American Hospital Supply v. Hospital Products Ltd.*[14] In that case Judge Posner adopted Leubsdorf's idea and put it in algebraic form, presumably to facilitate comparison with Learned Hand's famous formula for negligence adjudications.[15]

Critics and Evaluations

Critics. Some of the debate over Leubsdorf's formula centers on the question whether it changes anything and if so what. Leubsdorf himself thought his formula was similar in purpose to the traditional rules as they were variously stated. Leubsdorf gave those rules a rationale and a more precise form. Laycock, calling it a distillation,[16] seems to agree, although he emphasizes complexities of the judgments to be made in preliminary relief decisions.[17]

But some commentators have said the Leubsdorf formula changed things. Addressing the adoption of the Leubsdorf formula in *American Hospital,* Silberman suggested that the formula did indeed mark a change because the undifferentiated list of factors theretofore used in many decisions could be analyzed differently in different cases and with a variety of results.[18] That point may be well taken. Yet the difference in analysis of the same elements may only represent the confusion engendered by unstructured lists of factors that are given no particular weight and driven by no particular vision or rationale. Different treatment of similar factors can also represent the effects of equitable discretion; courts frequently invoke discretion in "equity" cases to avoid analysis.

Another writer claimed both that the Leubsdorf–Posner formula changed nothing and also that it changed everything.[19] The "changed

---

13. Friendship Materials, Inc. v. Michigan Brick, Inc., 679 F.2d 100 (6th Cir.1982) (quoting).

14. 780 F.2d 589 (7th Cir.1986).

15. The famous Hand formula appears in United States v. Carroll Towing Co., 159 F.2d 169 (2d Cir.1947). Judge Posner's English language explanation in *American Hospital* is clear and sharp, but some lawyers will find his formula hard to read. In his formula P stands for probability and H stands for irreparable harm, with subscripts to show which party's harm is referred to. The Posner formula is: "grant the preliminary injunction if but only if $P \times H_p > (1-P) \times H_d$ * * *." This formula achieves its elegance in part by using a single measurement of probability, the probability of the *plaintiff's* success instead of stating plaintiff's and defendant's probabilities separately. The probability that the *defendant* will succeed is equal to 100%, minus the probability that the plaintiff will succeed, or, as the formula has it, one minus P. It comes down to saying that if the plaintiff's probability of success is 60% (P in this formula), then the defendant's is 1 minus 60% or 40%.

16. Laycock, supra n. 2 at 119.

17. Laycock, supra n. 2 at 120–123. Laycock's discussion is straightforward, short, and to the point.

18. Silberman, Injunctions by the Numbers: Less than the Sum of Its Parts, 63 Chi–Kent L.Rev. 279, 283 (1987).

19. Mullenix, Burying (With Kindness) the Felicific Calculus of Civil Procedure, 40 Vand. L.Rev. 541, 547, 556 (1987) ("rewriting preliminary injunction law," an "effort to sever the preliminary injunction determination from its equitable roots," but at least as the formula is acted on in the cases, it adds only "an appearance of scientism * * * nothing has changed"). Laycock, supra n. 2, at 119 also points to these statements. The article rightly claims that the tough decisions under the formula lie in estimating probability and irreparable harm, but that is the same claim that John Leubsdorf himself made when he originally proposed the formula. It is not correct, however, that Leubsdorf or Posner proposed to require quantification.

nothing" version is probably closer to the truth. The change wrought by Leubsdorf's formula is not that it quantifies; judges have long and repeatedly sought to assess probabilities of success, as the list of factors shows; and they have also long tried to estimate and then to minimize the irretrievable loss of rights.[20]

Tune-up changes wrought by the Leubsdorf formula. Leubsdorf's formula, in its most immediate application, probably does change some of the traditional verbal formulas, but the change is a tune-up, not a trade-in. Even the tune-up is probably in line with what judges intend in most cases. The bare list of factors, however, is not so helpful as it might be, because the factors are presented with no particular weight, no particular order, and no clear set of estimates to be made.

One effect of the Leubsdorf approach is that it makes it clear why the plaintiff's probability of success is important: because that probability is part of estimating the net amount of irreparable harm resulting from error. It is the factor by which the plaintiff's irreparable harm is discounted. In the same way it makes it clear that the plaintiff with a less than 50% chance of success could still justly receive the chancellor's pre-trial assistance if it will prevent an enormous irreparable loss compared to a minimal loss for the defendant.

The second tune-up is that some traditional formulations overlooked the risk of irreparable harm to the defendant. Under one prong of the Second Circuit's formula, the plaintiff could have a preliminary injunction by showing irreparable harm plus a likelihood of success on the merits.[21] This statement taken literally does not direct the court to consider the defendant's risk of irreparable harm once the plaintiff proves a more than 50% chance of success. Leubsdorf's formula would serve to remind the judge that even if the plaintiff has a very good chance of success, a preliminary injunction cannot justly cause more harm than the good it can do. The formula provides a rational way of thinking about how to estimate that harm.

Significant change wrought by the Leubsdorf formula. The more significant change introduced by Leubsdorf's formula is not that it is "quantitative," which it is not. The significant change is that it gives us the basic requirements for adjudication: a rule that tells lawyers what arguments and proofs are relevant, a rule that helps judges decide by reminding them of the ultimate goal; a rule that permits the profession to evaluate the judge's decision because it can evaluate the judge's reasons. The judge's role in making choices and estimates is not changed but is given a rational purpose. Lawyers can make their own evaluation of a judge's decisions in a way that is impossible when a judge merely invokes discretion unconstrained by a rational process of analysis. What Leubsdorf's formula does is to bring adjudication back to its own best ideals.

What Counts as Irreparable Harm

Harm not preventable by permanent injunction and not compensable in damages. The irreparable harm to be estimated is not the entire harm a

---

20. See Harriman v. Northern Securities Co., supra n. 6.

21. See the formula set out in n. 5 supra.

plaintiff might suffer without preliminary relief. It is only the harm that could not be adequately compensated by damages, or averted by a decision on the merits at the permanent injunction stage, or limited by other available relief.[22]

Timber cutting example. Suppose the plaintiff believes she owns a certain disputed parcel of land and wishes to cut it over for timber. Defendant interferes with her access because defendant also claims ownership. If the plaintiff seeks access to the land by preliminary injunctive relief, she might be denied relief because courts are reluctant to decide title disputes on motions for preliminary injunction. If preliminary relief is potentially available, however, the plaintiff might show that she will incur substantial irreparable harm if no cutting is allowed. For example, she might need the cash flow that would be produced by lumbering operations in order to continue to finance her business, and might lose her business entirely if cash flow cannot be maintained.[23] On the other hand, if the preliminary relief is erroneously issued, the defendant will perhaps lose his entire forest, which he maintains for personal bird watching and hiking. Both kinds of losses are irreparable, because money payments later cannot satisfactory replace the values they represent.

Suppose, however, the defendant admits that he himself was going to spend a month thinning the forest, partly to produce funds and partly for the proper development of the forest itself. That means that one-month's cutting of this kind could be done by the plaintiff without producing any irreparable harm at all to the defendant. If the plaintiff cuts the timber the defendant himself would have cut, and it turns out that the defendant is the true owner of the land after all, the defendant can be made whole by payment of damages. So the losses to the defendant from the first month's cutting should not be considered irreparable at all and should not be included in the discounted estimate of the defendant's irreparable harm.

Timing of the final hearing as a factor. In the example above, the time of the final hearing is important, too. If the final hearing cannot be held for one-year, a lot of irreparable harm could accrue to the defendant as the plaintiff cut trees after the first month. On the other hand, if a final hearing can be scheduled two months from the preliminary injunction, the defendant faces an irreparable loss equal only to one-month's cutting and that is the loss to be estimated, not a two-month loss.

The museum example. In some situations the final hearing may prevent virtually *any* irreparable harm to the defendant. Suppose each of two museums claims to be the owner of a certain painting in the hands of the defendant or a stakeholder. The plaintiff museum seeks its recovery by way of preliminary injunction and needs it immediately because of an international exhibition to open next week.[24] The defendant museum, if it gets or retains possession, will keep the painting in storage for six months until its

---

22. See, considering a later election, when made available after federal administrative delays as other available relief, Adams County Election Com'n, By and Through McMillian v. Sanders, 586 So.2d 829 (Miss.1991).

23. If the plaintiff's cash flow problems are deemed remote from her claimed interest in the land, perhaps the harms accruing from disrupted cash flow should be excluded from consideration. See the paragraph "Remote irreparable harm" below.

24. See § 5.17(3) below.

new building is completed. If a final hearing can be held within the six month period and the plaintiff museum can be effectively prevented from transferring the painting to innocent purchasers, a temporary transfer to its possession can be effected with assurance that the defendant museum will get the painting back in time for the opening of its new building if it turns out that the defendant is indeed the owner.

Tailoring to avoid or limit irreparable harm. Whether the risk of irreparable harm can be completely avoided thus depends in part on the timing of the final hearing and the possibility of tailoring the preliminary relief. If the plaintiff museum has less reliable temperature and humidity controls or less reliable guards, the defendant museum will claim that even a temporary transfer of the painting to the plaintiff risks ultimate loss to both museums. If the court can draft a decree to minimize that risk, by requiring extra guards or an improved humidity control system as a condition to the relief, then that irreparable harm can be minimized.

Irreparable harm to public or third-party interests. Many people can be affected adversely by the decision to issue a preliminary injunction. A preliminary injunction that requires an automobile manufacturer or distributor to deliver a quota of cars to a dealer for resale may have the effect of depriving some other dealer of an appropriate allotment of cars.[25] A preliminary injunction that forces the defendant to accept the plaintiff's ad in the Yellow Pages even though the phone company excludes similar ads by others, might have a serious adverse effect on competition.[26] Some such damages to third persons or to the public interest will never be known to the trial judge or susceptible of estimation. Some might be excluded on the ground that third persons whose interests are not taken into account on the final hearing have no claim to be considered at the earlier preliminary injunction stage.[27]

Remote irreparable harm. Courts have usually said they would consider the interests of third persons and the public in determining whether to issue the permanent injunction.[28] If a court knows of legitimate interests of third persons, it would seem that *some* estimate of their potential irreparable harm should be made. The problem of remote irreparable harm is not that it is unlikely; it may be quite likely indeed. The problem is that we may doubt its legitimate connection with the plaintiff's rights. In such a case, perhaps the solution to the problem of remote irreparable harm is that it should be excluded from consideration, but not because it is harm to third persons. Courts deciding preliminary injunctions should give no weight to remote potential harm in the same way they give no weight to remote harm when they assess damages; the analogy is to the proximate cause rules.[29]

---

25. As in Leonard E. Warner, Inc. v. Nissan Motor Corp. in U.S.A., 66 N.C.App. 73, 311 S.E.2d 1 (1984).

26. See Triebwasser & Katz v. American Tel. & Tel. Co., 535 F.2d 1356 (2d Cir.1976) (telephone company rejected all ads by private detectives purporting to detect unwanted electronic surveillance because public would read the ads to mean the advertiser could provide illegal listening devices; a preliminary injunction favoring one plaintiff would leave that

detective agency with the only ad on point in the Yellow Pages).

27. This is Leubsdorf's argument. See Leubsdorf, The Standard for Preliminary Injunctions, 91 Harv.L.Rev. 525, 549 (1978).

28. E.g., Restatement Second of Torts § 936 (1977).

29. In specific performance cases a similar problem arises under the *Hadley v. Baxendale* rules and a similar suggestion is made about

Remote harm is thus excluded from the decision without regard to whether the irreparable harm is harm to the plaintiff, the defendant, or to third persons. Conversely, irreparable harm that results directly from loss of a right of one party should be considered in determining whether the preliminary injunction is to go.

§ 2.11(3) The Security Requirement [1]

General Rule

The standards for granting pre-trial injunctive relief discussed in the preceding subsection attempt to deal with the risk of irreparable harm resulting from decisions made without trial. The bond requirement discussed in this subsection mainly attempts to deal with the risk of *reparable* error—damages that may result to the defendant who has been erroneously enjoined before trial.

Bond required. Federal rule 65(c) and state counterparts rules and statutes [2] require the plaintiff who obtains provisional relief to post a bond or other security.[3] The bond guarantees the payment of damages and costs that may be suffered by the defendant if it turns out that the provisional injunction was erroneous and the defendant was "wrongfully enjoined." [4] The bond is usually limited so that the surety is not liable for more than the sum specified in the bond.

Under the federal rule and the rule applied in most states, the security requirement applies both to the temporary restraining order and the preliminary injunction.[5] The wording of rules and statutes usually appears to make a bond or other security mandatory, but courts sometimes claim the power to dispense with it, either as a matter of discretion or for some special reasons.[6] Most cases limit liability to the amount of the bond and exclude liability altogether if no bond is posted.[7]

their limits in specific performance cases in § 12.8(6) below.

§ 2.11(3)

1. See generally, Dobbs, Should Security Be Required as a Pre–Condition to Provisional Injunctive Relief?, 52 N.C.L.Rev. 1091, 1097–1099 (1974).; Note, Recovery for Wrongful Interlocutory Injunctions, 99 Harv.L.Rev. 828 (1986).

2. Virtually all states have statutes or court rules. Many replicate Rule 65(c) with some minor changes; others may derive from the New York Code of 1848 or may have been developed independently. Among statutes not based on Rule 65, see West's Ann.Cal.Civ.Code § 529; N.Y.–McKinney's Civ.Prac.L.Rule 6312. All statutes as they stood in 1974 are listed in Dobbs, Should Security Be Required as a Pre–Condition to Provisional Injunctive Relief?, 51 N.C.L.Rev. 1091, 1173–1174 (1974).

3. E.g., a certificate of deposit, as in Buddy Systems, Inc. v. Exer–Genie, Inc., 545 F.2d 1164 (9th Cir.1976). But Powell v. Home Run Inn, Inc., 202 Ill.App.3d 94, 147 Ill.Dec. 463,

559 N.E.2d 803 (1990) held that, under the Illinois statute, a bond could only mean a "bond," so that a deposit of irrevocable letters of credit would not suffice.

4. Rule 65(c), Federal Rules of Civil Procedure, provides:

> (c) *Security.* No restraining order or preliminary injunction shall issue except upon the giving of security by the applicant, in such sum as the court deems proper, for the payment of such costs and damages as may be incurred or suffered by any party who is found to have been wrongfully enjoined or restrained. No such security shall be required of the United States or of an officer or agency thereof.

5. California courts have held that the bond is not required for the temporary restraining order. See Wallace v. Miller, 140 Cal.App.3d 636, 189 Cal.Rptr. 637 (1983).

6. See segment *Discretion to Dispense with Bond or Refuse Claims against It,* below.

7. See Segment *Bond as Limit of Liability,* below.

Purposes. The main purpose of the bond requirement is to protect the defendant from *reparable* loss of rights due to a decision made before trial and without the usual development of evidence, cross examination, research, and arguments. Its secondary purpose is to assuage *irreparable* losses to the defendant so far as possible by money payments. The bond is needed for these purposes because ordinary rules do not make the plaintiff liable for the defendant's attorney fees or for collateral damages the defendant may suffer from litigation. The bond does not merely provide security for payment; it provides for compensation that otherwise is not available. A third purpose sometimes mentioned in the cases is that the bond serves to warn plaintiffs the price they may be compelled to pay if the injunction is wrongfully issued.[8]

The bond or other security is not a substitute for the high standards imposed to limit the grant of preliminary injunctions. Those standards attempt to minimize irreparable harm, while the bond requirement attempts to eliminate reparable harm or to provide reparations when, in spite of the high standards for preliminary relief, that relief proves to be erroneous and causes harm to the defendant. So it is not proper to reduce the standards because a bond can be given, or to reduce the bond because the standards have been met. The standards and the bond operate together.

Bond as Limit of Liability

Majority view: liability limited to amount of the bond. When the plaintiff procures a preliminary injunction but the defendant prevails at the permanent injunction stage or on appeal, the defendant is entitled to recover damages suffered as a result of losses erroneously imposed by the preliminary injunction.[9] The great majority of cases limit the damages recovery to the amount of the bond or other security.[10] Indeed, it is the bond or security that is liable, not the plaintiff himself. (Once the surety pays its obligation under the bond, it will have a claim over against the plaintiff, but the plaintiff is not directly liable to the erroneously enjoined defendant.) If for any reason the plaintiff has posted no bond, or if the trial judge has discharged it, then the defendant will recover no damages at all based on the preliminary injunction rule.[11] If a bond was provided as required by rule or

8. Instant Air Freight Co. v. C.F. Air Freight, Inc., 882 F.2d 797 (3d Cir.1989); Continuum Company v. Incepts, Inc., 873 F.2d 801 (5th Cir.1989).

9. As to damages see the segment *Damages Recoverable* below.

10. Instant Air Freight Co. v. C.F. Air Freight, Inc., 882 F.2d 797 (3d Cir.1989); First–Citizens Bank & Trust Co. v. Camp, 432 F.2d 481 (4th Cir.1970); Coyne–Delany Co., Inc. v. Capital Development Board of the State of Illinois, 717 F.2d 385 (7th Cir.1983); Adolph Coors Company v. A & S Wholesalers, Inc., 561 F.2d 807 (10th Cir.1977); Wallace v. Miller, 140 Cal.App.3d 636, 189 Cal.Rptr. 637 (1983); Parker Tampa Two, Inc. v. Somerset Development Corp., 544 So.2d 1018 (Fla.1989); Teel v. Hamilton–Wencham Regional Sch. Dist., 13 Mass.App.Ct. 345, 433 N.E.2d 907, 911 (1982); Tracy v. Capozzi, 98 Nev. 120, 642

P.2d 591, 30 A.L.R. 4th 266 (1982) (pointing out that the defendant may request a higher bond); Industrial Innovators, Inc. v. Myrick–White, Inc., 99 N.C.App. 42, 392 S.E.2d 425 (1990); DeSantis v. Wackenhut Corp., 793 S.W.2d 670, 686 (Tex.1990) ("The damages recoverable in an action on the injunction bond are, of course, limited to the amount of the bond;" see n. 12 below); see Dobbs, Should Security Be Required as a Pre–Condition to Provisional Injunctive Relief?, 51 N.C.L.Rev. 1091, 1122–1123 (1974).

11. Buddy Systems, Inc. v. Exer–Genie, Inc., 545 F.2d 1164 (9th Cir.1976) (trial judge discharged bond after granting permanent injunction; when appellate court reversed permanent injunction on legal issues, the defendant would have been entitled to claim against the bond if there had been one, but

statute, then the defendant can recover his damages, but only up to the amount provided by the bond.

Minority view: plaintiff is personally liable. A few courts have held that the plaintiff is personally liable and that the amount of the bond is not the limit of liability,[12] at least where the injunction is issued *ex parte* as a TRO rather than as a preliminary injunction.[13] In a Florida case, the plaintiff moved for a TRO and the court set a small bond of $1500. The defendant then moved for a hearing on the amount of the bond, but this was denied. After the *ex parte* temporary restraining order was dissolved, the defendant sought damages. The court held that because the defendant had never had an opportunity to be heard as to the bond's amount, a rule limiting liability to the amount of the bond would deny the defendant due process of law.[14] At the same time, the court recognized that in all other cases Florida law would limit liability to the bond. Whatever the personal liability of the plaintiff, the bond's limits reflect the limits of the surety's contractual liability.[15]

Expanding liability by a special undertaking. Although the plaintiff is not personally liable under the view adopted by the great majority of decisions, the judge might impose a different condition. The judge might, for instance, issue the preliminary injunction only on condition that the plaintiff accept personal liability. A Fifth Circuit case follows this procedure.[16] Where the plaintiff clearly has assets or income more than sufficient to pay predicted damages this solution is favorable to the defendant because it removes the limitation. If the plaintiff has a high probability of success on the merits, it is also favorable to the plaintiff, because it saves the cost of bonding. When very large sums of money are at issue, the savings may be

since it was discharged, the plaintiff had no claim at all).

12. Howard D. Johnson Company v. Parkside Development Corp., 169 Ind.App. 379, 348 N.E.2d 656, 663 (1976) ("Because of the purpose of the security and the unavoidable inexactitude by which it is fixed, no one, save the surety, should be bound by the amount thereof. If the damages are eventually ascertained to be less than the amount of the security given by the plaintiff, the defendant's recovery will be limited to the damages incurred. Accordingly, if the damages incurred by the defendant exceed the amount of the security, it is only logical that the defendant should be made whole again by recovery of the excess from the plaintiff"). Some older Texas cases are in this category, but in DeSantis v. Wackenhut Corp., 793 S.W.2d 670, 686 (Tex.1990) the court said "The damages recoverable in an action on the injunction bond are, of course, limited to the amount of the bond." Possibly this limit refers only to suits against the surety, but probably not because the court expressly analyzed all the claims possible, including malicious prosecution.

13. Smith v. Coronado Foothills Estates Homeowners Ass'n, Inc., 117 Ariz. 171, 571

P.2d 668 (1977) (possibly limiting liability above bond limits to temporary restraining order cases).

14. Seaescape, Ltd., Inc. v. Maximum Marketing Exposure, Inc., 568 So.2d 952 (Fla.App. 1990). A similar argument was rejected in Wallace v. Miller, 140 Cal.App.3d 636, 189 Cal.Rptr. 637 (1983).

15. See R.E.X., Inc. v. Trio Foods Enterprises, Inc., 183 W.Va. 217, 395 S.E.2d 217, 219 (1990) (bond language limits the surety's liability).

16. The Continuum Company v. Incepts, Inc., 873 F.2d 801 (5th Cir.1989). The court limited the bond to a relatively low level contingent upon the plaintiff's "filing an undertaking with this court that the amount of the bond will not limit the amount of damages for which it might be liable, should it be liable for any, as a result of a wrongful issuance of the injunction." The court went on to provide that "the parties are to meet within 48 hours after issuance of this order to attempt to agree jointly on the form of the undertaking," with further provisions in case agreement could not be reached.

significant.[17]

Alternative damages claims by the wronged defendant. Although the defendant is usually denied any damages in excess of the bond when the claim is based on the bond requirement, other money claims are possible. The most obvious is that the plaintiff, as losing party, is liable for the same costs as other losing parties. The plaintiff may also be liable in some cases for malicious prosecution or some similar tort, or for a Rule 11 violation.

Restitution claims by the wronged defendant. If the plaintiff gains something of value by reason of the erroneous provisional relief, the defendant has a restitutionary claim based on the amount the plaintiff gained. The restitution claim is not a damages claim, not based on the bonding requirement, and not limited to the amount of the bond.[18] For example, suppose a regulatory agency orders a public utility to lower its rates. The utility obtains a preliminary injunction to prohibit enforcement of the order and thus continues to charge higher rates. At the permanent injunction stage, however, the preliminary injunction is dissolved. The utility has gained payments at the higher rates and must disgorge them on restitutionary grounds, whether or not it has posted a bond and whether or not the bond is less than the amounts the utility has received.[19]

The same principle would apply to allow the defendant to recover restitution of the plaintiff's gains without regard to bond limits if the preliminary injunction required the defendant to pay royalties to the plaintiff as a patent owner and it turned out at the full trial that the patent was invalid.[20] Courts sometimes say, however, that they have discretion to permit the plaintiff to keep the gains from the wrongful injunction.[21]

Discretion to Dispense with Bond or Refuse Claims against It

Mandatory bond. The Federal Rule seems to be mandatory on its face. It provides that "No restraining order or preliminary injunction shall issue except upon the giving of security by the applicant * * *." Many state statutes are in the same form and some which are not appear to be even more emphatic in requiring a bond. For instance, California's general statute provides that the "judge *must* require an undertaking on the part of the applicant"[22] and goes on to specify permissible exceptions. In addition,

17. The costs of bonding explain why bonds themselves are not unlimited. Bonds in unlimited sums might obtain protection for the defendant, but it would be difficult or impossible to figure a sound basis for a premium, so the unlimited bond is likely to result from error, not planning. That seems in fact to have happened in R.E.X., Inc. v. Trio Foods Enterprises, Inc., 183 W.Va. 217, 395 S.E.2d 217, 219 (1990) (although surety apparently intended to provide an injunction bond, the language made it liable for all sums due on the merits, liability enforced).

18. See Dobbs, Should Security Be Required as a Pre–Condition to Provisional Injunctive Relief?, 51 N.C.L.Rev. 1091, 1136–1143 (1974); Restatement of Restitution § 74 (1937).

19. E.g., Middlewest Motor Freight Bureau v. United States, 433 F.2d 212 (8th Cir.1970).

20. Cf. Hartford–Empire Co. v. Shawkee Mfg. Co., 163 F.2d 474 (3d Cir.1947).

21. Teel v. Hamilton–Wencham Regional Sch. Dist., 13 Mass.App.Ct. 345, 433 N.E.2d 907 (1982) (school district required to keep children in school by preliminary injunction which proved erroneous, as a matter of discretion district can be denied recovery of tuition).

22. West's Ann.Cal.Code Civ.Proc. § 529 (emphasis added). New York's statute provides that "Except as provided in section 2512, prior to the granting of a preliminary injunction, the plaintiff shall give an undertaking * * *." N.Y.–McKinney's Civ.Prac.L. & R. 6312. Provision for statutory exceptions suggests a scheme that does not rely upon judicial discretion to carve out ad hoc exceptions.

some Justices of the Supreme Court have expressed the view that in some other cases of provisional remedies, a bond may be constitutionally required.[23] Not surprisingly, courts often treat the bond requirement as mandatory, at least to the extent of reversing orders when no bond is provided.[24] Courts in a few states go further, saying that the injunctive order is void if issued without a bond.[25]

Discretionary bond under state statutes. In some states, however, the statutes plainly call for the judge's discretion, or at least for the judge's decision, on the basis of facts in the individual case. Connecticut's statute, for example, seems to mandate a bond, but in a proviso adds that "a bond need not be required when, for good cause shown, the court or a judge is of the opinion that a temporary injunction ought to issue without bond." [26] The Illinois statute explicitly provides that the court "may" require a bond, but that it is a matter of the court's "discretion." [27]

Four stages or points for the exercise of discretion. The bond requirement or its purposes can be devalued by discretionary rulings at four stages of the proceeding. First, the court might refuse or omit to require a bond. Second, the court might set the amount of the bond so low that it will not protect against the defendant's potential loss. Third, the court may discharge the bond or surety at some later stage but before the defendant can recover on it. Fourth, the court may refuse to assess damages against the bond once the defendant has prevailed, or may artificially limit the damages recovery.

If the judge has any discretion on these matters, the facts that influence that discretion might differ depending on whether the judge is asked to dispense with the bond or whether the judge is merely asked to limit the damages claim against it. However, the same concern to effectuate the protection provided by the bond belongs to each of these stages. A decision to require a bond but deny damages undermines the protection just as much

23. See Connecticut v. Doehr, ___ U.S. ___, 111 S.Ct. 2105, 115 L.Ed.2d 1 (1991). Justice White, joined by Justices Marshall, Stevens, and O'Connor favored a bond requirement. The case involved a pre-trial attachment, not preliminary injunction, but the risks appear to be similar, at least when an injunction is used to affect property. Justice White stated:

Without a bond, at the time of attachment, the danger that these property rights may be wrongfully deprived remains unacceptably high even with such safeguards as a hearing or exigency requirement * * *. A defendant's property rights remain at undue risk even when there has been an adversarial hearing to determine the plaintiff's likelihood of recovery * * * neither a hearing nor an extraordinary circumstance limitation eliminates the need for a bond, no more than a bond allows waiver of these other protections. To reconcile the interests of the defendant and the plaintiff accurately, due process generally requires all of the above.

24. E.g., System Operations, Inc. v. Scientific Games Development Corp., 555 F.2d 1131

(3d Cir.1977) (at least where monetary loss to the defendant is threatened, "a district court commits reversible error when it fails to require the posting of a security bond by the successful applicant for a preliminary injunction"); Cutler Creek Village Townhouse Ass'n, Inc. v. Cutler Creek Village Condominium Ass'n, Inc., 584 So.2d 103 (Fla.App.1991); Carter v. Konstantatos, 156 A.D.2d 632, 549 N.Y.S.2d 131 (1989). See Dobbs, Should Security Be Required as a Pre–Condition to Provisional Injunctive Relief?, 51 N.C.L.Rev. 1091, 1096 1099 (1974).

25. Eichelberger v. Hayton, 814 S.W.2d 179 (Tex.App.1991) ("failure of the applicant to file such a bond renders the injunction void ab initio"); see Lawrence County v. Brenner, 135 Pa.Cmwlth. 619, 582 A.2d 79 (1990) ("Failure to post a bond * * * nullifies both the injunction and any disposition in the pending matter").

26. Conn.Gen.Stat.Ann. § 52–472.

27. Ill.—S.H.A. ch. 110 ¶ 11–103.

as a decision to dispense with the bond in the first place; a decision that undervalues the defendant's rights by setting the bond too low does the same. So for some purposes each of these decisions can be treated as raising the same issues of policy and statutory construction.[28]

Open-ended discretion. Some authority permits trial judges, as a matter of open-ended equitable discretion, to eliminate the bond in the first instance,[29] or to refuse to enforce the defendant's damages claim against it.[30] Sometimes this approach is taken on the theory that the judge could accomplish virtually the same result by setting a bond with a low limit and so must be permitted to ignore the bond requirement altogether.[31] The implicit predicate of that argument is that the judge is free to set the bond at a limit less than the good faith predicted damages that will be suffered by the defendant if the order is erroneous. While the judge is free to set the amount of the bond equal to the best estimate or judgment about probable damages, nothing in the rule suggests that the judge is free to require less than a fairly estimated sum. If this is correct, then the argument for open-ended discretion to dispense with the bond fails.

A second line of support for discretion to dispense with the bond purports to estimate the probable loss to the defendant and to reject the bond requirement when that loss appears to be small and the plaintiff would be unable to obtain critical relief if a bond were required.[32] But the bond is required for the very reason that estimates about hardship and irreparable loss before trial are notoriously unreliable.[33] To dispense with the bond

28. Possibly a judge could justify dispensing with the bond in the first instance, or limiting its amount, but would not be justified in refusing to award damages under a bond that was actually posted. See Note, Recovery for Wrongful Interlocutory Injunctions, 99 Harv.L.Rev. 828 (1986). Contrariwise, the decision not to grant damages against the bond because the plaintiff was right to begin with and only lost because of intervening change in law is a decision that could not have been made at the time the initial order was issued but one that might properly be made after the merits have been decided. However, the principles of discretion, if any, otherwise appear to be similar.

29. Continental Oil Co. v. Frontier Refining Co., 338 F.2d 780 (10th Cir.1964) ("Under this rule the trial judge has wide discretion in the matter of requiring security and if there is an absence of proof showing a likelihood of harm, certainly no bond is necessary"). Note that this reasoning puts the burden on the defendant to justify a bond, even though the rule appears in the first instance to require it. As to this shift of burdens, compare Page Communications Engineers, Inc. v. Froehlke, 475 F.2d 994 (D.C.Cir.1973) where the court excused the plaintiff from liability on the bond because the *defendant* had not produced evidence on the merits at the preliminary injunction hearing.

30. Page Communications Engineers, Inc. v. Froehlke, 475 F.2d 994 (D.C.Cir.1973) ("Al-

though rule 65(c) required a bond here, it does not follow that the district court was bound to award damages on the bond, without considering the equities of the case * * * the court * * * was exercising its equity powers, and was bound to effect justice between the parties"; major factor, semble, was the plaintiff's good faith); H & R Block, Inc. v. McCaslin, 541 F.2d 1098 (5th Cir.1976). Both cases inappropriately relied on Russell v. Farley, 105 U.S. (15 Otto) 433, 26 L.Ed. 1060 (1884), which dealt with discretion in the absence of a statute or rule like Rule 65(c).

31. See Dobbs, Should Security Be Required as a Pre–Condition to Provisional Injunctive Relief?, 51 N.C.L.Rev. 1091, 1099–1102 (1974).

32. Temple University v. White, 941 F.2d 201 (3d Cir.1991); cf. Crowley v. Local No. 82, Furniture and Piano Moving, Etc., 679 F.2d 978 (1st Cir.1982), rev'd on other grounds, 467 U.S. 526, 104 S.Ct. 2557, 81 L.Ed.2d 457 (1984).

33. See Connecticut v. Doehr, ___ U.S. ___, 111 S.Ct. 2105, 115 L.Ed.2d 1 (1991) ("At best, a court's initial assessment of each party's case cannot produce more than an educated prediction as to who will win. This is especially true when, as here, the nature of the claim makes any accurate prediction elusive") (Justice White for four members of the Court).

because the judge makes such an estimate without trial is to undermine the central purpose of the bond.[34]

A third line of reasoning is that the court may dispense with the bond at least in those cases in which the plaintiff is solvent and could pay damages. But in most courts, the bond is not merely security; it *is* the liability. Without the bond the plaintiff is not liable for damages at all. So the plaintiff's solvency and ability to pay damages is wholly irrelevant to the need for the bond unless the court is willing to overrule the general rule or to make the plaintiff his own surety. Recent decisions and writers have recognized the flaw just described.[35]

Limited discretion. Most cases seem to treat the bond as the norm; they begin from the position that a bond is required and that damages are to be assessed against it when the plaintiff ultimately loses on the merits. At the same time, a bond is not invariably required. In this approach, the trial judge has only a limited discretion to dispense with the bond in the first place or limit damages under it in the second. The discretion must be based upon a specific reason that can be stated objectively and that is consistent with the policy that requires a bond in the first place.[36]

For example, if the plaintiff had a good claim for relief when suit was brought but the plaintiff ultimately lost because of an intervening change in governing law, the court might properly limit the award of damages on the bond.[37] On the other hand, the fact that the plaintiff sued in good faith, or that some general balance of equities or hardships produces sympathy for the plaintiff is not enough. A corollary to this view would seem to be that the amount of the bond should be set in the first place at a figure that fairly estimates the defendant's probable damages, or possibly a figure that fairly estimates the upper limit of those damages.[38]

Triggering the Bond Liability

Liability upon the bond is appropriate when the provisional injunction has deprived the defendant of rights to which he was entitled. The injunction was wrongful at least when it is later authoritatively determined that it was erroneous and deprived the defendant of rights to which the defendant was otherwise entitled. It need not be wrongful in the sense that the

34. Distinguish a discretionary decision to dispense with the bond from a judgment that the defendant has no probable damages. See n. 50 below.

35. The Continuum Company v. Incepts, Inc., 873 F.2d 801 (5th Cir.1989); Note, Recovery for Wrongful Interlocutory Injunctions, 99 Harv.L.Rev. 828 (1986).

36. See Coyne–Delany Co., Inc. v. Capital Development Board of the State of Illinois, 717 F.2d 385 (7th Cir.1983) (damages ordinarily must be awarded against bond in absence of special reason to deny them, such as change in the law); State of Alabama ex rel. Siegelman v. United States Environmental Protection Agency, 925 F.2d 385 (11th Cir.1991) (error to discharge the bond; same good reasons as required to refuse damages under the bond); cf. System Operations, Inc. v. Scientific Games

Development Corp., 555 F.2d 1131 (3d Cir. 1977) (where monetary loss threatened, bond is required; "We do not decide whether a court may dispense with the posting of a bond in a case where the injunction raises no risk of monetary harm to the defendant").

37. Coyne–Delany Co., Inc. v. Capital Development Board of the State of Illinois, 717 F.2d 385 (7th Cir.1983).

38. See Eide v. Bierbaum, 472 N.W.2d 193 (Minn.App.1991) ("the trial court should attempt to determine the damages likely to accrue as a result of an erroneous injunction"); Note, Recovery for Wrongful Interlocutory Injunctions, 99 Harv.L.Rev. 828 (1986). If the point is to make a fair estimate of damages, judgment may be called for but not "discretion."

plaintiff was acting tortiously.[39] The determination on the merits may be a determination made by the trial judge at a later stage (such as the permanent injunction stage), or by the court on appeal. It may also be a determination made in some other tribunal with authority to decide, as where arbitrators properly decide the ultimate merits so that their determination triggers liability on the bond.[40]

Sometimes courts have found the injunction "wrongful" for reasons that do not go to the merits, as where the court had no jurisdiction over it. Although some such decisions have been criticized,[41] it does not necessarily seem wrong to expect the plaintiff to pay for harms done in selecting the wrong court.[42] The defendant has an especially strong case for claiming against the bond when the plaintiff voluntarily dismisses the case before the merits can be determined.

One small but nettlesome problem arises when the plaintiff prevails on the merits but only in part. As with claims for attorneys' fees by a prevailing party,[43] it may be difficult to feel confident about which party, if either, won the case. If the plaintiff lost in part, (as where the permanent injunction is much narrower than the preliminary injunction), then it may be possible to assess damages against the bond to the extent that harm was caused by the excessive force of the preliminary order.[44] If the bond statute does not require otherwise, this may be a situation in which the court would be justified in using discretion to deny relief otherwise due.[45] Massachusetts came up with a similar view, refusing to allow the defendant to claim damages against the bond for a preliminary injunction that was too broad, but allowing it to offset such damages against its own money liabilities to the plaintiff.[46] Possibly a court would simply treat the defendant who won in part as if he were a total victor and allow full damages.[47] The cases suggest a wide range of possible solutions, but no real rationale.

Damages Recoverable

Courts sometimes speak of assessing damages by an "equitable" standard, presumably meaning that they might in their discretion fix an award that is not actually an estimate of the defendant's losses.[48] However, courts actually appear to measure damages by the usual rules or approaches of

39. Blumenthal v. Merrill Lynch, Pierce, Fenner & Smith, Inc., 910 F.2d 1049 (2d Cir. 1990) ("A party has been "wrongfully enjoined" under Fed.R.Civ.P. Rule 65(c) if it is ultimately found that the enjoined party had at all times the right to do the enjoined act"); Parker Tampa Two, Inc. v. Somerset Development Corp., 544 So.2d 1018 (Fla.1989).

40. Blumenthal v. Merrill Lynch, Pierce, Fenner & Smith, Inc., 910 F.2d 1049 (2d Cir. 1990); Industrial Innovators, Inc. v. Myrick-White, Inc., 99 N.C.App. 42, 392 S.E.2d 425 (1990).

41. See Note, Recovery for Wrongful Interlocutory Injunctions, 99 Harv.L.Rev. 828 (1986).

42. See Quick, The Triggering of Liability on Injunction Bonds, 52 N.C.L.Rev. 1252, 1267 (1974).

43. See § 3.10 below.

44. Davis v. Champion Fibre Co., 175 N.C. 25, 94 S.E. 671 (1917); Clem v. Hunz, 132 Wash. 14, 231 P. 7 (1924); Annotation, 40 A.L.R. 987 (1926).

45. See Russell v. Farley, 105 U.S. (15 Otto) 433, 26 L.Ed. 1060 (1884) (suggesting so before the advent of Rule 65).

46. All Stainless, Inc. v. Colby, 364 Mass. 773, 308 N.E.2d 481 (1974).

47. See Blumenthal v. Merrill Lynch, Pierce, Fenner & Smith, Inc., 910 F.2d 1049 (2d Cir.1990).

48. E.g., State ex rel. Shatzer v. Freeport Coal Co., 145 W.Va. 343, 115 S.E.2d 164 (1960).

damages law. For instance, consequential damages must be proven with reasonable certainty, must be "proximate" results of the provisional relief, and must be reduced to the extent that the defendant fails to minimize.[49]

A major problem is assessing causation. The bond's liability is only for damages caused by the preliminary injunction or TRO. The bond is not liable for losses resulting from prosecution of the permanent injunction or for losses resulting from the defendant's voluntary and uncompelled choices,[50] nor, presumably, from the defendant's compliance with law.[51]

Attorney fees incurred in defending the motions for preliminary injunction or TRO, and those incurred in seeking to dissolve those orders or to obtain a higher bond, are recoverable in most states.[52] Arguably you could go further and say that if the preliminary injunction should have been dissolved, the defendant should recover fees incurred in the main action as well because he could have avoided these costs had the trial judge ruled correctly at the preliminary stage.[53] On the other hand, the plaintiff could have brought a permanent injunction suit without posting bond, so perhaps it is right to deny the defendant the fees he would have suffered in defending that suit.

An old decision of the Supreme Court in *Oelrichs v. Williams,*[54] decided before the adoption of Rule 65, denied any recovery for attorney's fees under the bond. The decision also influenced some state courts. On the surface, the *Oelrichs* rule would seem to have little intelligible application today. The *Oelrichs* rule applied in a regime that did not require a bond and one that did not recognize a distinction between provisional relief on the one hand and permanent injunctions on the other. A rule that denies attorney fees against a plaintiff who had posted no bond at all, or against one who merely sued for a permanent injunction and lost, does not seem to address the very different case in which the plaintiff is required to post a bond or the case in which the plaintiff obtains provisional relief without a trial. Nevertheless, some federal courts have carried *Oelrichs* over to deny attorney fee claims against the bond required in TRO and preliminary injunction cases.[55]

---

49. See generally Dobbs, Should Security Be Required as a Pre–Condition to Provisional Injunctive Relief?, 51 N.C.L.Rev. 1091, 1125–1133 (1974).

50. Suppose the defendant assures the court it has no intention of selling disputed antiques until ownership issues are resolved. In such a case, a preliminary injunction against selling the antiques threatens the defendant with no damages it would not suffer by its own decision. Republic of Lebanon v. Sotheby's, 167 A.D.2d 142, 561 N.Y.S.2d 566 (1990) (reducing bond from $14 million to $1 million); cf. DeSantis v. Wackenhut Corp., 793 S.W.2d 670, 686 (Tex.1990) ("Nor can he recover for having been prohibited from doing something which he agreed not to do * * *.").

51. Thus injunctions against violence and harassment by a spouse in the process of divorce may be exempted from the bond requirement; no legally cognizable damages could be found from the fact that a violent spouse is not allowed to beat the other spouse.

52. E.g., Saunders v. Sharp, 793 P.2d 927 (Utah App.1990) (accepting estimate that 4% of total fees in suit was the percentage attributable to defending the preliminary injunction); see Dobbs, Should Security Be Required as a Pre–Condition to Provisional Injunctive Relief?, 51 N.C.L.Rev. 1091, 1133 (1974); Annotation, 164 A.L.R. 1088 (1946).

53. See Youngs v. McDonald, 56 A.D. 14, 67 N.Y.S. 375, 378 (1900).

54. 82 U.S. (15 Wall.) 211, 21 L.Ed. 43 (1872).

55. See e.g., International Ladies' Garment Workers' Union v. Donnelly Garment Co., 147 F.2d 246 (8th Cir.1945); Dobbs, Should Security Be Required as a Pre–Condition to Provisional Injunctive Relief?, 51 N.C.L.Rev. 1091, 1135 (1974).

Comments on the Bond Requirement

Injunction bond cases raise many problems, not the least of which is the fact that judges often underestimate the potential harm to a defendant. This comment, however, only addresses two structural problems that suggest the need for a more comprehensive statutory scheme.

A bond requirement usually adds to the plaintiff's cost of litigating. Usually the plaintiff pays a premium (annually) for a commercial bond. Alternatives may be cheaper. The court may permit some other form of security; the plaintiff might be permitted to file a certificate of deposit with the clerk, so that if the plaintiff wins, all interest payable on the certificate will accrue to the plaintiff. Or the plaintiff might obtain a non-commercial bond, persuading friends to stand as surety.

Even these cheaper forms of providing security, however, cost something. Time to make such special arrangements may not be available to one who seeks a preliminary injunction. Those who do not have the funds to risk and those who do not have even the premium funds, may be excluded from access to courts by the bond requirement. Even those who have funds may be deterred from resort to court. So the decision to preserve the defendant's fair-trial/due process rights by a bond requirement has at least a degree of cost attached.

In addition, some of the potential plaintiffs who are short on funds are likely to be sympathetic; even more, they may at times represent important public interests, suing to enforce rights which, if vindicated, will aid many people or protect the environment from irreparable harm.[56]

When costs threaten to prevent litigation in the public interest, some courts have thought that the bond requirements should be meliorated.[57] But we do not know before trial that the plaintiff will vindicate public interest; the defendant might be innocent and victimized. Even if we think provisionally that the plaintiff is acting in the public interest to resolve an issue by litigation, it does not follow that the private defendant should pay for the public's chance. The public interest should be paid for by the public treasury, until we can determine that the defendant really was rightfully enjoined. So a more just solution to the defendants who prove in the end to be victims rather than wrongdoers is to invest public funds in a bond or other security, then to demand that those funds be repaid by defendants who are proven to be wrongdoers.

Public interest comes into bonding rules in another way, too. Public entities are often exempted from the bond requirement. Perhaps the exemption resulted because legislatures assumed that the public entity would be solvent and would pay damages it did to an innocent citizen by obtaining unjustified preliminary relief. But this is not the law in the federal system or in most states. Instead, recovery is allowed only against any security that is filed. Public entities, which are forbidden to take property without payment, should not be permitted to take other rights without a trial.

---

56. See Henson & Gray, Injunction Bonding in Environmental Litigation, 19 Santa Clara L.Rev. 541 (1979).

57. Crowley v. Local No. 82, Furniture and Piano Moving, Etc., 679 F.2d 978 (1st Cir. 1982), rev'd on other grounds, 467 U.S. 526, 104 S.Ct. 2557, 81 L.Ed.2d 457 (1984).

§ 2.11(4) Judicial Review of Injunctions

Appeals of Injunctive Orders

Under the collateral bar rule,[1] one must obey an injunction or risk liability for contempt; even if the injunction is reversed on appeal, it is ordinarily binding until that reversal actually occurs. The mere act of appeal does not suspend the injunction. For these reasons, the defendant who intends to seek review may seek that review immediately; alternatively, he may ask the trial judge or an appellate judge to stay the injunction pending appeal.

[*For discussion of stays, see this section in the Practitioner Treatise edition.*]

Chapter 3

PRINCIPLES OF DAMAGES

Analysis

Sec.
3.1 Introducing Damages Law: Terms, Goals and Methods.
3.2 Summarizing Damages Rules.
3.3 Basic Damages Measures or Approaches.
    3.3(1) Measures and Elements of Damages.
    3.3(2) Nominal Damages and Standardized Surrogate Damages.
    3.3(3) General Damages or Market Measures.
    3.3(4) Consequential Damages.
    3.3(5) Substitution Costs.
    3.3(6) Individuating Damages: Protecting the Plaintiff's Personal Values.
    3.3(7) Duplication of Damages.
    3.3(8) The Relative Accuracy of Damages Measures: A Comment.
3.4 Proving Consequential Damages: Special Requirements, Limited Alternatives.
3.5 Constructing Market Value: Definitions and Evidence.
3.6 Interest Adjustments.
    3.6(1) Interest and Prejudgment Interest.
    3.6(2) Sidestepping the Traditional Limitations.
    3.6(3) Attacking the Traditional Limitations.
    3.6(4) Computation of Interest.
    3.6(5) Other Limitations on Prejudgment Interest.
    3.6(6) Judgment Interest.
3.7 Damages and Variations in Dollar Value.
3.8 Benefits to the Plaintiff From the Defendant's Acts.
    3.8(1) Collateral Source Benefits.
    3.8(2) Direct Benefits.
3.9 Minimizing Damages: Avoidable Consequences Rules.
3.10 Recovery of Attorney Fees and Costs in Litigation.
    3.10(1) General Rule and Summary.
    3.10(2) The Common Fund, Substantial Benefit and Private Attorney General.
    3.10(3) Attorney Fees as Damages and Sanctions.
    3.10(4) Development of the Civil Rights Fee Statutes.
    3.10(5) Eligibility and Entitlement Generally.
    3.10(6) Eligibility and Entitlement: Prevailing Party Rules.
    3.10(7) Fee Measurement: In Summary.
    3.10(8) Fee Measurement: Basic Methods.
    3.10(9) Fee Measurement: Reduction for Partial Success.
    3.10(10) Fee Measurement: Enhancement and Multipliers.
    3.10(11) Fee Measurement: Effect of Client's Fee Contract.
3.11 Punitive Damages.
    3.11(1) Punitive Damages Allowable.
    3.11(2) Bases of the Traditional Punitive Damages Award.

Sec.

3.11(3) Deterrence and Other Purposes of Punitive Damages.
3.11(4) Proof Standards.
3.11(5) Financial Condition of Defendant.
3.11(6) Vicarious Liability for Punitive Damages.
3.11(7) Punitive Liabilities of Insurers for Wrongs of Insureds.
3.11(8) Multiple Punitive Liability.
3.11(9) Scope of Punitive Liability: Causation and Persons and Injuries Outside the Risk.
3.11(10) The Actual Damages Requirement.
3.11(11) The Ratio Rule.
3.11(12) Constitutional and Statutory Challenges to Punitive Damages.
3.11(13) Adjustments and Computations.
3.11(14) Factors in Fixing the Amount of Punitive Damages.
3.11(15) The Debate Over Punitive Damages.
3.12 Multiplied Damages.

§ 3.1 Introducing Damages Law: Terms, Goals and Methods

Terminology and Concepts

Money award and in rem enforcement. The damages[1] remedy is a judicial award in money, payable as compensation to one who has suffered a legally recognized injury or harm. The damages remedy is not conditional,[2] and it is not payable periodically as loss accrues unless a statute so provides.[3] So the damages award is traditionally made once, in a lump sum to compensate for all the relevant injuries, past and future.[4]

The damages award is not the only money award courts make.[5] Courts may also award restitution in money; they may also order money payments in the exercise of "equity" powers. Damages differs from restitution in that damages is measured by the plaintiff's loss; restitution is measured by the defendant's unjust gain.[6] Traditional damages awards differ from some "equitable" money awards in that the damages award is enforced where need be by seizure of the defendant's property, a sale of that property, and

§ 3.1

1. The term *damages* is frequently used where a singular form might be expected. We say the judgment is for *damages* and the remedy is the *damages* remedy. In contrast, we do not speak of the "restitutions" or "injunctions" remedy.

3. See § 8.5(5) below which discusses periodic payment alternatives.

5. Some kinds of money awards are not traditionally referred to as "damages," for historical reasons or because the award is limited to exclude some traditional elements of damages. Just compensation for taking of property by eminent domain or otherwise is usually called compensation or, with some irony, "just compensation" rather than damages. The

measures used are like those used in damages cases, except that consequential damages are resolutely denied as just compensation in the federal system. See §§ 3.5 & 5.2(6) below. Awards under the 1964 Civil Rights Act for job discrimination look precisely like damages, but because such relief did not include pain and suffering or punitive relief, courts tended to speak of this relief as something different. See § 6.10(4) below. "Compensation" in workers' compensation awards is likewise similar to damages but excludes some elements of harm and otherwise limits recovery; it is administered in a periodic payment system. Equitable distribution of marital property, although money awards may be made, may be regarded as something other than damages.

an application of the funds received to pay the judgment;[7] equitable money decrees may be enforced by the contempt power.[8]

Harm or loss distinguished. Courts and lawyers often use the term *damages* to mean either the harm or loss[9] suffered by the plaintiff or the legal remedy for that loss. Sometimes this usage leads to confusion. The amount of *harm* may be either more or less than the amount of *damages.* For example, suppose D enters on P's land and spends the weekend there, but without causing *harm:* observers could neither see nor measure a loss in value to P. Although P has suffered no *harm,* she may recover *damages.*[10] Conversely, suppose that D intentionally deprives P of a fundamental constitutional right, such as free speech or due process. P undoubtedly suffers *loss, harm,* or *injury,* but may have no *damages* unless P proves some consequence such as emotional harm.[11] The distinction between harm and damages does not depend on saying that the result in the example is necessarily correct. Because harm differs from damages in nature as well as in amount, the term damages is best reserved for the claim or the remedy rather than for the underlying loss or injury.

Specie remedies distinguished. The damages award is often a *substitutionary* remedy. That is, it substitutes money for the original condition or thing to which the plaintiff was entitled. The plaintiff was entitled to the tape deck in his car; the defendant stole the tape deck. *Specific* remedies might force the defendant to return the tape deck. *Damages* gives the plaintiff a money substitute. Frequently a substitutionary remedy in money is the only remedy available, as where the defendant causes physical injury to the plaintiff or the defendant breaches a contract to sell a pig but barbecues the subject matter of the contract instead.

Sometimes a money award is also a *specie* remedy. When the plaintiff was never entitled to anything but money, the recovery of an award of money is a kind of specie award. This occurs with indemnity, where the plaintiff is forced to pay an obligation for which the defendant is primarily liable. The plaintiff is entitled to indemnification from the defendant, that is, a money payment equal to the plaintiff's money loss. Another example occurs when the plaintiff recovers the price due on an account or on a contract of sale. In such cases money relief bears a close resemblance to specific performance.[13]

[margin note: Specie Remedies]

---

8. See § 2.8(1) above. Some awards made by use of equity or in personam powers are not usually conceived of as "damages". For instance, a court might order a property division between divorcing spouses. Other awards in equity look like ordinary damages except for the potential threat of contempt enforcement. When a court orders specific performance it may make money awards as necessary to give complete relief; sometimes a court will say this is an equitable adjustment, not damages. See Guard v. P & R Enterprises, Inc., 631 P.2d 1068 (Alaska 1981).

9. "Loss" as used in this chapter may include the failure to reap a gain to which the plaintiff is entitled. For example, if the plaintiff would have gained $1,000 by the defen-

dant's performance of a contract, we can say that the plaintiff has a "loss" of $1,000 when the defendant breaches and the plaintiff cannot obtain the contract gain.

10. See § 5.8(2) below.

11. Carey v. Piphus, 435 U.S. 247, 98 S.Ct. 1042, 55 L.Ed.2d 252 (1978) (due process denied, nominal damages only in the absence of proof of emotional harm or some other consequences); Memphis Community School Dist. v. Stachura, 477 U.S. 299, 106 S.Ct. 2537, 91 L.Ed.2d 249 (1986) (free speech denial); § 7.4(2) below.

13. See Bowen v. Massachusetts, 487 U.S. 879, 895, 108 S.Ct. 2722, 2732, 101 L.Ed.2d 749, 765 (1988) (states sued for money allegedly owed by government after government dis-

Restitution distinguished. Damages and restitution may happen to provide the same dollar recovery, but they are often triggered by different situations and always measured by a different yardstick. Damages always begins with the aim of compensation for the plaintiff, although that aim may be deflected by some special considerations to be mentioned later. Restitution, in contrast, begins with the aim of preventing unjust enrichment of the defendant. To measure damages, courts look at the plaintiff's loss or injury. To measure restitution, courts look at the defendant's gain or benefit.[14]

In many cases the defendant causes harm without getting a benefit at all, so restitution is not in issue. Defendant negligently causes a car collision, damaging the plaintiff's vehicle. The plaintiff has harm but the defendant has no benefit. In other cases, the harm to the plaintiff results in a benefit to the defendant. The defendant steals the plaintiff's tape deck; the plaintiff's loss and the defendant's benefit are the same because what the plaintiff lost, the defendant gains. In such cases it does not always matter whether one thinks of awarding damages as compensation for the plaintiff's loss or restitution as disgorgement of the defendant's gain. However, in a third group of cases the plaintiff's loss and the defendant's gain are not at all the same. If the defendant converts the tape deck and then sells it for more than its value at the time of the conversion, the plaintiff might recover the defendant's gains as restitution.[15] Such a recovery would not be a recovery of *damages* because it would be measured by the defendant's gain, not the plaintiff's loss.

The concepts of restitution and damages are quite distinct, but sometimes courts use the term damages when they mean restitution. The two concepts may be further confused by the fact that the amount of the defendant's gains may furnish some evidence about the plaintiff's probable losses.[16] But again, the damages remedy and the restitutionary remedies are always conceptually distinct and often distinct in dollar amount as well.

Compensatory and Non-compensatory Goals

The stated goal of the damages remedy is compensation of the plaintiff for legally recognized losses. This means that the plaintiff should be fully indemnified for his loss, but that he should not recover any windfall.[17] Stated in this way, damages is an instrument of corrective justice, an effort to put the plaintiff in his or her rightful position. But there are some important qualifications to these statements and perhaps some other goals as well.[18] First, the facts may be such that compensation cannot be figured. Courts may use non-compensatory measures or procedures to allow an award in such cases. Second, courts may adopt some non-compensatory purpose (usually in addition to the compensatory purpose). Third, the compensatory

---

allowed support for certain programs; held, not a "damages" claim but more akin to equitable claim for specific relief, hence district court could entertain the claim).

18. A thorough consideration of alternative goals or remedial theories is Leubsdorf, Remedies for Uncertainty, 61 B.U.L.Rev. 132 (1981). Leubsdorf begins by recognizing the uncertainties in obtaining corrective remedies, then considers the possibility that courts could administer remedies (1) as a "surrogate mar-

ket," seeking, not impossible-to-find corrective justice, but an economically efficient result; (2) to achieve an insurance effect emphasizing less the matter of past lost and its reparation and more the matter of what is to be done for the plaintiff now, perhaps allocating risks and standardizing loss payments; (3) to guarantee due process in some cases, for example, by giving damages for a violation of due process even if the plaintiff suffered no pecuniary harm.

purpose may be outweighed by other considerations, which may lead courts to award less than fully compensatory damages.

Non-pecuniary injury. When the plaintiff's proof fails to show the amount of damages with adequate certainty, courts usually deny the damages claim if the case is the kind in which plaintiffs generally would be able to quantify damages. On the other hand, when the plaintiff's claim is for non-pecuniary but legally recognized kind of harm, courts often allow the plaintiff to recover substantial damages. The most common case is the pain and suffering award in personal injury cases.[19] Substantial damages might also be permitted in cases of dignitary torts such as offensive but non-harmful batteries or the denial of important rights like the right to vote.[20] In the defamation area, the tradition, some of which remains,[21] was to "presume" damages to reputation when a libel was published.[22]

Non-compensatory characteristics of non-pecuniary injury damages. Can we say that damages awarded in non-pecuniary cases are "compensatory?" The award in non-pecuniary harm cases can never be quantified, that is, it can never be proven by reference to any evidence as to amount. One can prove the market price of a car, or the amount of a doctor's bill, or even the money value of perquisites that cannot be transferred to others.[23] A money recovery in these cases has two important characteristics: (1) it can be a replacement or substitute for what the plaintiff lost and (2) it can also be measured by the value of the original or cost of its replacement. For instance, a money recovery can be measured by the price of a substitute car or the cost of paying the doctor's bill. Awards for non-pecuniary injuries are not at all like this. They are not money awards for a loss measurable in money. Lawyers like to say that such awards are compensatory, perhaps because they believe the awards can only be justified on a theory of compensation. But it seems more straightforward to recognize that sometimes a money award may be justified even when it is *not* compensatory.

Three reasons for awarding non-compensatory damages. At least three reasons support the idea that damages could be awarded even when they are not compensatory. Those reasons would not apply in every case, but they would apply to some kinds of legally recognized but non-pecuniary harms. The most practical reason to permit such awards is that they fund attorney fees for the plaintiff.[24] Without fees, lawyers cannot maintain offices or the income necessary for their own livelihood. In some kinds of cases, non-pecuniary damages provide a major source of those fees through the contingent fee system. This is a pragmatic reason for allowing non-pecuniary damages and perhaps it is hard to justify on pure principle, but it probably is the most important single reason why non-pecuniary losses support large dollar recoveries.

A principled reason for allowing damages for non-pecuniary loss is the importance of providing a sense of public sympathy and fellow-feeling for a grievously injured person. This is not a reason that supports an unlimited amount of recovery, but neither is it a reason to disregard. A sense of justice and support for rights underlies much of the legal system and would certainly seem to justify an award for pain or for the loss of a valued constitutional right.

A third reason in support of non-compensatory damages for non-pecuniary injury lies in the capacity of the legal system to set standards and provide incentives by adjudicating particular cases. Even if the defendant is not subject to punitive damages, an ordinary "compensatory" damages judgment can provide an appropriate incentive to meet the appropriate standard of behavior.[25]

In any given case it may be appropriate to limit damages to purely compensatory elements, but it is hard to justify the position that damages must be denied in *all* cases of non-pecuniary injury. Some damages awards have never been truly "compensatory" and there is no essential reason why they must always be so.

Punitive damages. Almost all of the states award punitive damages, avowedly non-compensatory.[26] These awards probably have several purposes which are often confused. One of the major purposes is to provide an appropriate incentive for acceptable behavior in cases where compensatory damages (or non-pecuniary damages) are not likely to do so. The punitive damages topic comes in for a lot of discussion later. Here it is only important to recognize as one form of the non-compensatory damages award.

Proof, Convention and Substantive Policy in Damages Measurement

Even when an award of damages could be purely compensatory, principle and practicality may call for an award either larger or smaller than compensation. First, damages must always reflect the substantive policy or goal, which may require something more or less than compensation. Second, practical administration of the courts requires some conventions about the yardstick for measuring damages, and these conventions may result in an award that is not clearly compensatory.

Substantive goals guiding damages measurement. Compensatory damages attempt to provide compensation to the plaintiff, but only within the framework of substantive goals. Substantive law in turn does not recognize all harms as compensable. It is not true that full compensation is always the substantive-law goal. Some injuries are too remote in tort[27] or outside the scope of the parties' contemplation in contract.[28] Even injuries that are real and are also the direct result of tortious behavior may nevertheless not be compensable in damages. Some kinds of emotional distress are in this category.[29]

—Legal theory of the complaint. On the other hand, the legal theory of the plaintiff's claim is not important in and of itself. If the defendant runs his tractor trailer rig into the plaintiff's house, damage to the house will be measurable in the same way whether the plaintiff's claim is based on a negligence theory or on a trespass theory. Both theories recognize the

---

27. See, discussing proximate cause rules, Prosser & Keeton on Torts §§ 42–44 (5th ed. 1984).

28. The contemplation of the parties rule is discussed in §§ 12.4(4)–12.4(7) below.

29. E.g., Thing v. La Chusa, 48 Cal.3d 644, 257 Cal.Rptr. 865, 771 P.2d 814 (1989). Damages may also be limited in some cases of "wrongful birth" and related cases, as to which see § 8.2 below. Distinguish such limitations from cases in which the defendant infringes no rights at all.

plaintiff's legally protected interest in the house, and once that is recognized, compensation for that interest does not change with the theory asserted.

—Incentive damages; a nuisance example. The substantive goal may require more than compensation, as where the goal is to impose liabilities as incentives for proper conduct by the defendant. An incentive goal does not necessarily dictate punitive damages,[30] but it might dictate a generous measure of relief that would not be chosen for pure compensation. For example, suppose the defendant's factory is producing pollution that counts as a nuisance. Present technology does not permit elimination of the nuisance without closing the factory. The plaintiff might be allowed to recover a lump sum award covering all future harms, but such a recovery would leave the defendant with no incentives to seek a better technology. So a court might allow the plaintiff to sue for accrued damages and to continue to sue for damages as they accrue as a means of providing suitable incentives.[31] This approach may or may not represent an accurate compensation, but it definitely tends to serve other important purposes.

—Incentive damages; a contract example. Opinion differs whether incentives are appropriate in contract cases, but contract examples can be found even so. In one well-known case, *Groves v. John Wunder Co.,*[32] the defendant agreed to take gravel from the plaintiff's land, then restore the top soil. The defendant took the gravel but did not restore the land. The land was worth about $12,000 less as a result, but it would cost $60,000 to restore the soil. The court allowed the $60,000 recovery, partly, it seems, as an incentive to comply with contract promises.[33]

—Economic waste. Pushing in the opposite direction is a substantive policy that opposes economic waste and perhaps one that affirmatively seeks a degree of economic efficiency. Remedies law is largely concerned with making the best of a bad situation. Sometimes what the plaintiff claims as "compensation" is too wasteful of resources. In the *Groves* case, instead of focusing on incentives, the court might have focused on the economic waste entailed when the defendant is required to spend $60,000 in order to save $12,000 for the plaintiff. A court considering economic waste might be inclined to limit the damages rather than expand them.[34]

Whether a court should expand or contract damages awards to reflect incentives or economic waste concerns is a question that must be judged on the facts of each case. The immediate point is only that non-compensatory goals to provide suitable incentives and to avoid economic waste in others do in fact affect the damages measurement, which is not merely a matter of financial fact, but an amalgam of fact and policy.

Conventions in damages measurement. Substantive rules provide the goals of damages measurement, but a wide variety of practical considerations prompt courts and lawyers to settle for imperfection in measurement. In many, many instances, legal measures of damages reflect conventions, not actual measurements. One of the important conventions is discussed in

---

30. But some punitive damages serve this purpose. See § 3.11(3) below.

31. See §§ 5.6, 5.7 & 5.11(2) below.

32. 205 Minn. 163, 286 N.W. 235, 123 A.L.R. 502 (1939).

33. See § 12.19(1) below.

34. See Restatement Second of Contracts § 348(2)(b) (1981); §§ 12.2(2) & 12.19(1) below.

another section,[35] but an illustration of it is appropriate because it is important to see that the damages award is not purely a question of fact or compensation.

Suppose the plaintiff contracts to buy shares of stock in a small, closely held corporation for $1,000. The defendant seller reneges and the plaintiff is unable to buy the stock anywhere. On the date set for transfer, the stock was actually worth $1500 (which may be why the defendant did not want to sell). Suppose that one week later the corporation discovered that all of its property was a hazardous waste site and that cleanup costs would wipe out all the company's assets. The shares of stock were thereafter wholly without value. The plaintiff might be thankful that the defendant breached the sales contract, because, with hindsight, we know that the breach actually saved the plaintiff money.

Nevertheless, the plaintiff will almost certainly be allowed to recover. The conventional "measurement" is the difference between the contract price and the market price *on the date for performance.* On that basis, the plaintiff is entitled to $500. In reality the plaintiff seems to have had no loss at all, but as a matter of legal convention he recovers $500. Some writers have not much liked measures like this because they do not provide compensation.[36] But the point of such measures is not that they are truly or perfectly compensatory but that they are convenient conventions. In a sense, almost all damages are the product of conventions or convenient rules. The conventional nature of damages "measurement" is a central feature of damages law.

One other example can illustrate the pervasiveness and convenience of conventions in damages measurement. In permanent injury and wrongful death cases, damages must be based on a prediction about the victim's life expectancy. This could be avoided by using a total periodic payments system.[37] Or the issue could be resolved by the jury's or the expert's intuitions. In fact, most cases resolve the issue by resorting to statistical life expectancy tables. These are good conventions, but they are only conventions; they are used for convenience, definitely *not* because they tell us how long the individual victim would have lived.[38]

Major Issues in Damages Law

There are many important rules of damages. These are summarized in the next subsection. Beyond the rules already established, however, the profession is alive with a sense that some long accepted traditions in damages law are now up for serious reconsideration. Some of those broader issues are listed here.

The role of damages in the remedial scheme. Some issues of damages law are really issues about remedies law. For instance, should damages continue to be the single most important remedy, or should restitution and coercive remedies take a greater role in the remedial scheme of things? The traditions that made damages the primary remedy for most kinds of suits seem to be breaking down. Statutes may mark the way first, as suggested by the Annenberg proposals,[39] which would favor the heavy use of declaratory judgments instead of damages in defamation cases.

39. See § 7.2(14) below.

If the traditional "primacy" of damages breaks down, important new questions will arise. On what grounds should a court refuse damages that have been available under long-held legal traditions and substitute an injunction or restitution instead? Should courts consider, for example, the relative desirability of different remedial options? Remedial jurisprudence seldom compares relative desirability of remedies,[40] so new ground may be covered.

The role of compensation in damages remedies. Of the major issues that mainly concern the damages remedy standing alone, many are suggested by the discussion earlier in this section. Are non-pecuniary awards compensatory, and if not, how should they be measured?[41] More significantly, what is the role of compensation in figuring damages, as compared to incentive damages or considerations of economic waste and economic efficiency? Should conventional measures of damages be used more because of their convenience? Or less because they may not be accurate?

Caps on damages and multipliers of damages. Several issues closely relate to the question of conventional measures and accurate compensation. Statutes are now on the books setting caps on damages in various situations in the personal injury field.[42] On the other hand, statutes permit or require that actual damages be multiplied by a factor or two or three in a number of instances,[43] and of course punitive damages result in a similar extracompensatory award.[44] So a deliberate choice of less than compensation is made in some cases, while an equally deliberate choice for more than compensation is made in others.

Can the law really justify taking both of these approaches at the same time? This situation spawns at least three major questions for decision quite apart from the validity of either limiting or multiplying damages awards. When should damages be limited (and how)? When should damages be multiplied? When should damages be measured by convention, or measured as accurately as possible? Sooner or later such issues will have to be confronted.

The attorney fees issue. The American Rule holds that each side pays its own attorney fees and related litigation costs. This rule is under constant pressure and in the last generation enormous changes have been enacted by legislatures and adopted by courts, so that the prevailing party now can recover her attorney fees from the losing party in a number of particular cases, such as civil rights claims.[45] This situation gives rise to at least two major issues. First, should the fee recovery be limited to particular cases, or should it be more general? Second, what other rules of damages are logically affected by a rule that allows the winner to recover fees? For example, if the winner recovers her attorney fees, should pain and suffering awards or punitive awards be reduced?[46]

Damages administration: periodic payments. The lump sum rule has governed damages law throughout American history. The rule solves administrative problems and helps maintain a judicial atmosphere on future

40. Recall that the traditional comparison, invoked when the plaintiff seeks coercive equitable relief, is a comparison of *adequacy* of the legal remedy compared to the equitable. But that is a very limited comparison; it does not purport to compare relative desirability, all factors considered, only the adequacy for the plaintiff's purposes.

damages issues. Periodic payments made through the court system would create administrative problems and probably encourage a bureaucratic or administrative atmosphere. So the lump sum rule has real advantages. It also has real costs. Courts must figure inflation for the future and make reductions to present value for payments made now. Any given judgment may prove totally wrong tomorrow or ten years from tomorrow when the important facts bearing on future damages are known. With the appearance of some limited periodic payment schemes in the 1970s and 1980s, the question is again raised whether the lump sum rule is worth its costs and, related, whether a good periodic payment system can be designed that will improve matters.[47]

§ 3.2 Summarizing Damages Rules

This section summarizes some important general rules of damages and points to other sections where those rules are stated more fully. Because this is a summary section and a kind of narrative index, the limiting and qualifying rules are not stated here.

Measures of Damages

General or market damages.[1] Many kinds of harms are measured by market damages. Outside the personal injury field, the term "general damages" usually refers to market-measured damages. (In personal injury cases, "general damages" usually means non-pecuniary damages). Market measured damages are usually based on the idea that the plaintiff's balance sheet shows a loss[2] of net worth as a result of the defendant's tort or breach of contract.

For example, suppose the defendant negligently runs a bulldozer into the plaintiff's house. Market or general damages measures ask simple questions: how much was the property worth immediately before the harm? How much was it worth after? The difference is the plaintiff's market or general damages. If the property was worth $200,000 before and only $175,000 afterwards, the damages so measured would be $25,000.[3]

The market measure is pervasive. With slight adjustments, it works in contract cases[4] and fraud cases[5] just as well as in harm to property cases. When the defendant breaches his promise to sell Blackacre for $100,000, the market measure asks how much that property was worth at the relevant time. The plaintiff's general damages is the difference between the contract price and the market value. So if Blackacre was worth $140,000, the plaintiff's general damages come to $40,000.

Markets are not always available or trustworthy for measuring the value of the plaintiff's legal interests. In many instances, the supposed "market" value of the plaintiff's entitlement is merely a construct, that is, an effort to estimate what market value would be if there were a market. This is commonly a problem with real property, where opinion evidence and data are commonly used to prove value.[6]

§ 3.2

1. See § 3.3(3) below.

2. "Loss" encompasses a failure to make a gain to which the plaintiff is entitled by contract or otherwise.

Special or consequential damages.[7] Market damages may not suffice as fair compensation, either because there is no market or because the plaintiff has some losses not represented in the market value of the plaintiff's entitlement. To take the second instance, suppose the homeowner-plaintiff whose house is damaged by the bulldozer is forced to move out of the house while it is repaired. She rents an apartment for that period. Her claim for rental costs is a claim for consequential damages, which are sometimes called special damages. The rental cost represents a financial injury or harm that results as a consequence of the harm to her property, but this financial harm is not the same as the harm to the property. Consequential damages may be awarded in addition to [8] or instead of general damages if the facts make such an award appropriate. In a contract case, for example, the defendant's breach of a contract to sell goods to the plaintiff might cause the plaintiff a delay in opening his retail store and hence a loss of profits he would have made in operating the store. A claim for lost profits would be in addition to any added cost the plaintiff might have in purchasing substitute goods and would be a claim for consequential damages.

Consequential damages are almost always subjected to some limitations that do not directly apply to general or market damages.[9] Consequential damages are not ordinarily awarded unless the plaintiff has realized or will realize a loss. That is, paper losses, like those seen in market damages, are not enough when it comes to consequential damages.[10] In addition, most of the limiting rules summarized below apply only or especially to consequential damages.[11]

Substitution cost damages.[12] In some cases the plaintiff is allowed to recover the cost of obtaining a reasonable substitute for the thing to which he was entitled. For instance, if the defendant cuts down the cherry tree in the plaintiff's yard, the market measure might only give the plaintiff the diminished value of his land, but replacement of the tree might cost much more. Or if the defendant reneges on a promise to sell the plaintiff locks for resale in the plaintiff's hardware store, the plaintiff might reasonably buy locks from another manufacturer even if they are more costly.

In the lock example, the fact that substitution costs exceed the diminished value explains why the plaintiff may wish to base damages on substitution costs. However, substitution costs run the risk of overcompensation in many cases. That would be true with the cherry tree if the plaintiff really did not care about cherry trees, in which case the diminished value of the land would fully represent his loss. Substitution may also entail economic waste, if substitution requires destruction of existing structures.

Standardized and pattern damages. Although many measurements in the law of damages are highly conventional, they focus on the particular plaintiff's losses. When the plaintiff's entitlement is intangible or non-pecuniary in nature, no real "measurement" of the plaintiff's right is possible. A plaintiff who loses her pet cat may suffer something that cannot be measured by the market value of the cat. So far, American judges have not provided standardized damages, except in some cases in setting a formula for interest rates used in computation. However, statutes some-

---

7. See § 3.3(4) below.   **12.** See § 3.3(5) below.

times standardize damages. For example, an eavesdropping statute standardizes a damages minimum or floor at $100 per day for wiretapping.[13]

Punitive damages.[14] Punitive damages, also called exemplary damages, are available in most courts to condemn seriously bad conduct. Description of the conduct that warrants punitive damages is seldom very precise. Sometimes the conduct must be malicious and always it must involve some bad state of mind, as in the case of "reckless" conduct. Punitive damages resemble pain and suffering damages in that they have no established measure. However, they are unique in that the plaintiff is permitted to show the defendant's wealth to aid the trier in fixing an appropriate level of punitive damages. Punitive damages are routinely denied in contract cases, although there are exceptions.[15] Punitive damages are the oddest of all damages and raise many special issues. Statutes sometimes authorize or even require multiplication of actual damages by doubling or trebling.[16]

Litigation costs.[17] Damages awards in the American system are traditionally supplemented by an award of "costs," but costs award does not include attorney fees or indeed most other costs of litigation. The costs awarded the prevailing party are those specified by statute, usually such items as the charges of the sheriff or marshall for serving papers and the like. Otherwise the prevailing party does not recover anything for her attorney fees unless a special exception is found.

When the plaintiff's litigation results in the recovery of a fund of money that is to be shared by others, the others who share the proceeds must share in the attorney fee costs under the common fund rule.[18] In addition there are exceptions for some special cases,[19] and a number of particular statutes which allow recovery of the attorney fee against the losing adversary. Of the statutes, the most notable and most litigated involve civil rights, employment discrimination and environmental statutes. Under these, the prevailing plaintiff (but not usually the prevailing defendant) can recover a reasonable attorney fee.[20] The fee is usually based on a reasonable hourly charge for a reasonable number of hours.[21]

Adjustments for Time Differentials: Delay and Prepayment

Interest.[22] When the defendant litigates his liability, ultimate payment to the plaintiff always comes long after the original loss or injury. The defendant has the use of money during the litigation period that, it turns out, properly should have been paid to the plaintiff when the loss occurred. And, correspondingly, the plaintiff has lost the use of the money. The use value of money can be represented by interest, but courts were traditionally reluctant to permit interest to accrue until the judgment was entered. Prejudgment interest was traditionally allowed only when the underlying obligation was liquidated or ascertainable.

There are signs that courts are moving toward a better agreement with modern business practices by allowing interest more freely, but, apart from statute, the general rules still govern many cases.

---

13. 18 U.S.C.A. § 2520 (actual damages, but not less than $100 a day or $1,000, whichever is higher, plus punitive damages and attorney fee recovery). See § 3.3(2) below.

14. See § 3.11 below.

17. See § 3.10 below.

22. See § 3.6 below.

Reduction to present value.[23] The reverse of the interest problem occurs when the defendant must pay a lump sum now for all future damages, as in many personal injury cases. The lump sum awarded now for an expense expected to occur ten years from now can be invested with relative safety for ten years. In that time it can earn substantial interest that will help pay the defendant's obligation for the plaintiff's future expense. So courts have traditionally said that the amount the defendant should pay as compensation for future losses must be reduced to present value. Properly reduced, the award will give the plaintiff a sum which, when invested, will pay all future compensation when due by using both the interest and the invested capital.

Reduction to present value is right when future inflation is not a threat. When inflation is a threat, one way to be sure the plaintiff is fully compensated in spite of future inflation alters the way in which the reduction to present value is computed. Another way to adjust for inflation is to add a sum to the judgment in an amount estimated to cover prospective inflation over the period of the future losses.[24]

Adjustments for Benefits Reaped or Harms Avoided by the Plaintiff

Collateral source benefits.[25] In many instances the plaintiff who is injured by tort or breach of contract is able to reap some collateral benefits as a result of the same tort or breach. The plaintiff who is physically injured by tort may recover medical benefits from his insurer. The plaintiff victimized by contract breach may receive public benefits like unemployment insurance. The traditional collateral source rule is that these collateral benefits do not affect measurement of the plaintiff's damages. In one sense the plaintiff has no medical loss if his insurance coverage pays the whole medical bill. But courts do not generally accept this view. They say the plaintiff's collateral benefits (which are not necessarily in the form of insurance) are simply none of the defendant's business. So the plaintiff collects the collateral benefits *and* full damages from the defendant. In recent years tort defendants and their insurers have been able to modify this rule by statute for some kinds of tort cases; otherwise the rule remains in good standing.

Direct benefits.[26] The defendant gets no credit on his damages liability for collateral benefits, but does get credit for "direct" benefits, that is, for benefits which the defendant himself provided, intentionally or unintentionally, and for benefits that are concurrent with damage itself. For example, if the defendant's insurance policy pays the plaintiff's hospital bills, this is a direct benefit and the defendant's liability is reduced accordingly. What counts as a direct benefit, however, is itself subject to litigation in some cases.

Avoided and avoidable consequences.[27] Suppose the defendant contracts to sell goods to the plaintiff for the opening of the plaintiff's new store, but at the last minute the defendant reneges. To avoid the expense and

---

23. See §§ 3.7 & 8.5(3) below.
24. See § 8.5(4) below.
25. See § 3.8(1) below.

26. See § 3.8(2) below.
27. See §§ 3.9 & 12.6(2) below.

potential profit loss that might result if the opening is postponed, the plaintiff searches for, finds, and buys substitute goods. The defendant is not liable for lost profits; the plaintiff avoided those consequences. The avoidable consequences rules go further, however. If the plaintiff did not avoid the loss but *could* have done so by reasonable effort and expenses, the plaintiff's recovery of such consequential damages will still be denied. On the affirmative side, the plaintiff may recover the reasonable costs of avoiding the profit loss. In this example the reasonable costs might include any additional cost of the substitute goods and also the costs of locating appropriate substitutes.

§ 3.3 Basic Damages Measures or Approaches

§ 3.3(1) Measures and Elements of Damages

The Specific Element Approach: Personal Injury and Related Cases

To a large extent, damages must vary with the kind of harm suffered. For this reason, courts do not use a universal measure of damages. In some kinds of cases the practice is merely to state what is often called "elements" of damages. In personal injury cases, for example, damages are awarded for harms that include lost wages or earning capacity, medical and other expenses, and pain and suffering. This approach rarely attempts to suggest a formula for measuring damages but is usually content instead to list the kinds of harm for which the court will permit compensation.[1] The measures of damages discussed in this section have little to do with personal injury cases, which are considered separately in Chapter 8.

The Yardstick or Measured Approach: Property and Contract Cases

Three types of damages measurement. Personal injury and related cases aside, most claims involve harm to some kind of interest in tangible or intangible property, or some kind of contract right. In those cases, courts usually calculate damages by using one of three general measures of damages, or by combining two of the measures in some fashion. These broad measures, explained in more detail in the subsections that follow, are:

> (1) *General or market damages,* meaning market-measured compensation calculated by the value of the very thing to which the plaintiff was entitled.[2] (2) *Special or consequential damages,* meaning compensation for harms or losses resulting in *consequence* of harm to the very thing to which the plaintiff was entitled, often in the form of lost profits.[3] (3) *Substitution cost damages,* meaning the reasonable costs of

---

§ 3.3(1)

1. Personal injury measures can in fact be classified as consequential damages and substitutionary damages; but there is no room in personal injury cases (or breach of employment contract cases) for using a market measure.

2. For example: P's car is destroyed by tort. Its market value was $10,000. P's general or market damages are $10,000. See

§ 3.3(3) below. The term may have slightly different meanings for purposes of the pleading rule that requires specific pleading of special damages.

3. For example: When P's car was destroyed, he could not get to work for three days and lost $500 in income. His special damages, if any such damages may be recovered, come to $500. See § 3.3(4) below.

procuring a substitute for the very thing to which the plaintiff was entitled, rather than the value of the thing itself.[4]

§ 3.3(2) Nominal Damages and Standardized Surrogate Damages

Nominal Damages

Meaning. Nominal damages are damages in name only, trivial sums such as six cents or $1. Such damages are awarded both in tort[1] and contract[2] cases when the plaintiff establishes a cause of action against the defendant but is unable to prove damages under any of the measures listed above.

Where the plaintiff has no cause of action. In some kinds of cases the plaintiff has no cause of action at all unless and until damages can be shown. Negligence cases are in this category.[3] In those cases, nominal damages usually cannot be awarded because the plaintiff has no valid claim at all until a legally recognized loss is demonstrated.[4]

When substantial damages are recoverable. At the other extreme are cases in which a substantial, not merely nominal recovery is available without proof of pecuniary loss. Once some amount of loss is established, the plaintiff is entitled to recover non-pecuniary losses like pain and suffering or mental distress even in ordinary negligence cases. In some kinds of cases such as common law libel,[5] false imprisonment and others, substantial sums are awarded without any special proof of pecuniary loss.

When nominal damages are recoverable. Generalizations about the kind of cases in which nominal damages are available have not been very successful. It has been said that nominal damages could be awarded in tort cases that have their roots in the writ of trespass as distinct from the action on the case. Trespass to land,[6] assault,[7] battery[8] and false imprisonment[9] are trespassory claims and nominal damages can be awarded in all of them. Conversely, it was said that nominal damages could not be awarded in claims that traced their way back to Trespass on the Case. This is at least partly true with claims like negligence[10] and fraud,[11] where nominal damages are usually denied.

But the generalization does not hold up. Trespass to chattels, a trespassory tort, is actionable only if the plaintiff is dispossessed or actual harm is done or if the trespass amounts to a conversion.[12] A host of other torts that arise from the action on the case actually do permit nominal or even substantial damages without proof of harm. Libel[13] and malicious prosecution[14] are examples. Besides this, nominal damages are permitted in the contract action,[15] which is a descendant from the Writ of Trespass but one much more remote than Trespass on the Case.

Why nominal damages. Why award nominal damages? Few plaintiffs would sue for the privilege of recovering $1 or six cents, and certainly the lawyer who expected such a recovery would hardly take the case on a contingent fee. There are two kinds of reasons for nominal damages.

4. For example: P's car was worth $10,000 when destroyed, but it will cost $11,000 to procure a reasonably good substitute. P's substitution damages, if any such damages are recoverable, come to $11,000. See § 3.3(5) below.

First, some suits might be brought much as declaratory judgment suits are brought, to determine a right. A money recovery would not be the real object in such a suit. Lawyers might have asserted a claim for nominal damages to get the issue before the court in the days before declaratory judgments were recognized. Relatedly, a plaintiff might seek vindication of a right which is not economic in character and for which no substantial non-pecuniary award is available. A plaintiff might, for example, wish to establish a constitutional right, even if a large damage verdict is not possible.[16]

Second, the nominal damages award is, realistically, a rescue operation. The plaintiff has established a cause of action but has no damages or has been unable to prove the damages she does have. If that led to a judgment for the defendant, the plaintiff would normally be required to pay the court costs.[17] To avoid that and put the cost burden on the defendant, nominal damages are awarded.

Standardized Surrogate Damages

The common law has no concept that permits the award of substantial standardized sums of money. Nominal damages are more or less standardized sums, usually $1 or six cents, but they are far from substantial. Substantial sums are awarded for some kinds of non-pecuniary interests such as those associated with emotional distress, but these sums are not standardized. The plaintiff whose injury is intangible but real, and the plaintiff who has a pecuniary injury that is unprovable as to the amount may well need a recovery greater than nominal damages.

There are many instances in which justice and convenience might both be served if standardized damages were available, based on a pattern or formula. For example, suppose the plaintiff's pet is killed by the defendant's tort and the pet has no market value.[18] If no mental distress damages are available (and often they are not in property damages cases),[19] then a standard minimum award would be quite useful. The same could be said of almost any intangible harms, for example, defamation, invasion of privacy, or deprivation of civil rights.

One solution is to leave the matter to the jury and then allow judges to require a new trial if they feel damages are excessive. This is the expensive method actually used with such unmeasurable items as those just mentioned, as well as with pain and suffering and punitive damages and others. Because idiosyncratic values literally cannot be measured, this process does not guarantee accuracy of individuation, so it would be possible to standardize damages or provide patterns for damages in such cases.

One minor case of standardized damages appears in admiralty cases, some of which hold the ship liable to pay maintenance for injured seamen at a standardized rate such as $8 per day.[20] Some statutes provide standardized damages. Interest rates may be fixed by reference to a changing outside standard that can be readily checked.[21] The plaintiff's privacy rights

---

§ 3.3(2)

18. See § 5.16(3) below.

19. See § 5.15(3) below.

20. See, discussing the vicissitudes of this rule, Hansen v. Rothaus, 107 Wash.2d 468, 730 P.2d 662 (1986).

are protected under a federal statute which provides a standardized minimum recovery of $100 for each day of illegal wiretapping.[22]

Tradition is against the adoption of similar standardized rules by judges, but there probably are cases in which something of this kind is needed. A New Mexico case may have taken a step in the direction of standardized and substantial damages by holding that an award of $5,000 could count as "nominal" damages. Although the court did not discuss the standardization, to call such a sum nominal suggests that some such substantial awards could be granted more or less routinely.[23]

§ 3.3(3) General Damages or Market Measures

This subsection discusses the market or general damages measure used by courts when the plaintiff claims any kind of right in tangible or intangible property or almost any kind of contract right.

Sometimes the terms general and special damages are used in connection with a pleading rule that requires special damages to be pleaded specifically.[1] For present purposes the terms are more important in identifying methods or measures of damages.

Judicial definitions of general damages are usually vague or almost tautological,[2] but the actual decisions make it clear that the courts hold a fairly precise idea about general damages. General damages are market-measured damages. They value the plaintiff's entitlement by looking at its value on some real or supposed market.[3] Using a market or "general" damages measure, courts look at the plaintiff's assets, not at income lost or expenses incurred. The market measure attempts to make sure the defendant's tort or contract breach does not leave the plaintiff with assets or net worth less than that to which she is entitled.

The market measure is essentially the same both in contract and tort. To take a tort case first, suppose that the defendant negligently damages the plaintiff's airplane. Before the damage, the plane had a market value of $26 million. After the damage, its market value was only $24 million. The plaintiff's assets have dropped in value by $2 million as a result of the tort [4] and $2 million is thus its market measure of recovery.[5] (The plaintiff might also suffer other harms and might recover other damages, but the market

22. 18 U.S.C.A. § 2520 (actual damages, but not less than $100 a day or $1,000, whichever is higher, plus punitive damages and attorney fee recovery).

23. Ruiz v. Varan, 110 N.M. 478, 484, 797 P.2d 267, 273 (1990) ("We consider the award and amount of nominal damages to be a matter of discretion for the trial court,").

§ 3.3(3)

1. E.g., Hodges v. Gibson Products Co., 811 P.2d 151 (Utah 1991). Somewhat differently, the presence or absence of special damages in some kinds of cases determines whether the plaintiff has any cause of action at all. E.g., West's Ann.Cal.Civ.Code § 48a (in cases of newspaper libel where no correction has been demanded, and case of radio broadcast libels, plaintiff can recover only if special damages

are established). See also § 7.2(3) as to special damages in slander cases, where the term usually means pecuniary loss.

2. Denny v. Nutt, 189 Ga.App. 387, 388, 375 S.E.2d 878, 879 (1988) (generally damages arise in the normal course of things from defendant's breach); American List Corp. v. U.S. News and World Report, Inc., 75 N.Y.2d 38, 43, 550 N.Y.S.2d 590, 593, 549 N.E.2d 1161, 1164 (1989) (general damages are those that are natural and probable results of the defendant's acts, while special damages are not so direct); cf. Wall v. Pate, 104 N.M. 1, 715 P.2d 449 (1986) ("direct (or general) damage"). The definitions are reflected in some detail in C. McCormick, Damages § 8 (1935), but McCormick was mainly interested in the pleading purpose of this definition.

measure is based on diminished assets, as judged by a real or hypothetical market.)

Exactly the same process is used in contract cases. If the plaintiff had contracted to purchase a horse for $250,000 and the seller reneged, how could the plaintiff figure market damages? If the horse was worth $300,000 at the relevant time and the plaintiff had contracted to acquire the horse for $250,000, performance of the contract would have added to the plaintiff's assets on the date performance was due. Instead of $250,000 in cash, the plaintiff would have had a horse worth $300,000. The contract price-market price differential is $50,000 and represents the market measure of his expectancy damages.[6] Market measured damages are almost always recoverable in contract cases if the plaintiff wishes and the facts permit such a calculation.[7]

In some cases the plaintiff's loss is found in the fact that the plaintiff did not make the gain to which she was entitled. This is notably the case with expectancy damages in contracts. The horse purchaser has a loss in the sense that she failed to reap the $50,000 gain that contract performance would have given him. It is appropriate to say that the plaintiff failed to reap a "gain" or entitlement here but not helpful to say that he lost "profits," which would suggest that an expected income stream was lost or diminished.[9] Although lost profits may be recoverable in some cases, they will be recoverable as consequential damages, not as market damages.

Market or general damages measures have several especially notable characteristics. One of these is that market measured damages can be recovered even when no loss has been realized. To see this and some other characteristics, consider the plaintiff who contracts to purchase a house for $200,000, for use as her home. She likes the house and the neighborhood. The market value of the house is $210,000. The defendant reneges. General damages are represented by the contract-market price differential, $10,000. Notice that the plaintiff has not suffered a realized loss.

One way to see that the loss is not actually realized is to suppose that if the contract had been performed, the plaintiff's bookkeeping gain would not be taxable income and that when the contract was breached the failure to obtain the contract advantages is not a deductible loss. In fact, the loss as measured by general damages may never eventuate. Consider two examples.

First, suppose that the disappointed plaintiff finds another house in the same neighborhood which she actually likes better. In addition, the substitute house is selling for a much better price, $180,000. On top of that, the substitute house is worth at least $195,000. Plaintiff purchases the substitute house and admits that she would never have found or purchased it if the defendant had not breached. Clearly the plaintiff has no realized losses; in fact she has a gain, because she has spent less money and obtained a greater asset value and personal satisfaction at the same time.

Second, consider the possibility that the market price of the defendant's house falls shortly after the time for closing. Instead of getting a house worth $210,000 by paying $200,000, the plaintiff would have had a house worth only $190,000. If the plaintiff's position is considered a few days after the day performance was due, we could see that performance would not have been a good deal for the plaintiff at all.

The house purchase example reflects something of the conventional nature of general damages measurements and also shows that such damages may be measured by bookkeeping losses, not realized or liquidated losses. The plaintiff's rightful position under the contract was to have a paper gain of $10,000 on the house purchase; she did not get that gain, so she is entitled to general or market damages in that sum. The effect of the market measure in this example to give the plaintiff cash now for a gain that might never have been realized in cash.

Such a measure of damages is justified for several reasons.[10] The plaintiff might never have realized the loss, but she might also have sold the house the next day for an immediate gain. We do not know and cannot find out with certainty what the plaintiff would have done if the contract had been performed. It is far easier to treat the plaintiff's right to resell the house as equivalent to cash value when it comes to measuring damages even though it might not be equivalent to cash value for income tax purposes. Another reason for such a result is that the market price itself reflects the estimate of potential buyers about future price changes. If the house really can sell to buyers for $210,000, then buyers do not think prices will change dramatically in the foreseeable future. So the market price itself embodies *some* estimate about value than can be realized even in the future.

The same house purchase example reflects a second and related characteristic of market damages. Those damages are based on market value at a particular date. In effect, market or general damages close out the account between the parties on the date when performance was due[11] under the contract (or the date of the harm in the case of a tort). When market damages are used to measure loss, courts and lawyers are not required to estimate future losses. *All* loss is represented by the difference in market value before and after the tort or the contract-market differential at the relevant date and place.

A third characteristic of market measured damages awards is that they ignore transaction costs. If the defendant reneges on a contract to sell the plaintiff an amount of grain for $10,000 and the market price on the relevant date is $12,000, the plaintiff will recover $2,000 as market damages. Yet it is apparent that the plaintiff has at least *some* added costs in consummating a second transaction. When the plaintiff can recover consequential damages, transaction costs (and savings) are very much a part of the damage calculation. When the plaintiff recovers general damages (and general restitution), the market is the measure and the costs of calling the broker or finding a seller are almost always ignored.

Some of the reasons for using market measures of damages must be apparent. A date for closing the parties' accounting is as convenient as the date for closing a tax year or an inventory period. When there is an actual,

10. See Simon & Novack, Limiting the Buyer's Market Damages to Lost Profits: A Challenge to the Enforceability of Market Contracts, 92 Harv.L.Rev. 1395 (1979).

11. Under the UCC sales article, applicable to sales of goods, the date for measuring market damages in favor of the *buyer* is the date the buyer learned of the breach. See § 12.-16(2) below.

developed market, it is convenient also because it gives quick access to a dollar figure from which damages can be computed. It relieves courts and parties from the costs entailed in constructing a hypothetical value from a raw mass of data.[12]

A related advantage of the market measure may not always be obvious. The market measure is a good resolution of many uncertainties to which the parties fall prey when no market measure is available. A racehorse might or might not win important races in the future; no one knows for sure. If the defendant breaches a contract to sell the horse, or if someone negligently injures the horse so that he can no longer race, we might find it quite difficult to estimate the profits the horse would have earned in an uncertain future racing life.[13] If there really is a well-developed market for the horse or for horses that are closely similar in breeding and experience, the horse's market price will reflect the judgment of many potential buyers about his prospects. The market price incorporates the potential buyers' discount for the uncertainties of the future as well their hopes. Using that market price instead of guessing about profits he might have earned is one very useful way of dealing with the uncertainty of the future. These reasons apply, however, only if the market is a well-developed one in which relevant economic information is widely available.

Holmes thought that the stock market was about perfect as a means of providing accurate information about potential development of a property and locating the buyer who could best use it and pay the highest price. Sheer volume meant that the best price would tend to be paid. Even if the buyer who was most likely to pay the best price is not in the market when the stock is offered, nevertheless "there is an organized public ready to buy upon the anticipation that such a buyer will be found, and regulating the price which it will pay more or less by that anticipation." [14]

§ 3.3(4) Consequential Damages

The second measure attempts to estimate damages by gauging consequential harms to the plaintiff. Consequential damages are subjected to some special constraints or proof demands to be discussed later.[1] Recovery or denial of consequential damages in particular cases is discussed in the appropriate chapters.[2] The job of this subsection is to identify consequential damages as a measure or method for figuring the plaintiff's recovery.

The term special damages is almost always used in contrast to general damages. Apart from personal injury and similar cases which are outside the scope of this section, the term special damages means the same as consequential damages. Consequential (or special) damages in these cases refers to damages consequent upon but distinct from harm to the plaintiff's entitlement.

One common form of consequential damages is the claim for lost profits. For instance, when the plaintiff's airplane is tortiously damaged so that it is worth $2 million less than before, the harm to the plaintiff's entitlement is $2 million. But the plaintiff may also suffer extensive loss of income or profit because the harm to the plane prevented its use in carrying passen-

14. Bradley v. Hooker, 175 Mass. 142, 55 N.E. 848 (1900).

§ 3.3(4)

1. See § 3.4 below.

gers. The plaintiff's claim to lost income or profit is a claim for consequential damages and in a proper case is recoverable as such.[3]

Lost profit claims are also asserted in contract cases,[4] fraud cases,[5] or indeed almost any kind of case.[6] The plaintiff who contracts to purchase a horse for $25,000 might have a general damages loss of $5,000 if the seller refused to go through with the deal. But one consequence of not getting the horse might be that the plaintiff also lost earnings the horse could have produced. The plaintiff's claim to lost earnings the horse would have made is a claim for consequential damages, not based on the asset value of the horse but on its income production. Lost profit claims in contract cases are subject to the limiting rules discussed below, but are frequently successful.[7] One form of lost profit claim is the loss of goodwill in a business.[8]

Some losses cannot readily be characterized. In the damaged airplane case, the plaintiff lost the use of the plane during the repair period and might recover for any resulting loss of profit as consequential damages. If profit loss could not be proved, the plaintiff might claim rental value or interest on the tied up capital instead. Such claims have indeed been allowed in proper cases.[9] But their classification is not so clear. Sometimes the plaintiff claims the rental cost of obtaining a substitute, which definitely looks like consequential damages or substitute-cost damages. At other times the plaintiff claims, or gets, the rental value his own chattel would have had if it had not been harmed, a measure which bears some resemblance the market damages measure.[10] The classification is not critical, but it suggests something about whether the plaintiff should recover only actual expenses of renting a substitute or whether it could recover the market rental. When courts limit recovery to the plaintiff's actual reasonable expenditures, they seem to be awarding damages based on consequential or substitute cost measures. When they permit the plaintiff to recover rental value of his own chattel without actually leasing a substitute, they seem to be awarding something like market-measured damages without requiring any realized loss.[11]

3. E.g., Hardman Trucking, Inc. v. Poling Trucking Co., 176 W.Va. 575, 346 S.E.2d 551 (1986) (loss of hauling profits while triaxle truck being repaired). Harm to income producing property, personal or real, usually permits profit recovery during reasonable repair periods. E.g., Natural Soda Products Co. v. City of Los Angeles, 23 Cal.2d 193, 143 P.2d 12 (1943), cert. denied, 321 U.S. 793, 64 S.Ct. 790, 88 L.Ed. 1082 (1944) (land, lost profit recovery). See, among other sections, §§ 5.12 & 5.15 below.

7. E.g., Burnett & Doty Dev. Co. v. C. S. Phillips, 84 Cal.App.3d 384, 148 Cal.Rptr. 569 (1978) (contractor's delay in site preparation work, developer's lost profits recoverable); R.I. Lampus Co. v. Neville Cement Products Corp., 474 Pa. 199, 378 A.2d 288, 96 A.L.R.3d 290 (1977); see §§ 12.4(3) (consequential damages in contract cases generally); 12.16(4) (buyer's claim to lost profits) and particular types of contract, such as leases (§ 12.15 below).

8. Stott v. Johnston, 36 Cal.2d 864, 229 P.2d 348, 28 A.L.R.2d 580 (1951); Sol–O–Lite Laminating Corp. v. Allen, 223 Or. 80, 353 P.2d 843 (1960); AM/PM Franchise Ass'n v. Atlantic Richfield Co., 526 Pa. 110, 584 A.2d 915 (1990) (lost goodwill as a form of lost profits, recovery permissible where proof is adequate).

9. See § 5.15(2) below. See Brownstein, What's the Use? A Doctrinal and Policy Critique of the Measurement of Loss of Use Damages, 37 Rutgers L.Rev. 433 (1985).

10. Koninklijke Luchtvaart Maatschaapij, N.V. (KLM) v. United Technologies Corp., 610 F.2d 1052, 1056 (2d Cir.1979).

11. E.g., Public Serv. Co. of Ind., Inc. v. Bath Iron Works Corp., 773 F.2d 783 (7th Cir.1985). See § 5.15(2) below.

Direct loss of profit or income is not the only way in which consequential harm occurs. Instead of failing to gain income, the plaintiff's income may be diminished by increased expenses. So collateral expenses reasonably incurred because of the tort or breach of contract usually represent consequential harms. If the plaintiff in the airplane example had to store the plane until repairs could be begun, the storage costs that otherwise would not have been incurred would represent consequential harms for which damages would frequently be permitted. Almost any kind of collateral expense will count as consequential damages [12] and will be recoverable only under the special rules inhibiting consequential damages recovery. However, when the plaintiff's "expense" is repair or replacement of the entitlement itself, the expenditure is partly like consequential damages and partly like general damages; such expenditures are considered separately.[13]

These illustrations reflect some characteristics of consequential damages. While general or market damages attempt to protect the plaintiff's net worth by valuing the asset loss resulting from tort or contract breach, the consequential measure attempts to protect the plaintiff's income by awarding damages for losses of that income or, what is the same thing, for increases in expenses. General damages measures the losses in the very thing to which the plaintiff is entitled (an undamaged plane, a horse in the stable). Consequential damages measures something else; not the very thing the plaintiff was entitled to but income it can produce or losses it can avoid. Thus special or consequential damages are awarded for pecuniary losses that have been or will be realized.[14]

Lawyers often speak loosely about "profits," but not all lost gains are lost profits and not all lost gains are measured by consequential damages. Suppose the plaintiff contracts to purchase ten thousand bushels of Murg at $1 per bushel, delivery September 1. Defendant does not deliver as promised. On September 1 Murg is selling in well established markets for $1.50. Plaintiff's market measured damages would be 50 cents a bushel or $5,000. Sometimes lawyers say that the plaintiff is entitled to recover his expected $5,000 "profit" on the deal. But the recovery described is not a recovery of profit; it is a recovery of a market gain. It is a market or general damages measure.

Consequential damages seem appealing in many respects and sometimes people believe them to be more "accurate" than the market measures. The accuracy claim may be correct for any given case but it is doubtful if applied to cases as a whole.[15] Accurate or not, consequential damages often present problems. One of these lies in the fact that consequential damages may stretch infinitely in time. It is hard to be confident about proof of consequential losses, and it is easy to extend the claims. Consequential losses

---

12. See, for examples of expense incurred as consequential damages, e.g., U–Haul Intern., Inc. v. Jartran, Inc., 793 F.2d 1034 (9th Cir.1986) (cost of reestablishing goodwill damaged by defendant's tortious activity); Rogers v. Feltz, 163 Ariz. 462, 788 P.2d 1213 (App. 1989) (tenant's cost of relocating when landlord breached lease); Boehm v. French, 548 So.2d 12 (La.App.1989) (car owner's storage costs incurred when insurer failed to pay re-

pair bill, held recoverable); Schultz v. Sun Plastic, Inc., 1990 WL 72333 (Ohio App.1990) (not reported in N.E.2d) (added costs of financing in contract breach case); Reposa v. Buhler, 770 P.2d 235 (Wyo.1989) (telephone expense incurred to make arrangements minimizing damages after property was seriously damaged).

15. See § 3.3(8) below.

may easily exceed the risks created by the defendant's tort or those guaranteed by his contract. Consequential damages are costly to prove and litigate, both for parties and for courts. Consequential damages also run the risk of duplicated recoveries, if consequential damages are added to any other measures of relief. These problems prompt a series of rules which, effectively or not, attempt to guard against excessive consequential claims. These are discussed in the next section.

§ 3.3(5) Substitution Costs

Frequently a third kind of damages measurement is possible that resembles both market damages and consequential damages but differs from both. This is the substitution cost. Substitution cost does not measure the diminished net worth of the plaintiff as market damages would do. Instead it measures the cost of replacing the plaintiff's entitlement by repair or by obtaining a substitute. If the plaintiff's airplane is harmed by the defendant's tort, substitution cost would be the cost of repair, or, alternatively, the net cost of selling the damaged airplane and buying an undamaged plane of appropriate quality.[1] In breach of contract cases substitute costs would be the cost of procuring the contract goods or services elsewhere.[2]

Substitution cost may be introduced in a case either to measure damages or to limit damages. When it is used to limit damages under the avoidable consequences rules, it is offered as a least-cost measure, with no particular relationship to market damages measures at all. But sometimes substitution cost is introduced as a measure of rather than a limit on damages; the plaintiff wants such a measure because it will yield a higher recovery than market damages or because it is easier to prove. Sometimes the two uses of substitution cost become confused. This section deals only with substitution costs as a measure, not as a limit; that is, with cases in which the plaintiff, not the defendant, wants the case governed by substitution costs.

At first glance, substitution cost damages offer appealing and practical solutions to many cases. If your private car is damaged by the defendant's tort, your first thought is to recoup your repair cost. If the contractor does not complete the work on your house, you want to recover enough to pay a substitute contractor.

Actually, repair costs may be recovered de facto in some cases without adopting a substitution cost measure. In the car damage case this could happen because the diminished market value of your car was greater than the repair costs, so in recovering the market measure you would recover a sum more than sufficient to pay repairs. It could also happen because you used repair cost, not as a *measure* of damages, but as *evidence* about the probable diminution in market value. Because repair costs and market diminution are usually closely related, and because repair costs can often be identified easily and precisely, the evidence is practical and useful.

But cost of repair or substitution cost damages are not always the same or even approximately the same as diminished value measures. So in some cases the plaintiff who wishes to recover repair costs must establish grounds for departing from the market measure. Consider characteristics of substitution cost measures.

Substitution cost damages share characteristics with market or general damages on the one hand and with consequential damages on the other. Like market damages, substitution cost damages are normally measured by an objective standard; this is not market value of the plaintiff's entitlement, but it is market costs of repair, replacement or other substitution. By adverting to a market, we have some guarantee that the costs are genuine and not a subjective measure the plaintiff might adopt. Substitution damages resemble consequential damages in that they lack a firm closing date for the accounting between the parties and also in that they are usually invoked because the plaintiff claims some special or idiosyncratic value that cannot be compensated by a market measure.

Although substitution cost measures (or evidence) may be very practical in many cases, they often present some special problems. Some of the serious and common problems are these:

(1) Substitution costs may exceed the value of the property or the contract right. In the case of the damaged car, repairs to an old car might cost $5,000 even though the car itself was worth only $4,000. If we award repair costs of $5,000 might this be a windfall, that is, more than compensation?[3] If the plaintiff attached a special value to the particular car, we might conceivably be compensating for his subjective sense of loss; but if he does not in fact use the award to make repairs, we might doubt that there was any basis, even a subjective one, for giving more than market loss.[4]

(2) Substitution may provide the plaintiff with something more than his entitlement even if the cost of substitution is not great. This would occur if repair or replacement would give the plaintiff property more valuable than she was entitled to. For instance, suppose the plaintiff has a contract to purchase roofing material from the defendant for $5,000. The defendant reneges and the plaintiff purchases the only substitute roofing materials available, but it is more valuable, worth $10,000, and those materials add to the value of the plaintiff's house.[5]

(3) Substitution costs might not exceed the value of the plaintiff's right and might not give the plaintiff a greater value than that to which she is entitled, yet might contribute to economic waste if substitution is carried out, or alternatively to provide a windfall if it is not. Suppose the plaintiff's contract calls for installation of red tile in the bathroom but the defendant installs blue tile instead. When the error is discovered the plaintiff seeks to recover the cost of removing the work already done and installing red tile, even though the addition of red tile will add

§ 3.3(5)

3. See § 5.14(1) (reflecting cases going both ways); see also, on the same problem as to land, § 5.2(3).

4. If the "right" measure is a market measure and the substitution cost is allowed *only* because of the claimed subjective or special purpose of the plaintiff, then the plaintiff's post-award decision not to make repair or replacement might be understood to indicate that he had no such claimed subjective value. In that case, one might read the award as a

windfall. See United States v. 564.54 Acres of Land, Etc. (Lutheran Synod), 441 U.S. 506, 516, 99 S.Ct. 1854, 1859, 60 L.Ed.2d 435, 444 (1979) ("Awarding replacement cost on the theory that respondent would continue to operate the camps for a public purpose would thus provide a windfall if substitute facilities were never acquired, or if acquired, were later sold or converted to another use").

5. See the discussion of several kinds of "worth more" substitutes in § 12.16(3) below.

nothing to the value of the house. Destruction of the old tile and the work that went into it represents a loss of value forever, so substitution costs here create a problem of economic waste. Alternatively, if we imagine that the plaintiff will not use the damages recovery to install the red tile, then the plaintiff may have a windfall.[6]

(4) It is often difficult to determine what counts as a substitute for the plaintiff's entitlement. If defendant breaches his obligation to convey Blackacre to the plaintiff, is the plaintiff's purchase of Whiteacre a substitute?[7] If the defendant breaches a contract to sell 500 cows to the plaintiff, is the plaintiff's purchase of 500 cows elsewhere a substitute? Should the plaintiff's added cost of purchasing Whiteacre or 500 different cows be charged against the defendant? If so, what if it turns out that the plaintiffs also made a different and greater profit from these alleged substitutes?[8]

These problems suggest that substitution cost damages are not appropriate in every case, and the courts agree. The next subsection suggests that the courts avoid the substitution cost measure when it creates serious problems in particular cases, and use the measure when it seems needed to protect the plaintiff's idiosyncratic values.

§ 3.3(6) Individuating Damages: Protecting the Plaintiff's Personal Values

[*For the text of this section, see the unabridged Practitioner Treatise edition.*]

§ 3.3(7) Duplication of Damages

Adding Two Measures for One Loss or Wrong

Within the limits of practical damages measures, compensation remains the goal of damages. Overcompensation is undesirable, not only because it is unjust but also because it provides the wrong incentives to both parties. Yet overcompensation is sometimes hard to judge. When one measure of damages authorizes an award of $100 and another authorizes an award of $200, it is difficult to say that one measure is right and one is wrong. So it is hard to say that the plaintiff is overcompensated if she recovers $200. However, duplicated recoveries must count as overcompensation by any standard. In general, two different measures should not be used to compensate for the same underlying loss, even though the two measures produce different figures or use different calculations.

General damages plus substitution cost damages. One way damages recoveries can be duplicated occurs when both general market damages and substitution cost damages are awarded for the identical underlying loss.

Suppose the plaintiff claims the market damages of $100,000 but also the cost of drilling wells to provide the water, and that the well-drilling costs would come to $50,000. Can the plaintiff recover both sums? Such a recovery would duplicate some elements of damages. It would be like saying

---

6.　See, on facts like these, § 12.19(1) below.

7.　Cf. Mike Golden, Inc. v. Tenneco Oil Co., 450 N.W.2d 716, 718 (N.D.1990) (substitute mineral leases on same tract at a later and seemingly just as profitable a time, defendant should not be entitled to measure damages by the cost of these leases).

the plaintiff whose car is damaged can recover diminished value of the car *and* the cost of repairing it. If making repairs to the car or adding working wells to the farm would give the plaintiff what she was entitled to, then it will duplicate damages to award both measures.[1]

General damages and profits. Duplication can also occur if the plaintiff is allowed to recover both general damages and lost profits for the same underlying loss. Consider the plaintiff's contract to purchase a horse for $250,000. Suppose that the market value of the horse was $300,000 at time for performance and the seller reneges on the deal. Market damages would be $50,000, the difference between the contract price the plaintiff would have paid and the market value the plaintiff would have received. Suppose the plaintiff can put on evidence that the horse's winnings after the date for performance would have given the plaintiff a profit of $200,000. Can the plaintiff claim (a) $50,000 as the market measure plus (b) $200,000 as the lost profits? The answer should be no.

When you give the plaintiff a recovery calculated by using market value figures, you have given a recovery that is based on future profits as estimated by potential buyers who form the "market."[2] If you then give an award of future profits as estimated by the jury, you are giving part of the profits twice. It is true that the yardsticks are different because one estimate is made by looking at the market and one made by looking at individual forecasts of hoped-for profit. It is also true that the people doing the measurement are different; the buyers' estimates and the jury's estimates may be quite different. You might for these reasons prefer one estimate over the other, but you can't give the plaintiff both without duplication.

[*For discussion of other examples and other issues see this section in the Practitioner Treatise edition, vol. 1, pp. 313–316.*]

§ 3.3(8) The Relative Accuracy of Damages Measures: A Comment

Sometimes it is assumed that one measure of damages or the other is more "accurate." The assumption seems unwarranted for several different kinds of reasons.

First, a belief in accuracy of damages measurement can lead to confusion of *loss* with *damages*. In contracts cases the plaintiff may have losses that go "uncompensated" because they are excluded by the express terms of the contract or by the implied understandings of the parties. If you buy next-day parcel service and $100 insurance to cover you for a late delivery, you have a just claim when the service takes two days to deliver your parcel of factory parts. But even if the breach of contract causes your factory to stay closed an extra day and profits to be lost, you do not have a just claim for lost profits. You bought and paid for $100 in insurance, not insurance against lost profits. When writers say you are not accurately or fully compensated by the $100 recovery, they must mean that your *loss* is not

§ 3.3(7)

1. See Bechtel v. Liberty Nat. Bank, 534 F.2d 1335, 1342 n. 10 (9th Cir.1976); cf. Worthington v. Roberts, 304 Ark. 551, 803 S.W.2d 906, 910 (1991) (instruction that mentioned both replacement of trees damaged *and* differ-

ence in fair market value before and after damage would be error as "presenting a danger of double recovery"). Facts like those given in the text and some other duplication problems are discussed in § 9.2(3) below.

accurately measured. But the defendant, by contract, is not responsible for your loss, only for what it agreed to pay. The $100 (or perhaps the added cost you paid for the first-day service you didn't get). So the $100 recovery is an accurate measure of *compensation* based on your contractual entitlement, although it is not an accurate measure of loss. Accuracy is a concept that best addresses factual questions of loss, not the more complex questions about what counts as compensation.

Second, we can know that a measurement accurately reflects *compensation* only when we know what compensation is and how it is tested. But that is the very question at issue when one must choose among the market, consequential and substitution cost measures. We cannot say we know that consequential damages is a better measure than market damages except by assuming that consequential damages is the "right" test or by finding some higher, better, more authoritative test that validates consequential damages above others. But we don't have a higher, more authoritative test; we have three tests, each competing for acceptance. Unless we want to say that one test or another is more accurate because we know accuracy when we see it, it will be hard to prove that one of the measures is more accurate than the others in any general run of cases.

Third, even if the policy task of measuring damages were the same as empirically identifying losses, it is literally not possible to know when we have accurately identified a loss. We know the market measure may fail to identify all losses, because it closes out the account between the parties at the date the defendant's contract or tort duty was breached and we know that subsequent events could give a very different picture. But almost the same is true with consequential damages, to which is added the uncertainty involved in overt judicial speculation about the course of future events. With consequential damages we lose the convenience of "closing the account" in order to prove losses that occur later; the plaintiff can claim damages into the future as far as hope and fear can travel. But an estimate for the entire future must be made by trial time, and events the day after the trial may prove the estimate wholly wrong. Substitution cost damages may also be inaccurate. For instance, their accuracy depends in some cases on whether you think the award would be used to procure a substitute, or, if not, whether you think the award nevertheless is somehow equal to a subjective sense of loss for which "compensation" is required.

Accuracy in measurement is a desirable goal, but it should not lead us to forget the definitional and policy elements involved, nor the limits of the enterprise. Courts must choose among the measures as best they can, but they should not be faulted when they opt for the convenience and certainty of market damages. Nor should they be pushed into a regime of substitution cost damages by critics who believe they have the "accurate" answer.

§ 3.4 Proving Consequential Damages: Special Requirements, Limited Alternatives

Legal rules forbid consequential damages completely in some kinds of cases, notably in eminent domain takings cases.[1] In all other cases a

§ 3.4

1. See, United States v. Petty Motor Co., 327 U.S. 372, 66 S.Ct. 596, 90 L.Ed. 729 (1946); Yuba Natural Resources, Inc. v. United

number of rules impose added burdens on the claim for special or consequential damages. Occasionally a plaintiff will have limited opportunities to escape those burdens by formulating an alternative damages claim that is not regarded as a claim to consequential damages.

Rules Inhibiting Consequential Damages Claims

Pleading. It is traditionally said that special damages must be specifically pleaded, else they cannot be recovered.[2] This rule requires little comment. Although it impacts the damages claim (as do other procedural requirements) it is not itself a rule of damages. It is rather a pleading rule, and one of no great repute or standing at that.

Certainty: pecuniary loss must be realized. Consequential damages must be proved with reasonable certainty. This rule requires the plaintiff to show that any consequential damages claimed must have been caused in fact or at least reasonably likely to result in the future.[3] Another and maybe more revealing way to say the same thing is to say that consequential losses must have been realized or must be likely to be realized in the future. This differs from the rule about general damages, which as already shown,[4] may represent mere paper or bookkeeping losses.

A good illustration of a loss not realized occurs when the defendant publishes erroneous information about the plaintiff's shares of stock. The value of the stock drops as a result. But unless the plaintiff actually sells the stock at a loss, he cannot recover for the paper loss in value.[5] His claim is a consequential damages claim because he has the very thing to which he was entitled, the stock. The loss is unrealized, as we can see by remembering that the stock could rise again when correct information is published.

Certainty: proof as to amount. The reasonable certainty rule also requires proof to a reasonable certainty about the amount of loss that will be realized and requires rejection of the claim unless such proof is forthcoming.[6]

States, 904 F.2d 1577 (Fed.Cir.1990); see, relatedly, Risinger, Direct Damages: The Lost Key To Constitutional Just Compensation When Business Premises Are Condemned, 15 Seton Hall L.Rev. 483 (1985) (arguing that the "no business damages rule" is a myth). See also § 6.9(2) below (temporary and regulatory takings). Two qualifications: (1) In eminent domain cases the term "consequential damages" is sometimes given a unique meaning, referring to damages to un-taken land remaining in the original tract. (2) Some states have allowed consequential damages in eminent domain cases. See City of La Grange v. Pieratt, 142 Tex. 23, 175 S.W.2d 243 (1943) (compensation required not only for "taking," but also for "damage or destruction").

The UCC may contemplate that consequential damages will be denied to sellers of goods, except for those consequential damages called "incidental" and except for "lost profits" in a narrow category of cases. See §§ 12.17(4) & 12.17(5) below.

Outside the property-contract area, consequential damages are also sometimes excluded from whole classes of cases, such as employment discrimination cases under Title VII of the 1964 Civil Rights Act, as to which see § 6.10(4) below.

3. See e.g., West Haven Sound Dev. Corp. v. City of West Haven, 207 Conn. 308, 541 A.2d 858, 861 (1988). Causal rules, including liability for concurrent torts, is an elaborately developed subject in tort law. See Prosser & Keeton on Torts § 41 (5th ed. 1984). As to contracts, see § 12.4(2) below.

5. This illustration is taken from Malachy v. Soper, 3 Bing.N.C. 371, 121 Eng.Rep. 453 (1836).

6. Shannon v. Shaffer Oil & Ref. Co., 51 F.2d 878, 78 A.L.R. 851 (10th Cir.1931); St. Paul at Chase Corp. v. Manufacturers Life Ins. Co., 262 Md. 192, 278 A.2d 12 (1971), cert. denied, 404 U.S. 857, 92 S.Ct. 104, 30 L.Ed.2d 98 (1971).

The entrepreneur's "cheerful prognostications" are not enough.[7]

On this narrow rule courts usually take either a hard or a soft approach. The soft approach in effect says that the plaintiff must show he has realized or will realize actual losses, but that once he has made this proof, the court will not require precision as to amounts.[8] This soft approach is usually accompanied, however, with an escape clause in which the court warns that it will not permit speculation.[9]

The hard approach is more like the escape clause in the soft approach. It asserts in effect that the plaintiff must prove consequential damages with reasonable certainty, both as to their existence and amount.[10] Neither approach has much actual content. Both approaches reflect summaries of how the court feels about particular facts. As guiding rules they do little except to warn the plaintiff that bookkeeping losses do not count when it comes to consequential damages recoveries.

Courts once thought that the plaintiff could not recover for lost expected profits unless the plaintiff's business had a profit history; so new businesses could not recover for lost future profits.[11] Courts now recognize that recovery of profits in an appropriate case is a question of proof, not a rule of law. If the proof is persuasive, a lost profit recovery is appropriate, even with new businesses.[12] For instance, proof of sales and profits of comparable businesses, especially on the sale of mass produced, standardized goods at standard prices, may satisfy the proof requirements.[13] The plaintiff's own profit history in a comparable business, or in the same one at a different location, may also suffice.[14] The most persuasive evidence is often in the form of detailed business statistics [15] or marketing and production information, coupled with expert testimony.[16] But even statistics may turn out to be inadequate unless they are rigorously tested and conform to commonsense expectations.[17]

Proximate cause and Hadley limits. Consequential damages are also subject to the limitations expressed in rules of proximate cause or legal

---

7. Benham v. World Airways, Inc., 432 F.2d 359, 361 (9th Cir.1970) ("Those cheerful prognostications are worth no more than the factual data upon which they were based. The factual foundation was absent, and the opinions accordingly collapse").

8. E.g., Lam, Inc. v. Johns–Manville Corp., 718 F.2d 1056, 1065 (Fed.Cir.1983); Tull v. Gundersons, Inc., 709 P.2d 940, 943, 52 A.L.R.4th 699 (Colo.1985); Conrad v. Dorweiler, 189 N.W.2d 537 (Iowa 1971).

10. Sanchez–Corea v. Bank of Am., 38 Cal.3d 892, 902, 215 Cal.Rptr. 679, 689, 701 P.2d 826, 836 (1985).

11. Central Coal & Coke Co. v. Hartman, 111 Fed. 96 (8th Cir.1901).

12. See Comment, Remedies—Lost Profits as Contract Damages for an Unestablished Business: The New Business Rule Becomes Outdated, 56 N.C.L.Rev. 693, 714 (1978). For contract cases, see § 12.4(3) below.

13. Richfield Oil Corp. v. Karseal Corp., 271 F.2d 709 (9th Cir.1959), cert. denied, 361 U.S. 961, 80 S.Ct. 590, 4 L.Ed.2d 543 (1960);

Lehrman v. Gulf Oil Corp., 500 F.2d 659 (5th Cir.1974), cert. denied, 420 U.S. 929, 95 S.Ct. 1128, 43 L.Ed.2d 400 (1975). Comparable income or profits from service establishment is unlikely to suffice, because profit in those cases is likely to turn on individual characteristics of the entrepreneurs.

14. E.g., Petrie–Clemons v. Butterfield, 122 N.H. 120, 441 A.2d 1167 (1982).

15. E.g., Lexington Products Ltd. v. B.D. Communications, Inc., 677 F.2d 251 (2d Cir. 1982) (ratio of sales to advertising evidence helped justify award against defendant who breached contract to maintain certain level of advertising for product).

17. See University Computing Co. v. Management Science of America, Inc., 810 F.2d 1395 (5th Cir.1987) (statistics not rigorous or technical enough to permit profit recovery, at least where they were not buttressed by commonsense inferences).

cause [18] and in the analogous contemplation of the parties rules in contract cases.[19]   Neither the proximate cause issue nor the contemplation of the parties issue arises with general or market damages claims.   Indeed, *Hadley v. Baxendale*,[20] which limited contract damages to those within the contemplation of the parties, can be read as simply holding that market measures are to be used unless the parties' understanding contemplates the use of consequential damages.   So the plaintiff who claims consequential damages must reckon with the limitations imposed by proximate cause and contemplation of the parties rules, while the plaintiff who claims only general damages meets no such obstacle.

Avoidable consequences.   The avoidable consequences rules, which reduce the plaintiff's recovery to the extent he did or reasonably could have minimized loss,[21] apply preeminently to consequential damages.   Indirectly, market damages may be calculated in some cases supporting similar goals, but in general the avoidable consequences rules are aimed at consequential, not market damages.

Alternative Claims to Escape the Limitations

Objective substitutes for profit loss.   When the plaintiff is unable to mount sufficient evidence as to lost profits, alternative measures must be considered, among them the market and substitute cost measures.   Another possibility when profits cannot be proven is to claim what is essentially the opportunity cost of seeking profits.   For example, suppose the plaintiff's business is idled for a time because the defendant's tort or breach of a supply contract makes operation impossible.   If profits would have been likely but the amount cannot be shown, the plaintiff might be allowed to recover interest on the capital investment that was reduced to idleness [22] or perhaps rental value on equipment that had productive capabilities.[23]

Value of the chance; preponderance of the evidence.   Reality is increasingly perceived in terms of statistics.   Statistical outlooks encourage statistical solutions to proof of damages problems.   Suppose that the plaintiff cannot prove how much profit he lost to a reasonable certainty, but that he could prove that he had a 40% *chance* of making $100,000 except for the defendant's breach of contract or tort.   Traditional notions of proof hold that the plaintiff must prove not only damages but any element of his case by a preponderance of the evidence, meaning a greater weight of the evidence.   This would mean that the plaintiff would have to prove elements of his case to be true, more likely than not; and more likely than not, reduced to numbers, means anything more than a 50% chance.   So the plaintiff has not proved the loss of $100,000 in profits when he proves only a 40% likelihood that he would have earned such profits.

Value of chances that are bought and sold.   But we can reify "chance" and think of it as a kind of reality which itself can be won or lost, bought or sold.   Much of contemporary wealth exists in the form of chances or

---

18.   E.g., Keister v. Talbott, 182 W.Va. 745, 391 S.E.2d 895 (1990).

19.   See §§ 12.4(4)–12.4(7) below.

20.   9 Ex. 341, 156 Eng.Rep. 145 (1854); § 12.4(4) below.

22.   See Brooklyn Eastern Dist. Terminal v. United States, 287 U.S. 170, 174, 53 S.Ct. 103, 104, 77 L.Ed. 240, 242 (1932); Thornton & Warren v. Cordell, 8 Ga.App. 588, 70 S.E. 17 (1911); Foard v. Atlantic & N.C.R. Co., 53 N.C. 235 (1860).

opportunities. Some chances are represented, for example, by shares of stock. Such chances are bought and sold and so can be conveniently evaluated on a market. If I fail to buy the $1 lottery ticket for you as I promised, or if I destroy the one you have, I destroy a chance that can be valued in the market at one dollar. Some business opportunities might be viewed in this way.[24] Can this idea be carried over to chances that are *not* bought and sold? Or to chances that might be bought and sold but for which we have no estimate of a selling price?

Value of chances for which there is no market. The fact that there is no market for a given opportunity even when it has a statistical chance of success [25] warns against opting for this approach unless it is especially important to do so, perhaps for reasons not closely associated with compensation. Are there any cases compelling enough to warrant using the value of a chance approach where the plaintiff would otherwise be denied recovery for failure of proof?

Percentage chance without a market: the pig that missed the fair. Suppose the plaintiff can persuasively prove that the defendant breached a contract to transport the plaintiff's pig to the state fair, where it had a chance of winning first prize. The proof does not establish that the pig would be more likely to win than not, only that it had a one-in-three chance. If the first prize was $1,000, the plaintiff can argue that although he did not lose $1,000 he very definitely lost a one-third chance at the $1,000. *That* loss was certain. If we know that the chance was one-third, that certain loss of a chance can be valued at $333.

When we do not have any means of estimating the value of the lost chance, by its market value or by knowing that only three pigs showed up at the fair, the value of the chance seems as elusive as any traditional claim for lost profits that cannot be proved. Yet chance and risk, the hopeful and skeptical sides of probability, are constantly estimated both in courts and in every day life. To some extent, courts are themselves estimating business or economic risks when they attempt to value any property that has no market price.[26]

Authority for and against value of the chance. There is limited authority for allowing recovery in the pig case, although it may be based on the

24. Goodwill of a business may represent one possibility. The goodwill of a business is its prospects of receiving future income because of the favorable impressions of those who deal with the business. Those prospects may be represented in part by other, separately protected legal rights, such as trademarks. Either way, goodwill is not a thing but a projection of prospects. As such, it is a species of chance. Specifically, it is the chance to exploit favorable impressions of the public. Seen in this way, a claim for lost goodwill is just a claim for lost future profits. It is no more certain when it is called goodwill than when it is called consequential damages. In such a case, it would seem that the proof demands made on lost profit recoveries should also be imposed on lost goodwill recoveries.

When goodwill is actually bought and sold, as where a trademark is licensed at an established price, then it actually has a market price. In that case it can be valued as an asset so that market measured damages can be used. There would be no need to resort to uncertain evidence about the value of the chance of making profits. The same is true if experts can establish a goodwill value that is based on market estimates.

26. See Almota Farmers Elevator & Warehouse Co. v. United States, 409 U.S. 470, 93 S.Ct. 791, 35 L.Ed.2d 1 (1973) (chance that lease could be renewed was element to consider in fixing its market value); § 3.5 below.

assumption that the value of the chance could be accurately established.[27] Serious commentators have urged use of some version or another of the value of the chance technique.[28] A few courts have adopted the idea for what at present is a narrow class of cases. These are cases of medical neglect, in which the defendant physician fails to provide diagnosis or treatment for a patient who is already in serious condition. The patient dies, and was likely to die even if treatment had been given. But he is denied the chance of prolonged life, and some courts have said that was enough.[29] Others have refused to go along with this regime, even when the chance involved is the chance of life.[30]

Would value-of-the chance always limit the recovery to less than compensation? One problem may discourage wide adoption of the value of the chance approach. In the hypothetical pig example given above, the chance was one-third, so the plaintiff got one-third of the prize. If this is the right principle when the plaintiff's chance is one-third, is it not also the right principle when the plaintiff's chance is 60%? Traditional rules allow the plaintiff to recover full damages upon proof that more probably than not he would have made the profit or avoided the loss. A full-blown value of the chance rule would give the plaintiff only a percentage, even when loss was more likely than not and some commentators have argued for this.[31] It would also require estimates about the extent of the chance.

§ 3.5 Constructing Market Value: Definitions and Evidence

Constructing a Hypothetical Market

No market. In many instances no appropriate market can be found for the property or entitlement in question. This occurs for many reasons, ranging from the fact that no one is buying or selling property of the kind involved, to the fact that a monopoly may control prices. There would almost never be a "market" in real property, only sales of more or less

---

27. Kansas City, M. & O. Ry. Co. v. Bell, 197 S.W. 322, 323 (Tex.Civ.App.1917). By way of the defendant's railroad, the plaintiff shipped hogs to a stock show. The railroad delayed and the hogs did not look their best at the show. Even so they won second prize. Complaining that had they arrived on time they would have taken a first prize, the plaintiff sued. The court approved the argument for recovery saying:

> The chance might be worth little or nothing, or it might be worth, under some circumstances, the full amount of the premium offered for the best of the class in which the plaintiff was a competitor. In such a case, evidence as to all such matters as would tend to show the probability that the plaintiff would be successful in the competition would be admissible, and, as one of the judges in the English case says, it would then be left to the good sense of the jury * * *.

When a law student, Rick Bacal argued that the case be regarded as *sooey generis*. Perhaps *sooey generous* is closer.

28. Schaefer, Uncertainty and the Law of Damages, 19 Wm. & Mary L.Rev. 719 (1978); King, Causation, Valuation, and Chance in Personal Injury Torts Involving Preexisting Conditions and Future Consequences, 90 Yale J. 1353 (1981); cf. Leubsdorf, Remedies for Uncertainty, 61 B.U.L.Rev. 132 (1981) (suggesting some non-probabilistic solutions to some remedial problems, including damages that mimic a market or a social insurance fund or merely standardize a fixed recovery for certain situations).

29. E.g., McKellips v. Saint Francis Hosp., Inc., 741 P.2d 467, 81 A.L.R.4th 467 (Okl. 1987); cf. Herskovits v. Group Health Co-op., 99 Wash.2d 609, 664 P.2d 474 (1983).

30. E.g., Simmons v. West Covina Medical Clinic, 212 Cal.App.3d 696, 260 Cal.Rptr. 772 (1989); Gooding v. University Hosp. Bldg., Inc., 445 So.2d 1015 (Fla.1984).

31. Makdisi, Proportional Liability: A Comprehensive Rule to Apportion Tort Damages Based on Probability, 67 N.C.L.Rev. 1063 (1989).

comparable properties. Businesses, opportunities, and trade secrets might theoretically be bought and sold, but unique advantages and risks again make standard market prices unlikely. So in many cases, market value, one of the most common bases for damages decisions, is not an existing fact but a legal construct or even a convention.

Willing buyer and seller: looking for information to construct a "market". In the no-market situation, courts usually begin by saying that fair market value is the amount which a willing buyer would pay and for which a willing seller would sell, neither being under any special compulsion.[1] The definition does not help much in itself. It is indirectly useful, however, because it recognizes that market value "is no more than a summary expression of forecasts that the needs and attitudes which made up demand in the past will have their counterparts in the future."[2] In effect the willing dealers definition directs us to use information that buyers and sellers would use hypothetically, *if* they were interested in dealing, and in fact courts do attempt to use such information.

Sometimes the data for constructing a hypothetical market are introduced directly. Comparable sales,[3] income produced by the property,[4] its replacement costs,[5] cost of securing a functional substitute,[6] risks of loss and chances of gain[7] are all data that buyers and sellers would consider in negotiating a price, and all elements that courts may consider directly in trying to form an estimate of value. Very commonly these data are filtered through the opinion of an expert who is allowed to state an opinion as to value and also to state his basis in fact for that opinion.[8]

Scope and related material. No-market problems create a serious and costly problem for the parties and for a judicial system that attempts to restore the plaintiff to her or his rightful position.[9] At best courts must try to reconstruct information that would be quickly available and generally shared in a fully developed market.

Opinion Evidence of Value

Expert opinion. A common form of proving market value, especially of real property, relies on expert opinion, not only from professional appraisers, but from those who otherwise know the standards of value for the kind of property in question.[11] So one who knows sale prices of comparable property,[12] or knows the values in the vicinity and the property in question can give an opinion as to value.[13] An expert may be allowed on direct examination to state the basis of his or her opinion, even though the testimony would be hearsay if admitted independently.[14] The expert opinion is of course subject to cross examination and in extreme cases it might be excluded altogether where it is admittedly based upon calculations not supported by fact.[15] Even an expert who has never seen the property may testify to an

---

§ 3.5

1. Peterson v. Continental Boiler Works, Inc., 783 S.W.2d 896, 900 (Mo.1990); ITT Commercial Finance Corp. v. Riehn, 796 S.W.2d 248 (Tex.App.1990); Milwaukee Rescue Mission, Inc. v. Redevelopment Auth. of City of Milwaukee, 161 Wis.2d 472, 468 N.W.2d 663 (1991). But see Memphis Housing Auth. v.

Peabody Garage Co., 505 S.W.2d 719 (Tenn. 1974) and the comparable sale discussion below.

2. Kimball Laundry Co. v. United States, 338 U.S. 1, 69 S.Ct. 1434, 93 L.Ed. 1765, 7 A.L.R. 1280 (1949).

opinion on the basis of supposed facts about the property, where evidence about those facts has already been admitted through other witnesses.[16]

Most of the cases involve real property and many of those, aside from tax assessment disputes, arise in the context of eminent domain takings. But the same general ideas apply to permit expert valuation testimony not only to real property generally but also to valuation of personal property [17] and even to services.[18]

Owner opinion. A special rule has been applied to the testimony of property owners. In most states, owners are permitted to testify to the value of their own property, both real [19] and personal.[20] By analogy, one who performs services can testify as to the value of that service.[21] Under this rule, the owner is not required to establish qualifications as an expert. The owner's opinion testimony will be excluded only if the owner admits, or it affirmatively appears that the owner knows nothing about the value. Some authority is less generous and requires the owner either to qualify as an expert or to give some basis for an opinion before giving a conclusion as to value.[22] In the case of services, it is said that the opinion as to value is allowed only after the services have been described with reasonable particularity.[23]

Most of the cases involve common articles with which the owner was familiar, and in most of them the jury would also have at least a general notion about the range of values involved; and of course the jury is not obliged to believe the owner.[24] There are cases in which owners have given value testimony about esoteric or unusual items, such as literary property.[25] The current view seems to be that when it comes to unusual items, the owner must show he knows something about the value before he can state his conclusion as to value.[26]

Other opinion testimony. Sometimes non-owners are allowed to testify to the value of property without showing any special basis for knowledge, provided they are closely identified with ownership. The spouse may testify as to the value of property he or she uses, and relatives [27] and former owners may also testify.[28] Even a person buying the property under a contract has been allowed to testify.[29] This liberal approach has not been extended to corporate stockholders and officers, however. They are required to show some knowledge before their opinions are admissible.[30]

Data for Constructing a Value

Market reports. If there is in fact a market in items identical to the plaintiff's entitlement, that market furnishes the best guide to market value. Where necessary, an adjustment can be made for transportation costs. The UCC provides that where the price or value of goods is in issue, "reports in official publications or trade journals or in newspapers or periodicals of general circulation published as the reports of such market shall be admissible in evidence." [31] Similar rules have been applied in tort cases, where price lists, market reports, Blue Book prices and the like are admitted.[32]

Comparable sales. With unique property, which normally includes all real property, there can be no price lists or market reports because sale of one tract is not the equivalent of selling another. However, witnesses often testify as to "comparable sales," meaning sales of similar land, with adjustments for particular characteristics such as size and special improvements.[33] Courts often regard this as the best method for proving land value and may exclude less reliable methods when this one can be used.[34]

The comparable sales method requires proof that the properties compared are indeed similar.[35] The sales compared cannot have taken place at a remote time period.[36] If the terms of the compared sale are different, an adjustment would need to be made in the valuation accordingly.[37] The sale is not comparable if it is made under compulsion, as where the sale was compelled by foreclosure.[38] When the putative comparable sale was made to an entity with the power of eminent domain, the taking power might affect the price, even though the parties bargained for the sale and effectuated it by contract. So some courts have refused to admit evidence of such sales even though they are otherwise comparable.[39] However, other courts will treat such a purchase as a comparable sale if the contract was a bona fide transaction.[40]

The definition of market value posits a willing seller and buyer, neither of whom acts under compulsion. But the fact that one of the parties in the comparable sale acted under special need or compulsion may be irrelevant, depending on which party at trial seeks to introduce evidence. In a Tennessee case, the landowner whose property was taken by eminent domain wanted to prove a comparable sale. In the alleged comparable sale, the seller was "anxious to consummate the sale" for reasons of his own. This led the condemning authority to argue that the sale was "under compulsion," that it therefore did not reflect a free market, and hence that the evidence of such a sale could not be admitted. But because it was the *seller* who was pressed to sell, the price would not be *higher* as a result of his compulsion. If anything, the seller's anxiety to sell—the "compulsion"—might suggest that the sale price could be too low. If the landowner wanted to introduce this evidence, its weakness did not prejudice the condemning authority. So the Tennessee Court held the evidence to be admissible.[41]

The market measures are useful partly because it is often easy to find and prove the market. When comparable sales methods must be used, market value is unclear to begin with and costly to construct. In these cases, however, the alternatives are limited.

Offers and prior sales. Sometimes comparable sale evidence is not available but the land being valued has itself been sold in recent times. Sometimes its sale price, if not too remote in time, is accepted as admissible evidence of its present value.[42] Rental market value is not essentially different, so prior bona fide rental of the same land is good evidence about its rental value.[43] However, courts usually draw the line at mere offers to purchase. The usual practice is to exclude evidence of such offers.[44]

"Capitalization of income" or discounted cash flow. The market value of property is undeniably connected with its capacity for use. If it can produce income, that income will have an important bearing on what potential buyers would pay for the property, a fact that might be considered informally as one element among others in estimating value.[45]

---

45. See O'Brien Bros. v. The Helen B. Moran, 160 F.2d 502 (2d Cir.1947). The income would be relevant only if it were recent. See United States v. Toronto, Hamilton & Buffalo

But it might also be possible to work backward from known or projected income in a more systematic way and to come up with a firm estimate of what buyers would pay to have that income stream. This idea is referred to as the capitalization of income method, or the discounted cash flow method of estimating market value.[46] In essence, it seeks to establish the present worth of future income that could be derived from the property.[47] The idea is traditionally "suspect," but within limits this method has been used in valuing property, especially in eminent domain cases,[48] and some courts have even preferred it for some income producing properties when other methods fail.[49] It has received some approval in other kinds of cases as well.[50]

Capitalization: passive income requirement. If misused, the capitalization method might yield consequential damages in the form of lost profits rather than an estimate of market value of the property itself. This would happen if it were applied to income from the operation of a business on the property rather than to passive income from the land. So the method should not be used to calculate land value by estimating income from the owner's active operations or business.[51] Instead, capitalization properly considers only passive income that could be or is derived from the land itself, such as rental value or the royalty payable to the owner by someone else for the right to extract minerals.[52] The land itself is the main ingredient in producing such income, so it may be fair to value the land by the income it produces. Just the contrary is so when the income is derived from operations by the owner; the land does not produce the income, the owner does.

Capitalization: figuring the discount rate. But there are other difficulties in using the capitalization or cash flow method. The method requires one to project income from the land, which entails much the same difficulty that calls for caution in forecasting profits.[53] It then requires a reduction of the projected income to present value. Any present value reduction requires the court to select an appropriate "discount rate" or interest rate in order to calculate what award must be made now to produce the equivalent of the future income. For the purpose of valuing property which can earn money, the discount rate must reflect the risk that there would be no demand for the property at some later date and hence no income from it. So we would

Nav. Co., 338 U.S. 396, 70 S.Ct. 217, 94 L.Ed. 195 (1949).

48. Foster v. United States, 2 Cl.Ct. 426 (1983), aff'd, 746 F.2d 1491 (Fed.Cir.1984), cert. denied, 471 U.S. 1053, 105 S.Ct. 2112, 85 L.Ed.2d 478 (1985).

49. See In the Matter of Acquisition of Real Property by the City of Albany, 136 A.D.2d 818, 523 N.Y.S.2d 652, 653 (1988).

50. See O'Brien Bros. v. The Helen B. Moran, 160 F.2d 502 (2d Cir.1947); § 5.16(2) below (property damage cases).

51. See, e.g., Arkansas State Highway Com'n v. Wilmans, 236 Ark. 945, 370 S.W.2d 802 (1963).

52. Foster v. United States, 2 Cl.Ct. 426 (1983), aff'd, 746 F.2d 1491 (Fed.Cir.1984), cert.

denied, 471 U.S. 1053, 105 S.Ct. 2112, 85 L.Ed.2d 478 (1985).

53. In In re Blackwell's Island Bridge, 118 App.Div. 272, 103 N.Y.S. 441 (1907) the testimony offered was that vacant lots taken in a condemnation could best have been used to erect three apartment houses at a certain estimated cost, and that the apartment houses would produce a certain income. The court rejected so much "uncertainty and speculation." At the same time, the present income from the land is not necessarily controlling. If the claimant is obtaining rent, but comparable properties in the area obtain a higher rent, the higher figure can be used to project the future expected income. In the Matter of the Acquisition of Real Property by the City of Albany, 136 A.D.2d 818, 523 N.Y.S.2d 652 (1988).

need to know how to estimate the risks in order to translate them into an appropriate discount rate.

Suppose we know the royalty income that an owner can obtain by allowing an operator to quarry rock on the owner's land. That income is $10,000 a year and the quarry could produce rock for an indefinite period. We want to figure back from the income to estimate the value of the property. That will be very hard to do if the quarry and the income will last forever, but it will also be hard to do even if the quarry will last only a specified number of years. This is because in order to know the value of the land from the income it produces, we must know the rate of return expected. If the $10,000 annual income is a 10% return, then it is easy to believe the value is in the neighborhood of $100,000. But we don't know that the $10,000 income is a 10% return; maybe it is a 5% return and the land's value is $200,000, or maybe it is a 20% return and the land's value is therefore more like $50,000. If we knew the value, we would know the rate of return; if we knew the rate of return, we would know the value. Knowing neither, we can make no calculation.

For example, suppose the property is a mine. It has regularly produced gold. The owner wants to sell the right to work the mine for a period of twenty years and an investor and potential operator wants to buy that right. The price the investor would pay would turn on the investor's estimate of potential income and profit. How much gold is in there? What will the price of gold be over the next twenty years? If the investor thought that the risks were high that the price of gold would drop or that the mine would play out, then the price would be lower; the investor would want a greater return for the money because the risks were great. Greater return for the investor translates into a higher discount rate for the seller. As the risk goes up, the appropriate discount goes up, too, and the price of the property drops.

To construct market value from income, we must construct the discount rate, but we have no independent market source to establish either. The trier must construct a discount rate out of its guess about risks in order construct a market value. Since investors who know such risks did not invest in the property or any similar property—that is what is meant by saying there is no market—courts should be guarded in figuring the risks for themselves. Experts can give their own estimates, but we know that those experts did not themselves bid on the property in question or any similar property; had they done so, there would have been a market or at least comparable sales. Estimating risks in an effort to fix the discount rate which in turn is used to estimate the market value of property is a tricky business.[54] Courts use it where they must,[55] but they sometimes show

---

54. But some estimation of risks is implied in any estimate of market value that is not based on the market. This became explicit in a 5–4 decision in Almota Farmers Elevator & Warehouse Co. v. United States, 409 U.S. 470, 93 S.Ct. 791, 35 L.Ed.2d 1 (1973). The government condemned a lessee's interest in land. The lessee had built buildings on the land and the lease had only a few years to run; but the landlord had renewed the lease regularly for many, many years. So anyone buying the lessee's interest would probably be willing to pay more than the salvage value of the buildings; a buyer would pay for the expectation that the lease could be renewed. The Court held that this expectation of buyers should be taken into account in figuring what buyers would pay as fair market value. The risk of non-renewal would be the other side of the expectation or chance of renewal and both

55. See note 55 on page 244.

considerable reluctance to use it standing alone;[56] surely they are right to reserve it for cases when other methods are not reasonably possible,[57] or to use it along with other methods.[58]

Other methods. What if there is no market, no comparable sale and no income to capitalize? If capitalization were extended to property that had no income but that could be altered to produce income, there would be few if any cases in this category. But courts have not usually extended the capitalization idea to property that is not producing and never has produced income. There are many properties that presently have no market value and never would if present use is continued. Non-public or quasi-public property like churches, bridges, and shelters for the homeless are all like this. Many items of personal property have no market value, ranging from the faded picture of Great Aunts to the much loved but worthless cat.[59] Artistic items, too, may present problems for valuation.[60]

In some of these situations courts have resorted to a variety of other data that would be considered, directly or indirectly, by potential buyers and sellers in formulating a price. So original cost, replacement cost, and markets at other times and places may all be considered, subject to adjustments for depreciation where costs are used and for transportation where distant markets are used.[61] The cost to the claimant of obtaining a good functional substitute elsewhere is usually rejected by the Supreme Court in federal eminent domain cases.[62]

§ 3.6 Interest Adjustments

§ 3.6(1) Interest and Prejudgment Interest

Background and Summary

Interest as compensation, restitution and incentive. Interest is the sum paid or payable for the use or detention of money. Just as rent is money paid for the use of property, interest is money paid for the use of other money. As courts have repeatedly recognized, an award of interest, running from the time the plaintiff's claim arose, may be necessary to provide full compensation. Such an award may also serve other purposes, too, by forcing disgorgement of unjust enrichment or by removing incentives the defendant might otherwise have to delay payment.[1]

---

sides of that coin would influence the buyer. Other decisions as well have recognized that estimation of risks is part of the business of valuation. See Kimball Laundry Co. v. United States, 338 U.S. 1, 17, 69 S.Ct. 1434, 1443, 93 L.Ed. 1765, 7 A.L.R. 1280 (1949) (purchase might have measured certain values by "capitalizing" at a rate that takes into account the risks).

55. United States v. Eden Memorial Park Ass'n, 350 F.2d 933 (9th Cir.1965); Foster v. United States, 2 Cl.Ct. 426 (1983), aff'd, 746 F.2d 1491 (Fed.Cir.1984), cert. denied, 471 U.S. 1053, 105 S.Ct. 2112, 85 L.Ed.2d 478 (1985).

56. E.g., Ross v. Board of Review of the City of Iowa City, 417 N.W.2d 462 (Iowa 1988).

57. See Lataille v. Housing Auth. of City of Woonsocket, 109 R.I. 75, 280 A.2d 98 (1971).

58. As in Seravalli v. United States, 845 F.2d 1571 (Fed.Cir.1988) where the trier took evidence of comparable sales, capitalization, and replacement costs. The award, said to be based on capitalization, was in fact between the low and high estimates based on comparable sales.

59. See § 5.16(3) below.

60. See § 5.16(4) below.

61. See § 5.16(2) below.

62. See § 5.2(6) below.

Historic attitudes towards interest. Both Jewish and Christian thinkers and moralists of some periods thought it wrong to charge interest. The medieval Christian world called it evil and prelates proscribed it. All that has changed. The Medicis and the Rothschilds built great fortunes by putting money out at interest. Ordinary people pay and receive interest every day to buy time and goods that otherwise could not be available or to provide security for retirement. Beyond that, we can now see that the idea of rent and the idea of interest are virtually the same in principle, one no more objectionable than the other, and that at times interest is morally grounded in restitution and the protection of property.[2] Even so, the older prejudices against interest left a residue of common law rules restricting interest recoveries.

Residual reluctance to award interest for pre-judgment losses. In general, parties today may provide for interest in their contracts, and courts will award interest on judgments for money.[3] However, apart from contract, courts are more reluctant to award prejudgment interest running from the time of the plaintiff's loss or injury. This reluctance finds its main expression in the traditional rule that prejudgment interest will not be awarded unless the plaintiff's claim is liquidated or ascertainable.[4] Many of the rules and arguments discussed in these sections grow out of this rule. So do some of the strategies. For example, the plaintiff may avoid the limitation if he can recover for the delay in recovering his entitlement by claiming special damages, or rental value, or lost profits, all of which can take the place of interest.[5] Statutes and more recent judicial decisions may also reject the traditional limits.[6]

Computation. Even when the traditional limitations do not prevent recovery, full compensation is not assured. Sometimes the rate of interest is set artificially by courts or legislatures at a fixed percentage rather than at market rate, so that the plaintiff may recover 6% interest when he must pay 12% to borrow money during the delay period. Very commonly, interest is not compounded, either.[7] Other limitations may reduce interest to avoid overcompensation.[8]

Categories of Interest

Interest is classified as contract or conventional interest, judgment interest, and prejudgment interest. Interest prescribed by contract may be recovered according to the contract terms, subject to usury and other regulatory statutes. Judgment interest is interest provided by law; it accrues on money judgments from the time of verdict or judgment.[9]

Prejudgment interest is interest which is awarded in the judgment but which is calculated to begin accruing at some time before judgment is entered. For example, prejudgment interest might begin to accrue from the time the defendant breached a contract or committed a tort, or from the time suit was filed. Litigation about interest mainly concerns whether prejudgment interest should be awarded at all and if so how it should be measured.

§ 3.6(1)

8. See §§ 3.6(5) (duplication of damages by interest awards) & 3.6(4) (elements like puni-

tive damages that may be excluded from computation).

9. See § 3.6(3) below.

Courts have sometimes sought to distinguish between "interest as such" or "interest eo nomine" from "interest as damages."[10] They have loosely associated interest "as such" with interest provided by contract.[11] So limited, there is a kind of sense to the distinction, although it matters only occasionally. If a promissory note or loan contract provides that the borrower will pay interest on the loan, the payment of interest is the very performance required, not damages for nonperformance or delay.

In this situation a difference can be discerned between interest "as such" and interest "as damages." But very little need turn on the distinction. So far as valid, the contract establishes the parties' rights, including rights to interest, its rate, and its computation. So contractual provisions for interest authorize the award of interest or an amount of interest when the law would not do so in the absence of a contract. The distinction between "interest eo nomine" and "interest as damages" does not advance legal policy very much except so far as it respects the parties' valid contract. So far as the distinction merely creates a definition or conceptual scheme, it probably should have little use in resolving real issues.[12]

General Rules

Rule against interest on unliquidated sums. The most significant limitation on the recovery of prejudgment interest[13] is the general rule that, apart from statute,[14] prejudgment interest is not recoverable on claims that are neither liquidated as a dollar sum nor ascertainable by fixed standards. For example, suppose the plaintiff is injured by the defendant's negligence and suffers an immediate loss of $100,000. Judgment is not ultimately entered for the plaintiff until five years later, at which time the plaintiff recovers a large sum, including the $100,000 for the various losses that occurred before trial. The claim is an unliquidated claim. Under the common law rule, interest would not be recovered for the delay in payment from injury to judgment.[15]

Although personal injury actions were an obvious example of unliquidated damages, many other claims, both in tort and in contract, could fall in this category for which interest was denied. For instance, damages for nuisance may be unliquidated and unascertainable.[16] Even damages for destruction of property[17] or damages for back pay[18] may be unliquidated

---

10. Interest "as damages" is sometimes called "moratory" interest. See Allstate Ins. Co. v. Starke, 797 P.2d 14 (Colo.1990).

11. Frank B. Bozzo, Inc. v. Electric Weld Div. of Fort Pitt Div. of Spang Industries, Inc., 345 Pa.Super. 423, 498 A.2d 895 (1985). See American Enka Co. v. Wicaco Mach. Corp., 686 F.2d 1050, 1056 (3d Cir.1982) ("Pre-judgment interest, by name, is not awarded in Pennsylvania actions other than contract, but what is described as damages for delay may be awarded in other actions, including certain tort actions. Thus in these cases, Pennsylvania employs a charming legal fiction * * * and although disavowing pre-judgment interest by name allows a contract pre-judgment interest counterpart [as delay damages under specific conditions].").

15. Sagadin v. Ripper, 175 Cal.App.3d 1141, 221 Cal.Rptr. 675 (1985); see Phelps v.

Duke Power Co., 324 N.C. 72, 376 S.E.2d 238 (1989); Bond v. City of Huntington, 166 W.Va. 581, 276 S.E.2d 539 (1981) (recognizing rule and rejecting it under death statute).

16. City of Fayetteville v. Stanberry, 305 Ark. 210, 807 S.W.2d 26 (1991) (nuisance/inverse condemnation claim based on city's overflowing sewers, amount to be paid in "just compensation" depended on land value, date of taking, and for what period the taking covered, so claim was unliquidated).

17. Schenk v. Smith, 117 Idaho 999, 793 P.2d 231 (App.1990) (vandals destroyed house and contents, "Youth Ranch" responsible not liable for prejudgment interest because range

---

18. See note 18 on page 247.

and unascertainable if the defendant's obligation is not a fixed sum and not computable from a relatively precise formula. Attorney fees due the plaintiff in the litigation are normally not liquidated and no prejudgment interest is added to such fees.[19] Although contract damages are often liquidated or ascertainable,[20] some contract damages are not. When they are not, prejudgment interest will not be recoverable.[21]

Interest permitted on liquidated or "ascertainable" damages. The converse rule is that when the plaintiff is entitled to recover a liquidated sum of money, prejudgment interest is also recoverable, calculated on the liquidated sum. For example, if the defendant promises to pay the plaintiff $100 on June 1 and does not do so, the plaintiff has a liquidated claim for $100, on which interest runs from June 1. An insurance policy in a fixed amount would be similar.[22]

When the plaintiff is entitled to recover a sum that is not liquidated but that can be ascertained by application of arithmetic or by the application of "accepted standards of valuation,"[23] without reliance on opinion or discretion,[24] the case is treated like a liquidated damages case so as to permit prejudgment interest.[25]

Example of ascertainable damages. The most obvious case of ascertainable damages is one in which arithmetic applied to the facts will produce the right figure. Defendant's obligation is to pay $1 for each bushel of Murg accepted from the plaintiff by October 15, payment due November 8. Plaintiff delivers 1,000 bushels by October 15. The amount due is ascertainable by multiplication, so prejudgment interest is proper.[26] One further rule

of appraisal testimony on value of property and some of it, like used clothing, had no readily identifiable market; damages were unliquidated, no interest). But see §§ 3.6(2) & 5.15(2) below (rental value or interest recoverable for loss of use in many property damage cases).

18. Pannell v. Food Servs. of Am., 61 Wash.App. 418, 810 P.2d 952 (1991).

19. Simonetti v. Lovermi, 15 Conn.App. 722, 546 A.2d 331, 334 (1988); Hansen v. Rothaus, 107 Wash.2d 468, 477, 730 P.2d 662, 667 (1986) ("costs of defending and settling the injured crew member's suit are unliquidated"). Even a contingent fee based on a percentage of a liquidated sum might be unascertained until awarded so long as the judge has discretion about whether to make the award or not. See Bear Creek Planning Comm. v. Title Ins. & Trust Co., 164 Cal.App.3d 1227, 211 Cal.Rptr. 172 (1985). When the plaintiff is entitled to recover a fee for *prior* litigation, that fee may be liquidated. As to fees for prior litigation, see § 3.10(3) below.

21. City of Indianapolis v. Twin Lakes Enterprises, Inc., 568 N.E.2d 1073 (Ind.App.1991) (contractor's extra work recovery, damages were not liquidated or ascertainable because of wide disparity in alternative calculations).

22. Ginsburg v. Insurance Co. of N. Am., 427 F.2d 1318 (6th Cir.1970) (face amount of

insurance policy even though plaintiff had originally prayed for more).

23. E.g., among many cases, City of Indianapolis v. Twin Lakes Enterprises, 568 N.E.2d 1073, 1087 (Ind.App.1991); Hansen v. Rothaus, 107 Wash.2d 468, 472–473, 730 P.2d 662, 664–665 (1986).

24. E.g., among many cases, Starczewski v. Unigard Ins. Group, 61 Wash.App. 267, 810 P.2d 58 (1991).

25. Chesapeake & Ohio Ry. Co. v. Elk Refining Co., 186 F.2d 30, 36 A.L.R.2d 329 (4th Cir.1950); McLemore v. Alabama Power Co., 285 Ala. 20, 228 So.2d 780 (1969); Martinelli v. Merchant Oil Inc., 470 P.2d 55 (Colo.App. 1970); City of Indianapolis v. Twin Lakes Enterprises, 568 N.E.2d 1073 (Ind.App.1991); Schmidt v. Knox, 191 Neb. 302, 215 N.W.2d 77 (1974); Kamens v. Fortugno, 108 N.J.Super. 544, 262 A.2d 11 (1970); In re Manhattan Civil Centre Area, 57 Misc.2d 156, 291 N.Y.S.2d 656 (1968), aff'd, 32 A.D.2d 530, 299 N.Y.S.2d 675 (1969); Harris & Harris Const. Co. v. Crain & Denbo, Inc., 256 N.C. 110, 123 S.E.2d 590 (1962); Beck v. Lawler, 422 S.W.2d 816 (Tex.Civ.App.1967); Indust–Ri–Chem Laboratory, Inc. v. Par–Pak Co., Inc., 602 S.W.2d 282 (Tex.Civ.App.1980).

26. See Restatement Second of Contracts § 354, Illustration 3 (1981).

must be considered before turning to some less obvious cases of ascertainable damages.

Effect of disputes, defenses and counterclaims. Courts usually say that damages may be ascertainable and prejudgment interest proper even when the parties dispute the underlying liability or the facts on which damages are based. The fact that the defendant raises a defense, counterclaim or set-off, does not prevent ascertainment of damages under this rule.[27] For example, if the plaintiff claims $1,000 for delivery of as many bushels of Murg, the defendant might raise a defense that the Murg was spoiled and unmerchantable and a counterclaim for consequential damages resulting from this breach of warranty; or he might defend in part on the ground that he paid all or part of the price, or that the number of bushels delivered came only to 500, not 1,000. These pleadings raise factual issues which surely make it impossible to calculate damages until they are resolved. Nevertheless, courts have said that such pleadings do not cloud the ascertainment of damages or prevent the award of prejudgment interest. Even if the counterclaim is itself unliquidated, so that it may call for reduction of the plaintiff's claim in an uncertain amount, prejudgment interest will remain proper if the plaintiff's original claim was liquidated or ascertainable.[28] It is the character of that original claim that counts, not the vicissitudes of the lawsuit.

When the defendant's counterclaim or set-off is successful and reduces his liability for reasons arising out of the same facts that gave rise to the plaintiff's claim, the plaintiff's claim is still regarded as ascertainable and prejudgment interest still awarded, but in that case interest is computed on the net amount the plaintiff recovers after crediting the defendant.[29]

Other limitations on interest. When the sums due are liquidated or ascertainable, prejudgment interest may still be denied. It should be denied, for example, if it would merely provide a different measure for a loss already compensated by some other measure of damages,[30] or if the claim for interest precedes the liability for it.[31] When the standards for interest are met, however, the plaintiff is entitled to recover even if he has not realized any loss due to the delay in receiving payment.[32] On the other hand, the plaintiff may be limited to simple interest in many states and under many circumstances.[33]

§ 3.6(2) Sidestepping the Traditional Limitations

Extending the Realm of the Ascertainable

The most common method for avoiding the limiting rules in effect defines some of the plaintiff's claims as "ascertainable" in a very generous

27. Riggs Nat. Bank of Washington, D.C. v. District of Columbia, 581 A.2d 1229 (D.C.App. 1990); Ehrle v. Bank Bldg. & Equip. Corp. of Am., 530 S.W.2d 482 (Mo.App.1975); Hansen v. Rothaus, 107 Wash.2d 468, 730 P.2d 662 (1986). Occasionally courts make statements that appear to conflict with this rule, as in Atokad Agricultural and Racing Ass'n v. Governors of the Knights of Ak–Sar–Ben, 237 Neb. 317, 466 N.W.2d 73, 79 (1991) ("A claim is unliquidated where a reasonable controver-

sy exists either as to the right to recover or as to the amount of such recovery"); cf. Strand v. Courier, 434 N.W.2d 60, 65 (S.D.1988) ("Had the counterclaim been successful, then damages would not have been certain or capable of being made certain until the jury returned its verdict").

32. See § 3.6(2) below.

33. See § 3.6(4) below.

way. The primary illustration of an ascertainable sum is one that can be reduced to a liquidated sum by a mathematical calculation. When the agreed unit price is $1 per bushel and the number of bushels is 1000, the amount due is ascertainable. However, courts go far beyond this idea of what is ascertainable.

Generally. Although counter examples can be given for most expansive holdings,[1] courts have been ready to say that when the plaintiff sues for the deprivation of property by reason of its harm, destruction or taking, he has an ascertainable loss. The reason given is that the "value" of the property can be discovered objectively.[2] Courts are just about as ready to find that the sums due for services are ascertainable,[3] as are the sums due for construction or repairs.[4] Some courts have even ventured into the battleground of personal injury law and declared that while pain and suffering do not produce ascertainable damages, at least the pecuniary losses in death and injury cases do.[5]

Examples of extension. It seems apparent that as courts have come to accept interest as necessary for full compensation they have expanded the concept of ascertainable sums to permit the award in an increasingly larger group of cases. Suppose the defendant breaches a contract to sell stock to the plaintiff and the plaintiff has a "reasonable time" in which to consult a lawyer and make financial arrangements for purchasing a substitute. Damages are measurable by the added cost of the substitute, which can be determined by looking at the stock market price on the relevant day; but given a reasonable time for replacement, we cannot know which date is the relevant one until the judge tells us. Yet a court may conclude that the damages are ascertainable even if they are unknowable.[6]

In *Ridley v. VanderBoegh*,[8] the plaintiff was the surviving spouse of *A*, who had been in a business partnership with *B*. The plaintiff was entitled to compensation for the value of *A's* share in the business. Three appraisers estimated its value at sums ranging from $191,000 to $220,000. The trial court accepted the middle appraisal at $200,000, then made deductions and calculations based on various payments, ultimately holding that the widow was entitled to $64,000. Could the plaintiff recover prejudgment interest on the ground that the amount of her claim was ascertainable before trial? The court said so.

§ 3.6(2)

3. Beck v. Lawler, 422 S.W.2d 816 (Tex.Civ. App.1967) (interest awarded on sums due for services under an express contract, even though the amount of the plaintiff's recovery could not be ascertained until after a trial). Contra, Lockard v. City of Salem, 130 W.Va. 287, 43 S.E.2d 239 (1947) (quantum meruit claim, so far as based on services it was not liquidated; so far as it was based on supplying materials, interest allowable).

4. See Strand v. Courier, 434 N.W.2d 60, 64 (S.D.1988) (contractor's charges were ascertainable damages by calculating rate, costs, and number of hours); cf. Grynberg v. Roberts, 102 N.M. 560, 698 P.2d 430 (1985) (obligation of the defendant to share in unspecified tangible and "intangible" costs of drilling and completing wells became ascertainable when the work was done so that interest was due from that point); Hansen v. Rothaus, 107 Wash.2d 468, 475, 730 P.2d 662, 666 (1986) ("evidence was available which furnished data making possible the computation of the cost of repairs with exactness and without reliance upon opinion or discretion").

5. Bond v. City of Huntington, 166 W.Va. 581, 276 S.E.2d 539 (1981). Statutes may also permit interest in such cases. As to this see the segment *Statutes*, below.

6. Rauser v. LTV Electrosystems, Inc., 437 F.2d 800 (7th Cir.1971).

8. 95 Idaho 456, 511 P.2d 273 (1973).

The future of the "ascertainable" standard. The "ascertainable" standard as developed by the courts has left them free to grant prejudgment interest or to deny it as they feel moved to do at the moment of decision. Used this way the standard is not a good predictor of the outcome on the prejudgment interest issue, and it probably never did represent a policy consistent with compensation. Not surprisingly, the artificial limitations on prejudgment interest awards have been criticized not only by commentators but by distinguished judges and in important cases;[9] it has been criticized as well, although implicitly, by legislatures which have liberalized the standards in many instances.[10] Will courts continue to use the standard to deny prejudgment interest? The courts' own liberalization of the standard coupled with criticisms of it may suggest an answer.

Claiming Interest or Costs as Special Damages

When the plaintiff's underlying loss is liquidated or ascertainable, interest is awarded whether or not the plaintiff has realized any losses as a result of the delay in payment. For example, the plaintiff is not required to show that he had to borrow money and pay interest. In this respect the interest recovery, when available, is treated like market or general damages.

When the plaintiff has in fact incurred interest costs because of the defendant's delay in paying the underlying obligation, the plaintiff may recover those costs as consequential damages, provided his proof meets the rules for recovery of consequential loss.[11] Recovery of this kind of realized loss does not depend on the interest rules. So when actual interest or added financing costs are recoverable as special damages, the liquidated-ascertainable rules do not affect the case and recovery is allowed for these costs merely as special damages.[12]

Claiming Interest in Lieu of Rental Value or Lost Profits

When the plaintiff's property is harmed, destroyed or taken, the plaintiff may suffer a loss of use of the property during the period of repair or replacement. Rental value of the property for this period is often one element of damages he is allowed to recover. If his automobile is damaged and he loses the use of it for a month, he may be entitled to its rental value or the rental value of some substitute transportation, as well as to some recovery for the physical damage itself.[13]

But it is possible to measure the loss of use by interest on the cash value of the car instead of by rental value of the car or the cost of obtaining a substitute. Both rental value and interest are measures of the same loss of

9. See La Paz County v. Yuma County, 153 Ariz. 162, 735 P.2d 772 (1987) (Feldman, J. dissenting); Cavnar v. Quality Control Parking, Inc., 696 S.W.2d 549 (Tex.1985).

10. See Segment *Statutes,* below.

12. E.g., Nebraska Public Power Dist. v. Austin Power, Inc., 773 F.2d 960 (8th Cir. 1985); Farmers Ins. Co. of Arizona v. R.B.L. Inv. Co., 138 Ariz. 562, 675 P.2d 1381 (App. 1983); Billings Clinic v. Peat Marwick Main & Co., 244 Mont. 324, 797 P.2d 899, 914–915 (1990) (unascertainable loss, but prejudgment interest, called moratory interest, recoverable as a form of consequential damages); Schultz

v. Sun Plastic, Inc., 1990 WL 72333 (Ohio App.1990); Hansen v. Rothaus, 107 Wash.2d 468, 475–476, 730 P.2d 662, 666 (1986) ("The owner of the Sea Comber is also entitled to recover the interest on the money he had to borrow to pay for repairs, and to recover the interest charged on the unpaid repair bill. But for the [underlying harm] the owner would not have incurred these expenses. They are recoverable as a separate element of his damages").

13. See § 5.15(2) below.

use, so courts sometimes substitute one measure for the other.[14] The rental value measure, however, is likely to produce a higher figure. Two propositions stand out. *First,* interest is the more conservative of the two measures for loss of use. *Second,* when the plaintiff is entitled to recover rental value, he is entitled to recover interest in lieu of rental value.

Claiming Interest as Restitution

When the defendant is under a duty to pay the plaintiff as damages or otherwise, and during the period of nonpayment the defendant has a legally recognized benefit from use of the money retained, he is under an obligation to make restitution of that benefit to the plaintiff, whether the benefit is measured in profits or interest or some other form of use value.[18] Liability for interest under this rule does not depend upon whether the use value was "ascertainable." It is possible, however, that courts will not recognize a benefit to the defendant in some cases unless he has actually realized a gain or savings from his delayed payment. The remaining paragraphs in this segment explain and elaborate these statements.

Restitution, as distinct from damages, is an award made to remedy unjust enrichment of the defendant rather than loss of the plaintiff. The topic of restitution is considered generally in the next chapter. It is important in connection with interest, however, because when the defendant does not make a payment to the plaintiff as due, the plaintiff's loss is also the defendant's gain. Just as the plaintiff's loss can be conventionally measured in interest, so can the defendant's gain. In special cases, however, the use value gained by the defendant can be measured in other ways, too.

Suppose a corporate insider, a fiduciary, "borrows" company funds to make an investment for his own account. The investment proves profitable, the insider returns the "borrowed" money intact and keeps the profits he made with it. If the corporation would not have invested the money or earned interest on it in any event, it can be said that the corporation had no losses on the transaction. However, the insider received unjust gains by use of the company's money. The law requires the insider to make restitution of those gains, that is to disgorge them and pay them to the company.[19]

The profits of the fiduciary in this example represent one measure of use value of the money. It is capable of earning interest and it is capable of earning profits. In this kind of case the plaintiff is entitled to the profits measure if he prefers. Suppose the fiduciary merely deposits the company's money in an interest bearing account. Instead of profits, he reaps interest. There would hardly be any purpose in holding the fiduciary liable for profits he made in buying and selling stock with the company money if he is not also liable for interest earned.[20] It does not seem to matter in cases of this

---

14. E.g., Bellon v. Malnar, 808 P.2d 1089 (Utah 1991) (vendee of land defaulted, vendor entitled to fair rental value during vendee's occupancy, but held, interest on the contract could be substituted for rental value). The fact that both measure the same loss does not mean that they do so by the same standard or that the figures they produce will be the same.

18. See Restatement of Restitution § 157, Comment c (1937).

19. E.g., Marcus v. Otis, 168 F.2d 649 (2d Cir.1948), adhered to, 169 F.2d 148 (1948).

20. Martinez v. Continental Enterprises, 730 P.2d 308 (Colo.1986) ("When a court appropriately applies the doctrine of unjust enrichment, the unjustly enriched party is generally liable for interest on the benefits received. D. Dobbs, The Law of Remedies § 3.5 (1973). Failure to award such interest would

kind whether the defendant's gains are liquidated or ascertainable; the defendant is enriched if he reaps the gain and that is enough.

Because all of this was most obvious in fiduciary cases, and because those cases were decided in equity courts, the generalization often made was that interest would be permitted in equity, as a matter of the chancellor's discretion, even where not permitted at law because the claim was unliquidated. The principle behind this, however, is clearly broader than the scope of purely equitable actions: it is a principle based upon unjust enrichment notions. For that reason it should be stated, not as a rule about equity, but as a rule about restitution.[21] Whenever the defendant holds money or property that belongs in good conscience to the plaintiff, and the objective of the court is to force disgorgement of his unjust enrichment, interest upon the funds or property so held may be necessary to force complete restitution.

[*For additional material on interest as restitution see this section in the Practitioner Treatise edition.*]

Contract, Express or Implied

The most obvious way of creating liability for prejudgment interest is by a contract provision for such interest. Such a provision must comply with usury statutes, consumer protection statutes and others. If it does, it is enforceable and interest can be awarded according to contract terms. Promissory notes are common examples.

It is possible to find an implied in fact contract to pay interest.

[*For further discussion of implied in fact contracts for interest see this section in the Practitioner Treatise edition.*]

Statutes

Statutes may affect the right to recover prejudgment interest in several ways. First, statutes may specify a right to recover prejudgment interest in particular cases or in general categories of cases; second, statutes may fail to provide for interest, or provide for limited interest, in circumstances that suggest interest is to be denied except as specified; third, the statutes may affect the measure or incidents of the interest award, such as rates to be used. This last is considered in a separate section.[28]

Most states have now enacted statutes that affect interest rules in some classes of cases, invariably liberalizing the traditional common law "ascer-

result in incomplete restitution to the petitioner"); Sack v. Feinman, 489 Pa. 152, 163, 413 A.2d 1059, 1064–1065 (1980); cf. Arnold v. Burgess, 113 Idaho 786, 795, 747 P.2d 1315, 1324 (1987) (interest award substituted for award on share of profits and other benefits); Restatement of Restitution § 157 (1937). The *Sack* court said in part, quoting the first edition of this treatise:

[I]t seems clear that if the fiduciary must account for profits he has gained by the use of the plaintiff's money, he must likewise account for interest he gained by its use. There would hardly be any purpose in holding the fiduciary liable for profits he gains on sales of stock purchased with his benefi-

ciaries' funds, without also holding him liable for interest he earned by investment of his beneficiaries' funds. Hence, wherever the fiduciary's profits could be reached by the beneficiary, interest on the funds wrongly held by the fiduciary could be awarded as an alternative.

21. See, e.g., Martinez v. Continental Enterprises, 730 P.2d 308 (Colo.1986); Herrmann v. Gleason, 126 F.2d 936 (6th Cir.1942), awarding interest on quasi-contract basis. The *Herrmann* case is criticized below on other grounds.

28. See § 3.6(4) below.

tainable" standard. Some of these statutes are incentive measures, similar to offer of judgment rules. These are invoked only to encourage offers of settlement or their acceptance,[29] or sometimes as to deter or punish unreasonable delay.[30] Some statutes make interest accrue from commencement of the action or the date of demand rather than from the time of injury.[31] Others make prejudgment interest run from the time of injury or the date the cause of action accrued.[32] Some statutes cover only particular categories of cases, such as non-contract actions;[33] others appear to cover claims of all kinds.[34]

A few statutes attempt to provide more complicated rules, allowing interest or not, depending upon several contingencies.[35]

When the statute is not addressed to interest as such but is aimed instead at creating or enhancing a cause of action, its silence on the question of interest might be read to mean different things under different conditions. If the statute operates in a common law framework in which interest is traditionally denied, the statute's failure affirmatively to provide for interest might be read to confirm the common law practice. When the Supreme Court considered the question of prejudgment interest in FELA claims for negligent injury to railroad employees, it concluded, in line with general common law practice, that prejudgment interest could not be awarded. The statute's silence had the effect of leaving the field occupied by the limiting rules of the common law.[40]

In other cases, however, the statute's silence is "just silence," and does not impliedly exclude the court from developing or expanding interest rules.[41] When the statute creates a cause of action that has little common law framework, or has a strong remedial purpose, the court may be willing to award prejudgment interest in spite of the statute's silence on the subject if such interest is compatible with the statutory purpose.[42] Cases of this sort turn primarily on statutory construction.

29. E.g., West's Ann.Cal.Civ.Code § 3291 (plaintiff entitled to prejudgment interest if he makes an offer, if defendant does not accept it, and if plaintiff ultimately recovers a judgment more favorable than the offer).

30. E.g., Md.Ct. & Jud.Pro.Code Ann. § 11–301.

31. Iowa Code Ann. § 535.3; Me.Rev.Stat. Ann. tit. 14 § 1602 (sometimes a variable rate, always from "notice of claim setting forth under oath the cause of action"); M.G.L.A. c. 231, § 6B (personal injuries, consequential damages or damage to property, 12% from commencement date); Nev.Rev.Stats.Ann. § 17.130 (unless the law or the judgment itself specifies otherwise, "the judgment draws interest from the time of service of the summons and complaint until satisfied").

32. N.Y.—McKinney's Civ.Prac.LR § 5001(b) (contract, interference with title, possession enjoyment of property, "from earliest ascertainable date the cause of action existed or when damage incurred").

33. N.D.Cent.Code 32–03–05 (non-contractual cases and all those involving fraud, malice or oppression).

34. M.C.L.A. 600.6013 (12% after 1980); Nev.Rev.Stats.Ann. 17.130 (unless the law or the judgment itself specifies otherwise, "the judgment draws interest from the time of service of the summons and complaint until satisfied"); N.H.Rev.Stat.Ann. 524:1–a, 524:1–b; R.I.Gen.L. § 9–21–10.

35. West's Ann.Cal.Civ.Code § 3287 (interest on ascertainable damages generally, but if in contract, interest may be given on unliquidated damages in courts' discretion).

40. Monessen Southwestern Ry. Co. v. Morgan, 486 U.S. 330, 108 S.Ct. 1837, 100 L.Ed.2d 349 (1988).

41. Bond v. City of Huntington, 166 W.Va. 581, 276 S.E.2d 539 (1981).

42. See Kleier Advertising, Inc. v. Premier Pontiac, Inc., 921 F.2d 1036 (10th Cir.1990) (copyright statute).

§ 3.6(3) Attacking the Traditional Limitations

Compensation, restitution, and incentives. The courts have overwhelmingly and repeatedly said that an award of prejudgment interest is necessary to provide compensation.[4] They have also recognized that in many cases the interest award is necessary to avoid unjust enrichment of a defendant who has had the use of money or things which rightly belong to the plaintiff.[5] In some cases courts have also recognized a third reason for prejudgment interest awards: if interest is not awarded the defendant may be left with undesirable incentives to delay payment.[6] A fourth reason exists but has not had general application: interest may be awarded against a defendant who litigates obstinately, as a sanction.[7]

Given these purposes behind rules permitting or requiring interest, why is interest denied when the loss is not liquidated or ascertainable?

Plaintiff's real losses. Does the plaintiff have losses that can be compensated by interest when he has a claim in an amount that is not ascertainable? Consider the fact that the plaintiff does not have the principal sum to which he is entitled. He cannot earn interest on that sum because he does not have it; he may be compelled to borrow to replace it, or alternatively to do without what he would have bought if he had what he was entitled to in the first place. The same loss is present if the plaintiff is injured and incurs medical expense or wage loss, or if his property is damaged or his contract rights violated. He must advance money of his own to replace that to which he is entitled, or he must borrow money to do so, or he must do without his entitlement. If he uses his own money for the replacement or repair, he cannot invest that money at interest. If he borrows, he must pay interest to another.[8] If he does without goods or things to which he is entitled instead of replacing them, he still has a real loss and one for which interest is the least of the compensatory measures possible.[9] On a compensation standard,

---

§ 3.6(3)

4. General Motors Corp. v. Devex Corp., 461 U.S. 648, 655–656, 103 S.Ct. 2058, 2063, 76 L.Ed.2d 211, 218 (1983) (prejudgment interest necessary to put plaintiff patent-owner is rightful position); Funkhouser v. J.B. Preston Co., 290 U.S. 163, 168, 54 S.Ct. 134, 136, 78 L.Ed. 243, 246 (1933) ("a distinction * * * simply as between cases of liquidated and unliquidated damages, is not a sound one. Whether the case is of the one class or the other, the injured party has suffered a loss which may be regarded as not fully compensated if he is confined to the amount found to be recoverable as of the time of breach and nothing is added for the delay in obtaining the award of damages"); Franks Music Corp. v. Metro-Goldwyn-Mayer Inc., 886 F.2d 1545, 1550 (9th Cir.1989), cert. denied, 494 U.S. 1017, 110 S.Ct. 1321, 108 L.Ed.2d 496 (1990) ("Prejudgment interest compensates the injured party for the loss of the use of money he would otherwise have had"); Riggs Nat. Bank of Washington, D.C. v. District of Columbia, 581 A.2d 1229 (D.C.App.1990); Busik v. Levine, 63 N.J. 351, 307 A.2d 571 (1973); Hansen v. Rothaus, 107 Wash.2d 468, 730 P.2d 662 (1986); Allstate Ins. Co. v. Starke, 797 P.2d 14 (Colo.1990). Many cases expressly state that the interest is compensatory and *not* any kind of penalty. E.g., Federal Deposit Ins. Corp. v. British-American Corp., 755 F.Supp. 1314, 1328 (E.D.N.C.1991) ("Awarding prejudgment interest in this case does not penalize defendants, but rather puts each party in the same position it would now be in had the fraudulent transfer never occurred. As a matter of law, plaintiffs are entitled to prejudgment interest").

5. Martinez v. Continental Enterprises, 730 P.2d 308 (Colo.1986); Busik v. Levine, 63 N.J. 351, 307 A.2d 571 (1973) ("The fact remains that in both situations the defendant has had the use, and the plaintiff has not, of moneys which the judgment finds was the damage plaintiff suffered. This is true whether the contested liability is for a liquidated or for an unliquidated sum"), cf. Maryland Nat. Bank v. Cummins, 322 Md. 570, 600, 588 A.2d 1205, 1219 (1991) (trustee's liability, in some circumstances for compound interest); § 3.6(2) above.

then, the compensation is no less required merely because the loss is not ascertainable in amount.

The defendant's real gains. The plaintiff's real loss is matched by the defendant's real gain. When the defendant deprives the plaintiff of an entitlement of any kind, the defendant at that point owes the plaintiff the entitlement or its value. The money the defendant owes to the plaintiff remains in the defendant's hands. Where the plaintiff cannot invest the money, the defendant can. Where the plaintiff must incur the expense of borrowing money, the defendant has money without charge. This is no less true if the defendant has no cash at all on hand; he owes the plaintiff and saves the cost of immediate payment. So liability for interest is not only compensatory, it is also restitutionary.[10] The defendant's gains do not depend upon whether the plaintiff's losses were ascertainable or not. The defendant has exactly the same gains whether the plaintiff's loss is liquidated, ascertainable or wholly incapable of measurement. So denial of interest for unascertained claims does not comport with the restitutionary, unjust enrichment grounds for awarding interest.

Incentives to delay. If a defendant pays nothing in interest, he may have incentives to delay payment and even to delay trial, as some courts have recognized. This incentive is no less when the plaintiff's loss cannot be ascertained. In that case the defendant cannot be sure what the loss is, so disputes about the proper amount of payment are likely. Nevertheless, if the defendant is literally making money by nonpayment, he may have incentive to delay. Certainly he lacks affirmative incentive to negotiate a settlement quickly.

Reduction to present value argument. Sometimes the plaintiff recovers for losses that will be incurred in the future. For instance, a plaintiff who is totally and permanently disabled by injury may recover for wages that will be lost during the rest of the plaintiff's working life. But since the plaintiff will not suffer the losses at the time of judgment, the traditional rule requires a reduction of the claim to "present value." This reduction in present value is described in more detail later.[13] It is essentially the application of interest in reverse. The defendant's liability is reduced by the amount of interest that the award can earn before the loss occurs. (If the plaintiff will have a loss of $1,100 one year from the trial and can invest the award at 10% interest, the award can be $1,000, not $1100.)

Because reduction to present value is merely the obverse of prejudgment interest, a failure to grant prejudgment interest to the plaintiff for past pecuniary losses means that the parties are not being treated equally. In effect the defendant is "paid" interest for his early payment, but is not charged interest for his late payment. So the denial of prejudgment interest is not only a failure of compensation, it is also a failure to fairness.

Fairness to defendant arguments. Judged against the purposes for awarding interest, the ascertainable-liquidated rules seem plainly wrong. Courts sometimes suggest that it would be unfair to the defendant if he were required to pay interest on sums of money the amount of which he could not ascertain in advance. This implies that interest is a kind of penalty which should not be levied against the defendant unless he has an opportunity to stop the interest by paying the money due. But this idea does not hold up.

It is no more unfair to the defendant to hold him for compensatory interest on a sum he could not ascertain in advance than it is to hold him for the unascertainable sum itself. In addition, the defendant has money that he owes to the plaintiff. The theory is that he cannot "stop the running of interest" by paying the plaintiff because he does not know the amount to pay. But since he has the money, whatever its sum is, the money can be invested. Returns on the investment will help insure that the defendant never loses by prejudgment interest what was his to begin with.

§ 3.6(4) Computation of Interest

Courts have often assumed or held that, apart from contract, prejudgment interest should be calculated at a statutory or "legal" rate.[2] Sometimes this result is compelled by a specific statutory directive.[3] At other times courts simply import a statutory rate set for some other purpose, such as the rate set for interest on final judgments.

The main alternative is resort to an interest rate reflected in a market for loans. The merit of this approach is that it is more likely to reflect current charges in the real world. The difficulty is that shopping for money is more complicated than shopping for beans; not only may lenders differ as to rates and conditions, but the same lender will offer different rates to different borrowers, depending on risks and security. So resort to market rates of interest will be difficult unless some standardizing feature is used.

One kind of market rate that has been used and even prescribed by statute is the prime rate used by appropriate lenders.[4] Another market adopted by statute for judgment or prejudgment interest[5] and sometimes used by courts independently[6] is based on the average rate for fifty-two week Treasury bills, or some other similar market.

Market rates are probably preferable to statutory rates based on a fixed percentage. They are likely to be more accurate and they can be made to fit any particular time period, reflecting the interest rates actually charged during that period. On the other hand figuring the most proper of all proper market rates may provide greater accuracy only by incurring costs in litigation. Probably a standardized rate, like that for the Treasury bills, is a good compromise between accuracy and practicality. The plaintiff who actually must borrow at a higher than market rate would not be limited to

---

§ 3.6(4)

4. See General Facilities, Inc. v. National Marine Serv., Inc., 664 F.2d 672 (8th Cir.1981); Gluth Bros. Const., Inc. v. Union Nat. Bank, 166 Ill.App.3d 18, 116 Ill.Dec. 365, 518 N.E.2d 1345 (1988); Nev.Rev.Stat.Ann. § 17.130 (prime rate at largest bank in Nevada); Pa. R.Civ.Proc., Rule 238 ("prime rate as listed in the first edition of the Wall Street Journal published for each calendar year for which the damages are awarded, plus one percent, not compounded").

5. 28 U.S.C.A. § 1961(a) ("a rate equal to the coupon issue yield equivalent (as determined by the Secretary of the Treasury") of the average accepted auction price for the last auction of fifty-two week United States Trea-

sury bills); M.C.L.A. § 600.6013 ("a rate of interest which is equal to 1% plus the average interest rate paid at auctions of 5–year United States Treasury notes during the 6 months immediately preceding July 1 and January 1, as certified by the state treasurer"); 12 Okl. Stat.Ann., § 727(A)(2) and (B) (average United States Treasury Bill rate of preceding calendar year).

6. Frank Music Corp. v. Metro–Goldwyn– Mayer Inc., 886 F.2d 1545, 1552 (9th Cir.1989), cert. denied, 494 U.S. 1017, 110 S.Ct. 1321, 108 L.Ed.2d 496 (1990); Federal Deposit Ins. Corp. v. British–American Corp., 755 F.Supp. 1314, 1328 (E.D.N.C.1991) (rate is discretionary but court would adopt the federal judgment-interest statute as a guide).

the market rate under such a rule because he could recover his costs not as interest but as consequential damages.

The traditional rule is that in computing prejudgment interest, at whatever rate, the interest is not to be compounded.[7] In other words, prejudgment interest is traditionally simple interest.[8] Even where statutes have liberalized interest rules, they have sometimes been at pains to insist on simple interest.[9] When the parties have contracted for interest but have not prescribed compounding, simple interest seems to be the best rule because it seems most likely to respect the parties' expressed intentions in the absence of some custom in the trade that indicates otherwise. Perhaps these contract cases have led to overgeneralization of the simple interest rule. At any rate the simple interest rule has been carried over and applied in non-contracting situations as well.

Yet compounding interest is not a strange practice. It is the normal practice for many investment programs: the interest earned is itself reinvested so that once earned it becomes a part of the principal and earns additional interest. If compounding of interest is the practice in the relevant market for borrowing or lending money, a rule against compound interest will insure that the interest awarded will fall short of compensation or restitution. In that case, compounding should be permitted. The federal judgment-interest statute provides for compound interest,[10] and courts adopting that statute as a guide to prejudgment interest rates may also see fit to adopt its compounding feature. A few courts and statutes have favored compound prejudgment interest,[11] but without much impact so far.

[*For discussion of the types of compounding permitted, see this section in the Practitioner Treatise edition.*]

Accrual

Prejudgment interest does not accrue until the underlying obligation matures.[18] That principle raises a difficult problem where it is difficult to say when the obligation arose or whether it arose at all before a final judgment. That problem is discussed later.[19] The same principle raises a factual and practical problem when the plaintiff's past losses have occurred periodically over a long period. Personal injury cases are often like this, although there are others as well.[20] The plaintiff has wage loss over a five year period from injury to trial, but the wage loss does not occur all on one

7. Alyeska Pipeline Serv. Co. v. Anderson, 669 P.2d 956 (Alaska 1983) (even judgment interest must be simple interest); Fairway Builders, Inc. v. Malouf Towers Rental Co., 124 Ariz. 242, 603 P.2d 513, 536, 537 (App. 1979); Maryland Nat. Bank v. Cummins, 322 Md. 570, 588 A.2d 1205 (1991). See Big Bear Properties, Inc. v. Gherman, 95 Cal.App.3d 908, 913–914, 157 Cal.Rptr. 443, 446 (1979) (compound interest impermissible but judgment including award for prejudgment interest does not violate this rule).

8. See Restatement Second of Contracts § 354 Comment a (1981); Restatement Second of Trusts § 207(1) (1959); Restatement of Restitution § 156, Comment b (1937).

10. "Interest shall be computed daily [with certain exceptions] and shall be compounded annually." 28 U.S.C.A. § 1961(b).

11. See Stovall v. Illinois Cent. Gulf R. Co., 722 F.2d 190 (5th Cir.1984) (interpreting Mississippi statute); Palmer v. Palmer, 805 S.W.2d 326, 328 (Mo.App.1991) ("It is obvious from the findings of fact and conclusions of law that the trial court herein exercised its equitable powers, which it was authorized to do, and entered the compound interest as a means to fully compensate respondent herein"); Cavnar v. Quality Control Parking, Inc., 696 S.W.2d 549 (Tex.1985) established a compound interest regime, which, however, was quickly disestablished by Vernon's Ann.Tex. Civ.Stat. art. 5069–1.05 § 6(g).

day. Instead it accrues week by week or month by month. The formal rule for accrual of interest would require the court or trier to calculate a different set of interest for each week's or month's wage loss. The same would be true with medical expense. Although such calculations are possible, they add costs to the litigation and open the door for secondary disputes.[21]

Recognizing this problem, courts and legislatures may choose a single accrual date for all losses in cases of this kind. The Supreme Court of Texas set the accrual date in personal injury and wrongful death cases as a date six months after the incident giving rise to the cause of action.[22]

Elements of Damages Included

Traditional authority appeared to oppose prejudgment interest on awards for nonpecuniary losses,[24] and now that the issue is more often relevant, some contemporary cases have said expressly that prejudgment interest is not to be computed on nonpecuniary, noncompensatory awards such as pain, suffering and mental anguish [25] and punitive damages.[26] Some of the current statutes join this view by expressly excluding nonpecuniary damages from the interest calculation.[27]

[*For discussion of interest on non-pecuniary elements as restitution, see this section in the Practitioner Treatise edition.*]

§ 3.6(5) Other Limitations on Prejudgment Interest

Independent of the ascertainable-liquidated rules, prejudgment interest is to be denied (1) for any time period for which the underlying claim had not accrued or matured, and (2) to any extent that prejudgment interest would serve as compensation for an element of harm already compensated by some other measure. In addition, prejudgment interest is often held to be a matter of discretion, so that such interest might be denied for any reason that cannot be shown to be an abuse. Strong holdings of the Supreme Court are opposed to the award of interest against the United States unless the immunity is expressly waived.[1]

[*For discussion of interest on unmatured claims see this section in the Practitioner Treatise edition.*]

22. Cavnar v. Quality Control Parking, Inc., 696 S.W.2d 549 (Tex.1985). The Texas statutes now adopt a similar rule for personal injury, death, and property damages cases. Vernon's Ann.Tex.Civ.Stat. art. 5069–1.05 § 6(a) (180 days after written notice of claim or suit is filed).

25. Bond v. City of Huntington, 166 W.Va. 581, 276 S.E.2d 539, 548 (1981).

26. Cavnar v. Quality Control Parking, Inc., 696 S.W.2d 549, 555 (Tex.1985) ("Commentators are virtually unanimous in advocating that prejudgment interest not be awarded on future damages and punitive damages" and the plaintiff can be "made whole even if prejudgment interest is not awarded on punitive damages").

27. M.G.L.A. c. 231, § 6B (interest added to judgments for "pecuniary damages for personal injuries to the plaintiff or for consequential damages, or for damages to property"); M.S.A. § 549.09 Subd. 1(b)(4) ("punitive damages, fine, or other damages that are noncompensatory in nature" excluded from prejudgment interest); (R.I.Gen.Laws § 9–21–10 ("In any civil action in which a verdict is rendered or a decision made for pecuniary damages * * *" prejudgment interest is to be added). Cf. N.C.Gen.Stat. § 24–5(b) ("In an action other than contract, the portion of money judgment designated by the fact finder as compensatory damages bears interest from the date the action is instituted * * *.").

§ 3.6(5)

1. See Library of Congress v. Shaw, 478 U.S. 310, 106 S.Ct. 2957, 92 L.Ed.2d 250 (1986).

Prejudgment interest is awarded to compensate for the delay the plaintiff suffered in receiving his rightful due. If delay has been compensated by other portions of the judgment, prejudgment interest will be improper. Suppose the defendant wrongfully claims to own the plaintiff's apartment house. The defendant collects the rents and makes repairs as needed. When the plaintiff is able to establish title and regain possession by judicial proceedings, she demands a recovery of the rents received by the defendant, subject to a credit for the repairs he made. If the plaintiff recovers the net rents, she will have been put in her rightful position. To add interest for the period she was out of possession would be wrong because she recovered rents for that period instead.

[For discussion of additional problems of duplication see this section in the Practitioner Treatise edition.]

Equity courts always claim the power to withhold remedies in their discretion, and the discretion formula is frequently repeated when prejudgment interest is at issue in fiduciary and other equity cases. A regime of discretion rather than rights is more surprising when it comes to money judgments at law, but some courts [12] and statutes [13] have repeated the discretionary approach, perhaps because the conditions that ought to go into formulating rights and rules have not yet been fully identified and because courts traditionally distrusted interest in any event. Other courts [14] and a number of statutes [15] now appear to recognize interest as a right or entitlement, not merely a hope for which the plaintiff must go begging. Where prejudgment interest is not a right, discretion may operate as a substantial limitation on the recovery.

§ 3.6(6) Judgment Interest

Judgment interest is a creature of statute, routinely required or granted. Since the judgment liquidates the debt or obligation owed, problems encountered in the prejudgment interest cases on that score are of no concern once a judgment has been rendered. Interest from date of verdict or judgment is granted with almost no difficulty even where prejudgment interest is denied. Judgment interest is an admirably straightforward matter in many instances.

[For discussions of rates and compounding, of verdict vs. judgment accrual, and of modified or appealed judgments, see this section in the Practitioner Treatise edition.]

§ 3.7 Damages and Variations in Dollar Value

Topic and Scope

In some respects it is convenient to treat all dollars alike. We do not normally measure the value of dollars in damages suits; instead, dollars are the measure of value of all other things. For instance, if you agreed last year to buy an ounce of gold for $400 this week, but the value of the dollar

---

12. Wiegand v. Colbert, 68 Hawaii 472, 718 P.2d 1080 (1986).

13. E.g., West's Ann.Cal.Civ.Code § 3287(b) (unliquidated contract claims, judge has discretion to fix date on which interest begins to accrue); Mont.Code Ann. 27–1–212 ("interest may be given, in the discretion of the jury" in non-contract cases involving oppression, fraud, or malice).

has dropped and the price of gold has risen to $450, you are still entitled to enforce the contract by paying 400 cheaper dollars for an ounce of more valuable gold. This is a necessary concomitant of the rule that we enforce your bargain. When the contract is for dollars, the payment is for dollars, regardless whether the dollar has dropped or increased in value.

In other cases, however, fluctuations in money value must be considered, or, analogously, the different value money has when paid today instead of next year. This section introduces three such variations in money value as they may affect damages law.

Reduction to Present Value [1]

Reduction to present value required. The general rule requires that all awards for future pecuniary loss must be reduced to present value.[2] Suppose an injured plaintiff proves that, among his other injuries and losses, he will need a major medical operation ten years from now, and that the projected cost of such an operation is $20,000. Considering this item alone, he will be entitled to recover $20,000, reduced to present value. Present value is a sum of money that will suffice to provide the $20,000 when the loss or expense actually occurs ten years from now by using both the present award and the interest it can reasonably earn.

Reasons for rule. To illustrate with some unlikely but easy figures, suppose the plaintiff can earn 10% simple interest by investing any award he gets. If he obtains the entire $20,000 today for a cost he will not incur for ten years, he could invest the $20,000 and earn $20,000 in interest. When the cost must be paid, he would pay it from the interest generated and still have $20,000 left. The present value rule attempts to find the sum that will, when used with all the interest it produces, pay for the projected operation ten years from now but that will leave nothing left over.

Methods for computing. The present value can be easily computed or even found in tables once the correct interest rate is known. (The interest rate is usually called the discount rate in this context). Unless the discount rate is varied in order to account for inflation,[3] it should be the interest rate which a person unskilled in financial management can safely obtain on the investment. This is usually assumed to be a relatively low interest rate. Sometimes testimony is required or permitted to select a good rate. At other times, however, courts simply use statutory interest rates, which are not likely to produce accurate results. On these topics, more detail is provided in another section.[4]

Inflation [5]

Effect of future inflation on future losses considered. At one time courts took the position that the prospect of future inflation should be ignored in estimating the plaintiff's future losses. On this view, the plaintiff in the example above might be awarded $20,000 for the operation expected in ten

---

§ 3.7

1. This topic is developed in § 8.5(3) below.

2. E.g., Monessen Southwestern Ry. Co. v. Morgan, 486 U.S. 330, 108 S.Ct. 1837, 100 L.Ed.2d 349 (1988).

3. See below & § 8.5(4) below.

4. See § 8.5(3) below.

5. This topic is developed § 8.5(4) below.

years (with a reduction to present value), but he might find ten years later that inflation had driven the price up to $50,000. Put otherwise, the buying power of the dollars with which he is paid today may be eroded by inflation when the cost axe falls. With that in mind, courts have increasingly been willing to make adjustments for inflation since about 1970.

General methods for considering inflation. To take account of future inflation, courts have usually used one of two basic methods or some variation on one of them. (1) Courts have permitted experts to testify to projections of inflation and to give figures for adjusting the award in today's dollars to reflect the loss of buying power in the loss period. (2) Courts have sometimes recognized that future inflation and the discount to present value bear on each other in some reciprocal fashion, so that by adjusting the discount rate in calculating present value, one might also deal with inflation during the same period. Both approaches, properly applied, should yield about the same kind of adjustment for inflation, but they are not necessarily equally easy to apply.

Adjusting for inflation by finding the "real" interest rate. The second method for dealing with inflation works on the idea that interest rates really reflect two separate charges, one for use or rent of the money and another for the risk of inflation. By eliminating the part of the discount or interest rate that borrowers generally demand to cover risks of inflation, the "real," not merely the nominal interest rate can be discovered. Figures suggest that the real interest rate is quite low, maybe as little as 1%.[6] If you used 1% as the discount rate in figuring present value, the award would have to be relatively high because that would mean the plaintiff is not earning much real interest. In fact, of course, he would still be earning whatever the market pays, maybe 10%; but most of that 10% would be going to pay for future inflation. Because the interest actually earned is paying for the expected inflation, no other adjustment needs to be made.

Treating future inflation and present value reductions as a wash. In the extreme but simple version of the second method, the court treats the present value reduction and the inflation adjustment as a wash, so it makes no reduction to present value and no addition for inflation.[7]

Periodic payments. The common law traditionally gave a one-time judgment for all future damages. That is why reduction to present value and inflation adjustments are needed. It is not traditional but now possible under some statutes to provide for periodic payment of judgments, with adjustments in payments every few years. The periodic payment statutes are discussed in more detail in connection with personal injury damages.[8]

Distinguishing other adjustments from inflation adjustments. There are actually a number of adjustments that may be required in projecting a future loss, some of them having nothing to do with inflation. For example, the price of the required future operation might rise even if there were no inflation. Better technology may be developed that is more expensive but

6. See Jones & Laughlin Steel Corp. v. Pfeifer, 462 U.S. 523, 103 S.Ct. 2541, 76 L.Ed.2d 768 (1983) (approving rates between 1% and 3% when this method is used, so long as trial court has a basis for the choice); § 8.5(4) below.

7. Beaulieu v. Elliott, 434 P.2d 665 (Alaska 1967).

8. See § 8.5(5) below.

also more valuable because it saves more lives or produces better results; or hospitals may become less and less efficient; or paying patients may pay more because their payments must help absorb the costs of treating patients who do not pay. All of these things might drive the price of the operation up in the future, but none of them is the result of inflation. Similarly, the plaintiff might have earned more wages in the future if he had not been injured, partly because of wage increases, but partly also because of merit pay, promotions, or increased productivity in the industry as a whole.[9] It is important to make proof of such projections, but they are not proof of inflation.

Foreign Currency Fluctuations against the Dollar

A third kind of variation in dollar value occurs when obligations in foreign currency must be converted to dollars. In that case the variation of the dollar's value is taken into account. That is done by referring to the market exchange rate on the relevant date.

Dollar judgments; conversion from foreign currency. Money judgments in American courts are traditionally rendered in dollars, even though they may be based on obligations expressed in yen, pounds, or Deutschemarks.[10] As a result, a claim asserted in American courts based on obligations expressed in foreign currency (either contracts or judgments) traditionally is calculated in dollars before being reduced to judgment in the United States. Because the dollar varies in value from time to time as compared to any given foreign currency, the conversion to dollars must be made on some specific date and according to the currency values on that date. When currencies are fluctuating as compared to each other, the selection of one date rather than another can have an important effect on the real value of the plaintiff's recovery.

Example of conversion date options. An example illustrates how selection of a date for conversion can affect the ultimate cost to the defendant for paying his liability.[11] Suppose that defendant, an American, breaches a contract to pay 20,000 pounds sterling to a British company, that the British company recovers a judgment in Great Britain, and then sues on that judgment in the United States. Suppose that the value of the British pound declines steadily, so that the American defendant could buy £20,000 for $40,000 on the breach date, for $30,000 on the date the British judgment is entered, and for $20,000 on the date the American judgment is entered. Since the American judgment will be in dollars, the judge must decide which dollar amount to use.

No matter which amount the judge selects, a fourth possibility exists. Suppose the British pound continues to decline, so the American defendant postpones payment as long as possible. He ultimately purchases £20,000 for the very favorable price of $15,000 and pays the underlying debt (with accrued interest). Whatever the amount of the American dollar judgment, he claims it is satisfied by payment of the underlying obligation. If he is permitted to do this, his ultimate costs would be $15,000; if not, his costs

---

9. See § 8.5(4) below.

11. The example is a suggested by Competex, S.A. v. LaBow, 783 F.2d 333 (2d Cir.1986),

which is also the basis for a similar example in Prefatory Note, Uniform Foreign–Money Claims Act, 13 U.L.A. (Supp.).

would be either $20,000, $30,000 or $40,000, depending on the date used for converting currency.

The problem can arise without a foreign judgment. In the example above, the British plaintiff might have sued directly on the contract in the United States, without first obtaining a British judgment. Whether or not there is a foreign judgment, the courts have used three different rules:

Breach date rule. The breach date rule fixes the dollar obligation at the conversion rate applicable when the defendant breached his obligation to pay or the date at which a tort claim arose. In the example above, this would be either $40,000 or $30,000, depending on whether the defendant's obligation is identified with the contract or the British judgment.[12] This rule had substantial support.[13]

Judgment date rule. The judgment date rule fixes the dollar liability on the date the American court enters judgment, using the exchange rate at that time. In the example, this would be $20,000.[14]

Payment date rule. The payment date rule allows the defendant to pay the foreign judgment at any time by buying foreign currency and making payment; such a payment satisfies the underlying claim and therefore satisfies the American judgment. In the example above the defendant would buy £20,000 for $15,000 sometime after the judgment and pay the British judgment. Under the payment date rule the payment of the underlying obligation would satisfy the American judgment, even though that judgment was for $20,000 to $40,000.[15]

Criticizing the breach date rule. The breach date rule has been criticized because, although its purpose is to make the plaintiff whole, it allows the plaintiff the potential of speculation without risk. The breach date rule guarantees the plaintiff a minimum dollar recovery ($40,000 in the example). At the same time, the creditor still holds the underlying obligation in foreign currency (£20,000 in the example). If the pound falls, the plaintiff will take the dollar recovery, which will now buy more than £20,000; if the pound

---

12. If the American suit is brought upon the British judgment, then the date of the British judgment would be equivalent to the "breach date." See Competex, S.A. v. LaBow, 783 F.2d 333 (2d Cir.1986) (reflecting such a rationale in the trial court).

13. Parker v. Hoppe, 257 N.Y. 333, 178 N.E. 550, 80 A.L.R. 1359 (1931); Hoppe v. Russo–Asiatic Bank, 235 N.Y. 37, 138 N.E. 497 (1923). In diversity cases, federal court have followed this rule under governing state law. See Middle East Banking Co. v. State Street Bank Intern., 821 F.2d 897 (2d Cir.1987).

14. Die Deutsche Bank Filiale Nurnberg v. Humphrey, 272 U.S. 517, 47 S.Ct. 166, 71 L.Ed. 383 (1926); Agfa–Gevaert, A.G. v. A.B. Dick Co., 879 F.2d 1518 (7th Cir.1989) (applying pre-statutory New York law). In *Die Deutsche Bank Filiale Nurnberg,* Justice Holmes actually spoke of the "moment when the suit is brought," a term that may be considered to be a variation on the judgment date rule, but also one that might not be taken too literally.

15. Cf. Pecaflor Const., Inc. v. Landes, 198 Cal.App.3d 342, 243 Cal.Rptr. 605 (1988) (satisfaction of underlying Canadian judgment in Canadian dollars satisfied the enforcing judgment in California, although the enforcing judgment's American dollars were now worth more).

In *Pecaflor,* supra, the plaintiff brought the original action in Canada on a Canadian contract for work to be done there. The Canadian judgment was then entered in California under procedures for recognition of foreign judgments and a judgment in American dollars was then entered. After skirmishes, the defendant satisfied the Canadian judgment in Canadian dollars, but by that time the American dollars were worth more and the plaintiff argued to the California court that the California judgment should not be considered fully satisfied by the payment of the Canadian judgment. The court held the California judgment to be fully satisfied.

rises, the American judgment will be ignored and the plaintiff will enforce the British judgment. So the risk is all on one side and the opportunity on the other.[16] This "gamesmanship"[17] does not seem so likely, because the plaintiff would probably execute on assets in Great Britain in the first place if the defendant had assets there, but it is possible.

Supporting the payment date rule. The payment date rule, coupled with appropriate interest on the obligation, provides the plaintiff with the very currency and amount to which he was entitled. In the example, the underlying obligation was £20,000; the plaintiff will be fully compensated if it receives that sum with interest. Whether the plaintiff produces that sum by buying pounds at a favorable or unfavorable rate is of no consequence to the measure of compensation.

Making payment date work. If payment date is about the same as judgment date, courts could approximate the payment-date rule by making the conversion at the time of the judgment, that is, by using the judgment-date rule. To invoke a true payment-date rule, however, is difficult under the traditional assumptions that damages judgments must specify a sum certain in dollars at the time the judgment is rendered. There is no procedure for appointing a commissioner to revise the judgment when payment is made or to fill in the amount. An equitable in personam order to make payment of dollars equivalent to the foreign currency obligation might work, but this would be about the same as expressing the judgment in foreign currency in the first place. Rendering judgment in foreign currency would be the equivalent of a payment date rule.[18] The defendant would simply pay in foreign currency, which could be purchased with American dollars at the time of payment. This gist of the payment-date rule, then, is a revision of the dollar judgment rule and a provision for judgments expressed in foreign currency.

Judgments in foreign currency. The Uniform Foreign Money Claims Act directly supports the payment-date rule and provides explicitly that judgments are to be rendered in the foreign money.[19] Other statutory authority now provides for judgments in foreign currency.[20] Judgments in foreign currency are also used in some other countries, including at least one

---

19. Uniform Foreign Money Claims Act § 7(a). The judgment debtor may pay the judgment in either the foreign money or in "the amount of United States dollars which will purchase the foreign money on the conversion date at a bank-offered spot rate." Id., § 7(b). The Uniform Commercial Code provides for *payment* of obligations expressed in foreign currency in that currency. UCC § 3–107. See Annotation, Uniform Foreign–Money Judgments Act, Construction and Application of, 100 A.L.R.3d 792.

20. N.Y.—McKinney's Jud.Law § 27 provides:

(a) Except as provided in subdivision (b) of this section, judgments and accounts must be computed in dollars and cents. In all judgments or decrees rendered by any court for any debt, damages or costs, in all executions issued thereupon, and in all accounts arising from proceedings in courts the amount shall be computed, as near as may be, in dollars and cents, rejecting lesser fractions; and no judgment, or other proceeding, shall be considered erroneous for such omissions.

(b) In any case in which the cause of action is based upon an obligation denominated in a currency other than currency of the United States, a court shall render or enter a judgment or decree in the foreign currency of the underlying obligation. Such judgment or decree shall be converted into currency of the United States at the rate of exchange prevailing on the date of entry of the judgment or decree.

The provision for foreign-currency judgments would seem to imply that either the payment date or judgment-date rule is the proper one. The last sentence quoted above appears to provide for the judgment date as the most practical.

common law country, Great Britain.[21] An earlier impediment to foreign-money judgments seems to have been a federal statute which was read to forbid certain currency transactions. The statute may not have intended to forbid foreign money judgments, and in any event is now repealed. Another impediment may have been the fact that at one time markets for foreign exchange were not so accessible for information or for actual exchanges. This too has changed, and analysis has suggested that even without statutory authority, courts may award judgments in foreign currency when that currency expresses the rightful obligation,[22] unless a governing statute provides otherwise.[23]

Which currency is the rightful currency. The rules for conversion of foreign currency obligations to dollar obligations only apply when foreign currency is the rightful expression of the obligation. If a foreign seller were to invoice the American defendant by expressing the price in both Swiss francs and in American dollars, the contract might be understood to mean that the plaintiff could satisfy his obligation by paying the stated amount in either currency, in the amount stated. In that case there is nothing to convert because the parties themselves have in effect specified the conversion.[24] In other cases it may be necessary to recognize that different elements of the underlying claim are rightfully expressed in different currencies. For instance, if damage is done to a vessel in a foreign port and some repairs are made there, the foreign currency is appropriate in calculating damages for those repairs, but not for the additional repairs made in the United States.[25]

Making the plaintiff whole. Although the payment-date rule works well in most instances, it may not be the most appropriate rule in every case. It is unlikely to be satisfactory when the plaintiff has incurred consequential damages or substitution-cost damages in a foreign currency. For instance if the plaintiff's vessel is damaged by a tort in a foreign port and must be repaired there, with repairs paid for at that time in foreign currency, the plaintiff's loss is fixed at the time he must expend American dollars for the foreign currency required to pay the repair costs. At least if the governing law is American law,[26] there seems no reason to force the injured plaintiff to take a loss from foreign currency devaluation, and authority supports this view.[27] With cases like this in mind the Restatement of Foreign Relations provides that if money conversion is required, the date should be selected which will "make the creditor whole." [28]

Restitution. The conversion-date rules are constructed with damages, not restitution in mind. Because restitution is aimed at preventing unjust

---

22. Restatement Third of Foreign Relations § 823, Comment *b* (1987). No doubt this will complicate the sheriff's job when the plaintiff seeks to execute the judgment on assets of the defendant. Use of the court's equitable powers at this juncture may be helpful.

23. See West's Ann.Cal.Code Civ.Proc. § 577.5 ("In any judgment, or execution upon such judgment, the amount shall be computed and stated in dollars and cents, rejecting fractions").

25. Cf. The Gylfe v. The Trujillo, 209 F.2d 386 (2d Cir.1954) (date of expenditure for foreign repairs is date for conversion for their costs in foreign currency).

27. Jamaica Nutrition Holdings, Ltd. v. United Shipping Co., Ltd., 643 F.2d 376 (5th Cir.1981).

28. Restatement Third of Foreign Relations § 823(2) (1987).

enrichment of the defendant rather than compensation of the plaintiff, the emphasis in restitutionary claims might require a currency conversion that does not permit the defendant to retain any benefits to which he is not entitled.

For example, suppose that the defendant embezzles in marks worth at the time $10,000, converts the money to U.S. dollars and uses it in America. Suppose also that by the time the plaintiff is able to procure a judgment in the United States against the defendant, the dollar has rebounded, so that $7500 will now suffice to repay the embezzled marks and interest accrued. When the goal is compensation for the plaintiff's loss, it is of no concern that the defendant can pay off the debt cheaply.

When the goal is to deprive the defendant of his unjust gain, however, the payment date rule runs a risk that the embezzler will profit from his wrongdoing. In that case, the embezzler might be made to repay at the highest conversion rate if that is deemed necessary to prevent him from profiting from the wrong. On the other hand, if the embezzled marks were never converted to dollars and the embezzler's benefit was derived solely in terms of marks, restitutionary goals may be satisfied if the payment-date rule is used.

§ 3.8   Benefits to the Plaintiff From the Defendant's Acts

The defendant's tort or breach of contract may cause harm to the plaintiff but may also result in benefits the plaintiff would not otherwise receive. Does the defendant get a credit for benefits to the plaintiff resulting from his acts? The general rule is that the defendant does get such a credit when the benefits are direct benefits but that the defendant does not get such a credit when the benefits are collateral benefits.

Suppose the defendant negligently injures the plaintiff. The defendant accepts some of the blame and pays the plaintiff's medical expenses. That is a direct benefit for which the defendant is entitled to credit. When the plaintiff's employer pays the plaintiff's wages in spite of injury, however, that benefit is collateral. As to that benefit the defendant is entitled to no credit; he remains liable for the wage loss claim although in fact the plaintiff has continued to receive wages from his employer.

§ 3.8(1)   Collateral Source Benefits

General Rule

No credit to the defendant for collateral benefits to the plaintiff. The general rule is that benefits received by the plaintiff from a source collateral to the defendant may not be used to reduce that defendant's liability for damages.[1] The rule holds good even though the benefits are paid to the plaintiff because of the defendant's conduct, are measured by the plaintiff's loss, and would otherwise be unavailable to the plaintiff. Although the rule appears, at least initially, to be overcompensatory,[2] courts only differ about some applications of the rule, not about the rule itself. By far the most common application of the collateral source rule occurs in personal injury

§ 3.8(1)

1. Restatement Second of Torts §§ 920A & 920 (1979); see also Restatement Second of

Contracts § 347, Comment *e* (1981); §§ 8.6(3) & 12.6(4) below.

cases. The rule is discussed in more detail in that connection.[3] But according to many courts, it also applies to at least some contract cases.[4]

Insurance and similar benefits. The usual case is one in which the plaintiff is injured by the defendant's tort but suffers no actual medical expense loss because those expenses are paid for by the plaintiff's own medical insurance or paid for as part of government benefits to veterans. In these cases the rule is quite firm that the defendant must pay for the reasonable value of medical services reasonably required even though the plaintiff's own insurance has paid for such services.

Gifts and public benefits. In most courts, gifts to the plaintiff[5] and friendly help[6] that minimizes the plaintiff's actual loss or expenditure in tort or contract are in the same category as insurance, so the defendant gets no reduction. About public benefits there is a little more difference of opinion. A number of cases have allowed the plaintiff to recover full damages against the defendant, even though the plaintiff's loss has been reduced by some form of public benefit.[7]

Replacement of support and tax savings. Some other collateral benefits get the same treatment, although sometimes on different theories. A surviving spouse who claims loss of support as the result of the deceased's wrongful death can recover without reduction, even though the survivor has remarried and receives support from the new spouse.[9] The plaintiff who pays no taxes on a personal injury verdict traditionally recovers full damages, even though the recovery considered along with the tax savings put him in better financial position than before the injury.[10] The tax rule has now been rejected in certain federal tort cases,[11] but states have tended to maintain it.

Rationales

Donor's intent. When the collateral benefit comes in the form of a gratuity from friends or employers, courts sometimes say that the donor intends to benefit the plaintiff, not the defendant, and that therefore the defendant should have no credit for that benefit. To the extent that recovery from the defendant makes it possible for the plaintiff to pay back gratuities, the argument has the same basis as the subrogation rationale, or

3. See § 8.6(3) below.

4. See § 12.6(4) below.

5. A few courts have distinguished gifts to the plaintiff and have reduced a tortfeasor's liability by benefits received by the plaintiff in the form of donations. Thus the defendant might escape liability for medical expenses the plaintiff avoided because a friend rendered free medical services. Coyne v. Campbell, 11 N.Y.2d 372, 230 N.Y.S.2d 1, 183 N.E.2d 891 (1962).

6. See Hurd v. Nelson, 714 P.2d 767 (Wyo. 1986) (H breached contractual obligation to build a storage shed for W, whose friends at church donated time worth $8,000 to build it, held the defendant liable, although theorizing that this is not because of the collateral source rule).

7. Seibel v. Liberty Homes, Inc., 305 Or. 362, 752 P.2d 291 (1988) (contract claim: employer promised permanent job to injured worker, discharged him later; social security disability benefits would not reduce defendant's contract liability); Cates v. Wilson, 321 N.C. 1, 7, 361 S.E.2d 734, 738 (1987) (tort medical malpractice claim with substantial aid to permanently injured newborn: "forcing plaintiffs to depend on public coffers * * * stands at odds with the compensatory goal" of damages, in any event public aid may not last). For other torts cases, see § 8.6(3) below; for other contract cases, see § 12.6(4) below.

11. Norfolk and Western Ry. Co. v. Liepelt, 444 U.S. 490, 100 S.Ct. 755, 62 L.Ed.2d 689 (1980).

perhaps a better one. But this argument can apply only to benefits that come as gifts.

Subrogation. One of the reasons commonly given in support of the collateral source rule is that the rule preserves subrogation rights of any insurer who paid benefits to the plaintiff. Suppose the plaintiff's collision insurance pays $2,000 for full repair of the plaintiff's car after the defendant negligently damaged it. In the normal course of events, the insurer would stand in the shoes of the plaintiff to the extent it had paid the plaintiff's claim; so it could pursue a claim for $2,000 against the defendant. But if the defendant were entitled to a credit for the $2,000 on the ground that the plaintiff's insurer had paid it, the plaintiff would have no claim to which the insurer could be subrogated.

The argument is correct as far as it goes. But it can work only where the benefit is derived from one who would be subrogated to the plaintiff's claim. Further, it reinforces the use of the expensive subrogation mechanism for allocating ultimate responsibility among potential payors. It might be cheaper to craft a rule that allows the plaintiff a recovery against the insurer but not against the tortfeasor, or vice versa.[12]

Plaintiff paid. Courts sometimes offer other general grounds for the collateral source rule. They often say that the plaintiff is entitled to full recovery in spite of the collateral benefit because he paid for the benefit. At best, this reason can only work when the collateral benefit comes in the form of insurance for which the plaintiff paid. Those persons who pay for both liability and medical insurance thus have a chance of recovering twice, but they might prefer only one full recovery coupled with a reduced premium on one policy instead.[13]

Windfall. Finally it is argued that the wrongdoer should not have a windfall, which would be his if he got credit for a benefit that reduced the plaintiff's damages. This argument seems to assume what it sets out to prove. The credit to the defendant is a windfall only if he is not entitled to it. Whether the defendant is entitled to the credit is the very issue under consideration. In addition, it is hard to say the defendant gets a windfall if the plaintiff is fully compensated or if his injury is less by luck than one might expect from the defendant's tort.[14]

Measurement and prejudice. Two other grounds for the collateral source rule have been advanced. The first is that the plaintiff's proof of all damages, including damages paid for by collateral benefits, helps the jury estimate damages on other issues, at least in personal injury cases.[15] The second is that the introduction of evidence that the plaintiff received benefits is inherently prejudicial to the plaintiff.[16]

12. See Conard, The Economic Treatment of Automobile Injuries, 63 Mich.L.Rev. 279, 311 (1964) and the more extensive explanation in § 8.6(3) below.

13. See § 8.6(3) below.

14. See Imlay v. City of Lake Crystal, 453 N.W.2d 326, 332 (Minn.1990) ("The windfall argument generally is considered baseless * * * fault and cost have little relation to

each other"). Other arguments on the windfall issue are considered in § 8.6(3) below.

16. Denton v. Con–Way Southern Express, Inc., 261 Ga. 41, 402 S.E.2d 269 (1991); Cates v. Wilson, 321 N.C. 1, 361 S.E.2d 734 (1987); Sedler, The Collateral Source Rule and Personal Injury Damages, 58 Ky.L.J. 36 (1969). In Denton, supra, the Georgia Court appeared mainly concerned with insurance benefits for the plaintiff; it reasoned that since defen-

Unspoken rationales. Perhaps the strongest ties that bind many courts to the collateral source rule are not the stated rationales but the recognition that personal injury suits in particular are financed largely by the recovery through the contingent fee system. Reduction of the total recovery may significantly impact the plaintiff's ability to find counsel who will pursue the claim with vigor, because lawyers cannot afford to spend hundreds of hours on claims that will yield only a few dollars. Sometimes the concern that attorney fees are not recovered by plaintiffs are openly mentioned as grounds for support of the collateral source rule.[17] This rationale suggests, however, that where attorney fees are specifically recoverable by the prevailing plaintiff, or where they are readily absorbed by very high nonpecuniary awards, the collateral source rule has no place.

Statutory Changes

Statutes fostering a credit. In something like half the states, "tort reform" statutes have sought to change the collateral source rule in some particular group of personal injury cases, such as those involving medical malpractice claims. The statutes either credit the defendant with the collateral benefits received by the plaintiff or permit the defendant to introduce evidence of the benefit on the assumption that the jury will react to the evidence in fixing damages. Some of these statutes have been held unconstitutional,[18] others have not.[19]

Allocating and computing the credit. If they are valid, they will raise new questions. For example, suppose the plaintiff has an accident policy that pays $2,000 as a flat payment for a broken limb. The plaintiff's medical bill for setting her broken arm is only $500, but she also has $1500 in damage to her car. Where collateral sources benefits are to be credited to the defendant, the question will arise whether the accident policy, no doubt purchased as protection for medical and wage loss, should be credited against the defendant's liability for property damage.[20]

§ 3.8(2) Direct Benefits

General Rule

When the plaintiff benefits directly rather than collaterally from the defendant's breach of duty in tort or contract, then, subject to exceptions stated below, the plaintiff's recovery is reduced by the amount of the benefits

dant's liability or third-party insurance could not be admitted, the plaintiff's first-party insurance could not be admitted either.

17. See Helfend v. Southern Cal. Rapid Transit Dist., 2 Cal.3d 1, 84 Cal.Rptr. 173, 465 P.2d 61, 77 A.L.R.3d 398 (1970); cf. McConal Aviation, Inc. v. Commercial Aviation Ins. Co., 110 N.M. 697, 799 P.2d 133, 139–140 (1990) (Montgomery, J., specially concurring: "One of these losses—not insignificant in amount, I have no doubt—was the attorney's fees. Under the policy of the collateral source rule—that the 'windfall' is to be allocated to the innocent claimant rather than the arguably

culpable defendant * * *. I concur in giving the plaintiff the 'duplicate recovery' ").

18. Denton v. Con–Way Southern Express, Inc., 261 Ga. 41, 402 S.E.2d 269 (1991); Farley v. Engelken, 241 Kan. 663, 740 P.2d 1058, 74 A.L.R.4th 1 (1987).

19. Imlay v. City of Lake Crystal, 453 N.W.2d 326 (Minn.1990) (not unconstitutional as denying equal protection; rational basis standard).

20. See § 8.6(3) suggesting not. The order of credits will also present a problem in computation considered in the same section.

received.[1] A direct benefit is one that results from the defendant's breach of duty itself, or one that is derived from the defendant or someone who acts on the defendant's behalf.

The defendant's tort may create a benefit as well as a harm, as where the defendant trespasses to the plaintiff's land and digs a ditch. Although the defendant's act is a trespass and may cause pecuniary harm in some respects, it may also serve to drain the plaintiff's land and make it more productive or marketable. The defendant is entitled to a credit for the benefit.[2]

The defendant's tort may not in itself benefit the plaintiff, but some other act done by or on behalf of the defendant may do so. If the defendant's insurer pays the plaintiff, not under the liability provisions of its policy but under its medical payment provisions, this is a benefit to the plaintiff for which the defendant is entitled to a credit when the plaintiff later sues.[3]

Exceptions or Limitations

The defendant does not get credit for every direct benefit of his tort. In general, the exceptions to the credit correlate with the rules for recognizing and measuring benefits in restitution cases,[4] although the expression of the rules is different.[5] In particular, the credit is denied if the defendant's tort created a benefit to the plaintiff that (1) was common to the community, (2) affected some interest of the plaintiff different from the one harmed by the defendant, or (3) was of no value to the plaintiff for the plaintiff's own purposes and which the plaintiff could not effectively reject. The credit is also denied if the benefit is one (4) which is deemed not causally connected to the tort or one that accrues after the time for figuring tort damages; or (5) one that occurs after the time for valuation of the plaintiff's loss.

[*For discussion of each exception see this section and § 8.6(2) in the Practitioner Treatise edition.*]

§ 3.9 Minimizing Damages: Avoidable Consequences Rules

General Rule

General scope of avoidable consequences rules. The avoidable consequences rules, or rules for minimizing damages, are cardinal instruments of damages measurement. They are often instruments by which recovery is trimmed to reflect compensation. Minimizing damages rules apply in all kinds of cases, including contract,[1] tort,[2] and statutory claims.[3] But they do not apply to every kind of damages measurement. In general, avoidable consequences rules apply to require the plaintiff to minimize special or consequential damages, but do not usually affect measurement of general or market damages.[4]

§ 3.8(2)

1. Restatement Second of Torts §§ 920A(1), 920 (1979); § 8.6(2) below.

2. Restatement Second of Torts § 920, Illustration 3 (1979).

§ 3.9

1. See § 12.6(2).

2. See § 8.7(2) below.

3. E.g., § 6.10(4) below.

4. For example, if the plaintiff is entitled to the difference between the market price and the contract price upon the defendant's breach of a contract of sale, the fact that the plaintiff could have sold to another buyer at a

The four rules of avoidable consequences. Occasional skirmishes over the terminology aside,[5] three rules of avoidable consequences are generally accepted. A fourth rule may be implicit in the scheme reflected by the first three. The three main rules are:

(1) The defendant is entitled to a credit against liability for any consequential damages the plaintiff avoided or minimized.

(2) The defendant is entitled to a credit against liability for any consequential damages the plaintiff could have avoided or minimized by reasonable effort and expense, whether or not the plaintiff actually avoided or minimized such damages.

(3) The plaintiff is entitled to recover the reasonable costs of minimizing damages under Rule (1), whether or not the damages were successfully avoided or minimized.

The fourth rule, apparently not clearly established, would hold that

(4) when the plaintiff's recovery is reduced for failure to avoid harms that could have been reasonably avoided, the reduction is the net amount that the defendant would have benefitted by proper avoidance, after allowing credit to the plaintiff for the hypothetical costs of that avoidance.[6]

Example. The most common forms of minimizing damages are to repair harm done that would otherwise cause consequential losses, to locate property that has been taken, or to procure a substitute for performance owed by the defendant. For example, suppose the plaintiff's car is damaged by the defendant's negligence so that it cannot be used while it is being repaired. Repairs require four days. The plaintiff earns $100 per day in her job. On the first day of car repair, she is able to work half a day by telephone from home. For the remaining three and one-half days she earns nothing because the car is not available. However, for an expenditure of $20 for each day, she could have taken cabs to work and back without undue risk. The first rule credits the defendant with the $50 the plaintiff actually earned. The second rule credits the defendant with the amounts the plaintiff should reasonably have earned ($350).[7] Presumably, however, that credit is itself subject to a reduction, because it would have cost the plaintiff $80 to get substitute transportation necessary to earn the additional $350.

price above market is usually irrelevant. Market damages are fixed at some definite date, such as date for performance of a contract, so that subsequent events do not affect the plaintiff's rights as closed out on that date. The rule stated closely correlates with the rule that direct benefits resulting to the plaintiff after the date for calculation of market measures are not credited to the defendant. See § 3.8(2) above.

Market measures of damages, however, achieve some of the objectives of the minimizing damages rules and in some situations market measures *are* minimized damages.

5. The distinctions are truly minor. Courts often speak of a "duty" to minimize

damages. This literally cannot be right, since a duty is an obligation on which one can sue. A plaintiff's failure to minimize damages cannot give rise to a cause of action for the defendant. Even so, a "duty" to minimize is a convenient location and one unlikely to be misunderstood. Courts also speak of "mitigating" damages. This treatise uses the term "minimize" instead, to reflect the fact that the burden is upon the plaintiff to reduce the damages. This treatise reserves the term "mitigate" for situations in which the *defendant* can reduce his own liability, for example, by proving good faith. But "mitigating" is a well-accepted term and generally used, and again, no one is likely to be misled.

Burden of proof. The plaintiff has the burden of proving damages in the first place, but the defendant usually has the burden of proving that the plaintiff did in fact minimize or should have minimized damages.[8] In some situations, however, it has been suggested that the plaintiff will be required to prove at least the actual earnings she has received in substitute employment,[9] or that if the plaintiff failed to seek a job, then the failure made no difference because no jobs were available.[10] In extreme cases a literal application of the burden to require proof by the defendant, may permit the plaintiff who is wrongly discharged from employment to recover lost income for the rest of her life. Because the employer cannot show what jobs the plaintiff will be likely to have in the future, it may be unable meet the burden of proving the amount of damages that could be minimized. So an essentially speculative sum, a lifetime guaranteed wage without the work, is sometimes provided to the wrongly discharged plaintiff.[11]

Applications and Amplifications

First rule. The first rule reduces the plaintiff's damages by all amounts the plaintiff actually saved by minimizing or received in obtaining a replacement for the defendant's performance. The most common case is one in which the plaintiff obtains a new job when the defendant wrongfully discharges her. If the plaintiff actually obtains a job, and earns income, the defendant is entitled to credit, even if the job is so unsuitable that the plaintiff would not have been expected to minimize damages by accepting it. However, if the plaintiff accepts work that would have been consistent with the original job, such as part-time, at-home work, there is no reduction. In that case it is not possible to trace the new work back to the loss of the old job.[12]

Second rule: reasonableness assessments. The most common issues revolve around the second rule. The issue is often whether the plaintiff could have minimized damages by a reasonable effort or expenditure. Sometimes courts state the rule too broadly, saying that the plaintiff must make a diligent effort and that recovery must be denied where no effort is shown. The view consistent with the rule's philosophy and the general requirement of causation is narrower. It holds that diligence (or reasonable effort) by the plaintiff is only evidence and the ultimate issue is not the effort as such but whether damages could have been minimized by that effort. The plaintiff's lack of effort then becomes unimportant if effort would not have successfully reduced damages.[13]

The plaintiff is not required to accept great risks, undertake heroic measures, or accept great personal sacrifices to minimize damages for the benefit of the defendant. In personal injury cases, for example, surgery may reduce the plaintiff's damages, but the cost, the risk and the pain of surgery

---

8. E.g., Stark v. Shell Oil Co., 450 F.2d 994 (5th Cir.1971); Callander v. Sheridan, 546 N.E.2d 850 (Ind.App.1989); Ambassador Steel Co. v. Ewald Steel Co., 33 Mich.App. 495, 190 N.W.2d 275 (1971); Weaver v. Mitchell, 715 P.2d 1361 (Wyo.1986).

9. Horn v. Duke Homes, Etc., 755 F.2d 599, 607–608 (7th Cir.1985).

11. E.g., Goins v. Ford Motor Co., 131 Mich.App. 185, 347 N.W.2d 184, 191 (1983) (40–year expectancy with no offset for earnings elsewhere). In Frye v. Memphis State Univ., 806 S.W.2d 170 (Tenn.1991) a tenured professor did nothing towards securing alternate employment for seven years between termination and hearing. He was awarded $429,258. See §§ 6.10(2), 6.10(4) & 12.21(2).

are all to be considered in determining whether it should reasonably be required.[14] Very similarly, if the plaintiff is wrongly discharged from employment, she must seek a substitute job, and might be required to adapt with reason; but she is not required to accept substantially different employment, or a much lower salary, or a humiliating or demeaning position.[15]

In some instances, the issue is not merely simple reasonableness but also one of policy; or if it is a question of reasonableness, some important side issues affect what counts as reasonable. Suppose a tort-injured plaintiff has religious objections to blood transfusions, but his damages will be minimized if he accepts such a transfusion. Some authority has held that damages must be reduced if he does not.[16] The question is not merely one of reasonableness alone. Respect for an individual's personal choices is also important in resolving the issue. So is the idea that the individual must be the one to pay for those personal choices.

In contract cases, the reasonableness question is mixed with policy when the breacher offers the victim a less desirable substitute contract, but one that would minimize the victim's damages. In employment cases courts often insist that the victim accept re-employment if that does not impair his rights to sue.[17] In other cases courts often hold that the victim need not renegotiate with the breacher.[18]

Third rule. This is the affirmative side of avoidable consequences. If the plaintiff actually expends funds in a reasonable effort to minimize damages, the expenditures are recoverable under the third rule as a form of consequential damages. The key requirement is reasonableness. So the recovery for reasonable costs is appropriate, even if the effort to minimize was not successful and even if the costs incurred outran the savings.[19]

When minimizing adds assets. Sometimes the plaintiff's expenditure made to minimize damages has some additional effects. In particular, the plaintiff might reasonably expend money to obtain substitute performance when the defendant reneges on a contract, yet that substitute performance might turn out to be more valuable than the performance promised by the defendant. Suppose the defendant promised Grade 2 at 10 cents a unit, but the only reasonably available substitute was Grade 1, at 12 cents a unit. If Grade 1 represents an improvement the plaintiff can capture, the added 2 cent cost of minimizing for each unit should *not* be recoverable. On the other hand if the plaintiff reasonably obtains Grade 1 and cannot capture

15. E.g., See, e.g., Ford Motor Co. v. E.E.O.C., 458 U.S. 219, 231–232, 102 S.Ct. 3057, 3065–3066, 73 L.Ed.2d 721, 732–733 (1982); Parker v. Twentieth Century–Fox Film Corp., 3 Cal.3d 176, 89 Cal.Rptr. 737, 474 P.2d 689 (1970); §§ 6.10(4); 12.6(2) below.

16. Cf. Munn v. Southern Health Plan, Inc., 719 F.Supp. 525 (N.D.Miss.1989) (death action, no recovery at all because deceased could have avoided death by accepting transfusion).

17. See Small v. Springs Industries, Inc., 300 S.C. 481, 388 S.E.2d 808, 811 (1990); cf. Ford Motor Co. v. EEOC, 458 U.S. 219, 102

S.Ct. 3057, 73 L.Ed.2d 721 (1982) (employment discrimination claim, plaintiff should have minimized damages by accepting employer's offer of employment which did not fully comply with plaintiff's rights).

18. E.g., Zanker Dev. Co. v. Cogito Sys., Inc., 215 Cal.App.3d 1377, 264 Cal.Rptr. 76, 79–80 (1989); § 12.6(2) below.

19. E.g., Brandon & Tibbs v. George Kevorkian Accountancy Corp., 226 Cal.App.3d 442, 277 Cal.Rptr. 40 (1990) (but sometimes combining subjective, good faith tests with reasonableness tests); § 12.6(2) below.

the added benefits of Grade 1, the third rule permits a recovery as a net cost reasonably incurred to minimize damages.[20]

Special rule for leases. Under traditional rules, the lease of land was a conveyance of a property interest for a period of time. When the lessee failed to make rent payments, the lessor was *not* expected to minimize damages by seeking a new tenant; the property was not the lessor's during the period. This view was also consistent with a specific performance remedy. That is, it accomplishes a result similar to specific performance of the lease. The view might also be consistent with the idea that the non-paying tenant may be just as able to find a substitute tenant as the lessor and that the plaintiff should not suffer a reduction in damages where both parties could equally minimize the loss. Whether the parties are equally able to find a substitute in any given situation, is of course a factual question. In any event, the traditional rule came under severe attack, and a number of courts now require the lessor in some situations to minimize damages by seeking substitute tenants.[21]

Rationales and Limitations

Efficiency and fairness. The minimizing rules are grounded both in economic efficiency and in fairness. If the plaintiff can avoid a $10 loss by expending $1, efficiency suggests that the plaintiff should do so, at least when the defendant is no longer in position to avoid the harm so cheaply. The fairness basis for the rule can be expressed in terms of causal ideas. We could say that if the injured plaintiff fails to spend $1 when she knows it will reduce damages by $10, she is author of her own loss or that the defendant's tort is not a proximate cause of it. Both fairness and efficiency may require relaxation of the minimizing rules in some cases, however.

Relative fault or ability to minimize. If, after he has committed a tort or breached a contract, the defendant had an equal and continuing opportunity to minimize damages he has caused, and at a cost no greater than would be required of the plaintiff, the grounds for reducing his liability seem doubtful.[22] Under the Restatement's rule, even if the defendant does not maintain an ability to minimize damages after harm has been done, he may be denied the benefit of the minimizing rules if he was guilty of an intended harm.[23] This second rule seems to be the wrong way to get punitive damages, which can be more accurately measured and considered if they are identified as such and not confused with a measure of loss.

Substantial rights. In some cases the plaintiff's right seems to be too important to sacrifice to efficiency or apparent efficiency.[24] In some contract cases the plaintiff seems to be bargaining to avoid the kind of expense that minimizing would require; many insurance contracts are in this category, which may explain why many courts have created new actions for "bad

21. See § 12.15(3) below.

22. See S.J. Groves & Sons Co. v. Warner Co., 576 F.2d 524, 530 (3d Cir.1978); Paul Wartzman v. Hightower Productions, Ltd., 53 Md.App. 656, 456 A.2d 82, 40 A.L.R.4th 523 (1983). The best incentive structure to induce minimizing might be considered in some cases, however.

23. Restatement Second of Torts § 918(2) (1979).

24. See Camp v. Cohn, 151 Conn. 623, 201 A.2d 187 (1964) (plaintiff need not sacrifice important right of his own to minimize).

faith" in insurance cases. To require the plaintiff to minimize damages when his bargain with the defendant is that he will not have such expenditures is to deny him the core of his contract right. So at some point, perhaps illustrated by the next paragraph, the minimizing rule may go too far.

Strategically placed defendants. Sometimes minimizing rules should not be applied because the risk seems too high that the defendant will repeat misconduct if he gets the benefit of the minimizing rules. A defense must not routinely operate to negate duties already imposed. This point seems especially potent where the defendant's wrong is a continuing one and the defendant himself can minimize damages by ceasing his wrongful conduct. In *O'Brien v. Isaacs,*[25] a parking lot closed while plaintiff's car was parked there, then attempted to charge the plaintiff for the period in which he could not retrieve his car. The amount involved in this overcharge was only $1, but the plaintiff refused to pay it, using cabs instead. The plaintiff was allowed to recover the car and also for its loss of use, without reduction. This result may be efficient; without a rule like this, people probably would never succeed in correcting such misconduct. In addition, the defendant was in position to minimize damages at any time by recognizing the plaintiff's rights. Even if it is not efficient, however, the plaintiff's right might be deemed to outweigh the defendant's efficiency claim.

Comparative Fault vs. Avoidable Consequences

Are the avoidable consequences rules merely rules of contributory negligence or comparative fault? Descriptively speaking the answer is no.[26] Sometimes it is suggested that comparative fault or contributory negligence occurs *before* injury, while a failure to minimize damages occurs *after*. That observation is sometimes correct, but it does not touch the essence of the difference. The two doctrines are functionally different because they use radically different schemes for apportioning responsibility and for measuring that apportionment.

Comparative negligence rules reduce damages in proportion to the plaintiff's fault. Avoidable consequences rules reduce damages for discrete identifiable items of loss caused by the plaintiff's fault or unreasonableness. Although fault in some sense is involved in both cases, the response to that fault is quite different. Suppose the decedent decides that he will never accept a blood transfusion. After the defendant negligently injures him, the decedent refuses a transfusion and dies as a result. Had he accepted the blood, his life would have been saved. A comparative fault analysis of his refusal might hold him responsible for some percent of the total fault, low or high. It would reduce damages recoverable for his wrongful death, but would not bar all recovery.[27] The avoidable consequences rule, in contrast, will bar the entire wrongful death recovery if it applies.[28]

So there are two systems, one a fault-apportionment scheme and the other a causal apportionment scheme. Avoidable consequences rules work

25. O'Brien v. Isaacs, 17 Wis.2d 261, 116 N.W.2d 246 (1962).

27. Comparative fault could bar all recovery under a modified type comparative fault scheme where the plaintiff's or deceased's fault was more than (or in some states equal to) that of the defendant.

28. The recovery was held barred in Munn v. Southern Health Plan, Inc., 719 F.Supp. 525 (N.D.Miss.1989).

the same way as a decision that says, "the plaintiff's fault was the sole proximate cause" of some particular item of harm or loss. It is even possible to combine the two systems in a few cases. For example, a court might identify the plaintiff's *fault* in failing to attach a seat-belt at 5%, and then identify a bruised chest as the only damage resulting. The fault apportionment system alone would reduce the plaintiff's total damages by 5%; an avoidable consequences rule would only deduct the value of the bruised chest; a combined system would deduct 5% of the value of the bruised chest.[29]

There is no room for choice between the two systems, however, unless discrete and identifiable harms can be traced to the plaintiff's conduct. If the plaintiff suffers one harm, or harms that cannot be separated, apportionment if any must be based on fault rather than on causation, and this is true even if the plaintiff's fault occurs after the defendant's negligence.[30]

§ 3.10 Recovery of Attorney Fees and Costs in Litigation

§ 3.10(1) General Rule and Summary

The General Rule

The general rule. The general American rule is that the losing party in litigation is not liable to pay the winner's attorney fee.[1] Attorneys look to their own clients for payment of their fees. The losing litigant is normally charged with "costs," but these are relatively small items such as charges of the sheriff or marshall for service of papers and the like and they do not include either the attorney fees incurred or major litigation expenses. There are, however, a number of important exceptions which permit some prevailing parties to recover their reasonable attorney fees. These exceptions produce a substantial volume of secondary litigation over the entitlement to a fee award and over its measure.[2]

The American Rule against fee recovery has probably seen more change in the last quarter of the 20th century than any other remedial rule. There is now a large and important body of literature[3] and case decision on the

---

29. See § 8.7(4) below on seat-belt and analogous problems.

30. See Ostrowski v. Azzara, 111 N.J. 429, 545 A.2d 148 (1988). The facts in *Ostrowski* went something like this: plaintiff there had diabetes and she smoked. A doctor negligently operated on her toe. Against sound medical advice she refused to quit smoking. As a result of the doctor's negligence, the toe did not heal. Partly as a result of the plaintiff's failure to quit smoking and her preexisting diabetes, the circulation in the toe was poor. The infection did not heal and she eventually lost her leg. Smoking definitely contributed to her loss. Notice that it continued after the toe was injured by the doctor's negligence. Nevertheless, comparative negligence rather than avoidable consequences is the appropriate analysis, because no discrete element of loss can be separated out. Neither smoking nor medical negligence caused the loss of some particular part of the toe.

§ 3.10(1)

1. Alyeska Pipeline Serv. Co. v. Wilderness Soc., 421 U.S. 240, 95 S.Ct. 1612, 44 L.Ed.2d 141 (1975); Quealy v. Paine, Webber, Jackson & Curtis, Inc., 475 So.2d 756 (La.1985); State Farm Mut. Auto. Ins. Co. v. Royal Ins. Co. of Am., 222 Neb. 13, 382 N.W.2d 2 (1986); Hickey v. Griggs, 106 N.M. 27, 738 P.2d 899 (1987).

3. A partial list includes: M. Derfner & A. Wolfe, Court Awarded Attorney Fees (3 vols. supplemented various dates); S. Speiser, Attorney's Fees (2 vols. 1973 & Supp.); Berger, Court Awarded Attorney Fees: What is "Reasonable"?, 126 U.Pa.L.Rev. 281; Brand, The Second Front in the Fight for Civil Rights: The Supreme Court, Congress, and Statutory Fees, 69 Tex.L.Rev. 291 (1990) (reviewing major Supreme Court decisions on civil rights fee awards); Dobbs, Awarding Attorney Fees against Adversaries: Introducing the Problem, 1986 Duke L.J. 435; Dobbs, Reducing Attorneys' Fees for Partial Success: A Com-

attorney fee problem, and change in the scope of the rule and its exceptions continues to work throughout the legal system. These changes are likely to work a substantial impact on the way law is practiced, and indeed may have done so already.

Development of the American Rule. The rule against fee shifting is mainly a product of a special history. Early American legislatures, following the English practice, allowed the prevailing party to recover an attorney fee from the loser, but recovery was severely limited in amount.[4] The limits were so severe that lawyers sought and obtained the right to charge, not their adversaries, but their own clients, as to whom the fee limits were held not to apply.[5] The charge against the client became the standard American practice and the statutes allowing fees against adversaries became obsolete. The very existence of those statutes on the books, however, may have implied that no fee could be awarded against the losing adversary except pursuant to the statute's limited allowance. In any event, the "American rule" against fee shifting was well in place before 1800.[6] That rule may have served many purposes, including, perhaps, the indirect support of large commercial or industrial interests. Perhaps it was also viewed as providing incentives to keep litigation within cost-effective limits.[7]

Rationales. Rational support for the rule has concentrated mainly on the claim that any general regime of fee-shifting could punish litigants for the honest exercise of their rights to go to court and could discourage valid and even important claims and defenses. Less has been said about the effect of fee shifting on in-court strategy and fairness and about the possibility that claims or defenses will be overworked if someone else must pay for them. Yet any general liability for an adversary's attorney fees presents those problems, at least as an initial matter.

The Attacking Arguments

Other legal systems. It is often pointed out, sometimes with insidious intent, that most other Western countries follow a rule which permits fee shifting, charging the loser with the winner's attorney fees. But this is not an argument against the American Rule, only a fact that should open the mind to arguments. And no great significance necessarily attaches to practice in other legal systems, since the fee structure and the nature of litigation itself is often quite different both in Great Britain and in civil law countries.[8]

ment on Hensley and Blum, 1986 Wis.L.Rev. 935; Leubsdorf, Toward a History of the American Rule on Attorney Fee Recovery, 47 L. & Contemp. Probs. 9 (1984); Leubsdorf, Recovering Attorney Fees As Damages, 38 Rutgers L.Rev. 439 (1986); Leubsdorf, The Contingency Factor in Attorney Fee Awards, 90 Yale L.J. 473 (1981); Mureiko, A Public Goods Approach to Calculating Reasonable Fees under Attorney Fee Shifting Statutes, 1989 Duke L.J. 438; Rowe, The Legal Theory of Attorney Fee Shifting: A Critical Overview, 1982 Duke L.J. 651; Rowe, The Supreme Court on Attorney Fee Awards, 1985 and 1986 Terms: Economics, Ethics, and Ex Ante Analyses, 1 Geo. J. Leg. Ethics, 621 (1988).

5. See Leubsdorf, Toward a History of the American Rule on Attorney Fee Recovery, 47 L. & Contemp. Probs. 9 (1984).

6. Arcambel v. Wiseman, 3 U.S. (3 Dall.) 306, 1 L.Ed. 613 (1796).

8. Litigation in Europe often involves more predictable outcomes, and even so the allowance of fees against adversaries does not necessarily include much of the important litigation. See Pfennigstorf, The European Experience with Attorney Fee Shifting, 47 L. & Contemp.Probs. 37 (1984); Rowe, The Legal Theory of Attorney Fee Shifting: A Critical Overview, 1982 Duke L.J. 651. And all fees may

The main arguments. Putting aside cases in which fees may be recovered because of the adversary's bad faith litigation or because they are incorporated in punitive damages, several important arguments have been presented in favor of shifting [9] attorney fees and other litigation costs to the losing party. The design chosen for an alternative to the traditional American Rule depends on which argument is accepted. Professor Rowe has carefully analyzed the theories of fee shifting.[10] What follows here is a much abbreviated summary of some of the major arguments which appear to have influenced courts and legislators.

(1) Indemnity: two way fee shifting. "The prevailing party should not suffer financially for establishing a rightful position, whether the position is a vindicated claim or a vindicated defense." This argument supports two-way fee-shifting, meaning that if it is accepted, the prevailing plaintiff would recover fees from the losing defendant and equally the prevailing defendant would recover fees from the losing plaintiff. Any general regime of two-way fee shifting increases risks that citizens might not present just claims and just defenses because the threat of loss would be too great.

(2) Fees as damages: one way fee shifting. "A litigant in the role of a plaintiff [11] entitled to recover damages is also entitled to recover the reasonable costs of recovering those damages, because otherwise the aggrieved plaintiff is not made whole." This argument supports one-way fee shifting, meaning that if it is accepted, only litigants in the role of a prevailing plaintiff would recover their attorney fees from adversaries and only those in the role of losing defendants would pay them. A defendant victimized by bad faith or malicious claims could recover fees because with respect to such claims the defendant is an aggrieved party; with respect to such claims he is in the role of a plaintiff. Otherwise, however, the defendant would never recover fees and plaintiffs always would do so if they prevailed on the merits.

(3) Fees as incentives. "At least some litigation determines important public issues; where the benefits exceed the costs, that litigation should go forward. Yet if the costs to the individual plaintiff exceed the benefits that she can capture for herself, the litigation is unlikely to proceed unless a fee recovery is permitted. In such cases, a fee award should be granted against the losing defendant." The idea behind this argument is that if a plaintiff could recover only $100 at a litigation cost of $200, litigation should not ordinarily proceed; but that if the public in general receives $1,000 in benefits from the litigation, then the benefits may total $1,100 and far exceed the costs, in which case litigation *should* proceed. This argument favors holding the defendant liable for the fees in order to encourage the plaintiff to obtain the overall benefits.

---

not be recovered even under the English rule. See Goodhart, Costs, 38 Yale L.J. 849 (1929).

9. Fee *shifting* imposes liability for fees on the losing adversary. Fee *sharing* apportions liability for fees among those who participate in the fund produced by litigation.

10. Rowe, The Legal Theory of Attorney Fee Shifting: A Critical Overview, 1982 Duke L.J. 651.

11. "In the role of a plaintiff" means one who is entitled to recover for a grievance or breach of duty, not necessarily one who is the nominal plaintiff or in the procedural position of a plaintiff. One is in the role of a plaintiff if he is a defendant with a viable counterclaim, or a defendant who can assert a malicious prosecution or bad faith litigation claim.

One version of this idea emphasizes that benefits of litigation were received by persons represented by the defendant. This may be the case when the defendant is a public entity and the public in general benefits from the plaintiff's litigation. In that case it is fair to hold the defendant liable for the fees because the defendant's taxpayers receive the benefits.[12] The other version, stated in this paragraph, emphasizes the incentive purposes. Incentive purposes suggest that fees of the plaintiff should be paid, but not necessarily by the defendant. Public financing might be a more appropriate method, and it is interesting to notice that the most significant single change in the American Rule has actually come in civil rights cases, where the defendants who pay the plaintiffs' fees are usually in fact public entities. But there is at least some reason for insisting that the defendant bear the plaintiff's attorney fee because the defendant is a rights violator, regardless whether the defendant is a public entity or not.

Not much data has been generated about the actual strategy effects of fee shifting, especially in one-way fee shifting that permits fees to prevailing plaintiffs but denies them to prevailing defendants.[13] In such a system, institutional defendants such as cities, universities, and other public bodies, can be called into litigation at any time and will always have the unrecompensed costs of defending in such a system. In addition, they will sometimes be found liable and if so will bear additional costs of paying the fee of the prevailing plaintiff. Because plaintiffs (and some lawyers) have little to lose but at least some chance of winning, they may mount a sufficiently credible threat to induce a settlement even when they would not be entitled to win on the merits, partly because institutional defendants tend to attract many grievances. No one can really assess the costs of settlements to unmeritorious plaintiffs, but they may be heavy indeed.[14]

Perhaps the main problem with fees-as-incentives arguments is to identify cases in which benefits to persons other than the plaintiff are likely to outweigh costs of litigation. Because benefits other than those going to litigants are usually highly intangible, they are hard to count. One solution is to make ad hoc decisions after litigation is over. That is expensive and does not necessarily encourage the plaintiff's lawyers, who must decide whether to take the case before fees can be assured. The other solution is to identify in advance classes of cases in which fees may or must be awarded. This solution is adopted by legislation, such as civil rights legislation.[15]

§ 3.10(2) The Common Fund, Substantial Benefit and Private Attorney General

Fee Sharing under the Common Fund Rule

The common fund rule. When a prevailing plaintiff's litigation produces or preserves a fund in which others share, those who share in the fund must share as well in the cost of producing it. They are therefore responsible for a proportionate part of the attorney fee and other reasonable costs of the litigation.[1] This burden is imposed by deducting the fee from the fund itself

---

12. See § 3.10(2) below.   L.Rev. 1597 (1974).

§ 3.10(2)

1. See Dawson, Lawyers and Involuntary Clients: Attorney Fees from Funds, 87 Harv.

and then distributing the fund to those entitled to it. Recovery of fees under the common fund rule is special because it is a recovery against allies, not adversaries. It is not fee shifting but fee sharing.

Examples. Suppose that a trust is managed by a trustee for three beneficiaries. Believing that the trustee has siphoned off assets of the trust, one of the beneficiaries sues the trustee and recovers trust assets. The recovered assets constitute the common fund in which all trust beneficiaries will share. From the fund so produced, the plaintiff's attorney fees will be deducted, in effect charging each beneficiary proportionately.[2]

This kind of rule finds application in formal class action cases, but it is not limited to them. It can apply in any situation in which the work of the attorney has produced a fund or other tangible property and in which the benefits are accepted by others,[3] at least if those benefits can be accurately traced and the litigation costs can be shifted with "exactitude."[4] The ordinary automobile collision may produce a common fund if the car owner who has been paid by his collision insurer recovers sums from the tortfeasor that include car damages. In such a case the insurer is entitled to share in the recovery, up to the amount of its payments to the insured, but with a deduction for its share of the attorney fee.[5]

The beneficiaries may be liable for a fee even if the lawyer's work has not actually produced a fund, if that work protected a fund from improper disbursement,[6] or established, by stare decisis or otherwise, the rights of the beneficiaries to participate in that fund.[7] The special elements that justify an award in these cases are that those who must share in the fees (1) have received a benefit; (2) have received a specific fund (or had it protected from loss) and the attorney fee can be paid from that fund so that there is no personal obligation to pay fees from other sources; and (3) are not required to pay for benefits they do not want at the price.[8]

Restitutionary basis for fee sharing. The common fund rule is grounded in restitutionary considerations. Those who share the fund would be unjustly enriched if they could take the benefit without the burden.[9] Courts quickly extended the common fund rule to permit, not merely a recovery by plaintiffs who have paid their lawyers, but also a direct recovery by lawyers themselves; and the lawyer's recovery may be for fees in excess of the fee charged the client.[10] Even this recovery might be justified on unjust

2. Cf. Trustees v. Greenough, 105 U.S. (15 Otto) 527, 26 L.Ed. 1157 (1881) (recovery of land to be held as security for bondholders, the leading case). Much the same situation exists where a creditor sues to protect assets of a debtor; the fund created or protected by the plaintiff's suit, so far as it enures to the benefit of others, must bear the cost of the attorney's work. Central R.R. & Banking Co. v. Pettus, 113 U.S. 116, 5 S.Ct. 387, 28 L.Ed. 915 (1885).

5. Principal Casualty Ins. Co. v. Norwood, 463 N.W.2d 66 (Iowa 1990).

7. Sprague v. Ticonic Nat. Bank, 307 U.S. 161, 59 S.Ct. 777, 83 L.Ed. 1184 (1939). For explanation of the facts and why this decision is closer to the common fund than to the substantial benefit rule, n. 15 below.

8. These elements are important to preserve the beneficiaries' right of choosing her own benefits. See § 4.9.

9. See Lindy Bros. Builders, Inc. of Phila. v. American Radiator & Standard Sanitary Corp., 487 F.2d 161 (3d Cir.1973); Dawson, Lawyers and Involuntary Clients: Attorney Fees from Funds, 87 Harv.L.Rev. 1597 (1974).

10. Central R.R. & Banking Co. v. Pettus, 113 U.S. 116, 5 S.Ct. 387, 28 L.Ed. 915 (1885).

enrichment grounds, however, if the beneficiaries' liability is limited to the value of what they receive by sharing in the fund.

Restitution and the "volunteers" rule. The usual rule in restitution claims is that one person may not foist a benefit upon another and then demand payment, because to do so would interfere with the recipient's rights of choice and self-determination.[11] The common fund rule does not violate that principle, even though some of the beneficiaries may have refused to join in the litigation. They are not forced to accept the benefit of an augmented fund and if they reject it they are no worse off than they would be if no one had litigated at all. And just as important, the fund recovered generates a fund for payment of the fees; the beneficiary charged with liability will not be required to borrow money to pay the lawyer. These important characteristics do not exist when the common fund rule is extended.

Common fund and conflict of interest. When lawyers can collect a fee not formulated in advance and from "clients" who had not directly dealt with the lawyer, the lawyer becomes adverse to all the client-beneficiaries when it comes to figuring the amount of the fee. The greater the fee for the lawyer, the less fund for the involuntary clients. A certain amount of judicial supervision on the fee award might be desirable in such cases.[12] But conflict may be an unavoidable concomitant of settlement flexibility if fees are not determined in a liquidated or ascertainable sum in advance.[13]

In one well-known case,[14] lawyers represented a class of handicapped children. The defendant made them an offer that was favorable to the children-plaintiffs on the merits but that required, as part of the settlement, that the lawyers would waive all fees. When the lawyers accepted the offer for their clients and then asked the court to change the terms to permit a fee award, the Supreme Court held the settlement binding. One solution to the terrible dilemma for lawyers presented by this particular case is increased regulation of professional conduct by state bars. But no matter what the bar does or does not do, the case strikingly demonstrates a potential for conflict.

Fee Shifting under the "Substantial Benefit" Extension

Extending common fund ideas. The common fund rule allowed the plaintiff or the lawyers for the plaintiff to recover a fee from those who share in the fund recovered or protected by the litigation. The substantial benefit rule goes beyond this in significant ways. The substantial benefit rule permits the plaintiff's lawyer to recover from persons who share in a supposed benefit which is not a cash benefit and does not provide funds from

11. See § 4.9 below.

12. See Prandini v. National Tea Co., 557 F.2d 1015 (3d Cir.1977) (reflecting an effort to control this problem). In Ashley v. Atlantic Richfield Co., 794 F.2d 128, 137–138 (3d Cir. 1986) the court concluded that under decisions of the Supreme Court, no absolute ban on simultaneous negotiation of fees and merits could be imposed.

13. Professor Leubsdorf argued for a fixed percentage recovery, one advantage of which would be to avoid the conflict of interest and related problems. See Leubsdorf, Recovering Attorney Fees As Damages, 38 Rutgers L.Rev. 439, 477 (1986). The same result would seem to follow from any fee fixed in advance by rule of law.

14. Evans v. Jeff D., 475 U.S. 717, 106 S.Ct. 1531, 89 L.Ed.2d 747 (1986).

which the lawyer can be paid.[15] In the extreme version of the substantial benefit rule, the losing adversary is said to have received a benefit and accordingly made to pay the plaintiff's fees.

Hall v. Cole. In *Hall v. Cole,*[16] a union member, expelled from the union for comments made against the leadership, sued to establish his right to remain a member. The Court thought that when he won, he had established free speech rights for union members generally and that the membership, having benefited from the suit, should share in the costs of producing the benefit. This was accomplished by holding the union-defendant liable for the plaintiff's fee. A very similar case involved a corporate shareholder, whose suit against the corporation established intangible rights on behalf of other shareholders, with the result that the corporation itself was held liable for the shareholder's attorney fee.[17]

Potential coverage. Read literally, the substantial benefit rule might permit a fee recovery by almost any plaintiff who litigates against an institutional defendant. Every tenant who litigates against a lessor,[18] every taxpayer who litigates against a public entity,[19] can claim that intangible or even tangible benefits have been provided for all other tenants or taxpayers. Every employee who litigates against an employer[20] and every shareholder who litigates against the corporation[21] can make similar claims that other employees or shareholders must share in liability for the litigator's fees.

Criticizing the restitutionary argument in substantial benefit cases. It is difficult to justify these substantial benefit cases on the restitutionary grounds that applied in common fund cases. Because the benefits are intangible, the "beneficiaries" would have no method of rejecting the benefit as being too costly or even undesirable. For the same reason, the benefit does not provide the means by which to pay the lawyer without reaching funds that would otherwise be available to the "beneficiary" for the beneficiaries' own purposes. On both these counts the substantial benefit theory differs from the common fund rule, and on both these counts it runs afoul of the respect commonly accorded to citizens who receive benefits they did not ask for and do not want.[22] Increased union respect for free speech does not reduce union dues. Increased corporate respect for honest disclosure does not increase dividends. Perhaps union members or corporate shareholders would rather put up with authoritarian leaders or dishonest management than pay the cost of correction. If so, the restitutionary basis for the claim

---

15. An older case, Sprague v. Ticonic Nat. Bank, 307 U.S. 161, 59 S.Ct. 777, 83 L.Ed. 1184 (1939) is often identified as a substantial benefit case. The plaintiff there established her own rights in certain bonds; in so doing she established, by stare decisis or non-mutual collateral estoppel, the rights of some others similarly situated. The plaintiff was entitled to charge all of the bonds, including those belonging to others, with the legal expenses of her suit. The benefit was a realized cash benefit if the other owners would either have lost their rights in the bonds or had to pay for their own suits. So the other bond holders were not deprived of any right of choice. If their option was to lose the bonds and save the attorney fee, they could still exercise that option. They were not charged with costs for any benefit they did not want to pay for at the price charged, because, again, they could still choose to forfeit the bonds rather than to use their proceeds to pay attorneys. So *Sprague* probably is not a substantial benefit case in the ways that count.

16. 412 U.S. 1, 93 S.Ct. 1943, 36 L.Ed.2d 702 (1973).

17. Mills v. Electric Auto–Lite Co., 396 U.S. 375, 90 S.Ct. 616, 24 L.Ed.2d 593 (1970). But when the suit neither creates nor protects a fund, nor enforces a right, the fee is denied. Grace v. Ludwig, 484 F.2d 1262 (2d Cir.1973), cert. denied, 416 U.S. 905, 94 S.Ct. 1610, 40 L.Ed.2d 110 (1974).

that they must share in those costs seems to fail, although public interest in supporting such cases is another matter.

On a policy level, courts may simply believe that fees should be imposed on losing adversaries in certain kinds of cases, which was the end result in *Hall v. Cole* and in shareholder derivative suits. In some factual settings the substantial benefit theory does indeed look like a way station on the road to a more general theory of liability. If so, the trappings of "benefit" should be dropped.

The Private Attorney General

The substantial benefit rule is closely similar to a theory of fee shifting called the "private attorney general" theory. Sometimes it is regarded as identical.[23] The private attorney general doctrine says that in certain kinds of important litigation that will result in public benefits, the plaintiff should recover fees from the defendant, at least where such fees are necessary to finance important and beneficial litigation that otherwise might not be brought. The theory supports judicial fee awards even in the absence of statute, but it has much in common with some fee-shifting statutes.[24] It also has a little in common with the "restitutionary" arguments.

Serrano v. Priest. California judicially adopted a "private attorney general" theory in *Serrano v. Priest.*[25] The theory was later codified in California.[26] *Serrano* was a suit against the state treasurer and others based on the claim that the state's system of financing public education was unconstitutional as a denial of equal protection. The plaintiff's prevailed, then sought an attorney fee award for their efforts. The court thought that three factors should be considered in determining whether a fee would be appropriate:

> (1) the strength or societal importance of the public policy vindicated by the litigation, (2) the necessity for private enforcement and the magnitude of the resultant burden on the plaintiff, (3) the number of people standing to benefit from the decision.

Status of the private attorney general doctrine. In limited circumstances, usually when the state is the virtual defendant, a few other courts have given support to this theory, perhaps somewhat casually in the light of the major shift that it represents.[27] At this writing, only one or two states

25. 20 Cal.3d 25, 141 Cal.Rptr. 315, 569 P.2d 1303 (1977). The theory spread to cover legal fees incurred in administrative proceedings of a quasi-judicial type as well. See Consumers Lobby Against Monopolies v. Public Utilities Com'n, 25 Cal.3d 891, 160 Cal.Rptr. 124, 603 P.2d 41 (1979).

26. West's Ann.Cal.Code Civ.Proc. § 1021.5. The statute provides that fees may be awarded against opposing parties if the action enforced "an important right affecting the public interest" and

(a) a significant benefit, whether pecuniary or nonpecuniary, has been conferred on the general public or a large class of persons, (b) the necessity and financial burden of private enforcement are such as to make the

award appropriate, and (c) such fees should not in the interest of justice be paid out of the recovery, if any.

The statute refuses fee awards in favor of public entities.

27. Arnold v. Arizona Dept. of Health Servs., 160 Ariz. 593, 775 P.2d 521 (1989); see Brown v. State, 565 So.2d 585, 592 (Ala.1990) (class action against state to require it to comply with law in process of issuing traffic tickets, "litigation clearly resulted in a benefit to the general public," "public nature of the services rendered by these lawyers justifies an award of attorney fees," no discussion of the attorney fee rules generally or of private attorney general doctrine by name); Greensburg

outside California and apart from statutory authorization seem to have explicitly adopted the private attorney general rule.[28] Others have used the private attorney general analysis much more narrowly, only when perceived as a statutory policy or as a basis for construing a statute to authorize an award.[29] Most of the courts that have taken explicit judicial action on the issue have so far refused to apply the private attorney general theory.[30]

The benefit element. The benefit element in the *Serrano* formulation may be superfluous. That many people will benefit is evidentiary of the possible societal importance, and so encompassed in the first element. It also suggests that benefits are "externalized," so that no one person who sues will capture all the benefits of the litigation, which in turn suggests that costs may be reasonable in comparison to all the benefits of the litigation but still too high to be absorbed by any single plaintiff. So the benefit element may also be important on the second element in the *Serrano* formula—private enforcement may be economically infeasible, even though it would also be economically desirable from a public point of view.

Comparisons to substantial benefit rule. The benefit elements in the private attorney general rule suggests comparisons to, or identification with, the substantial benefit rule, although the California Court itself rejected any application of that rule in *Serrano.* In *Hall v. Cole,* discussed above as a substantial benefit case, the Court thought the union members benefited from the plaintiff's suit, so the union as an entity representing all the members, should pay the plaintiff's fees. This was possible because the union as an entity was also the defendant in the case.

Local No. 761 Printing Specialities v. Robbins, 549 N.E.2d 79, 80 (Ind.App.1990) (dictum recognizing American Rule exceptions to include bad faith, common fund and private attorney general rules); cf. Hellar v. Cenarrusa, 106 Idaho 571, 682 P.2d 524 (1984) (restricting litigation; statute authorized fee award, rule limiting awards did not apply where plaintiffs litigated public interest case and private attorney general doctrine applied).

28. *Arnold v. Arizona Dept. of Health Services,* and possibly *Hellar v. Cenarrusa,* both supra n. 27. The *Hellar* case is based at least in part on a statute. The *Arnold* case has the most discussion. However, the only reason given there for adopting of the rule was that the American Rule had been eroded by at least 73 state statutes which allowed fee shifting, as well as by common law exceptions. "Given the eroded status of the 'American Rule' and the benefit to Arizona citizens from public interest litigation, we adopt and apply the private attorney general doctrine here." Other states have reached the opposite conclusion from the presence of fee statutes, namely that the legislative policy was to create particular exceptions expressed by statute and no others. E.g., Doe v. State, 216 Conn. 85, 579 A.2d 37 (1990).

30. Doe v. State, 216 Conn. 85, 579 A.2d 37, 48 (1990) (legislature authorized fee awards in

particular statutes; regarding this as a legislative policy, court concluded "that it is inappropriate for the judiciary to establish under the private attorney general doctrine a broad rule permitting such fees whenever a private litigant has at substantial cost to himself succeeded in enforcing a significant social policy that may benefit others"); Pearson v. Board of Health of Chicopee, 402 Mass. 797, 802, 525 N.E.2d 400, 402 (1988) (seemingly not a general rejection for all cases; after viewing authorities, court stated a narrow conclusion that "in suits under [an open meeting statute], we should not depart from our general rule that each party bears its own legal costs"); Jones v. Muir, 511 Pa. 535, 547, 515 A.2d 855, 861 (1986) (fee awards based on vindication of public interests is exclusively a legislative matter); Blue Sky Advocates v. State, 107 Wash.2d 112, 727 P.2d 644 (1986); cf. Helena Elementary School Dist. No. 1 v. State, 236 Mont. 44, 769 P.2d 684 (1989) (rejecting "common fund" and substantial benefit claims to attorney fees because no fund or benefit was created); Dennis v. State, 234 Neb. 427, 451 N.W.2d 676, 687 (1990) (benefit without a fund is not ground for fee award). Alabama rejected the rule in Shelby County Com'n v. Smith, 372 So.2d 1092, 1097 (Ala.1979) ("not inclined to make such a drastic change") but may have given it at least some recognition since then. See Brown v. State, 565 So.2d 585, 592 (Ala. 1990).

In *Serrano* the configuration was similar. The state was a virtual defendant and like the union in *Hall*, it represented those who benefited, the citizens in *Serrano* and the union members in *Hall*. If a benefit could be found for the union members or citizens, then the defendant as their representative was a good entity to pay for that benefit. The criticism already given of the restitutionary theory would still apply, but at least if it is true that there is a benefit, then it is also true that the benefit received and the burden of paying for it would coincide in one entity.

Coincidence of burden and benefit. The coincidence of burden and benefit would be possible only when the defendant is an entity that can stand for the benefited people who would ultimately pay for the benefit through taxes or union dues or (in the case of shareholders) reduced dividends. If an individual were the defendant, or a small public entity that did not represent the benefited people, the private attorney general rule would lose its moral basis. For instance, in *Hall v. Cole,* if only a union official in his private capacity were the defendant, his personal liability for fees could not be justified on the ground that members of the union received the benefits. When the plaintiff's litigation costs exceed the plaintiff's own benefit but fall short of a benefit conferred upon the public, the plaintiff has a good claim against the public who receives the benefit, but not necessarily against the particular defendant.

The public policy elements. The *Serrano* decision emphasized two other elements in the private attorney general fee award. First, the issue had to involve the public interest—an issue of "societal importance." Second, the ability of the private sector to support the litigation through ordinary fees had to be at least in doubt. As already indicated, a guess about benefits to others may be important in determining both the social importance of litigation and the ability of the private sector to support it. But these policy elements can be determined without ad hoc guessing about benefits in particular cases. Legislation can establish definitionally whether certain kinds of litigation are important enough to warrant fee-shifting and also whether the benefits are likely to be so externalized that fee-shifting is desirable.

At any rate, statutory liability has increasingly focused on the fee award as either an element of damages to the plaintiff (not benefit to the defendant) or an element of public interest. These kinds of fee awards are considered in the succeeding subsections.

§ 3.10(3) Attorney Fees as Damages and Sanctions

Fee Recovery as Damages: The Principle

Under the American Rule, a plaintiff who prevails in ordinary tort or contract litigation does not recover the attorney fee expense incurred in the litigation, either as awardable court costs or as damages. However, when the defendant has breached a specific duty to protect the plaintiff from litigation expenses, the defendant is necessarily liable for those expenses, including attorney fees. The real problem is to determine when the defendant has a specific obligation to protect the plaintiff from litigation or litigation costs.

Although the rules are stated as insular expressions without a pattern, they all in fact reflect a willingness to award attorney fees to the plaintiff when the defendant should have protected the plaintiff from litigation or litigation costs. Linked to these cases are some that serve dual purposes, sanctioning some particular misbehavior while at the same time compensating the plaintiff.

When recovery of a fee award is permitted because the adversary has breached a duty to protect against just such costs, the fee award is *damages,* not *costs.* One implication of this statement is that statutes and rules affecting *costs* thus have no bearing on such cases.[1] A second implication is that only one who is in the role of a plaintiff can recover attorney fees under the rules stated in this subsection. Such a fee-claimant may occupy a formal role as defendant or intervenor, but must be asserting a grievance with respect to the matter on which fees are claimed; it is not enough to be a prevailing defendant to recover the fees discussed here.[2]

Contractual Obligations to Protect against Litigation Costs

Explicit contracts. Parties to a contract often provide explicitly that in the event of litigation between them, the losing party will pay the reasonable attorney fees of the prevailing party. Sometimes such provisions are more one-sided, only one party promising to pay the other. Provisions like this can run into trouble if they impose "penalties" by failing to figure fees properly,[3] but if they are valid as a matter of contract law, they impose a specific duty which justifies recovery of fees.[4] Other contractual obligations may be less explicit, yet may make it clear that their aim is to protect the plaintiff from litigation or its costs.

Injunction Bonds. Injunction bonds provide examples that are less obvious but squarely within the principle. If X seeks a temporary restraining order or a preliminary injunction against Y, he is usually required to post security guaranteeing payment of any damages suffered by the defendant in case this provisional remedy proves in the end to have been wrongly issued.[8] The context, if not the syntax, clearly shows that the undertaking is meant to protect the other party from litigation expense. So if it turns out on trial that the provisional relief was improper, the fees incurred in seeking dissolution of the provisional order are recoverable against the bond, although not necessarily those fees incurred in opposing the order in the first place, since the bond was not in effect at that time.[9]

---

§ 3.10(3)

2. See Leubsdorf, Recovering Attorney Fees As Damages, 38 Rutgers L.Rev. 439 (1986).

3. See Equitable Lumber Corp. v. IPA Land Dev. Corp., 38 N.Y.2d 516, 381 N.Y.S.2d 459, 344 N.E.2d 391, 98 A.L.R.3d 577 (1976); § 12.9(2) below.

4. See, e.g., Ocean West Contractors, Inc. v. Halec Constr. Co., 123 Ariz. 470, 600 P.2d 1102 (1979); Share v. Casiano Bel–Air Homeowners Ass'n, 215 Cal.App.3d 515, 521, 263 Cal.Rptr. 753, 757 (1989) (contract stipulation that in event of legal action between parties, "unsuccessful party" to pay successful party "such

court costs and attorneys' fees as the court deems just" was enforceable to permit recovery of fees for work done in contempt hearing).

8. See § 2.11(3) above.

9. Braun v. Intercontinental Bank, 452 So.2d 998, 999 (Fla.App.1984) ("Attorney's fees awarded as damages for the wrongful issuance of an injunction must be restricted to services rendered in undoing a wrongful injunction"); Devine v. Cluff, 110 Idaho 1, 713 P.2d 437 (App.1985); Beard v. Dugdale, 741 P.2d 968, 969 (Utah App.1987) ("only * * * the hours spent by * * * counsel as a result of the wrongfully issued injunction"). Wolverton v.

At one time, when no statute required an injunction bond, some authorities denied the attorney fee recovery, and these decisions continued to be applied even after statutes and rules required a bond. Federal law on this subject is confused because the language of Rule 65 differs from the language of some statutes, and because the language of a particular bond or court order approving a bond, may differ further. Rule 65 provides that the bond is "for payment of such costs and damages as may be incurred or suffered by any party who is found to have been wrongfully enjoined or restrained." It has been argued that the "costs and damages" language does not include attorney fees, and it is certainly true that federal courts have resisted the attorney fee award.[10] On the other hand, particular federal statutes may use broader language and even if they do not, the bond itself may do so, in which case the attorney fee award is appropriate even in federal courts.[11]

Title warranty. One important group of cases involves the vendor who warrants title to the land conveyed. A third person attacks the purchaser's title so that the purchaser is forced to defend the title if the vendor will not. The purchaser must ordinarily tender the defense to the vendor, that is, permit the vendor to take charge of defending the title. If the vendor refuses, or the purchaser is excused from offering the defense of the case to the vendor,[12] then the vendor is liable for the purchaser's litigation expenses, including reasonable attorney fee costs.[13]

[*For discussion of attorney fees as damages in cases of insurance and in arbitration cases, see this section in the Practitioner Treatise edition.*]

Other implicit agreements. The general principle that the defendant is liable for fees when he has agreed, explicitly or otherwise, to protect the plaintiff from litigation or its costs, can be found in a variety of cases, but courts often differ about the underlying obligation when that obligation is not explicit in the parties' contract. Suppose a purchaser releases a claim against a seller, or executes a covenant not to sue on it as part of a settlement, then later sues in violation of his agreement. The covenant not to sue looks like an implicit agreement to protect the seller against the costs of litigation, so if the purchaser violates the agreement it is not surprising to

Holcomb, 174 W.Va. 812, 329 S.E.2d 885, 889 (1985) ("In an action on an injunction bond, counsel fees and expenses expended in resisting the issuance of a preliminary writ of injunction are not damages sustained from the issuance of the writ; and are therefore not in the condition of the bond, and cannot be taken into account in determining the amount of damages that are caused by it"). Some courts once went further, attributing a part of the fees incurred in the main action to the fact that a provisional order was wrongly issued and allowing a recovery for those fees as well. See Dobbs, Should Security Be Required as a Pre-Condition to Provisional Injunctive Relief?, 52 N.C.L.Rev. 1091, 1133 (1974).

10. Matek v. Murat, 862 F.2d 720, 734 (9th Cir.1988) ("Attorney's fees are not recoverable as damages in an action on an injunction bond"); Dobbs, Should Security Be Required as a Pre-Condition to Provisional Injunctive

Relief?, 52 N.C.L.Rev. 1091, 1134 (1974) (tracing history).

11. International Ass'n of Machinist and Aerospace Workers v. Eastern Airlines, Inc., 925 F.2d 6 (1st Cir.1991) (Norris–LaGuardia Act requires bond covering losses as well as costs and expenses, and in addition the district court required the same coverage in the bond itself, liability for attorney fees imposed).

13. E.g., Rauscher v. Albert, 145 Ill.App.3d 40, 99 Ill.Dec. 84, 495 N.E.2d 149 (1986); Groves v. First Nat. Bank of Valparaiso, 518 N.E.2d 819 (Ind.App.1988); Welch v. LaGue, 141 Vt. 644, 451 A.2d 1133 (1982). The purchase price is normally the limit of damages in such cases, see § 12.11(1) below; this limit may also be applied to limit attorney fees. See Howard v. Clanton, 481 So.2d 272 (Miss. 1985).

find some authority that permits attorney fees as damages for that breach.[20] But other decisions have said that the agreement for fees must be explicit even in such cases.[21]

Tort, Indemnity, and Sanction: Obligations Imposed by Law

Indemnity without express contract. In all the cases outlined above, the fee-defendant had promised either to pay the claimant's fees or to protect the claimant from litigation or its costs, and either way liability for fees is proper, as the courts usually recognize. In some cases, however, the obligation to indemnify has a different source. It may arise as a matter of restitution law, simply because one person has paid the obligation of another.[22] Indemnity issues (and similar issues of contribution) commonly arise in tort cases.

In the traditional tort case, one person is primarily responsible for an injury to a victim, but another person is actually held liable to the victim (or settles the victim's full claim). For example, a victim might be negligently injured by *A*'s employee acting in the scope of his employment. If the victim recovers from *A* on the basis of vicarious liability, *A* is entitled to indemnity from the employee. Or a seaman is injured in the service of the ship so that the ship is strictly liable to pay for medical attention and support. If the injury was negligently caused by *T*, then the ship, having paid the obligation that should fall primarily on the negligent person, is entitled to indemnity. In such cases it is easy to find a right of indemnity in favor of one who is held strictly liable for practical reasons and against one who is actually negligent,[23] and indemnity of this kind carries with it the recovery of attorney fees incurred.[24]

The indemnity right that furnishes the ground for the fee recovery is not always clear. One kind of case that arises regularly is the products liability action in which a retailer is held liable to a consumer or victim for a product defect and then sues the manufacturer for indemnity, seeking not only to recover any sum the retailer may have had to pay the consumer but also the costs of defense. If the court concludes that the manufacturer should indemnify the retailer, then the retailer's attorney fees, incurred in defending the consumer's suit, are an appropriate part of the recovery. Some cases are difficult to interpret, but might be read to exclude the right to indemnity altogether in this setting.[26] A number of products liability statutes have now been passed to prescribe indemnity and to specifically

20. Anchor Motor Freight, Inc. v. International Broth. of Teamsters, Etc., 700 F.2d 1067 (6th Cir.1983), cert. denied, 464 U.S. 819, 104 S.Ct. 81, 78 L.Ed.2d 92 (1983).

21. Gruver v. Midas Intern. Corp., 925 F.2d 280 (9th Cir.1991); Bunnett v. Smallwood, 793 P.2d 157 (Colo.1990) (reviewing cases on both sides).

22. See § 4.3(2) below, as qualified by the rules stated in § 4.9 below. Some obligations to indemnify might be "implied in fact" obligations rather than obligations imposed purely as a matter of law. As to that distinction,

which does not appear to be important here, see § 4.2(3) below.

23. Flunker v. United States, 528 F.2d 239, 242 (9th Cir.1975) (purpose of strict liability of the ship coupled with right of indemnity is "to place ultimate liability on the party who was truly at fault who should mend his negligent ways to prevent future injury").

24. Flunker v. United States, supra n. 23.

26. Davis v. Air Technical Industries, Inc., 22 Cal.3d 1, 148 Cal.Rptr. 419, 582 P.2d 1010, 1012 (1978).

identify attorney fees as elements of the recovery.[27]

Third person litigation. It is commonly stated as a rule that when the defendant's breach of duty to the plaintiff involves the plaintiff in litigation with third parties, the defendant is held liable for the costs of that litigation, including attorney fees.[28] This might happen in contract cases, as where the vendor's breach of a deed warranty requires the purchaser to defend his would-be title by litigating with others. Or it might happen in tort cases, as where the negligence of a malpracticing lawyer requires the client to protect her interests by litigating with others; the lawyer is liable for the litigation expenses as consequential damages.[29]

Although the "third party litigation" rule factually describes many of the cases, including most of those summarized above in discussing contractual obligations, it fails to focus on the facts that create liability and delimit its scope. To illustrate the point: I have no claim against you merely because I must litigate with a third person. The claim against you must proceed from your duty to protect me from such litigation or from its costs. As shown above, such a duty might arise out of a contract between us or out of tort and a restitutionary obligation. But it is the contract, the tort, or the restitutionary duty that is important, not the fact that a third person is involved. So the critical questions are whether you owed me a duty to protect me from litigation expense and whether that duty was breached.

Beyond the third party limitation. The point just made is almost always overlooked. Courts often focus on whether the claim for fees is a claim for fees incurred in litigation with a third person rather than in litigation with the now-defendant or his privies,[31] or whether the litigation was "prior" rather than the current litigation, and they often deny the fee claim if it is based on litigation with the defendant himself. That result is often right, but not always. One could contractually agree, for example, to pay the plaintiff's attorney fees in litigation with the defendant. And as in other cases, the agreement might be implicit, to be found in a promise to protect the plaintiff from the litigation generally.[32] Likewise, a tort duty to protect the plaintiff from litigation with the defendant himself is found in some cases.[33] Any rational integration of the attorney fee rules requires us to recognize that what counts is the scope of the defendant's duty to protect the plaintiff from litigation.

27. E.g., Ariz.Rev.Stat. § 12–684; Idaho Code § 6–1407(2) [§ 6–1307(2)]. Cf. West's Ann.Cal.Code Civ.Proc. § 1021.6 (authorizing fee awards for a tort indemnitee once such a person prevails on the implied indemnity claim, but not establishing the indemnity right itself). Some statutes are aimed only at automobile manufacturers and dealers, e.g., Del.Code § 4905 (notwithstanding any franchise agreement to the contrary, indemnity to retailer, including attorney fees); Purdon's Pa.Stat.Ann. § 818.8(d); but sometimes these duplicate effects of broader statutes.

28. Leubsdorf, Recovering Attorney Fees As Damages, 38 Rutgers L.Rev. 439 (1986); Restatement Second of Torts § 914(2) (1979).

Some states offer only a constricted version of this rule. See West's Ann.Cal.Code Civ.Proc. § 1021.6 (implied indemnity, tort claims only).

29. E.g., Dessel v. Dessel, 431 N.W.2d 359 (Iowa 1988); Ramp v. St. Paul Fire & Marine Ins. Co., 263 La. 774, 269 So.2d 239, 55 A.L.R.3d 967 (1972). See § 6.11 below as to liabilities for lawyer malpractice.

32. See Peter Fabrics, Inc. v. S.S. "Hermes", 765 F.2d 306 (2d Cir.1985) (construing the indemnity agreement to cover prior claims by the indemnitor itself as well as claims by third persons); Manson–Osberg Co. v. State, 552 P.2d 654 (Alaska 1976).

Malicious prosecution and similar damages cases. A defendant who, without probable cause, instigates or institutes a criminal proceeding or a civil action against the now-plaintiff, may be held liable in tort for malicious prosecution or a civil analogue.[34] One of the main items of pecuniary harm caused by the wrongful institution or instigation of civil or criminal litigation is the cost of litigating. So to recognize malicious prosecution, wrongful civil proceedings or any similar tort is to recognize a claim for attorney fees reasonably incurred in the litigation as damages.[35] These torts are, so far, torts committed by people who are in the role of plaintiffs in the original litigation. If the defendant in the original case raises malicious defenses, not supported by any colorable grounds, he is not liable in these common law torts.[36]

No general principle limits the duty to protect the plaintiff from litigation expense to the case of the malicious prosecution. In *Liles v. Liles,*[37] an attorney representing the wife fraudulently induced her to enter into a property settlement which deprived her of assets to which she was entitled. When the wife discovered the facts, she sued both the husband and the attorney. She was allowed to recover her attorney fees for that suit against the attorney, who was in fact a party to the same suit. Although there were additional grounds in support of the recovery, the result seems clearly right even though the defendant was a party to the very litigation in which fees were sought.[38]

Litigation misconduct.[39] Judges may impose sanctions upon a party or an attorney guilty of some kinds of litigation misconduct. The sanction may take the form of an attorney fee award to the adversary for all or part of the adversary's fee costs. The power to do this is now usually invoked under Rule 11 of the Federal Rules or some counterpart provision,[40] but is also said to be an inherent power of courts,[41] and may include the power to impose the sanction upon either the adversary or his attorney.[42]

---

34. Prosser & Keeton on Torts §§ 119–121 (5th ed. 1984 & Supp.).

35. Bertero v. National General Corp., 13 Cal.3d 43, 118 Cal.Rptr. 184, 529 P.2d 608, 65 A.L.R.3d 878 (1974) (malicious prosecution); Vogtle v. Coleman, 259 Ga. 115, 376 S.E.2d 861 (1989) ("abusive litigation"). See also § 7.3(2) below.

36. Prosser & Keeton on Torts § 120, p. 893 (5th ed. 1984). Advocating recognition of the malicious defense tort: Van Patten & Willard, The Limits of Advocacy: A Proposal for the Tort of Malicious Defense in Civil Litigation, 35 Hast.L.Rev. 891 (1984).

37. 289 Ark. 159, 711 S.W.2d 447 (1986).

38. Sometimes courts say the litigation for which fees are sought must be a separate, earlier litigation. This supposed rule appears to be another version of the rule that litigation must be with third parties, and it falls on the same grounds. The *Liles* court did not expressly pass on that issue because it concluded that, as a trustee, the attorney there was subject to liability for the fees in any event.

39. Compare also the impact on fees under Rule 68, Federal Rules of Civil Procedure (offer of judgment provisions, see § 3.10(5) below).

40. E.g., Business Guides, Inc. v. Chromatic Communications Enterprises, Inc., 498 U.S. 533, 111 S.Ct. 922, 934, 112 L.Ed.2d 1140 (1991); Wang v. Gordon, 715 F.2d 1187 (7th Cir.1983). Attorney fee awards as Rule 11 sanctions are for improper trial court filings in the trial court and are limited to fees incurred as a result of the filings and in the trial court, so that fees on appeal are excluded. Cooter & Gell v. Hartmarx Corp., 496 U.S. 384, 110 S.Ct. 2447, 110 L.Ed.2d 359 (1990).

41. Chambers v. NASCO, Inc., __ U.S. __, 111 S.Ct. 2123, 115 L.Ed.2d 27 (1991) (inherent power permits courts to assess attorney fees and litigation costs against bad faith, vexatious litigant, even for conduct outside court and not covered by Rule 11); Actors' Equity Ass'n v. American Dinner Theatre Institute, 802 F.2d 1038, 1043 (8th Cir.1986); Winters v. City of Oklahoma City, 740 P.2d 724 (Okl.

Contempt of court. When the defendant disobeys an injunctive order, the plaintiff may seek remediation by asking the court to impose civil contempt sanctions in an effort to force compliance. If the plaintiff succeeds, some courts hold that the trial judge has discretion to order payment of the plaintiff's attorney fee for the work done in the contempt hearing,[47] and possibly even for fees in the entire litigation.[48] These cases are often supported by the authority of specific statutes,[49] but again, the contempt power is often said to be inherent, so that the same thing might be done whether a statute permits it or not.[50] These cases can be regarded as special versions of litigation misconduct; the non-complying defendant has not merely refused to pay a judgment, he has refused to obey an affirmative court order. Once again, his adversary suffers damages in the form of added fee costs. And once again, liability is imposed even though the damage involves no third party litigation.

§ 3.10(4) Development of the Civil Rights Fee Statutes

Fee Award Statutes Generally

Apart from the traditional common law exceptions, legislation now widely authorizes attorney fee awards against adversaries, not on any systematic basis, but in hundreds of statutes governing particular kinds of cases. Statutes are far too numerous even to list. Important federal statutes vary in detail and wording but provide for some kind of fee award in a wide range of cases, including those involving antitrust,[1] patent,[2] and securities[3] claims; and environmental,[4] civil rights,[5] and wage and hour suits.[6] The bankruptcy attorney fee award is something of a specialty of its own,[7] as are the awards under the Equal Access to Justice Act for citizens embroiled in litigation by truly unreasonable governmental action.[8] Some other statutes are listed in the footnote,[9] but they can only illustrate the point; the uncoordinated grind of legislation requires repeated statutory research.

1987) (inherent power of court to impose sanctions upon attorney personally, including a fee award).

47. Moran v. Rhode Island Broth. of Correctional Officers, 506 A.2d 542 (R.I.1986) (civil contempt, fee awarded against contemnor for attorney's work in the contempt proceeding, reflecting that courts differ on this topic); cf. McKiever v. McKiever, 305 Ark. 321, 808 S.W.2d 328 (1991) (contempt hearing arising out of marital settlement, fee awarded without discussion of reason). See Annotation, Allowance of attorneys' fees in civil contempt proceedings, 43 A.L.R.3d 793.

48. See Chambers v. NASCO, Inc., ___ U.S. ___, ___, 111 S.Ct. 2123, 2133, 115 L.Ed.2d 27 (1991) (courts have inherent power to impose contempt fine that includes "the entire cost of the litigation").

§ 3.10(4)

8. 5 U.S.C.A. § 504, 28 U.S.C.A. § 2412. Under § 2412(d)(1)(A) the award (except in tort claims) is to be made against the United States "unless the court finds that the position of the United States was substantially justified or that special circumstances make an award unjust." But under § 2412(d)(2)(A) the award is limited to $75 per hour "unless the court determines that an increase in the cost of living or a special fact, such as the limited availability of qualified attorneys * * * justifies a higher fee * * *." See, Pierce v. Underwood, 487 U.S. 552, 108 S.Ct. 2541, 101 L.Ed.2d 490 (1988) (discussing the statutory fee cap and the "substantially justified" limitation).

9. 5 U.S.C.A. § 552(a)(4)(E) (Freedom of Information Act); 5 U.S.C.A. § 552a(g)(4) (Privacy Act); 8 U.S.C.A. § 1964 (1984) ("threefold" damages, costs of suit and attorney fees under Racketeer Influenced and Corrupt Organizations (RICO) statute); 18 U.S.C.A. § 2520 (wiretapping, private cause of action, damages and attorney fees).

States have also enacted many fee award statutes, mostly providing for fees in particular and usually narrow instances. One somewhat general category covers consumer litigation. Most states have consumer protection legislation and most of that legislation authorizes attorney fees in favor of a prevailing consumer advocate.[10] In addition to many other particular statutes, state statutes frequently emulate federal legislation, including some of the federal statutes listed above.[11] But some state statutes now seem to tackle fee problems partly in principle. Arizona authorizes a limited fee award in any litigation arising out of contract,[12] including some torts claims that "arise" in contract.[13] Texas permits recovery of attorney fees in contract cases;[14] Nevada has a scheme for fee awards in small claims;[15] when states have not moved that far, they have nevertheless moved very definitely.[16] The sheer number of statutes suggests that the American Rule has been cut down to size one small chop at a time.

The statutes differ as to terminology and coverage and sometimes as to purpose. Even if they did not, they are too numerous to discuss separately. Accordingly, this subsection and those that follow will focus mainly on the development of civil rights attorney fee awards and issues of entitlement and measurement that arise when such awards are sought. To a large extent, the issues raised under civil rights fee statutes, and especially issues of entitlement and measurement, will shed light on similar issues under other statutes.

Development of the Civil Rights Fee Award

Narrow fee statutes. The 1964 Civil Rights Act included provisions for fee awards for plaintiffs who won public accommodation[17] and job discrimination (Title VII) cases.[18] No such statute permitted fees in other civil rights cases, such as those brought under the old mainstay, § 1983, which covered any violations of federal rights under color of state law.

The private attorney general rationale in Piggie Park. In this state of affairs a public accommodations case styled *Piggie Park*[19] went to the Supreme Court. The public accommodations statute allowed only an injunctive remedy and it provided for the award of attorney fees. The issue was whether fees should be awarded routinely under the statute and the Court said they should be. Fees might be especially important when only injunctive relief was available, since in that case no fund of money would be recovered from which fees could be paid. More importantly perhaps, the Court said that the plaintiff who pursued such a claim was conferring a benefit upon the public; such a plaintiff could be thought of as a kind of

12. Ariz.Rev.Stats. § 12–341.01.

13. See Sparks v. Republic Nat. Life Ins. Co., 132 Ariz. 529, 647 P.2d 1127 (1982).

14. V.T.C.A. Civ.Prac. and Rem.Code § 38.-001. The claimant must have been represented by an attorney, Id., § 38.002, and does not apply where other statutes govern the contract, Id., § 38.006.

15. Nev.Rev.Stat.Ann. 18.010.

16. See Alaska Rules of Civil Procedure, Rule 82 (unless court in its discretion directs otherwise, a fee schedule applies to fees "for the party recovering any money judgment,"

and a fee in a "reasonable amount" for the prevailing party if no recovery is obtained); Minn.Stat.Ann. § 8.31, Subd. 1 & Subd. 3a. See, discussing the Alaska rule and its history, McDonough v. Lee, 420 P.2d 459 (Alaska 1966).

17. 42 U.S.C.A. § 2000a–3.

18. 42 U.S.C.A. § 2000e–5(k).

19. Newman v. Piggie Park Enterprises, Inc., 390 U.S. 400, 88 S.Ct. 964, 19 L.Ed.2d 1263 (1968).

"private attorney general." [20] With these things in mind, the Court held that the fee should routinely be granted to the prevailing plaintiff in the absence of some special reason to deny it.

Attempts to extend the rationale. *Piggie Park* did not suggest that fees should be granted in the absence of statutory authority. It only held that they should be granted routinely where authorized. But some courts seized upon the phrase "private attorney general" to argue that when the plaintiff pursued the public good in civil rights or environmental cases, the losing defendant should pay the plaintiff's attorney fees, even in the absence of statutory authorization.[21] The argument was not wholly preposterous. Although *Piggie Park*'s language supported the result only when shorn of all its context and its meaning, some of the earlier "substantial benefit" decisions of the Court were easiest to explain as decisions of policy that favored a fee to one whose litigation provided important public benefits.[22]

Alyeska: the Supreme Court rejects the extension. When the question came before the Court in *Alyeska Pipeline Service Co. v. Wilderness Society,*[23] that Court squarely and firmly held that the fees could not be awarded except as authorized by statute or by traditional exceptions to the American Rule. That was in 1968, four years after the Civil Rights Act had been passed, but it should not have been especially surprising, because the Civil Rights Act had not authorized fees for suits brought under § 1983.

Section 1988. The decision in *Alyeska* appeared to rouse some members of Congress. Enthusiasts proposed broad statutes authorizing fee recoveries, but in the end Congress passed the Civil Rights Fee Award Act in 1976 to authorize fee awards only in certain civil rights cases.[24] The basis for the statute was a perceived need to encourage civil rights litigation by assuring winners that a reasonable fee could be collected from the adversary. The operative fee provisions are like those in Title VII but they cover actions brought under the older civil rights statutes such as § 1983, which prohibits violation of federal rights under color of state law.[25] The fee statute provides in part:

> In any action or proceeding to enforce a provision of sections 1981, 1982, 1983, 1985, and 1986 of this title, title IX of Public Law 92–318, or title VI of the Civil Rights Act of 1964, *the court, in its discretion, may allow the prevailing party, other than the United States, a reasonable attorney's fee as part of the costs.*[26]

§ 3.10(5) Eligibility and Entitlement Generally

The entitlement rules under the civil rights statutes can be summarized as follows:

21. See La Raza Unida v. Volpe, 57 F.R.D. 94 (N.D.Cal.1972).

22. See Hall v. Cole, § 3.10(2) above.

23. 421 U.S. 240, 95 S.Ct. 1612, 44 L.Ed.2d 141 (1975).

24. Codified as 42 U.S.C.A. § 1988.

25. 42 U.S.C.A. § 1983. These statutes literally cover any federal right, so they are not limited to claims traditionally viewed as civil rights claims. See Dennis v. Higgins, 498 U.S. 439, 111 S.Ct. 865, 112 L.Ed.2d 969 (1991).

26. The italicized words are identical to words also found in the Title VII (job discrimination) statute, 42 U.S.C.A. § 2000e–5(k).

(1) Routinely awarded to prevailing plaintiffs. The fee is granted routinely to the prevailing plaintiff and should not be denied except for special reasons peculiar to the case.[2]

(2) Routinely denied to prevailing defendants. The fee is granted as a one-way fee system, in favor of the prevailing plaintiff but not in favor of the prevailing defendant, unless the plaintiff is guilty of frivolous, vexatious or bad faith litigation.[3]

(3) Awarded as costs, not "damages". The civil rights fee is awarded as "costs" rather than as damages.[4] Some other statutes do not treat the fee award as costs.[5] Whatever statutes or procedures apply to "costs" thus apply to attorney fees under the civil rights statutes but not under some others.[6] When a governmental agency is a defendant, the classification of fee awards as damages might invite a sovereign immunity defense when classification as costs would not.[7]

(4) Fee awards can be claimed by clients' lawyers. The fee is recoverable by and for lawyers even if the client has not paid and will not pay a fee. Thus successful public interest and pro bono lawyering receives a fee.[8] Successful *pro se* lawyers, however, are to be denied a fee award, at least under civil rights statutes.[9]

§ 3.10(5)

2. See Blanchard v. Bergeron, 489 U.S. 87, 109 S.Ct. 939, 103 L.Ed.2d 67 (1989); Independent Federation of Flight Attendants v. Zipes, 491 U.S. 754, 109 S.Ct. 2732, 105 L.Ed.2d 639 (1989). The statute, 42 U.S.C.A. § 1988, quoted in § 3.10(4) above, provides that the court "in its discretion" "may" award fees. The Supreme Court decisions requiring a routine award for the plaintiff direct the manner in which that discretion is to be exercised.

3. Christiansburg Garment Co. v. EEOC, 434 U.S. 412, 98 S.Ct. 694, 54 L.Ed.2d 648 (1978). This rule is a judicial creation. Section 1988 itself refers to "prevailing party." Some other federal statutes, however, permit fees only to the prevailing plaintiff. E.g., 15 U.S.C.A. § 15; 29 U.S.C.A. § 216(b). Constitutional scruples about one-way fee shifting, see Gulf, Colo., & S.F. Ry. Co. v. Ellis, 165 U.S. 150, 165–166, 17 S.Ct. 255, 261, 41 L.Ed. 666, 672 (1897) (holding a one-way fee shifting statute denied railroads equal protection) appear to have evaporated. See Leubsdorf, Toward a History of the American Rule on Attorney Fee Recovery, Law & Contemp.Probs., Winter 1984 at 26.

4. 42 U.S.C.A. § 1988 (civil rights, "[T]he court, in its discretion, may allow the prevailing party, other than the United States, a reasonable attorney's fee as part of the costs"). Some others do the same, e.g., 17 U.S.C.A. § 505 (copyright, see § 6.3(7) below).

5. The patent and trademark attorney fees statutes do not specify the fee recovery as "costs," although the copyright statute does. See 35 U.S.C.A. § 285 (patent, "The court in

exceptional cases may award reasonable attorney fees to the prevailing party"); 15 U.S.C.A. § 1117(a) (one of the trademark statutory provision, same); 17 U.S.C.A. § 505 (copyright, "the court may also award a reasonable attorney's fee to the prevailing party as part of the costs").

6. Thus under Federal Rule 68 (and some state-law counterparts) the plaintiff who ultimately recovers a money judgment, but who rejected an earlier settlement offer for an even sum, is denied all recovery of "costs" incurred after the offer was rejected. Since "costs" in a civil rights action include attorney fees, the plaintiff is denied recovery of the attorney fees incurred after that point as well. Marek v. Chesny, 473 U.S. 1, 105 S.Ct. 3012, 87 L.Ed.2d 1 (1985). It does not follow that the defendant affirmatively recovers fees incurred from that point. Because the civil rights fee shifting is a one-way system, defendants have been denied recovery of their attorney fees incurred after the plaintiff refused an offer which proved to be better than the ultimate verdict. Crossman v. Marcoccio, 806 F.2d 329 (1st Cir.1986), cert. denied, 481 U.S. 1029, 107 S.Ct. 1955, 95 L.Ed.2d 527 (1987); O'Brien v. City of Greers Ferry, 873 F.2d 1115, 1120 (8th Cir.1989).

7. Cf. Hutto v. Finney, 437 U.S. 678, 98 S.Ct. 2565, 57 L.Ed.2d 522 (1978); Missouri v. Jenkins, 491 U.S. 274, 109 S.Ct. 2463, 105 L.Ed.2d 229 (1989).

8. See Blum v. Stenson, 465 U.S. 886, 104 S.Ct. 1541, 79 L.Ed.2d 891 (1984).

9. Kay v. Ehrler, ___ U.S. ___, 111 S.Ct. 1435, 113 L.Ed.2d 486 (1991) (implication of

(5) Only prevailing plaintiffs recover. Only a plaintiff who "prevails" can recover a fee.[10] The plaintiff is a prevailing party under this test if she succeeds on any significant issue in the case and achieves some of the relief she sought.[11]

§ 3.10(6) Eligibility and Entitlement: Prevailing Party Rules

General Rules

Standard. Under the civil rights fee shifting statutes, the plaintiff meets the threshold of entitlement by prevailing on any significant issue in the case and obtaining some relief. The plaintiff need not succeed on "the central issue," or recover all of the relief sought in order to recover fees.[1] This rule must be understood in connection with the rule that the *amount* of the fee may be affected by the plaintiff's relative lack of success.[2] Purely "de minimus" success may lead to a denial of the fee,[3] but fees have been awarded even though the plaintiff's recovery is for nominal damages only.[4]

Prevailing without relief. The plaintiff does not prevail unless she obtains some kind of relief. In *Hewitt v. Helms,*[5] the plaintiff was a prisoner who sued claiming he was denied due process in a punitive detention. The court agreed, but ultimately held that, the law having been uncertain, the defendants were entitled to immunity for past acts. The plaintiff then sought fees, arguing that he was successful because he established the new legal rule he had contended for. The Court held that this is not enough. A prevailing party, even in a declaratory judgment action, must get some relief affecting the behavior of the defendant in order to qualify for a fee recovery.

Relief without prevailing: interim success. The plaintiff is not a prevailing party when she prevails on some subsidiary ruling in the case. For example, she might successfully oppose a summary judgment motion, but that does not make her a prevailing party.[7] On the other hand, the rule

---

"attorney" in statute is that an agent is required and more significantly meritorious claims will more likely be successful if pursued by independent counsel). This decision will probably force a similar result under other statutes unless their language points toward a pro se award. Some other statutes strongly point to a denial of pro se awards. E.g., 5 U.S.C.A. § 552(a)(4)(E) (fees "incurred"). Dual representation of oneself and others might present a different case. See Hunt Inv. Co. v. Eliot, 154 Ariz. 357, 742 P.2d 858 (App.1987) (representing partnership of which lawyer was a member). Note, Pro Se Can You Sue? Attorney Fees for Pro Se Litigants, 34 Stan.L.Rev. 659 (1982) (recognizing that case is jeopardized by self-representation but supporting the award).

10. See Ruckelshaus v. Sierra Club, 463 U.S. 680, 103 S.Ct. 3274, 77 L.Ed.2d 938 (1983).

11. See § 3.10(6) below.

§ 3.10(6)

1. Texas State Teachers Ass'n v. Garland Indep. School Dist., 489 U.S. 782, 109 S.Ct. 1486, 103 L.Ed.2d 866 (1989); see Hensley v.

Eckerhart, 461 U.S. 424, 103 S.Ct. 1933, 76 L.Ed.2d 40 (1983).

4. E.g., Fast v. School Dist. of City of Ladue, 728 F.2d 1030 (8th Cir.1984) (plaintiff, who sought a right to a hearing before termination of employment, was denied this and given only a right to a post-termination meeting to state her views, and $1 damages; she waived the meeting, but fees were proper); Cf. Rosebrough Monument Co. v. Memorial Park Cemetery Ass'n, 736 F.2d 441 (8th Cir.1984), cert. denied, 469 U.S. 981, 105 S.Ct. 385, 83 L.Ed.2d 320 (1984) (antitrust plaintiff, nominal damages trebled, $3, fee award $51,293).

5. 482 U.S. 755, 107 S.Ct. 2672, 96 L.Ed.2d 654 (1987).

7. Cf. Hanrahan v. Hampton, 446 U.S. 754, 100 S.Ct. 1987, 64 L.Ed.2d 670 (1980) (appellate court's reversal of directed verdict gives plaintiff a trial but is not a determination on the merits, fee award not appropriate). Accord, under state law, Henderson v. Jantzen, Inc., 303 Or. 477, 737 P.2d 1244 (1987) (reversal of trial court's summary judgment for defendant created opportunity for plaintiff to become a prevailing party, but he was not one merely on the basis of "intermediate and pos-

since a 1974 decision has been that when the plaintiff succeeds on some definite substantive issue, as where liability is determined once and for all, the plaintiff is a prevailing party and eligible for an interim fee award.[8] This second rule fits well with the rule under which the plaintiff who has established a right to recover on the merits may be awarded some of her damages before a final determination of the total damages.[9]

The two rules read together may be viewed as illustrating the cases for denial and for grant of fees [10] but they do not make for easy solution of the cases in between. In addition, some doubt may be injected about the strength of the rule allowing fees. The second rule permits a fee award upon a determination of liability, but it might be difficult to square this with the Court's later insistence that a fee could not be awarded without some actual award of relief.[11]

Preliminary injunction shown to have been erroneous. Preliminary injunction fee awards fall into at least three distinct categories.[12] When a plaintiff is successful in obtaining a preliminary injunction or similar provisional relief, he may recover all of the relief he really wants. In such a case, is he a prevailing party entitled to fees if it is later determined that he was not entitled to that relief on the merits?

For example, in one case a high school student obtained a preliminary injunction that permitted him to enroll in a gymnastics program, theretofore available only to females. This lasted throughout the season, after which he graduated. So he literally obtained all the relief he wanted on the preliminary injunction. Although his own case was mooted by his graduation, a companion case ultimately decided that the preliminary injunction was erroneously issued. This and similar cases show that obtaining effective but legally provisional relief is not by itself enough when the plaintiff ultimately loses on the merits.[13] By definition, only litigation that enforces a federal right governed by the fee statute is covered for a fee award.[14] The plaintiff

---

sibly temporary success"; fee on appeal denied).

8. Bradley v. School Bd. of City of Richmond, 416 U.S. 696, 94 S.Ct. 2006, 40 L.Ed.2d 476 (1974). See also Hameed v. International Ass'n of Bridge, etc., 637 F.2d 506 (8th Cir. 1980).

9. See § 8.10 below.

10. See M. Derfner & A. Wolfe, Court Awarded Attorney Fees ¶ 9.03 for a helpful discussion.

13. See Dahlem v. Board of Educ. of Denver Pub. Schools, 901 F.2d 1508 (10th Cir. 1990) (male high school student obtained year in gymnastics by preliminary injunction); Palmer v. City of Chicago, 806 F.2d 1316 (7th Cir.1986), cert. denied, 481 U.S. 1049, 107 S.Ct. 2180, 95 L.Ed.2d 836 (1987); Frazier v. Board of Trustees of Northwest Miss. Regional Medical Center, 765 F.2d 1278 (5th Cir.1985), amended, 777 F.2d 329 (1985), cert. denied, 476 U.S. 1142, 106 S.Ct. 2252, 90 L.Ed.2d 697 (1986); Doe v. Busbee, 684 F.2d 1375, 1380 (11th Cir.1982) (abortion funding continued by preliminary injunction, 1800 women received

abortion funding; plaintiff's successes on preliminary injunction that was later dissolved did "not represent a vindication of * * * civil rights of the plaintiff against a violator of those rights"); Smith v. University of N.C., 632 F.2d 316, 347 (4th Cir.1980) (plaintiff retained job for one year by preliminary injunction; disentitlement on the merits was established at permanent injunction stage; fee award denied although plaintiff had been successful in prolonging job by one year through preliminary injunction; "what always must occur is the establishment of a right or the proscription of a wrong"). But cf. Grano v. Barry, 251 U.S.App.D.C. 289, 783 F.2d 1104 (1986) (treating case like mooted case, as to which see the paragraph, "Preliminary injunction mooted" below).

Cases sometimes mention that the plaintiff's success was merely temporary or not "enduring." The temporary nature of the plaintiff's success seems to be only an artifact, however. The plaintiff's success, temporary or otherwise, was not success *in establishing a right covered by the fee statute.*

who obtains preliminary relief to which he is not entitled is not awarded a fee.

Preliminary injunction mooted. A different kind of preliminary injunction issue arises when the plaintiff obtains a preliminary injunction and the defendant then voluntarily complies with the reform sought so that the claim is moot and no final or permanent injunction is required. For example, the plaintiff obtains a preliminary injunction against a city voting ordinance until it has been cleared by the attorney general as required by voting rights legislation. The city then clears the ordinance with the attorney general. The case is moot and dismissed on the city's motion. In this kind of case the plaintiff has received the relief sued for and no further hearing lies ahead that might reverse its effects. So the case is unlike the one in which the preliminary injunction is shown to have been erroneous. In this pattern of cases a fee award is proper.[15]

Preliminary injunction with immediate fees. What should be done about fee awards when a fee award is requested after the preliminary injunction issues in favor of the plaintiff and before the case is either mooted or determined in the defendant's favor? In *Deerfield Medical Center v. City of Deerfield Beach,*[16] the plaintiffs sought a preliminary injunction to force a city to permit them to begin operation of an abortion clinic. The trial judge denied the motion, but the Court of Appeals ordered the preliminary injunction to issue. It also ordered the trial court on remand to grant interim fees. Some other authority is in accord with a fee award in this situation.[17] Perhaps this rule is justified where the preliminary injunction appeal effectively resolves a determinative issue in the case, which may have been so in *Deerfield* itself. If applied to other preliminary injunction cases, however, such a rule creates problems.

Criticisms and limits on immediate fees. A preliminary injunction is not a final determination on the merits.[18] Although it forecasts that such a determination will probably be made on the permanent injunction hearing,[19] a full hearing frequently produces a different view of the facts and the law, so that the preliminary injunction is dissolved or reversed by controlling appellate action. To grant fees on an indecisive preliminary injunction is to invite potential difficulties later on. If the preliminary injunction turns out to be erroneous, the first rule discussed above would disentitle the plaintiff to fees. If the fees have been granted under an erroneous order, the normal

---

15. Maloney v. City of Marietta, 822 F.2d 1023 (11th Cir.1987) (the voting rights example); Taylor v. City of Fort Lauderdale, 810 F.2d 1551 (11th Cir.1987) (attack on ordinance restricting solicitation by religious group; after preliminary injunction, city passed new ordinance and parties agreed that plaintiff's case was moot because he had procured relief sought); Williams v. Alioto, 625 F.2d 845 (9th Cir.1980), cert. denied, 450 U.S. 1012, 101 S.Ct. 1723, 68 L.Ed.2d 213 (1981) (preliminary injunction to enjoin police stop and frisk operation carried out as part of search for killers; while preliminary injunction was on appeal, the killers were convicted and the police

stopped the operation, fees held proper). Cf. Grano v. Barry, 251 U.S.App.D.C. 289, 783 F.2d 1104 (1986) (treating case as mooted rather than lost).

16. 661 F.2d 328 (5th Cir.1981).

17. Chu Drua Cha v. Levine, 701 F.2d 750 (8th Cir.1983) (without discussion except to say that the plaintiff has gained a measure of success).

18. See § 2.11 above.

19. Some courts have relied on this *forecast* of liability to justify the fees awards at an early stage.

rule would also require the plaintiff or the attorney to make restitution of the fees received.[20]

If restitution will be due, the advance of fees before a decision on the merits will not be so advantageous to the plaintiff's side. The lawyer who receives a reversible fee must either retain it as undigested lump or risk disgorgement from funds committed elsewhere. On the other hand, the award is unjust if it is not to be repaid to the defendant who is ultimately shown to have been wrongly sued, wrongly enjoined, and wrongly wrested from its money. The purpose of the fee award is to make violators pay, not others. Finally, the fee award at the preliminary stage, when no issue on the merits has been finally decided, does not fit well with the normal requirement of a bond as a condition to preliminary injunction.[21] At a minimum, the defendant should be entitled to obtain an increase in the amount of the bond equal to the amount of interim fees it is required to pay.

These problems suggest that courts might well reject the *Deerfield* rule altogether. In fact, however, some courts have sought to make distinctions which in themselves are problematical. These decisions have said that if the preliminary injunction is a mere procedural maintenance of the status quo, the fee award is improper. But "status quo" in this rule turns out to include major changes in some cases.[22]

Prevailing by settlement. The plaintiff may be entitled to fees even if she settles the case,[23] so long as the fees are not waived in the settlement.[24] A formal settlement with no reference to fees could be read to settle the entire claim, including the fee claim.[25] But courts have been reluctant to read the settlement this way; silence of the parties on the question of fees after a "full" settlement is apt to be treated merely as some evidence about the parties' intent, and not controlling even there.[26]

20. Restatement of Restitution § 74 (1937).

21. See § 2.11(3) above.

22. See Webster v. Sowders, 846 F.2d 1032, 1036 (6th Cir.1988) where, at the instance of prisoners, the court preliminarily halted removal of asbestos in a prison, then employed an expert on asbestos removal before any issue of liability was determined even preliminarily, and arranged for plaintiffs' lawyers to monitor the "situation." Apparently restructuring or walling off was done, too. The trial judge ordered interim fees. On appeal the court said fees were improper because the preliminary injunction "must represent an unambiguous indication of probable success on the merits, and not merely a maintenance of the status quo ordered because the balance of equities greatly favors the plaintiff."

23. See Maher v. Gagne, 448 U.S. 122, 100 S.Ct. 2570, 65 L.Ed.2d 653 (1980). This rule has also been applied in settlements which produce a common fund or common benefit. Tandycrafts, Inc. v. Initio Partners, 562 A.2d 1162 (Del.1989). But under some other particular statutes fees may be due only if the case goes to judgment or if there is some independent ground for an award. Thus antitrust judgments justify a fee award, but antitrust settlements do so only if there is a class action and common benefit. See, e.g., In re Fine Paper Antitrust Litigation, 751 F.2d 562 (3d Cir.1984).

24. An express waiver, extracted by conditioning a favorable settlement for the clients on a waiver of all fees by their lawyer, was held valid in Evans v. Jeff D., 475 U.S. 717, 106 S.Ct. 1531, 89 L.Ed.2d 747 (1986).

25. See Jennings v. Metropolitan Gov't., 715 F.2d 1111 (6th Cir.1983).

26. Chicano Police Officer's Ass'n v. Stover, 624 F.2d 127 (10th Cir.1980); National Treasury Employees Union v. I.R.S., 735 F.2d 1277 (11th Cir.1984). But in El Club Del Barrio, Inc. v. United Community Corps., Inc., 735 F.2d 98 (3d Cir.1984) evidence showed that the original settlement draft contained a provision that settlement was without prejudice to a fee claim but that this clause was stricken by agreement. Nevertheless, the court thought "silence" should not be taken as a waiver of fees; settlement would have to contain a specific written waiver to bar the fee claim.

Suppose the settlement gives the plaintiff rights to which she is not constitutionally entitled. In the preliminary injunction cases, where the plaintiff obtains some temporary relief but ultimately loses on the merits, the fee is said to be inappropriate because even if the plaintiff obtained effective relief for a time, it was not relief to which the plaintiff was entitled and hence not covered by the fee statute. Is the same reasoning to be applied with settlements in which the plaintiff recovers something to which she is not entitled under federal law? The same reasoning is not applied because the value of the settlement will be lost if, after all, a trial on the merits is required. It is enough to entitle the plaintiff to a fee to show that the claim was colorable or even that it was simply not frivolous.[27]

Prevailing by defendant's unilateral reform; moot cases. As seen in the discussion of preliminary injunctions, the defendant may unilaterally make the reform the plaintiff seeks to require by injunction. In such cases the defendant's action may or may not be a response to the plaintiff's suit. Suppose the plaintiff sues under the Freedom of Information Act to obtain information from a government agency. After suit, the agency simply makes the information available.[28] The plaintiff must meet two conditions to recover fees in such cases.

First, the plaintiff's suit must have been a cause in fact of the reform.[29] Second, the reform must have been one to which the plaintiff was at least colorably entitled.[30] Courts use different verbal formulas in expressing the first point. A leading case on the point, *Nadeau v. Helgemoe*,[31] requires that the plaintiff's suit be a necessary and important factor in achieving the reform. If the suit qualifies, however, the fee may be awarded even if the reform was attributable in large part to constructive leadership by the defendant's officials. Sometimes courts say that it is sufficient if the suit is a "catalyst" in causing the reform.[32]

For discussion of fees for pre-litigation work, for related claims not covered by the fee statute, fees against intervenors, joint and several liability

---

27. Here is Judge Posner's explanation:

When a suit is settled, the district judge doesn't want to be bothered determining whether or not it has merit, merely to determine the ancillary question of attorney's fees; so he asks only whether the suit was nonfrivolous, a simpler inquiry. But when the suit is not settled and ultimately fails, the judge has no need to make a separate inquiry into its merit. Merit has been determined; that determination controls the issue of attorney's fees.

Palmer v. City of Chicago, 806 F.2d 1316, 1323 (7th Cir.1986), cert. denied, 481 U.S. 1049, 107 S.Ct. 2180, 95 L.Ed.2d 836 (1987).

28. Cf. Arevalo–Franco v. U.S. Immigration and Naturalization Serv., 889 F.2d 589 (5th Cir.1989) (similar facts, reversing district court holding that it had no jurisdiction to consider fees because of a venue problem).

29. Nadeau v. Helgemoe, 581 F.2d 275, 281 (1st Cir.1978).

30. Webster v. Sowders, 846 F.2d 1032 (6th Cir.1988); Hennigan v. Ouachita Parish School Bd., 749 F.2d 1148, 1153 (5th Cir.1985) ("plaintiff who brings an action that has no colorable, or even reasonable, likelihood of success on the merits is not entitled to recovery of attorney's fees" merely because of settlement).

31. 581 F.2d 275, 281 (1st Cir.1978).

32. See, e.g., Moore v. National Ass'n. of Securities Dealers, Inc., 762 F.2d 1093 (D.C.Cir.1985). In Disabled in Action v. Mayor & City Council, Etc., 685 F.2d 881, 886 (4th Cir.1982) a group of disabled persons seeking better access to Baltimore's Memorial Stadium settled their claim. The city argued that the improvements provided in the settlement were already being planned before the threat of suit, but, as an alternate ground for allowing fees in spite of this dubious causation, the court said it was enough that the suit "served to a limited extent to expedite the planning and achievement gained."

for fees and other matters, see this section in the Practitioner Treatise edition, vol. 1, pp. 423–427.]

§ 3.10(7) Fee Measurement: In Summary

This section summarizes the methods for measuring attorney fee awards, primarily based on the rules applied under the federal civil rights statutes. Most but not all of the rules apply under other statutes and to the common fund award. A more complete discussion appears in the next subsection.

Measurement of attorney fee awards against adversaries, like measurement of fees for masters,[1] has been a difficult problem. The measurement used may vary with the statutory authorization or the common law purpose.[2] Under the federal civil rights fee statutes the Supreme Court has fostered initial calculation of the fee by the hourly rate method—"the number of hours reasonably expended on the litigation multiplied by a reasonable hourly rate."[3] After this base fee is figured, adjustments may be required. This method is sometimes called the "lodestar" method. Public interest firms which charge less than other firms may recover at rates "prevailing in the community for similar services."[4] The hours for which fees are recovered include hours reasonably spent in preparing the fee petition itself.[5]

A different system of fee figuring permits the judge to consider a number of unquantified factors that have no precise content. For example, the court would consider the attorney's experience and skill and the time and labor involved, but would not necessarily rate the skill by objective standards or judge the labor by the number of billable hours. Instead, this approach, sometimes called the *Johnson* factors approach,[6] permits the judge to award a fee based on a kind of ball-park estimate. Percentage-of-recovery has not been a popular method in civil rights fee award cases, although it may be quite satisfactory in some common fund cases. Courts show some tendency to mix the hourly rate method with the *Johnson* factors method.

The reasonable fee calculated by an hourly rate method does not require a fee proportioned to the recovery as a percentage fee would. The fee may be larger than the actual recovery if the fee is "reasonable" as figured by a reasonable number of hours times a reasonable hourly rate.[7]

If the plaintiff only partially succeeds the fee must be reduced in the light of that limited success, even though, to begin with, the fee is based on a reasonable investment of hours.[8] How success is measured or how the fee reduction is to be calculated is so uncertain[9] that this rule may merely amount to a hortatory expression rather than an enforceable rule.

§ 3.10(7)

1. See Levine, Calculating Fees of Special Masters, 37 Hast.L.J. 141 (1985).

2. See § 3.10(8) below.

3. Hensley v. Eckerhart, 461 U.S. 424, 433, 103 S.Ct. 1933, 1939, 76 L.Ed.2d 40, 50 (1983).

4. Blum v. Stenson, 465 U.S. 886, 896, n. 11, 104 S.Ct. 1541, 1547, n. 11, 79 L.Ed.2d 891, 900 (1984).

5. E.g., Devine v. Sutermeister, 733 F.2d 892 (Fed.Cir.1984).

6. Based on Johnson v. Georgia Highway Express, Inc., 488 F.2d 714 (5th Cir.1974).

7. See City of Riverside v. Rivera, 477 U.S. 561, 106 S.Ct. 2686, 91 L.Ed.2d 466 (1986).

8. Blum v. Stenson, 465 U.S. 886, 104 S.Ct. 1541, 79 L.Ed.2d 891 (1984).

9. See Dobbs, Reducing Attorneys' Fees for Partial Success: A Comment on Hensley and Blum, 1986 Wis.L.Rev. 835.

If the lawyer contracts with the client for a fee, the fee contract limit is not the limit of the fee award against the adversary.[11] And vice versa: the fee award is not the limit of the client's liability on the fee contract.[12]

The civil rights statutes authorize an award of fees without mentioning other litigation costs. Some other statutes authorize the prevailing party or prevailing plaintiff to recover other litigation costs as well. In the absence of such an authorization, the Supreme Court has held that expert witness charges are not recoverable, even though the plaintiff has reasonably incurred charges for expert advice or testimony.[13] On the other hand, those expenses incidental to law office operations and normally included in overhead, are recoverable because the total hourly fee will reflect the sum of all overhead plus a charge for the service itself. Paralegal charges are examples. They are recovered if they are simply part of the overhead recouped by the fee charge. Beyond that, if the community practice is to bill separately for paralegal time, reasonable charges for paralegal work are recoverable. Not only are the actual costs of paying paralegals a recoverable item, the reasonable rate of billing is recoverable, even if that exceeds the actual cost to the plaintiff's lawyer.[14]

§ 3.10(8) Fee Measurement: Basic Methods

[*For discussion of measurement methods, the rate element and the time element in measurement, see this section in the Practitioner Treatise edition.*]

Evaluating Time Invested by Cost–Benefit Analysis: The Private Case Comparison

Disproportionate fees. In private cases involving paying clients, lawyers will seek to retain client satisfaction in many instances by using "billing judgment" and by limiting the number of hours for which they bill a client. The incentive is just reversed when the adversary pays the fee. Should courts attempt to judge reasonableness of hours invested in a case by looking at the private attorney model, discarding hours that a private client would not pay for? For example, in a job discrimination case the plaintiff recovered $1800, but the fee was $30,000.[49] In a property damage case, the city destroyed a house the plaintiff had purchased for $2700, but the plaintiff was awarded $17,000 in damages and almost $36,000 in attorney fees.[50]

Riverside. In *City of Riverside v. Rivera,*[51] several Chicano plaintiffs sued the city under state and federal laws, alleging that police had broken up a party without warrant and by using tear gas and other unnecessary

11. Blanchard v. Bergeron, 489 U.S. 87, 109 S.Ct. 939, 103 L.Ed.2d 67 (1989). Similarly, non-profit firms may recover fees although they charge nothing for their services. Blum v. Stenson, 465 U.S. 886, 104 S.Ct. 1541, 79 L.Ed.2d 891 (1984).

12. Venegas v. Mitchell, 495 U.S. 82, 110 S.Ct. 1679, 109 L.Ed.2d 74 (1990).

13. West Virginia Univ. Hospitals, Inc. v. Casey, ___ U.S. ___, 111 S.Ct. 1138, 113 L.Ed.2d 68 (1991).

14. Missouri v. Jenkins, 491 U.S. 274, 109 S.Ct. 2463, 105 L.Ed.2d 229 (1989).

§ 3.10(8)

49. Easley v. Empire Inc., 757 F.2d 923, 932 (8th Cir.1985).

50. Cunningham v. McKeesport, 753 F.2d 262 (3d Cir.1985), on further consideration after the decision in *Riverside,* 807 F.2d 49 (3d Cir.1986), cert. denied, 481 U.S. 1049, 107 S.Ct. 2179, 95 L.Ed.2d 836 (1987).

51. 477 U.S. 561, 106 S.Ct. 2686, 91 L.Ed.2d 466 (1986).

force, arresting some of those present. The plaintiffs recovered damages of about $33,000, of which about $13,000 represented damages for violation of federal civil rights. The attorney fee award, however, came to over $245,-000. The Supreme Court, divided three ways, upheld the award. Five of the Justices appeared to agree that the civil rights fee statutes impose no rule of proportionality, so fees could be disproportionate to the damages recovery, not only in nominal damages and injunction cases, but also in cases of a substantial damages recovery. All of the judges appeared to agree as well that a percentage fee was not required.

Riverside dissenters. The differences among the Justices were not precisely delineated. The four dissenters thought the fee was more or less obviously unreasonable because an attorney in private practice could not expect to charge more than winning the case could be worth to the client. Justice Rehnquist gave an example of an attorney examining title to land known to be worth $10,000. In such a case the attorney could not expect to be paid $25,000 even if he or she put in 200 hours of work at a reasonable rate of $125. Yet the dissenters appeared to recognize that proportionality would not always be required in civil rights litigation. First, some cases involve nonpecuniary rights and might result in only nominal damages, in which case, the dissenters implied, disproportionate fees might be appropriate. Second, civil rights litigation produces benefits to society as a whole in securing constitutional rights, so the costs in fees must be weighed not merely against the damages verdict but also against those external benefits. The dissenters, however, were apparently unwilling to weigh the social benefits produced by litigation unless that litigation "produces significant, identifiable benefits for persons other than the plaintiffs." This position is subject to the criticism that Congress itself made that decision for civil rights cases generally when it enacted the civil rights fees statutes.[52]

Riverside plurality; weighing social benefits against fee costs. Four other Justices seemed to think that Congress had already decided the question of social benefits; it passed the fee statute because it had decided that benefits from enforcement of federal rights exceeded fee costs. Indeed, it was because costs would often be high and many of the benefits of litigation could not be captured by the individual plaintiffs that private fee arrangements could not always be relied upon to provide redress for civil rights violations. So for four Justices, proportionality of costs and benefits had been determined by the Congress. Thus the proportion between the plaintiff's recovery and the fee would be irrelevant; proportion of total benefits to the fee would be relevant, but that had been decided by the legislation itself. Although the plurality did not stress it, these arguments also imply that incentives for future litigation will be correct if no proportionality is required.[53]

52. Brand, The Second Front in the Fight for Civil Rights: The Supreme Court, Congress, and Statutory Fees, 69 Tex.L.Rev. 291 (1990); cf. Dobbs, Awarding Attorney Fees Against Adversaries: Introducing the Problem, 1986 Duke L.J. 435, 483; Rowe, The Supreme Court on Attorney Fee Awards, 1985 and 1986 Terms: Economics, Ethics, and Ex Ante Analysis, 1 Geo.J.Leg.Ethics, 621, 627 (1988).

53. See Rowe, The Supreme Court on Attorney Fee Awards, 1985 and 1986 Terms: Economics, Ethics, and Ex Ante Analysis, 1 Geo.J.Leg.Ethics, 621 (1988).

Justice Powell, standing between the two groups of four, appeared to feel that although no rule of proportionality was required, such a disproportionate fee would not be reasonable unless the trial judge found that social benefits existed in the particular case, which was the case here. This position is significantly narrower because it would not provide any general incentive for future cases.[54]

Reciprocity in litigation costs. Aside from the external or social benefits point, a rule of proportionality would ignore the fluid and reciprocal characteristics of litigation costs. Litigation costs are fluid because each legal move, decision, or tactic in litigation has consequences that may change the lawyer's priorities and estimates. Original estimates about costs and benefits, reasonable when made, must be modified as new information comes in or as motions are won or lost. When a lawyer loses a critical motion, after which the chance of success is only one in five, a further investment of time may still be wise because it represents the only way to recover sunk costs. To know whether a litigation cost is reasonable, one must know the state of information available when the decision is made, and there will be a great many decision points.

Litigation costs are reciprocal as well as fluid, because the each party's litigation costs is responsive to the others party's acts in litigation as well as to his or her own changing perceptions of strategy and prospects. So a plaintiff's reasonable fee costs may in part reflect responses to the defendants' legal or factual arguments. Vigorous litigation by a defendant on points which it ultimately loses will tend to drive up the plaintiff's fee costs, just as the plaintiff's vigorous litigation will drive up the those of the defendant. Although vigorous litigation by a defendant is not to be condemned, it plays a role in the reasonableness of the plaintiff's fee costs that cannot be related mathematically to the size of the damages verdict.

Alternative grounds for attacking time invested. A proportionality rule would have favored defendants, in effect setting a cap on fees. A rejection of that rule does not mean, however, that defendants are without protection against claims of excessive hours. The plurality in *Riverside* allows the plaintiff's lawyer to invest the time necessary to win even claims known to be small, but it does not suggest that the time invested could be more than the time lawyers need to provide a reasonable development of facts and issues. Rejection of the proportionality rule focuses the defense on the first two types of objections to time-invested, asking whether resources were well used whether it was really necessary to invest hundreds of hours to present the case well.

Percentage Fees

Sometimes courts have evaluated a fee award in terms of contingent fee charges, a percentage of recovery. The percentage fee award or guideline could avoid many of the problems encountered in figuring hourly fees and at the same time avoid the subjective, untestable award under the *Johnson* factors. Its special merit is that it does not encourage the lawyer to

54. See Rowe, The Supreme Court on Attorney Fee Awards, 1985 and 1986 Terms: Economics, Ethics, and Ex Ante Analysis, 1 Geo.J.Leg.Ethics, 621, 627 (1988).

overwork the case or to claim excessive hours;[55] hours spent and risks undertaken are irrelevant if a pure percentage fee is used.

In spite of this advantage, percentage fees have serious limits and gross disadvantages in some cases. Percentage fees cannot be used at all in many civil rights cases, which seek injunction, declaratory relief, or nominal damages with the intent of establishing an important right rather than obtaining compensation. Even when a substantial sum is recovered, it may require work of quality and effort that could not be compensated by any percentage.

In spite of the disadvantages of percentage fees as a complete regime for fee shifting, they may still be useful in particular cases. The Supreme Court's decisions in *Blum* and *Hensley* appeared to state a strong preference for hourly rate computations. Although the Court stated an hourly rate formula, its preference seemed to be based on a desire to (1) obtain an objective standard and to move away from the unreviewable *Johnson* standards; (2) to require production of evidence about the propriety of a fee, however informal; and (3) to find confirmation in some kind of market, however loosely defined.[56] So the Court's real demand may not be an hourly rate but some kind of partially objective standard that meets these demands. A percentage fee might do that if one could find a "market" rate for percentage fees. Even so, many problems in picking the right percentage would remain.[57]

Standardized Fees

None of the fee-figuring methods is very good. All share the common problem in damages measurements that the measure is unlikely to be very precise. Market measures are often adopted in damages law, not for precision, but to facilitate closure and decision-making. When the market is thin, nonexistent, or skewed, the market measure may facilitate nothing but more litigation.[58] Secondary litigation over fee awards to be made for primary litigation should be minimized if reasonably possible, to say nothing of tertiary litigation over how to litigate the secondary litigation. Judges have noted the absence of "charts or grids into which all of the variables * * * can be neatly fitted." [59] In some areas of damages law sober thinkers have increasingly begun to consider standardized damages, or objective guidelines for figuring damages that are otherwise subject to quite varied awards, highly dependent on factors besides the merits.[60] The Equal Access to Justice Act actually sets a $75 an hour fee which is subject to increase

55. See Leubsdorf, Recovering Attorney Fees As Damages, 38 Rutgers L.Rev. 439 (1986).

56. See Dobbs, The Market Test for Attorney Fee Awards: Is the Hourly Rate Test Mandatory?, 28 Ariz.L.Rev. 1, 7 (1986).

57. The contingent percentage fee is relatively high because, in theory, it must pay out enough in winning cases to cover the lawyer's dead loss in losing or low return cases. If the civil rights lawyer can opt for the hourly fee rate in cases with a good win rate but a low damages rate, the contingency is altered, so that the "market" percentage rate would over value the risks and hence overpay the lawyer. See Dobbs, The Market Test for Attorney Fee Awards: Is the Hourly Rate Test Mandatory?, 28 Ariz.L.Rev. 1, 11 (1986).

58. See § 3.5 above.

59. Lightfoot v. Walker, 826 F.2d 516, 524 (7th Cir.1987).

60. See § 8.1(4) below.

under some circumstances.[61] Whether any fee guidelines could be developed that are both objective and reasonably accurate remains to be seen.

§ 3.10(9) Fee Measurement: Reduction for Partial Success [1]

General Rule

Under the Supreme Court's rule in *Hensley v. Eckerhart,*[2] the award to the plaintiff's lawyer must be reduced if the plaintiff's success on a claim is limited, partial or at a low level "in comparison to the scope of the litigation as a whole."[3] Success in litigation is the "most critical factor" in determining proper fee awards.[4]

Difficulty in Applying the Limited Success Rule

Judging success. The *Hensley* Court spoke in terms of results, which might suggest that it would judge success by judging remedies awarded rather than rights established. The distinction may not matter much under some standards for judging success. There are at least three major possible standards for determining whether a plaintiff who has obtained some results is fully or only partially successful. These are:

(1) The complaint-judgment test. The complaint-judgment test would compare what the plaintiff got as a remedy with what she sought in the complaint. If the plaintiff asked for $1 in damages and received $1 in damages, the plaintiff would be completely successful and entitled to an all-hours fee under this test. If the plaintiff asked for $10,000 and receives only $1,000, however, the plaintiff would not be fully successful. This test cannot serve the civil rights fee award purposes because if used it would provide plaintiff's lawyers with an incentive to reduce claims to maximize fee opportunities, an incentive that gives lawyer and client a serious conflict of interest and enhances the opportunity of wrongdoers to escape with less than full liability.[8]

(2) The reasonable expectation test. A reasonable expectation test would judge the plaintiff successful if she recovered all the relief she (or her lawyer) could reasonably have expected to recover, regardless whether it related to the amount claimed in the complaint. This test seems to be functionally equivalent to a rule allowing the plaintiff a fee for all reasonable hours invested in the case; but that is the very rule rejected by *Hensley's* requirement of a reduction.[9]

(3) Proportionality test. A third kind of test would judge the plaintiff's success by comparing the results or remedies, not with the demands or expectations, but with the *fee.* On its face the proportionality of a fee claim to a remedy does not sound like a test of "success."

61. 5 U.S.C.A. § 504(b), quoted in part, supra n. 1.

§ 3.10(9)

1. Some parts of this subsection draw on some parts of Dobbs, Reducing Attorneys' Fees for Partial Success: A Comment on Hensley and Blum, 1986 Wis.L.Rev. 835.

2. 461 U.S. 424, 103 S.Ct. 1933, 76 L.Ed.2d 40 (1983).

8. See Dobbs, Reducing Attorneys' Fees for Partial Success: A Comment on Hensley and Blum, 1986 Wis.L.Rev. 835, 844–846.

9. *Hensley* specifically rejected Brown v. Bathke, 588 F.2d 634 (8th Cir.1978), a case that had allowed recovery for all non-frivolous litigation hours and that seems equivalent to a reasonable expectation measure of success.

Possibly *Hensley* had some test of this sort in mind,[10] but if so, the Court's later decision in *City of Riverside v. Rivera*[11] seems for the moment[12] to foreclose any general use of such a test.

None of these tests appears to offer any sound ground for judging success, except possibly the second, which seems to undercut the *Hensley* demand for a reduction.

Reductions. The reduction for limited success is difficult because success itself has not been conceived with any precision. If success were defined, however, the problem of how to make a reduction would remain. Except for hours that can be identified as being separately devoted to a distinct, unrelated losing claim, the methods and standards for reduction have not been developed.

[*For additional analysis, see this section in the Practitioner Treatise edition.*]

§ 3.10(10) Fee Measurement: Enhancement and Multipliers

Enhancements for Quality, Difficulty, Results or Like Factors

Enhancements under Johnson factors approach. Under the *Johnson* factors approach to fee awards,[1] the fee was estimated in gross, taking into account, in unspecified ways, many factors. It was natural that courts using this approach would be impressed with the special difficulty of a case or with the skill of counsel in some instances and that they would take those impressions into account in setting a fee. Unfortunately, the comments they made on such matters suggested that they were awarding a reasonable fee and then adding something more to it. More quantitatively minded judges spoke of "multipliers" instead of enhancements, but probably none of these courts ever intended to provide a fee that was anything but a fee that was reasonable considering all the circumstances.

Enhancements/multipliers denied under hourly rate or lodestar approach. In 1984 the Supreme Court decided *Blum v. Stenson*.[2] It reaffirmed its then-recent ruling in the *Hensley* case[3] that the usual way to figure fees was to multiply the reasonable number of hours invested in the case by the reasonable hourly rate.[4] This was a market oriented shift away from the *Johnson* factors approach; it required proof about hours invested and rea-

---

10. See Dobbs, Reducing Attorneys' Fees for Partial Success: A Comment on Hensley and Blum, 1986 Wis.L.Rev. 835, 850.

11. 477 U.S. 561, 106 S.Ct. 2686, 91 L.Ed.2d 466 (1986), discussed in § 3.10(8) above.

12. *Riverside* was a 4–1–4 decision, the first five representing a plurality divided and perhaps uncertain as to grounds of decision. In Dobbs, Reducing Attorneys' Fees for Partial Success: A Comment on Hensley and Blum, 1986 Wis.L.Rev. 835, 848 it is suggested that a proportionality test would be inconsistent with the civil rights fee awards statutes, but that if proportionality were to be used, then a distinction should be drawn between expected and unexpected disproportion of fees (costs) to recovery (benefits). If disproportion is reasonably to be expected, so that properly measured costs (including fees) are expected to

exceed benefits (including the damages awarded), then the litigation does not seem desirable. On the other hand, lawyers charge full fees every day for work done that is reasonably expected to cost less than benefits produced but which in fact does not. All losing defense cases are in this category and there is nothing unreasonable about charging the full fee for a defense that did not work.

§ 3.10(10)

1. See § 3.10(8) above.

2. 465 U.S. 886, 104 S.Ct. 1541, 79 L.Ed.2d 891 (1984).

3. Discussed in § 3.10(8) above.

4. See § 3.10(8) above.

sonable hourly charges. When the fee is computed in this manner, would it be permissible to increased the fee by, say, 50% on the ground that the case was complex and novel and that the result was beneficial?

The *Blum* Court refused to permit the increase on these grounds. The novelty and complexity and other factors bearing on a fee were already accounted for by using the rate-times-hours formula. Complexity of the case, for example, would be "fully reflected in the number of billable hours recorded;" the special skill of counsel would be reflected in the hourly rate chosen.[5] The same reasoning applied to other factors, like "results obtained." Good results in the case did not warrant an increase in fees because the results "generally will be subsumed within other factors used to calculate a reasonable fee."[6] The Court has since confirmed this approach to fee assessment,[7] but sometimes courts of appeal continue to speak of enhancing the lodestar by taking into account the old *Johnson* factors,[8] and trial courts sometimes simply ignore the rules and order an enhancement.[9]

Blum reflects the substantial difference between the "factors" approach and the hourly rate approach. If courts look at factors without confining themselves to the actual prices lawyers charge, they can naturally award a fee and then add to it for novelty, complexity, skill and many other elements. But if courts must base a fee on hours times hourly rates, none of the factors affecting market need be examined separately; the market rates and the number of hours will together show the proper fee for the skill and the difficulties involved. Enhancements to that fee are improper because the grounds for enhancement have already been processed into the rate or into the number of hours.

Permissible enhancements under the hourly rate method. The *Blum* Court did not exclude all enhancements, however. The Court was willing to say that if the fee claimant could show that for any reason the hourly rate did not reflect the "quality of representation provided" then a fee enhancement might be proper. In that case, however, it would seem more appropriately consonant with the rate-times-hours approach to choose an hourly rate that reflected the quality of representation needed and provided.

---

5. Id. at 898, 104 S.Ct. at 1549, 79 L.Ed.2d at 902. The same point had been recognized in Lindy Bros. Builders, Inc. of Philadelphia v. American Radiator & Standard Sanitary Corp., 540 F.2d 102, 117 (3d Cir.1976), part of the litigation which initially established the lodestar method. Both *Blum* and *Lindy* left loopholes for the possibility of enhancements under some circumstances, however.

6. Id. at 900, 104 S.Ct. at 1549–1550, 79 L.Ed.2d at 903. This point in particular suggests that the rule in *Hensley v. Eckerhart,* discussed in § 3.10(8) above, should be confined to cases in which the *Johnson* factors are used rather than the hourly rate test.

7. Pennsylvania v. Delaware Valley Citizens' Council for Clean Air, 478 U.S. 546, 106 S.Ct. 3088, 92 L.Ed.2d 439 (1986).

8. E.g., Brown v. Sullivan, 917 F.2d 189, 192 (5th Cir.1990) ("the 'lodestar,' may be adjusted upward or downward based on the court's consideration of the circumstances surrounding the case. This process is guided by the twelve factors set forth by this court in Johnson"). The *Johnson* factors specifically included items such as novelty and difficulty and results obtained, all rejected in *Blum* as grounds for enhancement because they were covered in the lodestar.

9. See Hendrickson v. Branstad, 934 F.2d 158 (8th Cir.1991) (reversing trial court's enhancement); Alberti v. Klevenhagen, 896 F.2d 927 (5th Cir.1990), on rehearing, 903 F.2d 352 (1990) (first reversing, then affirming enhancement for "undesirability" of the case, conceivably a kind of contingency enhancement).

Contingency or Risk Enhancements

The risk problem. *Blum* did not decide the issue of contingency enhancement or contingency multiplier. The argument for the contingency multiplier is that it adheres to the market measures of fees which the Supreme Court fostered in *Hensley* and *Blum.* The market hourly rate is based on charges which lawyers normally collect from their clients, win or lose. Ten hours billed at $200 per hour normally yields $2,000 even if the billing lawyer has not won the case. The civil rights fee award, on the other hand, provides an hourly fee, but only when the plaintiff prevails.[10] If the lawyer prevails, say, in 50% of all civil rights cases she tries, she may recover what *appears* to be the correct hourly rate, but the appearance is deceiving: in her caseload as a whole, she is actually recovering half the rate that private litigants are able to charge clients.

The Leubsdorf proposal. Professor Leubsdorf, has written the best explanation of the risk enhancement or contingency multiplier and its problems.[11] His work has been cited in misleading ways at times,[12] so it should be understood immediately that he favored one particular kind of multiplier. He saw objections, however, to the case-by-case decision on multipliers in which different multipliers would be used, depending on the evidence. One objection to this is that if a multiplier were really to increase with the risk of loss as judged at some time prior to trial, the weakest case would garner the greatest fee, the most reasonable defendant would be the one liable for the most money. Professor Leubsdorf also foresaw that to gain the greatest multiplier, the lawyer would want to argue to the judge at the fee hearing that the case had been a weak one, a position that might put the lawyer in conflict with the client's interest if the case had to be retried later.

The Leubsdorf proposal was to abandon case-by-case decisions on multipliers in favor of a fixed multiplier to be selected in advance and used in all cases. He thought a multiplier of two, that is, one that would double the fee initially fixed by the lodestar method, would be about right. Such a multiplier should theoretically encourage cases in which the lawyer estimated at least a 50–50 chance of winning and provide an appropriate adjustment to achieve proper compensation in those cases. If the lawyer took riskier cases, the lawyer would sooner or later suffer financially, so she would not be encouraged by such a multiplier to take cases with a low chance of success and which probably should not be brought.

Judges have not traditionally adopted standardized damages, although they do adopt conventions for damages measurement.[13] But there are rules that serve as standardizing rules. For instance, Alaska adopted a rule by which the twin problems of future damages, inflation and reduction to present value, are deemed to offset one another, obviating proof on a case by case basis of the probable amount of inflation and the proper reduction to

---

10. This statement must be qualified to the extent that the client is liable to and actually does pay for the services at an hourly rate. See § 3.10(11) below.

11. Leubsdorf, The Contingency Factor in Attorney Fee Awards, 90 Yale L.J. 473 (1981).

12. Dobbs, Awarding Attorney Fees against Adversaries: Introducing the Problem, 1986 Duke L.J. 435, 471–472, may be an example, for which the author expresses apologies.

13. See § 3.1 above.

present value.[14] Damages, including attorney fee awards, are almost always inaccurate, so adoption of good standardized tools for measurement is highly desirable, and the Leubsdorf proposal should not be rejected merely because it uses a standard number.[15]

Pre–Blum decisions. Before *Blum* the federal courts solidly favored figuring a reasonable fee, then adding contingency or risk multipliers.[16] They might give as little as 110% of the fee or as much as 400%. The difference was sometimes in the millions.[17] A number of courts continued to do so after *Blum* as well.[18]

Delaware Valley II. In a case known as *Delaware Valley II,*[19] the Justices of the Supreme Court pooled their efforts to produce what one commentator called a "quagmire of opinions" on the topic,[20] coming to little agreement. One group of the Justices wanted to say that enhancement for risk or contingency is never to be awarded under ordinary fee statutes. Other groups, in various configurations, wanted to recognize enhancements in some cases, but not all. The decision is indecisive about the details, but it does mean that enhancement for contingency or risk must be rare and limited to exceptional cases.

As of late 1991, the District of Columbia Circuit, in *King v. Palmer,*[28] had concluded over the objection of substantial dissents, that the enhancement should always be denied, and invited the Supreme Court to clarify the whole matter. After this volume was set in type, the Supreme Court did so by holding that under federal statutes calling for a "reasonable fee" award, contingency enhancements are not to be permitted. The majority believed that enhancements could provide incentives to bring relatively meritless claims and would be difficult or impossible to administer. *City of Burlington v. Dague,* ___ U.S. ___, 112 S.Ct. 2638, 120 L.Ed.2d 449 (1992).

Delay Enhancement

Adjustments to account for delay in payment of attorney fees calculated on an hourly rate basis is proper even when other "enhancements" are not,

---

14. See § 8.5 below.

15. There might be other reasons for rejecting the Leubsdorf proposal. A decision maker might think, for example, that lawyer behavior would not always be rational; that low-risk cases would gravitate to a very few lawyers in any event (so that a multiplier at the level of 2 would systematically over-compensate those lawyers); and that high-risk cases would continue to be pursued by lawyers who have few clients because of the lawyers' unwarranted optimism, bad legal judgment, economic pressure, or true belief in the cause.

16. E.g., Lindy Bros. Builders, Inc. v. American Radiator & Standard Sanitary Corp., 540 F.2d 102 (3d Cir.1976) (doubling fee); Northcross v. Board of Education, 611 F.2d 624 (6th Cir.1979), cert. denied, 447 U.S. 911, 100 S.Ct. 2999, 64 L.Ed.2d 862 (1980). See M. Derfner & A. Wolf, Court Awarded Attorney Fees ¶ 16.04[2] (1991 & Supps.).

17. See In re Coordinated Pretrial Proceedings in Antibiotic Antitrust Actions, 410 F.Supp. 680 (D.Minn.1975); Berger, Court Awarded Attorneys' Fees: What Is "Reasonable"?, 126 U.Pa.L.Rev. 281, 290–291 (1977).

18. E.g., Wildman v. Lerner Stores Corp., 771 F.2d 605 (1st Cir.1985); LaDuke v. Nelson, 762 F.2d 1318 (9th Cir.1985), modified, 796 F.2d 309 (9th Cir.1986) (no discussion of the problem or analysis of *Blum* in the original, but modified to remand for consideration of multiplier in the light *Delaware Valley II*).

19. Pennsylvania v. Delaware Valley Citizens' Council for Clear Air, 483 U.S. 711, 107 S.Ct. 3078, 97 L.Ed.2d 585 (1987).

20. Brand, The Second Front in the Fight for Civil Rights: The Supreme Court, Congress, and Statutory Fees, 69 Tex.L.Rev. 291, 337 (1990).

28. 950 F.2d 771 (D.C.Cir.1991).

as the Supreme Court has held.[29]

[*For methods of delay enhancement, see this section in the Practitioner Treatise edition.*]

§ 3.10(11) Fee Measurement: Effect of Client's Fee Contract

[*For the text of this section, see the unabridged Practitioner Treatise edition.*]

§ 3.11 Punitive Damages *

THE GENERAL RULES

§ 3.11(1) Punitive Damages Allowable

Introduction and Summary

The topic of punitive damages is now a controversial one that invokes a full range of responses at every level, practical and political at one end and deeply philosophical at the other. Punitive damages are extracompensatory, at least in theory. They go beyond any obvious elements of ordinary compensation and are intended to punish or deter extreme departures from acceptable conduct.

Some observers believe that the number and amount of punitive awards have increased dramatically in recent decades.[1] This perception has heightened the debate over punitive damages. There are now several books [2] and

---

29. Missouri v. Jenkins by Agyei, 491 U.S. 274, 109 S.Ct. 2463, 105 L.Ed.2d 229 (1989).

§ 3.11

* *For extensive citation of authority, see this section and its subsections in the Practitioner Treatise edition.*

§ 3.11(1)

1. There is debate over the secondary issue whether the perception of increased awards is itself a correct one. The most enterprising studies leave somewhat undefined footprints in the shifting empirical sands: times change, places change. The RAND study, Peterson, Sarma, & Shanley, Punitive Damages: Empirical Findings 8–45 (Rand Institute 1986), suggests only modest changes, if any. In line with this is Daniels and Martin, Myth and Reality in Punitive Damages, 75 Minn.L.Rev. 1 (1990). Priest, Punitive Damages and Enterprise Liability, 56 So.Cal.L.Rev. 123 (1982) reflects one report of increased punitive damage awards. Harper, James & Gray, The Law of Torts § 25.5A (Supp.) discounts the idea that punitive awards play any serious role in the overall picture. Judge Posner and Professor Landes report a sample of products liability cases which indicated that punitive damages were ultimately approved in only about

5% of the cases that the plaintiffs won, that the amounts were moderate and that the ratios to actual damages were not disparate. W. Landes and R. Posner, The Economic Structure of Tort Law 302–307 (1987). See also ABA, Report of the Action Commission to Improve the Tort Liability System 17 (1987) reporting doubts whether there has been significant increase, based on preliminary empirical studies. Some data available suggests that the total amount of punitive damages awarded in the first years of the 1980s was four to six times more than the totals awarded in the last years of the 1970s. The number of awards also increased, but more or less in proportion to the increase in trials and verdicts for the plaintiff generally. Much of the increase seems to be found in economic tort cases, such as bad faith insurance or wrongful discharge cases. See American Bar Association, Report of the Special Committee on Punitive Damages, A Constructive Examination 17–26 (Litigation Section, 1986) (reporting on a study of awards in San Francisco County, California and Cook County, Illinois).

2. J. Ghiardi & J. Kircher, Punitive Damages Law and Practice (2 vols. 1984 & Supps.); K. Redden, Punitive Damages (1980 & Supp. 1987 (with L. Schlueter)).

many important articles,[3] as well as a heavy flow of decisions on the topic, and there is no assurance that the flood will abate.

A dozen or so simplified rules suggest its outlines and point to subsections where particular material can be located. After these "rules" are summarized, this subsection attempts to define punitive damages, sketch some characteristics, and illustrate the potential scope for such awards. The basic rules, allowing for simplified statement, are:

1. Punitive damages are awarded only for very serious misconduct coupled with a bad state of mind involving malice or at least a reckless disregard for the rights of others.[4]

2. The stated purposes of punitive damages almost always include (a) punishment or retribution and (b) deterrence. Sometimes the purpose encompasses (c) the desire to assist in financing useful litigation by providing a source from which fees and costs can be paid. The purposes are somewhat conflicting in that they do not necessarily call for the same amount of punitive recovery.[5]

3. If the judge decides that the facts warrant submission of the case to the jury on the punitive damages issue, the jury's discretion determines (a) whether to make the award at all, and (b) the amount of the award, as limited by its purposes, subject only to review as other awards are reviewed.

4. Punitive damages are not per se unconstitutional under the double jeopardy, excessive fines, or due process provisions of the United States Constitution. However, extreme awards, given without appropriate guidance to the jury and without adequate review by judges, may violate due process.[6]

5. Statutes in some states now limit the amount of punitive damages that can be awarded, or, alternatively, direct a portion of the award to some public entity.[7] In addition, some double and treble damages statutes may have the effect of precluding ordinary punitive damages.[8]

3. E.g., Ausness, Retribution and Deterrence: The Role of Punitive Damages in Products Liability Litigation, 74 Ky.L.J. 1 (1985–86); American Bar Association, Report of the Special Committee on Punitive Damages (Litigation Section 1986); American Bar Association, Report of the Action Commission to Improve the Tort Liability System (1987); Chapman and Trebilcock, Punitive Damages: Divergence in Search of a Rationale, 40 Ala. L.Rev. 741 (1989); Dobbs, Ending Punishment in "Punitive" Damages: Deterrence–Measured Remedies, 40 Ala.L.Rev. 831 (1989); Ellis, Fairness and Efficiency in the Law of Punitive Damages, 56 So.Cal.L.Rev. 1 (1982) (with Symposium comments by Cooter, Owen, Priest and Gary Schwartz); Galligan, Augmented Awards: The Efficient Evolution of Punitive Damages, 51 La.L.Rev. 3 (1990); Johnston, Punitive Liability: A New Paradigm of Efficiency in Tort Law, 87 Colum.L.Rev. 1385 (1987); Mallor & Roberts, Punitive Damages: Toward a Principled Approach, 31 Hast.L.J. 639 (1980); Owen, Punitive Damages in Products Liability Litigation, 74 Mich.L.Rev. 1258 (1976); Owen, Problems in Assessing Punitive Damages Against Manufacturers of Defective Products, 49 U.Chi. L.Rev. 1 (1982); Owen, The Moral Foundations of Punitive Damages, 40 Ala.L.Rev. 705 (1989); Wheeler, The Constitutional Case for Reforming Punitive Damages Procedures, 69 Va.L.Rev. 269 (1983); Note, Civil RICO is a Misnomer: The Need for Criminal Procedural Protections in Actions Under 18 U.S.C.A. § 1964, 100 Harv.L.Rev. 1288 (1987).

4. See below, this section & §§ 3.11(2), 3.11(3) below.

5. See §§ 3.11(2) & 3.11(3); see also § 3.11(15) below.

6. See § 3.11(12) below.

7. See § 3.11(12) below.

8. See § 3.12 below.

6. Punitive damages were traditionally proven by the ordinary civil standard of proof, a preponderance of the evidence. Some courts now demand clear and convincing evidence.[9]

7. The jury is normally allowed to hear evidence about the defendant's wealth, income, or profits as a basis for determining an appropriate amount of punitive damages.[10]

8. Under one rule, punitive awards may be levied against defendants who are only vicariously responsible. Under another rule, employers and others can be responsible for punitive damages for torts of agents or servants only if the employer participated in, encouraged, or ratified the tort.[11]

9. Under one view, probably the majority, liability insurers whose policies do not eliminate coverage for punitive damages are liable for punitive damages judgments against the insured. Under another view, the "punishment" will not be effective if the wrongdoer can insure, so insurance coverage for such awards is against public policy.[12]

10. A defendant whose wrongs have caused many harms to different people may be subjected to more than one punitive liability.[13]

11. Courts sometimes say that punitive damages cannot be awarded unless the plaintiff suffers actual harm or recovers actual damages. Some courts now read this rule to mean only that the plaintiff cannot recover punitive damages unless she first establishes a cause of action.[14]

12. Courts sometimes say that the amount of punitive damages must be in some reasonable proportion to actual damages, but normally this statement is no more than a rough guideline. It may conflict with some other rules.[15]

13. It appears that proximate cause and similar rules limit the recovery of punitive damages. If the defendant, without malice or wanton misconduct causes one harm, then he is not liable for punitive damages, even though, as to some other harm that did not in fact result, the defendant was malicious.[16]

Punitive Damages Generally

Definition, basis, and terms. Punitive damages are sums awarded in addition to any compensatory or nominal damages, usually as punishment or deterrent levied against a defendant found guilty of particularly aggravated misconduct,[17] coupled with a malicious, reckless or otherwise wrongful state of mind.[18] Sometimes these damages are called exemplary damages in reference to the idea that they make an example of the defendant.

Punitive damages may have some incidental compensatory effects; and "compensatory" damages may have some incidental punitive effects. When compensatory damages exceed pure compensation, some courts have said they were punitive.[19] But all remedies may have punitive effects, even

9. See § 3.11(4) below.
10. See § 3.11(5) below.
11. See § 3.11(6) below.
12. See § 3.11(7) below.
13. See § 3.11(8) below.

14. See § 3.11(10) below.
15. See § 3.11(11) below.
16. See § 3.11(9) below.

injunctive[20] and restitutionary remedies.[21] By the traditional understanding, however, the award is not punitive unless it is awarded apart from compensation and its amount is fixed as punishment for serious misconduct, or to deter such misconduct in the future.

Realistically, observers including judges have recognized that sometimes damages are called "punitive" when they appear covertly or even openly to serve non-punitive purposes such as compensation or deterrence. In recent years commentators have increasingly used terms like "extracompensatory" or "augmented" damages to reflect the fact that some "punitive" damages are intended for other purposes.[22]

In-court misconduct. Punitive damages respond to the defendant's out-of-court behavior, usually the same behavior that created the cause of action. In-court misbehavior, such as contempt of court or the presentation of frivolous claims or defenses, may also be subject to punishments under the rules of criminal contempt,[23] or under a rule such as Rule 11 of the Federal Rules of Civil Procedure. Typically the sanctions imposed for in-court misconduct are not called punitive damages,[24] but they serve similar purposes and sometimes go by the same name.[25]

Origin and discretion as to amount. Statutes sometimes authorize multiplication of actual damages as a form of punishment,[26] but the term punitive damages usually refers to an award discretionary as to the amount. In this sense, the modern origin of punitive damages is found in the 18th century English decisions in which punitive awards seem to have been initially a kind of compensation for mental distress or for intangible losses.[27] Retribution and deterrence were eventually identified as bases for a separate award and the compensatory and punitive awards became separated and remain so today in most courts.

State of authority for punitive damages. A handful of courts have opposed punitive damages as a form of civil punishment,[28] but even these states sometimes impose punitive damages under statutory provisions.[29] A few others have used punitive damage awards only as a species of compensa-

---

20. E.g., Valco Cincinnati, Inc. v. N & D Machining Serv., Inc., 24 Ohio St.3d 41, 492 N.E.2d 814, 59 A.L.R.4th 629 (1986) (injunction, prohibiting acts that would have been permissible had defendants not been guilty of misconduct).

21. E.g., Truck Equip. Serv. Co. v. Freuhauf Corp., 536 F.2d 1210 (8th Cir.1976), cert. denied, 429 U.S. 861, 97 S.Ct. 164, 50 L.Ed.2d 139 (1976) (liability for profits gained in trademark violation, either restitution or analogous to restitution; necessary as a deterrence). Cf. Gilchrist v. Perl, 387 N.W.2d 412 (Minn.1986) (fee of injury plaintiff's attorney may be forfeited to plaintiff if attorney breaches fiduciary duty, "the subtle, dual nature of the fee forfeiture remedy" has both punitive and non-punitive aspects).

27. See, among the historical discussions, Ellis, Fairness and Efficiency in the Law of Punitive Damages, 56 So.Cal.L.Rev. 1, 12–20 (1982) (early cases especially associated with intangible loss, with "honor" and with insult).

28. See Killebrew v. Abbott Laboratories, 359 So.2d 1275 (La.1978); Santana v. Registrars of Voters of Worcester, 398 Mass. 862, 502 N.E.2d 132 (1986); Miller v. Kingsley, 194 Neb. 123, 230 N.W.2d 472 (1975); Kammerer v. Western Gear Corp., 96 Wash.2d 416, 635 P.2d 708 (1981). A statute abolishes punitive damages for many cases in New Hampshire, which in any event had only a limited recognition of such damages. See N.H.Rev.Stat.Ann. 507:16.

29. E.g., LSA–Civil Code art. 2315.4 (injuries caused by driving motor vehicle while intoxicated); Mass.Gen.Laws Ann. ch. 111, § 199 (property owner notified of dangerous level of lead in paint subject to treble damages). Principled objections to punitive awards were analyzed in the classic article, Morris, Punitive Damages in Tort Cases, 44 Harv.L.Rev. 1173 (1931).

tion. Sometimes the "punitive" award compensates for the added mental distress caused when the defendant's conduct is egregious; [30] at other times it compensates for the plaintiff's attorney fee costs. [31]

However, in the courts of the great majority of states, [32] and in the federal courts, [33] punitive damages are fully approved as extracompensatory awards. The windfall to the plaintiff is tolerated as a means of securing public good through a kind of quasi-criminal punishment in the civil suit. [34] The assumption seems to be that the criminal law will be inadequate [35] and that neither the rules against double jeopardy nor other constitutional limitations prohibit the courts from imposing additional punishment in civil cases. [36] The punitive award may also serve non-punitive purposes, [37] but even so, it is inflicted only when the defendant is said to deserve punishment.

Traditional jury role and amounts. If the facts justify submitting the punitive damages issue to the jury, the jury is free to make the award, to limit it, or to deny it altogether, even if the facts show egregious misconduct by the defendant. [38] Perhaps the more common concern is that the punitive award may be excessive. Under the traditional rules, the amount of the award is usually not fixed in amount or by any precise formula. [39] Instead, the award has traditionally been determined largely in the jury's discretion, [40] subject only to judicial power to order a new trial if the verdict is excessive. [41]

Past practice has not only given the jury discretion in punitive awards but has also failed or refused to provide the jury meaningful instructions as to the purpose or limits of such damages. [42] Awards range from trivial amounts to quite large sums, sometimes millions of dollars. [43] New demands

30. See Eide v. Kelsey–Hayes Co., 431 Mich. 26, 427 N.W.2d 488 (1988) (Griffin, J., concurring in part) (reviewing the unusual Michigan position); Crowley v. Global Realty, Inc., 124 N.H. 814, 474 A.2d 1056 (1984).

41. The scope of judicial review and the court's powers to change the punitive award is itself an issue. Post-trial review of punitive awards is one process that helps guarantee fairness and defeat a claim that a punitive award violates due process. See Pacific Mutual Life Ins. Co. v. Haslip, ___ U.S. ___, 111 S.Ct. 1032, 1043, 113 L.Ed.2d 1 (1991). On the other hand, if the reviewing court's judgment is substituted for the jury's decision, the right to jury trial on punitive damages issues may be denied.

42. For example: *Recommended Arizona Jury Instructions:* "The law provides no fixed standards as to the amount of punitive or exemplary damages, but leaves the amount, if any, to your sound discretion." *Ohio Jury Instructions 23.70:* "If you award punitive damages, the amount should be fair and reasonable under all the facts and circumstances. It should not be excessive, nor actuated by passion or prejudice. The amount of punitive damages rests in the sound judgment of the jury and should be determined from all the evidence in the case." See Hospital Auth. of

Gwinnett County v. Jones, 261 Ga. 613, 409 S.E.2d 501 (1991) ("the 'guidance' to the jury provided by the admonition that it 'take into consideration the character and the degree of the wrong as shown by the evidence and necessity of preventing similar wrong'" is "not guidance but platitude").

See American College of Trial Lawyers, Report on Punitive Damages of the Committee on Special Problems in the Administration of Justice 28 (1989) (Roger C. Henderson, Reporter); Ghiardi, Punitive Damage Awards—An Expanded Judicial Role, 72 Marq.L.Rev. 33, 34–35 (1988).

43. E.g., Kelco Disposal, Inc. v. Browning–Ferris Industries of Vt., Inc., 845 F.2d 404 (2d Cir.1988), aff'd, 492 U.S. 257, 109 S.Ct. 2909, 106 L.Ed.2d 219 (1989) ($6 million punitive on interference with contract claim); O'Gilvie v. International Playtex, Inc., 821 F.2d 1438 (10th Cir.1987), cert. denied, 486 U.S. 1032, 108 S.Ct. 2014, 100 L.Ed.2d 601 (1988) ($10 million); Grimshaw v. Ford Motor Co., 119 Cal.App.3d 757, 174 Cal.Rptr. 348 (1981) (jury award, $125 million, reduced by trial court to $3.5 million and so reduced affirmed on appeal); Tetuan v. A.H. Robins Co., 241 Kan. 441, 738 P.2d 1210 (1987) ($7.5 million, intrauterine device); Flanigan v. Prudential Fed.

of due process may impose some limits on this permissive regime, at least to the extent of requiring jury instructions or better post-trial review.[44]

New limitations on or review of jury's role. Beginning in the 1980s, both courts and legislatures have tried to find new limits on punitive damages and on the jury's role in fixing them. The punitive award may be fixed by a treble damages statute,[45] capped by a "tort reform" statute,[46] or subjected to constitutional[47] or semi-constitutional scrutiny.[48] Some states have now ventured to exclude the jury from the punitive damages determination altogether, leaving that award to the court.[49] Although reviewing courts do limit punitive awards,[50] the potential for large punitive verdicts is threatening, and constitutional and other attacks on the amount of awards, which have begun to have some impact, will probably continue.[51]

Settings for Exclusion of Punitive Damages

Equity. In several classes of cases punitive damages are denied or carefully limited. The traditional rule was that equity would not award punitive damages, either because equity's sole province was to provide "complete relief," and compensatory damages marked the limit of that relief,[52] or because punishment or vengeance seemed vaguely inappropriate to a "benignant" equity.[53] Though this rule is rejected by contemporary decisions that have addressed it as a serious issue,[54] there are cases that still repeat it.[55]

Contract claims. Punitive damages are also ordinarily denied in contract cases,[56] but in a few special instances punitive liability has been imposed even there.[57]

Arbitration. The older judicial jealousies of arbitration tribunals have been expressed in a rule that prohibits the award of punitive damages in arbitration cases, even when a punitive award is authorized by the parties.[58] Increased respect for arbitration as an alternative mechanism for resolution of disputes, coupled with increased respect for party autonomy in contracting may open arbitration proceedings to punitive damages where the parties by their contract authorize such awards.[59]

Free speech areas. For quite different reasons, courts have denied or circumscribed punitive damages in defamation and other cases implicating a defendant's First Amendment rights, since punitive awards are especially likely to chill speech rights.[60]

Sav. & Loan Ass'n, 221 Mont. 419, 720 P.2d 257 (1986) (wrongful discharge, punitive award of $1.3 million affirmed); Texaco, Inc. v. Pennzoil, Co., 729 S.W.2d 768, 859–860 (Tex. App.1987) ($3 *billion* reduced to $1 *billion*).

48. Courts in imposing new limitations on punitive recoveries have sometimes hoisted the suggestion that, without limits, punitive damages might be unconstitutional. See Adams v. Murakami, 54 Cal.3d 105, 284 Cal. Rptr. 318, 813 P.2d 1348 (1991), discussed in § 3.11(5) below.

49. E.g., Conn.Gen.Stat.Ann. § 52–240b; Ohio Rev.Code § 2307.80; Ohio Rev.Code § 2315.21. See § 3.11(12) below.

54. Starkovich v. Noye, 111 Ariz. 347, 529 P.2d 698 (1974); I.H.P. Corp. v. 210 Central Park South Corp., 12 N.Y.2d 329, 239 N.Y.S.2d 547, 189 N.E.2d 812 (1963); Tideway Oil Programs, Inc. v. Serio, 431 So.2d 454, 461, 58 A.L.R.4th 819 (Miss.1983) ("A bona fide demand for punitive damages appeals to the conscience of the court"; also emphasizing the private attorney general basis of punitive damages); Gould v. Starr, 558 S.W.2d 755 (Mo.App.1977), cert. denied, Cady v. Gould, 436 U.S. 905, 98 S.Ct. 2236, 56 L.Ed.2d 403 (1978). See Nabours v. Longview Sav. & Loan Ass'n, 700 S.W.2d 901 (Tex.1985).

Statutory claims. Some statutory claims exclude punitive recoveries, either in express terms or by judicial interpretation. Although punitive damages are awarded in wrongful death actions in some states,[61] others refuse to permit punitive awards, sometimes on the ground that the death statute authorizes damages for pecuniary injury only.[62] In survival actions the decedent's estate can usually recover punitive damages against a living tortfeasor,[63] but the injured plaintiff is often denied punitive damages against the estate of the deceased tortfeasor.[64] Punitive damages were traditionally denied in job discrimination cases,[65] although discrimination claims brought on other theories sometimes yield punitive damages[66] and since 1991 Title VII itself does so for some cases.[67] Statutory construction has eliminated punitive damages in suits by a union member against the union for lack of fair representation,[68] in Jones Act and FELA suits,[69] in international air crash cases brought under the Warsaw Convention,[70] and others.[71] Federal statutory schemes may also preempt some claims that otherwise might present good cases for punitive damages.[72]

Settings for Grant of Punitive Damages

These special limits aside, punitive damages are available in a wide range of cases. The punitive award is not necessarily appropriate in every case of conscious wrongdoing,[73] but if the facts otherwise warrant the award, it may be made in a variety of tort cases, both intentional[74] and negligent,[75] and including civil rights torts.[76]

66. Some forms of job discrimination may amount to common law torts for which punitive damages may be awarded, as in Ford v. Revlon, Inc., 153 Ariz. 38, 734 P.2d 580 (1987) and Lewis v. Oregon Beauty Supply Co., 302 Or. 616, 733 P.2d 430 (1987). Likewise, punitive damages may be awardable under some state job discrimination statutes. See Levinson v. Prentice–Hall, Inc., 868 F.2d 558 (3d Cir.1989) (New Jersey, plaintiff had multiple sclerosis, handicap discrimination); Commodore Home Sys., Inc. v. Superior Court of San Bernadino County, 32 Cal.3d 211, 185 Cal. Rptr. 270, 649 P.2d 912 (1982). And some federal statutes other than Title VII may permit punitive damages for discrimination, as in Yarbrough v. Tower Oldsmobile, Inc., 789 F.2d 508 (7th Cir.1986) (42 U.S.C.A. § 1981 discrimination claim, punitive damages award affirmed); Smith v. United Technologies, Essex Group, Inc., 240 Kan. 562, 731 P.2d 871 (1987) (under 42 U.S.C.A. § 1981), overruled as to other points, in Coleman v. Safeway Stores, Inc., 242 Kan. 804, 752 P.2d 645 (1988); see Jones v. Western Geophysical Co., 761 F.2d 1158 (5th Cir.1985) (under 42 U.S.C.A. § 1981 punitive damages grantable for gross disregard of plaintiff's right, but in discretion of trial judge, discretion to deny affirmed on the facts).

67. The 1991 Civil Rights Act, PL 102–166, to be codified as 42 U.S.C.A. § 1981a, specifically provided that in cases of intentional job discrimination but not in the case of an employment practice that is unlawful because it has a disparate impact, punitive damages and full compensatory damages are now recoverable, but subject to a system of caps. See § 6.10 below.

75. Nast v. Lockett, 312 Md. 343, 539 A.2d 1113, 1122 (1988) ("As the degree of impairment by the voluntary consumption of alcohol increases, the need for other aggravating circumstances lessens, and vice versa"); Biswell v. Duncan, 742 P.2d 80 (Utah App.1987) (driving while intoxicated; listing states imposing punitive liability for drunken driving, including a handful which deny such liability); Booth v. Robertson, 236 Va. 269, 273, 374 S.E.2d 1, 3 (1988) ("The objective fact that the defendant in this case voluntarily consumed enough intoxicants to produce a reading of 0.22% blood alcohol content, causing him to drive as he did * * * provides sufficient proof of his conscious disregard of the rights of others"). See also La.Civil Code art. 2315.4 (injuries caused by driving motor vehicle while intoxicated).

76. E.g., Smith v. Wade, 461 U.S. 30, 103 S.Ct. 1625, 75 L.Ed.2d 632 (1983); Miga v. Holyoke, 398 Mass. 343, 497 N.E.2d 1 (1986). But public entities are not liable for punitive damages. See City of Newport v. Fact Concerts, Inc., 453 U.S. 247, 101 S.Ct. 2748, 69 L.Ed.2d 616 (1981) and the paragraph "Employers, public entities, public utilities," below. And job discrimination under Title VII did not permit punitive awards until the 1991 Civil Rights Act added a limited punitive relief, discussed in § 6.10 below.

Punitive liability has been imposed for professional malpractice [77] of physicians,[78] hospitals,[79] and lawyers.[80] Even nonfeasance or failure to act, if actionable as a tort, may be a basis for punitive damages.[81] Toxic tort cases, such as those involving reckless disposal of hazardous wastes which endanger the public, may be especially appropriate for the imposition of punitive damages.[82]

After publication of a groundbreaking article in 1976,[83] courts generally came to accept punitive damages in strict products liability cases, provided the defendant's conduct was found to be especially blameworthy.[84] Punitive awards have been granted in claims for restitution as well as in ordinary damages actions.[85]

Lawyers perhaps traditionally thought of punitive awards most commonly in cases of physical harms to person or property.[86] But punitive awards may also be made for violation of intimate rights such as those of privacy,[87] and for violation of civil rights [88] or constitutional rights that have nothing to do with physical security, such as free speech rights.[89] In the 1980s, most punitive awards seem to have been made in economic tort cases, such as cases of wrongful discharge,[90] bad faith business dealings [91] or interference with contract.[92] There may even be a trend to permit punitive awards by arbitrators in commercial arbitration cases.[93] Another case of non-physical injury for which some authority supports punitive awards is the case of persons who have derivative claims such as lost consortium or financial losses due to injury of another person.[94]

Persons Liable

Mental capacity. It is sometimes suggested that insane persons lack the mental capacity to form the "malice" or other egregiously bad intent that is prerequisite to punitive damages; but it might be more accurate to treat the question as one of fact: whether the particular defendant suffering from the particular mental disability could and did form the mental state necessary to

83. Owen, Punitive Damages in Products Liability Litigation, 74 Mich.L.Rev. 1258 (1976).

84. E.g., O'Gilvie v. International Playtex, Inc., 821 F.2d 1438 (10th Cir.1987), cert. denied, Playtex Holdings, Inc. v. O'Gilvie, 486 U.S. 1032, 108 S.Ct. 2014, 100 L.Ed.2d 601 (1988) (tampons, toxic shock syndrome); Fischer v. Johns–Manville Corp., 103 N.J. 643, 512 A.2d 466 (1986); Grimshaw v. Ford Motor Co., 119 Cal.App.3d 757, 174 Cal.Rptr. 348 (1981) (Ford Pinto case); Masaki v. General Motors Corp., 71 Hawaii 1, 780 P.2d 566 (1989).

85. Zippertubing Co. v. Teleflex Inc., 757 F.2d 1401 (3d Cir.1985); Thomas Auto Co. v. Craft, 297 Ark. 492, 498, 763 S.W.2d 651, 654 (1989) ("We can think of no reason why punitive damages should not accompany a restitutionary award if there is proof of the elements of deceit as a basis for revocation of acceptance or extrajudicial rescission"); see Davis v. Tyee Indus., Inc., 295 Or. 467, 668 P.2d 1186 (1983) (punitive damages in assumpsit if tortious conduct is alleged that would otherwise support punitive damages); Adams v. Crater

Well Drilling, Inc., 276 Or. 789, 556 P.2d 679 (1976).

91. Hawkins v. Allstate Ins. Co., 152 Ariz. 490, 733 P.2d 1073 (1987), cert. denied, Allstate Ins. Co. v. Hawkins, 484 U.S. 874, 108 S.Ct. 212, 98 L.Ed.2d 177 (1987) (bad faith insurance practices); Nicholson v. United Pac. Ins. Co., 219 Mont. 32, 710 P.2d 1342 (1985) (bad faith in performance of lease contract).

92. Rite Aid Corp. v. Lake Shore Investors, 298 Md. 611, 471 A.2d 735, 44 A.L.R.4th 1063 (1984) (interference with contract and injurious falsehood cases); cf. Murray v. Feight, 741 P.2d 1148 (Alaska 1987) (punitive damages against partner). One study suggests that punitive damages have become most common in business and contract litigation and that the increase in awards lies mostly in this area. See American Bar Association, Punitive Damages, A Constructive Examination 43 ff. (1986) (Special Committee on Punitive Damages, Section of Litigation).

justify punitive liability. Recent authority, not surprisingly, has taken this view.[95]

Minors. The same view has been taken as to the punitive liability of minors—where the facts of the particular case show the requisite states of mind, punitive liability is imposed.[96]

Employers, public entities, public utilities. Quite commonly, vicarious punitive liabilities are inflicted against employers, including corporate employers, for the evil deeds of their employees, though this liability is limited in some states to cases in which the misdeeds reflect corporate policy or managerial-level torts.[97] Public entities, on the other hand, are usually protected from punitive liabilities in the absence of a special statute,[98] and in some cases so are labor unions.[99] Traditionally, decedents' estates are likewise exempt from punitive liabilities.[100] Public utilities, on the other hand, have not been able to fortify themselves against punitive awards.[101]

Persons Who May Sue

Almost anyone who can claim an injury for which compensatory damages are awarded[102] can also claim punitive damages if the defendant's conduct is sufficiently egregious; but there are a few restrictions. Some courts have excluded plaintiffs whose compensatory claims are derivative,[103] and some authority prohibits recovery of punitive damages by public entities in the absence of statutory authorization.[104]

§ 3.11(2) Bases of the Traditional Punitive Damages Award

Punishment and Retribution: Just Deserts

Increasing attention to punitive damages has made it clear that there are several distinct rationales for inflicting punitive awards and that they are not very consistent with each other, either in underlying theory or in the measurement of damages each would entail. One rationale is punishment. Other quite different rationales—deterrence and compensation—are considered in the next subsection.

The punishment rationale holds that it is just to impose suffering upon a defendant who has engaged in extreme wrongdoing. By imposing the punishment, courts are somehow rectifying the wrong and restoring the rights of the victim.[1] In this view, the justice in punitive damages is not so much that the victim receives payment but that the defendant is made to suffer in a way that appropriately corresponds to his wrong. He gets his just deserts.

Punitive damages in this view would carry out corrective justice. Although punishment in this sense might effectively deter future wrongdoing,

98. City of Newport v. Fact Concerts, Inc., 453 U.S. 247, 101 S.Ct. 2748, 69 L.Ed.2d 616 (1981) (civil rights claim under 42 U.S.C.A. § 1983, no punitive damages); Metropolitan Atlanta Rapid Transit Auth. v. Boswell, 261 Ga. 427, 405 S.E.2d 869 (1991); Feingold v. Southeastern Pennsylvania Transportation Authority, 512 Pa. 567, 581, 517 A.2d 1270, 1277 (1986) ("punitive damages imposed on a municipality are in effect a windfall to a fully compensated plaintiff, and are likely accompa-

nied by an increase in taxes or reduction of public services for the citizens footing the bill"). Statutes regulating public entity liability are often explicit. E.g., 28 U.S.C.A. § 2674 (Federal Tort Claims Act).

§ 3.11(2)

1. See Owen, The Moral Foundations of Punitive Damages, 40 Ala.L.Rev. 705, 711 (1989).

deterrence is no part of the rationale of pure punishment. Instead, punishment is right because it is right. This viewpoint is probably closest to the traditional American rationale.[2] That rationale is important because it has the effect of controlling the basic grounds for punitive liability. This subsection considers those grounds.

The Mental State Required

Conduct. Courts agree that punishment should be deserved before the punitive award is made, but the conduct for which punishment is deserved is not defined, except that ordinary negligence alone will never qualify.[3] Punitive damages are awarded when the defendant is guilty of both a bad state of mind and highly serious misconduct. Conduct and state of mind are two different things, but the two are usually rolled up together in the discussions. For example, a court may say that the defendant's *conduct* must be malicious. But malice itself is a state of mind or a motive. Reference to conduct no doubt suggests extreme misbehavior, but the attention is usually given mainly to the mental state.

Tests for state of mind. Courts describe the conduct/state of mind in a wide variety of abstract and condemnatory terms. The defendant is subject to punitive damages if he is malicious; if he is reckless; if he is oppressive, evil, wicked, guilty of wanton or morally culpable conduct, or shows flagrant indifference to the safety of others.[4] A greater emphasis is laid on the conduct element if, with Professor Owen, one limits punitive damages to behavior "that constitutes an extreme departure from lawful conduct."[5]

State of mind: intentional risk-taking vs. intentional harm. Sometimes courts attempt to say that only truly malicious conduct justifies punitive damages[6] and that reckless or wanton conduct does not. This distinction, which is essentially a distinction between intentional risk-taking and intentional harm, is important for some purposes. For example, the defendant's liability insurance might protect him in cases of intentional risk-taking but not in cases of intentional harm.[7] Similarly, recent statutes have sometimes limited punitive liability in cases of intentional risk-taking but not in cases of intentional harms.[8]

The distinction is easy to draw in the abstract, but harder to draw in practice. It is not necessarily a good index to punitive liability. A manufacturer who markets a product it knows to be unreasonably dangerous is not guilty of intentional harm, but is definitely guilty of intentional risk-taking. If the risks are serious and the manufacturer is aware of them, punitive damages are surely appropriate. Not surprisingly, many decisions permit punitive damages when the plaintiff shows that the defendant was guilty of reckless or wanton misconduct involving conscious indifference to the rights of others.[9] This is not merely extreme negligence, however; the defendant must be consciously aware of the risk to others and willing to inflict that risk.[10]

2. Courts do not usually explain exactly what they mean by punishment, and certainly do not explain it in the stark terms of these paragraphs, but they appear to have in mind the idea of just deserts, as well as the distinct idea of deterrence.

5. Owen, The Moral Foundations of Punitive Damages, 40 Ala.L.Rev. 705, 730 (1989).

Limited value of tests. Most of the words used to describe the conduct/state of mind necessary to justify a punitive award do not point to objective evidence or reality. Instead, they suggest the kind of subjective reaction a judge or juror should have before punitive damages are awarded. For this reason the words cannot furnish very good guides either to the defendant or to the court. For the same reason, no one can say with confidence that there is a difference between the egregiously awful conduct which meets the "oppressive" standard and that which meets the "wanton" test. Although lawyers argue about these terms and many others like them, the terms are too abstract to guide resolution of serious issues. Significantly, however, all of the terms of opprobrium imply a bad state of mind as well as bad conduct.[11] The "inquiry focuses primarily upon the defendant's mental state, and to a lesser degree, the nature of his conduct." [12]

Illustrative cases. Examples of punishment-deserving conduct include serious intentional harms, such as batteries [13] breach of fiduciary duty [14] and fraud,[15] and even extremely dangerous motor vehicle driving.[16] Repeated misconduct,[17] or a policy of misconduct [18] intended to benefit the defendant at the expense of potential victims,[19] is often an element in punitive damages cases. For example, punitive damages would be appropriate against a trucking company which encourages its drivers in dangerous driving habits in order to speed company deliveries.[20] The defendant's attempts to conceal the fact of danger or causation in the first place,[21] and cover-ups or attempts to conceal the defendant's knowledge after harm has occurred, or to destroy evidence,[22] are all good indicators of the state of mind that will invoke punitive damages, with some authority that might be read to the contrary.[23] But the descriptive terminology is so abstract that in the end each case very largely requires individual analysis and examples can do no more than point to common patterns, some of which involve personal ill will or wilful conduct, while others involve an attempt to gain an economic benefit by imposing serious risks upon others.[24]

Gross Negligence and Mental States

Gross negligence, which traditionally did not imply any mental state but only highly negligent conduct, is said to be a sufficient basis for punitive liabilities in some states; but when the gross negligence standard is used, the court usually adds that it must be such as will indicate a bad mental state as well as bad conduct.[25] Thus in spite of the "gross negligence" terminology, the courts seem largely agreed in practice that bad conduct and bad states of mind are both required to justify punitive damages.[26] Some commentators, concerned that the threat of punitive liability might be economically inefficient because it might overdeter, or because it might be unfairly imposed to reflect jury bias, have suggested that the punitive award should be limited to cases of intentional torts or at least to cases of intentional fault.[27]

12. Masaki v. General Motors Corp., 71 Hawaii 1, 780 P.2d 566, 570 (1989) (citing original edition of this treatise).

27. See Ellis, Fairness and Efficiency in the Law of Punitive Damages, 56 S.Cal.L.Rev. 1 (1982) ("principles of fairness justify puni-

tive damages only when a wrongful act has been committed with the objective of harming another or when the utility of an act was unequivocally known by the actor to fall far short of the danger created"). Some commentators have suggested intention is required

Torts Based on Bad Faith, Malice or Serious Wrongs

In some instances the plaintiff must prove some element of serious misbehavior in order to establish even a claim for compensatory damages. The action of deceit at common law was like this, requiring proof of intentional fraud to establish any claim at all;[28] torts such as assault and battery usually require unjustified intent to interfere with another's person, and a number of economic torts are said to require an intent to interfere with another's rights, or bad faith.[29]

Courts have not always been willing to impose punitive damages in such cases.[30] In a few instances they have said that when the underlying cause of action itself requires egregious misconduct such as fraud or malice, punitive damages will be denied unless the plaintiff can show misconduct even worse than that required to establish compensatory damages.[31]

Other courts, however, have rejected any such limitation on the punitive award; they do not require more proof to support punitive damages than would be required in any other case.[32] The Supreme Court of the United States, in a civil rights case, has also rejected any such limitation.[33]

Deviant Applications of the Rules

Because terminology like "malicious, reckless and oppressive" is abstract and conclusory, it fails to describe kinds of conduct for which punishment can be imposed. Neither the defendant nor the lawyer is likely to know whether any but the most extreme conduct is subject to punitive liability.[34] Some cases have found malice or recklessness even where the defendant believes he is acting within his legal rights.[35] This rule is no doubt justified when the defendant acquires or maintains his belief by serious misconduct; but except for this, punitive liability when the defendant believes he is acting correctly seems to discard any requirement of serious fault.

Abuse of Power

One group of these cases may be especially justified. Some writers have followed the suggestion in the previous edition of this book[36] that punitive damages may be justified in some cases because the defendant has abused a special power rather than because of anything like "malice" or wanton misconduct.

This view, perhaps a supplement to the usual emphasis on malice, would emphasize that the power relationship of the parties must be considered. Insurers who do not pay off on their policies,[37] utilities who stop their

but define intention rather loosely, as in Cooter, Economic Analysis of Punitive Damages, 56 S.Cal.L.Rev. 79 (1982).

33. Smith v. Wade, 461 U.S. 30, 103 S.Ct. 1625, 75 L.Ed.2d 632 (1983).

34. Commentators have felt the uncertainty of these abstract condemnations to be a very serious problem with punitive damages. See, e.g., Ellis, Fairness and Efficiency in the Law of Punitive Damages, 56 S.Cal.L.Rev. 1 (1982); Mallor & Roberts, Punitive Damages: Toward a Principled Approach, 31 Hast.L.J.

639 (1980). Some judges have argued that the uncertainty of punitive awards may be desirable. See § 3.11(15), below.

36. See Owen, Civil Punishment and the Public Good, 56 S.Cal.L.Rev. 103, 104 (1982–83).

37. E.g., Hawkins v. Allstate Ins. Co., 152 Ariz. 490, 733 P.2d 1073 (1987), cert. denied, 484 U.S. 874, 108 S.Ct. 212, 98 L.Ed.2d 177 (1987); Eichenseer v. Reserve Life Ins. Co., 682 F.Supp. 1355 (N.D.Miss.1988), aff'd, 881 F.2d 1355 (5th Cir.1989). Cf. Breese v. AWI,

services,[38] or attempt to obtain the plaintiff's property without payment or use of their eminent domain powers,[39] employers guilty of wrongful discharge[40] are all in a position of special power, which can be seen to have been abused by their misdeeds, and all are held subject to punitive damages for such abuse.

§ 3.11(3) Deterrence and Other Purposes of Punitive Damages

Punitive damages awards do not represent one single legal response to the defendant's conduct. Instead they represent several distinct kinds of responses, the differences in which are hidden behind the common punitive label.[1] Punitive damages awards have at least three quite different effects on the defendant and on society[2] and at least three quite distinct rationales. These include the traditional punishment rationale, but also deterrence and some species of special compensation.

Although deterrence has long been recognized as one of the reasons for punitive awards, it was traditionally lumped with punishment as if the two were similar.[3] In fact, however, deterrence rationales of punitive damages sidestep some of the criticisms of punitive damages which are based on the punishment rationale and call for quite different amounts of punitive damages. "Punitive" damages may also serve as a kind of compensation on special occasions. Under either the deterrence or special compensation rationales, the label "punitive" becomes misleading, so that writers have now begun to speak of extracompensatory or augmented damages instead.

Deterrence

Deterrence as a goal and measure. The need to deter future misconduct is largely independent of the just deserts basis for punitive awards. If deterrence is an important purpose in "punitive" damages, that purpose would logically affect not only the occasions for imposing such damages, but also the amount or measure of the award,[4] the evidence that is appropriate,

Inc., 823 F.2d 100, 103 (5th Cir.1987) ("It is well settled that '(a) shipowner who arbitrarily and capriciously denies maintenance and cure to an injured seaman is liable to him for punitive damages and attorney's fees' ").

In Ainsworth v. Combined Ins. Co. of Am., 104 Nev. 587, 763 P.2d 673 (1988), cert. denied, 493 U.S. 958, 110 S.Ct. 376, 107 L.Ed.2d 361 (1989), the court explicitly referred to "oppression" as a standard for the grant of punitive damages, id. at 675, emphasized the relation of "special confidence" between insurer and insured in an accident policy, id. at 676, and the special "vulnerability" of the seriously injured plaintiff whose claim was denied, id. at 677.

§ 3.11(3)

1. See Chapman and Trebilcock, Punitive Damages: Divergence in Search of a Rationale, 40 Ala.L.Rev. 741 (1989).

2. In addition to the functions discussed in this text, punitive damages might function to require disgorgement of unjust enrichment. Professor Ausness, though he does not favor punitive damages in products liability cases,

has suggested that such damages might be related to unfair competition claims, though he thinks if so, the defendant's competitors should be the ones to recover. See Ausness, Retribution and Deterrence: The Role of Punitive Damages in Products Liability Litigation, 74 Ky.L.J. 1, 45 (1985–86). There is a casual reference to some such idea in Sturm, Ruger & Co., Inc. v. Day, 594 P.2d 38, 47 (Alaska 1979), opinion modified on reh'g, 615 P.2d 621 (Alaska 1980), cert. denied, 454 U.S. 894, 102 S.Ct. 391, 70 L.Ed.2d 209 (1981), overruled on other issues, in Dura Corp. v. Harned, 703 P.2d 396 (Alaska 1985) (" * * * if punitive damages could not be awarded in the products liability context, a reckless manufacturer might gain an unfair advantage over its more socially responsible competitors").

4. See Chapman and Trebilcock, Punitive Damages: Divergence in Search of a Rationale, 40 Ala.L.Rev. 741 (1989); Dobbs, Ending Punishment in "Punitive" Damages: Deterrence-Measured Remedies, 40 Ala.L.Rev. 831 (1989); Galligan, Augmented Awards: The Efficient Evolution of Punitive Damages, 51 La.

the procedures,[5] and even the taxability of the award.[6] Although the term "punitive" will be used because it is common, the term as used here does not imply a punitive rationale.

Deterrence by removing profit from profitable torts. Many commentators are skeptical about whether punitive damages actually do tend to deter,[7] or whether, if they do so, the deterrence is optimal.[8] Nevertheless, one ground for seeking deterrence-measured awards is that there are a number of cases in which, in the absence of such liability, the defendant would find it profitable to continue its misconduct because profits are high and compensatory damages are low.[9] This reason for adding to the compensatory recovery is very different from a simple desire to punish because the defendant is a bad actor who deserves to suffer. How would the defendant's continued tortious activity be profitable if the defendant had to pay damages for all harms done?

How tortious activity may continue to be profitable after paying compensatory damages. One reason why the defendant might profit from tortious activity even after paying compensatory damages is that the harms caused might be small and that compensatory damages would still leave the defendant with a profit. A manufacturer whose products cause small harms in some cases may still reap large profits from the product. In such a case,

L.Rev. 3 (1990). If the point is not deterrence but payment of litigation costs, then the measure of extra-compensatory liability would be litigation cost.

6. The current view seems to be that punitive damages are taxable, period. For an example see CIR v. Miller, 914 F.2d 586 (4th Cir.1990) (settlement for punitive damages in defamation/emotional distress claim taxable, though compensatory portion is not). A 1989 amendment to the governing tax statute, now seems to make this very clear. 26 U.S.C.A. § 104(a). But the rule may be too general; to the extent that punitive damages perform the same function as a non-taxable award, it may be changed. So recognition of some "punitive" damages as compensatory or something else might be important. See generally, L. Frolik, Federal Tax Aspects of Injury, Damage, and Loss 17–18 (1987); Morrison, Getting a Rule Right and Writing a Wrong Rule: The IRS Demands a Return on All Punitive Damages, 17 Conn.L.Rev. 39 (1984). This is most significant in personal injury cases, where the compensatory award is not taxable. As to this, see § 8.6(4) below.

7. Cf. Gary Schwartz, Deterrence and Punishment in the Common Law of Punitive Damages: A Comment, 56 S.Cal.L.Rev. 133 (1982) (pointing out a number of situations in which deterrence could not work but in which "punitive" damages are granted, and also some in which deterrence is needed but such damages must be denied). According to Tetuan v. A.H. Robins Co., 241 Kan. 441, 738 P.2d 1210 (1987), the A.H. Robins Company, instead of responding to earlier punitive awards for fail-

ing to warn about the dangers of the Dalkon Shield, merely burnt its records instead. This may merely reflect the extreme misbehavior of the Robins Company, but it may also reflect the fact that raising the stakes of the game by adding punitive damages or attorney fee liability may induce the defendant to resist liability more strongly rather than to comply. See Ausness, Retribution and Deterrence: The Role of Punitive Damages in Products Liability Litigation, 74 Ky.L.J. 1, 81 ff. (1985–86).

8. The question of optimal vs. over- or under-deterrence appears in most commentary. E.g., Ellis, Fairness and Efficiency in the Law of Punitive Damages, 56 S.Cal.L.Rev. 1 (1982); Ausness, Retribution and Deterrence: The Role of Punitive Damages in Products Liability Litigation, 74 Ky. L.J. 1, 84 ff. (1985–86); cf. American Bar Association, Report of the Special Committee on Punitive Damages, Punitive Damages, A Constructive Examination 8 (Litigation Section, 1986) (in spite of preference for statistics "it has proved impossible * * * to quantify the deterring force of the threat of punitive damages * * * we recognize that overdeterrence is a consequence to be avoided equally with underdeterrence. That is, if conduct which is potentially of social benefit is deterred by overthreat of punitive damages, society would be the loser. And we recognize that in the long run society pays for the sums that are actually transferred when a punitive award is paid to a victim.").

9. This is the explicit reason given for awarding punitive damages in some of the cases. See, e.g., recognizing this expressly, Sturm, Ruger & Co., Inc. v. Day, 594 P.2d 38,

the manufacturer may not be negligent at all and the product may not be defective because the level of profits suggests a high level of benefit which may more than offset the harm.[10] If, however, the product is proscribed by law or can otherwise be found to be defective or negligently made, a deterrent award will be required to remove the profits.

A more likely scenario is this: the manufacturer sells a product which in fact causes many harms, the total damages from which far outweigh any profits the manufacturer makes, but the manufacturer does not pay for all the harms it causes. This probably happens in a large number of cases. Many injured victims suffer harms too small to warrant a suit; or they do not know that their illness is connected with any product, or do not know it is connected with the defendant's product; or they cannot prove the connection. In some cases the law itself will forbid suit by the injured person because her injuries, though real and important, are nevertheless too remote.[11] In these cases, the compensatory liabilities do not fully reflect the true costs of the harms done. In situations like this, even if compensatory damages are expected to be very high they might not deter the misconduct if it is highly profitable.[12] In such cases, a surcharge on the compensatory award may be appropriate as a means of seeking deterrence.

Whether this surcharge can be calculated at the right level is another matter, but commentators have revealed an increasing interest in deterrence-measured awards.[13] Such awards may be measured quite differently from awards that seek to administer punitive just deserts and might be appropriate in any case where it is necessary to make the defendant pay full costs of harmful activity.

"General" deterrence by imposing costs of all harms done to everyone. The kind of deterrence indicated so far might be called specific deterrence, because it aims at removing the particular profits from tortious behavior. Professor Galligan poses the possibility of what might be called general deterrence, to be achieved by making sure the defendant pays *all* the costs his wrongful act imposes, at least within the limits of foreseeable harms. This does not turn on finding that the activity was profitable in any way

47 (Alaska 1979), opinion modified on reh'g, 615 P.2d 621 (Alaska 1980).

10. When the total harm done is less than the total benefits from the activity, the traditional Learned Hand risk-utility formula in United States v. Carroll Towing Co., 159 F.2d 169 (2d Cir.1947) suggests that the defendant is not negligent at all, much less punitively liable. However, some conduct may be identified as tortious even when the legally compensable harm done is small in comparison to the benefits to be reaped. This might be so by statute, for example.

11. See Galligan, Augmented Awards: The Efficient Evolution of Punitive Damages, 51 La.L.Rev. 3 (1990).

12. Where compensatory damages are high they may provide sufficient deterrence that punitive damages should not be awarded. But even very high punitive damages might not deter the defendant if profits were even high-

er. The New Jersey Court gave a second reason why high compensatory might be insufficient in a products liability case: the manufacturer-defendant might simply factor compensatory liabilities into the price of its product because they are reasonably predictable, in which case there would be no deterrence at all. Unpredictable punitive damages would not be so easy to factor in. Fischer v. Johns–Manville Corp., 103 N.J. 643, 512 A.2d 466 (1986). This argument may be based on an assumption that competition within the industry would be such that the malicious manufacturer could raise prices to cover punitive damages costs and still compete effectively in prices.

13. Dobbs, Ending Punishment in "Punitive" Damages: Deterrence–Measured Remedies, 40 Ala.L.Rev. 831 (1989); Galligan, Augmented Awards: The Efficient Evolution of Punitive Damages, 51 La.L.Rev. 3 (1990).

connected with the tort itself, or even on a finding that the defendant was guilty of serious misconduct.

Galligan gives an example similar to an oil spill which harms important bodies of water and some of the property on and around it.[14] One rule of tort law in common use permits recovery by those whose property was physically damaged, but not (apart from nuisance rules) by those who have economic losses. For instance, motel owners in the area might suffer a loss of business while the waters are polluted but would not be permitted to recover for that business loss. The economic harm is real, however. There might be a number of reasons to exclude liability for economic losses in such cases. However, assuming that the only reason to do so is to avoid the burden of handling so many small claims, then it is clear that the defendant has wrongfully imposed costs on others.

If such defendants need not pay those costs, then the defendants will not take them into account in deciding how much to spend on preventing oil spills. To make sure that defendants in such cases take the costs into account (and maybe as a result spend more in preventing the harm), Professor Galligan proposes that the plaintiffs who can recover (because their property was damaged) should also recover an augmented award equal to the sum of all harms done. The plaintiffs who can sue and recover stand "proxy" for those who cannot.

"Punitive" or augmented damages would be measured quite differently depending on which kind of deterrent was invoked. The general deterrence scheme potentially exposes the defendant to quite extensive harms, even when its activity is unprofitable. Owners of oil tankers do not really desire to discharge their valuable commodity into the public waters; this is not a profit-making activity for them. Yet under the general deterrence theory, they might be liable for extracompensatory awards anyway. This approach runs risks of collision with some other legal ideas, such as those associated with proximate cause. The procedural and computation side of this approach may also prove to be difficult.

The specific deterrence measure, however, would be more limited, aimed at removing the profit potential from the wrongful conduct. Both kinds of deterrence of course differ from the aims of retribution; just deserts punishment depends wholly on the eye of the beholder.

Injunctive deterrence with punitive awards. A different kind of deterrence might be achieved if a judge were to reduce a defendant's punitive liability in exchange for specific safer future conduct. This would operate much like an injunction against future misconduct, with a warning about the contempt fine that might be levied. But this form of deterrence has so far been disapproved.[15]

14. Galligan, Augmented Awards: The Efficient Evolution of Punitive Damages, 51 La. L.Rev. 3, 44 (1990).

15. O'Gilvie v. International Playtex, Inc., 821 F.2d 1438 (10th Cir.1987), cert. denied, 486 U.S. 1032, 108 S.Ct. 2014, 100 L.Ed.2d 601 (1988); cf. Weiner v. Ash, 157 Ariz. 232, 234, 756 P.2d 329, 331 (App.1988) (held, error to enter damages award conditioned on certain behavior of the defendant in the future). On the injunction and contempt comparison, see § 2.8(2) above. A reduction of punitive damages to achieve a kind of bargained-for deterrence is likely to be very effective in some kinds of cases, but it puts the judges in an unusual role. See the discussion in Note, Remedial Activism: Judicial Bargaining with Punitive Damage Awards, 19 Loy.L.A.L.Rev.

This point, however, raises the question whether an ordinary injunction might be substituted for punitive damages when the plaintiff has standing to seek it. Injunctions commonly aim at prevention of future harm, so they are also deterrent forces. A number of reasons have been suggested why the injunction will not be appropriate in many kinds of litigation. One is that the plaintiff, who has been paid and is not personally threatened with future harm, may have no standing to seek it. Another is that in the case of harms caused by enterprise defendants, the injunction may put the defendant in an unfair competitive posture as compared to other enterprises not subjected to the injunction, and may put the plaintiff in an unfair strategic position. Although none of these difficulties, nor others that have been suggested, would apply in every case, they do suggest some of the reasons why injunctions cannot be freely substituted for punitive awards.[16]

Deterrence by example to others. A third kind of deterrence might be achieved if the punitive damages award against the defendant served to discourage other persons from committing similar wrongdoings. Courts have often said that punitive damages are appropriate even if no deterrence of the defendant is needed or possible, because the infliction of such damages sets an example to others.[17] It is not so easy to justify this approach. If the only reason for imposing punitive, non-compensatory damages is to set an example for others, the defendant becomes merely a judicial hostage. No special misconduct or state of mind would be required. If other grounds exist for punitive awards, talk of setting an example seems extraneous.

Courts may not in fact really believe in the example-for-others approach. It is very hard to imagine the kind of proof that would have to be introduced to permit a judge to calculate the punishment that would have to be levied against the defendant in order to dissuade unknown persons from similar behavior. In fact, such proof is not made in the "example" cases. This is one indication that the deterrence of others may be more a linguistic convention than a real goal of the courts. Quite possibly the deterrence of others justification means only that, if the punitive award is fair enough because it is the defendant's just desert, it will be approved, and that the award can stand on just desert ground even if it has no deterrent effect upon the defendant.

Deterrence and just deserts. Courts usually invoke deterrence as a guide to the extent or *measure* of liability, or an added justification for it, rather than a sufficient *ground* for that liability in the first place. The stated ground for invoking punitive damages is that the defendant has committed a highly serious wrong. In the usual case, a basis for additional liability must

941 (1986). It also diminishes the recompense for the plaintiffs' attorneys who, in a complex and costly case, may count on a share of the punitive award to make the case financially feasible.

16. See Dobbs, Ending Punishment in "Punitive" Damages: Deterrence–Measured Remedies, 40 Ala.L.Rev. 831, 909–912 (1989). The reasons suggested, illustrated by a products liability case, are: (1) plaintiff may lack standing; (2) the risk of error, present in any judicial proceeding, may be magnified if injunc-tive relief is granted; (3) injunctions may not be possible because specific conduct (as distinguished from a desired result) may not be describable; (4) the injunction may put the defendant in an unfair position with respect to its competitors; (5) general regulation of an industry may be more appropriate by legislation than by injunctions; and (6) the plaintiff may simply use the injunctive threat as grounds for greater damages, dropping the threat when a good settlement is obtained.

exist in a truly punitive sense that such liability will be justly deserved. The mere fact that repetition of the wrong is possible or likely has not traditionally sufficed;[18] the wrong itself must be a serious one. The deterrence purpose of punitive damages, then, arises only after the court and trier conclude the defendant justly deserves punishment.

This is anomalous. If deterrence is the important point, the likelihood of repetition, not the seriousness of the wrong, is the most relevant issue.[19] If just deserts punishment is the important point, the measurement of punitive liability by the amount that is required to deter would be off the mark.[20] This anomaly no doubt affects the way courts try to define punishable misconduct. If a need for deterrence is perceived, it will be tempting to stretch the facts and to describe the defendant as a malicious actor so that punitive damages can be awarded to achieve deterrence.[21] It might be better to recognize deterrence damages as a separate heading for recovery, without resort to "punitive" theories.

Litigation Finance and Added Compensation

Litigation finance; compensation for attorney fees. A second non-punitive effect of an extracompensatory award is that it will help finance the litigation. Under the general American rule, the prevailing plaintiff will not ordinarily recover attorney fees or most other litigation expense.[22] A recovery of punitive damages may serve as a reservoir from which the plaintiff can pay attorney fees and litigation costs and in this sense may be compensatory.[23]

Litigation finance; incentives to sue. A very different idea and one that may be more significant, is that the hope of punitive damages may induce a contingent fee lawyer to take the case in the first instance and to devote adequate time to it. This might be especially important in cases involving only small compensatory damages, the recovery of which would provide an insufficient percentage fee and also in cases which might bring a large damage recovery but which would entail legal work worth even more.[24] If those cases also involve the public interest, or benefits to others besides the plaintiff, the prospect of punitive damages will work almost exactly like the award of attorney fees on a private attorney general theory.[25] Courts have increasingly mentioned the private attorney general idea explicitly in justifying the punitive award,[26] and before that terminology came into use they

19. Compensatory damages have a deterrent function and one of the theories for imposing such damages is in fact to deter undesirable conduct. See Gary Schwartz, Deterrence and Punishment in the Common Law of Punitive Damages: A Comment, 56 S.Cal. L.Rev. 133 (1982). Thus, it is in a sense anomalous to insist that the extreme wrongdoing required for punitive damages must be found in order to justify awards intended to deter.

25. See § 3.10(2), above. That is, the award would be made in those cases in which the plaintiff and her lawyer put in the work, but some of the benefits go to others, either to specific others or to the public in general.

26. Jackson v. Johns–Manville Sales Corp., 781 F.2d 394 (5th Cir.1986), cert. denied, 478

U.S. 1022, 106 S.Ct. 3339, 92 L.Ed.2d 743 (1986); Tideway Oil Programs, Inc. v. Scrio, 431 So.2d 454, 461, 58 A.L.R. 4th 819 (Miss. 1983) (punitive damages in equity justified partly because "plaintiff, at great trouble and personal expense, has rendered a public service by bringing the wrongdoer to account. The plaintiff in such cases is, and necessarily must be, acting as a private attorney general"); Thiry v. Armstrong World Indus., 661 P.2d 515 (Okl.1983); State ex rel. Young v. Crookham, 290 Or. 61, 618 P.2d 1268, 11 A.L.R.4th 1251 (1980); Biswell v. Duncan, 742 P.2d 80, 85 (Utah App.1987) ("The possibility of an award of punitive damages may induce the victim, not otherwise willing to proceed because of the trouble and expense, to take

sometimes used different language to express the same idea.[27]

Forcing a choice between attorney fee and punitive damages. The overlapping purposes of punitive damages and attorney fee awards in cases of this ilk suggest that it may be proper in some cases to limit the amount of punitive damages when attorney fees are awarded.[28] Alternatively the plaintiff might be allowed to elect between a fee award and punitive damages.[29] That the plaintiff may be forced to accept either the fee award or the punitive award is a good indication that the two serve the same function. But the exact amount of punitive damages required can never be shown with certainty, and there are no doubt cases in which it is proper to award both full punitive damages and full attorney fees.[30]

§ 3.11(4) Proof Standards

[For the text of this section, see the unabridged Practitioner Treatise edition.]

§ 3.11(5) Financial Condition of Defendant

Permitting Evidence of the Defendant's Finances

General rule admitting proof of financial condition. A second special rule for punitive damages is that the plaintiff may introduce evidence of the defendant's wealth or financial status. Although this rule is contrary to the general rule that wealth or status of the parties is irrelevant and inadmissible, and runs the risk of serious prejudice to the defendant, it is followed in most of the states that have considered the issue.[1]

action against the intoxicated driver"). Cf. Smith v. Wade, 461 U.S. 30, 103 S.Ct. 1625, 75 L.Ed.2d 632 (1983). See Mallor & Roberts, Punitive Damages: Toward a Principled Approach, 31 Hast.L.J. 639 (1980); Ellis, Fairness and Efficiency in the Law of Punitive Damages, 56 S.Cal.L.Rev. 1 (1982). The incentive basis for the award would not, of course, justify awards in every case. Not every form of litigation justifies or requires encouragement, but cases in which defendants act egregiously, when they are also cases costly to pursue or cases which produce substantial benefits to others, seem to be good candidates for some kind of fee award. Professor Redden, no friend at all of punitive damages, dismisses the incentive argument by characterizing the injuries in question as "petty," see K. Redden, Punitive Damages § 7.6(D). But the injuries are not always petty. They may be quite important in a civilized society even if compensatory damages are necessarily small; or the compensatory damages may be very high but too costly for most lawyers to pursue on a contingent fee without the hope of punitive recoveries; or they may produce benefits to many non-parties who do not share in the costs of producing them.

27. Walker v. Sheldon, 10 N.Y.2d 401, 404, 223 N.Y.S.2d 488, 490, 179 N.E.2d 497, 498 (1961) ("Moreover, the possibility of an award of such damages may not infrequently induce the victim, otherwise unwilling to proceed be-

cause of the attendant trouble and expense, to take action against the wrongdoer); Kink v. Combs, 28 Wis.2d 65, 80, 135 N.W.2d 789, 798 (1965) ("By allowing punitive damages the self interest of the plaintiff will lead to prosecution of the claim").

28. E.g., Dempsey v. Holiday Utilities Corp., 107 Ill.App.3d 467, 63 Ill.Dec. 45, 437 N.E.2d 694 (1982).

29. See Kelco Disposal, Inc. v. Browning-Ferris Indus. of Vt., Inc., 845 F.2d 404 (2d Cir.1988), aff'd, 492 U.S. 257, 109 S.Ct. 2909, 106 L.Ed.2d 219 (1989).

30. See Embassy/Main Auto Leasing Co. v. C.A.R. Leasing, Inc., 155 Ill.App.3d 427, 108 Ill.Dec. 170, 508 N.E.2d 331 (1987) (attorney fee award based on knowingly filing untrue pleadings rather than on the tortious conduct that gave rise to punitive damages). It should also be noticed that an award for deterrence purposes, for pure punishment, and for "rewarding" litigation are often inconsistent in purpose and would yield quite different calculations of amount. Cf. Cooter, Economic Analysis of Punitive Damages, 56 S.Cal.L.Rev. 79, 90 (1982).

§ 3.11(5)

1. E.g., Hawkins v. Allstate Ins. Co., 152 Ariz. 490, 733 P.2d 1073 (1987), cert. denied, 484 U.S. 874, 108 S.Ct. 212, 98 L.Ed.2d 177

Theory of the rule. The rule originated with the idea that when a defendant of wealth or high status abused the plaintiff, the actual damages, in the form of something like mental anguish, could be greater.[2] But the theory behind the rule today is that the trier must know something about the defendant's financial condition in order to inflict a liability that will have an appropriate sting,[3] and proof may show either a wealthy defendant or a poor one.[4] Punishment, in other words, is to fit the person, not the crime. Some kinds of financial information about the defendant, if it is an enterprise, would also be highly relevant in determining the amount necessary to achieve a deterrence.[5]

Is proof required? The plaintiff is permitted, but is not traditionally required to present evidence bearing on the defendant's wealth or financial condition.[6] A little authority goes the other way, holding that the plaintiff must show the defendant's financial condition if punitive damages are to be awarded.[7] A middle position might be that when there is no evidence of the defendant's wealth, punitive damages are still recoverable if the facts otherwise warrant, but that no affirmative instruction to consider the defendant's wealth should be given to the jury.[8]

California requirement of proof. There is some reason to think that in the backwash of tort reform statutes and constitutional attacks on punitive damages,[9] some courts will begin to require the plaintiff to prove the defendant's financial condition as an absolute prerequisite to a punitive recovery. A major California decision, *Adams v. Murakami*,[10] said that such evidence is necessary to permit appropriate judicial review. It hinted that a punitive award might be subject to constitutional doubts otherwise.

There may be some questions raised by this approach that will require clarification. One question that would be relevant in many states is whether the defendant's wealth is relevant at all when the defendant's liability insurance will cover the punitive award. If the defendant's wealth is

(1987) (punitive award of $3.5 million against an insurer for bad faith practices was justified in part on the ground that the insurer's net income was $346.7 million at about the time of the acts in question and the award was only $\frac{1}{25}$ of 1% of total assets and only 3½ days of net income); Independent Life & Accident Ins. Co. v. Peavy, 528 So.2d 1112, 1120 (Miss. 1988) ($250,000 punitive award justified in part because defendant's net worth was $130 million and award was "less than two tenth of one percent"); Ainsworth v. Combined Ins. Co. of Am., 104 Nev. 587, 763 P.2d 673 (1988), cert. denied, 493 U.S. 958, 110 S.Ct. 376, 107 L.Ed.2d 361 (1989) ($6 million punitive award justified in part because it was "only" 5% of defendant's "net operating gain" for year and only .4% of its "total assets"); Fischer v. Johns–Manville Corp., 103 N.J. 643, 512 A.2d 466 (1986). The rule is not of recent invention. See, e.g., Cumberland Tel. & Tel. Co. v. Poston, 94 Tenn. 696, 30 S.W. 1040 (1895). See also, Annotation, Punitive Damages: Relationship to defendant's wealth as factor in determining propriety of award, 87 A.L.R.4th 141 (1991).

A few cases reject the rule permitting evidence of wealth. Givens v. Berkley, 108 Ky. 236, 56 S.W. 158 (1900); First Nat. Bank of Marshall, Tex. v. Beavers, 619 S.W.2d 288 (Tex.Civ.App.1981) (error to admit evidence of number of acres owned by defendant as this would only bear on financial status). See generally J. Ghiardi & J. Kircher, Punitive Damages § 5.36 (1981 & Supps.).

7. Adams v. Murakami, 54 Cal.3d 105, 284 Cal.Rptr. 318, 813 P.2d 1348 (1991); Adel v. Parkhurst, 681 P.2d 886 (Wyo.1984). In Nelson v. Jacobsen, 669 P.2d 1207 (Utah 1983) the court seemed to say that if no evidence of the defendant's financial condition were offered, the plaintiff would be limited to a relatively small punitive award, but the court may have intended to rule out any punitive recovery without proof of wealth.

9. See § 3.11(12) below.

10. Adams v. Murakami, 54 Cal.3d 105, 284 Cal.Rptr. 318, 813 P.2d 1348 (1991).

relevant in spite of the fact that he is insured against punitive liability, then it must be said that in a sense liability insurance covering punitive damages *is* wealth. An absolute rule against recovery without proof of the defendant's wealth might be unfair if the plaintiff is not then permitted to show the most relevant form of wealth, but to permit the plaintiff to show the defendant's insurance would violate other rules.[11]

Other issues raised by an absolute requirement of proof may also cause difficulties. *Adams v. Murakami* was addressed to the proof required, not the consequences of making that proof. Suppose the plaintiff introduces the required evidence of the defendant's financial condition but that it shows him to have no assets and no income. If the California approach would still allow the plaintiff to recover punitive damages, the requirement of proof seems to add little or nothing. The same result could be obtained without requiring proof by reviewing the award on the strongest assumption against the plaintiff, namely, that the defendant had no wealth and no income. Since courts do not ordinarily require useless acts, the *Adams* Court may have assumed a rule that would bar all punitive recovery if proof showed no wealth. Yet that alternative also seems unlikely. It is hard to imagine that a court would overturn a punitive award in favor of a torture victim on the ground that his torturer had no wealth. A more tailored rule might be better: do not require proof of the defendant's financial condition, but in the absence of proof permit the punitive award to stand only if it is justified against a person of no wealth or income.

Countering Prejudice Resulting from Wealth Evidence

Defendant's introduction of financial evidence. Once the plaintiff introduces evidence of wealth, the defendant may introduce evidence to the contrary,[12] and perhaps should be permitted to do so in any event to allay any assumptions the jury might otherwise indulge that he is wealthy when in fact he is not, or to show that a large award might be excessive.[13]

Limits on wealth discovery. Because net worth is relevant evidence on the punitive damages claim, discovery of net worth is generally permitted.[14] At the same time, it is often recognized that the rule permitting financial evidence about the defendant is anomalous and that it represents potential for invasion of privacy and harassment.[15] These considerations have led some courts to place limits on discovery of financial information until the plaintiff has first established to the satisfaction of the trial judge that punitive damages are, prima facie, recoverable.[16] Until that is done, the trial judge under this rule is to protect financial information from discovery.[17] This rule does not directly affect trial of the case, only the order of discovery. Texas has rejected any formal rule that bars discovery of wealth until a right to punitive damages has been shown, but has recognized that a trial judge might bar discovery in particular cases if discovery would involve "unnecessary harassment or invasion of personal or property rights."[18]

Prejudice at trial; bifurcation. A second rule deals with the potential for prejudice to the defendant at trial when evidence of wealth is introduced.

11. See Garnes v. Fleming Landfill, Inc., 186 W.Va. 656, 413 S.E.2d 897 (1991) quoted   below at n. 40.

Evidence of the defendant's financial condition may potentially prejudice the trier on at least three major issues—the issue of liability as such, the issue of compensatory damages, and the issue of punitive damages itself. Evidence that the defendant is wealthy may make it easier for some triers to find that a tort was committed in the first place, or to award higher compensatory damages or to award punitive damages that otherwise would have been rejected.

As observers have noticed, the possibility for prejudice where the defendant is found to be wealthy is akin to the possibility of prejudice that arises when the trier learns that the defendant is insured.[19] Just as evidence of liability insurance is almost universally excluded in the absence of special circumstances,[20] some courts have initially excluded evidence of the defendant's financial condition until the jury first determines that the defendant is liable and that punitive damages should be awarded. But if the jury finds the defendant liable for punitive damages, the amount of the punitive award is considered in a second stage of the trial, at which time evidence of wealth is then admitted.[21] Fairness seems to require this or some similar procedure and it has been argued that Constitutional due process commands it as well.[22]

Types of Financial Information Admissible

Types of wealth—net worth, income. Courts seem not to have given extensive consideration as to the form of financial evidence. They have spoken at various times of annual income [23] or net income,[24] but also have said, usually without discussion, that net worth rather than net income would be the proper consideration.[25] In some cases both income evidence and net worth evidence is admitted or discussed.[26]

Since net worth is calculated by figuring the defendant's assets minus liabilities, there is the possibility of argument about what assets and liabilities should be counted. For example, should the defendant be considered poor, not wealthy, if he has given away many of his assets, or has liability for attorney fees in defending the punitive damages action itself?[27] Similarly, since both assets and liabilities will vary over time, there is room for argument about the controlling date for the net worth determination.[28]

---

21. The most thorough discussion is Campen v. Stone, 635 P.2d 1121, 32 A.L.R.4th 410 (Wyo.1981). It is usually said that Rupert v. Sellers, 48 A.D.2d 265, 368 N.Y.S.2d 904 (1975) led the way.

22. Wheeler, The Constitutional Case for Reforming Punitive Damages Procedures, 69 Va.L.Rev. 269, 300–302 (1983) (bifurcation of trial to separate all liability issues from all punitive issues). Bifurcation pursued in the cited cases separates the trial so that Part 1 covers liability, compensatory damages and liability for punitive damages; Part 2 then covers the amount of punitive damages.

A different bifurcation would be: Part 1: liability and compensatory damages issues; Part 2: all punitive issues, including liability for punitive damages. It would be possible to go further and "trifurcate" the trial: Part 1: liability and compensatory damages; Part 2: whether punitive damages should be awarded; Part 3: the amount of punitive damages. See American Bar Association, Punitive Damages: A Constructive Examination 59 (Special Committee on Punitive Damages, Section of Litigation, 1986). The report argues that bifurcation should be used in some cases and not others and that it should not be mandatory. Some of the "reform" statutes have made it mandatory. See § 3.11(12) below.

28. Welty v. Heggy, 145 Wis.2d 828, 429 N.W.2d 546 (App.1988) (net worth as of trial on remand rather than original trial date).

Although it seems clear that net rather than gross is the most appropriate measure of worth, it is not so clear whether the jury is to consider net income or net capital. If the defendant operates a business enterprise, emphasis on either form of wealth could be misleading in some cases. Some enterprises might have amassed great amounts of capital and yet have cash flow problems; others might have an enormous income in absolute terms, but that income might reflect a very poor earnings on the capital invested. Courts probably cannot devise a good solution to this problem; financial explanations by the defendant are not likely to be well understood and they run the risk as well that the jury would regard such explanations as admissions that punitive damages should be awarded.[29]

If all forms of evidence about the defendant's financial condition run the risk of serious misevaluation, some forms of financial evidence may be irrelevant as well as prejudicial in particular cases. If the purpose of the punitive award is purely retributive, net worth of the defendant, however prejudicial, is at least relevant to the purpose of inflicting a sting. But if the purpose of the punitive assessment is mainly one of deterrence, the defendant's net worth is at best only remotely relevant to the issue and perhaps not relevant at all.[30] Even net income seems fairly remote to the deterrence issue; the really relevant financial information would be the amount of profit the defendant might expect from continued wrongdoing.[31] If the real purpose of the punitive award is to provide some form of litigation finance, or compensation for the plaintiff's expenditure of attorney fees, financial condition of the defendant seems wholly out of place. In some cases it may be that no form of financial information introduced against a defendant would furnish a useful basis for fixing a punitive award; where a public entity is punitively liable its tax base or current budget would hardly be useful information without a comprehensive review of its entire range of services.[32]

Other uses of profits evidence. Even if net worth rather than income is the relevant inquiry in the ordinary case, profits of the defendant may be significant in some special situations. For one thing, the defendant's profits may be recoverable in themselves as restitution rather than damages.[33] For another, the profit made as a result of the tort itself, as distinct from the defendant's overall profits, may furnish some especially relevant evidence in determining the appropriate size of the extracompensatory award.[34] Indeed,

---

29. See Owen, Problems in Assessing Punitive Damages Against Manufacturers of Defective Products, 49 U.Chi.L.Rev. 1, 19–20 (1982).

30. See Gary Schwartz, Deterrence and Punishment in the Common Law of Punitive Damages: A Comment 56 So.Cal.L.Rev. 133 (1982).

31. See Dobbs, Ending Punishment in "Punitive" Damages: Deterrence–Measured Remedies, 40 Ala.L.Rev. 831 (1989).

32. Punitive damages are usually denied against public entities in the absence of a statute. Where a statute is read to authorize such damages, however, proof of the public entity's financial condition will be a problem, as the dissenters said in Jackson v. Housing Auth. of City of High Point, 316 N.C. 259, 341 S.E.2d 523 (1986). Perhaps a better case could be made for introducing evidence of the public entity's financial condition on behalf of the entity, to show that punitive damages could reduce services or increase taxes.

33. E.g., Zippertubing Co. v. Teleflex Inc., 757 F.2d 1401 (3d Cir.1985) (allowing both recovery of profits as restitution and punitive damages).

34. See Douglass v. Hustler Magazine, Inc., 769 F.2d 1128 (7th Cir.1985), cert. denied, 475 U.S. 1094, 106 S.Ct. 1489, 89 L.Ed.2d 892 (1986). Fischer v. Johns–Manville Corp., 103 N.J. 643, 512 A.2d 466, 486 (1986).

if the reason for imposing punitive liability is to deter conduct that otherwise would be profitable, the relevant evidence would not be net worth but rather the profit potential of the particular conduct.[35]

Surrogates for profits proof. When punitive awards most appropriately seek to deprive the defendant of profits made from a course of tortious conduct, proof of profits may become a difficult task. Proof of the defendant's profits is often undertaken in restitution cases but such proof has often proved difficult or impossible.[36] It has been suggested that when profits-from-the-tort cannot be proven, the punitive award may appropriately be based on the plaintiff's reasonable attorney fees, either as a measure of punitive damages or as an element in computing those damages.[37] Some courts have consciously permitted evidence of attorney fees on the punitive damages issue.[38] Such a measure would automatically place a limit on punitive awards. Although the limit might be very high in some cases where extraordinary legal efforts are required, the very fact that such efforts are reasonably required suggests that in such cases punitive damages based on fees are appropriate. In other cases, where the attorney fee is more moderate, the fee-measure of punitive damages would serve at least as a guideline limiting excessive awards.

Proof of insurance against punitive damages. Liability insurance could be regarded as a form of wealth, at least if it covers the punitive damages award itself. So far, however, the defendant's insurance has not been generally admissible in evidence, the general rule against insurance evidence prevailing over the rule permitting evidence of wealth in punitive damages cases.[39] One court has, however, made a strong statement which seems to suggest that a defendant cannot limit the punitive award by proving poverty if he is in fact insured for punitive damages.[40]

[*For discussion of wealth evidence in cases involving two or more parties, see this section in the Practitioner Treatise edition.*]

Many cases award punitive damages without the slightest regard to profits earned by the tort. See, specifically rejecting the limitation, Tetuan v. A.H. Robins Co., 241 Kan. 441, 738 P.2d 1210 (1987) ("how much Robins managed to profit by its fraud is not the ceiling of its punitive damage liability * * * if such were the case, punitive damages would have no deterrent effect * * *."). Cf. Hawkins v. Allstate Ins. Co., 152 Ariz. 490, 733 P.2d 1073 (1987), cert. denied, 484 U.S. 874, 108 S.Ct. 212, 98 L.Ed.2d 177 (1987) (research reveals no authority that proof of tort generated profit is necessary for award of punitive damages). The amount of profit resulting from the tort is of course the measure of liability for some kinds of restitution, as distinct from both compensatory and from punitive damages.

35. See Dobbs, Ending Punishment in "Punitive" Damages: Deterrence–Measured Remedies, 40 Ala.L.Rev. 831 (1989). Sometimes cases emphasize the need to deter the defendant from carrying on profitable conduct—manufacturing dangerous automobiles, for example—but at the same time justify the puni-

tive award by a consideration of net worth and net income generally. E.g., Grimshaw v. Ford Motor Co., 119 Cal.App.3d 757, 174 Cal. Rptr. 348 (1981). If deterrence of a specific activity is the only point, profit from that activity would seem more relevant, and net worth evidence might be particularly prejudicial. This issue probably is not isolated in the cases because in addition to deterrence there is usually some moral basis for pure punishment as well.

36. See § 4.5(3) below; see also Dobbs, Ending Punishment in "Punitive" Damages: Deterrence–Measured Remedies, 40 Ala. L.Rev. 831 (1989).

38. Afro–American Publishing Co. v. Jaffe, 366 F.2d 649 (D.C.Cir.1966); St. Luke Evangelical Lutheran Church, Inc. v. Smith, 318 Md. 337, 568 A.2d 35 (1990) (also reflecting the view of some courts that the attorney fee measure could not be punitive because it compensates).

40. Garnes v. Fleming Landfill, Inc., 186 W.Va. 656, 413 S.E.2d 897 (1991).

§ 3.11(6) Vicarious Liability for Punitive Damages

The Restatement Complicity Rule

It is ordinarily thought that there is no criminal liability without personal fault and accordingly vicarious criminal liability is based upon conspiracy or ratification which shows participation in the crime by the person charged, or approval of it.[3] To the extent that punitive damages are truly punitive in nature and thus to be assimilated to criminal responsibility, one would expect to find similar limits.

In line with this, the Restatements [4] and a number of courts [5] effectively exclude any pure vicarious liability for punitive damages. Under this rule, the principal may be held if he authorizes, ratifies or participates in the wrongdoing, but not otherwise. In the case of corporate principals, this means that managerial level employees must participate in or ratify the wrongdoing before punitive damages can be awarded.[6] The principal may also be held for punitive damages if it is itself egregiously at fault, as by retaining an employee known to be dangerous; but in this case liability is personal, not vicarious. Florida has adopted a variation under which the principal may be subjected to punitive awards if the employee is guilty of a wilful tort and the employer is guilty of any degree of fault.[7]

The Liberal Rule

The Restatement rule is logical if all punitive damages are really "punitive" and comparable to criminal punishment. As already indicated, however, damages denominated as punitive often seem to have quite different, and possibly non-punitive purposes, deterrence of future wrongs being the most commonly mentioned. It is not surprising, therefore, that many courts impose no special limits on vicarious punitive liability. Under this liberal view, consistent with the non-punitive aspects of "punitive damages," corporations and other principals are liable vicariously for punitive awards whenever they are liable for the underlying compensatory award.[8] The Supreme Court has upheld this approach against challenges on constitutional due process grounds.[9]

Alternatives

The ideal rule may lie somewhere in between. If the defendant has a financial incentive to continue the egregiously wrongful conduct and can pay

---

§ 3.11(6)

4. Restatement Second of Torts § 909 (1979); Restatement Second of Agency § 217C (1958).

6. See Loughry v. Lincoln First Bank, N.A., 67 N.Y.2d 369, 502 N.Y.S.2d 965, 494 N.E.2d 70 (1986) (ordinary bank officer not managerial level); Adams v. Zayre Corp., 148 Ill.App.3d 704, 102 Ill.Dec. 121, 499 N.E.2d 678 (1986) (manager of store's security division was at managerial level as to false imprisonment claim).

A thoughtful suggestion has been made that the employee's status ought to be of less sig-

nificance than the question whether the agent was carrying out corporate policy. See J. Ghiardi & J. Kircher, Punitive Damages § 24.-07. Perhaps courts would agree when the issue is actually raised.

7. Mercury Motors Express, Inc. v. Smith, 393 So.2d 545 (Fla.1981).

8. Alaskan Village, Inc. v. Smalley, 720 P.2d 945 (Alaska 1986) (semble); Stroud v. Denny's Restaurant, Inc., 271 Or. 430, 532 P.2d 790 (1975).

9. Pacific Mut. Life Ins. Co. v. Haslip, __ U.S. __, 111 S.Ct. 1032, 1041, 113 L.Ed.2d 1, 17 (1991).

all compensatory damages, continue its wrongful conduct and still make a profit, deterrence may be thought desirable.[10]　If so, vicarious punitive liability may be a useful means to secure appropriate deterrence.　But in cases where no further wrong is threatened or likely to occur, and where the punitive award would serve mainly to provide a criminal or quasi-criminal sanction,[11] punishment of the innocent principal would be pointless and also unjust.[12]　This suggests that neither of the rules is suitable for all cases.　It may not be feasible to distinguish the punitive from the non-punitive purposes in some cases; nevertheless, it may be that courts should limit vicarious punitive damages when it appears that such damages could only serve to punish the innocent.[13]

Differential in Punitive Awards Between Principal and Agent

When vicarious punitive liability is imposed upon a principal, a question may arise whether the liability is the same as, or might be greater than, that of the employee whose wrong engendered the liability in the first place.[14]　In part the question represents an aspect of the larger one whether, in the case of joint and several liability, punitive damages are joint and several or whether they are several only.[15]　So far as pure punishment goes, it would seem that the innocent employer, if subjected to punitive damages at all, should not be held for any punitive liability greater than that of the employee whose fault provides the basis for that award.[16]　But again, so far as the purpose is to deter the employer from engaging in a profitable but tortious activity, it may well be that the award against the employer should be fixed at a sum sufficient to deter that activity.　This sum might be quite a bit different from the sum necessary to punish the wrongdoing employee.　A little authority supports a differential in the punitive award, though the courts seem not to have worked out the appropriate applications for the idea.[17]　And it should go without saying that when the employer's liability is grounded in its own fault and is not merely vicarious, a differential award is justified on the basis of differences in fault or wealth.[18]

§ 3.11(7)　Punitive Liabilities of Insurers for Wrongs of Insureds

Insurers may be punitively liable for their own torts, as in the case of some bad faith refusals to pay on policies.[1]　Conceivably, insurers might also

---

16. See Wiper v. Downtown Dev. Corp., 152 Ariz. 309, 732 P.2d 200 (1987) (court disapproved jury's award of punitive damages against employer when none were awarded against employee); Kiser v. Neumann Co. Contractors, 426 S.W.2d 935, 937 (Ky.1967) ("By returning a verdict against Brownfield for compensatory damages alone the jury exonerated him of punitive damages. In circumstances under which the liability of the employer is purely derivative, he cannot be held liable while the employee at the same time is found not liable").

17.　Joab, Inc. v. Thrall, 245 So.2d 291 (Fla. App.1971) (zero punitive award against employee, $5,000 against employer approved explicitly, but opinion seemingly does not address the logical or moral problem); Ford Motor Credit Co. v. Johns, 269 So.2d 54 (Fla.App. 1972) (following Joab).

18.　E.g., Ford v. Revlon, Inc., 153 Ariz. 38, 734 P.2d 580 (1987) (reflecting a differential in awards where employer, on notice of supervisor's sexual harassment, did nothing to stop it).　Similarly in jurisdictions allowing vicarious punitive liability only in the case of employer fault, ratification or managerial misconduct.　See Greenfield v. Spectrum Inv. Corp., 174 Cal.App.3d 111, 219 Cal.Rptr. 805 (1985) (employer fault or ratification plus employer's attempted cover-up, employer's punitive liability $400,000, employee's punitive liability $42,500); O'Donnell v. K–Mart Corp., 100 A.D.2d 488, 474 N.Y.S.2d 344 (1984) (punitive damages of $70,000 against employer based on employee battery of obviously retarded customer, no punitive damages against employee).

be liable for punitive damages under uninsured motorist coverages.[2] Are insurers also responsible, under liability policies, for punitive damages assessed against their insureds? One question is whether the policy by its own provisions covers punitive damages, or is construed to do so.[3] If the policy does, the question is whether insurance against punitive awards is against public policy.

The cases are divided on the public policy question.[4] In a leading case, *Northwestern National Casualty Co. v. McNulty*,[5] Judge Wisdom reasoned that punitive damages were meant as a punishment and a deterrence, and that neither punishment nor deterrence could be achieved if the defendant were permitted to shift the punishment to the insurance company. Accordingly, insurance against punitive damages was said to be against public policy and the insurer would not be liable.

Although the *McNulty* view has its following,[6] it also has its detractors, and a number of courts have expressly rejected it in favor of a rule that holds insurers responsible for the punitive liabilities of their insureds, at least where that liability is based upon wanton misconduct rather than intended harm, and when the policy is construed to cover punitive damages in the first place.[7] Insurance policies may exclude not only punitive damages coverage but any coverage at all for some of the acts that lead to punitive damages—intentional torts, for example. Policy coverage may thus limit the insurer's liability even if the law does not do so.[8]

Perhaps the *McNulty* rule should apply to some but not all punitive damages awards. If punitive damages are awarded solely on a just deserts basis, insurance against those damages might allow a truly wicked defendant to wreak harm without punishment. If punitive damages are awarded as a deterrent remedy against an enterprise, however, coverage for punitive damages is not necessarily a bad idea. Premium costs would be insignificant to a one-time actor; but to enterprises engaged in repeated conduct, the

§ 3.11(7)

4. See J. Morrison, The Insurability of Punitive Damages (2d ed. 1986) (jurisdiction by jurisdiction survey).

5. 307 F.2d 432 (5th Cir.1962).

6. E.g., American Sur. Co. of N.Y. v. Gold, 375 F.2d 523, 20 A.L.R.3d 335 (10th Cir.1966); Beaver v. Country Mut. Ins. Co., 95 Ill.App.3d 1122, 51 Ill.Dec. 500, 420 N.E.2d 1058, 1061 (1981); In re Guardianship of Smith, 211 Kan. 397, 507 P.2d 189 (1973); Variety Farms, Inc. v. New Jersey Manufacturers Ins. Co., 172 N.J.Super. 10, 410 A.2d 696 (1980); Home Ins. Co. v. American Home Products Corp., 75 N.Y.2d 196, 551 N.Y.S.2d 481, 550 N.E.2d 930 (1990); Aetna Casualty & Sur. Co. v. Craig, 771 P.2d 212 (Okl.1989) (uninsured motorist insurance cannot be permitted to cover tortfeasor's punitive liabilities). See Allen v. Simmons, 533 A.2d 541, 544 (R.I.1987); Annot., 20 A.L.R.3d 343 (1968).

7. Whalen v. On–Deck, Inc., 514 A.2d 1072, 1074 (Del.1986) ("A wrongdoer who is insured against punitive damages may still be punished through higher insurance premiums or the loss of insurance altogether" and right of

parties to contract counts in favor of liability, too); First Bank (N.A.)–Billings v. Transamerica Ins. Co., 209 Mont. 93, 679 P.2d 1217, 1222 (1984) (at least in recklessness cases; insurers are more than capable of writing limited coverage if they wish); Harrell v. Travelers Indem. Co., 279 Or. 199, 567 P.2d 1013 (1977); Lazenby v. Universal Underwriters Ins. Co., 214 Tenn. 639, 383 S.W.2d 1 (1964) (a leading case); Hensley v. Erie Ins. Co., 168 W.Va. 172, 283 S.E.2d 227 (1981) (costs of insurance some deterrent, punishment not sole use of punitive damages, additional compensation for egregious conduct is part of the reason for the award); Sinclair Oil Corp. v. Columbia Casualty Co., 682 P.2d 975 (Wyo.1984) (not against public policy at least where punitive liability is based on wanton misconduct).

8. Hensley v. Erie Ins. Co., 168 W.Va. 172, 283 S.E.2d 227 (1981); Gleason v. Fryer, 30 Colo.App. 106, 491 P.2d 85 (1971) (liability insurer not liable for punitive damages due to intentional tort).

premium costs eventually factor in all the costs of the damages they must pay in tort judgments. So, indirectly, the punitive damage charge will have its effect even if it is covered by insurance.[9]

In either event, the insured may in good faith wish to insure against punitive damages, not so that he will be free to carry out evil deeds without punishment, but so that he will be able to carry out honest work without a ruinous liability erroneously imposed. The most obvious case for insurance against punitive liability is that of the employer whose liability is wholly vicarious and who is not even tacitly encouraging the employee's wrongdoing.[10] If such a potential defendant cannot insure against punitive liability, he may be held liable for a tort he did not commit and punished for a state of mind he never had. This same argument applies to the individual who might be held for punitive damages on a jury's error of judgment that his momentary lapse was a matter of reckless driving.[11]

These observations suggest that a *McNulty* rule might be right for some cases, not for others, and that to a large extent insurance policy coverage limits will approximate public policy limits.

§ 3.11(8) Multiple Punitive Liability

In some instances, a single wrongful act can cause injury to several persons at once or even to a very large number of people. Airline crashes and defectively designed products are examples. Such cases raise the question whether a defendant can be punitively charged more than once—perhaps in hundreds of cases. If the first verdict for punitive damages in an airline crash represents the appropriate level of punishment, it may be seriously unfair to inflict additional punishments in all subsequent cases. Besides the unfairness, such awards may destroy a valuable business and may exhaust its assets so that later victims of the same tort can collect nothing at all.

In a leading decision of 1967, the late Judge Friendly showed considerable sympathy with some of the arguments against multiple punitive damages.[1] With few exceptions,[2] other decisions in print at this writing have tended to discount them.[3]

Defendants have presented a long series of arguments against multiple punitive awards. They have said that subjecting the defendant to multiple

9. Cf. Galligan, Augmented Awards: The Efficient Evolution of Punitive Damages, 51 La.L.Rev. 3, 59–62 (1990) (also discussing possible differences in insurance pools).

§ 3.11(8)
1. Roginsky v. Richardson–Merrell, Inc., 378 F.2d 832 (2d Cir.1967) (but denial of punitive damages based on other grounds).

2. Juzwin v. Amtorg Trading Corp., 705 F.Supp. 1053 (D.N.J.1989) (multiple punitive damages held unconstitutional), order vacated, 718 F.Supp. 1233 (1989) (multiple punitive damages unconstitutional but no appropriate, practical remedy is available without nationwide uniformity).

3. Wammock v. Celotex Corp., 835 F.2d 818 (11th Cir.1988) (Georgia law before enact-

ment of 1987 statute); Awarding or approving punitive damages in multiple injury cases are, e.g.: Jackson v. Johns–Manville Sales Corp., 781 F.2d 394 (5th Cir.1986), cert. denied, 478 U.S. 1022, 106 S.Ct. 3339, 92 L.Ed.2d 743 (1986). Cathey v. Johns–Manville Sales Corp., 776 F.2d 1565 (6th Cir.1985), cert. denied, 478 U.S. 1021, 106 S.Ct. 3335, 92 L.Ed.2d 740 (1986). Moran v. Johns–Manville Sales Corp., 691 F.2d 811 (6th Cir.1982); Hanlon v. Johns–Manville Sales Corp., 599 F.Supp. 376 (N.D.Iowa 1984); Grimshaw v. Ford Motor Co., 119 Cal.App.3d 757, 174 Cal.Rptr. 348 (1981); Palmer v. A.H. Robins Co., Inc., 684 P.2d 187 (Colo.1984); Fischer v. Johns–Manville Corp., 103 N.J. 643, 512 A.2d 466 (1986).

punishments is unfair or unconstitutional in some respect, that innocent shareholders will be punished unfairly, that multiple punishments may destroy a valuable ongoing business, and that multiplication of punitive judgments may inflict liabilities far in excess of any sum needed to deter the defendant.

All of these arguments have been rejected in most of the courts that have considered them. Constitutional arguments have usually been dismissed on the ground that punitive damages do not come under double jeopardy or excessive fines clauses, which have been deemed to affect criminal cases only,[4] and that due process does not require protection either.[5] As to the innocent shareholder, he has bought into a corporate form of doing business and must take the sour with the sweet.[6] Although punitive liabilities might destroy a valuable business, courts have brushed aside this danger on the ground that it hasn't happened yet.[7] The possibility that multiple judgments for punitive damages will exceed anything necessary to deter the defendant has not often troubled the courts, partly because the defendant's excessive liabilities may operate to deter others.[8]

Up until 1989, the cases showed very little concern over the possibility that multiple punishments might be unfair and unjust, or that excessive punitive liabilities might really deter defendants from carrying on activities that are useful to society.[9] In 1989, a decision of a United States District Court held that the due process clause "places a limit on the number of times and the extent to which a defendant may be subjected to punishment for a single course of conduct." [10] On reconsideration, however, the court held that in spite of the unconstitutional deprivation worked by multiple punitive damages, it could not deny a recovery because it could not fairly provide access to litigation for all plaintiffs, past and potential.[11]

Multiple awards of punitive damages can create a problem for plaintiffs as well as defendants. Later plaintiffs may be deprived of all compensation if earlier plaintiffs are allowed to recover a series of punitive awards which exhaust the defendant's assets or insurance coverage.[12] The prospect here is

---

5. Grimshaw v. Ford Motor Co., 119 Cal. App.3d 757, 174 Cal.Rptr. 348, 383–384 (1981). The *Grimshaw* court reasoned that if due process objection to multiple damages were applied, "punitive damages could never be assessed against a manufacturer of a mass produced article," and also that the issue could be raised when a second punitive award was sought. *Grimshaw* was, however, in fact a case of multiple or continuing torts by the defendant, who could and should have withdrawn or modified the dangerous vehicle at any time. Due process arguments might be more plausible when urged by defendants who acted only once (as in a single airplane crash) but caused many injuries. Since the first bloom of these multiple punitive award cases, the Supreme Court has acknowledged that some kind of due process review of punitive damages is in order and that may serve to raise the issue again. See § 3.11(12) below.

6. Tetuan v. A.H. Robins Co., 241 Kan. 441, 738 P.2d 1210 (1987); Fischer v. Johns–

Manville Corp., 103 N.J. 643, 512 A.2d 466 (1986).

9. Commentators and legislatures have expressed more concern for these points, especially for the possibility that useful drugs might not be marketed because of the risk not only of compensatory liabilities but also punitive liabilities. See, e.g., Kuhlik and Kingham, The Adverse Effects of Standardless Punitive Damages Awards on Pharmaceutical Development and Availability, 45 Food Drug & Cosm. L.J. 693 (1990). There are data supporting this view, but sometimes it is hard to separate data from industry viewpoint.

10. Juzwin v. Amtorg Trading Corp., 705 F.Supp. 1053, 1064 (D.N.J.1989).

11. Juzwin v. Amtorg Trading Corp., 718 F.Supp. 1233 (D.N.J.1989).

12. See, recognizing this problem, American College of Trial Lawyers, Report on Punitive Damages of the Committee on Special Problems in the Administration of Justice 10 (1989) (Roger C. Henderson, Reporter).

that early plaintiffs may recover windfalls far in excess of compensation and that in doing so they may deprive later plaintiffs of any recovery whatever. Courts have displayed more sympathy for this problem than for the defendants' problems with multiple awards, but their practical response is the same.

With a brief-lived exception of a federal district court in New Jersey,[13] the courts have been unwilling so far to limit punitive awards to the first comer,[14] and have not thought it worthwhile to create a punitive damages escrow in which the punitive awards can be held until compensation for all victims is assured.[15] They have instead suggested increased judicial scrutiny for punitive awards [16] and have sometimes made the defendant an offer it probably could not accept—that the defendant could prove to the jury that other juries have already levied punitive awards against it.[17] Even in a bifurcated trial, with punitive issues tried only after a determination on the merits,[18] many defendants would undoubtedly feel that such proof would only enhance the jury's hostility.[19]

The courts have also suggested that class actions or consolidation of actions could be used as a device to force a single, classwide, punitive judgment, but again, have believed themselves unable to initiate any reforms along these lines.[20]

Although the courts may at times seem rather casual in their willingness to inflict repeated punishments for a single act, not all the cases that have raised these issues are in fact single act cases. Perhaps the most important cases so far are those in which a manufacturer knows of a product danger and deliberately conceals it or refuses to disclose it. The nondisclosure can be seen as a repeated act, deliberately taken to inflict a serious risk upon consumers or employees.[21] Every moment's nondisclosure creates a new and further risk. Most of the cases have been of this sort. In such cases, the arguments that multiple awards are unfair lose most of their logic. But this point has been blurred because courts and interest groups have repeatedly treated the defendant's repeated refusal to disclose as a single "course of conduct," [22] a phrase that makes it appear that there has been only one wrongdoing when in fact there are many wrongs.

But in other cases, the defendant's fault, though necessarily egregious if it is to engender a punitive award at all, is nevertheless fault confined to a single occasion. A bad product design of which the defendant is unaware or reckless maintenance of an airplane which causes a single crash but injures many people, might be like this.[23] In these cases, the unfairness of multiple punitive damage liabilities deserves more serious concern.

The mass tort problem cannot be concluded without a recognition that punitive damages may be upheld in some cases for reasons quite different from those most commonly mentioned. The multiple punitive awards have mostly been upheld in cases that require plaintiffs to expend enormous resources for litigation and that might not be financially feasible to litigate at all unless a punitive award were available to help pay for the efforts. The

21. See Tetuan v. A.H. Robins Co., 241 Kan. 441, 738 P.2d 1210 (1987). In such cases the defendant knows but does not reveal that its product—asbestos or the Dalkon Shield for examples—is dangerous and that the danger can be avoided if it will but give warning, which it then refuses to do.

effect is that the egregiously wrongful defendant may be compelled to pay for the costs of litigation against itself. If this, rather than pure punishment is the real goal of "punitive" damages, multiple awards may be more justified than they initially appear. If so, however, the potential for depleting assets that ought to be used to pay compensation to other victims cannot readily be ignored.

Most state legislation, proposed and enacted, has so far failed to recognize the complexities of the problem of multiple punitive awards. Caps on punitive damages may require the courts to impose awards that will not deter serious wrongdoing in the future.[24] A first comer rule limiting punitive liability to the plaintiff who first recovers a punitive award[25] may create its own inequities and in any event should have no application at all to cases in which the defendant commits more than one act or omission worthy of punishment. The Missouri statute which credits the defendant with prior payments of punitive damages[26] may be better than a first-comer rule, but its fairness may depend in large measure on whether a large or a small punitive damages verdict comes in first. From the plaintiffs' point of view, such statutes encourage a race to trial; from the defendants', they may not be helpful, since in the nature of the federal system they cannot limit liabilities beyond the borders of the state.[27]

The proposal for national legislation to permit punitive damages class actions at the insistence of a defendant[28] might minimize the present risks of unfair treatment of defendants. However, it is complex, adds legal work, and may discourage many just claims.[29] Another system for bringing all punitive damages claims together might include multi-district litigation procedures, with a kind of consolidation of all punitive claims.[30]

A third approach would be to expand federal interpleader[31] to permit injunction against enforcement of individual punitive damages judgments until they could all be consolidated for a single administration in the interpleader court. This would have the least intrusive effect, because the tort case would be tried in the court where it would normally be tried; and collection of the compensatory damages judgment would not be held up while a punitive fund is administered. Likewise, the plaintiff would not find

---

24. E.g., West's Colo.Rev.Stat.Ann. § 13–21–102 ("the amount of such reasonable exemplary damages shall not exceed an amount which is equal to the amount of the actual damages award to the injured party"; even this is subject to further reduction by the judge; the amount may be increased up to three-times actual damages in cases of continued misbehavior, or wanton misconduct while the action was pending); West's Fla.Stat.Ann. § 768.73(1) (three times the amount of compensatory damages awarded); Official Code Ga.Ann. § 51–12–5.1(g) (some torts, cap of $250,000); 23 Okl.Stat.Ann. § 9 (exemplary damages not to exceed actual damages awarded unless there is clear and convincing evidence of the misconduct that justifies punitive award).

25. Official Code Ga.Ann. § 51–12–5.1(e)(1). That section provides: "In a tort case in

which the cause of action arises from product liability, there shall be no limitation regarding the amount which may be awarded as punitive damages. Only one award of punitive damages may be recovered in a court in this state from a defendant for any act or omission if the cause of action arises from product liability, regardless of the number of causes of action which may arise from such act or omission."

26. V.A.M.S. § 510.263.

27. There is an excellent and succinct discussion of the limits of state law solutions in American College of Trial Lawyers, Report on Punitive Damages of the Committee on Special Problems in the Administration of Justice 21 (1989) (Roger C. Henderson, Reporter).

31. See § 2.9(4) above on interpleader.

herself in the hands of a committee of class-action lawyers she does not know and did not hire. Yet such a procedure is even less familiar than class-action procedure and might well be rejected for that reason.[32] A narrower change in legal process that has found some legislative support is a bifurcation or even trifurcation of trials, to separate the liability and damages issues from the punitive proof.[33]

Whether a just solution can be worked out in legislation or otherwise remains to be seen, but it seems safe to say that none of the solutions so far provided by either courts or legislatures seems satisfactory.

§ 3.11(9) Scope of Punitive Liability: Causation and Persons and Injuries Outside the Risk

[*For the text of this section, see the unabridged Practitioner Treatise edition.*]

§ 3.11(10) The Actual Damages Requirement

The Rule

Many cases have said, in one form or another, that punitive damages may not be recovered unless the plaintiff first shows actual loss or damages.[1] Other courts have rejected the rule in this bald form and have required only that the plaintiff show a breach of legal duty by the defendant.[2] Other courts have not yet adopted the rule and may not do so.[3] Sometimes the rule is discarded selectively, for one particular category of case, as when a court permits punitive damages in defamation cases without proof of any actual harm to reputation.[4]

Interpretations of the Rule

The ambiguity of the supposed rule has generated a lot of litigation. To some judges it has meant that the malicious defendant is immune from punitive liabilities unless the plaintiff proves and the jury actually awards pecuniary damages.[5] To other judges it has meant only that the plaintiff must show and the jury must make an award for some kind of loss, not necessarily a proven pecuniary loss [6] or one that could be included in a final judgment.[7] To others the actual damages requirement has meant that an award of nominal damages would suffice to support a punitive award,[8] though as to this there are opposing views.[9] To still others the rule is satisfied if the case is one in which actual damages may be presumed, or in which actual damage need not be shown to establish a cause of action.[10] Finally, to some judges the actual damages requirement only means that the

---

§ 3.11(10)

1. Oliver v. Raymark Indus., Inc., 799 F.2d 95 (3d Cir.1986); Olivetti Corp. v. Ames Business Sys., Inc., 319 N.C. 534, 356 S.E.2d 578 (1987); Shimola v. Nationwide Ins. Co., 25 Ohio St.3d 84, 495 N.E.2d 391 (1986). See Annot., 40 A.L.R.4th 11 (1985).

2. Ault v. Lohr, 538 So.2d 454 (Fla.1989). Wells v. Smith, 171 W.Va. 97, 297 S.E.2d 872 (1982) also supports this position, seems to

have been overruled. See the discussion of that point in n. 11 below.

4. Loftsgaarden v. Reiling, 267 Minn. 181, 126 N.W.2d 154 (1964), cert. denied, 379 U.S. 845, 85 S.Ct. 31, 13 L.Ed.2d 50 (1964) (when libel is per se, punitive damages can be recovered even though no actual damages exist). Punitive damages in defamation cases are to some extent now controlled by federal constitutional law. See § 7.2(4) below.

plaintiff must have proved some harm, even though the jury itself has made no award of compensatory damages of any kind, "actual" or otherwise.[11]

Criticisms of the Rule

The absence of recoverable compensatory damages—actual, presumed or otherwise—does not seem to have much bearing on the propriety of a punitive award,[12] except possibly to indicate that a punitive award may be needed as a deterrent because compensatory damages cannot perform that function. It is sometimes suggested that the rule finds a basis in the related notion that punitive damages should be limited to a sum bearing a reasonable ratio to compensatory damages; but this rule of commensurability or proportion is itself a doubtful rule [13] and at most is only one factor to be considered in determining whether punitive damages are excessive.[14] For these reasons, the proportion rule could not logically forbid all awards of punitive damages merely because compensatory damages are denied. No other reasons are readily apparent for it.[15]

Reinterpreting the Rule

The most reasonable interpretation of the supposed actual damages requirement is that it is really a defective formulation of an entirely different idea—that the plaintiff must establish a cause of action before punitive damages can be awarded.[16] Actual damages are required to establish a cause of action in the most common kinds of tort claims—those grounded in negligence—so it is quite understandable that a court might speak of an actual damages requirement as a kind of shorthand for the idea that punitives could not be awarded unless a claim were first established. Once the facts accepted by the trier show a valid cause of action, however, there seems no reason to deny punitive damages merely because the plaintiff's damages are not pecuniary, or because the jury awards nominal damages, or because it lumps all damages under the punitive label.[17] In-

11. Harris v. American General Life Ins. Co. of Delaware, 202 Mont. 393, 658 P.2d 1089, 40 A.L.R.4th 1 (1983); Wells v. Smith, 171 W.Va. 97, 297 S.E.2d 872 (1982), overruled in part, Garnes v. Fleming Landfill, Inc., 186 W.Va. 656, 413 S.E.2d 897 (1991).

The *Fleming Landfill* case states explicitly that *Wells* is overruled "to the extent that it stands for the proposition that a jury may return an award for punitive damages without finding any compensatory damages" and places this ruling on due process grounds. However, the rationale of *Fleming Landfill* does not suggest that overruling is required or appropriate. The court there also emphasized that "Punitive damages should bear a reasonable relationship to the *potential* of harm caused by the defendant's actions and that *generally* means that punitive damages must bear a reasonable relationship to actual damages because compensatory damages provide a reasonable measure of likely harm. However * * * where the actual harm was minimal but the potential harm was tremendous, a jury may reasonably find punitive damages com-

mensurate with the *potential* harm." This reasoning is consistent with the view that at least in some cases, punitive damages could be justified even when no compensatory award was made.

Some cases are difficult to interpret. Hawkins v. Hawkins, 101 N.C.App. 529, 400 S.E.2d 472 (1991), may mean that the existence of actual harm is sufficient, whether or not the jury awards damages, but the case might also mean that no actual harm need be proven when compensatory damages are presumed, as in cases of battery and some other "intentional torts." Cf. Equitable Life Leasing Corp. v. Abbick, 243 Kan. 513, 757 P.2d 304 (1988) (recovery of actual damages on a contract count justifies an award of punitive damages on a fraud count for which no actual damages are awarded).

16. See Ault v. Lohr, 538 So.2d 454, 456 (Fla.1989); Restatement Second of Torts § 908, comment c (1979).

17. An award the jury thinks of as punitive might be regarded by lawyers as compen-

deed, if the defendant's conduct otherwise warrants punitive liability, the need for punishment or deterrence may be increased by reason of the very fact that the defendant will have no liability for compensatory damages. If there is a need to limit punitive awards, then, the actual damages requirement is not a very good—or very effective—way to do so.

Case Development

The cases seem to be working toward an interpretation of this sort. Some of them have explicitly said that the actual damage requirement means only that the plaintiff must prove all the elements of a cause of action for damages.[18] Others support the idea by holding that presumed damages or nominal damages will suffice to support a punitive award. Whether movement in this direction will continue is uncertain, however, because of a renewed judicial interest in the claim that due process requires intensified judicial review of various factors affecting punitive awards, including the relationship of the punitive award to the compensatory award.[19]

§ 3.11(11) The Ratio Rule

Relationship of Punitive to Compensatory Damages

Courts have often said that any punitive award must be limited so that it bears some reasonable relationship to the amount of compensatory damages awarded.[1] This is the strict version of the ratio rule. The supposed rule has never been more than a very general idea, and no precise ratio is ever required.[2] In 1991 the United States Supreme Court upheld a punitive award that was 200 times the plaintiff's actual pecuniary loss.[3] As this holding suggests, the "rule" is now usually reduced to a guideline or discounted altogether.[4]

In the later 1980s, however, defendants began to argue that the excessive fines clauses of state or federal constitutions required some proportionality between actual and punitive damages as well as between wrongdoing and punitive damages.[5] Such arguments, and the companion arguments that unlimited punitive damages infringe due process, may breathe new life into the ratio rule.[6] The constitutional arguments are discussed in the next subsection.

---

satory, as where the plaintiff suffers intangible harms to reputation, privacy or emotional tranquility. If the jury makes such an award but calls it punitive, it might be upheld on this ground. See Clark v. McClurg, 215 Cal. 279, 9 P.2d 505, 81 A.L.R. 908 (1932).

§ 3.11(11)

1. See Palmer v. Ted Stevens Honda, Inc., 193 Cal.App.3d 530, 238 Cal.Rptr. 363 (1987); Nabours v. Longview Sav. & Loan Ass'n, 700 S.W.2d 901 (Tex.1985). Contemporary statements are frequently accompanied by mitigating statements that the ratio is only one factor to be considered.

2. Alaska Ins. Co. v. Movin' On Const., Inc., 718 P.2d 472 (Alaska 1986). In an earlier decision, the Alaska Court thought that, in determining whether the punitive award was either the result of passion and prejudice or was excessive, a comparison of the punitive amount with the compensatory amount was "better than nothing," see Sturm, Ruger & Co., Inc. v. Day, 594 P.2d 38 (Alaska 1979), cert. denied, 454 U.S. 894, 102 S.Ct. 391, 70 L.Ed.2d 209 (1981) but on rehearing modified its views somewhat: "We still believe that a comparison of actual damages with the punitive damages is a factor which may enter into the determination of excessiveness. However, there may be cases in which it is of only slight value or is totally inapplicable." Sturm, Ruger & Co., Inc. v. Day, 615 P.2d 621, 624 (Alaska 1980).

3. Pacific Mut. Life Ins. Co. v. Haslip, ___ U.S. ___, ___, 111 S.Ct. 1032, 1043, 113 L.Ed.2d 1 (1991).

Relationship of Punitive Damages to Potential Harm From Defendant's Conduct

A rule that is very different from the ratio rule states that the punitive award should bear some reasonable ratio or proportion to the harm threatened, risked, or potential from the defendant's misconduct. Although courts sometimes lump this rule together with the ratio rule, its effect is entirely different. Proportioning the punitive award to the risk or harm potential of the defendant's conduct is the same as proportioning it to the seriousness of the defendant's wrong. The seriousness of the defendant's wrongdoing is undoubtedly a proper factor for consideration in making a punitive award, but it is not the same as the strict ratio rule, which treats the damages awarded rather than the harm threatened as an index of the defendant's moral fault. When the issue has come to the fore, courts have recognized that the two "proportion" rules are not at all alike.[7]

Criticisms

Even as a guideline or a "factor" to be considered along with others, the ratio rule has little to recommend it. It is in direct conflict with the punitive purpose of the award, which requires that the award to be proportioned to the defendant's evil attitude and serious misconduct;[8] and it is equally in conflict with the deterrent purposes of the award, which requires that it be proportioned to the incentives for further wrongdoing.[9] It is likewise in direct conflict with the rule that proportions the award to the defendant's financial condition. As in the case of the actual damage requirement, the ratio rule may in fact minimize punitive damages in the very case

7. See Hosp. Auth. of Gwinnett County v. Jones, 261 Ga. 613, 409 S.E.2d 501 (1991) ("While comparison to the actual damages may be appropriate in one case, * * * it may not in another. We think Jones is one of the latter cases. The actual harm to O'Kelley was slight, but the potential harm to patients in other circumstances supports the punitive damages award here"). The best discussion is in Morris, Punitive Damages in Tort Cases, 44 Harv.L.Rev. 1173, 1181 (1931).

In Garnes v. Fleming Landfill, Inc., 186 W.Va. 656, 413 S.E.2d 897 (1991) the court recognized the distinction as follows: "Punitive damages should bear a reasonable relationship to the potential of harm caused by the defendant's actions and that generally means that punitive damages must bear a reasonable relationship to actual damages because compensatory damages provide a reasonable measure of likely harm. However * * * where the actual harm was minimal but the potential harm was tremendous, a jury may reasonably find punitive damages commensurate with the potential harm." Later in the opinion, however, the court held an award of compensatory damages was a prerequisite to the award of punitive damages.

8. See Morris, Punitive Damages in Tort Cases, 44 Harv.L.Rev. 1173, 1181 (1931) (in-

stancing a hunter who fires into a crowd of people but only breaks a ten-dollar pair of glasses; the admonition of punishment clearly should exceed the $10 figure or any likely multiple of that figure). Thus in State ex rel. Stephan v. GAF Corp., 242 Kan. 152, 747 P.2d 1326, 1334 (1987) the court upheld a $1 million punitive award where actual damage was $100,000 because the defendant "knowingly and wilfully led people—the State in this case—into building expensive roofs which were not durable, not watertight, and not satisfactory * * *." Seriousness of the misconduct may be expressed at least in part in terms of the misconduct's *potential* for harm, regardless of the actual harm caused. See Garnes v. Fleming Landfill, Inc., 186 W.Va. 656, 413 S.E.2d 897 (1991).

9. As to profits see Douglass v. Hustler Magazine, Inc, 769 F.2d 1128 (7th Cir.1985), cert. denied, 475 U.S. 1094, 106 S.Ct. 1489, 89 L.Ed.2d 892 (1986); Hawkins v. Allstate Ins. Co., 152 Ariz. 490, 733 P.2d 1073 (1987), cert. denied, Allstate Ins. Co. v. Hawkins, 484 U.S. 874, 108 S.Ct. 212, 98 L.Ed.2d 177 (1987); Tetuan v. A.H. Robins Co., 241 Kan. 441, 738 P.2d 1210 (1987). Some statutes also recognize profitability of the misconduct as a factor. See, e.g., N.J.Stat.Ann. 2A:58C–5d(2). On the defendant's financial condition generally, see § 3.11(5) above.

in which they would best serve their purpose.[10]

The Ratio Rule and Judicial Review

At best, the ratio guideline serves to prop up appellate review of excessive awards,[11] but for that purpose it is not needed at all, since such review in some form is always appropriate, ratio or no ratio.[12] Remission or reduction of punitive awards appears to be quite common,[13] and such reductions are often approved by appellate courts without reference to the ratio rule at all.[14]

Awards that cannot be verified or even estimated by reference to pecuniary loss run large risks of unfairness and inaccuracy, so punitive damages awards do in fact present a threat. If, in addition to punitive awards, a jury grants other unverifiable damages, such as pain and suffering damages or awards for invasion of privacy or mental distress, the total amount of the recovery that cannot be subjected to rational analysis and review may become very large. This presents a genuine concern and one that may on occasion call for judicial intervention by way of a remission of the punitive or other portions of the award; but it is not a concern about ratios.[15]

The Ratio Rule and Jury Instructions

Some courts have also insisted that the jury be instructed on the ratio rule, reversing awards when no instruction on it has been given.[16] As a means of guiding the jury, the ratio rule might at first glance seem to be useful or at worst harmless. Better guidance in instructions is a good idea.[17] But the ratio rule is inconsistent with all of the purposes of punitive damages, so the jury told to punish serious wrongdoing, to deter the defendant's propensity for future harm, and also to confine the award to some multiple of fortuitous actual damages might not find much guidance.

If the jury, uninstructed on the ratio rule returns a shockingly large verdict, a reduction or elimination of the punitive damages might be a better solution. If the verdict is not shockingly large, to require a new trial merely to allow another jury to hear an instruction inconsistent with the purposes of punitive damages piles irrationality and expense upon a bedrock of unreason.

§ 3.11(12) Constitutional and Statutory Challenges to Punitive Damages

Constitutional Attacks on Punitive Damages

Double jeopardy. Because punitive damages might be levied for purposes similar to those behind criminal punishment, and because the acts that subject the defendant to civil punishment may be the same as those that subject him to criminal punishment, defendants have sometimes claimed

---

10. See § 3.11(10); Mallor & Roberts, Punitive Damages: Toward a Principled Approach, 31 Hastings L.Rev. 639 (1980); Morris, Punitive Damages in Tort Cases, 44 Harv. L.Rev. 1173, 1181 (1931).

15. See Chandler v. Denton, 741 P.2d 855 (Okl.1987).

16. See Levinson v. Prentice–Hall, Inc., 868 F.2d 558 (3d Cir.1989) (large punitive award for handicap discrimination under New Jersey law).

that the infliction of punitive damages amounts to a constitutionally forbidden double jeopardy. At most, the argument seems plausible when the defendant has already been criminally prosecuted. (Or, if the argument is raised as a defense to the criminal prosecution, it seems plausible when the defendant has already been sued for punitive damages.)

State courts have almost always rejected the double jeopardy argument.[1] Sometimes they have done so on the ground that no prior criminal punishment had been sought. At other times they have said that the award of punitive damages to the aggrieved plaintiff distinguishes the two types of "punishment."[2] Indiana once purported to hold that punitive damages were not recoverable if the defendant was subject to criminal prosecution for the act on which punitive recovery would be based; but exceptions ate away at the rule,[3] and a statute now appears to authorize punitive damages even for criminal acts.[4]

It has been argued that punitive damages should not be awarded where the criminal law is adequately fulfilling its function.[5] If punitive damages are truly imposed as retribution and measured by the defendant's just deserts, the argument seems to be a very strong one indeed. However, courts have always recognized that the punitive damages award, which may not be well-named, performs several other functions that are not based on retributive justice at all. "Punitive" damages are sometimes not intended to inflict justly deserved suffering, but to provide deterrence by removing the defendant's profits[6] or to prevent the defendant from externalizing the costs of its enterprise.[7] Somewhat differently, they are sometimes invoked as a means to providing sufficient attorney fee financing for appropriate (and successful) contingent-fee suits.[8] In these instances the double jeopardy argument is no more relevant than it would be to a compensatory damages recovery or an award of attorney fees to the prevailing party.

Although at first glance one might expect that if the legislature has prescribed a criminal penalty for a given act, courts would not add to that penalty by prescribing a greater civil penalty. However, the difference between crime and tort functions has been persuasive even on this point. Courts have actually said that the legislature's limited penalty was an

§ 3.11(12)

1. See Generally, J. Ghiardi & J. Kircher, Punitive Damages Law and Practice § 3.02 (1985 & Supps.); see also Annotation, Assault: criminal liability as barring or mitigating recovery of punitive damages, 98 A.L.R.3d 870 (1979).

2. Wittman v. Gilson, 70 N.Y.2d 970, 972, 525 N.Y.S.2d 795, 796, 520 N.E.2d 514, 515 (1988) (convicted defendant still subject to punitive damages notwithstanding the double jeopardy argument because the sanction is not imposed "on behalf of all the people" but instead provides the "injured party a personal monetary recovery over and above compensatory loss"; punitive damages differs, too, as to the stigma attached).

3. See Nicholson's Mobile Home Sales, Inc. v. Schramm, 164 Ind.App. 598, 330 N.E.2d 785, 791 (Ind.App.1975) (rule does not forbid punitive damages for heedless disregard of consequences, if the statute of limitations has run on the criminal offense, or if the defendant is a corporation).

4. See Gosnell v. Indiana Soft Water Serv., Inc., 503 N.E.2d 879 (Ind.1987).

5. Mallor and Roberts, Punitive Damages: Toward a Principled Approach, 31 Hast.L.J. 639, 658 (1980).

6. Dobbs, Ending Punishment in "Punitive" Damages: Deterrence–Measured Remedies, 40 Ala.L.Rev. 831 (1989); § 3.11(3) above.

7. Galligan, Augmented Awards: The Efficient Evolution of Punitive Damages, 51 La. L.Rev. 3 (1990); § 3.11(3) above.

8. See § 3.11(3) above.

affirmative reason that justified the court in adding a greater penalty by way of punitive damages.[9]

Excessive Fines under the Eighth Amendment. Defendants have argued repeatedly in recent years that large punitive damages awards violate the Eighth Amendment's prohibition against excessive fines.[10] The Supreme Court has now flatly held that the Eighth Amendment has no application to punitive damages in civil actions between private parties.[11] This decision, however, merely opens the way for considering whether due process or other limitations apply.

Due Process. In 1991, the Supreme Court decided *Pacific Mutual Life Ins. Co. v. Haslip,*[12] to determine whether punitive damages would violate due process if the damages were assessed by the "common law method" in which juries are simply invited to exercise their judgment as to an appropriate amount in light of the enormity of the wrong. On this point the Court was convinced by two hundred years of history that the punitive award so casually invoked was not in itself a constitutional violation. Nevertheless, quoting Professor David Owen's observation,[13] the Court recognized that "punitive damages are a powerful remedy which itself may be abused, causing serious damage to public and private interests and moral values." [14] The Court then made it clear that although punitive damages would not be outlawed, particular awards might transgress Constitutional boundaries.

Due process and jury guidance. The *Haslip* Court thought due process required that the award be reasonable in amount. It also thought that the court was obliged to give the jury adequate guidance in the instructions. Guidance was thought to be sufficient in the *Haslip* case because the trial judge's instructions had told the jury that the purposes were retribution and deterrence and explained that the award was not compulsory. That does not seem like much guidance,[15] but perhaps it gives the jury no greater discretion than it did in awarding other non-pecuniary, unverifiable damages, such as those rendered for mental anguish.[16] Presumably, however, a more meaningful instruction would be permissible and even desirable; in the absence of strong post-trial review of the award, a more meaningful instruction might be required.[17]

Due process and post-trial review. The Court in *Haslip* also emphasized that post-trial review of punitive awards, in the trial court and on appeal, could provide an additional check on the jury's discretion, especially in the factors that could be considered by the reviewing court. These factors named by the Court included one version of the ratio rule,[18] the reprehensibility of the defendant's conduct, its profitability, the defendant's financial position, litigation costs, and the aggregate of all other civil and criminal

10. See Massey, The Excessive Fines Clause and Punitive Damages: Some Lessons from History, 40 Vand.L.Rev. 1233 (1987); Comment, Punitive Damages and the Eighth Amendment: An Analytical Framework for Determining Excessiveness, 75 Cal.L.Rev. 1433 (1987); Note, The Constitutionality of Punitive Damages under the Excessive Fines Clause of the Eighth Amendment, 85 Mich. L.Rev. 1699 (1987).

11. Browning–Ferris Indus. of Vermont, Inc. v. Kelco, 492 U.S. 257, 109 S.Ct. 2909, 106 L.Ed.2d 219 (1989).

12. __ U.S. __, 111 S.Ct. 1032, 1043, 113 L.Ed.2d 1 (1991).

13. Owen, The Moral Foundations of Punitive Damages, 40 Ala.L.Rev. 705, 739 (1989).

14. Pacific Mutual Life Ins. Co. v. Haslip, __ U.S. __, __, 111 S.Ct. 1032, 1043, 113 L.Ed.2d 1 (1991).

sanctions against the defendant.[19] The West Virginia Court has constructed a more elaborate diagram for control; in its version post-trial review by the judge takes into account factors that the jury is not allowed to consider at all, as for example, the costs of litigation.[20]

The Georgia Court has pointed out, quite correctly, that *Haslip* held that a consideration of the factors named to be *sufficient* to protect the punitive award from due process attack but that "sufficient" is not the same as "necessary." [21] Some of the factors are weak and even irrational in combination with others, and *Haslip* did not require that an award be justified on the basis of all such factors.[22]

There may be serious limitations on meaningful post-trial review. The Fourth Circuit has emphasized the limited grounds on which a federal judge can upset a jury verdict.[23] Somewhat similarly, the Alabama Court has held that while the legislature may provide for such review, it may not compel the judge to act without deference to the jury's findings.[24] Limitations on post-trial review, and deference to the jury's role, suggest that punitive damages awards should be controlled mainly by giving careful instructions to the jury in the first place. It may be possible to salvage a punitive award by post-trial review even when instructions tell the jury to award any sum it likes,[25] but the better practice is surely to give the jury appropriate limiting instructions, and when proper instructions are not given, more due process litigation can be expected.

First Amendment. Punitive damages imposed upon a defendant for good faith conduct which is arguably protected by free speech or religious freedom provisions of the First Amendment runs risks of chilling those freedoms. Even if it turns out the defendant has committed a legal wrong, if he is nevertheless subject to punitive damages, both he and those who see his example may engage in self-censorship in the future. For reasons somewhat like these, the Supreme Court has held that punitive damages are not

20. Garnes v. Fleming Landfill, Inc., 186 W.Va. 656, 413 S.E.2d 897 (1991).

21. Hosp. Auth. of Gwinnett County v. Jones, 261 Ga. 613, 409 S.E.2d 501 (1991).

22. The ratio rule, for example, was one of several factors used in Alabama to test the punitive award. These factors were listed by the Supreme Court as imposing "a sufficiently definite and meaningful constraint on the discretion of Alabama fact finders in awarding punitive damages"—that is, as providing a *sufficient* list, not a *necessary* one. However, before the year was out, at least one court seemed to conclude that the ratio rule was constitutionally required, at least for some cases. See Garnes v. Fleming Landfill, Inc., 186 W.Va. 656, 413 S.E.2d 897 (1991).

23. Defender Indus., Inc. v. Northwestern Mut. Life Ins. Co., 938 F.2d 502 (4th Cir.1991) (right to jury trial on punitive damages issues means judge cannot substitute her judgment as to proper amount, but is limited to remittitur as alternative to new trial); Mattison v. Dallas Carrier Corp., 947 F.2d 95 (4th Cir.

1991). The content of the *Mattison* instruction is discussed in § 3.11(14) below.

24. Armstrong v. Roger's Outdoor Sports, Inc., 581 So.2d 414 (Ala.1991). The Alabama statute provided for (a) post-trial and appellate review of punitive awards without a presumption in favor of the jury's verdict and also (b) for independent reassessment. The first provision was held unconstitutional because it violated constitutional separation of powers. The second provision was held construed to mean only that judges were to exercise their functions free from improper influences, and as so constructed regarded as a reiteration of what was required in any event. The decision is not directly based on jury trial rights but on the court's power to defer to the jury's findings.

25. See Johnson v. Hugo's Skateway, 949 F.2d 1338 (4th Cir.1991) (jury was told, "you may add to the award of actual damages such amount as you shall unanimously agree to be proper as punitive or exemplary damages," majority thought post-trial review would still sustain the award, dissenter disagreed).

appropriate in many libel cases brought by plaintiffs who are public figures or public officials.[26] Whether the same reasoning will protect the exercise of other freedoms from punitive awards remains to be seen.[27]

Legislative Limitations on Punitive Damages

Multiple damages statutes as caps. Antitrust statutes and a wide variety of others authorize treble damages or some other form of multiplied damages. Such statutes are sometimes punitive in purpose, and where they are, the effect of the treble damages provision may be to foreclose recovery of common-law punitive awards. The effect of this in turn is to put a cap on punitive awards. The cap effect, however, will depend upon construction of the statute.[28]

"Tort reform" legislative caps and limitations. A different and potentially more important limitation arises as a result of the "tort reform" movement of the mid–1980s. At that time, a number of states began passing general [29] statutes to limit tort remedies, including punitive damages. For the most part these statutes reflected an attempt to limit liabilities rather than an attempt to rectify some of the existing problems with punitive awards. At least one statute purports to abolish punitive damages altogether.[30] More commonly, statutes have placed some kind of cap on the recovery of punitive damages, sometimes naming a specific ratio between compensatory and punitive damages,[31] and sometimes setting a flat limit.[32]

26. See § 7.2(4) below.

27. Cf. Christofferson v. Church of Scientology of Portland, 57 Or.App. 203, 253, 644 P.2d 577, 608, 40 A.L.R.4th 1017 (1982) (even religious organization can be liable for punitive damages for fraudulent speech; "In order to be actionable at all, the statements alleged must be found to have been non-religious as made").

28. See § 3.12 below.

29. More specific statutes, aimed at narrow classes of cases antedate this movement. In addition, treble damages statutes, covering some particular torts, may have the effect of limiting the usual discretionary punitive damages in some cases. Some narrow or specific statutes also impose specific caps, as in 42 U.S.C.A. § 3612 (housing discrimination, punitive cap $1,000); 15 U.S.C.A. § 1691e(b) (consumer credit rights, defendant who violates is "liable to the aggrieved applicant for punitive damages in an amount no greater than $10,-000, in addition to any actual damages * * * except that in the case of a class action the total recovery under this subsection shall not exceed the lesser of $500,000 or 1 per centum of the net worth of the" defendant).

One recent addition is the system of caps imposed in the 1991 Civil Rights Act. This uses a graduated series of caps in job discrimination cases, depending on the number of employees the defendant has in a stated time period; caps apply to the combination of punitive and other non-pecuniary damages. The relevant provision is to be codified as 42 U.S.C.A. § 1981a(b)(3).

30. See N.H.Rev.Stat.Ann. 507:16. New Hampshire, however, already denied punitive damages by name and granted only liberal compensatory damages to reflect aggravated misconduct. See Crowley v. Global Realty, Inc., 124 N.H. 814, 474 A.2d 1056 (1984).

31. West's Colo.Rev.Stat.Ann. § 13–21–102 (no more than actual damages, but judge may increase up to three times actual damages if defendant's misbehavior continued during pendency of the case; West's Fla.Stat.Ann. § 768.73(1) (presumed that more than three times actual damages is excessive, but with clear and convincing evidence more can be allowed); 23 Okl.Stat.Ann. § 9 (punitive damages not to exceed actual damages unless there is clear and convincing evidence of reckless disregard or other conduct required for punitive damages).

32. Ala.Code § 6–11–21 ($250,000 limit unless the defendant is guilty of a "pattern or practice of intentional wrongful conduct," or "conduct involving actual malice other than fraud or bad faith" or, strikingly, defamation); West's Colo.Rev.Stat.Ann. § 13–21–102 (no more than actual damages, but judge may increase up to three times actual damages if defendant's misbehavior continued during pendency of the case; West's Fla.Stat.Ann. § 768.73(1) (presumed that more than three times actual damages is excessive, but with clear and convincing evidence more can be allowed); Official Code Ga.Ann. § 51–12–5.1

Statutes may also limit the substantive basis for punitive damages, by declaring that such damages may not be awarded without proof of actual fraud, malice, or oppression.[33] The effect of a statute of this kind may be to immunize serious risk-taking, as where a trucker takes serious safety risks to speed deliveries by encouraging drivers to speed or drive long hours. The trucker does not intend harm to anyone so he may not be punitively liable for malice or oppression. The statutes will undoubtedly require construction, however, and may be given a less radical interpretation.[34]

Constitutionality of caps. Capping statutes raises issues of constitutionality, but at this writing few decisions have been handed down. At least two courts have upheld a statutory cap on punitive damages without substantial discussion.[35]

Construction of capping statutes. One issue of construction arises when the plaintiff recovers compensatory damages from several defendants, or recovers on several different theories from a single defendant. One court has said that the cap applies to limit the plaintiff's total punitive damages, even if the plaintiff is successful against several distinct defendants or on several distinct theories arising out of the same underlying set of facts.[36] Another has held that the cap limits the total damages for *all* claims based on injury to one person, including the claims of plaintiffs who have derivative claims such as loss of consortium or the like.[37] So far, it appears that the cap will apply to protect the United States when it is sued under the Federal Tort Claims Act, because the government's liability, by terms of the

($250,000 limit, but limit inapplicable in products liability cases and cases of specific intent to harm); 23 Okl.Stat.Ann. § 9 (punitive damages not to exceed actual damages unless there is clear and convincing evidence of reckless disregard or other conduct required for punitive damages); V.T.C.A., Civ.Prac. & Rem.Code § 41.007 ($200,000 or four times actual damages in certain cases).

The Texas statute sets an alternative limit—either $200,000 or four times actual damages. V.T.C.A., Civ.Prac. & Rem.Code § 41.-007. As with most of these statutes, this one returns with the left hand much of what it had taken with the right. The limits so carefully imposed are removed when the defendant is guilty of malice or an intentional tort. But the limit appears to control unless there is specific intent to injure or reckless behavior threatening bodily injury. Thus the statute appears to exclude punitive liability for bad faith economic torts.

33. Ky.Rev.Stats.Ann. 411.184 (requiring oppression, fraud or malice).

34. The Kentucky statute requires the plaintiff to prove fraud, oppression, or malice, but then defines malice to mean *either* specific intent to cause injury to the plaintiff *or* conduct carried out "with a flagrant indifference to the rights of the plaintiff and with a subjective awareness that such conduct will result in human death or bodily harm." Ky.Rev.Stat. 411.184(1)(c). On the one hand, this could be

read as about the equivalent of the usual definitions of reckless or wanton misconduct. On the other, the statute might be read to immunize all flagrant indifference unless it is certain that harm *will* result to a particular plaintiff. If read in the latter way, the trucker in the example and the manufacturer of a product known to create horrible risks to consumers will escape punitive liability.

35. Bagley v. Shortt, 261 Ga. 762, 410 S.E.2d 738 (1991); Starns v. United States, 923 F.2d 34 (4th Cir.1991) reflects an unpublished decision of the Supreme Court of Virginia upholding its punitive damages cap in medical malpractice cases. Note that redirection of parts of the punitive award may face a different constitutional challenge. See the paragraph "Redirecting the award from plaintiff to the state" below.

36. Bagley v. Shortt, 261 Ga. 762, 410 S.E.2d 738 (1991).

37. Starns v. United States, 923 F.2d 34, 37–38 (4th Cir.1991) ("all claims arising out of Jeffrey's injuries are subject to one statutory cap. Since the damages awarded to Mr. and Mrs. Starns for the value of Mrs. Starns' past services, for lost wages of Mr. Starns, and for hospital and travel expenses incurred on behalf of Jeffrey are derivative, they must be included within Jeffrey's cap. Accordingly, the limit for all damages in this case is $750,-000").

statute, is the liability that would be applied to a private individual under state law.[38]

Redirecting the award from plaintiff to the state. Another statutory device technically does not limit the punitive recovery at all, but provides that a portion of the recovery is to be paid to the state or some specified agency.[39] This provision does not affect the fairness or efficiency issues of punitive damages at all, but simply attempts to reduce the incentive to claim such damages and thereby to reduce overall liability. At least one court has held that such redirection of a substantial part of the punitive recovery is a taking of property that is impermissible under the state and federal constitutions.[40]

Statutory confrontation of fairness issues. Some of the statutes do, however, address fairness issues. Some raise the standard of proof to require clear and convincing evidence on punitive damages issues.[41] Some require a bifurcated trial to separate punitive damages issues from other issues in the case, and thus to minimize the risk that punitive issues will prejudice the determination of liability itself or other issues in the case.[42] Georgia enacted a one-bite or first comer rule for some mass torts [43] although this may create more problems of unfairness than it resolves.

Statutory enhancement of judicial control. Some states have enacted statutes which purport to remove punitive awards from the jury altogether and to leave such awards exclusively to the judge.[44] Such provisions are probably efforts to control the amount of the award, on the assumption that the judge will be more modest as to the occasions for punitive damages and

38. Starns v. United States, 923 F.2d 34 (4th Cir.1991).

39. West's Colo.Rev.Stat.Ann. § 13–21–102(3)(b) (one-third to state general fund, two-thirds to plaintiff); West's Fla.Stat.Ann. § 768.(2) (40% payable to claimant, 60% to public medical assistance fund or general revenue fund); S.H.A. ch. 110, ¶ 2–1207 (apportioned in trial court's discretion among plaintiff, attorney and Department of Rehabilitation Services); Iowa Code Ann. § 668A.1 (75% of punitive recovery to be paid to fund for indigent civil litigation, with certain exceptions); Kan.Stat.Ann. 60–3402(e) (medical malpractice or "professional liability" cases, 50% to the plaintiff, 50% to health care stabilization fund); V.A.M.S. § 537.675 (50% to tort victim's compensation fund); Ore.Rev. Stat. 18.540 (half to Criminal Injuries Compensation Account).

40. Kirk v. Denver Pub. Co., 818 P.2d 262 (Colo.1991) (West's Colo.Rev.Stat.Ann. § 13–21–102(3)(b) unconstitutional).

41. Alaska Stat. 09.17.020 (clear and convincing); Montana Code Ann. 27–1–221(5). "Beyond a reasonable doubt" standard is used in Colorado. West's Colo.Rev.Stat.Ann. § 13–25–127. The clear and convincing standard has been adopted judicially in some states. See § 3.11(4) supra.

42. West's Cal.Civ.Code Ann. § 3295(d); Official Code Ga.Ann. § 105–2002.1(d); Mon-

tana Code 27–1–221. Some statutes require bifurcation in particular kinds of cases, such as products liability cases. E.g., N.J.Stat.Ann. 2A:58C–5b. An American Bar Association committee report has argued that though judges should be encouraged to bifurcate trials in many instances, mandatory bifurcation goes too far. See American Bar Association, Punitive Damages: A Constructive Examination 58–59 (Special Committee on Punitive Damages, Section of Litigation 1986).

43. Official Code Ga.Ann. § 105–2002.1(e) (in products liability cases). The statute's one-bite rule was held unconstitutional in McBride v. General Motors Corp., 737 F.Supp. 1563 (M.D.Ga.1990).

44. *In products cases:* Conn.Gen.Stat.Ann. § 52–240b ("If the trier of fact determines that punitive damages should be awarded, the court shall determine the amount of such damages not to exceed an amount equal to twice the damages awarded to the plaintiff"); Ohio Rev.Code § 2307.80 ("Whether the trier of fact is a jury or the court, if the trier of fact determines that a manufacturer or supplier in question is liable for punitive or exemplary damages in connection with a product liability claim, the amount of those damages shall be determined by the court"). *In punitive claims generally:* Ohio Rev.Code § 2315.21.

the amounts to be awarded. On their face, statutes like this appear to deprive the plaintiff of a jury trial on punitive damages,[45] a deprivation that may be quite significant when the function of punitive damages is to provide adequate financial basis for litigation against a wrongdoer.[46]

§ 3.11(13) Adjustments and Computations

It is sometimes argued that the gross punitive damages award should be augmented or reduced by the same factors used in adjusting compensatory damages. It may be argued, for example, that if prejudgment interest augments the compensatory award, it should also be added to the punitive award; or that if the compensatory award is subject to a comparative fault reduction, the same reduction should apply to the punitive award. For the most part, courts have usually rejected these and similar claims for adjustment in the punitive award, generally recognizing that punitive damages stand on an entirely different footing from the compensatory damages.

[*For discussion of cases on adjustments in punitive awards, see this section in the Practitioner Treatise edition.*]

§ 3.11(14) Factors in Fixing the Amount of Punitive Damages

"Factors"

Very little control over punitive awards can be asserted unless the award can be verified or audited by an objective standard. The traditional jury instruction approved in many courts seldom gave any guidance beyond the admonition to inflict just punishment or proper deterrence. Many such instructions were the moral equivalent to an instruction that the jury should do the right thing or whatever it thought best.[1] It now appears that such instructions, without more, may not meet due process challenges.[2] On the other hand, it appears that due process demands will be met if the jury,[3] or the court in post-trial review,[4] fixes the amount of the punitive award by referring to a number of relevant "factors" or "standards."[5]

---

45. See, recognizing a jury trial right on punitive damages, Defender Indus., Inc. v. Northwestern Mut. Life Ins. Co., 938 F.2d 502 (4th Cir.1991).

§ 3.11(14)

1. See Hospital Auth. of Gwinnett County v. Jones, 261 Ga. 613, 409 S.E.2d 501 (1991) ("the 'guidance' to the jury provided by the admonition that it 'take into consideration the character and the degree of the wrong as shown by the evidence and necessity of preventing similar wrong' * * * is not guidance but platitude").

2. See § 3.11(12) above.

4. See Pacific Mutual Life Ins. Co. v. Haslip, ___ U.S. ___, 111 S.Ct. 1032, 113 L.Ed.2d 1 (1991), holding that an Alabama post-trial review procedure to assess punitive awards shielded the award from due process attacks where that process evaluated the award in the light of a number of factors. Clarification may still be needed to determine whether a jury instruction that charged on those factors

would itself suffice to sustain the award without a post-trial review, or whether a post-trial review would suffice if the jury had been told to fix the amount as it thought best.

5. The factors considered in Alabama, and held sufficient in *Pacific Mutual Life Ins. Co. v. Haslip,* supra n. 4, were these:

(a) whether there is a reasonable relationship between the punitive damages award and the harm likely to result from the defendant's conduct as well as the harm that actually has occurred; (b) the degree of reprehensibility of the defendant's conduct, the duration of that conduct, the defendant's awareness, any concealment, and the existence and frequency of similar past conduct; (c) the profitability to the defendant of the wrongful conduct and the desirability of removing that profit and of having the defendant also sustain a loss; (d) the "financial position" of the defendant; (e) all the costs of litigation; (f) the imposition of criminal sanctions on the defendant for its conduct, these to be taken in mitigation; and

The Supreme Court's view of the relevant standards is similar to the traditional view as expressed by the Restatement and used both to fix the award in the first place and to test it for excessiveness.[6] These include principally the familiar direction that the award should reflect culpability and deterrence, the ultimate effort being to achieve liability commensurate with the wrongfulness of the act and also liability sufficient to deter without overdeterring.

Culpability factors. As to culpability, the appropriate factors include the nature of the wrongful act,[7] the motives and state of mind of the wrongdoer,[8] the relationship between the parties,[9] the provocation or lack of it,[10] the extent of harm actually inflicted[11] and the harm that was intended or could have resulted even if that harm did not result in fact.[12] The defendant's post-tort behavior, such as an attempt to cover up the evidence, has also been considered in determining the punitive award, perhaps on the theory that misbehavior afterward reflects something of the mental state at the time of the tort, or perhaps on the theory that post-tort behavior indicates a predisposition to continue wrongdoing that requires added deterrence.[13]

Deterrence factors. The amount needed to deter future misconduct is also a central factor, but one for which the parties offer little evidence. The wrongdoer's wealth or income are also to be considered as bearing both on the sums needed to secure appropriate punishment and on sums needed to deter wrongdoing in the future.[14] On the latter point, however, the actual profit or potential profit from the wrong would be a more relevant factor and it is one now being considered in the courts.[15] Relatedly, it has been argued that a punitive award exceeding the defendant's net worth is invalid as a confiscation of property.[16] Another factor of significance is whether the

(g) the existence of other civil awards against the defendant for the same conduct, these also to be taken in mitigation.

6. Restatement Second of Torts § 908, comment *e* (1979).

9. The relationship of the parties is usually mentioned as a factor in a formulaic recitation rather than in analysis. E.g., Safeco Ins. Co. v. Ellinghouse, 223 Mont. 239, 725 P.2d 217 (1986). The most obvious relevance of the parties' relationship, however, is that it may bear on culpability of the defendant. The defendant who abuses a position of power or trust to harm a vulnerable plaintiff may be more culpable than one who simply loses his temper. Vulnerability of the plaintiff was specifically singled out as a factor in Ace Truck and Equip. Rentals, Inc. v. Kahn, 103 Nev. 503, 746 P.2d 132 (1987).

13. E.g., Tetuan v. A.H. Robins Co., 241 Kan. 441, 738 P.2d 1210 (1987) (burning documents after suit filed); Greenfield v. Spectrum Inv. Corp., 174 Cal.App.3d 111, 219 Cal.Rptr. 805 (1985). Cover-up evidence may be regarded as relevant to deterrence. See State ex rel. Young v. Crookham, 290 Or. 61, 72, 618 P.2d 1268, 1274, 11 A.L.R.4th 1251 (1980) ("deterring future similar misconduct," factors in-

clude "the attitude and conduct of the wrongdoer upon learning of the hazard, the number and position of employees involved in causing or covering up the misconduct"). In *Haslip,* supra 4, the Supreme Court lumped concealment with the "degree of reprehensibility," but it also mentioned the disposition to continue wrongdoing, so it may have had deterrence in mind.

14. See § 3.11(5) above.

15. Profitability of the wrong was specifically named as a factor in Haslip, supra 3. See also Dobbs, Ending Punishment in "Punitive" Damages: Deterrence–Measured Remedies, 40 Ala.L.Rev. 831 (1989).

16. Elam v. Alcolac, Inc., 765 S.W.2d 42, 222–223 (Mo.App.1988), cert. denied, 493 U.S. 817, 110 S.Ct. 69, 107 L.Ed.2d 36 (1989) (but there was no evidence as to the defendant's net worth before the trier, hence the argument failed). In Mattison v. Dallas Carrier Corp., 947 F.2d 95, 110 (4th Cir.1991) the court thought "Any penalty must be limited to punishment and thus may not effect economic bankruptcy." This formula if taken literally would prevent a punitive award against one who had no net worth, regardless of how reprehensible his conduct. As stated, this rule

defendant has been or may be in the future, punished in other proceedings, as where mass tort claims generate many punitive awards.[17]

Litigation support factors. One justification for punitive awards is that they may help compensate for the plaintiff's attorney fees or, alternatively, provide encouragement to plaintiffs and their lawyers to act as "private attorneys general" by suing in cases in which punitive damages are appropriate.[18] This implies that one factor in fixing the punitive award would be to consider the amounts needed to provide appropriate incentives or to pay the fees incurred by the plaintiff.[19] This factor, if it is to be recognized, would focus on the costs of pursuing the case and the relative incentives to do so.

Criticisms

Disharmony among the factors. Lists of factors, no matter how long the lists may be, do not alone yield either controlled or predictable results. The major factors suggested by the underlying functions of the punitive award [20]—punishment, deterrence, and incentives to pursue socially useful litigation—are not always in harmony with each other. If the wrongdoing is very grave but not at all likely to be repeated, the punishment rationale suggests a relatively large award, but the deterrence rationale suggests little or no award. The incentive rationale might suggest still a third possibility.

When all these factors are lumped into a kind of mashed potato instruction to the jury, it is quite possible that neither the goals of punishment nor deterrence will be met. Heavy punishment in line with culpability may overdeter; heavy deterrence may overpunish. Limited punitive damages that may be in line with a small need for deterrence may fail to provide appropriate incentives to litigate financially small but socially serious wrongdoings. The factors approach, which has not been worked out in detail, tends to promote a kind of average in which none of the goals is necessarily achieved.

Absence of evidence. The other major criticism to be found in setting the amount of the punitive award is that although the underlying goals of punitive damages and the factors recognized by the courts often suggest the need for specific evidence, that evidence seldom appears in the cases. The award necessary to deter future misconduct, for example, would depend upon a number of facts, including the profitability of the misconduct by an enterprise or the psychological disposition of a bullying individual. But the absence of such evidence has not prevented courts from imposing punitive damages for the express purpose of deterring the defendant.

would bar punitive damages against a penniless person who expects to inherit millions. As long as reprehensibility of conduct is the basis for punitive liability, absolute rules like this one seem wrong.

17. See *Haslip,* supra n. 4. As to multiple liabilities, see § 3.11(8) above.

18. See § 3.11(3) above.

19. *Mattison v. Dallas Carrier Corp.,* 947 F.2d 95 (4th Cir.1991) ("the costs to the plaintiff of prosecuting the claim"). See also Dobbs, Ending Punishment in "Punitive" Damages: Deterrence–Measured Remedies, 40 Ala.L.Rev. 831 (1989).

§ 3.11(15) The Debate Over Punitive Damages

Criticizing, Defending and Reforming Punitive Damages

Punitive damages have been debated for a very long time, but the debated perception that awards have substantially increased in number and size [1] has recently brought the debate to the boiling point again. Critics have condemned punitive damages as both unfair and economically inefficient. Many of the particular criticisms are relevant to both points.

Fairness Criticisms

The criticisms of punitive damages on fairness grounds are many and detailed. Most of them fit under one of the following general charges:

(1) It is unfair to defendants to impose punishment without identifying in advance the acts that will entail such punishment.[2] At a minimum, the standard of liability should be more demanding,[3] more precise, or more uniform.

(2) Vicarious punitive liability is unjust.[4]

(3) It is unfair to defendants to impose punishment without specifying the penalty that can be imposed or otherwise setting limits to the penalty in advance.[5] Relatedly but distinctly, the amount of punitive damages is often unfairly high [6] or unfairly unpredictable and unmeasurable,[7] or even unconstitutionally high or disproportionate to the governing purposes.[8]

(4) It is unfair and perhaps unconstitutional to impose punishment unless the procedural safeguards required for criminal cases are applied to the punitive damages proceeding. This objection covers a host of sins.[9] One argument is that it is particularly unfair to introduce evidence of the defendant's wealth when it can be considered on issues of liability and compensatory damages.[10] Another is that multiple liabilities for a single act or at least a single course of conduct is grossly unfair.[11]

The analogy between punitive damages and Rule 11 sanctions and between punitive damages and criminal contempt of court suggests other arguments. In the case of contempt, the Court has said that criminal contempt is a crime like any other and that criminal process safeguards are required.[12] If the criminal contempt analogy is applicable there is a new problem arising from the Supreme Court's holding [13] that the judge could not appoint private counsel to prosecute the criminal contempt unless the private counsel was disinterested; that is, the plaintiff's attorneys should not prosecute the contempt charge. The plaintiff's attorney in the punitive claim lacks the disinterest required in the contempt case. Clarence Morris' classic article recognized this problem long ago and suggested that the plaintiff's attorneys' stake in

§ 3.11(15)

1. See § 3.11(1) above, reflecting the perception and studies that belie it.

12. See §§ 2.8(3) & 2.8(4) supra. Comment, Criminal Safeguards and the Punitive Damages Defendant, 34 U.Chi.L.Rev. 408 (1967) argues that punitive damages differ in stigma from ordinary criminal punishments and that at most only some of the criminal process safeguards are needed in punitive damages cases.

13. Young v. United States ex rel. Vuitton et Fils S.A., 481 U.S. 787, 107 S.Ct. 2124, 95 L.Ed.2d 740 (1987).

the case would be a problem only if punitive damages were shown to be generally excessive.[14]

(5) Even if punitive damages are not otherwise unfair, the inability to set appropriate constraints on those damages, coupled with the risk of jury bias and preferences for wealth distribution, operates to produce unfair and possibly unconstitutional results in too many cases.[15]

(6) It is unfair and offensive to give the plaintiff a windfall; if damages are invoked as punishment, the civil fine should be payable to the state, not to the plaintiff.[16]

Economic Criticisms

Other objections have been made in terms of efficiency. The principal objection can be summarized as a complaint that unlimited, discretionary punitive damages are very likely either to overdeter, underdeter, or not to deter at all.[17] Overdeterrence would occur if, for example, punitive damages were too high, leading a manufacturer-defendant to withdraw not only harmful but also socially useful products from the market out of its fear of punitive liabilities. A manufacturer struck by a heavy punitive award might, for example, decide not to market a demonstratively useful drug for fear that if anything went wrong it would be held for heavy punitive as well as compensatory damages. In other cases the infliction of punitive damages seems to have no deterrent effect at all; the A.H. Robins Company seems to have responded to the first punitive awards by burning all its relevant documents, not by giving appropriate warnings that its product was dangerous.[18] Uncertainty both as to the occasion and the amount of punitive damages could contribute to either over or under-deterrence. Either result could be described as economically inefficient.

Evaluating the Criticisms

All of the general criticisms listed above have some rational basis. Most of the fairness criticisms, however, are based on the assumption that punitive damages can be justified only as punishment in the sense of retribution, or that such damages are necessarily forms of criminal punishment. In fact, however, some portion of many awards of punitive damages is very likely to represent a hidden award of litigation costs. Many of the basic fairness objections would fail if the award now called punitive damages were openly called an award of attorney fees; yet the punitive award is sometimes just that, an award of litigations costs under a different name.

Other portions of the "punitive" award are clearly imposed, not as retribution, but as a kind of "tax" intended to remove the defendant's hope

14. Morris, Punitive Damages in Tort Cases, 44 Harv.L.Rev. 1173, 1178–79 (1934).

15. See, e.g., Ellis, Fairness and Efficiency in the Law of Punitive Damages, 56 So.Cal. L.Rev. 1 (1982).

17. Wheeler, The Constitutional Case for Reforming Punitive Damages Procedures, 69 Va.L.Rev. 269, 306 ff. (1983); Ellis, Fairness and Efficiency in the Law of Punitive Damages, 56 So.Cal.L.Rev. 1, 53 (1982); Ausness,

Retribution and Deterrence: The Role of Punitive Damages in Products Liability Litigation, 74 Ky.L.J. 1, 70–92 (1985–86).

18. See, Tetuan v. A.H. Robins Co., 241 Kan. 441, 484, 738 P.2d 1210, 1240 (1987) ("it consigned hundreds of documents to the furnace rather than inform women that the Dalkon Shield carried inside their bodies was a bacterial time bomb which could cause septic abortions, PID, and even death").

of future profit from continuing the wrongful activity and thus to deter the wrongful conduct. This portion of the "punitive" award devoted to a deterrence "tax" of this kind seems more like a license fee than a criminal proceeding. If so, many of the fairness criticisms are inapposite to this part of the punitive award.

Even so, criticisms remain. "Punitive" or augmented damages, even when courts consciously assess them as charges intended to help finance litigation, are not based on proof of litigation expense at all, but rather very often on prejudicial proof of the defendant's wealth. Similarly, although deterrence is always said to be a desired function of the punishment, courts do not demand proof that would suggest the amounts of damages needed to effectuate deterrence.[19] In brief, neither juries nor judges have before them any rational guidance in setting the amounts of punitive damages, and this criticism does not change even if one were to regard most punitive awards as deterrence taxes and litigation finance charges.

With these general criticisms and responses, as with many specific issues in punitive damages, a balanced assessment is difficult because the alternatives that have been identified so far are unattractive. Abolition of punitive damages would eliminate even the hope of deterrence, as well as support for litigation that otherwise would be financially impossible. Caps on punitive damages seem to present the same problems. Even a cap that is generous in a case against an individual may effect no deterrence at all in a case against a manufacturer whose income is millions or billions of dollars from a product it knows to be dangerous.[20]

The best reforms, as a result, may be less than satisfactory. Partial solutions, however, might include the following:

(1) Bifurcated trials, in which liability is determined first, with a separate determination of punitive damages.

(2) An increased role for judges in supervising and managing punitive awards.[21] Some thinkers have even suggested that the measure of punitive damages should be left wholly to the judge.[22] These sugges-

---

19. Both instructions to the jury and the evidence required to demonstrate appropriate levels of the punitive award are extremely weak. Instructions range from a kind of verbal shrug of the shoulders to pious and flabby abstractions. Rowlett v. Anheuser–Busch, Inc., 832 F.2d 194 (1st Cir.1987) may have signalled a purpose to require more helpful instructions.

As to evidence, the goals of deterrence and retribution—the goals overtly embraced—may call for quite different kinds of awards. Factors often named as critical in fixing the size of the punitive award seem at best only remotely relevant to deterrence, e.g., the character of the defendant's act and the extent of the harm done. See Ausness, Retribution and Deterrence: The Role of Punitive Damages in Products Liability Litigation, 74 Ky.L.J. 1, 78–79 (1985–86). Occasionally a jury will have before it one element of proof that does bear on the amount of award appropriate to deterrence, as where there is evidence of profit

defendant earns from the wrongdoing. This may occur where the evidence reveals that a defective product could have been corrected for a specified additional figure. See Sturm, Ruger & Co. v. Day, 594 P.2d 38 (Alaska 1979), modified on reh'g, 615 P.2d 621 (Alaska 1980), cert. denied, 454 U.S. 894, 102 S.Ct. 391, 70 L.Ed.2d 209 (1981) (jury apparently attempted to compute savings resulting from the defect on all products, award found excessive in ultimate appeal). Even so, the appropriate award to effectuate deterrence in "mass tort" cases would be almost impossible even to guess at unless all punitive awards were levied at the same time.

22. See, e.g., Owen, Problems in Assessing Punitive Damages Against Manufacturers of Defective Products, 49 U.Chi.L.Rev. 1, 52 (1982) Mallor & Roberts, Punitive Damages: Toward a Principled Approach, 31 Hast.L.J. 639, 663 (1980); Ausness, Retribution and Deterrence: The Role of Punitive Damages in

tions put in issue the whole question of the jury's role in punitive damages awards. One court held that the issue of punitive damages vel non was for the jury, but that the judge was free to fix the amount.[23] But the case was later overruled on the ground that its rule deprived the parties of a right to jury trial.[24] Even less intrusion on the jury's traditional role might encounter constitutional objections, perhaps under state constitutions, too.[25] Yet a number of courts have explicitly indicated that their standard of review for punitive awards is more demanding than for compensatory awards, and many have exhibited great care in analyzing punitive awards, often remitting them.[26] Indeed, due process may require some kind of judicial scrutiny of punitive damages.[27] This hodge-podge of holdings, with its potential conflict between jury trial ideals and due process, makes it difficult to draft a precise plan for judicial control of punitive awards, but increased judicial control in some form may be likely nevertheless.

(3) The use of criminal-process safeguards as to any element of punitive damages to be inflicted as retribution rather than as a means of providing litigation finance or a "deterrence tax." Such reforms would probably mean that most plaintiffs would drop retributive claims and concentrate on deterrence or litigation-finance grounds for punitive awards. As to those forms of "punitive" damages, perhaps the best reform would be to deny recovery unless the plaintiff proves some basis for calculating a reasonable attorney fee or other litigation expense some basis for estimating a sum needed for deterrence on the other.

§ 3.12 Multiplied Damages

Nature of Multiple Damages Statutes

Typical statutes. Many statutes now authorize[1] or require[2] the award of a double or treble damages, or occasionally some other added award.[3] The statutes are often aimed at only one specific act. For example, statutes may

Products Liability Litigation, 74 Ky.L.J. 1, 96 (1985–86).

§ 3.12

1. E.g., 35 U.S.C.A. § 284 (1984) (patent infringement cases, "[T]he court may increase the damages up to three times the amount found or assessed"); 15 U.S.C.A. § 1117 (trademark, similar). Cf. 42 U.S.C.A. § 9607(c)(3) (CERCLA) (one liable for release of hazardous substance who fails to take ordered remedial action "may be" liable for punitive damages, but amount must be "at least equal to, and not more than three times" the costs incurred by the government).

Connecticut has held that the defendant's right of jury trial is unconstitutionally abridged by a multiplied damages statute that left the decision to multiply to the judge rather than the jury. Bishop v. Kelly, 206 Conn. 608, 539 A.2d 108 (1988). Whether the plaintiff would have equal ground for complaint is not clear.

Sometimes a court's reference to a multiple damages provision as discretionary appears to mean only that a particular case is not within the statute's scope. See Patton v. Mohave County, 154 Ariz. 168, 741 P.2d 301 (App.1987) (under Ariz.Rev.Stat. § 23–355, authorizing treble damages for failure of employer to make payment of wages when due, "treble damages are discretionary and should not be awarded when there is a reasonable good-faith wage dispute").

2. See, e.g., Martin v. McKee Realtors, Inc., 663 S.W.2d 446 (Tex.1984) (statute requiring mandatory multiplication of first $1,000, discretionary multiplication of additional actual damages, but only where defendant was knowing wrongdoer); Sullivan v. Metro Productions, Inc., 150 Ariz. 573, 724 P.2d 1242 (App.1986), cert. denied, sub nom. Miller v. Sullivan, 479 U.S. 1102, 107 S.Ct. 1334, 94 L.Ed.2d 185 (1987) (State RICO treble damages mandatory).

authorize treble damages against motor vehicle dealers who alter a car's odometer reading.[4] Taken together, however, the statutes cover a wide range of cases. Among the more important groups of statutes are those that grant multiplied damages for violation of certain social or economic rights,[5] and those that aim at consumer protection or regulate various practices.[6] In the latter category antitrust statutes are perhaps the best known[7] but federal multiple damages statutes on trademarks[8] and patents[9] have also been important. Treble damages are also allowed under federal and state RICO statutes.[10] The states often have enacted multiple damages statutes covering timber trespass[11] and some kinds of forcible entry.[12] Consumer protection statutes also often provide for multiple damages,[13] and so do many others.[14] A somewhat different statute allows the court to make an award of "increased" damages in a certain dollars range when the defendant's conduct is wilful.[15]

Differences between multiplied and punitive damages. Multiplied damages statutes are often said to be punitive.[16] This is not always the whole story, however. In the first place, the statutory multiple damages differ from the common law punitive damages in that punitive damages involved no fixed sum or limit.[17] The fixed limit of multiple damages not only reduces their threat to the defendant and the potential for abuse, it also reduces the possibility of a measured deterrence. Likewise, because the enhancement of the award is fixed by the statutory multiple, there is no occasion for introducing evidence of the defendant's wealth as there is in the case of common law punitive damages.

Non-punitive purposes under some statutes. Perhaps a more important distinction is that multiple damages statutes may be enacted for entirely non-punitive purposes. Specifically, some double or treble damages statutes, and also specified "civil penalties," are intended to provide a kind of liquidated damages for actual losses that cannot be proved or that are otherwise unrecognized by the law.[18] Some may be intended to offer the carrot of multiplied damages as an inducement to sue on issues of public importance which might otherwise be financially unattractive to lawyers or litigants.[19] The statute that conditions multiple damages on serious wrongdoing will usually appear to be punitive;[20] the statute that provides multiple

---

16. E.g., Owen, Punitive Damages in Products Liability Litigation, 74 Mich.L.Rev. 1257, 1262, n. 17 (1976); Ausness, Retribution and Deterrence: The Role of Punitive Damages in Products Liability Litigation, 74 Ky.L.J. 1 (1985–86).

18. United States v. Bornstein, 423 U.S. 303, 96 S.Ct. 523, 46 L.Ed.2d 514 (1976); Overnight Motor Transp. Co., Inc. v. Missel, 316 U.S. 572, 62 S.Ct. 1216, 86 L.Ed. 1682 (1942).

Thus the statute may be intended to compensate for the inherent uncertainties and proof difficulties that beset some claims, or to provide a substitute for interest. See, giving both grounds, Trio Process Corp. v. L. Goldstein's Sons, Inc., 638 F.2d 661 (3d Cir.1981). See Note, Treble Damages Under RICO: Characterization and Computation, 61 Notre Dame L.Rev. 526, 533–34 (1986).

19. See Agency Holding Corp. v. Malley Duff & Associates, Inc., 483 U.S. 143, 107 S.Ct. 2759, 97 L.Ed.2d 121 (1987) (both Clayton Act and RICO use the "carrot of treble damages" to induce private suits as an enforcement mechanism). In Equitable Life Leasing Corp. v. Abbick, 243 Kan. 513, 757 P.2d 304 (1988) a civil penalty was held justified in addition to an award of punitive damages because the penalty was intended to encourage the plaintiff to act as a private attorney general and was thus remedial, not punitive. This is one of the recognized functions of the common law punitive award as well; but in that case the award is triggered only after a finding of serious wrongdoing. See § 3.11(3) above.

damages as a "liquidated" award will usually appear otherwise.[21] Similarly, a statute that imposes multiple damages in cases that involve no serious wrongdoing is by inference a non-punitive statute.[22]

Issues Affected by Punitive or Nonpunitive Nature

A number of remedial issues may turn on whether the award under any particular statute is regarded as punitive or as something else. If the statute is purely punitive, it may raise many of the important arguments raised about any other punitive damages,[23] including the argument that criminal process protections such as double jeopardy rules should apply,[24] or that due process imposes constraints in measurement.[25]

Punitive multiplication precluding common law punitive damages. Specifically remedial issues and computations may turn on how the multiple damages provision is characterized. If the statute is punitive, a recovery of multiplied damages under the statute presumably precludes any recovery of common law punitive damages, since two separate punitive awards would not ordinarily be justified.[26] Conceivably the plaintiff would have an option to choose between the statutory multiple and a common law punitive award,[27] but the very existence of a multiplied damages statute covering the case might be deemed to eliminate an option. Whether a treble damages statute is punitive, and whether it eliminates the more individualized award of punitive damages at common law, is usually a matter of construction under each statute.[28] Some statutes might be construed to permit both treble damages and a separate punitive award,[29] although such a construction might raise constitutional doubts.

Nonpunitive multiplication—effect on common law punitive damages. If the treble damage or civil penalty statute is not punitive but has a purely remedial purpose not served by punitive damages, then presumably both the statutory and the common law punitive damages award would be permissible.[30] But even here, punitive damages may be denied under a statutory cause of action if the statute sets up a comprehensive remedial scheme and makes no mention of punitive damages, because such a statute generates a

27. Eastern Star, Inc. v. Union Bldg. Materials Corp., 6 Hawaii App. 125, 712 P.2d 1148 (1985) (double recovery to allow both trebled damages and punitive damages, but plaintiff may take the greater of (a) common law punitive damages or (b) trebled damages); Birchfield v. Texarkana Memorial Hosp., 747 S.W.2d 361, 367 (Tex.1987) ("where the prevailing party fails to elect between alternative measures of damages, the court should utilize the findings affording the greater recovery and render judgment accordingly," hence plaintiff could recover treble damages if that was greater than the punitive damage award). See Kelco Disposal, Inc. v. Browning–Ferris–Indus., 845 F.2d 404 (2d Cir.1988), aff'd, 492 U.S. 257, 109 S.Ct. 2909, 106 L.Ed.2d 219 (1989) (plaintiff required to "elect" between accepting $6 million punitive recovery under state tort law or treble damages and attorney fees under federal antitrust laws).

29. E.g., Ariz.Rev.Stat. § 13–2314N (1978 & Supp.1987), after providing for treble damages specifies: "A civil action under this section is remedial and not punitive and does not limit and is not limited by any other previous or subsequent civil or criminal action under this title or any other provision of law. Civil remedies provided under this title are supplemental and not mutually exclusive." Even where both punitive and multiplied damages are authorized by the statute, however, the court may refuse to grant both on the ground that this would be doubling the punitive effect. See Marill Alarm Sys., Inc. v. Open Door Capital Corp., 68 B.R. 399 (Bkrtcy.Fla.1986), aff'd, 861 F.2d 725 (11th Cir.1988) (since trebled damages were sufficient to deter, no additional punitive award would be made, though it was authorized by statute).

30. Equitable Life Leasing Corp. v. Abbick, 243 Kan. 513, 757 P.2d 304 (1988).

negative inference.[31]

Nature of statutory damages as affecting compensatory award. Compensatory damages as well as punitive damages may be affected by the statute's purpose. If the statute's purpose is punitive, prejudgment interest might be appropriate for the basic award but not for the punitive portion that results from multiplication.[32] Some authority has treated prejudgment interest differently under multiple damages statutes, by adding the prejudgment interest to the base award and then multiplying the award so augmented.[33] If prejudgment interest is intended to provide a compensation for attorney fees, it might preclude or limit the award of any attorney fees otherwise recoverable.[34]

Nature of statutory damages as affecting other issues. A multiple damages statute is likely to affect still other issues, too, depending on whether it is punitive or not. In some jurisdictions punitive damages are not insurable,[35] or may be excluded by the terms of the defendant's insurance policy.[36] They may not survive the death of the tortfeasor.[37] The punitive character of the award may be critical in determining whether the award is taxable to the recipient.[38] And whether it is deductible as a business expense to the defendant who pays it.[39] As a result of all this, it becomes important to analyze the terms and purposes of the particular statute in question to determine whether it is punitive or not.

Computation under Multiple Damages Statutes

The other major problem under multiplied damages statutes is computation of the award. In the small number of cases two kinds of problems have appeared.

Which measure of damages is multiplied? In many instances the plaintiff may have choices among different damages claims. In a timber trespass case, for example, the plaintiff might claim the diminished land value resulting from the defendant's taking of timber; or the plaintiff might claim

---

31. Getty Petroleum Corp. v. Bartco Petroleum Corp., 858 F.2d 103 (2d Cir.1988), cert. denied, 490 U.S. 1006, 109 S.Ct. 1642, 104 L.Ed.2d 158 (1989) (trademark remedies spelled out in detail, no mention of punitive damages, no punitive award can be made even though multiple damages provisions are compensatory in nature).

32. Makino, U.S.A. v. Metlife Capital Credit, 25 Mass.App.Ct. 302, 518 N.E.2d 519 (1988) (citing many cases so holding).

33. See Lauder v. Peck, 11 Conn.App. 161, 526 A.2d 539 (1987); Midland–Guardian Co. v. United Consumers Club, Inc., 499 N.E.2d 792 (Ind.App.1986).

34. See Paper Converting Machine Co. v. Magna–Graphics Corp., 785 F.2d 1013, 1016 (Fed.Cir.1986) (reflecting trial judge's denial of counsel fees in patent infringement case because treble damage award was "adequate under the circumstances"). Cf. Ohio–Sealy Mattress Mfg. Co. v. Sealy Inc., 776 F.2d 646 (7th Cir.1985) (claim for fee enhancement denied partly because treble damages sufficed to encourage suit, so that fee enhancement was not required). But if the attorney fee is awarded as a sanction for bad faith rather than as an encouragement to sue, both the fee award and common law punitive damages have been allowed. White v. Kaufmann, 133 Ariz. 388, 652 P.2d 127 (1982).

38. L. Frolik, Federal Tax Aspects of Injury, Damage and Loss 17–18 (1987). Punitive damages were taxable under Commissioner v. Glenshaw Glass Co., 348 U.S. 426, 75 S.Ct. 473, 99 L.Ed. 483 (1955), which was a case in which compensatory damages, not being involved in personal injury under § 104, were also taxable. The IRS originally limited taxability of punitives to such a pattern, but now has held that punitive damages are taxable even if they arise in personal injury cases where the compensatory damages are not taxable. Frolik p. 17–18, citing Rev.Rul. 84–108, 1984–29 I.R.B.

39. See L. Frolik, Federal Tax Aspects of Injury, Damage and Loss (1987).

the value of the timber; or conceivably he might claim lost profits or special damages of some kind. If the multiple damages statute is aimed at punishment only, multiplication of any measure or element of damages the plaintiff actually establishes may be appropriate.[40] But if the statute is intended to provide enhanced damages only because actual losses may be difficult to prove,[41] perhaps it is intended to multiply only general damages and not to multiply consequential or special damages.[42] If the plaintiff actually proves special damages greater than the diminished land value, the multiplication may serve no compensatory purpose. The cases found have not addressed this issue clearly and it obviously requires analysis in terms of the particular statute.[43]

Order of credits and multiplication. The second major problem in computation occurs because in many instances the initial figure for damages requires adjustment to reflect the fact that the defendant is entitled to a credit or offset. For example, the plaintiff's recovery might be reduced under the rules for minimizing damages,[44] or because the plaintiff has settled with another tortfeasor.[45] Whether the statute is purely punitive or whether it is intended to provide liquidated compensation for unproven losses, its effects may be wiped out if the deductions for credits are made first.

The cases considering the point have largely agreed that the first operation should be the multiplication, with any credits deducted from the multiplied sum.[46] Thus under a treble damages statute, if the actual

---

40. Michigan has trebled both the value of the timber and the landowner's cost of cleanup. See Miller v. Wykoff, 346 Mich. 24, 77 N.W.2d 264 (1956). This appears to be clearly punitive. Cf. Blim v. Western Elec. Co., Inc, 731 F.2d 1473 (10th Cir.1984), cert. denied, 469 U.S. 874, 105 S.Ct. 233, 83 L.Ed.2d 161 (1984) (fringe benefits as well as cash pay lost doubled under Age Act).

41. Overnight Motor Transp. Co., Inc. v. Missel, 316 U.S. 572, 583–84, 62 S.Ct. 1216, 1223, 86 L.Ed. 1682, 1691 (1942) ("damages too obscure and difficult of proof for estimate other than by liquidated damages"). Timber trespass statutes that double damages even where the defendant acts in good faith seem to be in this category. See Hartland Cicero Mut. Ins. Co. v. Elmer, 122 Wis.2d 481, 363 N.W.2d 252 (App.1984).

42. In United States v. Aerodex, Inc., 469 F.2d 1003 (5th Cir.1972) the defendant had violated the False Claims Act by delivering and invoicing bearings that did not conform to the Government order. The government sustained $27,000 in general damages based on the fact that the delivered bearings were worth less than those contracted for. The government also sustained approximately $160,000 in consequential damages for the cost of removing the bearings. Although this statute requires "guilty knowledge" and thus seems punitive at least in part, the court held that only the general damages claim could be doubled. Thus the government recovered the

$27,000 and statutory penalties × 2, plus the $160,000. The result is generous to the defendant if the statute is purely punitive, but comports with the Supreme Court's announced view that the statute is at least partly compensatory. See United States v. Bornstein, 423 U.S. 303, 96 S.Ct. 523, 46 L.Ed.2d 514 (1976). But a high-measure damages was multiplied in Pearce v. G.R. Kirk Co., 92 Wash.2d 869, 602 P.2d 357 (1979) on the theory that the high-measure was compensatory, not punitive. The facts might have warranted the belief, however, that the consequential damages proven might not be fully compensatory. Michigan has trebled both the value of the timber and the landowner's cost of cleanup. Miller v. Wykoff, 346 Mich. 24, 77 N.W.2d 264 (1956).

43. Cf. Blim v. Western Elec. Co., Inc, 731 F.2d 1473 (10th Cir.1984), cert. denied, 469 U.S. 874, 105 S.Ct. 233, 83 L.Ed.2d 161 (1984), the court held that the Age Discrimination in Employment Act's double damages operates to double fringe benefits as well as cash pay lost. The Age Act is said to be punitive, see n. 19 supra; but the result would seem correct even if the act's purpose were to provide purely "liquidated" damages for unprovable harm.

46. United States v. Bornstein, 423 U.S. 303, 96 S.Ct. 523, 46 L.Ed.2d 514 (1976); United States v. Globe Remodeling Co, 196 F.Supp. 652 (D.Vt.1960); Vairo v. Clayden, 153 Ariz. 13, 734 P.2d 110 (App.1987). See Note, Treble

damages are $100 and the defendant is entitled to a credit of $90 because the plaintiff has received sums in settlement from other tortfeasors, the rule would allow the plaintiff to recover $100 × 3 = $300 − $90 = $210. The reverse order of computation would allow the plaintiff only $30.[47] The cases adopting the rule more favorable to the plaintiff seem justifiable on their facts. However, there may be cases in which the plaintiff's damages are to be reduced because of the plaintiff's own fault, as in comparative negligence, and if so, a less rather than a more liberal rule of computation would be preferable for those.

Damages Under RICO: Characterization and Computation, 61 Notre Dame L.Rev. 526, 533–34 (1986); Annot., 35 A.L.R. Fed. 805 (1977) (under False Claims Act).

47. The reverse order would give the plaintiff $100 − $90 = $10 × 3 = $30.

Chapter 4

RESTITUTION

Analysis

A. THE NATURE OF RESTITUTION

Sec.
4.1 Restitution and Unjust Enrichment.
    4.1(1) Core Ideas of Restitution.
    4.1(2) The Substantive Side of Restitution: Unjust Enrichment.
    4.1(3) Introducing the Procedural and Terminological Side of Restitution.
    4.1(4) The Measurement of Restitution—The Remedial Side of Restitution.
4.2 Restitution at Law—Terminology and Development.
    4.2(1) In Summary.
    4.2(2) Development of Restitution When Plaintiff Had Title: Ejectment and Replevin.
    4.2(3) Development of Restitution When Plaintiff Had No Title.
4.3 Restitution in Equity—Terminology and Procedure.
    4.3(1) Equitable Restitutionary Devices Generally.
    4.3(2) The Constructive Trust.
    4.3(3) The Equitable Lien.
    4.3(4) Subrogation.
    4.3(5) Accounting and Accounting for Profits.
    4.3(6) Rescission.
    4.3(7) Reformation.
    4.3(8) Equitable Conversion.
4.4 Specific and Substitutionary Restitution.
4.5 Measurement of Restitution.
    4.5(1) General Principles and Substantive Policy.
    4.5(2) Market Measures of Restitution.
    4.5(3) Consequential Benefits Measures of Restitution.
    4.5(4) Guides to and Limitations on Measures of Restitution.
    4.5(5) Combining Restitution With Other Remedies.

B. DEFENSES AND LIMITATIONS

4.6 Defendant's Change of Position.
4.7 Bona Fide Purchasers for Value and Discharge for Value.
    4.7(1) Bona Fide Purchasers.
    4.7(2) Discharge for Value.
4.8 The Requirement of Restoration or Tender by the Plaintiff.
4.9 Unsolicited Benefits—Volunteers and Intermeddlers.
    4.9(1) Rule, Background and Summary.
    4.9(2) Underlying Principles in Unsolicited Benefit Cases.
    4.9(3) Benefits in Cash or Specific Chattels.
    4.9(4) Intentionally Conferring Non–cash Benefits When Parties Could or Did Contract.
    4.9(5) Intentionally or Innocently Conferring Non–cash Benefits Where Bargaining Is Not Possible.

Sec.

4.9(6)   Acceptance or Opportunity to Reject: Lawyers and the
         Common Fund.

A. THE NATURE OF RESTITUTION

§ 4.1 Restitution and Unjust Enrichment

§ 4.1(1) Core Ideas of Restitution

Definitions and Goals

Defendant's gains, not plaintiff's losses. Restitution is a large, diverse and important topic with a significant literature of its own.[1] Most generalizations about restitution are trustworthy only so long as they are not very meaningful, and meaningful only so long as they are not very trustworthy. There are, however, some core ideas.

Although the term restitution is used in criminal as well as civil cases, this chapter deals with restitution only in the civil sense.[2] The word restitution means restoration. Restitution is a return or restoration of what the defendant has gained in a transaction. It may be a return of a specific thing or it may be a "return" of a money substitute for that thing. For example, if the defendant fraudulently obtains title to Blackacre from the

---

§ 4.1(1)

1. The leading contemporary work is Professor George Palmer's four-volume treatise. G. Palmer, Law of Restitution (4 vols. 1978 & Supps.). The Restatement of Restitution (1937) is still in use by the courts and writers. See also J. Dawson, Unjust Enrichment (1951); G. Douthwaite, Attorney's Guide to Restitution (1977); R. Goff and G. Jones, The Law of Restitution 60 (2d ed. 1978) (English); G. Fridman & J. McLeod, Restitution (1982) (Canadian, with some references to other North American authorities); International Encyclopedia of Comparative Law, Restitution—Unjust Enrichment and Negotiorum Gestio (Vol. X), including Palmer, History of Restitution in Anglo–American Law (Chapter 3) (1989); England, Restitution of Benefits Conferred without Obligation (Chapter 5) (1991); and Stoljar, Negotiorum Gestio (Chapter 1984). Other works are listed in Wade, The Literature of the Law of Restitution, 19 Hast. L.J. 1087 (1968).

Among recent articles dealing with broader issues in restitution are Dawson, The Self–Serving Intermeddler, 87 Harv.L.Rev. 1409 (1974); Dawson, Judicial Revision of Frustrated Contracts: The United States, 64 B.U.L.Rev. 1 (1984); Dawson, Restitution without Enrichment, 61 B.U.L.Rev. 563 (1981); Farnsworth, Your Loss or My Gain? The Dilemma of the Disgorgement Principle in Breach of Contract, 94 Yale L.J. 1339 (1985);

Friedmann, Restitution of Benefits Obtained Through the Appropriation of Property or the Commission of a Wrong, 80 Colum.L.Rev. 504 (1980); Kovacic, A Proposal to Simplify Quantum Meruit Litigation, 35 Am.U.L.Rev. 547 (1986); Laycock, The Scope and Significance of Restitution, 65 Tex.L.Rev. 1277 (1989); Levmore, Explaining Restitution, 71 Va.L.Rev. 65 (1985) (economic analysis of restitution issues); Litman, The Emergence of Unjust Enrichment as a Cause of Action and the Remedy of Constructive Trust, 26 Alberta L.Rev. 407 (1988).

A number of other articles deal with particular issues or settings in restitution, sometimes with useful observations about restitution in general. E.g., Galligan, Extra Work in Construction Cases: Restitution, Relationship, and Revision, 63 Tulane L.Rev. 799 (1989). Substantive aspects of restitution are often involved in articles on contracts and sometimes torts.

2. Judges and lawyers sometimes speak of a convicted criminal's duty to make restitution to his victim as a condition of probation or other leniency in the sentence. Restitution in this sense often only means compensation for actual losses suffered by the criminal's victim, not necessarily a restoration of gains received, although the two may come to the same thing in many instances. Restitution in criminal cases has little relationship to restitution in civil cases as covered in this chapter.

plaintiff, the plaintiff may be entitled to specific restitution of Blackacre itself. If the defendant has in the meantime sold Blackacre to an innocent purchaser, the plaintiff may be entitled to restitution in money.

Money restitution in excess of damages. Sometimes a restitutionary recovery is more desirable for the plaintiff than a recovery of damages. Suppose the defendant steals the plaintiff's watch, the value of which was admittedly only $10. The defendant is able to sell the watch for more than its value, say $20. The plaintiff's *loss* is a watch valued at $10 and his *damages* recovery measured by loss is $10. But the defendant's *gain* is $20 and the plaintiff's *restitutionary* recovery measured by that gain is $20. In this example, the plaintiff is entitled to restitution.[3] Not all restitution is in money as it is in the watch example. The watch example shows, however, that when restitution is made in money, the restitution remedy can yield results quite different from the money remedy called damages.

Unjust enrichment basis of restitution claims. Restitution is a simple word but a difficult subject, partly because restitutionary ideas appear in many guises.[4] In spite of their diversity, restitution claims are bound by a major unifying thread. Their purpose is to prevent the defendant's unjust enrichment by recapturing the gains the defendant secured in a transaction.[5]

Substantive and remedial sides of unjust enrichment. Unjust enrichment has both a substantive and a remedial aspect. The substantive question is whether the plaintiff has a right at all, that is, whether the defendant is unjustly enriched by legal standards. Sometimes unjust enrichment is so obvious that it is not important in the analysis: if the defendant steals the plaintiff's watch, he must restore it. The defendant in such a case is a wrongdoer and the plaintiff has title to the goods. Tort and title make the unjust enrichment clear.

When the defendant gains advantages without tort or breach of contract, the substantive question of unjust enrichment is often not so easy to answer. I might save your house by putting out a fire, thus giving you an advantage or benefit, but in the absence of additional facts it is not clear that you are unjustly enriched. The question raised by such cases is mainly substantive and only slightly remedial. The purely remedial questions are different. The remedial question is concerned first with whether, among the remedies possible, restitution is an appropriate or the most appropriate choice. Second, because the defendant's gains can often be measured in different ways, the remedial question is concerned with the appropriate measure or form of restitution.[6]

Applications

Contract breach; unenforceable contracts. Restitution is often an appropriate remedy for breach of an enforceable contract, whether or not there is

---

3. See § 5.18 below.

4. For example, a restitution claim may be familiar under another name. The claims for contribution and indemnity, which are restitutionary claims, are like this. See II G. Palmer, Law of Restitution § 10.6 (1978 & Supps.). Courts may allow a restitutionary recovery without mentioning restitution or any of the words associated with it. E.g., Popp v. Goun-

tanis, 221 Mont. 267, 718 P.2d 340 (1986). See § 4.1(2) below, classifying and illustrating a range of restitution cases.

5. Restatement of Restitution § 1 (1937).

6. The distinctions observed in this paragraph are developed in more detail in § 4.1(2) below.

a "rescission" of that contract.[7] Suppose the plaintiff partly performs a contract before the defendant breaches. Restitution for the value of the plaintiff's performance is an alternative to the ordinary damages remedy. When the contract itself is unenforceable, restitution is usually the *only* remedy available for benefits the plaintiff has conferred upon a defendant in part performance. For instance, if the plaintiff partly performs an agreement that is unenforceable because of the statute of frauds, the plaintiff may have restitution for the value of his performance.[8] The same is true when the contract is unenforceable because one party is a minor,[9] or because the contract has become impracticable of performance.[10] Sometimes restitution is available, too, when the contract is illegal.[11]

Mistake. Benefits conferred by mistake often provide grounds for restitution of the benefits. A plaintiff who enters into a contract with the defendant under an important mutual mistake may be able to avoid the contract altogether and recover back any benefits he has conferred in performing.[12] For example, the plaintiff might recover any prepayments he has made on the purchase price.

Quite aside from such mutual mistake, the plaintiff may transfer money or property under a unilateral mistake, as where he mistakenly overpays money due under a contract or mistakenly delivers a package to the wrong person. Restitution of the money overpaid or the package delivered is the normal rule in such cases.[13] A very similar rule is that the plaintiff is entitled to restitution of money paid to satisfy a judgment that is subsequently reversed or vacated.[14]

Torts and subtortious wrongs. One whose money or property is taken by fraud[15] or embezzlement,[16] or by conversion,[17] is entitled to restitution measured by the defendant's gain if the victim prefers that remedy to the damages remedy. Breach of fiduciary duty of any kind, if it yields gains to the fiduciary, is a favorite ground for restitution.[18] The plaintiff whose copyright[19] or trademark[20] is infringed is likewise commonly awarded restitution based on the gains to the infringer in the form of profits from the infringement.

Almost any kind of case in which the defendant gains from the plaintiff and in which it would be unjust or impolitic to permit the defendant to retain the gain is a good candidate for a restitutionary recovery. Defendant's gains from tortious interference with the plaintiff's contract,[21] or from

---

7. See generally § 12.7 below.

8. See § 13.2 below.

9. See § 13.4 below.

10. See § 13.3 below.

11. See § 13.6 below.

12. See §§ 11.3–11.5 below.

13. E.g., Blue Cross Health Servs., Inc. v. Sauer, 800 S.W.2d 72, 75 (Mo.App.1990); § 11.7 below (mistake in performance).

14. E.g., Mathison v. Clearwater County Welfare Dept., 412 N.W.2d 812 (Minn.App. 1987).

15. See § 9.3 below.

16. See § 6.1 below.

17. See § 5.18 below.

18. See Douthwaite, Profits and Their Recovery, 15 Vill.L.Rev. 346 (1970).

19. See § 6.3(4) below.

20. See § 6.4(4) below.

21. See § 6.6(3) below.

commercial or political bribery,[22] from undue influence or duress [23] are all recoverable as restitution in a proper case.

Other cases. Most restitution cases fall into one of the categories just listed; they provide a return to the plaintiff of benefits conferred in connection with contracts, enforceable or not, in connection with mistakes, and in connection with torts and wrongs. But restitution is open-ended; it is not limited definitionally to such cases. The plaintiff may confer a benefit upon the defendant without mistake and without wrongdoing or breach of an agreement by the defendant. In many such cases the plaintiff will be denied restitution in spite of the defendant's unjust enrichment because it will be important to protect the defendant's right to choose for himself what benefits he wants.[24] But if the defendant's right of choice is not in issue, the plaintiff may be entitled to restitution even when he has intentionally conferred a benefit, without mistake, tort or contract breach. For instance, the doctor who provides medical attention to an unconscious person she has never seen before is entitled to recover for the benefit conferred.[25]

Measuring Benefits for Restitution

Different measures. As with damages, restitution can be measured in different ways. Some of the different ways in which benefits to a defendant can be measured come in for discussion later in this chapter.[26] The most obvious benefit measure is the objective or market value of some asset which the defendant has but which in some relevant sense belongs to the plaintiff. However, restitution may be measured in some other ways. One of those ways must be explained here to show the basic scope and meaning of restitution.

Identifying benefits with the gains they produce. Suppose a thief takes the plaintiff's $10 watch and sells it for $20. The thief is liable for $20, as "restitution." One possible justification for this result is that we think the thief's sale price is good evidence of the actual value of the watch, in which case $20 would represent *damages* for the plaintiff's loss. But even if the plaintiff concedes that the watch was only worth $10, he can recover the $20 as restitution. Why is such a recovery considered to be restitution or "restoration"? How can the plaintiff be "restored" to $20 when what he had in the first place was a $10 watch? If the thief still had the watch, restoration might be in specie through the action of replevin which would give the watch itself back to the plaintiff. Since the thief no longer has the watch, one might think of restoration in terms of its money value, but that is only $10.

The defendant is liable for the $20 because the fund of $20 is perceived as a gain produced by the plaintiff's property. By identifying the $20 as a product of the plaintiff's property, we can think of it as a replacement or substitute for the property. The plaintiff entitled to recover the watch is equally entitled to recover whatever is produced by or substituted for the watch.

---

22. See § 10.6 below.
23. See § 10.2 below.
24. See § 4.9 below.

25. See § 4.1(2) below, analyzing this kind of case and giving further examples.
26. See §§ 4.1(4) & 4.5 below.

This is a potent principle of great value and wide application. It does not mean that the plaintiff will invariably be entitled to restitution or that restitution will always be measured so favorably. But when restitution is appropriate at all, this principle by which the plaintiff's entitlements are identified with the defendant's gains may provide the plaintiff with a remedy far superior to any other.[27]

Relation of Restitution to Damages

Remedial differences. Restitution measures the remedy by the defendant's gain and seeks to force disgorgement of that gain. It differs in its goal or principle from damages, which measures the remedy by the plaintiff's loss and seeks to provide compensation for that loss.[28] As the watch example shows, in some cases the defendant gains more than the plaintiff loses, so that the two remedies may differ in practice as well as in principle. The plaintiff may be able to claim whichever remedy is more advantageous.

Remedial similarities. Although restitution differs from damages, the two remedies can produce exactly the same result in some situations. In the watch example, damages and restitution would be exactly the same if the defendant's gain and the plaintiff's loss matched exactly. If the defendant sold the watch for its market value or if he did not sell it at all but merely kept it,[29] the plaintiff's claim can be seen as *either* restitution *or* as damages because it will perform both the compensatory purposes of damages law and the disgorgement purposes of restitution law. In such cases the claim is not "really" restitution or "really" damages.

Characterizing the award as restitution or damages. When restitution and damages would produce the same award, it is often unimportant to characterize the claim at all. But sometimes the claim must be characterized as one or the other. For example, if the statute of limitations has run on damages claims but not on claims for restitution, the plaintiff will assert unjust enrichment and claim restitution to take advantage of the statute. If a liability insurance company must pay "damages" for which its insured is legally liable, the insurer may argue that its coverage does not protect the insured against liability for "restitution." [30] How is the claim to be characterized when the damages recovery and the restitutionary recovery would be identical in amount and the recovery would serve both the purposes of compensation and disgorgement?

---

27. As the example in the text indicates, to recover the defendant's gains may be to recover a greater sum of money. Other advantages include the possibility of making a monetary recovery when the plaintiff cannot prove the amount of actual damages, the possibility of making a recovery of specific property, and the possibility of gaining priorities over other creditors of the defendant. These possibilities are illustrated in many different places in this treatise. Some of them can be seen in § 6.1 below.

28. Courts sometimes speak of "damages" measured by "restitution" or a "restitutionary measure of damages," but such locutions ignore that difference in principle between the two remedies. This treatise attempts to avoid such usages.

29. Some authority, based on the old forms of action, might refuse restitution in the absence of a sale.

30. E.g., Boeing Co. v. Aetna Casualty and Surety Co., 113 Wash.2d 869, 784 P.2d 507 (1990). *Boeing* reflects judicial differences of opinion as to whether response costs for which an insured entity is liable under CERCLA, 42 U.S.C.A. § 9601 et seq. count as damages covered under a liability policy or whether the insured's liability for response costs is a liability for "restitution."

The watch example presents this question. The plaintiff in that example has a good substantive claim grounded in the defendant's tort, so a remedy that provides compensation to the plaintiff can be viewed as a damages remedy even though the defendant will also disgorge his gains by paying the damages award. Unless a statute or public policy requires otherwise, the claim can equally be viewed as a restitution claim, because the award will force disgorgement of unjust gain even though it will also provide compensation. If the facts justify a substantive claim of restitution to prevent unjust enrichment, the existence of other remedies like damages is no impediment to restitutionary relief.[31] And correspondingly, if the facts justify a damages claim, that claim is not negated by the fact that the plaintiff could have chosen restitution instead. Substantive law and policy justifies either kind of claim and on the facts of the example, courts allow the plaintiff to treat the claim as either one for damages or one for restitution.[32]

On the other hand, if the plaintiff has *no* substantive claim grounded in tort, contract, or statute, then if the plaintiff's claim is viable at all, it *must* be one for restitution to prevent unjust enrichment. That is so because restitutionary ideals form the only substantive basis for the claim. In that case, the recovery will force disgorgement of the defendant's gains (restitution) and also provide the equivalent of compensation (damages). Even so, if unjust enrichment is the only substantive basis for that recovery, the claim is for restitution.

Relation of Restitution to Equity [33]

The substantive basis of restitution is related to substantive equity. That is, courts applying substantive equity and courts applying the law of unjust enrichment are both applying a law of "good conscience." Remedially and historically speaking, however, restitution might be either a purely legal claim or a purely equitable claim.

Restitution claims for money are usually claims "at law."[34] So are restitution claims for replevin and ejectment.[35] On the other hand, restitution claims that may require coercive intervention or some judicial action that is historically "equitable," may be regarded as equitable claims. For example, if the defendant fraudulently obtained title to Blackacre from the plaintiff, the plaintiff might ask the court to declare a "constructive trust," the upshot of which would be to order the defendant to reconvey Blackacre to the plaintiff. Such a claim is restitutionary and also historically regarded as equitable.[36]

If the same plaintiff merely asked for the money value of Blackacre or the sums gained by the defendant in selling that famous property, then the claim could still be restitutionary but it would now be a claim "at law."

Terminology

The terminology of restitution is abstruse and confusing and is no matter for amateurs. Some of the many special terms will appear in other

---

31. See I G. Palmer, Law of Restitution § 1.6 (1978 & Supps.).

32. See § 4.2(3) on waiver of tort and suit in assumpsit.

33. See § 4.3 below generally.

34. See § 4.2(3).

35. See § 4.2(2) below.

36. See § 4.3(2) below.

sections.[37] Because confusion has sometimes run very deep indeed, some major ways of talking about restitution should be understood immediately. Here are some basic points about the terms.

(1) As we have seen, *restitution* is not *damages;* restitution is a restoration required to prevent unjust enrichment.

(2) Restitution can be addressed by reference to the old forms of action in which restitutionary aims were pursued in the law courts. A judge can say that the plaintiff is entitled to recover in *assumpsit* as a reference to a form of action no longer in existence but one that might once have been used for restitutionary recoveries.[38] Special forms of assumpsit can also refer to restitution, the most familiar of these being *quantum meruit.* These and parallel terms refer to one form of restitution or one process of getting it. They are not something different from restitution.

(3) Restitution can also be addressed by reference to an older *theory* of relief (as distinct from the older forms of action). The older ways of speaking about restitutionary claims in law courts was to say that the law implied a contract between the parties although no contract existed. This in turn was called quasi-contract. So a judge who says the plaintiff has an implied in law contract claim could also say that the plaintiff has a quasi-contract claim or that the plaintiff has a restitution claim (for money).[39]

(4) Restitution can also be addressed by reference to the theory and form of the remedy used in equity. The terms constructive trust,[40] equitable lien,[41] accounting for profits [42] and subrogation [43] are terms that come to us from the equity side of the court. They reflect different measures or forms of restitution but they are all restitutionary.

§ 4.1(2) The Substantive Side of Restitution: Unjust Enrichment

Introducing the Meanings of Unjust Enrichment

Unjust enrichment as the basis of liability. The fundamental substantive basis for restitution is that the defendant has been unjustly enriched by receiving something, tangible or intangible, that properly belongs to the plaintiff. Restitution rectifies unjust enrichment by forcing restoration to the plaintiff.

Unjust enrichment cannot be precisely defined, and for that very reason has potential for resolving new problems in striking ways. But unjust enrichment is not as vague as it sounds for at least two kinds of reasons.

First, unjust enrichment refers to corrective justice, not distributive justice. It does not invite judgments about the fair distribution of wealth in society, but about what is right between two particular people, considering

---

37. See § 4.1(3) for further references to terms.

38. See § 4.2(3) below for details about assumpsit.

39. See § 4.2(3) below.

40. See § 4.3(2) below.

41. See § 4.3(3) below.

42. See § 4.3(5) below.

43. See § 4.3(4) below.

"equity and good conscience"[1] or by the ties of natural justice.[2] For example, one who is enriched by what he is entitled to under a contract or otherwise is not unjustly enriched.[3]

Second, some common patterns in the cases show that the unjust enrichment rationale is often only a unifying generalization about familiar kinds of cases, a way of protecting what we already believe to be the plaintiff's entitlements. Although factual details can be quite varied, many unjust enrichment cases fall in one of the groups described below.

Group 1 Cases: Benefits to defendant where title remains in the plaintiff. In some cases unjust enrichment is definitionally proved. Defendant takes the plaintiff's chattel. Title remains in the plaintiff under ordinary rules of law that a thief acquires no title. The defendant is unjustly enriched because he has something the law has already declared to be the plaintiff's property. The plaintiff is entitled to restitution of the chattel and he can enforce that right by the replevin action.[4]

Group 2 Cases: Benefits to defendant where title passes through misconduct. In other cases title does not remain in the plaintiff, but on the contrary the defendant takes good legal title. If the defendant takes that title by wrongdoing, however, the unjustness of his enrichment is shown by his wrongdoing. So if the defendant gets title to Blackacre or to a patent or to any other entitlement by fraud,[5] duress,[6] undue influence[7] or other

§ 4.1(2)

1. This is the standard of judgment repeatedly referred to in older cases. The use of the term equity has sometimes been confusing. It does not imply that all restitution cases are brought "in equity" or that equitable relief is given. It is not a jurisdictional statement but a standard about the goal or a standard for judging what counts as unjust enrichment. See Philpott v. Superior Court, 1 Cal.2d 512, 36 P.2d 635, 95 A.L.R. 990 (1934).

2. Moses v. MacFerlan, 2 Burr. 1005, 97 Eng.Rep. 676 (K.B.1760); Murdock–Bryant Const. Inc. v. Pearson, 146 Ariz. 48, 703 P.2d 1197, 1202 (1985).

3. *For example*: Under an agreement with a general contractor, a subcontractor improves the defendant's land but the general contractor goes out of business and does not pay him. The subcontractor has a loss and the landowner a gain, but the landowner's gain is one he bargained for in his contract with the general contractor. The landowner is not unjustly enriched at the expense of the subcontractor. E.g., Concrete Products Co. v. Salt Lake County, 734 P.2d 910 (Utah 1987). See § 4.9(4) below. Mechanics' and materialmen's lien statutes alter this result in some cases. As to those, see § 12.20(3) below.

The idea that one is not unjustly enriched by receiving what is due him is not necessarily an easy one to apply, however. In Lynch v. Deaconess Medical Center, 113 Wash.2d 162, 776 P.2d 681 (1989) a patient had received hospital treatment for which her insurer had paid over $8,000. The insurer then concluded that the treatment was not covered and de-

manded repayment from the hospital. The hospital made the repayment. The patient evidently believed she then owed the hospital, so she retained an attorney to sue the insurer. The attorney was successful and the insurer ended up paying the hospital. The attorney sought to recover attorney fees from the hospital, since his efforts had produced the gain to the hospital. Such a recovery is consistent with the rule applied in common fund cases, see § 3.10(2) above, and also with cases in which an insured pursues an insurer's subrogation claim, as in, e.g., Principal Casualty Ins. Co. v. Norwood, 463 N.W.2d 66 (Iowa 1990). Nevertheless, the *Lynch* court concluded that the hospital was not unjustly enriched because it was entitled to be paid for its services. If the hospital could have collected the debt against the patient, that conclusion seems right. But if, as perhaps was the case, the patient could not have paid the debt from her own resources, it seems arguable that the hospital was in fact enriched by the attorney's efforts, because, under the hypothesis that the debt was uncollectible, the hospital would never have recovered the payment except for the attorney's efforts.

4. As to replevin and its alternatives, see § 5.17, below.

5. Chapter 9 below.

6. See § 10.2 below. When conduct that counts as duress or undue influence is not actionable as a tort, there may be a major issue as to the wrongfulness and whether it

7. See note 7 on page 373.

misconduct,[8] the case for saying he is unjustly enriched is complete as soon as the actionable misconduct is established.[9] We can think of such cases as cases of "rescission" or avoidance of a transaction, or cancellation of a deed, but the underlying notion is one of unjust enrichment. We do not find the defendant to be unjustly enriched because the plaintiff has "rescinded." It is the other way around: we permit "rescission" or avoidance of the transaction because unless we did so the defendant would be unjustly enriched.

Group 3 Cases: Benefits to defendant resulting from breach of contract. Neither wrongdoing nor title is an essential element of a restitution claim. Restitution is an alternative remedy for an ordinary breach of contract with no wrongdoing and no title involved. If the plaintiff has partly performed his side of the contract, a breach or repudiation by the defendant will permit the plaintiff to recover either damages or restitution, at his option.[10] If damages are hard to prove he may choose restitution. He may also choose restitution if that would yield a larger recovery than damages. The plaintiff has no option to claim restitution where he has fully performed and the defendant only owes a liquidated sum of money.[11] Otherwise, however, restitution is available for breach of contract as one alternative remedy. The defendant in such cases is guilty of breach, not tort or wrongdoing. Nevertheless, the unjustness of allowing the defendant to retain the plaintiff's performance is established as soon as we know that he is liable for the breach.

Group 4 Cases: Benefits to defendant from money or services without misconduct—Mistakes and other disruptions in contracting. Not all unjust enrichment turns on tort, on tangible property, or on contract breach. Sometimes a plaintiff confers a benefit upon a defendant wholly apart from any breach of substantive duty. Parties attempting to enter a contract may be mistaken in their underlying assumptions about the subject matter of that contract,[12] or they may be faced with new conditions they never intended to contract about.[13] When the mistakes or new conditions become apparent, the best solution may be to call off the deal because it is not really the deal the parties attempted to make. In such cases, the plaintiff who has prepaid the price, is entitled to restitution of that price from the defendant. The defendant is excused from performance and he is no wrongdoer; but he would be unjustly enriched if he kept the prepayment, so must make restitution. The same is true if the plaintiff has performed some of the services due under the contract instead of paying part of the contract price. Restitution is also appropriate when the plaintiff mistakenly delivers the wrong goods or delivers the right goods to the wrong person.

suffices to support a restitution claim. When the conduct is shown to count as an actionable tort, the wrongfulness is established.

7. See § 10.3 below.

8. E.g., fiduciary breaches, see § 10.4 below.

9. When title has passed, however, a bona fide purchase by an innocent third person will ordinarily cut off the plaintiff's right to restitution.

10. See § 12.7(1) below.

11. See §§ 4.5(4), 12.7(5) below.

12. E.g., Beachcomber Coins, Inc. v. Boskett, 166 N.J.Super. 442, 400 A.2d 78 (1979) (buyer paid $500 for coin that proved to be counterfeit, rescission permitted on grounds of mistake); § 11.3 below generally.

13. See § 13.3 below.

Benefits conferred without mistake or contract. Cases of attempted contract often illustrate the Group 4 category, but contract is not an essential ingredient. What is essential is that the defendant receives a benefit without fault or breach of duty on his part, yet is at least arguably under a duty to give up that benefit on the ground that otherwise he will be unjustly enriched.

The absence of contract and wrongdoing can be seen in the case of the physician's medical attention to the unconscious plaintiff. Suppose the physician commits no wrong in administering medical treatment, but that the unconscious defendant made no contract to receive or pay for services. The physician can recover for the reasonable value of her services to the unconscious defendant, to prevent unjust enrichment, even though the defendant has committed no wrong and has entered no contractual relation with the physician.[14] Similarly, the plaintiff who performs the defendant's duties by providing necessaries to her minor children,[15] or who preserves the defendant's property at cost to himself,[16] has an unjust enrichment claim based neither in tort nor any kind of consensual relationship. Still another example can be seen in the claim of contribution by one who has paid more than his share of a joint obligation.[17]

Where restitution is the only basis of liability: substantive unjust enrichment issues. As Professor Laycock has pointed out,[18] restitution based on unjust enrichment is of great practical importance not only when restitution of the defendant's gains in a transaction would give the plaintiff a better recovery than compensatory damages, but also when unjust enrichment provides the *only* ground for any recovery at all. The cases in Group 4 are like this. They involve the substantive issue whether enrichment can be described as unjust. In contrast, the cases in the first three groups involved the remedial issue: what relief is available for breach of contract, tort, or dispossession?

It does not seem hard to decide cases like the one in which the physician renders services to an unconscious person in an emergency. The unconscious person should pay for benefits received. Yet all of us benefit constantly from efforts of others, so it is difficult to know in some of these cases what counts as an "unjust" enrichment or even what counts as "enrichment" at all. For instance, suppose my quarry and yours adjoin one another

14. See Cotnam v. Wisdom, 83 Ark. 601, 104 S.W. 164 (1907) (doctor entitled to recover restitution).

15. II G. Palmer, Law of Restitution § 10.4 (1978 & Supps.); Restatement of Restitution § 113 (1937).

16. Preservation of property cases might arise in emergency, or in the case of a finder of lost property, but also in other cases in which the plaintiff can avoid volunteer status. See Peterson v. Midland Nat. Bank, 242 Kan. 266, 747 P.2d 159 (1987) (holder of security interest in cattle asked debtor to have them fed; debtor asked plaintiff and plaintiff did so; the plaintiff could recover against the security holder who foreclosed on its lien on the cattle); Jacobs v. Andolina, 123 A.D.2d 835, 507 N.Y.S.2d 450 (1986) (occupier of property liable for rental value, but credited for expenses incurred in maintaining property, paying insurance and taxes).

17. E.g., Laura v. Christian, 88 N.M. 127, 537 P.2d 1389 (1975) (cotenant who paid off lien on cotenancy was entitled to contribution from other cotenant and a lien to secure contribution). As to contribution and similar claims see II G. Palmer, Law of Restitution § 10.6 (1978 & Supps.). Note that the right to contribution or "equitable indemnity" as some courts have called it, is not based on the defendant's breach of a tort duty toward the plaintiff, on contract, or on mistake.

18. Laycock, The Scope and Significance of Restitution, 67 Tex.L.Rev. 1277, 1284 (1989).

and both are filled with water; to make my quarry useful, I drain it at great expense, and the effect is to drain yours as well. You are advantaged, at least if you wish to quarry rock, but perhaps it would be unwise to say that you are unjustly enriched and must disgorge your gains.[19]

Or suppose that you are insured for liability by the defendant. You fall asleep while driving as a result of reading legal treatises all day; you crash into a house. You have the presence of mind, however, to hire a contractor to make a temporary foundation which prevents the house from collapsing. Your expense in hiring a contractor has the indirect effect of saving your liability company a large sum of money it would have had to pay if the house had fallen down. You have no contract or tort claim against your insurer; is the insurer nevertheless unjustly enriched? On difficult judgments of this kind, courts might be expected to differ.[20]

Finally, suppose that a corporate officer uses information he gains in his job to identify lucrative markets for a personal business of his own. If he has taken information that we know "belongs" to the corporation, we can say the officer is unjustly enriched.[21] The difficult question, and a substantive one, is whether any particular information should be regarded by the law as "belonging" to the corporation in the first place. Exactly the same issue arises when the plaintiff's former employee sets up in business and uses what he learned in working for the plaintiff to operate his own enterprise. Was the knowledge he gained protected information like a trade secret or was it merely part of the experience of life we are all free to use? [22]

Restitution/Unjust Enrichment Claims to Establish New Rights

Restitution as a means for recognizing rights in intangibles. Cases in which there is no tort or relevant contract are often the most difficult cases for determining unjust enrichment. We can see that the unjust enrichment conception of restitution will be most important in dealing with cases where title reasoning does not readily work—especially in cases in which the benefit to the defendant derives from services, money or other intangibles. Restitution in fact seems to be the tool that allowed law to move from the old medieval world of property and things to the modern world of contracts and by intangibles. Most wealth today is represented by intangibles like money, stock, trade secrets, or business opportunities. Restitution and unjust en-

19. Ulmer v. Farnsworth, 80 Me. 500, 15 A. 65 (1888) (denying liability) (discussed in Dawson, The Self–Serving Intermeddler, 87 Harv.L.Rev. 1409, 1418 (1974)). Cf. Dobson v. Arkansas Oil & Gas Com'n, 218 Ark. 160, 235 S.W.2d 33 (1950) (oil and gas unitization exceeded authority, majority cannot impose will on holdouts even though holdout benefits from majority improvements) (quoted in § 4.9(4) below).

20. Insurer liable on similar facts: Leebov v. United States Fidelity and Guar. Co., 401 Pa. 477, 165 A.2d 82 (1960). Insurer not liable on slightly different facts: McNeilab, Inc. v. North River Ins. Co., 645 F.Supp. 525 (D.N.J. 1986), aff'd, 831 F.2d 287 (3d Cir.1987) (Table) (product liability insurer not liable when man-

ufacturer recalled all of product after poison scare).

With *McNeilab* compare Lynch v. Deaconess Medical Center, 113 Wash.2d 162, 776 P.2d 681 (1989), discussed in n. 3, supra.

21. See e.g., Janigan v. Taylor, 344 F.2d 781 (1st Cir.1965), cert. denied, 382 U.S. 879, 86 S.Ct. 163, 15 L.Ed.2d 120 (1965), discussed in § 9.3(4) below; and see generally § 10.5 below. To say that information "belongs" to the company is to say it is intellectual property; once it is held that the information is property, the decision to grant restitution of benefits resulting from use of that is easy and the case would fall under either Group 1 or Group 2.

22. See § 10.5(3) below.

richment are often the terms in which rights in intangibles are recognized or rejected.

Is "unjust enrichment" too vague? Sometimes it is said that unjust enrichment is too vague a term and that rights should not depend upon it. The difficulty arises, not from the vagueness of unjust enrichment, but from the uncertainty about how to treat new forms of intangible value. We are often uncertain, for example, whether or not we should say that a given piece of business information "belongs" to anyone.

Difficulties of this kind are common with intangibles, whether the plaintiff seeks restitution or some other remedy. Tort law must face the same kinds of questions about the existence and scope of economic entitlements. For example, tort law must determine whether the opportunity to inherit, or to gain from a hoped-for contract with another person, or the opportunity to win a race is to be protected from interference.[23] In the same way, tort law must determine whether the plaintiff's characteristic voice or the manufacturer's package design is to be protected against imitation.[24] Although restitution may present the only possible money recovery in some situations, similar substantive issues arise in damages and injunction suits where the difficulties in reaching a decision are just as great.

The difficulty in Group 4 cases does not lie in the remedy or in the terminology of enrichment but in the substantive issues about what forms of intangible advantage deserve legal protection. Because most of the difficulty is substantive (deciding what enrichment should count as unjust) and only a little of it is remedial (deciding what should count as enrichment), many Group 4 cases come in for discussion in this treatise in only limited ways.

Qualifying and Limiting Unjust Enrichment Claims: Protecting Innocence and Autonomy

Courts refuse to permit recovery of restitution even when unjust enrichment is fully established if a restitutionary award would interfere with the defendant's own rights or would be unfair or inequitable on the particular facts of the case.

Protecting autonomy under the volunteers rules. The defendant's autonomy interests must be fully respected. Ordinarily at least, he must not be made to pay "restitution" for something he did not take, did not want, and did not bargain for. The housepainter cannot paint your house in your absence, then demand payment, even if you benefit from having a more valuable house.[25] An extension of the same principle holds that rights fixed by a contract between the parties must not be altered by an award of restitution.[26]

Protecting innocent purchasers. The innocent purchaser for value must be protected in most restitution cases where legal title has passed from the plaintiff. If *A* fraudulently gets title to Blackacre from the plaintiff, then

---

23. See §§ 6.6–6.9 below.

24. See § 6.5(3) below.

25. See § 4.9 below.

26. The point is pervasive. For one discussion, see § 12.7(5) below.

sells it to an innocent purchaser, the plaintiff is not entitled to recover Blackacre from that purchaser.[27]

Protecting defendants who have changed position. Innocent defendants must be protected where they have changed position after receiving the enrichment and where they would be placed under significant hardship if restitution is required of them.[28] Laches and estoppel[29] may be used as tools of this principle if needed.

Protecting public policy. Restitution may be bad policy in some cases even when unjust enrichment is shown. If a book invades the plaintiff's privacy she might find redress by damages, but if she is allowed to recover restitution based on some percentage of the author's profits, there is too much risk of over-restitution and too much risk to free speech interests.[30]

§ 4.1(3) Introducing the Procedural and Terminological Side of Restitution

Diversity and Unity

At one time the legal profession did not understand restitution to be a general legal topic at all. What we now call restitution was pursued through a whole host of actions, each of which was adapted to a single factual situation. These actions were often thought of as "remedies" rather than theories for a claim. They went under a splendid variety of names like Money Had and Received, Money Paid, Money Lent, Quantum Meruit and many others. Earlier lawyers thought of these narrow actions as essentially unrelated.

These same kinds of claims are now perceived to be merely subsets of restitution. The modern view is that unjust enrichment is a unifying principle for all such cases and restitution is the award made to vindicate that principle. Restitution today is applied both in cases that used to be brought at law and those that used to be brought in equity. The unity of the subject matter is now reflected in part by Professor Palmer's four-volume treatise of classic dimensions[1] and by the collection of many restitution cases under the topic of Implied and Constructive Contracts in the West Digests.[2] Even so, the history of restitution as a collection of insular and unrelated dooms or procedures is also still apparent in the diverse locutions of the courts[3] and in the fact that it cannot be fully captured in any single topic of the Digest.[4]

27. See § 4.7 below.
28. See § 4.6 below.
29. See §§ 2.3(5) & 2.4(4) above.
30. See § 7.2(13) (defamation cases).

§ 4.1(3)
1. G. Palmer, Law of Restitution (4 vols., 1978 & Supps.); Restatement of Restitution (1937).
2. The Westlaw numerical designation is 205h.
3. For instance, judges may still use a variety of terms such as "assumpsit" or "quantum meruit" although these terms are based on procedures that have been obsolete for over a

century. Judges very often use the term "damages" to refer to money restitution.
4. Before 1980 the Digest topic now consolidated as Implied and Constructive Contracts was divided into Money Lent, Money Paid, Money Received, Use and Occupation and Work and Labor. Consolidation of the fragments facilitated research, but because restitution is potentially a remedy in any situation in which the defendant receives benefits, restitutionary issues can appear in almost any digest topic. Because courts do not use a consistent terminology, even computer word searches can be difficult. Dean John Wade listed 31 Digest topics in which he found restitutionary materials. See Wade, The Litera-

Equity

Restitution claims are initiated in the same way that other claims are initiated, by a complaint, counterclaim, or set-off. Once the claim is initiated, many diverse terms and procedures may be invoked to enforce a restitutionary regime. Some of them derive from the old separate equity courts and are still distinguished by *in personam* orders.[5] Such procedures may operate to provide restitution in specie, that is, a return of a particular item of property such as Blackacre. The most notable equitable procedures to enforce restitution are the constructive trust,[6] the equitable lien,[7] and subrogation.[8] These procedures give the plaintiff restitution by giving the plaintiff title to, or a security interest in particular property; or, in the case of subrogation, by giving the plaintiff the rights formerly held by another person.

Law

Other restitutionary procedures are derived from the old separate "law" courts. Restitution in money was afforded at law by actions which, as a group, were referred to as quasi-contract actions or implied-in-law contract actions. The terminology was misleading; these claims did not necessarily have any relation whatever to contract claims. If a thief steals the plaintiff's watch and sells it, the plaintiff can have a "quasi-contract" claim for restitution, although the claim is based on a tort, not on a contract. Sometimes quasi-contract claims were discussed in terms of "assumpsit" because assumpsit was the ancient writ used in England to initiate such cases. Sometimes restitution was discussed in terms of assumpsit's subcategories, like quantum meruit. It is confusing to refer to the idea of restitution by such different terms as quasi-contract, assumpsit, and quantum meruit, and in contemporary usage the single term restitution may usually be substituted for the remedy and "unjust enrichment" is usually given as the substantive basis for it. Nevertheless, the old terms cannot be ignored if the cases are to be understood, and in fact they are discussed in more detail later.[9]

In Personam and in Rem Procedures

Law courts enforced specie restitution as well as money restitution. In particular the law courts allowed the plaintiff to recover his personal property through the action called replevin or one similar to such an action.[10] They allowed the plaintiff to recover his real property through the action in ejectment.[11] These actions differed from suits for constructive trust and from other equitable restitution in several ways.

The procedural difference lay in the fact that replevin and ejectment remedies operated directly on the property: the sheriff would seize it and restore it to the plaintiff (hence they were "in rem," about things). The

ture of the Law of Restitution, 19 Hast.L.J. 1087 (1968). For these reasons, treatises and articles are often the best beginnings for any restitution research.

5. See paragraph "In personam and in rem procedures" below, this section.

6. See § 4.3(2) below.

7. See § 4.3(3) below.

8. See § 4.3(4) below.

9. See § 4.2 below.

10. See § 5.17 below.

11. See § 5.10(1) below.

constructive trust imposed by equity courts on the other hand, operated on the "conscience of the defendant" by a direct order of the court which, for example, ultimately told the defendant to reconvey Blackacre to the plaintiff from whom it had been taken by fraud.

These procedures and old forms of action help us understand that the term restitution does not refer to a form of action or to a particular procedure. Instead, restitution is a general description of the relief afforded. It is thus *not* a parallel to terms like assumpsit, or trespass, or conversion, but a parallel to terms like damages, or injunction.

§ 4.1(4) The Measurement of Restitution—The Remedial Side of Restitution

Remedial Problems: Choosing Restitution and Its Measure

The remedial issues in restitution. Although it is important to understand the substantive and procedural sides of restitution, this book is primarily concerned with its remedial side. In other words, this book is concerned with the questions affecting the measurement of remedy, or its qualification, or the selection of some alternative remedy.

Measurement of defendant's benefits. The chief remedial problem of restitution is perhaps its measurement. Restitution is measured by the defendant's "benefits" in the relevant transactions. In damages law, losses to the plaintiff may be measured in a number of different ways. In restitution law, benefits to the defendant may be measured in different ways. Measurement of benefits should not be considered wholly apart from its context and purpose, but it is useful to recognize several possibilities. Those possibilities are discussed and illustrated later in this chapter, but they can be stated briefly now.

Major measures. If the alleged benefit to the defendant is a result of acts that call for restitution, the main options for measurement of the benefit are these:

(1) the increased assets [1] in the hands of the defendant from the receipt of property;

(2) the market value of services or intangibles provided to the defendant, without regard to whether the defendant's assets were actually increased; that is, the amount which it would cost to obtain similar services, whether those services prove to be useful or not.

(3) the use value of any benefits received, as measured by (i) market indicators such as rental value or interest or (ii) actual gains to the defendant from using the benefits, such as the gains identified in item (5) below;

(4) the gains realized by the defendant upon sale or transfer of an asset received from the plaintiff;

§ 4.1(4)

1. The term asset is meant to include anything of value, whether it is tangible or intangible. Information, for example, may be an asset if it can be directly used to produce income or a trading gain, as in corporate opportunity cases, or if it can be sold, as in trade secret cases.

(5) collateral or secondary profits earned by the defendant by use of an asset received from the plaintiff, or, what is much the same thing, the savings effected by the use of the asset.[2]

Choosing among the measures. In some cases the plaintiff might be allowed to choose among two or more of these optional methods for measuring restitution, but in many cases the measure of benefit, like the measure of compensatory damages, will be set by the court. Much of the remedial side of restitution law is about choosing an appropriate measure of the benefit received by the defendant. Some of the bases for choosing are discussed in a later section. This introductory section can appropriately notice in particular that the fourth measure—the defendant's profits[3]—can be compared to consequential damages in that they depart from market measures. To require a defendant to give up profits may operate with particular severity because at least some of the profits would almost always be attributable to the defendant's efforts or investment. So the profit recovery as a measure of restitution is extraordinary. In general, the defendant who is not a serious wrongdoer is held only to make restitution measured by actual gains in assets or in gains of services or intangibles which he in fact sought in the relevant transaction.[4]

Unjust enrichment and punitive damages. As shown in the example of the stolen watch,[5] the defendant's gains in a transaction may exceed the plaintiff's losses, so that if the plaintiff recovers the defendant's gains as restitution, the plaintiff is better off than if he had recovered compensation for his loss. In giving the plaintiff more than compensation, restitution suggests a punitive element, but that may be misleading. Restitution may be more than compensation to the plaintiff but under most measures of restitution it is not more than the defendant's unjust gain in the transaction. For this reason, such restitution is not punitive.

There are, however, cases in which restitution is measured in such a way that it exceeds both the plaintiff's loss and the defendant's gain. Such restitution can fairly be called punitive. This might occur if restitution is measured by the defendant's profits and he is forced to disgorge those profits without any credit for his own effort and investment.[6]

Remedy choice. The second major remedial problem with restitution is the selection or choice of a remedy. Sometimes courts can permit a plaintiff to have either damages or restitution but not both. For instance, the defrauded plaintiff might sue for damages or he might seek to rescind the

2. These measures are discussed in §§ 4.5(2) & 4.5(3) below.

3. Not all the defendant's gains are profits from operation of a business. Some gains are simple market gains, as in the watch hypothetical. See § 4.5(3) below.

4. Courts sometimes award profits made by a defendant and sometimes not. Professor Laycock succinctly states: "The Restatement and Professor Palmer explain such distinctions partly in terms of culpability and partly in terms of directness. The more culpable defendant's behavior, and the more direct the connection between the profits and the wrongdoing, the more likely that plaintiff can recov-er all defendant's profits." Laycock, The Scope and Significance of Restitution, 67 Tex. L.Rev. 1277, 1289 (1989). Laycock also recognizes that profits liability might serve some purposes of a more or less economic kind. Id. at 1290.

5. See § 4.1(1) above.

6. See §§ 4.3(3) & 4.5(3) below. Cf. Truck Equipment Serv. Co. v. Fruehauf Corp., 536 F.2d 1210 (8th Cir.1976), cert. denied, 429 U.S. 861, 97 S.Ct. 164, 50 L.Ed.2d 139 (1976); Warren v. Century Bankcorporation, Inc., 741 P.2d 846 (Okl.1987).

transaction and have restitution of what he gave. Conceivably, under modern procedures, a plaintiff might be permitted to have a combination of relief built in part from blocks of damages and in part from blocks of restitution.[7]

In many cases, however, courts limit the plaintiff to a restitutionary remedy. This might occur, for example, if the statute of frauds bars enforcement of a contract. In that case, damages is an inappropriate remedy because to allow damages would be to subvert the statute; but restitution is a perfectly acceptable remedy. Sometimes one remedy is precluded because of a supposed "election" of remedies resulting from the plaintiff's delay[8] in pursuing a claim or from his failure to restore benefits he himself has received in a transaction.[9] So the choice of remedy as well as a measure of it presents a common remedial issue.

Relation of Substance and Remedy

Substantive–remedial entanglement. It is convenient analytically to separate the substantive and remedial sides of restitution. Yet those two sides of restitution are at times virtually inseparable. The substantive question asks whether the defendant was unjustly enriched. Often enough, the focus here will be upon the question of justness or unjustness of the process by which defendant received some clear benefit, and in such cases the question is purely a substantive one. But the very question of the plaintiff's substantive right in a restitution case, the question of unjust enrichment, must turn on what one means by enrichment or benefit. The question of what one means by enrichment or benefit directly implicates the measurement question central to the remedial side of restitution law.

Example of services under an unenforceable contract. For instance, suppose a plaintiff, acting under an agreement that is unenforceable under the statute of frauds, spends the day as a salesperson for the defendant, attempting to sell encyclopedias door to door. Suppose she sells none and quits. Although the statute of frauds prohibits a recovery of damages "on the contract," the statute does not prevent a recovery of restitution. Can the plaintiff assert such a claim in light of the fact that she made no sales? In other words, did the defendant receive a benefit?[10]

The question is both substantive and remedial because its affirmative answer tells us both that the defendant is unjustly enriched and the measure of that enrichment. To decide that the defendant is unjustly enriched is also to decide that the proper measure of enrichment is the market value of the plaintiff's services, that is, what people charge for a day's work in similar jobs. The market value of services measure must be the right one if the court finds any enrichment at all, because by any other measure the defendant is not enriched. Enrichment could not be measured by the increase in the defendant's assets, for instance, because the defendant's assets were not increased by the plaintiff's unproductive work. So in this

7. Under traditional election of remedies this was not possible, but so long as the recovery does not either overcompensate the plaintiff nor exact more than restitution from the defendant, the combination is appropriate. A combination was allowed in Head & Seemann, Inc. v. Gregg, 107 Wis.2d 126, 318 N.W.2d 381 (1982).

8. See §§ 9.4 & 12.7(6) below.

9. See § 9.3(3) below.

10. See §§ 4.5(2), 13.2 below.

instance, the substantive decision that the defendant was "enriched" also decides most or all of the remedial question.

Which decision comes first, substantive or remedial? It is usually assumed that substantive law is determined first and that the remedy follows obediently like a dog on a leash. This is partly correct, because the remedy must indeed reflect the rule of substantive law and carry out its policy.

Substantive decisions influenced by existence of a mild remedy. On the other hand, the substantive rule must be made in the first place with an awareness of what it will do to the parties. For example, restitution can be either a radical remedy or a mild one because it may either upset a settled transaction or provide a modest restoration of the status quo ante. Judges may be willing to expand substantive liabilities when they are limited to mild forms of restitution, but may desire to constrict those liabilities when large damages might result. In fraud cases where loss of bargain damages are sought, traditional rules usually required the plaintiff to make his case by proving scienter, an intentional deception. But where restitution was sought on the same facts, the plaintiff was only required to prove a material misstatement by the defendant, and it was not necessary to show that the defendant intended to deceive.[11] The difference is not the difference between law and equity, but the difference between a remedy like damages that might be quite extensive, and a remedy like restitution that might be quite mild.

Substantive decisions influenced by radical remedy. Correspondingly, when the only possible measure of restitution is a radical one that captures the defendant's profits, courts might be reluctant to recognize any substantive right at all if recovery of the profits would be likely to capture the gains from the defendant's own legitimate efforts as well as the gains that fairly belong to the plaintiff.[12] This is not to say that courts always deny a recovery of the defendant's profits, only that courts may refuse to recognize any substantive wrong at all if the only remedial medicine available will be worse than the disease. If the wrong is bad enough, even a radical remedy that captures the defendant's own property to protect the plaintiff's rights may be acceptable.[13]

The point of these observations is that substantive and remedial issues often interact. Remedy should follow the right and reflect it, but courts cannot always proceed in such a direct manner. Sometimes the right is determined in the light of the remedy available.

---

11. See §§ 9.1 & 9.3 below.

12. See Simon & Schuster, Inc. v. Members of the New York State Crime Victims Board, ___ U.S. ___, 112 S.Ct. 501, 116 L.Ed.2d 476 (1991), discussed in § 8.9 below. In *Simon & Schuster* recovery of the defendant's profits from writing about his own crimes was unconstitutional as an infringement of free speech rights, seemingly because the statute authorizing such a recovery made no allocation of the profits resulting more or less directly from the crimes and the profits from the defendant's own ideas and effort or those from writing about other matters.

13. Hamilton–Brown Shoe Co. v. Wolf Bros. & Co., 240 U.S. 251, 261, 36 S.Ct. 269, 273, 60 L.Ed. 629 (1916) (all of defendant's profits on goods identified with the plaintiff's trademark), discussed in § 6.4(4) below; Snepp v. United States, 444 U.S. 507, 100 S.Ct. 763, 62 L.Ed.2d 704 (1980) (profits from book published in violation of "fiduciary duty" to submit for approval to author's employer, the Central Intelligence Agency); Janigan v. Taylor, 344 F.2d 781 (1st Cir.1965), cert. denied, 382 U.S. 879, 86 S.Ct. 163, 15 L.Ed.2d 120 (1965) (profits of corporate officer, a fiduciary, in concealing opportunities from stockholders), discussed in § 9.3(4) below.

§ 4.2   Restitution at Law—Terminology and Development

§ 4.2(1) In Summary

In the early development of restitution, no general principle of unjust enrichment was recognized. Restitution developed in association with various technical doctrines of the earlier law. Some doctrines were developed in equity, some at law. Both lines left their mark, so that the terminology of restitution even today is the terminology of the forms and fictions of a very different world.

This section sketches the development and terminology use in restitution cases brought in law courts. The next section sketches the development in equity.

Plaintiff Has Legal Title: Ejectment and Replevin

Restitution at law proceeded mainly in two large streams. The first dealt with cases in which the plaintiff had legal title to property or at least the right to immediate possession. If the plaintiff were the title owner to Blackacre with right to possession, he could bring ejectment to recover possession from the defendant who occupied the land. He recovered possession in such cases and hence recovered restitution of what was due him. What is today often called replevin allowed the plaintiff to recover possession of personal property to which he was entitled. In both the ejectment and replevin actions, the plaintiff was given possession by the sheriff, who physically seized the property for the plaintiff and ousted the defendant.

Plaintiff Has no Legal Title But Claims in Assumpsit on Analogy to Contract

The more significant stream of restitution derived from the writ of assumpsit. This kind of claim dealt with cases in which the plaintiff could *not* assert title or right to possession of particular property, but in which nevertheless he might be able to show just grounds for recovering money to pay for some benefit the defendant had received from him.

Assumpsit was the common law form of action by which contract claims were redressed. Sometimes the contract would be express, sometimes implied by the parties' actions, but in either event a genuine contract. However, the assumpsit action also came to be used when the parties had no contract at all, so long as the plaintiff could convince the court that he ought to recover something from the defendant as a matter of justice or good conscience.

Implying a Contract to do Justice

The connection to assumpsit is obscure to modern minds. The common law forced the plaintiff to sue under one of a limited number of forms of action or writs. Assumpsit was a good choice, but to make it work it was necessary for judges to relate the claim to some kind of contract, promise or undertaking. The common law judges were up to the task. They simply said that, although the defendant had promised nothing, if justice called for relief, then the law would imply a promise and then hold him liable on that implied promise.

An Example

For example, suppose the plaintiff paid money by mistake to the wrong person. He sues to recover the money. There is no contract, neither an express contract nor an implied fact contract. The money was not an identified object like a pony or a painting, and hence the plaintiff could not use replevin. In such cases the courts allowed restitution in the assumpsit action.

The Terminology

Courts explained liability in assumpsit for cases like the example by saying that the defendant was liable on an implied contract. Because the term "implied contract" might be confused with the idea of an implied in fact contract, judges sometimes use the term "implied in law contract" instead, tacitly recognizing that this kind of claim had nothing to do with a genuine contract. Another term for the implied in law contract is quasi-contract. So restitutionary claims of the kind involved in the second stream is still often referred to as claims for *assumpsit,* or claims based on *implied in law* or *quasi-contracts.* Because the writ of assumpsit had several different commonly used forms called the common counts, restitution in the second stream of cases might also be referred to by naming one of those common counts. The most familiar of these are the counts for *quantum meruit* and *money had and received.*

It should be understood that all of the forms of action have been abolished. Lawyers and judges today refer to restitution in these strange terms for convenience. But the incidents of assumpsit no longer control either the theory or the procedures for recovery of restitution, so words like assumpsit and quantum meruit should be used as reference only and not to suggest that restitution is limited by ghosts of ideas that were never more than fictions to begin with.

§ 4.2(2) Development of Restitution When Plaintiff Had Title: Ejectment and Replevin

[*In addition to this section in the Practitioner Treatise edition, see §§ 5.10 & 5.17.*]

§ 4.2(3) Development of Restitution When Plaintiff Had No Title

[*For the development of restitution at law through assumpsit, see this section in the Practitioner Treatise edition.*]

Implied in fact contracts. A good many contracts are never expressed in words, or at least not fully in words. These are genuine understandings between the parties even though they have not been spelled out. For instance, if a traveler goes to a hotel and asks for a room, he expects to pay for it at some more or less customary rate and the hotel expects to charge him. Both parties understand this and both understand that this reflects their agreement, even though the traveler has not promised to pay, much less named any amount of money. This kind of contract is sometimes called an implied in fact contract, a term that sometimes causes some confusion. The term only means that the parties had a contract that can be seen in their conduct rather than in any explicit set of words. In other words, the contract is proved by circumstantial evidence. As early as 1609, the English

Courts recognized exactly this kind of implied promise,[7] and Assumpsit came to be used to cover such cases as well as cases involving express undertakings and express bargains.

Implied in law contracts—quasi-contract and restitution in assumpsit. All of the development of Assumpsit to this stage had been concerned with genuine bargains, that is, enforcement of contracts the parties had actually made, either by express words or by clear indications in their conduct. The next step was to use Assumpsit where there was no contract at all between the parties, neither express nor implied in fact. This step was taken to prevent unjust enrichment of the defendant when "in equity and good conscience," he should not be permitted to keep gains he had received.[8] The form of Assumpsit used in these cases was called *general assumpsit,* or in many cases, *indebitatus assumpsit.*

Examples. Cases of this sort begin to arise sometime between around 1650 and 1700: the plaintiff has paid money by mistake to the wrong person and now seeks to recover it,[9] or someone else paid to the defendant money that should have been paid to the plaintiff.[10] It was clear in such cases that there is nothing like a contract between the parties, neither an express one nor one that might be reasonably inferred from their conduct. Nevertheless Assumpsit actions in such cases were sustained. The reason given was that "if any one received my money without my order, though it is a tort yet an indebitatus will lie, because by reason of the money the law creates a promise * * *."[11]

Quasi-contract: meaning, function and confusion. This law-created promise stands in stark contrast with the true contract implied in fact.[12] The implied in law contract is often called a quasi-contract. The most important thing about this implied in law or quasi contract is that it is not a contract in any sense. It is a rule of law that requires restitution to the plaintiff of something that came into defendant's hands but in justice belongs to the plaintiff.[13] Quasi contract is merely one way of discussing

§ 4.2(3)

8. The reference to "equity and good conscience" refers to a standard of judgment, not to equity jurisdiction. These cases are indisputably "law" cases. See Philpott v. Superior Court, 1 Cal.2d 512, 36 P.2d 635, 95 A.L.R. 990 (1934).

9. Bonnel v. Foulke, 2 Sid. 4, 82 Eng.Rep. 1224 (K.B. 1657). The report is in law French, which is a little difficult in places. There is a clear statement in this language, however: "Come si un vient a moy & dit, Pay me my rent, I am your landlord, & jeo respond give me your receipt and you shall have it & issint jeo ceo pay, & puis un auter q droit ad vient & demand & jeo luy pay, jeo poy aver indebitatus assumpsit ver il q done a moy le primer receipt."

10. Arris v. Stukely, 2 Mod. 260, 86 Eng. Rep. 1060 (1677).

11. Arris v. Stukely, 2 Mod. 260, 86 Eng. Rep. 1060 (1677) (argument of attorneys, probably accepted by the court).

12. The "law creates a promise" leads to the "implied-in-law" promise, another name for "quasi-contract." The contract terminology is misleading and it permits a more or less deliberate blending of claims based on actual agreements and those based on the judge's notion of justice. Thus where the Court of Claims was denied jurisdiction over quasi-contracts, it sometimes took cases that looked like quasi-contract cases but called them implied-in-fact contract cases. See Wall and Childres, The Law of Restitution and the Federal Government, 66 Nw.U.L.Rev. 587 (1971).

13. See e.g., Salamon v. Terra, 394 Mass. 857, 477 N.E.2d 1029, 1031 (1985) (unjust enrichment, not contract, is underlying basis); Cohen v. Home Ins. Co., 230 N.J.Super. 72, 82, 552 A.2d 654, 659 (1989) (quasi-contract liability based on unjust enrichment, not contract, and is sometimes imposed for benefits conferred over the "clear expression of dissent" by the defendant); Martin v. Little, Brown and Company, 304 Pa.Super. 424, 450 A.2d 984 (1981).

restitution based on unjust enrichment. Its function is to give the plaintiff a money judgment that will recover the defendant's unjust benefits. The contract language was natural at one time because to claim restitution the plaintiff on this kind of claim would use the writ of assumpsit and assumpsit of course meant undertaking or promise. So to justify the use of the assumpsit action judges associated the claim with contract by using the implied promise and quasi contract language.[14]

The terms quasi-contract and implied in fact contract sooner or later seem to confuse almost everyone. Sometimes courts seem to think quasi contract is different from restitution, when in fact quasi contract is only one form of it. It is possible to find courts that think a quasi-contract recovery is *damages* rather than restitution. Sometimes courts have said that *quantum meruit* is a term reserved for breach of contract cases.[15] Sometimes courts think that a case that begins with a tort is converted to contract when the plaintiff claims restitution, and hence invoke the contract statute of limitations.[16] All of these errors appear to result because lawyers sometimes focus on the contract language rather than its restitution content.

Unjust enrichment basis first recognized. What developed from this implied-in-law contract was a fairly detailed system of awarding restitution in cases where neither tort nor contract necessarily existed. In 1760 Lord Mansfield sought to explain the unjust enrichment policy behind all this in *Moses v. MacFerlan:* Quasi-contract actions in Assumpsit had a kind of equitable character, he said, and the action would lie when "the defendant, upon the circumstances of the case, is obliged by the ties of natural justice and equity to refund the money." [17]

The common counts. Lord Mansfield's broad policy statement in *Moses v. MacFerlan* has had considerable impact on the law of restitution. It laid the groundwork for establishing the principle against unjust enrichment as the central core of restitution claims. Nevertheless, quasi-contract was tied to the action in assumpsit and to the limited judicial powers of the law judges. The law of quasi-contract did not expand to encompass Lord Mansfield's principle, but instead developed in a group of very specific factual patterns. These patterns became so standardized that they acquired names as particular versions of the *General Assumpsit* form. These subordinate categories of assumpsit were called the common counts. The names of some of these are still in use today to describe certain standard situations for restitution claims.

There are a number of these counts, but only the major ones need be given attention here.[18] All of them are particular instances or forms of General Assumpsit; or put in slightly more modern terminology, all of them are particular kinds of quasi-contract. So all of them refer to fact patterns which may call for restitution to prevent unjust enrichment.

—*Money paid to the defendant's use.* The defendant owes money; the plaintiff, by mistake or otherwise, pays the defendant's debt. It might be

16. See Corbin, Waiver of Tort and Suit in Assumpsit, 19 Yale L.J. 221 (1910).

17. 2 Burr. 1005, 97 Eng.Rep. 676 (K.B. 1760).

18. See J. Koffler and A. Reppy, Common Law Pleading 349 (1969) for a list.

expected here that, since the defendant was "enriched" by the discharge of his debt, he would, under Lord Mansfield's rationale in *Moses v. MacFerlan*, be obliged to pay the plaintiff. In general, however, this has not been done in the absence of a request by the defendant for the plaintiff's help. The reasons for this, such as they are, are discussed elsewhere.[19] This means that the money paid count was really a count that applied mostly to implied in fact contracts, and did not do much service to enforce quasi-contract or purely restitutionary claims. As this would indicate, the common counts thus served as vehicles for both genuine contract claims and for restitutionary claims.

—*Money had and received.* When the defendant himself received money that belonged in good conscience to the plaintiff, for instance, if the plaintiff paid money to the defendant by mistake,[20] or under duress,[21] or by reason of fraud,[22] the plaintiff was entitled to restitution of the money, which is said to have been received by the defendant for the use of the plaintiff. The count includes money paid by a third person, so long as the money in good conscience belongs to the plaintiff.[23]

—*Use and occupation of land.* If the defendant occupied the plaintiff's land and derived any benefit from that occupation, one would again expect the principle in *Moses v. MacFerlan*, to force the defendant to disgorge the benefit to the landowner. For various highly technical reasons the common count for use and occupation of land by the defendant was not successful at common law. In the early 18th century a statute was passed that made the count available in cases of oral leases. By specifically including oral leases, the statute may have impliedly excluded all other cases of use and occupation. In general, liability was not extended in Assumpsit to any other cases of use and occupation.[24] But sometimes other forms of action would suffice to capture the benefits to the defendant resulting from his occupation of land. If the defendant were not on the land by permission, he might be liable to an ejectment suit, and to *Mesne profits*.[25] The differences between allowing the common count in assumpsit and the ejectment claim is not necessarily the difference between allowing restitution and damages; it is a difference in the form in which the claim is pursued, and hence, at common law, a difference in procedure, venue and other incidents. Thus a claim that has at least some of the characteristics of restitution does exist, for most kinds of land use by a defendant, though not a claim with the incidental characteristics of Assumpsit.

—*Goods sold and delivered.* If the plaintiff, acting under an agreement, delivered goods to the defendant for which he was to pay, there was a simple contract claim for their price; if the price was not agreed upon, there would still be an implied in fact agreement to pay the reasonable value. Here again, an implied in fact element in the contract could be brought under a common count. This count also could be used, according to some courts, where there was no contract between the parties, but where instead the defendant had converted the goods.[26] In such a case the plaintiff recovered

19. See § 4.9(3) below.

24. See generally, Ames, Assumpsit for Use and Occupation of Land, 2 Harv.L.Rev. 377 (1889).

25. See § 5.8 below.

the value of the goods on a restitutionary theory. As with many other cases of restitution, the plaintiff's loss and the defendant's gain may be equal in such a circumstance, and when this is so, the recovery serves all the purposes of both the law of damages and the law of restitution.

—*Quantum meruit.* The counts listed above and some others not discussed are called debt counts or indebitatus counts. Two major counts are called "value counts". The first of these is *quantum meruit,* a count used where the plaintiff has performed services for the defendant. As in many common count cases, the services may be performed at the defendant's request, so that an implied in fact contract might be found. However, services might be performed without the request of the defendant, but which nevertheless benefitted him in some way. If recovery is allowed for such unrequested services, it is clear that the recovery is the quasi-contract sort, that is, based upon the principle against unjust enrichment and not on contract. Most services rendered without request, however, are apt to be either given freely with no expectation of payment, or rendered officiously. If either of these things is true, restitution is denied on substantive rather than on formal grounds.[27]

There are other cases in which services are rendered by request, but in which, nevertheless, the parties have no valid and enforceable contract. This occurs, for example, where the parties have attempted to form a contract, but by reason of mistake have failed to do so.[28] It also occurs in cases where the statute of frauds or some similar impediment bars enforcement of the parties' agreement.[29] In such a case, the contract itself, whether express or implied in fact, is unenforceable, but the defendant may still be liable for the value of the plaintiff's services.

A recovery on *quantum meruit* usually appears to mean a recovery for the value of the services, measuring value in the labor market where the service itself was sought by the defendant. When the service was not sought by the defendant, if restitution is allowed at all it is usually measured by the increase in defendant's assets resulting from the service, not by the value of the service itself.[30]

—*Quantum valebant.* This is a count for the value of goods sold, and obviously resembles the indebitatus count for goods sold. The value counts were so called to distinguish them from the debt counts for reasons that ceased to have meaning even before the forms of action were abolished, and, like the other common counts, serve nowadays only as short expressions to identify some of the chief factual patterns in restitution cases at law.

Waiver of Tort and Suit in Assumpsit

Lamine v. Dorrell. Where the defendant acquired personal property by tort, the plaintiff ordinarily would have an action in trover, detinue or replevin. However—presumably to gain the various procedural incidents attached to the action in Assumpsit—plaintiffs began to sue in Assumpsit to redress such wrongs, and in 1706 the King's Bench approved such an action in *Lamine v. Dorrell.*[31]

31. 2 Ld.Raym. 1216, 92 Eng.Rep. 303 (K.B. 1706).

In that case the defendant had taken certain securities that belonged to the plaintiff, and had sold them. The plaintiff sought to recover the amount the defendant had received for the securities and brought an Assumpsit, counting for money had and received. His theory was that the defendant had received money that in good conscience belonged to the plaintiff, since the money was a product of the plaintiff's property. The defendant objected that there was no assumpsit or undertaking, only a plain tort. Clearly enough, any assumpsit or undertaking was of the implied in law kind; that is, it would be imposed by the judges to prevent the defendant's unjust enrichment. The judges were willing to do this, though with some mixed feelings. One of the judges expressed his feelings this way:

> "[W]hen the act that is done is in its nature tortious, it is hard to turn that into a contract, and against the reason of assumpsits. But the plaintiff may dispense with the wrong, and suppose the sale made by his consent, and bring an action for the money they were sold for, as money received to his use."

The agency theory. *Lamine v. Dorrell* was a case to which the count for money had and received was adapted. Furthermore it was a case in which some fairly persuasive analogies could be brought to mind. If the plaintiff was free to give the defendant permission to sell his goods for him, the defendant might be envisioned as something like a collecting agent. Such agents and others similarly situated had already been held liable even in the earlier common law for the sums he collected, under the action for Account.[32] Although the plaintiff had not in fact given such permission in advance, the court thought he could ratify the defendant's sale, and hence may have felt he could stand in much the same position as one claiming against his agent.

Limitations on waiver of tort. This idea came to be called a waiver of the tort and a suit in assumpsit. The particular fact situation shaped the idea strongly, however. Some courts denied that the tort of conversion could be waived except where the defendant had sold the converted goods and could thus be analogized to the collecting agent who would be liable for money had and received.[33] Others said that he could be liable for the value of the goods, even if he had not sold them, if the plaintiff used the common count for goods sold and delivered, rather than the count for money had and received.[34]

The waiver of tort idea has not been extended very far. One can't waive a libel and sue for the profits made by the defamer, for example.[35] The reluctance of courts to use assumpsit for use and occupation of land suggests limits in that direction, as well. The bulk of the cases have involved the taking of money or goods, or what is much the same, the severance and

---

32. T. Plucknett, A Concise History of the Common Law 635 (5th ed. 1956); A. Martin, Civil Procedure at Common Law 62–65 (1905). The action of *Account* was an action at law, to be distinguished from the equitable accounting that largely displaced it. As to equitable accounting see § 4.3(5) below.

33. See § 5.18 below.

34. Canepa v. Sun Pac., Inc., 126 Cal. App.2d 706, 272 P.2d 860 (1954).

35. See § 7.2(13) below.

taking of timber or the like.[36] When the assumpsit theory has been pursued
in tort cases, the purpose has usually been to get the advantage of some
procedural incident attached to contract claims, such as the contract statute
of limitations or some other advantageous rules that applied in contract
actions but not in tort.[37] Whatever sense this may have made before the
forms of action were abolished, it does not seem to make much sense today to
permit a plaintiff to call his case tort or contract to manipulate the statute of
limitations.

The other reason for bringing an assumpsit claim on the tort is to claim
the assumpsit measure of the remedy—that is to say, the gains resulting to
the defendant from his tort, such as any income he gets from sale of the
converted chattels. Where the defendant has sold the converted goods,
courts have usually been willing to give the plaintiff the sale price, without
inquiry into whether that price was greater than the value of the goods.
The usual assumption seems to be that where tangible goods are involved,
the sale price is entirely attributable to the goods themselves and not the
defendant's effort in finding customers, of his bargaining. Acting on this
assumption, it is entirely fair to deprive the defendant of the entire sale
price. The assumption, however, open to question in some cases, and where
the tort is an innocent one, allowance of more than the value of the
converted goods may be undesirable.[38]

The Future of Restitution Law

As a matter of history, restitutionary ideas developed mainly in the
particular forms of action discussed above. But those forms of action have
long since been abolished by modern procedural codes. In reading cases, one
must sometimes understand the archaic English terminology. But that
terminology is not necessary in today's decision-making process. In fact,
resort to terms like *quantum meruit* or *assumpsit* may do more to obscure
than to reveal the basis of a decision. It surely ought to be of supreme
irrelevance that the plaintiff's complaint speaks the ancient language of
money had and received rather than *goods sold and delivered*,[39] or that it
uses any such terms at all.

The significant questions today are very different. They ask whether
unjust enrichment should be redressed, and if so in what mode and by what
measure. There are many difficult questions about restitution, for example,
whether to allow the plaintiff to recover the profit made by a defendant in
excess of the plaintiff's loss. But such questions are not fairly or rationally
resolved by resort to half-understood and wholly archaic forms of action.
One who must learn about restitution must learn a little about the mysteries

---

36. See Corbin, Waiver of Tort and Suit in Assumpsit, 19 Yale L.J. 221 (1910).

37. Sometimes the tort rule may itself be doubtful, but rather than overrule it the court can treat the case as something else because of the restitutionary theory of the claim. See Barbouti v. Lysandrou, 559 So.2d 648 (Fla. App.1990) (rule denying garnishment in tort actions had no application where the plaintiff could claim quasi-contract or other unjust enrichment claim).

38. Restatement of Restitution § 128, Comment k (1937).

39. A point the court thought significant in Canepa v. Sun Pac., Inc., 126 Cal.App.2d 706, 272 P.2d 860 (1954). Later California decisions, however, observed that no particular form of pleading is necessary to invoke claim restitution. See Dinosaur Dev., Inc. v. White, 216 Cal.App.3d 1310, 265 Cal.Rptr. 525 (1989).

of the form; but no one needs to perpetuate them to resolve restitution issues.[40]

§ 4.3 Restitution in Equity—Terminology and Procedure

§ 4.3(1) Equitable Restitutionary Devices Generally

Law Courts' Limits: Protection of Legal Title

In property cases, a major limiting factor on restitution at law was the conception of formal title, beyond which courts could not examine. The ejectment claim was a restitutionary device, but not one that helped unless the plaintiff had good title at law. Equities in the plaintiff's favor were of no help at all. The plaintiff who was led by the defendant's fraud to convey his land had no remedy in ejectment because he had no title. The growth of restitution at law thus came in areas where title conceptions had not been significant in the first place—in areas involving money payments or the rendering of services where assumpsit was queen.[1]

Equity Courts' Ability to Ignore Legal Title

Equity's advantage in fashioning restitutionary remedies was exactly at this point: equity had developed a method of sidestepping title problems. Equity's theory was that it did not decide title but acted *in personam*. It did not act on title or property but upon the person of the defendant,[2] compelling him to follow good conscience rather than good title. If the defendant had secured legal title to Blackacre by unconscionable acts, the equity courts could simply order the defendant to reconvey Blackacre to the plaintiff. Equity's moral interest in conscience was coupled with an enormous power the law courts did not have, to act against the person rather than against the property. Equity courts would express the defendant's liability to reconvey by calling him a constructive trustee.

The distinctively equitable contributions to restitution, then, lies first, in the use of the personal order (ultimately enforceable by contempt powers) by which the court could ignore formalities of title; and second, in the flexible appeal to good conscience. Both aspects of equity represented a freedom from the purely legal order in which title or formal ownership governed all rights.

Major Restitutionary Remedies in Equity

Acting mainly on these foundations of the *in personam* power coupled with a flexible standard of "good conscience," the chancellors developed several similar restitutionary remedies of great consequence. These were: (1) the constructive trust; (2) the equitable lien; (3) subrogation; (4) the accounting for profits. These are sister remedies. They have several elements in common and all of them bore strong resemblance to, or can even be considered as forms of the constructive trust. Two other important equitable remedies were the (5) rescission in equity, with cancellation of instruments where that might be needed,[3] and (6) reformation of instru-

---

40. Cf. Laycock, The Scope and Significance of Restitution, 67 Tex.L.Rev. 1277, 1279 (1989) (common law writs little help to mod-ern lawyer, restitution both broader and nar-rower).

ments, to make them read as they should.[4] Any of these remedies might be granted without using the traditional terminology or stating its theory.[5]

Four Potential Effects of Tracing Remedies

Four major practical effects can result when a constructive trust is invoked, and to some extent the same can be said of its sister remedies, lien, subrogation and accounting. (1) Because these remedies are largely "equitable," a non-jury trial may be invoked.[11] (2) All the remedies named allow the plaintiff to trace funds or property taken from him into any new property or entitlement that is substituted for the plaintiff's property; the effect can be to give the plaintiff the gain a defendant makes from sale of the plaintiff's property and any reinvestment of the funds.[12] (3) Constructive trust may allow recovery of the specific property taken from the plaintiff, or any property substituted for it.[13] (4) The constructive trust, the equitable lien and the right of subrogation operate to give the plaintiff a priority over other creditors to the extent that the plaintiff can identify property or its substitutes as that which in equity and good conscience belongs to him.[14]

These mechanisms, their basis and effect, are explained in more detail in the subsections below, along with a closely related line of equity reasoning associated with the term "equitable conversion."[15]

§ 4.3(2) The Constructive Trust

In Summary

When equity imposes a constructive trust upon an asset of the defendant, the plaintiff ultimately gets formal legal title.[1] The effect is to allow the plaintiff to recover the asset in specie. For instance, the plaintiff may recover legal rights to Blackacre itself, or a particular bank account, or rights in an intangible such as a trademark, not merely a money judgment equal to the value of such assets. If the asset has increased in value, the plaintiff gets the increase. If the defendant has other creditors who might exhaust his assets in satisfying their claims, the plaintiff gains priority over them as to assets covered by the constructive trust. The constructive trust might be imposed upon any identifiable kind of property or entitlement in the defendant's hands if, in equity and conscience, it belongs to the plaintiff. This rule may be extended in some cases to cover not only property gained from the plaintiff directly, but also new property the defendant had substituted for it by sale or exchange. The constructive trust may also be imposed upon the property even after it has been transferred to third persons, so long as they are not bona fide purchasers. This subsection attempts to explain these rules.

The Mechanism of the Constructive Trust

The constructive trust and quasi-contract. Equity courts developed an equitable parallel to the law courts' quasi-contract.[2] Equity called this a

§ 4.3(2)

1. See, e.g., In re Marriage of Allen, 724 P.2d 651 (Colo.1986). The Restatement of Restitution, in a fling with esoteric metaphysics, delivered itself of the notion that there could be constructive trusts that had no effects whatever. Palmer carefully criticizes this notion. See I G. Palmer, Law of Restitution § 1.4 (1978 & Supps.). Even if there are such incorporeal and inoperative constructive trusts, they are of no account in procuring restitution. The text statement that title is ultimately passed when a constructive trust is declared is accurate both factually and theoretically.

constructive trust. The quasi-contract is imposed by courts to prevent unjust enrichment, not generated by contract. The constructive trust is likewise imposed by court to prevent unjust enrichment, and not generated by any trust.[3] The contract and trust language is the language of analogy or metaphor. Both quasi-contract and constructive trust aim at restitution of something that in good conscience belongs to the plaintiff.

One important difference between the quasi-contract and the constructive trust claim is that the quasi-contract claim is one for money and does not require the plaintiff to identify any particular asset as rightly "belonging" to him. The constructive trust, in contrast, restores to the plaintiff a particular asset, which is either the asset that rightly belongs to the plaintiff or one substituted for it. Although there are restitution claims "at law" which also restore the plaintiff to a particular asset, the constructive trust differs from these claims, too. Specific restitution at law is usually accomplished in ejectment and replevin actions. They restore to the plaintiff property which is legally his, not property which is only equitably his. If he has no legal title, he cannot recover the property.[4] The constructive trust allows the plaintiff to recover an asset even if he has no legal title to it, so long as that asset is regarded as "belonging" to him in an equitable sense.

Mechanisms and procedures of the constructive trust. Where the quasi-contract plaintiff wins a simple money judgment, enforceable by execution,[5] the constructive trust plaintiff who proves his claim by clear and convincing evidence [6] wins an *in personam* order that requires the defendant to transfer legal rights and title of specific property or intangibles to the plaintiff. When the court decides that the defendant is obliged to make restitution, it first declares him to be constructive trustee, then orders him as trustee to make a transfer of the property to the beneficiary of the constructive trust, the plaintiff.[7] For example, if the defendant, by fraud, induces the plaintiff to convey Blackacre to him, the court will declare that the defendant holds Blackacre on constructive trust for the plaintiff, and then order a conveyance to the plaintiff, on whatever conditions may be required to do justice.[8] The power to issue coercive or injunctive orders thus lies at the basis of the constructive trust.

Requirement of res or property. The constructive trust is only used when the defendant has a legally recognized right in a particular asset.[9] The asset may be an intangible entitlement such as a trademark. It may even be a fund of money like a bank account. But whatever it is, it must be an asset

3. See generally I G. Palmer, Law of Restitution §§ 1.3 & 1.4 (1978 & Supps.).

4. In the case of replevin of chattels by a seller of goods who was defrauded, there is something that seems to have come about because courts first thought that the buyer got no title when he acquired goods by fraud. Under that view, replevin of course would lie to permit recovery of the goods. Later, courts came to the view that the fraudulent buyer did get title that was voidable, but they kept the replevin procedure. See I G.

Palmer, Law of Restitution § 3.16 (1978 & Supps.).

5. See § 1.4 as to enforcement of money judgments.

7. See G. Bogert, Trusts and Trustees, § 471 et seq. (2d ed. 1960); 5 A. Scott, Trusts & 461 et seq. (3d ed. 1967); Restatement of Restitution § 160 Comment *e* (1937).

8. Restatement of Restitution § 160 Comments *e* & *f* (1937).

9. Restatement of Restitution § 160, Comments *i* & *j* (1937).

that can be identified as belonging in good conscience to the plaintiff in spite of the defendant's legal right to it.[10] If defendant obtains Blackacre from the plaintiff by fraud, he holds it on constructive trust and must ultimately reconvey to the plaintiff. But if the defendant sells the land and dissipates the money, the defendant is not a constructive trustee because he has nothing of the plaintiff's to hold in trust. The defendant may have other property of his own, but as to his own property he is not a constructive trustee.

Other liabilities not excluded. Although the defendant cannot be a constructive trustee when he no longer has an asset belonging in equity to the plaintiff, he may still be liable personally. If he gained Blackacre by fraud but no longer has Blackacre or any substituted property, he is still liable to the plaintiff for damages for the fraud. If he gave Blackacre to his children and they no longer own it, even the children as donees might owe restitution in money.[11] But neither the children nor the fraudfeasor himself are constructive trustees if they no longer own Blackacre or some substituted asset. In that case they are only debtors and the plaintiff is only an unsecured creditor.[12] Suing only as a creditor and without the constructive trust, the plaintiff will be unable to recover the specific property, unable to recover any gains that might once have been associated with that property, and will be unable to get the benefit of any automatic priority over other creditors.

Operation and Effects of the Constructive Trust

(1) Capturing the defendant's gains. The constructive trust has three or four especially important characteristics. One is that under the rules for following property or money into its product, the plaintiff may obtain, not merely what he lost, but gains received by the defendant from the property's increase in value,[13] from its transfer,[14] from its use in a business operation.[15] The defendant will also be liable for prejudgment interest on the plaintiff's

---

10. Identification is made by "tracing" the asset into its products or substitutes. See § 6.1 below.

11. See Otis v. Otis, 167 Mass. 245, 45 N.E. 737 (1897) (the plaintiff would have been entitled to a constructive trust against a fund that had been on deposit, but the defendant had withdrawn the money and given it to his daughters; the plaintiff was allowed a claim for "compensation" from all defendants to the extent of their respective misappropriations); I G. Palmer, Law of Restitution § 2.14 (1978 & Supps.); cf. United States v. Robilotto, 828 F.2d 940 (2d Cir.1987), cert. denied, 484 U.S. 1011, 108 S.Ct. 711, 98 L.Ed.2d 662 (1988) (RICO forfeiture not merely *in rem* against the property but also a personal liability of the wrongdoer for all his gains whether traceable to a particular res or not).

12. E.g., United States Fidelity and Guar. Co. v. Hiles, 670 S.W.2d 134 (Mo.App.1984); Aebig v. Commercial Bank of Seattle, 36 Wash.App. 477, 674 P.2d 696 (1984) (deposits with travel agency as prepayment on trips to

be taken created no identifiable fund, no constructive trust, only debt).

13. In re Rothko's Estate, 43 N.Y.2d 305, 401 N.Y.S.2d 449, 372 N.E.2d 291 (1977) ("damages" based on increased value of property still held by the defendant).

14. E.g., Janigan v. Taylor, 344 F.2d 781 (1st Cir.1965), cert. denied, 382 U.S. 879, 86 S.Ct. 163, 15 L.Ed.2d 120 (1965) (after wrongfully acquiring shares of stock for a certain amount of money, defendant sold the shares for a higher sum, recovery of the gain allowed as a remedy under federal securities laws); cf. G & M Motor Co. v. Thompson, 567 P.2d 80 (Okl.1977) (embezzled funds invested in life insurance, embezzler died, victim could have had entire insurance fund, in excess of its loss, if it had so claimed).

15. E.g., Zeller v. Bogue Elec. Mfg. Corp., 476 F.2d 795 (2d Cir.1973), cert. denied, 414 U.S. 908, 94 S.Ct. 217, 38 L.Ed.2d 146 (1973); Brooks v. Conston, 364 Pa. 256, 72 A.2d 75 (1950).

funds if use value is not otherwise accounted for.[16] These rules may give the plaintiff a considerable added sum.[17]

—*Example.* For instance, if the defendant secured Blackacre by fraud at a time when it was worth $10,000, and then traded it for Whiteacre which was worth $15,000, a constructive trust in the plaintiff's favor on Whiteacre would net him property worth considerably more than the property he lost. In this respect the constructive trust resembles the simple conversion case in which the plaintiff "waives the tort and sues in assumpsit", to get the price received by the converter,[18] but as shown in discussing the measures of restitution,[19] the constructive trust may be more potent in some cases.

—*Tracing.* The favorable rule that allows the plaintiff the gain produced by his property is often difficult to invoke. The plaintiff must trace his money or property to some particular funds or assets. Especially when the defendant has taken money, tracing is difficult. In such cases the plaintiff can often prove that the money was taken, but has difficulty in identifying that money with funds in the defendant's accounts. This leads to a series of special rules for tracing money.[20] If the tracing is incomplete, the rule that requires a *res* is invoked and the constructive trust is denied, with the result that the defendant is only a simple debtor.

(2) Preferences and priorities. The second especially important characteristic of the constructive trust is that it may function to give the plaintiff a priority over other creditors of the defendant.[21] A closely related advantage is that on the right facts it may also defeat a debtor's homestead or other exemption, allowing the plaintiff a satisfaction from assets of the defendant which are otherwise protected from creditors.[22]

—*Example.* For instance, suppose that X obtains Blackacre from the plaintiff by fraud. As is usually the case, X has many creditors with many valid claims against him. These creditors begin to file actions against X, asserting that he owes them debts, or has committed torts against them. In the ordinary course of events, such creditors, on getting a money judgment, would be entitled to enforce the judgment by forcing a sale of most or all of X's property, using the money to pay the judgments. Since X has legal title to Blackacre in his name, though he obtained it fraudulently, Blackacre might be sold in this way to satisfy the claims of X's creditors. If the

---

16. In re Estate of Wernick, 127 Ill.2d 61, 129 Ill.Dec. 111, 535 N.E.2d 876 (1989); Sack v. Feinman, 489 Pa. 152, 413 A.2d 1059 (1980). Interest would be inappropriate if use value were accounted for by an award of rent or earnings from the property.

17. See Ames, Following Misappropriated Property into Its Product, 19 Harv.L.Rev. 511 (1906).

18. See § 4.2 above.

19. See § 4.5 below.

20. See § 6.1 below.

21. E.g., Atlas, Inc. v. United States, 459 F.Supp. 1000 (D.N.D.1978); Estate of Liebman, 189 Misc. 282, 60 N.Y.S.2d 482 (1945); see Middlebrooks v. Lonas, 246 Ga. 720, 272 S.E.2d 687 (1980).

22. If the defendant purchases a home with money which belongs to the plaintiff in equity and good conscience, the constructive trust and its sister remedies are appropriate devices to avoid the exemption that would otherwise reserve the home to the defendant. American Ry. Express Co. v. Houle, 169 Minn. 209, 210 N.W. 889, 48 A.L.R. 1266 (1926); Annotations, 48 A.L.R. 1269 (1927); 47 A.L.R. 371 (1927); see also 43 A.L.R. 1415 (1926). Similarly, the constructive trust and sister remedies may allow the plaintiff to recover property that would otherwise be protected by the defendant's discharge in bankruptcy. See Leyden v. Citicorp Indus. Bank, 782 P.2d 6 (Colo.1989).

plaintiff is able to impose a constructive trust on Blackacre, however, the court will force the defendant to convey the land to the plaintiff. The land will not be used to satisfy other creditors' claims and the plaintiff will obtain what is his. This procedure treats the plaintiff better than other creditors, whose claims may have just as strong a moral basis. In theory such a result is justified because Blackacre, in the eyes of equity, has always been the plaintiff's property in all good conscience, though formal legal title was in X.

—*Combining profits and priorities.* When the constructive trust gives the plaintiff both priority over creditors *and* gains or profits, other creditors of X may suffer in order to give the plaintiff a windfall. Suppose X secures Blackacre by fraud, paying $10,000 for it when it was worth in fact $15,000, and then trades Blackacre for Whiteacre. Whiteacre proves to be worth $30,000, though X used no fraud to gain this extraordinary profit. X now has in his hands values of $30,000 for which he paid $10,000. The plaintiff's economic loss is only $5,000. He may have preferred to have Blackacre back, but if it was traded to a bona fide purchaser for value, he cannot have that in any event. The alternatives are to recompense the plaintiff by paying him $5,000, or to give him a constructive trust on Whiteacre. The latter course would give him a net gain of $15,000. On the other hand, if his claim is limited to a simple money recovery measured by his loss, the gains made by X's trade for Whiteacre will be available and may inure to the benefit of X's creditors.

While it would be improper to permit X himself to keep such gains, since they were the product of his own wrong, there is no similar reason against permitting the creditors of X to have the benefit of this property, once the plaintiff is restored. This is the kind of case, in other words, in which the preference worked by the constructive trust should not be permitted. Sometimes it is very difficult to see this, because in trying to right the wrong done to the plaintiff, one may forget that others, equally innocent, have a stake in the defendant's assets.

—*Priorities and tracing.* The problem of preference is especially acute when tracing is questionable. Indeed, a major reason for the rules requiring tracing is to avoid the unfairness that results to creditors of the defendant and other innocent persons when a preference is invoked without justification. Suppose X embezzles money from the plaintiff, then deposits it in his bank account. If the defendant opens an account with the plaintiff's money and neither added to it nor subtracted from it, it is fair to treat the account as a *res* held upon constructive trust. Any money that can be withdrawn from the deposit is precisely equivalent to the money originally deposited and belonging to the plaintiff. Imposing a constructive trust in such a case defeats claims the defendant's other creditors might have been able to collect from such funds, but that is fair enough because we can see by tracing that the funds have always belonged to the plaintiff.

However, if X withdraws all the funds and then at some other time opens another bank account, we cannot be sure that the second account contains money identifiable as the plaintiff's.[23] To impose a constructive trust upon the second account is to prefer the plaintiff's claim to those of

23. See § 6.1 below.

other creditors, and for no good reason. The plaintiff in such a case has a claim against the defendant, but he stands as an ordinary creditor and must take his chances with the rest by recovering a money judgment and enforcing it through execution, or sharing the limited funds with other creditors in an insolvency proceeding. Sympathy for the plaintiff's loss can distort these rules, but a court which imposes a trust without tracing the plaintiff's loss to the defendant's gain may simply be shifting the plaintiff's loss to a creditor of the defendant or to another innocent person.[24]

(3) Recovery of specific property. The third effect of a constructive trust in some cases is to permit recovery of specific property rather than a money substitute. The constructive trust is not the only remedy which permits specie recovery. Ejectment and replevin also permit such a recovery, but those remedies apply only, or at least most clearly, to cases in which legal title has remained in the plaintiff.[25] The constructive trust on the other hand permits the plaintiff to recover what equity regards as his. The very basis of the suit is that the defendant has legal title and must therefore be treated as a "trustee" who holds that title for the plaintiff. Although recovery of specific assets can be explained on other grounds besides constructive trust, the effect of a constructive trust is always to reach some specific asset.

(4) Equity trials—Nonjury trial. When the plaintiff asserts a constructive trust claim he asserts what is traditionally viewed as an equitable claim. The case is therefore tried as an equity case, without a jury.[26]

—Adequate remedy at law. Certain claims in equity were traditionally dismissed if the chancellor thought the plaintiff would have an adequate remedy at law.[27] Claims subject to the adequacy rule were claims based on rights the law courts recognized or created in the first place. The plaintiff in such cases resorted to equity only in hopes of a more effective remedy for a legal right. The constructive trust claim is different. It is not a claim based on a legal right. On the contrary, constructive trusts are needed because legal title is in the defendant. The plaintiff seeking a constructive trust does not assert a legal right but an equitable interest. In this setting, the adequacy of legal remedy seems irrelevant. Professor Palmer concludes that the adequacy rule has no effect when the claim is against a fiduciary, so that the case may proceed in equity even if there is an adequate remedy at law; but when the defendant is not a fiduciary, he believes the results are unpredictable.[28]

---

24. Cf. Rogers v. Rogers, 63 N.Y.2d 582, 483 N.Y.S.2d 976, 473 N.E.2d 226 (1984); Simonds v. Simonds, 45 N.Y.2d 233, 408 N.Y.S.2d 359, 380 N.E.2d 189 (1978). In *Simonds* a divorcing spouse promised to insure his life for the benefit of his first spouse; after he remarried he terminated the policy and procured a new policy in favor of the second spouse. A constructive trust was imposed in favor of the first spouse against the second, although it seems impossible to trace the second spouse's gain to the first spouse's loss. See § 6.1 below. New York has also been quick to equate loss on one side with gain on the other in statute of frauds cases. See Farash v. Sykes Datatronics, Inc., 59 N.Y.2d 500, 465 N.Y.S.2d 917, 452 N.E.2d 1245 (1983); § 13.2(2) below.

25. See § 4.2 above. As to replevin when title has passed, see note 4, supra.

26. See § 2.6 above.

27. See § 2.5(1) above.

28. I G. Palmer, Law of Restitution § 1.6 (1978 & Supps.).

At least some authorities support the view that a claim for a constructive trust may be pursued even if the legal remedy is adequate [29] and even if the trust would yield only money that could be recovered at law.[30] With the decline of the adequacy test generally,[31] an unhindered access to equity for restitution seems to be the most appropriate solution unless there are especially important needs for a jury trial. On the other hand, a claim for a constructive trust that does not attempt to identify particular property or fund subject to the alleged trust can sensibly be read as nothing but a claim at law for money had and received and hence as a jury trial case.[32]

Constructive trust effects without constructive trust terminology. The term constructive trust was once important because it denoted a theory that explained why equity courts would deny the defendant the benefits of his legal title in the assets. That no longer seems to lawyers to be a very significant issue and today the term constructive trust is remedially important only as a way of signifying the effects listed above. It is not important for courts to use the term constructive trust to achieve any given effect, such as restoration of specific property [33] or recovery of the defendant's gains.[34] Any of the effects for which constructive trust stands can be addressed without the slightest reference to constructive trust. A decision to award the plaintiff a recovery based on the defendant's profits, for example, is not a result of a constructive trust. Such an award is a result of a decision about the best way to remedy unjust enrichment in the particular case. Constructive trust is the name we give to that decision, not the reason for it. It is convenient to use the constructive trust terminology to stand for one or more of the potential effects, but the term has no mystical significance.

Grounds for the Constructive Trust

Basis in unjust enrichment. The constructive trust, like its counterpart

29. See Heckmann v. Ahmanson, 168 Cal. App.3d 119, 134, 214 Cal.Rptr. 177, 187 (1985) ("[A]n action in equity to establish a constructive trust does not depend on the absence of an adequate legal remedy"); Note 25 St. John's L.Rev. 253 (1951).

30. See Hochman v. Zigler's, Inc., 139 N.J.Eq. 139, 50 A.2d 97 (1946) (constructive trust to compel return of money exacted under duress, even though the court recognized that money could be recovered by an action at law).

31. See Laycock, The Death of the Irreparable Injury Rule, 103 Harv.L.Rev. 687 (1990); § 2.5 above.

32. Blue Cross Health Servs., Inc. v. Sauer, 800 S.W.2d 72 (Mo.App.1990).

33. See II G. Palmer, Law of Restitution § 11.5(c), p. 519 (1978 & Supps.). Restoration of specific property may be accomplished "at law" through ejectment and replevin, although usually only when legal title remains in the plaintiff. In equity, restoration might be accomplished even when title is not in the plaintiff through devices such as reformation and specific performance. A simple *in personam* order without the constructive trust terminology is also appropriate.

34. Defendant's gains, at least in certain forms, can be recovered at law under quasi-contract doctrines. Ablah v. Eyman, 188 Kan. 665, 365 P.2d 181, 90 A.L.R.2d 766 (1961) (business savings resulting to defendant from use of plaintiff's property); Edwards v. Lee's Adm'r, 265 Ky. 418, 96 S.W.2d 1028 (1936); cf. Olwell v. Nye & Nissen Co., 26 Wash.2d 282, 173 P.2d 652, 169 A.L.R. 139 (1946) (value of use of a machine). In this respect, note that net savings in a business operation are equivalent to increased profits (or, in a losing business, to diminished losses).

In Popp v. Gountanis, 221 Mont. 267, 718 P.2d 340 (1986) the defendant's gains were recovered by the plaintiff without reference to any restitutionary terms whatever. The plaintiff was a farm tenant. The defendants were landlords who had received federal payments for not raising crops on the land. The tenant was entitled to keep two-thirds of crops he raised. The court held he was entitled to two-thirds of the federal payments. The result must have seemed obvious because its only explanation was: "Popp had an estate in land for the duration of his tenancy, and the [federal payment] to Frank and Fountanis was in derogation of Popp's interest." Id. at 342.

remedies "at law," is a remedy for unjust enrichment.[35] It is not appropriate to every case because it can overdo the job or produce bad side effects such as unfair preferences. Where the constructive trust will produce the right measure and conditions of restitution, however, it is appropriate in any kind of unjust enrichment case and is in no way limited to cases of wrongdoing.[36]

Earlier limitations. At one time the constructive trust was closely associated with the violation of express trusts or with the violation of other fiduciary duties [37] and courts placed artificial limits on its use. One decision said that a thief could not be a trustee.[38] Sometimes it is still said that the constructive trust applies only to misdealings by fiduciaries or in cases of fraud.[39] But this is a misconception. The constructive trust is based on property, not wrongs. It proceeds on the notion that the defendant has legal title but that the plaintiff has the superior moral or equitable claim. The misconception probably arises in part from the trust language itself. The constructive trust terminology, like quasi-contract terminology at law, is an analogy only, but if taken literally can suggest a trust and hence a fiduciary.[40] It also probably arises in part from the fact that in a few special cases,[41] wrongdoing is indeed relevant to the constructive trust. At any rate, the constructive trust is no longer limited to misconduct cases; it redresses unjust enrichment, not wrongdoing.

Application of constructive trusts today. Restitution by way of constructive trust and similar remedies may be appropriate for embezzlement of money or for conversion of goods,[42] for benefits transferred because of fraud,[43] or duress,[44] or undue influence,[45] and for gains received by reason of misuse of position or information.[46] Analogous relief has been given for such torts as infringement of copyright and the like.[47] Even the murderer for gain may be a constructive trustee.[48] But wrongdoing is not required. Property transferred by mistake, for example, may be recovered in specie by

35. See I G. Palmer, Law of Restitution §§ 1.3 & 1.4 (1978 & Supps.).

36. Martin v. Kehl, 145 Cal.App.3d 228, 237, 193 Cal.Rptr. 312, 317 (1983) ("Section 2224 provides that '[o]ne who gains a thing by fraud, accident, mistake, undue influence, the violation of a trust, or other wrongful act, is, unless he has some other and better right thereto, an involuntary trustee of the thing gained, for the benefit of the person who would otherwise have had it"); Carr v. Carr, 120 N.J. 336, 352, 576 A.2d 872, 880 (1990) ("A constructive trust should 'be impressed in any case where to fail to do so will result in an unjust enrichment' "); see Petrie v. LeVan, 799 S.W.2d 632 (Mo.App.1990).

37. See J. Dawson, Unjust Enrichment 26–28 (1951); R. Goff and G. Jones, The Law of Restitution 60 (2d ed. 1978) (English law). Many kinds of fiduciary cases are categorized in Douthwaite, Profits and Their Recovery, 15 Vill.L.Rev. 346 (1970).

38. Campbell v. Drake, 39 N.C. (4 Ired.Eq.) 94 (1844).

39. Perry v. Wyeth, 25 Ill.2d 250, 184 N.E.2d 861 (1962).

40. See I G. Palmer, Law of Restitution § 1.3 (1978 & Supps.). Palmer and others have called the constructive trust a fiction. Analogy, metaphor, or conception might be more apt terms because nothing turns on the decision to use trust terminology; the term merely has the explanatory power of an analogy, and once accepted for that reason becomes a shorthand designation for a series of legal effects.

41. See paragraph *"When constructive trust is limited to cases of wrongdoing,"* below.

42. See § 6.1 below.

43. See § 9.3(4) below.

44. See § 10.2 below.

45. See § 10.3 below.

46. See §§ 10.4–10.6 below.

47. For example, recovery of the copyright infringer's profits is permitted, although the constructive trust terminology is not necessary to that recovery. See § 6.3(4) below.

48. See § 6.7 below.

way of constructive trust in appropriate cases.[49] The constructive trust or its tracing features has been used to provide for an equitable division of marital property when the facts called for relief but statutes did not cover the case,[50] and also to provide for such a division as between unmarried cohabitants, so that their respective economic contributions can be recognized.[51] Even nonpayment of a debt for specific property might suffice to warrant imposition of a constructive trust on the property under some circumstances.[52] The point is not that the defendant violated a fiducial duty, but that the plaintiff's money, services, or property can be traced to and identified as the asset the defendant now holds.

When constructive trust is limited to cases of wrongdoing. In a few cases the court cannot find unjust enrichment at all unless there is wrongdoing, and hence would have no basis for granting a constructive trust or any other restitutionary remedy. The statute of frauds cases are like this.[53] The plaintiff cannot indirectly enforce an oral contract and cannot enforce an oral trust, either. This rule would be defeated if the plaintiff could enforce the oral trust by simply resorting to constructive trust language. So when the plaintiff claims that the defendant orally promised to convey Blackacre, he has no claim for a constructive trust unless he can add some ingredient that makes the claim more than one to enforce an oral trust or contract. That ingredient is fiduciary breach or fraud. When the oral trust is accompanied by fraud or fiduciary breach, the constructive trust is imposed, otherwise usually not.[54] These rules are necessary to support the statute of frauds, but they have no application to cases generally.

Donees and purchasers. Since the constructive trust is not limited to cases in which the defendant is a wrongdoer, it may be applied to require restitution from transferees who are not bona fide purchasers of the assets.[55]

49. See Proctor v. Sagamore Big Game Club, 265 F.2d 196, 198 (3d Cir.1959), cert. denied, 361 U.S. 831, 80 S.Ct. 81, 4 L.Ed.2d 73 (1959) ("when Childs acquired the tax deed for Elk Tanning Company, the latter acquired title to a larger estate than was intended because of a mutual mistake of law as to the effect of the transaction"); Petrie v. LeVan, 799 S.W.2d 632, 634–635 (Mo.App.1990); II G. Palmer, Law of Restitution § 11.5(c); §§ 11.-6(3) & 11.7 below.

50. Carr v. Carr, 120 N.J. 336, 576 A.2d 872 (1990) (wife separated from husband who died before divorce was complete; she could not take an equitable distribution of the marital estate because that was available only upon divorce; she could not elect to take a surviving spouse's share of the decedent's estate because that was permitted only to a spouse living with the deceased at the time of death; constructive trust was held legally available to prevent unjust enrichment of the decedent's children). A constructive trust is of course appropriate as a means of capturing marital assets misappropriated by one of the partners. See Cottman v. Cottman, 56 Md. App. 413, 468 A.2d 131 (1983).

51. Goode v. Goode, 183 W.Va. 468, 396 S.E.2d 430 (1990); cf. Simonds v. Simonds, 45 N.Y.2d 233, 408 N.Y.S.2d 359, 380 N.E.2d 189 (1978); see also § 13.6 below.

52. See Middlebrooks v. Lonas, 246 Ga. 720, 272 S.E.2d 687 (1980) (promise to repay loan allegedly made without intention to perform; if so proved, constructive trust would be appropriate on funds, or equitable lien on property improved by them). In Leyden v. Citicorp Indus. Bank, 782 P.2d 6 (Colo.1989) the plaintiff transferred property to Howe in exchange for a promissory note. Howe never paid the note and Howe was eventually discharged in bankruptcy. In the meantime Howe had mortgaged the property to a bank in exchange for a loan and the bank took over the property. As against Howe, the court held that the plaintiff was entitled to an equitable lien on the property as a special form of constructive trust, and as against the bank and its transferees, she was entitled to the lien if they had notice of her claim.

53. See generally § 13.2(3) below.

54. See, e.g., King v. Uhlmann, 103 Ariz. 136, 437 P.2d 928 (1968).

55. See In re Marriage of Allen, 724 P.2d 651 (Colo.1986); § 4.7 below.

Suppose that, by fraudulent misrepresentations, the defendant secures title to Blackacre from the plaintiff, then gives Blackacre to his uncle, who needs a place to live. The uncle is a donee, not a purchaser. He is subject to the constructive trust, which is to say he must transfer Blackacre to the plaintiff as the person to whom it belongs in the eyes of equity and good conscience. The same would be true if the uncle had purchased Blackacre for valuable consideration, if he acted with notice of the plaintiff's interest.[56]

Constructive Trust in Relation to Other Trusts

The constructive trust is not in fact a trust, but a remedy which is explained by analogy to trusts. The differences and the similarities can be seen by considering an express trust and the so-called resulting trust.

[*For a brief comparison to express and resulting trusts, see this section in the Practitioner Treatise edition.*]

§ 4.3(3)　The Equitable Lien

Liens Generally

A lien is a charge against property that makes the property stand as security for a debt owed. A creditor who has a lien upon property of the debtor is entitled at a proper time to have the property sold and the proceeds used for payment of the debt. The lien creditor thus stands in a better position than a general, unsecured creditor of the same debtor, because he has a priority: the property subject to his lien is in effect set aside for the satisfaction of his claim first. Only after his claim is satisfied will the property or its proceeds become available for the payment of other creditors.[1] A lien is thus not merely a matter between the lien creditor and his debtor; it is a matter affecting other creditors as well, because it withdraws some of the debtor's resources that ordinarily would be available for satisfaction of the claims of those other creditors.

Agreements and Other Lien Sources

Most but not all liens are created by express agreement of the parties. Because other creditors or potential creditors of the debtor may be affected, most of these are recorded in some fashion. A creditor deciding whether to make a loan or whether to insist on immediate payment of a past debt can examine the official records of liens and other security devices and form some estimate of the debtor's assets for payment of his debts. A few liens, no longer of great commercial significance, are possessory—that is, the lien creditor has possession of some particular piece of property and the possession itself serves as notice to other creditors of the possessor's lien claim. A few others, some of the mechanics' and materialmen's liens, are based on complex statutory provisions.[2]

Equitable Liens by Agreement

The term "equitable lien" is used in at least two fairly disparate senses. In one sense it may refer to a lien created by express or at least implied-in-

56. See, e.g., Leyden v. Citicorp Indus. Bank, 782 P.2d 6 (Colo.1989) (equitable lien, a form of constructive trust, enforceable against transferees who were not unjustly enriched, since they had notice).

§ 4.3(3)

2. See § 12.20(3) below.

fact agreement of the parties, as where a borrower agrees that a certain fund or piece of property will stand as security for his debt. Such liens are "equitable" in the sense that they may have failed to comply with some requirement for establishment of a "common law" lien, but are recognized and enforced in the courts of equity. There is a real chance that such liens may be used to give one creditor a preference over others, on the basis of a simple agreement between creditor and debtor, and without notice to other creditors. But that is a matter of the substantive law of creditors' rights, not the law of remedies. The equitable lien created by express or implied-in-fact contract is mentioned here to distinguish it from the equitable lien imposed by the courts to prevent unjust enrichment.

Equitable Liens Judicially Implied to Prevent Unjust Enrichment

The equitable lien when imposed, not as a matter of contract, but to prevent unjust enrichment, is essentially a special, and limited, form of the constructive trust. The lien is imposed for reasons that, in principle, are the same as those that warrant the constructive trust, and it works in substantially the same way.[3] The difference is that restitution is measured differently. Where the constructive trust gives a complete title to the plaintiff, the equitable lien only gives him a security interest in the property, which he can then use to satisfy a money claim. Thus an equitable lien may be "foreclosed", so that the property that has been subjected to the lien is subjected to a forced sale and the proceeds of that sale applied to payment of the plaintiff's claim.[4] This results in only a money payment to the plaintiff and obviously does not carry with it the advantages of recovering specific property. On the other hand, it operates like the constructive trust in affording a preference over other creditors and in utilizing the rules for following property into its product.

Where Constructive Trust is Excessive

The equitable lien may be used when the constructive trust would work an overkill—in other words, when the property to which it attaches belongs only partly to the plaintiff. If the defendant secures money from the plaintiff by embezzlement and then uses that money to purchase a house and lot, the plaintiff is entitled to a constructive trust, which in the end will operate to give him title to the property purchased with his money. But if the defendant merely uses the plaintiff's money to add a house on a lot he already owns, it is clear that the plaintiff has no claim to a constructive trust on the house and lot because his money did not go into the lot. He is entitled instead to an equitable lien on the house and lot for the amount of money embezzled from him.[5] This will permit him to force a sale of the

3. See In re Marriage of Allen, 724 P.2d 651, 658 (Colo.1986) ("an equitable lien is a special and limited form of a constructive trust"); Martian v. Martian, 399 N.W.2d 849 (N.D.1987); J. Dawson, Unjust Enrichment 34 (1951); Restatement of Restitution § 161 (1937).

4. See Christiansen v. Strand, 82 S.D. 416, 147 N.W.2d 415 (1966); Restatement of Restitution § 161, Comment *b* (1937).

5. E.g., Warsco v. Oshkosh Sav. & Trust Co., 190 Wis. 87, 208 N.W. 886, 47 A.L.R. 366 (1926); cf. Middlebrooks v. Lonas, 246 Ga. 720, 272 S.E.2d 687 (1980) (if defendants made promise to repay loan without intent to perform and invested fund in home they already owned, equitable lien would be proper remedy); Laura v. Christian, 88 N.M. 127, 537 P.2d 1389 (1975) (cotenant paid off lien, entitled to contribution from other cotenant and a lien to secure contribution).

property if necessary and to use the proceeds of the same to reimburse himself. It will protect the embezzler and his family and his creditors, however, by leaving the remainder of the proceeds for them. In most instances this will work out to give the plaintiff the money stolen from him and the defendant will be left with approximately the value of the land he obtained with his own money.

Where the Constructive Trust Assets are Deficient

The reverse of the overkill situation occurs when the defendant invests the embezzled funds in assets that depreciate in value. In such a case a constructive trust would give the plaintiff property worth less than the defendant owes him. The plaintiff might therefore prefer an equitable lien on the property coupled with a money judgment. He could foreclose the lien and retain the unsatisfied portion of the money judgment for enforcement against any other assets the defendant might have.[6]

Lien and Trust Comparisons

Constructive trusts and equitable liens are invoked for the same reasons, to prevent unjust enrichment.[7] Neither remedy is limited to cases of wrongdoing or dishonorable conduct by the defendant. For example, suppose that the plaintiff and defendant decided to live together without marriage. They jointly purchase lumber and plaintiff uses his labor to build a house on the defendant's land. When the relationship cools and the parties separate, the defendant has a house which has improved the value of her land. She is not a wrongdoer, but she may be held liable to make restitution to the plaintiff for the value of his contribution to the house and the property may be subjected to an equitable lien to secure that restitution.[8] Another example of lien without wrongdoing occurs with the vendee's lien. A purchaser who pays a part of the price of a land purchase but who rescinds for breach by the vendor may have a lien on the land to secure repayment of his price.[9]

The constructive trust and equitable lien are also similar in the rule that neither remedy can be used unless some particular assets can be identified as belonging in good conscience to the plaintiff, and in the rule that permits any identified or traced assets, tangible or intangible, to qualify

---

6. See In re Marriage of Allen, 724 P.2d 651, 658 (Colo.1986); I G. Palmer, Law of Restitution § 1.5 (1978 & Supps.). It would be possible to speak of a constructive trust with a money judgment for any deficiency in value, but, perhaps because it seems illogical, the usual way of speaking uses the term equitable lien.

7. E.g., Leyden v. Citicorp Indus. Bank, 782 P.2d 6, 10 (Colo.1989) ("An equitable lien that is imposed by a court of equity to prevent unjust enrichment is a special form of constructive trust") and authorities cited note 3 above.

8. Cf. Robinson v. Robinson, 100 Ill.App.3d 437, 57 Ill.Dec. 532, 429 N.E.2d 183 (1981) (married couple built house on land belonging to husband's parents, upon couple's divorce, equitable lien in favor of wife was proper); Kuhlman v. Cargile, 200 Neb. 150, 262 N.W.2d 454 (1978) (on facts similar to text example, using constructive trust terminology but perhaps having equitable lien in mind).

9. See § 12.11(4) below. Cf. Leyden v. Citicorp Indus. Bank, 782 P.2d 6 (Colo.1989) (upon divorce, H kept marital residence but was ordered to pay W for her interest; after H's bankruptcy, the court recognized an equitable lien against the property that survived bankruptcy); Martian v. Martian, 399 N.W.2d 849, 850 (N.D.1987) (similar, lien imposed on property after H purported to transfer the property to the Mary Shrine as a result of his conversion to the "the lifestyle of St. Francis of Assisi: chastity, obedience, and poverty").

as particular assets.[10] Both remedies protect the rights of bona fide purchasers.[11] The two remedies are also alike in the way they affect the remedies of other creditors of the defendant: both have the effect of removing some of the defendant's assets from the pool of resources available to creditors generally.[12]

Lien and Trust Differences

The overkill and deficiency examples given above show two differences between the constructive trust and the equitable lien. First, the trust ultimately provides the plaintiff with title to specific assets, while the lien only attaches to the assets as security. Second, in the overkill situation, the trust would exact more than restitution, while the lien is proportioned to the unjust enrichment. Whenever security rather than title is to be the remedy, the term equitable lien is appropriate and the term constructive trust is not. As to the second kind of distinction between the two, however, it is possible to use either term so long as appropriate measurement qualifications are added. For example, if the defendant holds a share of stock worth $1,000, which he purchased with $500 of his own money and $500 embezzled from the plaintiff, we can talk of an equitable lien for $500 (and an accompanying money judgment). But it would also be possible to think of imposing a constructive trust on one-half interest. Sometimes decisions appear to use the constructive trust terminology in this way. If that terminology implies that the plaintiff and defendant would be forced into a tenancy in common, it seems wrong; otherwise, however, on facts like those in the share of stock example, it measures restitution in the same way.

§ 4.3(4) Subrogation

Subrogation as Substitution

Subrogation simply means substitution of one person for another; that is, one person is allowed to stand in the shoes of another and assert that person's rights against the defendant. Factually, the case arises because, for some justifiable reason,[1] the subrogation plaintiff has paid a debt owed[2] by the defendant. Having paid the defendant's creditor, the plaintiff stands in the creditor's shoes, becomes the real party in interest,[3] and "is entitled to exercise all the remedies which the creditor possessed" against the defendant.[4] The plaintiff takes all the rights and remedies the creditor had

---

10. See § 6.1 as to tracing to funds of money.

11. E.g., In re Marriage of Allen, 724 P.2d 651 (Colo.1986); § 4.7 below.

12. See §§ 4.3(2) above and 6.1 below.

§ 4.3(4)

1. The volunteers rules may bar the plaintiff's claim if the plaintiff simply pays the defendant's debt as an intermeddler. E.g., Scandinavian Mut. Ins. Co. v. Chicago B. & Q.R. Co., 104 Neb. 258, 177 N.W. 178 (1920). See § 4.9 below.

2. The defendant must have been legally benefitted by the payment. If the payment by the plaintiff does not satisfy an obligation of the defendant, it is not a benefit to him and

he is not liable. E.g., Prudential Ins. Co. of Am. v. Couch, 180 W.Va. 210, 376 S.E.2d 104 (1988) (insurer's mistaken payment of medical bills for defendant's son; the defendant was not unjustly enriched unless he owed a duty to pay the bills on behalf of his son).

3. American Nursing Resources, Inc. v. Forrest T. Jones & Co., Inc., 812 S.W.2d 790 (Mo.App.1991).

4. American Sur. Co. of New York v. Bethlehem Nat. Bank of Bethlehem, Pa., 314 U.S. 314, 317, 62 S.Ct. 226, 228, 86 L.Ed. 241, 244, 138 A.L.R. 509 (1941) (quoting Sheldon, Subrogation); Wilson v. Todd, 217 Ind. 183, 187, 26 N.E.2d 1003, 1005, 129 A.L.R. 192 (1940) ("Subrogation is the substitution of another person in the place of a creditor, so that the

against the defendant but no more; he takes rights subject to all the defenses to which the creditor was subject.[5] Subrogation can be compared to an assignment of the creditor's rights to the plaintiff, and sometimes subrogation is in fact referred to as an equitable assignment.[6] The "assignment," however, is made by the court, not by the parties.

Subrogation Based on Unjust Enrichment; Terminology

Subrogation is another equitable remedy in which tracing is used to prevent unjust enrichment and to give effective relief to the plaintiff. Subrogation, like lien, trust, and contract, may arise by express or implied-in-fact agreement of parties, in which case it is called conventional subrogation. Subrogation may also arise because it is imposed by courts to prevent unjust enrichment,[7] in which case it is called legal or equitable subrogation.[8] To prevent unjust enrichment, subrogation is appropriate in any case where restitution is warranted because one person pays the debt of another and the remedy can be given without working an injustice.[9] Liability is generated and measured by enrichment, not by wrongdoing.[10] Conversely, subrogation in this sense is to be denied when the court concludes that there is no unjust enrichment.[11] This subsection considers subrogation as a remedy to prevent unjust enrichment, not subrogation required by contract.

The Surety and Insurer Examples

The simplest case of subrogation occurs when one party pays the debt of another. This often occurs in the case of sureties and insurers. Suppose the bank agrees to lend money to a borrower only if a surety guarantees the borrower's promissory note. The borrower does not pay the note when it is due and the bank demands payment from the surety. The surety pays off the borrower's loan. He then steps into the bank's shoes and acquires the bank's right to enforce the promissory note against the borrower.[12]

The most familiar case of subrogation is that of the collision insurer, which contracts to pay its insured for damage to the insured's car in a

person in whose favor it is exercised succeeds to the rights of the creditor in relation to the debtor").

5. Hanover Ins. Co. v. Fireman's Fund Ins. Co., 217 Conn. 340, 586 A.2d 567 (1991).

6. E.g., Fidelity Nat. Title Ins. Co. v. Miller, 215 Cal.App.3d 1163, 264 Cal.Rptr. 17 (1989).

7. See generally I G. Palmer, Law of Restitution § 1.5 (1978 & Supps.).

8. See, e.g., American Nat. Bank & Trust Co. of Chicago v. Weyerhaeuser Co., 692 F.2d 455 (7th Cir.1982); Bachmann v. Glazer & Glazer, Inc., 316 Md. 405, 559 A.2d 365 (1989). When the term "legal" is used to refer to subrogation, it is not offered in contrast with "equitable" and in fact in this context the two words mean the same. The term "legal" subrogation merely refers to subrogation imposed by law rather than resulting from agreement.

9. Bachmann v. Glazer & Glazer, Inc., 316 Md. 405, 559 A.2d 365 (1989); see American Nat'l Bank & Trust Co. v. Weyerhaeuser Co.,

692 F.2d 455 (7th Cir.1982) (Illinois law, subrogation covers "every instance in which one person, not merely a volunteer, pays a debt for which another is primarily liable and which in equity and good conscience should have been discharged by the latter"); Principal Casualty Ins. Co. v. Norwood, 463 N.W.2d 66 (Iowa 1990); Cagle, Inc. v. Sammons, 198 Neb. 595, 254 N.W.2d 398 (1977).

10. Thus if a debtor uses the plaintiff's money to discharge a mortgage on land held by the debtor and his innocent spouse, subrogation resurrects the mortgage in favor of the plaintiff, even though it imposes a lien on the innocent as well as the guilty spouse. Wilson v. Todd, 217 Ind. 183, 26 N.E.2d 1003, 129 A.L.R. 192 (1940).

11. E.g., Lynch v. Deaconess Medical Center, 113 Wash.2d 162, 776 P.2d 681 (1989).

12. Cf. American Sur. Co. of New York v. Bethlehem Nat. Bank of Bethlehem, Pa., 314 U.S. 314, 62 S.Ct. 226, 86 L.Ed. 241, 138 A.L.R. 509 (1941).

collision. If the insured suffers damage to her car as the result of defendant's negligence, the insured would have a tort claim. If the damage is paid for by the insurer, the insurer steps into the insured's shoes, takes her rights to pursue the tort claim against the defendant.[13] The same principle applies in some other kinds of insurance cases.[14]

The Mortgage Example

A third example is less common but more central to the remedial issues. Suppose that the defendant fraudulently induces the plaintiff to purchase worthless shares of stock for $100,000. The defendant uses the money so obtained to pay off the bank's mortgage on the defendant's home. There is no surety and no insurance, but the defendant is enriched by receiving the $100,000 from the plaintiff. The money belonging in good conscience to the plaintiff cannot be traced into the purchase of a tangible asset, but it can be traced into satisfaction of the defendant's debt. It purchased the defendant's freedom from a debt to the bank and from the bank's mortgage lien. In so doing, the plaintiff's money did not add assets to the defendant's balance sheet but it did reduce his liabilities. So the plaintiff is permitted to stand in the bank's shoes and enforce the claim which the bank previously had. The plaintiff is "subrogated to the rights of the bank."

Priorities

In cases like that just described, the plaintiff might simply sue the defendant at law. He might claim damages for fraud or he might sue on a quasi-contract or "assumpsit" theory. Under either theory he could recover a money judgment for the $100,000 with whatever interest is appropriate. Subrogation will be more advantageous on the facts of the example and in any case in which the bank or other creditor had special rights against the debtor. In the example, the bank not only had a right to collect money from the defendant debtor but also a lien against his property as security for payment of the debt. Both the debt and the lien are resurrected and vested in the plaintiff,[15] allowing the plaintiff to stand in the creditor's shoes and enforce the same right and the same remedies that the creditor had[16] and that the plaintiff's money paid for. The effect is to give the plaintiff the bank's standing, security, and priority.[17] If the bank's mortgage is a first

13. E.g., Principal Casualty Ins. Co. v. Norwood, 463 N.W.2d 66 (Iowa 1990) (if insured recovers for damage which insurer was entitled to recover by subrogation, then insurer can recover from insured, less a proportionate share of insured's attorney fees); but cf. Lynch v. Deaconess Medical Center, 113 Wash.2d 162, 776 P.2d 681 (1989) (hospital patient's recovery from medical insurer, payable to hospital, hospital not liable for attorney fees).

14. Cf. Fidelity Nat. Title Ins. Co. v. Miller, 215 Cal.App.3d 1163, 264 Cal.Rptr. 17 (1989) (title insurance paid to land purchaser for defect in title, insurer subrogated to buyer's claim against vendor of land for breach of title warranty).

15. Bachmann v. Glazer & Glazer, Inc., 316 Md. 405, 412, 559 A.2d 365, 368 (1989) ("an obligation extinguished by a payment made by a third person is treated as still subsisting for the benefit of this third person").

16. American Sur. Co. of New York v. Bethlehem Nat. Bank of Bethlehem, Pa., 314 U.S. 314, 317, 62 S.Ct. 226, 228, 86 L.Ed. 241, 244, 138 A.L.R. 509 (1941) ("Succeeding to the creditor's right, the surety also succeeds to the creditor's means for enforcing it. The surety is a special kind of secured creditor. For its claim against the principal is secured by its right of subrogation to the remedies of the creditor which it has been compelled to pay").

17. Although the factual details vary, the following exemplify the pattern and the priorities just described: Banton v. Hackney, 557 So.2d 807 (Ala.1989) (similar to facts described in text); Wilson v. Todd, 217 Ind. 183, 26

mortgage, the plaintiff has a first mortgage and will prevail over other creditors of the defendant. In cases like this, subrogation represents one kind of equitable lien or a way of recognizing that the lien is an appropriate way to redress the unjust enrichment.[18]

Tracing

As with the constructive trust and the equitable lien, subrogation priorities are justified when, but only when, the payment made by the plaintiff can be traced to and identified with the payment and discharge of a claim against the debtor-defendant. Suppose the plaintiff pays money to the debtor by mistake and the debtor later happens to pay off his creditor. The plaintiff will be entitled to recover restitution of the money mistakenly paid, but it does not appear from these facts alone that the plaintiff's money went to pay the creditor's claim. In the absence of such tracing, it is improper to subrogate the plaintiff to the creditor's rights. Even where tracing is possible, a court may conclude that subrogation is not the most appropriate remedy on the particular facts, and might limit the plaintiff to a simple "quasi-contract" recovery instead.[19]

Garnishment and Subrogation

In some cases courts impose a kind of equitable garnishment[20] that resembles subrogation. When that is the case, tracing to a specific asset may not be important if there are good reasons to permit garnishment. For example, general building contractors may become insolvent while owing money to subcontractors who have worked on a job. If the landowner owes the general contractor money for the job, the subcontractor, to whom the landowner owes nothing, may nevertheless enforce his claim against the general contractor by reaching funds owing to that contractor.[21] This may not count as a full subrogation; no one subcontractor would have the right to exclude other subcontractors from the fund held by the landowner. The similarities to subrogation, however, suggest that some of the underlying ideas are pervasive in the law and useful in formulating remedies.

N.E.2d 1003, 129 A.L.R. 192 (1940) (H obtained money by fraud, discharged mortgage on land he held with W; victim of fraud could impose mortgage on both H and W by subrogation); Bachmann v. Glazer & Glazer, Inc., 316 Md. 405, 559 A.2d 365 (1989) (A promises to pay C and B guarantees the payment; P pays A's debt to C; by subrogation P is entitled to pursue C's claim against A and also against B as guarantor); Cagle, Inc. v. Sammons, 198 Neb. 595, 254 N.W.2d 398 (1977) (by subrogation contractor who had paid subcontractor's workers to finish incomplete job could stand in workers' shoes to claim on bond meant to protect workers); Leno v. Prudential Ins. Co., 228 N.C. 501, 46 S.E.2d 471, 1 A.L.R.2d 281 (1948) (long-term lessee paid off mortgage on premises when owner-landlord defaulted, lessee subrogated to mortgagee's rights). Cf. Haskel Engineering & Supply Co. v. Hartford Accident & Indem. Co., 78 Cal.App.3d 371, 144 Cal.Rptr. 189 (1978) (insurer which had reimbursed employer for employee's embezzlement

was subrogated to employer's constructive trust claim against employee to the extent of the insurer's payment, and could take the gains from the employee's investments under constructive trust principles).

18. See American Sur. Co. of New York v. Bethlehem Nat. Bank of Bethlehem, Pa., 314 U.S. 314, 317, 62 S.Ct. 226, 228, 86 L.Ed. 241, 244, 138 A.L.R. 509 (1941) ("In other respects a right of subrogation is as much in the nature of a security as is a mortgage").

19. Martinez v. Continental Enterprises, 730 P.2d 308 (Colo.1986).

20. The garnishment terminology is sometimes used in the contractor situation discussed in this paragraph. Flooring Sys., Inc. v. Radisson Group, Inc., 160 Ariz. 224, 772 P.2d 578 (1989).

21. See, e.g., Pearlman v. Reliance Ins. Co., 371 U.S. 132, 83 S.Ct. 232, 9 L.Ed.2d 190 (1962); § 12.20(3) below.

Contribution and Indemnity and Subrogation

The right to contribution from a co-obligor is also an equitable restitutionary claim which is enforced to prevent unjust enrichment.[22] The contribution claim based on unjust enrichment is closely similar to the subrogation claim based on unjust enrichment.[23] Suppose A and B are both sureties for a debtor. When the debtor defaults, the creditor enforces the debt claim against A, as he is entitled to do. A is entitled to contribution from B. Without such contribution, B would be unjustly enriched, because he would have escaped liability for his share. The close relationship to subrogation can be seen in such a case because it would be equally possible to reason that A, having paid the debt that B owes in equity and good conscience, is subrogated to the creditor's claim against B.

Indemnity claims are similar to contribution claims but seek a full recovery instead of a share. Suppose A has no obligation to pay the creditor; B is the sole obligor. But A mistakenly believes he must pay the creditor and he does so. Upon discovering the facts, A may seek indemnity from B. The unjust enrichment grounds for recovery are the same as in contribution; only the measure is different.

§ 4.3(5) Accounting and Accounting for Profits

The term accounting, or accounting for profits, is used in several ways. In its most important meaning, it is a restitutionary remedy based upon avoiding unjust enrichment. In this sense it reaches monies owed by a fiduciary or other wrongdoer, including profits produced by property which in equity and good conscience belonged to the plaintiff. It resembles a constructive trust in that tracing may be used to reach profits. But even if tracing fails, the plaintiff may recover a judgment for the profits due from use of his property.

Development of Common Law and Equitable Accounting

Common law action of account. A form of action known as Account was recognized by early common law. At the time this action was established, there was no simple contract action on the common law side. The action in Account was brought first against bailiffs of the manor to compel them to account for their stewardship, but it was later extended somewhat to include accountings between partners. Probably there were many occasions in which no complex accounting was required and the action was used to collect money owed by the defendant simply because no other form of action was

---

22. See generally I G. Palmer, Law of Restitution § 1.5(d) (1978 & Supps.).

23. Chenery v. Agri–Lines Corp., 115 Idaho 281, 284, 766 P.2d 751, 754 (1988).

The Chenery court explained:

Reimbursement, or the right of one party who has satisfied a claim to seek repayment from another party, can be pursued on any one of three interrelated common law principles: indemnity, contribution, or subrogation. All those principles are based on the concept that a party should be held respon-

sible for his own wrongs, and if another is compelled to pay damages caused by the wrongdoer, that party is entitled to recover from the wrongdoer * * *. Both indemnity and subrogation are equitable principles based on the general theory that one compelled to pay damages caused by another should be able to seek recovery from that party. The doctrines overlap in some cases and certainly the possessor of the right to indemnity may also possess the right of subrogation.

available.[1] But defects in enforcing the accounting led to the use of equitable claims for accounting and the common law action eventually fell into disuse.[2]

Equity accounting. As the limitations of the common law action of account became more apparent, the equity court began to entertain bills for accounting. Regular officers of the Chancery Court, the masters, could serve as auditors and work through complex accounts if necessary and report to the court. Chancery could use its powers of discovery to find hidden assets in the hands of the defendant, and altogether the chancery accounting worked out pretty well.

After the development of assumpsit at law,[3] with its recognition and enforcement of ordinary contract claims, it was clear that many money claims were actionable in the law courts, even though the amounts and offsets might be disputed. Thus equity was justified in compelling an accounting only where it could give some relief not available at law. The ability of the masters in Chancery to work out the details of complex accounts naturally meant that the equity trial was preferable to the jury trial where the accounting was complicated. This furnished one ground for equity jurisdiction, namely that the legal remedy was inadequate because of the complexity of the accounts.[4]

Equity might also intervene to compel an accounting where there was a pre-existing equitable duty to account. The duties of trustees and other fiduciaries were originally recognized and imposed only by equity courts, for example, and one of these equitable duties was to stand ready to account to the beneficiary. Naturally, equity courts were the only courts to enforce this duty to account at a time when they were the only courts to recognize it at all. In such cases, the complexity of the account was not the basis of equity action; the basis was instead the substantive equity rule, not enforced elsewhere.[5]

Accounting for Profits Today

In contemporary law the term accounting is sometimes confusing because it reflects disparate aspects of its history. Indeed, one writer thought that the grounds for invoking accounting and its effects could be so different that it should be regarded as three different remedies, not one.[6]

Accounting to deal with complex accounts. One version of accounting is invoked on the ground that questions of what one party owes the other is too complex for a jury's decision, either because the defendant has offsetting expenses that will have to be calculated to figure the net amount of profits, or because the defendant has claims of his own. This version of accounting can produce a non-jury equity trial in state courts.[7] The Supreme Court of the United States, however, has said that few accounts are likely to be

---

§ 4.3(5)

1. A more detailed and precise history is given in Eichengrun, Remedying the Remedy of Accounting, 60 Ind.L.J. 463 (1985).

2. Maitland, The Forms of Action at Common Law 63–64 (1954).

3. See § 4.2(3) above.

4. 4 J. Pomeroy, Equity Jurisprudence § 1421 (5th ed. 1941).

5. *J. Pomeroy,* supra note 4.

6. *Eichengrun,* supra note 1.

7. E.g., Van de Kamp v. Bank of American Nat. Trust & Savings Ass'n, 204 Cal.App.3d 819, 251 Cal.Rptr. 530 (1988).

complex enough to deny a jury trial right, since masters may assist as needed, without taking over the jury's function.[8]

Accounting as discovery. A second version of accounting was in effect hardly more than a discovery order, originating in equity at a time when discovery was not generally available otherwise. The defendant, once prima facie grounds for accounting was shown, was compelled to produce his books or other data needed. In the light of extensive modern discovery, this kind of accounting probably has little or no use today.[9]

Accounting to capture profits and force proof from the defendant. The terms "account" and "profits" are used in many common expressions that have little or no relationship to the accounting for profits discussed here,[10] so there is a risk of some confusion. The kind of accounting for profits discussed here has two main effects in current practice.[11] First it forces the fiduciary defendant to disgorge gains received from improper use of the plaintiff's property or entitlements. Second, it imposes upon the fiduciary defendant the burden of proving appropriate deductions for expenses he incurred in reaping those profits; that is, the plaintiff makes a prima facie case by showing a breach of fiduciary duty plus gross receipts resulting to the fiduciary, and the defendant must prove what deductions are appropriate to figure the net profit.[12]

Grounds for the accounting for profits; is accounting limited to fiduciaries? Equity traditionally took jurisdiction to enforce such an accounting because there was a substantive equitable duty to account on the part of the fiduciary. Today the accounting may be pursued as a separate cause of action or as incidental to some other claim.[13] Accounting holds the defendant liable for his profits, not for damages.[14] The ground of this liability is unjust enrichment. Can the accounting claim be extended to reach profits in the hands of wrongdoer's who are not fiduciaries? This question requires consideration.

8. See Dairy Queen, Inc. v. Wood, 369 U.S. 469, 82 S.Ct. 894, 8 L.Ed.2d 44 (1962); see § 2.6 above.

9. See *Eichengrun,* supra note 1. There are marginal discovery effects illustrated in cases like Reebok Intern. Ltd. v. Marnatech Enterprises, Inc., 737 F.Supp. 1521, 1523 (S.D.Cal.1989) where the court, preliminary to the merits, froze the defendant's assets to preserve them for an accounting for profits, entering an order enjoining all defendants from the transfer of any asset until "an accounting of all assets having a value of Five Thousand Dollars ($5,000) or more, and the location an identity thereof," was filed with the court.

10. For example, when a defendant occupies the plaintiff's land, it may be said that he is liable to "account for rents and profits," as in, e.g., Frankel v. Northeast Land Co., 391 Pa.Super. 226, 570 A.2d 1065 (1990). In such locutions, the term "account" does not refer to an equity suit for accounting but instead means only that the defendant is accountable or liable. The term "profits" in the occupation of land context is based on ancient usage

which has nothing to do with business profits. Today it ordinarily refers to net rents. See Van Ruymbeke v. Patapsco Indus. Park, 261 Md. 470, 276 A.2d 61 (1971); § 5.8(2) below.

11. There may be other less central elements associated with accounting. By treating accounting for profits like a constructive trust, a court might seek to justify a preliminary injunction freezing the defendant's assets until trial. See § 6.1(5) below.

12. *Eichengrun,* supra note 1.

13. See Hamilton–Brown Shoe Co. v. Wolf Bros. & Co., 240 U.S. 251, 36 S.Ct. 269, 60 L.Ed. 629 (1916) (accounting incidental to injunction); I G. Palmer, The Law of Restitution § 1.5(c) (1978 & Supps.).

14. Professor Yorio concludes that some courts have used equitable accounting fictionally and that they are really awarding consequential damages in some instances and undercutting damages rules in the process. E. Yorio, Contract Enforcement: Specific Performance and Injunctions § 9.2.2 (1989).

Profit recovery against non-fiduciaries. It is apparent that recovery of unjust enrichment gains in general is not limited to claims against fiduciaries.[15] For example, a wrongdoer[16] who is not a fiduciary may be forced to give up his gains when constructive trust[17] and subrogation theories are advanced.[18] Gains on resale are even recoverable in an ordinary quasi-contract action at law in appropriate cases.[19] So profits against non-fiduciaries are recoverable without the slightest reference to accounting or any other remedial theory.[20] Statutes specifically authorize profits recoveries in the case of copyright[21] and trademark infringement without reference to whether the defendant is a fiduciary.[22] A famous New York case even allowed the accounting suit itself against defendant who had received the plaintiff's goods from a thief, without mention of any restriction to fiduciaries.[23]

These instances do not show that the defendant's profits are invariably recoverable. They show that non-fiduciaries may be required to give up their gains and in some cases their business profits[24] where the merits of the case show that such an extreme remedy is justified.[25]

Burden of proof against non-fiduciaries. The discussion above shows that profits can be recovered against wrongdoers who are not fiduciaries. The only remaining question is whether accounting claims can be asserted

---

15. See generally Douthwaite, The Tortfeasor's Profits—A Brief Survey, 19 Hast.L.Rev. 1071 (1968).

16. When the substantive basis for the claim is merely breach of contract, restitution is almost never measured by the breacher's profits. See § 12.7(4) below. If the "breacher" also breaches a fiduciary duty, however, as where an employee takes the employer's trade secrets, the breacher-fiduciary may be made to disgorge his profits from the wrong. See § 10.5(3) below. In this setting, it is important to claim that the defendant is a fiduciary if the plaintiff wishes to recover the defendant's profits. The important ingredient added by the fiduciary status, however, is not that status in itself; what is added is wrongdoing as distinct from contract breach.

17. E.g., Zeller v. Bogue Elec. Mfg. Corp., 476 F.2d 795 (2d Cir.1973), cert. denied, 414 U.S. 908, 94 S.Ct. 217, 38 L.Ed.2d 146 (1973); Baxter House, Inc. v. Rosen, 27 A.D.2d 258, 278 N.Y.S.2d 442 (1967) (constructive trust applicable to converter, fiduciary relationship not required); see G & M Motor Co. v. Thompson, 567 P.2d 80 (Okl.1977) (embezzled funds invested in life insurance, embezzler died, victim could have had entire insurance fund, in excess of its loss, if it had so claimed); Restatement of Restitution § 202 (1937) (conscious wrongdoer).

18. Haskel Engineering & Supply Co. v. Hartford Accident & Indem. Co., 78 Cal. App.3d 371, 144 Cal.Rptr. 189 (1978).

19. Federal Sugar Ref. Co. v. United States Sugar Equalization Bd., 268 Fed. 575 (2d Cir. 1920) (interference with contract, recovery of defendant's profits); Ablah v. Eyman, 188

Kan. 665, 365 P.2d 181, 90 A.L.R.2d 766 (1961) (business savings resulting to defendant from use of plaintiff's property); Edwards v. Lee's Adm'r, 265 Ky. 418, 96 S.W.2d 1028 (1936); cf. Olwell v. Nye & Nissen Co., 26 Wash.2d 282, 173 P.2d 652, 169 A.L.R. 139 (1946) (value of use of a machine). In this respect, note that net savings in a business operation are equivalent to increased profits (or, in a losing business, to diminished losses).

20. See Popp v. Gountanis, 221 Mont. 267, 718 P.2d 340 (1986) (farm tenant entitled to ⅔ crops was entitled to recover ⅔ of federal payments made to landlord for non-production, no particular theory advanced).

21. See § 6.3(4) below.

22. See § 6.4(4) below.

23. Fur & Wool Trading Co. v. George I. Fox, Inc., 245 N.Y. 215, 156 N.E. 670, 58 A.L.R. 181 (1927).

24. For some purposes profits from a business operation may be distinguished from the gain in a simple market transaction in much the same way that income may be distinguished from capital gain. See § 4.5 below.

25. See § 4.5 below. In general, the wrongdoer may be required to give up (1) profits gained from dealing with property legal title to which remains in the plaintiff and (2) profits gained from dealing with property to which the plaintiff has no legal title but only an equitable claim based on good conscience. In the second case, however, it would seem that serious and conscious wrongdoing is required, and perhaps the same should be said about the first.

against non-fiduciaries to gain some additional advantage besides the recovery of profits. Specifically, is it appropriate to place the burden on a non-fiduciary wrongdoer to show expenses that would reduce the gross profit to a smaller net figure, once his serious wrongdoing and gross profit has been established? This is an issue that only arises with profits in the sense of income from an ongoing operation; there is no problem if the defendant simply reaped a gain in a simple market transaction. The defendant has the best access to his own business operations and for that reason it makes sense to place the burden on him to show appropriate deductions.[26] The trademark and copyright statutes places the burden in exactly this way against infringers,[27] and an even more extensive shift in the burden of proof has been used against some non-fiduciaries subjected to accounting.[28]

These authorities seem to show that profits can be awarded against non-fiduciaries and that the burden of proof can be shifted against non-fiduciaries. Any difference between awarding profits and shifting the burden of proof and an accounting for profits is presumably secondary.[29]

Burden to prove business expense deductions. It does not follow that every wrongdoing justifies a recovery of profits, under the rubric of accounting or otherwise, nor that the burden as to amounts should be shifted in every case. Serious and conscious wrongdoing should be required to justify a recovery of the defendant's profits except when a different rule is imposed by statute. As to the burden of proof, it seems fair to shift the burden of proving business expense deductions to reach a figure for net income.

Burden to prove basis for apportionment of profit between innocent and wrongful acts. When the problem is apportionment rather than calculation of net profits, a burden shifting is more dubious. In a trademark case, for example, if we are not sure what the defendant's gross profits were, or whether it profited at all from use of the plaintiff's trademark,[30] an award of the defendant's gross profits to the plaintiff exacts more than the pound of flesh to which the plaintiff is entitled. It also runs the risk that other creditors of the defendant will be too readily deprived of assets against which they can levy.

Perhaps the best solution is to recognize that profit recoveries may be justified to prevent unjust enrichment in a variety of wrongdoing cases, not just fiduciary cases. At the same time, what proof is acceptable to show the

26. See *Eichengrun,* supra n. 1 at 479–480 (1985).

27. "In assessing profits the plaintiff shall be required to prove defendant's sales only; the defendant must prove all elements of cost or deduction claimed." 15 U.S.C.A. § 1117(a). See § 6.4(4) below. A very similar statute covers copyrights. 17 U.S.C.A. § 504. See § 6.3(4) below.

28. Hamilton–Brown Shoe Co. v. Wolf Bros. & Co., 240 U.S. 251, 36 S.Ct. 269, 60 L.Ed. 629 (1916) shifted the burden to the defendant to show what share of profits from shoe sales were due to use of plaintiff's trademark on shoes; this goes beyond the statutory burden, which requires the defendant to prove any expense deductions. See § 4.5(3) below.

29. Against a non-fiduciary the case might not be considered to be an "equitable" one unless there is another basis for equitable jurisdiction. This classification could affect jury trial.

30. See the discussion of Hamilton–Brown Shoe Co. v. Wolf Bros. & Co., supra note 28. See also Warren v. Century Bankcorporation, Inc., 741 P.2d 846 (Okl.1987) (defendant's profits fully identified and defendant could show expenses incurred in generating those profits, but, held, the defendant can have no deductions for expenses at all, even though they are fully proven; seemingly a punitive decision).

defendant's profit, and how the burden is allocated on the matter of deductible expenses, could be a matter for cautious determination on a case-by-case basis.

Accounting for profits in law and equity. The fiduciary accounting for profits was traditionally an equitable claim. An equitable claim would ordinarily be tried to a judge, not to a jury. As already indicated, the plaintiff today may pursue at least some money claims against a defendant on a quasi-contract theory and thus have a jury trial if he prefers.[31] But the traditional view of the claim as equitable permits the converse as well: if the plaintiff prefers to treat the claim as a purely equitable one, he has been allowed to do so in some cases, even when the defendant is not a fiduciary and when a quasi-contract at law recovery would give him the relief he seeks.[32] The result, presumably, is a non-jury trial, at least in state courts. The famous *Dairy Queen* case seemed to say that the constitution required federal courts to grant a jury trial whenever the claim was one for money, even though the claim was one for accounting of profits.[33] If the accounting seeks to recover a fund that has been traced, so that it is in effect a constructive trust on a fund of money, the case might be classed as an equitable suit and tried without a jury. But accounting of profits is usually based on a much more limited tracing, in which the plaintiff merely shows that the defendant profited in some amount from use of the plaintiff's entitlement. The defendant is liable on the same unjust enrichment grounds as are involved in a constructive trust, but no particular fund is identified to which a trust or lien attaches. If the accounting merely results in a money judgment and not a trust or lien, it would seem to require a jury trial under the Supreme Court's decision in *Dairy Queen,* but some federal authority has insisted that a non-jury trial is appropriate.[34]

31. In addition to the preceding paragraphs, see I G. Palmer, The Law of Restitution § 1.5(c) (1978 & Supps.).

32. Fur & Wool Trading Co. v. George I. Fox, Inc., 245 N.Y. 215, 156 N.E. 670, 58 A.L.R. 181 (1927).

In *Fur & Wool Trading Co.* the plaintiff alleged that his goods were taken by force and then received by the defendant with knowledge of the facts. The defendant in turn allegedly sold the goods for a profit. The plaintiff sought an accounting and a recovery of the profits so gained. The lower courts dismissed the suit on the ground that the plaintiff could pursue a remedy at law. The Court of Appeals reversed, holding that the facts entitled the plaintiff to proceed in equity for an accounting. The Court thought that the plaintiff could get all the information he needed about the profits in an action at law. Traditional rules would also have allowed the plaintiff to recover the defendant's profits on the resale, since defendant was a converter without title and liable for the profits in a simple assumpsit claim at law. As to that, see § 4.2 above. So neither accounting as a means of discovery nor accounting as a means of capturing profits seems to add anything that the plaintiff could not get at law. The

Court of Appeals did not suggest complex accounts as a basis for relief. Perhaps the court only thought that the plaintiff should have the option of a non-jury trial. The case is discussed in I G. Palmer, The Law of Restitution § 1.5(c), pp. 24–25 (1978 & Supps.).

33. See Dairy Queen, Inc. v. Wood, 369 U.S. 469, 82 S.Ct. 894, 8 L.Ed.2d 44 (1962); see Tandy Corp. v. Malone & Hyde, Inc., 769 F.2d 362, 364 (6th Cir.1985), cert. denied, 476 U.S. 1158, 106 S.Ct. 2277, 90 L.Ed.2d 719 (1986); on jury trials in "equity" claims generally, see § 2.6 above.

In Hyatt Bros., Inc. v. Hyatt, 769 P.2d 329 (Wyo.1989) the court concluded that "stockholders' derivative actions, even if they include a request for an accounting, are not automatically considered actions purely in equity. Rather, the substance of the issues underlying the derivative action, as evidenced by the entire pleadings, will control the court's characterization of the derivative action as primarily legal or equitable in nature."

34. American Cyanamid Co. v. Sterling Drug, Inc., 649 F.Supp. 784 (D.N.J.1986). The *American Cyanamid* court reasoned that restitution was equitable in nature and that so long as the accounting claim was not com-

§ 4.3(6) Rescission

Meaning of Rescission

Rescission. A rescission is an avoidance of a transaction. Rescission will normally be accompanied by restitution on both sides. Rescission is thus less a remedy and more a matter of the conceptual apparatus that leads to the remedy: the contract is being unmade, so restoration of benefits received under the contract seems to follow. The rescission conception is not required to justify restitution,[1] but where rescission occurs, restitution is usually the next step. Rescission or avoidance is thus at least in the background of many claims for restitution.[2]

Avoidance. A contract may be avoided without reference to rescission. For example, a contract may be illegal or may become impossible of performance, and in either case the court might refuse enforcement. Such contracts are avoided, but it is not so common to say they are rescinded. Avoidance may or may not lead to restitution; it often does so in the case of contracts that have become impossible of performance,[3] but it often does not in the case of illegal contracts.[4] Another example of avoidance without "rescission" is the case of a will procured in favor of the defendant by fraud or duress. In such a case the court may simply declare the defendant to be a constructive trustee.[5]

Termination. A contract or rights under it, may be terminated pursuant to the contract itself, without rescission and without restitution as to past performance. A lessor might terminate a lease because of nonpayment of rent by a lessee. In such a case the future obligations on one or both sides might come to an end, but the termination is not necessarily a rescission, there is no restitution for past performances, and damages to the landlord might be in order.[6]

bined with a "legal" or damages claim, the case was an equitable one.

§ 4.3(6)

1. For examples: (1) P pays $100 to D under the mistaken belief that he owes D such a sum when in fact he owes only $50. P is entitled to restitution of the $50 overpayment unless D has a defense. There is no rescission. (2) A contract between P and D becomes impossible of performance. Impossibility discharges the responsibilities of the parties and may call for restitution and/or other adjustments, but the term rescission is not ordinarily used. (3) Rescission is an optional but unnecessary way of thinking about some cases. P partly performs a contract to build a house on D's land, rendering services as agreed. When the foundation is complete, D breaches by refusing to permit P to continue performance. P may recover restitution for the value of his services. This is an optional remedy for D's breach and does not depend on conceptualizing the case as one of rescission.

2. See, for example, the following sections on restitution following an avoidance or rescission: § 9.3 (misrepresentation); § 10.2(1) (duress, constructive trusts); § 10.3 (undue in-

fluence); § 11.3 (mutual mistake in contracting); § 11.11 (mistake in gifts); § 12.7 (breach of enforceable contract, restitution whether or not "rescission" is theory); § 12.11(2) (rescission for contract breach in favor of land purchaser); § 12.2(2) (rescission in care-of-grantor contracts); § 12.14 (rescission where property subject to contract is damaged before performance is due); §§ 12.15(2) & 12.15(3) (rescission in lease cases).

3. See § 13.3 below.

4. See § 13.6 below.

5. See § 6.7 below.

6. See § 12.15(3) below. The installment contract offers another example: the buyer's rights might be terminated for non-payment, but that is not necessarily a "rescission." Termination might leave the vendor with a damages or "deficiency" claim. See § 12.13 below. Palmer gives an example in which a patent license is terminated or canceled "without disturbing the performance on each side that had been previously rendered". See I G. Palmer, Law of Restitution § 4.6, p. 423 (1978 & Supps.).

Distinct from restitution. The term rescission refers to the avoidance of the transaction or the calling off of the deal, and not to the particular form of restitution that may be granted once the transaction is avoided.   To decide that a contract should be avoided is not to decide the form or measure of restitution.   Very commonly the restitution granted when the term rescission is used is restitution in money.   But a court could grant rescission and order a specie return of goods or real property.   The fact that the same thing could be done in terms of a constructive trust may suggest that we suffer from too many terms.   At any rate, the rescission is not the restitution that follows and it is the restitution that is remedially important.

Methods of Rescission

Mutual agreement. Rescission may be accomplished by agreement of the parties, and some writers prefer to use the term only to refer to such an agreement.   The professional usage, however, is broader, and includes both judicial and unilateral rescission.

Unilateral rescission; rescission at law. If the plaintiff has adequate grounds for doing so, she may unilaterally rescind a transaction against the will of the defendant.   If the plaintiff has paid $1,000 for goods and then discovers that the defendant fraudulently misrepresented their character, the plaintiff is entitled to rescind by declaring the transaction rescinded, offering to return the goods to the defendant, and demanding her money back.   If the defendant agrees, rescission is accomplished by agreement of the parties.   If he does not, rescission is still accomplished, but the plaintiff must bring suit to obtain restitution of her money.   In such a case there is no need for equity intervention, and the plaintiff may sue at law to recover the money she paid and which ought to be returned to her now that the contract is rescinded.   Such a suit, to use the older terminology, would be in assumpsit, based on quasi contract.   This whole process is sometimes called rescission at law.[7]

Judicial rescission; rescission in equity. Rescission "at law" is not always suitable, however, because it cannot always compel effective restitution.   If the plaintiff has paid for the goods with a negotiable note, the defendant may transfer the note to a holder in due course—who would be permitted to enforce it against the plaintiff, in spite of any rescission on the part of the plaintiff.   Effective restitution or restoration of the pre-existing state of affairs in such a case requires a method of destroying the note before the defendant transfers it.   This is a job that traditionally could be accomplished by equity courts because they could use their powers to issue an in personam order to compel the defendant to bring the note in to court for cancellation.   Thus a rescission that requires, for effective restitution, a cancellation or amendment of any document, normally is effected in equity courts.[8]   In equity rescission, the theory is that the rescission does not take place until the court declares it, while rescission "at law" takes place when

---

7. See Kracl v. Loseke, 236 Neb. 290, 461 N.W.2d 67 (1990); § 4.8 below.

8. Sometimes a suit of this kind was called a bill quia timet, that is, a bill "because he fears" the instrument will be negotiated or

used against him.   Instead of destruction or cancellation the court may merely enjoin transfer.   See, e.g., Yount v. Setzer, 155 N.C. 213, 71 S.E. 209 (1911).

the plaintiff makes a proper offer to restore the defendant and demands rescission.[9]

Equity rescission is also needed whenever the plaintiff wants a recovery of specific property having special or unique qualities. If the plaintiff has been induced to sell his land by the fraud of the defendant, the plaintiff is entitled to rescind and to seek the aid of equity. Here again, legal remedies for recovery of land may be inadequate, and equity may simply declare a rescission of the transaction and order restitution on both sides. This may be called a constructive trust, but whether it is or not, the result will be that the defendant is compelled to make restoration.

Since the plaintiff's power to rescind is often disputed, lawyers often resort to judicial or "equity" rescission. The equitable nature of rescission does not invoke the adequacy or irreparable harm test. Rescission can be granted or denied regardless whether the plaintiff has some other adequate remedy.[10]

Grounds for rescission and restitution. Rescission says a transaction must be undone; restitution says that performance received in the transaction must be returned. Neither term addresses the grounds or reasons for taking these steps. Rescission might be thought to be based on unjust enrichment in the same way that restitution is. For instance, if the parties have entered into a contract under a mutual mistake of basic facts, then it may be unjust to enforce such a contract. But rescission might also be thought to rest on firm grounds of policy or the logic of contracting: if one party is contracting about a horse named Sam and the other about a horse named Peerless, maybe there is no contract at all. So the decision to rescind might be grounded in either unjust enrichment or in the logic of contracting. But once rescission is granted it is easy to see why restitution must follow. If the defendant has received performance under a contract that is to be undone by rescission, he is unjustly enriched unless he is made to restore that performance or its value. The decision to rescind (and some other decisions to avoid a transaction) may itself be thought of as a decision based on something like unjust enrichment.

§ 4.3(7) Reformation

Reforming Documents to the Parties' Intent

Reformation is a restitutionary remedy invoked to avoid unjust enrichment, but in a special sense. When parties come to an agreement, but by fraud [1] or mistake [2] write it down in some fashion that does not truly reflect their contract, equity will reform the writing to make it reflect the parties' true intention. This is restitutionary in a limited sense that it restores the efficacy of the original agreement. It may also be restitutionary in the

---

9. "In equity, on the other hand, the rescission is effected by the decree of the equity court which entertains the action for the express purpose of rescinding the contract and rendering a decree granting such relief. In other words, a court of equity grants rescission or cancellation * * *." Kracl v. Loseke, 236 Neb. 290, 461 N.W.2d 67, 73 (1990). See § 4.8 below.

10. Cf. I G. Palmer, Law of Restitution § 4.7 (1978 & Supps.).

§ 4.3(7)

1. See § 9.4 below.

2. See § 11.6 below.

secondary sense that notions of unjust enrichment may lie behind some reformation cases.

Reformation is almost always sought so that some other remedy may then be pursued. For instance, the contract is reformed, and the plaintiff can then show that, as reformed, the contract was breached. He can then claim restitution, damages, or specific performance. Reformation is thus usually a way station, a precursor to some other and final remedy, which in turn may or may not be restitutionary.

Constructive Trust Compared

The restitutionary function of reformation can be seen in those cases in which it works like a constructive trust. Suppose the plaintiff contracts to convey Blackacre but by mistake prepares a deed which conveys both Blackacre and Whiteacre. The plaintiff might seek reconveyance of White-acre on a constructive trust theory, or he might seek reformation of the deed.[3] Reformation and constructive trust are two ways of thinking about the same ultimate restitution. The virtual identity of these two modes of relief indicates one of the ways in which reformation is restitutionary.

Rescission Compared

Reformation or constructive trust in the example just given had the effect of undoing the overconveyance, but not the effect of undoing the contract that led to that conveyance. Instead, it worked to enforce the contract as intended. Rescission is a contrasting remedy. Rescission calls the deal off. The mistake in writing the deed (or even the contract that led to it) would not justify rescission. The parties had a good contract and it should be enforced. A rescission would be justified if the parties thought they understood one another but did not, or acted under mistaken assumptions about the subject matter of the contract, but a rescission would not be justified if all that is needed is to express the contract properly. So rescission and reformation are not alternative remedies for the same kind of unjust enrichment. Instead they address very different problems. In some cases, however, it is very difficult to know whether the parties made a mistake in expression or a mistake in basic assumptions.[4]

Law and Equity; Reformation With or Without Physical Alteration

Reformation is traditionally an equitable remedy, requiring an in personam order of the chancellor. Sometimes, however, the effect of reformation can be achieved without an actual physical change in the document. For example, it can be directly construed to give it the effect the parties intended. This so-called reformation at law does not require equity's *in*

---

3. See Restatement of Restitution § 160 Comment *k* (1937); cf. Beasley v. Mellon Financial Services Corp., 569 So.2d 389 (Ala. 1990). The Restatement sometimes looks at the constructive trust as a state of being or a first premise leading to a remedy rather than as a remedy itself. Its conception of this situation is that the plaintiff is entitled to reformation *because* the defendant holds the property on constructive trust.

4. E.g., Brown v. County of Genesee, 872 F.2d 169, 173 (6th Cir.1989); cf. National Am. Corp. v. Federal Republic of Nigeria, 597 F.2d 314 (2d Cir.1979) (possibly invoking reformation to avoid hardship). A number of cases in which it is difficult to determine whether the facts justify rescission or reformation are discussed in § 9.5 below.

personam powers, because the court simply reads the parties' intention into document and enforces the document as read.[5]

In many other cases physical alternation or some kind of injunctive decree is necessary because of the possibility that third persons will act on the document. In the example of the plaintiff's conveyance of both Blackacre and Whiteacre, correction of the record and the deed itself is required to prevent the purchaser from selling to an innocent purchaser who might get good title. The correction might be made by physically altering the deed, issuing a decree that could be recorded in the title records, or by ordering the defendant to reconvey Whiteacre. But under no circumstances would a mere judicial interpretation suffice.

Some Nontraditional Reformation

Reformation in the broad sense refers to reformulation of a document such as a contract. A contract might be reformed or altered not only to reflect the parties' intent, but to some other standard. Within limits, some unconscionable contract provisions may be reformed to bring them within minimum legal standards of fairness [6] or to make them conform to rules against restraints on trade.[7] This is also reformation, but it is reformation to meet a legal standard, not to meet the parties' intent. A doctrine in insurance law in effect reads policies to meet the insureds' reasonable expectations, which may arise on the basis of brochures or other representations and in spite of printed policy provisions to the contrary.[8] The effect of this doctrine is also similar to reformation.

Reformation is also granted under other labels in some special cases. If the parties contract to buy and sell Blackacre at $1,000 per acre for a total price of $100,000, but it turns out that the acreage involved comes to only 90 acres, not 100, some courts might require the seller to accept $90,000. This is likely to go under the name of specific performance with abatement,[9] but it is a method of reforming the parties' contract, quite possibly not to their intentions.[10] Likewise insurance policies are in effect "reformed" to meet the insured's expectations, but not necessarily what the parties agreed upon.[11] Judicial adjustment for unexpected conditions in long-term contracts is not unheard of.[12] All these forms of nontraditional reformation have generated controversy. Although these forms of reformation are remedial—they attempt to make the best of a bad situation—they are not fundamentally restitutionary.

---

5. See Philippine Sugar Estates Dev. Co. v. Government of Philippine Islands, 247 U.S. 385, 38 S.Ct. 513, 62 L.Ed. 1177 (1918).

6. See § 10.7, below.

7. Karpinski v. Ingrasci, 28 N.Y.2d 45, 320 N.Y.S.2d 1, 268 N.E.2d 751 (1971); Rogers v. Runfola & Associates, Inc., 57 Ohio St.3d 5, 565 N.E.2d 540 (1991). See § 12.22(2) below.

8. See Roger Henderson, The Doctrine of Reasonable Expectations in Insurance Law after Two Decades, 51 Ohio St.L.J. 823 (1990).

9. These cases are discussed in § 12.12(3). A similar problem occurs when property sub-

ject to a contract to convey is damaged or destroyed before conveyance is made. As to this, see § 12.14 below.

10. See Dawson, Judicial Revision of Frustrated Contracts: The United States, 64 B.U.L.Rev. 1 (1984).

11. Roger Henderson, The Doctrine of Reasonable Expectations in Insurance Law after Two Decades, 51 Ohio St.L.J. 823 (1990).

12. See Aluminum Co. of Am. v. Essex Group, Inc., 499 F.Supp. 53 (W.D.Pa.1980).

§ 4.3(8) Equitable Conversion

Equitable conversion is not a remedy. The term refers only to a way of thinking about certain issues, a reasoning process that is similar to the reasoning process used in tracing for purposes of constructive trusts and equitable liens. Sometimes the results are similar too.

Raw Doctrine

The seller as trustee under a specifically performable contract. Stated illustratively, the equitable conversion doctrine holds that when parties enter into a sales contract that is subject to specific performance, the equity court will regard the seller as a kind of trustee. He holds legal title, but only for the purpose of performing the contract by conveying to the buyer. As to the title, the buyer in turn is analogized to a beneficiary of a trust. As to the purchase price, the same kind of reasoning applies to the buyer: the buyer holds the purchase price, but only as a kind of trustee for the purpose of paying the seller.[1] Having gone through this reasoning, the equity courts could then say that the buyer was a kind of equitable owner of the property and the seller was the equitable owner of the money. This is the "conversion"—the seller now equitably owns money and the buyer now equitably owns land. The dramatic form of the statement is that the realty is converted to personalty and vice versa.

The equitable conversion doctrine is not actually limited to sales contract cases. It may be invoked in any case in which a party is under a legal duty to convey. For example, it might be invoked when a will contains directions to sell property.[2] Legal duty to convey is the essential element, so in the case of a contract, the equitable conversion doctrine does not apply unless the contract is subject to specific enforcement. Normally this applies only to land sales.

The tracing element. The tracing element in equitable conversion reasoning may be obscure, but it is quite real and quite a lot like constructive trust tracing. If embezzled funds are used to purchase Blackacre, then the victim's property in the funds is traced to Blackacre and he recovers that property on a constructive trust theory. One could just as well use the language of conversion and say the victim's funds are "converted" into

---

§ 4.3(8)

1. Ruva v. Mente, 143 Ill.2d 257, 157 Ill. Dec. 424, 572 N.E.2d 888 (1991) ("as between the parties and those claiming through them, when the owner of land enters into a valid and enforceable contract for its sale he continues to hold the legal title, but in trust for the buyer; and the buyer becomes the equitable owner and holds the purchase money in trust for the seller. The conversion takes place at the time of entering into the contract"; quoting Shay v. Penrose, 25 Ill.2d 447, 449, 185 N.E.2d 218, 219 (1962)). See generally, Stone, Equitable Conversion by Contract, 13 Colum.L.Rev. 369 (1913).

2. Similar kinds of tracing are possible when a state condemns land and becomes indebted to the owner for a sum to be determined judicially. The sums payable could be viewed as substitutes for the land and as ac-

quiring its characteristics. If the land had been owned as a cotenancy, for example, the state's obligation to pay could be viewed in the same way, so that if one of the cotenants dies before the state pays the condemnation award, the other cotenant takes all. See Wilkins v. Oken, 157 Cal.App.2d 603, 321 P.2d 876 (1958) (dictum); Ronan v. Ronan, 339 Mass. 460, 159 N.E.2d 653 (1959) (tenancy by entireties, husband to have income from condemnation award for life, survivor takes the capital at death). The opposite view, that the taking destroys the cotenancy, is just as plausible and has its supporters too. E.g., Harbour v. Harbour, 229 Ark. 198, 313 S.W.2d 830 (1958) (tenancy destroyed by condemnation). Either result could be reached without resort to equitable conversion doctrines.

Blackacre. The equitable conversion doctrine does the same except that it is anticipatory; it gets a jump on reality by imagining the conversion or tracing in advance. The seller is obliged in equity to convey Blackacre in exchange for the price, so he will be treated as if he already had. Strangely enough, there is a retroactive as well as anticipatory feature to the equitable conversion doctrine: the judge treats the buyer as owner of the property retroactively, back to the time he entered into a specifically enforceable contract.

Such a medieval construct aids and abets surprising consequences.[3] Some are benign, some not. The benign consequences are the same that would be reached if no such doctrine had ever been invented.[4] Some of the consequences are restitutionary in nature and some not.[5] Usually the doctrine is invoked to aid the court in dealing with property rights of two or more parties when a disruptive event occurs. Three examples will suggest some of the potential of the doctrine.

Consequences of Equitable Conversion

Profit from the vendor's breach. Suppose that the defendant contracts to sell Blackacre to the plaintiff for $100,000. Suppose that the price reflects the market value of Blackacre, but that before the time for conveyance, the defendant finds an unusual opportunity to sell Blackacre for $150,000. Defendant does so. The plaintiff might claim damages, but if the market value really was only about $100,000, the damages recovery would be small or nonexistent. Can the plaintiff claim the defendant's gain of $50,000? This kind of question raises difficult policy issues. In some ways this case is similar to the stolen watch case, in which the owner of the watch was allowed to recover the thief's gains on resale of the watch.[6] But that case was a tort case. The general rule for contracts is that the plaintiff cannot recover profits made by the breacher of a contract.[7] On the basis of the normal contract rule, the defendant would keep the $50,000 gain he made from breaching his contract.

Now consider the potential impact of equitable conversion reasoning, which might apply in such a case because the contract, being for land, is probably subject to specific performance. The resemblance to the construc-

3. E.g., United States v. Big Value Supermarkets, Inc., 898 F.2d 493 (6th Cir.1990) (equitable conversion argument used to extend tax lien).

4. For example: O has the legal right to acquire title to Blackacre. He contracts to sell Blackacre to the plaintiff. Later he repudiates and the plaintiff sues for specific performance. The plaintiff is entitled to specific performance, the putative ground being that by equitable conversion O is, after all, the owner in the eyes of equity. Walgren v. Dolan, 226 Cal.App.3d 572, 276 Cal.Rptr. 554 (1990). Would it not be enough to say that O has breached and that he has it within his means to perform a contract that is otherwise subject to a specific performance decree?

5. The equitable conversion doctrine may affect a wide range of issues, including the admission of evidence and the question of proper or indispensable parties. In Security Mut. Ins. Ass'n of Iowa v. Board of Review of the City of Fort Dodge, Iowa, 467 N.W.2d 301 (Iowa App.1991) the doctrine was one of the reasons for holding that evidence was admissible. The issue was the value of land; the price paid for the land would be admissible only if the land had been sold in a certain time period. By equitable conversion, the land was "sold" when the contract was made, which meant that it was sold in the right time period so that the price was admissible. As to possible effects on parties see Coles v. Feeney, 52 N.J.Eq. 493, 29 A. 172 (1894) (contract to sell land, vendor died before conveyance, both executors and devisees had to be parties).

6. See § 4.1(1) above.

7. See § 12.7(4) below.

tive trust case will be clear. Equitable conversion reasoning says that from the time the contract was made, equity regarded the buyer as the equitable owner of the property, with the seller-defendant as a kind of trustee holding legal title only so he could convey at the proper time. Under this kind of reasoning, the plaintiff can say that the sale price, $150,000, was substituted for his equitable interest in Blackacre and that he should recover that price in much the same way one recovers a constructive trust. This kind of case has not often arisen, but there is authority that would support the plaintiff in this kind of equitable conversion argument.[8] Right or wrong, this kind of case reveals the tracing elements in equitable conversion and the close connection in some instances to constructive trust.

Risk of loss. A second kind of case to which equitable conversion reasoning can be applied is one in which the property contracted for is damaged or destroyed after the contract is made for sale and purchase but before time for conveyance. When property under contract of sale is damaged before conveyance one of the parties will bear the loss.[9] One solution is to avoid the contract under doctrines of frustration of purpose or impracticability.[10] The vendor would still hold title to the land and would bear the loss directly or through his insurance. Another solution is to put the risk of loss on the purchaser if he takes possession.[11] A third solution uses equitable conversion reasoning to put the risk of loss or damage on the purchaser from the date the contract was made. That reasoning says that the purchaser becomes the equitable owner at the time the contract is made and the vendor is a mere trustee, so the loss should fall on the purchaser.[12]

The tracing used in equitable conversion could continue. Suppose the vendor has insurance covering the loss. Under the equitable conversion doctrine the property belongs in equity to the purchaser. But some of that property has been converted into insurance funds. If the property itself was the purchaser's in the eyes of equity, then by tracing, anything substituted for that property must also belong in equity to the purchaser. Some authority has reached results consistent with this line of reasoning.[13]

Affecting nature of the property as personalty or realty. In the examples given above, the equitable conversion doctrine was important because it affected the question of timing—*when* title passed controlled the question of whether a vendor or a purchaser got the gains or bore the losses. The doctrine takes its name, however, from a different effect. When the contract calls for payment of money in exchange for land, it is said that by equitable

8. E.g., Coppola Enterprises, Inc. v. Alfone, 531 So.2d 334 (Fla.1988); Timko v. Useful Homes Corp., 114 N.J.Eq. 433, 168 A. 824 (Ch. 1933); see I G. Palmer, Law of Restitution § 4.9 (1978) and § 12.7(4) below.

9. These solutions are discussed in § 12.14 below.

10. See Dixon v. Salvation Army, 142 Cal. App.3d 463, 191 Cal.Rptr. 111 (1983); § 13.3 below. A price abatement would accomplish a similar result in many cases. See § 12.14 below.

11. This is the solution under the Uniform Vendor and Purchaser Risk of Loss Act.

12. E.g., Ross v. Bumstead, 65 Ariz. 61, 173 P.2d 765 (1946); Ridenour v. France, 442 N.E.2d 716 (Ind.App.1982). This is sometimes referred to as the rule in Paine v. Meller, (6 Ves.Jr. 349, 31 Eng.Rep. 1088 (1801)).

13. Skelly Oil Co. v. Ashmore, 365 S.W.2d 582 (Mo.1963) is the striking case. But cf. Edlin v. Security Ins. Co., 269 F.2d 159 (7th Cir.1959), cert. denied, 361 U.S. 932, 80 S.Ct. 370, 4 L.Ed.2d 354 (1960) (owner of land received both the condemnation award and insurance proceeds, condemning authority got only the fire-damaged property). See § 12.14 below.

conversion the land becomes personalty and vice versa. That is, the vendor, as legal title holder, is regarded in equity as holding the beneficial interest in the money to be paid for it (personalty). The purchaser holds equitable interests in the land.

Classification of property as realty or personalty is important for many purposes. For instance, suppose that a landowner makes a will devising Blackacre to her daughter *A* and all her personal property to her son *B*. Later the landowner contracts to sell Blackacre to a purchaser. The landowner dies before conveying Blackacre. One solution to this problem might be to say that when the purchaser enforces the contract, the money paid for Blackacre will substitute for Blackacre in the will, so the money would go to the daughter *A* in lieu of Blackacre itself. This sounds like familiar tracing: Blackacre produced the money as a substitute for Blackacre; *A* takes the substitute in the same way one might impose a constructive trust on substituted property. This is not the kind of tracing done under the equitable conversion doctrine, however. The equitable conversion doctrine starts with the proposition that once the contract is made, the landowner has, equitably speaking, become the owner of personalty, that is, the right to receive payment. In the eyes of equity Blackacre is not in her estate at all. The right to receive payment is the relevant asset and that being personalty, goes to the son *B*. This rule was actually applied in an 18th Century English decision, *Lawes v. Bennett.*[14] Most American decisions have rejected this rule, favoring an effort to find the testator's intent instead.[15] Some states have enacted statutes to exclude the conversion doctrine in this situation.[16]

Although the equitable conversion doctrine has been largely rejected in the ademption situation just discussed, it is potentially on call for use in any cases in which the classification of property matters. For example, if a creditor has a lien on all the debtor's personalty but not on any of the debtor's realty, the equitable conversion doctrine may be summoned to characterize the debtor's contract right to purchase land as an interest in real property.[17]

A Comment

Equitable conversion reasoning can work a great deal like constructive trust reasoning, tracing gains or losses in a familiar way. But constructive trust doctrine is not usually used to defeat the intention of the parties in

14. 1 Cox Eq.Cas. 167, 29 Eng.Rep. 1111 (1785).

15. Eddington v. Turner, 27 Del.Ch. 411, 38 A.2d 738, 155 A.L.R. 562 (1944); In re McDonough's Estate, 113 Ill.App.2d 437, 251 N.E.2d 405 (1969) (equitable conversion analysis in will case, but also recognizing that testator's intent should be given effect); Bauserman v. Digiulian, 224 Va. 414, 297 S.E.2d 671 (1982).

16. E.g., West's Ann.Cal.Prob.Code § 77. That statute provides: "An agreement made by a testator for the sale or transfer of property disposed of by a will previously made, does not revoke such disposal; but the property passes by the will, subject to the same remedies on the testator's agreement, for a specific performance or otherwise, against the devisees or legatees, as might be had against the testator's successors, if the same had passed by succession."

17. Dominion Bank, N.A. v. Wilson, 867 F.2d 203 (4th Cir.1989). Cf. In re Streets & Beard Farm Partnership, 882 F.2d 233 (7th Cir.1989) (installment land contract is not executory contract but a security device for bankruptcy purposes, reflecting a division of authority).

cases where that intention is the relevant legal standard. Nor is it used to capture profits for mere breach of contract.

Equitable conversion reasoning can do both of these things. Where the real question is the intention of the parties (as to who bears the risk of loss, or which child inherits, for example), the tracing of equitable conversion takes the analysis down the wrong path. When the question is whether to force a simple contract breacher to give up gains resulting from the contract, a serious policy issue is presented, but not one that can be resolved by tracing.

Equitable conversion doctrines can happenstantially produce the right result, but it is hard to imagine a case in which they are needed to do so.

§ 4.4　Specific and Substitutionary Restitution

[*For the text of this section, see the unabridged Practitioner Treatise edition.*]

§ 4.5　Measurement of Restitution

§ 4.5(1)　General Principles and Substantive Policy

Scope and Direction

This section discusses the potential measures of restitution and some of the grounds for choosing one measure or another. In all the cases discussed the assumption is that substantive grounds for restitution have been shown; the issue has been reduced to its measure. All of the measures and the illustrations are discussed in other sections where they are more factually relevant. Those involving fraud, mistake, or contract breach, for example, are discussed in the chapters on those topics, usually in more detail than here. The main optional measures and their examples are brought together in this section to facilitate comparison among them.

Unjust Enrichment

Restitution is measured by the defendant's unjust enrichment, not by the plaintiff's loss. But measurement of benefits to the defendant is no more cut and dried than measurement of the plaintiff's losses in compensatory damages cases. Benefits differ: some benefits take the form of property, some of profits, some of services. In addition, any particular benefit, such as property, often may be measured in different ways, for example, by its market value, by the income it produces, or by its subjective value to the defendant.

Types of Benefit and Measures

Most benefits arise when the plaintiff transfers money, property or services to the defendant under mistake, as the result of fraud, or in connection with a contract that is later avoided or repudiated. (The term property as used here includes any entitlement, including intangibles like trademark rights unless the context indicates otherwise). The principal kinds of benefits, each of which suggests its own measure, were summarized earlier [1] as follows:

(1) the increased assets[2] in the hands of the defendant from the receipt of property,[3]

(2) the market value of services or intangibles provided to the defendant, without regard to whether the defendant's assets were actually increased; that is, the amount which it would cost to obtain similar services, whether those services prove to be useful or not.

(3) the use value of any benefits received, as measured by (i) market indicators such as rental value or interest or (ii) actual gains to the defendant from using the benefits, such as the gains identified in item (5) below;

(4) the gains realized by the defendant upon sale or transfer of an asset received from the plaintiff;

(5) collateral or secondary profits earned by the defendant by use of an asset received from the plaintiff, or, what is much the same thing, the savings effected by the use of the asset.[4]

The first three benefits are measurable by the market in property, the rental market, and "market" or going rate for services. They may be unrealized, paper gains. The last two benefits are measurable by the actual gain received by the defendant, which may be more or less than the market-measured gain. Some variations may be recognized and limitations imposed. For example, the defendant's subjective valuation of a benefit, unrelated to its market value or any investment gain, may be important as a ceiling on liability if not a measure in the first instance.

Since two or more kinds of benefit may be perceived in a single case, courts are frequently put to a choice. For example, the defendant may receive property that belongs in good conscience to the plaintiff, increasing his assets by $1,000 as a result. The first measure would award the plaintiff $1,000 (or the property itself). But the defendant may also later sell that property for $2,000, in which case the fourth measure above would award the plaintiff $2,000.

Substantive Policy and Measurement

The choice between two competing measures of restitution must satisfy the requirements and policies of substantive law. Put differently, restitution should be measured to reflect the substantive law purpose that calls for restitution in the first place.[5] Some measurement problems can be resolved simply by respecting not only the general policy against unjust enrichment but the narrower situational policies that apply on the particular set of facts.

For example, suppose the plaintiff under a five year oral contract supplies business consulting services, and that these include giving the defendant information about business opportunities. The defendant uses some of this information and makes an enormous profit, then repudiates the contract. Respect for the statute of frauds' policy (and some other reasons) seems to exclude restitution based on the defendant's profit from the information. The measure of restitution for which he would be liable if the

---

§ 4.5(1)

4. These measures are discussed in §§ 4.5(2) & 4.5(3) below.

5. See Murdock–Bryant Const., Inc. v. Pearson, 146 Ariz. 48, 703 P.2d 1197, 1204 (1985).

statute of frauds' policy is respected might be the market value of the plaintiff's services. But a very different measure of restitution may be justified if the defendant obtained the information, not under contract, but in breach of a fiduciary duty or conscious wrongdoing. In that case restitution might well be measured by the defendant's profits. Substantive policy guides the measure of restitution.

No one could list all the relevant substantive policies. Some of the policies that are frequently involved in the decision granting or measuring restitution are named below. At times the courts may lose sight of the connection between policy and measure. They may lose sight of the policy itself on some occasions. In general, however, these policies are well accepted.

(1) Courts seek to respect the defendant's autonomy and right of choice. If the defendant does not want a benefit conferred upon him by the plaintiff, restitution in money may be inappropriate or if appropriate may be measured by the more conservative of the measures available.

(2) Courts seek to respect the joint autonomy of the parties as expressed in their contract. For instance they may sometimes deny a restitutionary remedy if it would relieve one party of a risk allocated to him by the contract. In many instances, however, courts find occasion to countermand the parties' own agreement; so this policy is intermittent in application even if it is constant in theory.

(3) Courts seek to respect statutory policy. The statute of frauds example given above indicates how a statutory policy may speak to the measurement of restitution.

(4) Courts oppose conscious wrongdoing or the violation of especially prized standards such as the standards of honesty imposed upon fiduciaries. When in doubt about which of two restitutionary measures is appropriate, the serious nature of conscious wrongdoing will at times justify the court in imposing the more radical measure. For instance, a fiduciary may be made to disgorge not only all immediate market gains but also any collateral profits.

§ 4.5(2) Market Measures of Restitution

Direct Money Payments

The simplest measurement is that for money. When the defendant who is not a wrongdoer has received money from or on behalf of the plaintiff, and is under an obligation to make restitution, restitution is normally measured by the amount of money the defendant received.[1] For example, if the plaintiff pre-pays part of the price on a contract purchase and the defendant later repudiates the contract, the plaintiff may recover a sum equal to that paid.

§ 4.5(2)　　　　　　　　157 (1937).

1. Restatement of Restitution §§ 150 &

Increase in Market Value of Defendant's Assets

General rule. When the defendant has received property which increases his assets, the increase in the defendant's assets is almost always a minimum measure of restitution. This is not to say that the defendant is always liable. If he has done nothing to capture the benefit and did what he reasonably could to reject it, he may not be liable for restitution at all.[2] But when, as a substantive matter, he owes restitution, the increase in his assets is almost always a minimum measure, and it is often the only measure.

Example: mistaken improvements to property add to its value. For example, suppose that, by mistake the plaintiff enters the defendant's land believing it to be his own. He drills a well and locates water. The well raises the value of the property by $10,000. The cost of services like those provided by the plaintiff in drilling the well would have been $20,000. When ownership of the land is clarified, the defendant moves onto the land and uses the well regularly. This might constitute an acceptance of the benefit so that the defendant could be liable to make restitution to the plaintiff.[3] Restitution will not be less than $10,000, the increase in the value of the defendant's assets.[4]

Defendant's subjective purpose affecting value. If the owner had not sought the well and did not use it, respect for his autonomy or right of self-determination argues that he should not be liable to make restitution at all.[5] If he uses the property (including the well) for its most valuable economic purposes, restitution can be based on the full value of the improvement. But suppose he uses the property and the well, but not for their most valuable economic purposes. How should restitution then be figured?

For example, suppose the reason why the well adds $10,000 to the value of the property is that it can produce enough water to permit a ranch for many head of cattle. But suppose that the defendant only uses the property as a personal home and only uses the well to produce drinking and bath water. A high regard for the defendant's right to reject the benefit he did not seek suggests that the benefit might be measured by the actual use to which he puts that benefit.

Measuring personal use value. How could the value of personal use be measured? Two basic measurement strategies might be possible. First, it might be possible to answer the question, "How much more would the property be worth if it had only a small well producing drinking and bath water quantities, as compared to having no well at all?" The answer, if one could be given, would be the increased asset value of the defendant's land *for*

---

2. See § 4.9 below.

4. When the benefits are not conferred in performance of the contract or at the defendant's request, the increased asset value is the proper limit. E.g., Wilson v. La Van, 22 N.Y.2d 131, 135, 291 N.Y.S.2d 344, 348, 238 N.E.2d 738, 740 (1968) (plaintiff entitled to "any improvements made in reliance upon the oral contract which enhanced the value of property").

In some other cases the increased value of the defendant's assets is a permissible but not necessarily exclusive measure of restitution.

It is permissible when the defendant breaches the contract and the plaintiff chooses to claim restitution instead of damages. See Restatement Second of Contracts § 371 (1981); § 12.-7(3) below. It is also permissible when the plaintiff has conferred benefits upon the defendant in the performance of a contract rendered unenforceable by the statute of frauds. See § 13.2(2) below. In both those instances the plaintiff may have the option to claim the value of the services rather than the increased asset value of the improved land.

his purposes resulting from the improvements. Second, it would be possible to depart from the increased asset measure altogether by asking how much the defendant saved by having the well. If the defendant, without the well, would have had to import bottle water, then the well saved him that cost and would be of value to him in at least the amount of money it saved.[6]

If restitution is proper at all, should courts attempt to measure the personal use value, or should they stick with the general market measure? Any answer may be unsatisfactory. Respect for the defendant's rights suggests that when he is not a wrongdoer and has not sought or used the benefits, he must never be held liable except for enrichment actually realized. But any realistic viewer must observe that, whatever the defendant's personal use at the moment, the value of his land has actually increased and that tomorrow the defendant might give up his ascetic life and sell the property to a cattle rancher who will pay its full market value.

Date for measurement. The normal date for measuring increased asset value is the date on which benefits were acquired by the defendant.[7] In the example above that date might be the date on which the defendant began using the well rather than the date on which the plaintiff struck water. The value the property would have had on that date without the well would be subtracted from the value the property has on that date with the well. The difference would reflect the increased assets in the defendant's hands.

In rare cases courts may use the date of trial for measurement of restitution. In a New York case the defendants were wrongdoers and the wrong was serious, a violation of fiduciary duty. The property for which defendants owed restitution, paintings of a famous modern artist, had substantially increased in value between the time of his wrong and the time of trial. The court allowed the plaintiff to recover the increased asset value measured at the time of trial.[8] Such cases are most unusual, however, when legal title has passed to and remains in the wrongdoer. (When legal title to property remains in the plaintiff, he can recover its value at trial by recovering the property itself.)

Unrealized gains. When restitution is measured by a market measure, it is not necessary for the defendant to realize the benefit. For example, if the defendant is liable for the increased asset value of his land resulting from the well, he is liable whether or not he liquidates the benefit by selling the land.[9] The gain is a gain on the defendant's balance sheet, not a cash gain. Consequential restitution differs in this respect. Consequential resti-

---

6. If the defendant has realized savings or will more likely than not realize savings in the future, those savings can form the basis for figuring restitution. The savings measure is not a market measure. To save an expense is to increase a profit or surplus. So this is a consequential restitution measure. See § 4.5(3) below.

7. Cf. Restatement of Restitution § 151 (1937) (benefits acquired by consciously tortious conduct, date of acquisition except that, to avoid injustice a different date may be used). The acquisition date in restitution

claims corresponds to the breach of duty date in damages claims for general or market measured damages. E.g., §§ 5.13(2) (chattel destruction), 12.2(3) (contracts general damages).

8. In re Rothko's Estate, 43 N.Y.2d 305, 401 N.Y.S.2d 449, 372 N.E.2d 291 (1977).

9. It may be arguable that in some unwanted benefit cases the defendant should nevertheless be liable if the unwanted benefit is realized in cash, as where he immediately sells the property at the higher price that the improvement justifies. See § 4.9 below.

tution is based on realized gains or those that are reasonably certain to be realized.[10]

The ability to measure gains that have not actually been realized has both advantages and disadvantages. If water becomes more valuable, the well may become more valuable, too. If we measured the increase in the defendant's assets at the date of trial instead of the date on which the defendant acquired the benefit, that increase might turn out to be $30,000 instead of $10,000. The opposite fluctuation is also possible: the increment in value due to the well might go down after the big dam is built. Both possibilities are usually ignored when restitution is measured by the market. The market itself values property by taking into account the possibility of further changes in value in both directions. So both the restitutionary and damages remedies usually close the accounting on market measures at the date of gain or loss respectively. In this respect the market measure of *restitution* mirrors the market measure of *damages*.[11] But because the defendant may be charged with and expected to pay for a benefit that he has not realized, restitution may impose a burden on the defendant when he never requested the benefit, although it would be a perfectly appropriate burden in those cases where the benefit was sought by the defendant.[12]

Value of Services in the Labor Market

Market value of services, regardless of assets they produce. When the defendant seeks the plaintiff's services by requesting or contracting for them, or by indicating an acquiescence in them, restitution if any may be measured by the value of those services in the labor market. Put otherwise, the measure of restitution is the costs that would be incurred by the defendant to purchase substantially similar services elsewhere.[13]

For example, suppose that the defendant, contracts to pay the plaintiff $100,000 for building a house on the defendant's land. When the plaintiff has completed the foundation and some of the framing, the defendant repudiates the contract. The foundation adds little value to the defendant's assets but the cost of hiring someone to do work like that done by the plaintiff would be $30,000. If the plaintiff seeks restitution instead of damages he may recover $30,000, even though the defendant's assets have increased by only a small fraction of that sum.[14] The same kind of rule applies if the contract is subject to the statute of frauds.[15] The defendant is benefitted when he gets what he wants, regardless of market value.

10. See § 4.5(3) below.

11. See for example, §§ 3.3(3) above, 12.-2(3) below.

12. Benefits sought by the defendant: The defendant may be liable to make restitution in ordinary contract breach cases where the plaintiff partially performs before the defendant's breach, and also in cases where the contract is not itself enforceable.

13. E.g., Matthews v. Neal, Greene & Clark, 177 Ga.App. 26, 338 S.E.2d 496 (1985) (defendants retained architect's service based on percentage of costs of building; after defen-

dants decided not to build, architect is entitled to recover reasonable (market) value of services, although the services resulted in no building for the defendants). See, discussing many cases, Kovacic, A Proposal to Simplify Quantum Meruit Litigation, 35 Am.U.L.Rev. 547 (1986).

14. E.g., Ramirez Co. v. Housing Auth. of City of Houston, 777 S.W.2d 167 (Tex.App. 1989); §§ 12.20(2) (contractor's restitutionary remedies) & 12.7 (restitution for breach of contract generally).

15. Blank v. Rodgers, 82 Cal.App. 35, 45, 255 P. 235, 238 (1927); § 13.2(2) below.

When increased asset value is a limitation. The corollary is that when the defendant does *not* seek the plaintiff's services (or accept them later), restitution may be denied in some circumstances altogether; if restitution is ordered, it is appropriately limited to the amount by which defendant's assets have increased.[16]

The limitation to increased asset value may be appropriate when the defendant did not know any services were being rendered and did not want them. The limitation might also apply to cases in which the defendant requests or contracts for benefits in the form of an end product, but does not want or agree to pay for the services needed to produce that product. Suppose the defendant contracts to pay the plaintiff $100,000 if she is able to synthesize a certain chemical for commercial use. The plaintiff invests much time, labor and skill in the project but is unable to synthesize the chemical. To hire services like those rendered by the plaintiff would cost $50,000. But the defendant did not request the services, only the end product. Although the defendant is enriched, it is not unjustly enriched. A part of the reason for this conclusion is that the contract itself allocates the risk of unsuccessful efforts to the plaintiff, not the defendant. To recover restitution for the value of her services, the plaintiff must show that the defendant requested the *service* and not merely the end product.[17]

Market rate for services includes normal "profits". When the plaintiff recovers the value of his services (and materials supplied) without regard to the increase in the defendant's assets, he recovers the "going rate" or market value of such services. There is no occasion to add an additional sum to give the plaintiff a profit. The reasonable value of services, if properly calculated by the going rate already includes whatever profits such providers of services normally make. If the plaintiff loses money when paid at the going rate it is because he is an inefficient or incompetent provider or because of extraneous factors. The plaintiff might recover on a contract for a higher sum if the contract so provides; but if his recovery is based on the defendant's unjust enrichment it cannot properly exceed the market value of the services and materials provided.

Market Use Value

Whenever the defendant receives something of value from the plaintiff—services, information, property—it may have a use value that is distinct from a market value. For instance, if the defendant receives Blackacre under a contract which he later avoids for fraud or otherwise, he may be

---

16. See Murdock–Bryant Const. v. Pearson, 146 Ariz. 48, 703 P.2d 1197, 1204 (1985) (distinguishing contractor sought benefits from later-joining venturer who did not); Passmore v. Woodard, 37 N.C.App. 535, 246 S.E.2d 795 (1978). Restatement Second of Contracts § 371, Comment *a* (1981) recognizes the point but says the measurement choice is purely a matter of discretion for the court. This Restatement is exceptionally supportive of discretion, however.

Professor Palmer, noting the varied and uncertain language in many of the cases thinks that the plaintiff should be entitled to full market value of his services even as to benefits the defendant did not request. 1 G. Palmer, The Law of Restitution § 4.18, pp. 524, 526 (1978). See § 12.7(3) below. Unless the defendant is guilty of wrongdoing, full respect for the defendant's rights of self-determination would seem to limit recovery for "benefits" the defendant did not seek to the increase in asset value, or possibly even to gains that have been or probably will be realized.

17. See § 13.2(4) below. It is not always easy to say how the parties allocated the risks or that the buyer was buying only an end product, not services.

required to make restitution of Blackacre; but that may not be enough because he has also had the use of the land. If he receives money from the plaintiff and must restore it, he will still have had the use of the money.

Unjust enrichment theory does not invariably require restitution for the use value of a benefit. For example, when a transaction is rescinded and each party gives back what he got, the use values on each side may be so similar that no separate calculation is necessary; or the parties to some transaction may intend to preclude use-value charges.[18] And conceivably an archaic technical doctrine might be applied to prevent some kinds of restitution for use value in certain trespass cases.[19] In general, however, when the defendant has received the use value of property or money, restitution will be owed for that value.

When restitution for use value is appropriate, that restitution may be measured by a market measure, rather than subjectively by the value the particular defendant got from use. (The same is true when *damages* for the plaintiff's loss of use is measured). In the case of land, the market measure[20] of restitution for use value is rental value,[21] at least where the defendant has actually used the property[22] and where rental value can be proven.[23] In the case of money it is interest.[24] Market measures of restitution for use value are often appropriate when the defendant's use has not produced gains or profits to which the plaintiff is entitled instead. Even when the use has produced gains or profits to the defendant, those gains may be impossible to measure. So a court might allow interest on money when it is unable to say what profits the defendant made by its use, and might adjust the rate of interest or permit compounding of interest as a market substitute for the supposed profits.[25]

18. Where a vendor of land permits a purchaser to move into the premises before closing, for example. E.g., Stapley v. American Bathtub Liners, Inc., 162 Ariz. 564, 785 P.2d 84 (App.1989); § 12.12(2) below.

19. See § 5.9, below. In any event, the plaintiff should be able to recover the rental value of his land from a trespasser as an ordinary, objective, market measure of damages. See § 5.8(2) below.

20. Since land is seldom auctioned either in the sale or rental markets, the "market" in land is usually a construct derived from transactions in similar parcels, or the same parcel at another time, or from various economic projections.

21. E.g., Metcalfe v. Talarski, 213 Conn. 145, 567 A.2d 1148 (1989); Smith v. Baldwin, 611 S.W.2d 611 (Tex.1980); Boris v. Heyd, 220 Neb. 569, 371 N.W.2d 268 (1985) (but placing the burden on the party claiming rental value to prove it and denying recovery where he has not done so); Malo v. Anderson, 76 Wash.2d 1, 454 P.2d 828 (1969) (one on land by mistake must make restitution of rental value of occupancy). Courts sometimes refer to use value without indicating precisely how they expect it to be measured. E.g., Wlaschin v. Affleck, 167 Neb. 403, 413, 93 N.W.2d 186, 192 (1958)

("reasonable value of plaintiff's use and occupation of the premises from the inception of her occupancy," mention of rental value without stating it as a standard).

22. See Miller v. Sears, 636 P.2d 1183 (Alaska 1981); McCoy v. West, 70 Cal.App.3d 295, 138 Cal.Rptr. 660 (1977). If the defendant had possession but did not use the property, restitution might be limited to gains he actually received from it, such as rents he received from others. See *Miller v. Sears,* supra.

23. In the case of vacant land used for a significant period of time, rental value would often be a very remote and untrustworthy construct, but option value might be quite provable. See § 6.9(2) as to option value in an analogous *damages* context.

24. E.g., Peterson v. Crown Financial Corp., 661 F.2d 287 (3d Cir.1981). On interest generally, see § 3.6 above. Conceivably one would be entitled to a recovery of money as restitution without being entitled to interest on it. Amiss v. State, 340 So.2d 1085 (La.App. 1976).

25. See Maryland Nat. Bank v. Cummins, 322 Md. 570, 588 A.2d 1205 (1991) (reflecting authority under which a trustee could be lia-

§ 4.5(3) Consequential Benefits Measures of Restitution

Consequential Damages and Consequential Benefits

Consequential benefits compared to consequential damages. The measures of restitution discussed in the preceding subsection are market measures. Restitution discussed there was measured by the increase in the market value of the defendant's assets, by the "market" value of the plaintiff's services, or by the market value of the use reflected in rental or interest rates. Restitution (like damages) can also be measured by consequences. In the case of damages, courts can take the measure of *consequential losses,* not the value of the thing itself, but the losses to the plaintiff consequent upon not having it.[1] In the case of restitution, courts can take the measure of *consequential benefits,* not the value of the thing itself but the value it produces in the hands of the defendant. Consequential benefits such as profits gained by the defendant which in good conscience belong to the plaintiff, are often associated with constructive trusts or with an accounting of profits. But if a consequential benefit measure is justified, it need not be pursued under either a trust or an accounting theory.

Distinctions between consequential and market measures. The differences between measurement based on the value of the thing and measurement based on consequences that happen to flow from its use are enormous, both in the case of damages and the case of restitution.

First, the thing-itself measurement, which in damages law is often referred to as general damages, is a measurement that takes place on a specific date, such as the date a contract was breached or a tort committed in damages law, or the date the benefit was received in restitution law. Consequential damages or restitution, in contrast, might be measured indefinitely into the future. The only limit is what can be proved at the time of trial as a future potential loss or gain.[2]

Second, the thing-itself measure is a market or objective measure. It asks about value of the thing on the relevant date and refers to outside standards to determine that value. The value of property, for instance, is what a buyer would pay for it, not what the seller would demand or what the seller could earn with it. Consequential measures on the contrary do not

ble for compound interest on trust funds if it made profits which could be roughly measured by compound interest). The traditional rule does not permit compound interest except in special circumstances. See § 3.6 above.

§ 4.5(3)

1. See §§ 3.3(3) & 3.3(4) above & 12.2(3) below.

2. If the point is unclear, consider this example: D, a fiduciary agent, violates her duty by using her employer's secret information about the probable location of a profitable vein of gold. She could sell the information to a mining company for $100,000 in the period immediately after she has taken it. However, she does not in fact sell the information but instead, one year after her illicit acquisition of the information, she purchases rights to mine the land in question for herself. Release of the information at that point would drive the price of the mining rights up to give her $500,000 gain. But she mines the gold herself, and within two years later she has net income gains of $1,000,000. If the employer brings suit at this point it could recover her $1,000,000 gains (perhaps with deductions for expenses and her own efforts) and would not be limited to a recovery of the $100,000 market value of the information at the date it was acquired. As to profits after trial, the employer would normally obtain those by getting a constructive trust on the property, which would permit it to operate the mine and earn its own future profits.

look at the market but at particular actual plaintiff-losses in the case of damages or defendant-gains in the case of restitution.

Third, market measures of relief are allowed even though the plaintiff has realized no loss in the case of damages and the defendant has realized no gain in the case of restitution. This is important, because today's unrealized gain may be tomorrow's actual loss. If the defendant is chargeable with a paper or bookkeeping gain because he has the plaintiff's shares of stock, the defendant may ultimately take a loss because the shares may drop in value after he has paid the plaintiff money restitution. In contrast, consequential measures of restitution or damages are based on proof that gains were in fact realized or that they will in fact be realized in the future.

Levels of consequential benefits. Several levels of consequences can be identified. The fact that the plaintiff is entitled to restitution at one of these levels does not necessarily mean that any of them would be equally suitable. This subsection first attempts to summarize, illustrate, and differentiate some of the major kinds of consequential benefits for which restitution might be ordered, then to discuss briefly some of the substantive grounds for such restitution.

Consequential Benefits from Transfer of Entitlements

Gains from transfer in a rising market. The simplest consequential benefit is almost like the market measure based on increased assets. It is the gain received by a defendant from selling at a higher price entitlements that equitably belong to the plaintiff, when that higher price results only from the fact that the market value has risen without input by the defendant.

Suppose that, by mistake, the plaintiff conveys Blackacre to the defendant, intending to convey Whiteacre instead. Blackacre has a market value of $500,000 (much more than Whiteacre). Before the plaintiff can discover the mistake, the market rises and the defendant takes advantage of the increase in market value to sell Blackacre at its new market value, $550,000. Because the plaintiff was entitled to recover Blackacre *in specie,* by way of a constructive trust if need be, it is easy to say he is also entitled to recover the gain produced by Blackacre.[3] In this instance, that conclusion is reinforced because the gain was produced by a rising market, not by any skill or enterprise of the defendant, whose only contribution was to make the sale.

Gains from a transfer above market rate. A potentially different case is one in which the defendant gains from the sale of assets that belong in equity to the plaintiff but the gain is not the result of a rising market. Instead, the gain is the result of selling above the market rate, raising the possibility that the defendant's information or skill contributed at least in some degree to the gain.

Suppose that the parties make a mistake similar to the one made with Blackacre except that the plaintiff transfers shares of stock to the defendant as the result of a mutual mistake in contracting. Suppose the shares are

---

3. Reformation might accomplish the same thing when Blackacre has not been transferred, but courts have used both constructive trust and reformation approaches. See III G. Palmer, Law of Restitution § 13.17 (1978 & Supps.). If the constructive trust can be used, then by tracing the gain is recoverable.

priced on a stock market at $100,000, and that the market never rises. Nevertheless, the defendant is able to take advantage of an opportunity to sell for a premium, $110,000. The opportunity to sell at a premium might be happenstantial or it might be the result of the defendant's skill, enterprise, or special information. The defendant must make restitution of the $100,000, but the case for restitution of the added $10,000 gain is not so clear as the first instance.

Elements that make a recovery of profits more doubtful in this case are these: the defendant is not shown to be a wrongdoer; the plaintiff was probably not entitled to recover the shares of stock *in specie* because they were not unique or special; and the $10,000 gain is only doubtfully traceable to the plaintiff's equity interest in the shares, because the defendant could presumably have sold other shares to capture the same gain. If we change the facts to say that the shares were unique so that the plaintiff would have been entitled to a *specie* recovery, the case for giving the plaintiff the $10,000 gain becomes stronger. If we change them further so that the defendant procures the shares by fraud, or violation of fiduciary, the case for giving the plaintiff the $10,000 gain becomes almost overwhelmingly strong.[4]

Consequential Benefits from Use

A third type of consequential gain to the defendant is income produced or increased by use of the plaintiff's property. Several distinct forms of such income can be identified.

Receipt of rental or interest income. If the defendant has the use of the plaintiff's property or money, the plaintiff may be entitled to restitution for the use value. The market measures have already been noted.[5] In some cases, however, restitution for use value might be measured by the gains the defendant actually realizes from use rather than by the more or less objectified market value. In the case of property, one owing restitution might be held for the rents he actually receives on the property, or in the case of money, for income actually received by its use.[6] If the defendant is a wrongdoer, the plaintiff may be able to recover the defendant's income from rents or interests even if that income exceeds rental value. If the defendant is innocent and the income is less than the rental value or going interest rates, then the shoe may be on the other foot and the defendant might insist that his liability is no greater than the amount he actually received.[7]

Savings from defendant's own use of the plaintiff's entitlement. If the defendant has the use of the plaintiff's property but instead of renting it out he uses it himself, it is possible to measure restitution by the savings realized by the defendant rather than by the market rental rate. Suppose the

4. E.g., Janigan v. Taylor, 344 F.2d 781 (1st Cir.1965), cert. denied, 382 U.S. 879, 86 S.Ct. 163, 15 L.Ed.2d 120 (1965); In re Rothko's Estate, 43 N.Y.2d 305, 401 N.Y.S.2d 449, 372 N.E.2d 291 (1977).

5. See § 4.5(2) above.

6. E.g., Woodling v. Garrett Corp., 813 F.2d 543 (2d Cir.1987) (interest actually earned on money received); see Maryland Nat. Bank v. Cummins, 322 Md. 570, 588 A.2d 1205 (1991) (trustee could be liable for compound interest on trust funds if it actually received such interest, or was under a duty to accumulate compound interest or made profits which can be estimated by amount of compound interest).

7. See Miller v. Sears, 636 P.2d 1183 (Alaska 1981); cf. Woodling v. Garrett Corp., 813 F.2d 543, 561–562 (2d Cir.1987) (rescission for fraud, plaintiff must restore what he got with such interest as he actually earned).

plaintiff owns a machine the rental value of which is $50 per month. The defendant tortiously uses the machine in his factory in such a way as to save $100 a month. The discrepancy between rental value and savings is not very likely but it is possible. At least if the defendant's tort justifies a recovery of the defendant's profit resulting from use of the machine, it also justifies a recovery of the savings, because the savings of expense in a business increases the profits.[8] The savings can be seen as a form of income and should be allowed or disallowed on that basis. For example, savings to the defendant should not measure his restitutionary liability unless the savings is or will be actually harvested or realized.

Collateral profit. A more significant kind of gain from the use of the plaintiff's money or property is the collateral profit. The term profit is usually used in this treatise to refer to net income from a business operation, as distinct from a gain in capital assets resulting from a single sale of property. Profit claims can be calculated out only by knowing what expenses should be deducted from the gross income. For example, suppose that the defendant is a trustee who wrongfully uses the plaintiff's trust fund of $5 million to purchase for himself a business which designs and manufactures fashion clothing. The business produces gross sales of $1 million annually but pays employee wages, rent, electricity and taxes. All these items and perhaps some others must be deducted to figure the net profit. The plaintiff can recover the $5 million that belonged to her trust fund by way of constructive trust on the business or by way of accounting or quasi-contract. This recovery will also give the plaintiff the investment gain, if any. If the business is now worth $6 million, the plaintiff will have recovered the assets equal to the trust fund plus $1 million in assets. More than this, however, the plaintiff will also recover from the defendant-trustee any net operating profits of the business. He was a serious wrongdoer who violated his fiduciary duty, and that will justify imposing a liability for profits as well as the asset gain.[9]

Adjustments and Problems in Collateral Profit Cases

Expense deductions. The profit case differs in significant degree if not in principle from some other consequential benefit cases. First, legitimate business expenses must be identified, calculated and deducted from the gross income.[10] No such adjustment for expenses is ordinarily made when the plaintiff claims market-measured restitution or even investment gains.[11]

8. The savings measure of restitution was used on similar facts in Olwell v. Nye & Nissen Co., 26 Wash.2d 282, 173 P.2d 652, 169 A.L.R. 139 (1946). That case is analyzed further and criticized in § 5.18(2) below.

9. Brooks v. Conston, 364 Pa. 256, 72 A.2d 75 (1950).

10. This is the normal rule with a *profits* recovery. E.g., Baker v. Simmons Co., 325 F.2d 580 (1st Cir.1963), aff'd, 342 F.2d 991 (1965), cert. denied, 382 U.S. 820, 86 S.Ct. 49, 15 L.Ed.2d 67 (1965). But in Warren v. Century Bankcorporation, Inc., 741 P.2d 846 (Okl.

1987) no deductions were allowed and the defendant was held liable for its gross profits.

11. For example, defendant obtains title to Blackacre by defrauding the plaintiff. The defendant pays $10,000 although its value is $20,000. The defendant then sells Blackacre for $30,000, more than its value. The defendant's costs of selling Blackacre must have included at least the value of his time or the cost of a telephone call, but no deduction is usually made for the expense of such single sales, either in restitution or in damages claims.

The process of proving and briefing issues about expense deduction can itself represent a significant expense. For example, a defendant might seek to reduce his liability for gross profits by deductions for income taxes paid on the illicit profits, or by deductions for some portion of his fixed overhead expense. Both kinds of issues raise difficult issues of accounting and also legal issues. So some taxes might be deducted and some not,[12] and some fixed overhead deducted and some not.[13] The defendant might also seek to offset profits in some years by losses in others,[14] or profits at one location with losses at another.[15]

The apportionment problem. Second, the gross income itself may have been produced in part by use of the plaintiff's property but also in part by investment, enterprise, and management skill of the defendant. In the case of the trustee who went into business manufacturing fashion clothing with the beneficiary's money, we may not much care because his wrongdoing is so central and significant. But if the trustee actually managed the business and put some of his own money in it, some of the profits must be fairly ascribed to the trustee's efforts and money, not to the beneficiary's.

The trademark-copyright examples. To see the difficulty when the defendant is not a trustee, consider the case of the trademark infringer. The defendant uses a mark which is confusingly similar to the plaintiff's trademark. Customers may be misled and may buy defendant's product when they intended to buy the plaintiff's. At least when the infringer is at fault in some degree, restitution of his profits is permitted. But not *all* the defendant's sales are due to the trademark; maybe none of them is. Even if some of the sales are the result of infringing the plaintiff's trademark, the defendant's management and investment in the enterprise counts for something in producing profits. Similar problems can be seen in copyright infringement cases. A song that infringes the plaintiff's copyrighted melody may sell well partly because the melody is attractive but also partly because the infringer's lyrics are better.

Apportionment required. Even the wilful wrongdoer should not be made to give up that which is his own; the principle is disgorgement, not plunder. So courts have recognized that some apportionment must be made between those profits attributable to the plaintiff's property and those earned by the defendant's efforts and investment, limiting the plaintiff to the profits fairly attributable to his share.[16] But sometimes courts have deviated from this

12. L.P. Larson, Jr., Co. v. William Wrigley, Jr., Co., 277 U.S. 97, 48 S.Ct. 449, 72 L.Ed. 800 (1928) (deduction impermissible); W.E. Bassett Co. v. Revlon, Inc., 435 F.2d 656 (2d Cir.1970) (deduction permissible).

13. See Maltina Corp. v. Cawy Bottling Co., Inc., 613 F.2d 582, 586 (5th Cir.1980) (trademark); Sheldon v. Metro–Goldwyn Pictures Corp., 106 F.2d 45, 54 (2d Cir.1939), aff'd, 309 U.S. 390, 60 S.Ct. 681, 84 L.Ed. 825 (1940) (copyright, "'Overhead' which does not assist in the production of the infringement should not be credited to the infringer; that which does, should be; it is a question of fact * * *.").

14. Duplate Corp. v. Triplex Safety Glass Co. of N.Am., 298 U.S. 448, 56 S.Ct. 792, 80 L.Ed. 1274 (1936) (deduction for lean-year losses in a patent infringement claim held denied); but cf. Burger King Corp. v. Mason, 855 F.2d 779 (11th Cir.1988).

15. Burger King Corp. v. Mason, 855 F.2d 779 (11th Cir.1988) (trademark infringement at 13 locations, profits at six locations, losses at seven, losses may not be used to offset profits).

16. See Speck v. North Carolina Dairy Found., Inc., 64 N.C.App. 419, 429, 307 S.E.2d 785, 792 (1983) ("where the defendant is not a conscious wrongdoer, equitable restitution should be limited to gains unjustly derived from the trade secret itself, as opposed to any share of profits attributable to the efforts,

principle by allowing the plaintiff to recover the defendant's full gross profits without either deduction for expenses or apportionment, a deviation that combines justice with punishment.[17]

Burden of proving apportionment. Perhaps more significantly, courts have sometimes placed the burden on the defendant to show the "right" amount of apportionment, holding him liable for the entire profits if he cannot do so.[18] This burden of proof rule is not like the rule that puts the burden on the defendant to show business expenses that should be deducted from gross profits. Business expenses are provable and the defendant is the right party to prove them because the defendant will know better than the plaintiff how much rent it paid on the factory and wages it paid to workers. But neither party can show how much of a manufacturer's profit results from the use of the plaintiff's trademark on the defendant's goods and how much is due to the defendant's own investment. The apportionment problem cannot be resolved by direct proof the way the problem of expense deductions can. An informed estimate about apportionment might be better than a liability we know exceeds the defendant's illicit gains.[19]

Counterpart problems in damages law. The two kinds of profits problems just discussed have counterparts in the law of damages. The first problem is paralleled in damages law by the rule requiring that consequential damages such as lost profits of the plaintiff be proven with reasonable certainty.[20] That is much harder in many damages cases than in restitution

---

capital, and skill of the defendant"); Brooks v. Conston, 364 Pa. 256, 72 A.2d 75 (1950). Even in the case of wilful confusion of fungible goods, the victim is entitled to his share of the goods, not to the whole mass. Indian Oil Corp. Ltd. v. Greenstone Shipping, S.A. (The Ypatianna), [1988] 1 Q.B. 345 (1987), 3 W.L.R. 869, 2 Lloyd's Rep. 286 (Q.B.1987) (crude oil in ship's tanks); R. Brown, Personal Property § 31 (1936).

17. Warren v. Century Bankcorporation, Inc., 741 P.2d 846 (Okl.1987). The amount of the punishment in such cases is only happenstantially the "right" amount. See § 4.5(5) below.

Some cases appear to regard the wrongdoer as if he were like a true trustee who owes his own best efforts to the beneficiary as well as the property itself. Justice Cardozo in Duplate Corp. v. Triplex Safety Glass Co. of N.Am., 298 U.S. 448, 457, 56 S.Ct. 792, 796, 80 L.Ed. 1274, 1281 (1936) commented:

'An infringer cannot be heard to say that his superior skill or intelligence enabled him to realize profits by his infringement which a person of less skill might not have realized.' * * *. Whatever is at his call in the service of the enterprise—brawn and intelligence, factories and lands, patents and machinery—will be viewed upon an accounting as if held upon a quasi trust to contribute what it can to the profits of the business. The wrongdoer must yield the gains begotten of his wrong.

It seems wrong in principle to treat the infringer like a trustee who must not only manage the property correctly but must devote his own time and efforts, and even his own "factories and lands" to the beneficiary. And the patent statute on which *Duplate* was based has been changed; it no longer authorizes a profits recovery. See § 6.2(4) below.

18. Hamilton–Brown Shoe Co. v. Wolf Bros. & Co., 240 U.S. 251, 36 S.Ct. 269, 60 L.Ed. 629 (1916) held that, unless the defendant could show a basis for a smaller recovery, the plaintiff could recover all the defendant's profits from the sale of shoes manufactured by the defendant but bearing a trademark deemed confusingly similar to the plaintiff's mark. This burden shift is not the same as one which requires the plaintiff to prove the defendant's gross profits and leaves to the defendant merely proof as to expense deductions. The *Hamilton–Brown* burden shift makes it possible for the plaintiff to recover the defendant's profits even if the defendant reaped *no* profits from use of the infringing mark, as would be the case if the mark did not cause the sale of any shoes. The *Hamilton–Brown* rule shifts the burden as to apportionment of profits to the wrongdoing; the narrower rule, represented in the statutes, shifts the burden to prove expense deductions.

19. As in Gaste v. Kaiserman, 863 F.2d 1061, 1069–1070 (2d Cir.1988) (defendant infringed music, but not lyrics, 12% of profits were found to be due to lyrics).

20. See §§ 3.4 above & 12.4(3) below.

cases because the plaintiff's loss of future profit is necessarily uncertain in some degree. The restitution claim for the defendant's gain, however, can usually start with some provable figure of actual gain. The second problem, the problem of tracing the defendant's profit back to the plaintiff's contribution, is paralleled in damages law by the rule of proximate cause and the rule in *Hadley v. Baxendale*.[21]

Profits recovery and the separation of risk from opportunity. The problem of tracing or apportionment of profits can be seen in another light. If the defendant is liable to make restitution of profits, the opportunity for gain and the risk of loss may be separated so that the plaintiff will have all the opportunity and none of the risk. For example, suppose that the defendant fraudulently induces the plaintiff to sell his business to the defendant. The defendant pays the plaintiff cash, so as to the cash in hand the plaintiff has no risk associated with the business at all. The defendant then manages the business. Because the business is now the defendant's, the defendant has the risk of loss if he makes bad management decisions and even if he merely has bad luck.[22] If the plaintiff can recover all the profits made in the business in such a case, he has economic opportunity without economic risk. If the separation of opportunity and risk is unwise because it is unjust or economically unsound, then tracing and apportionment is important for an additional reason.

Conversely, some cases do not involve the separation of risk and opportunity and they are much better candidates for a full profit recovery. In the trustee example given earlier, the trustee invested the beneficiary's money in the business. The beneficiary took the risk of loss, although he may not have known it at the time.[23] Taking the full risk of loss, he is entitled to the full profit, at least when the defendant is guilty of serious wrongdoing as he was there.

At least as an ideal, then, if profits are to be allowed as restitution, some effort must be made to apportion the profits between the investments that produce them. That is, the profits should be traceable to the plaintiff's contribution; when they are not traceable, considerations and concerns similar to those that actuate proximate cause rules suggest that recovery should be denied unless the defendant is a very serious wrongdoer.[24] Perhaps even then he should be compensated for his efforts.[25]

---

21. See §§ 12.4(4)–12.4(7) below.

22. The situation could be perceived otherwise. If the defendant's fraud leads to underpayment of the plaintiff, then it would be possible to think of the plaintiff as having some kind of claim against the business, for money or perhaps for money with an equitable lien as security. That limited claim for money is at risk. But even this perception suggests apportionment of profits, maybe in a ratio of the plaintiff's money claim to total capital investment.

23. If the trustee held net assets exceeding $5 million, then arguably the beneficiary was *not* taking the risk of loss because in that case

the trustee could repay the trust fund whether the business succeeded or not.

24. The innocent trademark infringer, for example, probably should not be liable to disgorge his profits at all. See Carl Zeiss Stiftung v. VEB Carl Zeiss Jena, 433 F.2d 686, 707 (2d Cir.1970), cert. denied, 403 U.S. 905, 91 S.Ct. 2205, 29 L.Ed.2d 680 (1971) ("Ordinarily it is necessary to show 'not only that the infringer infringed, but that he did so with the deliberate intent to cause confusion, mistake or to deceive purchasers * * *.'"). See § 6.4(4) below.

25. Brooks v. Conston, 364 Pa. 256, 72 A.2d 75 (1950).

The Breacher's Profits in Contract Cases

General rule.[26] Breach of contract by the defendant may give rise to a restitution claim by the plaintiff. For example, if the plaintiff has partly performed the contract he will be entitled to restitution for the value of his part performance when the defendant breaches. The general rule is that the plaintiff is not entitled to the gains made by the defendant through his breach.[27] Instead, the plaintiff will recover restitution under one of the market measures; for example, if his performance was in services, he can recover the value of those services; if his performance was in money, he can recover that.

The trust or equitable conversion exception. In one situation several courts have allowed the plaintiff to recover the gain the defendant made by reallocating contract resources after a breach of the contract. Defendant contracts to sell Blackacre to the plaintiff, but then repudiates and sells the property to a third person for a substantially higher price. Some courts have said that the plaintiff could seek restitution in such a case, measured by a sum that would return the plaintiff any payment he made and give him the defendant's added gain from the sale.[28] This has been based on a kind of trust reasoning under the equitable conversion doctrine.[29]

Fiduciary breach: the Snepp case. The United States Supreme Court has done something similar but not necessarily persuasive. In *Snepp v. United States*[30] a former CIA employee, Frank Snepp, Jr., had contracted not to publish any materials about his work in the CIA without prior approval. He breached this contract by publishing a work without such approval. The government was allowed to recover the profits Snepp made or would make on the book. Part of the Court's theory was that the contract breach was more than mere contract breach; it was a breach of a fiduciary relationship.

But Snepp's book did not reveal any improper information. If Snepp had sought approval as required by his contract, it would seem that approval would have to be given unless one can contract away his First Amendment rights to discuss government. And if approval would have been forthcoming, then it cannot be said that Snepp's profits are traceable to breach of contract—he would have had the profits even if he had sought approval as required. The CIA had good reasons for wanting Snepp to seek approval even if the CIA would be bound to give it; but Snepp's failure to seek it did not create the profits the government took from him, so liability without apportionment is most doubtful.[31]

26. This topic is covered generally in § 12.7 below.

27. See Farnsworth, Your Loss or My Gain? The Dilemma of the Disgorgement Principle in Breach of Contract, 94 Yale L.J. 1339 (1985); § 12.7(4) below.

28. Timko v. Useful Homes Corp., 114 N.J.Eq. 433, 168 A. 824 (Ch. 1933).

29. See § 4.3(8) above.

30. 444 U.S. 507, 100 S.Ct. 763, 62 L.Ed.2d 704 (1980).

31. Cf. Simon & Schuster, Inc. v. Members of the New York State Crime Victims Board, — U.S. —, 112 S.Ct. 501, 116 L.Ed.2d 476 (1991), (statutory scheme for paying crime victim out of profits earned by criminal in writing about his crime held unconstitutional under First Amendment, partly, semble, on the ground that no apportionment was made between profits from the crime and profits from the criminal's own efforts or discussion of non-criminal events), discussed in §§ 7.2(13) & 8.9 below.

The general rule against profit recovery for ordinary contract breach is probably sound, even if there are occasional exceptions. One case that may be a good candidate for a profit recovery is the one in which the contractor increases his profits by using substandard materials or otherwise violating specifications. In such a case the plaintiff might appropriately recover the contractor's savings/increased profits, but they are in no way collateral profits resulting from the dealings with third persons.[32]

When Is Restitution Properly Measured by Consequential Benefits?

Factors. Recovery of the defendant's consequential gains is not appropriate in every case. Major factors that bear on the allowance of consequential benefit measures are these: (1) Is the consequential benefit measure a limit on recovery or an expansion of it? (2) was the defendant a conscious or serious wrongdoer? (3) did the plaintiff have legal title to the asset or did he have only an equitable interest? (4) was the consequential benefit an investment gain or was it business profits? (5) Can the court be confident in tracing the defendant's profits to use of the plaintiff's entitlement, and in apportioning that profit between the plaintiff's and the defendant's respective contributions?

A generalization. Although few generalizations about restitution can explain every case, a good approximation about recovery of consequential benefits might go something like this:

(1) Restitution of gains from sale and investment may be awarded to expand liability against (a) defendants who gain from property to which the plaintiff had legal title, even if such defendants are innocent (as in the case of an innocent converter) *and* (b) defendants who gain from property to which plaintiff had no title but which belongs to the plaintiff "in equity and good conscience," if those defendants were conscious or serious wrongdoers. (2) Restitution of business profits, as distinct from investment gains, when used to expand liability, is proper only when the defendant is a conscious or serious wrongdoer.

Measure to limit vs. measure to expand liability. Consequential benefit measures can be used either as a limit on liability or as an expansion of liability. When the defendant's realized gains are less than the market would have produced, to award the consequential benefit measure is to limit liability. When the defendant's realized gains are more than the market would have produced, to award the consequential benefit measure is to expand liability. The first point is that the propriety of the consequential benefit measure should be judged in part by its function, whether it is limiting or expanding liability. The remainder of this discussion deals with the consequential benefit claim as used to expand liability.

Consequential benefits from property title to which remains in the plaintiff. (a) Gains from sale or investment. In some cases defendant uses, sells or invests property in which the plaintiff has legal title. If the defendant still has the plaintiff's property, the plaintiff can get it back by ejectment or replevin actions. Because he can recover the property *in specie,* he recovers

32. See Farnsworth, Your Loss or My Gain? The Dilemma of the Disgorgement Principle in Breach of Contract, 94 Yale L.J. 1339 (1985).

whatever enhanced value it has as a result of the defendant's efforts. This appears to be true whether or not the defendant is a conscious wrongdoer.[33] Because the plaintiff could recover the property itself on the basis of full legal title, he can also recover gains the defendant reaped in selling that property. This is illustrated in the simple case of the defendant who steals the plaintiff's watch and sells it for a grand price. The plaintiff might recover the defendant's gains from the sale. That might be so even if the defendant were an innocent converter, having taken the watch by reason of honest mistake.[34] As to such gains from simple sale of assets at a price above the market, the legal title owner seems to prevail and nothing much seems to turn on the defendant's state of mind. Such an approach is supported by the logic of legal title and maybe very little else. But it is a logic that is pervasive.

(b) Profits from business use. If the plaintiff claims the defendant's *profits* in the business sense of income from a business operation rather than a single sale of an asset, the case is harder. Profit-making in a business is a complex matter. If the defendant takes the plaintiff's machine and sells it, we are sure that the price he was paid was at least partly attributable to the machine. If the defendant uses the plaintiff's machine in producing goods, which he packages, distributes and sells to retail customers, he may increase his profits, but we are not so sure that the increase has much if any connection with the plaintiff's machine. We can be sure, however, that the defendant's profits relate in part to the defendant's own investments, efforts, or enterprising attitude.

Given the doubt that ought to be almost inevitable in such cases, conscious or very serious wrongdoing ought to be the only justification for reaching the defendant's business profits (as distinct from market gains). The major cases allowing business profits are in fact conscious wrongdoer cases.[35]

---

33. E.g., Austrian Motors, Ltd. v. Travelers Ins. Co., 156 Ga.App. 618, 275 S.E.2d 702 (1980) (thief took owner's car, ordered repairs from a mechanic, owner found and recovered car and was not liable for the repairs which added value to the car); Silsbury v. McCoon, 3 N.Y. 379, 53 Am.Dec. 307 (1850) (plaintiff's corn wrongfully taken and made into whiskey, plaintiff was the owner of the whiskey). The result may be reached by way of the law of accession.

34. Creach v. Ralph Nichols Co., 37 Tenn. App. 586, 267 S.W.2d 132 (1953) (A stole plaintiff's car, sold it to B, who sold it to C for $2,295, from which B paid a sales commission of over $100; plaintiff is entitled to recover $2,295 from B); see I G. Palmer, Law of Restitution § 2.2 (1978 & Supps.). The Restatement states that the innocent converter is not subject to a constructive trust, but that the owner may recover the highest value of the property in the hands of the converter. If the innocent converter sells the property, however, the owner gets no more than its value; he does not get the added gain the innocent con-

verter makes if he sells at a price higher than the value. Restatement of Restitution §§ 203 & 154 (1937). Palmer concludes succinctly that the cases do not support this limitation. I G. Palmer, Law of Restitution § 2.12 (1978 & Supps.).

35. Federal Sugar Ref. Co. v. United States Sugar Equalization Bd., 268 Fed. 575 (2d Cir. 1920) (intentional interference with contract); Edwards v. Lee's Adm'r, 265 Ky. 418, 96 S.W.2d 1028 (1936) (trespass in cave lying beneath the plaintiff's land, limited to its fact in Triple Elkhorn Mining Co. v. Anderson, 646 S.W.2d 725 (Ky.1983)); Raven Red Ash Coal Co. v. Ball, 185 Va. 534, 548, 39 S.E.2d 231, 238 (1946) ("intentional, deliberate and repeated" use of plaintiff's land to transport coal, plaintiff could recover savings effected); Olwell v. Nye & Nissen Co., 26 Wash.2d 282, 173 P.2d 652, 169 A.L.R. 139 (1946) (intentional conversion, cost saved to the defendant).

Conversely, profits recovery has been denied in one way or another where the defendant is not a conscious wrongdoer. See Ringele v. Terteling, 78 Idaho 431, 305 P.2d 314 (1956),

So plaintiff's legal title to the machine does not seem by itself to furnish a very good case for capturing the defendant's business profits, but it would be a very good basis, at least in logic, for capturing the defendant's gains from a sale of the asset or from enhancements of it. Reasoning in terms of title, however, works only on property. It does not work on many other forms of wealth and in particular it does not work on money. The plaintiff does not ordinarily have title to money except in the narrow and seldom-important sense that one might own a particular gold coin.

Consequential benefits from property or money, to which the plaintiff has no legal title. The distinctive "equitable" reach of restitution shows up when the plaintiff seeks to recover property (including money) to which the plaintiff no longer has legal title. This means that equity remedies like constructive trust and accounting for profits are especially adapted to the recovery of gains a defendant makes with money which in equity and conscience "belongs" to the plaintiff. The same remedies are potentially available for recovery of tangible property which in justice but not in law belongs to the plaintiff.

The logic of title gave the plaintiff at least the investment or sale gains in the case of conversion, but that logic does not work when the plaintiff has only an equitable interest and no legal title at all. So the typical basis for a recovery of an equitable remedy that captures either the defendant's investment gains or profit is not title but serious or conscious wrongdoing.[36] The embezzler, the fiduciary, the fraudfeasor may all be held liable for business profits made through their wrongdoing, but such liability is not appropriately imposed upon the innocent defendant who mistakenly uses the plaintiff's property. Even under trademark statutes which authorize a profits recovery against an infringer, courts have sometimes limited that recovery to cases in which the defendant is at fault.[37]

§ 4.5(4) Guides to and Limitations on Measures of Restitution

Contract Price As a Guide or Ceiling

Contract transactions permitting restitution. One case for restitution occurs when the plaintiff provides part of the performance due under the contract but the defendant repudiates. The plaintiff may recover damages in such a case; but if he prefers, he may recover restitution for the value of his performance. A very similar case arises when the parties discover that the contract was entered into by a serious mutual mistake, and when the defendant asserts the statute of frauds, or impossibility of performance to

cert. denied, 353 U.S. 988, 77 S.Ct. 1284, 1 L.Ed.2d 1142 (1957). Also in some cases where he is. In Moore v. Regents of the Univ. of Cal., 51 Cal.3d 120, 271 Cal.Rptr. 146, 793 P.2d 479 (1990), cert. denied, ___ U.S. ___, 111 S.Ct. 1388, 113 L.Ed.2d 444 (1991) the defendants removed human cells from a surgically removed organ, then used the unique cells to develop a profitable medical technology. The court refused to entertain the patient-plaintiff's claim as one for conversion, evidently to forestall a recovery of the defendant's profits.

36. See Warren v. Century Bankcorporation, Inc., 741 P.2d 846, 852 (Okl.1987) ("gross profits are recoverable" where "a wrongdoer is shown to have been a conscious, deliberate misappropriator of another's commercial values"); Parks v. Zions First Nat. Bank, 673 P.2d 590 (Utah 1983) (conscious wrongdoing standard).

37. Carl Zeiss Stiftung v. VEB Carl Zeiss Jena, 433 F.2d 686, 707 (2d Cir.1970), cert. denied, 403 U.S. 905, 91 S.Ct. 2205, 29 L.Ed.2d 680 (1971) ("Ordinarily it is necessary to show 'not only that the infringer infringed, but that he did so with the deliberate intent to cause confusion, mistake or to deceive purchasers * * *.' "). See § 6.4(4) below.

avoid liability. In all these cases the defendant is liable to make restitution. How should the value of the plaintiff's services be measured?

Contract price as evidence of amount of benefit. When contracting parties are mistaken about some basic matter, that mistake is likely to affect the price they would have been willing to pay under the contract. So when contracts are avoided for basic mistake,[1] the contract price is not usually a good evidence of anything. When the contract is unenforceable under the statute of frauds, however, courts have allowed the plaintiff to show the contract price as evidence of the value of his services.[2] Sometimes courts refuse to admit the contract price as evidence when the alleged contract is an oral one, especially if it is one under which the plaintiff will render nursing or other personal care services and the promisor will leave the plaintiff his entire estate.[3]

Contract price or expectancy not a ceiling on buyer's restitution. The contract price usually is not a ceiling on restitutionary recovery.[4] A sympathetic case for use of this rule can be seen in some cases in which a buyer of goods has made a downpayment. Suppose the buyer pays the seller $25,000 on the purchase of goods, the total price of which is $100,000. Suppose at the time for delivery of the goods the seller reneges; but on that date the goods are worth only $75,000. So when the seller reneges the buyer is in exactly the same financial position he would have been in if the goods had been delivered. He is out $25,000, his downpayment; but this is where he would be upon full performance, because upon full performance he would have paid $100,000 for $75,000 worth of goods. Almost everyone would agree that upon the seller's nonperformance, the buyer should recover back his $25,000 downpayment. Although the contract's risk allocations makes the buyer bear the risk that the price of goods will go down, the buyer avoids this allocation of the risk when he obtains restitution. It is in effect a way of saying the contract price or risk allocation is not the ceiling on his restitutionary recovery.[5]

Contract price or expectancy not a ceiling on seller's restitution? The rule may be less sympathetic in the case of sellers of goods[6] or services.[7] Suppose a lawyer contracts to provide services for $5,000. When he has performed one-half the contract obligation, the client repudiates or discovers some ground to avoid the contract. The value of the lawyer's part performance turns out to be $10,000, even though the contract price for full performance was half that. The lawyer-seller seems to have made a bad contract; he would lose money upon full performance. Nevertheless, the

§ 4.5(4)

1. As to avoidance for mistake, see Chapter 11.

2. E.g., Wise v. Midtown Motors, Inc., 231 Minn. 46, 42 N.W.2d 404, 20 A.L.R.2d 735 (1950); Bennett Leasing Co. v. Ellison, 15 Utah 2d 72, 387 P.2d 246, 21 A.L.R.3d 1 (1963). Some cases have given the price a conclusive or almost conclusive effect. See Exchange Bank of Commerce v. Meadors, 199 Okl. 10, 184 P.2d 458 (1947). See § 13.2(2) below.

3. Evans v. Mason, 82 Ariz. 40, 308 P.2d 245, 65 A.L.R.2d 936 (1957); Doub v. Hauser, 256 N.C. 331, 123 S.E.2d 821 (1962).

4. See § 12.7(5) below.

5. See §§ 12.16(6) & 12.7(5) below. For a case similar to the text example on its facts, see Bush v. Canfield, 2 Conn. 485 (1818).

6. See § 12.17(6) below.

7. See § 12.7(5) below.

lawyer is permitted to recover restitution measured by the value of his services. Again, the contract price is usually not a ceiling on recovery.[8]

A contract between the parties, at least when it is an enforceable one, allocates risks between them. A risk allocated to the seller is the risk that the seller is not charging enough. That is a risk that cannot appropriately be placed on the buyer. The buyer's breach does not reallocate the risks allocated by the parties. The buyer's breach only liquidates the risk by turning it into a damages claim in favor of the seller. So the buyer's breach does not seem a good occasion to relieve the seller of the risk he accepted under the contract by giving him more in "restitution" than he could have received by full performance.[9]

The full performance liquidated sum rule. There is an exception to the rule that the contract price is not a ceiling on restitutionary recoveries. If the plaintiff has fully (or almost fully) performed and all that remains due for him is a liquidated sum of money, he may not have restitution.[10] He is limited instead to the money due him, that is, the contract price. So in this kind of case the contract price is a ceiling on restitution because it is the only recovery available at all. The two examples given above may suggest that relief to the buyer beyond the contract price may be more sympathetic in some instances than similar relief for the seller. The full performance, liquidated sum rule operates only against sellers (whether of goods or services), since the seller is one to whom sums of money are paid. Perhaps the full performance, liquidated sum rule does not go far enough, but as far as it goes it is in line with the buyer-seller distinction.

Costs and Reliance Expenses

Restitution cannot be measured by the plaintiff's losses, only by the defendant's gains. Particularly in contract cases, the plaintiff may incur expenses in preparation for performance (reliance expenses) or in performance itself. For instance, the plaintiff may remodel its factory to accept special machinery the defendant has contracted to deliver. If the defendant later repudiates or avoids the contract and the plaintiff can find no substitutes, the plaintiff will have suffered damages at least equal to the special remodeling costs.[11] The plaintiff has no restitution claim however. His remodeling of his own building has conferred no benefit upon the defendant.

Suppose, however, that the plaintiff remodels his own building at the defendant's request and as part of an oral arrangement under which, when the building is remodeled, the defendant will lease it as an office building. The defendant then repudiates the oral contract and relies on the statutes of frauds to forestall any liability. The plaintiff has losses measured by reliance expenses, but reliance expenses are *damages* and he cannot recover

---

8. In re Montgomery's Estate, 272 N.Y. 323, 6 N.E.2d 40, 109 A.L.R. 669 (1936).

9. Alternatively it may be argued that if unjust enrichment overrides the contract allocations of risk, then its measure should be the increased assets of the defendant, not the market value of the services.

10. I G. Palmer, Law of Restitution § 4.3 (1978 & Supps.); Restatement Second of Contracts § 373(2) (1981); § 12.7(5) below.

11. E.g., L. Albert & Son v. Armstrong Rubber Co., 178 F.2d 182, 17 A.L.R.2d 1289 (2d Cir.1949). As to *damages* recoveries for reliance expense in contract cases, see § 12.3 below.

damages under the most traditional interpretation of the statute of frauds.[12] Nevertheless, he may be permitted to recover *restitution*.[13] If the remodeling of the factory in the first example does not justify a restitution why does remodeling of the office building? The difference, if there is one, is that the remodeling in the first case is not part of the plaintiff's performance due to the defendant. The remodeling of the office building is part of the performance due the defendant (or which would have been due if the contract had been enforceable); it is performance that the defendant has requested. Requested services are treated as benefits to the person who made the request.

So costs that count only as reliance expenses are not recoverable as restitution; but some costs, incurred at the defendant's request, will justify restitution. The measure would still not be the amount of the cost, however; it would be the market value of the services provided. If the plaintiff in the office building example were inefficient so that his costs exceeded the going rate for such work, he would recover only the going rate.

Benefits Passed on, Consumed, Destroyed or Offset by Losses

The value of any given benefit to the plaintiff may be diminished or destroyed by subsequent events. Three major kinds of subsequent events may be identified here: (1) The defendant passes the benefit on to someone with a better claim to it. (2) The defendant consumes the benefit so that it is no longer reflected in assets. (3) The defendant received the benefit, but in connection with the same transaction suffers damages, so that in a sense his net benefit is less the amount he received.

Benefits passed on. The general rule is that if the defendant passes the benefit on to someone who is entitled to it, the defendant is not treated as having received the benefit. A personal representative receives a check from the plaintiff which is a mistakenly overpayment of the plaintiff's debt to the estate. The personal representative distributes the proceeds to heirs before the mistake is discovered. The personal representative is not unjustly enriched.[14]

Benefits consumed or destroyed. The generally stated rule is that one who receives a benefit for which restitution is due does not escape or minimize liability because he has consumed all or part of the benefit. Consumption of the benefit is enjoyment of it.[15] Some cases consider that benefits destroyed after the defendant has received them are still benefits to the defendant at the time they were received, although the defendant has obtained no enjoyment of them. For example, if the plaintiff performs services in building a house for the defendant and the defendant must make restitution for those services, the defendant continues to owe restitution even though the house is destroyed by fire before it is completed. Other authorities have taken the opposite view.[16]

12. See § 13.2(4) below.

13. Trollope v. Koerner, 106 Ariz. 10, 470 P.2d 91, 64 A.L.R.3d 1180 (1970); Farash v. Sykes Datatronics, Inc., 59 N.Y.2d 500, 465 N.Y.S.2d 917, 452 N.E.2d 1245 (1983). See §§ 13.2(2) & 13.2(4) below.

14. See § 4.6 below.

15. See § 4.6 below.

16. Restatement of Restitution § 142, Comment *b* (1937).

Benefits offset by loss. The plaintiff buyer pays the defendant seller $10,000 in advance to make a unique machine for the plaintiff. The defendant expends $1,000 in labor and materials toward performance of the contract. At that point the parties discover that performance is impossible or for some other reason they avoid the contract. The materials acquired by the defendant for use in making the machine have no salvage value. The defendant has received the plaintiff's money and must return it. May the defendant have a credit for the expenditures he has made? Is he unjustly enriched by $10,000 or by $9,000?

When the defendant receives a benefit but suffers a corresponding loss, the loss may be used to offset the benefit and reduce liability for it if the loss, standing alone, would be an item the defendant could recover as damages. If the loss to the defendant is one that could not be recovered as damages, the traditional view is that it could not be indirectly recoverable by allowing it as an offset against the plaintiff's restitution claim. The result in the example would be that the defendant owes restitution of the full $10,000, because, the contract obligations being discharged by impossibility of performance, he has no claim against the plaintiff for the reliance expense incurred.[17] If the partially completed machine had been built on the plaintiff's premises, the answer might be different because it could then be seen as a "benefit" to the plaintiff which could be offset.

An opposing perception is that the defendant's loss has the effect of reducing the defendant's unjust enrichment in the first place, so that at the time of the contract was avoided, his unjust enrichment was only $9,000, not $10,000.[18] This way of looking at the case is not very consistent with the traditional view that restitution is simply a restoration to some earlier status quo. Instead it is consistent with the view that in unwinding contracts, courts must be free to make adjustments that neither fully enforce the contract nor fully reinstate the earlier state of affairs. Particularly in cases of impossibility, impracticability, or frustration of purpose, remedies aim at making the best of a bad situation, and might enforce some sharing of losses if necessary.[19]

17. Fibrosa Spolka Akcyjna v. Fairbairn Lawson Combe Barbour, Ltd., [1943] A.C. 32, [1942] 2 All.E.R. 122, 144 A.L.R. 1298 (H.L. 1942) (similar to facts in the text), discussed, § 13.3(2) below.

In City of Barnsdall v. Curnutt, 198 Okl. 3, 174 P.2d 596 (1945), the city retained an attorney on a 40% contingent fee contract to sue a polluter. The alleged polluter offered $25,000 in compromise. The city did not accept this sum and the attorney died. New lawyers concluded a settlement with the alleged polluter for $35,000 and the city paid their fee of $10,000. The original attorney's estate was then allowed to recover $10,000 as 40% of the original (unaccepted) settlement offer. No offset was given for the city's necessary payment to the substituted attorneys.

18. Cf. Edwards v. Miller, 102 Okl. 189, 228 P. 1105 (1924) (incompetent paid money to Edwards for work done in good faith; upon suit to rescind, Edwards claimed the right to keep some of the money because of expenses incurred, even though the expenses had not redounded to the benefit of the incompetent; the court sided with Edwards although it found he had no expenses that could be independently claimed).

19. See Harrison, A Case for Loss Sharing, 56 So.Cal.L.Rev. 573 (1983); Weiss, Apportioning Loss after Discharge of a Burdensome Contract, 69 Yale L.Rev. 1054 (1960). See also Sharpe, Promissory Liability, 7 U.Chi.L.Rev. 250, 269 (1951); Coons, Approaches to Court Imposed Compromise—The Uses of Doubt and Reason, 58 Nw.L.Rev. 750 (1964). Cf. Oglebay Norton Co. v. Armco, Inc., 52 Ohio St.3d 232, 556 N.E.2d 515 (1990) (court ordered renegotiation of prices after major shifts in the market and the failure of the primary pricing mechanisms specified in the contract). The concept of loss sharing and judicial adjustment is discussed in § 13.3(2) below.

§ 4.5(5) Combining Restitution With Other Remedies

Compensatory Damages and Restitution

Can restitution be combined with other remedies? There are two principled reasons to limit such a combination, but these reasons do not exclude the combination in all cases. First, restitution may not be combined with damages when no damage claim could be brought by itself. For example, if the statute of frauds prohibits a damages recovery but permits a restitutionary recovery, the plaintiff could not recover damages when the defendant breaches the contract, although she may recover restitution.[1] The combination of remedies would not be permitted because the damages remedy is excluded by the statute.

Second, restitution may not be combined with damages if the combination will produce an excess recovery. The familiar principle of *damages* law is that the remedy should not provide more than one full compensation. The analogous principle of *restitution* law is that restitution should not force disgorgement of more than the unjust enrichment. If the two remedies are to be combined in one recovery, those limiting principles require that the combined recovery must not exceed the greater of (a) full compensation or (b) full disgorgement. If the combination does not exceed full compensation, or full disgorgement of the unjust enrichment, then it should be permitted. In particular, either market measured restitution or specie restitution might leave the plaintiff with consequential damages. When neither damages nor restitution is a forbidden recovery, no principled reason requires courts to deny both forms of relief together for one complete recovery.

For example, suppose the defendant fraudulently induces the plaintiff to sell machinery from the plaintiff's factory for $10,000. The plaintiff expends $5,000 to remove the machinery. When the fraud is discovered the plaintiff may have specific restitution of the machinery. The court is not required to deny the plaintiff a recovery of the $5,000 removal expense (and the reinstallation expense) as well as a recovery of his machinery.[2]

On the other hand, there would be few if any occasions to permit recovery of consequential restitution and consequential damages; the higher of the two sums would by itself reflect the full justified recovery. For example, suppose the defendant steals the plaintiff's trade secret and sells it to the plaintiff's competitor for $50,000. Use of the trade secret allows the plaintiff's competitor to cut into the plaintiff's market for a two year period, causing the plaintiff to lose $100,000 in net profits. If the defendant is responsible for the plaintiff's damages, the damages recovery of $100,000 will serve fully to compensate the plaintiff and at the same time to disgorge the defendant's unjust enrichment. The single recovery is sufficient.[3]

§ 4.5(5)

1. See § 13.2(1) below.

2. See Head & Seemann, Inc. v. Gregg, 107 Wis.2d 126, 318 N.W.2d 381 (1982); § 9.4 below.

3. But conceivably the plaintiff could recover $100,000 as damages from the competitor if it knowingly took the trade secret and $50,000 against the defendant, since, although this would give the plaintiff more than its losses, it would accomplish one full disgorgement from each wrongdoer. See § 10.5(3) below as to trade secrets.

The election of remedies doctrines may operate against the principles of full compensation/full disgorgement. On facts like those in the machinery example, courts once said, and might say again, that if the plaintiff "elects" restitution of the machinery, he may not also have damages. That doctrine is explained elsewhere.[4] Where it is discarded or circumvented, recovery of both restitution and damages will be permitted if it does not exceed the justified amount.

Punitive Damages and Restitution

Can restitution be combined with punitive damages? The combination has been approved in some cases,[5] rejected in others.[6]

Here again, election of remedies doctrines may prevent the combined recovery. In addition, an ambiguous rule of punitive damages is sometimes read to mean that punitive damages cannot be awarded unless the plaintiff actually recovers compensatory damages too.[7] Such a reading is unfortunate, but given that reading of the rule, restitution could never form a basis for a punitive recovery.[8]

Some restitutionary recoveries already have a punitive element. The mere recovery of the defendant's profit in a wrongful transaction is not by itself punitive if it does no more than take from the defendant those gains that do not belong to him in good conscience. However, if the recovery of the defendant's profits includes not only the profits produced by the plaintiff's property or money but also those which depend upon the defendant's own effort or investment, it exceeds full disgorgement and therefore contains punitive elements.[9]

Such a result is not necessarily optimal. When the defendant has acquired gains by tortious actions, restitution helps remove incentives for tortious conduct by denying the defendant the hope of gain; but it does not

---

4. See §§ 9.4 & 12.7(6) below.

5. Thomas Auto Co., Inc. v. Craft, 297 Ark. 492, 763 S.W.2d 651 (1989) (citing first edition); Brown v. Techdata Corp., Inc., 238 Ga. 622, 234 S.E.2d 787 (1977); Indiana & Mich. Elec. Co. v. Harlan, 504 N.E.2d 301 (Ind.App. 1987); Coster v. Crookham, 468 N.W.2d 802 (Iowa 1991) (trustee could be held for profits resulting from self-dealing and also punitive damages).

6. Estate of Jones by Blume v. Kvamme, 449 N.W.2d 428 (Minn.1989).

7. See § 3.9(1) above.

8. This may be the basis for the decision in Hubbard v. Superior Court, 111 Ariz. 585, 535 P.2d 1302 (1975) (seeming to forbid punitive recovery in rescission claim, at least where no consequential damages were established).

9. Cf. Truck Equip. Serv. Co. v. Fruehauf Corp., 536 F.2d 1210 (8th Cir.1976), cert. denied, 429 U.S. 861, 97 S.Ct. 164, 50 L.Ed.2d 139 (1976). In some cases the professed reason for allowing a recovery of the full profit, including that portion fairly attributable to the defendant's efforts, is that the defendant should bear the burden of apportioning the profits between the plaintiff's property and the defendant's efforts and that if the defendant cannot do so, the entire sum must go to the plaintiff. But this doctrine is mainly invoked in cases of serious fault by the defendant, so its punitive element seems clear. See Carl Zeiss Stiftung v. VEB Carl Zeiss Jena, 433 F.2d 686, 707 (2d Cir.1970), cert. denied, 403 U.S. 905, 91 S.Ct. 2205, 29 L.Ed.2d 680 (1971) ("Ordinarily it is necessary to show 'not only that the infringer infringed, but that he did so with the deliberate intent to cause confusion, mistake or to deceive purchasers * * *.' "); § 6.4(4) below.

In Warren v. Century Bankcorporation, Inc., 741 P.2d 846 (Okl.1987) the court thought it proper to give the plaintiff all of the defendant's gross profits resulting from use of opportunities that rightfully belonged to the plaintiff, and it refused to allow a deduction for expenses the defendant reasonably incurred to generate those profits. The court insisted that it was granting restitution, but if, as defendant argued, its expenses outran its gross gains, the award is not restitution to prevent unjust enrichment at all and thus seems purely punitive.

affirmatively impose added costs. It is in no way proportioned to the malignity of the defendant's conduct and it does not necessarily recover the defendant's profits from all misconduct, only the profits related to the particular plaintiff. Since the same or similar misconduct might capture profits that fairly belong to other persons, and since some of those others might not be aware of their rights, or might not sue, the defendant who merely disgorges profits on a single transaction may not be fully deterred from similar misbehavior.[10]

In contrast, punitive damages might be fixed at a sum which forces disgorgement of profits made in the particular transactions and an additional sum to deter similar misconduct with respect to other people. In addition, punitive damages could be proportioned to the wrongfulness of the defendant's conduct. In these respects, punitive damages would be more flexible than restitution. These conclusions hold even in those cases where "punitive restitution" could be exacted. To take all the profits from defendant's business because the defendant imitated the plaintiff's trademark or packaging may be punitive, but the punishment does not necessarily fit the crime because the profits might be high or low and the wrongdoing might range from innocent to malicious. By the same token, restitution would often provide the right amount of deterrent, but it would not always do so.

B. DEFENSES AND LIMITATIONS

§ 4.6 Defendant's Change of Position

Changed Position May Defeat Restitution

If, after receiving a benefit, an innocent[2] defendant reasonably changes position in reliance on the benefit so that liability for restitution would be inequitable, his liability to make restitution is reduced or terminated accordingly.[3] The burden is upon the defendant to prove a change in position that would make it inequitable to require restitution.[4] Defendants who are conscious wrongdoers cannot claim the changed position defense, so most of the cases arise out of a mistaken payment to the defendant.

Related Rules

A defense called "discharge for value" bears some resemblance to both the changed position defense and to the bona fide purchaser defense. That defense is considered separately.[5] In addition, a number of other defenses may affect restitution. For instance, the plaintiff who wants to rescind a contract may be denied restitution against the defendant on the ground that what the plaintiff received in the deal has been damaged or destroyed and

---

10. Recapture of the defendant's overall profits is a good aim of punitive damages. See Dobbs, Ending Punishment in "Punitive" Damages: Deterrence–Measured Remedies, 40 Ala.L.Rev. 831 (1989).

Restatement of Restitution § 142 (1937). See generally, III G. Palmer, Law of Restitution § 16.8 (1978 & Supps.).

5. See § 4.7(2) below.

§ 4.6

3. See Prudential Ins. Co. of Am. v. Couch, 180 W.Va. 210, 376 S.E.2d 104, 108 n. 6 (1988);

cannot be restored.[6] The defendant might also be protected against restitutionary liability if the plaintiff has unreasonably delayed in seeking restitution and is thus guilty of laches[7] or can be thought to have ratified the transaction.[8] These cases are not covered by the changed position defense.

Types of Cases

The defense is raised mainly in three kinds of cases: (1) the defendant received a benefit but passed it on to someone with a better claim to the payment; (2) the defendant consumed the benefit by expenditures he would not otherwise have made; (3) the defendant received a benefit but it was lost, damaged or destroyed and cannot be returned. On the right facts, the defense may work in any of these cases, but on the whole it works best in the first kind of case.

Benefits Passed on

When the defendant is known[9] to be an intermediary or representative for another person, and receives a benefit in that capacity, then passes it on to the ultimate beneficiary or principal, the defendant has changed position and is not liable to make restitution.[10] For example, the plaintiff mistakenly transfers money to a bank for the account of a depositor. Without knowledge of the mistake, the bank duly credits the depositor's account. The bank is not liable thereafter to make restitution to the plaintiff.[11] Put more generally, the agent or trustee who receives monies for the principal or beneficiary by mistake, is protected from restitution after a good faith transfer to the funds, and often even if the transfer is a bookkeeping entry crediting the depositor, the principal or the beneficiary.[12]

Benefits Expended or Consumed

In general, the fact that the defendant has consumed or expended the benefits received does not show a change of position.[13] If she purchases assets or pays debts, for example, she is no less enriched than if she has cash. But the general rule is not invariably followed to the limit of its logic.

6. See § 9.3(3) below.

7. See § 2.4(4) above.

8. Westerland v. First Nat. Bank of Carrington, 38 N.D. 24, 31, 164 N.W. 323, 325, 7 A.L.R. 562 (1917) ("long delay tends to show a ratification").

9. When the defendant is an agent of an undisclosed principal so that the plaintiff deals with the defendant as if he were the principal, the defense may be rejected. See III G. Palmer, The Law of Restitution § 16.8, p. 519 (1978 & Supps.) (criticizing this rule).

10. III G. Palmer, The Law of Restitution § 16.8 (1978 & Supps.); § 11.9 below.

11. French Bank of California v. First Nat. Bank of Louisville, 585 S.W.2d 431 (Ky.App. 1979). Cf. Federal Ins. Co. v. First Nat. Bank of Boston, 633 F.2d 978, 982 (1st Cir.1980) (defendant bank paid a check drawn by plaintiff victimized by payee's fraud, plaintiff could not recover what was "lost by a payment over").

12. Weiner v. Roof, 19 Cal.2d 748, 122 P.2d 896 (1942) (trustee and agent treated the same, collections by innocent trustee had been disbursed by credits given to beneficial interests, no recovery).

13. United States v. Reagan, 651 F.Supp. 387 (D.Mass.1987) (erroneous tax refund, consumption no defense to government restitution claim); Western Casualty & Sur. Co. v. Kohm, 638 S.W.2d 798, 801, 37 A.L.R.4th 1042 (Mo.App.1982) (plaintiff insurer mistakenly paid defendant for destruction of his car, defendant bought a new one; "this type of change is not sufficient to bar restitution, since a purchaser generally receives something of value for his money"). Cf. Restatement of Restitution § 142, Comment b (1937) (not a change of position to pay debts, or expenses of living or business or to make gifts).

Hardships and equities may relieve the defendant in some expenditure-consumption cases. When the benefit is consumed or expended in ways that (a) do not increase assets or reduce liabilities and (b) the expenditure or consumption is one that the recipient would not have indulged except for the mistake, a strong equity appears in favor of the recipient and the defense may be effective to bar restitution,[14] but some decisions seem even more favorable to the defendant than the stated formula suggests.[15] In the case of overpayment of public benefits at least, the special vulnerability and needs of the defendant who is overpaid may justify the defense.[16]

Loss, Harm, or Destruction

Both Palmer and the Restatement take the position that when the plaintiff has conferred benefits upon the innocent defendant by mistake and, before the mistake is discovered, those benefits have been destroyed or damaged, lost or stolen, diminished or depreciated, the defendant's obligation to make restitution is reduced or terminated proportionately.[17] If the diminished value or damage results from the defendant's own consumption, decisions, or investments, reduction of the defendant's liability under this rule appears to conflict with the consumption-expenditure rule. However, the diminished value rule has been applied to reduce liability even when the loss in value results from the defendant's own investment decisions.[18]

The diminished value rule, if applied in mistaken benefit cases, does not necessarily apply when the benefit has been contracted for and is later destroyed or damaged. This occurs when the contractor does work on a building for the defendant but the work is later destroyed and the contract is avoided. In some such cases the defendant is held liable for the value of the contractor's work, although the defendant retains none of its benefits.[19]

§ 4.7 Bona Fide Purchasers for Value and Discharge for Value

§ 4.7(1) Bona Fide Purchasers

Rule Summary

The distinction between legal title and equitable interests which has already been observed, is again important when innocent third persons take

---

14. See Amalgamated Ass'n of Street Elec. Ry. & Motor Coach Employees of Am. v. Danielson, 24 Wis.2d 33, 128 N.W.2d 9 (1964) (after overpayment of insurance death benefits, daughter paid $50 debt of deceased father who left no assets, no restitution as to this sum).

15. Moritz v. Horsman, 305 Mich. 627, 9 N.W.2d 868, 147 A.L.R. 117 (1943) (defendant paid hospital bills with overpayment); Hilliard v. Fox, 735 F.Supp. 674 (W.D.Va.1990) (no restitution required if defendant invested benefit unwisely).

16. The social security statute, 42 U.S.C.A. § 404(b) provides:

In any case in which more than the correct amount of payment has been made, there shall be no adjustment of payments to, or recovery by the United States from, any person who is without fault if such adjust-

ment or recovery would defeat the purpose of this subchapter or would be against equity and good conscience. In making for purposes of this subsection any determination of whether any individual is without fault, the Secretary shall specifically take into account any physical, mental, educational, or linguistic limitation such individual may have (including any lack of facility with the English language).

17. III G. Palmer, Law of Restitution § 16.-8(f) (1978 & Supps.); Restatement of Restitution § 142, Comment b (1937).

18. Hilliard v. Fox, 735 F.Supp. 674 (W.D.Va.1990). This problem is considered more fully in § 11.9 below.

19. E.g., M. Ahern Co. v. John Bowen Co., Inc., 334 Mass. 36, 133 N.E.2d 484 (1956); Annotation, 170 A.L.R. 980 (1947). See § 13.-2(2).

property in which the plaintiff has either kind of interest. In general, if the original "owner," *O* still has legal title, *O* prevails over a bona fide purchaser, who acquires only equitable interests. On the other hand, if the purchaser acquires legal title and *O* has only an equity, the purchaser prevails. The principle is that when the conflict is between legal title and equitable interests, the legal title prevails. When both parties to the dispute have only equitable interests, equities are weighed; when they are equal, the first to acquire an equitable interest prevails.

General Rule—Legal versus Equitable Title

Where legal title remains in O. At common law, a bona fide purchase of goods from one who has no title gives the purchaser no title.[1] The principle is that no one could acquire good title to property without the owner's consent. There are some qualifications or exceptions discussed later, but the general rule remains as stated.

For example, *B,* in good faith and without reason to be suspicious, purchases a watch from Cellar, paying $100 cash. Later it turns out that the watch belonged to *O* and that Cellar had stolen it. The purchaser acquires no legal interest in the watch. To the logicians of property this seemed inevitable, since Cellar had no title pass to the purchaser. Thus Owner could sue Purchaser for conversion and recover the value of the watch from him,[2] or could sue in replevin for a return of the watch itself.[3] In either event Purchaser would be the loser unless he were able to recover over against Cellar, which was often impossible for practical reasons.

Where legal title passes to purchaser. In the situation just discussed, the Owner had legal title and the Purchaser had some equities in his favor. It would even be possible to think of the Purchaser as having an equitable title. The equitable title, however, must always bow to the legal title. In other words, if, somehow, the bona fide purchaser acquired *legal* title (not merely equitable one) he would prevail over earlier equitable title or interest.

Trust example. One situation in which this could come about involved the law of trusts. As equity courts conceptualized the law of trusts, the trustee held legal title to the property of the trust for the benefit of the beneficiary, whose title was purely equitable. Thus the trustee could convey legal title to a purchaser. If the trustee did convey legal title to the property in violation of the trust, the purchaser would be in a different position from the purchaser who took from a thief, since the purchaser from the trustee would be taking a legal title. If he was in good faith and had no notice of

§ 4.7(1)

1. E.g., Claybrooke Warehouse & Gin Co. v. Farmers Co-op. Warehouse & Gin Co., 260 Ala. 518, 71 So.2d 88 (1954); Panhandle Pipe & Supply Co. v. S.W. Pressey & Son, 125 Colo. 355, 243 P.2d 756 (1952); O'Keeffe v. Snyder, 83 N.J. 478, 416 A.2d 862 (1980); Mattson v. Commercial Credit Business Loans, Inc., 301 Or. 407, 723 P.2d 996 (1986).

The innocent purchaser might, however, acquire enough color of title to qualify as an insurable interest that would permit him to insure the property and claim against the insurer if it were damaged or destroyed. Butler v. Farmers Ins. Co. of Arizona, 126 Ariz. 371, 616 P.2d 46 (1980).

2. E.g., Peed v. Burleson's, Inc., 244 N.C. 437, 94 S.E.2d 351 (1956). As to remedies for conversion see §§ 5.13 et seq. below.

3. See §§ 5.17 (modern remedy of replevin) & 4.2(2) (historical development of replevin).

the legitimate claims of the beneficiary's equities, the purchaser's legal title from the trustee defeated the purely equitable title of the beneficiary.[4]

Fraudulent purchase example. Another situation in which this principle was applied involved the law of sales. It frequently occurred that an owner was induced by fraud to sell his goods to *A* who would thus acquire legal title. On the other hand, the owner, having been defrauded, would have a right to rescind the sale, and this was conceived of as an equity in his favor, or again, a sort of "equitable title." If, before this equity was exercised, *A* sold the goods to a bona fide purchaser for value who had no notice of the true owner's equities, the bona fide purchaser would take the legal title. This was so because the original purchaser, *A*, had legal title and could therefore pass it. As in the case of the trustee's conveyance, the legal title defeated the equitable one, and the bona fide purchaser was thus protected.[5]

Equitable remedies against bona fide purchasers who take legal title. The principles just stated lead in particular to the rule that purely equitable remedies do not lie to recover property or an interest therein from a bona fide purchaser for value who had no notice of the plaintiff's claim. Thus the right to a constructive trust or an equitable lien on the property,[6] or to subrogation,[7] or to reformation of an instrument[8] does not run against the bona fide purchaser. Conversely, the constructive trust and other equitable remedies will take precedence over subsequent takers who do *not* qualify as bona fide purchasers.[9] Donees,[10] as well as purchasers who have notice of the plaintiff's rights are among those who could not count as bona fide purchasers.

Restating the rule. The general rule, then, for these situations is that if legal title has passed to a bona fide purchaser for value and without notice of prior equities, that legal title will prevail over either equitable title or equitable interests. However, if the situation is reversed, and the bona fide

4. See Pilcher v. Rawlins, L.R. 7 Ch.App. 259 (1872). Maitland discusses and quotes this case in F.W. Maitland, Equity 114 (2d ed. 1947).

5. Baldwin v. Childs, 249 N.Y. 212, 163 N.E. 737 (1928). Courts sometimes say that a conveyance procured by forgery or "fraud in the factum" is absolutely void and conveys no title even to a bona fide purchaser. See Horvath v. National Mortgage Co., 238 Mich. 354, 213 N.W. 202 (1927); § 9.6 below.

6. In re Marriage of Allen, 724 P.2d 651 (Colo.1986); see Cottman v. Cottman, 56 Md. App. 413, 468 A.2d 131 (1983); Restatement of Restitution §§ 13 & 172–174 (1937).

Cf. In re Seaway Exp. Corp., 912 F.2d 1125, 1128, 1129 (9th Cir.1990) (trustee in bankruptcy as bona fide purchaser of debtor's assets prevailed over purely equitable security interest of a creditor). In *Seaway,* a debtor granted a lender a security interest in the debtor's accounts receivable. The debtor then sold one account for a parcel of real property. The debtor declared bankruptcy. It then in turn sold the real property for $1 million, which was placed in a separate account. The trustee

in bankruptcy was in the position of a bona fide purchaser of the debtor's assets. The lender's interest, became a purely equitable security interest when the account receivable was converted to real property. The trustee prevailed over the lender, essentially because under state law "a bona die purchaser who buys without notice cuts off a potential constructive trust."

7. Home Owners' Loan Corp. v. Murdock, 150 Pa.Super. 284, 28 A.2d 498 (1942).

8. Reformation must usually be denied as against a bona fide purchaser. See Beams v. Werth, 200 Kan. 532, 438 P.2d 957 (1968). This does not necessarily mean that reformation will be granted in favor of a bona fide purchaser. On both points see § 11.6 below.

9. See, e.g., Leyden v. Citicorp Indus. Bank, 782 P.2d 6, 12 (Colo.1989) (equitable lien is good against all those who acquire an interest with notice of the lien or the facts giving rise to it); Middlebrooks v. Lonas, 246 Ga. 720, 272 S.E.2d 687 (1980); Durham v. Creech, 32 N.C.App. 55, 231 S.E.2d 163 (1977).

10. In re Marriage of Allen, 724 P.2d 651 (Colo.1986).

purchaser has no legal title, but only an equitable one, he must lose to the title holder, and on the same principle—that legal title will prevail over the equitable one.

Purchase and value. The bona fide purchaser is not "bona fide" at all if he has knowledge or even notice of the equities in favor of the plaintiff and in that case cannot claim the defense. Two other important limitations are imposed. First, the party who claims as a purchaser must indeed acquire the property by "purchase." If he acquires property, or some interest in it, by a levy or attachment, he is not a purchaser, though he may qualify as a purchaser if he buys at an execution sale. Second, the purchaser must pay "value." This can be a term of art. Some courts traditionally held that value did not include the satisfaction of a pre-existing debts. Under the UCC this has been changed, and one who acquires property, paying in exchange the satisfaction of a debt, can nowadays generally be a bona fide purchaser for value,[11] although there may be some limits on this.

General Rule—Equitable Title versus Equitable Title

Conflicting equitable interests illustrated. It is possible to encounter situations in which the dispute is not between a legal title holder and an equitable title holder, but rather between the holders of two equitable titles. For instance, the trustee of an express trust might contract, in violation of his trust obligations, to convey trust property to a purchaser who has no notice of the trust. Before the contract to purchase is executed by a conveyance, it may be thought of as creating an "equity" in favor of the purchaser if he had paid the purchase money.[12] This would leave the purchaser competing with the beneficiary of the trust, each having an equity, but neither having a legal title, since that remained in the trustee until he actually executed a deed or other instrument of transfer. The rules previously discussed, in which legal title had passed to a bona fide purchaser for value under similar circumstances, clearly do not control this situation.

First in time, first in right. In situations like this, where two equitable titles clashed, courts sometimes fell back on the old equitable maxim that means "First in Time, First in Right."[13] The rule so expressed gave title or priority to the equitable interest that was created first in time. In the example just mentioned, the beneficiary of the trust would prevail over the person who had contracted to purchase trust property, since the beneficiary's interest was created first in time.[14]

Qualifying and limiting the First in Time rule. Although there are situations, such as the one just described, in which the prior equity will win simply because of its priority in time, courts and scholars have long recognized that the First in Time maxim is an oversimplification. In *Rice v.*

---

11. UCC § 2–402(1) read with 1–201(44).

12. A certain circularity is involved in describing the contract purchaser as having an equity here because under the equitable conversion doctrine he has that equity only when the contract would be specifically enforced. See, describing the purchaser's equitable interest in connection with the equitable conversion doctrine, § 4.3(8) above.

13. "Qui prior est tempore, potior est jure," is the Latin version. Pomeroy expressed it: "Where There are Equal Equities, The First in Order of Time Shall Prevail." See 2 J. Pomeroy, Equity Jurisprudence §§ 413–415 (5th ed. 1941).

14. See 4 A. Scott, Trusts § 285 (3d ed. 1967) describing this and other situations in which the equity first in time would prevail.

Rice,[15] decided in 1854, an English Vice–Chancellor declared flatly that the maxim "is an incorrect statement of the rule * * *." He went on to say that the correct rule was that "As between persons having only equitable interests, if their equities are *in all other respects equal*, priority of time gives the better equity * * *."

In the *Rice* case Michael purchased property from George and took the deeds. Michael had not in fact paid for the property, but he agreed to do so shortly. Nevertheless, the deeds recited that the purchase money had been paid. Michael took these deeds and offered them as security for a loan. On the strength of these deeds, Ede loaned Michael some money. Michael did not execute a formal mortgage, but this agreement and loan from Ede operated as a mortgage recognizable in equity. Michael then absconded. This left the vendor with an equity in the form of a vendor's lien for the sale price due,[16] and the money lender with an equity in the form of an equitable mortgage. The vendor's lien was clearly first in time, but the court held that it was not first in right. The chancellor thought that the equities were equal except for the fact that the money-lender had possession of the title deeds. This, he thought, was a sufficient additional circumstance to give priority to the money lender. Thus the equitable interest first in time was not given priority in the *Rice* case.

Where the bona fide purchaser for value acquires an equity only, and where the equity must compete with another equity rather than with a legal interest, no fixed, general rule establishes priority. On the contrary, though courts have settled rules for particular situations, for those situations not governed by precedent or statute, there must be a balancing of equities to determine which of the equitable interests will prevail.

Modifications and Exceptions: Commercial Sales, Land Titles and Security Transactions

Traditional rules undesirable in commercial sales. Where the conflict of claims is between a legal and an equitable title, the general rule refuses to protect the bona fide purchaser unless he has, somehow, acquired full legal title—and thus needs no additional protection. This may or may not be sound in some of the situations described, but it is certainly a rule of doubtful use in many commercial situations, and in many situations involving sales of goods and negotiable instruments the rules have in fact been modified.

In sales of goods cases, it would be most inconvenient if purchasers from a business establishment were required to check out the title to any goods they might purchase. Not only would this be difficult to do, it would be expensive, and very likely any rule that protected the "true owner" by holding the buyer liable—or requiring him to investigate title—would ultimately impede commercial activity and add to the cost of goods generally.

With some such considerations as these in mind, courts began to manipulate the bona fide purchaser rules in such a way as to get different

---

15. 2 Drew. 73, 61 Eng.Rep. 646 (1854).   **16.** See § 12.12(4) as to the vendor's (equitable) lien.

results in purely commercial cases, as Professor Gilmore's classic article shows.[17]

Voidable title technique. The main manipulative technique used was to find that, somehow, legal title had been passed to the bona fide purchaser. For example, Owner is induced by fraud to sell to Buyer. Before Owner discovers the fraud, Buyer sells to Bonafide, who pays valuable consideration and who buys in good faith. In this situation, courts treated the original Buyer as having acquired legal title to the goods. It was, to be sure, a title that was voidable by Owner, because of the fraud. However, this power to avoid the sale by Owner, until it was actually exercised, was a mere equity in the Owner. Since Buyer had legal title, he could pass legal title to Bonafide, whose legal title then prevailed over the equity of the original Owner.[18] This "voidable title" technique did not, of course, work in every case; but it had wide application in credit sales—in other words, in large commercial transactions.

Entrusting statutes. Various legislation, starting with the Factors' Acts in the 19th Century, has affected the bona fide purchaser rules in sales situations. The Factors' Acts provide, in one form or another, that an agent of the seller, who is entrusted with goods for the purpose of selling them, can pass good title to a bona fide purchaser.[19] The Uniform Commercial Code took over this idea. It provides in part: "Any entrusting of possession of goods to a merchant who deals in goods of that kind gives him power to transfer all rights of the entruster to a buyer in ordinary course of business." [20]

In addition to the general "entrusting" provision for sales cases, the UCC makes a number of provisions relevant to the bona fide purchaser in more complex transactions. It figures in the Code's regulation of Bulk Transfers,[21] Documents of Title,[22] and Secured Transactions.[23] The Code is, of course, a complex subject in itself and beyond the scope of this work, but it may be said that in general the Code has modified the older common law and equity rules about bona fide purchasers to put the bona fide purchaser on a somewhat better footing.

Land title recording. Another important modification of the bona fide purchaser rules—or rather a modification of how they operate—occurs under land title recording statutes, and to some extent under the certificate of title system for motor vehicle titles.

Under land recording statutes, many interests in land may be officially recorded in the county where the land lies. If A sells to B in fee, then B may record his deed in the proper office, and this recordation serves as notice to any purchaser from A that A no longer has any title. Under the statutes,

---

17. Gilmore, The Commercial Doctrine of Good Faith Purchase, 63 Yale L.J. 1057 (1954).

18. As to land: e.g., Strutt v. Ontario Sav. & Loan Ass'n, 11 Cal.App.3d 547, 90 Cal.Rptr. 69 (1970). As to chattels: the voidable title rule has been codified as UCC § 2–403. A similar principle applies to commercial paper partly through the conception of "holder in due course." For application of the voidable title principle to commercial paper see Manu-

facturers Hanover Trust Co. v. Eisenstadt, 64 Misc.2d 397, 315 N.Y.S.2d 19 (1970).

19. See 2 S. Williston, Sales §§ 317–320 (1948 & Supp.).

20. UCC § 2–403(2).

21. UCC Art. 6.

22. UCC Art. 7.

23. UCC Art. 9.

anyone who purchases from A is treated as having notice of this public record whether he actually examined it or not. Thus he cannot be in the position of a bona fide purchaser at all if B's title is properly recorded. The same sort of principle applies to other interests in land, such as mortgages.

Sometimes the converse situation arises under the recording statutes. A conveys to B and later to C, but C does not know of B's earlier deed and B's deed is not recorded. In this situation, where C records his deed first, he gets the title. This is an important modification of the common law rule as applied to the chattel cases described earlier.

Motor vehicle purchases. Purchasers of motor vehicles are protected by a different and perhaps more efficient device in most states. Each vehicle is represented by a certificate of title, issued by the state and identifying the vehicle particularly. There is no way to transfer legal title without a transfer of the certificate. Thus it is quite difficult to transfer the same legal interest twice, first to B and then to C, since the first transfer will carry with it the title certificate and the seller would be obliged to forge a new one if he wished to defraud a second purchaser. Security interests in motor vehicles are also endorsed directly on the certificate. Thus anyone lending money on the motor vehicle is already mortgaged or subject to other claims. This system tends to avoid many of the bona fide purchaser problems encountered with tangible chattels not represented by title certificates.

Modifications and Exceptions: Money, Choses in Action and Negotiable Instruments

Where the property involved is not tangible, problems of bona fide purchase become somewhat more complex. For immediate purposes, intangible property can be classified as (1) choses in action, (2) negotiable instruments and (3) money. Both money and negotiable instruments have special characteristics of free transferability, as will be indicated more fully. Choses in action—that is assignable rights not embodied in a negotiable instrument, such as a simple contract right—are not always freely transferable, and when they may be transferred at all, the purchaser usually takes such instruments without getting the status of a bona fide purchaser.

[*For discussion of the special rules applied to choses in action, money, and negotiable instruments, see this section in the Practitioner Treatise edition.*]

§ 4.7(2) Discharge for Value

Mistaken Payment Used to Satisfy a Valid Claim Against a Third Person

General rule. The defense of discharge for value is closely related to both the changed position [1] and the bona fide purchaser [2] defenses. In its primary version [3] the defense applies when a creditor of T receives a

---

§ 4.7(2)

1. See §§ 4.6 above & 11.8 below.

2. See § 4.7(1) above.

3. A secondary version of the rule governs cases in which C buys a chose in action, that

is, takes a right to sue as an assignee. One who takes a right to sue usually takes that right subject to the same defenses that would apply against the assignor. However, under the secondary version of the discharge for

payment in cash or cash equivalents from the plaintiff as a payment on T's debt. The creditor accepts the payment in complete or partial discharge of T's debt. Later the plaintiff discovers that his payment to the creditor was mistaken and he seeks restitution of the funds mistakenly [4] paid. Under the discharge for value rule, the creditor does not owe restitution because he has used the funds to discharge T's debt to him.[5] On the other hand if the creditor obtained the payment by misrepresentation or if the creditor knew of the plaintiff's mistake, restitution will be required.[6] Examples will show the potential scope of the discharge for value defense.

The example of Weiner v. Roof. In *Weiner v. Roof,*[7] some land developers financed the development by a loan from the bank. When someone bought a lot from one of the developers, payment had to be made to the bank, which would then credit the purchase price against the loan and against certain expenses. In this way the developer's debt would be reduced and the bank would be repaid as people bought lots. Mr. Weiner bought a lot from one of these developers and made appropriate payment to the bank. The bank applied the payment to reduce the developer's debt. After that, however, Mr. Weiner discovered that he had been induced to purchase by misrepresentations on behalf of the developer. So his payment was made under a mistake induced by misrepresentation. He sought recovery of his payment to the bank. But the California Supreme Court denied the claim. The bank in collecting the money was acting as agent for the seller, but in receiving the money it was acting as creditor of the seller. Because the bank had credited the seller by a bookkeeping entry,[8] the bank gave up something of value in exchange for the money. It was in effect a bona fide purchaser of the money.

The example of Banque Worms. In *Banque Worms v. BankAmerica Intern.,*[9] Spedley, a depositor of a Security Pacific Bank ordered electronic transfer of about $2 million to Banque Worms. Spedley owed Banque Worms and this transfer was to have been in partial payment of its debt. Later the same day, however, Spedley ordered Security Pacific to stop payment of this transfer and to make a $2 million to a different bank instead. Security Pacific mistakenly made the transfer to Banque Worms in

value rule, if the debtor on the chose in action mistakenly pays *C* in spite of the defense available, no restitution is permitted. See, e.g., Michelin Tires (Canada), Ltd. v. First Nat. Bank of Boston, 666 F.2d 673 (1st Cir.1981); and generally III G. Palmer, Law of Restitution § 16.7 (1978 & Supps.); Restatement of Restitution § 14(2) (1937).

4. The usual case is payment by mistake. The mistake is often induced by fraud of a third person. In Merchants Bank & Trust Co. v. Erdeljohn, 1990 WL 162018 (Ohio App.1990) the "payment" was merely a failure by the "payor" to object to garnishment of funds in which he had an interest. The discharge for value rule was applied to prevent recovery of the garnished funds because the recipient of the funds collected them to discharge a debt of another.

5. III G. Palmer, Law of Restitution § 16.6 (1978 & Supps.); Restatement of Restitution

§ 14 (1937). The defense seems to have been rejected in Firestone Tire & Rubber Co. v. Central Nat. Bank of Cleveland, 159 Ohio St. 423, 112 N.E.2d 636 (1953).

6. United Bank of Aurora v. Meaux, 761 P.2d 253 (Colo.App.1988).

7. 19 Cal.2d 748, 122 P.2d 896 (1942), also discussed in § 4.6 above.

8. Bookkeeping credits are clearly sufficient when they are irrevocable. See Equilease Corp. v. Hentz, 634 F.2d 850, 854 (5th Cir.1981). When the bookkeeping credit could be readily changed, there are still reasons to treat such credits as cash equivalents in commercial dealings. As to this, see § 11.8 below.

9. 77 N.Y.2d 362, 568 N.Y.S.2d 541, 570 N.E.2d 189 (1991) (answering a certified question). See also Banque Worms v. BankAmerica Intern., 928 F.2d 538 (2d Cir.1991) (applying the Court of Appeals decision).

spite of the stop payment. Then Spedley went into involuntary liquidation. The resulting claim was essentially a claim by Security Pacific to recover its mistaken payment to Banque Worms. Banque Worms resisted on the basis of the discharge for value rule. It had applied the payment to Spedley's debt to it, discharging Spedley to that extent. The New York Court of Appeals held that the discharge for value rule could be applied to protect Banque Worms. It was in the position of a bona fide purchaser of the money.

The example of Gaffner v. American Finance Co. In *Gaffner v. American Finance Co.,*[10] a man named Hughes stole a car in one state and took it to another, where he borrowed almost $500 by mortgaging the car. He later agreed to sell the car to Gaffner, who, as part of the deal, paid off the mortgage on the car. Later the true owner recovered the car from Gaffner, who then brought suit to recover the money he had paid to the finance company. Restitution was denied on the ground that the finance company discharged a bona fide indebtedness. Although the mortgage was void because it was not made by the owner, the thief's debt was valid, and that had been discharged by the finance company when Gaffner paid off the debt. There was no more reason to make the finance company the loser in this transaction than to make Gaffner the loser. The loss was thus left where it had fallen.

Mistaken Payment Used to Satisfy a Void Claim

In all of the examples given above, the recipient of the mistaken payment used it, in accord with the plaintiff's intention, to satisfy a valid claim against a third person. Suppose, however, the recipient of the payment uses the payment to satisfy a claim that is *not* valid. A leading case is *National Shawmut Bank v. Fidelity Mut. Life Ins. Co.,*[11] where Meissel, an insurance broker, got access to life insurance policies of Schneierson and, by forgery, borrowed money from the insurance company in Schneierson's name, using the policies as security. When the loan check arrived made out to Schneierson, Meissel forged an endorsement, cashed the check and kept the money. Schneierson knew nothing of all this. (At this point, the insurance company as lender thought it had a lien on the insurance policies owned by Schneierson. But it had no such lien, since the loan agreement was forged and absolutely void as far as Schneierson was concerned. Nor did the insurance company have any personal claim against Schneierson, since he did not agree to pay money and he did not receive any benefits from the loan.)

Some time later, Meissel, through another broker, borrowed money from a bank for the express purpose of paying off the insurance company's loan. This was again done by forging Schneierson's signature to a note and offering the policies as security. Meissel (in his role as Schneierson) authorized the bank to pay the insurance company directly from the proceeds of the loan, and the bank did so. (At this point the insurance company had been paid off and the bank held a void note to which Schneierson's name had been forged.)

10. 120 Wash. 76, 206 P. 916, 28 A.L.R. 624 (1922).

11. 318 Mass. 142, 61 N.E.2d 18, 159 A.L.R. 478 (1945).

When the bank discovered all this it sought to recover the money it had paid the insurance company on the ground that the payment had been made under a mistake induced by fraud. The bank believed it was paying a debt of Schneierson, when in fact there was no such debt. The insurer invoked the discharge for value defense, saying in effect that it was a bona fide purchaser of money, having given up its claim against Schneierson.

To this defense the Massachusetts Court answered that, since the insurance company's lien on the policies was void in any event, the company gave up nothing of value in giving up the lien. Perhaps more importantly, the company had no claim against Schneierson personally, so it gave up nothing in discharging his supposed debt. The insurer, then was "not a purchaser for value." Professor Palmer succinctly distinguishes *National Shawmut* from *Gaffner* by pointing out that the recipient of the payment in *Gaffner* did not have a valid lien but did have a valid personal claim against the thief-borrower; the recipient in *National Shawmut* on the other hand had neither a valid lien nor a valid personal claim against the person whose name was forged.[12]

The argument for restitution in *National Shawmut* is persuasive in some respects, but partly because its formal elements fit traditional lawyerly ways of thinking. A "void" claim against Schneierson seems like no claim at all, and against Schneierson that is true enough. Less formal analysis put the insurer and the bank on a par. Both paid out money, both were duped, both were innocent. Why exactly should courts prefer one over the other? Some authorities would deny restitution on *National Shawmut* facts as well as on *Gaffner* facts.[13]

Rationales and Policies

Discharge for value as a changed position rule. Some discharge for value cases may be viewed as changed position cases. *Weiner v. Roof* can be seen as a case in which the land purchaser makes a mistaken payment to an agent (bank), who then passes the payment on to his principal (land developer) by reducing the principal's debt.[14] The agent/bank/creditor is not benefitted at all because although it received a payment, it also discharged a debt claim worth an equal amount. Such a case can be viewed as a case in which the defendant has received "no benefit" at all; it got payment, but it was not unjustly enriched.[15] Such a case can also be viewed as one in which the defendant received a benefit but changed position by discharging the

---

12. III G. Palmer, Law of Restitution § 16.6, p. 494 (1978 & Supps.).

13. Restatement of Restitution § 14, Illustration 7 (1937); see III G. Palmer, Law of Restitution § 16.6, p. 494 (1978 & Supps.). In Strubbe v. Sonnenschein, 299 F.2d 185, 190, 97 A.L.R.2d 1386 (2d Cir.1962) the court said in part: "Both Metropolitan and Statford are innocent * * *. Since both were innocent parties and Stratford parted with its funds and extended its credit in reliance on the purported assignments, there is no equitable or ethical reason to consider its receipt of the funds unjust enrichment and prefer Metropolitan over Stratford in determining on whom the loss should fall. Nor is there any good reason for preferring one over the other victim of the same mistake." Professor Palmer implicitly criticizes this decision on the ground that the defendant did in fact have a valid claim against a third person. See III G. Palmer, Law of Restitution § 16.6, n. 28 (1978 & Supps.).

14. *Weiner v. Roof* was presented in this light in § 4.6 above.

15. See, taking this view, United States v. Bedford Associates, 713 F.2d 895 (2d Cir.1983) (tenant paid rent to landlord by paying landlord's mortgage; no recovery of overpayment from mortgagee because it was not enriched).

debt claim it would otherwise hold. So the discharge for value rule sometimes operates on the same facts as the changed position rule and yields the same results.

However, the discharge for value rule may go beyond the changed position rule, too. If the developer in *Weiner* had been insolvent, the bank's claim against him might be worth very little. If so, the bank's receipt of the mistaken cash payment might have been worth a great deal more than the discharge of a debt that might have been uncollectible in any event. In that case, the bank/creditor would have been enriched at least to some extent by the mistaken payment. Courts are right not to investigate the value of the right to recover from the debtor,[16] but in refusing to do so they necessarily go beyond any accurate measure of changed position.

Discharge for value as a bona fide purchaser rule. The discharge for value rule is more commonly understood as a special version of the bona fide purchaser rules,[17] or at least as a rule that expresses the same policies.[18] In *Banque Worms* when the creditor bank received Security Pacific's mistaken transfer of funds to pay Spedley's debt to it, it exchanged its right to collect the debt for the money. It "bought" the money with the debt, thus paying "value" by satisfying the antecedent debt. If the bank is not unjustly enriched it is because one is not unjustly enriched when one receives a payment due. The discharge for value rule, seen in this way as a version of the bona fide purchaser rules, also has a background in early negotiable instruments law.[19]

Policies. To some extent the discharge for value rule is congruent with unjust enrichment policies. But unjust enrichment is not itself a fact; unjust enrichment is only a perception or way of looking at facts. That perception sometimes varies with the beholder. Sometimes more significant policies are grounded in the need for stability or finality in commercial

---

16. See III G. Palmer, Law of Restitution § 16.6(b), p. 497 (1978 & Supps.).

17. Chase Manhattan Bank v. Burden, 489 A.2d 494, 497 (D.C.App.1985) (A ordered bank to pay B, who was A's creditor; bank made payment in mistaken belief that A had sufficient funds; on discovery of the error, the bank could not recover from B, who was "akin to a bona fide purchaser"); Banque Worms v. BankAmerica Intern., 77 N.Y.2d 362, 367, 568 N.Y.S.2d 541, 544, 570 N.E.2d 189, 192 (1991); Commonwealth, Dept. of Gen. Servs. v. Collingdale Millwork Co., 71 Pa.Cmwlth. 286, 454 A.2d 1176 (1983); Lincoln Nat. Life Ins. Co. v. Brown Schools, Inc., 757 S.W.2d 411 (Tex.App. 1988) (medical insurer for individual mistakenly continued to pay hospital bills after policy expired; held, no recovery against hospital, which was "in the position of a bona fide purchaser for value," citing the Restatement's discharge for value section); Restatement of Restitution § 14, Comment *a* (1937).

18. III G. Palmer, Law of Restitution § 16.5 (1978 & Supps.).

19. Price v. Neal, 3 Burr. 1354, 96 Eng. Rep. 221 (1762) developed a similar idea. A bill (somewhat like a check) purported to be drawn by one Sutton, directed Price to pay monies to Rudding. Rudding, for value, transferred the bill to Neal. Neal presented it to Price for payment, and Price paid according to its terms. Later, however, Price discovered that the bill had been forged by a man named Lee, who had by then gone on to his reward on the gallows. So Price had paid monies he did not owe under a mistake induced by fraud. Price sought to recover his mistaken payment from Neal, who had received them. But Neal himself had paid for the instrument. Lord Mansfield refused to permit Price's recovery. "It is a misfortune which has happened without the defendant's fault or neglect. If there was no neglect in the plaintiff, there is no reason to throw off the loss from one innocent man upon another innocent man." The rule is codified in the UCC § 3–418 where the recipient of the mistaken payment is a holder in due course analogous to a bona fide purchaser. The UCC provides in part that "payment or acceptance of any instrument is final in favor of a holder in due course, or a person who has in good faith changed his position in reliance on the payment."

transactions, and in particular in the need to permit money and money equivalents to flow freely.[20]   In general, these policies favor a denial of restitution based upon a payment of money in a commercial transaction, at least where that payment satisfies a claim of the recipient.

A different policy is grounded in the recognition that the law can do very little to improve matters when one of two innocent persons must bear the loss.   When the improvement is small and the cost of going to court to get it is large, it may be better to leave the loss where it falls.   In the *National Shawmut* case, for example, both the insurance company and the bank were innocent if such a state of grace properly can be attributed to corporate entities.   Meissel, the fraudfeasor, would no doubt be liable to whichever of the two suffered the ultimate loss, but in all probability persons in his position would be insolvent by the time the fraud is discovered.   The question in the case realistically, is whether the bank or the insurer should suffer the loss occasioned by Meissel's fraud.   But neither has been more at fault than the other and neither has been morally superior.

§ 4.8   The Requirement of Restoration or Tender by the Plaintiff

"At Law"

Pre-suit restoration or tender required for rescission "at law".   As this chapter shows, not all restitution involves unwinding a bargain.   When, however, restitution is given as part of unwinding a consensual transaction, as in the case of rescission, the plaintiff may be required to restore or tender what he got in the bargain as a condition of getting restitution himself.   The requirement of restoration or tender is a requirement when the plaintiff's claim is the kind which, for shorthand, is said to be "at law."   Such a requirement is not imposed when the plaintiff's suit is "in equity."

What is rescission "at law".   The rescission "at law" claim comes this way.   The plaintiff and defendant enter into a bargain which for any valid substantive reason, is subject to rescission.   For example, it might be subject to rescission for mutual mistake or because of the defendant's fraudulent representations.   When the plaintiff discovers such mistake or fraud, he may rescind by notice to the defendant that he has done so, if he also restores the defendant to what he gave in the transactions or tenders restoration.   When he has done that, the plaintiff has rescinded.[1]   If the defendant does not go

---

20. See Banque Worms v. BankAmerica Intern., 77 N.Y.2d 362, 372, 568 N.Y.S.2d 541, 547, 570 N.E.2d 189, 195 (1991).   The court said in part:

Establishing finality in electronic fund wire transactions was considered a singularly important policy goal (American Law Institute Approves UCC Article Governing Wire Transfers, 52 Banking Rep. 1150 [BNA] [June 5, 1989]).   Payments made by electronic funds transfers in compliance with the provisions of article 4A are to be the equivalent of cash payments, irrevocable except to the extent provided for in article 4A * * *.

and, quoting earlier authority,

[T]o permit in every case of the payment of a debt an inquiry as to the source from which the debtor derived the money, and a recovery if shown to have been dishonestly acquired, would disorganize all business operations and entail an amount of risk and uncertainty which no enterprise could bear.

§ 4.8

1. Savers Fed. Sav. & Loan Ass'n of Little Rock v. First Fed. Sav. & Loan Ass'n of Harrison, 298 Ark. 472, 474, 768 S.W.2d 536, 538 (1989) ("Rescission at law is accomplished when one party to a contract tenders or returns to the other party the benefits received under the contract.   It simply means a party, by his acts, rescinds the agreement * * *.   If

along, the plaintiff will then have to bring a suit to recover restitution for what the plaintiff gave to the defendant in the deal. At least if such a suit is for money or other legal relief, this is called rescission at law. If the plaintiff was right in thinking that he had grounds to rescind, the court will render an ordinary judgment for the plaintiff on the theory that because the deal is rescinded, the defendant owes the plaintiff restitution by way of replevin[2] or what used to be called assumpsit.[3] Under this "at law" procedure for restitution, the court does not effect the rescission upon which restitution is based; the plaintiff effects the rescission, and the court gives a judgment for restitution if that is needed.

What counts as a tender. In this kind of rescission at law, restoration by the plaintiff of what he received under the contract, or a tender of it and a refusal by the defendant, is normally required, simply because it would be unfair to insist that the defendant give up what he got without any assurance of getting back what he gave.[4] The tender may be conditional upon the defendant's restoring the plaintiff,[5] but, according to many courts, unless some exception applies, a tender must be made, and made "unequivocally."[6] Even a verbal offer may not qualify if some overt demonstration could be made.[7] The tender must also be made in good faith and with the

the plaintiff has adequate grounds for avoiding the transaction, his notice to the defendant that he has done so, accompanied by restoration to the defendant of benefits received by the plaintiff in the transaction, will itself amount to a rescission [at law]"); Brown v. Techdata Corp., Inc., 238 Ga. 622, 626, 234 S.E.2d 787, 791 (1977) ("In the rescission 'at law' the tender itself effectuates the rescission" after which plaintiff is "entitled to recover back the amount of the purchase price actually paid by him").

2. Thayer v. Turner, 49 Mass. (8 Metc.) 550 (1844).

3. Philpott v. Superior Court, 1 Cal.2d 512, 36 P.2d 635, 95 A.L.R. 990 (1934).

4. E.g., Metro Chrysler–Plymouth, Inc. v. Pearce, 121 Ga.App. 835, 175 S.E.2d 910 (1970) (car dealer sought to "rescind" sale of new car by repossessing the car without tendering buyer's trade-in car, tender is essential to rescission); Thayer v. Turner, 49 Mass. (8 Metc.) 550 (1844) (restoration or tender of it to the defendant must be made before a suit at law is commenced, plaintiff's action in replevin could not succeed without proof of this or waiver by the defendant); Perry v. Woodall, 20 Utah 2d 399, 438 P.2d 813 (1968).

5. Restatement of Restitution § 65, Comment *d* (1937). In Jeppson v. Jeppson, 75 Idaho 219, 270 P.2d 437 (1954) a land purchaser was allowed to rescind for fraud by tendering back a deed but remaining in possession as security for his own right of restitution. But some decisions would permit rescission by one who retains possession of land only if an "exception" is found. See Tanner v. McClure, 259 Ala. 142, 65 So.2d 709 (1952).

This procedure can risk an adverse election of remedies ruling later if it proves ineffective for any reason. See §§ 9.4 & 12.7(6) below. It can also risk a ruling that the tender was "equivocal" and of no effect.

6. Unequivocal and complete are words often used to emphasize insistence upon making a perfect offer of restoration. See Cruickshank v. Griswold, 81 R.I. 468, 471, 104 A.2d 551, 552 (1954). The attorney there wrote, after claiming to rescind: "Upon the payment of $1350 [his client's purchase price] to this office, I shall deliver to you a deed signed by Mr. and Mrs. Cruickshank conveying the land in question back to you." The court: "It did not amount to a definite and unequivocal tender * * *."

7. In Anson v. Grace, 174 Neb. 258, 260–261, 117 N.W.2d 529, 531 (1962) purchasers of real estate alleged fraud and sent the vendors a "notice of rescission," which said, after asserting a rescission: "[T]he undersigned hereby offer to reconvey such property to you and to restore everything of value which they have received from you, and to surrender the possession of said properties and to do and perform all acts and things which might be necessary or proper in order fully to restore to you all the properties and things of value * * *." The court: "[N]either by pleading nor evidence is it made to appear that the [purchasers] by their notice of rescission or otherwise ever tendered back to plaintiffs the property in its condition at the time the notice was given; and likewise no offer was made to restore it to its original condition and return it." Apparently the court felt that a deed should have been tendered.

present ability to make it good.[8] It is often said also that the tender must be kept good, that is, the plaintiff's ability to back up his offer must continue.

"In Equity"

Pre-suit tender or restoration not required for rescission "in equity".
Rescission in equity is a very different matter. Plaintiffs are frequently permitted to resort to equity courts for a rescission without much serious concern for the usual rule that equity jurisdiction is based upon the inadequacy of a legal remedy.[9] In equity the suit is not *on* rescission, but *for* rescission,[10] it is not a suit based upon the rescission already accomplished by the plaintiff, but a suit to have the court decree a rescission.[11]

Such a suit has many advantages, one of which is that the plaintiff need not guess about his legal rights to rescind, but can instead submit his demand to the court for decision. Obviously enough, this affects his obligation to make restoration. Since rescission is not accomplished "in equity" until the court so decrees, the plaintiff has no obligation before suit to make restitution of goods or money he received from the defendant.[12] In the equitable rescission cases it is sometimes said that the plaintiff should tender or offer restoration in his complaint, or show an ability to make restoration, but even this seems doubtful because of the court's capacity to protect the defendant by its decree and to condition rescission upon full restoration.[13]

Restoration ultimately determined at trial in equity rescission. This does not mean that the plaintiff is entitled to get back what he gave and keep what he got, too. It means only that he need not make formal tender before suit. Once the matter proceeds to trial, the judge must act to assure that each party is restored to his pre-contract position, at least as far as possible to do so.[14]

---

8. Bennett v. Emerald Serv., Inc., 157 Neb. 176, 59 N.W.2d 171 (1953) (buyer sought to rescind, offered to restore, and his offer was refused; however, offer was insufficient because he had mortgaged the item in question and could not restore it unmortgaged).

9. Rescission at law seems clearly inadequate if the rules stated above apply to hamper it. Laycock deals with rescission in equity in connection with harms resulting from uncertainty and regards both cancellation of instruments and rescission in this light. See D. Laycock, The Death of the Irreparable Injury Rule 80 (1991). In general courts have not bothered much with the adequacy issue when the plaintiff seeks rescission in equity, but there are exceptions. E.g., Laubengayer v. Rohde, 167 Mich. 605, 133 N.W. 535 (1911) (rescission at law adequate); cf. Brown v. Techdata Corp., Inc., 238 Ga. 622, 234 S.E.2d 787 (1977) (seemingly suggesting that tender is required before proceeding in equity as a means of showing that legal remedy is inadequate).

10. "He may bring an action in equity to rescind the contract, and in that action may have full relief. Such an action does not

proceed as upon a rescission, but proceeds for a rescission." Gould v. Cayuga County Nat. Bank, 86 N.Y. 75, 83 (1881).

11. See Masters v. Van Wart, 125 Me. 402, 134 A. 539 (1926); Annot., 105 A.L.R. 1003 (1936).

12. Knaebel v. Heiner, 663 P.2d 551 (Alaska 1983); Kracl v. Loseke, 236 Neb. 290, 461 N.W.2d 67 (1990); Lightner v. Karnatz, 258 Mich. 74, 77, 241 N.W. 841, 842 (1932) ("Restoration or tender before suit is a necessary element in legal rescission, but is wholly superfluous as a prerequisite to the commencement of a suit in equity for rescission or cancellation").

13. Compare Parker v. Baltimore Paint & Chem. Corp., 244 F.Supp. 267 (D.Colo.1965) (the court first thought a clear tender was required) *with* the decision on further motions in 39 F.R.D. 567 (D.Colo.1966) (the court recognized that no such thing was required because the court itself could condition and limit relief as needed).

14. E.g., Gnuse v. Garrett, 129 Neb. 265, 261 N.W. 143 (1935).

Qualifications to the Requirement of Tender at Law

Items the plaintiff is entitled to keep. Even the rigid rule of restoration at law has qualifications and exceptions. The first and most obvious is that the plaintiff who rescinds "at law" is not obliged to restore what he is in any event entitled to keep. For example, under the traditional rule an infant is permitted to rescind without restoring any property he obtained that had been destroyed.[15] Other rules forgive the obligation to restore or allow the plaintiff to substitute money for the goods he received.[16] When any of these rules apply, the tender requirement is adjusted accordingly.

Where tender would be useless. Some exceptions also relate to the uselessness of tender. The plaintiff need not tender back what he got in the transaction if it is utterly worthless,[17] or if the defendant would have refused it anyway,[18] or if he has offsetting money claims against the defendant in excess of the money he is obliged to restore.[19]

Amounts to be tendered indeterminate. In many rescission cases it is not really possible for either party to ascertain the amount to be restored to the other. For instance, during the period before avoidance of the contract, a purchaser will have had the use of goods or land and the seller will have been deprived of such a use. The seller, on the other hand, will have had the use of the purchaser's money and the purchaser will have been deprived of it. Rescission will require not only a restoration of the land to the seller and the money to the buyer, but also some adjustment for the use of the land and the use of the money, on each side. It will seldom be possible to identify before trial the amount of money that ought to be paid for the use of the land. Hence, if the rescission, whether at law or equity, involves the necessity for restoring unliquidated amounts, one cannot expect accurate restoration or tender. Thus, at least where there is fraud, some of the cases have even excused the plaintiff from tendering interest on a liquidated sum.[20] Although most of the cases involving the more complex adjustments and credits on both sides are probably brought for "equitable rescission," in which case no tender should be required in any event, courts would probably excuse the plaintiff's failure to make accurate offer of restoration even if the rescission were "at law" where such unliquidated sums are involved.

Where the adjustment remedy is not rescission. Finally, not all undoings or adjustments between the parties count as rescission. Termination of a contract or lease under a valid forfeiture clause is not a rescission, and the plaintiff in such a case is entitled to keep what is validly forfeited; no

---

15. See § 13.4(2) below.

16. For example, if the plaintiff cannot make restoration because defects which the defendant fraudulently concealed have now destroyed the property or made it inaccessible. Liland v. Tweto, 19 N.D. 551, 125 N.W. 1032 (1910); cf. Limoli v. Accettullo, 358 Mass. 381, 265 N.E.2d 92 (1970).

17. Nelson Realty Co. v. Darling Shop of Birmingham, Inc., 267 Ala. 301, 101 So.2d 78 (1957).

18. See Bennett v. Emerald Serv., Inc., 157 Neb. 176, 59 N.W.2d 171 (1953) (defendant would have refused but plaintiff did not have present ability to make restoration anyway; the present ability rule prevails, rescission denied).

19. Nuttall v. Holman, 110 Utah 375, 173 P.2d 1015 (1946); but see Block v. Block, 165 Ohio St. 365, 135 N.E.2d 857 (1956).

20. See Watson v. Bugg, 365 Mo. 191, 280 S.W.2d 67, 53 A.L.R.2d 743 (1955) (personal injury release, plaintiff tendered back amount received without interest, tender was sufficient, at least where basis for rescission was fraud).

rescission is involved at all.[21] A breach of warranty by a seller might justify relief without requiring restoration by the plaintiff.[22]

Reform of the Tender Rules

Tender rules are being reformed. A federal statute aimed at consumer credit protection permits a consumer to rescind a loan transaction in some circumstances, and puts the burden on the consumer to tender restoration of the loan proceeds only after the lender has appropriately released the consumer of liability.[23] Some states, by statute [24] or by court decision,[25] have reformed the tender rules by abandoning the requirement altogether and leaving all adjustments to the court.

This simpler approach is especially congruent with the merger of law and equity. Indeed, it has been said that because of that merger, there is no further need for the distinction between rescission at law and rescission in equity, because any court could issue a conditional judgment to protect the defendant's legitimate right to restoration.[26] This seems correct. Upon whatever theory the suit for rescission is brought, any court of general jurisdiction has both the law and equity powers necessary to condition and relief to make it fair to both parties.

There may be a few instances of provisional relief in which a tender should be required (or relief denied) because judicial supervision may come too late. Suppose, for example, the seller of a car decides to rescind the contract and get his car back. He brings a replevin action for this purpose and posts a bond, which will allow him to get possession of it. If this is permitted, the buyer has lost possession without an opportunity to get back what he gave in the transaction. He will be both without the car he bought and without the money he used to buy it; he may be required to bring a separate suit to enforce his restitutionary claim, to the additional burden of the judicial system. A rule requiring the seller to tender a return of the buyer's money before such a suit would be a welcome protection because under the traditional system of replevin the judge took no part in the initial repossession and could give the buyer no protection. Even here tender rules may not be necessary because the reform of replevin statutes under the

21. See §§ 12.13 & 12.15 (installment land sales and forfeitures and lease forfeitures respectively).

22. Cf. Phillips v. Ripley & Fletcher Co., 541 A.2d 946 (Me.1988).

23. 15 U.S.C.A. § 1635(b) ("Upon the performance of the creditor's obligations under this section, the obligor shall tender the property to the creditor, except that if return of the property in kind would be impracticable or inequitable, the obligor shall tender its reasonable value").

24. NY—McKinney's CPLR 3004. The tender requirement is sometimes eliminated especially for the purpose of certain consumer protection legislation. E.g., 14A Okl.Stat. Ann. § 5–204(2) (Uniform Consumer Credit Code).

25. Nab v. Hills, 92 Idaho 877, 884, 452 P.2d 981, 988 (1969) ("we believe that the

necessity for restoration of benefits prior to maintaining an action or defense based on fraud is an outmoded concept, the effect of which is to further injure the innocent party").

26. See P. Keeton, Cases on Fraud and Mistake 487 (1954). The idea that separate equity powers are a part of the natural order of the universe dies hard. An old New York decision, now happily obsolete because of statutory reform, asserted that it was

idle to say that the distinction between legal and equitable actions has been wiped out by modern practice * * *. [T]he distinction between legal and equitable actions is as fundamental as that between actions *ex contractu* and *ex delicto,* and no legislative fiat can wipe it out.

Gould v. Cayuga County Nat. Bank, 86 N.Y. 75, 83 (1881).

impact of constitutional decisions may put the judge in the picture at an early stage.[27] If so, the judge can make provision as needed for appropriate restoration.

Measure of Restoration Required of the Plaintiff

If tender is required, what is it that must be tendered? If it is not required, what is it that the judge will require to be restored?

The general rule, entirely distinct from the tender requirement, is that the plaintiff must, at some point, whether before or after the judgment or decree, make restoration to the defendant of whatever the plaintiff himself received in the transaction between them. If he received tangible items of property, such as land or chattels, he is ordinarily required to make restoration in specie.[28] No such requirement can be imposed where he has received services rather than tangible goods, and in that case, he makes restoration by substituting money value for the services and restoring that.[29]

It is often difficult to be certain what a plaintiff who is himself entitled to restitution must restore or in what form the restoration must be made. Rules stated too firmly can be misleading here. Suppose the plaintiff has purchased insurance and paid premiums, then seeks restitution of the premiums because of a substantial breach by the insurer. If it is felt that the plaintiff was insured until the insurer's breach, the plaintiff has received something which he must restore if he is to get restitution of his premiums. If, additionally, it is felt that the value of what he received—coverage—is equal to the premiums paid in, he will recover nothing.[30] Most courts have recognized in this situation, however, that it is unfair to deny recovery altogether, and that restitution of premiums could be permitted, perhaps less as a matter of unjust enrichment and more as a matter of policy, or as a convenient surrogate measure of damages for breach of the insurance contract.[31]

Where the plaintiff finds it impossible to make restoration in specie in the case of tangible benefits, as for example, because the property he received has been transferred or destroyed, he is sometimes allowed to substitute money values for the property and make his restoration in money, especially if the ground for rescission and restitution lies in the defendant's fraud. Whether such a substitutionary restoration will suffice will depend on several factors, such as the defendant's fault or lack of it, the adequacy of other remedies available to the plaintiff, and the nature of the inability to restore. These are discussed in more detail elsewhere, particularly in connection with the problem of rescission for fraud.[32]

27. See § 5.17 below.

28. Restatement of Restitution § 66 (1937).

29. Restatement of Restitution § 66, Comment *d* (1937).

30. Some cases have so held. See Watson v. Massachusetts Mut. Life Ins. Co., 78 U.S.App.D.C. 248, 140 F.2d 673 (1943), cert. denied, 322 U.S. 746, 64 S.Ct. 1156, 88 L.Ed. 1578 (1944).

31. "As to the measure of damages * * * where the insurer has breached the contract [it] is the amount of premiums paid, or premiums with interest where there has been a wrongful repudiation of the contract by the insurer. This is the majority rule." Kentucky Home Mut. Life Ins. Co. v. Rogers, 196 Tenn. 641, 644–645, 270 S.W.2d 188, 190 (1954). See Annotation, 34 A.L.R.3d 245 (1970).

32. See § 9.3(3) below.

§ 4.9 Unsolicited Benefits—Volunteers and Intermeddlers [1]

§ 4.9(1) Rule, Background and Summary

Factual Context

In many cases the plaintiff confers a benefit which the defendant did not seek and for which he did not bargain. Unsolicited benefits may be conferred in cases of mistake, as where the plaintiff erroneously pays the defendant monies [2] or builds her house on the defendant's lot. [3] They may also be conferred intentionally, as where the plaintiff repairs the defendant's fire-damaged roof in the defendant's absence, [4] cares for a neighbor during years of illness, [5] or builds a road that gives access to the defendant's house as well as the plaintiff's. [6] In these cases and in a splendid variety of others, the defendant or the neighbor is enriched, but he did not seek the enrichment and may not want it.

This section considers when the plaintiff can recover in spite of the fact that the benefits were unsolicited. Even if the plaintiff is not barred from recovery on the ground that benefits were unsolicited, she may be barred for other reasons, such as the defendant's changed position. [7] So the question here is whether to deny recovery even when the defendant has not changed position by passing on the benefit or otherwise.

Denial of Restitution to "Volunteers and Intermeddlers"

If there is a black-letter rule for unsolicited benefits it is that "volunteers" [8] and "officious intermeddlers" [9] cannot recover restitution. The Restatement says a volunteer is one who confers a benefit without mistake, coercion or request. [10]

Both the rule and its terms may be misleading. The mistaken plaintiff is not always allowed to recover unsolicited benefits, [11] and the plaintiff who

---

§ 4.9(1)

1. The leading general works on materials covered in this section are II G. Palmer, Law of Restitution Ch. 10 (1978 & Supps.); Restatement of Restitution (1937); Dawson, The Self-Serving Intermeddler, 87 Harv.L.Rev. 1409 (1974); Dawson, Negotiorum Gestio: The Altruistic Intermeddler, 74 Harv.L.Rev. 817 (1961); Levmore, Explaining Restitution, 71 Va.L.Rev. 65 (1985); Wade, Restitution for Benefits Conferred without Request, 19 Vand. L.Rev. 1183 (1966).

2. See § 4.9(3) below.

3. See § 4.9(5) below.

4. Berry v. Barbour, 279 P.2d 335 (Okl. 1954); see § 4.9(5) below.

5. See § 4.9(4) below.

6. Dinosaur Dev., Inc. v. White, 216 Cal. App.3d 1310, 265 Cal.Rptr. 525 (1989); see § 4.9(4) below.

7. See § 4.6 above. The volunteers defense discussed in this section is closely related to the change of position defense; both rest in part on respect for the defendant's autonomy or right of choice; both attempt to recognize hardships to the defendant.

8. E.g., Glanz Contracting Co. v. General Elec. Co., 379 So.2d 912, 917 (Miss.1980) ("[A] voluntary payment can not be recovered back"); Martin v. Little, Brown and Co., 304 Pa.Super. 424, 431, 450 A.2d 984, 988 (1981) ("As a general rule, volunteers have no right to restitution * * *. Appellant was a volunteer. It was he who made the unsolicited suggestion" resulting in benefit to the defendant).

9. Restatement of Restitution § 2 (1937). "Officiousness" says the Restatement, "means interference in the affairs of others not justified by the circumstances * * *." Id., Comment *a*.

10. Restatement of Restitution § 112 (1937).

11. For example, mistaken builders on the land of others, as in Producers Lumber & Supply Co. v. Olney Bldg. Co., 333 S.W.2d 619 (Tex.Civ.App.1960); see §§ 4.9(5) & 5.8(3) below. The text does not imply that all mistakes are equal or alike. Sometimes the plaintiff's mistake is such that she believes she is conferring no benefit upon anyone else, as where she builds a house thinking the land

is not mistaken sometimes is.[12] The terms of the rule—"volunteer," "intermeddler," "officious"—are usually regarded as equivalent to one another, but they may suggest the wrong inquiry. The defense does not really turn in most cases on the plaintiff's meddlesome attitude as "officiousness" might suggest, nor upon his intention to voluntarily give up legal rights, as "volunteer" suggests. On top of this, some decisions deal with unsolicited benefits without ever mentioning the rule.[13] To a large extent the terms are merely conclusory aphorisms; they are alternate and easy ways of stating the end result, not reasons for that result.[14]

Arguing and Resolving Cases

For these reasons unsolicited benefit cases can seldom be resolved in an intelligible way by adverting to the volunteers rule alone. Particular cases can be resolved by one of two strategies. First, the underlying principles or policies can be identified and then applied to the facts of the case; or second, rules for particular kinds of cases might be located and applied. Both methods are summarized here and then considered separately in the subsections that follow.

Unifying Principles

The unsolicited benefits cases treated as a unit may yield "surprising results and inconsistent maxims" as one commentator says.[15] Some cases do indeed seem to lose sight of governing principles, and conflicting demands of principle may produce some divergent results. There are, however, consistent currents and meaningful principles. In their light, the decisions as a whole provide a core of understandable applications.

Many of the cases and particular practices make sense if understood as a judicial effort to respect the defendant's autonomy or rights of choice and self-determination, and at the same time to minimize his unjust enrichment. In close cases, the plaintiff's moral posture—whether he was meddling or acting with bad motives—may be important,[16] but frequently this is not the issue. In attempting to effectuate these ideals, courts have implicitly recognized that not all benefits are alike, and restitution is better ordered for some kinds of benefits than for others. So inevitably the cases must be factually categorized to some degree.

is her own when it is not. Sometimes the plaintiff knows she is conferring a benefit but mistakenly believes that the benefit is conferred upon the person with whom she has contracted when in fact the benefit goes to someone who never agreed to pay.

12. E.g., Trustees v. Greenough, 105 U.S. (15 Otto) 527, 26 L.Ed. 1157 (1881) (lawyers fees payable from common fund so that all beneficiaries of litigation share in fee), discussed in §§ 3.10(2) above & 4.9(6) below; Leebov v. United States Fidelity & Guar. Co., 401 Pa. 477, 165 A.2d 82 (1960), discussed in § 4.9(4) below.

13. E.g., Callano v. Oakwood Park Homes Corp., 91 N.J.Super. 105, 219 A.2d 332 (1966) (defendant held to be enriched by unsolicited benefits, but not unjustly).

14. Because it is easy to call a plaintiff a volunteer and hard to attack that conclusion, a decision-maker may find it convenient to invoke the "volunteers" rule to justify the results in the case, especially if everyone would agree on the result and would not be much tempted to argue about reasons. The easier the case, the easier it is to give a bad reason or, in the case of "volunteers," a non-reason. Easy cases make bad law.

15. Levmore, Explaining Restitution, 71 Va.L.Rev. 65 (1985).

16. E.g., cases in which the plaintiff pays another's debt in an effort to get control of that other's property by mortgage foreclosure or the like. See Stein v. Simpson, 37 Cal.2d 79, 85, 230 P.2d 816, 821 (1951), discussed in § 4.9(3) below.

Categorizing Cases

The trouble with categorizing cases is that too many categories can be found. Cases can be categorized, for instance, according to the kind of benefit conferred (services, cash, property), or according to the plaintiff's motive or reason for conferring the benefit, or according to the ability of the parties to bargain or not. This introduction is not the place to work through the classification process. Several general observations may point to some possibilities, however.

(1) Restitution is usually easier to recover for benefits conferred in cash or cash equivalents.[17] The plaintiff mistakenly overpays the telephone bill by $100. He is entitled to recover the $100.

(2) Restitution is relatively difficult to recover where the benefit intentionally conferred is neither cash nor a cash equivalent *and* where the parties are in position to bargain in advance. In this setting, the parties' implicit understandings are often most important. These implicit understandings include those revealed by the parties' failure to provide for payment. The plaintiff notifies a publisher that T is infringing the publisher's copyright in a certain book. The publisher enjoins T's infringement and recovers damages from T. The information plaintiff provided has thus been useful to the publisher, but the publisher does not owe the plaintiff restitution.[18] Restitution will be proper in submission-of-idea cases only if the plaintiff submits a useful idea with the understanding that he will be paid if it is used and in circumstances that permit the defendant to reject its use, may call for compensation because the parties so understand.[19]

(3) Restitution is troubling and the cases divided when the plaintiff does not intend to confer a benefit upon the defendant *and* there is no opportunity to bargain *and* the benefit is not in cash. The plaintiff builds her home on the defendant's lot by mistake. Nothing else appearing, traditional authority refuses to permit restitution to the plaintiff,[20] but a number of contemporary cases allow it.[21]

§ 4.9(2) Underlying Principles in Unsolicited Benefit Cases

Incidental Reasons for Denying Relief

Sometimes restitution should be denied for reasons that bear only an indirect relationship to the volunteers rule or to the fact that benefits were unsolicited. For example, even if the volunteers rule does not prohibit recovery, the change of position rule might do so. The common elements of the two rules might cause some confusion; the volunteers rule might be invoked when the issues would be more coherently analyzed under the

---

17. See § 4.9(3) below. Perhaps arguably, a benefit that is not initially in cash should be treated as a cash benefit once it is realized in cash by the recipient. Two major exceptions occur when the benefit is payment of another's debt without "justification," and overpayment of taxes.

18. Martin v. Little, Brown and Co., 304 Pa.Super. 424, 431, 450 A.2d 984, 988 (1981), discussed in § 4.9(4) below.

19. For more detail on submission-of-idea cases, see § 6.5(2) below.

20. E.g., Foltz v. Alford, 102 Ark. 191, 143 S.W. 905 (1912); §§ 4.9(5), 5.8(3) below.

21. E.g., Somerville v. Jacobs, 153 W.Va. 613, 170 S.E.2d 805 (1969); §§ 4.9(5) & 5.8(3) below.

changed position rule. This section attempts to focus solely on reasons, apart from changed position, that bear on grant or denial of restitution for unsolicited benefits.

Economic and Moral Reasons

Apart from the defendant's changed position, why do courts hesitate to grant restitution for unsolicited benefits? More than one principled explanation can be given. Economic analysis may suggest such policies as "market encouragement" as well as others.[1] Some cases (but not so many) might be explained by a moral analysis that focuses on the plaintiff's bad purposes or attitude, or conversely on his lack of enterprising purpose.

Personal Autonomy: the Defendant's Right of Free Choice

Underlying most of the cases, however, seems to be a strong double commitment to prevent unjust enrichment on the one hand and to protect the defendant's right of free choice on the other. Where the defendant has a right to choose for himself whether to receive a benefit, and where restitution would deprive him of this choice by requiring payment for a "benefit" the defendant may not want, restitution is often denied. The right of self-determination through personal choices—that is, personal autonomy—is central to personal being and growth as well as to the concept of a free society.

Respect for the individual's autonomy is not limited to volunteer cases or even to restitution. It can be seen throughout the law. For example, tort rules of informed consent attempt to respect the patient's rights to decide on medical procedures for himself by assuring relevant information.[2] Property rules attempt to respect the owner's rights by holding that title cannot be changed without his consent, no matter how innocent the buyer. On the remedial side, damages rules also reflect the same principle. For instance, if a defendant negligently destroys the plaintiff's garden, the defendant is liable even if the harm does not affect the land's market value; the damages rule is constructed to reflect the plaintiff's own personal valuations and choices.[3] Similarly, the plaintiff who sues for breach of the defendant's contract is not to have damages reduced for "benefits" he does not want.[4]

Free Choice in Non-consensual Transactions

The easiest cases for restitution of unsolicited benefits are those in which the plaintiff mistakenly gives the defendant cash or a specific chattel.

---

§ 4.9(2)

1. Levmore, Explaining Restitution, 71 Va. L.Rev. 65 (1985).

2. In the informed consent setting it is easier to see that one value is the right to decide for oneself. Doctors on the whole are better decision makers than patients, but it is the patient's body and the patient's decision. Similarly in the unsolicited benefit cases, the right to decide for oneself when to make an improvement, who to hire for it, how to arrange payment, what form the liability should take, and where payment is to be made are rights that go with freedom. Even if the landowner would have made the same improvement that the volunteer made, the landowner's right to decide for himself deserves respect.

3. See § 5.2(2) below.

4. Handicapped Children's Education Bd. of Sheboygan County v. Lukaszewski, 112 Wis.2d 197, 332 N.W.2d 774 (1983) (defendant teacher-defendant breached, school was forced to hire a better qualified teacher at a higher salary, school could recover the higher cost even though it "got more;" it did not "want more").

In the absence of a changed position, the defendant's autonomy or right of choice is simply not involved when he returns the cash or the identical chattel. So in that case the unjust enrichment principle prevails because the autonomy principle simply does not come into play.

One of the hardest tests for the autonomy principle occurs with the mistaken improver. I cannot paint your house, knowing it is yours and knowing we have no agreement, and then recover compensation. You have the right to choose for yourself whether to have your house painted. If I paint it by mistake, my moral position is stronger but it would still impair your right of choice if you were forced to pay. My attitude or motive is important in judging my character but not in judging your right of choice. The limits of the autonomy principle are tested when you are enriched by my acts, I acted under a forgivable mistake, and my motive is not bad.

Choice in Contracts and Consensual Transactions

When the parties engage in a consensual transaction, the concern for the defendant's autonomy becomes a concern for the joint autonomy of the parties or their choices as expressed in their contract or understanding. Respect for the joint autonomy of the parties requires courts to respect the risk-allocations of the contract or understanding, including those allocated by silence. The most obvious application of this point is that when the plaintiff intends to make a gift of the benefits, as where a neighbor helps you put out a grass fire, restitution for the value of her efforts is improper because courts should respect the making and acceptance of a gift.

Almost as obviously, respect for the contract means that the plaintiff cannot recover restitution of benefits to which the defendant was entitled under the contract. Even if the plaintiff mistakenly confers benefits under a contract, restitution is inappropriate when the contract allocated the risk of mistake to the plaintiff.[5] The failure of the contract to provide for liability may itself point to a decision against liability. So we see courts saying that restitution will be denied when the parties have a contract on the same subject matter.[6] When the parties are in a consensual or bargaining relationship, then, the most central element in deciding on restitution lies in the parties' own understandings. The plaintiff cannot seek compensation for benefits she gave without charge, or more compensation than she agreed to accept.[7] Interpreting the parties' understanding is not easy; allocation of

---

5. See Indianapolis Raceway Park, Inc. v. Curtiss, 179 Ind.App. 557, 386 N.E.2d 724 (1979); Salamon v. Terra, 394 Mass. 857, 477 N.E.2d 1029, 1032 (1985) (plaintiff built houses on defendant's land under contract contemplating sale of improved land to third parties; neither party expected defendant to pay for improvements on his land, and when houses could not be sold in contract period, plaintiff was not entitled to recover value of improvements from defendant as the express contract showed no such thing was contemplated).

6. E.g., City of Indianapolis v. Twin Lakes Enterprises, Inc., 568 N.E.2d 1073, 1079 (Ind. App.1991) ("As a general rule, there can be no constructive contract where there is an express contract between the parties in refer- ence to the same subject matter"); Julien J. Studley, Inc. v. New York News, Inc., 70 N.Y.2d 628, 518 N.Y.S.2d 779, 512 N.E.2d 300 (1987) (no implied-in-fact contract when an express contract on the same subject matter).

7. When the defendant breaches or the deal is called off, restitution in excess of the price is usually said to be recoverable. As to this see § 12.7(5) below. When the deal is not called off but the plaintiff must do more work than expected (hence in a sense confers more benefits), risk allocations of the parties be- come critical. In an excavation contract, for example, did the parties intend to allocate to the plaintiff the full cost of completing the work, regardless of unexpected difficulties? Or only the full cost of completing the work if

risks is often implicit or vague or even temporary. But if the parties have allocated risks by expression, implication, or silence, their choices should govern and restitution should not be awarded inconsistent with those choices.

Limits of Choice

Respect for the defendant's autonomy does not mean that restitution must always be denied. No one has unlimited choices. I cannot chose to park my car in the parking space already occupied by your car. I cannot (legally) choose to refuse food for my minor children. When the defendant's choice is limited by law or fact, restitution may not interfere with any choice he legally or practically has. For example, if the defendant refuses to feed his children and I do so in his stead, I may have restitution for the benefits I have conferred upon him by performing his duty.[8] Restitution in such a case does not interfere with any choice the defendant rightfully has.

Sometimes restitution for unsolicited benefits may be permissible because the defendant is in a position to reject the benefit. If he can either accept the benefit and pay for it or reject the benefit altogether, no significant right of choice is involved. The same is true if the benefit is liquidated; restitution of a cash overpayment to the defendant, in the absence of a change of position, does not interfere with any legitimate right of choice.

Limits of Principle

The autonomy principle does not explain all the cases. One or two lines of cases may be wrong (and may be on the way out as authority, too) or at least explicable only on the basis of some other grounds. Other cases, however, simply refuse to give primacy to the autonomy principle when it comes into conflict with too many other demands. Both kinds of deviation are considered in connection with the discussion of particular factual settings below.

§ 4.9(3) Benefits in Cash or Specific Chattels

When the plaintiff confers unsolicited benefits upon another person in the form of cash (or specific recoverable chattels to which the plaintiff retains title), he is usually able to recover restitution. Although the benefit in such cases is unsolicited, recovery of cash does not affect any right of choice in the defendant.[1] The defendant might have defenses that would bar restitution, but they would be based on changed position or on the plaintiff's

conditions proved to be those supposed by the parties? Recovery beyond the contract price here depends on how the risks were allocated by the parties. See Galligan, Extra Work in Construction Cases: Restitution, Relationship, and Revision, 63 Tulane L.Rev. 799 (1989); § 12.20(2) below.

8. Restatement of Restitution § 113 (1937) (performing another's non-contractual duty to supply necessaries).

§ 4.9(3)

1. A similar idea, embedded in an economic analysis of the unsolicited benefit problem,

can be seen in Levmore, Explaining Restitution, 71 Va.L.Rev. 65, 74–79 (1985) (discussing "wealth dependency" and taste as factors that might make defendant unwilling to "buy" a benefit, noting that the problem "disappears and restitution need not be denied where the nonbargained benefit is easily translated into wealth," id. at 77, and giving cash benefits as an example).

inequitable conduct, not on the volunteers rule. Even when the defendant has not proved a change of position, some exceptions prevent the plaintiff's recovery of cash overpayments; but these turn upon other considerations entirely, such as a desire to protect or overprotect governmental entities that have collected too much for taxes.

Restitution Generally Allowed

Mistaken cash payments. The general principles discussed above appear to mean that the defendant is not required to restore non-cash benefits by paying cash. To do that would be forcing the defendant to "buy" the benefit. But if the benefit conferred upon the defendant is in the form of cash or cash equivalents,[2] restitution does not infringe his right of choice. He is not being forced to buy a benefit he may not want but on the contrary is asked to return it. The cases are in accord with this view; they allow restitution of mistaken cash payments or overpayments in the absence of some independent reason to deny it.[3] Changed position, discharge for value, or a special policy in favor of finality in the transaction might all be good reasons to deny restitution, but those grounds are connected to the unsolicited character of the benefit only by a factual thread, not by the web of reason.

Specific chattels. Suppose the plaintiff owns a TV set. He intends to give it to Haley, but the delivery service takes to it Williams instead. Getting restitution of the specific chattel from Williams creates no legal problem. Title has not passed. Williams is obliged to give up the TV set in a replevin suit.[4] Even if he has changed position by giving the set away or otherwise, he will be liable in money. If he sells it for a very favorable price, he will be liable to make restitution of the sale price.[5] So in cases of specific chattels, restitution is the usual and very standard rule.

Such cases work under the general choice principles in exactly the same way that mistaken cash payments work. The defendant in returning the chattel is not being asked to buy a benefit he may not want, only to return the one he has. When he changes position by giving or selling the TV set, there are good reasons to argue that he should escape liability for restitution, but that would turn on changed position or some other defense. The cases awarding restitution of cash and specific chattels are in accord with each other and with the defendant's right of choice.

Contribution for cotenant improvements later realized in cash. Forms of shared ownership of property give rise to several different kinds of claims for restitution by way of contribution from other owners for improvements or payments made by one.[6] The case of cotenant improvements illustrates the difference between a cash and a non-cash benefit. Suppose one cotenant improves the shared property, adding to its book value by the improvements.

---

2. What is equivalent to cash is a question of what is so accepted commercially. A credit to one's account at the bank would suffice.

3. E.g., Dickens v. First Am. Title Ins. Co. of Ariz., 162 Ariz. 511, 784 P.2d 717 (App. 1989).

The general rule permitting restitution for mistaken payments rests on this idea. See § 11.7 below.

4. See § 4.2(2) above.

5. This is the so-called waiver of tort introduced earlier in this chapter. See §§ 4.2(3) & 4.1 above.

6. See II G. Palmer, Law of Restitution § 10.7(c) (1978 & Supps.).

The other cotenant does not agree to the improvement and, since he has no realized gain, he is not liable to contribute.[7] When the tenancy is later partitioned and sold, so that cash is produced,[8] however, the improver reaps restitution for the improvement costs he bore.[9] This does not mean that later-realized cash will always result in liability,[10] but in the joint-ownership instance represented by cotenants, it does.

Restitution Sometimes Denied

In two groups of cases especially, restitution may be denied in spite of the fact that the benefit was conferred in the form of cash. Both, however, turn on special considerations only fortuitously connected to the unsolicited nature of the benefit.

Payment of another's debt. When, without request, the plaintiff knowingly pays a debt owed by the defendant to a third person, *T,* the plaintiff is traditionally denied any recovery of restitution [11] unless he was acting under mistake,[12] compulsion or legal duty [13] or for reasons of justifiable self-interest.[14] If the plaintiff can justify his payment, he may be subrogated to the creditor's claim. For example, if the plaintiff was defendant's surety on a note and was called upon to pay the creditor when the defendant defaulted, the plaintiff will stand in the shoes of the creditor and can enforce the note against the defendant.[15] In most cases he could also pay the debt and

7. Collier v. Collier, 73 Ariz. 405, 242 P.2d 537 (1952) (lien on the property for contribution to the improvement but no personal judgment); Higgins v. Eva, 204 Cal. 231, 267 P. 1081 (1928); II G. Palmer, Law of Restitution § 10.7(c) (1978 & Supps.); Dawson, The Self-Serving Intermeddler, 87 Harv.L.Rev. 1409, 1424 (1974).

8. Levmore, Explaining Restitution, 71 Va. L.Rev. 65, 70, 83 (1985) agrees that the case for restitution is strong because the benefit is "easily or already monetized," but gives a more complex analysis.

9. Kelley v. Acker, 216 Ark. 867, 228 S.W.2d 49 (1950). The improvement must be in good faith and the enhancement of the land's value must be shown. Graham v. Inlow, 302 Ark. 414, 790 S.W.2d 428 (1990).

10. For example, A drains his own quarry, making quarry operations possible; his pumping inevitably drains an adjoining quarry as well. The adjoining quarry owner, receiving this non-cash benefit, is not liable in the first instance, and seemingly not liable even when he realizes the opportunity in cash sales. The quarry case is Ulmer v. Farnsworth, 80 Me. 500, 15 A. 65 (1888) discussed in § 4.9(4) below. See also, on acceptance of benefits as a ground of liability, § 4.9(6) below.

11. E.g., Hanover Ins. Co. v. Fireman's Fund Ins. Co., 217 Conn. 340, 586 A.2d 567 (1991) (no contribution in favor of payor who could not have been compelled to pay entire liability, noting that some courts have created exceptions in favor of insurers to encourage prompt payment); In re Marriage of Milliken, 199 Ill.App.3d 813, 145 Ill.Dec. 821, 557

N.E.2d 591 (1990). Restitution is sometimes denied even when the payment is made under a mistake. E.g., Scandinavian Mut. Ins. Co. v. Chicago, B. & Q. R. Co., 104 Neb. 258, 177 N.W. 178 (1920) (insurer paid insured farmer for fire losses, some of which were beyond its policy liability; insurer then sued railroad which had caused the fire but was barred as to overpayments because it was a volunteer); see II G. Palmer, Law of Restitution § 10.2 (1978 & Supps.).

12. Nationwide Mut. Ins. Co. v. American Mut. Liab. Ins. Co., 89 N.C.App. 299, 301, 365 S.E.2d 677, 678 (1988) (insurer mistook coverage, paid an injured victim monies; this redounded to the benefit of the victim's workers' compensation carrier, recovery allowed; "a party making payments in good faith 'under a moral obligation, or in ignorance of the real state of facts, or under an erroneous impression of one's legal duty' is not a mere volunteer").

13. See In re Marriage of Milliken, 199 Ill.App.3d 813, 145 Ill.Dec. 821, 557 N.E.2d 591, 595 (1990) ("Illinois courts have stressed the necessity for a legal liability to exist in order to invoke the subrogation doctrine. [ ]. The voluntary assumption of the payment of a debt, irrespective of the motives of the payor, does not confer upon the payor the status of subrogee").

14. Stein v. Simpson, 37 Cal.2d 79, 85, 230 P.2d 816, 821 (1951); Chenery v. Agri–Lines Corp., 115 Idaho 281, 766 P.2d 751 (1988).

15. See § 4.3(4) above.

take an assignment from the creditor, in which case he would become the creditor by assignment. Why can he not recover without an assignment? Is it because of the unsolicited nature of the benefit? If so, wouldn't the fact that the benefit is in cash still support a recovery?

The reasons for the rule probably do not lie in the unsolicited character of the benefit. First, there was a time in which choses in action, such as ordinary debt claims, could not be assigned. As long as that rule held, restitution had to be denied; otherwise the plaintiff could do without an assignment what he could not do with one.[16] That rule against assignments is long gone for most obligations, but its secondary consequence remains. A second reason is from a 19th century melodrama: Villain pays a debt to extort the Heroine's hand: having become the Creditor, he will foreclose the homestead unless Father yields up his Daughter.[17] The first reason was a good one in its day, but no longer applies. The second reason might still be a good one if we wish to deny villains the right to be creditors, but it does not justify denying restitution when the plaintiff is not a villain. Neither reason is founded on the defendant's right of choice. In some other cases courts have used the doctrine where it was not needed for the result[18] or where the relationship between the parties made restitution improper on other grounds.[19]

Would the defendant's right of choice be diminished if the plaintiff were allowed restitution by way of subrogation? The plaintiff allowed to subrogate himself to the creditor's position could recover exactly what the creditor could recover and when. He could not recover more or sooner. The plaintiff's right of choice does not seem diminished, because he owes the debt whether the creditor is A or B. Even if the original creditor is forgiving and likely to grant extensions for payment, the defendant debtor has no complaint. If the creditor could assign the debt, that necessarily means that the debtor had no right to choose who his creditor might be. His rights of choice are simply not involved.

It is also possible to think of the payment of another's debt as conferring a cash benefit, or at least one that would be realized in a cash savings at the

16. See II G. Palmer, Law of Restitution § 10.2, p. 364 (1978 & Supps.).

17. Cf. Stein v. Simpson, 37 Cal.2d 79, 86, 230 P.2d 816, 821 (1951) (Simpson treated as volunteer in paying Stein's debt because his conduct was "tantamount to fraud, * * * an endeavor to unlawfully obtain plaintiffs' property for less than its value"); Norton v. Haggett, 117 Vt. 130, 85 A.2d 571 (1952) (plaintiff and defendant had quarreled, plaintiff paid off the defendant's note to gain power over him, but got no assignment or endorsement of the note; no restitution from defendant).

18. In some other cases courts have appealed to the doctrine as one step in reasoning about something else altogether, where the doctrine is not needed to obtain the correct result. See, e.g., Blackford v. Dickey, 302 Ark. 261, 789 S.W.2d 445 (1990) (doctrine mentioned in determining priority of creditors and rights to proceed against a homestead).

19. In Smart v. Tower Land and Inv. Co., 597 S.W.2d 333 (Tex.1980) a mortgagee foreclosed on the property and bought it in. The mortgagor had failed to pay taxes on the mortgaged property and the mortgagee paid them. The mortgage transaction did not permit the mortgagee to recover taxes from the mortgagor in a personal judgment (as distinct from making the land pay them); the court held that the mortgagee could not recover by subrogation to the taxing authorities' lien, either. As in cases discussed in § 4.9(4), this result makes sense because it is the most consistent result with the way the parties themselves allocated responsibilities in their contract. The result was also consistent with the fact that the mortgagee in bidding for the property could set his price in light of the taxes due. In any event, the "volunteer" rule here does not turn on the unsolicited nature of the benefit.

moment when, but for the plaintiff's payment, the defendant would have been forced to make a payment. This may sometimes be the case and when it is, the debtor's savings is an added ground for allowing the payor to recover. However, in practical fact, the benefit may never be realized by a debtor who cannot pay; the "benefit" may simply become the occasion for the payor to foreclose a mortgage.

Overpayment of taxes. When the plaintiff overpays taxes, by mistake or under protest, recovery has often been denied [20] unless the court is willing to find duress.[21] It is hard to see the justice of this position or its role in the constitutional effort to protect citizens from government. In any event, recovery can hardly be denied because the citizen intends to make a gift of an overpayment of taxes, or on the ground that recovery would interfere with government autonomy. But in the days of smaller governments a recovery of tax payments might indeed disrupt fiscal planning, and no doubt courts worried about that. To the extent that this non-recovery rule hangs on, it probably should be seen as a reflection of an independent ground for denying restitution, not as a reflection of the volunteers rule. Levmore suggests that in fact many taxing authorities refund overpayments in any event.[22]

§ 4.9(4) Intentionally Conferring Non-cash Benefits Where Parties Could or Did Contract

Situations and Principles

This section sketches several kinds of cases in which the parties can identify each other and either have bargained with each other or could have done so. Unsolicited, the plaintiff takes soup every day to his bedridden neighbor; the plaintiff builds a road to her own property and this also serves the defendant's, saving him the cost of a similar road; the plaintiff manufacturer recalls a potentially dangerous product, saving its insurer the cost of defending claims. In each of these cases, the plaintiff has intentionally conferred a non-cash benefit and in each of them the parties either have a contract or were in a position to contract about the benefit.

The form of the benefit matters. If the plaintiff delivers a television set to his bedridden neighbor who never expected to pay, the neighbor can return the set when the plaintiff later demands payment. If the plaintiff simply performs services, however, the neighbor will not be able to return the services. If he is liable, he will be liable to make restitution in cash. He might be disappointed if he must return the television but he will be financially harmed if he must pay cash for services he did not bargain for.

If the parties could have contracted but did not, the plaintiff generally is denied recovery of the non-cash benefit.[1] If they contracted or had a tacit

---

20. See generally III G. Palmer, Law of Restitution § 14.20 (1978 & Supps.).

21. As it did in In re New Jersey State Bd. of Dentistry, 84 N.J. 582, 423 A.2d 640 (1980) (duress because the taxpayers would lose right to practice their profession unless the tax was paid).

22. Levmore, Explaining Restitution, 71 Va.L.Rev. 65, 94 (1985).

§ 4.9(4)

1. Even if the plaintiff believes the parties have a contract and that the defendant wants the benefits, restitution is not appropriate where the defendant does not in fact want them and did not in fact contract for them, if the benefits cannot be realized as an economic gain to the defendant. Thus in Blue Ridge Sewer Improvement District v. Lowry and As-

understanding, then recovery is granted or denied in accord with that understanding. If they contracted with each other about the general subject matter but were silent about the specific benefits in question, the question is whether their contract permits liability or implies the contrary. The absence of a contract between parties in a position to bargain suggests that in the ordinary case we need have no special sympathy for the plaintiff who confers a non-cash benefit. In the other cases the presence of some kind of understanding between the parties is more positive: liability should follow that understanding or the implications of their dealings with one another.

Tacit, Vague or Ambiguous Understandings

Implications derived from parties' dealings. Two parties deal with each other informally and without express contract but probably with vague understandings on both side; one knowingly provides benefits and the other knowingly receives them. Their informal dealings may imply that benefits provided by one party are to be paid for by the other. Or their dealings and relationship may imply the contrary. In cases of this kind, the defendant is not unjustly enriched if he has what was given to him without charge because the plaintiff intended a gift of the benefit, or the defendant could reasonably have so understood. Unjust enrichment and restitution for it turns, then, on the parties' informal understandings, and those are often hard to fathom.

Family and neighborly services. One example is the case of non-professional services. Family members, neighbors,[2] and unmarried cohabitants often render services to each other. Often the services involve long-term care for elderly or ill persons. The plaintiff cares for an ailing neighbor for ten years, bringing food daily and doing wash once a week. When the neighbor dies, the plaintiff asserts a claim against the estate. The law does not forbid the spontaneous and caring donation of services, and the only question is whether the services were donated or whether the parties' relationship and dealings reasonably indicates that compensation was expected.

Because the dealings are informal and may change over time as the burden of care lengthens and increases, interpreting that understanding is difficult; but it is the central question. Most of the trier's estimate about that understanding may come from the relationship rather than from spoken words. Courts say that if family members render services of this kind, it is "presumed" that no payment is expected and the services were a gift.[3] But what counts is the understanding of the parties, so courts may

sociates, Inc., 149 Ariz. 373, 718 P.2d 1026, 1029 (1986) property owners in an improvement district rejected proposed work, but the contractor mistakenly believed that a majority had signed the required petitions. The contractor then rendered design services in accord with its mistaken belief. Restitution was ultimately denied on the ground that the property owners had implicitly chosen to reject the services and hence were not unjustly enriched.

2. Bartholomew v. Jackson, 20 John. 28, 11 Am.Dec. 237 (N.Y.Sup.Ct.1822) (neighbor saved defendant's property from fire). Regarding this decision as "devastating" to the plaintiff, see Comment, Restitutionary Recovery for Rescuers of Human Life, 74 Cal.L.Rev. 85, 89 (1986).

3. E.G. Grout v. Solon, 131 Ind.App. 650, 174 N.E.2d 593 (1961). In many of these cases the recipient of the services dies and leaves an estate, not to the long-suffering child who nursed him for years but to someone else. The recipient's ingratitude or incompetence, or the difficulty of making formal wills, may

draw the same inference based on a long and friendly relationship between non-family members.[4] And equally the presumption may disappear if the services go beyond those normally rendered freely, or if the family members live apart, or otherwise demonstrate a relationship in which gratuitous aid would not be expected.[5]

Submission of ideas. Another example of informal dealings that may be difficult to interpret occurs when people submit ideas or suggestions to businesses, often ideas for new or improved products. If a business uses the idea, does it become liable to pay the plaintiff? Liability in such cases is circumscribed by considerations described elsewhere.[6] The question here is whether the plaintiff is barred from recovery because the idea was not solicited. If the defendant has not committed a tort or breach of confidence in using the idea, the plaintiff's recovery must be based on contract or quasi-contract. Palmer favors the view that liability is quasi-contractual, imposed to prevent unjust enrichment[7] rather than based on an implied in fact contract. Yet here again the parties' understanding, as best as can be construed from the appearances, seems to control. If the plaintiff does not suggest compensation and nothing about the idea itself implies that compensation would be expected, compensation is to be denied.[8] If the plaintiff makes it clear that compensation is expected, the plaintiff may be required to clear some other hurdles as a condition of recovery, but he will not be barred merely because the benefit was unsolicited.[9]

Business or professional services. When professionals intentionally provide services and the recipient knowingly receives them, the tacit expectation of compensation is usually clear and indeed in some cases the recipient of the services may even tacitly request them.[10] The expectation of compensation, and from whom it is expected, is a question of fact, not a question of unjust enrichment doctrine.

press courts to stretch some inferences to find an implied promise to pay.

4. See Schanz v. Terry's Estate, 504 S.W.2d 653, 92 A.L.R.3d 719 (Mo.App.1974) (Ella Schanz went to work for the Terry family at the age of 13, lived with them and worked for them for 40 years, she was a "family" member); Annotation, Recovery for services rendered by persons living in apparent relation of husband and wife without express agreement for compensation, 94 A.L.R.3d 552 (1979).

5. "The plaintiff in this case is an adult daughter who married, left her father's house and established a home of her own. Therefore, no presumption arises that any services he rendered to her father were gratuitous." Johnson v. Sanders, 260 N.C. 291, 293, 132 S.E.2d 582, 584 (1963).

6. See § 6.5(2) below.

7. See II G. Palmer, Law of Restitution § 10.11 (1978 & Supps.).

8. Martin v. Little, Brown and Co., 304 Pa.Super. 424, 431, 450 A.2d 984, 988 (1981) ("As a general rule, volunteers have no right to restitution * * *. Appellant was a volunteer. It was he who made the unsolicited

suggestion" resulting in benefit to the defendant).

9. Hamilton Nat. Bank v. Belt, 210 F.2d 706, 93 U.S.App.D.C. 168 (1953); § 6.5(2) below. Some of the cases have been preoccupied with the concept of ideas as property and have emphasized that in order to qualify for protection the idea must be concrete. If the parties have implicitly contracted that does not seem to matter, but concreteness might be significant on the question whether they *have* contracted and whether the plaintiff expected payment. Presumably the plaintiff does not expect compensation for the general suggestion that a manufacturer should make its products better.

10. E.g. Dunn v. Phoenix Village, Inc., 213 F.Supp. 936 (W.D.Ark.1963) (loan broker); Tibbetts Contracting Corp. v. O. & E. Contracting Co., 21 A.D.2d 915, 251 N.Y.S.2d 725 (1964) (subcontractor recovered against landowner who continued to accept subcontractor's beneficial work on the land after the main contractor had breached), rev'd on other ground, 15 N.Y.2d 324, 258 N.Y.S.2d 400, 206 N.E.2d 340 (1965).

The defendant's right of choice is not implicated in any of these tacit agreement cases so long as the court imposes liability in accordance with the parties own understandings. The parties' understanding may fall short of a contract, but it is no less entitled to respect. If the plaintiff's services were gratuitous, recovery is barred for that reason. These understandings based on relationships, the silent communications, and the assumptions of everyday life are very hard to interpret. When the facts are confusing courts may seek refuge in more talk of doctrine; but in these cases, there is no occasion for doctrine at all, only the best interpretation possible of what the parties thought the deal was.

No Contract Between Parties Who Are in Position to Bargain

Non-liability. A well-known case is *Ulmer v. Farnsworth,*[11] where, quarries owned by different parties were interconnected, and where, to drain the water from his own quarry, the plaintiff necessarily drained the defendant's as well. The plaintiff sought a recovery which was denied. Although his *purpose* was not to benefit the defendant, the benefit was nonetheless intentionally conferred in the sense that the plaintiff knew with certainty that it would result. Nothing in the nature of the circumstances prevented bargaining: the parties knew each other and knew the interests involved; parties were not so numerous that bargaining was infeasible. Where the benefit is intentionally conferred, is not in cash or specific chattels, and the parties are in a position to bargain about compensation, the cases, in line with *Ulmer v. Farnsworth,* deny restitution.[12]

The same principle is applied to deny restitution when a tenant is permitted to make improvements, which revert to the landlord at the end of the term,[13] when a would-be purchaser improves the property, then cancels

---

11. 80 Me. 500, 15 A. 65 (1888), discussed in Dawson, The Self–Serving Intermeddler, 87 Harv.L.Rev. 1409, 1418 (1974) and Levmore, Explaining Restitution, 71 Va.L.Rev. 65, 111–112 (1985).

12. Dobson v. Oil & Gas Com'n, 218 Ark. 160, 166, 235 S.W.2d 33, 36 (1950) ("Almost any improvement a man makes on his own land is likely to make that of his neighbor either more or less valuable. But, with a notable exception involving nuisances, the courts have never undertaken to require payment for such incidental benefits or to award compensation for such incidental damage"); Dinosaur Dev., Inc. v. White, 216 Cal.App.3d 1310, 265 Cal.Rptr. 525 (1989) (defendant adjoining owner induced government agency to require plaintiff developer to build a road to defendant's landlocked parcel as a condition of permitting plaintiff to develop his own land further, no restitution).

13. E.g., Hayward Lumber & Inv. Co. v. Graham, 104 Ariz. 103, 449 P.2d 31 (1968); Lafary v. Lafary, 522 N.E.2d 916, 919 (Ind. App.1988) ("John as a tenant may not charge Inez, his landlord, for improvements to the property in the absence of an express contract"); Schmeckpeper v. Koertje, 222 Neb.

800, 388 N.W.2d 51 (1986) (no right of restitution for value of improvements made by tenant in possession, and improvements that become part of real estate cannot be removed by the tenant). Contractors who work for the tenant are in the same position, e.g., Alaska Sales & Serv. Inc. v. Millett, 735 P.2d 743 (Alaska 1987) (chattel lease); Indianapolis Raceway Park, Inc. v. Curtiss, 179 Ind.App. 557, 386 N.E.2d 724 (1979).

Distinguish improvements made by the tenant under a mistake or misunderstanding. In that case the tenant is a mistaken improver and may be permitted to recover the value of the improvements. Farese v. McGarry, 237 N.J.Super. 385, 568 A.2d 89 (1989). The tenant may also recover if he is entitled to the value of the improvements under an actual contract or an implicit understanding of the parties, or as part of a larger contract which is later breached or terminated. Cf. Gheen v. Gheen, 276 S.C. 404, 279 S.E.2d 361 (1981) (son's substantial improvements as "tenant;" "a tenant who in good faith makes improvements to the leasehold, with knowledge and consent of the lessor, with the intent of enjoying them in the event he becomes the owner, is entitled to reimbursement").

the contract,[14] and when a lawyer does unauthorized work for client.[15]

Freeriders problems. Neighbor cases like *Ulmer* might prompt some economists to note the possibility that the defendant is merely holding out to get a free ride. Each neighbor in fact might seek to outwait the other, with the result that no production is undertaken. If this were true, the defendant is not one who would like to avoid the benefit; he is one who actually wants the benefit but is trying to get it without cost to himself. Although some thinkers approve of judicial intervention when the freerider problem is pressing, this is not an especially convincing case for such intervention. Professor Levmore thinks that economic arguments lie on both sides of the restitution issue here.[16] In addition, we cannot be sure that we have a freerider; the defendant may *not* want the benefit, and the courts are rightly reluctant to compel him to buy it at the plaintiff's instance.[17]

Contract Between Parties on General Subject Matter

Existence of an express contract. Where the parties did in fact contract with reference to the same general subject matter, the contract itself, interpreted in the light of its gaps and silences as well as in the light of its express provisions, should control. This principle is frequently given a shorthand expression in the statement that where there is an express contract dealing with the subject matter, no implied contract or restitution claim will be permitted.[18] The shorthand statement is inaccurate, because the express contract may not allocate all risks. The statement points in the right direction, however. If the contract and context, fully and fairly interpreted, show that the parties' allocated a given risk to the plaintiff or advantage to the defendant, then restitution should not be permitted to undermine that allocation.

Example of the failed land purchase. For example, in *Salamon v. Terra*,[19] the defendant wanted to sell his land. The plaintiff, a builder, wanted land upon which to build houses for resale. They came to a financing arrangement under which the plaintiff builder, with a small downpayment, would be permitted to enter the defendant's land and build

14. Cf. Callano v. Oakwood Park Homes Corp., 91 N.J.Super. 105, 219 A.2d 332 (1966) (contractor who improved lot for would-be purchaser cannot recover from landowner-vendor when purchaser canceled contract).

15. Swan v. Dolphin Lane Assocs., Ltd., 92 A.D.2d 608, 610, 459 N.Y.S.2d 801, 803 (1983) (plaintiff "knew that he had no express agreement to be compensated for the services claimed in this lawsuit," and "continued performing services in the face of warnings" that he would not be paid).

16. See Levmore, Explaining Restitution, 71 Va.L.Rev. 65, 112–113 (1985).

17. In Dobson v. Oil & Gas Com'n, 218 Ark. 160, 235 S.W.2d 33 (1950) a gas field could be developed for its best potential only if the entire field were treated as one unit and all individual owners accepted less present production in order to be sure that all the gas could be captured. The efforts of the Oil & Gas Commission to unitize the entire field

were unconstitutional. The court specifically recognized the freerider problem (in fact the litigation was brought by an owner who would get a free ride because other owners would agree to limit production and thus preserve the capacity to capture the gas, while he would get full production *and* the benefit of other owners' self restraint). But the court said that voluntary cooperation was the only solution.

18. City of Indianapolis v. Twin Lakes Enterprises, Inc., 568 N.E.2d 1073, 1079 (Ind. App.1991) ("As a general rule, there can be no constructive contract where there is an express contract between the parties in reference to the same subject matter); Julien J. Studley, Inc. v. New York News, Inc., 70 N.Y.2d 628, 518 N.Y.S.2d 779, 512 N.E.2d 300 (1987) (no implied-in-fact contract when an express contract on the same subject matter).

19. 394 Mass. 857, 477 N.E.2d 1029, 1032 (1985).

houses. The parties contemplated that upon completion the houses would be resold and that the proceeds would be used to pay the defendant for the land, and to give the plaintiff-builder a profit from the remainder. It did not work. Hard times made it impossible for the builder to complete the houses and they could not be sold. The defendant extended the time provided for payment, but still the houses could not be completed or sold. Finally the builder sued the landowner claiming restitution.

The landowner had acquired the added value of the partially complete houses on his land. Yet examination of the contract suggests that the landowner never undertook to take enterprise risks of the building trade; he undertook to sell his land and to finance the purchase by delaying his claim for payment. He expected cash income, not cash outlay. The Massachusetts Court accordingly thought that the express contract precluded restitution.

Example of the insured's expense saving the insurer liability. The parties' express contract is often difficult to interpret, and when that is the case, application of the principle is commensurately difficult. In *McNeilab, Inc. v. North Rivers Ins. Co.,*[20] the plaintiffs were producers of the drug Tylenol. They withdrew all packages of the product from the market after a cyanide scare. They destroyed these and replaced them with tamper-resistant containers, then carried out a major advertising campaign to rehabilitate the drug in the public's eye. It was successful. The plaintiffs were insured for liability by the defendants. The defendants were not liable under the policy for any of the plaintiff's costs, but the plaintiffs argued that they should be liable on a restitutionary theory. Acting as a kind of agent for the insurers, they said, they reduced the insurers' almost certain liability to defend cyanide-related suits; so the insurer would be unjustly enriched unless it shared some of the costs.

The court denied recovery on the ground that the plaintiffs were volunteers and some other cases have said the same in similar situations.[21] Since the parties had contracted about the subject matter of liability, it seems doubtful that the insurer undertook any more than it expressly promised. It is not simply that the parties did not think of this kind of case. It is rather that insurers wish to exclude all risks not specifically included, and this one was not. Courts have something like this in mind when they say that in contracting expressly, the parties exclude any unjust enrichment or quasi-contract recovery on the same subject matter.[22]

20. 645 F.Supp. 525 (D.N.J.1986), aff'd, 831 F.2d 287 (3d Cir.1987) (Table).

21. J.L. Simmons Co. v. Lumbermens Mut. Ins. Co., 84 Ill.App.2d 98, 107, 228 N.E.2d 227, 232, 33 A.L.R.3d 1254 (1967) ("Nowhere in the insuring agreement is plaintiff empowered to make an ex parte determination of its obligation to pay. Accordingly, plaintiff acted as a mere volunteer and is thus not entitled to the cost of mitigating a damage, which damage it may not have been legally obligated to pay initially"). *Distinguish* cases in which the injured victim (not the insured) minimizes damages by an expenditure. Those damages would be recoverable against the tortfeasor-insured, and the tortfeasor's insurer would be liable for them if they were the kind of damages covered in the policy. See Marley Orchard Corp. v. Travelers Indem. Co., 50 Wash. App. 801, 750 P.2d 1294 (1988).

22. Julien J. Studley, Inc. v. New York News, Inc., 70 N.Y.2d 628, 518 N.Y.S.2d 779, 512 N.E.2d 300 (1987) (no implied contract where express contract on subject matter); City of Indianapolis v. Twin Lakes Enters., 568 N.E.2d 1073, 1079 (Ind.App.1991) ("As a general rule, there can be no constructive contract where there is an express contract between the parties in references to the same subject matter"). The point is exemplified in cases that never mention this rule, e.g., Smart v. Tower Land and Inv. Co., 597 S.W.2d 333

Variations on the insurer example. Variations on the facts of *McNeilab* might produce some different results. The answer would be different if, for some good reason, the insureds had performed the very obligations the insurer had undertaken, by defending suits when the insurer could not, for example. But in *McNeilab* the insured performed acts the insured was not obliged to perform, although they were acts the insurer might have wanted. On facts slightly different from those in *McNeilab, Leebov v. United States Fidelity & Guaranty Co.,*[23] went for the insured. In that case a building contractor was insured for liability by the defendant. While he was excavating, he caused a landslide which damaged a house. To prevent further landslides and damages, he expended sums to shore up the slide area. He then claimed these costs against the insurer. The court imposed liability.

No doubt the specificity of the damages and the identification of a particular potential claimant in *Leebov* make the case easier than *McNeilab* for imposing liability.[24] Some other cases have also taken this route, but focusing on the contract provisions.[25] Some decisions have also found the insurance policy to cover some slightly similar kinds of claims by victims (not insureds). These cases attempted to use *Leebov* by analogy, but even as analogy it seems unhelpful. Not only were the claims different but the issue was policy coverage, not restitution.[26]

Three–Party Dealings; Improvement by Subcontractors

Implications of non-contracting. In more complicated transactions involving three parties, *A* may contract with *B* but not with *C,* although the three are involved in a single project. The parties *could* have contracted each with both others, but they did not. The separate contracts convey clearly the limited kinds of liability and exposure each party has in mind. Each party may benefit by the work or payments of both other parties, but the parties understand that their responsibilities and rights are only those set up by the contract. Respect for that contract arrangement requires the courts to refuse restitution between the parties who did not contract with each other.

Examples. A simple example is the broker. A broker's services in placing a product for its owner may also benefit the buyer, conceivably even more than the seller. But if the parties all understand that the broker's fee

(Tex.1980) (mortgage transaction did not permit mortgagee to collect taxes due from mortgagor personally, and mortgagee could not obtain restitution by way of subrogation to the government's tax lien either).

23. 401 Pa. 477, 165 A.2d 82 (1960).

24. Palmer supports liability in *Leebov* on the ground that the insurer would owe restitution if the insured had satisfied the insurer's liability and ought to be liable equally if he forestalled it. See III G. Palmer, Law of Restitution § 10.6, pp. 409–410 (1978 & Supps.). He does not discuss the effect of the insurance contract in prescribing the risks for which the insurer is liable, nor does he distinguish between performing the insurer's duties by satisfying legal liabilities from performing other

acts that may affect those liabilities. Forestalling liability, were that to be the test, might occur even before an accident identifies a victim. The insured driver might repair his brakes, thus forestalling liability of his insurer, but almost certainly his brake repair cannot be charged to the insurer.

25. Slay Warehousing Co. v. Reliance Ins. Co., 471 F.2d 1364 (8th Cir.1973).

26. Goodyear Rubber & Supply, Inc. v. Great Am. Ins. Co., 545 F.2d 95 (9th Cir.1976) (insured may have been responsible for damages to a vessel; insurer obliged to defend claim of salvor who towed vessel); Aetna Casualty and Sur. Co. v. Eberheim, 41 Conn. Supp. 125, 556 A.2d 1067 (1988) (salvage claim covered by policy).

is to come from the seller, the broker is not entitled to restitution from the buyer in spite of the buyer's benefit, even if the seller has become insolvent and unable to pay the fee.[27] In the same way, if a department store issues charges cards to A, relying on A's credit alone, and permits A's family members to charge goods on those cards, it would seem that the family members would not be liable; they are enriched but never promised to pay, and the store knows it.[28]

Subcontractors enriching a landowner. Perhaps a more common kind of case involves a subcontractor's contribution of benefits to a landowner. Suppose a landowner contracts with a general contractor for construction on the land. As the landowner knows, subcontractors may be hired, but the landowner's contract is solely with the general contractor, whose responsibility it is to pay any subcontractors he hires. Suppose the subcontractor does the work, thus improving the landowner's property, but the general contractor does not pay the sub, usually because he has become insolvent. Can the sub recover from the landowner on the ground that he is unjustly enriched by the sub's work? This kind of case resembles the case of the tenant who makes improvements, to the enrichment of the landlord at the end of the term. It differs, however, in that in the contractor case, we can be sure that the landowner-defendant did in fact want the benefit because he sought that benefit in his contract with the general contractor.

Statutes aside, the cases deny recovery.[29] Somewhat similar cases, those in which improvements are ordered by a tenant [30] or someone who is not the owner,[31] also deny recovery to the hapless contractor. The subcontractor

27. Eckert v. Soverel Marine, Inc., 380 So.2d 569 (Fla.App.1980) (yacht purchaser not liable for broker's commission); Kagan v. K–Tel Entertainment, Inc., 172 A.D.2d 375, 568 N.Y.S.2d 756 (1991) (plaintiff brokered a TV series to MGM/UA on behalf of a client who became insolvent, held, MGM/UA not liable for benefits it may have received, "if services were performed at the behest of someone other than the defendant, the plaintiff must look to that person for recovery").

28. Liability was denied in Sears, Roebuck & Co. v. Stover, 32 Ohio Misc.2d 1, 513 N.E.2d 361 (1987) but imposed in Sears, Roebuck & Co. v. Ragucci, 203 N.J.Super. 82, 495 A.2d 923 (1985).

29. E.g., Premier Elec. Const. Co. v. La-Salle Nat. Bank, 132 Ill.App.3d 485, 87 Ill.Dec. 721, 477 N.E.2d 1249 (1984); Custer Builders, Inc. v. Quaker Heritage, Inc., 41 A.D.2d 448, 344 N.Y.S.2d 606 (1973); see § 12.20(3) below. See also Restatement of Restitution § 110 (1937); cf. Dawson, The Self–Serving Intermeddler, 87 Harv.L.Rev. 1409, 1454 (1974). Many cases are collected and analyzed in II G. Palmer, Law of Restitution § 10.7(2) (1978 & Supps.).

30. E.g., Indianapolis Raceway Park, Inc. v. Curtiss, 179 Ind.App. 557, 386 N.E.2d 724 (1979); contra, even where the landlord gave the contractor notice of non-liability, Frank M. Hall & Co. v. Southwest Properties Venture, 747 P.2d 688 (Colo.App.1987). When a contract purchaser of land orders improvements from a contractor, then cancels his purchase, the contractor is again denied restitution from the owner. Callano v. Oakwood Park Homes Corp., 91 N.J.Super. 105, 219 A.2d 332 (1966).

31. Dalton v. Bundy, 666 S.W.2d 443 (Mo. App.1984) (owner's parents ordered improvements).

In Murdock–Bryant Const. v. Pearson, 146 Ariz. 48, 703 P.2d 1197 (1985) a contractor was induced to do excavating work on the basis of certain misrepresentations by A. After the misrepresentations and the contract, A entered into a joint venture with B, the effect of which was to create an A–B partnership. The excavation proved to be more extensive than expected and the contractor sued for restitution for the value of his added work, naming both A and B as defendants. B was held liable though he had not been a partner at the time the representations or the contract had been made, on the ground that he received benefits. But the facts given do not show whether he received benefits at all, since that would depend on the terms of the partnership or joint venture. If, for example, he had paid a price for entry that excluded liability for existing obligations, his benefit would not be clear. It would also seem that as to a later-joining partner's individual account, the bene-

cases sometimes say that the landowner is not unjustly enriched and this seems accurate, because the landowner got no more than what he contracted for. He remains liable for the payments due the contractor if he has not already paid. Indeed, this liability redounds to the benefit of the sub, who can, using garnishment or subrogation, enforce his claim against the general contractor against any funds retained by the landowner. In addition, the parties almost certainly contemplated that their contractual arrangements constituted the full set of liabilities. The subcontractor relied on the credit of the general contractor, not the owner, and it is not unfair to him or enriching to the landowner to respect the contractual arrangement.

Although one might not want to call the subcontractor a volunteer, a successful claim against the landowner would impair the landowner's choice about important matters, and in particular about his exposure to liability through the agency of the general contractor. The landowner *has* bargained about the extent of his liabilities for work by bargaining only with a general contractor; the subcontractor *could* bargain for added security from the landowner. The fact that it would take a considerable inducement to persuade the landowner to guarantee that the general contractor would pay the sub is a good indication how significant the bargain was and why courts are right to respect it.

Mechanics' lien laws make some important but limited changes in these rules, one effect of which is often to force the landowner to force the general contractor to purchase a bond to guarantee payment.[32]

Non-cash Benefits Realized in Cash Later

In some cases the benefit is conferred as a non-cash benefit but is readily realized as cash without impairing other rights of the recipient. This might be true in *Ulmer* if the defendant immediately opened his quarry and began profitable production as soon as it was drained.[33] Even if the defendant would never have spent the money on his own, the savings begins to be realized as a cash benefit from the time the defendant begins to reap income from the quarry which, without the plaintiff's effort, he would not have reaped. When the benefit is realized as cash, the unsolicited character of the benefit no longer poses a reason to deny restitution. Such consequential restitution, like consequential damages, may be difficult and costly to estimate. In any event, courts have not shown any desire to treat saved expenses as cash, even when that saving will surely be realized.

§ 4.9(5) Intentionally or Innocently Conferring Non–cash Benefits Where Bargaining Is Not Possible

In some instances the plaintiff confers an unsolicited non-cash benefit upon the defendant where bargaining is not possible. It might not be

fits were unsolicited. However, neither of these issues seems to have been raised and the court imposed restitutionary liability on B. See Comment, Liability for Incidental Beneficiaries: Creating Third Party Liability in Quasi–Contract, 28 Ariz.L.Rev. 83 (1986) (regarding non-liability under the traditional rule as an "injustice" because "an obvious recipient of benefits" would escape liability).

32. See § 12.20 below.

33. The defendant's use of the quarry, profitable or not, might suggest acceptance of the benefit and liability might conceivably be imposed on that ground. See § 4.9(6) below. The point here is a little different. It is that the cost saved to the defendant might be treated as the equivalent of a cash benefit when the saving is actually realized.

possible because practical action is needed immediately and the defendant cannot be reached for negotiation. Or it might not be possible because the plaintiff is mistaken about the ownership of the benefitted property. When the benefit in such cases is not cash, that fact pushes toward a denial of restitution. On the other hand, in some of the cases the choice principle is not involved because the defendant either had no right to reject the benefit, or had a full choice about doing so.

Emergency, Preservation of Property or Life, Necessaries

Cases involving emergency preservation of property or life and those involving the provision of "necessaries" illuminate the choice element in the choice principle and show something about its limits.

Suppose the defendant is injured and unconscious. A doctor stops, sees his condition, and administers appropriate treatment. The doctor cannot bargain for a fee unless the defendant has an agent on the scene. The doctor's assistance is in line with the wishes of the great majority of people, so the doctor-plaintiff is acting in accord with the bargain we believe would have been struck. The doctor is entitled to restitution for the value of her services.[1] Such an award does not offend the choice principle. At no relevant time did the defendant have a meaningful choice, because he was unconscious or mentally incapacitated. Indeed, the treatment represents our best guess about what his choice would be.

When the plaintiff performs the defendant's legal duty to another person by providing necessaries, he can recover from the defendant. Although the benefit is again a non-cash benefit, the defendant is under a legal duty to provide necessaries (for family members, for instance). About that duty the law definitely does *not* seek to permit the defendant any choice; instead it affirmatively requires him to make provision. When the plaintiff intentionally provides benefits after the defendant has defaulted, the plaintiff is entitled to recover their value.[2]

A third case is similar to or perhaps one version of the emergency rule. In *Chase v. Corcoran*,[3] the plaintiff rescued a boat that was adrift with holes in it. He stored it after seeking to find the owner, and made repairs necessary to preserve it. After the owner took the boat, the plaintiff was allowed to recover. Here again the owner is deprived of no choice. In the absence of repairs the boat would have been destroyed. If the owner preferred the destroyed boat, he need not take it back. In a sense, "the boat could be said to finance the repairs."[4]

§ 4.9(5)

1. Cotnam v. Wisdom, 83 Ark. 601, 104 S.W. 164 (1907); Restatement of Restitution § 116 (1937).

2. Restatement of Restitution § 113 (1937).

3. 106 Mass. 286, 288 (1871). The court said that liability was for "the reasonable expenses incurred in keeping and repairing it." This is a reliance damages measure, not a restitutionary measure. One would not expect the court to award restitution equal to the value of the boat, but restitution might be measured by its increase in value due to repair or by the value of the plaintiff's services. Reliance expense might not suffice to encourage salvors (at least not enough to encourage them to find the true owner). On the other hand, it offers a manageable measure that might be especially useful in cases where a rescuer saves human life.

4. Levmore, Explaining Restitution, 71 Va. L.Rev. 65, 121–122 (1985).

When the repair does not save the property from utter destruction, however, the case is harder. In *Berry v. Barbour* [5] a contractor was working on a home when a fire burned the roof. The owner was out of the country and could not be consulted, so the contractor acted sensibly and repaired the roof to prevent further damage. The court held the owner liable, apparently for labor and materials costs rather than full market value of the services. In the boat case, if the owner's choice would have been to let the boat sink, he can accomplish that preference by not taking the boat back; but in *Berry* the homeowner could not do that without giving up that part of the house he would have had without repairs. The difference does not seem very important on the facts, however. The homeowner's choice could not be predictably furthered any better by leaving the roof open to the elements than it would by making reasonable repairs. Respect for his choice might even best be achieved by making the repair, since that is far and away the most likely choice.

Maybe a formal emergency, rescue, or preservation is not really the key in these cases. Maybe it is enough if we do the best we can to uphold the defendant's rights of self-determination. When the defendant is absent, and cannot be reached, his rights are not more jeopardized by doing the sensible thing than by doing nothing. Maybe not just anyone should be privileged to make the decision about what to do, but if the plaintiff is a reasonable person to make the decision and he makes it reasonably in accord with a good objective guess about the defendant's probably preferences, life will move along more smoothly and restitution is appropriate. In *United States v. Summitt Constr. Co.,* [6] a contractor arrived at a remote job site ready to work. The preparation work, which was to have been done by another contractor, had not been done. The contractor could go home and come back another day or he could do some of the preparation work and proceed. It was a good decision and he was allowed to recover for the added labor. Again, it is hard to see how the owner's choice could have been furthered if the contractor had done nothing.

Improvers of Chattels, Extenders of Credit

Sometimes the plaintiff will extend credit to one person while providing the corresponding benefit to another. The subcontractor cases and some others already discussed [7] were like this. In those cases, however, the subcontractor knew he was providing a benefit to the landowner but expecting payment only from the general contractor. But suppose an improver takes an order for extensive repairs on a car from a person he believes to be the owner. He makes the repairs, but the person he dealt with proves to have been a thief. The true owner recovers the car and refuses to pay for the repairs. Unlike the landowner in the subcontractor cases, the car owner has *not* contracted with anyone to have work done.

The orthodox view is that the repairer cannot recover restitution, whether he is an innocent converter who believes he is improving his own

---

5. 279 P.2d 335 (Okl.1954).

6. 892 F.2d 788 (9th Cir.1989).

7. See § 4.9(4) above.

property or a professional repairer who simply mistook the thief for the owner.[8] That view is in line with complete respect the defendant-owner's right of property and right of choice. The benefit is unsolicited as far as the owner is concerned and it is not in cash. So to require restitution is to require the owner to buy a benefit he did not ask for and may not want.

The only factor that might weigh against protecting the owner's right of choice is that the parties were in no position to bargain. The fact that the owner was not identified meant that bargaining was impossible. This may be a weak factor in spite of sympathy for the repairer, because the repairer was in position to determine the ownership of the car or to demand cash or security for payment. There are good practical reasons why the repairer is not likely to do either of those things, but those reasons usually reflect business decisions of the repair trade that it is cheaper to take some losses than to verify ownership in every case.[9] Having taken the best business decision, the repairer does not come with great equity when he seeks to saddle the defendant with the loss that decision entails. Nevertheless, some decisions can be found that approve a recovery for the repairer.[10]

8. Bank of Am. v. J. & S. Auto Repairs, 143 Ariz. 416, 694 P.2d 246 (1985) (repairer has no claim against bank holding purchase money mortgage unless repairer is sued in conversion); Austrian Motors, Ltd. v. Travelers Ins. Co., 156 Ga.App. 618, 275 S.E.2d 702 (1980) (owner may retake automobile with accessions thereto, repairer's lien cannot be asserted against owner who did not authorize repairs); United States Fidelity and Guar. Co. v. Marshall, 4 Kan.App.2d 9, 601 P.2d 1169 (1979) (one who repaired at the instance of a thief has no claim against owner); Eddie's Auto Body Works, Inc. v. Lumbermen's Mut. Casualty Co., 28 A.D.2d 995, 283 N.Y.S.2d 306, 307 (1967) ("plaintiff, deriving its title from a thief, may not assert against the true owner or one standing in privity with the owner any claim for the automobile or the cost of repairs or improvements thereto made without the consent of the owner"). In accord with this view, common law and statutory mechanics' liens are not applied unless the owner has authorized the would-be lienor to deal with the property. Bob Ryan Leasing v. Sampair, 125 Wis.2d 266, 371 N.W.2d 405 (App.1985). See generally II G. Palmer, Law of Restitution § 10.9, pp. 454–455 (1978 & Supps.); Restatement of Restitution § 42(2). Some cases are dealt with under the law of personal property accession, which generally coincides with restitutionary doctrine but which may not use the terminology of restitution.

Additions by a repairer that can be severed without damage to the whole may be retaken by him. Bank of Am. v. J. & S. Auto Repairs, supra (even engine might be severable). If an innocent good faith purchaser-converter completely remakes a stolen hull, adding engine, transmission, wheels, shocks, and seats—a kind of one-horse shay in reverse—then the good faith purchaser is the owner under the principle that the owner of the principal part owns the whole. Capital Chevrolet Co. v. Earheart, 627 S.W.2d 369 (Tenn.App.1981). In re Marriage of Allen, 724 P.2d 651 (Colo. 1986) the court said that an innocent donee of property illicitly taken would be subject to a constructive trust or equitable lien as appropriate, but only to the extent of her unjust enrichment; so she would be entitled to credit for improvements or contributions to the property.

9. Sometimes the repairer is especially careful to check title and is still misinformed, as in Bank of Am. v. J. & S. Auto Repairs, 143 Ariz. 416, 694 P.2d 246 (1985); but the rule remains the same, just as it does when an innocent person purchases rather than repairs.

10. Iacomini v. Liberty Mut. Ins. Co., 127 N.H. 73, 497 A.2d 854 (1985); cf. Walden v. Vera's Auto Body Serv., 94 Misc.2d 792, 405 N.Y.S.2d 400, 401–402 (City Ct.1978) (repairer could recover even though he dealt with owner and owner declared he did not want repairs). Neither case examined authorities on this point or discussed the owner's rights of choice. Walden seems far out of line with even a mild respect for the owner. The court's discussion of the point is as follows:

Notwithstanding the defendant's fraud upon the plaintiff, it would be unfair and grossly inequitable to allow the plaintiff to have the benefit of the repairs which have already been made to his automobile, without paying for them. This is especially so since there is no proof that the defendant participated in the fraud perpetrated by its employees, and since the plaintiff anticipated making these repairs.

Mistaken Improvers of Land [11]

Sometimes, as part of a living or family arrangement, one person will intentionally build a house on the land of another; when the relationship between the parties sours, some kind of restitution may be required in favor of the builder, the nature of which will depend upon the parties informal understanding or relationship.[12] When the improver believes he is building on his own land, the situation is more difficult. Given that belief, no tacit understanding between the improver and the true owner is possible.

A mistaken improver of land may believe he has title to an identified parcel when in fact title lies in another; or he may know he has title to described land but may be mistaken about where that land lies. If he makes the first kind of mistake, he may own nothing; if he makes the second, he owns something, but not the parcel he has improved. The difference is important because Betterments Statutes or Occupying Claimants Acts may help the improver in cases involving the first kind of mistake, at least if he occupies the land under color of title.[13] But they do not assist the improver who owns Lot A but builds on Lot B by mistake. Nor do they protect one who knows he does not own the land but mistakenly believes he is under a contractual duty to improve it.[14]

The improver who makes the location mistake was traditionally [15] denied any restitution.[16] The true owner of the lot acquired title to the fixtures on the land and was not required to pay for them unless he made the mistake of suing in equity, in which case he was required to "do equity" by paying for the value of the improvements.[17] In the last half of the twentieth century, a number of courts have shown a distinct willingness to seek other kinds of solutions, by awarding restitution to the improver, or even forcing the owner to sell the land to the improver,[18] just as they might force a sale of a small strip of property when one neighbor mistakenly builds so that his house sits a few inches across the property line.[19]

The mistaken improver is normally an intentional improver in a sense; he is mistaken only about ownership. He does not believe that he is conferring a benefit upon anyone. He has no opportunity to bargain and the improvement is likely to be substantial, so hardship is great if he is denied restitution. On the other hand, the benefit is a non-cash benefit and one to which people customarily attach specific significance. The conflict between

11. See generally § 5.8(3) below.

12. E.g., Robinson v. Robinson, 100 Ill. App.3d 437, 57 Ill.Dec. 532, 429 N.E.2d 183 (1981).

13. The different kinds of statutes and their limitations are discussed in II G. Palmer, Law of Restitution § 10.9(b) (1978 & Supps.).

14. See Blue Ridge Sewer Improvement District v. Lowry and Associates, Inc., 149 Ariz. 373, 718 P.2d 1026, 1029 (App.1986).

15. There was a period of slight vacillation in earlier 19th century, but later the decisions fell into line with the rights of the true owner. See II G. Palmer, Law of Restitution § 10.9(a) (1978 & Supps.).

16. E.g., Foltz v. Alford, 102 Ark. 191, 143 S.W. 905 (1912); Graham v. Ashley, 74 N.M. 251, 392 P.2d 667 (1964); Casad, The Mistaken Improver—A Comparative Study, 19 Hast.L.J. 1039 (1968); Merryman, Improving the Lot of the Mistaken Improver, 11 Stan.L.Rev. 456 (1959); Annot., 57 A.L.R.2d 263 (1958); see § 5.8(3) below.

17. E.g., Beavers v. Weatherly, 250 Ga. 546, 299 S.E.2d 730 (1983) (incompetent avoiding deed as against an innocent purchaser would be required to pay for improvements made by purchaser).

18. See Manning v. Wingo, 577 So.2d 865, 868–869 (Ala.1991); § 5.8(3) below.

19. See § 5.10(4) below.

the urge to prevent unjust enrichment and the urge to protect the owner-defendant's rights of self-determination is strong and it is not surprising that the cases show support for both sides. Some remedial flexibility, however, may meliorate the hardships and perhaps also reduce the infringement of the defendant's choice. For example, use of a lien with enforcement postponed until the landowner voluntarily transfers the property might sometimes offer an appropriate compromise.[20] Unfortunately, many other solutions seem extreme in one direction or the other.[21]

§ 4.9(6)   Acceptance or Opportunity to Reject: Lawyers and the Common Fund

If the plaintiff confers an unsolicited benefit upon the defendant who is not initially required to make restitution, it is possible that the plaintiff could still obtain restitution if the defendant meaningfully "accepts" the benefit. This might conceivably be done with tangible goods, or even, perhaps by using an improvement on property. The idea has not been very well developed in the cases,[1] maybe because it is so similar to some other ideas which may also tend to show that the defendant's choice rights were not infringed. Specifically, this section distinguishes (1) acceptance of a benefit, (2) realization of a non-cash benefit in cash at some later date, and (3) the ability to reject the benefit before received. In each case it is possible to argue that the defendant's choice rights are not infringed or at least not infringed in a substantial way, and that restitution is therefore appropriate.

Acceptance of a Benefit

Consider the plaintiff mistakenly builds a house on the defendant's property. The defendant moves in and lives in the house, then sells it a year later for a sum much higher than the bare land. It seems plausible to say that the defendant has accepted the benefit and should pay for it. Indeed, "acceptance" is a plausible argument even if the defendant merely lives in the house.

Realization of a Benefit in Cash

A related but different point is that if the house was sold by the defendant before suit was brought for restitution, the defendant has realized a cash benefit. Since cash benefits are generally subject to restitution,[2] it could then be argued that once a benefit is realized, restitution is owed.

Ambiguities in Acceptance and Realization

Ambiguities lurk in both the acceptance by use and the realization scenarios. Quite possibly the defendant did not want the house but, afraid to raze it and build his dreamhouse until legal issues are resolved, he lives in it. On that take of the situation, the defendant's choice has been violated.

---

20. This is discussed in § 5.8(3) below.

21. Sometimes courts seek to justify the traditional rule against restitution by saying that to allow the landowner to keep the improvements will be compensation for rental value owed by the occupying plaintiff, Lindvig v. Lindvig, 385 N.W.2d 466 (N.D.1986), or compensation for his trespass. Skelton v. Doble, 347 N.W.2d 81, 84 (Minn.App.1984). The re-sult, however, is the same extreme result unless the value of the improvements happens to equal the damages or rents due.

§ 4.9(6)

1. II G. Palmer, Law of Restitution § 10.10 (1978 & Supps.).

2. See § 4.9(3) above.

With the postponed realization of cash from sale of the house it is still possible that the defendant would have preferred a world in which no one but himself built houses on his land and that he is merely making the best of a disappointingly bad situation.

In spite of these ambiguities, triers of fact might well conclude that use of the house reflected a substantial willingness to have it and that the sale of the house reflected a cash benefit which should be restored for similar reasons. The infringement of choice in those cases might be so minor in comparison to the extreme unjust enrichment involved that restitution should be ordered.

Ability to Reject the Benefit and the Common Fund Attorney Fee Rule

Both the acceptance and realization arguments are intimately related to the idea that the defendant's choice is never infringed in the first place if he has a choice of either accepting or rejecting the benefit without interfering with any of his other rights. The common fund rule presents an important example. That rule was discussed in the preceding chapter [3] so it is only briefly sketched here.

Suppose that Wilbur leaves two heirs at law, his daughters A and B, but by a will of doubtful provenance leaves all his fortune to a recent friend. Daughter A wishes to contest the will, since if she is successful she and B will take $1 million each. Daughter B takes the principled, self-sacrificing, and worshipful approach: if Daddy Wilbur wanted to leave everything to someone else that was his right. So A sues and B does not. A is successful, the will is found to have been induced by undue influence, and the $2 million, less attorney fees, goes entirely to A and B. But A wants B to pay one-half the substantial attorney fee. B resists: "I opposed your whole suit, why should I pay half the fee for the attorney *you* engaged?"

The common fund rule makes B pay one-half if she is going to take one-half of the estate.[4] She may renounce her share and take nothing. That was, remember, her initially stated wish. And she can still have her wish, in which case she is not charged the costs of procuring the benefit of inheritance. Her right of choice is fully preserved. In this instance, it is doubly clear because the estate in this example was treated as being composed of cash. However, even if the estate were composed of $2 million in beef cattle and a stamp collection, the principle would still apply. B never had a right to choose a cost-free trial; she had a choice to join in the suit and pay her share, or to reject its costs and its benefits. That choice remains to her so long as she can renounce the inheritance her sister procured for her. Her choice rights are preserved and she takes the costs with the benefits, both exactly as they are supposed to be in a perfect world.

If the litigation benefit is one that might be obtained in other ways, however, or is thrust upon the defendant against her will, to allow attorney fees as restitution cannot be justified, although the fee might be justified on

3. See § 3.10(2) above.

4. See Trustees v. Greenough, 105 U.S. (15 Otto) 527, 26 L.Ed. 1157 (1881) (all bondhold-ers who benefitted from plaintiff's litigation to recover dissipated security share in fees).

other, non-restitutionary grounds. In *Hall v. Cole*[5] the plaintiff sued his union, which had ousted him for criticism of union officials. The plaintiff won the right to be reinstated and asked for attorney fees. The Court was unwilling to recognize any basis outside the common fund or common benefit rule, but it was willing to find a benefit to the union resulting from the plaintiff's litigation. The litigation had established rights of union members to free speech so they and hence the union benefitted. Maybe so, provided the union does get to judge for itself what it considers a benefit. But the union obviously did *not* consider the plaintiff, his ideas, his speech or his litigation to be a benefit; that's why the union fought him. More importantly, however, the union is in a position quite different from the position of Sister B. Sister B could reject the benefit; the whole point of the litigation was to force the union to accept the "benefit."

So the restitutionary basis for the common fund rule lies in the fact that the defendant has a right to reject the benefit. If attorney fees are to be awarded against one who resists the "benefit" thrust upon him, there must be a better basis than the one urged in *Hall v. Cole*.

5. 412 U.S. 1, 93 S.Ct. 1943, 36 L.Ed.2d 702   (1973).

Chapter 5

HARMS TO INTERESTS IN TANGIBLE PROPERTY

Analysis

A. LAND

(1) In General

Sec.
5.1 Harms to Interests in Land Generally.

(2) Interests in Physical Integrity of Land and Structures

5.2 Harms to Interests in Physical Integrity of Land and Structures: Damages.
    5.2(1) Basic Measures of Damages for Physical Harm to Property: Diminished Value vs. Repair Costs.
    5.2(2) Choosing Between Diminished Value and Repair Costs: The Permanency Test and Restatement Test.
    5.2(3) Ceilings on Repair Costs Recoveries.
    5.2(4) Repair Costs as a Ceiling on Diminished Value Claim.
    5.2(5) Allowance of Repair Costs in Environmental Damage Cases.
    5.2(6) Limits on Replacement Costs in Analogous Eminent Domain Cases.
    5.2(7) Adjustments Required When Repair Costs Are Allowed.
    5.2(8) Waste.
5.3 Harms to Interests in Physical Integrity of Land and Structures: Damages for Severance.
    5.3(1) Severance Cases Generally.
    5.3(2) Good Faith Trespassers.
    5.3(3) Bad Faith Trespassers: Three Punitive Approaches.
    5.3(4) Traders Who Purchase Severed Articles.
5.4 Harms to Interests in Physical Integrity of Land and Structures: Restitution for Severance.
5.5 Harms to Interests in Physical Integrity of Land and Structures: Injunctive Relief.

(3) Interests in Use and Enjoyment

5.6 Harms to Interests in Use and Enjoyment: Damages for Nuisance.
    5.6(1) Substantive Background: Nuisance and Trespass.
    5.6(2) Nuisance Damages Generally.
    5.6(3) Damages Incentives to Abate.
    5.6(4) Regulatory Takings.
5.7 Harms to Interests in Use and Enjoyment: Injunctive Relief.
    5.7(1) Substantive Background and Summary.
    5.7(2) Doctrine Limiting Nuisance Injunctions.
    5.7(3) The Remedial Options in Nuisance Cases.

Sec.

5.7(4)   Economic and Other Perspectives.
5.7(5)   Effects of Statutes on Nuisance Injunctions.
5.7(6)   Easements.

(4) Harms to Interests in Exclusive Possession

5.8   Harms to Interests in Exclusive Possession: Damages for Non-harmful Trespasses, Use, or Occupation of Land.
      5.8(1)   In General.
      5.8(2)   Damages and Mesne Profits.
      5.8(3)   Improvements Added by Trespasser.
5.9   Dispossession—Restitution for Use and Occupation.
5.10   Harms to Interests in Exclusive Possession—Injunction, Ejectment and Summary Relief.
      5.10(1)   Ejectment.
      5.10(2)   Forcible Entry and Detainer, Summary Ejectment.
      5.10(3)   Injunctive Protection of Possession Generally.
      5.10(4)   Injunctive Protection Against Encroaching Structures.

(5) Procedural and Remedial Impacts of Permanent Invasions

5.11   Statutes of Limitations, Res Judicata and the Permanent Harm Doctrines.
      5.11(1)   General Rules for Permanent Invasions.
      5.11(2)   What Invasions Are "Permanent"?
      5.11(3)   Incentives in the Permanent Nuisance Issue.
      5.11(4)   The Plaintiff's Dilemma.

(6) Consequential and Punitive Measures in Land Cases

5.12   Consequential, Multiple and Punitive Damages.
      5.12(1)   General Rules.
      5.12(2)   Duplicative Recoveries: Recovering Both Consequential and General Damages.
      5.12(3)   Punitive Damages.

B. PERSONAL PROPERTY

5.13   General Damages: Diminished Market Value.
      5.13(1)   General Rules.
      5.13(2)   Time for Assessment of Market Value.
      5.13(3)   Place or Market for Assessment of Market Value.
      5.13(4)   Evidence of Value.
5.14   Replacement and Repair Costs.
      5.14(1)   Replacement and Repair Costs as Alternative Measures of Damages or as Limits on Recovery.
      5.14(2)   Accounting for Overhead in Repairs Cases.
      5.14(3)   Credits for Appreciation in Value Resulting From Repair or Replacement.
      5.14(4)   Credits for Return of Converted Chattel or Its Use in Plaintiff's Interest.
5.15   Special or Consequential Damages for Harm to, Taking or Destruction of Personal Property.
      5.15(1)   Special or Consequential Damages Generally.
      5.15(2)   Loss of Profits and Other Loss of Use Claims.
      5.15(3)   Intangible and Sentimental Losses; Emotional Harms and Punitive Damages.
5.16   Unique Goods and Those Without Market Value.
      5.16(1)   In General.
      5.16(2)   Property Used in Production of Income.
      5.16(3)   Property Held for Personal Use.
      5.16(4)   Property With Artistic or Historic Value.
5.17   Specific Recovery of Chattels.

Sec.
5.17(1) Generally.
5.17(2) Replevin: Recovery at Law and Due Process.
5.17(3) Injunction: Equitable Recovery of Chattels.
5.18 Restitution in Money.
5.18(1) Waiver of Tort and Suit in Assumpsit for Conversion.
5.18(2) Measure of Recovery in Assumpsit for Converted Chattels.
5.18(3) Constructive Trusts and Equitable Liens.

A. LAND

(1) IN GENERAL

§ 5.1 Harms to Interests in Land Generally

Elements in Selecting and Measuring Remedies

Types of remedies. As in many other cases, remedies for invasion of interests in land fall into three large categories—damages, restitution and injunctive or other equitable relief. The shape and extent of the remedy afforded is very largely a result of the harm perceived. This means that the extent and shape of the remedy is determined mainly by the interest invaded.

Interests in land. Interests in land can be categorized in many different ways and the categories are likely in any event to overlap. However, it is useful to recognize that there are at least three major kinds of interests in land and that remedies will vary according to which of those interests has been invaded as well as according to the extent of the invasion.

Physical security, use and enjoyment and pure possession interests. There is first of all the interest in physical integrity of the land and its structures.[1] Damage or threatened damage to buildings on the land, dumping on the land or ditching it are examples of an invasion of this interest.[2] Second, there is the interest in use and enjoyment of land. Pollution by odors or noises or possibly even inchoate dangers are examples of invasions of this second interest.[3] Third, there is the interest in the exclusive right to possession. The trespasser who occupies an owner's vacation cottage or farmhouse in the owner's absence and the neighbor whose garage encroaches six inches on the owner's property are examples. They invade the right to possession without harming the physical structure of the land and without necessarily affecting its use and enjoyment.[4]

Role of legal theory. If the nature of the interest invaded is important in shaping remedies, the nature of the plaintiff's legal theory most commonly is not. A good many legal theories may be invoked in land cases. These theories include trespass, nuisance, negligence, strict liability for hazardous

§ 5.1

1. See §§ 5.2 and 5.3 (damages); 5.4 (restitution) and 5.5 (injunctive relief).

2. See §§ 5.2–5.5 below.

3. See §§ 5.6 (damages) and 5.7 (injunctive relief).

4. See §§ 5.8 (damages), 5.9 (restitution) and 5.10 (injunctive relief).

activities, and even breach of warranty or breach of contract.[5] But except so far as the legal theory of the case evidences something else, such as the defendant's state of mind or the nature of the interest invaded, the substantive-law theory is not usually very helpful in determining remedies.[6] The present chapter is thus organized, not according to the theory asserted but according to the general nature of the interest harmed or threatened. There are, however, certain statutory claims, some of which may add to or limit elements of damage otherwise recoverable.[7]

Means of harm. The same ideas apply to the means by which the plaintiff's interest is invaded. Land may be invaded by negligent driving of a vehicle or negligent operation of a marine vessel; it may be shaken or pummelled with rocks from blasting; it may be ditched by a trespasser, or buildings may be torn down. But again, except so far as the means of harm prove something else, they are less important than the kind of harm done.

Defendant's state of mind. The state of mind of the defendant is also generally less important than the harm done. There are, of course, punitive damages claims, in which the defendant's state of mind is important.[8] And it is certainly true that the defendant who intends harm or who acts as a conscious wrongdoer may be subjected to liabilities for general damages[9] or injunction[10] or restitution[11] that otherwise would not be imposed. But the majority of harms in the cases do not seem to arise from such unmitigated evil doing. For the ordinary cases, the problems will be to identify the interest invaded and the extent of the invasion with a view to providing compensation without waste or windfalls.

Damages Generally

Physical harms to the land. It is unsafe to rely on a single general statement of damages for harms to property interests. Quite commonly, however, in the case of physical harms to the property itself, the measure is

5. For example, in Gully v. Southwestern Bell Tel. Co., 774 F.2d 1287 (5th Cir.1985) the defendant agreed by a condition in the easement granted to it that it would remove its cable upon 90 days notice. It refused to remove the cable and was held liable not as a trespasser but "on the contract."

6. There is a helpful discussion in Laurin v. DeCarolis Const. Co., Inc., 372 Mass. 688, 363 N.E.2d 675, 97 A.L.R.3d 1214 (1977).

7. Many statutes provide for double or treble damages in cases of bad faith trespass or waste. See § 5.2 and 5.3 below. Under civil rights statutes, an improper entry upon land may be actionable in some cases but with special limits on damages rules. See Tyree v. Keane, 400 Mass. 1, 507 N.E.2d 742 (1987) applying Carey v. Piphus, 435 U.S. 247, 98 S.Ct. 1042, 55 L.Ed.2d 252 (1978) and the rules discussed in § 7.3 below. There are also cases in which the plaintiff may indirectly focus attention on a particular way of measuring damages by selecting a theory of recovery, as where the plaintiff sues for conversion of timber rather than for trespass to land. As to this, see § 5.3 below.

8. As to punitive damages generally see § 3.11 above; in land cases, see § 5.12(4) below.

9. Doubts about whether to use the repair cost or the diminished value measure of damages might be resolved against a defendant who acts with intent to harm. See § 5.2 below. Bad faith of a trespasser also figures in multiple damages awards.

10. Bad faith of one who builds an encroaching building partly on the plaintiff's land would always warrant a mandatory injunction for removal, while the injunction may be denied as to a good faith builder. See § 5.8 below.

11. The measure of restitution may include profits made by the tortfeasor who is in bad faith or is a conscious wrongdoer, while it might be limited to the market or rental value of the land used if the trespass is in good faith. See § 5.9 below.

the diminished value of the land caused by the trespass.[12] In some cases, perhaps especially where the land has special personal uses, the owner may be allowed a repair cost measure of damages in excess of the diminished value.[13] When an item is taken from the land, as where timber is taken or ore mined, courts often use the value of the item itself as a measure;[14] but if the trespass is in bad faith, they may allow the plaintiff to recover its value at a later date, perhaps when it has been given added value by manufacture.[15]

Interference with possession. When the injury is to possession alone, damages are typically measured by rental value.[16]

Interference with use and enjoyment. If the invasion interferes with use and enjoyment, as in nuisance cases, then the damages may be measured either by reduced market value of the land or reduced rental value,[17] depending on whether the harm is permanent or temporary.[18] The plaintiff in such cases may also recover for personal illness or inconvenience caused by the nuisance.[19]

Adjustments. In all these cases adjustments may be made to accommodate particular facts. For example, if repair cost is allowed as a measure of recovery, but repairs increased the value of the land, an adjustment must be made to take that fact into account.[20]

Restitution Generally

A trespasser who uses the plaintiff's land or takes something of value from it may at times be held liable for restitution in lieu of damages—that is, for the benefit to the trespasser rather than for the harm to the landowner.[21] Depending upon how this unjust enrichment is to be measured, a restitutionary liability might at times be considerably greater than a liability for pure damages.

Injunction and Possessory Relief

Threat of future harm, inadequate remedy at law. Where the issue is raised at all, courts generally say that an injunction against trespass to land will not issue unless the plaintiff shows that future harm is threatened [22] and further shows that unless an injunction issues, there will be irreparable injury. That is to say, the legal remedy must be shown to be inadequate before an injunction will issue.[23] Special limits on injunctive relief are found in some cases, such as those involving certain kinds of waste.[24]

---

12. See generally § 5.2(1) below; Restatement Second of Torts § 929 (1979).

13. E.g., Andersen v. Edwards, 625 P.2d 282 (Alaska 1981). See § 5.2(3) below.

14. See Restatement Second of Torts § 929(2) (1979).

15. E.g., Payne v. Consolidation Coal Co., 607 F.Supp. 378 (W.D.Va.1985). See § 5.3(3) below.

16. E.g., Uhlhorn v. Keltner, 723 S.W.2d 131 (Tenn.App.1986). See § 5.8(2) below.

17. Compare, e.g., Exxon Corp., U.S.A. v. Dunn, 474 So.2d 1269 (Fla.App.1985) (reduced market value) with Earl v. Clark, 219 N.W.2d 487 (Iowa 1974) (reduced rental value). See generally § 5.6(2) below.

18. See generally §§ 5.6 and 5.11 below.

19. E.g., Ayers v. Township of Jackson, 106 N.J. 557, 525 A.2d 287, 76 A.L.R.4th 571 (1987); see generally § 5.6(2) below.

20. See generally § 5.2(7) below.

21. See generally § 5.9 below.

Injunction to affect title and possession. Equity courts were likewise loath to determine title [25] or possession [26] in injunction cases, preferring to leave those matters to jury trials available in ejectment. Equity shows less reluctance about considering such matters than it once did.[27] However, where the plaintiff is out of possession, the legal action of ejectment may lie to restore possession without injunction;[28] and in many cases a summary form of this relief known as a forcible entry and detainer action may be available more or less like a provisional remedy.[29]

Encroachment cases. Not all possession problems can be remedied without injunctive relief however. An injunction may be required in the encroachment cases, in which defendant's structure such as a house is built so that a portion stands on the plaintiff's property. In these cases the primary concern of the courts is usually to arrive at a solution that equitably balances the rights of both parties and takes into account the absolute right of the landowner without compelling substantial economic waste or economic dislocation.[30]

Costs and benefits of injunctive relief. Assessment of injunction cases increasingly requires economic analysis, as where it is necessary to consider the costs and benefits of an injunction,[31] and public policy analysis, as where there are environmental harms as well as harm to the plaintiff's property.[32] Injunction is very often a prime remedy in pollution cases causing a nuisance.[33]

(2) INTERESTS IN PHYSICAL INTEGRITY OF LAND AND STRUCTURES

§ 5.2 Harms to Interests in Physical Integrity of Land and Structures: Damages

§ 5.2(1) Basic Measures of Damages for Physical Harm to Property: Diminished Value vs. Repair Costs

Alternative Measures

When compensation is sought for physical harm to real property or to structures upon it, courts usually choose between two different general damages measures.[1] The choice is the same one that arises in contract cases when the contractor fails to complete the work required or leave the work in need of repairs.[2] The diminution measure permits the plaintiff to recover the difference between the reasonable sale value of the property immediate-

---

28. See generally § 5.10(1).

29. See generally § 5.10(2).

30. See generally § 5.10(4) below.

31. See e.g., § 5.7(2) below.

32. See, e.g., §§ 5.2(5), 5.7(4), 5.11(3) all below.

33. See generally § 5.7 below.

§ 5.2(1)

1. "General" damages are usually market damages, see § 3.3(3), above. Such damages are contrasted with consequential or special damages, as to which see §§ 3.3(4) above and 5.12 below. The cost measure of damages bears some resemblance to both, as explained in connection with contract cases. As to that, see § 12.2(2) below.

2. See § 12.19(1) below.

ly before the harm was done and the value immediately [3] afterward.[4] This measurement permits the use of accounting conventions and other devices for estimating value.

The repair-cost measure gives the plaintiff the reasonable cost of repairing the damage done.[5] "Repair" in this sense may be defined to include replacement and salvage adjustment when the context makes that reasonable. Consequential or special damages or even other measures of general damages may be used when the facts dictate.[6] It is even possible to combine the repair and diminished value measures in a way that provides one single complete compensation.[7]

Windfall and Waste

Each measure has its advantages and disadvantages. The repair-cost measure may best provide full compensation in many cases, but if the value of the property is reduced very little by the tort and the repairs would cost a great deal, the most economic thing for the landowner to do would be to sell the property rather than to repair it. If the plaintiff takes this route, an award of repair cost damages can be seen as a windfall[8] since the plaintiff will not have suffered the costs of repairs but only the smaller loss represented by the diminished value.[9] On the other hand, if the plaintiff actually

---

3. The value of land at any given moment depends in part on its present potential for future development. But its value at any given moment is not *equivalent* to its potential future value. Costs, risks and delay in developing its potential will always be entailed, so its present value is less than its potential. In Thorsen v. Johnson, 745 P.2d 1243, 1244 (Utah 1987) defendant did substantial damage to portions of the plaintiff's land. The plaintiff had made plans to develop the land as a subdivision and had spent some $15,000 for surveying and platting and attempting to drill a well for water. He expected to expend about $171,000 or more to develop the lots for sale. The trial judge awarded the value of nine lots destroyed by the defendant's excavations of an irrigation ditch, estimating that value as "lots" in the subdivision that was planned but did not yet exist. The court held this to be error, saying that "the measure of damages is the diminution of the fair market value of the land immediately following the infliction of the damages—not what the property may be worth when and if substantial sums of money are expended to turn it into an improved subdivision." It quoted from Pennsylvania S.V.R. Co. v. Cleary, 125 Pa. 442, 17 A. 468 (1889), to the effect that present value is based in part on the purposes for which the land might be adapted "but it is the tract, and not the lots into which it might be divided, that is to be valued * * *. [The jury is to decide] what a present purchaser would be willing to pay for it in the condition it is now in."

4. E.g., McKinney v. Christiana Community Builders, 229 Cal.App.3d 611, 280 Cal.Rptr.

242 (1991); Copiah Dairies, Inc. v. Addkison, 247 Miss. 327, 153 So.2d 689 (1963).

5. E.g., Falcone v. Perry, 68 Wash.2d 909, 416 P.2d 690 (1966). Restoration (cleanup) may be a preferred measure in the case of environmental harm from hazardous substances. See Comprehensive Environmental Response, Compensation and Liability Act (CERCLA), 42 U.S.C.A. § 9607(a).

7. Reasonable repair costs plus any diminished value remaining after repair would be entirely appropriate in any case in which repair costs alone would be permissible. An award based on a combination of the two measures was affirmed in Wade v. S.J. Groves & Sons Company, 283 Pa.Super. 464, 424 A.2d 902 (1981).

8. See United States v. 564.54 Acres of Land, Etc., 441 U.S. 506, 99 S.Ct. 1854, 60 L.Ed.2d 435 (1979); McKinney v. Christiana Community Builders, 229 Cal.App.3d 611, 280 Cal.Rptr. 242 (1991) ("Courts normally will not award costs of repair which exceed diminution in value because the basic objective of compensatory damages is to make an injured party whole, but no more than that"); Board of County Com'rs of Weld County v. Slovek, 723 P.2d 1309 (Colo.1986).

9. *Example:* Land originally worth $100,000 is damaged by defendant's unauthorized grading. It will cost $10,000 to restore the original contours of the land, but the land is diminished in value only by $500. If the plaintiff can use the cost of repair measure, recovery will be $10,000. It will be worth $9,500 to the plaintiff to learn to love the land as graded, or alternatively to sell the land at a

makes the more expensive repairs, an award of repair costs as damages does not provide a windfall, but it does seem uncomfortably like economic waste. To make expensive repairs would be to maximize rather than to minimize the loss.[10] These considerations suggest that, for many cases, the diminution rule would prove more satisfactory than the cost of repair rule.

Idiosyncratic and Personal Uses

There are cases, however, in which costly repairs might be justified even though the land's value has been reduced only slightly. In many instances the plaintiff is using land in a way that suits the plaintiff very well but that does not maximize its economic value. This is often the case when a landowner uses land as a residence when it would be worth much more for commercial development. If the defendant bulldozes the plaintiff's trees or his garden, it may be that there is no economic harm at all: the land may be worth as much or more than before because it can be readily used for a housing development.[11] If that is the case, the diminution measure would give the plaintiff no more than nominal recovery.

For cases of this sort, the diminution measure seems unacceptable, at least if the plaintiff really wants the property as a homestead or for some special purpose such as use for a church [12] rather than as an economic investment [13] and if repair is in fact likely to be carried out.[14] A variation on the same theme might be seen in those cases in which damage is done to natural resources without harming present market value.[15] Even so, an extensive repair that costs more than the diminution in value should not be granted lightly. A California court establishes careful limitations on repair cost recovery, insisting that cost of repair is not an appropriate measure even under the "personal reason" rule "where only slight damage has occurred and the cost of repair is far in excess of the loss in value." [16]

loss of $500 in order to keep the $10,000 damages award.

11. See, e.g., Garey Const. Co., Inc. v. Thompson, 697 S.W.2d 865 (Tex.App.1985) (shrubs, no reduction in land value, recovery for "intrinsic" value).

12. See, e.g., Trinity Church in the City of Boston v. John Hancock Mut. Life Ins. Co., 399 Mass. 43, 502 N.E.2d 532 (1987) (damage to church caused no immediate expense but hastened the day when major rebuilding would be required, percentages of replacement cost used). As to the problem in eminent domain cases, however, see § 5.2(6) below.

13. Since there may be no way to find out whether the plaintiff really wants to make repairs or only to obtain the highest possible damage award, the parties might be forced into bargaining over damages by ordering the defendant to make the repairs. If the plaintiff does not really want the repairs but only the money, he can bargain to let the defendant pay a smaller sum, but one still greater than the diminution in value. This approach has been suggested for the somewhat analogous case of the encroaching building. See Note, Injunction Negotiations: An Economic, Moral and Legal Analysis, 27 Stand.L.Rev.

1563 (1975). But it is too optimistic to think that this solution will get the plaintiff just the sum she would have been willing to take for the damage and no more. Cost and cash flow pressure, which may be wholly disproportionate to the defendant's legal wrong, are more likely to influence the outcome.

14. See Andersen v. Edwards, 625 P.2d 282, 289 (Alaska 1981); McKinney v. Christiana Community Builders, 229 Cal.App.3d 611, 280 Cal.Rptr. 242, 245 (1991).

15. See Ohio v. United States Department of Interior, 880 F.2d 432 (D.C.Cir.1989) (under federal environmental statute).

16. McKinney v. Christiana Community Builders, 229 Cal.App.3d 611, 280 Cal.Rptr. 242, 245 (1991) (quoting earlier authority). The court spelled out proof it apparently would require:

"substantial evidence (1) [the landowners] had a personal reason to repair the damages caused to their residence; (2) they intended to make those repairs; and (3) costs of repair bore a reasonable relationship to both the value of their home before harm and to the level of damages actually suffered due to the defendants' tortious acts."

§ 5.2(2) Choosing Between Diminished Value and Repair Costs: The Permanency Test and Restatement Test

The Restatement rule provides that if repair cost disproportionately exceeds the diminished value of the land, then the measure of damages is limited to the diminished value. However, this ceiling does not apply under the Restatement rule if the land is used for a "purpose personal to the owner." [17] The owner who wishes to restore her land to its pre-injury condition is thus allowed repair costs under this rule even if those costs far exceed the amount by which the land's value has been diminished, at least where repair is possible [18] and likely to be carried out. [19]

The Restatement illustrates its approach by a case in which a garden in a city lot is destroyed, but its destruction does not reduce the value of the lot. [20] The owner would be permitted to recover the cost of restoring the garden. The Restatement has support of judicial authority on principle. [21] It also finds support in the results of cases in which the cost of repairing homes [22] or replacing trees [23] or even restoring the grade or contour of land [24] has been awarded. When repair costs can be recovered, the plaintiff may also be permitted to recover for loss of use of the property during repairs. [25]

The Restatement rule is exceedingly difficult to apply in some cases. If repair costs exceed diminished value, many owners will claim repair costs even if they intend to make no repairs at all, so that the "windfall" problem may remain. And equally the economic waste problem may remain. If the owner insists on repairing a damaged house which only clutters the land and is worth nothing, the fact that his purpose is "personal" will not eliminate the waste entailed in making repairs rather than adapting the land to its best purposes.

§ 5.2(3) Ceilings on Repair Costs Recoveries

Courts sometimes formulate the damages measure by saying that repair costs can be recovered, but that the recovery is limited to the diminished value of the land. [1] This is equivalent to a diminished value rule; but unlike some formulations, it rather clearly recognizes that the plaintiff may prove damages by introducing evidence of repair costs, which is undoubtedly correct in any event. [2] With this point recognized, it may be said that the rule in this form seems in substance no different from any other rule using diminished value as a basis, and it is presumably subject to the same exceptions allowing repair costs in special cases.

§ 5.2(2)

17. Restatement Second of Torts § 929 (1979).

20. Restatement Second of Torts § 929, Comment *b* (1979).

21. Andersen v. Edwards, 625 P.2d 282, 288 (Alaska 1981); Moulton v. Groveton Papers Co., 114 N.H. 505, 323 A.2d 906 (1974); see Hanset v. General Const. Co., 285 Or. 101, 589 P.2d 1117 (1979) (dictum supporting First Restatement, no actual proof of diminished value).

23. E.g., Worthington v. Roberts, 304 Ark. 551, 803 S.W.2d 906 (1991) (cost of replacement proper for destroyed trees, hence cost of treatment proper for damaged trees, without regard to whether land value was or was not diminished); Malerba v. Warren, 108 Misc.2d 785, 438 N.Y.S.2d 936 (1981), modified on other points, 96 A.D.2d 529, 464 N.Y.S.2d 835 (1983) (replacement of shrubs and beach grass); Garey Const. Co., Inc. v. Thompson, 697 S.W.2d 865 (Tex.App.1985). See Annots., 95 A.L.R.3d 508 (1979) (shade, ornamental trees); 90 A.L.R.3d 800 (1979) (fruit or other productive trees).

Some cases allow repair costs subject to a very different ceiling or maximum. These cases hold that the plaintiff may recover cost of repairs in excess of the diminished value of the property, so long as the repair costs are less than the total pre-injury value of the property.[3]

§ 5.2(4) Repair Costs as a Ceiling on Diminished Value Claim

Defendants occasionally argue that when repair costs are less than the diminished value, repair costs should be the ceiling on recovery or even that repair cost is the only acceptable measure. The effect of a rule like this would be to compel the plaintiff to accept repair or restoration costs even if diminished value were much greater.

There is a surface plausibility to the argument, which relies on the policy applied, as to special damages, in the rule requiring a plaintiff to minimize damages.[1] However, if the testimony is that repair costs are significantly less than diminished value, something is likely to be wrong. If damage to real property can be made good by repairs costing $1,000, it is not quite credible that the market value of the property is diminished by $10,000. Either the repair cost estimate or the diminished value estimate is likely to be wrong in such a case.

An example will show why. Suppose the plaintiff's property is valued at $100,000. Defendant, by mistake, begins doing construction work on the plaintiff's land, grading and hauling dirt. The mistake is soon discovered and the testimony shows that the land can be restored to its initial condition for $1,000, but there is also testimony that the land is diminished in value by $10,000. Willing land buyers, however, knowing that the land could be made worth $100,000 again by the expenditure of $1,000 would offer any sum up to something close to $99,000 in order to get the land. If the buyer were to pay $99,000 plus $1,000 for repair, she would obtain value equal to what she paid. If she paid anything less, she would gain from the deal. Thus willing buyers would tend to pay, if necessary, a sum only slightly less than the total of pre-injury value minus repair costs. If repairs are economical then the diminished value is correspondingly less, too. So when repair costs estimates and diminished value estimates are wildly disparate, one of those estimates is likely to be wrong.

One explanation for testimony that reflects an unlikely discrepancy between repair costs and diminished value measures is that the repair costs envisioned by a witness would not fully restore the property, or would restore it for its best economic use but not necessarily for the "personal" use to which the plaintiff intends to put it. Another explanation is that the repair cost testimony may not take into account repairs that may be required in the future.[2]

Although there are some decisions that appear to adopt a repair cost measure for some class of cases, and hence to support the idea that cost of repair, if less than diminished value, would be a ceiling,[3] courts have not ordinarily forced a cost of repair measure upon an unwilling plaintiff.[4] But as in other cases, cost of repairs should usually be admissible as evidence bearing on the diminished value even though repair cost is not itself a measure or a ceiling.

§ 5.2(5) Allowance of Repair Costs in Environmental Damage Cases

Repair or Restoration Costs to Prevent or Minimize External Harm

In some cases damage to the plaintiff's land also causes harm to others or to the public. Injunctive remedies may furnish the best relief in such cases. For example, a defendant might deposit toxic wastes on the plaintiff's land. As long as the wastes remain, they may be a source of secondary pollution that affects a neighbor's well or public waters. In such a case, the diminution in the value of the plaintiff's land does not represent all of the damage done. Instead, some of the costs are externalized or placed upon other victims. Although the costs are real,[1] many of them would be difficult to measure, even if appropriate plaintiffs could be identified. So injunctions will often be appropriate and desirable in such cases, because the injunction can stop conduct that causes harms to the public at the same time it stops conduct that causes harm to the plaintiff.

Injunctions will not solve all such problems, however. The defendant may no longer add to the pollution, yet toxic substances may be left behind that continue to cause threats to the landowner and also to others. If the defendant cannot remove the hazards, or should not be trusted to do so safely, the question will be one of damages.

In this situation, damages should not usually be limited to the diminished market value of the land. Instead, the landowner should be permitted to recover full restoration costs and all consequential damages that are properly established, at least if he can give the court assurance that repair, restoration or cleanup will actually take place. Such a scenario gives the landowner no windfall and it entails no waste. Because costs of the pollution affect others, or the public at large, the diminished value of the plaintiff's land is no guide to the actual costs imposed by the pollution. Cost of repair or cleanup are thus appropriate, even if they exceed the diminished value of the land. As indicated below, this result is supported by analogy to environmental laws, even if those laws do not apply to the particular case.

Analogies under Environmental Statutes

Environmental statutes do not attempt to provide direct protections for landowners as such. Such statutes may occasionally assist a landowner's claim against someone who, like a trespasser, contaminates the land,[2] but

---

§ 5.2(5)

1. See Cross, Natural Resource Damage Valuation, 42 Vand.L.Rev. 269 (1989).

2. 42 U.S.C.A. § 9607(a)(4)(B) provides for recovery of "any other necessary costs of response incurred by any other person consistent with the national contingency plan." See Wickland Oil Terminals v. Asarco, Inc., 792 F.2d 887 (9th Cir.1986) (action under CERCLA, private plaintiff allowed to recover from predecessor who left hazardous wastes; damages include cleanup and testing costs, even though government had not incurred costs or approved cleanup). One who suffers from environmental damages in some capacity other than as a landowner may not have a CERCLA claim. See Artesian Water Co. v. Government of New Castle Co., 851 F.2d 643 (3d Cir.1988).

Recovery includes only costs actually incurred to the time of trial. "Under CERCLA's scheme for private action, response costs may not be recovered when there has been no commitment of resources for meeting these costs. Section 9607(a)(4)(B) permits an action for response costs 'incurred'—not 'to be incurred.' Moreover, CERCLA expressly provides for declaratory actions for determining liability as to future response costs. Section 9613(g)(2) provides that in actions under § 9607, 'the court shall enter a declaratory judgment on liability for response costs * * * that will be binding on any subsequent action or actions to recover further response costs * * *.'" Dant & Russell, Inc. v. Burlington N.R.R. Co., 951 F.2d 246 (9th Cir.1991). 42 U.S.C.A. § 9613(f) specifically provides for

their main impact is a double analogy. First, environmental statutes deal with harms to land that cause harms to the public or to others outside the land and hence raise the problem presented in this subsection. Second, the government which claims for damages to natural resources is in a position similar to the landowner who claims damages to the land itself.[3]

The Superfund Act.   The Superfund Act, also known as CERCLA,[4] authorizes government identification of hazardous substance sites and government cleanup. The government in turn is given the right to recover certain costs from those responsible for any "release" of hazardous substances. There are many environmental statutes and some of them address similar problems and contain somewhat similar provisions,[5] but only the CERCLA provisions are discussed here. CERCLA liability represents a specialized field, so arcane terminology is common in most discussions. Some of the common and puzzling acronyms are given in a footnote.[6]

Persons liable.   Costs of cleaning up a hazardous substance site are typically very high and run into many millions for each site. The Superfund statute contemplates that in most instances the government will clean up the hazardous substance site, and then recover from responsible persons. There are four classes of responsible persons: (1) the present owner, (2) the operator of the facility at the time the substances were disposed of, (3) any person who arranged for disposal, and (4) any person who accepted hazardous substances for disposal or transportation.[7]

Elements of recovery.   Parties held responsible under CERCLA are liable for two different kinds of harms. *First* they are liable for "response costs," incurred by the government (state, federal, or tribal). These costs include "all costs of removal or remedial action." *Second* they are liable for "damages for injury to, destruction of, or loss of natural resources, including the reasonable costs of assessing such injury, destruction, or loss resulting from such a release." [8]

contribution actions among responsible parties.

3. CERCLA provides that certain national and state officials may be designated as trustees for the natural resources and that the trustees shall "act on behalf of the public." 42 U.S.C.A. § 9607. The trustee conception helps explain the relevance of this material to the present chapter but it does not mean that all the problems are identical. In particular, market value measurement is virtually impossible in the case of public interests in natural resources like uncontaminated rivers or oceans.

4. The Comprehensive Environmental Response, Compensation, and Liability Act, 42 U.S.C.A. § 9601 et seq.

5. The Clean Water Act (CWA) and the Oil Pollution Act of 1990, 33 U.S.C.A. § 2701 et seq. (other materials from the act are scattered in places indicated in the notes to § 2701).

6. A "reauthorization" and amending statute passed in 1986 is known as SARA (Super-

fund Amendment and Reauthorization Act). Some but not all of the hazardous substances covered are listed in the Resource Conservation and Recovery Act (RCRA). The Superfund administration is carried out by the Environmental Protection Agency (EPA). It studies hazard sites and follows procedures it has established in the National Contingency Plan (NCP). It then, after administrative hearings or public comment, lists sites for cleanup on the National Priorities List (NPL). As explained in the text, several classes of persons including many individuals or companies, may be held liable for the costs incurred by the government. Some of these may be ordered, in some circumstances, to remove hazardous substances directly. The persons who may be so liable are known as potentially responsible parties or PRPs.

7. 42 U.S.C.A. § 9701(a)(1)–(4).

8. 42 U.S.C.A. § 9607(a)(4)(C). The Act defines damages to mean "damages for injury or loss of natural resources as set forth in section 9607(a) or 9611(b) of this title." 42 U.S.C.A. § 9601. Thus in the Act's terminology, dam-

Response costs. The response costs recoverable are analogous to repair costs and consequential damages that a private landowner-plaintiff might recover in similar situations. Response costs include (1) costs of removing the hazardous materials themselves and (2) costs of remedial action to prevent further damage. Physical removal of contaminated soil might be an example of the first category. Cost of repairing leaking containers or collecting contaminated rainfall to prevent further damage might be in the second category. Costs of remedial action also include relocation of endangered residents or businesses,[9] "any other necessary costs of response incurred by any other person," and even "the costs of any health assessment or health effects study" under certain circumstances.[10] Such items are closely analogous to common law consequential damages. Remedial actions generally operate like minimizing damages rules, to prevent further harm, although the harm may be harm to others rather than to the government itself. Response costs are very high, but in spite of the terminology, they closely resemble familiar common law types of damages.

Natural resource damage. Natural resource damage includes residual harms the effects of which are not eliminated by removal of hazardous substances or taking remedial action. Natural resources include the land, water and wildlife.[11] To take an example from a judicial opinion,[12] a hazardous substance or oil that destroys a rookery for fur seals and destroys their habitat is damage to natural resources. Environmental lawyers have had difficulties with this item of damages. Although public resources like seal habitats do have great importance, many such items are not bought and sold, so the common law "market value" measure is not directly helpful.

Thinkers have argued that resources could be valued for their uses by humans, for their existence value regardless of actual present use,[13] and for their intrinsic value, regardless of human existence.[14] Federal regulations, however, have approached the matter with a heavy emphasis on methodology—establishing the nature of the injury, then quantifying it, and at last estimating damages.[15] Regulations attempt to measure the damages by

ages does not mean any of the named compensatory recoveries, but only the recovery for loss of natural resources.

9. The definitional section, 42 U.S.C.A. § 9601(23)–(25) defines remove/removal, remedy/remedial, and response. Removal and remove mean the cleanup or removal of the substances. Remedy or remedial action mean actions "consistent with permanent remedy taken instead of or in addition to removal actions," specifically, to prevention of escape of substances and including the "costs of relocation of residents and businesses and community facilities" where necessary. Respond and response mean removal or remedy.

10. 42 U.S.C.A. § 9607(a).

11. 42 U.S.C.A. § 9601(16) defines natural resources to include "land, fish, wildlife, biota, air, water, ground water, drinking water supplies, and other such resources belonging to, managed by, held in trust by, appertaining to, or otherwise controlled by the United States

* * * any State or local government, any foreign government, any Indian tribe * * *."

12. State of Ohio v. United States Dept. of Interior, 880 F.2d 432, 442 (D.C.Cir.1989).

13. Ability to use in the future or option value, either for existing humans or future generations might be included in this category. Thus experimental economics has indicated that people would pay something to preserve, say, whales, even though they never expect to see one.

14. Cross, Natural Resource Damage Valuation, 42 Van.L.Rev. 269 (1989).

15. A brief description of the general process is found in 43 C.F.R. § 11.13. Critics believe that heavy emphasis on "scientific" methodologies makes for sluggish and delayed response to real problems and that for the moment at least efficiency is less important now than actual effectiveness. See Guruswamy, Integrating Thoughtways: Re-Opening of the Environmental Mind?, 1989 Wis.L.Rev. 463, at n. 193.

either restoration costs [16] or by diminished use value. If use value measurement is used, the regulations prefer measurement by market price of use values where that is possible,[17] or standardized appraisals, where it is not.[18]

Sometimes, as in the case of public recreational areas, no market prices can be attached to use values. In that case, economic values may be established in a variety of other ways. For example, the added travel costs people incurred to visit the resource indicate something about its purely economic value, as does the price people pay for a substitute.[19]

Restoration costs in excess of resource value? The efficiency argument. If restoration is possible, should it be carried out even when it will cost more than the natural resource is worth? The Interior Department, defending an earlier version of its regulations, argued that it was economically inefficient to restore a natural resource if it would cost more than the value of the resource. It argued, therefore in favor of an earlier regulation that valued the resource at the lesser of restoration or diminished use value.

The District of Columbia Circuit concluded that a rule always favoring the measure that produced the least amount of damages violated the statute.[20] Although the court accepted efficiency as a goal, it rejected the argument that economic efficiency argument compelled assessment of damages as the lesser of the two measures. It said: " 'Efficiency,' standing alone, simply means that the chosen policy will dictate the result that achieves the greatest value to society. Whether a particular choice is efficient depends on *how the various alternatives are valued.*"[21] The court thought Congress favored efficiency but that it also thought the value of the natural resources was presumptively greater than the cost of restoration, and hence preferred the cost measure as a starting point.

Restitution or damages. The normal terminology of the law would probably treat the recovery for natural resource damages and also the recovery of response costs as damages. Both compensate for loss incurred. It often happens, however, compensation and restitution turn out to yield the same dollar amount. That may be the case with response costs. One

16. 43 C.F.R. § 11.81.

17. 43 C.F.R. § 11.83(c): "(1) A determination shall be made as to whether the market for the resource is reasonably competitive. Unless the authorized official determines that the market for the resource is not reasonably competitive, the diminution in the market price of the resource shall be used to estimate the damages to the injured resource. This methodology shall be referred to as the market price methodology." Many resources, or components of them, have market values. Forests, for example, can be valued as lumber if nothing else.

18. 43 C.F.R. § 11.83(c)(2).

19. See 43 C.F.R. § 11.83(d)(3); Cross, Natural Resource Damage Valuation, 42 Van. L.Rev. 269, 387 (1989). Regulations also recognize the possibility of "Hedonic" valuation. See 43 C.F.R. § 11.83(d)(4). In spite of its name, hedonic valuation is a market-oriented method. Here the idea is that the value of resources that are not marketed may be indicated by the value attached to similar resources that are marketed. Cross gives the example of declining land values in areas suffering increased pollution as a way of measuring the value of clean air. See Cross, supra at n. 234. Contingent valuation is a third way of attempting to get at use value. See 43 C.F.R. § 11.83(d)(5) (authorizing only a limited use). Contingent valuation is a kind of poll which asks how much the interviewees would pay to keep the resource (or alternatively how much they would charge to sell it). Although some experimental economists have used ingenious games and real money payoffs in an attempt to keep answers honest, there are obviously some difficulties with these methods.

20. Ohio v. United States Dept. of Interior, 880 F.2d 432 (D.C.Cir.1989).

21. Id. at 456–457.

analysis of those costs emphasizes that the government is expending costs to fulfill the duty of the owner operator of the facility. A person who has fulfilled another's duty, for example, by providing necessaries for another's children, is entitled to restitution. So some writers and judges have viewed the response costs as restitution rather than as damages.

However, apart from the self-interest of a party, it is important to characterize a liability as restitutionary only if restitution differs in amount from damages or if there is no substantive basis for recovery as damages. Under the statute, there is a substantive basis for recovery of "response costs," which are not otherwise characterized by the statute. The amount to be recovered does not differ according to the characterization as restitution or damages. Attempts to characterize the recovery of response costs as either restitution or damages do not seem helpful. Usually the attempt is made only to determine whether an insurance policy covers liability for release of hazardous substance.[22] It is doubtful that the term "damages" in an insurance policy carries with it any such inchoate set of distinctions and the question whether response costs are covered by the policy probably cannot not turn on proposed definitions of those costs as restitution without distorting the remedial concepts involved.

§ 5.2(6) Limits on Replacement Costs in Analogous Eminent Domain Cases

If repair or restoration costs are favored in environmental cases, the opposite has been true in federal eminent domain cases. A governmental taking of property requires just compensation and is closely analogous to the problem of damages for harms done to property. But in the taking cases the Supreme Court has often insisted on measuring damages or just compensation by the market value of the property taken.[1] Neither personal uses nor individual attachments increase the compensation due; nor is the landowner generally entitled to a cost of replacement measure of compensation.[2] The landowner is instead entitled to the fair market value of the land with whatever opportunities and risks that would represent to buyers.[3]

Courts generally have recognized that when there is no meaningful market for property, replacement cost is at least a datum that can be considered as evidence on the question of market value. Sometimes in eminent domain cases this rule is invoked only by finding that the property is a "special use" property, having a value to the owner he could not realize

---

22. E.g., Boeing Company v. Aetna Casualty and Sur. Co., 113 Wash.2d 869, 784 P.2d 507, 87 A.L.R.4th 405 (1990) (reflecting a division in the court and in the cases as to whether response costs are "damages" or "restitution").

§ 5.2(6)

1. See, e.g., United States v. 564.54 Acres of Land, Etc. (Lutheran Synod), 441 U.S. 506, 99 S.Ct. 1854, 60 L.Ed.2d 435 (1979) ("we have recognized the need for a relatively objective working rule * * *. The Court therefore has employed the concept of fair market value to determine the condemnee's loss").

2. Kimball Laundry Co. v. United States, 338 U.S. 1, 5, 69 S.Ct. 1434, 1437, 93 L.Ed.

1765, 7 A.L.R. 1280 (1949) (compensation limited to transferable value "as opposed to such personal and variant standards as value to the particular owner whose property has been taken," a rule that provides "an external validity" to the award). See also, discussing the related "no business damage" rule, Risinger, Direct Damages: The Lost Key To Constitutional Just Compensation When Business Premises Are Condemned, 15 Seton Hall L.Rev. 483 (1985).

3. See Almota Farmers Elevator & Warehouse Co. v. United States, 409 U.S. 470, 93 S.Ct. 791, 35 L.Ed.2d 1 (1973); § 3.5 above.

in a sale.[4] Supposed examples are churches and bridges, for which the market would not reflect the "real" value to the owner. Replacement cost is relevant, not as a measure, but as a piece of evidence in determining value in a variety of cases when value cannot be established by direct reference to an existing market.[5]

Replacement or reproduction costs as an element in figuring value of the plaintiff's property will differ from the cost of procuring a substitute elsewhere. Replacement cost evidence might look to the value of the land plus the cost of building a replacement building on it, then making a depreciation deduction.[6] The focus on replacement cost or the "cost method" as it is often called in eminent domain literature, is on the plaintiff's (or condemnee's) property; it is valued by estimating the cost to replace it. When one considers substitute property as a measure of payment, the focus is shifted to the cost of acquiring the substitute, which may be quite different indeed from the hypothetical cost of building the same facility on the condemned land. So to permit use of replacement costs as one element in estimating value of the plaintiff's own property is not necessarily like permitting evidence of substitute facility costs.

In federal eminent domain cases the Supreme Court has insisted that the cost of substitute facilities cannot be used as a measure of just compensation unless (a) the plaintiff's land has no ascertainable market value[7] and (b) the plaintiff is under a duty to replace the facility.[8]

In the *Duncanville, Texas* case[9] the federal government took a landfill used by a Texas city. The city was forced to construct waste disposal facilities elsewhere, at a cost of $700,000. But the landfill taken by the government was worth only $200,000, so the city suffered an immediate cash loss of about half a million dollars. As there was a market value for the city's property, however, the Court concluded that the substitute facilities measure of compensation could not be used.[10]

---

4. See J. Sackman, Nichols' Law of Eminent Domain § 12C.01[1] (1990 and Supps.).

5. The Supreme Court has directly or indirectly approved use of replacement cost evidence on the issue of value in damages claims, and in public utility rate determinations. See Standard Oil Co. of New Jersey v. Southern Pacific Co., 268 U.S. 146, 45 S.Ct. 465, 69 L.Ed. 890 (1925) (damages action; "by numerous decisions of this court it is firmly established that the cost of reproduction as of the date of valuation constitutes evidence properly to be considered in the ascertainment of value"); Ohio Utilities Co. v. Public Utilities Com'n, 267 U.S. 359, 45 S.Ct. 259, 69 L.Ed. 656 (1925) (public utility rate hearing; reproduction cost in valuing utility must include overhead allowance).

6. E.g., Milwaukee Rescue Mission, Inc. v. Redevelopment Authority of City of Milwaukee, 161 Wis.2d 472, 468 N.W.2d 663 (1991) (expert testimony estimating bare land, cost of building new building, fixtures, and depreciation adjustment).

7. United States v. 50 Acres of Land, (Duncanville, Texas), 469 U.S. 24, 105 S.Ct. 451, 83 L.Ed.2d 376 (1984).

8. The federal standard is that there must be a "legal or factual obligation to replace" the facility before replacement or "substitute facilities" costs can be considered. See United States v. 564.54 Acres of Land, Etc. (Lutheran Synod), 441 U.S. 506, 99 S.Ct. 1854, 60 L.Ed.2d 435 (1979).

9. Supra note 7.

10. Testimony showed that there was a market for landfill sites. However, it would seem that a market for the same site for apartment house purposes would also show a market value. Indeed, if apartment house purposes would be the highest and best use for the landfill, and the plaintiff were using the land only as a landfill, the market would very likely provide fine compensation. Only if the plaintiff were somehow putting the land to better use than that for which there was a market would there really be no market.

The other half of the rule is illustrated in the *Lutheran Synod* case.[11] A church operated a camp on land taken by the government. The church had owned the land before certain code requirements had been imposed, so it was able to avoid the costs of meeting code. This was not an advantage is could sell or transfer, however. When the land was taken, the church, if it replaced the camp, would be compelled to purchase or construct a substitute facility that could not avoid those costs. So the church would have a realized cash loss, but only if it actually constructed a substitute camp. The Court worried that the church might *not* construct a substitute, in which case, there would be no real loss. If substitute facility costs were awarded against the government, and the church did not actually construct a new facility, the church would have a windfall. So the Court imposed a rule that substitute facilities could measure compensation only if the condemnee were under an obligation to replace the property.

The problem encountered in *Duncanville* is a very common problem in the law of damages. If the city paid more for the substitute facility, it presumably also got more. Justice might require us to take this fact into account in deciding just compensation.[12] This point is worth some careful distinctions, however.

Suppose the city paid $500,000 more for the substitute than its original landfill was worth, but at that point held an asset worth $700,000. The city's balance sheet in such a case is the same as it was before; although it has spent money, it has acquired an equal value. In such a case the market value approved by the *Duncanville* court would be the same as allowing the cost of substitute facilities with a deduction for the increased value the city received. That would leave the city with what might be a serious cost of financing the new expense; perhaps it would be required to float bonds at great expense. That expense, however, would easily be in the category of consequential damages, long ruled out in federal condemnation cases. So on facts like these, *Duncanville* may not make much difference.

Suppose, however, Duncanville had to buy expensive property for $700,-000 but did *not* get an asset equal to the money it spent. Suppose it had to purchase land very well suited for expanding suburbs and hence very expensive, but that upon acquisition by the city the land's value immediately dropped because land used for sanitary landfills is worth less (and so is the land around it).[13] In that case the decision in *Duncanville* makes a big difference. If the real problem is to prevent a windfall to the city, a rule that allows substitution cost with a deduction for the fact that the city got assets worth more would represent a good solution to just compensation. The Court in *Duncanville*, however, thought that such a rule would be too complicated.[14] Yet it is probably not as complicated as some of the efforts to

11. Supra note 8.

12. See § 5.2(7) immediately below; § 12.-16(3) (disappointed buyer obtains substitute goods at greater cost but worth more).

13. Schill, Intergovernmental Takings and Just Compensation: A Question of Federalism, 137 U.Pa.L.Rev. 829 (1989), n. 281 reports cases of takings of local government office buildings by the federal government. He points out that if the taken building is in an inner city neighborhood where depressed values prevail, comparable sales methods of figuring market value (see § 3.5 above) will yield a small amount of "just compensation" in comparison to the cost of rebuilding.

14. "This approach would add uncertainty and complexity to the valuation proceeding without any necessary improvement in the process * * * the fact-finder would have to figure market value itself.[15]

Not surprisingly, some writers have criticized *Duncanville*. One argument is that the undercompensation effect interferes with the integrity of the federal system.[16] The other argument is that it promotes "fiscal illusion." Government projects are inefficient and undesirable if they cost more than the benefits they provide. If government overestimates benefits or underestimates costs, the project may seem to be a good expenditure of public funds when it is not. The same inefficiency or wasteful expenditure results if the government externalizes costs, that is, makes the landowner bear part of the real costs of the project. This would be the case whenever the landowner is undercompensated for his losses. So *Duncanville* and some other rules limiting compensation in eminent domain cases can be seen as a rule that encourages wasteful and expensive governmental projects.[17]

As already indicated, cases recognize that physical replacement costs as distinct from substitute facility or equal utility costs can be considered in figuring market value when other methods are less satisfactory. This rule applies in state courts as well. In addition, some states apparently would allow the plaintiff (or condemnee) to claim full substitute facility costs.[18] If so, an allowance should be made for the added value or appreciation the plaintiff or condemnee captures.[19]

§ 5.2(7) Adjustments Required When Repair Costs Are Allowed

Deduction for Appreciated Value

If repair costs are to be awarded as damages, some further adjustments may be required. Some repairs to land or structures will provide the owner with property more valuable than it was before the injury. For example, if the plaintiff's roof is 15 years old, and, when new, had a normal expected life of 20 years, replacement of the damage may give the plaintiff an effectively new roof with a 20 year expected life. If the plaintiff recovers the full costs of this new roof, he will certainly have a windfall. (Sometimes a very similar problem occurs in the contract setting, when the victim of a breach

make at least two determinations: (i) the reasonable (rather than the actual) replacement cost, which would require an inquiry into the fair market value of the second facility; and (ii) the extent to which the new facility is superior to the old, which would require an analysis of the qualitative differences between the new and the old. It would also be necessary to determine the fair market value of the old property in order to provide a basis for comparison." United States v. 50 Acres of Land (Duncanville, Texas), 469 U.S. 24, 35, 105 S.Ct. 451, 458, 83 L.Ed.2d 376 (1984).

15. See § 3.5 above.

16. See Schill, supra note 13.

17. See Durham, Efficient Just Compensation as a Limit on Eminent Domain, 69 Minn. L.Rev. 1277 (1985).

18. State By and Through Alabama State Docks Department v. Atkins, 439 So.2d 128, 131 (Ala.1983) ("public need * * * which made it reasonably necessary for the condemnee to

provide substitute facilities"); Moulton v. Groveton Papers Co., 114 N.H. 505, 323 A.2d 906 (1974) (town recovered cost of replacing bridge destroyed by defendant); City of Chester v. Commonwealth, 495 Pa. 382, 434 A.2d 695 (1981).

19. When *replacement* costs are used to fix the value, *depreciation* of the original property must be considered. See Roman Catholic Archbishop of Boston v. Commonwealth, 364 Mass. 486, 306 N.E.2d 254 (1974) (replacement cost less depreciation method used); Milwaukee Rescue Mission, Inc. v. Redevelopment Authority of City of Milwaukee, 161 Wis.2d 472, 468 N.W.2d 663, 667–668 (1991) ("fair market value of special use properties" can be usefully determined under a cost approach which uses "replacement or reproduction costs, minus depreciation"). When *substitute facility* costs are used, the appropriate and analogous consideration is whether the substitute facility adds value to the plaintiff/condemnee's holdings.

obtains substitute performance which costs more but is worth more.)[1] For most cases, then, the full cost of installing a new, 20–year roof will be denied. The general rule, "rather universally applied," "denies the plaintiff recovery for expenditures that enhance the value of his property."[2]

[*For discussion of methods for figuring adjustments, consult § 5.14(3) below, and see this section in the Practitioner Treatise edition.*]

§ 5.2(8) Waste

[*For the text of this section, see the unabridged Practitioner Treatise edition.*]

§ 5.3 Harms to Interests in Physical Integrity of Land and Structures: Damages for Severance

§ 5.3(1) Severance Cases Generally

In some instances harm is done to the physical integrity of land by damaging or removing some part of the realty that can be valued separately. Examples include removal of minerals like coal and ores, removal of timber or crops, and even removal of water.[1] Physical harm to such resources is in the same category as removal in most instances.[2]

Cases of severance may differ from other cases of physical harm in at least three ways. First, it is possible to measure damages by the value of the severed thing itself rather than by the diminished value of the land or by replacement costs. Second, statutes frequently permit double or treble damages in cases of bad faith severance.[3] Third, restitution may be measured by the wrongdoer's profits on the severed goods rather than, say, by rental value of the land.[4]

The cases usually apply a "mild" or modest measure of damages as against a good faith trespasser but an enhanced measure against willful or bad faith trespassers. Cases state the modest measure of damages against good faith trespassers in a variety of ways, but this appears to be because the measure is stated in terms of the evidence or proof in the particular case or proof the court has in mind and not because of any difference as to principle. The principle seems to be the one expressed by the Restatement Second of Torts,[5] namely, that the plaintiff may, at his or her election, recover either the diminished value of the land,[6] or the value of the article severed or

---

§ 5.2(7)

1. E.g., 525 Main Street Corp. v. Eagle Roofing Co., Inc., 34 N.J. 251, 168 A.2d 33 (1961); see §§ 12.6(2); 12.15(1); 12.19(1) below.

2. Freeport Sulphur Co. v. S/S Hermosa, 526 F.2d 300 (5th Cir.1976); Trinity Church in the City of Boston v. John Hancock Mut. Life Ins. Co., 399 Mass. 43, 502 N.E.2d 532 (1987) ("the cost of reproduction less depreciation"). The point is often recognized without resort to technical language of depreciation or appreciation, as in Bluemlein v. Szepanski, 101 Mich. App. 184, 300 N.W.2d 493 (1980) ("The destroyed barn was eight years old and may not have been as valuable as a new one would have been"); Tortolano v. DiFilippo, 115 R.I. 496, 349 A.2d 48 (1975) ("The defendant has not alleged * * * that plaintiff would somehow profit from an award" based on repair costs).

§ 5.3(1)

2. Whitaker v. Earnhardt, 289 N.C. 260, 221 S.E.2d 316 (1976) (damage to crops rather than severance); Wilson v. Brand S Corporation, 27 Wash.App. 743, 621 P.2d 748 (1980) (damage to slate rather than severance).

3. E.g., West's Ann.Cal.Civ.Code § 3346 (1970) (double for innocent, treble for willful trespass); N.C.Gen.Stat. § 1–539.1 (1983).

4. See § 5.4 below.

5. Restatement Second of Torts § 929(2) (1979).

damaged, so long as it in fact has a provable separate value. Some courts may still expect to see a claim for the value of the severed article asserted as one for "conversion."[7]

§ 5.3(2) Good Faith Trespassers

[*For the text of this section, see the unabridged Practitioner Treatise edition.*]

§ 5.3(3) Bad Faith Trespassers: Three Punitive Approaches

Harsh Measure of Damages

Bad faith trespassers who sever minerals or timber from the soil are usually subjected to a "harsh" measure of damages—the value of the severed article itself, not merely the value of the right to mine or harvest it. This value is figured at some point after the article is severed, perhaps even after it is in some manufactured state, and the bad faith trespasser is given little or no credit for costs of mining or transporting or milling the article.[1]

[*For additional discussion, see this section in the Practitioner Treatise edition.*]

Punitive Approaches Compared Generally

Of these three methods of punishment, the harsh measure of damages is probably the least correlated with the trespasser's punishable behavior and state of mind. It deprives the trespasser of a profit by imposing liability for the full market value of the article severed; but it goes further and imposes also a loss to the extent of costs incurred in producing the article. There is no necessary relationship between the amount of those unrecouped costs—which represent the punitive element—and the trespasser's state of mind or bad behavior. The behavior might be moderately bad, the costs immoderately high, for example. The multiple damages solution is likewise not necessarily related to the degree of the trespasser's wrongdoing, but it has the merit of great convenience, and it also serves to provide an advance estimate of the potential recovery that is likely to encourage attorneys to take the case on contingent fees. The common law punitive damage award is the one capable of the most tailoring to the facts, since it can be adjusted downward or upward to fit the defendant's misconduct; but it may be the most uncertain of the three and the least useful in prospectively financing litigation costs for the plaintiff.

§ 5.3(4) Traders Who Purchase Severed Articles

[*For the text of this section, see the unabridged Practitioner Treatise edition.*]

§ 5.4 Harms to Interests in Physical Integrity of Land and Structures: Restitution for Severance

Trespasses That Do Not Justify Restitution

Since restitution is based upon unjust enrichment of a defendant and measured by benefits to the defendant rather than losses to the plaintiff,[1] there is no occasion at all for restitution in the case of a trespass that causes

§ 5.4
1. See §§ 4.1(1), 4.5 above.

harm to the plaintiff but yields no benefit to the defendant.[2] For somewhat different reasons, some kinds of restitution was traditionally denied when the trespass consisted merely of use or occupation of the land.[3]

Restitution for Taking

When the trespasser actually takes items of value from the land, it is said that restitutionary recovery is readily allowed.[4] Restitution is also allowed against third persons. If the trespasser takes timber from the land and sells it to the defendant, the defendant is liable to make restitution. If the trespasser sells the timber to *A* and uses the proceeds to pay a debt to *B*, *B* may also be liable to make restitution unless he is a bona fide "purchaser" of the proceeds without notice that the proceeds had their source in the plaintiff's property.[5]

Restitution to Capture the Defendant's Gains

There is another potential advantage of a restitution claim in cases of severance. It is possible, as in the case of any conversion, that the defendant will derive some benefit from the resources severed that exceeds their market value.[9] The pure damages recovery would ordinarily [10] be limited to market value of the items severed, perhaps with a credit for the cost of severance; but restitution, measured by the benefit to the defendant, might capture for the plaintiff any gains the defendant is able to reap beyond market value of the severed goods. It is not so likely that the defendant will profit from the severed goods in a sum much in excess of their market value, but if he does, analogous cases support a recovery of his gains where he is an intentional wrongdoer.[11]

§ 5.5 Harms to Interests in Physical Integrity of Land and Structures: Injunctive Relief

Injunctions are often sought to protect all of the interests in land—use and enjoyment interests,[1] possession and title interests,[2] and interests in the physical integrity of the land itself. This section deals only with the possibility of injunctive relief to protect physical integrity.

When a defendant threatens harm to the physical integrity of the land, the remedy at law will usually be inadequate [3] because the land itself and its characteristics are typically regarded as unique and valued in themselves, so that money is no substitute.[4]

Consequently the defendant may be enjoined, even by preliminary injunction,[5] from cutting ornamental trees or timber [6] on the plaintiff's land or discharging waters [7] upon it, removing its ore,[8] or disturbing the surface by open pit mining.[9] The same concerns justify injunctive relief in the case

---

2. Marauders or vandals who damage property but gain nothing from their acts are not appropriate targets for a restitutionary claim, though they undoubtedly obtain some kind of psychic "benefit" from their depredations. Similarly, the causal trespasser who takes a short cut across the plaintiff's lot probably does not acquire a marketable benefit. It is far easier to talk of damages than of restitution in such cases.

3. See § 5.9 below.

§ 5.5

5. Cameron v. Bartels, 214 Ill.App.3d 69, 157 Ill.Dec. 855, 573 N.E.2d 273 (1991) (timber); Madison Fork Ranch v. L & B Lodge Pole Timber Products, 189 Mont. 292, 615 P.2d 900 (1980); Wiederspiel v. Bernholz, 163 A.D.2d 774, 558 N.Y.S.2d 739 (1990) (irreplaceable trees); Christensen v. Chromalloy American Corp., 99 Nev. 34, 656 P.2d 844 (1983).

of ditching the land [10] or dumping rocks or debris on it,[11] and it seems safe to say that any threat of serious physical harm to the land or its resources will be protected in the same way.[12] Since the remedial problem is to assess the harm done and tailor relief to that harm, the injunction may issue for harm to the physical integrity of land or its waters regardless whether the substantive law theory is one of trespass or one of nuisance.[13]

If the defendant has already carried out some such serious invasion, the court's order may be a mandatory injunction to make appropriate repairs or to remove trespassing objects.[14] Although in many such cases the plaintiff can have repairs done and claim damages, courts have been willing to find reasons why this remedy at law would not be adequate.[15] Even preliminary mandatory injunctions may be issued in some cases.[16]

Sometimes courts say that the remedy at law for damages is inadequate in trespass cases when multiple or repeated trespasses are likely to occur. The reasoning is that the plaintiff's damages claim at law would entail a "multiplicity" of suits and hence would be inadequate.[17] In the case of substantial physical harms to the land, however, threats of repeated trespass are not necessary to establish that the legal remedy is inadequate. Because the land is considered unique, even the threat of a single invasion of this kind warrants the injunction.[18]

(3) INTERESTS IN USE AND ENJOYMENT

§ 5.6 Harms to Interests in Use and Enjoyment: Damages for Nuisance

§ 5.6(1) Substantive Background: Nuisance and Trespass

The use and enjoyment interest in land might be invaded both by trespass and by nuisance.[1] The balancing of hardships in injunction cases

14. Shattles v. Field, Brackett & Pitts, Inc., 261 So.2d 795 (Miss.1972) (mandatory injunction to fill ditch defendant had dug on property); Wheelock v. Noonan, 108 N.Y. 179, 15 N.E. 67 (1888) (boulders dumped on land); Tortolano v. DiFilippo, 115 R.I. 496, 349 A.2d 48 (1975) (mandatory injunction to correct condition on defendant's land that led to washing of debris onto plaintiff's land). The fact that the plaintiff proceeds on a nuisance theory, as where the defendant discharges surface waters on the plaintiff's land, does not change the remedy for this physical invasion, and a mandatory injunction may issue to compel removal of the damaging condition. E.g., Wilmont Homes, Inc. v. Weiler, 42 Del.Ch. 8, 202 A.2d 576 (1964).

15. For example, one court speculated that the plaintiff would have no place to put rocks that had been dumped on his land by defendant and thus could not pay for removal and sue for damages. Wheelock v. Noonan, 108 N.Y. 179, 15 N.E. 67 (1888). Another court speculated that the plaintiff could not stop flooding of his land and sue for damages be-

cause that would require the plaintiff to enter the land of another. Wilmont Homes, Inc. v. Weiler, 42 Del.Ch. 8, 202 A.2d 576 (1964). In both cases, therefore, the legal remedy was regarded as inadequate and injunction proper.

16. Doré v. Jefferson Guaranty Bank, 543 So.2d 560 (La.App.1989) (preliminary mandatory injunction requiring removal of trash and objects deposited on the plaintiff's land).

§ 5.6(1)

1. Although trespass always involves some theoretical interference with possession and thus some entry of a person or thing upon the land, microscopic particles might now count for a trespass in some jurisdictions. See Bradley v. American Smelting and Refining Co., 104 Wash.2d 677, 709 P.2d 782 (1985); Lunda v. Matthews, 46 Or.App. 701, 613 P.2d 63 (1980). More importantly, the interest in exclusive possession is itself often secondary to the interest in use and enjoyment. Interference with easements is also an interference with use and enjoyment (since there is no

may at times differ according to whether the theory of the plaintiff's claim is trespass or nuisance;[2] but the measurement of harm to the landowner's enjoyment interest is much the same in either case, once it is established that the owner's legal right has been violated. Even so, the most common way in which use and enjoyment interests are violated is through a private nuisance.

As a matter of substantive law, a nuisance is in fact defined as an unreasonable interference with the use and enjoyment of land[3] as distinct from an interference with possession, which has traditionally been allocated to the trespass action. Pollution of the air or water,[4] or excessive noise or lights,[5] if extreme enough, can count as nuisances. So may certain invasions, like the backup of waters or sewage,[6] which may be considered too indirect to qualify as trespasses. Even dangerous conditions outside the land,[7] or unpleasant ones,[8] might at times qualify. The distinction between nuisance and trespass may be less significant than it once was, and today it may be possible for a plaintiff to claim a trespass when pollution of the land occurs—a micro-trespass.[9]

Damages for nuisance vary with the facts. If the effects of the nuisance are more or less permanent, the diminution in land value due to the nuisance will be recoverable; if temporary, the diminished rental value during the period of harm. Cost of repair and personal discomfort or inconvenience may also form bases for recovery.[10] Where the nuisance causes harm besides that claimed by the plaintiff personally, damages awards can be structured to provide incentives to cease pollution.[11]

§ 5.6(2)　Nuisance Damages Generally

Objective or Market Measures

Diminished market value. Apart from special and punitive damages,[1] the measures most commonly invoked when the plaintiff has lost use and enjoyment of land are the diminished land value, the diminished rental value and the cost of repairing the condition in question. These measures are appropriate when the nuisance or trespass actually involves physical harm to the land. The same measures of damages are invoked when the nuisance does no physical harm at all, but affects use and enjoyment directly. Noise, air pollution and sight nuisances are in this category. Interference with easements is treated in the same way as nuisances. If the nuisance is significant and the effects more or less permanent, the diminished use and enjoyment will be reflected in diminished market value and the plaintiff may recover an award based on that diminution.[2]

---

possessory interest in easement rights), and may also be regarded as a nuisance. See Mondelli v. Saline Sewer Co., 628 S.W.2d 697 (Mo.App.1982).

2. See § 5.9 below.

3. See Prosser & Keeton on Torts § 87 (5th ed. 1984).

§ 5.6(2)

1. See § 5.12 below.

2. Exxon Corp., U.S.A. v. Dunn, 474 So.2d 1269 (Fla.App.1985). As to diminished value where the nuisance is an interference with easement rights, see Mondelli v. Saline Sewer Co., 628 S.W.2d 697 (Mo.App.1982); cf. 487 Elmwood, Inc. v. Hassett, 107 A.D.2d 285, 486 N.Y.S.2d 113 (1985) (diminished value of leasehold).

Diminished rental value. If the effects of the nuisance are transitory, as in the case of a pollution which has now been stopped at its source and the effects of which will abate with time, then the damages are not measured by depreciation in market value but by depreciation in rental value of the property for the period in which the nuisance has been or will be in existence.[3] This is a market measure, but it is one based on the rental rather than the sales market; it reflects the fact that the harm will last only a limited period of time.

Costs of repair or abatement. In some cases it will be appropriate for the plaintiff to recover costs reasonably incurred in abating the nuisance[4] or in preventing future injury.[5] For example, the plaintiff who has sewer lines relaid after a sewage backup, may avoid future damage and if the expense was reasonably incurred to that end, it is a recoverable element in the nuisance action.[6] In the case of hazardous substances controlled by federal law under CERCLA,[7] liability is for the cost or removal or remedial action,[8] but remedial action is site clean-up, not necessarily full compensation for consequential damages.[9] On the other hand, CERCLA also authorizes recovery by the state or other governmental entity for damage to natural resources themselves.[10] To the extent the nuisance is abated, permanent damages are not to be assessed.[11]

Ceilings on recovery of repair or abatement costs. There are limits to damages recovered to remove the nuisance or minimize future harm. The expense incurred for such purposes must be reasonable. In addition, some cases have said that the recovery of damages based on the cost of repair or the like may not exceed the sum by which the property value has been diminished.[12] There are no doubt cases for which this rule is correct, as suggested by the rules concerning physical harms of land.[13] But if the expenditure is reasonably made to forestall future damages, that expenditure should qualify as an item recoverable under the affirmative version of the avoidable consequence rule;[14] this in turn seems to imply that the plaintiff could recover for the expenditures reasonably made even if hindsight shows that the attempt to minimize damages cost more than it saved.

Damages Not Based on Property Value or Repair

Personal discomfort, illness and anguish. Plaintiffs often emphasize personal discomfort, illness or mental anguish resulting from the nuisance. These are recoverable elements of damages, as is simple inconvenience

---

3. Earl v. Clark, 219 N.W.2d 487 (Iowa 1974) (one year lost rental value of pasture land due to nuisance, $30 rental value recoverable); Fletcher v. City of Independence, 708 S.W.2d 158 (Mo.App.1986); Coty v. Ramsey Associates, Inc., 149 Vt. 451, 546 A.2d 196 (1988). As to diminished rental value where the nuisance is an interference with easement rights, see M.H. Siegfried Real Estate, Inc. v. Renfrow, 633 S.W.2d 272 (Mo.App.1982).

4. Earl v. Clark, 219 N.W.2d 487 (Iowa 1974) ($9600 recovered as special damages incurred in removing offensive deposits that

constituted a nuisance). In interference with easement cases, see Harthcock v. Hurst, 413 So.2d 636 (La.App.1982).

6. Stratford Theater, Inc. v. Town of Stratford, 140 Conn. 422, 101 A.2d 279, 41 A.L.R.2d 1060 (1953), Annot., 41 A.L.R.2d 1064 (1955).

7. The Comprehensive Environmental Response, Compensation and Liability Act (CERCLA), 42 U.S.C.A. § 9601 et seq. (also known as the Superfund Act). References here include the amendments known as SARA. See § 5.2(5) for further explication of CERCLA.

caused by the nuisance.[19]   In contrast, courts usually compensate only for pecuniary losses when the tort physically harms the property or dispossess the plaintiff.   In those cases, as distinct from nuisance cases, the plaintiff might recover the diminished value of the property or the cost or repair, or (in dispossession cases) the use value of the property, but no damages for emotional distress.[20]   Where serious personal injury results from a nuisance, as in some toxic torts cases, the damages emphasis tends to become an emphasis on personal injury rather than property damage.[21]

Combining claims for discomfort and claims for diminished value.   In many cases plaintiffs claim both discomfort damages and diminished value damages.   But since the diminished value award is itself a reflection of the discount that potential buyers would require to be willing to live with the discomforts of the nuisance in question, it may be quite inappropriate to award both a sum for diminished value and an additional sum for discomfort the plaintiff will suffer from a continuance of the nuisance in the future. Many writers wish to see the law expand liability for the plaintiff's subjective sense of loss in addition to liability for market diminution,[22] so perhaps plaintiffs should have a choice of either measure but not both.

Most decisions, however, seem to have gone further by routinely allowing the plaintiff to recover both depreciated value *and* discomfort or illness,[23] with a little authority to the contrary.[24]   The recovery of both seems right enough where the sums are trivial or where the plaintiff's illness is idiosyncratic and unlikely to be reflected in diminished value,[25] where the illness is likely to continue even if the plaintiff were to correct the nuisance or leave it, and where the recovery for illness or discomfort is limited to that which

---

19.   Ayers v. Jackson Tp., 106 N.J. 557, 525 A.2d 287, 76 A.L.R.4th 571 (1987) (damages for inconvenience, quality of life lost when drinking water was polluted, costs of continuing medical check-ups to monitor risk of cancer, but no damages for fear of future harm).

20.   Compare Day v. Montana Power Co., 242 Mont. 195, 789 P.2d 1224 (1990) (defendant negligently caused fire and explosion which destroyed plaintiff's restaurant, no mental distress damages) with French v. Ralph E. Moore, Inc., 203 Mont. 327, 661 P.2d 844 (1983) (nuisance, mental anguish damages permitted).

21.   For personal injury damages, including those arising from toxic torts and nuisances, see generally Chapter 8 below.

22.   E.g., Lewin, Compensated Injunctions and the Evolution of Nuisance Law, 71 Iowa L.Rev. 775 (1986) (subjective values to be protected by special injunctive remedies, as to which see § 5.7); Hiley, Involuntary Sale Damages in Permanent Nuisance Cases: A Bigger Bang from Boomer, 14 B.C. Envtl.Aff. L.Rev. 61 (1986) (arguing for damages in excess of market diminution in order to protect subjective values).

23.   Exxon Corp., U.S.A. v. Dunn, 474 So.2d 1269 (Fla.App.1985) (awarding $90,250 for di-

minished value of house, which was regarded as zero after the nuisance, plus $100,000 in "personal damages" to owner, and over $100,-000 more to other occupants); Fletcher v. City of Independence, 708 S.W.2d 158 (Mo.App. 1986); Coty v. Ramsey Associates, Inc., 149 Vt. 451, 546 A.2d 196 (1988); Wilson v. Key Tronic Corp., 40 Wash.App. 802, 701 P.2d 518 (1985) (hazardous wastes nearby, drinking water dangerous).

24.   Swift v. Broyles, 115 Ga. 885, 42 S.E. 277 (1902) held it error to submit to the jury both the discomfort and the loss of rental value elements on the express ground that to award both would be to visit duplicative liabilities upon the defendant.   It is not clear that this view has survived, however.   A Kentucky statute appears to stake out a middle ground, refusing to permit personal injury or discomfort claims based on a private nuisance, but permitting them if the plaintiff can make out an ordinary case for recovery on negligence grounds.   Ky.Rev.Stat. 411.560(3).   ("No damages shall be awarded for annoyance, discomfort, sickness, emotional distress, or similar claims for a private nuisance * * *.   [L]iability for such personal injury or damage shall be determined on the basis of applicable principles of tort law independent of whether the defendant's use of property is found to constitute a nuisance").

occurs before judgment. Otherwise a recovery of both diminished value and future discomfort seems duplicative.

§ 5.6(3) Damages Incentives to Abate

In many instances a defendant carries on an activity that is both useful and harmful at the same time. A factory that produces goods people wish to have and that contributes significantly to the local economy might at the same time pollute the atmosphere and cause a nuisance. Injunction against the nuisance is a possibility in such a case, but the injunction may be denied on the ground that the benefits outweigh the harm,[1] in which case the plaintiff will be remitted to the damages claim. If the defendant's liability in damages is based on the reduced market value of the plaintiff's property, the defendant will have no incentive to reduce the nuisance in the future; it will have already paid for the right to continue the pollution.[2]

Consequently, damage awards in cases of this kind may often best be constructed as damages for a temporary license to commit the nuisance. Such an award is constructed to give damages for past harms only, leaving the plaintiff to sue again in the future. The threat of future liability will tend to encourage the defendant to minimize the costs by minimizing the nuisance where that is financially reasonable.

The award for past harms only, however, runs the risk of many repeated suits. To avoid this, a damage award for past harms plus a sum representing future damage to a specified time in the future would be possible. A defendant who pays for a five year license to cause the harm will have every incentive to find a means to avoid such a liability again when the five-year period is over. In short, the use of some form of "temporary" damages award, perhaps one based on diminished rental value or personal discomfort, seem preferable if there is a chance that an environmental nuisance can be reduced in the future.[3]

§ 5.6(4) Regulatory Takings

[*For the text of this section, see the unabridged Practitioner Treatise edition.*]

§ 5.7 Harms to Interests in Use and Enjoyment: Injunctive Relief

§ 5.7(1) Substantive Background and Summary

The use and enjoyment interest in land is very largely an interest in the quality of life.[1] As such it differs from the interest in physical integrity of the land and from the interest in exclusive possession. The use and enjoyment interest is quite frequently protected by the injunctive remedy.

Substantively, the use and enjoyment interest is traditionally protected under the law of nuisance;[2] but today environmental statutes,[3] restrictive covenants,[4] and zoning ordinances[5] all add their own protections. Even the law of trespass sometimes protects use and enjoyment as well as possession and physical integrity.[6] Easements, which establish a right of use, also come in for their share of attention under this heading.[7] Likewise, some governmental actions may affect use and enjoyment of land and may constitute partial takings of property subject to judicial remedies.[8]

In general, the plaintiff suing for a nuisance injunction is usually able to show that the legal remedy is inadequate. However, even though the defendant is clearly maintaining a nuisance, the injunction may still be denied because of the "relative hardship" it may impose upon the defendant. In determining relative hardship, courts often balance the hardships of the parties, the equities such as good faith, and public interests.[9] Environmental concerns become significant in determining whether to issue the injunction or to rely on damages, and sometimes statutes may require an injunction regardless of the hardships.[10] Economic analysis of the relative costs and incentives also may become especially significant in balancing hardships and equities.[11]

§ 5.7(2) Doctrine Limiting Nuisance Injunctions

Adequacy of Legal Remedy, Irreparable Harm

Adequacy test. The injunction is usually regarded as an appropriate remedy in nuisance cases [1] if the nuisance would be likely to continue in the absence of an injunction.

Balancing Hardships and Equities

Threshold, rights, and remedies types of balancing. The discretion in equity to deny, limit or shape relief is reflected in the flexible process of balancing hardships and equities. Relief is limited or expanded in accord with that balance. Balancing occurs in several distinct ways. There is some "threshold balancing," as it has been called,[17] to determine whether the plaintiff has standing in equity in the light of unclean hands, estoppel, laches or the like. Another kind of balancing occurs on the substantive issues themselves in some cases. Nuisance cases, for example, are largely a matter of degree, so a discretionary kind of weighing of relative hardships is almost always involved in such cases. A third level of balancing occurs when the court, having found a nuisance or statutory violation to exist, must determine whether to use a damages remedy or an injunctive remedy. And finally, a similar balancing or discretion is invoked at a fourth stage when the court fixes the exact scope and commands of the injunction issued.[18]

Rights-balancing. In determining whether the defendant's activity is a nuisance at all, courts traditionally balanced the benefits derived from that activity with the harm it caused. A balance of harms, costs, utilities and hardships suggests, for example, that a very valuable industry which is causing annoyance to neighbors might not be a nuisance at all in the light of

---

§ 5.7(1)

8. Corrigan v. City of Scottsdale, 149 Ariz. 538, 720 P.2d 513 (1986), cert. denied, 479 U.S. 986, 107 S.Ct. 577, 93 L.Ed.2d 580 (1986) (city would be liable for a temporary taking when it passed an unconstitutional zoning ordinance).

§ 5.7(2)

17. Plater, Statutory Violations and Equitable Discretion, 70 Calif.L.Rev. 524 (1982).

18. See, with a slightly different description of the balancing and "tailoring" of remedies, Schoenbrod, The Measure of an Injunction: A Principle to Replace Balancing the Equities and Tailoring the Remedy, 72 Minn. L.Rev. 627 (1988).

the relative utilities.[19] In such a case there are no remedial issues at all because there are no rights to be redressed.

The "modern" view taken by the Restatement would hold that some conditions constitute a nuisance even if the nuisance is the result of a socially useful activity.[20] In this view, a balancing of utilities, costs or hardships would be important, but only on the choice of remedies, not on the initial question whether a nuisance existed. The two approaches are quite different, but both recognize that a balancing of utilities or hardships on the remedies issue is distinct from a balancing of utilities on the question whether a nuisance exists at all. The main concern of this text is the balance of utilities or hardships in determining the appropriate remedy and in determining its scope.

Remedies balancing generally. When a nuisance is found to exist, either on the balance of utilities or otherwise, it is still important to balance or re-balance the relative costs and hardships in determining the appropriate remedy. At the remedies stage of the claim, courts routinely reconsider the balance to determine whether an injunction should be granted or whether the plaintiff should be limited to some other remedy such as damages.

Specifically, courts consider the public benefit derived from the defendant's operations,[21] the public benefits that might result from a grant of the injunction,[22] the relative hardships or the economic costs the parties would be likely to suffer if the nuisance is or is not enjoined,[23] and the equities between the parties such as laches,[24] bad faith or misconduct.[25] This new balancing of public and private benefits and harms may lead the court to deny an injunction and leave the plaintiff to a damages remedy [26] on the ground that an injunction would do more harm than good.

A similar balancing may be done in cases that do not necessarily involve a nuisance but where use and enjoyment interests are invaded by violation of a restrictive covenant [27] or zoning ordinance.[28] The traditional terms for this balancing at the remedial stage refer to relative hardships, but it is clear that the balancing includes a broad consideration of utilities and is not limited to "hardship" in any narrow sense. It is also clear that it includes fairness considerations of the "equities."

Equities and misconduct. Courts consider a number of equities between the parties in exercising discretion whether to grant the injunction. Misconduct,[29] bad faith,[30] elements of estoppel,[31] or laches [32] can all be considered.

19. See Prosser & Keeton on Torts § 88 (5th ed. 1984); Restatement (Second) of Torts §§ 826, 941, Comment c (1979).

20. See Restatement (Second) of Torts § 826(b) (1979).

26. E.g., City of Harrisonville, Mo. v. W.S. Dickey Clay Mfg. Co., 289 U.S. 334, 53 S.Ct. 602, 77 L.Ed. 1208 (1933).

29. E.g., willful violation of a deed restriction. See Moore v. McDaniel, 48 Ill.App.3d 152, 5 Ill.Dec. 911, 362 N.E.2d 382 (1977).

30. E.g., knowingly "taking a chance" that conduct would be nuisance or violation of deed restrictions. See Swaggerty v. Petersen, 280

Or. 739, 572 P.2d 1309 (1977); Restatement (Second) of Torts § 941 Comment b (1979).

31. See Scott v. Jordan, 99 N.M. 567, 661 P.2d 59 (App.1983) (acquiescence defense is for trier to determine).

32. Barbian v. Lindner Bros. Trucking Co., 106 Wis.2d 291, 316 N.W.2d 371 (1982). Madison v. Ducktown Sulphur, Copper & Iron Co., 113 Tenn. 331, 83 S.W. 658 (1904). See generally Restatement (Second) of Torts § 939 (1979).

Laches may be no defense against a claim of public as distinct from private nuisance. Liller v. State Highway Administration, 25 Md.

If the defendant's conduct is a deliberate infliction of an unjustified harm, as in the case of a spite fence nuisance, there is a strong equity in favor of the plaintiff and an injunction will probably issue.[33] Even a decision to set up a factory in proximity to personal residences may count against the defendant and in favor of the injunction.[34] When the defendant's conduct is less egregious and has social values, as in the case of factory nuisances, the plaintiff's misconduct if any, or delay in bringing suit, may be the critical equity: the plaintiff who stands by while a factory is built next door and then complains of a nuisance may have a nuisance claim for damages, but the injunction may be denied.[35]

Hardships and economic waste. Courts also take into account the relative hardships of the parties. The hardship that may be worked upon the defendant if the injunction goes is compared to the hardship that may be wreaked upon the plaintiff if it does not. The plaintiff's hardship in nuisance cases is often expressed as an intangible impairment of enjoyment of the quality of living on the property; but this impairment, if substantial, will be reflected in diminished property values as well. In any event, if sufficiently proven, the hardship may outweigh the tangible economic losses the defendant will suffer if its business is enjoined.[36]

The hardship attributed to the defendant is often more frankly economic, and courts often mention the investment that would be lost if the injunction goes.[37] This calls, however, for a practical judgment. If there are reasonable alternatives available to the defendant that will accomplish his goals without causing a nuisance, the supposed hardship counts for little.[38] The same point can be recognized in decisions that grant an injunction against a full-scale operation by the defendant but leave it open to him to operate in ways that cause less harm.[39]

App. 276, 333 A.2d 644 (1975) (quoting, 'There is no such thing as a prescriptive right or any other right to maintain a public nuisance * * *.'); City of Lee's Summit v. Browning, 722 S.W.2d 114 (Mo.App.1986). The same with estoppel. City and County of San Francisco v. City Investment Corp., 15 Cal.App.3d 1031, 93 Cal.Rptr. 690 (1971). However, in Matter of Chicago, Rock Island and Pac. R.R., 756 F.2d 517 (7th Cir.1985) Judge Posner was moved to say that the public entity, though not necessarily guilty of laches, had slept on its rights and that this played at least an indirect part in denial of injunctive relief against a prospective nuisance.

33. Schork v. Epperson, 74 Wyo. 286, 287 P.2d 467 (1955).

34. As in Helmkamp v. Clark Ready Mix Co., 214 N.W.2d 126, 82 A.L.R.3d 997 (Iowa 1974).

35. See Staton v. Atlantic Coast Line R. Co., 147 N.C. 428, 61 S.E. 455 (1908).

36. Affirmative hardship to plaintiff is often the very thing complained of, such as the smells from the piggery. Pendoley v. Ferreira, 345 Mass. 309, 187 N.E.2d 142, 2 A.L.R.3d 924 (1963). This hardship, though

personal, does translate into economic terms and is reflected in lowered property values. The courts' concern to maximize the economic condition of the community in these cases is often expressed in the initial determination that a nuisance does or does not exist.

Correspondingly, a lack of hardship to the plaintiff often figures in denial of relief. Hunsicker v. Katz, 310 Pa.Super. 213, 456 A.2d 576 (1983) (defendant's building partly in easement for street, but no prospect that street would be opened so plaintiff not materially affected by the encroachment).

37. Hargreaves v. Skrbina, 662 P.2d 1078 (Colo.1983) (zoning violation balanced like nuisance, "defendants would lose a $150,000 investment if forced to comply with the setback requirements"); Boomer v. Atlantic Cement Co., 26 N.Y.2d 219, 309 N.Y.S.2d 312, 257 N.E.2d 870, 40 A.L.R.3d 590 (1970).

38. Rose v. Chaikin, 187 N.J.Super. 210, 453 A.2d 1378, 36 A.L.R. 4th 1148 (1982) ("the availability of alternative means of achieving the defendant's objective has been found to be relevant").

39. See below § 5.7(3).

Public interests and social utility. Courts have long said that public as well as private interests are to be weighed in determining whether the injunction will go.[40] The term seems to include all social utility, not merely interests of an identified governmental body.[41] The interests of individual third persons as well as the interests of the public as a whole may also be given weight.[42] The public interest thus broadly defined may weigh against the issuance of an injunction in some cases and in favor of its issuance in others.

Public interests against the injunction. A public interest in favor of the defendant and against the injunctive remedy is sometimes found in the fact that the defendant's nuisance is a business or factory that employs individuals and brings economic well-being to the community.[43] Much of what goes under the name of hardship is economic cost. Economic costs, though they do not directly harm the whole community, may do so indirectly. If an injunction closing or limiting the operation of the defendant's business will cause the loss of an investment, courts weigh this factor against the injunction, or at least against it in its broadest and most destructive form.[44]

Courts are sometimes also leery of injunctions against firms deemed to be affected with the public interest, as in the case of a public utility or common carrier.[45] There are also practical constraints that may be thought of as a kind of public interest. A state court might refuse to enjoin a noise nuisance committed by an airport partly in deference to federal regulation of the airline industry,[46] just as a federal court might refuse injunctions in some cases out of deference to state courts.[47]

Public interests favoring the injunction. On the other hand, there may be a public interest in terminating a nuisance causing environmental pollu-

40. City of Harrisonville, Mo. v. W.S. Dickey Clay Mfg. Co., 289 U.S. 334, 53 S.Ct. 602, 77 L.Ed. 1208 (1933); Virginian Ry. Co. v. System Federation No. 40, 300 U.S. 515, 57 S.Ct. 592, 81 L.Ed. 789 (1937).

41. See Rose v. Chaikin, 187 N.J.Super. 210, 453 A.2d 1378, 36 A.L.R. 4th 1148 (1982) ("So, also, might the social utility of defendant's conduct, judged in light of prevailing notions of progress and the demands of modern life, be relevant").

42. E.g., the injury to workers from loss of jobs if a plant is closed, Madison v. Ducktown Sulphur, Copper & Iron Co., 113 Tenn. 331, 83 S.W. 658 (1904). See Restatement (Second) of Torts § 942 (1979).

43. Riter v. Keokuk Electro–Metals Co., 248 Iowa 710, 82 N.W.2d 151 (1957) (factory furnishing work in the community); Madison v. Ducktown Sulphur, Copper & Iron Co., 113 Tenn. 331, 83 S.W. 658 (1904) (jobs in community plus enormous increase in tax assessments in county due to defendants' smelters). Cf. Boomer v. Atlantic Cement Co., 26 N.Y.2d 219, 309 N.Y.S.2d 312, 257 N.E.2d 870 (1970).

44. State of Oregon ex rel. Cox v. Davidson Industries, Inc., 291 Or. 839, 635 P.2d 630 (1981) ("If the fill had to be completely removed, the $24,000 cost of erecting it would be

lost. The cost of removal was estimated to be $30,000 to $40,000, and the plaintiff would incur significantly greater costs in transporting logs and agricultural products by a longer route," narrower injunction used); Madison v. Ducktown Sulphur, Copper & Iron Co., 113 Tenn. 331, 83 S.W. 658 (1904) (investment of $2 million by defendant, plaintiffs' aggregate lands worth less than $1,000).

45. Loma Portal Civic Club v. American Airlines, Inc., 61 Cal.2d 582, 39 Cal.Rptr. 708, 394 P.2d 548 (1964) ("It is well established that public policy denies an injunction and permits only the recovery of damages where private property has been put to a public use by a public service corporation and the public interest has intervened"); Goldstein v. Potomac Elec. Power Co., 285 M.D. 673, 404 A.2d 1064, 19 A.L.R.4th 442 (1979); see, Reppun v. Board of Water Supply, 65 Hawaii 531, 656 P.2d 57 (1982), cert. denied, 471 U.S. 1014, 105 S.Ct. 2016, 85 L.Ed.2d 298 (1985) (recognizing public interest balancing in injunctions generally, fashioning a special version of the doctrine where public agency has diverted water for public use).

47. See Shreve, Federal Injunctions and the Public Interest, 51 Geo.Wash.L.Rev. 382 (1983).

tion, even if that nuisance is caused by a conduct that otherwise contributes to the public weal.[48] Poisoning the water supply of a town could hardly be justified even by the most important of industries. Much serious environmental pollution will generate strong public interest reasons in support of an injunction.[49] In less obvious cases, public interest balancing may be controversial and is likely to involve at least some element of political or social decision-making outside the traditional judicial role.[50]

However, the political or social balancing may have been done before trial by the legislature itself. When the defendant's conduct violates a statute, it is possible that the legislature has already weighed the competing interests and has reflected its judgment in the statute. In such a case the court may be willing to discount its own assessment of public interests and issue the injunction authorized by statute.[51] Somewhat similarly, where the defendant's conduct violates a deed restriction, the balancing has been done by the parties or their predecessors in title and the balance struck in the covenant itself, so that if one neighbor violates the covenant it should be no defense to the injunction that his violation serves some public good.[52]

With the development of intense economic analysis in the law, some of it focused directly on the question of nuisance remedies,[53] the issues about balancing of utilities have become more complex. Some of the developing perspectives on balancing can best be appreciated, however, only when the remedial options are understood.

§ 5.7(3) The Remedial Options in Nuisance Cases

Four Basic Remedial Choices

Traditional choices. Until 1973 it was thought that a chancellor faced with a claim of nuisance might have three basic remedial choices:

(1) Deny any relief on the ground that there was no nuisance at all. This would be equivalent to saying that the defendant was entitled to conduct the activity in question.

(2) Grant an injunction abating the nuisance. This might be a partial abatement, but to the extent granted it would be equivalent to saying that the plaintiff was entitled to be free from the activity in question and that the plaintiff's entitlement would be protected as a property right—that is, by an injunction.

48. Cf. Rose v. Chaikin, 187 N.J.Super. 210, 453 A.2d 1378, 36 A.L.R.4th 1148 (1982) (defendant's windmill served public interest in developing alternate sources of energy, but it also caused noise pollution in an otherwise quiet natural environment, balancing favored injunction).

51. See Little Joseph Realty, Inc. v. Town of Babylon, 41 N.Y.2d 738, 395 N.Y.S.2d 428, 363 N.E.2d 1163 (1977) (injunction to run against zoning violation harmful to private plaintiff without balancing of hardships, etc.). The effect of statutes is complex, however. See § 5.7(5) below.

52. See Wier v. Isenberg, 95 Ill.App.3d 839, 51 Ill.Dec. 376, 420 N.E.2d 790 (1981).

53. Calabresi & Melamed, Property Rules, Liability Rules, and Inalienability: One View of the Cathedral, 85 Harv.L.Rev. 1089 (1972); Ellickson, Alternatives to Zoning: Covenants, Nuisance Rules, and Fines as Land Use Controls, 40 U.Chi.L.Rev. 681 (1973); Polinksy, Resolving Nuisance Disputes: The Simple Economics of Injunctive and Damages Remedies, 32 Stan.L.Rev. 1075 (1980); Edward Rabin, Nuisance Law: Rethinking Fundamental Assumptions, 63 Va.L.Rev. 1299 (1977); Lewin, Compensated Injunctions and the Evolution of Nuisance Law, 71 Iowa L.Rev. 775 (1986). See § 5.7(4) below.

(3) Deny the injunction but grant damages to the plaintiff. This would be equivalent to saying that the defendant was entitled to continue his activity (hence no injunction), but only on payment of damages caused by it. Except for fine-tuning these remedies, it was thought that there were no other remedial choices.

The Fourth option: a compensated injunction. In 1972, a remarkable article and a remarkable case appeared at almost the same moment to suggest a fourth option. In the article, Calabresi and Melamed suggested that the nuisance victim might in some cases be entitled to an injunction abating the nuisance, but only if he paid the defendant for the costs of the abatement.[1] The plaintiff under the fourth option would be entitled to the injunction, but in contrast with the traditional "free" injunction, the plaintiff would obtain the injunction only if paid for it.[2]

Spur Industries. The case which appeared on the heels of the Calabresi and Melamed article furnished an example of the "compensated injunction." In *Spur Industries, Inc. v. Del Webb Development Co.,*[3] homes had been built in a widening gyre into the desert until they approached the defendant's feed lot, which processed enormous numbers of animals and created seriously unpleasant conditions for the homeowners. The Arizona Court held that the feed lot could be enjoined, thus forcing it to move to a new location, but that the plaintiffs who sought this remedy could have the injunction only if they paid the costs of the move.

Acceptance of Spur Industries. The case was an appealing one on its facts because the feed-lot had been constructed originally in a place far from any dense habitation and the homebuilder had built up to the nuisance. It was also appealing because it was feasible to consider moving the whole operation to a more suitable place. Commentators have liked the idea[4] and sometimes have sought to extend it to less obvious candidates for this form of relief.[5] So far, however, other courts have not had occasion to employ the compensated injunction, much less to extend it.[6] The compensated injunction has been used, however, in a completely different factual setting to enjoin competition by one in possession of trade secrets.[7]

Form and Terms of the Remedy: Fine–Tuning Injunctions

Nebulous injunctions. In many simple nuisance cases it is clear enough that an injunction should go and the only problem will be its form. The leaking sewer might be enjoined in terms that tell the defendant specifically

§ 5.7(3)

1. Calabresi & Melamed, Property Rules, Liability Rules, and Inalienability: One View of the Cathedral, 85 Harv.L.Rev. 1089 (1972).

2. Discussed in detail in Lewin, Compensated Injunctions and the Evolution of Nuisance Law, 71 Iowa L.Rev. 775 (1986). See also § 5.7(4) below.

3. 108 Ariz. 178, 494 P.2d 700, 53 A.L.R.3d 861 (1972).

4. Ellickson, Alternatives to Zoning: Covenants, Nuisance Rules, and Fines as Land Use Controls, 40 U.Chi.L.Rev. 681 (1973); Edward Rabin, Nuisance Law: Rethinking Fundamental Assumptions, 63 Va.L.Rev. 1299 (1977); Lewin, Compensated Injunctions and the Evolution of Nuisance Law, 71 Iowa L.Rev. 775 (1986).

5. Rabin proposed to allow even a plaintiff who could not otherwise recover for a nuisance to have an injunction if he could pay for it. See Edward Rabin, Nuisance Law: Rethinking Fundamental Assumptions, 63 Va. L.Rev. 1299 (1977). This view was attacked in Lewin, Compensated Injunctions and the Evolution of Nuisance Law, 71 Iowa L.Rev. 775 (1986).

7. Emery Industries, Inc. v. Cottier, 202 U.S.P.Q. 829 (S.D.Ohio 1978); see § 10.5(3).

what to do [8] and even in terms that provide for monitoring his compliance; [9] or it might be enjoined by an injunction that tells him merely to cease maintaining a nuisance.[10] The latter form—a "nebulous" injunction [11] or an injunction to "be good"—runs the risk of constitutional violation.[12] It may also violate Federal Rule 65 [13] and its state counterparts.[14] In any event such an injunction can be quite unfair to the defendant.[15] But in simple cases the terms of the injunctive order will seldom present a serious problem.

Scope and limits of injunction. In more complex or difficult cases, however, it may be necessary to invest considerable effort in the exploration of the remedial options. As already indicated, the chancellor may issue either an injunction, or damages, or possibly both. But these are not the only choices, because each remedy presents its own spectrum of measurement or scope. Damages might be based on diminished market value, on the cost of eliminating the nuisance effects, or on subjective, personal elements such as illness or diminished enjoyment of the property.[16] Injunctions also may range widely in their scope. The injunction might compel complete abatement of the offending condition,[17] but equally it might only compel some adjustment in operating conditions.

Often a balance of the hardships and equities leads to the conclusion that the defendant may continue the activity, but only for limited periods during the day or only on certain days of the week,[18] or only when specified

8. E.g., Valasek v. Baer, 401 N.W.2d 33 (Iowa 1987) (injunction to dispose of wastes 80 rods farther from plaintiffs' houses).

9. Miller v. Cudahy Co., 592 F.Supp. 976 (D.Kan.1984).

10. See McCastle v. Rollins Environmental Services of Louisiana, Inc., 415 So.2d 515 (La. App.1982) (defendant enjoined to stop emitting odors that made the plaintiff ill or uncomfortable).

11. The term derives from Durfee, Nebulous Injunctions, 19 Mich.L.Rev. 83 (1920).

12. It would seem that due process would be violated if the defendant could be punished for violating a decree that could not be understood. Cf. International Longshoremen's Ass'n v. Philadelphia Marine Trade Ass'n, 389 U.S. 64, 88 S.Ct. 201, 19 L.Ed.2d 236 (1967) ("The most fundamental postulates of our legal order forbid the imposition of a penalty for disobeying a command that defies comprehension"); Schmidt v. Lessard, 414 U.S. 473, 94 S.Ct. 713, 38 L.Ed.2d 661 (1974) ("basic fairness requires that those enjoined receive explicit notice of precisely what conduct is outlawed").

13. See International Longshoremen's Ass'n v. Philadelphia Marine Trade Ass'n, 389 U.S. 64, 88 S.Ct. 201, 19 L.Ed.2d 236 (1967) (Rule 65 requires specific terms and one is not in violation of an order that does not meet this requirement).

14. See Banker v. Bath Iron Works Corp., 507 A.2d 602 (Me.1986) (in a state substantially adopting Federal Rule 65), the requirement of specific and reasonably detailed terms is "codified" and mandatory.

15. Although nebulous injunctions have been and still are issued, state-court decisions have long condemned them, independent of the commands of procedural rules or constitutions. In Baldwin v. Miles, 58 Conn. 496, 20 A. 618 (1890) the court said: "Such an order should be clear and certain in its terms, so that the party upon whom it is served may readily know what he can or cannot do thereunder, seeing that the consequences of a breach may subject him to loss of property and imprisonment. As this court said * * * 'Injunctions ought to be made plain and distinct. No respondent is to be entrapped into a contempt by vague or general orders.'" On this ground the Baldwin court overturned a contempt sentence.

18. Daugherty v. Ashton Feed and Grain Co., 208 Neb. 159, 303 N.W.2d 64 (1981) (operating of drying fans on certain days and during certain hours enjoined); Mercer v. Brown, 190 So.2d 610 (Fla.App.1966) (no cooking of offal and garbage except between 11:00 p.m. and 2:00 a.m.); Sherrod v. Dutton, 635 S.W.2d 117 (Tenn.App.1982) (night time races enjoined); Hopkins v. Stepler, 315 Pa.Super. 372, 461 A.2d 1327 (1983) (time of day when dogs allowed out).

steps have been taken to ameliorate the harm that it does.[19] Intractable cases may call for continued experiment, perhaps under court supervision,[20] in an effort to find a way to minimize the harm. Or the injunction might be issued with a proviso for delay in enforcement to give the defendant time to comply as efficiently as possible, or perhaps to give a defendant incentive to find better means of compliance than are now possible.[21] Both injunction and damages are thus flexible remedies in this context, and because they can be used together in various combinations, the flexibility is even greater than might be achieved by one remedy alone.

Incentive injunctions and incentive damages. The preferred combination of remedies is likely to be that which reflects the court's balance of interests and utilities and which at the same time provide appropriate incentives to the parties. For example, in the case of the factory that serves social purposes but also unavoidably pollutes, the court might refuse an absolute abatement but order research or experiment into means of reducing the pollution; or it might injunctively proscribe the operation effective at some future time unless the defendant is able to show the court before the cut-off date that the nuisance has been materially reduced. In the case of widespread pollution, an order of this kind might be preferable to a decision that denies the injunction altogether.

As has been indicated elsewhere,[22] there is similar room for shaping the damages award to provide incentives. This can be done mainly by awarding temporary rather than permanent damages, because to do so subjects the defendant to the threat of continued future suits unless the nuisance is reduced. A combination remedy might be an award of temporary damages to the plaintiff covering a time-period of two years after the trial, coupled with an injunction to eliminate the nuisance at the end of the two-year period. Variations of this kind of injunction can be structured as the facts demand.[23]

§ 5.7(4) Economic and Other Perspectives

A balance of the benefits of the nuisance against its costs cannot be realistic unless total costs are estimated. This may be difficult because data is difficult to obtain and because some of the economic costs of a nuisance may be inflicted upon persons who are not parties to the suit and who may not be identified.

A different complication in estimating costs arises from the limited array of solutions which the court or the parties can imagine. The costs will seem very high if the court imagines that a cement factory which deposits loads of dust on its residential neighbors would be compelled to close down if

---

19. Flansburgh v. Coffey, 220 Neb. 381, 370 N.W.2d 127 (1985) (hog raising and odors, injunction permitted continued raising of hogs but prohibited particular confinement buildings and accumulation of manure); West v. National Mines Corp., 168 W.Va. 578, 285 S.E.2d 670, 25 A.L.R.4th 1179 (1981) (dust from trucks hauling coal, preliminary injunction to issue, terms of which might merely require watering the road or similar steps to keep dust down without stopping traffic).

20. Restatement (Second) of Torts § 941 Comment *e* (1979).

21. See Reserve Mining Co. v. EPA, 514 F.2d 492, 541, n. 1, 29 A.L.R.Fed. 73 (8th Cir.1975). The textual discussion of the postponed injunction suggests that postponement here might be three years, but evidently it might have been as much as seven or even ten years. See Plater, Statutory Violations and Equitable Discretion, 70 Calif.L.Rev. 524, 572 (1982).

enjoined. But the costs would not be so high if the cement factory were merely compelled to move 1000 yards away or to buy out the neighbors' properties.

A third and related complication is one often discussed by economic analysts. If the cement factory is enjoined from further operation, the factory owners will almost certainly attempt to buy the injunction back from the plaintiff, a process that might simply mean buying the plaintiff's property at a high price.[1] Estimating all the costs of an injunction in the light of this possibility would be very difficult indeed, and would require an estimate of the costs of bargaining itself.

The potential for party bargaining is central to most economic analysis. Some commentators have thought that private bargaining would generally be the best solution to nuisance problems in any event, and that if a nuisance is found to exist, then an injunction should run automatically without any balance of hardships.[2] This would serve to allow the injured plaintiff to insist on his rights to enjoyment of property until the defendant offers him a price he is subjectively willing to accept. This gives him what a judgment for damages does not, since the damages judgment compels him to suffer the invasion of his property at a price fixed by others.

Other commentators, however, have taken the view that while balancing of hardships is not a good idea, the more or less automatic rule should be to deny rather than to grant the injunction. Such commentators are concerned about the economic inefficiency that would result if the costs imposed by the injunction exceeded the benefits the injunction could bring to the plaintiff.[3]

§ 5.7(4)

1. Sometimes it is suggested that the plaintiff is engaging in extortionate behavior if he sells his injunction back to the defendant for any price greater than the damages he has suffered as measured by the legal rules of damages. But the plaintiff is doing no more than he would have a right to do without a nuisance—refuse to sell property or any of the rights in it at any but the price that suits him. Some writers have emphasized that his subjectively held values can only be protected by giving the aggrieved property owner some method for terminating the nuisance, either allowing him the right to a compensated injunction or allowing him the injunction with the right to sell it back for a high price. See Lewin, Compensated Injunctions and the Evolution of Nuisance Law, 71 Iowa L.Rev. 775 (1986); Note, Injunction Negotiations: An Economic, Moral, and Legal Analysis, 27 Stan. L.Rev. 1563 (1975).

The extortion argument turns on a perception of fairness or unfairness, not on economic efficiency. See Polinsky, Resolving Nuisance Disputes: The Simple Economics of Injunctive and Damages Remedies, 32 Stan.L.Rev. 1075 (1980). The extortion can work in either direction if extortion is the right word. The plaintiff can "extort" if the injunction will cost the defendant more than the good it will

do the plaintiff; but the defendant can extort if it is held liable only for damages and the damages are set lower than the cost of abatement; in this case the defendant can offer to stop the nuisance for "extortionate" sums. Neither case will arise except as a result of fallible decision-making by the courts. But a court decision to grant an injunction allocates the possibility for being unreasonable to the plaintiff, while any decision to grant damages only allocates the possibility for being unreasonable to the defendant in the event the court's decision is erroneous as to the relative costs. With this in mind the extortion argument may be given only moderate weight, even by those who do not believe protection of the landowner's subjective valuation of his rights is the highest priority.

2. Note, Injunction Negotiations: An Economic, Moral, and Legal Analysis, 27 Stan. L.Rev. 1563 (1975). Cf. O. Fiss, The Civil Rights Injunction (1978).

3. See Ellickson, Alternatives to Zoning: Covenants, Nuisance Rules, and Fines as Land Use Controls, 40 U.Chi.L.Rev. 681 (1973); Edward Rabin, Nuisance Law: Rethinking Fundamental Assumptions, 63 Va.L.Rev. 1299 (1977).

Cf., Shreve, Federal Injunctions And the Public Interest, 51 Geo.Wash.L.Rev. 382 (1983): "Remission of plaintiff to a damage

For example, the plaintiff's property value might be diminished by $1,000 as a result of the nuisance. But the costs to the defendant and others in complying with the injunction might be much more. The defendant might be compelled to cut production and lose profits, with additional resulting losses to workers and to the community in taxes. If the total of all such losses were $100,000, then the relative hardships would seem to weigh heavily in favor of the defendant, so one would not expect the injunction to issue under a balancing test. But these commentators point out that there is a risk of error because information about costs is incomplete, and also that the balancing process itself is expensive and introduces uncertainty into the case.[4] The cost of balancing itself plus the risk of erroneously imposing costs greater than benefits lead such critics to oppose any general balancing of hardships.

A very different view is that if the court, perhaps because of incomplete information, issues an injunction that will do more harm than good, the parties' ability to bargain for a different result can correct the resulting inefficiency; the enjoined cement factory can buy out the aggrieved neighbor.[5] But because bargaining is not always feasible and because in any event it has costs of its own, it may be that the court should choose a remedy with a view to minimizing the risk of error, or choose a remedy that would be most easily corrected by party-bargaining if the remedy turns out to be the economically wrong solution. These points suggest that whether an injunction or damages will be most efficient will depend on the facts of individual cases.[6]

Finally, some economically oriented thinkers have focused on the compensated injunction as a partial solution to some of the problems. Although they differ among themselves as to some important details, these thinkers have argued that the main remedies should be limited to damages in favor of the plaintiff, or a compensated injunction in which the plaintiff can obtain an injunction only if he pays its costs.[7] Detailed economic analysis has convinced these writers that such a system is, overall, more efficient.

The compensated injunction has received support on another ground. The plaintiff who is entitled to damages for a nuisance but not entitled to an injunction because of relative hardship, may feel himself seriously undercompensated by market-measured damages. To say his property is reduced

---

proceeding may debase the value of his right, but the issuance of an injunction may exact an exaggerated cost from the defendant. The injunction's purpose is to avert harm to the plaintiff by incapacitating the defendant. Incapacitation poses the threat of adjusting more aspects of the defendant's behavior than those that would wrong the plaintiff if the injunction were not issued."

4. Ellickson, Alternatives to Zoning: Covenants, Nuisance Rules, and Fines as Land Use Controls, 40 U.Chi.L.Rev. 681 (1973).

5. See Polinsky, Resolving Nuisance Disputes: The Simple Economics Of Injunctive And Damages Remedies, 32 Stan.L.Rev. 1075 (1980). The price achieved by bargaining may not be the price an appraiser would fix; but if bargaining is complete, with perfect information, the price will not result in a less-than-optimum output at the factory. Put differently, the plaintiff might "extort" a good price not to enforce the injunction, but although this would cut the defendant's share of the economic pie, it would not be like throwing a part of the pie away. Closing the factory WOULD be like throwing a part of the pie away.

6. See Polinsky, Resolving Nuisance Disputes: The Simple Economics of Injunctive and Damages Remedies, 32 Stan.L.Rev. 1075 (1980).

7. Ellickson, Alternatives to Zoning: Covenants, Nuisance Rules, and Fines as Land Use Controls, 40 U.Chi.L.Rev. 681 (1973); Edward Rabin, Nuisance Law: Rethinking Fundamental Assumptions, 63 Va.L.Rev. 1299 (1977).

in value by $1,000 is not to say he would be willing to take $1,000 for the defendant's right to continue the nuisance. For the plaintiff, the cement dust from the defendant's plant may be well-nigh unbearable even though most people would put up with the dust for a cash payment of $1,000. The compensated injunction has been advanced as a solution to the problem perceived in this set of facts. The plaintiff who finds the nuisance subjectively damages him to the extent of $5,000 can afford to pay anything up to $5,000 to induce the defendant to move. The compensated injunction relieves him of bargaining with a plant owner who may be unreasonable by letting the court fix the cost of abatement and charging it to the plaintiff (with an offset for the plaintiff's damages).[8]

Economic analysis, which is far too complex to summarize adequately here, has contributed enormously to the understanding of remedies and it should be taken quite seriously in any kind of case. Nevertheless, as a practical matter it is best adapted for dealing with cases of serious pollution caused by a significant economic activity. Such cases occur, but many of the nuisance cases in the books are much more mundane affairs; they display claims in which feelings and a sense of right and wrong predominate over economic concerns. The defendant's Christmas decorations attract unwanted traffic to the neighborhood;[9] the defendant proposes to build a fence or a gable on his house that will block a view;[10] the defendant's sewer stinks.[11] Such cases are the quotidian fare of nuisance litigation. Economic thinking will perhaps be helpful in many cases, but it may seem less cogent in these neighborhood disputes which still form the basis for a large number of cases involving nuisance, deed restriction, and even zoning claims. The time has not yet arrived when the feelingful side of the law can be ignored in these cases.

§ 5.7(5) Effects of Statutes on Nuisance Injunctions

[*Consult § 2.10 above in addition to this section in the Practitioner Treatise edition as to adequacy and balancing; for preemption and exhaustion of remedies, see this section in the Practitioner Treatise edition.*]

§ 5.7(6) Easements

[*For the text of this section, see the unabridged Practitioner Treatise edition.*]

(4) HARMS TO INTERESTS IN EXCLUSIVE POSSESSION

§ 5.8 Harms to Interests in Exclusive Possession: Damages for Non-harmful Trespasses, Use, or Occupation of Land

§ 5.8(1) In General

The interest in exclusive possession of land is distinct from the interests in physical integrity and actual enjoyment of the land. The right to

8. Lewin, Compensated Injunctions and the Evolution of Nuisance Law, 71 Iowa L.Rev. 775 (1986).

9. As in Rodrigue v. Copeland, 475 So.2d 1071 (La.1985), cert. denied. 475 U.S. 1046, 106 S.Ct. 1262, 89 L.Ed.2d 572 (1986).

10. E.g., Leonard v. Stoebling, 102 Nev. 543, 728 P.2d 1358 (1986).

11. E.g., Kriener v. Turkey Valley Community School District, 212 N.W.2d 526 (Iowa 1973).

exclusive possession is the right to exclude others from the land. The rightful possessor may insist that others not enter the land even if the possessor is not physically present on the land, is not using it, and is not harmed in any tangible way by another's entry or use. This rather technical right is intimately related to the interest in protecting title from any activity that could cast doubt on its validity or extent. When the landowner is actually physically present, the possessory interest also reflects interests in privacy, self-determination, and the right to decide for oneself who shall enter and upon what terms.[1]

The possessory interest thus has some of the qualities of an intangible right. It is protected by a variety of remedies that vary with the kind of harm done to possession. The trespass action will support a claim for at least nominal damages even when the trespass causes neither harm to the land nor any loss of possession.[2] Restitution for the value of things taken by the trespasser is recoverable as a modern equivalent of assumpsit.[3] Damages based on rental value of land wrongfully possessed by the trespasser is recoverable in other cases.[4] The ejectment action will return a dispossessed owner to actual possession,[5] and a summary form of ejectment with limited trial and speedy results, is often available to the same end.[6] In some cases the injunction might be used to gain full possessory rights.[7]

§ 5.8(2) Damages and Mesne Profits

Nominal Damages

Even the slightest trespass entitles the plaintiff to recover at least nominal damages for the invasion of the plaintiff's possessory rights.[1] This gives the plaintiff the status of prevailing party, a status which in turn will usually control his right to recover court costs and any awardable attorney fees.[2]

Rental Value or Mesne Profits

Generally. When the trespasser's presence is substantial enough to count as a possession, or even as temporary use, damages for the invasion can be measured by rental value of the land during the period of the trespass.[8] The rental value recovery can be made in the action of ejectment, where it was traditionally known as a recovery of "mesne profits" but the measure was nevertheless a rental value measure.[9] The same measure of damages is used in the general trespass action. Rental value is also an appropriate measure for temporary takings under eminent domain powers, that is, for taking the land for a limited period of time.[10]

§ 5.8(2)

8. Kruvant v. 12–22 Woodland Ave. Corp., 138 N.J.Super. 1, 350 A.2d 102 (1975), aff'd, 150 N.J.Super. 503, 376 A.2d 188 (1977); Salesian Society, Inc. v. Village of Ellenville, 121 A.D.2d 823, 505 N.Y.S.2d 197 (1986) (rental value "taking the property as is and as zoned," lease in effect is some evidence of that value); Uhlhorn v. Keltner, 723 S.W.2d 131 (Tenn.App.1986) (rental value, but rental value does not include improvements made by defendants).

10. See Kimball Laundry Co. v. United States, 338 U.S. 1, 69 S.Ct. 1434, 93 L.Ed. 1765, 7 A.L.R. 1280 (1949) (United States had

The rental market value of the land in these cases represents the value of possession or use. If the defendant does not take the whole of the property, the recovery is for the amount by which rental value has been diminished by the defendant's acts. In some cases, interest on the diminished value resulting from taking or dispossession might furnish an alternative to the diminished rental value measure.[11] The rental value measure has no application if the defendant's trespass is not measurable in terms of use or possession or taking; it is not appropriate to the case of a single, transitory trespass.[12] If there is physical damage or destruction, separate damages will be required for that harm.[13]

Objective or market measure; irrelevance of defendant's losses. Rental value is ordinarily an objective measure, based on an estimate of the price others would pay to rent the land,[14] not on what the trespasser personally would pay. Although it may be possible to assert a restitution claim in some trespass cases,[15] the claim here is for damages based on the objective rental value of the land used by the trespasser. Thus whether the trespasser actually gained any benefit from the land is not controlling and he remains liable for rental value even if he lost money in his use of the land.[16]

Objective measure; irrelevance of plaintiff's lack of loss. Use of the objective rental value measure also means that the plaintiff is entitled to recover rental value even if the plaintiff himself could not reach the land, did not intend to use it, and would not have rented it to others.[17] The

---

taken right to use a laundry for a limited period, rental value).

11. See Wheeler v. City of Pleasant Grove, 833 F.2d 267 (11th Cir.1987) (fair return on diminished value in case of a regulatory taking of property by unconstitutional zoning ordinance).

However, in Freidus v. Eisenberg, 123 A.D.2d 174, 510 N.Y.S.2d 139, 143 (1986), a case in which the plaintiff was delayed in getting possession of land under a contract, the court refused to consider interest that might have been earned on the capital value of the land. "While this approach might establish what a fair return on the cash value of the property might have been had it been sold each successive year in question—a conversion theory—it was not evidence at all of the reasonable rent that a tenant or occupant of the property might pay." The case was modified on appeal on other grounds, which did not dispose of the interest question. Freidus v. Eisenberg, 71 N.Y.2d 981, 529 N.Y.S.2d 69, 524 N.E.2d 423 (1988).

14. The rental market in some cases appears to be entirely hypothetical and rental value is often proved by opinion testimony, e.g., Kruvant v. 12–22 Woodland Ave. Corp., 138 N.J.Super. 1, 350 A.2d 102 (1975), aff'd, 150 N.J.Super. 503, 376 A.2d 188 (1977), though in some cases it may be proved by actual leasing price or standard prices for similar property. In any case, however, the objective rental value differs in kind from a

subjective measure based merely on what the plaintiff would like to charge or how much he cares about it. The plaintiff can, however, testify to his opinion of the objective rental value.

17. See generally Restatement Second of Torts § 931, Comment *b* (1979).

In De Camp v. Bullard, 159 N.Y. 450, 54 N.E. 26 (1899) the defendants who had used a river for floating logs were liable to the plaintiff for rental value of the stream. There was no proof of lost rental value, but the court was unmoved by this fact. It said in part: "If a man's house is vacant, with no prospect of a tenant and no intention on his part of occupying it himself, and a trespasser occupies it, he must pay as damages for the trespass the value of the use and occupation." At least this is so in the case of a deliberate trespass.

In Steel Creek Development Corp. v. James, 58 N.C.App. 506, 294 S.E.2d 23 (1982) the court held that the defendant would be responsible for rental value of submerged lands over which defendants had placed floats and into which it had sunk anchors.

Distinguish the case in which the plaintiff can recover rentals as special or consequential damages but not otherwise. In that case actual loss of rentals or tenants would have to be proven. Such a case would arise if the defendant's entry upon the land was transient or trivial only, so that rental value as general damages would be inappropriate. In those cases the plaintiff could still prove lost ten-

plaintiff must, however, prove what the objective rental value is and the appropriate time period for calculating it.[18]

Trespasser's profits; damages and restitution distinguished. When the trespasser's profits from occupation of the land exceed the rental value, a recovery of the profits instead of the rental value is sometimes preferable to the plaintiff and sometimes, as indicated elsewhere, is actually allowed as restitution.[19] Such cases raise difficult problems in determining how much of the "profit" is due to the defendant's labor and how much is due to the plaintiff's property.[20] This difficulty makes it doubtful whether the court should allow recovery of business profits earned by the defendant in the course of his trespass. But there are some important distinctions in the cases.

It seems right to say that the defendant's business profits are recoverable when, but only when (1) they reflect gains attributable to the property itself and not to the defendant's enterprise or when (2) they reflect the plaintiff's recoverable special or consequential damages.[22] This is in accord with the cases allowing recovery for rents collected by the defendant,[23] since those items are mainly or wholly a product of the property, not the operation of a business enterprise and they clearly reflect losses to the plaintiff as well as gains to the defendant. The view stated is also in accord with the cases which deny a recovery of the defendant's business profits as such, but permit such a recovery where the plaintiff and defendant were operating similar businesses; in that case the defendant's profits would be some evidence of the plaintiff's probable loss.[24] So rental value and not the defendant's profits would be the appropriate normal recovery. Some authority, however, fails to recognize these distinctions.[25]

Subjective tests. Finally, cases sometimes speak of "actual worth" or "actual value" of the property to the plaintiff. In many of these it is most uncertain whether the phrase is meant to authorize a recovery of subjective value to the plaintiff.[26] If the "actual value" refers to consequential dam-

ants, but if he did not, rental value recovery would be denied. Cf. Malerba v. Warren, 96 A.D.2d 529, 464 N.Y.S.2d 835 (1983).

There are cases that have allowed only nominal damages rather than rental value, apparently because the rental value rule was overlooked rather than because it was weighed and rejected. See Vecchiotti v. Tegethoff, 745 S.W.2d 741 (Mo.App.1987).

19. See Edwards v. Lee's Adm'r, 265 Ky. 418, 96 S.W.2d 1028 (1936), discussed in § 5.9 below.

20. Thus the court must consider whether the defendant is entitled to any deductions for expenses incurred in making the "profit." See London v. Bear, 84 N.C. 266 (1881); Dime Sav. Bank of Brooklyn v. Altman, 275 N.Y. 62, 9 N.Ed.2d 778 (1937). The trespasser's own contributions may also be difficult to evaluate. For instance, did a trespasser who operated a service station on the land sell a lot of gasoline because the property was valuable or because he was a good salesperson? Pritchard

Petroleum Co. v. Farmers Co–op Oil & Supply Co., 121 Mont. 1, 190 P.2d 55 (1948) (evidence attempting to measure value of use by 1 cent per gallon improper). Cf. Van Ruymbeke v. Patapsco Industrial Park, 261 Md. 470, 276 A.2d 61 (1971) (extensively quoting trial judge, that profits of defendant "are so interrelated with the ownership of equipment and with management * * * [and] matters of personal management and general business skill, that [they bear] no relationship whatsoever to the specific use of this property").

22. This may be the explanation of Capital Garage Co. v. Powell, 98 Vt. 303, 127 A. 375 (1925).

25. See the broad statements in Sabourin v. Woish, 117 Vt. 94, 85 A.2d 493 (1952).

26. The term "value to the plaintiff" suggests a subjective measure. But the cases cast doubt on this interpretation. In Stokes v. Van Seventer, 355 P.2d 594 (Alaska 1960) the court said the test was "actual worth of the property to the plaintiff," suggesting a subjec-

ages, they are certainly recoverable if the appropriate kind of proof is made. If it refers to a plaintiff's subjective feeling that the possession is worth a thousand dollars when rental value is only $100, such a recovery seems unjustified.

[*For a discussion of a trespass on part of a tract, see the Practitioner Treatise edition.*]

Periodic and Sub-optimal Uses

The defendant's use or occupation might be less than complete in still other ways. The defendant who builds a road across a tract of 500 acres and hauls out coal or timber might be thought of as occupying the fee for the whole 500 acres or as occupying the fee of that portion of the tract occupied by the road. But such a defendant could also be thought to be taking an easement on the way. If he is considered to have taken an easement or license only, the value would ordinarily be relatively small. Some awards have been made based at least in part on the value of the easement,[28] but the issue seems not to have been generally considered.

A closely analogous problem in fixing rental value occurs when the trespasser does not use the land for its highest and best use. In a New Jersey case the defendant conducted its stable horses across a very valuable but unimproved commercial area. The commercial building value of the lot was very high, and with that in mind the rental value would also be very high. Its value for the use to which the trespasser put the lot, however, would be much less. Although no final decision was reached in the reported decision, the court appeared to have in mind a rental value recovery based on the highest and best use for the land, not one based on the limited and relatively trivial use.[29]

If the plaintiff actually suffers special damages in the form of a lost rental at the higher value, that should of course be recoverable. When the claim is one for general damages based on rental value, perhaps it would be better to limit the plaintiff's recovery to a sum equal to the rental value of the property for the purpose to which the trespasser used it. The family that once picnicked on a vacant lot that later became the World Trade Center should not be paying for that trespass at the rates for a commercial lessee.

§ 5.8(3) Improvements Added by Trespasser

[*Consult § 4.9(5) above in addition to this section in the Practitioner Treatise edition.*]

§ 5.9 Dispossession—Restitution for Use and Occupation

When a trespasser appropriates tangible property in the course of a trespass—minerals or timber, for example,—the reasonable value of the

tive approach, but added that this was the same as "its rental value."

28. See Raven Red Ash Coal Co. v. Ball, 185 Va. 534, 39 S.E.2d 231, 167 A.L.R. 785 (1946), discussed in § 5.9 below. In that case the trespasser already had an easement and was guilty of trespass only because he overburdened it.

29. Kruvant v. 12–22 Woodland Ave. Corp., 138 N.J.Super. 1, 350 A.2d 102 (1975), aff'd, 150 N.J.Super. 503, 376 A.2d 188 (1977). The court took testimony as to the rental value of a tract valued at $250,000 and zoned for office/research. There seems to have been no evidence offered as to the value of an easement for riding horses on the empty lot.

property so taken by be recovered on a conversion theory.[1] In addition, the plaintiff may recover on a theory that the plaintiff waives the tort and sues in assumpsit to recover the trespasser's ill-gotten gains.[2]

When the trespasser has not taken tangible things from the land but has merely used or occupied the premises, the traditional view was that whatever the measure of recovery in trespass or ejectment, the plaintiff could not sue in assumpsit in the absence of a landlord-tenant relationship.[3]

The effect of this was that the plaintiff could recover the objective rental value of the land in an ordinary trespass or ejectment action,[4] but could not obtain restitution of any special benefits that accrued to the defendant from use of the land. The rule had other effects, too: the plaintiff's claim would not take on the character of the assumpsit (or contract) action and thus would not be governed by any of the rules special to assumpsit or contract cases. The plaintiff's claim would not, for example, be governed by the joinder rules,[5] venue rules,[6] survival of actions rules,[7] or statute of limitations rules[8] for contract claims since he could not sue in "assumpsit."

With the abolition of the writ system in the years around 1850, the rule seems somewhat less than relevant on such matters as fixing venue, which is now presumably determined by a fair interpretation of the statute rather than by invocation of "assumpsit" claims. The measure of recovery, however, is another matter. The reasons for the rule against assumpsit for use and occupation of land are obscure,[9] but the resulting limit on recovery might nonetheless be a wise one in at least some of the cases.

Since the plaintiff is entitled to recover rental value for use and occupation as an objective measure of damages[10] the use of an "assumpsit" or restitutionary claim could only be of assistance in affecting the amount of recovery if it could serve to capture special values gained by the defendant from the occupation.[11] This would most typically be profits from operation of a business or alternatively special savings from use of the particular parcel of land. But operating profits or analogous special savings in a business operation are not products of the land; they are at most joint products of the land and the defendant's investment of time, money and enterprise. If the defendant should be liable to make restitution of gains, they should be gains identified with the land, not gains resulting from his enterprise. The rule against "assumpsit" for use and occupation has the effect of precluding a recovery of the defendant's business profits.

Some authorities, however, have departed from the traditional rule and have allowed the "assumpsit" measure of recovery—that is, restitution—in use and occupation cases. One of the two most important cases involved a cave in Kentucky, the entrance to which was on the defendant's land. The cave extended beneath the plaintiff's land, as well, though the plaintiff had no means of access to the cave. The defendant operated a business showing sightseers the wonders of the cavern, including the wonders under the plaintiff's land. The plaintiff was allowed to recover, not merely rental value for the use of the land, but a share of the profits earned by defendant.[12]

Although a recovery of the defendant's profits might be justified on the ground that the defendant who is a wilful tortfeasor should not be allowed to keep the profits of his tort, the amount of profits that result from the tort itself rather than from the defendant's perfectly legitimate activity, are not readily discernible. Punishment of a wilful tort might better be accomplished through punitive damages. In any event, the Kentucky Court has now recognized that the decision is peculiar and has said it is "sui generis." [13]

The second case, *Raven Red Ash Coal Co. v. Ball*,[14] involved a defendant who deliberately overburdened an easement. The defendant had a right to use a way across the plaintiff's land, but only for limited purposes. Defendant carried some 50,000 tons of coal for which there was no such authorization. This was a trespass. The rental value for a completely new easement was one cent per ton, but rental value for the additional burden would have been only a small fraction of that price. The court nevertheless allowed the plaintiff to recover the one-cent per ton rate as value to the defendant.

Although *Raven Red Ash* did not allow a recovery of the defendant's business profits, it did allow a recovery in excess of rental value for the plaintiff's easement. Consequently the case cannot be seen as merely an award of objective or market-based damages. In addition, the defendant was actually enriched by one-cent per ton only if, but for the trespass, it would have been required to rent an entirely new easement at the one-cent rate.[15] But the defendant certainly did not save the one-cent per ton cost if, but for the trespass, he could have purchased rights to haul additional coal from the plaintiff at the fractional rate. The defendant who engorged one apple may have been required to disgorge two.

The problems with the unjust enrichment or "assumpsit" measure of recovery in these cases suggests that an objective measure of the defendant's gains would be preferable. This would be similar to the ordinary damages rule in trespass and ejectment cases. Punitive damages could be added if the defendant's conduct is truly blameworthy. The punitive damages approach could be more flexible than a simple confiscation of all the defendant's profits.

§ 5.10 Harms to Interests in Exclusive Possession—Injunction, Ejectment and Summary Relief

§ 5.10(1) Ejectment

When a defendant's invasion of the land is not merely casual or transient but constitutes a substantial presence on the land or a possession of it, the true owner usually wishes three kinds of remedy. He wishes to be restored to possession, to have his title officially recognized and declared, and to recover damages for the dispossession. The traditional method for achieving these remedies was the action of ejectment.

Ejectment was a species of trespass claim,[1] open to the plaintiff who

---

§ 5.9

13. See Triple Elkhorn Mining Co., Inc. v. Anderson, 646 S.W.2d 725 (Ky.1983). Speaking of *Edwards:* "Under these peculiar circumstances, the court permitted profits as a method of measuring damages but took great pains to declare that it was sui generis and peculiar on its facts, setting out that reasonable rental value was impossible to compute under the facts of that case."

14. Raven Red Ash Coal Co. v. Ball, 185 Va. 534, 39 S.E.2d 231, 167 A.L.R. 785 (1946).

15. So-called negative unjust enrichment, negative because it represents a cost saved rather than affirmative income.

§ 5.10(1)

1. See 7 W. Holdsworth, History of English Law 4–23 (1926).

could show legal title and a right to immediate possession.[2] At one time, due to the maze of fictions used in the common law development of the ejectment action,[3] the plaintiff had to bring a separate suit for damages, which were traditionally called *mesne profits*. The second action is not now required and the damages claim can be asserted in the ejectment action.[4]

The ejectment action is an action at law, for which a jury is a matter of right.[5] When the plaintiff prevails in the ejectment action, his right to possession is then enforced in rem rather than in personam. This means that the sheriff is ordered, through the writ of possession, to put the plaintiff in possession of the premises.[6] This is a strong contrast with the injunction, which is in personam and would order the defendant to give possession to the plaintiff.[7] The in rem enforcement by the sheriff suggests some limits to the ejectment action. The sheriff would not be likely to put the plaintiff in possession of his land by removing a four-story building that encroached four inches on the land, for example.[8] Similarly, ejectment would be inappropriate as a remedy for transient trespasses that could not be affected by the sheriff's efforts at putting the plaintiff in possession.[9]

The ejectment action is oriented towards the tangible and immediate. If the defendant casts doubt on the plaintiff's title but does not deprive the plaintiff of possession, ejectment is not the traditional remedy; to remove a cloud of title when there is no dispossession, the plaintiff must resort to an equitable remedy like injunction or to a statutory procedure.[10]

§ 5.10(2) Forcible Entry and Detainer, Summary Ejectment

[*For the text of this section, see the unabridged Practitioner Treatise edition.*]

§ 5.10(3) Injunctive Protection of Possession Generally

As already shown, injunctions will issue to protect interests in the physical integrity of the land and its structures [1] and interests in the use and enjoyment.[2] Many injunctions operate to protect interests in use and enjoyment and purely possessory interests at the same time, as in the case of injunctions against protestors who trespass on the property and prevent its use.[3] Injunctions also issue to protect purely possessory interests even

2. An equitable interest in the plaintiff is said to be an insufficient ground to maintain ejectment. Smith's Lessee v. McCann, 65 U.S. (24 How.) 398, 16 L.Ed. 714 (1860).

3. See 7 W. Holdsworth, History of English Law 15 (1926).

4. Statutes expressly so provide, e.g., Ark. Code Ann. § 18–60–209; N.Y.—McKinney's Real Prop. A. & P. Law § 601.

5. See Berger v. Malneut Realty Corp., 174 A.D.2d 308, 570 N.Y.S.2d 53 (1991); § 2.6(3) above as to jury trial; § 4.2(2) as to the history of ejectment as a claim "at law."

6. See, discussing the writ of possession, and the parallel writ of assistance used by the Chancellors in equity, Fuller v. Gibbs, 122 Mont. 177, 199 P.2d 851 (1948); Southern State Bank v. Leverette, 187 N.C. 743, 123 S.E. 68 (1924).

7. The injunction would then be enforced, if necessary, through contempt powers in contrast to the in rem enforcement through the sheriff. See §§ 1.4 (enforcement devices compared) and 2.8 (contempt) above.

8. See Hahl v. Sugo, 169 N.Y. 109, 62 N.E. 135 (1901).

9. Marder v. Realty Const. Co., 84 N.J.Super. 313, 202 A.2d 175 (1964), aff'd, 43 N.J. 508, 205 A.2d 744 (1964) (isolated trespasses, damages rather than ejectment proper remedy).

§ 5.10(3)

3. E.g., Planned Parenthood League of Massachusetts, Inc. v. Operation Rescue, 406 Mass. 701, 550 N.E.2d 1361 (1990).

where there is no threat to physical integrity or use and enjoyment. But when injunction is sought purely to protect possession there are some added impediments and special problems which are the concern of this section.

Adequacy and Irreparability Rules

General rules. Two rules are invoked when the plaintiff seeks an injunction based on a single, transitory trespass that causes no physical change in the land. *First,* injunctive relief will be denied unless future harm is threatened.[4] The threat of repeated future trespass can be found either in the defendant's actual words [5] or in the nature of his past trespasses and the motives for them.[6] But past trespass does not always imply a threat to repeat the invasion, and if it does not, the injunction will not issue.

Second, under traditional views, injunctive relief will be denied if the plaintiff fails to prove [7] that the legal remedy is inadequate or the harm irreparable.[8] Even if an additional trespass is threatened for the future, it might be regarded as a threat that could be adequately redressed by a damages recovery.[9] Contemporary cases for the most part have deemphasized the adequacy test, however, or have applied it liberally to permit the injunction.[10]

Repeated or continuing trespasses. When the defendant by words or conduct expressly or impliedly threatens repeated future trespasses, the injunction will go.[11] Courts have said that the adequacy rule is satisfied in such cases, because without an injunction the true owner would be required to sue repeatedly at law for damages for the repeated trespasses and that equity should issue the injunction to prevent a multiplicity of suits.[12]

[*For further rules and analysis, see this section in the Practitioner Treatise edition.*]

Injunctions Where Title to Land Is in Issue

General rule. Equity will not try title to land; that is for the law courts with their jury trials in ejectment suits. There are exceptions, mainly in the bill to remove a cloud on title,[22] but at least where the title issue can be

4. Perley v. Town of Effingham, 94 N.H. 120, 48 A.2d 484 (1946).

6. E.g., Kugler v. Ryan, 682 S.W.2d 47 (Mo. App.1984) (abortion protestor on plaintiff's premises enjoined; "frequency and pattern" of conduct warranted inference that trespasses would continue unless enjoined). Another kind of case that would justify the inference is one in which the defendant has created a structure that will continue to cause invasions unless altered, as where the defendant ditches his own land in a way to cast waters on the plaintiff's. Cf. Cobai v. Young, 679 P.2d 121 (Colo.App.1984) (defendant's roof so constructed as to pitch snow onto plaintiff's land).

9. See McRaven v. Culley, 324 Ill. 451, 155 N.E. 282, 283 (1927), taking the view that repeated trespasses would be adequately redressed by a damages recovery unless the trespasses would yield damages recoveries "so small and disproportionate to the vexation

and expense of the action as to render the remedy at law inadequate."

11. E.g., Lanier v. Ocean Pond Fishing Club, Inc., 253 Ga. 549, 322 S.E.2d 494 (1984).

12. Reproductive Health Services v. Lee, 712 S.W.2d 718 (Mo.App.1986); Kugler v. Ryan, 682 S.W.2d 47 (Mo.App.1984); Cobai v. Young, 679 P.2d 121 (Colo.App.1984). See Gregath v. Bates, 359 So.2d 404, 408 (Ala.Civ. App.1978) (proper to "restrain a repeated or continuing trespass when the remedy at law is inadequate because of the nature of the injury or because of multiplicity of actions necessary to obtain relief").

22. Where the plaintiff is not in possession he lacks grounds for ejectment, if defendant's claims cloud the plaintiff's title, he may induce equity to settle the dispute. See Suplee v. Eckert, 35 Del.Ch. 428, 120 A.2d 718 (1956). Equity courts may sometimes change the inci-

resolved in an ejectment suit, equity will not determine a substantial and disputed issue of title by issuing a permanent injunction.[23]

Provisional relief. Provisional relief, however, may be available to protect the property from permanent injury until the law courts can reach and determine the title issue. For example, a preliminary injunction might issue to prohibit the defendant from cutting timber on the land until title is decided in the pending ejectment action.[24] Beyond this, courts may even use the preliminary injunction to protect the "last peaceable possession" or the status quo from trespass until title can be decided.[25] This is a kind of judicial hot pursuit rule, protecting the landowner who has been recently dispossessed. It is important, because without such a rule the landowner would be required to resort to ejectment and to carry the burden of proof. If, on the other hand, his possession is protected by the injunction, it will be the attacker who has the burden of proof.

Enjoining economic activity while title is in issue. An injunction, even if it is limited to the period necessary to determine title at law, may have important economic consequences. Although the older policy of rapid exploitation of natural resources [26] has largely given way to a policy of conservation and concern for the environment,[27] it remains true that injunction against economic activity on the land may cause permanent losses, at least if it turns out that the defendant had good legal title after all. For this reason the injunction to protect property until a legal determination of title has been rendered will not issue automatically and the chancellor should not act unless the plaintiff shows irreparable harm and a fairly clear claim to title.[28]

dents of title, as by altering a deed restriction. See McClure v. Leaycraft, 183 N.Y. 36, 75 N.E. 961 (1905); Hill v. Ogrodnik, 83 R.I. 138, 113 A.2d 734 (1955). Equity might also recognize an interest in land not recognized "at law." In this kind of case, instead of enjoining the trespass until the case can be decided at law, the equity court might enjoin the proceeding at law until the plaintiff's equitable interests are be determined in equity. See Stanardsville Volunteer Fire Co., Inc. v. Berry, 229 Va. 578, 331 S.E.2d 466 (1985) (plaintiff, sued at law for trespass, could seek injunction in equity against legal proceeding until plaintiff could have equity court determine his right to easement based on estoppel). And where equity has independently taken jurisdiction on some other ground, such as fraud, it may involve itself in title issues. Goings v. Shafer, 214 Mo.App. 419, 253 S.W. 133 (1923).

23. Anderson v. Turner, 133 Colo. 453, 296 P.2d 1044 (1956); Williams v. Bridy, 391 Pa. 1, 136 A.2d 832 (1957).

24. Erhardt v. Boaro, 113 U.S. 537, 5 S.Ct. 565, 28 L.Ed. 1116 (1885).

25. Deisenroth v. Dodge, 350 Ill.App. 20, 111 N.E.2d 575 (1953) (preliminary mandatory injunction to remove barricade on right of way to protect last peaceable status); Owens v. Texaco, Inc., 368 S.W.2d 780 (Tex.Civ.App.

1963) (injunction to protect in boundary dispute).

26. Earlier cases refusing to enjoin timber cutting, even by preliminary injunction to protect the land until title could be decided, was apparently largely due to the assumption that resources ought to be exploited as rapidly as possible. In Gause v. Perkins, 56 N.C. 177, 179 (1857) the court refused an injunction against timber cutting because it would cause "not only much private loss, but great detriment to the public. Fields already cleared would lie idle, woodland that, in a country like ours, ought to be cut down and cultivated, would stand wild and unproductive, and the valuable products of our forests would no longer swell in the tide of trade."

27. Compare Gause v. Perkins, 56 N.C. 177, 179 (1857) with Pardee v. Camden Lumber Co., 70 W.Va. 68, 74, 73 S.E. 82, 85 (1911). *Gause* emphasized the need for removing timber to "swell in the tide of trade," but *Pardee,* noting that "In early days [timber] was regarded as an incumbrance," went on to point out that "It takes half a century or more to regrow it * * *."

28. See Williams v. Bridy, 391 Pa. 1, 136 A.2d 832 (1957) (plaintiff's title not cleary enough established to support preliminary injunction); Dobbs, Trespass to Land in North Carolina, Part II, 47 N.C.L.Rev. 334 (1969).

Exceptions to the title rules. The rule against trying title in equity does not prevent relief in all cases. If the plaintiff remains in technical possession and the defendant's acts on the land, or his claims, constitute a cloud on title, equity may take jurisdiction to remove the cloud because ejectment will not furnish a remedy at law for the plaintiff.[29] And incident to the suit to remove cloud, equity may issue a declaratory judgment[30] or even an injunction as ancillary relief.[31] If jury trial rights are the most significant reason for the title rules, then the injunction should also be available when the title issue turns on rules of law rather than on factual disputes, since the judge, not the jury, would decide the purely legal issues in any event.[32]

As with other restrictive rules in equity, the rule against equity's deciding title issues is likely to be enforced much less strictly today than in the 19th century,[33] and there are certainly cases in which courts grant the injunction in the face of a title dispute when irreparable damage is convincingly shown[34] and others in which injunction and title issues mix freely without the slightest mention of the supposed rule.[35]

Injunctions Transferring Possession of Land

No transfer of possession by preliminary injunction. It is sometimes stated as a rule that equity will not transfer possession[36] of land by preliminary injunction,[37] a rule often coupled with the rule against title decisions in equity but one that is also distinct from the title rule. To shift possession by injunction, on the other hand, is to shift the burden of proof on the title issue, since the party who is out of possession will be the party who must bring the ejectment suit at law and who must sustain the burden of proof. The rule against shifting possession by injunction is thus the twin sister to the rule that restores possession to the last (recent) peaceable possession. Read together, the two rules protect against a fortuitous or forcible shifting of the burden of proof on the title in the subsequent ejectment action.

Broader rule statements. Sometimes courts have stated the rule more broadly by saying that no injunction—presumably not even a permanent one—will be used to affect possession.[38] If the legal remedy is adequate that will be ground enough for denying the injunction and an additional rule against transferring possession would not be needed.[39] If there is a title issue, that alone might suffice to exclude injunctive relief, and again the additional rule about possession would not be needed. If the legal remedy is

---

31. Suplee v. Eckert, 35 Del.Ch. 428, 120 A.2d 718 (1956); Comstock v. Little, 359 P.2d 704 (Okl.1961).

32. See Boerner v. McCallister, 197 Va. 169, 89 S.E.2d 23 (1955) (trespass on stream enjoined, court construed grant and made one finding of fact, that the stream was non-navigable).

33. See Simpson, Fifty Years of American Equity, 50 Harv.L.Rev. 171, 176 (1936).

34. Sikes v. Turner, 212 Mo.App. 419, 425, 247 S.W. 803, 805 (1923) (timber cutting; "the law does not require that a person shall submit to the stripping of his timber land of its forest trees * * * the nature of the property

involved and the inconvenience of suiting for continuous trespasses constitute a basis for equitable relief" though title is in dispute).

35. E.g., Vecchiotti v. Tegethoff, 745 S.W.2d 741 (Mo.App.1987).

37. See State ex rel. Janus v. Ferriss, 344 S.W.2d 656 (Mo.App.1961) (alleged tenants locked out by "landlord," could not regain possession by preliminary injunction); Taylor v. Gulf Oil Corp., 303 S.W.2d 541 (Tex.Civ. App.1957). See also Knower v. Atkins, 273 A.D. 356, 77 N.Y.S.2d 559 (1948), aff'd without opinion, 298 N.Y. 750, 83 N.E.2d 150 (1948).

not adequate and there is no title issue, however, the broad statement that equity would not act seems wrong. And in fact courts do transfer possession by permanent injunction in some cases, notably those in which the defendant has erected a structure on the plaintiff's land.[40] Probably the rule against transferring possession by a permanent injunction is too broadly stated and should be discarded as either unnecessary or wrong or both.

Easements

Easements are not estates in land.[41] One who enjoys an easement such as a right of way has no possessory rights. Even the owner of the underlying estate does not have the right of exclusive possession of the way, since it is subject to another's right to use. The pure rules of trespass, which are founded on possessory rights, thus do not apply to easements.[42] The rules invoked in pure trespass cases, seem to create no impediment to injunctions in easement cases. Preliminary injunctions may issue to prevent obstruction or to restore access;[43] injunctions may issue to require removal of substantial structures[44] or to regulate the extent and nature of use.[45] Indeed, as in nuisance cases, the injunction suit is frequently used to define the nature and extent of the rights of use,[46] and courts appear to have no hesitation about doing so.

§ 5.10(4) Injunctive Protection Against Encroaching Structures

One kind of trespass has posed special problems and produced special solutions. This is the trespass by an encroaching structure, in which the defendant has built a substantial structure such as a house or factory in such a way that a part of it is on the plaintiff's land—eaves overhang slightly,[1] or footings project into the plaintiff's land a few inches underground,[2] or the structure is actually built in part on the surface of the plaintiff's land[3] or on his easement.[4]

Adequacy, Title and Possession in Encroachment Cases

Adequacy. The adequacy of legal remedy rule has presented little problem to plaintiffs in encroachment cases. The trespass claim for damages is regarded as inadequate because the trespass is continuing and might require a multiplicity of suits for damages.[5] And if the defendant's building remains on the plaintiff's land long enough the defendant may acquire title by adverse possession.[6] The ejectment suit, which is aimed at putting the

40. Blood v. Cohen, 330 Mass. 385, 113 N.E.2d 448 (1953); Pile v. Pedrick, 167 Pa. 296, 31 A. 646, 46 Am.St.Rep. 677 (1895).

41. R. Cunningham, W. Stoebuck & D. Whitman, The Law of Property 435 (1984).

43. See Hancock v. Moriarity, 215 Ga. 274, 110 S.E.2d 403 (1959); Deisenroth v. Dodge, 350 Ill.App. 20, 111 N.E.2d 575 (1953) (preliminary mandatory injunction to remove barricade); Hoffman Hardware Co. v. Naame, 18 N.J.Super. 234, 86 A.2d 832 (1952) (preliminary mandatory injunction to remove obstruction of right of way).

44. See Arkansas Louisiana Gas Co. v. Cutrer, 30 So.2d 864 (La.App.1947) (building on fee but over gas line easement ordered removed since it might someday interfere with

effort to reach buried pipeline); Carolina Power & Light Co. v. Bowman, 229 N.C. 682, 51 S.E.2d 191, 6 A.L.R.2d 194 (1949).

45. Sampson v. Grooms, 230 Mont. 190, 748 P.2d 960 (1988) (parties enjoined from further long-term parking on easement but allowed short-time parting and ingress and egress, no discussion of any rules limiting remedies).

46. E.g., Alburger v. Philadelphia Electric Co., 112 Pa.Cmwlth. 441, 535 A.2d 729 (1988) (defining limits of flowage easement and enjoining upper riparian owner from artificially augmenting flowage, no issue of limits on injunctive power discussed).

plaintiff in actual possession,[7] is not adequate to force a removal of a substantial structure, since ejectment is enforced by the physical actions of the sheriff, who cannot be expected to put the plaintiff in possession by removing a building.[8]

Title and possession. Although equity has shown itself reluctant to deal with issues of title and possession in other kinds of trespass cases,[9] the reluctance is invisible when encroaching structures are in issue.[10] The encroachment cases thus usually go directly to the merits—whether an injunction should issue to compel removal of the structure.

Hardships and Equities

Balancing hardships. The dominant approach in the encroachment cases is to balance the relative hardships and equities and to grant or deny the injunction as the balance may seem to indicate. If the injunction is denied, the plaintiff is left with defendant's encroaching structure partly on his land and he will be entitled to damages in lieu of the injunction. If the hardship of removal is not too great, a mandatory injunction will issue to require removal, leaving the plaintiff in complete possession.

Guiding policies. Courts seem mainly moved by two central considerations. *First,* no one should be permitted to take land of another merely because he is willing to pay a market price for it. This would amount to a private eminent domain; one should not be permitted to accomplish such a taking indirectly by intentionally trespassing with the hope that he would be permitted to remain on the land because of the hardship or cost of removing the structure.[11]

Second, although private eminent domain cannot be sanctioned, neither extortion nor economic waste that may be entailed in destroying a structure is desirable. If the encroachment can be removed only by destroying a part of the defendant's large building, but the harm it does to the plaintiff is quite small, the mandatory injunction would compel economic waste or else put the plaintiff in position to demand an unconscionably high price to let the building stay in place. Conscionability and economic arguments may combine to disfavor this kind of result.[12] These two general principles point in different directions; it is this fact that prompts courts to seek resolution through a balancing of hardships and equities.[13]

Equities. The equities to be balanced include such items as good faith, laches and estoppel. The defendant who intentionally or recklessly builds his structure partly on the plaintiff's land will be compelled to remove it,

§ 5.10(4)

8. See Hirschberg v. Flusser, 87 N.J.Eq. 588, 101 A. 191 (1917); Cutrona v. Columbus Theater, 107 N.J.Eq. 281, 151 A. 467 (1930); Hahl v. Sugo, 169 N.Y. 109, 62 N.E. 135 (1901); Restatement Second of Torts § 945, Comment *d* (1979) (not clear how far sheriff can be compelled to remove items, adequacy test judged accordingly).

11. See Christensen v. Tucker, 114 Cal. App.2d 554, 250 P.2d 660 (1952); Ottavia v. Sevarese, 338 Mass. 330, 155 N.E.2d 432, 2 A.L.R.3d 997 (1959).

12. See Restatement Second of Torts § 941, Comment *c* (1979); Keeton & Morris, Notes on "Balancing the Equities,", 18 Tex. L.Rev. 412, 416 (1940). This point about "balancing" is developed at greater length in con-

even at great cost, to avoid giving him a right of private eminent domain.[14] Even if the defendant is merely negligent, that will weigh as one factor against him and in favor of the mandatory injunction.[15] Laches or unreasonable delay by the plaintiff in asserting his right,[16] will weigh against the plaintiff as a factor that tends to or does bar the injunction. If the plaintiff's conduct has misled the defendant, the plaintiff may be estopped from obtaining an injunction, even if it would otherwise go.[17]

Hardships or economic costs.[18] The economic costs of an injunction as compared to damages was traditionally considered by the courts under the "balance of hardships" rubric. If the total cost of removal of the encroachment, including the loss in value of the defendant's remaining building, was very high in comparison to the harm done to the plaintiff because the building encroached on his property, that disparity in economic consequences would be a significant factor in determining whether to issue the injunction. Unless the equities ran in the other direction, the injunction in such a case would not issue, and the plaintiff would be allowed to recover damages instead.[19]

The injunction is not to be withheld merely because to remove the structure will be inconvenient or even because it will be costly. Rather, the injunction is to be withheld only when the hardship to the defendant is not only great but disproportionate compared with the hardship or loss of rights the plaintiff would suffer if the structure is allowed to remain.[20] If the injunction is denied, the defendant in effect acquires either title or an easement in the land [21] and pays damages accordingly. In such a case, the defendant must take care to be sure the resulting decree has an adequate description of the land which is being acquired and becomes a part of the title record.[22]

Refusing to balance hardships and equities. There are a few decisions that refuse to balance the hardships.[23] These purport to say that an injunction should always issue, or at least almost always. There are others that have issued the injunction in the face of severe hardship.[24] These more stringent views seem largely to have passed,[25] and in any event they leave room for balancing of such equities as estoppel and laches.[26] However, when

---

nection with the distinct but analogous case of nuisance. See §§ 5.7(2) and 5.7(4) above.

14. See Waterbury Trust Co. v. G.L.D. Realty Co., 124 Conn. 191, 199 A. 106 (1938); Ottavia v. Sevarese, 338 Mass. 330, 155 N.E.2d 432, 2 A.L.R.3d 997 (1959); Calhoon v. Communications Sys. Const., Inc., 140 Ill.App.3d 1012, 95 Ill.Dec. 71, 489 N.E.2d 23 (1986) (television cable run over the plaintiff's land; the "encroachment will be deemed deliberate if made after due warning" and public interest is not sufficient to induce equity to stay its hand in the case of intentional invasion of a clear legal right); Van De Carr v. Schloss, 277 A.D. 475, 101 N.Y.S.2d 48 (1950).

15. Christensen v. Tucker, 114 Cal.App.3d 554, 250 P.2d 660 (1952); Kershishian v. Johnson, 210 Mass. 135, 96 N.E. 56, 36 L.R.A.,N.S. 402 (1911).

16. Dolske v. Gormley, 58 Cal.2d 513, 25 Cal.Rptr. 270, 375 P.2d 174 (1962) (8 year delay a factor); Pomilio v. Caserta, 42 Del.Ch. 535, 215 A.2d 924 (1965) (7 year delay, plaintiffs should have sought relief sooner).

17. Dunn v. Fletcher, 266 Ala. 273, 96 So.2d 257 (1957) (neighbor helped locate line, made no objection to construction of building erected in reliance); Brandhagen v. Burt, 117 N.W.2d 696 (N.D.1962); cf. Ollig v. Eagles, 347 Mich. 49, 78 N.W.2d 553 (1956) (estoppel as to improvements wholly on another's land). As to estoppel generally see § 2.3 above.

18. A more detailed discussion of the balancing of hardships is given in the distinct but analogous case of nuisances, § 5.7(2) above. Some of the economic commentary is also discussed in connection with balancing in nuisance cases. See § 5.7(4) above.

the defendant's structure is built entirely upon the plaintiff's land, the problem becomes more intense on both sides. The problem of mistaken improvements entirely on the land of another is treated elsewhere.[27]

(5) PROCEDURAL AND REMEDIAL IMPACTS OF PERMANENT INVASIONS

§ 5.11 Statutes of Limitations, Res Judicata and the Permanent Harm Doctrines

§ 5.11(1) General Rules for Permanent Invasions

When an interest in land is invaded by a nuisance or trespass that will continue to cause harm indefinitely[3] into the future, general damages[4] are measured by the diminished value rule.[5] Even though harm will continue, its future effects are captured all at one time by this measure, which gives to the plaintiff the loss in value attributable to the future continuance of the invasion. In a sense, all of the harm is completed when the nuisance first occurs, because the diminished land value is all measurable from that time. In contrast, if an invasion is temporary, general damages will be measured for the harm that has been done up until judgment, with more damages to come in later suits if they are necessary.[6] For example, diminished value that will continue only for one year can be measured by the diminished rental value of the land for one year.

This way of thinking about permanent nuisances and trespasses implies rules for the statute of limitations and for res judicata. If the nuisance is permanent, all harm is done when the nuisance first occurs, and there is but one cause of action for the nuisance, not a series of potential actions. An example is the harm caused when the defendant builds an embankment that periodically causes water to flood the plaintiff's land. Where the embankment is considered to be a permanent nuisance,[7] all of that harm is legally measurable in one cause of action, even though the harm will continue indefinitely into the future. If the plaintiff sues on that cause of action, res judicata doctrines will prevent a second suit later[8] (unless there is a new and greater invasion).[9] By the same token, if permanent damage is done, the owner at the time has the claim for that damage, not a subsequent purchaser.[10] The same sort of analysis can be applied to inverse condemnation or eminent domain cases.[11]

Similarly, the cause of action will accrue for statute of limitations purposes when the permanent nuisance or trespass first occurs.[12] Given a two-year statute, the plaintiff will be barred after two years from the first injury, even though the nuisance is still in effect and still causing harm at

---

27. See §§ 4.9 and 5.8(3).

§ 5.11(1)

8. North Counties Hydro–Electric Co. v. United States, 138 Ct.Cl. 380, 151 F.Supp. 322 (Ct.Cl.1957), cert. denied, 355 U.S. 882, 78 S.Ct. 149, 2 L.Ed.2d 112 (1957). The text statement is the result of saying that there is but one cause of action, the action for permanent damages. Once a suit has gone to judgment on that cause of action, the action is extinguished under the ordinary res judicata rules.

12. Bowen v. City of Kansas City, 231 Kan. 450, 646 P.2d 484 (1982); Rebel v. Big Tarkio Drainage Dist. of Holt City, Mo., 602 S.W.2d 787 (Mo.App.1980).

the time suit is filed. Inverse condemnation suits for informal "takings" by public entities can be analyzed in the same fashion.[13]

Conversely, if a harm from a nuisance or trespass is "temporary"—one that will not last indefinitely—general damages would be based on diminished rental value rather than diminished market value.[14] The invasion would be seen as a series of invasions, each one giving rise to a new claim or cause of action. Res judicata doctrines might require the plaintiff to sue on all those accrued when suit is brought or to be barred, but as to damages accrued after suit or judgment, new claims could be brought [15] up until such time as the new harms became permanent.[16] And, in parallel reasoning, the statute of limitations might have run on claims that accrue two years earlier, but not on claims accruing within the last two years.[17] The fact that a nuisance or trespass continues over a period of time does not prevent the application of these "continuing trespass" rules, so long as the invasion is not a permanent one.

§ 5.11(2) What Invasions Are "Permanent"?

[*For the text of this section, see the unabridged Practitioner Treatise edition.*]

§ 5.11(3) Incentives in the Permanent Nuisance Issue

It is unlikely, even when injunction against an invasion is denied, that physical permanency alone will determine the issues. The practical and policy side of the "permanency" decision involves some other issues. If the nuisance is one affecting not only the plaintiff but others as well—air pollution is a common example—then there is much to be said for using an injunction. When, on balance of hardships or for other reasons,[1] the nuisance is not to be enjoined, the defendant should be given incentive to minimize the nuisance and to correct it altogether if technology becomes available to do so.

If the nuisance is found to be "permanent" so that a single cause of action exists for diminished value damages, the defendant will have no incentive to reduce the effects in the future even if it becomes technically possible to do so. The defendant will have bought, by payment of the permanent damages, a permanent easement or a permanent right to pollute.[2] At least this is so as far as the plaintiff is concerned.[3]

On the other hand, if the nuisance is found to be temporary, the defendant will pay only diminished rental value up until judgment and will have every incentive to adopt such efficient technologies that may become available in the future to avoid any further liabilities.[4] An important California case has applied this kind of reasoning to permit a plaintiff to recover on a temporary nuisance basis long after the statute of limitations would have run if the nuisance had been treated as a permanent one.[5] Probably these considerations have been in the background in many other cases.

§ 5.11(3)

4. There is a good, detailed discussion in Baxter & Altree, Legal Aspects of Airport Noise, 15 J.L. & Econ. 1 (1972).

5. Baker v. Burbank–Glendale–Pasadena Airport Auth., 39 Cal.3d 862, 218 Cal.Rptr. 293, 705 P.2d 866 (1985).

But the incentive arguments do not apply to every possible set of facts and there will be room for judgment in some instances. The court's refusal to grant an injunction against the nuisance bespeaks hardships or community interests that call for continued operation. An infinite series of temporary nuisance actions by the plaintiff might well undermine the court's decision to allow the operation to continue. If, in addition, the nuisance causes harm mainly to the plaintiff and not to others, incentives are not likely to correct the problem, and if the community benefits from the operation, the court might well insist on a permanent damage recovery in spite of the disincentive this creates for future improvement.[6]

§ 5.11(4) The Plaintiff's Dilemma

Plaintiffs may face a dilemma when the invasion could turn out to be permanent. If they sue for and recover permanent nuisance damages, a disincentive for improvement results. If they sue for temporary damages but the court believes the nuisance to be permanent, the single recovery of temporary damages may be res judicata and prevent other recoveries later. Similarly, if plaintiffs believe the nuisance to be temporary they may not sue immediately; and if it turns out that the court believes the nuisance to be permanent, the plaintiffs may be barred by the statute of limitations. Writers have proposed to solve this dilemma and its variations by giving the plaintiff an election or option to sue for either temporary or permanent damages.[1] Some of the case decisions have gone along with this idea.[2]

On the other hand, as already suggested, an election to claim repeated suits for temporary damages may undermine the court's decision not to grant an injunction; and an election to claim permanent damages may undercut the need for incentives to minimize the nuisance with future technologies. Given these public interests affected by the damages measures, the plaintiff's power to elect one or the other probably should be limited by those interests as they apply in particular cases.

(6) CONSEQUENTIAL AND PUNITIVE MEASURES IN LAND CASES

§ 5.12 Consequential, Multiple and Punitive Damages

§ 5.12(1) General Rules

[*For the text of this section, see the unabridged Practitioner Treatise edition.*]

§ 5.12(2) Duplicative Recoveries: Recovering Both Consequential and General Damages

[*For the text of this section, see the unabridged Practitioner Treatise edition.*]

§ 5.11(4)

1. 4 J. Sutherland, Damages § 1048 (4th ed. 1916); McCormick, Damages for Anticipated Injury to Land, 37 Harv.L.Rev. 574 (1924).

2. Reynolds Metals Co. v. Wand, 308 F.2d 504 (9th Cir.1962); Spaulding v. Cameron, 38 Cal.2d 265, 239 P.2d 625 (1952). Short of election, a court might simply interpret doubtful cases in the plaintiff's favor. See Rebel v. Big Tarkio Drainage Dist. of Holt City, Mo., 602 S.W.2d 787 (Mo.App.1980) (where allegations doubtful, court would favor right of successive actions).

§ 5.12(3) Punitive Damages

[*For the text of this section, see the unabridged Practitioner Treatise edition.*]

B. PERSONAL PROPERTY

§ 5.13 General Damages: Diminished Market Value

§ 5.13(1) General Rules

General Damages Rules

Damages for harm to, or destruction or conversion of personal property are quite commonly measured by general damages measured based on market value of the property. The main topic of the present section is the market value measure. Damages based on repair or replacement costs and consequential damages are considered in succeeding sections.[1]

Taking and destruction. A permanent taking of property, as in a conversion case, and a destruction of property as in a negligence case, both involve the same general type of damage to the owner. In both cases, damages are based on permanent deprivation of the property.[2] The usual measure of general damages for either taking or destruction is the market value of the item taken or destroyed[3] at the time[4] and place[5] of the taking or destruction, with alternate or supplementary measures allowed in special instances.

Taking: supplementary measures. Supplementary measures may include the cost of reasonable efforts to recover the chattel in the case of a taking.[6] In the case of conversion by the holder of a security interest who fails to provide appropriate notice or to dispose of the goods in a reasonable manner, the owner may find it difficult to establish damages, but the Uniform Commercial Code provides for a minimum statutory recovery.[7] And a willful tortfeasor may be held liable in some instances for the value of the goods as enhanced by his own labor in removing them or preparing them for market.[8] In the case of destruction, an adjustment is made for any

---

§ 5.13(1)

3. Chlopek v. Schmall, 224 Neb. 78, 396 N.W.2d 103 (1986). See Cooper v. Feency, 34 Ohio App.3d 282, 518 N.E.2d 46 (1986); Denby v. North Side Carpet Cleaning Co., 257 Pa.Super. 73, 390 A.2d 252 (1978).

Where the plaintiff owns less than a complete interest, the value of his interest is the measure of his recovery. E.g., Contrail Leasing Partners, Ltd. v. Consolidated Airways, 742 F.2d 1095 (7th Cir.1984) (good illustration of purchaser's interest in repossessed chattel where owner of security interest improperly resells); See Restatement Second of Torts § 927 (1979). Improper repossession or sale by a holder of a security interest may be a conversion in which damage of the purchaser are difficult to determine. The Uniform Com-

mercial Code § 9–507(1) provides special minimum recovery in this situation.

6. E.g., Haines v. Parra, 193 Cal.App.3d 1553, 239 Cal.Rptr. 178 (1987). See the discussion below on special and punitive damages.

7. The Uniform Commercial Code provides a minimum, in the case of consumer goods, of "not less than the credit service charge plus ten per cent of the principal amount of the debt or the time price differential plus ten per cent of the cash price." UCC § 9–507(1).

8. Wronski v. Sun Oil Co., 89 Mich.App. 11, 279 N.W.2d 564 (1979); see, Western Nat. Bank of Casper v. Harrison, 577 P.2d 635, 641 (Wyo.1978). This rule is most commonly seen in the case of severance of articles from land. See § 5.3 supra. But it can have striking application to other articles under the doc-

salvage value.[9]

Harm to chattels. Analogous rules of general damages apply when a chattel is harmed but not taken or destroyed. Although there are alternatives to be considered below,[10] the usual measure of damage for a chattel that is damaged is not the entire market value of the chattel but the sum by which its market value has been diminished.[11] This is sometimes referred to as the before and after rule because the plaintiff recovers the value of the chattel immediately before the harm was done, less the value immediately afterwards. As in the case of destruction, value is ordinarily judged at the time and place the damage is done.[12]

Applications. These rules apply to a wide variety of personal property [13] including pet dogs,[14] cattle,[15] household goods,[16] art objects,[17] commercial items, and even some intangibles such as shares of stock and cash.[18] In some instances, however, the general measures of damages are thought to be inadequate and they are supplemented or supplanted by rules allowing special damages or some other measure.

Alternatives and Special Damages

Repair or replacement costs. In some instances, courts consider and apply alternative or additional measures of damages. If the chattel is only damaged, the plaintiff may be permitted to recover the reasonable costs of repairs [19] plus any remaining diminution in value.[20] If it is taken or destroyed, the plaintiff may be allowed to recover the reasonable costs of replacing the item.[21] Occasionally courts not only permit repair costs recoveries but require them in preference to the diminished value recovery, a rule that may result in serious undercompensation.[22]

Adjustments when repair or replacement costs are awarded. When repair or replacement costs are allowed in lieu of the ordinary market value measure, subsidiary issues arise. Some courts hold, for example, that replacement costs ordinarily may not be allowed in excess of the value of the goods at the time of taking or destruction. And adjustments must be made to allow for the fact that replacement goods are worth more than the original. When the plaintiff repairs its own goods or manufactures a substitute good, an allowance may be made not only for the plaintiff's direct costs of repair but also for a share of its fixed overhead costs. These adjustments complicate the damage assessment considerably and are given further attention below.[23]

trine of accession. See Silsbury v. McCoon, 3 N.Y. 379 (1850) (owner's corn used to make whiskey, allegedly by conscious wrongdoer, whiskey regarded as original owner's).

9. E.g., Brooks Transp. Co. v. McCutcheon, 154 F.2d 841 (D.C.Cir.1946); New York State Elec. & Gas. Corp. v. Fischer, 24 A.D.2d 683, 261 N.Y.S.2d 310 (1965); Nelson v. Boulay Bros. Co., 27 Wis.2d 637, 135 N.W.2d 254 (1965).

11. E.g., Lynn Strickland Sales and Service, Inc. v. Aero–Lane Fabricators, Inc., 510 So.2d 142 (Ala.1987); Martin v. Rieger, 289 Ark. 292, 711 S.W.2d 776 (1986); Huff v. Thornton, 287 N.C. 1, 213 S.E.2d 198 (1975);

Merrill v. Tropoli, 414 S.W.2d 474 (Tex.Civ. App.1967); Bartlett v. Menard, 126 Vt. 215, 227 A.2d 300 (1967); Younger v. Appalachian Power Co., 214 Va. 662, 202 S.E.2d 866 (1974); Duggan v. Board of Com'rs of County of Weld, 747 P.2d 6 (Colo.App.1987); McCurdy v. Union Pac. R. Co., 68 Wash.2d 457, 413 P.2d 617 (1966); Krueger v. Steffen, 30 Wis.2d 445, 141 N.W.2d 200 (1966); see, Daughhetee v. Shipley, 282 Ark. 596, 669 S.W.2d 886 (1984).

22. As in Romco, Inc. v. Broussard, 528 So.2d 231 (La.App.1988).

23. See § 5.14(2) below.

Unique goods, goods without market value. Some items are unique. When such items are destroyed, replacement with any reasonable substitute may be impossible, and if so, replacement costs cannot be used as a measure of damages. When the same item has no known market value and produces no income,[24] the courts are challenged to provide a damages award that respects the plaintiff's property rights without providing a windfall. Here courts have sometimes resorted to largely vague or even meaningless abstractions, such as "intrinsic value," or "value to the owner," or else have allowed the trier to come up with a figure by examining various unquantified "factors" supposed to affect value.[25]

Special and punitive damages. In some cases plaintiffs have claimed other special damages such as profits or reputation [26] lost because the chattel was not available,[27] emotional distress resulting from its loss,[28] and costs of attempting a reasonable repair.[29] Although a conversion is routinely regarded as an event that forces a sale of the chattel and thus terminates the owner's interests in it, there are situations in which the owner may have some residual interests affecting the damages claim. He might recover the cost of reasonable attempts to regain the chattel, for example,[30] and in some cases might even recover for loss of its use during a reasonable period for replacing it.[31] Punitive damages may also be awarded in some cases.[32]

Every element in these rules has generated subsidiary issues and rules to be surveyed in the remaining subsections.

§ 5.13(2)   Time for Assessment of Market Value

Steady Markets

The general rule requires the courts to assess market value of a damaged, destroyed or converted chattel at the time of the harm. In the

---

24. Income producing property can often be assigned a monetary value. See § 5.16(2) below and § 3.5 above.

25. See § 5.16(3) below.

26. Fine art represents a special kind of property which has a market value belonging to the owner and a capacity for affecting the reputation of the artist. Destruction of art may prevent the artist from enhancing or developing reputation, and this may (or may not) affect the artist's future income. The artist's interests are known in civil law countries as "moral rights;" where those interests are recognized in America, as under the California statute, damages for destruction or harm to paintings or other fine arts may be adjusted accordingly. See Pelletier v. Eisenberg, 177 Cal.App.3d 558, 223 Cal.Rptr. 84 (1986).

27. "Fair market value generally includes a component for present valuation of future profits," McPherson v. Schlemmer, 230 Mont. 81, 749 P.2d 51 (1988), hence the lost profits claim will often duplicate elements in the fair market value claim and will not be allowed in every case. As to profits lost, see § 5.15 below.

28. As to emotional distress, see § 5.15(3) below.

29. Thus veterinary expenses for attempting to save a pet dog in Zager v. Dimilia, 138 Misc.2d 448, 524 N.Y.S.2d 968 (1988).

30. The cost of pursuit includes costs of investigation and other pursuit by an attorney, but not the attorney fee in the conversion action itself. Haines v. Parra, 193 Cal.App.3d 1553, 239 Cal.Rptr. 178 (1987); see Welch v. Kosasky, 24 Mass.App.Ct. 402, 509 N.E.2d 919 (1987).

Statutes may provide explicitly for "the time and money properly expended in pursuit of the property." West's Ann.Cal.Civ.Code § 3336.

31. As to loss of use generally, see § 5.15(2) below. Loss of use of property during period needed for replacement may take several forms—rental value, loss of profits during the replacement period, interest, and subjective values.

32. Punitive damages: see Lane v. Dunkle, 231 Mont. 365, 753 P.2d 321 (1988); Blades v. White Motor Credit Corp., 90 Or.App. 125, 750 P.2d 1198 (1988).

case of damage, this takes the familiar before-and-after form: the plaintiff recovers the value of the chattel as it stood immediately before the harm, less the value as it stood immediately afterward. In the case of destruction or conversion of the chattel, the time rule gives the plaintiff the value of the chattel immediately before the destruction or conversion,[1] usually with interest.[2]

Delayed Replacement and Fluctuating Markets

The problem. The time rule works well in many cases, but if the plaintiff does not discover the harm for a long period, or is unable to replace the chattel at approximately the time the harm occurred, the plaintiff may be victimized by a fluctuation in the market value. The chattel damaged in February might have to be replaced in June when the market price is much higher. Put the other way around, the plaintiff could not sell the chattel at the higher price he might have reaped had it not been converted. For these reasons, if the chattel has appreciated in value, a recovery of its value at the time of the tort will not compensate the plaintiff for the loss. This problem most frequently arises in conversion cases and is perhaps most serious in the case of conversion of stocks or other securities.

An indirect approach to the problem is sometimes available. The time of conversion may itself be debateable. When the converter rightfully has possession of the goods as a bailee, a demand for a return of the goods may be required, followed by his refusal. So the converter who has lost or taken the goods at an earlier time when prices were low, may still be held liable for the higher value at the time a demand is made.[3]

Once the time of conversion is established by substantive law, courts have taken several different approaches to the damages rule.

The stand-pat rule. First, some courts stand pat with the time rules, insisting that market fluctuation changes nothing.[4] In this group, some decisions may work a great deal of hardship on the plaintiff. But some decisions manipulate the time rule to help provide compensation. One method of doing this is to find that the conversion did not occur when the property is taken but at some later time, for example, when the defendant refuses to return it on demand or when the defendant sells the property to another; this gives the plaintiff the higher value at the later date.[5] Another

---

§ 5.13(2)

1. E.g., Fremont Nat. Bank and Trust Co. v. Collateral Control Corp., 724 F.2d 1410 (8th Cir.1983); Ocean Nat. Bank of Kennebunk v. Diment, 462 A.2d 35 (Me.1983). The rule is stated repeatedly in many cases.

2. As to interest and other loss of use damages see § 5.15(2).

3. Cf. American Enka Company v. Wicaco Machine Corp., 686 F.2d 1050 (3d Cir.1982) (holding the bailee liable from the time a demand was made on the ground that this is the best damages rule when prices are rising).

4. Many of the cases that repeat the rule do so in contexts in which there has been no appreciation in value. E.g., Ocean Nat. Bank of Kennebunk v. Diment, 462 A.2d 35 (Me. 1983). Such cases are not authority for a stand-pat rule. Other cases state the stand-pat rule but as the following text shows, find means to avoid its effects. Courts that do not stand pat on the old time rule may nevertheless impose artificial limits on a rule that allows the plaintiff the value at a later time. In Texas one must plead that the property was of changing or fluctuating value in order to invoke a later date. See Prewitt v. Branham, 643 S.W.2d 122 (Tex.1982).

method is to award restitution under the name of damages, that is, to award the plaintiff any money the defendant has received in selling the property.[6]

Highest value to trial rule. Second, some courts modify the time rules to permit recovery of the highest value of the property between conversion and the date of trial,[7] or some similar date.[8] This is a rule by statute in some instances.[9] This formula is sometimes invoked only in the case of wilful or reckless torts, leaving the ordinary conversion case to be covered by the more traditional rule.[10] In some states the plaintiff may be allowed to invoke the rule to take advantage of post-conversion appreciation only if he prosecutes the suit with reasonable diligence.[11]

New York rule: highest value in reasonable time. Third, some courts modify the time rules to permit recovery of the highest value of the property between the time of conversion and a reasonable time for replacing the property.[12] This rule seeks to achieve full compensation without allowing the plaintiff to speculate at the defendant's expense, which cannot always be avoided under the second rule.[13] New York itself has followed a version of the third rule under which the property is assigned its highest value between the time plaintiff had notice of conversion and a reasonable time for replacement. By emphasizing the date of plaintiff's notice, rather than the date of conversion itself, and by emphasizing the plaintiff's need for consultation and planning, the New York courts have sought to create a situation in which the plaintiff can effectively recoup the real cost of replacing the converted property.[14] No doubt this rule is subject to adjustment when the property is not replaceable or when there is reason to use some other time period.[15] Likewise, if the property is ultimately recovered rather than

---

6. Cf. Welch v. Kosasky, 24 Mass.App.Ct. 402, 509 N.E.2d 919 (1987) (recognizing that, under restitution decisions, the plaintiff's "damages" are not necessarily capped by value of property at time of conversion). As to this kind of restitution see generally § 4.2(3) above.

7. Brown v. Campbell, 536 So.2d 920 (Ala. 1988); Gowan v. Wisconsin–Alabama Lumber Co., 215 Ala. 231, 110 So. 31 (1926); Quealy v. Paine, Webber, Jackson & Curtis, Inc., 475 So.2d 756 (La.1985) (mentioning a date "within a few months" after conversion, but approving judgment based on value at time of trial); Ludwig v. Kowal, 419 A.2d 297 (R.I.1980) (under statute doubling liability for larcenous takings, value at time plaintiff made summary judgment affidavit).

8. Time of trial, time of verdict, time of filing suit are all expressions courts have used. E.g., Merritt v. Williams, 214 Ala. 427, 108 So. 257 (1926) (verdict); Cochran v. Wool Growers Central Storage Co., 140 Tex. 184, 166 S.W.2d 904 (1942) (filing suit).

When conversion takes place over a period of time, the analogous problem is to determine which of the prices during the conversion period should govern. See, using the highest, Wronski v. Sun Oil Co., 89 Mich.App. 11, 279 N.W.2d 564 (1979).

9. See Official Code Ga.Ann. § 107–103; Mont.Code Ann. § 17–404 (if suit is prosecuted with reasonable diligence); 23 Okl.Stat.Ann. § 64 (if prosecuted with reasonable diligence); N.D.Century Code of 1943 § 32–0323 (similar).

12. Newburger Cotton Co. v. Stevens, 167 Ark. 257, 267 S.W. 777, 40 A.L.R. 1279 (1925); Mayer v. Monzo, 221 N.Y. 442, 117 N.E. 948 (1917); Ahles v. Aztec Enterprises, Inc., 120 A.D.2d 903, 502 N.Y.S.2d 821 (1986); Mohoff v. Northrup King & Co., 234 Or. 174, 380 P.2d 983 (1963); Parks v. Yakima Valley Production Credit Ass'n, 194 Wash. 380, 78 P.2d 162 (1938) (if wilful). Statutes may call for the same result. See, e.g., 68 Pa.Stat. § 481.

14. See Gelb v. Zimet Bros., Inc., 34 Misc.2d 401, 228 N.Y.S.2d 111 (1962), aff'd, 18 A.D.2d 967, 237 N.Y.S.2d 989 (1963). The rule is closely similar to the option created by the UCC for an aggrieved buyer of goods. The buyer is allowed to cover, that is, purchase substitute goods, and charge any excess price to the breaching seller. See § 12.15(1) below.

15. In Wronski v. Sun Oil Co., 89 Mich. App. 11, 279 N.W.2d 564 (1979) there were serial conversions of oil under the plaintiff's land from 1970 to 1974. The total oil taken was discovered but the dates on which any given amount was taken could not be shown. The prices ranged from $.17 to $5.02 per bar-

replaced, the time of recovery should govern if the plaintiff was reasonable in seeking recovery rather than replacement.[16]

§ 5.13(3) Place or Market for Assessment of Market Value

Any given chattel might conceivably be sold or bought in a variety of different markets. Geographically, the Los Angeles market for antique furniture is quite different from the New York market and the geographic difference may also entail a price difference. Markets might also differ economically even in the same locale. Economically, the wholesale market usually is quite different from the retail market and the antique market quite different from the second-hand furniture market. When personalty has been damaged, destroyed or taken, so that damages are assessed with reference to "market value" or market price, to what market does the court refer?

Geographical Markets

"*No market*". In some sense, there may be a market at the exact spot in which personal property is damaged. A car wrecked at the corner of Broadway and 42d Street might be auctioned off at the very site in its wrecked state, and crops damaged in the field might be sold where they stand; and if removal or severance diminishes the value of the property, a valuation at the very site of injury may be desirable.[1] But in a practical sense, it is often much easier to say that there is no market at that very spot. This requires assessment in some practical market elsewhere, usually the nearest one,[2] with adjustments for transportation costs.

Adjustments for transportation costs. The adjustment may be either upward or downward, depending on the facts.[3] For example, if the plaintiff buys cars in New York and transports them to Los Angeles for sale, destruction of a car when half the trip is completed might justify alternative damages measures. In line with the rule stated below,[4] the value of the car could be based on the market in which the plaintiff buys (New York) with an addition of special damages equal to the costs of transporting the car to the place where it was damaged.[5] Alternatively, the value of the car might be based, not on the value in New York, but on the value in Los Angeles where it would be sold. If so, then the cost of transporting the car from the site of destruction to the market has been saved, so the adjustment would not add transportation costs but rather would subtract them.[6] Similarly, subtraction

rel during the period in which conversions were taking place. The court rejected use of a weighted average, and awarded the highest price, $5.02. The governing date in this case was the date on which conversions ended.

§ 5.13(3)

5. Restatement Second of Torts § 911, Comment *b* (1979); 2 T. Sedgwick, Damages § 434 (9th ed. 1920). See also Barton v. Borit, 316 F.2d 550 (3d Cir.1963).

The value in a distant market may, if known at home, affect the price at home; if sufficiently known, it may create a market at home which is based on the expectation that the goods in question could be resold in the distant market. See United States v. Toronto, Hamilton & Buffalo Nav. Co., 338 U.S. 396, 70 S.Ct. 217, 94 L.Ed. 195 (1949).

The rule stated in the text would also work appropriately in the case of a consumer. If the plaintiff is a desert prospector and his car is destroyed in the desert, the Los Angeles market, if the closest, would furnish a good guide to the value of the car; the adjustment for transportation would be the addition of transportation costs.

6. This example as it appeared in the First Edition of this treatise was specifically approved in Newbery Alaska, Inc. v. Alaska Constructors, Inc., 644 P.2d 224 (Alaska 1982).

of saved transportation costs is the rule in figuring damage to standing crops—market value less the cost of harvest and the cost of transporting to the market.[7]

Economic Markets—Wholesale versus Retail Markets

Retailer and consumer. At least where the damaged or destroyed goods are replaceable in a market, the usual rule, with a little authority to the contrary,[8] values the goods in the market in which the plaintiff buys as retailer or consumer.[9] The rule gives the merchant only the value of the taken or converted goods in the wholesale market;[10] this will ordinarily suffice to permit replacement with goods of like kind and quality. The rule gives the ultimate consumer the value of the goods in the retail market,[11] and this, too, suffices to permit appropriate replacement.

Manufacturer, maker or shipper. On the other hand, when goods are owned by the manufacturer or artist who made them in the first place, they are usually valued in the market in which the owner sells them rather than the market in which he buys.[12] If the manufacturer sells to dealers at wholesale, it is the wholesale price; if he sells directly at retail, it is the retail price. If he has a contract to sell the particular goods in issue, that will govern.[13] This rule as to manufacturers is often applied to shippers in their suits against carriers for damaged or destroyed goods.[14] Since the

---

See also Gore Products v. Texas & N.O.R. Co., 34 So.2d 418 (La.App.1948), adhered to, 38 So.2d 233 (1949); Restatement Second of Torts § 911, Comment *b* (1979); cf. Felder v. Reeth, 34 F.2d 744, 97 A.L.R. 244 (9th Cir.1929) (mining machinery stranded in the Territory of Alaska, owner "waived the tort" of conversion and sued in assumpsit, transportation costs to market deducted).

7. See, e.g., Peterson v. Hager, 724 F.2d 851 (10th Cir.1984). As to crops generally, see § 5.3(2) above.

8. "The proper measure of tort damages for a plaintiff holding personalty for sale in the retail market is the total diminution in the retail market value proximately caused by the defendant's tort * * *." Ishee v. Dukes Ford Co., 380 So.2d 760, 761 (Miss.1980). The court cited no cases for the quoted proposition and gave no reasons for it. Cf. Pelletier v. Eisenberg, 177 Cal.App.3d 558, 223 Cal.Rptr. 84 (1986).

9. Restatement Second of Torts § 911, Comment *d* (1979) (market to which the plaintiff resorts, retail price for consumer, wholesale price for retailers).

10. Illinois Cent. R. Co. v. Crail, 281 U.S. 57, 50 S.Ct. 180, 74 L.Ed. 699, 67 A.L.R. 1423 (1930); Rudd Construction Equipment Co., Inc. v. Clark Equipment Co., 735 F.2d 974 (6th Cir.1984); Whaley v. Crutchfield, 226 Ark. 921, 294 S.W.2d 775 (1956); Dubiner's Bootery, Inc. v. General Outdoor Advertising Co., 10 A.D.2d 923, 200 N.Y.S.2d 757 (1960).

12. Gunn v. Burghart, 47 N.Y.Super. 370 (1881); H.K. Porter Co. v. Halperin, 297 F.2d 442 (7th Cir.1961); Gore Products v. Texas &

N.O.R. Co., 34 So.2d 418 (La.App.1948), adhered to, 38 So.2d 233 (1949); Restatement Second of Torts § 911, Comment *d* (1979).

14. E.g., Polaroid Corporation v. Schuster's Express, Inc., 484 F.2d 349 (1st Cir.1973); Gore Products v. Texas & N.O.R. Co., 34 So.2d 418 (La.App.1948), adhered to, 38 So.2d 233 (1949); see Oak Hall Cap and Gown Co. v. Old Dominion Freight Line, Inc., 899 F.2d 291 (4th Cir.1990). When the claim against the carrier is brought by a retailer or middleman, the rule is to value the property at replacement or wholesale cost, in line with the rule as to retailers generally. See Illinois Cent. R. Co. v. Crail, 281 U.S. 57, 50 S.Ct. 180, 74 L.Ed. 699, 67 A.L.R. 1423 (1930).

Shippers vs. carriers. The claim of the shipper against the carrier subject to the jurisdiction of the Interstate Commerce Commission is governed by federal statute which provides in part that the relevant carriers and freight forwarders "are liable to the person entitled to recover under the receipt or bill of lading. The liability imposed under this paragraph is for the actual loss or injury to the property caused by (1) the receiving carrier, (2) the delivering carrier, or (3) another carrier over whose line or route the property is transported in the United States or from a place in the United States to a place in an adjacent foreign country * * *." 49 U.S.C.A. § 11707. The "actual loss" provision as to damages was derived from old 49 U.S.C.A. § 20(11), under which cases such as *Polaroid*, supra, were decided. The actual loss provision has generated a small discrete jurisprudence of its own.

retail value is usually much higher than the manufacturer's cost of replacement, this rule is usually advantageous to the shipper or manufacturer. In particular cases, however, the retail value of the goods does not appropriately represent the actual loss. For this reason, the facts of particular cases may dictate use of replacement costs rather than retail value,[15] or the addition of special damages to the retail valuation.[16]

§ 5.13(4) Evidence of Value

[Consult § 3.5 above in addition to this section in the Practitioner Treatise edition.]

§ 5.14 Replacement and Repair Costs

§ 5.14(1) Replacement and Repair Costs as Alternative Measures of Damages or as Limits on Recovery

[Consult the summary in § 5.13(1) above in addition to this section in the Practitioner Treatise edition.]

§ 5.14(2) Accounting for Overhead in Repairs Cases

Direct Costs of Repairs

In some cases, principally when there is no market for the damaged property used in the plaintiff's business, the plaintiff may make its own repairs or manufacture its own replacement. One of the most common instances is the utility company which replaces a utility pole damaged by the defendant's vehicle.[1] In such a case the plaintiff may recover reasonable expenses of making the repairs, including all reasonable direct costs such as the wages[2] and fringe benefits[3] paid to workers employed in making the

In *Oak Hall,* supra, the court summarized some of the rule as follows:

In an action to recover from a carrier for damages to a shipment, the shipper establishes a prima facie case under the ICA when he shows "delivery [of the goods] in good condition, arrival in damaged condition, and the amount of damages." [ ]. The liability imposed on a common carrier is the "actual loss or injury to the property caused by [the responsible carrier]." [ ]. It is well established, however, that when damaged but salvageable goods are tendered to the owner, the carrier's liability for further damages terminates. Thus, when the damaged goods arrive at the shipper's destination, the consignee has a duty to accept them and mitigate damages unless the goods are deemed "totally worthless." *Oak Hall* at 291.

15. Oak Hall Cap and Gown Co. v. Old Dominion Freight Line, Inc., 899 F.2d 291 (4th Cir.1990); Acme Delivery Service, Inc. v. Samsonite Corp., 663 P.2d 621 (Colo.1983); Meletio Sea Food Co. v. Gordons Transports, 191 S.W.2d 983 (Mo.App.1946).

In the *Acme* and *Meletio* cases, supra, the plaintiff had consigned the goods to a buyer who purchased the substitute goods in lieu of the destroyed goods, so that the seller did not lose the anticipated profit. There was reason to speculate in either case that the seller's manufacturing capacity was limited or that it lost volume in sales elsewhere in replacing the goods in question.

Replacement cost or wholesale value or the like would be appropriate also under the rules for retailers if the plaintiff is a retailer or middleman. See Illinois Cent. R. Co. v. Crail, 281 U.S. 57, 50 S.Ct. 180, 74 L.Ed. 699, 67 A.L.R. 1423 (1930).

§ 5.14(2)

1. E.g., Public Service Elec. & Gas Co. v. Stone, 184 N.J.Super. 504, 446 A.2d 578 (1982).

2. Wisconsin Tel. Co. v. Reynolds, 2 Wis.2d 649, 87 N.W.2d 285 (1958) (average hourly rates for repair crews rather than actual pay to particular repair crew); Southwestern Elec. Power Co. v. Canal Ins. Co., 121 So.2d 769 (La.App.1960); Gulf States Utilities Co. v. Guidry, 183 So.2d 122, 130 (La.App.1966).

3. Baltimore & O.R. Co. v. Commercial Transport, Inc., 273 F.2d 447 (7th Cir.1960); Central Ill. Light Co. v. Stenzel, 44 Ill.App.2d 388, 195 N.E.2d 207 (1963). Sometimes fringe

repairs. The disputed question is whether the plaintiff is also entitled to recover an added sum for fixed overhead expenses.

Overhead Costs Attributable to Repairs

The overhead claim. The fixed overhead claim is supported by usual accounting practice and by the idea that every activity of the company should bear its proportionate share of the costs of administering the company. When a utility replaces a damaged pole in Springfield, a payroll clerk in Peoria has no direct connection with the cost of paying the workers who replaced the pole. Yet the Peoria clerk and all others are necessary because of all the paperwork of the company. A tiny fraction of the clerk's salary is thus fairly attributable to payments to the repair workers. The same is true with many other costs incurred by the company. The replacement pole, for example, might have been stored on a rented lot. Though the lot would have been rented in order to store all the other poles used by the company, as a matter of accounting it can be seen that the rental cost can be attributed to all the poles as a group and thus that a fraction can be attributed to each particular pole.

Accountants have worked out ways to figure the appropriate fractions, sometimes based on a ratio of administrative costs to labor costs, sometimes based on a ratio of administrative (or rental) costs to costs of property used. When overhead is allowed as a part of the damages, it reflects the appropriate share of fixed costs attributable to the repair or replacement of the property damaged by the defendant's tort.[4]

Rejection of overhead claims. Recovery of overhead costs in addition to direct labor costs is not a recovery of profit and, at least from an accounting standpoint, it is not a recovery of more than compensation. Some courts, however, have been unwilling to permit an overhead recovery.[5] It is sometimes argued that overhead costs, being fixed, have not been increased by the harm to the property in question and that the defendant should not be expected to pay them, or, more obscurely, that the overhead costs are not a "proximate result" of the defendant's tort.[6] Probably the fact that most

---

benefits are lumped with overhead charges and recovery is denied where the court denies recovery of overhead. See, e.g., Public Service Co. of New Mexico v. Jasso, 96 N.M. 800, 635 P.2d 1003 (App.1981).

5. Houston Oil & Minerals Corp. v. American Intern. Tool Co., 827 F.2d 1049 (5th Cir. 1987), cert. denied, AMF Tuboscope, Inc. v. Houston Oil & Minerals Corp., 484 U.S. 1067, 108 S.Ct. 1031, 98 L.Ed.2d 995 (1988) (seemingly using "overhead" in two different senses, approving some "overhead" as direct costs, but disallowing what is usually referred to as fixed overhead); Central Ill. Light Co. v. Stenzel, 44 Ill.App.2d 388, 195 N.E.2d 207 (1963); Ohio Power Co. v. Huff, 12 Ohio Misc. 214, 231 N.E.2d 897, 41 Ohio Ops.2d 296 (1967). See Carolina Power & Light Co. v. Paul, 261 N.C. 710, 136 S.E.2d 103 (1964) ("actual, out-of-pocket expenses * * *.").

In Public Service Co. of New Mexico v. Jasso, 96 N.M. 800, 635 P.2d 1003 (App.1981)

the court rejected a power company's claim for overhead after it replaced a pole damaged by the defendant. Part of the reason was that the utility, having incurred the expense, was able to pass it on to its customers. Such a rule of law means that the purchasers of electricity will be forced to bear the costs in the future as well, and that the tortfeasor's insurer will not. Although the sums involved are no doubt relatively small, this ruling means that a poor person with no car may pay incrementally for electricity, perhaps enough more that she will find it necessary to cut down heat in the winter. At the same time, those who drive cars will not find their liability insurance dollars charged with these costs. The real question probably should be whether it is good accounting or just law to charge the tortfeasor with an appropriate share of overhead.

lawyers and judges are not accountants and may feel uncomfortable with the accountant's proof in these cases contributes to the view of several courts that overhead recoveries are impermissible.

Acceptance of overhead claims. In recent years particularly, a larger number of courts have supported the recovery of appropriately proved or conceded overhead expenses.[7] Some courts have suggested that it is unrealistic to ignore business practice.[8] In addition, if a third person had been hired to repair the property, his charges, for which the defendant would be liable, would always properly include not only his direct costs, but also a charge for overhead, for otherwise the charges would not suffice to keep him in business.[9]

Overhead and profits recovery. Sometimes the defendant's tort damages property so that it must be repaired and cannot produce income during the repair period. When this is the case, the defendant may recover for lost income as well as for repair costs. In such a case, recovery of gross profits lost may fully account for fixed overhead as well.

For example, suppose that the defendant's tort causes harm to a retail store so that it must close down for one month, losing all its normal business income during that period. At the same time, the store's owner must pay rent on the building. The rent is part of fixed overhead. Suppose the store's lost income was $20,000, the average monthly income. Suppose that the store would have had these expenses: (1) cost of goods sold, $10,000; (2) manager's salary, $3,000; (3) rental costs, $1,000; and (4) wages for hourly workers, $2,000. Suppose that the $2,000 for hourly workers is saved because the store is shutdown but that all other costs would remain.

The simple calculation. The simplest calculation is to give the store the (gross) "profit" it would normally have made. If that is done no separate overhead calculation is needed. First this requires a subtraction for the $10,000 the goods themselves cost. Then it requires a subtraction for the $2,000 in wage costs the store owner has saved during the shutdown. The result is an award of $8,000, from which the owner can pay the fixed salary of the manager and the rent and still have her normal monthly net profit of $4,000. In this case nothing is added because a recovery of the gross profit covers all the losses and in effect allows the store owner to recover her net profits after paying all the obligations.

The cumbersome calculation. It is possible to make the calculation more cumbersome. The plaintiff could be allowed her net profits. On these figures her net profits will be only $4,000 for the month's shutdown. In this case, it will be necessary to compute fixed overhead separately and make a separate award for that. The fixed overhead is rent, $1,000 plus the manager's salary, $3,000. So by this method the store owner adds up $4,000

7. Freeport Sulphur Co. v. S/S Hermosa, 526 F.2d 300 (5th Cir.1976); Curt's Trucking Co. v. City of Anchorage, 578 P.2d 975 (Alaska 1978); Board of Public Utilities v. Fenton, 669 S.W.2d 612 (Mo.App.1984); Public Service Elec. & Gas Co. v. Stone, 184 N.J.Super. 504, 446 A.2d 578 (1982); Columbus & Southern Ohio Elec. Co. v. J.P. Sand & Gravel Co., 22 Ohio App.3d 98, 489 N.E.2d 830 (1985); Miller Pontiac, Inc. v. Osborne, 622 P.2d 800 (Utah 1981) (repairer, whose business included re-

as net profits, plus $4,000 in fixed overhead, and recovers $8,000.[10] Put otherwise, "net profit plus overhead" is equivalent to "gross profit" (which already includes the overhead figure).[11]

Why the gross profit recovery is right. The plaintiff properly recovers the $8,000 as part of the income lost from the shutdown caused by the defendant's tort. Although the plaintiff must use some of that income to pay fixed expenses, every dollar of that income is exactly as valuable as any other dollar of that income. If the plaintiff cannot recoup the $4,000 in fixed expenses, her net profits of $4,000 will be lost, too, because she will be obliged to use the net profit recovery to pay the fixed expenses. This is a point well recognized in the law of contract damages under the UCC, and it applies equally in tort.[12] Either method of calculation produces the right sum, $8,000. The simpler method requires no separate overhead award because it awards all the gross lost profit less any expenses saved.

Proof; spurious overhead. Although most courts appear now to accept overhead claims in principle, such claims must still be proven in each case by appropriate testimony of accountants or at least by proof of customary overhead of the industry.[13] And not all of the plaintiff's costs can count as overhead. The plaintiff which maintains a sprinkler system on its property cannot charge the costs of the sprinkler system to the defendant who negligently sets a fire.[14] The plaintiff which maintains its own legal staff cannot charge legal expense of collecting the claim for property damage as "overhead," at least in the absence of a rule that otherwise permits attorney fees.[15]

§ 5.14(3)　Credits for Appreciation in Value Resulting From Repair or Replacement

In some instances repair to or replacement of damaged property may enhance the value of the property so that after repair it is worth more than before the damage was done. If the plaintiff's recovery is limited to the diminished value of the property, the fact that repairs enhance the value of the property is of no concern to the defendant, since in that instance the defendant's liability is no more than the diminution in value.[1] The fact that repairs enhance the value of the property in such a case is no windfall to the plaintiff, either, since his recovery is limited to the diminished value.[2] Put differently, the diminished value measure of damages automatically takes into account any depreciation of the property before it was harmed and never gives the plaintiff any value added by repairs or replacement.

pairs, was entitled to recover overhead but not profit).

10. See Champs Convenience Stores, Inc. v. United Chemical Co., Inc., 329 N.C. 446, 406 S.E.2d 856 (1991).

11. Bead Chain Mfg. Co. v. Saxton Products, Inc., 183 Conn. 266, 439 A.2d 314 (1981). See § 12.17(5) below.

12. See § 12.17(5) below. Somewhat more detail is provided in that section.

13. See Columbus & Southern Ohio Elec. Co. v. J.P. Sand & Gravel Co., 22 Ohio App.3d 98, 489 N.E.2d 830 (1985) ("when established

by sound accounting principles" overhead is recoverable).

14. Cf. United States v. Denver & Rio Grande Western R. Co., 547 F.2d 1101 (10th Cir.1977) (government maintained fire protection resources as part of its land management, held, this was not an item chargeable to defendant as "overhead" because of the specific fire).

15. Curt's Trucking Co. v. City of Anchorage, 578 P.2d 975 (Alaska 1978).

General Rule: Deduction for Increased Value

Deduction allowable. When the plaintiff seeks to recover repair or replacement costs rather than diminished value, the story is different. When the repairs enhance the value of the damaged property and the measure of damages is the cost of repairs, the general rule is that the defendant's liability for repair costs must be reduced by any enhancement or appreciation in value resulting from the repair.[3] The plaintiff is not entitled, it is said, to get "new for old."[4]

Types of increased value. Perhaps most commonly the gain in value due to repairs or replacement of parts results because the repair extends the expected useful life of the property.[5] Repairs may also increase the use value of the chattel by making it more productive or by making it operate more cheaply,[6] or the asset value by making it more attractive to potential buyers. Increase in value for any of these reasons would warrant an appropriate deduction from the liability that would otherwise be imposed for repair costs.

Qualifications to the rule. The general rule allowing a deduction for enhanced value of the property resulting from repairs is subject to the qualifications discussed below. In general, it may be said that if the increase in value is not wanted by the plaintiff and not captured by him, he is not to be charged with it, and hence that the defendant will not get any deduction from repair or replacement costs in such a case. In addition, some courts accept the general rule but do not permit the defendant to show that repairs enhanced the plaintiff's property by showing that the property had been depreciated before damage.

[*For discussion of unwanted appreciation and appreciation not captured by the plaintiff, see this section in the Practitioner Treatise edition.*]

§ 5.14(3)

3. E.g., United States v. Ebinger, 386 F.2d 557 (2d Cir.1967) (saved maintenance costs); Sigue Trucking, Inc. v. Insured Lloyds, 417 So.2d 97 (La.App.1982); Strzelecki v. Blaser's Lakeside Industries of Rice Lake, Inc., 133 Mich.App. 191, 348 N.W.2d 311 (1984) (replacement cost alone would not be evidence of market value, but replacement cost less depreciation would).

The deduction for enhancement is implicitly required by the rule that the recoverable cost of repair is the cost of repairing the property "to make it as serviceable and good for plaintiff's purposes as it was before the accident." See, e.g., State v. Urbanek, 177 N.W.2d 14, 17 (Iowa 1970), quoting Board of Jackson County Road Com'rs v. O'Leary, 326 Mich. 570, 40 N.W.2d 729 (1950).

In many instances the enhancement of value is shown by showing replacement or repair with new parts and by showing that the damaged property had depreciated. As to depreciation, see below.

Some older cases appear to reject the deduction not only when it is sought in the form of conventional depreciation but also when there is proof of actual enhanced market value. See The Baltimore (U.S.) 75 U.S. (8 Wall.) 377, 385–386, 19 L.Ed. 463 (1869).

4. E.g., Midwest Indus. Painting of Fla., Inc. v. United States, 4 Cl.Ct. 124 (1983); Creole Shipping Ltd. v. Diamandis Pateras, Ltd., 410 F.Supp. 313 (S.D.Ala.1976).

5. As in, e.g., Freeport Sulphur Co. v. S/S Hermosa, 526 F.2d 300 (5th Cir.1976); Younger v. Appalachian Power Co., 214 Va. 662, 202 S.E.2d 866 (1974).

6. United States v. Ebinger, 386 F.2d 557, 561 (2d Cir.1967) (Friendly J.) (new cooling tower installed to replace damaged tower would save maintenance expenses of more than $2,000 a year on the average, defendant entitled to a credit not exceeding the "capitalized value" of the savings).

Proof of Enhanced Value: Accounting Depreciation vs. Market Value

Accounting for enhancement by use of diminished market value test. In the easiest cases it can be shown that repairs have increased the value of the plaintiff's property because it now has a market value greater than the market value it had immediately before it was injured. But the cost-of-repairs measure is used in many cases only because market value is difficult or impossible to establish.

Accounting for enhancement by use of depreciation formulas. If market value cannot be shown, either before the injury or after the repairs, courts are generally willing to use accepted accounting formulas [16] to figure depreciation and to make the award on the basis of original costs [17] minus depreciation,[18] although in special circumstances some courts reject the use of standardized depreciation proof.[19] The idea behind accounting formulas for depreciation is that any given kind of property suffers a regular or predictable loss in value with the passage of time and with use,[20] and that the loss in value may be estimated by one of the several methods for computing depreciation. If the property's original cost or value is known, along with the property's normal expected life, it then becomes possible to estimate the current value at any given point by applying the depreciation formula.

Depreciation formulas. The cases have mostly applied a straight line depreciation formula, one that assumes a continuous and equal loss in value as time goes on. Under this kind of depreciation formula, property with a ten year life expectancy has lost half its value when it is five years old. If such property is damaged and then replaced with property that has a ten-year life, one-half the value of the new property is then considered to be an enhancement. Other formulas for figuring depreciation may be more suited to particular facts, and if so can be used.[21]

---

16. The straight-line depreciation method, sketched in the text below, is the most readily grasped method, but there are forms of accelerated depreciation as well. In accelerated depreciation formulas, more depreciation is allocated to earlier years. One's newly purchased automobile might lose half its original value in the first two years, for example, but thereafter depreciate in value only at 10% each year. For a concise and clear explanation, see S. Siegel and D. Siegel, Accounting and Financial Disclosure, A Guide to Basic Concepts, pp. 56–60 (1983). Since depreciation formulas are used in business partly as a means of effecting tax savings, they are not necessarily appropriate for accurate computation of damages. Courts should require either assurance by either stipulation or proof that the depreciation formula proposed for use in a damage suit is an appropriate one.

17. This statement, like others about accounting, is simplified to convey the general idea. Actual calculations must of course take into account any salvage value that would remain when the property's useful life is exhausted.

18. Freeport Sulphur Co. v. S/S Hermosa, 526 F.2d 300 (5th Cir.1976) (dock damaged, leading case); Weyerhaeuser Co. v. Atropos Island, 777 F.2d 1344 (9th Cir.1985); Orange Beach Water, Sewer, and Fire Protection Auth. v. M/V Alva, 680 F.2d 1374 (11th Cir. 1982); Community Television Serv., Inc. v. Dresser Industries, Inc., 435 F.Supp. 214, 217 (D.S.D.1977) (South Dakota law) (television and radio broadcast tower collapsed during blizzard; in owner's claim against designer-builder, plaintiff should not recover a windfall, hence repair and replacement costs should be allowed with a deduction for "reasonable depreciation for the use plaintiff had enjoyed prior to the damage"); Central Ill. Light Co. v. Stenzel, 44 Ill.App.2d 388, 195 N.E.2d 207 (1963); Ohio Power Co. v. Huff, 12 Ohio Misc. 214, 231 N.E.2d 897, 41 Ohio Ops.2d 296 (1967); New York State Elec. & Gas Corp. v. Fischer, 24 A.D.2d 683, 261 N.Y.S.2d 310 (1965); Younger v. Appalachian Power Co., 214 Va. 662, 202 S.E.2d 866 (1974) ("used life credit," essentially a straight-line depreciation).

The rate of depreciation may be standardized within an industry or as to a given product, and expert evidence showing that rate has been used in the courts.[22] The fact that a given rate of depreciation is allowed by tax authorities, or that the property has been "depreciated out" on the plaintiff's own books is not necessarily controlling.[23] No deduction for depreciation is called for unless the repaired or replaced property has more value than the property as it stood immediately before damage,[24] and it would seem that the burden should be on the defendant to show the depreciation of the old property or the enhanced value of the new.[25]

Intuitive and other adjustments for depreciation. The amount of depreciation, or the absence of depreciation,[26] might be estimated by considering the physical condition of the damaged property itself as it stood immediately before the damage was inflicted.[27] Some adjustments of this kind seem to be intuitive guesses rather than informed decisions.[28]

Depreciation formulas represent conventions that are accepted for convenience; they do not represent proof of any actual market value. And they cannot work without proof that shows the reasonably expected useful life of the property before damage and the useful life of the replacement. Nevertheless, depreciation formulas are very useful and for the most part recognized in the decisions.

Cases demanding extraordinary proof or extreme degrees of depreciation. There is, however, a line of authority, mostly relying on an older view,[29] that severely limits the use of the repair-minus-depreciation measure. Courts following this view are disinclined to accept accounting practice as a basis for estimating the useful life of the property. Some insist that a deduction can be justified only if the defendant can show a market value increase in the particular item of property so that proof of depreciation in an accounting sense is regarded as insufficient.[30] Or they may insist that depreciation can

---

22. See Denby v. North Side Carpet Cleaning Co., 257 Pa.Super. 73, 390 A.2d 252 (1978) (carpet expert testifying as to rate of depreciation of carpets by reference to industry's "Gray Guide").

23. See Petition of M/V Elaine Jones, 480 F.2d 11, 27 (5th Cir.1973), modified on other points, 513 F.2d 911 (5th Cir.1975), cert. denied, 423 U.S. 840, 96 S.Ct. 71, 46 L.Ed.2d 60 (1975) (bridge, "fully depreciated in accordance with governing rates" nevertheless had indefinite life expectancy, no deduction allowed for depreciation).

24. See Board of Public Utilities v. Fenton, 669 S.W.2d 612, 616 (Mo.App.1984) (transformer, proof that it would last indefinitely, no proof as to age, no deduction for depreciation; "Such being the case, we agree with Professor Dobbs that use of the replacement cost 'seems fair enough,'" citing First Edition at 394).

25. See Chemical Express Carriers, Inc. v. French, 759 S.W.2d 683 (Tex.App.1988) (defendant does not have burden of pleading the "betterment," but does have the "burden of proceeding" with the evidence to show that the betterment has occurred). Presumably the defendant must show some basis for mak-

ing a calculation, which seems to have been the real problem in *Chemical Express, supra.*

28. Cf. Standard Oil Co. of New Jersey v. Southern Pac. Co., 268 U.S. 146, 45 S.Ct. 465, 69 L.Ed. 890 (1925) (court appeared to think that an unspecified reduction in normal depreciation rates on ship should be applied because trend of reproduction costs was upward, shipyards were working at full capacity, and these facts should result in lower depreciation rate, though the amount by which it should be lowered was not clear).

29. See The Baltimore, 75 U.S. (8 Wall.) 377, 385–386, 19 L.Ed. 463 (1869).

30. New Jersey Power & Light Co. v. Mabee, 41 N.J. 439, 197 A.2d 194 (1964) is the leading case. It took the position that a utility company, suing for the cost of replacing a pole, should recover full cost without a deduction for the depreciation of the pole that was destroyed. The pole was 20 years old and had an expected life of 36 years. The court reasoned that not *every* pole had a 36–year expected life and that "the pole that was destroyed might well have served for a much longer period and the new pole may last for

be used to reduce the defendant's liability only if there is some extraordinary discrepancy between the pre-tort value of the property and the repaired value.[31]

Calculating Depreciation Adjustments

Depreciation. Although courts often speak in terms of depreciation of the replaced or repaired property, depreciation is merely one element in estimating the enhanced value of the repaired property. The ultimate goal is only to avoid giving the plaintiff a windfall gain or benefit. In some situations, the enhancement can be figured by taking the original cost of the damaged property, figuring the percentage of depreciation, and deducting the same percentage from the replacement or repair cost. For example, if the property originally had a ten-year expected life and was four years old when destroyed, a straight-line depreciation formula shows that it is 40% depreciated. If the property is replaced with property otherwise identical to the original and the replacement property had a 10–year expected life, then the 40% depreciation deduction is appropriate. This accounts for the four added years of useful life that otherwise would be a windfall to the plaintiff.

"Appreciation". But this method does not work properly in every factual situation, as Judge Wisdom long ago pointed out. When the replacement property increases the property's value but does not restore it to its original value, the kind of calculation represented in the preceding paragraph does not yield an appropriate adjustment. For instance, if the replacement or repair gives the property, not a 6–year expected life but an 8–year expected life, the 40% deduction represented by the depreciation of the old property will not reflect the enhanced value of the newly repaired property. Instead, the adjustment to the repair or replacement cost should allocate an appropriate portion of the repair cost to the enhanced value of the property as reflected by its increased expected life. The useful life was extended from six to eight years by the repairs. Of those eight years, two represented an enhancement. Thus $2/8$ ($1/4$) of the repair costs is attributable to enhanced value. If the repairs cost $10,000, one-fourth of that cost should thus fall upon the plaintiff who will get the enhancement. This reflects the real point of the "depreciation" adjustment—to credit the defendant with any appreciation or enhancement in value captured by the plaintiff.

Additional adjustment when plaintiff will not realize enhanced value immediately. Many cases call for one further adjustment. If the plaintiff will not capture the enhanced value of the property until some time in the future, then to allow a full credit for the enhancement now would be to deny complete compensation. In effect, the plaintiff would be financing the premature replacement of his property, by crediting the defendant now for

but a few years * * * we cannot say with reasonable assurance that the installation of a new pole did more than remedy the wrong done." 197 A.2d at 195. This language, if read literally, appears to reject the use of depreciation formulas which the plaintiff itself might use in its own business.

On the utility-pole facts, a number of courts have followed Mabee. Mississippi Power & Light Co. v. Tillman, 291 So.2d 736 (Miss.

1974); Carolina Power & Light Co. v. Paul, 261 N.C. 710, 136 S.E.2d 103 (1964); Appalachian Power Co. v. Morrison, 152 W.Va. 638, 165 S.E.2d 809 (1969); Hartford Elec. Light Co. v. Beard, 3 Conn.Cir. 323, 213 A.2d 536 (1965); Horton v. Georgia Power Co., 149 Ga. App. 328, 254 S.E.2d 479 (1979); Board of Public Utilities v. Fenton, 669 S.W.2d 612 (Mo.App.1984).

benefits or enhancement the plaintiff will not realize until later.[32] For example, if the plaintiff's property had an expected life of 10 years when it was damaged and the repairs give it an expected life of 20 years, the plaintiff will clearly get a very substantial benefit. But the benefit will not be realized for ten years, until the time at which he would normally have had to replace the property in question. At that time, but not until then, he will begin saving money because he will not have to replace the property. For this reason, the credit to the defendant for enhanced value must represent the present value of the future savings on replacement. Alternatively, the credit to the defendant must be reduced by the interest charges the plaintiff could incur in presently financing "his" share of the repair costs.

Integral parts of a larger whole. The issues about enhancement of property value are largely issues of fact—does the property in question depreciate in value,[33] and if so is there adequate evidence as to the amount of depreciation in this case? When the damaged property is an integral part of a larger unit of property, the question of depreciation or enhanced value becomes more factually more complex; but if the plaintiff's property is in *fact* enhanced in value and the plaintiff has captured that enhancement or will do so in the future, a credit remains appropriate.[34] At the same time, it must be recognized that the repair of a ceiling fan in large office building is not likely in fact to increase the building's value and that the building owner will realize the enhanced value of the fan itself only if the fan would otherwise have to be repaired or replaced at a determinable time in the future. If the fan itself would last indefinitely, repair constitutes no enhancement at all.[35] The fact that damaged property is an integral part of a larger whole is also relevant on another factual issue. In some cases there might be little doubt that replacement of one unit of a large property enhances the useful life of the larger unit to which it is attached. But, as already observed, the enhancement is not relevant unless the plaintiff will be able to capture it. The plaintiff cannot be expected to capture the

32. United States v. Ebinger, 386 F.2d 557 (2d Cir.1967).

33. In Jay–Ox, Inc. v. Square Deal Junk Co., 208 Kan. 856, 494 P.2d 1103, 1107 (1972) the court found gas cylinders were virtually indestructible and that depreciation "is not a significant factor in determining their value." Hence replacement cost without a deduction was appropriate.

34. Some of the references to the property as an "integral part" of a larger unit may be read to mean that there is a rule of law about integral parts. Cf. Weyerhaeuser Co. v. Atropos Island, 777 F.2d 1344, 1352 (9th Cir.1985) ("There is no deduction for depreciation, however, when 'the repair or replacement adds nothing of substance to the overall value of the structure of which it is an integral part' "); United States v. Commercial American Barge Line Co., 424 F.Supp. 453, 456 (E.D.Mo.1977) ("The lower land wall miter gate was an integral part of the Lock and the Lock itself had an exceedingly long life expectancy. The repairs to the gate added nothing to the life expectancy of the Lock itself. Accordingly, a depreciation formula should not be applied"). Read literally the quoted comments might suggest that even if the repair added value to the damaged unit, there would be no credit unless value was also added to the larger unit. If the issue is a factual one—compensation—then this "rule" would be right only in those cases in which there is no added value, or no realizable added value, to the repaired unit standing alone. The real question is one of fact here—whether there has been enhancement and whether that enhancement is likely to be realized in fact by the plaintiff and if so in what amount.

35. This idea seems to be the explanation for Oregon v. Tug Go–Getter, 468 F.2d 1270 (9th Cir.1972) where the defendant damaged a pier supporting a bridge. It seems that the pier would not require replacement unless the state as owner continued to allow barge traffic to batter the pier. The court alluded to the "integral part" rule, but seems only to have meant that depreciation of the old pier could not be taken as a fact in the light of the possibility that the state would insist on better protection for it in the future.

enhancement of a cooling tower on a 20–story building by selling the building as soon as the tower is repaired.[36] But the mere fact that the property damaged is a component part of a larger whole does not in itself foreclose a deduction for depreciation if that component part has a life expectancy less than the whole and if that life expectancy is increased by repair or replacement.[37] Decisions that make a rule of law which forecloses depreciation adjustments when small parts of large properties are damaged appear to miss the point that the plaintiff should not obtain an enhanced value as a result of the court's award.

§ 5.14(4) Credits for Return of Converted Chattel or Its Use in Plaintiff's Interest

[*For the text of this section, see the unabridged Practitioner Treatise edition.*]

§ 5.15 Special or Consequential Damages for Harm to, Taking or Destruction of Personal Property

§ 5.15(1) Special or Consequential Damages Generally

[*For the text of this section, see the unabridged Practitioner Treatise edition.*]

§ 5.15(2) Loss of Profits and Other Loss of Use Claims

Measures: Loss of Profits, Increase of Expense

Profits and increased expenses recoverable. The owner who uses a chattel in the production of income is always entitled to claim profits lost when the chattel is unavailable during a reasonable period for repair or replacement as a result of tortious destruction, damage,[1] or conversion.[2] The claim may be that inability to use the chattel reduced the plaintiff's income [3] or that it increased his expenses,[4] either way reducing his net profit, which is recoverable if the proof is adequate.

Proof required. But the claim of reduced profits is undoubtedly one for special damages and as such it must meet the requirements for special damages claims by proving actual lost profits with reasonable certainty. This means, for one thing, that abstract proof of potential earning power is not good enough; the proof must show the probability of actual lost earnings.[5] It means as well that proof of a reduction in gross income is not itself sufficient, because as in all pure lost profit claims it is the plaintiff's net loss that counts.[6] In the same way, the plaintiff must prove that the losses were

---

36. See United States v. Ebinger, 386 F.2d 557 (2d Cir.1967).

37. Thus in Midwest Indus. Painting of Fla., Inc. v. United States, 4 Cl.Ct. 124 (1983) a contractor negligently damaged the seals in government jet fuel pumps and repair or replacement was required, but the government was not entitled to recover replacement cost. "The government received seals with a useful life of 20 additional years in exchange for seals which had exceeded their useful life by over 40 percent" and in addition the government got a uniform seal system because before replacement the pumps had used different

kinds of seals. "It was just such windfalls that the 'new for old' rule was designed to prevent." Id. at 135.

§ 5.15(2)

1. Allowing lost profit claims, e.g., McPherson v. Schlemmer, 230 Mont. 81, 749 P.2d 51 (1988) (death of cows, replacement delayed, expected profits from sale of expected calves); Hardman Trucking, Inc. v. Poling Trucking Co., 176 W.Va. 575, 346 S.E.2d 551 (1986) (loss of hauling profits while triaxle truck being repaired).

actually incurred because he would have used the chattel to increase income or reduce expense,[7] and the amounts must be pleaded and proved with a reasonable degree of certainty.[8] It is often difficult to produce persuasive proof of profit loss and the claim must sometimes be denied as too speculative.[9]

The avoidable consequences rules. To say that the claim is one for special damages is also to say that it is subject to the avoidable consequences rule.[10] One side of the rule means that if the profits could be maintained at their earlier level by reasonable effort or expense on the part of the plaintiff, he will have no claim for losses he could have avoided by such reasonable means.[11] The other side of the rule means that expenditures reasonably made to minimize profit losses will be recoverable as special damages even if it turns out that the costs were greater than the savings.[12]

Duplication. When the chattel destroyed is used in the production of income, a complete recovery of lost profits (or increased operating expense) will usually provide full compensation. Thus it would ordinarily be improper to allow recovery of both lost profits and interest or rental value.[13]

Measures: Cost of Hiring a Substitute Chattel—"Lease-in" Costs

Rental value distinguished; rule. A number of cases have stated that the reasonable cost of renting a substitute chattel is the measure of damages for loss of use,[14] or at least one optional measure.[15] The reasonable cost of renting a substitute is to be distinguished from the rental value of the plaintiff's own chattel, because the two values are not necessarily identical. Although the reasonable cost [16] of a substitute is actually the measure of the loss of use in the eyes of some courts, in others it is merely evidence of the rental value of the plaintiff's own chattel,[17] or evidence of his inconvenience.[18] Unfortunately the opinions do not always make it clear which the court has in mind.[19] But either way, evidence of the reasonable costs of renting a substitute is at least relevant and admissible whenever an appropriate substitute is actually rented.

Recovery when no substitute is actually hired. The cost of renting a substitute chattel, where that is a measure of damages and not merely evidence of something else, is clearly an element of special damages.[20] Under the usual rules applied to special damages claims, this would mean

7. Koninklijke Luchtvaart Maatschaapij, N.V. (KLM) v. United Technologies Corporation, 610 F.2d 1052 (2d Cir.1979) (plaintiff would not have used commercial airplane during repair period to save fuel and to increase the number of profitable flights, hence no claim for profits based on such flights); CTI Intern., Inc. v. Lloyds Underwriters, 735 F.2d 679 (2d Cir.1984) (plaintiff in business of leasing containers could not recover for lost rentals of destroyed containers because it had sufficient inventory to meet all demands); Berry Contracting, Inc. v. Coastal States Petrochemical Co., 635 S.W.2d 759 (Tex.App.1982) (plaintiff oil refinery shut down because defendant negligently broke a pipeline, would not have rented the refinery for the repair period, no recovery).

14. See, e.g., stating the substitute cost as a general test, Nashban Barrel and Container Co. v. G.G. Parsons Trucking Co., 49 Wis.2d 591, 182 N.W.2d 448 (1971); Allanson v. Cummings, 81 A.D.2d 16, 439 N.Y.S.2d 545 (1981); Little v. Rose, 21 N.C.App. 596, 205 S.E.2d 150, 153 (1974), aff'd, 285 N.C. 724, 208 S.E.2d 666 (1974).

17. Antokol v. Barber, 248 Mass. 393, 143 N.E. 350, 32 A.L.R. 703 (1924).

18. Camaraza v. Bellavia Buick Corp., 216 N.J.Super. 263, 523 A.2d 669 (1987).

20. It is not based on the market value of the very chattel to which the plaintiff is entitled. See § 3.3(4) above.

that if no substitute chattel is actually hired by the plaintiff, he could not recover the purely hypothetical costs of the purely potential substitute. Actual loss, as distinct from the paper or book loss that suffices in general damages claims, is the essential requisite of special damages awards. Nevertheless, many cases have said that the plaintiff may recover the reasonable cost of hiring a substitute chattel even when one has not in fact been hired.[21]

Limited recovery for overworked substitutes. This anomaly is qualified by a subsidiary rule. If the plaintiff, not hiring a substitute, in fact makes up for the lost use of the chattel by overworking other equipment, he cannot recover the cost of renting a substitute chattel for the loss of use. Instead he can recover only for the added wear and tear on the overworked chattels and any other actual losses he can demonstrate satisfactorily. At least the federal courts sitting in Admiralty, following English cases, have so held.[22] One way to state this subsidiary rule is to say that although substitute chattel costs are recoverable even when no substitute chattel is obtained, if a substitute is in fact used, then actual costs of the substitute will ordinarily limit damages. The plaintiff who uses his own existing equipment overtime to make up for lost use of the damaged chattel is in fact using a substitute chattel, though not one obtained from a third party. Either way, it is appropriate to limit recovery to the actual losses.

The spare boat doctrine. The rule just stated is subject to an exception. Under the spare boat doctrine, if the plaintiff keeps a spare chattel specifically for the purpose of replacing those out of service, he may, after all, recover the cost of the substitute and he is not limited to the wear and tear on the substitute chattel.[23] As Professor Brownstein points out,[24] the plaintiff's maintenance of back-up equipment is a form of self-insurance and the rule allowing full recovery of substitute chattel costs works exactly like the collateral source rule.[25] The fact that the plaintiff has purchased protection against the defendant's tort by insurance or by back-up equipment does not reduce the damages otherwise recoverable in either case. Perhaps most equipment is maintained with many purposes in mind, including use as a back-up. If so, a rule that distinguishes equipment intended solely as back-up from equipment intended partly as back-up may not be wholly practical or wholly just.

Measures: Rental Value—The "Lease-Out" Value

Rental value vs. substitute chattel cost. An alternative measure of lost use damages uses the rental value of the very chattel that was damaged, destroyed or converted, as it stood immediately before the harm was done.

21. E.g., Public Service Co. of Indiana, Inc. v. Bath Iron Works Corp., 773 F.2d 783 (7th Cir.1985). See, Chemical Express Carriers, Inc. v. French, 759 S.W.2d 683 (Tex.App.1988).

The text statement appears correct even for those cases which regard the cost of a substitute merely as some evidence that bears on some other measure, since the trier of fact could accept that evidence and make the award on the basis of it.

22. Brooklyn Eastern Dist. Terminal v. United States, 287 U.S. 170, 53 S.Ct. 103, 77

L.Ed. 240 (1932); The Susquehanna, [1926] A.C. 655 (H.L.).

23. Brooklyn Eastern Dist. Terminal v. United States, 287 U.S. 170, 53 S.Ct. 103, 77 L.Ed. 240 (1932); Mountain View Coach Lines, Inc. v. Storms, 102 A.D.2d 663, 476 N.Y.S.2d 918 (1984).

24. Brownstein, What's the Use? A Doctrinal and Policy Critique of the Measurement of Loss of Use Damages, 37 Rutgers L.Rev. 433, 486 (1985).

25. See § 3.8(1) above.

The cost of renting a substitute might be good evidence of the rental value of the plaintiff's own family automobile, but the cost of a substitute would not necessarily be the same as rental value of the plaintiff's car. A substantial number of courts have used the rental value or "lease-out" measure of damages,[26] though within a given jurisdiction the decisions accepting this measure may be matched by decisions that reject or limit it,[27] or by those that cloud the measure in ambiguity.[28]

Rental value as general damages. The claim of rental value—what a chattel like the plaintiff's could be leased out for—is formulated like a general damages claim.[29] That is, the claim represents the market value of the very item to which the plaintiff is entitled. In this kind of claim the plaintiff recovers paper losses or reductions in value that might or might not ultimately be realized. One justification for this is that general damages represent the value of an opportunity the plaintiff has to sell (or rent) the property and that in depriving him of the opportunity, the defendant has deprived him of something worth at least as much as the market says it is. Another justification is that although the plaintiff may have lost no opportunity to sell or rent his property, he at least has intangible losses that can better be measured by the market value than by claims for mental anguish.[30]

But cases discussing rental value are often unclear about whether they refer to rental value in this general damages sense or to the rental costs of getting a substitute chattel. Some cases which speak of rental value measures appear to be using some measure of special damages. For example, instead of figuring the market rental value they may attempt to figure net lost profits,[31] or the number of days the plaintiff might actually have used the chattel rather than the number of days he had a right to use it.[32] In addition to such uncertainties and confusions, there are no doubt many cases in which there is no rental market for the plaintiff's chattel or one reasonably like it, so that in some cases rental value is nothing more than a construct, easy to write about but hard to cope with in an actual trial.

Measures: Interest

Mandatory or optional measure. When the plaintiff's chattel was converted[33] and sometimes when it was destroyed and beyond repair,[34] courts historically allowed interest on the value of the chattel as the measure of

---

26. Antokol v. Barber, 248 Mass. 393, 143 N.E. 350, 352, 32 A.L.R. 703 (1924): "In the absence of an allegation of special damages of that nature, the plaintiff was entitled to recover as one element of damage the fair value of the use of his own automobile, while it was being repaired, not the hire paid for a different automobile."

See Koninklijke Luchtvaart Maatschaapij, N.V. (KLM) v. United Technologies Corporation, 610 F.2d 1052, 1056 (2d Cir.1979) ("the rental value to be found is * * * that of * * * the damaged vehicle itself during its time of idleness").

27. Compare Cottrell v. Gerson, 296 Ill. App. 412, 16 N.E.2d 529, 538 (1938), aff'd, 371 Ill. 174, 20 N.E.2d 74 (1939) (reasonable rent for the property in question) with International Harvester Credit Corp. v. Helland, 151 Ill. App.3d 848, 104 Ill.Dec. 833, 503 N.E.2d 548, 554 (1986) (rental value appropriate only if plaintiff would have leased, *Cottrell* court must have "assumed" that the property would have been leased out by the plaintiff).

28. E.g., Allen v. Fox, 51 N.Y. 562, 565 (1873), allowing "value of the use" in the case of property having usable value. That phrase could readily be defined to mean rental value of the property, substitute chattel costs, or loss of profits that could have been earned by use of the chattel, but the court did not define the term. Current New York authority lends support to the substitute chattel measure. See Allanson v. Cummings, 81 A.D.2d 16, 439 N.Y.S.2d 545, 546 (1981).

damages for loss of use, and usually rejected alternate measures such as rental value.[35] Today, there appears to be no reason to deny the plaintiff interest on the value of his chattel for the loss of use period merely on the ground that the chattel was converted or destroyed rather than damaged.[36] Even more clearly when the chattel is merely damaged, the plaintiff should be permitted to measure his loss of use by the interest on the chattel's value if he so wishes.[37] The plaintiff might prefer the interest measure of damages when rental value or the cost of a substitute chattel cannot be shown, or when rental value is less, or when a rental value award would violate public policy.[38] In addition, the plaintiff might properly claim interest expense incurred if he reasonably borrows funds to hire a substitute or to buy a replacement vehicle.[39] If interest is allowed as a measure of lost use, it should not be awarded again for the same time period under the rubric of prejudgment interest.[40]

Prejudgment interest rules. Interest in these cases is a substitute for other lost use measures. As a result, courts traditionally granted interest in conversion cases [41] even though, in some other kinds of cases prejudgment

---

36. See Brownstein, What's the Use? A Doctrinal and Policy Critique of the Measurement of Loss of Use Damages, 37 Rutgers L.Rev. 433, 443 (1985) ("No other damage measure provides such ease of application," interest is simple and certain; on balance, there are advantages to each measure, but interest is the most sensible measure when no substitute is hired).

37. In Farmers Insurance Co. of Arizona v. R.B.L. Investment Co., 138 Ariz. 562, 675 P.2d 1381, 1384 (App.1983) the court quoted the first edition of this treatise with approval as follows:

"Where plaintiff has a claim for rental value or other loss of use. In cases where the plaintiff's claim is one for the loss of use of his property, the rental value of the property during the period in which the plaintiff was deprived of it is often one element of damages he is allowed to recover. If his automobile is damaged and he loses the use of it for a month, he may be entitled to its rental value or the rental value of some substitute transportation, as well as to some recovery for the physical damage itself. But it would be possible, if the occasion arose, to mentally convert the car into cash. Instead of talking of renting the car, it would then be possible to talk of 'renting' the cash—that is, to talk of paying interest for the use of money in a sum equal to the value of the car. The amount of interest on the cash value of the car is not necessarily the same as the amount of rental value of the car itself. Nevertheless, rental value of the car and interest on the cash value of the car can be seen as two measurement of the same underlying value, since it is almost always acceptable to express the value of property in terms of money * * * if for any reason he is willing to base his loss of use

claim on interest rather than rental values of the tangible form of his property, there is no reason to deny it, and sometimes this is convenient to both parties."

39. Farmers Insurance Co. of Arizona v. R.B.L. Inv. Co., 138 Ariz. 562, 675 P.2d 1381 (App.1983); Spreader Specialists, Inc. v. Monroc, Inc., 114 Idaho 15, 752 P.2d 617 (App. 1987); cf. Wallace v. American Manufacturers Mut. Ins. Co., 22 Mass.App.Ct. 938, 494 N.E.2d 35 (1986) (insurer failed to settle claim for stolen car, both rental costs for substitute vehicle and interest expense on funds borrowed would be recoverable).

40. See Brownstein, What's the Use? A Doctrinal and Policy Critique of the Measurement of Loss of Use Damages, 37 Rutgers L.Rev. 433, 505 (1985). Cf. State v. Stanley, 506 P.2d 1284, 1295 (Alaska 1973) (to award both interest and lost profits "constitutes a double recovery" which is not permitted). But prejudgment interest on the lost profit or rental value itself may be appropriately recoverable to compensate for the delay in payment of lost use damages. See ERA Helicopters, Inc. v. Digicon Alaska, Inc., 518 P.2d 1057 (Alaska 1974); Hardman Trucking, Inc. v. Poling Trucking Co., 176 W.Va. 575, 346 S.E.2d 551 (1986).

41. See T. Sedgwick, Damages § 178 (9th ed. 1920); Annot., 36 A.L.R.2d 337, 377 (1954). According to some decisions this is not invariable and interest may be withheld in some instances. See Jensen v. Chicago and Western Indiana R. Co., 94 Ill.App.3d 915, 50 Ill. Dec. 470, 419 N.E.2d 578 (1981) (good faith of defendant who had converted plaintiff's locomotive and rolling stock). Whether it was correct to withhold interest in *Jensen* or not, it was not withheld on the basis of the rule that prejudgment interest must be liquidated.

interest would ordinarily be denied unless the claim was liquidated.[42] But some decisions, seemingly losing sight of this traditional rule, have imported the rule that interest can be granted only if the claim is liquidated.[43]

Probable Use—Market Value of the Use or Actual Loss?

Three types of limited loss. In some sense the plaintiff has no actual loss of use damage if the chattel would not have been used in any event during the period of repair, replacement or detention of the chattel.[44] Similarly, if the chattel would have been used but the plaintiff managed to get the same work done without it, perhaps by better management or perhaps by added use of other equipment, the plaintiff may have some loss of use expenses, but the actual loss would not be represented by rental value.[45] And much the same can be said if the chattel would have been used but its use would not in fact have proved profitable.[46] The question in such cases is whether the plaintiff is to be denied all damages, to be limited to some particular measure of damages, or to be allowed a full recovery such as rental value.

Brooklyn Terminal. The best-known American case is probably *Brooklyn Eastern District Terminal v. United States,*[47] where the plaintiff's tug was damaged and where the plaintiff was able to make do during the repair by using its other boats overtime. The District Court awarded demurrage or rental value of the laid-up tug during its 78–day repair period. The Supreme Court held this to be "erroneous and extravagant," not an award for losses at all. The Court thought that if a substitute vessel had been rented to minimize damages, the cost of that substitute would perhaps be a good measure of damages; and that if the plaintiff had kept a spare boat

42. See § 3.6 above.

43. Compare Otto Farms, Inc. v. First National Bank of York, 228 Neb. 287, 422 N.W.2d 331 (1988) (no prejudgment interest allowable on conversion because claim did not meet Nebraska's restrictive standards as to what constituted liquidated claim) with Mapledge Corporation v. Coker, 167 Neb. 420, 93 N.W.2d 369, 374 (1958) ("the measure of damage is the value of such pins at the time and place of conversion with interest from the date of conversion").

44. *Examples*: (1) Plaintiff, on vacation in Europe, would have garaged her car had it not been damaged and would not have used it during the repair period. See International Harvester Credit Corp. v. Helland, 151 Ill. App.3d 848, 104 Ill.Dec. 833, 503 N.E.2d 548, 555 (1986) ("a party who intended to keep the property * * * in a garage should not be entitled to recover damages for its rental value merely because the property was absent from his garage").

(2) The telephone company's underground cable is cut and circuits are out. There is no proof that the circuits would have been used by the company or its customers during the three hours it takes to repair the cable. Cf. American Tel. & Tel. Co. v. Connecticut Light & Power Co., 470 F.Supp. 105 (D.Conn.1979).

(3) Plaintiff owns a valuable jewel. Defendant has converted the jewel but the plaintiff, who keeps the jewel in his safe and examines it once a year, does not know of the conversion for many months. The conversion has not affected his use during the months before discovery.

45. Brooklyn Eastern Dist. Terminal v. United States, 287 U.S. 170, 53 S.Ct. 103, 77 L.Ed. 240 (1932).

46. See Brownstein, What's the Use? A Doctrinal and Policy Critique of the Measurement of Loss of Use Damages, 37 Rutgers L.Rev. 433, 501 (1985), discussing an unreported litigation involving loss of use of a commercial aircraft which would have been operated on commercial routes but which, because of "extraneous events" during the lost-use period, could not have been operated profitably. Cf. International Harvester Credit Corp. v. Helland, 151 Ill.App.3d 848, 104 Ill.Dec. 833, 503 N.E.2d 548, 555 (1986) ("a party who intended to rent the property at the time when no market existed for such rented property should not be entitled to recover damages [based on rental value]").

47. 287 U.S. 170, 53 S.Ct. 103, 77 L.Ed. 240 (1932).

"specifically reserved" for such use, the value of its use would be a good measure of damage. But neither of those conditions was met. A recovery of rental value of the tug might have been acceptable if the plaintiff had intended to rent it out, just as a recovery of substitute chattel costs might be acceptable if the plaintiff had actually needed to get a substitute. But the plaintiff had *not* intended to rent out its tugs and hence it could not charge the defendant with liability for rental value.[48] In other words, loss would be measured by the probable use of the chattel, not by its rental market value.[49]

Private automobile cases. Applied to private automobile cases, the *Brooklyn Terminal* case would deny the car owner a recovery of rental value unless he would have rented out his car. But in the automobile cases the courts have not followed the *Brooklyn Terminal* case. Instead, as already indicated, they have frequently allowed the owner to recover the cost of renting a substitute vehicle while the damaged vehicle is being repaired, and have made this allowance even if no substitute vehicle is in fact hired. Indeed, the fact that the owner intended to use the car for pleasure driving only did not defeat lost use recovery. Perhaps courts feel the automobile cases, with the high incidence of private use, are different from cases of large commercial chattels; or perhaps courts feel ambivalent about the whole issue.

Other commercial chattels. Although *Brooklyn Terminal* has its following,[50] some courts have rejected it even in some cases of commercial chattels. In a claim for loss of use of a commercial airliner the Second Circuit in the *KLM* case thought *Brooklyn Terminal* distinguishable because that case involved a tug with a limited number of floats to be towed; it was relatively certain that the owner could cover his loss by working other boats over-time.[51] But it would be difficult to make a similar assumption about airliners and passengers. More importantly, the court appears to reject the central view of the *Brooklyn Terminal* court that hypothetical losses could not be used to measure damages; it said rental value of the plaintiff's chattel would be an acceptable measure of damages.[52]

48. Professor Brownstein summarizes: "Neither lease-out [rental value] nor lease-in [substitute chattel costs] was appropriate when the 'lost' chattel could not or would not have been rented out and there was insufficient need for the services of a substitute to justify hiring one * * *." Brownstein, What's the Use? A Doctrinal and Policy Critique of the Measurement of Loss of Use Damages, 37 Rutgers L.Rev. 433, 491 (1985).

49. See also International Harvester Credit Corp. v. Helland, 151 Ill.App.3d 848, 104 Ill.Dec. 833, 503 N.E.2d 548, 555 (1986) ("rule is to require the injured party to establish by competent evidence the use to which the property would have been put had it remained in his possession," rental value only if plaintiff intended to rent out the chattel).

Cf. Story v. Gateway Chevrolet Co., 237 Cal. App.2d 705, 47 Cal.Rptr. 267 (1965) (plaintiff recovered "rental value," of private boat during detention period, but only for those weekends he would actually have used the boat).

Some cases that might be read to limit rental value recovery to actual days of lost use may in fact be lost profit rather than rental value cases. See Parmalee v. Bartolomei, 106 Cal.App.2d 68, 234 P.2d 1019 (1951), in which case actual loss would always be the limit of recovery.

50. International Harvester Credit Corp. v. Helland, 151 Ill.App.3d 848, 104 Ill.Dec. 833, 503 N.E.2d 548 (1986).

51. Koninklijke Luchtvaart Maatschaapij, N.V. (KLM) v. United Technologies Corporation, 610 F.2d 1052, 1057 (2d Cir.1979).

52. "[A]n owner or lessee of a commercial vehicle may recover loss of use damages based on rental value without proving that he suffered actual financial loss * * *." Koninklijke Luchtvaart Maatschaapij, N.V. (KLM) v. United Technologies Corporation, 610 F.2d 1052, 1057 (2d Cir.1979).

A later Second Circuit case, *CTI International,*[53] applying its view of New York law, held that a claimant whose business was to lease cargo containers for international shipping could not recover the lease-out value for loss of use when the proof showed it had an excess of containers on hand and could not actually have leased any of the containers in dispute. The court thought that the facts fell between *Brooklyn Terminal* on the one hand and the *KLM* case on the other. The potential market for the tug boat work was quite limited in *Brooklyn Terminal* but financial loss was uncertain but quite possible in *KLM.* The court thought that, at the least, the defendant should be permitted to show that no loss would occur because there would be no customers for the containers even if they had not been damaged or lost.

One difference between *CTI International* and the other cases is that the *CTI* plaintiff was in the business of leasing out containers, not operating a service business in which containers were a part. The *KLM* plane in contrast was not leased out at all, but used as a significant instrumentality in a business operation. In *KLM* recovery represented the property; but a recovery in *CTI* would have represented lost business profits that the plaintiff did not suffer. That is so because CTI was in the business of leasing out the containers and its profits were derived from the lease of property. Normal rules of special damages might be thought to apply where the lease-out value and the business "profit" is substantially the same.[54]

General damages/special damages dichotomy and the actual loss problem. In a way *Brooklyn Terminal* is an anomaly. Although the plaintiff cannot recover special or consequential damages such as claims for lost profits without proof of actual loss,[55] there are many instances in which a plaintiff can recover under the rules of general damages when he has no actual loss at all. He would recover for the defendant's use or occupancy of his real property, for example, even if the plaintiff himself would not have used the property at all during the relevant time period.[56] He can recover for his own lost earning capacity when he is personally injured even if he would never have worked.[57]

The anomaly in lost use cases. In the case of loss of use, both rental (lease-out) value and interest are, at least in form,[58] general damages measures. Lost profits, increased expenses, and substitute chattel costs are plainly special damages. This general-special dichotomy suggests that the plaintiff could always recover rental value of his own chattel during the appropriate repair or replacement period, or, alternatively interest on its value, and that such a recovery would not be dependent upon a showing that

53. CTI International, Inc. v. Lloyds Underwriters, 735 F.2d 679 (2d Cir.1984).

54. See the discussion of the *AT & T* case, n. 62 below.

55. The loss must be actual in the sense that it has been realized or that there is proof to a reasonable certainty that it will be realized. Bookkeeping or "paper" losses are not recoverable as special damages. See § 3.3(4).

56. See § 5.8(2) above.

57. See § 8.1(2) below. The problem of earning capacity/lost earnings is exactly parallel to the problem of rental value/actual

losses here. See Antokol v. Barber, 248 Mass. 393, 143 N.E. 350, 32 A.L.R. 703 (1924).

58. "In form," because in substance one might regard all loss of use claims as special damages. General damages based on diminished value of the chattel resulting from the harm done might be viewed as the only general damage claim available, and all claims for lost use viewed as consequential. This would not be an unrealistic view. This text does *not* suggest that the loss of use problem can be resolved merely by defining the claims as general or special damages.

he would actually have used the chattel at all. *Brooklyn Terminal* is at odds with the general damages half of the traditional dichotomy.

The same general-special division also suggests that neither lost profits nor substitute chattel costs could be recovered unless the profits were actually diminished because the chattel was unavailable or a substitute chattel was actually rented. Many cases permit a recovery of substitute chattel costs regardless whether a substitute is hired. These cases are at odds with the special damages half of the dichotomy.

Choosing a measure of damages. Rules in line with the familiar general-special damages division would suggest that the plaintiff could recover either rental value (lease-out) *or* interest on the capital value of the chattel during the appropriate period and that such a recovery could be made on the basis of market value without deduction for the costs of leasing or investing.

Similarly, the plaintiff could not recover for lost profits or substitute chattel costs except under the rules for special damages: the plaintiff would be required to show actual, not bookkeeping losses. And the award would also be reduced by deductions for saved expenses. Perhaps this rule should apply to claims by plaintiffs who are essentially in the business of leasing out the chattels in question rather than in business that merely use the chattel.[59] A set of rules of this kind would bring the lost use recovery in chattel cases into line with traditional (but not invariable) understandings of damages law.

The interest compromise. But just and efficient rules of damages are more important than the formal structure of damages law, however useful that formal structure may be. The *Brooklyn Terminal* Court rejected rental value where the plaintiff would not have rented out the chattel and where it had no substitute chattel costs; but that Court suggested that "interest on the capital value tied up in the disabled boat during the term of disability and thus unfruitfully employed" might be an acceptable measure.[60]

Although both rental value and interest can be thought of as general damages measures, it may be practical good sense to reject the rental value recovery in favor of an interest recovery where there are no provable specials such as the rental of a reasonable substitute chattel or lost profits. The most intensive study of the whole area has reached some such conclusion.[61] Yet, whatever the measure, substitute rental costs and rental value will surely have some bearing on the matter as evidence, and even if interest were widely adopted as the main measure of general damages, in particular cases some other measure may be better. In this area adaptability and certainty cannot always go hand in hand.

59. See the discussion of the *CTI* case, supra n. 53.

60. Brooklyn Eastern Dist. Terminal v. United States, 287 U.S. 170, 174, 53 S.Ct. 103, 104, 77 L.Ed. 240 (1932).

61. Brownstein, What's the Use? A Doctrinal and Policy Critique of the Measurement of Loss of Use Damages, 37 Rutgers L.Rev. 433, 443 (1985) ("No other damage measure provides such ease of application," interest is simple and certain; there are advantages to each measure, but interest is the most sensible measure when no substitute is hired). Professor Brownstein's conclusions are based first on exclusion of the rental value recovery, which he finds particularly undesirable, and second on an extended fairness-efficiency analysis of the remaining optional measures.

Characterization and the Question of Deductions

A plaintiff may seek to recover "rental value" of a chattel during its repair period because he cannot prove any actual loss of profit or any actual expenditure. As already indicated, *Brooklyn Terminal* is opposed to such a recovery, but some other cases appear to favor it, thus allowing the plaintiff to recover in effect a general damages recovery based on rental value even when no actual loss has been or will be realized.

Erroneous characterizations as rental value claims. But some claims are wrongly characterized as rental value claims in this general damages sense; they are in reality claims for special damages such as lost profits masquerading as general damages claims. Where this is the case, the rules limiting special damages recoveries to losses that have been or will be actually realized should apply even if a court would be willing to allow a general damages recovery for a true rental value claim.

AT & T v. Connecticut Light. A good example is *American Tel. & Tel. Co. v. Connecticut Light & Power Co.,*[62] where the defendant cut the telephone company's underground cable, putting a number of circuits out of commission for a period of several hours. The telephone company claimed "rental value" of the circuits, perhaps because it would have been difficult to establish that any customer failed to make a call that otherwise would have been made.

But the company's claim was not a true general damages claim, though it was dressed to look like one. It did not claim rental value in the sense that it could have rented the cable in gross to another company. Such a claim might have been one for general damages. Instead, the telephone company claimed the "rental value" of its hundreds of individual circuits, based on charges it would have made if customers had placed calls on those circuits. This is essentially a claim for special damages for lost profits and it is not proved by showing that if there had been customers a given charge could have been made. It was as if the owner of a restaurant who lost its use for a day claimed losses based on all the meals it could have served without regard to whether it would have had any customers. It also bears a resemblance to the *CTI* case discussed above.[63]

The deduction problem. The telephone case also illustrates the problem of deductions. If the claim is one for general damages based on the hypothetical possibility of a single sale—or single rental—courts simply award the market (or rental market) value. They make no deduction for the fact that the plaintiff would necessarily incur expense in getting to the market, perhaps delay in effectuating the sale, or any other transaction costs.

When the claim is one for special damages in the form of lost profits, however, courts insist that only net profits are recoverable. Thus when the supposed income is to result from an ongoing business with many sales rather than a single market transaction, the courts deduct expenses of operating the business from the gross profit claim. The same rule applies when the plaintiff seeks to recover lost profits as a measure of lost use of a

---

62. 470 F.Supp. 105 (D.Conn.1979).

63. See the text discussion following n. 53, supra.

chattel, and characterization of the claim as one for "rental value" should not avoid the rule. In the telephone cable case, this meant that the company could not recover lost use of its circuits unless, in addition to proof of lost custom, it proved the amount of business expenses it would have incurred to reap the lost income.

Thus the characterization of the claim as one for general damages or special damages is important both in establishing the basic loss and in determining whether expense deductions are to be made. As the cable case shows, the plaintiff's characterization of the claim as one for general damages based on rental value need not be accepted by the court.

Conversion and Destruction Cases

Traditional conversion rule. In the absence of proven lost profits, the older conversion cases measured loss of use solely by interest; neither the cost of renting a substitute nor the rental value of the plaintiff's own chattel were optional measures for the plaintiff.[64] The reasons for limiting the recovery to interest were not very convincing. One was that interest provided full compensation for the lost use, which might be true enough in some cases but clearly enough not all.[65] The other was that once a chattel was converted, the plaintiff lost title and was not entitled to the use of the chattel but only to money compensation, with interest for the time-value of the money.

Destruction rules. By extension, some courts carried this same argument over to the case of destruction, and some went even further by denying interest as well as rental value as a measure of lost use. One theory for doing so was that loss of use damage is included in the award of damages for destruction;[66] another was that the market value of the chattel is an absolute ceiling on any recovery, so that when such a sum is recovered for the destruction, no further amount is recoverable.[67] The first reason to exclude even an interest recovery may be theoretically sound but probably is not a realistic reflection of actual loss. The second reason may be the same as the first, restated in an altered form, or it may be a purely conceptual construct. Perhaps the real reason for this view is that courts were assuming an immediate replacement of the chattel in the market, with the replacement providing all the use or profits that the original did.[68]

Contemporary rules. In any event, with some notable lapses,[69] courts today appear to have very generally allowed rental value claims even in cases of complete destruction of the chattel.[70] There is even some authority for allowing rental value in pure conversion cases.[71] Correlatively, the idea

---

70. Long v. McAllister, 319 N.W.2d 256 (Iowa 1982); Chlopek v. Schmall, 224 Neb. 78, 396 N.W.2d 103 (1986); DTS Tank Service, Inc. v. Vanderveen, 683 P.2d 1345 (Okl.1984); Nashban Barrel & Con. Co. v. G.G. Parsons Trucking Co., 49 Wis.2d 591, 182 N.W.2d 448 (1971); Allanson v. Cummings, 81 A.D.2d 16, 439 N.Y.S.2d 545 (1981). See Fairchild v. Keene, 93 Ill.App.3d 23, 48 Ill.Dec. 475, 416 N.E.2d 748, 750 (1981) (rental value recoverable during replacement period for destroyed chattel).

71. Henderson v. For–Shor, 757 P.2d 465 (Utah App.1988) (rental value of converted goods recoverable in lieu of interest where plaintiff was actually leasing goods out prior to conversion, where defendant knew it, and where defendant itself leased the goods out after conversion). Cf. France v. Nelson, 292 Ark. 219, 729 S.W.2d 161 (1987) (property plaintiff was in the business of leasing out, "rental value" allowed, issue bypassed by majority on appeal).

that the market value of the property is a ceiling on the recovery for loss of use has been firmly rejected in strong opinions of recent years.[72]

Time Period

Whatever measure of damages is used, the lost use claim is limited to the time reasonably required for repair or replacement [73] that will return the property to the plaintiff in an appropriate condition.[74] In a conversion this may include time reasonably used to attempt to locate and recapture the property.[75]

When the plaintiff has options to handle the damages in different ways—to repair or to trade in the damaged chattel on a new one—some authority has limited the lost-use recovery to the shorter time.[76] Such a rule may give too little weight to the plaintiff's property interest—to the fact that the plaintiff did not agree to accept damages in lieu of his chattel. It is far from clear that the plaintiff should be compelled by the defendant's tort either to accept a repaired car when he would prefer to trade in the damaged vehicle or else to suffer unrecompensed cost of renting a substitute while the trade is effected. In other words, the "reasonable time" rule should not necessarily mean the shortest time possible; it should mean the time that is reasonable in the light of appropriate protection for the plaintiff's legitimate interests.

The reasonable time rule does not mean a short time, either. A long period is acceptable where it is reasonable in light of exigencies. In some cases the owner cannot recover possession of the repaired chattel for many months because he is financially unable to pay the repair bill. If he can obtain a loan to pay for repairs, he can recover the expense of borrowing money;[77] but if he cannot, the loss of use period may extend until he can financially manage to effectuate repairs and recover use of the chattel.[78] The loss of use period may also extend to cover the time reasonably necessary to determine what repair or replacement is required,[79] and to obtain parts or replacements necessary for the repair.[80] A few cases have refused to allow loss of use recoveries when the period has been abnormally long, even though the delay in recovering use of the chattel is in no way attributable to the plaintiff's fault.[81]

§ 5.15(3) Intangible and Sentimental Losses; Emotional Harms and Punitive Damages

In general, one whose property is damaged, converted or destroyed is not entitled to recover for emotional distress or sentimental attachment to the

---

72. See Long v. McAllister, 319 N.W.2d 256 (Iowa 1982); Chlopek v. Schmall, 224 Neb. 78, 396 N.W.2d 103 (1986).

76. Roberts v. Pilot Freight Carriers, Inc., 273 N.C. 600, 160 S.E.2d 712 (1968); Glass v. Miller, 44 Ohio Law Abs. 278, 51 N.E.2d 299 (Ohio App.1940).

81. A very restrictive case is Magnolia Petroleum Co. v. Harrell, 66 F.Supp. 559 (D.Okl. 1946), where, because of conditions at the end of World War II, replacement parts could not be obtained for six months. The court found several reasons to deny loss of use recovery under Oklahoma law. One of these grounds has since been eliminated. See DTS Tank Service, Inc. v. Vanderveen, 683 P.2d 1345 (Okl.1984). Another ground was that the loss of use was brought about by a six-month delay in getting replacement parts which in turn was brought about by war conditions rather than by the defendant's tort, so that recovery was denied on proximate cause grounds. Somewhat similar is Parsons v. Lambert, 209 Miss. 649, 48 So.2d 143 (1950), criticized in Note, 8 Wash. & Lee L.Rev. 209 (1951).

property. But one may recover for intentional infliction of mental distress regardless whether property is involved; and in some states and under some circumstances one may recover for negligent infliction of emotional distress as well. Thus the plaintiff may be able to show a tort that warrants emotional distress damages independent of the property damage claim. Somewhat relatedly, punitive damages may be awarded in cases of bad faith conversion of [1] or damage [2] to property. In addition, courts tend to allow some relatively small special damage claim for the plaintiff's emotional distress when the property damaged has little or no market value and is of a personal, non-functional nature, as in the case of pets or family photographs.

A defendant who damages property as a means of, or in the course of intentionally inflicting emotional harm on its owner may be held liable for mental anguish damages if the emotional injury is severe [3] and if his conduct constitutes the outrage necessary to establish the tort of intentional infliction of mental distress to the person.[4] The mental distress damages recoverable in such cases are a part of the personal injury claim, not a part of the property damage claim.

When the defendant damages or destroys property by negligent rather than intentional misconduct, most cases deny any recovery for the owner's mental anguish or emotional harm based solely on the injury to or destruction or loss of property.[6]

While mental distress damages are usually denied in simple property damage cases, sometimes the claim for mental distress damages is based, not on damage to the property as such, but on a shocking event that caused the damage. If the event is shocking enough to warrant mental distress damages under the state's rules for such claims, those damages are no less recoverable merely because, along with the shock to the plaintiff's person, there is also damage to his property. For example, the sudden intrusion of an automobile into one's home has been enough to allow the plaintiff mental distress damages along with a recovery for the damage to property, as long as the plaintiff is personally present or nearby.[9] In such a case it is the shocking event in which the plaintiff was significantly involved that supports the mental distress claim if there is one, not merely the fact that there is property damage. When the shocking event implicates the plaintiff personally, courts are willing to approve mental distress damages provided

§ 5.15(3)

1. Lane v. Dunkle, 213 Mont. 365, 753 P.2d 321 (1988) (conversion of commissions due); McCarthy v. General Electric Co., 151 Or. 519, 49 P.2d 993, 100 A.L.R. 1370 (1935); Grant v. Clinkscales, 230 S.C. 416, 95 S.E.2d 854 (1957); Winkler v. Hartford Acc. & Indem. Co., 66 N.J.Super. 22, 168 A.2d 418 (1961); Blades v. White Motor Credit Corp., 90 Or.App. 125, 750 P.2d 1198 (1988). In some cases punitive damages have been imposed even when the defendant appears to have held a subjectively honest belief that he had a right to hold the property, where, objectively speaking, his conduct appears outrageous. See, e.g., France v. Nelson, 292 Ark. 219, 729 S.W.2d 161 (1987); Daly v. Wolfard Bros., 204 Or. 241, 282 P.2d 627, 54 A.L.R.2d 1355 (1955).

2. E.g., Ultimate Chemical Co. v. Surface Transportation International, Inc., 232 Kan. 727, 658 P.2d 1008 (1983) (defendant bulldozed plaintiff's equipment).

3. See Richardson v. Fairbanks North Star Borough, 705 P.2d 454, 456 (Alaska 1985) (recognizing tort of intentional infliction of mental distress for killing of a pet dog, and the recoverability of mental anguish damages if, but only if, emotional harm is severe).

4. The tort is explained in Prosser & Keeton on Torts § 12 (5th ed. 1984).

9. Hunsley v. Giard, 87 Wash.2d 424, 553 P.2d 1096 (1976).

the local prerequisites are met.[10] When the mental distress results solely from property damage that does not implicate the plaintiff in any personal way, only scant authority allows recovery for emotional distress,[11] and courts are generally agreed that mental distress damages are not to be allowed. If the plaintiff is not present when the defendant drives his automobile into the bedroom, the plaintiff has a claim for property damage but not one for mental distress;[12] distress at the property damage is not enough for the mental distress claim if the plaintiff's person is not involved in the event, through shock or otherwise. To a large extent the distinction between a personal claim based on shock and a property claim based on emotional attachment to the property is a matter of degree, but the distinction at least marks the main guidelines for decision.

Special Property: Pets and Other Animals

Animals, in spite of the fact that they are living beings and sometimes treated almost as part of the family, are given the legal status of property. Consequently, the general rule is that the owner of an animal negligently killed or harmed is entitled to recover general damages based on market value or diminished market value of the animal,[13] but nothing for the owner's mental distress[14] at the animal's injury or for the "loss of consortium" that might be appropriate with a human family member.[15]

In practice this rule may be ameliorated somewhat in five distinct ways that may tend to yield special damages to the owner. (1) Courts may find that an intentional injury to a pet is an intentional infliction of mental

---

10. As applied to personal (not property) claims based on ordinary negligence, the structure of mental distress law is complex. Some courts require physical impact to the person as a predicate for the mental distress claim. Others require only a physical symptom resulting from the defendant's non-impacting conduct. A few courts have eliminated the latter requirement, following Molien v. Kaiser Foundation Hospitals, 27 Cal.3d 916, 167 Cal.Rptr. 831, 616 P.2d 813, 16 A.L.R. 4th 518 (1980).

11. In Campbell v. Animal Quarantine Station, 63 Hawaii 557, 632 P.2d 1066 (1981) the defendant transported the plaintiffs' pet dog in an unventilated van and the dog died of heat prostration. Emotional harm damages were held recoverable, though there was no malice and though the plaintiffs did not witness either the transportation or the dog's death. The theory was the same used when the plaintiff witnesses a serious injury to a family member. Even here one might conclude that there was something more than property damage, but the decision is certainly a liberal one no matter how it is viewed.

Some recovery for affect is permitted in some jurisdictions when the property is of a special kind having value primarily in satisfaction of highly personal and subjective wants. Pets, heirlooms and photographs are in this category, as to which see the text below.

12. See Farr v. Johnson, 308 So.2d 884 (La.App.1975) (automobile crashed into lawn and bedroom, damaging home and contents, but as plaintiff was not present, no mental anguish damages were recoverable; "[s]uch minimal worry over consequences of damage to one's property is not 'damage'" for which the defendant is liable); Smith v. Clough, 106 Nev. 568, 796 P.2d 592 (1990).

13. Ponder v. Angel Animal Hospital, Inc., 762 S.W.2d 846 (Mo.App.1988) (plaintiff's dog, taken to vet for "grooming and clipping" was "negligently" castrated instead, no loss of market value, no damages; and since case was in negligence, where actual damages are required to sustain the cause of action, plaintiff could not recover nominal damages, either). See also Barton & Hill, How Much Will You Receive in Damages from the Negligent or Intentional Killing of Your Pet Dog or Cat?, 34 N.Y.L.Sch.L.Rev. 411 (1989).

14. Paul v. Osceola County, 388 So.2d 40 (Fla.App.1980) (absent allegation of malice or intentional destruction of seven-toed cat, no claim for mental distress); Young v. Delta Air Lines, Inc., 78 A.D.2d 616, 432 N.Y.S.2d 390 (1980).

15. Daughen v. Fox, 372 Pa.Super. 405, 539 A.2d 858 (1988); cf. Jankoski v. Preiser Animal Hosp., Ltd., 157 Ill.App.3d 818, 110 Ill. Dec. 53, 510 N.E.2d 1084 (1987). Brousseau v. Rosenthal, discussed in n. 19 below appears contrary.

distress, thus allowing a recovery of distress damages independent of the harm to the property.[16] (2) Courts may grant punitive damages against one who intentionally harms an animal,[17] and these damages may serve many of the same purposes as mental distress damages. (3) Courts may hold that intentional harm to an animal, without intentional infliction of mental distress upon its owner, is sufficient to warrant distress damages.[18] (4) Courts in some jurisdictions may allow mental distress or some other form of non-economic damage to the aggrieved animal owner by the use of the fiction that damages do not include emotional harm or sentimental value but can include a special "value to the owner" award that includes elements for the owner's feelings for the property.[19] (5) One court, Hawaii, allows the pet owner to recover for his own mental anguish when the pet is negligently injured or killed.[20]

Other Personal Property

Courts have treated damage to or destruction of other highly personal chattels in much the same way they have treated harm to animals, denying in one breath that sentimental value or emotional harm damage can be recovered, but awarding special damages for the personal value to the owner, specifically including the owner's feelings as a part of this value.[21]

§ 5.16 Unique Goods and Those Without Market Value

§ 5.16(1) In General

[For the text of this section, see the unabridged Practitioner Treatise edition.]

16. Gill v. Brown, 107 Idaho 1137, 695 P.2d 1276 (App.1985); see Richardson v. Fairbanks North Star Borough, 705 P.2d 454, 456 (Alaska 1985) (recognizing tort of intentional infliction of mental distress for killing of a pet dog, and the recoverability of mental anguish damages if, but only if, emotional harm is severe).

Cf. La Porte v. Associated Independents, Inc., 163 So.2d 267, 1 A.L.R.3d 992 (Fla.1964) (court's theory of the case may not have been intentional infliction of mental distress, but facts seem consistent with that theory).

17. In Wilson v. City of Eagan, 297 N.W.2d 146, 8 A.L.R.4th 1277 (Minn.1980) municipal employees, impounding a cat, could find no place to hold it the requisite five days; when attempts to asphyxiate the cat were unsuccessful, an officer took it to the rifle range and shot it three times with a shotgun. That seems to have done the trick. Although the officers involved did not know the owner and had no malice toward him, punitive damages were held proper against the officers who knew that the cat had not been impounded for the statutory period.

18. See La Porte v. Associated Independents, Inc., 163 So.2d 267 (Fla.1964); Knowles Animal Hospital, Inc. v. Wills, 360 So.2d 37 (Fla.App.1978) ("great indifference" by vet toward's dog in his care, resulting in severe burn, warranted recovery of owners' mental

pain and suffering, on authority of La Porte); Fredeen v. Stride, 269 Or. 369, 525 P.2d 166 (1974) (veterinarian, to "put to sleep" a dog in pain, gave it away instead). Cf. Gill v. Brown, 107 Idaho 1137, 695 P.2d 1276 (App.1985) (intentional infliction theory, facts stated did not show that plaintiff's witnessed the killing of the donkey).

In La Porte v. Associated Independents, Inc., supra, the court said that mental suffering of the owner was an appropriate element of damage for which the owner should recover for the malicious destruction of a pet. The facts suggest that serious mental suffering might have been substantially certain to follow from the attack on a tethered dog, and if so the case factually fits the tort of intentional infliction of mental distress. But if the case does not fit the tort, it seems rightly decided nonetheless.

19. See, e.g., Jankoski v. Preiser Animal Hospital, Ltd., 157 Ill.App.3d 818, 110 Ill.Dec. 53, 510 N.E.2d 1084 (1987) (dog death); Brousseau v. Rosenthal, 110 Misc.2d 1054, 443 N.Y.S.2d 285 (Civil Court 1980) (same).

20. Campbell v. Animal Quarantine Station, 63 Hawaii 557, 632 Pa.2d 1066 (1981).

21. Harvey v. Wheeler Transfer & Storage Co., 227 Wis. 36, 277 N.W. 627 (1938); Campins v. Capels, 461 N.E.2d 712 (Ind.App.1984).

§ 5.16(2) Property Used in Production of Income

Major Factors in Valuing No–Market Income Property

When the damaged property is valuable because of its actual or potential use in producing income, but there is no market established for property of this type, courts consider a number of factors in estimating "value." These include: (1) original cost of the property;[1] (2) cost of labor and materials in constructing it;[2] (3) past earnings of the property[3] and the likelihood that those earnings will continue;[4] (4) cost of repair or replacement[5] with adjustments for depreciation;[6] (5) market value at a different place with suitable adjustments for transportation;[7] (6) market value at a

---

§ 5.16(2)

1. Standard Oil Co. of N.J. v. Southern Pac. Co., 268 U.S. 146, 45 S.Ct. 465, 69 L.Ed. 890 (1925); Rhodes v. Ritz Camera Centers, 151 A.2d 262 (D.C.Mun.App.1959). The time elapsed between original purchase and trial is relevant and in some cases the evidence might be deemed so remote that it should be excluded. See Jensen v. Chicago and Western Indiana R.R. Co., 94 Ill.App.3d 915, 50 Ill.Dec. 470, 419 N.E.2d 578, 595 (1981).

2. Leard v. Breland, 514 So.2d 778 (Miss. 1987) (expenses incurred to raise crop to point of destruction where lost profits not proved); Redwine v. Fitzhugh, 78 Wyo. 407, 329 P.2d 257, 72 A.L.R.2d 664 (1958), rehearing denied, 78 Wyo. 407, 330 P.2d 112 (1958) (destruction of immature crops or seed in the ground warrants at least a recovery for the value of the seed and labor expended in sowing and cultivating). But "Original cost is well termed the 'false standard of the past' where, as here, present market value in no way reflects that cost." United States v. Toronto, Hamilton & Buffalo Navigation Co., 338 U.S. 396, 70 S.Ct. 217, 222, 94 L.Ed. 195 (1949).

3. Monongahela Nav. Co. v. United States, 148 U.S. 312, 13 S.Ct. 622, 37 L.Ed. 463 (1893) (toll charges on canal and lock relevant to fixing value when lock condemned). See O'Brien Bros. v. The Helen B. Moran, 160 F.2d 502 (2d Cir.1947) ("capitalization of earning capacity" one possible method of proving value); cf. United States v. Eden Mem. Park Ass'n, 350 F.2d 933 (9th Cir.1965) ("value which the property's net earning power will support, based upon a capitalization of net income" is one factor in appraisal for condemnation).

Cf. Seravalli v. United States, 845 F.2d 1571 (Fed.Cir.1988) (capitalization of income method used to fix value of apartment complex defendant contracted to sell to plaintiff for the purpose of fixing damages under the contract-market differential measure).

4. United States v. Toronto, Hamilton & Buffalo Nav. Co., 338 U.S. 396, 70 S.Ct. 217, 94 L.Ed. 195 (1949).

5. Standard Oil Co. of N.J. v. Southern Pac. Co., 268 U.S. 146, 45 S.Ct. 465, 69 L.Ed. 890 (1925); King Fisher Marine Service, Inc. v. NP Sunbonnet, 724 F.2d 1181 (5th Cir.1984) (factors include replacement cost, depreciation and "the amount of insurance"). Cost of repair or replacement is a factor in judgment about value rather than a measure of damages in itself. In the federal eminent domain decisions, at least, the cost of physical replacement may be distinguished from cost of obtaining a substitute facility elsewhere that has the same utility to the plaintiff. See § 5.2(6) above.

In King Fisher, supra, the plaintiff purchased a barge for $30,000, intending to convert it to a drydock. Two days after purchase the barge sank and could not be recovered. The defendant was responsible but insisted that the market value was $30,000, since it had just been purchased for that sum. The court rejected this and allowed the most economical replacement cost, which came to more than $232,000. "[T]he market did not value the barge's use as a drydock platform * * *. The district court correctly found that the price paid by King Fisher for the now lost barge did not represent its value as a drydock platform." (724 F.2d at 1186). "While the barge may only have been a large steel box to some, King Fisher recognized and took advantage of an opportunity to purchase a suitable drydock platform at low cost. The value of the barge was not reflected by its cost * * *." (724 F.2d at 1187).

6. As to adjustments for depreciation, see § 5.14(3) above.

7. Standard Oil Co. of N.J. v. Southern Pac. Co., 268 U.S. 146, 45 S.Ct. 465, 69 L.Ed. 890 (1925); cf. Woonsocket Machine & Press Co. v. New York, N.H. & H.R. Co., 239 Mass. 211, 131 N.E. 461 (1921) (contracts of other manufacturers with sole buyer of such goods).

different time; [8] (7) comparable sales. [9] Subsidiary items of relevance would include evidence of the age and condition of the property.

Depreciation

"New for old". When repair or replacement costs become important in fixing "value" of personal property, additional calculations are required. First, the court must determine whether repair or replacement will provide property worth more than the plaintiff's property at the time of damage or destruction. Second, it must reduce the damages accordingly to avoid overcompensation that would result if the plaintiff got "new for old." [10] But if the problem in the first place is that the property is unique, that there is no market, and that the value of the property is unknown, it will not be easy to discover whether the replacement property provides the plaintiff with something of greater value or not. In this situation, courts may fall back on formal accounting notions of depreciation in an attempt to estimate the current value of the property. [11]

Depreciation and the Standard Oil Case. Even conventional accounting depreciation may not present a convincing answer to this difficulty. In *Standard Oil Co. of N.J. v. Southern Pac. Co.,* [12] an old vessel had been requisitioned by the government for the duration of the first world war. Because it and like ships were under requisition, there was no immediate market at all. When it was destroyed in a collision, the owner was faced with a problem in proving value. The original cost, in 1900, was $557,000. Cost of reproducing a similar ship in 1918 was at least $1,750,000. Normal depreciation rates would indicate that the vessel had little value, but a conclusion that it was worth nothing when shipyards were working at full capacity to provide new vessels seemed improbable. The Supreme Court concluded that the depreciation rates were wrong in failing to account for the high cost of reproduction and on this basis approved an award of $1,225,000.

[*For discussion of valuation by "capitalization if income," consult § 3.5 above in addition to this section in the Practitioner Treatise edition.*]

§ 5.16(3) Property Held for Personal Use

When clothing or household goods are destroyed the courts have departed from the market value formula in favor of one that gives the plaintiff the

---

8. Routine in the case of immature crops or animals, see Tennessee Corp. v. Barnett, 269 Ala. 450, 114 So.2d 135 (1959) (fair market value of crop at maturity, not at date of injury). Sometimes the date of injury to crops is taken as the measure, but in a way that requires advertence to the value of the mature crop less cultivation costs. E.g., Burke v. Thomas, 313 P.2d 1082 (Okl.1957). As to crops generally, see § 5.3(2) above.

9. Comparable sales of personal property may tend to establish a market price. Comparable sales of comparable property is a test most often used in fixing a value of real prop-

erty because each parcel is unique and hence almost never has a "market." E.g., United States v. 179.26 Acres of Land in Douglas Cty., Kan., 644 F.2d 367 (10th Cir.1981).

10. See § 5.14(3) above.

11. Some courts in some circumstances have refused to take depreciation into account when the only method of estimating depreciation in the record is through some accounting formula. Others appear to pick a figure intuitively; others accept the accounting formulas for depreciation. See § 5.13(7), supra.

12. 268 U.S. 146, 45 S.Ct. 465, 69 L.Ed.2d 890 (1925).

"value to the owner" or "real value," [2] frequently adding that this does not include "sentimental value." [3] Such statements provide a goal but not a measure of damages. "Value to the owner" cannot yield any dollar figure by computation, by analysis or by empirical investigation. The point seems to be to give the plaintiff something more than the market value, but something less than the full replacement cost of a new item.

However, the cost of replacement new is relevant in assessing value to the owner, and evidence of full replacement cost new is admissible, though if replacement cost is the only evidence, it may be necessary to calculate a deduction for depreciation.[4] As with income-producing property, age, original cost, and general condition of the property is each relevant.[5] The owner himself may give opinion evidence of value.[6]

Since value to the owner is stated as a measure but cannot function as one, all this is very unsatisfactory in theory. But the cases are usually small ones in which detailed accounting evidence would be unwelcome as too elaborate for the modest occasion. Perhaps the value to the owner rule suffices to invite some help from the jury and at the same time to provide a tool for control if the award becomes too generous; if so, maybe no more should be demanded.

The primary value of many highly personal items is their affect or associational value. Many items of this kind have no market value at all; the faded photograph of the owner's mother, for example. Other items, like great grandfather's watch, may have a market value, but if so it is one that does not represent the special significance to the owner.

In these cases, as in the household goods cases, the courts have said, somewhat contradictorily, that recovery is to be measured by value to the owner, but that it may not include anything for sentimental value.[7] Since the value to the owner *is* sentimental value, this formula should not be understood too literally. Rather it is a means of warning the jury away from enormous awards for affect value and a way of permitting the courts to limit awards if they do go too far. Thus courts have had to explain that they do not exclude all claims based on the owner's special attachment but only those based on a "mawkish and unreasonable attachment," [8] and have allowed limited recoveries for sentimental value or something that seems indistinguishable from sentimental value in cases of pets,[9] family photo-

§ 5.16(3)

2. Wall v. Platt, 169 Mass. 398, 48 N.E. 270 (1897); Spackman v. Ralph M. Parsons Co., 147 Mont. 500, 414 P.2d 918 (1966); DeSpirito v. Bristol County Water Co., 102 R.I. 50, 227 A.2d 782, 34 A.L.R.3d 809 (1967); McCurdy v. Union Pac. R. Co., 68 Wash.2d 457, 413 P.2d 617 (1966); Broyles v. Broyles, 711 P.2d 1119, 1124 (Wyo.1985).

3. E.g., Nelson v. Coleman Co., 249 S.C. 652, 155 S.E.2d 917 (1967).

4. See Rafal v. Rafal, 41 Del.Ch. 434, 198 A.2d 177 (1964).

5. Rutherford v. James, 33 N.M. 440, 270 P. 794, 63 A.L.R. 237 (1928).

6. Nelson v. Coleman Co., 249 S.C. 652, 155 S.E.2d 917 (1967); Bangert v. Emmco Ins. Co.,

349 Ill.App. 257, 110 N.E.2d 528 (1953). This may be especially appropriate in the case of household goods or personal items. See Nickens v. McGehee, 184 So.2d 271 (La.App.1966).

7. Furlan v. Rayan Photo Works, 171 Misc. 839, 12 N.Y.S.2d 921 (1939); Harvey v. Wheeler Transfer & Storage Co., 227 Wis. 36, 277 N.W. 627 (1938).

8. Mieske v. Bartell Drug Co., 92 Wash.2d 40, 593 P.2d 1308, 6 A.L.R.4th 923 (1979); Campins v. Capels, 461 N.E.2d 712 (Ind.App. 1984).

9. E.g., Jankoski v. Preiser Animal Hospital, Ltd., 157 Ill.App.3d 818, 110 Ill.Dec. 53, 510 N.E.2d 1084 (1987) (dog death); Brousseau v. Rosenthal, 110 Misc.2d 1054, 443 N.Y.S.2d

graphs,[10] heirlooms [11] and personal trophies.

As indicated elsewhere,[12] the general rule is that the owner does not recover for mental or emotional distress merely because property has been damaged or destroyed or converted. The practice of allowing some sentimental value but not too much can be understood best as a rule that allows, in addition to "value" of destroyed property, a modest recovery for relatively minor mental distress at its loss.

To recover substantial sums for mental distress, the plaintiff will ordinarily be required to make out an intentional or negligent tort to himself and not merely a tort to his property,[13] although in some cases they may be one and the same, as where the evil defendant intentionally inflicts distress by maiming the pet dog in the owner's presence.[14]

§ 5.16(4) Property With Artistic or Historic Value

Use of Market Value

Markets for unique historical and artistic items. Many items of property are like heirlooms or family photographs in that their value lies in the feelings and attitudes they engender rather than in commercial use, but are different from heirlooms in that the feelings they engender are reflected in a market price. Works of art and objects associated with historical events or famous persons are like this. Their unique qualities may affect the right to equitable relief,[1] but if there is a market in historical or art objects, the plaintiff is entitled to base his claim for damage or destruction on that market. This point seems to have been overlooked in one case dealing with the weapons used in the assassination of President Kennedy,[2] but a later decision properly reverted to the market value.[3]

Where there is no market. There is, however, a question whether market value can be established for unique items of historical or artistic value. A market for unique items, like a market for land, could only be established by holding an auction for that item. If repair is feasible, repair costs may furnish at least an optional measure for recovery in the case of art.[4] Destruction cases may be more difficult. As in other cases where there is no established market for the goods, it may be necessary to resort to

---

285 (Civ.Ct.1980) (same). See Barton & Hill, How Much Will You Receive in Damages from the Negligent or Intentional Killing of Your Pet Dog or Cat?, 34 N.Y.L.Sch.L.Rev. 411 (1989); § 5.15(3) above.

10. Mieske v. Bartell Drug Co., 92 Wash.2d 40, 593 P.2d 1308, 6 A.L.R.4th 923 (1979); Furlan v. Rayan Photo Works, Inc., 171 Misc. 839, 12 N.Y.S.2d 921 (1939); Bond v. A.H. Belo Corporation, 602 S.W.2d 105, 9 A.L.R.4th 1236 (Tex.Civ.App.1980).

11. Brown v. Frontier Theatres, 369 S.W.2d 299 (Tex.1963) (grandfather's pistol, grandmother's wedding veil).

12. See § 5.15(3).

13. As explained more fully in § 5.15(3).

14. La Porte v. Associated Independents, Inc., 163 So.2d 267, 1 A.L.R.3d 992 (Fla.1964).

§ 5.16(4)

1. See § 5.17 below, for example.

2. King v. United States, 292 F.Supp. 767 (D.Colo.1968) held that the plaintiff could recover the intrinsic or "value to the owner" value of weapons but not "historical value" as that might affect market price.

3. Porter v. United States, 473 F.2d 1329 (5th Cir.1973) (widow of assassin of President Kennedy sought compensation for personal effects taken by act of Congress; value to collectors of such effects to be taken into account).

4. In the case of a destroyed manuscript the cost of reproducing it might be a ceiling on recovery as Judge Posner has suggested, see Taliferro v. Augle, 757 F.2d 157, 162 (7th Cir.1985), but perhaps this would not be so with a unique work of visual art.

evidence of earlier sales of the same property or to sales of comparable property. Factors such as original cost of materials and cost of reproduction, sometimes helpful in connection with property used in producing income, seem largely irrelevant in establishing the affect value of an historical object, since the reproduction would be merely an imitation. The same can be said for a destroyed work of art, except, perhaps, works by living artists or authors who could reproduce their own works.[5] For the artist who has not established the value of his or her works by past sales, it will be very difficult indeed to prove damages for destruction of a work of art.

Artist's Remedies for Alteration of Art after Sale: "Moral Rights" Legislation

Common law and civil law. The common law rule was that once an artist sells a tangible work of visual art,[6] he has no further property in it and the purchaser is free to alter the work in any way, for example, by painting the work a different color, or destroying it.[7] Civil law countries, on the contrary, recognize a right in the artist to prevent alterations of art works even after sale.[8] The artist is said to have "moral rights" in the art work, meaning that the artist retains intangible rights in the property.[9]

---

5. To the extent that a destroyed painting could be reproduced by the very artist who painted it, it would be possible to fix damages by estimating the cost of reproduction, based on materials and the average income of the artist. This could create the problem of estimating lost volume and in addition it might be thought seriously to infringe upon the artistic process and the integrity of the work itself. The "moral rights" statutes, discussed below, do not seem to address this issue directly, but the concept of artistic integrity on which they are based might imply that the artist should not be compelled to reconstruct his work. And if he does not reconstruct the damaged work, then it would be wrong to base damages on the cost of reconstruction despite the artist's objection.

In the case of manuscripts, Judge Posner has suggested that though "an author may prove nonmarket damages for the tortious destruction of a manuscript," proof of value would be required and that value could not exceed the cost in time or materials of reconstructing it. Taliferro v. Augle, 757 F.2d 157, 161–162 (7th Cir.1985). Other courts have suggested that the cost of "hours of labor" put into a manuscript would be at least relevant as to value. Seth v. British Overseas Airways Corp., 329 F.2d 302, 306 (1st Cir.1964), cert. denied, 379 U.S. 858, 85 S.Ct. 114, 13 L.Ed.2d 61 (1964).

6. Written works are of course protected by the copyright laws. Tangible art works also receive protection from copying, publication and display, but not from alteration.

7. E.g., Crimi v. Rutgers Presbyterian Church, 194 Misc. 570, 89 N.Y.S.2d 813 (1949). See generally F. Feldman, S. Weil and S.

Biederman, Art Law, Rights and Liabilities of Creators and Collectors Chapter 5 (1986).

8. See F. Feldman, S. Weil and S. Biederman, Art Law, Rights and Liabilities of Creators and Collectors Chapter 5 (1986); Roeder, The Doctrine of Moral Right: A Study in the Law of Artists, Authors and Creators, 53 Harv.L.Rev. 554 (1940); Gantz, Protecting Artists' Moral Rights: A Critique of the California Art Preservation Act as a Model for Statutory Reform, 49 Geo.Wash.L.Rev. 873, 874 (1981).

9. The civil law doctrine includes several components: the right to decide whether and when to publish or display the work, the right to withdraw it if it no longer represents the artist's thought, the right to protect the integrity of the work (as from physical alteration), and the right to be recognized as the "author" of the work. These components are summarized as the rights of disclosure, retraction, integrity, and attribution. See Damich, The New York Artists' Authorship Rights Act: A Comparative Critique, 84 Colum.L.Rev. 1733 (1984). All of these "moral rights" are distinguished from the economic rights of artists. Other components are sometimes mentioned, for example, the right to prevent excessive criticism. See Kwall, Copyright and the Moral Right: Is an American Marriage Possible?, 38 Vand.L.Rev. 1, 5 (1985).

In American law there is room for some kind of right to display based on First Amendment free speech rights, but the right does not necessarily guarantee the artist any particular forum for display. See Piarowski v. Illinois Community College Dist. 515, 759 F.2d 625 (7th Cir.1985), cert. denied, 474 U.S. 1007, 106 S.Ct. 528, 88 L.Ed.2d 460 (1985) (sexually

Statutory changes. Federal copyright legislation did not traditionally recognize these moral rights in tangible art works,[10] but incidental protection of those rights may occasionally result under other theories.[11] A number of states once enacted statutes which specifically prohibited intentional alteration of fine art [12] or else prohibited the knowing display of altered work.[13] They typically provided that "legal and injunctive relief," or "actual damages" and punitive damages could be recovered by the artist for violation.[14] Whether these statutes are desirable or well-drafted, they present difficult problems in remedies as well as in their substantive provisions. These statutes, however, now appear to be preempted largely or wholly by the federal Visual Artists Rights Act, effective in 1991 as an amendment to the Copyright Act, so comment on the state statutes is limited to an appended note to this section.

The federal Visual Artists Act. As a part of the Copyright Act, but distinct from the rights it otherwise provides, the federal statute now provides for limited recognition of moral rights theories.[15] It recognizes the

explicit works of college professor on exhibit on his campus moved to less frequented exhibit room, no violation of civil rights). There have been serious incidents reported in which pressure groups successfully forced even previously well-regarded art institutions to remove paintings offensive to their political symbols. There have also been instances in which artists have been aggrieved because their work has allegedly been published without attribution. It is usually said that apart from contract there is no American right to credit for one's art once it is sold. Vargas v. Esquire, Inc., 164 F.2d 522 (7th Cir.1947). But in some cases the artist has been successful in stating a claim for attribution on the basis of the Lanham Trademark Act. See Smith v. Montoro, 648 F.2d 602 (9th Cir.1981) (actor whose name was removed from film credits, "reverse passing off"); Dodd v. Fort Smith Special School Dist. No. 100, 666 F.Supp. 1278 (W.D.Ark.1987) (one Farrar credited as "author" of book on local war hero William O. Darby, while journalism teacher and students who prepared initial materials were not credited; preliminary injunction against advertising and distribution of book). Of these claims, only the right to prevent alteration is within the purview of the present chapter, which deals with harms to tangible property. Even that component of the moral rights claim fits only strangely here, since ultimately the claim for damages focuses on the artist rather than the property.

10. Tangible visual art is given protection by the Copyright Revision Act but this does not extend to protection from physical alteration by an owner of the work of art. See 17 U.S.C.A. §§ 102, 106 (copyrightable works include "pictorial, graphic, and sculptural works," and "author" has exclusive right to reproduce, to prepare derivative works, to distribute and to display publicly).

11. For example under copyright, unfair competition or trademark laws. See Gilliam v. American Broadcasting Companies, Inc., 538 F.2d 14 (2d Cir.1976). Supporters of moral right claims often believe that existing theories for relief are insufficient. See Kwall, Copyright and the Moral Right: Is an American Marriage Possible?, 38 Vand.L.Rev. 1 (1985).

12. E.g., West's Ann.Cal.Civ.Code § 987 ("no person, except an artist who owns and possesses a work of fine art which the artist has created, shall intentionally commit, or authorize the intentional commission of, any * * * alteration * * *.").

13. E.g., N.Y.—McKinney's Arts & Cultural Affairs Law § 14.03 (where damage to reputation from display of altered work is "reasonably likely;" "legal relief" authorized); R.I.Gen.Laws § 5–62–2 ("no person other than the artist * * * shall knowingly display in a public exhibition a work of fine art * * * in an altered * * * form, if the work is displayed * * * as being the work of the artist * * *.").

14. West's Ann.Cal.Civ.Code § 987 (actual damages); La.Rev.Stat. 51:2156 ("legal and injunctive relief"); M.G.L.A. ch. 231, § 85 S (actual damages); Me.Rev.Stat.Ann. tit. 27 § 303 (public display of altered work, and damage to reputation is reasonably likely, "legal relief" authorized); N.J.Stat.Ann. 2A:24A–8 ("legal and injunctive relief"); N.Y.—McKinney's Arts & Cultural Affairs Law § 14.03 (where damage to reputation from display of altered work is "reasonably likely;" "legal relief" authorized); 73 Pa.Stat. § 2104 (injunctive relief, actual damages and punitive damages); R.I.Gen.Laws § 5–62–6 ("legal and injunctive relief").

15. 17 U.S.C.A. §§ 106A & 113.

less controversial right of the artist to attribution, that is, to claim author-ship of works the artist created and to avoid attribution of works the artist did not create. More importantly, it recognizes the right in the author of works of visual art, even after the work is unconditionally sold, to prevent intentional modification or distortion of the work that is prejudicial to the artist's "honor or reputation." In the case of works of recognized stature, the artist's rights are violated by either intentional or grossly negligent destruction as well. The artist is permitted to waive these rights in writing, but they are not transferable. The federal statute preempts state laws that provide "equivalent" rights.

Remedies under the federal statute. Once a work of art is sold, the artist has no traditional property interest in the work and hence would not have a plausible claim to traditional damages based on diminished value. Recogniz-ing this remedial problem, the federal statute provides that the artist's moral rights claims are independent of copyright ownership and that the artist may recover statutory damages even if the copyright is not registered. Statutory damages may be awarded in sums not less than $1,000 nor more than $20,000, or larger sums if the violation is wilful.[16]

Salvage Value of Art and "Moral Rights of Artists"

Diminished value rule. Some of the same concerns about the artist's personal standards in creating anything as personal as serious art lead to a further difficulty. If a defendant negligently damages but does not destroy an artist's painting, conventional damages measures would award the dimin-ished value of the painting.[17] If it had been worth $100,000 whole, but was worth only $80,000 after damage, the artist would be awarded $20,000 as the diminished value.

Dilution of artist's standards or goodwill by sales of damaged work. But the artist might reasonably take the view in some instances that he does not wish to market his work in a damaged condition any more than he would wish to permit it to be painted over or to be cut into segments for separate sales. He could regard sale of damaged work as a kind of dilution of his tradename, but perhaps more importantly he might regard it as an infringe-ment of his personal integrity. If the artist's wishes are to prevail, then the usual rule of damages could not be applied. Rather, the artist would be allowed to destroy the damaged art and recover its full market value.

Moral right and economic waste. This kind of claim seems to assert rights quite similar to those protected, or partly protected, by the moral rights statutes.[18] Perhaps where those statutes are in force in a strong form,

---

16. 17 U.S.C.A. § 504(c).

17. As to the general rule of law, see § 5.13. It seems on its face applicable to works of art. Cf. Gates v. LaBelle's Distribut-ing of Arizona, Inc., 147 Ariz. 23, 708 P.2d 114 (App.1985) (market value of art work de-stroyed in fire was not a claim for lost profits for statute of limitations purposes); Klein v. General Elec. Co., 714 S.W.2d 896 (Mo.App. 1986) (owner testimony was sufficient to show diminished value of real estate and art result-ing from fire). As to the facts, however, it

may be that any damage to some art is equiva-lent to economic destruction. See Merchants Fire Assurance Corp. v. Lattimore, 263 F.2d 232 (9th Cir.1959) (insurance claim for de-struction of insured art, accepting testimony that non-unique "art objects" such as molded porcelains lose their value as art when dam-aged). But that is an economic question on the facts of each case.

18. The moral rights doctrine is consistent with the idea that the artist should be permit-ted to destroy the work once it is altered

the artist's claim would get sympathetic attention. But to destroy the art is to maximize rather than to minimize damages. Under ordinary damages rules the destruction of art that still has value would count as economic waste and the recovery could not be based on the artist's destruction of a work that was economically valuable. A broad view of the artist's integrity rights is thus at odds with the traditional view that economic waste should be avoided.

Wholesale or Retail Value of Art

Still another special problem arises when art still owned by the artist is damaged or destroyed. The general rule is that a manufacturer of destroyed goods recovers the value of the goods in the market in which he sells, that is, the price at which he sells those goods.[19] The artist is, economically speaking, the manufacturer of the work and under this rule would be entitled to value the work in the market where it would be sold. If he sells to a dealer who exacts a 50% commission, his "price" is what the dealer pays him. This may seriously undercompensate the artist because exhibition and sales of a painting may be necessary to maintain or establish a reputation which in turn may be necessary to maintain appropriate price levels for his work. With such concerns in mind, a California court has allowed the artist to recover the full retail value of the destroyed painting.[20] However, this will only fortuitously approximate the loss of goodwill or reputation and it may not be the best solution to the problem.

———

Appended Note to § 5.16(4)

Note on Remedies under State Moral Rights Statutes
Possibly Preempted under Federal Law

[*For this appendix, see the Practitioner Treatise edition.*]

§ 5.17 Specific Recovery of Chattels

§ 5.17(1) Generally

[*For the text of this section, see the unabridged Practitioner Treatise edition.*]

§ 5.17(2) Replevin: Recovery at Law and Due Process

Traditional Procedure

Replevin of chattels, both a provisional remedy and a permanent one, had its own peculiar common law development.[1] At the same time, it is one of a whole range of provisional remedies granted before trial on the merits. It may be compared to or contrasted with such other remedies as pre-judgment attachment and garnishment[2] and with those preliminary injunc-

---

intentionally, but the doctrine does not apply under the statutes to negligently caused damage. The doctrine might thus point to a solution it does not compel.

19. See § 5.13(3) above.

20. Pelletier v. Eisenberg, 177 Cal.App.3d 558, 223 Cal.Rptr. 84 (1986).

tions that are used to freeze a bank account before trial.[3]

The procedure under the traditional replevin statutes[4] was somewhat peculiar. The plaintiff, having filed the action to recover an identified chattel, could then claim the right to immediate possession by posting a bond. The bond was treated as standing for the property; it guaranteed that the defendant would be reimbursed for damages if, at a hearing on the merits, the court decided that the property belonged to the defendant. The bond and any formal orders necessary would then be exhibited to the sheriff, who on this basis would seize the chattel.

The sheriff usually held the property for a stated period of time to allow the defendant to demand a higher bond or better sureties on it. In addition, many states allowed the defendant to post a counter bond or redelivery bond. This would allow the defendant to keep the chattel pending a decision on the merits, with the bond as a guarantee that the plaintiff would be paid damages if it turned out that the plaintiff was entitled to the chattel.

Constitutional Limitations

In *Fuentes v. Shevin,*[5] the Supreme Court appeared to hold, as a matter of due process, that some kind of hearing was required in a replevin action prior to seizure of the property. *Fuentes* was one of a series of Supreme Court decisions making similar requirements of a hearing in provisional remedy cases.[6] But in another case, *Mitchell,* which was sandwiched uncomfortably among those decisions, the Supreme Court seemed to imply that replevin procedure could meet constitutional standards if the total balance of several factors provided adequate protections. In this view, a pre-seizure hearing would not necessarily be required, provided (1) a post-seizure hearing was immediately available to the defendant and (2) a judge passed on the case in some meaningful way and (3) evidence or at least affidavits were factual and not merely conclusory.[7] Other factors that appear to be important are whether (4) the plaintiff had a pre-existing interest in the property seized or attached, and (5) the dispute would lend itself to documentary proof

§ 5.17(2)

3. See § 6.1(5) below.

4. Many traditional statutes, some of which have now been amended as a result of the constitutional decisions and which are now mainly of interest in understanding the development of the problem, are cited in the first edition of this treatise, p. 400.

5. 407 U.S. 67, 92 S.Ct. 1983, 32 L.Ed.2d 556 (1972).

6. Sniadach v. Family Finance Corp. of Bay View, 395 U.S. 337, 89 S.Ct. 1820, 23 L.Ed.2d 349 (1969) (garnishment of wages without notice or hearing violates due process); Fuentes v. Shevin, 407 U.S. 67, 92 S.Ct. 1983, 32 L.Ed.2d 556 (1972) (provisional relief under replevin statutes without a hearing before seizure violates due process); North Georgia Finishing, Inc. v. Di–Chem, Inc., 419 U.S. 601, 95 S.Ct. 719, 42 L.Ed.2d 751 (1975) (gar-

nishment of corporate bank account without hearing, with no provision for early hearing after garnishment violates due process). Mitchell v. W.T. Grant Co., 416 U.S. 600, 94 S.Ct. 1895, 40 L.Ed.2d 406 (1974) took a more lenient view where a lienholder sequestered property without notice, but where there was judicial supervision and a factual rather than a conclusory affidavit. In Connecticut v. Doehr, __ U.S. __, 111 S.Ct. 2105, 115 L.Ed.2d 1 (1991) Connecticut's pre-trial, ex parte attachment statute was held unconstitutional for want of notice and opportunity to be heard before the attachment, where the plaintiff could attach property in which it had no pre-existing interest.

7. Mitchell v. W.T. Grant Co., 416 U.S. 600, 94 S.Ct. 1895, 40 L.Ed.2d 406 (1974) (lienholder sequestered property without notice, but there was judicial supervision and a factual rather than a conclusory affidavit).

rather than highly factual determination.[8]

The constitutional requirements are not limited to cases in which possession of property is given to the plaintiff. They apply as well to cases in which the defendant is merely enjoined from disposing of disputed property, since in either kind of case he is deprived of the use of his property.[9] Presumably the hearing requirement does not apply to self-help repossession by a creditor who is otherwise empowered to repossess the chattel.[10] If it is given that a hearing before seizure of property is required, there remains the question whether the hearing must be an adversary one or whether a hearing before the judge without notice to the defendant will suffice.[11] But the central rule is clear enough to condemn the traditional statutes even if it is not clear enough to permit confident drafting of new ones.

As a result of the constitutional decisions a number of states—but not all—have revised their replevin statutes, sometimes only after the state court applied the Supreme Court decisions.[12] The revised statutes are quite varied, and local statutes must be consulted individually. Some of the statutes were written to comply with the lenient *Mitchell* test, under which a post-seizure hearing is good enough if a judge passes on the plaintiff's right to recover in an ex parte hearing prior to seizure.[13] This kind of statute if not one even more lenient, would presumably be favored by those emphasizing economic efficiency, because the tangible gains from a pre-seizure hear-

---

8. See Connecticut v. Doehr, ___ U.S. ___, 111 S.Ct. 2105, 115 L.Ed.2d 1 (1991).

9. See United States v. Spilotro, 680 F.2d 612, 617 (9th Cir.1982) (freeze of assets by order restraining defendant from selling, transferring, encumbering or otherwise disposing of the property during pendency of *RICO* case; due process protections apply generally, but where government seizes for forfeiture and preseizure notice might defeat purposes of the statute by creating opportunity in defendant to destroy, conceal, or remove the property, the preseizure hearing is not required).

10. One problem is whether state action can be found. See, discussing a number of cases holding that there is no state action, Catz & Robinson, Due Process and Creditor's Remedies: From Sniadach and Fuentes to Mitchell, North Georgia and Beyond, 28 Rutgers L.Rev. 541, 568 (1975).

But where a police officer is in attendance in an act of repossession, this has been found to imply state action, so that the hearing requirement is invoked, with the result that the repossession was constitutionally impermissible without notice and hearing. Walker v. Walthall, 121 Ariz. 121, 588 P.2d 863 (App. 1978). See also Del's Big Saver Foods, Inc. v. Carpenter Cook, Inc., 795 F.2d 1344, 1346 (7th Cir.1986) ("A state cannot avoid its obligations under the due process clause by delegating to private persons the authority to deprive people of their property without due process of law. If * * * the effect of Wisconsin's law of

repossession is to arm creditors with the state's power to dispossess debtors of their property, Del's can challenge the law in a suit against the creditor under" federal civil rights acts).

11. Thus an ex parte hearing may suffice in temporary restraining order cases, see § 5.16(3) below, and perhaps in some others. See Mitchell v. W.T. Grant Co., 416 U.S. 600, 94 S.Ct. 1895, 40 L.Ed.2d 406 (1974).

12. See First National Bank of Santa Fe v. Southwest Yacht & Marine Supply Corp., 101 N.M. 431, 684 P.2d 517, 520 (1984) (reflecting earlier decision holding statute unconstitutional, statutory response, and view that current statute met constitutional requirements); General Electric Credit Corp. of Tenn. v. Hatch, 3 Ohio App.3d 80, 443 N.E.2d 1054 (1982) (traditional statute unconstitutional) (statute later reformed to permit hearing, see Ohio Rev.Code §§ 2337.03 & 2737.04).

13. See, e.g., N.M.Stat.Ann. § 2–8–18; Wis. Stat.Ann. 810.02, 810.05. The New Mexico statute is specifically grounded in *Mitchell* rather than in the *Sniadach–Fuentes* line of cases. See First National Bank of Santa Fe v. Southwest Yacht & Marine Supply Corp., 101 N.M. 431, 684 P.2d 517 (1984). Judge Posner justified the Wisconsin statute by emphasizing that it met the *Mitchell* factors—availability of an immediate post-seizure hearing, a judge passing on the facts. See Del's Big Saver Foods, Inc. v. Carpenter Cook, Inc., 795 F.2d 1344 (7th Cir.1986).

ing, at least in most creditor-debtor cases, are likely to be small compared to the added cost of holding hearings in all cases.[14]

Other statutes respond to the constitutional problem by requiring an adversary hearing on the question whether to transfer possession of the disputed chattel, followed by an order of the judge. Some go on to allow the plaintiff to recover possession without notice to the defendant or a hearing at which he is present, but unlike the traditional procedure, require an *ex parte* hearing before the judge, who must hear evidence and make explicit findings.[15] This procedure also differs from the traditional procedure in that the transfer of possession is the result of a judicial order, not merely the seizure by an officer of the court. Statutory changes of this kind come close to converting the common law in rem actions into equity claims for the transfer of possession by injunction.

§ 5.17(3) Injunction: Equitable Recovery of Chattels

Inadequate Legal Remedy

"Equitable replevin" is merely a form of injunction compelling the defendant to hand over a chattel. As in most other injunction cases, such relief was not available unless it could be said that legal relief was inadequate, as where the chattel is unique. In such a case replevin would prove inadequate if the defendant secreted the chattel, or removed it from the jurisdiction, so that the sheriff could not seize it. The defendant's ability to retain possession by posting a redelivery bond would defeat even the most urgent need in a replevin action. With these inadequacies of replevin in mind, the late Professor Van Hecke supported wide use of equitable replevin.[1] There are in fact occasional cases in which injunctions have been used to give the plaintiff possession of an unique or unusual chattel where the legal remedy is inadequate.[2] Where the legal remedy is perceived to be

---

14. See Del's Big Saver Foods, Inc. v. Carpenter Cook, Inc., 795 F.2d 1344, 1349 (7th Cir.1986); Robert E. Scott, Constitutional Regulation of Provisional Creditor Remedies: The Cost of Procedural Due Process, 61 Va.L.Rev. 807 (1975).

In *Del's Big Saver Foods,* supra, Judge Posner said in part:

A predeprivation hearing would confer benefits as well as impose costs; it would reduce the likelihood of an erroneous repossession order that might work a hardship to the debtor. But this danger is small where the creditor is required to put up a substantial bond * * *. Considering the importance of summary repossession as a creditor's remedy (and hence its value to nondefaulting debtors, who pay lower interest rates than they would have to do if creditors lacked good remedies in the event of default), [and other elements] we would be inclined * * * to hold that a procedure which provides for a bond and entitles the debtor to a prompt postdeprivation hearing is constitutionally adequate.

The excerpt is highly compressed.

15. § 34–1–9.1–4; N.Y.C.P.L.R. 7102(d).

§ 5.17(3)

1. Van Hecke, Equitable Replevin, 33 N.C.L.Rev. 57 (1954).

2. Yeargin Const. Co., Inc. v. Parsons & Whittemore Alabama Mach. & Serv. Corp., 609 F.2d 829 (5th Cir.1980); Burton v. Rex Oil & Gas Co., 324 Mich. 426, 36 N.W.2d 731 (1949) (goods not available in market, defendant refused to disclose whereabouts so that sheriff could not take them on a replevin writ); Steggles v. National Discount Corp., 326 Mich. 44, 39 N.W.2d 237, 15 A.L.R.2d 208 (1949) (return of car from finance company, court purported to see a risk of multiplicity of suits justifying equitable intervention); McGowin v. Remington, 12 Pa. 56 (1849); Pressed Steel Car Co. v. Standard Steel Car Co., 210 Pa. 464, 60 A. 4 (1904).

Cf. Ferry–Morse Seed Co. v. Food Corn, Inc., 729 F.2d 589 (8th Cir.1984) (preliminary mandatory injunction requiring defendant to turn over 6000 bags of unique seed corn pursuant to a contract).

The classic case is McGowin v. Remington, 12 Pa. 56 (1849). The chattels involved were maps and plans. Damages could not be mea-

adequate, on the other hand, the injunction is denied and plaintiff left to damages or replevin under the statutes.[3] The adoption of the revised replevin statutes with provisions for pre-seizure hearings, however, may eliminate the need for any separate equitable kind of claim. Indeed, there may be a general blending of equitable and legal approaches.[4]

Provisional Equitable Relief and Constitutional Requirements

If the plaintiff needs injunctive relief in recovering a chattel he usually needs immediate relief as well, so the claim is usually one for a temporary restraining order or a preliminary injunction. The preliminary injunction motion requires notice to the defendant and an opportunity to be heard, and hence clearly meets the constitutional requirement of notice and hearing.[5]

The temporary restraining order, however, is issued without notice to the defendant and without a hearing at which he takes part. As to such orders there may be at least a degree of constitutional doubt. But the restraining order under most procedures [6] is issued by a judge after taking at least informal evidence, and is followed by an almost immediate right to a hearing. These factors are probably sufficient to justify the temporary restraining order as a means of affecting possession.[7] Conversely, if notice could be given but is not,[8] or if a bond could have been posted but is not,[9] or if the defendant could have been provided with a prompt opportunity to seek dissolution of the order but was not,[10] the restraining order will be improper.

sured adequately for any dispossession period; the plans could not be replaced and damages would therefore not be adequate even if measurable; and the defendant was in the role of a trustee against whom equity was especially willing to act.

3. Charles Simkin & Sons, Inc. v. Massiah, 289 F.2d 26 (3d Cir.1961) (tools); Alger v. Davis, 345 Mich. 635, 76 N.W.2d 847 (1956) (merchandise); Haavik v. Farnell, 264 Ala. 326, 87 So.2d 629 (1956) (personal items).

4. Thus statutes may authorize not only a hearing in a replevin suit at law but also the use of in personam restraining orders. See West's Ann.Ind.Code 34–1–9.1–4(b). Under a revised-type replevin statute the court may invoke discretion to refuse a seizure order just as an equity court might. See Consolidated Edison Co. of New York, Inc. v. Haymer, 139 Misc.2d 95, 527 N.Y.S.2d 941 (1988). And conversely a restraining order may be used to initiate a seizure of property by the sheriff, so that what was traditionally an in rem action throughout can now begin in personam and end in rem. See Gozelski v. Wyoming County, 115 A.D.2d 1000, 497 N.Y.S.2d 562 (1985).

5. City of Signal Hill v. Owens, 154 Cal. App.3d 118, 200 Cal.Rptr. 925 (1984); cf. Attorney General v. Thomas Solvent Co., 146 Mich.App. 55, 380 N.W.2d 53 (1985) (defendant who received notice and had several hearings on preliminary injunction motion suffered no denial of due process merely because it could not take discovery).

6. See § 2.11 above.

7. State v. B Bar Enterprises, Inc., 133 Ariz. 99, 649 P.2d 978, 981 (1982) (abatement of bawdy house nuisance, specific facts must be shown, "only a court can issue the temporary restraining order, the order is of limited duration, and the restrained party can obtain an expeditious hearing"). The same idea has been used in support of the ex parte temporary restraining order where the defendant is prohibited from exercising a personal, as distinct from a property right. Marquette v. Marquette, 686 P.2d 990 (Okl.App.1984) (former husband enjoined from communicating with former wife, depriving him of visitation rights with children, but fact of hearing, fact that judge issues order, and fact that it is of limited duration together defeat due process argument).

8. Thompson v. Ramirez, 597 F.Supp. 726 (D.Puerto Rico 1984) (plaintiff must show, prior to the restraining order, that notice could not or should not have been given to the defendant, and if plaintiff fails to make this showing, issuance of the restraining order would violate due process).

9. Simpson v. Simpson, 524 So.2d 1124 (Fla.App.1988) (injunction reversible when no bond posted).

10. United States v. Spilotro, 680 F.2d 612 (9th Cir.1982); United States v. Perholtz, 622 F.Supp. 1253 (D.D.C.1985). See Gozelski v. Wyoming County, 115 A.D.2d 1000, 497 N.Y.S.2d 562, 563 (1985) ("The fact that the order was issued ex parte does not, by itself, deny plaintiff his property without due pro-

§ 5.18   Restitution in Money

§ 5.18(1)   Waiver of Tort and Suit in Assumpsit for Conversion

If the defendant converts chattels of the plaintiff and sells them, he is enriched by the sum he receives from the sale. If the defendant converts a gold watch worth $100 but sells it for $200, the plaintiff is allowed to recover not merely the $100 value of his watch, but the $200 gained by the tortfeasor. The recovery is allowed, not as compensation for loss but as restitution to prevent unjust enrichment.[1] It has been applied even against joint tortfeasors.[2] The right to recover for unjust enrichment is a substitute for the right to sue for tort damages, and presumably the right invested in the very person who could have maintained the claim for tort damages—that is, the person at whose expense the defendant was unjustly enriched.[3] The principle under which the tort victim may substitute an unjust enrichment recovery has been extended to the "conversion" of intangibles in some cases [4], and similarly, to the case of one who merely uses a chattel without converting it. In the latter case, the value of the use rather than market value is the measure of unjust enrichment.[5]

The option is with the plaintiff: he may sue for ordinary tort damages if that suits him, but he may obtain restitution of the proceeds if he prefers, as he presumably would when the tortfeasor's gain exceeds the plaintiff's loss.

cess of law" because plaintiff could have moved to vacate the restraining order).

§ 5.18(1)

1. "The touchstone of the rule is the moral obligation arising out of unjust enrichment to the tortfeasor." Western Nat. Bank of Casper v. Harrison, 577 P.2d 635, 642 (Wyo.1978). See generally, I G. Palmer, Law of Restitution § 2.2 (1978 & Supps.). Traditional expressions asserted that there is an implied in law promise to make payment, or by that the plaintiff is entitled to sue in assumpsit. These expressions are still used as ancient references to restitution. As to restitution for unjust enrichment generally, see §§ 4.1 et seq.

2. See Western Nat. Bank of Casper v. Harrison, 577 P.2d 635 (Wyo.1978). In that case a secured creditor and one who helped him avoid debtor's right to notice were joint converters of the chattel, a mobile home. The court held that the plaintiff-debtor's claim could proceed on a theory of waiver of tort and suit in assumpsit, with recovery measured by benefits to tortfeasors. It looks as if the court had in mind separate measurement of liabilities, however, based on separate net benefits.

3. The owner of the converted chattel would have the right to sue for tort damages and thus the right to sue for unjust enrichment instead.

The principle may have been overlooked in John A. Artukovich & Sons, Inc. v. Reliance Truck Co., 126 Ariz. 246, 614 P.2d 327 (1980), where temporary use of a chattel was in issue.

The owner of a crane who had leased it to another, was allowed to recover on an unjust enrichment from one who had used the crane without permission of either the owner-lessor or of the lessee. Since the owner-lessor had no right to use the crane while it was under lease, he was denied a tort recovery. But, without explanation, he was allowed a recovery for unjust enrichment, even though it would appear that defendant enriched himself at the expense of the lessee rather than the expense of the lessor. The court did not explain why the lessor was the proper plaintiff. However, the lessee had told the defendant-user that he would have to get permission from the plaintiff to use the crane, so perhaps the claim for unjust enrichment from use of the crane had passed back to the lessor.

4. Cablevision of Breckenridge, Inc. v. Tannhauser Condominium Ass'n, 649 P.2d 1093 (Colo.1982) ("conversion" of cable television feeds). But cf. Moore v. Regents of University of California, 51 Cal.3d 120, 271 Cal.Rptr. 146, 793 P.2d 479 (1990), cert. denied, ___ U.S. ___, 111 S.Ct. 1388, 113 L.Ed.2d 444 (1991) (no conversion of body cells could be found where patient knew body tissue was removed, even though he did not suspect it was removed for research and commercial development and subsequent cell-products; subsequently developed products from cells treated as not owned by patient).

5. See John A. Artukovich & Sons, Inc. v. Reliance Truck Co., 126 Ariz. 246, 614 P.2d 327 (1980); § 5.18(2).

Cases of this sort actually do arise because the tortfeasor has made a good bargain or has sold in a market that rose after the time at which conversion damages are figured.[6]

[*For additional discussion consult § 4.2(3) above and see this section in the Practitioner Treatise edition.*]

§ 5.18(2) Measure of Recovery in Assumpsit for Converted Chattels

Sale Price and Market Value

General rules. When the plaintiff is entitled to "waive the tort" and sue for restitution in a case of converted chattels, the normal measure of recovery is the benefit received by the defendant, not the loss to the plaintiff.[1] The benefit to the defendant in turn is generally measured by the proceeds from the defendant's sale of those chattels.[2] If the goods were not sold, the measure of recovery is the value of the goods [3] at the time and place of conversion,[4] or if the defendant uses the goods, then the value of their use by the defendant.[5] As in the claim for damages from conversion,[6] the plaintiff may be entitled to prejudgment interest from the time the duty to make restitution first arose—that is, from the time of conversion.[7] However, where the plaintiff recovers profits made by the defendant and not merely the defendant's gain from a single market transaction, the use-value of the plaintiff's converted property is represented by the profit recovery; a separate interest award on the profits themselves would be appropriate only from the time each unit of profit should have been paid to the plaintiff.

---

6. As reflected in § 5.13(2), conversion damages are traditionally measured at the time of conversion. This would leave the defendant with a gain if the value of the property rose after conversion. That section also reflects the fact that some but not all states adjust the time-of-conversion rule for damages claims when the value of the property has risen. A state may insist on the time-of-conversion rule for *damages* but still allow a waiver-of-tort-and-suit in assumpsit claim based on the tortfeasor's gains.

§ 5.18(2)

1. The benefit must be derived from the plaintiff's interests in the goods, but there need not be a corresponding loss to the plaintiff, or any realized loss at all. See, e.g., Olwell v. Nye & Nissen Co., 26 Wash.2d 282, 173 P.2d 652, 169 A.L.R. 139 (1946) where the plaintiff claimed restitution for the defendant's use of a machine which had been in storage. The plaintiff was not using the machine and was not aware of the defendant's use for years. Restitution for the benefit of the use was granted. See generally I.G. Palmer, The Law of Restitution § 2.10 (1978).

2. Rock–Ola Mfg. Corp. v. Music & Television Corp., 339 Mass. 416, 159 N.E.2d 417 (1959); Brittain v. Payne, 118 N.C. 989, 24 S.E. 711 (1896). See Shahood v. Cavin, 154 Cal.App.2d 745, 316 P.2d 700, 702 (1957)

("price received at such sale or * * * the value of the property * * *."); Welch v. Kosasky, 24 Mass.App.Ct. 402, 509 N.E.2d 919, 922 (1987); Annot., 97 A.L.R. 250, 274 (1935).

3. Conaway v. Pepper, 30 Del. (7 Boyce) 511, 108 A. 676 (1919); Hagberg v. Haas, 237 Or. 34, 390 P.2d 361 (1964); Walker v. Norfolk & W.R. Co., 67 W.Va. 273, 67 S.E. 722 (1910).

4. Felder v. Reeth, 34 F.2d 744, 97 A.L.R. 244 (9th Cir.1929); Bowen v. Detroit United Ry., 212 Mich. 432, 180 N.W. 495 (1920).

5. E.g., Olwell v. Nye & Nissen Co., 26 Wash.2d 282, 173 P.2d 652, 169 A.L.R. 139 (1946).

6. See § 5.15(2).

7. See § 3.6(2) above. Cf. Davis Cattle Co., Inc. v. Great Western Sugar Co., 544 F.2d 436 (10th Cir.1976) (defendant received plaintiffs' sugar beets under contract but failed to use good faith to estimate amounts immediately owing, prejudgment interest proper). But cf. Restatement of Restitution, § 156 (1937) (importing the narrow rules of damages law as to prejudgment interest but allowing interest when it is "required to avoid injustice"). When use rather than sale is the basis for restitution, interest might run from the different times at which the goods were used rather than from the date of conversion.

Variations: market value of goods sold. The rules are subject to variation as the facts warrant. In the leading case, *Felder v. Reeth,*[8] the converter had sold goods of substantial value for only $550. Since there was actually a sale, the normal recovery would be the sale price. But the plaintiff was allowed to claim the market value in an assumpsit suit rather than the limited sale price. In a narrow sense the defendant's benefit was only the $550 received rather than the more substantial value of the goods. A more realistic view, however, might be that the defendant had a benefit in his hands equal to the value of the goods; he merely chose to discard some of that benefit by selling the goods cheaply.[9] Consequently, the plaintiff can reasonably claim restitution measured by the value of the goods [10] and not by the sale price, at least where the defendant is a conscious wrongdoer.

Variations: subjective value to converter. The market value of goods converted is an objective measure; the sales price, though it might differ from market value, is in a sense also objective. But the goods might have special value to the converter that is not represented by market value or sales price. Some cases speak of "the value of the benefit" to the converter, which suggests that any special value to him would be an appropriate measure as well.[11] Where the special value is less than the exchange value of the goods, the plaintiff should be and presumably is entitled to recover the larger sum based on market value.[12] Some courts have said that special value to the converter is an inappropriate measure,[13] but others appear to have used special value when that value exceeded market.

Savings to the Defendant

The Olwell Case. The leading case involving special value to the converter was based on the special use value of the converted goods. In *Olwell v. Nye & Nissen Co.,*[14] the defendant used an egg-washing machine belonging to the plaintiff. The defendant made no claim of ownership and did not have the plaintiff's permission to use the machine. The defendant saved $10 per week in its production costs by using the machine for a total of 156 weeks, so that the use value to the converting defendant was $1560.

8. 34 F.2d 744, 97 A.L.R. 244 (9th Cir. 1929). Cf. Matter of Rothko's Estate, 43 N.Y.2d 305, 401 N.Y.S.2d 449, 372 N.E.2d 291 (1977) (fiducial breach, fiduciary liable for current value of paintings held as a result of self-dealing, not merely for market value at the time it took the paintings), discussed in § 9.3(4) below.

9. See Bowen v. Detroit United Ry., 212 Mich. 432, 180 N.W. 495 (1920), treating market value as a benefit, apparently on the ground that the converter could sell at market whether in fact he does so or not. This view treats "benefit" in restitution claims in a way analogous to damages in a *general* damages claim.

10. Shipman v. Penney, 268 Ark. 1096, 598 S.W.2d 450, 453 (1980) (Newbern, J. concurring, "I agree with Professor Dobbs that a fair result can be reached by refusing to limit assumpsit * * * and permitting recovery of the value of the converted item", concurring

views apparently actually a majority); see Bowen v. Detroit United Ry., 212 Mich. 432, 180 N.W. 495 (1920).

11. L.B. Menefee Lumber Co. v. McDonald, 122 Or. 579, 260 P. 444, 447 (1927).

12. See Bowen v. Detroit United Ry., 212 Mich. 432, 180 N.W. 495 (1920) where the defendant contracted to purchase coal from T at $6.10 per ton but unintentionally used the plaintiff's coal, which had a market value of $9.25 per ton. The plaintiff recovered at market rate of $9.25 rather than the $6.10 per ton rate, though the latter was the value to the defendant in the sense that it could purchase for this price.

13. Felder v. Reeth, 34 F.2d 744, 97 A.L.R. 244 (9th Cir.1929). Objective market measurement is supported in Woodward, Quasi–Contracts § 292 (19–13).

14. 26 Wash.2d 282, 173 P.2d 652, 169 A.L.R. 139 (1946).

The trial court awarded this sum and in principle [15] this was affirmed, although it appeared that the machine was never worth more than $600 and might have been worth as little as $50 on the market.

Observations on Olwell. *Olwell* may not have reached the best result. First, the plaintiff in *Olwell* had no realized losses and the recovery was in no sense a measure of the plaintiff's damages. Second, the defendant in *Olwell* was not held liable for rental value of the machine, which would have been a market or objective measure of recovery. Instead the defendant's liability was purely a subjective measure, based on "negative unjust enrichment" or the savings reaped by the particular defendant. And third, the benefit charged the defendant may not be the one it received. It saved $10 per week in comparison to the alternative of hand washing eggs. But if similar machines could be purchased on the market, the defendant's use of the machine did not save it more than the market cost of the machine itself.[16] If *Olwell* is wrong, it is not necessarily wrong because it used a subjective measure of the defendant's benefit but because there may have been no such benefit at all. If *Olwell* is meant to be punitive, the better method would be to impose punitive damages separately, since only quite accidentally could the unjust enrichment measure match the defendant's fault.

The Ablah case. In *Ablah v. Eyman,*[17] a case similar to *Olwell,* the converter took an accountant's working papers, using them to save very substantial sums he otherwise would have been required to spend for accountant's fees in connection with an Internal Revenue Service audit. The plaintiff lost no use of the papers and indeed they had no market value; but the plaintiff recovered the special subjective benefit reaped by the defendant in saving the costs of hiring an accountant. *Ablah* and *Olwell* are alike in using subjective measures of benefit and restitution, but they differ in one important respect. Since there was no alternative market for similar papers in *Ablah,* the converter there really did reap a benefit. Compared to the realistic alternatives, use of the papers saved him money. If the converter in *Olwell* saved money, it was probably no more than the market cost of the machine.

Profits of the Defendant From Use of Goods

Profits generally. If the converter does not merely sell the converted goods, but uses them in production of income, it is arguable that part of the profit can be identified as derived from the plaintiff's goods and that the profit is therefore the measure of the benefit. For example, if the defendant converts the plaintiff's machinery and uses it to increase production at a

---

15. The trial court limited the number of weeks to those within the statute of limitation period and the Supreme Court made a further adjustment to limit the recovery to the amount prayed in the complaint.

16. It might have saved the defendant even less than the market value, since the defendant might have purchased the machine, paid the price, used it for 156 weeks and still had an operating machine. That is, had the defendant purchased a machine, the defendant might have reaped the same savings in production for a cost of, say, $50, and might then still have had the machine which would allow it to reap even further savings. It is possible to imagine facts in which the defendant could not have purchased the machine on the market because of limitations in its financing, but that does not appear to be the case in *Olwell.*

17. 188 Kan. 665, 365 P.2d 181, 90 A.L.R.2d 766 (1961).

mine or factory, profits on the increased production may measure the benefit to the defendant. There are no doubt cases in which profits to the defendant from use of the plaintiff's goods would be an appropriate recovery, but claims for profits present two problems.

Measuring the benefit. First, as indicated in connection with the *Olwell* case, if the converted goods could have been purchased in the market, then the defendant may have benefitted by saving the market price of the goods; but it does not look as if he benefitted by making profits because the profits would have been equally available by purchasing goods. If the defendant is a conscious wrongdoer who has committed a serious wrongdoing, however, an appropriate measure of punitive damages—as distinct from restitution— may be disgorgement of all profits.

Attributing benefit to plaintiff's goods rather than to defendant's labor. Second, if the defendant does not merely sell the goods but uses them in a business, the "profit" earned by the defendant may have been the result of his own labor, investment, or ingenuity rather than the value of the plaintiff's goods. Even if the goods are actually sold, but the sale entails services, the sale price may reflect the defendant's services as well as the value of the goods. In such a case the sale price or profit should furnish no measure of the value of the plaintiff's goods and is not recoverable.[18]

§ 5.18(3) Constructive Trusts and Equitable Liens

Equitable Relief and Its Advantages

The ordinary action for conversion is one for damages "at law," and so is the assumpsit claim.[1] But in some instances the victim of conversion may be permitted to seek a purely equitable remedy such as a constructive trust or equitable lien.[2] Such remedies may be granted for the same underlying reason that applies in assumpsit claims—to prevent unjust enrichment of the converter. However, the claim for equitable relief may differ from the claims at law in important ways. The measure of recovery may be affected because the constructive trust may allow the plaintiff to trace his goods into new forms,[3] and to capture all the converter's gains, including profits.[4] The forum for trial may be affected because the constructive trust will ordinarily

---

18. See Ringele v. Terteling, 78 Idaho 431, 305 P.2d 314 (1956), cert. denied, 353 U.S. 988, 77 S.Ct. 1284, 1 L.Ed.2d 1142 (1957). Cf. Laurin v. DeCarolis Const. Co., Inc., 372 Mass. 688, 363 N.E.2d 675, 97 A.L.R.3d 1214 (1977) (vendor removed gravel and other items after contracting to sell, market value of gravel recoverable but not value added by defendant's labor in removing it). Where courts hold a converter liable in *damages* for the value of the converted property as enhanced by the converter's efforts, the same rule might be carried over to the restitution claim. As to the damages claim based on enhanced value see, e.g., Western Nat. Bank of Casper v. Harrison, 577 P.2d 635 (Wyo.1978).

An unusual example of the problem is suggested by Moore v. Regents of the University of California, 51 Cal.3d 120, 271 Cal.Rptr. 146, 793 P.2d 479 (1990), cert. denied, __ U.S. __, 111 S.Ct. 1388, 113 L.Ed.2d 444 (1991) where the defendants, acting as physicians and medical attendants, took unusual cells from the plaintiff's body and developed them into cell line of great potential commercial value, allegedly without the plaintiff's knowledge or consent. The court held that this was not a conversion.

§ 5.18(3)

1. See generally § 4.2 above.

2. Described generally in § 4.3 above.

3. As to tracing generally, see §§ 4.3(1), 4.3(2), and 6.1; also, among others, 4.5(3).

4. Operating profits are distinct from the gain made on a single sale or the rental value of the use. The assumpsit claim is usually thought of as allowing the plaintiff to get the proceeds of a sale of the converted goods, but not as allowing the plaintiff to recover profits earned by their use in a business.

invoke an equity trial without a jury.[5] The enforcement of any recovery may be affected because equitable decrees might be enforced by contempt powers.[6]

Relief Against Fiduciaries

The easiest case for equitable relief is that of the fiduciary who converts the beneficiary's goods. There is no difficulty in holding such a converter as a constructive trustee for the proceeds [7] of the converted goods and even for profits [8] made by his tortious activities. All of the rules of the constructive trust will apply, often to the plaintiff's advantage. He may, for instance, trace the converted goods into a new and more valuable product and in addition may gain relative advantages over other creditors.[9] Perhaps most important, he will have the advantage of a secured claim, a priority over other creditors as to any assets on which the constructive trust or equitable lien is imposed.[10] As already indicated, he has in addition whatever advantage that goes in his particular facts in having a non-jury trial.

Non-fiduciary Cases

English law tends to restrict the constructive trust remedy to cases of fiduciaries,[11] but in American law the constructive trust and other appropriate equitable relief can also be given when the converter is not a fiduciary but gains the plaintiff's property through fraud or duress.[12] Where the conversion is accomplished by out-and-out thievery, or by innocent mistake of a non-fiduciary, some early American authority held that a constructive trust could not be imposed on the proceeds of the converted property,[13] but the argument that a thief cannot be a trustee seems naive today and

5. As to jury trial in equity, see § 2.6.

6. See § 2.8 above.

7. Gray v. Sutherland, 124 Cal.App.2d 280, 268 P.2d 754 (1954) (corporate officers withdrawing corporate funds); Adams v. Fleck, 171 Ohio St. 451, 172 N.E.2d 126 (1961) (attorneys); Restatement of Restitution, § 138 (1937); Comment, Constructive Trusts, Thieves and Embezzlers as Constructive Trustees, 35 Mich.L.Rev. 798 (1937).

8. See Regal Ins. Co. v. Summit Guar. Corp., 324 N.W.2d 697, 705 (Iowa 1982); Restatement of Restitution § 202, especially Illustration 11 (1937). Most of the cases involve misuse of intangible, rather than conversion of tangible property. For example, an insider uses the employer's confidential business information. See, e.g., § 10.5 below. However, negative unjust enrichment—savings effected in a business—represent a form of profits. This kind of recovery has been allowed even in an action at law. See Olwell v. Nye and Nissen Co., 26 Wash.2d 282, 173 P.2d 652, 169 A.L.R. 139 (1946), discussed supra § 5.18(2).

9. See § 4.5.

10. See generally § 4.3 above. To illustrate briefly in the conversion context: Defendant converts plaintiff's horse, Sam, worth $5,000. Defendant sells Sam for $8,000 and invests the proceeds in the ABC Computer Company. It is now worth $10,000. Defendant owes creditors A and B a total of $20,000. Defendant has few assets other than the shares in ABC. If plaintiff pursues his claim at law, he and the other creditors will compete equally for the limited funds. If he is able to gain a constructive trust, he will be entitled to the proceeds of the horse; he will probably also be able to trace those to the stock and obtain that. The constructive trust (or equitable lien) on the stock will make him the owner or the holder of a claim fully secured by the stock. This will exclude creditors A and B from any participation in that fund, thus giving the plaintiff a priority.

11. See I George Palmer, Law of Restitution § 1.3 (1978).

12. E.g., Peoples Nat. Bank v. Waggoner, 185 N.C. 297, 117 S.E. 6 (1923) (gain achieved by inducing another to breach fiduciary obligation); Wallach v. Joseph, 420 S.W.2d 289 (Mo.1967), cert. denied, 389 U.S. 953, 88 S.Ct. 335, 19 L.Ed.2d 362 (1967) (land); Restatement of Restitution § 166 (1937).

13. Campbell v. Drake, 39 N.C. (4 Ired.Eq.) 94 (1844).

probably would not be followed.[14]

Reasons for Limiting Equitable Relief

There are, however, reasons in particular cases for denying or limiting equitable relief. Invocation of equitable remedies will ordinarily mean that a jury trial is denied; to say the least, this should not be done lightly.[15] If the policy against unjust enrichment can be served in an assumpsit action at law, it may be undesirable to use the constructive trust. In some cases the constructive trust or equitable lien remedies may operate to impair interests of other creditors against the defendant. It may be undesirable to give all of the thief's profit to the plaintiff if that will exhaust his assets and prevent his paying other creditors. These are reasons for caution about extension of the constructive trust, but they are not reasons for invariably limiting that remedy. When its value in preventing unjust enrichment outweighs its disadvantages, or when the disadvantages do not exist on the facts, there is no reason not to use such a remedy against a converter of any stripe.

Adequacy of Legal Remedy

Some equitable remedies, such as the injunction and the specific performance decree, have traditionally been denied when there is an adequate remedy at law. In contemporary law the adequacy test is chiefly important as a means of furthering policies like those just mentioned above.[16] For example, if the legal remedy is adequate, the plaintiff is left to pursue the claim at law where there will be a jury trial.[17] The adequacy test would also be one means of insuring that the victim of conversion does not, by claiming a constructive trust or equitable lien, obtain unfair priorities against other, equally deserving creditors.

Adequacy Test in Fiduciary Cases

The adequacy test is usually invoked when law (not equity) created the substantive right asserted by the plaintiff. In such a case the equity court added nothing to the right but did supplement the legal remedy if that remedy was inadequate. But in some instances equity (not law) created the substantive right on which the plaintiff relies. In those instances there was no need to discuss the legal remedy at all and the adequacy test could not be invoked to bar equitable intervention. Because equity created the substantive rights against fiduciaries, equity has always taken jurisdiction in claims against them without regard to the adequacy test. Thus if the plaintiff seeks a constructive trust against a fiduciary who converts goods, that claim will not be denied merely because the plaintiff might have done just as well by claiming in assumpsit.[18]

Is the Legal Remedy Adequate in Non-fiduciary Cases?

As against converters who are not fiduciaries, perhaps the equitable remedy should be denied when the claims at law will sufficiently serve the policy against unjust enrichment. If the converter has not sold the converted property at all, the plaintiff can ordinarily use replevin to recover the

14. See Newton v. Porter, 69 N.Y. 133 (1877); I George Palmer, The Law of Restitution § 1.3 (1978).

18. See I George Palmer, The Law of Restitution § 2.19 (1978); Note, 25 St. Johns L.Rev. 283 (1951).

goods in specie,[19] and this will capture any increase in the value of the goods. Even if the converter has passed the goods on to a third person, the remedy at law against that person is usually adequate or at least no worse than the constructive trust itself.[20] If the converter has sold the goods for a price in excess of their value, the plaintiff can capture this gain in the assumpsit action.[21] Though tracing is traditionally associated with the constructive trust or equitable lien, there is no reason why the plaintiff could not trace proceeds of his goods into the hands of third persons in a purely legal action in assumpsit.[22] The legal remedy is clearly not adequate compared to the equitable remedy whenever the trust or lien would give the plaintiff a priority, or when the trust would give the plaintiff a return of specific unique property not reachable at law, but in such cases there is a question whether the more effective equitable remedy appropriately protects the interests of third-party creditors.[23]

Judicial Response to Adequacy Test in Non-fiduciary Cases

In fact, some courts have declared broadly that the adequacy test is no barrier to a constructive trust,[24] and others have actually granted both the constructive trust [25] and the equitable lien.[26] Only scanty concern has been shown for the adequacy rule,[27] and the most important scholar in the field of restitution has concluded that relief will be granted without regard to it.[28] It does not seem likely that courts will withhold a constructive trust against a non-fiduciary, even though the assumpsit remedy might serve just as well in some cases.

21. See §§ 5.18(1) & 5.18(2) above.

22. Cf. Otis v. Otis, 167 Mass. 245, 45 N.E. 737 (1897). In *Otis* a trustee gave away his beneficiary's funds to Samuel, who gave the funds to his four daughters; none of these persons paid value. The original bill sought to recover an identified fund, presumably on a lien or trust theory. But the identity of the monies had been lost and it was no longer possible to trace the proceeds to any particular fund or res. The court, Holmes, J., nevertheless held that the plaintiff had a right to money compensation against those who had received parts of the fund. If the plaintiff had proceeded at law for a money judgment against the four daughters, it would presumably have been granted and it would have been adequate, too, except so far as it might fail to give the plaintiff an unfair priority over other creditors.

24. See Heckmann v. Ahmanson, 168 Cal. App.3d 119, 214 Cal.Rptr. 177 (1985).

25. See Newton v. Porter, 69 N.Y. 133 (1877); Fur & Wool Trading Co. v. George I. Fox, Inc., 245 N.Y. 215, 156 N.E. 670, 58 A.L.R. 181 (1927).

26. Humphreys v. Butler, 51 Ark. 351, 11 S.W. 479 (1889). In Lamb v. Rooney, 72 Neb. 322, 100 N.W. 410 (1904) Lamb knowingly purchased the plaintiff's stolen cattle and sold them along with cattle of his own. Some $600 of the proceeds was used to purchase other cattle. The court awarded the plaintiff an equitable lien for $600 on the newly purchased cattle, calling it a "resulting trust" lien.

27. In United States v. Bitter Root Development Co., 200 U.S. 451, 26 S.Ct. 318, 50 L.Ed. 550 (1905) the plaintiff sought a constructive trust and an equitable accounting. Plaintiff alleged that defendants stole its timber. The court held that a case for accounting had not been made out because defendants' books could be "perfectly well obtained by an inspection * * * in an action at law," and that no other ground existed for equity jurisdiction because "it is clear that the complainant has a plain, adequate and complete remedy at law * * * *."

28. I George Palmer, The Law of Restitution 2.19 (1978).

Chapter 6

INTERFERENCE WITH ECONOMIC RIGHTS

Analysis

Sec.
6.1   Misappropriation of Money—Tracing.
     6.1(1)   Conversion and "Assumpsit".
     6.1(2)   Constructive Trusts, Equitable Liens and Subrogation in General.
     6.1(3)   The Necessity of Tracing.
     6.1(4)   Mingled Funds.
     6.1(5)   Injunctive Recovery of Money—Freezing Assets.
6.2   Patent Infringement.
     6.2(1)   Substantive Background.*
     6.2(2)   Summary of Remedies.*
     6.2(3)   Compensatory Damages.*
     6.2(4)   Restitution, Including Infringer's Profits.*
     6.2(5)   Injunctive Relief and Destruction of Infringing Articles.*
     6.2(6)   Equitable Defenses.*
     6.2(7)   Attorney Fees.*
     6.2(8)   Punitive and Multiple Damages.*
6.3   Copyright Infringement.
     6.3(1)   Substantive Background.*
     6.3(2)   Summary of Remedies.*
     6.3(3)   Compensatory Damages.*
     6.3(4)   Restitution, Including the Infringer's Profits.*
     6.3(5)   Injunctive Relief and Destruction.*
     6.3(6)   Equitable Defenses.*
     6.3(7)   Attorney Fees.*
     6.3(8)   Punitive and Multiple Damages.*
6.4   Trademark Infringement.
     6.4(1)   Substantive Background.*
     6.4(2)   Summary of Remedies.*
     6.4(3)   Compensatory Damages.*
     6.4(4)   Restitution, Including the Infringer's Profits.*
     6.4(5)   Injunctive Relief and Destruction of Infringing Goods.*
     6.4(6)   Equitable Defenses.*
     6.4(7)   Attorney Fees.*
     6.4(8)   Punitive and Multiple Damages.*
6.5   Misappropriation of Intangible Work Product Not Protected by Copyright or Patent.
     6.5(1)   Misappropriation: Scope and Substantive Background.*
     6.5(2)   Privately Communicated Ideas: Submission of Ideas in Expectation of Payment.

* For the text of this section, see Dobbs, Law Treatise, Vol. 2 (§§ 6.1-11.10). of Remedies, Second Edition, Practitioner

Sec.

6.5(3) Publicly Communicated Ideas or Work Products: Misappropriation.

6.6 Interference With Contracts and Opportunities Generally.

6.6(1) Scope and Substantive Background.*

6.6(2) Damages.

6.6(3) Restitution.

6.6(4) Injunction and Specific Performance.

6.6(5) Efficient Breach and Remedies for Interference With Contract or Opportunities.*

6.7 Interference by Wrongful Acquisition of Property at Death of Another.

6.8 Interference by Commercial Disparagement or Injurious Falsehood.

6.8(1) Substantive Background.*

6.8(2) Damages.*

6.8(3) Injunctions.*

6.9 Interference by Unconstitutional Regulation of Land Use: "Regulatory Takings".

6.9(1) Substantive Background.*

6.9(2) Taking by Regulation.

6.9(3) Civil Rights Theories—Due Process or Equal Protection.*

6.9(4) Limiting Recoveries to Special Damages.*

6.10 Wrongful Discharge and Job Discrimination.

6.10(1) Scope, Background and Summary.

6.10(2) Common Law Wrongful Discharge.*

6.10(3) Statutory Wrongful Discharge: The Legislative Background.*

6.10(4) ____ The Remedies.*

6.10(5) Statutory Job Discrimination and Equity: Jury Trial.*

6.10(6) Statutory Job Discrimination and Equity: Discretion.*

6.10(7) Statutory Job Discrimination and Equity: Equitable Defenses.*

6.11 Lawyer Malpractice.

6.12 Bad Faith Breach of Contract.*

---

§ 6.1 Misappropriation of Money—Tracing

§ 6.1(1) Conversion and "Assumpsit"

Economic rights are most directly interfered with when money is misappropriated, by embezzlement, theft, forgery or otherwise. As a result of purely formal considerations no longer of any great consequence, some of the common law courts took the position that an action of trover for conversion of money would not lie unless there was an obligation to return some specific pieces of gold or the like.[1]

---

* For the text of this section, see Dobbs, Law of Remedies, Second Edition, Practitioner Treatise, Vol. 2 (§§ 6.1-11.10).

§ 6.1(1)

1. Orton v. Butler, 5 B. & Ald. 652, 106 Eng.Rep. 1329 (K.B.1822). But Lord Mansfield entertained an action in trover for conversion of a bank note in Miller v. Race, 1 Burr. 452, 2 Keny. 189 (1758).

In *Orton,* supra, Abbott, C.J., said: "The law has provided certain specific forms of action for particular cases, and it is of importance that they should be preserved; we ought therefore, to look with great jealousy to an innovation of this sort." Bayley, J.: "This is an innovation upon the old forms established by law, and therefore ought not to be allowed." The abolition of the forms of action and the adoptions of procedural codes and

The common law rule is still occasionally repeated, though usually with substantial qualification.[2] For the most part it is ignored altogether, and suits for "conversion" of money [3] and sometimes for "conversion" of even less tangible values,[4] are entertained in the courts. Even where the conversion action was not entertained, the plaintiff was not necessarily out of court; the "conversion" label could be disregarded [5] and the claim treated as a claim in assumpsit for money had and received.[6] This means that in some jurisdictions the plaintiff can simply recover on a conversion theory when money is improperly taken, while in others he can recover, but must do so on an assumpsit theory.

To say that one may be liable either in conversion or in assumpsit for misappropriation of money is not to say one in possession of another's money is invariably a converter or even that he is liable in assumpsit. Money is the lingua franca of trade and if it is to do its job, sellers of goods must feel free to accept it without determining its provenance. Consequently, one who takes stolen money in good faith is not a converter at all, even though that same one is a converter if he innocently buys a stolen watch.

It is also true that the plaintiff's right to recover on a conversion theory does not imply a right to use replevin for money. First, replevin cannot be used unless the particular tangible property can be identified.[8] Money represented by an account is not a tangible good at all; and though bills identifiable by serial number might be replevied, fungible goods, including monies that are not distinguishable from all other monies, is not subject to replevin.[9] Second, the plaintiff may not be entitled to specific monies even if he is entitled to their cash equivalent. The bank, as is often repeated, is not a bailee of the depositor's money and does not owe the depositor any specific res; it is merely a debtor for an equivalent sum, and consequently replevin would not lie to recover a deposit.[10]

§ 6.1(2) Constructive Trusts, Equitable Liens and Subrogation in General

[*For the text of this section, see the unabridged Practitioner Treatise edition.*]

rules in their place makes this observation obsolete.

3. Republic of Haiti v. Crown Charters, Inc., 667 F.Supp. 839 (S.D.Fla.1987) (funds of Haitian government allegedly taken by former President Duvalier); Haines v. Parra, 193 Cal.App.3d 1553, 239 Cal.Rptr. 178 (1987) ($4,000 in cash taken on pretense it would be used to recover property stolen from plaintiff by others); cf. Lane v. Dunkle, 231 Mont. 365, 753 P.2d 321 (1988) (checks payable to plaintiff forged by defendant); Shonberger v. Oswell, 365 Pa.Super. 481, 530 A.2d 112 (1987) (conversion of "proceeds" of sale of consigned goods; seemingly a conversion of credits).

4. Ocean Nat. Bank of Kennebunk v. Diment, 462 A.2d 35 (Me.1983).

6. Shahood v. Cavin, 154 Cal.App.2d 745, 316 P.2d 700 (1957); Hull v. Freedman, 383 S.W.2d 236 (Tex.Civ.App.1964).

8. Williams Management Enterprises, Inc. v. Buonauro, 489 So.2d 160 (Fla.App.1986).

9. "[A]s Blackstone noted, normally money is fungible property, like grain, cotton, etc., which, if commingled with other similar money, is incapable of specific identification and not the proper subject of replevin. When specific bills and coins are identifiable because of serial numbers or special markings, or because they are located uncommingled at a specific exclusive place or contained within [an] identifiable container, the bills and coins, so identifiable can be replevied." Williams Management Enterprises, Inc. v. Buonauro, 489 So.2d 160 (Fla.App.1986).

§ 6.1(3) The Necessity of Tracing

Tracing or Identification Required

The purpose of constructive trust, equitable lien and even subrogation, is to require restitution to prevent unjust enrichment. The idea is that the plaintiff's property has been found in the hands of the defendant and must be restored to the plaintiff, even if legal title has passed, and even if the property has undergone a change in form by reason of an exchange or otherwise.[1]

Although this "tracing" or identification of the plaintiff's property in a new form has been subjected to serious attacks and many proposals for reform,[2] its core applications are well accepted. In addition, ideas about tracing may be important in determining whether one remedial award duplicates another,[3] in determining a secured creditor's rights under the Uniform Commercial Code,[4] and in determining rights or liabilities in a variety of other cases.[5]

Tracing Monies; Debt vs. Constructive Trust

The conception behind the claim of constructive trust is that the property subjected to the trust (including property in the form of money) is somehow the plaintiff's property in spite of its changed form; and this naturally implies that the plaintiff must identify specific property which can be regarded by equity as belonging to him. If the only evidence is that the defendant obtained the plaintiff's money, the plaintiff has established a debt claim that can be pursued by an ordinary judgment at law but has not established a basis for a constructive trust or equitable lien on particular property.[6] On the contrary, the constructive trust or equitable lien may be

---

§ 6.1(3)

1. Typically there is a simple exchange: defendant uses plaintiff's funds to purchase property of some kind. Three situations may suggest the variations on simple exchange:

(1) *Subrogation situations.* When the funds are used to pay the defendant's debts to *T*, subrogation theories will find the plaintiff's property in the hands of *T* and restore the plaintiff by reviving *T*'s earlier claim against the defendant and giving it as an asset to the plaintiff. E.g., Wilson v. Todd, 217 Ind. 183, 26 N.E.2d 1003, 129 A.L.R. 192 (1940); Whalen v. Schumacher, 176 Wis. 441, 187 N.W. 169 (1922).

(2) *"Equitable conversion" situations.* Where the plaintiff has a contract right to receive title to Blackacre, which is destroyed by fire before the right can be exercised, it is sometimes argued that the insurance proceeds should go to the plaintiff. This argument entails tracing similar to the tracing used in constructive trust cases—plaintiff was entitled to Blackacre, and therefore entitled to the funds that have been substituted for Blackacre—but usually it will be presented in different terminology, namely, the terminology of equitable conversion. Cf. Skelly Oil Co. v. Ashmore, 365 S.W.2d 582 (Mo.1963).

(3) *Income situations.* The property is not fully exchanged but its *use* is exchanged for income, e.g., interest, in the case of money. The view is that interest or other earnings is the property of the owner of the fund in the same way that a calf is property of the owner of the cow.

2. See Oesterle, Deficiencies of the Restitutionary Right to Trace Misappropriated Property in Equity and in UCC § 9–306, 68 Corn. L.Rev. 172 (1983). Professor Oesterle develops the most thoroughgoing disapproval of tracing. He classes some other modern commentators as revisionists who seek more modest reforms, especially to prevent the victim from gorging on unearned gains while other creditors go hungry. He includes the first edition of this treatise and G. Palmer, Law of Restitution (1978) in the revisionist category. See Id. at 194. Tracing by UCC secured creditors, where constructive trust analogies are sometimes used, has been specifically criticized by other commentators. See Henning, Article Nine's Treatment of Commingled Cash Proceeds in Non–Insolvency Cases, 35 Ark.L.Rev. 191 (1982).

6. Money is treated differently from tangible property in this respect. If plaintiff deposits a book with defendant, the book still belongs to the plaintiff. If the plaintiff deposits

imposed only where the plaintiff's funds are themselves located and identified [7] or where they are traced into other funds or property.[8]

The rule is often expressed by saying that there must be a specific res, an identifiable thing or fund that can be regarded as the plaintiff's.[9] In modern law, tracing does not require a showing that specific coins or bills belong to the plaintiff,[10] but it does ordinarily [11] require a showing that plaintiff's funds can be identified by ordinary commercial practices in a specific account,[12] credit, property, or chose in action, which can be regarded not merely as a source from which the debt to the plaintiff can be paid, but as being in itself property of the plaintiff or property substituted for the plaintiff's funds or property.[13]

Swollen Assets

Under the rules just stated, a constructive trust or equitable lien is not warranted by a showing that the defendant obtained the plaintiff's monies and that he paid debts with it or is generally wealthier in some unspecified way.[14] There is some authority taking a more liberal view, holding that if

funds with a bank, the money becomes the bank's money and the bank is merely the debtor to the plaintiff. The depositor thus has no claim to a constructive trust on monies deposited in a general bank account. Huston v. Exchange Bank, 376 N.W.2d 624 (Iowa 1985); cf. Aebig v. Commercial Bank of Seattle, 36 Wash.App. 477, 674 P.2d 696 (1984) (deposits with travel agency toward trips, no constructive trust).

7. For example, defendant deposits A's funds in an account, but later withdraws the entire fund. Still later defendant deposits B's fund to the account. A has no equity in the account; B has an equity in the account enforceable by equitable lien or constructive trust. See Estate of Reece, 122 Misc.2d 517, 470 N.Y.S.2d 974 (Sur.1983).

11. A striking contemporary departure from ordinary tracing requirements has been authorized to favor the first spouse over the second when the remarrying spouse breaches his contract to insure himself in favor of the first spouse. Funds saved by allowing the lapse of the policy in favor of the first spouse cannot be traced to the purchase of a policy in favor of the second spouse. Nevertheless, in this and similar situations, important New York cases have imposed a constructive trust in favor of the first spouse and to the exclusion of the second. Rogers v. Rogers, 63 N.Y.2d 582, 483 N.Y.S.2d 976, 473 N.E.2d 226 (1984); Simonds v. Simonds, 45 N.Y.2d 233, 408 N.Y.S.2d 359, 380 N.E.2d 189 (1978).

12. A hotel uses 12 separate bank accounts for its operations. Sometimes funds from one account are moved to another as may be convenient. The plaintiff's funds are deposited to one account, which is then depleted. The plaintiff sought a constructive trust on the accounts as a group on the theory that they

should be considered to be "one general 'cash-in-banks' account." But held not in Connecticut General Life Ins. v. Universal Ins. Co., 838 F.2d 612 (1st Cir.1988). Cf. In re United Cigar Stores Co., 70 F.2d 313 (2d Cir.1934) (multiple bank accounts, tracing inadequate).

13. Aebig v. Commercial Bank of Seattle, 36 Wash.App. 477, 674 P.2d 696 (1984) is a good example. A travel agency received advance deposits from customers, long before any travel services were delivered. These were deposited in the agency's bank account. The agency owed money to the bank and the bank eventually used the agency's account as partial payment on the debt to the bank. The case essentially involved a claim by the agency's customers whose funds had gone to the agency and had been deposited in the bank account, that they were entitled to a constructive trust on the deposits, so that the bank had no right to use the account in payment of the agency's debt to the bank. The customers would be right if they had a right to recover the specific fund or account they deposited, see Gluth Bros. Const. v. Union Nat. Bank, 166 Ill.App.3d 18, 116 Ill.Dec. 365, 518 N.E.2d 1345 (1988); but they would be wrong if they had a right to recover only an equal sum of money as a debt. The court thought the latter to be the case, and accordingly there was no ground for a constructive trust. Customers paid money to the agency and the agency paid money to the bank, but the customers not being entitled to particular accounts or funds but only to a sum of money, could not trace "their" funds into the bank's hands. Once the customer paid the deposit they had no right to that particular deposit, though they did have a right to recover an equal sum.

14. Hoffman v. Rauch, 300 U.S. 255, 57 S.Ct. 446, 81 L.Ed. 629 (1937); In re United

the plaintiff's money has come into the defendant's hands, and he has paid debts with it, the defendant's assets were swollen or "augmented" by the plaintiff's money, and this would be sufficient for a trust or lien.[15]

If the swollen assets approach only operated to redress a wrong to the plaintiff, that approach would be accepted without dispute. But the effect of imposing a trust or lien is to give the plaintiff a priority over other creditors as to the property in question. A priority over other creditors can be justified if the property can be identified as a product of the plaintiff's funds. But if specific property cannot be identified as having been produced by use of the plaintiff's monies, there is no basis for giving the plaintiff a preference over all other creditors, whose funds at one time or another have likewise swollen the defendant's assets. The general rule that requires tracing of the plaintiff's funds into identifiable property, then, seems correct.

Circumstantial Evidence in Tracing

At the same time, circumstantial evidence may be sufficient to convince the trier of fact that the plaintiff's funds were in fact used to purchase identified property. The rule that requires tracing does not require the trier to eschew all rational inferences.[16]

§ 6.1(4) Mingled Funds

Tracing to a Commingled Fund

Proportionate share in the fund. A special tracing problem occurs when the plaintiff's monies are mingled with funds of the defendant or funds of others.[1] In the simplest situation, plaintiff's money is placed in defendant's bank account, along with defendant's funds and there are no withdrawals or additions to the account. The plaintiff is entitled to a lien on the commin-

---

Cigar Stores Co., 70 F.2d 313 (2d Cir.1934); Slater v. Oriental Mills, 18 R.I. 352, 27 A. 443 (1893); Want v. Alfred M. Best Co., 233 S.C. 460, 105 S.E.2d 678 (1958); State, Dept. of Nat. Resources v. Benjamin, 41 Colo.App. 520, 587 P.2d 1207 (1978).

15. Jones v. Chesebrough, 105 Iowa 303, 75 N.W. 97 (1898) (limited to cases where the misappropriated money paid debts that otherwise would have been paid from other funds of the wrongdoer). But reasons may be found not to apply this rule. See Huston v. Exchange Bank, 376 N.W.2d 624 (Iowa 1985).

One case is special. If the plaintiff's funds can be traced to the payment the defendant's debt to a specific person, *A*, then the plaintiff can claim whatever lien or other special right *A* might have had. This is the principle of subrogation. See Whalen v. Schumacher, 176 Wis. 441, 187 N.W. 169 (1922).

16. Thus in Atlas, Inc. v. United States, 459 F.Supp. 1000 (D.N.D.1978) Arlene Dohn embezzled funds, for a total of almost $400,-000, which she deposited in a bank account. During the embezzlement period, she made a

payment of $13,849.35 to pay off principal due on her home mortgage. During the embezzlement period she also made improvements of over $5,000, paid for by personal check. The trial judge as trier concluded that monthly payments on her house during the embezzlement period had to be treated as coming from her salary, but that the check of almost $14,-000, incommensurate with her salary, probably came from the embezzled funds, and likewise the improvements. To this extent, the victim of embezzlement was entitled to a lien or trust which gave it priority over the government's tax lien on the same house.

§ 6.1(4)

1. Analogous but distinct problems arise under the Uniform Commercial Code. See Barnes, Tracing Commingled Proceeds: The Metamorphosis of Equity Principles into U.C.C. Doctrine, 51 U.Pitt.L.Rev. 281 (1990) (arguing that courts should be suspicious of doctrines that create superior rights in a secured creditor at the expense of general creditors in insolvency, and that while commingling of proceeds is similar to commingling in

gled fund in the amount of his own monies traced to it.[2] The plaintiff is not ordinarily entitled to the entire fund; it is not a product of his money merely because it is mingled with his money, even though the defendant may have the burden of proving which segment belongs separately to him.[3]

Property purchased by use of the entire fund. A situation only slightly more complex arises when the defendant uses the entire[4] commingled fund to purchase property. In such a case, the plaintiff is not entitled to a constructive trust on the entire property purchased, but he is entitled to a trust for a share in the property proportionate to his share in the fund.[5] The rule simply carries into the property the characteristics of the fund that purchased it.

Rules for Tracing After Withdrawals

If the wrongdoer's account contains $100 of his own money plus $100 misappropriated from the plaintiff, "whose money"[6] is left when the wrongdoer spends $100 from the account? Courts have developed several different rules, fictions or presumptions[7] for dealing with this situation.

(1) First in, first out rule. The original English solution to this was to formulate a more or less arbitrary rule of First In, First Out.[8] Under this rule the rights of the parties depended on whether the victim's monies or the wrongdoer's monies were first deposited. If the wrongdoer deposited $100 of his own money first, then $100 of the victim's money, the first withdrawal was subtracted from the wrongdoer's money, as the first deposit. But if it happened that the first deposit was the victim's money, the first withdrawal was deemed to be a withdrawal of that money.

(2) Hallett Rule: wrongdoer's funds withdrawn first. A second rule was then developed by Jessel, M.R. in *Hallett's Estate*.[9] Under the *Hallett* rule the money withdrawn was presumed to be the money of the wrongdoer and not trust funds, regardless of the order in which deposits were made. Many cases support use of the *Hallett* presumption,[10] at least when the plaintiff

trust cases, there is a difference in duties owed in the commercial setting).

2. Estate of Liebman, 189 Misc. 282, 60 N.Y.S.2d 482 (1945) (insurance agent banked premium monies with own monies, insurance company had a charge against the funds so as to give priority over creditors; in addition, the fund, always owned by the insurance company, was not part of the agent's estate and hence not required to bear a share of administration expense); Restatement of Restitution § 209 (1937).

3. The cases have said the burden is on the defendant to show which portion of the fund is his. See Leigh v. Engle, 727 F.2d 113 (7th Cir.1984); Simonson v. McInvaille, 42 Wis.2d 346, 166 N.W.2d 155 (1969); 1 George Palmer, Law of Restitution § 2.13, p. 167 (1978).

5. See Provencher v. Berman, 699 F.2d 568 (1st Cir.1983); Marcus v. Otis, 169 F.2d 148 (2d Cir.1948).

8. Pennell v. Deffrell, 4 De G. M. & G. 372, 43 Eng.Rep. 551 (1853). The rule was derived

from Clayton's Case, a completely different factual setting. See McConville, Tracing and the Rule in Clayton's Case, 79 L.Q.Rev. 388 (1963).

9. Knatchbull v. Hallett, 13 Ch.Div. 696 (1880).

10. E.g., Central National Bank v. Connecticut Life Insurance Co., 104 U.S. (14 Otto 54) 54, 26 L.Ed. 693 (18–81); Hurricane Elkhorn Coal Corporation II, 32 B.R. 737 (W.D.Ky.1983) (bankruptcy); Peterson v. Redpath, 224 Neb. 845, 402 N.W.2d 648 (1987).

In addition to more traditional settings, the rule has been used regularly in UCC cases when a creditor's security has been sold but the creditor can identify the proceeds of the sale in a bank account which has been partially depleted. C. O. Funk & Sons, Inc. v. Sullivan Equipment, Inc., 89 Ill.2d 27, 59 Ill.Dec. 85, 431 N.E.2d 370 (1982) (UCC tracing claim by secured creditor after collateral was sold and proceeds deposited in active account, there is "a presumption that proceeds remain

seeks to impose a lien or trust on the fund itself [11] as distinct from the withdrawals. This rule worked satisfactorily when the victim was seeking to reach the bank account in which $100 remained. However, it might not seem so satisfactory a rule where the wrongdoer drew out $100 (presumed under *Hallett* to be his own) and invested it in securities whose value rose. The wrongdoer might later dissipate the remaining $100 in gambling, so that the only assets remaining would be those produced by the withdrawals. In this kind of case the *Hallett* presumption would mean that it was the wrongdoer's own money that was successfully invested while it was the victim's that was dissipated.[12]

(3) "Evidence" tracing to withdrawals. It would be possible to create a rule that reverses the *Hallett* presumption. Such a rule would always allow the plaintiff to trace his funds through withdrawals from the commingled account but would presume that the balance remaining in the account represents funds of the wrongdoer. No such rule of law seems to have been adopted, but courts do at times appear to suggest that tracing withdrawals is permitted on some occasions because evidence in the particular case warrants such a tracing.[13] The problem arises in the first place, however, because evidence does not in fact show (and is never likely to show) which particular dollars belong to the plaintiff. At most, the evidence may show that a withdrawal was treated as, or regarded as, a withdrawal of the plaintiff's funds. Whether such evidence of the wrongdoer's state of mind indicates anything more than his abstract conceptions about how the bookkeeping ought to run is doubtful, though there are no doubt cases in which it is entirely fair to trace to withdrawals rather than to the balance in the original commingled account.

(4) Option rule. In *In re Oatway* [14] the English court allowed the victim of misappropriated monies to trace them into a bank account and thence into a purchase of securities. The approach seems in effect to have fur-

---

in the account as long as the account balance is equal to or greater than the amount of the proceeds deposited"); Bank of Kansas v. Hutchinson Health Services, Inc., 12 Kan. App.2d 87, 735 P.2d 256 (1987) (similar). See also Aluminum Industrie Vaassen V.B. v. Romalpa Aluminum Ltd., [1976] 2 All.E.R. 552, [1976] 1 W.L.R. 676 (C.A.1976). See generally, Barnes, Tracing Commingled Proceeds: The Metamorphosis of Equity Principles into U.C.C. Doctrine, 51 U.Pitt.L.Rev. 281 (1990). In some of the UCC cases the courts have stated the *Hallett* rule and the lowest intermediate balance rule together in a collapsed form and have labeled the rule so stated as the lowest intermediate balance rule. In fact the rules stated in the cases are the rule in *Hallett's* case and the lowest balance rule.

When bankruptcy intervenes, and a secured creditor claims against a fund which includes proceeds of the security and other funds, the UCC provides a special and somewhat peculiar rule which has been described as "the malformed mouse." See Weinberg, The Malformed Mouse Meets the LIBR: Secured and Restitutionary Claims to Commingled Funds, 8 Annual Review of Banking Law 269 (1989)

(discussing the lowest balance rule and UCC § 9–306(e)(d)).

11. See, e.g., Estate of Redpath, 224 Neb. 845, 402 N.W.2d 648 (1987) (balance in account is subject to trust but withdrawals from account used to pay life insurance premiums was not); Moody v. Pitts, 708 S.W.2d 930, 937 (Tex.App.1986) ("When a trustee has commingled funds and has expended funds, the money expended is presumed to be the trustee's own").

12. If the desire is to hold the commingled account liable for the plaintiff's loss, and to do so in a way that gives the plaintiff a priority over other creditors, an equitable lien on the account would reach the same result without implying any inability to trace withdrawals from the account. See 5 A. Scott, Trusts § 517 (1967).

13. United States v. Banco Cafetero Panama, 797 F.2d 1154 (2d Cir.1986); In re Preston, 76 B.R. 654 (Bkrtcy.D.Ill.1987); Mitchell v. Dunn, 211 Cal. 129, 294 P. 386 (1930).

14. In re Oatway, Hertslet v. Oatway, [1903] 2 Ch. Div. 356.

nished the victim an option. If the wrongdoer deposited $100 of his own money with $100 of the misappropriated money and later spent $100 on securities that increased in value, the victim could treat the investment as having been made with his money and impose a constructive trust on the stock. On the other hand, if the wrongdoer withdrew $100 and made a bad investment or dissipated it, the victim could regard the remaining $100 in the account as his own and impose a lien on it. It is possible to interpret the *Hallett* rule as being in reality merely an option rule.[15] Some cases support this view under some circumstances, and there can be no fair objection to it even by unsecured creditors if the plaintiff is limited to a proportionate share of the asset purchased on withdrawal.[16] But some cases refuse to recognize even an option to trace to a proportionate share of the withdrawal; from *Hallett*'s fictional premise that funds on deposit after a withdrawal are the plaintiff's, these courts draw the fictional conclusion that the withdrawn funds are not the plaintiff's at all, even in part.[17] A federal decision[18] may have adopted a kind of modified option rule in determining whether monies were "traceable proceeds" from illegal drug transactions.

(5) The Restatement Proportionate Shares Rule. The Restatement of Restitution,[19] which has received some support in the cases,[20] has it that the plaintiff has an option to impose an equitable lien on the fund and any monies traced out of it, or in the alternative to impose a constructive trust instead. The trust may be imposed on the fund itself and on traceable monies withdrawn from it, but in either case, the constructive trust is

---

15. Professor Palmer believes that the *Hallett* rule does not prevent the plaintiff from tracing to withdrawals and that he should be permitted to do so. In his view, the *Hallett* rule is really a rule that the wrongdoer acted rightly, so that if he purchased an asset with the withdrawn funds instead of dissipating them, he is to be regarded as doing so on behalf of the victim or beneficiary. The effect is that the victim can "trace" his monies into a commingled fund and also through any withdrawals. George Palmer, 1 The Law of Restitution § 2.16, p. 203 ff. (1978).

16. See Republic Supply Co. of California v. Richfield Oil Co., 79 F.2d 375 (9th Cir.1935) (tracing to assets purchased with mingled fund, limited only by fund's low balance).

Hallett itself would clearly give the plaintiff an option when the commingled fund is so reduced by withdrawals that under the *Hallett* rule only the plaintiff's funds remain when the final withdrawal is made for the purchase of the asset which the plaintiff now claims. See Bell v. Killian, 266 Ala. 12, 93 So.2d 769 (1957).

The Restatement proportionate share rule would clearly give the plaintiff the option to trace to assets purchased with withdrawals, but only a proportionate share. See Massachusetts Bonding & Ins. Co. v. Josselyn, 224 Mich. 159, 194 N.W. 548 (1923).

17. E.g., Covey v. Cannon, 104 Ark. 550, 149 S.W. 514 (1912). See generally, V.A. Scott, Trusts § 517.1 (1967). Cf. Loring v.

Baker, 329 Mass. 63, 106 N.E.2d 434 (1952) (commingling of funds of different beneficiaries).

Estate of Redpath, 224 Neb. 845, 402 N.W.2d 648 (1987) involved a conversion of over $45,000, the commingling of these funds with personal monies, and the payment of insurance premiums from the commingled account. The court rejected the plaintiff's effort to trace the withdrawal into the premiums and hence into the insurance proceeds. It gave two reasons, one of which was that the withdrawal should be attributed to the funds of the wrongdoer so far as possible, that is, the *Hallet* rule as narrowly construed. It approved a judgment for the amount of the conversion, but not the constructive trust sought against the life insurance proceeds.

18. United States v. Banco Cafetero Panama, 797 F.2d 1154 (2d Cir.1986).

19. Restatement of Restitution §§ 211, 212 (1937).

20. Cf. Provencher v. Berman, 699 F.2d 568 (1st Cir.1983) ("The [plaintiff] is entitled to an undivided share of the property equivalent to the proportion which his funds bore to the total amount * * * used by the [defendants] to buy the house"); Marcus v. Otis, 169 F.2d 148 (2d Cir.1948) ("he is liable only for a proportionate part of the profits realized based upon the ratio of the amount of money misappropriated to the original commingled mass").

imposed only to the extent of the plaintiff's proportionate share of the fund. For example, if the embezzler takes $5,000 of the plaintiff's monies and deposits them in an account containing $10,000 of the embezzler's own funds, the plaintiff's share is $^5/_{15}$ or $^1/_3$. If the embezzler withdraws $6,000 and invests it in a winning horse which pays 10 to one, the plaintiff may have a constructive trust on the $60,000 proceeds (if they are traced), but only for his proportionate share, one-third. He likewise gets a proportionate share of the bank balance. Professor Palmer has pointed out that the Restatement position is not clear, however, about how to work the proportion rule when there have been untraceable withdrawals and new deposits.[21]

Limits on Tracing to a Fund Partially Depleted and Restored—The Lowest Balance Rule

Trust or lien on fund's lowest balance. When the plaintiff's funds are commingled in deposit with funds of the defendant who first makes withdrawals and then deposits of his own funds, a special problem arises. The lowest balance rule states that the plaintiff can never trace to a sum greater than the lowest balance in an account between the time of the deposit and the time of the tracing. The wrongdoer deposits $1,000 of his own money and $1,000 of the plaintiff's in an account. (At this point, any of the rules would give the plaintiff at least an equitable lien for $1,000.) The wrongdoer then withdraws all but $100. The wrongdoer then makes a new deposit of $1900. The account balance is exactly as it was when the commingling first took place. But under the lowest intermediate balance rule, the plaintiff is not entitled to a lien for the $1,000; all but $100, of the plaintiff's monies have been withdrawn. The new deposits do not belong to the plaintiff. They are funds of the wrongdoer (or perhaps untraceable funds from other victims). The plaintiff in such a case is entitled to claim the full $1,000 as a general creditor, but not entitled to claim a lien or trust for any more than the lowest balance, $100.[22]

Denial of recovery where low balance not provable. An additional consequence of the lowest balance rule is that, unless there is evidence to show the amount of the low balance, the plaintiff may recover nothing at all, on the view that without such evidence, the plaintiff's funds have not been identified in the account.[23]

Computing low balance. In active accounts it may be literally impossible to determine the low balance because the exact times of deposits and withdrawals cannot be known. One way to figure the lowest balance is to

21. I George Palmer, Law of Restitution §§ 2.16, 2.17 (1978).

22. E.g., Connecticut General Life Ins. v. Universal Ins. Co., 838 F.2d 612 (1st Cir.1988); Powell v. Missouri & Arkansas Land & Min. Co., 99 Ark. 553, 139 S.W. 299 (1911).

23. C.O. Funk & Sons, Inc. v. Sullivan Equipment, Inc., 89 Ill.2d 27, 59 Ill.Dec. 85, 431 N.E.2d 370 (1982); see Republic Supply Co. of California v. Richfield Oil Co. of California, 79 F.2d 375, 378 (9th Cir.1935) (prima facie case made when claimant showed misappropriation, commingling, lowest intervening

balance and certain elements peculiar to the case). Contra, Ex parte Alabama Mobile Homes, Inc., 468 So.2d 156 (Ala.1985) (allocating the burden to the debtor to show an intervening low balance less than the amount claimed). As to the special UCC rule for "insolvency proceedings," see Weinberg, The Malformed Mouse Meets the LIBR: Secured and Restitutionary Claims to Commingled Funds, 8 Annual Review of Banking Law 269 (1989) (discussing the lowest balance rule and UCC § 9–306(e)(d)).

examine detailed bank records for early posting of debits and credits,[24] but in a well-known federal case, the court took the practical view that where there are many deposits and withdrawals on a daily basis, daily closing balances would accurately enough measure the lowest balance.[25] Beyond this, however, any given series of credits and debits to an account may be ambiguous or capable of various interpretations. Some charges against an account are treated as depleting or reducing the account, but others may be treated as mere bookkeeping entries that do not reflect the underlying reality.[26] But since the tracing involved in this section does not involve any tracing of tangible goods, there *is* no "underlying reality"; the bookkeeping entries are everything and the only reality is an accountant, dancing on the point of a pen. This is, in fact, the difficulty of constructing a rational tracing scheme in this area.

Wrongdoer's purpose to restore trust funds. An exceptional case arises when the wrongdoer declares that he makes the new deposit in satisfaction of his duty to restore the plaintiff's funds. In such a case the wrongdoer may become a sort of trustee of the new deposit as well as the lower balance, with the result that the plaintiff has a trust or lien on the low balance plus the newly declared trust funds.[27] Such a declaration, actual or implied, however, may simply operate to allow the wrongdoer to choose which among his victims and creditors will be fully repaid, and probably should not be given automatic effect if the wrongdoer is insolvent, which is very often the case.

Mingling Funds of Several Victims

When the wrongdoer commingles funds of several victims with the funds of each other rather than with his own funds, some of the complexities of tracing may be diminished. It may be that an account will contain funds traceable to victims as a class but not traceable to any particular victim. In such a case, funds belonging to victims as a class may be treated as a unit subject to a constructive trust or equitable lien and unavailable to general creditors.[28] The portion of the fund identifiable to the victims can then be pro rated among the victims on the ground that they are all in the same boat and that there is no basis for rescuing one at the expense of the others.[29]

24. Utica Sheet Metal Corp. v. J.E. Schecter Corp., 53 Misc.2d 284, 278 N.Y.S.2d 345 (1967).

25. Republic Supply Co. v. Richfield Oil Co., 79 F.2d 375 (9th Cir.1935). But in In re Seneca Oil Co., 76 B.R. 813 (W.D.Okl.1987) the court treated a deposit as part of the account when it was evidenced by the bank's records but not actually posted until the following day.

26. E.g., In re Seneca Oil Co., 76 B.R. 813 (W.D.Okl.1987).

27. See Mickelson v. Barnet, 390 Mass. 786, 460 N.E.2d 566 (1984) (embezzled funds; the embezzler's documents, as reformed by court, amounted to declaration of trust in certain of his assets; this may establish priority over United States' claim for taxes); Baker v. New York Nat. Exchange Bank, 100 N.Y.

31, 2 N.E. 452, 53 Am.Rep. 150 (1885) (bank account designed as trust account).

28. See In re Teltronics, Ltd., 649 F.2d 1236 (7th Cir.1981); In re Heston Oil Co., 63 B.R. 711, 715 (Bkrtcy.N.D.Okl.1986) ("withdrawals drew upon the monies of all trust claimants in the account").

29. See In re Walter J. Schmidt & Co., 298 F. 314 (S.D.N.Y.1923); United States v. Benitez, 779 F.2d 135 (2d Cir.1985); Ruddle v. Moore, 134 U.S.App.D.C. 3, 411 F.2d 718 (1969) (victims of a confidence man, who mingled their contributions, to share pro rata); Estate of Reece, 122 Misc.2d 517, 470 N.Y.S.2d 974 (Surr.1983); Annot., 17 A.L.R.3d 937 (1968). The ground for this result is arguably applicable as well to any case in which the tracing presumptions are used to the disadvantage of general creditors. The Supreme

When the commingled fund has increased in value, however, there may be reasons in the facts of particular cases to share the gains among some contributors to the fund while allowing others to recover only a lien for what they have lost.[30]

Assessing the Tracing Problem

The limits set by the lowest balance rule cause no serious problems, but every one of the methods for tracing commingled funds can present a problem on some sets of facts. It makes sense in all cases to force the wrongdoer to disgorge his profits, even when that puts the plaintiff in a better position than if he had never been wronged at all. But in many instances a plaintiff's recovery of profits is *not* at the wrongdoer's expense but at the expense of other creditors.[31] If the wrongdoer has limited assets, it may be best to use them to pay actual claims of all creditors, rather than to pay the plaintiff a "profit," the effect of which is to exhaust assets and to deny other creditors any recovery at all.[32] Professor Sherwin has argued in line with this that the constructive trust in bankruptcy should be limited to cases in which, without the constructive trust, the bankruptcy's creditors would be unjustly enriched, which would ordinarily require tracing to specific assets.[33]

To deny the plaintiff a recovery of the wrongdoer's profit in order to save assets for other creditors is not necessarily to refuse appropriate punishment of the wrongdoer.[34] The court, denying a constructive trust that would give the plaintiff the embezzler's profits and defeat the hopes of other creditors, could still render a money judgment against the wrongdoer for those profits, so that if he acquired other assets, he would be liable to pay the plaintiff. The court might most appropriately, therefore, focus on the particular situation it faces in a particular case, in an effort, especially appropriate to remedial law, to maximize everyone, or at least all innocent parties.[35]

§ 6.1(5) Injunctive Recovery of Money—Freezing Assets

Statutes authorizing attachment, garnishment, or *lis pendens*, sometimes permit the plaintiff to attach property or funds of the defendant before

Court has held that the *Hallett* rule cannot be applied to permit some of the victims to "trace" funds at the expense of others. Cunningham v. Brown, 265 U.S. 1, 44 S.Ct. 424, 68 L.Ed. 873 (1924). See, discussing *Cunningham*, Sherwin, Constructive Trusts in Bankruptcy, 1989 U. of Ill.L.Rev. 297, 318 (1989).

31. "It is wrong to begin analysis of a constructive trust claim in bankruptcy, as bankruptcy courts often do, with the assumption that the claimant is entitled to priority as the equitable owner of the property she claims. The claimant does not own the property unless the court grants the remedy. If the court places her ahead of general creditors, it must be because general creditors would be unjustly enriched by sharing the property." Sherwin, Constructive Trusts in Bankruptcy, 1989 U. of Ill.L.Rev. 297, 339 (1989).

32. See Sherwin, Constructive Trusts in Bankruptcy, 1989 U. of Ill.L.Rev. 297, 339 (1989). The policy becomes more technically complex when creditors are divided into two classes in bankruptcy, secured and unsecured. Conceivably one might wish to provide more protection for secured creditors in cases of doubt generated by commingling. See Weinberg, The Malformed Mouse Meets the LIBR: Secured and Restitutionary Claims to Commingled Funds, 8 Annual Review of Banking Law 269 (1989) (discussing the lowest balance rule and UCC § 9–306(e)(d)).

33. Sherwin, Constructive Trusts in Bankruptcy, 1989 U. of Ill.L.Rev. 297 (1989).

34. See In re Heston Oil Co., 63 B.R. 711, 716 (Bkrtcy.N.D.Okl.1986) ("the result is *not* to reward Heston for its own wrongdoing, for Heston remains liable to these claimants as well as to other creditors").

trial and before the plaintiff has judicially established any rights against the defendant. A suit to put defendant's assets in receivership may accomplish the same thing.[1] So may an injunction requiring the defendant to create a fund for payment of a potential tort judgment.[2]

One effect of such relief is to freeze the defendant's funds or hold the other property until a decision can be reached on the merits and thus to prevent dissipation or removal from the jurisdiction. Another is to put the defendant under great hardship and perhaps under considerable pressure to pay off the claim whether it is just or not.[3] Attachment statutes normally permit such provisional relief only under extremely limited circumstances. For example, attachment might be permitted to reach funds or property of a defendant who is about to remove property from the state to defraud creditors, but not permitted for a general money claim against a resident defendant.[4]

The plaintiff may seek to avoid the limits of the attachment statute by applying for a temporary restraining order or preliminary injunction and claiming that the remedy under the statute is inadequate. But the argument that the attachment statute is inadequate is an invitation to subvert the authority and protective limits of the statute. Courts have often refused to grant freeze orders when the plaintiff claims an ordinary tort or debt claim and cannot prove the special grounds for attachment or garnishment under the statute,[5] even though the attachment remedy might be "inadequate." Nor have courts been quick to find special statutory authorization for any general sequestration of funds.[6] The principle applies regardless of the parties' alignment procedurally or the terminology invoked: a party cannot impose a judicial "escrow" on disputed funds any more readily than he can impose an injunctive freeze order.[7]

Occasionally the plaintiff will succeed in securing a provisional freeze order to protect his potential general money claim, merely on the ground that the remedy at law under an attachment or similar statute is inadequate,[8] or on the ground that the court is enforcing a regulatory statute

§ 6.1(5)

4. E.g., West's Ann.Cal.Civ.Proc.Code § 485.010 (great or irreparable harm if attachment not issued); West's Fla.Stat.Ann. § 76.04 (danger of fraudulent transfer of property, removal from state); S.H.A. ch. 110, ¶ 4–101 (debtor concealing him or herself, about to depart the state or remove property and similar grounds); N.H.Rev.Stat.Ann. 511–A:8 (danger that property would be damaged, destroyed, concealed or removed); N.Y.—CPLR 6201; S.D. Codified L. 21–17A–3.

5. De Beers Consol. Mines v. United States, 325 U.S. 212, 65 S.Ct. 1130, 89 L.Ed. 1566 (1945); In re Fredeman Litigation, 843 F.2d 821 (5th Cir.1988); Exchange Nat. Bank of Chicago v. Harris, 126 Ill.App.3d 382, 81 Ill.Dec. 277, 466 N.E.2d 1079 (1984) (no injunction against distribution of trust when the plaintiff's claim was general debt claim rather than claim against particular identified funds).

Similarly, an equitable order to pay a debt before liability is finally established is refused. Sims v. Stuart, 291 Fed. 707 (S.D.N.Y.1922) (L. Hand, J.). But cf. Friends for All Children, Inc. v. Lockheed Aircraft Corp., 241 App.D.C. 83, 746 F.2d 816, 46 A.L.R.4th 1113 (1984) (defendant ordered to create fund for payment where liability but not amount had been adjudicated).

8. EBSCO Industries, Inc. v. Lilly, 840 F.2d 333 (6th Cir.1988). Some cases might be read to support the award of preliminary relief, but their facts differ materially from the usual freeze-order cases. See Tri–State Generation and Transmission Ass'n, Inc. v. Shoshone River Power, Inc., 805 F.2d 351 (10th Cir.1986) (provisional injunctive order to prevent sale of entire assets to particular buyer in regulated industry situation). Cf. Foltz v. U.S. News & World Report, 760 F.2d 1300 (D.C.Cir.1985) (recognizing that it might be proper to enjoin a cash distribution from a profit-sharing plan if that distribution would jeopardize plaintiffs'

which in general terms authorizes injunctive relief.[9] But the attachment statute itself is limited by constitutional rights of the defendant to receive due process, so to say that a freeze order is justified because attachment cannot be used may raise serious constitutional questions.[10] The most that can usually be said in favor of the freeze order to secure the plaintiff's debt claim is that the "inadequate remedy" reasoning is not enough; preliminary relief of this kind is not to be given in private cases unless there is a serious threat of loss to the plaintiff,[11] unless the defendant's property[12] and due process rights[13] can be respected, and the freeze order will not interfere with rights or priorities of other creditors or subvert a clear policy of the statutes.[14]

When the plaintiff can assert, not merely that the defendant owes him money and may dissipate his assets, but that the plaintiff equitably owns the funds in issue through a constructive trust or otherwise,[15] courts appear to be open to the need for provisional relief, and in such cases may issue a temporary restraining order[16] or a preliminary injunction[17] barring expenditure of the disputed trust funds. On the same principle, if the plaintiff has funds which are payable to the defendant under an agreement which the plaintiff seeks to rescind, the court may relieve the plaintiff of any obligation to pay those funds to the defendant until a decision can be made as to

retirement rights under a federal statute, ERISA).

9. Securities and Exchange Com'n v. Unifund SAL, 910 F.2d 1028, 1041 (2d Cir.1990) ("Congress has authorized the Commission to obtain preliminary injunctive relief upon a 'proper showing' "). The *Unifund SAL* case also bore a little resemblance to the constructive trust cases discussed below, in that the plaintiff claimed disgorgement of the defendant's profits from insider trading.

10. Major factors in justifying pre-trial provisional remedies have been (1) whether a serious threat was shown that the defendant might transfer, encumber, or secrete the fund or property in the absence of provisional relief; (2) whether the plaintiff claimed a preexisting interest in the fund or property, see the paragraph "Grant of injunctive orders to freeze funds in equitable ownership claims," below; (3) whether judicial supervision or adjudication is provided; (4) whether effective post-deprivation hearings are available to undo the attachment; (5) whether the dispute was highly factual or on the contrary lent itself to documentary proof. See Connecticut v. Doehr, ___ U.S. ___, 111 S.Ct. 2105, 115 L.Ed.2d 1 (1991); § 5.17(2) above.

11. See Connecticut v. Doehr, ___ U.S. ___, 111 S.Ct. 2105, 2115, 115 L.Ed.2d 1 (1991) (recognizing that a serious threat to transfer property or encumber it would be an exigent circumstance warranting ex parte attachment in some cases, but insisting that without the threat such an attachment was unconstitutional).

12. As where the plaintiff posts adequate security and the assets frozen represent no unique opportunity for the defendant. E.g., Deckert v. Independence Shares Corp., 311 U.S. 282, 61 S.Ct. 229, 85 L.Ed. 189 (1940).

13. See § 5.17(2) supra.

14. Cf. Douglas Laycock, The Death of the Irreparable Injury Rule 76–77 (1991).

15. It would seem that the plaintiff must claim specific, identifiable assets or funds, but the term "constructive trust" is not always necessary to such a claim. The Supreme Court has spoken of a "preexisting interest" in the property or fund as a factor helping to justify a provisional ex parte remedy. See Connecticut v. Doehr, ___ U.S. ___, 111 S.Ct. 2105, 115 L.Ed.2d 1 (1991).

16. Silverman v. Blaustein, 369 So.2d 86 (Fla.App.1979) (plaintiff claimed virtual ownership of funds and that defendant had "secreted" the funds in her personal bank account through use of a power of attorney); cf. Teferi v. Dupont Plaza Associates, 77 Md.App. 566, 551 A.2d 477 (1989) (ex parte order issued and continued, not clear whether plaintiff claimed that embezzled funds were traceable to frozen accounts).

17. Republic of Philippines v. Marcos, 806 F.2d 344 (2d Cir.1986); Federal Sav. & Loan Ins. Corp. v. Dixon, 835 F.2d 554 (5th Cir. 1987); USACO Coal Co. v. Carbomin Energy, Inc., 689 F.2d 94 (6th Cir.1982); Heckmann v. Ahmanson, 168 Cal.App.3d 119, 214 Cal.Rptr. 177 (1985).

ownership.[18]

This idea seems to have been extended in some cases to hybrid claims like those for equitable accounting. Equitable accounting for profits resembles the constructive trust in that the plaintiff traces the defendant's profits to the use of the plaintiff's property. But they differ in that the plaintiff need not identify any particular account or fund of money as representing those profits. So the plaintiff does not own any particular account of the defendant. The resemblance to the constructive trust, however, leads to the belief or the fiction that the case is an equitable ownership case so that a freeze order is justified.[19]

In addition, statutes such as those dealing with marital rights of divorcing parties may authorize freeze orders to preserve marital assets pending the divorce decree or settlement.[20] When the defendant's liability is established and only the amount remains in question, the plaintiff does not own any particular fund or portion of the defendant's assets. Nevertheless, an injunction that secures the plaintiff's rights or even requires payment, might be justified if the amount funds frozen or paid were clearly less than the defendant's total obligation.[21]

The terms of the injunction may present additional issues. Sometimes the bank or other depositary is made a party and is enjoined from paying out the funds until the issue can be resolved in court. When the assets in question are used in trade, as with the stock of goods or with funds used by a defendant in the business of buying and selling, care must be exercised in drafting the injunction so as to avoid destroying working capital.[22] In any event some provision for daily expenses and even extraordinary expenses

18. American Re–Insurance Co. v. MGIC Inv. Corp., 73 Ill.App.3d 316, 29 Ill.Dec. 269, 391 N.E.2d 532 (1979) (permitting plaintiff to deposit in court all funds due defendant under an agreement which plaintiff was seeking to rescind, noting that the funds in issue were the very funds covered by the agreement, not "irrelevant" collateral monies, i.e., the plaintiff claimed the specific funds in issue, not merely a general debt).

19. In Reebok International Ltd. v. Marnatech Enterprises, Inc., 737 F.Supp. 1521 (S.D.Fla.1989) the court froze the defendant's assets pending trial in order to preserve its power to order an effective accounting for profits in a counterfeit trademark case. In distinguishing *De Beers*, supra note 5, the court appeared to say that tracing in the accounting claim was like that in a constructive trust claim and that the plaintiff was entitled to the specific funds being frozen:

> In this case, plaintiffs are entitled to an accounting of profits, which is an equitable remedy creating a right of the claimant to "his" money which has been inequitably retained by the defendant. It creates under the law a "fund" of money which the plaintiff is recovering, his diverted profits. Thus the assets sought to be frozen are part of the subject of the action. The *De Beers* court

acknowledged that pre-judgment orders freezing assets can be issued when the injunction is granted "with respect to a fund or property which would have been the subject of the provisions of any final decree" in the case.

20. See, e.g., Leibowits v. Leibowits, 93 A.D.2d 535, 462 N.Y.S.2d 469 (1983). This kind of statutory authorization seems to fit the same general pattern—that is, the plaintiff is claiming equitable ownership. The plaintiff is not, however, normally limited to an order freezing assets that can be identified as hers or his. Instead, the statute may authorize a freeze of all, or substantially all the marital assets until a determination can be made.

21. Friends for All Children, Inc. v. Lockheed Aircraft Corp., 241 App.D.C. 83, 746 F.2d 816, 46 A.L.R.4th 1113 (1984). See § 8.10 below.

22. See, e.g., Securities and Exchange Com'n v. Unifund SAL, 910 F.2d 1028, 1041 (2d Cir.1990) (frozen securities account must allow trading in securities; the plaintiff can seek an order requiring replenishment of the account if securities traded drop in value, and time is limited to 30 days); Richter v. Richter, 131 A.D.2d 453, 515 N.Y.S.2d 876 (1987) (funds used in business).

must be made in the injunctive order.[23] Sometimes the injunction permits use of funds for payment of attorneys,[24] but even here, courts sometimes limit the fees that can be paid from the frozen funds.[25] And in RICO actions, the Supreme Court has interpreted the statute to permit not only a freeze of the defendant's assets, but a freeze that prevents payment of attorney fees from them.[26]

When the plaintiff asserts a claim against real property instead of against funds or other assets the general rules are closely similar. The form in which protection is given is different, however, and no injunction is ordinarily required. If the plaintiff has a claim against specific real property, he may, when he files suit on the merits, also file a *lis pendens* or formal notice of his claim in the recorder's office. This serves to preserve his claim against the property even if the property is sold to third persons, since, by the *lis pendens,* they have notice of his claim. The *lis pendens* may impose the same pressures on the defendant as a freeze order,[27] and accordingly it is limited by similar rules.

A general money claim will not warrant a freeze of real property through the *lis pendens* any more than a general money claim will warrant an injunctive freeze of assets.[28] But correlatively, the *lis pendens* is fully justified when the plaintiff can trace his funds into the property and can assert a constructive trust[29] or equitable lien,[30] on the specific realty. The effect is much like that of the injunctive freeze of assets. Although the defendant is not forbidden by the *lis pendens* to sell the property, the record shows that the property is subject to the plaintiff's claim and hence buyers would seldom pay a full price. If they did so, the plaintiff will have a good claim against the property in the hands of the buyer. So the *lis pendens* is a

23. See, e.g., Teferi v. Dupont Plaza Associates, 77 Md.App. 566, 551 A.2d 477, 480, n. 2 (1989).

24. Cf. Federal Savings & Loan Ins. Corp. v. Dixon, 835 F.2d 554, 565 (5th Cir.1987) (adversary system threatened if one party gains control of other's defense by freezing funds; some kind of allowance for attorney fee payments from the fund must be made if defendant shows he cannot pay fees otherwise).

25. See FTC v. World Wide Factors, Ltd., 873 F.2d 1235 (9th Cir.1989) (attorney fees limited to $90 per hour).

26. United States v. Monsanto, 491 U.S. 600, 109 S.Ct. 2657, 105 L.Ed.2d 512 (1989).

27. See McKnight v. Superior Court, 170 Cal.App.3d 291, 215 Cal.Rptr. 909, 915 (1985) (expungement of *lis pendens* necessary remedy "to alleviate the problem of unscrupulous plaintiffs misusing the *lis pendens* procedure to force the settlement of groundless or malicious lawsuits"); 5303 Realty Corp. v. O & Y Equity Corp., 64 N.Y.2d 313, 486 N.Y.S.2d 877, 476 N.E.2d 276, 48 A.L.R.4th 715 (1984) (emphasizing that a *lis pendens* notice retards alienability of property, New York courts must be strict in limiting *lis pendens* to cases directly affecting real property, claim to stock in company holding real property not enough).

28. E.g., Brownlee v. Vang, 206 Cal.App.2d 814, 24 Cal.Rptr. 158, 160 (1962) (the underlying claim must affect "the title or right of possession of the specific real property described in the *lis pendens* * * *. [Otherwise] any litigant could effectively tie up the title of another litigant in an ordinary action for money, with complete immunity to the requirement for posting attachment bonds").

29. Vilone v. Sea & Pines Consolidation Corp., 541 A.2d 135, 137–138 (Del.Ch.1988); Keen v. Keen, 140 A.D.2d 311, 527 N.Y.S.2d 817 (1988).

In *Vilone,* supra, the court recognized that a *lis pendens* could properly be recorded on the basis of a constructive trust claim, but concluded that it could set aside the *lis pendens* on the basis of equitable considerations applicable to the particular case. It remarked:

Since *lis pendens* impairs the marketability of the subject land and the litigation may be prolonged, there is a prospect that, "unscrupulous plaintiffs (will misuse) the *lis pendens* procedure to force the settlement of groundless or malicious law suits."

30. Coventry Homes, Inc. v. Scottscom Partnership, 155 Ariz. 215, 745 P.2d 962 (App. 1987).

kind of unilateral attachment, without benefit of judicial supervision, and at the very least must be subject to expungement when it is inappropriately used.[31]

§ 6.2   Patent Infringement

[*For the text of this section, see the unabridged Practitioner Treatise edition.*]

§ 6.3   Copyright Infringement

[*For the text of this section, see the unabridged Practitioner Treatise edition.*]

§ 6.4   Trademark Infringement

[*For the text of this section, see the unabridged Practitioner Treatise edition.*]

§ 6.5   Misappropriation of Intangible Work Product Not Protected by Copyright or Patent

[*For the text of this section, see the unabridged Practitioner Treatise edition.*]

§ 6.5(2)   Privately Communicated Ideas: Submission of Ideas in Expectation of Payment

Elements of a Claim

Submission of ideas. In a number of cases a person submits an unsolicited idea, work-product or collection of information to a business, which then uses the idea in its products or its advertising or otherwise.[1] A leading case, *Hamilton Nat. Bank v. Belt,*[2] held that one who submits such an idea may recover under certain circumstances. That was a case in which the plaintiff suggested to a bank that it sponsor a radio program of his design, to be based on high school performances. The bank did promote and sponsor such a program, but did not compensate Belt for the idea. The court affirmed a recovery.

Elements of the claim. Hamilton held a recovery to be proper where the following elements are established: (1) the idea is original, (2) the idea is concrete and useful and (3) it was submitted in circumstances that "clearly indicate that compensation is contemplated if it is accepted and used."[3] Two other qualifications might be added. (4) The idea must have been used in fact by the defendant, unless the circumstances or explicit agreement indicates that the defendant was paying for the opportunity to use the idea regardless of actual use.[4] Use of the same idea is not enough if the defendant did not obtain the idea from the plaintiff or with knowledge of the plaintiff's rights.[5] (5) The idea must not have been published generally, else

---

31. In Connecticut v. Doehr, ___ U.S. ___, 111 S.Ct. 2105, 115 L.Ed.2d 1 (1991) the Supreme Court described the effect of an attachment of real property: "[A]ttachment ordinarily clouds title; impairs the ability to sell or otherwise alienate the property; taints any credit rating; reduces the chance of obtaining a home equity loan or additional mortgage;

and can even place an existing mortgage in technical default where there is an insecurity clause."

§ 6.5(2)

2. 210 F.2d 706, 93 U.S.App.D.C. 168 (1953).

it will be in the public domain.[6] The same principles of liability embodied in these five rules seem to apply, with appropriate shifts in the verbal formulation, when the plaintiff's idea is acquired by improper means, such as fraud or breach of fiduciary duty.[7]

[For complete discussion of theories and remedies see this section in the Practitioner Treatise edition.]

§ 6.5(3) Publicly Communicated Ideas or Work Products: Misappropriation

Substance and Remedy

Substantive and remedial interaction. When ideas or work products are publicly communicated without the protection of patent, copyright or trademark, a number of serious substantive issues are raised and only a few remedial ones. Because some of the substantive matters derive in part from historic notions of unjust enrichment and because others may affect measurement of remedy, the present subsection cannot wholly set aside the theories of liability and defense.

General rule. When a work product is published or communicated generally, it becomes a part of the public domain unless it is protected by patent, copyright, or trademark/unfair competition law. This is the general rule for trade secrets, for example. Once they are divulged publicly they are no longer protectible.[1] It is also the general rule applied by the Supreme Court as to unpatented designs or inventions. Once the invention is available to the public, the defendant is usually free to copy it freely if he can do so without violating trademark[2] or patent rights.[3] A similar rule is applied to writings; the defendant is free to copy them once they are published without copyright protection and once the copyright has expired.[4]

However, when the publicly revealed work product is more personal a different legal attitude appears; a public figure's style, pose, voice or the like is often protectible. Protection is also afforded when the defendant does not merely use the plaintiff's work product or persona, but uses it in a way that is misleading to the public or defamatory to the plaintiff.

[For discussion of the governing cases see this section in the Practitioner Treatise edition.]

§ 6.6 Interference With Contracts and Opportunities Generally

[For text of this section, see the unabridged Practitioner Treatise edition.]

§ 6.6(2) Damages [1]

Injunction[2] and restitution[3] claims aside, the plaintiff who establishes a valid tort claim for interference with contract or opportunity may recover in an appropriate case: (1) general damages based on the difference between contract price and market value of the thing promised, where the interference prevents the performance of the thing promised; (2) special or consequential damages subject to the rules of proximate cause, or, in some jurisdictions, the limits of *Hadley v. Baxendale,* and subject also to the requirements of the reasonable certainty and avoidable consequences rules; (3) punitive damages where the defendant's conduct and state of mind warrant punishment; and (4) emotional distress damages in a limited class of cases.

[*For discussion of these rules and of other issues, see this section in the Practitioner Treatise edition, vol. 2, pp. 134–146.*]

§ 6.6(3) Restitution

Wrongdoer's Gains Recoverable

If the interfering tortfeasor has made profits or other gains by his wrongful interference with contract or opportunity, the plaintiff may be allowed an option to recover those gains instead of his own losses.[2] Not all interference cases are necessarily alike, however; it may be appropriate to deny restitution in some cases that involve neither wrongful means nor independently tortious conduct[3] as well as in cases in which the defendant's profits cannot be fairly traced to the tort.[4]

[*For discussion and applications see this section in the Practitioner Treatise edition, vol. 2, pp. 146–148.*]

§ 6.6(4) Injunction and Specific Performance

Against the Contracting Party

In some instances a plaintiff whose contract is disrupted by an interfering defendant may have an opportunity to avoid the harm by obtaining a specific performance decree against the contracting party,[1] and the cases sometimes reflect such decrees in interference cases.[2] It is almost never suggested, however, that the plaintiff must minimize the damages claim against the interfering tortfeasor by demanding specific performance against the promisor.[3]

§ 6.6(3)

2. Federal Sugar Ref. Co. v. United States Sugar Equalization Board, 268 Fed. 575 (2d Cir.1920); National Merchandising Corp. v. Leyden, 370 Mass. 425, 348 N.E.2d 771, 5 A.L.R.4th 1266 (1976) (reviewing literature on older "hesitation" to award restitution for contract interference). See generally 1 George Palmer, The Law of Restitution § 2.6 (1978); Annot., 5 A.L.R.4th 1276 (1981).

Contra: American Air Filter Co. v. McNichol, 527 F.2d 1297 (3d Cir.1975). The *American Air Filter* court took the older view that the restitution claim for profits was associated with "accounting," which was an equitable remedy and which would only arise if there was "some particular relationship between" the plaintiff and defendant, and that the plaintiff could recover the defendant's profits "at law" only if those profits were equal to the plaintiff's losses. The court did not discuss *Federal Sugar*, supra.

3. Efficient breach considerations would tend to oppose restitution in many cases that do not involve acts that are themselves tortious or that interfere with the plaintiff's existing property rights. See § 6.6(5) below.

The Restatement of Restitution §§ 136, 133 (1937) recognized recovery of the tortfeasor's profits in some kinds of interference but wrote a Caveat as to others. Inducing breach of a fiduciary or similar duty would perhaps be an easy case for awarding the wrongdoer's profits, as would any case in which a contract was interfered with by means independently tortious. Economic perspectives and assumptions may be quite different.

4. There are legitimate and serious concerns that a recovery of the defendant's profits may take not only what resulted from the tort but also what resulted from the defendant's independent efforts.

§ 6.6(4)

2. See Duff v. Engelberg, 237 Cal.App.2d 505, 47 Cal.Rptr. 114 (1965); Handy Andy Home Improvement Centers, Inc. v. American Nat. Bank and Trust Co. of Chicago, 177 Ill. App.3d 647, 126 Ill.Dec. 852, 532 N.E.2d 537 (1988) (injunction against lessor who had given the plaintiff the exclusive right to sell certain kinds of goods in shopping center lease and then gave similar lease to a competitor).

3. Stopford v. Boonton Molding Co., 56 N.J. 169, 265 A.2d 657 (1970), not an interference with contract case, held that the plaintiff could not recover certain consequential dam-

When the promisor is an employee, specific performance is not possible, because courts will not compel performance of personal services.[4] But the breaching employee may, in some instances, be enjoined from providing his or her unique services to a competitor.[5]

The adequacy test. Against the tortfeasor, an injunction is very frequently sought. When the tort interferes with economic opportunity not represented by a specific contract, the adequacy or irreparable harm test[6] is often met because damages are likely to be impossible to prove or to measure, and the injunction will go in many cases without difficulty.[7] Even when the tort interferes with a specific contract, the legal remedy may not be adequate because the contract represents unique opportunities or profit opportunities difficult to measure, and again injunctions may go without difficulty in many of the cases.[8]

§ 6.6(5) Efficient Breach and Remedies for Interference With Contract or Opportunities

[*For discussion of the effect of efficient breach theories and of cases outside the efficient breach regime, see this section in the Practitioner Treatise edition, vol. 2, pp. 151–154.*]

§ 6.7 Interference by Wrongful Acquisition of Property at Death of Another

Types of Claims

Forms of interference: murder, fraud, and other wrongs. In some instances the wrongdoer may interfere with a plaintiff's economic opportunity by interfering with his reasonable expectancy of inheriting or otherwise taking property at the death of another person. Interference with one's expected acquisition of property may be accomplished through murder[1] of the deceased in order to take property by inheritance,[2] devise,[3] trust,[4] life insurance[5] or survivorship.[6] Interference is perhaps more commonly accomplished through manipulation of legal title, by preventing the decedent from changing a will, or by inducing him to make a new one through fraud, duress, or undue influence.[7] Interference may also take the form of inducing a property holder to make gifts of the property during his lifetime, so as to deplete the estate and leave heirs or devisees with nothing at the property holder's death.[8]

---

ages against a contract breacher where those damages could have been avoided by obtaining specific performance.

4. See § 12.22(2) below.

5. Lumley v. Wagner, 1 De G.M. & G. 604, 42 Eng.Rep. 687 (1852); Hart, Nininger and Campbell Associates, Inc. v. Rogers, 16 Conn. App. 619, 548 A.2d 758 (1988). See § 12.22(2) below.

In cases like this, the breaching party is also in the role of the tortfeasor. That is, he is in breach of his employment contract by violating a covenant not to compete or by taking trade secrets; the same acts also interfere with the employer's economic opportunities in pursuit of its business. Some cases have said that in this sense it is possible for a contracting party also to be guilty of interference. Probably, however, those cases are best considered as involving the "bad faith" tort. See § 6.12 below. Some courts might simply deny a separate tort claim against a contracting party where the contract claim redresses the employer's interests fully. See Mallory Factor Inc. v. Schwartz, 146 A.D.2d 465, 536 N.Y.S.2d 752 (1989).

7. Davis v. New England Ry. Pub. Co., 203 Mass. 470, 89 N.E. 565 (1909); Tuscarora Warriors Bingo Com'n v. Clause, 137 A.D.2d 259, 271, 529 N.Y.S.2d 917, 924 (1988) (difficulty in proving monetary damages because of difficulty in proving how many individuals would be deterred from patronizing plaintiff's business).

Potential remedies. Depending on the facts, the remedy may be a claim in tort for damages for interference with an economic expectancy,[12] a claim for constructive trust against property gained by the wrongdoer,[13] or a probate proceeding to contest or set aside probate of a will.[14] Somewhat rarely, an equity proceeding may be brought to set aside probate on the ground of extrinsic fraud.[15] To the extent that the damages or trust claim contradicts a will, the policies behind the statute of frauds or statutes requiring formalities in wills may be undermined, so rather clear evidence may be required to assert the interference claim independent of a will contest in probate.[16]

[*For discussion of alternative remedies, relative advantages, and measurement, see this section in the Practitioner Treatise edition, vol. 2, pp. 154–166.*]

§ 6.8 Interference by Commercial Disparagement or Injurious Falsehood

[*For the text of this section, see the unabridged Practitioner Treatise edition.*]

§ 6.9 Interference by Unconstitutional Regulation of Land Use: "Regulatory Takings"

[*For the text of this section, see the unabridged Practitioner Treatise edition.*]

§ 6.9(2) Taking by Regulation

Diminished Rental Value or Equivalent

When a public entity unconstitutionally regulates land use, the kinds of harm suffered by the landowner may be quite varied and no single damages measure is likely to properly cover all cases.[1] Under traditional rules of compensation for takings of property, if the property was taken completely for a period of time, rental value for that period was the appropriate measure.[2] A regulatory taking may be both partial and temporary—partial because the regulation prohibits only some uses, not all; and temporary because the regulation may be rescinded when it is found to constitute a taking for which compensation is required; indeed, its enforcement may be enjoined in some instances.[3]

Because the taking is temporary, the award should compensate only for the period in which the regulation was in effect. Because the taking is partial, the award should reflect only the diminution in value resulting from

§ 6.7

13. E.g., Pope v. Garrett, 147 Tex. 18, 211 S.W.2d 559 (1948). For most practical purposes it does not matter whether the wrongdoer takes the estate but holds it on constructive trust or whether he is regarded as never taking title to the estate at all.

§ 6.9(2)

1. See Note, Measuring Damages for Temporary Regulatory Takings: Against Undue Formalism, 32 Ariz.L.Rev. 985 (1990).

2. Cf. Kimball Laundry Co. v. United States, 338 U.S. 1, 69 S.Ct. 1434, 93 L.Ed. 1765 (1949) (eminent domain taking for limited period, rental value).

the regulation.[4] In situations of this description, the traditional general damages measures would be diminished rental value during the period covered by the regulation, and some authority supports this measure in the regulatory taking cases.[5]

Rental value might be somewhat theoretical in the case of undeveloped land;[6] an alternative method of measuring the same loss would be interest on a sum of money which represents diminution in the land's value, interest to run for the period in which the regulation is in effect.[7] It is possible that other methods could be devised to measure the same elements of loss. One such method might use the option value of the land for the period in question.[8] It would also be possible to use consequential or special damages measures, projecting the loss of actual expected income during the period of impermissible regulation.[9]

[*For discussion of special damages, theories of recovery, attorney fees and other issues, see this section in the Practitioner Treatise edition, vol. 2, pp. 181–190.*]

§ 6.10   Wrongful Discharge and Job Discrimination

§ 6.10(1)   Scope, Background and Summary

Traditional At–Will Employees and Common Law Wrongful Discharge

The traditional rule was that an "at will" employee could be discharged at any time and for any reason. In the 1970s and 1980s a number of cases developed a wedge of common law exceptions[1] from a small body of earlier

---

4. "Resulting from the regulation": The market value of the property or the rental value could be assessed by comparing the value as regulated and the value as unregulated. This might give the landowner a considerable windfall since the alternative to an unconstitutional regulation is not necessarily no regulation at all. Unregulated land in an area otherwise heavily regulated might be worth a very considerable premium. Nevertheless in Sheerr v. Evesham Township, 184 N.J.Super. 11, 445 A.2d 46, 74 (1982) the court rejected the suggestion that damages should be based in part on the difference between the value the land would have as it was regulated in fact and the value it would have had regulations been at the maximum constitutional level. See also Kmiec, Regulatory Takings: The Supreme Court Runs Out of Gas in San Diego, 57 Ind.L.J. 45 (1982).

5. See Keystone Associates v. State, 45 N.Y.2d 894, 411 N.Y.S.2d 8, 383 N.E.2d 560 (1978) (approving the dissent in the Appellate Division, 55 A.D.2d 85, 389 N.Y.S.2d 895 (1976)); Brazil v. City of Auburn, 23 Wash. App. 672, 598 P.2d 1 (1979) (plaintiff entitled to "reasonable rents," a position taken en passant and without definitions), rev'd on other grounds, 93 Wash.2d 484, 610 P.2d 909 (1980). Cf. Herrington v. Sonoma County, 834 F.2d 1488 (9th Cir.1987), amended, 857 F.2d 567 (1988), cert. denied, 489 U.S. 1090, 109

S.Ct. 1557, 103 L.Ed.2d 860 (1989); Wheeler v. City of Pleasant Grove, 833 F.2d 267 (11th Cir.1987) ("market rate of return" on difference between land's value with and without the impermissible regulation).

City of Austin v. Teague, 570 S.W.2d 389 (Tex.1978) speaks in two voices. One uses the language of rental value or general damages; the other uses the language of actual losses or special damages. The actual decision appears similar in effect to a rule requiring proof of special damages.

6. "Neither expert testified that the raw, undeveloped land would earn anything before it was sold, rented, or developed." On this basis, proof of diminished rental value was held inadequate to sustain the landowner's judgment in City of Austin v. Teague, 570 S.W.2d 389, 395 (Tex.1978).

8. Sheerr v. Evesham Township, 184 N.J.Super. 11, 445 A.2d 46, 74 (1982).

§ 6.10(1)

1. See Monge v. Beebe Rubber Co., 114 N.H. 130, 316 A.2d 549 (1974) (female employee refused to see superior socially); Nees v. Hocks, 272 Or. 210, 536 P.2d 512 (1975) (discharged for accepting jury duty); Harless v. First Nat. Bank in Fairmont, 162 W.Va. 116, 246 S.E.2d 270 (1978) (discharged for reporting

authority.[2] For example, if an employer discharges an employee because the employee will not perjure himself or because the employee reports serious law violations of the employer, the courts which apply an exception to the common law rule recognize a cause of action on behalf of the employee.[3]

Advent of Statutory Law

About the same time that exceptions were developing to the "at will" rule, courts began dealing with important statutory provisions against retaliatory[4] and discriminatory discharges as well as with provisions against other forms of employment discrimination.[5] A patchwork of some complexity has resulted. Common law job rights, federal statutory rights and state statutory rights[6] must all be made to work with each other[7] and also with preexisting systems such as workers' compensation[8] and union-management grievance and arbitration procedures.[9] Because statutes protect against several forms of job discrimination and not merely against discharge,[10] they are broader in scope than the present section, which considers discharge and closely analogous actions, such as discriminatory refusal to hire or promote.

Strategy Issues

Many strategy issues lurk in these materials, because remedies may be quite different depending on the claim asserted. For example, the common law claims usually do not carry with them any award of attorney fees to the prevailing plaintiff, but the statutory claims routinely provide for such awards.[11] On the other hand, some of the statutory claims did not traditionally permit punitive damages or mental distress damages or even consequential damages, while such damages are recoverable in some common law cases[12] and under other statutes.[13]

or threatening to report employer law violations).

2. E.g., Petermann v. International Brotherhood of Teamsters, Etc., 174 Cal.App.2d 184, 344 P.2d 25 (1959).

3. See generally Prosser & Keeton on Torts, § 131 (5th ed. 1984 and Supp.).

4. E.g., 42 U.S.C.A. § 7622; 42 U.S.C.A. § 5851; N.Y.—McKinney's Labor Law § 740. See § 6.10(3) below.

5. E.g., 42 U.S.C.A. 2000e et seq. (Title VII of the 1964 Civil Rights Act). See § 6.10(3) below.

6. E.g., Iowa Code Ann. § 601A.6.

7. See Froyd v. Cook, 681 F.Supp. 669 (E.D.Cal.1988) (state Fair Employment Housing Act did not preempt or displace state common law wrongful discharge action); Chrisman v. Philips Industries, Inc., 242 Kan. 772, 751 P.2d 140 (1988) (plaintiff contended he was discharged in part because he refused to approve the employer's defective products to be used in nuclear industry, claim held preempted by a federal anti-retaliatory statute dealing with nuclear industry); Lally v. Copygraphics, 85 N.J. 668, 428 A.2d 1317 (1981) (administrative remedy for retaliatory

firing attributable to employee's workers' compensation claim does not bar tort suit).

8. See Note, Workers' Compensation Exclusivity and Wrongful Termination Tort Damages: An Injurious Tug of War?, 39 Hast. L.J. 1229 (1988).

9. See Korn, Collective Rights and Individual Remedies: Rebalancing the Balance after Lingle v. Norge Division of Magic Chef, Inc., 41 Hastings L.J. 1149 (1990).

10. Wage and hour legislation, labor-management relations legislation for example. Particular statutes of narrow scope may also dictate remedies. 29 U.S.C.A. § 2002 prohibits employers generally from requiring or even requesting employees to take a lie detector test. Section 2005 provides remedies similar to but broader than many of the remedies provided in job discrimination statutes: "legal or equitable relief as may be appropriate, include, but not limited to, employment, reinstatement, promotion, and the payment of lost wages and benefits."

11. See § 6.10(4) below.

12. See § 6.10(2) below.

13. Under 42 U.S.C.A. §§ 1981 and 1983 in particular. See §§ 6.10(3) and 6.10(4) below.

Law and Equity

Part of the remedial complexity in this particular area derives from the separation of law and equity. The common law claims and those derived from older civil rights statutes are at least partly claims at law, with the normal right to jury trial. But some important statutory claims, especially under Title VII before the 1991 Civil Rights Act, were said to be equitable, even when they involve money awards. This invoked a rule against jury trial and a good deal of equitable discretion in fashioning remedies when the claim is based on such statutes.[14] Somewhat similarly, a Title VII claim may have to await action by the federal agency charged with enforcement, the Equal Employment Opportunity Commission, while a common law claim and some others will not.

Given these remedial and procedural differences, good strategy for plaintiffs requires an assessment of the different remedies and procedures available under the different actions as well as the different substantive rules. Consequently, general statements about remedies have limited use.

Summary

Nevertheless, the following summary may guide entrance into the materials that follow.

(1) Under common law wrongful discharge claims, the damages are normally tort damages, including lost pay, provable consequential damages, emotional distress damages, and punitive damages where appropriate. Some cases, however, limit recovery to "contract" damages, and thus exclude punitive damages and emotional distress damages. Reinstatement is not a common law remedy for wrongful discharge.[15]

(2) Under some federal statutes, employment discrimination that produces a wrongful discharge, refusal to hire, or refusal to promote, is remedied mainly by back pay and reinstatement. Under these statutes, of which Title VII is the main exemplar, neither punitive damages nor emotional distress damages could be recovered before the 1991 Civil Rights Act.[16]

(3) Under certain civil rights statutes which are not aimed exclusively at employment discrimination, the remedies can include the complete list of remedies—back pay, reinstatement, emotional harm damages and punitive damages where appropriate, as well as any provable consequential damages.[17]

(4) In almost all the statutory claims prejudgment interest is permitted, and an award of reasonable attorney fees to the prevailing plaintiff is required.[18]

(5) The back pay and reinstatement remedies are usually considered equitable. For this reason there was no jury trial right under Title VII before 1991, and still may be no jury in some instances. But claims for compensatory, punitive, or emotional harm damages under the general civil rights statutes are "legal" and a jury trial is granted as to these.[19]

---

14. See § 6.10(5) below.

15. See § 6.10(2) below.

16. See § 6.10(4) below.

[For a discussion of common law theories of relief, a survey of statutes, the available remedies, jury trial, and equitable defenses, see this section in the Practitioner Treatise edition, vol. 2, pp. 190–239.]

§ 6.11 Lawyer Malpractice [1]

Primarily an economic tort. What constitutes lawyer malpractice is of course a question of tort law, not remedies law, as is the question of privity and the attorney's potential liability to third persons. On the remedial side, it can be said that lawyer malpractice, unlike most medical malpractice, is largely an economic rather than personal tort. It is true that in some situations there are substantial personal elements, as where malpractice leads to imprisonment and consequent emotional distress.[2] But lawyer malpractice is commonly a specific instance of interference with economic opportunities, and in line with the rules for that tort generally,[3] the courts have mostly said that there is no cause of action at all unless the plaintiff has actual damages.[4]

Non-representational lawyer torts. Lawyers can commit a variety of torts against their clients. A lawyer might invade a client's privacy, or batter a client, for example, and in some sense any of these things might be malpractice. But such claims lie outside the scope of this section, which focuses primarily upon remedies invoked when the lawyer's malpractice lies in the way he or she represents the client. Cases in which lawyers defraud clients,[5] or breach their fiduciary duty to clients in management of their property,[6] are of only peripheral concern here. Lawyer torts to adversaries and other non-clients—tortious debt collection, for example [7]—are equally outside the scope of this section.

Representational settings. Lawyer malpractice can occur in many ways. For example, a lawyer might draft a will that fails to pass the estate to the intended beneficiary,[8] or might negotiate a contract that fails to protect the client's interest; [9] or the lawyer might perform a title search without discovering a lien or encumbrance [10] or a title deficiency; [11] or the lawyer might improperly record the client's own mortgage or other security interest.[12] A conflict of interest may or may not be part of the malpractice claim.[13] All of these situations raise damages issues which have been addressed in the literature,[14] but they cannot be covered separately here. This section addresses instead the case of litigation malpractice.

Litigation malpractice. The most common examples of litigation malpractice are probably cases in which the lawyer fails to assert the client's claim in a timely manner,[15] or fails to assert all the claims or defenses to which the client is entitled,[16] or fails to investigate or otherwise prepare the case properly.[17] Such malpractice raises difficult causal issues, namely whether non-negligent behavior by the lawyer would have resulted in a favorable or more favorable judgment or other outcome for the client. It is also remedially complex because there are several layers of damages which must be distinguished one from another.

§ 6.11

1. See generally, R. Mallen & J. Smith, Legal Malpractice (3d ed. 1989); Bauman, Damages for Legal Malpractice: An Appraisal of the Crumbling Dike and the Threatening Flood, 61 Temple L.Rev. 1127 (1988).

Depending somewhat upon exact proof, the malpracticing lawyer is potentially liable for these three layers of damages:

(1) Substituted liability damages: Damages based on what the client would have recovered from his adversary in the original litigation, had there been no malpractice there (or losses he would have avoided as a defendant in the original litigation); the lawyer substitutes for the client's original adversary and takes on his liabilities.

(2) Consequential damages: additional collateral damages caused by loss of the original litigation but that would not have been part of the original adversary's liability; for example, the client's loss of credit standing.

(3) Malpractice suit damages: damages based on the malpractice suit itself, for example, attorney fees incurred in pursuing the malpractice claim.

[For discussion of each type of damages, proof, credits and other issues, see this section in the Practitioner Treatise edition, vol. 2, pp. 239–251.]

§ 6.12   Bad Faith Breach of Contract [1]

[For the text of this section, see the unabridged Practitioner Treatise edition.]

Chapter 7

INVASION OF CIVIL RIGHTS AND DIGNITARY INTERESTS

Analysis

Sec.
7.1 Dignitary Invasions Generally.
    7.1(1) Background and Scope.
    7.1(2) Presumed and General Damages.
7.2 Remedies for Defamation.
    7.2(1) Substantive Background.
    7.2(2) Summary of Remedies.
    7.2(3) Presumed or General Damages Under Common Law Rules.
    7.2(4) Constitutional Limits on Presumed and Punitive Damages.
    7.2(5) Presumed or General Damages: Relationship to Emotional, Reputational, and Nominal Damages.*
    7.2(6) The Free Standing Claim for Emotional Distress Damages.
    7.2(7) Reputational Harm Generally.*
    7.2(8) Reputational Harm—Understanding and Belief of Accusations.*
    7.2(9) Reputational Harm—Prior Reputation, Prior Publications, and the Libel Proof Plaintiff.*
    7.2(10) Reputational Harm—Retraction.*
    7.2(11) Economic Damages.
    7.2(12) Punitive Damages.*
    7.2(13) Restitution.
    7.2(14) Non-monetary Relief: Injunction, Reply, and Declaratory Judgment and Reform Proposals.
7.3 Remedies for Other Dignitary Claims.
    7.3(1) Dignitary Torts Generally.*
    7.3(2) Dignitary Torts: Damages.
    7.3(3) Constitutional Limits Generally.*
    7.3(4) The Special Case of Privacy Invasion.*
    7.3(5) Injunctive Relief.
7.4 Constitutional Civil Rights Torts.
    7.4(1) Scope and Substantive Background.*
    7.4(2) Presumed General Damages.
    7.4(3) Compensatory and Punitive Damages.*
    7.4(4) Injunctive Relief.
    7.4(5) Attorney Fees and Remedial Strategy Issues.*

---

* For the text of this section, see Dobbs, Law of Remedies, Second Edition, Practitioner Treatise, Vol. 2 (§§ 6.1–11.10).

§ 7.1 Dignitary Invasions Generally

§ 7.1(1) Background and Scope

The injuries considered in this chapter can be called dignitary injuries or injuries to the personality. This means that, though economic or physical loss may be associated with the injury in some cases, the primary or usual concern is not economic at all, but vindication of an intangible right.

Many dignitary claims are recognized torts that involve some confrontation with the plaintiff in person or some indirect affront to his personality—assault, battery, false imprisonment, malicious prosecution, intentional infliction of mental distress, libel and slander, invasion of privacy, and alienation of affections are all in this category.[1] In addition, these torts have their statutory and constitutional analogues so that essentially the same sort of interests may be protected under a variety of statutes, including federal or state civil rights statutes. Dignitary interests may also be vindicated incidentally, in the course of protecting some other interest, as where mental distress damages are awarded incident to some other tort.

All these dignitary harms may cause economic harm as well as affront to personality. If so, economic damages may be recovered. However, in a great many of the cases, the only harm is the affront to the plaintiff's dignity as a human being, the damage to his self-image, and the resulting mental distress. It does not follow that recovery is limited to nominal damages, however, even if the extent of emotional distress is not proved. On the contrary, the traditional rule for "trespassory" cases like assaults and batteries, was that "general damages" or "presumed damages" of a substantial amount can be recovered merely upon showing that the tort was committed at all. In other cases, including some cases of defamation[2] and some of the civil rights cases,[3] this liberal rule of damages has been rejected in favor of a rule that demands proof of actual damages as a prerequisite to an award.

Some dignitary claims are based in whole or in part on the defendant's communicative acts. Libel is but one example. Where liability is based upon a communication of publication, new concerns arise. Older doctrines of equity against the protection of personal rights have largely disappeared and no longer stand as a serious barrier to injunctive relief.[4] On the other hand, as the old barriers against protection of personal rights have disappeared, new sensitivity to problems of free speech has erected new and more formidable barriers that affect both injunctive relief and the damages award.

In the free speech cases in particular, substantive rule and remedial limit have been married to produce unique limits on some dignitary claims that otherwise might infringe free speech rights. Thus the constitutionalization of libel law in the years since 1964 has in part produced new limits on damages remedies.[5]

It is somewhat impractical to discuss the remedies for each dignitary tort separately. Consequently, after a further analysis of "presumed" and "general" damages below,[6] most of the torts are grouped for discussion in a single section.[7] Libel, however, has been treated to intense constitutional scrutiny and that tort exemplifies many of the constitutional and other remedial problems that can arise. Because libel can be an exemplar, the discussion of that tort is in an important way an introduction to the discussion of the other dignitary torts and it is given separate treatment.[8]

§ 7.1(2) Presumed and General Damages

Courts have used several terms to express the idea that substantial damages could be awarded for unproven harms. They have said (1) the violation of the right is a harm in itself, (2) that the plaintiff can recover "general damages," or (3) that the plaintiff can recover "presumed damages." It looks as if there are at least several distinct purposes represented in these terms, purposes that are almost always blurred in practice. One purpose is to compensate for harm which exists but is not proven. Another quite different purpose is to ascribe a value to the right in question irrespective of the plaintiff's actual harm beyond loss of the right itself. A third purpose might be to encourage suits to vindicate important rights, especially when any citizen's loss of the right may tend to diminish the rights of others as well.

Because these purposes are seldom spelled out in the cases, they sometimes lend an air of confusion to the subject. The Supreme Court decisions, which use the term "presumed damages,"[3] are sometimes difficult to analyze without first recognizing some of the different purposes that may be involved in allowing damages without proof of "actual" harm.

The first purpose in granting awards of unproven damages is most clearly illustrated when we believe from the facts that the plaintiff has pecuniary loss but that it is unprovable. For example, if a contractor is libeled by the report that he uses shoddy materials in his work, he may lose business without being able to prove it. If the report is widespread and the plaintiff's customers are diverse, one-time customers, the court may be willing to believe that *in fact* there is pecuniary loss even when none is provable.

Although less clear, the same idea works when the harm done by the tort is intangible, as in the case of emotional distress. If one is threatened with jail by a police officer who acts without probable cause, or maliciously prosecuted on a charge of serious crime, some distress in greater or lesser degree follows. Since emotional distress is a recognized "harm," in these cases, it is a short step to presume that the plaintiff suffers that distress when the facts show that ordinary persons would do so.

§ 7.1(2)

3. A series of opinions by Justice Powell deals with and generally condemn "presumed" damages. The terminology has been consistently that of "presumed damages," and the discussion has concentrated exclusively on the first purpose stated in the text above—compensation for "real" but unprovable harm. The opinions sidestep the idea that violation of some rights *is* harm for which compensation should be payable. The main decisions are Gertz v. Robert Welch, Inc., 418 U.S. 323, 94 S.Ct. 2997, 41 L.Ed.2d 789 (1974) (no presumed damages when plaintiff in libel does not prove knowing or reckless falsehood); Car-

ey v. Piphus, 435 U.S. 247, 98 S.Ct. 1042, 55 L.Ed.2d 252 (1978) (no presumed damages in civil rights claim based on denial of due process); Memphis Community School Dist. v. Stachura, 477 U.S. 299, 106 S.Ct. 2537, 91 L.Ed.2d 249 (1986) (no presumed damages in civil rights claim based on denial of First Amendment rights); Dun & Bradstreet, Inc. v. Greenmoss Builders, Inc., 472 U.S. 749, 105 S.Ct. 2939, 86 L.Ed.2d 593 (1985) (plaintiff in libel who does not prove knowing or reckless falsehood can recover presumed damages if he is a private person and the issue in the libel is not of public concern).

In both the illustrations just given it is possible to speak of the presumed damages as *compensatory* even though they are presumed.[4] This is common usage in the legal profession, although it muddies the meaning of compensation, since the damage award does not ordinarily provide substantial reduction in distress beyond the vindication of one's right.

The second purpose is quite different. It is better captured by the term "general damages" or more precisely by the statement that a violation of a dignitary right is harm in itself. Here the idea does not seem to be that the plaintiff really has pecuniary loss and that the only problem is proving it. Nor does it seem to be that the plaintiff has actual substantial emotional harm that is unproven. Rather the idea seems to be that some rights are "valuable" in an important although intangible way, even if their loss does *not* lead to either pecuniary loss or compensable emotional harm. The invasion of such a right *is* harm for which damages are recoverable.

The idea that invasion of a right is harm in itself is not so unusual in the law. If defendant withholds the plaintiff's automobile from him, the plaintiff's right to use it has been invaded and he has a good claim even if he had no need to use the automobile at the time. The right of exclusive use has been invaded and that is enough to justify substantial damages. What is difficult about this idea as applied to dignitary right is that the damages are not readily measurable. For deprivation of a right to use one's car, damages can readily be pegged as rental value. For deprivation of a right to free speech there is no ready measure.

It could be said that some rights, such as rights to participate in society equally with others, should be vindicated in courts and that an award of money should be made to make this vindication possible. The right to vote might be a good example of this type of right. One who is tortiously excluded from voting may have no pecuniary loss or even emotional harm, but vindication of voting rights is nonetheless significant. Where attorney fees are awarded to the prevailing plaintiff, as in most civil rights cases, this third purpose of the "general damages" award might justify a smaller award than otherwise.

The Critical Problem of Damages Measurement or Limit

The second and third purposes reflect a desire to value some rights in themselves and not because they are instruments of physical safety or emotional tranquility. They also reflect a desire to provide suitable incentives for individuals to vindicate rights that are important to the whole community. To adopt these purposes, however, is not to deal with the difficult matter of putting a value on the right or to fix a suitable incentive level.

The traditional view on this was to leave the matter of such intangible damages to the jury, which was no more uncertain than leaving to the jury other intangible damages such as emotional harm damages and punitive damages. This approach has seemed less and less satisfactory, partly because of the high costs involved, partly because of the uncertainty, partly because of the unfairness of some awards, and partly because of the uneven enforcement of rights at the hands of diverse juries who have no guide to intangible damages beyond their own subjective feelings.

A different solution is seen in some statutes. This is to prescribe a minimum award in a set sum or in a formula. For example, the award might be $1,000 minimum plus an award of attorney fees to the successful plaintiff who vindicates a dignitary right.[5] Or it might be based on some formula such as "treble damages." The number of statutes utilizing such a formula is increasing, but their appearance is sporadic and their solutions are still rudimentary. They do, however, have the merit of providing for some degree of recovery for intangible rights and the additional merit of providing a limit on unmeasurable damages.

A very different solution, but one that has not been tried in this country, is to permit the courts themselves to set minimum damages and/or limits on damages awardable without proof. The present system is an all-or-nothing system: courts allow juries to award more or less unlimited damages that cannot be measured and hence cannot readily be reviewed; or else they foreclose the claim to unproven damages altogether. By expanding the concept of nominal damages, and by coupling this with a high level of judge-control over limits on unproven damages, it would be possible to effectuate the second and third purposes in the case of some dignitary torts.

As it is, the judicial solutions are complex. Presumed damages are unconstitutional in some defamation cases,[6] simply not available in some civil rights cases,[7] and sporadically awarded in some state-law tort cases. Where presumed damages are not awarded, the main technique is to permit recovery of emotional distress damages, often in very high amounts, with very scanty proof about what the emotional distress really is.[8]

§ 7.2 Remedies for Defamation

§ 7.2(1) Substantive Background

The law of defamation attempts to protect the plaintiff's interest in reputation through the torts of libel and slander.[1] The law is unusually complex. It is also closely related to such slightly different torts as privacy invasion[2] and malicious prosecution,[3] and it is quite easily confused with commercial disparagement or trade libel.[4]

Both libel and slander require a "publication" or communication by the defendant to someone other than the plaintiff. Libel is traditionally written, tangible or permanent defamation; slander is traditionally oral, intangible, or impermanent. One important consequence of the distinction between

---

5. E.g., 18 U.S.C.A. § 2520 (wiretapping, actual damages, but not less than $100 a day or $1,000, whichever is higher, plus punitive damages and attorney fee recovery). This technique is used in economic tort statutes as well. E.g., the Copyright Act, 17 U.S.C.A. § 504(c)(1).

6. See § 7.2(4) below.

7. See § 7.4 below.

8. E.g., Keehr v. Consolidated Freightways of Delaware, Inc., 825 F.2d 133 (7th Cir.1987) (testimony of husband that plaintiff was "shocked" and "upset," only testimony mentioned by court, warranted $20,000 emotional distress recovery).

§ 7.2(1)

1. See generally R. Smolla, The Law of Defamation (1986 & Supps.); 2 F. Harper, F. James & O. Gray, The Law of Torts, Chapter 5 (1986 and Supps.); Prosser & Keeton on Torts, Chapter 18 (5th ed. 1984 & Supp. 1988).

2. See § 7.3(4) below.

3. See Dobbs, Belief and Doubt in Malicious Prosecution and Libel, 21 Ariz.L.Rev. 607 (1979).

4. See § 6.8, supra.

libel and slander was that substantial recoveries could be allowed in most libel cases without proof of any loss at all.[5] This is the doctrine of presumed or general damages. It did not apply to ordinary slander cases; pecuniary loss was required in those.[6]

The common law of defamation imposed a kind of strict liability upon publishers or communicators of material that was derogatory to others. Even if the publisher reasonably believed the material was true, he could be held liable. Although truth was a defense, along with some other "privileges," the burden was upon the defendant to persuade the jury that the defamatory publication was true in the substance of its sting.[7]

The United States Supreme Court has eliminated strict liability aspects of libel in order to prevent an undue chill on free speech as guaranteed by the First Amendment.[8] Public figure and public official plaintiffs must now prove that the defamatory publication was false in fact and that the defendant published knowing it was false, or in reckless disregard of falsity.[9] Private plaintiffs must prove at least some degree of fault,[10] and usually must prove actual damages as well.[11] Additional substantive protections are provided by the constitutional rules which put the burden of proving falsity, at least in some cases, on the plaintiff,[12] and which provide at least a degree of protection for expression in the principle that in American tradition there is "no such thing as a false idea." [13]

§ 7.2(2) Summary of Remedies

Remedies for libel and slander are traditionally damages remedies. Restitutionary remedies have not been applied to defamation cases,[1] and injunction against libel raises the fear of censorship, so injunction is seldom sought and usually denied.[2] The idea of giving the defamed plaintiff a right of reply in the same medium that defamed him proved unconstitutional.[3]

5. Prosser & Keeton on Torts § 112 (5th ed. 1984).

6. See § 7.2(2) below; Prosser & Keeton on Torts § 112 (5th ed. 1984).

7. Prosser & Keeton on Torts § 116 (5th ed. 1984 & Supp.1988).

8. Gertz v. Robert Welch, Inc., 418 U.S. 323, 94 S.Ct. 2997, 41 L.Ed.2d 789 (1974) (some degree of fault is required, even when a private person sues).

9. New York Times v. Sullivan, 376 U.S. 254, 84 S.Ct. 710, 11 L.Ed.2d 686, 95 A.L.R.2d 1412 (1964); Curtis Pub. Co. v. Butts, 388 U.S. 130, 87 S.Ct. 1975, 18 L.Ed.2d 1094 (1967); St. Amant v. Thompson, 390 U.S. 727, 88 S.Ct. 1323, 20 L.Ed.2d 262 (1968).

10. Gertz v. Robert Welch, Inc., 418 U.S. 323, 94 S.Ct. 2997, 41 L.Ed.2d 789 (1974).

11. Plaintiffs are exempted from the requirement of proof when (a) they are private (not public) persons and (b) the defamatory assertions involved no public issues. See Dun & Bradstreet, Inc. v. Greenmoss Builders, Inc., 472 U.S. 749, 105 S.Ct. 2939, 86 L.Ed.2d 593 (1985).

12. Philadelphia Newspapers, Inc. v. Hepps, 475 U.S. 767, 106 S.Ct. 1558, 89 L.Ed.2d 783 (1986) (even private plaintiffs must shoulder the burden of proving falsity when the issue under discussion is one of public concern).

13. See Gertz v. Robert Welch, Inc., 418 U.S. 323, 94 S.Ct. 2997, 41 L.Ed.2d 789 (1974). Until the decision in Milkovich v. Lorain Journal, 497 U.S. 1, 110 S.Ct. 2695, 111 L.Ed.2d 1 (1990), a number of decisions protected expressions of opinion against liability. Ollman v. Evans, 750 F.2d 970 (D.C.Cir.1984), cert. denied, 471 U.S. 1127, 105 S.Ct. 2662, 86 L.Ed.2d 278 (1985); Janklow v. Newsweek, 788 F.2d 1300 (8th Cir.1986), cert. denied, 479 U.S. 883, 107 S.Ct. 272, 93 L.Ed.2d 249 (1986); Dairy Stores, Inc. v. Sentinel Publishing Co., Inc., 104 N.J. 125, 516 A.2d 220 (1986). *Milkovich* appeared to retain protection for expression of ideas and the use of hyperbole, but rejected any separate protection for opinion. Although *Milkovich* limited federal protection for some expressions of "opinion," states may continue to protect them. E.g., Immuno AG. v. Moor–Jankowski, 77 N.Y.2d 235, 566 N.Y.S.2d 906, 914, 567 N.E.2d 1270, 1278 (1991).

As of the late 1980s, reformers have been suggesting some form of declaratory judgment as a partial solution to the many serious problems in defamation cases.[4]

The plaintiff is ordinarily entitled to recover damages for all the harmful consequences reasonably to be anticipated from the publication.[5] This includes harm caused when the initial audience republishes the defamation to others, so long as republication is reasonably foreseeable.[6]

The plaintiff is entitled to recover his pecuniary losses resulting proximately from the defamatory publication. For example, he is entitled to recover for earnings lost as a result of the defamation, provided the loss is reasonably proven.[7] If no pecuniary loss can be proved, then the plaintiff is entitled at least to nominal damages.[8]

A major issue on the damages claim is whether damages can be "presumed" in defamation cases, so that the plaintiff can recover without proof of any harm. The common law rule allowed recovery of presumed damages in many cases,[9] and it was the central means by which the dignitary or personality right was traditionally vindicated. Both common law and constitutional[10] law place limits—very different kinds of limits—on the recovery of presumed damages, but there remain cases in which presumed damages can be recovered, and even when they cannot, the plaintiff may be able to recover substantial sums for emotional harm resulting from the defamation.[11]

The main function of defamation law is usually said to be the redress of reputational loss. Apart from the economic damages caused by harms to reputation, those harms seem ultimately important because they inflict emotional or mental distress; but damages are usually estimated on the basis of evidence about reputation nonetheless. For this reason, evidence of the plaintiff's preexisting bad reputation is important. In some cases—the libel-proof plaintiff cases—the plaintiff's reputation may be so bad that the court, as a matter of law, dismisses the claim.[12] In others the reputation is merely a piece of evidence on the issue of damages. Retraction of the defamation by the defendant is similarly relevant on damages; but under statutes, retraction may have the effect of precluding all but actual or special damages.[13]

Although punitive damages can be recovered in extreme cases, the Constitutional concern to protect free speech has limited recovery to those cases in which the publisher is guilty of a knowing or reckless falsehood and to those in which the plaintiff is a private person and the defamatory material is of no public concern.[14] Once the constitutional standard is met, punitive damages are usually recoverable under the ordinary rules for punitive damages, although there are some special rules in some states.[15]

§ 7.2(3) Presumed or General Damages Under Common Law Rules

The disputed topic of "presumed" damages, on which both common law and constitutional law have a great deal to say, generates many of the remedial issues in defamation cases. Constitutional rules are stated in the next subsection.

A kind of strict liability was imposed for libelous publications at common law. Once defamatory content was shown, courts "presumed" that the defendant was at fault, which is to say they held the defendant liable even if his publication was honest and reasonable. They also presumed that the plaintiff had suffered damages.[1] Plaintiffs were allowed to recover large sums as "general damages" without proof of either economic loss or any actual mental distress.[2] Indeed, it has been said that the plaintiff could recover even for a libel that no one believed.[3] Under the presumed damages rule, the plaintiff would get to the jury even if the defendant proved there were no damages in fact, although the defendant's proof would be considered as bearing on the amount of damages.[4]

The doctrine of presumed damages has even been extended to allow corporate plaintiffs, whose harm is entirely economic, to recover "presumed" damages that would be condemned as utterly speculative in other circumstances.[5] The plaintiff could, of course, recover proven economic losses as well,[6] and also damages for mental distress.[7]

Slander, as distinct from libel, ordinarily required proof of "special damages," meaning the loss of something having pecuniary value.[8] This meant that the plaintiff who had emotional distress but not pecuniary damages from a publication, could not recover; but once the cause of action was established by some pecuniary loss, damages for emotional distress were recoverable, and so were presumed damages.[9] Slander per se was different. If a statement were slanderous per se, the plaintiff was not required to prove pecuniary loss and damages could be presumed.[10] Slander per se usually involved statements imputing a serious crime to the plaintiff, or imputing some personality trait or characteristic seriously inconsistent with the plaintiff's trade, profession or business.[11]

At some relatively recent time, a disputed number of common law courts began to require proof of pecuniary loss in cases of "libel per quod."[12]

The courts were quite ambiguous about what counted as libel per quod, but the category included cases in which the defamatory content of the publication could not be recognized by a mere reading of the publication, that is, cases in which some added information was required to see that the statement defamed someone. For example, to print news that the plaintiff gave birth to twins yesterday is not defamatory on its face even if it is false, but may become defamatory if coupled with the information that the plaintiff was only married yesterday.[13]

Most states have statutes that appear to forbid the recovery of presumed damages under specified circumstances. Presumed damages are commonly abrogated in suits against the electronic media where the plaintiff shows no fault on the part of a radio station which has leased time to someone else. Similarly, presumed damages are eliminated in suits against the print media where the defendant has published an appropriate retraction, and also where the plaintiff has failed to demand one.[20]

§ 7.2(4) Constitutional Limits on Presumed and Punitive Damages

If the plaintiff is a public official or public figure, he may recover only if he proves that the statement is false in fact, and in addition that the defendant published the statement knowing it to be false or in reckless disregard whether it was false or not. This is the rule of *New York Times v.*

Sullivan.[1] Under this rule the plaintiff has not been forbidden to recover presumed damages.[2] In such cases, states are also free to award punitive damages if the facts of the case otherwise warrant such a recovery.

If the plaintiff is not a public figure but is purely a private person, he need not prove knowing or reckless falsehood but must prove that the defendant was guilty of some degree of fault (usually negligence) with respect to the falsity of the statement.[3] The private-person plaintiff is permitted to go beyond proving negligence if he can; and if he proves knowing or reckless falsehood, he can recover full damages under the *Times–Sullivan* rules, just as a public figure plaintiff can.[4] However, if the private figure plaintiff proves only negligence or some other fault less than knowing falsehood, he is subject to important remedial limitations. In that case, he must prove "actual" damages. This is one of the important rules of *Gertz*.[5] It means that the plaintiff can recover neither presumed nor punitive damages when he proves only such ordinary fault as negligence. The constitutional rule does not, however, require proof of pecuniary loss as the old slander rules did.[6] The constitutional rule permits the plaintiff to recover any "actual" damages he proves, including "actual" nonpecuniary damages for such intangible elements as emotional distress.[7]

When a private person plaintiff sues for defamation that involves no issue of public concern, the Constitution is now held to permit a recovery of presumed damages if such damages are otherwise recoverable under the governing state law.[8] It would seem that because private concern speech about a private person plaintiff is not covered by the constitutional rules, punitive damages could be freely awarded under state law rules in that situation.[9]

§ 7.2(5) Presumed or General Damages: Relationship to Emotional, Reputational, and Nominal Damages

[*For the text of this section, see the unabridged Practitioner Treatise edition.*]

§ 7.2(6) The Free Standing Claim for Emotional Distress Damages

Emotional Distress without Defamation: Constitutional Concerns

Constitutionally permissible. When mental distress results from actionable defamation, mental distress can be claimed as one item of damages in the defamation action.[1] When the distress results from nondefamatory publications, the First Amendment provides the same protections it provides for libel cases.[2] But no constitutional rule prohibits recovery for mental distress resulting from a publication solely on the ground that the distress is not a result of harm to reputation. In the famous *Firestone* case[3] the plaintiff dropped her claims for injury to reputation and asked only for

---

§ 7.2(4)

1. 376 U.S. 254, 84 S.Ct. 710, 11 L.Ed.2d 686, 95 A.L.R.2d 1412 (1964).

3. Gertz v. Robert Welch, Inc., 418 U.S. 323, 94 S.Ct. 2997, 41 L.Ed.2d 789 (1974).

8. Dun & Bradstreet, Inc. v. Greenmoss Builders, Inc., 472 U.S. 749, 105 S.Ct. 2939, 86 L.Ed.2d 593 (1985); Great Coastal Express,

Inc. v. Ellington, 230 Va. 142, 334 S.E.2d 846 (1985).

§ 7.2(6)

2. Hustler Magazine v. Falwell, 485 U.S. 46, 108 S.Ct. 876, 99 L.Ed.2d 41 (1988).

3. Time, Inc. v. Firestone, 424 U.S. 448, 96 S.Ct. 958, 47 L.Ed.2d 154 (1976).

damages for mental anguish. Since she was regarded as a private person rather than a public figure, and since her evidence was deemed adequate to show fault in the publisher, the mental anguish recovery was constitutionally permissible, even though there was no claim for defamation.

§ 7.2(7)　Reputational Harm Generally

[*For the text of this section, see the unabridged Practitioner Treatise edition.*]

§ 7.2(8)　Reputational Harm—Understanding and Belief of Accusations

[*For the text of this section, see the unabridged Practitioner Treatise edition.*]

§ 7.2(9)　Reputational Harm—Prior Reputation, Prior Publications, and the Libel Proof Plaintiff

[*For the text of this section, see the unabridged Practitioner Treatise edition.*]

§ 7.2(10)　Reputational Harm—Retraction

[*For the text of this section, see the unabridged Practitioner Treatise edition.*]

§ 7.2(11)　Economic Damages

Although defamation is very largely a dignitary harm or harm to personality, defamation may also proximately cause economic losses. If such losses are adequately proven, they are recoverable items of damages. The same causal elements logically necessary to support a claim of reputational loss are logically necessary to support the claim of economic loss.[1]

Specifically, the plaintiff who prevails in a defamation claim is entitled to show that the defamation disrupted an employment or business relationship with another, so that the plaintiff lost wages and fringe benefits,[2] commission income,[3] profits or customers,[4] or contract or business opportunities,[5] and entitled to recover such items if they are properly proven.

The plaintiff is also entitled to recover for expenses incurred or losses suffered as a result of the libel. For example, if the libel results in the loss of his job, the plaintiff may incur costs of borrowing money or may lose his investment in his house when he is unable to meet payments.[6] In addition, the plaintiff is entitled to recover for actual expenses incurred in reasonable efforts to defend against or to counter the defamatory statements.[7] This includes corrective advertising, so long as that is a reasonable method of minimizing the loss,[8] and even attorney fees incurred in litigating with third parties to clear the plaintiff's name or preserve his economic opportunities.[9]

The plaintiff is also entitled to recover medical expenses reasonably incurred when mental distress or physical ill-health is a proximate result of the defamation.[10]

All economic loss is special damage and subject to the requirement that the loss be proven with reasonable certainty and that it be limited to losses that are not reasonably avoidable.[11]

If a libel causes the plaintiff to lose a job, and he cannot obtain substitute employment, he can recover for lost wages. It is not necessary to show that his inability to obtain substitute employment was caused by the libel as long as his original job loss was caused by it.

§ 7.2(12) Punitive Damages

[For the text of this section, see the unabridged Practitioner Treatise edition.]

§ 7.2(13) Restitution

It is possible to argue that the plaintiff in a defamation action should have the option to claim either (1) damages based on his own losses or (2) restitution, based on the publisher's gain from the defamatory portion of the publication. The issue has almost never been litigated. The very limited authority on point has denied the restitutionary claim altogether.[1]

One reason to deny the restitution claim is the threat it presents to free speech. Another is the difficulty of apportioning the publisher's profit between his own effort and investment and the defamatory material.[2] The difficulty of making an apportionment is itself an added threat to free speech rights, because an unapportioned recovery of profits from a libel would very likely capture profits from socially desirable speech as well.[3]

Publisher's Profits in Non-defamation Cases

Outside the context of defamation, the Supreme Court in the *Snepp* case has permitted recovery of all the gains from publication of a book where publication was found to violate a fiduciary duty and where national security was thought to be involved.[4] And Judge Posner has suggested that in the analogous case of privacy invasion by publication, the publisher's profits might furnish some guide to punitive damages.[5] So it may be that under some circumstances, free speech concerns would not forbid restitution of the defamer's profits, but at the same time the narrow and special circumstances in *Snepp* suggest that there is little room for expanding the traditional liability in an ordinary defamation case.[6]

§ 7.2(14) Non–monetary Relief: Injunction, Reply, and Declaratory Judgment and Reform Proposals

Injunctions denied. Courts have generally refused to enjoin simple

---

§ 7.2(13)

1. Hart v. E.P. Dutton & Co., 197 Misc. 274, 93 N.Y.S.2d 871 (1949), aff'd, 277 A.D. 935, 98 N.Y.S.2d 773 (1950), rearg. den., 277 A.D. 962, 99 N.Y.S.2d 1014 (1950).

3. Cf. Simon & Schuster, Inc. v. Members of the New York State Crime Victims Board, ___ U.S. ___, 112 S.Ct. 501, 116 L.Ed.2d 476 (1991) (statute allocating profits from criminal's book about crime to crime victims was unconstitutionally too broad, semble, since book might cover non-crime materials and thus a burden on free speech).

4. Snepp v. United States, 444 U.S. 507, 100 S.Ct. 763, 62 L.Ed.2d 704 (1980) (constructive trust on royalties from a book written in

violation of a covenant with the CIA to give the CIA a chance to censor the book).

5. Douglass v. Hustler Magazine, Inc., 769 F.2d 1128 (7th Cir.1985), cert. denied, 475 U.S. 1094, 106 S.Ct. 1489, 89 L.Ed.2d 892 (1986). In a less likely analogy, Son of Sam statutes also require convicted felons to disgorge profits from books or other productions based on their felonies. E.g., Fla.Stat.Ann. § 944.512.

6. Cf. Simon & Schuster, Inc. v. Members of the New York State Crime Victims Board, ___ U.S. ___, 112 S.Ct. 501, 116 L.Ed.2d 476 (1991) (statute burdened free speech in capturing all of criminal's book profits), discussed in § 8.9 below.

personal defamation, leaving the plaintiff to his claim for damages.[1] At one time the reasons for this rule lay largely in the idea that equity would not protect personal rights as distinct from property rights, an idea that was never very sound and is obsolete today.[2] The rule has also been supported on the arguments that equity should not enjoin a crime and that the damages remedy is adequate. These reasons do not suffice, however, to support a per se rule against the injunction; at best they cover some particular cases.

Free speech. The rule against enjoining libel or slander is supported today primarily by free speech concerns. Whether or not the First Amendment of the federal Constitution forbids the injunction,[3] state constitutions sometimes do so,[4] and independent of either of those grounds, the courts themselves are most reluctant to stop speech. Suppression of libel sounds proper enough, but as Chafee pointed out long ago,[5] judges are not infallible and can be mistaken about what is true and what is false. If true statements are suppressed by injunction, the truth may not be available for use by citizens. In addition, as Chafee went on to say, truth and falsehood are seldom so separate as milk and cream, so that suppression of falsehood is likely also to suppress truth. A somewhat different aspect of free speech arises when the issues discussed are of public concern. Issues of public concern are committed, in a democratic society, to the decision of the public through votes or through the market, not to judges or legislatures. The idea of an official truth is deeply inconsistent with a democratic society.[6]

Expungement. Expungement claims usually arise in connection with public records, often records of crime or arrest. In some cases, statutes specifically permit the court to seal or sequester records to prevent disclosure, or to expunge them altogether, with much the same effect as an injunction.[16] Some courts, without specific statutory authority, have actually ordered expungement or deletion of public records relating to a particular person, again with much the same effect as an injunction against defamation.[17] Not surprisingly, other courts have been reluctant to expunge public

---

§ 7.2(14)

1. Kramer v. Thompson, 947 F.2d 666 (3d Cir.1991) (even though jury has first found statements libelous and awarded damages, no injunction and no compulsory retraction); High Country Fashions, Inc. v. Marlenna Fashions, Inc., 257 Ga. 267, 357 S.E.2d 576, 577 (1987) ("we follow the general rule that 'equity will not enjoin libel and slander' "); Greenberg v. De Salvo, 254 La. 1019, 229 So.2d 83 (1969), cert. denied, 397 U.S. 1075, 90 S.Ct. 1521, 25 L.Ed.2d 809 (1970); Prucha v. Weiss, 233 Md. 479, 197 A.2d 253 (1964), cert. denied, 377 U.S. 992, 84 S.Ct. 1916, 12 L.Ed.2d 1045 (1964); Koussevitzky v. Allen, Towne & Health, Inc., 188 Misc. 479, 68 N.Y.S.2d 779 (1947); Willing v. Mazzocone, 482 Pa. 377, 393 A.2d 1155 (1978); Pirmantgen v. Feminelli, 745 S.W.2d 576 (Tex.App.1988); Annotation, Injunction as remedy against defamation of person, 47 A.L.R.2d 715 (1956).

2. Pound, Equitable Relief against Defamation and Injuries to Personality, 29 Harv.

L.Rev. 640 (1916) launched a strong attack against the idea. Civil rights cases in the second half of the twentieth century have made it clear that equity no longer protects only property rights.

5. Z. Chafee, Government and Mass Communications 91–92 (1947).

6. "The First Amendment bars the State from imposing upon its citizens an authoritative vision of truth." Herbert v. Lando, 441 U.S. 153, 184, 99 S.Ct. 1635, 1653, 60 L.Ed.2d 115 (1979) (Brennan, J.). Cf. Cahn, Defamation Control v. Press Freedom: A Current Chapter in Israel, 13 J.Pub.L. 3 (1964).

16. E.g., 18 U.S.C.A. § 5038. See Franklin & Johnsen, Expunging Criminal Records: Concealment and Dishonesty in an Open Society, 9 Hofstra L.Rev. 733 (1981) (concentrating on adult rather than juvenile offenders).

17. Police Com'r of Boston v. Municipal Ct., Etc., 374 Mass. 640, 374 N.E.2d 272 (1978) (but this requires a balancing of law enforce-

records in spite of their libelous possibilities.[18]

Retraction and Right of Reply

Many states have retraction statutes, but these statutes emphatically do not require the publisher to retract defamatory materials.[20] Instead, they usually limit the publisher's liability *if* a retraction is published. They offer the carrot of reduced liability, not the stick of an injunction.

At one time some thinkers hoped that a right of reply remedy could be developed. Such a remedy was allowed in a Florida statute, which purported to require the publisher to give space to a reply written by the accused person. This statute, however, has been held unconstitutional because it invaded the editorial functions of a free press.[21] This decision does not appear on its face to affect retraction statutes.

The Annenberg Proposals

The declaratory judgment idea is now part of the Annenberg proposals for libel reform,[25] invoked after an unsuccessful "stage I effort to resolve the controversy through retraction or reply." [26] If the plaintiff elected to use the declaratory judgment procedure (when it is permitted), the Annenberg proposal would exclude the recovery of damages, either in that or in a later suit. In the declaratory judgment suit the plaintiff would have a clear advantage—he would not be required to prove either fault of the defendant or the defendant's state of mind. What he would have to prove instead would be only falsity and the defamatory quality of the publication. In the declaratory judgment action, the loser would pay the winner's reasonable attorney fees.

Under this proposal, the plaintiff might opt instead to claim damages, but in that case he would be required to prove by clear and convincing evidence that the defendant was negligent and the claim might be defeated even so by a privilege. In any event, damages would be limited to "actual injury" and no punitive damages would be allowed. The prevailing party in the declaratory judgment action recovers reasonable attorney fees, but if the plaintiff sues for damages, "each side shall bear its own attorneys' fees * * *."

The damage suit becomes very unattractive to the plaintiff and to plaintiffs' lawyers under these proposals, because the two main sources of

---

ment needs with dangers to the juvenile in question and trial court must also consider less drastic alternatives); In re Smith, 63 Misc.2d 198, 310 N.Y.S.2d 617 (1970) (physical obliteration of the names from all records to prevent employer's knowledge that juveniles had been arrested).

In some cases even those litigating against a person may be denied access to relevant arrest records, see State ex rel. Herget v. Circuit Court for Waukesha Co., 84 Wis.2d 435, 267 N.W.2d 309 (1978), but this may deny due process in some instances. Cf. Davis v. Alaska, 415 U.S. 308, 94 S.Ct. 1105, 39 L.Ed.2d 347 (1974).

18. Roth v. Reagen, 422 N.W.2d 464 (Iowa 1988). Cf. Monroe v. Tielsch, 84 Wash.2d 217,

525 P.2d 250, 71 A.L.R.3d 736 (1974) (although records may not be released to prospective employers, automatic expungement for all purposes would be denied). See Annotation, Expungement of Juvenile Court Records, 71 A.L.R.3d 753 (1976).

20. See § 7.2(10), supra.

21. Miami Herald Pub. Co. v. Tornillo, 418 U.S. 241, 94 S.Ct. 2831, 41 L.Ed.2d 730 (1974).

25. See R. Smolla, The Law of Defamation § 9.13(4) (1989).

26. See Smolla, The Annenberg Libel Reform Proposal: The Case for Enactment, 31 Wm. & Mary L.Rev. 25 (1989).

attorney fee payment, general or presumed damages and punitive damages, are no longer available and they are not replaced by an attorney fee recovery.

The Annenberg proposals proceed in part on the theory that finding the truth in a dispute about the plaintiff's reputation is not only a judicial task but a central one.[27] But the difficulty of being sure about the truth is one of the reasons why remedies have been limited in the first place. When the issue is one of public concern, there may be a much more important issue. Who decides, the courts or the citizens, whether an assertion of public importance is true or not? If the issue is committed to the voters, a declaratory judgment, which may shut off debate and establish an official truth, may be an undesirable as a damages judgment. Maybe even more so.

§ 7.3 Remedies for Other Dignitary Claims

§ 7.3(1) Dignitary Torts Generally

[*For the text of this section, see the unabridged Practitioner Treatise edition.*]

§ 7.3(2) Dignitary Torts: Damages [1]

Presumed General Damages

Presumed damages rules. The common law dignitary torts[2]—a technical assault without physical harm, for example—are comparable to libel and slander in that they have traditionally supported damages for intangible injuries even when little or no economic or physical harm is done. The tort is said to be damage in itself,[3] or as more commonly put, the plaintiff can

---

27. See R. Smolla, The Law of Defamation § 9.13(4)(b) (Supp.1989) ("what ought to be the heart of the matter: a determination of the truth or falsity of what was published").

§ 7.3(2)

1. Money remedies for dignitary torts are almost invariably damages rather than restitution. See York, Extension of Restitutional Remedies in the Tort Field, 4 U.C.L.A. Law Rev. 499, 540–46 (1957); Friedmann, Restitution of Benefits Obtained Through the Appropriation of Property or the Commission of a Wrong, 80 Colum.L.Rev. 504, 511 (1980).

2. Some of the torts are listed in § 7.3(1) above.

3. Phillips v. District of Columbia, 458 A.2d 722, 725 (D.C.App.1983); Sutherland v. Kroger Co., 144 W.Va. 673, 110 S.E.2d 716, 724 (1959) ("damage flows from the wrongful act, itself injurious to another's right, although no perceptible loss or harm accrues therefrom"); Smith v. Whalen, 613 S.W.2d 868, 870 (Mo.App.1981); see Miles v. F.E.R.M. Enterprises, Inc., 29 Wash.App. 61, 627 P.2d 564, 570 (1981); Harris v. B & M Groceries, 1983 WL 5611 (Ohio App.1983) (Allfeds library).

In *Phillips,* supra, the court said:

"Given the very nature of the tort, then, it is in our view appropriate for a jury in a false arrest case to consider loss of liberty per se as a basis for the award of compensatory damages * * *. We therefore must reject appellees' contention that because appellant had withdrawn his claims for mental anguish and emotional distress and failed to present any evidence regarding such damage elements as physical discomfort and injury or loss of business opportunities, the jury necessarily was limited to compensating appellant only for his out-of-pocket expenses. The trial court may have entertained the view * * * that the loss of liberty itself, stripped of the appellant's emotional or mental reaction to such loss, is not compensable. We disagree, and take the view that the single fact of imprisonment, the deprivation of one's right to move about, is compensable."

The idea that some invasions of legal right are in themselves harmful is not limited to money claims or even to torts. If the defendant proposes to park his mobile home on his lot in violation of a restrictive covenant, the court may enjoin the violation even if the violation causes no damage. The court is not likely to ask whether the plaintiff claims emotional harm or distress from the violation, only

recover "general" or "presumed" damages in substantial or more-than-nominal amounts.[4]

This rule is quite different from the rule applied to many other torts, such as ordinary negligence torts, in which no damages may be recovered unless physical or economic harm is first shown.[5] It also differs from some civil rights cases, in many of which only nominal damages are recoverable unless "actual damage" is shown.[6]

Some common law decisions also approach dignitary torts without invoking any general or presumed damages rule. This could leave the plaintiff with no substantial recovery; but usually when the common law court fails to invoke presumed damages it will emphasize other unmeasurable damages, such as emotional distress or punitive damages.[7]

Application to particular torts. Under the presumed or general damages rule, substantial damages have been recovered even when neither physical harm nor mental anguish proved in cases of trespassory [8] torts such as assault,[9] battery,[10] and false imprisonment.[11]

Non-trespassory torts that warrant awards of substantial damages without proof of actual harm include malicious prosecution [12] and some kinds of privacy invasion. The kind of privacy invasion that focuses on appropriation

whether there is a violation and the plaintiff had rather enforce his right than not. See, e.g., Reetz v. Ellis, 279 Ala. 453, 186 So.2d 915 (1966).

4. Wayne v. Venable, 171 C.C.A. 100, 260 Fed. 64, 66 (8th Cir.1919) (right to vote "is so valuable that damages are presumed from the wrongful deprivation of it").

5. Prosser & Keeton on Torts § 30 (5th ed. 1984). Thus mental distress damages might be recoverable in many cases once a tort is established, but it will be "parasitic," that is, an element of damage recoverable only if the tort is first established. Even an intentional tort such as trespass to land that does not involve personal intrusion or privacy invasion is not a dignitary claim; such a claim does not support a substantial damages recovery in and of itself. Trespass does of course support a nominal damage claim in all cases.

6. See § 7.4(2) below.

7. Courts which do not use the presumed damages approach, or do not use it with a particular dignitary tort, sometimes stretch a point of law or a point of evidence in order to allow damages on some other ground. For instance, in Donnel v. Lara, 703 S.W.2d 257 (Tex.App.1985) the jury awarded $1 in damages for a privacy invasion. The reviewing court thought itself bound by the rule that punitive damages could not be awarded on the basis of a merely nominal verdict, but then spent a good deal of effort to conclude that a $1 award was not "nominal" so that punitive damages could be awarded. In Keehr v. Consolidated Freightways of Delaware, Inc., 825 F.2d 133 (7th Cir.1987) the court found that

actual emotional distress damages of $20,000 were adequately proven by testimony of the plaintiff's husband that when plaintiff heard of the defendant's privacy-invading words, the plaintiff was "shocked" and "greatly upset." This was the entire basis for the award so far as reflected in the opinion. It is at least pardonable to think that these are cases of presumed or general damages under other names.

8. In the formal sense of a direct and forcible act by the defendant. See Prosser & Keeton on Torts § 6 (5th ed.1984).

9. I de S et ux. v. W de S, Y.B.Lib.Ass. f. 99, pl. 60 (1348); Allen v. Hannaford, 138 Wash. 423, 244 P. 700 (1926) (pointing gun that was in fact unloaded but which plaintiff feared might be loaded, $750).

10. McCandless v. State, 3 A.D.2d 600, 162 N.Y.S.2d 570 (1957), aff'd mem., 4 N.Y.2d 797, 173 N.Y.S.2d 30, 149 N.E.2d 530 (1958) (abortion performed on mental patient without her consent, though pain was less than labor would have been and mental condition was improved as result of abortion, $2,000 in damages).

11. Peak v. W.T. Grant Co., 386 S.W.2d 685 (Mo.App.1964) ("general damages," including mental suffering); Stowers v. Wolodzko, 386 Mich. 119, 191 N.W.2d 355 (1971) ($40,000, no dollar value can be assessed accurately, there was pain and humiliation).

12. See Montgomery Ward & Co. v. Morris, 273 F.2d 452, 453 (6th Cir.1960) ("intangible factors to be weighted," $17,500); Progressive Life Ins. Co. v. Doster, 98 Ga.App. 641, 106 S.E.2d 307 (1958) (recovery not limited to "ac-

of a celebrity's personality for entertainment or other gain seems to be partly an economic rather than a dignitary tort.[13]   However, other kinds of privacy invasion, including some uses of the plaintiff's name or photograph in advertisements, appear to involve dignitary claims for which general or presumed damages can be awarded [14] where constitutional limits permit.[15] The same is true for some statutory privacy claims such as those protected by anti-wiretapping acts.[16] Voting rights cases have also allowed substantial damages without proof of actual harm.[17]

Courts have also approved the use of presumed or general damages in alienation of affection and criminal conversation cases.[18] Intentional infliction of mental distress should be mentioned as a tort which permits substantial damages, although in the nature of things mental distress is always proven or inferred in such cases, so the "presumption" of damages is unnecessary.[19]

[*For discussion of emotional distress damages, punitive damages and other issues, see this section in the Practitioner Treatise edition, vol. 2, pp. 307–312.*]

§ 7.3(3) Constitutional Limits Generally

[*For the text of this section, see the unabridged Practitioner Treatise edition.*]

tual damages"); Barnes v. Culver, 192 Ky. 10, 232 S.W. 39 (1921) ("presumed in law," $500).

13. See § 6.5(3), supra. This category ordinarily involves celebrity plaintiffs who have an economic market for aspects of their personality in endorsements and otherwise.

14. On the different types of privacy invasion, see § 7.3(4) below.

Olan Mills, Inc. of Tex. v. Dodd, 234 Ark. 495, 353 S.W.2d 22 (1962) (plaintiff's picture used by mistake in photographer's ads, $2500 approved); Fairfield v. American Photocopy Equip. Co., 138 Cal.App.2d 82, 291 P.2d 194, 198 (1955) ("The fact that damages resulting from an invasion of the right of privacy cannot be measured by a pecuniary standard is not a bar to recovery. [ ] While special damages may be recovered if sustained, general damages may be recovered without a showing of specific loss").

15. Where the privacy invasion entails publication, constitutional standards of fault may apply to bar recovery and constitutional remedial limits may apply to bar presumed damages in some cases. See §§ 7.3(1) and 7.2(4) supra.

16. 18 U.S.C.A. § 2520 (actual damages, but not less than $100 a day or $1,000, whichever is higher, plus punitive damages and attorney fee recovery); see Ribas v. Clark, 38 Cal.3d 355, 212 Cal.Rptr. 143, 696 P.2d 637, 49 A.L.R.4th 417 (1985) (applying West's Ann. Cal. Penal Code § 637.2, $3,000 for each violation). See also Fair Debt Collection Practices Act, 15 U.S.C.A. § 1692; The Privacy Act, 5

U.S.C.A. § 552a(g); but cf. 29 U.S.C.A. §§ 2002, 2005 (lie detectors improperly used, but no minimum damages specified).

17. Wayne v. Venable, 171 C.C.A. 100, 260 Fed. 64 (8th Cir.1919); Lane v. Mitchell, 153 Iowa 139, 133 N.W. 381 (1911). Cf. Schwartz v. Heffernan, 304 N.Y. 474, 109 N.E.2d 68 (1952) (upholding cause of action by candidate whose name was not placed on the ballot in a primary election, right is correlative to citizen's right to vote).

18. Smith v. Whalen, 613 S.W.2d 868, 870 (Mo.App.1981) (criminal conversation, only *injuria*, not damage, is required; put otherwise, damages are presumed).

Intangible, mental distress elements are often mentioned along with references to general damages, but it looks as if courts are not in fact requiring proof of mental distress. See, e.g., Eubank v. Hayden, 202 Va. 634, 119 S.E.2d 328, 331 (1961) ("lost affections, assistance, aid and companionship"); Fennell v. Littlejohn, 240 S.C. 189, 125 S.E.2d 408, 413 (1962) ("The violation of plaintiff's marital rights is sufficient * * * to justify an allowance of compensatory damages, and whether they are more than nominal rests within the discretion of the jury"). Damages have been allowed for future losses, too, including those to be suffered after a divorce between the spouses. Vogel v. Sylvester, 148 Conn. 666, 174 A.2d 122, 96 A.L.R.2d 893 (1961).

19. E.g., Ford v. Revlon, Inc., 153 Ariz. 38, 734 P.2d 580 (1987) (employer recklessly permitted one employee to harass another in

§ 7.3(4)   The Special Case of Privacy Invasion

[*For the text of this section, see the unabridged Practitioner Treatise edition.*]

§ 7.3(5)   Injunctive Relief

General Rules

Contemporary view.   The old view that equity would not protect personal rights has become largely obsolete.   Although vestiges of the old tradition occasionally make fleeting appearances in some cases,[5] the general idea has been authoritatively repudiated [6] or grandly ignored in most decisions.   With the advent of the civil rights injunction to enforce a wide variety of personal rights,[7] it has become clear that equity will in fact injunctively protect personal or dignitary rights that have no pecuniary or property foundation at all.

Adequacy of legal remedy.   Another traditional bar to equitable relief is the adequacy rule—that equitable relief will be denied if a legal remedy is adequate.[8]   This rule, however, seems irrelevant in the case of personal rights.   The fact that the plaintiff asserts a right that cannot be readily valued in money—a privacy right, for example—is a good warrant for equitable intervention; the legal remedy for money damages would necessarily be inadequate to replace a right that is not grounded in money or property interests in the first place.   Put differently, a personal right is necessarily unique.

Grounds for denial of injunction.   However, there are reasons to deny the injunction in particular cases.   An injunction may not be needed because there is no threat of future harm; or it may be impractical; or it may interfere with orderly resolution of the dispute by other means; or it may interfere with important interests of the defendant, such as the defendant's rights of free speech and association.   Consequently, rejection of the traditional view that personal rights would not be protected is not equivalent to a rule that the injunction will issue.   Each case must be considered on its own merits.

[*For a summary of problems in enjoining criminal prosecutions, civil litigation, privacy invasion, interference with family relations, and other particular personal wrongs, consult §§ 2.9(3), 2.9(4) & 2.9(5) above, and this section in the Practitioner Treatise edition, vol. 2, pp. 323–334.*]

§ 7.4   Constitutional Civil Rights Torts

§ 7.4(1) Scope and Substantive Background

[*For the text of this section, see the unabridged Practitioner Treatise edition.*]

§ 7.4(2)   Presumed General Damages

The Federal Rule against Presumed Damages

The rule in Carey v. Piphus.   State courts may redress state-law civil rights claims as they see fit, through presumed damages[1] or claims for emotional distress.[2] Federal civil rights claims, although clearly dignitary in nature, are subject to special limitations. For these claims, the Supreme Court has foreclosed the recovery of what Professor Jean Love has called presumed general damages[3] in at least some federal civil rights cases. In *Carey v. Piphus*[4] the Court held that "presumed damages"[5] could not be awarded in favor of school children who had been suspended without a hearing. Denial of the hearing was a denial of due process, but had a hearing been given, the plaintiffs would have been suspended anyway because there was evidence that they deserved suspension under the appropriate rules. The Court held that nominal damages could be recovered, and also said that civil rights plaintiffs could recover emotional distress damages where such damages were adequately proven. But presumed general damages were not to be recovered.

Some of the language in *Carey* opposed presumed damages in broad and general terms; but other portions of the opinion suggested that presumed damages might be acceptable in the case of some kinds of constitutional violation. Because the exact scope and meaning of *Carey* was unclear, some jurists held that presumed damages could still be recovered when *substantive* constitutional rights were violated;[6] in this view, *Carey* prohibited presumed damages only in claims involving procedural due process.[7]

Resolving the ambiguity: Stachura. However, in 1986 the Court in *Memphis Community Sch. Dist. v. Stachura*[8] held that the kind of damages the Court had earlier called "presumed damages" should be denied even when the claim was a substantive constitutional claim, a denial of free speech rights rather than a denial of process rights.[9] On the same idea it seems that substantial damages could not be recovered for a warrantless, unconstitutional search of one's home, unless the plaintiff proved actual damages.[10] The Court thought that "some form of presumed damages may possibly be appropriate," but only when the injury in question "is likely to have occurred but difficult to establish." The plaintiff was not entitled to recover for the abstract or intrinsic value of the constitutional right of which he was deprived,[11] and jury instructions must not authorize such an award.[12]

search of sexual favors, $10,000 compensatory, $100,000 punitive).

§ 7.4(2)

1. See Miles v. F.E.R.M. Enterprises, Inc., 29 Wash.App. 61, 627 P.2d 564 (1981) (citing the first edition of this treatise, § 7.3). In addition, a civil rights violation may be redressed in some instances through common law tort actions of the kind that presumed damages. See § 7.3 above.

2. E.g., Herman v. State, 78 Misc.2d 1025, 357 N.Y.S.2d 811 (Ct. Claims 1974) (police entrance in home, substantial damages recovered for distress of occupants).

3. See Love, Damages: A Remedy for the Violation of Constitutional Right, 67 Cal. L.Rev. 1242 (1979).

For the distinction between general damages or damages based on the inherent value of the right on the one hand and presumed damages in the narrow sense of damages that can be inferred from the facts, see § 7.1(2), supra.

4. 435 U.S. 247, 98 S.Ct. 1042, 55 L.Ed.2d 252 (1978). There is a good discussion in Love, Damages: A Remedy for the Violation of Constitutional Right, 67 Cal.L.Rev. 1242, 1259 (1979).

5. As to possible difference between presumed damages and damages based on the inherent value of a constitutional right, see § 7.1(2), supra.

8. 477 U.S. 299, 106 S.Ct. 2537, 91 L.Ed.2d 249 (1986).

What Counts as Actual Injury?

No injury in rights violation. Under the *Carey–Stachura* requirements, one of the critical questions is what counts as "injury." The Court's whole assumption in *Carey* and *Stachura,* as well as in the libel cases which raise similar issues,[13] has been that there is no such thing as intangible or dignitary injury based on violation of a constitutional right alone.[14] "Injury" requires something personal to the plaintiff, such as pecuniary loss, pain or emotional distress.[15] In addition, the Court has said that even if the facts warranted presumed damages otherwise, such damages were not to be recovered except as a rough estimate of compensation and hence they were not to be recovered if compensation is otherwise provided for.[16]

Emotional and other consequences of a rights violation. Nevertheless, the Court has not required a showing of pecuniary loss. Emotional distress may count as actual injury, but beyond that it may still be possible even after *Carey* and *Stachura* to say that although violation of a constitutional right is not damage in itself, specific consequences of that violation can count as actual damages. For instance, in a case of unconstitutional punitive segregation of a prisoner, Judge Seitz wrote that the prisoner's loss of visiting and phone privileges, rights to recreation and library use, and loss of job wages counted as actual injury for which more than nominal damages could be recovered.[17] On the same basis, loss of freedom would seem to be an actual injury without proof of anything more.[18]

[*For further analysis and comment see this section in the Practitioner Treatise edition, vol. 2, pp. 339–341.*]

§ 7.4(3) Compensatory and Punitive Damages

[*For the text of this section, see the unabridged Practitioner Treatise edition.*]

§ 7.4(4) Injunctive Relief

"Private" or Individual Injunctions

Injunctive relief is important in many civil rights claims. The civil rights injunction is not barred by the adequacy-of-legal remedy rule[1] merely because the plaintiff might have a damages or habeas corpus remedy for violation of his rights.[2] An injunction might run, for example, against a sheriff's deputy to forbid harassment of black persons,[3] or against a city to forbid a racially motivated denial of building permits,[4] or against a public employer to forbid unreasonable search and seizure of employees in the form

17. Brooks v. Andolina, 826 F.2d 1266, 1270 (3d Cir.1987).

18. See Drake v. Lawrence, 524 N.E.2d 337 (Ind.App.1988) (§ 1983 action based on police officer's acts similar to malicious prosecution; loss of plaintiff's freedom until bond was posted was one element justifying damages award).

§ 7.4(4)

1. See, on the adequacy test, § 2.5 above.

2. E.g., Wyatt v. Aderholt, 503 F.2d 1305, 1316 (5th Cir.1974).

3. Lance v. Plummer, 353 F.2d 585 (5th Cir.1965).

4. Dailey v. City of Lawton, Okla., 425 F.2d 1037, 12 A.L.R.Fed. 956 (10th Cir.1970) (city enjoined from denying building permit, proof supported finding that denial was racially motivated).

of drug testing.[5]　Reinstatement of the plaintiff in a public job from which he was unconstitutionally discharged is another form of civil rights injunction.[6]　Typically in these traditional injunctions, the injunctive order requires or prohibits a discrete, unitary act; when the injunction is issued, the case is over.

Structural or Institutional Injunctions

Re-structuring institutions.　Some civil rights injunctions are quite different in that their goal is not merely to halt a single wrongful practice, but to halt a group of wrongful practices by restructuring a social institution such as a mental hospital, school, or prison.　Structural injunctions are not limited to civil rights cases; one might restructure a private corporation in an effort make its compliance with legal rules more likely.[7]　But structural injunctions have a special prominence in civil rights cases.

A structural injunction in a civil rights case might attempt to prevent cruel and unusual punishment in a state's prison system by requiring the prison to institute programs permitting personal hygiene and adequate diet and to cease tortures and killings of prisoners.[8]　Or it might attempt to require public schools to provide equal educational opportunity to all ethnic groups by drawing new boundaries in school attendance districts.[9]　Or it might attempt to require actual treatment of persons held involuntarily in mental hospitals.[10]

Because there are a great many ways in which school district lines could be drawn or cruel and unusual punishments eliminated from prisons, the structural injunction may invoke a high degree of discretion in the judge [11] and produce a high degree of complexity in the ultimate orders.

Bi-polar vs. representative or "legislative" litigation.　Structural injunction cases differ from the traditional ones in other ways besides their purpose to restructure institutions.　One difference is that the traditional injunction case, like the traditional damages case, is "bipolar," [12] focusing on the rights of two parties vis-a-vis each other.　Structural injunction cases tend to involve wider interests of society, not only in the sense that the judge may consider those interests in fashioning remedies, but also in the sense that they are represented in the litigation itself as intervenors or amici, and in the additional sense that third parties will surely be affected in substan-

5.　E.g., Caruso v. Ward, 131 A.D.2d 214, 520 N.Y.S.2d 551 (1987).

6.　Santiago–Negron v. Castro–Davila, 865 F.2d 431 (1st Cir.1989).　See § 6.10 for discussion of reinstatement under employment discrimination statutes.

7.　Stone, Large Organizations and the Law at the Pass: Toward a General Theory of Compliance Strategy, 1981 Wis.L.Rev. 861.

8.　Cf. Hutto v. Finney, 437 U.S. 678, 683, 98 S.Ct. 2565, 57 L.Ed.2d 522 (1978).

9.　Cf. Brown v. Board of Education, 349 U.S. 294, 75 S.Ct. 753, 99 L.Ed.2d 1083 (1955) (requiring lower courts to order a "prompt and reasonable start" toward full compliance with the desegregation order, then to monitor compliance, taking into account problems of administration, physical conditions, school transportation systems, and other details).

10.　Wyatt v. Aderholt, 503 F.2d 1305 (5th Cir.1974).

11.　See Fletcher, The Discretionary Constitution: Institutional Remedies and Judicial Legitimacy, 91 Yale L.J. 635 (1982).　Professor Fletcher recognizes that most of the remedial problems are polycentric, adding that to the extent that they are also not controlled by legal rule, they invoke the judge's "uncontrolled discretion."　See id. at 645–49.

12.　Chayes, The Role of the Judge in Public Law Litigation, 89 Harv.L.Rev. 1281, 1282 (1976).　Professor Chayes also uses *bipolar* to mean that the winner takes all.

tial ways by affirmative injunctive relief. In this respect the judge's work in fashioning a new structure resembles the work of the legislator.[13]

Terminal remedies vs. ongoing administration. Relatedly, the injunctive remedies in the traditional case are discrete and particular; typically the remedy is granted and the case is terminated. Occasionally a contempt sanction is required, but no more. Remedies in the structural or "public law" injunction can be quite different. Jurists expect remedies in such litigation to change over time, to be flexible, and to involve a measure of negotiation and mediation.[14] Professor Fiss described the usual structural injunction as a cycle in which the court issues a general injunctive decree, which is followed by disobedience or unsatisfactory compliance, which is followed by further hearings, and a supplemental decree stating in more detail what is required of the defendant. The cycle is then repeated several times, with each decree becoming more precise in its demands.[15] This description is borne out, with variations, in the reported cases.[16]

Judicial supervision of institutional reform; masters and receivers. The judge in such litigation becomes involved to a high degree in administration of the institution. The judge's decrees may prescribe the staff to be required in the institution, the types of food to be served, the temperatures to which inmates are subjected, the occasions and times permitted for solitary confinement and many other details.[17] The judge's supervision continues for a long period as the process of change continues. For this purpose, it may be necessary to appoint masters or receivers to supervise, enforce or monitor compliance,[18] and further additional hearings may be held on the master's reports. A judge might even go so far as to appoint a receiver to operate a public institution such as a school system if this is the only feasible way to secure compliance with the degree.[19]

Changes in the community—demographic changes in school desegregation cases, for example,—and even changes in the Supreme Court's constitutional interpretation, may require additional re-structuring. As all this

13. See Chayes, The Role of the Judge in Public Law Litigation, 89 Harv.L.Rev. 1281, 1294 (1976). Effects on non-parties appear in many affirmative relief cases, including some very private litigation. For example, if a manufacturer is ordered to allocate a portion of his product to one distributor, another distribution may be given short supply. See Leonard E. Warner, Inc. v. Nissan Motor Corp. in U.S.A., 66 N.C.App. 73, 311 S.E.2d 1 (1984). Professor Chayes, however, addresses much broader impacts on large aggregates of people. In this situation, the "public law" type litigation resembles legislation. See Chayes, supra, at 1297.

14. Chayes, The Role of the Judge in Public Law Litigation, 89 Harv.L.Rev. 1281, 1284, 1298–1302 (1976).

15. Owen Fiss, The Civil Rights Injunction, 36 (1978).

16. See Hutto v. Finney, 437 U.S. 678, 683, 98 S.Ct. 2565, 57 L.Ed.2d 522 (1978) (describing the orders issued at various times in that case).

17. See, giving a short description of such decrees, Fletcher, The Discretionary Constitution: Institutional Remedies and Judicial Legitimacy, 91 Yale L.J. 635, 639 (1982).

18. E.g., Ruiz v. Estelle, 679 F.2d 1115, 1159–1163 (5th Cir.1982) (with direction to the district judge to limit authority of the special master and to consider whether six monitors to assist the master were really necessary).

19. Morgan v. McDonough, 540 F.2d 527 (1st Cir.1976), cert. denied, 429 U.S. 1042, 97 S.Ct. 743, 50 L.Ed.2d 755 (1977). The possibility of using receivers or masters in such roles has excited a great deal of comment. See Owen Fiss and Doug Rendleman, Injunctions 827–830 (2d ed. 1984) for a two-page bibliography as of 1984. Sometimes courts or writers use nontraditional terms like ombudsman or institutional reform receiver. Sometimes they use the term master but include within that term powers traditionally assigned to receivers for management of property or operations.

suggests, the work of the judge in monitoring the structuring injunction resembles the work of a high level administrator.[20]

Right-remedy: correlation vs. dis-correlation. Traditional litigation, equitable and legal, attempted to provide a remedy which correlated with the right asserted and reflected or enforced that right, no more, no less.[21] If the plaintiff had a right to a due process hearing before discharge from public employment, an injunction might compel the defendant to provide such a hearing.

Structural injunctions sometimes go beyond this kind of right-remedy correlation. For instance, if a governmental agency had a history of discharging employees without a due process hearing, a structural injunction might not only order the hearing for aggrieved plaintiffs, but also order that employees be given notices of hearing rights, or that a grievance system be instituted.

Such remedial orders, though simple in comparison to many larger structural injunction cases, provide a remedy that goes beyond the right in question. The remedy helps enforce the constitutional right but it also has other effects, some of which may be good for employees generally and even for the management, but in any event something more than the hearing which is the only constitutional right in issue. Professor Chayes in particular noted this feature of public law litigation, of which structural injunctions are one part.[22]

In the example given, the discrepancy between the scope of the right and the scope of the remedy is relatively small and so is the intrusion on the operations of the defendant. But there is a limit somewhere; at some point the remedy is so different that it does not address the wrong done by the defendant but some wrong that has not been committed at all. When that point is reached, the remedy that exceeds the defendant's wrong or the plaintiff's right becomes unacceptable, partly because it is too intrusive,[23] partly because it opens up too much discretion,[24] and partly perhaps because it is unacceptable in principle to force a defendant to do more than rectify his wrong.[25]

---

20. See Chayes, The Role of the Judge in Public Law Litigation, 89 Harv.L.Rev. 1281, 1302 (1976).

21. See Schoenbrod, The Measure of an Injunction: A Principle to Replace Balancing the Equities and Tailoring the Remedy, 72 Minn.L.Rev. 627 (1988). Professor Schoenbrod argues that in some cases balancing or tailoring has led to injunctive relief that gives the plaintiff more than his entitlement.

22. Chayes, The Role of the Judge in Public Law Litigation, 89 Harv.L.Rev. 1281 (1976).

23. Rizzo v. Goode, 423 U.S. 362, 96 S.Ct. 598, 46 L.Ed.2d 561 (1976). In *Rizzo*, a pattern of police misconduct led the trial court to order city officials to implement a comprehensive program for handling citizen complaints. Although the low-level police misconduct was real enough, it was in no way affirmatively sponsored by the defendant officials. In this light, the injunction was thought too intrusive

on state affairs. An incidental burden on those who committed no violation, on the other hand, would be acceptable. Compare Zipes v. Trans World Airlines, Inc., 455 U.S. 385, 102 S.Ct. 1127, 71 L.Ed.2d 234 (1982) with General Building Contractors Ass'n, Inc. v. Pennsylvania, 458 U.S. 375, 102 S.Ct. 3141, 73 L.Ed.2d 835 (1982).

24. See Schoenbrod, The Measure of an Injunction: A Principle to Replace Balancing the Equities and Tailoring the Remedy, 72 Minn.L.Rev. 627 (1988); Fletcher, The Discretionary Constitution: Institutional Remedies and Judicial Legitimacy, 91 Yale L.J. 635, 679–83 (1982).

25. See, reflecting a corrective rather than a retributive view of civil remedies, Swann v. Charlotte–Mecklenburg Bd. of Educ., 402 U.S. 1, 16, 91 S.Ct. 1267, 1276, 28 L.Ed.2d 554, 566 (1971), where the Court said: "The task is to correct * * * the condition that offends the

Even so, pragmatic concerns may lead a court to approve some remedies that exceed the plaintiffs' rights because more modest or less specific remedies are less likely to succeed in the real world. Prisoners have no constitutional right to a system that limits solitary confinement to 30 days; but a court order limiting such confinement to 30 days may still be justified as a practical means for achieving constitutional conditions when prison administrators have been unwilling or unable to bring the prison into compliance in other ways.[26] Put differently, an injunction that gives the plaintiff more than the relief to which he is entitled, but only to assure that he gets his entitlement, is justified.[27]

Remedies for rights vs. remedies against social attitudes. Traditional injunctions attempted to provide a remedy for a right. The defendant's attitudes or his quality as a human being or as an institution, were seldom if ever at issue. But structural injunctions attempt to attack a social attitude as expressed in institutionalized unconstitutionality, sometimes institutionalized barbarism.[28]

Comment on Structural Injunctions

Structural injunctions raise important issues about remedies and especially about the appropriate role of the judge and the appropriate scope and structure of remedies. Some commentators have criticized the structural injunction, or at least warned that it requires caution. It has been argued that the structural injunction may inject judges too much into political or policy decisions that should be left to the political branches,[29] or somewhat relatedly, that separation of powers values are undermined.[30] It has also been argued that at least some of the discretion in fashioning remedies that attends the structural injunction is itself political and illegitimate in consti-

Constitution * * * judicial powers may be exercised only on the basis of a constitutional violation." See also Toussaint v. McCarthy, 801 F.2d 1080, 1086–1087 (9th Cir.1986) ("relief against a state agency or official must be no broader than necessary to remedy the constitutional violation").

26. See Hutto v. Finney, 437 U.S. 678, 688, 98 S.Ct. 2565, 2572, 57 L.Ed.2d 522, 532–533 (1978); Toussaint v. McCarthy, 801 F.2d 1080, 1087 (9th Cir.1986) (emphasizing that remedy must be limited to correct the wrong done, but that "a federal court may order relief that the Constitution would not of its own force initially require if such relief is necessary to remedy a constitutional violation," and that the defendant's history of noncompliance with prior orders is a relevant factor in this determination); Fletcher, The Discretionary Constitution: Institutional Remedies and Judicial Legitimacy, 91 Yale L.J. 635, 686 (1982).

27. See Schoenbrod, The Measure of an Injunction: A Principle to Replace Balancing the Equities and Tailoring the Remedy, 72 Minn.L.Rev. 627, 679 (1988).

28. See Hutto v. Finney, 437 U.S. 678, 683, 98 S.Ct. 2565, 57 L.Ed.2d 522 (1978).

29. See Mishkin, Federal Courts as State Reformers, 23 Wash. & L.L.Rev. 949, 966 (1978). Cf. Fletcher, The Discretionary Constitution: Institutional Remedies and Judicial Legitimacy, 91 Yale L.J. 635, 694 (1982) ("a federal judge is not controlled by the elements of the [polycentric] problem that he resolves. This control by the problem's constituent parts is what legitimates the exercise of discretion by a political body").

30. Professor Fiss has responded to the separation of powers argument in part by saying that all three branches of government exercise different functions and that the judiciary's involvement in structural litigation will not compromise its capacity to resolve disputes. Fiss, The Supreme Court 1978 Term, Foreward: The Forms of Justice, 93 Harv.L.Rev. 1, 32 (1979). But Professor Fiss view may be affected by the limited weight he attaches to the judge's role in dispute resolution. "I doubt," he says, "whether dispute resolution is an adequate description of the social function of courts. To my mind courts exist to give meaning to our public values, not to resolve disputes." Id. at 29.

tutional litigation.[31]

All the criticisms, which can be extended and expressed in various forms, have some merits. As many criticisms themselves suggest, however, structural injunctions must be given a place in the remedial armory if constitutional rights are to be vindicated in a realistic way. Caution rather than condemnation seems the right approach. If remedies are matched specifically to the rights they are intended to support, or in the alternative, if good reasons can be articulated for providing a remedy greater than the right itself, the structural injunction should hold its place as an occasional, troubling and complex remedy, which nevertheless must sometimes be invoked.

§ 7.4(5) Attorney Fees and Remedial Strategy Issues

[*For the text of this section, see the unabridged Practitioner Treatise edition.*]

---

31. See Fletcher, The Discretionary Constitution: Institutional Remedies and Judicial Legitimacy, 91 Yale L.J. 635 (1982). Similar and broader criticisms are made in Schoenbrod, The Measure of an Injunction: A Principle to Replace Balancing the Equities and Tailoring the Remedy, 72 Minn.L.Rev. 627 (1988).

Chapter 8

PERSONAL INJURY AND DEATH

Analysis

Sec.
8.1 Damages for Personal Injury.
    8.1(1) Elements of Damages for Personal Injury.
    8.1(2) Earning Capacity and Lost Income.
    8.1(3) Medical and Other Expenses.
    8.1(4) Mental and Physical Pain and Suffering.
    8.1(5) Consortium.
    8.1(6) Punitive Damages.*
    8.1(7) Future Damages.*
8.2 The Special Cases of Wrongful Pregnancy, Wrongful Birth, and Wrongful Life Claims.
8.3 Wrongful Death and Survival Actions.
    8.3(1) Substantive Background and Remedial Summary.
    8.3(2) Survival Statute Damages.
    8.3(3) Wrongful Death Statute Damages—Summary.
    8.3(4) ___ Economic Damages.*
    8.3(5) Non-economic Damages.*
    8.3(6) Nominal Damages, Punitive Damages, Interest.*
    8.3(7) Death Damages—Damages Affected by Events Subsequent to Death.
8.4 Adjustments: Delayed Payment of Past Damages—Interest.*
8.5 Adjustments: Future Damages: Reduction to Present Value and Inflation Adjustment.
    8.5(1) Summary.*
    8.5(2) Adjustments for Future Damages Generally: Establishing the Loss Period.
    8.5(3) Reduction to Present Value.*
    8.5(4) Inflation and Loss of Increased Future Income.*
    8.5(5) Periodic Payments, Structured Settlements and Court Ordered Funds.*
8.6 Adjustments: Benefits to the Plaintiff.
    8.6(1) Summary.*
    8.6(2) Direct Benefits to the Plaintiff.*
    8.6(3) Collateral Source or Collateral Benefit Rule.*
    8.6(4) Plaintiff's Income Tax Benefits.
8.7 Adjustments: Avoidable Consequences and Comparative Negligence.
    8.7(1) Apportionment Systems: Causal Apportionment, Avoidable Consequences and Comparative Fault.
    8.7(2) Avoidable Consequences Rules: Minimizing Damages.*
    8.7(3) Comparative Negligence.
    8.7(4) "Seat Belt" Defenses.
8.8 Statutory Caps on Damages—"Tort Reform" Limits.
8.9 Restitution in Personal Injury Cases.
8.10 Equitable Relief in Personal Injury Claims.

* For the text of this section, see Dobbs, Law   Treatise, Vol. 2. of Remedies, Second Edition, Practitioner

§ 8.1 Damages for Personal Injury

§ 8.1(1) Elements of Damages for Personal Injury

Compensation Elements Generally

Compensatory, lump-sum awards. The traditional theory is that, except for punitive damages imposed as punishment for more serious wrongdoings,[1] awards for personal injury are aimed at compensating the victim or making good the losses proximately resulting from the injury. Personal injury awards are lump-sum awards; unlike workers' compensation awards, they are not paid out in weekly or monthly sums. For this reason all damages for personal injury, including damages expected to accrue in the future, traditionally must be proved and calculated at the trial.[2]

Elements. Plaintiffs prove three basic elements of recovery in personal injury actions. (1) Time losses. The plaintiff can recover loss or wages or the value of any lost time or earning capacity where injuries prevent work.[3] (2) Expenses incurred by reason of the injury. These are usually medical expenses and kindred items.[4] (3) Pain and suffering in its various forms, including emotional distress and consciousness of loss.[5]

Permanent or future harm. One characteristic or attribute of each element of damage is that it may be permanent, or if not permanent, may continue to cause harm for some period in the future. Permanency and continuation of harm in the future are not logically elements of harm in themselves.[6] They are not losses but they are characteristics that reflect the degree of loss which the plaintiff suffers. If an injury is permanent or will continue in the future, the plaintiff may lose time from her job, may have additional medical expense, or may suffer pain long after the trial is over. The plaintiff is entitled to recover for such future losses with respect to each of the elements. Proof of future loss may be especially difficult or uncertain in many cases, however. In addition, adjustments must be made when future losses are estimated to account for inflation and the effects of prepayment.

§ 8.1(1)

1. See generally § 3.11 above.

2. Periodic payment statutes and structured settlements may provide for payment of damages over a period of time, but nevertheless rely primarily on an up-front determination of the amount of damages. See § 8.5(5) below.

3. See § 8.1(2) below.

4. See § 8.1(3) below.

5. See §§ 8.1(5) & 8.1(6) below.

6. A few cases, however, have spoken as if permanency were an entity in itself for which damages could be recovered irrespective of pain and suffering, lost earning capacity or expenses of injury. See Thompson v. National R.R. Passenger Corp., 621 F.2d 814 (6th Cir. 1980), cert. denied, 449 U.S. 1035, 101 S.Ct. 611, 66 L.Ed.2d 497 (1980); Flannery v. United States, 171 W.Va. 27, 297 S.E.2d 433, 34 A.L.R.4th 281 (1982). This does not seem to be a tenable position. Permanency is not a thing in spite of syntax that permits a noun to express it; permanency is the property or characteristic of something (else) such as pain or diminished earning capacity. Judge Posner gave a brief and clear statement of the semantic analysis of such words in Posner, Art for Law's Sake, 58 American Scholar 513, 514 (1989).

Elements apply in injury claims generally. Although details may differ in particular jurisdictions, the basic elements just listed are always recognized as recoverable items in some form, not only in the various states, but also under federal tort systems such as the FELA[7] and Jones Act.[8] The same elements are recognized as recoverable in any kind of tort claim for personal injury. Pain and suffering, for example, is equally recoverable in a strict products liability claim,[9] in an ordinary negligence case,[10] and in a civil rights action.[11] Even wrongful death actions, with their statutory peculiarities, take into account the same general kinds of elements of damage and the same general kinds of adjustments in the award.[12] The identity of the elements in all tort cases flows from the compensatory theory of recovery. That is, since the law attempts to measure compensation for losses, differences in losses require a different recovery but differences in the tort that leads to those losses do not.

Limits and Adjustments

Limits; attorney fees. The compensatory aim of personal injury awards is not always honored by the rules. Under the general American Rule, each side in litigation must pay its own attorney fees.[17] The injured plaintiff typically pays his attorney between one-fourth and one-half of the recovery as the "contingent fee." The result is that if the award was not excessive, the plaintiff will not receive full compensation; or put the other way around, only by giving awards that exceed pure compensation for injury can the jury assure the plaintiff full compensation in fact. In recent years "tort reform" legislation, aimed broadly at cutting the tort costs to defendants and insurers, has sometimes set limits or caps on recovery or some element of the recovery, usually intangible elements like pain and suffering.[18]

Adjustments for delayed payment. Any payment for past damages that comes only after a trial and judgment is delayed payment. Although interest on delayed payments might be expected as a matter of course, the traditional interest rule denies prejudgment interest except on liquidated sums. Under this rule interest runs from the time of the judgment. Judges sometimes show a good deal of dissatisfaction with this rule, but they have not generally abandoned it. However, statutes in some jurisdictions have altered the rule to permit recovery of some prejudgment interest.[19]

Adjustments for inflation and present value. Any payment at the time of judgment for damages that will not occur until some future date is a prepayment of damages. A downward adjustment is ordinarily required to allow for the fact that the plaintiff will have the money before it is needed to compensate for the injury sustained. This is merely the reverse case of interest; but although prejudgment interest is denied to the plaintiff, the defendant is allowed a credit for the prepayment.[20] This is called reduction to present value. Two other adjustments may or must be made when the judgment includes elements of future damages. An adjustment may be

7. 45 U.S.C.A. § 51. See, reflecting damage elements, Chesapeake & O.R. Co. v. Carnahan, 241 U.S. 241, 243, 36 S.Ct. 594, 594, 60 L.Ed. 979 (1916) (FELA damages include pain and mental anguish, bodily injury, pecuniary loss including "loss of power and capacity for work" and its effect upon plaintiff's future).

8. 46 U.S.C.A. § 688. See, reflecting damage elements, Allen v. Seacoast Products, Inc., 623 F.2d 355 (5th Cir.1980) (pain, earning power, medical).

made for future inflation.[21] In addition, an upward adjustment may be made to account for increase of losses in the future due to factors other than inflation.[22]

Comparative fault reductions. Still other adjustments in the award are possible. The most obvious adjustment today is the reduction in damages under comparative negligence regimes to account for the plaintiff's own contributory fault.[23]

Tax savings adjustments. Injury awards are not subject to income tax, even though they may be used to replace taxable wages lost. For this reason, some courts now require a downward adjustment to recognize that the award is economically worth more than the wages it replaces. The traditional rule is the opposite; it gives the defendant no credit for the fact that the plaintiff will have a tax-free award. Many courts still follow this traditional rule.[24]

Avoidable consequences and collateral sources. The avoidable consequences rule requires the plaintiff to make reasonable efforts to minimize damages. It applies to injury cases as well as to others, and it may be the occasion for a further reduction if the plaintiff could have limited her damages by a reasonable effort.[25]

On the other hand, the collateral source rule traditionally applies personal injury claims, so that *no* adjustment is made for the fact that the plaintiff's injury was partly compensated for from sources "collateral" to the defendant.[26] For example, the defendant's liability is not reduced if the plaintiff's losses are partly compensated by her own insurance or by public benefits. "Tort reform" statutes in some states have affected this rule and may require or permit a reduction in the defendant's liability if the plaintiff's injury is partly compensated from other sources.

§ 8.1(2) Earning Capacity and Lost Income

Earning Capacity—Wage Distinction

The injured plaintiff may recover either specific income loss, past and future, *or* loss of earning capacity.

Recovery for wage and other income loss. The plaintiff is entitled to recover past and future losses in income resulting from the injury if the losses are reasonably proved.[1] In many instances the plaintiff claims or the court discusses only wage loss.[2] However, recovery is not limited to paycheck wages. The plaintiff is entitled to recover any kind of income lost as a result of injury, including the value of fringe benefits.[3]

Recovery for impaired earning capacity. If he prefers, the plaintiff is entitled to recover for lost or diminished earning capacity rather than for specific wage loss. An estimate of lost earning capacity is not an estimate of specific present or future wage loss; it is rather an estimate of lost present ability to work in appropriate occupations,[4] now and in the future. It might be thought of as loss of human capital[5] and the opportunity it represents.[6] Thus one who is earning the same wages after the injury as before might still have a loss of earning capacity, representing a likely diminution in earnings at some point in the future,[7] or an increase in the effort required to keep earnings at the same level.[8] In a real sense it may even be said that even if capacity for work remains the same but injury reduces the chance of being hired, the plaintiff has a measurable loss.[9]

Rules applied. A religious person who has taken a vow of poverty and will accept no wages is a striking but not unique example of the earning capacity rule. Such a person may recover for lost earning capacity, even though he or she has no wages to lose.[17] In the same way, a school child,[18] an infant,[19] an unemployed person,[20] or one whose wages have not actually been reduced at the time of trial,[21] may suffer lost earning capacity and recover for it, even though there is no present wage loss and no way to quantify the loss that will occur in the future.[22]

Homemakers. One important category of cases involves a homemaker who is not a wage earner but whose earning capacity is devoted to providing household services, either for other family members[23] or for himself alone.[24]

The injured homemaker may claim the cost of replacement services as special damages,[25] using the testimony of experts such as economists or employment experts to show the replacement cost for each type of service provided.[26] Typically, testimony of this kind would break down the services into many components, some of which might be replaced cheaply, as in the case of baby-sitting, while others such as governess or chauffeur services might come at a very high price. Sometimes the plaintiff will prefer to claim the cost of replacement services.[27]

If the homemaker prefers, he is entitled to claim diminished or lost earning capacity instead. This is based on the value of the work he could have performed in the home but for the injury,[28] or on the value of the work he could have done outside the home if that is higher.[29] In either case, the fact that the homemaker was not in fact working outside the home before injury and never intended to do so does not limit the recovery if diminished capacity is in fact established.[30] And for the same reasons, it is irrelevant that the injured plaintiff would marry and terminate outside employment.[31]

§ 8.1(3) Medical and Other Expenses

Expenses Generally

General rule. The value of medical and related treatment reasonably necessary[1] to minimize or alleviate injury itself or the pain or disability that results from it are almost always recoverable as items of damage against the tortfeasor who causes personal injury. In the same way, the plaintiff is entitled to recover the value of treatment or care likely to be reasonably

§ 8.1(2)

7. See Bishop v. Poore, 475 So.2d 486 (Ala. 1985) (plaintiff not working at time of injury); Henry v. National Union Fire Ins. Co., 542 So.2d 102, 106 (La.App.1989) (plaintiff making more now than before, but injury will prevent advances and moonlighting of which she would otherwise have been capable, award for lost earning capacity is required as a matter of law); cf. Peterson v. Western World Ins. Co., 536 So.2d 639 (La.App.1988) (though plaintiff's business increased its profits after

injury, he might still have lost earning capacity).

8. "A tort feasor is not entitled to a reduction in his financial responsibility because, through fortuitous circumstances or *unusual application on the part of the injured person,* his wages following the accident are as high or even higher than they were prior to the accident." Bochar v. J.B. Martin Motors, Inc., 374 Pa. 240, 97 A.2d 813 (1953) (emphasis added).

necessary in the future. The value of care provided by doctors,[2] dentists,[3] nurses,[4] and hospitals [5] and nursing homes [6] is recoverable; so is the cost or value of any appropriate diagnostic tests,[7] drugs [8] and medical appliances such as braces or artificial limbs.[9]

Recovery is not limited to expenses of treatment or even to expenses for relief of pain. Any reasonable expense, adequately proved to be the result of the injury, is an item of damage.[10] Housekeeping service required because the plaintiff is injured is one example.[11] Another is the extraordinary expenses of rearing a child who suffers genetic defects and is born as a result of medical malpractice.[12]

Diagnostic, Medical Monitoring or Medical Surveillance Expenses

Recovery for diagnosis in absence of symptoms. No rule of law excludes recovery for expenses of diagnosis or limits the recovery to expenses of treatment. Indeed, diagnostic tests such as X–rays and many others are routinely part of the medical recovery.[26] The rule is that future medical harms, like other future harms, must be proven with reasonable certainty. But the rule does not, even taken literally, exclude recovery for expenses of minimizing damages or of determining the nature and extent of the plaintiff's injury.

Defendants have sometimes argued, however, that when the plaintiff has no symptoms, he cannot recover for expenses of a diagnosis. In some instances the defense may have a good argument that it would not be reasonable to incur the expense of diagnosis and recovery might be appropriately denied if that is the case. The argument that diagnosis expense is not recoverable, however, has mainly been based on a misunderstanding of a tort-law rule. If there is no injury at all, the negligent defendant simply is not a tortfeasor and he is liable for neither diagnostic nor any other costs. "Injury," however, does not necessarily require physical symptoms. There is no reason to doubt that the airline passenger who miraculously walks away after an explosive crash of the plane has an "injury" and can proceed with a negligence claim, even if there are no symptoms at all. Such a plaintiff can recover the expense of obtaining X–rays and other reasonable diagnostic information even if no broken bones are showing. Thus where a tort has occurred and is complete, the plaintiff may recover any expense of diagnosis, so long as that expense is reasonably incurred.[27] Future expenses might even be provided for by creation of a court administered fund, or some form of insurance fund.[28]

The more difficult cases arise when there is an exposure to or ingestion of a chemical which may at some future time cause cancer or other difficulties but which has not done so at the time of trial. In some such cases, depending on how the exposure occurs, the tort may be complete upon exposure, and if so, again, the answer would seem to be that diagnosis expense is an appropriate element of recovery. On the other hand, if, under appropriate tort law, the exposure itself is not regarded as harm and the tort is not complete, the defendant is not liable for any damages at all.

Medical surveillance. In some cases the plaintiff claims not merely a one-time expense for a diagnosis, but expenses of continually medical monitoring or medical surveillance. This has typically occurred in toxic tort cases where plaintiffs have been exposed to carcinogens or other chemicals that may cause serious future harm. Early detection of such harm is important and the expense of medical monitoring is reasonably incurred.[29] Recovery of monitoring expense, once a tort has been established, appears to be in accord with the usual rules of personal injury damages for diagnosis expenses [30] and also with the rule that permits recovery of expenses incurred to minimize damages.[31] In such cases some courts have not only allowed for such periodic future monitoring expenses,[32] but, in line with commentators,[33] have sometimes suggested that the defendant might be required to set up a special fund to finance such medical checkups as they arise.[34] At least one intermediate court, however, has rejected such monitoring costs as elements of damages, saying that to allow them would be to create a new cause of action that should be recognized only by the Supreme Court.[35]

§ 8.1(4) Mental and Physical Pain and Suffering

Recoverability

All forms of suffering recoverable generally. The third element of damages for personal injury is pain and suffering. Infliction of pain is not always a tort,[1] but where the tort is established, the pain for which recovery is allowed includes virtually any form of conscious suffering,[2] both emotional [3] and physical.[4] Recovery is not limited to suffering or distress directly resulting from the tort; it may include pain or distress resulting from subsequent medical treatment so long as it is a proximate result.[5] Even self-inflicted pain, if it is indeed a proximate result of the injury, is compensable.[6]

Pain award required. Some courts will not merely permit but will actually require an award for pain once the jury determines that physical injury has been inflicted.[9] For example, a zero verdict for pain, coupled with a verdict for the plaintiff on medical expenses, is thus often regarded as insupportable or inadequate, since the award for medical expense must reflect a jury finding that there was also pain for which at least some compensation is due.[10] Proof of future pain is to a large extent a matter of inference from proof that the physical or emotional injury claimed will continue and that medical attention cannot alleviate it.

Emotional states produced by injury. Perhaps more significantly, pain and suffering include mental or emotional anguish or distress resulting from injury.[22] Any form of unpleasant emotional reactions to the injury or its consequences, so long as it is proximately related to the tort, is a basis for the pain and suffering recovery. Disfigurement, for example, may cause mental pain or embarrassment, even if the disfigurement could not normally be seen by others.[23] The loss of pleasure as well as the actual sensation of pain is likewise recoverable.[24]

§ 8.1(3)

34. Friends for All Children, Inc. v. Lockheed Aircraft Corp., 241 App.D.C. 83, 746 F.2d 816, 46 A.L.R.4th 1113 (1984) (preliminary injunction ordered defendant to fund medical monitoring program); see Ayers v. Jackson Tp., 106 N.J. 557, 525 A.2d 287 (1987) (medical surveillance costs for those exposed to toxic chemicals, courts should be encouraged to use court-ordered medical surveillance funds, but lump-sum award here because case was tried that way).

Pain and suffering also includes such negative emotional states as those associated with terror the plaintiff felt at an approaching injury, and the anxiety about the future course of an injury. For example, the plaintiff may recover for the terror he felt when he became aware that the aircraft in which he was a passenger would crash.[25] Worry about whether a dog bite will lead to rabies or a burn to cancer [26] are examples of suffering over the future course of an injury already inflicted. Apprehension and even guilt that comes with awareness of impending death is another form of the same thing.[27]

Not surprisingly, pain also includes various forms of depression, anxiety,[28] and hysterical or conversion reaction.[29] The results of personality changes, such as altered relationships with family members and friends are also included.[30] Some compensable emotional states resulting from injury fall into identifiable psychological patterns, which may in turn facilitate expert testimony, as in the case of post-traumatic stress disorder.[31]

Loss of enjoyment of life. In some cases a plaintiff without physical pain is nevertheless unable to pursue the normal activities of life or a career for which she has prepared herself. Such a plaintiff is not in pain in the narrow sense that she feels the immediate sensation of physical pain, but the balance of pain and pleasure in life has been drastically altered for the worse. Many of the traditional elements of mental distress in personal injury cases are in this category.[32]

In particular, to injure a victim so that he can no longer play the violin, bowl, engage in sexual activity or any of hundreds of other aspects of normal life is to cause pain and suffering in a legal sense, and almost without exception, loss of enjoyment of life in this sense is as compensable as any other emotional state.[33] The same is true when the victim's injury makes it impossible to pursue some specialized activity, such as a chosen vocation, provided the proof adequately demonstrates the loss.[34] Indeed, it would be a surprise if the tortfeasor who leaves the plaintiff blinded or with impaired hearing but without pain could escape liability for the suffering that would follow.[35]

A few older cases, some of which are now in doubt, denied recovery for loss of enjoyment of life or some specific activities on the ground that the damage is speculative.[36]

Is loss of enjoyment independent of pain and suffering? The most common view is that loss of enjoyment of life or the inability to pursue normal pursuits and pleasures of life is an element to be recovered as one form of pain and suffering.[38] Loss of enjoyment of particular pursuits is exactly parallel to reduction in life expectancy, which also induces forms of pain and suffering when the plaintiff is aware that his life expectancy has

§ 8.1(4)

33. Thompson v. National Railroad Passenger Corp., 621 F.2d 814 (6th Cir.1980); Yosuf v. United States, 642 F.Supp. 432 (M.D.Pa. 1986); Leiker By and Through Leiker v. Gafford, 245 Kan. 325, 778 P.2d 823 (1989); Kenton v. Hyatt Hotels Corp., 693 S.W.2d 83 (Mo. 1985) (emphasizing plaintiff's loss of ability to play tennis, ski, jog, and carry on other athletic activities); Swiler v. Baker's Super Market, Inc., 203 Neb. 183, 277 N.W.2d 697 (1979); Judd v. Rowley's Cherry Hill Orchards, Inc., 611 P.2d 1216 (Utah 1980); Mariner v. Marsden, 610 P.2d 6, 15 A.L.R.4th 276 (Wyo.1980). See Annotation, Loss of Enjoyment of Life As A Distinct Element or Factor in Awarding Damage for Bodily Injury, 34 A.L.R.4th 293 (1984).

been cut short.[39] Some discussions have referred to loss of enjoyment of life as being in some sense a "separate element" of damages unrelated to the pain and suffering recovery, but what is meant by "separate element" is not always clear.

Most of the cases cited as recognizing lost enjoyment as a separate element appear to mean only that loss of enjoyment is a recoverable item under some heading or another, or that it may be mentioned to the jury, either in counsel's argument or an instruction defining pain and suffering.[40] Thus many of the cases cited as supporting lost enjoyment as a "separate element," do *not* support a charge to the jury that lost enjoyment is to be added to pain and suffering damages, or that a lost enjoyment recovery is due even if the plaintiff is unaware of the loss. Such cases seem to be merely versions of the general principle that pain and suffering covers a wide range of proximately resulting emotional responses to injury.

Some cases, however, have gone further by permitting instructions to the jury to make an award first for pain and suffering generally and then to make an additional award for loss of enjoyment of life.[41] Such instructions may run some risk that jurors will render an award for pain and suffering based on all of its feelings for the injured person and then make another award for lost enjoyment, based on some of the same feelings of loss. This seems to be a risk even if, definitionally, pain and suffering did not include lost enjoyment. But pain and suffering does include lost enjoyment of life's activities because by universal agreement it includes mental distress.[42] On the surface it would seem that given the broad legal understanding of pain and suffering, an instruction that treats loss of enjoyment as an element separate from pain and suffering runs the risk of duplicative recoveries.

However, any particular jury might understand a normal pain and suffering instruction in a much narrower sense, and to avoid such a misunderstanding, some specific mention of loss of enjoyment seems desirable. Perhaps the best solution is not to treat loss of enjoyment as a separate element but to instruct the jury that pain and suffering is a recoverable element *and* that pain and suffering includes all forms of mental distress and a sense of lost enjoyment or lost opportunities in life. This approach actually seems consistent with most of the cases, including many of those sometimes listed as supporting a separate claim for loss of enjoyment.[43]

Is consciousness of pain or loss required? Courts have rejected a pain and suffering claim when the plaintiff is not aware of pain, as where he is comatose.[44] Most courts apparently would also reject the claim for lost enjoyment if the plaintiff is not sentient and not aware of his loss.[45] This

41. Andrews v. Mosley Well Service, 514 So.2d 491 (La.App.1987); Eyoma v. Falco, 247 N.J.Super. 435, 589 A.2d 653 (1991); Kirk v. Washington State University, 109 Wash.2d 448, 746 P.2d 285 (1987).

44. Leiker By and Through Leiker v. Gafford, 245 Kan. 325, 778 P.2d 823 (1989); cf. McDougald v. Garber, 73 N.Y.2d 246, 538 N.Y.S.2d 937, 536 N.E.2d 372, 376 (1989).

45. McDougald v. Garber, 73 N.Y.2d 246, 538 N.Y.S.2d 937, 536 N.E.2d 372, 376 (1989);

see Willinger v. Mercy Catholic Medical Center of Southeastern Pennsylvania, 482 Pa. 441, 447, 393 A.2d 1188, 1191 (1978) ("this Court has never held that loss of life's pleasures could be compensated other than as a component of pain and suffering. Indeed, the two types of loss are interrelated * * * to a large extent it has been the plaintiff's consciousness of his or her inability to enjoy life that we have compensated under the rubric of 'loss of life's pleasures' ").

approach in part rests on the view that lost enjoyment is a species of the pain and suffering award and in part on the view that such an award would be punitive rather than compensatory.[46]

West Virginia has given a different answer, holding that a comatose patient has a loss of enjoyment though he has no awareness and never will have.[47] At this writing a New Jersey court has come to the same conclusion.[48] In effect the court separated lost enjoyment from pain, suffering and mental distress by reifying it. That is, lost enjoyment is treated as if it were a thing, or as if it were property, so that the plaintiff is entitled to recover for its "diminished value" even if the plaintiff does not know of it.[49] As a realistic assessment of damages, such a recovery does not appear to be compensatory, not even in the limited sense in which pain and suffering damages are compensatory. Some justification has been offered for the recovery as providing an "incentive" to defendants.[50] Awards added to compensation to produce incentives, however, would be properly measured by the need for incentive, not by an imputed loss.[51]

Recovery for distress at reduced life expectancy. The loss of enjoyment of life problem finds a variation in the "lost years" case—where the plaintiff's injury shortens his life expectancy so that he can be expected to die sooner than he would have without the injury. Shortened expectancy may have several effects. One is that it reduces the period of actual pain and suffering, and the period for which medical expense is required, though it may be difficult to take this into account.[52] On the positive side, pecuniary losses resulting from those "lost years"—lost earning capacity, for example—are recoverable.[53] In addition, if the plaintiff is aware that his life expectancy has been shortened, he can recover for distress that results,[54] in exactly the same way he can recover for the distress that results when his activities are cut short by injury. Indeed, the shortened life expectancy case may be an instance of loss of enjoyment, though it may also involve increased anxiety and depression, too.

Traditional view: no additional independent recovery for reduced expectancy. The traditional American authority permits the plaintiff to recover for emotional distress and pecuniary loss resulting from shortened life

---

The text statement is supported by the logic and the assumption of some decisions that do not actually state that consciousness is required. For example, in Leiker By and Through Leiker v. Gafford, 245 Kan. 325, 778 P.2d 823 (1989) the court held that (1) loss of enjoyment damages could be recovered but only as part of pain and suffering or disability, and (2) that pain and suffering damages could not be recovered unless the plaintiff was conscious of pain and suffering. Since loss of enjoyment is, under this view, merely one aspect of pain and suffering, the pain and suffering rules logically apply to it, including the rule that the plaintiff must be conscious of the pain.

47. Flannery v. United States, 171 W.Va. 27, 297 S.E.2d 433, 34 A.L.R.4th 281 (1982) (answering certified questions from federal court).

The federal court refused to apply *Flannery* to a claim against the United States government because it regarded liability for lost enjoyment as illicitly punitive in any case in which the victim was unaware of the loss. See Flannery v. United States, 718 F.2d 108, 111 (4th Cir.1983). The United States Supreme Court later held that the Federal Tort Claims Act's provision barring punitive awards against the United States did not bar loss of enjoyment claims by a permanently comatose plaintiff on the ground that an award was not punitive unless based on intentional or egregious misconduct and its purpose was to punish. However, the Court did not pass on the question whether such damages were recoverable. Molzof v. United States, — U.S. —, 112 S.Ct. 711, 116 L.Ed.2d 731 (1992).

expectancy, but it denies recovery for shortened life expectancy as an element of damages independent of the emotional or pecuniary impact.[55] This view is exactly congruent with the usual view that lost enjoyment of life is not an element recoverable in the absence of the plaintiff's awareness.

Cases allowing recovery for reduced expectancy independent of emotional or pecuniary harm. Some cases, however, appear to have moved toward a non-compensatory award for diminished life expectancy, that is, toward an award to be made even when the plaintiff (or decedent) is not aware this injury curtailed his life.[56] In *Sherrod v. Berry*,[57] a death case decided in 1985, a trial judge made an award for the decedent's loss of the pleasure of living, as distinct from any conscious pain or awareness of loss. The court said this loss represented moral and philosophical values.

The *Sherrod* court also said that such an award, though novel, was not unheard of, because English courts had recognized such an award. This is misleading for two reasons, however. First, the English recognition of the non-compensatory award for loss of expectation of life was limited to a conventional sum,[58] increased with the years to reflect inflation and reaching as high as £1750,[59] but never awarded in any significant amount. Second, the award was actually abolished by the Administration of Justice Act of 1982,[60] but even if the award had been retained, it was never comparable to an award of damages in American law.

Fear of Future Harm

Types of recovery for future harm. When a present tort to the plaintiff makes him more susceptible to future harm, three different theories for recovery must be distinguished. These are:

(1) The future harm has been proved to a reasonable degree of certainty by a preponderance of the evidence, so that the plaintiff is entitled to recover all damages for that harm, including future loss of earnings, future medical expense, and future pain and suffering.[61]

(2) The future harm is not proved to be more likely than not, but there is still a substantial chance that future harm will occur, so that the plaintiff should recover for the value of the lost *chance* of living a normal life in the future, presumably a percentage of future damages equal to the percentage chance of incurring those damages.[62]

(3) Future harm cannot be proved under either of the above theories, but the plaintiff nevertheless suffers present fear and anxiety about potential for future harm and may recover for such fear as one item of suffering or distress, provided always that the defendant has committed a tort and that such fear is a proximate result.

Fear recovery permissible. Courts have usually been willing to allow recovery for the fear of future harm as a form of mental anguish or suffering,[63] so long as the fear itself is reasonable and a proximate result of the defendant's tort. Future harm may be a fearful prospect even when it is

---

57. 629 F.Supp. 159 (N.D.Ill.1985), rev'd on other grounds, 856 F.2d 802 (7th Cir.1988).

63. See Sterling v. Velsicol Chem. Corp., 855 F.2d 1188, 1206, n. 24 (6th Cir.1988) ("Cancerphobia is merely a specific type of mental anguish"); Mauro v. Raymark Industries, Inc., 116 N.J. 126, 561 A.2d 257, 263 (1989) ("damages for emotional distress based on a reasonable concern that he or she has an enhanced risk of future disease").

not very likely to occur.[64] Fear of rabies after a dog bite,[65] fear of cancer after an exposure to carcinogens,[66] fear of losing vision after one eye has been blinded [67] are good examples.[68]

Where there is no present injury or tort. Confusion arises when the plaintiff has been exposed to a harmful substance but there is either no tort or no injury at the time. The usual tort rule is that when the claim against the defendant is based upon negligence then "harm" must be done, else there is no tort at all. In some instances, mental distress, including distress based on fear of future harm, may count as harm under the tort rule; [71] but when this is the case, courts often require physical manifestation of the distress or otherwise limit the claim under substantive tort rules.

If the plaintiff did not suffer a physical contact with toxic materials and no discernable physical harm, damages based on his fear of future health hazards might be denied because as to him there has been no personal injury tort at all.[72] In contrast, a plaintiff who is actually victimized by contact with a toxic chemical,[73] by actual invasion of harmful bacteria in his body,[74] by burns,[75] by medical equipment left in her body,[76] or by other actual physical impacts or injuries, not only has a tort action for the physical harm inflicted but may successfully claim mental distress based on fear of future complications or disease.

[*For discussion of the per diem or unit of time argument see this section in the Practitioner Treatise edition, vol. 2, pp. 394–396.*]

Abolishing or Limiting Pain and Suffering Awards

Proposals and statutes. A number of critics have expressed disapproval of the pain and suffering award as it is now made. The American Law Institute's Reporter's Study on Enterprise Responsibility for Personal Injury has proposed significant limitations [91] and so have several eminent teachers of torts,[92] sometimes in connection with proposals to supplant or supplement the tort system with other reparative arrangements such as no-fault insurance or increased employment benefits.[93]

Professor Plant proposed a maximum limit on pain and suffering awards, which he suggested tentatively might be at 50 per cent of the medical and related expenses.[94] Another proposal is that pain and suffering damages be limited according to a fixed schedule of amounts for each kind of injury [95] or at least subjected to guidelines analogous to federal sentencing

91. II American Law Institute, Enterprise Responsibility for Personal Injury Chapter 8 (Reporter's Study 1991).

92. Ingber, Rethinking Intangible Injuries: A Focus on Remedy, 73 Calif.L.Rev. 772 (1985); Jaffe, Damages for Personal Injury: The Impact of Insurance, 18 L. & Contemp.Prob. 219 (1953); James, Some Reflections on the Bases of Strict Liability, 18 La. L.Rev. 293 (1958); Clarence Morris, Liability for Pain and Suffering, 59 Colum.L.Rev. 476 (1959); Seavey, Torts and Atoms, 46 Calif.L.Rev. 3 (1958).

93. E.g., Sugarman, Serious Tort Law Reform, 24 San Diego L.Rev. 795 (1987) (propos-

ing a threshold of six month disability before pain damages could be recovered and also a cap, but only in connection with a non-tort system for providing benefits).

94. Plant, Damages for Pain and Suffering, 19 Ohio St.L.J. 200 (1958).

95. Zelermyer, Damages for Pain and Suffering, 6 Syracuse L.Rev. 27 (1955); cf. Bovbjerg, Sloan, & Blumstein, Valuing Life and Limb in Tort: Scheduling "Pain and Suffering", 83 Nw.U.L.Rev. 908 (1989) (three types of "scheduling" with different emphases on numerical controls).

guidelines or otherwise.[96] One group of policy analysts have recently proposed a "common law" of damages, in which consistent records are kept of jury awards and juries are instructed in severity-of-injury guidelines based on this past experience.[97]

In recent years, "tort reform" statutes, aimed at minimizing the costs of insurance and other defense costs, have sometimes imposed caps on damage recovery,[98] although some of these caps have been held to be unconstitutional,[99] and they are, standing alone, a crude means of controlling the award. A more finely tuned but still workable possibility is a low-end limit or threshold which would require a serious disability before any pain and suffering damages could be awarded.[100] A serious injury threshold could be coupled with a scale-down rule which sets a ceiling or cap on total recovery for the most significant injuries such as quadriplegia but requires the jury to reduce the award progressively for lesser injuries.[101]

Criticisms: overdeterrence without compensatory function. A number of criticisms can be made of pain and suffering damages. The awards contribute to the high cost of doing business and buying insurance without appearing to provide much if any desirable benefit to the plaintiff.[102] They are not compensatory in any ordinary sense of that term [103] and it is not clear what

96. See Levin, Pain and Suffering Guidelines: A Cure for Damages Measurement "Anomie", 22 U.Mich.J.L.Ref. 303 (1989) (advocating descriptive rather than prescriptive guidelines to model past practices and achieve coherence in line with general community values rather than to impose limits); see also Bovbjerg, Sloan, & Blumstein, Valuing Life and Limb in Tort: Scheduling "Pain and Suffering", 83 Nw.U.L.Rev. 908 (1989); cf. American Law Institute Reporter's Study, Enterprise Responsibility for Personal Injury 230 (1991) (recommending pain awards only for "significant" injury, with use of guidelines based on disability profiles).

97. Blumstein, Bovbjerg & Sloan, Beyond Tort Reform: Developing Better Tools for Assessing Damages for Personal Injury, 8 Yale J. on Reg. 171 (1991).

98. Hawaii Sess.L.Act 1 § 19 (1986); Md. Code, Ct. & Jud.Proc., § 11–108(b) ($350,000). As to caps generally, see § 8.8 below.

99. Smith v. Department of Ins., 507 So.2d 1080 (Fla.1987); Lucas v. United States, 757 S.W.2d 687 (Tex.1988); Brannigan v. Usitalo, 134 N.H. 50, 587 A.2d 1232 (1991) ("unfair and unreasonable to impose the burden of supporting the [insurance] industry solely upon those persons who are [even more] severely injured and therefore [even more] in need of compensation" (quoting earlier authority). For additional materials on caps, see § 8.8 below.

100. Sugarman, Serious Tort Law Reform, 24 San Diego L.Rev. 795, 823 (1987) (six months disability, serious disfigurement or impairment as a condition of any pain and suffering damages, in connection with a non-tort system of benefits).

101. See American Law Institute, Enterprise Responsibility for Personal Injury, Chapter 8 (Reporter's Study) (1991) (recommending pain awards only for "significant" injury, with use of inflation adjusted guidelines based on disability profiles).

102. One problem, not adequately investigated, is whether the award may actually tend to reinforce the plaintiff's pain. This is a psychological question as to which the law may have made an unjustified assumption. At least in some cases, to pay a person for pain may be unconsciously interpreted as a reward for continued pain with the result that the victim unconsciously feels obliged to suffer. If such cases exist, the award would have a negative rather than a positive impact on the plaintiff. Compare, exploring the individual's role in experiencing and perpetuating pain, Peck, Compensation for Pain: A Reappraisal in Light of New Medical Evidence, 72 Mich.L.Rev. 1355 (19–74).

103. Thus in McDougald v. Garber, 73 N.Y.2d 246, 538 N.Y.S.2d 937, 536 N.E.2d 372, 375 (1989) the New York Court of Appeals said that recovery for "noneconomic losses such as pain and suffering * * * rests on 'the legal fiction that money damages can compensate for a victim's injury' [ ]. We accept this fiction, knowing that although money will neither ease the pain nor restore the victim's abilities, this device is as close as the law can come in its effort to right the wrong. We have no hope of evaluating what has been lost, but a monetary award may provide a measure of solace * * *." See Monessen Southwestern Ry. Co. v. Morgan, 486 U.S. 330, 349, n. 5, 108 S.Ct. 1837, 1849, n. 5, 100

function they are intended to serve for the plaintiff personally. It is sometimes suggested that these damages can be used by an injured plaintiff to purchase distractions, but it is clear that the price of distractions is not the measure of these damages and it is equally clear that no plaintiff's attorney has ever argued to the jury that he only wanted $1000 to buy a new TV set. Although pain and suffering damages would no doubt be justified in the case of conscious wrongdoing, as a deterrent if nothing else, this argument will hardly support such damages where there is merely negligence, especially since the "wrongdoing" in many negligence cases is virtually nonexistent.

Criticisms: no measurement, unfairly inconsistent awards. Since pain and suffering damages have no restorative purpose, there is no way to measure the amounts that should be given, and the result is that verdicts vary enormously, raising substantial doubts whether the law is evenhanded in the administration of damage awards or whether in fact it merely invites the administration of biases for or against individual parties.[104]

Limited symbolic value of pain award. Even where the wrongdoing of the defendant is minor or nonexistent, as in negligence cases generally, there may be justification in awarding a small sum for pain and suffering to assuage the plaintiff's sense of outrage when his bodily security is violated and as a legal symbol of society's commitment to recognize the dignity and bodily security of each individual. However, if this is the function of pain and suffering damages, the purpose is purely symbolic, and though such symbolism is often important in the legal system, it hardly commands the unlimited verdicts for pain and suffering we are now accustomed to finding.

Compelled purchase of insurance. As tort liability has expanded, many observers have seen the tort system as increasingly like compulsory insurance. Victims of injury recover from defendants who are not always at fault in any meaningful way. The cost of the defendant's goods or services is then raised to pay the new costs of tort judgments. Consumers must then pay the increased costs of the goods or services. Ideally, consumers should be able to opt for cheaper goods in exchange for giving up the right to sue for pain and suffering; but as there is no practical way to achieve that solution at present, the consumer is compelled to buy the pain and suffering "insurance" if he buys the goods, because the cost of paying pain and suffering judgments will be included in the cost.[105]

Financing litigation costs with pain awards. Whatever weight should be given to the criticisms of pain and suffering awards, they serve an eminently practical and important purpose in providing a fund from which

L.Ed.2d 349 (1988) (Blackmun, J. concurring and dissenting); James, Damages in Accident Cases, 41 Corn.L.Q. 582 (1956).

104. There is a good discussion of the variability and unfairness in Blumstein, Bovbjerg & Sloan, Beyond Tort Reform: Developing Better Tools for Assessing Damages for Personal Injury, 8 Yale J. on Reg. 171 (1991).

105. A good short explanation of this idea is found in American Law Institute, Enterprise Responsibility for Personal Injury, Chapter 8 (Reporter's Study) (1991). For a thorough economic analysis of similar ideas, see S. Shavell, Economic Analysis of Accident Law Chapter 10 (1987); Alan Schwartz, Proposals for Products Liability Reform: A Theoretical Synthesis, 97 Yale L.J. 353 (1988); Stewart, Crisis in Tort Law? The Institutional Perspective, 54 U.Chi.L.Rev. 184 (1987). But such economic thinkers have also expressed concern that some kind of liability for intangible harm may be necessary to provide appropriate safety incentives to defendants.

the plaintiff's attorney's fee can be paid without drawing too heavily on that portion of the award actually needed to pay medical bills or replace lost earnings. Increased use of attorney fee awards in other kinds of litigation suggests the possibility that other means for financing litigation are possible. If attorney fees are paid through separate awards, then the pain and suffering award could be appropriately limited or perhaps substantially eliminated in some cases. However, raw caps on noneconomic damages in the absence of a provision for attorney fee awards may have the effect of excluding just but expensive litigation from the courts. Any effective limitation on pain and suffering awards must accordingly be accompanied by a provision for the recovery of attorney fees against the losing defendant.[106]

§ 8.1(5) Consortium

When one person is injured or killed,[1] the spouse may suffer a loss of consortium—that is, loss of the injured person's services, society, companionship, affection or sexual relations. The old common law rule, grounded in the husband's right to his wife's services, allowed the husband to claim consortium when his wife was injured, but did not make any similar allowance for the wife when the husband was injured, since she was never entitled to his services.[2]

The blatant discrimination of the common law, which would obviously raise constitutional issues if applied today,[3] has now been rejected almost everywhere, so that the wife may recover for lost consortium when the husband is injured.[4] In addition, a few courts have allowed children to recover for loss of parental society,[5] companionship and guidance, when the parent is injured, and parents to recover for loss of similar elements when a child is injured.[6] They have, however, rejected consortium claims by unmarried cohabitants[7] and also those by spouses based on premarital injury.[8] The traditional rule holds the consortium claim to be "derivative," so that it is lost, diminished or barred when the injured person's claim is so affected.[9] Some courts have permitted a full recovery of consortium by the non-injured spouse even when the claim by the injured spouse would be barred.[10]

The claim for lost services is really two kinds of claims. First it represents the claim that, but for the injury, the non-injured spouse would have received services having an economic value. For example, the injured spouse might have kept the house in repair or might have helped rear children before injury but can no longer do so after the injury. The non-injured spouse in some sense has "lost" these services,[11] but in another sense has not. The common law gave the husband the "right" to a wife's services, and when the common law rule was in effect, the husband of an injured wife had indeed lost something. But today each spouse has the right to her or his own efforts and the fruits of those efforts. The loss of services therefore is the loss of the injured, not the non-injured spouse. That loss in fact is compensable, as part of the injured spouse's lost earning capacity. Consequently it should not be compensated again by paying the non-injured spouse

---

106. E.g., O'Connell, A Proposal to Abolish Defendants' Payment for Pain and Suffering in Return for Payment of Claimants' Attorneys' Fees, 1981 U.Ill.L.Rev. 333; Sugarman, Serious Tort Law Reform, 24 San Diego L.Rev. 795, 834 (1987); cf. American Law Institute Reporter's Study, Enterprise Responsibility for Personal Injury, 229, 315 (1991) (proposing to retain but limit pain and suffering damages and to add attorney fees respectively).

for loss of these same services for which the injured spouse already recovers.[12] To avoid the potential for duplication of damages, courts may require that the consortium claim of the non-injured spouse be joined with the bodily injury claim of the injured spouse.[13]

The second aspect of the consortium claim is in reality a claim of mental or emotional distress or loss of enjoyment, that is, distress or suffering resulting from the diminished quality of the marital relationship itself. The right to consortium includes, in the case of spouses, rights to "society, services, sexual relations and conjugal affection which includes companionship, comfort, love and solace." [14] Thus the right of consortium is a right to an unimpaired relationship, and damages can be shown by proof of any impairment to that relationship or reduction in its satisfactions.

§ 8.1(6) Punitive Damages

[*Consult § 3.11 above and see this § in the Practitioner Treatise edition, vol. 2, pp. 403–406.*]

§ 8.1(7) Future Damages

[*For the text of this section, see the unabridged Practitioner Treatise edition.*]

§ 8.2 The Special Cases of Wrongful Pregnancy, Wrongful Birth, and Wrongful Life Claims

Substantive Background

Three kinds of injury claims present special problems which have troubled courts and writers and which have led to remodeled damages rules and an extensive commentary and analysis.[1] All three of these injuries involve the claim that the defendant, usually a medical doctor, was negligent in permitting a child to be conceived or born.

Wrongful conception or pregnancy. In the wrongful pregnancy claim, the defendant is responsible for a negligent birth control procedure, such as a vasectomy. As a result, the patients who sought to avoid having further children have a normal, healthy child who is not wanted and for whom the family may be unable to care emotionally or economically. A large number of courts have recognized such a claim.[2] In a few cases, the failure to prevent pregnancy has in fact resulted in the birth of a genetically defective child.[3]

Wrongful birth. In the wrongful birth claim, the defendant is responsible for negligent genetic testing. Because no tests were made or they were made negligently, the defendant fails to reveal to the parents that a fetus suffers genetic defects. And because the parents do not know of the defect,

§ 8.2

1. Among many articles and notes, see Collins, An Overview and Analysis: Prenatal Torts, Preconception Torts, Wrongful Life, Wrongful Death, and Wrongful Birth: Time for a New Framework, 22 J.Fam.L. 677 (1984); Rogers, Wrongful Life and Wrongful Birth: Medical Malpractice in Genetic Counseling and Prenatal Testing, 33 S.C.L.Rev. 714 (1982); Note, One More Mouth To Feed, 25 Ariz.L.Rev. 1069, 1075 (1983).

2. See Prosser & Keeton on Torts § 55, p. 372 (5th ed. 1984).

3. See Gallagher v. Duke University, 852 F.2d 773 (4th Cir.1988); Ochs v. Borrelli, 187 Conn. 253, 445 A.2d 883 (1982).

they have no option to terminate the pregnancy. A child, sometimes suffering horrible maladies and great pain, is born. A number of cases have allowed the parents to recover in such cases.[4] There is also a closely analogous situation; a public or private adoption agency negligently or fraudulently places a genetically defective child with adoptive parents, who learn only much later of the difficulty and the expense. Here again the parents may have a good claim.[5]

Wrongful life. The third claim, that for wrongful life, is a claim against the doctor who failed to discover genetic defects but is brought by the child himself for having been allowed to be born at all. In this claim and in the wrongful birth claim, early discovery of the genetic defect would not permit treatment or correction; the only additional option gained by early discovery would have been termination of the pregnancy. Thus the child's wrongful life claim is literally a claim that he should never have been allowed to be born at all. Most courts have rejected the wrongful life claim.[6] Where it is recognized, it has been a claim only for special expenses of treatment, in effect allowing the child to make a recovery that otherwise would be made by the parent.[7]

Wrongful Birth, Wrongful Life and Misadoption

Child-rearing expense. Courts that have recognized the wrongful birth claims have allowed a recovery for the some of the expenses of rearing the child.[8] The same rule has been applied to the liability of an adoption agency which misrepresents the adoptive child's health.[9] Recovery is usually limited, however, to the "extraordinary" expenses, those over and above the ordinary expenses of child rearing.[10] This element of recovery is probably not subject to offset for the "benefits" supposedly received by the parents in

4. See generally Prosser & Keeton on Torts § 55, pp. 370–72 (5th ed. 1984); Annotation, Tort Liability for Wrongfully Causing One To Be Born, 83 A.L.R.3d 15 (1978). Anti-abortion legislatures have passed several statutes curtailing or eliminating this cause of action. E.g., Idaho Code § 145.424; Minn. Stat.Ann. § 5–334. See Note, Wrongful Birth Actions: The Case against Legislative Curtailment, 100 Harv.L.Rev. 2017 (1987). Some of the cases cited in this section would be affected by any validly enacted statute of this kind, though their authority as to issues of damages might remain intact. At this writing the scope of constitutional abortion rights is in considerable doubt, and if permitted to do so more states may eliminate the wrongful birth claim.

5. See Meracle v. Children's Serv. Soc. of Wis., 149 Wis.2d 19, 437 N.W.2d 532 (1989); Burr v. Board of County Com'rs of Stark County, 23 Ohio St.3d 69, 491 N.E.2d 1101, 56 A.L.R.4th 357 (1986).

6. E.g., Siemieniec v. Lutheran General Hosp., 117 Ill.2d 230, 111 Ill.Dec. 302, 512 N.E.2d 691 (1987); Smith v. Cote, 128 N.H. 231, 513 A.2d 341, 348–349 (1986).

7. Turpin v. Sortini, 31 Cal.3d 220, 182 Cal.Rptr. 337, 643 P.2d 954 (1982); Harbeson

v. Parke–Davis, Inc., 98 Wash.2d 460, 656 P.2d 483 (1983).

8. Phillips v. United States, 575 F.Supp. 1309 (D.S.C.1983); Smith v. Cote, 128 N.H. 231, 513 A.2d 341 (1986); Schroeder v. Perkel, 87 N.J. 53, 432 A.2d 834 (1981); Becker v. Schwartz, 46 N.Y.2d 401, 413 N.Y.S.2d 895, 386 N.E.2d 807 (1978); Speck v. Finegold, 497 Pa. 77, 439 A.2d 110 (1981); Naccash v. Burger, 223 Va. 406, 290 S.E.2d 825 (1982); Harbeson v. Parke–Davis, Inc., 98 Wash.2d 460, 656 P.2d 483 (1983); James G. v. Caserta, 175 W.Va. 406, 332 S.E.2d 872 (1985).

See Proffitt v. Bartolo, 162 Mich.App. 35, 412 N.W.2d 232, 236 (1987) ("medical expenses").

9. Meracle v. Children's Serv. Soc. of Wis., 149 Wis.2d 19, 437 N.W.2d 532 (1989).

10. E.g., Phillips v. United States, 575 F.Supp. 1309 (D.S.C.1983); Siemieniec v. Lutheran General Hosp., 117 Ill.2d 230, 111 Ill. Dec. 302, 512 N.E.2d 691 (1987); Smith v. Cote, 128 N.H. 231, 513 A.2d 341, 348–349 (1986). Contra: Robak v. United States, 658 F.2d 471 (7th Cir.1981).

having the child.[11]

So far, the significance of allowing a "wrongful life" claim has only been that the extraordinary expenses of the child are awarded to the child himself rather than to the parents.[12] In some of the wrongful birth cases the child's life expectancy is terribly short, and in those cases it may make little difference whether the extraordinary expenses are recovered by the child or by the parent, so long as the parent actually pays the bills. But if the child may live past the age of 18, recovery in the child's name may be important, because the parental liability to provide medical care may terminate at that time; hence the parental recovery for medical expense may be limited to the period of the child's minority[13] or to the period of the parent's life expectancy rather than the child's.[14] Such a limitation seems clearly wrong as a matter of damages measurement.[15] Some courts, without allowing recovery in the child's name, have allowed full damages for the child's lifetime in the parents' name.[16]

Pain and emotional distress. Physical pain of the mother in labor and delivery is an appropriately recoverable item of damages.[17] When it comes to mental or emotional distress, the usual rule allows free recovery of emotional distress damages to any victim of a personal tort. There are special restrictions on emotional distress recovery, but only in cases when the *only* tort to the plaintiff is the infliction of emotional distress. For example, if no other tort has been committed to the plaintiff, the plaintiff can usually recover emotional distress damages only when he suffers some physical manifestation of that distress; and when the plaintiff's distress is based on shock at seeing injury or suffering of another person, the plaintiff can recover emotional distress only if he himself is in the zone of danger in most states.

These restrictive rules, however, have no logical bearing on the parents' wrongful birth claim, because in the wrongful birth claim a tort has already been committed to the parents; they do not assert a freestanding emotional distress claim, but merely assert emotional distress as an item of damages for a personal tort. For these reasons, the physical manifestation and zone-of-danger rules offer no occasion to reject mental distress damages in wrongful birth cases any more than they would do so in the case of libel or invasion of privacy.[18] Most courts appear to be more than willing to award

---

11. See "Offsets" below.

12. Turpin v. Sortini, 31 Cal.3d 220, 182 Cal.Rptr. 337, 643 P.2d 954 (1982); Harbeson v. Parke–Davis, Inc., 98 Wash.2d 460, 656 P.2d 483 (1983).

13. As in Bani–Esraili v. Lerman, 69 N.Y.2d 807, 513 N.Y.S.2d 382, 505 N.E.2d 947 (1987); see Siemieniec v. Lutheran General Hosp., 117 Ill.2d 230, 111 Ill.Dec. 302, 512 N.E.2d 691 (1987).

14. As in Gallagher v. Duke University, 852 F.2d 773 (4th Cir.1988).

15. See, arguing for damages to the child or to the family as a unit in wrongful life cases, Kelly, The Rightful Position in "Wrongful Life" Actions, 42 Hast.L.J. 505 (1991).

16. Smith v. Cote, 128 N.H. 231, 513 A.2d 341, 348–349 (1986); James G. v. Caserta, 175 W.Va. 406, 332 S.E.2d 872 (1985) (based on parental duty to support past majority where child is physically or mentally infirm).

17. Gallagher v. Duke University, 852 F.2d 773 (4th Cir.1988). The claim for pain in labor and delivery is most obviously suited to the wrongful pregnancy claim; but so far as that pain exceeds the pain the mother would have undergone in avoiding wrongful birth, it the claim is also appropriate in wrongful birth cases.

18. See Phillips v. United States, 575 F.Supp. 1309, 1317–1319 (D.S.C.1983).

damages for the parents' emotional distress,[19] subject to offsets for emotional benefits the parents may gain in having the child.[20]   Several important states, however, have denied emotional distress damages altogether.[21]

Wrongful Conception or Pregnancy

Generally: expense, wage loss, pain and distress.   Most courts have allowed the plaintiff in wrongful conception or wrongful pregnancy claims to recover the expenses of the negligently performed pregnancy-avoidance procedure,[22] or the cost of repeating the procedure later.[23]   They have also allowed recovery for pregnancy-related medical expenses, including wages lost because of pregnancy or delivery,[24] and expenses or wage lost in the post-natal period in appropriate cases.[25]   Most courts have also recognized the mother's pain and suffering in pregnancy, labor and delivery, and the emotional distress of both parents at the birth of an unplanned, unwanted, or unaffordable child,[26] and the father's loss of consortium,[27] subject in most cases to offsets for benefits and joys of child-rearing.[28]

Child-rearing expense—the majority.   Most courts have refused to allow parents to recover the expenses of rearing the healthy child, even when they agree that the defendant was guilty of a negligent sterilization.   Most of the reasons given for this position reflect strong feelings and a firm conclusion, but they may not quell all doubts.   "The parents of a normal, healthy child whom they now love have not suffered any injury or damage," the Kentucky

19. Phillips v. United States, 575 F.Supp. 1309 (D.S.C.1983); Berman v. Allan, 80 N.J. 421, 404 A.2d 8 (1979); Eisbrenner v. Stanley, 106 Mich.App. 357, 308 N.W.2d 209 (1981). Cf. Gallagher v. Duke University, 852 F.2d 773 (4th Cir.1988) (handicapped child, but court analyzed case as wrongful conception or wrongful pregnancy case on the facts; emotional distress damages allowed based on distress at having handicapped child).   See Annotation, Recoverability of Compensatory damages for mental anguish or emotional distress for tortiously causing another's birth, 74 A.L.R.4th 798 (1989).

20. See "Offsets" below.

21. Siemieniec v. Lutheran General Hosp., 117 Ill.2d 230, 111 Ill.Dec. 302, 512 N.E.2d 691 (1987); Smith v. Cote, 128 N.H. 231, 513 A.2d 341, 348–349 (1986); Becker v. Schwartz, 46 N.Y.2d 401, 413 N.Y.S.2d 895, 386 N.E.2d 807 (1978).   In some authorities the distinction between emotional distress as *damages* and emotional distress as a freestanding *tort* seems to have been overlooked.

22. Smith v. Gore, 728 S.W.2d 738, 751 (Tenn.1987).

23. Lovelace Medical Center v. Mendez, 111 N.M. 336, 805 P.2d 603 (1991).

24. Pitre v. Opelousas General Hosp., 530 So.2d 1151 (La.1988) (expenses of pregnancy and delivery).

25. Smith v. Gore, 728 S.W.2d 738, 751 (Tenn.1987).

26. Pitre v. Opelousas General Hosp., 530 So.2d 1151 (La.1988); Burke v. Rivo, 406 Mass. 764, 551 N.E.2d 1 (1990).   See Gallagher v. Duke University, 852 F.2d 773 (4th Cir.1988) (treated as a wrongful conception case but involving handicapped child).   See Annotation, Recoverability of Compensatory damages for mental anguish or emotional distress for tortiously causing another's birth, 74 A.L.R.4th 798 (1989).

Tennessee has said that pain and suffering awards would be limited to the period of time from discovery of pregnancy until recovery from childbirth and that mental distress recovery is limited to the period from discovery of pregnancy to its termination.   Smith v. Gore, 728 S.W.2d 738, 751 (Tenn.1987).   The same court has recognized that mental distress might vary, and that age, marital status of the plaintiff-parent, the number of other children and other considerations would be relevant in assessing the distress.   New Mexico, foreseeing unseemly arguments over the appropriate offsets if emotional distress damages are allowed, concluded that emotional distress damages should not be allowed. Lovelace Medical Center v. Mendez, 111 N.M. 336, 805 P.2d 603 (1991).

27. Pitre v. Opelousas General Hosp., 530 So.2d 1151, 1161–1162 (La.1988); Burke v. Rivo, 406 Mass. 764, 551 N.E.2d 1 (1990); Smith v. Gore, 728 S.W.2d 738, 751 (Tenn. 1987).

28. See "Offsets" below.

Court said.[29] The parents demonstrated their desire not to rear a child by seeking the sterilization, and they will undoubtedly incur enormous economic costs,[30] so the court's statement seems to be a way of expressing legal policy,[31] not a way of describing either harm or a measure of damages.

Most courts considering the question have made statements similar to Kentucky's, or have argued that damages are out of proportion to the defendant's fault, that they are speculative, that the avoidable consequences rule would require the plaintiff-mother to put the child up for adoption rather than claim the expense of rearing, or that the benefits outweigh the harms as a matter of law, or in any event that the benefits should not be weighed by courts.[32]

Child-rearing expense—the minority. Several important decisions have taken a different position, allowing the jury to award child-rearing costs, at least where the parents sought to avoid having children in part for economic reasons.[33] In most cases, however, such recoveries may be subject to an offset for the emotional benefit the parents receive in having the child.

In a Connecticut case, Justice Peters pointed out that the normal liability of the tortfeasor is for all damages proximately caused. She suggested that an exception in wrongful pregnancy cases would run head-on into the mother's constitutional rights to employ contraceptive techniques.[34] In an Arizona case, Justice Feldman pointed to normal tort rules allowing an offset for benefits the parents might have from the birth of the child, and

29. Schork v. Huber, 648 S.W.2d 861 (Ky. 1983).

30. Justice Wilkins for the Massachusetts Court observing that the reasons for the limitation "are outstandingly unimpressive," added his reasons:

The judicial declaration that the joy and pride in raising a child always outweigh any economic loss the parents may suffer * * * simply lacks verisimilitude. The very fact that a person has sought medical intervention to prevent him or her from having a child demonstrates that, for that person, the benefits of parenthood did not outweigh the burdens, economic and otherwise, of having a child * * *.

Burke v. Rivo, 406 Mass. 764, 551 N.E.2d 1 (1990).

31. Cf. Kelly, The Rightful Position in "Wrongful Life" Actions, 42 Hast.L.J. 505, 525–535 (1991) (addressing the "no injury" conclusion in wrongful life cases as a policy expression).

32. See Cockrum v. Baumgartner, 95 Ill.2d 193, 69 Ill.Dec. 168, 447 N.E.2d 385 (1983); Pitre v. Opelousas General Hosp., 530 So.2d 1151, 1162 (La.1988) ("Absent unusual circumstances, a child is presumed to be a blessing not offset by the inconvenience of redistributing the family income and patrimony * * *."); O'Toole v. Greenberg, 64 N.Y.2d 427, 488 N.Y.S.2d 143, 477 N.E.2d 445 (1985); Johnson v. University Hospitals of Cleveland, 44 Ohio St.3d 49, 540 N.E.2d 1370 (1989); Miller v.

Johnson, 231 Va. 177, 343 S.E.2d 301 (1986); James G. v. Caserta, 175 W.Va. 406, 332 S.E.2d 872 (1985); Beardsley v. Wierdsma, 650 P.2d 288 (Wyo.1982).

Tennessee denied child-rearing costs on an entirely different and wholly non-remedial theory, namely that since parents have the responsibility for support of the child, others cannot have that responsibility; hence the defendant cannot be liable. Smith v. Gore, 728 S.W.2d 738, 751 (Tenn.1987). The usual view, of course, is that if the plaintiff incurs a financial responsibility as a result of the defendant's tort, this is grounds in favor of the defendant's liability rather than grounds against that liability. Thus when a tortfeasor injures a child, the parent's responsibility for the medical expenses of the child is grounds for allowing the parent to recover.

33. University of Arizona Health Sciences Center v. Superior Court, 136 Ariz. 579, 667 P.2d 1294 (1983); Ochs v. Borrelli, 187 Conn. 253, 445 A.2d 883 (1982); Jones v. Malinowski, 299 Md. 257, 473 A.2d 429 (1984); Burke v. Rivo, 406 Mass. 764, 551 N.E.2d 1 (1990); Lovelace Medical Center v. Mendez, 111 N.M. 336, 805 P.2d 603 (1991); Marciniak v. Lundborg, 153 Wis.2d 59, 450 N.W.2d 243 (1990). Offsetting emotional benefits against out-of-pocket expense raises another problem, however. See "Offsets" below.

34. Ochs v. Borrelli, 187 Conn. 253, 445 A.2d 883, 885 (1982).

concluded that the jury, representing a cross section of the community, could best assess those benefits in the light of the plaintiff's reasons for seeking a sterilization in the first place.[35]

Genetic defects in wrongful pregnancy cases. The usual wrongful pregnancy case involves birth of a normal, healthy child. The defendant's negligent failure to prevent the plaintiff's pregnancy may, however, lead happenstantially to the birth of a child suffering genetic defects. If the reason for seeking to prevent pregnancy in the first place was a risk of genetic defects, there seems no reason to deny recovery for the extraordinary expense of rearing the child.[36] On the other hand, if the reasons for preventing pregnancy were not based on genetic risks but on financial, emotional or personal considerations of the parents, the risk the doctor creates by a negligent sterilization procedure is the risk of a normal pregnancy and a healthy child, not the risk of a child suffering genetic defects. In that kind of case, the defendant may not be regarded as a "legal cause" or proximate cause of the damages resulting from the genetic problems, even though he is a legal cause of other harms. The Louisiana Court has so held.[37]

Offsets

Offsets; the "benefits" rule. The general rule of damages is that benefits to the plaintiff that result directly from the tort must be offset against the damages otherwise due.[38] Most courts have professed to believe that the parents will have benefits in having a child, whether it is a "wrongful birth" child with a handicap or a "normal" but unwanted child. On this basis, and on the added ground that the benefits and joys of parenthood were unmeasurable if not infinite, some earlier decisions rejected the wrongful birth claims altogether. Although both wrongful birth and wrongful pregnancy claims are now usually entertained, the courts continue to use the offset in several different ways.

Wrongful pregnancy and presumed benefit. In wrongful pregnancy cases some courts use the offset under a rule that presumes the parents' emotional benefits to be in excess of all child-rearing costs, the effect being to say that the cost of rearing the child cannot be recovered in wrongful pregnancy cases.[39] But the presumed blessing is *not* usually presumed to outweigh the

35. University of Arizona Health Sciences Center v. Superior Court, 136 Ariz. 579, 667 P.2d 1294, 1299–1301 (1983).

36. Cf. Gallagher v. Duke University, 852 F.2d 773 (4th Cir.1988) (pregnancy would have been prevented if doctor had correctly diagnosed genetic problem, extraordinary costs recoverable).

37. Pitre v. Opelousas General Hosp., 530 So.2d 1151, 1161–1162 (La.1988). Justice Dennis wrote:

"[W]e conclude that as a general principle that the same criterion of foreseeability and risk of harm which determined whether a physician in this kind of situation was negligent in the first instance should determine the extent of his liability for that negli-

gence; and that the doctor should not be held liable for consequences which no reasonable practitioner would expect to follow from the conduct * * *. The parents may not recover for the special expenses regarding the child's deformity, or for emotional and mental distress associated with the child's deformity. These are not consequences which were caused by an impact on the person of the mother or which a reasonable practitioner would expect to follow from the conduct as alleged * * *."

38. See §§ 3.8(2) above and 8.6(2) below.

39. See Schork v. Huber, 648 S.W.2d 861, 862 (Ky.1983) ("The benefits conferred by the child's existence clearly outweigh any economic burden involved"); Pitre v. Opelousas General Hosp., 530 So.2d 1151, 1162 (La.1988).

costs of pregnancy and delivery, emotional and mental distress and consortium interests.[40] The presumption and the compulsory offset seem to reflect a policy decision, not an actual measuring of damages in cases following these views.

Wrongful pregnancy and "actual" benefit. On the other hand, in those courts which allow recovery of child-rearing costs in wrongful pregnancy claims, no presumption is indulged that the emotional benefits exceed the costs. These courts allow a recovery of child-rearing costs, and allow the trier to reduce that recovery by the amount of emotional benefits actually accruing to the parents. In these cases the trier must estimate the intangible benefit on the basis of the facts of the case, and similarly must estimate the intangible costs in the form of mental distress.

Wrongful pregnancy: emotional benefits offsetting economic loss? In this category of cases, an additional question arises. Should the emotional benefits of unwanted parenthood be offset only against the parent's emotional distress claims? Or should the emotional benefits be offset against the economic losses of the parents' as well? Decisions in this category have usually concluded that the economic losses and the emotional harm were "inextricably related to each other," and that the trier should be allowed to offset emotional benefits against both emotional distress and economic costs.[41]

The effect of the offset in this situation is to credit the defendant with benefits to the plaintiff in one category against losses in another. This seemingly violates the normal rules that benefits from a tort are to be offset only against losses to the same "interest."[42] The idea of the normal rule is that if the defendant negligently burns down your trees, reducing the value of your land, he does not get any credit for the pleasures you might get because your view is enhanced at the same time your shade is lost.[43] Although those pleasures might be real, they do not diminish the economic loss.

Wrongful pregnancy: undiminished recovery of child-rearing expenses. A New Mexico case follows the logic of the general rule for offsetting benefits by holding that the emotional benefits to the parents from having

40. Pitre v. Opelousas General Hosp., 530 So.2d 1151, 1161–1162 (La.1988).

41. University of Arizona Health Sciences Center v. Superior Court (Heimann), 136 Ariz. 579, 667 P.2d 1294, 1299, n. 4 (1983); Jones v. Malinowski, 299 Md. 257, 473 A.2d 429, 435 (1984) (child rearing costs to the age of the child's majority, offset by the benefits derived from the child's aid, society and comfort). Cf. Morris v. Frudenfeld, 135 Cal.App.3d 23, 185 Cal.Rptr. 76 (1982) (plaintiff requested offset instruction based on prior authority, under which emotional benefits would be offset against costs of child-rearing and could not object when jury awarded only medical expenses); Ochs v. Borrelli, 187 Conn. 253, 445 A.2d 883 (1982) (trial court so instructed with

concurrence of plaintiff, perhaps with tacit approval on appeal). See Note, One More Mouth To Feed, 25 Ariz.L.Rev. 1069 (1983).

42. Restatement Second of Torts § 920 and Comments *a* and *b* (1979) ("benefit to the interest of the plaintiff that was harmed").

43. The enhancement of a view might also tend to reduce economic loss because while the property may be worth less without the trees, its loss in value may not be as great as it would otherwise be if the felled trees open to a beautiful view. The normal rule does not ignore this effect. Nor does it ignore the landowner's pleasure at having a view if he claims emotional harm damages. Instead, it simply prohibits reduction of his economic harm claim by his non-economic benefits.

the child must not be used to offset their economic losses.[44] The same court held, however, that emotional harms to the parents resulting from having the child would have to be offset by emotional benefits. In its view, the task of making such an offset would be so unseemly that damages for emotional harms to parents of healthy children should simply be denied altogether. The effect of that decision is to permit a full recovery for economic loss without offset, but to deny the emotional harm claim altogether. A Wisconsin case appears to go further by allowing full recovery of child-rearing expenses without constricting any other damages to which the plaintiff might be entitled.[45]

Wrongful birth. In wrongful birth cases, where the defendant's liability in the first place includes the extraordinary costs of rearing the handicapped child, it seems clear that if the parents are found or presumed to have emotional benefits from having the child, the benefits should be offset only against the parents' claims for emotional distress. Otherwise, the expense recovery aimed primarily at providing medical and related attention for the child would be absorbed by the purely non-economic "benefit" to the parents.[46]

The courts seem to agree with this point, and usually allow the offset in wrongful birth cases only against the emotional distress claim.[47] One theoretical basis for this conclusion lies in the Restatement view that benefits may be offset only against the same kinds of losses.[48] But as indicated above, the Restatement theory has not been much applied in the case of wrongful *pregnancy* claims. Whatever is right in the wrongful pregnancy cases, however, it must be recognized that the offset in wrongful birth cases could have devastating consequences because its practical effect is to take support and care from the child because of the parent's supposed joys.

Comment. The offset required for direct benefits resulting from tort is often in conflict with the very general principle of personal autonomy that no one is required to pay for unsolicited benefits.[49] Perhaps the best case for requiring one to pay for an unwanted "benefit" is the case in which the

44. Lovelace Medical Center v. Mendez, 111 N.M. 336, 805 P.2d 603 (1991).

45. Marciniak v. Lundborg, 153 Wis.2d 59, 450 N.W.2d 243, 249 (1990) ("It was precisely to avoid that 'benefit' that the parents went to the physician in the first place * * * it hardly seems equitable to not only force this benefit upon them but to tell them they must pay for it as well as by offsetting it against their proven emotional damages").

46. Where "wrongful life" claims have been recognized, this error is automatically avoided because the child would recover the extraordinary economic costs in his own name; the parents' joys could not, presumably, be offset against the child's loss.

47. Phillips v. United States, 575 F.Supp. 1309 (D.S.C.1983) (wrongful birth, judge as trier of fact offset emotional benefits only against emotional distress damages); Blake v. Cruz, 108 Idaho 253, 698 P.2d 315, 320 (1984)

("In determining damages for emotional injury, countervailing emotional benefits attributable to the birth of the child should also be considered and the award adjusted accordingly").

Some cases have used broader language but do not appear to be addressing the issue. In Eisbrenner v. Stanley, 106 Mich.App. 357, 308 N.W.2d 209 (1981) the court literally says that the plaintiff can recover medical and hospital expenses, lost wages, child-rearing costs, pain and anxiety, "to be offset by the value to plaintiffs of the child's services and companionship," but the court is alluding to earlier authority not involving wrongful birth and appears to be addressing only the issue whether mental distress is recoverable.

48. Restatement Second of Torts § 920 and Comments *a* and *b* (1979) ("benefit to the interest of the plaintiff that was harmed").

49. See § 4.9 above.

benefit provides the means of payment. A class-action class member who benefits in cash from an attorney's services can easily be held for a share of the attorney's fee, even if the class member did not seek the attorney's work. In such a case the unsolicited benefit produces the cash with which to pay it.

In the wrongful birth and wrongful pregnancy cases the emotional benefit most definitely does *not* produce the cash with which to pay for it. Instead, the wrongdoer is given an immediate cash deduction from his liability, while the victim pays a cash outlay for the unwanted benefit for perhaps the rest of his or her life.[50] The restrictive recovery rules applied in many courts thus seem to be completely out of line with general rules of tort law, which hold tortfeasors for all proximate damage, and just as opposed to the principles of personal autonomy. The decisions may be justified on some basis of policy[51] but they do not seem explicable under the ordinary principles of tort or damages law.

Avoidable Consequences—"Mitigation" of Damages

The avoidable consequences rule excludes recovery for any damages that could have been reasonably avoided by the plaintiff.[52] This rule has raised the question whether a plaintiff suffering from an unwanted pregnancy as the result of the defendant's negligence must seek an abortion to minimize damages. Although courts have sometimes played with the idea as an argument for denying any claim at all, or severely limiting the claim, almost no court seems to have actually applied such an idea.[53] As the Tennessee Court observed, any such requirement might "infringe upon Constitutional rights to privacy in these matters," and in addition would fail the reasonableness test which is built into the avoidable consequences rule.[54]

In wrongful birth cases, the nature of the case is that there is no opportunity for terminating the pregnancy, but there remains the possibili-

---

50. Perhaps this is the problem the Restatement intended to reach, although somewhat circuitously, in providing the benefit to the victim was not credited to the defendant unless the benefit acquired was to the very same "interest" damaged by the defendant. Restatement Second of Torts § 920 and Comments *a* and *b* (1979).

51. Perhaps the restrictive rules grow out of a concern that the courts can no longer use directed verdicts or new trial orders in an effective way to control irrational verdicts on the merits and that an innocent physician might be held liable for stunning sums without justification. If this is the real reason it is no surprise that the courts do not wish to discuss it.

52. See §§ 3.9 above and 8.7 below.

53. The possibility of abortion to minimize damages has been suggested as a ground for denying recovery of normal child-rearing expenses. See Robak v. United States, 658 F.2d 471, 479, n. 23 (7th Cir.1981) ("Because they freely chose not to have an abortion, they should be responsible for the costs of a normal child"); Sorkin v. Lee, 78 A.D.2d 180, 434 N.Y.S.2d 300 (1980) (normal child-rearing expenses were avoidable because abortion was

possible, but "We do not suggest that the mother was obliged to terminate the pregnancy"). These cases appear to adopt a rule of damages that excludes the normal costs of child-rearing for the very purpose of *avoiding* the issue of minimizing damages and some of the decisions have spelled this point out in detail. See Flowers v. District of Columbia, 478 A.2d 1073 (D.C.App.1984). In Cowe v. Forum Group, Inc., 541 N.E.2d 962 (Ind.App. 1989) the child-plaintiff had in fact been adopted. His wrongful life claim for support was denied from the time of adoption on the ground that the adoptive parents assumed the liability; but the adoptive parents were not parties and were not themselves asserting a claim. On appeal, the entire claim was rejected. 575 N.E.2d 630 (Ind.1991).

54. Smith v. Gore, 728 S.W.2d 738, 751–752 (Tenn.1987). See also Ochs v. Borrelli, 187 Conn. 253, 445 A.2d 883, 885 (1982) (constitutional rights of mother require allowance of child-rearing costs, too); Marciniak v. Lundborg, 153 Wis.2d 59, 450 N.W.2d 243, 247 (1990) (not reasonable under ordinary rules to require abortion to minimize damages)

ty, also open in wrongful pregnancy cases, that damages could be minimized by relinquishing the child for adoption. Relinquishment might indeed work a sound economic result, but the tort is not in the first instance an economic tort. The defendant having deprived the mother of one choice has no right to force upon her another choice she does not want to make. With these ideas in mind, it seems unlikely that courts will require a mother to give up her legitimate claim or her child, one or the other.[55]

§ 8.3 Wrongful Death and Survival Actions

§ 8.3(1) Substantive Background and Remedial Summary

Substantive Common Law Rules [1]

Three rules. Three distinct and basic common law rules bore on recovery of damages in death cases. These rules remain important today as the reasons for modern statutory changes. These rules were: (1) If the tortfeasor died after committing a tort against his victim, the victim's claim died as well.[2] (2) If the tort *victim* died, his cause of action was at an end, "drowned," in the larger matter of a crime against the Crown.[3] (3) The victim's survivors had no independent claim of their own against the tortfeasor for the loss of their support or for their grief and sorrow.[4] There has never been any good explanation for all these rules.[5]

---

55. Courts have sometimes emphasized the plaintiff's probable pleasure in keeping the normal child, and that it would outweigh the costs of rearing, by pointing out that the parents had not or would not put the child up for adoption, even though there would be many available adoptive parents. E.g., Rieck v. Medical Protective Co. of Fort Wayne, Ind., 64 Wis.2d 514, 219 N.W.2d 242, 245 (1974); Ball v. Mudge, 64 Wash.2d 247, 391 P.2d 201, 204 (1964). Those cases seem only to use the usual rule that the "benefits" of the unwanted child outweigh the doctor's potential liability; adoption or lack of adoption is mentioned only as a means of demonstrating a basis for that conclusion.

In Smith v. Cote, 128 N.H. 231, 513 A.2d 341, 348–349 (1986) the court limited recovery of economic damages to the "extraordinary" costs on the theory such a limitation was an appropriate trade for the gain the parents make in wrongful birth cases because the avoidable consequences rule is not applied. The court reasoned that the avoidable consequences rule forbids recovery of damages that could have been avoided, and that this would normally require the parents to put the child up for adoption. Out of "respect for sanctity of the family," the court was unwilling to require a mandatory adoption. Since the parents would be relieved of the mandates of the avoidable consequences rule, the court thought their damages should be limited. The court then suggested a more direct reason for limiting damages. In wrongful birth cases the parents want a child, so that economically speaking, the harm suffered is only that represented by the extraordinary child-rearing expenses. It suggested that this line of reasoning was supported by contract-damages concepts. But the core of the court's point is that the harm is represented accurately by comparing the cost of a normal, healthy child with the cost of the plaintiffs daughter; if that point is well-taken, the damage measure is consistent with any damages measure, either tort or contract.

§ 8.3(1)

1. See generally, Prosser & Keeton on Torts §§ 125A–127 (5th ed. 1984).

2. The reason for this may have been that tort and crime were not distinct categories in the early law and there seemed little point in punishing the tortfeasor's successors in an action that seemed as much "criminal" in nature as it did tortious. See Winfield, Death as Affecting Liability in Tort, 29 Colum.L.Rev. 237, 242 (1929); Smedley, Wrongful Death— Bases of the Common Law Rules, 13 Vand. L.Rev. 605 (1960).

3. See Higgins v. Butcher, Yelv. 89, 80 Eng.Rep. 61 (K.B. 1607). There was early statutory limitation on this rule, however, and some tort actions, such as those for conversion of or damage to personal property did survive the victim's death, even though torts to his person or real property did not. See Winfield, Death as Affecting Liability in Tort, 29 Colum.L.Rev. 237, 242–43 (1929).

4. Baker v. Bolton, 1 Camp. 493, 170 Eng. Rep. 1033 (Nisi Prius 1808).

5. At one time they were said to reflect the Latin maxim, *action personalis moriturcum*

Effect. Taken together these three rules meant that if a tortfeasor killed a person, neither the victim's losses before death nor the losses to dependents who were deprived of support would be compensable. And if the victim lived but the tortfeasor died, the victim could get no compensation from the tortfeasor's estate.

American Survival and Death Statutes

Judge-made claims. After a period in which American courts permitted recovery of death damages at common law,[6] a reversal set in,[7] perhaps triggered by the existence of spotty legislation recognizing death claims in narrow instances.[8] From 1848 on, American common law courts repeatedly rejected any judge-made wrongful death claim.[9] American Admiralty courts, perhaps out of inertia or perhaps out of reluctance to compete with common law courts for suitors, originally did the same.[10] Only many years later, in 1970, did the Supreme Court recognize a death action in Admiralty.[11] Today federal civil rights claims for wrongful death seem to be edging toward recognizing a right that is an amalgam of the Constitution, federal and state statutes, and judge-made civil rights death actions.[12]

Wrongful death statutes. Most states now create a new action in favor of certain beneficiaries, usually intended to afford recompense for the pecuniary loss of those survivors dependent upon the deceased[14] and hence measuring damages by the loss of their support.[15] For example, if the deceased was supporting a spouse and children by providing food, shelter and medical care, the economic value of those provisions would be the main measure of damages. Today, most statutes go beyond this to cover at least some non-pecuniary claims of survivors as well.[16] These statutes address the Third Rule of the common law and reverse it; they are usually known as wrongful death statutes or "death statutes" to distinguish them from the "survival" statutes.

---

persona, that is, that personal actions die with the person. But even if that maxim explained anything, which it does not, it could not explain why contract actions survive and tort actions do not, or why some tort actions, like those for harm to personal property survive.

6. Malone, The Genesis of Wrongful Death, 17 Stan.L.Rev. 1043 (1965).

7. Carey v. Berkshire R.R., 55 Mass. (1 Cush.) 475, 48 Am.Dec. 616 (1848).

9. E.g., Miller v. Wellman Dynamics Corp., 419 N.W.2d 380 (Iowa 1988). But cf. Gaudette v. Webb, 362 Mass. 60, 284 N.E.2d 222, 62 A.L.R.3d 893 (1972) (death action is now a common law right with statute regulating procedures and remedies).

10. The Harrisburg, 119 U.S. 199, 7 S.Ct. 140, 30 L.Ed. 358 (1886).

11. Moragne v. States Marine Lines, Inc., 398 U.S. 375, 90 S.Ct. 1772, 26 L.Ed.2d 339 (1970).

12. See Gilmere v. City of Atlanta, 864 F.2d 734 (11th Cir.1989) (rejecting state wrongful death statute's measure of damages

because constitutional tort requires compensatory measure); § 7.4(3) above. Since the state wrongful death statute, unlike the survival statute, is considered to create a new cause of action, by definition it cannot be the cause of action created by federal civil rights statutes. Federal civil rights statutes, on the other hand, do not in themselves explicitly create a wrongful death action.

14. Many of the statutes were modeled on Lord Campbell's Act, the English statute that introduced the wrongful death action in that country. 9 & 10 Vict. Ch. 93 (1846). It read in part:

"That whensoever the Death of a Person shall be caused by wrongful Act, Neglect, or Default, and the Act, Neglect, or Default is such as would (if Death had not ensued) have entitled the Party injured to maintain an Action and recover Damages in respect thereof, then and in every such Case the Person who would have been liable * * * shall be liable to an action for Damages, notwithstanding the Death of the Person injured * * *."

Survival statutes. Survival statutes differ from wrongful death statutes; they do not provide for an independent action in favor of the deceased's dependents. Instead, they provide for the survival of whatever action the deceased himself would have had if he had lived—for example, for his pain and suffering, loss of wages, and medical expenses between the time of injury and death. Survival statutes do not address the Third Rule of the common law as the death statutes do; they address and reverse the First and Second Rules. Almost all states appear to have both death and survival statutes in some form, so that it is frequently possible that a tortfeasor will be liable for any losses the decedent had before his death as well as for the loss of support of the decedent's dependents.[17]

Hybrid statutes. Several statutes seem to involve some combination of objectives in a single statute—protection of dependents and also revival of the claim the victim would have had if he had lived. Because a single statute is left to do the work of both the death and survival actions, the measure of damages in such cases may not quite reflect either. In these cases, damages are not measured by the losses suffered by dependents, nor by the claims the deceased would have had for his own injury. Rather, the damages are measured, with local differences in the exact formulation, by the amount the deceased victim could have accumulated in the remainder of his lifetime.[18]

Changing Purposes and Enduring Problems

Social welfare purposes. The wrongful death statutes as a whole have often presented shameful injustices. In part this has been because the statutes have seldom been clearly conceived, precisely drafted or consistently executed. The initial purpose was undoubtedly more related to a limited version of social welfare than to corrective justice. The idea was to protect dependents from lost support when a breadwinner was killed; damages were based on the loss of income. This narrowly defined purpose provided no recovery when the deceased was not a breadwinner—when he was a home-maker, a retired person, or a child. The ensuing cases reflected a choice between a raw sense of injustice or judicial manipulation of the statute.[19]

Property protection purposes. From time to time and in some states the purpose of the death statutes shifted, sometimes unconsciously, to a property purpose—protection of heirs' inheritance rights rather than dependents' sustenance rights. This purpose is reflected in the loss-to-the-estate measure of damages, based on the estate the deceased could have amassed over a normal life span. In the grip of this purpose, one could overlook the income loss of dependents and there was no provision that dependents would get first call on the recovery. In fact, damages based on the inheritance the deceased could have provided might actually be paid to those who would never have inherited from the deceased or taken under his will.

Maldistribution of dependents' recoveries. When recovery is based on a loss-to-the-estate measure but beneficiaries are those living now rather than those who would have taken at the end of the decedent's normal life span, the damages are either mismeasured or maldistributed. If the measure is right, the distribution seems wrong. If the distribution is right, the measure is wrong. Similarly, if the object of the statute is to protect dependents from lost support, a requirement that damages be based on or paid to "heirs" or other categories, may prevent distribution to a real dependent with a real loss. Because little attention has been paid in the statutes to appropriate distribution of the recovery, some statutes seem literally to require damages to be measured by the support lost by one person and at the same time to require distribution of the recovery to someone else altogether. At best, statutes may prevent recovery by dependents who do not fall within pre-established categories, such as "heirs."

Pecuniary vs. non-pecuniary claims. Part of the difficulty in administration of death and survival statutes has arisen because the social vision behind the statutes has imperceptibly changed and expanded. The original social welfare notion was the protection of family dependents, which meant protection against their pecuniary loss. One mutation, toward a property concept which meant an emphasis on inheritance rather than on sustenance, has already been observed. A very different change has been perhaps more conscious. This is the increased emphasis on the personal rather than the financial losses of dependents, with resulting increased availability of non-pecuniary awards.[20]

§ 8.3(2) Survival Statute Damages

Two forms of survival actions. The survival statute, as distinct from the wrongful death action, can cover two kinds of cases. In the first, the victim has died without making a recovery against the tortfeasor. If the survival statute applies to this case, it allows the victim's estate to collect the damages the victim himself could have collected had he been able to pursue the tort claim for his injuries before his death. In the second kind of case, it is the tortfeasor who has died, not the victim. The survival statute, if it applies at all, allows the victim to proceed against the estate of the tortfeasor, again to collect his tort damages. In both cases the victim's damages are based on his own injury, not on losses of survivors. For the most part, the damages in the two kinds of survival action are the same. For convenience, the discussion here is based on the first kind of case, in which the injured victim had died and the tortfeasor remains alive.

General rule. The survival action (of the first type) is usually brought by the decedent's personal representative on behalf of the estate in the same way the personal representative might bring suit to collect a debt owed the deceased. Because the claim is regarded as a continuation of the claim the deceased brought or could have brought during his lifetime, the damages are usually measured by the damages the decedent himself suffered and, with certain exclusions and adjustments, they are the same as the damages in an ordinary personal injury action.

Exclusion of particular elements. Most states exclude recovery of *future* lost earnings from the survival action.[1] In addition, individual statutes exclude or condition specific elements of recovery. For example, a statute may forbid recovery of pain and suffering damages,[2] or may forbid recovery of punitive damages.[3] As with all statutory matters, the latest version of the governing statute must be consulted.

Recovery of particular elements. In the absence of a statutory exclusion, recovery in the survival action usually includes (1) the tort victim's medical expenses resulting from the injury,[4] (2) conscious[5] pain and suffering resulting from the injury,[6] (3) any earnings lost between the time of injury and the death [7]; (4) punitive damages against a living tortfeasor,[8] and (5) funeral expenses,[9] when such expenses are not allocated to [10] or actually recovered in the wrongful death action.[11]

Punitive damages. Punitive damages are usually denied in the second type of survival action; they are denied, that is, in claims against the estate of the deceased tortfeasor.[22] Under the view that punitive damages serve only to punish or deter misconduct, this result is logical. If, however, punitive damages are to be denied not only in the survival but also in the wrongful death actions, lawyers may find it financially infeasible to bring some actions that should in all justice be pursued.[23]

§ 8.3(3) Wrongful Death Statute Damages—Summary

Damages under wrongful death statutes are quite distinct from those recoverable under survival statutes. The principle item of damages under wrongful death statutes is the economic loss to survivors. Apart from relatively minor items such as funeral expense,[1] most states measure economic loss by the loss of support to dependents. Some measure it differently, by the loss of projected lifetime savings of the deceased. The first measure is usually called loss to survivors or loss to dependents measure, while the second is called the loss to the estate measure.[2]

The original wrongful death statutes limited recovery to pecuniary loss and some still do. This meant that the death of someone not earning money—a child, an older person, a homemaker—resulted in little or no recovery. In particular, mental anguish recoveries for the dependents or heirs were not allowed. However, over the years, through legislative change and through judicial opinions, courts have come to allow substantial non-economic recoveries in death cases, usually as some kind of consortium claim for loss of services or society of the deceased.[3]

Punitive damages were likewise generally excluded under the pecuniary loss standard of most of the earlier statutes. Punitive damages may be recovered today where the statute is construed to permit such a recovery, otherwise they are still excluded.[4]

Most of the economic portions of wrongful death damages represent future loss. Contributions of the decedent to survivors, for example, would take place over a period of years, so that damages can be fixed only when the trier of fact estimates the amount and interval of contributions and also the normal life-span of the deceased or the period in which he would normally earn money and make contributions. Reduction to present value, or some substitute adjustment, is then required.[5]

[For detailed rules and analysis consult §§ 8.3(4) & 8.3(5) in the Practitioner Treatise edition, vol. 2, pp. 430–445.]

§ 8.3(4) Wrongful Death Statute Damages—Economic Damages

[For the text of this section, see the unabridged Practitioner Treatise edition.]

§ 8.3(5) Non–economic Damages

[*For the text of this section, see the unabridged Practitioner Treatise edition.*]

§ 8.3(6) Nominal Damages, Punitive Damages, Interest

[*For the text of this section, see the unabridged Practitioner Treatise edition.*]

8.3(7) Death Damages—Damages Affected by Events Subsequent to Death

Post-death Changes in Damages Generally

Are damages fixed at the time of death? Courts often say that damages for wrongful death are measured at the time of death and fixed at that point, implying that subsequent effects cannot affect the amount of the recovery. The cases are not fully consistent with this proposition, however. At best the proposition works in some contexts but not in others.

Events bearing on damages to survivors. A number of events after the death of the decedent might occur to minimize losses of the beneficiaries. For instance, the spouse might remarry, or a child might be adopted, or the survivors themselves might die. In addition, their needs for support might change.

Remarriage of a spouse, death of a survivor and altered needs of dependents. Remarriage of a surviving spouse after the death is usually ignored in fixing damages; the remarried spouse recovers as if support and consortium would be lost for the rest of the plaintiff's life. This can be expressed as a rule that damages are fixed at the time of death, not at some later time. But death of the same surviving spouse at some point after the primary decedent's death and before judgment is usually considered as a basis for reducing damages, or as a basis for computing damages on the loss to different beneficiaries, or even as a basis for abating the wrongful death action altogether. This practice can be expressed as a rule contrary to the first, namely, as a rule that damages are *not* fixed at the time of death. When the financial circumstances of beneficiaries change after the death, so that either more or less support might be needed, the results are mixed but limited. If there is a principle that explains all these cases it is not that damages are fixed at death.

[*For discussion and analysis of these rules see this section in the Practitioner Treatise edition, vol. 2, pp. 448–454.*]

§ 8.4 Adjustments: Delayed Payment of Past Damages—Interest

[*For the text of this section, see the unabridged Practitioner Treatise edition.*]

§ 8.5   Adjustments: Future Damages: Reduction to Present Value and Inflation Adjustment

§ 8.5(1) Summary

[*For the text of this section, see the unabridged Practitioner Treatise edition.*]

§ 8.5(2)   Adjustments for Future Damages Generally: Establishing the Loss Period

Loss Periods Generally

Relevance of loss period. To permit computation of damages for future losses such as continuing wage loss or future medical expense, the plaintiff must establish not only the probability that such damages will occur, but also the time period over which they will accrue. The loss period is also an important element in two adjustments—the reduction to present value [1] and the adjustment for potential future inflation.[2]

Loss periods in permanent injury cases. The harm may be temporary, in which case the loss period will ordinarily be for a limited time in the future as established by medical evidence. Or the harm may be permanent. In that case two types of loss period may be in issue, and both of them are likely to be resolved in part by reference to statistical compilations. The first period is the plaintiff's life expectancy (or, in a wrongful death action, the life expectancy of the deceased or of a beneficiary). The second period is the plaintiff's work-life expectancy, the period of time in the future in which she or he is likely to be both living and working. This second loss period is relevant to the claim for lost wages or earning capacity. Mortality tables may be used to show life expectancy; work-life tables to show work-life.

The Life Expectancy Loss Period

Mortality tables admissible. The plaintiff who claims permanent injury—pain, medical expense, or wage loss—must establish the life expectancy period. Sometimes life expectancy is also relevant in wrongful death cases.[3] Mortality tables, which are relevant in valuing property at divorce and for many other such purposes,[4] are almost always admitted in some form to show the plaintiff's or decedent's life expectancy.[5] They are usually introduced through the testimony of an economist or other expert,[6] but sometimes they are simply given to the jury in a judge's instruction.[7]

Nature of mortality tables. A mortality table attempts to show the average future life at any given age. Mortality tables are based on experience with a particular group of people at a particular time and place in history. If a table were made up on the basis of experience with poor people with inadequate medical care or nourishment, it would show a shorter life expectancy at some ages than a table made up on the basis of experience with people who are well nourished and medically well cared for. A table made up by studying the lives of people who buy life insurance is likely to show longer life expectancy than one made up by studying the lives of jobless

§ 8.5(2)

5. Harlow v. Chin, 405 Mass. 697, 545 N.E.2d 602 (1989); Teegarden v. Dahl, 138 N.W.2d 668, 46 A.L.R.3d 708 (N.D.1965) (judicial notice of mortality tables, trial judge could instruct on life expectancy on basis of known age); Annotation, Admissibility of mortality tables in personal injury action as dependent upon showing of permanency of injury, 50 A.L.R.2d 419 (1956).

or homeless persons. Tables made up from data in 1900 in general will show a shorter life expectancy than tables made up from data today.[8]

Limits of mortality tables. Though mortality tables are helpful in some ways, they are not conclusive and they may be misleading. Professor Immel long ago pointed out that the average future lifetime shown by such a table is not the same as the most *likely* future lifetime, so that one may in all likelihood expect to live 43 years even though the mortality table shows an average expectancy of only 35 years.[9] In addition, mortality tables are necessarily out of date when life expectancy is in fact increasing.

Individualized health information. Individuals are all different, and no matter how accurate the mortality table, it cannot predict a single individual's life span. Accordingly, the plaintiff is permitted to show that the decedent in a death case was in excellent health just before the mortal injury; and likewise the defendant might show, if it is not a tactical error to do so, that the decedent or plaintiff was in poor health and unlikely to live long in any event.[10] So the ultimate estimate about probable life expectancy may be made by combining statistical data with more personalized estimates.

Prejudicial health information. If the personalized facts about the plaintiff only vaguely bear on his health and life expectancy, and at the same time is highly prejudicial, courts may exclude testimony about those facts. For instance, the plaintiff's (or deceased's) habitual use of drugs or abuse of alcohol,[11] or status as an illegal alien whose statistical life expectancy may not be the same as that of American citizens,[12] may all be kept from the jury.

Policy Issues on Mortality Tables

Ethnic and gender distinctions. Most mortality tables are likely to show that some national, ethnic or racial groups—African–Americans, for example—have a much shorter average life than some other groups.[13] In addition, the tables usually show that there is also a significant gender difference in life expectancy.[14] A white woman in mid-life may expect to outlive a black male of the same age by perhaps ten years.[15] Other figures might be produced to show differences in life expectancy among those who live in different states or communities. Whether a plaintiff or deceased with a shorter life expectancy must accept the table that most particularly describes that plaintiff, or whether the plaintiff can use the general average of

---

9. See Immel, Actuarial Tables and Damage Awards, 19 Ohio St.L.J. 240, 244 (1958).

13. As of 1986 the government figures showed, for example, that white persons in the 35–40 age range had an average life expectancy of 42.5 years, but that black persons in the same age range had an expectancy of only 37.8 years. See II Vital Statistics of the United States, 1986, Sec. 6, Life Table, Pages 7 and 9 (1988). *Caveat:* The figures given are for illustration only. Data changes over time; the latest available statistics should be consulted for actual use.

14. The "All Races" category shows that males in the 35–40 year age range have an average life expectancy of 39.1; females in the same category and at the same age have an expectancy of 44.9. See II Vital Statistics of the United States, 1986, Sec. 6, Life Table, Page 6 (1988).

15. A black male in the 35–40 age range has an average life expectancy of 34.3 years, while a white female in the same age range has an average life expectancy of 45.3 years. At some other ages the difference may be greater. At birth, the black male has an average expectancy of 65.2 years, the white female 78.8 years. See II Vital Statistics of the United States, 1986, Sec. 6, Life Table Pages 7 and 9 (1988).

all groups to show life expectancy is a point that is both troubling and unclear.

Implications of a compensatory purpose. The compensatory purpose of damages suggests that liability should be limited to actual loss. Conceivably society at large is responsible for the fact that some groups are afflicted with a relatively short life expectancy. But the defendant is not responsible for the life expectancy the plaintiff had before the injury, nor has the defendant caused the loss of anything more than that life expectancy.[16] Whatever reparation society as a whole should make, there seems little basis for inflicting liability upon the defendant for a harm he did not cause, so long as the purpose of the damage award is purely compensatory. If the best evidence of actual loss of life expectancy is reflected in a table that groups people by gender or race or nationality, compensatory principles suggest that such a grouping should be used; but the question remains whether the groupings do represent the best evidence, or even acceptable evidence of life expectancy.[17]

Gender discrimination rulings on mortality tables. In certain sex discrimination cases under Title VII,[18] the Supreme Court has required a unisex mortality table for pension benefits, even though use of a unisex table may mean that men as a class will pay more for the same benefit, or pay the same for less benefit, because women as a class live longer, or at least have done so in the past.[19] These decisions are based on a statute[20] which is interpreted to make any formal distinction between men and women illegal; for this reason they do not technically control the question in personal injury suits. Sometimes gender-based and race-based tables are used in trials without objection,[21] or used to give the plaintiff the more favorable table that applies particularly to him.[22] In a federal estate tax matter, gender-based mortality tables were approved as promoting accuracy in valuing the interests in question.[23] They have also been used in valuing pension rights upon divorce.[24]

On the analogous question whether nationality or ethnic status can be considered as affecting life expectancy, the Wisconsin Court found it possible to skirt the issue, but the effect of its holding was to allow a Mexican citizen to claim the life expectancy shown by mortality tables for citizens of the United States.[25] Massachusetts allowed the use of ordinary mortality tables in the case of a quadriplegic plaintiff, even though the life expectancy of such a seriously injured person is less than normal.[26] The Massachusetts case differs enormously from the Wisconsin case, however, because the Wisconsin courts prevented the jury from hearing evidence of the plaintiff's nationality, which would probably affect his life expectancy. In the Massa-

16. See Follett v. Jones, 252 Ark. 950, 481 S.W.2d 713 (1972) (defendant responsible for death of man who was already dying of cancer, liability limited to actual life expectancy); Dillon v. Twin State Gas & Elec. Co., 85 N.H. 449, 163 A. 111 (1932) (if deceased, who has fallen from bridge, would die when he hit the ground, defendant who was responsible for deceased's electrocution as he fell would be liable only for the time deceased had left to live).

17. Cf. Brilmayer, Hekeler, Laycock and Sullivan, Sex Discrimination in Employer–Sponsored Insurance Plans: A Legal and Demographic Analysis, 47 U.Chi.L.Rev. 505 (1980).

18. Los Angeles Dept. of Water & Power v. Manhart, 435 U.S. 702, 98 S.Ct. 1370, 55 L.Ed.2d 657 (1978); Arizona Governing Committee, Etc. v. Norris, 463 U.S. 1073, 103 S.Ct. 3492, 77 L.Ed.2d 1236 (1983).

chusetts case, the trier knew of the plaintiff's quadriplegia and could take that into account, especially if the defendant shouldered the burden of proving its effect on life expectancy.

[*For discussion of work-life expectancy, reduction to present value, inflation, periodic payments and structured settlements, see this section in the Practitioner Treatise edition, vol. 2, pp. 466–488.*]

§ 8.6 Adjustments: Benefits to the Plaintiff

[*Consult the summary in §§ 3.8(1) & 3.8(2) above, and see this section in the Practitioner Treatise edition, vol. 2, pp. 488–501.*]

§ 8.6(4) Plaintiff's Income Tax Benefits

[*For the text of this section, see the unabridged Practitioner Treatise edition.*]

§ 8.7 Adjustments: Avoidable Consequences and Comparative Negligence

§ 8.7(1) Apportionment Systems: Causal Apportionment, Avoidable Consequences and Comparative Fault

Adjustments in damages awards discussed in the preceding sections were measurement adjustments. When those adjustments were made, they were made to make the measurement of compensation more accurate. This was the case, for example, with adjustments attempted to account for interest, for inflation, for tax benefits, and others.

Adjustments discussed in the present section differ. These adjustments do not reflect an effort to *measure* damages but to determine responsibility for damages that are known to exist. They attempt to apportion responsibility in tort between plaintiff and defendant. When responsibility is apportioned, the defendant is liable for some portion of the plaintiff's damages, but the plaintiff himself is liable for another portion.

There are two main systems currently used for apportionment of damages or allocation of responsibility. Which system is used depends on the facts and somewhat on legal policy. One system is the system that can be called causal apportionment. The other is comparative fault. Sometimes the two can be combined.[1]

Causal apportionment. Where causal apportionment is used, responsibility for damages is divided by determining which party caused which element of harm.[2] As a matter of but-for cause, it usually turns out that each party was one of several but-for causes of all the harms. But it is sometimes possible to say that one defendant was the legal, proximate, or most significant cause of the plaintiff's broken arm while some other party was the legal cause of the plaintiff's broken leg. In such a case it is possible to assign legal responsibility according to this perception of "causation" or the separation of injuries.

The avoidable consequences rule[3] is one specific form of causal apportionment.[4] For example, that part of the plaintiff's injury that occurs because he unreasonably refused medical attention is causally apportioned to the plaintiff, as if he were the only relevant cause of that injury. Indeed, some of the avoidable consequences cases proceed expressly on a theory of proximate cause.

Comparative fault. In contrast, comparative fault rules attempt to apportion liability by assessing the respective *fault* of the relevant actors. As between the plaintiff and the defendant, one may be much more at fault than the other, but the faultier party does not necessarily cause more harm. If a speeding driver runs over a pedestrian who is not keeping a proper lookout, the trier will probably estimate that the driver was guilty of greater fault. If the pedestrian suffers a broken leg it is not even possible to apportion some of the injury to the driver and some to the pedestrian, since there is but one indivisible injury. But it is quite possible and quite routine to apportion *fault* and to divide responsibility for damages on that basis.

Because the causal apportionment system must identify separate *injuries* to permit apportionment, while the comparative fault system need only identify the separate *conduct* of the parties,[5] the comparative fault system is more versatile. It can be used both in cases where injuries can be separated and attributed separately and in cases where they cannot. Where comparative negligence is adopted, it is routinely used for both kinds of cases. Causal apportionment between plaintiff and defendant[6] is usually reserved for special cases—strict liability cases in which fault plays no part,[7] cases in which a defendant's conduct enhances a pre-existing injury[8] or makes a contemporaneous injury worse,[9] and avoidable consequences cases in which the plaintiff's post-accident conduct enhances the harm he suffers.[10] Sometimes, in addition, causal apportionment is used in seat belt cases in which the plaintiff's failure to use a protective device enhances injury that otherwise results from the defendant's fault.[11]

§ 8.7(2) Avoidable Consequences Rules: Minimizing Damages

[Consult § 3.9 above and see this section in the Practitioner Treatise edition, vol. 2, pp. 510–515.]

§ 8.7(3) Comparative Negligence

Comparative fault is a large topic and the subject of several large books.[1] Although the topic involves substantive, procedural, and strategic issues, as well as more fundamental attitudes about responsibility,[2] the issues about the remedial side of comparative negligence are quite limited.

The simplest form of comparative negligence divides damages equally between the plaintiff and defendant. This approach, once used in Admiralty, is no longer in use. Instead, comparative negligence rules today, when they apply at all,[3] ask the trier of fact to assess the seriousness of each actor's negligence and to divide damages in proportion to that fault.

§ 8.7(3)

1. V. Schwartz, Comparative Negligence (2d ed. 1986); H. Woods, Comparative Fault (2d ed. 1987 and Supp.).

2. See e.g., Dobbs, Accountability and Comparative Fault, 47 La.L.Rev. 939 (1987).

3. In "modified" comparative negligence states the plaintiff is barred if his negligence is equal to defendant's, or at least if his negligence is greater than the defendant's. In addition, some of the situations in which contributory negligence was no bar, such as those involving last clear chance or wanton misconduct by a defendant, are no bar under comparative negligence regimes in some states.

Mechanically, the trier of fact estimates the extent to which each actor departed from appropriate standards of conduct. Taking the total relevant negligence as 100%, the trier then expresses its estimate of relative fault by assigning responsibility to each party in a percentage figure. The process calls for the trier's judgment, as does the process of determining the very existence of negligence. Although the ultimate percentage figures are precise expressions, they do not reflect any quantifiable data or a precise estimate; they are only a mode of expressing the trier's judgment.

Once the trier has assigned percentage figures to the fault of each party, and determined damages of the plaintiff, the award is computed. Computation is completed by awarding the plaintiff the actual damages multiplied by the defendant's percentage of fault. For example, if the plaintiff's damages are $100,000 and the defendant's fault is assessed at 90% of the total, the plaintiff will recover .90 × $100,000 or $90,000.[4]

If the plaintiff's claim is barred by the application of comparative negligence rules, as it may be under the modified systems discussed below, the entire claim is barred, including any punitive damages claim.[5] If the plaintiff can recover compensatory damages, even though they are reduced under comparative negligence, punitive damages against a defendant guilty of outrageous misconduct are still appropriate.[6] And it would seem that punitive damages, meant to provide a disincentive to the defendant, should not be reduced by comparative negligence rules.[7] Not only would the reduction fail to provide proper deterrence,[8] it would complicate the effort to find appropriate punitive levels.

Two different systems of comparative negligence or comparative fault are presently in use in the United States. In both systems, the plaintiff who is guilty of contributory negligence may recover, but damages are reduced to reflect his fault. In the pure comparative negligence system the plaintiff may recover even if his fault far exceeds that of the defendant.[9] In the modified comparative fault system the plaintiff may not recover if his

---

4. The Uniform Comparative Fault Act, for example, provides that the plaintiff's contributory fault "diminishes proportionately the amount awarded as compensatory damages for an injury attributable to the claimant's contributory fault." The comments provide the following illustrations:

"*Illustration No. 1. (Simple 2–party situation).* A sues B. A's damages are $10,000. A is found 40% at fault. B is found 60% at fault. A recovers judgment for $6,000.

"*Illustration No. 2. (Multiple-party situation).* A sues B, C and D. A's Damages are $10,000. A is found 40% at fault. B is found 30% at fault. C is found 30% at fault. D is found 0% at fault. A is awarded judgment jointly and severally against B & C for $6,000 * * *."

Local law differs on many points, but the basic reduction suggested by the first illustration reflects the usual practice. In some states the plaintiff could not recover on facts like those in the second illustration because the plain-tiff's negligence exceeds that of each separate defendant. On that point there is a division, even among those states that adopt the modified form of comparative fault. The syntax used in the illustrations "A is found 40% at fault" is commonly used for convenience; but it does not mean that A's conduct amounts to something less than fault. It means that A is negligent, but that his negligence is only 40% of the total relevant negligence in the case.

5. Tucker v. Marcus, 142 Wis.2d 425, 418 N.W.2d 818 (1988).

6. Champagne v. Raybestos–Manhattan, 212 Conn. 509, 562 A.2d 1100 (1989).

7. Godbersen v. Miller, 439 N.W.2d 206 (Iowa 1989); see Tucker v. Marcus, 142 Wis.2d 425, 418 N.W.2d 818 (1988) (punitive damages are not "damages" covered by comparative negligence statute). See Ghiardi, Comparative Negligence: Effect on Punitive Damages, 37 Def.L.J. 297 (1988). Contra, City of San Antonio v. Hamilton, 714 S.W.2d 372 (Tex. App.1986).

negligence is greater than that of the defendant, or, in some states, if it is equal to that of the defendant.

Because the comparative fault system of apportionment is so different from causal apportionment, it is important in many cases to distinguish between the two. But it may be especially important in the modified comparative negligence scheme because a seriously faulty plaintiff might be barred under the modified comparative negligence rule but only denied recovery of the damages he aggravates under the avoidable consequences rule.[10]

§ 8.7(4) "Seat Belt" Defenses

The seat belt debate originated with the plaintiff's failure to use automobile safety harness or restraint systems, but the issues it raises are potentially applicable to any kind of case in which the plaintiff fails to take safety precautions that would minimize injury when it occurs.

At least three basic methods can be used for apportioning responsibility in seat belt and other protective device cases. The results under any one method are not necessarily uniformly favorable to one party or another. For simplification, the basic methods described will assume that the plaintiff is not at all guilty of negligence in causing the collision, but that he could have avoided some identifiable injury by wearing a restraint.

(1) The avoidable consequences solution. The avoidable consequences solution excludes any recovery of the damages traceable to the plaintiff's failure to wear a seat belt. For example, if the plaintiff's damages are $40,000 plus $20,000 additional damages that result from the failure to use a restraint, the plaintiff would recover $40,000, no more.

The rule cuts two ways. It eliminates the $20,000 seat belt injury from any recovery at all and in some cases the seat belt injury might be much higher. On the other hand, it has three substantial advantages for some plaintiffs. Any plaintiff whose seat belt injuries could not be segregated would presumably make a full recovery if comparative fault were ignored and only the avoidable consequences rule were used.[18] And any plaintiff whose comparative fault would be rated very high might be better off under an avoidable consequences/causal apportionment scheme.

(2) A comparative negligence solution. One kind of comparative negligence solution would be to treat the plaintiff's failure to wear a seat belt as fault, to be compared with all the defendant's fault in the case. The plaintiff's total losses, from seat belt injuries as well as others would then be reduced in proportion to the negligence assessed against the plaintiff.[19]

This solution would also be advantageous to the plaintiff in some cases. If seat belt injuries were very heavy but the plaintiff's negligence in failure to use the restraint is rated at a very small percentage, the comparative negligence solution would be preferable to the plaintiff. On the other hand, this solution has two strong disadvantages for the plaintiff. First, damages might be reduced in *any* case, not merely those in which separate injuries can be identified and evaluated. Second, in modified comparative fault jurisdictions, the plaintiff might not only suffer a reduction in damages but might be barred altogether under a comparative fault approach.

(3) A dual or combined approach. A third approach could be thought of as a dual approach which combines features of the first two. It was articulated with great care by the New Jersey Court in 1988 in *Waterson v. General Motors Corp.*[20] and enjoys the support of some of the most thorough decisions,[21] as well as the Uniform Comparative Fault Act,[22] among other authorities.[23] Under this approach, the plaintiff's failure to use protective devices is regarded as evidence of contributory fault under the comparative negligence regime. But that fault goes to reduce *only* the injuries that result from failure to use the restraining device. The first half of the procedure adopts the comparative fault approach; the second, in segregating damages to which the comparative fault rule applies, resembles the avoidable consequences or causal apportionment approach.

§ 8.8   Statutory Caps on Damages—"Tort Reform" Limits

Summary

The tort reform movement. Limitations on the kinds of harm for which damages may be awarded at all, or on the amount of recovery,[1] are not new in tort law. But the tort reform movement of the 1980s was a large, systematic and sustained movement to impose a number of new limitations on liability. That movement was a renewal and a broadening of an earlier effort which was intended to limit medical malpractice liabilities.

Both waves of tort reform argued that a crisis had erupted because claims had increased in volume and amount, that insurance costs were excessive as a result, that insurance was not even available in some instances, and that some valuable goods or services were being driven from the market by the threat of tort liability. The tort reform movement was a political effort to reduce tort liability by a variety of means, with the expectation that reduced liability would mean reduced insurance premiums and sufficient financial safety to engage in production of appropriate goods and services.

Tort reform changes. Tort reform initiatives of the 1980s produced a wide range of enactments. Some statutes attacked the substantive tort law rules by changing rules of liability or adding defenses.[2] Others launched procedural initiatives, limiting joint and several liability[3] or imposing more stringent statutes of limitations. Many of the tort reform packages affected

§ 8.7(4)

20. 111 N.J. 238, 544 A.2d 357 (1988).

21. Law v. Superior Court, 157 Ariz. 147, 755 P.2d 1135 (1988) (approving the view that "failure to use a seat belt would reduce damages solely for those injuries directly attributable to the lack of seat belt restraint").

22. Uniform Comparative Fault Act, § 1(b) defines fault to include "unreasonable failure to avoid an injury or to mitigate damages." The comment adds:

" 'Injury attributable to the claimant's contributory fault' refers to the requirement of a causal relation for the particular damage. Thus, negligent failure to fasten a seat belt would diminish recovery only for damages in which the lack of a seat-belt restraint played a part * * *."

23. See Wemyss v. Coleman, 729 S.W.2d 174, 175 (Ky.1987) (quoting the Uniform Comparative Fault Act comment); See Prosser & Keeton on Torts § 65, p. 459 (5th ed. 1984) ("plaintiff's recovery should be reduced to the extent that [damages] have been aggravated by his own antecedent negligence," better rule than one placing "artificial emphasis upon the moment of impact"); Note, A Compromise between Mitigation and Comparative Fault?, 14 Hofstra L.Rev. 319, 345 (1986), relying on Twerski, The Use and Abuse of Comparative Negligence in Products Liability, 10 Ind. L.Rev. 797 (1977).

remedies, notably by modifying the collateral source rule[4] by instituting periodic payment systems,[5] and by limiting punitive damages in some instances.[6]

The most direct attack on the plaintiff's claim has been to impose a "cap" or dollar limit on the amount that can be recovered. As a direct limit on recoverable damages, this is a new thing in the law and quite distinct even from those few cases in which the legislature created a special cause of action and placed a dollar limit on it.[7] The idea of a direct dollar cap on damages is even more strongly opposed to the common law, which attempted to provide compensation for injury and to estimate that compensation on a case by case basis.

Types of statutes. Statutes imposing direct caps on damages differ along two lines of cleavage. *First,* they differ as to the kind of claim or defendant to which they apply. Some apply only to cases involving particular subject matter, such as those involving medical malpractice. *Second,* they differ as to the kind or element of damage that is subject to a cap. Some caps apply only to damages for pain and suffering or other intangible damages. An indirect cap may be imposed by shunting certain cases out of the tort system altogether, much as workers' compensation does, or by setting up a public compensation system to handle larger claims. By 1990, some kind of direct cap had been imposed in at least half the states, though in some cases the statute has been held to be unconstitutional.[8]

Types of Damages Capped

(1) Noneconomic limits only. Many of the statutes limit or cap recovery of "noneconomic", "general", or non-pecuniary damages, but leave the plaintiff a full recovery for all actual pecuniary harms. The noneconomic cap limits damages for pain and suffering, loss of consortium, and mental distress.[9] Some states have also capped punitive damages.[10]

(2) Limit on recovery of actual damages. Some statutes go far beyond the first group by limiting the recovery of damages for pecuniary or "economic" harm as well as for intangible harms. Statutes which contain these absolute limits, however, usually apply only to a specified group of defendants, such as health care providers.[11]

(3) Dual caps. Some statutes impose two caps—first on noneconomic damages, and second on total recovery.[12]

Types of Cases or Defendants to Which Cap Applies

(1) Application to cases generally. Perhaps a dozen statutes by 1990 had been enacted to cap damages in personal injury cases generally, subject

§ 8.8

7. E.g., W.Va.Code, § 57–7A–2 ($2500 cap on special liability of parents for certain acts of children).

8. See segment "Constitutionality" below.

9. E.g., West's Ann.Cal.Civ.Code § 3333.2.

10. See, upholding a punitive damages cap, Bagley v. Shortt, 261 Ga. 762, 410 S.E.2d 738 (1991).

11. E.g., West's Colo.Rev.Stat.Ann. § 13–64–302 ($1 million cap on medical malpractice damages of any kind); La.Rev.Stat. 1299.42(B)

(total cap $500,000 plus interest and costs); West's Ann.Ind.Code 16–9.5–2–2 ($100,000 for a single health care provider, but added compensation systems); Va.Code § 8.01–581.15 ($1 million).

12. E.g., West's Colo.Rev.Stat.Ann. § 13–21–102.5 ($250,000 on non-economic damages in any injury case) *and* West's Colo.Rev.Stat. Ann. § 13–64–302 ($1 million cap on medical malpractice damages of any kind).

sometimes to relatively narrow exceptions.[13] When the statute applies to personal injury cases generally, it usually imposes a cap only on noneconomic damages.

(2) Application of specified claims or defendants. The remainder of the statutes apply a cap to specified claims, most commonly to claims against health care providers,[14] governmental entities,[15] alcohol providers[16] and other groups[17] which had been generally favored at common law by limited duty rules or by immunities.

Indirect Caps and Substitute Compensation Systems

Caps are imposed indirectly when a public compensation scheme with a non-tort measure of recovery is substituted for tort liability. The Federal Childhood Vaccine Injury Act provides a semi-compulsory, strict-liability compensation system for certain vaccine injuries with substantial but not unlimited compensation.[18] California has enacted a similar statute to cover any prospective injury from an AIDS vaccine.[19] Some state statutes provide a cap on damages against health care providers but then add a public compensation scheme on top of the cap to guarantee the victim additional recovery when damages exceed the cap.[20]

13. Alaska Stat. 09–17.010 (500,000); West's Colo.Rev.Stat.Ann. § 13–21–102.5 (250,000); Haw.Rev.Stat.Ann. § 663–8.7 (375,000); Idaho Code § 6–1603 (400,000); Md.Code, Cts. & Jud.Proc.Code § 11–108 (350,000); Minn. Stat.Ann. § 549.23 (400,000); N.H.Rev.Stat. Ann. 508:4–d (875,000); Or.Rev.Stat. 18.560 (500,000). As to those held unconstitutional, see segment "Constitutionality" below.

14. E.g., Ala.Code § 6–5–544 (400,000); West's Ann.Cal.Civ.Code § 3333.2 (250,000); West's Colo.Rev.Stat.Ann. § 13–64–302 ($1,000,00); LSA–Rev.Stat. 1249.42 (100,000/500,00); West's Ann.Ind.Code 16–9.5–2–2 (100,000); Mass.Gen.Laws Ann. ch 231, § 60h (500,000); M.C.L.A. § 27a.1483 (225,000); Vernon's Ann.Mo.Stat. § 538.210 ($350,000 for noneconomic damages) (passed 1986); N.M.Stat.Ann. § 41–5–6 (500,000); Ohio Rev. Code § 2307.43 (200,000); S.D.Codified Laws 21–3–12 (1,000,000); Utah Code Ann. 78–14–7.1 (250,000); Va.Code § 8.01–581.15 (1,000,000); W.Va.Code, 55–7b–8 (1,000,000); Wis. Stat.Ann. 893.55(4)(d) (1,000,000).

15. Me.Rev.Stat.Ann. § 8105 ($300,000 cap on all claims against government entity or employees); Mont.Code Ann. 2–9–108 ($750,000 for public entity, scheduled to terminate June 30, 1991).

16. Utah Code Ann. 32A–14–1(4) ($100,000 cap).

17. S.D.Codified Laws 33–55–210 ($200,000 cap on "actual damages" recovery from charitable organization and this recovery bars suit against the negligent employee as well).

18. 42 U.S.C.A. § 300aa–1. The plaintiff is compelled to seek an award under the scheme before resorting to tort law. The plaintiff may then take the cash in hand and waive the rest or he may reject the certain award and hope for a tort judgment. The drafters obviously have in mind that the plaintiff will ordinarily accept the substitute scheme. The idea is that this protection will help to guarantee that vaccine makers will not be forced from the market by tort liability. See generally Victor Schwartz & Liberty Mashigian, National Childhood Vaccine Injury Act of 1986: An Ad Hoc Remedy or a Window for the Future?, 48 Ohio St.L.J. 387 (1987).

19. West's Ann.Cal.Health & Safety Code §§ 199.48–199.51. In some instances tort liability against the vaccine maker is preserved. Where it is not, the plaintiff must claim against the state-created fund. But the fund compensation, although it caps damages, allows up to $550,000 in pain and suffering claims.

20. See, e.g., Williams v. Kushner, 549 So.2d 294 (La.1989) (reflecting a cap of $100,000 against health care providers with an added claim against a public compensation fund, which in turn was capped at $400,000). The Virginia Birth–Related Neurological Injury Compensation Act, Va.Code Ann. § 38.2–5001 covers a narrow range of birth-related injuries with the object of maintaining available insurance for obstetricians, providing for strict liability against a state-created fund, which in turn is created by assessments against medical professionals generally. See, describing the system, Note, Innovative No–Fault Tort Reform for an Endangered Specialty, 74 Va.L.Rev. 1487 (1988). See also comments in Epstein, Market and Regulatory Approaches to Medical Malpractice: The Virginia Obstetrical No–Fault Statute, 74 Va. L.Rev. 1451 (1988); O'Connell, Pragmatic Con-

Constitutionality

Statutes unconstitutional. A fair number of states have found cap statutes to be unconstitutional on various grounds including denial of due process and equal protection,[21] especially where the statute capped damages for an interest group such as health care providers and where no substitute compensation scheme was provided.[22] Sometimes the statute has been found unconstitutional on rather narrow or local grounds not necessarily convincing to outsiders, as in a decision that caps on damages somehow interfered with jury trial rights.[23] But the most central argument against the caps for health care providers is that if there is a crisis for health care providers, the problem is theirs and not that of an individual victim of their negligence; and that while government might provide assistance to the providers, the individual victim should not be forced to do so.[24]

Statutes constitutional. Although the caps appear to be invoked to aid the tortfeasor at the expense of the victim, they have been upheld in important decisions,[25] especially where the legislature seems to have sought to provide the victim with substitutes for full tort compensation.[26] Where

straints on Market Approaches: A Response to Professor Epstein, 74 Va.L.Rev. 1475 (1988). Cf. 40 Pa.Stat. § 1301.701 (providers to purchase insurance only for $100,000 per occurrence, state fund to cover excess).

21. Smith v. Department of Insurance, 507 So.2d 1080 (Fla.1987); Wright v. Central Du Page Hospital Ass'n, 63 Ill.2d 313, 347 N.E.2d 736, 80 A.L.R.3d 566 (1976); Kansas Malpractice Victims Coalition v. Bell, 243 Kan. 333, 757 P.2d 251 (1988); Carson v. Maurer, 120 N.H. 925, 424 A.2d 825, 12 A.L.R.4th 1 (1980) (medical malpractice damages cap); Brannigan v. Usitalo, 134 N.H. 50, 587 A.2d 1232 (1991) (general personal injury damages cap); Morris v. Savoy, 61 Ohio St.3d 684, 576 N.E.2d 765 (1991); Lucas v. United States, 757 S.W.2d 687 (Tex.1988); Sofie v. Fibreboard Corp., 112 Wash.2d 636, 771 P.2d 711, 780 P.2d 260 (1989). See also White v. State, 203 Mont. 363, 661 P.2d 1272, 43 A.L.R.4th 1 (1983) (governmental entity cap unconstitutional); Condemarin v. University Hospital, 775 P.2d 348 (Utah 1989) (governmental liability limits unconstitutional as applied to university hospital, divided court). See Annotation, Validity and construction of state statutory provisions relating to limitations on amount of recovery in medical malpractice claim and submission of such claim to pretrial panel, 80 A.L.R.3d 583 (1977).

22. See Lucas v. United States, 757 S.W.2d 687 (Tex.1988).

23. Sofie v. Fibreboard Corp., 112 Wash.2d 636, 771 P.2d 711, 780 P.2d 260 (1989) (state constitution's jury trial right). The claim that the jury must decide the measure of damages does not seem in line with the usual notion that the law prescribes the remedy and its measure. See Boyd v. Bulala, 877 F.2d 1191 (4th Cir.1989) (rejecting the argument that caps interfere with federal jury trial rights);

cf. Davis v. Omitowoju, 883 F.2d 1155 (3d Cir.1989) (also rejecting jury trial argument, on ground that federal jury trial rights guarantee the jury against interference by judge, not against legislation); Peters v. Saft, 597 A.2d 50 (Me.1991) ("Although it is conceivable that a statute could limit the measure of tort damages so drastically that it would result in a denial of the right to trial by jury and the denial of a remedy, the $250,000 cap before us is not such a measure. In the present context, the right 'to a jury trial means that, with respect to those questions of fact that the substantive law makes material, the party has the right to have a determination made by the jury' ").

24. See Carson v. Maurer, 120 N.H. 925, 424 A.2d 825, 12 A.L.R.4th 1 (1980); Morris v. Savoy, 61 Ohio St.3d 684, 576 N.E.2d 765, 771 (1991) (denial of due process: "[I]t is irrational and arbitrary to impose the cost of the intended benefit to the general public solely upon a class consisting of those most severely injured by medical malpractice" (quoting an unreported case).

25. Davis v. Omitowoju, 883 F.2d 1155 (3d Cir.1989); Franklin v. Mazda Motor Corp., 704 F.Supp. 1325 (D.Md.1989); Fein v. Permanente Medical Group, 38 Cal.3d 137, 211 Cal. Rptr. 368, 695 P.2d 665 (1985), cert. denied, 474 U.S. 892, 106 S.Ct. 214, 88 L.Ed.2d 215 (1985); Potomac Elec. Power Co. v. Smith, 79 Md.App. 591, 558 A.2d 768 (1989) (constitutional at least in death cases); Etheridge v. Medical Center Hospitals, 237 Va. 87, 376 S.E.2d 525 (1989).

26. See Lucas v. United States, 757 S.W.2d 687 (Tex.1988) (no viable quid pro quo for the seriously injured victim of medical malpractice). The *Lucas* court thought it "significant" "that in two of the jurisdictions in

the statute merely caps damages for intangible harm, there may be justifications quite different from those aimed at aiding a special group of defendants, because intangible harms are hard to measure and because their unmeasurable nature may in effect compel all citizens to pay the high costs for goods and services.[27] The constitutionality of a cap is probably also easier to sustain when the statute merely provides protection for a defendant which was once immune altogether, as in the case of a public entity.[28] Similarly, where the legislature creates a cause of action that did not previously exist, courts are likely to sustain legislative caps.[29]

Construction

Because direct caps on damages are almost entirely new to the law, problems of interpretation and application will arise. For instance, cap statutes may apply to reduce the recovery in cases that also require other reductions. Reductions in the plaintiff's recovery might be made under comparative negligence rules or under a statute which requires a reduction in damages to reflect insurance or other benefits the plaintiff has received from other sources. The order in which reductions are computed may make an enormous difference in the actual net judgment. In *McAdory v. Rogers*,[30] a California appellate court held it would be wrong to cap the award at $250,000 first and then to further reduce the award by the percentage of fault attributable to the plaintiff. In that case, the comparative fault reduction was first made, and since this left a sum in excess of the cap, the cap was applied. Had the order of deduction been the other way around, the plaintiff would have recovered less than the capped damages. But this solution will not invariably produce a better recovery for the plaintiff, and other ways of computing multiple reductions are possible and presumably will eventually reach litigation.[31]

which damages caps were upheld, the fact that alternative remedies were provided weighed heavily in the decision," Id. at 691, citing Johnson v. St. Vincent Hospital, Inc., 273 Ind. 374, 404 N.E.2d 585, 601 (1980); Sibley v. Board of Supervisors of Louisiana, 462 So.2d 149, 156 (La.1985). In Williams v. Kushner, 549 So.2d 294 (La.1989) the court upheld a cap on the public compensation fund, but did not address the cap on liability of a private health care provider.

27. Cf. Schweich v. Ziegler, Inc., 463 N.W.2d 722 (Minn.1990) ("underwriting challenges" presented by such damages; upholding cap of $400,000 on various intangible injury damages, including loss of consortium, on attack regarded as similar to due process attack under state law and on standards similar to minimal scrutiny standard).

28. See Annotation, Validity and construction of statute or ordinance limiting the kinds or amount of actual damages recoverable in tort action against governmental unit, 43 A.L.R.4th 19 (1986). Contra, holding such a statute unconstitutional, White v. State, 203 Mont. 363, 661 P.2d 1272, 43 A.L.R.4th 1 (1983); cf. Condemarin v. University Hospital, 775 P.2d 348 (Utah 1989) (governmental cap

unconstitutional as applied to university hospital).

29. See Potomac Elec. Power Co. v. Smith, 79 Md.App. 591, 558 A.2d 768 (1989); Owen v. Meserve, 381 Mass. 273, 408 N.E.2d 867, 870 (1980), cert. denied, 449 U.S. 1082, 101 S.Ct. 866, 66 L.Ed.2d 806 (1981) (death actions); cf. Peters v. Saft, 597 A.2d 50 (Me.1991) (where liability of alcohol server was not established, legislature could rationally impose liability and cap it).

30. 215 Cal.App.3d 1273, 264 Cal.Rptr. 71 (1989).

31. Examples: (1) *Some different computations possible.* Assume a cap of $250,000 on nonpecuniary damages and only on such damages. *P* recovers, gross, $2 million in actual and $1 million in pain and suffering. *P* is guilty of 50% of the fault, but is entitled to recover with a reduction. *Comparative fault reduction first.* Total damages would be reduced to $1.5 million. This might be interpreted in one of two ways: (a) as a pro rata reduction, so that at this stage of the computation the plaintiff would have $1 million in actual damages and $500,000 in nonpecuniary damages, to which the cap would then be

There are also likely to be issues about how caps are to be applied in cases of multiple injuries by one defendant and cases of multiple defendants causing one injury. Many of the statutes attempt to address some of these issues, but their exact scope will probably leave room for more litigation.

Effects

At this writing extensive data about the effect of caps is not available. But the most obvious effects are likely to be that recoveries will be reduced and that reduced recoveries may serve the purposes of the tort reform movement by making insurance more readily available and affordable.

At the same time, by cutting liability, the tort reform statutes may have several other less obvious effects. One might be that deterrence levels are reduced too far, even if they were too high before; in other words, the caps might not be pegged at the best level for optimum safety even if caps in principle are a good idea. Another is that since the plaintiff's claim is pursued by lawyers paid on contingent fees, a reduction of potential damages will reduce the fee. A reduced fee will almost certainly mean that some complicated cases will simply be too costly to pursue. This has led to the proposal that if caps are imposed, lawyer's fees should then be paid by the losing defendant.[32]

Effects might be quite different depending on whether the statute caps all damages or only intangible damages. There is no way to determine the appropriate dollar award for intangible harm and no guarantee that present awards are even remotely "accurate" by any standard. Awards of hundreds of thousands for a broken arm cannot be shown to offer the proper level of deterrence; nor can they be shown to be the right amount of compensation. So the statutes which cap intangible damages of this kind might represent no reduction in appropriate levels of deterrence. And, for much the same reason, awards of nonpecuniary damages may have a compulsory insurance effect or a "tort tax" effect, because they probably help drive up the cost of goods and services to everyone, including the very poor. In this state of affairs, it has been argued that after some minimum amount of intangible damages are provided, it might be best to let people buy first party insurance if they felt it worth their while to be assured of payments for pain.[33] But even if this is correct, intangible damages like others serve a function in

---

applied to leave a net judgment of $1,250,000. Or: (b) The reduction ate up all of the $1 million in nonpecuniary damages plus $500,-000 of the pecuniary damages, leaving the plaintiff with $1,500,000 net recovery. *Comparative fault reduction after caps.* A different order of the first computation would be to cap the damages first. This would produce $2 million in pecuniary loss plus $250,000 in nonpecuniary (capped) damages. A comparative fault reduction at the 50% rate would reduce the pecuniary loss to $1 million and the nonpecuniary loss to $112,500. This would provide a net recovery of only $1,112,500. (2) *Cap first favorable to the plaintiff.* Assume the same cap but a plaintiff guilty of only 10% of the fault. The plaintiff has $1 million pecuniary damages and $7 million pain and suffer-

ing. If the cap is first imposed, and the plaintiff's fault reduction figured on the resulting $1,250,000, the recovery is reduced to $1,125,-000 ($1,250,000–.10 × $1,250,000). If the reduction is made first, then the total $7,000,000 figure is reduced by 10%, leaving $6.3 million. If the cap is then applied to the noneconomic damages only, the plaintiff's net recovery is $1,250,000 (all the pecuniary damages plus the capped nonpecuniary loss).

32. See Hicks, Statutory Damage Caps Are an Incomplete Reform: A Proposal for Attorney Fee Shifting in Tort Actions, 49 La.L.Rev. 763 (1989).

33. See Schwartz, Proposals for Products Liability Reform: A Theoretical Synthesis, 97 Yale L.J. 353 (1988).

financing litigation, so that capping these damages, however justified in theory, may preclude appropriate recoveries because no one can afford to sue in expensive cases with caps. Again, however, a cap with an attorney fee award would present a different picture.

All the effects of caps will not be clear for some time. Some of the effects may turn out to be a surprise. For example, courts which are now reluctant to permit open-ended emotional distress damages might find it easier to support a broader tort rule for recovery if a cap set an upper limit. It may turn out that although recoveries will not be as high as in the past, there may be more of them. No one knows all the effects of this new legislative venture in caps; perhaps no one even knows for sure that they will narrow the total costs of defense.

Alternatives

Because the problems of open-ended awards are indeed substantial, some kinds of caps deserve serious consideration. But because flat caps are in the nature of things arbitrary and not even-handed, other forms of setting limits will probably be developed. Schedules are used for the estimation of pecuniary loss in a number of situations, sometimes directly as in the case of workers' compensation, and sometimes indirectly, as where a physician converts a limited motion in a limb to a percentage disability which in turn can be converted into a highly conventionalized dollar figure.[34]

There are now proposals on the floor for development of several types of schedules for limiting (and guaranteeing) the award of non-pecuniary awards.[35] One type of schedule would use variable limits on damages, depending on stated levels of injury, and age grouping of the plaintiff.[36] The limits could be based on past experience with the same type of claim or could be based on some other judgment about the appropriate amount. Other types of schedules are possible. No doubt comparisons could be made with sentencing "guidelines" adopted for federal criminal sentencing,[37] and also with the "grids" used in social security disability determinations.[38] Very probably these options will be debated and refined, with due effort to avoid building bias or discrimination into the schedules. If non-pecuniary awards are to be limited, those limits may be found in the future through some means other than flat caps.

§ 8.9   Restitution in Personal Injury Cases

Murder-and-inherit cases. In two groups of personal injury cases, however, the tortfeasor may derive a gain or profit, although sometimes quite indirectly, from the injury. In the first group, the tortfeasor murders in

---

34. See Pryor, Flawed Promises: A Critical Evaluation of the American Medical Association's Guides to the Evaluation of Permanent Impairment (Book Review), 103 Harv.L.Rev. 964 (1990) (reviewing American Medical Ass'n, Guides to the Evaluation of Permanent Impairment (1988)).

36. See Bovbjerg, Sloan & Blumstein, Valuing Life and Limb in Tort: Scheduling "Pain and Suffering", 83 Nw.U.L.Rev. 908 (1989).

37. See Mistretta v. United States, 488 U.S. 361, 109 S.Ct. 647, 102 L.Ed.2d 714 (1989) (upholding the statutory requirement of determinate sentence under guidelines against a delegation and separation of powers arguments).

38. See 20 C.F.R. Pt. 404, Subpt. P, App. 2 (4–1–89 ed.).

hope of gain by inheritance, insurance, or otherwise. In this situation, "restitution" by way of a constructive trust or a similar statutory remedy may be imposed to prevent the tortfeasor from profiting from his wrong, and to force allotment of the inheritance or insurance funds to others.[4]

Murder-and-publish cases. The second group is illustrated by cases in which the tortfeasor commits a dramatic crime, causing injury or death, then takes advantage of the publicity by writing a book about his crime or selling his story for media exploitation. A restitution claim by the tortfeasor's victim would seek to recover the wrongdoer's profits or earnings from materials produced about the crime.

Adoption of "Son of Sam" statutes. Almost all states, by statute, have attempted to provide some crime victims with a kind of right against the profits otherwise payable to the tortfeasor who exploits his crime in the media.[7] Because the original New York statute was inspired by the case of David Berkowitz, whose random crimes were known at the time as "Son of Sam" murders,[8] the statutes are often known by the same picturesque name. The initial idea was to deprive the wrongdoer of his profits from exploitation of his crime in the media.

The statutes differ, as to many details. For instance, one statute may permit part of the exploitation gains to go to the criminal's dependents [9] while others do not. Or some statutes may indirectly seize the gains before judgment,[10] while others do not.[11] The statutes also differ in the rigor with which they pursue the stated purpose.

Effect on wrongdoer's profits. There are two sides to the ordinary restitution equation. One side takes the profit from the wrongdoer. The other gives it to the victim. The statutes vary somewhat in their approach to both sides. Some statutes appear to contemplate that after the claims of the victims and other statutory claims have been satisfied, any remaining proceeds from the exploitation will be paid over to the wrongdoer himself.[12] If this is done, the wrongdoer would be allowed to profit at least somewhat from his crime. Other statutes contemplate that any balance remaining after paying victims will be [13] or may be [14] paid to a fund for crime victims generally or to some other state fund.

Effect on victim's recovery. For the injured victims, the statutes might be disappointing in one respect. They mostly provide that the funds received from exploitation of the crime are subjected to a trust or an escrow and may be reached by levy or by court order to pay the judgments obtained by the victim.[15] Because the judgments obtained by victims would be for damages or loss rather than for restitution, such provisions do not on their face award the victim the profit or gain from the crime.[16] Perhaps in a high percentage of the cases it would not matter because the damages judgment will exceed the profit or gain in any event. However, the statutes do have the effect of creating something like an equitable lien in favor of the victim, so that, with respect to some creditors of the wrongdoer, the victim may have first priority.[17]

Constitutional challenges to the statutes. Until 1991, the few cases to consider the point upheld the prospective operation [18] of Son of Sam statutes

§ 8.9
4. See § 6.7 above.

against constitutional attacks.[19] But from the beginning, free speech interests have been asserted against the Son of Sam statutes on the ground that they chill the wrongdoer's right to speak and the public's right to know and on other less central grounds.[20]

The Supreme Court itself was once very quick to confiscate an author's royalties earned by publishing a book in breach of a contract not to do so.[21] Nevertheless, in 1991, the Court held that some Son of Sam statutes were unconstitutional.[22] The New York statute at issue there was drawn so broadly that it would impound the royalties on books like those written by St. Augustine and Henry David Thoreau about their crimes and convictions. The First Amendment's free speech provisions prohibit content-based impediments to speech, at least in the absence of a compelling state interest, so prima facie the statute was unconstitutional.

Although the Court agreed that the state has a compelling interest in compensating crime victims from the fruits of the crime, the Court thought the New York's statute covered too much territory. The statute captured fruits of the criminal's activities that were not criminal, since events that were not criminal may also be reported in books that are partly about crime.

The Court left it open to consider other, and more narrowly drawn statutes, presumably those that attempt to apportion profits and allow recovery only from those attributable to the crime itself. Courts have long had the problem of apportioning the wrongdoer's profits so that the victim recovers only that share attributable to the wrong;[23] and they could no doubt do so with criminal profits as well. However, even a more narrowly drawn statute may run into trouble, on the argument that a criminal's thoughts, feelings, or analysis about his crimes cannot be fairly called the fruits of the crime.

A point not considered in the Supreme Court's decision is that some of the statutes do not confiscate all gains from publication, but merely use the criminal-author's gains to secure the victim's claim for damages. If *all* of the criminal's assets could be subjected to a lien in favor of the victim, it is not so obvious that it burdens speech to place a lien on those assets most closely derived from the victim's suffering, especially if the criminal is allowed to keep the profits in excess of the victim's damages.

Another constitutional issue may lie in the provision of some of the statutes that requires exploiters such as publishers to submit copies of their contracts and to make royalty or other payments directly to the state or to a trust or escrow account. This is no doubt also a burden of sorts, but the statutes do not appear to reach the profits of the publisher or others who exploit the crime material.[24]

21. Snepp v. United States, 444 U.S. 507, 100 S.Ct. 763, 62 L.Ed.2d 704 (1980).

22. Simon & Schuster, Inc. v. Members of the New York State Crime Victims Board, ___ U.S. ___, 112 S.Ct. 501, 116 L.Ed.2d 476 (1991).

23. See, e.g., §§ 6.3(4) and 6.4(4) above.

24. Fasching v. Kallinger, 211 N.J.Super. 26, 510 A.2d 694, 60 A.L.R.4th 1189 (1986); see Comment, The Expansion of Victim Compensation Programs: Today's "Son of Sam" Legislation and Its Susceptibility to Constitutional Challenge, 18 Toledo L.Rev. 155 (1986). Distinguish the constructive trust applied to life insurance or inheritance in the murder for gain case. Those who innocently gain from the murder as well as those who gain guiltily may be deprived of the proceeds so that they can be paid to the proper parties. See § 6.7 above.

§ 8.10 Equitable Relief in Personal Injury Claims

Summary

In the traditional personal injury practice, plaintiffs sought money judgments for injuries already inflicted or for wrongful death. Injunctions against the wrongful conduct, either before injury or afterward, were not used. Changing attitudes in recent years have made it possible to consider use of injunctions to prevent ongoing risky practices. For example, injunctions may be used increasingly to prevent continued mismanagement of toxic wastes, or to reform institutions such as prisons. In both cases, the plaintiffs may have aims unrelated to personal injury concerns; nevertheless the injunction in such cases may be aimed in part at preventing injury or death.

It is also possible that injunctions or other equitable relief can be used in the enforcement stage of personal injury claims. For example, injunctions have been used to require the defendant to create special funds for payment of periodic medical expenses, even before final judgment has been rendered.

[*For discussion of injunctions against risky activities, see this section in the Practitioner Treatise edition, vol. 2, pp. 535–538.*]

Injunctive Enforcement of Liability—Enjoining Payment

The American legal system has frowned on the use of injunctions to compel the payment of money. The money judgment at law is normally enforced by execution; assets are seized and sold, and the judgment is paid from the funds so produced. The injunction is normally enforced by contempt powers which are subject to abuse in many ways and which may lead to extreme measures, such as jailing the defendant who has not paid. Damages suits for personal injury, like most others, have traditionally involved no injunctive relief at the enforcement stage.[16]

Securing payment before judgment. One problem that plagues many tort victims is that they must bear costs inflicted by the defendant until the suit is over. A separate problem is that the defendant's finances may be shaky; even if the victim ultimately secures a judgment, the defendant by that time may be in bankruptcy.

A possible solution to both problems might lie in a preliminary injunction requiring payments by the defendant before trial or judgment. Courts have traditionally expressed caution about preliminary injunctions generally, and about freeze orders or seizures before judgment in particular.[17] Some preliminary seizures of money or property certainly run the risk of constitutional infraction, as a deprivation of procedural due process if not a taking of property.

Injunctive creation of medical monitoring funds. In a quite unusual

§ 8.10

16. As indicated in § 8.9 above, a constructive trust or equitable lien might be invoked to secure enforcement in the case of some torts, but not typically in personal injury

cases. However, as the same section indicates, something like an equitable lien could secure the victim's damages claim under any valid "Son of Sam" statute.

17. See § 6.1(5) above.

decision in 1984,[18] the court granted an injunction to require the defendant to create a fund for payment of its liability before final judgment. The defendant had been held liable for diagnostic expenses of a class of children, but the amount of expense for each child remained undetermined. Because the case had been pending for years, because trials to determine amounts might take years more, and because without immediate diagnosis irreparable harm could be done to some of the children, the court required the defendant to create a fund for payment of expenses, to be claimed by submission of vouchers. In a few decisions since then, similar medical monitoring funds have been approved in class actions, at least in principle.[19]

The case is remedially unusual in three respects. First, the court used equity powers to order payments of money; second, it created a fund for payment of damages rather than the definitive liability of the traditional system. Third, the defendant was ordered to make payments before a final judgment. The court did not, however, order payments to be made before *liability* of the defendant had been determined, though it has been argued that even this would be justified.[20]

18. Friends for All Children, Inc. v. Lockheed Aircraft Corp., 241 U.S.App.D.C. 83, 746 F.2d 816, 46 A.L.R.4th 1113 (1984).

19. Barth v. Firestone Tire & Rubber Co., 673 F.Supp. 1466 (N.D.Cal.1987); Ayers v. Jackson Tp., 106 N.J. 557, 525 A.2d 287 (1987).

20. Wasserman, Equity Transformed: Preliminary Injunctions to Require the Payment of Money, 70 B.U.L.Rev. 623 (1990).

Chapter 9

FRAUD AND MISREPRESENTATION

Analysis

Sec.
9.1 Substantive Background and Remedial Summary.*
9.2 Damages for Deception.
    9.2(1) Damages Measure in Intentional Fraud Cases.
    9.2(2) Measures of Damages for Negligent or Innocent Repre-
        sentations.
    9.2(3) Consequential or Special Damages.
    9.2(4) Emotional Distress Damages in Misrepresentation
        Cases.
    9.2(5) Punitive Damages in Misrepresentation Cases.*
    9.2(6) Limitations of Damages Under Causation and Proximate
        Causation Doctrines.
9.3 Restitutionary Remedies for Deception: Rescission, Construc-
    tive Trusts and Other Remedies.
    9.3(1) Rescission and Restitution.*
    9.3(2) Is Damages Causation Required to Support Rescission?
    9.3(3) Restoration Required of the Plaintiff.*
    9.3(4) Restitution Required of the Defendant.
9.4 Restitution Plus Damages: Election of Remedies.
9.5 Reformation as a Remedy for Deception.
9.6 Equitable Defenses in Misrepresentation Cases.*

§ 9.1 Substantive Background and Remedial Summary

[*For the text of this section, see the unabridged Practitioner Treatise edition.*]

§ 9.2 Damages for Deception

§ 9.2(1) Damages Measure in Intentional Fraud Cases

In General

Misrepresentation cases are varied. In some cases the defendant is simply a seller of tangible property and misrepresents its characteristics. Because this pattern is both common and simple, it is convenient to state the damages rules as if the plaintiff were always the buyer. The rules stated below should be understood in that context; but it must also be understood that sellers and those engaged in more complex economic transactions may recover damages on the basis of the same principles.

* For the text of this section, see Dobbs, Law   Treatise, Vol. 2.
of Remedies, Second Edition, Practitioner

The "Out-of-Pocket" Measure

General damages: out of pocket measure. The out of pocket measure allows the plaintiff to recover the price paid for property he was induced to buy as a result of the misrepresentation, less the market value of the property[4] and with suitable adjustment by way of interest.[5] The out of pocket measure is the limit of general damages recovery in a small group of states, even in cases of intentional fraud.[6] It is also the measure most commonly adopted under federal securities laws.[7] Anomalously, where this limit applies, the plaintiff will be better off to recover for contract or warranty breach than for deliberate fraud.

Special meaning of "out-of-pocket". The out of pocket measure is a general damages measure, that is, one computed with reference to the value of the very thing purchased or sold.[8] The term thus does not refer to collateral expenses the plaintiff may have incurred as a result of the misrepresentation, although such expenses may be recoverable as consequential damages.[9]

Example of out-of-pocket measure. The defendant, by falsely representing authorship, induces the plaintiff to purchase a painting. The plaintiff pays $100,000 for the painting in reliance on the representation. In fact, because the painting was not authored by the artist named by the defendant, it is worth only $50,000. The out of pocket measure allows the plaintiff to recover $50,000 as the difference between the value and the price paid. The effect of this measure of damages is to leave the plaintiff with assets equal to those he had before the fraudulent transaction took place. In this respect, the out of pocket measure resembles restitution, although it differs in that it does not require a restoration in specie.[16]

The "Loss of Bargain" Measure

General damages: the benefit of the bargain or loss of bargain measure. The other measure of general damages is the loss of bargain measure,[17] which is exactly like the expectancy measure of contract damages.[18] The loss of bargain measure attempts to put the plaintiff in the economic position he would have been in had the representations been true. This rule not only guarantees that the plaintiff will have no loss; it also guarantees that the plaintiff will achieve any economic gains he would have had if the representations had been correct. The loss of bargain measure in some form has been used in most states, at least when the fraud is intentional,[19] but it may

---

§ 9.2(1)

4. R. Dunn, Recovery of Damages for Fraud § 2.5 (1988); Restatement Second of Torts § 549(1)(a) (1977); Annotation, "Out of pocket" or "Benefit of bargain" as proper rule of damages for fraudulent representations inducing contact for the transfer of property, 13 A.L.R.3d 875 (1967).

6. Reno v. Bull, 226 N.Y. 546, 124 N.E. 144 (1919); Strouth v. Wilkison, 302 Minn. 297, 224 N.W.2d 511 (1974). The rule is mandated by statute in California, West's Ann.Cal.Civ. Code § 3343, but the limits of the rule have been avoided in some of the cases. See Continental Airlines, Inc. v. McDonnell Douglas

Corp., 216 Cal.App.3d 388, 264 Cal.Rptr. 779 (1989). Other jurisdictions usually listed are the District of Columbia, Idaho, Montana, Pennsylvania and Texas. Oregon has a peculiar history and may or may not be in the out of pocket category. Compare Galego v. Knudsen, 281 Or. 43, 573 P.2d 313 (1978) with Selman v. Shirley, 161 Or. 582, 85 P.2d 384, 91 P.2d 312 (1939).

19. E.g., Bechtel v. Liberty Nat. Bank, 534 F.2d 1335 (9th Cir.1976); Turnbull v. LaRose, 702 P.2d 1331 (Alaska 1985); Slack v. Sodal, 190 Colo. 411, 547 P.2d 923 (1976); Miller v. Appleby, 183 Conn. 51, 438 A.2d 811 (1981); Gerill Corporation v. Jack L. Hargrove Build-

be rejected in favor of the more conservative out of pocket rule when the misrepresentation is merely negligent.[20]

The "value" form of the loss of bargain measure. The traditional loss of bargain measure allows the plaintiff to recover the difference between (a) the value the thing would have had if the false representations had been true and (b) the price paid.[21] This formulation is clearly a general damages measure; it is based on the value of the very thing purchased as a result of the misrepresentation. Although additional special damages for loss of profits in the operation of a business might also be recovered in some cases, the loss of bargain measure does not deal with profits. It captures only the gains the plaintiff should have had in the value of the property itself.

Example of the value form. For example, the defendant seller represents that spring water on Blackacre is pure, has been sold commercially and is of unlimited quantity. The plaintiff is induced to purchase Blackacre for $100,000, intending to bottle its water. Had the representations been true Blackacre would have been worth $150,000. In fact Blackacre's market value is only the price paid. The plaintiff is entitled to recover $50,000 under the loss of bargain rule. This represents the difference in the price value and the asset value actually received. This measure is not a special damages measure; it does not measure lost profits from the water business except so far as the potential for profits might be captured in the market value of the land itself.[22]

The "cost" form of the loss of bargain measure. An alternative measure of recovery awards the plaintiff the reasonable cost of putting the property in a condition that conforms to the representation. Courts have sometimes regarded this cost rule as merely one form of the loss of bargain rule.[23] But like repair and replacement costs in other circumstances, it could also be considered to be a form of special damages. In any event, the cost of putting the property into a condition that conforms to the representation is a permissible measure of recovery if costs are reasonable and appropriately proven.

Example of the cost form. The cost form of the rule can be illustrated by the spring water case. If the representation that the spring water was pure

ers, Inc., 128 Ill.2d 179, 131 Ill.Dec. 155, 538 N.E.2d 530 (1989); LeFlore v. Reflections of Tulsa, Inc., 708 P.2d 1068 (Okl.1985); Danca v. Taunton Sav. Bank, 385 Mass. 1, 429 N.E.2d 1129 (1982); Terry v. Panek, 631 P.2d 896 (Utah 1981); Kramer v. Chabot, 152 Vt. 53, 564 A.2d 292 (1989). See Restatement Second of Torts § 549 (1977) (providing for either lost bargain or out of pocket at plaintiff's option); Annotation, 13 A.L.R.3d 875 (1967).

A California statute seems to adopt an out of pocket rule, but California courts have found means of avoiding that limit in at least some instances. See Continental Airlines, Inc. v. McDonnell Douglas Corp., 216 Cal. App.3d 388, 264 Cal.Rptr. 779 (1989) (suggesting that the UCC lost bargain measure would supersede the out of pocket rule when "goods" were sold, including in that case the sale of a fleet of DC–10 airplanes); cf. Ward v. Taggart, 51 Cal.2d 736, 336 P.2d 534 (1959) (unjust enrichment recovery in excess of any out of pocket loss).

21. Bechtel v. Liberty Nat. Bank, 534 F.2d 1335 (9th Cir.1976); Slack v. Sodal, 190 Colo. 411, 547 P.2d 923 (1976).

22. Lost profits might be recovered separately as special or consequential damages if they do not duplicate the loss of bargain recovery. See § 9.2(3) below.

23. Bechtel v. Liberty Nat. Bank, 534 F.2d 1335 (9th Cir.1976); Slack v. Sodal, 190 Colo. 411, 547 P.2d 923 (1976). This alternative was regarded as a form of the loss of bargain measure in *Slack.* As with cost of repair measures in other cases, it might also be regarded as a form of special damages. All special damages recoveries tend to further the loss of bargain principle.

and of satisfactory quantity could be made good by building a filter system and drilling a well, the cost rule would allow the plaintiff to recover the costs of doing so, provided that solution was a reasonable one.[24] If costs of achieving conformity with the representation exceed the loss of bargain as measured by the "value" method, the value method should be preferred in many but probably not all instances.[25]

Flexible Measures

Measure optional with the plaintiff or flexibly applied by the court. In most instances the loss of bargain measure favors the plaintiff's interests, but when the plaintiff made a very bad bargain and would have lost money even if the representations had been true, recovery of the bad "bargain" is no solace. In such a case the plaintiff prefers rescission or the out of pocket measure of damages.[26] The Restatement[27] and some of the courts[28] have expressly adopted a rule that permits the plaintiff to use either measure in intentional fraud cases (but not in negligent misrepresentation cases). Somewhat differently, it must be said that courts themselves take a flexible view of damages in misrepresentation cases, adapting as circumstances seem to dictate, but according to the court's view of appropriate damages rather than at the plaintiff's option.[29]

Consequential Damages

Special or consequential damages. In appropriate cases, special damages are recoverable in addition to the recovery of general damages,[30] provided they are proved with reasonable certainty. Special damages, however, present some problems which require further discussion elsewhere.[31]

§ 9.2(2) Measures of Damages for Negligent or Innocent Representations

The Restatement takes the position that when the misrepresentation is merely negligent rather than fraudulent, the liability if any is limited to the out-of-pocket measure,[1] even though, in the case of fraudulent misrepresentations, liability extends to the loss of bargain.[2]

Liabilities for innocent misrepresentation. Traditional common law made innocent misrepresentations actionable for damages only when they counted as warranties or contract promises.

Rescission for innocent misrepresentations. Rescission (as distinct from damages) was granted at law or equity for innocent misrepresentation.[9] Perhaps this is understandable as a variation on rescission for mistake. As measured by the balance sheets of the parties, the effect of an out-of-pocket damages recovery is the same as the effect of a rescission, at least in the case of simple buy-sell contracts in stable markets.[10] The financial identity of these two remedies—rescission and out-of-pocket damages—suggests that they might be more or less interchangeable, so that if rescission would be permissible, a recovery of out-of-pocket damages would be equally so in the

27. Restatement Second of Torts § 549 and Comment *g* (1977).

§ 9.2(2)

1. Restatement Second of Torts § 552A (1977).

2. Restatement Second of Torts § 549 (1977).

absence of special reasons to require the specie restoration entailed by rescission.

Recovery of out-of-pocket damages for innocent representations. Based on the similarity of financial effects between rescission and out-of-pocket damages, the Restatement provides that (1) the plaintiff is to be allowed out-of-pocket damages for innocent representation whenever he would be allowed rescission for innocent representation; and (2) that the damages for innocent representation, when allowed, must not exceed the out-of-pocket measure.[11] Because this liability is grounded in restitutionary thought rather than in a policy of strict liability, consequential damages are to be denied; the damages claim, like its restitutionary analogue, simply equalizes the exchange of values and goes not further.[12] This is not to say that every innocent misstatement should be actionable for damages or rescission,[13] but that when it is actionable, damages are limited.

§ 9.2(3) Consequential or Special Damages

Specials Recoverable in Addition to General Damages

In most jurisdictions, the victim of fraud may recover special or consequential damages caused by the misrepresentation, in addition to the recovery under the appropriate general damages measure.

Although there is no rule against the recovery of both general and consequential damages, in some cases a recovery of both will permit duplication of awards because the consequential damages claimed will have been accounted for already by the general damages recovery. To avoid the duplication in such cases, the court must award either the general or the special damages, but not both. If such a choice must be made, the plaintiff's preference probably should be honored, as it sometimes is when the plaintiff claims only special or consequential damages in the first place.[16]

Because the way in which general and consequential damages are measured are quite different, it is not always obvious that the two measures are duplicative. An example will show the problem. If Blackacre, a farm, would be worth $500,000 with the good water supply represented by the seller, but is worth only $400,000 with the water that in fact exists, then the buyer who has paid $400,000 for the farm has $100,000 general damages under the loss of bargain measure. This sum reflects, as a capital sum, the expectation that, with limited water, the farm will produce fewer crops and that it will therefore earn less money. If the plaintiff is permitted to recover *both* $100,000 *and* the estimated value of the future crops themselves, the value of the diminished crops will have been counted twice.[17]

§ 9.2(4) Emotional Distress Damages in Misrepresentation Cases

Interests Protected—General Rule

Emotional distress recovery denied. Fraud, deceit and negligent misrepresentation are economic torts. Although the invasion of an economic interest by tort or by contract breach will often cause the plaintiff personal distress, the interest ordinarily protected in such cases is purely an economic interest and does not include interests in personality. Accordingly, the usual rule is that the plaintiff must show pecuniary loss in misrepresentation cases and the damages are limited to such pecuniary loss, with no recovery for emotional distress.[1]

Emotional distress recovery allowed. Mental distress recoveries are allowed where the fraud also amounts to some other tort.[2] A few cases allow the recovery even on an outright fraud theory.[3] Some writers have perceived substantial support in the recent cases in favor of an emotional distress recovery on a fraud theory [4] although as indicated more fully below, most of the cases seem to be in reality cases of punitive damages,[5] or cases of intentional infliction of emotional distress, or cases in which the court simply has not seriously addressed the general rule.[6]

Scope of the rule against emotional distress recovery. In recent years, both courts and writers have repeatedly urged expansion of liability for the invasion of economic interests.[7] Whether or not this is a good idea, it should be understood that the traditional rule in misrepresentation cases does not bar all recovery of intangible damages. First, punitive damages, which perform many of the same functions as mental distress damages, are recoverable in many fraud cases.[8] Second and more importantly, fraudulent statements or acts may be the basis for direct recovery of emotional distress damages in many cases because the fraudulent statement is an element in some tort besides fraud. The rule against mental distress recovery, in other words, is not a rule against recovery of such damages for *acts* of fraud but only a rule against such damages on a fraud *theory*. The rule is an analytical directive to consider elements besides a bare misrepresentation if the plaintiff is to recover for emotional distress.

§ 9.2(5) Punitive Damages in Misrepresentation Cases

[*For the text of this section, see the unabridged Practitioner Treatise edition.*]

§ 9.2(6) Limitations of Damages Under Causation and Proximate Causation Doctrines

Scope of Risk and Loss Problems

Special or consequential damages are always subject to the rule that the damages awarded must be caused in fact by the misrepresentation and in addition must be of the kind risked or "contemplated" by the parties. The tort version of the rule speaks of proximate cause; the contract version

---

§ 9.2(4)

1. Sierra Nat. Bank v. Brown, 18 Cal. App.3d 98, 95 Cal.Rptr. 742 (1971); Cornell v. Wunschel, 408 N.W.2d 369 (Iowa 1987) (quoting first edition of this treatise, "deceit is an economic not a dignitary tort"); Jourdain v. Dineen, 527 A.2d 1304 (Me.1987) (citing first edition of this treatise); see Durant v. Surety Homes Corp., 582 F.2d 1081, 1085 (7th Cir. 1978) (concealment of structural defects in home, to recover on mental distress the plaintiff must show defendant intended to cause severe emotional distress); Restatement Second of Torts § 549 (1977).

4. See R. Dunn, Recovery of Damages for Fraud § 4.8 (1988) (describing the courts as

being "divided sharply", but listing cases with only casual comments and those which seem to fit patterns discussed below).

7. *Fraud:* Merritt, Damages for Emotional Distress in Fraud Litigation: Dignitary Torts in a Commercial Society, 42 Vand.L.Rev. 1 (1989); *contracts:* Sebert, Punitive and Nonpecuniary Damages in Actions Based upon Contact: Toward Achieving the Objective of Full Compensation, 33 UCLA Law Rev. 1565 (1986); as to bad faith breach as a tort, see § 6.12, above; *tortious interference with contract:* Mooney v. Johnson Cattle Co., 291 Or. 709, 634 P.2d 1333 (1981); § 6.6(2) above.

speaks of the parties' contemplation. Both locutions are used in fraud cases,[1] and it probably does not matter much which one is chosen. Fraud has both tort and contract elements, but technically at least it is a tort, so the proximate cause language seems fitting and is used here. Causation problems are found both in common law and in statutory cases, such as those involving federal securities frauds. This section does not consider the intricacies of federal securities fraud rules, but does mention some of the cases selectively.[2]

The proximate cause problem is primarily a problem of special or consequential damages and has little application to general damages. In fraud cases, however, even general damages may be limited or denied in some instances because the court concludes that the representation is not a proximate or actual cause of the harm. Conversely, in restitution cases, the problem is to determine what portions of the defendant's gain is causally related to the misrepresentation.[3]

Cause in Fact

The but-for rule. The defendant's liability ordinarily extends only to pecuniary losses caused in fact by the plaintiff's reliance on the misrepresentation. Under the familiar but-for test,[4] if the plaintiff did not rely on the misrepresentation, then the misrepresentation is not a cause in fact of harm. If the plaintiff did rely on the misrepresentation but would have suffered the same loss even without any misrepresentation, the misrepresentation is still not a cause in fact of any harm.

Transaction causation where same loss would have occurred anyway. For instance, suppose an investor wishes to invest in domestic oil stocks and is led by a lie to invest in Company *A's* stock. The Company *A* stock becomes worthless as oil prices fall below production costs. Suppose further that if the plaintiff had been told the truth about Company *A* stock, he would have invested in oil stocks of Company *B*, which, as it turns out, also goes bankrupt because of the same fall in oil prices. Some judges would conclude that the misrepresentation in fact caused no harm even though the plaintiff did in fact rely upon it, because some similar harm[5] would have resulted anyway; and on this basis would deny relief.[6] Special statutes may, however, sometimes permit the plaintiff to rescind even when the fraud has not caused any loss.[7]

Transaction causation where loss causation can also be fairly assumed. In most cases, it seems safe and also fair to assume that had the plaintiff not invested in the defendant's misrepresented transaction, he would not have suffered a loss at all and hence that the misrepresentation was a cause in fact. For instance, suppose the plaintiff buys a home from the defendant on

---

§ 9.2(6)

6. See Bastian v. Petren Resources Corp., 892 F.2d 680 (7th Cir.1990), cert. denied, 496 U.S. 906, 110 S.Ct. 2590, 110 L.Ed.2d 270 (1990) (securities act and RICO case, Posner, J., concluding on similar facts that the rule is not one of "proximate cause," but "cause, period;" but also suggesting that the plaintiffs could have provided a basis for a causal inference in their favor by showing that most alternative investments survived the fall in prices).

But see Merritt, Loss Causation and Securities Fraud, 66 Tex.L.Rev. 469, 530 (1988) ("The used car dealer who defrauds a car buyer should have no defense that the gullible buyer otherwise would have wasted her money betting on horses").

7. See Rousseff v. E.F. Hutton Co., 867 F.2d 1281 (11th Cir.1989) (following a Florida decision under a Florida securities statute).

the basis of a lie about the condition of the roof and later suffers great pecuniary loss because the roof falls in and must be replaced. There is no reason to imagine that the plaintiff, had he known the truth, would have forsaken the fraudulent deal but would have purchased a house with an equally bad roof from another seller. And if the plaintiff would not have made a bad deal elsewhere, then all of the defendant's misrepresentation did in fact cause all the plaintiff's loss under the but-for test.

When defendant could have fulfilled his duty by either a causal or non-causal act. One puzzling situation for but-for cause cases of any kind arises when the defendant could have fulfilled his duty to the plaintiff by either two different acts, one of which would have led to the same loss the plaintiff suffered and one of which would have avoided that loss. For instance, some federal securities fraud cases impose upon insiders a duty *either* to disclose private information publicly, *or* to abstain from trading in the shares affected by that information.[8]

Suppose the insider has nonpublic information that a company's earnings has gone down and knows that the stock price will fall when the information is publicly announced. The insider sells his shares, taking advantage of the preannouncement price. Buyers on the stock exchange who lack the information, buy at current prices, but find that their newly acquired shares immediately drop in value when the information is made public a day later. The insider is a violator of securities law, but it is not clear that he caused a loss. Buyers through a stock exchange did not buy the seller's shares.

Did the insider seller cause their losses? The insider could have fulfilled his duty to the buyer by divulging the inside information, in which case the buyer would presumably not have bought. In this scenario, the buyer's loss is caused by the seller's breach of duty. However, the seller probably would have violated duties to others if he had divulged the inside information. If he were to comply with his duty to the buyer, the most probable and most legal way to comply would be to abstain from trading. Had he abstained from trading, however, the buyer would still have had no information and would still have suffered the loss. In *this* scenario, the seller's violation is not a cause of loss at all.

As always, but-for causation is tested by considering the hypothetical alternative that never came about. In this situation, there are two hypothetical alternatives, one of which leads to the conclusion that the seller was a cause and one of which leads to the opposite conclusion. Not surprisingly, some federal authority supports a finding of causation in such cases[9] and some does not.[10] A 1988 federal statute seems to adopt a compromise position, permitting recovery by contemporaneous traders in the stock but limiting their recovery not to exceed the profits made by the inside trader.[11]

---

8. Some of the insider information material is discussed in § 10.5(2) below.

9. Shapiro v. Merrill Lynch, Pierce, Fenner & Smith, Inc., 495 F.2d 228 (2d Cir.1974) (similar to the facts of the example).

10. Fridrich v. Bradford, 542 F.2d 307 (6th Cir.1976).

11. 15 U.S.C.A. § 78t–1(a) & (b). The statute provides in part:

(a) Any person who violates any provision of this chapter or the rules or regulations thereunder by purchasing or selling a security while in possession of material, nonpublic information shall be liable in an action

Proximate Cause: Losses Outside the Risks Associated With the Representation

Cause-in-fact with unrelated losses. The defendant's misrepresentation may in fact cause the plaintiff to enter a transaction and may also in fact cause the resulting loss to the plaintiff. Even if cause in fact is established, however, the loss that occurs may be due to factors that seem unrelated in any significant way to the fraud which induced the loss.

The factory explosion example. For example, the defendant may induce the plaintiff to purchase shares of stock on the representation that corporate management has just entered into a valuable contract for producing rockets. If the statement is untrue, the shares may be worth less than the plaintiff bargained for; if the plaintiff takes a loss as a result, it is a recoverable item of damages. But suppose that, immediately after the plaintiff purchases the shares, the company's factory is destroyed by an explosion and the shares of stock become worthless for *that* reason.

Transaction causation, price causation. In cases of which this is an example, the plaintiff might have had no loss at all if he had not been fraudulently induced to enter the contract. He might not have entered the transaction and might have saved his investment.[12] But it is also possible that the plaintiff, had he not been victimized by the fraud, would have entered the transaction anyway, but would have paid a lower price. Given that possibility, analysis may emphasize that the loss in cases like the factory example proceeds from facts as to which there was *no* representation and from risks that would *not* have affected the price. Not surprisingly, there is a certain amount of conflict about what to do with cases of this sort. Some of the different results may depend on assumptions about what the plaintiff, or a reasonable person, would have done in the absence of misrepresentation.

Four Approaches to the "Proximate Cause" Problem

In cases like that of the factory explosion, the damages result may depend upon several factors. The defendant guilty of actual fraud might be distinguished from the defendant guilty of only negligent misrepresentation, for example. The plaintiff who would never have entered into the transaction at all if fully informed might be distinguished from the plaintiff who would have entered into the transaction, but would have done so at a different price. Without parsing all the permutations, four major approaches to such cases can be stated:

(1) Allowing full recovery. In *Fottler v. Moseley,*[13] the plaintiff purchased stock on the misrepresentation that there was an active market in the shares. The plaintiff took a loss because a corporate officer embezzled

---

in any court competent jurisdiction to any person who, contemporaneously with the purchase or sale of securities that is the subject of such violation, has purchased (where such violation is based on a sale of securities) or sold (where such violation is based on a purchase of securities) securities of the same class.

(b)(1) The total amount of damages imposed under subsection (a) of this section shall not exceed the profit gained or loss avoided in the transaction or transactions that are the subject of the violation.

13. 185 Mass. 563, 70 N.E. 1040 (1904). See also David v. Belmont, 291 Mass. 450, 197 N.E. 83 (1935); cf. Chasins v. Smith, Barney & Co., 438 F.2d 1167 (2d Cir.1970).

corporate funds, which had the effect of removing much of the value of the shares. The Massachusetts Court permitted the stockholder to recover against the defendant for the drop in the value of his stock due to the embezzlement of corporate funds by an officer, even though the broker's representation was on another matter altogether. Though less dramatic, the case is an almost exact parallel to the factory explosion example. The same result may be achieved by the grant of either rescission or out of pocket damages.[14] In that case the plaintiff gets his money back and avoids losses from both the misrepresentation and the explosion. The effect is to give him protection against risks as to which there was no misrepresentation.[15]

(2) Denying all recovery. It would be possible to deny *all* recovery in cases like the factory explosion case.[16] But unless the plaintiff's claim can be dismissed on cause-in-fact grounds because he would have suffered the same loss even in the absence of misrepresentation, denial of *all* recovery as a rule of law seems insupportable.[17] However, doctrines that are nominally independent of causal rules may lead to a denial of all relief when the plaintiff is unable to segregate losses caused by the misrepresentation from those caused by other forces.[18]

14. E.g., Olney Sav. & Loan Ass'n v. Trinity Banc Sav. Ass'n, 885 F.2d 266 (5th Cir.1989) (rescission); cf. Wallace v. Hallowell, 56 Minn. 501, 58 N.W. 292 (1894) (out of pocket).

In *Wallace,* supra, the plaintiff, in a single transaction, purchased certain notes from defendant. The notes had been executed by *A* and *B* respectively. The defendant, to induce plaintiff to buy the notes, told plaintiff that *A* was financially sound. The plaintiff, relying on this, bought both notes. It turned out that both *A* and *B* were unable to pay the notes. Since the misrepresentation was about *A's* notes only, it might be thought that the loss suffered as to *B's* notes ought not be recoverable. However, the plaintiff was allowed a recovery of his investment as to both notes. The court treated the case much as a rescission and restitution case—and indeed the out of pocket damages recovered do amount to just that. In *Wallace* the different *risks* are represented by different *persons*. The misrepresentation was only to one risk (the rocket contract, the financial stability of *A*); the losses came from both.

15. See In re Washington Public Power Supply System Securities Litigation, 650 F.Supp. 1346, 1355 (W.D.Wash.1986).

17. It might be argued that the plaintiff was merely a *potential* loser, and that the potential for loss was wiped out by the loss from the explosion. The case might be analogized to the case of a person who has swallowed slow-acting poison but who is killed by a train one day before the poison would have killed him anyway. It would be possible to regard the train as "the" relevant cause of death, not the poison. In such a case the negligently operated railroad would be liable only for hastening the plaintiff's death by one day. Dillon v. Twin State Gas & Elec. Co., 85

N.H. 449, 163 A. 111 (1932). Given that rule, it becomes very difficult to be content with the view that the poisoner has no liability at all. And actually, if the poisoned plaintiff is no where near an operating train when the poison is swallowed, the poisoner might be held fully liable on the ground that subsequent events do not affect recovery unless their forces were in operation at the time. Cf. Baker v. Willoughby, [1970] A.C. 467, [1970] 2 W.L.R. 50, [1969] 3 All.Er. 1528 (H.L.1969); but cf. Jobling v. Associated Dairies, Limited, [1982] A.C. 794, [1981] 3 W.L.R. 155, [1981] 2 All E.R. 752 (H.L.1981). If the new force is a force of nature instead of a new tortfeasor (or in fraud cases, a force such as an economic downturn), the case is more like the case of a person who is killed on July 4 but who, if not killed, would have gone trekking in Nepal with a group all of whom were killed by an avalanche. Almost certainly one would not say the killer escapes all liability because a force not present at the time would later have killed the plaintiff anyway. These analogies suggest why it would be difficult to justify a rule denying all liability unless it can be shown that the plaintiff would have suffered the same loss even without the misrepresentation. As to that argument, see Bastian v. Petren Resources Corp., supra n. 6, which, however, does not seem applicable to a case like the explosion case. But if it is difficult to justify a rule denying all liability, it is perhaps much easier to justify a finding that the plaintiff had not adequately segregated the losses due to the misrepresentation from those due to other causes. See the discussion of Edwards v. Wilcoxen, note 18 below.

18. Edwards v. Wilcoxen, 278 Or. 91, 562 P.2d 1207 (1977) is instructive. The plaintiffs purchased a restaurant, allegedly as a result

(3) Full recovery in limited cases: misrepresentation interpreted broadly to cover all risks. In a very few cases, the misrepresentation might be interpreted to be material on a wide range of factors affecting value, with the result that losses from quite obscure and apparently unrelated sources might be recoverable. In an old New York case, *Hotaling v. A.B. Leach & Co.,*[19] the defendant broker made representations that a company was financially sound. The plaintiff, in reliance on these statements, purchased the company's bond. Later, there was an industry-wide depression that affected, not merely that particular company, but others as well. As a result of this intervening financial situation, the corporation was unable to pay off the bond and the plaintiff sued the broker for misrepresentation. Although the loss seemed more the result of the depression than the misrepresentation, the plaintiff was allowed to recover. The judge's reasoning in allowing recovery was elliptical,[20] but he may have taken the view that the representation covered the economic soundness of the company to withstand even a world-wide depression, or that the representation "continued" and induced the buyer to retain his securities in the face of signs that they should be sold.[21] Perhaps few representations could be interpreted so broadly as to cover risks of a general depression,[22] so this third approach appears to offer no solution for most cases.

(4) Proximate cause approach: allowance of true general damages. Perhaps most courts,[23] with the support of the Restatement,[24] would allow a

of a misrepresentation about its income. But the plaintiffs themselves change the mode of operation, atmosphere, food style, and prices. When they lost money they sought rescission. The court refused relief partly because of the plaintiffs' delay, partly because of the changed restaurant operation. There was no direct discussion of causal rules, but it was clear that rescission would avoid not only losses caused by the misrepresentation but those due to the plaintiffs' own mode of operation. Had the plaintiffs to sue for damages instead of rescission, the form of the problem would change but its substance would remain, so that a court might deny damages unless the plaintiffs could segregate the losses due to the misrepresentation from the losses due to their own management.

19. 247 N.Y. 84, 159 N.E. 870, 57 A.L.R. 1136 (1928).

20. Judge Lehman explained this result on the ground that "loss of the investment was due to weakness inherent in the investment concealed by the defendant. That weakness might not under all circumstances have produced the ruin of the company. It did produce that ruin when conditions demanding greater strength arose in the oil trade * * *. [V]alue [of the bond] must be determined in the light of subsequent events." Hotaling v. A.B. Leach & Co., 247 N.Y. 84, 159 N.E. 870, 873, 57 A.L.R. 1136 (1928).

21. See Marbury Management, Inc. v. Kohn, 629 F.2d 705 (2d Cir.1980), (representation that defendant was a portfolio specialist and licensed representative induced purchase

but did not cause loss in stock value, but induced plaintiff to continue holding stock, good discussion of cases, liability), cert. denied Wood Walker & Co. v. Marbury Management, Inc., 449 U.S. 1011, 101 S.Ct. 566, 66 L.Ed.2d 469 (1980).

22. See People v. S.W. Straus & Co., 156 Misc. 642, 282 N.Y.S. 972 (1935) where the court rejected the opportunity to get the same result on similar facts. Cf. Bastian v. Petren Resources Corp., supra n. 6. The court's reasoning in *Hotaling* was not inconsistent in form with the Restatement view that limits liability to losses associated with the misrepresentations; but its notion about the range of economic factors to which the misrepresentation related was certainly an expansive one. If the proximate cause issue is skirted on the *Hotaling* theory, there will likely be a second line of defense on cause in fact grounds, as in *Bastian,* supra.

23. Boatmen's Nat. Co. v. M.W. Elkins & Co., 63 F.2d 214 (8th Cir.1933); Waddell v. White, 56 Ariz. 420, 108 P.2d 565, 572 (1940); see People v. S.W. Straus & Co., 156 Misc. 642, 282 N.Y.S. 972 (1935); see, Bruschi v. Brown, 876 F.2d 1526, 1530 (11th Cir.1989) (federal securities law).

In *Waddell,* supra, the court said:

"[I]t should * * * be remembered that defendant cannot be held responsible for depreciation in the value of the stock of the development company caused by the general depressed condition of the country, nor

24. See note 24 on page 705.

partial recovery, limiting damages to those which were "foreseeable" as a result of the misrepresentation, or to damages the risk of which was hidden or falsely minimized by the misrepresentation.[25] Statutes, too, may incorporate this view.[26] This approach excludes recovery of damages resulting from extraneous sources such as the factory explosion but should not exclude damages that can be identified as derived from the misrepresentation. Nor should it necessarily exclude a greater recovery as restitution to prevent the defendant's unjust enrichment.[27]

Segregating Misrepresentation Damages From Extraneous–Force Damages

Market value at purchase date as basis. The proximate cause approach is appealing, if at all, only if there are convenient and practical ways to segregate the "foreseeable" damages from those which are not. Such segregation can be accomplished by allowing any consequential damages specifically risked by the misrepresentation[28] plus general damages calculated as of the date of sale rather than as of a later date after some unrelated

the inability to find purchasers for the citrus land * * * He is liable only for such damages as reasonably resulted to the value of the stock from his [fraud and misconduct]."

24. Restatement Second of Torts § 548A (1965).

The Restatement states the rule in terms of foreseeability and limits liability to losses that might reasonably be expected to result from the plaintiff's reliance. This may be too narrow in some cases. If a representation affecting value is in fact material to several factors affecting value, it may not be important whether the intentional fraudfeasor should have or did foresee its materiality on one factor, two factors or many factors.

25. See Huddleston v. Herman & MacLean, 640 F.2d 534, 549 (5th Cir.1981) ("The causation requirement is satisfied in a Rule 10b–5 [securities act] case only if the misrepresentation touches upon the reasons for the investment's decline in value"), rev'd as to other issues, Herman & MacLean v. Huddleston, 459 U.S. 375, 103 S.Ct. 683, 74 L.Ed.2d 548 (1983).

26. Under federal securities law, liability for false statements in a registration statement, excludes any depreciation in value of the security "other than" the depreciation resulting from the misstatement or omission. The burden is upon the defendant, however, to demonstrate what portion of damages falls in this category. 15 U.S.C.A. § 77k.

27. See Thompson, The Measure of Recovery under Rule 10b–5: A Restitution Alternative to Tort Damages, 37 Vand.L.Rev. 349 (1984). In the absence of any gain to the defendant that results from the misrepresentation, however, the proximate cause rule, if otherwise desirable, should not be circumvented by a rescission theory. See § 9.3(2) below.

28. When the defendant sells the plaintiff securities worth the price paid but engages in excessive trading or "churning" so that added transaction costs or commissions are incurred, the fraud has caused the plaintiff no general damages, if the securities are worth the price paid; but it has caused special or consequential damages which should be recoverable. See T. Hazen, The Law of Securities Regulation § 10.11 (1985 & Supps.) (stating the usual rule to be recovery of damages for excessive commissions, with some possible liability for more remote consequential damages).

In Hatrock v. Edward D. Jones & Co., 750 F.2d 767 (9th Cir.1984) the court said that in such a case the plaintiff should not be required to prove loss causation because "the evil is not the price the investor paid for a security, but the broker's fraudulent inducement of the investor to purchase the security." Id. at 773. It might be more accurate as a matter of loss measurement to say that causation of damages must indeed be proven, but that such damages can be seen in the excessive commission charges. In *Hatrock,* the court went on to say that the excessive commission charges would not be the limit of recovery if the value of the securities fell. In that case the plaintiff could recover the decline in the value of his portfolio to the extent that the decline resulted from excessive transactions. "The recoverable decline in portfolio value is 'the difference between what [the plaintiff] would have had if the account ha[d] been handled legitimately and what he in fact had at the time the violation ended.'" Id. at 773–74. This appears to be a requirement of causation in fact, though it may not fully honor the proximate causation requirement, because it seems not to limit the recovery to a decline that was within the scope of the risk created by excessive trading.

disaster has struck.[29] An approach like this would consider the market value of the plaintiff's purchase immediately after sale,[30] *or* in some cases, the market value a reasonable time after discovery of the fraud;[31] but it would not consider the market value after the explosion or other extraneous force affecting price.[32] Such an approach makes it practical to segregate losses that result from the misrepresentation from losses that result from extraneous forces, but it does not guarantee that the plaintiff will always be able to make appropriate proof.[33]

General (unrealized) damages. In the factory explosion case, the defendant represented that the company had an important contract to build rockets; relying on this, the plaintiff paid $10,000 for shares in the company. The shares became worthless after the factory was destroyed, but a full recovery of the $10,000 would give the plaintiff not only damages resulting from the misrepresentation but also those resulting from the explosion (as to which no representation was made). Although the plaintiff had no special damages—no realized loss—at the time the shares were purchased, he had general damages at that time if the shares were worth less than he paid or bargained for.[34] Such damages, calculated as of the time the transaction took place, will automatically exclude extraneous factors like the explosion.

Out-of-pocket measure example. Applying the fourth approach to the factory explosion case with an out of pocket measure, the court would note that the plaintiff paid $10,000 for shares that are now worthless. But their present value is not relevant. The question is their value at the time of purchase. If the shares were worth only $8,000 when the plaintiff paid $10,000, the recovery is $2,000.[35] This is exactly what it would be under the

29. See 1 George Palmer, Law of Restitution § 3.8 (1978 & Supp.).

30. Special damages might also be recoverable between the time of purchase and discovery of the fraud as stated in § 9.2(3) above.

31. See the careful discussion in Thompson, The Measure of Recovery under Rule 10b–5: A Restitution Alternative to Tort Damages, 37 Vand.L.Rev. 349 (1984) (valuable for its general-law analysis as well as for discussion of securities cases in particular).

32. See In re Washington Public Power Supply System Securities Litigation, 650 F.Supp. 1346, 1354 (W.D.Wash.1986).

33. See Edwards v. Wilcoxen, 278 Or. 91, 562 P.2d 1207 (1977), discussed supra note 18.

34. General damages need not be realized. They are based on asset-value held by the owner, not on actual expenditures. The plaintiff's balance sheet immediately after the transaction in question, if it accurately reflected value, would show his net worth to be less than immediately before if he made a bad bargain. If there is an informed market for the shares in the example, that market will reflect what buyers would pay for the shares when they know all the facts. If the fraud is widely disseminated, so that there is no informed market and every potential buyer is misled in the same way as the plaintiff, the value of the shares would have to be constructed hypothetically as of the time of the transaction. Most "market" measured damages have a large element of convention and construction, so this is nothing new.

35. See Bruschi v. Brown, 876 F.2d 1526, 1531 (11th Cir.1989) (proof of overvaluation of securities due to misrepresentation); In re Washington Public Power Supply System Securities Litigation, 650 F.Supp. 1346, 1353–1354 (W.D.Wash.1986). In the *Washington Public Power Supply System Securities Litigation* (known as *WPPSS* or *Whoops* litigation), the court took the following example from another case:

[A]n investor might purchase stock in a shipping venture involving a single vessel in reliance on a misrepresentation that the vessel had a certain capacity when in fact it had less capacity than was represented in the prospectus. However, the prospectus does disclose truthfully that the vessel will not be insured. One week after the investment the vessel sinks as a result of a casualty and the stock becomes worthless.

The *Whoops* court commented:

By misrepresenting the capacity of the ship, the investor was induced to pay a certain price for stock in the venture. As a result of the misrepresentation, the investor paid more for the stock than it was worth.

out of pocket measure if the plaintiff discovered the fraud and sued before the explosion. The recovery would not repair the plaintiff's losses resulting from the explosion, but it would repair losses associated with the risks created by the misrepresentation.

Loss of bargain measure example. Under the loss of bargain measure the fourth approach would consider the (hypothetical) value the shares would have had if the representation had been true. And again the relevant date would be the date of the transaction, not the date of the explosion. If it is reasonably estimated that the shares would have been worth $15,000 had the representation been true, but the plaintiff received shares worth only $8,000, then the recovery on a loss of bargain measure would be $7,000. And again, damages from risks as to which there was no representation are excluded.

Comment

In the case of negligent misrepresentation, perhaps it would be unwise to impose upon the defendant any risks not undertaken by the contract or encompassed without the representation. Since any given transaction imposes risks upon the plaintiff-purchaser as well as risks upon the defendant-seller, the plaintiff should not be permitted too readily to escape the risks he accepted in the transaction merely because he also suffers losses from risks he did not accept. In a case without misrepresentation, a purchaser must accept risks of extraneous injury to the property he purchases—the risk that the property will be destroyed, for example—and such a risk should not be readily avoided merely because some other risk has caused some other loss. If any liability is to be imposed for representations that are merely negligent, then the fourth approach, with its limitation that general damages are to be measured as of date of the transaction, should probably furnish a ceiling on liability in the ordinary case.[36]

But it is at least arguable that liability should be more extensive in cases of actual fraud.[37] Full liability, including liability for the loss caused by the explosion, may be arguably proper where:

(1) the defendant is guilty of actual fraud; and

(2) the defendant's fraud induced the plaintiff to enter the transaction, (not merely to pay a higher price than otherwise would have been the case); and

(3) the plaintiff, had he not been deceived, would not have entered into similar transactions and lost similar sums.

When the ship sank, the entire investment was lost. The investor, however, was injured by more than the true value of the investment because he paid an inflated price for the stock. His damages thus consist of two components: the value lost due to the casualty and the amount lost because he overpaid for the stock. This latter component of damages is related directly to the initial misrepresentation. Hence, this [latter] amount should be recoverable in an action for securities fraud.

§ 9.3 Restitutionary Remedies for Deception: Rescission, Constructive Trusts and Other Remedies

§ 9.3(1) Rescission and Restitution

[*For the text of this section, see the unabridged Practitioner Treatise edition.*]

§ 9.3(2) Is Damages Causation Required to Support Rescission?

Existence of Damage as a Prerequisite to Restitution

General rule. The ordinary rule is that the plaintiff must demonstrate the existence of actual damages to have a common law [1] action for damages based on misrepresentation.[2] Restitution claims are different. Most courts seem to have rejected any pecuniary damages requirement as a pre-condition to restitution where the misrepresentation was clearly material even though it did not bear on economic value,[3] and even where the misrepresentation *under*stated the value of goods involved.[4]

Some cases, however, have carried over to restitution claims the damage-suit requirement of pecuniary loss.[6] These courts have said that rescission is to be denied unless the plaintiff demonstrates actual damages.

"Proximate cause" limits. If the plaintiff claims *damages* for misrepresentation, the usual rule limits his recovery to harms proximately caused by the misrepresentation. The case put in discussing the damages rule was this: the plaintiff buys stock in a company in reliance on the false representation that the company has just entered into a valuable contract, but the company's stock becomes worthless because its entire plant is destroyed in an explosion. In such a case the plaintiff is not usually permitted to recover for the loss in value due to the explosion. As to that, there was no misrepresentation. He might instead recover any provable pre-explosion damages, based on the difference between the market value as represented at the date of purchase and the price he actually paid. Possibly some other date could be used as well, but in any event it would be a date that would exclude a recovery for the unrelated harms from the explosion.[9]

Avoiding proximate cause limits by claiming rescission? A number of cases have permitted the plaintiff to rescind for a misrepresentation, and thus to avoid all losses associated with the transactions, including those losses not resulting from the misrepresentation.[10] In a Minnesota case,[11] for example, the plaintiff, in a single transaction, purchased two notes from the defendant, one executed by *A* and one executed by *B*. The defendant misrepresented the financial foundation of *A*, but made no representation as to *B*. When it turned out that both *A* and *B* were unable to pay the notes the plaintiff sought out of pocket damages, which is the financial equivalent of rescission. The court permitted this relief. Other courts have done the same in similar cases on a rescission theory.[12]

§ 9.3(2)

4. Earl v. Saks & Co., 36 Cal.2d 602, 226 P.2d 340 (1951) (donor wanted a gift not exceeding a certain value, allowed to rescind his purchase when he discovered that the seller had taken the difference from the donee and had fraudulently sold him an item worth more).

6. E.g., Mott v. Tri–Continental Financial Corp., 330 F.2d 468 (2d Cir.1964) (New York law); see McCleary, Damage as Requisite to Rescission for Misrepresentation (Pts. 1 and 2), 36 Mich.L.Rev. 1, 227 (1937).

10. See 1 G. Palmer, Law of Restitution § 3.8 (1978).

11. Wallace v. Hallowell, 56 Minn. 501, 58 N.W. 292 (1894).

The damages solution. The effect of rescission in such cases is to allow the plaintiff to avoid losses as to which there was no misrepresentation at all. If this is a bad idea in ordinary damages claims, it would seem to be an equally bad idea in rescission claims. If the proximate cause rules are right, the better solution is to deny rescission and restitution but to award out of pocket damages figured as of the transaction date. Out of pocket damages would put the plaintiff in the position he would have been in had he rescinded immediately after the transaction was completed rather than at a later date after unrelated loss has occurred.[13]

For example, if the plaintiff paid $10,000 for shares of stock because of the misrepresentation, but they were worth only $8,000 at the time they were sold, then given knowledge of the facts, the plaintiff could rescind at that point and be better off by $2,000 than if he affirmed the transaction. Similarly, he could recover $2,000 in out of pocket damages. When the shares become worthless at a later date from forces that were not misrepresented, the appropriate adjustment is still $2,000. Rescission after the shares have become worthless, however, would give the plaintiff back his consideration $10,000, in exchange for worthless stock. The simple solution, if the proximate cause rules are right, is to deny rescission and restitution and to permit the out of pocket damages.

§ 9.3(3) Restoration Required of the Plaintiff

[*For the text of this section, see the unabridged Practitioner Treatise edition.*]

§ 9.3(4) Restitution Required of the Defendant

Restitution Allowable

Benefits to be restored to the plaintiff generally. The plaintiff who is entitled to avoid a transaction because of misrepresentation is entitled to have restitution of all values which he transferred in the transaction as a result of the misrepresentation. The equities and the particular facts count heavily in measuring such restitution, but in a claim based on actual fraud or fiduciary breach the court would normally award as restitution,

(1)(a) in specie, all unique tangible and intangible property transferred to the defendant if it is capable of specific return,[1] and if that property is still in the defendant's hands; *or*

(b) the market value of that property as held by the defendant at the time of judgment;[2] *or*

§ 9.3(4)

1. E.g., patent rights that can be reassigned to the plaintiff, as in Roberts v. Sears, Roebuck and Co., 617 F.2d 460 (7th Cir.1980), cert. denied, 449 U.S. 975, 101 S.Ct. 386, 66 L.Ed.2d 237 (1980); or real property which the defendant's fraud prevent the plaintiff from obtaining. Nguyen v. Scott, 206 Cal.App.3d 725, 253 Cal.Rptr. 800 (1988).

2. See Restatement of Restitution § 151 (1937) (value at time of taking, retention or disposal, depending on facts). If value is fixed at the time of trial or judgment, and the value so fixed reflects an appreciation in value after the time of taking, the equities in particular cases may indicate that the plaintiff who elects to take such value should not also recover interest from the time of the taking. The plaintiff might appropriately be denied value-at-judgment if he has delayed in pursuing his rights so as to raise the suspicion that he was speculating in price fluctuations. See § 9.6 below.

(c) gains reaped by the defendant from his re-sale of property transferred to him by the plaintiff;[3] *or*

(d) the value of money or non-returnable intangibles transferred by the plaintiff, the value of services rendered by the plaintiff and the value of non-unique personal property transferred by him;[4] *and*

(2) any benefits defendant derived from the use of the property or intangibles transferred, measured by rental value, rents received, market interest rates, or interest actually received, as may be appropriate.[5]

Appropriate credits to the defendant for gains received by the plaintiff in the same transaction, may be offset against the defendant's liability for restitution.[6] Where several different measures of restitution are possible, equitable considerations may apply to limit the defendant's liability to the less stringent measure, but usually not less than the plaintiff's actual loss. In addition, the same "proximate cause" limitations that apply to damages may limit a recovery of the defendant's profits to those that result from the specific matters misrepresented.[7]

Third person liability for restitution. Because the plaintiff's rights are grounded in unjust enrichment, they run against any person who is unjustly enriched as a result of the defendant's fraud and not merely against the other party to the transaction. Thus a real estate broker may be liable to make restitution of benefits he receives in fraudulently fostering a transaction between the plaintiff and others;[8] and the donee of land which the defendant obtained by fraud may likewise be required to disgorge it.[9]

[*For discussion of these rules, see this section in the Practitioner Treatise edition, vol. 2, pp. 594–603.*]

Recovering defendant's gains from a sale. When the plaintiff transfers property to the defendant as a result of fraud and the defendant sells that property at a gain, the plaintiff can no longer recover the property in specie, but he is entitled to recover the sale price. If he can identify specific funds as those produced by his property, he will be entitled to a constructive trust upon those funds which will give him the gains those funds represent and also priority over other creditors.[26] Very often the recovery of the defendant's gains is accomplished by imposition of a constructive trust theory. But there is no reason why the plaintiff cannot sue for the gains in an

---

3. E.g., Estate of Jones v. Kvamme, 449 N.W.2d 428 (Minn.1989).

4. See 1 George Palmer, Law of Restitution (1978).

5. E.g., Blaising v. Mills, 176 Ind.App. 141, 374 N.E.2d 1166, 99 A.L.R.3d 1238 (1978) (rents actually collected).

6. In many instances the defendant's liability is stated in terms that incorporate the principle behind an offset in the measure of restitution itself. For example, *D*, a broker, tells *P* that land can be purchased for no less than $5,000 per acre. *P* bids $5,000 per acre and the broker delivers title. In fact, however, the broker has purchased the land himself at $4,000 per acre and taken a secret profit of $1,000 per acre. Instead of awarding *P* $5,000

per acre and then crediting *D* with $4,000 per acre for property received by *P,* the court can simply say that *D* is liable for his secret profit of $1,000 per acre. See Ward v. Taggart, 51 Cal.2d 736, 336 P.2d 534 (1959).

7. See Rowe v. Maremont Corp., 850 F.2d 1226, 1241 (7th Cir.1988) (buyer misrepresented intent to make a tender offer for corporate stock; had seller known, seller would have sold, but at a higher price; buyer's unjust enrichment measurable only by the premium it would have paid if truth had been told, not by its profits later made from shares).

8. Ward v. Taggart, 51 Cal.2d 736, 336 P.2d 534 (1959); Harper v. Adametz, 142 Conn. 218, 113 A.2d 136, 55 A.L.R.2d 334 (1955).

9. See § 9.6 below.

ordinary legal action, so long as he is not attempting to impress a trust upon a specific fund of money, such as an identified bank account.[27]

Gains the plaintiff would not have made. The plaintiff is not limited to the value of the property as of the time he transferred it to the defendant. Nor is he limited to the gains he would personally have made had he retained the property. In appropriate cases, the defendant may be required to disgorge illicit gains in a transaction even when the transaction has caused no loss at all.[28]

A well-known case is *Janigan v. Taylor*,[29] where the defendant, who was president and general manager of a corporation, had inside knowledge of a company opportunity. Concealing this knowledge, he induced the stockholders to sell him virtually all the outstanding stock for $40,000. Taking advantage of opportunities, the defendant made the company so valuable that two years later he sold the same stock for $700,000. In spite of the fraud, the plaintiffs may have had no loss; there was reason to think that the stock in their hands would not have risen so dramatically in value. Even so, the plaintiffs were entitled to recover the defendant's gains from resale of the stock to prevent his unjust enrichment. "It is more appropriate to give the defrauded party the benefit even of windfalls than to let the fraudulent party keep them."

Janigan arose under federal securities laws, but state-law fraud remedies produce the same kind of results, with the plaintiff recovering the defendant's market price gain at a much later date.[30]

Gains the defendant would have made anyway. The reverse of the *Janigan* case is one in which the defendant made gains from the fraudulently induced transaction but would have made them even without fraud. For example, suppose the defendant, by a misrepresentation, induces the plaintiff to sell her share of stock for $100. Had the defendant told the truth, the plaintiff would have sold and the defendant would have bought for $175. After the defendant buys the share, conditions change and the defendant sells the share for $400. Although the defendant in such a case has made a profit from the sale, it is a profit the defendant would have made even if it had made no misrepresentation. The defendant's profit cannot be seen to derive from the misrepresentation, since the transaction would have proceeded in any event. The defendant's liability in such a case, in line with the proximate cause type limits used in damages cases,[31] is limited to the plaintiff's loss, $75.[32]

Recovering appreciation in value in excess of defendant's gains—possible options. If the plaintiff is entitled to recover money restitution, he can no doubt measure that restitution by the value of the property he transferred at the date of transfer, with adjustments in interest or rental value to reflect the defendant's use.[33] A money recovery would be the only form of restitution available if the defendant has sold the property. In such a case, as shown in the preceding materials, the plaintiff might seek restitution of the

29. Janigan v. Taylor, 344 F.2d 781 (1st Cir.1965), cert. denied, 382 U.S. 879, 86 S.Ct. 163, 15 L.Ed.2d 120 (1965).

30. Estate of Jones v. Kvamme, 449 N.W.2d 428 (Minn.1989) ($5500 paid by defendant for 10 shares of stock in 1966, over $678,-000 paid for stock in 1978 when business was bought out).

32. Rowe v. Maremont Corp., 850 F.2d 1226 (7th Cir.1988).

gains defendant took from the sale, by constructive trust or otherwise. Conceivably the plaintiff could claim more. The plaintiff might claim, at least against a disloyal fiduciary, (1) the amount by which the defendant *could* or *should* have gained from use of the property transferred, or somewhat more modestly, (2) the value of the property at the time of the judgment even though the defendant no longer holds it. The first kind of claim has been denied,[34] but there is some support for the second.

—The Rothko case. A recovery of the current market value at time of trial was allowed in a well-known New York decision, but the defendants there were fiduciaries and third persons who knew the fiduciaries violated their trust. Executors of Mark Rothko's estate sold off his paintings to Marlborough. One of the executors was a director of one of the Marlborough companies, and thus had a conflict of interest. Other directors knew the facts, as did Marlborough itself. The price paid appeared to be inadequate—less than $2 million over a 12–year period—and the commission charged was more than the Marlborough charged Rothko in his lifetime. By the time of trial the value of the paintings was found to be about $10 million and the defendants were held liable for that sum, with credits for past payments.[35]

§ 9.4 Restitution Plus Damages: Election of Remedies

Traditional Rules Generally

General rule. Under traditional doctrine, by no means limited to misrepresentation cases,[1] a plaintiff who has two "inconsistent" remedies must "elect" between them and pursue only one of them. Alternatively, courts often say the plaintiff has in fact made an election of one remedy or another by some act before trial, often described as a ratification or affirmance of the transaction.[2] Remedies are traditionally found to be "inconsistent" when one of the remedies results from "affirming" a transaction and the other results from "disaffirming" a transaction. Most typically the plaintiff has elected, or is forced to elect, between rescission and damages remedies, but the election rule may apply to any pair of affirming and disaffirming remedies, such as replevin and damages.[3] The election of remedies terminology is also sometimes invoked in very different cases that appear in reality to be based on res judicata or satisfaction of the plaintiff's claim rather than on election as such.[4]

Examples. The traditional election doctrine has a surprising range of results. For example, the plaintiff who was induced by fraud to trade Blackacre for Whiteacre could not claim rescission for fraud and also reliance expense incurred in traveling to Whiteacre. He could rescind and get his property back (disaffirm) or he could sue for damages (affirm). He could not rescind *and* get reliance expense incurred, even if both remedies were necessary to make him whole. He was instead required to "elect" one or the other; or his action in suing was treated as an election he himself made.[5] On the same principle, the plaintiff who elects to rescind for fraud

---

34. See Marcus v. Otis, 168 F.2d 649 (2d Cir.1948), adhered to, 169 F.2d 148.

35. In re Rothko's Estate, 43 N.Y.2d 305, 401 N.Y.S.2d 449, 372 N.E.2d 291 (1977). The claim proceeded as one for damages. Profes-

sor Palmer thought the same result would be reached if the claim had been presented as one for restitution. See 1 George Palmer, Law of Restitution § 3.15 (Supp.1984).

may be denied a recovery of punitive damages, since all damages remedies are considered to "affirm" the contract while rescission disaffirms it.[6]

Or again, the plaintiff who has sued for damages cannot change his mind and ask for replevin instead; he has "elected" a remedy.[7] More commonly, the plaintiff who has sued for damages cannot change his mind and seek rescission instead.[8] Sometimes courts even hold that the plaintiff who sues for both rescission and damages in one complaint will be forced to make an election at the pleading or some other pre-trial stage,[9] in effect subverting liberal joinder and alternative pleading rules now common in most procedural systems.

Election rules inapplicable to inconsistent theories. The election doctrine does not apply to preclude the plaintiff from pursuing inconsistent theories or even inconsistent factual assertions. Modern procedure permits alternative and inconsistent claims and also alternative and inconsistent defenses.[10] No objection can be raised, for example, to the plaintiff's claim of both common law fraud and statutory misrepresentation, or to the claim of both fraud and contract breach, even though the plaintiff will be entitled to but one satisfaction.[11]

Rationales for Election Doctrine

The duplication theory of election doctrine. Courts often suggest that the election of remedies doctrine is based on a policy to avoid duplication of relief.[12] It is true that many cases avoid duplication of remedies by invoking the language of election. But many other cases invoke the language of election when duplication of relief is not a problem. The election is forced upon the plaintiff on the ground that the remedies are logically inconsistent, not on the ground that they are duplicative.

The first rule: the either/or rule. Traditional courts felt that two subsidiary legal rules followed from the idea that affirmance and disaffirmance remedies were inconsistent. First, the rule was that the plaintiff could not actually recover both kinds of remedies. He could not, for example, obtain damages for fraud and also rescind and get his money back.[19] He cannot have his cake and eat it too, one court said.[20] This is one of the two "election of remedies" rules only in the sense that *ultimately* the plaintiff cannot recover both kinds of remedies. Standing alone, the either/or rule does not require the plaintiff to make any choice or election before judgment.[21]

The second rule: pre-trial election forced. The either/or rule standing alone could permit a verdict in the plaintiff's favor for both restitution and damages, so long as both claims are not enforced by judgment. The second rule, however, imposes an election before trial in many instances. Under the pre-trial election rule, the plaintiff's conduct before trial can be treated as an "election" to affirm the transaction even when that is not the plaintiff's intent.[22] More rarely, the plaintiff's conduct might be treated as an "election"[23] to *dis*affirm.[24] Some courts have even required the plaintiff to announce an election at or before trial, and then have held that the forced election, once made, is binding.[25] Potentially, as explained in more detail below, any act that can be seen as a ratification of the transaction may be regarded as an affirmance which precludes rescission.

Critics have roundly and rightly condemned such rules.[29] The foremost scholar of restitution has said the forced election rule is "pernicious"[30] and courts have increasingly sought to circumscribe it.[31] The rule is not needed to protect the defendant from unjust or misleading conduct of the plaintiff. If the plaintiff's changed or delayed decision to sue for rescission rather than damages is a problem to the defendant, the defendant is fully protected by a whole catalog of doctrines and rules. Doctrines of laches and estoppel, the court's discretion to deny rescission to prevent hardship, procedural rules conditioning the amendment of complaints on court approval, and Rule 11 sanctions against strategic or harassing misbehavior all secure the defendant against actual harm that might otherwise result if the plaintiff attempts to harm the defendant by delay or change of pleading.

Nontraditional Recoveries

Allowing both restitution and compensatory consequential damages. When the misrepresentation is fraudulent or negligent and thus capable of remediation by either rescission or damages,[34] a number of cases have allowed recovery of both restitution and damages[35] and the Uniform Commercial Code expressly permits both kinds of recovery.[36] Some of the cases allowing a full recovery by way of a combination of restitution and damages do not mention the traditional rule to the contrary,[37] but others confront the old rules, find them wanting, and directly overrule them.[38] Still others formally adhere to the traditional either/or rule, but redefine restitution to require the defendant to "restore" not only the consideration received by the defendant, but to "restore" also any collateral damages the plaintiff may have suffered.[39] These cases all appear to contemplate the recovery of restitution plus consequential or out-of-pocket damages rather than restitution plus loss-of-bargain damages.

Restitution plus loss-of-bargain damages. There appears little occasion to permit the plaintiff to recover both restitution and loss-of-bargain dam-

§ 9.4

35. E.g., Seekings v. Jimmy GMC of Tucson, Inc., 130 Ariz. 596, 638 P.2d 210 (1981) ("[C]onsequential damages may be awarded in a case where revocation of acceptance is granted"); Landin v. Ford, 151 Ariz. 278, 727 P.2d 331, 332 (1986) ("A plaintiff electing rescission is entitled to those damages that are necessary to make him whole"); Robison v. Katz, 94 N.M. 314, 610 P.2d 201 (App.1980); Head & Seemann, Inc. v. Gregg, 107 Wis.2d 126, 318 N.W.2d 381 (1982); First Equity Investment Corp. v. United Service Corp. of Anderson, 299 S.C. 491, 386 S.E.2d 245 (1989).

36. UCC § 2–711 (buyer's revocation of acceptance, analogous to rescission, permits recovery of any price paid and damages for non-delivery).

38. Head & Seemann, Inc. v. Gregg, 107 Wis.2d 126, 318 N.W.2d 381 (1982), adopting the opinion in 104 Wis.2d 156, 311 N.W.2d 667 (App.1981) (traditional election of remedies doctrine modified to permit the plaintiff to recover all consistent "restorative" costs or damages, including out of pocket expenses and rental value of land involved in this transaction).

39. Indiana & Mich. Elec. Co. v. Harlan, 504 N.E.2d 301 (Ind.App.1987); First Equity Investment Corp. v. United Service Corp. of Anderson, S.C., 299 S.C. 491, 386 S.E.2d 245 (1989) ("Rescission entitles the party to a return of the consideration paid as well as any additional sums necessary to restore him to the position occupied prior to the making of the contract").

The court in *Indiana & Mich. Elec. Co. v. Harlan*, supra, said: If he elects to rescind the contract he may not recover general damages, but is only entitled to be returned to the status quo, which usually necessitates a return of money or other things received or paid under the contract, plus reimbursement as special damages, for any reasonable expenditure incurred as a proximate result of the fraudulent conduct. However, the rescinding party must restore all benefits received under the contract.

ages and such recoveries have been rejected not only by courts which recite the traditional election doctrine,[40] but also by courts that allow both restitution and consequential damages.[41]

Restitution, election and punitive damages. A rule denying both restitution and punitive damages is comprehensible as a part of the traditional election of remedies or ratification doctrine, since the claim of restitution disaffirms the transaction and with it the defendant's bad conduct. Contemporary thinking seems to be departing from the old conceptual thinking involved in election doctrine. With the contemporary concern chiefly to avoid duplicated remedies, some courts have flatly said that restitution and punitive damages should be permitted.[44] Others, without discussing election, have approved the award of both punitive damages and a restitutionary remedy such as constructive trust or accounting for profits.[45] But some courts have said that punitive awards should not be granted in rescission cases.[46] Even some of the same courts that have abolished the either/or rule in its traditional form by approving the recovery of both restitution and special damages, have insisted upon retaining the either/or rule when it comes to punitive damages. These courts have held that the claim for restitution is an election to disaffirm and that it operates to bar the recovery of punitive damages.[47]

§ 9.5 Reformation as a Remedy for Deception [1]

Reformation Generally

Reformation to reflect the true agreement. Reformation is the judicial reforming or re-writing of a document to make that document reflect the true agreement of the parties. Reformation may be granted if the requisite fraud or mistake is found to exist, even when the writing is wholly unambiguous.[2] For example, a deed might be reformed to correct a misdescription,[3] to convey share of the land agreed upon,[4] or to convey the kind of tenancy agreed upon.[5] Or a contract might be reformed to provide for the kind of goods agreed upon or the amount of the payment.[6] The principle applies to any kind of document, including personal injury releases[7] and divorce settlements.[8]

---

40. Boris v. Heyd, 220 Neb. 569, 371 N.W.2d 268 (1985); cf. Schlange–Schoeningen v. Parrish, 767 F.2d 788, 792–793 (11th Cir. 1985) (seemingly reflecting a Georgia rule that would have the effect of denying loss of bargain damages for fraud where there is a merger clause).

41. See Landin v. Ford, 151 Ariz. 278, 727 P.2d 331, 332 (1986) ("The election of remedies doctrine merely prevents a plaintiff from 'both repudiating [a] contract and then suing on it to gain the benefit of the bargain.' ").

44. Thomas Auto Co., Inc. v. Craft, 297 Ark. 492, 763 S.W.2d 651 (1989) (citing first edition); Brown v. Techdata Corp., Inc., 238 Ga. 622, 234 S.E.2d 787 (1977); Indiana & Mich. Elec. Co. v. Harlan, 504 N.E.2d 301 (Ind.App.1987).

45. Coster v. Crookham, 468 N.W.2d 802 (Iowa 1991) (trustee could be held for profits

resulting from self-dealing and also punitive damages).

46. Estate of Jones by Blume v. Kvamme, 449 N.W.2d 428 (Minn.1989); Roberts v. Estate of Barbagallo, 366 Pa.Super. 559, 531 A.2d 1125 (1987).

47. First Equity Investment Corp. v. United Service Corp. of Anderson, S.C., 299 S.C. 491, 386 S.E.2d 245 (1989) ("The election of rescission does not bar the rescinding party from receiving damages to make the party whole, but prevents him from receiving damages that presuppose a valid contract"). Compare Landin v. Ford, 151 Ariz. 278, 727 P.2d 331, 332 (1986) (rescission plus make-whole damages permitted) with Hubbard v. Superior Court, 111 Ariz. 585, 535 P.2d 1302 (1975) (seeming to forbid punitive recovery in rescission claim, at least where no consequential damages were established).

Reformation to reflect legal standard. There are some special instances in which courts will "reform" a writing to make it conform to a legal requirement rather than to the parties' actual intent,[9] or at least enforce the writing in conformity with the legal standards rather than the parties' intent. This section does not deal with such cases. It deals rather with the traditional purpose of reformation to make the writing reflect the true agreement of the parties.

Reformation vs. rescission. Reformation is the appropriate remedy,[10] and the only appropriate remedy for fraud or mistake in the written expression of the agreement.[11] And reformation must ordinarily be denied if the writing actually reflects the parties' prior agreement,[12] since courts do not change the parties' agreement but only correct their erroneous expression of it.[13] If there is no agreement, or if the agreement itself is voidable for fraud, then the remedy is traditionally one of rescission, not reformation.[14]

Reformation in Law and Equity

Physical reformation as equitable remedy. Reformation is normally an equitable remedy, to be accomplished by a chancellor whose *in personam* powers can command the physical presence of the writing so that it may be literally rewritten if need be.[23]

"Reformation" without physical re-writing. Reformation can be effected at times without any physical rewriting of the instrument, and if so, there is no reason why there cannot be reformation "at law," without resort to equity.[24] Such a reformation "at law," without an *in personam* order, might take place where fraud in the integration of a contract is asserted as a defense to a suit on that contract. Without physically re-writing the document, the court can simply recognize the defense.[25] Reformation is also achieved affirmatively at law in some suits for damages that are allowed to proceed *as if* the instrument sued upon had been reformed, so that the plaintiff can recover damages for breach of the original agreement even though it was improperly written down, or alternatively could recover constructive trust or specific performance in accord with the original agreement.[26]

Rescission or Reformation—Fraud in Forming or Fraud in Expressing the Contract?

The formation-integration distinction. Fraud or mistake in expressing or writing down the agreement warrants reformation. Rescission is not permitted in such cases,[27] because rescission would deny one of the parties the benefit of a bargain actually made. Fraud in inducing the *formation* of an agreement, on the other hand, warrants rescission or damages, but it does not warrant reformation,[28] because reformation in such a case could only impose a contract the parties did not agree to.

The formula or principle vs. the application as embodying the agreement. Some of the cases point to a deep ambiguity about the definition of "agreement." Parties often agree on a general formula at one stage of the "agreement," then at a later stage on a precise term which they take to result from an application of the formula. The formula "all my land" becomes "lots 1 and 2." In such a case the judge may think the agreement is "all my land" so that the deed conveying lots 1 and 2 should be reformed if the grantor in fact owns more.[33] On the other hand, the judge may think that the agreement for "all my land" was induced by mistake or misrepresentation as to how much land was involved, so that rescission but not reformation would be appropriate.[34]

[*For the full discussion of this topic as well as other reformation issues, see this section in the Practitioner Treatise edition, vol. 2, pp. 618–623.*]

§ 9.6 Equitable Defenses in Misrepresentation Cases
Equitable Defenses and Equitable Discretion Generally

[*For the text of this section, see the unabridged Practitioner Treatise edition.*]

§ 9.5

33. E.g., Long v. Vielle, 549 So.2d 968 (Ala. 1989) (all land between points x and y intended, conveyance of Lots 1 and 2 in belief that this covered all owned land reformed to include Lot 3 which fell within points x and y); cf. Cleghorn v. Zumwalt, 83 Cal. 155, 23 P. 294 (1890) (similar except that purchaser learned of seller's erroneous belief as to her holdings and did not disclose, reformation); Dettor v. BHI Property Co., No. 101, 324 N.C. 518, 379 S.E.2d 851 (1989) (was intent to deal with all grantor's land, assumed to be about 12 acres, or only to deal with tract of about 12 acres even if grantor owned more, summary judgment inappropriate).

34. See Russell v. Shell Petroleum Corp., 66 F.2d 864 (10th Cir.1933); cf. Metzler v. Bolen, 137 F.Supp. 457 (D.N.D.1956) (similar, mistake).

Chapter 10

DURESS, UNDUE INFLUENCE, AND OTHER UNCONSCIONABLE CONDUCT

Analysis

Sec.
10.1 Substance and Remedy in Misconduct Cases.
10.2 Duress and Economic Compulsion.
    10.2(1) Avoidance for Duress Generally.
    10.2(2) What Threats Are Wrongful Generally.*
    10.2(3) Threats in Particular Settings.
10.3 Undue Influence.
10.4 Breach of Fiduciary Obligation or Abuse of Confidential Relationship.
10.5 Misuse of Confidential Economic Information.
    10.5(1) Duties of Loyalty and Confidentiality and the Real Estate Broker's Secret Profits.
    10.5(2) Insider Transactions in Securities.*
    10.5(3) Trade Secrets and Confidential Information.
10.6 Liabilities for Commercial and Political Bribery and Related Wrongs.
10.7 Unconscionable Conduct and the UCC.*

§ 10.1 Substance and Remedy in Misconduct Cases

Scope the Substantive Wrongs

This chapter covers a group of varied, almost miscellaneous kinds of misconduct. Particular acts of misconduct in this chapter may also count as torts in some instances, but in general the misconduct covered here is wrong but not tortious. The rules here characteristically aim at preventing stated results but do not aim at identifying particular acts of misconduct.

The kinds of misconduct covered are mainly these: (1) duress, the use of improper threats or economic pressure to secure a contract or some other action;[1] (2) undue influence, the use of a position of special influence and respect to gain some purely personal advantage;[2] (3) breach of fiduciary or confidential relationship by failing to reveal information;[3] (4) breach of fiduciary duty by misuse of confidential information "belonging" to another;[4] (5) bribery of another's employee,[5] and (6) "unconscionable" conduct or the use of "unconscionable" contract provisions.[6]

---

* For the text of this section, see Dobbs, Law of Remedies, Second Edition, Practitioner Treatise, Vol. 2.

As different as these forms of misconduct may be, they do have one or two salient features in common. They all involve misconduct that, like deceit, affects economic relations and opportunities, but that, unlike deceit, does not involve actual misrepresentation of fact.[7]

§ 10.2   Duress and Economic Compulsion

§ 10.2(1)   Avoidance for Duress Generally

General Rule

Coercion occurs in many dealings and in many legal claims. Duress is a form of coercion. Duress "overcomes the will."[1] Transactions entered into under duress may be avoided. To show duress, one must show (1) a wrongful act or threat, (2) that left the victim no reasonable alternative, and (3) to which the victim in fact acceded, and that (4) the resulting transaction was unfair to the victim.[2]

[*For additional discussion, see this section in the Practitioner Treatise edition, vol. 2, pp. 636–639.*]

The plaintiff's remedies in a case of a transaction induced by duress are essentially restitutionary. Generally they are the same as the restitutionary remedies available to the victim of fraud.[9] The transaction may be avoided by affirmative action of the injured party and he may obtain restitution where it is appropriate.[10] If the plaintiff gave up property as a result of duress applied by the defendant, he can recover that property as restitution; and if the property is no longer available it would seem that he can recover its value as substitutionary restitution.

§ 10.2(2)   What Threats Are Wrongful Generally

Wrongful Threat Required

Duress requires some kind of wrongful act or threat of wrongful act by the defendant. The threat may be implied rather than explicit, as where the defendant makes a show of force that is inexplicable except as a threat.[1] Wrongfulness of the threat is not by itself enough to show duress; the threat must leave the victim no reasonable alternative and he must in fact be coerced. It is equally true, however, that coercion without a wrongful threat is not duress at all.

[*For discussion of what threats one wrongful, see this section in the Practitioner Treatise edition, vol. 2, pp. 639–642.*]

§ 10.2(3)   Threats in Particular Settings

[*For discussion of duress to person and to goods, of threats by railroads, utilities, and taxing authorities, threats of prosecution, threats of civil litigation, and threats to breach a contract, see this section in the Practitioner Treatise edition, vol. 2, pp. 642–655.*]

§ 10.3   Undue Influence

General Rules[1]

Influence by dominant party. A dominant or influential party on one side may exert influence against a dependent or submissive one on the other. The parties are frequently in a relationship that justifies the dependent party in trusting the other, in relying on his judgment, and in assuming that the dominant party will be motivated by the dependent party's welfare and interests.[2] The dominant party's conduct counts as undue influence when he uses his position to sway the judgment of the other by advice or suggestion, or even by implication. Much of the law of undue influence appears to be part of the law of confidential relationships.[3] When a person is induced by undue influence of another to make a gift or enter into some other transaction, the transaction may be avoided by the victim or by his personal representative.

[*For examples, rules of evidence and presumptions and related materials, see this section in the Practitioner Treatise edition, vol. 2, pp. 655–661.*]

§ 10.4 Breach of Fiduciary Obligation or Abuse of Confidential Relationship

Fiduciary obligations. A fiduciary obligation is an obligation arising out of equity's demands on the conscience to act for the benefit of another person rather than one's self. The fiduciary must, in dealing with those to whom he owes such an obligation, reveal fully all circumstances that might affect the transaction and is thus under a duty of disclosure not imposed upon others.[5] In addition, the fiduciary must not take secret profits derived from her position as a fiduciary, either at the expense of the beneficiary, or even by use of the beneficiary's confidential information.[6] The fiduciary must not put herself in a conflict of interest position.[7] The fiduciary also owes a duty of considerable care in dealing with the property or funds of the beneficiary. The fiduciary who is administering an estate as a trustee, guardian or executor, owes a duty of administration, loyalty, care, and skill. She is also under a duty to keep trust property separate from her own or that of others, and to make the property productive.[8] A frequently quoted aphorism is that the trustee owes "[n]ot honesty alone, but the punctilio of an honor the most sensitive."[9]

These obligations differ from the obligations owed between those who deal at arms' length. Although certain good faith performance of contracts may be required even between those who deal at arms' length,[10] that good faith does not require one party to subordinate her own interests to those of the other.[11] The land buyer may purchase Blackacre without informing its owner that oil has been found nearby,[12] but the fiduciary in the same situation must disclose the fact to the vendor.[13]

The fiduciary obligation falls upon a number of persons in determinate, long recognized relationships. Trustees are fiduciaries for their beneficiaries.[14] So are guardians;[15] and so, for their respective obligees, are personal representatives of estates,[16] attorneys,[17] agents,[18] partners,[19] and corporate directors and officers.[20] The fiduciary concept has been used as a basis for legislatively created duties in a variety of situations,[21] and it is a major

---

§ 10.4

8. As to these duties and some related ones, see Restatement Second of Trusts §§ 169–185 (1959). For cases demonstrating many of these duties, see generally Deborah DeMott, Fiduciary Obligation, Agency and Partnership: Duties in Ongoing Business Relationships (1991).

9. Meinhard v. Salmon, 249 N.Y. 458, 464, 164 N.E. 545, 546, 62 A.L.R. 1 (1928).

10. See § 6.12 above.

ingredient in specialized fields of contemporary litigation, for example, litigation over the duties of majority shareholders to minority shareholders in a corporation.

Confidential relationship. Sometimes courts use the term "confidential relationship" as a synonym for fiduciary relationship. Perhaps it is most often used to indicate a relationship deemed analogous to a fiduciary relationship, but having no definite well-defined status, and having less rigid duties.[22] The existence of actual, reasonably warranted trust and confidence is characteristic of this relationship. A stockholder in a corporation may totally distrust his directors and regard them as a pack of ill-begotten thieves, but he is nevertheless entitled to performance of their fiduciary obligations. In other words, the fiduciary relationship in such cases may be recognized by law independent of actual confidence reposed in the fiduciary.

In confidential relationship cases, on the other hand, the courts demand that one party act for the benefit of the other because the other reasonably expects it from past conduct showing concern for the other's best interest and an intent to act for those interests.[23] For example, if *A*, rightly reposing trust and confidence in *B*, as friend and financial advisor, reveals a unique investment opportunity to *B* for the purpose of getting his advice, *B* cannot rightly use the information to secure the investment for himself.[24] Equally, *B* must disclose facts he knows to bear on the wisdom of the investment.[25] One person frequently reposes special confidence in another when they are related by blood or other family ties,[26] or where one party is highly dependent, or disadvantaged.[27] But the confidential relationship is not limited to such cases. The important thing is that trust and confidence are actually reposed and that the person in whom they are reposed knows it.

Beyond this, principles against unjust enrichment require a fiduciary to disgorge any improper gain he has received as a result of the relationship, even if the beneficiary has no corresponding loss. One kind of case like this is the dual agency case. In *Spratlin, Harrington & Thomas, Inc. v. Hawn,*[41] a developer of a shopping center, in search of capital, sought the services of a loan broker. The broker agreed to seek a loan commitment from a commercial lender in return for a substantial fee. The developer never went through with the loan, though the loan commitment was made through the service of the broker. The broker sued to recover the contracted-for fee. The developer defended successfully on the ground that, unbeknownst to the developer, the broker was also getting a "finder's fee" from the commercial lender. Thus the broker was representing both the lender and borrower and taking a fee from both. Since this was a violation of his fiduciary duty as an agent, it was held a good defense when the broker sued on the contract.

In cases of this sort the beneficiary of the relationship does not necessarily prove that he would have refused the contract had he been given full information. He does not even prove that the contract is disadvantageous to him or that the broker's profit was made at his expense in any sense. He merely proves the disloyalty, and that is enough to operate as a defense on the contract or as grounds for restitution.

---

41. 116 Ga.App. 175, 156 S.E.2d 402 (1967).

In *Sears, Roebuck & Co. v. American Plumbing & Supply Co.,*[42] an employee of a retail chain store was hired to buy all the store's plumbing supplies for resale at retail. He bought from American Plumbing & Supply, apparently because American was willing to pay him additional fees, not because American's supplies were cheaper or better. American paid over $26,000 to the employee, who, of course, was also on Sears' payroll. Sears sued American, who had paid the commissions and thus led its agent to violate his fiduciary relationship. Sears was allowed to recover. The defendant argued that Sears marked-up supplies at 20% regardless of original cost, and hence, even if the agent, because of his violation of fiduciary duty, bought items at a higher cost than need be, the net result was to give Sears more, rather than less, profit. The court rejected this argument on the ground that Sears might have been damaged by having its competitive position weakened. This is undoubtedly true, but the fact, if it was one, was not proven. The case illustrates the willingness of courts to condemn fiduciary breaches and retrieve all gains that result from them, even when such gains are not proved to be at the expense of the beneficiary. The case also illustrates a potential double recovery by the wronged beneficiary, one recovery against the agent and one against the party who induced the agent's breach of trust.[43]

Special relationships and unclean hands or pari delicto. The normal rules permit courts to deny equitable relief to a plaintiff who is guilty of unclean hands,[44] and to bar all relief to a plaintiff who participates in equal fault with the defendant in an illegal transaction.[45] For example, the plaintiff who conveys her land to the defendant to avoid creditors, with the understanding that the defendant will reconvey when creditors have been eluded, may be denied all relief against the defendant who refuses to recovery, on the grounds that the plaintiff comes into equity with unclean hands or is guilty of illegal conduct. Although the defendant is also guilty, the court may refuse to give its aid to a peccant plaintiff. These rules do not apply when the defendant is in a confidential relationship and owes special duties to the plaintiff. The lawyer who helps the plaintiff avoid creditors by taking title to the plaintiff's property may be forced to return it. In that case, it is said, the parties are not in equal fault and the plaintiff's unclean hands will not bar her recovery.[46]

Remedies for Breach of Fiduciary Obligation or Abuse of Confidential Relationship

Since a breach of fiduciary relationship or abuse of confidential relationship can amount to a tort, such as fraud, it is quite possible to claim damages on the basis of the fiduciaries' misconduct in such cases.[47] It is, however, much more common to find the victim asserting restitutionary remedies or asserting the breach of confidence as a defense to contract suit by the other party. The restitutionary rules governing fraud, duress and undue influence

42. 19 F.R.D. 334 (E.D.Wis.1956).

43. See Seavey, Problems in Restitution, 7 Okla.L.Rev. 257 (1954). This problem is discussed in § 10.6 below.

44. See § 2.4(2) above.

45. See § 13.6 below.

46. Dillon v. Dean, 158 A.D.2d 579, 551 N.Y.S.2d 547 (1990).

47. E.g., Nichols–Morris Corp. v. Morris, 174 F.Supp. 691 (S.D.N.Y.1959) (corporate officer induced a third person to terminate valuable corporate contract, then resigned, loss of profits estimated and allowed).

usually apply here as well, and with the same aim—prevention of unjust enrichment of the wrongdoer. Innocent third parties who receive the profit are, of course, equally liable to disgorge the benefit if they have not paid value for it,[48] again in accord with the rules applied in fraud cases.

Quite frequently the remedy asserted is the constructive trust. The fiduciary who uses inside information to profit for himself is thus liable to make "restitution" of the profits produced with that information. This is often expressed by saying that he holds those profits on a constructive trust for the beneficiary of the special relationship.[49]

A Massachusetts case is a good example.[50] Some lawyers in a partnership left the firm and secretly induced certain clients to retain them rather than remain as firm clients. The firm brought suit against the leaving lawyers and under all the circumstances the court found the leaving lawyers breached their fiduciary duties to the firm. Unless the defendant lawyers could prove that the clients would have left the firm even without fiduciary breach, the court thought they should be liable for all "profits" or fees on these clients' cases, with two exceptions. First the defendant lawyers should get a share of fee from the cases they would have received had the firm kept the cases. Second the defendant lawyers could deduct reasonable overhead expenses, but that deduction did not include a fee for the lawyers' own time.

One of the most extreme and unusual cases is *Snepp v. United States*,[51] where Snepp, as an agent of the CIA, contracted as part of his employment (a) not to reveal classified information and (b) not to publish anything at all, classified or not, without prior approval of the CIA. After he left employment with the CIA, he wrote a book about his experiences. The book did not reveal any classified information but it was in fact published without prior approval by the CIA. Under ordinary breach of contract rules, the CIA would be permitted to recover damages if it could prove any, but it would not be permitted to recover the royalties Snepp earned from the book.[52] The Supreme Court, however, refused to view the case as a breach of contract. Instead, the Court considered it to be a case of breach of fiduciary duty. The Court allowed the CIA to recover Snepp's royalties, even though, as it would seem, the CIA would have had no basis for refusing permission to publish the book once it had exercised its censorial powers.

Snepp may not be a good guide to results in cases that do not raise the specter of national insecurity. If an employee at an armed camp of survivalists were to breach his promise to publish no books without prior approval, it seems likely that First Amendment free speech considerations would outweigh the employer's claim to the book's profits. Perhaps more significantly for present purposes, it might be said that even a fiduciary can make promises the breach of which may not warrant appropriating of the fiduciary's own property. If an employee of a prudential employer promises not to gamble, but invests $1 in the lottery and wins a large sum, it would be

48. Hesthagen v. Harby, 78 Wash.2d 934, 481 P.2d 438 (1971) (distributees of estate must disgorge in favor of true next of kin where administrator failed to notify them of the administration).

49. E.g., Funderburg v. Shappert, 23 Ill.2d 220, 177 N.E.2d 845 (1961).

50. Meehan v. Shaughnessy, 404 Mass. 419, 535 N.E.2d 1255, 1270 (1989).

51. 444 U.S. 507, 100 S.Ct. 763, 62 L.Ed.2d 704 (1980).

52. See § 12.7(4) below.

surprising indeed if the employer were allowed to recover the winnings on the ground that the employee was a fiduciary.

The fiduciary profit rules are generally like those used in fraud cases. The transaction can be rescinded or a constructive trust can be imposed to prevent enrichment of the wrongdoer. However, there is a potential difference. In an ordinary fraud case, the wrongdoer never had any fiduciary duties with respect to the money or property he got from his victim; a fiduciary on the other hand has affirmative duties that might affect the remedy. Suppose a corporate officer, using a corporate opportunity to buy shares at a favorable price, does buy them, and shortly thereafter re-sells at a handsome profit. If he were treated like the fraudfeasor, he is liable for the profits, on a constructive trust or in assumpsit, but he has no obligation to invest the profits prudently for the benefit of the corporation. If, on the other hand, he is to be treated as a fiduciary for the profits as well as for the initial opportunity, he owes a duty to maximize their productiveness within the limits of prudent management and might be liable for failing to do so.

A famous case, *Marcus v. Otis,*[53] involved this point. Judge Learned Hand would have held that the wrongdoer owed the same duty with respect to the profits he got as he would have owed with respect to the same profits in the hands of the corporation where they belonged. The other two judges—Augustus N. Hand and Judge Chase—held otherwise. In their view, liability of the fiduciary was limited to the profits he actually made from misuse of corporate property. The majority of the court did, however, hold that the fiduciary was liable for interest on the corporate funds while they were out of the hands of the corporation.

§ 10.5 Misuse of Confidential Economic Information

§ 10.5(1) Duties of Loyalty and Confidentiality and the Real Estate Broker's Secret Profits

Special Duties of Loyalty and Confidentiality

Private, confidential, or inside information covers a large legal territory and many different legal doctrines attempt to map parts of it. For instance, the right of privacy and some analogous rights may protect against some revelations.[1] On the other hand, the law of confidential and fiduciary relationships determines many of the rights in private information of an economic character. If economically valuable information has been revealed and is no longer private or confidential, protection against use must be found in contract or in doctrines of intellectual property.[2]

A confidential or fiduciary relationship imposes two diverse duties about confidential or inside information. The person who owes special duties because of a confidential or fiduciary relationship will be called the fiduciary for convenience, and the other will be called the beneficiary. Under the first duty, the fiduciary must disclose relevant private information he possesses to

---

53. 168 F.2d 649 (2d Cir.1948), adhered to, 169 F.2d 148 (1948).

§ 10.5(1)

1. E.g., Humphers v. First Interstate Bank of Oregon, 298 Or. 706, 696 P.2d 527 (1985) (duty of confidence, not "privacy," warrants liability of doctor who released adopted child's identity). As to remedies for privacy invasions, see § 7.3(4) below.

2. See §§ 6.2–6.5 above (patents, copyrights, trademark, misappropriation of ideas, performances, etc.).

his beneficiary.[3] Under the second, the fiduciary must neither reveal nor use private, inside, or confidential information held by the beneficiary. Along with this, the fiduciary must remain loyal to the beneficiary and must not put himself in a position of conflict of interest.

The subsections here illustrate rather than define the second duty and the remedies available for it. In general, the use of the beneficiary's inside information by a fiduciary is a violation of his duty. If he gains from the use, he must disgorge his gain to the beneficiary. Sometimes the fiduciary uses the beneficiary's inside information to the detriment of others who are not themselves beneficiaries. Those cases raise much more complicated problems.[4]

The Broker's Profit Cases

Agent's duty to principal. An agent is a fiduciary to his principal. Where an agent uses information gained in his agency for personal profit rather than to aid his principal, the agent is liable to disgorge the secret profit. As a fiduciary, he is obliged to take no profit from the transaction except that disclosed to and approved by his principal.[5] The same rule has been applied where the agent represents two principals, *P* and *T*.[6]

Agent's duty to buyers or third persons. Suppose the agent of *P* takes a profit, but not at the principal's expense. Instead the agent takes a profit from a third person, *T*, with whom the principal deals. Because the agent for *P* is not a fiduciary to the third person, it seems plausible to argue that the third person has no claim; and because the profit was not at the expense of the principal, it seems plausible to argue that the principal has no claim. Yet some of the cases hold *P*'s agent liable to *T*.

The Harper case. In *Harper v. Adametz*[7] the owner of land, Tesar, listed it with Adametz, a real estate agent, for sale. The parcel consisted of an 80 acre farm and a colonial house. Adametz ascertained that the owner would sell the entire farm of 80 acres for $6500. Harper, a potential buyer, offered $7,000 for the entire farm. Adametz pretended to communicate this offer to the seller but in fact did not do so. Instead he reported to Harper a fictitious counter offer to sell the house and 17 acres to Harper for $6,000. Harper accepted this supposed offer. Adametz arranged with the owner to transfer the entire 80 acres to straw purchasers for $6,500. Tesar in turn executed a deed for the house and 17 acres to Harper, and conveyed the remainder of the farm, at Adametz' direction, to Adametz' son, who paid nothing for it. Thus for the price of $500, less a real estate agent's commission, Adametz got 63 acres of land for his son. Harper, discovering this, sued.

One difficulty for Harper is that he got the land he was promised and it is not worth less than it was represented to be worth, nor less than he paid

3. See § 10.4 above. One in a fiducial relation may be under a broad duty of disclosure about many items. One in a confidential relationship may be under a narrower duty, but it includes at least the disclosure of relevant private information in any transactions between the parties. The exact range of the disclosure required is a matter of substantive law.

4. See § 10.5(2) below as to traders in the stock market who use inside information of one corporation to the detriment of others.

5. Restatement Second of Agency §§ 388 and 395 (1984).

6. See Siler v. Gunn, 117 Ga.App. 325, 160 S.E.2d 427 (1968).

7. 142 Conn. 218, 113 A.2d 136, 55 A.L.R.2d 334 (1955).

for it. Ordinary damages rules for fraud would thus give Harper no recovery.[8] If Adametz is seen as an agent of Harper, then the agent's duty of loyalty can be invoked, and Adametz as agent will not be permitted to profit in a transaction with his principal. The information that the owner would accept Harper's offer, or one substantially like it, can be seen as information that belongs to Harper as the principal, and the broker should not be permitted to withhold such information or to deal in such information for his own account.

The difficulty with this analysis is that it is usually said that a broker represents only one of the parties, and that is usually the one who hired him in the first place. This would mean, on the facts given, that Adametz was a fiduciary to Tesar, the seller, but not to Harper, the buyer. In turn, this would imply that Adametz is liable for his misdeeds, but only to Tesar. Indeed, there would not be any difficulty in finding liability to Tesar if he were to sue. All this would seem to point toward a conclusion that Adametz is not liable to Harper. Yet liability was imposed and Adametz and his son were required to disgorge the land they acquired.

The Ward case. There are a number of cases on similar or analogous facts also imposing liability. In *Ward v. Taggart*,[9] a California case, Taggart fraudulently represented to a potential buyer that he was the real estate agent for a landowner. He was not, but pretended to submit the buyer's offer of $4,000 per acre for some 72 acres of land. He then pretended that the offer had been rejected, but that the owner would accept $5,000. The buyer agreed to this price, whereupon Taggart purchased the land himself at $4,000 per acre and resold it to the buyer, Ward, for $5,000. Taggart thus took a profit of some $72,000. There was, as Justice Traynor recognized in his opinion, no claim based on fraud, because there were no damages under the fraud damages rules. Furthermore, Taggart and Ward were clearly not in a fiduciary relationship and they bargained at arms' length. Nevertheless, Ward was allowed to recover Taggart's "secret profit." The California Court reasoned that recovery should be permitted simply to prevent unjust enrichment.

The meanings of Harper and Ward. What is the explanation for decisions like *Harper* and *Ward*? Professor Palmer sees *Harper* as an interference with contractual prospects. The court merely protected the contract expectancy Harper probably would have had if the dishonest broker had not interfered.[10] It might be added that even if the broker's representations were not actionable as fraud or deceit, they were easily improper enough to warrant liability for the tort of interference with prospective advantage.[11] In that analysis, it is unimportant that the broker had no fiducial or other special relationship to the purchaser. Consistent with this analysis, negligence by the broker in failing to communicate an offer to the vendor is not enough,[12] just as negligent interference with contracts or

8. See § 9.2(1) above.

9. 51 Cal.2d 736, 336 P.2d 534 (1959).

10. See I George Palmer, Law of Restitution § 3.18 (1978 and Supps.). See § 6.6 above.

11. See § 6.6 above generally.

12. See Carroll v. Action Enterprises, Inc.,

prospects is usually not enough.[13]

The interference with prospects theory may be the best explanation for the *Harper* case, but it does not work so well with some others. In *Nguyen v. Scott*,[14] the buyer did not allege any representations at all by the broker, only that the broker did not submit the buyer's offer and instead bought the property himself. If true, the allegations surely show a violation of the broker's fiduciary duty to his principal, but not to the buyer. Yet the court thought the buyer stated a claim, seemingly with the suggestion that the broker owes at least some duties of honesty to the buyer as well as to his principal.[15]

Agent's misrepresentation of the vendor's price. Where the vendor's agent's only misdealing is that he misrepresents the vendor's minimum price, and thus sells to the purchaser at a higher figure and pockets the differential, the courts have divided about the agent's liability to the purchaser. A number have taken the view that there is no liability in such a case. Such a result is perhaps supportable where the vendor and broker agree that the broker will be entitled to what he can get over a specified sum. In some of these cases, the selling price has been only slightly higher than the minimum price demanded by the vendor. In those cases, the agent received a profit that at least roughly compensated him for his services, and the vendor was aware of and approved this. Thus where there is nothing more than a misrepresentation of the vendor's price which results in compensation to the broker in a fair amount, some of the cases have refused to impose liability.[16]

On the other hand, some of the cases impose liability for restitution upon the vendor's agent who misrepresents the minimum sale price and thus takes a personal "profit" when he sells at a higher figure. This is especially so where the profit obviously exceeds any reasonable compensation for services and where the vendor himself did not authorize this form of sale.[17]

Remedies

Restitution. Remedies in the broker cases have been varied. Perhaps the prime remedy is the restitutionary one, that is, a recovery of the secret profit gained by the tricky broker.[18] Where the broker has gained land itself rather than a cash profit, a constructive trust has been imposed upon the land so gained, with the result that the purchaser has obtained the addition-

---

206 Neb. 204, 292 N.W.2d 34, 37 (1980).

13. Prosser & Keeton on Torts §§ 129–130 (5th ed. 1984 and Supp.).

14. 206 Cal.App.3d 725, 253 Cal.Rptr. 800 (1988).

15. For instance, the court said "Following the Ward decision, the principle that a broker owes a duty of honesty and fairness to all parties to a transaction has been reiterated in other cases * * *." 253 Cal.Rptr. at 806, and emphasized statutory duties that would re-dound to the benefit of buyers as well as vendor-principals.

16. Sanders v. Stevens, 23 Ariz. 370, 203 P. 1083 (1922); H & H Farms, Inc. v. Hazlett, 6 Kan.App.2d 263, 627 P.2d 1161 (1981); Aronowitz v. Woollard, 166 A.D. 365, 152 N.Y.S. 11 (1915).

17. Lear v. Bawden, 75 Colo. 385, 225 P. 831 (1924).

18. Ward v. Taggart, 51 Cal.2d 736, 336 P.2d 534 (1959) specifically grounded its allow-

al land.[19]

Effect of vendor's rights to restitution in same property. In cases like *Harper,* the broker's acts are first and foremost a violation of duty owed to the vendor. The purchaser in *Harper* was allowed to obtain the entire tract of land which the court supposed he would have bought from the vendor had the broker not been fraudulent. Suppose, however, the vendor himself sought to undo the whole transaction on the ground that his fiduciary had defrauded him? Presumably the vendor would be permitted to recover the acreage the broker had obtained. If the vendor recovers the acreage that went to the broker, then the purchaser could not get that same acreage. Should the court deny the purchaser the acreage on the ground that the vendor has a better right to it? Palmer thinks this question is not so embarrassing that the purchaser should be denied relief when the vendor has not in fact claimed the acreage for himself.[20]

In *Nguyen v. Scott,*[21] a California court dealt with facts somewhat like those in *Harper.* The court agreed with *Harper* that the purchaser's remedy should not be foreclosed merely because the vendor might have a better claim against the broker. Nevertheless, it thought the vendor's potential right to avoid the transaction posed a practical problem. By the time of the law suit, the purchasers were on notice of the vendor's rights and equities; so if the court allowed them to make the purchase according to their original offer, they might take the property subject to the vendor's superior right to avoid the whole transaction. The California court's solution was to give the plaintiffs time to negotiate with the vendor or to seek clarification of the vendor's rights through declaratory judgment.

When the agent's or insider's gain is in the form of money. The problem is most pointed for those cases in which the agent gets legal title to property by use of inside information. But it also arises when the agent gets money gains from use of such information. If the agent or insider is required to make restitution of money gained by use of the information, more than one person may have a legitimate claim to it, just as, in *Harper,* both the seller and buyer might claim the excess acreage. This problem has arisen in securities cases, when the agent or insider uses confidential information to profit in the purchase or sale of stocks.[22] Instead of suggesting negotiation or declaratory judgment as the California court did, a federal court simply required the wrongdoer to deposit the unjust gains in escrow, bearing interest, with payment to be made to the plaintiff if no other claimants appeared.[23] Another court simply said the agent could implead other potential claimants if he wished.[24]

ance of restitution in unjust enrichment theory.

19. Harper v. Adametz, 142 Conn. 218, 113 A.2d 136, 55 A.L.R.2d 334 (1955). A similar remedy was envisioned in Nguyen v. Scott, 206 Cal.App.3d 725, 253 Cal.Rptr. 800 (1988).

20. See I George Palmer, Law of Restitution § 3.18, p. 342 (1978 and Supps.).

21. 206 Cal.App.3d 725, 253 Cal.Rptr. 800, 809 (1988).

22. Discussed in § 10.5(2) below.

23. SEC v. Texas Gulf Sulphur Co., 446 F.2d 1301 (2d Cir.1971), discussed in § 10.5(2) below.

24. Diamond v. Oreamuno, 24 N.Y.2d 494, 301 N.Y.S.2d 78, 248 N.E.2d 910 (1969), discussed in § 10.5(2) below * * *. This solution focuses on the potential double liability of the agent and protects against such liability. It does not secure the money gains for possible additional claimants, however, and if such other claimants are likely the escrow solution,

Damages. Sometimes the plaintiff recovers money, not property, and sometimes the cases speak of "damages," rather that restitution. If the broker is liable in money to someone other than his principal because he has committed a tort—fraud or interference with prospects—then damages rather than restitution may be the right recovery, with damages being measured by the plaintiff's loss rather than by the defendant's gain.

In *Collins v. Philadelphia Oil Co.,*[25] the buyer agreed with the vendor's agent to pay $5,500 for an oil and gas lease. The vendor executed that lease and gave it to the agent, who then represented that his principal would not transfer the lease without receiving another $5,000. In fact he held the executed lease in his pocket. The purchaser had contracted to assign the lease to another and was therefore under pressure to pay the additional $5,000, which he did. He then sued to recover this overpayment, and recovery was allowed. On the facts, the recovery may be considered either as damages or as restitution. It could be considered as damages because the agent was guilty of a fraud and the overpayment measures the plaintiff's loss. It could be considered as restitution, because it also represents the defendant's unjust enrichment.

Punitive damages. Courts have allowed exemplary damages in the broker cases. This has been justified on the ground that if the defendant's behavior is sufficiently improper to warrant restitution, it is improper enough to warrant a legal response that will deter such conduct in the future, and that such a deterrence can be effected by imposing a punitive liability.[26]

§ 10.5(2) Insider Transactions in Securities

[*For the text of this section, see the unabridged Practitioner Treatise edition.*]

§ 10.5(3) Trade Secrets and Confidential Information

[*For discussion of trade secrets and covenants not to compete generally, see this section in the Practitioner Treatise edition, vol. 2, pp. 686–690.*]

Remedies: Restitution

The wrongdoer's profits. One liable for the use of trade secrets may be held liable for any gains made by the use of that information. The defendant may thus be liable to disgorge any profits made from its use.[25] A similar remedy has been imposed when the defendant breaches a covenant not to compete.[26] The courts may or may not use the language of constructive trust or accounting for profits in requiring such a disgorgement. The fact that the employee is a conscious wrongdoer, if that is in fact the case, may have its effects in calculating the profits, and where there are two or more ways in which profits could be figured, the conscious wrongdoer will be charged with the larger figures.[27]

The wrongdoer's savings. One form of "profit" or benefit is savings. If the defendant uses a trade secret to save a production expense, thus reducing the cost of manufacturing goods, the defendant adds to its profit or

although cumbersome, might be more effec-   **25.** 97 W.Va. 464, 125 S.E. 223 (1924).
tive.

reduces its losses, and either way has a gain that must be disgorged.[28] Alternatively, it would be possible to measure the benefit received from use of the trade secret by estimating the cost of independent development of the trade secret, without regard to whether or not the secret proved to be of economic value.[29]

Adjustments in profit recoveries: apportionment and deductions. When a wrongdoer's collateral profits are recoverable as restitution, the aim is to force full disgorgement but no more.[30] If a competitor makes profits by use of the plaintiff's trade secrets, he must disgorge them, but he cannot properly be made to give up earnings that result from his own investment, skills, or ingenuity, or that to which he was entitled by contract.[31] How much of the profit was due to the trade secret and how much to the defendant's own legitimate acts and skills is the problem of apportionment. Apportionment is largely a question of evidence, with doubts resolved against intentional wrongdoers.[32] The defendant who is liable to disgorge profits is also usually entitled to deductions for expenses incurred in earning the profit.[33] In other words, the liability is normally for net profits, not gross earnings.[34]

[*For discussion of the damages remedy, see this section in the Practitioner Treatise edition, vol. 2, pp. 691–693.*]

Remedies: Injunctions

Both permanent and preliminary injunctions[57] are issued to protect trade secrets and confidential information. The scope, terms, and duration of the injunction are of the greatest practical significance.

Be-good injunctions. An employee in possession of trade secrets resigns and intends to set up in competition with the employer or accept employment with a competitor. The weakest injunctive weapon for protection of trade secrets will be an injunction that forbids disclosure by the former employee or use by the new employer.[58] Such an injunction formally respects all the rights of all the persons involved. But it may be difficult to show that disclosure or use of trade secrets is threatened or has actually taken place. Even if circumstantial evidence convinces the trier that the defendants have disclosed or used trade secrets,[59] enforcement of a be-good injunction may be difficult or impossible. Employees do not divulge trade secrets in public and the manufacturer of a product made by use of the secret may claim that the product was made independently, without using the plaintiff's trade secrets. In addition, courts have recognized in many cases that disclosure will be inevitable, even when the former employee acts in good faith.[60] In fact, courts do issue be-good injunctions that forbid disclosure of trade secrets or use of them by competitors;[61] but except that such injunctions define the arena of protected material, they may not provide much comfort to the employer who originally held the trade secret.

No-competition injunctions against former employee. In contrast, the strongest injunctive weapon the employer could wield would be an injunc-

§ 10.5(3)

60. E.g., Emery Industries, Inc. v. Cottier, 202 U.S.P.Q. 829 (S.D.Ohio 1978). See Lowry, Inevitable Disclosure Trade Secret Disputes: Dissolutions of Concurrent Property Interests, 40 Stan.L.Rev. 519 (1988).

61. B.F. Goodrich Co. v. Wohlgemuth, 117 Ohio App. 493, 192 N.E.2d 99 (1963).

tion against the employee's engagement in competitive employment at all. In a suit against the competitor who hires the employee with trade secrets, the strong weapon would be an injunction to prevent manufacture or distribution of any product that could be made by use of the trade secrets. Such an injunction would tend to remove economic incentive for disclosure or use of the secret, but it would also seriously impinge important personal and competitive freedoms.

A strong injunction against the employee who is in possession of trade secrets is justified when the employee has validly contracted by negative covenant not to compete for a period. In that case, a non-competition injunction is issued, not only because it will tend to protect against loss of the secret, but also because the employee contractually agreed to it.

What about injunctions against the competing employment when no covenant exists? Where the nature of the employee's knowledge is such that disclosure of trade secrets in the new job is "inevitable," and especially where that is the apparent purpose for which he was hired in the new job, there is some judicial authority for enjoining acceptance of the new job at all, at least by way of temporary restraining order or preliminary injunction.[62]

On the other hand, the injunction in the absence of a noncompetition covenant operates to protect trade secrets by forcing the defendant to give up personal freedoms, including the right to work. If the employer had exacted a noncompetition covenant in the first place, the employee's compensation might have been adjusted upward in exchange. If the court imposes a non-competition injunction when no covenant not to compete was given, it imposes a duty upon the defendant he never undertook, and for which no compensation was given. On reasoning something like this, at least one court concluded that if disclosure would be inevitable because of the nature of the new job, a preliminary injunction should issue, but only if the plaintiff compensated the defendant at a specified rate.[63]

Injunctions against competitor. Sometimes an injunction may run against a hiring employer or competitor who has appropriated the trade secret. In the most extreme form, the injunction may forbid manufacture of the products in which the trade secret is an essential ingredient and the manufacturer of the product is a wrongful appropriator.[64] Such injunctions have issued against former employees who set up their own business in competition with the plaintiff.

Scope and duration of injunctions. When legal rights in the secret terminate, the injunction against use or disclosure should also terminate, except that if the defendant has improperly used the trade secret, the injunction appropriately continues for a period of time to reflect the period of his improper use.[65] The injunction can be limited by its terms to reflect

65. The Uniform Trade Secrets Act essentially so provides. E.g., West's Ann.Cal.Civ. Code § 3426.2 ("Upon application to the court, an injunction shall be terminated when the trade secret has ceased to exist, but the injunction may be continued for an additional period of time in order to eliminate commercial advantage that otherwise would be derived from the misappropriation").

this principle, or it can be terminated upon application of a defendant who shows that the trade secret protection has ceased to exist.

The reason for terminating injunctions lies in the fact that the trade secret may be properly discovered by the defendant without any breach of duty or may simply become public and in either case the trade secret protection is lost. For instance, in *Schulenburg v. Signatrol, Inc.,*[66] the employee set up a competing business, using copied or memorized copies of blueprints from which he made a virtually identical product. The employee could have legally duplicated the product, produced and marketed it all quite legally by simply measuring its parts from an actual item purchased in the market. His liability stemmed from the fact that he used blueprints belonging to the employer instead. The trial court responded by enjoining further manufacture of the product. The Supreme Court of Illinois reversed, as to this remedy, pointing out that such an injunction put the defendant out of business for all time, in spite of the fact that he could have legally manufactured the product by other means. The Illinois Court thus indicated that on remand, an injunction should issue against the defendant's manufacture for the time required to duplicate the product by lawful means.

If the court doubts the defendant's ability to manufacture the product by reverse engineering,[67] a permanent injunction might issue, but even then, the injunction could presumably be terminated or modified at a later time if the defendant shows reverse engineering has actually succeeded.

Almost the same kind of problem has arisen where the defendant pirates trade secrets that are later made public by patent or otherwise. The public disclosure destroys any further right to protection of the information. Nevertheless, the defendant who obtains trade secrets before public disclosure gets an advantage in the head start. In these situations courts usually issued "head start" injunctions, forbidding the defendant from manufacturing a product or otherwise using the trade secret for a period equal to the head start, no more, no less.[68] Once the head start period is over, even the wrongdoer will be free to use the information available to the public,[69] although at least one notable decision perpetually bans the wrongdoer's use.[70]

A parallel problem appears when the plaintiff seeks to enforce a non-

66. 33 Ill.2d 379, 212 N.E.2d 865 (1965), cert. denied, 383 U.S. 959, 86 S.Ct. 1225, 16 L.Ed.2d 302 (1966).

67. See Curtiss–Wright Corp. v. Edel–Brown Tool & Die Co., Inc., 381 Mass. 1, 407 N.E.2d 319, 11 A.L.R.4th 1 (1980).

68. E.g., Lamb–Weston, Inc. v. McCain Foods, Ltd., 941 F.2d 970 (9th Cir.1991); Winston Research Corp. v. Minnesota Min. & Mfg. Co., 350 F.2d 134 (9th Cir.1965).

69. Cf. Conmar Products Corp. v. Universal Slide Fastener Co., 172 F.2d 150, 156 (2d Cir.1949) (headstart injunctions not actually considered, but perpetual injunction rejected as having "no support in principle", Learned Hand, J.).

70. Shellmar Products Co. v. Allen–Qualley Co., 87 F.2d 104 (7th Cir.1936); cf. Curtiss–

Wright Corp. v. Edel–Brown Tool & Die Co., Inc., 381 Mass. 1, 407 N.E.2d 319, 11 A.L.R.4th 1 (1980) (termination of the secret through reverse engineering is but one factor, commercial morality is another; a permanent injunction may be warranted in some cases). *Distinguish* Warner–Lambert Pharmaceutical Co. v. John J. Reynolds, Inc., 178 F.Supp. 655 (S.D.N.Y.1959), aff'd per curiam, 280 F.2d 197 (2d Cir.1960) (as a matter of contract interpretation, not trade secret law, one who is required to pay royalties for use of a formula was held not, under contract, entitled to cease payments because formula had been made public). *Distinguish also* Valco Cincinnati, Inc. v. N & D Machining Service, Inc., 24 Ohio St.3d 41, 492 N.E.2d 814, 59 A.L.R.4th 629 (1986) (supporting the *Shellmar* rule only where the defendant's conduct was egregiously bad, a punitive injunction).

competition covenant. In a Minnesota case,[71] for example, the employees signed a two-year non-competition covenant, then, taking confidential information, went into competition. By the time the case was ripe for an injunction, however, the two-year period had expired. Nevertheless, the court issued an injunction prohibiting competition for two years, in effect substituting the two year period after the injunction for the two year period following the defendants' termination of employment.

§ 10.6   Liabilities for Commercial and Political Bribery and Related Wrongs

Bribing Seller's Liability to Buyer—Common Law Damages and Restitution

As the preceding sections in this chapter have emphasized, employees owe fiduciary duties to employers and accordingly are liable if they use confidential information to their own gain, if they disclose trade secrets, and if they take a business opportunity for themselves.[1] The preceding sections focused primarily on the agent or fiduciary who breached the duty of confidence. But in many instances outsiders induce or participate with the fiduciary in the breach of confidence. This section addresses the liability of those who induce or participate in the fiduciary's breach even though they are not themselves fiduciaries. In the most common case, the defendant bribes the employee, directly or indirectly, to do an act that violates his duty.

Illustrative cases; the fiduciary's liability. The factual situation in which commercial bribery arises can be illustrated by a case in which an employee is a purchasing agent for his employer. A manufacturer of goods wishes to sell them, but is unsuccessful by ordinary means. He bribes the purchasing agent, thus inducing him to purchase the goods for his employer. The employee who accepts the bribe is in violation of his fiduciary duty to the employer, even if the goods he purchases are exactly what the employer wants and even if the price is a fair and reasonable one. The employer is thus entitled to recover the amount of the bribe from the employee.[2] Similar principles apply to selling as well as to buying agents. The selling agent, for example, may not secretly purchase his employer's goods for himself and re-sell them at a profit. If he does, he must disgorge the profit to his employer, on the same principle that requires the disgorgement of the bribe.[3]

Basis in fiduciary rules. The fiduciary rules call for such stringent results because the acceptance of the bribe deprives the employer of the unbiased judgment and undivided loyalty of his employee, both things to

---

71. Cherne Industrial, Inc. v. Grounds & Associates, Inc., 278 N.W.2d 81 (Minn.1979). Not only had the two-year period specified in the covenant expired, but the trade secrets had become public information.

§ 10.6

2. Sears, Roebuck & Co. v. American Plumbing & Supply Co., 19 F.R.D. 334 (E.D.Wis.1956); Canadian Ingersoll–Rand Co. v. D. Loveman & Sons, Inc., 227 F.Supp. 829 (N.D.Ohio 1964); Spratlin, Harrington &

Thomas, Inc. v. Hawn, 116 Ga.App. 175, 156 S.E.2d 402 (1967); cf. Hunter v. Shell Oil Co., 198 F.2d 485 (5th Cir.1952) (employee's profits from the employer's information must be disgorged even though employer would not have used the information).

3. Gutting v. Jacobson, 184 Neb. 402, 167 N.W.2d 762 (1969); Anderson Cotton Mills v. Royal Mfg. Co., 221 N.C. 500, 20 S.E.2d 818 (1942). See also § 10.5(1) (brokers' secret profits cases).

which the employer is entitled; alternatively, or in addition, the bribe deprives the employer of a pecuniary gain to which it was entitled. For example, if the seller of goods to the employer would kickback a percentage to the disloyal purchasing agent, it would presumably also discount the price to the employer directly. In this presumptive sense, what the disloyal agent took is what the employer lost.

Briber's liability. The briber who suborns the fiduciary is probably guilty of the tort of inducing breach of contract, but whether he is or not, he is guilty of aiding and abetting a fiduciary breach.[4] In addition, he may have violated a criminal statute against commercial bribery in some jurisdictions.[5] From the briber, the victimized employer may recover either (1) proven damages or (2) restitution. In addition, if the briber has sold goods to the victimized employer as a result of the bribes, the briber may find that, as a result of illegality,[6] he cannot recover for their value; that is, his bribery is a defense to the claim.[7] Nor, unless he was himself victimized,[8] can he recover the bribe money itself.[9]

4. Many such broad statements can be found when the fiduciary pays out funds or other tangible benefits to a knowing recipient. See Sexton v. Sword S.S. Line, Inc., 118 F.2d 708 (2d Cir.1941) (" 'others who knowingly join a fiduciary in such an enterprise likewise become jointly and severally liable with him for such profits,' i.e., 'all the profits obtained by him and those who were associated with him in the matter' "); Republic of Haiti v. Crown Charters, Inc., 667 F.Supp. 839 (S.D.Fla.1987) (commission for selling yacht for former president for life of Haiti, allegedly with knowledge that it had been obtained originally with funds embezzled from Haiti; bona fide purchase would be an affirmative defense, no summary judgment); Hirsch v. Schwartz, 87 N.J.Super. 382, 209 A.2d 635 (1965) ("One who causes or assists an agent to violate his duty to a principal may be subject to liability to the principal * * *."); Restatement Second of Agency § 312 (1959); Restatement of Restitution § 138 (1937) (one who colludes with fiduciary and obtains a benefit thereby must make restitution).

5. E.g., 18 U.S.C.A. § 201; La.Stat.Ann. 14:73; N.Y.—McKinney's Penal L. § 439; see Annotation, Validity and Construction of Statutes Punishing Commercial Bribery, 1 A.L.R.3d 1350 (1965).

6. See § 13.6 below.

7. See Jaclyn, Inc. v. Edison Bros. Stores, Inc., 170 N.J.Super. 334, 406 A.2d 474, 485 (1979) (but allowing recovery for goods sold to victimized employer after employer knew of bribes; "The party which interposes the defense must establish that the payments to the agent were made secretly, i.e., without the knowledge and consent of the principal, and must be attended with the intent to influence the agent's action with respect to his employer's business").

8. The briber often claims to have been a victim of duress and argues that the bribe can be recovered for that reason. In City of New York v. Corwen, 165 A.D.2d 212, 565 N.Y.S.2d 457 (1990) a city sued the briber to recover "damages" equal to bribe defendant paid to city employees. The briber defended on the ground that one who is victimized by extortion will not be held civilly liable. The court held the defense could not be excluded. See also Karpinski v. Collins, 252 Cal.App.2d 711, 60 Cal.Rptr. 846 (1967) (illegal rebate paid by dairy farmer to dominant creamery is recoverable where rebate was only means of selling milk); Hornstein v. Paramount Pictures, 292 N.Y. 468, 55 N.E.2d 740, 741 (1944) (dictum that union officials' threat to call strike unless they were paid $100,000 would be "extortion" which victimized business and restitution would be owed). As to illegality generally, see § 13.6 below; as to duress generally see § 10.2 above.

9. In a number of cases a briber or would-be briber has paid money in exchange for expected favors from a judge, officer, or witness in connection with a trial. If the money was paid, it is usually not recoverable even if the bribery failed and the payment was part of a sting operation. See State v. Pierro, 192 Conn. 98, 470 A.2d 240 (1984) (money paid as attempted bribe was not retained by state as "seized property" and need not be returned after claimant was acquitted of bribery, sovereign immunity); State v. Gunzelman, 200 Kan. 12, 434 P.2d 543 (1967) (no recovery of attempted bribe, pari delicto and other grounds); State v. Strickland, 42 Md.App. 357, 400 A.2d 451 (1979) ("Parties of that ilk are left where they are found, to stew in their own juice", and public policy forbids return of the money to the briber "whether his efforts be a success or failure"); Bruder v. State, 601 S.W.2d 102 (Tex.Civ.App.1980), cert. denied,

[For discussion of the briber's liability for damages and restitution, and recovery against both briber and bribee, and other liabilities, see this section in the Practitioner Treatise edition, vol. 2, pp. 699–703.]

Political bribery. Public employees are fiduciaries within the scope of their employment, so their liability to disgorge bribes is the same as that of other employees, both under state and federal law.[17] A number of cases attest to that liability.[18] The briber of government employees has also been held liable to the government for the amount of his bribes without proof of any particular item of damage.[19] As in other cases, the "bribe" may be disguised, but if it in fact is a bribe, it is recoverable.[20]

§ 10.7   Unconscionable Conduct and the UCC

[For the text of this section, see the unabridged Practitioner Treatise edition.]

452 U.S. 940, 101 S.Ct. 3084, 69 L.Ed.2d 954 (1981) (claim cannot be founded on illegal act, assignee's claim rises no higher); State v. Konchesky, 166 W.Va. 57, 272 S.E.2d 452 (1980) (money paid to witness who turned it over to state, not recoverable, pari delicto rule).

Chapter 11

MISTAKE IN CONTRACTING AND GIFT TRANSACTIONS

Analysis

Sec.
11.1   Varieties of Mistake and Remedies for Mistake.
11.2   The Meaning of Mistake—Erroneous Belief, Misunderstand-
       ing and Conscious Ignorance.
11.3   Mistake in the Attempted Formation of a Contract—Mutual
       Mistake.
11.4   ____ Unilateral Mistake.
11.5   Restitution as a Remedy for Mistake in Formation of a
       Contract—Measurement of Restitution.
11.6   Reformation for Mistake in Expression.
       11.6(1) Grounds and Cases for Reformation.*
       11.6(2) Reformation and the Alternatives.*
       11.6(3) Effectuating, Extending and Defending Reformation
               Claims.
11.7   Mistake in the Performance of an Obligation—Restitution
       Remedies.
11.8   Change of Position.*
11.9   Settlement of Claims and Personal Injury Releases.*
11.10 Mistake in Gift Transaction.*

---

§ 11.1 Varieties of Mistake and Remedies for Mistake

Mistakes are pervasive in life and in legal problems. A mistake may lead to such personal and legal problems as personal injury, to conversion of property, or to infringement of a trademark. Some of those problems of mistake lead to remedies issues discussed in other chapters. The present chapter addresses the problems of mistakes in forming a contract or in making a gift, but not, say, mistakes in building a house on the wrong lot.[1]

Much of the law of mistake as a ground for avoiding a contract is not remedial law. It is substantive law because it concerns primary rights and duties and possible ways of avoiding them. Professor Palmer's great work on substantive and remedial restitution[2] provides a full exploration of substantive rules of mistake, with emphasis on mistake as a means of

---

* For the text of this section, see Dobbs, Law of Remedies, Second Edition, Practitioner Treatise, Vol. 2.

§ 11.1

1. See § 5.8(2) as to mistaken improvements.

2. See II George Palmer, Law of Restitution Chapters 11 and 12, pp. 479–714 (1978 and Supps.).

preventing unjust enrichment.[3] Standard works on contracts also cover the substantive side of mistake. That is, they consider the question whether a given kind of mistake justifies any relief at all. This chapter summarizes the main substantive rules of mistake, but primarily as a prelude to understanding remedies for different kinds of mistake and remedies in the enforcement of contracts.

A party to a contract who confronts unexpected potential for loss or diminished potential for gain often seeks to escape the contract altogether. Such a party might attempt to argue that conditions have changed in ways that make the contract impossible or impracticable of performance, or that makes its performance useless. These arguments are very similar to claims that the parties were profoundly mistaken when they entered the contract or that they entered it upon assumptions that were incorrect. Both kinds of argument turn on the idea that the contract allocates some more or less identified risks as between the parties; each is liable for the risks he or she shouldered by the express or implicit terms of the contract, but neither should not be liable for risks allocated to the other party or not allocated at all.[4] In this respect impracticability and mistake are similar. But impracticability and frustration problems are treated in another chapter.[5] The present chapter focuses on mistake, because it is important to recognize that the kind of mistake that resembles impracticability is only one of several kinds which may implicate restitutionary remedies, and because it is important to separate the different kinds of mistake recognized in the courts.

Because the rules about restitution for mistake differ according to the kind of mistake involved, no universal set of requirements can be stated. But it is useful to recognize that in some situations mistake must be a mutual mistake shared by the parties if it is to justify relief.[6] It is also useful to recognize that a misestimation about what the future holds is not traditionally regarded as a mistake of fact.[7] Finally, and much less importantly, it is also useful to acknowledge that the traditional rule excluded relief for mistakes of law, although this is probably no longer a good generalization.[8] Assuming for present simplicity that the mistake in question is one of "fact" and is mutual, there are three general kinds of mistake to be identified.

First, the parties may be mistaken in their basic assumptions of fact forming the contract. This is the kind of mistake in which the parties believe themselves to be buying and selling certain goods that in fact have been destroyed without the parties' knowledge. If the buyer pays $500 toward the price of such goods, and it later appears that the goods had burned in a fire before the contract was made, the buyer may "rescind" the

---

3. In the case of mistakes made in forming a contract, the account given in this chapter puts less emphasis on unjust enrichment and more emphasis on the parties' own risk allocations.

4. The same general idea seems to lie behind the familiar rule in *Hadley v. Baxendale,* limiting contract damages to the kinds of risks "contemplated" by the parties. As to that, see § 12.4 below.

5. See § 13.3 below. The similarities between impracticability-frustration on the one hand and mistake on the other are very great, but there are also important differences arising from the fact that most risks of the future are usually implicitly allocated by the parties to one or the other of them.

6. Unilateral mistakes in formation, § 11.4 below; unilateral mistakes in integration, § 11.6 below; unilateral mistakes in performance, § 11.7 below.

contract for the mistake in its formation.[9] Sometimes the theory is that no contract was ever formed at all in such cases. At other times the theory may be that a valid contract was formed, but that other considerations require its rescission.[10] In either event, if the mistake is deemed sufficiently significant, the court will refuse to give the contract any effect and will allow restitution of any sums the buyer may have paid toward the price.[11] A "misunderstanding" about the subject matter of the contract may have somewhat the same effect under certain circumstances,[12] and the remedy will be the same—restitution of all values received.

The second type of mistake is the mistake in performance of a valid obligation, contractual or otherwise.[13] This kind of mistake does not involve rescission of any contract or any mistake in its formation. The mistaken performance is illustrated by the case in which a buyer overpays a seller for the goods by mistake. There was no mistake in the amount due; it was clearly agreed upon by the parties, and the contract is valid and not subject to rescission. However, there was a mistake in performance when the buyer overpaid. In such a case the mistaken party is usually entitled to restitution, absent change of position by the other party. This does not involve cancellation of any instrument nor any "rescission," since the contract between the parties remains valid. It does, however, involve restitution of benefits retained by the party who is overpaid—a disgorgement of values he has improperly received. Whatever may be the requirement of mutuality of mistake where it goes to the formation of the contract, no such requirement is imposed where the mistake is one going to performance.

The third kind of mistake is quite different and so is the remedy. This is a mistake in integration of the contract, that is, a mistake in writing it down.[14] The parties bargain for the sale of "Lot 1," but write "Lot 10" by error. If their intent to bargain over "Lot 1" is clear and it is established that the expression was an error, the writing ought to be reformed, if need be, to reflect their true intent. This is the remedy of reformation, and it is, of course, quite distinct from the rescission or restitution remedies. It does not involve cancellation of the contract, but on the contrary, rewording of it to reflect the parties' agreement.

The mistakes described here—mistakes in the formation, in the performance, and in the integration of a contract—are not the only mistakes that arise in a transaction, nor are the remedies of rescission, restitution and reformation the only remedies. There are other mistakes in life and other remedies for them. The manufacturer who mistakenly uses the wrong wood for a ladder's rungs may be liable for the customer's injury if the wrongly chosen wood weakens the ladder and causes it to collapse. But although mistake underlies the manufacturer's conduct, the legal claim is not for mistake but for negligence, breach or warranty, or strict tort liability. The mistake at the root of those claims has no special interest in this chapter.

§ 11.2 The Meaning of Mistake—Erroneous Belief, Misunderstanding and Conscious Ignorance

Mistake of Fact or Law

Mistake as state of mind. A mistake is a state of mind not in accord with the facts.[1]   A mistake of fact may be induced by representations of others,[2] or by one's own forgetfulness,[3] but it is no less a mistake in either case.   A mistake of law may be counted as a mistake of fact.[4]

Legal policy: respecting parties' risk allocations.   In many cases the legal definition of mistake coincides very well with the policy in issue.   If the parties agree to buy and sell widgets at $1 each, they may believe that the price will change, or that competition will not introduce a cheaper substitute in the market.   Such a belief may turn out to be a poor prophecy.   Yet the contract should not be rescinded because of this misjudgment about the future, because the parties' contract allocated the risks on those very matters.   The parties understood, for example, that the buyer who agrees to pay $1 runs the risk that, by the time of performance, the market price may have dropped to 50 cents so that he could have purchased more cheaply. The seller runs the risk that by the time for performance the market price may have risen, so that the seller could have sold the goods at a higher price. Among traders, this allocation of risks is much of what the contract is about. The mistake rule protects the parties' risk allocations without referring to them.   It does so definitionally rather than by pointing to the policy.   It says that there is no mistake of fact at all when the parties misestimate the future.[17]

Conscious Ignorance, Assumed Risk and Doubt

One who acts, knowing that he does not know certain matters of fact, makes no mistake as to those matters, whether they are matters of fact or law.[19]   He is consciously ignorant and thus has no state of mind at variance with facts.   Only if he believes he knows facts or acts on a tacit assumption about the facts can he be mistaken.   The question of conscious ignorance may arise in the formation, performance or expression of a contract, as the following examples show.

Formation of the contract.   A contractor agrees to move dirt from a borrow pit; he knows there has been flooding in the area and that the pit may be flooded at the time he executes the agreement.   Having such notice and knowing his own uncertainty, the contractor makes no mistake; or, put differently, he assumes the risk.[20]

§ 11.2

1. Restatement Second of Contracts § 151 (1981); Restatement of Restitution § 6 (1937). Sometimes courts attempt to apply a mistake analysis to conduct rather than a state of mind. See, e.g., Krieger v. Iowa Dept. of Human Services, 439 N.W.2d 200 (Iowa 1989) ("failure to list the insurance policy" and "failure to follow through with a second inquiry" discussed as "mistakes"). Although conduct may result from a mistake about facts that motivates the conduct, conduct is not itself the mistake.

19. Restatement Second of Contracts § 154, Comment *c* (1981); Restatement of Restitution § 6, Comment *e* (1937); Gerard v. Almouli, 746 F.2d 936, 939 (2d Cir.1984) (parties believed approval required could be obtained in six months, but knew they did not

know; no mutual mistake because "the contract was entered into on the known assumption of a doubtful fact"); Gannett v. Merchants Mut. Ins. Co., 131 N.H. 266, 552 A.2d 99 (1988) (mistake of law is grounds for rescission, but mistake about future course of the law is not); cf. Prince v. Friedman, 202 Ga. 136, 139, 42 S.E.2d 434, 437 (1947) ("mistake of fact presupposes some knowledge thereof. Lack of knowledge or ignorance of a fact is not the same as mistake").   In many instances parties are aware that they cannot be certain of the law or its future course.

20. Tombigbee Constructors v. United States, 190 Ct.Cl. 615, 420 F.2d 1037, 1043 (1970) ("plaintiff assumed the risk of flood, or, at least, did not put in the contract the risk on the government"); Deans v. Layton, 89 N.C.App. 358, 366 S.E.2d 560, 564 (1988) ("A

Performance of a contract. A mistake in performance may be illustrated by any overpayment of an obligation. One who overpays but knows he is uncertain about whether the obligation exists, is consciously ignorant and in a sense makes no mistake at all. A fire insurance policy, for example, might require payment in case of a fire, but with an exception for arson. If the company is unable to prove arson, but suspects it might exist, and pays the policy anyway, it operates under no mistake, since it is aware of its own ignorance.[22] If the insurance company pays the full amount of the policy, that fact might be construed as some evidence that the company was *not* consciously ignorant since normally factual doubts produce a compromise rather than a full payment. Some courts have given great weight to this factor and have readily allowed rescission for mistake where full payment was made, sometimes emphasizing also a judicial policy to encourage early payment by insurers.[23] However, where the facts are known to be doubtful, even full payment should have no bearing on the case except as evidence of the parties' state of mind. If they are in fact aware of serious uncertainties a mistake does not seem to exist at all.

Expression or integration of a contract. The same sort of analysis can be made in cases where reformation is sought to change the wording of a written contract. In *Harley v. Magnolia Petroleum Co.,*[24] deeds were given subject to a recorded lease. The parties knew they did not know the exact contents of the lease, though they probably did make some basic assumptions about its contents. Their conscious ignorance was held to prevent reformation.

Assumed risks formulation of the principle. The notion that where the parties are consciously ignorant, they are not mistaken can be expressed in quite different terms. Sometimes courts speak of this situation as an assumption of the risk.[25]

Misunderstanding

Negotiating parties often make no mistake of fact at all, but do have problems in communicating with sufficient accuracy. The kind of mischance involved in communication failures is sometimes called misunderstanding to distinguish it from mistake of an external fact. Misunderstanding is characterized by the fact that the parties attach different meanings to their manifestations of assent.[30]

The classic case of misunderstanding is *Raffles v. Wichelhaus.*[31] The plaintiff in that case agreed to sell cotton to arrive on a ship named *Peerless,* and the buyer agreed to buy cotton to arrive on a ship named *Peerless.* It

party assumes the risk of mistake where: (a) the risk is allocated to him by agreement of the parties, or (b) he is aware, at the time the contract is made that he has only limited knowledge with respect to the facts to which the mistake relates but treats his limited knowledge as sufficient").

22. Meeme Mut. Home Protection Fire Ins. Co. v. Lorfeld, 194 Wis. 322, 216 N.W. 507 (1927).

23. Phoenix Indem. Co. v. Steiden Stores, Inc., 267 S.W.2d 733 (Ky.1954); see Restate-

ment of Restitution § 11 (1937). For more details, see § 11.7 below.

24. 378 Ill. 19, 37 N.E.2d 760, 137 A.L.R. 900 (1941). See Annotation, Conscious Ignorance of Fact as Ground for Reformation, 137 A.L.R. 908 (1942).

25. E.g., New York Life Ins. Co. v. Chittenden & Eastmen, 134 Iowa 613, 112 N.W. 96 (1907).

31. 2 Hurl. & C. 906, 159 Eng.Rep. 375 (1864).

turned out that there were two ships by the same name. The seller had in mind the ship sailing in December; the buyer had in mind the ship sailing in October. Apparently both parties were reasonable in their interpretation of the agreement and neither knew of the other ship by the same name. The English Court of Exchequer held there was no contract under these circumstances. Basic mistakes in communication—reasonable misunderstandings—will often have this effect. Courts that use a more subjective theory of contract formation may say, with the *Raffles* court, that there was no *consensus ad idem* or no "meeting of the minds." [32] Courts that talk in more objective language may say there was no manifestation of mutual assent in the reasonable misunderstanding cases. [33]

§ 11.3　Mistake in the Attempted Formation of a Contract— Mutual Mistake

The contract enforcing principle. Contracting parties should not be made to bear obligations they did not undertake. When parties contract under a mutual mistake of facts which makes the contract more burdensome or less valuable to one party, that party may avoid the contract if enforcement would impose burdens not allocated to him by the contract. The contract may not be avoided merely because it is more burdensome than expected; it is avoided only when the increased burden is outside the risks allocated to the complaining party. One who buys a used car with no guarantees is accepting the risk that unexpected repairs may be required. The same principles of respecting the whole contract apply when the doctrinal basis for relief is impossibility or frustration rather than mistake.[1]

Example. For example, suppose that a sales representative for a large manufacturer believes he owns a kind of dealership which can be sold. He contracts to sell it to a buyer and the buyer pays him $50,000. The parties then discover that the sales representative-seller had no power to sell his dealership rights. The buyer can avoid the contract and the seller must return the buyer's payments.[5] The buyer did not contract to pay $50,000 for nothing, so if it were not given restitution of this sum it would suffer a liability it never contracted for. Put in terms of the evidence, the buyer and seller operated under a basic mistake and the contract did not place the risk of error on the buyer.

Requiring mistake as to identity or existence of subject matter. Some cases, especially older ones, concentrated exclusively on the nature of the parties' mistake rather than on their implicit risk allocations. These cases in effect said that to obtain relief the plaintiff would be required to show that (1) the mistake was basic, that is, that it went to the basis of the bargain,[12] the essence,[13] or the root of the matter; [14] (2) a basic mistake is a mistake that goes to the identity or existence of the subject matter; [15] (3) conversely, a mistake that merely goes to the value or quality of the subject matter is not basic or vital and does not warrant relief.[16] In short, these rules held that a mistake about the identity or existence of the subject

§ 11.3

5. E.g., E.B. Sherman, Inc. v. Mirizio, 556 So.2d 1143 (Fla.App.1989) (parties mistakenly believed that would-be seller had power to transfer his rights as sales representative; when the mistake was revealed, the would-be buyer could recover payments made to effect the purchase).

matter warranted relief,[17] but no other mistake did. These rules were somewhat attractive only because they suggested evidence that would often be important in judging risk allocations of the parties, not because they stated the ultimate policy or principle.

Mistake as to existence example. When the parties were in fact mistaken about the identity of the subject matter, or its existence, the case is indeed a good one for avoiding the contract. Seller contracts to sell a horse named Sam and buyer contracts to buy that horse. Both parties believe the horse is alive and well in Paris, but in fact the horse has died. The parties made a mistake about the existence of the subject matter,[18] so the contract would be avoided.

The identity-existence rule works well when the parties are in fact mistaken about the identity or existence of the subject matter. A direct address to the principle would have worked just as well: the risk that the horse would not be alive was *not* allocated to the buyer; the parties did *not* contract to sell and buy a dead horse. When the mistake is serious but not one about identity or existence of subject matter, the rule does not work so well, because the contract may have implicitly allocated risks that have nothing to do with existence or identity of the subject matter.

In the famous pregnant cow case, *Sherwood v. Walker,*[23] the seller of the cow had owned it for breeding purposes, but he came to the conclusion that the cow was barren. The buyer, said to have shared this belief, bought the cow at the price prevailing for beef cattle. In due course the mistake of the parties became apparent—the cow was in fact with calf at the time the contract had been made and she was worth ten times the agreed price. The mistake prevented the formation of any contract, according to the Michigan Court. The Michigan Court admitted that the very animal the parties had in mind did in fact exist and her physical identity was not in doubt. Nevertheless, the court said that the parties' mistake "went to the very nature of the thing," and that the "thing sold and bought had in fact no existence." Of course this was not true; the cow in *fact* had existence. The only thing that lacked existence was the parties' *idea* of the cow. The idea of the cow became in the court's eye, more real than the cow itself. Thus the court avoided the contract since the mistake went to the very "existence" of the cow.

Although there may be reasons to question the decision in *Sherwood v. Walker,* the court's insistence that the mistake was about the "existence" of the cow has an appeal for pragmatic Americans, who may think that a thing *is* what a thing *does* and that in operational terms a cow that produces calves is indeed a different cow from the cow that produces barbecue and beef Wellington.

Comment. The rule which limits contract avoidance to cases of mistake about the identity or existence of the subject matter puts the emphasis in the wrong place; it elevates evidence to the status of a rule. The point is not that mistakes about subject matter have independent significance. The point is rather that mistakes about identity of the subject matter are likely to be outside the risks allocated expressly or impliedly by the parties. The

23. 66 Mich. 568, 33 N.W. 919 (1887).

identity-existence rules represent a dead-end. To ask whether a mistake is "basic" is a little better than asking whether it is a mistake about identity or existence of subject matter. To ask how the parties, expressly or impliedly allocated risks would be best of all.

§ 11.4 Mistake in the Attempted Formation of a Contract— Unilateral Mistake

General Rules

Unilateral mistake alone insufficient. Mutual mistake of a basic fact may warrant avoidance of the transaction induced by that mistake,[1] but the same mistake by only one of the parties is not ordinarily sufficient to do so. A strong common law tradition grants relief from unilateral mistakes in the formation of contracts [2] only with caution if at all.[3] Two different mistakes by the two parties to a transaction are not mutual mistakes; they are two different one-party or unilateral mistakes, and the same caution applies. But commentators and case decisions have recognized that relief may be appropriate if, besides the unilateral mistake, substantial additional grounds for relief are shown.[4]

The additional Restatement rule: unconscionable hardship plus a favorable allocation of risk of mistake. The Second Contracts Restatement proposes a rule which allows the mistaken party to avoid the contract if (1) the mistaken party does not bear the risk of mistake, and (2) the effect of the mistake would make enforcement of the contract unconscionable,[8] and (3) enforcement is not required to provide appropriate protection to the non-mistaken party.[9] Some cases have adopted the Restatement rule in its entirety.[10]

§ 11.5 Restitution as a Remedy for Mistake in Formation of a Contract—Measurement of Restitution

When a contract is avoidable for mistake, the party aggrieved by the mistake may defend the other's suit for damages or performance. If the aggrieved party has delivered some or all of the performance due under the contract before discovering the mistake, he may not only defend a suit but may also avoid the contract by rescission or otherwise and recover restitution for the benefits he has conferred. Although he may recover the benefits he has conferred, he must likewise restore to the other party any benefits he has received.

For example, if a buyer has paid $100 toward a purchase and a seller has delivered merchandise, avoidance of the contract normally requires the buyer to restore the merchandise or its value and the seller to return the $100 payment.

When restitution is due it may be effectuated by any appropriate legal or equitable remedy, or by defense, or set-off. For example, the plaintiff might sue in equity, asking the court to rescind the contract for mistake and to compel restitution.[1] If the restitution claim is a simple money claim, the plaintiff might simply declare the contract rescinded and sue at law for the

§ 11.4
8. Restatement Second of Contracts § 153 (1981).

money due him, asserting a quasi-contract theory of restitution.[2] If the plaintiff is entitled to restitution of specific property, he may seek injunctive relief or a constructive trust.

Reliance expenses generally unrecoverable. Measurement of restitution may be more difficult if the plaintiff has performed services. First, when the basis of restitution is only mistake rather than breach, the plaintiff is not entitled to recover restitution for the value of labor he has invested in reliance on the contract unless those services were part of the performance due under the contract or those services conferred economic benefits upon the other party which can be restored to the plaintiff without prejudice to the other party. For example, if the plaintiff, in reliance on the contract to purchase Blackacre, expends $2,000 to purchase rose bushes for planting, but before doing so avoids the contract for mistake and loses his investment in the roses, he cannot recover the investment loss from the defendant vendor. In that case the vendor has not received bargained for performance or indeed any benefit at all.

Benefits conferred but not as part of bargained for performance. When the party aggrieved by a mistaken formation of contract has conferred benefits incidental to performance but not as a part of the performance required by contract, he is entitled to restitution in the same way that a stranger would be entitled to restitution for benefits mistakenly conferred.[6] Restitution in such a case is measured by the actual economic benefit to the recipient for his own purposes.[7]

In the example of the roses, suppose the buyer of Blackacre had actually been permitted to enter and plant the roses before discovering the mistake and rescinding the contract to purchase Blackacre. The roses were no part of the performance due from him and the vendor had not requested the plantings. Suppose the rose bushes as saleable items were worth $2,000, and the labor to put them in the ground or remove them is also $2,000, but that the property value is increased only by $500. The vendor's maximum liability in this kind of case is $500, the most that can be said to be actual economic benefit to him.[8] If we go further and say that he decides to pave the rose garden for a parking lot, so that gets no benefit at all, then it would seem that he is not liable for restitution at all.

Benefits conferred as part of the performance under the contract. In contrast, the defendant may be liable for the full market value of any benefits he received as part of the plaintiff's performance under the contract, because these are benefits the defendant sought and valued. That is, restitution may be measured by what it would cost the defendant to receive the same performance from other persons, and is not limited to the increase in defendant's assets.[13]

For example, suppose that instead of contracting to sell the land, the defendant contracts to have the plaintiff plant 2,000 rose bushes on the defendant's land. After the plaintiff plants the roses, he discovers that the parties had entered the contract under a misunderstanding or a mistake, and the plaintiff wants to rescind and have restitution for the benefits he has conferred. In this instance, the rose bushes *are* the performance called for by the contract; the defendant wanted rose bushes and bargained for them. If the rose bushes increased the value of the land by only $1,000 but the reasonable value of the plaintiff's services plus the bushes themselves was $10,000, the defendant may be held for the $10,000 as the reasonable value of the plaintiff's goods and services, not merely for the $1,000 increased land value.[14]

§ 11.6 Reformation for Mistake in Expression

§ 11.6(1) Grounds and Cases for Reformation

[*For the text of this section, see the unabridged Practitioner Treatise edition.*]

§ 11.6(2) Reformation and the Alternatives

[*Consult § 9.5 above and see these subsections in the Practitioner Treatise edition, vol. 2, pp. 743–751.*]

§ 11.6(3) Effectuating, Extending and Defending Reformation Claims

[*For discussion of methods for effectuating reformation, and defenses, see this section in the Practitioner Treatise edition, vol. 2, pp. 751–755.*]

Equities and hardships. Some equitable remedies are denied when courts believe that the remedy would impose more costs than the benefits it provides, or when the hardships and equities favor the defendant. If such discretion were applied in reformation cases, it would warrant the court in denying restitution, not in granting it. However, in *National American Corp. v. Federal Republic of Nigeria*,[9] the court appeared to impose a contract the parties never agreed to rather than to rescind for mistake, and may have been actuated by considerations of equity and hardship.

In that case Nigeria had ordered over 20 millions of metric tons of cement to be delivered by many different suppliers at its one port and within a year. The port could only unload one million tons a year. Congestion, confusion, and delay resulted. The contract called for a payment to suppliers of $3500 per day for each supplier. It turned out that many ships carried loads of many suppliers, so the $3500 per day for each supplier represented a great sum and more than the time loss for delay of a ship. Nigeria then renegotiated contracts to alleviate some of the ruin threatened by these payments. NAC was a supplier under the original contract. Nigeria negotiated a new contract with NAC for a price for its 12 shiploads of cement, plus a reduced figure for delay time. This new contract was based on an error; NAC had not dispatched 12 ships, but was instead still loading half of them in New York and only actually managed to put six of them in Nigerian territorial waters.

The trial judge "reformed" the renegotiated contract, using the figures the parties had agreed upon for 12 ships, but only for the six ships that had actually reached Nigeria. A divided panel of the Second Circuit affirmed. If the parties intended to cover six ships but erroneously wrote 12, that decision would clearly be in line with traditional views of reformation. Likewise, if the parties agreed to cover "ships actually in the harbor when this agreement is signed," but wrote "all ships," reformation would be proper. The underlying mistake seems to be different, however. It seems to

§ 11.6(3)

9.   597 F.2d 314 (2d Cir.1979).

have been a mistake by the Nigerians about the status or location of the ships, probably coupled with awareness of the mistake by NAC. If so, it was a mistake that induced the contract, not one that led to its wrong expression and in that case rescission would be the appropriate remedy.

The hardship on one side and seeming inequity on the other suggest that the court might have used reformation in a non-traditional way. If that is so, it is very non-traditional indeed, because it does not deny or limit a remedy to account for hardship; it grants affirmative relief to do so. But unorthodox reformation to deal with a disastrous mistake that could ruin a small emerging nation might not signal a willingness to give the same relief for private parties in more ordinary business situations.

§ 11.7 Mistake in the Performance of an Obligation—Restitution Remedies

Mistakes in performance differ from mistakes in formation and mistakes in expression. A mistake in attempting to perform a contract may result in underperformance or overperformance. Underperformance of the contract may constitute a breach, remedies for which are considered in Chapter 12. A mistaken overperformance may have the effect of conferring benefits upon the other party. This section deals with mistakes in performance of a contract that confer a benefit upon the other party.

Most of the cases involve overpayment of money. When that is so, restitution is measured in money, by the amount overpaid. The bank that pays the overdraft for the customer,[11] or pays the customer too much when it closes his account,[12] the buyer of goods that overpays the purchase price,[13] the insurance company that pays on an expired policy,[14] or twice the amount it owes [15]—all these are entitled to restitution in money. On similar principle, the executor or administrator of an estate, or trustee of a trust will be entitled to restitution in money from an overpaid legatee or beneficiary.[16]

But other restitutionary remedies may be appropriate, too. It is conceivable that one might mistakenly perform her contract with another in such a way as to discharge the other's debt to a secured creditor. In such a case, subrogation would be an appropriate remedy.[17]

In other situations specific restitution, rather than restitution in money, will be appropriate. If the plaintiff delivers two motorcycles when she was only obliged by contract to deliver one, she can recover one of them by replevin.[18] If the plaintiff has overconveyed land, she may recover the overconveyance by way of reformation or by constructive trust.[19]

§ 11.8 Change of Position

[Consult the summary in § 4.6 above and see this section in the Practitioner Treatise edition, vol. 2, pp. 761–772.]

§ 11.9 Settlement of Claims and Personal Injury Releases

[For the text of this section, see the unabridged Practitioner Treatise edition.]

§ 11.10 Mistake in Gift Transaction

[For the text of this section, see the unabridged Practitioner Treatise edition.]

Chapter 12

REMEDIES FOR BREACH
OF CONTRACT

Analysis

A. GENERAL REMEDIAL RULES

Sec.
12.1   Contract Remedies Generally.
    12.1(1)   Damages, Restitution and Specific Performance.
    12.1(2)   Policy and Practicality in Selecting and Measuring
            Contract Remedies.

(1) Money Remedies

12.2   Damages to Compensate for Expectancy.
    12.2(1)   Expectancy and Compensation Generally.
    12.2(2)   Market Value vs. Cost Expectancy Measures.
    12.2(3)   General vs. Special Measures of Expectancy.
12.3   Damages to Compensate for Reliance Loss and Opportunity
    Costs.
    12.3(1)   Reliance Loss as Measure of Damages.
    12.3(2)   Expectancy as a Cap on Reliance Damages.
12.4   The Special Problems of Consequential Damages.
    12.4(1)   Special or Consequential Damages: Limiting Rules.
    12.4(2)   Causation Requirements.
    12.4(3)   Proof Requirements.
    12.4(4)   The Contemplation of the Parties Rule.
    12.4(5)   The Contemplation of the Parties Rule: Rationales.
    12.4(6)   The Contemplation of the Parties Rule: Formula-
            tions.
    12.4(7)   Contemplation of the Parties: Applications and Sub-
            sidiary Principles.*
12.5   Extracontractual Damages: Emotional Distress and Punitive
    Damages.
    12.5(1)   Emotional Distress Damages.
    12.5(2)   Punitive Damages for Breach of Contract.
12.6   Adjustments in Damages.
    12.6(1)   Summary of Adjustments.
    12.6(2)   The Avoidable Consequences Rules.*
    12.6(3)   Must General Damages Be Minimized?*
    12.6(4)   The Collateral Source Rule.*
12.7   Money Awards as Restitution for Breach of Contract.
    12.7(1)   General Rules Permitting Restitution.
    12.7(2)   Form of Restitution—Specific vs. Monetary.
    12.7(3)   Mode of Measurement for Money Restitution.
    12.7(4)   Restitution Based on Defendant's Profits in Connec-
            tion With Breach.

* For the text of this section, see Dobbs, Law   Treatise, Vol. 3.
of Remedies, Second Edition, Practitioner

747

Sec.

12.7   Money Awards as Restitution for Breach of Contract—Cont'd
    12.7(5) Expectancy or Price as a Limit on Restitution.
    12.7(6) Recovery of Both Restitution and Damages: Election of Remedies.*
    12.7(7) Restitution Claims Against Non-parties.

(2) Specie and Non-monetary Remedies

12.8   Non-monetary Remedies—Specific Performance and Declaratory Judgment.
    12.8(1) Specific Performance Generally.
    12.8(2) The Adequacy Test.
    12.8(3) Practicability and Policy Limitations.
    12.8(4) Fairness and Hardship Limitations.
    12.8(5) Discretion and the Effect of Equitable Defenses on Legal Relief.*
    12.8(6) Specific Performance and Contemplation of the Parties.*
    12.8(7) Declaratory Judgment.*
12.9   Agreed Remedies.
    12.9(1) Summary.
    12.9(2) Liquidated Damages and Penalties: General Rules.
    12.9(3) Liquidated Damages: Rationales and Critiques.*
    12.9(4) Liquidated Damages: Alternative Analysis, Alternative Clauses.
    12.9(5) Liquidated Damages: Drafting and Interpretation.
    12.9(6) Agreements for or Against Specific Performance and Other Remedies.

B. PARTICULAR CONTRACTS

(1) Land Contracts

12.10   Vendor and Purchaser of Land: Remedies and Risk of Loss in Summary.
12.11   Purchaser's Remedies for Vendor's Breach.
    12.11(1) Purchaser's Damages.
    12.11(2) Rescission and Restitution for the Purchaser.
    12.11(3) Specific Performance in Favor of the Purchaser.*
    12.11(4) The Purchaser's Lien.
12.12   Vendor's Remedies for Purchaser's Breach.
    12.12(1) Vendor's Damages Remedy.
    12.12(2) Restitution to the Vendor.
    12.12(3) Specific Performance in Favor of the Vendor.
    12.12(4) The Vendor's Lien.
12.13   Some Problems of Installment Contracts Remedies.*
12.14   Loss or Damage to Property Before Conveyance.
12.15   Leases and Lease Contracts.
    12.15(1) Background and Scope.*
    12.15(2) Lessee's Remedies for Lessor's Breach Affecting Use Premises.
    12.15(3) Lessor's Remedies Against Lessee Who Defaults or Abandons the Premises.

(2) Chattel Sales Contracts

12.16   Buyer's Remedies for Breach of Chattel Sales Contract.
    12.16(1) Buyer's Remedies: Background and Summary.
    12.16(2) Buyer's Market Measured Damages.*
    12.16(3) Buyer's Cover Damages Under the Code.

* For the text of this section, see Dobbs, Law   Treatise, Vol. 3.
of Remedies, Second Edition, Practitioner

Sec.
12.16 Buyer's Remedies for Breach of Chattel Sales Contract—
     Cont'd
     12.16(4) Buyer's Incidental and Consequential Damages.*
     12.16(5) Buyer's Damages After Seller's Anticipatory Repu-
         diation.
     12.16(6) Buyer's Restitutionary Claims.*
     12.16(7) Buyer's Specific Performance Remedy.*
12.17 Seller's Remedies for Breach of Chattel Sales Contract.
     12.17(1) Seller's Remedies—Background and Summary.
     12.17(2) Seller's Market Measured Damages.*
     12.17(3) Seller's Resale Measured Damages.*
     12.17(4) Seller's Incidental and Consequential Damages.*
     12.17(5) Seller's "Lost Profit" Damages.*
     12.17(6) Seller's Restitutionary Remedies.*
     12.17(7) Seller's Specific Performance Remedy: The Price
         Action.*
12.18 Remedies for Breach of Lease of Goods.*

(3) Building Contracts

12.19 Owner's Remedies for Breach of Building or Repair Contract.
     12.19(1) Owner's Damages Remedy.
     12.19(2) Owner's Restitutionary Remedies.*
     12.19(3) Owner's Specific Performance Remedy.*
12.20 Contractor's Remedies for Owner's Breach of Construction or
     Repair Contract.
     12.20(1) Contractor's Damages Remedies.
     12.20(2) Contractor's Restitutionary Remedies.
     12.20(3) Third Party Restitution Claims of Subcontractors
         and Others: Mechanics' Liens and Other De-
         vices.

(4) Other Contracts

12.21 Employee's Remedies for Employer's Breach of Employment
     Contract.
     12.21(1) Scope and Related Materials.*
     12.21(2) Employee's Damages Remedy.*
     12.21(3) Employee's Restitutionary Remedies.
     12.21(4) Specific Performance and Injunction in Favor of
         Employee.
12.22 Employer's Remedies for Employee's Breach of Employment
     Contract.
     12.22(1) The Employer's Money Remedies.*
     12.22(2) The Employer's Equitable Remedies.
12.23 Remedies Under Arbitration Contracts.*

A. GENERAL REMEDIAL RULES

§ 12.1 Contract Remedies Generally

§ 12.1(1) Damages, Restitution and Specific Performance

Contract Remedies Generally

This section is a small-scale road map. It sketches the basic remedies and remedial limitations in contract breach cases and points to the location

* For the text of this section, see Dobbs, Law   Treatise, Vol. 3.
of Remedies, Second Edition, Practitioner

of more complete discussion later in the chapter. The first part of the chapter considers the principles of contract remedies and their limitations. The last part examines those remedies in the context of several particular kinds of contracts, such as those for the sale or purchase of land or chattels, leases, construction and employment contracts and others.

Traditional remedies. Remedies against a contract-breacher usually fall into one of three major categories. First, a plaintiff might recover damages, aimed at providing compensation to the promisee or "victim" of the breach. Several different kinds of damages might be asserted and also several different measures of damages may be used.[1]

Second, the plaintiff might recover restitution, aimed at depriving the defendant of unjust enrichment or improper gains resulting from the breach. This recovery is often but not always associated with the idea that the contract, being breached, can be rescinded.[2]

Third, the plaintiff might recover the very performance promised, that is, specific performance.[3] In some cases, the specific performance effect might be achieved through imposition of a constructive trust to obtain title to property promised under the contract.

Flexible remedies. A fourth kind of remedy, arbitration, opens the possibility of more flexible adjustments.[4] In addition, a mounting body of scholarly literature suggests that in some instances court-ordered or other adjustments in the parties' obligations may be appropriate,[5] although the courts have not usually gone this far [6] by direct or overt action.[7]

§ 12.1(1)

1. See § 12.2 below.

2. See §§ 12.2 and 12.7(1)–(7) below.

3. See § 12.8 below.

4. See § 12.23 below.

5. This body of work deals with the idea that many contracts today mainly establish long-term relationships or a framework rather than a discrete transaction. As Professor Kidwell puts it, this view sees "contract-as-relation" rather than "contract-as-transaction." Kidwell, A Caveat, 1985 Wis.L.Rev. 615 (1985). From the relational viewpoint, contracts establish relationships rather than transactions or particular promises; adjustments within the framework of the relationship may be more appropriate than traditional damages or other judicial remedies. Although the relational contract idea has deep roots, see Symposium, Law, Private Governance and Continuing Relationships, 1985 Wis.L.Rev. 461 (1985), it is mainly associated with the extensive scholarship of Professor Ian Macneil. See among his many writings, Macneil, Contracts: Adjustments of Long–Term Economic Relations under Classical, Neoclassical, and Relational Contract Law, 72 Nw.L.Rev. 854 (1978).

6. See Hillman, Court Adjustment of Long–Term Contracts: An Analysis under Modern Contract Law, 1987 Duke L.J. 1 (1987); Speidel, Court–Imposed Price Adjustments under Long–Term Supply Contracts, 76 Nw.L.Rev. 369 (1981). See generally § 13.3 below.

Professor Hillman proposes adjustments in long-term contracts when substantial unanticipated changes take place (such as an oil embargo) if the parties have implicitly agreed on adjustment or if there is a gap in their risk allocations so that it becomes fair to allocate losses between them which they have not themselves allocated. Professor Speidel proposed a different limitation; the adjustment would be justified only if the fortuitously advantaged party failed to engage in good faith post-calamity negotiations.

7. Indirectly, courts may re-write contracts in limited ways under a theory of reformation, as where the vendor has more land than he knew and is allowed to claim at the contract rate for any excess conveyed. See §§ 12.12(3) and 12.11(1) below; 3 George Palmer, Law of Restitution §§ 14.25 and 14.26 (1978); Dawson, Judicial Revision of Frustrated Contracts: The United States, 64 B.U.L.Rev. 1, 9–11 (1984). Some other doctrines that may meliorate the parties' obligations are discussed in Hillman, The Crisis in Modern Contract Theory, 67 Tex.L.Rev. 103 (1988). See also § 13.-3(2) below (remedies when performance is impossible or contract goals frustrated).

Combining and "electing" remedies. Sometimes remedies can be combined without duplication of recoveries. For instance, the plaintiff may obtain specific performance of a land purchase contract, and in addition may obtain an award of damages for the delay suffered in receiving the conveyance.[8] Less often, the plaintiff might recover both restitution and damages.[9] At other times, the plaintiff may be subjected to election of remedy doctrines. These may require the plaintiff to "elect" one remedy or another, or to give up one remedy because he has already claimed another.[10]

Damages—Compensation and Convention

Compensation goals. Damages for contract breach, like damages in other cases, theoretically aim at compensation of the plaintiff.[11] Sometimes the question of compensation is less a matter of legal rule than it is a matter of factual measurement.

Practical constraints and conventional limits. For practical reasons—the costs and uncertainties of proof, for example—pure compensation is often not feasible. When this is the case, the plaintiff may recover nominal damages in lieu of compensation.[12] But more often the courts seek a substitute for compensation by finding an acceptable convention for structuring an award.[13] Market value of the goods, service or property promised, for example, is often a basis for computing damages even though it may only imperfectly reflect the ideal of compensation.[14]

Policy constraints: defining compensation. A money award intended as "compensation" may turn out to be more or less than one would expect because of the practical constraints and the measurement conventions adopted in response to those constraints. Money awards might also be more or less than expected because of the way compensation is defined in some settings or because legal policies expand or contract the award.

To some extent, compensation is defined by the parties' own promises and the risks they undertook. The defendant's promise to dig a well at a certain price might be a guarantee that the plaintiff can have the necessary labor without paying a higher price; or it might be a guarantee that the plaintiff's cattle will have water. If the defendant breaches, what counts as compensation to the plaintiff will depend on which guarantee the defendant made, that is, upon which risk he undertook to protect against. If he guaranteed the water, compensation may require him to pay for the loss of the plaintiff's cattle when water was not produced. If he only guaranteed against the risk of a higher price for the labor, then compensation will be based on the cost of getting the well dug by another driller.[15] The parties' relationship, the economic setting, and the business structure[16] and even business culture[17] are all relevant in determining the scope of the promise and the legal policy.

---

8. See § 12.8(1) below.

9. See § 12.7(6) below.

10. See § 12.7(6); see also §§ 12.12(1) and 12.13 below and 9.4 above.

15. See § 12.4(4) below. Cf. Hadley v. Baxendale, 9 Exch. 341, 156 Eng.Rep. 145 (1854).

16. See Cooter and Eisenberg, Damages for Breach of Contract, 73 Cal.L.Rev. 1432 (1985).

17. See Macaulay, An Empirical View of Contract, 1985 Wis.L.Rev. 465, 467.

Expectancy damages. Damages remedies most frequently aim at protecting the plaintiff's expectation or expectancy interest. This means that the damages remedy attempts to give the plaintiff the kind of gains he would have made if the contract had been performed, no more, no less.[19] (The expectation interest may be protected also by specific performance.)[20] Because factual settings, business structures, and contract purposes differ enormously, the expectancy interest is not always measured in the same way.[21]

General and consequential measures of expectancy. Expectancy damages are sometimes measured by "general damages" or market measures. Such measures use the market value of the very thing promised, at the time of performance, as a basis for calculation. When the defendant reneges on a promise to sell the plaintiff certain shares of stock for $10,000, the plaintiff's recovery can be measured by the difference between the contract price and the market price of the shares.[22] (There are usually also some adjustments to account for delays, prepayment or special savings.)[23] "Special damages" (consequential damages) are measured, not by the value of the promised performance alone but by the gains such performance could produce for collateral reasons, or the loss that is produced by the absence of such performance. When the defendant fails to repair the plaintiff's factory machinery as promised, the factory cannot operate and the plaintiff cannot make the profit that otherwise would have been made. Expectation damages could be measured by either general or special damages measures, but special damages are subject to several limiting rules.[24]

Certainty and foreseeability limitations on consequential damages. The recovery of consequential damages is limited by two important rules. First, consequential damages must be proven with reasonable certainty, a rule that sometimes prevents recovery of such items as future profits.[25] Second, consequential damages must be of the general kind contemplated by the parties at the time of contracting. Damages not within the parties' contemplation are not recoverable, even when they are clearly proven.[26]

Attorney fees. One item of special damages is forbidden by an independent rule. In line with the "American rule" for litigation generally, the parties in contract litigation pay their own attorneys' fees and many other litigation costs unless the contract itself provides otherwise or one of the other traditional exceptions applies.[27]

Reliance damages. Instead of aiming to protect the expectancy, the damages remedy may aim more modestly to prevent losses. Such an aim attempts to protect the plaintiff's reliance interest. The plaintiff who promises to design custom software for the defendant will expend time and money doing so. If he cannot sell the software elsewhere, he will have reliance damages based on his expenditures. In general, the plaintiff might opt to claim reliance damages when he cannot prove consequential expectancy damages with reasonable certainty. As will be indicated more fully, however, limitations may apply.[28]

Liquidated damages. When the parties contract not only about performance but also about the damages payable upon breach, the agreement is said to call for either liquidated damages or a "penalty." Courts refuse to enforce the provision for such damages if they are viewed as a penalty. If the provision is regarded as "liquidated damages" rather than a penalty, it may be enforced as the applicable measure of damages in the case. However, courts have been grudging about enforcement liquidated damages clauses. In general, they have refused to enforce the parties' agreement as to the measure or amount of damages when the damages agreed upon exceed the traditional measures used by courts and when the traditional measure would not be too difficult to figure.[29] The parties' agreement for damages may also be disregarded when the damages they provide for differ too much from the "actual" damages expected at the time of contracting or those actually incurred.[30] On the other hand, in most jurisdictions today the parties are free to limit damages and also to provide for arbitration of claims arising under a contract. The arbitrator in turn may award remedies quite different from the traditional judicial remedies.[31]

Punitive damages and mental anguish damages. Contract rights are mostly economic [32] rights, so contract remedies are mostly economic remedies—that is, remedies based on objective economic loss. Punitive damages and mental anguish damages are thus considered "extracontractual," and usually denied in pure contract cases.[33] In some instances, however, breach of a contract may constitute a tort, in which case punitive damages or mental anguish damages may be appropriate.[34] In some other instances, the contracted-for promise may have such strong personal elements that "non-economic" or mental anguish damages may be permissible.[35]

Avoidable consequences and collateral sources. The avoidable consequences rules forbid recovery of any consequential damages that the plaintiff could reasonably have avoided; put differently, the plaintiff must make reasonable effort to minimize damages. The costs of such reasonable efforts then become themselves an item of recovery.[36] If the plaintiff's damages are minimized by insurance, or public benefits, however, the court may invoke the collateral source rules rather than the avoidable consequences rule; if so the plaintiff will be allowed to recover full damages without regard to the fact that payments from a collateral source have reduced his net loss.[37]

Other adjustments. Several accounting adjustments may also be required. Damages awarded now for losses expected to occur in the future traditionally require a reduction to present value. The prospects of future inflation may be considered in making this adjustment. Conversely, damages awarded now for losses that occurred before trial may require an upward adjustment by way of interest for the delay in payment.[38]

Restitution

Defendant's gain. Restitutionary recoveries are based on the defendant's gain, not on the plaintiff's loss.[39] Restitution is thus distinct from damages, which measures compensation for loss rather than disgorgement of the defendant's gain. Like damages, restitution may depend in part on conventions of measurement, but in the case of restitution, the convention will relate to the measure for the defendant's gain rather than the plaintiff's loss.[40]

Specific restitution. Restitution may be specific or in money. Specific restitution restores the very thing given by the plaintiff in the exchange. For example, the plaintiff who exchanged land in return for a promise of lifetime support is often entitled to rescission and cancellation of the deed if the defendant breaches the promise.[41]

Money restitution. Restitution can also be in money, either because the plaintiff gave money in the exchange or because money can be substituted for the specific thing the plaintiff gave. Money restitution may or may not be equivalent in dollar amount to compensation or damages. If the theory for the claim is "restitution" based upon the defendant's unjust enrichment, then the recovery is not "damages" even if, in dollar amount, it is equivalent to a compensatory damages recovery. Courts sometimes reinforce the money restitution remedy by giving the plaintiff security, such as a lien on property involved in the transaction.[42]

Defendant's collateral gains or profits. In rare cases, the plaintiff might recover some collateral gain or "profit" the defendant has received as a result of the breach.[43] More commonly, however, the plaintiff's restitutionary recovery for breach is a simple recovery of what he gave. The defendant not having performed his part of the bargain, the plaintiff can treat the contract as being at an end and recover any performance he has delivered to the defendant. In this kind of case restitution may be thought of as following "rescission" of the contract for breach. However, it is not necessary to theorize a rescission to obtain restitution of benefits the defendant holds by reason of his breach. Partial breach, for example, might benefit the defendant, even though the contract was otherwise fully performed.[44] In such a case it is especially difficult to think about "rescission." The point of restitution is simpler than undoing the whole contract; it is only to deprive the defendant of the unjust gain resulting from breach.[45]

Specific Performance

Generally; adequacy test. Injunctive enforcement of the contract is usually called specific performance. Such enforcement is another way of enforcing the plaintiff's expectancy. It does so by requiring actual performance rather than a money valuation of that performance. Specific performance was traditionally an equitable remedy, an in personam order requiring the defendant to perform. As an equitable remedy it was subject to the supposed rule that equity would deny relief if the legal remedy was adequate.[46] Under this regime, specific performance was most often used to enforce contracts to convey land, for which it was thought that money could be no substitute.[47] It has been used in other kinds of cases, but probably more sparingly.[48] Changing attitudes among the bar, or changing perceptions about the adequacy rule, may lead to broader availability of specific performance as a remedy in the future.[49]

Equitable discretion and equitable defenses. Because specific performance grew out of equity, that remedy might be denied in the chancellor's discretion. Special concerns for hardship, inequitable conduct, and even unfair provisions of the contract might lead a chancellor to deny specific performance,[50] even though, at least theoretically, damages would still be available.[51] Equity courts also insisted at one time on "mutuality" of remedy, denying specific performance to a deserving plaintiff if they thought the defendant—in the event of a hypothetical breach by the plaintiff—would be denied specific relief. The doctrine is applied much less rigorously today, but it may still have important effects on the way the specific performance decree is written.[52]

The chancellor may also deny the specific performance remedy for reasons of practicability rather than fairness or hardship. For example, courts have sometimes said that they would not order specific performance of contracts that would require long continued supervision by the court; and on this ground have often denied specific performance of building contracts.[53] It is, however, a matter of degree and the practical problem must be balanced against the urgency of the need for relief.[54]

Equitable conversion based on specific performability. Because specific performance was almost routinely granted at the behest of the purchaser in land cases, equity courts thought of the land contract in a special way. They treated the promise to convey as equivalent to a conveyance in the eyes of equity. The general idea found expression in the doctrine of "equitable conversion."[55] The idea has a common sense root, but some exotic and even bizarre flowers. At root the idea is similar to the notion that when one deposits a paycheck in the bank, one "has the money," even though the bank may not actually credit the account for several days. The equitable conversion doctrine, however, in treating the land as if it were already conveyed, sometimes put the burden of a fire loss on the purchaser, even though the vendor had not in fact conveyed; in the eyes of equity, the land was already owned by the buyer, and the owner bears the loss.[56] The equitable conversion doctrine produced other, somewhat similar results, all of which turned on the idea that in land cases, specific performance was routinely available. Equitable conversion can also have strange effects on restitutionary recoveries.[57]

Security for Performance: Liens

Security as remedy. Many consensual arrangements provide one of the parties some kind of security as a guarantee of performance. For instance, a lender might require the borrower to execute a mortgage of property as security for the debt. When the contract does not provide for security, the non-breaching party may often claim a kind of equitable security interest in any tangible property involved and enforce his claims against that security. The paragraphs below illustrate some of the other ways in which security interests may be enforced and some of the remedial options that may result when such interests are established and suggest other sections for additional detail.

Mechanic's and materialman's lien. Perhaps the most familiar instance is the mechanic's or materialman's lien. That is the lien of the contractor or supplier whose work or labor has gone to construct improvements on the land of another. Statutes commonly give various subcontractors, suppliers and workers a lien against the improved land to secure their right of payment for work done. The most striking element of this lien is that it may run in favor of a subcontractor who contracted only with a general contractor. The landowner, whose only contract is with the general contract, may thus indirectly incur liability to the subcontractor. This in turn leads to further legal arrangements to protect the landowner against having to pay twice.[58]

Liens for the vendor and purchaser of land. If the non-breaching party is given a security interest, it is an interest in the property subject to the contract. Sometimes it is an interest in the property the defendant contracted to transfer. Sometimes it is an interest in the property the plaintiff contracted to transfer. For instance, a purchaser of real property who takes title to the property may discover grounds for avoiding the transaction and recovering the price he has paid. In such a case, he may have a lien on the property conveyed to him to secure his restitutionary right.[59] If a vendor of real property conveys title before all the purchase price is paid, the vendor may have an implied lien on the property so conveyed to secure full payment.[60]

Dealing in the property for the breacher's account. Other forms of security may be seen in cases of landlords and installment land contract sellers. If the tenant abandons a lease, the landlord may traditionally demand that the tenant continue to pay rent until the term is completed. To secure his right to the rent, the landlord may lease the premises to others "for the tenant's account." That is, the landlord is exercising a kind of security interest in the property, holding any payments received to apply to the tenant's rent obligation.[61] This is a kind of indirect specific performance with the income from the lease applied to the payments owed by the tenant.

Options and issues. The possibility of proceeding against security may open remedial options, strategy choices, and legal issues. Using the landlord-tenant example to stand for other cases as well, consider the possible strategies of the landlord when the tenant abandons the premises and refuses to pay further rent: (1) The landlord may insist on full payment of all rents, but re-let the premises for the tenant's account, crediting the tenant with any rents paid by a new tenant. (2) The landlord may terminate the lease as a remedy for the tenant's breach. This releases the tenant of any responsibility for future rent and leaves the landlord free to use the property as he likes. If he re-lets the property to another tenant, the new rents belong to the landlord, not the tenant. (3) The landlord may seek to make the best of both worlds by terminating the lease and re-letting, holding the tenant responsible if the new rent is less than that owed by the tenant but keeping any gain made if the new rent is greater.

The most central and pertinent issue raised by cases similar to the landlord-tenant example is whether the non-breaching party can claim a security interest and also claim to use the property for his own account— that is, claim the right to a deficiency when the substitute transaction falls short, but keep the gain when the substitute transaction is a good one.[62] Solutions vary not only with the jurisdiction but with the factual setting. In the landlord's case, some jurisdictions permit the landlord of a commercial tenant to have the best-of-both-worlds remedies, recovering a deficiency as needed but keeping the gain from a re-letting if there is any.[63] When the tenant is a residential tenant instead, the courts may be quick to treat any act by the landlord as a flat termination, eliminating any further liability of the tenant.

The same general kind of issue arises in installment land sales. In such cases the vendor keeps title to the land and thus has security by title. After the purchaser has made some of the payments, he defaults. Some courts in effect say that the security—the land—and the retained payments together constitute the whole remedy: no deficiency judgment is available.[64]

The same general issue can also arise in sales-of-goods cases. In a New York sales case the Court of Appeals divided on an issue of security.[65] The buyer contracted to receive goods by a specified date. As the seller knew, time was of the essence because the buyer had a forward contract to sell the goods in Baghdad. When it appeared that the delivery would be late, the buyer purchased new substitute goods elsewhere, but the substitute goods cost $700,000 more than the originals—in effect, leaving the buyer with a "deficiency." When the seller's goods arrived late the buyer did not reject them, even though it had already purchased substitute goods. It had prepaid the price of the original contract goods and it was afraid to reject them, because that would leave it with neither the purchase money nor the goods. Several months later, it sold the contract goods for a price some $450,000 more than it had paid the seller. Since the buyer had purchased substitute goods and had a good damages claim for the increased cost of those goods, it might seem that the buyer's interest in the late-delivered goods could only be a security interest. That would mean he could trade in the goods for the account of the seller, giving the seller a credit against his liability for any gains received by selling the goods. A majority of the Court, however, was willing to permit the buyer to buy substitute goods and charge the seller with their added cost and to treat the late-delivered goods as its own. With some adjustments to account for other figures, this permitted the buyer to recover the $700,000 added costs of substitute goods without crediting the seller for gains made on the late-delivered goods.[66]

Recognition of a security interest, or even the possibility of one, immediately creates new issues and requires that all of the options be expressly considered, both by lawyers planning remedial strategy and by courts adjudicating remedial limits.

§ 12.1(2) Policy and Practicality in Selecting and Measuring Contract Remedies

Contract Policy and Remedial Outlook

The values of enforcement. Within limits, enforcement of promises by some measure is itself a legally recognized good. Unless the parties' agreement is impeached by fraud, unconscionability, or illegality, enforcement of the promise by its own terms, no more, no less, is a way of respecting the parties as autonomous human beings. In addition, enforcement of promises probably encourages efficient economic activity to the benefit of the community generally.[1]

65. Fertico Belgium S.A. v. Phosphate Chemicals Export Ass'n, Inc., 70 N.Y.2d 76, 517 N.Y.S.2d 465, 510 N.E.2d 334 (1987).

§ 12.1(2)

1. Among many economic writings, see Richard Posner, Economic Analysis of Law § 4.8 (3d ed 1986).

Contract policy affecting remedial attitudes. The measure of enforcement one deems appropriate may vary, not only with the facts of cases, but with the policy one finds in contract law. Moral analysis of contract, grounded on promise, consent and autonomy of the contracting parties,[2] may yield, at least for some thinkers, a different measure of relief from an economic analysis that is grounded in either efficiency or distributional concerns. One's outlook is likely to vary considerably depending on whether one emphasizes the contract's pragmatic effect as an allocation of price and supply risks between the parties[3] or the contract's importance in imparting information about the future and encouraging future promises.[4]

Relational contracts. The view that contracts mainly establish a framework or relationship, within which the parties must and do make many adjustments as circumstances change,[6] is at odds with the view that contracts mainly allocate particular risks such as risks of price change or supply. Some writers have suggested that remedies are in fact adjusted by courts in a way that reflects at least some acceptance of the relational contract viewpoint. If this is correct, then fairness-as-judged by the particular promise may sometimes be less important than the relationship as a whole. The contract is assimilated to a narrow and limited version of a joint enterprise, in which the best economic results will be achieved if the parties cooperate both in the performance and in making adjustments when breach occurs or is imminent.[7]

This viewpoint affects how one thinks about many particular remedial problems, such as those that arise in the rules for minimizing damages[8] or how one measures restitution for extra work in a building contract,[9] or what remedies should be devised when performance becomes impossible but one party has expended money in partial performance.[10] It is pervasively different from the traditional outlooks; in supporting a more flexible ap-

---

2. See C. Fried, Contract as Promise (1981); Barnett, A Consent Theory of Contract, 86 Colum.L.Rev. 269 (1986).

3. Most writings recognize the risk-allocating function of contracts. The parties provide in the contract for many future contingencies. See A. Polinsky, An Introduction to Law and Economics 25 (1983). Of the future contingencies, change in cost or value of performance are often high on the list. Most contracts implicitly deal with at least some price risks. Much of the writing deals with the fact that the parties cannot anticipate every future contingency nor allocate every conceivable risk, so that legal rules are necessary as a kind of default setting, else some non-legal forms of adjustment must be made. See Goetz & Scott, Principles of Relational Contracts, 67 Va. L.Rev. 1089 (1981).

4. Goetz & Scott, Enforcing Promises: An Examination of the Basis of Contract, 89 Yale L.J. 1261 (1980) (treating promise as "information" about the future, on the basis of which the recipient is able to engage appropriately "adaptive behavior").

6. See among many writing, Macneil, Contracts: Adjustments of Long-Term Economic Relations under Classical, Neoclassical, and Relational Contract Law, 72 Nw.L.Rev. 854 (1978); Symposium, Law, Private Governance and Continuing Relationships, 1985 Wis. L.Rev. 461 (1985); Hillman, Court Adjustment of Long-Term Contracts: An Analysis under Modern Contract Law, 1987 Duke L.J. 1 (1987).

7. See, e.g., Goetz & Scott, The Mitigation Principle: Toward a General Theory of Contractual Obligation, 69 Va.L.Rev. 967 (1983) (seeking rules to minimize joint costs when breach occurs or is threatened, by "cooperative readjustments by both parties" in some cases); Harrison, A Case for Loss Sharing, 56 So.Cal.L.Rev. 573, 585 (1983) (analogizing to partnership, both partnership and contract law seek "to foster the sharing of a jointly created surplus").

8. See Goetz & Scott, The Mitigation Principle: Toward a General Theory of Contractual Obligation, 69 Va.L.Rev. 967 (1983).

9. Galligan, Extra Work in Construction Cases: Restitution, Relationship, and Revision, 63 Tulane L.Rev. 799 (1989); § 12.20(2) below.

10. See § 13.3(2) below.

proach to contract obligations, it potentially affects a wide range of remedial issues.[11] Perhaps the relational and cooperative viewpoint reflects a shift in American commercial activity from the emphasis on risk-taking enterprisers to efficiency-capturing managers. But rescissionary remedies remind us that there must remain situations in which the freedom to get out of a relationship will be more important than the gains to be captured by remaining in an unwanted relationship.[12]

Rigorous enforcement attitudes. At the opposite end of the spectrum is the view that contracts must be fully enforced, and exactly as written—that specific performance should be granted in every case in which it is sought if it is practical to do so. The most insistent version of this view is derived from economic thought,[13] but the same idea might be based on an unyielding "moral" view of contract as well.[14]

Economic considerations. Economic concerns may substantially affect contract remedies. Courts and writers have advanced these economic ideas: (1) Contract remedies should promote economic efficiency in performance[15] and should encourage economic actors to make the economically desirable promises.[16] (2) Contract remedies should not require economic waste.[17] (3) Contract remedies should permit or even encourage at least some efficient breach of contract—that is, permit or encourage breach when the breach is so productive that the breacher can pay all the victim's damages and still profit from the breach.[18] (4) Contract remedies should promote efficient

---

11. Thus, consistent with preserving the economic relationship, the court in Oglebay Norton Co. v. Armco, Inc., 52 Ohio St.3d 232, 556 N.E.2d 515 (1990) ordered the parties to a long-term shipping contract with a high level of mutual dependence to negotiate prices after major shifts in the market and the failure of the primary pricing mechanisms specified in the contract. In other cases, an increased emphasis on "cure" of defective performance and on legal rules promoting renegotiation of the contract when breach occurs may demonstrate a greater respect for the business relationship as a whole. See Hillman, Keeping the Deal Together After Material Breach—Common Law Mitigation Rules, The UCC, And The Restatement (Second) of Contracts, 47 U.Colo.L.Rev. 553 (1976); Sebert, Rejection, Revocation, and Cure under Article 2 of the Uniform Commercial Code: Some Modest Proposals, 84 Nw.L.Rev. 375 (1990). Although some of these examples are nominally substantive rather than remedial, even those also operate to expand means of minimizing damages. See § 12.6(2) below. Or they may require adjustments in the remedial scheme; for example, if the deal is enforced in spite of small defects in performance, it may be necessary to allow damages for those defects. See Sebert, supra, 84 Nw.L.Rev. 375, 431.

12. This is most obviously true of personal service contracts. See § 12.22(2) below. In those cases more than others, the analogy is to marriage. See McKnight v. General Motors

Corporation, 908 F.2d 104 (7th Cir.1990) (an industrial equivalent of matrimonial squabbles). Preserving some relationships, including some that are not purely personal, may thus move in the wrong direction where freedom is important.

13. Alan Schwartz, The Case for Specific Performance, 89 Yale L.J. 271 (1979).

14. Cf. C. Fried, Contract as Promise 117–18 and n. 7 (1981).

15. See Cooter & Eisenberg, Damages for Breach of Contract, 73 Cal.L.Rev. 1432, 1468 (1985) (summarizing detailed analysis).

18. See R. Posner, Economic Analysis of Law § 4.8 (3d ed 1986); Birmingham, Breach of Contract, Damages Measures, and Economic Efficiency, 24 Rutg.L.Rev. 273 (1973); Birmingham, Damages Measures and Economic Rationality: The Geometry of Contract Law, 1969 Duke L.J. 49; Birmingham, Notes on the Reliance Interest, 60 Wash.L.Rev. 217 (1985); Goetz & Scott, Liquidated Damages, Penalties and the Just Compensation Principle: Some Notes on an Enforcement Model and a Theory of Efficient Breach, 77 Colum.L.Rev. 554 (1977). See, on counting costs and benefits of remedies, § 1.9 above. It is suggested in § 12.22(2) below that a social corollary of efficient breach recognizes that freedom of the breacher is itself a social good, so that if the breacher values freedom (from a personal services contract, for example), he should not be forced to continue a relationship.

investment in reliance on the contract promises.[19]

The efficient breach idea in particular has been a powerful force in thinking about contract remedies, among courts [20] as well as among academic commentators.[21] The idea works properly, however, only if all of the damages due the plaintiff from the breach are in fact recoverable under the legal rules, and some damages may not be recoverable because they cannot be proven.[22] In addition to this problem, there is a question whether the breaching defendant should retain all the gain or "surplus" resulting from the breach. It is possible to imagine that all the desirable efficient breaches would take place if, when the breach-opportunity is presented, the defendant renegotiated with the plaintiff to escape the contract obligation by paying damages and sharing some of the surplus. This idea in turn has created a literature concerned with the possibility that renegotiation costs will be so high that at least some efficient breaches would be discouraged.[23]

It is also possible to accept the efficient breach idea for contracts among enterprisers while rejecting the idea in some consumer contracts.[24] Likewise the frequent suggestion that the efficient breach idea is "immoral" because it is morally wrong to breach promises,[25] might be a good criticism in some cases but not others. Not all contracting parties believe the deal is to keep all promises no matter what. Given the fact that most contracts have not traditionally been enforced by specific performance, parties must often understand that the promise simply requires either performance or payment of damages. In such a case the efficient breach idea is not necessarily "immoral" and at least conceivably it may encourage the "right number" of breaches unless practical constraints on damages assessment undercut the idea. Indeed, if the parties themselves understand that they are free to breach and pay damages, it would be "immoral" to impose specific performance.

On the other hand efficient breach ideas may not solve particular cases or point unerringly to a single remedy.[26] Some economists suggest that rules obtaining the right amount of efficient breach may not obtain the right amount of efficient reliance investment or vice versa.[27] Others have doubted the values or assumptions of economic analysis.[28] Economic ideas may affect remedial thinking in the courts, but they are not the only ideas in play.[29]

Remedial Purposes and Limits

Practical constraints. All remedial principles and purposes may be limited in their operation by practical constraints. Only so much judicial

19. See A. Polinsky, An Introduction to Law and Economics, 32–36 (1983).

23. See, reviewing literature and argument, Craswell, Contract Remedies, Renegotiation, and the Theory of Efficient Breach, 61 S.Cal.L.Rev. 629 (1988).

24. See Farber, Reassessing the Economic Efficiency of Compensatory Damages for Breach of Contract, 66 Va.L.Rev. 1443, 1444 (1980).

25. Cf. Marschall, Willfulness: A Crucial Factor in Choosing Remedies for Breach of Contract, 24 Ariz.L.Rev. 733 (1982).

26. See Mather, Restitution as a Remedy for Breach of Contract: The Case of the Partially Performing Seller, 92 Yale L.J. 14 (1982).

27. See *Polinsky,* supra n. 19.

28. E.g., Harrison, Egoism, Altruism, and Market Illusions: The Limits of Law and Economics, 33 U.C.L.A.L.Rev. 1309 (1986).

29. See also § 1.9 above.

time can be used to investigate the precise losses suffered or the gains received from a contract breach. The evidence available, time and effort required to make proof, doubts about the inferences to be drawn from the proof actually offered in court—all these things play a role in conventionalizing contract remedies, especially contract damages. So contract remedies often furnish only a stylized representation of actual loss, not a perfect image.[30]

Contracting purposes. All of these considerations operate in a complex contracting world. Contracts are made for vastly different purposes—to acquire an investment, as where one buys shares of stock; to obtain capital goods for the production of income, as where one buys a machine for a factory; to procure inventory for trade or manufacture, as where one buys flour for resale at retail or flour in bulk for making bread at a bakery; to secure personal wants as an end-use consumer, as where one buys a computer game for entertainment. Sometimes purposes are combined, as where one buys a home as an end-user, but expecting appreciation in value to guarantee a comfortable retirement.

It is probably undesirable to fashion remedies by attempting to guess exactly what the plaintiff would have done if she had received the defendant's performance. Yet the general purposes of the contract cannot be ignored in framing remedies. If you are buying a home you would ordinarily be entitled to specific performance; if you were buying the same property for resale, specific performance might still be a good remedy, but if there were reasons to deny it, the court might feel free to do so. If you order red tile for resale in your retail store, you might have little loss if the seller delivered blue tile instead; but if you order red tile for your own kitchen and blue tile is installed instead, your loss might be very different. In both examples, the understood purpose of your contract would help the court know what remedy is most appropriate.

Subjective vs. objective measurement. The difference in the parties' purposes in contracting is highlighted at the remedies stage if the court must consider a remedy that will protect the plaintiff's non-monetary interests by a subjective measure of damages. If the plaintiff contracts to purchase a Picasso painting or a prize pig, he can reasonably claim that his personal satisfaction at owning or admiring such works of art and nature has value to him not represented by the market value of either. The courts have clearly found it useful to measure damages objectively, by market value in many such cases. At the same time, market measures do not always reflect what courts consider to be "compensation." Some commentators have increasingly favored protection of highly subjective interests in contract, through increased awards of consequential damages, or mental anguish, or punitive damages for breach.[31]

Type of breach. Appropriate remedies are affected not only by such general purposes in contracting, but also by the different ways in which breach may occur. The remedial setting created by non-delivery of promised goods is quite different from the remedial setting created by defective

---

31. Sebert, Punitive and Nonpecuniary Damages in Actions Based upon Contract: Toward Achieving the Objective of Full Compensation, 33 U.C.L.A.L.Rev. 1565 (1986). See §§ 12.2(4), 12.5 below.

performance of a home-building contract. The possible remedies for non-delivery of goods would seldom raise the possibility that performance already rendered must be destroyed; a possible remedy for defective building might be based upon destruction of the performance already rendered and the economic loss that such a destruction could entail. Breach of a contract to sell for investment or a contract to sell for trade in the market strongly suggests a market measure of damages. Delay in providing goods used in income production suggests the possibility of such different remedies as rental value for the delay period, interest, or lost profits.

Economic setting. The economic setting in which the contract is made or performed may be remedially significant as well. In estimating remedies it may be important to know in some cases whether the contract deals with goods in a competitive market or in one that is only imperfectly competitive and how, economically speaking, breach victims adjust to breach.[32]

Remedial implications. For many observers, some of these diverse considerations of substance and remedy converge to suggest that some form of expectancy recovery is an appropriate measure of contract enforcement,[33] although observers favor either a greater[34] or a more limited remedy.[35] Where the liability is derived from promise alone, without a basis in tort, the implication is that the remedy should be limited to the kinds of harms or losses the defendant guaranteed against,[36] and that the scope of the promise or guarantee should be judged less by purely formal words and more by the business culture and setting; but thinkers who emphasize what is "right" rather than what is agreed upon, may favor wider liabilities. On the other hand, different philosophies, policies and outlooks do not necessarily lead to different remedial conclusions. Respect for the parties' agreement as an expression of their joint autonomy suggests that liquidated damages clauses and agreed-upon specific performance clauses should be enforced, but economic analysis might result in the same conclusion.[37]

So the diversity and complexity of policy, facts and attitudes has ultimate impact on remedies. That very diversity and complexity suggest that it is important to keep simple and central guidelines like compensation and practicality in sight. The same complexity suggests that such guidelines cannot fully determine appropriate remedies in particular cases without consideration of more particular settings, policies and practicalities.

(1) MONEY REMEDIES

§ 12.2 Damages to Compensate for Expectancy

§ 12.2(1) Expectancy and Compensation Generally

General Rules of Expectation Damages

A rough rule. In general, expectation damages for a complete breach of contract attempt to give the plaintiff the difference between the price he was to pay and the value he was to get from performance, with a return of any part of the price he has already paid, and with additions for certain collateral or consequential damages, and reductions for damages that were or could reasonably have been avoided.[1]

A buy-sell contract. Seller agrees to sell and Buyer agrees to buy a particular load of steel, price $100,000. On the date for delivery, Seller refuses to deliver. On that date the market value of equivalent steel in the same quantity is $110,000. The buyer can recover $10,000 as his market damages, plus properly established collateral damages such as any costs he may incur in delay as a result of the seller's breach.[2] Subject to some special variations, a similar result would be reached if Seller were selling real property instead of a commodity.[3]

A services contract. An executive contracts with a corporation for employment for two years as vice-president in charge of sales, with a base salary of $200,000 annually. At the end of one year the corporation terminates her employment in breach of contract (but not in violation of any statute). The executive is unable to find substitute employment for six months. She then finds comparable employment paying $180,000 annually. The executive is entitled to recover $110,000. This represents the $100,000 salary loss during the six months plus the salary reduction suffered in the substitute for the remaining six months of her contract period. She is also entitled to any properly proven consequential damages, such as any special costs of seeking substitute employment.[4]

Although these two illustrations indicate the general attitude about contract damages, they do not reflect the fact that contracts come in all sizes and colors. The general rule and the illustrative models can be applied to other kinds of cases and to help flesh out details of computation only when the general aims of expectation damages, and the practicalities that limit them, are also understood.

Compensation as a Goal

The goal of "compensation". The traditional goal in awarding damages for breach of contract is to provide "compensation" for the breach victim, not merely reliance loss,[5] restitution,[6] or nominal damages.[7] The goal is to avoid either overcompensation or undercompensation.

Putting plaintiff in the performance position. Subject to limitations on damages that the parties themselves provide or assume,[8] the contract idea of money[9] compensation has been to award a sum that will put the plaintiff as a nonbreaching party in as good a position as he would have been in had the contract been performed,[10] and no better.[11] The objective is not to put the plaintiff in the position he would have been in with no contract at all,[12] but instead to give him the benefit of the bargain he in fact made, that is, the "profit" or gain the plaintiff would have made upon performance. Particular "rules" or formulas for computing damages should be read flexibly, in the light of the general goal.[13]

Defining "compensation". Although the law aims at compensation in a general way, some writers have thought that the law systematically undercompensates contract-breach plaintiffs.[14] Whether this is the case depends

---

§ 12.2(1)

1. Cf. Restatement Second of Contract § 347 (1981). The Restatement's formula would give the plaintiff the "loss in the value to him of the other party's performance," but this appears to state a subjective measure that will not always apply.

in part on how you define "compensation" and whether you think there are other remedial goals that must be accommodated.[15] If "compensation" means a sum of money necessary to place the plaintiff in the same financial position as full performance, no more and no less,[16] then indeed it is likely that many breach victims are undercompensated, if for no other reason than because some losses cannot be proven adequately.

Compensation, with its connotation of corrective justice, might instead be taken to mean the amount of money necessary to put the plaintiff in the rightful contract position, but not necessarily the full performance position. Under this conception of compensation, the plaintiff must be awarded damages only (a) with respect to those losses against which the contract was meant to guarantee (that is, those in the contemplation of the parties),[18] and (b) with respect to those losses that caused by the breach and are provable in amount.[19] This means that compensation might be understood *not* to require payments of losses that were not reasonably proven or those that were not guaranteed by the contract. Because the price of the contract is likely to go up as the promisor assumes greater risks of loss, and to go down as the promisor assumes smaller risks of loss, damages will be compensatory if they reflect the kinds of losses the plaintiff paid the defendant to assume. This would exclude losses the parties did not contemplate.

Practical limits on the compensation goal. In any event it is probably fair to say that the law does not aim to give the plaintiff a perfect substitute for full performance. Damages estimates are almost always imprecise and are conditioned by practical limitations of proof and understanding. Conventions are used which sometimes undercompensate and sometimes overcompensate. Damages remedies are default remedies provided by the law, but subject to limits the parties themselves choose. Because the parties can control the contract provisions, including some of the damages provisions, it may not be necessary or desirable to attempt perfect compensation. In line with this, the overall aim of the cases seems to be to find an approximately right and reasonably usable legal rule of damages, which the parties may modify if they choose. The goal of compensation should probably be understood in this light.

§ 12.2(2) Market Value vs. Cost Expectancy Measures

Market and Cost Measures of Expectancy

Market measures. In the contract setting, the market measure allows the breach victim to recover the market value of the very performance he should have had, less the contract price. If a seller commits a total breach, the buyer would recover the market value of the property contracted for, less the contract price. For example, if the seller contracts to sell land for $10,000, but when performance is due the land is worth $15,000, the buyer would be entitled to recover $5,000 under the market-contract differential measure.[5] The buyer will be able to show damages under this measure whenever he can show a contract price less than market value at the relevant time and place. The relevant time is almost always the date when performance was due,[6] even in cases of anticipatory repudiation.[7] The relevant place is usually where the seller's performance was due.[8] A limited degree of flexibility in the contract-market differential is sometimes achieved by varying the date or place for determining the market price where special circumstances call for it.[9]

When the tables are turned and the buyer commits a total breach, the same principle applies to the seller's damages claims, but the seller shows damages by showing that the contract price is *greater than* the market value on the relevant date.[10]

Market measures are applied in chattel sales contracts (subject to some special rules of the UCC),[11] real estate sales,[12] and to analogous single-shot market transactions.[13]

Conventions in market measures. Market measures tend to be conventional. That is, they do not always appear to be accurate measurements of the plaintiff's subjective loss, but they seem to be allowed as a kind of minimum damage award, usually with no requirement that the plaintiff minimize damages. In addition, market measures are usually applied without counting any transaction costs that might be entailed in buying or selling in the market. In the most obvious contrast, special or consequential damages will almost always be reduced if the plaintiff should have minimized the consequential damages[14] and all manner of transaction costs will be considered in coming to a net consequential damages figure.[15]

Cost measures. A cost measure would award the plaintiff the cost of obtaining substitute performance and in some instances might limit the plaintiff to such an award if it is less than the market-based award. One common law example is the case in which a builder contracts to build or repair a structure on the plaintiff's land. If the performance is incomplete or defective, a market measure can be used to give the landowner the difference between the value of the land-and-building as contracted for and the value as received. Quite frequently, however, landowners may wish to contract with another builder to repair or replace the defective work. The reasonable costs of such substitute performance, is usually an alternative measure of the landowner's damages in such cases,[16] with accounting adjustments to reflect any savings to the landowner resulting from the breach.[17]

In chattel purchase cases the buyer is specifically permitted by the UCC to claim the cost of any cover actually made—that is, the cost of purchasing commercially reasonable substitute goods.[18] Similarly, the chattel seller is permitted a cost measure based on his losses on resale.[19]

Although in many instances these cost measures may yield the same recovery as a market measure, they do not always do so. Some of the cases in which market and cost measure produce different results are sketched in the following paragraphs.

How Market and Cost Measures May Yield Different Awards

Market measures might yield either more or less than cost measures of damages, both in contract and in tort cases. The choice between these measures becomes clearer when some of the specific differences can be identified.

(1) Measurement date: rising cost of substitute performance. One situation in which market and cost measures will yield different awards occurs when the price of performance is rising or falling. Market-contract differen-

tial damages are usually computed as of the date for performance.[20] The cost of substitute performance, on the other hand, may be measured by the reasonable costs incurred, which is likely to be at a date after the original performance was due. If prices rise after the defendant breaches and before substitute performance can be obtained, damages would be higher under a substitute-performance standard than under the market-contract differential. If prices fall in the same period, however, damages would be higher under a market-contract differential.

(2) Acceptable similar but different substitute performance under UCC. Another situation in which market and cost measures will yield different awards occurs when the substitute performance is not literally the same performance. On some occasions under the UCC,[21] when a seller breaches a contract to sell goods, the buyer may base his damages claim on the added costs of "cover." Cover is the purchase of a commercially reasonable substitute for the promised performance. The substitute might function in the same way as the contract goods but might be physically different and might actually cost more. Since the substitute need not be physically identical, it is easy to see why it might cost more or less than the original performance. If the substitute costs more but nevertheless counts as a substitute, an award based on the cost of the substitute would be higher than an award based on the market value of the original performance.[22] If the substitute costs a great deal more than the promised performance, it may not qualify as a commercially reasonable substitute at all.

(3) Substitute performance at less than market price. In some instances, the victim of a breach appears to have a loss as measured by market damages, but is in fact able to obtain alternative performance at the original contract price. For example, if the buyer's contract price is $100 and market value is $110 after seller breaches, market damages are $10. But the buyer may nevertheless find a bargain in the same or substitute goods for the original $100 price. Such bargains in market goods are not very likely, first because the seller of substitute goods is likely to raise his price to the market, and second because we tend to form an opinion about what the market value is from actual sales prices. However, enterprising actors do find bargains. If the buyer actually found a bargain at a below market price, and if damages were measured by the cost of substitute performance, the buyer would have no damages award (other than incidental damages); the defendant, not the buyer, would get the fruits of the bargain. Whether the buyer in such an example should be denied market damages may be a difficult question. The buyer in such a case might, for example, have gained the advantages of the second deal even if the defendant had not breached. If so, to limit recovery may be to deny him enterprise opportunities.[23] Whatever the answer, however, the facts illustrate one reason why a cost and market measure may work differently.

(4) Repair-replacement with destruction of existing work as a substitute performance. Another situation might occur when the defendant delivers performance that is equal in market value to the performance called for in the contract but is not actually identical, as where a builder uses red tile in the bathrooms of a home built to specification when the plans called for blue tile. If the defective performance constitutes a breach, the market measure might yield a zero award: a house with red-tiled bathrooms is likely to be as

valuable in the real estate market as a house with blue-tiled bathrooms. The cost of substitute performance, however, may be substantial, since it will require removal of the red tile and an installation of the blue tile.[24]

(5) Idiosyncratic values. The plaintiff's preference for blue tile in the preceding illustration suggests another and similar problem. The plaintiff may contract for performance that would not add to the plaintiff's assets. Landowners frequently seem to contract for features in buildings or for landscaping work that adds nothing to the land's value. If the contractor builds a building to specifications except that the work omits an oddly shaped and ugly window, the work done may have as much value in the real estate market as the work called for by the contract. If so, the market-contract differential measure will give the landowner nothing. The cost of completing performance, however, might be quite substantial. Such a case resembles the red tile/blue tile case, except that it does not actually entail destruction of economic values.

Choosing Between Market and Cost Measures

Cost measures not invariably available at the plaintiff's option. The plaintiff will usually be permitted to choose the market measure if that suits him. Is the cost of substitute performance treated in the same way, always available if the plaintiff wishes? The answer seems to be no. Cost of substitute performance must be justified on the ground that it is less than the market measure, or that it is likely to provide an accurate measure of the expectancy or that it is specifically authorized by statute. Even if the cost measure is an accurate measure of expectancy, courts often express the view that the cost measure cannot be used to yield an award disproportionate to the market measure.[30] The reasons for this apparently different treatment of the cost measure lies in the problems that measure sometimes engenders.

"Economic waste" and associated dilemmas. Not all cases of substitute performance raise the possibility of economic waste, but some of them may do so. When the substitute performance requires destruction of the original performance or the values it produces, courts often concern themselves with the economic waste that can result. An example is the red tile vs. blue tile bathroom. An award of damages based on the cost of removing the red tile and installing blue tile might lead the aggrieved plaintiff to destroy the red tile even though home buyers generally would pay as much for the house with red as with blue tile. This would be economically wasteful. As Professor Farnsworth has pointed out, however, the award of damages on such a basis does not necessarily lead to actual destruction. The homeowner might keep the red tile and regard the damages award as a sufficient compensation for the aesthetic offense.[31]

Windfall or compensation? But if the homeowner does not redress his aesthetic offense by the economically wasteful act of destroying the old tile, then courts must wonder whether the aesthetic offense really exists, whether

§ 12.2(2)

30. E.g., Keppel v. BaRoss Builders, Inc., 7 Conn.App. 435, 509 A.2d 51 (1986); Anchor Coatings, Inc. v. Marine Industrial Residential Insulation, Inc., 490 So.2d 1210 (Miss.1986); Mathis v. Glover, 714 S.W.2d 222 (Mo.App. 1986) (none limiting the plaintiff's cost recovery on the facts).

31. E.A. Farnsworth, III Farnsworth on Contracts § 12.13, p. 238 (1990).

protection of the homeowner's aesthetics was a part of the real bargain of the parties, whether the aesthetic offense is appropriately measured by cost of destruction and replacement, and whether the difference between cost to the defendant and gain to the plaintiff puts the plaintiff in too good a strategic position in the litigation.[32] So there is a risk in at least some cases of either economic waste or of overcompensation. Because it is *only* a risk, courts must consider each case on its own facts. The result is a guideline rather than a bright-line rule: the cost of replacement in such cases may be awarded if necessary for compensation, provided it is not unreasonably disproportionate to the loss as measured by the market measure.[33] On the other hand, if the property is used solely for income production and the breach does not affect the property's value or the income it produces, a recovery of large sums to provide substitute performance is likely to be windfall or waste.[34]

Added benefits or useful life from substitute performance. In many cases the plaintiff who obtains substituted performance at a higher cost is not better off by reason of that performance.[35] But in other cases the plaintiff who obtains the cost of substituted performance is indeed better off than if the defendant had not breached. *For example:* a builder provides a defective roof on the plaintiff's business building. Five years later the defect becomes apparent and a new roof is required. The new roof—the substitute—will last twenty years. The original roof would have lasted twenty years if it had not been defective. If the damages award is the cost of the new roof, the result will be that the plaintiff is better off than if there were no breach. The plaintiff in such a case will have twenty-five years of roofing when he was only entitled to a 20–year roof under the contract. This is a problem that does not arise under market value tests.[36] However, the overcompensation raised by use of substitute performance measures in such a case can be addressed in some cases by an adjustment in the damages to reflect the appreciated value the plaintiff would get. So if the new (substitute) roof costs $20,000 and will last twenty years, five of which the plaintiff is not entitled to, a reduction in the plaintiff's award of approximately $5,000 is appropriate.[37] In other cases it is hard to know how much adjustment to make or whether to make any at all.[38]

Determining what counts as a substitute performance. In some cases, a third problem may arise when the cost of substitute performance is sought. It may not be reasonably possible to determine what counts as a substitute

34. See Crisman v. Stidd, 396 Pa.Super. 335, 578 A.2d 542 (1990) (tenant's alteration to premises, restoration costs would be $18,000, cost of putting premises in condition to produce same income would be $3,000, damages limited to latter sum).

35. If the plaintiff is purchasing goods for use as components in a product it manufactures, for example, the defendant's breach may drive the plaintiff to purchase substitute goods at a higher price, but the substitute may not affect the price the plaintiff can charge for the manufactured product. So the recovery of substitute-performance damages does not per-

mit the plaintiff to be better off than it would have been had the defendant performed.

38. See, St. Joseph's Hospital v. Corbetta Const. Co., 21 Ill.App.3d 925, 316 N.E.2d 51 (1974) (liability for added costs not reflected in added value); Handicapped Children's Education Bd. of Sheboygan County v. Lukaszewski, 112 Wis.2d 197, 332 N.W.2d 774 (1983) (after employee breached, employer had to hire better qualified employee at higher salary but did not want the "excess" qualifications, employer could recover full added cost). Some of these problems are analyzed in connection with "cover" under the UCC in § 12.-16(3).

for the contract performance. Defendant contracts to sell a quantity of wheat to the plaintiff, delivery in September. The defendant does not deliver and the plaintiff goes into the market and makes several purchases. The plaintiff pays different prices at different times as the market fluctuates. Which price is to be used in computing the added cost of getting substitute performance? Which purchase counts as the substitute purchase? Because any bushel of wheat is like any other of the same grade, there is little objective basis for determining that one purchase was and one was not the substitute performance. Any solutions will be conventional rather than precise.

Advantageous use of the cost measure. Although the cost measure is difficult and perhaps undesirable in some cases, in others it works extremely well. If the defendant has promised performance to be used in the plaintiff's business, the plaintiff may be able to minimize profit loss that would result from the breach if he promptly procures substitute performance elsewhere. In such a case the substitute performance cost may be the quickest, most convenient and most fair measure. It might also accord with the affirmative version of the avoidable consequences rule, which compensates for the cost of minimizing damages.[40] In the landowner-vs-builder cases, substitute performance may be the *only* practical redress if the landowner is in the role of a consumer such as a homeowner. In addition, in such cases the "market" is largely a construct, based on expert opinion and an amalgam of past sales and projections rather than a reality based on observations of many purchases.[41] So in the construction cases, use of the cost measure may be and is highly preferred.

§ 12.2(3) General vs. Special Measures of Expectancy

Expectancy Via General or Special Damages

Recovery of both general and special damages. Courts sometimes distinguish between "general" and "special" damages. In this context, special damages is also referred to as consequential damages and the terms are used interchangeably here. Either general or special damages might be used as measures of expectancy. In fact, both measures may be used in the same case to capture different elements of compensation. Readers of cases sometimes misunderstand this point because courts habitually refer to "the" measure of damages when they state a general damages measure. Yet to say that a general measure of damages is "the" measure does not ordinarily also mean that special damages are precluded.[1] On the contrary, both general and special damages may be recovered so long as the two measurements do not duplicate elements of the recovery and so long as the special damages do not run aground on the limitations imposed on them.

41. Market value is a construct or an imaginative emulation when the promised performance is not identical with substitutes. This is the case with land, for example. The same problem arises when there is in fact no regular market but only sporadic sales. The market measure may be useful even in such cases. Experts may be able to plausibly construct what a market would look like by examining sales of comparable land, for example, and by examining prices in similar contracts at different times with adjustments for known changes in price or demand. But the trial time necessary to do this and to permit appropriate counter demonstrations from adversaries does not approximate the time required to show stock prices on the New York Stock Exchange. Nor is the result so reliable.

Limitations on consequential or special damages. The rules impose three important limitations upon the recovery of consequential damages. *First,* special or consequential damages must ordinarily be pleaded and they must be proven with reasonable certainty.[2] *Second,* the plaintiff must make reasonable effort to minimize consequential damages (perhaps by seeking a substitute for the defendant's promised performance).[3] *Third,* the plaintiff cannot recover consequential damages at all unless those damages reflect the general kinds of harm against which the defendant's promise guaranteed.[4] This rule is often expressed as a rule that consequential damages are not recoverable unless they are within the contemplation of the parties at the time of contracting, or "foreseeable" to them.[5] These limitations usually have little or no direct application to general damages. One effect of this is that general damages are often easier to recover than special damages.

[*For discussion of the general-special distinction, consult §§ 3.3(3) & 3.3(4) above, and this section in the Practitioner Treatise edition.*]

Special or consequential damages: benefits that would have resulted from performance. In the present context,[12] consequential or "special" damages are not based on the capital or present value of the promised performance but upon benefits it can produce or losses that may be caused by its absence.[13] Usually these consequential benefits are somewhat peculiar to the plaintiff individually and therefore not well reflected in the market price for the commodity. In the usual case, the use of consequential damages measures means that the court is not measuring the plaintiff's net gain or loss in assets at a fixed date as it is with general damages. To renew the accounting metaphor, you could say that instead of a focus on the plaintiff's balance sheet, the consequential measure would suggest a focus on a profit and loss statement, but if so, it is one that covers an indefinite future as well as a certain past. The consequential damages measure emphasizes income or loss, or cash flow, including losses that may result far into the future. In certain cases the plaintiff will be entitled to have the expectancy recovery measured by an estimate of consequential damages.

Consequential damages illustrated. To see an example of consequential damages, suppose the defendant reneges on a promise to deliver a specified computer system for $150,000. The computer is worth $160,000. A general or market measure of damages would give the plaintiff an award in such a case, ($10,000). But suppose the plaintiff is unable to use the computer as planned to calculate factory production schedules for maximum efficiency. This in turn may cause a reduction in profits compared to those that would have been earned had the computer been available. Damages based on the market value of the computer will not compensate the plaintiff for the profits lost in this way. Nor would the general damages measure provide compensation for the added expense the plaintiff might suffer in hiring added workers to do customer billing by hand that the computer could do more efficiently. The added expense and the loss of profits are real losses not based directly on the market value of the computer. They are losses in *consequence* of not having the computer.

"Profits" and consequential damages. As the above example suggests, consequential damages are often identified with lost profits. However, the two terms are not equivalent. Some consequential damages claims are

based on added expenses, not on lost profits as such. More importantly, not all profits claims are alike. It may be helpful to distinguish several kinds or levels of lost profit claims.

(1) First, some writers might use the term "lost profit" to describe the loss of expected market gain in the very performance promised. This usage may tend to confuse general and special damages, however. For instance, if the plaintiff contracts to purchase Blackacre for $10,000 and at the time of performance its market value is $20,000, then the plaintiff surely has an expectancy; but since that expectancy reflects a market gain in the very performance contracted for, it is an item of general damages, so the "profit" label might best be avoided.

(2) The clear case of damages truly based on lost profits that also count as consequential damages is the case of lost operating profits of a business. If the plaintiff contracts to buy flour for his bakery and cannot get substitute flour when the defendant reneges, the plaintiff might assert a claim for damages based on the profits he would have made by making bread and selling it. Whether or not he can prove such a claim and justify it, such a claim is a claim for lost operating profits in a business and it is indisputably a special damages claim. There are many potential levels of lost profits claim like this because one loss can cause another. The baker may lose the profits he would have made on the bread he could have made with the flour, and the fact that he cannot supply customers may lead them to take their patronage elsewhere, so that the baker loses profits on *other* loaves as well.[14]

(3) The third kind of "lost profit" claim may seem to be a hybrid. Suppose that A leases a building to B Company, promising to consent to an assignment to any reasonable party. The B Company immediately contracts to sell the business and assign the lease at a sum that will give the B Company a $45,000 gain. But A refuses to consent to the assignment and the sale falls through.[15] B Company has no loss of operating profits; its loss is a loss of a market gain from sale of the whole business. So the loss bears some resemblance to general damages. But the loss is not based on the market value of the very performance promised; the lessor did not promise the business sale, only to consent to the lease assignment. Such lost profit claims are treated as predominantly consequential damages claims in this treatise, but their hybrid character suggests that the consequential damages rule be applied leniently in such cases.[16]

[*For discussion of the cost measure in the general-special scheme, and the functions of general damages, see this section in the Practitioner Treatise edition.*]

§ 12.3 Damages to Compensate for Reliance Loss and Opportunity Costs

§ 12.3(1) Reliance Loss as Measure of Damages

Recoverability of Reliance Damages

Reliance loss damages generally. When the defendant breaches an enforceable, bargained-for promise,[1] the plaintiff has the option of claiming

§ 12.3(1)

1. Distinguish the substantive question whether to impose liability upon the plain-

tiff's reasonable reliance. The remedial question is whether, given an enforceable, bargained-for promise, the plaintiff can claim re-

and recovering reliance expense or loss rather than the expectancy.[2] The reliance recovery is a reimbursement for losses the plaintiff suffers in reliance on the defendant's contractual promise.[3] Some particular kinds of reliance damages may be identified by other names.[4]

The object of reliance damages awards is to protect the plaintiff against actual losses resulting from contracting even while denying him the gains or expectancy he would have had upon performance.[5] The definition of reliance and the rules limiting special damages[6] operate to limit the recovery to reasonable reliance expenses.[7] In addition, the reliance damages recovery is a recovery for *net* reliance loss, so that the defendant is credited with any benefit the plaintiff receives from the expenditures in reliance.[8]

Illustration. A typical illustration of recoverable reliance damage is the plaintiff's expense of performance or of preparing for performance.[9] A retailer contracts to receive a shipment of popular but difficult-to-obtain blue jeans from a manufacturer, and in reliance upon the contract conducts extensive advertising. The advertising cost is a recoverable reliance expense as an alternative to an expectancy recovery.

Motivation to claim. The traditional assumption is that unless the plaintiff expects to lose money on the contract, the expectancy claim would normally yield a greater recovery than the reliance loss claim (because expectancy would give the plaintiff the gains that would be made on the contract while reliance would merely protect against losses).[10] Nevertheless, the reliance claim must be considered as an option when the plaintiff cannot prove expectancy damages with reasonable certainty. In such a case, a recovery of actual expenditures may be the best the plaintiff can hope for. As indicated below, the plaintiff may have another motive in seeking reliance expense if that expense exceeds his expectancy.

⚹ Reliance and Expectancy

Recoupment through performance: pre-contract expenses and fixed overhead. Given an enforceable set of promises, perhaps the most important reason for allowing recovery for some kinds of reliance expense is that they represent a kind of partial expectancy; they would have been recouped by

---

imbursement for expenses in lieu of expectancy.

2. E.g., L. Albert & Son v. Armstrong Rubber Co., 178 F.2d 182 (2d Cir.1949) (expense of building footings to accommodate machines never delivered); Vecco Construction Industries, Inc. v. Century Const. Co. of Washington, D.C., Inc., 30 B.R. 945 (Bkrtcy.E.D.Va. 1983) (subcontractor could not establish lost profits, entitled to claim reliance expenses in performing, less any progress payments), modified on other grounds, 33 B.R. 757 (1983); Herbert W. Jaeger & Associates v. Slovak American Charitable Ass'n, 156 Ill.App.3d 106, 107 Ill.Dec. 710, 507 N.E.2d 863 (1987) (cost of demolishing structure when building contractor did not complete it rather than the

cost of completing the structure); Wartzman v. Hightower Productions, Ltd., 53 Md.App. 656, 456 A.2d 82, 40 A.L.R.4th 523 (1983) (venture to promote profits from flagpole sitter could not proceed because lawyer improperly prepared securities work, extensive costs of promotion, consultants, and other expenses recoverable); Mistletoe Express Service of Oklahoma City v. Locke, 762 S.W.2d 637 (Tex. App.1988) (plaintiff's investment in capital goods in reliance on contract, loss on goods when contract was breached and goods sold); Reimer v. Badger Wholesale Co., Inc., 147 Wis.2d 389, 433 N.W.2d 592 (1988) (moving expenses). See, analyzing the concept and collecting a number of cases, Hudec, Restating the "Reliance Interest", 67 Cornell L.Rev. 704 (1982).

the gain the plaintiff would have made if the defendant had performed.[15] If this is correct, it would be perfectly sound to award the plaintiff any reasonably proven "partial expectancy." On this basis one might justify an award of pre-contract expenditures, even though they could not possibly be said to have been made in reliance on a non-existent promise.[16] If such expenditures were directed toward a hoped-for contract, the contract was in fact made and breached, and the expenditures would have been recouped had it been performed, it is difficult to see any objection to recovery. Whether it is called "reliance" expense or partial expectancy does not seem to matter very much when enforceable, bargained-for promises were exchanged.

Opportunity cost. Reliance and expectation are entangled again in the case of opportunity costs. Some writers have even defined reliance losses to include the losses attributable to the fact that the plaintiff, entering into the defendant's contract, had to forego another contracting opportunity,[19] and one that might well have been performed. The opportunity lost in such a case is a reliance loss because, but for the defendant's contract the plaintiff would have accepted the alternative. It is a lost opportunity because he relied upon the defendant's promise to perform instead. At the same time, this kind of lost opportunity also represents part or perhaps substantially all of the plaintiff's expectancy.[20] Courts and writers usually do not consider lost opportunities when they discuss reliance expenses; reliance expenses are roughly "out of pocket" expenses in the traditional view. However, if the lost opportunity would have been offset by the defendant's performance, it should be subject to recovery. If it is the same as the defendant's performance, it is the expectancy itself; if it is less, then it is a kind of partial expectancy. The earlier comments apply: whether it is called reliance or not may not matter much in the case of bargained-for promises. On the other hand, unless the lost opportunity was merely an opportunity to deal in an established market, the opportunity cost will be special damages and subject to the limitations that apply to such claims.

Reliance and Restitution

The reliance damages formula also contrasts with the restitution formula, but not enough to prevent confusion and resignation. Reliance recoveries may restore the plaintiff to his pre-contract financial position (without affording an expectancy recovery). Restitutionary recoveries often restore the plaintiff to a pre-contract financial position; in this respect they resemble the reliance damages recovery. However, restitution theoretically "restores" the plaintiff only by returning consideration he gave under the contract, or at least by forcing the defendant to disgorge unjust gains. As the advertising example shows, reliance expense recoveries are not limited to recovery of something the plaintiff gave the defendant under the contract, nor to any financial benefit received by the defendant. However, as many observers have noticed since Fuller and Perdue first analyzed the reliance

---

19. Goetz & Scott have called "reimbursement damages." Goetz & Scott, Enforcing Promises: An Examination of the Basis of Contract, 89 Yale L.J. 1261 (1980).

20. See Cooter and Eisenberg, Damages for Breach of Contract, 73 Calif.L.Rev. 1432, 1445 (1985).

damages idea,[22] courts have often confused the two and awarded reliance damages under the name of restitution.[23]

The Other Relevance of Reliance—Transactions Unenforceable as Contracts

The question of reliance damages for breach of an enforceable contract is the topic of this section. There are, however, other issues about reliance damages which may become confused.

First, the plaintiff's reliance upon some conduct of the defendant is the essential ingredient of promissory estoppel liability under Restatement § 90.[24] Many authors who address the substantive question—should there be liability based upon reliance?—also address the remedial question—how should reliance damages be calculated?[25] The reliance damages question in turn may deal with cases in which reliance rather than bargain is the basis of liability in the first place. Or the reliance question may deal with cases in which the promises have been bargained for and the plaintiff simply cannot prove expectancy damages. This section deals only with the last question. However, in general the mode of estimating damages is the same. For example, the plaintiff's reliance damages are necessarily limited to expenses incurred after the promise is made.[26]

Second, in many cases the parties come to a bargained-for agreement that is or becomes unenforceable—it does not meet with the statute of frauds requirements, or it is illegal, or its purposes have become frustrated and liability discharged.[27] In such cases, given the impetus to compromise or to find damages that do not seem extreme for the setting, reliance damages may be arguably justified, even when expectancy damages would not be. Again, the issue in such cases is quite different from the straightforward cases in this section, where there is no special occasion to seek a compromise or in-between damages measure.

§ 12.3(2) Expectancy as a Cap on Reliance Damages

General Rules: Expectancy Caps Reliance

Zero expectancy cases. In some cases the plaintiff has no expectancy under the applicable measure of damages, but nevertheless has suffered reliance expenses. This would occur in any case in which the plaintiff has a losing contract. He contracts to buy the defendant's performance for $10,000, but when performance is due, the defendant's performance is worth only $8,000. In such a case the expectancy is actually negative, an expectation of loss. So the expectancy recovery would be zero and the plaintiff's best hope[1] in many instances would be to recover reliance expenses, if any.

Recovery of reliance expenses when they exceed expectancy. To allow reliance recovery in excess of the appropriate measure[2] of expectancy would mean that the plaintiff would be better off by reason of the breach and recovery than he would have been upon full performance. Such a result might be justified if the reliance claim is properly regarded as a tort claim,[3] or at any rate as something other than a contract claim.[4] But if the reliance claim is to be justified as a contract claim, then a recovery that makes the plaintiff better off by reason of breach seems wrong: the plaintiff should not be put in *better* position by reason of breach than by performance. In accord with this view, the Restatement [5] and the leading decisions have taken the position that the expectancy is a ceiling on reliance damages.[6]

Burden of proof rule. An expectancy ceiling or cap on reliance claims could operate to eliminate reliance damages in the very instance when they are most needed—when the amount of the expectancy is speculative or too uncertain to be awarded. A kind of compromise position seeks to evade this problem by allowing the plaintiff to recover reliance damages unless the defendant shoulders the burden of proving the expectancy as a cap. This was the holding in an influential decision,[7] and it is followed by the Restatement [8] and some other cases.[9] The plaintiff makes a case for reliance damages without proving anything at all about expectancy; but the defendant can defeat or diminish the reliance damages recovery by showing that the expectancy would be less than the reliance expense. The cases have not shown exactly how this rule will operate when there are two or more potential measures for expectancy damages.[10]

Reliance as Special Damages: Essential and Incidental Reliance

The kind of reliance expense usually envisioned is a form of special damages, not based on market value but on an actual outlay of funds. Fuller and Perdue in their classic article on the subject of reliance, identified two kinds of reliance: essential and incidental.[11]

Essential reliance expenses as specials. Essential reliance is that reliance necessary or essential for the plaintiff's performance of his promises under the contract. If he contracted to produce unique machinery for the defendant, then expenses in making dies for the machinery would be essential reliance expenses. Essential reliance expense would normally be within the contemplation of the parties, so its recovery would not be forbidden under the *Hadley v. Baxendale* rule limiting consequential damages.[12]

Essential reliance and the expectancy cap. On the other hand, essential reliance expenses are elements in the computation of the plaintiff's expectancy; the amount that the plaintiff will gain from completion of the contract on both sides depends on the amount of these essential expenses. So the plaintiff must not recover *both* essential reliance expenses *and* expectancy damages. By the same token, the market measured expectancy in such a case should furnish the ceiling on reliance damages recovery.

Incidental reliance expense as consequential damage. Incidental reliance expenses could include any kind of collateral outlay by the plaintiff, but it would not include expenses of performing his own promises to the defendant. For instance, in reliance on the defendant's promise to sell special machinery to the plaintiff, the plaintiff expends funds to remove a wall of his factory so that the machinery can be installed. When the defendant breaches and no comparable machines can be purchased, the plaintiff can recover the cost of removing and rebuilding the wall as *incidental* reliance expense. It is "incidental" or consequential, because it is

§ 12.3(2)

11. Fuller & Perdue, The Reliance Interest in Contract Damages (pt. 1), 46 Yale L.J. 52, 78 (1936).

no part of the price the plaintiff is paying for the defendant's performance. Incidental reliance expenses might or might not be within the contemplation of the parties and hence might or might not be barred under the rule limiting consequential damages.[13] Whether they are barred will depend on the facts, not on a rule.

Incidental reliance and the expectancy cap. Is the expectancy a ceiling or cap on *incidental* reliance damages? The logical answer is yes, they are capped by the expectancy if other reliance damages are so capped and if consequential damages are recognized as one measure of expectancy. If the expectancy measure which is the ceiling on reliance recovery is a consequential damages measure, such as lost profits, then the ceiling in such a case is the same ceiling imposed by the rules that limit consequential damages—the contemplation of the parties rules and others.[14]

[*For a discussion of measurement of reliance expenditures against caps and the basis of expectancy caps, see this section in the Practitioner Treatise edition.*]

§ 12.4 The Special Problems of Consequential Damages

§ 12.4(1) Special or Consequential Damages: Limiting Rules

Consequential or special damages for breach of contract are those claimed to result as a secondary consequence of the defendant's non-performance. They are distinguished from general damages, which are based on the value of the performance itself, not on the value of some consequence that performance may produce.[1] For example, if the defendant contracts to supply feed for cattle and fails to do so, general damages would be based on the value of the feed itself and might be calculated by giving the plaintiff the difference between the contract price and the market value. Consequential damages, in contrast, might be based on the loss of cattle from starvation, or diminished profits because the cattle could not be properly fattened before selling them. Whether such consequential damages would be recoverable depends on several rules stated below.

One type of consequential damage—emotional harm resulting from contract breach—is usually excluded altogether, along with punitive damages.[3] For other consequential damages claims, there are four categories of limitation.

First, the plaintiff is denied recovery of consequential damages if proof does not show that the breach in fact caused the losses claimed. Causation in fact is seldom a concern in general damages claims.[4]

Second, the plaintiff is denied recovery of consequential damages if they cannot be shown to be reasonably certain in amount. The qualifier, "reasonably," imports into the adjudication all the attitudes of the particular judges about contracts in general and about the merits of the particular case. It is a safe bet that the reasonably certain proof requirement is an elastic rule that reflects the era in which it is applied as well as the merits of the particular case. However elastic, the rule is one that seldom if ever has any application to market damages.[5]

Third, the plaintiff is denied recovery of consequential damages that are not shown to be within the contemplation of the parties at the time the contract was made. This is the rule of *Hadley v. Baxendale.*[6] Several formulations of the rule are in use and may expand the range of damages available.[7] The *Hadley* rule is in large part another way of stating the distinction between general damages and consequential damages. The effect of the rule is that general damages are always recoverable, representing as they do the value of the very performance promised. Special or consequential damages may be or may not be recoverable, depending on whether the risks of those special damages were part of the basis of the parties' bargain. Most contract suppliers of cattle feed, for example, probably mean to guarantee price, but perhaps do not mean to provide life insurance for the herd. If not, the rancher's cattle losses incurred when the feed supply is interrupted would not be recoverable.[8]

Fourth, in several particular situations the governing rules eliminate consequential damages altogether, or limit those damages in accordance with a provision of the contract,[9] or in accordance with a tariff or schedule of liabilities established by law.[10] Common carriers[11] and innkeepers[12] are groups often protected by statutes or contract provisions limiting liability for goods carried or stored. Vendors of land enjoy the protection of a rule that excludes consequential damages for breach of their deed warranties.[13] In addition, it is usually thought that the UCC excludes certain kinds of consequential damages for sellers aggrieved by a buyer's breach,[14] and similarly for lessors of chattels.[15]

The first three rules attempt to assure that consequential damages awards will be denied when they are outside the parties' agreement, when they are not properly proven, and when they duplicate other awards in the case. The fourth category is different because cases in that category fall under the ax of a rule of law that simply forbids consequential damages or narrows their scope. Presumably a rule of law against consequential damages for specified cases reflects a belief that such damages are not within the parties' contemplation, or can never be adequately proven, or should be minimized or avoided by other, more efficient means. Such cases aside, there is no reason to deny consequential damages if the limiting rules are met. When proof meets the standards imposed by the limiting rule, courts regularly approve the award or potential award of lost collateral earning losses or profits,[16] and many forms of collateral out-of-pocket expenses resulting from the breach.[17]

§ 12.4(2) Causation Requirements

The causation in fact requirement prevents the plaintiff's recovery for any losses not proven to have occurred at all,[5] for losses which in fact occurred but as a result of factors wholly other than the defendant's breach,[6] and for losses which in fact occurred but which would have resulted even if the defendant had not breached. For instance, if the defendant contracts to supply tomatoes to the plaintiff's cannery, breach of the contract to supply does not cause loss of profits from canning if the plaintiff's plant was incapacitated and could not process tomatoes anyway.[7] The requirement of cause in fact or but for cause also means that when two defendants breach separate contracts, the plaintiff cannot recover from one of them the losses caused solely by the other.[8]

In some instances the defendant's breach appears to be a sufficient but not a necessary cause of the loss. That is, the breach, isolated from other relevant events, would have caused the loss, but other events, isolated from the breach, would also have sufficed to cause it. Two subcontractors, working on a hotel, are both in breach by their delay. The hotel cannot open on time and the owner loses profits as a result. As in comparable tort cases, courts may well be reluctant here to allow each contractor to escape liability by pointing to the fact that even if he had not breached, the other contractor's breach would have prevented opening the hotel on time.[12] As one court said, "The continued default of both parties would operate to take each of them off the hook. That cannot be the law."[13] But in some cases courts seem to have regarded one contractor's default as somehow primary, with the result that the second breach is considered to be not causal at all.[14]

Where the defendant's breach does not combine with the breach of other contractors to cause harm, the argument for liability is harder to sustain. In *Lekas & Drivas, Inc. v. Goulandris*,[15] the owners of cheese shipped by sea sued the carrier when the cheese arrived at its destination in a spoiled condition. The carrier was responsible for improper ventilation, but because the ship had been forced by a wartime emergency to take an especially long route through hot climates, the cheese would have spoiled even had ventilation been proper. Applying the but-for test, the court rejected the claim that the carrier was liable. But other authority is more forgiving. A distinguished panel of federal judges applied the "substantial factor" rather than a rigorous but-for test in *Krauss v. Greenbarg*.[16] The effect was that the plaintiff recovered for breach of a supplier's contract to supply raw materials, even though the plaintiff had been evicted from its factory and might not have been able to use the materials. The court upheld an instruction that the plaintiff could recover if the breach was the primary, real and chief cause.[17]

---

§ 12.4(2)

13. California and Hawaiian Sugar Co. v. Sun Ship, Inc., 794 F.2d 1433, 1437 (9th Cir. 1986), cert. denied, 484 U.S. 871, 108 S.Ct. 200, 98 L.Ed.2d 151 (1987). In this case *A* was to deliver specially built barge to fit tug specially built by *B*. Both *A* and *B* were in breach by their separate substantial delays. The court concluded that in case of "concurrent causation each defaulting contractor is liable for the breach and for the substantial damages which the joint breach occasions."

14. Husman Construction Co. v. Purolator Courier Corp., 832 F.2d 459 (8th Cir.1987) (one delivery service failed to deliver a contractor's base bid, the second failed to deliver the modification; the first contractor "had a duty to perform 'first,' and if it failed to do so, then Western Union's actions would be, in all cases, irrelevant").

15. 306 F.2d 426 (2d Cir.1962).

16. 137 F.2d 569 (3d Cir.1943), cert. denied, 320 U.S. 791, 64 S.Ct. 207, 88 L.Ed. 477 (1943). The plaintiff was a manufacturer with a contract to supply goods to the government. It contracted with the defendant to supply raw materials. When the defendant was late in providing the materials, the plaintiff became liable to the government for liquidated damages. The plaintiff sued the defendant supplier for this loss. The manufacturer, however, had been evicted from its factory and also encountered a shortage of other necessary materials for completion of its government contract. The trial judge charged the jury that the plaintiff could recover from the supplier if the delay would have been sufficient in itself to cause the loss and was the primary, real and chief cause of it. A distinguished panel upheld this charge on appeal, saying that "substantial factor" was enough to impose liability.

See also Bruckman v. Parliament Escrow Corp., 190 Cal.App.3d 1051, 235 Cal.Rptr. 813 (1987).

§ 12.4(3) Proof Requirements

General Rule

Certainty rule. When the plaintiff claims special or consequential damages rather than general market-based damages, the requirement is that the damages must be proven with reasonable certainty, and must not be "speculative."[1] The certainty rule is important but it does not go very far. It invites and requires good proof[2] but it does not say what form that proof should take. So far as this issue is concerned, the plaintiff's recovery is likely to turn less on rules and analysis than on vigorous presentation of evidence. It is distinct from the contemplation-of-the-parties rule discussed in the next subsection, although the two rules are sometimes conflated.[3]

Hard and soft approaches. The cases reflect both hard and soft approaches to the evidence. Hard approaches demand proof not only that damage was caused in fact by the breach but also that the amount can be inferred with reasonable certainty.[4] Soft approaches may be demanding in the proof required to show that damage was in fact caused by the breach, but forgiving in the proof required to show the amount of damages. The soft formula is that once the plaintiff has proved the *existence* of damages, the amount need not be proven with precision.[5] These approaches, however, express attitudes, rather than rules. Even the soft approach does not countenance speculation or an irrational guess about damages.[6]

[*For additional discussion of consequential damages, with emphasis on lost profits, see this section in the Practitioner Treatise edition.*]

§ 12.4(4) The Contemplation of the Parties Rule

In 1854 an English court initiated limits on contract damages in a decision which has dominated all discussions on the topic ever since. In *Hadley v. Baxendale,*[1] the court in effect stated a preference for general damages[2] by imposing a limit upon the recovery of consequential damages[3] in pure contract cases.[4] Under *Hadley,* the breaching defendant was held to be liable only for such consequential damages that were within "the contemplation of both parties" at the time of contracting. There are, however, other formulations of the rule, to be discussed later.[5]

The *Hadley* case itself is a good illustration of the rule. In that case, a miller whose flour mill was stopped when a shaft was broken, contracted with a common carrier, which was to take the broken shaft to Greenwich where engineers could use it as a pattern for a new shaft. He told the carrier that his mill was stopped and that the shaft must be shipped immediately. The evidence was that the carrier promised next-day delivery,

§ 12.4(4)

1. 9 Ex. 341, 156 Eng.Rep. 145 (1954).

2. That is, damages based on the value of the very performance promised rather than on the value of consequences that performance might produce, with calculation ordinarily based on market rates. See § 12.2(3) above.

The verbal definition of general damages is often rendered differently: those which arise naturally, or which normally follow from breach. The "arising naturally" definition is unhelpful at best and misleading at worst.

However, if it is taken to be a shorthand expression for the idea that the market value of the very performance to which the plaintiff was entitled, then it can provide a useful category. The "general damages" terminology, if not taken to mean market damages based on the value of the very thing to which the plaintiff is entitled may justifiably be dismissed. See A. Farnsworth, Contracts § 12.-14, p. 874, n. 5 (1982). The Restatement Second of Contracts generally avoids analysis of damages in which the term plays a part.

but in fact the carrier delayed for many days. The carrier's delay meant that the plaintiff's mill was inoperable and the plaintiff lost his normal profits during that period. The claim was for these lost profits and the trial court allowed the jury to make a profits award.[6] The *Hadley* court reversed because the profits should not have been allowed; the loss of profits claim was a special damages claim and was not in the "contemplation of the parties" at the time of contracting.[7]

Another example is found in *Kerr S.S. Co. v. Radio Corp. of America.*[8] In that case the plaintiff paid the defendant to transmit a business cable in cipher. The defendant understood that the cable related to business but did not understand the particular message. The defendant failed to transmit the cable and the plaintiff suffered business losses as a result. In an opinion by Judge Cardozo, the court held that, under the principle in *Hadley*, the defendant was not liable for the plaintiff's lost profits.

In much the same way, an Arkansas case[9] took the position that the seller of a tractor who failed to provide the promised lighting equipment needed for night work would not be liable for the losses incurred by the farmer-buyer due to his inability to work at night. The seller knew the farmer wanted to work at night—that was the reason for the lighting equipment—but the court nonetheless thought the seller had never contemplated liability based on loss of profits.

The *Hadley* rule, in some form or another, is consistently recognized by the courts today,[10] and sometimes codified in statutes.[11] The rule is applied in a wide variety of cases. For example, courts invoke *Hadley* as a basis for rejecting mental anguish and loss-of-reputation damages in many contract cases.[12] The principle finds ample expression not only in explicit discussions but in many cases that incorporate it indirectly by defining a measure of damages that excludes the special damages claimed by the plaintiff.[13] For instance, grantors are not liable for most consequential damages resulting from the breach of their deed covenants;[14] buyer's of goods are not liable for most kinds of seller's lost collateral profits.[15] In some situations the parties' expectations about the limits of their guarantees is so well understood that claims for consequential damages are extremely rare; employers rarely claim lost profits from employees who merely quit on their contracts, even from rich employees.[16] The parties may make the scope of their contemplation or guarantee clear by spelling it out, too, providing express rather than implied limits on contract liability.[17] In its most general form the *Hadley* principle is in fact a pervasive and central one.

---

7. It would seem that a general damages claim would be for the difference between the contract price for the carriage and the market value of the carriage. If the plaintiff paid $5 for next-day service, but the market for such service was $10, the plaintiff would seem to have a general damages claim for $5 when he got next-week instead of next-day service.

8. 245 N.Y. 284, 157 N.E. 140, 55 A.L.R. 1139 (1927), cert. denied, 275 U.S. 557, 48 S.Ct. 118, 72 L.Ed. 424 (1927).

9. Lamkins v. International Harvester Co., 207 Ark. 637, 182 S.W.2d 203 (1944). The Arkansas Court used the tacit agreement test, which is now largely rejected, see § 12.4(6) below. In addition, the UCC would normally control such cases today. But the result is approved in Restatement Second of Contracts § 351, Illustration 18 (1982) because of the extreme disproportion between contract price and lost profit claim and because of the informality of contracting.

§ 12.4(5)   The Contemplation of the Parties Rule: Rationales

The Moral Basis for a Contemplation of the Parties' Limitation

Scope of liability determined by scope of promise. The moral basis for limiting contract liability lies in the idea that the boundaries of contract liability are determined by the contract itself; the scope of the risks assumed by the defendant delineate the scope of his liability. His liability originates in contract and is thus bounded by contract.[1] The seller is not liable for flour when he has promised corn; he is not liable for lost profits when he has only guaranteed the price of goods against a market rise; he is not liable for mental distress when he has only guaranteed a cash payment.[2] Although the promise of a contract is almost always written in terms of performance required—to sell goods, to provide services—the parties usually have some ideas about the kinds of risks which performance is meant to guard against. Their understanding of the contract's purposes conditions their understanding of the liabilities they undertake.

The moral understanding of *Hadley* is that it attempts to respect those understandings of the parties. Damages are not, in other words, measured by a rule of law imposed from above, but by the parties' own agreement.[3] This idea is in line with the usual rule that general damages—based on the value of the very performance promised—are always recoverable, while special or consequential damages may be denied unless the defendant explicitly or impliedly undertook to guarantee against consequential damages. The idea is also part of a web of principles that relieve parties from obligations when they did not contemplate supervening events that frustrate the contract's purposes or make performance impracticable.[4] If this moral rationale is sound, then it may be misleading to say that *Hadley* leads to undercompensation;[5] instead, it leads to exactly the compensation for which the plaintiff paid.[6]

Necessary conditions: party autonomy. The moral argument for a limitation imposed by the contract itself can be sustained only if two or possibly three conditions are met. First, the parties must be reasonably free to prescribe the limits of their liability, as the *Hadley* court thought.[7] For instance, although a carrier may be required to accept a shipper's goods for delivery and may be required to accept liability, the carrier is permitted to limit that liability; and correspondingly, it may accept higher liability only upon condition that the shipper pay a higher shipping charge or premium.[8] Any legal rule of damages, as this treatise and other commentators have observed repeatedly, is thus a default rule, to be applied when the parties make no separate provision limiting or expanding relief. In the absence of fraud, unconscionability or other abuse, and in the absence of tortious acts,

---

§ 12.4(5)

1. See generally Epstein, Beyond Foreseeability: Consequential Damages in the Law of Contract, 18 J.Legal Stud. 105, 122 (1989). Professor Sebert puts it succinctly:

> "Thus, damage rules recognize the consensual basis of contract liability by limiting a contracting party's potential liability to those risks that might reasonably be deemed to have been assumed upon entering the contract."

Sebert, Punitive and Nonpecuniary Damages in Actions Based upon Contract: Toward Achieving the Objective of Full Compensation, 33 U.C.L.A.L.Rev. 1565, 1567 (1986).

4. See § 13.3 below. Similarly as to mistake, see Chapter 11 generally.

5. See Wolcher, The Accommodation of Regret in Contract Remedies, 73 Iowa L.Rev. 797, 859, n. 279 (1988); Narasimhan, Modification: The Self–Help Specific Performance Remedy, 97 Yale L.J. 61 (1987) (*Hadley* often results in "significant undercompensation").

the idea that the parties can set the scope of their own promises seems inherently correct in the context of a free society.[9]

Necessary conditions: parties' implicit understandings can be determined. Second, the moral argument for limited consequential damages depends on the belief that the parties' assumption about limits of liability can be ascertained even when the contract itself speaks only in terms of the performance required. For a very large number of cases this belief is well warranted. No one thinks the cabby's contract to drive you to the airport covers the profits lost when you missed the plane and missed the business deal; no amount of notice to the cabbie is likely to make anyone think the cabbie guarantees the entrepreneur's profits.

But not every case is so clear. Probably courts should feel unsure of the parties' assumptions about liability limits in a good many cases, in the absence of good evidence about the implicit understandings in the particular business culture. The moral rationale for *Hadley's* limits is weakest when the evidence is uncertain about the risks covered by the contract. Although it is morally right to limit liability to the kinds of damages for which the defendant contracted a responsibility, it is not so clear that the burden must be upon the plaintiff to mark those limits. It might be equally consistent with the moral rationale to put the burden upon the defendant to show that a promise of specified performance is a promise to pay only some of the damages that result from nonperformance. So the moral basis for *Hadley* suggests clear guidelines for the many cases in which it is possible to say that defendant probably never undertook to guarantee the plaintiff against special damages claimed; but it leaves delicate, debateable areas for judgment when the scope of the defendant's guarantee is not so clear.

A qualification: contract as risk assignment. A kind of limit or qualification may be implied in one or both of the two conditions described above. The moral rationale for *Hadley* works most obviously if the contract is regarded as an allocation of risks between the parties. For instance, if buyer agrees to buy grain for $1 to be delivered next September and seller agrees to sell at that price, the contract can be regarded as an allocation or assumption of risks of price fluctuation. The buyer assumes the risk that the price will go down so that he ends up paying more than he would have if he had no contract at all. The seller assumes the risk that the price will go up so that he ends up selling for less than the actual market price when the performance date arrives. The moral rationale for *Hadley* fits this view very well. If the only risk allocated to the buyer is the risk of a price fluctuation, the buyer in breach will not be liable to the seller for consequential damages the seller may suffer, such as interest cost on a loan the seller must take out because he does not receive the buyer's payment.

This risk allocation conception of a contract fits many discrete contracts very well, but scholarship on "relational" contracts shows that other contracts are not aimed so much at risk allocation as they are at establishing a framework for further dealing or a long-term relationship.[11] Although there are no doubt limits on liability in relational contracts as well as others, it may turn out with experience that the kinds of limitations imposed in such cases are not so easy to determine.

9. However, courts have often taken a restrictive view of liquidated damages clauses which *increase* the defendant's liability. See § 12.9 below.

The Economic Basis for a Contemplation of the Parties' Limitation

Increased costs, cross-subsidies, efficient use of resources. Economic thinkers have usually supported a *Hadley*-like limitation on contract damages. One suggestion is that unrestricted liability for all provable consequential damages would tend to (a) raise the price of the goods or services the defendant provides, (b) "cross subsidize" some users of the goods or services at the expense of other users, and (c) sometimes produce an "inefficient" use of resources.[12] Another economic idea suggests that *Hadley* encourages efficient use of resources. It may do so by getting relevant information on the table, since the would-be plaintiff must reveal and bargain about his special needs if he wants those needs guaranteed in potential damages liability;[13] it might also do so by encouraging efficient ways of dealing with actual or potential loss, since the miller who finds the price too high for guaranteed next-day service may find it more efficient to have a spare crankshaft.[14]

The business trip example. Some economic ideas are easily illustrated. Consider the purchaser of an airline ticket, bound for Vancouver to close a

12. See Note, Contract Damages and Cross–Subsidization, 61 S.Cal.L.Rev. 1125 (1988). The topic can also be considered in terms of setting appropriate incentives to deal with the potential loss. See R. Posner, Economic Analysis of Law § 4.9 (3d ed. 1986). One writer has suggested, however, that if unrestricted damages were allowed in cases like *Hadley*, the carrier might increase its charges for the carriage of goods, but that this new cost might be "offset" by increased consumer usage of the carrier, generated because people who were afraid to contract before because they knew they would be "undercompensated" in the event of the carrier's breach might now lug their mill shafts to the railroad, secure in the knowledge that the law would require full damages. See Wolcher, The Accommodation of Regret in Contract Remedies, 73 Iowa L.Rev. 797, 859, n. 279 (1988).

13. Goetz & Scott, Principles of Relational Contracts, 67 Va.L.Rev. 1089, 1114–1115 (1981) ("it compels a party with unanticipatable interests to supply the information necessary for economically efficient behavior"). The reverse argument is that revealing special needs may be undesirable to the would-be plaintiff, who may wish to conceal his plans for fear that once they are perceived by the other, a higher price will be extorted. See Wolcher, The Accommodation of Regret in Contract Remedies, 73 Iowa L.Rev. 797, 859, n. 279 (1988).

14. Judge Posner has advanced this kind of idea in several cases. See EVRA Corp. v. Swiss Bank Corp., 673 F.2d 951 (7th Cir.1982), cert. denied, 459 U.S. 1017, 103 S.Ct. 377, 74 L.Ed. 511 (1982); Afram Export Corp. v. Metallurgiki Halyps, S.A., 772 F.2d 1358 (7th Cir.1985). In Husman Construction Co. v. Purolator Courier Corp., 832 F.2d 459 (8th Cir. 1987) the plaintiff sent a construction bid by a delivery service. The contract specifically excluded consequential damages and went on to advise the shipper:

> If the shipment involves a bid or other similar extremely time-sensitive material, the loss or delay of which might result in consequential, incidental or special damages. [sic] Purolator Courier will accept such shipments, but subject to the limitations contained herein. The shipper should prominently identify such shipment as a bid or similar document and call Purolator Courier's attention to the special nature of the shipment. In view of Purolator Courier's limitation on consequential damages, the shipper is advised to contact its own insurance broker, agent or company to obtain coverage against such risk.

The bidder-plaintiff did not obtain insurance or use back-up services available, though he was sending the bid only one day before it was due.

Rules limiting liability of land grantor's for breach of deed covenants may have the same effect. The covenantee, knowing that lost profits are not recoverable if title fails for breach of a deed warranty, can procure title insurance or perform its own title search. See Booker T. Washington Const. & Design Co. v. Huntington Urban Renewal Authority, 181 W.Va. 409, 383 S.E.2d 41 (1989); § 12.11(1) below.

business deal. Time is of the essence; if the purchaser misses the plane, she
will be out of the deal. For whatever reasons, the plane does not fly. If the
failure to fly is a breach of contract (and is not governed by regulations or
tariffs), the business passenger will claim damages for the breach. The
moral interpretation of the *Hadley* rule suggests that the airline would not
be liable for lost profits, but only for return of the fare, or for any price
advantage the intending passenger had gained by purchasing the ticket at a
lower-than-market rate. Economic interpretations may suggest the same.

The economic point can be seen by asking what would happen if the
airline were liable for lost profits of business passengers when the flight did
not proceed properly. The airline might provide a limit on its liability in its
contract or ticket, or, if it were concerned that such a limitation might not
be effective, it might lobby the Congress for a statute or regulation providing
such protection. One way or another it would almost certainly succeed in
limiting liability, and indeed it should if the limit accords with the parties'
expectations. If the airline can properly succeed in limiting liability and
will do so, the imposition of liability in the first place seems not merely
bootless but actually wasteful and wrong because it will generate costs of
shedding the liability through lobbying Congress or otherwise.

Increased costs. If the airline can*not* successfully limit its liability for
business profits of passengers who are delayed, then the airline might
attempt to identify the passengers whose economic risks are especially high.
The airline might demand a higher ticket price from business passengers.
Identification of those passengers who stood to lose most from a delayed or
canceled flight, however, would itself be costly and would add to the cost of
the ticket even more.[15] Furthermore, if it would be permissible for the
airline to charge more to the flyer who has more at risk from a late flight,
we can see that the extra charge works much like an insurance premium:
those subject to special risks must pay more. If such a plan is permissible,
why not permit at-risk fliers to buy their own insurance, in the form of a
policy, in the form of a chartered flight or otherwise?[16] So charging higher
prices to passengers with more at stake seems to be either costly in itself
(because the passengers must be identified) or merely a form of insurance

15. Identification of the at-risk passengers (or goods) would only be the first step. Explaining the costs that would be imposed upon the carrier in *Hadley* if no limitations applied, Judge Posner noted: "The defendants were not privy to the mill's finances and hence could not form an accurate estimate of how costly delay would be and therefore how much care to take to prevent it." Rardin v. T & D Machine Handling, Inc., 890 F.2d 24, 26 (7th Cir.1989).

16. Compare Judge Posner's suggestion that the plaintiff in *Hadley* might have protected himself by having a spare shaft and that such precautions, because they would protect against losses besides those caused by a contract breach, might be more efficient and prudent in any event. Afram Export Corp. v. Metallurgiki Halyps, S.A., 772 F.2d 1358 (7th Cir.1985).

In Husman Construction Co. v. Purolator Courier Corp., 832 F.2d 459 (8th Cir.1987) the court said:

Those using delivery services to transmit bids are in the best position to procure insurance for their time-sensitive cargo or to otherwise proceed at their own risk. It is unreasonable to subject a carrier to liability for enormous and unforeseeable consequential damages in return for an $11.75 shipment fee. See J. Calamari & J. Perillo, Contracts s 14–6, at 598 (3d ed. 1987). As succinctly stated by the Third Circuit in denying relief to a shipper under similar circumstances: "They made a business judgment when they decided not to explore the possibility of obtaining greater protection from the airline at a higher rate, or even of taking out a policy themselves with an insurance company to cover their exposure. Having made their bed they must lie in it."

which could be left to the passenger in the first place by adopting a rule like that in *Hadley v. Baxendale.*

Cross-subsidies. Because of the cost of identifying special passengers, the airline might try a third strategy if courts insisted on imposing profits liability. It might simply raise the price of all tickets to reflect the costs of paying lost profits damages. If this happens, then the grandfather will pay more for his annual cross-country flight to visit his grandchildren. The increased cost will be imposed on him as a ticket purchaser even though he has no profits at risk from canceled flights and could never possibly recover for more than the low-value of his lost time. So the non-business travelers, and business travelers who have no special profit at stake, will subsidize those in the fast lane.[17] If there are ever good subsidies, this does not seem to be one of them. As with the other possible airline strategies in response to extended liability, this one seems to lead to added or badly distributed costs.

The Pragmatic Limitation

A final rationale for *Hadley*-type limitations is skimpier and pragmatic rather than principled. It simply says that liability must stop somewhere and that courts must have a language for stating the stopping place. This rationale supports *any* kind of limitation, not merely a *Hadley* limitation. It is in fact probably the basis for the contemporary formulation of the limitation, which states only that defendants are not liable for "unforeseeable" damages, which is discussed in the following subsection.

§ 12.4(6)   The Contemplation of the Parties Rule: Formulations

Tests Based on the Moral Rationale of Hadley

Contemplation of the parties formulation. *Hadley v. Baxendale* did not use the term "foreseeability." It formulated the rule by insisting that the defendant would be liable for (a) general damages and (b) any special damages within the contemplation of the parties, although it did not use the term "general" or "special," either.[1] The defendant would not be liable, however, for special damages not within the "contemplation of the parties" at the time of contracting.[2] This formulation probably should be read like other early statements of a new rule: it is a first approximation and subject to refinement; it is not a final legislative act. So read, it seems loosely to express the idea that the defendant's liability is congruent with his undertaking; the scope of liability is limited to the risks or types of losses which the parties meant his performance to protect against.[3] The principle is that

---

17. See the more detailed analysis of other examples in Note, Contract Damages and Cross–Subsidization, 61 S.Cal.L.Rev. 1125 (1988).

§ 12.4(6)

3. Kenford Co. v. County of Erie, 73 N.Y.2d 312, 540 N.Y.S.2d 1, 537 N.E.2d 176 (1989); cf. Epstein, Beyond Foreseeability: Consequential Damages in the Law of Contract, 18 J.Legal Stud. 105, 122 (1989).

A scope-of-risk formulation reveals the connection between tort law limitations (often expressed as proximate cause or duty limitations) and the contract rule. See, recognizing the connection, Overseas Tankship (U.K.) Limited v. Morts Dock & Engineering Co., Limited (The Wagon Mound), [1961] A.C. 388 (Privy Council 1961). But courts delineate the relevant scope of risk in tort cases as a matter of law and policy; courts should delineate the relevant scope of risk in contract cases by enforcing the parties' agreement or its underlying assumptions. See Richmond Medical Supply Co. v. Clifton, 235 Va. 584, 369 S.E.2d 407, 409 (1988) ("Contracting parties are en-

liability based on contract must be limited by the contract. This is the "moral" rationale already discussed. Foreseeability would not be the ultimate test of liability; whether the parties expected to shift the particular risk to the defendant would be the test.[4]

Tacit agreement formulation and its liberalization. Earlier courts sometimes applied the *Hadley* rule in line with the moral rationale by saying that the defendant would be liable only for consequential damages for which the defendant explicitly or tacitly agreed to accept liability.[5] In a particular trade or business reasonable people might understand the contract to protect against only specified risks, or the parties's own negotiations and purposes might reflect the limits to the defendant's guarantees. If the tacit agreement rule meant only this, it was entirely in line with the moral rationale for the *Hadley* rule. But many writers, reformers, and courts have been intermittently hostile to the *Hadley* limits. In general, judicial decisions[6] and even statutes[7] have moved away from the tacit agreement formulation in favor of a more liberal formula based on "foreseeability."[8]

Foreseeability Tests

Foreseeability formulation. The rule advanced in *Hadley* is often formulated today in terms *Hadley* itself never used. Instead of saying that the defendant is liable for the kinds of losses the contract was intended to protect against, courts and writers often say that the defendant is not liable for "unforeseeable" damages resulting from the breach of contract[9] and concomitantly that he *is* liable for any "foreseeable" harms.[10]

tirely capable of assuming duties toward one another beyond those imposed by general law, and, in fact, do so in nearly every contractual arrangement. It follows that those authorities which define the duties imposed by general law do not restrict the enforcement of additional duties assumed by contract"); Koufos v. C. Czarnikow Ltd (The Heron II), [1967], 1 A.C. 350, 3 W.L.R. 1491, 3 All.E.R. 111 (H.L.) (judgment of Lord Reid) (in contract, as distinct from tort, "if one party wishes to protect himself against a risk which to the other party would appear unusual, he can direct the other party's attention to it").

7. Comments to UCC provisions for buyer's damages expressly repudiate the tacit agreement rule. UCC § 2–715(2). See J. White & R. Summers, Uniform Commercial Code § 10–4, p. 516 (3d ed. 1988). On the other hand, the UCC may have imposed a tacit agreement rule with a vengeance when it comes to seller's damages. It is at least possible that sellers are denied *all* consequential damages under the Code. See J. White & R. Summers, supra § 7–16, p. 382.

8. Professor Farnsworth, the distinguished reporter of the Restatement Second of Contracts, has said that the tacit agreement rule is "discredited" and doctrinally unsound. A. Farnsworth, Contracts § 12.14 (1982); Farnsworth, Contracts Scholarship in the Age of

Anthology, 85 Mich.L.Rev. 1406, 1412 (1987). A good short statement of the rule and its history is found in J. Calamari & J. Perillo, Contracts § 14–5, p. 595–96 (3d ed. 1987). The tacit agreement rule seems, however, to come closer to the moral rationale for the *Hadley* rule than any other formula. See Epstein, Beyond Foreseeability: Consequential Damages in the Law of Contract, 18 J.Legal Stud. 105 (1989). Hostility to the tacit agreement rule may be grounded in the belief that the law rather than the parties must provide a damages rule. See J. Calamari & J. Perillo, supra at 596 ("The 'tacit agreement' test was based on the dubious assumption that damages for breach of contract are based upon the contracting parties' implied or express promise to pay damages in the event of a breach, rather than based upon a secondary duty imposed by law as a consequence of the breach"). Some decisions reject the tacit agreement rule as only to general damages, as to which *Hadley* has no application. E.G., Twin City Fire Ins. Co. v. Philadelphia Life Ins. Co., 795 F.2d 1417, 1426 (9th Cir.1986) ("imposition of contract-market price damages does not depend upon an agreement (express or implied) between the parties that such damages will be imposed upon breach").

9. See Restatement Second of Contracts § 351 (1981).

Foreseeability as a misinterpretation? Courts probably did not adopt the foreseeability formula as a result of any conscious rejection of the contemplation of the parties test, as both are often mentioned in the same case. *Hadley* had recognized that damages "arising naturally * * * according to the usual course of things, from such breach of contract itself * * * " would be recoverable, as well as those special damages in the contemplation of the parties. Read as a first approximation of a new rule and subject to refinement, this language can be taken as a description of what today we might call general or market damages. The claim in *Hadley* was not a claim for market or general damages and it was not allowed. Courts adopting a foreseeability test, however, may have read the "arising naturally" language as the equivalent to "natural and probable" language and thus as equivalent to foreseeability language. Such a reading does not seem justified, but it does seem understandable.

Non-literal applications of foreseeability. If the foreseeability test is applied simply and literally, it opens the way to much more extensive liability than would be suggested by the moral rationale for *Hadley* and by its formulation in the contemplation of the parties and tacit agreement tests. But courts often recognize that if "foreseeability" is to be the test at all, it must not be understood as a simple factual term but as a term of art, a kind of shorthand for the more complex idea that damages should be limited as the parties intended.

A New York decision, *Kenford Co. v. County of Erie,*[11] illustrates this point well. The defendant, a public entity, promised to build a domed stadium on land supplied by the plaintiff and to give the plaintiff the right to manage the dome for a period of time. Both the parties counted on an increase in the value of surrounding lands; in fact an expected increase in the land value was central to the financing method used. The defendant counted on the increase to supply an additional tax base; the plaintiffs counted on it to raise the value of their own nearby landholdings. Each party knew of the other's expectation in this regard, so it was entirely foreseeable to the defendant that if it failed to build the dome, the plaintiff would lose the expected increase in land value. When the defendant breached by failing to build, the plaintiffs sought damages for the loss suffered because their land did not increase in value as it would have with the nearby domed stadium. This was an item of special or consequential damages because it was not based on the market value of the very performance to be delivered to the plaintiff, the right to manage the building and to have concessions there. So the rule of *Hadley* was invoked. The plaintiff argued, however, that the loss in the value of the plaintiff's land was foreseeable. As a simple fact, foreseeability seemed indisputable. But the New York Court of Appeals denied liability even so, because the defendant's promise was understood to guarantee against the risk of losing the concession and management rights, not a guarantee against the risk of losing peripheral land values.

The same kind of observations can be made more simply about those cases in which the plaintiff claims mental distress damages for breach of contract. Such damages are generally denied, though they have their

---

11. 73 N.Y.2d 312, 540 N.Y.S.2d 1, 537 N.E.2d 176 (1989) is a good illustration.

proponents.[12] As a matter of simple foreseeability, it seems almost inescapable that a promisee will be upset by breach of any contract favorable to him and certainly by breach of such contracts as those of employment. Yet *Hadley* is invoked as a ground for denying mental distress damages in such cases in spite of the obvious foreseeability that such harms will occur. Because such harms are not within the risks guaranteed by the promise, however, liability is denied.

If "foreseeability" is a test in such cases, it must therefore be understood in a special sense, as shorthand for more complex ideas about the scope of the parties' bargain. This is well understood when the issue is broadened to consider whether performance is to be excused altogether under doctrines of impracticality or frustration. In the impracticality and frustration cases, which also turn on the scope of the parties' risk allocations,[13] foreseeability of a frustrating event is important evidence,[14] but it does not necessarily show how the parties intended to allocate that risk.[15] Perhaps it would be better to return to the "contemplation of the parties" terminology as a means of helping us to remember that foreseeability is not itself a test or rule but a piece of evidence.

The Restatement Second of Contracts Formulations

Discretionary limits on damages. The Second Restatement of Contracts attempted a completely different formulation of the limitations. Its first rule was that unforeseeable damages were not recoverable.[16] So far as it goes, this rule is in accord with all other formulations and all rationales. Perhaps the Restatement also meant to imply that foreseeable losses would ordinarily be recoverable, but it does not so state in the black letter. Instead, it provides a new kind of limitation on damages recovery. It provides that a court may limit damages as a matter of discretion. It may, for example, exclude particular elements such as lost profits or consequential damages if "justice so requires."[17] This new limitation would permit the exclusion of damages that were wholly foreseeable.

Unassumed risks and disproportionate pricing. The Restatement suggests that its new discretionary damages recovery would be appropriate when the parties assumed that the defendant would not bear the risk of the particular loss.[18] It also suggests that disproportion between the contract price and the potential liability might furnish strong evidence that the disproportionate risk was not assumed.[19] These comments in turn put the

---

12. See § 12.5 below.

13. See § 13.3 below.

14. See Lloyd v. Murphy, 25 Cal.2d 48, 153 P.2d 47 (1944) ("If [a supervening event] was foreseeable there should have been provision for it in the contract, and the absence of such a provision gives rise to the inference that the risk was assumed").

15. See Transatlantic Financing Corp. v. United States, 124 U.S.App.D.C. 183, 363 F.2d 312 (1966) (the parties "are not always able to provide for all the possibilities of which they are aware * * * often simply because they are too busy * * *."). See E.A. Farnsworth, Farnsworth on Contracts § 9.6, p. 554 (1990).

16. Restatement Second of Contracts § 351(1) (1981).

17. Restatement Second of Contracts § 351(3) (1981).

18. Restatement Second of Contracts, § 351, Comment *f* (1981).

19. The actual wording of the Restatement does not seem right. The Restatement speaks of "an extreme disproportion between the loss and the price charged" by the defendant. But price charged probably should be compared to the type of loss, not the actual dollar claim. When the cabbie makes the executive late for business conference, thus causing the executive to lose a profitable deal, the cabbie proba-

Restatement closer to the moral rationale for *Hadley* than a pure foresee-ability rule. However, the Restatement deviates from that rationale in important respects. The Restatement does not expressly address the burden of proof issue, but its wording suggests that damages would be recoverable unless circumstances affirmatively show the defendant did not agree to assume particular risks. This, coupled with the Restatement's rejection of the distinction between general and special damages in this context,[20] seems to reverse the burden that *Hadley* put upon the plaintiff to show that the defendant had assumed the risks of special damages. The Restatement differs, too, in making damages a matter of discretion rather than a matter of right.

Unallocated risks, judicial discretion. Finally, the Restatement departs significantly from *Hadley* limitations and other damages rules in providing for cases in which, because of informality of the contracting situation, the parties did not attempt to allocate risks in any clear way. Instead of assuming, with *Hadley,* that the risk was not allocated to the defendant if it reflected consequential damages, the Restatement discards the distinction between special and general damages. It then invites the judge to deal with the uncertainty, not through proof burdens, but by judicial allocation of risks in whatever way seems fair to the judge, or possibly the jury.

§ 12.4(7) Contemplation of the Parties: Applications and Subsidiary Principles

[*For the text of this section, see the unabridged Practitioner Treatise edition.*]

§ 12.5 Extracontractual Damages: Emotional Distress and Punitive Damages

§ 12.5(1) Emotional Distress Damages

Rule and Exceptions Generally

General rule. The general rule is that no award may be made for emotional or mental distress resulting from contract breach alone.[1] The rule normally excludes intangible damages for loss of reputation as well.[2]

Escaping the rule under contract theory. In addition to a series of traditional exceptions listed below, there are two separate routes that may be used to escape the proscription against emotional distress damages. *First,* the plaintiff can show that emotional distress damages were contemplated by the parties in the particular case, as where the contract is for some highly

bly should not be liable for the profit loss because his undertaking did not include any such risks. A literal application of the Restatement formula seems to suggest that the cabbie might be held liable if the executive's profit loss was $100 but not if it was $10,000. The evidence that makes us think the cabbie never contemplated the assumption of a profit-loss risk is not the dollar disproportion between cab fare and the actual profit lost, but the disproportion of a (standard) cab fare to *any* profit claim. It is the fact that cabbies do not vary their fare with the passenger's poten-tial loss or gain, not the amount of loss the particular passenger actually suffered.

20. Restatement Second of Contracts § 351, Comment *b* (1981).

§ 12.5(1)

1. Marcella v. ARP Films, Inc., 778 F.2d 112 (2d Cir.1985); Westwater v. Rector of Grace Church, 140 Cal. 339, 73 P. 1055 (1903); Rubin v. Matthews International Corp., 503 A.2d 694 (Me.1986); Restatement Second of Contracts § 353 (1981).

personal, intangible benefit. Such a showing is unusual but possible. A funeral director who contracts with the deceased's mother to keep punk rockers out of the funeral ceremonies is probably on notice that the mother will suffer distress if he breaches the contract by allowing abusive rockers to attend the funeral at all, and certainly if he allows them to take drugs, abuse the mourners and to express their feelings at the cemetery by wearing dresses made of live rats.[6]

Escaping the rule under tort theory. Emotional distress damages may be recovered if the plaintiff can show that the defendant breached the contract by conduct that also amounts to a tort.

[*For discussion of the tort and contract exceptions and a critique, see this section in the Practitioner Treatise edition.*]

§ 12.5(2) Punitive Damages for Breach of Contract

General Rules

Rule against punitive awards. The firmly established common law rule holds that punitive damages are not to be awarded for simple breach of contract.[1] The Uniform Commercial Code calls for the same rule except where punitive damages are specifically authorized.[2] The rule against punitive damages prevails even if the breach is wilful or malicious, so long as the breach does not amount to an independent tort.[3] To these rules there is almost no stated dissent in the courts.[4]

The "exceptions" to the rule. If a breach of contract also constitutes a violation of fiduciary duties[5] or other tort[6] for which punitive damages may be awarded, such damages are recoverable for that reason. Punitive damages may also be awarded for fraud in inducing the contract in the first place, as distinct from a breach that is tortious.[7] These rules are closely parallel to those applied in claims for emotional distress in contract cases.[8] As in the emotional distress cases, public utilities and carriers may be subject to punitive damages for breach of contract, although such cases usually involve at least some tortious elements as well.[9] In addition there is

---

6. Ross v. Forest Lawn Memorial Park, 153 Cal.App.3d 988, 203 Cal.Rptr. 468, 42 A.L.R.4th 1049 (1984).

§ 12.5(2)

1. Thyssen, Inc. v. S.S. Fortune Star, 777 F.2d 57 (2d Cir.1985) (admiralty, simple contract breach, no punitive damages); L.L. Cole & Son, Inc. v. Hickman, 282 Ark. 6, 665 S.W.2d 278 (1984); Walker v. Signal Companies, Inc., 84 Cal.App.3d 982, 149 Cal.Rptr. 119 (1978) ("Punitive damages are not recoverable in an action for breach of contract no matter how wilful, malicious or fraudulent the breach"); Berryhill v. Hatt, 428 N.W.2d 647 (Iowa 1988) ("A breach of contract alone, even if intentional, will not form the basis of punitive damages * * *. Rather, the breach must also constitute an intentional tort, or other wrongful act, committed with legal malice, that is with willful or reckless disregard for another's rights"); Halpin v. Prudential Ins. Co. of America, 48 N.Y.2d 906, 425 N.Y.S.2d

48, 401 N.E.2d 171 (1979); Stack Electric Inc. v. DiNardi Const. Corp., 161 A.D.2d 416, 555 N.Y.S.2d 346 (1990); International Bank, N.A. v. Morales, 736 S.W.2d 622 (Tex.1987); Restatement Second of Contracts § 355 (1981).

2. UCC § 1–106(1) provides that "neither consequential or special nor penal damages may be had except as specifically provided in this Act or by other rule of law."

9. See Sullivan, Punitive Damages in the Law of Contract: The Reality and the Illusion of Legal Change, 61 Minn.L.Rev. 207, 224–25 (1977). In Ft. Smith & W.R. Co. v. Ford, 34 Okl. 575, 126 P. 745 (1912) a train carried a ticketed passenger beyond his stop and he sued. The court concluded that the contract of carriage was merely in the background of the case and that the essence of the case was tort for which punitive damages could be awarded because its duty to stop was recklessly disregarded.

the old rule, bizarre in today's world, that one is subject to punitive damages for breach of a contract to marry, perhaps in reality a displaced recognition of emotional distress damages.[10] Punitive damages, usually in limited amounts, may also be permitted under statutes governing particular transactions.[11]

Rationales. One stated basis for the rule is simply definitional: contract remedies are intended to provide compensation and hence punishment is inappropriate.[12] More fundamentally, however, the rule against punitive damages for contract breach is usually thought to represent the efficient breach principle that one should be permitted to breach the contract so long as he pays the damages required to put the non-breaching party in his rightful position.[13]

[*For discussion of the expanding liability issue, see this section in the Practitioner Treatise edition.*]

§ 12.6 Adjustments in Damages

§ 12.6(1) Summary of Adjustments

Almost all damages measures, whether in contract cases or not, are subject to the possibility of several adjustments. Aside from those special limitations imposed when consequential damages are sought,[1] the main adjustments in the contract award are as follows:

(1) Credits for Prepayments and Benefits Bestowed

When the defendant commits a total breach after the plaintiff has made prepayments, the plaintiff is entitled to recover the prepayment as well as additional expectation damages such as those measured by a market-contract differential. When the defendant has made prepayments or has partly performed to the benefit of the plaintiff, the defendant, though liable as a breacher, is normally entitled to a credit for prepayments or the value of part performance delivered.[2]

(2) Savings Effected

To the extent that the defendant's breach obviates the necessity for the plaintiff's own performance or some part of it, the breach gives the plaintiff an element of savings, since the plaintiff will not have the expense of completing performance. Much the same is true if the breach leaves the plaintiff holding salvageable materials. The savings thus effected to the plaintiff by reason of the breach are deducted from the damage otherwise due the plaintiff. The rule is mainly applicable to contracts involving a substantial element of personal services. For example, if landowner repudiates a building contract when the contractor has completed half the work, the contractor may be entitled to recover the contract price, with a deduction for savings he makes because he need not perform the remainder of the contract.[3]

(3) Interest

Interest is always awarded on money damages from the time of judgment. In addition, if the contract itself provides for interest, as is common in the case of loan contracts and the like, those provisions are generally enforceable.[7] Indeed, general damages for breach of a lender's contract to lend money are based on the difference between interest rate promised and market interest rate.[8] The common law rule also permitted prejudgment interest, running from the time the obligation fell due, if the obligation was liquidated, that is, for a certain sum of money, and even if it was not liquidated but could be reduced to a liquidated sum [9] by use of a formula that required no discretion.[10] These rules apply generally in contract cases. In addition, statutes are sometimes more generous in the provision for interest.

(4) *Reduction to Present Value*

So far as damages represent losses that are expected to occur in the future, those damages are traditionally reduced to present value. The rule applies in contract cases as well as others.[11] The idea is that if the plaintiff recovers money today that is not needed to replace a loss until sometime in the future, the plaintiff can invest the money and reap the interest. Full compensation does not require an award of the money when due plus the interest it can presently earn. The reduction to present value attempts to provide an award that gives the plaintiff an amount of present capital which, with the interest it can safely earn, will provide a total sufficient to compensate for the loss when the loss occurs.

(5) *Attorney Fees*

The "American rule" does not include attorney fees as part of the prevailing party's damages.[15] That rule recognizes that a contract may provide for attorney fees going to the prevailing party.[16] Such a contract provision, however, may be subject to the rules which limit the parties' power to provide their own damages measures, because in some instances an attorney fee provision might be regarded as a "penalty" rather than as liquidated damages.[17] In addition to the possibility of a contract provision for attorney fees, statutes may sometimes provide for attorney fee awards to the prevailing party in cases arising out of contract.[18] More modest statutes merely equalize attorney fee provisions in the contract, so that a fee provision favoring only the prevailing seller is applied by the statute to award the fee to the prevailing buyer as well.[19] Otherwise, recovery of attorney fee costs in contract cases is relatively rare.

(6) *Avoidable Consequences, Minimizing Damages*

The plaintiff's contract damages are adjusted to exclude special damages that were actually avoided by the plaintiff's post-breach efforts to minimize damages. In addition, the damage recovery is reduced to the extent that the plaintiff could reasonably have avoided damages he claims and is otherwise entitled to. On the other hand, the plaintiff's damages are adjusted upward to reflect all the reasonable costs he incurs in attempting to avoid losses, whether or not he was successful in doing so.[20] This topic is developed further in the following subsection.

(7) *Collateral Source Payments*

The common law collateral source rule, most often seen in injury litigation, holds that the defendant gets no credit on the liability otherwise incurred merely because the plaintiff's net damages are reduced by donations or payments from others. The rule is now being affected by statutes.[21]

The most frequent case is the one in which the injury victim's losses are meliorated by insurance. Under the collateral source rule, the defendant pays the plaintiff's damages as though plaintiff had collected no insurance at all.

Some cases have refused to apply the collateral source rule in contract claims, at least in the absence of tort-like elements. Others have applied it, notably where the plaintiff has been discharged from employment in breach of contract and is able to reduce his net loss by collecting unemployment or other public benefits. In those cases, courts have usually applied the collateral source rule to deny the defendant any credit for the public benefit.[22]

§ 12.6(2)   The Avoidable Consequences Rules

[*Consult the summary in § 3.9 above and see this section in the Practitioner Treatise edition. As to anticipatory repudiation and avoidable consequences, see the appendix to this section in the Practitioner Treatise edition.*]

§ 12.6(3)   Must General Damages Be Minimized?

[*For the text of this section, see the unabridged Practitioner Treatise edition.*]

§ 12.6(4)   The Collateral Source Rule

[*Consult the summary in § 3.8(1) above and see this section in the Practitioner Treatise edition.*]

§ 12.7   Money Awards as Restitution for Breach of Contract

§ 12.7(1)   General Rules Permitting Restitution

Roles of Restitution in Contracting

Restitution. Restitution—recovery of benefits conferred—is permitted to prevent unjust enrichment.[1] Restitution is an important remedy in connection with contracting. Sometimes, because of the way "benefit" is defined in practice,[2] decisions ostensibly based on "restitution" may operate in fact to fill gaps in the parties' bargain, or to adjust their obligations in ways that go beyond any simple return of benefits.[3]

Avoidable or unenforceable contracts. Restitution is most commonly sought, not as a remedy for breach of a fully enforceable contract, but when the contract is avoided for fraud,[4] mistake,[5] duress[6] or the like, or when the contract is not enforceable because of the statute of frauds,[7] or because of impracticability or frustration.[8] In all of those situations, the party who has by performance conferred benefits on the other may have a claim for restitution of those benefits or their value, even though he may not enforce the contract.

Restitution to the party in default. In some cases, even the party in breach of a contract may be entitled to restitution. The traditional rule was otherwise, but the modern view, favored by the Restatement[9] and by the Uniform Commercial Code,[10] requires the innocent party to make restitution of benefits he has received so far as those benefits exceed his damages.

§ 12.7(1)

1. Restatement of Restitution § 1 (1937).

Adoption of the modern view permitting restitution to the party in default raises new questions whether the innocent party can keep the defaulting party's payments of earnest money [11] or installments.[12] Although these questions are considered in other sections, rights of the defaulting party are not the main focus of this chapter.

Restitution for breach of enforceable contract. This chapter is principally concerned with remedies for breach of fully enforceable contracts. Restitution is sometimes an alternative remedy for a substantial breach of contract as well as a device for dealing with unenforceable agreements. That is the topic of this section. Restitution is not normally granted for trivial breaches.

General Rules Permitting Restitution for Contract Breach

Restitution vs. damages. A damages award focuses on the victim's loss and seeks compensation (or partial compensation); the restitution award focuses on the breacher and seeks to prevent his unjust enrichment by forcing restitution of gains he received under the contract. In many instances the dollar amount of damages would be the same as the dollar amount of restitution. In other cases the amounts are not the same. The plaintiff will prefer restitution when it is easier to prove than damages and when it will yield a greater recovery than damages.

General rules. The general principle is that upon the defendant's substantial breach or repudiation of an enforceable contract, the plaintiff is entitled to recover restitution of any benefits he has conferred in performance of the contract,[13] for example, any part of the price which he has prepaid,[14] or the reasonable value of any services rendered as contract performance.[15] In those rare cases in which a policy reason prevents the plaintiff's recovery of expectancy damage, restitution is still available.[16] More commonly, a restitutionary recovery is merely an alternative remedy [17] for total or substantial breach [18] of contract. In such cases restitution is given in lieu of expectancy damages, not in addition to such damages.[19] If, however, the plaintiff has separate incidental reliance losses, recovery of both restitution and reliance loss may be proper.[20]

The restitutionary claim can be conceived as simply an alternative remedy for contract breach; or it can be conceived as the second of two steps consisting of rescission or avoidance of the contract for breach, followed by restitution. In line with a "rescission" conception, even the breaching party may be entitled to restitution in some cases, if the benefits he has conferred by performance exceed the loss of the other party.[21]

Restitution illustrated. Although restitutionary issues may be complex in some cases, in others they are simple and the results intuitive and predictable. Suppose the plaintiff contracts to purchase an automobile for $20,000 and pays $5,000 toward its price. When the plaintiff tenders the balance of the price, the defendant repudiates the contract and refuses to transfer the car. The plaintiff may recover the $5,000 as restitution.

Restitution and expectancy. In the car purchase illustration it is easy to distinguish restitution from expectancy. To obtain restitution the plaintiff need only establish the amount of the benefits conferred upon the defendant, the $5,000. To establish expectancy damages, however, the plaintiff would be required to show the market-contract differential, or else some consequential damages. If the expectancy was a loss, perhaps because the car was worth only $18,000, the plaintiff would prefer restitution and would always seek that remedy rather than the expectancy. Even if the expectancy was not a loss, the restitution claim may be easier to assert as a practical matter; it raises no doubts about the facts and it is morally and intuitively a compelling claim. Recovery of restitution in cases like this is usually permitted, even though the recovery puts the plaintiff in a better position than performance would have done.[22]

Restitution and reliance. The plaintiff's prepayment of $5,000 in the car purchase illustration may also be compared to reliance claims. In fact, the plaintiff's payment fits the definition of reliance damages, because the prepayment is an expense incurred in performance of his obligations under the contract.[23] In the car purchase illustration the plaintiff could recover the $5,000 as reliance damages just as well as he could recover that sum as restitution. But there is a difference between reliance and restitution that can be important in many cases.

The heart of the difference is that the claim qualifies as one for restitution *only* if it is a claim to recover benefits conferred upon the defendant.[24] In the car purchase case, the $5,000 is restitution only because the defendant has received that sum of money. If the plaintiff had ordered custom equipment for the car from another source, the lost expense of that equipment would count as reliance damages, but it would not count as restitution because the special equipment order would not represent a benefit or enrichment in the hands of the defendant. The moral claim for restitution of benefits received by the defendant is emphatically more compelling than the claim for reliance. It represents—in this instance at least—both a loss to the plaintiff *and* a benefit to the breacher.

The moral stature of the restitution claim makes a practical difference when the expectancy is negative. The plaintiff may not recover mere reliance expenses in excess of the expectancy.[25] But a restitution claim stands on better ground, at least in cases like the car purchase. The plaintiff can recover the $5,000 prepayment even if, upon performance, he would have taken a loss of $10,000.[26] Restitutionary claims do not invariably produce such a dramatic result. But when the plaintiff can recover benefit to the defendant in excess of the plaintiff's own lost expectancy, the practical difference between restitution and reliance is quite clear.

§ 12.7(2) Form of Restitution—Specific vs. Monetary

Restitution for breach of contract ordinarily takes the form of a money recovery. However, when the plaintiff has transferred a specific thing that

24. Professor Perillo argues that restitution in fact is not limited to prevention of unjust enrichment—benefits conferred—but that it really aims at restoration of the status quo ante. See Perillo, Restitution in a Contractual Context, 73 Colum.L.Rev. 1208 (1973); see also J. Calamari & J. Perillo, The Law of Contracts § 15–2 (3d ed. 1987). As the terms are used here in this treatise, restitution describes return to the status quo ante where that return is accomplished by depriving the defendant of unjust gain; and the term reliance describes return to the status quo ante where that is accomplished by imposing liabilities in excess of the defendant's unjust enrichment. The different terminology signals a different treatment of the two kinds of claims when those claims exceed the plaintiff's expectancy and also when those claims are asserted in the absence of an enforceable contract. The point is less important when the contract is enforceable and more important when enforcement is forbidden by the statute of frauds. See § 13.2 below.

can be returned, specific restitution is sometimes appropriate. The plaintiff can plausibly claim restitution of specific goods or property that she gave as her performance of the contract when the property is unique or has special qualities. For example, if the plaintiff contracted to exchange a Picasso for a Van Gogh, the plaintiff should surely recover the Picasso she transferred when the defendant breaches his contract to transfer the Van Gogh. Courts would grant specific performance of a contract to transfer property with such special qualities, so they should equally grant specific restitution for breach.

The plaintiff can also plausibly claim specific restitution when she holds a security interest in the goods which she has transferred; in that case, she is simply enforcing her security interest by recovering the goods when the defendant breaches by nonpayment or otherwise.

The contracts Restatement, following Professor Palmer,[1] takes a much broader view than this line of reasoning suggests. Those authorities would permit specific restitution[2] in favor of the non-breaching party[3] without the traditional adequacy requirement[4] imposed in specific performance cases.

The wider availability of specific restitution under the Restatement might be justified on the broad ground, sometimes urged, that specific performance itself should be granted freely.[5] It might also be justified on the narrower ground that the breach victim has a better claim to specific return of his own performance than he has to the performance promised by the other party.

The Uniform Commercial Code does not appear to adopt the liberal stance of the Restatement in favor of a seller of goods whose buyer breaches. Specific restitution under the Code, which goes by the name of "reclamation" in that document, seems to be permitted only in certain cases of buyer-insolvency unless the seller has retained a security interest in the goods.[6] So the liberalizing effect of the Restatement may be limited, and in fact its illustrations involve specific restitution of land or unique values, such that a promise to transfer such items would be specifically enforced.[7]

Even under the Restatement position, rejection of an adequacy test does not guarantee specific restitution. Leading commentators have recognized

§ 12.7(2)

1. I George Palmer, Law of Restitution § 4.7 (1978 & Supps.).

2. Restatement Second of Contracts § 372 (1981). The Restatement formulation authorizes refusal of specific restitution in the court's discretion when specific restitution would unduly interfere with certainty of land title or "otherwise cause injustice."

3. Although money restitution is available even to the breacher in some cases under the Restatement, specific restitution is not. Restatement Second of Contracts § 372(1)(b) (1981).

4. See § 2.5, above.

5. See § 12.8 as to specific performance generally.

6. Uniform Commercial Code § 2–702 provides for reclaiming the specific goods sold after buyer breaches where the buyer received goods on credit while insolvent. See J. White & R. Summers, Uniform Commercial Code §§ 7–17 and 25–14 (1988).

7. Restatement Second of Contracts § 372, Illustrations 2–4 all involve the plaintiff's transfer of land (in some of which specific restitution is defeated or conditioned by other equities). Illustration 5 involves the plaintiff's transfer of half of his stock to defendant, who promises to organize a holding company to control the corporation and to protect the plaintiff's interest as a shareholder. If the parties were reversed so that the defendant had promised to deliver the land or the shareholder rights, specific performance would be granted even under very restrictive notions of the adequacy test.

that courts are more reluctant to order specific restitution in cases of contract breach than in cases of contract rescission or avoidance.[8] The Restatement accommodates this reluctance, not by the traditional adequacy test, but by recognizing discretion to deny specific restitution. That discretion is informed by a desire to protect certainty in land titles, a desire to protect innocent third persons, and a desire to assure restitution by the plaintiff as well as to him.

§ 12.7(3)   Mode of Measurement for Money Restitution

Generally

Benefits Conferred in Performance of the Contract

Restitution of price. When the plaintiff has conferred a benefit upon the breaching defendant by paying a price or part of a price in money, the usual measure of restitution is recovery of the price, plus interest.[7]

Restitution of the defendant's profits. The general rule is that restitution is *not* measured by the benefits defendant obtains collateral to his breach but by the value of the plaintiff's performance. Under this rule the defendant who reneges on his contract with the plaintiff in order to render the same performance elsewhere at a higher price is not liable for the advantage thus secured. Although there are a few qualifications and exceptions to this rule,[8] it remains the rule of general application.

Value of performance bargained for. When the plaintiff's performance is not payment of money, one possible measure of restitution is the value of that performance by some more or less objective measure. For instance, if the plaintiff is hired to paint the defendant's house, the plaintiff's partial performance can be valued, at least approximately, in the "market" for such services, so that the plaintiff can recover the value of his services even if the partial performance adds nothing to the value of the house.[9] The principle is a general though not inflexible one; it is not limited to service contracts as such. When the plaintiff's performance represents the very acts bargained for and no special equities counsel otherwise,[10] the defendant is liable to make restitution for the value of the very thing bargained for, even when the performance adds nothing to the defendant's wealth.[11]

Because restitution aims at preventing unjust enrichment of the defendant, the plaintiff's *cost* in providing that enrichment is not the measure of restitution. Somewhat similarly, the plaintiff's efforts that do not count as performance of the bargain but are merely part of the plaintiff's preparation, would not count as benefits conferred on the defendant.[12] On the other

8. See I George Palmer, Law of Restitution § 4.7, (1978 & Supps.) (recognizing some situations in which a party should be held to the terms of the contract and thus recover money payments due under that contract rather than the performance he has delivered); Allan Farnsworth, Contracts § 12.19, p. 907 (1982).

§ 12.7(3)

12. Professor Palmer explains the difference in I George Palmer, Law of Restitution § 4.2 (1978). If the contract is that the plaintiff will sell the defendant a dog house, and

the plaintiff decides to build the house himself, his work on the house is not performance of the promise, which is only to sell a dog house to the defendant. If the contract is to *build* a dog house for the defendant, the plaintiff's work and expense on the house is truly performance toward the promise and would count as a benefit. In the first instance the plaintiff may recover for his efforts, not as restitution but as reliance expense, but subject to the limits applied to reliance claims.

hand, once part performance takes place, the cost of that performance to the plaintiff may at times furnish good evidence about the value of the performance and may be admissible and even persuasive on that ground.[13]

Additions to the defendant's wealth from plaintiff's performance. When the plaintiff sues for expectancy damages he might claim the value of the very performance he was promised, or he might claim the value of some desirable consequence the promised performance might bring. When the plaintiff sues for restitution, the same dichotomy applies in estimating benefits. Instead of suing for the value of his services, the house painter in the example above might consider suing for the consequential benefits his services brought to the defendant—added value to the defendant's house, for example. It is unlikely on the facts of this example that the value of the defendant's land is improved by a sum greater than the reasonable value of the plaintiff's services, so the plaintiff would normally prefer to measure restitution by the market value of his service. But if the plaintiff's work added more value to the house than the services were themselves worth in the market for house-painting services, then the Restatement would invite the court to give the more generous measure if that comported with its judgment about the justice of the case.[14]

Benefits Conferred in Reliance but not in Performance

The measures of restitution discussed above deal with restitution for performance or part performance by the plaintiff. However, it is also possible for the plaintiff to confer a benefit by acting in incidental reliance on the contract—that is, by some means other than performance of his contract obligation. For example, the defendant contracts to convey Blackacre to the plaintiff and permits the plaintiff to make improvements on the land before title is passed. If the defendant then breaches, and retains the land and the improvements, he may be unjustly enriched because he holds improvements made by the plaintiff.

The measure of restitution in that kind of case differs from the ones earlier discussed. In the house painter example, the defendant bargained for and got the performance, the paint work. That being so, it is fair to hold him liable for restitution and maybe even for the higher measure of restitution. In the case of the defendant who fails to convey Blackacre as promised, however, the defendant has not asked for the improvements and may not want them; if he wants them, he may not value them at market value. In this setting, the plaintiff seeking restitution may properly be limited to the less generous method of measuring restitution. If his time and labor could have brought him $10,000 but the land is improved only by $2,000, then the defendant's liability should be limited to the $2,000 figure.[18]

14. Restatement Second of Contracts § 371 (1981). Cf. A. Corbin, Contracts § 1112 (1964 and Supps.) (doubts and difficulties to be resolved against the defendant, on the view that would be rejected by many, that the contract breacher is a "wrongdoer").

18. Passmore v. Woodard, 37 N.C.App. 535, 246 S.E.2d 795 (1978). See Restatement Second of Contracts § 371, Comment *a* (1981).

Professor Palmer recognizes that "benefits" resulting from collateral reliance rather than from performance differ in that benefits conferred in performance were requested or bargained for. He thinks, nevertheless, that the plaintiff should be entitled to restitution measured by the market value of his labor, even though that exceeds any increase in the land's value. I George Palmer § 4.18, p. 526 (1978). Palmer notes that language of the cases al-

§ 12.7(4)   Restitution Based on Defendant's Profits in Connection With Breach

General Rule

Wrongdoer's profits recoverable in tort cases.   One who obtains another's property by fraud or embezzlement and sells or invests it at a gain is liable to make restitution to the fraud victim.[1]   In the same way, a fiduciary who uses the beneficiary's business opportunity or property to make a gain must make restitution of any profits he obtains from use of the opportunity or property.[2]   Even an ordinary tortfeasor who converts the plaintiff's chattel and sells it at a profit is liable for the profit.[3]

Breacher's profits generally denied in contract cases.   Writers sometimes argue for applying the tort rules to contract cases, or to some particular kinds of contract cases.[4]   But the practice in contract cases is to the contrary: one who merely breaches a contract is not required to restore collateral profits or gains facilitated by the breach.[5]   It is convenient to speak of this strong practice as a rule.   The rule of course does not preclude damages based upon the plaintiff's loss, nor even all restitution.   The breacher is liable for restitution of any price the plaintiff has paid on the contract, or the market value of any performance the breacher has received. In some circumstances, the breacher may also be liable to make restitution based on consequential value of performance received as his due under the contract.[6]   The "rule" merely permits the breacher to retain gains or profits that result from [7] his own breach but that are not the result of the plaintiff's own performance.

Illustration of the contract rule.   If these distinctions are puzzling in the abstract they may be entirely understandable in the concrete.   Suppose the defendant promises to sell the plaintiff widgets for $10,000.   At the time for performance $10,000 is the market value of the widgets, but the defendant finds a special opportunity to sell his warehoused widgets for $15,000. Although there is a market, he cannot replace them in time for performance of his contract with the plaintiff.   The plaintiff purchases substitute widgets in the market at the same price and suffers no damages based on the market-contract differential and little or no damage based on delay.   Although it may seem to some that the defendant has gained at the plaintiff's expense,[8] the general rule means that the defendant is not obliged to make "restitution" to the plaintiff of the $5,000 gain he made by selling the widgets to a better buyer.   If the parties are reversed and the buyer breaches, using his money to invest in a winning race horse rather than to pay the contract price the no-restitution result becomes even more obvious.

[*For discussion of the bases for the rule, see this section in the Practitioner Treatise edition.*]

Scope of or Exceptions to the Rule

(1) Contract combined with tort or fiduciary breach.   Some torts and some fiducial breaches might arise in a contractual setting and might even entail breach of a contract as well as breach of a tort or fiduciary duty.   An

ludes variously to costs of the improvement, market value of labor and materials, enhanced land value or some combination.   Id. at p. 524.

employee's use of a trade secret or inside information might at the same time violate contractual provisions and fiduciary duties. Similarly, property agreements between spouses might raise equitable duties as well as purely contractual ones. Restitution of the wrongdoer's profits in such cases may be awarded even though the wrongdoing is also a breach of contract.[13]

A much-doubted decision but one that strikingly illustrates the point is *Snepp v. United States.*[14] Snepp, as part of his work for the Central Intelligence Agency, contracted with that body (a) not to reveal classified information and (b) not to publish *any* information about the agency without prepublication clearance. Snepp wrote a book, published by a distinguished publisher. He revealed no classified information but publication of the book violated the agreement not to publish without clearance. The Supreme Court forced Snepp to disgorge all profits earned for him by publication, on the ground that the contract violation was also a breach of fiduciary duty. It may be unwise to require restitution of profits in some such cases,[15] or to characterize all employee contract violations as fiducial breaches; but *Snepp* shows that if restitution should be forbidden on those facts, it is not forbidden by the rule against restitution from contract breachers.

(2) Plaintiff acquires a property right in the defendant's promised performance: equitable conversion. If the defendant profits by converting and using the plaintiff's goods, the plaintiff is entitled to recover restitution from the defendant measured by his profits. The contract rule does not apply to cases in which the plaintiff's own property is used to generate profits for the defendant. In a contract setting a seller might sell the plaintiff goods or real property in such a way that the plaintiff has become not merely a promisee but the owner (at least for some purposes). If the buyer has become the owner in any relevant sense and the seller *then* manages to deprive the plaintiff of possession or ownership, the seller seems to be in the role of a converter of the goods or a constructive trustee of the realty. Either way, the seller would be liable for profits he takes from use or resale of the plaintiff's property. The basis for liability would be the ordinary liability of the tortfeasor to make restitution of gains achieved through his wrong.

The strange doctrine of equitable conversion enters the picture here to create a similar situation. Suppose the plaintiff contracts to buy Blackacre. Contracts to purchase land are traditionally enforced by specific performance almost routinely. This routine availability of specific performance led equity courts to regard the contract purchaser of land as obtaining an equitable interest in the land from the time the contract was made.[16] In the eyes of equity, the purchaser was the owner, even though legal title remained for the nonce in the vendor. The division of legal title and equitable interest was the same as seen in cases of trust, which equity had also

§ 12.7(4)

14. Snepp v. United States, 444 U.S. 507, 100 S.Ct. 763, 62 L.Ed.2d 704 (1980).

15. Professor Farnsworth criticizes *Snepp* on the ground that if the CIA could not properly have refused permission, Snepp could have made the same profits without breach of the contract, so that breach was not a cause in fact of the profits earned. He also points out that the Court made no apportionment of the profits, even though they must have been earned not merely from breach alone but also from Snepp's non-breaching efforts. See Farnsworth, Your Loss or My Gain? The Dilemma of the Disgorgement Principle in Breach of Contract, 94 Yale L.J. 1339, 1359 (1985).

created. Under this familiar idea, equity would regard the plaintiff-purchaser of the land as the "real" owner of it, and if the defendant vendor then sold the land to some third person, he might be held liable to make restitution of his profit from the sale. But not because he was a contract breacher; rather, because he interfered, in the eyes of equity, with the plaintiff's existing property rights.

There are a few cases that support this view and thus permit restitution of the breacher's profits where the purchaser has become the equitable owner of the land.[17] Because the whole structure of this rule is based on routine availability of specific performance, and because goods contracts were not so readily given such enforcement, the same line of reasoning is not as likely to be persuasive in sales of goods cases.[18] It is even more unlikely that one who breaches a contract to provide services to the plaintiff would be liable to make restitution for better wages earned elsewhere in breach of the contract.[19]

(3) Plaintiff's own performance used to generate profits for breaching defendant. The discussion so far has considered cases like that in the illustration—the breacher does not deliver the goods he promised, but instead sells those very goods to another buyer for a better price, reaping a gain of $5,000 by doing so. This kind of case can be described as a case in which the defendant breaches by not performing his own promise.

An arguably different case occurs if the defendant not only has not delivered his own performance but has taken the plaintiff's performance and used it to obtain collateral gains. For example, suppose the vendor of land conveys title to the purchaser. The purchaser, who is to pay later, breaches by nonpayment, but sells the land at a great profit. Or the parties could be reversed. The buyer might pay money without getting title and the vendor might then use the purchaser's money to make a very profitable investment. In either of these two instances the breacher has profited by resale of the plaintiff's performance, not by the resale of his own performance. There seems to be little authority or even discussion.[20]

(4) "Abuse of contract". Professor Farnsworth proposed a limited exception to the rule against restitution of breacher's profits.[21] He envisioned a situation in which a building contractor substitutes materials cheaper than those called for in the contract, saving costs and thus enhancing profit. The switch also results in a building worth less.[22] Expectancy measured by cost of completion might resolve the problem in some cases, but such a measure probably would not be used if the cost of undoing the work and replacing it would substantially exceed the value such effort would produce. With this situation in mind, Professor Farnsworth proposes a rule allowing restitution

17. Defeyter v. Riley, 671 P.2d 995 (Colo. App.1983); Coppola Enterprises, Inc. v. Alfone, 531 So.2d 334 (1988); Timko v. Useful Homes Corp., 114 N.J.Eq. 433, 168 A. 824 (Ch.1933); cf. Popp v. Gountanis, 221 Mont. 267, 718 P.2d 340 (1986) (farm lease required lessee to pay one-third crops to landlord and entitled him to keep two-thirds; when federal program paid landlord not to plant crops, lessee was entitled to recover two-thirds of that payment). See generally 1 George Palmer, Law of Restitution § 4.9 (1978).

20. Palmer opposes restitution of profits in such cases. See I George Palmer, Law of Restitution § 4.9, p. 451 (1978).

21. Farnsworth, Your Loss or My Gain? The Dilemma of the Disgorgement Principle in Breach of Contract, 94 Yale L.J. 1339, 1382 (1985).

of the breacher's gains from the breach when the breacher abuses the contract. The breacher abuses the contract, he suggests, when "you, the injured party, are left with a defective performance and no opportunity to use your return performance to obtain a substitute." [23] On the facts of this illustration, the idea that restitution of profits is appropriate when the plaintiff acquires a property right in the defendant's performance might suggest the same result.

But in at least some of the cases falling under the Farnsworth proposal, the measure of restitution would be limited. His limit would apply to the kind of case in which a contractor leases land from the owner to mine minerals and promises to restore its surface at the end of the lease. It turns out that cost of restoration will be $60,000 but that expenditure of this sum will only increase the land's value by $10,000. The contractor who breaches will save (profit) by $50,000 even after paying expectancy damages based on the market-contract differential. Although this case fits the proposed abuse of contract rule, Professor Farnsworth argues that only gains caused in fact should be recoverable. In his analysis, the only gain caused in fact is not the $50,000 that performance would have cost the contractor. The contractor, instead of performing, could have bargained with the landowner for payment of some price between the $10,000 market-contract differential and the $60,000 savings. Although we cannot know what that sum would have been, it is only that sum which has been saved by the breach and courts should attempt to estimate it. The result would be that the gain resulting from breach would be shared in some proportion by the breacher and the victim.

§ 12.7(5) Expectancy or Price as a Limit on Restitution

Rule summary. In general, restitution, when allowable for breach of an enforceable contract,[1] is recoverable in amounts that may exceed the plaintiff's expectancy damages, (or the rate of expectancy damages for part performance) in two situations: (1) when the plaintiff has prepaid a price and seeks its recovery, or, similarly, when the plaintiff is entitled to recover tangible property in specie; and (2) when the plaintiff has partly performed a contract for services and/or goods and seeks to recover the value of the performance after breach. Some decisions reflect a contrary view by refusing to allow restitution in excess of expectancy in part performance cases.[2]

In general, restitution in excess of the plaintiff's expectancy is denied when (1) the plaintiff seeks to recover the defendant's collateral profits resulting from the defendant's breach; and (2) when the plaintiff has fully performed and the defendant's only remaining obligation is to pay a sum of money.

The full performance/liquidated sum rule in effect makes expectancy a ceiling in the cases to which it applies. In a California case,[4] an attorney contracted to represent the defendant in a certain matter for $750. The matter dragged on and the attorney eventually performed work valued at $5,000, before being discharged by the client-defendant. In retrospect it could be seen that the lawyer had a losing contract. Five thousand dollars

§ 12.7(5)
4. Oliver v. Campbell, 43 Cal.2d 298, 273 P.2d 15 (1954).

in services would be delivered in exchange for a mere $750 payment. Restitution for the value of the services would far exceed the contract price. But the court considered that the attorney had substantially performed. Because all that remained was then payment of a liquidated sum of money, the client was liable for the contract price, not for the value of the services.

Restitution for value of non-money partial performance. Restitution in excess of the plaintiff's expectancy is also allowed when the plaintiff's performance consists of non-monetary benefits such as services, so long as the plaintiff's performance is incomplete.[6] (Once the performance is complete, the full performance/liquidated sum rule will limit recovery to the contract price.) The rule allowing the plaintiff to recover restitution in excess of the contract price or the plaintiff's expectancy even though he has only partly performed is remarkable. If full performance were completed, the plaintiff's expectancy would be the limit of the recovery. With part performance, he may recover more.

Another example is found in a well known case, *Boomer v. Muir.*[8] There a subcontractor recovered restitution for the value of his services—"quantum meruit"—of more than $250,000 against the general contractor. Under the contract price he probably would have recovered no more than $20,000. Perhaps even more striking, the plaintiff appears to have lost money each step of the way, so that a termination of the plaintiff's performance before completion might actually have saved the plaintiff from further losses.[9] A number of other construction[10] and manufacturing cases[11] are in accord.

[*For additional discussion, see this section in the Practitioner Treatise edition.*]

§ 12.7(6)　Recovery of Both Restitution and Damages:　Election of Remedies

[*Consult the summary in § 9.4 above and see this section in the Practitioner Treatise edition.*]

§ 12.7(7)　Restitution Claims Against Non-parties

Sometimes the plaintiff's performance of an enforceable contract with *A* results in a benefit to *B*, with whom the plaintiff had no contract at all. If *A* becomes insolvent or prudently disappears, does the plaintiff have a restitution claim against *B?*

For example, suppose that the plaintiff is a contractor who has agreed to repair or remodel a building for *A,* who is a long-term lessee. After the work is done *A* becomes insolvent. The lease reverts to *B* the lessor, who now has a repaired or improved building.[1] Or the plaintiff extends a charge

---

8. 24 P.2d 570 (Cal.App.1933).

9. Professor Laycock, noting the court's omission of figures, worked up figures based on inferences from the case. On his figures, the plaintiff had completed 95% of the work at a cost of $571,000 and it would have cost another $29,999 to finish. He had been paid $313,000 of a contract price of $333,000. The plaintiff recovered about $258,000 as restitution, so the effect was that the defendant's breach converted the plaintiff's losing con- tract to a no-loss contract. See D. Laycock, Modern American Remedies, Cases and Materials 522–23 (1985).

§ 12.7(7)

1. See Dawson, The Self–Serving Intermeddler, 87 Harv.L.Rev. 1409, 1454 (1974); Annotations, Lessee as agent of lessor within contemplation of mechanic's lien laws, 79 A.L.R. 962 (1932), 163 A.L.R. 992 (1946).

account to *A,* who allows *B* to charge goods to the account; and again *A* becomes insolvent, so that the plaintiff's only hope of collection is to claim that *B* is unjustly enriched by having what *A* gave him.[2] Or the plaintiff repairs a car brought to him by *A,* who agrees to pay for the repair, but it turns out that *A* is merely a thief who is not only insolvent but is sent to prison, and that *B* is the real owner.[3] The question in such cases is whether the plaintiff can claim against *B* with whom there was no contract at all.

There are substantial impediments to the plaintiff's claim against *B.* The bases for *B's* liability, if any, would lie in a contract between the plaintiff and *B,* or, what is much the same, in an acceptance or ratification by *B,*[4] or in statutory provisions protecting some contractors and suppliers in such cases.[5] Absent such theories, *B's* liability may be doubtful, because of the very general principle that liability without wrongdoing or consent would seriously infringe personal freedom and autonomy.[6] In addition, almost all contracts create benefits for people other than the parties; so if such claims are to be allowed, a device for narrowing them would be required.

In spite of these difficulties, the plaintiff is occasionally allowed a restitution recovery against a non-party to the contract who benefits from its performance.[7] Yet it is clear that the *contract* with *A* cannot be the basis of *B's* liability.[8] Even if the plaintiff and *A* expressly contracted that *B* would pay for benefits, *B,* who made no such promise, could not be held on the contract. If *B* is liable for restitution, then, it is not as a remedy for *A's* breach of contract, but on some other basis. Accordingly, further consideration of the claims against *B* is left for other sections.[9]

2. Recovery was allowed in Sears Roebuck & Co. v. Ragucci, 203 N.J.Super. 82, 495 A.2d 923 (1985); it was denied in Sears, Roebuck & Co. v. Stover, 32 Ohio Misc.2d 1, 513 N.E.2d 361 (1987).

3. Cf. Iacomini v. Liberty Mut. Ins. Co., 127 N.H. 73, 497 A.2d 854 (1985) (car repair at instance of non-owner).

4. See, discussing the terms under which some such claims are analyzed, Kovacic, A Proposal to Simplify Quantum Meruit Litigation, 35 Am.U.L.Rev. 547 (1986).

5. The statutes usually make it possible for workers and suppliers in construction or in automobile repair to establish a "mechanic's" or "materialmen's" lien by following specified procedures. The statutes do not cover all cases, do not apply if the procedures are not followed in a timely manner, and do not apply in some exempt cases. So they provide no complete solution. See § 12.20(3) below.

6. See § 4.9 (volunteers and intermeddlers' rules); cf. Mather, Restitution as a Remedy for Breach of Contract: The Case of the Partially Performing Seller, 92 Yale L.J. 14 (1982).

7. Murdock–Bryant Const., Inc. v. Taylor Pearson Co., 146 Ariz. 48, 703 P.2d 1197 (1985); Frank M. Hall & Co. v. Southwest Properties Venture, 747 P.2d 688 (Colo.App. 1987); Iacomini v. Liberty Mut. Ins. Co., 127 N.H. 73, 497 A.2d 854 (1985); Sears Roebuck & Co. v. Ragucci, 203 N.J.Super. 82, 495 A.2d 923 (1985). In none of these cases did the courts advert to the principle of individual autonomy (as seen for example in the volunteers and intermeddler rules). It may have been overlooked in some of the cases; in others it may be that the court thought there was some kind of implied in fact contract between the plaintiff and *B,* or an act of acceptance or ratification of the benefit by *B.* The confusion of the analytic terminology in restitution claims probably adds to the difficulty of getting all the issues on the table. See Kovacic, A Proposal to Simplify Quantum Meruit Litigation, 35 Am.U.L.Rev. 547 (1986).

8. Restatement of Restitution § 110 (1937).

9. See §§ 12.20(3) (contractors-subcontractors and others); 4.9 (intermeddlers).

(2) SPECIE AND NON–MONETARY REMEDIES

§ 12.8 Non-monetary Remedies—Specific Performance and Declaratory Judgment

§ 12.8(1) Specific Performance Generally

Specific Performance Generally

Elements in grant or denial of relief. One remedy that fulfills the plaintiff's expectancy interest is specific performance. It may at the same time serve certain restitutionary functions.[1] A specific performance decree is a court order compelling the defendant to perform the contract. The main advantage to the plaintiff is that it provides the very performance contracted for, not a money substitute. This remedy is almost routinely available to enforce contracts for the purchase of land.[2] In other cases, the court's decision to grant or deny specific performance is ordinarily a product of several considerations—practicalities, equities and hardships.

Under the traditional views, specific relief will be denied when (1) the legal remedy is regarded as adequate or the plaintiff is not subjected to irreparable harm by the breach;[3] (2) the hardship to the defendant outweighs the plaintiff's legitimate interest in specific performance;[4] (3) the "equities" or ethical considerations favor the defendant; for example, specific relief may be denied because the contract is too one-sided, because the plaintiff is estopped or has unclean hands, because the plaintiff delayed too long in pursuing the claim, or because remedies are not "mutual";[5] (4) specific performance is deemed impractical because it will require too much judicial supervision or for other reasons.[6] Equitable defenses like hardship, unfairness, laches and others, theoretically work to deny specific performance but to leave open the remedies "at law" for damages.[7]

[*For a discussion of characteristics of specific performance, see this section in the Practitioner Treatise edition.*]

The Role of Specific Performance

Remedial role for the plaintiff. The plaintiff's principled reason for seeking specific performance is that the performance itself is more important to her than its money value. The most obvious and also the most common illustration is the contract to purchase a particular parcel of land or a particular house for personal use. If the plaintiff does not regard all equally valuable houses or parcels as equivalent but wants the very house she bargained to get, she will seek specific performance, not damages.

Strategic role in litigation. The procedural and strategic reasons for seeking specific performance are different. The plaintiff may fear the difficulty of proving money damages or collecting them. Or the plaintiff may wish to avoid a jury trial that might be invoked if the suit were "at law" for damages.

§ 12.8(1)

1. See Levmore and Stuntz, Remedies and Incentives in Private and Public Law: A Comparative Essay, 1990 Wis.L.Rev. 483, 487.

Specific performance against a defendant who threatens to breach in order to gain greater profits by contracting elsewhere prevents the gain and is thus analogous to disgorgement.

In addition, specific performance may have strategic values for the plaintiff. The defendant who proposes to breach may do so because the performance promised has become more expensive than expected or because the performance promised would be more valuable elsewhere. In either case, actual performance may be more costly to him than payment of damages. The plaintiff's claim for specific performance in such a case imposes potential costs upon the defendant that would not be imposed by a claim for damages. This in turn is likely to increase the defendant's willingness to settle the claim. If specific performance in fact adds a cost in excess to legal damages, the defendant may seek to avoid that cost by settling for more than the sums he would be required to pay as damages.[30]

A more subtle and less likely strategic use can be made of specific performance if the plaintiff really wishes to recover future damages and doubts whether proof can be made sufficiently certain. In such a case a claim for specific performance might be asserted merely to lure the defendant into making the claim that damages will be adequate. Once having made that claim, the defendant may find it difficult to say that the damages are conjectural, so the way may then be opened for the plaintiff to recover damages that otherwise might be doubtful.[31]

Strategic role in price speculation. The plaintiff may also find a strategic advantage in having an option to claim either specific performance or damages. Suppose a plaintiff contracts to purchase Blackacre, closing on July 1. General damages are normally determined as of the date performance is due even if suit is not brought until months or years later. So the market-contract differential as of July 1 determines the damages once and for all. Specific performance is different. The speculator plaintiff may wait for months or perhaps years to watch prices on comparable land. If prices go up, he may demand specific performance. If prices go down, the damages remedy is his best bet, and the choice is normally his.[32] Courts may seek to defeat the buyer's ability to speculate by using election of remedies or laches doctrines,[33] but at least to a degree, a party having the option to claim either damages or specific performance may have speculative opportunities. Even if the defendant, holding land that is rising in value, refuses to comply with the specific performance decree, the specific performance decree will have an important effect. When specific performance is ordered but for some reason fails, courts measure damages differently. Instead of figuring the value of the land on the date of breach, they figure it on the date the specific performance decree failed, thus giving the plaintiff-purchaser the increase in land value from the time of breach to the time of trial or thereafter.[34]

Implications of Specific Performance—Equitable Conversion

The fact that the remedy of specific performance is, or might be, available to the plaintiff in any given case may have more or less logical implications that would be more important in determining collateral issues than in actually giving the remedy.

34. See Beard v. S/E Joint Venture, 321 Md. 126, 581 A.2d 1275 (1990); Cameron v. Benson, 295 Or. 98, 664 P.2d 412 (1983).

Implication for damages measurements. The least likely argument of this kind is that the plaintiff who claims special damages should have minimized damages by claiming specific performance if that remedy was available. The argument does not seem justified and it has scant support.[35] More plausibly, it can be said that if the plaintiff is entitled to specific performance then she is entitled to any financially equivalent remedy. For instance, if the plaintiff were entitled to compel a contractor to complete work on a building, that would imply that the plaintiff should be permitted to sue for cost-of-completion damages instead, since the two remedies would be substantially similar in cost to the defendant. And if the plaintiff would be denied specific performance only for reasons that do not go to the merits, then the same argument can be made. For example, the plaintiff might be entitled to compel a contractor to complete a building contract except for the fact that the court would be reluctant to compel a performance that would require supervision. If that is the only reason to deny specific performance, the implication would be that cost-of-completion damages should be allowed, not merely the amount by which the property is diminished in value. Such an argument is not always needed or even helpful, but in some instances it sheds light on the plaintiff's damages claim to recognize that specific performance would (or would not) be granted.

Implications of equitable "ownership" affecting risks and opportunities. The most significant "logical" argument derived from the conclusion that a contract would be subject to specific performance is the "trustee" or equitable conversion argument.[36] This argument says that when the plaintiff would be entitled to specific performance of a contract, then equity will treat the contract as if it were already executed in heaven though not on earth, in equity though not at law. Thus the landowner who contracts to sell Blackacre is owner of the legal title until the deed is delivered, but in the eyes of equity he holds that title as a trustee for the buyer, who is the equitable "owner." If this were only a way of looking at the relationship between buyer and seller of a specifically performable contract it might be quaint but otherwise of little interest. However, in some instances the "logic" of this conception has important bearing on other issues.

Two effects of "equitable ownership" theory. Two effects worth singling out are these. First, the seller who could be made specifically to perform might be liable in a few states to disgorge his profits to the buyer if he breaches by selling to another. Since he is a "trustee," in the eyes of equity, he must account for his default. The plaintiff being the "owner" is entitled to the gain from the property.[37] Second, if the property is damaged before time for conveyance to the buyer, the buyer rather than the seller may have to bear the loss. The theory is exactly the same; since the buyer is the equitable "owner" he must bear the loss or damage to the property just as he obtains the gains when the vendor sells the property. These effects occur principally in land-purchase cases and are discussed in that connection.[38] Neither of these effects is necessary and courts often ignore the "logic" of the doctrine. A better solution to the problems of contract remedy is based on the parties' own contractual understandings where it is possible to fathom it, and upon policy considerations where it is not.

§ 12.8(2) The Adequacy Test

[Consult § 2.5(1) above and see this section in the Practitioner Treatise edition for additional materials.]

What remedies are inadequate. A legal remedy may be inadequate, and specific performance thus justified, if the contract calls for unique[5] performance such as transfer of a work of art or an heirloom.[6] Even if the performance is not literally unique, it is now regarded as effectively unique if monopoly or shortage make it impossible to obtain substitute goods, in which case the money remedy is inadequate and specific performance permitted.[7] The legal remedy may also be inadequate if the plaintiff would have substantial difficulty finding substitute in the market,[8] or substantial difficulty in proving the amount of damages.[9] Loss of a business or substantial business income (as distinct from a loss on a market transaction) is likely to be unquantifiable, and hence a money remedy for such a loss would be inadequate.[10] Even difficulty in collecting damages that are entirely provable may suffice in some cases to show that the money remedy is less desirable.[11]

When the plaintiff's argument shifts from uniqueness to difficulty, the chancellor's judgment, attitude, and discretion become the significant determinants of the issue about adequacy. Some chancellors will find difficulties of getting substitute performance to be a sufficient basis for believing the legal remedy inadequate. Others will not be so readily convinced. The plaintiff in such cases must depend more upon the advocate's persuasion about the facts and their importance than upon the legal rules.

The traditional adequacy test operated to bar specific performance of most contracts for the sale or purchase of ordinary goods[16] and specific performance of most contracts in which the plaintiff was entitled merely to receive a money payment.[17]

The traditional adequacy test did not bar specific performance of contracts to purchase interests in land, however, because each parcel of land was regarded as unique,[18] and because some interests are not reasonably measurable in money damages.[19] Perhaps courts have also felt more comfortable about specific performance of land transfers because title can be transferred in the usual case without use of the contempt power.[20] Contemporary cases go further in land cases and give the land *seller* specific performance as well, even though the seller's only entitlement is to receive money.[21]

§ 12.8(3) Practicability and Policy Limitations

Generally

Courts will not specifically enforce contracts if they regard enforcement as futile, impractical, or too demanding upon judicial resources. Traditionally the practicality idea has been used to deny the plaintiff's claim for specific

---

§ 12.8(2)

16. Klein v. PepsiCo, Inc., 845 F.2d 76 (4th Cir.1988) (specific performance denied in contract to purchase second-hand aircraft, although there were only three others "roughly comparable;" money damages would be adequate); Weathersby v. Gore, 556 F.2d 1247 (5th Cir.1977) (cotton output contract, no specific performance even under UCC's liberalizing provision). See § 12.16(7) below.

performance in three major kinds of cases, although it can be applied in others as well. The main cases are:

(1) Cases in which the court might be required to supervise enforcement of the decree, perhaps for a long period of time. This form of the practicality rule is typically invoked when a landowner seeks specific performance of the defendant's contract to do construction or substantial repair work,[1] but it is not limited to building or construction cases.

(2) Cases in which important terms of the contract are uncertain and where the court might be unable to formulate a decree with sufficient precision.

(3) Cases in which the plaintiff seeks to provide personal service to the defendant as prescribed in the contract, but where enforcement might not be practical because the parties' ability to work together cannot be guaranteed by a decree and where either party might withhold quality of service in ways that are difficult to monitor.[2]

Enforcement and Supervision Problems

Traditional refusal to enforce. Even if the plaintiff's money remedies are deemed inadequate in some cases, judges may refuse specific performance if they fear that the court will be repeatedly drawn into further controversies in attempting to enforce the decree. They seek to avoid, as the saying is, "long continuous supervision" of their decrees.

For example, to prevent cavernous and unattractive vacancies, shopping centers often contract with tenant stores that the tenant will continuously operate the store's business during the lease period. But courts have often refused to enforce such lease covenants on the ground that to do so would require long supervision.[3] Sometimes courts have refused to enforce franchise or exclusive dealership contracts on the same ground.[4] The case most commonly discussed is the case of the building, construction or repair contract. Courts have often taken the position that the landowner cannot compel the contractor to perform a building or other construction contract,[5] even though the legal remedy is inadequate,[6] since undue supervision might be required.

Meliorating rules. The Restatement rationalizes and meliorates this heavy-handed rule. Its version of the rule has it that specific performance will be refused if the performance is so extensive that the burdens of supervision would outweigh the plaintiff's advantages in having specific performance.[7] Important writers agree that the issue is to be governed by

§ 12.8(3)

5. Besinger v. National Tea Co., 75 Ill. App.2d 395, 221 N.E.2d 156 (1966); Caddo Oil & Mining Co. v. Producers' Oil Co., 134 La. 701, 708, 64 So. 684, 687 (1913) ("One cannot be forced to drill a well for oil, as such operation would not be within the power of the courts to enforce. It would be subject to many contingencies. It is entirely impracticable"); Beck v. Allison, 56 N.Y. 366 (1874) ("[T]he power of enforcing the specific performance of contracts for repairs is not now exercised by courts of equity [in England], and there is no authority for its exercise by the courts of this State"). See Axelrod, Judicial Attitudes Toward Specific Performance of Construction Contracts, 7 Dayton L.Rev. 33 (1981); Annotation, Specific performance of lease of, or binding option to lease, building or part of building to be constructed, 38 A.L.R.3d 1052 (1971).

7. Restatement Second of Torts § 366 (1981).

such a balance of costs and benefits rather than by an absolute rule.[8] So do a number of modern cases.[9] Some cases grant relief without even mentioning the supposed rule against it.[10]

[*For additional rules and analysis, see this section in the Practitioner Treatise edition.*]

Personal Service Contracts

Traditional rule against compulsion. Courts will not compel an employee to work, but at least conceivably they could compel an employer to accept work from an employee who has contract rights to a job. Even in the employee's suit, however, many concerns counsel caution in enforcement of personal service contracts. Most of those concerns are addressed elsewhere.[30] The immediate point is that practical reasons may justify a court in refusing to enforce a job contract for an employee. Cooperation cannot be readily compelled; friction cannot be readily prohibited. As with other continuing performance cases, courts worry about the possibility that they will be dragged into the case again and again to resolve recurring disputes.[31] So the general rule of judge-made law is that specific performance will not be granted to an employee, even if the job has special significance besides the wage or salary.[32] The rule is calcified as statute in some states.[33]

Legislative and judicial change. On the other hand, victims of unfair or discriminatory practices are often given specific job rights by statute and those rights are enforced by courts by orders to hire, pay, reinstate and the like.[34] As Professor Laycock has said, a judge-made rule against reinstatement coupled with a legislative rule in favor of it looks like "an unstable combination." [35] Perhaps courts of the future will specifically enforce contracts at the behest of the employee where the particular dispute does not imply serious supervisory or friction problems and where the irreparable harm claim is strong because of potential reputational damages or otherwise.[36]

§ 12.8(4) Fairness and Hardship Limitations

In General

In the chancery tradition, judges enjoyed discretion to deny specific relief. The plaintiff who had a contract right might be denied specific performance even if the contract was valid and even if the money remedy at

---

8. Edward Yorio, Contract Enforcement: Specific Performance and Injunctions § 13.2.3 (1989); Laycock, The Death of the Irreparable Injury Rule, 103 Harv.L.Rev. 687, 762 (1990).

9. Laclede Gas Co. v. Amoco Oil Co., 522 F.2d 33, 39 (8th Cir.1975) ("While a court may refuse to grant specific performance where such a decree would require constant and long-continued court supervision, this is merely a discretionary rule of decision which is frequently ignored when the public interest is involved"); City Stores Co. v. Ammerman, 266 F.Supp. 766, 776 (D.D.C.1967), aff'd, 394 F.2d 950, 38 A.L.R.3d 1042 (D.C.Cir.1968) ("Some jurisdictions in the United States have opposed granting specific performance of contracts for construction of buildings and other

contracts requiring extensive supervision of the court, but the better view, and the one which increasingly is being followed in this country, is that such contracts should be specifically enforced unless the difficulties of supervision outweigh the importance of specific performance to the plaintiff"); Link v. State, 180 Mont. 469, 591 P.2d 214 (1979) (defendant compelled to construct and operate a mountain railroad in a state park for remainder of long term lease); cf. Travellers International AG v. Trans World Airlines, Inc., 722 F.Supp. 1087 (S.D.N.Y.1989) (enforcing tour company's contract with airline, minimizing supervision problems and emphasizing that tour business would be destroyed without enforcement).

law was inadequate. This theoretically left the plaintiff with a remedy "at law" for money damages, because "law" judges did not enjoy the same discretion. Law judges enforced rights; equity judges enforced conscience. At least in form, this tradition still holds.

The exact scope of equitable discretion is doubtful. The reasons usually given for invoking discretionary refusal to award specific performance are in fact limited. They fall into three or four somewhat fluid categories that are not always distinguishable and that often run together.[1] Courts have discretion to refuse specific enforcement, even though the contract itself is valid and enforceable for damages, when:

(1) the contract itself is found to be unfair or unconscionable in its own terms or because of the plaintiff's limited experience or capacity or because of unfair practices of the defendant in securing the contract;

(2) the plaintiff is guilty of bad faith, or unethical, misleading or dilatory conduct, so that specific enforcement risks serious unfairness to the defendant or else would put the court in the position of lending a kind of tacit approval to the plaintiff's misconduct;

(3) specific enforcement may work a disproportionately large hardship upon the defendant even though the contract was fair and honorable when made;

(4) the defendant's legitimate rights under the contract cannot be secured or protected by the court, so that specific performance in favor of the plaintiff might be one-sided.

Specific performance may be denied for any one of these reasons when it is strong enough to be persuasive, and equally may be denied when no one factor is convincing but in combination the court is left with the feeling that equitable relief should be withheld.[2] The equitable defenses are notoriously fact-specific; their rule-content is extremely low.

[*For more detailed discussion of unconscionable contracts, hardship defenses, estoppel and unclean hands, see this section in the Practitioner Treatise edition.*]

§ 12.8(5) Discretion and the Effect of Equitable Defenses on Legal Relief

[*For the text of this section, see the unabridged Practitioner Treatise edition.*]

§ 12.8(6) Specific Performance and Contemplation of the Parties

[*For the text of this section, see the unabridged Practitioner Treatise edition.*]

§ 12.8(7) Declaratory Judgment

[*For the text of this section, see the unabridged Practitioner Treatise edition.*]

§ 12.9 Agreed Remedies

§ 12.9(1) Summary

Contract law generally attempts to respect the parties' self-determination by permitting the parties to contract and then by enforcing their promises. In the absence of fraud, mistake, unconscionability or similar impediment, the parties are free to promise much or little, fast delivery or slow, superior quality or mediocre. When it comes to the parties' agreement for remedies, however, courts have been more intrusive and less willing to respect the parties' agreement. This had led to uncertainty and expense, as well as to litigation over the question whether a remedial provision is one for liquidated damages, or for a penalty, or for something else altogether, such as a fee for an option or a forfeiture. The rules are stated more fully in the following subsections. The main rules can be summarized as follows.

The parties may contract for liquidated damages in the event of a breach. This may be a fixed sum or a formula for figuring damages. The parties may also limit damages and other remedies so that they would be less valuable than the relief that courts would give.

However, the parties may not stipulate for damages that would be a "penalty."[1] In general, the contract provision for damages will be considered a penalty unless it either (a) aims at or (b) achieves an award approximately like an award the court would make. In something of a contradiction, the rule also says that the actual damages must be uncertain or difficult to ascertain, and that if they can be easily ascertained, the plaintiff will be permitted to recover only actual damages, not those the parties agreed upon.[2]

The parties' agreement is usually now said to be a valid and enforceable one if it was a good approximation of actual damages either at the time of contracting or at the time of breach, so long as there is some difficulty in determining the amount of those actual damages. However, the Restatement[3] and some of the cases refuse to enforce the liquidated damages clause even if it was a good approximation when it was made if, on breach, it turns out that the defendant had no damages at all.[4]

The penalty rules resulted from a particular history of doubtful relevance in present-day life, and specifically from oppressive and unfair contracts enforced in a medieval, non-market economy. The penalty rules developed primarily to deal, albeit in a crude way, with unconscionable contracts. There are now many other methods for identifying and controlling unconscionable contracts and the penalty rules may not be needed for this purpose except in the most unusual cases.[5]

It has also been argued that the penalty rules are desirable to prevent compulsion to perform and thus to permit efficient breach. If this were the reason for the penalty rules, one would expect to find that penalties would be permitted whenever specific performance would be permissible, since the two remedies would represent merely different forms of compulsion. But this is not the case, and some economic writers who support efficient breaches of contract, believe that it would be at least equally efficient to permit sophisticated parties to contract freely for liquidated damages.[6]

Not all contract provisions fall within the ambit of the liquidated damages/penalty rules. Some contract provisions for deposits call for a forfeiture when the depositor defaults, and sometimes these provisions are upheld without respect to the penalty rules. Sometimes, too, a provision is simply a contract debt, not a sum paid for breach, and if so it will again escape the demands imposed by the penalty rules.[7]

Problems of drafting and interpretation frequently arise, chiefly over the question whether a valid stipulated damages clause will preclude specific performance or the actual damages remedy. In general, this is a question of the parties' intent as revealed by the contract itself and any admissible surrounding circumstances.[8]

Parties may attempt to agree on remedies other than damages. Agreements to arbitrate and to accept the arbitrator's remedies are now commonly enforced. Agreements that the contract will be specifically enforced, however, run into difficulty with the courts, which wish to decide on specific performance for themselves.[9]

§ 12.9(2) Liquidated Damages and Penalties: General Rules

Contract provisions for *limitation* upon recovery are treated differently. Unless a limitation is unconscionable,[4] the limitation is usually enforceable.[5] Thus a sum specified as damages that is *less* than the estimated and actual loss is never a penalty. Otherwise, a specified sum of damages is usually[6] regarded as a penalty unless the sum named either aims at or hits the "right" amount of damages.

The "right" amount of damages is not always the amount that would be fixed by judges in the absence of such a provision. One of the best uses for liquidated damages clauses is to permit a recovery for losses that otherwise would go uncompensated because they cannot be proved or because they are intangibles not ordinarily recoverable in contract.[7]

Even so, courts often assume that the right amount of damages is the amount that the judges would fix under existing legal rule. For example, it has been held that the liquidated damages provision must aim at the measures of damages supported by law and may even be required to take into account the plaintiff's potential for minimizing damages.[8]

As formulated by the Restatement, the liquidated damages clause is valid if the amount specified is reasonable at the time of contracting, in light of the anticipated loss; or alternatively, it is valid if the amount specified is reasonable in the light of the actual loss caused by breach.[12] Similar

---

§ 12.9(2)

7. Thus in Koenings v. Joseph Schlitz Brewing Co., 126 Wis.2d 349, 377 N.W.2d 593 (1985) the employee's liquidated damages upon breach of an employment contract could permit a recovery for loss in professional status that otherwise would go uncompensated.

8. Gary Outdoor Advertising Co. v. Sun Lodge, Inc., 133 Ariz. 240, 650 P.2d 1222 (1982) (clause void because it provided for full payments when in fact plaintiff might be able to minimize damages). On the other hand, since a reasonable aim is as good as a direct hit, a clause that awards full damages minus a discount for the uncertain potential of minimiz-

ing is valid. Truck Rent–A–Center, Inc. v. Puritan Farms 2d, Inc., 41 N.Y.2d 420, 425, 361 N.E.2d 1015, 1019, 393 N.Y.S.2d 365, 370 (1977); Weinstein v. Griffin, 241 N.C. 161, 84 S.E.2d 549 (1954).

Distinguish the question whether liquidated damages under a clause found to be valid must be minimized or "mitigated." As to that point, Judge Posner has said that the certainty liquidated damages are intended to give is impaired if minimizing were to be required. Lake River Corp. v. Carborundum Co., 769 F.2d 1284, 1291 (7th Cir.1985).

provisions were enacted in the Uniform Commercial Code [13] and other statutes,[14] and there is case support for the same rule.[15] For example, if a contract calls for a one-year salary in the event an employment contract is breached, that sum will be reasonable and enforceable if it was a reasonable estimate of probable loss at the time the contract was made, even if it turns out that the plaintiff suffered no actual loss from breach because he immediately obtained substitute employment elsewhere.[16] The parties' aim was good in such a case and that is enough. It is also enough if the parties aim was bad but they in fact hit a sum that approximates actual damages.[17]

According to the Restatement, the more difficult it is to prove the loss, the "easier it is to show that the amount fixed is reasonable." [24] The Restatement does not actually say that liquidated damages are impermissible when proof of actual damages is easy, but it does make it clear that the specified sum may be hard to justify in such a case; that is also the traditional view.[25] But some courts might treat difficulty of proving "actual" loss as a precondition to a valid agreed remedies clause.[26] Other courts have said flatly that if damages are ascertainable at the time of contracting, then any specified damages clause is a penalty.[27]

Besides these limitations, courts sometimes seem to say that the liquidated damages clause will fail, even if it is objectively in accord with all the rules, unless in addition the parties held appropriate subjective attitudes about the clause—that is, unless they intended to make a fair estimate of probable actual damages.[28]

A liquidated damages clause may also be found insufficiently related to actual damages forecasts and hence voided where the defendant is under several distinct contractual obligations but there is only one provision for liquidated damages. If the defendant's obligation are of different value, a single damages provision might represent a good forecast of damages likely to accrue from breach of one clause, but it is not likely to represent such a good forecast of damages that would result from breach of the other. In *Seidlitz v. Auerbach*,[30] a tenant held under a rental agreement that called for payment of rent and also subjected him to a duty to clear sidewalks of snow and other duties of maintenance. The court held the liquidated damages clause was unreasonable and denied enforcement of it. The liquidated damages, though appropriate for some breaches, would be disproportionate to others. The same principle might operate to void a liquidated damages clause in a contract calling for continuous performance, where the sum provided is the same for both early and late breaches.[31] This approach takes the view that if the liquidated damages is "invariant to the gravity of the breach," [32] it is a penalty. Such approaches would seem inconsistent with tests of reasonableness advanced by the Restatement and the UCC, which seems more concerned with reasonableness of the liquidated sum in comparison to the breach that actually occurred rather than the abstract

13. UCC § 2–718(1) approves liquidated damages for either buyer or seller of goods in "an amount which is reasonable in the light of the anticipated or actual harm caused by the breach [and] the difficulties of proof of loss * * *." UCC § 2A–504 provides a standard

the drafters sought to make more liberal in cases of leases of goods, expressly approving liquidation by formula. See § 12.18 below.

32. Lake River Corp. v. Carborundum Co., 769 F.2d 1284, 1290 (7th Cir.1985).

reasonableness in comparison to all breaches that might occur, and some of the cases are now reaching the same conclusion.[33]

[*For additional discussion, see this section in the Practitioner Treatise edition.*]

§ 12.9(3) Liquidated Damages: Rationales and Critiques

[*For the text of this section, see the unabridged Practitioner Treatise edition.*]

§ 12.9(4) Liquidated Damages: Alternative Analysis, Alternative Clauses

Clauses that are typically considered to be liquidated damages or penalty clauses can very often be thought of in quite different terms. When considered apart from the traditional penalty analysis, the clauses in issue often appear right and reasonable. These different ways of perceiving payment clauses may all rest on the same kind of understanding: In all cases of sophisticated-party contracting it looks as if the plaintiff who demands a liquidated payment clause is buying the right to receive payment, since presumably the plaintiff must give up something in price or other terms to get it. But the language and the circumstances engendering these different perceptions are different, so some of them are illustrated here separately.

Noncompetition covenants by a defendant are closely analogous to liquidated damages; they exact a cost from the defendant that may or may not be related proportionately to the damages of the plaintiff. Yet covenants not to compete, by seller of a business, for example, are not necessarily seen as penalties. They may be upheld on the ground that such a covenant is the means by which the goodwill is sold,[1] or even simply on the ground that they are reasonable means of protecting the plaintiff's interests.[2] Such covenants in effect describe what is sold in the first place and are enforced specifically by injunction to prevent the seller from taking back some of what he sold. If, instead of an injunction, the seller were to use a payment clause, the effect would be to say he has an option to buy back the goodwill and to set the price on the buy-back. Sometimes courts see obligations to pay damages in excess of "actual" loss as a right the plaintiff has paid for and see the defendant's effort to avoid liabilities, not as a just resistance to a penalty, but as an effort to take back something he "sold" in fixing the original contract price.[3]

Stipulated sums in a contract are not necessarily subjected to the penalty analysis. First, some dollar amounts due under a contract may not be damages at all because they are not payable upon breach; they are rather simply the payment or performance called for by the contract. A promisso-

---

§ 12.9(4)

3. See Farrell Lines, Inc. v. City of New York, 30 N.Y.2d 76, 330 N.Y.S.2d 358, 281 N.E.2d 162 (1972). *Farrell* was not a case of liquidated damages. The court fixed damages on the basis of a landlord's hypothetical cost of repairing premises left in bad condition by a tenant, even though the landlord had decided to and did demolish the entire structure to make room for a different project. The landlord thus had no loss, but the court enforced damages as if it did. Its reason was exactly the one given in the text. Limiting liability to "actual" loss would be "unfair to the lessor who, in return for such covenants, charges a rental that is far less than he could have received."

ry note for $100 and stipulated interest simply obligates the debtor to pay the $100 and the stipulated interest. The obligation to pay is the substance of the contract, not merely a measure of damages for breach of some other provision.

In *Ditommaso Realty, Inc. v. Moak Motorcycles, Inc.,*[5] the plaintiff was a realtor with an exclusive contract for sale of property, under which he was entitled to 10% of the sales price, no matter who sold the property within the contract term. The plaintiff said this was a penalty clause and invalid; the court said it was not a provision for damages for breach and hence not either a liquidated damages clause or a penalty clause. Instead, it was simply the debt created when a contract term was satisfied. Accordingly, it was enforceable without resort to the penalty analysis. Other courts have reached similar results, sometimes on similar reasoning.[6]

Somewhat obliquely, the Restatement recognizes that the parties may legitimately provide for alternative performances.[9] The promisor may thus be subjected to an obligation to supply 500 almond cakes or 500 walnut cakes, and either performance will satisfy the obligation. In some instances a price differential might be warranted as an alternative. A contract that calls for 500 almond cakes at $2.00 each *or* 500 walnut cakes at $1 each might reflect the difference in value of the two kinds of product. Somewhat similarly, a supplier who wishes to sell goods or services may waive the charge for preliminary samples or designs if the defendant buys the goods in question but insist upon it if no purchase is made.[10] In other cases the alternative performance permitted may simply reflect an option the defendant wishes to have because he cannot be sure of commercial needs when he contracts.

A price difference like these, that reflects a cost or value difference, would hardly count as a penalty, so calling this a contract for alternative performance does not seem to have much effect. It would have a great effect, however, if the parties could avoid the "penalty" rules by treating all provisions for stipulated sums as contracts for alternative performance. For example, if the parties who are forbidden to create a "penalty" are allowed to say that the defendant has the option of *either* delivering 500 almond cakes *or* paying $10,000, the "penalty" rules would be subverted. So not surprisingly the Restatement insists that the provision must be "a true alternative performance" provision. Professor McCormick added that it would not be a true alternative performance provision unless it would constitute a rational choice,[11] a view the California Court has accepted as well.[12]

Even if contract provisions were readily interpreted to call for options or alternative performances rather than penalties, such provisions may offer very little assistance to a party who wishes to prescribe damages. Damages would be based on the less valuable of the alternatives,[13] so that if one alternative is to deliver 500 cakes worth $1,000 and the other is to pay $10,000, the defendant's breach would make him liable only for the value of

5.   309 Or. 190, 785 P.2d 343 (1990).

9.   Restatement Second of Contracts § 361, Comment *b* (1981). The Restatement is mainly addressing the question whether a liqui-

dated damages provision forecloses specific performance, and in this connection distinguishes a provision for alternative performance.

the cakes. This would defeat any hoped-for liquidation of damages. Even so, there are some cases in which the defendant finds himself held for the liquidated sum rather than for an optional and cheaper alternative.[14]

Contracts often provide that deposits of money made at the time of contracting are to be forfeited in the event of breach or repudiation by the depositor. This is an especially common practice with earnest money deposits in real estate purchase transactions. A forfeiture of the deposit operates like an award of liquidated damages,[15] but differs from a claim for liquidated damages or penalty in that the fund is already in the hands of the aggrieved party at the time of breach and suit must be brought by the breacher. Courts once treated forfeitures differently from penalty clauses partly because of the supposed rule that a party in breach could not seek restitution.[16] Consequently some decisions have upheld forfeitures without regard to whether they would otherwise count as penalties.[17]

The rule against allowance of restitution to a breacher is now somewhat moribund, but the practice of permitting earnest money forfeitures is an ingrained practice in the real estate market, so courts that would allow restitution to the breacher may still uphold the forfeiture deposits on the ground that they are valid, or presumptively valid [18] as liquidated damages even though forfeiture of later installments on the price would be penalties. Forfeitures of initial deposits may also be upheld on the ground that the earnest money deposit operates like a fee for an option to purchase and is not a forfeiture at all,[19] or on the similar ground that it represents performance due under the contract rather than damages for breach.[20]

The drafter who considers a liquidated damages clause might hope that it would be accepted, or that it could pass as an alternative contract or forfeiture provision. Still another possibility for the drafter is to provide payments or pricing that encourages full performance. Professor Levmore gives the example of a traveler who wishes to hire a companion for a long trip for a total payment of $1000. Fearing that the companion will become bored after a few weeks and leave the employment, the traveler might simply arrange an "end-loaded" payment schedule, a higher weekly wage as the trip progressed. Although it might seem just as permissible to use an economic stick as it is to use an economic carrot, judges so far seem more willing to permit the carrot.[27]

§ 12.9(5) Liquidated Damages: Drafting and Interpretation

[*For a discussion of the exclusiveness or non-exclusiveness of liquidated damages, see this section in the Practitioner Treatise edition.*]

If the liquidated damage clause by its terms specifies a deposit or a stipulated sum as the sole remedy for the plaintiff, or declares that its payment terminates the obligations of the parties, then of course the plaintiff cannot have specific performance any more than he could have actual damages; the remedy would be limited to the stipulated damages.[13] But if the liquidated damages clause is not the sole remedy and not intended to give the defendant the option of buying out of the contract at the price

---

19. See Macneil, Power of Contract and Agreed Remedies, 47 Cornell L.Rev. 495, 515 (1962).

27. Levmore, Explaining Restitution, 71 Va.L.Rev. 65 (1985).

specified, specific performance remains an option for the plaintiff.[14]   A liquidated damages or forfeiture clause that limits the liability of one party does not necessarily limit the liability of the other. The land buyer whose only liability upon default is to lose his earnest money deposit may still have specific performance against the seller unless the seller's liability is also limited by the agreement.[15]

But even if, as a matter of contract interpretation, the liquidated damages clause did not foreclose specific performance, courts at one time worried that provision for liquidated damages might be inconsistent with the underlying premises of specific performance. If a land buyer or seller provides for liquidated damages, it may seem that the contract only signifies money, not a unique thing, hence that specific performance should be or could be denied. This view attaches too much significance both to the liquidated damages clause and to the specific performance adequacy rules. Some courts have avoided the impact of this viewpoint by finding that the clause was not a true liquidated damages clause.[16] But such a ruling is distortive. The easy answer is that even if the adequacy test is still dominant, the option to use liquidated damages might be a prudent provision to have at the time the contract is made and one not at all inconsistent with a genuine desire to enforce the contract for its unique qualities. So the presence of a non-exclusive liquidated damages clause does not in itself preclude specific performance. The liquidated damages clause precludes specific performance only if the clause was intended to be an exclusive remedy.[17]

What Breaches Are Covered; Delay

A liquidated damages clause might be written to cover any kind of breach that might occur or only some particular kind of breach. If the clause is not precisely drafted, interpretation may be required. In construction contracts with a completion date, damages for delay are often fixed at a specified sum for each day of delay. Such provision may be valid as a liquidated damages clause rather than a penalty,[20] but its scope may still be uncertain. For example, when a contractor totally abandons the work after the time for completion, it has been held that he is liable for the specified delay payments from the date completion was due until a reasonable time for completing the job.[21] The clause may not apply, however, if the contractor abandons the project before time for completion. This and similar cases raise issues of construction that may prevent a summary judgment as to liquidated damages.[22]

§ 12.9(6) Agreements for or Against Specific Performance and Other Remedies

General rule. May the parties effectively stipulate that specific performance will be granted where the courts would not normally give such relief? May they stipulate against such relief where the courts would normally grant it? The decisions do not appear to be numerous but they are generally opposed to the parties' power to contract freely for or against specific performance.[2] The Restatement[3] and a distinguished commentator agree.[4]

§ 12.9(6)
3. Restatement Second of Contracts § 359, Comment *a* (1981).

4. E. Yorio, Contract Enforcement: Specific Performance and Injunctions, §§ 19.1–19.4 (1989).

Melioration of the general rule. The cases do not seem overwhelming; they are few in number and the results they reach may sometimes be justified on other grounds.[5] Even if these restrictive views are maintained, three forms of melioration are possible. First, the parties might agree contractually that predicate facts exist in support of specific performance. For instance, they might agree that performance has unique qualities or spell out reasons why damages would be inadequate. Even the Restatement would permit the court to "take appropriate notice of the facts recited in the contract" in determining whether to grant specific relief.[6] Such a rule is not necessarily effective, since the court may decide that the recital is not factually correct or that it does not comport with the court's exercise of discretion.[7]

Second, the parties might provide for arbitration as a remedy and the arbitrator in some instances may grant specific performance.[8]

Third, the court may consider the contract provision in favor of specific performance, not as binding, but as an important influence in the exercise of discretion.[9] Some language suggests that some judges are prepared to give significant weight to the parties' provisions for equitable relief.[10]

[*For a discussion of rationales and other remedial agreements, see this section in the Practitioner Treatise edition.*]

B.   PARTICULAR CONTRACTS

(1) LAND CONTRACTS

§ 12.10   Vendor and Purchaser of Land: Remedies and Risk of Loss in Summary

Land Contract Types

Earnest money contracts. The ordinary contract to sell or purchase land, sometimes called an earnest money contract, contemplates that the deal will close and the purchaser will take title within a relatively short time. The vendor will be fully paid at the closing and the purchaser will take the deed. At the same time the vendor's mortgage debt, if any, will usually be paid off with part of the purchase price, and the purchaser will use the property to generate a loan with which to purchase. All this must be done more or less simultaneously in many transactions, but once it is completed the vendor and purchaser have no further contract relationship.

Installment contracts. An installment contract is different. The vendor in the installment contract retains title and accepts installment payments from the purchaser, with a contract to give a deed when the purchase price is fully paid. The relationship between the vendor and the purchaser continues, often for many years. If the purchaser stops making payments, the vendor will typically attempt to keep the property (title has not passed) and also keep the payments made. The installment contract raises more difficult and complicated remedial and substantive issues.

Scope. The sections that follow immediately are primarily concerned with remedies for breach of the earnest money contract. A separate section then considers some of the special remedial problems of the installment contract,[1] but a complete understanding of the installment contract problem must be gained from the field of real estate finance law.[2]

Purchaser's Remedies

Damages. Where the vendor breaches his contract to convey land to the purchaser, the purchaser's normal damages remedy gives her the loss of bargain, plus consequential damages in the contemplation of the parties. This is usually the difference between the contract price and the market value of the land on date of breach. Some states, however, limit recovery to a restoration of any sum paid on the purchase price when the vendor's breach is not wilful and results only from an unintended failure of title.[3]

Restitution. Restitution to the purchaser normally contemplates repayment of the purchase price. When the purchaser rescinds for breach and thus becomes entitled to a recovery of the price paid, he may be given a purchaser's lien on the land to secure the repayment.[4] In addition, the purchaser normally can obtain specific performance of the contract,[5] a remedy that has led a few courts to conclude that the vendor is essentially like a "trustee" of the land after the contract has been made and consequently that the vendor must make restitution of any profits she might make from resale of the land in breach of the contract.[6]

Specific performance. The purchaser is routinely granted specific performance of land purchase contracts in the absence of some special reason to deny the relief, such as hardship or unfairness in the contract.[7] If deficiencies in title or in acreage occur, specific performance is sometimes granted with a money adjustment, but such cases require care to avoid a judicial rewriting of the parties' contract. When adjustment or "abatement" in the price is allowed, further problems arise in determining how it is to be computed.[8]

Deed covenants. Running throughout the various remedial situations involved in the purchaser's suit based on the vendor's breach is the distinction between the executed and executory contract—that is, between the bare contract to buy and sell on the one hand and the executed deed on the other. It is at least arguable that the vendor's liability in damages for breach of the executory contract ought not to be the same as his liability for breach of a covenant in the deed, and courts frequently distinguish between the contract and the deed. Thus damages are limited for a vendor's breach of a deed covenant in a way they are not limited for breach of the executory contract.[9]

§ 12.10

1. See § 12.13 below.
2. See G. Nelson & D. Whitman, Real Estate Finance Law §§ 3.26–3.37 (2d ed. 1985 and Supp.)
3. See § 12.11(1) below.
4. See § 12.11(4) below.
5. See § 12.11(3) below.
6. See § 12.11(2) below.
7. See § 12.11(3) below.
8. See § 12.11(1) below.
9. See § 12.11(1) below.

Rescission of an executed deed for failure of the purchaser to perform a part of his agreement is likewise usually denied except in the special case of care-for-grantor contracts.[10]

Vendor's Remedies

Damages. The vendor's remedies for the purchaser's breach of her obligation to buy land are often analogous to the purchaser's remedies for a corresponding default by the vendor. The vendor normally recovers loss of bargain damages. This usually means the difference between the market value and the contract price plus the vendor's reasonable cost of resale.[11] Sometimes courts allow an action for the purchase price, contemplating that the vendor will deliver the deed if the price is recovered, a recovery that is cumbersome in form but that resembles specific performance in its ultimate result. Rental value of the land during the purchaser's occupancy and/or interest for delayed payment of the price may also be appropriate on the facts of particular cases. In addition, the vendor is entitled to such consequential damages as fit the formula of *Hadley v. Baxendale.*[12] Besides these remedies, the vendor is entitled to retain earnest money as a forfeiture in most states, on analogy to liquidated damages.[13] In installment contracts, the vendor may be entitled to retain installment payments as well, but this remedy may be subject to the purchaser's claim for restitution of installment payments so far as they exceed the vendor's actual damages.[14]

Specific performance. The vendor's recovery of the purchase price (with delivery of the deed by the vendor) is almost identical to specific performance, which is also readily granted to the vendor, even though there may at times exist technical arguments to the effect that the legal remedy is adequate.[15] In many instances, however, the contract limits the vendor's remedy to a retention of the earnest money deposit. Such a limit is valid and may preclude both compensatory damages and specific performance.

Restitution. The vendor is also entitled to rescind the contract at the executory stage for the purchaser's breach, but once a deed is delivered, rescission or forfeiture of the land is granted only for breach of a condition or for a very serious breach of a covenant in the deed.[16]

Vendor's lien. Like the purchaser, the vendor may enjoy a judicially created lien on the land to secure the other party's obligations.[17]

Risk of Loss

Well-advised parties usually provide by contract for the possibility that the property will be substantially damaged or destroyed before title passes. Where they do not do so, the risk of loss may be cast upon the purchaser on the theory that he becomes the equitable owner at the time of contracting, by virtue of the thinking behind the equitable conversion doctrine. The Uniform Vendor and Purchaser Risk Act casts the loss upon the purchaser only after possession or title has passed. Both these solutions leave substan-

---

10. See § 12.12(2) below.
11. See § 12.12(1) below.
12. As to Hadley v. Baxendale, see generally § 12.4 above.
13. See generally § 12.9(4) above.

14. See § 12.13 below.
15. See § 12.2(3) below.
16. See § 12.12(2) below.
17. See § 12.2(4) below.

tial problems in their wake. Sometimes the purchaser is allowed either a price abatement as a result of the damage or a credit for any insurance the vendor has collected. A separate section summarizes the authority on these issues.[18]

§ 12.11 Purchaser's Remedies for Vendor's Breach

§ 12.11(1) Purchaser's Damages

Breach Because of Innocent Title Defect

The English rule: Flureau v. Thornhill. When the total breach by the vendor results from a defect in his title and the vendor is in good faith in attempting to perform, the English courts under the rule of *Flureau v. Thornhill*[5] limited the purchaser to a recovery of prepayment he had made on the purchase price, plus expenses incurred. This rule denied the purchaser his expectancy damages, allowing instead a kind of restitution measure with the addition of some items of reliance expense. The result is similar to the result of a rescission for mistake, with the addition of reliance costs that are usually minor. The rule received the blessing of a Uniform Act which has never been enacted in any state,[6] but something less than half of the American states seem to accept it,[7] and the number may be declining.[8]

Limitations on the Flureau rule. The English rule, where otherwise applicable, does not limit restitutionary recoveries, only damages.[13] When the rule is applied to damages claims, everything turns on the vendor's "good faith." If the vendor has good title or can make it, or breaches in bad faith, liability for expectancy is imposed.[14] The vendor who knew or should have known that he could not make good title is not in good faith,[15] nor is the vendor who has title but intentionally refuses to convey,[16] or fails to use his best efforts to make a good conveyance. In these cases the plaintiff is allowed to recover full expectancy damages even under the *Flureau* rule. Even a vendor who believed he could get good title has been held liable for the loss of bargain or expectancy, since he knew at the time of contracting that he did not have the present means of performance.[17]

Partial Breach

Deficiencies. The vendor of land may commit a partial breach of the contract to convey because the land contains less acreage or square footage than promised, because the vendor owns less than a fee, because there are encumbrances, or because the vendor delays conveyance beyond the time promised. Not every deficiency amounts to a breach; a contract to convey a described parcel containing 100 acres more or less is not ordinarily breached

18. See § 12.14 below.

§ 12.11(1)

5. 2 W.Bl. 1078, 96 Eng.Rep. 635 (C.P. 1776).

6. The Uniform Land Transaction Act § 2–510, 13 U.L.A. 558, provides in part:

(a) * * * the measure of damages for a seller's repudiation or wrongful failure to convey is the difference between the fair market value at the time for conveyance and the contract price and any incidental and consequential damages, less expenses avoided because of the seller's breach. (b) Unless the title defect is an encumbrance * * * which could be discharged by application of all or a portion of the purchase price, if a seller is unable to convey because of a title defect of which the seller had no knowledge at the time of entering into the contract, the buyer is entitled only to restitution of any amounts paid on the contract price and incidental damages.

by tendering the described parcel, even if it contains only 98 acres.[25] If, on the other hand, the deficiency is severe, courts may properly hesitate to order a price abatement, because to do so may be to enforce a contract very different from the one the parties themselves made. In some cases, however, the purchaser is allowed to accept the defective performance and demand damages by way of price abatement to reflect the deficiency. Depending on which party has the risk of loss, similar options may be afforded when property is damaged by fire before conveyance.[27]

Acreage deficiencies. Acreage deficiencies most frequently amount to a contract breach when the sale is "by the acre," that is, based on a price-per-acre (or square foot) and not on a price by the tract as a whole. The division between the American and English rules seen in the case of a total breach can be carried over to the case of partial breach by a good faith vendor whose title covers fewer acres than originally believed. Some of the cases give the purchaser a price abatement proportioned to the contract price; others give the purchaser a price abatement proportioned to the land's value. The former mimics the *Flureau* or English rule, the latter gives the plaintiff the expectancy.[28]

Under an English–rule approach—reduction proportioned to price. If the English rule of *Flureau v. Thornhill* is applied to partial breach of this kind, the purchaser would be entitled to an abatement in price equal to the part of the contract price allocable to the missing acreage. For example, in a sale of 10 acres at $10,000 per acre, if the vendor can deliver only nine acres, the price would be reduced to a total of $90,000 instead of $100,000. If the English rule is to be applied to partial breach cases, this is the kind of reduction courts [29] and writers [30] seem to have in mind, that is, a deduction based on the price of the missing acreage, not a deduction based on the value of the missing acreage. One way to look at this kind of reduction would be to say that, as to the missing acreage, the breach is total. Just as in a *Flureau*–total–breach case the plaintiff recovers the purchase price, the plaintiff in a deficiency case recovers the purchase price of the missing acreage. If the land is worth more than the contract price, the plaintiff obtains his "bargain" or expectancy as to the nine acres conveyed, but does not as to the missing acre. Put differently, as to the missing land, the plaintiff who has paid the price recovers the price, but no more. The plaintiff who has not paid the price is forgiven the price, but no more.

—Reduction only as needed to equalize value on contract as a whole. The expressions of courts are not invariably clear with it comes to calculations. It would be possible to read the *Flureau* rule to require an equaliza-

27. This comparable but distinct topic is considered in § 12.14 below.

28. See Annotation, Measure and Elements of Damages Recoverable from Vendor where there Has Been Mistake as to Amount of Land Conveyed, 94 A.L.R.3d 1091 (1979) (reflecting variations on these formulas as well).

29. E.g., Terry v. Rich, 197 Ala. 486, 73 So. 76 (1916) (sale by tract); Forbes v. Wells Beach Casino, Inc., 409 A.2d 646 (Me.1979); Queen v. Sisk, 238 N.C. 389, 78 S.E.2d 152

(1953) ("value of the deficiency at the agreed price per acre"); Ewing v. Bissell, 105 Nev. 488, 777 P.2d 1320 (1989) ("abatement is to be determined by multiplying the quantity of the deficiency by the price per acre"); Arrott v. Smith, 225 S.W.2d 639 (Tex.Civ.App.1949); Hepler v. Atts, 201 Pa.Super. 236, 192 A.2d 138 (1963) (value of missing acreage over value of whole tract times purchase price); Flygare v. Brundage, 76 Wyo. 350, 302 P.2d 759 (1956) (sale by tract).

tion of exchange in terms of market value rather than a return of proportionate contract price. In the ten-acre example above, if the nine acres have a market value in excess of the $100,000 contract price, one way to deny the plaintiff a loss-of-bargain recovery would be to allow no abatement at all in the price. The plaintiff would pay $100,000 for fewer acres than expected but would be getting equal value. This kind of approach would look at the contract price and received value as a whole, not as to individual missing acreage. As long as the total land received is worth as much as or more than the price, the plaintiff would be entitled to no abatement at all. Some of the courts' expressions may permit, or at least do not clearly exclude this method of measuring damages under an English–rule approach.[31]

Under an American–rule approach. A court which follows the American rule in cases of total breach would logically reject proportionate abatement in the price under either of the methods outlined above. It would instead give the plaintiff the loss of bargain or expectancy, by providing a price abatement equal to the *value* of the missing acres, not merely one equal to the *price* of those acres. This approach is stated in a substantial portion of the cases.[34]

Improvements and variably valued acres. When some of the land is improved, it is not so easy to calculate missing acres by a simple proportionate reduction. In *Denman v. Stuart,*[35] the buyer got land with valuable improvements, including two houses, a water well, and outbuildings, but about $1/15$ of the total acreage was missing. The court allowed an abatement in price of $1/15$ even though it recognized that the purchaser had received the more valuable improved acres. The court reasoned that the parties had spread the price over the total acreage by assigning a per acre price. The Wyoming court in *Flygare v. Brundage,*[36] handled the problem differently. The court there deducted the value of the improvements, then allowed an abatement of the remaining sum in proportion to the deficiency. If the land is sold by the tract or as a unit rather than by the acre, there is no reason to use the average per acre price in figuring the abatement, since the parties themselves did not do so in figuring the price. In such a case it is appropriate to figure the abatement on the basis of either the actual price charged for, or the market value of the missing acres.[37]

[*For a discussion of qualitative defects and other matters, see this section in the Practitioner Treatise edition.*]

Vendor's Breach of Deed Covenants [75]

Merger in deed; covenants. The contract to convey usually requires the vendor to furnish a warranty deed. Once such a deed is executed, the rights of the parties, at least in theory, turn on the deed and its covenants, not on the contract that preceded it.[76] Of the six usual covenants in the warranty deed, three are especially important. These are the covenants, *first,* that the grantor is lawfully seized, *second,* that there were no encumbrances, and *third,* that the grantor will warrant and defend the title.[77] The first two are *"in praesenti,"* and if title is not good when the deed is made, they are breached at that time. The covenant of warranty, on the other hand, is said

75. R. Cunningham, W. Stoebuck & D. Whitman, The Law of Property § 11.13 (1984)   provides excellent coverage of the covenants and also of the damages for breach.

to operate prospectively and is not breached until the grantee suffers such actual loss as eviction or expense in clearing title.[78]   Whether a covenant is breached when made or only when harm occurs is important in determining whether a claim is actionable and hence in determining the statute of limitations.   Various other substantive incidents attach to each of these different covenants.   For instance, some of them may run with the land and some may not.[79]

Damages limited to contract price.   Breach of any of the named covenants could result in the purchaser's complete loss of the land, either because someone with better title ousts the purchaser or because the land is sold to enforce an encumbrance.   Where there is such a total failure of title, most courts permit the grantee to recover only the purchase price.[80]   This rule means the purchaser would take a significant loss if she had built on the land or if land values had risen when the ouster takes place.[81]   But any other rule would hold grantors liable indefinitely into the future.[82]   In this respect the limitation may be appropriate for deed covenants even when a similar limitation would not be appropriate for the executory contract. Sometimes the price limitation has been applied to limit the grantor's liability even further by holdings that if the title failed only to some percentage of the land, then liability would be limited to that percentage of the price.[83]

Measures of damages.   Various measures of damages may be appropriate, depending upon the facts, but usually all of the measures are subject to the price limit already stated.   When a covenant is breached by an encumbrance such as a lien on the property, the cost of removing the encumbrance is often the appropriate measure of damages.[84]   When the covenant is breached by partial title failure that cannot be cured, the damages measure is the difference between the value of the property without breach of the covenant and the property with the breach or defect.[85]   If the breach requires the purchaser to litigate title issues, the costs of doing so, including the purchaser's attorney fees, are also items of damage.[86]   Finally, the purchaser may recover interest from the time of eviction.[87]   These rules have the effect of excluding recovery of consequential damages such as the grantee's loss of profits.[88]

§ 12.11(2) Rescission and Restitution for the Purchaser

Executory Contracts

In the case of an executory contract, the vendor's total breach always gives the purchaser the option of claiming restitution in the amount of any sum paid on the purchase price.[3]   This may be conceptualized as a "rescission" or avoidance of the contract coupled with restitution; or it may be thought of more simply as a restitutionary alternative to the damages claim for breach.   However conceptualized, the claim is subject to the requirement that the purchaser take prompt action [4] if he wishes to avoid the contract.

[*For a discussion of minor breaches and recovery of the vendor's profits, see this section in the Practitioner Treatise edition.*]

Executed Contracts: Deed Covenants

Once the land sale contract is executed by delivery of a deed, the contract provisions are merged in the deed and the vendor's liability if any is based on breach of the deed covenants, not on the original contract. Fraud by the vendor may justify "rescission" (or constructive trust), with a restoration of both parties to their pre-contract position. Breach of the deed covenants alone, however, is not usually remedied by avoiding the transaction and giving restitution. Instead the purchaser is limited to the recovery of damages.[29] Damages for breach of a deed covenant are hardly adequate for the purchaser, but the rule against restitution may reflect a strong policy favoring security of transactions once a deed has been delivered.

§ 12.11(3) Specific Performance in Favor of the Purchaser

[*For the text of this section, see the unabridged Practitioner Treatise edition.*]

§ 12.11(4) The Purchaser's Lien

The purchaser to whom the vendor owes any remaining obligations is entitled to a lien to secure fulfillment of those obligations. Sometimes the parties provide for the lien by express terms of the contract,[1] and sometimes the lien is codified by statute.[2] Ordinarily, however, the lien is created or recognized by the courts as a "natural equity,"[3] and courts shape the lien even in states where it is codified.[4]

For example, if the vendor has not conveyed all of the land, the purchaser holds a lien on the land covered by the contract to secure its proper conveyance.[5] If the purchaser has a right to terminate or rescind for any reason, including for fraud,[6] or failure of a condition,[7] then he must hold the land he received for the vendor and stand ready to reconvey it, but he holds a lien on that land to secure repayment by the vendor[8] payment for any improvements, taxes and insurance,[9] and perhaps for costs and fees as well.[10]

The lien can likewise attach to the property itself in the hands of a purchaser or encumbrancer who has notice of the plaintiff's rights,[13] and also against general creditors and even judgment creditors.[14] The lien is not effective against an encumbrancer or a subsequent purchaser who takes or encumbers the land in good faith, for value, and without notice of the first purchaser's lien,[15] and it may be cut off by delay in asserting it.[16]

§ 12.12 Vendor's Remedies for Purchaser's Breach

§ 12.12(1) Vendor's Damages Remedy

General Damages

In summary. Putting aside installment contracts which are discussed in a separate section,[1] the measure of the vendor's damages for the purchaser's total breach of an executory contract to purchase land is (a) the difference between the market price of the land at breach and the contract price, plus special damages; or (b) the forfeiture of any reasonable earnest money deposit under the rules for liquidated damages; or, in some states, (c) an action for the price, which is similar to specific performance.

Rental value recoveries. Rental value claims must not duplicate delay damages already given in the form of interest. Subject to that qualification, the vendor may have several distinct types of rental value claims against the breaching purchaser. *First,* the vendor may hold herself ready to perform even after the purchaser's breach in order to pursue her specific performance suit; and in so doing she may refuse to rent the land to others. Such a loss is recoverable as special damages.[30] *Second,* if the purchaser commits a partial breach by delayed performance, damage for delay might plausibly be measured by interest on the purchase price, but alternatively by rental value of the land during the delay period.[31] *Third,* the purchaser has occupied the land under an installment contract on which the purchaser later defaults, rental value of the land during his occupancy is one element of the vendor's damages which may justify the vendor in retaining the payments already made.[32] *Fourth,* the vendor may be unable either to resell or re-rent the land immediately after default, in which case rental value from the time of default to the time of re-sale (or re-renting) may be an element of special damages. *Fifth,* the purchaser may have gone into occupancy of the land before closing, not under provisions of the contract but simply by informal permission of the vendor given after the contract has been made. If the purchaser later breaches or repudiates, the question arises whether he will be liable for rental value during his period of occupancy. Conceivably, the vendor might have a claim for rental value as reliance damages associated with such an occupancy;[33] but if there is no detrimental reliance by the vendor,[34] then the claim might be one for restitution rather than damages.[35]

Care of grantor contracts. The vendor of land sometimes conveys or contracts to convey in exchange for the purchaser's promise, covenant or condition to support the grantor for the remainder of the grantor's life. A whole arsenal of remedies is available to the grantor where the grantee commits a substantial breach of such a contract, including, for one, the ordinary damages remedy. The measure of the vendor's damages in such a case is usually the reasonable value of the support or other services contracted for, or the cost of getting the support or services elsewhere.[44] Most courts hold that the grantor can recover not only past damages for lost support but also reasonably proven future damages.[45]

[*For additional materials, see this section in the Practitioner Treatise edition.*]

§ 12.12(2) Restitution to the Vendor

Purchaser's Pre-closing Occupancy

After contracting for the sale, the vendor often informally permits the purchaser to occupy the land without charge in anticipation of closing in the near future. In such a case, occupancy can be no part of the contract itself, since it was arranged afterward. The purchaser is not a trespasser, since he had permission to be there; he did not breach any contract as to occupancy, since he never agreed to pay for use of the land. Indeed, it seems clear that the parties understand that no rental will be paid in such cases, so liability for restitution is equally inappropriate, at least if the contract is ultimately performed. Such is the traditional view.[7]

§ 12.12(2)

7.   Carpenter v. United States, 84 U.S. (17 Wall.) 489, 21 L.Ed. 680 (1873); Stapley v. American Bathtub Liners, Inc., 162 Ariz. 564, 785 P.2d 84 (App.1989); Marshall v. Bare, 107 Idaho 201, 687 P.2d 591 (App.1984). Cf. Weeks v. Standish Hardware & Garage Co., 145 Me. 307, 75 A.2d 444 (1950) (when ven-

Does breach of the purchase agreement affect the rental value claim? Should the same rule apply when the purchaser totally breaches or repudiates the contract or when the closing is postponed? If the contract itself provides for occupancy as a part of the quid pro quo, it is easy to say that the purchaser who repudiates must upon rescission or termination make restitution. When the purchaser occupies by permission but not as a part of what he gets under the contract, breach of the contract seems irrelevant to the question of occupancy. Upon rescission or termination, the parties must restore to each other what they received under the contract, but not benefits they received apart from the contract performance. So some authority has opposed restitution even when the purchaser himself is in breach and has obtained free use of the land without ever going through with the purchase.[8]

No assumpsit for use rule and implicit contractual exclusion. This result fits with the antique notion that *assumpsit* would not lie for use and occupation of land alone. But this occult expression of obscure anxieties has little bearing on the case in a modern remedial system.

Bases for liability for the pre-closing rental. If the parties contemplate no rent when they expect the contract to go through, it does not follow that they have made any contract at all about what is to happen if the contract is breached by the purchaser. The actual scope of the particular contract or assumptions of the parties may suggest that rental liability is appropriate in some cases as pure restitution. So some cases—rather sketchily—have permitted the vendor to recover restitution of rental value for pre-closing occupancy,[11] and others have done so where the vendor himself breaches and the contract is rescinded.[12] There are also statutes in some states that permit restitution in such cases.[13] In addition, it may be plausible today for the vendor to assert, not restitution, but a claim of reliance damages.[14]

dor's successor had right to disaffirm contract, purchaser in possession would owe rental value for use but only from the time of disaffirmance); Jacobs v. Andolina, 123 A.D.2d 835, 507 N.Y.S.2d 450 (1986) (no obligation to make restitution for rental value while defendant was a contract purchaser in possession, but when he became bidder at foreclosure sale that status terminated and from that time he became liable for rental value, less any contributions toward taxes, insurance and repairs).

In *Carpenter,* supra, The government agreed to purchase land from the vendor, but later found it had no authority to make the purchase. Before its want of authority was discovered, however, it went into possession by the vendor's agreement, and actually made improvements. Thereafter authority was secured and money appropriated for the purchase which eventually took place. Plaintiff vendor then sued for the rental value of the occupancy that took place before the purchase was completed. The Court denied recovery, saying that the plaintiff, had he done so before transfer of title, might have claimed interest of the money due, but not rental value. The concession of interest might be fatal to

the principle, since interest, like rent, is a measure of time-value; the only question would be whether the plaintiff is entitled to the time-value of money or the time-value of the property.

In various contexts, courts frequently state that upon a contract to purchase, the parties do not stand in the relationship of landlord and tenant. E.g., MacKenna v. Jordan, 123 Ga.App. 801, 182 S.E.2d 550 (1971); Panhandle Rehabilitation Center, Inc. v. Larson, 205 Neb. 605, 288 N.W.2d 743 (1980). As applied to the restitution claim and taken literally, such statements seem obviously true but also irrelevant to the question of remedies, since one might owe rental value not as "rent" but as restitution. See Tompkins v. Sandeen, 243 Minn. 256, 259, 67 N.W.2d 405, 408, n. 4, 49 A.L.R.2d 1162 (1954) ("the purchaser is charged with the benefit from the use of the property and not rent, although reasonable rental value is the accepted standard of determining the beneficial use"). Taken as a metaphor for the view that there should be no restitutionary liability, the statements that the parties do not stand in a landlord tenant relationship furnish a conclusion but do not in themselves give a reason for it.

Executed Contracts

Denial of rescission for purchaser's breach of money obligation. Except for the case of a contract to convey land in return for support or care,[15] the grantee's breach or the "failure of consideration" does not warrant rescission or cancellation of the deed.[16] If the grantee breaches by failure to pay the price, the vendor may have a damages action or even a vendor's lien on the land,[17] but traditionally does not have a claim for restitution when the only performance remaining due is payment of a liquidated sum of money.[18]

Support of Grantor Contracts

Rescission and cancellation granted. In many instances landowners convey land to a grantee in return for a promise of lifetime support. This is not either an entrepreneurial contract or an ordinary contract for end consumption. The grantee is often a family member or long-time friend or neighbor and the arrangement often assumes that the grantor will continue to live on the land along with the grantee. Close living arrangements coupled with the irritations of dependency and whatever crotchets of personality the parties bring with them often disrupt the arrangement.

Courts have often recognized that rescission and cancellation of the deed given in exchange for support is an appropriate remedy for breach by the grantee (or "failure of consideration").[29] Sometimes the theory is that care-for-grantor contracts warrant an exception to the general rule against deed cancellation;[30] sometimes it is that the covenant to care for the grantor is a condition subsequent or an implied trust.[31] Sometimes courts purport to require "fraud" or other misdealing by the grantee, but the real reasons in such cases often appear to be nothing more than breach.[32] Indeed, Professor Palmer has noted that cancellation seems to be granted in fact not only when the grantee breaches by non-performance, but also when the arrangement simply does not work.[33] Even when the promise of support is oral, relief is given if the evidence is sufficiently convincing.[34] And when the support covenants appear in the deed itself or subsequent purchasers otherwise have notice, purchasers are themselves subject to the grantor's cancellation remedy.[35]

Perhaps the remedy is granted partly because courts sympathize deeply with the elderly and afflicted who are usually the grantors in these cases,[36] and because courts are reluctant to keep the parties in a close relationship that has turned unpleasant. In this respect, grant of rescission and cancellation is quite like the refusal to grant specific performance in contracts that require a close working relationship:[37] the grant of a remedy in the one case and its denial in the other both relieve the parties of impinging personal relationships.

§ 12.12(3) Specific Performance in Favor of the Vendor

If applied to the vendor's claim for specific performance of a contract to sell land for money, the adequacy rule would almost always lead courts to refuse relief. Specific performance in favor of the vendor would merely order the purchaser to pay money which is in no sense unique, and which can be provided adequately by a legal action. In spite of the supposed adequate-legal-remedy rule, courts have generally been willing to grant specific performance to the vendor,[3] subject only to the usual equitable defenses.[4]

[*For substantial discussion of the vendor's specific performance remedy, see this section in the Practitioner Treatise edition.*]

§ 12.12(4) The Vendor's Lien

If a vendor of land sells on an installment contract, she retains the title to the land even though the purchaser occupies the land. The retained legal title furnishes good security for the payments due in the future. If the vendor delivers the deed to the purchaser before the vendor has received payments due, the vendor can secure herself by taking a mortgage or expressly reserving a lien on the land. When the vendor makes neither of these arrangements, a substantial number of courts nevertheless "imply" a lien in favor of the grantor.[1] Others refuse to do so, limiting themselves instead to the enforcement of liens created by the parties.[2]

[*For additional discussion of the vendor's lien, see this section in the Practitioner Treatise edition.*]

§ 12.13 Some Problems of Installment Contracts Remedies

[*For the text of this section, see the unabridged Practitioner Treatise edition.*]

§ 12.14 Loss or Damage to Property Before Conveyance

What happens when the property is substantially damaged by fire or condemned under eminent domain powers after the contract is made but before conveyance? May either party rescind or otherwise avoid the contract obligation? May either party enforce it? If it is enforced, is there to be a price abatement? Is fire insurance (or compensation for the eminent domain taking) payable or credited to the buyer? These questions rightly suggest that a number of variables might influence decisions. Although the damaged-property case resembles the acreage deficiency case in important ways,[1] the damaged-property case adds new and more complicated elements. Not surprisingly, the answers are not entirely uniform.

It is usually assumed that if one of the parties is guilty of actionable fault in causing the loss, that liability will be allocated by tort law. Even contract provisions allocating the risk of loss probably are not intended to cover the case in which one party is guilty of negligence in causing it.[2] Lawyers drafting contracts usually provide for the contingency of a casualty loss by fire or otherwise. If such provisions exist, they will control.[3] When the contract does not provide a solution, a statute such as the Uniform Vendor and Purchaser Risk of Loss Act may do so.[4]

In the absence of contract or statute governing the point, some courts have tried to resolve the problem by using the equitable conversion doctrine,

---

§ 12.14

3. Caulfield v. Improved Risk Mutuals, Inc., 66 N.Y.2d 793, 497 N.Y.S.2d 903, 488 N.E.2d 833 (1985); Bryant v. Willison Real Estate Co., 177 W.Va. 120, 350 S.E.2d 748 (1986); see Hawkes v. Kehoe, 193 Mass. 419, 79 N.E. 766 (1907).

4. E.g., N.Y.—McKinney's Gen. Obligations Law § 5–1311 (from the Uniform Vendor and Purchaser Risk Act). See discussing the history of the act in detail, Lucenti v. Cayuga Apartments, Inc., 48 N.Y.2d 530, 423 N.Y.S.2d 886, 399 N.E.2d 918 (1979).

under which a purchaser of land is treated in equity as the equitable owner from the time he enters into a specifically performable contract.[5] Treating the purchaser as owner means that he cannot call off the deal on the ground that the property was destroyed; it also means he bears the loss.[6] Sometimes courts get this result without theorizing an equitable conversion, especially where the purchaser has taken up possession or other incidents of ownership.[7]

A different solution would be to leave the risk of loss upon the vendor as owner until legal title has passed. The appeal of the equitable conversion solution is that it puts the burden on the buyer who takes charge of the property and who can therefore be expected to protect his own interests by insurance or otherwise. The equitable conversion solution, however, is a crude device; it allocates risks to the purchaser from the time the contract is made and whether or not the purchaser takes charge of the property. The Uniform Act is more precise. It provides that unless the parties expressly contract otherwise, the risk shifts to the purchaser when he *either* takes title *or* takes possession,[8] but not in any event merely because a contract has been signed.

To say that the risk of loss falls upon the vendor is necessarily to say that the purchaser may either rescind or have a price abatement. Some courts have taken the view that a casualty that substantially damages the property is ground for a rescission or avoidance by either party, so that neither can enforce the contract against the other's will.[9] The theory advanced by the Massachusetts court many years ago was that the contract was impliedly conditioned on the continued existence of the property.[10] Although this solution is appealing where the purchaser has not taken possession or title and where there is no fund payable for the loss, it may not be so compelling where the loss is fully insured or where the purchaser has actually gone into possession and taken charge of the property.

When one of the parties has collectible insurance, it would be possible to view the insurance proceeds as a substitute for the destroyed land or as a credit on the price, at the option of one of the parties. If the risk of loss is upon the vendor under any of the rules discussed above, it may be plausible to argue that the purchaser can still treat the proceeds of the vendor's policy as a substitute for the loss and enforce the contract with a credit for the policy's proceeds. Even if the risk of loss is upon the purchaser rather than the vendor, the purchaser should have the insurance proceeds or a credit for them,[11] if the proceeds of the policy are identified with or treated as a substitute for the land. In such a case the purchaser must make an appropriate contribution to the vendor for the cost of premiums.[12] But some judicial opinion has taken the view that the insurance policy should be identified with the premiums paid for it, not with the land it stands for, and hence that the insurance proceeds paid to the vendor are not to be credited against the purchase price.[13]

9. Dixon v. Salvation Army, 142 Cal. App.3d 463, 191 Cal.Rptr. 111 (1983) (vendor's performance is excused and he could not be compelled to convey with a price abatement); Hawkes v. Kehoe, 193 Mass. 419, 79 N.E. 766 (1907). Doctrines of frustration of purpose or impracticability would suggest this solution. As to these, see § 13.3 below.

13. Long v. Keller, 104 Cal.App.3d 312, 163 Cal.Rptr. 532 (1980).

In *Skelly Oil Co. v. Ashmore,*[14] the building was destroyed by fire and the vendor collected the insurance. The purchaser was allowed to enforce the contract, with a full credit for the insurance collected by the vendor. The case is striking because the property was actually worth more to the purchaser *after* the fire, partly because it intended to raze the building in any event. A dissent argued that the purchaser should be permitted only to cancel the contract if it so chose, not to proceed with a credit for the vendor's insurance. This solution would force a re-bargaining and would allocate any windfall to the vendor rather than to the purchaser.

A California case [15] was slightly different because the vendor was grossly underinsured. The purchaser wanted to proceed with the purchase but to have an abatement in the price representing the full value of the destroyed premises. The court refused on the ground that neither purchaser nor vendor had ever agreed to a lesser price for lesser value. The effect was to leave the risk of loss on the vendor and to excuse performance.

If the loss falls upon the purchaser under any of the rules stated above, then the purchaser cannot escape the contract obligation to pay full price; that seems to be a necessary result of saying the loss falls upon him. If performance is excused on both side, then the purchaser escapes liability but cannot impose liability upon the vendor. If, however, the vendor must bear the loss under the applicable rule, then the purchaser might be allowed the option of enforcing the contract with a price abatement, as in some of the land deficiency cases. An abatement might reflect the loss in value from casualty or from an eminent domain taking.[16]

§ 12.15   Leases and Lease Contracts

§ 12.15(1)   Background and Scope

[*For the text of this section, see the unabridged Practitioner Treatise edition.*]

§ 12.15(2)   Lessee's Remedies for Lessor's Breach Affecting Use Premises

General Damages. The lessee of real property usually stands in a position closely analogous to the purchaser of real property and the damages measures available to the lessee are substantially the same as those available to the purchaser, with appropriate adjustments in the form of words used. If the lessor deprives the tenant of use of the premises by failing to provide possession in the first instance or by any actionable conduct later, the tenant is entitled to his expectancy measured by general damages. Where rent has not been paid, the general damages measure is the difference between the rental value of the premises and the agreed upon rent for the relevant period, a species of the familiar market-contract differential.[2]

14.   365 S.W.2d 582 (Mo.1963).

15.   Dixon v. Salvation Army, 142 Cal. App.3d 463, 191 Cal.Rptr. 111 (1983).

16.   Lucenti v. Cayuga Apartments, Inc., 48 N.Y.2d 530, 423 N.Y.S.2d 886, 399 N.E.2d 918 (1979).

§ 12.15(2)

2.   Birge v. Toppers Menswear, Inc., 473 S.W.2d 79 (Tex.Civ.App.1971); R. Schoshinski, American Law of Landlord and Tenant, § 3.2 (1980 and Supp.).

The Restatement of Property calls this calculation "the fair market value of the lease."[3]

A different formulation for the same measurement says that the tenant recovers the rental value less any rents saved by the breach. For example, if the rent is $1,000 and the rental value is $1200, the tenant would be entitled to $200, the rental value of $1200 less the $1,000 in rents saved.

If rent has already been paid for the period, the plaintiff is entitled to the rental value of the premises without a deduction. If the rent is $1,000, which has been paid by the tenant, and the value is $1200, and the plaintiff gets no possession, the tenant is entitled to recover the whole rental value, $1200.[4]

In the same way, the lessor's failure to repair or maintain essential services required by the lease may reduce the value of the premises. In that case, if the tenant does not actually repair the default himself, he may recover the difference between the value of the premises as with the proper maintenance and the value as received.[5]

Consequential damages generally. In addition to general damages, the lessor may be held liable for consequential damages that do not duplicate compensation already afforded by general damages, provided such damages are within the contemplation of the parties[6] and proven with sufficient certainty.[7] In some states a warranty of habitability claim may permit recovery of damages for emotional distress.[8] These aside, consequential damages may include the tenant's cost of relocating if the lease is terminated,[9] the reasonable cost of substitute premises if the leased premises become temporarily unusable,[10] or the reasonable costs of making the premises usable if the tenant remains in possession.[11] Reliance damages—expenses incurred before the lessor's breach and in reliance upon her performance—may also be awarded when the evidence supports such losses.[12] For instance, if the tenant, in reliance on the lease incurs costs in surveying equipment for the new premises, those costs are recoverable as reliance expense damages.[13]

Rent withholding and abatement. Suppose the lessor fails to maintain the leased property as required by the lease and violates a warranty of habitability. In some jurisdictions, the tenant is sometimes permitted to withhold payment of rent instead of relying on the damages or termination remedies. This has a two-fold direction. It may compensate the tenant for reduced use value of the premises, and the prospect of recovering the rent may induce the landlord to make the necessary repairs promptly. Procedurally, the issue may arise when the tenant withholds rent and the landlord

3. Restatement Second of Property § 10.2 and Illustration 1 (1976).

4. Zais v. CF West Florida, Inc., 505 So.2d 577 (Fla.App.1987) (fair rental value of the apartment during the uninhabitable period).

5. Miller v. Ritchie, 45 Ohio St.3d 222, 543 N.E.2d 1265 (1989). As to evidence, the *Miller* court observed:

"Evidence showing reduction-in-use is relevant. But damages should be computed by measuring the effect of such reduction-in-

use (together with any other defect in the leasehold) on the rental value of the property * * *. The stipulated rent amount is presumptive evidence of the rental value of the property without defects. [ ]. The tenant's undisputed testimony as to the extent of defects, even if not accompanied by the tenant's opinion on the monetary value of the defective property, is sufficient evidence on which to base a damages award."

sues to evict. In such a case the tenant proves the breach of warranty or constructive eviction and the right to withhold rent or the right to abate it.[18]

Measure of abatement based on general damages or expectancy. The measure of abatement in these circumstances, according to the Restatement, aims to give the tenant the benefit of his original bargain and this is to be accomplished by a "proportional" abatement. For example, premises might have been leased for a restaurant with two dining rooms, but one of the rooms may have been left in such disrepair that it cannot be used. If the full rent in the lease was $1,000 but the rental value is only $750 under the conditions existing, then the abatement reduces the rent owed to $750. If the rising rental market is such that the premises have a rental value of $2,000 for the two dining rooms but only $1500 with one of them in disrepair, the same proportion is used to respect the plaintiff's bargain. Under this rule the plaintiff would pay only in rent $750, even though the defective premises have a rental value of $1500.[19]

Measure of abatement based on cost of substitute performance. A different measure of abatement might be possible if the tenant actually and reasonably makes repairs necessary to cure the lessor's default. This measure would be analogous to "cover" or cost of procuring substitute performance seen in other contracting situations.[20] It is based on the cost of making the obligation good, not on the market value of the premises. It may be more justified than some types of cover because the cost incurred inures to the lessor's benefit in the form of repaired property. When the tenant actually uses the rent withheld to make the necessary improvements, the remedy is also comparable to specific performance in that the end result is actual repair, although it is a unilateral and indirect version of that relief.

Rescission. The executory contract to enter a lease is subject to rescission for a total breach by the landowner. Once a lease is executed, the traditional view was that the lessee was a property owner, albeit only for a term. If the lessee's status were analogized to that of a purchaser who bought the fee, rescission would not be allowed.[21] Indeed, the traditional common law view was that the tenant's covenant to pay rent was independent of the landlord's covenants of maintenance or service, so the landlord's breach did not release the tenant from obligations to pay unless the tenant was actually or constructively evicted.[22]

Contemporary view permitting rescission. However, the lease has always had contractual elements to it and the view today emphasizes that those elements are more significant than the property elements. The independent covenant rule is thus rejected today,[23] with the result that the tenant can pursue any appropriate remedy upon the lessor's breach. This view permits the tenant to rescind or terminate for the lessor's breach,[24] provided the default is a significant one,[25] not promptly cured, and the tenant vacates the premises.

18. See Javins v. First Nat. Realty Corp., 428 F.2d 1071 (D.C.Cir.1970), cert. denied, 400 U.S. 925, 91 S.Ct. 186, 27 L.Ed.2d 185 (1970) (leading case, warranty of habitability breach justifies withholding rent and furnishes a defense to eviction proceeding); Teodori v. Werner, 490 Pa. 58, 415 A.2d 31 (1980).

19. Restatement Second of Property § 11.1, Comment d & Illustration 1 (1976). Compare the similar problem that arises with acreage and other deficiencies in land sales contracts. See § 12.11(1) above.

20. See Restatement Second of Property § 11.2 (1976).

The modern view of the lease as a contract suggests that the lease "gives rise to the usual remedies for breach of contract" [32] including specific performance. In line with this, specific performance of the underlying contract may be ordered even after the lease is executed and tenant takes possession.[33] Specific performance is perhaps more commonly achieved by way of injunction to compel the landlord to comply with the lease terms or with covenants therein. For example, an injunction might go to prevent the landlord from interfering with possession or from removing amenities [34] or from interfering with a permissible sublease.[35] Injunctive (or declaratory) relief is also used to prevent a forfeiture or termination by a landlord when the tenant disputes an obligation.

§ 12.15(3) Lessor's Remedies Against Lessee Who Defaults or Abandons the Premises

Recovery of accrued rental and repair costs. Tenants may default on rental payment in two potentially different situations. In the first, the tenant defaults on rental payments but continues to occupy the premises. In the second, the tenant defaults on rental payments but vacates the premises, abandoning the lease altogether. The first situation is the simplest. In that situation, the lessor is entitled to recover rental payments due, with interest, and may in addition be entitled to terminate the lease.[1] The landlord may also have a recovery for the tenant's breach of covenants to repair or to return the premises in good condition.[2]

Remedies when tenant abandons the lease. When the tenant ceases payment of rent and abandons the lease, the traditional view gives the landlord three options: (1) continue to collect (or sue for) the rent as it becomes due, with interest,[3] and without any obligation to minimize damages by re-letting;[4] (2) accept the abandonment as a surrender of the lease

33. Guinn v. Holcombe, 29 Ark.App. 206, 780 S.W.2d 30 (1989).

34. Bargain Mart, Inc. v. Lipkis, 212 Conn. 120, 561 A.2d 1365 (1989) (injunction to continue furnishing heat affirmed); Union City Union Suit Co., Ltd. v. Miller, 162 A.D.2d 101, 556 N.Y.S.2d 864 (1990) (reflecting trial court order restraining lessor from removing essential freight elevator).

35. Med Mac Realty Co., Inc. v. Lerner, 154 A.D.2d 656, 547 N.Y.S.2d 65 (1989) (requiring landlord to execute necessary documents to permit renovations for a sublessee and enjoining landlord's interference in relationship between lessee and sublessee).

§ 12.15(3)

1. Restatement Second of Property § 12.-1(2) (1977). Traditional thought had it that the landlord was recovering "rent" as such. With the advent of a contractual view of the lease, it is possible to think of the recovery merely as damages for breach of the covenant to pay rent.

2. See Crisman v. Stidd, 396 Pa.Super. 335, 578 A.2d 542 (1990) (reasonable repair costs necessary to return the premises to full rental value, but not the added costs necessary to

undo some changes that would not affect rental value). The tenant's covenant to return the premises in good repair is closely analogous to a contractor's contract to build or repair, and damages rules for the two kinds of cases are the same, usually the cost of repair, but sometimes the cost of repair recovery is subjected to a ceiling equal to the diminished value of the premises. E.g., Missouri Baptist Hospital v. United States, 213 Ct.Cl. 505, 555 F.2d 290 (1977). The cost of repair measure as compared to the diminished value measure is discussed in connection with contractors and leases in § 12.19(1) below. As to the remedies for waste, see § 5.2(8) above.

3. National Advertising Co. v. Main Street Shopping Center, 539 So.2d 594 (Fla.App. 1989); Miller v. Vineyard, 765 S.W.2d 865 (Tex.App.1989). Procedurally, the landlord may of course wait until all installments are due and bring a single suit for all past due rents. E.g., N.J. Industrial Properties, Inc. v. Y.C. & V.L., Inc., 100 N.J. 432, 495 A.2d 1320, 50 A.L.R.4th 369 (1985).

4. Love, Landlord's Remedies When the Tenant Abandons: Property, Contract, and Leases, 30 U.Kan.L.Rev. 533, 550 (1982); R.

and a termination of all future obligations on both sides;[5] or (3) with proper notice to the tenant, treat the abandonment as a breach, re-let the premises *for the account of the tenant*; credit the tenant with the amounts received from re-letting but hold the tenant liable for any deficiency,[6] and, presumably, any appropriate costs of re-letting.[7] All of these remedies remain intact today, except that some courts today would require the landlord to minimize damages under the first remedy.[8] In some jurisdictions today a fourth option is available in some circumstances. The fourth option permits the landlord to sue on a contract theory for anticipatory repudiation, measuring damages by the difference between the rent due and the fair rental value of the premises for the balance of the term, with appropriate reductions to present value.[9]

[*For discussion of termination vs. the tenant account remedy, accelerated rents, future loss, see this section in the Practitioner Treatise edition.*]

Minimizing or "mitigating" damages. The would-be lessor in a *contract* to lease was of course required to minimize damages.[38] But the traditional view held that once a lease was executed, the landlord, confronted with the tenant's default and abandonment, could "stand idly by," do nothing to find a substitute tenant, and simply collect the rent installments as they were due.[39] If the landlord did in fact install a new tenant, he would be required to credit the first tenant with the rents received; but he would not be required to seek the new tenant or to accept him if offered. The effect is that the first rule of avoidable consequences is not applied but the second rule is.[40] This result was thought to follow from the view of the lease as a conveyance of property for a period of time. The landlord was no more required to maximize the tenant's use of the property any more than he would be required to do so if the tenant had purchased the fee and then failed to use the property or resell it.

Modern view. Many contemporary cases, following Dean McCormick's suggestion,[41] have rejected the traditional rule and have said that the landlord must credit the defaulting tenant with any rent the landlord could reasonably have obtained from a substitute tenant.[42] Some statutes adopt the same position.[43] This view may be limited, however, to residential leases in some cases.

Rationales: lease as conveyance. It is often said that this rule violates the avoidable consequences rule in failing to require the landlord to minimize damages, and indeed that it is unique in permitting such wasteful behavior. Such comments evidently assume that the property conception of the lease is "wrong" and the contract conception "right." If the lease can rightly be regarded in the same light as conveyance, then a rule that absolves the landlord of any duty is exactly what would be expected from comparable cases. A grantor of a fee, for example, is not required to minimize the grantee's damages by finding a new buyer when the grantee abandons the land he bought.

Rationales: lease as contract with specific performance. Even if the lease is viewed as a contract, the criticisms do not hold. Victims of contract

---

Schoshinski, American Law of Landlord and Tenant § 10:12 (1980 and Supp.); Restatement Second of Property § 12.1(3) (1977).

5. Restatement Second of Property § 12.-1(3) (1977).

breach are often required to use reasonable efforts to minimize consequential damages,[44] but this is never the case when the court grants specific performance. Specific performance forces the breacher to perform the contract. The necessary effect of the breacher's forced performance is that the other party need not minimize. This fact may properly lead courts to scrutinize the options and to deny specific performance when the plaintiff can achieve the contract objectives more cheaply.[45] Procedure and form aside, any recovery of full price by a seller is a form of specific performance. This is true in ordinary land sale contracts, as noted elsewhere.[46] Given the almost-routine award of specific performance to either party to a land sale contract, a routine award of specific performance in a land lease case is not only plausible but to be expected. The action for rent due, with somewhat less efficiency, obtains the same thing for the lessor.

Computing Credits to the Tenant

The problem of excess substitute rents. When, before judgment against the tenant for rent or damages, the landlord lets to a new tenant for some of the time remaining on the original lease, all of the rules require that the landlord credit the new tenant's rent to the original tenant in some way.[47] How much credit should the original tenant receive if the premises are vacant for some time period before a new tenant can be found but the new tenant pays a higher rent overall, but not rent for some of the vacant months? Should the excess portion of the new rent be credited against those months in which there was no tenant at all?

For example, suppose the tenant vacates the premises and ceases rent payments with a year remaining on his lease and rent accruing at $1,000 per month. The landlord finds no new tenant for six months, then obtains a tenant who pays $2,000 for the remaining six months of the original lease. The original tenant is entitled to full credit for six months, month by month, when the new tenant occupied and paid all of the rents originally due and then some. Does the original tenant also get credit for the excess on the ground that for the balance of the term taken as a whole, the landlord received the full $12,000 to which he was originally entitled?

Choice of termination vs. tenant's account remedy determining credit. The courts have gone both ways on the matter of crediting the tenant for the excess rent, sometimes influenced by specific lease clauses or statutes.[48] One line of thought attempts to reconcile the decisions by distinguishing between the termination and the tenant's account remedy. Under this view, where the lease is terminated but the landlord nevertheless is entitled to recover rents (or damages) for the unexpired term, the courts have mostly held that the tenant does not get credit for the excess rent paid.[49] Instead, the new tenant's rental for any given month is credited only against the first tenant's obligation for that month. The new tenant's payment in July offsets the

48. See Annotation, Landlord and Tenant: Respective Rights in Excess Rent When Landlord Relets at Higher Rent During Lessee's Term, 50 A.L.R. 4th 403 (1986).

49. N.J. Industrial Properties, Inc. v. Y.C. & V.L., Inc., 100 N.J. 432, 495 A.2d 1320, 50

A.L.R. 4th 369 (1985); Liqui–Box Corp. v. Estate of Elkman, 238 N.J.Super. 588, 570 A.2d 472 (1990); Hargis v. Mel–Mad Corp., 46 Wash.App. 146, 730 P.2d 76 (1986).

first tenant's liability for July, but no part of the higher rent paid offsets the first tenant's liability for January when the premises were vacant.[50]

On the other hand, when the landlord pursues the tenant's account remedy or some similar remedy provided in the lease itself, the landlord collects rents as "agent" for the tenant and whatever is collected in whatever amounts must be fully credited to him.[51] The same is true if the claim is regarded as a claim for simple breach of contract rather than a claim for "rent," in which case the tenant is entitled to a credit under the principle that limits the plaintiff to full compensation.[52]

(2) CHATTEL SALES CONTRACTS

§ 12.16 Buyer's Remedies for Breach of Chattel Sales Contract

§ 12.16(1) Buyer's Remedies: Background and Summary

The Uniform Commercial Code (UCC) now governs virtually all sales transactions.[8] For non-delivery of goods,[9] or anticipatory repudiation[10] of the contract, the Code retains the expectancy measure of damages based on the contract-market differential,[11] plus any appropriate and separate consequential damages.[12] The Code provides that the buyer can recover (a) any portion of the price paid[13] and (b) the contract-market differential,[14] less any expenses saved as a result of the breach.[15] A contract-market differential is also the measure of damages when accepted goods are in breach of warranty.[16] As to consequential damages, the Code retains the substance of the traditional rules, for instance by requiring the buyer to make reasonable effort to minimize damages.

Code differences. However, the Code makes three obvious changes, one of which raises new difficulties.

(1) The UCC adds a new measure of damages called "cover." This allows the buyer to recover any actual cost of getting a substitute performance to replace the goods the seller did not provide, so long as the new performance really is a substitute and is commercially reasonable.[17]

(2) The UCC provides a somewhat more liberal standard for awarding consequential damages than the traditional common law standard.[18]

(3) The UCC changes the relevant date for computing market damages; it is no longer the date on which performance was due, but is now the date the buyer learned of the breach.[19] Code language in different scattered sections has also raised some doubts about how anticipatory repudiation should be treated.

Liquidated damages. The Code makes one general provision for liquidated damages by either buyer or seller. Under that provision, damages "may be liquidated in the agreement but only at an amount which is reasonable". What is reasonable is judged in the light of either "anticipated or actual harm caused by the breach, the difficulties of proof of loss, and the inconvenience or non-feasibility of otherwise obtaining and adequate remedy." The Code retains the common law rule that "A term fixing unreasonably large liquidated damages is void as a penalty." [20]

The UCC also permits recovery of one form of restitution. The buyer may recover any part of the price paid. The recovery of the price does not prevent recovery of any appropriate damages in addition.[22] Price recovery is permitted even though the buyer is better off by reason of the breach, as where the buyer would have lost money upon full performance.[23] Even the breaching buyer may be entitled to recover the price paid (minus the seller's damages). Although courts force a fiduciary to make "restitution" of any profits resulting from breach of a fiduciary duty, they ordinarily do not force this kind of "restitution" for mere contract breach.[24] The Code does not change this traditional rule.

The traditional rule stated that if legal remedies were adequate, specific performance would be denied.[26] This rule ordinarily operated to prevent specific performance of contracts to purchase common goods available in the market. A contract to buy a "unique" good, however, was specifically enforceable. The Code's attitude is more liberal, but it provides few directions. It authorizes specific performance on traditional grounds and also in any other "proper circumstances." [27] Inability to find substitute goods is strong evidence that specific performance is to be granted.[28] In addition, if title has passed or even if the goods are merely "identified to the contract," the buyer may be able in some circumstances to possess the goods through a replevin action.

§ 12.16(2) Buyer's Market Measured Damages

[*For the text of this section, see the unabridged Practitioner Treatise edition.*]

§ 12.16(3) Buyer's Cover Damages Under the Code

Cover Under the Code Generally

Damages measured by added cost of getting substitute performance. "Cover" under the UCC is largely a new concept. When the seller fails to deliver the contract goods and in some other circumstances, the buyer is permitted to cover "by making in good faith and without unreasonable delay any reasonable purchase of or contract to purchase goods in substitution for those due from the seller." Cover as a measure of damages is not mandatory; it is an option for the buyer which he may use or not as he chooses.[1] If the buyer's purchase of substitute goods counts as a cover, then he may opt to measure damages by the increased cost—"the difference between the cost of cover and the contract price" along with incidental and consequential damages.[2] In other words the buyer is permitted to measure damages by the contract-cover differential rather than the contract-market differential, if he actually covers. So long as cover is reasonable, it is a permissible option to the buyer. Conceivably cover could be a more expensive option and still be reasonable and if so, it is permitted.

What counts as cover? To count as cover the buyer's new purchases must be in good faith and reasonable. However, the new purchases need not be identical items; it is enough if they are good commercial substitutes.[3] Beyond this point, definition is sparse and problems plentiful. In many of its forms this problem resembles the problem of tracing seen in constructive trust cases and elsewhere.[4] If Seller breaches a contract to deliver Murg and thereafter Buyer buys Murg in some quantity, under what circumstances we can rightly attribute the purchase to the breach? For example, is the buyer's intent to cover (or not to do so) relevant in determining whether the purchase counts as cover?[5] Or his disposition of the goods?[6]

[For a discussion of cover as a measure that is worth more than the original performance, see this section in the Practitioner Treatise edition.]

Two remedial meanings of cover. One of the difficulties surrounding cover arises from the fact that cover has two aspects and that they are not clearly identified as such in the Code's structure. One aspect is quite familiar at common law: cover is one way of minimizing consequential damages. The buyer who is about to lose profits because of the seller's breach should attempt to minimize that loss. Buying substitute goods is one way to do that.[8] The other aspect of cover under the Code is quite different and mostly new: the added costs of procuring appropriate substitute goods, so far as they exceed the contract price, is an optional measure of damages.

Cover in the second aspect is quite different from cover in the first. Although this second aspect of cover also has roots in the common law,[9] it is important to distinguish cover as damages from cover as a mode of minimizing damages, a mental operation made more difficult by use of the same word for both. An example of the difference lies in the rule that cover (as a measure of damages) is not mandatory, but that cover (as a means of minimizing damages) may be required if the plaintiff is to be awarded consequential damages. What counts as cover is also likely to be different, depending on whether the buyer claims cover as a measure of damages or as a form of minimizing damages. The discussion below first considers cover as a damages measure and then as a means of minimizing.

§ 12.16(4) Buyer's Incidental and Consequential Damages

[For the text of this section, see the unabridged Practitioner Treatise edition.]

§ 12.16(5) Buyer's Damages After Seller's Anticipatory Repudiation

When the seller repudiates the contract before performance is due, § 2–610 of the UCC authorizes the buyer to wait for a reasonable time for performance or, in the alternative, to sue for breach.[1] If, at any time after repudiation, he sues for breach and claims the contract-market differential, what is the relevant date for determining the market price? Section 2–713 says in so many words that the "measure of damages for nondelivery or repudiation by the seller is the [contract-market differential] at the time when the buyer learned of the breach * * *." Given the historical and practical difference between anticipatory repudiation and breach, however, "learned of the breach" is not very instructive. It might mean "learned of the repudiation." It might also mean quite literally some date after performance was due when the buyer actually learned that performance had not been rendered, or, practically, the date performance was due. Because the Code also says the buyer may wait a reasonable time for performance after a repudiation, the language as applied to repudiation might also mean that the

date is one that falls at the end of a reasonable time to await performance. Other sections of the Code cast deeper shadows on the problem.[2]

Some courts have adopted the view that in cases of anticipatory repudiation, "learned of the breach" means "learned of the repudiation."[3] Although this may work well for buyers in some cases, it may also force a buyer to accept a date for damages that is not the date named in the contract and one that is wholly within the control of the breacher; alternatively it may force the buyer to cover at some date before performance is due. Either way, the buyer subjected to a "learned of the repudiation" date is in effect forced to accept a unilateral amendment of his contract.

There is also case support for the view that "learned of the breach" means the time performance was due[4] and still other support for the view that it means time of repudiation plus a reasonable time thereafter.[5] The "reasonable time thereafter" period, however, most obviously relates to cover, either as a means of minimizing damages or as a measure of damages in itself. To use this uncertain period in figuring a *market* measure of damages is to give up the certainty and convenience advantage that market measures offer. So time that performance was due seems to be the best date for figuring market damages in anticipatory repudiation cases. White and Summers reach the same conclusion from the somewhat different viewpoint of Code language and Code schematics,[6] although Sebert believes that the end of a reasonable time for awaiting performance is the right answer.[7]

Anticipatory repudiation is probably most important on the issue of cover. The buyer may cover immediately[8] or may await performance for a reasonable time. The Code is not specific, but evidently means to say that if the buyer does not cover within a reasonable time after repudiation, the right to measure damages by cover is lost. If so, the buyer will lose the right to assert cover-as-a-measure and will also lose consequential damages that could have been reasonably avoided by cover.[9] This line of thought suggests that the time for measurement of damages in anticipatory repudiation cases depends on the damages sought. If the market measure is sought, the time and place for performance would be the correct measure; if cover costs measure damages, the time of any actual cover would necessarily govern. If consequential damages were sought, the time when the buyer should have covered would govern.

§ 12.16(6) Buyer's Restitutionary Claims

[*For the text of this section, see the unabridged Practitioner Treatise edition.*]

§ 12.16(7) Buyer's Specific Performance Remedy

[*For the text of this section, see the unabridged Practitioner Treatise edition.*]

§ 12.16(5)

6. 1 James White & Robert Summers, Uniform Commercial Code § 6-7, p. 324 (3d ed. 1988 and Supp.). These authorities conclude that time of performance is the right way to read the Code's unfortunate language partly because it will jibe with the corresponding rule for seller's recoveries when buyers breach, partly because it is the traditional rule.

7. Sebert, Remedies under Article Two of the Uniform Commercial Code: An Agenda for Review, 130 U.Pa.L.Rev. 360, 372–380 (1981).

§ 12.17 Seller's Remedies for Breach of Chattel Sales Contract
§ 12.17(1) Seller's Remedies—Background and Summary

Common Law Damages

When the buyer of goods breaches or repudiates, the seller's damages closely parallel those afforded the buyer when the shoe is on the other foot. The common law rule gave the seller his market expectancy by using the ordinary market-contract differential. If the contract price was $100 but the market value was only $75, the seller's market gain in the transaction would be $25 and that would be his recovery. The common law also recognized the possibility of special or consequential damages, but those claims were, as usual, subject to demands of the rules for certainty, damage minimizing, and contemplation of the parties.[3] In a few instances the seller might be entitled to sue for the price, a virtual specific performance recovery which is discussed in connection with that remedy.[4]

Basic measures under the Code: market and resale measures. The Uniform Commercial Code (UCC) tracks these common law rules in a general way and adds another. In most cases, the seller may choose between

 (1) the difference between the market price and the contract price (the market-contract differential);[5] *or,*

 (2) the difference between the price the seller obtains in a good faith and reasonable resale of the goods to another buyer and the contract price (the resale-contract differential).[6] This resale remedy radically changes the common law, which relied on the market-contract differential.

Special-case measures: lost profits and price recovery. Two additional measures are available for special circumstances. When the market-contract differential measure is inadequate to fully compensate, the seller may recover

 (3) what the Code calls "lost profit," that is, the gain or "profit" the seller would have made on the particular contract plus reasonable reliance expenses incurred in trying to perform.[7]

When the buyer has actually accepted the goods and in very few other cases, the seller may recover

 (4) the price of the goods, more or less the substantive equivalent of specific performance.[8]

Incidental damages. In addition to whatever basic measure is applied, the seller may recover incidental damages for most breaches.[9] Incidental damages are characteristically costs incurred in attempting to deal with the goods after a breach, as for example, the costs of returning rejected goods to the seller.[10]

Consequential damages. There is no general category of consequential damages allowable to the seller,[11] but some kinds of damages that can be described as "consequential" are recoverable as incidental damages or as lost profits. The Code does not specifically state any version of *Hadley v. Baxendale's* contemplation-of-the-parties rule for seller's recoveries, even though it did state a liberal version of that rule for buyer's damages.[12]

Consequential damages for the *seller* are instead limited definitionally: the only consequential damages he recovers are those in the form of incidental damages or possibly lost profits. Incidental damages are defined (by illustrations) to cover what appears to be a limited range of expenses: those incurred in dealing with the rejected goods. Lost profits recoveries may be mis-named; the lost "profit" the Code envisions is seemingly limited to the profit on the very deal at hand. The Code's structure and methods for computing lost profits imply that no recovery for the seller's collateral lost profits is to be permitted. Because these rules and calculation methods limit the recovery of consequential damages, no contemplation of the parties principle is needed for that purpose.

Liquidated damages, limited remedies. The Code enacted a general freedom of contract provision under which the parties could vary the Code provisions by agreement, except as specifically provided otherwise and except for obligations of good faith, reasonableness and the like.[13] The Sales Article adds a specific direction to the effect that damages may be liquidated, but then imposes a version of the common law limitation [14] that is only slightly liberalized. Damages may be liquidated "only at an amount which is reasonable in the light of the anticipated or actual harm caused by the breach, the difficulties of proof of loss, and the inconvenience or nonfeasibility of otherwise obtaining and adequate remedy." [15]

Restitution. Restitution was not a major remedy for the goods seller at common law, but it was allowed on occasion. If the buyer refuses payment and the seller has not fully performed, the seller might recover restitution for the *value* of the goods; this would be useful if the value exceeded the contract price. Specie recovery would also be useful if it turned out that the buyer was insolvent. The Code does not speak of restitution as such. It is quite possible that the seller would be limited to an action for the price or, under restrictive rules, to a recovery of the goods themselves.[16]

Specific performance. The Code does not recognize a seller's right to specific performance as such. It provides instead that the seller may recover the price of the goods once the buyer has accepted them and also when the goods are identified to the contract and cannot be resold at any reasonable price. The price action performs the function of specific performance; both remedies will yield a recovery of the price. The price action is procedurally different, however.[17]

§ 12.17(2)   Seller's Market Measured Damages

[*For the text of this section, see the unabridged Practitioner Treatise edition.*]

§ 12.17(3)   Seller's Resale Measured Damages

[*For the text of this section, see the unabridged Practitioner Treatise edition.*]

§ 12.17(4)   Seller's Incidental and Consequential Damages

[*For the text of this section, see the unabridged Practitioner Treatise edition.*]

§ 12.17(5) Seller's "Lost Profit" Damages

[*For the text of this section, see the unabridged Practitioner Treatise edition.*]

§ 12.17(6) Seller's Restitutionary Remedies

[*For the text of this section, see the unabridged Practitioner Treatise edition.*]

§ 12.17(7) Seller's Specific Performance Remedy: The Price Action

[*For the text of this section, see the unabridged Practitioner Treatise edition.*]

§ 12.18 Remedies for Breach of Lease of Goods

[*For the text of this section, see the unabridged Practitioner Treatise edition.*]

(3) BUILDING CONTRACTS

§ 12.19 Owner's Remedies for Breach of Building or Repair Contract

§ 12.19(1) Owner's Damages Remedy

General Rules—Nonperformance or Defective Performance

Basic alternative rules. When a building or repair contractor breaches by nonperformance, or by incomplete or defective performance, the general goal is to put the owner in the performance position by providing a damages equivalent.[1] The owner's damages are usually measured either by (1) the cost of completing performance properly[2] or (2) the difference between the asset value of the land with proper performance and the asset value of the land with the incomplete or improper work.[3]

Factors in choosing. The cost of completion rule is generally favored where it does not create windfall or waste. If the cost measure is disproportionately high compared to the value lost, the loss in asset value is the limit of recovery.[5] When the contract requirement was bargained for to serve the owner's personal or aesthetic values, that fact may be considered in determining whether the cost of repair or completion is disproportionately high. When the defendant's breach is "wilful," some courts also consider that fact as supporting the cost measure. These rules and attitudes are discussed more fully below.

Related situations and claims. The problem under discussion is not literally limited to landowners' claims against contractors or even to pure contract claims. Architects and engineers sometimes have similar liabilities for failure to supervise contractor-performance[6] and sub-contractors may incur similar liability to general contractors.[7] In the same way, tenants who return leased premises in a damaged condition,[8] and trespassers who damage

---

§ 12.19(1)

5. See Restatement Second of Contracts § 348(2)(b) (1981) (if "cost is not clearly dispro- portionate to the probable loss in value to" the owner).

real property [9] come under similar damages rules, which do not differ significantly with the injection of warranty, negligence or fraud theories that sometimes appear in contract cases.

The Cost Rule: Conditions and Qualifications

Completion or repair must be a substitute for contract performance. The rule permitting recovery of the cost of completion or repair is a rule measuring loss by the cost of substitute performance. It is thus somewhat analogous to "cover" by a disappointed buyer of goods who purchases substitute goods.[10] The building contract case is a particularly good case for such a measure, because the land is a fixed site and the owner wants only one performance. If a new roof meeting proper specifications is added because the contractor did a poor job of installing the first one, the new roof is a substitute. In contrast, the buyer of goods who contracts to buy ten cows from *A* might, after *A's* breach buy ten cows from *B,* but it is not so easy to say that *B's* cows were substitutes for *A's,* because they might be alternatives or additions rather than substitutes. Such problems do not usually confront the court in building contract cases.

[*For a discussion of more beneficial substitute performance, see this section in the Practitioner Treatise edition.*]

Waste, windfall and expectancy. Completion or repair may have two undesirable effects. First, completion or repair may require "undoing" work already done, that is, destroying its economic value. Second, the completion or repair may be costly without adding a commensurate value to the structure. A contractor installs tile of the wrong color in the bathroom of a new home. The home is worth no less, but the specifications are clear and the contractor is in breach. Under the cost rule the landowner recovers the cost of repair, based on ripping out the tile and reinstalling the same kind of tile with a different color. If she actually does rip out the old, unsalvageable tile and actually installs new tile that adds nothing to the value of the house, there will be in some important way a kind of economic waste. If she does not do so but does recover the cost of doing so, there will be no economic waste, but she arguably has a windfall.[21] Neither waste nor windfall is desirable; but protection of the owner's bargained for expectancy is not only desirable but central. These are the main concerns that have actuated the decisions.

Disproportion: costs to lost value. The Restatement's solution,[26] in which the courts generally concur, is to say that the reasonable cost of completion or repair is generally recoverable, but only if the "cost is not clearly disproportionate to the probable loss in value" to the landowner.

In some cases the contract seems to be wholly pecuniary in nature, involving no aesthetic preference by the plaintiff. In some such cases courts have held that the recovery may not exceed the diminished value of the premises resulting from the breach.[32] For example, suppose a contractor is to install a composition flooring of a specified design and color, Grade A. The contractor breaches by installing flooring of the same color and design but Grade B. Grade B looks and feels the same as Grade A, but will need

26. See Restatement Second of Contracts § 348(2)(b) & Comment *c* (1981).

replacement in four years, while Grade A would last for five years. Although the color and design parts of the specification relate to aesthetic preference, the quality specification is primarily pecuniary. If a five-year floor cost $5,000, the four-year floor ought to cost about $4,000, so damages should not exceed about $1,000. The cost of repairs should not be used if those costs (including the losses of the unsalvageable Grade B flooring) would exceed $1,000 by any appreciable sum.

Role of wilfulness in the breaching. Some courts and writers would resolve the problem for many cases by asking whether the contractor's breach was wilful.[41] If it was, then the contractor would be liable for the higher cost of repair or completion measure. *Groves v. John Wunder Co.*[42] is a famous case that continues to provoke discussion.[43] The contractor there was to take gravel from the land and then to grade the land to a specified level and make it uniform. The contractor took the gravel but did not grade the land as required by the contract. Evidence was that it would require $60,000 to grade the land but that such grading would not increase the land's value by more than $12,160. This meant that measured by the value rule, the owner's damages came to $12,160, the difference in value of the land in the condition required by the contract and the value of the land as it actually stood after breach. However, the Minnesota Court refused to apply the value rule. Instead it held the contractor subject to liability for $60,000, the cost of completing the contract. Any other approach, according to the court, "handsomely rewards bad faith and deliberate breach of contract." The "transgressor" must be made to pay for his sins. It is no surprise that other authority has rejected punitive reasoning on similar facts and insisted that damages must be limited to the value or market diminution measure.[44]

Criticizing wilfulness analysis. If a contractor is both wilful and in bad faith, that fact might be relevant to the question whether a damages measure is too harsh or not; but it does not seem relevant to any estimate of pure compensation. Contract damages are normally compensatory; punitive damages are normally not permitted.[45] If that rule is right, then wilfulness of the breach cannot have much appropriate effect in choosing the measure of damages. The cost of completion measure of damages may be justified in many cases for other reasons, but if it is justified by reason of the contractor's wilful breach, then it becomes merely a punitive measure, forbidden by the general rule. Its use in cases like *Groves* may give the owner unjust leverage because she can present to the jury evidence that the contractor was a "bad man" as well as a breacher, with the probably result

41. See Marschall, Willfulness: A Crucial Factor in Choosing Remedies for Breach of Contract, 24 Ariz.L.Rev. 733 (1982). Discussions of wilfulness or the like may take the view that unexcused and intentional breach of a contract is a moral wrongdoing; they may discuss whether a breacher acted "honorably" or not in breaching. See J. Calamari & J. Perillo, The Law of Contracts § 14–29, p. 635 (3d ed. 1987); *Marschall,* supra, at 740. However, an argument that makes damages higher when breach is wilful seems inescapably an argument for punishment or deterrence. Professor Marschall wants courts to be concerned about wilful breaches because she believes that contract law should deter breach and that remedies based on assessment of wilfulness will promote deterrence. Id. at 734.

44. Peevyhouse v. Garland Coal & Min. Co., 382 P.2d 109 (Okl.1962), aff'd on rehearing, 382 P.2d 116 (1963), cert. denied, 375 U.S. 906, 84 S.Ct. 196, 11 L.Ed.2d 145 (1963). Judge Posner thought the result in *Groves* to be "incorrect from an economic standpoint" because efficiency dictated breach, given the $60,000 cost to comply compared to the $12,000 value those costs would produce. See R. Posner, Economic Analysis of Law 108–109 (3d ed. 1986).

that the jury will favor the plaintiff on any disputed issue in the case from liability to damages. In addition, when the plaintiff is able to claim a cost measure that far exceeds his balance sheet losses, as in *Groves*, the plaintiff increases the defendant's risk of litigation without increasing his own, and acquires a strong strategic position in bargaining. These considerations suggest that a completely straight effort at compensation would be preferable to one which turns on supposed wilfulness of the defendant.

Unjust enrichment of the contractor. In some cases the contractor's breach may save him substantial costs. If so, one may be tempted to approve a cost of completion measure that is highly disproportionate to the difference between the land's contracted-for value and the value provided by performance. However, the contractor's gain from breach may be far less than the cost of completion. If the cost to complete or repair is disproportionately high, the gain itself rather than the cost of completion should measure liability.[46]

It is possible that *Groves* involves something similar. If the going price was $165,000 for gravel rights like those contracted for, then the contractor's price in *Groves* was $105,000 plus a $60,000 obligation to regrade the land after the gravel was removed. If that is so, one might think of the $12,000 value-type recovery as leaving the contractor unjustly enriched. The contractor would have obtain gravel rights worth $165,000 by breaching and paying legal damages of only $117,000. The court may have had something like this in mind in deciding *Groves*,[47] but if the contractor's unjust enrichment is to be the basis of liability, it should also be the limit of liability, so the recovery should be in the amount of the enrichment not in some other amount. Another possibility is that the going rate for the right to take gravel was, say, $200,000, and that the landowner purchased the right to have the land restored by reducing the price. If so, the price would reflect a strong subjective preference to have the land restored and would also provide an objective value for that preference, so that a cost measure would be justified on that ground.[48]

Four solutions. When the cost of completion or repair measure respects an owner's subjective preferences and those preferences were a part of the bargain, there is no windfall in making the award, at least where it is limited by the disproportionality rule. If the court knows the subjective preferences and the cost measure is not disproportionate, there is no problem to solve. On the other hand, when the contract is purely pecuniary in nature, aimed at improving assets rather than vindicating his aesthetics, a cost measure that exceeds the market loss might be deemed to give the owner a windfall to the extent that it exceeds the owner's "real" losses. At least four solutions arise.

(1) *The aggrieved party would get the "windfall".* The cost of completion award might be regarded, as market measured damages are usually

---

46. See Farnsworth, Your Loss or My Gain? The Dilemma of the Disgorgement Principle in Breach of Contract, 94 Yale L.J. 1339, 1381–86 (1985); § 12.19(2) below.

47. See Dawson, Restitution or Damages, 20 Ohio St.L.J. 175, 188 (1959).

48. See Muris, Cost of Completion or Diminution in Market Value: The Relevance of Subjective Value, XII J.Leg.Studies 379 (1983).

regarded; they are rules of convenience, not attempts at perfect measurement. In that light, the cost rule is no windfall; it might even be built into the price of some contracts. (2) *The breacher would get the "windfall".* Alternatively, the court might insist on the traditional view that contract damages are intended to put the non-breaching party in as good a position as performance but no better. If applied here, that view would lead the court to refuse to apply the cost of completion measure on the ground that it would make the non-breacher party better off than would full performance. (3) *The breacher would get the "windfall" but would be liable for any unjust enrichment directly resulting from the breach.* This solution may provide a middle ground in some cases, but it may also try to put too much weight on the uncertain pillar of "unjust enrichment." (4) *The "windfall" if any could be divided.* Cases like *Groves,* if they do not reflect the owner's aesthetic preferences, may be regarded as cases in which the parties find they can get what they want at a cheaper price than either had imagined. The expense of grading is saved because it is no longer the best economic move. The savings can be regarded as equally allocable to both parties. This kind of reasoning has been suggested but not, seemingly, actually used to decide cases.[49]

[*For a discussion of consequential damages, see this section in the Practitioner Treatise edition.*]

§ 12.19(2) Owner's Restitutionary Remedies

[*For the text of this section, see the unabridged Practitioner Treatise edition.*]

§ 12.19(3) Owner's Specific Performance Remedy

[*For the text of this section, see the unabridged Practitioner Treatise edition.*]

§ 12.20 Contractor's Remedies for Owner's Breach of Construction or Repair Contract

§ 12.20(1) Contractor's Damages Remedies

Full performance and no performance cases. When a contractor has fully performed, his expectancy damages are measured by the contract price as with any other liquidated debt.

Price less saved expenses. When the owner terminates the work after it has begun but before it is completed, the measure of damages is the contract price less savings effected by the contractor by not doing the remaining work,[6] or put differently, the contract price less the cost the contractor would incur to complete the job.[7] A similar rule applies when the owner repudiates before the contractor has performed at all.[8] As with other general measures of damages, this one is subject to adjustments.[9] For example, the recovery will be reduced to the extent of any part of the price already paid.[10]

Alternate calculations: profits plus costs incurred and proportionate payment for proportionate work. Two other methods are sometimes used for doing the actual calculations of the contractor's expectancy, and they almost always produce the same results. First, courts can award the expected "profit" or gain on the contract, plus the costs already incurred.[11] Second, courts can attempt to estimate the total proportion of the work done, using the proportion of costs incurred to the total costs required to complete the job, than adding a proportionate share of the profit due on the uncompleted work. If the total cost is to be $8,000 and the work done has cost $5,000, the contractor is deemed to have done $5/8$ of the work. His damages are then taken to be $5/8$ of the total price, plus the profit on the uncompleted work.[12]

Sometimes the aim of these rules is expressed by saying that the contractor is entitled to recover reasonable costs plus his lost "profit." [13] In the building contractor cases, as in the case of sellers of goods,[14] the reference to "profits" usually has a restricted connotation. It means the gain the contractor would have made on the particular contract, not the loss of collateral profits in the business as a whole or on other jobs. Loss of collateral profits would be consequential damages and would be required to meet the standards for proving such damages.[15]

When the rules are equivalent. The three means of computation all work out to produce the same result in damages when the contractor can obtain proof of each element and when he is in fact making a profit. The differences in these computations are chiefly significant because they show that there are different mathematical methods for proving the expectancy. Any of these should be acceptable to courts; if the proof fits any one of them, that should be sufficient, so long as the contract is profitable.

Losing contracts. When the contractor is losing money, the three different methods of computation can produce three widely disparate results. Suppose the contract price is $10,000 and the work done cost $5,000. But now suppose that the cost to complete the work will be $10,000. The contractor would have lost money upon full performance because he would have spent $15,000 and would have been paid only $10,000. The first formula—contract price minus expenses saved by the breach—gives the contractor a zero recovery because price minus savings comes to $-$ $5,000. The second formula—profits plus costs incurred—gives the contractor $5,000 because he has no profits recovery but does recover for expenditures actually made. The third formula would give him one-third of the contract price of $3333.33 if the $5,000 costs represent one-third of the total work to be done. As to compensatory *damages,* the first formula gives the right result; the contractor has lost nothing by reason of the breach. But to say he has no *damages* is not to say he has no recovery. His potential recovery of *restitution* based on unjust enrichment is considered in the next subsection.

[*For a discussion of the contractor's reliance and consequential damages, see this section in the Practitioner Treatise edition.*]

§ 12.20(2) Contractor's Restitutionary Remedies

General Rules

Restitution allowable for benefits conferred on owner or general contractor.[1] The contractor's normal remedy for a simple breach by the owner is to recover damages based on losses to the contractor.[2] In some cases, however, the contractor may consider claiming restitution instead. The restitution claim is often invoked with the terminology of quasi-contract, implied-in-law contract, or *quantum meruit.*[3] Restitution is justified to prevent unjust enrichment of the breaching party and in theory is measured by that party's gain rather than by the victim's losses.[4] In general, upon the landowner's breach, a contractor may recover, as restitution, the value of the direct benefits he has conferred upon the landowner by his part performance of the contract, with deductions for any payments he has received from the landowner and further deduction for any damages he himself has caused the landowner by his own breach.

Measures of restitution. Two ways of measuring benefit to the landowner predominate. One measures the market value of the labor and materials package—what it would cost the owner to purchase such services and materials in the market. The other measures the landowner's gain in asset value. The usual measure of restitution for breach of an enforceable contract is the market value of the labor and materials.[5] Where the contractor himself is in default and where the work is misdirected or unwanted, the actual gain in asset value to the owner is a fairer measure.

Restitution to put contractor in better position by reason of breach. Suppose that the builder has agreed to do a job for $10,000, but after he has incurred $5,000 in costs he realizes that the complete project will cost him a total of $15,000. In other words, he will lose $5,000 if he completes the work. At this point the landowner repudiates and excludes the contractor from all work on the land. Although the contractor will have lost money if the contract is performed, he has lost nothing more by reason of the landowner's breach. Quite literally he has no damages resulting from the breach.[11] Nevertheless, the landowner may have benefitted from the contractor's work. To the extent that the breaching landowner has actually benefitted, courts generally hold him liable to the contractor for the value of those benefits, even if that liability puts the contractor in better position than he would be by full performance.[12] A few cases go the other way, limiting the contractor's quantum meruit recovery to the contract price or rate.[13]

In a leading case, the contractor came out far ahead: he recovered over $250,000 in restitution, although the contract payment apparently would have been about $20,000.[15] Some courts might not go along with such an award; they might invoke the proportion-of-the-price *damages* measure as a kind of ceiling on restitution that would prevent such a recovery.[16] But the allowance of restitution without the ceiling is more common.[17]

[*For discussion of restitution measurements in accord with contract risk allocations and restitution to the defaulting contractor, see this section in the Practitioner Treatise edition.*]

§ 12.20(3) Third Party Restitution Claims of Subcontractors and Others: Mechanics' Liens and Other Devices

Subcontractors', Laborers' and Suppliers' Claims Generally

The third party situations. Owners usually contract for construction work with a general contractor, who in turn subcontracts particular parts of the job to one or more independent subcontractors. The subcontractors, however, have no contract with the owner for whom the project is carried out. To the subcontractors, the general contractor is in much the same position as owner: their work must satisfy his specifications and he must pay them. This situation creates a potential problem. Suppose the subcontractor performs his contract with the general contractor and that his work improves the owner's premises in some measurable way. Suppose also that the general contractor becomes insolvent and cannot pay the subcontractor. The subcontractor has performed and the owner has benefitted. Does the subcontractor have a restitution or any other claim against the owner?

The same question can be raised for the general contractor's workers and suppliers who may go unpaid when the contractor defaults, even though they have performed work that creates improvements on the land. These situations and others similar to them all raise the question whether the landowner who has the improvements is obliged to pay third parties with whom he has no direct contract. The rules apply in similar ways to other third parties such as workers and suppliers whose labor or goods have gone into the improvement. Contractors are usually required to post bonds to assure performance, and when their bond sureties perform the contractor's obligations, by paying laborers, for example, the sureties become parties to the litigation with claims of their own. For simplicity this section will usually state the rules in terms of the subcontractor, with the understanding that similar reasoning applies to other third party claimants.

Three general rules. Three general rules stake out the subcontractor's remedies: (1) the subcontractor is generally not entitled to a restitution claim against the landowner; (2) the subcontractor contractor is, however, entitled to enforce his claim against any funds still held by the landowner but which are owed to the general contractor; (3) the subcontractor is entitled to enforce a lien against the improved land (or a bond substituted for the land) where the subcontractor has met the requirements of a mechanic's lien statute.

The subcontractor's subrogation claim against retained funds. Landowners usually pay the general contractor a percentage of the price as work proceeds, retaining the remainder until completion. When the landowner has retained funds owing the general contractor for work completed, the subcontractor may sue the landowner demanding payment from the funds held by the landowner. He may legitimately claim against the funds on a theory of subrogation or simply by way of garnishment. The subcontractor's work in such a case has helped to create the landowner's debt to the general contractor, so the subcontractor may "stand in the shoes" of the general contractor to the extent he has not been paid.[1] (A contractor's surety who has discharged the contractor's obligations is in the same way subrogated to the contractor's claims against retained funds.[2])

General rule against restitution. An owner is not generally liable for improvements made to his property without his assent.[7] Nor is he liable to a subcontractor for making improvements for which the owner contracted only to pay the general contractor.[8] The owner may of course be held if he contracts directly with a subcontractor or supplier, as where he asks the subcontractor to continue work after a general contractor has withdrawn from the job[9] or otherwise accepts responsibility.

The rule is an outgrowth of the underlying policy that protects personal autonomy and rights of choice: no one incurs an obligation on the say-so of another. The rules against recovery by "officious" actors [13] reflect this policy of supporting the landowner's choice.

Landlord's benefit from tenant's improvements at the expense of contractors or materialmen. Sometimes an individual who is not the owner orders improvements on the owner's land, then fails to pay the contractor or supplier. In a Missouri case,[18] the owner's parents ordered improvements; in a Tennessee case the owner's daughter ordered them.[19] More commonly a tenant does so. The same problem can arise when the lessee of a chattel orders improvements on it which the lessor will enjoy when the lease is terminated.[20] Such cases are usually governed by the general rule that the owner is not liable to the contractor or supplier unless he agreed to pay them.[21]

Statutory liens against the owner. Mechanics' and materialmen's lien statutes in most states make it possible under some circumstances for subcontractors, workers and suppliers to impose liens against the landowner to secure their rights of payment.[27] The lien threat gives the owner incentive to be sure that if he pays the general contractor, the general contractor in turn pays those whose work has improved the premises; and if this incentive is ineffective, the subcontractor and other persons covered by the statute may foreclose their liens against the property.

Local statutes must always be consulted, but in general, the statutes prescribe procedures for claiming the lien and time limits. The subcontractor or other claimant must notify the owner and must file the lien within a certain period. Only specified persons come within the benefits of the statutes; and some who come within the statute may not come within the contractual provisions of the payment bond. For instance, the statute [29] or the bond [30] or both may exclude suppliers who do not themselves work on the land, or suppliers of suppliers, so that it is necessary to determine whether a lien claimant who makes doors for a building but does not install them is a "subcontractor" or merely a supplier.

Some landowners may be exempted from the lien provisions. Statutes sometimes impose a lien on owners generally but exempt homeowners who reside in the premises being improved; and public entity owners are generally not subject to the lien but may be required to secure payment bonds. Sometimes courts have recognized additional defenses as well.[31]

The Miller Act and state counterparts. Public entities are not ordinarily subject to lien claims. When contractors work on public construction projects the subcontractors, suppliers and workers do not have the protection afforded by mechanics' and materialmen's lien statutes. To remedy this, the Miller Act [33] provides that, with exceptions, government contractors must furnish a payment bond before construction begins.[34] Those who furnish

§ 12.20(3)

33. 40 U.S.C.A. §§ 270a–270d.

34. "Before any contract, exceeding $25,-000 in amount, for the construction, alteration, or repair of any public building or public work of the United States is awarded to any person, such person shall furnish to the United States the following bonds, which shall become binding upon the award of the contract to such person, who is hereinafter designated as 'contractor': * * *. A payment bond with a surety or sureties satisfactory to such officer for the protection of all persons supplying labor and material in the prosecution of the work provided for in said contract for the use of each such person. Whenever the total amount payable by the terms of the contract

work or materials in the project are entitled to sue on the bond,[35] not only when they claim on an express contract, but also when they sue for quantum meruit.[36] Suit is brought only in the United States District Court where the work was performed, regardless of the amount in controversy. States often have Little Miller Acts or other similar provisions.

(4) OTHER CONTRACTS

§ 12.21 Employee's Remedies for Employer's Breach of Employment Contract

§ 12.21(1) Scope and Related Materials

[For the text of this section, see the unabridged Practitioner Treatise edition.]

§ 12.21(2) Employee's Damages Remedy

[For the text of this section, see the unabridged Practitioner Treatise edition.]

§ 12.21(3) Employee's Restitutionary Remedies

[For the text of this section, see the unabridged Practitioner Treatise edition.]

§ 12.21(4) Specific Performance and Injunction in Favor of Employee

[For the text of this section, see the unabridged Practitioner Treatise edition.]

§ 12.22 Employer's Remedies for Employee's Breach of Employment Contract

§ 12.22(1) The Employer's Money Remedies

[For the text of this section, see the unabridged Practitioner Treatise edition.]

§ 12.22(2) The Employer's Equitable Remedies

Negative promises: covenants not to compete. Many contracts of employment contain two distinct kinds of promises. The first is the affirmative promise to perform services; the second is the negative promise not to perform those services for others or to compete with the employer. The negative covenant can be enforced in some cases even when the affirmative covenant cannot be. However, it is important not to enforce the negative covenant as a means of coercing the employee to perform the affirmative promise to work.

The Lumley v. Wagner case. The best known case is *Lumley v. Wagner.*[6] In that case Miss Wagner agreed to sing at the plaintiff's theatre for three

shall be not more than $1,000,000 the said payment bond shall be in a sum of one-half the total amount payable by the terms of the contract [with a declining percentage as the total construction price rises]." 40 U.S.C.A. § 270a(a).

§ 12.22(2)

6. Lumley v. Wagner, 1 De G.M. & G. 604, 42 Eng.Rep. 687 (1852).

months. The contract contained a negative covenant as well: she would not sing elsewhere during this period. The plaintiff sued for specific enforcement of the negative covenant, that is, sought an injunction to prevent her performance elsewhere. The court rejected the defendant's argument that the contract had to be enforced all or nothing.

Enforcement of the negative against skilled employees. Enforcement of negative covenants is important today where the employee has special skills or knowledge that, but for enforcement, would not only be denied to the employer but would also be used in competition against him. If the covenant is valid, an injunction may issue to prevent a physician from practicing in the same locality in violation of the negative covenant;[7] to prevent a sports star from switching teams in the middle of a contract;[8] to exclude a television celebrity from a competitor's broadcasts;[9] to forbid a skilled scientist or technician from selling her skills to the employer's competitors.[10] Prospective employers, whose acts of employment might aid and abet the employee's breach, might also be enjoined.[11]

Negative injunctions against sellers of good will. Similar negative injunctions issue in comparable cases that do not involve actual employment. Buyers of businesses often want to buy the good will of the business, not merely its equipment or real property. So they buy the name, the trademarks and other intangibles. The good will so purchased may all be lost if the seller goes into business next door. The seller's only means of selling the good will, then, is to provide assurance that he will not compete in the relevant locality. Such negative covenants are enforced,[12] and somewhat more readily than employee covenants,[13] because they are essential if the seller is to be able to sell the good will.[14] (If the seller cannot validly promise not to compete, the buyer will have no assurance that he will get the good will for which he is paying; so he may not pay for it and the seller will not be able to sell it.)

Limiting considerations. The negative injunction is limited by two major considerations. First, enforcement of the negative promise should not be used to coerce performance of the affirmative promise. So it should not be enforced at all unless there is an apparent need for such a clause, such as the need to prevent competitors from tapping the employee's special skills that are under contract to the employer.[15] It may be that courts do not observe this requirement as meticulously as they should.[16] Second, the negative promise may operate as an improper restraint on trade. It will not be enforced if it is unreasonable in its restrictions or in its geographical or temporal scope,[17] or goes beyond what is reasonably required to protect the legitimate interests of the employer.[18] Reasonableness judgments take into account many factors, including public interest, hardship to the employee,

7. E.g., Brian McDonagh S.C. v. Moss, 207 Ill.App.3d 62, 151 Ill.Dec. 888, 565 N.E.2d 159 (1990).

8. Lemat Corp. v. Barry, 275 Cal.App.2d 671, 80 Cal.Rptr. 240 (1969).

9. Cf. Beckman v. Cox Broadcasting Corp., 250 Ga. 127, 296 S.E.2d 566, 36 A.L.R. 4th 1132 (1982) (declaratory judgment).

10. Cf. E.I. duPont de Nemours & Co. v. American Potash & Chem. Corp., 41 Del.Ch. 533, 200 A.2d 428 (1964).

11. Winnipeg Rugby Football Club, Ltd. v. Freeman, 140 F.Supp. 365 (N.D.Ohio 1955).

14. See Purchasing Associates, Inc. v. Weitz, 13 N.Y.2d 267, 246 N.Y.S.2d 600, 196 N.E.2d 245 (1963).

and whether the employer's heavy investment in providing skill to the employee would be exported to a competitor before the investment could be recouped.[19] Sometimes it is said that the negative injunction will not issue without an express negative covenant,[20] but in fact this rule is sometimes ignored.[21]

§ 12.23 Remedies Under Arbitration Contracts

[*For the text of this section, see the unabridged Practitioner Treatise edition.*]

Chapter 13

UNENFORCEABLE CONTRACTS

Analysis

Sec.
13.1 Restitution in Unenforceable Contracts: Scope and Summary.
13.2 Restitution for Benefits Conferred Under Contracts Unenforceable for Lack of a Writing.
  13.2(1) Restitution Permitted Under Statute of Frauds Policy.
  13.2(2) Restitution and Its Measure.
  13.2(3) Restitution in Specie.
  13.2(4) Reliance Expenses vs. Restitution.
  13.2(5) Estoppel and Part Performance.
13.3 Remedies When Performance Is Excused Under Doctrines of Frustration or Impracticality.
  13.3(1) Substantive Framework.
  13.3(2) Remedial Alternatives and Problems.
13.4 Remedies for Benefits Conferred Under Contracts Avoided for Defective Capacity.
  13.4(1) Power of Avoidance.*
  13.4(2) Infancy.
  13.4(3) Mental Incompetency.
13.5 Attorney's Remedy When Client Avoids Contract.*
13.6 Restitution in Connection With Illegal Contracts and Activities.

§ 13.1 Restitution in Unenforceable Contracts: Scope and Summary

This chapter deals with situations in which the parties have attempted to regulate their relations by an agreement, which, however, turns out to be unenforceable. Typically the contract is unenforceable because it is not in writing as required by the statute of frauds,[1] or because performance has become frustrated or impracticable,[2] or because one of the parties lacked capacity to contract because he was a minor[3] or because of mental disability.[4] In the most extreme cases, the contract is unenforceable because it is illegal in some important way.[5] In one special kind of case, involving the lawyer-client contract, the contract may be subject to the client's power of avoidance simply for reasons of public policy, so that no client is pressed to use a lawyer in whom he has lost faith.[6]

* For text of this section, see Dobbs, Law of Remedies, Second Edition, Practitioner Treatise, Vol. 3.

§ 13.2 Restitution for Benefits Conferred Under Contracts Unenforceable for Lack of a Writing

§ 13.2(1) Restitution Permitted Under Statute of Frauds Policy

General Rules

A number of statutes are designed to require written evidence of certain important transactions. Statutes usually require that wills be in writing and refuse to give effect to most oral testamentary transactions. Statutes of frauds in most states will provide against enforcement of oral contracts to transfer any interest in land, to sell goods priced at more than $500, to marry, to stand surety for another person, or to do work that cannot be fully completed within one year. Other statutes may forbid enforcement of various other oral contracts.

The rules that sometimes permit recovery are discussed in the following subsections. Their thrust may be summarized as follows, but all of these summary statements are subject to qualifications.

(1) When an oral contract falls within the statute of frauds and has not already been fully performed, it may not be enforced except under the special rules of part performance, equitable estoppel and promissory estoppel.[1]

(2) Unless one of these estoppel doctrines applies, the fact that the plaintiff had expended money or labor in reliance upon the contract is not sufficient to permit a recovery.[2]

(3) However, the plaintiff whose reliance represents not only an expense to himself but also a benefit to the defendant, is entitled to restitution for the value of the benefits conferred.

(4) The remedial question under the restitution rule is usually whether to measure the benefit by what it would cost the defendant to buy such a benefit elsewhere, or whether to measure it by the net increase it produces in the defendant's wealth. When the benefit is conferred at the defendant's request or is part of the performance required by the oral contact, the plaintiff usually has the option to select the higher measure. For example, if the contract is for the plaintiff to act as a salesperson for defendant's business and the plaintiff does so, the defendant may be held to make restitution measured by the cost of getting those services elsewhere, even if the plaintiff sold no goods and produced no income for the defendant. When the plaintiff conferred a benefit but it was not one sought by the defendant, the defendant's liability to make restitution is limited to his net increase in wealth.[3]

(5) Restitution is typically limited to money-value restitution. Only in special cases is the plaintiff allowed to recover specific restitution by way of constructive trust or otherwise merely because the defendant breached the unenforceable contract. If the defendant's breach is accompanied by fraud or fiduciary breach, however, restitution in specie is usually allowed.[4]

Restitution and the Statute of Frauds Policy

Statutory policy does not prevent a recovery of the defendant's unjust enrichment. As will be seen, even if the plaintiff can circumvent the statute of frauds by estoppel, recovery may be limited to restitution. So restitution is a central idea in dealing with most efforts to recover in the statute of frauds cases. Why do courts permit recovery of restitution in the face of the statute? The answer is that recovery of restitution does not violate the statute or frauds or its policy. The policy of these statutes permits either party to avoid *enforcement* of such oral contracts, that is, to avoid the other's expectancy interest or the hoped-for gain or exchange. But this policy does not extend to the restitutionary interest. The statute may deny the plaintiff his expectancy without approving the defendant's unjust enrichment.

Example. For example, suppose that *A* orally agrees to sell Blackacre in exchange for *B's* services, and that *B* in fact renders those services. Because the contract is not in writing, *B* may not enforce it by getting specific performance of the promise to convey Blackacre. Nor may *B* enforce the contract by obtaining damages equal to Blackacre's value. Either form of enforcement would impinge upon the statute of frauds' policy (in the absence of estoppel or part performance). But, although *B* will not be permitted to enforce the contract and get his expectancy, he will be permitted to recover the value of his services to *A,* who, otherwise, would be unjustly enriched. "When a landowner relies upon the Statute of Frauds as a basis for repudiating his agreement, it is unjust to permit him to retain payments or services that he has received and to transfer nothing in return." [5]

Relevance of the contract. This restitutionary recovery is clearly different in purpose and effect from enforcement of the contract. The contract in such a case is admitted in evidence for a limited purpose, to be sure—to show that *B* is not a volunteer. But, at least in theory, it does not measure *B's* rights, and he is not entitled to whatever bargain the contract gave him. He is only entitled to a recovery of whatever values he has transferred to *A.* If theory is followed in practice, then, this kind of restitutionary claim does not violate the statute of frauds policy, at least in the ordinary case.

§ 13.2(2) Restitution and Its Measure

Measures of Restitution

General rule permitting restitution. When the plaintiff has conferred a benefit upon the defendant in reliance upon an agreement which is unenforceable under the statute of frauds, the plaintiff is entitled to restitution of the benefit conferred to prevent unjust enrichment of the defendant at the plaintiff's expense.[1] For example, if the plaintiff has paid a part of the purchase price for land covered by an unenforceable oral contract, he is entitled to recover the amount so paid. As to this general rule there seems to be no dissent, but there is an exception.

Exception where plaintiff is in default. When the plaintiff defaults or invokes the statute as a defense to enforcement of an oral contract, courts have routinely denied him restitution of payments he has made.[2] For

§ 13.2(2)

1. E.g., Trollope v. Koerner, 106 Ariz. 10, 470 P.2d 91, 64 A.L.R.3d 1180 (1970); Blank v. Rodgers, 82 Cal.App. 35, 255 P. 235, 238 (1927); Farash v. Sykes Datatronics, Inc., 59 N.Y.2d 500, 465 N.Y.S.2d 917, 452 N.E.2d 1245 (1983); cf. Weeks v. Standish Hardware & Garage Co., 145 Me. 307, 75 A.2d 444 (1950) (remainderman had right to disaffirm life ten-

ant's oral contract, would-be buyer can recover price paid from life tenant's estate); Tompkins v. Sandeen, 243 Minn. 256, 67 N.W.2d 405, 49 A.L.R.2d 1162 (1954) (recognizing rule applied in statute of frauds cases and analogizing to it); II G. Palmer, Law of Restitution Chapter 6 (1978 and Supps.).

2. E.g., Durham Consolidated Land & Improvement Co. v. Guthrie, 116 N.C. 381, 21

instance, a land purchaser under an oral contract may have made payments on the price before defaulting; he is denied recovery even if the payments he has made exceed the vendor's damages. This exception has been criticized.[3] The older rule in the parallel situation denied restitution to the purchaser in default even under an enforceable contract. That parallel rule seems to be on its way out as courts increasingly award restitution to the defaulter.[4] Conceivably a similar change will occur to permit restitution in favor of the party who defaults on an oral contract or invokes the statute of frauds to prevent enforcement of it.

Measurement options. Benefits may be measured in several different ways. The principal measurements of benefits are: (1) money paid by or on behalf of the plaintiff; (2) the market value of the plaintiff's performance, that is, what it would cost to obtain that performance elsewhere; (3) the increased value of the defendant's net worth resulting from the plaintiff's performance; (4) the subjective value to the defendant of the plaintiff's performance; (5) the contract price. A major distinction is drawn between item (2) and item (3). For example, if the plaintiff makes improvements upon the defendant's land in performance of a contract subject to the statute of frauds, the value of the land might be improved by $1,000 while the market value of the plaintiff's services might be $2,000. The subjective worth to the defendant might be zero; the contract price might be still another figure.

Benefits Conferred in Performance of the Contract Obligation

Payments made, market value of performance, or increase in defendant's wealth. When the benefit conferred is a payment of money as all or part of the price, the plaintiff is entitled simply to recover that payment.[5] When the plaintiff has conferred non-cash benefits in performance of his obligations under the unenforceable contract, the plaintiff may ordinarily recover *either* the value of his performance [6] *or* the increase in the defendant's

S.E. 952 (1895); Schweiter v. Halsey, 57 Wash.2d 707, 359 P.2d 821 (1961); Annotation, 169 A.L.R. 187 (1947); see Tompkins v. Sandeen, 243 Minn. 256, 259–261, 67 N.W.2d 405, 408–409, 49 A.L.R.2d 1162 (1954) (vendor who disaffirms under statute of frauds cannot have restitution for value of purchaser's occupancy, but if purchaser seeks a recovery, vendor may have a set off); cf. Weeks v. Standish Hardware & Garage Co., 145 Me. 307, 311, 75 A.2d 444, 446 (1950) ("If the vendee disaffirms the law implies an obligation to pay for use and occupation ab initio, whereas if the vendor disaffirms, the implied obligation is to pay only for use and occupation subsequent to disaffirmance").

3. II G. Palmer, Law of Restitution § 6.6 (1978 and Supps.).

4. See § 12.13 above. The non-defaulting party is protected even though he must make restitution, because he is allowed to deduct his damages from the restitutionary obligation. If damages exceed restitution, he will of course be entitled to recover damages and the defaulter will be denied all restitution.

5. See II G. Palmer, Law of Restitution § 6.5 (1978 and Supps.); Restatement of Restitution § 150 (1939) (general rule measures restitution of money payments by the amount paid); Jeanblanc, Restitution under the Statute of Frauds: What Constitutes a Legal Benefit, 26 Ind.L.J. 1, 8 (1950).

6. Misisco v. La Maita, 150 Conn. 680, 192 A.2d 891 (1963); Williams v. Mason, 556 So.2d 1045, 1049 (Miss.1990) (care for decedent in return for promise to devise, the plaintiff is entitled to the "monetary equivalent of the reasonable value of the services rendered to the decedent for which payment has not been received"); Theuerkauf v. Sutton, 102 Wis.2d 176, 306 N.W.2d 651 (1981) (implied in fact contract by attorney to pay for accountant's services in client's file, statute of frauds does not bar recovery for actual value of services); see Bingham v. Bridges, 613 F.2d 794 (10th Cir.1980).

wealth, whichever is higher.[7] Offsets in favor of the defendant may be appropriate to make the recovery reflect the defendant's net benefit.[8]

Rationale. The basis for this rule is that when the defendant has requested performance, the market value of that performance is the measure of benefit. Even though such performance adds nothing to the defendant's wealth, the performance is worth something to one who actively seeks that performance with the expectation of paying,[9] and both fairness and practicality suggest that such a benefit be measured by its market value. The performance does in fact have subjective value in "advancing the purposes of the recipient."[10] As Professor Palmer says, there is nothing fictional about finding a benefit in performance which the defendant has sought and placed a money value upon.[11] Put differently, the plaintiff's performance has saved the defendant the cost of getting the work done elsewhere, presumably at market prices.[12]

This is the same measure of restitution used when defendant breaches a fully enforceable contract.[13] The principle is invoked in statute of frauds cases only by noticing that the defendant has requested or bargained for the performance. That is to say that courts must consider the existence of the contract to justify invoking the more generous measure of benefit. But, at least in a literal sense, the statute of frauds does not say that contracts cannot be considered; it only says they cannot be enforced.

Improvements on land by vendor or lessor. One example of the point is the case of the lessor's folly. A would-be lessor orally agrees with a would-be tenant that the lessor will make changes in the premises especially designed to suit the tenant and the tenant orally agrees to lease. The tenant never moves into occupancy of the premises and thus never receives any obvious benefit. The lessor may be left with premises that do not suit other tenants or do not suit them any better than the unimproved version. In cases like these, courts have permitted the lessor to recover his expenditures.[14] Simi-

---

7. E.g., Trollope v. Koerner, 106 Ariz. 10, 470 P.2d 91, 64 A.L.R.3d 1180 (1970) (oral agreement to lease; unique improvements made by would-be lessor at request of would-be lessee, restitution to the lessor for their value); Blank v. Rodgers, 82 Cal.App. 35, 42–43, 255 P. 235, 238 (1927) (oral agreement to lease; improvements made pursuant to contract terms by would-be lessee, who was then ejected; restitution to lessee for their value, not limited to enhancement of land's value); Kearns v. Andree, 107 Conn. 181, 139 A. 695, 59 A.L.R. 599 (1928) (oral agreement to sell, with changes designed for purchaser, contract too indefinite for enforcement, but purchaser liable for reasonable value of services); Farash v. Sykes Datatronics, Inc., 59 N.Y.2d 500, 465 N.Y.S.2d 917, 452 N.E.2d 1245 (1983).

11. See II George Palmer, Law of Restitution § 6.3 generally and n. 6 in particular (1978 and Supps.).

12. See Jeanblanc, Restitution under the Statute of Frauds: What Constitutes a Legal Benefit, 26 Ind.L.J. 1, 14–18 (1950). This could be viewed as a form of "negative unjust enrichment", see Thurston, Recent Develop-

ments in Restitution: 1940–1947, 45 Mich. L.Rev. 935, 946 (1947), that is, enrichment by way of savings. However, the defendant may or may not have saved expenses by inducing the plaintiff to act. The alternatives might be that he would have obtained the same services on another oral and unenforceable contract, or that he would not have obtained any services at all. Certainly if the alternative was to obtain no services, then he saved no expenses by reason of the plaintiff's efforts. So the savings argument might be viewed as merely a way of emphasizing that value should be attributed to services the defendant actually desires and induces.

13. See § 12.7(3) above.

14. Trollope v. Koerner, 106 Ariz. 10, 470 P.2d 91, 64 A.L.R.3d 1180 (1970); Farash v. Sykes Datatronics, Inc., 59 N.Y.2d 500, 465 N.Y.S.2d 917, 452 N.E.2d 1245 (1983). Cf. Minsky's Follies of Florida v. Sennes, 206 F.2d 1 (5th Cir.1953) (oral agreement to lease, would-be lessor allowed to recover cost of nightwatchman and liquor license, perhaps procured at request of would-be tenant, who never occupied).

lar cases involving vendors rather than lessors of land get similar results.[15]

Improvements on land by purchaser or lessee. The point is not limited to those in the position of lessors or vendors, however; any plaintiff who incurs expenses performing the very acts requested by the defendant can assert the claim for the reasonable (market) value of the promised performance. So the buyer or lessee rather than the vendor or lessor may be the party who has made the improvements. The critical question is whether they are improvements made in performance of the promise. If they are, restitution for the value of labor and materials and not merely the land's increase in value is warranted.[16] (The landowner in such a case may be entitled to a set off equal to the value of the purchaser's or lessee's use and occupancy.[17])

Services rendered under employment and care contracts. Another example is the case of an employment contract subject to the statute of frauds because it cannot be performed within one year. The employee in such a case may work hard but add nothing to the defendant's wealth; the salesperson might produce no orders, or orders might be filled at a loss. Nevertheless, the employer is liable for the market value of the employee's services as restitution.[18]

One kind of case makes it especially easy to see that the benefit from desired services is real even when the services do not increase the defendant's assets. This is case in which the plaintiff cares for a disabled or elderly person in return for a promise of a conveyance or will of property. When no conveyance or will is forthcoming, the plaintiff is entitled to the value of her services.[19] It is usual to present opinion evidence about the value of the services rendered and such evidence may be necessary if the plaintiff is to have more than a nominal recovery.[20] However, there may be some cases in which a mere description of the services will suffice to permit a trier's finding about their value.[21]

Contract Price as Evidence of Benefit

Contract price and restitution measures. It is plausible to permit the plaintiff to recover benefits conferred upon the defendant in spite of the statute of frauds. It is also plausible to go further and permit the plaintiff to measure those benefits by their market value even if the defendant cannot

---

If the lessor's expenditures improve the value of her land, that improved value should be offset against the claim. See II G. Palmer, Law of Restitution § 6.3, n. 4 (Supplement) (1978 and Supps.).

15. Kearns v. Andree, 107 Conn. 181, 139 A. 695, 59 A.L.R. 599 (1928).

16. E.g., Blank v. Rodgers, 82 Cal.App. 35, 42–43, 255 P. 235, 238 (1927) (would-be lessee's claim where oral agreement contemplated that he would make the improvement he in fact made, higher recovery allowable).

17. E.g., Tompkins v. Sandeen, 243 Minn. 256, 67 N.W.2d 405, 49 A.L.R.2d 1162 (1954). In some cases it is plausible simply to regard the landowner's claim of rental for use and occupancy as equivalent to the interest on any

paid portions of the purchase price and to allow neither of these adjustments.

18. Fabian v. Wasatch Orchard Co., 41 Utah 404, 125 P. 860 (1912).

19. E.g., Boyher v. Gearhart's Estate, 367 S.W.2d 1 (Mo.App.1963); II G. Palmer, Law of Restitution § 6.10 (1978 and Supps.).

20. Veluzat v. Janes, 462 S.W.2d 194 (Ky. 1970); Succession of Dolsen, 129 La. 577, 56 So. 514 (1911); Johnson v. Sanders, 260 N.C. 291, 132 S.E.2d 582 (1963).

21. See Boyher v. Gearhart's Estate, 367 S.W.2d 1 (Mo.App.1963) (common knowledge of the value of the services obviated any need for opinion evidence as to their value).

realize such value. It is not so plausible to permit the plaintiff to recover the contract price for the performance. The contract price represents the plaintiff's full expectancy, which seems to be the very thing barred by the statute of frauds. Accordingly, some courts refused to admit the contract price even as evidence on the issue of the value of the plaintiff's services, though it may be relevant on some other issue in case.[25] This has been particularly the case when the plaintiff claims to have rendered nursing or similar services and seeks to introduce the value of the defendant's estate as evidence of their value.[26] For the most part, however, courts admit the contract price at least as evidence of the value of the performance.[27] Sometimes they go further and treat the contract price as not merely evidence but as the measure of liability.[28]

Contract price as a ceiling on recovery. Can the restitutionary recovery exceed the contract price? Suppose the decedent orally promised to leave the plaintiff one-half of his estate at death in return for care during his lifetime. The plaintiff faithfully cares for the decedent for ten years, but is left nothing in the will. The reasonable value of the services as services comes to $25,000, but one-half of the decedent's estate is worth only $15,000. Courts have permitted the plaintiff to recover the higher sum, or $25,000 in this example, even though such a recovery puts him in better position than full performance of the contract.[29] The leading commentator on restitution believes this is correct.[30]

§ 13.2(3) Restitution in Specie

When the statute of frauds bars enforcement of a contract, restitution in specie by way of constructive trust or otherwise is appropriate only in a limited group of cases. Even in contracts affecting land or unique goods, the role for specific restitution is limited. For instance, if the plaintiff is a land purchaser who has paid the money price for land, he is entitled to recover the price paid. If he is the vendor of land who has conveyed the land itself, his full performance makes the contract enforceable, so that he recovers the

---

25. Evans v. Mason, 82 Ariz. 40, 308 P.2d 245, 65 A.L.R.2d 936 (1957) (contract to pay for services by leaving part of estate to plaintiff, value of decedent's estate not admissible on value of services but was admissible to help persuade jury that the decedent had the means to and did make the promise).

26. See Annotation, Admissibility of evidence of value or extent of decedent's estate in action against estate for reasonable value of services furnished decedent, 65 A.L.R.2d 945 (1959).

27. Mangione v. Braverman, 234 Md. 357, 199 A.2d 225 (1964); Bennett Leasing Co. v. Ellison, 15 Utah 2d 72, 387 P.2d 246, 21 A.L.R.3d 1 (1963); Annotation, Price fixed in contract violating statute of frauds as evidence of value in action on quantum meruit, 21 A.L.R.3d 9 (1968).

28. See Exchange Bank of Commerce v. Meadors, 199 Okl. 10, 184 P.2d 458 (1947). Some of the cases that might support this view are vague or ambiguous. See Cline v. Fountain Rock Lime and Brick Co., 210 Md. 78, 122 A.2d 449 (1956).

29. E.g., In re Estate of Moore, 802 S.W.2d 192 (Mo.App.1991). The argument is that one who uses the statute of frauds to deny his obligation under the contract cannot claim the contract price as a limit on liability. See Williams v. Bemis, 108 Mass. 91, 93 (1871) ("[the contract] cannot be treated as a nullity for one purpose, and as a contract for another"); Wise v. Midtown Motors, 231 Minn. 46, 42 N.W.2d 404, 20 A.L.R.2d 735 (1950).

30. II George Palmer, Law of Restitution § 6.3, p. 27 (1978 and Supps.).

price due as damages,[1] and does not recover restitution of the land.[2]

When a grantor conveys land in exchange for a personal promise of support or care, restitution in specie is appropriate to permit the grantor to recover the land.[3] If the contract has become fully enforceable by reason of the conveyance, restitution in specie is appropriate as a remedy for breach; in the exchange of unique land for unique services, the grantor should not lose both the unique thing he held before the contract and the unique thing he bargained for. If the contract is not enforceable, restitution in specie is the most appropriate form of restitution if it is desired by the grantor. The grounds for denying restitution and the adjustments required to account for the services received by the grantor are discussed in another section.[4]

§ 13.2(4) Reliance Expenses vs. Restitution

Distinguishing Reliance Expense From Restitution

Contracting for process vs. contracting for end-result. When a contract is subject to the statute of frauds defense and no estoppel makes the contract enforceable,[1] the promisee is not permitted either to enforce the contract or to recover expenses incurred in reliance on the contract, except so far as the plaintiff has conferred a benefit upon the promisor. A benefit can be found and recovery allowed when the plaintiff does something requested or contracted-for by the defendant, but not when the plaintiff merely expends money or effort in preparing to perform.[2] The rule is not always easy to apply because it is sometimes difficult to determine whether the defendant was contracting for an end-result (which he has not received) or for the work necessary to produce that end result (some of which he has received). This subsection illustrates the difficulty of drawing that distinction.

Contracting for manufactured product not for steps in manufacture. Suppose the defendant orally agrees to convey land in return for construction of a monument by the plaintiff. The plaintiff constructs the monument but the defendant refuses to accept it or to convey the land. In this case it is not clear that the defendant has received any benefit he bargained for. Probably he did not bargain for *services,* although services were necessary to produce the monument. Instead, he probably bargained for the end product. He does not have that end product (and under the statute of frauds is not required to accept it). On such facts the Massachusetts Court held in *Dowling v. McKenney*[3] that the plaintiff who constructed the monument had no claim for restitution. The plaintiff's expenses were reliance expenses, but they produced no benefit to the defendant. The rule that allows the plaintiff the market value of his services has no application because that rule works only when the defendant gets the thing or part of the thing bargained for.

---

§ 13.2(3)

1. Restatement Second of Contracts § 125(3) (1981). Once the contract is found to be enforceable because of the full performance by the grantor, restitution is forbidden under the full performance-liquidated sum rule explained in § 12.7(5) above.

2. See II George Palmer, Law of Restitution § 6.4 (1978 and Supps.).

3. See Dietz v. Dietz, 244 Minn. 330, 335, 70 N.W.2d 281, 285–286 (1955); II G. Palmer, Law of Restitution §§ 4.20 & 6.4 (1978 and Supps.).

§ 13.2(4)

3. Dowling v. McKenney, 124 Mass. 478 (1878).

Contracting to employ, not employee's preparation to work. Other cases have denied reliance damages relief and can be explained in the same way. One well known example is *Boone v. Coe*,[4] where the defendant orally promised to provide the plaintiff and his family a farm for sharecropping in Texas if they would move from Kentucky. The plaintiff moved but the defendant repudiated the oral contract, leaving the plaintiff with the losses incurred in the move. But these were reliance losses. Although the move was essential to performance, it was not the very performance required by the contract. (The performance required was sharecropping, not moving.) So the plaintiff had no restitutionary claim.

Doubting the distinction. These cases raise doubts and they might well be treated quite differently if the plaintiff's argument is estoppel instead of restitution.[5] There is indeed a difference between bargained-for performance on the one hand and collateral or incidental reliance expenses on the other. The plaintiff who improves the defendant's land because he relies on receiving a deed to it later is not performing any act required by the contract; his reliance is incidental and in such a case the defendant should be liable only for actual benefits received, not the value of the plaintiff's services. But the *Dowling* and *Boone* cases are not like this. You cannot order a custom-made monument without ordering as well the work necessary to create it; you cannot have the dance without the dancer. It may or may not be true that the defendant in *Dowling* bargained only for the end result, but it is certainly true that the plaintiff's effort was a necessary ingredient or step in what was bargained for and in that sense one that was intended by the defendant.[6]

Three levels of reliance. These comments suggest that there are at least three levels of reliance expense that could be distinguished, conceivably with different results when it comes to measuring "benefits" to the defendant. *First*, the plaintiff might rely on the unenforceable contract by getting ready to exploit the defendant's performance for his own purposes. This is incidental reliance, illustrated by the case of the would-be land purchaser who makes improvements without receiving a deed. *Second*, the plaintiff might rely on the contract by taking steps necessary to perform it, although performance is never completed because of the defendant's repudiation. This is essential reliance, illustrated perhaps by the case of services rendered in constructing the monument. *Third*, the plaintiff might rely by expending resources to actually deliver some of the very performance requested by the defendant. This is performance itself, illustrated by cases like the lessor's folly, in which the lessor makes the unmarketable improvements requested by the prospective tenant.[7] Cases like *Dowling* and *Boone* treat the middle

4. 153 Ky. 233, 154 S.W. 900 (1913).

5. Where the employee relies by making a costly move, liability may be imposed today under promissory estoppel doctrines, as in McIntosh v. Murphy, 52 Hawaii 29, 469 P.2d 177, 54 A.L.R.3d 707 (1970), but liability may be denied if the reliance is not substantial enough, as in Munoz v. Kaiser Steel Corp., 156 Cal.App.3d 965, 203 Cal.Rptr. 345 (1984). See § 13.2(5) below.

6. The tort rule is that one is deemed to intend that which is substantially certain to result from one's act, even if the result is not desired. See Prosser & Keeton on Torts § 8 (1984 and Supp.).

7. See Trollope v. Koerner, 106 Ariz. 10, 470 P.2d 91, 64 A.L.R.3d 1180 (1970), discussed in § 13.2(2) above.

category, essential reliance, as if it were the same as purely incidental reliance.

Recognizing essential steps as requested performance. If it is right to recognize a benefit to the defendant in receiving bargained-for performance, it might be equally right to recognize a benefit to him when he "receives" the acts he knows necessary to that performance. There is an element of convention in many restitutionary measurements, just as there is in damages measurements. In line with these thoughts, the UCC would apparently reverse the holding in the monument case. The UCC provides that the oral contract to specially manufacture goods for the buyer will be enforceable if the goods would not be "suitable for sale to others."[8]

Direct or Indirect Allowance of Reliance Damages

A New York decision, *Farash v. Sykes Datatronics, Inc.,*[9] is somewhat difficult to interpret, but it might suggest that restitution can be defined broadly enough to encompass all reliance expenses. Restitution is already defined broadly to cover cases in which a defendant requests performance, even though that performance yields no assets or income to the defendant. The *Farash* opinion suggests a much greater extension. It apparently would define restitution as the restoration of the plaintiff to his pre-contract position. This differs widely from the traditional conception of restitution, which would limit the plaintiff to restoration of the benefits he has conferred upon the defendant, that is, to a return of what he has given. If the *Farash* opinion is to be so interpreted, it will be more difficult than ever to provide a coherent picture of restitution and easier than ever to ignore the statute of frauds.

The distinctions between reliance and performance, to say nothing of the distinction between incidental and essential reliance, are difficult. Arguably, they are too fine to reflect any actual assumptions that knowledgeable parties themselves would make, and too fine as well for practical use by judges and lawyers. When cases like *Farash* are added to this mix of difficulties, it may seem easier to resolve doubtful cases under the Restatement's liberal estoppel formula discussed in the next subsection.

§ 13.2(5) Estoppel and Part Performance

The statute of frauds defense nurtures creative lawyering. When the plaintiff is faced with a potent statute of frauds defense, counsel may consider tort theories that may be plausible on the facts. For instance, the potential statute of frauds defense has generated claims based on the tort of interference with contract[1] and claims of deceit or fraud.[2] More directly, two substantive contract doctrines may make an oral contract fully or partly enforceable in spite of the statute of frauds and without regard to the restitutionary limits.

Part Performance

Incorporated in UCC. First, part performance may suffice to take the case out of the statute of frauds. Sometimes the statute may itself incorporate a part performance doctrine. The UCC does this in sales of goods cases

---

8. UCC § 2-201. See also § 13.2(5) on estoppel solutions.

9. 59 N.Y.2d 500, 465 N.Y.S.2d 917, 452 N.E.2d 1245 (1983).

by providing that contracts for the manufacture of custom goods for a buyer are enforceable once the manufacturer has made either a substantial beginning in their fabrication or procurement.[3]   It also provides that when payment has been made and accepted, the contract is enforceable.[4]

Judicial doctrine of part performance.   Otherwise the part performance doctrine is a judicial creation, frequently raised in land sale cases.   Part performance by the plaintiff might be regarded as one form of estoppel.   Most commonly, however, part performance is regarded as an independent means of escaping the statutory ban and based on the idea that some performances may serve the same purpose as the writing required by the statute, namely, a guarantee that the alleged contract is genuine.[5]   Because courts seek such a guarantee from the part performance, they usually require that the performance be referable to the contract.   Actions will not count as part performance if those actions are most readily explicable on some ground other than the contract claimed.[6]   If the plaintiff claims to have an oral contract to purchase land, the part performance he offers to make the contract enforceable must be at least as consistent with a contract to purchase as with a contract to lease.[7]

Limitations.   If a would-be land buyer pays the price under an oral contract, specific performance does not follow; because he can be protected by restitution of the payment, full enforcement may be denied.   Many actions short of payment of the price, such as actions to arrange financing of a land purchase, are similarly not enough.[8]   In the land cases, a purchaser's occupancy coupled with improvement or payment is likely to suffice to satisfy the part performance doctrine.[9]   The result of the part performance doctrine in the land cases is that specific performance may be ordered (usually for the purchaser).   Strangely enough, part performance is applied only "in equity," so that while it justifies specific performance, it does not justify a damages action.[10]

Estoppel, Equitable and Promissory

Equitable estoppel.   Equitable estoppel rules originated in equity but are

---

§ 13.2(5)

3.   UCC § 2–201(3)(a).

4.   UCC § 2–201(3)(c).

5.   See Note, Parol Purchasers of Land— Equitable Remedies in Tennessee, 10 Mem.St. U.L.Rev. 107 (1979).

6.   E.g., A & R Co. v. Union Air Trans., Inc., 738 P.2d 73 (Colo.App.1987) ("A party relying on part performance to defeat a defense based on the statute of frauds must show that the partial performance is more consistent with the terms of the contract than with some other arrangement, such as a month-to-month tenancy or a tenancy at will.")

7.   Wilson v. La Van, 22 N.Y.2d 131, 291 N.Y.S.2d 344, 238 N.E.2d 738 (1968) (a divided court, with the majority taking the hard line that the plaintiff's payments on the mortgage and improvements could be explicable by a lease and hence that those acts did not count as part performance).

8.   E.g., Weale v. Massachusetts General Housing Corporation, 117 N.H. 428, 432, 374 A.2d 925, 928 (1977) ("incurring expenses for a search of title and preparation of conveyances; measuring or surveying the land; securing estimates of the costs of improvements; arranging for financing for the purchase does not constitute sufficient part performance to take the case out of the requirements of the Statute of Frauds").

9.   E.g., Bank of Alton v. Tanaka, 247 Kan. 443, 799 P.2d 1029 (1990); Ojeda v. Ojeda, 461 S.W.2d 487 (Tex.Civ.App.1970); but see Wilson v. La Van, 22 N.Y.2d 131, 291 N.Y.S.2d 344, 238 N.E.2d 738 (1968) (possession, payments on mortgage, improvements, not enough because all this is consistent with a lease).

10.   Trollope v. Koerner, 106 Ariz. 10, 470 P.2d 91, 64 A.L.R.3d 1180 (1970).

now applied in legal actions as well.[11] When the defendant misrepresents a
fact, either by conduct or by words that create a misleading appearance, and
the plaintiff foreseeably relies upon this appearance to his detriment, the
defendant is estopped to deny the truth of the representation. An equitable
estoppel rule of this kind might be invoked in a statute of frauds case, for
example, if the defendant who has orally promised to lease or sell land to the
plaintiff represents that he has in fact signed a lease or deed and the
plaintiff in reliance then invests in improvements. The defendant will not
be heard later to speak the truth; he is estopped to deny his representation
or to invoke the statute of frauds.[12] A representation of a present intent to
execute a document in the future is also regarded as a representation of a
present fact and not merely a promise.[13] So a representation that the
promisor has the present intent to (and thus will) sign may be treated like a
representation that he has already done so, thus invoking the equitable
estoppel doctrine.[14]

Promissory estoppel. Promissory estoppel is different. Promissory estoppel is not invoked by a factual representation but by a promise, coupled
with foreseeable reliance by the plaintiff. The doctrine began as a substitute
for more formal kinds of consideration [15] but was expanded for use as a
weapon against the statute of frauds beginning about the mid-twentieth
century. For courts that accept the full implications of promissory estoppel,
it is no longer necessary to find that the defendant represented existing
facts; it is enough that he made the contract promise, that the plaintiff
reasonably and expectably relied to his detriment, and that other remedies
are not adequate to protect the plaintiff.[16] Some cases that are ostensibly
based on restitution or unjust enrichment may in reality be promissory
estoppel cases.[17] On the other hand, some cases that ostensibly recognize

---

11. See generally § 2.3 above.

12. Combined Network, Inc. v. Equitable
Life Assurance Soc. of the United States, 805
F.2d 1292 (7th Cir.1986).

13. "Fact" includes past and present conditions and events but not those of the future, so
one cannot either misrepresent or mistake a
"fact" about the future. See § 11.2 distinguishing present facts from future expectations. However one can misrepresent the fact
of a present intention with the result that
some misrepresentations of present intention
can count as actionable fraud. See Prosser &
Keeton on Torts § 109 (1984 and Supp.).
Equally, a misrepresentation of present intention can count as an equitable estoppel.

14. See Seymour v. Oelrichs, 156 Cal. 782,
106 P. 88 (1909). But some authorities approach this situation as a promise rather than
a representation of an existing state of mind,
and hence treat it under the promissory estoppel doctrine discussed below. See Johnson v.
Gilbert, 127 Ariz. 410, 621 P.2d 916 (App.
1980).

15. See Alaska Airlines, Inc. v. Stephenson, 15 Alaska 272, 279, 217 F.2d 295, 298 (9th
Cir.1954) (quoting Restatement of Contracts
§ 90, the court observed: "The foregoing section, not mentioning promissory estoppel, is

addressed not to the statute of frauds but to
promissory estoppel as a substitute for consideration").

16. See Hoffius v. Maestri, 31 Ark.App. 13,
786 S.W.2d 846 (1990) (employee move on
promise of job and medical insurance); McIntosh v. Murphy, 52 Hawaii 29, 469 P.2d 177,
54 A.L.R.3d 707 (1970) (employee move on
promise of job, following the Restatement earlier draft); J. Calamari & J. Perillo, The Law
of Contracts § 19–47 (3d ed. 1987); E.A.
Farnsworth, Farnsworth on Contracts § 6.12
(1990); Restatement Second of Contracts
§§ 129, 139 (1981); Comment Note, Promissory estoppel as basis for avoidance of statute of
frauds, 56 A.L.R.3d 1037 (1974); Annotation,
Action by employee in reliance on employment contract which violates statute of frauds
as rendering contract enforceable, 54 A.L.R.3d
715 (1974).

17. Cf. Farash v. Sykes Datatronics, Inc.,
59 N.Y.2d 500, 465 N.Y.S.2d 917, 452 N.E.2d
1245 (1983). As indicated below, the promissory estoppel approach may not be used if
restitution fully protects the plaintiff. If restitution is not available (as where the plaintiff
made expenditures in reliance but those expenditures did not benefit the defendant) the

promissory estoppel do not appear to go substantially beyond the old equitable estoppel.[18]

Promissory estoppel examples. The leading case was *Monarco v. Lo Greco,*[19] where the defendant had promised to leave property to the plaintiff if the plaintiff would stay on the farm and work it. The plaintiff did stay and Justice Traynor found the reliance sufficient to justify enforcement. The Court emphasized that it was no longer necessary to find that defendant had promised to reduce the contract to writing. The oral promise that constituted the contract itself would be enough if there was reliance. "[W]here either an unconscionable injury or unjust enrichment would result from refusal to enforce the contract, the doctrine of estoppel has been applied whether or not plaintiff relied upon representations going to the requirements of the statute itself." [20]

In *Alaska Airlines, Inc. v. Stephenson,*[21] the plaintiff was working temporarily with Alaska Airlines, but held job security with Western Airlines. Alaska wanted to keep the plaintiff and promised him a long term job and also promised to sign a written contract later. The plaintiff gave up his job security with Western. The court found a promissory estoppel. The case might have been decided on narrow grounds, because the defendant promised to execute a written contract that would comply with the statute of frauds. But the court generalized its reasons to suggest that any foreseeable, definite, and substantial reliance on any kind of promise would suffice to permit enforcement in the face of the statute if justice would require.

Limitations on the Doctrine and the Remedy

Limiting remedy to restitution or to reliance damages. Although the estoppel doctrine potentially erodes the statute of frauds, the doctrine as developed in *Monarco* and the Restatement is hedged with important limitations. The logical effect of the estoppel doctrine is to prevent the defendant

---

estoppel theory may be available to cover the plaintiff's reliance losses.

18. See Tiffany Inc. v. W.M.K. Transit Mix, Inc., 16 Ariz.App. 415, 493 P.2d 1220, 56 A.L.R.3d 1028 (1972). The *Tiffany* court held that promissory estoppel applied to avoid the statute of frauds only "where a promise has been made not to rely on the Statute." This sounds essentially like the liberal version of the old equitable estoppel, virtually equivalent to a representation of a present state of mind. The court thought it differed from equitable estoppel in that equitable estoppel could be used only as a shield or defense, not as a sword or cause of action. The "shield, not a sword" principle, however, hangs from a linguistic thread. The *Tiffany* court thought the plaintiff there was asserting a cause of action based on estoppel, thus using estoppel as a sword. But the use of estoppel could equally have been explained as a shield: plaintiff sues on the contract, defendant pleads the statute of frauds, plaintiff interposes the estoppel, not as a "cause of action" but to prevent the defense.

19. 35 Cal.2d 621, 220 P.2d 737 (1950).

20. Monarco v. Lo Greco, 35 Cal.2d 621, 625, 220 P.2d 737, 741 (1950). The court went on:

> [I]t is not the representation that the contract will be put in writing or that the statute will not be invoked, but the promise that the contract will be performed that a party relies upon when he changes his position because of it. Moreover, a party who has accepted the benefits of an oral contract will be unjustly enriched if the contract is not enforced whether his representations related to the requirements of the statute or were limited to affirmations that the contract would be performed.

The last quoted sentence may suggest that the estoppel doctrine might not be triggered unless the defendant is unjustly enriched; but if that were the case, the estoppel doctrine would not be necessary because restitution could be claimed.

21. Alaska Airlines, Inc. v. Stephenson, 15 Alaska 272, 217 F.2d 295 (9th Cir.1954).

from effectively using the statute of frauds defense at all. That would mean the plaintiff could obtain full enforcement, not merely a restitutionary recovery or a recovery of reliance expenses, and in fact full enforcement is sometimes granted.[22] However, the Restatement [23] and *Monarco*[24] support the position that if restitutionary remedies are adequate, or if reliance expenses furnish an adequate measure, one of those remedies may be used in lieu of expectancy damages or specific enforcement; the estoppel doctrine will not be invoked at all if injustice can be avoided by other means.

§ 13.3 Remedies When Performance Is Excused Under Doctrines of Frustration or Impracticality

§ 13.3(1) Substantive Framework

Discharging Liability for Risks Outside the Scope of the Contract

In general, the substantive law of contract excuses performance or discharges the obligations of a contract when performance would require the promisor to bear a risk not allocated to him by the contract.[4] For example, supervening events may make performance of the contract literally impossible or substantially impractical. Or post-contracting events may frustrate the contract's purposes, leaving performance possible and practical but eliminating the benefits contemplated by the parties. If the parties bargained in contemplation of possible and practical performance, and supervening events make it impossible or impractical, then the obligation is discharged because it is not one the parties undertook to deal with.[5]

§ 13.3(2) Remedial Alternatives and Problems

Restitution Generally[1]

"Rescission ab initio" vs. excuse of future performance. If contracting parties are mutually mistaken about an existing and basic fact at the time they bargain, it may be that the mistake prevents them from forming an enforceable contract at all.[2] When the parties actually bargain to an enforceable contract, but supervening events make performance impractical or frustrate its purposes, the outlook may be different. In that case they have a contract; only future performance is excused.[3] These views might logically affect remedies available when part of the performance has been rendered. In a mistake case, when mistake in contracting is discovered, the contract might be avoided or rescinded, with the result that each party must return the benefits he received from the other. But in the case of supervening events that frustrate the contract's purpose, future performance could be excused without requiring restitution of performance already given.

The future excuse rule of Chandler v. Webster. In *Chandler v. Webster,*[4]

---

23. See generally, Restatement Second of Contracts § 139 (1981) (remedy limited as justice requires in light of other potential remedies such as restitution); also Id. § 129 (similar as to land). The Restatement here as elsewhere eschews rules in favor of discretion. Judges are said to have the power to limit the remedy as justice may require in the particular case. Factors include the availability of other remedies, the character of the reliance, its foreseeability, the reasonableness of the action in reliance, and the usefulness of the action in reliance as some guarantee that the claimed contract was genuine. See § 139(2)(a)–(e).

§ 13.3(2)

4. Chandler v. Webster, [1904] 1 K.B. 493, 501 (C.A.).

one of the coronation cases,[5] a judge said that when the supervening event occurred each party was "thenceforth free from all further obligations under the contract" but that the contract was not "rescinded ab initio. That being so, any legal right which had previously accrued to either party remained in force * * *." If you made a downpayment on rooms for the purpose of viewing the King's Coronation procession, but the procession was later cancelled, you would not have to pay any balance due on your contract; but you could not get back your downpayment.

The full restitution rule of Fibrosa. Chandler v. Webster seems to be the logical result if supervening events only excuse future performance. However, courts have not limited the remedy as *Chandler v. Webster* suggests. Instead, they have often allowed restitution of any performance delivered. A famous decision of the House of Lords in the *Fibrosa* case [6] overruled or limited *Chandler v. Webster*. In *Fibrosa* a Polish company contracted to purchase special machinery to be manufactured by the English seller. The machinery was to be delivered to Poland and the English seller was to supervise its installation there. The price was 3200 pounds, 1600 of which was to have been paid immediately, although the Polish buyer in fact paid only £1,000.

The contract was dated July 12, 1939. Hitler, the Chancellor of Germany, had occupied the Rhineland in violation of limits imposed on Germany by treaties after World War I. He had also taken a hunk of Czechoslovakia (with the approval of the English government at Munich). He had taken another hunk, all of Bohemia and Moravia, by force. He had annexed Austria in toto. Throughout all of 1939 he had been demanding a part of Poland. As some evidence of his probable intent, he repudiated the Polish–German non-aggression pact. In spite of these ominous signs, the contract in *Fibrosa* made no mention of war except to say that if war delayed performance a reasonable extension would be granted. Six weeks after the contract was signed Hitler attacked Poland. Britain, in compliance with her treaty obligation to Poland, went to war with Germany when Poland was attacked. Performance of the contract was impossible so far as delivery in Poland was required.

What should be done with the £1,000 pounds prepayment? If the buyer was entitled to restitution of the prepayment, should the seller be entitled to any damages based on its reliance expense? The House of Lords allowed the Polish buyer to recover its 1,000 pounds, but it also denied the seller any offsetting recovery for its reliance expense.

If the case is to be treated like a mistake case with rescission or avoidance of the contract, then each party recovers for the performance it has delivered to the other party. In unjust enrichment terminology, the seller is unjustly enriched by 1,000 pounds if the contract is "rescinded ab initio." [7] On this analysis, the seller is not entitled to recover for its reliance expense, a point that calls for further comment later.

5. See § 13.3(1) above.

6. Fibrosa Spolka Akeyjna v. Fairbairn Lawson Combe Barbour, Ltd., [1943] A.C. 32,

[1942] All.E.R. 122, 144 A.L.R. 1298 (H.L. 1942).

American rule generally. The American view is like that in *Fibrosa.* Restitution is available in the event of excusing impracticality or frustration, and restitution is usually measured by value of all performance completed.[8] However, if the court understands the case to be one of illegality rather than impracticability or mistake, the result is equivalent to the future excuse rule: restitution is denied, but no further performance will be enforced.[9]

Restitutionary Measures

Money payments and the value of services generally. Under the general rule, if the benefit conferred is in the form of money, the amount of money paid with interest is the measure of restitution.[10] If the performance confers a benefit in the form of services, then restitution is generally owed for the market value of the services, that is, what it would cost the recipient to get the same services elsewhere.[11]

Contract rate; divisible contracts. The contract rate may also be used to measure restitution in some cases.[12] The contract rate is in fact the measure of restitution in "divisible" contracts, in which each unit of performance can reasonably be regarded as an equivalent for a unit of the price, as where one party is to deliver supplies on a weekly basis with payment for each delivery. In such cases a supervening event may discharge future obligations, but as to completed units of performance, the plaintiff's performance is compensated at the contract price.[13]

Benefit received but its value lost. When a contractor provides services and materials in performing a building contract but a fire destroys the property, the destruction of the subject discharges the obligations of the parties. The landowner has nothing to show for the labor and materials furnished by the contractor. What restitution does he owe? Some cases deny any relief to the contractor.[14] Others say that the contractor is entitled to recover for the market value of services and materials so long as they were "wrought into" the building.[15] No restitution is given for work that did not go into the building but went only into plans or into materials delivered to the job but not incorporated as fixtures because in these instances the owner does not even theoretically receive benefits, even though the contractor has suffered reliance expenses. These decisions seem right. The landowner can insure for fire whether or not she has actually done so in the particular case. For this reason it is probably practical or efficient to put the risk of loss on the landowner. Perhaps the parties would have put it there had they thought about the matter.[16]

8. Restatement Second of Contracts §§ 272, 377 (1981).

13. See II George Palmer, Law of Restitution § 7.5, p. 125 (1978 and Supps.); Restatement Second of Contracts §§ 240, 272(1) (1981) (price recovery in "agreed equivalents" contracts).

14. See, reviewing authorities, Harrison, A Case for Loss Sharing, 56 So.Cal.L.Rev. 573 (1983); 6 A. Corbin Contracts § 1338 (1951). Compare the case of benefits conferred by mistake rather than in performance of a contract. In that case destruction of the benefit before the mistake is discovered may be a defense to restitution. See §§ 4.6 & 11.9 above.

15. Bell v. Carver, 245 Ark. 31, 431 S.W.2d 452, 28 A.L.R.3d 781 (1968); Ahern v. John Bowen Co., Inc., 334 Mass. 36, 133 N.E.2d 484 (1956); Annotation, 170 A.L.R. 980 (1947).

16. A rationale for this is provided by Judge Posner in the following language: "All are doctrines for shifting risk to the party better able to bear it, either because he is in a better position to prevent the risk from materializing or because he can better reduce the disutility of the risk (as by insuring) if the risk does occur * * *. [I]mpossibility and related

Unrealized benefit. Some personal services do not confer any realizable benefit until they have been fully performed or result in tangible values. In the building-fire cases just discussed, the contractor is allowed to recover for services or materials that have resulted in a tangible improvement even though the improvement is destroyed before it is completed. But the contractor is not allowed recovery for other parts of his performance such as making plans or purchases. Suppose a lawyer performs services for a client by preparing files and thinking carefully about her plans for trial, but then dies before creating any tangible benefit. Impossibility of performing the contract personally excuses the lawyer and that in turn allows the client to terminate or avoid the contract. Has the client received any benefit? The building contractor cases suggests that the lawyer's performance would be like the contractor's plans. Thinking about the case *is* part of the performance but nothing useable has been delivered to the client. The next lawyer would have to do her own thinking about the case and would have to be paid accordingly.

But impracticality and frustration cases lead to some strange decisions. In *City of Barnsdall v. Curnutt,*[17] a lawyer promised to render his services to the city in conjunction with a lawsuit. He was to be paid a contingent fee of 40% of any recovery made by the city against a polluter. The polluter offered the city $25,000 in settlement. Shortly after the offer and before any settlement was concluded, the lawyer died. The city was compelled to secure services of other attorneys, who ultimately secured a settlement for $35,000. The client paid the attorneys a reasonable fee of $10,000. Then the estate of the first lawyer sued for "restitution." The Oklahoma Court allowed recovery at the contract rate or 40% of the offer in hand at the time the lawyer died. So the client paid $10,000 to the estate and another $10,000 to the lawyers who actually obtained the settlement. In all it paid $20,000 for a $35,000 claim.

It is not possible to believe the client actually benefited from the first lawyer's work to the extent of $10,000. The court's decision allocates all the risk of impossibility to the client and then charges the client the contract rate[18] for benefits that may have had no practical use at all. The case differs enormously from the building contractor/fire case. In the fire case the claimant (who unlike the lawyer, is not the party claiming impossibility) has produced a tangible benefit. If the building contractor were to quit work, some other contractor could take over and make full use of the existing work. This is not so in the lawyer case. Nor is it the case that the client can readily insure as the landowner can. Professor Palmer thinks

doctrines are devices for shifting risk in accordance with the parties' presumed intentions, which are to minimize the costs of contract performance * * *." Northern Indiana Public Service Co. v. Carbon County Coal Co., 799 F.2d 265 (1986).

17. 198 Okl. 3, 174 P.2d 596 (1945).

18. In another lawyer's quantum meruit claim, the court appeared to use a market value rate based on the number of hours expended rather than a percentage figure. See Gaines, Gaines & Gaines, P.C. v. Hare, Wynn,

Newell & Newton, 554 So.2d 445 (Ala.Civ.App. 1989) (semble). In that case the quantum meruit fee would apparently operate to reduce the fee of the lawyers who actually pursued the case. Note that even if the lawyer's fee is measured by the cost of purchasing similar services elsewhere rather than by a percentage of the total recovery in the case, it may not represent any actual benefits to the erstwhile client, much less benefits to the other law firm.

with the dissenter in *City of Barnsdall* that equity was outraged by the decision.[19]

Reliance Damages and Net Value Restitution

Reliance expense award inappropriate. The lawyer's time investment in *City of Barnsdall* looks like a reliance expense but not like any real benefit delivered to the possession of the client. Should reliance expenses be recoverable when the contract obligation is terminated for impracticality or frustration of purpose? The comments above suggest that a recovery by the lawyer's estate in *City of Barnsdall* would be inappropriate whether it is regarded as reliance expense or restitution because the parties probably never expected to make the client bear the expenses resulting from the lawyer's death, even though death excused future performance by the lawyer.

In other cases, however, the best adjustment of the deal would be to award reliance expenses as well as restitution. The logic of damages and excuse make an award of reliance damages conceptually difficult even when such an award seems right. In the *Fibrosa* case discussed above, the Polish buyer had prepaid 1,000 pounds. When the seller's performance became impossible, the buyer was entitled to a return of the prepaid monies, but the seller in the meantime had expended unrecoverable sums in preparing to make the custom machinery required by the contract. Neither party was in breach because their obligations were discharged by the impossibility of performance, so damages are logically inappropriate—restitution is justified without breach, but not damages. Reliance expense claims that do not result in a benefit to the other party are necessarily damages claims, not restitution claims. That being so, there was no logical basis for a damages award.

Reliance expense award appropriate. Nevertheless, reliance recovery is right in some cases. It is right to order restitution to prevent unjust enrichment, but unjust enrichment is not the only consideration. Courts must also allocate risks and losses the parties did not expressly allocate for themselves. Courts are engaged in contract adjustment in such cases not merely in ordering mechanical restitution. A fair adjustment of a deal that has gone awry might appropriately award restitution to one party with an offset for reliance expense of the other. Such a solution might work well in a case like *Fibrosa*.[20] At any rate the Second Restatement,[21] supported by case authority,[22] provides for the recovery of reliance expenses in appropriate cases. The counterbalance to this, however, is that neither reliance

---

19. II George Palmer, Law of Restitution § 7.7, p. 142 (1978 and Supps.).

20. See Comment, 46 Mich.L.Rev. 401 (1948).

21. Restatement Second of Contracts §§ 272(2), 377 (1981). The Second Restatement leans heavily on the subjective and the discretionary. Section 272(2) would permit courts to "grant relief on such terms as justice requires." Such a formulation might suggest a great deal of discretion to re-write the contract, but Professor Dawson thought that the Restatement offered no such "ephemeral equi-

ty." See Dawson, Judicial Revision of Frustrated Contracts: The United States, 64 B.U.L.Rev. 1, 8–9 (1984).

22. See Chugach Elec. Ass'n v. Northern Corp., 562 P.2d 1053 (Alaska 1977), the controlling facts and theories of which are reflected in Northern Corp. v. Chugach Elec. Ass'n, 518 P.2d 76 (Alaska 1974), rehearing, Northern Corp. v. Chugach Elec. Ass'n, 523 P.2d 1243 (1974); Albre Marble and Tile Co. v. John Bowen Co., 338 Mass. 394, 155 N.E.2d 437 (1959).

damages nor any other adjustment should be made if it is inconsistent with the parties' own risk allocations.[23]

Other Remedial Solutions

Economic efficiency vs. division of losses. Some writers have offered different solutions in cases of frustration and impossibility. They have proposed some kind of loss-sharing by the parties, so that the court would not award either pure restitution or pure reliance losses, but would instead divide the reliance losses between the parties, an idea that has appeared in other contexts as well.[24] Professor Harrison has developed such a proposal based in part on the perception of a contract as a kind of mini-partnership, which, because of gaps, has come before the court for unwinding.[25] He proposes a presumption in favor of equal sharing of all reliance losses on both sides, which he believes the parties might have agreed to under proper conditions. Essential reliance losses[26] would be divided and any remaining "actual" unjust enrichment would be dealt with by a restitutionary award. Professor Harrison's approach opposes a simple all-or-nothing approach. It also opposes the approach which allocates all of the loss to one of the parties on economic efficiency grounds in which the superior risk bearer is identified and made to bear the loss.[27]

Court-made adjustments. Some writers have suggested the possibility of affirmative adjustments in the contract obligations that go beyond awards of restitution, reliance or shared losses. Some of these have concentrated in particular on relational contract or long-term arrangements,[28] trying to find a way to salvage the core relationship when supervening events make performance impracticable.[29] Sometimes courts have ordered adjustments that are hard to fit with the parties' own apparent risk allocations, but which may be efficient in preserving a relationship it would be too costly to lose.[30]

23. Cf. Albre Marble and Tile Co. v. John Bowen Co., 338 Mass. 394, 155 N.E.2d 437 (1959) (contract expressly required preparatory work by subcontractor, general contractor held liable for its value even though performance of general contract became impossible, semble, parties so allocated risks). City of Barnsdall v. Curnutt, 198 Okl. 3, 174 P.2d 596 (1945) discussed in the text above, was really a case of a reliance loss recovery that was not consistent with the probable intent or risk-allocations of the parties.

24. See Weiss, Apportioning Loss after Discharge of a Burdensome Contract, 69 Yale L.J. 1054 (1960). See also § 4.5(4) above.

25. See Harrison, A Case for Loss Sharing, 56 So.Cal.L.Rev. 573 (1983).

26. That is, reliance expenses incurred in doing acts necessary to perform contract obligations, but not "incidental" reliance expenses that might be incurred collaterally. As to the distinction see § 12.3(2) above.

27. See Harrison, A Case for Loss Sharing, 56 So.Cal.L.Rev. 573, 585 (1983). For a succinct statement of the economic view, but one that also incorporates the parties' intent, see

Northern Indiana Public Service Co. v. Carbon County Coal Co., supra n. 16 (quoting Judge Posner).

28. See § 12.1(2) above.

29. Cf. Speidel, Court–Imposed Price Adjustments under Long–Term Supply Contracts, 76 Nw.L.Rev. 369 (1981) (adjustment justified if party who is fortuitously advantaged by a supervening event refuses to re-bargain in good faith).

30. In Oglebay Norton Co. v. Armco, Inc., 52 Ohio St.3d 232, 556 N.E.2d 515 (1990) the court ordered the parties to a long-term shipping contract with a high level of mutual dependence to negotiate prices after major shifts in the market and the failure of the primary pricing mechanisms specified in the contract. Cf. City of Vernon v. City of Los Angeles, 45 Cal.2d 710, 290 P.2d 841 (1955) (City of Vernon, which had contract to dispose of its sewage through Los Angeles system, had to negotiate a new price when performance became impossible; but this was a result of two separate decrees and some choices by the City of Vernon).

§ 13.4 Remedies for Benefits Conferred Under Contracts Avoided for Defective Capacity

§ 13.4(1) Power of Avoidance

[For the text of this section, see the unabridged Practitioner Treatise edition.]

§ 13.4(2) Infancy

Substantive rules: contracts voidable. A contract made with a minor [1] is voidable at the minor's option,[2] even though the minor has capacity to marry and is in fact married.[3] Minors may disaffirm even during infancy, and also within a reasonable time after reaching majority.[4] Sometimes it is said that conveyances can be disaffirmed only after reaching majority. An unseasonable delay in disaffirmance after majority will operate to ratify the contract.[5] The minor disaffirms by any act or declaration.[6] Most commonly the disaffirmance is accomplished simply by raising the infancy defense when the other party sues on the contract, but it is also possible for minors themselves to bring suit to recover what they have paid.[7] The minor's contract is usually voidable, not void. So minors can enforce contracts that turn out to be advantageous but disaffirm those which do not.

Exceptions. The minor's right to disaffirm is qualified in several ways. First, minors (and their parents or guardians) may be held liable for "necessaries" such as food, clothing, lodging, and some kinds of medical care. This liability is not technically an exception because it is a restitutionary liability to prevent unjust enrichment, not a contract liability.[8] The "necessaries" rule has been given a grudging interpretation, so that provisions are not considered "necessary" if the minor could get them from his own parents.[9]

Second, some courts deny the minors the power of avoidance when they misrepresent their age and the other party relies on the representation,[10] although most immunize the minor from this fraud as well as from the contract obligations.[11] Presumably also there would be limits to disaffirmance by a minor who has a statutory or constitutional right to contract for the particular services,[12] and statutes sometimes provide that specified contracts cannot be disaffirmed.[13] Finally, the requirement of restitution as applied in some courts may operate as a de facto exception that prevents disaffirmance in particular cases.[14]

Restitution to the Minor

When minors successfully disaffirm their contracts, they are entitled to restitution for what they have given in the transaction. If they have paid money, they are entitled to that; if they have rendered services or transferred a chattel, they are entitled to recover the value of the services or chattel.[15] Minors have been allowed to recover property from bona fide purchasers. If the minor transferred property to *A*, who sold it to *B*, a purchaser for value without notice of the minor's claim, *B* was forced to give up the property he paid for.[16] This runs contrary to the usual rule that an equitable right to avoid a transaction is cut off by a bona fide purchase,[17] but it is in line with other extreme rules favoring minors. Statutes may alter the rule and provide protection for the bona fide purchaser.[18]

Restitution From the Minor

The harsh rule for damaged or depreciated property. The minor must also make restitution, but the measure of restitution owed by the minor is quite different. Upon disaffirmance, the minor must restore what remains in her hands. If she has wasted or consumed property she obtained under the contract, she is not obliged to make restitution;[19] if the property is damaged, she need only restore it in its damaged condition.[20] She recovers restitution but makes no restitution to the other party in return. For example, she may buy a car, wreck it, then disaffirm the contract and recover back her payments on the car, restoring to the seller only the scrap that remains as a souvenir of her adventure.[21]

Moderate rules requiring restitution. Not all courts follow the harsh rules. Some require the minor to make full restitution of what she actually received under the contract.[27] She might also be required to make restitution for any use value she got from having the purchased chattel between the time of purchase and disaffirmance.[28] Statutes sometimes prompt the same kind of result, either because they change the disaffirmance rules as to certain minor's contracts[29] or because they provide for full value restitution.[30]

§ 13.4(3)   Mental Incompetency

One who lacks a minimum degree of mental capacity may avoid his "contracts."

At one time it was said that contracts with incompetents were absolutely void, because if the incompetent had no mind in a legal sense, there could be no "meeting of the minds."[3] This is still correct when one has been adjudicated incompetent and a guardian appointed. In that case, the incompetent has no power to contract at all; all power to do so with respect to the incompetent's estate is vested in the guardian.[4] Sometimes the transaction is also said to be void even when an incompetent has not been so adjudicated, if the capable party knows of the incompetence.[5] With respect to persons

---

§ 13.4(2)

20. Halbman v. Lemke, 99 Wis.2d 241, 298 N.W.2d 562 (1980).

21. Bowling v. Sperry, 133 Ind.App. 692, 184 N.E.2d 901 (1962) (minor may have failed to put oil in car, main bearing burned out, return of car in damaged condition sufficient); Star Chevrolet Co. v. Green, 473 So.2d 157 (Miss.1985) (car destroyed in collision, minor could recover purchase price although he kept insurance which was in excess of the purchase price); Fisher v. Taylor Motor Co., 249 N.C. 617, 107 S.E.2d 94 (1959) ($750 car wrecked due to minor's negligence and unlawful acts, reducing its value to $400; further depreciation in value to $50, minor could recover full consideration paid less the value of the fully depreciated car remaining in his hands); Hines v. Cheshire, 36 Wash.2d 467, 474, 219 P.2d 100, 104 (1950) (car wrecked and repaired several times, perhaps not repaired at all the

last time, but "this is entirely immaterial," since minor only needs to return any property not lost or wasted).

27. Berglund v. American Multigraph Sales Co., 135 Minn. 67, 160 N.W. 191 (1916); Porter v. Wilson, 106 N.H. 270, 209 A.2d 730, 13 A.L.R.3d 1247 (1965); Boyce v. Doyle, 113 N.J.Super. 240, 273 A.2d 408 (1971).

28. Rice v. Butler, 160 N.Y. 578, 55 N.E. 275 (1899); Annotation, 12 A.L.R.3d 1274 (1967).

29. See West's Ann.Cal.Civil Code §§ 34.5–34.10.

30. Ark.Code Ann. § 9–26–101 provides that the "infant over 18" must make full restitution of property received in substantially the same condition as it was when received; but the statute may be obsolete because the age of majority has been lowered to 18 since the statute was passed.

who have not been adjudicated to be incompetent, however, the current view holds the contract voidable, not void.[6]

To say that a transaction is void is to say that the transaction can be disaffirmed even as against a bona fide purchaser who has in good faith purchased from the capable party.[7] To say that the transaction is voidable, not void, is to say that the incompetent loses his power to avoid the transaction once the rights of a bona fide purchaser have intervened.

When incompetency is demonstrated, the incompetent party may disaffirm and avoid the contract, but typically is required to make full restitution of what he has received by way of performance. The mental incompetent does not usually get the benefit of the favorable rule lavished on minors.[10] He must restore what he received in the deal, not merely what he has left of it. If the incompetent has used or destroyed the consideration he received under the contract and if he cannot restore it or its value, he is not entitled to avoid the contract.[11] A few cases have gone the other way, requiring only restitution of what remains in the incompetent's hands.[12]

When the capable party has imposed upon the incompetent, by entering the transaction with knowledge of the incompetent's disability, then the restitutionary rule is different. In that case the incompetent need restore only the consideration that remains in his hands.[13] Even in that case, however, the incompetent is liable to make restitution for the value of necessaries received.

§ 13.5 Attorney's Remedy When Client Avoids Contract

[*For the text of this section, see the unabridged Practitioner Treatise edition.*]

§ 13.6 Restitution in Connection With Illegal Contracts and Activities

General rule against restitution. Can one who has performed under an illegal contract "rescind" or otherwise recover restitution of what he has given in performance even though he may not enforce the contract for damages? The general rule is that when a contract cannot be enforced because it is illegal, then restitution will also be denied.[3] As a matter of locution, the rule is often referred to as the *pari delicto* defense which literally means that if the parties are *in pari delicto*—equal fault—then recovery will be denied.[4] At other times the rule is stated by saying the familiar equitable doctrine that bars recovery in favor of one with unclean hands.[5]

Rationale and extensions. Sometimes the rule against enforcement, like the unclean hands doctrine, seems to reflect moral distaste without instrumental purpose. In many of the cases, however, the courts explicitly base the rule on the theory that by refusing restitution in illegality cases, they

§ 13.4(3)

11. Young v. Lujan, 11 Ariz.App. 47, 461 P.2d 691 (1969) (recognizing rule); Davis v. Colorado Kenworth Corp., 156 Colo. 98, 396 P.2d 958 (1964); Sjulin v. Clifton Furniture Co., 241 Iowa 761, 41 N.W.2d 721 (1950); Lawson v. Bennett, 240 N.C. 52, 81 S.E.2d 162 (1954).

12. Reaves v. Davidson, 129 Ark. 88, 195 S.W. 19 (1917).

13. Sjulin v. Clifton Furniture Co., 241 Iowa 761, 41 N.W.2d 721 (1950).

can discourage illegal transactions. The rule may go beyond its rationale. Although both parties are engaged in the illegal contract, one of them is enriched by the other's performance and is allowed to retain that enrichment under the rule. One party may thus find illegality unprofitable but the other, quite the contrary, is allowed to keep the fruits of illegality under the general rule, so the actual deterrent effect of the rule against restitution is sometimes debatable.[6]

Exceptions generally. Courts have recognized exceptions to the rule against restitution in a number of cases. Restitution is often measured by the money value of the plaintiff's performance, but it may be made in specie by way of a constructive trust or the like when appropriate.[24] The way in which exceptions are stated is not completely standardized. Situational elements may be far more important in determining the result than the stated exceptions, but the exceptions are important as the tools through which moral and policy elements are occasionally uncovered. Disregarding overlapping elements among the stated exceptions, it can be said that the plaintiff is permitted to enforce the contract or at least to have restitution in all of the following cases.

(1) The plaintiff is ignorant of the illegality. The plaintiff may be "excusably" ignorant either because he does not know facts that would make the transaction or its purpose illegal, or because he is unaware of some relatively minor legal requirement.[25]

(2) The plaintiff is the victim of fraud, duress, or similar misconduct. The plaintiff may recover the value of his performance when the illegal contract was induced by the defendant's fraud, duress, undue influence or oppression.[26] The formal exception does not refer expressly to the plaintiff's status; but the plaintiff's inferior or vulnerable position [27] and the defendant's dominant role [28] in the illegality are clearly relevant and clearly favorable to the plaintiff's recovery. The point seems to be that the plaintiff is more a victim than a wrongdoer, or else that those in the position of the defendant would ordinarily be in better position to avoid the wrongdoing.

In line with that idea, some plaintiffs who have paid bribes or kickbacks have been allowed to recover on the view that they were victims of economic coercion rather than direct wrongdoers.[29] Most often, however, the general rule leads courts to deny the briber any restitution of his bribe, even when he got nothing in return for it.[30]

(3) Recovery will prevent unjust enrichment of a fiduciary. Even if a fiduciary is not guilty of fraud or misconduct in inducing an illegal transaction to begin with, the duty of loyalty requires that he restore to the beneficiary any gains he has received.[31]

(4) The plaintiff is within a class of persons for whose protection the transaction was made illegal.[32] Sometimes the statute which makes a transaction illegal does so in order to protect persons like the plaintiff. In such cases the statute itself has recognized that the plaintiff, like the plaintiff under the fraud and the fiduciary exceptions, is more the victim than the wrongdoer.

For example, the borrower at an illegal rate of interest may be regarded as the victim and entitled to the courts' aid; [33] an investor who buys stock on the basis of inside information illegally provided by a broker is permitted to recover when the information turns out to be misleading; the main fault is with the tipper, not the tippee.[34]

(5) The illegality is not closely related to the plaintiff's claim or is a segment in a "divisible" contract. When the illegality is collateral or incidental to the plaintiff's claim, the plaintiff may recover in spite of that illegality.[39] Sometimes the incidental or collateral nature of the illegality is determined mechanically by saying that if the plaintiff can state the claim without mentioning the illegality, then the illegality is remote or irrelevant.[40] A very similar idea is that the contract is "divisible," made up of a series of pairs of performances on each side, and that illegality in one pair or segment of the contract does not necessarily preclude enforcement of other segments.[41] Again, similar notions arise in cohabitation cases, in which one party allegedly agrees to provide benefits to another in connection with joint living arrangements, often also involve sexual relations. If the contractual rights to benefits rests on a promise to provide sexual relations in return, then the contract is regarded as one for prostitution and it is illegal and unenforceable. But the contract is not illegal at all if there are no sexual promises. If there are sexual promises and they are "outside the scope of the agreement"[42] for a division of property or other benefits, then the contract can be enforced or restitution can be granted for the value of the services performed by the promisee.[43]

(6) Restitution is consistent with preventing accomplishment of the illegality. When the illegal acts have not themselves been performed, a termination of the deal with restitution to the plaintiff is consistent with the deterrent goals. When, in addition, the plaintiff has "repented" before the illegality has been carried out, the old equity emphasis on personal morality suggests that restitution should be permitted to encourage and reinforce the repentance. Thus the doctrine of *locus poenitentiae* allows restitution in some of the cases in which the plaintiff stops short before committing an illegal act, awarding restitution for the "legal" part of the performance he has already rendered.[44]

(7) Public policy will be served by granting restitution or enforcement. The public policy "exception" is often stated or exemplified in the cases and commentaries.[45] For the most part, however, it seems to be a way of generalizing the particular exceptions already named above or the idea that courts should aim at granting or denying restitution depending on which is the most effective deterrence.[46]

Generalizing and reformulating exceptions. Sometimes the exceptions operate to protect the party in inferior status[47] or to deny relief to the party who is most subject to deterrence. But such results often coincide with the *pari delicto* principle. Almost all of the stated exceptions can be brought under the umbrella rule that restitution (or enforcement) is permitted when the parties are not *in pari delicto*, that is, when the plaintiff is not in a position of equal fault.[48]

Pari delicto and unclean hands. Unclean hands[57] and *pari delicto* doctrines are often mentioned in the same judicial opinions. Sometimes courts seem to use the terms as if they were distinct doctrines,[58] sometimes as if they were about the same.[59] If they are not the same, there are probably two important differences here. First, the unclean hands doctrine may simply appeal to equity's traditional discretion to deny equitable relief; if so, that doctrine would leave the plaintiff free to claim his legal rights even if he is denied an equitable remedy for them. The *pari delicto* doctrine, in contrast, would bar the plaintiff's entire claim, not merely one of the possible remedies for it.

Second, the unclean hands doctrine relies heavily on equity's claim of moral superiority, not on a policy of discouraging wrongdoing. The classic position when unclean hands doctrine is explicated is that the maculate plaintiff is banished from the court in order to maintain the court's own robes free from blemish,[60] not because he is morally worse than the defendant. Because the court in such cases seems not to be considering the moral position of the parties at all, it is not weighing the relative fault of the parties.

Appendix

REMEDIES LAW RESEARCH
ON WESTLAW

Analysis

Sec.
1. Introduction.
2. Databases for Remedies Law Research.
3. Menu–Driven WESTLAW: EZ ACCESS™.
4. Retrieving a Document With a Citation: Find and Jump.
5. Query Formulation.
   5.1 Terms.
   5.2 Alternative Terms.
   5.3 Connectors.
   5.4 Restricting Your Search by Field.
   5.5 Restricting Your Search by Date.
6. Verifying Your Research With Citators.
   6.1 Insta–Cite®.
   6.2 Shepard's® Citations.
   6.3 Shepard's PreView™.
   6.4 QuickCite™.
   6.5 Using WESTLAW as a Citator.
   6.6 Citator Commands.
7. Research Examples.
   7.1 Retrieving Law Review Articles.
   7.2 Retrieving Statutes.
   7.3 Retrieving Federal Regulations.
   7.4 Retrieving Restatement Provisions.
   7.5 Retrieving Employment Discrimination Decisions.
   7.6 Using Citator Services.

Section 1. Introduction

Dobbs' *Remedies* provides a strong base for analyzing even the most complex remedies problem. Whether your research requires examination of case law, statutes, administrative materials or commentary, West books and WESTLAW are excellent sources of research materials.

In the area of remedies, WESTLAW expands your library by giving you access to documents issued by state and federal courts, legislatures and administrative agencies. In addition, WESTLAW provides the Restatements of the Law, including the *Restatement (Second) of Conflicts*, the *Restatement (Second) of Contracts*, the *Restatement (Second) of Judgments*, the *Restatement (Second) of Restitution* and the *Restatement (Second) of Torts*. Texts and periodicals databases contain information and publications such as *Punitive Damages*. DIALOG on WESTLAW databases provide you with vast amounts of additional information necessary for a complete analysis of possible remedies. The West Topic and Key Number System allows you to search for case law specifically on your point of law. With WESTLAW, unparalleled resources are at your fingertips.

Additional Resources

If you have not used WESTLAW or have questions not addressed in this appendix, see the *WESTLAW Reference Manual* or contact the West Reference Attorneys at 1–800–688–6363. The West Reference Attorneys are trained, licensed attorneys, available throughout the work day and on weekends to answer your WESTLAW or West book research questions.

Section 2. Databases for Remedies Law Research

Each database on WESTLAW is assigned an abbreviation called an identifier, which you use to access the database. You can find identifiers for all databases in the WESTLAW Directory and in the *WESTLAW Database List.* When you need to know more detailed information about a database, use the Scope command; type **sc** followed by the database identifier. Scope displays coverage, unique commands and related databases for each database and service.

The chart below lists WESTLAW databases that contain information on remedies law. Because new information is continually being added to WESTLAW, you should check the WESTLAW Directory for any new database information.

Description	Database Identifier	Coverage (see Scope for more specific information)
FEDERAL DATABASES		
Case Law		
Combined Federal Cases	ALLFEDS	Varies by court
U.S. Supreme Court Cases	SCT	From 1945 *
U.S. Courts of Appeals Cases	CTA	From 1945 *
Individual Courts of Appeals	CTA1–CTA11 CTAF CTADC	Varies by court
U.S. District Court Cases	DCT	Varies by court
Statutes and Regulations		
U.S. Code Annotated®	USCA	Current
Federal Register	FR	From July 1980
Code of Federal Regulations	CFR	Current
STATE DATABASES		
Case Law from all 50 states and the District of Columbia	ALLSTATES	Varies by state
Individual State Cases **	XX–CS	Varies by state
State Statutes–Annotated Statutes and annotations from all available states, the District of Columbia, Puerto Rico and the Virgin Islands	ST–ANN–ALL	Varies by state
State Statutes–Unannotated Statutes from all 50 states, the District of Columbia, Puerto Rico and the Virgin Islands	STAT–ALL	Current
Individual State Statutes–Annotated **	XX–ST–ANN	Current

Description	Database Identifier	Coverage (see Scope for more specific information)
Individual State Statutes–Unannotated **	XX–ST	Current
Individual State Statute Indexes **	XX–ST–IDX	Varies by state
General index references for the statutes and constitutions of all available states and the District of Columbia		

TEXTS & TREATISES

Law Reviews, Texts and Bar Journals	TP	Varies by title
Restatements of the Law	REST	
Restatement–Agency	REST–AGEN	
Restatement–Conflicts	REST–CONFL	
Restatement–Contracts	REST–CONTR	
Restatement–Judgments	REST–JUDG	
Restatement–Property	REST–PROP	
Restatement–Restitution	REST–RESTI	
Restatement–Security	REST–SEC	
Restatement–Torts	REST–TORT	
Restatement–Trusts	REST–TRUST	

* Cases dated before 1945 are contained in databases whose identifiers end with the suffix –OLD. For example, the identifier for the Federal Energy–Supreme Court Cases–Before 1945 database is FEN–SCT–OLD. Coverage for federal databases whose identifiers end with the suffix –OLD is 1789–1944. Coverage for the ALL-STATES–OLD database varies by state.

** XX is a state's two-letter postal abbreviation.

Section 3. Menu–Driven WESTLAW: EZ ACCESS™

EZ ACCESS is West Publishing Company's menu-driven research system. It is ideal for new or infrequent WESTLAW users because it requires no experience or training on WESTLAW.

To access EZ ACCESS, type **ez.** Whenever you are unsure of the next step, or if the choice you want is not listed, simply type **ez;** additional choices will be displayed. Once you retrieve documents with EZ ACCESS, use standard WESTLAW commands to browse your documents. For more information on browsing documents, see the *WESTLAW Reference Manual.*

Section 4. Retrieving a Document With a Citation: Find and Jump

Find is a WESTLAW service that allows you to retrieve a document by entering its citation. Find allows you to retrieve documents from anywhere in WESTLAW without accessing or changing databases or losing your search result. Find is available for many documents including case law (federal and state), state statutes, the *United States Code Annotated,* the *Code of Federal Regulations,* the *Federal Register,* and state and federal public laws.

To use Find, type **fi** followed by the document citation. Below is a list of examples.

To Find This Document:	Type:
California Federal Bank v. Matreyek, 1992 WL 165766	**fi 1992 wl 165766**
Grill v. Hunt, 7 Cal.Rptr.2d 768	**fi 7 cal.rptr.2d 768**
15 U.S.C.A. § 78u–2	**fi 15 usca 78u–2**

To Find This Document:	Type:
57 Federal Register 8964	**fi 57 fr 8964**
1 Code of Federal Regulations	**fi 1 cfr 305.82–6**
§ 305.82–6 *	
United States Public Law 102–306 *	**fi us pl 102–306**

> * To retrieve historical versions of the U.S.C.A., C.F.R. or public laws using a citation, access the appropriate database and search for your terms in the citation field.

Use Jump to retrieve a case or U.S.C.A. section cited in a case you are viewing. Click your mouse on the > or ► symbol displayed before the citation, or press the **Tab** key until the cursor reaches the desired location, then press **Enter.** The cited document will be displayed automatically.

Section 5.   Query Formulation

Overview: A query is a request you make to WESTLAW specifying the information you wish to retrieve. The terms in a query are words or numbers that you include in your request so that WESTLAW will retrieve documents containing those words or numbers. These terms are linked together by connectors, which specify the relationship in which the terms must appear.

5.1   Terms

Plurals and Possessives: Plurals are automatically retrieved when you enter the singular form of a term. This is true for both regular and irregular plurals (e.g., **child** retrieves *children*). If you enter the plural form of a term, you will not retrieve the singular form.

If you enter the non-possessive form of a term, WESTLAW automatically retrieves the possessive form as well. However, if you enter the possessive form, only the possessive form is retrieved.

Automatic Equivalencies: Some terms have alternative forms or equivalencies; for example, 5 and *five* are equivalent terms. WESTLAW automatically retrieves equivalent terms. The *WESTLAW Reference Manual* contains a list of equivalent terms.

Compound Words and Acronyms: When a compound word is one of your search terms, use a hyphen to retrieve all forms of the word. For example, the term **long-term** retrieves *long-term, long term* and *longterm.*

When using an acronym as a search term, place a period after each of the letters in the acronym to retrieve any of its forms. For example, the term **t.r.o.** retrieves *tro, t.r.o, t r o* and *t. r. o.*

Root Expander and Universal Character: Placing a root expander (!) at the end of a root term generates ALL other terms with that root. For example, adding the ! symbol to the root *develop* in the query

develop! /s covenant

instructs WESTLAW to retrieve such words as *develop, develops, developed, developer, developing* and *development.*

The universal character (*) stands for one character and can be inserted in the middle or at the end of a term. For example, the term

s**holder**

will retrieve *shareholder* and *stockholder*. But adding only two asterisks to the root *jur* in the query

jur**

instructs WESTLAW to retrieve all forms of the root with up to two additional characters. Terms like *jury* or *juror* are retrieved by this query. However, terms with more than two letters following the root, such as *jurisdiction,* are not retrieved. Plurals are always retrieved, even if more than two letters follow the root.

Phrase Searching: To search for a phrase on WESTLAW, place it within quotation marks. For example, to search for references to the American Rule for paying attorney fees, type **"american rule"**. You should use phrase searching only when you are certain that the phrase will not appear in any other form.

5.2 Alternative Terms

After selecting the terms for your query, consider which alternative terms are necessary. For example, if you are searching for the term *contract,* you might also want to search for the term *agreement.* You should consider both synonyms and antonyms as alternative terms.

5.3 Connectors

After selecting terms and alternative terms for your query, use connectors to specify the relationship that should exist between search terms in your retrieved documents. The connectors you can use are described below:

Use:	To retrieve documents with:	Example:
& (and)	search terms in the same document	**estop! & interven!**
or (space)	one search term or the other	**punitive exemplary treble**
/p	search terms in the same paragraph	**lessee /p damages**
/s	search terms in the same sentence	**prescrip! /s easement**
+s	one search term preceding the other within the same sentence	**trespass +s case**
/n	search terms within "n" words of each other (where "n" is a number)	**attorney /5 fee**
+n	one search term preceding the other by "n" words (where "n" is a number)	**42 +5 1983**

Use:	To exclude documents with:	Example:
% (but not)	search terms following the % symbol	**cloud /s title % to (318)**

5.4 Restricting Your Search by Field

Overview: Documents in each WESTLAW database consist of several segments, or fields. One field may contain the citation, another the title, another the synopsis, and so forth. A query can be formulated to retrieve only those documents that contain search terms in a specified field. Not all databases contain the same fields. Also, depending on the database, fields of the same name may contain different types of information.

To view the fields and field content for a specific database, type **f** while in the database. Note that in some databases, not every field is available for every document. To restrict your search to a specific field, type the field name or abbreviation followed by search terms enclosed in parentheses. For example, to retrieve a case entitled *Alexander v. McKnight,* restrict your search to the title field:

ti(alexander & mcknight)

The fields discussed below are available in WESTLAW databases you might use for remedies law research.

Digest and Synopsis Fields: The digest and synopsis fields, provided in case law databases by West Publishing Company's editors, summarize the main points of a case. A search in these fields is useful because it retrieves only cases in which a search term was significant enough to be included in a summary.

Consider restricting your search to one or both of these fields if

- you are searching for common terms or terms with more than one meaning, and you need to narrow your search; or

- you cannot narrow your search by moving to a smaller database.

For example, to retrieve New York cases that discuss whether a buyer of real estate can rescind the purchase if the seller fraudulently misrepresented the property, access the New York Real Property Cases database (NYRP–CS) and type a query such as the following:

sy,di(buy! purchas! /s estate home house /p fraud!
misrepresent! represent! /p resci!)

Headnote Field: The headnote field is a part of the digest field, but does not contain the topic number, the key number, the case citation or the title. The headnote field contains only the one-sentence summary of the point of law and any supporting statutory citations given by the author of the opinion. A headnote field search is useful when you are searching for specific code sections or rule numbers. For example, to retrieve headnotes that cite 17 U.S.C.A. § 502, type the following query:

he(17 +5 502)

Topic Field: The topic field is also a part of the digest field. It contains the West digest topic name and number, the key number, and the key line text. You should include a topic field search in your query if

- a digest field search retrieves too many documents; or

- you want to retrieve cases with digest paragraphs classified under more than one topic.

When a digest search retrieves too many cases, search for a topic by its number, e.g., type **to(212)** to search for topic 212, *Injunction.* To retrieve federal antitrust cases that discuss the requirement that there be no adequate remedy at law in order for an injunction to issue, access the Federal Antitrust & Trade Regulation—Federal Cases database (FATR–CS) and type a query like the following:

to(212) /p damages /p adequa! inadequa!

Use the second type of topic field search to retrieve West headnotes classified under more than one topic. Search for the topic name in the topic field; for example, to search for state cases that discuss damages assessed against brokers who fraudulently misrepresent real estate, access the Multistate Real Property Cases database (MRP–CS) and type a query like the following:

to(damages) /p fraud! misrepresent! represent! /p land "real estate" property /p broker! realtor realty

The TOPIC database contains a complete list of West Digest topics and their corresponding topic numbers. Some West Digest topics that might be of use to you in remedies law research are listed below:

93	Contempt	279	Nuisance
150	Equity	313a	Products Liability
156	Estoppel	328	Reformation of Instruments
212	Injunction	358	Specific Performance
250	Mandamus	379	Torts

Be aware that slip opinions and cases from looseleaf services do not contain the synopsis, digest, headnote or topic fields.

Prelim and Caption Fields: When searching in a database containing statutes or regulations, restrict your search to the prelim and caption fields to retrieve documents in which your terms are important enough to appear in a section name or heading. For example, to retrieve Illinois statutes discussing the payment of attorney fees in actions for violation of the state's electronic funds transfer act, access the Illinois Statutes—Annotated database (IL–ST–ANN) and type the following:

pr,ca(bank savings fund & electronic & attorney /3 fee)

5.5 Restricting Your Search by Date

You can instruct WESTLAW to retrieve documents *decided or issued* before, after, or on a specified date, as well as within a range of dates. The following are examples of queries that contain date restrictions:

da(bef 1991 & aft 1986) & delay +2 rental

da(1990) & delay +2 rental

da(4/26/90) & delay +2 rental

You can also instruct WESTLAW to retrieve documents *added to a database* on or after a specified date, as well as within a range of dates. The following are examples of queries that contain added date restrictions:

ad(aft 1–1–89) & delay +2 rental

ad(aft 2–1–91 & bef 3–1–91) & delay +2 rental

Section 6. Verifying Your Research With Citators

Overview: WESTLAW contains four citator services that assist you in checking the validity of cases and statutes you are relying on. These four citator services—Insta–Cite®, Shepard's® Citations, Shepard's PreView™ and Quick*Cite*™—help you perform many valuable research tasks, saving you hours of manual research. Sections 6.1 through 6.4 provide further information on these services.

For citations that are not covered by one of these services, a fifth technique, called *using WESTLAW as a citator,* can assist you. Section 6.5 explains how to use this technique.

6.1 Insta–Cite

Insta–Cite is West Publishing Company's case history and citation verification service. It is the most current case history service available. Use Insta–Cite to see if your case is still good law. Insta–Cite provides the following types of information about a citation:

Direct History. In addition to reversals and affirmances, Insta–Cite gives you the complete reported history of a litigated matter including any related cases. Insta–Cite provides the federal direct history of a case from 1754 and the state direct history from 1879. Related references (cases related to the litigation) are provided from 1983 to date.

Negative Indirect History. Insta–Cite lists subsequent cases that have a substantial negative impact on your case, including cases overruling your case or calling it into question. Cases affected by decisions from 1972 to date will be displayed on Insta–Cite. To retrieve negative indirect history prior to 1972, use Shepard's Citations (discussed in Section 6.2).

Secondary Source References. Insta–Cite also provides references to secondary sources that cite your case. These secondary sources currently include the legal encyclopedia *Corpus Juris Secundum* ®.

Parallel Citations. Insta–Cite provides parallel citations for cases including citations to *U.S. Law Week* ®, *The Labor Relations Reference Manual* ® and many other looseleaf reporters.

Citation Verification. Insta–Cite confirms that you have the correct volume and page number for a case. Citation verification information is available from 1754 for federal cases and from 1879 for state cases.

6.2 Shepard's Citations

Shepard's provides a comprehensive list of cases and publications that have cited a particular case or statute. Shepard's also includes explanatory analysis to indicate how the citing cases have treated the case, e.g., "followed," "explained". For statutes, Shepard's includes analysis codes such as "amended," "repealed," "constitutional" or "unconstitutional."

In addition to citations from federal, state, and regional citators, Shepard's on WESTLAW includes citations from specialized citators, such as *Product Liability Citations.*

6.3 Shepard's PreView

Shepard's PreView gives you a preview of citing cases from West's® National Reporter System® that will appear in Shepard's Citations. Depending on the citation, Shepard's PreView provides citing information days, weeks or even months before the same information appears in Shepard's online. Use Shepard's PreView to update your Shepard's results.

6.4 Quick*Cite*

Quick*Cite* is a citator service that enables you to update case law by retrieving the most recent citing cases on WESTLAW, including slip opinions, automatically.

There is a four- to six-week gap between a citing case's availability on WESTLAW and its listing in Shepard's PreView. This gap occurs because cases go through an editorial process at West before they are added to Shepard's PreView. To retrieve the most recent citing cases, therefore, you need to search case law databases on WESTLAW for references to your case. Quick*Cite* does this for you automatically by retrieving and displaying the complete text of recent citing cases.

Quick*Cite* formulates a query using the title, the case citation(s), and an added date restriction. Quick*Cite* then accesses the appropriate database, either ALLSTATES or ALLFEDS, and runs the query for you. Quick*Cite* also allows you to choose a different date range and database for your query so you can tailor it to your specific research needs.

Quick*Cite* is designed to retrieve documents that cite cases. To retrieve citing references to other documents, such as statutes and law review articles, use WESTLAW as a citator (discussed below).

6.5   Using WESTLAW as a Citator

Using WESTLAW as a citator, you can search for documents citing a specific statute, regulation, rule, agency decision or other authority. To retrieve Pennsylvania cases citing Restatement (Second) of Torts § 905, for example, access the Pennsylvania Cases database (PA–CS) and search for the citation alone:

rest restatement /s torts /9 905

If the citation is not a unique term, add descriptive terms. For example, to retrieve cases citing injunctive relief under California Government Code § 12900, the California Fair Employment and Housing Act, access the California Civil Rights–Cases database (CACIV–CS) and type a query like the following:

12900 /p injunct! enjoin!

6.6   Citator Commands

The following are some of the commands that can be used in the citator services. For a complete list, see the *WESTLAW User Guide* or the *WESTLAW Reference Manual.*

Type:	To retrieve:
ic xxx or **ic**	an Insta–Cite result when followed by a case citation (where xxx is the citation), or when entered from a displayed case, Shepard's result or Shepard's PreView result.
sh xxx or **sh**	a Shepard's result when followed by a case or statute citation (where xxx is the citation), or when entered from a displayed case, Insta–Cite result or Shepard's PreView result.
sp xxx or **sp**	a Shepard's PreView result when followed by a case citation (where xxx is the citation), or when entered from a displayed case, Insta–Cite result or Shepard's result.
qc xxx or **qc**	a Quick*Cite* result when followed by a case citation (where xxx is the citation), or when entered from a displayed case, Insta–Cite result, Shepard's result or Shepard's PreView result.
sc xx	the scope of coverage (where xx is the citator).
sh sc xxx	the scope of coverage for a specific publication in Shepard's, where xxx is the publication abbreviation (e.g., **sh empl prac dec**).
xx pubs	a list of publication abbreviations available with the citator (where xx is the citator).

Type:	To retrieve:
xx cmds	a list of commands (where xx is the citator).

Section 7.   Research Examples

7.1   Retrieving Law Review Articles

A colleague refers you to a law review article by R.B. Graves, III, *Bad–Faith Denial of Insurance Claims: Whose Faith, Whose Punishment? An Examination of Punitive Damages and Vicarious Liability,* 65 Tul.L.Rev. 395 (1990).   How can you retrieve the article on WESTLAW?

Solution

• If you know the citation, access the Tulane Law Review database (TLNLR). Search for terms from the citation in the citation field:

ci(65   +5   395)

• If you know the title of the article, but not which journal it appears in, access the Insurance—Law Reviews, Texts and Bar Journals database (IN–TP).   Search for key terms in the title field:

ti(bad-faith   &   punitive)

7.2   Retrieving Statutes

You need to retrieve any California statutes that discuss injunctions and attorneys fees for filing suit to force release of personal information from the government.

Solution

• Access the California Statutes—Annotated database (CA–ST–ANN). Search for your terms in the prelim and caption fields:

pr,ca(inform! data   &   injunct! enjoin! & attorney   /3   fee)

• When you know the citation for a specific section of a state statute, use Find to retrieve the statute.   (Note: For more information on Find, see Section 4 of this appendix.)   For example, to retrieve California Civil Code § 3336, discussing damages for conversion of personal property, type

fi ca civil s 3336

• To look at surrounding statutory sections, use the Documents in Sequence command.   To retrieve the section preceding § 3336, type **d-**.   To retrieve the section immediately following § 3336, type **d**.

• To see if a statute has been amended or repealed, use the Update service. Simply type **update** while viewing the statute to display any legislation that amends or repeals the statute.

Remember that because slip copy versions of laws are added to WESTLAW before they contain full editorial enhancements, they are not retrieved with Update.   To retrieve slip copy versions of laws, access the United States Public Laws database by typing **db us-pl** (or access the appropriate state legislative service database by typing **db xx-legis**, where xx is the state's two-letter postal abbreviation) and then type **ci(slip)** and descriptive terms, e.g., **ci(slip) & civil +5 3336**.   Slip copy documents are replaced by the editorially enhanced versions within a few working days.

Update also does not retrieve legislation that enacts a new statute or covers a topic that will not be incorporated into the statutes. To retrieve this legislation, access US–PL (or access the appropriate state legislative service database, e.g., the California Legislative Service database (CA–LEGIS)) and enter a query containing terms that describe the new legislation.

7.3 Retrieving Federal Regulations

Your client is concerned that the Resolution Trust Corporation (RTC) is going to rescind its contract with him. You know that 12 C.F.R. § 1606.15 governs the RTC's contract rescission powers. You want to look at this regulation to see if it can help your client.

Solution

- Because you have the citation, use Find; type **fi 12 cfr s 1606.15**.

- After retrieving this regulation, use Update to display any document from the *Federal Register* that amends or repeals this regulation; type **update**.

7.4 Retrieving Restatement Provisions

Your client lives in a house with several housing code violations. He has contacted the landlord and asked for repairs, but the landlord has not responded. Your client wants to know if he can withhold rent until the problems are fixed. According to the *Restatement (Second) of Property,* what options does your client have?

Solution

- Access the Restatement of the Law–Property database (REST–PROP) by typing **db rest-prop**. Formulate a query to search for documents that discuss rent withholding. Limit your search to the title and prelim fields to retrieve documents specifically addressing your issue, and type a query like the following:

    ti,pr(rent! & abat! withh*ld!)

7.5 Retrieving Employment Discrimination Decisions

Your client, a resident of California, alleges she was terminated from her job in retaliation for her complaints about her work environment. She wants to know if she can be reinstated and receive punitive damages.

Solution

- Access the California Labor & Employment–Cases database (CALB–CS) by typing **db calb-cs**; then type a query containing descriptive terms:

    retaliat! /s discharg! fir*** terminat! /p reinstat!
    damages exemplary punitive treble

7.6 Using Citator Services

One of the cases retrieved with your query is *Garcia v. Rockwell International Corp.,* 187 Cal.App.3d 1556. You wish to see if this case is still good law and if other cases have cited this case.

Solution

- Use Insta–Cite to retrieve the direct history and negative indirect history of *Garcia*.   While viewing the case, type **ic**.
- You want to Shepardize *Garcia*.   Type **sh**.

    Limit your Shepard's result to decisions containing a reference to a specific headnote, such as headnote one.   Type **Loc 1**.

    - Check Shepard's PreView for more current cases citing *Garcia*.   Type **sp**.

    - Check Quick*Cite* for the most current cases citing *Garcia*.   Type **qc** and follow the online instructions.

Table of Cases

A

Ablah v. Eyman—§ 4.3(2), n. 34; § 4.3(5), n. 19; § 5.18(2); § 5.18(2), n. 17.

Ace Truck and Equipment Rentals, Inc. v. Kahn—§ 3.11(14), n. 9.

Acme Delivery Service, Inc. v. Samsonite Corp.—§ 5.13(3), n. 15.

Acquisition of Real Property by the City of Albany, Matter of—§ 3.5, n. 49, 53.

Actors' Equity Ass'n v. American Dinner Theatre Institute—§ 3.10(3), n. 41.

Adams v. Crater Well Drilling, Inc.—§ 3.11(1), n. 85.

Adams v. Fleck—§ 5.18(3), n. 7.

Adams v. Murakami—§ 3.11(1), n. 48; § 3.11(5); § 3.11(5), n. 7, 10.

Adams v. Zayre Corp.—§ 3.11(6), n. 6.

Adams County Election Com'n v. Sanders—§ 2.9(5), n. 10; § 2.11(2), n. 4, 22.

Adel v. Parkhurst—§ 3.11(5), n. 7.

Adolph Coors Co. v. A & S Wholesalers, Inc.—§ 2.11(3), n. 10.

Adolph Rub Trust, First Trust Co. of North Dakota v. Rub—§ 2.6(4), n. 26.

Adoption of W.A.T., Matter of—§ 2.4(2), n. 7.

Aebig v. Commercial Bank of Seattle—§ 4.3(2), n. 12; § 6.1(3), n. 6, 13.

Aerodex, Inc., United States v.—§ 3.12, n. 42.

Aetna Cas. and Sur. Co. v. Craig—§ 3.11(7), n. 6.

Aetna Cas. and Sur. Co. v. Eberheim—§ 4.9(4), n. 26.

Afram Export Corp. v. Metallurgiki Halyps, S.A.—§ 12.4(5), n. 14, 16.

Afro-American Pub. Co. v. Jaffe—§ 3.11(5), n. 38.

Agency Holding Corp. v. Malley–Duff & Associates, Inc.—§ 3.12, n. 19.

Agfa-Gevaert, A.G. v. A.B. Dick Co.—§ 3.7, n. 14.

Ahern Co. v. John Bowen Co., Inc.—§ 4.6, n. 19; § 13.3(2), n. 15.

Ahles v. Aztec Enterprises, Inc.—§ 5.13(2), n. 12.

Ainsworth v. Combined Ins. Co. of America—§ 3.11(2), n. 37; § 3.11(5), n. 1.

Alabama ex rel. Siegelman, State of v. United States E.P.A.—§ 2.11(3), n. 36.

Alabama Mobile Homes, Inc., Ex parte—§ 6.1(4), n. 23.

Alaska Airlines v. Stephenson—§ 13.2(5), n. 15, 21.

Alaska Ins. Co. v. Movin' On Const., Inc.—§ 3.11(11), n. 2.

Alaskan Village, Inc. v. Smalley, for and on Behalf of Smalley—§ 3.11(6), n. 8.

Alaska Sales and Service, Inc. v. Millet—§ 4.9(4), n. 13.

Alberti v. Klevenhagen—§ 3.10(10), n. 9.

Albre Marble and Tile Co., Inc. v. John Bowen Co., Inc.—§ 13.3(2), n. 22, 23.

Alburger v. Philadelphia Elec. Co.—§ 5.10(3), n. 46.

Aldrich v. Geahry—§ 2.5(2), n. 5.

Alemite Mfg. Corporation v. Staff—§ 2.8(5); § 2.8(5), n. 13.

Alexander v. Alexander—§ 2.8(8), n. 7.

Alger v. Davis—§ 5.17(3), n. 3.

Allanson v. Cummings—§ 5.15(2), n. 14, 28, 70.

Allcard v. Skinner—§ 2.4(4), n. 30.

Allen, In re Marriage of—§ 4.3(2), n. 1, 55; § 4.3(3), n. 3, 6, 11; § 4.7(1), n. 6, 10; § 4.9(5), n. 8.

Allen v. Fox—§ 5.15(2), n. 28.

Allen v. Hannaford—§ 7.3(2), n. 9.

Allen v. Seacoast Products, Inc.—§ 8.1(1), n. 8.

Allen v. Simmons—§ 3.11(7), n. 6.

Allied Industries Intern., Inc. v. AGFA–Gevaert, Inc.—§ 2.8(1), n. 36.

Allis v. Allis—§ 2.7, n. 22.

All Stainless, Inc. v. Colby—§ 2.11(3), n. 46.

Allstate Ins. Co. v. Starke—§ 3.6(1), n. 10; § 3.6(3), n. 4.

Almota Farmers Elevator & Warehouse Co. v. United States—§ 3.4, n. 26; § 3.5, n. 54; § 5.2(6), n. 3.

Alpern v. Coe—§ 2.8(1), n. 15.

Aluminum Co. of America v. Essex Group, Inc.—§ 4.3(7), n. 12.

Aluminum Industrie Vaassen V.B. v. Romalpa Aluminum Ltd.—§ 6.1(4), n. 10.

Alyeska Pipeline Service Co. v. Anderson—§ 3.6(4), n. 7.

Alyeska Pipeline Service Co. v. Wilderness Soc.—§ 3.10(1), n. 1; § 3.10(4); § 3.10(4), n. 23.

Amalgamated Ass'n of St. Elec. Ry. and Motor Coach Employees of America, Division 998 v. Danielson—§ 4.6, n. 14.

Ambassador Steel Co. v. Ewald Steel Co.—§ 3.9, n. 8.

American Academy of Pediatrics v. Van de Kamp—§ 2.11(2), n. 12.

American Air Filter Co., Inc. v. McNichol—§ 6.6(3), n. 2.

American Cyanamid Co. v. Sterling Drug, Inc.—§ 4.3(5), n. 34.

American Enka Co. v. Wicaco Mach. Corp.—§ 3.6(1), n. 11; § 5.13(2), n. 3.

American Hosp. Supply Corp. v. Hospital Products Ltd.—§ 2.11(2); § 2.11(2), n. 12, 14.

American List Corp. v. United States News and World Report, Inc.—§ 3.3(3), n. 2.

American Nat. Bank and Trust Co. of Chicago v. Weyerhaeuser Co.—§ 4.3(4), n. 8, 9.

American Nursing Resources, Inc. v. Forrest T. Jones & Co., Inc.—§ 4.3(4), n. 3.

American Re–Insurance Co. v. MGIC Inv. Corp.—§ 6.1(5), n. 18.

American Ry. Exp. Co. v. Houle—§ 4.3(2), n. 22.

American Sur. Co. of New York v. Gold—§ 3.11(7), n. 6.

American Surety Co. v. Bethlehem Nat. Bank—§ 4.3(4), n. 4, 12, 16, 18.

American Tel. & Tel. Co. v. Connecticut Light & Power Co.—§ 5.15(2); § 5.15(2), n. 44, 62.

Amiss v. State—§ 4.5(2), n. 24.

Amoco Production Co. v. Village of Gambell, AK—§ 2.10, n. 20.

AM/PM Franchise Ass'n v. Atlantic Richfield Co.—§ 3.3(4), n. 8.

Anchor Coatings, Inc. v. Marine Indus. Residential Insulation, Inc.—§ 12.2(2), n. 30.

Anchor Motor Freight, Inc. v. International Broth. of Teamsters, Chauffeurs, Warehousemen & Helpers of America, Local Union No. 377—§ 3.10(3), n. 20.

Andersen v. Edwards—§ 5.1, n. 13; § 5.2(1), n. 14; § 5.2(2), n. 21.

Anderson v. St. Mary's Hospital—§ 2.8(3), n. 6.

Anderson v. Turner—§ 5.10(3), n. 23.

Anderson Cotton Mills v. Royal Mfg. Co.—§ 10.6, n. 3.

Andre v. Morrow—§ 2.7, n. 22.

Andrews v. Mosley Well Service—§ 8.1(4), n. 41.

Anson v. Grace—§ 4.8, n. 7.

Antokol v. Barber—§ 5.15(2), n. 17, 26, 57.

Appalachian Power Co. v. Morrison—§ 5.14(3), n. 30.

Aradia Women's Health Center v. Operation Rescue—§ 2.8(3); § 2.8(3), n. 21.

Arcambel v. Wiseman—§ 3.10(1), n. 6.

A & R Co. v. Union Air Transport, Inc.—§ 13.2(5), n. 6.

Arevalo–Franco v. United States I.N.S.—§ 3.10(6), n. 28.

Arizona Governing Committee for Tax Deferred Annuity and Deferred Compensation Plans v. Norris—§ 8.5(2), n. 18.

Arkansas Louisiana Gas Co. v. Cutrer—§ 5.10(3), n. 44.

Arkansas State Highway Commission v. Wilmans—§ 3.5, n. 51.

Armstrong v. Dantoni—§ 2.1(2), n. 12.

Armstrong v. Roger's Outdoor Sports, Inc.—§ 3.11(12), n. 24.

Arnold v. Arizona Dept. of Health Services—§ 3.10(2), n. 27, 28.

Arnold v. Burgess—§ 3.6(2), n. 20.

Aronowitz v. Woollard—§ 10.5(1), n. 16.

Arris v. Stukely—§ 4.2(3), n. 10, 11.

Arrott v. Smith—§ 12.11(1), n. 29.

Artesian Water Co. v. Government of New Castle County—§ 5.2(5), n. 2.

Artist M. v. Johnson—§ 2.5(2), n. 3; § 2.11(1), n. 26.

Asbestos School Litigation, In re—§ 2.9(4), n. 35.

Ashley v. Atlantic Richfield Co.—§ 3.10(2), n. 12.

Associated Truck Lines, Inc. v. Baer—§ 2.8(1), n. 15.

Atlas, Inc. v. United States—§ 4.3(2), n. 21; § 6.1(3), n. 16.

Atokad Agr. and Racing Ass'n v. Governors of the Knights of Ak–Sar–Ben—§ 3.6(1), n. 27.

Attorney General v. Thomas Solvent Co.—§ 5.17(3), n. 5.

Ault v. Lohr—§ 3.11(10), n. 2, 16.

Austin, City of v. Teague—§ 6.9(2), n. 5, 6.

Austrian Motors, Ltd. v. Travelers Ins. Co.—§ 4.5(3), n. 33; § 4.9(5), n. 8.

Ayers v. Jackson Tp.—§ 5.1, n. 19; § 5.6(2), n. 19; § 8.1(3), n. 34; § 8.10, n. 19.

B

Bachmann v. Glazer & Glazer, Inc.—§ 4.3(4), n. 8, 9, 15, 17.

Bagley v. Shortt—§ 3.11(12), n. 35, 36; § 8.8, n. 10.

Bailey v. Tully—§ 2.7, n. 22.

Baker v. Bolton—§ 8.3(1), n. 4.

Baker v. Burbank–Glendale–Pasadena Airport Authority—§ 5.11(3), n. 5.

Baker v. Carr—§ 2.9(5), n. 5.

Baker v. Willoughby—§ 9.2(6), n. 14.

Baker v. New York Nat. Exch. Bank—§ 6.1(4), n. 27.

Baker v. Simmons Co.—§ 4.5(3), n. 10.

Baldwin v. Childs—§ 4.7(1), n. 5.

Baldwin v. Miles—§ 2.8(7), n. 12; § 5.7(3), n. 15.

Baldwin–United Corp. (Single Premium Deferred Annuities Ins. Litigation), In re—§ 2.8(5), n. 27.

Ball v. Mudge—§ 8.2, n. 55.

Balter v. Regan—§ 2.8(6), n. 2.

Baltimore, The—§ 5.14(3), n. 3, 29.

Baltimore and Ohio R. Co. v. Commercial Transport, Inc.—§ 5.14(2), n. 3.

Banco Cafetero Panama, United States v.—§ 6.1(4), n. 13, 18.

Bangert v. Emmco Ins. Co.—§ 5.16(3), n. 6.

Bani–Esraili v. Lerman—§ 8.2, n. 13.

Banker v. Bath Iron Works Corp.—§ 5.7(3), n. 14.

Bank of Alton v. Tanaka—§ 13.2(5), n. 9.

Bank of America v. J. & S. Auto Repairs—§ 4.9(5), n. 8, 9.

Bank of Kansas v. Hutchinson Health Services, Inc.—§ 6.1(4), n. 10.

Banque Worms v. BankAmerica Intern., 928 F.2d 538—§ 4.7(2), n. 9.

Banque Worms v. BankAmerica Intern., 568 N.Y.S.2d 541—§ 4.7(2); § 4.7(2), n. 9, 17, 20.

Banton v. Hackney—§ 4.3(4), n. 17.

Barbian v. Lindner Bros. Trucking Co., Inc.—§ 5.7(2), n. 32.

Barbouti v. Lysandrou—§ 1.3, n. 5; § 4.2(3), n. 37.

Bardwell v. Parish Council of Parish of East Baton Rouge—§ 2.9(5), n. 10.

Bargain Mart, Inc. v. Lipkis—§ 12.15(2), n. 34.

Barnes v. Culver—§ 7.3(2), n. 12.

Barnsdall, City of v. Curnutt—§ 4.5(4), n. 17; § 13.3(2); § 13.3(2), n. 17, 23.

Barrois v. Nelda Faye, Inc.—§ 2.4(4), n. 38.

Barth v. Firestone Tire and Rubber Co.—§ 8.10, n. 19.

Bartholomew v. Jackson—§ 4.9(4), n. 2.

Bartlett v. Menard—§ 5.13(1), n. 11.

Barton v. Borit—§ 5.13(3), n. 5.

Bastian v. Petren Resources Corp.—§ 9.2(6), n. 6.

Baumann, People v.—§ 2.8(2), n. 6.

Bauserman v. Digiulian—§ 4.3(8), n. 15.

Baxter House, Inc. v. Rosen—§ 4.3(5), n. 17.

B Bar Enterprises, Inc., State v.—§ 5.17(3), n. 7.

Beachcomber Coins, Inc. v. Boskett—§ 4.1(2), n. 12.

Beacon Theatres, Inc. v. Westover—§ 1.2, n. 3; § 2.6(3), n. 45; § 2.6(4); § 2.6(4), n. 25.

Bead Chain Mfg. Co. v. Saxton Products, Inc.—§ 5.14(2), n. 11.

Beams v. Werth—§ 4.7(1), n. 8.

Bear Creek Planning Committee v. Title Ins. & Trust Co.—§ 3.6(1), n. 19.

Beard v. Dugdale—§ 3.10(3), n. 9.

Beard v. S/E Joint Venture—§ 12.8(1), n. 34.

Beardsley v. Wierdsma—§ 8.2, n. 32.

Beasley v. Mellon Financial Services Corp.—§ 4.3(7), n. 3.

Beaulieu v. Elliott—§ 3.7, n. 7.

Beaver v. Country Mut. Ins. Co.—§ 3.11(7), n. 6.

Beavers v. Weatherly—§ 4.9(5), n. 17.

Bechtel v. Liberty Nat. Bank—§ 3.3(7), n. 1; § 9.2(1), n. 19, 21, 23.

Beck v. Allison—§ 12.8(3), n. 5.

Beck v. Lawler—§ 3.6(1), n. 25; § 3.6(2), n. 3.

Becker v. Schwartz—§ 8.2, n. 8, 21.

Beckman v. Cox Broadcasting Corp.—§ 12.-22(2), n. 9.

Bedford Associates, United States v.—§ 4.7(2), n. 15.

Beech v. Ragnar Benson, Inc.—§ 2.4(4), n. 9.

Beesley v. Hartford Fire Ins. Co.—§ 2.6(3), n. 61.

Bell v. Carver—§ 13.3(2), n. 15.

Bell v. Killian—§ 6.1(4), n. 16.

Bellon v. Malnar—§ 3.6(2), n. 14.

Bendick v. Cambio—§ 2.6(4), n. 20.

Benedict v. Little—§ 2.3(5), n. 2.

Benham v. World Airways, Inc.—§ 3.4, n. 7.

Benitez, United States v.—§ 6.1(4), n. 29.

Bennett v. Emerald Service, Inc.—§ 4.8, n. 8, 18.

Bennett Leasing Co. v. Ellison—§ 4.5(4), n. 2; § 13.2(2), n. 27.

Berger v. Malneut Realty Corp.—§ 5.10(1), n. 5.

Berglund v. American Multigraph Sales Co.—§ 13.4(2), n. 27.

Berman v. Allan—§ 8.2, n. 19.

Berry, In re—§ 2.8(6), n. 9, 12, 15.

Berry v. Barbour—§ 4.9(1), n. 4; § 4.9(5); § 4.9(5), n. 5.

Berry Contracting, Inc. v. Coastal States Petrochemical Co.—§ 5.15(2), n. 7.

Berryhill v. Hatt—§ 12.5(2), n. 1.

Bertero v. National General Corp.—§ 3.10(3), n. 35.

Besinger v. National Tea Co.—§ 2.5(4), n. 10; § 12.8(3), n. 5.

B.F. Goodrich Co. v. Wohlgemuth—§ 10.5(3), n. 61.

B.G.H. Ins. Syndicate, Inc. v. Presidential Fire & Cas. Co.—§ 2.5(1), n. 12.

Big Bear Properties, Inc. v. Gherman—§ 3.6(4), n. 7.

Big Value Supermarkets, Inc., United States v.—§ 4.3(8), n. 3.

Billings Clinic v. Peat Marwick Main & Co.—§ 3.6(2), n. 12.

Bingham v. Bridges—§ 13.2(2), n. 6.

Birchfield v. Texarkana Memorial Hosp.—§ 3.12, n. 27.

Birge v. Toppers Menswear, Inc.—§ 12.15(2), n. 2.

Bishop v. Bishop—§ 2.8(3), n. 6.

Bishop v. Kelly—§ 3.12, n. 1.

Bishop v. Poore—§ 8.1(2), n. 7.

Bishop Processing Co. v. Davis—§ 2.4(6), n. 5.

Biswell v. Duncan—§ 3.11(1), n. 75; § 3.11(3), n. 26.

Bitter Root Development Co., United States v.—§ 5.18(3), n. 27.

Blackford v. Dickey—§ 4.9(3), n. 18.

Blackwell's Island Bridge in City of New York, In re—§ 3.5, n. 53.

Blades v. White Motor Credit Corp.—§ 5.13(1), n. 32; § 5.15(3), n. 1.

Blaising v. Mills—§ 9.3(4), n. 5.

Blake v. Cruz—§ 8.2, n. 47.

Blanchard v. Bergeron—§ 3.10(5), n. 2; § 3.10(7), n. 11.

Blank v. Rodgers—§ 4.5(2), n. 15; § 13.2(2), n. 1, 7, 16.

Blim v. Western Elec. Co., Inc.—§ 3.12, n. 40, 43.

Block v. Block—§ 4.8, n. 19.

Blood v. Cohen—§ 5.10(3), n. 40.

Bloom v. Illinois § 2.8(4), n. 3, 16.

Blue Cross Health Services, Inc. v. Sauer—§ 2.6(3), n. 18; § 4.1(1), n. 13; § 4.3(2), n. 32.

Bluemlein v. Szepanski—§ 5.2(7), n. 2.

Blue Ridge Sewer Imp. Dist. v. Lowry and Associates, Inc.—§ 4.9(4), n. 1; § 4.9(5), n. 14.

Blue Sky Advocates v. State—§ 3.10(2), n. 30.

Blum v. Stenson—§ 3.10(5), n. 8; § 3.10(7), n. 4, 8, 11; § 3.10(8); § 3.10(10); § 3.10(10), n. 2, 5.

Blumenthal v. Merrill Lynch, Pierce, Fenner & Smith, Inc.—§ 2.11(3), n. 39, 40, 47.

Board of County Com'rs of Weld County v. Slovek—§ 5.2(1), n. 8.

Board of Public Utilities of City of Springfield v. Fenton—§ 5.14(2), n. 7; § 5.14(3), n. 24, 30.

Board of Road Com'rs of Jackson County v. O'Leary—§ 5.14(3), n. 3.

Boatmen's Nat. Co. v. M. W. Elkins & Co.—§ 9.2(6), n. 23.

Bob Ryan Leasing v. Sampair—§ 4.9(5), n. 8.

Bochar v. J. B. Martin Motors, Inc.—§ 8.1(2), n. 8.

Boehm v. French—§ 3.3(4), n. 12.

Boeing Co. v. Aetna Cas. and Sur. Co.—§ 4.1(1), n. 30; § 5.2(5), n. 22.

Boerner v. McCallister—§ 5.10(3), n. 32.

Boffard v. Barnes—§ 2.11(1), n. 27.

Bond v. A. H. Belo Corp.—§ 5.16(3), n. 10.

Bond v. City of Huntington—§ 3.6(1), n. 15; § 3.6(2), n. 5, 41; § 3.6(4), n. 25.

Bonnel v. Foulke—§ 4.2(3), n. 9.

Booker T. Washington Const. & Design Co. v. Huntington Urban Renewal Authority—§ 12.4(5), n. 14.

Boomer v. Atlantic Cement Co.—§ 2.9(2), n. 13; § 5.7(2), n. 37, 43.

Boomer v. Muir—§ 12.7(5); § 12.7(5), n. 8.

Boone v. Coe—§ 13.2(4); § 13.2(4), n. 4.

Booth v. Robertson—§ 3.11(1), n. 75.

Boris v. Heyd—§ 4.5(2), n. 21; § 9.4, n. 40.

Bornstein, United States v.—§ 1.5, n. 4; § 3.12, n. 18, 42, 46.

Borom v. City of St. Paul—§ 2.5(1), n. 12.

Bowen v. City of Kansas City—§ 5.11(1), n. 12.

Bowen v. Detroit United Ry.—§ 5.18(2), n. 4, 9, 10, 12.

Bowen v. Massachusetts—§ 3.1, n. 13.

Bowling v. Sperry—§ 13.4(2), n. 21.

Boyce v. Doyle—§ 13.4(2), n. 27.

Boyd v. Bulala—§ 8.8, n. 23.

Boyher v. Gearhart's Estate—§ 13.2(2), n. 19, 21.

Boyls v. Boyls—§ 2.8(6), n. 3.

Bradley v. American Smelting and Refining Co.—§ 5.6(1), n. 1.

Bradley v. Hooker—§ 3.3(3), n. 14.

Bradley v. School Bd. of City of Richmond—§ 3.10(6), n. 8.

Brandhagen v. Burt—§ 5.10(4), n. 17.

Brandon & Tibbs v. George Kevorkian Accountancy Corp.—§ 3.9, n. 19.

Brannigan v. Usitalo—§ 8.1(4), n. 99; § 8.8, n. 21.

Braun v. Intercontinental Bank—§ 3.10(3), n. 9.

Brazil v. City of Auburn—§ 6.9(2), n. 5.

Breese v. AWI, Inc.—§ 3.11(2), n. 37.

Brian McDonagh S.C. v. Moss—§ 12.22(2), n. 7.

Brittain v. Payne—§ 5.18(2), n. 2.

Broadworth Realty Associates v. Chock 336 B'way Operating, Inc.—§ 2.3(5), n. 6.

Brooklyn Eastern District Terminal v. United States—§ 3.4, n. 22; § 5.15(2); § 5.15(2), n. 22, 23, 45, 47, 60.

Brooks v. Andolina—§ 1.5, n. 7; § 7.4(2), n. 17.

Brooks v. Conston—§ 4.3(2), n. 15; § 4.5(3), n. 9, 16, 25.

Brooks Transp. Co. v. McCutcheon—§ 5.13(1), n. 9.

Brousseau v. Rosenthal—§ 5.15(3), n. 19; § 5.16(3), n. 9.

Brown v. Bathke—§ 3.10(9), n. 9.

Brown v. Board of Education of Topeka, Kansas, 75 S.Ct. 753—§ 1.5, n. 1, 8; § 2.9(5); § 2.9(5), n. 4; § 7.4(4), n. 9.

Brown v. Board of Education of Topeka, Shawnee County, Kan., 74 S.Ct. 686—§ 1.5; § 1.5, n. 1.

Brown v. Brown—§ 2.6(1), n. 18; § 2.8(2), n. 6.

Brown v. Campbell—§ 5.13(2), n. 7.

Brown v. County of Genesee—§ 4.3(7), n. 4.

Brown v. Frontier Theatres, Inc.—§ 5.16(3), n. 11.

Brown v. State—§ 3.10(2), n. 27, 30.

Brown v. Sullivan—§ 3.10(10), n. 8.

Brown v. Techdata Corporation, Inc.—§ 4.5(5), n. 5; § 4.8, n. 1, 9; § 9.4, n. 44.

Brown v. Trustees of Boston University—§ 2.4(6), n. 1.

Brownfield v. Daniel Freeman Marina Hosp.—§ 2.5(1), n. 12.

Browning–Ferris Industries of Vermont, Inc. v. Kelco Disposal, Inc.—§ 3.11(12), n. 11.

Brownlee v. Vang—§ 6.1(5), n. 28.

Broyles v. Broyles—§ 5.16(3), n. 2.

Bruckman v. Parliament Escrow Corp.—§ 12.-4(2), n. 16.

Bruder v. State—§ 10.6, n. 9.

Bruschi v. Brown—§ 9.2(6), n. 23, 35.

Bryant v. Willison Real Estate Co.—§ 12.14, n. 3.

Buddy Systems, Inc. v. Exer–Genie, Inc.—§ 2.11(3), n. 3, 11.

Bunnett v. Smallwood—§ 3.10(3), n. 21.

Burger King Corp. v. Mason—§ 4.5(3), n. 14, 15.

Burke v. Rivo—§ 8.2, n. 26, 27, 30, 33.

Burke v. Thomas—§ 5.16(2), n. 8.

Burlington, City of v. Dague—§ 3.10(10).

Burnett & Doty Development Co. v. C. S. Phillips—§ 3.3(4), n. 7.

Burr v. Board of County Com'rs of Stark County—§ 8.2, n. 5.

Burton v. Rex Oil & Gas Co.—§ 5.17(3), n. 2.

Bush v. Canfield—§ 4.5(4), n. 5.

Busik v. Levine—§ 3.6(3), n. 4, 5.

Business Guides, Inc. v. Chromatic Communications Enterprises, Inc.—§ 3.10(3), n. 40.

Butler v. Farmers Ins. Co. of Arizona—§ 4.7(1), n. 1.

Byron v. Clay—§ 2.4(2), n. 9, 24.

C

Cablevision of Breckenridge, Inc. v. Tannhauser Condominium Ass'n—§ 5.18(1), n. 4.

Caddo Oil & Mining Co. v. Producers' Oil Co.—§ 12.8(3), n. 5.

Cagle, Inc. v. Sammons—§ 4.3(4), n. 9, 17.

Calcote v. Calcote—§ 2.4(2), n. 12.

Calhoon v. Communications Systems Const., Inc.—§ 5.10(4), n. 14.

California and Hawaiian Sugar Co. v. Sun Ship, Inc.—§ 12.4(2), n. 13.

Callander v. Sheridan—§ 3.9, n. 8.

Callano v. Oakwood Park Homes Corp.—§ 4.9(1), n. 13; § 4.9(4), n. 14, 30.

Camaraza v. Bellavia Buick Corp.—§ 5.15(2), n. 18.

Cameron v. Bartels—§ 1.3, n. 1; § 2.11(1), n. 11; § 5.5, n. 5.

Cameron v. Benson—§ 12.8(1), n. 34.

Camp v. Cohn—§ 3.9, n. 24.

Campbell v. Animal Quarantine Station—§ 5.15(3), n. 11, 20.

Campbell v. Drake—§ 4.3(2), n. 38; § 5.18(3), n. 13.

Campbell Soup Co. v. Wentz—§ 2.4(3); § 2.4(3), n. 3.

Campen v. Stone—§ 3.11(5), n. 21.

Campins v. Capels—§ 5.15(3), n. 21; § 5.16(3), n. 8.

Canadian Ingersoll–Rand Co. v. D. Loveman & Sons, Inc.—§ 10.6, n. 2.

Canepa v. Sun Pacific, Inc.—§ 4.2(3), n. 34, 39.

Capital Garage Co. v. Powell—§ 5.8(2), n. 22.

Capitol Chevrolet Co. v. Earheart—§ 4.9(5), n. 8.

Capraro v. Lanier Business Products, Inc.—§ 2.5(2), n. 1.

Carey v. Berkshire—§ 8.3(1), n. 7.

Carey v. Piphus—§ 1.5, n. 21; § 2.11(2), n. 11; § 3.1, n. 11; § 5.1, n. 7; § 7.1(2), n. 3; § 7.4(2); § 7.4(2), n. 4.

Carl Zeiss Stiftung v. VEB Carl Zeiss Jena—§ 4.5(3), n. 24, 37; § 4.5(5), n. 9.

Carolina Power & Light Co. v. Bowman—§ 5.10(3), n. 44.

Carolina Power & Light Co. v. Paul—§ 5.14(2), n. 5; § 5.14(3), n. 30.

Carpenter v. United States—§ 12.12(2), n. 7.

Carr v. Carr—§ 4.3(2), n. 36, 50.

Carroll v. Action Enterprises, Inc.—§ 10.5(1), n. 12.

Carroll Towing Co., United States v.—§ 2.11(2), n. 15; § 3.11(3), n. 10.

Carson v. Maurer—§ 8.8, n. 21, 24.

Carter v. Konstantatos—§ 2.11(3), n. 24.

Caruso v. Ward—§ 7.4(4), n. 5.

Casale, State ex rel. v. McLean—§ 2.4(4), n. 8.

Catalano v. Catalano—§ 2.8(5), n. 8.

Catena v. Seidl—§ 2.8(3); § 2.8(3), n. 26, 29.

Cates v. Wilson—§ 3.8(1), n. 7, 16.

Cathey v. Johns–Manville Sales Corp.—§ 3.11(8), n. 3.

Caulfield v. Improved Risk Mutuals, Inc.—§ 12.14, n. 3.

Cavnar v. Quality Control Parking, Inc.—§ 3.6(2), n. 9; § 3.6(4), n. 11, 22, 26.

Central Coal & Coke Co. v. Hartman—§ 3.4, n. 11.

Central Illinois Light Co. v. Stenzel—§ 5.14(2), n. 3, 5; § 5.14(3), n. 18.

Central Nat. Bank v. Connecticut Mut. Life Ins. Co.—§ 6.1(4), n. 10.

Central Railroad & Banking Co. of Georgia v. Pettus—§ 3.10(2), n. 2, 10.

Cerrito v. Kovitch—§ 2.6(4), n. 20.

Chambers v. NASCO, Inc.—§ 2.8(2), n. 20; § 2.11(1), n. 5; § 3.10(3), n. 41, 48.

Champagne v. Raybestos–Manhattan, Inc.—§ 8.7(3), n. 6.

Champs Convenience Stores, Inc. v. United Chemical Co., Inc.—§ 5.14(2), n. 10.

Chandler v. Denton—§ 3.11(11), n. 15.

Chandler v. Webster—§ 13.3(2); § 13.3(2), n. 4.

Channell v. Applied Research, Inc.—§ 2.8(5), n. 16.

Charles Simkin & Sons, Inc. v. Massiah—§ 2.5(1), n. 23; § 5.17(3), n. 3.

Charlett, Commonwealth v.—§ 2.8(3), n. 5.

Chase v. Corcoran—§ 4.9(5); § 4.9(5), n. 3.

Chase Manhattan Bank v. Burden—§ 4.7(2), n. 17.

Chasins v. Smith, Barney & Co.—§ 9.2(6), n. 13.

Chauffeurs, Teamsters and Helpers, Local No. 391 v. Terry—§ 2.6(3), n. 69; § 2.6(4), n. 17.

Chavez, State v.—§ 2.8(6), n. 17.

Cheff v. Schnackenberg—§ 2.8(4), n. 15.

Chemical Bank v. Washington Public Power Supply System—§ 2.3(5), n. 5.

Chemical Exp. Carriers, Inc. v. French—§ 5.14(3), n. 25; § 5.15(2), n. 21.

Chemical Specialties Mfrs. Ass'n, Inc. v. Deukmejian—§ 2.4(4), n. 28.

Chenery v. Agri–Lines Corp.—§ 4.3(4), n. 23; § 4.9(3), n. 14.

Cherne Indus., Inc. v. Grounds & Associates, Inc.—§ 10.5(3), n. 71.

Chesapeake & Ohio Ry. Co. v. Elk Refining Co.—§ 3.6(1), n. 25.

Chesapeake & O. R. Co. v. Carnahan—§ 8.1(1), n. 7.

Chester, City of v. Commonwealth, Dept. of Transp.—§ 5.2(6), n. 18.

Chicago, City of v. Hart Bldg. Corp.—§ 2.8(2), n. 23.

Chicago, Rock Island and Pacific R. Co., Matter of v. Iowa Dept. of Transp.—§ 2.4(4), n. 26; § 5.7(2), n. 32.

Chicago & W. I. R. Co. v. Brotherhood of Ry. and S. S. Clerks, Freight Handlers, Exp. and Station Emp.—§ 2.4(2), n. 23.

Chicano Police Officer's Ass'n v. Stover—§ 3.10(6), n. 26.

Chlopek v. Schmall—§ 5.13(1), n. 3; § 5.15(2), n. 70, 72.

Chrisman v. Philips Industries, Inc.—§ 6.10(1), n. 7.

Christensen v. Chromalloy American Corp.—§ 5.5, n. 5.

Christensen v. Tucker—§ 5.10(4), n. 11, 15.

Christiansburg Garment Co. v. E.E.O.C.—§ 3.10(5), n. 3.

Christiansen v. Strand—§ 4.3(3), n. 4.

Christofferson v. Church of Scientology of Portland—§ 3.11(12), n. 27.

Chu Drua Cha v. Levine—§ 3.10(6), n. 17.

Chugach Elec. Ass'n v. Northern Corp.—§ 13.-3(2), n. 22.

Circuit Court for Waukesha County, State ex rel. Herget v.—§ 7.2(14), n. 17.

Citizens State Bank of Sealy, Tex. v. Caney Investments—§ 2.6(2), n. 5.

City and County of (see name of city)

City of (see name of city)

City Stores Co. v. Ammerman—§ 2.5(4), n. 11; § 12.8(3), n. 9.

C & K Engineering Contractors v. Amber Steel Co., Inc.—§ 2.6(3), n. 52.

Clark v. McClurg—§ 3.11(10), n. 17.

Claybrooke Warehouse & Gin Co. v. Farmers Co-op. Warehouse & Gin Co.—§ 4.7(1), n. 1.

Clayton v. Deverell—§ 2.6(2), n. 4.

Cleghorn v. Zumwalt—§ 9.5, n. 33.

Clem v. Hunz—§ 2.11(3), n. 44.

Cleveland Newspaper Guild, Local 1 v. Plain Dealer Pub. Co.—§ 2.4(4), n. 9, 39.

Cliett v. Hammonds—§ 2.8(4), n. 1.

Cline v. Fountain Rock Lime & Brick Co.—§ 13.2(2), n. 28.

Cobai v. Young—§ 5.10(3), n. 6, 12.

Cochran v. Wool Growers Central Storage Co.—§ 5.13(2), n. 8.

Cockrum v. Baumgartner—§ 8.2, n. 32.

Coe, State v.—§ 2.8(6), n. 16.

C. O. Funk & Sons, Inc. v. Sullivan Equipment, Inc.—§ 6.1(4), n. 10, 23.

Cohen v. County of San Francisco Board of Sup'rs—§ 2.9(3), n. 17.

Cohen v. Home Ins. Co.—§ 4.2(3), n. 13.

Coleman v. Safeway Stores, Inc.—§ 3.11(1), n. 66.

Coles v. Feeney—§ 4.3(8), n. 5.

Collier v. Collier—§ 4.9(3), n. 7.

Collins v. Philadelphia Oil Co.—§ 10.5(1); § 10.5(1), n. 25.

Cologne v. Westfarms Associates—§ 2.8(6), n. 2, 14.

Columbus & Southern Ohio Elec. Co. v. J.P. Sand & Gravel Co.—§ 5.14(2), n. 7, 13.

Combined Network, Inc. v. Equitable Life Assur. Soc. of the United States—§ 13.2(5), n. 12.

Commercial American Barge Line Co., United States v.—§ 5.14(3), n. 34.

Commodore Home Systems, Inc. v. Superior Court of San Bernardino County—§ 3.11(1), n. 66.

Common Council of City of Peru v. Peru Daily Tribune, Inc.—§ 2.9(5), n. 8; § 2.10, n. 4.

Commonwealth v. _____ (see opposing party)

Commonwealth, Dept. of General Services v. Collingdale Millwork Co.—§ 4.7(2), n. 17.

Community Television Services, Inc. v. Dresser Industries, Inc.—§ 5.14(3), n. 18.

Competex, S.A. v. LaBow—§ 3.7, n. 11, 12.

Comstock v. Little—§ 2.6(4), n. 26; § 5.10(3), n. 31.

Conaway v. Pepper—§ 5.18(2), n. 3.

Concrete Products Co., a Div. of Gibbons & Reed v. Salt Lake County—§ 4.1(2), n. 3.

Condemarin v. University Hosp.—§ 8.8, n. 21, 28.

Conmar Products Corp. v. Universal Slide Fastener Co.—§ 10.5(3), n. 69.

Connecticut v. Doehr—§ 2.11(3), n. 23, 33; § 5.17(2), n. 6, 8; § 6.1(5), n. 10, 11, 15, 31.

Connecticut General Life Ins. Co. v. Universal Ins. Co.—§ 6.1(3), n. 12; § 6.1(4), n. 22.

Connolly v. J.T. Ventures—§ 2.8(2), n. 23.

Conrad v. Dorweiler—§ 3.4, n. 8.

Consolidated Edison Co. of New York, Inc. v. Haymer—§ 5.17(3), n. 4.

Consolidated Gold Fields PLC v. Minorco, S.A.—§ 2.11(2), n. 5.

Consumers Lobby Against Monopolies v. Public Utilities Commission—§ 3.10(2), n. 25.

Contempt of Dougherty, In re—§ 2.8(3); § 2.8(3), n. 17; § 2.8(4), n. 2, 22.

Contempt of Reeves, In re—§ 2.8(6), n. 3, 19.

Continental Airlines, Inc. v. McDonnell Douglas Corp.—§ 9.2(1), n. 6, 19.

Continental Oil Co. v. Frontier Refining Co.—§ 2.11(3), n. 29.

Continuum Co., Inc. v. Incepts, Inc.—§ 2.11(3), n. 8, 16, 35.

Contrail Leasing Partners, Ltd. v. Consolidated Airways, Inc.—§ 5.13(1), n. 3.

Cooley v. Scarlett—§ 2.8(1), n. 16.

Cooper v. Feeney—§ 5.13(1), n. 3.

Coordinated Pretrial Proceedings in Antibiotic Antitrust Actions, In re—§ 3.10(10), n. 17.

Cooter & Gell v. Hartmarx Corp.—§ 3.10(3), n. 40.

Copiah Dairies, Inc. v. Addkison—§ 5.2(1), n. 4.

Coppola Enterprises, Inc. v. Alfone—§ 4.3(8), n. 8; § 12.7(4), n. 17.

Cornell v. Wunschel—§ 9.2(4), n. 1.

Corrigan v. City of Scottsdale—§ 5.7(1), n. 8.

Coster v. Crookham—§ 4.5(5), n. 5; § 9.4, n. 45.

Cotnam v. Wisdom—§ 4.1(2), n. 14; § 4.9(5), n. 1.

Cottman v. Cottman—§ 4.3(2), n. 50; § 4.7(1), n. 6.

Cottrell v. Gerson—§ 5.15(2), n. 27.

Coty v. Ramsey Associates, Inc.—§ 5.6(2), n. 3, 23.

County of (see name of county)

Courtesy Temporary Service, Inc. v. Camacho—§ 2.11(1), n. 18.

Coventry Homes, Inc. v. Scottscom Partnership—§ 6.1(5), n. 30.

Covey v. Cannon—§ 6.1(4), n. 17.

Cowe by Cowe v. Forum Group, Inc.—§ 8.2, n. 53.

Coyne v. Campbell—§ 3.8(1), n. 5.

Coyne–Delany Co., Inc. v. Capital Development Bd. of State of Ill.—§ 2.11(3), n. 10, 36, 37.

Creach v. Ralph Nichols Co.—§ 4.5(3), n. 34.

Credit Bureau of Laredo, Inc., State v.—§ 2.6(2), n. 6.

Crenshaw, State v.—§ 2.8(6), n. 7.

Creole Shipping Ltd. v. Diamandis Pateras, Ltd.—§ 5.14(3), n. 4.

Crimi v. Rutgers Presbyterian Church, City of New York—§ 5.16(4), n. 7.

Crisman v. Stidd—§ 12.2(2), n. 34; § 12.15(3), n. 2.

Crookham, State ex rel. Young v.—§ 3.11(3), n. 26; § 3.11(14), n. 13.

Crossman v. Marcoccio—§ 3.10(5), n. 6.

Crowley v. Global Realty, Inc.—§ 3.11(1), n. 30; § 3.11(12), n. 30.

Crowley v. Local No. 82, Furniture and Piano Moving, Furniture Store Drivers, Helpers, Warehousemen, and Packers—§ 2.11(3), n. 32, 57.

Crozer–Chester Medical Center v. Moran—§ 2.8(3), n. 20.

Cruickshank v. Griswold—§ 4.8, n. 6.

CTI Intern., Inc. v. Lloyds Underwriters—§ 5.15(2), n. 7, 53.

Cumberland Tel. & Tel. Co. v. Poston—§ 3.11(5), n. 1.

Cunningham v. Brown—§ 6.1(4), n. 29.

Cunningham v. City of McKeesport—§ 3.10(8), n. 50.

Curtis v. Loether—§ 2.6(3), n. 55; § 2.6(4), n. 17.

Curtis Pub. Co. v. Butts—§ 7.2(1), n. 9.

Curtiss-Wright Corp. v. Edel–Brown Tool & Die Co., Inc.—§ 10.5(3), n. 67, 70.

Curt's Trucking Co. v. City of Anchorage—§ 5.14(2), n. 7, 15.

Custer Builders, Inc. v. Quaker Heritage, Inc.—§ 4.9(4), n. 29.

Cutler Creek Village Townhouse Ass'n, Inc. v. Cutler Creek Village Condominium Ass'n, Inc.—§ 2.11(3), n. 24.

Cutrona v. Columbus Theater—§ 5.10(4), n. 8.

D

Dahlem v. Board of Educ. of Denver Public Schools—§ 3.10(6), n. 13.

Dailey v. City of Lawton, Okl.—§ 7.4(4), n. 4.

Dairy Queen, Inc. v. Wood—§ 2.6(3); § 2.6(3), n. 25; § 2.6(4); § 2.6(4), n. 15; § 4.3(5), n. 8, 33.

Dairy Stores, Inc. v. Sentinel Pub. Co., Inc.—§ 7.2(1), n. 13.

Daley, People ex rel. v. Warren Motors, Inc.—§ 2.6(3), n. 19.

Dalton v. Bundy—§ 4.9(4), n. 31.

Daly v. Wolfard Bros.—§ 5.15(3), n. 1.

Danca v. Taunton Sav. Bank—§ 9.2(1), n. 19.

Dant & Russell, Inc., In re—§ 5.2(5), n. 2.

Daughen v. Fox—§ 5.15(3), n. 15.

Daugherty v. Ashton Feed and Grain Co., Inc.—§ 5.7(3), n. 18.

Daughhetee v. Shipley—§ 5.13(1), n. 11.

David v. Belmont—§ 9.2(6), n. 13.

David Steed and Associates, Inc. v. Young—§ 2.6(4), n. 20.

Davis v. Air Technical Industries, Inc.—§ 3.10(3), n. 26.

Davis v. Alaska—§ 7.2(14), n. 17.

Davis v. Champion Fibre Co.—§ 2.11(3), n. 44.

Davis v. Colorado Kenworth Corp.—§ 13.4(3), n. 11.

Davis v. New England Ry. Pub. Co.—§ 6.6(4), n. 7.

Davis v. Omitowoju—§ 8.8, n. 23, 25.

Davis v. Tyee Industries, Inc.—§ 3.11(1), n. 85.

Davis Cattle Co., Inc. v. Great Western Sugar Co.—§ 5.18(2), n. 7.

Day v. Montana Power Co.—§ 5.6(2), n. 20.

Deans v. Layton—§ 11.2, n. 20.

De Beers Consol. Mines v. United States—§ 6.1(5), n. 5.

De Camp v. Bullard—§ 5.8(2), n. 17.

Deckert v. Independence Shares Corporation—§ 6.1(5), n. 12.

Deerfield Medical Center v. City of Deerfield Beach—§ 3.10(6); § 3.10(6), n. 16.

Defender Industries, Inc. v. Northwestern Mut. Life Ins. Co.—§ 3.11(12), n. 23, 45.

Defeyter v. Riley—§ 12.7(4), n. 17.

Deisenroth v. Dodge—§ 5.10(3), n. 25, 43.

Del's Big Saver Foods, Inc. v. Carpenter Cook, Inc.—§ 5.17(2), n. 10, 13, 14.

Dempsey v. Holiday Utilities Corp.—§ 3.11(3), n. 28.

Denby v. North Side Carpet Cleaning Co.—§ 5.13(1), n. 3; § 5.14(3), n. 22.

Dennis v. Higgins—§ 3.10(4), n. 25.

Dennis v. State—§ 3.10(2), n. 30.

Denny v. Nutt—§ 3.3(3), n. 2.

Denton v. Con-Way Southern Exp., Inc.—§ 3.8(1), n. 16, 18.

Denver & R. G. W. R. Co., United States v.—§ 5.14(2), n. 14.

Department of Revenue v. Jarvenpaa—§ 2.6(3), n. 55, 56.

DeSantis v. Wackenhut Corp.—§ 2.11(3), n. 10, 12, 50.

DeSpirito v. Bristol County Water Co.—§ 5.16(3), n. 2.

Dessel v. Dessel—§ 3.10(3), n. 29.

Dettor v. BHI Property Co. No. 101—§ 9.5, n. 33.

Devine v. Cluff—§ 3.10(3), n. 9.

Devine v. Sutermeister—§ 3.10(7), n. 5.

Diamond v. Oreamuno—§ 10.5(1), n. 24.

Dick v. Dick—§ 2.6(3), n. 22; § 2.6(4), n. 3, 14.

Dickens v. First American Title Ins. Co. of Arizona—§ 4.9(3), n. 3.

Die Deutsche Bank Filiale Nurnberg v. Humphrey—§ 3.7, n. 14.

Dietz v. Dietz—§ 13.2(3), n. 3.

Dillon v. Dean—§ 2.4(2), n. 6; § 10.4, n. 46.

Dillon v. Twin State Gas & Electric Co.—§ 8.5(2), n. 16; § 9.2(6), n. 17.

Dime Sav. Bank of Brooklyn v. Altman—§ 5.8(2), n. 20.

Dinosaur Development, Inc. v. White—§ 4.2(3), n. 39; § 4.9(1), n. 6; § 4.9(4), n. 12.

Disabled in Action v. Mayor & City Council of Baltimore—§ 3.10(6), n. 32.

Ditommaso Realty, Inc. v. Moak Motorcycles, Inc.—§ 12.9(4); § 12.9(4), n. 5.

Diver v. Diver—§ 2.8(7), n. 4.

Dixon v. Salvation Army—§ 4.3(8), n. 10; § 12.-14, n. 9, 15.

Dixon v. Thatcher—§ 2.5(2), n. 4.

Dobson v. Arkansas Oil & Gas Commission—§ 4.1(2), n. 19; § 4.9(4), n. 12, 17.

Dodd v. Fort Smith Special School Dist. No. 100—§ 5.16(4), n. 9.

Doe v. Busbee—§ 3.10(6), n. 13.

Doe v. State—§ 3.10(2), n. 28, 30.

Dolan v. Hudson—§ 2.8(1), n. 30.

Dollar Systems, Inc. v. Avcar Leasing Systems, Inc.—§ 2.6(4), n. 35.

Dolsen, Succession of—§ 13.2(2), n. 20.

Dolske v. Gormley—§ 5.10(4), n. 16.

Dombrowski v. Pfister—§ 2.5(4), n. 18.

Dominion Bank, N.A. v. Wilson—§ 4.3(8), n. 17.

Donnel v. Lara—§ 7.3(2), n. 7.

Dore' v. Jefferson Guar. Bank—§ 2.11(1), n. 13; § 5.5, n. 16.

Doub v. Hauser—§ 4.5(4), n. 3.

Douglass v. First Nat. Realty Corp.—§ 2.8(4), n. 21.

Douglass v. Hustler Magazine, Inc.—§ 3.11(5), n. 34; § 3.11(11), n. 9; § 7.2(13), n. 5.

Dowling v. McKenney—§ 13.2(4), n. 3.

Doyle v. Clark—§ 2.9(5), n. 2.

Drake v. Lawrence—§ 7.4(2), n. 18.
Drake v. National Bank of Commerce of Nor-
    folk—§ 2.8(7), n. 7.
DTS Tank Service, Inc. v. Vanderveen—
    § 5.15(2), n. 70, 81.
Dubiner's Bootery, Inc. v. General Outdoor
    Advertising Co.—§ 5.13(3), n. 10.
Duff v. Engelberg—§ 6.6(4), n. 2.
Duggan v. Board of County Com'rs of County
    of Weld—§ 5.13(1), n. 11.
Dun & Bradstreet, Inc. v. Greenmoss Builders,
    Inc.—§ 7.1(2), n. 3; § 7.2(1), n. 11; § 7.2(4),
    n. 8.
Duncan v. Louisiana—§ 2.8(4), n. 16.
Dunn v. Fletcher—§ 5.10(4), n. 17.
Dunn v. Phoenix Village, Inc.—§ 4.9(4), n. 10.
Duplate Corp. v. Triplex Safety Glass Co. of
    North America—§ 4.5(3), n. 14, 17.
Durant v. Surety Homes Corp.—§ 9.2(4), n. 1.
Durham v. Creech—§ 4.7(1), n. 9.
Durham Consol. Land & Imp. Co. v. Guthrie—
    § 13.2(2), n. 2.
Duvall v. Duvall—§ 2.5(1), n. 15.

                              E

Earl v. Clark—§ 5.1, n. 17; § 5.6(2), n. 3, 4.
Earl v. Saks & Co.—§ 9.3(2), n. 4.
Easley v. Empire Inc.—§ 3.10(8), n. 49.
Eastern Star, Inc., S.A. v. Union Bldg. Materi-
    als Corp.—§ 3.12, n. 27.
Eavenson, Auchmuty & Greenwald v. Holtz-
    man—§ 2.8(7), n. 14.
Eberle v. Greene—§ 2.8(2), n. 21.
Ebinger, United States v.—§ 5.14(3), n. 3, 6,
    32, 36.
EBSCO Industries, Inc. v. Lilly—§ 6.1(5), n. 8.
E.B. Sherman, Inc. v. Mirizio—§ 11.3, n. 5.
Eckerd Drugs of New Jersey, Inc. v. S. R. 215,
    Rite-Aid Corp.—§ 2.6(4), n. 6.
Eckert v. Soverel Marine, Inc.—§ 4.9(4), n. 27.
Eddie's Auto Body Works, Inc. v. Lumber-
    men's Mut. Cas. Co.—§ 4.9(5), n. 8.
Eddington v. Turner—§ 4.3(8), n. 15.
Edelman v. Jordan—§ 1.8, n. 2; § 1.10, n. 6.
Eden Memorial Park Ass'n, United States v.—
    § 3.5, n. 55; § 5.16(2), n. 3.
Edison Illuminating Co. v. Eastern Pennsylva-
    nia Power Co.—§ 2.5(4), n. 7.
Edlin v. Security Insurance Company—
    § 4.3(8), n. 13.
Edwards v. Lee's Adm'r—§ 4.3(2), n. 34;
    § 4.3(5), n. 19; § 4.5(3), n. 35; § 5.8(2), n. 19.
Edwards v. Miller—§ 4.5(4), n. 18.
Edwards v. Wilcoxen—§ 9.2(6), n. 18, 33.
E.E.O.C. v. Radiator Specialty Co.—§ 2.4(4), n.
    8.
Ehrle v. Bank Bldg. & Equipment Corp. of
    America—§ 3.6(1), n. 27.
Eichelberger v. Hayton—§ 2.11(3), n. 25.
Eichenseer v. Reserve Life Ins. Co.—§ 3.11(2),
    n. 37.
Eide v. Bierbaum—§ 2.11(3), n. 38.
Eide v. Kelsey–Hayes Co.—§ 3.11(1), n. 30.
E. I. duPont de Nemours & Co. v. American
    Potash & Chemical Corp.—§ 12.22(2), n. 10.
Eisbrenner v. Stanley—§ 8.2, n. 19, 47.

Elam v. Alcolac, Inc.—§ 3.11(14), n. 16.
El Club Del Barrio, Inc. v. United Community
    Corporations, Inc.—§ 3.10(6), n. 26.
Eldredge v. Gourley—§ 2.6(4), n. 27.
Embassy/Main Auto Leasing Co. v. C.A.R.
    Leasing, Inc.—§ 3.11(3), n. 30.
Emery Industries, Inc. v. Cottier—§ 2.4(6), n.
    11; § 5.7(3), n. 7; § 10.5(3), n. 60.
Equilease Corp. v. Hentz—§ 4.7(2), n. 8.
Equitable Life Leasing Corp. v. Abbick—
    § 3.11(10), n. 11; § 3.12, n. 19, 30.
Equitable Lumber Corp. v. IPA Land Develop-
    ment Corp.—§ 3.10(3), n. 3.
ERA Helicopters, Inc. v. Digicon Alaska,
    Inc.—§ 5.15(2), n. 40.
Erhardt v. Boaro—§ 5.10(3), n. 24.
Estate of (see name of party)
Etheridge v. Medical Center Hospitals—§ 8.8,
    n. 25.
Eubank v. Hayden—§ 7.3(2), n. 18.
Evans v. Evans—§ 2.6(4), n. 20.
Evans v. Jeff D.—§ 3.10(2), n. 14; § 3.10(6), n.
    24.
Evans v. Mason—§ 4.5(4), n. 3; § 13.2(2), n. 25.
Everett v. Harron—§ 2.9(3), n. 24.
Evra Corp. v. Swiss Bank Corp.—§ 12.4(5), n.
    14.
Ewing v. Bissell—§ 12.11(1), n. 29.
Exchange Bank of Commerce v. Meadors—
    § 4.5(4), n. 2; § 13.2(2), n. 28.
Exchange Nat. Bank of Chicago v. Harris—
    § 6.1(5), n. 5.
Ex parte (see name of party)
Exxon Corp., U.S.A. v. Dunn—§ 5.1, n. 17;
    § 5.6(2), n. 2, 23.
Eyoma v. Falco—§ 8.1(4), n. 41.

                              F

Fabian v. Wasatch Orchard Co.—§ 13.2(2), n.
    18.
Fairchild v. Keene—§ 5.15(2), n. 70.
Fairfield v. American Photocopy Equipment
    Co.—§ 7.3(2), n. 14.
Fairway Builders, Inc. v. Malouf Towers Rent-
    al Co., Inc.—§ 3.6(4), n. 7.
Falcone v. Perry—§ 5.2(1), n. 5.
Fall v. Eastin—§ 2.7, n. 21.
Farash v. Sykes Datatronics, Inc.—§ 4.3(2), n.
    24; § 4.5(4), n. 13; § 13.2(2), n. 1, 7, 14;
    § 13.2(4); § 13.2(4), n. 9; § 13.2(5), n. 17.
Farese v. McGarry—§ 4.9(4), n. 13.
Farley v. Engelken—§ 3.8(1), n. 18.
Farmers Ins. Co. of Arizona v. R.B.L. Inv.
    Co.—§ 3.6(2), n. 12; § 5.15(2), n. 37, 39.
Farr, In re—§ 2.8(3), n. 26.
Farr v. Johnson—§ 5.15(3), n. 12.
Farrell Lines, Inc. v. City of New York—
    § 12.9(4), n. 3.
Fasching v. Kallinger—§ 8.9, n. 24.
Fast v. School Dist. of City of Ladue—
    § 3.10(6), n. 4.
Fayetteville, City of v. Stanberry—§ 3.6(1), n.
    16.
Federal Deposit Ins. Corp. v. British–Ameri-
    can Corp.—§ 2.8(1), n. 36; § 3.6(3), n. 4;
    § 3.6(4), n. 6.

Federal Ins. Co. v. First Nat. Bank of Boston—§ 4.6, n. 11.

Federal Sav. & Loan Ins. Corp. v. Dixon—§ 6.1(5), n. 17, 24.

Federal Sugar Refining Co v. United States Sugar Equalization Bd—§ 4.3(5), n. 19; § 4.5(3), n. 35; § 6.6(3), n. 2.

Fein v. Permanente Medical Group—§ 8.8, n. 25.

Feingold v. Southeastern Pennsylvania Transp. Authority—§ 3.11(1), n. 98.

Felder v. Reeth—§ 5.13(3), n. 6; § 5.18(2); § 5.18(2), n. 4, 8, 13.

Fennell v. Littlejohn—§ 7.3(2), n. 18.

Fenner v. Fenner—§ 2.7, n. 21, 22.

Ferriss, State ex rel. Janus v.—§ 5.10(3), n. 37.

Ferry-Morse Seed Co. v. Food Corn, Inc.—§ 2.11(1), n. 19; § 5.17(3), n. 2.

Fertico Belgium S.A. v. Phosphate Chemicals Export Ass'n, Inc.—§ 12.1(1), n. 65.

Fibrosa Spolka Akcyjna v. Fairbairn Lawson Combe Barbour, Ltd.—§ 4.5(4), n. 17; § 13.3(2), n. 6.

Fidelity Nat. Title Ins. Co. v. Miller—§ 4.3(4), n. 6, 14.

Fiesta Mall Venture v. Mecham Recall Committee—§ 2.11(1), n. 12.

50 Acres of Land (Duncanville, Texas), United States v.—§ 5.2(6), n. 7, 14.

Fine Paper Antitrust Litigation, In re—§ 3.10(6), n. 23.

Firestone Tire & Rubber Co. v. Central Nat. Bank of Cleveland—§ 4.7(2), n. 5.

First Bank (N.A.)-Billings v. Transamerica Ins. Co.—§ 3.11(7), n. 7.

First-Citizens Bank and Trust Co. of South Carolina v. Hucks—§ 2.6(3), n. 46; § 2.6(4), n. 28.

First-Citizens Bank & Trust Co. v. Camp—§ 2.11(2), n. 4; § 2.11(3), n. 10.

First Equity Inv. Corp. v. United Service Corp. of Anderson—§ 9.4, n. 35, 39, 47.

First Family Mortg. Corp. of Florida v. White—§ 2.1(2), n. 12.

First Federal Sav. & Loan Ass'n of Toledo v. Perry's Landing, Inc.—§ 2.3(5), n. 5.

First Nat. Bank of Marshall v. Beavers—§ 3.11(5), n. 1.

First Nat. Bank of Meeker v. Theos—§ 2.6(3), n. 42.

First Nat. Bank of Santa Fe v. Southwest Yacht & Marine Supply Corp.—§ 5.17(2), n. 12, 13.

First Western Bank, Sturgis v. Livestock Yards Co.—§ 2.6(4), n. 28.

Fischer v. Brombolich—§ 2.5(1), n. 13.

Fischer v. Johns-Manville Corp.—§ 3.11(1), n. 84; § 3.11(3), n. 12; § 3.11(5), n. 1, 34; § 3.11(8), n. 3, 6.

Fisher v. Taylor Motor Co.—§ 13.4(2), n. 21.

564.54 Acres of Land, Etc. (Lutheran Synod), United States v.—§ 3.3(5), n. 4; § 5.2(1), n. 8; § 5.2(6), n. 1, 8.

525 Main St. Corp. v. Eagle Roofing Co.—§ 5.2(7), n. 1.

5303 Realty Corp. v. O & Y Equity Corp.—§ 6.1(5), n. 27.

Flanigan v. Prudential Federal Sav. & Loan Ass'n—§ 3.11(1), n. 43.

Flannery v. United States—§ 8.1(1), n. 6; § 8.1(4), n. 47.

Flannery for Flannery v. United States—§ 8.1(4), n. 47.

Flansburgh v. Coffey—§ 5.7(3), n. 19.

Fletcher v. City of Independence—§ 5.6(2), n. 3, 23.

Flooring Systems, Inc. v. Radisson Group, Inc.—§ 4.3(4), n. 20.

Flowers v. District of Columbia—§ 8.2, n. 53.

Flunker v. United States—§ 3.10(3), n. 23.

Flureau v. Thornhill—§ 12.11(1); § 12.11(1), n. 5.

Flygare v. Brundage—§ 12.11(1); § 12.11(1), n. 29.

Foard v. Atlantic & N.C.R. Co.—§ 3.4, n. 22.

Follett v. Jones—§ 8.5(2), n. 16.

Foltz v. Alford—§ 4.9(1), n. 20; § 4.9(5), n. 16.

Foltz v. U.S. News & World Report—§ 6.1(5), n. 8.

Forbes v. Wells Beach Casino, Inc.—§ 12.11(1), n. 29.

Ford v. Blue Cross and Blue Shield of Connecticut, Inc.—§ 2.6(3), n. 56.

Ford v. Revlon, Inc.—§ 3.11(1), n. 66; § 3.11(6), n. 18; § 7.3(2), n. 19.

Ford Motor Co. v. E.E.O.C.—§ 3.9, n. 15, 17.

Ford Motor Credit Co. v. Johns—§ 3.11(6), n. 17.

Foster v. United States—§ 3.5, n. 48, 52, 55.

Fottler v. Moseley—§ 9.2(6); § 9.2(6), n. 13.

487 Elmwood, Inc. v. Hassett—§ 5.6(2), n. 2.

Fowler v. Ross—§ 2.6(3), n. 46.

France v. Nelson—§ 5.15(2), n. 71; § 5.15(3), n. 1.

Francis Edward McGillick Foundation, In re—§ 2.4(2), n. 17.

Frank v. United States—§ 2.8(4), n. 19.

Frank B. Bozzo, Inc. v. Electric Weld Div. of Fort Pitt Div. of Spang Industries, Inc.—§ 3.6(1), n. 11.

Frankel v. Northeast Land Co.—§ 4.3(5), n. 10.

Franklin v. Mazda Motor Corp.—§ 8.8, n. 25.

Frank M. Hall & Co. v. Southwest Properties Venture—§ 4.9(4), n. 30; § 12.7(7), n. 7.

Frank Music Corp. v. Metro-Goldwyn-Mayer Inc.—§ 3.6(3), n. 4; § 3.6(4), n. 6.

Frazier v. Board of Trustees of Northwest Mississippi Regional Medical Center—§ 3.10(6), n. 13.

Fredeen v. Stride—§ 5.15(3), n. 18.

Fredeman Litigation, In re—§ 6.1(5), n. 5.

Freeport Coal Co., State ex rel. Shatzer v.—§ 2.11(3), n. 48.

Freeport Sulphur Co. v. S/S Hermosa—§ 5.2(7), n. 2; § 5.14(2), n. 7; § 5.14(3), n. 5, 18.

Freidus v. Eisenberg—§ 5.8(2), n. 11.

Fremont Nat. Bank and Trust Co. v. Collateral Control Corp.—§ 5.13(2), n. 1.

French v. Ralph E. Moore, Inc.—§ 5.6(2), n. 20.

French Bank of California v. First Nat. Bank of Louisville—§ 4.6, n. 11.

Fridrich v. Bradford—§ 9.2(6), n. 10.

Friends for All Children, Inc. v. Lockheed Aircraft Corp.—§ 6.1(5), n. 5, 21; § 8.1(3), n. 34; § 8.10, n. 18.

Friendship Materials, Inc. v. Michigan Brick, Inc.—§ 2.11(2), n. 4, 12, 13.

Froyd v. Cook—§ 6.10(1), n. 7.

Frye v. Memphis State University—§ 3.9, n. 11.

F.T.C. v. World Wide Factors, Ltd.—§ 6.1(5), n. 25.

Ft. Smith & W. R. Co. v. Ford—§ 12.5(2), n. 9.

Fuentes v. Shevin—§ 5.17(2); § 5.17(2), n. 5, 6, 13.

Fuller v. Gibbs—§ 5.10(1), n. 6.

Funderburg v. Shappert—§ 10.4, n. 49.

Funkhouser v. J. B. Preston Co.—§ 3.6(3), n. 4.

Furlan v. Rayan Photo Works—§ 5.16(3), n. 7, 10.

Furtado v. Furtado—§ 2.8(4), n. 9.

Fur & Wool Trading Co. v. George I. Fox, Inc.—§ 4.3(5), n. 23, 32; § 5.18(3), n. 25.

G

GAF Corp., State ex rel. Stephan v.— § 3.11(11), n. 8.

Gaffner v. American Finance Co.—§ 4.7(2); § 4.7(2), n. 10.

Gaines, Gaines & Gaines, P.C. v. Hare, Wynn, Newell & Newton—§ 13.3(2), n. 18.

Galego v. Knudsen—§ 9.2(1), n. 6.

Galella v. Onassis—§ 1.7, n. 13; § 2.4(6), n. 12.

Gallagher v. Duke University—§ 8.2, n. 3, 14, 17, 19, 26, 36.

Gannett v. Merchants Mut. Ins. Co.—§ 11.2, n. 19.

Gardco Mfg., Inc. v. Herst Lighting Co.— § 2.6(4), n. 12.

Garey Const. Co., Inc. v. Thompson—§ 5.2(1), n. 11; § 5.2(2), n. 23.

Garnes v. Fleming Landfill, Inc.—§ 3.11(5), n. 11, 40; § 3.11(11), n. 7, 8; § 3.11(12), n. 20, 22.

Garrett v. Garrett—§ 2.8(2), n. 26.

Gary Outdoor Advertising Co. v. Sun Lodge, Inc.—§ 12.9(2), n. 8.

Gaste v. Kaiserman—§ 4.5(3), n. 19.

Gates v. La Belle's Distributing of Arizona, Inc.—§ 5.16(4), n. 17.

Gaudette v. Webb—§ 8.3(1), n. 9.

Gause v. Perkins—§ 5.10(3), n. 26, 27.

Geddes v. Rosen—§ 2.6(3), n. 29.

Gee v. Pritchard—§ 2.9(5), n. 2.

Gelb v. Zimet Bros., Inc.—§ 5.13(2), n. 14.

General Bldg. Contractors Ass'n, Inc. v. Pennsylvania—§ 1.7, n. 1; § 1.8, n. 5; § 7.4(4), n. 23.

General Elec. Credit Corp. of Tennessee v. Hatch—§ 5.17(2), n. 12.

General Facilities, Inc. v. National Marine Service, Inc.—§ 3.6(4), n. 4.

General Motors Corp. v. Devex Corp.—§ 3.6(3), n. 4.

Georgia Power Co. v. Hudson—§ 2.9(4), n. 17.

Gerard v. Almouli—§ 11.2, n. 19.

Gerill Corp. v. Jack L. Hargrove Builders, Inc.—§ 9.2(1), n. 19.

Gertz v. Robert Welch, Inc.—§ 7.1(2), n. 3; § 7.2(1), n. 8, 10, 13; § 7.2(4); § 7.2(4), n. 3.

Getty Petroleum Corp. v. Bartco Petroleum Corp.—§ 3.12, n. 31.

Gheen v. Gheen—§ 4.9(4), n. 13.

Gilchrist v. Perl—§ 3.11(1), n. 21.

Gill v. Brown—§ 5.15(3), n. 16, 18.

Gilliam v. American Broadcasting Companies, Inc.—§ 5.16(4), n. 11.

Gilmere v. City of Atlanta, Ga.—§ 8.3(1), n. 12.

Ginsburg v. Insurance Co. of North America— § 3.6(1), n. 22.

Ginsburg v. Kovrak—§ 2.9(3), n. 23.

Givens v. Berkley—§ 3.11(5), n. 1.

Glantz Contracting Co. v. General Elec. Co.— § 4.9(1), n. 8.

Glass v. Miller—§ 5.15(2), n. 76.

Gleason v. Fryer—§ 3.11(7), n. 8.

Glenshaw Glass Co., Commissioner v.—§ 3.12, n. 38.

Glenwood Bridge, Inc. v. City of Minneapolis— § 2.11(1), n. 22.

Globe Remodeling Co., United States v.— § 3.12, n. 46.

Gluth Bros. Const., Inc. v. Union Nat. Bank— § 3.6(4), n. 4; § 6.1(3), n. 13.

G & M Motor Co. v. Thompson—§ 4.3(2), n. 14; § 4.3(5), n. 17.

Gnuse v. Garrett—§ 4.8, n. 14.

Godbersen v. Miller—§ 8.7(3), n. 7.

Goings v. Shafer—§ 5.10(3), n. 22.

Goins v. Ford Motor Co.—§ 3.9, n. 11.

Gold v. Ziff Communications Co.—§ 2.11(1), n. 21.

Golden State Bottling Co., Inc. v. N. L. R. B.— § 2.8(5), n. 17.

Goldstein v. Potomac Elec. Power Co.— § 5.7(2), n. 45.

Gompers v. Buck's Stove & Range Co.— § 2.8(2), n. 16; § 2.8(3); § 2.8(3), n. 19; § 2.8(4), n. 4, 7.

Goode v. Goode—§ 4.3(2), n. 51.

Gooding v. University Hosp. Bldg., Inc.—§ 3.4, n. 30.

Goodman v. Goodman—§ 2.8(2), n. 13.

Goodman v. McDonnell Douglas Corp.— § 2.4(4), n. 36.

Goodyear Rubber & Supply, Inc. v. Great American Ins. Co.—§ 4.9(4), n. 26.

Gorena, Ex parte—§ 2.8(2), n. 13.

Gore Products v. Texas & N. O. R. Co.— § 5.13(3), n. 6, 12, 14.

Gosnell v. Indiana Soft Water Service, Inc.— § 3.11(12), n. 4.

Gould v. Cayuga County Nat. Bank—§ 4.8, n. 10, 26.

Gould v. Starr—§ 3.11(1), n. 54.

Gowan v. Wisconsin–Alabama Lumber Co.— § 5.13(2), n. 7.

Gozelski v. Wyoming County—§ 5.17(3), n. 4, 10.

Grace v. Ludwig—§ 3.10(2), n. 17.

Graham v. Ashley—§ 4.9(5), n. 16.

Graham v. Inlow—§ 4.9(3), n. 9.

Grand Jury Investigation, In re—§ 2.8(3), n. 28.

Grand Jury Proceedings (Freligh)—§ 2.8(3), n. 30.

Granfinanciera, S.A. v. Nordberg—§ 2.6(3); § 2.6(3), n. 6, 30, 32, 39, 58.

Grano v. Barry—§ 3.10(6), n. 13, 15.

Grant v. Clinkscales—§ 5.15(3), n. 1.

Gray v. City of Billings—§ 2.6(4), n. 21.

Gray v. Sutherland—§ 5.18(3), n. 7.

Great Coastal Exp., Inc. v. Ellington—§ 7.2(4), n. 8.

Green v. United States—§ 2.8(4), n. 14.

Greenberg v. De Salvo—§ 7.2(14), n. 1.

Greenfield v. Spectrum Inv. Corp.—§ 3.11(6), n. 18; § 3.11(14), n. 13.

Greensburg Local No. 761 Printing Specialties v. Robbins—§ 3.10(2), n. 27.

Gregath v. Bates—§ 5.10(3), n. 12.

Griffin, In re Marriage of—§ 2.6(1), n. 18.

Grimshaw v. Ford Motor Co.—§ 3.11(1), n. 43, 84; § 3.11(5), n. 35; § 3.11(8), n. 3, 5.

Grout v. Solon—§ 4.9(4), n. 3.

Groves v. First Nat. Bank of Valparaiso—§ 3.10(3), n. 13.

Groves v. John Wunder Co.—§ 1.9, n. 10; § 3.1; § 3.1, n. 32.

Gruver v. Midas Intern. Corp.—§ 3.10(3), n. 21.

Grynberg v. Roberts—§ 3.6(2), n. 4.

Guard v. P & R Enterprises, Inc.—§ 3.1, n. 8.

Guardianship of Smith, In re—§ 3.11(7), n. 6.

Guilfoyle, Commonwealth v.—§ 2.6(3), n. 57.

Guinn v. Holcombe—§ 12.15(2), n. 33.

Gulesian v. Newton Trust Co.—§ 2.6(4), n. 9.

Gulf, C. & S. F. R. Co. v. Ellis—§ 3.10(5), n. 3.

Gulf States Utilities Company v. Guidry—§ 5.14(2), n. 2.

Gully v. Southwestern Bell Telephone Co.—§ 5.1, n. 5.

Gunn v. Burghart—§ 5.13(3), n. 12.

Gunzelman, State v.—§ 10.6, n. 9.

Gutting v. Jacobson—§ 10.6, n. 3.

Gylfe, The v. The Trujillo—§ 3.7, n. 25.

H

Haavik v. Farnell—§ 5.17(3), n. 3.

Habib v. Thurston—§ 2.6(4), n. 20.

Hadley v. Baxendale—§ 3.4; § 3.4, n. 20; § 4.5(3); § 6.6(2); § 12.1(1), n. 15; § 12.3(2); § 12.4(2); § 12.4(4); § 12.4(6); § 12.10; § 12.17(1).

Hagberg v. Haas—§ 5.18(2), n. 3.

Hahl v. Sugo—§ 5.10(1), n. 8; § 5.10(4), n. 8.

Haines v. Parra—§ 5.13(1), n. 6, 30; § 6.1(1), n. 3.

Halbman v. Lemke—§ 13.4(2), n. 20.

Hall v. Cole—§ 3.10(2); § 3.10(2), n. 16; § 4.9(6); § 4.9(6), n. 5.

Hall, United States v.—§ 2.8(5); § 2.8(5), n. 23.

Halpin v. Prudential Ins. Co. of America—§ 12.5(2), n. 1.

Hameed v. International Ass'n of Bridge, Structural and Ornamental Iron Workers, Local Union No. 396—§ 3.10(6), n. 8.

Hamer Holding Group, Inc. v. Elmore—§ 2.11(1), n. 23.

Hamilton–Brown Shoe Co. v. Wolf Bros. & Co.—§ 4.1(4), n. 13; § 4.3(5), n. 13, 28; § 4.5(3), n. 18.

Hamilton Nat. Bank v. Belt—§ 4.9(4), n. 9; § 6.5(2); § 6.5(2), n. 2.

Hammond Packing Co. v. State of Arkansas—§ 2.8(2); § 2.8(2), n. 25.

Hancock v. Moriarity—§ 5.10(3), n. 43.

Handicapped Children's Educ. Bd. of Sheboygan County v. Lukaszewski—§ 4.9(2), n. 4; § 12.2(2), n. 38.

Handy Andy Home Imp. Centers, Inc. v. American Nat. Bank & Trust Co. of Chicago—§ 6.6(4), n. 2.

Hanks, Matter of—§ 2.8(3), n. 4.

Hanlon v. Johns–Manville Sales Corp.—§ 3.11(8), n. 3.

Hanover Ins. Co. v. Fireman's Fund Ins. Co.—§ 4.3(4), n. 5; § 4.9(3), n. 11.

Hanrahan v. Hampton—§ 3.10(6), n. 7.

Hansen v. Rothaus—§ 3.3(2), n. 20; § 3.6(1), n. 19, 23, 27; § 3.6(2), n. 4, 12; § 3.6(3), n. 4.

Hanset v. General Const. Co.—§ 5.2(2), n. 21.

Harbeson v. Parke–Davis, Inc.—§ 8.2, n. 7, 8, 12.

Harbour v. Harbour—§ 4.3(8), n. 2.

Hardman Trucking, Inc. v. Poling Trucking Co., Inc.—§ 3.3(4), n. 3; § 5.15(2), n. 1, 40.

Hargis v. Mel–Mad Corp.—§ 12.15(3), n. 49.

Hargreaves v. Skrbina—§ 5.7(2), n. 37.

Harkless v. Sweeny Independent School Dist.—§ 2.6(3), n. 61.

Harless v. First Nat. Bank in Fairmont—§ 6.10(1), n. 1.

Harley v. Magnolia Petroleum Co.—§ 11.2; § 11.2, n. 24.

Harlow v. Chin—§ 8.5(2), n. 5.

Harper v. Adametz—§ 9.3(4), n. 8; § 10.5(1); § 10.5(1), n. 7, 19.

Harrell v. Travelers Indem. Co.—§ 3.11(7), n. 7.

Harriman v. Northern Securities Co.—§ 2.11(2), n. 6.

Harris v. American General Life Ins. Co. of Delaware—§ 3.11(10), n. 11.

Harris v. B & M Groceries—§ 7.3(2), n. 3.

Harris & Harris Const. Co. v. Crain & Denbo, Inc.—§ 3.6(1), n. 25.

Harrisburg, The—§ 8.3(1), n. 10.

Harrisonville, Mo., City of v. W.S. Dickey Clay Mfg. Co.—§ 2.4(5), n. 20; § 5.7(2), n. 26, 40.

Hart v. E. P. Dutton & Co.—§ 7.2(13), n. 1.

Hartford Elec. Light Co. v. Beard—§ 5.14(3), n. 30.

Hartford–Empire Co. v. Shawkee Mfg. Co.—§ 2.11(3), n. 20.

Harthcock v. Hurst—§ 5.6(2), n. 4.

Hartland Cicero Mut. Ins. Co. v. Elmer—§ 3.12, n. 41.

Hart, Nininger and Campbell Associates, Inc. v. Rogers—§ 6.6(4), n. 5.

Harvey v. Prall—§ 2.9(3), n. 25.

Harvey v. Wheeler Transfer & Storage Co.—§ 5.15(3), n. 21; § 5.16(3), n. 7.

Hashem v. Taheri—§ 2.6(4), n. 20.

Haskel Engineering & Supply Co. v. Hartford Acc. & Indem. Co.—§ 4.3(4), n. 17; § 4.3(5), n. 18.

Hatrock v. Edward D. Jones & Co.—§ 9.2(6), n. 28.

Hawkes v. Kehoe—§ 12.14, n. 3, 9.

Hawkins v. Allstate Ins. Co.—§ 3.11(1), n. 91; § 3.11(2), n. 37; § 3.11(5), n. 1, 34; § 3.11(11), n. 9.

Hawkins v. Hawkins—§ 3.11(10), n. 11.

Hayward Lumber & Inv. Co. v. Graham—§ 4.9(4), n. 13.

Head & Seemann, Inc. v. Gregg—§ 4.1(4), n. 7; § 4.5(5), n. 2; § 9.4, n. 35, 38.

Heath v. DeCourcy—§ 2.8(8), n. 11.

Hecht Co. v. Bowles—§ 2.4(7), n. 12; § 2.10; § 2.10, n. 1, 17.

Heckmann v. Ahmanson—§ 2.5(1), n. 28; § 4.3(2), n. 29; § 5.18(3), n. 24; § 6.1(5), n. 17.

Helena Elementary School Dist. No. 1 v. State—§ 3.10(2), n. 30.

Helfend v. Southern California Rapid Transit Dist.—§ 3.8(1), n. 17.

Hellar v. Cenarrusa—§ 3.10(2), n. 27, 28.

Helmkamp v. Clark Ready Mix Co.—§ 5.7(2), n. 34.

Hendershot v. Handlan—§ 2.8(5), n. 6.

Henderson v. For–Shor Co.—§ 5.15(2), n. 71.

Henderson v. Jantzen, Inc.—§ 3.10(6), n. 7.

Hendrickson v. Branstad—§ 3.10(10), n. 9.

Hennigan v. Ouachita Parish School Bd.—§ 3.10(6), n. 30.

Henry v. National Union Fire Ins. Co.—§ 8.1(2), n. 7.

Hensley v. Eckerhart—§ 3.10(6), n. 1; § 3.10(7), n. 3; § 3.10(8); § 3.10(9); § 3.10(9), n. 2, 9; § 3.10(10); § 3.10(10), n. 6.

Hensley v. Erie Ins. Co.—§ 3.11(7), n. 7, 8.

Hepler v. Atts—§ 12.11(1), n. 29.

Herbert v. Lando—§ 7.2(14), n. 6.

Herbert W. Jaeger & Associates v. Slovak American Charitable Ass'n—§ 12.3(1), n. 2.

Herget, State ex rel. v. Circuit Court for Waukesha County—§ 7.2(14), n. 17.

Herman v. State—§ 7.4(2), n. 2.

Herrington v. Sonoma County—§ 6.9(2), n. 5.

Herrmann v. Gleason—§ 3.6(2), n. 21.

Hershey v. Hershey—§ 2.3(5), n. 11.

Herskovits v. Group Health Co-op. of Puget Sound—§ 3.4, n. 29.

Hesthagen v. Harby—§ 10.4, n. 48.

Heston Oil Co., In re—§ 6.1(4), n. 28, 34.

Hewitt v. Helms—§ 3.10(6); § 3.10(6), n. 5.

H & H Farms, Inc. v. Hazlett—§ 10.5(1), n. 16.

Hibbett Sporting Goods v. Biernbaum—§ 2.5(2), n. 1.

Hickey v. Griggs—§ 3.10(1), n. 1.

Hicks on Behalf of Feiock v. Feiock—§ 2.6(1), n. 18; § 2.8(2), n. 4; § 2.8(3); § 2.8(3), n. 5, 7, 9, 32; § 2.8(4), n. 6; § 2.8(7), n. 3, 5.

Higgins v. Butcher—§ 8.3(1), n. 3.

Higgins v. Eva—§ 4.9(3), n. 7.

High Country Fashions, Inc. v. Marlenna Fashions, Inc.—§ 2.9(5), n. 17; § 7.2(14), n. 1.

Hill v. Ogrodnik—§ 5.10(3), n. 22.

Hilliard v. Fox—§ 4.6, n. 15, 18.

Hines v. Cheshire—§ 13.4(2), n. 21.

Hirsch v. Schwartz—§ 10.6, n. 4.

Hirschberg v. Flusser—§ 5.10(4), n. 8.

H. J. Heinz Co. v. Superior Court—§ 2.8(2), n. 21.

H. K. Porter Co. v. Halperin—§ 5.13(3), n. 12.

Hochman v. Zigler's, Inc.—§ 4.3(2), n. 30.

Hodges v. Gibson Products Co.—§ 3.3(3), n. 1.

Hoffius v. Maestri—§ 13.2(5), n. 16.

Hoffman v. Rauch—§ 6.1(3), n. 14.

Hoffman Hardware Co. v. Naame—§ 5.10(3), n. 43.

Holden v. Holden—§ 2.8(2), n. 12.

Home Ins. Co. v. American Home Products Corp.—§ 3.11(7), n. 6.

Home Owners' Loan Corporation v. Murdock—§ 4.7(1), n. 7.

Hopkins v. Price Waterhouse—§ 2.4(6), n. 2.

Hopkins v. Stepler—§ 5.7(3), n. 18.

Hoppe v. Russo–Asiatic Bank—§ 3.7, n. 13.

Horn v. Duke Homes, Etc.—§ 3.9, n. 9.

Hornstein v. Paramount Pictures—§ 10.6, n. 8.

Horton v. Georgia Power Co.—§ 5.14(3), n. 30.

Horvath v. National Mortg. Co.—§ 4.7(1), n. 5.

Hospital Authority of Gwinnett County v. Jones—§ 3.11(1), n. 42; § 3.11(11), n. 7; § 3.11(12), n. 21; § 3.11(14), n. 1.

Hotaling v. A. B. Leach & Co.—§ 9.2(6); § 9.2(6), n. 19, 20.

Houston Oil & Minerals Corp. v. American Intern. Tool Co.—§ 5.14(2), n. 5.

Hovey v. Elliott—§ 2.8(2); § 2.8(2), n. 24.

Howard v. Clanton—§ 3.10(3), n. 13.

Howard D. Johnson Co. v. Parkside Development Corp.—§ 2.11(3), n. 12.

H & R Block, Inc. v. McCaslin—§ 2.11(3), n. 30.

Hubbard v. Superior Court of Maricopa County and American Life Insurance Company—§ 4.5(5), n. 8; § 9.4, n. 47.

Huddleston v. Herman & MacLean—§ 9.2(6), n. 25.

Huff v. Thornton—§ 5.13(1), n. 11.

Hull v. Freedman—§ 6.1(1), n. 6.

Humphers v. First Interstate Bank of Oregon—§ 10.5(1), n. 1.

Humphreys v. Butler—§ 5.18(3), n. 26.

Hunsicker v. Katz—§ 5.7(2), n. 36.

Hunsley v. Giard—§ 5.15(3), n. 9.

Hunter v. Shell Oil Co.—§ 10.6, n. 2.

Hunt Inv. Co. v. Eliot—§ 3.10(5), n. 9.

Hurd v. Nelson—§ 3.8(1), n. 6.

Hurricane Elkhorn Coal Corp. II, In re—§ 6.1(4), n. 10.

Husman Const. Co. v. Purolator Courier Corp.—§ 12.4(2), n. 14; § 12.4(5), n. 14, 16.

Hustler Magazine v. Falwell—§ 7.2(6), n. 2.

Huston v. Exchange Bank—§ 6.1(3), n. 6, 15.

Hutto v. Finney—§ 1.8, n. 2; § 1.10, n. 6; § 2.9(5), n. 12; § 3.10(5), n. 7; § 7.4(4), n. 8, 16, 26, 28.

Hyatt Bros., Inc. v. Hyatt—§ 2.6(4), n. 20; § 4.3(5), n. 33.

I

Iacomini v. Liberty Mut. Ins. Co.—§ 4.9(5), n. 10; § 12.7(7), n. 3, 7.

Ickowitz v. Iowa Dist. Court for Polk County—§ 2.8(7), n. 5.

I. H. P. Corp. v. 210 Central Park South Corp.—§ 3.11(1), n. 54.

Illinois Cent. R. Co. v. Crail—§ 5.13(3), n. 10, 14, 15.

Imlay v. City of Lake Crystal—§ 3.8(1), n. 14, 19.

Immuno AG. v. Moor–Jankowski—§ 7.2(1), n. 13.

Imperial County, Cal. v. Munoz—§ 2.5(4), n. 20; § 2.8(5), n. 27; § 2.9(3), n. 16; § 2.9(4), n. 12, 15.

Independent Federation of Flight Attendants v. Zipes—§ 3.10(5), n. 2.

Independent Life & Acc. Ins. Co. v. Peavy—§ 3.11(5), n. 1.

Indian Oil Corp. Ltd. v. Greenstone Shipping, S.A. (The Ypatianna)—§ 4.5(3), n. 16.

Indiana & Michigan Elec. Co. v. Harlan—§ 4.5(5), n. 5; § 9.4, n. 39, 44.

Indianapolis, City of v. Twin Lakes Enterprises, Inc.—§ 3.6(1), n. 21, 23, 25; § 4.9(2), n. 6; § 4.9(4), n. 18, 22.

Indianapolis Raceway Park, Inc. v. Curtiss—§ 4.9(2), n. 5; § 4.9(4), n. 13, 30.

Industrial Innovators, Inc. v. Myrick–White, Inc.—§ 2.11(3), n. 10, 40.

Indust–Ri–Chem Laboratory, Inc. v. Par–Pak Co., Inc.—§ 3.6(1), n. 25.

Infusaid Corp. v. Intermedics Infusaid, Inc.—§ 2.8(7), n. 16.

In re (see name of party)

Instant Air Freight Co. v. C.F. Air Freight, Inc.—§ 2.11(3), n. 8, 10.

International Ass'n of Machinists and Aerospace Workers v. Eastern Airlines, Inc.—§ 3.10(3), n. 11.

International Bank, N.A. v. Morales—§ 12.5(2), n. 1.

International Harvester Credit Corp. v. Helland—§ 5.15(2), n. 27, 44, 46, 49, 50.

International Longshoremen's Ass'n, Local 1291 v. Philadelphia Marine Trade Ass'n—§ 2.4(6), n. 9; § 2.8(7), n. 13; § 5.7(3), n. 12, 13.

Internnational Ladies' Garment Workers' Union v. Donnelly Garment Co.—§ 2.11(3), n. 55.

Ishee v. Dukes Ford Co.—§ 5.13(3), n. 8.

Isuani v. Manske–Sheffield Radiology Group, P.A.—§ 2.5(1), n. 13.

IT Corp. v. County of Imperial—§ 2.10, n. 4; § 2.11(2), n. 12.

ITT Commercial Finance Corp. v. Riehn—§ 3.5, n. 1.

J

Jackson v. Housing Authority of City of High Point—§ 3.11(5), n. 32.

Jackson v. Johns–Manville Sales Corp.—§ 3.11(3), n. 26; § 3.11(8), n. 3.

Jaclyn, Inc. v. Edison Bros. Stores, Inc.—§ 10.6, n. 7.

Jacobs v. Andolina—§ 4.1(2), n. 16; § 12.12(2), n. 7.

Jamaica Nutrition Holdings, Ltd. v. United Shipping Co., Ltd.—§ 3.7, n. 27.

Jamaica Sav. Bank v. M. S. Investing Co.—§ 2.6(3), n. 41.

James v. Grand Trunk Western R. Co.—§ 2.5(4), n. 15, 16; § 2.9(4), n. 9, 10.

James G. v. Caserta—§ 8.2, n. 8, 16, 32.

Janigan v. Taylor—§ 4.1(2), n. 21; § 4.1(4), n. 13; § 4.3(2), n. 14; § 4.5(3), n. 4; § 9.3(4); § 9.3(4), n. 29.

Janklow v. Newsweek, Inc.—§ 7.2(1), n. 13.

Jankoski v. Preiser Animal Hosp., Ltd.—§ 5.15(3), n. 15, 19; § 5.16(3), n. 9.

Janus, State ex rel. v. Ferriss—§ 5.10(3), n. 37.

Javins v. First Nat. Realty Corp.—§ 12.15(2), n. 18.

Jay–Ox, Inc. v. Square Deal Junk Co.—§ 5.14(3), n. 33.

Jennings v. Metropolitan Government of Nashville—§ 3.10(6), n. 25.

Jensen v. Chicago and Western Indiana R. Co.—§ 5.15(2), n. 41; § 5.16(2), n. 1.

Jeppson v. Jeppson—§ 4.8, n. 5.

J. L. Simmons Co. v. Lumbermens Mut. Ins. Co.—§ 4.9(4), n. 21.

Joab, Inc. v. Thrall—§ 3.11(6), n. 17.

Jobling v. Associated Dairies, Limited—§ 9.2(6), n. 14.

John A. Artukovich & Sons, Inc. v. Reliance Truck Co.—§ 5.18(1), n. 3, 5.

John A. McCarthy & Co. v. Hill—§ 2.6(3), n. 24.

Johnson v. Georgia Highway Exp., Inc.—§ 3.10(7), n. 6.

Johnson v. Gilbert—§ 13.2(5), n. 14.

Johnson v. Hugo's Skateway—§ 3.11(12), n. 25.

Johnson v. Johnson—§ 2.8(2), n. 8.

Johnson v. Sanders—§ 4.9(4), n. 5; § 13.2(2), n. 20.

Johnson v. South Carolina Nat. Bank—§ 2.6(3), n. 47.

Johnson v. St. Vincent Hospital, Inc.—§ 8.8, n. 26.

Johnson v. University Hospitals of Cleveland—§ 8.2, n. 32.

John W. Cowper Co., Inc. v. Buffalo Hotel Development Venture—§ 2.6(4), n. 7, 21, 24.

Jolly v. Wright—§ 2.8(3), n. 4.

Jones v. Chesebrough—§ 6.1(3), n. 15.

Jones v. Malinowski—§ 8.2, n. 33, 41.

Jones v. Muir—§ 3.10(2), n. 30.

Jones, United States v.—§ 2.8(3), n. 34.

Jones v. Western Geophysical Co.—§ 3.11(1), n. 66.

Jones v. Wolf—§ 2.9(5), n. 15.

Jones by Blume, Estate of v. Kvamme—§ 4.5(5), n. 6; § 9.3(4), n. 3, 30; § 9.4, n. 46.

Jones & Laughlin Steel Corp. v. Pfeifer—§ 3.7, n. 6.

Jourdain v. Dineen—§ 9.2(4), n. 1.

Judd v. Rowley's Cherry Hill Orchards, Inc.—§ 8.1(4), n. 33.

Julien J. Studley, Inc. v. New York News, Inc.—§ 4.9(2), n. 6; § 4.9(4), n. 18, 22.

Juzwin v. Amtorg Trading Corp., 718 F.Supp. 1233—§ 3.11(8), n. 11.

Juzwin v. Amtorg Trading Corp., 705 F.Supp. 1053—§ 3.11(8), n. 2, 10.

K

Kagan v. K–Tel Entertainment, Inc.—§ 4.9(4), n. 27.
Kahle v. John McDonough Builders, Inc.— § 2.6(3), n. 42, 44.
Kaiser Hawaii Kai Development Co. v. City and County of Honolulu—§ 2.9(5), n. 10.
Kamberos v. GTE Automatic Elec., Inc.— § 2.4(4), n. 24.
Kamens v. Fortugno—§ 3.6(1), n. 25.
Kammerer v. Western Gear Corp.—§ 3.11(1), n. 28.
Kandt, State ex rel. v. North Platte Baptist Church of North Platte—§ 2.8(3), n. 6.
Kansas City M. & O. Ry. Co. v. Bell—§ 3.4, n. 27.
Kansas Malpractice Victims Coalition v. Bell—§ 8.8, n. 21.
Kanter & Eisenberg v. Madison Associates— § 2.9(4), n. 7; § 2.11(2), n. 12.
Karpinski v. Collins—§ 10.6, n. 8.
Karpinski v. Ingrasci—§ 4.3(7), n. 7.
Karras v. Gannon—§ 2.8(6), n. 3.
Katchen v. Landy—§ 2.6(3), n. 33.
Kay v. Ehrler—§ 3.10(5), n. 9.
Kearns v. Andree—§ 13.2(2), n. 7, 15.
Keehr v. Consolidated Freightways of Delaware, Inc.—§ 7.1(2), n. 8; § 7.3(2), n. 7.
Keen v. Keen—§ 6.1(5), n. 29.
Keister v. Talbott—§ 3.4, n. 18.
Kelco Disposal, Inc. v. Browning–Ferris Industries of Vermont, Inc.—§ 3.11(1), n. 43; § 3.11(3), n. 29; § 3.12, n. 27.
Kelley v. Acker—§ 4.9(3), n. 9.
Kelly v. City of Cape Girardeau—§ 2.8(5), n. 16.
Kenford Co., Inc. v. County of Erie—§ 12.4(6); § 12.4(6), n. 3, 11.
Kenney v. Scientific, Inc.—§ 2.6(4), n. 21.
Kenton v. Hyatt Hotels Corp.—§ 8.1(4), n. 33.
Kentucky Home Mut. Life Ins. Co. v. Rogers— § 4.8, n. 31.
Kenyon v. City of Chicopee—§ 2.9(4), n. 39; § 2.9(5), n. 3.
Keppel v. BaRoss Builders, Inc.—§ 12.2(2), n. 30.
Kerr S. S. Co. v. Radio Corporation of America—§ 12.4(4); § 12.4(4), n. 8.
Kershishian v. Johnson—§ 5.10(4), n. 15.
Keystone Associates v. State—§ 6.9(2), n. 4.
Killebrew v. Abbott Laboratories—§ 3.11(1), n. 28.
Kimball Laundry Co. v. United States—§ 3.5, n. 2, 54; § 5.2(6), n. 2; § 5.8(2), n. 10; § 6.9(2), n. 2.
King v. Palmer—§ 3.10(10); § 3.10(10), n. 28.
King v. Uhlmann—§ 4.3(2), n. 54.
King v. United States—§ 5.16(4), n. 2.
King Fisher Marine Service, Inc. v. NP Sunbonnet—§ 5.16(2), n. 5.
Kink v. Combs—§ 3.11(3), n. 27.
Kirk v. Denver Pub. Co.—§ 3.11(12), n. 40.

Kirk v. Washington State University— § 8.1(4), n. 41.
Kiser v. Neumann Co. Contractors, Inc.— § 3.11(6), n. 16.
Kleier Advertising, Inc. v. Premier Pontiac, Inc.—§ 3.6(2), n. 42.
Klein v. General Elec. Co.—§ 5.16(4), n. 17.
Klein v. PepsiCo, Inc.—§ 2.5(1), n. 21; § 12.-8(2), n. 16.
Knaebel v. Heiner—§ 2.4(2), n. 12; § 2.5(1), n. 12; § 4.8, n. 12.
Knatchbull v. Hallett—§ 6.1(4), n. 9.
Knighton v. Knighton—§ 2.9(5), n. 3.
Knower v. Atkins—§ 5.10(3), n. 37.
Knowles Animal Hospital, Inc. v. Wills— § 5.15(3), n. 18.
Koenings v. Joseph Schlitz Brewing Co.— § 12.9(2), n. 7.
Konchesky, State v.—§ 10.6, n. 9.
Koninklijke Luchtvaart Maatschaapij, N. V. (KLM) v. United Technologies Corp.— § 3.3(4), n. 10; § 5.15(2), n. 7, 26, 51, 52.
Koufos v. C. Czarnikow Ltd. (The Heron II)— § 12.4(6), n. 3.
Koussevitzky v. Allen, Towne & Heath— § 7.2(14), n. 1.
Kracl v. Loseke—§ 4.3(6), n. 7, 9; § 4.8, n. 12.
Kramer v. Chabot—§ 9.2(1), n. 19.
Kramer v. Thompson—§ 2.9(5), n. 17; § 7.2(14), n. 1.
Krauss v. Greenbarg—§ 12.4(2); § 12.4(2), n. 16.
Krieger v. Iowa Dept. of Human Services— § 11.2, n. 1.
Kriener v. Turkey Valley Community School Dist.—§ 5.7(4), n. 11.
Krueger v. Steffen—§ 5.13(1), n. 11.
Kruvant v. 12–22 Woodland Ave. Corp.— § 5.8(2), n. 8, 14, 29.
KSM Fastening Systems, Inc. v. H.A. Jones Co., Inc.—§ 2.5(2), n. 1.
Kugler v. Ryan—§ 2.5(1), n. 8; § 5.10(3), n. 6, 12.
Kuhlman v. Cargile—§ 4.3(3), n. 8.

L

Labbadia v. Bailey—§ 2.8(7), n. 11.
Labor Relations Commission v. Fall River Educators' Ass'n—§ 2.8(3), n. 4.
Laclede Gas Co. v. Amoco Oil Co.—§ 12.8(3), n. 9.
LaDuke v. Burlington Northern R. Co.— § 2.9(4), n. 13.
LaDuke v. Nelson—§ 3.10(10), n. 18.
Lafary v. Lafary—§ 4.9(4), n. 13.
La Grange, City of v. Pieratt—§ 3.4, n. 1.
Laker Airways Ltd. v. Sabena, Belgian World Airlines—§ 2.9(4), n. 8, 11.
Lake River Corp. v. Carborundum Co.—§ 12.-9(2), n. 8, 32.
L. Albert & Son v. Armstrong Rubber Co.— § 4.5(4), n. 11; § 12.3(1), n. 2.
Lally v. Copygraphics—§ 6.10(1), n. 7.
Lamb v. Rooney—§ 5.18(3), n. 26.
Lambert v. Montana—§ 2.8(3), n. 26.

Lamb–Weston, Inc. v. McCain Foods, Ltd.— § 10.5(3), n. 68.

Lam, Inc. v. Johns–Manville Corp.—§ 3.4, n. 8.

Lamine v. Dorrell—§ 4.2(3); § 4.2(3), n. 31.

Lamkins v. International Harvester Co.— § 12.4(4), n. 9.

La Mothe, People v.—§ 2.8(2), n. 10.

Lance v. Plummer—§ 2.8(2); § 2.8(2), n. 27; § 7.4(4), n. 3.

Landin v. Ford—§ 9.4, n. 35, 41, 47.

Landis v. Hodgson—§ 2.4(4), n. 8.

Lane v. Dunkle—§ 5.13(1), n. 32; § 5.15(3), n. 1; § 6.1(1), n. 3.

Lane v. Mitchell—§ 7.3(2), n. 17.

Lanier v. Ocean Pond Fishing Club, Inc.— § 5.10(3), n. 11.

La Paz County v. Yuma County—§ 3.6(2), n. 9.

La Porte v. Associated Independents, Inc.— § 5.15(3), n. 16, 18; § 5.16(3), n. 14.

La Raza Unida v. Volpe—§ 3.10(4), n. 21.

Lash Furniture Co. of Barre v. Norton— § 2.6(1), n. 4.

Lataille v. Housing Authority of City of Woonsocket—§ 3.5, n. 57.

Laubengayer v. Rohde—§ 4.8, n. 9.

Lauder v. Peck—§ 3.12, n. 33.

Laura v. Christian—§ 4.1(2), n. 17; § 4.3(3), n. 5.

Laurin v. DeCarolis Const. Co., Inc.—§ 5.1, n. 6; § 5.18(2), n. 18.

Law v. Superior Court In and For Maricopa County—§ 8.7(4), n. 21.

Law v. Texas Delivery Service, Inc.—§ 2.9(5), n. 2.

Lawes v. Bennett—§ 4.3(8); § 4.3(8), n. 14.

Lawrence County v. Brenner—§ 2.11(3), n. 25.

Lawson v. Bennett—§ 13.4(3), n. 11.

Lazenby v. Universal Underwriters Ins. Co.— § 3.11(7), n. 7.

L. B. Menefee Lumber Co. v. MacDonald— § 5.18(2), n. 11.

Lear v. Bawden—§ 10.5(1), n. 17.

Leard v. Breland—§ 5.16(2), n. 2.

Leebov v. United States Fidelity & Guaranty Co.—§ 4.1(2), n. 20; § 4.9(1), n. 12; § 4.9(4); § 4.9(4), n. 23, 24.

Lee's Summit, City of v. Browning—§ 5.7(2), n. 32.

LeFlore v. Reflections of Tulsa, Inc.—§ 9.2(1), n. 19.

Lehrman v. Gulf Oil Corp.—§ 3.4, n. 13.

Leibowits v. Leibowits—§ 6.1(5), n. 20.

Leigh v. Engle—§ 6.1(4), n. 3.

Leiker By and Through Leiker v. Gafford— § 8.1(4), n. 33, 44, 45.

Lekas & Drivas, Inc. v. Goulandris—§ 12.4(2); § 12.4(2), n. 15.

Leman v. Krentler–Arnold Hinge Last Co.— § 2.8(2), n. 23.

Lemat Corp. v. Barry—§ 12.22(2), n. 8.

Leno v. Prudential Ins. Co. of America— § 4.3(4), n. 17.

Leonard v. Stoebling—§ 5.7(4), n. 10.

Leonard E. Warner, Inc. v. Nissan Motor Corp. in U.S.A.—§ 2.8(1), n. 11; § 2.11(2), n. 25; § 7.4(4), n. 13.

Levinson v. Prentice–Hall, Inc.—§ 3.11(1), n. 66; § 3.11(11), n. 16.

Lewis v. Oregon Beauty Supply Co.—§ 3.11(1), n. 66.

Lexington Products Ltd. v. B. D. Communications, Inc.—§ 3.4, n. 15.

Leyden v. Citicorp Indus. Bank—§ 4.3(2), n. 22, 52, 56; § 4.3(3), n. 7, 9; § 4.7(1), n. 9.

Library of Congress v. Shaw—§ 3.6(5), n. 1.

Liebman, Estate of—§ 4.3(2), n. 21; § 6.1(4), n. 2.

Life for God's Stray Animals, Inc. v. New North Rockdale County Homeowners Ass'n—§ 2.6(4), n. 20.

Lightfoot v. Walker—§ 3.10(8), n. 59.

Lightner v. Karnatz—§ 4.8, n. 12.

Liland v. Tweto—§ 4.8, n. 16.

Liles v. Liles—§ 3.10(3); § 3.10(3), n. 37.

Liller v. State Highway Administration— § 2.4(4), n. 27; § 5.7(2), n. 32.

Limoli v. Accettullo—§ 4.8, n. 16.

Lincoln Nat. Life Ins. Co. v. Brown Schools, Inc.—§ 4.7(2), n. 17.

Lindvig v. Lindvig—§ 4.9(5), n. 21.

Lindy Bros. Builders, Inc. of Phila. v. American Radiator & Standard Sanitary Corp.— § 3.10(2), n. 9.

Lindy Bros. Builders, Inc. of Philadelphia v. American Radiator & Standard Sanitary Corp.—§ 3.10(10), n. 5, 16.

Link v. State By and Through Dept. of Fish and Game—§ 12.8(3), n. 9.

Linville v. Wilson—§ 2.6(4), n. 22.

Liqui–Box Corp. v. Estate of Elkman—§ 12.15(3), n. 49.

Little v. Rose—§ 5.15(2), n. 14.

Little Joseph Realty, Inc. v. Town of Babylon—§ 2.10, n. 4; § 5.7(2), n. 51.

L.L. Cole & Son, Inc. v. Hickman—§ 12.5(2), n. 1.

Lloyd v. Murphy—§ 12.4(6), n. 14.

Lloyd Corp., Ltd. v. Whiffen—§ 2.4(5), n. 24.

Lockard v. City of Salem—§ 3.6(2), n. 3.

Loftsgaarden v. Reiling—§ 3.11(10), n. 4.

Loma Portal Civic Club v. American Airlines, Inc.—§ 2.4(5), n. 22; § 2.10, n. 27; § 5.7(2), n. 45.

London v. Bear—§ 5.8(2), n. 20.

Long v. Keller—§ 12.14, n. 13.

Long v. McAllister—§ 5.15(2), n. 70, 72.

Long v. Vielle—§ 9.5, n. 33.

Long v. Zirkle—§ 2.9(4), n. 6.

Loring v. Baker—§ 6.1(4), n. 17.

Los Angeles, City of v. Lyons—§ 2.9(5), n. 11.

Los Angeles, Dept. of Water and Power, City of v. Manhart—§ 8.5(2), n. 18.

Loughran v. Loughran—§ 2.4(2), n. 13.

Loughry v. Lincoln First Bank, N.A.— § 3.11(6), n. 6.

Lovejoy Specialty Hosp., Inc. v. Advocates For Life, Inc.—§ 2.8(3), n. 25.

Lovelace Medical Center v. Mendez—§ 8.2, n. 23, 26, 33, 44.

L. P. Larson, Jr., Co. v. William Wrigley, Jr., Co.—§ 4.5(3), n. 12.

Lucas v. United States—§ 8.1(4), n. 99; § 8.8, n. 21, 22, 26.

Lucenti v. Cayuga Apartments, Inc.—§ 12.14, n. 4, 16.

Ludwig v. Kowal—§ 5.13(2), n. 7.

Lumley v. Wagner—§ 12.22(2), n. 6.

Lunda v. Matthews—§ 5.6(1), n. 1.

Lynch v. Deaconess Medical Center—§ 4.1(2), n. 3, 20; § 4.3(4), n. 11, 13.

Lynn Strickland Sales and Service, Inc. v. Aero–Lane Fabricators, Inc.—§ 5.13(1), n. 11.

Lytle v. Household Mfg., Inc.—§ 2.6(4); § 2.6(4), n. 31.

M

Mabry v. Howington—§ 2.8(4), n. 4.

MacArtor v. Graylyn Crest III Swim Club, Inc.—§ 2.4(6), n. 7.

MacKenna v. Jordan—§ 12.12(2), n. 7.

Madden v. Rosseter, 192 N.Y.S. 113—§ 2.8(1), n. 25.

Madden v. Rosseter, 187 N.Y.S. 462—§ 2.8(1), n. 24.

Madison v. Ducktown Sulphur, Copper & Iron Co.—§ 5.7(2), n. 32, 42, 43, 44.

Madison Fork Ranch v. L & B Lodge Pole Timber Products—§ 5.5, n. 5.

Magnolia Petroleum Co v. Harrell—§ 5.15(2), n. 81.

Maher v. Gagne—§ 3.10(6), n. 23.

Majmundar v. Veline—§ 2.9(4), n. 41.

Makino, U.S.A., Inc. v. Metlife Capital Credit Corp.—§ 3.12, n. 32.

Malachy v. Soper—§ 3.4, n. 5.

Malerba v. Warren, 464 N.Y.S.2d 835—§ 5.8(2), n. 17.

Malerba v. Warren, 438 N.Y.S.2d 936—§ 5.2(2), n. 23.

Mallory Factor Inc. v. Schwartz—§ 6.6(4), n. 5.

Malo v. Anderson—§ 4.5(2), n. 21.

Maloney v. City of Marietta—§ 3.10(6), n. 15.

Maltina Corp. v. Cawy Bottling Co., Inc.— § 4.5(3), n. 13.

Maness v. Meyers—§ 2.8(4), n. 7; § 2.8(6), n. 7.

Mangione v. Braverman—§ 13.2(2), n. 27.

Manhattan Civic Centre Area, In re—§ 3.6(1), n. 25.

Manning v. Wingo—§ 4.9(5), n. 18.

Manson–Osberg Co. v. State—§ 3.10(3), n. 32.

Manufacturers Hanover Trust Co. v. Eisenstadt—§ 4.7(1), n. 18.

Mapledge Corp. v. Coker—§ 5.15(2), n. 43.

Marbury Management, Inc. v. Kohn—§ 9.2(6), n. 21.

Marcella v. ARP Films, Inc.—§ 12.5(1), n. 1.

Marciniak v. Lundborg—§ 8.2, n. 33, 45, 54.

Marcus v. Otis, 169 F.2d 148—§ 6.1(4), n. 5, 20.

Marcus v. Otis, 168 F.2d 649—§ 3.6(2), n. 19; § 9.3(4), n. 34; § 10.4; § 10.4, n. 53.

Marder v. Realty Const. Co.—§ 5.10(1), n. 9.

Marek v. Chesny—§ 3.10(5), n. 6.

Marill Alarm Systems, Inc. v. Open Door Capital Co.—§ 3.12, n. 29.

Mariner v. Marsden—§ 8.1(4), n. 33.

Markley v. State—§ 2.8(4), n. 22.

Marley Orchard Corp. v. Travelers Indem. Co.—§ 4.9(4), n. 21.

Marquette v. Marquette—§ 5.17(3), n. 7.

Marriage of (see name of party)

Marshall v. Bare—§ 12.12(2), n. 7.

Martian v. Martian—§ 2.8(1), n. 18; § 2.8(7), n. 8; § 4.3(3), n. 3, 9.

Martin v. Herzog—§ 2.8(8), n. 9.

Martin v. Kehl—§ 4.3(2), n. 36.

Martin v. Little, Brown and Co.—§ 4.2(3), n. 13; § 4.9(1), n. 8, 18; § 4.9(4), n. 8.

Martin v. McKee Realtors, Inc.—§ 3.12, n. 2.

Martin v. Rieger—§ 5.13(1), n. 11.

Martinelli v. Merchants Oil Inc.—§ 3.6(1), n. 25.

Martinez v. Continental Enterprises—§ 3.6(2), n. 20, 21; § 3.6(3), n. 5; § 4.3(4), n. 19.

Maryland Nat. Bank v. Cummins—§ 3.6(3), n. 5; § 3.6(4), n. 7; § 4.5(2), n. 25; § 4.5(3), n. 6.

Masaki v. General Motors Corp.—§ 3.11(1), n. 84; § 3.11(2), n. 12.

Mason Furniture Corp. v. George—§ 2.8(3), n. 4.

Massachusetts Bonding & Insurance Co. v. Josselyn—§ 6.1(4), n. 16.

Masters v. Van Wart—§ 4.8, n. 11.

Matawan Regional Teachers Ass'n v. Matawan–Aberdeen Regional Bd. of Educ.— § 2.10, n. 6.

Matek v. Murat—§ 3.10(3), n. 10.

Mathis v. Glover—§ 12.2(2), n. 30.

Mathison v. Clearwater County Welfare Dept.—§ 4.1(1), n. 14.

Matter of (see name of party)

Matthews v. Neal, Greene & Clark—§ 4.5(2), n. 13.

Mattison v. Dallas Carrier Corp.—§ 2.4(7), n. 1; § 3.11(12), n. 23; § 3.11(14), n. 16, 19.

Mattson v. Commercial Credit Business Loans, Inc.—§ 4.7(1), n. 1.

Mauro v. Raymark Industries, Inc.—§ 8.1(4), n. 63.

Mayberry v. Pennsylvania—§ 2.8(4), n. 11.

Mayer v. Monzo—§ 5.13(2), n. 12.

McAdory v. Rogers—§ 8.8; § 8.8, n. 30.

McBride v. General Motors Corp.—§ 3.11(12), n. 43.

McCall v. Atchley—§ 2.4(3), n. 9.

McCandless v. State—§ 7.3(2), n. 10.

McCarthy v. General Electric Co.—§ 5.15(3), n. 1.

McCastle v. Rollins Environmental Services of Louisiana, Inc.—§ 5.7(3), n. 10.

McClure v. Leaycraft—§ 2.4(5), n. 11; § 5.10(3), n. 22.

McConal Aviation, Inc. v. Commercial Aviation Ins. Co.—§ 3.8(1), n. 17.

McCoy v. West—§ 4.5(2), n. 22.

McCurdy v. Union Pacific Railroad Company—§ 5.13(1), n. 11; § 5.16(3), n. 2.

McDonough v. Lee—§ 3.10(4), n. 16.

McDonough's Estate, In re—§ 4.3(8), n. 15.

McDougald v. Garber—§ 8.1(4), n. 44, 45, 103.

McElreath v. McElreath—§ 2.7, n. 22.

McGowin v. Remington—§ 5.17(3), n. 2.

McIntosh v. Murphy—§ 13.2(4), n. 5; § 13.2(5), n. 16.

McKellips v. Saint Francis Hosp., Inc.—§ 3.4, n. 29.

McKiever v. McKiever—§ 3.10(3), n. 47.

McKinney v. Christiana Community Builders—§ 5.2(1), n. 4, 8, 14, 16.

McKnight v. General Motors Corp.—§ 12.1(2), n. 12.

McKnight v. Superior Court (Faber)—§ 6.1(5), n. 27.

McLean, State ex rel. Casale v.—§ 2.4(4), n. 8.

McLemore v. Alabama Power Co.—§ 3.6(1), n. 25.

McNeilab, Inc. v. North River Ins. Co.—§ 4.1(2), n. 20; § 4.9(4); § 4.9(4), n. 20.

McPherson v. Schlemmer—§ 5.13(1), n. 27; § 5.15(2), n. 1.

McRaven v. Culley—§ 5.10(3), n. 9.

Med Mac Realty Co., Inc. v. Lerner—§ 12.-15(2), n. 35.

Meehan v. Shaughnessy—§ 10.4, n. 50.

Meeme Mut. Home Protective Fire Ins. Co. v. Lorfeld—§ 11.2, n. 22.

Meinhard v. Salmon—§ 10.4, n. 9.

Meletio Sea Food Co. v. Gordons Transports—§ 5.13(3), n. 15.

Memphis Community School Dist. v. Stachura—§ 3.1, n. 11; § 7.1(2), n. 3; § 7.4(2); § 7.4(2), n. 8.

Memphis Housing Authority v. Peabody Garage Co.—§ 3.5, n. 1.

Menard v. Woonsocket Teachers' Guild–AFT 951—§ 2.8(6), n. 2.

Meracle v. Children's Service Soc. of Wisconsin—§ 8.2, n. 5, 9.

Mercer v. Brown—§ 5.7(3), n. 18.

Merchants Bank & Trust Co. v. Erdeljohn—§ 4.7(2), n. 4.

Merchants Fire Assurance Corporation v. Lattimore—§ 5.16(4), n. 17.

Mercury Motors Exp., Inc. v. Smith—§ 3.11(6), n. 7.

Merrill v. Tropoli—§ 5.13(1), n. 11.

Merritt v. Williams—§ 5.13(2), n. 8.

Messenger v. Messenger—§ 2.8(1), n. 30.

Metcalfe v. Talarski—§ 4.5(2), n. 21.

Metro Chrysler–Plymouth, Inc. v. Pearce—§ 4.8, n. 4.

Metropolitan Atlanta Rapid Transit Authority v. Boswell—§ 3.11(1), n. 98.

Metzler v. Bolen—§ 9.5, n. 34.

Meyers v. Kissner—§ 2.4(4), n. 30, 37.

M. H. Siegfried Real Estate, Inc. v. Renfrow—§ 5.6(2), n. 3.

Miami Herald Pub. Co. v. Tornillo—§ 7.2(14), n. 21.

Michelin Tires (Canada), Ltd. v. First Nat. Bank of Boston—§ 4.7(2), n. 3.

Mickelson v. Barnet—§ 6.1(4), n. 27.

Microsoftware Computer Systems, Inc. v. Ontel Corp.—§ 2.9(4), n. 13.

Middlebrooks v. Lonas—§ 4.3(2), n. 21, 52; § 4.3(3), n. 5; § 4.7(1), n. 9.

Middle East Banking Co. v. State Street Bank Intern.—§ 3.7, n. 13.

Middlesex County Sewerage Authority v. National Sea Clammers Ass'n—§ 2.10, n. 25.

Middlewest Motor Freight Bureau v. United States—§ 2.11(3), n. 19.

Midland–Guardian Co. v. United Consumers Club, Inc.—§ 3.12, n. 33.

Midland Steel Prods. Co. v. International Union, United Auto, Aerospace and Agricultural Implement Workers of America Local 486—§ 2.8(4), n. 5; § 2.8(5), n. 3.

Midwest Indus. Painting of Florida, Inc. v. United States—§ 5.14(3), n. 4, 37.

Mieske v. Bartell Drug Co.—§ 5.16(3), n. 8, 10.

Miga v. City of Holyoke—§ 3.11(1), n. 76.

Mika Timber Co., Inc., People v.—§ 2.10, n. 13; § 2.11(1), n. 28.

Mike Golden, Inc. v. Tenneco Oil Co.—§ 3.3(5), n. 7.

Miles v. F.E.R.M. Enterprises, Inc.—§ 7.3(2), n. 3; § 7.4(2), n. 1.

Milkovich v. Lorain Journal Co.—§ 7.2(1), n. 13.

Miller v. Appleby—§ 9.2(1), n. 19.

Miller v. Cudahy Co.—§ 5.7(3), n. 9.

Miller v. Johnson—§ 8.2, n. 32.

Miller v. Kingsley—§ 3.11(1), n. 28.

Miller v. Race—§ 6.1(1), n. 1.

Miller v. Ritchie—§ 12.15(2), n. 5.

Miller v. Sears—§ 4.5(2), n. 22; § 4.5(3), n. 7.

Miller v. Vineyard—§ 12.15(3), n. 3.

Miller v. Wellman Dynamics Corp.—§ 8.3(1), n. 9.

Miller v. Wykoff—§ 3.12, n. 40, 42.

Miller, Commissioner v.—§ 3.11(3), n. 6.

Miller Pontiac, Inc. v. Osborne—§ 5.14(2), n. 7.

Milliken, In re Marriage of—§ 4.9(3), n. 11, 13.

Milling v. Berg—§ 2.4(6), n. 6.

Mills v. Electric Auto–Lite Co.—§ 3.10(2), n. 17.

Milwaukee Rescue Mission, Inc. v. Redevelopment Authority of City of Milwaukee—§ 3.5, n. 1; § 5.2(6), n. 6, 19.

Minsky's Follies of Fla., Inc. v. Sennes—§ 13.-2(2), n. 14.

Misener, In re—§ 2.8(6), n. 9.

Misisco v. La Maita—§ 13.2(2), n. 6.

Mississippi Power & Light Co. v. Tillman—§ 5.14(3), n. 30.

Missouri v. Jenkins—§ 3.10(5), n. 7; § 3.10(7), n. 14; § 3.10(10), n. 29.

Missouri Baptist Hosp. v. United States—§ 12.15(3), n. 2.

Mistletoe Exp. Service of Oklahoma City, Okl. v. Locke—§ 12.3(1), n. 2.

Mistretta v. United States—§ 8.8, n. 37.

Mitchell v. Dunn—§ 6.1(4), n. 13.

Mitchell v. W. T. Grant Co.—§ 5.17(2); § 5.17(2), n. 6, 7, 11, 13.

Mitchell Bros. Film Group v. Cinema Adult Theater—§ 2.4(2), n. 19.

Mohoff v. Northrup King & Co.—§ 5.13(2), n. 12.

Molien v. Kaiser Foundation Hospitals—§ 5.15(3), n. 10.

Molzof v. United States—§ 8.1(4), n. 47.

Monarco v. Lo Greco—§ 13.2(5); § 13.2(5), n. 19, 20.

Mondelli v. Saline Sewer Co.—§ 5.6(1), n. 1; § 5.6(2), n. 2.

Monessen Southwestern Ry. Co. v. Morgan—§ 3.6(2), n. 40; § 3.7, n. 2; § 8.1(4), n. 103.

Monge v. Beebe Rubber Co.—§ 6.10(1), n. 1.

Monongahela Nav. Co. v. United States—§ 5.16(2), n. 3.

Monroe v. Tielsch—§ 7.2(14), n. 18.

Monsanto, United States v.—§ 6.1(5), n. 26.

Montgomery's Estate, In re—§ 4.5(4), n. 8.
Montgomery Ward & Co. v. Morris—§ 7.3(2), n. 12.
Moody v. Pitts—§ 6.1(4), n. 11.
Mooney v. Johnson Cattle Co., Inc.—§ 9.2(4), n. 7.
Moore, In re Estate of—§ 13.2(2), n. 29.
Moore v. McAllister—§ 2.5(1), n. 15.
Moore v. McDaniel—§ 5.7(2), n. 29.
Moore v. National Ass'n of Securities Dealers, Inc.—§ 3.10(6), n. 32.
Moore v. Regents of University of California—§ 4.5(3), n. 35; § 5.18(1), n. 4; § 5.18(2), n. 18.
Moragne v. States Marine Lines, Inc.—§ 8.3(1), n. 11.
Moran v. Johns–Manville Sales Corp.—§ 3.11(8), n. 3.
Moran v. Rhode Island Broth. of Correctional Officers—§ 3.10(3), n. 47.
Morey v. Sings—§ 2.4(2), n. 20.
Morgan v. Foretich—§ 2.8(3), n. 27.
Morgan v. McDonough—§ 1.4, n. 25; § 7.4(4), n. 19.
Moritz v. Horsman—§ 4.6, n. 15.
Morris v. Frudenfeld—§ 8.2, n. 41.
Morris v. Savoy—§ 8.8, n. 21, 24.
Morris v. Whitehead—§ 2.8(2), n. 21.
Moses v. MacFerlan—§ 4.1(2), n. 2; § 4.2(3); § 4.2(3), n. 17.
Motor Vehicle Mfrs. Ass'n of United States, Inc. v. O'Neill—§ 2.6(4), n. 2, 22.
Motor Vehicle Mfrs. Ass'n of United States, Inc. v. State—§ 2.6(3), n. 47; § 2.6(4), n. 22.
Mott v. Tri–Continental Financial Corp.—§ 9.3(2), n. 6.
Moulton v. Groveton Papers Co.—§ 5.2(2), n. 21; § 5.2(6), n. 18.
Mountain View Coach Lines, Inc. v. Storms—§ 5.15(2), n. 23.
Muniz v. Hoffman—§ 2.8(4), n. 20.
Munn v. Southern Health Plan, Inc.—§ 3.9, n. 16, 28.
Munoz v. Kaiser Steel Corp.—§ 13.2(4), n. 5.
Murdock–Bryant Const., Inc. v. Taylor Pearson Co.—§ 4.1(2), n. 2; § 4.5(1), n. 5; § 4.5(2), n. 16; § 4.9(4), n. 31; § 12.7(7), n. 7.
Murray v. Feight—§ 3.11(1), n. 92.
M/V Elaine Jones, Petition of—§ 5.14(3), n. 23.

N

Nab v. Hills—§ 4.8, n. 25.
Nabours v. Longview Sav. & Loan Ass'n—§ 3.11(1), n. 54; § 3.11(11), n. 1.
Naccash v. Burger—§ 8.2, n. 8.
Nadeau v. Helgemoe—§ 3.10(6); § 3.10(6), n. 29, 31.
Nashban Barrel & Container Co. v. G. G. Parsons Trucking Co.—§ 5.15(2), n. 14, 70.
Nast v. Lockett—§ 3.11(1), n. 75.
National Advertising Co. v. Main Street Shopping Center—§ 12.15(3), n. 3.
National American Corp. v. Federal Republic of Nigeria—§ 4.3(7), n. 4; § 11.6(3); § 11.6(3), n. 9.

National Merchandising Corp. v. Leyden—§ 6.6(3), n. 2.
National Shawmut Bank of Boston v. Fidelity Mut. Life Ins. Co.—§ 4.7(2); § 4.7(2), n. 11.
National Treasury Employees Union v. I.R.S.—§ 3.10(6), n. 26.
National Union of Marine Cooks & Stewards v. Arnold—§ 2.8(2), n. 26.
Nationwide Mut. Ins. Co. v. American Mut. Liability Ins. Co.—§ 4.9(3), n. 12.
Natural Soda Products Co. v. City of Los Angeles—§ 3.3(4), n. 3.
NBA Properties, Inc. v. Gold—§ 2.8(5); § 2.8(5), n. 28; § 2.8(7), n. 14.
Nebraska Public Power Dist. v. Austin Power, Inc.—§ 3.6(2), n. 12.
Nebraska Public Power Dist. v. Lockard—§ 2.5(1), n. 12.
Nees v. Hocks—§ 6.10(1), n. 1.
Nelson v. Boulay Bros. Co.—§ 5.13(1), n. 9.
Nelson v. Coleman Co.—§ 5.16(3), n. 3, 6.
Nelson v. Jacobsen—§ 3.11(5), n. 7.
Nelson Realty Co. v. Darling Shop of Birmingham, Inc.—§ 4.8, n. 17.
Neu v. Miami Herald Pub. Co.—§ 2.10, n. 4.
Nevitt, In re—§ 2.8(2), n. 2.
Newbery Alaska, Inc. v. Alaska Constructors, Inc.—§ 5.13(3), n. 6.
Newburger Cotton Co. v. Stevens—§ 5.13(2), n. 12.
New Hampshire v. Gross—§ 2.8(5), n. 25.
New Jersey Highway Authority v. Renner—§ 2.6(4), n. 23, 29.
New Jersey Power & Light Co. v. Mabee—§ 5.14(3), n. 30.
New Jersey State Bd. of Dentistry, Matter of—§ 4.9(3), n. 21.
Newman v. Piggie Park Enterprises, Inc.—§ 1.5, n. 3; § 3.10(4), n. 19.
Newport, City of v. Fact Concerts, Inc.—§ 3.11(1), n. 76, 98.
Newton v. Porter—§ 5.18(3), n. 14, 25.
New York, City of v. Corwen—§ 10.6, n. 8.
New York Life Ins. Co. v. Chittenden & Eastmen—§ 11.2, n. 25.
New York State Elec. & Gas Corp. v. Fischer—§ 5.13(1), n. 9; § 5.14(3), n. 18.
New York State Nat. Organization for Women v. Terry—§ 2.8(2), n. 18; § 2.8(3), n. 24.
New York Times Co. v. Sullivan—§ 7.2(1), n. 9; § 7.2(4); § 7.2(4), n. 1.
Nguyen v. Scott—§ 9.3(4), n. 1; § 10.5(1); § 10.5(1), n. 14, 19, 21.
Nichols–Morris Corp. v. Morris—§ 10.4, n. 47.
Nicholson v. United Pacific Ins. Co.—§ 3.11(1), n. 91.
Nicholson's Mobile Home Sales, Inc. v. Schramm—§ 3.11(12), n. 3.
Nickens v. McGehee—§ 5.16(3), n. 6.
N.J. Indus. Properties, Inc. v. Y.C.& V.L., Inc.—§ 12.15(3), n. 3, 49.
Norfolk & Western Ry. Co. v. Liepelt—§ 3.8(1), n. 11.
North Counties Hydro–Elec Co. v. United States—§ 5.11(1), n. 8.
Northcross v. Board of Ed. of Memphis City Schools—§ 3.10(10), n. 16.

Northeast Women's Center, Inc. v. McMonagle, 939 F.2d 57—§ 2.8(3), n. 24.

Northeast Women's Center, Inc. v. McMonagle, 868 F.2d 1342—§ 2.4(2), n. 2, 21; § 2.8(5), n. 4.

Northern Corp. v. Chugach Elec. Ass'n—§ 13.-3(2), n. 22.

Northern Indiana Public Service Co. v. Carbon County Coal Co.—§ 13.3(2), n. 16.

North Georgia Finishing, Inc. v. Di–Chem, Inc.—§ 5.17(2), n. 6.

North Pac. Lumber Co. v. Oliver—§ 2.4(2), n. 10, 16.

North Platte Baptist Church of North Platte, State ex rel. Kandt v.—§ 2.8(3), n. 6.

Northwestern Nat. Cas. Co. v. McNulty—§ 3.11(7); § 3.11(7), n. 5.

Norton v. Haggett—§ 4.9(3), n. 17.

Novak, In re—§ 2.8(3), n. 15; § 2.8(6), n. 6.

Nuttall v. Holman—§ 4.8, n. 19.

O

Oak Hall Cap and Gown Co., Inc. v. Old Dominion Freight Line, Inc.—§ 5.13(3), n. 14, 15.

Oatway, Hertslet, In re v. Oatway—§ 6.1(4), n. 14.

O'Brien v. City of Greers Ferry—§ 3.10(5), n. 6.

O'Brien v. Isaacs—§ 3.9, n. 25.

O'Brien Bros. v. The Helen B. Moran—§ 3.5, n. 45, 50; § 5.16(2), n. 3.

Ocean Nat. Bank of Kennebunk v. Diment—§ 5.13(2), n. 1, 4; § 6.1(1), n. 4.

Ocean West Contractors, Inc. v. Halec Const. Co., Inc.—§ 3.10(3), n. 4.

Ochs v. Borrelli—§ 8.2, n. 3, 33, 34, 41, 54.

O'Donnell v. K–Mart Corp.—§ 3.11(6), n. 18.

Oelrichs v. Williams—§ 2.11(3); § 2.11(3), n. 54.

O'Gilvie v. International Playtex, Inc.—§ 3.11(1), n. 43, 84; § 3.11(3), n. 15.

Oglebay Norton Co. v. Armco, Inc.—§ 2.8(8), n. 10; § 4.5(4), n. 19; § 12.1(2), n. 11; § 13.3(2), n. 30.

Ohio v. Kovacs—§ 1.8; § 1.8, n. 4; § 2.5(2), n. 9.

Ohio Power Co. v. Huff—§ 5.14(2), n. 5; § 5.14(3), n. 18.

Ohio–Sealy Mattress Mfg. Co. v. Sealy Inc.—§ 3.12, n. 34.

Ohio, State of v. United States Dept. of Interior—§ 5.2(1), n. 15; § 5.2(5), n. 12, 20.

Ohio Utilities Co v. Public Utilities Commission of Ohio—§ 5.2(6), n. 5.

Ojeda v. Ojeda—§ 13.2(5), n. 9.

O'Keeffe v. Snyder—§ 4.7(1), n. 1.

Olan Mills, Inc. of Tex. v. Dodd—§ 7.3(2), n. 14.

Olivares, Ex parte—§ 2.8(6), n. 3.

Oliver v. Campbell—§ 12.7(5), n. 4.

Oliver v. Raymark Industries, Inc.—§ 3.11(10), n. 1.

Olivetti Corp. v. Ames Business Systems, Inc.—§ 3.11(10), n. 1.

Ollig v. Eagles—§ 5.10(4), n. 17.

Ollman v. Evans—§ 7.2(1), n. 13.

Olney Sav. & Loan Ass'n v. Trinity Banc Sav. Ass'n—§ 9.2(6), n. 14.

Olwell v. Nye & Nissen Co.—§ 4.3(2), n. 34; § 4.3(5), n. 19; § 4.5(3), n. 8, 35; § 5.18(2); § 5.18(2), n. 1, 5, 14, 16; § 5.18(3), n. 8.

179.26 Acres of Land in Douglas County, Kan., United States v.—§ 5.16(2), n. 9.

Orange Beach Water, Sewer, and Fire Protection Authority v. M/V Alva—§ 5.14(3), n. 18.

Oregon By and Through State Highway Commission, State of v. Tug Go–Getter—§ 5.14(3), n. 35.

Oregon ex rel. Cox, State of v. Davidson Industries, Inc.—§ 2.10, n. 21; § 5.7(2), n. 44.

Oregon State Bar v. Wright—§ 2.4(4), n. 35; § 2.8(7), n. 2.

Orton v. Butler—§ 6.1(1), n. 1.

Ostrowski v. Azzara—§ 3.9, n. 30.

Otis v. Otis—§ 4.3(2), n. 11; § 5.18(3), n. 22.

Otis Oil & Gas Corporation v. Maier—§ 2.7, n. 18.

O'Toole v. Greenberg—§ 8.2, n. 32.

Ottavia v. Sevarese—§ 5.10(4), n. 11, 14.

Otto Farms, Inc. v. First Nat. Bank of York—§ 5.15(2), n. 43.

Overnight Motor Transp. Co. v. Missel—§ 3.12, n. 18, 41.

Overseas Tankship (U.K.) Limited v. Morts Dock & Engineering Co., Limited (The Wagon Mound)—§ 12.4(6), n. 3.

Owen v. Meserve—§ 8.8, n. 29.

Owens v. Texaco, Inc.—§ 5.10(3), n. 25.

Ozark Bi–Products v. Bohannon—§ 2.8(8), n. 6.

P

Pacific Mut. Life Ins. Co. v. Haslip—§ 3.11(1), n. 41; § 3.11(6), n. 9; § 3.11(11), n. 3; § 3.11(12); § 3.11(12), n. 12, 14; § 3.11(14), n. 4.

Packaging Industries Group, Inc. v. Cheney—§ 2.11(2), n. 12.

Page Communications Engineers, Inc. v. Froehlke—§ 2.11(3), n. 29, 30.

Paine v. Meller—§ 4.3(8), n. 12.

Palmer v. A.H. Robins Co., Inc.—§ 3.11(8), n. 3.

Palmer v. City of Chicago—§ 3.10(6), n. 13, 27.

Palmer v. Palmer—§ 3.6(4), n. 11.

Palmer v. Ted Stevens Honda, Inc.—§ 3.11(11), n. 1.

Panhandle Pipe & Supply Co. v. S. W. Pressey & Son—§ 4.7(1), n. 1.

Panhandle Rehabilitation Center, Inc. v. Larson—§ 12.22(2), n. 7.

Pannell v. Food Services of America—§ 3.6(1), n. 18.

Paper Converting Mach. Co. v. Magna–Graphics Corp.—§ 3.12, n. 34.

Paramount Pictures Corp. v. Davis—§ 2.9(1), n. 10.

Pardee v. Camden Lumber Co.—§ 5.10(3), n. 27.

Parker v. Baltimore Paint & Chemical Corp.—§ 4.8, n. 13.

Parker v. Hoppe—§ 3.7, n. 13.
Parker v. Twentieth Century–Fox Film Corp.—§ 3.9, n. 15.
Parker Tampa Two, Inc. v. Somerset Development Corp.—§ 2.11(3), n. 10, 39.
Parklane Hosiery Co., Inc. v. Shore—§ 2.6(4); § 2.6(4), n. 30.
Parks v. Yakima Valley Production Credit Ass'n—§ 5.13(2), n. 12.
Parks v. Zions First Nat. Bank—§ 4.5(3), n. 36.
Parmalee v. Bartolomei—§ 5.15(2), n. 49.
Parsons v. Lambert—§ 5.15(2), n. 81.
Passmore v. Woodard—§ 4.5(2), n. 16; § 12.-7(3), n. 18.
Patton v. Mohave County—§ 3.12, n. 1.
Paul v. Osceola County—§ 5.15(3), n. 14.
Paulsen v. County of Nassau—§ 2.5(2), n. 2; § 2.11(1), n. 25.
Paul Wartzman v. Hightower Productions, Ltd.—§ 3.9, n. 22; § 12.3(1), n. 2.
Payne v. Consolidation Coal Co.—§ 5.1, n. 15.
Peak v. W. T. Grant Co.—§ 7.3(2), n. 11.
Pearce v. G. R. Kirk Co.—§ 3.12, n. 42.
Pearlman v. Reliance Ins. Co.—§ 4.3(4), n. 21.
Pearson v. Board of Health of Chicopee—§ 3.10(2), n. 30.
Pecaflor Const., Inc. v. Landes—§ 3.7, n. 15.
Peed v. Burleson's, Inc.—§ 4.7(1), n. 2.
Peevyhouse v. Garland Coal & Min. Co.—§ 1.9, n. 10; § 12.19(1), n. 44.
Pelletier v. Eisenberg—§ 5.13(1), n. 26; § 5.13(3), n. 8; § 5.16(4), n. 20.
Pendoley v. Ferreira—§ 5.7(2), n. 36.
Pennell v. Deffrell—§ 6.1(4), n. 8.
Pennsylvania v. Delaware Valley Citizens' Council for Clean Air, 107 S.Ct. 3078—§ 3.10(10); § 3.10(10), n. 18, 19.
Pennsylvania v. Delaware Valley Citizens' Council for Clean Air, 106 S.Ct. 3088—§ 3.10(10), n. 7.
Pennsylvania S. V. R. Co. v. Cleary—§ 5.2(1), n. 3.
Pennzoil Co. v. Texaco, Inc.—§ 2.5(4), n. 19.
People v. _____ (see opposing party)
People ex rel. v. _____ (see opposing party and relator)
People's Nat. Bank v. Waggoner—§ 5.18(3), n. 12.
Perholtz, United States v.—§ 5.17(3), n. 10.
Perilli v. Board of Educ., Monongalia County—§ 2.6(4), n. 20.
Perley v. Town of Effingham—§ 5.10(3), n. 4.
Perry v. Woodall—§ 4.8, n. 4.
Perry v. Wyeth—§ 4.3(2), n. 39.
Peter Fabrics, Inc. v. S.S. "Hermes"—§ 3.10(3), n. 32.
Petermann v. International Broth. of Teamsters, Chauffeurs, Warehousemen and Helpers of America Local 396—§ 6.10(1), n. 2.
Peters v. Saft—§ 8.8, n. 23, 29.
Peterson v. Continental Boiler Works, Inc.—§ 3.5, n. 1.
Peterson v. Crown Financial Corp.—§ 4.5(2), n. 24.
Peterson v. Hager—§ 5.13(3), n. 7.
Peterson v. Midland Nat. Bank—§ 4.1(2), n. 16.

Peterson v. Redpath—§ 6.1(4), n. 10.
Peterson v. Western World Ins. Co.—§ 8.1(2), n. 7.
Petition of (see name of party)
Petrie v. LeVan—§ 4.3(2), n. 36, 49.
Petrie–Clemons v. Butterfield—§ 3.4, n. 14.
Petty Motor Co., United States v.—§ 3.4, n. 1.
Phelps, Estate of v. Odekerken—§ 2.6(3), n. 50.
Phelps v. Duke Power Co.—§ 3.6(1), n. 15.
Phelps v. Williams—§ 2.7, n. 22.
Philadelphia Newspapers, Inc. v. Hepps—§ 7.2(1), n. 12.
Philippine Sugar Estates Development Co. v. Government of Philippine Islands—§ 4.3(7), n. 5.
Phillips v. District of Columbia—§ 7.3(2), n. 3.
Phillips v. Iowa Dist. Court for Johnson County—§ 2.8(4), n. 4.
Phillips v. Kaplus—§ 2.6(3), n. 22.
Phillips v. Ripley & Fletcher Co.—§ 4.8, n. 22.
Phillips v. United States—§ 8.2, n. 8, 10, 18, 19, 47.
Philpott v. Superior Court In and For Los Angeles County—§ 4.1(2), n. 1; § 4.2(3), n. 8; § 4.8, n. 3.
Phoenix Indem. Co. v. Steiden Stores—§ 11.2, n. 23.
Phoenix Mut. Life Ins. Co. v. Conway—§ 2.6(3), n. 47.
Phoenix Newspapers, Inc. v. Superior Court—§ 2.8(6), n. 3, 16.
Piarowski v. Illinois Community College Dist. 515—§ 5.16(4), n. 9.
Pierce v. Underwood—§ 3.10(4), n. 8.
Pierro, State v.—§ 10.6, n. 9.
Pilcher v. Rawlins—§ 4.7(1), n. 4.
Pile v. Pedrick—§ 5.10(3), n. 40.
Pirmantgen v. Feminelli—§ 7.2(14), n. 1.
Pitre v. Opelousas General Hosp.—§ 8.2, n. 24, 26, 27, 32, 37, 39, 40.
Planned Parenthood Ass'n of Cincinnati, Inc. v. City of Cincinnati—§ 1.3, n. 8; § 2.9(3), n. 16; § 2.11(2), n. 4, 10.
Planned Parenthood League of Massachusetts, Inc. v. Operation Rescue—§ 2.8(7), n. 15; § 5.10(3), n. 3.
Polaroid Corp. v. Schuster's Exp., Inc.—§ 5.13(3), n. 14.
Police Com'r of Boston v. Municipal Court of Dorchester Dist.—§ 7.2(14), n. 17.
Pomilio v. Caserta—§ 5.10(4), n. 16.
Ponder v. Angel Animal Hosp., Inc.—§ 5.15(3), n. 13.
Pons v. Lorillard—§ 2.6(3), n. 61.
Pope v. Garrett—§ 6.7, n. 13.
Popp v. Gountanis—§ 4.1(1), n. 4; § 4.3(2), n. 34; § 4.3(5), n. 20; § 12.7(4), n. 17.
Porter v. United States—§ 5.16(4), n. 3.
Porter v. Wilson—§ 13.4(2), n. 27.
Posey v. Leavitt—§ 2.6(2), n. 7.
Poss v. Franklin Federal Sav. & Loan Ass'n of Russellville, Alabama—§ 2.6(3), n. 29.
Post v. Commissioner of Dept. of Environmental Quality Engineering—§ 2.3(5), n. 4.
Potomac Elec. Power Co. v. Smith—§ 8.8, n. 25, 29.
Powell v. Home Run Inn, Inc.—§ 2.11(3), n. 3.

Powell v. Missouri & A. Land & Min. Co.—§ 6.1(4), n. 22.

Prandini v. National Tea Co.—§ 3.10(2), n. 12.

Premeaux v. Smith—§ 2.8(4), n. 12.

Premier Elec. Const. Co. v. La Salle Nat. Bank—§ 4.9(4), n. 29.

Presbyterian Church in United States v. Mary Elizabeth Blue Hull Memorial Presbyterian Church—§ 2.9(5), n. 14.

Presley, Estate of v. Russen—§ 2.11(1), n. 17.

Pressed Steel Car Co. v. Standard Steel Car Co.—§ 5.17(3), n. 2.

Preston, Ex parte—§ 2.8(2), n. 8; § 2.8(7), n. 6.

Preston, In re—§ 6.1(4), n. 13.

Presto–X–Company v. Ewing—§ 2.5(1), n. 12.

Prewitt v. Branham—§ 5.13(2), n. 4.

Price v. Neal—§ 4.7(2), n. 19.

Prince v. Friedman—§ 11.2, n. 19.

Principal Cas. Ins. Co. v. Norwood—§ 3.10(2), n. 5; § 4.1(2), n. 3; § 4.3(4), n. 9, 13.

Pritchard Petroleum Co. v. Farmers Co-op. Oil & Supply Co.—§ 5.8(2), n. 20.

Processed Plastic Co. v. Warner Communications, Inc.—§ 2.11(1), n. 16.

Proctor v. Sagamore Big Game Club—§ 4.3(2), n. 49.

Producers Lumber & Supply Co. v. Olney Bldg. Co.—§ 4.9(1), n. 11.

Proffitt v. Bartolo—§ 8.2, n. 8.

Progressive Life Ins. Co. v. Doster—§ 7.3(2), n. 12.

Provencher v. Berman—§ 6.1(4), n. 5, 20.

Prucha v. Weiss—§ 7.2(14), n. 1.

Prudential Ins. Co. of America v. Couch—§ 4.3(4), n. 2; § 4.6, n. 3.

Public Service Co. of Indiana, Inc. v. Bath Iron Works Corp.—§ 3.3(4), n. 11; § 5.15(2), n. 21.

Public Service Co. of New Mexico v. Jasso—§ 5.14(2), n. 3, 5.

Public Service Elec. & Gas Co. v. Stone—§ 5.14(2), n. 1, 7.

Purchasing Associates, Inc. v. Weitz—§ 12.22(2), n. 14.

Q

Quealy v. Paine, Webber, Jackson & Curtis, Inc.—§ 3.10(1), n. 1; § 5.13(2), n. 7.

Queen v. Sisk—§ 12.11(1), n. 29.

R

Radich v. Kruly—§ 2.5(4), n. 6.

Rafal v. Rafal—§ 5.16(3), n. 4.

Raffles v. Wichelhaus—§ 11.2; § 11.2, n. 31.

Ramirez Co., Inc. v. Housing Authority of City of Houston—§ 4.5(2), n. 14.

Ramp v. St. Paul Fire and Marine Insurance Company—§ 3.10(3), n. 29.

Rardin v. T & D Mach. Handling, Inc.—§ 12.4(5), n. 15.

Rauscher v. Albert—§ 3.10(3), n. 13.

Rauser v. LTV Electrosystems, Inc.—§ 3.6(2), n. 6.

Raven Red Ash Coal Co. v. Ball—§ 4.5(3), n. 35; § 5.8(2), n. 28; § 5.9; § 5.9, n. 14.

Reagan, United States v.—§ 4.6, n. 13.

Reaves v. Davidson—§ 13.4(3), n. 12.

Rebel v. Big Tarkio Drainage Dist. of Holt City—§ 5.11(1), n. 12; § 5.11(4), n. 2.

Redpath, In re Estate of—§ 6.1(4), n. 11, 17.

Redwine v. Fitzhugh—§ 5.16(2), n. 2.

Reebok Intern. Ltd. v. Marnatech Enterprises, Inc.—§ 4.3(5), n. 9; § 6.1(5), n. 19.

Reece, Estate of—§ 6.1(3), n. 7; § 6.1(4), n. 29.

Reetz v. Ellis—§ 7.3(2), n. 3.

Reeves v. Crownshield—§ 2.8(2), n. 11.

Regal Ins. Co. v. Summit Guar. Corp.—§ 5.18(3), n. 8.

Regal Knitwear Co. v. N.L.R.B.—§ 2.8(5), n. 5, 17.

Reich v. United States—§ 2.8(5), n. 8.

Reimer v. Badger Wholesale Co., Inc.—§ 12.3(1), n. 2.

Reno v. Bull—§ 9.2(1), n. 6.

Reposa v. Buhler—§ 3.3(4), n. 12.

Reppun v. Board of Water Supply—§ 5.7(2), n. 45.

Reproductive Health Services v. Lee—§ 5.10(3), n. 12.

Republic Molding Corp. v. B. W. Photo Utilities—§ 2.4(2), n. 14.

Republic of Haiti v. Crown Charters, Inc.—§ 6.1(1), n. 3; § 10.6, n. 4.

Republic of Lebanon v. Sotheby's—§ 2.11(3), n. 50.

Republic of Philippines v. Marcos—§ 6.1(5), n. 17.

Republic Steel Corp., United States v.—§ 2.4(6), n. 15.

Republic Supply Co. of California v. Richfield Oil Co. of California—§ 6.1(4), n. 16, 23, 25.

Reserve Min. Co. v. E.P.A.—§ 5.7(3), n. 21.

R.E.X., Inc. v. Trio Foods Enterprises, Inc.—§ 2.11(3), n. 15, 17.

Rexnord, Inc. v. Ferris—§ 2.6(4), n. 21.

Reynolds Metals Co. v. Wand—§ 5.11(4), n. 2.

Rhodes v. Ritz Camera Centers—§ 5.16(2), n. 1.

R. H. Sanders Corp. v. Haves—§ 2.5(2), n. 8.

Ribas v. Clark—§ 7.3(2), n. 16.

Rice v. Butler—§ 13.4(2), n. 28.

Rice v. Norman Williams Co.—§ 2.9(3), n. 17.

Rice v. Rice—§ 4.7(1); § 4.7(1), n. 15.

Richardson v. Fairbanks North Star Borough—§ 5.15(3), n. 3, 16.

Richfield Oil Corporation v. Karseal Corporation—§ 3.4, n. 13.

Richmond Medical Supply Co., Inc. v. Clifton—§ 12.4(6), n. 3.

Richter v. Richter—§ 6.1(5), n. 22.

Ridenour v. France—§ 4.3(8), n. 12.

Ridley v. VanderBoegh—§ 3.6(2); § 3.6(2), n. 8.

Rieck v. Medical Protective Co. of Fort Wayne, Ind.—§ 8.2, n. 55.

Rigas v. Livingston—§ 2.8(5); § 2.8(5), n. 10.

Riggs Nat. Bank of Washington, D.C. v. District of Columbia—§ 3.6(1), n. 27; § 3.6(3), n. 4.

R. I. Lampus Co. v. Neville Cement Products Corp.—§ 3.3(4), n. 7.

Ringele v. Terteling—§ 4.5(3), n. 35; § 5.18(2), n. 18.
Rite Aid Corp. v. Lake Shore Investors—§ 3.11(1), n. 92.
Riter v. Keokuk Electro–Metals Co.—§ 2.4(5), n. 23; § 5.7(2), n. 43.
Riverside, City of v. Rivera—§ 3.10(7), n. 7; § 3.10(8); § 3.10(8), n. 51; § 3.10(9); § 3.10(9), n. 11, 12.
Rizzo v. Goode—§ 1.7, n. 1; § 1.8, n. 5; § 2.9(5), n. 11; § 7.4(4), n. 23.
Roach v. Roach—§ 1.4, n. 2.
Robak v. United States—§ 8.2, n. 10, 53.
Roberts v. Estate of Barbagallo—§ 9.4, n. 46.
Roberts v. Pilot Freight Carriers, Inc.—§ 5.15(2), n. 76.
Roberts v. Sears, Roebuck & Co.—§ 9.3(4), n. 1.
Robilotto, United States v.—§ 4.3(2), n. 11.
Robinson v. Robinson—§ 4.3(3), n. 8; § 4.9(5), n. 12.
Robison v. Katz—§ 9.4, n. 35.
Rock–Ola Mfg. Corp. v. Music & Television Corp.—§ 5.18(2), n. 2.
Rodrigue v. Copeland—§ 5.7(4), n. 9.
Roe v. Operation Rescue—§ 2.8(3), n. 24; § 2.8(5), n. 5.
Rogers v. Feltz—§ 3.3(4), n. 12.
Rogers v. Rogers—§ 4.3(2), n. 24; § 6.1(3), n. 11.
Rogers v. Runfola & Associates, Inc.—§ 4.3(7), n. 7.
Rogers v. State ex rel. Robinson—§ 2.8(5), n. 20.
Roginsky v. Richardson–Merrell, Inc.—§ 3.11(8), n. 1.
Roman Catholic Archbishop of Boston v. Commonwealth—§ 5.2(6), n. 19.
Romco, Inc. v. Broussard—§ 5.13(1), n. 22.
Ronan v. Ronan—§ 4.3(8), n. 2.
Rondeau v. Mosinee Paper Corp.—§ 2.10, n. 1, 19.
Rose v. Chaikin—§ 5.7(2), n. 38, 41, 48.
Rose v. Rose—§ 2.5(2), n. 8.
Rosebrough Monument Co. v. Memorial Park Cemetery Ass'n—§ 3.10(6), n. 4.
Rosenberg v. Rosenberg—§ 2.6(4), n. 27.
Ross v. Bernhard—§ 2.6(1), n. 9; § 2.6(3); § 2.6(3), n. 26; § 2.6(4), n. 17.
Ross v. Board of Review of City of Iowa City—§ 3.5, n. 56.
Ross v. Bumstead—§ 4.3(8), n. 12.
Ross v. Forest Lawn Memorial Park—§ 12.5(1), n. 6.
Roth v. Reagen—§ 7.2(14), n. 18.
Rothko's Estate, Matter of—§ 4.3(2), n. 13; § 4.5(2), n. 8; § 4.5(3), n. 4; § 5.18(2), n. 8; § 9.3(4), n. 35.
Rousseff v. E.F. Hutton Co.—§ 9.2(6), n. 7.
Rowe v. Maremont Corp.—§ 9.3(4), n. 7, 32.
Rowlett v. Anheuser–Busch, Inc.—§ 3.11(15), n. 19.
Rozan v. Rozan—§ 2.7, n. 22.
Rubin v. Matthews Intern. Corp.—§ 12.5(1), n. 1.
Ruckelshaus v. Sierra Club—§ 3.10(5), n. 10.
Rudd Const. Equipment Co., Inc. v. Clark Equipment Co.—§ 5.13(3), n. 10.

Ruddle v. Moore—§ 6.1(4), n. 29.
Rufo v. Inmates of Suffolk County Jail—§ 2.8(8), n. 12.
Ruhsam v. Ruhsam—§ 2.8(2), n. 9.
Ruiz v. Estelle—§ 1.4, n. 23; § 7.4(4), n. 18.
Ruiz v. Varan—§ 3.3(2), n. 23.
Rupert v. Sellers—§ 3.11(5), n. 21.
Russell v. Farley—§ 2.11(3), n. 30, 45.
Russell v. Shell Petroleum Corporation—§ 9.5, n. 34.
Rutherford v. James—§ 5.16(3), n. 5.
Ruva v. Mente—§ 4.3(8), n. 1.
R. Y., In re—§ 2.6(3), n. 51.
Ryan, State v.—§ 2.8(1), n. 5.

S

Sabourin v. Woish—§ 5.8(2), n. 25.
Sack v. Feinman—§ 3.6(2), n. 20; § 4.3(2), n. 16.
Safeco Ins. Co. v. Ellinghouse—§ 3.11(14), n. 9.
Sagadin v. Ripper—§ 3.6(1), n. 15.
Salamon v. Terra—§ 4.2(3), n. 13; § 4.9(2), n. 5; § 4.9(4); § 4.9(4), n. 19.
Salesian Soc., Inc. v. Village of Ellenville—§ 5.8(2), n. 8.
Salinger v. Random House, Inc.—§ 2.11(1), n. 14.
Sampson v. Grooms—§ 5.10(3), n. 45.
Sampson v. Murray—§ 1.1, n. 51.
Sanchez–Corea v. Bank of America—§ 3.4, n. 10.
Sanders v. Stevens—§ 10.5(1), n. 16.
San Francisco, City and County of v. City Inv. Corp.—§ 5.7(2), n. 32.
Santana v. Registrars of Voters of Worcester—§ 3.11(1), n. 28.
Santiago–Negron v. Castro–Davila—§ 7.4(4), n. 6.
Saunders v. Sharp—§ 2.11(3), n. 52.
Savers Federal Sav. and Loan Ass'n of Little Rock v. First Federal Sav. and Loan Ass'n of Harrison—§ 4.8, n. 1.
Scandinavian Mut. Ins. Co. v. Chicago, B. & Q.R. Co.—§ 4.3(4), n. 1; § 4.9(3), n. 11.
Schanz v. Terry's Estate—§ 4.9(4), n. 4.
Scheldrup v. Gaffney—§ 2.8(2), n. 13.
Schenk v. Smith—§ 3.6(1), n. 17.
Schlange–Schoeningen v. Parrish—§ 9.4, n. 40.
Schmeckpeper v. Koertje—§ 4.9(4), n. 13.
Schmidt v. Knox—§ 3.6(1), n. 25.
Schmidt v. Lessard—§ 2.8(7), n. 13; § 5.7(3), n. 12.
Schork v. Epperson—§ 5.7(2), n. 33.
Schork v. Huber—§ 8.2, n. 29, 39.
Schroeder v. Perkel—§ 8.2, n. 8.
Schulenburg v. Signatrol, Inc.—§ 10.5(3); § 10.5(3), n. 66.
Schultz v. Sun Plastic, Inc.—§ 3.3(4), n. 12; § 3.6(2), n. 12.
Schwartz v. Heffernan—§ 7.3(2), n. 17.
Schweich v. Ziegler, Inc.—§ 8.8, n. 27.
Schweiter v. Halsey—§ 13.2(2), n. 2.
Scott v. Jordan—§ 5.7(2), n. 31.
Scott v. Neely—§ 2.6(4), n. 13.
Scott v. Woods—§ 2.6(4), n. 21.

Seaescape, Ltd., Inc. v. Maximum Marketing Exposure, Inc.—§ 2.11(3), n. 14.

Sears, Roebuck & Co. v. American Plumbing & Supply Co.—§ 10.4; § 10.4, n. 42; § 10.6, n. 2.

Sears Roebuck & Co. v. Ragucci—§ 12.7(7), n. 2, 7.

Sears, Roebuck & Co. v. Stover—§ 4.9(4), n. 28.

Seaway Exp. Corp., In re—§ 4.7(1), n. 6.

S.E.C. v. Texas Gulf Sulphur Co.—§ 10.5(1), n. 23.

S.E.C. v. Unifund SAL—§ 2.10, n. 13; § 2.11(2), n. 5; § 6.1(5), n. 9, 22.

Security Mut. Ins. Ass'n of Iowa v. Board of Review of City of Fort Dodge, Iowa—§ 4.3(8), n. 5.

Seekings v. Jimmy GMC of Tucson, Inc.—§ 9.4, n. 35.

Seibel v. Liberty Homes, Inc.—§ 3.8(1), n. 7.

Selby Constructors v. McCarthy—§ 2.6(4), n. 20.

Selman v. Shirley—§ 9.2(1), n. 6.

Seneca Oil Co., In re—§ 6.1(4), n. 25, 26.

Sequoia Books, Inc., People v.—§ 2.8(6), n. 14, 18.

Seravalli v. United States—§ 3.5, n. 58; § 5.16(2), n. 3.

Serrano v. Priest—§ 3.10(2); 3.10(2), n. 25.

Seth v. British Overseas Airways Corp.—§ 5.16(4), n. 5.

Sexton v. Public Service Coordinated Transport—§ 2.5(4), n. 8.

Sexton v. Sword S. S. Line—§ 10.6, n. 4.

Seymour v. Oelrichs—§ 13.2(5), n. 14.

Shaffer v. Heitner—§ 2.7, n. 20.

Shahood v. Cavin—§ 5.18(2), n. 2; § 6.1(1), n. 6.

Shannon v. Shaffer Oil & Refining Co.—§ 3.4, n. 6.

Shapiro v. Merrill Lynch, Pierce, Fenner & Smith, Inc.—§ 9.2(6), n. 9.

Share v. Casiano Bel-Air Homeowners Ass'n—§ 3.10(3), n. 4.

Shattles v. Field, Brackett & Pitts, Inc.—§ 5.5, n. 14.

Shatzer, State ex rel. v. Freeport Coal Co.—§ 2.11(3), n. 48.

Shay v. Penrose—§ 4.3(8), n. 1.

Sheerr v. Evesham Tp.—§ 6.9(2), n. 4, 8.

Sheila's Shine Products, Inc. v. Sheila Shine, Inc.—§ 2.6(2), n. 7.

Shelby County Commission v. Smith—§ 3.10(2), n. 30.

Sheldon v. Metro-Goldwyn Pictures Corp.—§ 4.5(3), n. 13.

Shellmar Products Co. v. Allen-Qualley Co.—§ 10.5(3), n. 70.

Sherrod v. Berry—§ 8.1(4); § 8.1(4), n. 57.

Sherrod v. Dutton—§ 5.7(3), n. 18.

Sherwood v. Walker—§ 11.3; § 11.3, n. 23.

Shillitani v. United States—§ 2.8(3), n. 16; § 2.8(4), n. 17.

Shimola v. Nationwide Ins. Co.—§ 3.11(10), n. 1.

Shipman v. Penney—§ 5.18(2), n. 10.

Shonberger v. Oswell—§ 6.1(1), n. 3.

Shukovsky, People v.—§ 2.8(6), n. 7.

Sibley v. Board of Sup'rs of Louisiana State University—§ 8.8, n. 26.

Siemieniec v. Lutheran Gen. Hosp.—§ 8.2, n. 6, 10, 13, 21.

Sierra Nat. Bank v. Brown—§ 9.2(4), n. 1.

Signal Hill, City of v. Owens—§ 5.17(3), n. 5.

Sigue Trucking, Inc. v. Insured Lloyds—§ 5.14(3), n. 3.

Sikes v. Turner—§ 5.10(3), n. 34.

Silbury v. McCoon—§ 4.5(3), n. 33; § 5.13(1), n. 8.

Siler v. Gunn—§ 10.5(1), n. 6.

Silverman v. Blaustein—§ 2.11(1), n. 20; § 6.1(5), n. 16.

Silvers v. Traverse—§ 2.8(5), n. 21.

Simineo, Matter of v. Kelling—§ 2.3(5), n. 6.

Simler v. Conner—§ 2.6(4), n. 19.

Simmons v. West Covina Medical Clinic—§ 3.4, n. 30.

Simonds v. Simonds—§ 4.3(2), n. 24, 51; § 6.1(3), n. 11.

Simonetti v. Lovermi—§ 3.6(1), n. 19.

Simon & Schuster, Inc. v. Members of New York State Crime Victims Bd.—§ 4.1(4), n. 12; § 4.5(3), n. 31; § 7.2(13), n. 3, 6; § 8.9, n. 22.

Simonson v. McInvaille—§ 6.1(4), n. 3.

Simpson v. Simpson—§ 5.17(3), n. 9.

Sims v. Stuart—§ 6.1(5), n. 5.

Sinclair Oil Corp. v. Columbia Cas. Co.—§ 3.11(7), n. 7.

S. J. Groves & Sons Co. v. Warner Co.—§ 3.9, n. 22.

Sjulin v. Clifton Furniture Co.—§ 13.4(3), n. 11, 13.

Skelly Oil Co. v. Ashmore—§ 4.3(8), n. 13; § 6.1(3), n. 1; § 12.14; § 12.14, n. 14.

Skelton v. Doble—§ 4.9(5), n. 21.

Slack v. Sodal—§ 9.2(1), n. 19, 21, 23.

Slater v. Oriental Mills—§ 6.1(3), n. 14.

Slay Warehousing Co., Inc. v. Reliance Ins. Co.—§ 4.9(4), n. 25.

Small v. Springs Industries, Inc.—§ 3.9, n. 17.

Smart v. Tower Land and Inv. Co.—§ 4.9(3), n. 19; § 4.9(4), n. 22.

Smith, In re—§ 7.2(14), n. 17.

Smith v. Baldwin—§ 4.5(2), n. 21.

Smith v. Clough—§ 5.15(3), n. 12.

Smith v. Coronado Foothills Estates Homeowners Ass'n Inc.—§ 2.11(3), n. 13.

Smith v. Cote—§ 8.2, n. 6, 8, 10, 16, 21, 55.

Smith v. Department of Ins.—§ 8.1(4), n. 99; § 8.8, n. 21.

Smith v. Gore—§ 8.2, n. 22, 25, 26, 27, 32, 54.

Smith v. Montoro—§ 5.16(4), n. 9.

Smith v. Smith, 427 A.2d 928—§ 2.8(2), n. 8.

Smith v. Smith, 484 P.2d 409—§ 2.5(1), n. 12.

Smith v. Staso Milling Co.—§ 2.4(6), n. 8.

Smith v. State—§ 2.9(5), n. 3.

Smith v. United Technologies, Essex Group, Inc., Wire and Cable Div.—§ 3.11(1), n. 66.

Smith v. University of North Carolina—§ 3.10(6), n. 13.

Smith v. Wade—§ 3.11(1), n. 76; § 3.11(2), n. 33; § 3.11(3), n. 26.

Smith v. Whalen—§ 7.3(2), n. 3, 18.

Smith Intern., Inc. v. Hughes Tool Co.—§ 2.11(1), n. 15.

Smith's Lessee v. McCann—§ 5.10(1), n. 2.

Snepp v. United States—§ 4.1(4), n. 13; § 4.5(3); § 4.5(3), n. 30; § 7.2(13), n. 4; § 8.9, n. 21; § 10.4; § 10.4, n. 51; § 12.7(4); § 12.-7(4), n. 14.

Sniadach v. Family Finance Corp. of Bay View—§ 5.17(2), n. 6, 13.

Sofie v. Fibreboard Corp.—§ 8.8, n. 21, 23.

Sol-O-Lite Laminating Corp. v. Allen—§ 3.3(4), n. 8.

Solow v. Liebman—§ 2.11(2), n. 3.

Somerville v. Jacobs—§ 4.9(1), n. 21.

Sonoma, County of v. Rex—§ 2.3(5), n. 4.

Sorkin v. Lee—§ 8.2, n. 53.

Southern State Bank v. Leverette—§ 5.10(1), n. 6.

Southwestern Electric Power Co. v. Canal Ins. Co.—§ 5.14(2), n. 2.

Southwestern Newspapers Corp. v. Curtis—§ 2.9(3), n. 21; § 2.9(5), n. 9.

Sovereign Camp W.O.W. v. O'Neill—§ 2.9(4), n. 17.

Spackman v. Ralph M. Parsons Co.—§ 5.16(3), n. 2.

Spallone v. United States—§ 2.8(5), n. 12; § 2.9(5), n. 6.

Sparks v. Republic Nat. Life Ins. Co.—§ 3.10(4), n. 13.

Spaulding v. Cameron—§ 5.11(4), n. 2.

Speck v. Finegold—§ 8.2, n. 8.

Speck v. North Carolina Dairy Foundation, Inc.—§ 4.5(3), n. 16.

Spilotro, United States v.—§ 5.17(2), n. 9; § 5.17(3), n. 10.

Sprague v. Ticonic Nat. Bank—§ 3.10(2), n. 7, 15.

Spratlin, Harrington & Thomas, Inc. v. Hawn—§ 10.4; § 10.4, n. 41; § 10.6, n. 2.

Spreader Specialists, Inc. v. Monroc, Inc.—§ 5.15(2), n. 39.

Spur Industries, Inc. v. Del E. Webb Development Co.—§ 2.4(6), n. 11; § 5.7(3); § 5.7(3), n. 3.

Stack Elec. Inc. v. DiNardi Const. Corp.—§ 12.5(2), n. 1.

St. Amant v. Thompson—§ 7.2(1), n. 9.

Stanardsville Volunteer Fire Co., Inc. v. Berry—§ 2.6(1), n. 3; § 2.6(2), n. 7; § 5.10(3), n. 22.

Standard Oil Co. of New Jersey v. Southern Pac. Co.—§ 5.2(6), n. 5; § 5.14(3), n. 28; § 5.16(2); § 5.16(2), n. 1, 5, 7, 12.

Stanley, State v.—§ 5.15(2), n. 40.

Stapley v. American Bathtub Liners, Inc.—§ 4.5(2), n. 18; § 12.12(2), n. 7.

Star Chevrolet Co. v. Green by Green—§ 13.-4(2), n. 21.

Starczewski v. Unigard Ins. Group—§ 3.6(1), n. 24.

Stark v. Borner—§ 2.10, n. 6.

Stark v. Hamilton—§ 2.9(5), n. 2.

Stark v. Shell Oil Co.—§ 3.9, n. 8.

Starkovich v. Noye—§ 3.11(1), n. 54.

Starns v. United States—§ 3.11(12), n. 35, 37, 38.

State v. ——— (see opposing party)

State Bank of Lehi v. Woolsey—§ 2.6(3), n. 41; § 2.6(4), n. 22.

State By and Through Alabama State Docks Dept. v. Atkins—§ 5.2(6), n. 18.

State, Dept. of Natural Resources, Division of Wildlife v. Benjamin—§ 6.1(3), n. 14.

State ex rel. v. ——— (see opposing party and relator)

State, Fall River County v. Dryden—§ 2.8(3), n. 4.

State Farm Fire & Cas. Co. v. Tashire—§ 2.9(4), n. 33.

State Farm Mut. Auto. Ins. Co. v. Royal Ins. Co. of America—§ 3.10(1), n. 1.

State of (see name of state)

Staton v. Atlantic Coast Line R. Co.—§ 5.7(2), n. 35.

Stearns v. Emery-Waterhouse Co.—§ 2.1(3), n. 8.

Steel Creek Development Corp. v. James—§ 5.8(2), n. 17.

Steffel v. Thompson—§ 2.9(4), n. 40.

Steggles v. National Discount Corp.—§ 5.17(3), n. 2.

Stein v. Simpson—§ 4.9(1), n. 16; § 4.9(3), n. 14, 17.

Steinberg v. McKay—§ 2.9(4), n. 4.

Stephan, State ex rel. v. GAF Corp.—§ 3.11(11), n. 8.

Sterling v. Velsicol Chemical Corp.—§ 8.1(4), n. 63.

St. Joseph Hospital v. Corbetta Const. Co., Inc.—§ 12.2(2), n. 38.

St. Luke Evangelical Lutheran Church, Inc. v. Smith—§ 3.11(5), n. 38.

Stokes v. Johnston—§ 2.6(3), n. 42.

Stokes v. Van Seventer—§ 5.8(2), n. 26.

Stopford v. Boonton Molding Co.—§ 6.6(4), n. 3.

Story v. Gateway Chevrolet Co.—§ 5.15(2), n. 49.

Stott v. Johnston—§ 3.3(4), n. 8.

Stovall v. Illinois Central Gulf R. Co.—§ 3.6(4), n. 11.

Stowers v. Wolodzko—§ 7.3(2), n. 11.

St. Paul at Chase Corp. v. Manufacturers Life Ins. Co.—§ 3.5, n. 8.

Strand v. Courier—§ 3.6(1), n. 27; § 3.6(2), n. 4.

Strande v. Mershon—§ 1.3, n. 6.

Stratford Theater, Inc. v. Town of Stratford—§ 5.6(2), n. 6.

Stratton Finance Co., Commonwealth v.—§ 2.9(3), n. 26.

Strauss, In re Marriage of—§ 2.5(1), n. 12.

Streeter v. Brogan—§ 2.9(5), n. 3.

Streets & Beard Farm Partnership, In re—§ 4.3(8), n. 17.

Strickland, State v.—§ 10.6, n. 9.

Stroud v. Denny's Restaurant, Inc.—§ 3.11(6), n. 8.

Strouth v. Wilkison—§ 9.2(1), n. 6.

Strubbe v. Sonnenschein—§ 4.7(2), n. 13.

Strutt v. Ontario Sav. & Loan Ass'n—§ 4.7(1), n. 18.

Strzelecki v. Blaser's Lakeside Industries of Rice Lake, Inc.—§ 5.14(3), n. 3.

Sturm, Ruger & Co., Inc. v. Day, 615 P.2d 621—§ 3.11(11), n. 2.

Sturm, Ruger & Co., Inc. v. Day, 594 P.2d 38—§ 3.11(3), n. 2, 9; § 3.11(11), n. 2; § 3.11(15), n. 19.
Suburbia Pools, Inc. v. Fischer—§ 2.6(3), n. 43; § 2.6(4), n. 1.
Succession of (see name of party)
Sullivan v. Metro Productions, Inc.—§ 3.12, n. 2.
Summit Const. Co., United States v.—§ 4.9(5); § 4.9(5), n. 6.
Sunbeam Corporation v. Golden Rule Appliance Co.—§ 2.8(2), n. 14.
Suplee v. Eckert—§ 5.10(3), n. 22, 31.
Sutherland v. Kroger Co.—§ 7.3(2), n. 3.
Swaggerty v. Petersen—§ 5.7(2), n. 30.
Swan v. Dolphin Lane Associates, Limited—§ 4.9(4), n. 15.
Swann v. Charlotte–Mecklenburg Bd. of Ed.—§ 7.4(4), n. 25.
Sweeney v. Hoff—§ 2.8(8), n. 3.
Swift v. Broyles—§ 5.6(2), n. 24.
Swift & Co., United States v.—§ 2.8(8); § 2.8(8), n. 8.
Swiler v. Baker's Super Market, Inc.—§ 8.1(4), n. 33.
S. W. Straus & Co., People v.—§ 9.2(6), n. 22, 23.
System Federation No. 91, Ry. Emp. Dept. v. Wright—§ 2.8(8), n. 2.
System Operations, Inc. v. Scientific Games Development Corp.—§ 2.11(3), n. 24, 36.

T

Taliferro v. Augle—§ 5.16(4), n. 4, 5.
Tami v. Pikowitz—§ 2.4(2), n. 14.
Tandy Corp. v. Malone & Hyde, Inc.—§ 4.3(5), n. 33.
Tandycrafts, Inc. v. Initio Partners—§ 3.10(6), n. 23.
Tanner v. McClure—§ 4.8, n. 5.
Taylor v. City of Fort Lauderdale—§ 3.10(6), n. 15.
Taylor v. Gulf Oil Corp.—§ 5.10(3), n. 37.
Teegarden v. Dahl—§ 8.5(2), n. 5.
Teel v. Hamilton–Wencham Regional School Dist.—§ 2.11(3), n. 10, 21.
Teferi v. Dupont Plaza Associates—§ 6.1(5), n. 16, 23.
Teltronics, Ltd., In re—§ 6.1(4), n. 28.
Temple University v. White—§ 2.4(6), n. 14; § 2.6(1), n. 22; § 2.9(3); § 2.9(3), n. 20; § 2.11(3), n. 32.
Tempo Music, Inc. v. Myers—§ 2.4(2), n. 10.
Tennessee Corp. v. Barnett—§ 5.16(2), n. 8.
Tennessee Valley Authority v. Hill (Snail Darter Case)—§ 2.4(7); § 2.4(7), n. 9; § 2.10, n. 22.
Teodori v. Werner—§ 12.15(2), n. 18.
Terrace v. Thompson—§ 2.5(1), n. 13.
Terry v. Panek—§ 9.2(1), n. 19.
Terry v. Rich—§ 12.11(1), n. 29.
Tetuan v. A.H. Robins Co.—§ 3.11(1), n. 43; § 3.11(3), n. 7; § 3.11(5), n. 34; § 3.11(8), n. 6, 21; § 3.11(11), n. 9; § 3.11(14), n. 13; § 3.11(15), n. 18.
Texaco, Inc. v. Pennzoil, Co.—§ 3.11(1), n. 43.

Texas State Teachers Ass'n v. Garland Independent School Dist.—§ 3.10(6), n. 1.
Thayer v. Turner—§ 4.8, n. 2, 4.
Theuerkauf v. Sutton—§ 13.2(2), n. 6.
Thing v. La Chusa—§ 3.1, n. 29.
Thiry v. Armstrong World Industries—§ 3.11(3), n. 26.
Thomas v. Given—§ 2.1(3), n. 2.
Thomas Auto Co., Inc. v. Craft—§ 3.11(1), n. 85; § 4.5(5), n. 5; § 9.4, n. 44.
Thompson v. First Mississippi Nat. Bank and Mut. Sav. Life Ins. Co.—§ 2.6(4), n. 21.
Thompson v. National R. R. Passenger Corp.—§ 8.1(1), n. 6; § 8.1(4), n. 33.
Thompson v. Ramirez—§ 5.17(3), n. 8.
Thornton & Warren v. Cordell—§ 3.4, n. 22.
Thorsen v. Johnson—§ 5.2(1), n. 3.
Thyssen, Inc. v. S.S. Fortune Star—§ 12.5(2), n. 1.
Tibbetts Contracting Corp. v. O. & E. Contracting Co.—§ 4.9(4), n. 10.
Tideway Oil Programs, Inc. v. Serio—§ 3.11(1), n. 54; § 3.11(3), n. 26.
Tiffany Inc. v. W. M. K. Transit Mix, Inc.—§ 13.2(5), n. 18.
Time, Inc. v. Firestone—§ 7.2(6), n. 3.
Times Pub. Co. v. Williams—§ 2.10, n. 4, 6.
Timko v. Useful Homes Corporation—§ 4.3(8), n. 8; § 4.5(3), n. 28; § 12.7(4), n. 17.
Tombigbee Constructors v. United States—§ 11.2, n. 20.
Tompkins v. Sandeen—§ 12.12(2), n. 7; § 13.2(2), n. 1, 17.
Toronto, Hamilton & Buffalo Nav. Co., United States v.—§ 3.5, n. 45; § 5.13(3), n. 5; § 5.16(2), n. 2, 4.
Torphy v. Reder—§ 2.6(4), n. 14.
Tortolano v. DiFilippo—§ 5.2(7), n. 2; § 5.5, n. 14.
Toussaint v. McCarthy—§ 7.4(4), n. 25, 26.
T.R., In re—§ 2.4(5), n. 21.
Tracy v. Capozzi—§ 2.11(3), n. 10.
Transatlantic Financing Corp. v. United States—§ 12.4(6), n. 15.
Travellers Intern. AG v. Trans World Airlines, Inc.—§ 12.8(3), n. 9.
Tribbette v. Illinois Cent. R. Co.—§ 2.9(4), n. 18.
Triebwasser & Katz v. American Tel. & Tel. Co.—§ 2.11(2), n. 5, 26.
Trinity Church in City of Boston v. John Hancock Mut. Life Ins. Co.—§ 5.2(1), n. 12; § 5.2(7), n. 2.
Trio Process Corp. v. L. Goldstein's Sons, Inc.—§ 3.12, n. 18.
Triple Elkhorn Mining Co., Inc. v. Anderson—§ 4.5(3), n. 35; § 5.9, n. 13.
Triple J Cattle, Inc. v. Chambers—§ 2.9(4), n. 6.
Tri–State Generation and Transmission Ass'n, Inc. v. Shoshone River Power, Inc.—§ 6.1(5), n. 8.
Trollope v. Koerner—§ 4.5(4), n. 13; § 13.2(2), n. 1, 7, 14; § 13.2(4), n. 7; § 13.2(5), n. 10.
Truck Equipment Service Co. v. Fruehauf Corp.—§ 3.11(1), n. 21; § 4.1(4), n. 6; § 4.5(5), n. 9.

Truck Rent–A–Center, Inc. v. Puritan Farms 2nd, Inc.—§ 12.9(2), n. 8.
Trustees v. Greenough—§ 3.10(2), n. 2; § 4.9(1), n. 12; § 4.9(6), n. 4.
Tucker v. Marcus—§ 8.7(3), n. 5, 7.
Tull v. Gundersons, Inc.—§ 3.4, n. 8.
Tull v. United States—§ 2.6(3); § 2.6(3), n. 6, 56, 67, 68; § 2.6(4), n. 17.
Tully v. State—§ 2.9(5), n. 10.
Turnbull v. LaRose—§ 9.2(1), n. 19.
Turner v. Turner—§ 2.8(8), n. 4.
Turpin v. Sortini—§ 8.2, n. 7, 12.
Tuscarora Warriors Bingo Com'n v. Clause—§ 6.6(4), n. 7.
Twin City Fire Ins. Co. v. Philadelphia Life Ins. Co.—§ 12.4(6), n. 8.
Tyree v. Keane—§ 5.1, n. 7.

U

U–Haul Intern., Inc. v. Jartran, Inc.—§ 3.3(4), n. 12.
Uhlhorn v. Keltner—§ 5.1, n. 16; § 5.8(2), n. 8.
Ulmer v. Farnsworth—§ 4.1(2), n. 19; § 4.9(3), n. 10; § 4.9(4); § 4.9(4), n. 11.
Ultimate Chemical Co. v. Surface Transp. Intern., Inc.—§ 5.15(3), n. 2.
Umphrey, In re Marriage of—§ 2.3(5), n. 5.
Union City Union Suit Co., Ltd. v. Miller—§ 12.15(2), n. 34.
United Bank of Aurora v. Meaux—§ 4.7(2), n. 6.
United Cigar Stores Co. of America, In re—§ 6.1(3), n. 12, 14.
United Factory Outlet, Inc. v. Jay's Stores, Inc.—§ 2.8(7), n. 9.
United Mine Workers of America, United States v.—§ 2.7; § 2.7, n. 13; § 2.8(2), n. 17; § 2.8(3), n. 8, 14; § 2.8(6); § 2.8(6), n. 10.
United Shoe Machinery Corp., United States v.—§ 2.11(1), n. 1.
United States v. ____ (see opposing party)
United States Catholic Conference v. Abortion Rights Mobilization, Inc.—§ 2.8(6), n. 7, 8.
United States ex rel. v. _____ (see opposing party and relator)
United States Fidelity and Guar. Co. v. Hiles—§ 4.3(2), n. 12.
United States Fidelity & Guaranty Co. v. Marshall—§ 4.9(5), n. 8.
United States Jaycees v. Cedar Rapids Jaycees—§ 2.5(2), n. 1, 10.
University Computing Co. v. Management Science America, Inc.—§ 3.4, n. 17.
University of Arizona Health Sciences Center v. Superior Court of State In and For Maricopa County—§ 8.2, n. 33, 35, 41.
Urbanek, State v.—§ 5.14(3), n. 3.
USACO Coal Co. v. Carbomin Energy, Inc.—§ 6.1(5), n. 17.
Utica Sheet Metal Corp. v. J. E. Schecter Corp.—§ 6.1(4), n. 24.

V

Vairo v. Clayden—§ 3.12, n. 46.

Valasek v. Baer—§ 5.7(3), n. 8.
Valco Cincinnati, Inc. v. N & D Machining Service, Inc.—§ 3.11(1), n. 20; § 10.5(3), n. 70.
Van De Carr v. Schloss—§ 5.10(4), n. 14.
Van de Kamp v. Bank of America Nat. Trust & Sav. Ass'n—§ 2.6(3), n. 22; § 4.3(5), n. 7.
Van Ruymbeke v. Patapsco Indus. Park—§ 4.3(5), n. 10; § 5.8(2), n. 20.
Vargas v. Esquire—§ 5.16(4), n. 9.
Variety Farms, Inc. v. New Jersey Mfrs. Ins. Co.—§ 3.11(7), n. 6.
Vecchiotti v. Tegethoff—§ 5.8(2), n. 17; § 5.10(3), n. 35.
Vecco Const. Industries, Inc. v. Century Const. Co. of Washington, D.C., Inc.—§ 12.3(1), n. 2.
Veluzat v. Janes—§ 13.2(2), n. 20.
Venegas v. Mitchell—§ 3.10(7), n. 12.
Vernon, City of v. City of Los Angeles—§ 13.3(2), n. 30.
Vilone v. Sea & Pines Consolidation Corp.—§ 6.1(5), n. 29.
Virginian Ry. Co. v. System Federation—§ 2.5(4), n. 5; § 5.7(2), n. 40.
Vogel v. Sylvester—§ 7.3(2), n. 18.
Vogtle v. Coleman—§ 3.10(3), n. 35.

W

Waddell v. White—§ 9.2(6), n. 23.
Wade v. S. J. Groves & Sons Co.—§ 5.2(1), n. 7.
Waggoner v. Johnston—§ 2.6(3), n. 29.
Walden v. Vera's Auto Body Service—§ 4.9(5), n. 10.
Walgren v. Dolan—§ 4.3(8), n. 4.
Walker v. City of Birmingham—§ 2.8(6); § 2.8(6), n. 4, 8.
Walker v. Norfolk & W. Ry. Co.—§ 5.18(2), n. 3.
Walker v. Sheldon—§ 3.11(3), n. 27.
Walker v. Signal Companies, Inc.—§ 12.5(2), n. 1.
Walker v. Walthall—§ 5.17(2), n. 9.
Wall v. Pate—§ 3.3(3), n. 2.
Wall v. Platt—§ 5.16(3), n. 2.
Wallace v. American Mfrs. Mut. Ins. Co.—§ 5.15(2), n. 39.
Wallace v. Hallowell—§ 9.2(6), n. 14; § 9.3(2), n. 11.
Wallace v. Miller—§ 2.11(3), n. 5, 10, 14.
Wallach v. Joseph—§ 5.18(3), n. 12.
Walter J. Schmidt & Co., In re—§ 6.1(4), n. 29.
Walton v. Eaton Corp.—§ 2.6(3), n. 61.
Wammock v. Celotex Corp.—§ 3.11(8), n. 3.
Wang v. Gordon—§ 3.10(3), n. 40.
Want v. Alfred M. Best Co.—§ 6.1(3), n. 14.
Ward v. Taggart—§ 9.2(1), n. 19; § 9.3(4), n. 6, 8; § 10.5(1); § 10.5(1), n. 9, 18.
Warehouse Carpet Sales & Service, Inc. v. S.C.J. Associates, Inc.—§ 2.8(1), n. 32.
Warner–Lambert Pharmaceutical Co. v. John J. Reynolds, Inc.—§ 10.5(3), n. 70.
Warren v. Century Bankcorporation, Inc.—§ 4.1(4), n. 6; § 4.3(5), n. 30; § 4.5(3), n. 10, 17, 36; § 4.5(5), n. 9.

Warren Motors, Inc., People ex rel. Daley v.—§ 2.6(3), n. 19.

Warsco v. Oshkosh Savings & Trust Co.—§ 4.3(3), n. 5.

Washington Public Power Supply System Securities Litigation, In re—§ 9.2(6), n. 15, 32, 35.

Waterbury Trust Co. v. G. L. D. Realty Co.—§ 5.10(4), n. 14.

Waterson v. General Motors Corp.—§ 8.7(4); § 8.7(4), n. 20.

Watson v. Bugg—§ 4.8, n. 20.

Watson v. Massachusetts Mut. Life Ins. Co.—§ 4.8, n. 30.

Wayne v. Venable—§ 7.3(2), n. 4, 17.

Weale v. Massachusetts General Housing Corp.—§ 13.2(5), n. 8.

Weathersby v. Gore—§ 12.8(2), n. 16.

Weaver v. Mitchell—§ 3.9, n. 8.

W. E. Bassett Co. v. Revlon, Inc.—§ 4.5(3), n. 12.

Webster v. Sowders—§ 3.10(6), n. 22, 30.

Weeks v. Standish Hardware & Garage Co.—§ 12.12(2), n. 7; § 13.2(2), n. 1, 2.

Weinberg v. Commonwealth, State Bd. of Examiners of Public Accountants—§ 2.4(4), n. 8, 11, 25.

Weinberger v. Romero–Barcelo—§ 2.4(7), n. 11; § 2.10, n. 19.

Weiner v. Ash—§ 3.11(3), n. 15.

Weiner v. Roof—§ 4.6, n. 12; § 4.7(2); § 4.7(2), n. 7.

Weinstein v. Griffin—§ 12.9(3), n. 8.

Weisman v. Hopf–Himsel, Inc.—§ 2.6(3), n. 42; § 2.6(4), n. 2.

Weiss v. State ex rel. Cardine—§ 2.8(5), n. 7.

Welch v. Kosasky—§ 5.13(1), n. 30; § 5.13(2), n. 6; § 5.18(2), n. 2.

Welch v. LaGue—§ 3.10(3), n. 13.

Wells v. Smith—§ 3.11(10), n. 2, 11.

Welty v. Heggy—§ 3.11(5), n. 28.

Wemyss v. Coleman—§ 8.7(4), n. 23.

Wernick, In re Estate of—§ 4.3(2), n. 16.

West v. National Mines Corp.—§ 5.7(3), n. 19.

Westerland v. First Nat. Bank of Carrington—§ 4.6, n. 8.

Western Cas. & Sur. Co. v. Kohm—§ 4.6, n. 13.

Western Nat. Bank of Casper v. Harrison—§ 5.13(1), n. 8; § 5.18(1), n. 1, 2; § 5.18(2), n. 18.

West Haven Sound Development Corp. v. City of West Haven—§ 3.4, n. 3.

West Virginia University Hospitals, Inc. v. Casey—§ 3.10(7), n. 13.

Westwater v. Rector of Grace Church—§ 12.5(1), n. 1.

Westwood Corp. v. Bowen—§ 2.6(4), n. 26.

Weyerhaeuser Co. v. Atropos Island—§ 5.14(3), n. 18, 34.

Whalen v. On–Deck, Inc.—§ 3.11(7), n. 7.

Whalen v. Schumacher—§ 6.1(3), n. 1, 15.

Whaley v. Crutchfield—§ 5.13(3), n. 10.

Wharton, Matter of—§ 2.8(6), n. 3.

Wheeler v. City of Pleasant Grove—§ 5.8(2), n. 11; § 6.9(2), n. 5.

Wheelock v. Noonan—§ 2.1(1), n. 5; § 5.5, n. 14, 15.

Whitaker v. Earnhardt—§ 5.3(1), n. 2.

White v. Kaufmann—§ 3.12, n. 34.

White v. State—§ 8.8, n. 21, 28.

White v. White—§ 2.8(1), n. 30.

Wickland Oil Terminals v. Asarco, Inc.—§ 5.2(5), n. 2.

Wides v. Wides—§ 2.8(3), n. 6.

Wiederspiel v. Bernholz—§ 5.5, n. 5.

Wiegand v. Colbert—§ 3.6(5), n. 12.

Wier v. Isenberg—§ 5.7(2), n. 52.

Wilcox v. Timberon Protective Ass'n—§ 2.5(1), n. 13.

Wildman v. Lerner Stores Corp.—§ 3.10(10), n. 18.

Wilkins v. Oken—§ 4.3(8), n. 2.

Williams v. Alioto—§ 3.10(6), n. 15.

Williams v. Bemis—§ 13.2(2), n. 29.

Williams v. Bridy—§ 5.10(3), n. 23, 28.

Williams v. Greene—§ 2.11(2), n. 12.

Williams v. Kushner—§ 8.8, n. 20, 26.

Williams v. Mason—§ 13.2(2), n. 6.

Williams v. Overstreet—§ 2.6(3), n. 29.

Williams v. Owens–Illinois, Inc.—§ 2.6(4), n. 18.

Williams Management Enterprises, Inc. v. Buonauro—§ 6.1(1), n. 8, 9.

Willing v. Mazzocone—§ 2.5(2), n. 8; § 7.2(14), n. 1.

Willinger v. Mercy Catholic Medical Center of Southeastern Pennsylvania, Fitzgerald Mercy Division—§ 8.1(4), n. 45.

Wilmont Homes, Inc. v. Weiler—§ 5.5, n. 14, 15.

Wilson v. Brand S Corp.—§ 5.3(1), n. 2.

Wilson v. City of Eagan—§ 5.15(3), n. 17.

Wilson v. Key Tronic Corp.—§ 5.6(2), n. 23.

Wilson v. La Van—§ 4.5(2), n. 4; § 13.2(5), n. 7, 9.

Wilson v. Todd—§ 4.3(4), n. 4, 10, 17; § 6.1(3), n. 1.

Winkler v. Hartford Acc. & Indem. Co.—§ 5.15(3), n. 1.

Winnipeg Rugby Football Club, Ltd v. Freeman—§ 12.22(2), n. 11.

Winston Research Corp. v. Minnesota Min. & Mfg. Co.—§ 10.5(3), n. 68.

Winters v. City of Oklahoma City—§ 3.10(3), n. 41.

Wiper v. Downtown Development Corp. of Tucson—§ 3.11(6), n. 16.

Wisconsin Telephone Co. v. Reynolds—§ 5.14(2), n. 2.

Wise v. Midtown Motors—§ 4.5(4), n. 2; § 13.2(2), n. 29.

Wittman v. Gilson—§ 3.11(12), n. 2.

Wlaschin v. Affleck—§ 4.5(2), n. 21.

Wolverton v. Holcomb—§ 3.10(3), n. 9.

Wood, United States v.—§ 2.9(4), n. 39.

Woodling v. Garrett Corp.—§ 4.5(3), n. 6, 7.

Woonsocket Machine & Press Co. v. New York, N. H. & H. R. Co.—§ 5.16(2), n. 7.

Worden v. Searls—§ 2.8(3), n. 14, 15.

Worthington v. Roberts—§ 3.3(7), n. 1; § 5.2(2), n. 23.

Wright v. Central Du Page Hospital Ass'n—§ 8.8, n. 21.

Wronski v. Sun Oil Co.—§ 5.13(1), n. 8; § 5.13(2), n. 8, 15.

W. T. Grant Co. v. Srogi—§ 2.9(3), n. 19; § 2.11(2), n. 3.
Wyatt v. Aderholt—§ 7.4(4), n. 2, 10.

Y

Yarbrough v. Tower Oldsmobile, Inc.— § 3.11(1), n. 66.
Yeargin Const. Co., Inc. v. Parsons & Whittemore Alabama Machinery & Services Corp.—§ 5.17(3), n. 2.
Yoho, In re—§ 2.8(3), n. 4.
Yosuf v. United States—§ 8.1(4), n. 33.
Young v. Delta Air Lines, Inc.—§ 5.15(3), n. 14.
Young v. Lujan—§ 13.4(3), n. 11.
Young, State ex rel. v. Crookham—§ 3.11(3), n. 26; § 3.11(14), n. 13.
Young v. United States ex rel. Vuitton et Fils S.A.—§ 2.8(4), n. 13; § 3.11(15), n. 13.

Younger v. Appalachian Power Co.—§ 5.13(1), n. 11; § 5.14(3), n. 5, 18.
Younger v. Harris—§ 2.5(4), n. 17; § 2.9(4), n. 37.
Youngs v. McDonald—§ 2.11(3), n. 53.
Yount v. Setzer—§ 4.3(6), n. 8.
Yuba Natural Resources, Inc. v. United States—§ 3.4, n. 1.

Z

Zager v. Dimilia—§ 5.13(1), n. 29.
Zais v. CF West Florida, Inc.—§ 12.15(2), n. 4.
Zanker Development Co. v. Cogito Systems, Inc.—§ 3.9, n. 18.
Zeller v. Bogue Elec. Mfg. Corp.—§ 4.3(2), n. 15; § 4.3(5), n. 17.
Zipes v. Trans World Airlines, Inc.—§ 7.4(4), n. 23.
Zippertubing Co. v. Teleflex Inc.—§ 3.11(1), n. 85; § 3.11(5), n. 33.

Index

For complete coverage, this index references the three-volume edition. In most instances, the referenced material will appear in this abridgment, although in shorter form. In rare cases the reader may find that the referenced material has been edited out of this abridgment. In that case, please turn to the subsection referred to as it appears in the unabridged edition.

ABATEMENT
Death of party in personal injury cases, 8.3(1)
Nuisance, see Injunction; Nuisance
Wrongful death action as abating when dependent dies, 8.3(7)

ABUSIVE LITIGATION
Injunction against, 2.9(4)

ACCELERATION CLAUSES
Enforceability,
 Generally, 12.9(2)
 Leases, 12.15(3)

ACCEPTANCE OF BENEFITS
Restitution claim, 4.9(6)

ACCOUNT
Common law account action, 4.3(5)
Lessor's re-letting for account of tenant, 12.15(3)

ACCOUNTING FOR PROFITS
Cost of outweighs probable profits, where, 6.4(4)
Equitable defenses, 6.4(6)
Injunction freezing assets and, 6.1(5)
Introduced, 4.3(1)
Jury trial and, 2.6(3), 4.3(5)
Restitutionary claim, generally, 4.3(5)
Trademark cases, 6.4(4)

ACCOUNTS
 See also Money
Trusts or liens on, 6.1(2)

ACCRUAL
Interest, personal injury cases, 8.4

ACQUIESCENCE
Estoppel and, 2.3(5)
Laches and, 2.4(4)
Trademark cases, 6.4(6)

ACREAGE DEFICIENCY OR EXCESS
Land sales contract, 12.12(3)

ADEQUACY OF LEGAL REMEDY
Building contracts, 12.19(1)
Civil rights claims for wrongful discharge, 6.10(4)
Constructive trusts,
 Generally, 4.3(2)

ADEQUACY OF LEGAL REMEDY—Cont'd
Constructive trusts—Cont'd
 Chattels, 5.18(3)
Damages,
 Collection difficulty, 2.5(2)
 Measurement difficulty, 2.5(2)
Debate over, 2.5(3)
Easements, 5.7(6)
Economic interpretations, 2.5(3)
Efficient breach of contract, and, 2.5(3)
Employment contracts, 12.21(3)
Equity, rule generally, 2.5(1)
Establishing inadequate remedy, 2.5(2)
Fiduciary cases, 5.18(3)
Injunction,
 Encroaching structures, 5.10(4)
 Interference with contract, 6.6(4)
 Nuisance, 5.7(2)
 Trespass,
  Physical harm, 5.5
  Possession, 5.10(3)
Irreparable harm,
 Formulation of adequacy test, 2.5(1)
 Remote, 2.11(2)
Judgment at law uncollectible, 2.5(2)
Land purchaser's suit for performance, 12.11(3)
Land seller's suit for performance, 12.12(3)
Merger and, 2.6(1)
Multiplicity of suits, 2.5(2)
Personal rights, 7.3(5)
Preliminary injunction,
 Employment rights, 6.10(4)
 Standards, 2.10, 2.11(2)
Remote irreparable harm, 2.11(2)
Repeated acts, 2.5(2)
Repeated invasions, 5.10(3)
Sale of goods, 12.16(7)
Specific performance,
 Generally, 2.5(2), 12.8(2)
 Building contracts, 12.19(1)
 Employee v. employer, 12.21(3)
 Moral theory of, 2.5(3)
Specific restitution and, 9.3(4)
Statutes, effect on, nuisance cases, 5.7(5)
Statutory injunction cases, 2.10
Temporary restraining order standards, 2.11(2)
Threat of harm requirement confused, 2.5(1)

922

INDEX

ADEQUACY OF LEGAL REMEDY—Cont'd
Uniqueness test, 2.5(2)
Wrongful discharge, preliminary injunction, 6.10(4)

ADJUSTMENTS IN ATTORNEY FEE AWARDS
Contingency or risk of loss, 3.10(10)
Delay in receiving payment, 3.10(10)
Success limited, 3.10(7)

ADJUSTMENTS IN DAMAGES AWARDS
Appreciation of assets,
    Nuisance, 5.6(2)
    Repair adds value, 5.2(6), 5.6(2), 5.14(3)
    Taking or eminent domain cases, 5.2(6)
Avoidable consequences, see Avoidable Consequences
Benefit to plaintiff,
    Rule summary, 8.6(1)
    Wrongful birth etc. cases, 8.2
Benefit to plaintiff from tort, 8.6(2)
Benefits offset, wrongful birth etc. cases, 8.2
Caps on damages, order of credits, 8.8
Chattel damage, appreciation in value from repair or replacement, 5.14(3)
Collateral source rule,
    Generally, 3.8(1)
    Personal injury cases, 8.6(3)
Comparative fault, personal injury cases, summary, 8.7(1)
Contracts,
    Avoidable consequences, 12.6(2), 12.6(3)
    Collateral source rule, 12.6(4)
    Summary, 12.6(1)
Converter's use of plaintiff's chattel to plaintiff's benefit, 5.14(4)
Credits, order of,
    Collateral source payments credited, 8.6(3)
    Damages capped, when, 8.8
Direct benefits rule, credits, 3.8(2)
Foreign currency conversion, 3.7
Inflation, 3.7, 8.5(4)
Interest, personal injury cases, 8.4
Interest generally, 3.6(1)
Mitigation, see Avoidable Consequences
Punitive damages addition, 3.11(13)
Reduction to present value adjustment, 3.7, 8.6(2)
Repair appreciating value, trespass, 5.2(7)
Summary, 3.2
Tax savings to plaintiff on non-taxable injury award, 8.6(4)
Transportation costs to or from market, 5.13(3)

ADJUSTMENTS IN RESTITUTION AWARDS
Apportionment, 4.5(3)
Expense deductions, 4.5(3)

ADMINISTRATIVE PROCEEDINGS
Attorney fees in, 3.10(6)

ADMINISTRATIVE RELIEF, 1.1

ADOPTION OF CHILDREN
Wrongful death, 8.3(7)

ADVISORY JURIES
Equity, 2.6(2)

AFFIRMATIVE MUTUALITY OF REMEDY, 2.4(3)

AGE DISCRIMINATION ACT, 6.10(3)

AGENTS
See Vicarious Liability

AGREED REMEDIES
Acceleration clauses, 12.9(2), 12.15(3)
Actual and liquidated damages, both recovered, 12.9(5)
Alternatives to traditional analysis, 12.9(4)
Building contract, 12.19(1)
Chattel leases, 12.18
Delayed performance, covered or not, 12.9(5)
Drafting, 12.9(5)
Employment contracts, 12.21(2)
Incentive to induce breach argument against enforcement, 12.9(3)
Interpretation of provisions, 12.9(5)
Liquidated damages, enforceable, when, 12.9(2)
Option as alternative analysis, 12.9(4)
Penalty, unenforceable, when, 12.9(2)
Present value discount in liquidated damages clauses, 12.15(3)
Rationales for rules limiting parties' power to agree on remedies, 12.9(3)
Specific performance affected by agreement for another remedy, 12.9(5)
Specific performance as agreed remedy, 12.9(5)
Summary, 12.9(1)
UCC, buyer's remedies, 12.16(1)

AIDERS AND ABETTERS
Contempt liability of, 2.8(5)

ALIENATION OF AFFECTIONS
Damages presumed, 7.3(2)
Injunction against, 7.3(5)

ALTERNATIVE DISPUTE RESOLUTION, 1.1, 12.23

ALYESKA CASE
Attorney fee awards, American Rule, 3.10(4)

AMERICAN RULE
Attorneys fees, 3.10(1)

ANALYSIS OF REMEDIAL ISSUES
Costs and benefits, 1.9
Equivalent remedies, 1.8
Right and remedy, 1.7
Strategic issues, 1.10

ANIMALS
Harm to, damages, 5.15(3)

APPEAL
Injunction reversed, contempt liability for disobedience, 2.8(6)
Injunctive orders generally, 2.11(4)
Interest on judgment, effect, 3.6(6)
Mandatory injunction, 2.11(4)
Prerogative writs to review, 2.11(4)

APPORTIONMENT OF DAMAGES
See also Apportionment of Profits; Joint and Several Liability
Damages,
Attorney fee awards apportioned, 3.10(6)
Causal apportionment, 3.3(9), 8.7(1)—8.7(4)
Comparative fault vs. avoidable consequences methods, 8.7(3)
Injury cases, summary, 8.7(1)
Seat belt defenses, 8.7(4)

APPORTIONMENT OF PROFITS
Accounting claims, 4.3(5)
Innocent and wrongful acts, between,
Generally, 4.3(5), 4.5(3)
Copyright infringer, 6.3(4)
Trademark infringer, 6.4(4)
Restitution, generally, 4.5(3)

APPRECIATION
Assets appreciated by repair, replacement, 5.2(6), 5.2(7), 5.6(2), 5.14(3)

ARBITRATION
Generally, 12.23
Attorney fee liability for breach of contract to arbitrate, 3.10(3)
Punitive damages in, 3.11(1)

ART AND ARTISTS
Harm to art, damages, retail vs. wholesale market, 5.16(4)
Moral rights,
Generally, 5.16(4)
Copyright statute protection, 6.3(3)
Shipping goods, measure of damages for harm to goods, 5.13(3)
Taking, alteration, or destruction of art, 5.16(4)

ASCERTAINABLE SUMS
Prejudgment interest rule for, 3.6(2)

ASSAULT
Damages, 7.3(2)
Injunction, 7.3(5)

ASSISTANCE
Writ of, 2.8(1)

ASSOCIATIONS
Injunction to protect rights in, 7.3(5)

ASSUMED RISK
Mistake excluded by, 11.2

ASSUMPSIT
Common counts and, 4.2(3)
Goods sold and delivered count, 4.2(3)
Historical development, 4.2(3)
Implied in law contracts, 4.2(3)
Money, appropriation of, 6.1(1)
Money had and received count, 4.2(3)
Money paid count, 4.2(3)
Quantum meruit count, 4.2(3)
Quantum valevant count, 4.2(3)
Restitution, terminology for, 4.1(1), 4.2(1)
Trespass and case writs, relation, 4.2(3)
Use and occupation of land count, 4.2(3)

ASSUMPSIT—Cont'd
Waiver of tort,
Generally, 4.2(3)
Chattels taken, 5.18(1)–5.18(2)

AT–WILL EMPLOYEES
See Employment Discrimination

ATTACHMENT
Economic compulsion by, 10.2(3)
Provisional remedy, as, 1.3, 6.1(5)

ATTORNEY FEES
Personal injury cases, 8.1(1)
Punitive damages, relation to, 3.11(3)

ATTORNEY FEES AWARDS
Administrative proceedings, 3.10(6)
Against adversary, denied generally, 3.10(1)
Amount,
Contingency, 3.10(10)
Contract with client, effect, 3.10(7), 3.10(11)
Disproportion to success, 3.10(8)
Hourly rate method, 3.10(8)
Limited success, effect, 3.10(7)
Quality of service, 3.10(1)
Reduction for partial success, 3.10(9)
Risks of litigation, effect, 3.10(7)
Standard of measurement, 3.10(7)
Success limited, effect, 3.10(7)
Apportionment of liability for, 3.10(6)
Arbitration contract breached, 3.10(3)
Civil rights fee awards to prevailing plaintiff, 3.10(4)–3.10(11), 7.4(5)
Civil rights statutes, 3.10(4)
Collateral disputes within the controversy, 3.10(6)
Common fund rule, 3.10(2)
Contempt cases, 3.10(3)
Contingency multipliers, 3.10(10)
Contracts imposing liability to pay, 3.10(3)
Copyright litigation, 6.3(7)
Costs,
Recovery as, 3.10(5)
Recovery as not, 6.4(7)
Costs and benefits for time invested as affecting amount, 3.10(8)
Damages, recovery as, 3.10(3)
Declaratory judgment, prevailing party status, 3.10(6)
Delay enhancement, 3.10(10)
Discretion,
Amount of award, statutes permitting, 3.10(8)
Limited, statutory award routine, 3.10(5)
Disparagement, 6.8(2)
Disproportionate fees, 3.10(8)
Employment discrimination, 6.10(4)
Enhancements, 3.10(10)
Entitlement under statutes, 3.10(5)
Exceptions to American Rule,
Common fund rule, 3.10(2), 4.9(6)
Contempt of court, 3.10(3)
Contract liability for, 3.10(3)
Indemnity agreements, 3.10(3)
Injunction bond, 3.10(3)
Insurer's promise to defend, 3.10(3)
Litigation misconduct, 3.10(3)

ATTORNEY FEES AWARDS—Cont'd
Exceptions to American Rule—Cont'd
    Malicious prosecution, 3.10(3)
    Sanctions, 3.10(3)
    Statutes, 3.10(4)
    Third party litigation, 3.10(3)
        Lawyer malpractice cases, 6.11
    Title warranty cases, 3.10(3)
Factors in fixing award of, 3.10(7), 3.10(8),
        3.10(10)
False imprisonment, 7.3(2)
General rule, 3.10(1)
    Introduction to, 3.2
Hall v. Cole rule, 3.10(2), 4.9(6)
Hensley case, 3.10(9)
Hourly rate method of fixing, 3.10(8)
Injunction bonds, recoverable under or not,
        2.11(3)
Injurious falsehood, 6.8(2)
Insurers, liability for, 3.10(3)
Interest and, 3.6(5)
Interim success as grounds for, 3.10(6)
Intervenors, 3.10(6)
Issue in damages generally, 3.1
Johnson factors,
    Amount, 3.10(8)
    Enhancements under, 3.10(10)
Joinder of fee and non-fee claims, 3.10(6)
Joint and several liability, 3.10(6)
Leubsdorf proposal, 3.10(10)
Lodestar method,
    Generally, 3.10(8)
    Factors approach contrasted, 3.10(10)
Malicious prosecution, 7.3(2)
Malpractice, lawyer's, 6.11
Market rate, 3.10(8)
Measurement generally, 3.10(7)
Moot cases, 3.10(6)
Multipliers, 3.10(10)
Non-fee claims joined with fee claims, 3.10(6)
Non-pecuniary losses and, 3.1
One-way fee shifting, 3.10(5)
Partial success, effect on amount awarded,
        3.10(9)
Patent infringement cases, 6.2(7)
Percentage fees awards, 3.10(8)
Preliminary injunction with immediate fee
        award, 3.10(6)
Prevailing party status, standard, 3.10(6)
Prevailing plaintiff statutes, 3.10(5)
Private attorney general rule, 3.10(2)
Public interest lawyers, 3.10(8)
Quality of service, 3.10(10)
Rates used in hourly rate method, 3.10(8)
Reduction for limited success, 3.10(7)
Restitution, basis in, 4.9(6), 3.10(2)
Risk multipliers, 3.10(10)
Riverside case, 3.10(8)
Settlement, prevailing by, 3.10(6)
Social benefits of litigation, 3.10(8)
Standardized fees awards, 3.10(8)
Statutes,
    Development, civil rights, 3.10(4)
    Entitlement, 3.10(5)
Substantial benefit rule, 3.10(2)
Success in litigation affecting, 3.10(9)

ATTORNEY FEES AWARDS—Cont'd
Success on the merits affecting amount award-
        ed, 3.10(7)
Summary, 3.10(1)
Third person litigation exception, 3.10(3)
Time claimed in hourly rate method, 3.10(8)
Trademark cases, 6.4(7)
Wrongful discharge, 6.10(4)

ATTORNEYS
    See also Lawyer Malpractice
Client avoids contracts, restitution, 13.5
Client's liability for contempt based on attor-
        ney's violation of order, 2.8(5)
Punitive damages against, 3.11(1)
Restitution, common fund attorney fee
        awards, 4.9(6)
Unauthorized services, restitution, 4.9(4)

AUTHORS
    See also Art and Artists
Attribution rights, injunction to protect,
        5.16(4)
Gains from publications about their torts, 8.9

AUTOMOBILES
    See also Chattels; Conversion of Property;
        Damages
Damages to,
        Generally, 5.13–5.16
    Loss of use, 5.15(2)
Unauthorized repair, liability to repairer,
        4.9(5)

AUTONOMY
See Unsolicited Benefits

AVOIDABLE CONSEQUENCES
    See also Cover
Acts that minimize damages add to plaintiff's
        assets, 3.9, 12.16(3)
Anticipatory repudiation, minimizing dam-
        ages after, 12.6(2)
Business ventures minimizing harm from em-
        ployment loss, 12.21(2)
Contract cases, 12.6(2)
Contracts, general damages, 12.6(3)
Cover under UCC and, 12.16(3)
Employment contracts, 12.21(2)
Employment discrimination, statutory claims,
        6.10(4)
Generally, summary, 3.2
Injunction undercutting rule of, 2.9(2)
Leases, special rule for, 3.9
Leases and contracts to lease, 12.6(2), 12.15(3)
Libel and slander cases, 7.2(11)
Limitation on consequential damages general-
        ly, 3.4
Measuring and tracing savings, lease cases,
        12.15(3)
Minimizing damages adds to plaintiff's assets
        or income, 3.9, 12.16(3)
Personal injury, summary, 8.7(1)
Personal injury cases, rule, 8.7(2)
Rules generally, 3.9
Seat belt defenses, 8.7(4)
Specific performance to minimize damages,
        12.6(2)

AVOIDABLE CONSEQUENCES—Cont'd
Substitution costs and, 3.3(5)
UCC cover distinguished, 12.16(3)
UCC resale distinguished, 12.17(3)
Unsuccessful efforts compensated, 12.6(2)
Wrongful birth, wrongful pregnancy cases, 8.2, 8.7(2)
Wrongful discharge,
Common law, 6.10(2)
Statutory claims, 6.10(4)

AVOIDANCE
See Rescission

BACKPAY
Wrongful discharge,
Common law, 6.10(2)
Statutory claim, 6.10(4)

BAD FAITH
Contract breach claim, damages, 6.12
Punitive damages, 3.11(1)
Tort claim alternative, damages affected, 12.15(1), 12.5(2)
Wrongful discharge, common law, 6.10(2)

BALANCING
Third persons' interests, introduction, 2.4(1)

BALANCING EQUITIES AND HARDSHIPS
Changed position defense in restitution claims, 11.8
Equity approach generally, 2.4(5)
Injunction, 2.9(2)
Encroachments, 5.10(4)
Nuisance, 5.7(2)
Introduction, 2.4(1)
Reformation cases, 11.6(3)
Rights balancing vs. remedies balancing, 5.7(2)
Specific performance, 12.8(4)

BALANCING PUBLIC INTERESTS
Clean hands defense, patent infringement, 6.2(6)
Equity approach generally, 2.4(5)
Introduction, 2.4(1)
Nuisance, 5.7(2)

BANKRUPTCY
Automatic stay as injunctive form, 2.9(1)
Jury trial in, 2.6(3)

BANKS
Dishonor of check,
Mental distress, 12.5(1)
Punitive damages, 12.5(2)

BATTERY
Damages, 7.3(2)

BEACON THEATRES CASE
Equitable claim with legal counterclaim, 2.6(4)

BENEFITS
See also Restitution; Unsolicited Benefits
Attorney fees recoverable, substantial benefit rule, 3.10(2)
Collateral source or benefit rule, 3.8(1), 8.6(3)
Conversion of plaintiff's chattel, 5.18(2)–5.18(3)

BENEFITS—Cont'd
Credit card charges permitted by one who did not agree to pay, 4.9(4)
Damages,
Benefits to plaintiff, effect on generally, 3.8(2)
Collateral sources, 3.2, 3.8(1), 8.6(3)
Credits to defendant for benefits to plaintiff and to community generally, 3.8(2)
Credits to defendant for benefits to plaintiff's different interests, 3.8(2)
Credits to defendant for plaintiff's benefits, collateral sources, 3.8(1), 8.6(3)
Direct benefits to plaintiff from defendant's act, credit, 3.8(2), 8.2, 8.6(2)
Unwanted benefits to the plaintiff, 3.8(2)
Direct source rule, 3.8(2), 8.2
Offset,
Credit limited to same type of damages, 8.2, 8.6(3)
Wrongful birth or pregnancy, 8.2
Order of credits for collateral source payments, 8.6(3)
Public benefits,
Natural resources, 1.9
Reduction of damages for, 8.6(2)
Remedies, element in choosing, 1.9
Restitution,
Acceptance of benefits, 4.9(6)
Benefits consumed, 4.5(4)
Benefits destroyed, 4.5(4)
Benefits lost or destroyed, see Changed Position
Benefits passed on, 4.5(4)
Bona fide purchaser, 4.6
Defense, 4.6
Discharge for value rule, 4.6
Mistake cases, 11.8
Benefits to non-contracting third person, 4.9(4)
Brokers, benefit to non-contracting party, 4.9(4)
Consequential benefits generally, 4.5(3)
Constructive trust, 4.3(2)
Consumption of benefits, 4.6
Contract breach, benefits from, 4.1(2)
Cotenant improvement, unsolicited benefits rules and, 4.9(3)
Debt paid, unsolicited benefit, restitution, 4.9(3)
Defendant acquires title through misconduct, 4.1(2)
Destruction of benefits, 4.6
Discharge for value and benefits passed on rules, 4.6
Evidence, contract price as evidence of benefit received, 4.5(4)
Frustrated and impracticable contracts, 13.3(2)
Liability of another minimized at plaintiff's expense, 4.9(4)
Losses as offsets, 4.5(4)
Measure,
Contract cases, 12.7(3)

BENEFITS—Cont'd
Restitution—Cont'd
    Measure—Cont'd
        Contract price as ceiling or evidence, 13.2(2)
        Measurement, statute of frauds cases, 13.2(2)
        Measurement introduced, 4.1(1)
        Money or cash, unsolicited benefits rule, 4.9(3)
        Money or services, without misconduct, 4.1(2)
        Non-cash benefits, unsolicited benefit rule, 4.9(4)
        Offset by losses, 4.5(4)
        Possession in defendant, title in plaintiff, 4.1(2)
        Profits, see Profits
        Quarry case, 4.9(4)
        Realization of, 4.5(2), 4.9(6)
        Reliance expense, qualifying as, when, 4.5(4)
        Requested and unrequested benefits, 13.2(2)
        Services requested, 4.5(4)
        Services unsolicited, 4.9(4)
        Specific chattels, unsolicited benefits rules and, 4.9(3)
        Statute of frauds cases, 13.2(2)
        Subcontractors work, landowner's liability, 4.9(4)
        Subjective purpose and, 4.5(2)
        Taxes overpaid, 4.9(3)
        Unrealized benefits, 13.3(2)
        Unrealized gains, restitution, measure affected, 4.5(2), 4.9(6)
        Unsolicited,
            Effect of acceptance, 4.9(6)
            See also Unsolicited Benefits
        Value received but lost, 13.3(2)
  Services, unsolicited benefit from, 4.9(4)
  Substantial benefit rule, attorney fee recoveries, 3.10(2)
Tax savings to plaintiff on non-taxable injury award, 8.6(4)
Tort, plaintiff's benefits from, 8.2, 8.6(1), 8.6(2)
Unsolicited, see Unsolicited Benefits
Value of plaintiff's chattel increased by repair or replacement, 5.14(3)
Value of plaintiff's land increased by repair or replacement, 5.2(7)
Wrongful birth, etc. cases, 8.2
Wrongful death, survivor's benefits from death, 8.3(7)

BENEFITS RULE
See Direct Benefits Rule

BETTERMENT STATUTES, 5.8(3)

BILLS OF PEACE, 2.9(4)

BIRTH CONTROL,
Wrongful pregnancy, 8.2

BONA FIDE PURCHASER
Articles severed from land, 5.3(4)
Defense, discharge for value compared, 4.7(2)

BONA FIDE PURCHASER—Cont'd
Misrepresentation, 9.6
Restitution,
    Generally, 4.7(1)
  Benefits in restitution cases, 4.6
Transactions with incompetent parties, 13.4(3)

BOND
Attorney fee liability on, 3.10(3)
Preliminary injunctions,
    Limiting plaintiff's liability to, 2.11(3)
    Required, 2.11(3)

BOOTSTRAP JURISDICTION, 2.7, 2.8(6)

BRIBES
Liability for giving or receiving, 10.6

BROKERS
Diversion of benefits, 10.5(1)
Duties generally, 10.5(1)
Restitution, benefits conferred on non-contracting party, 4.9(4)
Secret profits, 10.5
Securities, 10.5(2)

BUILDING CONTRACTS
Additional work claims, 12.20(2)
Contractor's damages remedy, 12.20(1)
Contractor's restitutionary remedies, 4.9(4), 12.20(2)
Delay, contractor's damages for, 12.20(1)
Losing contracts, 12.20(1)
Owner's damages remedy, 12.19(1)
Owner's liability to laborers and suppliers for benefits received without contract, 4.9(4), 12.20(3)
Owner's restitutionary remedies, 12.19(1)
Owner's specific performance remedy, 12.19(1)
Reliance damages, contractor's remedy, 12.20(1)
Subcontractors, work enriching landowner, 4.9(4), 12.20(3)
Third persons' claims for benefits conferred upon owner, 12.20(3)
Total cost method, contractor's delay losses, 12.20(1)

BUILDING RESTRICTIONS
Equitable discretion to enforce, 2.4(5)
Injunctive enforcement, 2.9(2), 5.7(2)

BURDEN OF PROOF
Apportionment of profits,
    Copyright, 6.3(4)
    Trademark, 6.4(4)
Avoidable consequences,
    Generally, 3.9
    Employment contracts, 12.21(2)
    Personal injury cases, 8.7(2)
Bad faith trespass, punitive damages compared, 5.3(3)
Changed position, mistake cases, 11.8
Constructive trust claim, 4.3(2)
Contempt, inability to comply with order, 2.8(7)
Defaulting plaintiff, 12.13
Liquidated damages or penalty clauses, 12.9(2)
Present value, 8.5(3)

BURDEN OF PROOF—Cont'd
Punitive damages,
    Multiple damages compared, 5.3(3), 6.3(8)
    Proof standard generally, 3.11(4)
    Statutory requirements, 3.11(12)
Punitive damages compared to accounting for
    profits, 4.3(5)
Reformation, 9.5, 11.6(1)
Reliance damages caps, 12.3(2)
Restitution, defaulting plaintiff's burden,
    12.13

BUSINESS EXPENSE DEDUCTIONS
Accounting for profits, 4.3(5)

BUYER'S REMEDIES
See Sales

CAMPBELL SOUP V. WENTZ
Equity unconscionability case, 2.4(3), 12.8(5),
    12.8(6)

CAPACITY
Comotose patient insensitive to pain, 8.1(4)
Earning capacity, loss of, injury affecting,
    8.1(2)
Incapacity of party to contract, restitution,
    generally, 13.4(1)
Punitive damages, defendant's limited capaci-
    ty, 3.11(1)
Restitution,
    Mental incompetent's contracts, 13.4(3)
    Minor's contracts, 13.4(2)
Undue influence claim, 10.3

CAPITALIZATION OF INCOME
Constructing estimate of market value by, 3.5,
    5.16(2)

CAPS AND CEILINGS
    See also Adjustments in Damages Awards
Consequential damages or substitution costs,
    ceiling on market measured damages or
    not, 5.1(7), 5.6(2), 5.14(1), 5.14(3),
    12.16(4), 12.16(6), 12.17(3), 12.17(6)
Contract price, attorney's restitution claim,
    13.5
Contract price or expectancy as ceiling on
    recovery, 9.2(1), 12.7(5), 12.16(6),
    12.21(3)
Cover as a ceiling, 12.16(3)
Damages,
    Legislative limits,
        Generally, 3.1
        Wrongful death, 8.3(4)
    Order of credits and caps, 8.8
    Personal injury cases, 8.8
Full-performance-liquidated-sum rule, 4.5(4),
    12.7(5)
Punitive damages, 3.11(12)
Resale losses as a ceiling, 12.17(3)
Restitution, contract expectancy a cap, when,
    9.2(1), 12.7(5), 12.16(6), 12.21(3)
Sanctions for contempt, Rendleman proposal,
    2.8(3)
Warsaw Convention, 3.11(1), 8.3(4), 8.8

CARRIERS
Damages, measure for harm to shipped goods,
    5.13(3)
Delay, *Hadley v. Baxendale* rule,
    12.4(4)–12.4(7)
Harm to property carried, damages measures,
    5.13(3)

CASH
See Foreign Currency; Money

CATS
Injury or destruction, damages, 5.15(3)

CAUSAL APPORTIONMENT
Personal injury damages, 3.3(9), 8.7(1)–8.7(4)

CAUSATION
Consequential damages,
    Generally, 3.4
    Contract cases, 12.4(2)
Punitive damages, 3.11(9)

CELEBRITIES
Property in performance or persona, 6.5(3)

CERCLA, 5.2(5)

CERTAINTY
Consequential damages, requirement in claim
    for,
    Generally, 3.4
    Contracts, 12.4(3)
Specific performance, certainty of contract,
    2.5(4)

CHANCE
Value of,
    Generally, recovery, 3.4
    Personal injury cases, recovery, 8.1(7)

CHANCELLOR
Judge in equity, 2.2

CHANCELLOR'S FOOT
Epigram, 2.2 n.

CHANGED POSITION
Defense, discharge for value compared, 4.7(2)
Defense to restitution for mistake, 11.8
Reformation cases, 11.6(3)
Restitution, defense to, 4.6

CHATTELS
    See also Market Measured Damages
Affect value, damages for, 5.16(3)
Artistic or historical value, 5.16(4)
Damages,
    Diminished value, 5.13
    Punitive damages, 5.15(3)
    Summary, 5.13(1)
    Unique goods, 5.16(1)
Harms or takings, generally, 5.13–5.18
Income-producing chattels, 5.16(2)
Injunction to recover, 5.17(3)
Loss of use, 5.15(2)
Nominal damages, 5.16(1)
Personal-use chattels, 5.16(3)
Repair, unauthorized, liability to repairer,
    4.9(5)

CHATTELS—Cont'd
Repair or replacement costs,
    Generally, 5.14(1)
    Overhead expenses, 5.14(2)
Replevin, 5.17(2)
Restitution for taking,
    Generally, 5.18(1)
    Measure, 5.18(2)
Specific recovery, 5.17(2)–5.17(3)

CHILDREN
    See also Capacity; Parent and Child; Spouses
Adoption, wrongful death, 8.3(7)
Earning capacity lost, 8.1(2)
Expense of rearing, wrongful birth and pregnancy cases, 8.2
Punitive damages awards against, 3.11(1)
Support,
    Contempt enforcement of support orders, 2.8(2)
    Decrees subject to modification for future payments, 2.8(8)
Wrongful death, 8.3(7)

CHOICE OF REMEDY, 1.7

CHOSES IN ACTION
Bona fide purchaser rules and, 4.7(1)

CHURCHES
Injunction affecting doctrine or procedure, 7.3(5)
Property interests, injunctive protection, 7.3(5)

CIVIL CONTEMPT
See Contempt

CIVIL LITIGATION
Injunction against, 2.9(4)
Threat of, 10.2(3)

CIVIL RIGHTS
    See also Personal Rights
Actual injury test, meaning, 7.4(2)
Attorney fee awards, 3.10(4)–3.10(11), 7.4(5)
Attorney fees,
    Development, 3.10(4)
    Entitlement, 3.10(5), 3.10(6)
    Measurement, 3.10(7)–3.10(11)
    Strategy, 7.4(5)
Contempt enforcement of injunctions, 2.8(2)
Damages,
    Mental distress, 7.4(3)
    Physical harms, 7.4(3)
    Presumed damages rejected, 7.4(2)
Injunction to protect, 7.4(4)
Institutional restructuring injunction, 7.4(4)
Jury trial, Title VII,
    Generally, 6.10(5)
    Equitable characterization or not, 2.6(3)
Punitive damages, 3.11(1), 7.4(3)
Regulatory takings as violation of, 6.9(3)
Substantive background, 7.4(1)
Unconstitutional order disobeyed, contempt, 2.8(6)
Wrongful death, 7.4(3)
Wrongful discharge, statutes affecting, 6.10(3)

CLAIM AND DELIVERY
See Replevin

CLASS ACTIONS
Common fund rule for attorney fees, 3.10(2)
Proposed solutions to multiple punitive damages awards, 3.11(8)

CLEAN HANDS
See Unclean Hands

CLEAN UP DOCTRINE
Incidental jurisdiction in equity, 2.6(4), 2.7

CLEAR AND CONVINCING EVIDENCE STANDARD
Constructive trust, 4.3(2), 6.1(2)
Estoppel,
    Generally, 12.8(4)
    Promissory, 13.2(5)
Libel and slander,
    Punitive damages, 7.2(12)
    Reform proposals, 7.2(14)
    Substantive rule, 7.2(4)
Mistake, gift, restitution claim, 11.10
Promissory estoppel, 13.2(5)
Punitive damages,
    Generally, 3.11(4)
    Libel and slander, 7.2(12)
    Multiple claim for, 3.11(8)
    Statutory requirements, 3.11(12)
Reformation, 9.5, 11.6(1)

CLOTHING
Taking, harm, or destruction, measure of damages, 5.16(3)

CO–MINGLING
See Mingled Funds

COERCIVE EFFECTS
Contempt sanctions, 2.8(3)

COERCIVE REMEDIES
    See also Injunction; Specific Performance
Basic relief, 1.1
Equity, adequacy test, debate, 2.5(3)
Equity generally, 2.1(2)

COLLATERAL BAR RULE
Contempt, 2.8(6)

COLLATERAL SOURCE RULE
    Generally, 3.8(1)
Computing credit when rule is rejected, 3.8(1)
Contract cases, 12.6(4)
Credits limited to same type of damages, 8.6(3)
Efficient breach and, 12.6(4)
Introduced, 3.2
Order of credits, personal injury cases, 8.6(3)
Personal injury cases, 8.6(3)
Public benefits, 8.6(2), 12.6(4)
Remarriage after death of spouse, 8.3(7)
Statutory changes, 3.8(1)
Tort reform, 8.6(3)
Wrongful discharge, statutory claims, 6.10(4)

COMMERCIAL APPROPRIATION
    See also Misappropriation of Intangible Property; Privacy

COMMERCIAL APPROPRIATION—Cont'd
Privacy invasion, 7.3(4)

COMMERCIAL BRIBERY, 10.6

COMMERCIAL DISPARAGEMENT
See Injurious Falsehood

COMMISSIONS
Fiduciary's secret profits or, 10.5(1), 10.6
Value of goods, effect of sales commission on, 5.13(3)

COMMON COUNTS
Assumpsit and, 4.2(3)

COMMON FUND RULE
Attorney fees,
        Generally, 3.10(2)
        Restitutionary theory and critique, 4.9(6)

COMPARABLE SALES
Evidence of market value, 3.5

COMPARATIVE FAULT
Avoidable consequences rules and, 3.9, 8.7(4)
Causal apportionment contrasted, 8.7(3), 8.7(4)
Personal injury,
        Generally, 8.7(3)
        Summary, 8.7(1)
Punitive damages and, 3.11(13), 8.7(3)
Reducing award for, 8.1(1), 8.8
Seat belt defenses, 8.7(4)

COMPENSATED INJUNCTION
Nuisance cases, 5.7(3), 5.7(4)
Trade secret cases, 10.5(3)

COMPENSATION
Damages,
        Compensatory goals,
                Generally, 3.1
                Contracts, market measures and, 12.2(1)
        Convention and, 1.7, 3.1, 3.5, 8.1(2)

COMPENSATION SYSTEMS AWARDS
Personal injuries, 8.1(1)

COMPLEX ACCOUNTS
Accounting, 4.3(5)

COMPOUND INTEREST
        Generally, 3.6(4), 3.6(6)
Injury cases, 8.4

COMPROMISE AND SETTLEMENT
See Release

COMPUTATION
        See also Adjustments in Attorney Fee
                Awards; Adjustments in Damages
                Awards; Avoidable Consequences;
                Credits; Multiple Damages
Benefits to plaintiff from defendant's act, 3.8(1)
Comparative fault reductions, 8.1(1), 8.8
Interest, 3.6(4)

CONDEMNATION
See Eminent Domain; Regulatory Takings

CONFIDENTIAL RELATIONSHIPS
        See also Fiduciaries; Principal and Agent
Brokers, 10.5
Duties arising from, 10.4
Securities transactions, 10.5(2)
Trade secrets, 10.5(3)
Undue influence based on, 10.3

CONFLICT OF INTEREST
Common fund rule and, 3.10(2)

CONSCIOUS IGNORANCE
Mistake excluded by, 11.2

CONSENT DECREES
Contempt, 2.8(2)
Modification, 2.8(8)

CONSEQUENTIAL BENEFITS
Restitution, 4.5(3)

CONSEQUENTIAL DAMAGES
        Generally, 3.3(4)
Accuracy of measurement, 3.3(8), 12.2(3)
Added to general damages, duplication risks, 3.3(7)
Alternative to claims for, 3.4
Avoidable consequences, limitation on generally, 3.4
Bad faith breach of contract, 6.12
Building contracts,
        Contractor's claim, 12.20(1)
        Owner's claim, 12.19(1)
Buyer's claim, UCC, 12.16(4)
Causation or realized loss requirement, 3.4
Certainty rule, 3.4
Characteristics of, 3.3(4)
Chattel leases, 12.18
Chattels, summary, 5.15(1)
Chattels harmed or taken, 5.15
Contracts,
        Generally, 12.4
        Contemplation of parties rules, 12.4(4)–12.4(7)
        Market measures vs., 12.2(2)
        Proof standards, 12.4(3)
Cost of minimizing damages recoverable, 3.9
Duplication, adjustments to prevent, 12.4(3)
Efficiency loss suffered by plaintiff as a result of contract breach, 12.20(1)
Eminent domain, 3.4, 5.2(6)
Employment contracts, 12.21(2)
Employment discrimination, statutory claims, 6.10(4)
Hadley v. Baxendale limits on, 3.4
Interest as, 3.6(4)
Interest as alternative to, 3.4
Introduction to, 3.2
Land sales contract, purchaser's damages, 12.11(1)
Land seller's, 12.12(1)
Lessee's claim against landlord, 12.15(2)
Lessor's claim against tenant, 12.15(3)
Loan agreements, 12.4(4), 12.4(7)
Malpractice, lawyer's, 6.11
Market measures distinguished, 3.3(6)
Misrepresentation, 9.2(1), 9.2(3)
Proof required generally, 3.4

CONSEQUENTIAL DAMAGES—Cont'd
Proximate cause limitations generally, 3.4
Realized loss requirement, 3.4
Regulatory takings, limits proposed, 6.9(4)
Rental value as alternative, 3.4
Repair costs or substitution costs as ceiling on market measured damages, 5.1(7), 5.6(2), 5.14(1), 5.14(3), 12.16(4), 12.17(3), 12.17(6)
Sales, buyer's, 12.16(4)
Trespass to land, 5.12(1)–(2)
Value of the chance alternative, 3.4
Wrongful discharge, statutory claims, 6.10(4)

CONSORTIUM
See also Mental Distress
Lawyer malpractice, 6.11
Libel and slander, 7.2(6)
Personal injury damages, 8.1(5)
Punitive damages, 3.11(1), 3.11(9)
Wrongful death damages, 8.3(5)
Wrongful discharge, 6.10(2)

CONSTITUTIONAL LIMITATIONS
Dignitary torts, presumed damages, 7.3(3)
Presumed damages,
    Civil rights cases, 7.4(2)
    Libel and slander, 7.2(4)
Privacy claims, 7.3(4)
Provisional remedies, 5.17(2)
Punitive damages, libel and slander, 7.2(12)
Religious interests, interference in, 7.3(5)

CONSTITUTIONAL RIGHTS
See also Civil Rights
Attorney fee awards in litigation, 3.10(4)–3.11, 7.4(5)
Damages generally, 7.4(3)
Injunctive relief, 7.4(4)
Regulatory takings, 6.9(3)

CONSTRUCTION CONTRACTS
See Contractors

CONSTRUCTIVE MARKETS
Damages measured by, 3.5, 5.16(1)–(2)

CONSTRUCTIVE TRUST
    See also Accounting for Profits; Equitable Lien; Restitution, Subrogation; Tracing
  Generally, 4.3(2)
Adequacy of legal remedy, 4.3(2), 5.18(3)
Basis for, 4.3(2)
Chattels converted, 5.18(3)
Clear and convincing evidence required, 6.1(2)
Debt distinguished, 4.3(2), 6.1(3)
Donees and purchasers, 4.3(2)
Equitable conversion and, 4.3(8)
Equitable lien compared and distinguished, 4.3(3)
Equity trial, 4.3(2)
Exemptions, defeating, 4.3(2)
Express trust and, 4.3(2)
Freezing funds, 6.1(5)
Gains or profits of the defendant captured by, 4.3(2)
Hallet rule, withdrawals from fund, 6.1(4)

CONSTRUCTIVE TRUST—Cont'd
Insurance, see Insurance
Introduced, 1.4, 4.3(1)
Jury trial, 2.6(3), 4.3(2)
Mechanisms of, 4.3(2)
Mingled funds, 6.1(4)
Misrepresentation, 9.3(4)
Operation and effect, 4.3(2)
Priorities gained by, 4.3(2)
Profits gained by, 4.3(2)
Property wrongfully acquired at another's death, 6.7
Reformation compared, 4.3(7), 4.5(3)
Res requirement, 4.3(2)
Rescission compared, 4.4
Resulting trust and, 4.3(2)
Specific property recovery, 4.3(2)
Statute of frauds cases, 13.2(3)
Swollen assets, 6.1(3)
To enforce claim, equity generally, 2.8(1)
Tracing, see Tracing
Unjust enrichment basis, 4.3(2)
Withdrawals from account, 6.1(4)
Wrongdoing required, when, 4.3(2)

CONTEMPLATION OF THE PARTIES
See Contracts

CONTEMPT
Agents, 2.8(5)
Aiding violation of court order, liability to, 2.8(5)
Ambiguous orders, 2.8(7)
Attorney fee liability, 3.10(3)
Civil vs. criminal, 2.8(3)
Classification as civil or criminal,
    Generally, 2.8(3)
    Consequences of, 2.8(4)
Coercive sanctions,
    Generally, 2.8(2)
    Diminished or exhausted coercion, effect, 2.8(3)
Collateral bar rule, 2.8(6)
Consent decrees, 2.8(2)
Contemnor's profits, patent cases, 6.2(4)
Court's order reversed on appeal, permissible sanctions for earlier disobedience, 2.8(3)
Criminal,
    Incidents of criminal trial, 2.8(4)
    Jury in, 2.8(4)
    Punishment limited, 2.8(4)
Defenses to charge, 2.8(7)
Determinate sanctions as criminal, 2.8(2)
Direct contempt, n., 2.8(1)
Enforcement device generally, as, 1.4
Enforcement of coercive decrees generally, 2.8(1)
Equity jurisdiction and the *Mineworkers* case, 2.7
Erroneous order, disobedience punishable, 2.8(6)
Fines, 2.8(2)
Imprisonment for debt, 2.8(2)
Inability to comply, 2.8(7)
Indeterminate sanctions as civil, 2.8(2)
Injunction against protests, 2.8(3)
Introductory summary, 2.1(1)

CONTEMPT—Cont'd
Jury trial rights, 2.8(4)
Keys to the jail test of civil contempt, 2.8(2)
Media restraints violating First Amendment, 2.8(6)
Michigan rule, 2.8(3)
Mineworkers case, 2.8(6)
Nebulous injunction defense, 2.8(7)
Orders to testify, enforcement of, 2.8(3)
Pennsylvania rule, 2.8(3)
Persons subject to, 2.8(5)
Profits of contemnor, recovery as sanction for, 2.8(2)
Punitive damages analogy, 3.11(15)
Removal from office as sanction for, 2.8(2)
Right to litigate denied as sanction for, 2.8(2)
Sanctions,
    Generally, 2.8(2)
    Civil or criminal character determined by, 2.8(3)
    Coercive effects, civil contempt, 2.8(3)
    Ineffective, 2.8(3)
    Profits of contemnor, 2.8(2)
    Punishment function, 2.8(3)
Support orders enforced by, 2.8(2)
Third persons acts, 2.8(5)
Unconstitutional order disobeyed, 2.8(6)
Vague decree, defense, 2.8(7)
Witnesses, 2.8(3), 2.8(6)

CONTRACTORS
See Building Contracts; Contracts

CONTRACTS
    See also Agreed Remedies; Building Contracts; Capacity; Employment Contracts; Frustration; Illegality; Impracticability; Landlord and Tenant; Land Sales Contracts; Loan Contracts; Statute of Frauds
Abuse of contract theory, 12.7(4)
Alternative contracts, 12.9(4)
Anticipatory repudiation,
    Buyer's damages after seller's, 12.16(4)
    Minimizing damages after, 12.6(2)
Arbitration, 12.23
Assumed risk vs. mistake, 11.2
Attorney fee awards, effect of client's contract, 3.10(11)
Attorneys, restitution to discharged attorney, 13.5
Avoidable consequences, general or market damages, 12.6(3)
Bad faith tort alternative, 12.5(1), 12.5(2)
Bidding mistakes, 11.4
Breach,
    Deed covenants, 12.11(1)
    Goodwill lost, 12.16(4)
    Restitution for improvements, 12.11(2)
Breacher's profits, restitution generally, 4.5(3)
Building contracts, see Building Contracts
Chattel buyer's remedies, 12.16
Chattel seller's remedies, 12.17
Collateral source rule, 12.6(4)
Contemplation of the parties,
    Generally, 12.4(4)–12.4(7)
    Application of cap, 12.4(7)

CONTRACTS—Cont'd
Contemplation of the parties—Cont'd
    Chattel buyer's damages, 12.16(4)
    Employment contracts, 12.21(2)
    Foreseeability version, 12.4(6)
    Formulations of rule, 12.4(6)
    Land sales contract, 12.11(1)
    Market damages, inapplicable to, 12.4(4), 12.4(7)
    Mental distress damages, 12.5(1)
    Rationales, 12.4(4), 12.4(5)
    Reliance damages limit, 12.4(7)
    Specific performance and, 12.8(6)
    Specific performance exceeding risks guaranteed, employment contracts, 12.21(3)
    Tacit agreement version, 12.4(6)
    UCC version, 12.4(7)
Damages,
    Compensation goal, 12.2(1)
    Consequential damages,
        Causation requirement, 12.4(2)
        Proof standards, 12.4(3)
        Summary, 12.4(1)
    Contemplation of parties,
        See Contemplation of the Parties, this topic
    Date for measurement, 12.2(1)
    Duplication, adjustments to prevent, 12.4(3)
    Expectancy,
        Market vs. cost measures of, 12.2(2)
        Reliance damages cap, 12.3(2)
    Expectancy goal, generally, 12.2(1)
    Introduced, 3.3(1)
    Limited to risks allocated by parties, 12.4(5), 12.4(6)
    Limits,
        Buy-sell contracts, 12.4(7)
        Loan contracts, 12.4(7)
        Standardized goods, 12.4(7)
        Telegraphic transmissions, 12.4(7)
        Vacation cases, 12.5(1)
    Market measured damages, substitution costs compared, 12.2(2)
    Punitive damages, 12.5(2)
    Reliance damages,
        Generally, 12.3(1)
        Contemplation of parties' cap, 12.4(7)
        Expectancy cap on, 12.3(2)
            Incidental vs. essential reliance, 12.3(2)
            Restitution contrasted, 12.3(1)
    Restitution and, 12.7(6)
    Substitution costs, market measure compared, 12.2(2)
    Summary, 12.1(1)
    Wilful breach, effect, 12.19(1)
Declaratory judgments, 12.8(7)
Defenses in equity, 2.4(3)
Deposits and forfeitures, 12.9(4)
Economic considerations, 12.1(2)
Efficient breach, see Efficient Breach of Contracts
Election of remedies, 12.7(6)

CONTRACTS—Cont'd

Employment contracts, see Employment Contracts

Expectancy damages,
    Generally, 12.2(1)
    Market vs. costs measures of, 12.2(2)
    Restitution compared, 12.7(1)

Express contract precluding restitution on implied contract theory, 4.9(4)

Formation of, mistake in, 11.3

Full-performance-liquidated-sum rule, 12.7(5)

Good will lost, 12.4(3)

Impossibility of performance, see Impracticability

Land contracts, see Land Sales Contracts

Lease,
    Chattels, remedies, 12.18
    Real property, remedies, 12.15

Lien summary, 12.1(1)

Liquidated damages, see Agreed Remedies

Loan contracts, see Loan Contracts

Losing contract,
    Building contractor losing money, 12.20(1), 12.20(2)
    Chattel's buyer's, 12.16(6)
    Limits of restitution, 12.7(5)

Mental distress damages, 12.5(1)

Misrepresentation compared, 9.1

Mistake,
    Cause or condition of breach, 11.1
    Rescission for generally, 11.1, 11.3, 11.4, 11.5

Performance, mistake in, 11.2, 11.7

Personal services, specific performance denied, 12.8(3)

Price abatement,
    Acreage deficiency, 12.12(3)
    Injury to property before closing, 12.14

Punitive damages, 3.11(1), 12.5(2)

Relational, 12.1(2)

Reliance expense, benefit conferred, qualifying as, 4.5(4)

Remedies policy, 12.1(2)

Remedies summary, 12.1(1)

Reputation harmed by breach, 12.5(1), 12.21(2)

Restitution,
    Generally, 12.7(1)
    Chattel buyer's claim to, 12.16(6)
    Damages and, 12.7(6)
    Deed covenant breached, 12.11(2)
    Expectancy as a limit or not, 12.7(5)
    Farnsworth theory, 12.7(4)
    Full-performance-liquidated-sum rule, 4.5(4), 12.7(5)
    Measurement, 12.7(3)
    Price or expectancy as limit, 4.5(4)
    Profits of breacher, 12.7(4), 12.11(2)
    Reliance expense as benefit for restitution claim, 4.5(2)
    Specific restitution, 12.7(2)
    Subcontractors, 4.9(4), 12.20(3)
    Summary, 12.1(1)
    Third persons, claims against, 12.7(6)

Risk allocation by,
    Generally, 12.4(5), 12.4(6)
    Risk of mistake allocated, 11.3

CONTRACTS—Cont'd

Sales,
    Buyer's remedies generally, 12.16
    Seller's remedies generally, 12.17

Sales contracts, see Sales

Specific performance,
    Generally, 12.8(1)
    Summary, 12.1(1)

Subcontractors, work enriching landowner, 4.9(4), 12.20(3)

Support of grantor covenant, 12.12(2)

Third persons' claims, building contracts, 12.20(3)

Threat to breach as economic compulsion, 10.2(3)

To pay prevailing party's attorney fees, 3.10(3)

UCC claims, 12.16–12.18

Unenforceable contracts, summary, 13.1

CONTRIBUTION

Cotenant improvement, 4.9(3)

Restitutionary claim,
    As, 4.3(4)
    Subrogation and, 4.3(4)

CONVENTIONS

Damages measurement,
    Hypothetical markets, 3.5
    Introduced, 3.1
    Misrepresentation, 9.2(6)
    Personal injury, 8.1(2)

Remedial law generally, 1.7

CONVERSION

See Conversion of Foreign Currency; Conversion of Property; Equitable Conversion

CONVERSION OF FOREIGN CURRENCY

Obligations in foreign currency, dates for, 3.7

CONVERSION OF PROPERTY

Assumpsit for, 4.2(3), 5.18(2)

Consequential damages for, generally, 5.15(1), 5.15(2)

Constructive trust, 5.18(3)

Contract breach, as conversion of property, 12.5(2)

Credit for return, 5.14(4)

Credit for using to plaintiff's benefit, 5.14(4)

Damages measured, 5.13(2)

Equitable relief, 5.17(3), 5.18(3)

Evidence of market value, 5.13(4)

Fiduciary breach compared to, 9.3(4)

Injunction to compel return, 5.17(3)

Interest, 3.6(2)

Loss of use damages when property is converted, 5.15(2)

Mental distress resulting from, 5.15(2)

Money, of, 6.1(1)

Place for assessing market value, 5.13(3)

Prejudgment interest, 3.6(2)

Profits, loss of, 5.15(2)

Punitive damages for, 3.11(1), 5.15(3)

Purchaser of goods, measure of liability, 5.3(4)

Repair to converted property, restitution, 4.9(5)

Replevin, 5.17(1) & 5.17(2)

CONVERSION OF PROPERTY—Cont'd
Restitution,
    Generally, 5.18(1)
    Measure, 5.18(2)
Severance, items taken from real property, 5.3(1), 5.4
Time for assessing market value, 5.13(2)
Waiver of tort and suit in assumpsit for, 4.2(3), 5.18(2)

CONVEYANCES
Executed, restitution denied, 12.7(2), 12.11(2), 12.12(2)

COORDINATION OF BENEFITS
Collateral source payments, 8.6(3)

COPYRIGHT
    See also Misappropriation of Intangible Property
Apportionment of profits, burden of proof, 6.2(6)
Free speech and, 6.3(1)
Increased damages, 6.3(8)
Infringement,
    Damages, 6.3(3)
    Equitable defenses, 6.3(6)
    Injunction, 6.3(5)
    Profits apportionment, 6.3(4)
    Remedies summarized, 6.3(2)
    Restitution for, 6.3(4)
Litigation, attorney fee awards, 6.3(7)
Moral rights, 5.16(4)
Profits, infringer's, 6.2(6)
Punitive damages, 6.3(8)
Substantive background, 6.3(1)

COST
Entitlement costs as damages measure, see Substitution Costs

COSTS
Attorney fee awards, attorney fees as not costs, 6.4(7)
Attorney fees as, 3.10(5)
Items included in when statute authorizes fee award, 3.10(7)

COSTS AND BENEFITS
Balancing in injunction cases, 2.9(2)
Balancing third persons' interests in equity, 2.4(1), 2.4(5)
Element in choosing remedy, 1.9

COTENANTS
Improvement by one, restitution, 4.9(3)
Surviving cotenant acquiring property by wrongdoing, 6.7

COUNTERCLAIMS
Effect on prejudgment interest, 3.6(1)

COURTS
Injunction against proceedings in, deference, 2.5(4)

COVENANT
    See also Building Restrictions
Deed covenants, breach, damages, 12.11(1)
Historical action of, 4.2(3)

COVER
Buyer's damages measure under UCC, 12.16(3)
Chattel leases, 12.18
Tracing new purchases as substitutes, 12.16(3)

CREDIT CARDS
Benefits from charging by one who did not agree to pay, 4.9(4)

CREDITOR'S BILL
Supplemental proceedings to find and reach debtor's assets, 2.8(1)

CREDITS
    See also Adjustments in Damages Awards
Benefit to plaintiff, limited to same type of damage, 8.2, 8.6(3)
Damages,
    Benefits to the plaintiff, 3.8(2)
    Collateral source payments to plaintiff, 3.8(1)
    Conversion, return of chattel, 5.14(4)
    Prior punitive damages payments, 3.11(8)
Direct benefits from torts,
    Generally, 3.8(2)
    Personal injury generally, 8.6(2)
Order of,
    Caps imposed on damages award, 8.8
    Collateral source credits, 8.6(3)
Punitive damages, payment of to other claimants, 3.11(8)
Repair or replacement appreciating value,
    Chattels, 5.14(3)
    Eminent domain or takings cases, 5.2(6)
    Nuisance, 5.6(2)
    Trespass, 5.2(7)
Restitution,
    Benefits offset by losses, 4.5(4)
    Expense deductions against profits liability, 4.5(3)
Return of converted property, 5.14(4)
Tax benefits to personal injury plaintiff, credit or not, 8.6(4)

CRIMES
Injunction against, 2.9(3)

CRIMINAL CONTEMPT
See Contempt

CRIMINAL PROSECUTION
Injunction against, 2.9(4), 7.3(5)

CROPS
Injury to, damages, 5.3(2)

CURRENCY
See Foreign Currency; Money

DAIRY QUEEN CASE
Characterizing issues as equitable or not, 2.6(3)
Employment discrimination jury trials and, 6.10(5)
Jury trial in equity, incidental jurisdiction, 2.6(4)

DAMAGES

See also particular kinds of damages such as Consequential Damages; Interest; Punitive Damages; particular damages issues; such as Avoidable Consequences; Evidence; and particular settings such as Contracts; Libel and Slander; Sales; Trademark; Trespass to Land

Accuracy of measurement, 3.3(8)

Adjustments,
See also Adjustments in Damages Awards
Summarized, 3.2

Art, 5.16(4)

Assault, 7.3(2)

Attorney fee awards,
See also entries under, Attorney Fees Awards
Issue generally, 3.1
Rules generally, 3.10(1)–3.10(11)

Avoidable consequences,
See also Avoidable Consequences
Generally, 3.9
Consequential damages limits, 3.4
Contract cases, 12.6(2), 12.6(3)
Introduced, 3.2

Bad faith breach of contract, 6.12

Bad faith trespassers, 5.3(3)

Basic remedy, characteristics, 1.1

Battery, 7.3(2)

Benefits, direct, adjustment for introduced, 3.2

Benefits rule,
Generally, 3.8(2)
Wrongful birth, etc. cases, 8.2

Building contracts, 12.19, 12.20

Caps,
Generally, 3.1
Personal injury, 8.8
Punitive damages, 3.11(12)

Characteristics and nature of award, 3.1

Chattels, see Chattels

Civil rights, 7.4(2), 7.4(3)

Clothing and personal chattels, 5.16(3)

Collateral source rule, see Collateral Source Rule

Compensation goal, contracts, 12.2(1)

Compensatory goals, 3.1

Consequential, see Consequential Damages

Contracts,
Collateral sourse rule, 12.6(4)
Consequential damages, 12.4
Contemplation of parties cap, 12.4(4)–12.4(7)
Expectancy, 12.2(1)
Generally, 12.2(1)
Introduced, 3.3(1)
Reliance damages, 12.3
Summary, 12.1(1)

Conventions in, 3.1

Conversion of property, 5.13, 5.14(4)

Copyright infringement, 6.3(3)

Credits, see Credits

Crops, 5.3(2)

Date, measurement date, contracts, 12.2(2)

DAMAGES—Cont'd

Date for measuring, personal property taking or damage, 5.13(2)

Deed covenant, breach, 12.11(1)

Depreciation, accounting for,
Chattel cases, 5.14(3)
Trespass cases, 5.2(7)

Disparagement, 6.8(2)

Dollar value variations, 3.7

Double damages statutes, 3.12

Duplication of elements,
See also Duplication
Generally, 3.3(7)
Trespass to land, 5.12(2)

Economic waste and, 3.1

Efficiency and, eminent domain measures, 5.2(6)

Election of remedies, contracts, 12.7(6)

Environmental harm, 5.2(5)

Evidence, see Evidence

False imprisonment, 7.3(2)

Foreign currency, 3.7

Fraud, 9.2

Future losses, see Future Harm or Loss

General, market measure, 3.2, 3.3(3)

General rules, 3.1–3.12

Heirlooms, 5.16(3)

Household goods, 5.16(3)

Hypothetical markets, 3.5

Idiosyncratic values, 3.3(6)

In rem enforcement of damages award, 3.1

Incentives and,
Generally, 3.1
Nuisance abatement, 5.6(3), 5.11(3)
Punitive damages, 3.11(3), 3.11(14)

Incidental damages, UCC concept, 12.16(4)

Individuating damages, 3.3(6)

Inflation, effect on claims for future loss, 3.7

Injunction bond, items recoverable, 2.11(3)

Injurious falsehood, 6.8(2)

Interest, see Interest

Interference with contract or prospects, 6.6(2)

Judgment interest generally, 3.6(6)

Just compensation distinguished, 3.1

Land, see Nuisance, Trespass to Land, Waste

Land sales contracts, 12.11(1), 12.12(1)

Landlord and tenant claims, 12.15

Lawyer malpractice, 6.11

Legal theory of complaint, relevance to, 3.1

Libel and slander, generally, 7.2

Loss of use, chattels generally, 5.15(2)

Loss or harm distinguished, 3.1

Lump sum or periodic payment, 3.1, 3.7

Major issues in law of, 3.1

Malicious prosecution, 7.3(2)

Malpractice, lawyers, 6.11

Manufacturer of goods, measure of damages for harm to goods, 5.13(3)

Marital distributions distinguished, 3.1

Market gains distinguished from profits, 3.3(3)

Market measures, see also Market Measured Damages

Market measures of damages generally, 3.2, 3.5

Market vs. consequential,

Measures generally, 3.3(1)

DAMAGES—Cont'd

Mental distress,
　　Contract breach, 12.5(1)
　　Interference with contract cases, 6.6(2)
　　Libel and slander, 7.2(5), 7.2(6)
　　Nuisance, 5.6(2), 5.12(2)
　　Property damage, 5.15(3)
Minerals removed from land, 5.3(2)
Misappropriation of intangible property, public revelation cases, 6.5(3)
Misrepresentation, 9.2
Money awards that are not damages awards, 3.1
Multiple damages awards, 3.12
Natural resource damage, 5.2(5)
Nominal damages, 3.3(2)
Non-compensatory goals, 3.1
Nuisance generally, 5.6(2)
Objective measures of, 3.3(6)
Opinion evidence, 3.5
Patent infringement, 6.2(3)
Pattern damages, introduced, 3.2
Periodic payments award, 3.1, 3.7
Permanent nuisance, harm or invasion, 5.11
Personal injury damages, generally, 3.3(1)
Personal property generally, 5.13–5.18
Pets, harm to, 5.15(3)
Pleading, 3.3(3), 3.4
Possession, interference with, land, 5.8(2)
Prejudgment interest, see Interest
Present value, see Present Value
Presumed, generally, 7.1(2)
Profits distinguished from market gains, 3.3(3)
Property damages,
　　Introduced, 3.3(1)
　　Value of property generally, 3.5
Property wrongfully acquired at another's death, 6.7
Proximate cause limits, consequential damages, 3.4
Punitive damages,
　　　　See also Punitive Damages
　　Generally, 3.11(1)–3.11(15)
　　As non-compensatory award, 3.1
　　Chattel damage, 5.15(3)
　　Libel and slander, 7.2(12)
　　Restitution compared, 4.1(4)
　　Summary introduction, 3.2
　　Trespass to land, 5.12(2)
Reduction to present value, see Present Value
Regulatory taking of property, 5.6(4), 6.9
Regulatory takings, 6.9(2), 6.9(4)
Rental value, alternative to consequential damages, 3.4
Repair or replacement, chattels generally, 5.13–5.14
Repair or replacement costs, adjustments required, 5.2(7)
Repair or replacement vs. diminished value, trespass cases, 5.2(2)–5.2(7)
Restitution,
　　Compared, 4.1(1)
　　Distinguished, 3.1
　　Punitive damages compared, 4.1(4)
Restitution vs., Superfund Act, 5.2(5)
Retail price, 5.13(3)

DAMAGES—Cont'd

Role of in remedial scheme, 3.1
Sales,
　　Buyer's remedies, 12.16
　　Seller's remedies, 12.17
Sand, gravel or dirt removed, 5.3(2)
Slander of title, 6.8(2)
Special damages, see Consequential Damages
Specie remedies distinguished, 3.1
Specific performance and, land seller's suit, 12.12(3)
Standardized damages, generally, 3.2, 3.3(2)
Substantive goals, 3.1
Substitute for equitable relief, jury trial, 2.6(5)
Substitution costs,
　　　　See also Contracts; Cover
　　Generally, 3.3(5)
　　Introduction to, 3.2
Superfund Act, 5.2(5)
Terminology of, generally, 3.3
Timber cutting, 5.3(2)
Title VII awards distinguished, 3.1
Trade secret use, 10.5(2)
Trademark infringement, 6.4(3)
Transaction costs, ignored in market damages, 3.3(3)
Treble damages statutes, 3.12
Trespass,
　　Consequential damages, 5.12(1)–(2)
　　Diminished value rule, 5.2(1), 5.2(2)
　　Repair or replacement costs, 5.2(1)–5.2(7)
Uncollectible, equitable remedies triggered, 2.5(2)
Unconstitutional regulation, 6.9(2)
Unique goods, generally, 5.16(1)
Unrealized losses, 3.3(3), 3.4
Value of the chance, 3.4, 8.1(7)
Voting right, 7.3(2)
Waste to a future estate, 5.2(8)
Wholesale price, 5.13(3), 5.16(4)
Workers' compensation payments distinguished, 3.1
Wrongful birth, wrongful life, wrongful pregnancy, 8.2
Wrongful death, 8.3
Wrongful discharge,
　　Common law, 6.10(2)
　　Statutory remedies, 6.10(4)

DATE

Buyer's market measured damages, UCC, date for measurement, 12.16(2)
Cover rule affecting date for damages measurement, 12.16(3)
Damages, measurement date, 12.2(2)
Damages measurement, ignoring subsequent events, 12.19(1)
Measuring value,
　　Misrepresentation, 9.2(1)
　　Personal property, when, 5.13(2)
Seller's market measured damages, date, 12.17(2)

DEATH

See Wrongful Acquisition of Property at Death of Another; Wrongful Death

DEBT
Constructive trust claim distinguished, 4.3(2), 6.1(3)
Credit card benefits to one who did not agree to pay, 4.9(4)
Equitable lien to secure, 4.3(3)
Historical action of, 4.2(3)
Imprisonment for, 2.8(2)
Paying another's, restitution, 4.3(4), 4.9(3)
Writ of, 4.2(3)

DEBT COLLECTION
Improper, damages, 6.11, 7.3(4)

DECEDENTS' ESTATES
Punitive damages denied against, 3.11(1)

DECLARATORY REMEDIES
Attorney fee entitlement, 3.10(6)
Basic remedy, 1.1
Contract cases, 12.8(7)
Equity generally, 2.1(2)
Legal or equitable, jury trial, 2.6(3)

DECREES
See also Injunction; Judgments and Decrees; Specific Performance
Modification, 2.8(8)

DEEDS
Care-for-grantor covenants, 12.12(1), 12.12(2)
Covenant breached,
    Damages, 12.11(1)
    Restitution denied, 12.11(2)
Fraud, 9.5
Gift, mistake, 11.10
Mistake, reformation, 9.5, 11.10
Rescission for vendor denied, 12.12(2)
Restitution, executed conveyance rule, 12.7(2), 12.11(2), 12.12(2)

DEFAMATION
See Libel and Slander

DEFAULTING PLAINTIFF
Restitution,
    Building contractor, 12.20(2)
    Land sale contract, 12.13
    Purchase of goods contract, 12.16(6)
    Statute of frauds cases, 13.2(2)

DEFERENCE
Injunction against judicial proceedings, caution, 2.5(4)

DEFICIENCY JUDGMENT
Equitable lien and, 4.3(3)
Equitable lien with, 4.3(3), 9.3(4)
Installment land sales contract, 12.13
Lessor's claim to, 12.15(3)

DELAY
See also Interest; Laches; Rental Value
Building contract, contractor's increased costs resulting from, 12.20(1)
Defeats equity, equitable maxim, 2.3(4)
Finance charged, 12.20(1)
Hidden compensation for in jury verdicts, 3.6(5)
Idled equipment, 12.20(1)

DELAY—Cont'd
Interest compensation for, 3.6(5)
Laches generally, 2.4(4)
Land sales contract, damages for, 12.11(1)
Prejudgment interest rule incentives, 3.6(3)
Total cost method, building contracts, 12.20(1)

DEMONSTRATIONS AND PROTESTS
Injunction against trespasses, 2.8(3)

DEPRECIATION
Accounting for in repair cost award, 5.2(7), 5.14(3)
Effect in estimating market value, 5.16(2)

DERIVATIVE CLAIMS
Punitive damages, 3.11(1), 3.11(9)

DERIVATIVE SUITS
Jury trial, character of issue as equitable or not, 2.6(3)

DESTRUCTION
Injunction to destroy infringing devices,
    Copyright cases, 6.3(5)
    Patent cases, 6.2(5)
    Trademark cases, 6.4(5)

DESTRUCTION OF PROPERTY
See Conversion; Damages

DETERMINATE SANCTIONS FOR CONTEMPT
Criminal character, 2.8(3)

DETERRENCE
See Injunction; Punitive Damages

DETINUE
Historical claim in, 4.2(2)

DIAGNOSTIC EXPENSES
Personal injury, 8.1(3)

DIGNITARY TORTS
See also Civil Rights and particular torts such as Assault; Libel and Slander; Privacy
Generally, 7.1–7.4; 7.3(1)
Injunction, 7.3(5)
Presumed or general damages, 7.1(2)
Punitive damages, 7.3(2)

DILUTION
See Trademark

DIMINISHED RENTAL VALUE
Nuisance damages measure, 5.6(2)

DIMINISHED VALUE
Art, harms to, 5.16(4)
Chattels,
    Ceiling on recovery, 5.14(1)
    Damage or destruction of, 5.13
Damages measure, trespass, 5.2(1)–5.2(7)
Nuisance damages measure, 5.6(2)
Trespass, ceilings on recovery, 5.2(4)

DIRECT BENEFITS RULE
See also Benefits
Generally, 3.8(2)
Personal injury cases generally, 8.6(2)

DIRECT BENEFITS RULE—Cont'd
Plaintiff benefits from tort, rule summary, 8.6(1)
Public benefits and, 8.6(2)
Tracing benefit back to plaintiff, 8.6(2)
Wrongful birth and pregnancy cases, 8.2

DISCHARGE FOR VALUE
Defense to restitution generally, 4.6, 4.7(2)
Restitution, relation to benefits-passed-on rule, 4.6

DISCOUNT RATE
Adjusting to reflect future inflation, 8.5(4)
Reduction to present value, 8.5(3)
Role in capitalization of income to estimate market value, 3.5

DISCOVERY
Accounting claim as, 4.3(5)
Defendant's financial condition, punitive damages claims, 3.11(5)

DISCRETION
Attorney fee awards,
    Amount, statutes granting discretion as to, 3.10(8)
    Employment discrimination, 6.10(5)
    Limited discretion to deny, civil rights and similar statutes, 3.10(5)
    Trademark cases, 6.4(7)
Balancing in equity generally, 2.4(5)
Bond requirement in preliminary injunction cases, dispensing with, 2.11(3)
Damages increased, copyright, 6.3(8)
Equitable, employment discrimination cases, 6.10(5)
Equity,
    Generally, 2.4(7)
    Jury trial rights affecting, 2.6(5)
Expanding rights by, 2.4(7)
Injunction bonds, 2.11(3)
Interest awards and, 3.6(5)
Limiting equitable relief on ethical grounds, summary, 2.4(1)
Limiting rights by, 2.4(7)
Merger of law and equity and, 2.6(1)
Modifying injunctive decrees, 2.8(8)
Reformation, 11.6
Restitution limited by, contract cases, 12.7(2)
Specific performance, 12.8(1), 12.8(5)
Statutory rights and, 2.4(7), 2.10
To deny statutory injunction, 2.10
Types of, employment discrimination cases, 6.10(5)
Unclean hands, barring rights in exercise of discretion, 2.4(2)

DISCRIMINATION
    See also Employment Discrimination
Employment, 6.10
Ethnic and gender, mortality and other tables, effect, 8.5(2)

DISPARAGEMENT
See Injurious Falsehood

DISTRAINT OR DISTRESS
Historical remedy of, 4.2(2)

DIVESTITURE
Injunctive form, 2.9(1)

DOGS
Injury or destruction, 5.15(3)

DOLLAR
Fluctuation in value, effect on damages, 3.7

DONEES
Bona fide purchaser contrasted, 4.7(1)
Constructive trust generally, 4.3(2)

DOUBLE DAMAGES
Statutes, 3.12

DOUBLE JEOPARDY
Punitive damages and, 3.11(12)

DROIT MORAL, 5.16(4)

DRUG EXPENSE
Personal injury, 8.1(3)

DUE PROCESS OF LAW
Injunction, nebulous injunction, 2.8(7)
Provisional remedies, limitations on, 5.17(2)
Punitive damages,
    Limits generally, 3.11(12)
    Multiple liability cases, 3.11(8)

DUPLICATION
Damages,
    Election of remedies and, 9.4
    Elements, 3.3(7)
    Interest and, 3.6(5)
    Land seller's, 12.12(1)
    Misrepresentation cases, 9.2(3)
    Other remedies combined, 3.3(7)
    Trespass to land, 5.12(2)

DURESS
Duress of goods, 10.2(3)
Duress of person, 10.2(3)
Prosecution threatened, 10.2(3)
Railroads, utilities, taxing authorities, 10.2(3)
Restitution, basis for, 10.2(1)
Taxes overpaid, restitution, 4.9(3)
Threats, wrongfulness required, 10.2(2)

EARNING CAPACITY
Child's loss of, damages, 8.1(2)
    Libel and slander, 7.2(11)
    Personal injury damages generally, 8.1(2)
    Wrongful birth, etc. type claims, 8.2

EARNINGS
Survival statutes, lost earnings, 8.3(2)

EASEMENTS
Injunctive protection of, 5.7(6), 5.10(3)

ECONOMIC COMPULSION
    See also Duress
Duress of goods, 10.2(3)
Duress of person, 10.2(3)
Prosecution threatened, 10.2(3)
Railroads, utilities, taxing authorities, 10.2(3)
Restitution, basis for, 10.2(1)
Threats, wrongfulness required, 10.2(2)

ECONOMIC EFFICIENCY
See also Analysis of Remedial Issues; Economics; Efficiency; Efficient Breach of Contract
Frustrated and impracticable contracts, 13.3(2)

ECONOMIC HARM
Negligently causing generally, 6.6(2)

ECONOMIC LOSS
Emotional benefits offset against, 8.2

ECONOMIC RIGHTS
Injunctions to protect generally, 2.9(3)

ECONOMIC TORTS
See particular torts such as Bad Faith Breach of Contract; Fraud; Injurious Falsehood; Interference with Contract; Lawyer Malpractice; Wrongful Discharge
Punitive damages in, 3.11(1)

ECONOMIC WASTE
Art and, 5.16(4)
Building contracts and, 12.19(1)
Damages awards and, 3.1
Destruction of infringing goods, 6.2(5), 6.3(5), 6.4(5)

ECONOMICS
Adequacy of legal remedy, economic interpretations, 2.5(3)
Nuisance, analysis, 5.7(4)
Remedies law and, generally, 1.9
Specific performance, analysis, 12.8(2), 12.8(4)

EFFICIENCY
Avoidable consequences rule and, 3.9
Damages measures affecting, eminent domain, 5.2(6)
Moral rights in art and, 5.16(4)
Nuisance, economic perspectives, 5.7(4)
Nuisance injunctions and, 5.7(2)
Remedies role generally, 1.9

EFFICIENT BREACH OF CONTRACT
Generally, 1.9, 12.1(2), 12.2(1)
Adequacy of legal remedy, 2.5(3)
Bad faith breach of contract and, 6.12
Collateral source rule and, 12.6(4)
Economic compulsion and, 10.2(3)
Equitable conversion and, 6.6(5)
Interference with contract and, 6.6(4), 6.6(5)
Penalty clauses, rationale for non-enforcement, 12.9(1), 12.9(3)
Punitive damages and, 12.5(2)
Restitution measures and, 12.7(4)
Specific performance and,
        Generally, 12.8(2)
        Employee contracts, 12.22(2)

EJECTMENT
See also Trespass to Land
Enforcement procedure, 1.4, 5.10(1)
Historical background, 4.2(2)
Mesne profits, 5.8(2)

EJECTMENT—Cont'd
Restitution,
    As form of, 4.2(1)
    History, 4.2(2)
Summary ejectment, 5.10(2)
Trespass to land, remedy, 5.10(1)
Unlawful detainer, 5.10(2)

ELECTION OF REMEDIES
Contract breach, 12.7(6)
Land sales contracts, 12.13
Misrepresentation cases, 9.4
Ratification and, 9.4, 12.7(6)
Restitution and damages combined, 4.5(5)

EMBEZZLEMENT, 6.1(1), 6.1(2)

EMERGENCY
Services, restitution, 4.9(5)

EMINENT DOMAIN
Capitalization of income, 3.5
Consequential damages and, 3.4
Measure of compensation generally, 5.2(6)
Taking by illegal regulation of land, 5.6(4), 6.9

EMOTIONAL BENEFITS
Offset against economic loss, 8.2

EMOTIONAL DISTRESS
See Mental Distress

EMPLOYMENT CONTRACTS
Employee's damages remedy, 12.21(2)
Employee's restitution remedy, 12.21(3)
Employee's specific performance remedy, 12.21(3)
Employer's damages remedy, 12.22(1)
Employer's restitution remedy, 12.22(1)
Employer's specific performance remedy, 12.22(2)
Negative covenants, 10.5(3), 12.22(2)

EMPLOYMENT DISCRIMINATION
See also Wrongful Discharge
Attorney fees, 6.10(5)
Avoidable consequences, 6.10(4)
Consequential damages, statutory claims, 6.10(4)
Discretionary remedies, 6.10(5)
Equitable defenses, 6.10(8)
Jury trial, 6.10(5)
Laches, 6.10(8)
Preliminary injunction, 6.10(4)
Punitive damages, 3.11(1)
Title VII generally, 6.10(3)

ENCROACHMENTS
Structures trespassing on land, 5.10(4)

ENFORCEMENT OF REMEDIES
See also Judgments and Decrees
Generally, 1.4, 2.8

ENJOINING
See Injunction

ENJOYMENT OF LIFE
Loss of, personal injury, 8.1(4)

ENTRUSTING STATUTES
Bona fide purchasers, 4.7(1)

ENVIRONMENTAL HARM
Natural resource damage, Superfund Act, 5.2(5)
Nuisance or pollution, 5.7(2)
Trespass damages, 5.2(5)

EQUAL PAY ACT, 6.10(3)

EQUALITY IS EQUITY
Equitable maxim, 2.3(4)

EQUITABLE CONVERSION
Generally, 4.3(8)
Contract for sale of property, injury before closing, 12.14
Equity history, 2.3(4)
Hardships, specific performance and, 12.8(4)
Personalty or realty, character affected by, 4.3(8)
Profits, contract breacher's, and, 4.5(3), 12.7(4), 12.11(2), 12.12(2)
Restitution and, 12.7(4), 12.11(2), 12.12(2)
Risk of loss, 4.3(8), 12.10, 12.14
Specific performance,
    A product of, 12.8(1)
    UCC and, 12.16(7)
Tracing and, 4.3(8), 6.1(3)
UCC specific performance and, 12.16(7)

EQUITABLE DEFENSES
See also Balancing Equities and Hardships; Estoppel; Laches; Unclean Hands
Copyright cases, 6.3(6)
Employment discrimination, 6.10(8)
Introductory summary, 2.1(1)
Laches, 2.4(4)
Land sales contracts, 12.11(3)
Misrepresentation cases, 9.6
Patent infringement, 6.2(6)
Trademark infringement, 6.4(6)
Unclean hands, 2.4(2)

EQUITABLE DISCRETION
See Discretion

EQUITABLE LIEN
Accounts or funds, 6.1(2)
Chattels converted, 5.18(3)
Constructive trust compared and distinguished, 4.3(3)
Deficiency judgment and, 4.3(3)
Introduced, 1.4, 4.3(1)
Misrepresentation, 9.3(4)
Restitution, generally, 4.3(3)

EQUITABLE RELIEF
See also Equity; Injunction; Specific Performance and specific equitable remedies such as Constructive Trust, Interpleader and others; and specific topics such as Contracts
Basic remedy, 1.1
Liability of one who has not violated plaintiff's rights, 2.4(7)
Personal injury cases, 8.10

EQUITABLE REPLEVIN, 5.17(3)

EQUITIES
See also Balancing Equities and Hardships
Balancing,
    Injunction cases, 2.9(2)
    Reformation cases, 11.6(3)
Equal, equitable maxim, 2.3(4)
Hardships, balancing in equity generally, 2.4(5)

EQUITY
See also Contempt; Injunction; Interpleader; Specific Performance
Accounting, restitution, 4.3(5)
Adequacy of legal remedy, see Adequacy of Legal Remedy
Advisory juries, 2.6(2)
Aids the vigilent, equitable maxim, 2.3(4)
Balancing introduced, 2.4(1)
Bankruptcy, jury trial, 2.6(3)
Be good epigram, 2.2
Characteristics, 2.1(3)
Characterizing claims as equitable, 2.1(3)
Clean up jurisdiction, 2.7
Codifying all laws epigram, 2.2
Coercive remedies,
    Generally, 2.1(2)
    Introductory summary, 2.1(1)
    Overview, 2.1(1)
Compelling act in foreign state, jurisdiction, 2.7
Constructive trust, 4.3(2)
Contempt, introductory summary, 2.1(1)
Contract defenses in, 2.4(3)
Discretion,
    Generally, 2.4(7)
    Employment discrimination cases, 6.10(5)
    Jury trial, effect on, 2.6(5)
    Limiting relief on ethical grounds, summary, 2.4(1)
    Summary, 2.1(1)
    Unclean hands, 2.4(2)
Enforcement of decrees generally, 2.8(1)
Epigrams, 2.2
Equitable defenses, introductory summary, 2.1(1)
Equitable interests conflicting, 4.7(1)
Equity in mortgaged land, 2.3(3)
Equity of redemption, 2.3(3)
Estoppel generally, 2.3(5)
Ethical principles, summary introduction, 2.3(1)
Foreign land titles, jurisdiction to affect, 2.7
Forfeitures, 2.1(3)
Forms of action, no use of, 2.9(2)
Full faith and credit to decrees in, 2.8(1)
Hardships, balancing, introduction, 2.4(1)
History,
    Generally, 2.2
    Adequacy rule, 2.5(1)
    Introductory summary, 2.1(1)
    Mortgages, 2.3(3)
    Trusts, 2.3(2)
In personam orders, 2.2
Incidental jurisdiction,
    Clean up jurisdiction, 2.7

EQUITY—Cont'd
Incidental jurisdiction—Cont'd
  Jury trial and, 2.6(4)
Injunction, see Injunctions
Interpleader, 2.9(1), 2.9(4)
Interstate decrees, 2.7
Irreparable harm rule, summary, 2.1(1)
Jurisdiction and adequacy test, 2.5(1)
Jurisdiction generally, 2.7
Jurisdiction in separate courts, 2.2
Jury trial,
  Characterization of issues as equitable, 2.6(3)
  Discretion, effect on, 2.6(5)
  Employment discrimination claims, 6.10(5)
  Equitable claim with legal counterclaim, 2.6(4)
  Introductory summary, 2.1(1)
  Mixed law and equity issues, 2.6(4)
  No constitutional right generally, 2.6(2)
  Res judicata affecting, 2.6(4)
Laches defense, 2.4(4)
Law and equity classification, 1.2
Limiting speech, policy against, 2.5(4)
Maxims of, 2.3(4)
Meanings of term, 2.1(3)
Measuring equitable relief, 2.4(6)
Merger of law and equity,
  Generally, 2.6(1)
  Summary introduction, 2.1(1)
Modification of decrees, jury trial rights and, 2.6(5)
Money obligations, merger of law and equity and, 2.6(1)
Mutuality of remedy, 2.4(3)
Nature of equity issue for jury trial purposes, 2.6(3)
Personal services, policy against compelling, 2.5(4)
Policy limits on remedies, 2.5(4)
Practicality as limit on remedies, 2.5(4)
Procedure in separate courts, 2.2
Public interests, balancing, introduction, 2.4(1)
Punitive damages in, 3.11(1)
Reformation, 4.3(7)
Remedial vs. substantive equity, 2.3(1)
Remedies distinctively equitable, 2.1(3)
Remedies exceeding rights, 2.4(6)
Rescission,
  Restitutionary remedy generally, 4.3(6)
  Restoration required of the plaintiff, 4.8
Restitution, relationship, 4.1(1)
Restitution in, generally, 4.3(1)
Restitutionary remedies in generally, 2.1(2)
Right and remedy, congruence, 2.4(6)
Roguish thing, chancellor's foot epigram, 2.2
Specific performance as species of injunction, 2.1(2)
Substantive equity,
  Adequacy rule inapplicable, 2.5(1)
  Remedial equity distinguished, 2.3(1)
Summary overview, 2.1(1)
Supervision or enforcement of decrees, 2.5(4)
Tailoring remedies,
  Generally, 2.4(6)
  Jury trial rights and, 2.6(5)

EQUITY—Cont'd
Theory of in separate courts, 2.2
Title in equity vs. title at law, bona fide purchasers, 4.7(1)
Unclean hands generally, 2.4(2)
Unconscionability, 2.4(3)

EQUIVALENT REMEDIES
Arguments based upon, 1.8
Costs and benefits, 1.9
Externalized costs, 1.9
Remedy to reflect the right, 1.7

ERRONEOUS ORDERS
Contempt and, 2.8(6)

ESCROW
Disputed royalty funds, 6.2(5)

ESSENTIAL RELIANCE, 12.3(2)

ESTOPPEL
Copyright cases, 6.3(6)
Election of remedies doctrine and, 9.4
Jury trial, equitable characterization or not, 2.6(3)
Laches and, 2.3(5), 2.4(4)
Law actions, applied in, 2.3(5)
Misrepresentation, 9.6
Patent infringement, 6.2(6)
Promissory estoppel, 2.3(5)
  Statute of frauds and, 13.2(5)
Ratification and, 2.3(5)
Restitution and, 2.3(5)
Specific performance cases, 12.8(4)
Statute of frauds, against, 13.2(5)
Trademark cases, 6.4(6)
Waiver and, 2.3(5)

ETHICAL PRINCIPLES
Equity, summary introduction, 2.3(1)

EVIDENCE
Clear and convincing standard,
  Constructive trust, 6.1(2)
  Libel, 7.2(4), 7.2(12)
  Promissory estoppel, 13.2(5)
  Punitive damages, 3.11(4)
  Undue influence, 10.3
Comparable sales evidence, value of property, 3.5
Contract price, benefits received shown by, 4.5(4)
Costs to one as evidence of benefits to another, 4.5(4)
Financial condition of defendant, punitive damages cases, 3.11(5)
Profit loss,
  Generally, 3.4
  Contract cases, 12.4(3)
Punitive damages,
  Financial condition of defendant, 3.11(5)
  Standard of proof, 3.11(4)
Reliance expense as evidence of benefits to other person, 4.5(4)
Value of property, 3.5
Value of property, opinion testimony, personal property, 5.13(4)

EVIDENCE—Cont'd
Wealth, punitive damages cases, defendant's, 3.11(5)

EX PARTE ORDERS, 2.11(1)

EXECUTION
Enforcing judgments by, 1.4
Enforcing money decrees in equity by, n., 2.8(1)

EXEMPLARY DAMAGES
See Punitive Damages

EXEMPTIONS
Constructive trust defeating, 4.3(2)

EXHAUSTION OF REMEDIES
Nuisance cases, 5.7(5)

EXPECTANCY
Consequential or substitute cost measure as ceiling on, chattel buyer's claims, 12.16(4)
Contract damages,
    Cap on reliance damages recovery, 12.3(2)
    Costs and market measures of, 12.2(2)
    Goal, 12.2(1)
    Market vs. consequential measures of, 12.2(2)
    Restitution compared, 12.7(1)
    Restitution in excess of, 12.7(3)
Election of remedies doctrine impinging, installment land sales contract, 12.13
Losing contract, a limit on restitution or not, 9.2(1), 12.7(5), 12.16(6), 12.21(3)

EXPENSE DEDUCTIONS
Restitution of profits, 4.5(3)

EXPENSES INCURRED
As consequential damages, 3.3(4)

EXTERNALIZED COSTS, 1.9

FAIRNESS
Morality, flexibility, equity as, 2.1(3)

FALSE IMPRISONMENT
Damages, 7.3(2)

FALSE LIGHT
Privacy invasion, 7.3(4)

FAMILY RELATIONSHIPS
Injunction protecting, 7.3(5)

FARNSWORTH, E. ALAN
Restitution for breach of contract, 12.7(4)

FAULT
Comparative, avoidable consequences rule and, 3.9

FEAR OF FUTURE HARM
Damages element, personal injury, 8.1(4), 8.1(7)
Libel and slander cases, 7.2(5)

FEDERAL COURTS
Injunction against state litigation, 2.5(4), 2.9(4)

FEE SHIFTING
See Attorney Fees Awards

FELA ACTIONS
Punitive damages, 3.11(1)

FIDUCIARIES
    See also Accounting; Constructive Trust and other related topics
Accounting for profits, 4.3(5)
Bribery, 10.6
Chattels taken, restitution, 5.18(3)
Contempt, imprisonment for failure to pay money due, 2.8(2)
Conversion, fiducial breached compared to, 9.3(4)
Duties generally, 10.4
Inside information, 10.4, 10.5
Profits from breach of duty, 4.5(3)
Punitive damages, 3.11(2)

FIERI FACIAS
Execution by, 1.4

FINES
Contempt sanctions, 2.8(2)

FIRST AMENDMENT
Injunction, media restraint, contempt, 2.8(6)
Injunction against defamation, 2.9(5)
Libel and slander,
    Presumed damages, 7.2(4)
    Substantive limitations on, 7.2(1)
Privacy, presumed damages and fault requirement, 7.3(4)
Punitive damages limits to avoid chill, 3.11(12)

FIRST IN TIME, FIRST IN RIGHT
Equity maxim, 4.7(1)

FISS, OWEN
Adequacy of legal remedy generally, 2.5(3)
Structural injunction, 2.9(1)

FLUREAU v. THORNHILL
Defect in contract vendor's title, 12.11(1)

FORCIBLE ENTRY AND DETAINER
Summary ejectment remedy, 5.10(2)

FORECLOSURE
Equity, historic role in, 2.3(3), 2.6(3)
Installment land contract, 12.13
Jury trial in, 2.6(4)
Loss of land at sale, special damages for contract breach, 12.4(7)
Mechanic's or materialman's lien, 12.20(3)
Mortgages, equity role in, 2.3(3)
Oral promise to buy in at sale, specific restitution, 13.2(3)

FOREIGN CURRENCY
Damages, awards based on foreign obligations, 3.7

FOREIGN LAND TITLES
Equitable remedies affecting, 2.7

FORFEITURES
Contract breach, penalty distinguished, 12.9(4)
Equitable maxims, 2.3(4)

FORFEITURES—Cont'd
Installment land sales contracts, 12.13
Land sales contract deposit, 12.12(1)

FORGERY, 9.6

FORMS OF ACTION
Equity, not used in, 2.9(2)

FRAUD
See also Fraudulent Conveyances; Misrep-
resentation
Acquisition of property at another's death by,
6.7
Estoppel and, 2.3(5)

FRAUD IN THE FACTUM, 9.6

FRAUDULENT CONVEYANCES
Illegality, restitution, 13.6
Jury trial, characterizing litigation as equita-
ble or not, 2.6(3)
Supplementary proceedings to reach assets,
2.8(1)

FREE SPEECH
Copyright and, generally, 6.3(1)
Dignitary torts and, 7.3(3)
Injunction,
Adequacy test and, Fiss view, 2.5(3)
Copyright infringement, 6.3(5)
Irreparable harm, loss of as, 2.5(2)
Libel and slander, 2.9(5), 7.2(14)
Personal torts, generally, 7.3(5)
Protests and, 2.11(1), 5.10(3)
Trade secrets, 6.6(4)
Trademark, disclaimer required, 6.4(5)
Injurious falsehood, 6.6(4), 6.8(3)
Libel and slander, 7.1(1), 7.2(1), 7.2(4), 7.2(14)
Mental distress damages without defamation,
7.2(6)
Misappropriation doctrine and, 6.5(3)
Moral rights of artists and, 5.16(4)
Policy against equitable interference with,
2.5(4)
Punitive damages for violation of, 3.11(1)
Punitive damages limits to protect, 3.11(1),
3.11(12)
Trade secrets, 6.6(4)
Wrongful discharge for exercising, 6.10(4)

FREEZING ASSETS
Escrow of royalty funds, patent cases, 6.2(5)
Injunction to hold funds, 6.1(5)

FRONT PAY
Employment discrimination, statutory claims
for, 6.10(4)

FRUSTRATION
Mistake compared, 11.1
Reliance expenses, 13.3(2)
Restitution for benefits conferred in frustrated
contracts,
Generally, 13.3(1)
Measures, 13.3(2)

FULFILLING ANOTHER'S DUTY
Restitution for, 4.9(2)

FULL FAITH AND CREDIT
Equitable decrees, 2.8(1)

FUTURE HARM OR LOSS
Damages,
Personal injury, 8.1(7)
Reduction to present value, 3.7
Fear of, element of damages, personal injury,
8.1(4)
Frontpay, wrongful discharge,
Common law, 6.10(2)
Statutory claims for, 6.10(4)
Inflation, 3.7, 8.5(1), 8.5(4)
Interest on, injury cases, 8.4
Lease breached, measure, 12.15(3)
Libel and slander cases, 7.2(5)
Lump sum awards,
Generally, 3.1
Incentives to correct harmful condition,
5.6(3)
Periodic payments, 8.5(5)
Personal injury, generally, 8.5(1)
Reduction to present value, personal injury,
8.5(1)
Structured settlements, 8.5(5)
Toxic tort cases, 8.1(7)
Value of chance, personal injury cases, 8.1(7)

GAINS
See Benefits

GALLIGAN, THOMAS
Punitive damages, general deterrence proposals, 3.11(3)

GAMBLING CONTRACTS
Restitution and, 13.6

GARNISHMENT
Provisional remedy, 1.3
Subrogation compared, 4.3(4)

GENDER
See also Employment Discrimination
Effect in mortality and work life tables, 8.5(2)

GENERAL DAMAGES
See also Market Measured Damages
Added to consequential damages, duplication
risks, 3.3(7)
Added to substitution costs, duplication risks,
3.3(7)
Introduction to, 3.2
Market measure, as, 3.3(3)

GENETIC DEFECTS
Wrongful birth, wrongful pregnancy, 8.2

GEOGRAPHICAL MARKET
Valuing property, which market, 5.13(3)

GIFTS
Benefits from as collateral source not credited
to defendant, 3.8(1)
Credit card charge privilege, donee's liability
to pay for charges, 4.9(4)
Mistakes in making, restitution, 11.10
Presumption from gift to a dominant party,
10.3

INDEX 943

GIFTS—Cont'd
Services as gifts, unsolicited benefits rules, 4.9(4)

GOLDEN RULE ARGUMENT
Personal injury, 8.1(4)

GOOD WILL
Capital value, as, 3.4
Chattel buyer's loss of, 12.16(4)
Consequential damages, 3.4, 12.4(3), 12.16(4)
Copyright infringement causing loss, 6.3(4)
Dilution as loss to, 6.8(3)
General or market damages, capital value of, 3.4
Moral rights of artists and, 5.16(4)
Rehabilitation of, expenses, consequential damages for, 3.3(4)
Trademark infringement, harm to, 6.4(3)
Value of chance and, 3.4

GOODS SOLD AND DELIVERED
Assumpsit count, 4.2(3)

GRANTORS
Support or care for grantors, covenants to, 12.12(1), 12.12(2)

GROVES v. JOHN WUNDER CO.
Contract damages, costs of completing contract, 12.19(1)

HABEAS CORPUS
Prerogative writ of, 2.9(1)

HADLEY v. BAXENDALE
Contract damages limits, 3.4, 12.4(4)–12.4(7)

HALL v. COLE
Rule of in attorney fee cases, 4.9(6), 3.10(2)

HALLET RULE
Tracing withdrawals from fund, 6.1(4)

HARDSHIPS
See also Balancing Equities and Hardships
Balancing,
Injunction cases, 2.9(2)
Reformation cases, 11.6(3)
Balancing in exercise of equitable discretion, introduction, 2.4(1)

HARM
Damages award distinguished, 3.1

HARPER v. ADAMETZ
Broker profit case, 10.5(1)

HAZARDOUS SUBSTANCES
See Superfund Act

HEDONIC DAMAGES
Environmental damages measure, n., 5.2(5)
Personal injury, 8.1(4)
Wrongful death cases, 8.3(5)

HEIRLOOMS
Taking, harm, or destruction, measure of damages, 5.16(3)

HISTORICAL BACKGROUNDS
Accounting action or suit, 4.3(5)

HISTORICAL BACKGROUNDS—Cont'd
Adequacy of legal remedy test, 2.5(1)
Assumpsit, 4.2(3)
Attorney fee awards, 3.10(1)
Debt, form of action in, 4.2(3)
Debtinue, 4.2(3)
Distress, 4.2(3)
Ejectment, 4.2(2), 5.10(1)
Enforcement, 2.8(1)
Equity, 2.2
Interest, 3.6(1)
Interpleader, 2.9(4)
Jury trial in equity, 2.6(2)
Mortgages, 2.3(3)
Punitive damages, 3.11(1)
Replevin, 4.2(2)
Trusts, 2.3(2)
Uses, 2.3(2)

HOMEMAKERS
Lost earning capacity, personal injury, 8.1(2)
Wrongful death, 8.3(4)

HOUSEHOLD GOODS
Taking, harm, or destruction, measure of damages, 5.16(3)

HOUSEKEEPING SERVICES EXPENSES
Personal injury, 8.1(3)

HUSBAND AND WIFE
See Spouses

IDEAS
No property in, 6.5(1)
Unsolicited submission of, 4.9(4)

IDIOSYNCRATIC VALUES
Damages for harm to, 3.3(6)

ILLEGALITY
Agreement reformed to meet legal rules, 11.6(3)
Restitution for benefits conferred in illegal contract, 13.6
Unclean hands and, 2.4(2)

IMPLIED IN FACT CONTRACT
Assumpsit and, 4.2(3)
Quasi contract contrasted, 4.2(3)
Terminology for restitution, 4.1(1), 4.2(1)

IMPOSSIBILITY OR IMPRACTICABILITY
Mistake compared, 11.1

IMPOUNDMENT
Infringing devices,
Copyright cases, 6.3(5)
Patent cases, 6.2(5)

IMPRACTICABILITY
Reliance expenses, 13.3(2)
Restitution for benefits conferred in contracts discharged for impracticability, 13.3(1)

IMPRISONMENT
Contempt sanction, 2.8(2)
Debt, constitutionality contempt sanction, 2.8(2)

IMPROVEMENTS
Chattels, services not authorized by owner, 4.9(5)
Cotenant improvement, restitution, 4.9(3)
Land sales contract, breach and restitution, 12.11(2)
Statute of frauds, benefits conferred by, restitution, 13.2(2)
Subcontractor's work improving land, 4.9(4)
Tenant's improvements reverting to landlord, restitution, 4.9(4)
Trespasser's improvements to land, 5.8(3)

IN PERSONAM
Enforcement, judgments or remedies, generally, 1.4, 2.8(1)
Equity orders, characteristic, 2.2
Restitution generally, 4.1(3)

IN REM
Enforcement,
Judgments or remedies, generally, 1.4, 2.8(1)
Sheriff's role, replevin and ejectment, 4.2(2)
Injunction in rem or against the world, 2.8(5)
Restitution generally, 4.1(3)

INCIDENTAL DAMAGES
Chattel leases, 12.18
UCC measure for buyer, 12.16(4)
UCC measure for seller, 12.17(4)

INCIDENTAL JURISDICTION
Equity power, jury trial not eliminated by, 2.6(4)

INCIDENTAL RELIANCE EXPENSES
Damages for contract breach, 12.3(2)

INCOME LOSS
See also Earning Capacity
Consequential damage, as, 3.3(4)
Personal injury, 8.1(2)

INCOME-PRODUCING PROPERTY
Damages for, 5.16(2)

INCOME TAXES
See Taxes

INCONSISTENT REMEDIES
See Election of Remedies

INDEMNITY
Attorney fees, third person litigation, 3.10(3)
Restitutionary claim, subrogation and, 4.3(4)

INDETERMINATE SANCTIONS FOR CONTEMPT
Civil character, 2.8(3)

INFANCY
See Capacity; Children

INFLATION
Adjustment for,
Damages award generally, 3.7
Personal injury cases, summary, 8.5(1)
Interest and, personal injury cases, 8.5(4)
Methods of accounting for, 3.7

INFLATION—Cont'd
Periodic payments approaches to, 3.7
Personal injury cases generally, 8.5(4)
Productivity increases distinguished, 3.7
Proof methods, injury cases, 8.5(4)

INHERITANCE
Acquisition by wrongdoing, 6.7
From decedent, effect on wrongful death damages, 8.3(4)
Lost inheritance claims, 8.3(4)
Wrongful death, survivor's inheritance affecting damages, 8.3(7)

INJUNCTION
See also Adequacy of Legal Remedy; Contempt; Specific Performance
Acts in other states, 2.5(4)
Adequacy of legal remedy,
Generally, 2.9(2)
Encroaching structures, 5.10(4)
Nuisance cases, 5.7(2)
Statutory injunction, 2.10
Trespass,
Physical harm cases, 5.5
Possession cases, 5.10(3)
Administrative proceeding, against, 2.5(4)
Agents of defendant bound by, contempt, 2.8(5)
Aiding violation, contempt liability, 2.8(5)
Alternative remedies as benchmark for measuring costs and benefits of, 2.9(2)
Ambiguous, contempt defense, 2.8(7)
Appeal,
Generally, 2.11(4)
Contempt liability for disobedience before reversal, 2.8(6)
Attorney fees awards, 3.10(6)
Balancing equities and hardships, 2.9(2)
Bankruptcy, automatic stay, form of injunction, 2.9(1)
Basic equitable remedy, 2.1(2)
Bills of peace, 2.9(4)
Bond, preliminary injunction or TRO, 2.11(3)
Chattel recovered by, 5.17(3)
Civil rights cases, 7.4(4)
Classifications generally, 2.9(1)
Compensated injunctions,
Nuisance,
Generally, 5.7(3)
Economic perspective, 5.7(4)
Trade secret cases, 10.5(3)
Copyright infringement, 6.3(5)
Costs and benefits balancing, 2.9(2)
Crimes, against, 2.9(3)
Criminal prosecution, against, 2.9(4), 7.3(5)
Demonstrations with trespass prohibited by, 2.8(3)
Destruction compelled by,
Infringing devices,
Copyright cases, 6.3(5)
Patent cases, 6.2(5)
Trademark cases, 6.4(5)
Dignitary torts, 7.3(5)
Dilution, trademark, 6.4(3), 6.8(3)
Discretion,
Denial or grant, 2.4(1)—2.4(7)

INJUNCTION—Cont'd
Discretion—Cont'd
  Modification of, 2.8(8)
  Statutory, 2.10
Disparagement, 6.8(3)
Divestiture as, 2.9(1)
Easements, 5.7(6)
Economic perspectives, nuisance cases, 5.7(4)
Economic rights protected by, 2.9(3)
Encroaching structures, to remove, 5.10(4)
Erroneous, contempt and, 2.8(6)
Executive, against, 2.5(4)
Existing legal rights enforced by, 2.9(2)
Family relationships, protection by, 7.3(5)
Federal injunction against state proceedings, 2.5(4), 2.9(4)
First Amendment, defamation, 2.9(5), 7.2(14)
Freezing assets by, 6.1(5)
Grounds for generally, 2.9(2)
In rem injunction binding the world, 2.8(5)
Incentive injunctions, nuisance, 5.7(3)
Injunctive remedies under other names, 2.1(2)
Injurious falsehood, 6.8(2)
Institutional restructuring by, 2.9(1)
Interference with contract, 6.6(4)
Interpleader,
  Generally, 2.9(4)
  As, 2.9(1)
Irreparable harm, generally, 2.9(2)
Judicial proceedings, against, 2.5(4), 2.9(4)
Litigation, against, 2.9(4), 7.3(5)
Mandamus writ compared, 2.9(1)
Mandatory,
  Generally, 2.9(1)
  Trespass to land cases, 5.5
Media publications, against, contempt, 2.8(6)
Medical care, requiring, 7.3(5)
Minimizing damages, injunction undercutting rule of, 2.9(2)
Misappropriation of intangible property,
  Private submission of ideas, 6.5(2)
  Public revelation cases, 6.5(3)
Modification of, 2.8(8)
Name change prohibited by, 2.9(2)
Ne exeat regno, 2.9(1)
Nebulous,
  Contempt defense, 2.8(7)
  Nuisance cases, 5.7(3)
New rights created by, 2.9(2)
Nuisance, generally, 5.7
Patent infringement, 6.2(5)
Payment of money compelled,
  Merger of law and equity, 2.6(1)
  Personal injury, 8.10
Permanent, generally, 2.9(1)
Personal rights, 2.9(5), 7.3(5)
Persons bound, 2.8(5)
Political rights or relations, 2.9(5), 7.3(5)
Possession of land, transfer by, 5.10(3)
Preliminary,
  Generally, 2.11(1)
  Statute authorizing, 2.10
Prerogative writs compared, 2.9(1)
Preventive,
  Generally, 2.9(1)
  Threat of future harm required, 2.5(1)

INJUNCTION—Cont'd
Privacy invasions, 7.3(5)
Prohibition, writ of compared, 2.9(1)
Prohibitory, 2.9(1)
Property rights protected by, 2.9(3)
Protests and trespasses, against, contempt, 2.8(3)
Public accommodations, 7.3(5)
Public information rights, protecting, 7.3(5)
Punitive damages and, 3.11(3), 8.10
Reinstatement, wrongful discharge,
  Common law, 6.10(2)
  Statutory claims, 6.10(4)
Reinstatement in job as, 2.9(1)
Religious interests, protecting, 2.9(5), 7.3(5)
Reparative, 2.9(1)
Reversal on appeal, contempt liability, 2.8(6)
Review, agencies and other decisions, by, 2.9(4)
Right-remedy discorrelation, 1.7, 7.4(4)
Risk of error, 2.9(2)
Scope,
  Acts covered, 2.4(6)
  Discretion and, 2.4(7)
  Freezing funds, terms, 6.2(5)
  Patent infringement, 6.2(5)
  Persons covered, 2.4(7), 2.8(5)
  Trademark cases, 6.4(5)
Segregation in schools, example of, 2.9(5)
Slander of title, 6.8(3)
Smoking prohibited by, 2.9(2)
Social relations, 7.3(5)
Specific performance as form of, 2.9(1), 12.8(1)
Spur injunctions, 5.7(3)
Standards,
    See also Adequacy of Legal Remedy; Balancing Equities and Hardships
  Preliminary injunction, 2.11(2)
  Temporary restraining order, 2.11(2)
Statutes, effect,
  Generally, 2.10
  Nuisance cases, 5.7(5)
Stay of, 2.11(4)
Strategic position effected by, 2.9(4)
Strike, excessive injunction, contempt, 2.8(6)
Structural, 1.5, 2.9(1), 7.4(4)
Successors and privities to, contempt liability for violation, 2.8(5)
Tactical position effected by, 2.9(4)
Temporary restraining order, generally, 2.11(1)
Threat of future harm, when required, 2.9(1)
Title in issue, 5.10(3)
Trade secret use, 10.5(2)
Trademark infringement, 6.4(5)
Transferring possession of land by, 5.10(3)
Trespass,
  Adequacy of legal remedy,
    Physical harm cases, 5.5
    Possession cases, 5.10(3)
  Physical harm to land, 5.5
  Possessory interests, 5.10(3)
Unconstitutional orders disobeyed, contempt, 2.8(6)
Vague terms, contempt defense, 2.8(7)

INJUNCTION—Cont'd
Violation, see Contempt
Voting rights, example of, 2.9(5)
Waste to a future estate, 5.2(8)
Zoning violations, against, 5.7(2)

INJURIOUS FALSEHOOD
Attorney fee awards, 6.8(2)
Damages, 6.8(2)
Free speech limits on claim, 6.8(3)
Libel compared, 6.8(1)
Substantive background, 6.8(1)

INS CASE
Misappropriation doctrine, 6.5(3)

INSIDE INFORMATION
Corporate insider's liability for short swing
profits, 10.5(2)
Fiduciaries and others, 10.4
Securities, dealing in, 10.5(2)
Trade secrets, 10.5(3)

INSTALLMENT CONTRACTS
See Land Sales Contracts

INSTITUTIONAL RESTRUCTURING
Injunction, 1.5

INSURANCE
Bad faith failure to pay benefits due, attorney
fee liability, 3.10(3)
Benefits from, collateral source not credited to
defendant, 3.8(1)
Constructive trust on policy or proceeds,
Fire policy, 12.14
Life policy, n., 4.3(2), 6.1(2)
Insurer's contract to defend, liability for attor-
ney fees, 3.10(3)
Insurer's liability minimized by insured ac-
tion, restitution or not, 4.9(4)
Insurer's punitive liability for own torts, poli-
cy coverage distinguished, 3.11(7)
Land sales contract, injury to property before
closing, 12.14
Life insurance, constructive trust on, 6.1(2)
Overpayment of benefits, 11.7
Punitive damages, coverage, 3.11(7)
Reformation of policy, 11.6(3)
Restitution,
Insured minimizes insurer's liability, 4.9(4)
Overpayment of benefits, 11.7
Wealth in punitive damages claim, 3.11(5)

INTANGIBLE INTERESTS
Economic, see Chapter 6 generally and entries
under Misappropriation of Intangible
Property
Personal, see Chapter 7 generally and entries
under Civil Rights; Dignitary Torts;
and particular torts such as Assault,
Libel and Slander; Privacy

INTELLECTUAL PROPERTY
See also Copyright; Misappropriation of
Intangible Property; Patents;
Trademark; Unfair Competition
Unsolicited submission of ideas, 4.9(4)

**INTENTIONAL INFLICTION OF MENTAL DIS-
TRESS**
See also Mental Distress
Property damage claim distinguished, 5.15(3)

INTEREST
See also Judgment Interest; Prejudg-
ment Interest
Generally, 3.6(1)–3.6(6)
Accrual,
Generally, 3.6(4)
Interest accrual vs. claim accrual, 3.6(5)
Personal injury cases, 8.4
Adjustment of damages, introduced, 3.2
Alternative to consequential damages, 3.4
Attorney fees and, 3.6(5)
Building contract, delayed performance,
12.19(1)
Capital tied up, 3.4
Compound,
Generally, 3.6(4), 3.6(6)
Personal injury cases, 8.4
Computation, 3.6(4), 8.4
Consequential damages, as, 3.6(4)
Copyright infringement, 6.3(3)
Damages adjustment generally, 3.6(1)–3.6(6)
Death cases, 8.3(6)
Discount rate,
Inflation and, 8.5(4)
Reduction to present value, 8.5(3), 8.5(4)
Discretion to award, injury cases, 8.4
Duplication of awards and, 3.6(5)
Elements of damages on which interest is
awarded, 3.6(4)
Future losses, 8.4
Inflation and,
Generally, 3.7
Personal injury cases, 8.5(4)
Judgment,
Generally, 3.6(6)
Personal injury cases, 8.4
Lawyer malpractice, 6.11
Loss of use, substitute measure for rental,
5.15(2)
Modification of judgment, 3.6(6)
Multiple judgments, 3.6(6)
Nonpecuniary losses, interest on, 8.4
Pain and suffering damages, 3.6(4)
Patent infringement cases, 6.2(3)
Personal injury cases, 8.4
Prejudgment,
Generally, 3.6(1)–3.6(5)
Personal injury cases, 8.4
Punitive damages,
Generally, 3.6(4), 3.11(13)
Interest on denied, patent infringement,
6.2(3)
Rate,
Generally, 3.6(4), 3.6(6), 8.4
Personal injury cases, 8.4
Real rate of, figuring inflation, 3.7
Rent, relation to, 3.6(2)
Simple, 3.6(4), 3.6(6)
Trademark infringement, 6.4(3)
Wrongful discharge, statutory claims, 6.10(4)

INTERFERENCE WITH CONTRACT

See also particular means for interfering with contract, such as Injurious Falsehood; Wrongful Acquisition of Property at Death of Another; Wrongful Discharge; see also, particular types of rights interfered with, such as Trade Secrets

Damages, 6.6(2)
Disparagement or trade libel, by, 6.6(4), 6.8
Efficient breach, property not contract interference, 6.6(4)
Efficient breach and, generally, 6.6(5)
Independent tort, by, 6.6(4)
Injunction against and efficient breach, 6.6(4)
Mental distress damages, 6.6(2)
Negligent interference, damages calculations, when allowed, 6.6(2)
Punitive damages, 6.6(2)
Restitution, 6.6(3)
Soliciting employees, 6.6(4)
Specifically performable contract, 6.6(2), 6.6(4)
Substantive background, 6.6(1)
Trade secrets, 6.6(4)

INTERFERENCE WITH OPPORTUNITIES OR PROSPECTS

See Interference with Contract

INTERMEDDLERS

See Unsolicited Benefits

INTERPLEADER

Generally, 2.9(4)
Injunction, form of, 2.9(1)
Punitive damages, multiple awards, proposed solution, 3.11(8)

INTERSTATE DECREES

Equity, 2.7

INTERVENORS

Attorney fees awards, 3.10(6)

INTRUSION

Privacy invasion, 7.3(4)

INVERSE CONDEMNATION

See Eminent Domain; Regulatory Takings

INVESTMENT INCOME LOSSES

Personal injury, 8.1(2)

IRREPARABLE HARM

See Adequacy of Legal Remedy

JOB DISCRIMINATION

See Employment Discrimination

JOINT AND SEVERAL LIABILITY

Attorney fees, 3.10(6)
Punitive damages, 3.11(5), 3.11(6)

JOINT TENANTS

See Cotenants

JONES ACT

Punitive damages, 3.11(1)

JUDGMENTS AND DECREES

See also Res Judicata

JUDGMENTS AND DECREES—Cont'd

Ambiguous or vague decrees, contempt impermissible, 2.8(7)
Consent decrees,
Contempt, 2.8(2)
Modification, 2.8(8)
Contempt, see Contempt
Damages, currency in which expressed, 3.7
Disobedience of, see Contempt
Enforcement generally, 1.4, 2.8
Injunction against enforcement of, 1.5(4)
Interest on,
Generally, 3.6(6)
Accrual from time of verdict vs. time of judgment, 3.6(6)
Affirmance after appeal, 3.6(6)
Modification of judgment, 3.6(6)
Multiple judgments, which of, 3.6(6)
Verdict or judgment triggering, 3.6(6)
Title, transfer by decree, 2.8(1)

JURISDICTION

Compelling act in foreign state, 2.7
Contempt and, 2.8(6)
Equity, generally, 2.7
Error distinguished, 2.7
Third person's standing to attack, 2.8(6)
To preserve jurisdiction, 2.7

JURY

Punitive damages, role in, 3.11(1)

JURY ROLE

Equity,
Advisory juries, 2.6(2)
Introductory summary, 2.1(1)
Punitive damages, instructions, 3.11(12)

JURY TRIAL

Accounting for profits and, 2.6(3), 4.3(5)
Advisory juries, equity, 2.6(2)
Bankruptcy, equitable proceeding, when, 2.6(3)
Civil rights, Title VII, characterizing as equitable or not, 2.6(3)
Constitutional right, equity cases excluded, 2.6(2)
Constructive trust, 2.6(3), 4.3(2)
Contempt, 2.8(4)
Damages substitutes for equitable relief, 2.6(5)
Declaratory remedies, 2.6(3), 12.8(7)
Employment discrimination claims, equitable or legal, 6.10(5)
Equitable claim with legal counterclaim, 2.6(4)
Equity,
Discretion affecting right to, 2.6(5)
Equitable characterization of issues, 2.6(3)
Modification of decrees and, 2.6(5)
No right to, 2.6(2)
Improvements, claim for as equitable, n., 5.8(3)
Law and equity issues mixed, 2.6(4)
Merger and, generally, 2.6(1)
Mixed law and equity issues, 2.6(4)
Remedies sought govern equitable characterization, 2.6(3)
Res judicata and, 2.6(4)
Restitution claims, 2.6(3)

JURY TRIAL—Cont'd
Statutory actions as equitable or not, 2.6(3)
Substantive equity governs equitable charac-
    terization, 2.6(3)
Title VII, 6.10(5)

KALDOR–HICKS EFFICIENCY, 1.9

LACHES
    Generally, 2.4(4)
Employment discrimination, 6.10(7)
Estoppel and, 2.3(5), 2.4(4)
Law, application to actions in, 2.4(4)
Merger of law and equity and, 2.6(1)
Patent cases, 6.2(6)
Specific performance cases, 12.8(4)
Trademark cases, 6.4(6)

LAND
See Improvements; Trespass to Land; Nui-
    sance; Regulatory Takings and other
    particular topics

LAND SALES CONTRACTS
    See also Deeds
Acreage deficiency, 12.11(1), 12.11(3), 12.12(3)
Earnest money contracts, 12.10–12.12
Equitable conversion, see Equitable Conver-
    sion
Grantor support covenant, 12.12(2)
Improvements, effect of breach and rescission,
    12.11(1)
Injury to property before closing, 12.14
Installment contracts, 12.13
Insurance, injury to property, 12.14
Lien of purchaser, 12.11(4)
Mortgages and installment contracts, 12.12(4)
Price abatement,
    Acreage deficiency, 12.12(3)
    Injury to property before closing, 12.12(3)
Purchaser's cover or substitute property cost
    12.11(1)
Purchaser's damages for delayed performance,
    12.11(1)
Purchaser's damages for vendor's total breach,
    12.11(1)
Purchaser's lost profits, 12.11(1)
Purchaser's reliance expense, 12.11(1)
Remedies, summary, 12.10
Rental value, purchaser's pre-closing occupan-
    cy, 12.12(2)
Rescission,
    Injury to property before closing, 12.14
    Purchaser's, 12.11(2)
Restitution,
    Defaulting purchaser, favoring, 12.13
    Executed contract, purchaser's breach,
        12.12(2)
    Vendor, favoring, 12.12(2)
Specific performance,
    Purchaser's claim, 12.11(3)
    Vendor's claim, 12.12(3)
Title clearing after purchaser breaches,
    12.12(2)
Title defect, purchaser's claim for, 12.11(1)
Vendor's damages for purchaser's breach,
    12.12(1)
Vendor's lien, 12.12(4)

LAND TITLES
    See also Constructive Trust; Specific Per-
        formance
Constructive trust to compel transfer general-
    ly, 4.3(2)
Decretal transfer,
    Generally, 2.8(1)
    Foreign land, 2.7
Foreign land titles, equity's power over, 2.7
Specific performance to compel transfer,
    12.11(3)

LAND–USE REGULATIONS
    See also Zoning
Taking property by, damages, 5.6(4), 6.9

LANDLORD AND TENANT
Avoidable consequences, special rule of, 3.9,
    12.6(2)
Background, 12.15(1)
Lessee's remedies, 12.15(2)
Lessor's remedies, 12.15(3)
Restitution for tenant's improvements, 4.9(4)

LATENT DISEASE OR INJURY
See Future Harm or Loss

LAW
Equity and,
        See also Equity
    Classification of remedies, 1.2
Reformation at law, 4.3(7), 9.5
Rescission at law, 4.3(6)
Restitution, role of law courts in generally,
    4.3(1)

LAWYER MALPRACTICE
Damages, 6.11

LAYCOCK, DOUGLAS
Adequacy of legal remedy,
        Generally, 2.5(3)
        Specific performance cases, 12.8(2)

LEASE–IN COSTS
Measure of loss of use, chattels, 5.15(2)

LEASE–OUT VALUE
Measure of loss of use, chattels, 5.15(2)

LEASES
    See also Landlord and Tenant
Chattels, 12.18

LEGAL ACTIONS
See Equity

LEGAL THEORY OF COMPLAINT
Relevance in assessing damages, 3.1

LEUBSDORF, JOHN
Attorney fee awards, contingency multiplier,
    3.10(10)
Preliminary injunction standard reformulat-
    ed, 2.11(2)
Temporary restraining order standard refor-
    mulated, 2.11(2)

LEVMORE, SAUL
Agreed remedies, alternative drafting, 12.9(4)
Earning capacity, limits on recovery of, 8.1(2)

LIABILITY OF ANOTHER MINIMIZED
Restitution, 4.9(4)

LIBEL AND SLANDER
Avoidable consequences, 7.2(11)
Clear and convincing evidence requirement,
  7.2(4), 7.2(12)
Constitutional rules of, 7.2(1), 7.2(4)
Damages,
    Economic harms, 7.2(11)
    Expenses incurred to counter defamation,
      7.2(11)
    Mental distress, 7.2(5), 7.2(6)
    Presumed, common law rules, 7.2(3)
Economic harms from, 7.2(11)
Injunction, 2.9(5)
Injurious falsehood compared, 6.8(1)
Libel per quod, 7.2(3)
Libel-proof plaintiff, 7.2(9)
Mental distress, 7.2(5), 7.2(6)
Nominal damages, 7.2(5)
Pecuniary loss from, 7.2(3), 7.2(11)
Punitive damages, 3.11(12), 7.2(12)
Remedies summary, 7.2(2)
Reputational harm,
      Generally, 7.2(5), 7.2(7)
    Evidence of, 7.2(7)
    Prior reputation of plaintiff, 7.2(9)
    Retraction, effect, 7.2(10)
    Understanding and belief of accusations,
      7.2(8)
Retraction, effect, 7.2(10)
Slander per se, damages rule for, 7.2(3)
Substantive background, 7.2(1)
Truth, damages and, 7.2(9)

LICENSING VIOLATIONS
Restitution and, 13.6

LIE DETECTORS
Privacy invasion, 7.3(5)

LIENS
    See also Equitable Lien; Mechanic's Lien
Chattel leases, 12.18
Equitable lien to enforce remedy, 2.8(1)
Laborers, subcontractors and suppliers,
      12.20(3)
Land sales contract,
    Purchaser's, 12.11(4)
    Vendor's, 12.12(4)
Mistaken trespasser, lien or postponed lien,
      5.8(3)

LIEPELT RULE
Tax benefits to plaintiff credited to defendant,
      8.6(4)

LIFE EXPECTANCY
Constructive trust on, 6.1(2)
Mortality tables, 8.5(2)
Reduction as element of damages, personal
      injury, 8.1(4)
Time period, proof, personal injury and death
      cases, 8.5(2)

LIMITATIONS
Statute of,
    Laches and, 2.4(4)

LIMITATIONS—Cont'd
Statute of—Cont'd
      Permanent harms and, 5.11

LIQUIDATED DAMAGES
See Agreed Remedies

LIQUIDATED SUMS
Prejudgment interest rules for, 3.6(1)

LIS PENDENS
Damages claim precluding, 9.4
Duress by filing, 10.2(3)
Enforcement of, 12.8(1), 12.12(11)
Provisional remedy, as, 6.1(5)
Strategic use, 1.10
Third party affected by, injunction to enforce,
      12.8(1)

LITIGATION
Injunction against, 2.9(4), 7.3(5)

LITIGATION COSTS OR FINANCE
See Attorney Fees Awards; Punitive Damages

LOAN CONTRACTS
Consequential damages, 12.4(4), 12.4(7)
Interest, 12.6(1)
Mental distress, 12.5(1)
Option for, 12.9(4)
Specific performance, 12.8(2)

LODESTAR
Attorney fee awards computation method,
      3.10(8)

LOSS
Damages award distinguished, 3.1

LOSS OF BARGAIN DAMAGES
Misrepresentation, 9.2(1)

LOSS OF CONSORTIUM
Personal injury cases generally, 8.1(5)
Wrongful death cases generally, 8.3(5)

LOSS OF ENJOYMENT OF LIFE
Personal injury, 8.1(4)

LOSS OF USE
    See also Interest; Rental Value
Diminished value rule not a ceiling, 5.14(1)
Market value or actual probable use, 5.15(2)
Repair cost rule not a ceiling, 5.14(1)

LOSS PERIOD COVERED
Personal injury cases, 8.5(2)

LOST EARNINGS OR INCOME
Personal injury, 8.1(2)

LOST INHERITANCE, 8.3(4)

LOST VOLUME SELLERS, 12.17(5)

LOST YEARS
Personal injury, 8.1(4)

LOWEST BALANCE RULE
Tracing funds, 6.1(4)

LUMP SUM AWARDS
General practice, 3.1

LUMP SUM AWARDS—Cont'd
Incentives to abate nuisance lost, 5.6(3)

MACNEIL, IAN
Relational contracts conception, 12.1(1), 12.1(2)

MAGISTRATE
Federal, master in equity, 2.8(1)

MALICIOUS PROSECUTION
Attorney fee liability in, 3.10(3)
Damages, 7.3(2)
Injunction against, 7.3(3)

MALPRACTICE
See also Lawyer Malpractice
Punitive damages, 3.11(1)

MANDAMUS
Prerogative writ of, 2.9(1)

MANDATORY INJUNCTION
Generally, 2.9(1)
Appeals of, 2.11(4)
Preliminary, 2.11(1)
Trespass to land, restoration or repair required, 5.5

MANUFACTURER
Harm to goods of, measure of damages, 5.13(3)

MARKET DAMAGES
See General Damages; Market Measured Damages

MARKET GAINS
Consequential damages distinguished, 3.3(4)
Profits distinguished, 3.3(3)

MARKET MEASURED DAMAGES
See also Evidence; General Damages
Absence of market, 3.5, 5.16(2)
Accuracy of measurement, 3.3(8), 12.2(3)
Avoidable consequences rule and, 12.6(3)
Capitalization of income, 3.5
Ceiling on,
 Contemplation of the parties cap inapplicable as, 12.4(4)
 Repair or substitution costs as, 5.1(7), 5.6(2), 5.14(1), 5.14(3), 12.16(4), 12.17(3)
Characteristics of, 3.3(3)
Chattel leases, 12.18
Collateral source rule and, 12.6(4)
Comparable sales, 3.5
Compensation goals and, 3.3(8), 12.2(2)
Consequential damages distinguished, 3.3(6)
Consequential damages or substitute cost measure as a potential ceiling on, 5.1(7), 5.6(2), 5.14(1), 5.14(3), 12.16(4), 12.17(3)
Constructive markets, 3.5, 5.16(1), 5.16(2)
Contemplation of the parties cap, inapplicable, 12.4(7)
Contracts, cost measure compared, 12.2(2)
Date for measure,
 Damage to property, 5.13(2)
 Subsequent events, 12.19(1)
Fluctuating market prices, 5.13(2)
Hypothetical markets, 3.5

MARKET MEASURED DAMAGES—Cont'd
Income-producing chattels, 5.16(2)
Interest, 3.6(4)
Introduction to, 3.2
Loss of use, market vs. consequential measures, 5.15(2)
Markets, types, 5.13(3)
Opinion evidence, 3.5
Personal use chattels, 5.16(3)
Place for measure, damage to property, 5.13(2)
Repair or substitution costs as ceiling on, 5.1(7), 5.6(2), 5.14(1), 5.14(3), 12.16(4), 12.17(3)
Resale costs as a ceiling on, 12.17(3)
Retail vs. wholesale market price, 5.13(3), 5.16(4)
Substitution costs and, generally, 3.3(5)
Substitution or repair costs as ceiling on, 5.1(7), 5.6(2), 5.14(1), 5.14(3), 12.16(4), 12.17(3)
Transportation cost adjustment, 5.13(3)
UCC, buyer's damages, 12.16(2)
Unique goods, 5.16(1)
Wholesale vs. retail markets, 5.13(3), 5.16(4)

MARKET MEASURED RESTITUTION
Generally, 4.5(2)
Asset value increased, 4.5(2)
Consequential benefit measure distinguished, 4.5(3)
Increased asset value, when a limit, 4.5(2)
Money payments, 4.5(2)
Services, 4.5(2)
Use value, 4.5(2)

MARKET REPORTS
Evidence of market value, 3.5

MARKET–SHARE LIABILITY, 8.1(7)

MARKET VALUE
See Market Measured Damages

MASS TORTS
Punitive damages, 3.11(8)

MASTER AND SERVANT
See Principal and Agent

MASTERS
Judicial officers,
 Enforcement of decrees, 1.4
 Hearing case or enforcing remedies, 2.8(1)

MATERIALMAN'S LIEN
See Mechanic's Lien

MAXIMS OF EQUITY
Generally, 2.3(4)
Delay defeats equity, 2.3(4)
Equality of equity, 2.3(4)
One who seeks equity must do equity, 5.8(3)

MEASUREMENT
See also Damages; Market Measured Damages; Market Measured Restitution; Punitive Damages; Restitution and particular contexts or topics, such as Contracts
Damages, introduced, 3.3(1)

MEASUREMENT—Cont'd
Restitution, introduced, 4.5(1)

MECHANIC'S LIEN
Unauthorized repair, mechanic's claim for, 4.9(5)
Unsolicited benefits and, 4.9(4), 12.20(3)

MEDICAL CARE
Damages, reasonable cost of for injury, 8.1(3)
Injunction, requiring care, 7.3(5)

MEDICAL EXPENSE
Libel and slander cases, 7.2(11)
Personal injury claim, 8.1(3)
Wrongful birth, etc., cases, 8.2

MEDICAL MONITORING
Injunction creating funds for, 8.1(3), 8.10

MENTAL ANGUISH
See Mental Distress

MENTAL CAPACITY
See Capacity

MENTAL DISTRESS
Bad faith breach of contract, 6.12
Civil rights, 7.4(2), 7.4(3)
Consortium loss,
    Compared, personal injury, 8.1(5)
    Libel and slander, 7.2(6)
Contract breach, 12.5(1)
Dishonor of check, 12.5(1)
Fear of future harm, 7.2(5), 8.1(4), 8.1(7)
Intentional infliction of, property damage claim distinguished, 5.15(3)
Interference with contract cases, 6.6(2)
Libel and slander, 7.2(5), 7.2(6)
Malpractice, lawyer's, 6.11
Misrepresentation, 9.2(4)
Negligent infliction of, property damage claim distinguished, 5.15(3)
Nuisance, 5.6(2), 5.12(2)
Personal injury, 8.1(4)
Presumed damages, relationship to, libel and slander cases, 7.2(5)
Property damage cases, 5.15(3)
Wrongful birth and pregnancy cases, 8.2
Wrongful death, 8.3(5)
Wrongful discharge, statutory claims for, 6.10(4)

MENTAL INCOMPETENCY
See Capacity

MERGER OF LAW AND EQUITY
Adequacy of legal remedy, effect of, 2.6(1), 12.8(2)
Equity and law systems, 2.6(1)
Injunction to compel money payments after, 2.6(1)
Jury trial, mixed law and equity issues, 2.6(4)
Jury trial and, generally, 2.6(1)
Money obligations in equity after, 2.6(1)
Summary introduction, 2.1(1)

MESNE PROFITS
Ejectment, 5.8(2)
Use value recovery in ejectment, 4.2(3)

MILLER ACT
Government construction, bonds for payment of laborers, subcontractors and suppliers, 12.20(3)

MINERALS
See Trespass to Land

MINEWORKERS CASE
Contempt, 2.8(6)
Jurisdiction in equity and contempt, 2.7

MINGLED FUNDS
Rights in, 6.1(4)

MINIMIZING DAMAGES
See Avoidable Consequences

MINORS
See Capacity; Children; Parent and Child; Spouses

MISAPPROPRIATION DOCTRINE
See Misappropriation of Intangible Property

MISAPPROPRIATION OF INTANGIBLE PROPERTY
Bonito case, 6.5(3)
Ideas,
    No property in, 6.5(1)
    Submission in expectation of payment, 6.5(2)
INS case, 6.5(3)
Private submission of ideas,
    Damages, 6.5(2)
    Injunction, 6.5(2)
    Punitive damages, 6.5(2)
    Restitution, 6.5(2)
Public revelation of ideas,
    Generally, 6.5(3)
    Celebrity characteristics, 6.5(3)
    Damages, 6.5(3)
        Injunction to protect property interests, 6.5(3)
        Restitution, 6.5(3)
        Right of publicity, 6.5(3)
Sears and *Compco* cases, 6.5(3)
Substantive background, 6.5(1)
Works performed in public, 6.5(3)
Zacchini Case, 6.5(3)

MISAPPROPRIATION OF MONEY
Assumpsit for, 6.1(1)
Constructive trusts and liens on funds,
        Generally, 6.1(2)
        Tracing required, 6.1(3)
Injunctive recovery, freezing funds, 6.1(5)
Mingling monies, 6.1(4)

MISREPRESENTATION
    See also Brokers; Fiduciaries; Principal and Agent
Bona fide purchasers, 9.6
Broker's misrepresentation of vendor's price, 10.5(1)
Consequential damages, 9.2(1), 9.2(3)
Constructive trust, 9.3(4)
Cost making representation good, damages measure, 9.2(1)

MISREPRESENTATION—Cont'd
Damages,
    Generally, 9.2(1)
    Limitations on, 9.2(6)
    Loss of bargain, 9.2(1)
    Negligent and innocent, 9.2(2)
    Out of pocket measure, 9.2(1)
    Restitution and, 9.4
Date for valuation, 9.2(1)
Deceit vs. negligence, 9.1
Disclaimers and merger clauses, 9.5
Duplicative damages measures, 9.2(3)
Election of remedies, 9.4
Equitable defenses, 9.6
Equitable lien, 9.3(4)
Financial loss requirement, 9.2(1)
Forgery, 9.6
Fraud in the factum, 9.6
Innocent representation, damages, 9.2(2)
Losing contract, 9.2(1)
Loss causation, 9.2(6)
Loss of bargain damages, 9.2(1)
Mental distress damages, 9.2(4)
Negligence vs. deceit, 9.1
Negligent, damages, 9.2(2)
Out of pocket damages,
    Generally, 9.2(1)
    Rescission compared, 9.2(2)
Profits lost, 9.2(3)
Proximate cause limits, 9.2(6)
Punitive damages,
    Generally, 9.2(5)
    Restitution and, 9.4
Reformation, 9.5
Releases secured by, restoration required of
    plaintiff seeking rescission, 9.3(3)
Restitution,
    Generally, 9.3(1)
    Actual harm prerequisite, 9.3(2)
    Damages and, 9.4
    Restoration required of defendant, 9.3(4)
    Restoration required of plaintiff, 9.3(3)
    Specie restitution, 9.3(3)
    Use value, 9.3(4)
Scope of risk of misrepresentation, 9.2(6)
Specie restitution, 9.3(3)
Summary, 9.1
Transaction causation, 9.2(6)
Value of representation, damages measure,
    9.2(1)

MISTAKE
Assumed risk,
    Generally, 11.2
    Compromise, 11.7
    Release-of-claim, 11.9
Assumptions of parties mistaken, 11.2, 11.3,
    11.4
Bids, 11.4
Changed position defense, 11.8
Compromise, conscious ignorance negating
    mistake, 11.2, 11.7
Contract allocating risk of, 11.3
Contract formation,
    Mutual mistake in, 11.3
    Unilateral mistake in, 11.4
Contract formed by, restitution, 11.6

MISTAKE—Cont'd
Defenses, 11.8
Defined, 11.2
Donative intent, 11.10
Fact, of, 11.2
Formation of contract, 11.2
Future expectation, 11.2
Gift transactions, 11.10
Identity or existence of subject matter, 11.3
Impossibility, impracticability compared, 11.1
Improvements by mistaken trespasser, 5.8(3)
Insurance,
    Overpayment of benefits, 11.7
    Reformation of policy, 11.6(3)
Law, of, 11.2
Meaning, 11.2
Misunderstanding distinguished, 11.2
Negligence, relation to, 11.2
Overpayment generally, 11.7
Ownership,
    Improvement of chattel, unsolicited bene-
        fits rules, 4.9(5)
    Improvement of land, unsolicited benefits
        rules, 4.9(5)
Ownership of chattel mistaken, improvements
    authorized by apparent owner, 4.9(5)
Payment by, restitution, unsolicited benefits
    rule and, 4.9(3)
Payment of another's debt, restitution, 4.9(3)
Payment to agent, 11.8
Performance of contract, in, 11.2, 11.7
Personal injury, nature or extent of injury
    mistaken, 11.9
Price, 11.5
Reformation, 11.6(1)
Releases, avoidance, 11.9
Rescission for, generally, 11.1, 11.5, 11.6
Restitution, measurement, 11.5
Taxes, 10.2(3)
Unilateral,
    Contract formation, rescission, 11.4
    Contract performance, restitution, 11.7

MISUNDERSTANDING
Mistake distinguished, 11.2

MITIGATING DAMAGES
See Avoidable Consequences

**MODIFICATION OF INJUNCTION OR DE-
CREES**
Grounds generally, 2.8(8)

MONEY
    See also Foreign Currency; Payment;
        Tracing
Assumpsit for misappropriation of, 6.1(1)
Cash, bona fide purchaser rules and, 4.7(1)
Constructive trust on fund or account, 6.1(2)
Conversion of, 6.1(1)
Decrees for payment of,
    Contempt, imprisonment, 2.8(2)
    Enforcement in equity, 2.8(1)
Embezzlement, 6.1(1)
Equitable lien on fund or account, 6.1(2)
Foreign currency, damages and restitution,
    3.7
Freezing accounts, 6.1(5)

MONEY—Cont'd
Mingled funds, 6.1(4)
Misappropriation of, 6.1(1)
Replevin for, 6.1(1)
Restitution, 6.1
    Unsolicited benefits rule and, 4.9(3)
Tracing, after withdrawal from account, 6.1(4)

MONEY HAD AND RECEIVED
Assumpsit count, 4.2(3)

MONEY OBLIGATIONS
Equity role in enforcing, merger of law and
    equity, 2.6(1)
Injunction to compel payment, personal injury
    obligations, 8.10

MONEY PAID
Assumpsit count, 4.2(3)

MONEY REMEDIES
Damages awards generally, 3.1
Non-damages money remedies, 3.1

MOOT CASES
Attorney fee awards in, 3.10(6)

MORAL RIGHTS
Artist's rights in integrity of art, 5.16(4)
Copyright protection for, 6.3(3)

MORTALITY TABLES
Ethnic or gender discrimination in use of,
    8.5(2)
Personal injury and death cases, 8.5(2)

MORTGAGES
    See also Foreclosure
Equity historic role in law of, 2.3(3)
Foreclosure, equity's role, 2.3(3)
Installment land contract and, 12.12(4)
Jury trial, equitable characterization or not,
    2.6(3)
Subrogation, 4.3(4)

MOSES v. MACFERLAN
Restitution, unjust enrichment basis estab-
    lished, 4.2(3)

MULTIPLE DAMAGES
    Generally, 3.12
Copyright, 6.3(8)
Misrepresentation, 9.2(5)
Patent infringement, 6.2(8)
Trademark cases, 6.4(8)
Trespass to land, 5.3(2), 5.3(4), 5.12(3)

MULTIPLICITY OF SUITS
Legal remedy inadequate, 2.5(2)

MUNICIPAL CORPORATIONS
Restitution against, ultra vires or improper
    contracts, 13.6

MURDER
Acquisition of property by, 6.7

MUTUAL MISTAKE
See Mistake

MUTUALITY OF REMEDY
Equity rule generally, 2.4(3), 12.8(4)
Land seller, specific performance, 12.12(3)

NAMES
Property right in, 6.5(3)

NATURAL RESOURCE DAMAGE
Superfund Act, 5.2(5)

NE EXEAT REGNO
As injunction, 2.9(1)

NEBULOUS INJUNCTIONS
Due process, 2.8(7)
Nuisance cases, 5.7(3)
Patent cases, 6.2(5)

NECESSARIES
Restitution for supply of, 4.9(2), 4.9(5)

NEGATIVE COVENANTS
Employment contracts, 10.5(3), 12.22(2)

NEGATIVE MUTUALITY OF REMEDY, 2.4(3)

NEGATIVE UNJUST ENRICHMENT, 5.9

NEGLIGENCE
    See also Personal Injury and other particu-
        lar topics
Economic loss caused, physical harm distinc-
    tions, 6.6(2)
Negligent misrepresentation, 9.1, 9.2(2)

**NEGLIGENT INFLICTION OF MENTAL DIS-
    TRESS**
See Mental Distress

NEGOTIABLE INSTRUMENTS
Bona fide purchaser rules and, 4.7(1)

NET WORTH
Evidence of defendant's, punitive damages
    claims, 3.11(5)
Increased by minimizing damages, 3.9

NOMINAL DAMAGES
    Generally, 3.3(2)
Chattels, 5.16(1)
Contracts, 12.1(1)
Libel and slander, 7.2(5)
Wrongful death, 8.3(6)

NON–COMPENSATORY GOALS
Damages, 3.1

NON–JUDICIAL REMEDIES, 1.1

NON–PECUNIARY LOSSES
Attorney fees and damages recovery for, 3.1
Functions of damages recovery for, 3.1
Interest on, 8.4

NON–WORKING PERSONS
Injury or death, 8.1(2), 8.3(4)

NUISANCE
Abatement, see Injunction; del Nuisance
Balancing equities and hardships, 5.7(2)
Compensated injunction, 5.7(3)

NUISANCE—Cont'd
Damages,
      Generally, 5.6(2)
   Incentives to abate, 5.6(3), 5.11(3)
Economic perspectives, 5.7(4)
Injunction,
      Generally, 5.7
   Adequacy of legal remedy, 5.7(2)
   Statutes, effect, 5.7(5)
Mental distress damages, 5.6(2), 5.12(2)
Permanent nuisance, 5.11(1)
Remedial options in, 5.7(3)
Substantive background, 5.7(1)
Temporary nuisance, 5.11(1)
Trespass and, generally, 5.6(1)

OCCUPYING CLAIMANTS STATUTES
Improvements on land, restitution, 5.8(3)

OFFERS
Evidence of, probative of property value, 3.5

OFFICIOUS INTERMEDDLERS
See Unsolicited Benefits

OFFSETS
See Adjustments in Damages Awards; Credits

OPEN MEETINGS
Injunctive protection of, 7.3(5)

OPEN RECORDS
Injunctive protection of, 7.3(5)

OPINION EVIDENCE
Market value, 3.5, 5.13(4)
Owner opinion, 3.5, 5.13(4)

ORDERS
See Injunction; Judgments and Decrees

OVERCOMPENSATION
See Duplication

OVERHEAD COSTS
Repair of chattels, 5.14(2)
Restitution for trademark infringer's profits,
    deductions for, 6.4(4)
Seller's claims, 12.17(5)

OWEN, DAVID
Punitive damages observations, 3.11(12)

OWNER OPINION
Evidence of value, 3.5

PAIN AND SUFFERING
Attorney fees, proposals to substitute fee lia-
    bility for pain awards 8.1(4)
Civil rights, 7.4(3)
Fear of future harm, 8.1(4), 8.1(7)
Hedonic damages and, 8.1(4)
Interest on, 3.6(4)
Personal injury generally, 8.1(4)
Wrongful birth, wrongful pregnancy cases, 8.2

PALMING OFF
Unfair competition, 6.4(1)

PARENT AND CHILD
Services, society, companionship loss, personal
    injury, 8.1(5)

PARETO EFFICIENCY, 1.9

PARI DELICTO
Illegality and restitution, 13.6
Unclean hands and, 2.4(2)

PAROL EVIDENCE RULE
Reformation and, 9.5
Reformation for mistake and, 11.6(1)

PASSIVE INCOME
Requirement in using capitalization of income
    method, 3.5

PATENTS
Infringement,
   Attorney fee awards, 6.2(7)
   Contempt, contemnor's profits, 6.2(4)
   Damages, 6.2(3)
   Equitable defenses, 6.2(6)
   Injunction against, 6.2(5)
   Interest, 6.2(3)
   Punitive awards, 6.2(3), 6.2(8)
   Remedies
      Generally, 6.2
      Summary, 6.2(2)
   Restitution for denied, 6.2(4)
Substantive background, 6.2(1)

PATTERN DAMAGES
Introduction to, 3.2

PAYMENT
   See also Foreign Currency; Money
Debt of another paid, restitution, 4.9(3)
Mistake in,
   Restitution,
      Generally, 11.7
      Unsolicited benefits rule and, 4.9(3)
Surety's payment of another's debt, restitu-
    tion, 4.9(3)

PER DIEM ARGUMENTS
Personal injury, 8.1(4)

PERCENTAGE DISABILITIES
Earning capacity loss rated by, 8.1(2)

PERFORMANCE
Property right in, 6.5(3)

PERIODIC PAYMENTS
Damages remedy, 3.1, 3.7
Future loss paid periodically, personal injury
    cases, 8.5(1), 8.5(5)

PERMANENT HARM
   Generally, 2.9(1)
Personal injury, 8.1(1)

PERMANENT INJUNCTION
Preliminary and temporary injunction con-
    trasted, 2.9(1), 2.11(1)

**PERMANENT NUISANCE, HARM, OR INVA-
SION**
   Generally, 5.11(1)

PERMANENT NUISANCE, HARM, OR INVA-
SION—Cont'd
Dilemma for plaintiff, 5.11(4)
Incentives, 5.11(3)
Tests of permanence, 5.11(2)

PERMANENT REMEDIES
Provisional remedies contrasted, 1.3

PERMISSIVE WASTE
Future estate, to, 5.2(8)

PERSONA
Property in, 6.5(3)

PERSONAL INJURY
See also particular topics such as Collater-
al Source Rule or particular ele-
ments of loss such as Earning Capac-
ity
Damages measures generally, 3.3(1)
Injunction to compel payment for, 8.10
Injunction to prevent, 8.10
Nuisance, illness caused, damages, 5.6(2)
Release, mistake and avoidance, 11.9

PERSONAL PROPERTY
See Chattels

PERSONAL RIGHTS
See also Civil Rights
Injunction protecting generally, 2.9(5), 7.3(5)
Property rights distinguished, injunction,
2.9(5)

PERSONAL SERVICES
See also Employment Contracts
Policy against equitable interference, 2.5(4)
Specific performance, 12.8(3)
Statute of frauds, benefits conferred by, resti-
tution, 13.2(2)

PERSONALTY VS. REALTY
Equitable conversion and 4.3(8)

PETS
Harm to, damages, 5.15(3)

PHYSICIANS
Benefit conferred by tort, wrongful concep-
tion, etc. cases, 8.2
Patient's body parts, secret use of, 10.4
Quantum meruit for services rendered, 4.9(5)
Undue influence on patient, 10.3

PLACE
Buyer's market measured damages, UCC,
place for measurement 12.16(2)
Valuing property for damages award, where,
5.13(3)

PLEADING
Consequential damages, 3.4

POLICY LIMITATIONS ON REMEDIES
Equitable remedies, 2.5(4)

POLITICAL BRIBERY
Public recovery of bribe, 10.6

POLITICAL RELATIONS
Injunction to protect, 7.3(5)

POLITICAL RIGHTS
Injunctive protection, 2.9(5)

POLLUTION
See Environmental Harm; Nuisance

POSNER, RICHARD
Preliminary injunction or TRO formula,
2.11(2)

POSSESSION
Injunction to transfer, 5.10(3)
Writ of, 2.8(1)

PRACTICALITY
Equity, limits on remedies, 2.5(4)

PREEMPTION
Punitive damages, claim preempted by federal
law, 3.11(1)
Statutes in nuisance cases, 5.7(5)

PREFERENCES
Jury trial, characterizing litigation as equita-
ble or not, 2.6(3)
Priorities, 4.3(2)

PREGNANCY
Wrongful, 8.2

PREJUDGMENT INTEREST
See also Interest
Accrual issues, 3.6(5)
Ascertainable sums due, 3.6(2)
Attacks on traditional rule, 3.6(3)
Attorney fees awards, on, 3.6(5)
Consequential damages, as, 3.6(2)
Contract express or implied affecting, 3.6(2)
Copyright infringement, 6.3(3)
Counterclaims or defenses, effect on, 3.6(1)
Employment discrimination, statutory claims,
6.10(4)
Hidden compensation in jury verdicts, 3.6(5)
Implicit awards of in verdicts, 3.6(5)
Patent infringement cases, 6.2(3)
Punitive damages, 3.11(13)
Reduction to present value and, 3.6(3)
Rental value, in lieu of, 3.6(2)
Restitution, as, 3.6(2)
Statutes, 3.6(2)
Summary, 3.6(1)
Trademark infringement, 6.4(3)
When claim does not accrue until judicial
decision, 3.6(5)

PRELIMINARY INJUNCTIONS
Generally, 2.11(1)
Attorney fee awards before permanent relief,
3.10(6)
Bond requirement, 2.11(3)
Employment discrimination, 6.10(4)
Factors in granting, 2.11(2)
Irreparable harm,
Remote, 2.11(2)
Specially required, 2.11(2)
Mandatory injunctions, 2.11(1)
Posner formula, 2.11(2)

PRELIMINARY INJUNCTIONS—Cont'd
Probability of success on merits, 2.11(2)
Provisional remedy, as, 1.3
Reinstatement in job by, 6.10(4)
Risk of error, formulas to account for, 2.11(2)
Standards for granting, 2.11(2)
Tailoring to avoid irretrievable loss of rights, 2.11(2)
Third persons, harm to, 2.11(2)
Transfer of possession of land by, 5.10(3)
Wrongful discharge, 6.10(4)

PREROGATIVE WRITS, 2.9(1), 2.11(4)

PRESENT VALUE
Burden of proving, 8.5(3)
Damages adjustment, introduced, 3.2
Discount rate, 8.5(3)
Discount required in liquidated damages clauses, 12.15(3)
Punitive damages, reduction to not required, 3.11(13)
Reduction to,
    Generally, 3.7
    Injury cases, 8.5(3)

PRESUMED DAMAGES
Generally, 7.1(2)
Civil rights violations, 7.4(2)
Constitutional limitations, libel and dignitary torts, 7.3(2)
Libel and slander, common law, 7.2(3)
Mental distress, relation to, libel and slander, 7.2(5)
Privacy invasions, 7.3(4)
Statutory allowances as, 7.3(4)
Wiretapping, 7.3(4)

PREVENTIVE INJUNCTIONS, 2.9(1)

PRICE
Action for, land seller, 12.12(1)
Building contracts, price less saved expenses, 12.20(1)
Land vendor's action on installment contract, 12.13

PRICE SPECULATION
Specific performance right facilitating, 12.8(1)

PRINCIPAL AND AGENT
Agent's liability for use of principal's confidential information or opportunity, 10.4
Bribes, liability for giving or accepting, 10.6
Brokers, secret profits, 10.5
Contempt, agent's violation of court order, 2.8(5)
Discharge for value generally, 4.6, 4.7(2)
Fiduciary duty to principal, 10.4
Mistaken payment to known intermediary, 11.8
Punitive damages liability of principal, 3.11(1), 3.11(6)

PRIOR SALES
Evidence of market value, 3.5

PRIORITIES
Constructive trust establishing, 4.3(2)

PRIORITIES—Cont'd
Subrogation and, 4.3(4)

PRIVACY
    See also Misappropriation of Intangible Property
Constitutional limitations on claims, 7.3(4)
Injunction to protect, 7.3(5)
Remedies, 7.3(4)

PRIVATE ATTORNEY GENERAL
Attorney fees,
    Limited rationale in early cases, 3.10(4)
    Theory of, 3.10(2)

PRIVATE FACTS
Privacy invasion, 7.3(4)

PROBABILITY
Preliminary injunction, success on merits, 2.11(2)
Temporary restraining order, success on merits, 2.11(2)
Value of the chance, 3.4, 8.1(7)

PROCEDURAL LAW
Remedies and, 1.1

PROCEDURE
Equity courts, historical, 2.2

PRODUCTS LIABILITY
Punitive damages, 3.11(1)

PROFITS
    See also Consequential Damages and particular subject matter
Accounting for generally, 4.3(5)
Apportionment of profits between innocent and wrongful acts,
    Generally, 4.3(5), 4.5(3)
    Copyright infringement, 6.3(4)
    Trademark infringement, 6.4(4)
Building contracts,
    Contractor's expected profits plus costs already incurred, 12.20(1)
    Delay, owner's loss, damages, 12.19(1)
Buyer's lost profit on seller's breach, 12.16(4)
Capital and income versions, 12.4(3)
Chattel leases, 12.18
Constructive trust to capture, 4.3(2)
Contemnor's profits,
    Patent infringement cases, 6.2(4)
    Recovery as sanction for contempt, 2.8(2)
Contract breach,
    Consequential damages, proof required, 12.4(3)
    Restitution, 4.5(3), 12.7(4)
    Types of profit loss, generally, 12.2(2)
Copyright, infringer's profits recoverable, 6.3(4)
Credit to defendant for plaintiff's profits after defendant's breach of employment contract, 12.21(2)
Defendant's contempt, recovery as sanction for, 2.8(2)
Defendant's profits, punitive damages role in eliminating, 3.11(3)

PROFITS—Cont'd
Employer's lost profit on employee's breach, 12.22(1)
Evidence of value of profitable property, as, 3.5, 5.16(2), 6.5(2)
Gains from rising market, 4.5(3)
Interference with contract,
    Damages, 6.6(2)
    Restitution, 6.6(3)
Loss of as consequential damages,
        Generally, 3.3(4)
    Buyer of goods, 12.16(4)
    Contractor vs. landowner, 12.20(1)
    Copyright infringement, 6.3(3)
    Employer vs. employee, 12.22(1)
    Injurious falsehood, 6.8(2)
    Interference with contract, 6.6(2)
    Land sale contract, 12.11(1)
    Landowner vs. builder, 12.19(1)
    Lessee of goods, 12.18
    Lessee of land, 12.15(2)
    Loss of use, 5.15(2)
    Patent infringement, 6.2(3)
    Personal injury, 8.1(2)
    Property damage, 5.15(2)
    Seller of goods, 12.17(4), 12.17(5)
    Trademark infringement, 6.4(3)
Market gain distinguished, 3.3(3)
Market rate for restitution for services includes, 4.5(2)
Measurement of, trademark examples, 6.4(4)
Mesne profits terminology for use value recovery in ejectment, 4.2(3)
Misrepresentation cases, damages, 9.2(3)
Occupation of another's land, restitution, 5.9
Overhead, deduction for in calculating, 6.4(4)
Overhead and, seller's claims, 12.17(5)
Patent infringement,
    Denied as restitution, 6.2(4)
    Lost profits damages, 6.2(3)
Personal injury, loss of, 8.1(2)
Personal injury cases, victim's loss as damages, 8.1(2)
Publication of libel or privacy-invading material, 8.9
Restitution,
    Breaching seller's profit, 12.16(6)
    Chattels used by defendant, 5.18(2)–5.18(3)
    Collateral profits, 4.5(3)
    Contract breach,
        Generally, 12.7(4)
        Vendor's breach of land sale contract, 12.11(2)
    Overhead calculations, 6.4(4)
    Trespass and profit-making activity, 5.4
    Vendor of land breaching contract, 12.11(2)
Seller's loss, damages, 12.17(5)
Taxes, deduction in calculating, 6.4(4)
Trade secret use, 10.5(3)
Trademark, infringer's profits recoverable, 6.4(4)
Trespasser's profit in occupation of land, 5.8(2)
Vendor's profit from breach of land sale contract, equitable conversion doctrine and, 4.3(8)

PROFITS—Cont'd
Wrongdoer's profits in personal injury cases, 8.9

PROHIBITION
Prerogative writ of, 2.9(1)

PROHIBITORY INJUNCTION, 2.9(1)

PROMISSORY ESTOPPEL
Clear and convincing evidence of, 13.2(5)
Equitable estoppel and, 2.3(5)
Statute of frauds and, 13.2(5)

PROOF METHODS
Future expected inflation affecting damages, 8.5(4)

PROPERTY
Salvage, restitution, 4.9(5)

PROPERTY DAMAGE
See also Trespass to Land; Chattels and other particular topics introduced, 3.3(1)

PROPERTY RIGHTS
Injunctions to protect generally, 2.9(3)
Personal rights distinguished, injunction, 2.9(5)

PROPERTY VALUE
Element in damages generally, 3.5

PROTESTS AND DEMONSTRATIONS
Injunction against, 2.8(3)

PROVISIONAL REMEDIES
        See also, Freezing Assets; Preliminary Injunctions; Temporary Restraining Order
    Generally, 1.3
Attachment, 6.1(5)
Bond requirement in, 2.11(3)
Economic compulsion by, 10.2(3)
Equitable replevin, 5.17(3)
Freezing accounts, 6.1(5)
Interference with possession of land, 5.10(3)
Lis pendens, 6.1(5)
Preliminary injunctions, generally, 2.11
Seizure of infringing articles, trademark cases, 6.4(5)
Summary ejectment, unlawful detainer, 5.10(2)

PROXIMATE CAUSE
Consequential damages, 3.4
Misrepresentation cases, 9.2(6)
Punitive damages, 3.11(9)
Rescission remedy to avoid limits of, 9.3(2)

PUBLIC ACCOMMODATIONS
Injunction to protect rights to, 7.3(5)

PUBLIC BENEFITS
Application of benefits rule to, 8.6(2)
Assessed in choosing remedy, 1.9
Plaintiff's receipt, credit to defendant or not, 3.8(1), 12.6(4)

PUBLIC ENTITIES
Bond requirement in preliminary injunction cases, 2.11(3)
Contracts, irregularities, restitution, 13.6
Laches, 2.4(4)
Punitive damages, 3.11(1)

PUBLIC FIGURES OR OFFICIALS
Libel cases, 7.2(4)

PUBLIC INFORMATION
Injunction to protect right to, 7.3(5)

PUBLIC INTERESTS
Balancing in equity,
    Introduction to, 2.4(1)
    Nuisance injunctions, 5.7(2)

PUBLIC LAW REMEDIES, 1.5

PUBLIC UTILITIES
Punitive damages, 3.11(1)

PUBLICATIONS
Profits from tortfeasor's publications about tort, 8.9

PUNITIVE DAMAGES
Abuse of power, 3.11(2)
Actual damages factor in fixing, 3.11(10)
Adjustments in, 3.11(13)
Amount, actual damage factor, 3.11(10)
Arbitration cases, 3.11(1), 12.23
Attorney fees, relation to, 3.11(3)
Attorney fees as a measure of, 3.11(5)
Attorney liability for, malpractice, 3.11(1)
Bad faith breach cases, 3.11(1), 6.12
Bad faith or malice standard for award of, 3.11(2)
Bad faith trespasser damages compared, 5.3(3)
Bank dishonors check, 12.5(2)
Bases for award of, 3.11(1)–3.11(3)
Bifurcation of trials, 3.11(5)
Brokers, 10.5(1)
Burden of proof,
    Generally, 3.11(4), 3.11(15)
    Bad faith trespasser rule contrasted, 5.3(3)
Caps on, 3.11(12)
Causation and, 3.11(9)
Civil rights claims, 3.11(1), 7.4(3)
Class actions solution to multiple awards, 3.11(8)
Clear and convincing evidence standard, 3.11(4)
Comparative fault and, 3.11(13)
Comparative fault reduction, personal injury cases, 8.7(3)
Compensatory award reduced, effect on, 3.11(3)
Compensatory awards, distinguished, 3.1
Computations, 3.11(13)
Concealment of facts after injury, 3.11(2), 3.11(9)
Consortium claims, 3.11(1)
Constitutional limitations generally, 3.11(12)
Constitutional limitations on, libel and slander cases, 7.2(12)
Contract cases, 12.5(2)
Contracts claims, denied generally, 3.11(1)

PUNITIVE DAMAGES—Cont'd
Copyright infringement,
    Generally, 6.3(8)
    Added damages, 6.3(3)
Cover-ups, 3.11(2), 3.11(9)
Credit to defendant, prior punitive payments, 3.11(8)
Criminal contempt analogy, 3.11(15)
Criminal punishment vs. deterrence tax views, 3.11(15)
Criticisms, 3.11(15)
Culpability factor in fixing amount, 3.11(14)
Death, survival statutes, 8.3(2)
Deceased tortfeasor, against, 3.11(1)
Decedents' estates, no liability for, 3.11(1)
Defined, 3.11(1)
Derivative claims, 3.11(1), 3.11(9)
Deterrence,
    Example to others, 3.11(3)
    Factor in fixing amount, 3.11(14)
    Injunctive deterrence compared, 3.11(3)
    Insurance coverage and, 3.11(7)
    Measuring by, 3.11(3), 3.11(14)
    Rationale for, 3.11(3)
    Tax to deter vs. criminal punishment, 3.11(15)
Differential in awards against employer and employee, 3.11(6)
Dignitary tort cases, 7.3(2)
Discovery, defendant's financial condition, 3.11(5)
Disparagement, 6.8(2)
Diverting award from plaintiff, 3.11(12)
Double damages statutes, 3.12
Double jeopardy and, 3.11(12)
Drunk driving, 3.12
Due process,
    Limits imposed by, 3.11(12)
    Multiple liability cases, 3.11(8)
Economic criticisms, 3.11(15)
Economic tort cases, 3.11(1)
Efficient breach of contract and, 12.5(2)
Employer-employee, differential in punitive awards, 3.11(6)
Employer's vicarious liability for, 3.11(1)
Employment discrimination, 3.11(1)
Equity cases, 3.11(1)
Evidence,
    Defendant's financial condition, 3.11(5)
    Standard of proof, 3.11(4)
Example to others, 3.11(3)
Excessive fines clause and, 3.11(12)
Factors in fixing amount, 3.11(14)
Fairness criticisms, 3.11(15)
FELA, 3.11(1)
Fiduciary breach, 3.11(2)
Financial condition of defendant, evidence of admitted, 3.11(5)
First amendment limits, 3.11(12)
First-comer rule against multiple claims, 3.11(8)
Free speech,
    Restrictions to protect speech rights, 3.11(1)
    Rights violated, award of, 3.11(1)
General deterrence, 3.11(3)

PUNITIVE DAMAGES—Cont'd
Gross negligence insufficient, 3.11(2)
Grounds for, 3.11(1)
Haslip limits, 3.11(12)
Incentive to sue, high-cost, low-compensation cases, 3.11(3)
Income of defendant, relevance, 3.11(5)
Inconsistent factors in measuring, 3.11(11), 3.11(14)
Injunction and, 3.11(3), 8.10
Injunctive deterrence and, 3.11(3)
Injuries within the risk, 3.11(9)
Injurious falsehood, 6.8(2)
Insurance coverage for, 3.11(7)
Insurance of defendant as wealth, 3.11(5)
Interest on,
　　Generally, 3.6(4), 3.11(13)
　　Patent infringement cases, 6.2(3)
Interference with contract cases, 6.6(2)
Interpleader solution to multiple awards, 3.11(8)
Joint and several liability, 3.11(5), 3.11(6)
Jones Act, 3.11(1)
Judicial review,
　　Constitutional requirement possible, 3.11(12)
　　Ratio rule, effects, 3.11(11)
Jury,
　　Instructions,
　　　　Due process, 3.11(12)
　　　　Ratio rule, 3.11(11)
　　Traditional role, 3.11(1)
Just deserts,
　　Deterrence rationale compared, 3.11(3)
　　Insurance coverage and, 3.11(7)
　　Punishment rationale generally, 3.11(2)
　　Punishment rationale vs. deterrence rationale, 3.11(3), 3.11(15)
Lawyer malpractice, 6.11
Legislative limits on, 3.11(12)
Libel and slander, 7.2(12)
Literature of, 3.11(1)
Litigation finance effects, 3.11(3)
Litigation support factor in fixing amount, 3.11(14)
Malice or bad faith, 3.11(2)
Malpractice cases, 3.11(1)
Mass tort cases, 3.11(8)
Measure,
　　Actual damages factor, 3.11(10)
　　Deterrence goals, 3.11(3)
　　Factors generally, 3.11(14)
　　Harm to third persons, 3.11(9)
　　Ratio rule, 3.11(11)
Mental capacity of defendant, 3.11(1)
Mental state of defendant required for, 3.11(2)
Minors, liability for, 3.11(1)
Misappropriation of intangible property, private submission of ideas, 6.5(2)
Misrepresentation cases, 9.2(5)
Multiple damages,
　　Patent infringement, 6.2(8)
　　Statutes generally, 3.12
　　Trespass to land, 5.12(3)
Multiple defendants, 3.11(5)
Multiple liability for, 3.11(8)

PUNITIVE DAMAGES—Cont'd
Negligence insufficient, 3.11(2)
Net worth of defendant, 3.11(5)
Nonfeasance cases, 3.11(1)
Overdeterrence claims, 3.11(15)
Patents, infringement, 6.2(8)
Personal injury cases, 8.1(6)
Persons liable, 3.11(1)
Persons within the risk, 3.11(9)
Physician liability, malpractice, 3.11(1)
Post-trial review, 3.11(12)
Preemption, 3.11(1)
Preponderance of the evidence standard, 3.11(4)
Present value reduction, 3.11(13)
Products liability,
　　Award available, 3.11(1)
　　Multiple claims for, 3.11(8)
Profits, defendant's,
　　Collateral to plaintiff's harm, 3.11(9)
　　Evidence or measure of award, generally, 3.11(3), 3.11(5)
Proof standard, 3.11(4)
Property damage cases, 5.15(3)
Proximate cause issues, 3.11(9)
Public entities, liability for, 3.11(1)
Public utilities, liability for, 3.11(1)
Punishment or retribution rationale,
　　Generally, 3.11(2)
　　Deterrence rationale compared, 3.11(3), 3.11(15)
Ratio rule,
　　Generally, 3.11(11)
　　Constitutional relevance, 3.11(12)
　　Inconsistency with other factors, 3.11(14)
Rationales,
　　Generally, 3.11(2)–3.11(3)
　　Added compensation rationale, 3.11(3)
　　Deterrence, 3.11(3)
　　Punishment or just deserts, 3.11(2)
Reasonable doubt standard, 3.11(4)
Reduction when compensatory award is reduced, 3.11(13)
Repeated liability for, 3.11(8)
Restitution and, 9.4
Restitution cases, when awardable, 4.5(5)
Restitution compared, 4.1(4)
Risk, scope of, affecting punitive award, 3.11(9)
Rule 11 analogy, 3.11(15)
Sexual harassment, 3.11(1), 3.11(6)
Slander of title, 6.8(2)
Standards of proof, 3.11(4)
State of mind required for, 3.11(2)
Summary, 3.2, 3.11(1)
Survival actions, 8.3(6)
Taxability of award, 8.6(4)
Title VII, 3.11(1)
Toxic torts, 3.11(1)
Trademark cases, 6.4(8)
Treble damages statutes, 3.12
Trespass to land, 5.12(3)
Union fair representation suits, 3.11(1)
Vicarious liability for,
　　Generally, 3.11(1), 3.11(6)

PUNITIVE DAMAGES—Cont'd
Vicarious liability for—Cont'd
　Separate negligence of two different
　　agents, 3.11(9)
Warsaw Convention limitations, 3.11(1)
Wealth of defendant, 3.11(5)
Wrongful death, 8.3(4), 8.3(6)
Wrongful discharge, 3.11(2)

PUNITIVE DENIAL OF RELIEF, 12.8(4)

PUNITIVE RESTITUTION, 3.11(1), 12.11(2)

QUANTUM MERUIT
Assumpsit count, 4.2(3)
Restitutionary terminology, 4.1(1), 4.2(1)

QUANTUM VALEBANT
Assumpsit count, 4.2(3)

QUASI CONTRACT
　See also Restitution
Assumpsit and, 4.2(3)
Constructive trust compared, 4.3(2)
Implied in fact contract contrasted, 4.2(3)
Terminology for restitution, 4.1(1), 4.2(1)

RATIFICATION
Election of remedies and, 9.4, 12.7(6)
Estoppel and, 2.3(5)

RATIO RULE
Punitive damages, 3.11(11), 3.11(12)

REAL PROPERTY
See Deeds; Land Sales; Land Titles; Trespass
　to Land and similar topics

REALTY VS. PERSONALITY
Equitable conversion and, 4.3(8)

RECEIVERS
Enforcement of remedies through, 1.4, 2.8(1)

REDUCED LIFE EXPECTANCY
Personal injury, 8.1(4)

REDUCTION TO PRESENT VALUE
　See also Capitalization of Income
　Generally, 3.7
Future loss, personal injury, 8.5(1), 8.5(3)
Prejudgment interest and, 3.6(3)
Relation to inflation, 8.5(4)

REFORMATION
Alternatives to, 11.6(2)
Bona fide purchasers and, 11.6(3)
Changed position, 11.6(3)
Conscionability standards, reforming to meet,
　4.3(7)
Constructive trust compared, 4.3(7), 4.5(3)
Defenses to, 11.6(3)
Disclaimers and, 9.5
Downwriting agreements to conform to law,
　11.6(3)
Equitable discretion, 11.6(3)
Implicit, 11.6(3)
Interpretation of document in lieu of, 11.6(3)
Law courts and, 4.3(7)
Misrepresentation cases, 9.5
Mistake cases, 11.6(1)

REFORMATION—Cont'd
Negative covenants, reformed to meet legal
　restrictions, 12.22(2)
Physical alteration of instrument, 11.6(3)
Rescission compared or contrasted, 4.3(7), 9.6,
　11.6(2)
Restitution by, generally, 4.3(7)
Third persons and, 11.6(1)

REGULATORY TAKINGS
Compensation for, 5.6(4), 6.9
Damages,
　　Generally, 6.9(2)
　　Limits proposed, 6.9(4)
Unconstitutional regulation as civil rights vio-
　lation, 6.9(3)

REINSTATEMENT
Injunction, as form of, 2.9(1)
Wrongful discharge,
　　Reinstatement remedy,
　　　Common law, 6.10(2)
　　　Statutory claims, 6.10(4)

RELATIONAL INJURIES
　See also Dignitary Torts
Reputational harm and, libel and slander
　cases, 7.2(5)

RELEASE
Misrepresentation, restoration required of the
　plaintiff, 9.3(3)
Mistaken, 11.9

RELIANCE DAMAGES OR EXPENSE
　Generally, 12.3
Benefit conferred, qualifying as restitution,
　4.5(4)
Building contractor, 12.20(1)
Essential form of, 12.3(2)
Evidence of benefit conferred, as, 4.5(4)
Frustrated and impracticable contracts,
　13.3(2)
Incidental form of, 12.3(2)
Land sales contract, purchaser's, 12.11(1)
Restitution distinguished or compared, 4.5(4),
　12.7(1), 12.7(3), 13.2(2)
Statute of frauds, and, 13.2(2), 13.2(3)

RELIGION
Injunction, religious interests affected, 2.9(5),
　7.3(5)

REMARRIAGE
Death of a spouse, effect of, wrongful death
　damages, 8.3(7)

REMEDIAL ANALYSIS
See Analysis of Remedial Issues

REMEDIAL EQUITY
Substantive equity distinguished, 2.3(1)

REMEDIAL EQUIVALENCE, 1.8

REMEDIES
　See also particular remedies such as Con-
　　structive Trust; Damages; Injunc-
　　tion; Interpleader; Replevin; Spe-
　　cific Performance; Restitution; and
　　particular topics such as Contracts;
　　Mistake, etc.

REMEDIES—Cont'd
Basic types, 1.1
Classification, legal and equitable, 1.2
Costs and benefits of as factor in choosing among, 1.9
Damages,
    Generally, 3.1–3.12
    Introduced, 1.1
Equivalent remedies, analysis, 1.8
Exceeding rights, 1.7, 2.4(6)
Injunction,
    Generally, 2.1–2.11
    Introduced, 1.1
Public law remedies, 1.5
Restitution, introduced, 1.1
Rights compared to, 1.7
Rights congruent with, 1.7
Rights violated by others, defendant not liable, 2.4(7)
Scope, 1.6

RENDLEMAN, DOUG
Adequacy of legal remedy generally, 2.5(3)
Contempt and collateral bar rule, 2.8(6)
Contempt sanctions, caps proposed, 2.8(3)

RENT
Lessor's remedy for against tenant, 12.15(2)
Tenant's remedy of abatement or withholding, 12.15(2)

RENTAL VALUE
Alternative to consequential damages claim, 3.4
Automobiles, loss of use during repair, 5.15(2)
Building contract,
    Equipment idled, 12.20(1)
    Occupation delayed or limited, 12.19(1)
Chattels, lost use, 5.15(2)
Consequential damages compared and contrasted, 3.3(4), 3.4, 6.6(2), 12.4(7)
Conversion, restitution based on, 5.18(1)
Crop damage, diminished rental value of land as alternative measure, 5.3(2)
Duplication with other elements, nuisance cases, 5.12(2)
Easement obstructed, diminished rental value of plaintiff's lots, 5.7(6)
Extorted use of property, 10.2(3)
General damages, as,
    Hadley limits inapplicable to, 12.4(7)
    Robins Dry Dock limits inapplicable, 6.6(2)
Improver, mistaken addition of improvements, liability for, 5.8(3)
Interest and, 3.6(2), 3.6(4)
Interference with contract or prospects, 6.6(2)
Land sales,
    Installment contracts, 12.13
    Vendor's claim for after purchaser's breach, 12.12(1)
    Vendor's delay,
        Damages measured by, 12.11(1)
        Restitution of vendor's gains, 12.7(4)
Landlord and tenant,
    Landlord's general damages, 12.15(3)
    Tenant's general damages, 12.15(2)

RENTAL VALUE—Cont'd
Lease of goods, element in measuring damages for breach, 12.18
Loss of use, damaged chattel, 5.15(2)
Mesne profits as, 5.8(2)
Nuisance cases, 5.6(2), 5.11(3), 5.12(2)
Occupation of land by defendant, 5.8(2)
Regulatory taking damages, 5.6(4), 6.9(2), 6.9(4)
Restitution,
    Defendant uses chattel, 5.18(2)
    Defendant uses land, 5.8(2), 5.8(3), 5.9, 12.7(4), 9.3(3), 9.3(4), 12.11(2), 12.12(2)
    Measures, alternative, 4.5(3)
Restitution of,
    Contract breach after pre-closing occupancy, 12.11(2), 12.12(2)
    Misrepresentation cases, 9.3(3), 9.3(4)
    Purchaser's pre-closing occupancy, 12.11(2), 12.12(2)
Trespass, owner deprived of use, 5.2(1)
Use and occupation of land by defendant, 5.8(2), 5.8(3), 5.9, 12.7(4), 9.3(3), 9.3(4), 12.11(2), 12.12(2)
Use of chattel by defendant, 5.18(2)

REPAIR
Homeowner's liability for unauthorized expense to preserve house, 4.9(1), 12.20
Mechanic's claim against owner for repairs authorized by thief, 4.9(5)

REPAIR OR REPLACEMENT COSTS
See also Cover; Substitution Costs
Assets increased by repair or replacement, 5.2(7), 5.6(2), 5.14(1)
Chattels, ceiling on recovery, 5.14(1)
Eminent domain and taking cases, 5.2(6)
Environmental harm cases, 5.2(5)
Nuisance damages measure, 5.6(2)
Trespass,
    Adjustments required when a damages measure, 5.2(7)
    Ceilings, 5.2(3)
    Injunction to repair or replace, 5.5

REPARATIVE INJUNCTION, 2.9(1)

REPEATED ACTS
Legal remedy inadequate, 2.5(2)

REPLACEMENT COSTS
See Repair or Replacement Costs; Substitution Costs

REPLACEMENT SERVICES
Personal injury, 8.1(2)

REPLEVIN
Chattel recovery, 5.17(2)
Constitutional limitations on process, 5.17(2)
Historical background, 4.2(2)
Money, action for, 6.1(1)
Provisional remedy, as, 1.3
Restitution, history, 4.2(2)
Restitutionary goals, 4.2(1)

REPUTATION
See also Libel and Slander

REPUTATION—Cont'd
Artist's, work altered, 5.16(4)
Harm to, contract breach,
     Generally, 12.5(1)
     Employment contracts, 12.21(2)

RES JUDICATA
Equitable relief denied, effect, 12.8(5)
Equity jury trial and, 2.6(4)
Permanent nuisance or the like, 5.11(1)
Splitting cause of action for future loss, 8.1(7)
Unlawful detainer or summary ejectment action, 5.10(2)

RESALE
Seller's remedy under UCC, 12.17(3)

RESCISSION
    See also other remedies that may be equivalent such as Constructive Trust; Restitution; see also settings such as Contracts
Collateral breaches, land purchaser, 12.11(2)
Constructive trust compared, 4.4
Equity courts' role in, 4.3(6), 9.3(3)
Jury trial, equitable characterization or not, 2.6(3)
Land contracts,
    Purchaser's breach, 12.12(2)
    Vendor's breach, 12.11(2)
Law courts' role in, 4.3(6), 9.3(3)
Lessee's remedy, 12.15(2)
Out of pocket damages equivalence, 9.2(2)
Reformation compared, 4.3(7)
Reformation contrasted, 9.6, 11.6(2)
Restitution generally, 4.3(6)
Restoration required of plaintiff, 4.8, 9.3(3), 11.9
Termination contrasted, 4.3(6), 12.13
Unilateral, 4.3(6)

RESPONSE COSTS
Superfund Act, 5.2(5)

RESTITUTION
    See also Benefits; Confidential Relationships; Constructive Trust; Equitable Lien; Fiduciaries; Principal and Agent; Profits; Reformation; Rescission; Subrogation and related topics
    Generally, 4.1(1)
Accounting for profits, generally, 4.3(1), 4.3(5)
Applications introduced, 4.1(1)
Apportionment of profits between innocent and wrongful acts, see Apportionment of Profits
Assumpsit,
    Historical background, 4.2(3)
    Reference to, as, 4.1(1), 4.2(1)
Attorney fees, common fund rule, 3.10(2), 4.9(6)
Attorneys,
    Client-avoided contract, 13.5
    Unauthorized services, 4.9(4)
Autonomy rights generally protected, 4.1(2)
Bargaining possible between parties, where, 4.9(4)

RESTITUTION—Cont'd
Basic remedy, 1.1
Benefits,
    Measure, statute of frauds cases, 13.2(2)
    Measurements introduced, 4.1(1)
    Passed on, 4.6
    Statute of frauds cases, reliance expense distinguished, 13.2(2)
    Subjective purpose and, 4.5(2)
Benefits consumed or passed on, 4.5(4)
Bona fide purchaser generally, 4.7(1)
Bribes, 10.6
Brokers, benefit to non-contracting party, 4.9(4)
Building contracts, owner's remedy, 12.19(1)
Burden of proof,
    Apportionment of profits, see Apportionment of Profits; Burden of Proof
    Defaulting plaintiff, 12.13
Ceilings on, 4.5(4), 12.7(5)
Changed position,
    Defense generally, 4.6
    Mistake cases, 11.8
Characterizing award, restitution vs. damages, 4.1(1)
Chattel buyer's claim to, 12.16(5)
Chattel converted, waiver of tort,
    Generally, 5.18(1)
    Measure, 5.18(2)
Chattel improved, unauthorized improvement, 4.9(5)
Combining other remedies, 4.5(5)
Common counts in assumpsit, 4.2(3)
Common fund rule, attorney fees, 3.10(2), 4.9(6)
Consequential benefits generally, 4.5(3)
Constructive trust,
    Generally, 4.3(2)
    Chattels converted, 5.18(3)
    Introduced, 4.3(1)
    Terminology introduced, 4.1(1)
    Tracing to funds of money generally, 6.1
Contract avoided for incapacity of a part, 13.4(1)
Contract between parties, effect on, 4.9(4)
Contract breach,
    Generally, 12.7
    Election of remedies, 12.7(6)
    Executed conveyances, 12.7(2)
    Expectancy as a limit or not, 12.7(5)
    Farnsworth theory, 12.7(4)
    Full-performance-liquidated-sum rule, 12.7(5)
    Measurement, generally, 12.7(3)
    Summary, 12.1(1)
Contract price, when relevant to restitution, 4.5(4)
Contracts,
    Full-performance-liquidated-sum rule, 4.5(4), 12.7(5)
    Price or expectancy as ceiling, 4.5(4)
Contribution,
    Claim as, 4.3(4)
    Cotenant improvement, 4.9(3)
Conversion of property, 5.18
Copyright infringement, 6.3(4)

RESTITUTION—Cont'd
Cotenant improvements, 4.9(3)
Credit cards, benefits to one who did not contract to pay debt, 4.9(4)
Credits,
    Benefits offset by losses, 4.5(4)
    Expense deductions against profits liability, 4.5(3)
Damages and, recovery of both, 4.5(5)
Damages compared, 4.1(1)
Damages vs., Superfund Act, 5.2(5)
Defaulting plaintiff,
    Defaulting buyer of goods, 12.16(6)
    Installment land sale contract, 12.13
Defenses,
        Generally, 4.6
    Bona fide purchaser, 4.7(1)
    Discharge for value, 4.7(2)
Defined, 4.1
Discharge for value defense, 4.7(2)
Duress basis for, 10.2(1)
Economic compulsion basis for, 10.2(1)
Efficient breach and measure of, 12.7(4)
Ejectment,
    History, 4.2(2)
    Terminology, 4.2(1)
Election of remedies,
    Combining restitution and damages, 4.5(5)
    Contracts, 12.7(6)
    Misrepresentation, 9.4
Emergency services or supplies, 4.9(5)
Employment contracts, employee's remedy, 12.21(3)
Equitable conversion and, 4.3(8)
Equitable lien,
        Generally, 4.3(3)
    Chattels converted, 5.18(3)
    Introduced, 4.3(1)
Equities in conflict, 4.7(1)
Equity and, 4.1(1), 4.1(3)
Equity courts' administration of generally, 4.3(1)
Estoppel and, 2.3(5)
Executed deeds, denied generally, 12.7(2), 12.11(2), 12.12(2)
Express contract precluding restitution, 4.9(4)
Family and neighborly services, 4.9(4)
Foreclosure, oral promise to buy in at sale, 13.2(2)
Foreign currency, benefits in, 3.7
Fraudulent conveyances, 13.6
Frustration of contract purposes, generally, 13.3(1)
Fulfilling another's duty, 4.9(2)
Full-performance-liquidated-sum rule, 12.7(5)
Gain in market transaction or appreciation,
        See also Constructive Trust; Profits and related topics
    Misrepresentation cases 9.3(4)
    Trespass, 5.4
Gambling contracts, 13.6
Gifts, 11.10
Historical development, 4.2
Illegal contracts, 13.6
Implied in fact contract, and, 4.2(3)

RESTITUTION—Cont'd
Implied in law contract,
    Assumpsit and, 4.2(3)
    Terminology, 4.1(1), 4.2(1)
Impracticability of contract performance, generally 13.3(1)
Improvements,
    Breached land sale contract, 12.11(2)
    Chattel, unauthorized, 4.9(5)
    Mistaken trespasser, 5.8(3)
Indemnity claim as, 4.3(4)
Innocent purchasers,
    Bona fide purchaser doctrines, 4.7(1)
    Protected generally, 4.1(2)
    Reformation and, 4.3(7)
Insurer's liability minimized by insured's action, 4.9(4)
Interest, role in summarized, 3.6(1)
Interference with contract, 6.6(3)
Intermeddlers, see Unsolicited Benefits
Introduced generally, 4.1(1)–4.1(4)
Jury trial or not, 2.6(3)
Land sales contract,
    Purchaser's breach, denied, 12.12(2)
    Vendor's breach, 12.11(2)
Law courts administration of, 4.1(3), 4.2
Liability for improvements authorized by apparent owner, 4.9(5)
Licensing violations, 13.6
Lien for mistaken improver of land, 5.8(3)
Losing contracts or transactions, expectancy a limit or not, 9.2(1), 12.7(5), 12.16(6), 12.17(6), 12.20(2), 12.21(3)
Measure,
    Attorneys' claims against client, 13.5
    Benefits consumed, passed on or destroyed, 4.5(4)
    Contract price,
        Limit on or not, generally, 4.5(4)
        Mistake cases, 11.5
    Contracts,
        Generally, 12.7(3)
        Avoided for incapacity, 13.4(2)
    Dividing gains, 11.5
    Dividing losses, 11.5, 13.3(2)
    Frustrated and impracticable contracts, 13.3(2)
    Income gained, 4.5(3)
    Increased value of defendant's assets, 4.5(2)
    Introduced, 4.1(1), 4.5(1)
    Limits, 4.5(4)
    Market measures, 4.5(2)
    Mistake cases, 11.5
    Offsets, 4.5(4)
    Rental or interest received, 4.5(3)
        See also Rental Value
    Requested service, 4.5(4)
    Sale in a rising market, 4.5(3)
    Savings effected, 4.5(3)
    Services rendered, 4.5(2)
    Shared gains or losses, 11.5
    Summarized, 4.1(4)
    Use value, 4.5(2)
        See also Rental Value
Misappropriation of intangible property,
        Private submission of ideas, 6.5(2)

RESTITUTION—Cont'd
Misappropriation of intangible property
—Cont'd
  Public revelation cases, 6.5(3)
Misrepresentation cases generally, 9.3
Mistake,
  Measurement of, 11.5
  Payment of another's debt, 4.9(3)
  Remedy for generally, 11.4, 11.5, 11.7
Money or accounts, 6.1(2)
Money or cash, unsolicited benefits rule and, 4.9(3)
Money payments, 4.5(2)
Necessaries supplied, 4.9(5)
Negative unjust enrichment, 5.9
No title in plaintiff, 4.2(3)
Non-cash benefits, unsolicited benefits rule and, 4.9(4)
Oral promises, statute of frauds, generally, 13.2
Other remedies combined, 4.5(5)
Patent infringement, unavailable, 6.2(4)
Payment of another's debt, unsolicited, 4.9(3)
Personal injury and death cases, 8.9
Prejudgment interest as, 3.6(2)
Price received by defendant for sale of plaintiff's chattel, 5.18(2)
Procedural aspects introduced, 4.1(3)
Profits,
  Adjustments, 4.5(3)
  Chattels used by defendant, 5.18(2)–5.18(3)
  Constructive trust to capture defendant's, 4.3(2)
  Contempt sanction, 2.8(2)
  Contract breach, 12.7(4)
  Copyright infringement, 6.3(4)
  Seller's, 12.16(6)
  Trespasser's severance of items, 5.4
  Trespasser's use and occupation of land, from, 5.9
Property saved, 4.9(5)
Property wrongfully acquired at another's death, 6.7
Public entity contracts irregular, 13.6
Punitive, as, 3.11(1), 12.11(2)
Punitive damages, compared to, 4.1(4)
Punitive damages and, recovery, 4.5(5)
Quantum meruit as reference to, 4.1(1)
Quasi contracts, assumpsit and, 4.2(3)
Quasi-contract terminology, 4.1(1), 4.2(1)
Real property, executed conveyance rule, 12.7(2)
Reformation, generally, 4.3(7)
Release avoided, restoration required of plaintiff, 9.3(3)
Reliance damages or expense,
  Benefit conferred, qualifying as, 4.5(4)
  Contrasted or compared, 4.5(4), 12.3(1), 12.7(1), 12.7(3), 13.2(2)
Remedial side generally, 4.1(4)
Rental value, see Rental Value
Replevin,
  History, 4.2(2)
  Terminology, 4.2(1)
Requested services, 4.5(4)
Rescission generally, 4.3(6)

RESTITUTION—Cont'd
Restoration required of the plaintiff,
  Generally, 4.8
  Misrepresentation cases, 9.3(3)
  Mistaken release cases, 11.9
Rights established on substantive theory of, 4.1(2)
Savings to defendant, use of chattel, 5.18(2)
Securities transactions, gains from inside information, 10.5(2)
Seller's remedy, 12.17(6)
Services,
  Requested, 4.5(4)
  Unsolicited, 4.9(4)
Specific chattels,
  Replevin, see Replevin
  Unsolicited delivery of, 4.9(3)
Specific property, constructive trust to recover, 4.3(2)
Specific restitution,
  Generally, 4.4
  Contract breach, 12.7(2)
  Defendant's obligation, 9.3(4)
  Plaintiff's obligation, 9.3(3)
Statute of frauds,
  Constructive trust, 13.2(3)
  Reliance distinguished, 13.2(3)
Statute of frauds cases, generally, 13.2(1)
Subcontractor's claim against landowner for improvements, 4.9(4), 12.20(3)
Subrogation,
  Generally, 4.3(4)
  Introduction, 4.3(1)
  Payment of another's debt, 4.9(3)
Substantive restitution generally, 4.1(2)
Substantive vs. remedial restitution, 4.1(1)
Substitutionary restitution generally, 4.4
Superfund Act, 5.2(5)
Support of grantor covenant, 12.12(2)
Taxes, deduction for in computing defendant's profits, trademark cases, 6.4(4)
Taxes overpaid, for, 4.9(3)
Tenant's claim against landlord for improvements, 4.9(4)
Terminology, summary, 4.2(1)
Third persons,
  Claims against, 12.7(6)
  Laborers, subcontractors and suppliers, building contracts, 12.20(3)
Title in plaintiff protected by restoration of possession, 4.2(2)
Tracing introduced, 4.3(1)
Trade secret use, 10.5(3)
Trademark infringement, 6.4(4)
Trespass, physical harm to land, 5.4
Ultra vires acts, 13.4, 13.6
Undue influence basis, 10.3
Unenforceable contracts, summary, 13.1
Unjust enrichment,
  Basis, 4.1(1), 4.1(2)
  Vagueness of concept, 4.1(2)
Unjust enrichment patterns,
  Benefits to defendant from contract breach, 4.1(2)
  Benefits to defendant from money or services without misconduct, 4.1(2)

RESTITUTION—Cont'd
Unjust enrichment patterns—Cont'd
    Possession in defendant, title in plaintiff, 4.1(2)
    Title passes to defendant through misconduct, 4.1(2)
Unsolicited benefits, see Unsolicited Benefits
Use value,
        See also Rental Value
    Benefit, 4.5(2)
    Consequential benefits from, 4.5(3)
Vendor of land, to, 12.12(1)
Volunteers, see Unsolicited Benefits
Waiver of tort and suit in assumpsit, 4.2(3)

RESTORATION REQUIRED OF THE PLAINTIFF
Misrepresentation cases, 9.3(3)
Mistaken release cases, 11.9
Restitution cases, generally, 4.8

RESTRUCTURING INSTITUTIONS BY INJUNCTION, 1.5, 2.9(1)

RESULTING TRUST
See Constructive Trust

RETAIL MARKET
Damages based on, when, 5.13(3)

RETALIATORY DISCHARGE
See Wrongful Discharge

RETIRED PERSONS
Wrongful death, 8.3(4)

RIGHT OF PRIVACY
See Privacy

RIGHT OF PUBLICITY
See Misappropriation of Intangible Property

RIGHTS AND REMEDIES
Compared, 1.7
Congruence, 1.7
Correlation, 1.7

RISK ALLOCATION CONTRACTS
Contracts as risk control devices generally, 11.2, 12.1(1), 12.1(2), 12.4(5), 12.4(6), 12.4(7)
Emotional distress, risk of allocated, 12.5(1)
Employment contracts, risks allocated, 12.21(3)
Hardship and, 12.8(4)
Impracticability, judicial reallocation of risks, 13.3(2)
Land sales, property damaged before closing, 12.14
Loss sharing and, 11.5
Mistake, and,
    Generally, 11.3, 11.4, 11.7
    Releases, 11.9
Price, evidence of risks allocated, 12.4(7)
Punitive damages and, 12.5(2)
Relational contracts contrasted, 12.1(2)
Restitution, availability or measure affected by, 12.7(5), 12.20(2), 13.3(1)
Specific performance and, 12.8(6)

RISK OF LOSS
Equitable conversion solutions, 4.3(8)
Land sales contract, 12.14

ROYALTY
Patent infringement damages measure, 6.2(3)

SALES
Ancitipatory repudiation, seller's, 12.16(4)
Buyer's cover measured damages, 12.16(3)
Buyer's damages, anticipatory repudiation by seller, 12.16(4)
Buyer's goodwill loss claim, 12.16(4)
Buyer's market measured damages,
    Generally, 12.16(2)
    Ceiling on, 12.16(4)
Buyer's remedies, summary, 12.16(1)
Buyer's restitution remedy, 12.16(6)
Buyer's specific performance remedy, 12.16(7)
Common law and UCC compared, 12.16(1)
Damages,
    Ceiling on market damages, 12.16(4)
    Ceiling on market measured recovery, 12.16(4)
Incidental damages, buyer's claim for, 12.16(4)
Losing contract, expectancy as a limit on restitution or not, 12.16(6)
Lost volume sellers, 12.17(5)
Overhead, seller's, 12.17(5)
Reclamation, seller's remedy, 12.17(6)
Resale contract, expectancy as ceiling on buyer's market measured damages, 12.16(4)
Restitution,
    Buyer's claim, 12.16(6)
    Seller's profits, 12.16(6)
Seller's consequential damages, 12.17(3)
Seller's incidental damages, 12.17(3)
Seller's lost profit damages, 12.17(5)
Seller's market measured damages, 12.17(2)
Seller's remedies, summary, 12.17(1)
Seller's resale remedy, 12.17(3)
Seller's restitutionary and reclamation remedies, 12.17(6)
Seller's specific performance remedy, 12.17(6)
Specific performance, buyer's remedy, 12.16(7)

SALVAGE
Property saved, restitution claims for, 4.9(5)

SANCTIONS FOR CONTEMPT
    See also Contempt
    Generally, 2.8(2)
As determining civil or criminal character, 2.8(3)
Coercive, 2.8(2)
Ineffective sanctions lifted, 2.8(3)
Keys to the jail test, 2.8(2)
Profits of contemnor, 2.8(2)
Remedial sanctions as civil, 2.8(3)
Right to litigate denied, 2.8(2)

SAND
Gravel, dirt, removal, damages, 5.3(2)

SCHEDULED INJURIES
Caps on damages distinguished, 8.8
Personal injury, 8.1(2)

SCHOENBORD, DAVID
Statutory injunctions, when remedy can be withheld, 2.10

SCOPE OF REMEDIES, 1.1

SEARS AND COMPCO CASES, 6.5(3)

SEAT BELT DEFENSES
Damages rules, 8.7(4)

SEBERT, JOHN
Mental distress damages in contract cases, 12.5(1)

SECURITIES
See also Misrepresentation
Inside information in securities transactions, 10.5(2)

SEIZURE OF GOODS
Enforcement of remedies, 2.8(1)

SELDEN, JOHN
Chancellor's Foot epigram, 2.2 n.

SELECTION OF REMEDY, 1.7

SELF–HELP REMEDIES, 1.1

SENTIMENTAL VALUE
Property damage cases, 5.15(3)

SERVICES
Chattel improvements, unauthorized, 4.9(5)
Emergency services, restitution, 4.9(5)
Loss of, see Consortium
Restitution, professional services, 4.9(4)
Restitution for requested, 4.5(4)
Restitution for unsolicited, 4.9(4)
Saving property, restitution for, 4.9(5)
Unsolicited, restitution, 4.9(4)

SETTLEMENT
Attorney fee awards, prevailing party status achieved by, 3.10(6)

SEVERANCE
Items taken from land, 5.3(1)

SEXUAL HARASSMENT
Punitive damages, 3.11(1)

SEXUAL RELATIONS
Loss of, see Consortium

SHERIFF
In rem enforcement, role in, ejectment or replevin, 1.4, 4.2(2), 5.10(1)

SHIPPER
Harm to goods shipped, measure of damages, 5.13(3)

SHORT SWING PROFITS
Corporate insider's liability, 10.5(2)

SLADE'S CASE, 4.2(3)

SLANDER OF TITLE
See Injurious Falsehood

SNAIL DARTER CASE, 2.4(7), 2.10, 5.7(5)

SNEPP CASE
Breacher's or fiduciary's profits, 4.5(3)

SOCIAL RELATIONS
Injunctive protection, 7.3(5)

SOCIETY
Loss of, see Consortium

SON OF SAM STATUTES
Criminal's gains from crime, security for victim's damages, 8.9

SPARE BOAT DOCTRINE
Loss of use claims, 5.15(2)

SPECIAL ACTIONS
Substituted for prerogative writs, 2.11(4)

SPECIAL DAMAGES
See Consequential Damages

SPECIFIC CHATTELS
Restitution by replevin, see Replevin
Restitution of, unsolicited benefits rule, 4.9(3)

SPECIFIC PERFORMANCE
See also Injunction
Generally, 12.8(1)
Adequacy of legal remedy,
    Generally, 2.5(2), 12.8(2)
    Building contracts, 12.19(1)
    Land purchase, 12.11(3)
    Land sale, 12.12(3)
    Sales of goods, 12.16(7)
Agreed remedies and right to, 12.9(5)
Arbitration,
    As arbitrator's remedy, 12.23
    Enforcement by, 12.23
Building contract, owner's remedy, 12.19(1)
Buyer's remedy, UCC, 12.16(7)
Certainty of contract rule, 2.5(4)
Chattel leases, 12.18
Contemplation of the parties test and, 12.8(5)
Damages and, land seller's suit, 12.12(3)
Discretion, 12.8(1), 12.8(5)
Economic arguments for and against, 12.8(2)
Efficient breach and,
    Generally, 12.8(2)
    Employee contracts, 12.22(2)
Employee's remedy against employer, 12.21(3)
Equitable conversion and, 12.8(1)
Estoppel, 12.8(4)
Fairness limitations on, 12.8(4)
Hardship limitations on, 12.8(4)
Injunction, as form of, 2.1(2), 2.9(1), 12.8(1)
Installment land vendor's claim terminated, 12.13
Interference with contract subject to, 6.6(2)
Judicial supervision problem, 12.8(3), 12.19(3)
Laches, 12.8(4)
Land sales contract,
    Acreage deficiency or excess, 12.12(3)
    Purchaser's claim, 12.11(3)
Lessee's claim against landlord for, 12.15(2)
Loan contracts, 12.8(2)
Minimizing damages by, 12.6(2)

SPECIFIC PERFORMANCE—Cont'd
Moral theory of, effect on adequacy rule, 2.5(3)
Mutuality of remedy, 12.8(4)
    Equity rule, 2.4(3)
Partial, 12.8(1), 12.11(3)
Personal service contracts, 12.8(3)
Practicability, policy and supervision,
        Generally, 12.8(3)
    Building contracts, 12.19(3)
    Employment contracts, 12.21(3)
Price speculation and, 12.8(1)
Reformation compared, 11.6(2)
Res judicata, 12.8(5)
Seller's specific performance remedy, UCC,
        12.17(6)
Strategic goals of claim, 12.8(1)
Summary, 12.8(1)
Supervision of performance by court, 2.5(4)
Uncertainty of contract terms, 12.8(3)
Unclean hands, 12.8(4)
Unconscionability, equity rule, 2.4(3)
Unconscionable contracts, 12.8(4)

SPECIFIC PROPERTY
Constructive trust to recover, 4.3(2)

SPECIFIC RESTITUTION
    Generally, 4.4
Contract breach, 12.7(2)

SPLITTING CAUSE OF ACTION
Future damages, personal injury, 8.1(7)

SPOUSES
See also Consortium; Personal Injury;
        Wrongful Death
Consortium loss, personal injury, 8.1(5)
Remarriage after death of a spouse, 8.3(7)

STANDARDIZED DAMAGES
Copyright infringement, 6.3(3)
Introduction to, 3.2, 3.3(2)

STANDING TO SUE
Equity accords standing, merger of law and
        equity effect, 2.6(1), 2.6(3)
Injunction, 5.7(5), 8.10
Plaintiff compensated or uninjured, injunction
        denied, 8.10
Punitive damages, injunction in lieu of, 8.10

STATISTICAL TABLES
Mortality and work life tables, injury cases,
        8.5(2)

STATUTE OF FRAUDS
Constructive trust, 13.2(3)
Estoppel to invoke, 13.2(5)
Part performance, 13.2(5)
Reformation and, 9.5, 11.6(1)
Restitution,
    Agreements for acts distinguished from
            agreements for end product, 13.2(3)
    Benefits conferred in performing unen-
            forceable agreement, generally,
            13.2(1)
    Measure, 13.2(1)
    Reliance expense distinguished, 13.2(4)
    Specie, 13.2(3)

STATUTE OF FRAUDS—Cont'd
UCC, 13.2(5)

STATUTE OF LIMITATIONS
Laches and, 2.4(4)
Permanent nuisance or harm, 5.11(1)

STATUTES
Attorney fee award statutes, generally, 3.10(4)
Collateral source rule, changes in, 3.8(1)
Discretion affecting statutory rights, 2.4(7)
Injunction, nuisance, 5.7(5)
Injunction authorized or required, 2.10
Interest rates, 3.6(4)
Jury trial, equitable characterization or not,
        2.6(3)
Limitation of actions, laches and, 2.4(4)
Multiple damages, 3.12
Nuisance injunctions, effect on, 5.7(5)
Prejudgment interest, 3.6(2)
Punitive damages and, 3.11(1)

STAYS
Injunction stay pending appeal, 2.11(4)

STRATEGY
Injunction to improve litigation position, 2.9(4)
Remedies avoiding remedy-specific defenses,
        1.10
Remedies enhancing enforcement, 1.10
Remedies enhancing procedural advantage,
        1.10
Remedies imposing high costs on adversaries,
        1.10
Specific performance, 12.8(1)

STRICT LIABILITY
Punitive damages, 3.11(1)

STRUCTURAL INJUNCTION, 2.9(1)

STRUCTURED SETTLEMENTS, 8.5(5)

STUMPAGE
Damages, timber trespass, 5.3(2)

SUBCONTRACTORS
See Contractors

SUBROGATION
Building contracts, subcontractor's claim
        against owner, 12.20(3)
Collateral source rule rationale, injury cases,
        3.8(1), 8.6(3)
Contribution compared, 4.3(4)
Garnishment and, 4.3(4)
Indemnity compared, 4.3(4)
Introduced, 4.3(1)
Restitution, generally, 4.3(4)
Surety's payment, 4.9(3)
Tracing and, 4.3(4)
Unjust enrichment basis, 4.3(4)

SUBSTANTIAL BENEFIT RULE
Attorney fee awards, 3.10(2)

SUBSTANTIVE EQUITY
Adequacy rule inapplicable, 2.5(1)
Equitable conversion doctrine, 2.3(4)
Mortgages, 2.3(3)

SUBSTANTIVE EQUITY—Cont'd
Remedial equity distinguished, 2.3(1)
Trusts, 2.3(2)

SUBSTANTIVE LAW
Remedies and, 1.1

SUBSTITUTE FACILITIES
Eminent domain and takings cases, 5.2(6)

SUBSTITUTION COSTS
    See also Repair or Replacement Costs
Building contracts, 12.19(1)
Consequential damages or as ceiling on mar-
    ket damages, damaged chattels, 5.1(7),
    5.6(2), 5.14(1), 5.14(3), 12.16(4)
Contracts,
    As general or as special damages, 12.2(2)
    Market measure compared, 12.2(2)
Cover, 12.16(3)
Damages measure,
    Characteristics, 3.3(5)
    Compensation goals and, 12.2(2)
    Introduction to, 3.2
General damages and, duplication risks, 3.3(7)
Loss of use, lease-in measure, 5.15(2)
Substitute worth more,
    Building contract cases, 12.19(1)
    Property damage cases, 5.2(7), 5.6(2),
    5.14(1)
    UCC cover, 12.16(3)

SUCCESSORS
Liability for violation of order against prede-
    cessor, 2.8(5)

SUMMARY EJECTMENT, 5.10(2)

SUMMERS, ROBERT
Cover under UCC, 12.16(3)

SUPERFUND ACT
Damages vs. restitution, 5.2(5)

SUPERVISION
Specific performance, practicality issue, 2.5(4)

SUPPLEMENTAL PROCEEDINGS
Debtor's assets reached through, 1.4, 2.8(1)

SUPPORT
Contract to support grantor, 12.12(2)

SUPPORT ORDERS
Contempt enforcement, 2.8(2)

SURETIES
Subrogation, 4.3(4)

SURROGATE DAMAGES
See Standardized Damages

SURVIVAL
Wrongful death action, survival of after de-
    pendent's death, 8.3(7)

SURVIVAL ACTIONS
    See also Wrongful Death
    Generally, 8.3(2)
Lost earnings, 8.3(2)
Punitive damages, 8.3(6)

SURVIVAL ACTIONS—Cont'd
Summary, 8.3(1)

SURVIVORSHIP
Cotenant acquisition of property by wrongdo-
    ing, 6.7

SWOLLEN ASSETS
Tracing problems, 6.1(3)

TACTICAL POSITION
Injunction to improve, 2.9(4)

TAILORING
Damages,
    See also Consequential Damages
    Individuating, 3.3(6)
Equitable remedies,
    Generally, 2.4(6)
    Jury trial rights and, 2.6(5)
Injunctions,
    Preliminary injunction, limiting risk of er-
    ror by, 2.11(2)
    Temporary restraining order limiting risk
    of error by, 2.11(2)

TAKINGS
See Eminent Domain; Regulatory Takings

TAXES
Credit to defendant denied on plaintiff's tax
    benefits, injury cases, 8.6(4)
Overpayment, restitution, 4.9(3), 10.2(3)
Personal injury cases generally, 8.6(4)
Restitution of profits, deductions for in com-
    puting, trademark cases, 6.4(4)
Structured settlements, 8.5(5)

TEMPORARY NUISANCE
Harm or invasion, 5.11(1)

TEMPORARY RESTRAINING ORDER
    Generally, 2.11(1)
Bond requirement, 2.11(3)
Factors in granting, 2.11(2)
Irreparable harm,
    Remote, 2.11(2)
    Specially required, 2.11(2)
Leubsdorf formula, 2.11(2)
Posner formula, 2.11(2)
Probability of success on merits, 2.11(2)
Provisional remedy, as, 1.3
Risk of error, formulas to account for, 2.11(2)
Standards for granting, 2.11(2)
Tailoring to avoid irretrievable loss of rights,
    2.11(2)
Third persons, harm to, 2.11(2)
Trademark infringement, 6.4(5)

TENDER
Release cases, 11.9
Required in rescission, when, 4.8

TERMINATION
Lessee's remedy against landlord, 12.15(2)
Lessor's remedy against tenant, 12.15(3)
Rescission distinguished, 4.3(6)

TEXAS GULF SULPHUR CASE
Securities litigation, 10.5(2)

THEORY OF THE CLAIM
Damages under different theories, duplication, 3.3(7)

THIRD PERSONS
See also Bona Fide Purchaser; Discharge for Value
Balancing interests of in equity generally, 2.4(1), 2.4(5)
Benefits to consider in choosing remedy, 1.9
Contempt liability of named defendant for acts of, 2.8(5)
Defendant responsible for litigation with, attorney fee liability, 3.10(3)
Equitable relief affecting, 2.4(7)
Incidental effect upon, 2.4(7)
Injunction, persons bound, 2.8(5)
Irreparable harm to in preliminary injunctions, 2.11(2)
Irreparable harm to in temporary restraining orders, 2.11(2)
Liens against, land purchaser's, 12.11(4)
Litigation with, attorney fee recovery as damages, 3.10(2)
Payment of another's debt to, restitution, 4.9(3)
Punitive damages,
  Harm to, bearing on amount awarded, 3.11(9)
  Wealth of, 3.11(5)
Reformation in favor of 11.6(1)
Restitution,
  Absence of contracts among all parties, effect, 4.9(4)
  Claims against, 12.7(6)
  Credit card charges, restitution for benefits received by one who did not agree to pay, 4.9(4)
  Restitution to, labor and supplies provided to building contractor creating benefits to landowner, 12.20(3)
  Standing to attack jurisdiction to defeat contempt sanction, 2.8(6)

THREATS
See also Duress; Economic Compulsion
Preventive injunction, threat required, 2.5(1)

TIMBER CUTTING
Damages, 5.3(2)

TIME
See Date

TITLE
See Deeds; Land Titles

TITLE VII
Discretionary remedies, 6.10(5)
Employment discrimination, statutes compared, 6.10(3)
Jury trial, equitable characterization or not, 2.6(3)
Jury trial or not, 6.10(5)

TORT REFORM
Caps,
  Damages, 8.8
  Punitive damages, 3.11(12)

TORT REFORM—Cont'd
Collateral source rule, and, 3.8(1), 8.6(3)
Punitive damages generally, 3.11(12)
Scheduled injuries, 8.8

TORTS
See also particular torts, such as Injurious Falsehood; Interference with Contract; Libel and Slander; Misappropriation; Misrepresentation; Privacy; Unfair Competition; and particular settings such as Personal Injury
Mistake as cause or condition of liability, 11.
Toxic torts,
  Future harm anticipated, 8.1(7)
  Punitive damages, 3.11(1)

TRACING
Direct benefit rule, tracing benefit to plaintiff, 8.6(2)
Effect introduced, 4.3(1)
Equitable conversion and, 4.3(8)
Mistaken payment, tracing to benefit received, 11.8
Money,
  After withdrawal from account, 6.1(4)
    Generally, 6.1(3)
  Lowest balance rule, 6.1(4)
Restitutionary tracing introduced, 4.3(1)
Subrogation and, 4.3(4)
Swollen assets theory, 6.1(3)
Tortfeasor's profits from publishing accounts of his wrong, 8.9

TRADE LIBEL
See Injurious Falsehood

TRADE SECRETS
See also Interference with Contract
Generally, 10.5(3)

TRADEMARK
Dilution, injunction remedy only, 6.4(3)
Dilution and injurious falsehood, 6.8(3)
Infringement,
  Attorney fee awards, 6.4(7)
  Damages, 6.4(3)
  Equitable defenses, 6.4(6)
  Injunction, 6.4(5)
  Interest, 6.4(3)
  Overhead deductions in computing infringer's profits, 6.4(4)
  Punitive damages, 6.4(8)
  Remedies summarized, 6.4(2)
  Restitution, 6.4(4)
  Seizure or destruction of marks or goods, 6.4(5)
  Substantive background, 6.4(1)
  Taxes deductions in computing infringer's profits, 6.4(4)

TRANSACTION COSTS
Considered in choosing remedy, 1.9
Market damages, ignored in, 3.3(3)

TRANSPORTATION COSTS
Adjustment for, market measured damages, 5.13(3)

TREBLE DAMAGES STATUTES, 3.12

TREES
Damages for removal, 5.3(2)

TRESPASS AND CASE
Assumpsit relation to, 4.2(3)

TRESPASS TO CHATTELS
See Chattels

TRESPASS TO LAND
   See also Nuisance
Bad faith trespassers, 5.3(3)
Consequential damages, 5.12(1)–5.12(2)
Crops injured or destroyed, 5.3(2)
Damages,
   Diminished value,
      Ceilings on, 5.2(4)
      Rule, 5.2(1), 5.2(2)
   Environmental damage, 5.2(5)
   Idiosyncratic uses, 5.2(1)
   "Permanent" harm test, 5.2(2)
   Repair or replacement costs,
      Generally, 5.2(2)–5.2(7)
      Ceilings on, 5.2(3)
Ejectment remedy, 5.10(1)
Encroaching structures, 5.10(4)
Forcible entry and detainer remedy, 5.10(2)
Good faith trespassers, 5.3(2)
Improvements by trespasser, 5.8(3)
Injunction,
   Interference with possession, 5.10(3)
      Interference with enjoyment, 5.7
      Physical harm, 5.5
Injury or removal of trees, shrubs, 5.3(2)
Interests protected, 5.1(1)
Mesne profits, 5.8(2)
Minerals removed, 5.3(2)
Multiple damages,
      Generally, 5.12(1), 5.12(3)
   Severance cases, 5.3(2)
Natural resources, harm to, 5.2(5)
Permanent damages, 5.2(2)
Permanent harm or invasion,
   Statute of limitations, 5.11(1)
   Res judicata, 5.11(1)
Physical harms to land,
   Damages, 5.2–5.3
      Generally, 5.2–5.5
     Injunction, 5.5
     Restitution, 5.4
Possessory interests,
   Damages, 5.8(2)
   Ejectment, 5.10(1)
   Injunction, 5.10(3)
   Protected generally, 5.8–5.10
   Provisional relief, 5.10(1)
   Restitution, 5.9
   Specific relief, 5.10
Punitive damages, 5.12(3)
Purchasers of articles severed from the land, 5.3(4)
Remedies generally, 5.1(1)
Repeated trespass, injunction, 5.10(3)
Restitution for use and occupation, 5.9
Sand, gravel or dirt removed, 5.3(2)
Severance generally, 5.3(1)

TRESPASS TO LAND—Cont'd
Superfund Act, 5.2(5)
Timber cutting, good faith, 5.3(2)
Title in issue, effect on injunction, 5.10(3)

TROVER
See Conversion of Property

TRUSTS
   See also Constructive Trust
Equity's historic role in, 2.3(2)
Jury trial, equitable characterization or not, 2.6(3)

UCC
Buyer's remedies, 12.16
Chattel leases, 12.18
Contemplation of parties limit, 12.4(7)
Cover measure of damages, 12.16(3)
Seller's anticipatory repudiation, 12.16(4)
Seller's remedies, 12.17
Specific performance,
   Buyer's remedy, 12.16(7)
   Seller's remedy, 12.17(6)
Statute of frauds and part performance doctrine, 13.2(5)

ULTRA VIRES
Restitution, benefits conferred, 13.4

UNCLEAN HANDS
Copyright cases, 6.3(6)
Equity, defense or factor in balancing, 2.4(2)
Equity maxim, 2.3(4)
Merger of law and equity and, 2.6(1)
Misrepresentation, 9.6
Obscene materials, copyright enforced, 6.3(6)
Pari delicto compared, 2.4(2), 13.6
Patent infringement, 6.2(6)
Specific performance cases, 12.8(4)
Trademark cases, 6.4(6)
Unrelated bad conduct, 2.4(2)

UNCOLLECTIBLE JUDGMENT
Effect on adequacy of legal remedy, 2.5(2)

UNCONSCIONABILITY
Equity rule, 2.4(3)
Rationale for denying enforcement of contract's "penalty" clause, 12.9(1), 12.9(3)

UNCONSCIONABLE CONDUCT
Equity and UCC unconscionability, 10.7

UNCONSCIONABLE CONTRACTS
Specific performance, 12.8(4)

UNCONSTITUTIONAL ORDERS
Contempt for disobedience, 2.8(6)

UNCONSTITUTIONAL REGULATION
Taking for which compensation is required, 6.9

UNDUE INFLUENCE
Restitution, basis for, 10.3

UNEMPLOYED PERSONS
Personal injury, 8.1(2)

UNENFORCEABLE CONTRACTS, 13.1–13.6

UNFAIR COMPETITION
See Misappropriation of Intangible Property;
    Trade Secrets; Trademark

UNILATERAL MISTAKE
Formation of agreement, 11.4
Performance of obligation, 11.7

UNIQUE ENTITLEMENTS
Inadequate legal remedy, 2.5(2)

UNJUST ENRICHMENT
See Restitution

UNLAWFUL DETAINER, 5.10(2)

UNLIQUIDATED SUMS
Prejudgment interest rules for, 3.6(1)

UNMARRIED COHABITANTS
Consortium, personal injury, 8.1(5)

UNREALIZED GAINS
Restitution, measure affected, 4.5(2)

UNREALIZED LOSSES
Damages for, 3.3(3), 3.4

UNSOLICITED BENEFITS
Building contracts, mechanic's and supplier's
    liens, 12.20(3)
Chattel value increased by repair or replace-
    ment, 5.14(3)
Converter's use of plaintiff's property for
    plaintiff's benefit, 5.14(4)
Mistaken trespasser's improvements, 5.8(3)
Restitution,
    Ability to reject, 4.9(6)
    Attorney fees from common funds and,
        4.9(6)
    Autonomy basis of rule denying restitution
        for, 4.9(2)
    Brokers, benefit to non-contracting party,
        4.9(4)
    Choice principle or autonomy basis for rule
        against restitution of, 4.9(1)
    Cotenant improvement, restitution for,
        when, 4.9(3)
    Credit card charges permitted by one who
        did not agree to pay, 4.9(4)
    Denial of recovery for, 4.9(2)
    Effect of contract on general subject mat-
        ter, 4.9(4)
    Emergency services, 4.9(5)
    Express contract on related matters pre-
        cluding restitution for, 4.9(4)
    Freeriders problems, 4.9(4)
    Fulfilling another's duty, 4.9(2)
        Generally, 4.9
    Gifts intended, 4.9(4)
    Ideas submitted and used, 4.9(4)
    Improvements authorized by apparent
        owner, 4.9(5)
    Laborers etc. for general contractor bene-
        fiting landowner, 12.20(3)
    Liability of another minimized, 4.9(4)
    Mechanic's lien statutes, 4.9(4)

UNSOLICITED BENEFITS—Cont'd
Restitution—Cont'd
    Mistake as to property ownership, im-
        provements made, 4.9(5), 5.8(3)
    Money or cash, restitution permitted, 4.9(3)
    Necessaries supplied, restitution granted,
        4.9(2)
    Payment of another debt, 4.9(3)
    Presumption of gift, family service cases,
        4.9(4)
    Property saved, restitution for, 4.9(5)
    Quarry case, 4.9(4)
    Realized gains, 4.5(2), 4.9(6)
    Subcontractor's work, no agreement to pay
        subcontractor, 4.9(4)
    Subrogation, 4.9(3)
    Taxes overpaid, 4.9(3)
    Trespasser's improvements, 5.8(3)
    Unrealized gains, 4.5(2), 4.9(6)
    Volunteers rule generally, 4.9(1)

USE AND ENJOYMENT OF LAND
See also Nuisance
Assumpsit count, 4.2(3)
Contract land purchaser's pre-closing occupan-
    cy, 12.12(2)
Damages, 5.8
Mesne profits in ejectment compared, 4.2(3)
No assumpsit rule, 12.12(2)
Restitution, 5.9

USE VALUE
See also Rental Value
Damaged chattel, recovery, 5.15(2)
Loss of use, chattels, 5.15(2)
Misrepresentation, 9.3(4)
Restitution, consequential benefits from, 4.5(3)
Restitution for, 4.5(2)

USES
Equity's historic role in, 2.3(2)

VALUE
See also Market Measured Damages; Pres-
    ent Value
Property generally, 3.5
Sentimental value, property damage case,
    5.15(3)
Willing buyer and willing seller test, 3.5

VALUE OF THE CHANCE
Damages,
    Future damages, personal injury, 8.1(7)
    Recovery, 3.4

VENDOR AND PURCHASER
See Land Sales Contracts

VERDICT
Interest from verdict or from judgment, 3.6(6)

VICARIOUS LIABILITY
Punitive damages, 3.11(1), 3.11(6)

VISUAL ARTISTS RIGHTS ACT, 5.16(4)

VOID ORDERS
Contempt and, 2.8(6)

VOLUNTARY WASTE (TO A FUTURE ES-TATE), 5.2(8)

VOLUNTEERS
See Unsolicited Benefits

VOTING RIGHTS
Damages, presumed or general, 7.3(2)

WADE, JOHN
Solution to illegality-restitution problem, 13.6

WAGES LOST
See Earning Capacity

WAIVER
Estoppel and, 2.3(5)

WAIVER OF TORT AND SUIT IN ASSUMPSIT
Generally, 4.2(3)
Conversion of chattels,
    Generally, 5.18(1)
    Measure of recovery, 5.18(2)

WARD v. TAGGART
Broker profit case, 10.5(1)

WARRANTY
Title, attorney fee liability, 3.10(3)

WARSAW CONVENTION
Caps on damages, 8.8
Punitive damages, 3.11(1)
Wrongful death, 8.3(4)

WASTE
Effect of remedy causing, 1.9

WASTE TO A FUTURE ESTATE
Damages, 5.2(8)
Injunction, 5.2(8)

WEALTH
Punitive damages, defendant's financial condition, relevance, 3.11(5)

WHISTLEBLOWERS
Wrongful discharge, 6.10(3)

WHITE, JAMES
Cover under UCC, 12.16(3)

WHOLESALE MARKET
Damages based on, when, 5.13(3), 5.16(4)

WIFE AND HUSBAND
See Spouses

WILLING BUYER
Value of property and, 3.5

WILLING SELLER
Value of property and, 3.5

WIRETAPPING
Damages, 7.2(2), 7.3(2), 7.3(4)
Standardized or surrogate damages, exemplifying, 3.3(2)

WITNESSES
Order to testify,
    Attack on court's jurisdiction, 2.8(6)

WITNESSES—Cont'd
Order to testify—Cont'd
    Contempt liability, 2.8(3), 2.8(6)

WORK LIFE EXPECTANCY
Personal injury cases, 8.5(2)

WORK LIFE TABLES
Ethnic or gender discrimination in, 8.5(2)

WRONGFUL ACQUISITION OF PROPERTY AT DEATH OF ANOTHER
Restitution, 6.7

WRONGFUL BIRTH
Generally, 8.2
Wrongful pregnancy cases, avoidable consequences, 8.7(2)

WRONGFUL CONCEPTION, 8.2

WRONGFUL DEATH
Civil rights violations, 7.4(3)
Tax savings on award, credits for, 8.6(4)

WRONGFUL DISCHARGE
Attorney fees, 6.10(4), 6.10(8)
Avoidable consequences,
    Common law, 6.10(2)
    Statutory claims, 6.10(4)
Collateral source rule, 6.10(4)
Consequential damages, statutory claims, 6.10(4)
Contract vs. tort theory of, common law, 6.10(2)
Damages or compensation,
    Common law, 6.10(2)
    Statutory remedies, 6.10(4)
Discretion, statutory claims, 6.10(7)
Equitable defenses, statutory claims, 6.10(8)
Frontpay, common law, 6.10(2)
Jury trial, 6.10(5)
Laches, statutory claims, 6.10(8)
Minimizing damages, common law, 6.10(2)
Preliminary injunction to prevent, 6.10(4)
Punitive damages awards, 3.11(2)
Reinstatement,
    Common law, 6.10(2)
    Form of injunction, as, 2.9(1)
    Statutory claims, 6.10(4)
Statutory bases for claim of, 6.10(3)
Substantive background, 6.10(1)
Whistleblower statutes, 6.10(3)

WRONGFUL LIFE, 8.2

WRONGFUL PREGNANCY, 8.2

YORIO, EDWARD
Adequacy of legal remedy,
    Generally, 2.5(3)
    Specific performance, 12.8(2)
Specific performance, purchase of goods contracts, 12.16(7)

ZONING
Injunction,
    Standing to sue for violation, 5.7(5)
    Violation, against, 5.7(2)
Taking of property by, damages, 5.6(4), 6.9

0–314–01123–4

90000